Chuck Klassen

MOTOR
AUTO REPAIR MANUAL

46th Edition

First Printing

Louis C. Forier, SAE
Editorial Director

Michael J. Kromida, SAE
Editor

Dan Irizarry, SAE • Warren Schildknecht, SAE
Senior Editors

Michael E. Pallien, SAE • Mark E. Flynn, SAE
Associate Editors

Daniel E. Doku • Patrick Peyton, SAE • Robert R. Savasta
Derek K. Long, SAE • Mark Sharrock • Russell Macrae
Denver Steele • John R. Lypen • John J. Glynn
Assistant Editors

Rose-Ellen Lorber-Termaat
Editorial Assistant

Published by
MOTOR

224 West 57th St., New York, N.Y. 10019

The Automotive Business Magazine

Printed in the U.S.A. © Copyright 1982 by The Hearst Corporation
Library of Congress Catalog Number: 75-643020

ISBN 0-87851-553-4

Books Published by MOTOR

The nature of the automobile we know today makes it economically impractical to cover all phases of servicing in one book. A brief descriptive list of all titles is provided below for your convenience.

Auto Repair Manual—*Early Model Edition*

Mechanical specifications and service procedures for 1969–76 American built cars. Special sections on Alternators, Carburetors, Starting Motors and Switches, Transmissions, Tune Up, Emission Controls, Brakes, Headlamps, etc.

Auto Repair Manual—*Vintage Car Edition*

A must for the owner or restorer of old cars. Has mechanical specifications and service procedures for most 1935–61 American built cars.
Vol. I covers 1935–53 and includes 23 popular makes. Special service includes information on such systems as Automatic Seat Adjusters, Automatic Transmissions, Tops, Automatic Window Lifts, Carburetors, Generators, Hill Holder, Ignition, Overdrives and much more.
Vol. II covers 1953–61 and covers 31 popular makes. Includes service on Air Conditioning, Alternators, Brakes, Distributors, Non-Slip Differentials, Starting Motors and more, plus a special service section on Automatic Transmissions.

Imported Car Repair Manual

For the "Imported Car" owner who is totally involved with his car and is interested in Do-It-Yourself car repairs: the maintenance of peak performance . . . and in saving money.
Includes specifications and service procedures for 27 popular imported cars and pickups. Over 1,300 pages and 2,600 plus illustrations and diagrams.

Truck Repair Manual

Service and repair is surprisingly easy with this new edition that covers 2,800 Truck Models, 1973 through 1982. Over 1,400 pages of step-by-step instructions, 2,000 cutaway pictures, 3,000 service and repair facts, specs and adjustments. Covers all popular makes of trucks. Manual also includes specs for gasoline and diesel engines used in off-highway equipment and farm tractors.

INDEX

This Edition Covers Mechanical Specifications and Service Procedures on 1977–83 Models available at time of publication.

———— CAR INFORMATION SECTION—1 ————

———— GENERAL SERVICE INFORMATION SECTION—2* ————

*For your convenience in locating this section, a black bar has been positioned beneath all odd page numbers.

American Motors

INDEX OF SERVICE OPERATIONS

NOTE: Refer to the back of this manual for vehicle manufacturer's special service tool suppliers.

VEHICLE IDENTIFICATION NUMBER LOCATION:

1977–83: Plate is attached to top of instrument panel, on driver's side.

ENGINE IDENTIFICATION

4-121 (1977–79): The engine code is located on a machined flange at the left rear of the cylinder block adjacent to the oil dipstick. The letter "G" denotes the 4-121 engine.

4-151 (1980–83): The engine code is located on a pad at the right front of the cylinder block below the cylinder head. The letter B denotes the 4-151 engine.

6-232 & 6-258 (1977–83): The engine code is located on a pad between number two and three cylinders. The letter "A" denotes the 258 engine with one barrel carburetor. The letter "C" denotes the 258 engine with two barrel carburetor. The letter "E" denotes the 232 engine.

V8-304, & 360 (1977–79): The engine code is located on a tag attached to the right bank rocker cover. The letter "H" denotes the 304 engine. The letter "N" denotes the 360 engine with 2 barrel carburetor.

GRILLE IDENTIFICATION

1977 Hornet

1977 Pacer

1977–78 Matador 2 Door

1977–78 Matador 4 Door

1977 AMX

1977–78 Gremlin

1978 AMX

1978 Concord

1978–80 Pacer

1979–80 AMX

1979 Concord

1979–80 Spirit

1980 Concord

1980 Eagle

1980 Eagle Sport

1981–83 Concord

1981–83 Spirit

GRILLE IDENTIFICATION—Continued

1981–83 Eagle

1981–83 Eagle SX/4 Sport

GENERAL ENGINE SPECIFICATIONS

Year	Engine CID①/Liter	V.I.N. Code②	Carburetor	Bore and Stroke	Compression Ratio	Net H.P. @ R.P.M.③	Maximum Torque Ft. Lbs. @ R.P.M.	Normal Oil Pressure Pounds
1977	4-121, 2.0L	G	5210, 2 Bbl.⑩	3.41 × 3.32	8.1	80 @ 5000	105 @ 2800	28½
	6-232, 3.8L	E	YF, 1 Bbl.④⑤	3.75 × 3.50	8.0	90 @ 3050	163 @ 2200	37–75
	6-258, 4.23L	A	YF, 1 Bbl.④⑤	3.75 × 3.90	8.0	95 @ 3050	179 @ 2100	37–75
	6-258, 4.23L	C	BBD, 2 Bbl.④	3.75 × 3.90	8.0	120 @ 3600	200 @ 2000	37–75
	V8-304, 5.0L	H	2100, 2 Bbl.⑧⑨	3.75 × 3.44	8.4	120 @ 3200	220 @ 2000	37–75
	V8-360, 5.9L	N	2100, 2 Bbl.⑧⑨	4.08 × 3.44	8.25	140 @ 3300	251 @ 1600	37–75
1978	4-121, 2.0L	G	5210, 2 Bbl.⑩	3.41 × 3.32	8.2	80 @ 5000	105 @ 2800	28.5
	6-232, 3.8L	E	YF, 1 Bbl.④	3.75 × 3.50	8.0	90 @ 3400	168 @ 1600	37–75
	6-258, 4.23L	A	YF, 1 Bbl.④	3.75 × 3.90	8.0	100 @ 3400	200 @ 1600	37–75
	6-258, 4.23L	C	BBD, 2 Bbl.④	3.75 × 3.90	8.0	120 @ 3600	201 @ 1800	37–75
	V8-304, 5.0L	H	2100, 2 Bbl.⑧⑨	3.75 × 3.44	8.4	130 @ 3200	238 @ 2000	37–75
	V8-360, 5.9L	N	2100, 2 Bbl.⑧⑨	4.08 × 3.44	8.25	140 @ 3350	278 @ 2000	37–75
1979	4-121, 2.0L	G	5210, 2 Bbl.⑩	3.41 × 3.32	8.2	80 @ 5000	105 @ 2800	28.5
	6-232, 3.8L	E	YF, 1 Bbl.④	3.75 × 3.50	8.0	90 @ 3400	168 @ 1600	37–75
	6-258, 4.23L	A	YF, 1 Bbl.④	3.75 × 3.90	8.3	100 @ 3400	200 @ 1600	37–75
	6-258, 4.23L	C	BBD, 2 Bbl.④	3.75 × 3.90	8.3	110 @ 3200	210 @ 1800	37–75
	V8-304, 5.0L	H	2100, 2 Bbl.⑧	3.75 × 3.44	8.4	125 @ 3200	220 @ 2400	37–75
1980	4-151, 2.5L⑪	B	2SE, 2 Bbl.⑫	4.0 × 3.0	8.24	—	—	36–41
	6-258, 4.23L	C	BBD, 2 Bbl.④	3.75 × 3.90	8.3	—	—	37–75
1981	4-151, 2.5L⑪	B	2SE, 2 Bbl.⑫⑬	4.0 × 3.0	8.24	—	—	36–41
	6-258, 4.23L	C	BBD, 2 Bbl.④	3.75 × 3.90	8.0	—	—	37–75
1982	4-151, 2.5L⑪	B	2SE, 2 Bbl.⑫	4.0 × 3.0	8.24	—	—	36–41
	4-151, 2.5L⑪	B	E2SE, 2 Bbl.⑫⑭	4.0 × 3.0	8.24	—	—	36–41
	6-258, 4.23L	C	BBD, 2 Bbl.④	3.75 × 3.90	8.6	—	—	37–75
1983	4-151, 2.5L⑪	B	2 Bbl.	4.0 × 3.0	8.2	—	—	36–41
	6-258, 4.23L	C	BBD, 2 Bbl.④	3.75 × 3.90	9.2	—	—	37–75

①—CID—cubic inch displacement.
②—On 1977–80 models, the seventh digit denotes engine code. On 1981–83 models, the fourth digit denotes engine code.
③—Ratings are net-as installed on vehicle.
④—Carter.
⑤—High altitude, YFA.
⑥—Except Matador.
⑦—Matador.
⑧—Motorcraft.
⑨—High altitude V8, 2150.
⑩—Holley.
⑪—Refer to the Chevrolet Monza, Buick Skyhawk, Olds. Starfire, Pontiac Sunbird chapter for service procedures on this engine.
⑫—Rochester.
⑬—Calif. vehicles equipped with E2SE.
⑭—Calif. & auto. trans. only.

TUNE UP SPECIFICATIONS

The following specifications are published from the latest information available. This
data should be used only in the absence of a decal affixed in the engine compartment.

★ When using a timing light, disconnect vacuum hose or tube at distributor and plug opening in hose or tube so idle speed will not be affected.

● When checking compression, lowest cylinder must be within 80 percent of highest.

▲ Before removing wires from distributor cap, determine location of the No. 1 wire in cap, as distributor position may have been altered from that shown at
the end of this chart.

Spark plug types shown in this chart are recommendations of the original vehicle manufacturer and not MOTOR.
Check local sources for other spark plug manufacturers listings.

Year & Engine/V.I.N.	Spark Plug Type	Gap	Ignition Timing BTDC ① ★ Firing Order Fig. ▲	Man. Trans.	Auto. Trans.	Mark Fig.	Curb Idle Speed ② Man. Trans.	Auto. Trans.	Fast Idle Speed Man. Trans.	Auto. Trans.	Fuel Pump Pressure
1977											
4-121/G ⑨	N8L	.035	F	12°	⑩	G	900	800D	1600⑪	1600⑪	4–6
6-232/E Exc. Calif.	N12Y	.035	A	⑫	10°	E	600	550D	1500④	1600④	4–5
6-232/E Calif.	N12Y	.035	A	10°	10°	E	850	700D	1500④	1600④	4–5
6-258/A 1 Barrel Exc. Calif. ⑬	N12Y	.035	A	6°	⑭	E	600	550D	1500④	1600④	4–5
6-258/A 1 Barrel Calif.	N12Y	.035	A	—	8°	E	—	700D	—	1600④	4–5
6-258/A 1 Barrel High Alt.	N12Y	.035	A	10°⑮	10°⑯	E	600	550D	1500④	1600④	4–5
6-258/C 2 Barrel	N12Y	.035	A	6°	8°	E	600	⑰	1500④	1600④	4–5
V8-304/H Exc. Calif.	RN12Y	.035	B	—	10°	C	—	600D	—	1600④	5–6½
V8-304/H Calif.	RN12Y	.035	B	—	5°	C	—	700D	—	1800④	5–6½
V8-360/N Exc. Calif. & High Alt.	RN12Y	.035	B	—	10°	C	—	600D	—	1600④	5–6½
V8-360/N Calif.	RN12Y	.035	B	—	5°	C	—	700D	—	1600④	5–6½
V8-360/N High Alt.	RN12Y	.035	B	—	10°	C	—	700D	—	1800④	5–6½
1978											
4-121/G ⑨	N8L	.035	F	12°	⑩	G	900	800D	1600⑪	1600⑪	4–6
6-232/E	N13L	.035	H	8°	10°	E	600	550D	1500④	1600④	4–5
6-258/A 1 Barrel	N13L	.035	H	6°	8°	E	850	700D	1500④	1600④	4–5
6-258/C 2 Barrel	N13L⑱	.035	H	6°	8°	E	600	600D	1500④	1600④	4–5
V8-304/H Exc. Calif. & High Alt.	N12Y	.035	I	—	10°	D	—	600D	—	1600④	5–6½
V8-304/H Calif.	N12Y	.035	I	—	5°	D	—	700D	—	—	5–6½
V8-304/H High Alt.	N12Y	.035	I	—	10°	D	—	700D	—	1600④	5–6½
V8-360/N Exc. Calif. & High Alt.	N12Y	.035	I	—	10°	D	—	600D	—	1600④	5–6½
V8-360/N Calif.	N12Y	.035	I	—	10°	D	—	650D	—	1800④	5–6½
V8-360/N High Alt.	N12Y	.035	I	—	10°⑲	D	—	700D	—	1800④	5–6½
1979											
4-121/G Exc. Calif. ⑨	N8L	.035	F	⑳	12°	G	㉑	800D	1800⑪	1800⑪	4–6
4-121/G Calif. ⑨	N8L	.035	F	—	8°	G	—	800D	—	1800⑪	4–6
6-232/E	N13L	.035	H	8°	10°㉒	E	600	550D	1500④	1600④	4–5
6-258/A 1 Barrel	N13L	.035	H	—	8°	E	—	700D	—	—	4–5
6-258/C 2 Barrel	N13L	.035	H	4°	8°	E	700	600D	1500④	1600④	4–5
V8-304/H	N12Y	.035	I	5°	8°	D	800	600D	1500④	1600④	5–6½
1980											
4-151/B Exc. Calif.	R44TSX㉓	.060	J	10°	12°	K	900	700D	2400㉔	2600㉔	6½–8
4-151/B Calif.	R44TSX㉓	.060	J	12°	10°	K	㉕	㉖	2400㉔	2600㉔	6½–8
6-258/C Exc. Eagle	N14LY⑥	.035	H	6°	⑦	E	700	600D	1700④	1850④	4–5
6-258/C Eagle Exc. Calif.	N13L⑥	.035	H	—	10°	E	—	600D	—	1850④	4–5
6-258/C Eagle Calif.	N13L⑥	.035	H	—	8°	E	—	600D	—	1850④	4–5

TUNE UP SPECIFICATIONS—Continued

The following specifications are published from the latest information available. This data should be used only in the absence of a decal affixed in the engine compartment.

★ When using a timing light, disconnect vacuum hose or tube at distributor and plug opening in hose or tube so idle speed will not be affected.

● When checking compression, lowest cylinder must be within 80 percent of highest.

▲ Before removing wires from distributor cap, determine location of the No. 1 wire in cap, as distributor position may have been altered from that shown at the end of this chart.

Spark plug types shown in this chart are recommendations of the original vehicle manufacturer and not MOTOR. Check local sources for other spark plug manufacturers listings.

Year & Engine/V.I.N.	Spark Plug		Ignition Timing BTDC①★				Curb Idle Speed②		Fast Idle Speed		Fuel Pump Pressure
	Type	Gap	Firing Order Fig. ▲	Man. Trans.	Auto. Trans.	Mark Fig.	Man. Trans.	Auto. Trans.	Man. Trans.	Auto. Trans.	
1981											
4-151/B Concord & Spirit Exc. Calif.	R44TSX㉓	.060	J	10°	12°	K	500/900	500/700D	2400㉔	2600㉔	6½–8
4-151/B Concord & Spirit Calif.	R44TSX㉓	.060	J	10°	10°	K	500/900	500/700D	2400㉔	2600㉔	6½–8
4-151/B Eagle Exc. Calif.	R44TSX㉓	.060	J	11°	12°	K	500/900	500/700D	2400㉔	2600㉔	6½–8
4-151/B Eagle Calif.	R44TSX㉓	.060	J	10°	8°	K	500/900	500/700D	2400㉔	2600㉔	6½–8
6-258/C Concord & Spirit Exc. High Alt.	RFN14LY⑥	.035	H	6°	6°	E	650③	550D⑧	1700④	1850④	4–5
6-258/C Eagle Exc. Calif. & High Alt.	RFN14LY⑥	.035	H	8°	8°	E	650③	550D⑧	1700④	1850④	4–5
6-258/C Eagle Calif.	RFN14LY⑥		H	4°	6°	E	650③	550D⑧	1700④	1850④	4–5
6-258/C High Alt.	RFN14LY⑥		H	—	15°	E	—	550D⑧	—	1850④	4–5
1982											
4-151/B Concord & Spirit Exc. Calif. & High Alt.	R44TSX㉓	.060	J	10°	10°	K	900㉘	700D㉙	2400	2400⑤	6½–8
4-151/B Eagle Exc. Calif. & High Alt.	R44TSX㉓	.060	J	12°	12°	K	900㉘	700D㉙	2400	2500	6½–8
4-151/B Concord & Spirit Calif.	R44TSX㉓	.060	J	8°	8°	K	900㉘	700D㉙	2400	2400⑤	6½–8
4-151/B Eagle Calif.	R44TSX㉓	.060	J	8°	8°	K	900㉘	700D㉙	2500	2500	6½–8
4-151/B Concord & Spirit High Alt.	R44TSX㉓	.060	J	15°	15°	K	900㉘	700D㉙	2400	2400⑤	6½–8
4-151/B Eagle High Alt.	R44TSX㉓	.060	J	15°	15°	K	900㉘	700D㉙	2500	2500	6½–8
6-258/C Exc. High Alt.	RFN14LY⑥	.035	H	15°㉗	15°㉗	L	600③	500D⑧	1850	1850	4–5
6-258/C Concord & Spirit High Alt.	RFN14LY⑥	.035	H	19°㉗	19°㉗	L	600③	500D⑧	1850	1850	4–5
6-258/C Eagle High Alt.	RFN14LY⑥	.035	H	21°㉗	21°㉗	L	600③	500D⑧	1850	1850	4–5
1983											
4-151/B Exc. Calif.	R44TSX	.060	J	10°	10°	K	650/900	550/700D	—	—	6½–8
4-151/B Calif.	R44TSX	.060	J	10°	10°	K	650/900	550/700D	—	—	6½–8
6-258/C Concord & Spirit Exc. High Alt.	RFN14LY	.035	H	6°	6°	L	650㉚	550D㉛	—	—	5–6½
6-258/C Eagle Exc. Calif. & High Alt.	RFN14LY	.035	H	6°	6°	L	600㉚	500D㉛	—	—	5–6½
6-258/C Eagle Calif.	RFN14LY	.035	H	6°	6°	L	650㉚	550D㉛	—	—	5–6½
6-258/C High Alt.	RFN14LY	.035	H	13°	13°	L	700㉜	650D	—	—	5–6½

①—BTDC—Before top dead center.
②—Idle speed on man. trans. vehicles is adjusted in Neutral & on auto. trans. equipped vehicles is adjusted in Drive unless otherwise specified. When two idle speeds are listed, the higher speed is with the A/C or idle solenoid energized.
③—With holding solenoid energized, 750 RPM; with vacuum actuator energized, 900 RPM.

TUNE UP NOTES—Continued

④—With stop screw on 2nd step of fast idle cam, TCS & EGR disconnected.

⑤—Models with A/C, 2600 RPM.

⑥—Champion.

⑦—Concord & Spirit, 10° BTDC; Pacer, 8° BTDC.

⑧—With holding solenoid energized, 650D RPM; with vacuum actuator energized, 800D RPM.

⑨—Point gap, .018"; dwell angle, 44–50°.

⑩—Except Calif., 12° BTDC; California, 8° BTDC.

⑪—With stop screw on low step of fast idle cam against shoulder of high step & EGR disconnected.

⑫—Except high altitude, 8° BTDC; high altitude, 10° BTDC.

⑬—Except high altitude.

⑭—Except Matador, 8° BTDC; Matador, 6° BTDC.

⑮—When operating at altitudes below 4000 ft., set to 6° BTDC.

⑯—When operating at altitudes below 4000 ft., set to 8° BTDC.

⑰—Except Calif., 600D RPM; California, 700D RPM.

⑱—On models with auto. trans. & 2.53 rear axle ratio, use N12Y

⑲—When operating at altitudes below 4000 ft., set to 5° BTDC.

⑳—Except emission control label code EH, 12° BTDC; emission control label code EH, 16° BTDC.

㉑—Except emission control label code EH, 900 RPM; emission control label code EH; 1000 RPM.

㉒—On models with 2.37 rear axle ratio, set at 12° BTDC.

㉓—AC.

㉔—With fast idle screw on highest step of fast idle cam.

㉕—With A/C, 900/1250 RPM; less A/C, 500/900 RPM.

㉖—With A/C, 700/950 RPM; less A/C, 500/700 RPM.

㉗—With ignition module electronic retard (two wire) connector disconnected and a jumper wire connected between the two module wire connector terminals.

㉘—On models equipped with A/C, with A/C off & solenoid disconnected, 500 RPM; with A/C on & solenoid connected, 950 RPM.

㉙—On models equipped with A/C, with A/C off & solenoid disconnected, 500D RPM; with A/C on & solenoid connected, 1250D RPM.

㉚—With holding solenoid energized, 750 RPM; with vacuum actuator energized, 950 RPM.

㉛—With holding solenoid energized, 650D RPM; with vacuum actuator energized, 850D RPM.

㉜—With holding solenoid energized, 950 RPM; with vacuum actuator energized, 1000 RPM.

㉝—With holding solenoid energized, 750D RPM; with vacuum actuator energized, 850D RPM.

Fig. A

Fig. B

Fig. C

Fig. D   Fig. E

Fig. F

Fig. G

Fig. I

Fig. J

Fig. H

Fig. K

Fig. L

American Motors

STARTING MOTOR SPECIFICATIONS

Year	Engine Model/V.I.N. ②	Rotation ①	Brush Spring Tension, Ounces	No Load Test			Torque Test		
				Amperes	Volts	R.P.M.	Amperes	Volts	Torque, Ft. Lbs.
1977	All/②	C	40	65	12	9250	600	3.4	13
1978–79	4-121/G	—	—	69	12	6709–10843	—	—	—
	6-232, 258/②	—	—	67	12	7380–9356	—	—	—
	V8-304/H	—	—	67	12	7380–9356	—	—	—
	V8-360/N	—	—	77	12	8900–9600	—	—	—
1980–83	4-151/B	—	—	45–70	9	7000–11900	—	—	—
	6-258/C	—	—	67	12	7380–9356	—	—	—

①—As viewed from drive end. C—Clockwise. ②—For V.I.N. code, refer to the "General Engine Specifications" at the front of the chapter.

DRIVE AXLE SPECIFICATIONS

Year	Model	Carrier Type ②	Ring Gear & Pinion Backlash		Pinion Bearing Preload			Differential Bearing Preload		
			Method	Adjustment	Method	New Bearings Inch-Lbs.	Used Bearings Inch-Lbs.	Method	New Bearings Inch-Lbs.	Used Bearings Inch-Lbs.
1977–79	7 9/16" Dr. Gr.	Integral	Shims	.005–.009	Sleeve	15–25①	15–25①	Shims	.008	.008
	8 7/8" Dr. Gr.	Integral	Shims	.005–.009	Sleeve	17–28①	17–28①	Shims	.008	.008
1980–83	7 9/16" Dr. Gr.③	Integral	Shims	.005–.009	Sleeve	15–25①	15–25①	Shims	.008	.008
	MODEL 30④	Integral	Shims	.005–.010	Shims	20–40①	15–25①	Shims	.015	.015

①—Adjust at drive pinion flange nut with inch-pound torque wrench. ②—Rear axle shaft end play .006 inch. Eagle front axle shaft end play .003 inch. ③—Rear Axle. ④—Eagle front axle.

DISTRIBUTOR SPECIFICATIONS

★If unit is checked on vehicle, double the RPM and degrees to get crankshaft figures.

Distributor Part No.①	Centrifugal Advance Degrees @ RPM of Distributor					Vacuum Advance		Distributor Retard	
	Advance Starts	Intermediate Advance			Full Advance	Inches of Vacuum to Start Plunger	Max. Adv. Dist. Deg. @ Vacuum	In. of Mercury Start Retard	Max. Retard Dist. Deg. @ Vacuum
1977									
3228263	0–2.8 @ 500	2.8–4.85 @ 750	4.2–6.25 @ 1000	7.05–9.05 @ 1500	11–13 @ 2200	4–6	8½ @ 12.7	—	—
3228264	0–2.4 @ 500	3.4–6.4 @ 750	6.3–8.3 @ 1000	9.3–11.3 @ 1500	13½–15½ @ 2200	5–7	8½ @ 12.5	—	—
3228265	0–2.7 @ 500	2.4–4.4 @ 750	3.3–5.3 @ 1000	5.1–7.1 @ 1500	7½–9½ @ 2200	4–6	8½ @ 12.7	—	—
3228266	0–3¾ @ 500	4.4–6.4 @ 750	5.4–7.4 @ 1000	7.3–9.3 @ 1500	10–12 @ 2200	4–6	8½ @ 12.7	—	—
32229719	0–1.8 @ 500	1–3 @ 750	4–6 @ 1000	6–8 @ 1500	9–11 @ 2200	5–7	9 @ 13	—	—
1977–78									
3250163	0 @ 550	4 @ 800	8 @ 1000	11 @ 1500	17 @ 2200	2–4	9 @ 9.5	—	—
3230443	−¾ @ 400	4.5 @ 800	6.5 @ 1200	9.5 @ 1800	13 @ 2200	5.5–6.5	9¼ @ 12½	—	—
3231340	−¾ @ 400	5.5 @ 800	8.5 @ 1200	12 @ 1800	15.5 @ 2200	6.5–8.5	9⅛ @ 12	—	—
3231341	−¾ @ 400	3.5 @ 800	5 @ 1200	7 @ 1800	9.5 @ 2200	5.5–6.5	9¼ @ 12½	—	—
3231915	−1 @ 400	3 @ 800	5.5 @ 1200	7.5 @ 1800	10.5 @ 2200	3.5–5.5	13¼ @ 11½	—	—
3232434	−¾ @ 400	2¾ @ 800	5¼ @ 1200	7 @ 1600	10.5 @ 2200	6.5–8.5	9½ @ 13	—	—
3233173	−⅝ @ 400	4 @ 800	6¼ @ 1200	9.5 @ 1800	13 @ 2200	4–6	13⅛ @ 11¼	—	—
3233174	−¾ @ 400	3.5 @ 800	4¾ @ 1200	6⅞ @ 1800	9.5 @ 2200	4–6	13⅛ @ 11	—	—
1979									
3231915	−1 @ 400	3 @ 800	5.5 @ 1200	7.5 @ 1800	10.5 @ 2200	3.5–5.5	13¼ @ 11.5	—	—
3232434	−¾ @ 400	2¾ @ 800	5¼ @ 1200	7 @ 1600	10.5 @ 2200	6.5–8.5	9.5 @ 13	—	—
3233959	−1 @ 400	2 @ 800	5¼ @ 1200	10 @ 1800	14.5 @ 2200	1.5–3	17¼ @ 12	—	—
3234693	−¾ @ 400	3¾ @ 800	6.5 @ 1200	9 @ 1600	14.5 @ 2200	2–3.5	12¾ @ 12	—	—
3250163	0 @ 550	4 @ 800	8 @ 1000	11 @ 1500	17 @ 2200	2–4	9 @ 9.5	—	—
3250497	0 @ 500	2 @ 700	4 @ 900	7 @ 1400	10¾ @ 1800	2–4	17 @ 13	—	—

Continued

DISTRIBUTOR SPECIFICATIONS—Continued

★If unit is checked on vehicle, double the RPM and degrees to get crankshaft figures.

Distributor Part No.①	Centrifugal Advance Degrees @ RPM of Distributor					Vacuum Advance		Distributor Retard	
	Advance Starts	Intermediate Advance			Full Advance	Inches of Vacuum to Start Plunger	Max. Adv. Dist. Deg. @ Vacuum	In. of Mercury Start Retard	Max. Retard Dist. Deg. @ Vacuum
1980									
1110560	−½ to 0 @ 400	1–3 @ 800	3–5 @ 1200	4–6 @ 1600	8 @ 2200	3.5–4.5	11 @ 9.5	—	—
1110561	−½ to 0 @ 400	1–3 @ 800	3–5 @ 1200	4–6 @ 1600	8 @ 2200	2.5–3.5	8 @ 6	—	—
1110650	−½ to 0 @ 400	1–3 @ 800	3–5 @ 1200	4–6 @ 1600	8 @ 2200	3.5–4.5	10¼ @ 9.5	—	—
3235141	−½ to +½ @ 400	1–3 @ 800	2¾–5 @ 1200	3¼–5½ @ 1600	6½ @ 2200	3–5	13¼ @ 15.5	—	—
3238428	−½ to +½ @ 400	1–3¼ @ 800	3–5 @ 1200	3½–5½ @ 1600	6½ @ 2200	4.5–5.5	12½ @ 19	—	—
1981									
1110560	−½ to 0 @ 400	¾–3 @ 800	3–5 @ 1200	4¼–6¼ @ 1600	8 @ 2200	3½–4½	10½ @ 9½	—	—
1110561	−½ to 0 @ 400	¾–3 @ 800	3–5 @ 1200	4¼–6¼ @ 1600	8 @ 2200	2½–3½	8 @ 6	—	—
1110595	−½ to 0 @ 400	¾–3 @ 800	3–5 @ 1200	4¼–6¼ @ 1600	8 @ 2200	2½–3½	10½ @ 7	—	—
1111393	−½ to 0 @ 400	¼–2 @ 800	2½–4½ @ 1200	4¼–6¼ @ 1600	8¼ @ 2050	2½–3½	10½ @ 7	—	—
3235141	−½ to ½ @ 400	1½–3½ @ 800	3–5 @ 1200	3½–5½ @ 1600	6½ @ 2200	3–5	13½ @ 15½	—	—
3239829	−¾ to ½ @ 400	2–4½ @ 800	3–5¼ @ 1200	3¼–5½ @ 1600	6¼ @ 2200	3–5	12½ @ 15	—	—
3239833	−½ to ½ @ 400	1–3½ @ 800	3–5 @ 1200	3½–5½ @ 1600	6½ @ 2200	3–5	12½ @ 15	—	—
1982									
1103491	−½ to 0 @ 400	¼–2½ @ 800	2½–4¾ @ 1200	4¼–6¼ @ 1600	8 @ 2200	3½–5	9¾ @ 8¾	—	—
1103492	−½ to 0 @ 400	1–2½ @ 800	2½–5½ @ 1200	4¼–6¼ @ 1600	8 @ 2200	3–4½	10½ @ 7	—	—
1110598	−½ to 0 @ 400	⅛–2⅛ @ 800	2½–4½ @ 1200	4⅛–6⅛ @ 1600	8⅛ @ 2200	2¼–3¾	10½ @ 7	—	—
3241333	−1 to ¾ @ 600	—	—	—	7¼ @ 1050	2½–4¾	12½ @ 18	—	—
1983									
1110598	−½ to 0 @ 400	⅛–2⅛ @ 800	2½–4½ @ 1200	4⅛–6⅛ @ 1600	8 @ 2050	2½–5	9¾ @ 8¾	—	—
3242409	−½ to ½ @ 400	2–4 @ 800	—	—	7 @ 2050	3–5	12½ @ 18	—	—

①—Stamped on distributor housing plate.

AMERICAN MOTORS

VALVE SPECIFICATIONS

Year	Model/V.I.N.	Valve Lash Int.	Valve Lash Exh.	Valve Angles Seat	Valve Angles Face	Valve Spring Installed Height	Valve Spring Pressure Lbs. @ In.	Stem Clearance Intake	Stem Clearance Exhaust	Stem Diameter Intake	Stem Diameter Exhaust
1977	6-232, 258/⑩⑥	Hydraulic③	⑦	②		1²⁵/₃₂	195 @ 1¹³/₃₂	.001–.003	.001–.003	.3715–.3725	.3715–.3725
	6-258/C⑤	Hydraulic③	⑦	②		1²⁵/₃₂	205 @ ²⁵/₆₄	.001–.003	.001–.003	.3715–.3725	.3715–.3725
	V8-304, 360/⑩	Hydraulic③	⑦	②		1¹³/₁₆	213 @ 1²³/₆₄	.001–.003	.001–.003	.3715–.3725	.3715–.3725
1977–79	4-121/G	⑧		45	45	①	⑨	.031	.039	.3526–.3531	.3522–.3528
1978–79	6-232, 258/⑩	Hydraulic③	⑦	②		1²⁵/₃₂	195 @ 1¹³/₃₂	.001–.003	.001–.003	.3715–.3725	.3715–.3725
	V8-304, 360/⑩	Hydraulic③	⑦	②		1²⁵/₃₂	④	.001–.003	.001–.003	.3715–.3725	.3715–.3725
1980–83	4-151/B	Hydraulic③		46	45	1.66	176 @ 1.254	.0010–.0027	.0010–.0027	.3418–.3425	.3418–.3425
	6-258/C	Hydraulic③	⑦	②		1.786	195 @ 1.411	.001–.003	.001–.003	.3715–.3725	.3715–.3725

①—Inner 1¹/₂"; outer 1⁴⁵/₆₄".
②—Intake 29°, exhaust 44°.
③—No adjustment.
④—1978, 211 @ 1²³/₆₄; 1979, 195 @ 1¹³/₃₂.
⑤—2 Barrel carburetor.
⑥—1 Barrel carburetor.
⑦—Intake 30°, exhaust 44¹/₂°.
⑧—Intake, .006–.009 in. H; exhaust, .016–.019 in. H.
⑨—Intake, inner 39 lbs. @ 1³/₃₂"; outer 166 lbs. @ 1⁵/₁₆". Exhaust, inner 37 lbs. @ 1⁷/₆₄"; outer 160 lbs. @ 1²¹/₆₄".
⑩—For V.I.N. code, refer to the "General Engine Specifications" at the front of chapter.

PISTONS, PINS, RINGS, CRANKSHAFT & BEARINGS

Year	Model/V.I.N.	Piston Clearance Top of Skirt	Ring End Gap① Comp.	Ring End Gap① Oil	Wrist-pin Diameter	Rod Bearings Shaft Diameter	Rod Bearings Bearing Clearance	Main Bearings Shaft Diameter	Main Bearings Bearing Clearance	Thrust on Bear. No.	Shaft End Play
1977	4-121/G	.0009–.0015	.010	.010	.945	1.888–1.889	.0008–.0028	2.1581–2.1587	.0008–.0031	3	.0039–.0075
	6-232, 258/④	.0009–.0017	.010	.010	.9307	2.0934–2.0955	.001–.0025	2.4986–2.5001	.001–.003	3	.0015–.0065
	V8-304/H	.0010–.0018	.010	.010	.9311	2.0934–2.0955	.001–.003	②	④	3	.003–.008
	V8-360/N	.0012–.0020	.010	.015	.9311	2.0934–2.0955	.001–.003	②	④	3	.003–.008
1978–79	4-121/G	.007–.0017	.010	.010	.9448	1.8882–1.8888	.0007–.0029	2.1581–2.1587	.00098–.00311	3	.0039–.0075
	6-232, 258/④	.0009–.0017	.010	.010	.9307	2.0934–2.0955	.001–.0025	2.4986–2.5001	.001–.003	3	.0015–.0065
	V8-304/H	.0010–.0018	.010	.010	.9311	2.0934–2.0955	.001–.003	②	④	3	.003–.008
	V8-360/N	.0012–.0020	.010	.015	.9311	2.0934–2.0955	.001–.003	②	④	3	.003–.008
1980–83	4-151/B	.0025–.0033	.010	.015	.92725	2.000	.0005–.0026	2.2998	.0005–.0022	5	.0035–.0085
	6-258/C	.0009–.0017	.010	.010	.9307	2.0934–2.0955	.001–.003	2.4986–2.5001	.001–.003	3	.0015–.0065

①—Fit rings in tapered bores for clearance listed in tightest portion of ring travel.
②—Rear main 2.7464–2.7479", others 2.7474–2.7489".
③—Rear main, .002" to .004"; all others, .001" to .003".
④—For V.I.N. code, refer to the "General Engine Specifications" at the front of chapter.

ENGINE TIGHTENING SPECIFICATIONS★

★Torque specifications are for clean and lightly lubricated threads only. Dry or dirty threads produce increased friction which prevents accurate measurement of tightness.

Year	Engine Model/V.I.N.	Spark Plugs Ft. Lbs.	Cylinder Head Bolts Ft. Lbs.	Intake Manifold Ft. Lbs.	Exhaust Manifold Ft. Lbs.	Rocker Arm Shaft Bracket Ft. Lbs.	Rocker Arm Cover Ft. Lbs.	Connecting Rod Cap Bolts Ft. Lbs.	Main Bearing Cap Bolts Ft. Lbs.	Flywheel to Crankshaft Ft. Lbs.	Vibration Damper or Pulley Ft. Lbs.
1977–79	4-121/G	22	⑥	18	18	—	①②	41	⑦	65	—
1980	4-151/B	11	92	37	39	20④	7	30	65	68	160
1981–82	4-151/B	11	92	37	37	20④	7	30	65	68	160
1983	4-151/B	—	92	26	37	20	7	30	65	68	162
1977–80	6-232, 258/⑨	28	105	23	23	19③	50①	33	80	105	80⑤
1981–83	6-258/C	11	85	23	23	19③	28①	33	65	105	80⑤
1977–79	V8-304, 360/⑨	28	110	43	⑧	19③	50①	33	100	105	90⑤

①—Inch pounds.
②—1977–78 50 in.-lb.; 1979, 35 in.-lb.
③—Rocker arm cap screw.
④—Rocker arm stud nut.
⑤—Lubricate bolt threads lightly before assembly.
⑥—Cold, 65 ft. lbs.; warm, 80 ft. lbs.
⑦—Hex head, 58 ft. lbs.; rear main bearing socket head cap screw, 47 ft. lbs.
⑧—1977–78, 25 ft. lbs.; 1979, 3/8 inch bolts, 25 ft. lbs., 5/16 inch bolts, 15 ft. lbs.
⑨—For V.I.N. code, refer to the "General Engine Specifications" at the front of chapter.

WHEEL ALIGNMENT SPECIFICATIONS

Year	Model	Caster Angle, Degrees		Camber Angle, Degrees				Toe In. Inch	Toe Out on Turns, Deg.①	
		Limits	Desired	Limits		Desired			Outer Wheel	Inner Wheel
				Left	Right	Left	Right			
1977	Hornet, Gremlin	−1/2 to +1/2	Zero	+1/8 to +5/8	0 to +1/2	+3/8	+1/4	1/16 to 3/16	③	38
	Others	+1/2 to +1 1/2	+1	+1/8 to +5/8	0 to +1/2	+3/8	+1/4	1/16 to 3/16	③	②
1978	Pacer	+1 to +3	+2	+1/8 to +5/8	0 to +1/2	+3/8	+1/4	1/16 to 3/16	③	35
	Except Pacer	0 to +2	+1	+1/8 to +5/8	0 to +1/2	+3/8	+1/4	1/16 to 3/16	③	38
1979	Pacer	+1 to +3 1/2	+2	0 to +3/4	0 to +3/4	+3/8	+3/8	1/16 to 3/16	③	35
	Except Pacer	0 to +2 1/2	+1	0 to +3/4	0 to +3/4	+3/8	+3/8	1/16 to 3/16	③	38
1980	Eagle	+3 to +5	+4	−3/8 to +3/8	−3/8 to +3/8	Zero	Zero	1/16 to 3/16	③	38
	Pacer	+1 to +3 1/2	+2	0 to +3/4	0 to +3/4	+3/8	+3/8	1/16 to 3/16	③	35
	AMX, Concord & Spirit	0 to +2 1/2	+1	+1/8 to +3/4	−1/8 to +1/2	+3/8	+1/8	1/16 to 3/16	③	38
1981	Concord & Spirit	0 to +2 1/2	+1	+1/8 to +3/4	−1/8 to +1/2	+3/8	+1/8	1/16 to 3/16	③	38
	Eagle	+2 to +3	+2 1/2	−1/8 to +5/8	−1/8 to +5/8	+3/8	+3/8	④	③	38
1982–83	Concord & Spirit	+3 1/2 to +5	+4 1/2	+1/8 to +3/4	−1/8 to +1/2	+3/8	+1/8	1/16 to 3/16	—	—
	Eagle	+3 to +5	+4	−1/8 to +5/8	−1/8 to +5/8	+3/8	+3/8	1/16 to 3/16	③	38

①—Incorrect toe-out when other adjustments are correct, indicates bent steering arms.
②—Matador 38°; Pacer 35°.
③—Wheels at full turn.
④—With Select Drive System, 1/8" toe-in; less Select Drive System 1/8" toe-out.

ALTERNATOR SPECIFICATIONS

Year	Alternator							Regulator			
	Make	Model	Ground Polarity	Rated Output		Field Current		Model	Regulator Test @ 120°F.		
				Amperes	Volts	Amperes ①	Volts		Ampere Load	Altern. R.P.M.	Volts
1977	Delco	—	Negative	37	—	4.0–4.5	—	1116387④	10③	3000③	14.0–14.3③
	Delco	—	Negative	55	—	4.0–4.5	—	1116387④	10③	3000③	14.0–14.3③
	Delco	—	Negative	63	—	4.0–4.5	—	1116387④	10③	3000③	14.0–14.3③
1977–78	Motorcraft	—	Negative	40	—	2.5–3.0	—	—	—	—	13.4–14.2
	Motorcraft	—	Negative	60	—	2.5–3.0	—	—	—	—	13.4–14.2
1978–79	Delco	—	Negative	37	—	4.0–5.0	—	1116387④	—	—	13.4–14.4
	Delco	—	Negative	55	—	4.0–5.0	—	1116387④	—	—	13.4–14.4
	Delco	—	Negative	63	—	4.0–5.0	—	1116387④	—	—	13.4–14.4
1979	Bosch	—	Negative	45	—	3.5–5.0	—	④⑤	—	—	13.4–14.4
	Bosch	—	Negative	55	—	3.5–5.0	—	④⑤	—	—	13.4–14.4
1980	Delco	—	Negative	42	—	4.0–5.0	—	1116387④	—	—	13.4–14.4
	Delco	—	Negative	55	—	4.0–5.0	—	1116387④	—	—	13.4–14.4
	Bosch	—	Negative	65	14	3.5–5.0	—	②	—	—	13.4–14.4
1981–82	Delco	—	Negative	42	—	4.0–5.0	—	1116387④	—	—	13.4–14.4
	Delco	—	Negative	55	—	4.0–5.0	—	1116387④	—	—	13.4–14.4
	Delco	—	Negative	63	—	4.0–5.0	—	1116387④	—	—	13.4–14.4
	Delco	—	Negative	70	—	4.0–5.0	—	1116387④	—	—	13.4–14.4
1983	Delco	—	Negative	42	—	4.0–5.0	—	1116387④	—	—	
	Delco	—	Negative	56	—	4.0–5.0	—	1116387④	—	—	
	Delco	—	Negative	66	—	4.0–5.0	—	1116387④	—	—	
	Delco	—	Negative	78	—	4.0–5.0	—	1116387④	—	—	

①—Excessive current drawn indicates shorted field winding. No current draw indicates an open winding.
②—B192052193B B14V3.
③—At 80° F.
④—Integral regulator.
⑤—B 192052 193 EE 14v3.

AMERICAN MOTORS

BRAKE SPECIFICATIONS

Year	Model	Brake Drum Inside Diameter	Wheel Cylinder Bore Diameter			Master Cylinder Bore Diameter		
			Disc Brake	Front Drum Brake	Rear Drum Brake	Disc Brakes	Drum Brakes	Power Brakes
1977	Pacer	10	2.6	—	13/16	.945	—	.945
	Gremlin②	9	2.6	—	.94	.945	—	.945
	Gremlin, Hornet①	10	2.6	—	13/16	.945	—	.945
	Matador	10	3.1	—	⑤	1 1/8	—	1 1/8
1978	Pacer	10	2.6	—	.812	.945	—	.945
	Gremlin②	9	2.6	—	.94	.945	—	.945
	AMX, Concord	10	2.6	—	.812	.945	—	.945
	Matador	10	3.1	—	⑤	1 1/8	—	1 1/8
1979	Pacer	10	2.6	—	.81	.94	—	.94
	AMX	10	2.6	—	.94	.94	—	.94
	Concord②	10	2.6	—	.94	.94	—	.94
	Spirit②	9	2.6	—	.94	.94	—	.94
	Concord & Spirit①	10	2.6	—	.81	.94	—	.94
1980	AMX	10	2.6	—	.94	.94	—	.94
	Pacer	10	2.6	—	.81	.94	—	.94
1980–81	Concord	9④	2.6	—	.94	.94	—	.94
	Eagle	10	2.6	—	.94	.94	—	.94
	Spirit	9③	2.6	—	.94	.94	—	.94
1982–83	Concord	9④	2.6	—	.94	.94	—	.94
	Eagle	10	2.6	—	.94	.94	—	.94
	Spirit	9③	2.6	—	.94	.94	—	.94

① —Models equipped w/6 cyl. or V8 engines.
② —Models equipped w/4 cyl. engine.
③ —Spirit GT models w/rally tuned suspension, 10".
④ —Concord sta. wag. w/6 cyl. engine, 10."
⑤ —Exc. sta. wag., 7/8"; sta. wag. 15/16".

COOLING SYSTEM & CAPACITY DATA

Year	Model or Engine/V.I.N.	Cooling Capacity, Qts.		Radiator Cap Relief Pressure, Lbs.	Thermo. Opening Temp.	Fuel Tank Gals.	Engine Oil Refill Qts. ①	Transmission Oil			Rear Axle Oils Pint
		Less A/C	With A/C					3 Speed Pints	4 & 5 Speed Pints	Auto. Trans. Qts. ②	
1977	4-121/G Gremlin	6 1/2	6 1/2	14	189	15	4	—	2.4	7.1	3
	6-232, 258/⑲ Gremlin	11	14	15	195	21	4	3 1/2	3 1/2	8 1/2	3
	6-232, 258/⑲ Hornet	11	11 1/2	15	195	22	4	3 1/2	3 1/2	8 1/2	3
	6-232, 258/⑲ Matador	⑪	⑪	15	195	⑫	4	—	—	8 1/2	4
	6-232, 258/⑲ Pacer	14	14	15	195	22	4	3 1/2	3 1/2	8 1/2	3
	V8-304/H Hornet	16	16	15	195	22	4	3 1/2	3 1/2	8 1/2	4
	V8-304/H Matador	⑭	⑭	15	195	⑫	4	—	—	8 1/2	4
	V8-360/N Matador	⑭	⑭	15	195	⑫	4	—	—	9 1/2	4
1978	4-121/G Gremlin	6 1/2	6 1/2	14	190	④	3 1/2⑤	—	2.4	7.1	3
	6-232, 258/⑲ Gremlin	11	14	14	195	⑬	4	3	3.3	8.5	3
	6-232, 258/⑲ Concord & AMX	11	14	14	195	⑬	4	3	3.3	8.5	3
	6-232, 258/⑲ Matador	⑪	⑪	14	195	⑯	4	—	—	8.5	4
	6-232, 258/⑲ Pacer	14	14	14	195	20	4	3	3.3	8.5	3
	V8-304/H Concord & AMX	18	18	14	195	22	4	3	—	8.5	4
	V8-304/H Pacer	18	18	14	195	20	4	—	—	8.5	4
	V8-360/N Matador	⑧	⑧	14	195	⑯	4	—	—	8.2	4

Continued

COOLING SYSTEM & CAPACITY DATA—Continued

Year	Model or Engine/V.I.N.	Cooling Capacity, Qts.		Radiator Cap Relief Pressure, Lbs.	Thermo. Opening Temp.	Fuel Tank Gals.	Engine Oil Refill Qts. ①	Transmission Oil			Rear Axle Oils Pint
		Less A/C	With A/C					3 Speed Pints	4 & 5 Speed Pints	Auto. Trans. Qts. ②	
1979	4-121/G AMX, Spirit	6½	6½	14	190	21	3½⑤	3	2.4	7.1	3
	4-121/G Concord	6½	6½	14	190	22	3½⑤	3	2.4	7.1	3
	6-232, 258/⑲ AMX, Spirit	11	14	14	195	21	4	3	3.3	8.5	3
	6-232, 258/⑲ Condord	11	14	14	195	22	4	3	3.3	8.5	3
	6-232, 258/⑲ Pacer	14	14	14	195	21	4	3	3.3	8.5	3
	V8-304/H AMX & Spirit	18	18	14	195	21	4	—	3.3	8.5	3
	V8-304/H Concord	18	18	14	195	22	4	—	3.3	8.5	3
	V8-304/H Pacer	18	18	14	195	21	4	—	3.3	8.5	3
1980	4-151/B Spirit & Concord	6.5	6.5	14	195	13⑦	4⑨	—	3.3	7.1	3
	6-258/C Spirit, AMX & Concord	11	14	14	195	21⑦	4	—	3.3	8.5	3
	6-258/C Pacer	14	14	14	195	21	4	—	3.3	8.5	3
	6-258/C Eagle	11	14	14	195	22	4	—	—	8.5⑥	3③
1981	4-151/B Spirit & Concord	6.5	6.5	15	195	21⑦	3⑨	—	3.3	7.1	3
	4-151/B Eagle	6.5	6.5	15	195	22⑰	3⑨	—	3.3⑥	7.1⑥	3③
	6-258/C Spirit & Concord	11⑮	14	15	195	21⑦	4	—	3.3	8.5	3
	6-258/C Eagle	14	14	15	195	22⑰	4	—	3.3⑥	8.5⑥	3③
1982	4-151/B Spirit & Concord	6.5	6.5	15	195	21⑦	3⑨	—	⑱	7.1	3
	4-151/B Eagle	6.5	6.5	15	195	22⑰	3⑨	—	⑱⑥	7.1⑥	3③
	6-258/C Spirit & Concord	11⑮	14	15	195	21⑦	4	—	⑱	8.5	3
	6-258/C Eagle	11⑮	14	15	195	22⑰	4	—	⑱⑥	8.5⑥	3③
1983	4-151/B Eagle	6.5	6.5	15	195	⑩	3⑨	—	⑱⑥	7.1⑥	3③
	6-258/C Spirit & Concord	11⑮	14	15	195	21⑦	4	—	⑳	8.5	3
	6-258/C Eagle	14	14	15	195	⑩	4	—	⑱⑥	8.5⑥	3③

①—Add one quart with filter change.
②—Approximate. Make final check with dipstick.
③—Front Axle, 2.5 pts.
④—With man. trans., 13 gals.; with auto. trans., 15 gals.
⑤—Add ½ qt. with filter change.
⑥—Transfer Case, 3.0 qts.
⑦—Concord, 22 gal.
⑧—Coupe 17½ qts.; Sedan & Sta. Wag., 15½ qts.

⑨—With or without filter change.
⑩—Except SX-4, 22 gals.; SX-4, 21 gals.
⑪—Coupe, 13½ qts.; sedan & wagon 11½ qts.
⑫—Except wagon, 24½ gals.; wagon, 21 gals.
⑬—Gremlin, 21 gals.; Concord, 22 gals.
⑭—Sedan & wagon: V8-304 16½ qts. V8-360 15½ qts. Add 2 quarts with coolant recovery system; Coupe models: V8-304 18½ qts. V8-360 17½ qts.
⑮—With heavy duty cooling system, 14 qts.

⑯—Except Sta. wag., 25 gals.; sta. wag., 21 gals.
⑰—Kammback & SX-4, 21 gals.
⑱—Four speed man. trans., 3.5 pts.; five speed man. trans., 4.0 pts.
⑲—For V.I.N. code, refer to the "General Engine Specifications" at the front of chapter.
⑳—Four speed man. trans., 4 pts.; five speed man. trans., 4.5 pts.
㉑—Includes filter.

Electrical Section

STARTER, REPLACE

1980–83 4-151

1. Disconnect battery ground cable, then remove starter motor to engine brace. On Eagle models it may be necessary to remove an additional brace to remove starter motor.
2. Remove two starter motor to engine attaching bolts, then lower starter motor and disconnect wiring from solenoid.
3. Remove starter motor from vehicle.
4. Reverse procedure to install. Reinstall any shims that were removed.

Except 1980–83 4-151

1. Disconnect battery ground cable.
2. Disconnect cable from starter motor terminal.
3. Remove attaching bolts and remove starter.
4. Reverse procedure to install.

IGNITION LOCK, REPLACE

1. Remove turn signal switch as described further on.
2. Place key lock in "Lock" position and using a small flat blade screwdriver to depress the lock cylinder retaining tab, remove the lock cylinder, Fig. 1.
3. Reverse procedure to install.

IGNITION SWITCH, REPLACE

NOTE: On Pacer models, it may be necessary to remove steering tube cover and A/C duct to gain access to ignition switch. On Concord, Eagle, Gremlin, Hornet and Spirit models, remove package tray, if equipped.

Fig. 1 Lock cylinder removal

The ignition switch, Fig. 2, is mounted on the lower section of the steering column of all models and is connected to the steering lock by a remote control rod.

Removal

1. Disconnect battery ground cable.
2. Place ignition lock in "Off-Lock" position and remove switch attaching screws.
3. Disconnect switch from control rod and wiring connectors from switch, then remove switch from steering column.

Installation

1. On standard steering columns, move slider to extreme left and on tilt steering columns, move slider to extreme right. This places the switch in the "Accessory" position.
2. Place actuator rod in slider hole and install switch on steering column without moving slider out of detent. Hold key in "Accessory" position and push switch downward to remove slack in linkage and tighten screws.
3. Connect battery ground cable and check for proper operation.

LIGHT SWITCH, REPLACE

1977–83 Concord, Eagle, Gremlin, Hornet & Spirit

1. Disconnect battery ground cable.
2. Remove package tray, if equipped, and disconnect speedometer cable.
3. Remove instrument cluster bezel attaching screws and tilt bezel away from instrument panel.
4. With switch in full "On" position, press release button on switch and remove shaft and knob assembly.
5. Remove switch mounting sleeve nut.
6. Disconnect electrical connectors from switch and remove switch from vehicle.
7. Reverse procedure to install.

1977–80 Pacer

1. Disconnect battery ground cable.
2. Remove switch overlay attaching screws and pull overlay assembly rearward.
3. With switch in full "On" position, press release button on switch and remove shaft and knob assembly.
4. Remove switch mounting sleeve nut.
5. Disconnect electrical connectors from switch and remove switch from vehicle.
6. Reverse procedure to install.

1977–78 Matador

1. Disconnect battery ground cable.
2. Remove instrument cluster bezel.
3. Remove screws attaching light switch and wiper-washer bracket to instrument panel.
4. With switch in full "On" position, press release button on switch and remove shaft and knob assembly.
5. Remove switch mounting sleeve nut.
6. Disconnect electrical connectors from switch and remove switch from vehicle.
7. Reverse procedure to install.

STOP LIGHT SWITCH, REPLACE

1. Disconnect battery ground cable.
2. On Concord, Eagle, Gremlin, Hornet and Spirit models, remove package tray, if equipped.

Fig. 2 Ignition switch installation (typical)

Fig. 3 Stoplight switch. (typical)

Fig. 4 Compressing lock plate & removing retaining ring

3. On Pacer models, remove steering column tube cover and intermediate duct under instrument panel, if equipped with A/C.
4. On all models, disconnect wire connector from switch.
5. Remove brake pedal pivot bolt, nylon retaining rings, sleeve, and remove switch.
6. When installing switch, be sure dimple on switch is opposite the bushing collar, Fig. 3.

NOTE: On 1977–83 models, there are two bolt holes on the brake pedal. On models equipped with power brakes, install bolt in lower hole. On models less power brakes, install bolt in upper hole.

7. Reverse procedure to install.

NEUTRAL SAFETY SWITCH, REPLACE

Except 1980–83 4-151

1. Raise and support vehicle.
2. Disconnect wiring from switch and unscrew from transmission. Allow fluid to drain into a container.
3. Move shift linkage to park and neutral positions and check switch operating fingers for proper positioning.
4. Reverse procedure to install. Correct transmission fluid level as required.

TURN SIGNAL SWITCH, REPLACE

1977–83

1. Disconnect battery ground cable, then remove steering wheel.
2. Using lock plate compressor tool No. J-23653, depress lock plate and remove and pry round wire snap ring from steering shaft groove, Fig. 4.

NOTE: On some models, the steering shaft has metric threads and is identified by a blue colored steering wheel nut and/or a groove cut into the steering shaft splines. If shaft has metric threads, replace compressor forcing screw with metric forcing screw J-23653-4 to depress lock plate.

Fig. 5 Taping turn signal connector & wires

3. Remove lock plate compressor tool, snap ring, lock plate and directional signal canceling cam from steering shaft.
4. Place directional signal lever in the right turn position, then remove lever and directional signal switch mounting screws, Fig. 6.
5. Depress hazard warning switch and remove button by turning in counter clockwise direction.

Fig. 6 Turn signal switch

6. Remove directional signal switch wiring connector from mounting bracket on right side of lower column.
7. On Concord, Eagle, Gremlin, Hornet, Pacer & Spirit models, remove steering tube cover.

Fig. 7 Instrument cluster (typical). 1978–83 Concord, Eagle, Gremlin & Spirit

ILLUMINATING
CLUSTER SOCKET LAMP

BULB

HEADLAMP/WIPER
SWITCH ILLUMINATION
ASSEMBLY

HEADLAMP
SWITCH GROUND
TERMINAL

HEADLIGHT/WIPER
SWITCH
ILLUMINATION PRISM

HEADLAMP
SWITCH

PRINTED
CIRCUIT
BOARD

CLUSTER
LENS MASK

INTERMITTENT
WIPER SWITCH
GROUND
STRAP

FUEL GAUGE

CLUSTER
CASE

WIPER
SWITCH

TEMPERATURE
GAUGE/CVR

CLOCK

SPEEDOMETER/ODOMETER
ASSEMBLY

Fig. 8   Instrument cluster (typical). 1977 Gremlin & Hornet

8. On Matador models, remove lower finish panel.
9. Remove steering column lower bracket bolts, then loosen steering column bracket nuts.
10. Fold connector over harness and wrap with tape to avoid snagging, Fig. 5. Raise column and pull harness out of column.

NOTE: On models with tilt column, raise column and remove plastic wiring harness protector.

11. On Concord and Hornet models, with column shift, automatic transmission, use stiff wire, such as a paper clip, to depress lock tab which retains shift quadrant light wire to wiring harness connector. The shift quadrant light wire is the grey wire connected to terminal D on wiring harness connector.
12. Reverse procedure to install.

HORN SOUNDER & STEERING WHEEL, REPLACE

1. Disconnect battery ground cable.
2. On steering wheels with horn buttons, remove button by first lifting button upward, and then pulling button out. On steering wheels equipped with horn ring or bar, remove screws from back of steering wheel, then pull wire plastic retainer out of directional signal canceling cam and remove horn ring or bar.
3. Remove steering wheel nut and washer. Note alignment marks on steering wheel and shaft for use during installation. If marks are not present, paint alignment marks on shaft and steering wheel.

NOTE: Some steering shafts have metric steering wheel nut threads. Metric steering wheel nuts are color coded blue for identification and steering shafts will have an identifying groove on shaft steering wheel splines.

4. Using a suitable puller, remove steering wheel.
5. Reverse procedure to install.

INSTRUMENT CLUSTER, REPLACE

1978–83 AMX, Concord, Eagle, Gremlin & Spirit

1. Disconnect battery ground cable.
2. On 1979–83 Concord, Eagle and Spirit models, remove lower steering column cover. On models equipped with column shift automatic transmission, remove gear selector dial actuator cable from steering column shift shroud.
3. On all models, remove instrument cluster bezel attaching screws across top of bezel, above radio and behind glove box door.
4. Tip top of bezel outward and disengage tabs along bottom edge of bezel.
5. If equipped, disconnect glove box lamp wire connector.
6. Depress speedometer cable locking tab and disconnect speedometer cable.
7. Push downward on three illumination lamp housings above bezel, until lamp housings are clear of instrument panel.
8. Disconnect headlamp switch and wiper control connectors and switch lamp.

NOTE: To disconnect headlamp switch connector, lift two locking tabs.

9. Twist and remove cluster illumination lamp sockets, then disconnect instrument cluster wire connectors.
10. Remove clock or tachometer attaching screws, if equipped. It is not necessary to remove clock adjusting knob.
11. Disconnect clock or tachometer feed wires from circuit board, if equipped.
12. Remove cluster housing and circuit board to bezel attaching screws.
13. Remove cluster housing and circuit board assembly from bezel, Fig. 7. If equipped with clock or tachometer, position aside as necessary.

14. Reverse procedure to install.

1977 Gremlin & Hornet

1. Disconnect battery ground cable.
2. Remove package tray if equipped to gain access speedometer cable.
3. Remove speedometer cable.
4. Remove top and side screws from instrument panel and tilt panel forward to gain access to headlamp and wiper control switch harness connectors.
5. Disconnect fiber-optic ashtray lamp if equipped.
6. Disconnect harness connectors and fuel economy gauge vacuum line if equipped and remove instrument cluster, Fig. 8.
7. Reverse procedure to install.

1977–80 Pacer

1. Disconnect battery ground cable.
2. Remove cluster bezel.
3. Remove radio knobs and nuts, then remove radio overlay.
4. Remove headlamp switch overlay retaining screws, then pull overlay back so that speedometer cable can be removed.
5. Remove cluster retaining screws, disconnect wiring harness and gear selector cable if equipped, then remove cluster assembly, Fig. 9.

NOTE: On models equipped with automatic transmission, remove steering tube cover.

6. Reverse procedure to install.

1977–78 Matador

1. Disconnect battery ground cable.
2. Remove radio knobs, attaching nuts and bezel retaining screws.
3. Remove right hand remote control mirror control from instrument panel, if equipped.
4. Tilt bezel forward and disconnect wiring.
5. Remove bezel, then remove clock or economy fuel gauge (if used) attaching screws, pull assembly away from cluster and disconnect bulbs and electrical leads. If equipped with fuel economy gauge, disconnect vacuum line and remove assembly.
6. Using clock opening, disconnect speedometer cable from instrument cluster, and disconnect gear selector dial cable from steering column.
7. Remove cluster mounting screws, disconnect any remaining electrical connections and remove cluster, Fig. 10.
8. Reverse procedure to install.

W/S WIPER MOTOR, REPLACE

1977–80 Pacer

1. Disconnect battery ground cable and disconnect linkage drive arm from motor crankpin.
2. Remove vacuum canister and mounting bracket assembly, if necessary.
3. On models equipped with air conditioning, remove two nuts from left side of heater housing and one nut from the right side of the housing.
4. On models not equipped with air condi-

Fig. 9   Instrument cluster (typical). 1977–80 Pacer

PRINTED CIRCUIT BOARD

FUEL AND TEMPERATURE GAUGES

INDICATOR BULB LENS

SPEEDOMETER

MASK

GEAR SELECTOR DIAL (AUTO. TRANS)

CLUSTER HOUSING

LENS

Fig. 10   Instrument cluster (typical). Matador

tioning, remove two nuts and one screw from left side of heater housing and one nut from the right side of the housing.
5. On all models, remove screw from heater housing support.
6. Pull heater housing forward.
7. Remove screws from wiper motor mounting plate and disconnect wiring harness.
8. Remove attaching screws and wiper motor.
9. Reverse procedure to install.

NOTE: Ensure output arm is in parked position before installing wiper motor.

1977–78 Matador Coupe

1. Disconnect battery ground cable. Remove wiper arms and cowl screen.
2. Remove retaining clip from linkage drive arm and disconnect electrical connectors from motor.
3. Remove wiper motor retaining screws and wiper motor.

NOTE: If output arm contacts dash panel, preventing wiper motor removal, hand turn output arm so arm clears dash opening.

4. Before installing motor, be sure output arm is in park position.
5. Reverse procedure to install.

1977–83 Exc. Matador Coupe & Pacer

1. Disconnect battery ground cable. Remove wiper arms and blades.
2. Remove four screws holding motor to dash.

3. Separate harness connector at the motor.
4. Pull motor and linkage out of opening to expose the drive link to crank stud retaining clip. Raise up the lock tab of the clip with a flat bladed screwdriver and slide clip off stud.
5. Reverse procedure to install.

LIFTGATE WIPER MOTOR, REPLACE

1. Disconnect battery ground cable. Remove wiper arm and blade.
2. Remove liftgate trim pad.
3. Disconnect wiring harness and ground wire.
4. Remove nut and pad securing wiper motor shaft to liftgate.
5. Remove screws securing wiper motor bracket, then separate bracket from motor.
6. Reverse procedure to install.

W/S WIPER TRANSMISSION, REPLACE

1977–80 Pacer

1. Disconnect battery ground cable and remove wiper arms and blades.
2. Remove pivot shaft bodies to cowl screws using tool No. J-25359-02.
3. Disconnect linkage from motor output arm, then remove pivot shaft body assembly.
4. Reverse procedure to install.

1977–78 Matador Coupe

1. Disconnect battery ground cable.
2. Remove wiper arm and blade assemblies, then remove cowl screen.
3. Remove screws attaching right and left pivot bodies to cowl using tool No. J-25359-02.
4. Disconnect linkage drive arm from motor output arm crankpin by removing retaining clip.
5. Remove pivot shaft body assembly through cowl opening.
6. Reverse procedure to install.

1977–78 Matador Exc. Coupe

1. Disconnect battery ground cable. Remove wiper arms and blades.
2. Remove cowl air intake cover.
3. Disconnect link-to-motor retainer and link from wiper arm through cowl top opening.
4. Remove screws holding each pivot shaft body to cowl top.
5. Remove both pivot body and link assemblies through cowl top opening.
6. Reverse procedure to install.

AMERICAN MOTORS

Fig. 11 Heater & blower housing assembly. Pacer (Typical)

1977-83 AMX, Concord, Eagle, Hornet, Gremlin & Spirit

1. Disconnect battery ground cable. Remove wiper arms and blades.
2. Remove pivot shaft-to-cowl top nuts.
3. Remove wiper motor.
4. Slide pivot shaft body and link assembly to the left to clear right pivot shaft opening and move assembly to the right side of car to remove as a unit.
5. Reverse procedure to install.

NOTE: When installing pivot shafts to cowl top, flat side of pivot shaft indexes flat side of hole in cowl top when pivot shaft is in up position.

W/S WIPER SWITCH REPLACE

1978-80 Pacer

1. Disconnect battery ground cable. Using a small screwdriver, remove knob from switch by releasing tension on clip.
2. Remove bezel from instrument cluster by pulling toward rear of vehicle.
3. Remove four screws attaching headlamp switch overlay, then pull toward rear of vehicle to gain access to rear of w/s wiper switch.
4. Remove connector from rear of switch.
5. Remove two screws attaching switch to instrument panel, then remove switch.
6. Reverse procedure to install.

1977 Pacer

1. Disconnect battery ground cable.
2. Remove instrument cluster bezel, then the four screws from headlamp overlay.
3. Remove control knob, using a small screw driver to release spring tension on clip.
4. Remove wire connector, then the two screws attaching switch to instrument panel.
5. Reverse procedure to install.

1977-83 All Exc. Pacer

1. Disconnect battery ground cable.
2. Locate small notch at base of knob and insert a small screwdriver and apply pressure to release spring and pull knob from shaft.
3. Remove slotted trim nut from front of switch.
4. Push switch through instrument panel, then disconnect wiring harness and remove switch.
5. Reverse procedure to install.

RADIO, REPLACE

NOTE: When installing radio, be sure to adjust antenna trimmer for peak performance.

1979-83 Concord, Eagle & Spirit

1. Disconnect battery ground cable.
2. Remove radio knobs and retaining nuts.

On models equipped with C.B. radio, remove radio bezel.
3. Remove instrument cluster center housing retaining screws, then remove center housing.
4. Disconnect power and speaker wiring and antenna lead, then remove radio.
5. Reverse procedure to install.

1977-80 Pacer

1. Disconnect battery ground cable.
2. Remove radio knobs, nuts and bezels, then the radio overlay.
3. Loosen radio attaching screws and lift radio from mounting bracket.
4. Disconnect antenna lead and wire connectors and remove radio.
5. Reverse procedure to install.

1977-78 Matador

1. Disconnect battery ground cable.
2. Remove radio knobs, retaining nuts and instrument cluster bezel.
3. Loosen upper radio retaining screw and lift radio disengaging bracket from screw, and pull radio slightly forward.
4. Disconnect antenna lead, electrical wiring and remove radio.
5. Reverse procedure to install.

1977-78 AMX, Concord, Gremlin & Hornet

1. Disconnect battery ground cable.
2. Remove package tray, if equipped.
3. Disconnect fiber-optic ash tray lamp from instrument cluster, if equipped.
4. Remove ash tray and bracket.
5. Remove radio knobs and shaft nuts.
6. Remove bezel retaining screws and bezel.
7. On 1977-78 models equipped with A/C, remove instrument panel center housing and attaching screws and center housing.
8. Disconnect antenna, speaker and power lead.
9. Remove radio.
10. Reverse procedure to install.

HEATER CORE, REPLACE

1977-80 Pacer, Fig. 11

1. Disconnect battery ground cable.
2. Drain approximately 2 qts. from cooling system.
3. Remove heater hoses and install plugs in hoses and core openings.
4. Position vacuum hoses away from core housing.
5. On models with A/C, disconnect outside air door vacuum hose from vacuum motor.
6. Remove core housing cover screws, disconnect overcenter spring and remove cover.
7. Remove screws attaching core to housing and remove core.
8. Reverse procedure to install.

1977-78 Matador, Fig. 12

Less Air Conditioning
1. Disconnect battery ground cable.

Fig. 13 Centering adjusting screw location. 1978—83

Fig. 14 Centering spring adjustment. 1977

Fig. 12 Heater and blower housing assembly. Matador (Typical)

2. Drain about 2 quarts of coolant then disconnect heater houses and plug ends of hoses and core openings, Fig. 16.
3. Remove lower instrument finish panel and glove box.
4. Disconnect control cables and vacuum motor hoses.
5. On 1977–78 models, remove right side windshield reveal moulding to gain access to upper right housing attaching screw.
6. On all models, remove retaining screws and remove heater core housing assembly.
7. Remove heater core from housing.
8. Reverse procedure to install.

With Air Conditioning

1. Disconnect battery ground cable and drain cooling system.
2. Disconnect heater hoses from core and plug core tubes, Fig. 12.
3. Remove glove box and door.
4. Remove blend-air door cable from core housing and remove fuse panel.
5. Remove lower instrument finish panel.
6. Remove right windshield pillar and corner finish mouldings.
7. Remove vacuum motor hoses.
8. Remove screw attaching instrument panel to right "A" pillar.
9. Pull out right side of instrument panel and remove heater core housing assembly.
10. Remove heater core from housing.
11. Reverse procedure to install.

1977–83 AMX, Concord, Eagle, Hornet, Gremlin & Spirit

1. Disconnect battery ground cable, then drain about 2 qts. from cooling system.

2. Disconnect heater hoses and plug heater core tubes.
3. Remove blower motor and fan.
4. Remove housing attaching nut(s) from inside engine compartment.
5. Remove package tray if so equipped.
6. Disconnect wire connector at resistor.
7. On models with A/C, remove instrument panel bezel, outlet and duct.
8. Disconnect control cables from damper levers.
9. Remove right side windshield pillar moulding and the instrument panel upper attaching screws and right side cap screw at the door hinge post.
10. Remove right side kick panel and heater housing attaching screws.
11. Pull the right side of the instrument panel slightly rearward and remove the housing.
12. Remove cover and screws attaching heater core to housing, then remove heater core from housing.
13. Reverse procedure to install.

BLOWER MOTOR, REPLACE

1977–80 Pacer

Less Air Conditioning

1. Disconnect battery ground cable.
2. Remove right side windshield moulding, then the instrument panel crash pad.
3. Remove right scuff plate and cowl panel.
4. Remove lower instrument panel to pillar attaching screws, then pull instrument panel rearward and reinstall attaching screws, allowing panel to rest on screws.
5. Remove heater core housing attaching nuts and screw, position vacuum lines aside, disconnect air door, then pull hous-

ing forward and position on upper control arm.
6. Remove blower motor attaching screws, disconnect relay ground wire and resistor wiring.
7. Remove blower motor brace.
8. Loosen heater housing to instrument panel attaching nuts.
9. Pull blower motor housing rearward and downward, disconnect vacuum hoses from motors and remove blower housing.
10. Remove housing cover, disconnect wire and remove blower to housing attaching screws.
11. Remove blower from housing, then separate fan and mounting bracket from motor.
12. Reverse procedure to install.

With Air Conditioning

1. Disconnect battery ground cable.
2. Remove right scuff plate and cowl panel.
3. Remove radio overlay, then the instrument panel crash pad.
4. Remove instrument panel to right pillar attaching screws, then the upper to lower instrument panel attaching screws, located above glove box.
5. Disconnect air door cable from heater core housing and remove housing to floor pan brace screw.

6. Disconnect wires from blower motor resistor and vacuum lines from vacuum motors.
7. Remove heater core housing attaching nuts and screw, position vacuum lines aside, then pull housing forward and position on upper control arm.
8. Remove floor duct.
9. Disconnect wires from blower motor relay and remove blower motor housing attaching screw from firewall.
10. Loosen evaporator housing to dash panel attaching nuts, remove blower motor housing attaching screw from dash panel, then pull blower housing rearward and downward.
11. Pull right side of instrument panel rearward and remove blower motor.
12. Remove blower housing cover.
13. Remove blower motor from housing, the separate fan and mounting bracket from motor.
14. Reverse procedure to install.

1977–78 Matador, Fig. 12

1. Disconnect battery ground cable.
2. Disconnect blower motor wiring and cooling hose.
3. Remove blower motor attaching screws and remove blower motor.
4. Reverse procedure to install.

1977–83 AMX, Concord, Eagle, Gremlin, Hornet & Spirit

1. Disconnect battery ground cable.
2. Working in engine compartment, disconnect blower motor wire.
3. Remove three retaining nuts for blower scroll cover to which blower assembly is attached and remove blower motor and fan.
4. Reverse procedure to install.

SPEED CONTROL, ADJUST

1978–83

Centering Adjustment

This adjustment is made by turning the centering adjusting screw on the regulator, Fig. 13. If speed control engages at two or more mph higher than selected speed, turn centering adjusting screw counter clockwise a small amount. If engagement speed is two or more mph below selected speed, turn centering adjusting screw clockwise a small amount. Check for proper centering adjustment on a level road after making each adjustment.

Vacuum Dump Valve

While holding brake pedal in the depressed position, move vacuum dump valve toward pedal bracket as far as possible, then release brake pedal.

1977

Chain Linkage, Adjust

Chain linkage should never be taut. To adjust, start engine and set carburetor at hot idle with anti-stall plunger backed off so as not to affect idle speed and disconnect idle stop solenoid. Hook chain to accelerator linkage, pull taut, then loosen one ball at a time until a slight chain deflection is obtained without moving carburetor throttle or servo. After chain has been adjusted, bend servo hook tabs together and chain must be free in hook.

NOTE: Whenever adjusting chain linkage, be sure chain does not hold carburetor throttle open.

Centering Springs, Adjust

If speed control system holds speed three or more mph higher than selected speed, turn centering spring adjusting screw (C) toward (S) 1/32" or less, Fig. 14.

If speed control system holds speed three or more mph below selected speed, turn centering spring adjusting screw (C) toward (F) 1/32" or less. *Do not move adjustment screw (R).*

4-121 Engine Section

ENGINE MOUNTS, REPLACE

1. Remove nut from cushion upper stud, Fig. 1.
2. If replacing right side cushion, remove TAC flexible hose.
3. Raise engine until engine bracket clears cushion stud.
4. Remove nut from lower cushion and the cushion.
5. Reverse procedure to install.

ENGINE, REPLACE

1. Scribe hood hinge locations and remove hood.
2. Remove air cleaner and TAC flexible hose.
3. Drain coolant and disconnect battery ground cable from battery and alternator mounting bracket.
4. Remove fuel line, vapor return and canister lines.
5. Disconnect engine wiring at dash panel connectors.
6. Disconnect throttle cable and, if equipped with automatic transmission, the throttle valve linkage.
7. Disconnect upper radiator hose from radiator.
8. On models equipped with A/C, remove service valve covers and front seat valves. Loosen nuts attaching service valve to compressor head and allow compressor charge to bleed off. Remove service valves and cap compressor ports and service valves.
9. Raise vehicle and remove starter.
10. Remove exhaust pipe support backet and the bellhousing shield.
11. On automatic transmission vehicles, remove torque converter to flywheel nuts.
12. On all models, disconnect exhaust pipe from manifold.
13. Disconnect back-up light switch wire from switch and clips.
14. Disconnect the lower radiator hose and heater hose from radiator.
15. On automatic transmission vehicles, disconnect transmission oil cooler lines at flexible hose.
16. On all models, disconnect wiring harness from alternator.
17. Remove all bellhousing bolts except the top center.
18. Lower vehicle.

Fig. 1 Engine mounts. 4-121

19. Remove screw securing cold air induction manifold to radiator.
20. Remove radiator attaching screws and move radiator approximately one inch toward the left side. Rotate radiator and remove with shroud attached.
21. Remove tie from upper heater hose, then disconnect hose from heater and secure to engine.
22. Pull back-up light harness upward and secure to engine.
23. Disconnect hoses from power steering gear, if equipped, and secure to engine.
24. On automatic transmission vehicles, remove transmission filler tube support screws.
25. On all models, remove engine mount cushion nuts on both sides.
26. Raise engine with suitable lifting equipment to clear support cushion studs.
27. Support transmission with a suitable jack and remove the top center bolt from bellhousing.

CYLINDER HEAD, REPLACE

1. Disconnect battery ground cable and drain coolant.
2. Remove air cleaner, TAC vacuum motor and valve assembly, and flexible hoses.
3. Disconnect upper radiator hose from radiator.
4. Remove bypass hose from bottom of thermostat housing.
5. Remove accessory drive belts.
6. Remove camshaft drive belt guard and the camshaft drive belt.
7. Remove fan spacer and pulley.
8. Remove air pump.
9. Remove alternator pivot screw.
10. Remove air pump front bracket.

Fig. 2 Cylinder head tightening sequence

Fig. 3 Valve train

11. Disconnect exhaust pipe from manifold and the air hose from diverter valve.
12. Disconnect heater hose from rear of head.
13. Remove EGR tube to bellhousing screw.
14. Disconnect the following wiring connectors: temperature sender, oil pressure sender, electric choke, throttle solenoid, PCV valve solenoid, distributor primary and ignition secondary to coil.
15. Disconnect fuel line at bottom of intake manifold bracket, then remove screw from bottom of bracket.
16. Disconnect accelerator cable.
17. Disconnect power brake booster vacuum hose, if equipped.
18. Disconnect fuel return line from filter.
19. Disconnect intake manifold inlet and outlet hoses.
20. Disconnect canister to carburetor hoses from carburetor and the PCV hose from block.
21. Remove cylinder head cover.
22. Remove cylinder head bolts in reverse order of tightening sequence, Fig. 2.
23. Remove cylinder head from engine.
24. Reverse procedure to install. Torque cylinder head bolts in sequence, Fig. 2

VALVE ARRANGEMENT

Front to Rear
4-121 .... I-E-I-E-I-E-I-E

CAM LOBE LIFT SPEC.

Year	Engine	Intake	Exhaust
1977–78	4-121	.400	.380
1979	4-121	.396	.366

Cylinder head assembly

VALVE TIMING

Intake Opens Before TDC

Year	Engine	Degrees
1977–78	4-121	41.8
1979	4-121	25

TAPPETS, ADJUST

These mechanical tappets are provided with a clearance adjusting screw, Fig. 3. The adjusting screw is threaded into a hole drilled into the tappet at an angle of approximately 86° to the valve stem. A flat is milled onto the screw perpendicular to the valve stem. The flat is moved .002 inch relative to the valve stem each time the adjusting screw is rotated one complete turn.

1. Remove TAC flexible hose.
2. Disconnect harness clip from cylinder head cover.
3. Disconnect ignition wires from spark plugs and remove distributor cap and position aside.
4. Remove cylinder head cover.
5. Rotate crankshaft to position No. 1 piston at top dead center, compression stroke.
6. Check clearance of the following tappets,

Fig. 4: No. 1 intake and exhaust, No. 2 intake and No. 3 exhaust.
7. If tappet adjustment is required, perform the following precedure:
   a. With adjusting screw bit, J-26810, and wrench rotate adjusting screw one complete turn until it clicks, Fig. 5. Continue to rotate the adjusting screw in complete turns until clearance is within specifications.
   b. When clearance is within specifications, check position of adjusting screw in tappet with tappet adjusting screw gauge, J-26860, Fig. 6. The gauge is marked with a band. The outside edge of the tappet must be within the band. If the gauge indicated that the adjusting screw is turned too far into the tappet, the next thicker adjusting screw must be installed. Five sizes of tappet adjustings are available and are identified by grooves on the end of the screw opposite the wrench socket, Fig. 7. The tappet must be removed to replace the adjusting screw.
8. Rotate crankshaft 360° and check and adjust the clearance of the following tappets: No. 2 exhaust, No. 3 intake and No. 4 intake and exhaust. Perform step 7 if tappet adjustment is required.

Fig. 4 Checking tappet clearance

Fig. 5 Adjusting tappet clearance

Fig. 6 Checking tappet adjusting screw position

TAPPETS, REPLACE

1. Remove camshaft as outlined under "Camshaft, Replace" procedure.
2. Remove tappets from bores by lifting upward.
3. Lubricate new tappets with AMC Engine Oil Supplement or suitable equivalent.
4. Install new tappets in bores.
5. Install camshaft.
6. Adjust tappet clearance.
7. Pour the remaining AMC Engine Oil Supplement or equivalent over the valve train.

NOTE: The engine oil supplement should remain in the engine for at least 1000 miles.

CYLINDER HEAD COVER, REPLACE

1. Remove TAC flexible hose.
2. Remove PCV valve hose from cylinder head cover.
3. Disconnect ignition wires from spark plugs, then the harness clip from the cover.
4. Remove cylinder head cover nuts and washers.
5. Clean gasket material from cylinder head and cover.
6. Install end pieces of replacement gasket in grooves of bearing caps at both ends of head, Fig. 8. Ensure the end pieces fit into

Fig. 7 Tappet adjusting screw markings

GROOVE MARKING	DIMENSION X-mm
NONE	3.00
I	3.45
II	3.57
III	3.69
IIII	3.81

the side seal slots. Also, apply silicone gasket material to all joints.
7. Install side pieces of gasket over cylinder head studs.
8. Install cylinder head cover, reinforcement strips, washers and nuts. Torque nuts to specifications.
9. Install PCV valve hose into cylinder head cover.
10. Connect ignition wires to spark plugs, then the harness clip to cover.
11. Install TAC flexible hose.

CAMSHAFT DRIVE BELT, REPLACE

1. Rotate engine to position crankshaft timing mark at "0". The camshaft sprocket timing mark should be aligned with the pointer on the cylinder head cover, Fig. 9.

NOTE: If camshaft timing mark is 180°

out of position, rotate the crankshaft 360°. The camshaft mark should then align with the pointer.

2. Loosen front pulley retaining screws.
3. Remove drive belts from alternator and power steering pump.
4. Remove cam drive belt guard.
5. Loosen tensioner retaining screw, Fig. 10.
6. Remove camshaft drive belt.
7. Install new drive belt on crankshaft sprocket.
8. Position belt in tensioner pulley and install belt on camshaft sprocket.
9. Rotate tensioner adjusting nut counterclockwise to increase tension, Fig. 10. The belt is properly tensioned when the drive side of the belt can be twisted 90° with the fingers. When checking belt tension, apply force to the crankshaft with a wrench in the counter-clockwise direction. This is done to position the belt slackness on the side of the belt being checked.
10. Maintain pressure to the tensioner pulley nut and torque the retaining screw to 29 ft. lbs. Recheck belt tension.
11. Install cam belt drive guard.
12. Install and tension alternator and power steering pump drive belts.

CAMSHAFT DRIVE SPROCKETS, REPLACE

Upper

1. Remove cam drive belt as outlined previously.

Fig. 8 Cylinder head cover gasket installation

Fig. 9 Camshaft sprocket timing mark

Fig. 10 Camshaft drive belt tensioner

Fig. 11   Replacing camshaft sprocket

2. Remove sprocket retaining bolt. Use a suitable tool wrapped in a shop cloth to prevent the sprocket from turning, Fig. 11.
3. Remove sprocket, key and washer.
4. Reverse procedure to install. Torque sprocket retaining bolt to 58 ft. lbs.

Lower

1. Raise vehicle and support on jack stands.
2. Loosen crankshaft pulley screws.
3. Remove accessory drive belts.
4. Remove crankshaft pulley.
5. Remove cam drive belt guard.
6. Loosen tensioner retaining screw.
7. Attach crankshaft holding tool, J-26867, Fig. 12, to crankshaft sprocket with the six pulley attaching screws. Remove crankshaft sprocket retaining bolt and the sprocket.
8. Remove tool from sprocket and attach to new sprocket, if replacing sprocket.
9. Install sprocket.

NOTE: The hole in the sprocket must index with the crankshaft locating pin.

10. Install and torque crankshaft sprocket retaining bolt to 181 ft. lbs.
11. Remove tool from sprocket and install crankshaft pulley.
12. Rotate crankshaft to position crankshaft timing mark at "0".
13. Rotate camshaft sprocket to align timing

Fig. 15   Front oil seal removal

Fig. 12   Replacing crankshaft sprocket

Fig. 14   Distributor drive housing installation

mark with pointer on cylinder head cover.
14. Install and tension camshaft drive belt.
15. Remove crankshaft pulley.
16. Install cam drive belt guard.
17. Install crankshaft pulley and torque attaching bolts to 15 ft. lbs.
18. Install accessory drive belts.

CAMSHAFT, REPLACE

Removal

1. Remove TAC flexible hose.
2. Disconnect ignition wires from spark plugs, then the clip from cylinder head cover.
3. Remove distributor cap with wire attached.
4. Remove accessory drive belts.
5. Remove cam drive belt guard.
6. Loosen tensioner attaching bolt and remove camshaft drive belt.
7. Remove camshaft sprocket.

Fig. 16   Front oil seal installation

Fig. 13   Camshaft & bearings

8. Disconnect the distributor primary wire and the vacuum advance hose.
9. Remove distributor housing and distributor assembly.
10. Disconnect PCV valve hose from cylinder head cover and remove the cylinder head cover.
11. Remove two 10mm screws from the No. 5 bearing cap, Fig. 13.
12. Remove nuts from bearing cap Nos. 1, 2, 3, 4 and 5.
13. Remove oil pipe, Fig. 13.
14. Remove bearing caps and the camshaft.
15. Remove distributor drive gear from camshaft with a suitable puller and install on replacement camshaft, if replacing camshaft.

Installation

1. Install camshaft.
2. Lubricate and install bearing caps.
3. Install oil pipe.
4. Install and torque nuts on cap Nos. 2 and 4 to 13 ft. lbs.
5. Install and torque nuts on cap Nos. 3 and 5 to 13 ft. lbs.
6. Install and torque the 10mm screws on cap No. 5 to 7 ft. lbs.
7. Install replacement seal on camshaft.
8. Install and torque nuts on cap No. 1 to 13 ft. lbs.
9. Install camshaft sprocket.
10. Install cylinder head cover seals and gaskets.
11. Install cylinder head cover and install

Fig. 17   Piston & rod assembly

nuts finger tight.
12. Align camshaft timing mark with pointer on cylinder head cover.
13. Install distributor housing, Fig. 14, with distributor rotor pointing to the No. 1 cylinder firing position. Install distributor cap.
14. Connect distributor primary wire and the vacuum advance hose.
15. Rotate crankshaft to position crankshaft timing mark at "0".
16. Install and tension camshaft drive belt.
17. Install cam drive belt guard.
18. Install pulley, spacer and fan.
19. Install and tension accessory drive belts.
20. Remove cylinder head cover and adjust tappets.
21. Install cylinder head cover.
22. Connect ignition wires to spark plugs and the harness clip to cylinder head cover.
23. Install TAC flexible hose and the PCV valve hose.

FRONT OIL SEAL, REPLACE

1. Remove accessory drive belts, cam drive belt guard and accessory drive pulley.
2. Loosen camshaft drive belt tensioner and remove drive belt.
3. Remove crankshaft sprocket.
4. Remove front oil seal from oil pump recess with tool J-26868, Fig. 15.
5. Lubricate seal inner lip with engine oil. Do not apply sealant to outer edge of seal.
6. Drive seal into oil pump recess with tool J-26877, Fig. 16.
7. Reverse procedure to assemble.

Fig. 18 Crankshaft rear oil seal installation

PISTON & ROD ASSEMBLY

Assemble piston to rod as shown in Fig. 17. Check side clearance between connecting rod and crankshaft journal. Clearance should be .002–.120 inch.

MAIN & ROD BEARINGS

Main bearings are available in undersizes of .25mm, .50mm and .75mm.
Rod bearings are available in undersizes of .25mm, .50mm and .75mm.

CRANKSHAFT REAR OIL SEAL, REPLACE

1. Remove transmission.

2. If equipped with a manual transmission, remove pressure plate and flywheel.
3. On all models, remove seal with tool J-26868.
4. Lubricate new seal lips with engine oil.
5. Drive new seal into position with tool J-26834, Fig. 18, until bottomed in bore. The seal should be positioned approximately 1/32 inch below the surface of the cylinder block.
6. Install flywheel and pressure plate, if removed.
7. Install transmission.

OIL PAN, REPLACE

1. Raise vehicle and support on jackstands.
2. Drain oil pan.
3. Install suitable engine lifting equipment.
4. Remove engine bracket to cushion nuts.
5. Loosen strut and bracket screws.
6. Raise engine approximately two inches.
7. Remove crossmember to sill attachments.
8. Remove steering gear idler bracket.
9. Pry crossmember loose and insert wooden blocks between crossmember and sill on both sides.
10. Remove oil pan attaching bolts and the oil pan.
11. Reverse procedure to install. Torque oil pan attaching bolts to 70 inch lbs. for side bolts and 90 inch lbs. for end bolts.

OIL PUMP, REPLACE

Removal

1. Remove fan shroud.
2. Raise and support vehicle on jackstands.
3. Remove accessory drive belts.
4. Remove accessory drive pulley and the cam drive belt guard.
5. Remove crankshaft sprocket and camshaft sprocket.
6. Remove oil pump screws and front oil pan screws.
7. Remove oil pump by prying in slot provided with a suitable screwdriver, Fig. 19.
8. Remove gasket and crankshaft seal.

Installation

1. Install new gasket.
2. Rotate crankshaft to position; oil pump lugs either vertically or horizontally to ease alignment with oil pump.
3. Cut off oil pan gasket flush with front of block.
4. Apply marking material to crankshaft lugs and install pump. Then, remove

Cylinder block assembly

Fig. 19 Oil pump removal

Fig. 20 Oil pump

Engine oiling system. 4-121

pump and observe markings and orient gears accordingly.
5. Apply silicone material to pump sealing surface and the edges of pump and oil pan.
6. Install oil pump and torque attaching screws to 87 inch lbs.
7. Install crankshaft and camshaft sprockets and the camshaft drive belt.
8. Install cam drive belt guard and accessory drive pulley.
9. Install accessory drive belts.
10. Install fan shroud.
11. Lower vehicle.

Relief Valve Replacement
1. Remove relief valve from pump, Fig. 20.
2. Remove spring and piston from pump, if not removed with valve body.
3. Install spring and piston into valve body.
4. Install valve body into pump and torque to 35 ft. lbs.

BELT TENSION DATA

	New lbs.	Used lbs.
1977–79		
Air Pump	40–60	40–60
A/C, Fan & Alternator	125–155	90–115
Power Steering	125–155	90–115

WATER PUMP, REPLACE

1. Drain coolant.
2. Rotate crankshaft to place No. 1 piston at TDC, compression stroke.
3. Remove power steering drive belt, if equipped.
4. Loosen the alternator and air pump.
5. Remove fan, spacer and pulley.
6. Remove cam drive belt guard.
7. Remove air pump bracket.

8. Remove camshaft drive belt idler pulley.
9. Remove all hoses from water pump except the thermostat hose.
10. Remove water pump attaching screws and the water pump, pulling the pump from thermostat hose.
11. Reverse procedure to install.

FUEL PUMP, REPLACE

1. Disconnect fuel lines from pump.
2. Remove pump retaining screws.
3. Remove pump, spacer and gaskets.
4. Reverse procedure to install.

NOTE: Ensure the pushrod is properly positioned against the pump actuating lever. If positioned improperly, the pump may be damaged when the screws are tightened.

4-151 Engine Section

NOTE: Refer to the "Chev. Monza • Buick Skyhawk • Olds Starfire • Pont. Sunbird chapter" for Service procedures not covered in this section.

ENGINE MOUNTS, REPLACE

NOTE: Remove fan shroud to radiator attaching screws to prevent damage to shroud.

1980–82 Concord & Spirit

Removal or replacement of any cushion can be accomplished by supporting the weight of the engine at the area of the cushion to be replaced.

1980–83 Eagle
Left Side
1. Disconnect heated air tube from air cleaner and exhaust manifold.
2. Remove bolts attaching engine cushion bracket to axle housing.
3. Remove engine mount through bolt, then

support engine using a suitable jack.
4. Remove engine cushion support bracket, then remove engine mount attaching bolts and engine mount.
5. Reverse procedure to install. Torque engine mount to engine bolts to 33 ft lbs., cushion support bracket to engine bolts to 40 ft. lbs. and engine mount through bolt to 45 ft. lbs.

Right Side
1. Disconnect battery ground cable, then loosen left hand side engine mount through bolt.
2. Loosen bolts attaching engine cushion bracket to axle housing.
3. Remove right side engine mount through bolt, then remove engine cushion to bracket attaching bolts.
4. Disconnect axle tube at right hand side, then disconnect axle at pinion support.
5. Position a suitable jack under engine and raise engine slightly, then remove engine mount.
6. Reverse procedure to install. Torque en-

gine mount to engine bolts to 33 ft. lbs., cushion bracket bolts to 40 ft. lbs. and engine mount through bolts to 45 ft. lbs.

ENGINE, REPLACE

1980–82 Concord & Spirit

NOTE: On these models, the engine and transmission are removed as an assembly.

1. Disconnect battery ground cable, then drain cooling system.
2. Disconnect upper and lower radiator hoses at radiator.
3. Mark location of hinges on hood, then remove hood.
4. Remove air cleaner, fan and fan shroud.
5. On models equipped with automatic transmission, disconnect fluid cooler lines from radiator.
6. Remove radiator to support attaching

bolts, then remove radiator.

7. Remove power steering pump drive belt, if equipped.
8. On models less A/C, disconnect wire connector from alternator.
9. On models with A/C, remove compressor and condenser attaching bolts, then position compressor and condenser out of way with refrigerant lines connected. Remove evaporator to dryer line from sill clips.
10. Disconnect heater hose from intake manifold, then remove throttle cable clip and remove cable from bracket.
11. On models with A/C, disconnect wire connector from alternator and pull wiring through tube.
12. Disconnect pressure and return hoses from power steering gear, if equipped.
13. Disconnect module control solenoid, choke heater, idle speed solenoid and temperature sending unit wire connectors.
14. Detach dipstick tube from exhaust manifold, then remove tube and dipstick from block.
15. Remove engine mount nuts at crossmember and ground cable from left hand engine cushion bracket at engine.
16. Disconnect fuel hose from steel tube on right hand frame side rail.
17. Disconnect wiring from starter solenoid, distributor and oil pressure sending unit.
18. Loosen crossmember attaching bolts and lower crossmember slightly, then remove transmission oil cooler lines, if equipped, speedometer cable from transmission, transmission linkage, backup light switch wire connector, transmission rear mount and crossmember.
19. Disconnect exhaust pipe from exhaust manifold, then suspend exhaust pipe from strut rod bushing with wire.
20. On models equipped with manual transmission, disconnect clutch linkage.
21. Mark propeller shaft and pinion flange so they can be installed in the same position, then remove propeller shaft.
22. Using a suitable engine lifting device, remove engine and transmission from vehicle.
23. Reverse procedure to install.

1980–83 Eagle

NOTE: On these models, the engine is removed separately from the transmission.

1. Refer to the 1980–82 Concord and Spirit Engine, Replace procedure and perform steps 1 through 14.
2. Remove left front engine mount bracket

to axle housing attaching bolts.

3. Raise and support vehicle, then remove splash shield and disconnect both half shafts from front axle. Compress half shafts inward, toward wheels and secure to frame side sills with wire.
4. Mark front drive shaft so it can be installed in the same position, then remove front driveshaft.
5. Using a suitable jack, support front axle, then disconnect axle at right hand tube support and at pinion end of axle.
6. Disconnect axle vent tube, then remove front axle.
7. Remove axle support bracket from cylinder block, then remove starter motor and shims.
8. Disconnect wiring from distributor, oil pressure sending unit and backup light switch.
9. Disconnect fuel hose from steel line.
10. On models with manual transmission, disconnect clutch release cylinder from clutch housing. Position a wooden block between transfer case and skid plate, then remove clutch housing to engine attaching bolts.
11. On models with automatic transmission, disconnect manual linkage, then remove converter housing inspection cover and remove converter to flywheel attaching nuts. Remove converter housing to engine attaching bolts.
12. Disconnect exhaust pipe from exhaust manifold, then lower vehicle.
13. Remove engine mount attaching bolts, then attach a suitable engine lifting device and raise engine slightly.
14. Remove left engine mount bracket, then remove engine from vehicle.
15. Reverse procedure to install.

OIL PAN, REPLACE

1. Disconnect battery ground cable, then remove fan shroud attaching screws and slide shroud toward engine.
2. Raise vehicle and support at frame side sills, then drain crankcase.
3. On Eagle models proceed as follows:
   a. Using a suitable jack, support front axle.
   b. Mark front drive shaft so it can be installed in the same position, then remove drive shaft.
   c. Disconnect both half shafts from axle. Compress shafts inward, toward wheels, and secure to frame side sills with wire.
   d. Disconnect axle assembly at right hand axle tube, at left hand engine mount and at pinion mount.
   e. Lower axle assembly slightly and dis-

connect vent tube, then remove axle assembly.

4. Remove starter motor, then remove flywheel housing inspection cover.
5. Remove engine mount to crossmember attaching nuts.
6. Position a suitable jack under vibration damper and raise engine approximately 1 to 2 inches.
7. Remove crossmember right hand nut and screws and loosen left hand nut, then lower right side of front crossmember.
8. Remove oil pan attaching bolts, then pry crossmember downward on right side and remove oil pan.
9. Reverse procedure to install.

FUEL PUMP, REPLACE

1981–83 Eagle

1. Disconnect battery ground cable.
2. Remove alternator and harness as an assembly and position aside, then disconnect mounting bracket from cylinder block and intake manifold.
3. Loosen bottom bolt of intake manifold-to-right side engine cushion bracket and move bracket toward fender panel.
4. Disconnect carburetor vent hose and position aside.
5. Temporarily move coolant hoses to heater core to gain clearance, then disconnect vacuum hoses after tagging them.
6. Disconnect fuel inlet pipe at fuel pump, then disconnect fuel pump-to-carburetor pipe at pump.
7. Install engine holding fixture and remove right engine cushion through bolt and raise engine slightly.
8. Raise and support vehicle.
9. Disconnect right side engine cushion bracket from block and axle bracket, then lower vehicle.
10. Raise engine and position bracket to gain access clearance to fuel pump bolts, then remove fuel pump bolts and fuel pump.
11. Clean all gasket material from fuel pump-to-block mating surface, then install new gasket and fuel pump and torque to 15 ft. lbs.
12. Connect fuel pipes to fuel pump.
13. Connect engine cushion bracket to cylinder block and axle bracket, then lower engine onto cushion and remove holding fixture.
14. Install engine cushion through bolt and nut, then connect vacuum hoses and route heater hoses to original locations.
15. Install intake manifold-to-cushion bracket.
16. Install alternator mounting bracket and alternator, then install and adjust belts and reconnect battery ground cable.

Six Cylinder & V8 Engine Section

Fig. 1   Engine mounts. 1978-79 Pacer V8-304

Fig. 2   Engine mounts. 1977-79 V8 except Pacer (typical)

ENGINE MARKINGS

A letter code is used to denote size of the bore, main bearings and rod bearings. On V8 engines, this code is stamped on the engine code tag. On six cylinder engines, this code is located on a boss above the oil filter. This letter code is as follows:

Letter "B"
  Cyl. bore .010″ oversize
Letter "M"
  Main bearings .010″ undersize
Letter "P"
  Rod bearings .010″ undersize
Letter "C"
  Camshaft block bore .010″ oversize
Letters "PM"
  Main and rod bearings .010″ undersize

ENGINE MOUNTS, REPLACE

1978-79 Pacer V8-304

NOTE: The right side mount must be removed before removing the left side mount.

Right Side
1. Remove air cleaner and ignition electronic control unit.
2. Attach suitable engine lifting equipment to engine and raise engine slightly.

3. Remove engine mount, Fig. 1.
4. Remove cushion from brackets.
5. Install cushion to brackets.
6. Install engine mount to engine and crossmember.

ENGINE REAR
SUPPORT CUSHION

WITH OVERDRIVE

REAR
CROSSMEMBER

ENGINE
FRONT
SUPPORT
MOUNTING
BRACKET

ENGINE FRONT
SUPPORT CUSHION

FRONT

FRONT
CROSSMEMBER

Fig. 3   Engine mounts. 1977-83 6 cyl. except Pacer (typical)

REAR CROSSMEMBER

CUSHION

CUSHION

BRACKETS—ENGINE-TO-CUSHIONS

CUSHION

FRONT CROSSMEMBER

Fig. 4   Engine mounts. 1977-80 6 cyl. Pacer

7. Lower engine and remove lifting equipment.
8. Install ignition electronic control unit and air cleaner.

Left Side

1. Remove right side engine mount as outlined previously, Fig. 1.
2. Remove nuts and screw attaching upper left bracket to engine block.
3. Position engine toward right side of vehicle.
4. Remove engine mount from crossmember.
5. Remove cushion from brackets.
6. Install cusion to brackets.
7. Install engine mount to crossmember.
8. Position engine to left side of vehicle.
9. Attach upper bracket to engine block.
10. Install right side engine mount.

Exc. Pacer w/V8-304

Removal or replacement of any cushion can be accomplished by supporting the weight of the engine or transmission at the area of the cushion to be replaced, Figs. 2, 3 & 4.

ENGINE, REPLACE

1978-79 Pacer V8-304

NOTE: The engine and transmission is removed as an assembly.

1. Scribe hood hinge locations and remove hood. If equipped, disconnect underhood lamp wire.
2. Drain cooling system.
3. Remove grille, air cleaner and battery.
4. Disconnect transmission oil cooler lines from radiator, then remove the shroud and radiator assembly.
5. Remove fan attaching nuts and the fan.
6. If equipped with air conditioning, turn service valves clockwise to front seated position. Bleed refrigerant from compressor by slowly loosening the service valve fittings. Disconnect and cap the condenser and evaporator lines from compressor. Cap compressor service valve outlets. Disconnect receiver outlet at the coupling. Remove condenser and receiver assembly.
7. On all models, disconnect vacuum hoses, cable and heater hoses from heater housing.
8. Remove heater housing.
9. Disconnect the wiring at the following locations: alternator, oil pressure sending unit, ignition coil, A/C compressor, temperature sending unit, distributor, solenoid vacuum valve, TCS solenoid control switch and throttle solenoid.
10. Disconnect the hoses or lines at the following locations: fuel pump, power brake booster, fuel filter return, carburetor vapor vents, intake manifold heater vacuum hose and power steering pump.
11. Disconnect throttle cable and bracket.
12. Attach suitable engine lifting equipment to engine.
13. Raise vehicle and drain oil pan.
14. Disconnect neutral safety switch harness, starter motor wiring and speedometer cable.
15. Remove propeller shaft from vehicle.
16. Disconnect throttle valve and shift linkage.
17. Disconnect oil cooler lines from transmission.

18. Disconnect exhaust pipes from exhaust manifolds.
19. Loosen engine rear support crossmember to body retaining nuts. Do not remove the nuts.
20. Disconnect transmission linkage at shift lever.
21. On left side of engine, disconnect engine mount from engine block.
22. On right side of engine, disconnect engine mount from crossmember.
23. Disconnect steering shaft flexible coupling and position aside.
24. Support tramsmission with a suitable jack and remove the engine rear support crossmember to body nuts loosened previously.
25. Raise engine and transmission assembly from vehicle. Remove oil cooler lines when engine is moved forward.
26. Reverse procedure to install.

1977-79 V8 AMX, Concord, Gremlin, Hornet, Matador & Spirit

The engine is removed without the transmission.
1. Mark hood hinge locations, disconnect underhood lamp, if equipped, and remove hood.
2. Drain cooling system.
3. Disconnect transmission oil cooler lines, if equipped.
4. Disconnect radiator hoses from radiator.
5. Remove fan shroud screws, then the radiator and shroud.
6. Remove fan and spacer.
7. Remove air cleaner and disconnect purge hose at canister, TAC vacuum hose at manifold and TAC heat tube.
8. Install a 5/16 × 1/2 inch capscrew through the fan pulley, into the water pump flange.
9. Disconnect alternator wiring.
10. Disconnect neutral safety switch harness at cowl and the TCS harness at solenoid control switch and solenoid vacuum valve. Open clip on intake manifold and position harness on cowl.
11. Disconnect heater hoses from heater core and intake manifold.
12. Disconnect heater and A/C system vacuum hose from intake manifold.
13. Disconnect throttle cable and remove from bracket, then position aside.
14. Remove power brake vacuum check valve from power brake unit.
15. Disconnect temperature sender wire and throttle stop solenoid wire from connector near ignition coil.
16. Disconnect TCS solenoid control switch and the transmission cooler lines, if equipped.
17. Disconnect distributor leads, primary leads at coil and ground wire from coil bracket.
18. Remove fuel return hose from fuel filter.
19. Remove vapor canister and bracket.
20. Disconnect flexible fuel line from steel fuel line and plug lines.
21. If equipped with air conditioning:
    a. Remove service valve covers and front-seat valves.
    b. Loosen nuts attaching service valves to compressor head.
    c. Bleed compressor refrigerant charge.
    d. Remove service valves and cap compressor ports and service valves.
    e. Disconnect clutch feed wire.
22. If equipped with power steering, disconnect hoses from steering gear, drain res-

ervoir and cap hose fittings and gear ports.
23. On all models, raise and support vehicle on jackstands.
24. Remove starter.
25. Remove exhaust flange nuts, seals and heat valve.
26. Remove converter housing spacer cover.
27. Remove lower throttle valve bellcrank and inner manual linkage support. Disconnect throttle valve rod at lower end of bellcrank.
28. Remove converter attaching screws.
29. Remove exhaust support screws at transmission extension housing bracket, then lower the exhaust system.
30. Remove front motor mount to block attaching bolts.
31. Remove the four upper converter housing screws and loosen the lower screws.
32. Remove throttle cable housing retainer bracket.
33. Install suitable engine lifting equipment.
34. Slightly raise engine and support transmission with a suitable jack.
35. Remove the remaining converter housing screws.
36. Remove engine from vehicle.
37. Reverse procedure to install.

1977-83 Six Cyl. AMX, Concord, Eagle, Hornet, Matador & Spirit

The engine is removed without the transmission as follows:
1. Drain cooling system.
2. Mark hood hinge locations, disconnect underhood lamp, if equipped, and remove hood.
3. Disconnect battery cables and remove battery.
4. Disconnect alternator wiring and the ignition coil, distributor and oil pressure sender leads.
5. Remove TCS switch bracket from cylinder block, if equipped.
6. Disconnect flexible fuel line from fuel pump and plug line and pump port.
7. Disconnect engine ground strap.
8. Remove the right front engine support cushion to bracket screw.
9. If equipped with air conditioning:
    a. Remove service valve covers and front-seat valves.
    b. Loosen service valve to compressor attaching nuts.
    c. Bleed compressor refrigerant charge.
    d. Remove service valves and cap compressor ports and service valves.
    e. Disconnect clutch feed wire.
10. Remove starter.
11. Remove air cleaner and disconnect purge hose from canister and TAC vacuum hose from manifold, if equipped.
12. Disconnect throttle stop solenoid lead, if equipped.
13. Disconnect fuel return hose from fuel filter and the carburetor bowl vent hose from canister.
14. Disconnect throttle cable and remove from bracket. Disconnect throttle valve rod at carburetor and the bellcrank.
15. Disconnect heater and air conditioning system vacuum hose from intake manifold.
16. Disconnect temperature sender wire and TCS vacuum solenoid wiring harness.
17. Disconnect radiator hoses from radiator and the heater hoses from engine.
18. Disconnect transmission oil cooler lines from radiator, if equipped.
19. Remove fan shroud attaching screws,

Fig. 5 Cylinder head tightening sequence 6-232, 258 engines. The No. 11 bolt must be sealed to prevent coolant leakage.

Fig. 6 Manifold tightening sequence. 1977–80 6-232 & 258

Fig. 7 Manifold tightening sequence. 1981–83 6-258

then the radiator and shroud.
20. Remove fan and spacer. Install a 5/16 × 1/2 inch capscrew through fan pulley, into water pump flange.
21. Remove power brake vacuum check valve from power brake unit, if equipped.
22. If equipped with power steering, disconnect hoses from gear and drain reservoir. Cap gear ports and hoses.
23. Remove transmission filler tube bracket screw, if equipped.
24. Raise and support vehicle on jackstands.
25. If equipped with automatic transmission:
    a. Remove converter housing spacer cover.
    b. Remove converter attaching screws.
    c. Remove exhaust pipe support from converter housing. This also supports the inner end of the transmission linkage.
26. If equipped with manual transmission:
    a. Remove clutch housing cover and clutch bellcrank inner support screws.
    b. Disconnect springs and remove bellcrank.
    c. Remove outer bellcrank to strut rod bracket retainer.
    d. Disconnect back-up lamp switch wiring harness under hood at dash panel to gain access to clutch housing screw.
27. On all models, remove engine mount cushion to bracket screws.
28. On Eagle models proceed as follows:
    a. Support axle assembly, then remove half shaft to axle flange attaching bolts.
    b. Compress half shafts inward, toward wheels, and secure to frame side sills with wire.
    c. Remove axle bracket attaching bolts at axle tube and right hand engine mount, then remove axle bracket.
    d. Remove axle bracket attaching bolts at pinion end of axle.
    e. Remove left engine mount support to front axle bracket attaching bolts.
    f. Disconnect axle vent hose, then lower axle assembly and remove from vehicle.
29. Disconnect exhaust pipe from manifold.
30. Remove upper converter or clutch housing screws and loosen the bottom screws.
31. Raise vehicle and support on jackstands.
32. Remove air conditioning compressor drive belt idler pulley and the compressor mounting bracket, if equipped.
33. Install suitable engine lifting equipment and slightly raise engine. Support transmission with a suitable jack.
34. Remove remaining converter or clutch housing screws.
35. Remove engine from vehicle.
36. Reverse procedure to install.

1977–80 Six Cyl. Pacer

The engine and transmission are removed as an assembly.
1. Mark hood hinge locations, disconnect underhood lamp, if equipped, and remove hood.
2. Drain cooling system and oil pan.
3. Disconnect heater and radiator hoses from engine.
4. Park W/S wiper at center of windshield to provide clearance for valve cover removal.
5. Remove battery.
6. Disconnect and cap transmission oil cooler lines, if equipped.
7. Remove fan shroud and radiator.
8. If equipped with air conditioning:
    a. Remove service valve covers and front-seat the valves.
    b. Bleed refrigerant charge from compressor by loosening service valve fittings.
    c. Disconnect and cap condenser and evaporator lines from compressor. Cap the service valves.
    d. Disconnect receiver outlet at coupling.
    e. Remove condenser and receiver assembly.
9. Remove air cleaner assembly.
10. Disconnect wiring at the following components, if equipped: starter, ignition coil, distributor, alternator, A/C compressor, temperature sensing unit, oil pressure sending unit, solenoid vacuum valve, TCS solenoid control switch, throttle stop solenoid and brake warning lamp switch.
11. Disconnect the following lines, if equipped: fuel pump suction, power brake vacuum supply from manifold, fuel filter return, heater and A/C system vacuum supply from manifold, carburetor pressure vent and power steering.
12. Remove carburetor and cover intake manifold opening.
13. Remove valve cover and vibration damper.
14. Disconnect accelerator cable at control cable bracket.
15. Raise and support vehicle with jackstands.
16. Disconnect exhaust pipe at manifold.
17. Disconnect transmission linkage and, if equipped, clutch linkage.
18. Disconnect speedometer cable from transmission.
19. Remove propeller shaft and cap transmission output shaft.
20. Support transmission with a suitable jack and remove rear crossmember.
21. Install suitable engine lifting equipment and support engine weight.
22. Remove engine mount bracket to front support cushion attaching bolts, then the front support cushions.

23. Lower jack from transmission.
24. Raise vehicle with a suitable positioned under front crossmember until bottom of front bumper is approximately three feet from floor, then support vehicle at that height with jackstands.
25. Remove oil filter and starter.
26. Raise front of engine and partially remove assembly by pulling upward until rear of cylinder head clears cowl.
27. Lower the vehicle and remove engine-transmission assembly.
28. Reverse procedure to install.

CYLINDER HEAD, REPLACE

Tighten cylinder head bolts a little at a time in three steps in the sequence shown in the illustrations. Final tightening should be to the torque specifications listed in the *Engine Tightening* table.

6-232 & 258

NOTE: On Pacer models, park windshield wiper blades at center of windshield to aid in removal cylinder head.

1. Drain cooling system and disconnect hoses at thermostat housing.
2. Remove air cleaner and disconnect fuel line and vacuum advance line.
3. Remove valve cover and gasket.
4. Remove rocker arms and bridged pivot assemblies. Alternately loosen each cap screw one turn at a time to prevent damage to bridge.

NOTE: Label push rods, rocker arms and bridge pivots so they can be installed in the same position.

5. Disconnect power steering pump and air pump and position pumps and brackets aside. Do not disconnect hoses from pumps.
6. Remove intake and exhaust manifold assembly from cylinder head.
7. On models equipped with A/C, remove A/C drive belt idler bracket from cylinder head. Loosen alternator drive belt, then remove alternator bracket to cylinder head mounting bolt. Remove bolts from compressor mounting bracket and position compressor aside.
8. Disconnect ignition wires and remove spark plugs.
9. Disconnect temperature sending unit wire and battery ground cable.
10. Remove ignition coil and bracket assembly.

THREADS MUST BE SEALED
TO PREVENT COOLANT LEAKAGE

Fig. 8 Cylinder head tightening sequence on V8-304 & 360. The No. 7 bolt indicated (second from front on left bank only) must be sealed to prevent coolant leakage.

ROCKER ARM

BRIDGED PIVOT

Fig. 9 Rocker arms, push rod and pivot assembly. Six cylinder & V8

LUBRICATION SUPPLY
TO PUSH ROD

Fig. 10 Hydraulic lifter identification. Six cylinder & V8

11. Remove cylinder head bolts, cylinder head and gasket.
12. Reverse procedure to install. Torque cylinder head bolts in sequence shown in Fig. 5 and torque manifold bolts in sequence shown in Figs. 6 and 7.

V8-304 & 360

1. Drain cooling system and cylinder block.
2. Remove valve cover and gasket.
3. Remove rocker arm, bridged pivot assemblies and push rods. Alternately loosen cap screws one turn at a time to prevent damage to bridge pivots.

NOTE: Label push rods, rocker arms and bridged pivot assemblies so they can be installed in the same position.

4. Disconnect ignition wires and remove spark plugs.
5. Remove intake and exhaust manifolds, then loosen all drive belts.
6. If right hand cylinder head is to be removed, remove battery ground cable from cylinder head. Detach alternator support brace from cylinder head. On models equipped with A/C, remove compressor mounting bracket from cylinder head.
7. If left hand cylinder head is to be removed, detach air pump and power steering pump mounting bracket, if equipped, from cylinder head.
8. Remove cylinder head bolts, cylinder head and gasket.
9. Reverse procedure to install. Torque cylinder head bolts in sequence shown in Fig. 8.

VALVE ARRANGEMENT

Front to Rear

All V8s	E-I-I-E-I-I-E
6-232, 258	E-I-I-E-I-E-E-I-E-I-I-E

VALVE LIFT SPECS.

Year	Engine	Intake	Exhaust
1977–79	6-232 & 258		
	1 Bbl. Carb.	.375	.375
1977–79	6-258		
	2 Bbl. Carb.	.400	.400
1980–83	6-258	.405	.405
1977–79	V8-304, 360	.430	.430

VALVE TIMING

Intake Opens Before TDC

Year	Engine	Degrees
1977–80	Six①	12.12
1977–80	Six②	14.58
1981–83	Six②	9
1977–78	V8-304, 360	14¾

①—1 barrel carb.
②—2 barrel carb.

ROCKER ARMS

All engines have the intake and exhaust rocker arms pivoting on a bridged pivot assembly which is secured to the cylinder head by two cap screws, Fig. 9. When installing cap screws, turn each screw one turn at a time to avoid breaking the bridge. Torque cap screws to 19 ft. lbs.

Lock Ring
Plunger Cap
Push Rod Socket
Metering Disc
Plunger
Valve Seat
Valve
Valve Spring
Valve Retainer
Plunger Return Spring
Tappet Body

Fig. 11 Hydraulic valve lifter

The push rods are hollow, serving as oil galleries for lubricating each individual rocker arm assembly. Prior to installing, the push rods should be cleaned thoroughly, inspected for wear and deposits which may restrict the flow of oil to the rocker arm.

The push rods also serve as guides to maintain correct rocker arm to valve stem relationship; therefore, a contact pattern on the push rods where they contact the cylinder head is normal.

Lubrication to each rocker arm is supplied by the corresponding hydraulic valve lifter. A metering system located in each valve lifter consists of a stepped lower surface on the push rod cap that contacts a flat plate, causing a restriction, Fig. 10. The restriction meters the amount of oil flow through the push rod cap, hollow push rod, and upper valve train components. A loss of lubrication to the rocker arm could be caused by a restricted or plugged push rod or a defective hydraulic valve lifter.

CAUTION: Correct installation of push rods in these engines is critical and more than normal care must be taken upon installation. When placing the push rods through the guide hole in the cylinder head, it is important that the push rod end is inserted in the plunger cap socket. It is possible that the push rod may seat itself on the edge of the plunger cap which will restrict valve lifter rotation and lubrication to rocker arms.

It is recommended that, just prior to installation of the cylinder head covers, the engine be operated and the supply of lubrication to each rocker arm be visually inspected. If inspection reveals that an individual rocker arm is not being supplied with lubrication, the push rod and/or valve lifter must be inspected to determine the cause.

VALVE GUIDES

Excessive valve stem-to-guide clearance will cause lack of power, rough idling and noisy valves, and may cause valve breakage. Insufficient clearance will result in noisy and sticky functioning of valves and disturb engine smoothness of operation.

Fig. 12 Timing chain cover assembly. V8-304, 360 engines

Timing Chain Cover Gasket

Timing Chain Cover

Vibration Damper

Engine Accessory Drive Pulley

Oil Slinger

Timing Chain Cover Oil Seal

Valve stem-to-guide clearances are listed in the *Engine Valve Specifications* table. By using a micrometer and a suitable telescope hole gauge, check the diameter of the valve stem in three places (top, center and bottom). Insert telescope hole gauge in valve guide bore, measuring at the center. Subtract the highest reading of valve stem diameter from valve guide bore center diameter to obtain valve-to-guide clearance. If clearance is not within specified limits, use the next oversize valve and ream bore to fit. Valves with oversize stems are available in .003", .015" and .030".

HYDRAULIC LIFTERS

Valve lifters may be removed from their bores after removing the cylinder head. Adjustable pliers with taped jaws may be used to remove lifters that are stuck due to varnish, carbon, etc. Fig. 11 illustrates the type of lifter used.

TIMING CASE COVER, REPLACE

6-232, 258

1. Remove drive belts, fan and pulley.
2. Remove vibration damper.
3. Remove oil pan-to-timing chain cover screws and cover-to-block screws.

TIMING MARKS

Fig. 13 Valve timing. V8 engines

4. Raise the cover and pull the oil pan front seal up enough to pull the retaining nibs from the holes in the cover.
5. Remove timing chain cover gasket from block. Cut off seal tab flush with front face of cylinder block. Clean gasket surfaces.
6. Remove oil seal.
7. Place gasket in position on cylinder block. Install new oil pan front seal, cut off protruding tab of seal to match portion of the original seal.
8. Insert suitable aligning tool in cover seal bore and on crankshaft. Install cover-to-oil pan screws and tighten lightly. Install cover screws and tighten.
9. Retighten all screws and install new cover seal.

V8-304, 360

The timing chain cover is a die casting incorporating an oil seal at the vibration damper hub, Fig. 12. On 1977 models, the crankshaft front seal is installed from the back side of the cover, therefore it is necessary to remove the cover when replacement of the seal is required. On 1978–79 models, the oil seal may be installed from either side of the timing case cover, therefore it is not necessary to remove the cover to replace the oil seal. To remove cover, proceed as follows:
1. Drain cooling system completely.
2. Remove radiator hoses and bypass hose from cover.
3. Remove distributor, fuel pump, drive belts, fan and hub assembly, alternator, air pump and vibration damper, using a suitable puller.

NOTE: It is not necessary to disconnect power steering or discharge air conditioning system (if equipped). Remove units from their mounting brackets and place them aside.

4. Remove two front oil pan bolts and the eight hex head bolts retaining the cover to the cylinder block.

NOTE: Timing chain cover bolts are of various lengths. Note location of bolts during disassembly so they can be installed in original position.

5. Pull cover forward until free from locating dowel pins.

6. Remove used seal and clean seal bore and gasket surface of cover.
7. Apply sealing compound to outer surface of seal and a film of Lubriplate or equivalent to seal lips. Drive seal into cover bore until seal contacts outer flange of cover.

Installation of Cover
1. Prior to installation of cover, remove lower dowel pin from cylinder block.
2. Using a sharp knife or razor blade, cut oil pan gasket flush with cylinder block on both sides of oil pan.
3. Cut corresponding pieces of gasket from the replacement oil pan gasket set. Cement gasket to cover. Install replacement Neoprene oil pan seal into cover and align cork gasket tabs to the pan seal.
4. Apply a strip of sealing compound to both the cut-off oil pan gaskets at the oil pan to cylinder block location.
5. Place cover in position, install oil pan bolts in cover, tighten evenly and slowly until cover aligns with upper dowel. Then install lower dowel through cover. Drive dowel in corresponding hole in cylinder block.
6. Install cover attaching bolts and torque to 25 ft-lbs.

TIMING CHAIN

When installing a timing chain, see that the timing marks on the sprockets are in line as shown in Figs. 13, 14 and 15.

NOTE: All V8-360 heavy duty engines use a new double row roller type timing chain to improve timing chain durability. This new timing chain is available as a service replacement item and should be installed when timing chain failures occur to eliminate recurrence of the problem. Installation of the new timing chain requires the use of a new heavy duty camshaft sprocket and crankshaft sprocket.

CAMSHAFT, REPLACE

6-232, 258

1. Remove distributor and ignition wires and the fuel pump.

TIMING MARKS (SHOWN IN ALIGNMENT)

Fig. 14 Valve timing. V8-360 with double row roller timing chain

AMERICAN MOTORS

Fig. 15 Valve timing. 6-232, 258 engines

2. Remove radiator from vehicle. If equipped with A/C, remove condenser and receiver with refrigerant lines attached and position out of way.
3. Remove cylinder head and valve lifters.
4. Remove timing chain cover.
5. Rotate crankshaft until timing marks on sprockets are aligned, Fig. 15.
6. Remove sprockets and chain.
7. On all models except Pacer, remove front bumper or grille as required to remove camshaft.
8. On Pacer models, remove hood and raise engine sufficiently to permit camshaft removal.

NOTE: Mark hinge locations on hood panel for alignment during installation.

9. Remove camshaft.
10. Reverse procedure to install.

V8-304, 360

1. Disconnect battery ground cable.
2. Disconnect transmission cooler lines at radiator if so equipped.
3. Remove radiator and A/C condenser if equipped.
4. Remove distributor, wires and coil.
5. Remove intake manifold and carburetor as an assembly.
6. Remove valve covers, loosen rocker arms and remove push rods and lifters.

Fig. 17 Piston and rod assembly. 6-232, 258 engines

7. Dismount power steering pump.
8. Remove fan and hub, fuel pump and heater hose at water pump.
9. Remove alternator.
10. Remove vibration damper and pulley and lower radiator hose at water pump.
11. Remove timing chain cover, distributor-oil pump drive gear, fuel pump eccentric, sprockets and chain.

NOTE: Remove camshaft sprocket, crankshaft bracket and timing chain as an assembly.

12. Remove hood latch support bracket upper retaining screws and move bracket as required to allow removal of camshaft.
13. Reverse procedure to install.

PISTONS & RODS, ASSEMBLE

V8 Engines

Assemble piston to connecting rod as shown in Fig. 16. Check side clearance between connecting rod and crankshaft journals. Clearance should be .006–.018 inch.

6 Cyl. Engines

Pistons are marked with a depression notch or arrow on the top perimeter, Fig. 17. When installed in the engine, this notch or arrow must be toward the front of the engine. Always assemble rods and caps with the cylinder numbers facing the camshaft side of engine. Check side clearance between connecting rod and crankshaft journals. Clearance should be .005–.014 inch on 1977–80 models and .010–.019 inch on 1981–83 models.

PISTONS, PINS & RINGS

Pistons are furnished in standard sizes and oversizes of .002, .005, .010 and .020".
Piston pins are furnished in oversizes of .003 and .005".
Piston rings are available in .020" oversizes.

MAIN & ROD BEARINGS

Both main and rod bearings are supplied in undersizes of .001, .002, .010 and .012".

CRANKSHAFT REAR OIL SEAL, REPLACE

1. To replace the seal, Fig. 18, remove oil pan and scrape oil pan surfaces clean.
2. Remove rear main bearing cap.
3. Remove and discard old seals.
4. Clean cap thoroughly.
5. Loosen all remaining main bearing cap screws.
6. With a brass drift and hammer, tap upper seal until sufficient seal is protruding to permit pulling seal out completely with pliers.
7. Wipe seal surface of crankshaft clean, then oil lightly.

Fig. 16 Piston and rod assembly. V8-304, 360

8. Coat back surface of upper seal with soap, and lip of seal with engine oil.
9. Install upper seal into cylinder block. *Lip of seal must face to front of engine.*
10. Coat cap and cylinder block mating surface portion of seal with RTV Silicone or equivalent, being careful not to apply sealer on lip of seal.
11. Coat back surface of lower seal with soap, and lip of seal with No. 40 engine oil. Place into cap, seating seal firmly into seal recess in cap.
12. Place RTV Silicone or equivalent on both chamfered edges of rear main bearing cap.
13. Install main bearings and install cap. Tighten all caps to correct torque as listed in the *Engine Tightening Specifications* table.
14. Cement oil pan gasket to cylinder block with tongue of gasket at each end coated with RTV Silicone or equivalent before installing into rear main bearing cap at joint of tongue and oil pan front neoprene seal.
15. Coat oil pan rear seal with soap. Place into recess of rear main bearing cap, making certain seal is firmly and evenly seated.
16. Install oil pan and tighten drain plug securely.

Fig. 18 Rear main bearing sealing

Fig. 19 Engine lifting fixture

OIL PAN, REPLACE

1977–80 Pacer 6 Cyl.

1. Drain oil, then install engine holding fixture.
2. Disconnect steering shaft flexible coupling and position out of way.
3. Raise vehicle and support on side sills.
4. Remove front engine mount through bolts.
5. Disconnect brake lines from front wheel cylinders, then disconnect upper ball joints from spindles.

NOTE: Ensure shock absorber is securely attached.

---

6. Remove upper control arm and position aside.
7. Support front crossmember with jack, then remove nuts from rear mounts and swing crossmember forward.
8. Remove starter.
9. Remove oil pan and front and rear oil pan seals.
10. Reverse procedure to install.

1978–79 Pacer V8-304

Removal

1. Disconnect battery ground cable.
2. Remove air cleaner and ignition control unit.
3. Attach suitable engine lifting equipment to engine and lift engine.
4. Raise and support vehicle.
5. Remove front wheels.
6. Remove brake calipers and suspend caliper with a wire.
7. Remove upper ball joint nuts, then the upper control arms.
8. Disconnect steering shaft flexible coupling and position aside.
9. On left side of engine, disconnect engine mount from engine block.
10. On right side of engine, remove engine mount.
11. Disconnect transmission oil cooler lines.

12. Remove sway bar.
13. Lower vehicle and support crossmember with a suitable jack.
14. Remove nuts from rear crossmember insulators and lower the crossmember.
15. Raise and support vehicle.
16. Drain oil pan and remove starter motor.
17. Remove torque converter inspection cover, then the oil pan.
18. Remove gaskets and seals.
19. Clean gasket surface of oil pan and cylinder block.
20. Clean oil pan sump.

Installation

1. Install oil pan front seal to timing case cover.
2. Apply an adequate amount of RTV sealer to end tabs.
3. Apply an adequate amount of RTV sealer to gasket contacting surface of seal end tabs.
4. Install seal in recess of rear main bearing cap, seating the seal fully.
5. Apply engine oil to oil pan contacting surface of front and rear oil pan seals.
6. Cement oil pan side gaskets onto cylinder block.
7. Apply an adequate amount of RTV sealer to gasket ends.
8. Install oil pan. Torque 1/4-20 screws to 7 ft. lbs. and the 5/16-18 screws to 11 ft. lbs.
9. Install and tighten oil pan drain plug.
10. Install torque converter inspection cover and starter motor.
11. Install right side engine mount.
12. Lower vehicle and install crossmember.
13. Lower engine and connect engine mounts.
14. Remove engine lifting equipment.
15. Install ignition control unit and air cleaner.
16. Raise vehicle and install upper control arms and the upper ball joint nuts.
17. Install brake calipers and front wheels.
18. Install sway bar.
19. Connect transmission oil cooler lines.
20. Connect steering shaft flexible coupling.
21. Connect battery ground cable.

1977–83 All Exc. Pacer & Eagle

6 Cyl.

1. Disconnect battery ground cable.
2. Turn steering wheel to full left lock.
3. Support engine using a suitable holding fixture.
4. Raise vehicle and support on side sills.
5. Disconnect steering idler arm at side sill.
6. Disconnect engine front support cushions at engine brackets.
7. Loosen sway bar link nuts to end of threads, if equipped.
8. Remove front crossmember to side sill attaching bolts, then pull crossmember down.
9. Remove engine right support bracket from engine.
10. Loosen strut rods at lower control arms; do not remove screws.
11. Remove starter motor.
12. Drain crankcase, then remove oil pan attaching bolts and oil pan.
13. Clean gasket surfaces of oil pan and engine block. Remove all sludge and dirt from oil pan sump.
14. Reverse procedure to install.

1980–83 Eagle

6 Cyl.

1. Disconnect battery ground cable.
2. Drain engine oil.
3. Lock steering wheel and remove air cleaner.
4. Support engine using a suitable holding fixture.
5. Raise vehicle and support on side sills.
6. Mark for assembly reference and disconnect front driveshaft.
7. Remove engine cushion bolts.
8. Remove bolts from sill-to-crossmember and position bar aside.
9. Loosen pitman arm at gear, then loosen idler arm at steering linkage.
10. Remove bolt from steering damper at crossmember.
11. Loosen sway bar bolts and lower sway bar bolts and lower sway bar.
12. Disconnect half shafts from axle.

NOTE: Compress half shafts in toward wheels, secure in compressed position with wire attached to frame sills.

---

14. Remove bolts from right bracket at axle tube bolt bars, then remove bolts from left upper axle bracket at upper end, and bolts from pinion end bracket at pinion.
15. Remove vent hose and remove axle assembly.
16. Support crossmembers with jack and remove crossmember nuts and bolts, then lower crossmember assembly for clearance.
17. Remove starter motor, then the torque converter housing access cover.
18. Remove oil pan screws and remove oil pan.
19. Reverse procedure to install.

1977–79 All Exc. Pacer

V8-304 & 360

1. Disconnect battery ground cable.
2. Support engine using a suitable holding fixture.
3. Raise vehicle and support on side sills.
4. Drain engine oil, then disconnect steering idler arm and sway bar brackets at side sills.

Engine oiling system. 6-232, 258

Engine oiling system. V8-304, 360 engines

5. Disconnect strut rods at lower control arms.
6. Disconnect engine to body ground cable.
7. Disconnect engine support cushions at crossmember.
8. Remove crossmember to side sill attaching bolts, then pull crossmember down.
9. Remove starter motor, then remove oil pan attaching bolts and oil pan.
10. Remove oil pan front and rear oil seals. Clean engine and pan gasket surfaces.
11. Remove all sludge and dirt from oil sump.
12. Reverse procedure to install.

OIL PUMP
6-232, 258 & V8s

NOTE: When servicing oil pump on 6 cylinder engines if inlet tube is moved out of position a new inlet tube and screen assembly must be installed.

The oil pump on six cylinder models is located in the oil pan thus necessitating removal of the pan to gain access to the pump. The pump on V8 engines is an integral part of the timing case cover and it can be serviced after removal of the oil filter adapter body.

Oil pump removal or replacement will not affect distributor timing as the distributor drive gear remains in mesh with the camshaft gear.

Upon disassembly of the oil pump, place a straightedge across gears and pump body and check clearance between straightedge and pump body which should be .004–.008 inch for 1977 engines, and 1978–80 6 cyl. engines and .004–.0065 inch for 1978–79 V8 engines and .006–.004 inch for 1981–83 6 cyl. engines. Clearance between gears and pump housing should be .0005–.0025 for 1977–79 V8 engines and all 6 cylinder engines.

NOTE: The pump cover should be installed with the pump out of the engine and pump checked for freedom of operation before installation.

The oil pressure relief valve, which is built into the pump, is not adjustable, the correct pressure being built into the relief valve spring.

BELT TENSION DATA

	New Lbs.	Used Lbs.
1977–83		
Air Condition	125–155	90–115
Air Pump—		
Except 6 cyl.	125–155	90–115
With P.S.		
6 cyl. with P.S. (3⁄8 inch belt)	65–75	60–70
Fan and Power Steering	125–155	90–115

WATER PUMP, REPLACE

NOTE: On 1981–83 6-258 California engines equipped with a serpentine drive belt, the water pump and fan drive assembly will operate in the reverse rotation of an engine not equipped with a serpentine drive belt. Water pumps for use on these engines can be identified by the letters "REV" cast into the pump body, while fan components can be identified by the word "REVERSE" stamped on the fan drive and on the inner side of the fan.

1. Disconnect battery ground cable.
2. Drain cooling system and disconnect radiator and heater hoses from pump.
3. Remove drive belts.

4. On V8 models, remove power steering pump, air pump and mounting bracket assembly from engine and position aside. Do not disconnect hoses.
5. On V8 models, remove A/C compressor and bracket as an assembly and position aside if equipped. Do not discharge system.

NOTE: On some models it will be necessary to remove alternator front bracket and place alternator aside, without disconnecting wires.

6. Remove fan shroud attaching bolts, then remove fan, hub and shroud.
7. Remove water pump and gasket.
8. Reverse procedure to install.

FUEL PUMP, REPLACE

1. Disconnect fuel lines from pump.
2. Remove retaining screws and fuel pump.
3. Remove all gasket material from the pump and block gasket surfaces. Apply sealer to both sides of new gasket.
4. Position gasket on pump flange and hold pump in position against its mounting surface. Make sure rocker arm is riding on camshaft eccentric.
5. Press pump tight against its mounting. Install retaining screws and tighten them alternately.
6. Connect fuel lines. Then operate engine and check for leaks.

NOTE: When installing pump, crank engine to place camshaft eccentric in a position as to place the least amount of tension on fuel pump rocker arm. This will ease pump installation.

Clutch, Transmission & Transfer Case Section

CLUTCH PEDAL, ADJUST

Pedal Free Play

1980–83 4-151

These models are equipped with a hydraulic actuated clutch and no adjustment is required.

1977–79 4-121

1. Raise vehicle and remove screw attaching throwout lever boot to clutch housing, then the boot.
2. Loosen clutch cable locknut at transmission side of clutch housing, Fig. 1, View A.
3. Pull cable housing toward front of vehicle until throwout lever free play is eliminated, then rotate the adjuster nut toward rear of vehicle until adjuster nut face tabs contact housing boss, Fig. 1, View B.
4. Release cable housing and rotate adjuster nut until adjuster nut tabs engage clutch housing slots.
5. Torque clutch cable locknut to 25 ft. lbs.
6. Install throwout lever boot and attaching screw.
7. Lower vehicle.

Exc. 4-121 & 151

In order to provide sufficient free movement of the clutch release bearing when the clutch is engaged and pedal fully released, free pedal play should be 7/8" to 1 1/8" with desired free play of 1 1/8" for 1977–83.

Adjustment for free pedal play is made by varying the length of the beam or link to the release lever rod. Lengthening this rod reduces pedal travel; shortening it increases pedal play, Fig. 2.

CLUTCH, REPLACE

4-121

Removal

1. Remove gearshift lever bezel and slide outer and inner boots toward top of lever.
2. Fold carpet and straighten all gearshift lever lock tabs bent downward.
3. Remove gearshift lever locknut and the gearshift lever.
4. Raise and support vehicle, then remove propeller shaft.
5. Disconnect speedometer cable and adapter from transmission.
6. Disconnect back-up lamp switch wires and disengage wire harness from clips on transmission top cover.
7. Remove starter motor.
8. Loosen clutch cable locknut and back off adjuster nut to slacken cable. Slide cable toward clutch housing until cushion and cable ball can be disengaged from throwout lever, Fig. 3.
9. Remove inspection cover at front of clutch housing.
10. Remove bolts attaching catalytic converter support bracket to transmission rear support bracket.
11. Support engine with a suitable jack.
12. Remove nuts and bolts attaching transmission support cushion to rear crossmember.
13. Remove rear crossmember.
14. Support transmission with a suitable jack and remove clutch housing to engine bolts.
15. Remove clutch housing and transmission.
16. Mark clutch cover and flywheel alignment.
17. Remove clutch cover bolts, then the cover and driven plate.

NOTE: Loosen the clutch cover-bolts evenly and alternately to prevent cover distortion.

Installation

NOTE: The clutch cover is positioned on dowel pins located on the flywheel face.

When installing the driven plate and cover, the cover must be indexed with the alignment marks and be properly engaged with the dowel pins.

1. Position clutch driven plate and cover, then install the attaching bolts finger tight.
2. Align clutch driven plate with tool J-5824-01 or equivalent.
3. Torque clutch cover bolts to 23 ft. lbs. and remove alignment tool.
4. Install transmission and clutch housing assembly and torque attaching bolts to 54 ft. lbs.
5. Install rear crossmember, then the support cushion to crossmember attaching bolts and torque to 25 ft. lbs. Torque rear crossmember stud nuts to 35 ft. lbs.
6. Connect clutch cable to throwout lever and adjust as outlined previously.
7. Connect speedometer cable and adapter to transmission.
8. Connect back-up lamp switch wires and engage harness in retaining clips at top of transmission cover.

Fig. 1 Clutch adjustment. 4-121

Fig. 2 Typical clutch linkage. 6 Cyl. & V8

9. Install clutch housing inspection cover.
10. Install catalytic converter support bracket bolts, then the starter.
11. Install propeller shaft.
12. Lower vehicle.
13. Install gearshift lever. Ensure shift rail insert is facing downward and that offset side of lever fork is facing right side of extension housing before lever installation. Bend at least three lock tabs down to retain lever.
14. Install inner and outer lever boots, then the bezel.

4-151 & 1981–83 6-258

Except Eagle
1. Remove transmission as described under Transmission, Replace.
2. Remove clutch housing to engine attaching bolts, then the clutch housing.
3. Remove throwout bearing, then mark pressure plate and flywheel for reassembly.
4. Remove pressure plate to flywheel attaching bolts, then remove pressure plate and clutch disc.

NOTE: Loosen pressure plate to flywheel bolts alternately and evenly to prevent distorting pressure plate.

5. Reverse procedure to install. Position clutch and pressure plate on flywheel and install attaching bolts finger tight. Align clutch disc using a suitable alignment tool, then tighten pressure plate attaching bolts alternately and evenly to 23 ft. lbs. Torque clutch housing to engine and transmission to clutch housing attaching bolts to 54 ft. lbs.

Eagle
1. Remove transmission as described under Transmission, Replace.
2. Remove right hand brace rod and starter motor, then disconnect clutch release cylinder spring from clutch fork.
3. Remove clutch release cylinder, with hydraulic line attached, and clutch housing inspection cover.
4. Disconnect exhaust pipe at exhaust manifold, then remove clutch housing to engine attaching bolts and remove clutch housing.
5. Mark pressure plate and flywheel for reassembly, then remove pressure plate attaching bolts and remove pressure plate and clutch disc.

NOTE: Loosen pressure plate attaching bolts alternately and evenly to prevent distorting pressure plate.

6. Reverse procedure to install. Position clutch disc and pressure plate on flywheel and install attaching bolts finger tight. Align clutch disc using a suitable alignment tool, then tighten pressure plate attaching bolts alternately and evenly to 28 ft. lbs. Torque clutch housing to engine upper attaching bolts to 27 ft. lbs. Torque clutch housing lower attaching bolts and dowel bolts to 43 ft. lbs. Torque transmission to engine attaching bolts to 55 ft. lbs.

6 Cyl. & V8

Removal
1. Remove transmission as described further on.

Fig. 3 Clutch cable removal. 4-121

2. Remove starter, clutch housing, throwout lever, bearing and sleeve assembly.

NOTE: Mark clutch cover, pressure plate and flywheel to insure correct alignment during installation.

3. Remove clutch cover and pressure plate assembly.

NOTE: When removing clutch cover and pressure plate assembly from flywheel, loosen screws evenly until spring tension is released, as cover could be warped by improper removal, resulting in clutch chatter when reassembled.

4. Remove pilot bushing lubricating wick and soak in engine oil.

NOTE: Unless special clutch rebuilding equipment is available, it is recommended that the clutch assembly be exchanged for a rebuilt unit should the clutch require rebuilding. The driven disc, however, may be replaced without special equipment. If clutch rebuilding equipment is available, follow the equipment manufacturer's instructions.

Installation
1. Inspect clutch release lever height and correct as necessary. If used, lubricate pilot bushing wick with engine oil.
2. Install clutch disc and cover on flywheel and loosely install bolts. Using clutch aligning tool or transmission clutch shaft, align clutch disc.
3. Tighten cover retaining bolts several turns at a time to prevent cover distortion, then torque bolts to 28 ft. lbs.
4. Install throwout lever, bearing and sleeve assembly, clutch housing and starter.

MANUAL TRANS., REPLACE
Except Eagle

4-121
Refer to Clutch, Replace 4-121 for manual transmission removal and installation procedures.

4-151 & 1981–83 6-258
1. Remove console, if equipped, then remove gearshift lever, bezel and boot.
2. Mark propeller shaft and rear axle pinion flange so they can be installed in the same position, then remove propeller shaft.
3. Disconnect speedometer cable and back-up lamp switch wire connector.
4. Disconnect exhaust pipe, if necessary.
5. Remove starter motor, then disconnect clutch release cylinder spring at clutch fork.
6. Remove inspection cover from clutch housing, then remove bolts attaching catalytic converter support bracket to transmission rear support bracket, if equipped.
7. Place support under front of engine, then remove bolts attaching transmission mount to rear crossmember.
8. Remove nuts attaching rear crossmember to frame side sills, then remove crossmember.
9. Remove transmission to clutch housing attaching bolts, then remove transmission.
10. Reverse procedure to install. Torque transmission to clutch housing attaching bolts to 54 ft. lbs.

6 Cyl. & V8 Engines

1977–80
1. Remove knob, bezel, boot and gear shift lever.
2. Open hood and raise vehicle.
3. Mark rear universal joint and propeller shaft to ensure proper alignment at time of installation, then remove propeller shaft.
4. Disconnect speedometer cable and back-up lamp switch and TCS switch wires, if equipped.
5. If equipped with four speed transmission, release back-up lamp switch wires from clip on transmission top cover.
6. Install support stand under clutch housing to support engine when crossmember and transmission are removed.
7. On Pacer models, disconnect ground strap at support cushion bolt.
8. On all models, remove rear crossmember to frame side sill attaching nuts.
9. Remove catalytic converter support bracket, if equipped.
10. On AMX, Concord, Gremlin, Hornet and Spirit models, remove rear support cushion to crossmember attaching bolts and remove crossmember.

NOTE: On Pacer models, crossmember is removed with transmission.

11. On all models remove two lower transmission to clutch housing attaching bolts.

NOTE: On 1977–78 models, install two guide pins in place of the lower housing bolts.

12. Remove two upper transmission to clutch housing attaching bolts and remove transmission.

NOTE: Care must be taken not to damage clutch shaft, pilot bushing or clutch disc.

Eagle

4-151 & 6-258

1. Place transmission shift lever in the neutral position, then remove console, if equipped.
2. Remove gearshift lever bezel and boot, then remove gearshift lever from mounting cover on transmission.
3. Remove skid plate, then mark position of speedometer adapter for reassembly, then disconnect speedometer cable. Plug adapter opening in transfer case to prevent lubricant spillage.
4. Mark propeller shafts and axle yokes for reassembly, then disconnect propeller shafts at transfer case.
5. Disconnect backup lamp switch wire connector, then support engine using a suitable jack.
6. Support transmission and transfer case using a suitable transmission jack, then remove rear crossmember.
7. Remove catalytic converter support bracket from transfer case.
8. Remove transmission to clutch housing attaching bolts, then remove transmission and transfer case as an assembly.
9. Remove nuts from transfer case mounting studs, then separate transfer case from transmission.
10. Reverse procedure to install. Torque transfer case to transmission adapter housing stud nuts to 33 ft. lbs. Torque transmission to clutch housing bolts to 55 ft. lbs.

TRANSFER CASE, REPLACE

1980-83 With Auto. Trans.

1. Raise and support vehicle.
2. Support engine and transmission with a suitable jack or jack stand.
3. Disconnect catalytic converter support bracket from adapter housing.
4. Remove skid plate.
5. Disconnect speedometer cable and adapter from transfer case. Discard adapter "O" ring.
6. Mark propeller shafts and transfer case yoke for assembly reference. Then, disconnect propeller shafts from yokes. Secure shafts aside.
7. Disconnect gearshift and throttle linkage from transmission.
8. Remove rear crossmember.
9. Remove transfer case to adapter housing nuts.
10. Remove transfer case from vehicle.
11. Install transfer case on adapter housing.
12. Install and torque transfer case to adapter housing nuts to 33 ft. lbs.
13. Install rear crossmember.
14. On 1981-83 models, install rear brace

rod.
15. Remove jack or jack stand, supporting engine and transmission.
16. Connect gearshift and throttle linkage to transmission.
17. Connect propeller shafts to transfer case yokes.
18. Install new "O" ring on speedometer adapter, then the adapter and speedometer cable to transfer case.
19. Install skid plate.
20. Connect catalytic converter support bracket to adapter housing.
21. Check transfer case lubricant level and adjust, if necessary. Also, check transmission linkage adjustments.

MANUAL TRANS. SHIFT LINKAGE, ADJUST

1977-79 Three Speed Floor Shift

1. Place transmission shift levers in neutral and loosen second-third transmission lever retaining nut and adjustment bolt.
2. Place first-reverse shift rod in neutral position, then align second-third shift rod so shift notch is exactly aligned with first-reverse shift rod notch. Tighten adjustment bolt and nut.
3. Actuate shifter lever to assure a smooth crossover between first and second speed and for proper engagement in all gears.
4. If equipped with tilt steering column on a steering column lock which is actuated by the transmission shift linkage on 1976 models, loosen steering column reverse lockup rod trunnion locknuts to allow free movement of trunnion on rod.
5. Shift transmission into reverse and lock steering column.

NOTE: It may be necessary to rotate lower column shifter lever upward until it is in locked position.

6. Tighten lower trunnion locknut until it contacts trunnion, then tighten upper locknut while holding trunnion centered in column lever.
7. Shift through all gears to check for freedom of operation. Shift into reverse and lock column. Column must lock without any binding.

1980-83 With Manual Trans.

1. Shift transmission into neutral.
2. Remove screws attaching gear shift lever bezel to floorpan or console, (if equipped).
3. Slide bezel and boot up on gear shift lever to gain access to lever attaching bolts,

then remove bolts and remove lever.
4. Remove bolts attaching gear shift lever mounting cover to transmission adapter housing and remove cover.
5. Remove nut from transfer case mounting stud from inside transmission adapter housing.
6. Raise and support vehicle.
7. Remove skid plate and stiffening brace, or rear brace rod on 1982-83 models.
8. Remove speedometer adapter retainer attaching bolt and remove retainer, adapter and cable, then plug adapter opening in transfer case to avoid excessive oil leakage.

NOTE: Before removing speedometer adapter, mark position for reference during assembly.

9. Mark propeller shafts and axle yokes for assembly reference and disconnect propeller shafts at transfer case.
10. On 1981-83 models only, remove transfer case shift motor vacuum harness.
11. Support transfer case with transmission jack, then remove nuts from transfer case mounting studs and remove transfer case.
12. Align transmission output and transfer case input shafts and install transfer case on transmission adapter housing, then install and torque transfer case mounting stud nuts to 33 ft. lbs.
13. Remove jack supporting transfer case.
14. Connect propeller shafts to axle yokes and torque clamp strap bolts to 15 ft. lbs.
15. Install new O-ring on speedometer adapter, then install adapter and cable and retainer, torque retainer bolt to 100 inch lbs.
16. Install skid plate and stiffening brace, or rear brace rod on 1982-83 models, and torque retaining bolts to 30 ft. lbs.
17. On 1981-83 models only, install transfer case shift motor vacuum harness.
18. Check and correct fluid levels in transmission and transfer case, then lower vehicle.
19. Install nut on transfer case mounting stud inside transmission adapter housing, torque nut to 33 ft. lbs.
20. Install gear shift lever mounting cover on transmission adapter housing, then install gear shift lever on mounting cover.
21. Position gear shift lever boot and bezel on floorpan of console (if equipped), and install bezel attaching screws.

NOTE: On 1982-83 models, steps 1 through 5 and 19 through 21 apply to SR-4 transmission only.

Rear Axle, Propeller Shaft & Brakes

REAR AXLES

Figs. 1 and 2 illustrate the rear axle assembly used on these cars. When necessary to overhaul the unit, refer to the *Rear Axle Specifications* table in this chapter.

DESCRIPTION

In these rear axles, Figs. 1 and 2, the drive pinion is mounted in two tapered roller bearings. These bearings are preloaded by a washer behind the front bearing. The pinion is positioned by shims located in front of the rear bearing. The differential is supported in the carrier by two tapered roller side bearings. These bearings are preloaded by shims located between the bearings and carrier housing. The differential assembly is positioned for proper ring gear and pinion backlash by varying the position of these shims. The differential case houses two side gears in mesh with two pinions mounted on a pinion shaft which is held in place by a lock pin. The side gears and pinions are backed by thrust washers.

It is not necessary to remove the rear axle assembly. However, the underbody should be washed to prevent particles of road dirt from contaminating the parts.

REAR AXLE & PROP. SHAFT, REPLACE

1977–83

1. Remove cotter pins and remove axle shaft nuts.
2. Raise vehicle and position support stands under rear frame side sills.
3. Remove wheels and brake drum retaining screws.
4. Remove brake drums, then disconnect brake lines at wheel cylinders.
5. Using a suitable puller, remove support plates, oil seal, retainer and end play shims.

NOTE: Axle shaft end play shims are installed at left side of axle only.

---

6. Using a suitable puller, remove axle shafts.
7. Remove axle housing cover and drain lubricant, then reinstall cover.
8. Disconnect parking brake cables at equalizer.
9. Mark universal joint and rear axle yokes for reassembly, then disconnect propeller at rear yoke.
10. Remove stabilizer bar, if equipped.
11. Disconnect brake hose at body floor pan bracket.
12. Disconnect vent tube from axle tube.
13. Support axle assembly using a suitable jack.
14. On all except Matador models:
    a. Disconnect shock absorbers at spring plates.
    b. Remove rear spring U-bolts and spring plates.
    c. Rotate axle until it clears springs, then lower axle assembly and remove from vehicle.

1. BOLT
2. WASHER
3. AXLE SHAFT OIL SEAL AND RETAINER ASSEMBLY
4. AXLE SHAFT BEARING SHIM
5. AXLE SHAFT BEARING CUP
6. AXLE SHAFT BEARING
7. AXLE SHAFT
8. AXLE SHAFT INNER OIL SEAL
9. NUT
10. AXLE HOUSING
11. COLLAPSIBLE SPACER
12. PINION BEARING CUP-FRONT
13. PINION BEARING-FRONT
14. PINION OIL SEAL
15. UNIVERSAL JOINT YOKE
16. PINION NUT
17. BREATHER
18. BREATHER HOSE
19. BREATHER
20. PINION DEPTH ADJUSTING SHIM
21. PINION REAR BEARING CUP
22. PINION BEARING-REAR
23. PINION GEAR
24. DIFFERENTIAL BEARING
25. DIFFERENTIAL BEARING CUP
26. DIFFERENTIAL BEARING SHIM
27. DIFFERENTIAL BEARING CAP
28. DIFFERENTIAL BEARING CAP BOLT
29. RING GEAR
30. DIFFERENTIAL CASE
31. RING GEAR BOLT
32. DIFFERENTIAL PINION WASHER
33. DIFFERENTIAL PINION
34. DIFFERENTIAL SIDE GEAR
35. DIFFERENTIAL SIDE GEAR THRUST WASHER
36. DIFFERENTIAL PINION SHAFT THRUST BLOCK
37. DIFFERENTIAL PINION SHAFT PIN
38. DIFFERENTIAL PINION SHAFT
39. AXLE HOUSING COVER GASKET
40. AXLE HOUSING COVER
41. AXLE IDENTIFICATION TAG
42. BOLT
43. AXLE HOUSING COVER FILL PLUG
44. WASHER

Fig. 1 Rear axle assembly (typical). 7⁹⁄₁₆ in. axle

15. On Matador models:
    a. Disconnect shock absorbers from lower control arms. If equipped with air shocks, release all air pressure by opening valves before disconnecting.
    b. Lower jack and disconnect upper control arms from axle housing brackets.
    c. Pull left side axle tube downward and remove coil spring, then pull right side axle tube downward and remove coil spring.
    d. Disconnect lower control arms from axle tube brackets, then lower axle assembly and remove from vehicle.
16. On all models, reverse procedure to install.

AXLE SHAFTS, REPLACE

The hub and drum are separate units, and the hub and axle shaft are serrated to mate and fit together on the taper. Both are punched marked to insure correct assembly,

Fig. 3. The axle shaft and bearing may be removed as follows:

1. Remove rear wheel, drum and hub, then disconnect parking brake cable at equalizer.
2. Disconnect brake tube from wheel cylinder and remove brake support plate assembly, oil seal and axle shims from axle shaft.

NOTE: Axle shaft end play shims are located on the left side only.

---

3. Using suitable puller, pull axle shaft and bearing from axle tube, then remove and discard inner oil seal.

NOTE: The bearing cone must be pressed off the shaft, using an arbor press.

CAUTION: On models equipped with Twin Grip differential, do not rotate differential unless both axle shafts are in place.

SERRATIONS

1-3/16 (30.14 mm) (7 9/16 AXLE)
1-5/16 (33.32 mm) (8 7/8 AXLE)

Fig. 3   Installing hub on axle

1. BOLT
2. WASHER
3. AXLE SHAFT OIL SEAL RETAINER
4. AXLE SHAFT OIL SEAL
5. AXLE SHAFT BEARING SHIM
6. AXLE SHAFT BEARING CUP
7. AXLE BEARING
8. AXLE SHAFT
9. AXLE SHAFT INNER OIL SEAL
10. PINION COLLAPSIBLE SPACER
11. FILLER PLUG
12. FRONT PINION BEARING CUP
13. PINION OIL SEAL
14. UNIVERSAL JOINT YOKE
15. PINION NUT

16. FRONT PINION BEARING
17. BREATHER
18. BREATHER HOSE
19. NUT
20. REAR AXLE HOUSING
21. DRIVE PINION DEPTH ADJUSTING SHIM
22. REAR PINION BEARING CUP
23. REAR PINION BEARING
24. PINION GEAR
25. DIFFERENTIAL BEARING
26. DIFFERENTIAL BEARING CUP
27. DIFFERENTIAL BEARING SHIM
28. DIFFERENTIAL BEARING CUP
29. BOLT
30. BOLT

31. HOUSING COVER
32. HOUSING COVER GASKET
33. DIFFERENTIAL PINION SHAFT
34. DIFFERENTIAL PINION GEAR THRUST WASHER
35. DIFFERENTIAL SIDE GEAR THRUST WASHER
36. DIFFERENTIAL PINION GEAR
37. DIFFERENTIAL SIDE GEAR
38. DIFFERENTIAL PINION SHAFT THRUST BLOCK
39. BOLT
40. DIFFERENTIAL CASE
41. DIFFERENTIAL PINION SHAFT PIN
42. RING GEAR

Fig. 2   Rear axle assembly (typical). 8⅞ in. axle

When installing hub onto axle, install two well lubricated thrust washers and axle shaft nut. Tighten axle shaft nut until hub is installed to the dimensions shown in Fig. 3. Remove axle shaft nut and one thrust washer. Reinstall axle shaft nut and tighten to 250 ft. lbs. If cotter pin hole is not aligned, tighten the nut to the next castellation and install cotter pin.

NOTE: Do not use an original hub on a replacement axle shaft; use a new hub. A new hub may be installed on an original axle shaft providing the serrations on the shaft are not worn or damaged. Be certain that the hub and axle shaft are punch marked to insure proper alignment on installation. A replacement hub, which is not serrated, can be installed and serrations will be cut in the hub when installed on the shaft due to the difference in hardness of the shaft and the hub.

Assembly

Replace the parts in the reverse order of their removal. If the old parts are replaced and the shims have not been disturbed, the axle shaft end play should be correct when the parts are assembled. However, if a new shaft, bearing, differential carrier or housing has been installed, it will be necessary to check the end play.

The end play can be checked when all parts have been replaced except the wheel and hub. To make this check, rap each axle shaft after

the nuts are tight to be sure the bearing cups are seated. Then place a dial indicator so that its stem contacts the end of the shaft and work the shaft in and out to determined the amount of existing end play. If an adjustment is necessary, remove the outer oil seal and brake support and add or remove shims as required. When making this adjustment, add or subtract shims on left side of axle only.

NOTE: *The application of a bead of sealing material such as "Pliobond" or "Permatex" to the outer diameter of axle tube flange and the brake support contact area is recommended. The sealing material will be used in addition to the gasket for improved sealing.*

PROPELLER SHAFT VIBRATION

1. Raise and support the rear of the car at the axle and remove rear wheels.
2. Remove all undercoating and accumulated dirt from shaft.
3. With the use of an electronic wheel balancer, the propeller shaft can be balanced as follows:
   a. Place electronic pick up unit under axle housing as close as possible to pinion yoke. Use crayon or chalk to mark four equally spaced horizontal lines on the propeller shaft. To aid in identifying lines, it is suggested they be of unequal length.

NOTE: On models with an aluminum extension housing, it will be necessary to install a steel hose clamp on rear of extension housing to accommodate the magnetic pickup.

   b. Operate the car in gear at the speed of greatest vibration. Locate the heavy spot.

NOTE: Do not operate in gear for long periods as overheating may occur.

4. If electronic wheel balancer is not available, proceed as follows:
   a. Operate vehicle in gear at about 40 mph.
   b. Using a jack stand as a steady rest, slowly advance a chalk toward the spinning propeller shaft. At the instant of first contact with propeller shaft, withdraw chalk. This mark indicates the heavy spot.

NOTE: Do not operate in gear for long periods as overheating may occur.

5. Place two worm type hose clamps on propeller shaft with heads of clamps located 180° from heavy spot noted previously. Slide clamps as far to rear as possible.
6. Again operate car in gear and if vibration still exists move both clamp heads an equal distance in opposite directions to-

ward the heavy spot until vibration is at a minimum.

7. Replace rear wheels and road test car.

BRAKE ADJUSTMENTS

These brakes, Figs. 4 and 5, have self-adjusting mechanisms that assure correct lining-to-drum clearances at all times. The automatic adjusters operate only when the brakes are applied as the car is moving rearward.

Although the brakes are self-adjusting, an initial adjustment is necessary after the brake shoes have been relined or replaced, or when the length of the star wheel adjusting screw has been changed during some other serivce operation.

Frequent usage of an automatic transmission forward range to half reverse vehicle motion may prevent the automatic adjusters from functioning, thereby inducing low pedal heights. Should low pedal heights be encountered on these models, it is recommended that numerous forward and reverse stops be made until satisfactory pedal height is obtained.

NOTE: If a low pedal condition cannot be corrected by making numerous stops (provided the hydraulic system is free of air) it indicates that the self-adjusting mechanism is not functioning. Therefore, it will be necessary to remove the brake drum, clean, free up and lubricate the adjusting mechanisms. Then adjust the brakes as follows, being sure the parking brake is fully released.

Adjustment

1. Remove access slot cover from brake support plate.
2. Using brake adjusting tool or screwdriver, rotate adjuster screw until wheel is locked.
3. Back off adjuster screw one complete turn.

NOTE: To back off adjuster screw, insert a piece of 1/8 inch rod past adjuster screw and force adjusting lever off adjuster screw.

4. Install rubber access slot cover.
5. Following the initial adjustment and final assembly, check the brake pedal height to insure brake operation. Then drive the car forward and reverse, making 10 to 15 brake applications prior to road testing. This action balances the adjustment of the four brake units and raises the brake pedal.

PARKING BRAKE, ADJUST

1977–80 Pacer

1. Make sure service brakes are properly adjusted.
2. Apply and release parking brake several times.
3. Place parking lever in first notch from fully released position and place transmission in neutral.
4. Raise and support vehicle at rear axle using jack stands.
5. Loosen locknut and tighten cable adjuster until there is a heavy brake drag at rear wheels.
6. Loosen adjuster until heavy drag is just eliminated and tighten locknut.

Fig. 4 9 Inch drum brake assembly

Fig. 5 10 Inch drum assembly

1977—83 Exc. Pacer

With Adjustment Gauge J-23462
1. Make sure service brakes are properly adjusted.
2. Apply and release parking brake several times.
3. Raise and support vehicle at rear axle using jack stands.
4. Place parking brake in first notch from fully released position.
5. Place an inch lb. torque wrench on Parking Brake Cable Adjustment Gauge J-23462 and place gauge on from parking brake cable, centered between cable housing ferrule and cable equalizer.
6. Apply 50 inch lbs. of torque and note indicator reading. If reading is not within the green band, adjust parking brake at equalizer until satisfactory reading is obtained.
7. Release parking brake and check for brake drag. If brake drag is evident, inspect actuating cables and equalizer for freedom of movement and proper operation. Inspect cable condition, especially at areas where cable passes near exhaust components. Correct as necessary and readjust parking brake cable.

Without Adjustment Gauge J-23462
1. With service brakes properly adjusted, set parking brake pedal on the first notch from fully released position.
2. Tighten parking brake cable at equalizer to a point where the rear wheels are locked in forward rotation.
3. Release pedal and check for rear wheel drag—wheels should rotate freely.

BRAKE MASTER CYLINDER, REPLACE

1. Disconnect brake lines from master cylinder. Cap lines and master cylinder ports.
2. On models with manual brakes, disconnect master cylinder push rod at brake pedal.
3. On all models, remove nuts or bolts attaching master cylinder to dash panel or brake booster and remove master cylinder. On Matador and Pacer models, remove mounting bracket and boot retainer plate.
4. Install in the reverse order of removal and bleed the brake system.

POWER BRAKE UNIT, REPLACE

1. Disconnect booster push rod from brake pedal.
2. Remove vacuum hose from check valve.
3. Remove nuts and washers securing master cylinder to booster unit, then separate master cylinder from booster unit.

NOTE: Do not disconnect brake lines from master cylinder.

4. Remove booster unit to firewall attaching nuts and remove booster unit.
5. Reverse procedure to install.

Rear Suspension

SHOCK ABSORBER, REPLACE

1. With the rear axle supported properly, disconnect lower end of shock absorber from stud on mounting bracket.
2. Remove upper mounting bracket from underbody.
3. Reverse procedure to install.

LEAF SPRINGS, REPLACE

1. Support rear axle, removing tension from springs.
2. Disconnect lower end of shock absorber from stud on mounting bracket.
3. Remove "U" bolts securing spring plate and spring to axle tube.
4. Disassemble rear shackle and remove eye bolt from spring forward mounting bracket.

NOTE: On Pacer, remove nuts attaching rear hanger bracket to mounting studs on side sill and remove spring.

5. Reverse procedure to install. Replace bushings as necessary.

COIL SPRINGS, REPLACE

1. Support vehicle at frame and support rear axle with a suitable jack.
2. Disconnect shock absorbers from lower mountings.
3. On 1977–78 models disconnect upper control arm at axle housing.
4. On all models, lower axle assembly until spring can be removed, Fig. 1.
5. Reverse procedure to install.

Fig. 1 Coil spring suspension (typical)

CONTROL ARMS & BUSHINGS, REPLACE

NOTE: Replace control arms one at a time to prevent axle assembly misalignment, making installation difficult.

Upper Control Arms

1. Support vehicle at frame.
2. Remove control arm bolts from frame crossmember and axle tube bracket.
3. To replace axle tube bracket bushings, refer to Figs. 2 & 3.
4. Reverse procedure to install.

Lower Control Arms

1. Support vehicle at rear axle.
2. Remove stabilizer bar, if equipped.
3. Remove control arm mount bolts from frame and axle tube brackets.
4. Reverse procedure to install.

NOTE: Lower control arm bushings are not serviceable.

STABILIZER BAR, REPLACE

Matador

1. Raise and support rear of vehicle.

Fig. 2 Upper control arm rear bushing removal

Fig. 3 Upper control arm rear bushing installation

Fig. 4 Rear stabilizer bar. 1977-78 Matador

Fig. 5 Rear stabilizer bar. 1979-83 Concord & Spirit

2. Remove bolts attaching stabilizer bar to lower control arms, then remove stabilizer bar, shims (if used) and spacing sleeves, Fig. 4.
3. Install spacing sleeves in lower control arms.
4. Position stabilizer bar on lower control arms, then install attaching bolts and nuts. Hand tighten bolts and nuts only.
5. Install shims, if used, then torque stabilizer bar attaching bolts to 75 ft. lbs.

1979-83 Concord, Eagle & Spirit

1. Raise and support rear of vehicle, then remove nuts and grommets attaching stabilizer to connecting links, Figs. 5 and 6.
2. Remove bolts attaching stabilizer bar mounting clamps to spring clip plates and remove stabilizer bar.
3. Reverse procedure to install. Torque link lock nuts to 7 ft. lbs. and mounting clamp bolts to 25 ft. lbs.

Fig. 6 Rear stabilizer bar. 1980-83 Eagle

Front End & Steering Section

DESCRIPTION

1980-83 Eagle

These models use an independent front coil spring suspension system, Fig. 1. The wheels are suspended on upper and lower control arms with a coil spring located between the upper control arm and a spring seat beneath the wheel housing panels.

Direct acting telescoping shock absorbers are located inside the coil springs. A stabilizer bar attached to each control arm with stabilizer links provides stability, and a dampener dampens steering oscillations.

1977-80 Pacer

These models have an independent front coil spring front suspension system using unequal length upper and lower control arms, Fig. 2. The coil springs are mounted between the lower control arms and the front crossmember with the lower arm functioning as the loaded member.

1977-83 Exc. Eagle & Pacer

The front suspension, Figs. 3 & 4 is an independent linked type, with the coil springs located between seats in the wheel house panels and seats attached to the upper control arms.

Directing acting telescoping shock absorbers are located inside the coil springs.

Each upper control arm assembly has two rubber bushings attached to the wheel house panel and a ball joint attached to the steering knuckle.

Each lower control arm has a rubber bushing attached to the front crossmember and a Ball joint attached to the steering knuckle.

The lower control arm strut rods are attached to the lower control arms and body side sill brackets.

WHEEL ALIGNMENT

1977-80 Pacer

Caster is adjusted by rotating the rear pivot bolt eccentric, Fig. 5. After adjustment, torque locknut to 110 ft. lbs.

Camber is adjusted by rotating both front and rear lower control arm pivot bolt eccentrics, Fig. 5. After adjustment, torque locknut to 110 ft. lbs.

1977-83 Exc. Pacer

Caster is obtained by moving the two adjusting nuts on the threaded strut rod, Fig. 6. One nut is on each side of the mounting bracket. Therefore, moving the nuts on the rod will move the lower control arm to front or rear for desired caster angle. After adjustment, torque adjusting nuts to 65 ft. lbs. Torque locknuts to 75 ft. lbs.

Camber is obtained by turning on the eccentric lower control arm bolt, Fig. 7. After adjustment, torque lock nut to 110 ft. lbs.

TOE-IN, ADJUST

To adjust toe-in, loosen the clamps at both ends of the adjustable tubes on each tie rod. Turn the tubes an equal amount until the toe-

Fig. 1 Front suspension view. 1980–83 Eagle

Fig. 2 Front suspension. 1977–80 Pacer (Typical)

clamp bolts.

NOTE: In performing service operations on the steering linkage or when adjusting toe-in, be sure to square the tie rod ball sockets on the studs and align the tie rod stud in the center, or slightly above center, of the cross tube opening, before tightening the steering linkage adjusting tube. This will prevent the stud from contacting the side of the cross tube opening, which would otherwise result in noise problems or damage.

WHEEL BEARINGS, ADJUST

1977–83 Exc. Eagle

1. To adjust bearings tighten spindle nut to 25 ft. lbs. while rotating the wheel to seat bearings.
2. Then loosen spindle nut 1/3 turn and with wheel rotating, retorque spindle nut to 6 inch pounds.
3. Place the nut retainer on spindle nut with the slots of the retainer aligned with the cotter pin hole on the spindle.
4. Install cotter pin and dust cap.

WHEEL BEARINGS, REPLACE

(Disc Brakes)

Exc. Eagle
1. Remove two thirds of the total fluid capacity of the master cylinder reservoir to prevent fluid overflow when the caliper pistons are pushed back on their bores.
2. Raise car and remove front wheels.
3. Disconnect hydraulic tube from mounting bracket. Do not disconnect any hydraulic fitting.
4. Holding the lower edge of the caliper, remove the lower bolt. Any shims that fall out at this point should be labeled to insure that they be replaced in their original position.
5. Holding the upper edge of the caliper, remove the upper bolt, tag these shims.
6. Hang caliper from upper suspension to prevent strain being placed on brake hose.
7. Remove spindle nut and hub and disc assembly. Grease retainer and inner bearing can now be removed.
8. Reverse procedure to install.

CHECKING BALL JOINTS FOR WEAR

1977–80 Pacer

Lower Ball Joint
1. Position vehicle on level surface and remove lower ball joint lubrication plug.
2. Insert a 2 to 3 in. piece of stiff wire or thin rod into plug hole until it contacts ball stud, then accurately scribe mark on wire or rod at outer edge of plug hole.
3. If distance from ball stud to outer edge of plug hole is 7/16 in. or more, replace ball joint.

in is correct. Turning the right tube in the direction the wheels revolve when the car is going forward increases the toe-in and turning the left tube in the opposite direction increases toe-in. To decrease toe-in turn the right tube backward and the left tube forward. It is important that both tubes be turned an equal amount in order to maintain the correct position of the steering wheel. When adjustment is complete, tighten all

Fig. 3 Front suspension upper control arm components. Exc. Eagle & Pacer

Fig. 4 Front suspension lower control arm components. Exc. Eagle & Pacer

Fig. 5 Caster and camber adjustment. Pacer

Upper Ball Joint

1. Position suitable jack under lower control arm and raise vehicle until wheel is off floor.
2. Move top of wire toward and away from center of vehicle, if any looseness or play is present, replace ball joint.
3. Using a suitable tool, move uppper control arm up and down. If looseness or play is present, replace ball joint.

1977–83 Except Pacer

Before checking ball joints for wear, make sure the front wheel bearings are properly adjusted and that the control arms are tight.

Referring to Fig. 8, raise wheel with a jack placed under the frame as shown. Then test by moving the wheel up and down to check axial play, and rocking it at the top and bottom to measure radial play.

The upper ball joint should be replaced if total travel when rocking and tire exceeds .160″.

The lower ball joint is spring loaded and should be replaced if there is any noticeable lateral shake.

NOTE: On Eagle models, if lower ball joint is worn excessively, the lower control arm and ball joint must be replaced as an assembly.

BALL JOINTS, REPLACE

1977–80 Pacer

Upper Ball Joint

1. Raise vehicle and remove wheel and tire assembly.
2. Using suitable jack, raise lower control

arm approximately 1 in.
3. Remove cotter pin and retaining nut from upper ball joint stud.
4. Install tool J-9656 onto ball joint stud.
5. Lower jack supporting control arm slightly, then strike tool with hammer to loosen ball stud in steering knuckle.
6. Chisel heads from rivets attaching ball joint to upper control arm, then drive rivets out using a punch.
7. Remove tool from ball stud, then remove ball joint assembly.
8. Position ball joint on upper control arm and install nuts and bolts.

NOTE: Install bolts from bottom with nuts on top. Torque nuts to 25 ft. lbs.

9. Reverse procedure to assemble. Torque ball joint stud to 75 ft. lbs.

Fig. 6 Caster adjustment, Exc. Pacer

Lower Ball Joint

1. Raise vehicle and remove wheel and tire assembly.
2. Remove brake drum or caliper and rotor assembly.

NOTE: When removing caliper do not damage brake tubing or hose. Secure caliper to frame with wire.

3. Remove steering arm to steering knuckle attaching bolts and position steering arm aside.
4. Disconnect stabilizer bar link bolt at lower control arm, if equipped.
5. Support lower control arm with a suitable jack and remove cotter pin and nut from lower ball joint stud.
6. Install tool No. J-9656 on ball stud and remove jack.
7. Strike tool with hammer to loosen ball stud in steering knuckle.
8. Support lower control arm with jack and remove tool.
9. Disengage ball stud from steering knuckle and position components aside.

NOTE: Use wire to suspend components from upper control arm.

10. Chisel heads from rivets attaching ball joint to lower control arm, then drive rivets out using a punch and remove ball joint.

Fig. 7 Camber adjustment.
Exc. Pacer

11. Position ball joint on lower control arm and install nuts and bolts.

NOTE: Install bolts from top with nuts on bottom. Torque bolts to 25 ft. lbs.

12. Reverse procedure to assemble. Torque lower ball joint stud nut to 75 ft. lbs., steering arm to knuckle bolts to 55 ft. lbs., and the stabilizer bar link bolt to 7 ft. lbs.

1977-83 Exc. Pacer

UPPER BALL JOINT
1. Position a 2x4x5 in. block of wood on side sill under upper control arm.
2. Raise vehicle and support at frame side sills.
3. Remove wheel and brake drum or caliper and rotor assembly.

Fig. 10 Compressing spring. Pacer

Fig. 8 Check ball joints for wear. Exc. Pacer

NOTE: When removing caliper do not damage brake tubing or hose. Secure caliper to frame with wire.

4. Remove cotter pin and retaining nut from upper ball joint stud.
5. Install tool No. J-9656 on ball stud, then using a hammer strike tool to loosen ball stud in steering knuckle.
6. Support lower control arm with a suitable jack.
7. Chisel heads from rivets attaching ball joint to upper control arm, then drive rivets out using a punch.
8. Remove tool from ball stud and ball joint from steering knuckle.
9. Position ball joint on control arm and install nuts and bolts. Torque bolts to 25 ft. lbs.
10. Reverse procedure to assemble. Torque ball joint stud nut to 75 ft. lbs.

LOWER BALL JOINT
Exc. Eagle
1. Position a 2x4x5 in. block of wood on side sill under upper control arm.
2. Raise vehicle and support at frame side sills.
3. Remove wheel and brake drum or caliper and rotor assembly.

NOTE: When removing caliper do not damage brake tubing or hose. Secure caliper to frame with wire.

Fig. 9 Installing Spring compressor.
Pacer

4. Disconnect strut rod from lower control arm and steering arm from steering knuckle.
5. Remove lower ball joint stud cotter pin and retaining nut.
6. Install tool No. 9656 on ball stud, then strike tool with hammer to loosen ball stud in steering knuckle.
7. Support lower control arm with a suitable jack.
8. Chisel heads from rivets attaching ball joint to upper control arm, then drive rivets out using a punch.
9. Remove tool from ball stud and ball joint from steering knuckle and lower control arm.
10. Position ball joint on lower control arm and install attaching bolts loosely.
11. Connect strut to lower control arm and torque bolts to 75 ft. lbs.

Fig. 11 Installation of spring compressor
Exc. Pacer

1. HALF-SHAFT ASSEMBLY
2. AXLE MOUNTING BRACKETS
3. VENT HOSE
4. PINION AND FRONT BEARING CUP
5. WASHER
6. YOKE AND SEAL
7. OUTER BOOT AND RETAINER
8. RZEPPA JOINT ASSEMBLY
9. SPINDLE
10. HALF-SHAFT
11. INNER BOOT AND RETAINER

12. TRI-POT JOINT ASSEMBLY
13. TRI-POT HOUSING
14. AXLE SHAFT (SHORT)
15. BALL BEARING AND SEAL
16. AXLE HOUSING
17. AXLE SHAFT (LONG)
18. NEEDLE BEARING AND SEAL
19. PRELOAD SHIM
20. WASHER
21. DEPTH SHIM
22. PINION REAR BEARING AND CUP

23. SLINGER
24. PINION GEAR
25. COVER
26. DIFFERENTIAL BEARING AND CUP
27. DIFFERENTIAL PINION AND THRUST
    WASHER
28. PINION MATE SHAFT
29. SIDE GEAR, THRUST WASHER AND
    LOCKRING
30. BEARING CAP
31. RING GEAR
32. DIFFERENTIAL CASE

Fig. 12   Front axle assembly. Eagle less Select Drive System

12. Torque ball joint to lower control arm attaching bolts to 25 ft. lbs.
13. Lubricate steering stop, then install ball stud on steering knuckle. Torque stud nut to 75 ft. lbs. Install cotter pin.
14. Install wheel and brake drum or caliper and rotor and lower vehicle.

Eagle

NOTE: On these models, the lower control arm and lower ball joint must be replaced as an assembly.

1. Remove cotter pin, nut lock and hub nut, then raise and support front of vehicle.

2. Remove wheel, caliper and rotor.
3. Remove lower ball joint cotter pin and retaining nut.
4. Using tool No. J-9656, disconnect lower ball joint from steering knuckle.
5. Remove half shaft flange bolts, then remove half shaft.
6. Remove bolts attaching strut rod to lower control arm, then disconnect stabilizer bar from lower control arm.
7. Remove inner pivot bolt, then remove lower control arm from crossmember.
8. Position control arm on cross member, then install inner pivot bolt. Do not tighten inner pivot bolt at this time.
9. Position lower ball joint on steering knuckle, then install ball joint stud nut.

Torque ball joint stud nut to 75 ft. lbs., then install cotter pin.
10. Connect stabilizer bar to lower control arm and torque lock nut to 7 ft. lbs.
11. Connect strut rod to lower control arm and torque attaching bolts to 75 ft. lbs.
12. Install half shaft to axle flange and torque bolts to 45 ft. lbs.
13. Position a suitable jack under control arm and raise control arm slightly to compress coil spring, then tighten inner pivot bolt to 110 ft. lbs.
14. Install rotor, caliper and hub nut. Torque hub nut to 180 ft. lbs., then install nut lock and cotter pin.
15. Install wheel and tire assembly, then lower vehicle and check wheel alignment.

SHOCK ABSORBER, REPLACE

Pacer

1. Disconnect shock absorber at upper mounting.
2. Raise and support vehicle.
3. Disconnect shock absorber at lower mounting.
4. Remove shock absorber.
5. Reverse procedure to install.

Exc. Pacer

After disconnecting shock absorber from wheelhouse panel at top and lower spring seat at the bottom, withdraw shock absorber out of top of wheelhouse.

SPRING, REPLACE

1977–80 Pacer

1. Remove shock absorber, then the stabilizer bar link bolt at lower control arm, if equipped.
2. On models with drum brakes, remove wheel, tire and drum. On disc brake models, remove wheel, tire, caliper and rotor.
3. Remove steering arm to knuckle attaching bolts and position arm aside.
4. Compress spring, Figs. 9 and 10.
5. Remove cotter pin and nut from lower ball joint, then using tool J-9656 and a hammer, disengage stud from steering knuckle and position knuckle aside.

NOTE: Use wire to support steering knuckle otherwise brake hoses may be damaged.

6. Position lower control arm aside and relieve spring tension. When all tension is relieved, remove tool and spring.
7. Reverse procedure to install.

1977–83 Exc. Pacer

1. Remove shock absorber.
2. Install spring compressor (J-23474) through upper spring seat opening, Fig. 11. Place tool lower attaching screws through shock absorber mounting holes in the lower spring seat. Install tool lower retainer.
3. Remove lower spring seat pivot retaining nuts.
4. Tighten compressor until spring is compressed approximately 1″.
5. Raise and support front of car under frame allowing control arms to fall free of lower spring seat. Remove wheel.
6. Pull lower spring seat away from car. Loosen compressor and allow lower spring seat to come out.
7. When all spring tension is released, remove tool lower retainer spring seat and spring.
8. Reverse procedure to install.

STEERING GEAR, REPLACE

1977–80 Pacer

1. Unlock steering column, then raise and support vehicle.
2. Remove reinforcement brace to crossmember and left engine support bracket attaching bolts, then remove brace.

3. On models with power steering, position a drain pan under steering gear housing and disconnect power steering hoses at gear.

NOTE: Cap hoses and connections to prevent entry of dirt.

4. Remove flexible coupling pinch bolt, then disconnect coupling from steering pinion shaft.
5. Turn wheels in direction of tie rod to be disconnected, then using a floor jack, raise lower control arm at least 2 in. Remove cotter pin and retaining nut from tie rod end and using tool J-3295, disconnect tie rod from steering arm.
6. Remove bolts attaching steering gear mounting clamp to right side of crossmember.
7. Remove steering gear housing to crossmember attaching nuts, then using a blunt punch, remove bolts, washers, sleeves and grommets from gear housing.
8. Rotate bottom of gear housing toward front of front of vehicle until pinion shaft is parallel with skid plate, then slide gear toward right side of vehicle until housing and tube clear mounting plate.
9. Reverse procedure to install.

1977–83 Except Pacer

Manual Steering
1. Remove flexible coupling bolts.
2. Remove pitman arm, using a suitable puller.
3. Remove mounting screws and lower steering gear from vehicle.
4. Reverse procedure to install.

Power Steering
1. Disconnect pressure and return hoses from gear. Raise hoses above pump level to keep oil from draining out of pump.
2. Remove flexible coupling bolt nuts, noting the different nut sizes to insure correct assembly.
3. On Eagle models, remove skid plate, if equipped, then remove left hand crossmember to sill support brace and stabilizer bar bracket from frame.
4. Remove pitman arm with a suitable puller.
5. Remove gear attaching bolts.
6. Slide lower shaft free of coupling flange, then remove gear.
7. Reverse procedure to install.

POWER STEERING PUMP, REPLACE

Models W/ 4 Cyl. Engine

1977–79 4-121
1. Remove adjuster lock nuts and washers attaching power steering pump and pivot bracket to pump mounting bracket. The lower adjuster assembly is accessible from underneath vehicle.

NOTE: To remove adjuster lock nuts, a 9/16 inch box wrench having a 45° offset must be used. All other power steering pump mounting bolts are of metric sizes.

2. Move power steering pump toward engine and remove drive belt, then loosen return hose clamp and slide clamp back along hose.

3. Pull power steering pump forward and disconnect pressure and return lines.
4. Remove bolts attaching power steering pump front mounting bracket to rear mounting bracket and engine, then remove pump, pivot bracket and front mounting bracket as an assembly.
5. Reverse procedure to install.

1980–83 4-151
1. Remove air induction hose, then remove power steering pump adjusting bracket mounting bolts.
2. Move power steering pump toward engine and remove drive belt.
3. Loosen return hose clamp and slide back along hose, then pull power steering pump forward and disconnect both pressure and return lines.
4. Remove bolts attaching power steering pump front mounting bracket to rear mounting bracket and engine.
5. Remove power steering pump, pivot bracket and front mounting bracket as an assembly.
6. Reverse procedure to install.

Models W/ 6 Cyl. Engine

Less A/C
1. Remove air pump drive belt, then remove air pump pivot stud nut.
2. Remove power steering pump adjusting stud nuts and pivot bolt, then remove pump drive belt.
3. Disconnect pressure and return lines, then remove bolts attaching power steering pump bracket to engine and remove pump.
4. Reverse procedure to install.

With A/C
1. Remove air induction hoses
2. Remove air pump adjusting bolt and pivot stud, then remove air pump drive belt.
3. Remove A/C compressor drive belt, then remove compressor pulley and pulley bracket as an assembly.
4. Remove power steering pump pivot bolt attaching lower edge of pump to engine.
5. Remove power steering pump adjusting bracket stud nuts and bolt attaching pump to rear bracket, then slide drive belt from pulley.
6. Pull power steering pump and front mounting bracket forward until bracket clears air pump pivot stud.
7. Remove air pump pivot stud and position air pump aside.
8. Disconnect power steering pump pressure and return lines, then remove pump.
9. Reverse procedure to install.

Models W/ V8 Engine

1. Remove fuel vapor charcoal canister, then disconnect pressure and return lines from power steering pump. Cap lines and fitting.
2. Remove air pump belt adjusting strap, then remove drive belt.
3. Remove two power steering pump mounting stud nuts from rear of pump mounting bracket, then remove drive belt.
4. Remove bolts attaching air pump support bracket to air pump and front of power steering pump mounting bracket.
5. Remove nut securing front of power steering pump bracket to water pump housing.
6. Remove power steering pump and front half of mounting bracket as an assembly.
7. Reverse procedure to install.

EAGLE FRONT AXLE SERVICE, FIGS. 12 & 12A

Axle, Replace

Removal
1. Raise and support vehicle.
2. Install half shaft boot protectors J-28712 onto boots.
3. Remove half shaft to axle flange bolts and secure half shaft to vehicle underbody.
4. Insert wire through half shaft flange bolt holes, then compress half shaft and wrap wire between boots to prevent half shaft from separating.
5. Mark propeller shaft and axle yoke for reference during reassembly and remove propeller shaft.
6. Support axle assembly using suitable jack.
7. On models equipped with Select Drive System, remove brace rod and shift motor shield.
8. On all models, remove axle mounting bolts. On models less Select Drive System, the axle is secured to the engine block with five bolts. On models with Select Drive System, the axle is secured to the engine block by five bolts on the left hand side and one bolt on the right hand side.
9. On models equipped with Select Drive System, disconnect vacuum hose from axle shift motor, then partially lower axle assembly and disconnect vent hose.
10. On all models, lower axle assembly to allow access to vent hose and remove hose.
11. Remove axle assembly from vehicle.

NOTE: Do not apply any load or weight on the hub assembly whenever the half shafts are not securely attached to the axle shaft flanges.

Installation
1. Support axle assembly on suitable jack and position assembly under vehicle.
2. Raise axle assembly slightly and install vent hose.
3. Continue raising axle assembly until properly positioned and install axle mounting bolts. Torque bolts to 50 ft. lbs.
4. Connect propeller shaft to axle yoke. Ensure shaft and yoke are aligned.
5. Remove wire used to prevent half shafts from separating, then install half shaft to axle flange bolts and torque to 45 ft. lbs.
6. On models equipped with Select Drive System, connect vacuum harness on axle shift motor shield.
7. On all models, remove half shaft boot protectors.
8. On models equipped with select drive, connect brace rod to axle.

Axle Shaft Seal, Replace

1. Remove axle assembly.
2. Remove axle housing cover and drain lubricant.
3. Remove axle shaft retaining clip, then the axle shaft.
4. Remove axle shaft seal using suitable screwdriver.
5. Install replacement axle shaft seal using Installer J-29152 for right hand side axle shaft and Installer J-29154 for left hand

Fig. 12A Front axle assembly. Eagle models w/Select Drive System

side axle shaft.
6. Install axle shaft, then the axle shaft retaining clip.
7. Apply suitable sealant to axle housing cover and install cover. Torque cover bolts to 20 ft. lbs.
8. Fill axle with 2½ pints of SAE 85W-90 lubricant, then install assembly onto vehicle. Refer to Axle, Installation for procedures.

Axle Hub & Bearing

Removal
1. Raise and support vehicle, then remove wheel, caliper and rotor.
2. Remove bolts attaching axle shaft flange to half shaft.

NOTE: Insert wire through half shaft flange bolt holes, then compress half shaft and wrap wire between boots to prevent half shaft from separating.

3. Remove cotter pin, lock nut and axle shaft nut, then the half shaft.
4. Remove steering arm from steering knuckle.
5. Remove caliper anchor plate from steer-

ing knuckle, then the three torx head bolts retaining hub assembly using tool J-26359.
6. Remove hub assembly from steering knuckle and clean grease from steering knuckle cavity.

Disassemble
1. Press hub from bearing carrier, then remove bearings, hub spacer, steering knuckle pin seal, carrier to hub seal, carrier O-ring and bearing spacer, if equipped, Fig. 13.
2. Clean all components and inspect for wear and damage and replace as necessary.

NOTE: If hub incorporates ball bearings, the entire hub assembly must be replaced if damage to internal components is indicated. If hub incorporates tapered bearings, internal hub components may be replaced as necessary. Bearings and races must be replaced in matched sets.

3. Press bearing races from hub carrier, if necessary. Install replacement bearing races using a brass drift or suitable press.

Fig. 13 Disassembled view of axle hub. 1980–83 Eagle

Fig. 14 Half shaft identification. 1980–83 Eagle

Assemble

1. Fill steering knuckle pin, hub, bearing carrier and lip type seal cavities with lithium base wheel bearing lubricant.
2. Pack bearings with lithium base wheel bearing lubricant, then install bearings into hub carrier, Fig. 13.
3. Install seal onto hub side of bearing carrier, then press hub into carrier and install hub spacer on end of hub shaft.

NOTE: Do not install bearing carrier O-ring at this time.

4. Install inner seal into steering knuckle pin.
5. Install splash shield onto hub and bearing carrier, then install bearing carrier O-ring.
6. Install splash shield and bearing carrier into steering knuckle pin, then install carrier attaching bolts and torque to 75 ft. lbs.

Installation

1. Partially fill hub cavity of steering knuckle with chassis lubricant and install hub assembly onto steering knuckle. Torque hub torx head bolts to 75 ft. lbs.
2. Install caliper anchor plate and torque plate retaining bolts to 100 ft. lbs.
3. Install steering arm onto steering knuckle and torque retaining bolts to 100 ft. lbs.
4. Install half shaft, then the axle flange to shaft bolts and hub nut. Torque half shaft to flange bolts to 45 ft. lbs and hub nut 175 ft. lbs.
5. Install lock nut, replacement cotter pin, rotor, caliper and wheel.

Axle Shaft, Replace

1. Refer to Axle Shaft Seal, Replace. Perform steps 1 thru 3 for axle shaft removal and steps 6 thru 8 for axle shaft installation.

Axle Shaft Bearing, Replace

NOTE: Two different style axle shaft bearings are used on the Eagle front axle. The left side axle shaft uses a ball bearing. The right side axle shaft uses a needle bearing.

1. Remove axle assembly. Refer to Axle, Removal for procedure.

2. Remove axle housing cover and drain lubricant.
3. Remove axle shaft retaining clip, then the axle shaft.
4. Remove axle shaft seal using suitable screwdriver.
5. Remove needle bearing using Tools J-29173 and J-2619-1. Remove ball bearing using suitable brass punch and hammer.

NOTE: If needle bearing tools are not available, then remove the differential, then remove the bearing using a 15/16 in. socket and three foot extension bar.

6. Install axle shaft bearings. Use tool J-29153 to install needle bearing and tool J-29154 to install ball bearing.
7. Install axle shaft seals using Installer J-29152 for the right hand side axle shaft and Installer J-29154 for left hand side axle shaft.
8. Install axle shafts, then the retaining clips.
9. Apply suitable sealant to axle housing cover and install cover. Torque cover bolts to 20 ft. lbs.
10. Fill axle with 2½ pints of SAE 85W-90 lubricant, then install asembly onto vehicle. Refer to Axle, Installation for procedure.

Half Shaft Service

NOTE: Three different types of half shafts are used on these models. When performing half shaft service, refer to Fig. 14 to identify type of half shaft installed in vehicle. The half shafts are identified by the different configurations of tripod housings and inner boots.

TYPE A
Disassemble
1. Using a suitable tool cut small boot clamp from outer boot.
2. Using a brass punch, separate outer boot from metal retainer. Tap evenly around retainer to remove from boot, then slide boot from constant velocity joint.
3. Using snap ring pliers, remove snap ring, then remove constant velocity joint from shaft.
4. Remove outer boot and retainer from shaft.

5. Using a brass punch, tap constant velocity joint cage until cage is tilted outward far enough to remove first ball. Remove remaining balls in the same manner.
6. Rotate constant velocity cage outward until cage is at a 90° angle from the installed position and remove cage and inner race, then rotate inner race upward and out of cage.
7. Remove small clamp from inner boot, then using a brass punch separate inner boot from metal retainer. Tap evenly around retainer to remove, then slide boot and retainer from tripod housing.
8. Remove tripod and shaft from housing, then using snap ring pliers, remove inner snap ring from groove. Slide tripod joint onto shaft to expose outer snap ring, then remove outer snap ring and tripod joint.
9. If necessary, remove inner snap ring from shaft and remove boot.

Inspection
Clean all components in a suitable solvent and dry with compressed air. Check all components for wear and damage and joints for rough operation, replace components as necessary.

NOTE: Outer constant velocity joint and inner tripod joint are replaced as an assembly.

Assemble
1. Pack spindle hub with chassis grease.
2. Install outer constant velocity joint inner race into cage, then position cage 90° from the installed position and insert cage and race into hub.
3. Using a brass punch, tilt cage outward until first ball can be installed in cage, then install remaining balls in the same manner.
4. Pack outer constant velocity joint with chassis grease, then install outer boot and retainer on half shaft.
5. Install inner race snap ring into inner race snap ring groove, then install constant velocity joint onto shaft until race snap ring seats in groove.
6. Using a brass punch, seat metal retainer on spindle, then install boot into retainer. If difficulty is encountered, support metal portion of boot on wooden blocks and press retainer into boot.
7. Using tool No. J-22610, install small outer boot clamp.
8. Pack tripod joint housing with chassis

grease, then install inner boot and retainer onto half shaft.

9. If removed, install inner snap ring onto shaft, past snap ring groove.

10. Install tripod joint onto shaft, then install outer snap ring into outer snap ring groove. Slide tripod joint toward outer snap ring, then slide inner snap ring into groove.

11. Install inner tripod joint and shaft into tripod housing, then seat inner boot retainer on tripod housing.

12. Using a brass punch, seat boot into metal retainer, then install small inner boot clamp using tool No. J-22610.

TYPES B & C
Disassemble

1. Using a suitable tool cut and remove both outer boot clamps, then roll outer boot from constant velocity joint.

2. Position a wooden block against constant velocity joint inner race and drive joint from shaft. If half shaft is to be positioned in a vise, use protective vise jaws.

3. Using a brass drift, tap constant velocity joint cage until cage is tilted outward far enough to remove first ball, then remove remaining balls in the same manner.

4. Align two outer constant velocity joint oblong holes with slots located on interior wall of spindle housing and remove cage and inner race.

5. Align shoulder between race grooves with inside of oblong cage holes, then rotate inner race out of cage using the larger of the two openings.

6. Remove two snap rings from shaft, then remove outer boot.

7. Remove rubber retaining ring from small end of inner boot, then using a brass drift, tap evenly around retainer to separate from boot. Slide boot and retainer from tripod joint housing.

8. Remove tripod joint and shaft assembly from housing, then remove snap ring that retains tripod joint to shaft and remove tripod joint.

9. If necessary, remove inner boot.

Inspection

Clean all components in a suitable solvent and dry with compressed air. Check all components for wear and damage and joints for rough operation, replace components as necessary.

NOTE: Outer constant velocity joint and inner tripod joint are replaced as an assembly.

Assemble

1. Pack spindle hub with chassis grease.

2. Install outer constant velocity joint inner into cage, then install cage and race assembly into spindle hub. The smaller diameter of the cage and stopping groove of race must face outward.

3. Using a brass drift, tilt cage outward until first ball can be installed into cage, then install remaining balls in the same manner.

4. Pack constant velocity joint with chassis grease, then install outer boot on half shaft.

5. Install inner and outer snap rings, then constant velocity joint onto shaft until inner race contacts inner snap ring.

6. Position boot over constant velocity joint, then install both boot clamps using tool No. J-22610.

7. Pack tripod joint housing with chassis grease, then install inner small retainer

In 4WD Mode

MAINSHAFT DRIVING DIFFERENTIAL

ENGINE POWER INPUT

SPLINE CLUTCH CONNECTS CHAIN SPROCKET TO DIFFERENTIAL

OUTPUT TO FRONT DRIVETRAIN THROUGH DRIVE CHAIN

2 WD / 4 WD

FRONT DRIVE CHAIN SPROCKET DRIVEN FROM DIFFERENTIAL

OUTPUT TO REAR DRIVETRAIN FROM DIFFERENTIAL

In 2WD Mode

2 WD / 4 WD

MAINSHAFT, DIFFERENTIAL AND REAR OUTPUT SHAFT TURN TOGETHER AS A UNIT

ENGINE POWER INPUT

SPLINE CLUTCH RELEASES CHAIN SPROCKET FROM DIFFERENTIAL

FRONT OUTPUT SHAFT, CHAIN AND SPROCKETS STATIONARY

DIRECT OUTPUT TO REAR DRIVETRAIN

Fig. 15 Transfer case operation. 1981–83 Eagle W/ Select Drive System

ring, boot and large retainer ring onto half shaft.

8. Install tripod joint and snap ring onto shaft, then install tripod joint and shaft into housing.

9. Install boot and metal retainer over tripod housing, then using a brass drift, carefully seat boot and retainer.

10. Install rubber retaining ring over small end of boot.

Intermediate Shaft, Outer Axle Shaft & Shift Housing, Replace

Models W/Select Drive System

1. Raise and support front of vehicle.

2. Remove front axle assembly, then drain lubricant.

3. Remove bolts securing shift housing and remove shift housing and shift motor as an assembly, Fig. 12A.

4. Working through access hole in the outer axle shaft flange, remove screws securing axle tube cover.

5. Remove outer axle shaft assembly by tapping shaft flange with a rubber or plastic mallet.

6. Remove intermediate shaft snap ring, then remove intermediate shaft and shift collar.

7. Using a suitable puller and slide hammer, remove outer axle shaft bearing race.

8. Using adapter tool No. J-26225 and slide hammer J-6471-2, remove intermediate shaft needle bearing from axle tube end.

9. Using spreader tool No. J-29369-1 and slide hammer No. J-2619-01, remove intermediate shaft gear bearing.

NOTE: The intermediate shaft gear is retained on the axle shaft by an internal type expandable snap ring. When removing the bearing from the gear be sure to support the gear face on vise jaws to avoid pulling the gear off the shaft. The gear and shaft are serviced only as an assembly.

---

10. Remove outer axle shaft retaining "E" ring.

11. Make a reference mark on outer axle

Front View

RIGHT SIDE   CIRCLE A   DIFFERENTIAL SIDE GEARS   LEFT SIDE

RIGHT HALF SHAFT AND AXLE ENGAGED BY SPLINE CLUTCH

RIGHT HALF SHAFT AND AXLE DISCONNECTED BY SPLINE CLUTCH

◀ 4WD Mode   2WD Mode ▶

Select Drive Axle Disconnect

From Circle A Above

Fig. 16 Front drive axle assembly. 1981—83 Eagle W/ Select Drive System

shaft gear (for assembly purposes) and remove gear from shaft.
12. Remove outer axle shaft bearing using an arbor press.
13. Remove axle oil seal and tube cover.
14. Clean and carefully inspect all components for wear or damage. Replace all necessary components.
15. Install axle oil seal and tube cover on axle shaft.
16. Using an arbor press, install axle shaft bearing and race on shaft.
17. Install axle shaft gear on shaft using an arbor press. Be sure to align reference

mark. Also ensure gear splines are facing outward.
18. Install axle shaft "E" ring.
19. Using tool No. J-29153, install intermediate shaft needle bearing.
20. Install intermediate shaft gear needle bearing in gear bore using an arbor press.
21. Install intermediate shaft, then install shift collar, and seat shaft in differential.
22. Install intermediate shaft lock ring.
23. Install outer axle shaft assembly, torque axle tube cover bolts evenly and in a cross

sequence. Torque bolts 144 inch-pounds.
24. Install gasket on shift housing cover and install.

NOTE: Check to ensure the shift fork and tabs are aligned in the shift collar.

25. Torque shift housing cover bolts to 108 inch-pounds.
26. Install axle cover using a new gasket. Torque bolts to 20 ft. lbs.
27. Fill shift housing with five ozs. of specified lubricant, then fill axle housing.

Select Drive System

The Select Drive is a system which permits the full time four wheel drive power train to be operated in a two wheel drive mode. When the vehicle is stopped, the system can be changed from two wheel drive to four wheel or four wheel drive to two wheel drive, by pulling the instrument panel control switch pull release pin downward and moving the control switch lever to the desired position. The two major components of this system are a shifting device in the transfer case and a disconnecting mechanism in the front axle, which are controlled by the instrument panel switch through a series of vacuum actuators.

The vacuum actuated shifter mechanism located on the transfer case, Fig. 15, slides a splined clutch, located on the transfer case main shaft, rearward to engage or forward to disengage power to the front drive chain sprocket. In the two wheel drive position, the shifter mechanism also locks the transfer case differential. Also the main shaft and differential assembly will turn as a unit, transferring power to the rear driveshaft, while front output shaft, chain and sprocket remain stationary.

A vacuum actuated disconnect device, Fig. 16, is used to engage or disengage a splined clutch that connects the right hand driveshaft to the right hand half shaft. When four wheel drive is selected, the spline clutch is engaged and the front drive axle operates in a normal manner. When two wheel is selected, the vacuum actuator releases the spline clutch, which releases drive to the right hand half shaft and allows the right hand driveshaft to rotate freely. Due to the design of the differential, to equalize torque between left and right axle shafts, disconnecting the right axle shaft will allow the left axle shaft to rotate freely. The axle disconnect will not release all front drive components in the two wheel drive mode. Half shafts and different side gears will continue to rotate with the front wheels as the vehicle is driven.

AXLE SHIFT MOTOR, REPLACE
Models W/ Select Drive System
1. Make a reference mark on fork and housing for assembly purposes.
2. Rotate shift motor and remove retaining snap rings using a suitable screwdriver.
3. Remove shift motor from housing and remove O-ring from motor.
4. Reverse procedure to install.

BUICK
EXC. SKYHAWK, 1980–83 SKYLARK & 1982–83 CENTURY
INDEX OF SERVICE OPERATIONS

NOTE: Refer to the back of this manual for vehicle manufacturer's special service tool suppliers.

ENGINE IDENTIFICATION

Buick engines are stamped with two different sets of numbers. One is the engine production code which identifies the engine and its approximate production date. The other is the engine serial number which is the same number that is found on the vehicle identification plate. To identify an engine, look for the production code prefix letters, then refer to the following table for its identification.

Buick built engines have the distributor located at the front of the engine. On 1977–79 and 1980 V8 models, the engine production code is located on the right front of block. On 1980–83 V6 models, the production code is located on the left rear of block. On 1977–80 vehicles, the fifth digit in the VIN denotes engine code. On 1981–83 vehicles the eighth digit in the VIN denotes engine code.

Chevrolet built V8 engines have the distributor located at rear of engine with clockwise rotor rotation; the code is stamped on the engine case pad located below the cylinder head on the right hand side of the engine.

Oldsmobile built engines have the distributor located at the rear of the engine with counter-clockwise rotor rotation and right side mounted fuel pump. The engine production code is located on the oil filler tube on early 1978 engines or the left side valve cover on late 1978 and 1979–83 engines.

Pontiac built V8 engines, have the distributor located at the rear of the engine with counter-clockwise rotor rotation and left side mounted fuel pump. The engine production code is located on the right front of the cylinder block.

ENGINE CODES

Engine	VIN	Code Prefix
1977		
V6-231⑩	C	RA, RB
V6-231⑩	C	SG, SI, SJ, SK, SL
V6-231⑩	C	SM, SN, ST, SU
V6-231⑫	A	RC, RD
V8-301①	Y	YF, YJ, YW, YX
V8-305②	U	CPA, CPY
V8-350③	H	FA, FB, FK
V8-350④	J	FC, FD, FG
V8-350④	J	FH, FL
V8-350⑤	R	QK, QL
V8-350⑤	R	QP, QQ, Q2, Q3, Q6, Q7
V8-350⑤	R	Q8, Q9, TK, TL, TN
V8-350⑤	R	TO, TQ, TX, TY
V8-350②	L	CKM, CKR
V8-403⑤	K	UA, UB, U2, U3
V8-403⑤	K	VA, VB, VJ, VK
1978		
V6-196	C	PA, PB
V6-231③⑥	A	EA, EG, OH, OK
V6-231③⑥	A	EG, EI, EJ, EK, EL
V6-231③⑦	G	EO, OL
V6-231④⑦	3	EP, ER, ES
V8-301①	Y	XA, XC
V8-305②③	U	CEK, CPZ, CRU, CRX
V8-305②③	U	CRX, CRZ, CTM, CTR
V8-305②③	U	CTW, CTX, C3P
V8-350④	X	MA, MB
V8-350④⑤	R	Q2, Q3, TO
V8-350④⑤	R	TP, TQ, TS
V8-350②④	L	CHM, CKM, CMC
V8-403⑤	K	UA, UB, U2
V8-403⑤	K	U3, VA, VB
1979		
V6-196③⑧	C	FA, FB, FE, FG, FH
V6-231③⑥	A	RA, RJ, RB, RW, NJ, RC RG, WL, RX, RY
V6-231④⑦	3	RR, RU, RV, RO, RS, RP, RT
V6-231③⑨	2	RM, RN
V8-301①③⑧	Y	XP, XR
V8-301①④⑧	W	PXL, PXN
V8-305②③	G	DNJ

Engine	VIN	Code Prefix
V8-305②④	H	DNX, DNY, DTA
V8-350②④	L	DRJ, DRY
V8-350④⑤	R	UA, UZ, U9, VK
V8-350④⑧	X	SA, SB
V8-403④⑤	K	QB, Q3, TB, GB, G3
1980		
V6-231③⑥	A	EA, EB, EC, ED, EK, EM, EP, OV, OW, OX, OY
V6-231④⑦	3	EE, EH, EJ, ER, EU, EV, EW, OS
V6-252④	4	MF
V8-301①④	W	X3, XT, XW
V8-305②④	H	CEC, CMM
V8-350②④	X	MB, MT, MU
V8-350④⑤	R	UAD, UAF, UAS, UAT
V8-350⑤⑪	N	VBM, VBN, VBS, VBT, VBU, VCD, VCH
1981		
V6-231③⑥	A	NA, NB, NC, ND, NF, NJ, NK, NL, NZ, LZ, RA, RB, RK, RL, RC, RD
V6-231④⑦	3	NE, NR, NG, RO, RR
V6-252④	4	SA, SB, SC, SD, SF, SG, SJ, SK, SL, SM, SN, SP, SQ
V8-265①③	S	AW, DB, DC, AZ, BA, DH, DJ
V8-307④⑤	Y	TKA, TKB, TKC, TKL, TKM, TKP, TKT, TKU, TKX, TKY, TKZ, TLA, TLB, TLD, TLF, TLH, TLJ, TLK, TLL, TLM, TLN, TLP, TLR, TLT, TMF, TMH, TMJ
V8-350⑤⑪	N	VKB, VKC, VKH, VKJ, VKN, VKR

Engine	VIN	Code Prefix
		VKU, VKY, VLA, VLC, VLD, VLK, VLL, VLN, VLP, VL8, VLY, VMJ, VMT, VMX, VMY, VNA, VNB, VNC, VND, VNE, VNF, VNJ, VNK, VNL, VNR, VNT, VNV, VNZ, VPA, VPK, VPL, VPR, VPS, VPT, VPV, VPX, VPY, VPZ, VRP, VRH
1982		
V6-231③⑥	A	MA, MC, MG, MK, ML, MM
V6-231④⑦	3	MB, MF, MH
V6-252④	4	FA, FB, FC, FD, FE, FF, FG, FH, FJ, FK
V6-262⑤⑪	V	UAA, UAD, UAJ
V8-307④⑤	Y	TAA, TAB, TAC, TAD, TAF, TAK, TAM, TAW, TAX, TAY, TAZ, TBA, TBB
V8-350⑤⑪	N	VAB, VAC, VAD, VAK, VAL, VAM, VAN, VAP, VAS, VAU, VAW, VAX, VAY, VAZ, VBA, VBB, VBC, VBP, VBU, VBW

①—Pontiac built engine.
②—Chevrolet built engine.
③—Two barrel carb.
④—Four barrel carb.
⑤—Oldsmobile built engine
⑥—Except turbocharged engine.
⑦—Turbocharged engine
⑧—Except California
⑨—California
⑩—Except even fire engine.
⑪—Diesel
⑫—Even fire engine.

GRILLE IDENTIFICATION

1977 Skylark

1977 Century Sedan

1977 Century Special Sport

Continued

GRILLE IDENTIFICATION—Continued

1977 Regal

1977 LeSabre & Estate Wagon

1977 Electra

1977 Riviera

1978 Skylark SR

1978 Skylark Custom

1978 Regal

1978 Century

1978 Century Sport Coupe

1978 LeSabre

1978 Limited & Estate Wagon

1978 Riviera

1979 Skylark

1979 Century

1979 Regal

1979 LeSabre & Estate Wagon

1979 Electra

1979–80 Riviera

1980 Century

1980 Century Ltd.

1980 Regal

Continued

GRILLE IDENTIFICATION—Continued

1980 LeSabre

1980 Electra

1981 Century

1981 Regal Limited

1981–83 Regal Sport Coupe

1981 LeSabre

1981 Electra & Estate Wagon

1981–82 Riviera
1983 Riviera Exc. "T" Type

1982 Regal Limited Sedan &
Estate Wagon
1983 Regal "T" Type

1982–83 Electra

1982–83 LeSabre

1983 Regal Limited

1983 Riviera "T" Type

GENERAL ENGINE SPECIFICATIONS

Year	Engine		Carburetor	Bore and Stroke	Com-pression Ratio	Net H.P. @ R.P.M.③	Maximum Torque Lbs. Ft. @ R.P.M.	Normal Oil Pressure Pounds
	CID①/Liter	V.I.N. Code②						
1977	V6-231, 3.8L⑰	C	2GE, 2 Bbl.④	3.80 × 3.40	8.0	105 @ 3200	185 @ 2000	37
	V6-231, 3.8L⑱	A	2GE, 2 Bbl.④	3.80 × 3.40	8.0	105 @ 3200	185 @ 2000	37
	V8-301, 4.9L⑧	Y	M2MC, 2 Bbl.④	4.00 × 3.00	8.2	135 @ 4000	250 @ 1600	38–42
	V8-305, 5.0L⑨	U	2GC, 2 Bbl.④	3.736 × 3.48	8.5	145 @ 3800	245 @ 2400	32–40
	V8-350, 5.7L	H	2GE, 2 Bbl.④	3.80 × 3.85	8.1	140 @ 3200	280 @ 1400	37
	V8-350, 5.7L	J	M4MC, 4 Bbl.④	3.80 × 3.85	8.0	155 @ 3400	275 @ 1800	37
	V8-350, 5.7L⑨	L	M4MC, 4 Bbl.④	4.00 × 3.48	8.5	170 @ 3800	270 @ 2400	32–40
	V8-350, 5.7L⑥	R	M4MC, 4 Bbl.④	4.057 × 3.385	8.5	170 @ 3800	275 @ 2400	30–45
	V8-403, 6.6L⑤	K	M4MC, 4 Bbl.④	4.351 × 3.385	8.5	185 @ 3600	315 @ 2400	30–45

GENERAL ENGINE SPECIFICATIONS—Continued

Year	Engine			Carburetor	Bore and Stroke	Compression Ratio	Net H.P. @ R.P.M.[3]	Maximum Torque Lbs. Ft. @ R.P.M.	Normal Oil Pressure Pounds
	CID[1]/Liter	V.I.N. Code[2]							
1978	V6-196, 3.2L	C		2GE, 2 Bbl.[4]	3.50 × 3.40	8.0	90 @ 3600	165 @ 2000	37
	V6-231, 3.8L	A		2GE, 2 Bbl.[4]	3.80 × 3.40	8.0	105 @ 3400	185 @ 2000	37
	V6-231, 3.8L[10]	G		M2ME, 2 Bbl.[4]	3.80 × 3.40	8.0	150 @ 3800	245 @ 2400	37
	V6-231, 3.8L[10]	3		M4ME, 4 Bbl.[4]	3.80 × 3.40	8.0	165 @ 3800	265 @ 2800	37
	V8-301, 4.9L[8]	Y		M2MC, 2 Bbl.[4]	4.00 × 3.00	8.2	135 @ 4000	245 @ 2000	30–40
	V8-305, 5.0L[9]	U		2GC, 2 Bbl.[4]	4.736 × 3.48	8.5	145 @ 3800	245 @ 2400	30–40
	V8-305, 5.0L[9]	H		4GC, 4 Bbl.[4]	3.736 × 3.48	8.5	160 @ 4000	235 @ 2400	30–40
	V8-350, 5.7L[5]	X		M4MC, 4 Bbl.[4]	3.80 × 3.85	8.0	155 @ 3400	275 @ 1800	37
	V8-350, 5.7L[5]	R		M4MC, 4 Bbl.[4]	4.057 × 3.385	8.0	170 @ 3800	275 @ 2000	30–45
	V8-350, 5.7L[9]	L		M4MC, 4 Bbl.[4]	4.00 × 3.48	8.5	170 @ 3800	270 @ 2400	32–40
	V8-403, 6.6L[5]	K		M4MC, 4 Bbl.[4]	4.351 × 3.385	8.0	185 @ 3600	320 @ 2200	30–45
1979	V6-196, 3.2L	C		M2ME, 2 Bbl.[4]	3.50 × 3.40	8.0	105 @ 3800	160 @ 2000	37
	V6-231, 3.8L	A		M2ME, 2 Bbl.[4]	3.80 × 3.40	8.0	115 @ 3800	190 @ 2000	37
	V6-231, 3.8L[7]	2		E2ME, 2 Bbl.[4]	3.80 × 3.40	8.0	—	—	37
	V6-231, 3.8L[10]	3		M4ME, 4 Bbl.[4]	3.80 × 3.40	8.0	170 @ 4000	265 @ 2400	37
	V6-231, 3.8L[11][10]	3		M4ME, 4 Bbl.[4]	3.80 × 3.40	8.0	175 @ 4000	275 @ 2600	37
	V6-231, 3.8L[12][10]	3		M4ME, 4 Bbl.[4]	3.80 × 3.40	8.0	185 @ 4000	280 @ 2400	37
	V8-301, 4.9L[8]	Y		M2MC, 2 Bbl.[4]	4.00 × 3.00	8.2	140 @ 3600	235 @ 2000	35–40
	V8-301, 4.9L[8]	W		M4MC, 4 Bbl.[4]	4.00 × 3.00	8.2	150 @ 4000	240 @ 2000	35–40
	V8-305, 5.0L[9]	G		M2MC, 2 Bbl.[4]	3.736 × 3.48	8.5	130 @ 3200	245 @ 2000	32–40
	V8-305, 5.0L[9]	H		M4MC, 4 Bbl.[4]	3.736 × 3.48	8.5	160 @ 4000	235 @ 2400	32–40
	V8-350, 5.7L	X		M4MC, 4 Bbl.[4]	3.80 × 3.85	8.0	155 @ 3400	280 @ 1800	34
	V8-350, 5.7L[9]	L		M4MC, 4 Bbl.[4]	4.00 × 3.48	8.5	160 @ 3800	260 @ 2400	32–40
	V8-350, 5.7L[12]	R		M4MC, 4 Bbl.[4]	4.057 × 3.385	8.0	170 @ 3800	275 @ 2000	30–45
	V8-403, 6.6L[5]	K		M4MC, 4 Bbl.[4]	4.351 × 3.385	8.0	185 @ 3600	320 @ 2000	30–45
1980	V6-231, 3.8L	A		M2ME, 2 Bbl.[4]	3.80 × 3.40	8.0	110 @ 3800	190 @ 1600	37
	V6-231, 3.8L[10]	3		E4ME, 4 Bbl.[4]	3.80 × 3.40	8.0	170 @ 4000	265 @ 2400	37
	V6-252, 4.1L	4		M4ME, 4 Bbl.[4]	3.97 × 3.40	8.1	—	—	37
	V8-265, 4.3L[8]	S		M2ME, 2 Bbl.[4]	3.75 × 3.00	8.2	120 @ 3600	210 @ 1600	40
	V8-301, 4.9L[8]	W		M4ME, 4 Bbl.[4]	4.00 × 3.00	8.2	150 @ 4000	240 @ 2000	38–42
	V8-305, 5.0L[9]	H		E4ME, 4 Bbl.[4]	3.736 × 3.48	8.5	155 @ 4000	230 @ 2400	32–40
	V8-350, 5.7L	X		M4MC, 4 Bbl.[4][13]	3.80 × 3.85	8.0	—	—	34
	V8-350, 5.7L[5][12]	R		M4MC, 4 Bbl.[4][13]	4.057 × 3.385	8.3	160 @ 3600	270 @ 2000	30–45
	V8-350, 5.7L[5][14]	N		Fuel Injection	4.057 × 3.385	22.5	105 @ 3200	205 @ 1600	30–45
1981	V6-231, 3.8L	A		M2ME, 2 Bbl.[4]	3.80 × 3.40	8.0	110 @ 3800	190 @ 1600	37
	V6-231, 3.8L[10]	3		E4ME, 4 Bbl.[4]	3.80 × 3.40	8.0	[15]	[16]	37
	V6-252, 4.1L	4		E4ME, 4 Bbl.[4]	3.97 × 3.40	8.0	125 @ 4000	205 @ 2000	37
	V8-265, 4.3L[8]	S		M2ME, 2 Bbl.[4]	3.75 × 3.00	8.0	119 @ 4000	204 @ 2000	37
	V8-307, 5.0L[5]	Y		M4MC, 4 Bbl.[4]	3.80 × 3.385	8.0	150 @ 3600	245 @ 1600	37
	V8-350, 5.7L[5][14]	N		Fuel Injection	4.057 × 3.385	22.5	105 @ 3200	205 @ 1600	30–45
1982	V6-231, 3.8L	A		E2ME, 2 Bbl.[4]	3.80 × 3.40	8.0	110 @ 3800	190 @ 1600	37
	V6-231, 3.8L[10]	3		E4ME, 4 Bbl.[4]	3.80 × 3.40	8.0	[15]	[16]	37
	V6-252, 4.1L	4		E4ME, 4 Bbl.[4]	3.97 × 3.40	8.0	125 @ 4000	205 @ 2000	37
	V6-262, 4.3L[5][14]	V		Fuel Injection	4.057 × 3.385	21.6	85 @ 3600	165 @ 1600	35
	V8-307, 5.0L[5]	Y		E4ME, 4 Bbl.[4]	3.80 × 3.385	8.5	140 @ 3600	240 @ 1600	35
	V8-350, 5.7L[5][14]	N		Fuel Injection	4.057 × 3.385	22.5	105 @ 3200	200 @ 1600	35
1983	V6-231, 3.8L	A		2 Bbl.[4]	3.80 × 3.40	8.0	110 @ 3800	190 @ 1600	37
	V6-231, 3.8L[10]	8		4 Bbl.[4]	3.80 × 3.40	8.0	180 @ 4000	[19]	37
	V6-252, 4.1L	4		4 Bbl.[4]	3.965 × 3.40	8.0	125 @ 4000	205 @ 2000	37
	V6-262, 4.3L[5][14]	V		Fuel Injection	4.057 × 3.385	22.5	85 @ 3600	165 @ 1600	30–45
	V8-307, 5.0L[5]	Y		4 Bbl.[4]	3.80 × 3.385	8.0	140 @ 3600	240 @ 1600	30–45
	V8-350, 5.7L[5][14]	N		Fuel Injection	4.057 × 3.385	22.5	105 @ 3200	200 @ 1600	30–45

Continued

GENERAL ENGINE NOTES—Continued

①—CID-cubic inch displacement.
②—The fifth digit in the V.I.N. denotes engine code on 1977–80 vehicles. The eight digit in the V.I.N. denotes engine code on 1981–83 vehicles.
③—Ratings are net—as installed in the vehicle.
④—Rochester.
⑤—See Oldsmobile chapter for service procedures on this engine.

⑥—Except California.
⑦—California.
⑧—See Pontiac chapter for service procedures on this engine.
⑨—See Chevrolet chapter for service procedures on this engine.
⑩—Turbocharged engine.
⑪—Dual exhaust.

⑫—Riviera.
⑬—Vehicles equipped with C-4 system-E4ME.
⑭—Diesel.
⑮—Regal, 170 @ 4000; Riviera, 180 @ 4000.
⑯—Regal, 275 @ 2400; Riviera, 270 @ 2400.
⑰—Except even firing engine.
⑱—Even firing engine.
⑲—Regal, 280 @ 2400; Riviera, 290 @ 2400.

TUNE UP SPECIFICATIONS

The following specifications are published from the latest information available. This data should be used only in the absence of a decal affixed in the engine compartment.

★ When using a timing light, disconnect vacuum hose or tube at distributor and plug opening in tube or hose so idle speed will not be affected.

● When checking compression, lowest cylinder must be within 70 percent of highest.

▲ Before removing wires from distributor cap, determine location of the No. 1 wire in cap, as distributor position may have been altered from that shown at the end of this chart.

Spark plug types shown in this chart are recommendations of the original vehicle manufacturer and not MOTOR.
Check local sources for other spark plug manufacturers listings.

Year & Engine/V.I.N.	Spark Plug Type	Gap	Firing Order Fig. ▲	Ignition Timing BTDC①★ Man. Trans.	Auto. Trans.	Mark Fig.	Curb Idle Speed② Man. Trans.	Auto. Trans.	Fast Idle Speed Man. Trans.	Auto. Trans.	Fuel Pump Pressure
1977											
V6-231/C⑫	R46TS	.040	J	12°	12°	K⑬	⑭	600D	—	—	3 Min.
V6-231/C⑮	R46TSX	.060	A	—	15°	B⑬	—	600/670D	—	—	3 Min.
V8-301/Y	R46TSX	.060	N	—	12°	G	—	550/650D	—	1700⑯	7–8½
V8-305/U	R45TS	.045	E	—	8°	D	—	500/650D	—	—	7½–9
V8-350/H, 2 Barrel⑰	R46TS	.040	H	—	12°	K⑬	—	600D	—	—	3 Min.
V8-350/J, 4 Barrel⑰	R46TS	.040	H	—	12°	K⑬	—	550D	—	1800⑧	3 Min.
V8-350/L, 4 Barrel	R45TS	.045	E	—	8°	D	—	⑲	—	1600⑳	7½–9
V8-350/R, 4 Barrel Exc. Calif. ㉑㉒	R46SZ	.060	L	—	20°⑦	M	—	550/650D④	—	900㉓	5½–6½
V8-350/R, 4 Barrel Calif.㉑	R46SZ	.060	L	—	㉔	M	—	550/650D④	—	1000㉓	5½–6½
V8-350/R, 4 Barrel High Alt.㉑	R46SZ	.060	L	—	20°⑦	M	—	600/650D④	—	1000㉓	5½–6½
V8-403/K, Exc. Calif. & High Alt.	R46SZ	.060	L	—	24°⑦	M	—	550/650D④	—	900㉓	5½–6½
V8-403/K, Calif. & High Alt.	R46SZ	.060	L	—	20°⑦	M	—	④㉕	—	1000㉓	5½–6½
1978											
V6-196/C	R46TSX	.060	A	15°	15°	B⑬	600/800	600D	—	—	3 Min.
V6-231/A㉖	R46TSX	.060	A	15°	15°	B⑬	600/800	600/670D	—	—	3 Min.
V6-231㉗㊹	R44TSX	.060	A	—	15°	B⑬	—	650D	—	—	5
V8-301/Y	R46TSX	.060	N	—	12°	G	—	550/650D	—	2200	7–8½
V8-305/U, 2 Barrel Exc. Calif.㉒	R45TS	.045	E	—	4°	C	—	500/600D	—	—	7½–9
V8-305/U, 2 Barrel Calif.	R45TS	.045	E	—	6°	C	—	600/700D	—	—	7½–9
V8-305/U, 2 Barrel High Alt.	R45TS	.045	E	—	8°	C	—	600/700D	—	—	7½–9
V8-305/U, 4 Barrel	R45TS	.045	E	—	4°	C	—	500/600D	—	—	7½–9
V8-350/X⑰	R46TSX	.060	H	—	15°	B⑬	—	550D	—	1550	3 Min.
V8-350/L⑱	R45TS	.045	E	—	8°	C	—	㉘	—	1600	7½–9
V8-350/R㉑	R46SZ	.060	L	—	20°⑦	M	—	㉙	—	1000	5½–6½
V8-403/K, Exc. Calif. & High Alt.	R46SZ	.060	L	—	20°⑦	M	—	550/650D	—	900	5½–6½
V8-403/K, Calif. & High Alt.	R46SZ	.060	L	—	20°⑦	M	—	㉙	—	1000	5½–6½

Continued

TUNE UP SPECIFICATIONS—Continued

The following specifications are published from the latest information available. This
data should be used only in the absence of a decal affixed in the engine compartment.

★ When using a timing light, disconnect vacuum hose or tube at distributor and plug opening in tube or hose so idle speed will not be affected.

● When checking compression, lowest cylinder must be within 70 percent of highest.

▲ Before removing wires from distributor cap, determine location of the No. 1 wire in cap, as distributor position may have been altered from that shown at the end of this chart.

☞ Spark plug types shown in this chart are recommendations of the original vehicle manufacturer and not MOTOR.

Check local sources for other spark plug manufacturers listings.

Year & Engine/V.I.N.	Spark Plug Type ☞	Spark Plug Gap	Ignition Timing BTDC①★ Firing Order Fig. ▲	Ignition Timing BTDC①★ Man. Trans.	Ignition Timing BTDC①★ Auto. Trans.	Ignition Timing BTDC①★ Mark Fig.	Curb Idle Speed② Man. Trans.	Curb Idle Speed② Auto. Trans.	Fast Idle Speed Man. Trans.	Fast Idle Speed Auto. Trans.	Fuel Pump Pressure
1979											
V6-196/C	㉚	.060	A	15°	15°	B⑬	600/800	550/670D	2200	2200	3 Min.
V6-231/A, Exc. Calif.㉒㉖	㉚	.060	A	15°	15°	B⑬	600/800	550/670D	2200	2200	3 Min.
V6-231/A, Calif.㉖	㉚	.060	A	15°	15°	B⑬	600/800	㉛	2200	2200	3 Min.
V6-231/A, High Alt.㉖	㉚	.060	A	—	15°	B⑬	—	600D	—	2200	3 Min.
V6-231㉗㊺	R44TSX	.060	A	—	15°	B⑬	—	㉜	—	2500	5
V8-301/Y, 2 Barrel	R46TSX	.060	N	—	12°	G	—	500/650D	—	2000	7–8½
V8-301/W, 4 Barrel	R45TSX	.060	N	—	12°	G	—	500/650D	—	2200	7–8½
V8-305/G, 2 Barrel	R45TS	.045	E	—	4°	C	—	㉝	—	1600	7½–9
V8-305/H, 4 Barrel Calif.	R45TS	.045	E	—	4°	C	—	500/600D	—	1600	7½–9
V8-305/H, 4 Barrel High Alt.	R45TS	.045	E	—	8°	C	—	600/650D	—	1750	7½–9
V8-350/X⑰	㉚	.060	H	—	15°	B⑬	—	550D	—	1500	3 Min.
V8-350/L, Calif.⑱	R45TS	.045	E	—	8°	C	—	500/600D	—	1600	7½–9
V8-350/L, High Alt.⑱	R45TS	.045	E	—	8°	C	—	600/650D	—	1750	7½–9
V8-350/R, Exc. Calif.㉑	R46SZ	.060	L	—	20°⑦	M	—	㉙	—	900	5½–6½
V8-350/R, Calif.㉑	R46SZ	.060	L	—	20°⑦	M	—	500/600D	—	1000	5½–6½
V8-403/K, Exc. Calif. & High Alt.	R46SZ	.060	L	—	20°⑦	M	—	550/650D	—	900	5½–6½
V8-403/K, Calif.	R46SZ	.060	L	—	20°⑦	M	—	500/600D	—	1000	5½–6½
V8-403/K, High Alt.	R46SZ	.060	L	—	20°⑦	M	—	600/700D	—	1000	5½–6½
1980											
V6-231/A, Exc. Calif.㉒㉖	R45TSX	.060	A	15°	15°	B⑬	600/800	③	2200	2000	3 Min.
V6-231/3, Exc. Calif.㉒㉗	R45TS	.040	A	—	15°	B⑬	—	㉜	—	2200	5
V6-231/A, Calif.㉖	R45TSX	.060	A	—	15°	B⑬	—	⑥	—	2200	3 Min.
V6-231/3, Calif.㉗	R45TS	.040	A	—	15°	B⑬	—	㉜	—	⑩	5
V6-252/4, Exc. Calif.	R45TSX	.060	A	—	15°	B⑬	—	㉞	—	2000	3 Min.
V8-265/S, Exc. Calif.	R45TSX	.060	N	—	10°	G	—	㉟	—	2200	7–8½
V8-301/W, Exc. Calif.	R45TSX	.060	N	—	12°	G	—	㊱	—	2500	7–8½
V8-305/H	R45TS	.045	E	—	4°	⑤	—	㉟	—	2200	7½–9
V8-350/X, Exc. Calif.⑰	R45TSX	.060	H	—	15°	B⑬	—	③	—	1850	3 Min.
V8-350/R, Exc. Calif.㉑	R46SX	.080	L	—	18°⑦	M	—	500/600D	—	700D	5½–6½
V8-350/R, Calif.㉑	R46SX	.080	L	—	㊲	M	—	550/650D	—	700D	5½–6½
V8-350 Diesel/N㉒	—	—	—	—	4½°㊳㊴㊽	—	—	600/750D	—	750D	—
V8-350 Diesel/N㊻	—	—	—	—	5½°㊳㊴㊽	—	—	600/750D	—	750D	—

Continued

TUNE UP SPECIFICATIONS—Continued

The following specifications are published from the latest information available. This data should be used only in the absence of a decal affixed in the engine compartment.

★ When using a timing light, disconnect vacuum hose or tube at distributor and plug opening in tube or hose so idle speed will not be affected.

● When checking compression, lowest cylinder must be within 70 percent of highest.

▲ Before removing wires from distributor cap, determine location of the No. 1 wire in cap, as distributor position may have been altered from that shown at the end of this chart.

Spark plug types shown in this chart are recommendations of the original vehicle manufacturer and not MOTOR.

Check local sources for other spark plug manufacturers listings.

Year & Engine/V.I.N.	Spark Plug Type	Gap	Firing Order Fig. ▲	Ignition Timing BTDC① ★ Man. Trans.	Auto. Trans.	Mark Fig.	Curb Idle Speed② Man. Trans.	Auto. Trans.	Fast Idle Speed Man. Trans.	Auto. Trans.	Fuel Pump Pressure
1981											
V6-231/A㉖	R45TX8	.080	A	15°	15°	B⑬	800	⑪	2200	1800	3 Min.
V6-231/3㉗	R45TS	.040	A	—	15°	B⑬	—	650D	—	2200	5
V6-252/4	R45TS8	.080	A	—	15°	B⑬	—	550/690D	—	2200	3 Min.
V8-265/S	R45TSX	.060	N	—	12°	G	—	450D	—	2300	7–8½
V8-307/Y	R46SX	.080	L	—	15°⑦	M	—	⑪	—	650D	5½–6½
V8-350 Diesel/N㉒	—	—	—	—	4°㊳㊴	—	—	600/750D	—	750D	—
V8-350 Diesel/N㊻	—	—	—	—	5°㊳㊴	—	—	600/750D	—	750D	—
1982											
V6-231/A㉖	R45TS8	.080	A	—	15°	B⑬	—	500D⑪	—	2000	5½–6½
V6-231/C㉗	R45TSX	.060	A	—	15°	B⑬	—	500D	—	2000	5½–6½
V6-252/4	R45TS8	.080	A	—	15°	B⑬	—	500D⑪	—	2000	5½–6½
V6-262 Diesel/V㉒	—	—	—	—	7°㊳㊵	—	—	650D	—	725D	—
V6-262 Diesel/V㊻	—	—	—	—	7°㊳㊶	—	—	650D	—	725D	—
V8-307/Y	R46SX	.080	L	—	20°⑦	M	—	⑪	—	650D	5½–6½
V8-350 Diesel/N㉒	—	—	—	—	4°㊳㊷	—	—	600D	—	725D	—
V8-350 Diesel/N㊻	—	—	—	—	4°㊳㊸	—	—	600D	—	725D	—
1983											
V6-231/A㉖	R45TS8	.080	A	—	15°	B⑬	—	⑪	—	2200	5½–6½
V6-231/8㉗	R45TSX	.060	A	—	15°	B⑬	—	⑪	—	2200	5½–6½
V6-252/4	R45TS8	.080	A	—	15°	B⑬	—	⑪	—	㊼	5½–6½
V6-262 Diesel/V㉒	—	—	—	—	7°㊳㊵	—	—	650D	—	725D	—
V6-262 Diesel/V㊻	—	—	—	—	7°㊳㊶	—	—	650D	—	725D	—
V8-307/Y	R46SX	.080	L	—	20°⑦	M	—	⑪	—	900D	5½–6½
V8-350 Diesel/N㉒	—	—	—	—	4°㊳㊷	—	—	600D	—	725D	—
V8-350 Diesel/N㊻	—	—	—	—	4°㊳㊸	—	—	600D	—	725D	—

①—BTDC—Before top dead center.
②—Idle speed on man. trans. vehicles is adjusted in Neutral & on auto. trans. equipped vehicles is adjusted in Drive unless otherwise specified. Where two idle speeds are listed, the higher speed is with the A/C or idle solenoid energized.
③—Models less idle solenoid, 550D RPM; models w/idle solenoid, 550/670D RPM.
④—With A/C on & Compressor clutch wires disconnected.
⑤—Early models, Fig. C; late models, Fig. I.
⑥—Models less idle solenoid, 550D RPM; models w/idle solenoid, 550/620D RPM.
⑦—At 1100 RPM.
⑧—On low step of fast idle cam with vacuum hose to EGR disconnected & plugged & A/C off.
⑨—Injection timing at 800 RPM.
⑩—Except Riviera, 2200 RPM; Riviera, 2500 RPM.
⑪—Idle speed is controlled by the idle speed control (ISC) motor or idle load compensator (ILC).
⑫—Except Even-Fire engine.

⑬—The harmonic balancer on these engines has two timing marks. The timing mark measuring 1/16 in. is used when setting timing with a hand held timing light. The mark measuring 1/8 in. is used when setting timing with magnetic timing equipment.
⑭—Except Calif., 500/800 RPM; California, 600/800 RPM.
⑮—Even fire engine.
⑯—On 2nd step against high step of fast idle cam.
⑰—Buick built engine. Distributor located at front of engine.
⑱—Chevrolet built engine. Distributor located at rear of engine, clockwise rotation.
⑲—Except high altitude, 500/650D RPM; high altitude, 600/650D RPM.
⑳—On high step of fast idle cam.
㉑—Oldsmobile built engine. Distributor located at rear of engine, counterclockwise rotation.
㉒—Except high altitude.
㉓—On low step of fast idle cam with vacuum hose to EGR disconnected & plugged & A/C off.

㉔—Except sta. wag. 18° BTDC at 1100 RPM; sta. wag., 20° BTDC at 1100 RPM.
㉕—Except high altitude, 550/650D RPM; high altitude, 600/650D RPM.
㉖—Except turbo charged engine.
㉗—Turbo charged engine.
㉘—Except high altitude, 500/600D RPM; high altitude, 600/700D RPM.
㉙—Except high altitude, 550/650D RPM; high altitude, 600/700D RPM.
㉚—R45TSX or R46TSX.
㉛—Models less idle solenoid, 600D RPM; models with idle solenoid, 580/670D RPM.
㉜—Except Riviera, 650D RPM; Riviera, 600/650D RPM.
㉝—Less A/C, 500/600D RPM; with A/C, 550/650D RPM.
㉞—Models less idle solenoid, 550D RPM; models w/idle solenoid, 550/680D RPM.
㉟—Models less idle solenoid, 550D RPM; models w/idle solenoid, 550/650D RPM.
㊱—Models less idle solenoid, 500D RPM; models w/idle solenoid, 500/650D RPM.
㊲—Electra & LeSabre, 18° BTDC at 1100 RPM; Riviera, 16° BTDC at 1100 RPM.

Continued

TUNE UP NOTES—Continued

③⑧—ATDC—After top dead center.
③⑨—At 1200 RPM.
④⓪—At 1300 RPM. When operating at altitudes above 4000 ft., 8° ATDC.
④①—At 1300 RPM. When operating at altitudes below 4000 ft., 6° ATDC.

④②—At 1250 RPM. When operating at altitudes above 4000 ft., 5° ATDC.
④③—At 1250 RPM. When operating at altitudes below 4000 ft., 3° ATDC.
④④—V.I.N. code G denotes 2 Bbl. carb.; V.I.N. code 3 denotes 4 Bbl. carb.

④⑤—V.I.N. code 2 denotes 2 Bbl. carb.; V.I.N. code 3 denotes 4 Bbl. carb.
④⑥—High altitude.
④⑦—Except Riviera, 2200 RPM; Riviera, 2100 RPM.
④⑧—Using diesel timing meter J-33075.

Fig. A

Fig. B

Fig. C

Fig. D

"O" is TDC Marks 2° Increments

Fig. E

Fig. F

Fig. G

Fig. H

Fig. I

Fig. J

Fig. K

Fig. L

Continued

TUNE UP NOTES—Continued

Fig. M

Fig. N

REAR AXLE SPECIFICATIONS

Year	Model	Carrier Type	Ring Gear & Pinion Backlash		Pinion Bearing Preload			Differential Bearing Preload		
			Method	Adjustment	Method	Adjustment New Bearings Inch-Lbs.	Adjustment Used Bearings Inch-Lbs.	Method	Adjustment New Bearings Inch-Lbs.	Adjustment Used Bearings Inch-Lbs.
1977–83	All	Integral	Shims	.006–.008	Spacer	20–25①	10–15①	Shims	35–40②	20–25②

①—Measured with torque wrench at pinion flange nut. ②—Total preload measured with torque wrench at pinion flange nut with new seal installed.

DISTRIBUTOR SPECIFICATIONS

★ Note: If unit is checked on the vehicle, double the RPM and degrees to get crankshaft figures.

Distributor Part No.①	Centrifugal Advance Degrees @ RPM of Distributor				Vacuum Advance	
	Advance Starts	Intermediate Advance		Full Advance	Inches of Vacuum to Start Plunger	Max. Adv. Dist. Deg. @ Vacuum
1977						
1103275②	0 @ 725	—	—	—	10 @ 2200	5½–7½	12 @ 14
1110677②	0 @ 766	8.9–11 @ 1800	—	—	7.95–11 @ 2500	6	12.7 @ 20
1110686②	0 @ 888	3.15–5.45 @ 1300	8.8–11 @ 1800	—	8.7–11 @ 2500	6	4.7 @ 20
1110694②	0 @ 764	8.9–11 @ 1800	—	—	7.95–11 @ 2500	3.5	15.5 @ 20
1978						
1103281②	0 @ 500	5 @ 850	—	—	10 @ 1900	4	9 @ 12
1103282②	0 @ 500	5 @ 850	—	—	10 @ 1900	4	10 @ 10
1103285②	0 @ 600	6 @ 1000	—	—	11 @ 2100	4	5 @ 8
1103314②	0 @ 412	5 @ 900	—	—	10.7 @ 1700	4	12½ @ 12
1103322②	0 @ 300	5½ @ 600	—	—	14½ @ 2000	6	12 @ 13
1103323②	0 @ 500	—	—	—	9½ @ 2000	5	8 @ 11
1103324②	0 @ 300	5½ @ 600	—	—	11½ @ 1800	6	12 @ 13
1103325②	0 @ 500	—	—	—	6½ @ 1800	5	8 @ 11
1103342②	2 @ 1000	—	—	—	9½ @ 2200	7	12 @ 13
1103346②	0 @ 500	—	—	—	9½ @ 2000	6	12 @ 14
1103347②	0 @ 500	—	—	—	6½ @ 1800	6	12 @ 13
1103353②	0 @ 550	6 @ 800	—	—	8 @ 1100	4	10 @ 10
1110695②	0 @ 1000	—	—	—	9 @ 1800	3–6	12 @ 13
1110723②	—	—	—	—	6 @ 2000	4–6	4 @ 7
1110728②	—	—	—	—	9 @ 1600	1–5	10 @ 8
1110730②	—	—	—	—	11½ @ 2000	4–6	12 @ 10
1110731②	0 @ 1000	—	—	—	9 @ 1800	4–6	8 @ 9
1110732②	0 @ 1000	—	—	—	9 @ 1800	4–6	7 @ 13
1110735②	—	—	—	—	11½ @ 2000	2–4	10 @ 13
1110739②	—	—	—	—	8½ @ 1800	2–4	10 @ 13

Continued

DISTRIBUTOR SPECIFICATIONS—Continued

★ Note: If unit is checked on the vehicle, double the RPM and degrees to get crankshaft figures.

Distributor Part No. ①	Centrifugal Advance Degrees @ RPM of Distributor					Vacuum Advance	
	Advance Starts	Intermediate Advance			Full Advance	Inches of Vacuum to Start Plunger	Max. Adv. Dist. Deg. @ Vacuum
1979							
1103281②	0 @ 500	5 @ 850	—	—	10 @ 1900	4	9 @ 12
1103314②	0 @ 412	5 @ 900	—	—	10.7 @ 1700	4	12½ @ 12
1103322②	0 @ 300	5.5 @ 600	—	—	14.5 @ 2000	6	12 @ 13
1103323②	0 @ 500	—	—	—	9½ @ 2000	5	8 @ 11
1103324②	0 @ 600	5.5 @ 600	—	—	11½ @ 1800	6	12 @ 13
1103325②	0 @ 500	—	—	—	6½ @ 1800	5	8 @ 11
1103342②	—	—	—	—	9 @ 2200	5–7	12 @ 13
1103346②	0 @ 500	—	—	—	9½ @ 2000	6	12 @ 13
1103347②	0 @ 500	—	—	—	12½ @ 1800	6	12 @ 13
1103368②	0 @ 500	5 @ 850	—	—	10 @ 1900	4	5 @ 8
1103379②	0 @ 500	5 @ 850	—	—	10 @ 1900	3	10 @ 7½
1103399②	1 @ 575	4 @ 700	—	—	10 @ 2200	4	12½ @ 13
1103400②	1 @ 525	4.5 @ 1000	—	—	8½ @ 2350	4	12½ @ 12
1110765②	—	—	—	—	9 @ 2200	2–4	10 @ 13
1110766②	0 @ 840	—	—	—	7½ @ 1800	4–3	12 @ 11
1110767②	0 @ 840	—	—	—	7½ @ 1800	3	10 @ 12
1110768②	0 @ 500	2½ @ 800	3 @ 1200	—	7½ @ 1800	3	10 @ 12
1110769②	0 @ 500	—	—	—	7½ @ 1800	4	12 @ 11
1110770②	0 @ 840	—	—	—	7½ @ 1800	3	10 @ 9
1110772②	—	—	—	—	9 @ 1800	2–4	12 @ 11
1110774②	—	—	—	—	6 @ 1800	2–4	10 @ 13
1110775②	—	—	—	—	9 @ 1800	3	10 @ 10
1110779②	0 @ 840	—	—	—	7½ @ 1800	3	12 @ 9½
1980							
1103379②	0 @ 600	4–6 @ 850	—	—	11 @ 1900	2–4	10 @ 9
1103384②	0 @ 500	5–8 @ 800	—	—	11 @ 2000	3–6	12 @ 13
1103386②	0 @ 600	4–6 @ 850	—	—	11 @ 1900	3–5	8 @ 8
1103398②	0 @ 550	7–10 @ 1200	—	—	14 @ 2200	—	—
1103407②	0 @ 600	7–9 @ 1300	—	—	13 @ 2200	4–5	10 @ 11
1103412②⑤	—	—	—	—	—	—	—
1103413②⑤	—	—	—	—	—	—	—
1103414②⑤	—	—	—	—	—	—	—
1103417②	0 @ 1100	—	—	—	9 @ 2200	5–6	12 @ 14
1103425②	—	—	—	—	—	—	—
1103444②	0 @ 700	—	—	—	9 @ 1000	7–8	10 @ 15
1103447②	0 @ 1100	—	—	—	9 @ 2200	—	—
1103449②	—	—	—	—	—	—	—
1103450②	0 @ 650	—	—	—	11 @ 1600	2–4	7 @ 7
1110550②	0 @ 500	4–8 @ 600	—	—	9 @ 2200	2–4	10 @ 13
1110551②	0 @ 500	—	—	—	6 @ 2200	—	—
1110554②	0 @ 1000	—	—	—	9 @ 1800	2–4	12 @ 13
1110555②	1 @ 800	2–4 @ 1200	—	—	12 @ 1800	3–5	12 @ 12
1110571②	0 @ 500	2–4 @ 600	—	—	9 @ 2200	2–4	10 @ 10
1110572②	0 @ 500	—	—	—	6 @ 2200	—	—
1110573②⑤	—	—	—	—	—	—	—
1110576②	—	—	—	—	—	—	—
1110784②⑤	—	—	—	—	—	—	—
1981							
1103443②③	—	—	—	—	—	—	—
1103451②③	—	—	—	—	—	—	—
1103453②③	—	—	—	—	—	—	—
1103466②③	—	—	—	—	—	—	—

Continued

DISTRIBUTOR SPECIFICATIONS—Continued

★ Note: If unit is checked on the vehicle, double the RPM and degrees to get crankshaft figures.

Distributor Part No.①	Centrifugal Advance Degrees @ RPM of Distributor					Vacuum Advance	
	Advance Starts	Intermediate Advance			Full Advance	Inches of Vacuum to Start Plunger	Max. Adv. Dist. Deg. @ Vacuum
1981—Continued							
1110567②③	—	—	—	—	—	—	—
1110573②③	—	—	—	—	—	—	—
1110579②③	—	—	—	—	—	—	—
1111381②③	—	—	—	—	—	—	—
1982							
1103457②③	—	—	—	—	—	—	—
1103470②③	—	—	—	—	—	—	—

①—Stamped on distributor housing plate.
②—High Energy Ignition.
③—On vehicles equipped with EST (Electronic Spark Timing), refer to Tune Up Chapter.
④—Except California.
⑤—On vehicles equipped with EMR (Electronic Module Retard) or ECM (Electronic Control Module), refer to Tune Up Chapter.

ALTERNATOR & REGULATOR SPECIFICATIONS

Year	Alternator					Regulator						
	Model	Rated Hot Output Amps.	Field Current 12 Volts @ 80 F.	Cold Output @ 14 Volts		Model	Field Relay			Voltage Regulator		
				2000 R.P.M. Amps.	5000 R.P.M. Amps.		Air Gap In.	Point Gap In.	Closing Voltage	Air Gap In.	Point Gap In.	Voltage @ 125° F.
1977	1101016	80	4.0–4.5	—	80②	Integral	—	—	—	—	—	13.5–14.5①
	1101024	80	4.0–4.5	—	80②	Integral	—	—	—	—	—	13.6–14.2
	1102389	42	4.0–4.5	—	42②	Integral	—	—	—	—	—	13.6–14.2
	1102391	61	4.0–4.5	—	61②	Integral	—	—	—	—	—	13.6–14.2
	1102392	63	4.0–4.5	—	63②	Integral	—	—	—	—	—	13.6–14.2
	1102394	37	4.0–4.5	—	37②	Integral	—	—	—	—	—	13.6–14.2
	1102478	55	4.0–4.5	—	55②	Integral	—	—	—	—	—	13.6–14.2
	1102479	61	4.0–4.5	—	55②	Integral	—	—	—	—	—	13.6–14.2
	1102485	42	4.0–4.5	—	42②	Integral	—	—	—	—	—	13.6–14.2
	1102486	61	4.0–4.5	—	61②	Integral	—	—	—	—	—	13.6–14.2
	1102491	37	4.0–4.5	—	37②	Integral	—	—	—	—	—	13.6–14.2
	1102492	37	4.0–4.5	—	37②	Integral	—	—	—	—	—	13.6–14.2
	1102495	55	4.0–4.5	—	55②	Integral	—	—	—	—	—	13.6–14.2
	1102841	42	4.0–4.5	—	42②	Integral	—	—	—	—	—	13.6–14.2
	1102842	63	4.0–4.5	—	63②	Integral	—	—	—	—	—	13.6–14.2
	1102854	63	4.0–4.5	—	63②	Integral	—	—	—	—	—	13.6–14.2
	1102881	37	4.0–4.5	—	37②	Integral	—	—	—	—	—	13.6–14.2
	1102882	37	4.0–4.5	—	37②	Integral	—	—	—	—	—	13.6–14.2
	1102902	61	4.0–4.5	—	61②	Integral	—	—	—	—	—	13.6–14.2
	1102905	55	4.0–4.5	—	55②	Integral	—	—	—	—	—	13.6–14.2
	1102906	61	4.0–4.5	—	61②	Integral	—	—	—	—	—	13.6–14.2
	1102913	61	4.0–4.5	—	61②	Integral	—	—	—	—	—	13.6–14.2
1978	1101016	80	4.0–5.0	—	—	Integral	—	—	—	—	—	13.6–14.2
	1101024	80	4.0–5.0	—	—	Integral	—	—	—	—	—	13.6–14.2
	1102389	42	4.0–5.0	—	—	Integral	—	—	—	—	—	13.6–14.2
	1102391	61	4.0–5.0	—	—	Integral	—	—	—	—	—	13.6–14.2
	1102392	63	4.0–5.0	—	—	Integral	—	—	—	—	—	13.6–14.2
	1102394	37	4.0–5.0	—	33	Integral	—	—	—	—	—	13.6–14.2
	1102479	55	4.0–4.5	—	51	Integral	—	—	—	—	—	13.6–14.2
	1102485	42	4.0–5.0	—	—	Integral	—	—	—	—	—	13.6–14.2
	1102486	61	4.0–4.5	—	57	Integral	—	—	—	—	—	13.6–14.2
	1102495	55	4.0–5.0	—	—	Integral	—	—	—	—	—	13.6–14.2
	1102841	42	4.0–5.0	—	—	Integral	—	—	—	—	—	13.6–14.2
	1102842	63	4.0–5.0	—	—	Integral	—	—	—	—	—	13.6–14.2

ALTERNATOR & REGULATOR SPECIFICATIONS—Continued

Year	Model	Rated Hot Output Amps.	Field Current 12 Volts @ 80 F.	Cold Output @ 14 Volts 2000 R.P.M. Amps.	Cold Output @ 14 Volts 5000 R.P.M. Amps.	Model	Air Gap In.	Point Gap In.	Closing Voltage	Air Gap In.	Point Gap In.	Voltage @ 125° F.
	1102854	63	4.0–5.0	—	60	Integral	—	—	—	—	—	13.6–14.2
	1102901	61	4.0–5.0	—	—	Integral	—	—	—	—	—	13.6–14.2
	1102904	63	4.0–5.0	—	—	Integral	—	—	—	—	—	13.6–14.2
	1102906	61	4.0–5.0	—	—	Integral	—	—	—	—	—	13.6–14.2
	1102913	61	4.0–5.0	—	—	Integral	—	—	—	—	—	13.6–14.2
	1103033	42	4.0–5.0	—	—	Integral	—	—	—	—	—	13.6–14.2
1979	1101024	80	—	—	—	Integral	—	—	—	—	—	—
	1101043	80	—	—	—	Integral	—	—	—	—	—	—
	1102389	42	—	—	—	Integral	—	—	—	—	—	13.9–14.5
	1102392	63	—	—	—	Integral	—	—	—	—	—	13.9–14.5
	1102394	37	4.0–4.5	—	33	Integral	—	—	—	—	—	13.9–14.5
	1102479	55	4.0–4.5	—	51	Integral	—	—	—	—	—	13.9–14.5
	1102495	55	4.0–5.0	—	—	Integral	—	—	—	—	—	13.9–14.5
	1102841	42	—	—	—	Integral	—	—	—	—	—	13.9–14.5
	1102860	63	—	—	—	Integral	—	—	—	—	—	13.9–14.5
	1102904	63	—	—	—	Integral	—	—	—	—	—	—
	1103033	42	—	—	—	Integral	—	—	—	—	—	13.9–14.5
	1103055	42	—	—	—	Integral	—	—	—	—	—	—
	1103056	63	—	—	—	Integral	—	—	—	—	—	—
	1103058	63	—	—	—	Integral	—	—	—	—	—	13.9–14.5
1980	1100110	42	—	—	—	Integral	—	—	—	—	—	—
	1100111	63	—	—	—	Integral	—	—	—	—	—	—
	1101038	70	—	—	—	Integral	—	—	—	—	—	—
	1101044	70	—	—	—	Integral	—	—	—	—	—	—
	1101080	80	—	—	—	Integral	—	—	—	—	—	—
	1101071	70	—	—	—	Integral	—	—	—	—	—	—
	1103088	55	—	—	—	Integral	—	—	—	—	—	—
	1103100	55	—	—	—	Integral	—	—	—	—	—	—
	1103101	37	—	—	—	Integral	—	—	—	—	—	—
	1103102	63	—	—	—	Integral	—	—	—	—	—	—
	1103103	63	—	—	—	Integral	—	—	—	—	—	—
	1103104	42	—	—	—	Integral	—	—	—	—	—	—
	1103105	42	—	—	—	Integral	—	—	—	—	—	—
	1103106	63	—	—	—	Integral	—	—	—	—	—	—
	1103112	63	—	—	—	Integral	—	—	—	—	—	—
	1103186	63	—	—	—	Integral	—	—	—	—	—	—
1981	1100110	42	—	—	—	Integral	—	—	—	—	—	—
	1100121	63	—	—	—	Integral	—	—	—	—	—	—
	1100156	55	—	—	—	Integral	—	—	—	—	—	—
	1100164	55	—	—	—	Integral	—	—	—	—	—	—
	1100167	63	—	—	—	Integral	—	—	—	—	—	—
	1101037	70	—	—	—	Integral	—	—	—	—	—	—
	1101045	85	—	—	—	Integral	—	—	—	—	—	—
	1101082	70	—	—	—	Integral	—	—	—	—	—	—
	1101084	85	—	—	—	Integral	—	—	—	—	—	—
	1101085	85	—	—	—	Integral	—	—	—	—	—	—
	1101437	70	—	—	—	Integral	—	—	—	—	—	—
	1103088	55	—	—	—	Integral	—	—	—	—	—	—
	1103119	63	—	—	—	Integral	—	—	—	—	—	—
1982	1100110	42	—	—	—	Integral	—	—	—	—	—	—
	1100111	63	—	—	—	Integral	—	—	—	—	—	—
	1100121	63	—	—	—	Integral	—	—	—	—	—	—
	1100156	55	—	—	—	Integral	—	—	—	—	—	—
	1100164	55	—	—	—	Integral	—	—	—	—	—	—

Continued

ALTERNATOR & REGULATOR SPECIFICATIONS—Continued

Year	Alternator					Regulator							
				Cold Output @ 14 Volts				Field Relay			Voltage Regulator		
	Model	Rated Hot Output Amps.	Field Current 12 Volts @ 80 F.	2000 R.P.M. Amps.	5000 R.P.M. Amps.	Model	Air Gap In.	Point Gap In.	Closing Voltage	Air Gap In.	Point Gap In.	Voltage @ 125° F.
	1100165	60	—	—	—	Integral	—	—	—	—	—	—
	1100190	76	—	—	—	Integral	—	—	—	—	—	—
	1100194	70	—	—	—	Integral	—	—	—	—	—	—
	1100198	38	—	—	—	Integral	—	—	—	—	—	—
	1100281	63	—	—	—	Integral	—	—	—	—	—	—
	1100284	85	—	—	—	Integral	—	—	—	—	—	—
	1101037	70	—	—	—	Integral	—	—	—	—	—	—
	1101045	85	—	—	—	Integral	—	—	—	—	—	—
	1101056	—	—	—	—	Integral	—	—	—	—	—	—
	1101082	70	—	—	—	Integral	—	—	—	—	—	—
	1101084	85	—	—	—	Integral	—	—	—	—	—	—
	1101088	70	—	—	—	Integral	—	—	—	—	—	—
	1101098	70	—	—	—	Integral	—	—	—	—	—	—
	1103119	63	—	—	—	Integral	—	—	—	—	—	—

①—At 2000 engine R.P.M.　　　②—At 5500 R.P.M. & 80°F.

ENGINE TIGHTENING SPECIFICATIONS★

★ Torque specifications are for clean and lightly lubricated threads only. Dry or dirty threads produce increased friction which prevents accurate measurement of tightness.

Year	Engine/V.I.N.	Spark Plugs Ft. Lbs. ①	Cylinder Head Bolts Ft. Lbs.	Intake Manifold Ft. Lbs.	Exhaust Manifold Ft. Lbs.	Rocker Arm Shaft Bracket Ft. Lbs.	Rocker Arm Cover Ft. Lbs.	Connecting Rod Cap Bolts Ft. Lbs.	Main Bearing Cap Bolts Ft. Lbs.	Flywheel to Crankshaft Ft. Lbs.	Vibration Damper or Pulley Ft. Lbs.
1977–78	V6-196, 231⑲	⑫	80	45	25	30	4	40	100	60	⑬
	V8-301/Y	15	90	40	35	20⑯	7	35	⑤	95	160
	V8-305/U	15	65	30	20	—	3¾	45	70	60	60
	V8-350/⑥⑲	⑫	80	45	25	30	4	40	100	60	⑬
	V8-350/L⑦	15	65	30	20⑧	—	3¾	45	70⑨	60	60
	V8-350/R⑩	25	130	40⑮	25	25④	7	42	③	⑪	260
	V8-403/K	25	130	40⑮	25	25④	7	42	③	⑪	260
1979–83	V6-196, 231⑲	15	80	45	25	30	4	40	100	60	225
	V8-265, 301⑲	15	95	40	35	20⑯	6	35	②	95	160
	V8-305⑲	22	65	30	20	—	4	45	70	60	60
	V8-350/L⑦	22	65	30	20	—	4	45	70	60	60
	V8-350/X⑥	15	80	45	25	30	4	40	100	60	225
	V8-350/R⑩	25	130⑮	40⑮	25	28④	⑰	42	③	⑪	255
	V8-403/K	25	130	40⑮	25	28④	⑰	42	③	⑪	255
1980–83	V6-252/4	15	80	45	25	30	4	40	100	60	225
	V8-307/Y⑩	25	130⑮	40⑮	25	28④	⑰	42	③	60	200–310
	V8-350/N⑭	—	130⑮	40⑮	25	28④	⑰	42	120⑮	60	200–310
1982–83	V6-262/V⑭	—	⑱	41	29	29④	⑰	42	106	65	160–350

①—Dry threads.
②—Rear main 100 ft. lbs; all others, 70 ft. lbs.
③—Nos. 1, 2, 3, 4—80 ft. lbs., No. 5—120 ft. lbs.
④—Rocker arm pivot bolt to head.
⑤—Rear main, 100 ft. lbs.; all others, 60 ft. lbs.
⑥—Buick built engine. Distributor located at front of engine.
⑦—Chevrolet built engine. Distributor located at rear of engine, clockwise rotation.

⑧—1977 only; Inside bolts; 30 ft. lbs.
⑨—Outer bolts on engines with 4 bolt caps, 65 ft. lbs.
⑩—Oldsmobile built engine. Distributor located at rear of engine, counterclockwise rotation.
⑪—Auto. trans. 60 ft. lbs.; man. trans., 90 ft. lbs.
⑫—1977; 20 ft. lbs. & 1978; 15 ft. lbs.
⑬—1977; 175 ft. lbs. & 1978; 225 ft. lbs.
⑭—Oldsmobile built diesel engine.

⑮—Clean and dip entire engine bolt in engine oil before installing and tightening.
⑯—Rocker arm to stud nut.
⑰—Fully driven, seated and not stripped.
⑱—Torque inner 8 bolts to 142 ft. lbs. Torque outer 6 bolts (bolts nearest intake & exhaust manifolds to cylinder head mating surfaces) to 59 ft. lbs.
⑲—For V.I.N. code identification refer to the "General Engine Specifications" at the beginning of the chapter.

BRAKE SPECIFICATIONS

Year	Model	Brake Drum Inside Diameter	Wheel Cylinder Bore Diameter			Master Cylinder Bore Diameter		
			Front Disc Brake	Front Drum Brake	Rear Drum Brake	With Disc Brakes	With Drum Brakes	With Power Brakes
1977	Century, Regal	10.997–11.007	2 15/16	—	15/16	1 1/8	—	1 1/8
	Electra, Riviera, Estate Wagon	10.997–11.007	2 15/16	—	15/16	1 1/8	—	1 1/8
	LeSabre	9.5	2 15/16	—	7/8	1 1/8	—	1 1/8
	Skylark	9.5	2 15/16	—	15/16	1 1/8	—	1 1/8
1978	Skylark	9.5	2 15/16	—	15/16	1 1/8	—	1 1/8
	Century, Regal	9.45	2 7/16	—	3/4	7/8	—	15/16
	Electra, Riviera, Estate Wagon	10.997–11.007	2 15/16	—	15/16	1 1/8	—	1 1/8
	LeSabre	9.5	2 15/16	—	7/8	1 1/8	—	1 1/8
1979	Skylark	9.5	2 15/16	—	15/16	1 1/8	—	1 1/8
	Century, Regal	9.45	2 7/16	—	3/4	7/8	—	15/16
	LeSabre	9.5	2 15/16	—	①	1 1/8	—	1 1/8
	Electra, Estate Wagon	11	2 15/16	—	15/16	1 1/8	—	1 1/8
	Riviera	9.45	2 1/2	—	3/4 ⑤	15/16 ⑥	—	15/16 ⑥
1980	Century, Regal	9.45	2 7/16	—	3/4	7/8	—	15/16
	LeSabre ②	9.5	2 15/16	—	7/8	1 1/8	—	1 1/8
	LeSabre, LeSabre Estate Wagon ③	11	2 15/16	—	15/16	1 1/8	—	1 1/8
	Electra, Electra Estate Wagon	11	2 15/16	—	15/16	1 1/8	—	1 1/8
	Riviera	9.45	2 1/2	—	3/4 ⑤	15/16 ⑥	—	15/16 ⑥
1981	Century, Regal	9.5	2 7/16	—	3/4	15/16	—	15/16
	LeSabre ②	9.5	2 15/16	—	7/8	1 1/8	—	1 1/8
	LeSabre, LeSabre Estate Wagon ③	11	2 15/16	—	15/16 ④	1 1/8	—	1 1/8
	Electra, Electra Estate Wagon	11	2 15/16	—	15/16 ④	1 1/8	—	1 1/8
	Riviera	9.5	2 1/2	—	3/4 ⑤	15/16 ⑥	—	15/16 ⑥
1982–83	Regal	9.5	2 1/2	—	3/4	15/16	—	15/16
	LeSabre, LeSabre Estate Wagon	⑦	2 15/16	—	① ④	1 1/8	—	1 1/8
	Electra, Electra Estate Wagon	⑦	2 15/16	—	15/16 ④	1 1/8	—	1 1/8
	Riviera	9.5	2 1/2	—	3/4 ⑤	15/16	—	15/16

①—7/8" or 15/16".
②—Models w/V6 engine.
③—Models w/V8 engine.
④—Estate Wagon 1".
⑤—Rear disc brake caliper bore, 2 1/8".
⑥—Models w/4 wheel disc brakes, 1".
⑦—Except heavy duty & Estate Wagon, 9 1/2"; heavy duty & Estate Wagon, 11".

PISTONS, PINS, RINGS, CRANKSHAFT & BEARINGS

Year	Engine/V.I.N.	Piston Clearance	Ring End Gap①		Wrist-pin Diameter	Rod Bearings		Main Bearings			
			Comp.	Oil		Shaft Diameter	Bearing Clearance	Shaft Diameter	Bearing Clearance	Thrust on Bear. No.	Shaft End Play
1977	V6-196, 231⑯	.0008–.0020	.010	.015	.9393	1.9991–2.000	.0005–.0026	2.4995	.0004–.0015	2	.004–.008
	V8-301/Y⑦	.0025–.0033	.010	.035	.927	2.25	.0005–.0025	3.00	.0004–.0020	4	.003–.009
	V8-305/U②	.0007–.0017	.010	.015	.9272	2.099–2.100	.0013–.0035	⑪	⑫	5	.002–.006
	V8-350⑯	.0008–.0020	.010	.015	.9393	1.9991–2.000	.0005–.0026	3.00	.0004–.0015	3	.003–.009
	V8-350/L②	.0007–.0017	.010	.015	.9272	2.099–2.100	.0013–.0035	⑪	⑫	5	.002–.006
	V8-350/R④	.001–.002	.010	.015	.9805	2.1238–2.1248	.0005–.0026	⑤	.0005–.0021⑥	3	—
	V8-403/K④	.001–.002	.010	.015	.9805	2.1238–2.1248	.0005–.0026	⑤	.0005–.0021⑥	3	—
1978	V6-196, 231⑯	.0008–.0020	.010	.015	.9393	2.2487–2.2495	.0005–.0026	2.4995	.0003–.0018	2	.004–.008
	V8-305/U②	.0007–.0017	.010	.015	.9272	2.099–2.100	.0013–.0035	⑪	⑫	5	.002–.006
	V8-350⑯	.0008–.0020	.010	.015	.9393	1.991–2.000	.0005–.0026	3.00	.0004–.0015	3	.003–.009
	V8-350/L②	.001–.002	.010	.015	.9272	2.099–2.100	.0013–.0035	⑪	⑫	5	.002–.006
	V8-350/R④	.001–.002	.010	.015	.9805	2.1238–2.1248	.0004–.0033	⑤	.0005–.0021⑥	3	.0035–.0135
	V8-403/K④	.001–.002	.010	.015	.9805	2.1238–2.1248	.0004–.0033	⑤	.0005–.0021⑥	3	.0035–.0135
1978–79	V8-301⑦⑯	.0025–.0033	.010	.035	.927	2.25	.0005–.0025	3.00	.0004–.0020	4	.006–.020
1979–80	V6-196, 231⑯	.0008–.0020	.013	.015	.9393	2.2487–2.2495	.0005–.0026	2.4995	.0003–.0018	2	.003–.009
	V8-305②⑯	.0007–.0017	.010	.015	.9272	2.099–2.100	.0013–.0035	⑪	⑫	5	.002–.006

Continued

PISTONS, PINS, RINGS, CRANKSHAFT & BEARINGS—Continued

Year	Engine/V.I.N.	Piston Clearance	Ring End Gap① Comp.	Oil	Wrist-pin Diameter	Rod Bearings Shaft Diameter	Bearing Clearance	Main Bearings Shaft Diameter	Bearing Clearance	Thrust on Bear. No.	Shaft End Play
	V8-350/X	.0008–.0020	.013	.015	.9393	1.991–2.000	.0005–.0026	3.0000	.0004–.0015	3	.003–.009
	V8-350/L②	.0007–.0017	.010	.015	.9272	2.099–2.100	.0013–.0035	⑪	⑫	5	.002–.006
	V8-350/R④	.00075–.00175	.010	.015	.9805	2.1238–2.1248	.0004–.0033	⑤	.005–.021⑥	3	.0035–.0135
	V8-403/K④	.0005–.0015	.010	.015	.9805	2.1238–2.1248	.0004–.0033	⑤	.005–.021⑥	3	.0035–.0135
1980	V8-265, 301⑦⑯	.0017–.0025	.010	.035	.940	2.00	.0005–.0025	3.00	.0002–.0018	4	.003–.009
1980–81	V6-252/4	.0008–.0020	.013	.015	.9393	2.2487–2.2495	.0005–.0026	2.4995	.0003–.0018	2	.003–.009
	V8-350/N⑧	.005–.006	.015	.015	1.0951	2.1238–2.1248	.0005–.0026	2.9998	.005–.0021⑥	3	.0035–.0135
1981	V6-231⑯	.0008–.0020	.013	.015	.9393	2.2487–2.2495	.0005–.0026	2.4995	.0003–.0018	2	.003–.009
	V8-265/S⑦	.0017–.0025	.010	.035	.940	2.00	.0005–.0025	3.00	.0002–.0018	4	.003–.009
	V8-307/Y④	.00075–.00175	.010	.015	.9805	2.1238–2.1248	.0004–.0033	⑨	⑩	3	.0035–.0135
	V8-350/N⑧	.005–.006	.015	.015	1.0951	2.1238–2.1248	.0005–.0026	2.9998	.005–.0021⑥	3	.0035–.0135
1982	V6-231/A⑬	.0008–.0020	.013	.015	.9393	2.2487–2.2495	.0005–.0026	2.4995	.0003–.0018	2	.003–.009
	V6-231/3⑭	.0022–.0034	.013	.015	.9393	2.2487–2.2495	.0005–.0026	2.4995	.0003–.0018	2	.003–.009
	V6-252/4	.0008–.0020	.013	.015	.9393	2.2487–2.2495	.0005–.0026	2.4995	.0003–.0018	2	.003–.009
	V6-262/V⑧	.003–.004	.015	.015	1.0950	2.2490–2.2510	.0003–.0035	2.9993–3.0003	⑮	3	.0035–.0135
	V8-307/Y④	.00075–.00175	.010	.015	.9805	2.1238–2.1248	.0004–.0033	⑨	⑩	3	.0035–.0135
	V8-350/N⑧	.003–.004	.015	.015	1.0951	2.1238–2.1248	.0005–.0026	2.9993–3.0003	⑮	3	.0035–.0135
1983	V6-231/A⑬	.0008–.0020	.010	.015	.9393	2.2487–2.2495	.0005–.0026	2.4995	.0003–.0018	2	.003–.009
	V6-231/8⑭	.0022–.0034	.010	.015	.9393	2.2487–2.2495	.0005–.0026	2.4995	.0003–.0018	2	.003–.009
	V6-252/4	.0008–.0020	.010	.015	.9393	2.2487–2.2495	.0005–.0026	2.4995	.0003–.0018	2	.003–.009
	V6-262/V⑧	.0035–.0045	⑰	.015	1.0950	2.2490–2.2510	.0003–.0025	2.9993–3.0003	⑮	3	.0035–.0135
	V8-307/Y④	.00075–.00175	.010	.015	.9805	2.1238–2.1248	.0004–.0033	⑨	⑩	3	.0035–.0135
	V8-350/N⑧	.003–.004	.015	.015	1.0951	2.1238–2.1248	.0005–.0026	2.9993–3.0003	⑮	3	.0035–.0135

①—Fit rings in tapered bores for clearance given in tightest portion of ring travel. Clearances specified are minimum gaps.
②—Chevrolet built engine. Distributor located at rear of engine, clockwise rotation.
③—No. 1 .010; No. 2, .013.
④—Oldsmobile built engine. Distributor located at rear of engine, counterclockwise rotation.
⑤—No. 1: 2.4988–2.4998 inch; Nos. 2, 3, 4, 5: 2.4985–2.4995 inch.
⑥—Rear, .0015–.0031 inch.
⑦—Pontiac built engine. Distributor located at rear of engine, clockwise rotation.
⑧—Olds. built diesel engine.
⑨—No. 1, 2.4993–2.4998 inch; Nos. 2, 3, 4, 5, 2.4990–2.4995 inch.
⑩—No. 5, .0015–.0031 inch; Nos. 1, 2, 3, 4, .0005–.0021 inch.
⑪—No. 1: 2.4484–2.4493 inch; Nos. 2, 3, 4: 2.4481–2.4490 inch; No. 5: 2.4479–2.4488 inch.
⑫—No. 1: .0008–.0020 inch; Nos. 2, 3, 4: .0011–.0023 inch; No. 5: .0017–.0032 inch.
⑬—Except turbocharged engine.
⑭—Turbocharged engine.
⑮—Nos. 1, 2 & 3, .0005–.0021 inch; No. 4, .0020–.0034 inch.
⑯—For V.I.N. code, refer to the "General Engine Specifications" at the beginning of the chapter.
⑰—Top ring, .019 inch; 2nd ring, .015 inch.

VALVE SPECIFICATIONS

Year	Model/V.I.N.	Valve Lash Int.	Exh.	Valve Angles Seat	Face	Valve Spring Installed Height①	Valve Spring Pressure Lbs. @ In.	Stem Clearance Intake	Exhaust	Stem Diameter Intake	Exhaust
1977	V8-305/U④	¾ turn⑤		46	45	③	②	.0010–.0027	.0010–.0027	.3410–.3417	.3410–.3417
	V8-350/L④	¾ turn⑤		46	45	③	②	.0010–.0027	.0010–.0027	.3410–.3417	.3410–.3417
1977–78	V6-196, 231⑮	Hydraulic⑥		45	45	1.727	168 @ 1.327	.0015–.0032	.0015–.0032	.3405–.3412	.3405–.3412
	V8-301/Y⑩	Hydraulic⑥		46	45	1.69	170 @ 1.26	.0017–.0020	.0017–.0020	.3400	.3400
	V8-350⑪⑮	Hydraulic⑥		45	45	1.727	⑬	.0015–.0035	.0015–.0032	.3720–.3730	.3723–.3730
	V8-350/R⑦	Hydraulic⑥		⑧	⑨	1.67	187 @ 1.27	.0010–.0027	.0015–.0032	.3425–.3432	.3420–.3427
	V8-403/K⑦	Hydraulic⑥		⑧	⑨	1.67	187 @ 1.27	.0010–.0027	.0015–.0032	.3425–.3432	.3420–.3427
1978	V8-305/U④	1 Turn⑤		46	45	1.70	200 @ 1.25	.0010–.0027	.0010–.0027	.3410–.3417	.3410–.3417
	V8-350/L④	1 Turn⑤		46	45	1.70	200 @ 1.25	.0010–.0027	.0010–.0027	.3410–.3417	.3410–.3417

VALVE SPECIFICATIONS—Continued

Year	Model/V.I.N.	Valve Lash Int.	Valve Lash Exh.	Valve Angles Seat	Valve Angles Face	Valve Spring Installed Height ①	Valve Spring Pressure Lbs. @ In.	Stem Clearance Intake	Stem Clearance Exhaust	Stem Diameter Intake	Stem Diameter Exhaust
1979–80	V6-196, 231, 252⑮	Hydraulic⑥		45	45	1.727	⑭	.0015–.0035	.0015–.0032	.3401–.3412	.3405–.3412
	V8-265, 301⑮	Hydraulic⑥		46	45	1.69	170 @ 1.26	.0017–.0020	.0017–.0020	.3400	.3400
	V8-305④⑮	1 Turn⑤		46	45	1.70	200 @ 1.25	.0010–.0027	.0010–.0027	.3410–.3417	.3410–.3417
	V8-350/X⑪	Hydraulic⑥		45	45	1.727	⑬	.0015–.0035	.0015–.0032	.3720–.3730	.3723–.3730
	V8-350/L④	1 Turn⑤		46	45	1.70	200 @ 1.25	.0010–.0027	.0010–.0027	.3410–.3417	.3410–.3417
	V8-350/R⑦	Hydraulic⑥		⑧	⑨	1.67	187 @ 1.27	.0010–.0027	.0015–.0032	.3425–.3432	.3420–.3427
	V8-403/K⑦	Hydraulic⑥		⑧	⑨	1.67	187 @ 1.27	.0010–.0027	.0015–.0032	.3425–.3432	.3420–.3427
1980	V8-350/N⑦⑫	Hydraulic⑥		⑧	⑨	1.67	152 @ 1.30	.0010–.0027	.0015–.0032	.3425–.3432	.3420–.3427
1981	V6-231⑮	Hydraulic⑥		45	45	1.727	⑭	.0015–.0035	.0015–.0032	.3402–.3412	.3405–.3412
	V6-252/4	Hydraulic⑥		45	45	1.727	⑭	.0015–.0035	.0015–.0032	.3402–.3412	.3405–.3412
	V8-265/S⑩	Hydraulic⑥		46	45	1.66	187 @ 1.296	.0010–.0027	.0010–.0027	.3418–.3425	.3418–.3425
	V8-307/Y⑦	Hydraulic⑥		⑧	⑨	1.67	189 @ 1.27	.0010–.0027	.0015–.0032	.3425–.3432	.3420–.3427
	V8-350/N⑦⑫	Hydraulic⑥		⑧	⑨	1.67	⑭	.0010–.0027	.0015–.0032	.3425–.3432	.3420–.3427
1982–83	V6-231⑮	Hydraulic⑥		45	45	1.727	182 @ 1.34	.0015–.0035	.0015–.0032	.3401–.3412	.3405–.3412
	V6-252/4	Hydraulic⑥		45	45	1.727	182 @ 1.34	.0015–.0035	.0015–.0032	.3401–.3412	.3405–.3412
	V6-262/V	Hydraulic⑥		⑧	⑨	1.670	210 @ 1.220	.0010–.0027	.0015–.0032	.3425–.3432	.3420–.3427
	V8-307/Y	Hydraulic⑥		⑧	⑨	1.670	187 @ 1.27	.0010–.0027	.0015–.0032	.3425–.3432	.3420–.3427
	V8-350/N	Hydraulic⑥		⑧	⑨	1.670	210 @ 1.220	.0010–.0027	.0015–.0032	.3425–.3432	.3420–.3427

①—Outer spring
②—Intake 200 @ 1.25; exhaust 200 @ 1.16
③—Intake, 1.70 inch; exhaust, 1.61 inch.
④—Chevrolet built engine. Distributor located at rear of engine, clockwise rotation.
⑤—Turn rocker arm stud nut until all lash is eliminated, then tighten nut the additional turn listed.
⑥—No adjustment.
⑦—Oldsmobile built engine. Distributor located at rear of engine, counterclockwise rotation.
⑧—Intake, 45°; exhaust 31°.
⑨—Intake 44°; exhaust, 30°.
⑩—Pontiac built engine. Distributor located at rear of engine, clockwise rotation.
⑪—Buick built engine. Distributor located at front of engine.
⑫—Diesel engine.
⑬—Intake, 180 @ 1.34; exhaust, 177 @ 1.45.
⑭—Intake, 164 @ 1.34; exhaust, 182 @ 1.34.
⑮—For V.I.N. code, refer to the "General Engine Specifications" at the beginning of the chapter.

STARTING MOTOR SPECIFICATIONS

Year	Model/V.I.N.	Starter Number	Brush Spring Tension Oz①	Free Speed Test Amps.	Free Speed Test Volts	Free Speed Test R.P.M.	Resistance Test② Amps. ①	Resistance Test② Volts
1977	V6-231/C	1108797	—	55–80③	9	5500–10000	—	—
	V8-301/Y	1108758	—	55–80③	9	3500–6000	—	—
	V8-305/U, Auto. Trans.	1109056	—	50–80③	9	5500–10500	—	—
	V8-305/U, Man. Trans.	1108799	—	50–80③	9	5500–10500	—	—
	V8-350④⑫	1108762	35	55–80③	9	3500–6000	—	—
	V8-350/L⑤	1109052	—	65–95③	9	7500–10500	—	—
	V8-350/R⑥	1108765	—	55–80③	9	3500–6000	—	—
	V8-403/K	1108794	—	65–95③	9	7500–10000	—	—
1978	V8-350/X④	1109061	—	60–85③	9	6800–10300	—	—
	V8-350/L⑤	1109065	—	65–95③	9	7500–10500	—	—
	V8-350, 403⑥⑫	1109072	—	65–95③	9	7500–10500	—	—
1978–80	V6-196, 231⑩⑫	1109061	—	60–85③	9	6800–10300	—	—
	V8-265, 301⑫	1109523	—	45–70③	9	7000–11900	—	—
	V8-305 2 Bbl. Carb.⑫	1109064	—	60–85③	9	6800–10300	—	—
	V8-305/H, 4 Bbl. Carb.	1109524	—	45–70③	9	7000–11900	—	—
1979–80	V6-231⑪⑫	1998204	—	60–85③	9	6800–10300	—	—
	V8-350/X④	1109062	—	65–95③	9	7500–10500	—	—
	V8-350/L⑤⑧	1109524	—	45–70③	9	7000–11900	—	—
	V8-350/L⑤⑨	1109065	—	65–95③	9	7500–10500	—	—
	V8-350, 403⑥⑩⑫	1109072	—	65–95③	9	7500–10500	—	—
	V8-350⑪⑫	1998205	—	65–95③	9	7500–10500	—	—

Continued

STARTING MOTOR SPECIFICATIONS—Continued

Year	Model/V.I.N.	Starter Number	Brush Spring Tension Oz[1]	Free Speed Test			Resistance Test[2]	
				Amps.	Volts	R.P.M.	Amps. [1]	Volts
1980	V6-252/4	1109062	—	65–95[3]	9	7500–10500	—	—
	V8-350/N[7][10]	1100215	—	—	—	—	—	—
	V8-350/N[7][11]	1100214	—	—	—	—	—	—
1981	V6-231[10][12]	1109061	—	60–85[3]	9	6800–10300	—	—
	V6-231[11][12]	1998204	—	60–85[3]	9	6800–10300	—	—
	V6-252/4[10]	1998227	—	65–95[3]	9	7500–10500	—	—
	V6-252/4[11]	1998205	—	65–95[3]	9	7500–10500	—	—
	V8-265, 301[12]	1109523	—	45–70[3]	9	7000–11900	—	—
	V8-307/Y	1998205	—	65–95[3]	9	7500–10500	—	—
	V8-350/N[7][10]	1109216	—	120–210[3]	10.6	9000–13400	—	—
	V8-350/N[7][11]	1109218	—	120–210[3]	10.6	9000–13400	—	—
1982	V6-231[12]	1998236	—	60–85[3]	9	6800–10300	—	—
	V6-252/4[10]	1998234	—	65–95[3]	9	7500–10500	—	—
	V6-252/4[11]	1998237	—	65–95[3]	9	7500–10500	—	—
	V8-262/U[7]	1998552	—	160–220	9	4000–5500	—	—
	V8-307/Y	1109544	—	45–70	9	7000–11900	—	—
	V8-350/N[7][10]	1998552	—	160–220	9	7000–11900	—	—
	V8-350/N[7][11]	1109495	—	120–210	11	9000–13400	—	—

[1]—Minimum.
[2]—Check capacity of motor by using a 500 ampere meter and a carbon pile rheostat to control voltage. Apply volts listed across motor with armature locked. Current should be as listed.
[3]—Includes solenoid.
[4]—Distributor at front of engine.
[5]—Distributor at rear of engine, clockwise rotation.
[6]—Distributor at rear of engine, counter-clockwise rotation.
[7]—Diesel engine.
[8]—Exc. Skylark.
[9]—Skylark.
[10]—Exc. Riviera.
[11]—Riviera.
[12]—For V.I.N. code, refer to the "General Engine Specifications" at the beginning of the chapter.

COOLING SYSTEM & CAPACITY DATA

Year	Model or Engine/V.I.N.	Cooling Capacity, Qts.		Radiator Cap Relief Pressure, Lbs.	Thermo. Opening Temp.	Fuel Tank Gals.	Engine Oil Refill Qts. [1]	Transmission Oil			Rear Axle Oil Pints
		Less A/C	With A/C					3 Speed Pints	4 Speed Pints	Auto. Trans. Qts. [2]	
1977	V6-231/C[7]	12.7	12.8	15	[17]	21	4	3½	—	[15]	3.5
	V6-231/C[11]	12.8	12.7	15	[17]	22	4	3½	—	[15]	4¼
	V6-231/C[10]	12.7	12.7	15	[17]	21	4	—	—	[15]	4¼
	V8-301/Y[7]	18.6	19.2	15	195	21	4	—	—	[15]	3.5
	V8-301/Y[10]	18.2[22]	18.1[22]	15	195	21	4	—	—	[15]	4¼
	V8-305/U[7]	17	18	15	195	21	4	—	—	[15]	3.5
	V8-350/V[11][23]	14.3[24]	14.9[24]	15	195	22	4	—	—	[15]	4¼
	V8-350/V[6][10][23]	14.2[25]	14.1[25]	15	195	[26]	4	—	—	[15]	[20]
	V8-350[7][18][28][54]	15.6	15.6	15	195	21	4	—	—	[15]	3.5
	V8-350[11][18][28][54]	15.3[29]	15.9[29]	15	195	22	4	—	—	[15]	4¼
	V8-350[6][10][28][54]	14.6[30]	14.5[30]	15	195	[26]	4	—	—	[15]	[20]
	V8-350[7][28][54]	17	18	15	195	21	4	—	—	[15]	3.5
	V8-350[11][28][54]	14.8	15.4	15	195	22	4	—	—	[15]	4¼
	V8-403/K[11]	16.4[31]	17[31]	15	195	22	4	—	—	[15]	4¼
	V8-403/K[6][10]	15.7[32]	15.6[32]	15	195	[26]	4	—	—	[15]	[20]
1978	V6-196/C	13.1	13.2	15	195	17.5	4	3½	—	[15]	4¼
	V6-231[7][54]	13.6	13.7	15	195	21	4	3½	—	[15]	4¼
	V6-231[11][54]	13.1	13.2	15	195	17.5	4	—	3½	[15]	4¼
	V6-231[10][54]	12.9	12.9	15	195	21	4	—	—	[15]	4¼
	V8-301/Y	20.9[5]	20.9[5]	15	195	21	4	—	—	[15]	4¼

COOLING SYSTEM & CAPACITY DATA—Continued

Year	Model or Engine/V.I.N.	Cooling Capacity, Qts. Less A/C	With A/C	Radiator Cap Relief Pressure, Lbs.	Thermo. Opening Temp.	Fuel Tank Gals.	Engine Oil Refill Qts. (1)	Transmission Oil 3 Speed Pints	4 Speed Pints	Auto. Trans. Qts. (2)	Rear Axle Oil Pints
	V8-305/U(7)	15.9(33)	16.3(33)	15	195	21	4	3½	—	(15)	4¼
	V8-305/U(11)	19.2(34)	18.9(34)	15	195	17.5	4	—	—	(15)	4¼
	V8-305/U(10)	16.6	16.7	15	195	21	4	—	—	(15)	4¼
	V8-350(7)(54)	16.1	16.9	15	195	21	4	—	—	(15)	4¼
	V8-350(11)(54)	19.2(34)	18.9(34)	15	195	17.5	4	—	—	(15)	4¼
	V8-350/X(6)(10)(23)(39)	14.1(35)	14.1(35)	15	195	(19)	4	—	—	(15)	4¼
	V8-350/R(6)(10)(18)(28)(40)	14.6(30)	14.5(30)	15	195	(19)	4	—	—	(15)	4¼
	V8-350/L(6)(10)(28)	16.6(36)	16.7(36)	15	195	(19)	4	—	—	(15)	4¼
	V8-403/K	15.7	16.6	15	195	(19)	4	—	—	—	4¼
1979	V6-196, 231(11)(54)	13.5	13.5	15	195	18.1	4	3.5	3.5	(41)	(38)
	V6-231(10)(14)(54)	12.9	12.9	15	195	25.3	4	—	—	(15)	(38)
	V6-231(7)(54)	13.8	13.9	15	195	21	4	3.5	—	(15)	(38)
	V6-231 Turbo/3(11)(37)	13.7(43)	13.8(43)	15	195	18.1	4	—	—	(41)	(38)
	V6-231 Turbo/3(13)(37)	—	14(4)	15	195	20	4	—	—	(9)	3.2(8)
	V8-301(11)(54)	20.3(27)	21(27)	15	195	18.1	4	3.5	3.5	(41)	(38)
	V8-301(10)(14)(54)	21(5)	21(5)	15	195	21(3)(42)	4	—	—	(15)	(38)
	V8-305(7)(54)	15.9(33)	16.3(33)	15	195	21	4	3.5	—	(15)	(38)
	V8-305(11)(54)	17.6(36)	17.6(36)	15	195	18.1	4	3.5	3.5	(41)	(38)
	V8-350(11)(54)	17.6(36)	18.1	15	195	18.1	4	3.5	3.5	(41)	(38)
	V8-350(7)(54)	16.1(33)	16.9	15	195	21	4	3.5	—	(15)	(38)
	V8-350/X(10)(14)(23)(39)	14.1(25)	14.1(25)	15	195	21(3)(42)	4	—	—	(15)	(38)
	V8-350/R(10)(14)(28)(40)	14.6(30)	14.5(30)	15	195	21(3)(42)	4	—	—	(15)	(38)
	V8-350(13)(54)	—	14.9(30)	15	195	20	4	—	—	(9)	3.2(8)
	V8-403/K(10)(14)	15.7(32)	16.6	15	195	21(3)(42)	4	—	—	(15)	(38)
1980	V6-231(11)(54)	13.3	13.3	15	195	18.1	4	3.5	3.5	(45)	(38)
	V6-231(10)(54)	13	13	15	195	25	4	3.5	—	(45)	(38)
	V6-231 Turbo/3(11)	13.7(43)	13.8(43)	15	195	18.1	4	3.5	—	(45)	(38)
	V6-231 Turbo/3(10)	13.4(44)	13.4(44)	15	195	25	4	—	—	(45)	(38)
	V6-231 Turbo/3(13)	—	13.66(47)	15	195	21	4	—	—	(9)	3.2(8)
	V6-252/4(10)(14)	13	13	15	195	25	4	—	—	(45)	(38)
	V8-301/W(11)	20.3(27)	21	15	195	18.1	4(46)	3.5	—	(45)	(38)
	V8-301/W(10)(14)	18.9	18.9	15	195	25(3)	4(46)	3.5	—	(45)	(38)
	V8-305/H(11)	—	17.6(36)	15	195	18.1	4	—	—	(45)	(38)
	V8-350/X(10)(14)(23)(39)	14.3(48)	14.2(48)	15	195	25(3)	4	—	—	(45)	(38)
	V8-350/R(10)(14)(28)(40)	—	14.5(49)	15	195	25(3)	4	—	—	(45)	(38)
	V8-350(13)(54)	—	15.5	15	195	21	4	—	—	(9)	3.2(8)
	V8-350 Diesel/N(10)(14)	18.3	18	15	195	27(3)	7(21)	—	—	(45)	(38)
1981	V6-231/A(11)	13	13	15	195	18.1	4	3.5	—	(12)	3½
	V6-231/A(10)	13	13	15	195	25	4	3.5	—	(12)	3½
	V6-231 Turbo/3(11)	13.4(44)	13.4(44)	15	195	18.1	4	—	—	(12)	3½
	V6-231 Turbo/3(13)	13.6(43)	13.6(43)	15	195	21	4	—	—	(12)	3.3(8)
	V6-252/4(10)(14)	13	13	15	195	25	4	—	—	(12)	3½
	V6-252/4(13)	13	13	15	195	21	4	—	—	(12)	3.3(8)
	V8-265/S(11)	20.2(27)	20.2(27)	15	195	18.1	4(46)	3.5	—	(12)	3½
	V8-307/Y(10)(14)	18.9	18.9	15	195	25(3)	4	—	—	(12)	3½
	V8-307/Y(13)	16.4	16.4	15	195	22	4	—	—	(12)	3.3(8)
	V8-350 Diesel/N(10)(14)	17.3	17	15	195	27(3)	7(21)	—	—	(12)	3½
	V8-350 Diesel/N(13)	18.2	18.2	15	195	27	7(21)	—	—	(12)	3½
1982	V6-231/A(50)	12.98	13.02	15	195	18	4	—	—	(51)	(16)
	V6-231/A(10)	13	13	15	195	25(3)	4	—	—	(51)	(16)
	V6-231 Turbo/3(50)	13.44(44)	13.44(44)	15	195	25(3)	4	—	—	(51)	(16)
	V6-231 Turbo/3(13)	13.6(43)	13.6(43)	15	195	21	4	—	—	(51)	3.2(8)
	V6-252/4(50)	12.98	13.02	15	195	18	4	—	—	(51)	(16)

Continued

COOLING SYSTEM & CAPACITY DATA—Continued

Year	Model or Engine/V.I.N.	Cooling Capacity, Qts. Less A/C	With A/C	Radiator Cap Relief Pressure, Lbs.	Thermo. Opening Temp.	Fuel Tank Gals.	Engine Oil Refill Qts. [1]	Transmission Oil 3 Speed Pints	4 Speed Pints	Auto. Trans. Qts. [2]	Rear Axle Oil Pints
	V6-252/4 [10][14]	13	13	15	195	25[3]	4	—	—	[51]	[16]
	V6-252/4 [13]	13	13	15	195	21	4	—	—	[51]	3.2[8]
	V6-262 Diesel/V [50]	14.8	14.8	15	195	20	6.5[21]	—	—	[51]	[16]
	V8-307/Y [10][14]	18.9	18.9	15	195	25[3]	4	—	—	[51]	[16]
	V8-307/Y [13]	18.8	18.95	15	195	21	4	—	—	[51]	3.2[8]
	V8-350 Diesel/N [50]	17.33	17.33	15	195	20	7[21]	—	—	[51]	[16]
	V8-350 Diesel/N [10][14]	17	17	15	195	27[3]	7[21]	—	—	[51]	[16]
	V8-350 Diesel/N [13]	18.2	18.2	15	195	23	7[21]	—	—	[51]	3.2[8]
1983	V6-231/A [50]	12.9	13	15	195	[53]	4	—	—	[51]	[38]
	V6-231/A [10]	12.9	13	15	195	25[3]	4	—	—	[51]	[38]
	V6-231 Turbo/8 [50]	13.4	13.4[44]	15	195	19.8	4	—	—	[51]	[38]
	V6-231 Turbo/8 [13]	—	13.6[43]	15	195	21.1	4	—	—	[51]	3.2[8]
	V6-252/4 [50]	12.9	13	15	195	[53]	4	—	—	[51]	[38]
	V6-252/4 [10][14]	12.9	13	15	195	25[3]	4	—	—	[51]	[38]
	V6-252/4 [13]	—	13	15	195	21.1	4	—	—	[51]	3.2[8]
	V6-262 Diesel/V [50]	—	14.7	18.5	195	[53]	6.5[21]	—	—	[51]	[38]
	V8-307/Y [10][14]	15.4[52]	16[52]	15	195	25[3]	4	—	—	[51]	[38]
	V8-307/Y [13]	—	16[52]	15	195	21.1	4	—	—	[51]	3.2[8]
	V8-350 Diesel/N [50]	—	17.3	15	195	[53]	6.5[21]	—	—	[51]	[38]
	V8-350 Diesel/N [10][14]	—	17.9	15	195	26[3]	6.5[21]	—	—	[51]	[38]
	V8-350 Diesel/N [13]	—	18	15	195	22.8	6.5[21]	—	—	[51]	3.2[8]

①—Add one quart with filter change.
②—Approximate. Make final check with dipstick.
③—Estate Wagon 22 gallons.
④—With heavy duty cooling system, 14.5 qts.
⑤—With heavy duty cooling system, 21.6 qts.
⑥—Estate Wagon, Electra & Riviera.
⑦—Skylark.
⑧—Final drive.
⑨—Total 12 qts. Oil pan only 5 qts.
⑩—LeSabre.
⑪—Century & Regal.
⑫—THM 200C—total 9½ qts., pan only 3½ qts.; THM 325—total 12 qts., pan only 5 qts.; THM 250C—total 10¾ qts., pan only 4 qts.; THM 350C—total 10 qts., pan only 3⅛ qts.; THM 2004R—total 11 qts., pan only 3½ qts.
⑬—Riviera.
⑭—Electra.
⑮—Total 10 qts.; pan only 3 qts.
⑯—With 7½ inch ring gear, 3.5 pints; with 8¾ inch ring gear, 5.4 pints.
⑰—Exc. Calif., 195°; Calif., 180°.
⑱—Oil filler tube located on engine front cover.
⑲—LeSabre, 21; Estate Wagon, 22.5; Electra, Riviera, 25.3.
⑳—Exc. wagon, 4¼ pts.; wagon, 5.4 pts.

㉑—Includes oil filter. For 1980 models, use recommended diesel oil, designated SE/CC. For 1981 models use recommended diesel oil designated SF/CC, SF/CD or SE/CC. For 1982–83 models use recommended diesel oil designated SF/CC or SF/CD.
㉒—With heavy duty cooling system, 19.1 qts.
㉓—Distributor at front of engine.
㉔—With heavy duty cooling system, 16.4 qts.
㉕—With heavy duty cooling system, 15 qts.
㉖—LeSabre, 21 gal.; Electra & Riviera, 24.5 gal.; Estate wagon, 22 gal.
㉗—With heavy duty cooling system, 20.8 qts.
㉘—Distributor at rear of engine.
㉙—With heavy duty cooling system, 17.4 qts.
㉚—With heavy duty cooling system, 15.4 qts.
㉛—With heavy duty cooling system, 18.5 qts.
㉜—With heavy duty cooling system, 16.6 qts.
㉝—With heavy duty cooling system, 16.9 qts.
㉞—With heavy duty cooling system, 19.6 qts.
㉟—With heavy duty cooling system, 14.9 qts.
㊱—With heavy duty cooling system, 18.0 qts.
㊲—4 Barrel Carb.
㊳—7½ inch axle, 3.5 pts.; 8½ inch axle, 4.25 pts.; 8¾ inch axle, 5.4 pts.
㊴—Buick built engine.
㊵—Oldsmobile built engine.
㊶—THM 200—total 9.5 qts.; oil pan only 3.5 qts. THM 350—total capacity 10 qts; oil pan only 3 qts.

㊷—Electra, 25.3 gal.
㊸—With heavy duty cooling system, 14.1 qts.
㊹—With heavy duty cooling system, 13.7 qts.
㊺—THM 200—total 9.5 qts., pan only 3.5 qts.; THM 250C—total 10 qts., pan only 4 qts.; THM 350—total 12¼ qts., pan only 3¼ qts.; THM 400—total 10 qts., pan only 3 qts.
㊻—With or without filter change.
㊼—With heavy duty cooling system, 14.17 qts.
㊽—With heavy duty cooling system, 14.8 qts.
㊾—With heavy duty cooling system, 15.2 qts.
㊿—Regal.
(51)—THM 250C—total 9.4 qts.; pan only 3.48 qts. THM 2004R—total 11.05 qts., pan only 3.48 qts. THM 250C—total 10.04 qts., pan only 4.0 qts. THM 3254L—total 11.75 qts., pand only 4.86 qts. THM 350C—total 10.04 qts.; pan only 3.17 qts.
(52)—With heavy duty cooling system, 16 qts.
(53)—Exc. wagon, 19.8 gals.; wagon, 18.2 gals.
(54)—For V.I.N. code, refer to the "General Engine Specifications" at the beginning of the chapter.

WHEEL ALIGNMENT SPECIFICATIONS

Year	Model	Caster Angle, Degrees Limits	Desired	Camber Angle, Degrees Limits Left	Right	Desired Left	Right	Toe-In. Inch	Toe Out on Turns, Deg. Outer Wheel	Inner Wheel
1977	Skylark[1]	−½ to −1½	−1	+¼ to +1¼	+¼ to +1¼	+¾	+¾	0 to ⅛	—	—
	Skylark[2]	+½ to +1½	+1	+¼ to +1¼	+¼ to +1¼	+¾	+¾	0 to ⅛	—	—
	Century, Regal[4]	+½ to +1½	+1	+½ to +1½	0 to +1	+1	+½	0 to ⅛	—	—
	Century, Regal[5]	+1½ to +2½	+2	+½ to +1½	0 to +1	+1	+½	0 to ⅛	—	—
	Others	+2½ to +3½	+3	+¼ to +1¼	+¼ to +1¼	+¾	+¾	1/16 to 3/16	—	—
1978	Skylark[1]	−.5 to −1.5	−1	+.3 to +1.3	+.3 to +1.3	+.8	+.8	1/16 to 3/16	—	—

WHEEL ALIGNMENT SPECIFICATIONS—Continued

| Year | Model | Caster Angle, Degrees | | Camber Angle, Degrees | | | | Toe-In. Inch | Toe Out on Turns, Deg. | |
| | | Limits | Desired | Limits | | Desired | | | Outer Wheel | Inner Wheel |
				Left	Right	Left	Right			
	Skylark②	+.5 to +1.5	+1	+.3 to +1.3	+.3 to +1.3	+.8	+.8	1/16 to 3/16	—	—
	Century, Regal①	+.5 to +1.5	+1	0 to +1	0 to +1	+.5	+.5	1/16 to 3/16	—	—
	Century, Regal②	+2.5 to +3.5	+3	0 to +1	0 to +1	+.5	+.5	1/16 to 3/16	—	—
	Others	+2.5 to +3.5	+3	+.3 to +1.3	+.3 to +1.3	+.8	+.8	1/16 to 3/16	—	—
1979	Skylark①	−.5 to −1.5	−1	+.3 to +1.3	+.3 to +1.3	+.8	+.8	1/16 to 3/16	—	—
	Skylark②	+.5 to +1.5	+1	+.3 to +1.3	+.3 to +1.3	+.8	+.8	1/6 to 3/16	—	—
1979–80	Century, Regal①	+.5 to +1.5	+1	0 to +1	0 to +1	+.5	+.5	1/16 to 3/16	—	—
	Century, Regal②	+2.5 to +3.5	+3	0 to +1	0 to +1	+.5	+.5	1/16 to 3/16	—	—
	Riviera	+2 to +3	+2.5	−.5 to +.5	−.5 to +.5	Zero	Zero	⑥	—	—
	Others	+2.5 to +3.5	+3	+.3 to +1.3	+.3 to +1.3	+.8	+.8	1/16 to 3/16	—	—
1981	Century, Regal②	+2.5 to +3.5	+3	0 to +1	0 to +1	+.5	+.5	1/16 to 3/16	—	—
	Riviera	+2 to +3	+2.5	−.5 to +.5	−.5 to +.5	Zero	Zero	⑥	—	—
	Others	+2.5 to +3.5	+3	+.3 to +1.3	+.3 to +1.3	+.8	+.8	1/16 to 3/16	—	—
1982	Regal	+2.5 to +3.5	+3	0 to +1	0 to +1	+.5	+.5	1/16 to 3/16	—	—
	Riviera	+2 to +3	+2.5	−.5 to +.5	−.5 to +.5	Zero	Zero	⑥	—	—
	Others	+2.5 to +3.5	+3	+.3 to +1.3	+.3 to +1.3	+.8	+.8	1/16 to 3/16	—	—
1983	Regal	+2.5 to +3.5	+3	0 to +1	0 to +1	+.5	+.5	1/16 to 3/16	—	—
	Riviera	+2 to +3	+2.5	−.5 to +.5	−.5 to +.5	Zero	Zero	⑥	—	—
	Others	+2.5 to +3.5	+3	+.3 to +1.3	+.3 to +1.3	+.8	+.8	1/16 to 3/16	—	—

①—Manual steering.
②—Power steering.
③—Manual steering & all Sta. Wag.—right turn, 19³/₁₆°; left turn, 18³/₁₆°: power steering Exc. Sta. Wag.—right turn, 19°; left turn, 18¹¹/₁₆°.
④—Equipped with bias belted tires.
⑤—Equipped with radial tires.
⑥—1/16" toe-in to 1/16" toe-out.

Electrical Section

STARTER, REPLACE

To remove the starter, disconnect battery cable from battery. Disconnect cable and solenoid lead wire from solenoid switch. Remove flywheel inspection cover. Remove starter attaching bolts and remove starter.

LIGHT SWITCH, REPLACE

1977–83

1. Disconnect battery ground cable.
2. On intermediate models equipped with A/C, remove left hand duct.
3. On all models except 1978–81 Century and 1978–83 Regal, pull switch knob to full "On" position, depress latch button on rear of switch and pull knob and rod from switch. On 1978–81 Century and 1978–83 Regal, depress retainer tab behind switch knob and remove knob from stem. On all models, remove switch escutcheon or retaining nut, if used.
4. Pull switch down, disconnect electrical connector and remove switch.
5. Reverse procedure to install.

COLUMN-MOUNTED DIMMER SWITCH, REPLACE

1977–83 Full Size; 1978–81 Century & Regal; 1982–83 Regal

1. Disconnect battery ground cable.
2. Remove instrument panel lower trim and on models with A/C, remove A/C duct extension at column.
3. Disconnect shift indicator from column and remove toe-plate cover screws.
4. Remove two nuts from instrument panel support bracket studs and lower steering column, resting steering wheel on front seat.
5. Remove dimmer switch retaining screw(s) and the switch. Tape actuator rod to column and separate switch from rod.
6. Reverse procedure to install. To adjust switch, depress dimmer switch slightly and install a 3/32 inch twist drill to lock the switch to the body. Force switch upward to remove lash between switch and pivot. Torque switch retaining screw(s) to 35 inch lbs. and remove tape from actuator rod. Remove twist drill and check for proper operation.

Fig. 1 Lock cylinder removal. 1979–83 models

Fig. 2 Ignition lock removal. 1977–78

Fig. 3 Clutch start switch in start position. 1977—81

1977 Intermediates

1. Remove switch cover.
2. Remove three switch to column attaching screws.
3. Disconnect switch lead at lower end of column and attach a wire to lead end of harness for ease of installation.
4. Hold switch and pull harness from column.
5. Reverse procedure to install.

IGNITION LOCK, REPLACE

1979—83

1. Remove steering wheel as described under Horn Sounder and Steering Wheel, Replace.
2. Remove turn signal switch as described under Turn Signal Switch, Replace, then remove buzzer switch.
3. Place ignition switch in Run position, then remove lock cylinder retaining screw and lock cylinder.
4. To install, rotate lock cylinder to stop while holding housing, Fig. 1. Align cylinder key with keyway in housing, then push lock cylinder assembly into housing until fully seated.
5. Install lock cylinder retaining screw. Torque screw to 40 in. lbs. for standard columns. On adjustable columns, torque retaining screw to 22 in. lbs.
6. Install buzzer switch, turn signal switch and steering wheel.

1977—78

1. Follow procedure to remove turn signal switch as described further on.
2. Place lock cylinder in "run" position.
3. Place a thin tool (small screw-driver or knife blade) into the slot next to the switch mounting screw boss (right hand slot) and depress spring latch at bottom of slot which releases lock Fig. 2. Remove lock.
4. To install lock, hold lock cylinder sleeve and rotate knob clockwise against stop, then insert cylinder with key on cylinder sleeve aligned with keyway in housing. Push in to abutment of cylinder and sector, then rotate knob counterclockwise, maintaining a light inward push on cylinder until drive section of cylinder mates with drive shaft.

Fig. 4 Turn signal and hazard warning flasher switch assembly. 1977—83

Fig. 6 Taping turn signal connector & wiring

IGNITION SWITCH, REPLACE

1977—83

The ignition switch is located on the top of the steering column under the instrument panel. To replace it the steering column must be lowered as follows:
1. Disconnect shift indicator link.
2. Remove nuts securing bracket to dash panel and carefully lower column.
3. Disconnect electrical connector from switch. On models equipped with standard column and key release feature or tilt column except key release, ensure switch is in "Accessory" position. On models equipped with standard column except key release or tilt column with key release, ensure switch is in "Off-Unlock" position.
4. Remove two screws securing switch, then remove switch.
5. On models equipped with standard column and key release feature or tilt column except key release, position switch slider and lock in the "Accessory" position. On models equipped with standard column except key release or tilt column with key release, position switch slider and lock at "Accessory" position, then move slider and lock two detents to the "Off-Unlock" position.
6. Fit actuator rod into switch and assemble to column.

Fig. 5 Compressing lock plate & removing snap ring

7. Complete assembly in reverse of removal procedure.

STOP LIGHT SWITCH, REPLACE

1977—83

The stop lights are controlled by a mechanical switch mounted on the brake pedal bracket. This spring loaded switch makes contact whenever the brake pedal is applied. When the brake pedal is released it depresses the switch to open the contacts and turn brake lights off.

CLUTCH START SWITCH

1977—81

A clutch start switch is installed on all manual transmission cars. The switch is mounted on the clutch pedal bracket and it prevents the car from being started until the clutch pedal is depressed, Fig. 3.

TURN SIGNAL SWITCH, REPLACE

1977—83

As shown in Fig. 4, the assembly is a turn signal switch and hazard warning switch. It is mounted in a housing at the upper end of the steering column mast jacket, just below the steering wheel. Therefore to get at the switch the steering wheel will have to be removed.

Also, on models equipped with tilt steering columns, it is necessary to lower the column assembly from instrument panel.
1. Disconnect battery ground cable.
2. Remove steering wheel and lock plate cover. On tilt columns, remove tilt lever.
3. With a suitable compressor, compress lock plate and spring, then remove snap ring from shaft, Fig. 5.
4. Remove lock plate cover with a suitable screwdriver.
5. Remove lock plate, cancelling cam, preload spring and thrust washer.
6. Remove turn signal lever and hazard warning switch knob.
7. Disconnect switch wiring connector and wrap a piece of tape around connector

Fig. 7 Mechanical neutral start system with standard column. 1977–83 Full Size; 1978–81 Century, Regal; 1982–83 Regal

Fig. 8 Mechanical neutral start system with tilt column. 1977–83 Full Size; 1978–81 Century, Regal; 1982–83 Regal

Fig. 9 Mechanical neutral start system in Park position. 1977–83 Full Size; 1978–81 Century, Regal; 1982–83 Regal

upper end and wiring harness, preventing snagging when removing switch, Fig. 6.
8. Remove three switch retaining screws and switch.
9. Reverse procedure to install.

NEUTRAL START SWITCH

1977–83 Full Size; 1978–81 Century, Regal; 1982–83 Regal

Actuation of the ignition switch is prevented by a mechanical lockout system, Figs. 7 and 8, which prevents the lock cylinder from rotating when the selector lever is out of Park or Neutral. When the selector lever is in Park or Neutral, the slots in the bowl plate and the finger on the actuator rod align allowing the finger to pass through the bowl plate in turn actuating the ignition switch, Fig. 9. If the selector lever is in any position other than Park or Neutral, the finger contacts the bowl plate when the lock cylinder is rotated, thereby preventing full travel of the lock cylinder.

NEUTRAL START & BACK-UP LIGHT SWITCH, REPLACE

NOTE: Some models use a combination neutral start & back-up light switch, while other models use a back-up light switch. Both type switches are serviced by the following procedures.

1977–81 Models

1. On automatic transmission equipped models, place gear selector in "Neutral" for column shift, or "Park" for console shift. On manual transmission models, place gearshift in "Reverse".
2. Remove screws attaching switch to steering column, then remove switch.
3. Disconnect wiring connectors. Connect wiring connectors to new switch.
4. Position new switch on steering column, aligning the switch carrier tang in the switch tube slot.
5. Install attaching screws and tighten.

NOTE: No adjustment is required. The switch is pinned in the proper position with a plastic shear pin.

6. If adjustment is required:
   a. On 1977–78 models with automatic transmission, place gear selector in "Neutral" position. On 1979–81 models with automatic transmission, place gear selector in "Neutral" for column shift, or "Park" for console shift. On all models with manual transmission, place gearshift in "Reverse".

   b. Loosen switch adjusting screws.
   c. On 1977–79 models and 1980–81 models with column shift, while rotating switch on column, insert a .096 inch gage pin in neutral gage hole a depth of 3/8 inch, Fig. 10. On 1980–81 models with console shift, while rotating switch on column, insert .096 inch gage pin in park gage hole a depth of 3/8 inch, Fig. 10.
   d. Tighten attaching screws and remove gage pin.

1982–83 Models

1. Place gear selector in "Neutral".
2. Gently rock switch out of steering column.
3. Disconnect wiring connectors. Connect wiring connectors to new switch.
4. Align switch actuator with hole in shift tube, Fig. 11.
5. Position connector side of switch into lower jacket cut out.
6. Push down front of switch, ensuring switch tangs snap into holes in steering column jacket.
7. Adjust switch by placing gear selector in "Park" position. The switch main housing and housing back should ratchet, providing proper adjustment.

Fig. 10 Neutral start & back-up light switch adjustment. 1977–81 models

Fig. 11 Neutral start & back-up light switch installation. 1982–83 models

Fig. 12 Disassembled view of tilt & telescope steering wheel. 1977–83 models

Fig. 13   Instrument cluster trim cover. 1979–83 Riviera

Fig. 14   Speedometer & telltale assembly. 1977 Century & Regal

STANDARD HORN SOUNDER & STEERING WHEEL, REPLACE

1977–83

1. Remove horn cap or actuator bar.
2. Remove steering wheel nut retainer, if used.
3. On all models, back off nut until flush with top of steering shaft.
4. Use a suitable puller to remove wheel.

TILT & TELESCOPE STEERING WHEEL, REPLACE

1977–83

Removal
1. Disconnect battery ground cable.
2. Remove screws, Fig. 12, and lift pad assembly up, then disconnect horn wiring electrical connector by pushing in and turning counterclockwise.
3. Push locking lever counterclockwise until full release position is obtained.
4. Scribe plate assembly where the two screws secure plate assembly to locking lever.
5. Remove screws and plate assembly.
6. Remove steering wheel nut retainer and nut.
7. Using tool No. J185903, remove steering wheel assembly.

NOTE: Use of a steering wheel puller other than the one recommended in Step 7, or a sharp blow on the end of the steering shaft or shift lever could shear or loosen the plastic fasteners which maintain steering column rigidity.

Installation
1. Install a suitable set screw into upper shaft at the full extended position and lock.
2. Align scribe mark on steering wheel hub with mark on end of shaft and install steering wheel. Ensure unsecured end of horn upper contact assembly is complete-

ly seated against top of horn contact carrier assembly.
3. Install nut onto upper steering shaft and torque to 30 ft. lbs. Install nut retainer.
4. Remove set screw and install plate assembly and screws. Tighten screws finger tight.
5. Position locking lever in vertical position and move lever counterclockwise until plate holes align with holes in lever. Install plate securing screws.
6. Align pad assembly with holes in steering wheel and install screws.
7. Connect battery ground cable. Ensure locking lever securely locks steering wheel travel and that steering wheel travel is free in the unlocked position.

INSTRUMENT CLUSTER, REPLACE

1979–83 Riviera

1. Disconnect battery ground cable.
2. Remove left hand trim cover, Fig. 11.
3. Remove headlamp and windshield wiper switches.
4. Disconnect headlamp and windshield wiper switch wire connectors from cluster carrier.
5. Disconnect speedometer cable, and wire connectors from cluster carrier.
6. Remove cluster carrier to instrument panel attaching screws, then remove cluster carrier.

1978–81 Century & Regal; 1982–83 Regal

1. Disconnect battery ground cable.
2. Remove headlamp switch knob and escutcheon.
3. Carefully pry out and remove clutch trim plate.
4. Remove five cluster lens attaching screws, then remove cluster lens.
5. To remove speedometer, remove two speedometer retaining screws. Disconnect speedometer cable and wire connector, then lift speedometer from instrument cluster.
6. To replace fuel gauge or clock, remove attaching screws, then slide gauge or clock from cluster and disconnect wire connector.

1977–83 Full Size Except 1979–83 Riviera

1. Disconnect battery ground cable.
2. Remove glove box door and glove box.
3. Remove trim plates and the steering column opening filler.
4. Disconnect electrical and vacuum connectors from gauges or controls.
5. Remove wiring harness from instrument panel carrier clips.
6. Remove instrument panel carrier attaching nuts and screws, then the carrier from vehicle.
7. Reverse procedure to install.

1977–79 Skylark

1. Disconnect battery ground cable.
2. Disconnect heater or A/C control panel from the instrument panel carrier.
3. Remove radio control knobs, bezels and nuts, leaving the radio attached to the instrument panel reinforcement.
4. Disconnect instrument panel pad from the carrier and disconnect the shift quadrant indicator cable at the shift bowl. On automatic transmission equipped vehicles remove the two nuts securing the steering column to instrument panel.
5. Remove toe plate cover and disconnect from cowl.
6. Lower steering column from instrument panel and use a protective cover (such as shop towel).
7. Disconnect the ground wire from left side of instrument panel pad followed by the speedometer cable.
8. With carrier and cluster assembly tilted rearward, disconnect printed circuit and cluster ground connectors.
9. Rest assembly on top of column and disconnect cluster from carrier assembly.
10. Reverse procedure to install.

1977 Century & Regal
Speedometer Cluster
1. Disconnect battery ground cable.
2. Place transmission selector lever in "L" position and disconnect shift indicator cable from steering column.
3. Pry trim plate from instrument panel.
4. Remove speedometer retaining screws, Fig. 14, disconnect speedometer cable and wiring connector, then remove speedometer.
5. Reverse procedure to install.

Fuel Gauge & Telltale Assembly

1. Disconnect battery ground cable.
2. Pry trim plate from instrument panel.
3. Remove retaining screws, Fig. 14, disconnect wiring connectors, then remove assembly.

NOTE: If equipped with temperature and oil pressure gauges and one gauge of the assembly is defective, all three gauges must be replaced since the cluster is serviced as an assembly.

4. Reverse procedure to install.

W/S WIPER MOTOR, REPLACE

1977–83

1. Disconnect battery and remove cowl screen.
2. Loosen nuts on wiper drivelink to motor cranking arm and slip drivelink off cranking arm.
3. Disconnect washer hoses and electrical connections.
4. Unfasten motor and remove.

NOTE: On models with round motor, the motor must be in "Park" position when assembling crank arm to transmission drive link.

W/S WIPER TRANSMISSION, REPLACE

1977–83

1. Disconnect battery ground cable and remove cowl vent screen or grille.
2. Disconnect wiper motor electrical connector.
3. Remove wiper arm and blade assemblies.
4. Loosen transmission drive link to motor crankarm attaching nuts, then disconnect drive link from crankarm.
5. Remove right and left transmission to body retaining screws and guide transmission and linkage through cowl opening.

NOTE: On full size models equipped with round motor, remove transmission retaining screws from transmission being removed.

6. Reverse procedure to install.

W/S WIPER SWITCH, REPLACE

1982–83 Full Size

1. Remove steering wheel as described under "Horn Sounder and Steering Wheel, Replace."
2. Remove turn signal switch as described under "Turn Signal Switch, Replace."
3. Remove ignition lock and buzzer as described under "Ignition Lock, Replace."
4. Remove and install cover and wiper switch as shown in Fig. 15.
5. Reverse remaining procedure to install.

Fig. 15 Windshield wiper switch removal & installation. 1982–83 models

1979–81 Riviera

1. Disconnect battery ground cable.
2. Remove left hand trim cover, Fig. 13.
3. Remove two switch to cluster attaching screws.
4. Pull switch rearward and remove.

1978–81 Century & 1978–83 Regal

1. Remove headlamp switch knob and escutcheon.
2. Remove trim plate.
3. Remove two switch attaching screws, then disconnect wire connector and remove switch.
4. Reverse procedure to install.

1977–81 Full Size Except 1979–81 Riviera

1. Remove left trim plate.
2. Remove switch attaching screws.
3. Disconnect electrical connector from switch and remove switch from vehicle.
4. Reverse procedure to install.

1977–79 Skylark

1. Remove electrical connector, three attaching screws and switch.

1977 Century & Regal

1. Insert blade of a small screwdriver into slots above knobs, bend retaining clips down and pull top of switch outward.
2. Remove electrical connector from switch.

RADIO, REPLACE

NOTE: When installing radio, be sure to adjust antenna trimmer for peak performance.

1981–83 Riviera

1. Disconnect battery ground cable.
2. Remove center trim plate by grasping firmly and pulling rearward.
3. Remove six screws from radio mounting bracket.
4. Remove six screws from instrument panel lower cover assembly, then pull cover assembly out from instrument panel enough to gain access to two screws attaching radio bracket to instrument panel lower tie bar. Remove screws.
5. Carefully pull radio assembly rearward to remove.
6. Disconnect radio harness connectors and antenna lead.
7. Reverse procedure to install.

1979–80 Riviera

1. Disconnect battery ground cable.
2. Remove center trim cover.
3. Remove four screws attaching radio mounting plate to instrument panel.
4. Disconnect radio wire connector and antenna lead.
5. Pull radio and mounting plate rearward and remove radio.

1978–81 Century & Regal; 1982–83 Regal

1. Disconnect battery ground cable.
2. Remove cigar lighter knob, radio knobs and escutcheons by pulling rearward.
3. Remove center trim plate by grasping firmly and pulling rearward.

NOTE: A flat blade screwdriver or putty knife can be used to pry up a corner of the center trim plate to aid in removal.

4. Remove four screws attaching radio bracket to instrument panel.
5. Open glove box door and release spring retainers, then allow door to open fully.
6. Working through glove box door, loosen holding bracket nut on right rear side of radio, then remove antenna lead.
7. Carefully pull radio assembly rearward to remove.
8. Disconnect radio harness connectors, then remove bracket.
9. Reverse procedure to install.

1981–83 Full Size Except 1981–83 Riviera

1. Disconnect battery ground cable.
2. Remove radio knobs, escutcheons and if equipped with rear defogger, rear defogger knob.
3. Remove left hand instrument panel trim plate by removing headlight knob, then place gear selector in low. Using a suitable flat bladed screwdriver or putty knife, remove trim plate by gently prying edge, then lifting straight out.
4. Remove four center trim plate attaching screws, then trim plate.
5. Remove four screws attaching radio to radio bracket, then carefully pull radio rearward out of instrument panel.
6. Disconnect radio harness connectors and antenna lead.
7. Reverse procedure to install.

1977–80 Full Size Except 1979–80 Riviera

1. Disconnect battery ground cable.
2. Remove ash tray and bracket.
3. Remove radio knobs and escutcheons from shafts.
4. Remove lower left-hand air duct.
5. Remove retaining nuts from radio control shafts.

6. Disconnect electrical connections from radio.
7. Remove rear radio attaching nut, then the radio from vehicle.
8. Reverse procedure to install.

1977-79 Skylark

1. Remove radio knobs, bezels, nuts and side brace screw.
2. Disconnect antenna and leads.
3. Remove radio from under dash.
4. Reverse procedure to install.

1977 Century & Regal

1. Remove radio knobs and escutcheons. If equipped with center air duct assembly control, remove screws.
2. Disconnect antenna and leads.
3. Remove radio support nut.
4. Remove attaching nuts and slide radio to front of car and downward.
5. Reverse procedure to install.

HEATER CORE, REPLACE

1979-83 Riviera

1. Disconnect battery ground cable and drain cooling system.
2. Disconnect heater hoses from heater core and install plugs in heater core outlets.
3. Remove instrument panel sound absorbers, then lower steering column.
4. Remove instrument cluster as described under Instrument Cluster, Replace.
5. Remove radio front speakers.
6. Remove screws attaching manifold to heater case.
7. Remove upper and lower instrument panel attaching screws.
8. Disconnect parking brake release cable.
9. Disconnect instrument panel wiring harness from dash wiring harness.
10. Disconnect right hand remote control mirror cable from instrument panel pad.
11. Disconnect speedometer cable and temperate control cable at heater case.
12. Disconnect radio, A/C wiring and vacuum lines, and all wiring necessary to remove instrument panel assembly. If equipped with pulse wiper, remove wiper switch, unlock wire connector from cluster carrier and separate pulse wiper jumper harness from wiper switch wire connector.

Fig. 16   Heater core. 1979-83 Riviera

13. Remove instrument panel and harness assembly.
14. Remove defroster ducts, then remove blower motor resistor.
15. Remove A/C-heater housing to dash panel nuts, Fig. 16.
16. Remove housing to dash screw and clip from inside vehicle, then remove housing assembly from dash.
17. Remove heater core from housing assembly.

1978-81 Century & Regal; 1982-83 Regal

Without Air Conditioning

1. Disconnect battery ground cable and partially drain cooling system.
2. Disconnect hoses from heater core, then the electrical connectors.
3. Remove front module retaining screws and module cover.
4. Remove heater core.
5. Reverse procedure to install.

With Air Conditioning

1. Disconnect battery ground cable and partially drain cooling system.
2. Disconnect hoses from heater core, then the electrical connectors from module.
3. Remove retaining bracket, ground strap, module rubber seal and screen.
4. Remove right hand windshield wiper arm.
5. Remove retaining screws from diagnostic connector, hi-blower relay and thermostatic switch.
6. Remove module top cover, then heater core.
7. Reverse procedure to install.

1977-83 Full Size Except 1979-83 Riviera

Without Air Conditioning

1. Disconnect battery ground cable and drain radiator.
2. Disconnect heater hoses from module, then the electrical connections from module front case.
3. Remove module front case attaching screws, then the heater core, Fig. 17.

Fig. 17   Heater core & blower motor. 1977-83 Full Size Except 1979-83 Riviera without air conditioning

Fig. 18   Heater core & blower motor. 1977-83 Full Size Except 1979-83 Riviera with air conditioning

Fig. 19   Heater core. 1977–79 Skylark (Typical)

4. Reverse procedure to install.

With Air Conditioning
1. Disconnect battery ground cable and drain radiator.
2. Disconnect heater hoses from module.
3. Remove diagnostic connector and thermostatic switch from module.
4. Remove weather seal from top of module cover, then the cowl screen and windshield washer nozzle.
5. Remove module cover attaching screws.
6. Remove heater core retaining clip and the heater core from vehicle, Fig. 18.
7. Reverse procedure to install.

1977–79 Skylark

Without Air Conditioning
1. Disconnect battery ground cable and drain radiator.
2. Disconnect heater hoses from core and plug hoses and core openings to prevent coolant spillage.
3. Remove core case retaining nuts from engine side of dash, Fig. 19.
4. Remove glove compartment and door.
5. Using a ¼ inch twist drill, drill out lower right hand heater case stud from inside vehicle.
6. Pull heater core and case assembly from dash.
7. Disconnect heater cables and blower motor resistor connector from case, then remove heater core and case assembly from vehicle.
8. Remove core tube seal and retaining strips, then heater core from case.
9. Reverse procedure to install.

With Air Conditioning
1. Disconnect battery ground cable and drain radiator.

2. Disconnect upper heater hose and plug hose and core openings. Remove accessible heater core and case attaching nuts.
3. Remove right front fender skirt bolts, lower skirt and disconnect lower heater hose from core tube. Plug hose and core openings.
4. Remove lower right hand heater core and case attaching nuts, Fig. 19.
5. Remove glove compartment and door.
6. Remove right hand kick panel recirculation vacuum diaphragm.
7. Remove heater outlet from bottom of heater case, then cold air distributor duct.
8. Remove heater case extension screws, then separate extension from heater case.
9. Disconnect heater cables and electrical connectors from heater case, then remove heater core and case assembly. Separate core from case.
10. Reverse procedure to install.

1977 Century & Regal

Without Air Conditioning
1. Disconnect battery ground cable.
2. Drain cooling system and disconnect heater hoses from heater core.
3. Disconnect control cables from door levers.
4. Remove four nuts securing heater to dash, Fig. 20.
5. Remove screw securing defroster outlet to heater.
6. Work heater assembly rearward until studs clear dash.
7. Reverse procedure to install.

With Air Conditioning
1. Disconnect battery ground cable.
2. Drain cooling system and disconnect heater hoses from heater core.
3. Disconnect control cables from temperature door guides and vacuum hoses from actuator diaphragms.
4. Remove resistor assembly and reach through opening and remove one attaching nut to dash. Remove one attaching nut to dash directly over transmission and two attaching nuts to upper and lower inboard evaporator case half.
5. From inside car remove one screw in lower righthand corner on passenger side.
6. Remove lower attaching outlets and work assembly rearward until studs clear dash.
7. Reverse procedure to install.

BLOWER MOTOR, REPLACE

1979–83 Riviera
1. Disconnect battery ground cable.
2. Remove right fender skirt to provide clearance for blower motor removal.
3. Disconnect wire connector and cooling hose.
4. Remove blower motor attaching screws and blower motor.

1982–83 Regal; 1978–81 Century & Regal; 1977–83 Full Size Except 1979–83 Riviera
1. Disconnect blower motor wiring.
2. Remove blower motor attaching screws and the blower motor, Figs. 17 and 18.

Fig. 20   Heater core. 1977 intermediate models exc. Skylark (Typical)

1977 Century & Regal
1. Disconnect blower motor wire.
2. Remove screws securing motor to air inlet and remove blower motor, Fig. 21.

1977–79 Skylark
1. Disconnect battery ground cable and raise vehicle on hoist.
2. Remove fender skirt attaching bolts except those attaching skirt to radiator support.
3. Pull skirt out and down, then place a block of wood between skirt and fender to provide clearance for motor removal.
4. Disconnect blower motor electrical connections and remove motor attaching screws and blower motor.
5. Remove blower motor retaining nut and separate impeller from motor.
6. Reverse procedure to install.

Fig. 21 Blower motor. 1977 Century & Regal (Typical)

SPEED CONTROL

Power Unit, Adjust

Units With Bead Chain
1. Make sure that engine hot idle speed is properly adjusted, then shut off engine and set carburetor choke to hot idle position.
2. Check slack in chain by disconnecting swivel from ball stud and holding chain taut at ball stud. Center of swivel should extend 1/8 inch beyond center of ball stud.
3. To adjust bead chain slack, remove retainer from swivel and chain assembly, then place chain into swivel cavities which permits chain to have slight slack.
4. Install retainer over swivel and chain assembly.

Units With Servo Rod
1. Make sure that engine hot idle speed is properly adjusted, then shut off engine and set carburetor choke to hot idle position.

2. Remove servo rod retainer, then adjust rod and install retainer in hole which provides some clearance between retainer and servo bushing. Clearance must not exceed width of one hole.

Units With Cable
1. Make sure that engine hot idle speed is properly adjusted, then shut off engine and set carburetor choke to hot idle position.
2. Remove cable pin retainer, then pull power unit end of cable toward power unit as far as it will go. If one of four holes in power unit tab aligns with cable pin, connect pin to tab with retainer.
3. If tab does not align with pin, move cable away from power unit until next closest tab hole aligns and connect pin to tab with retainer.

CAUTION: Do not force cable to make adjustment, as this will prevent engine from returning to idle.

Cruise Speed Adjustment
The cruise speed adjustment can be set as follows:
1. If car cruises below engagement speed, screw orifice tube on transducer outward.
2. If car cruises above engagement speed, screw orifice tube inward.

NOTE: Each 1/4 turn of the orifice tube will change cruise speed about one mile per hour. Snug up lock nut after each adjustment.

Brake Release Switch Adjustment
Fully depress brake pedal, then push switch and valve forward to contact bracket or arm. Pull pedal rearward with approximately 15 to 20 pounds of force to adjust switch and valve properly.

Gasoline Engine Section

NOTE: For service procedures see Chevrolet Chapter for V8-305 and V8-350 with the distributor located at the rear of engine, clockwise distributor rotor rotation; Oldsmobile Chapter for V8-307, V8-350 and V8-403 with distributor located at the rear of engine, counter clockwise distributor rotor rotation; Pontiac Chapter for V8-265 and V8-301.

ENGINE MOUNTS, REPLACE

1. Raise car and provide frame support at front of car.
2. Support weight of engine at forward edge of pan.
3. Remove mount to engine block bolts. Raise engine slightly and remove mount to mount bracket bolt and nut, Figs. 1 and 2. Remove mount.
4. Reverse above procedure to install.

Fig. 1 Engine mounts. V6-196 & 231

ENGINE, REPLACE

1979–83 Riviera
1. Remove hood. Scribe alignment marks on hood around hinge areas for alignment during installation.
2. Disconnect battery ground cable and remove air cleaner.
3. Drain cooling system and disconnect heater hoses.
4. Remove fan, pulleys and belts.
5. Remove upper and lower radiator hoses

Fig. 2   Engine mounts. V8-350

Fig. 3   Cylinder head tightening sequence V8-350

Fig. 4   Cylinder head tightening sequence V6-196, 231, 252

and fan shroud.

6. Disconnect transmission cooler lines from radiator, then remove radiator.
7. Remove air conditioning compressor.
8. Disconnect all electrical wires and vacuum hoses.
9. On turbocharged engines:
   a. Disconnect accelerator cable at carburetor.
   b. Disconnect fuel pump lines and plug lines to prevent spilling fuel.
   c. Remove power steering pump mounting bolts and position pump assembly aside.
   d. Remove alternator, then disconnect engine to body ground straps.
   e. Disconnect turbocharger outlet exhaust pipe from turbocharger.
10. On all except turbocharged engines:
    a. Disconnect accelerator rod and throttle valve cable.
    b. Disconnect fuel lines and plug lines to prevent spilling fuel.
    c. Remove power steering pump.
    d. Remove transmission cooler line bracket.
    e. Disconnect left exhaust pipe.
11. Raise and properly support vehicle.
12. Drain engine oil, then remove starter.
13. Remove converter shield, then the flywheel to converter bolts.
14. On all except turbocharged engines, disconnect right exhaust pipe and remove splash shield.
15. Remove the right transmission to engine bolts.
16. Remove right output shaft support bolts.
17. Remove front motor mount support bolts.
18. Support the final drive using a chain, then remove the remaining transmission to engine bolts.

19. Remove final drive to engine bracket.
20. Remove engine using a suitable hoist.
21. Reverse procedure to install.

Exc. 1979–83 Riviera

1. Remove hood and drain radiator.
2. Disconnect battery ground cable.
3. Remove fan shroud, radiator and air cleaner.
4. If equipped with A/C, disconnect compressor brackets and position out of way.
5. Remove power steering from bracket and position out of way.
6. Disconnect all hoses, linkages and electrical connections from engine.
7. Disconnect exhaust pipes and remove converter cover.
8. Remove flywheel to converter or pressure plate bolts, engine to transmission bolts and motor mount bolts.
9. Support transmission and remove engine.

CYLINDER HEAD, REPLACE

Prior to reinstalling the cylinder head bolts on V6 engines, coat the head bolts with a suitable heavy body thread sealer. This is to prevent coolant leakage, as the head bolt holes extend into the water jacket.

An accurate torque wrench should be used when installing head bolts. Uneven tightening of the head bolts can distort the cylinder bores, causing compression loss and excessive oil consumption.

1. Drain coolant and disconnect battery.
2. Remove intake manifold.
3. When removing right cylinder head, remove Delcotron and/or A/C compressor

with mounting bracket and move out of the way. *Do not disconnect hoses from A/C compressor.*

4. When removing left cylinder head, remove oil dipstick, power steering pump and move out of the way with hoses attached.
5. Disconnect exhaust manifold from head to be removed.
6. Remove rocker arm shaft and lift out push rods.
7. On 1977–79 Skylark models equipped with V6-231 and V8-350 engines, to replace left cylinder head, disconnect power brake unit hose at rear of cylinder head. Remove left front engine mount bolt and loosen right front engine mount bolt. Raise engine until exhaust manifold clears steering gear.
8. Remove cylinder head.
9. Reverse procedure to install and tighten bolts gradually and evenly in the sequence shown in Figs. 3 and 4.

NOTE: When installing intake manifold, refer to Figs. 5 and 6 for bolt tightening sequence.

ROCKER ARMS
V6-196, 231, 252; V8-350

A nylon retainer is used to retain the rocker arm. Break them below their heads with a chisel, Fig. 7, or pry out with channel locks.

Fig. 5   Intake manifold tightening sequence. V8-350

Fig. 6   Intake manifold tightening sequence. V6-196, 231, 252

Fig. 7   Removing nylon retainer. V6-196, 231, 252 & V8-350

Fig. 8   Service rocker arms identification. V6-196, 231, 252 & V8-350

Fig. 9   Service rocker arms installation. V6-196, 231, 252 & V8-350

Fig. 10   Hydraulic valve lifter parts

⑥—Distributor located at rear of engine, clockwise distributor rotor rotation.
⑦—Distributor located at rear of engine, counter distributor rotor clockwise rotation.
⑧—Diesel engine.

Production rocker arms can be installed in any sequence since the arms are identical.

Replacement rocker arms for all engines are identified with a stamping, right (R) and left (L), Fig. 8 and must be installed as shown in Fig. 9.

To install rocker arms, position arm on rocker shaft, centering it over the 1/4 inch hole in the rocker shaft. Install new rocker arm retainers in the provided holes using a 1/2 inch or larger drift to seat them.

VALVE ARRANGEMENT

Front to Rear

V6-196, 231, 252 . . . . E-I-I-E-I-E
V8-350 . . . . E-I-I-E-E-I-I-E

VALVE LIFT SPECS.

Engine	Year	Intake	Exhaust
V6-196	1978	.3230	.3660
V6-196	1979	.3410	.3660
V6-231	1977–78	.3830	.3660
V6-231①	1979–83	.3570	.3660
V6-231②	1979–81	.3410	.3660
V6-252	1980–83	.3570	.3660
V6-262⑧	1982	.3750	.3750
V8-265	1980–81	.3570	.3660
V8-301③	1977	.3770	.3770
V8-301④	1977–79	.3640	.3640
V8-301	1980	.3570	.3660
	1981	.3500	.3500
V8-305	1977–80	.3727	.4100
V8-307	1981	.4000	.4000
V8-350⑤	1977–79	.3230	.3390
V8-350⑤	1980	.3570	.3390
			.3660
V8-350⑥	1977–79	.3900	.4100
V8-350⑦	1977–79	.4000	.4000
V8-350⑧	1980–83	.3750	.3760
V8-403	1977–79	.4000	.4000

①—Exc. turbo charged engine.
②—Turbo charged engine.
③—Man. trans.
④—Auto. trans.
⑤—Distributor located at front of engine.

VALVE TIMING

Intake Opens Before TDC

Engine	Year	Degrees
V6-196	1978	18
V6-196	1979	16
V6-231	1977–78	17
V6-231	1979–83	16
V6-252	1980–83	16
V6-262⑧	1982	16
V8-265	1980	27
	1981	16
V8-301①	1977	31
V8-301②	1977–78	27
V8-301⑥	1979	16
V8-301①⑦	1979	27
V8-301②⑦	1979	16
V8-301	1980	16
V8-305	1977–80	28
V8-307	1981	20
V8-350③	1977–79	13.5
V8-350③	1980	16
V8-350④	1977–79	28
V8-350⑤	1977–79	16
V8-350⑧	1980–83	16
V8-403	1977–79	16

①—Man. trans.
②—Auto. trans.
③—Distributor located at front of engine.
④—Distributor located at rear of engine, clockwise distributor rotor rotation. Refer to Chevrolet chapter for engine service procedures.
⑤—Distributor located at rear of engine, counter clockwise distributor rotor rotation. Refer to Oldsmobile chapter for engine service procedures.
⑥—2 Bar. Carb.
⑦—4 Bar. Carb.
⑧—Diesel engine.

VALVE GUIDES

The valve guides are an integral part of the cylinder head and cannot be replaced.

If valve stem clearance is excessive, the valve guide must be reamed and an oversize valve installed. On 1977–78 engines, valves are available in the oversizes of .010 inch for V8-350 and .006 inch for V6-196, 231, 252. On 1979–83 engines, valves are available in the oversize of .010 inch.

HYDRAULIC VALVE LIFTERS

Failure of an hydraulic valve lifter, Fig. 10, is generally caused by an inadequate oil supply or dirt. An air leak at the intake side of the oil pump or too much oil in the engine will cause air bubbles in the oil supply to the lifters, causing them to collapse. This is a probable cause of trouble if several lifters fail to function, but air in the oil is an unlikely cause of failure of a single unit.

The valve lifters may be lifted out of their bores after removing the rocker arms, push rods and intake manifold. Adjustable pliers with taped jaws may be used to remove lifters that are stuck due to varnish, carbon, etc. Fig. 10 illustrates the type of lifter used.

TIMING CASE COVER, REPLACE

V6-196, 231, 252 & V8-350

1. Drain cooling system and remove radiator and heater return hose.
2. Remove fan, pulleys and belts.
3. Remove crankshaft pulley and balancer.
4. If equipped with power steering, remove any pump bracket bolts attached to timing chain cover and loosen and remove any other bolts necessary that will allow pump and brackets to be moved out of the way.
5. Remove fuel pump.
6. Remove Delcotron and brackets.
7. Remove distributor cap and pull spark plug wire retainers off brackets on rocker arm cover. Swing distributor cap with wires attached out of the way. Disconnect distributor primary lead.
8. Remove distributor. *If chain and sprockets are not to be disturbed, note position of distributor rotor for installation in the same position.*
9. Loosen and slide clamp on thermostat bypass hose rearward.
10. Remove bolts attaching chain cover to block.
11. On V6-196, 231, 252 and V8-350 engines, remove two oil pan-to-chain cover bolts and remove cover.
12. Reverse procedure to install, noting data shown in Figs. 11 and 12.

Fig. 11 Timing chain cover installation.
V6-196, 231 & 252

Fig. 12 Timing chain cover installation.
V8-350

Fig. 13 Valve timing marks.
V6-196, 231, 252 & V8-350

IMPORTANT: Remove the oil pump cover and pack the space around the oil pump gears completely full of vaseline. There must be no air space left inside the pump. Reinstall the cover using a new gasket. This step is very important as the oil pump may lose its prime whenever the pump, pump cover or timing chain cover is disturbed. If the pump is not packed it may not begin to pump oil as soon as the engine is started.

TIMING CHAIN, REPLACE

V6-196, 231, 252 & V8-350

1. With the timing case cover removed as outlined above, temporarily install the vibration damper bolt and washer in end of crankshaft.
2. Turn crankshaft so sprockets are positioned as shown in Fig. 13. Use a sharp rap on a wrench handle to start the vibration damper bolt out without disturbing the position of the sprockets.

3. On 1977–79 V6 engines, remove the oil pan.
4. Remove oil slinger.
5. On V6-196, 231, 252 and V8-350 remove camshaft distributor drive gear and fuel pump eccentric.
6. Use two large screwdrivers to alternately pry the camshaft sprocket then the crankshaft sprocket forward until the camshaft sprocket is free. Then remove camshaft sprocket and chain, and crankshaft sprocket off crankshaft.
7. To install, assemble chain on sprockets and slide sprockets on their respective shafts with the "O" marks on the sprockets lined up as shown.
8. Complete the installation in the reverse order of removal.

CAMSHAFT, REPLACE

NOTE: If engine is in the car, the radiator, grille and A/C components will have to be removed. If engine is out of car, proceed as follows:

1. To remove camshaft, remove intake manifold, rocker arm shaft assemblies, push

rods and valve lifters.
2. Remove timing chain and sprockets.
3. Slide camshaft out of engine, using care not to mar the bearing surfaces.

PISTONS & RODS, ASSEMBLE

Rods and pistons should be assembled and installed as shown in Figs. 14 and 15.

Measure connecting rod side clearance using a suitable feeler gauge. Clearance obtained should be .006–.027 inch for 1977–78, .006–.023 for 1979–83.

PISTONS, PINS & RINGS

Pistons are available in standard sizes and oversizes of .005, .010 and .030 inch.

Rings are furnished in standard sizes and oversizes of .010 and .030 inch.

Piston pins are supplied in standard sizes only.

Fig. 14 Piston and rod assembly.
V6-196, 231, 252

Fig. 15 Piston and rod assembly.
V8-350

Fig. 16 Location of undersize mark on main and rod bearing shell

VALVE LIFTER OIL GALLERIES

MAIN OIL GALLERY

OIL PICKUP SCREEN AND HOUSING

OIL PUMP

OIL FILTER

Engine lubrication system. V8-350

OIL PUMP COVER

VALVE SPRING

GASKET

VALVE CAP

Fig. 17 Oil pump cover and by-pass valve. V6-196, 231, 252 & V8-350

CHECK CLEARANCE BETWEEN STRAIGHT EDGE & GASKET SURFACE SHOULD BE BETWEEN .002" & .006"

Fig. 18 Checking oil pump gear and clearance. V6-196, 231, 252 & V8-350

MAIN & ROD BEARINGS

Main bearings are available in standard sizes and undersizes of .001, .002, and .010 inch.

Rod bearings are furnished in standard sizes and undersizes of .001, .002 and .010", Fig. 16.

CRANKSHAFT OIL SEAL REPAIR

Since the braided fabric seal used on these engines can be replaced only when the crankshaft is removed, the following repair procedure is recommended.

1. Remove oil pan and bearing cap.
2. Drive end of old seal gently into groove, using a suitable tool, until packed tight. This may vary between 1/4 and 3/4 inch depending on amount of pack required.
3. Repeat previous step for other end of seal.
4. Measure and note amount that seal was driven up on one side. Using the old seal removed from bearing cap, cut a length of seal the amount previously noted plus 1/16 inch.
5. Repeat previous step for other side of seal.
6. Pack cut lengths of seal into appropriate side of seal groove. A guide tool, J-21526-1, and packing tool, J-21526-2, may be used since these tools have been machined to provide a built-in stop.
7. Install new seal in bearing cap.

OIL PAN, REPLACE

V6-196, 231, 252

Exc. 1981–83 Riviera
1. Raise and support front of vehicle.
2. Remove flywheel cover and exhaust crossover pipe. On 1982–83 models, raise engine with a suitable lifting device to gain clearance.
3. Drain engine oil into a suitable contain-

er.
4. Remove oil pan bolts, then pan.
5. Reverse procedure to install.

NOTE: Some 1981–83 engines use R.T.V. silicone sealer instead of a cork gasket for oil pan to crankcase sealing. When replacing the oil pan or sealing material on these engines, either R.T.V. sealer or a cork gasket can be used during reassembly. If R.T.V. sealer is used, the pan rail and block sealing surfaces should be cleaned thoroughly and a 1/4 inch bead of sealant applied evenly to the pan rail, avoiding any breaks or gaps in the sealer during application.

1981–83 Riviera
1. Disconnect battery ground cable.
2. Remove one final drive to transmission bolt.
3. Install suitable engine support fixture.
4. Raise and support vehicle.
5. Remove idler arm bracket from frame, then position steering wheel at left lock.
6. Disconnect drive axles from output shafts, then battery cable support from output shaft support.
7. Disconnect output shaft support from engine block.
8. Remove remaining final drive to transmission bolts.
9. Position suitable transmission jack under final drive, then remove final drive cover and final drive unit.
10. Remove starter, then flywheel cover.
11. Remove oil pan bolts, then oil pan.
12. Reverse procedure to install.

NOTE: Some 1981–83 engines use R.T.V. silicone sealer instead of a cork gasket for oil pan to crankcase sealing. When replacing the oil pan or sealing material on these engines, either R.T.V. sealer or a cork gasket can be used during reassembly. If R.T.V. sealer is used, the pan rail and block sealing surfaces should be cleaned thoroughly and a 1/4 inch bead of sealant applied evenly to the pan rail, avoiding any breaks or gaps in the sealer during application.

1977–80 V8-350

NOTE: On 1977–78 models except Skylark, it is no longer necessary to disconnect the idler arm. Otherwise, proceed as follows:

1. Disconnect battery and drain oil.
2. Remove fan shroud to radiator tie bar screws.
3. Remove air cleaner and disconnect linkage to throttle.
4. Raise and support car on stands.
5. With manual transmission, loosen clutch equalizer bracket to frame bolts. Disconnect crossover pipe at engine.
6. With automatic transmission, remove lower flywheel housing. Remove shift linkage attaching bolt and swing out of way. Disconnect crossover pipe at engine. Disconnect idler arm at frame and push steering linkage forward to crossmember. Remove front engine mount bolts and raise engine by placing jack under crankshaft pulley mounting.

NOTE: If car is air conditioned, at this point it will be necessary to place a support under right side of transmission prior to raising engine to prevent transmission from cocking to the right when raised.

7. Remove oil pan. It may be necessary to position crankshaft so 1 and 2 crankpin and counterweight will not interfere with front of pan.

OIL PUMP

NOTE: On some 1978–79 General Motors models with V6-196, 231 engines, the oil pressure indicator light also serves as the electric choke defect indicator. If Oil or Eng. indicator light does not light, check to ensure electric choke is not disconnected at carburetor. Also check for defect in electric choke heater, blown gauge fuse or defect in lamp or wiring circuit. If indicator light stays on with engine running possible causes are: oil pressure is low, switch to indicator light wiring has an open circuit, oil pressure switch wire connector has disconnected or on some models, gauge or radio fuse has blown.

V6-196, 231, 252 & V8-350

1. To remove pump, take off oil filter.
2. Disconnect wire from oil pressure indicator switch in filter by-pass valve cap (if so equipped).
3. Remove screws attaching oil pump cover to timing chain cover. Remove cover and slide out pump gears. Replace any parts not serviceable.
4. Check relief valve in its bore in cover. Valve should have no more clearance than an easy slip fit. If any perceptible side shake can be felt, the valve and/or cover should be replaced.
5. The filter by-pass valve should be flat and free of nicks and scratches.

Assembly & Installation

1. Lubricate and install pressure relief valve and spring in bore of pump cover. Install cap and gasket. Torque cap to 30–35 ft-lbs.
2. Install pump gears and shaft in pump body section of timing chain cover to check gear end clearance. Check clearance as shown in Fig. 18. If clearance is less than .002" for 1977–83 models, check timing chain cover for evidence of wear.
3. If gear end clearance is satisfactory, remove gears and pack gear pocket *full* of vaseline, not chassis lube.
4. Reinstall gears so vaseline is forced into every cavity of gear pocket and between teeth of gears. *Unless pump is packed with vaseline, it may not prime itself when engine is started.*
5. Install cover and tighten screws alternately and evenly. Final tightening is 10–15 ft-lbs. torque. Install filter in nipple.

BELT TENSION DATA

	New lbs.	Used lbs.
1980–83—		
5/16 in.	80	50
3/8 in. exc. cogged belt	140	70
3/8 in. cogged belt		60
15/32 in.	165	90
1977–79—		
Alternator	130	75
Air Condition	155	90
A.I.R. Pump	70	60
Power Steering	155	90

WATER PUMP, REPLACE

Drain cooling system, being sure to drain into a clean container if antifreeze solution is to be saved. Remove the fan belt and disconnect all hoses from water pump. Remove water pump.

FUEL PUMP, REPLACE

NOTE: Before installing the pump, it is good practice to crank the engine so that the nose of the camshaft eccentric is out of the way of the fuel pump rocker arm when the pump is installed. In this way there will be the least amount of tension on the rocker arm, thereby easing the installation of the pump.

1. Disconnect fuel lines from fuel pump.
2. Remove fuel pump mounting bolts and the fuel pump.
3. Remove all gasket material from the pump and block gasket surfaces. Apply sealer to both sides of new gasket.
4. Position gasket on pump flange and hold pump in position against its mounting surface. Make sure rocker arm is riding on camshaft eccentric.
5. Press pump tight against its mounting. Install retaining screws and tighten them alternately.
6. Connect fuel lines. Then operate engine and check for leaks.

Diesel Engine Section

REFER TO THE OLDSMOBILE CHAPTER FOR SERVICE PROCEDURES ON THE V6-262 & V8-350 DIESEL ENGINES, NOT FOUND IN THIS SECTION.

ENGINE, REPLACE

V8-350 Engine

Exc. Riviera
1. Disconnect ground cable from batteries and drain cooling system.
2. Remove air cleaner.
3. Scribe hood hinge locations and remove hood.
4. Disconnect ground wires at inner fender and the engine ground strap at right cylinder head.
5. Disconnect radiator hoses, oil cooler lines, heater hoses, vacuum hoses, power steering hoses from gear, A/C compressor with brackets and hoses attached, fuel pump hose from fuel pump and the wiring.
6. Remove hairpin clip from bellcrank.
7. Remove throttle and throttle valve cables from intake manifold brackets and position cables aside.
8. Remove upper radiator support and the radiator.
9. Raise and support vehicle.
10. Disconnect exhaust pipes from exhaust manifold.
11. Remove torque converter cover and the three bolts securing torque converter to flywheel.
12. Remove engine mount bolts or nuts.
13. Remove three engine to transmission bolts on the right side.
14. Disconnect starter wiring and remove starter.
15. Lower vehicle.
16. Attach suitable engine lifting equipment to engine. Support transmission with a suitable jack.
17. Remove the three engine to transmission bolts on the left side.
18. Remove engine from vehicle.
19. Reverse procedure to install.

Riviera
1. Disconnect battery ground cable and drain cooling system.
2. Remove radiator upper support.
3. Remove air cleaner assembly.
4. Scribe hood hinge locations and remove hood.
5. Disconnect engine ground strap.
6. Disconnect upper and lower radiator hoses from engine.
7. Disconnect transmission oil cooler lines from radiator.
8. Disconnect heater hoses from water pump and water control valve.
9. Remove radiator, fan and the shroud.
10. Disconnect power steering pump bracket from engine and position aside without disconnecting lines.
11. Disconnect A/C compressor bracket from engine and position aside without disconnecting lines.
12. Disconnect fuel lines.

13. Disconnect throttle cable, vacuum hoses and electrical connections.
14. Disconnect left hand exhaust pipe from manifold.
15. On left side of engine, remove through bolt and bracket securing final drive to engine.
16. Raise and support engine.
17. Remove flywheel shield.
18. Disconnect right hand exhaust pipe from manifold.
19. Disconnect starter motor wiring and remove starter motor.
20. Remove converter to flywheel bolts. Mark location of converter on flywheel for alignment during installation.
21. Remove splash shield.
22. Remove engine front mounting attaching nuts.
23. Remove two bolts securing right hand output shaft support brackets. Using a sharp tool, scribe a mark around the washers as far as possible. Use these scribe marks to position bracket upon installation.

24. Remove lower right hand transmission to engine attaching bolts. One bolt retains the modulator line clip.
25. Use a suitable length of chain to retain final drive in vehicle.
26. Lower vehicle and attach suitable engine lifting equipment to engine.
27. Remove the remaining transmission to engine bolts. It may be necessary to raise or lower transmission with a suitable jack to facilitate bolt removal.
28. Raise engine and remove from vehicle.
29. Reverse procedure to install.

V6-262 Engine

1. Disconnect battery ground cable and drain cooling system.
2. Scribe reference marks, then remove hood from vehicle.
3. Disconnect all hoses, lines and electrical connectors from engine.

NOTE: Do not disconnect wires from the starter.

4. Disconnect throttle cable, transmission T.V. or detent cable at injection pump and engine brackets.
5. Remove upper radiator support and radiator from vehicle.
6. Raise and support vehicle.
7. Disconnect exhaust pipes at exhaust manifold.
8. Remove torque converter flywheel cover and three torque converter to flywheel bolts.
9. Remove starter and two engine mount bolts.
10. From the right side of the vehicle, remove three engine to transmission bolts.
11. Lower vehicle and position suitable lifting equipment onto engine.
12. Using a suitable jack, raise transmission enough to gain access to the other three transmission to engine bolts. Remove bolts and lift engine from vehicle.
13. Reverse procedure to install. Torque flywheel to torque converter bolts to 35 ft. lbs. Torque two engine mount bolts to 55 ft. lbs.

Turbocharger Section

DESCRIPTION

The turbocharger, Fig. 1, is used to increase engine power on a demand basis, therefore allowing a smaller, more economical engine to be used. The turbocharged V6-231 is available with either two or four barrel carburetion.

As engine load increases and the throttle opens, more air-fuel mixture is drawn into the combustion chambers. As the increased volume is burned, a larger volume of high energy exhaust gasses enters the engine exhaust system and is directed through the turbocharger turbine housing, Fig. 2. Some of the exhaust gas energy is used to increase the speed of the turbine wheel which is connected to the compressor wheel. The increased speed of the compressor wheel compresses the air-fuel mixture from the carburetor and delivers the compressed air-fuel mixture to the intake manifold, Fig. 2. The high pressure in the intake manifold allows a denser charge to enter the combustion chambers, in turn developing more engine power during the combustion cycle.

The intake manifold pressure (Boost) is controlled to a maximum value by an exhaust gas bypass valve (Wastegate). The wastegate allows a portion of the exhaust gas to bypass the turbine wheel, thereby not increasing turbine speed. The wastegate is operated by a spring loaded diaphragm device sensing the pressure differential across the compressor. When intake manifold pressure reaches a set value above ambient pressure, the wastegate begins to bypass the exhaust gas.

An Electronic Spark Control System, Figs. 3 and 4, is used to retard ignition timing up to 20° to minimize detonation. The 1978 two barrel application uses a turbocharger vacuum bleed valve (TVBV) and the 1978 four barrel application uses a power enrichment control valve (PECV). These valves assist in proper vacuum control during boost. On 1979–80 applications, the power enrichment vacuum regulator (PEVR) is used to control vacuum flow to the carburetor power piston. On 1981–83 models, no vacuum control is required, the carburetor power enrichment circuit is controlled by the Electronic Control Module (ECM).

NOTE: Engine oil on 1978–81 turbocharged engines must be changed every 3000 miles, otherwise, turbocharger bearing damage may occur from oil contamination. On 1982–83 turbocharged engines the recommended oil and oil filter change interval is every 7500 miles or 12 months, whichever comes first. This change is due to increased oil capacity, a higher output oil pump and a revised turbocharger oil passage.

DIAGNOSIS & TESTING

Prior to performing any diagnostic or testing procedure check all vacuum hoses and wiring for proper routing and connections, carburetor linkage for freedom of movement, wastegate linkage for damage or any problems which may occur in a non-turbocharged engine.

Fig. 1 Turbocharger assembly

Fig. 2 Turbocharged V6 engine schematic

CAUTION: A turbocharged engine has exhaust pipes located high in the engine compartment. Care must be taken to avoid accidental contact with hot exhaust pipes since personal injury may occur.

Engine Diagnosis

Refer to Fig. 5 for engine diagnosis.

Wastegate-Boost Pressure Test

1. Inspect actuator linkage for damage.
2. Check tubing from compressor housing to actuator assembly and on 1978–80 models, the return tubing from the actuator to the PCV tee. Replace if necessary.
3. Remove compressor housing to actuator assembly hose, then attach vacuum-pressure pump J-23738, in series with compound gauge J-28474, to actuator assembly.
4. On 1978–80 models apply pressure to actuator assembly. At approximately 8 psi on 1978 models or 9 psi on 1979–80 models, the actuator lever should move .008 inch on 1978 models or .015 inch on 1979–80 models, actuating the wastegate. On 1981–83 models, apply vacuum to the actuator assembly. At approximately 3 in. Hg., the actuator lever should move .015 inch, actuating the wastegate. On all models, if the actuator did not respond properly, it should be replaced. Prior to installing actuator, test as outlined above, then crimp threads on actuator rod to maintain calibration.
5. Remove vacuum-pressure pump and reinstall hose.

Road Test
1. Tee compound gauge J-28474 into tubing between compressor housing and boost gauge switches with a sufficient length of hose to place the gauge in the passenger compartment.

NOTE: Ensure gauge and hose are in good condition to prevent possible leakage of air/fuel mixture.

2. With conditions and speed limits permitting, perform a zero to 40–50 mph, wide open throttle acceleration and maintain speed for two to three seconds. Boost pressure should reach 7–8 psi on 1978 2 barrel engines, 8–9 psi on 1978 4 barrel engines and 1981–83 engines and 9–10 psi on 1979–80 engines.
3. If boost is not satisfactory, replace actuator assembly. Prior to installation, test actuator as outlined in step 4 of Wastegate-Boost Pressure Test.

1979–80 Power Enrichment Vacuum Regulator (PEVR) Test

1. Inspect PEVR and attaching hoses for deterioration, cracking or other damage and replace as necessary.
2. Tee one hose of manometer J-23951 between yellow stripped input hose and input port. Connect other hose directly to PEVR output port.
3. Start engine and operate at idle speed. There should be no more than 14″ H₂O difference between manometer readings. If difference is greater than 14″ H₂O, replace PEVR.
4. Remove PEVR from intake manifold and install a plug in intake manifold PEVR

bore. Connect input and output hoses to PEVR.
5. Tee gauge J-28474 into output hose of PEVR.
6. Start engine and operate at idle speed. The gauge reading from the output port should be 7–9″ Hg.
7. Apply 3 psi. to manifold signal port of PEVR. Vacuum reading from output port should be 1.4–2.6″ Hg. If difficulty is encountered in measuring level of vacuum, apply 5 psi. to manifold signal port of PEVR. There should be no vacuum output from PEVR.
8. If PEVR does not perform as described above, replace PEVR.

1978 Turbocharger Vacuum Bleed Valve (TVBV) Test

1. Inspect valve and attaching hoses deterioration, cracking or other damage and replace, if required.
2. Disconnect and plug the vacuum hose to the remote power enrichment port on the carburetor. Tee one hose from J-23951 manometer into the distributor vacuum hose between the carburetor and the TVBV. Tee the other hose into the hose between the TVBV and the distributor. Start and idle engine. There should be no more than a 14 inch H₂O difference on the manometer scale.
3. Repeat step 2 with the manometer teed into the vacuum hose from the Thermac sensor to the TVBV and the vacuum hose from the TVBV to the hot air door actuator.

NOTE: If the engine is at normal operating temperature, the hot air door may not have an applied vacuum signal. If so, connect manifold vacuum to port and recheck.

4. Plug the EGR hose at the EGR valve and install one hose from the manometer into the hose from the carburetor EGR signal port to the TVBV. Install the other manometer hose into the hose from the TVBV to the EGR-EFE switch. Start the engine and open the throttle slightly. There should be no more than a 14 inch H₂O difference on the manometer scale.
5. Disconnect all hoses from the TVBV. Connect one side of the manometer to the center vent port and vent the other side of the manometer to the atmosphere. Start and idle engine. There should be no vacuum signal at the port.
6. If conditions in steps 2, 3, 4 and 5 are not met, replace the TVBV and install all hoses.
7. If the TVBV tests normally but is still suspect, remove the TVBV from intake manifold. Plug the intake manifold and connect all hoses to the TVBV. Using J-23738, apply at least 6 inch Hg (3 psi) to the manifold signal port of the TVBV. Start and idle engine. Attach one side of the manometer to the output port of each pair of ports described in steps 2, 3 and 4, in turn, and vent the other side of the manometer to the atmosphere. If the manometer indicates any pressure difference, replace the TVBV.

Fig. 3   Electronic spark control (ESC) system. 1978–79 models

1978 Power Enrichment Control Valve (PECV) Test

1. Inspect the valve and attaching hoses for deterioration, cracking and other damage. Replace, if necessary.
2. Tee one side of manometer J-23951 into the input port and the other side into the output port of the PECV. Start and idle engine. There should be no more than a 12 inch H_2O difference on the manometer scale.
3. Disconnect all hoses from the PECV and plug the vacuum source hose. Connect one side of the manometer to the vent port and vent the other side to the atmosphere. Start and idle engine. The manometer should not indicate any pressure differential.
4. If conditions in steps 2 and 3 are not met, replace the PECV.
5. If the PECV tests normally but is still suspect, remove the PECV from intake manifold. Plug the intake manifold and connect hoses to the PECV. Tee one side of the manometer into the output port and vent the other side to the atmosphere. Apply at least 6 inch Hg (3 psi) to the manifold signal port of the PECV. Start and idle engine. If manometer indicates any pressure differential, replace the PECV.

1978–79 Electronic Spark Control (ESC) System Diagnosis

Engine Detonation Or Poor Performance

1. Check all vacuum hoses and wires for proper connections and routing.
2. With ignition switch "On," check for voltage between light blue wire to black wire across ESC relay. If no voltage reading is obtained, replace ESC relay.
3. If voltage reading is obtained in step 2, check initial ignition timing and correct, if necessary.
4. With engine at normal operating temperature, install a tachometer and timing meter, if available, to engine. Place air conditioner in "Off" position and the fast idle cam on high step. Run engine above 1800 RPM. Using a steel rod, tap intake manifold near detonation sensor with light to medium taps and observe tachometer or timing metering. Engine RPM should drop 300–500 RPM and timing should retard 18–22 degrees. Engine should return to original RPM and timing within 20 seconds after tapping stops.
5. If conditions are not met in step 4, check connection between ESC controller and detonation sensor, Fig. 3. Check detonation sensor for proper installation. Connect an ohmmeter between detonation sensor and the ground, Fig. 3. If resistance is not 175–375 ohms, replace detonation sensor. If these checks and correction do not correct the problem, replace the ESC controller.
6. If conditions in step 4 are met, disconnect the four wire connector from ESC controller to distributor, Fig. 3. Using a jumper wire, connect socket No. 2 to pin No. 4 on the distributor side of the harness connector, Fig. 3. Test H.E.I. distributor as outlined in the "Electronic Ignition Systems" chapter. After distributor repair, remove jumper wire and connect ESC controller.

Engine Cranks But Does Not Start

1. Check all vacuum hoses and wires for proper connections and routing.
2. Check for spark at spark plug.
3. If spark is present at spark plug, refer to the "Trouble-Shooting Chapter" and the "Electronic Ignition Systems" chapter.
4. If spark is not present at spark plug, check ESC relay voltage between light blue wire and black wire while cranking. If voltage is present, replace ESC relay.
5. If no voltage was present in step 4, check voltage between the distributor "BAT" terminal and the ground with ignition "On". If voltage is under 7 volts, check for open circuit between distributor "BAT" terminal and ignition switch.
6. If voltage in step 5 is 7 volts or over, check voltage at "A" terminal, pink wire, on engine harness side of two wire connector from ESC controller to engine wiring harness, Fig. 3. If voltage is under 7 volts, check for open circuit between "A" terminal and the ignition switch.
7. If voltage in step 6 was 7 volts or over, disconnect four wire connector from ESC controller to distributor, Fig. 3. Connect a jumper wire between socket No. 2 and pin No. 4 on distributor side of harness connector, Fig. 3. Check for spark at spark plug while cranking engine. If spark is present at spark plug, replace ESC controller.
8. If spark is not present at spark plug in step 7, leave the jumper wire connected and test the H.E.I. distributor as outlined in the "Tune-Up Chapter, Electronic Ignition Section". After distributor repair, remove the jumper wire and connect the ESC controller.

1980–83 Electronic Spark Control (ESC) System Diagnosis

Engine Detonation

1. Check all vacuum hoses and wires for proper connections and routing.
2. Check engine coolant for proper concentration and level.
3. Check initial timing.
4. With engine thoroughly warmed up, A/C off, install tachometer to engine.
5. Set throttle on high step of fast idle cam.

NOTE: Engine speed must be above 1800 RPM.

Fig. 4 Electronic Spark Control (ESC) system. 1980–83 models

Condition	Possible Cause	Correction
ENGINE DETONATION	1. Electronic Spark Control.	1. Refer to ESC Diagnosis.
	2. EGR	2. Requires Emission Control diagnostic equipment.
	3. Carburetor or Turbocharger.	3. Correct air inlet restrictions. a. Air cleaner duct. b. Thermac door operation. c. Air cleaner dirty. Eliminate actuator overboost. a. Mechanical linkage jammed or blocked. b. Hose from compressor housing to actuator assembly or return hose from actuator to PCV tee damaged or loose. c. Wastegate not operating-Refer to Wastegate-Boost Pressure Test. Service Carburetor Power System. a. Refer to TVBV/PECV or PEVR Test. b. Refer to Carburetor Chapter elsewhere in this manual. c. Refer to Trouble-Shooting Chapter elsewhere in this manual. Inspect turbocharger-Refer to Turbocharger Internal Inspection.
	4. Other causes.	4. Refer to Trouble-Shooting Chapter elsewhere in this manual.
ENGINE LACKS POWER	1. Air inlet restriction.	1. Air cleaner duct. Thermac door operation. Air cleaner element dirty.
	2. Exhaust system restriction.	2. Repair exhaust pipes if damaged. Repair or replace catalytic converter if damaged.
	3. Transmission.	3. Check for correct shifting. Refer to Automatic Transmission Chapter elsewhere in this manual.
	4. Electronic spark control.	4. Refer to ESC Diagnosis.
	5. EFE	5. Requires Emission Control diagnostic equipment.
	6. EGR	6. Requires Emission Control diagnostic equipment.
	7. Carburetion	7. Refer to Carburetor Chapter elsewhere in this manual. Refer to Trouble-Shooting Chapter elsewhere in this manual.
	8. Turbocharger	8. Check for exhaust leaks or restrictions. Refer to TVBV/PECV or PEVR test procedure. Inspect for collapsed or kinked plenum coolant hoses (if equipped). Check wastegate operation. a. Refer to Wastegate-boost pressure test. b. Remove exhaust pipe from elbow assembly. Using a mirror, observe movement of wastegate while manually operating actuator linkage. Replace elbow assembly if valve does not open or close. Refer to Turbocharger Internal Inspection.
	9. Other causes.	9. Refer to Trouble-Shooting Chapter elsewhere in this manual.
ENGINE SURGES	1. Electronic Spark Control.	1. Refer to ESC diagnosis.
	2. Carburetion.	2. Refer to TVBV/PECV or PEVR Test Procedure. Refer to Carburetor Chapter elsewhere in this manual. Refer to Trouble-Shooting Chapter elsewhere in this manual.
	3. EGR	3. Requires Emission Control diagnostic equipment.
	4. Turbocharger.	4. Inspect turbocharger for loose bolts on compressor side of assembly, tighten.
	5. Other causes.	5. Refer to Trouble-Shooting Chapter elsewhere in this manual.

Fig. 5 Engine Diagnosis (part 1 of 2)

Condition	Possible Cause	Correction
EXCESSIVE OIL CONSUMPTION OR BLUE EXHAUST SMOKE	1. External turbocharger oil leaks.	1. Inspect turbocharger oil inlet for proper connection. Inspect turbocharger oil drain hose for leaks or restriction.
	2. PCV	2. Requires Emission Control diagnostic equipment.
	3. Other causes.	3. Refer to Trouble-Shooting Chapter elsewhere in this manual.
	4. Turbocharger.	4. Refer to Turbocharger Internal Inspection.
BLACK EXHAUST SMOKE	1. Carburetion.	1. Refer to TVBV/PECV or PEVR Test. Refer to Carburetor Chapter elsewhere in this manual.
	2. Other causes.	2. Refer to Trouble-Shooting Chapter elsewhere in this manual.
EXCESSIVE ENGINE NOISE	1. EFE	1. Requires Emission Control diagnostic equipment.
	2. Exhaust System.	2. Inspect for incorrect or loose mountings.
	3. AIR System.	3. Requires Emission Control diagnostic equipment.
	4. Other causes.	4. Refer to Trouble-Shooting Chapter elsewhere in this manual.
	5. Turbocharger.	5. Check for exhaust leaks. Inspect for restriction of turbocharger oil supply. Refer to Turbocharger Internal Inspection.

Fig. 5 Engine Diagnosis (part 2 of 2)

6. Using a suitable steel bar (a socket wrench breaker bar will do), tap the front area of the left exhaust manifold rapidly with medium to heavy taps.
7. Observe tachometer for RPM drop. RPM should drop 200 RPM and return to original RPM within 20 seconds. If RPM drops as indicated, problem is ignition or carburetor related. If RPM does not drop, inspect detonation sensor for any signs of physical damage.

NOTE: Detonation sensor is extremely sensitive to physical damage.

8. Check detonation sensor for proper installation and torque. Correct torque is 14 ft. lbs.
9. Disconnect detonation sensor connector at firewall. On the sensor side of the connector, connect the positive lead of a suitable ohmmeter to the connector terminal attached to the center conductor of the sensor lead. While grounding the negative ohmmeter lead to a suitable ground, measure resistance. Resistance should be 175–375 ohms.
10. If sensor failed any of the above tests, replace. If sensor passed all the above tests, substitute a known good sensor and repeat steps 4 through 7. If RPM drops, replace sensor.
11. If RPM does not drop in step 10, remove ESC 10 pin connector at controller (located under dashboard), then jump pins A and B with a suitable jumper wire, Fig. 4. Disconnect detonation sensor wire connector from area of firewall, then using a suitable ohmmeter, check continuity across sensor connector. If continuity exists, replace sensor and sensor harness between firewall and sensor. If no continuity exists, repair detonation sensor wire.
12. Repeat steps 4 through 7. If RPM does not drop, replace ESC controller.

Engine Cranks But Will Not Start
1. Check for spark at cylinder number 2 spark plug.

2. If spark is present, ESC system is operating. Refer to the "Electronic Ignition Systems" chapter.
3. If spark is not present at spark plug, check ESC controller (located under dashboard) connector for proper connection, then check distributor 4 pin connector. Repair as necessary.
4. Turn ignition "On", then, using a suitable voltmeter, check voltage from pin F to pin K of the ESC controller connector, Fig. 4.
5. If voltage obtained is under 7 volts, check for and repair open circuit between pin F of ESC connector and ignition switch. If engine will not start, proceed to step 6.
6. If voltage obtained is over 7 volts, disconnect distributor 4 pin connector, then ESC 10 pin connector. Using a suitable ohmmeter, check continuity of wires at pins G, H, J & K.
7. If continuity exists, repair wire or wires causing trouble.
8. If continuity does not exist, check wiring harness for possible opens, then on distributor side of 4 pin connector, jump pins A and C together and attempt to start engine.
9. If engine does not run, check distributor. Refer to "Electronic Ignition Systems" chapter. If distributor is satisfactory, replace ESC controller.
10. If engine runs, replace ESC controller.

NOTE: When running engine with distributor 4 pin connector disconnected and pins A and C jumped, do not race engine. Run at idle only.

11. If, after completing step 10, the engine will not run, check distributor. Refer to "Electronic Ignition Systems" chapter.

Poor Engine Performance
1. Check all vacuum hoses and wires for proper connections and routing.
2. Check engine coolant for proper concentration and level.
3. Check initial timing.

4. With engine running, use a suitable voltmeter to measure voltage between pins F and K of the ESC controller 10 pin connector, Fig. 4.

NOTE: The ESC controller is located under the dashboard.

5. If voltage obtained is 11.6 volts or less, check and repair alternator and charging system. If problem still remains, proceed to step 6.
6. If voltage obtained is 11.6 volts or more, refer to "Engine Detonation" procedure and perform steps 4 through 7.
7. If RPM does not drop, perform remaining "Engine Detonation" procedure.
8. If RPM drops, disconnect distributor 4 pin connector, then jump pins A and C of the connector on the distributor side, Fig. 4.
9. Check distributor. Refer to "Electronic Ignition Systems" chapter.
10. If problem still remains, problem is ignition or carburetor related.

TURBOCHARGER INTERNAL INSPECTION

1. Remove the turbocharger assembly but do not separate the center housing rotating assembly from the turbine housing.
2. Manually operate the wastegate linkage and using a small mirror, observe wastegate movement in the elbow assembly. Replace the elbow assembly if the wastegate fails to open or close.
3. Check for loose backplate to center housing rotating assembly bolts and tighten, if necessary.
4. Spin the compressor wheel. If rotating assembly binds or drags, replace the center housing rotating assembly.
5. Inspect center rotating housing assembly for sludge in the oil drain area. Clean, if minor, or replace center housing rotating assembly if excessively sludged or caked.
6. Inspect compressor oil seal for damage or

leakage on the compressor wheel side of the backplate. Replace center housing rotating assembly if oil seal damage or leakage is present.

7. If compressor wheel is damaged or severely caked, replace center housing rotating assembly.

8. If center housing rotating assembly is being replaced, pre-lubricate with engine oil.

9. Inspect compressor housing and turbine housing. If either housing is gouged, nicked or distorted, replace if necessary.

10. Remove turbine housing from center housing rotating assembly and check the journal bearing radial clearance and thrust bearing axial clearance as follows:

a. Journal bearing radial clearance.

(1) Attach a rack and pinion type dial indicator (Starrett model 656-517 or equivalent with a two inch long, 3/4 to 1 inch offset extension rod) to the center housing so the indicator plunger extends through the oil output port and contacts the turbine wheel assembly shaft, Fig. 6. If required, a dial indicator mounting adapter can be utilized, Fig. 6.

(2) Manually apply pressure equally and at the same time to both the compressor wheel and turbine wheel as required to move the turbine wheel assembly shaft away from the dial indicator as far as possible.

(3) Zero the dial indicator.

(4) Manually apply pressure equally and at the same time to both the compressor and turbine wheels as required to move the turbine wheel assembly shaft toward the dial indicator plunger as far as possible. Note maximum reading on dial indicator.

NOTE: To ensure that the dial indicator reading is the maximum obtainable, roll the wheels slightly in both directions while applying pressure.

(5) Manually apply pressure equally and at the same time to both the compressor and turbine wheels as required to move the turbine wheel assembly shaft away from the dial indicator as far as possible. The dial indicator should return to zero.

(6) Repeat steps 2 through 5 as required to ensure the maximum clearance between the center housing bores and the shaft bearing diameters, as indicated by the maximum shaft travel, has been obtained.

(7) If the maximum bearing radial clearance is less than .003 inch or greater than .006 inch, replace the center housing rotating assembly.

NOTE: Continued operation of a turbocharger having excessive bearing radial clearance will result in severe damage to the compressor and turbine wheels and the housings.

b. Thrust bearing axial clearance.

(1) Mount a dial indicator (Starrett

Fig. 6 Journal bearing clearance check

Fig. 7 Thrust bearing clearance check

model 25-141 or equivalent) at the turbine end of the turbocharger so the dial indicator plunger contacts the end of the turbine wheel assembly, Fig. 7.

(2) Manually move the compressor wheel and turbine wheel assembly in each direction shown on the indicator dial.

(3) Repeat step 2 to ensure the maximum clearance between the thrust bearing components, as indicated by the maximum turbine wheel assembly travel, has been obtained.

(4) If the maximum thrust bearing axial clearance is less than .001 inch or greater than .003 inch, replace the center housing rotating assembly.

NOTE: Continued operation of a turbocharger having excessive thrust bearing axial clearance will result in severe damage to the compressor and turbine wheels and the housings.

SERVICE

Before performing turbocharger service, note the following general cautions:

1. Clean area around turbocharger assembly with a non-caustic solution before service. Cover openings of engine assembly connections to prevent entry of foreign material.

2. When removing the assembly, do not bend, nick or in any way damage the compressor or turbine wheel blades. Any damage may result in rotating assembly imbalance, failure of the center housing rotating assembly, and failure of the compressor and/or turbine housings.

3. Before disconnecting center housing rotating assembly from either compressor housing or turbine housing, scribe location of components for assembly in original position.

Wastegate Actuator Assembly, Replace

1. Disconnect two vacuum hoses from actuator.

Fig. 8 Wastegate actuator assembly

2. Remove clip from wastegate linkage to actuator rod, Fig. 8.
3. Remove two bolts attaching actuator and the actuator.
4. Reverse procedure to install.

Elbow Assembly, Replace

1. Raise vehicle.
2. Loosen exhaust pipe at catalytic converter.
3. Lower the vehicle.
4. Disconnect turbocharger exhaust outlet pipe from elbow, Fig. 9.
5. Disconnect actuator rod from wastegate linkage.
6. Remove elbow from turbine housing.
7. Reverse procedure to install.

Turbine Housing & Elbow Assembly, Center Housing Rotating Assembly

1. Disconnect turbocharger exhaust outlet pipe from elbow.
2. Raise vehicle.
3. Disconnect catalytic converter from exhaust pipe and move pipe aside.
4. Lower vehicle.
5. Disconnect turbocharger exhaust inlet pipe from turbine housing, Fig. 10.
6. Disconnect turbocharger exhaust inlet pipe from right exhaust manifold, Fig. 10.
7. Disconnect turbine housing from bracket.
8. Disconnect turbocharger oil feed pipe, Fig. 11, and oil drain hose, Figs. 12 and 13 from center housing rotating assembly.
9. Disconnect actuator rod from wastegate linkage.
10. Remove six bolts and three clamps attaching center housing rotating assembly backplate to compressor housing.
11. Remove six bolts, three lockplates and three clamps attaching turbine housing to center housing rotating assembly, Fig. 14.
12. Reverse procedure to install.

Compressor Housing

1. Remove turbine housing and elbow assembly/center housing rotating assembly as outlined previously, however do not separate the turbine housing from the center housing rotating assembly.
2. Remove six bolts attaching compressor housing to the plenum, Figs. 15 and 16.
3. Remove clamp attaching compressor to actuator hose, then the hose from connector.
4. Remove three bolts attaching compressor housing to intake manifold.
5. Reverse procedure to install.

Turbo Charger Assembly, Replace

1979–83 Riviera
1. Remove nut attaching air intake elbow to carburetor stud.

Fig. 9 Elbow assembly

BOLT (3)
19.5 N·m (15 lb. ft.)

ELBOW ASSEMBLY

GASKET

COMPRESSOR HOUSING, TURBINE HOUSING, AND CENTER HOUSING ROTATING ASSEMBLY

Fig. 10 Turbocharger exhaust inlet pipe

BOLT
19 N·m (14 lb. ft.)

TURBO CHARGER EXHAUST INLET PIPE

VIEW - A

1.20°

BOLT & WASHER
27 N·m (20 lb. ft.)

BOLT & L WASHER
27 N·m (20 lb. ft.)

BOLT & L WASHER (2)
27 N·m (20 lb. ft.)

BOLT (2)
31 N·m (23 lb. ft.)

CROSSOVER PIPE

BOLT (2)
19 N·m (14 lb. ft.)

2. Disconnect inlet pipe from turbine housing and exhaust outlet pipe from elbow assembly.
3. Raise vehicle and disconnect turbocharger exhaust outlet pipe at catalytic converter.
4. Lower vehicle and two bolts attaching turbocharger adjustment bracket to turbocharger support bracket on right cylinder head.
5. Disconnect oil feed line from turbocharger.
6. Disconnect choke wire connector and remove choke cover.
7. Remove five plenum chamber attaching bolts and gasket.
8. Tip turbocharger assembly upward and away from intake manifold. Disconnect vacuum line from plenum at actuator. Disconnect oil drain hose from pipe.
9. Remove turbocharger from adapter on intake manifold, Fig. 16.

Except 1979–83 Riviera
1. Disconnect turbocharger exhaust inlet and outlet pipes at turbocharger.
2. Disconnect oil feed pipe from center housing rotating assembly.
3. Remove nut attaching air intake elbow to carburetor and remove elbow.

Fig. 12 EGR valve & turbocharger oil drain. Except 1979–83 Riviera

Fig. 11 Turbocharger oil feed pipe (typical)

Fig. 13 Oil drain collector. 1979–83 Riviera

Fig. 14 Center housing rotating assembly

Fig. 15 Compressor housing

4. Disconnect accelerator, cruise control and detent linkages at carburetor, then remove linkage bracket from plenum.
5. Remove two bolts attaching plenum to side bracket.
6. Disconnect fuel line and necessary vacuum hoses.
7. Disconnect coolant hoses and power brake vacuum hose from plenum.
8. Disconnect plenum front bracket from intake manifold.
9. Remove two bolts attaching turbine housing to bracket on intake manifold.
10. Remove two bolts attaching EGR valve manifold to plenum, then remove AIR

bypass hose from pipe.
11. Remove three bolts attaching compressor housing to intake manifold.
12. Remove turbocharger and actuator with carburetor and plenum assembly attached from engine.
13. Remove six bolts attaching turbocharger and actuator assembly to plenum assembly and carburetor Fig. 17.
14. Drain oil from center housing rotating assembly.

EGR Valve Manifold, Replace

1. Disconnect vacuum line.

2. Remove two bolts attaching EGR valve.
3. Remove bolts attaching EGR manifold, Figs. 18 and 19.
4. Reverse procedure to install.

ESC Detonation Sensor, Replace

1. Disconnect wire connector from sensor. Do not pull on wire.
2. Remove the sensor with a deep socket, Figs. 20 & 21.
3. Reverse procedure to install. Torque ESC detonation sensor to 14 ft. lbs.

Fig. 17   Plenum & turbocharger assembly. Except 1979–83 Riviera

Fig. 16   Turbocharger assembly. 1979–83 Riviera

Fig. 18   EGR valve manifold. Except 1979–83 Riviera

Fig. 19   EGR manifold. 1979–83 Riviera

Fig. 20   ESC detonation sensor (typical). 1979–80 models

Fig. 21   ESC detonation sensor (typical). 1981–83 models

Clutch and Transmission Section

CLUTCH PEDAL, ADJUST

1. Disconnect return spring from clutch fork.
2. Rotate clutch lever and shaft assembly until pedal is against rubber bumper on dash brace.
3. Push outer end of clutch fork rearward until throwout bearing lightly contacts pressure plate fingers.
4. Install lower push rod in gauge hole and increase length until all lash is removed.
5. Install swivel or rod in hole furthest from centerline of lever and shaft assembly, then install retainer.
6. Tighten lock nut and spacer against swivel and connect clutch fork return spring.
7. Check clutch pedal free travel. Free play should be 55/64 to 1 29/64 for 1977 Skylark, 45/64 to 1 5/16 in. for 1977–81 Century and 1 45/64 to 2 5/16 in. for 1978–79 Skylark.

CLUTCH, REPLACE

1. Remove transmission.
2. Remove pedal return spring from clutch fork and *disconnect rod assembly from clutch fork.*
3. Remove flywheel housing.
4. Remove clutch throw-out bearing from clutch fork.
5. Disconnect clutch fork from ball stud by moving it toward center of flywheel housing.
6. Mark clutch cover and flywheel so it can be installed in the same position.

7. Loosen clutch cover to flywheel bolts one turn at a time to avoid bending of clutch cover flange until spring pressure is released.
8. Support pressure place and cover assembly while removing last bolts, then remove pressure plate and driven plate.
9. Reverse procedure to install being sure to line up marks made in removal.

3 SPEED TRANS. REPLACE

1. Disconnect speedometer cable from driven gear fitting.
2. Disconnect shift control rods from shifter levers at transmission.
3. Remove propeller shaft.
4. Support rear of engine and remove transmission crossmember.
5. Remove two top transmission attaching bolts and insert guide pins in these holes.
6. Remove two lower bolts and slide transmission straight back and out of vehicle.
7. Reverse procedure to install.

3 SPEED TRANS. SHIFT LINKAGE

Column Shift
1. Place column selector lever in Reverse detent, making sure the steering column selector plate engages lower most column lever (1st-reverse).
2. Loosen 1st-reverse adjusting clamp.
3. Shift transmission lever into reverse and tighten the 1st-reverse clamp.

4. Shift transmission levers into neutral and loosen 2nd-3rd clamp.
5. Install 3/16" diameter rod through 2nd-3rd lever selector plate and the 1st-reverse lever and alignment plate.
6. Tighten 2nd-3rd shift rod clamp.

Floor Shift
1. Place transmission levers in Neutral.
2. Loosen shift rod adjusting clamp bolts on shifter assembly.
3. Insert 1/4" drill rod through shift assembly and shift levers.
4. Tighten clamp bolts.

4 SPEED TRANS. REPLACE

1. Disconnect speedometer cable and remove driven gear.
2. Disconnect shift control rods from transmission.
3. Remove propeller shaft.
4. Support rear of engine and remove transmission support.
5. Remove two top transmission-to-flywheel housing bolts and insert guide pins.
6. Remove two lower bolts.
7. Slide transmission back and out.
8. Reverse procedure to install.

4 SPEED TRANS. SHIFT LINKAGE

Floor Shift
1. Place transmission in neutral.
2. Adjust all three shift rods so a 1/4" drill rod can be installed through shifter assembly and shift levers.
3. Tighten swivel nuts.

Rear Axle, Propeller Shaft & Brakes

REAR AXLES

Figs. 1 and 1A illustrate the type rear axle assemblies used on Buicks. When necessary to overhaul any of these units, refer to the *Rear Axle Specifications* table in this chapter.

1977–83

In this rear axle, Figs. 1 and 1A the drive pinion is mounted in two tapered roller bearings which are preloaded by two selected spacers at assembly. The pinion is positioned by shims located between a shoulder on the drive pinion and the rear bearing. The front bearing is held in place by a large nut.

The differential is supported in the carrier by two tapered roller side bearings. These are preloaded by inserting shims between the bearings and the pedestals. The differential assembly is positioned for proper ring gear and pinion backlash by varying these shims. The ring gear is bolted to the case. The case houses two side gears in mesh with two pinions mounted on a pinion axle which is anchored in the case by a spring pin. The pinions and side gears are backed by thrust washers.

REAR AXLE ASSEMBLY, REPLACE

1977–83

It is not necessary to remove the rear axle assembly for any normal repairs but if the housing must be replaced the assembly may be removed as follows:
1. Raise vehicle and support using jack stands under both frame side rails.
2. Mark rear universal joint and flange for proper reassembly and disconnect rear joint.
3. Push propeller shaft as far forward as possible and wire up out of way.
4. Disconnect parking brake cables and rear brake hose. Cover brake hose opening to prevent entrance of dirt.
5. Support axle with jack and disconnect shock absorbers at lower ends. On 1977–79 Skylark models, remove leaf springs as outlined under "Leaf Spring, Replace" procedure in the Rear Suspension section.
6. Disconnect upper control arms at axle housing, then lower axle and remove coil springs.
7. Disconnect lower control arms and remove axle assembly.

AXLE SHAFT, REPLACE

NOTE: Design allows for axle shaft end play of .018" on 1977 "B" axle, .002 to .020" on 1978–79 "B" axles, .022" on 1977 "C", "G", "K", and "O", .025" on 1978–83 "C", "G", "K", "O" and "P" (7½") and .032" on 1977–83 "P" (except 7½"). These axles may be identified by the third letter located on the right rear tube on the forward side. This end play can be checked with the wheel and brake drum removed by measuring the difference between the end of the housing and the axle shaft flange while moving the axle shaft in and out by hand.

End play over this is excessive. Compensating for all the end play by inserting a shim inboard of the bearing in the housing is not recommended since it ignores the end play of the bearing itself, and may result in improper seating of the gasket or backing plate against the housing. If end play is excessive, the axle shaft and bearing assembly should be removed and the cause of the excessive end play determined and corrected.

Removing Axle Shaft

1977–83 C, G, K, O & P Axles
1. Remove wheels and brake drums.
2. Remove bolts and differential cover and allow lubricant to drain.
3. Remove pinion shaft lock bolt and pinion shaft then push axle shafts inward, remove C-lock and axle shaft.

1977–79 B Axles
1. Remove wheels and brake drums.
2. Remove retainer plate nuts. Pull retainers clear of bolts and reinstall two opposite nuts to hold brake backing plate in place.
3. Pull axle shaft assembly using a puller.

Replacing Axle Shaft Bearings & Seals

1977–83 C, G, K, O & P Axles
1. Using a suitable pry bar, remove seal from housing.

NOTE: Do not damage axle housing.

2. Position tool No. J-23689 behind bearing bore so tangs on tool engage bearing outer race, then using a suitable slide hammer attached to tool No. J-23689, remove bearing.
3. Using suitable gear lubricant, lubricate bearing. Then, using axle bearing installer J-23690, install bearing. Bearing is properly seated when tool bottoms against housing shoulder.
4. Lubricate seal with suitable gear lubricant, then using seal installer J-21128, tap seal into position until seal is flush with axle tube.
5. Install axle.

1977–79 B Axle
1. Place axle shaft in a vise so that the retainer ring rests on vise jaws. Use a chisel and a hammer to crack the ring, Fig. 2.
2. Press bearing off shaft and remove seal. Inspect seal running surface for bad spots and replace if necessary.

NOTE: Before installing seal, apply grease between seal lips to avoid damaging the seal.

3. Press bearing against shoulder on shaft and retainer ring against bearing using Installer tool J-21022 for intermediate models and J-8609 for full size models.

Axle Shaft, Install

1. Apply a coat of wheel bearing grease in wheel bearing and seal recess.
2. For C, G, K, O and P axles:
   a. Install axle shaft through seal and bearing and through side gear as far in as possible.

   NOTE: Do not let shaft drag across seal lip and apply grease between seal lips.

   b. Install C-lock and move axle shaft outward to bottom C-lock in recess of side gear.
   c. Install pinion shaft and torque lock bolt to 15 ft. lbs.
   d. Install gasket and cover and torque bolts to 30 ft. lbs. After 20 minutes, retorque bolts to 30 ft. lbs.

Fig. 1   Rear axle assembly (Typical). 1977–79 type "B"

Fig. 1A   Rear axle assembly (Typical). 1977–83 type "C, G, K, O & P"

e. Install correct type and amount of lubricant.
3. For B axle, insert axle shaft through housing and install retaining nuts. Torque retaining nuts to 55 ft. lbs. on 1977 full size models, 35 ft. lbs. on 1978–79 full size, Century and Regal models.
4. Install drum and wheel.

REAR WHEEL BEARING & SPINDLE, REPLACE 1979–83 Riviera

NOTE: The rear wheel bearing is a sealed unit. This bearing is not serviceable for repacking or adjustment. The bearing must not be subjected to heat or early bearing failure may result.

Rear Disc Brakes

Removal
1. Raise and support rear of vehicle.
2. Remove tire and wheel assembly.
3. Mark a wheel stud and a corresponding place on the rotor to assist in installation if bearing is not replaced.
4. Disconnect brake line at bracket on control arm.
5. Remove caliper and rotor assembly.
6. Remove four nuts and bolts securing the spindle to the control arm and remove bearing assembly, Fig. 3.

Installation

NOTE: Before installing bearing, remove all rust and corrosion from bearing mounting surfaces. Lack of a flat surface may result in early bearing failure. A slip fit must exist between the bearing and the control arm assembly.

1. Install rear spindle, shield and plate to lower control arm. Torque nuts to 35 ft. lbs., Fig. 3.
2. If bearing was not replaced, install rotor using reference marks made at time of removal.
3. Install brake caliper assembly.
4. Connect brake line at bracket on control

Fig. 2 Removing axle shaft bearing retainer

Outer Retainer (Plate)
Bearing
Inner Retainer (Ring)

arm, tighten and bleed brake system.
5. Install wheel and tire assembly.
6. Remove support and lower car.

Rear Drum Brakes

Removal
1. Raise and support rear of vehicle.
2. Remove tire and wheel assembly.
3. Remove brake drum.
4. Remove four nuts attaching rear wheel bearing assembly to control arm.
5. Remove wheel bearing and four attaching bolts Fig. 4.

Installation

NOTE: Before installing bearing, remove all rust and corrosion from bearing mounting surfaces. Lack of a flat surface for any reason may result in early bearing failure. A slip fit must exist between the bearing and the control arm assembly.

1. Install four nuts and bolts attaching wheel bearing to rear control arm assembly Fig. 4. Torque nuts to 35 ft. lbs.

2. Install brake drum.
3. Install wheel and tire assembly.
4. Remove supports and lower car.

PROPELLER SHAFT, REPLACE

NOTE: When service is required, the propeller shaft must be removed from the car as a complete assembly. While handling it out of the car, the assembly must be supported on a straight line as nearly as possible to avoid jamming or bending any of the parts.

1977–83

NOTE: Two attachment methods are used to secure the propeller shaft to the pinion flange or end yoke, a pair of bolted straps or a set of bolted flanges.

1. Scribe alignment marks between propeller shaft and pinion flange or end yoke to aid reassembly.
2. Remove strap or flange bolts at rear of propeller shaft. Tape bearing cups to prevent loss of needle bearings.
3. Slide shaft assembly rearward, disengaging front yoke from transmission output shaft splines and lower from vehicle.
4. Reverse procedure to install.

NOTE: Prior to installing propeller shaft, lubricate all shaft splines with engine oil. When installing propeller shaft, do not attempt to drive in place with hammer. If shaft will not slip into place, inspect for burrs on transmission output shaft splines, twisted slip yoke splines or the wrong U-joint yoke. Repair as necessary.

PROPELLER SHAFT BALANCE

A wheel balancer of the type equipped with a strobe light can be used to facilitate balancing of the driveshaft. The pick-up unit should be placed directly under the nose of the rear axle carrier and as far forward as possible.
1. Place car on twin post lift so rear of car is supported on the rear axle housing and rear wheels are free to rotate.

NUT 47 N·m (35 LB. FT.)
CONTROL ARM ASSEMBLY
SCREW 41 N·m (30 LB. FT.) DO NOT LUBRICATE
SLEEVE DO NOT LUBRICATE
COVER
CALIPER ASSEMBLY
SCREW 10 N·m (7 LB. FT.)
SHIELD
UPPER BOLT
CALIPER ASSEMBLY
PLATE ASSEMBLY
"O" RING
SCREW
SLEEVE
SECTION THRU PIN & CALIPER ASSEMBLY TWO PLACES
"O" RING
PLATE ASSEMBLY
LOWER BOLT
ROTOR
PAD
BEARING ASSEMBLY
NUT
ROTOR

BOLT - UPPER
ACCESS HOLE
BEARING ASSEMBLY
BRAKE ASSEMBLY
BOLT - LOWER
VIEW A (DISC 902)
VIEW A (DRUM 903)

Fig. 3 Rear wheel bearing. 1979–83 Riviera with rear disc brakes

Fig. 4 Rear wheel bearing. 1979–83 Riviera with rear drum brakes

2. Remove both rear wheels and tire assemblies and reinstall wheel lug nuts with flat side next to drum.
3. Mark and number driveshaft at four points 90° apart at rear of shaft just forward of balance weights.
4. Place strobe light pick-up under nose of differential.
5. With car running in gear at car speed where unbalance is at its peak, allow driveline to stabilize by holding at constant speed. Point strobe light at spinning shaft and note position of one of the reference marks.
6. Shut off engine and position shaft so reference mark will be in position noted when car was running.

CAUTION: Do not run car on hoist for extended periods due to danger of overheating transmission or engine.

7. When strobe light flashed, the heaviest point of the shaft was down. To balance shaft it will be necessary to apply weight 180° away. Screw type hose clamps can be used as weights as shown in Fig. 5.

STEP 1
DETERMINE POINT OF UNBALANCE

STEP 2
ADD HOSE CLAMPS 180° FROM POINT OF UNBALANCE UNITL THEY BECOME HEAVY SPOT

STEP 3
ROTATE TWO CLAMPS EQUALLY AWAY FROM EACH OTHER UNTIL BEST BALANCE IS ACHIEVED

Fig. 5 Positioning hose clamps to balance shaft

BRAKE ADJUSTMENTS

1977–83 Self-Adjusting Drum Brakes

These brakes, Figs. 6, 7 and 8 have self-adjusting shoe mechanisms that assure correct lining-to-drum clearances at all times. The automatic adjusters operate only when the brakes are applied as the car is moving rearward.

Although the brakes are self-adjusting, an initial adjustment is necessary after the brake shoes have been relined or replaced, or when the length of the adjusting screw has been changed during some other service operation.

Frequent usage of an automatic transmission forward range to halt reverse vehicle motion may prevent the automatic adjusters from functioning, thereby inducing low pedal heights. Should low pedal heights be encountered, it is recommended that numerous forward and reverse stops be made until satisfactory pedal height is obtained.

NOTE: If a low pedal condition cannot be corrected by making numerous reverse stops (provided the hydraulic system is free of air) it indicates that the self-adjusting mechanism is not functioning. Therefore, it will be necessary to remove the brake drum, clean, free up and lubricate the adjusting mechanism. Then adjust the brakes as follows, being sure the parking brake is fully released.

Adjustment

1. Remove adjusting hole cover from backing plate. Turn brake adjusting screw to expand shoes until wheel can just be turned by hand.
2. Using suitable tool to hold actuator away from adjuster, Fig. 9, back off adjuster 30 notches. If shoes still drag, back off one or two additional notches.

NOTE: Brakes should be free of drag when adjuster has been backed off approximately 12 notches. Heavy drag at this point indicates tight parking brake cables.

3. Install adjusting hole cover and check parking adjustment.

CAUTION: *If finger movement will not turn the screw, free it up. If this is not done, the actuator will not turn the screw during subsequent vehicle operation. Lubricate the screw with oil and coat with wheel bearing grease. Any other adjustment procedure may cause damage to the adjusting screw with consequent self-adjuster problems.*

4. Install wheel and drum, and adjusting hole cover. Adjust brakes on remaining wheels in the same manner.
5. If pedal height is not satisfactory, drive the vehicle and make sufficient reverse stops until proper pedal height is obtained.

PARKING BRAKE, ADJUST

1977–83 W/Rear Disc Brakes

1. Lubricate parking brake cables at equalizer and underbody rub points. Check all cables for freedom of operation.
2. Fully release parking brake and raise vehicle.
3. Hold cable stud from turning and tighten equalizer nut until cable slack is removed and levers are against stops on caliper housing. If levers are off stops, loosen cable until levers return to stop.

Fig. 6 Right rear drum brake assembly. 1977–83 except 1978–81 Century & Regal & 1979–83 Riviera & 1982–83 Regal

Fig. 7 Left rear drum brake assembly. 1978–81 Century & Regal; 1982–83 Regal

Fig. 8 Left rear drum brake assembly. 1979–83 Riviera

Fig. 9 Adjusting drum brakes

4. Operate parking brake several times to check adjustment. When properly adjusted, the parking brake pedal should move 5¼ inch to 6¾ inch when a force of approximately 125 pounds is applied on all except Riviera. On Riviera, the parking brake pedal should move 4 inch to 5½ inch when a force of approximately 125 pounds is applied.

1977–83 W/Rear Drum Brakes

Need for parking brake adjustment is indicated if the service brake operates with good pedal reserve but the parking brake pedal can be depressed a minimum of 9 ratchet clicks but not more than 16 on 1977–83 models, under heavy foot pressure. After making sure that the service brakes are properly adjusted, adjust the parking brake as follows:
1. Depress parking brake exactly three ratchet clicks on 1977 models except Skylark, two ratchet clicks on Skylark

and all 1978–83 models.
2. Loosen jam nut, and tighten adjusting nut until rear wheels can just be turned rearward using both hands but are locked when forward motion is attempted.
3. Tighten jam nut and release parking brake. Rear wheels should turn freely in either direction with no brake drag.

MASTER CYLINDER, REPLACE

1977–83

1. Disconnect brake pipes from master cylinder and tape end of pipes to prevent entrance of dirt.
2. On manual brakes, disconnect brake pedal from master cylinder push rod.
3. Remove two nuts holding master cylinder to dash or power cylinder and remove master cylinder from car.

POWER BRAKE UNIT, REPLACE

1977–83

1. Remove two nuts attaching master cylinder to brake unit, then position master cylinder away from brake unit with brake lines attached.

NOTE: Use care not to bend or kink brake lines.

2. Disconnect vacuum hose from check valve. Plug vacuum hose to prevent dirt from entering.
3. Remove four nuts holding power unit to dash.
4. Remove retainer and washer from brake pedal pin and disengage push rod eye or clevis.
5. Remove power unit from car.

Rear Suspension

SHOCK ABSORBER, REPLACE

1. With the rear axle supported properly, disconnect shock absorber from lower mounting bracket. On models equipped with automatic level control, disconnect air hose from shock absorber.
2. Disconnect shock absorber upper end from underbody attachment.
3. Reverse procedure to install.

LEAF SPRINGS & BUSHINGS, REPLACE

1977–79 Skylark

1. Support vehicle at frame and rear axle, relieving tension from spring.

2. Disconnect shock absorber from lower mounting.
3. Loosen spring front mount bolt.
4. Remove spring front mounting bracket attaching screws, lower axle and remove bracket.
5. Disconnect parking brake cable from spring plate bracket.
6. Remove "U" bolts and spring plate.
7. Support spring, remove front mount bolt and disassemble rear shackle.
8. Replace rear shackle and spring eye bushings as necessary, Figs. 1 and 2.
9. Reverse procedure to install.

LEAF SPRING SERVICE

1977–79 Skylark

NOTE: The spring leaves are not serviced sep-

arately, however, the spring leaf inserts may be replaced.

1. Clamp spring in a vise and remove spring clips.
2. File peened end of center bolt to permit nut removal, remove nut and open vise slowly, allowing spring to expand.
3. Replace spring leaf inserts as necessary.
4. Use a drift to align center bolt holes, compress spring in vise and install new center bolt and nut. Peen end of bolt to retain nut.
5. Align springs and bend spring clips into position.

NOTE: Overtightening of spring clips will cause spring binding.

Fig. 1   Leaf spring bushings removal. 1977—79 Skylark

Fig. 2   Leaf spring bushings installation. 1977—79 Skylark

Fig. 3   Leaf spring suspension (typical)

A LOCATE BOTTOM END OF SPRING BETWEEN DIMPLES ON CONTROL ARM ASSEMBLY.

B USE EITHER ALL HIGH LIMIT, OR ALL LOW LIMIT SPRINGS. DO NOT INTERMIX BETWEEN LEFT AND RIGHT REAR POSITIONS. (LOW LIMIT SPRINGS HAVE A CIRCLE AROUND THE CODE LETTERS. HIGH LIMIT SPRINGS DO NOT.)

Fig. 4   Coil spring suspension. 1979—83 Riviera

COIL SPRINGS, REPLACE

1979—83 Riviera

1. Raise and support rear of vehicle.
2. Using a suitable jack support lower control arm.
3. Disconnect automatic level control air hose from shock absorber. If removing spring from left hand side of vehicle, disconnect level control link from control arm.
4. Disconnect shock absorber from upper mounting.
5. Lower the control arm until all spring tension is relieved, then remove spring.
6. Reverse procedure to install. Locate spring as shown in Fig. 4.

Except 1979—83 Riviera

1. Support vehicle at frame and support rear axle with a suitable jack.
2. Disconnect shock absorbers from lower mounting brackets, Fig. 5, then the brake hose from the axle housing.
3. Disconnect upper control arms at differential.
4. Lower jack fully, extending springs, then remove springs.

NOTE: Do not allow the brake hose to become kinked or stretched.

5. Reverse procedure to install. Refer to Fig. 6, for correct coil spring staggering. After installation, bleed brakes.

CONTROL ARMS, REPLACE

NOTE: Remove and replace one control arm at a time as axle assembly may slip sideways, making installation difficult.

Fig. 5   Coil spring suspension. Except 1979—83 Riviera

Fig. 6   Coil spring suspension. Except 1979—83 Riviera

Fig. 7   Control arm assembly. 1979–83 Riviera

Fig. 8   Rear Stabilizer installation. 1979–83 Riviera

1979–83 Riviera

1. Raise and support rear of vehicle, then remove wheel and tire assembly.
2. Disconnect brake line at bracket on control arm.
3. Remove stabilizer bar. Refer to "Stabilizer Bar, Replace".
4. Remove rear wheel bearing and spindle. Refer to "Rear Wheel Bearing And Spindle, Replace" in Rear Axle, Propeller Shaft and Brakes Section.
5. If removing left hand control arm, disconnect automatic level control link from control arm.
6. Using a suitable jack, support control arm.
7. Disconnect air hose from shock absorber, then detach shock absorber from upper and lower mountings.
8. Lower control arm until all spring tension is relieved, then remove spring and insulators.
9. Remove two bolts attaching control arm to frame and remove control arm, Fig. 7.

Except 1979–83 Riviera

Upper Control Arms
1. Support vehicle at frame and rear axle.

2. Remove control arm mount bolts from frame and axle housing attachments, Fig. 5.
3. Reverse procedure to install.

NOTE: Control arm bolts must be tightened with vehicle at curb height.

Lower Control Arm
Lower control arms may be removed and replaced using the "Upper Control Arms" procedure. However, it may be necessary to reposition the jack farther forward under carrier to aid in removing rear mount bolt. Also, a brass drift may be needed to remove mount bolts.

STABILIZER BAR, REPLACE

1977–79 Skylark

1. Support vehicle at rear axle.
2. Disconnect stabilizer bar from spring

plate brackets, Fig. 9.
3. Disconnect stabilizer bar from body brackets.
4. Reverse procedure to install. Tighten attaching bolts with vehicle at curb height.

1979–83 Riviera

1. Raise and support rear of vehicle, Fig. 8.
2. Remove bolts attaching front of stabilizer bar to control arms.
3. Remove inside nut and bolt from each side of stabilizer bar link, then loosen nut and bolt on outside of link.
4. Rotate bottom parts of link to one side and slide stabilizer bar out of bushings.

Except 1977–79 Skylark & 1979–83 Riviera

1. Support vehicle at rear axle.
2. Remove stabilizer bar attaching bolts from brackets on lower control arms, Fig. 10.
3. Reverse procedure to install.

Fig. 9   Stabilizer bar installation. 1977–79 Skylark

Fig. 10   Stabilizer bar installation exc. 1977–79 Skylark & 1979–83 Riviera (Typical)

Front Suspension & Steering Section

For service procedures on 1979—83 Riviera, refer to Cadillac, "Front End & Steering Section, Eldorado & 1980—83 Seville."

FRONT SUSPENSION

On this type front suspension, Fig. 1, each wheel is connected independently to the vehicle frame by upper and lower control arms, ball joints and a steering knuckle. The upper and lower control arms are designed and positioned to allow the steering knuckles to move in a prescribed three dimensional arc. Tie rods, connected to the steering knuckles, ensure the front wheels are held in the proper relationship to each other.

A ball joint is riveted to the outer end of the upper arm and is spring loaded to insure proper alignment of the ball in the socket.

The inner end of the lower control arm has pressed-in bushings. Two bolts, passing through the bushings, attach the arm to the frame. The lower ball joint is a press fit in the arm and attaches to the steering knuckle with a castellated nut that is retained with a cotter pin.

Rubber seals are provided on upper and lower shafts and at ball socket assemblies to exclude dirt and moisture from bearing surfaces. Grease fittings are provided at all bearing locations.

WHEEL ALIGNMENT

NOTE: Prior to checking or resetting caster and camber angles, bounce the front end at least twice to allow vehicle to return to normal trim height.

Caster and camber are adjusted by shimming at the upper control arm shaft attaching points.

Adding shims at the front locations will change caster toward negative with practically no change in camber. Adding shims at the rear locations will change caster toward positive and camber toward negative. Adding equal shims at both front and rear locations will not change caster but will change camber toward negative.

To adjust, loosen both front and rear nuts to free shims for removal or addition. After installing or removing shims, torque shaft nuts to 75 ft. lbs. on all 1977 models and 1978—83 models except Century and Regal and 46 ft. lbs. for 1978—81 Century and Regal and 1982—83 Regal.

NOTE: A normal service shim pack should leave at least two threads exposed beyond the shaft nuts after final tightening. The difference between front and rear shim packs should not exceed .40 inch.

TOE-IN, ADJUST

NOTE: Prior to checking or resetting toe-in, bounce the front end at least twice to allow vehicle to return to normal trim height.

1. Ensure wheel bearings are adjusted properly. Refer to "Wheel Bearings, Adjust".
2. Using suitable alignment equipment, with steering wheel in the straight ahead position, check toe-in.
3. If toe-in is not within specifications, loosen tie rod adjustable sleeves clamp bolts.
4. Turn tie rod adjustable sleeves an equal amount of turns but in opposite directions to bring toe-in within specifications.
5. Ensure tie rod end housings are at right angles to the steering arm, then position and torque tie rod adjustable sleeves and clamps as shown in Fig. 2.

WHEEL BEARINGS, ADJUST

1. Raise and support front of vehicle.
2. Remove wheel hub dust cap.
3. Remove spindle nut cotter pin, then while rotating wheel assembly forward, torque spindle nut to 12 ft. lbs. to seat bearings.
4. Loosen spindle nut slightly to "the just loose" position.
5. Hand tighten spindle nut, then install cotter pin. If cotter pin cannot be installed, loosen spindle nut until hole in the spindle lines up with a slot in the nut. Do not loosen more then 1/2 flat of the nut.
6. With wheel bearings properly adjusted, end play should be .001 to .005 inch.

WHEEL BEARINGS, REPLACE

1. Raise car and remove front wheels.
2. Remove brake tube support bracket bolt. Do not disconnect hydraulic tube or hose.
3. Remove caliper to mounting bracket bolts. Hang caliper from upper suspension.

NOTE: Do not place strain on brake line.

4. Remove spindle nut and hub and disc assembly. Inner wheel bearing and grease retainer can now be removed.

CHECKING BALL JOINTS FOR WEAR

If loose ball joints are suspected, first be sure front wheel bearings are properly ad-

Fig. 1 Front suspension (typical). 1977—83

justed and that control arms are tight. Then check ball joints as follows:

Upper Ball Joint

1. Raise front of vehicle with jacks placed between coil spring pockets and ball joint of lower control arm.
2. On 1977–79 models, grasp wheel at top and bottom and shake top of wheel in and out. On 1980–83 models, position a suitable dial indicator at top of wheel rim, then grasp wheel top and bottom, while pulling out top, push in bottom and read dial indicator. Reverse the push-pull procedure and read dial indicator.
3. On 1977–79 models, if any looseness is detected, replace ball joint. On 1980–83 models, if dial indicator reading exceeds .125 inch, the upper ball joint should be replaced.

Lower Ball Joint

A wear indicator is built into the ball joint. Remove dirt deposits around service plug and observe position of nipple. Refer to Fig. 3 for wear tolerance.

BALL JOINTS, REPLACE

NOTE: On all models the upper ball joint is spring-loaded in its socket. If the ball stud has any perceptible shake or if it can be twisted with the fingers, the ball joint should be replaced.

On all models, the lower ball joint is not spring-loaded and depends upon car weight to load the ball. The lower ball joint should never be replaced merely because it "feels" loose when in an unloaded condition.

Upper ball joints on all models are riveted to the control arm and can be replaced.

Lower ball joints on all models are pressed into the control arm and can be replaced with a suitable ball joint tool.

CAUTION: When servicing lower ball joints, be sure to support lower control arm with a suitable jack. If lower control arm is not supported and steering knuckle is disconnected from control arm, the heavily compressed front spring will be completely released.

BOLTS MUST BE INSTALLED IN DIRECTION SHOWN, ROTATE BOTH INNER AND OUTER TIE ROD HOUSINGS REARWARD TO THE LIMIT OF BALL JOINT TRAVEL BEFORE TIGHTENING CLAMPS. WITH THIS SAME REARWARD ROTATION ALL BOLT CENTERLINES MUST BE BETWEEN ANGLES SHOWN AFTER TIGHTENING CLAMPS.

FRONT OF CAR

CLAMP ENDS MAY TOUCH WHEN NUT IS TORQUED TO SPECIFICATIONS, BUT GAP MUST BE VISIBLE ADJACENT TO ADJUSTER SLEEVE.

50°
10°

CLAMP

ADJUSTER TUBE

GAP

DO NOT LOCATE ADJUSTER TUBE SLOT IN THIS AREA

TIE ROD INNER

TIGHT

STEERING KNUCKLE

TIE ROD OUTER

20 N·m (15 FT. LBS.)

CLAMP MUST BE BETWEEN AND CLEAR OF DIMPLES. TORQUE NUTS TO SPECIFICATION.

Fig. 2   Tie rod adjustable sleeve & clamp installation

Upper Ball Joint

1. Support vehicle at frame and remove wheel assembly.
2. Remove cotter pin from upper ball joint stud, loosen nut approximately 2 turns, do not remove nut.
3. Position tool as shown in Fig. 4, turn threaded end of tool until stud disengages knuckle.
4. Position jack under lower control arm at spring seat, raise jack until compression is relieved from upper control arm bumper.
5. Remove stud nut, lift control arm from steering knuckle and place a block of wood between control arm and frame.
6. On all models,
   a. Center punch rivet head as close to center as possible.
   b. Using a 1/8 inch twist drill, drill through center of rivet approximately 1/2 rivet length deep.
   c. Enlarge hole using a 7/32 inch drill.
   d. Using a chisel, remove rivet heads, then drive rivets out using a suitable punch.
7. Position ball joint on upper control arm. Install bolts through bottom of control arm with nuts on top, torque to 8 ft. lbs.
8. On all models, position ball joint stud so

cotter pin hole is facing forward and remove wooden block from between control arm and frame.

9. Place wheels in straight ahead position, raise jack under lower control until ball joint stud can be installed in steering knuckle.
10. Install castellated nut on ball joint stud. Torque nut to 60 ft. lbs. on 1978 Skylark, 50 ft. lbs. on all 1977 models, 61 ft. lbs. on 1978–79 models except Skylark, 63 ft. lbs. on 1979 Skylark and 65 ft. lbs. on all 1980–83 models.

NOTE: If cotter pin holes do not align, do not loosen nut, however, tighten until cotter pin can be installed.

11. Install wheel assembly and lower vehicle.

Lower Ball Joint

1. Support vehicle under frame side rails.

NOTE: Position jack under lower control at outboard end, raise jack until it is 1/2 inch below control arm.

2. Remove cotter pin, loosen ball joint stud nut approximately 2 turns, do not remove nut.
3. Position tool as shown in Fig. 4, turn threaded end of tool until ball joint stud is disengaged from steering knuckle.
4. Position jack under lower control arm at spring seat and raise jack until compression is removed from upper control arm bumper.
5. Remove lower ball joint stud nut and position steering knuckle aside.
6. Using tool No. J-9519-10, remove ball joint from lower control arm.
7. Position ball joint on control arm with bleed vent on rubber boot facing inward.
8. Install tools J-9519-17 and J-9519-10 and turn threaded end of tool until ball joint is fully seated in lower control arm.
9. Position new ball joint stud so cotter pin hole is facing forward.
10. Place wheels in the straight ahead position and install ball joint stud on steering knuckle.
11. Install stud nut and cotter pin. Torque nut to 70 ft. lbs. on all 1977 models and 85 ft. lbs. on 1978–79 all models, except Skylark, and 81 ft. lbs. on 1979 Skylark and all 1980–83 models.

NOTE: If cotter pin holes do not align do not loosen stud nut, tighten nut until cot-

Fig. 3   Lower ball joint check

Fig. 4   Removing ball joint stud from steering knuckle

ter pin can be installed.

12. Install wheel assembly.

SHOCK ABSORBER, REPLACE

Unfasten shock absorber at top and bottom and remove it through the spring seat. Check shock absorber for obvious physical damage or oil leakage. Push and pull shock absorber in an upright position. If smooth hydraulic resistance is not present in both directions, replace shock absorber.

COIL SPRING, REPLACE

1. Raise and support vehicle at frame.
2. Remove shock absorber lower mount, then push shock up through control arm and into spring.
3. Remove stabilizer shaft from lower control arm. Refer to "Stabilizer Shaft, Replace".
4. Position a tool No. J-23028 at lower control arm pivot bolts, Fig. 5.
5. Position a suitable jack under tool installed in step 4 and chain together, then raise jack slightly to remove tension from lower control arm pivot bolts.
6. Using a suitable chain, secure lower control arm and coil spring together.
7. Remove rear lower control arm pivot bolt, then front bolt.
8. Slowly lower jack with lower control arm and spring attached.
9. When spring compression is relieved, remove spring.
10. Reverse procedure to install. Refer to Figs. 6 and 7, for proper installation.

Fig. 5 Removing front coil spring

STABILIZER BAR, REPLACE

1. Raise and support front of vehicle.
2. Remove nut, link bolt, retainers, grommets, spacer and stabilizer linkage from lower control arms.
3. Remove bracket to frame bolts, then remove stabilizer shaft, rubber bushings and brackets. On 1978–81 Century and 1978–83 Regal models, use tool No. J-25359-20 to remove stabilizer shaft bolt.
4. Reverse procedure to install. Note the following:
   a. When installing rubber bushings, bushings should be positioned squarely in the brackets with the bushing slit facing front of vehicle.
   b. Torque stabilizer link nut to 13 ft. lbs. and bracket bolts to 25 ft. lbs.

MANUAL STEERING GEAR, REPLACE

1977–80 All Models

1. Remove two nuts or pinch bolt securing lower coupling to steering shaft flange.
2. Use a suitable puller to remove pitman arm.
3. Unfasten gear (3 bolts) from frame and remove from car.
4. Reverse procedure to install.

POWER STEERING, GEAR REPLACE

1977–83

1. Disconnect pressure and return line hoses at steering gear and elevate ends of hoses higher than pump to prevent oil from draining out of pump.
2. Remove pinch bolt securing coupling to steering gear.
3. Jack up car and remove pitman shaft nut, then use a suitable puller to remove pitman arm.
4. On full size models, remove sheet metal baffle that covers frame-to-gear attaching bolts, if equipped.
5. Loosen the three frame-to-steering gear bolts and remove steering gear.
6. Reverse procedure to install.

POWER STEERING PUMP, REPLACE

1. Disconnect battery ground cable.
2. Remove steering pump belt, alternator belt and air conditioning compressor belt, if equipped.
3. On 1977–79 models, remove steering pump bracket from engine. On 1980–81 models, remove steering pump pulley using tool J-25304 or equivalent.
4. Disconnect steering pump hoses from pump and plug all open lines and fittings to prevent entry of dirt.
5. Remove pump or pump with brackets from engine.
6. Reverse procedure to install.

SPRING

FORWARD

A

NOTE SPRING TO BE INSTALLED WITH TAPE AT LOWEST POSITION. BOTTOM OF SPRING IS COILED HELICAL, AND THE TOP IS COILED FLAT WITH A GRIPPER NOTCH NEAR END OF WIRE (TAPE LOCATION OPTIONAL)

NOTE: AFTER ASSEMBLY, END OF SPRING COIL MUST COVER ALL OR PART OF ONE INSPECTION DRAIN HOLE. THE OTHER HOLE MUST BE PARTLY EXPOSED OR COMPLETELY UNCOVERED.

SPRING

FORWARD

WHEN A PORTION OF COILS ARE COMPRESSED THE COIL TO COIL GAP MUST NEVER BE LESS THAN 23.3mm. (29/32")

FORWARD

VIEW A

WHEN ENTIRE SPRING IS COMPRESSED THE OVERALL DIMENSION MUST NEVER BE LESS THAN 205.5 mm. (3.2/32")

VIEW B

Fig. 6 Coil spring installation. All exc. Full size models

INSULATOR FRAME NOTE: INSTALL SPRING SO THAT TAPED END IS AWAY FROM FRAME AS SHOWN.

SPRING

WHEN A PORTION OF THE COILS ARE COMPRESSED, THE COIL-TO-COIL GAP MUST NEVER BE LESS THAN 20.0 mm (.78").

LOWER CONTROL ARM

MAXIMUM SPRING COMPRESSION

WHEN THE ENTIRE SPRING IS COMPRESSED, THE OVERALL DIMENSION MUST NEVER BE LESS THAN 241.3 mm (9.5").

WITH SUSPENSION ASSEMBLED, THE BOTTOM END OF COIL SPRING MUST SHOW IN FIRST HOLE AND NOT COVER SECOND HOLE.

Fig. 7 Coil spring installation. Full size models

CADILLAC
EXC. CIMARRON

INDEX OF SERVICE OPERATIONS

NOTE: Refer to the back of this manual for vehicle manufacturer's special service tool suppliers.

SERIAL NUMBER LOCATION:

On top of instrument panel, left front.

ENGINE NUMBER LOCATION:

On all engines except V6-252, V8-250 and V8-350, engine unit number is located on cylinder block behind left cylinder head. V.I.N. derivative is located on cylinder block behind intake manifold.

The engine identification number on V6-252 engines is stamped on the left rear of cylinder block.

On 1977–78 V8-350, engine identification number is located on left hand side of cylinder block at front below cylinder head. On 1979–82 V8-350, engine code label is located on top of left hand valve cover and engine unit number label is located on top of right hand valve cover. On 1983 V8-350, engine code label is located on front left side of crankcase below the cylinder head.

On 1982–83 V8-250 engines, the engine identification plate is located on a pad at the lower left side of the crankcase.

ENGINE IDENTIFICATION

Year/Engine	V.I.N	Engine Code
1977		
V8-350①②	R	—
V8-425③	S	—
V8-425②	T	—
1978		
V8-350①②	B	—
V8-350④	N	—
V8-425③	S	—
V8-425②	T	—
1979		
V8-350④⑤	N	C2, C3, C4, C5, C6
V8-350④⑥	N	E2, E3, E4, E5, E6
V8-350④⑦	N	K2, K3, K4, K5, K6
V8-350②⑥	B	EA, EC
V8-350②⑦	B	KA, KB
V8-425②⑤	T	JAA, JBA, JCA, JDA, JFA
V8-425③⑤	S	JHA

Year/Engine	V.I.N.	Engine Code
1980		
V6-252⑦	4	MF, MZ
V8-350④⑤	N	VCJ, VCS, VBW
V8-350④⑥⑦	N	VBK, VCK
V8-350②⑥⑦	8	HFA, VBX
V8-368③⑤	6	HAA, HBA, KA
V8-368②⑥	9	HDA
V8-368②⑦	9	HHA
1981		
V6-252⑧	4	SA, SB, SC, SD, SF, SG, SJ, SK, SL, SM, SN, SP, SQ
V8-350④	N	VKB, VKC, VKH, VKJ, VKN, VKR, VKU, VKY, VLA, VLC, VLD, VLK, VLL, VLN, VLP, VL8, VLY, VMJ, VMT, VMX, VMY, VNA, VNB, VNC, VND, VNE, VPB, VPC, VPD, VPF

Year/Engine	V.I.N.	Engine Code
V8-368②	9	AA, BA, CA, DA, FA, HA, RA, SA, TA
1982		
V6-252⑧	4	FA, FB, FC, FD, FE, FF, FG, FH, FJ, FK
V8-250②	8	AA, AB, AD, AF
V8-350④	N	VAB, VAC, VAD, VAK, VAL, VAM, VAN, VAP, VAS, VAU, VAW, VAX, VAY, VAZ, VBA, VBB, VBC, VBP, VBU, VBW
1983		
V8-250②	8	—
V8-350④	N	—

①—Oldsmobile built engine.
②—Fuel injected engine.
③—Carbureted engine.
④—Oldsmobile built diesel engine.
⑤—Brougham & DeVille.
⑥—Eldorado.
⑦—Seville.
⑧—Buick built engine.

GRILLE IDENTIFICATION

1977 Exc. Eldorado & Seville

1977 Eldorado

1978 Eldorado

1979 Exc. Eldorado & Seville

1979 Eldorado

1979 Seville

1980 Exc. Eldorado & Seville

1980 Eldorado

1980–81 Seville

GRILLE IDENTIFICATION—Continued

1981 Exc. Eldorado & Seville   1981 Eldorado   1982 Exc. Eldorado & Seville

1982 Eldorado   1982 Seville   1983 Exc. Eldorado & Seville

1983 Eldorado   1983 Seville

GENERAL ENGINE SPECIFICATIONS

Year	Engine CID①/Liter	Engine VIN Code②	Carburetor	Bore and Stroke	Compression Ratio	Net H.P. @ R.P.M.③	Maximum Torque Ft. Lbs. @ R.P.M.	Normal Oil Pressure Pounds
1977	V8-350, 5.7L	R	Fuel Injection	4.057 × 3.385	8.5	180 @ 4400	275 @ 2000	30–35
	V8-425, 7.0L	S	M4ME, 4 Bbl④⑤	4.082 × 4.060	8.2	180 @ 4000	320 @ 2000	35 Min.
	V8- 425, 7.0L	T	Fuel Injection	4.082 × 4.060	8.2	195 @ 3800	320 @ 2400	35 Min.
1978	V8-350, 5.7L⑥	N	Fuel Injection	4.057 × 3.385	22.5	120 @ 3600	220 @ 1600	30–45
	V8-350, 5.7L	B	Fuel Injection	4.057 × 3.385	8.0	170 @ 4280	270 @ 2000	30–35
	V8-425, 7.0L	S	M4ME, 4 Bbl④	4.082 × 4.060	8.2	180 @ 4000	320 @ 2000	35 Min.
	V8-425, 7.0L	T	Fuel Injection	4.082 × 4.060	8.2	180 @ 4000	320 @ 2000	35 Min.
1979	V8-350, 5.7L⑥	N	Fuel Injection	4.057 × 3.385	22.5	125 @ 3600	225 @ 1600	30–45
	V8-350, 5.7L	B	Fuel Injection	4.057 × 3.385	8.0	170 @ 4200	270 @ 2000	30–45
	V8-425, 7.0L	S	M4ME, 4 Bbl④	4.082 × 4.060	8.2	180 @ 4000	320 @ 2000	35 Min.
	V8-425, 7.0L	T	Fuel Injection	4.082 × 4.060	8.2	195 @ 3800	320 @ 2400	35 Min.
1980	V6-252, 4.1L⑧	4	M4ME, 4 Bbl④	3.96 × 3.40	8.0	125 @ 4000	205 @ 2000	37
	V8-350, 5.7L⑥	N	Fuel Injection	4.057 × 3.385	22.5	105 @ 3200	205 @ 1600	30–45
	V8-350, 5.7L	8	Fuel Injection	4.057 × 3.385	8.0	160 @ 4400	265 @ 1600	30–45
	V8-368, 6.0L	9	Fuel Injection	3.800 × 4.060	8.2	145 @ 3600	270 @ 2000	30–45
	V8-368, 6.0L	6	M4ME, 4 Bbl④⑦	3.800 × 4.060	8.2	150 @ 3800	265 @ 1600	30–45
1981	V6-252, 4.1L⑧	4	E4ME, 4 Bbl④	3.96 × 3.40	8.0	125 @ 3800	210 @ 2000	37
	V8-350, 5.7L⑥	N	Fuel Injection	4.06 × 3.38	22.5	105 @ 3200	200 @ 1600	30–45
	V8-368, 6.0L	9	Fuel Injection	3.80 × 4.06	8.2	140 @ 3800	265 @ 1400	30–45
1982	V6-252, 4.1L⑧	4	E4ME, 4 Bbl④	3.96 × 3.40	8.0	125 @ 4000	205 @ 2000	37
	V8-250, 4.1L	8	Fuel Injection	3.465 × 3.307	8.5	135 @ 4600	200 @ 1600	30
	V8-350, 5.7L⑥	N	Fuel Injection	4.06 × 3.38	22.5	105 @ 3200	200 @ 1600	30–45
1983	V8-250, 4.1L	8	Fuel Injection	3.465 × 3.307	8.5	135 @ 4200	200 @ 2200	30
	V8-350, 5.7L⑥	N	Fuel Injection	4.06 × 3.38	22.5	105 @ 3200	200 @ 1600	30–45

①—CID—Cubic inch displacement.
②—On 1977–80 vehicles, the fifth digit in the VIN denotes the engine code. On 1981–83 vehicles, the eighth digit in the VIN denotes the engine code.
③—Net rating—as installed in the vehicle.
④—Rochester.
⑤—On 1977 high altitude vehicles, M4MEA.
⑥—Oldsmobile built diesel engine.
⑦—DeVille and all vehicles with C-4 system, E4ME.
⑧—Buick built engine.

TUNE UP SPECIFICATIONS

The following specifications are published from the latest information available. This data should be used only in the absence of a decal affixed in the engine compartment.

★ When using a timing light, disconnect vacuum hose or tube at distributor and plug opening in hose or tube so idle speed will not be affected.

● When checking compression, lowest cylinder must be within 70 percent of highest.

▲ Before removing wires from distributor cap, determine location of No. 1 wire in cap, as distributor position may have been altered from that shown at the end of this chart.

☞ Spark plug types shown in this chart are recommendations of the original manufacturer and not MOTOR.

Check local sources for other spark plug manufacturers listings.

Year & Engine/V.I.N.	Spark Plug Type ☞	Gap	Firing Order Fig. ▲	Ignition Timing BTDC① ★ Man. Trans.	Auto. Trans.	Mark Fig.	Curb Idle Speed Man. Trans.	Auto Trans.②	Fast Idle Speed Man. Trans.	Auto. Trans.③	Fuel Pump Pressure
1977											
V8-350/R, Exc. Calif.	R47SX	.060	B	—	10°	A	—	600D	—	—	—
V8-350/R, Calif.	R47SX	.060	B	—	8°	A	—	600D	—	—	—
V8-425/S, Exc. Calif. & E.F.I.	R45NSX	.060	C	—	18°⑤	D	—	⑥	—	1400⑦	5¼—6½
V8-425/S, Calif. Exc. E.F.I.	R45NSX	.060	C	—	18°⑤	D	—	⑥	—	1500⑦	5¼—6½
V8-425 E.F.I./T	R45NSX	.060	D	—	18°⑤	D	—	650D	—	—	—
1978											
V8-350 E.F.I./B, Exc. Calif.	R47SX	.060	B	—	10°	A	—	650D	—	—	—
V8-350 E.F.I./B, Calif.	R47SX	.060	B	—	8°	A	—	650D	—	—	—
V8-350 Diesel/N, Exc. High Alt.	—	—	—	—	4½°⑬⑭⑮	—	—	575D	—	650D	—
V8-350 Diesel/N, High Alt.	—	—	—	—	5½°⑬⑭⑮	—	—	575D	—	650D	—
V8-425/S, Exc. E.F.I.	R45NSX	.060	C	—	⑨	D	—	600D	—	⑦⑩	—
V8-425 E.F.I./T	R45NSX	.060	C	—	18°⑪	D	—	600D	—	—	—
1979											
V8-350 E.F.I./B	R47SX	.060	B	—	10°	A	—	600D	—	—	—
V8-350 Diesel/N, Exc. High Alt.	—	—	—	—	4½°⑬⑭⑮	—	—	575D	—	650D	—
V8-350 Diesel/N, High Alt.	—	—	—	—	5½°⑬⑭⑮	—	—	575D	—	650D	—
V8-425/S, Exc. E.F.I.	R45NSX	.060	C	—	23°⑪	D	—	550/650D	—	⑦⑫	—
V8-425 E.F.I./T	R45NSX	.060	C	—	18°⑤	D	—	650D	—	—	—
1980											
V6-252/4, 4 Barrel	R45TSX	.060	E	—	15°	F	—	550/680D	—	2000	3 Min.
V8-350 E.F.I./8	R47SX	.060	B	—	10°	A	—	600D	—	—	—
V8-350 Diesel/N, Exc. High Alt.	—	—	—	—	4½°⑬⑭⑮	—	—	600D	—	750D	—
V8-350 Diesel/N, High Alt.	—	—	—	—	5½°⑬⑭⑮	—	—	600D	—	750D	—
V8-368/6, 4 Barrel Exc. Calif.	R45NSX	.060	C	—	18°⑤	D	—	500/650D	—	1450	5¼—6½
V8-368/6, 4 Barrel Calif.	R45NSX	.060	C	—	18°⑤	D	—	575/650D	—	1350	5¼—6½
V8-368 D.E.F.I./9	R45NSX	.060	C	—	10°④	D	—	550D	—	—	—
1981											
V6-252/4	R45TS8	.080	E	—	15°	F	—	550/690D	—	2200	3 Min.
V8-350 Diesel/N, Exc. High Alt.	—	—	—	—	4°⑬⑭⑮	—	—	600D	—	750D	—
V8-350 Diesel/N, High Alt.	—	—	—	—	5°⑬⑭⑮	—	—	600D	—	750D	—
V8-368 D.E.F.I./9	R45NSX	.060	C	—	10°	D	—	550D	—	—	—

Continued

TUNE UP SPECIFICATIONS—Continued

The following specifications are published from the latest information available. This
data should be used only in the absence of a decal affixed in the engine compartment.

★ When using a timing light, disconnect vacuum hose or tube at distributor and plug opening in hose or tube so idle speed will not be affected.
● When checking compression, lowest cylinder must be within 70 percent of highest.
▲ Before removing wires from distributor cap, determine location of No. 1 wire in cap, as distributor position may have been altered from that shown at the end of this chart.

Spark plug types shown in this chart are recommendations of the original manufacturer and not MOTOR.
Check local sources for other spark plug manufacturers listings.

Year & Engine/V.I.N.	Spark Plug Type	Gap	Ignition Timing BTDC①★ Firing Order Fig. ▲	Man. Trans.	Auto. Trans.	Mark Fig.	Curb Idle Speed Man. Trans.	Auto Trans.②	Fast Idle Speed Man. Trans.	Auto. Trans.③	Fuel Pump Pressure
1982											
V6-252/4	R45TS8	.080	E	—	15°	F	—	⑧	—	—	4.5 PSI.
V8-250 D.E.F.I./8	R43NTS6	.060	G	—	10°	—	—	⑧	—	—	—
V8-350 Diesel/N, Exc. High Alt.	—	—	—	—	4°⑬⑭⑮	—	—	600D	—	750D	—
V8-350 Diesel/N, High Alt.	—	—	—	—	4°⑬⑭⑮	—	—	600D	—	750D	—
1983											
V8-250 D.E.F.I./8	R43NTS6	.060	G	—	10°	—	—	⑧	—	—	—
V8-350 Diesel/N	—	—	—	—	—	—	—	—	—	—	—

①—B.T.D.C.—Before top dead center.
②—Where two idle speeds are listed, the higher speed is with idle solenid energized. Curb idle speed is adjusted with A/C off, while solenoid idle speed is adjusted with A/C on. Idle speed is adjusted in Drive unless otherwise specified.
③—With transmission in Park position & parking brake fully applied.
④—Engine wiring harness test lead, green connector, must be grounded.
⑤—At 1400 RPM.
⑥—Except Eldorado, 600/675D RPM; Eldorado,

600D RPM.
⑦—With cam follower on 2nd step of fast idle cam, distributor vacuum hose & EGR vacuum hose disconnected & plugged & A/C off.
⑧—Idle speed is controlled by an idle speed control motor or idle load compensator.
⑨—Except Eldorado, except high altitude, 21° BTDC at 1600 RPM; high altitude, 23° BTDC at 1600 RPM. Eldorado, except Calif. & high altitude, 21° BTDC at 1600 RPM; California, 18° BTDC at 1600 RPM; high altitude, 23° BTDC at 1600 RPM.
⑩—Except carburetor No. 17058230, 1500 RPM;

carburetor No. 17058230, 1400 RPM.
⑪—At 1600 RPM.
⑫—Except carburetor No. 17059230, 1500 RPM; carburetor No. 1705923, 1000 RPM.
⑬—ATDC—After top dead center.
⑭—The injection pump timing specifications listed are for use with Diesel Timing Meter J-33075.
⑮—At 1200 RPM.
⑯—At 1250 RPM. When operating at altitudes above 4000 ft., set at 5° ATDC.
⑰—At 1250 RPM. When operating at altitudes below 4000 ft., set at 3° ATDC.

Fig. A

Fig. B

Fig. D

Fig. E

Fig. F

Fig. G

VALVE SPECIFICATIONS

Year	Engine/V.I.N.	Valve Lash	Valve Angles Seat	Valve Angles Face	Valve Spring Installed Height	Valve Spring Pressure Lbs. @ In.	Stem Clearance Intake	Stem Clearance Exhaust	Stem Diameter Intake	Stem Diameter Exhaust
1977–79	V8-350/R,B	Hydraulic①	②	③	1⁴³/₆₄	187 @ 1⁹/₃₂	.0010–.0027	.0015–.0032	.3425–.3432	.3420–.3427
1977–79	V8-425/S,T	Hydraulic①	45	44	1⁶¹/₆₄	160 @ 1³¹/₆₄	.0010–.0027	.0010–.0027	.3413–.3420	.3413–.3420
1978–79	V8-350/N④	Hydraulic①	②	③	1.670	151 @ 1.30	.0010–.0027	.0015–.0032	.3425–.3432	.3420–.3427
1980	V8-350/8	Hydraulic①	②	③	1.670	187 @ 1.27	.0010–.0027	.0015–.0032	.3425–.3432	.3420–.3427
1980–81	V6-252/4⑤	Hydraulic①	45	45	1.727	⑥	.0015–.0035	.0015–.0032	.3401–.3412	.3405–.3412
	V8-350/N④	Hydraulic①	②	③	1.670	210 @ 1.3	.0010–.0027	.0015–.0032	.3425–.3432	.3420–.3427
	V8-368/6,9	Hydraulic①	45	44	1.946	160 @ 1.496	.0010–.0027	.0010–.0027	.3413–.3420	.3413–.3420
1982	V8-250/8	Hydraulic①	45	44	1.73	182 @ 1.28	.001–.003	.001–.003	.3413–.3420	.3411–.3418
	V6-252/4⑤	Hydraulic①	45	45	1.727	220 @ 1.34	.0015–.0035	.0015–.0032	.3401–.3412	.3405–.3412
	V6-350/N④	Hydraulic①	②	③	1.670	210 @ 1.22	.0010–.0027	.0015–.0032	.3425–.3432	.3420–.3427
1983	V8-250/8	Hydraulic①	45	44	1.73	182 @ 1.28	.001–.003	.001–.003	.3413–.3420	.3411–.3418
	V8-350/N④	Hydraulic①	②	③	1.670	210 @ 1.22	.0010–.0027	.0015–.0032	.3425–.3432	.3420–.3427

①—No adjustment
②—Intake 45°; exhaust 31°.
③—Intake 44°; exhaust 30°.
④—Diesel engine.
⑤—Buick built engine.
⑥—Intake, 164 @ 1.34; Exhaust, 182 @ 1.34

DISTRIBUTOR SPECIFICATIONS

★ Note: If unit is checked on the vehicle, double the RPM and degrees to get crankshaft figures.

Distributor Part No.①	Advance Starts	Intermediate Advance			Full Advance	Vacuum Advance Inches of Vacuum to Start Plunger	Vacuum Advance Max. Adv. Dist. Deg. @ Vacuum
1103307④	0 @ 200	−½ to +1³/₅ @ 450	4¹/₅–7³/₁₀ @ 700	11½–13⁴/₅ @ 1450	22 @ 2500	9½	9½ @ 20.7
1103307⑤	0 @ 200	−³/₆₄ to 0 @ 400	4³/₄–7⁷/₈ @ 725	6¹/₈–8³/₈ @ 790	22 @ 3000	9	9½ @ 17
1103331	0 @ 200	½–3½ @ 450	5½–8 @ 700	7½–9½ @ 1450	9½ @ 2500	3½	14½ @ 20.7
1103332④	0 @ 200	½–3½ @ 450	5½–8 @ 700	7½–9½ @ 1450	9½ @ 2500	3½	10½ @ 20.7
1103332⑤	0 @ 200	−½ to +2½ @ 400	5¼–8 @ 775	7½–9½ @ 1450	9½ @ 2400	3	10½ @ 13
1103334④	0 @ 200	½–3½ @ 450	4¹/₅–6³/₁₀ @ 700	6–8 @ 1450	9½ @ 2500	4²/₅	14½ @ 20.7
1103334⑤	0 @ 200	−½ to +2½ @ 400	3–6 @ 575	4–6¹/₈ @ 613	9½ @ 2500	4	14½ @ 16
1103335④	0 @ 200	−½ to +1³/₅ @ 450	1¹/₅–3³/₁₀ @ 700	3–5³/₁₀ @ 1450	8 @ 2500	3½	10½ @ 20.7
1103335⑤	0 @ 200	−½ to +1⁵/₈ @ 463	⁷/₈–3 @ 600	3½–5⁵/₈ @ 1600	8 @ 2900	3	10½ @ 13
1103345	0 @ 200	½–3½ @ 450	5½–8 @ 700	7½–9½ @ 1450	9½ @ 2500	3½	8½ @ 20.7
1103348	0 @ 200	−½ to +1³/₅ @ 450	4¹/₅–7³/₁₀ @ 700	11½–13⁴/₅ @ 1450	22 @ 2500	5³/₅	12½ @ 20.7
1103349	0 @ 200	−½ to +1³/₅ @ 450	4¹/₅–7⁴/₅ @ 700	11½–13⁴/₅ @ 1450	22 @ 2500	5³/₅	14½ @ 20.7
1103352	0 @ 200	½–3½ @ 450	5½–8 @ 700	7½–9½ @ 1450	9½ @ 2500	5³/₅	5½ @ 20.7
1103389④	0 @ 200	½–3½ @ 450	5½–8 @ 700	7½–9½ @ 1450	9½ @ 1450	4	14½ @ 20
1103389⑤	0 @ 200	−½ to +2½ @ 400	5–8 @ 675	6–8¹/₁₆ @ 712	9½ @ 2000	3	14½ @ 16
1103392④	−¼–0 @ 275	—	7 @ 700	—	8½ @ 1450	6	10 @ 13.5
1103392⑤	0 @ 200	−½ to 2½ @ 400	5–8 @ 725	7½–9½ @ 1450	9½ @ 2400	3	10½ @ 14
1103393④	0 @ 450	—	7 @ 750	—	21 @ 2500	5	12 @ 12
1103393⑤	0 @ 200	−½ to 0 @ 400	4³/₄–7³/₄ @ 725	8–10 @ 1000	22 @ 3000	4	12½ @ 13
1103394④	0 @ 450	—	7 @ 750	—	21 @ 2500	5	14 @ 15.5
1103394⑤	0 @ 200	−½ to 0 @ 400	4³/₄–8 @ 725	7⁷/₈–10 @ 1000	22 @ 3000	4	14½ @ 16
1103395④	0 @ 350	—	7 @ 700	—	8½ @ 1450	8	5 @ 12
1103395⑤	0 @ 200	−½ to +2½ @ 400	6–8 @ 712	7½–9½ @ 1000	9½ @ 2400	7	5½ @ 12
1103401⑥⑦	—	—	—	—	—	—	—
1103405⑥⑦	—	—	—	—	—	—	—
1103415⑥⑦	—	—	—	—	—	—	—
1103416⑥⑦	—	—	—	—	—	—	—
1103455⑦②	—	—	—	—	—	—	—
1103540⑦⑧	—	—	—	—	—	—	—
1103541⑦⑧	—	—	—	—	—	—	—
11103462⑦③	—	—	—	—	—	—	—
11103472⑦③	—	—	—	—	—	—	—

Continued

DISTRIBUTOR SPECIFICATIONS—Continued

★ Note: If unit is checked on the vehicle, double the RPM and degrees to get crankshaft figures.

Distributor Part No.①	Centrifugal Advance Degrees @ RPM of Distributor				Full Advance	Vacuum Advance	
	Advance Starts	Intermediate Advance				Inches of Vacuum to Start Plunger	Max. Adv. Dist. Deg. @ Vacuum
1110555⑦②③	—	—	—	—	—	—	—
1112891	0 @ 200	8 @ 600	—	—	9 @ 2500	4½	14½ @ 13
1112892	−¼–0 @ 330	−½ to +2½ @ 450	2½–5 @ 600	5–7 @ 1400	10 @ 000	5.5	9.5–10.5 @ 14
1112954	−¼–0 @ 330	−½ to +2½ @ 450	2½–5 @ 600	5–7 @ 1400	10 @ 3000	4.5	13.5–14.5 @ 16
1112897	0 @ 200	−½ to +2½ @ 450	2½–5 @ 600	5–7 @ 1400	10 @ 2500	5½	9½–10½ @ 13½
1112924	0 @ 200	−1 to +1¾ @ 450	1½–3 @ 800	4–6 @ 1700	8 @ 2500	5	13½–14½ @ 16
1112931	0 @ 200	½ to 1¾ @ 450	6¼–8½ @ 800	13½–15¾ @ 1700	22 @ 2500	5	13½–14½ @ 18
1112932	0 @ 200	½ to 1¾ @ 450	6¼–8½ @ 800	13½–15¾ @ 1700	22 @ 2500	5	8½–9½ @ 18
1112954	−¼–0 @ 330	−½ to +2½ @ 450	2½–5 @ 600	5–7 @ 1400	10 @ 3000	4½	13½–14½ @ 16
1113202	0 @ 200	4 @ 600	—	—	9 @ 2500	4½	10½ @ 13

①—Stamped on distributor housing plate.
②—1981 Models.
③—1982 Models.
④—1978 units.
⑤—1979 units.
⑥—1980 Models.
⑦—On models equipped with E.S.S. or E.S.T. refer to Tune-up chapter for specifications.

PISTONS, PINS, RINGS, CRANKSHAFT & BEARINGS

Year	Model/ V.I.N.	Piston Clearance	Ring End Gap①		Wrist-pin Diameter	Rod Bearings		Main Bearings			Shaft End Play
			Comp.	Oil		Shaft Diameter	Bearing Clearance	Shaft Diameter	Bearing Clearance	Thrust on Bear. No.	
1977–78	V8-350/R,B	.0010–.0020	.010	.015	.9805	2.1238–2.1248	.0005–.0026	④	⑤	3	.004–.008
1977–79	V8-425/S,T	.0006–.0014	.013	.015	.9997	2.500	.0005–.0028	3.250	.0001–.0026	3	.002–.012
1978–79	V8-350/N⑥	.0050–.0060	.015	.015	1.0951	2.1238–2.1248	.0005–.0026	2.9998	⑤	3	.0035–.0135
1979	V8-350/B	.0010–.0020	.010	.015	.9805	2.1238–2.1248	.0004–.0033	④	⑤	3	.0035–.0135
1980	V8-350/8	.0010–.0020	.010	.015	.9805	2.1238–2.1248	.0004–.0033	④	⑤	3	.0035–.0135
1980–81	V6-252/4⑦	.0008–.0020	.013	.015	.9394	2.2495	.0005–.0026	2.4995	.0003–.0018	2	.003–.009
	V8-350/N⑥	.0050–.0060	.015	.015	1.0951	1.877–1.887	.0005–.0026	2.9993–3.0003	⑤	3	.0035–.0135
	V8-368/6,9	.0006–.0014	.013	.015	.9997	2.500	.0005–.0028	3.250	.0005–.0026	3	.002–.013
1982	V6-252/4⑦	.0008–.0020	.013	.015	.9393	2.2487–2.2495	③	2.4995	.0003–.0018	2	.003–.009
1982–83	V8-250/8	.0010–.0018	.009	.010	.8658	1.93	.0005–.0028	2.64	.0004–.003	—	.001–.007
	V8-350/N⑥	.0030–.0040	.015	.015	1.0951	2.1238–2.1248	.0005–.0026	2.9993–3.0003	⑤	3	.0035–.0135

①—Fit rings in tapered bores for clearance given in tightest portion of ring travel.
②—See text under "Pistons".
③—No. 1, .0005–.0025 inch; Nos. 2, 3, 4, .0005–.0035 inch.
④—Exc. No. 1, 2.4985–2.4995; No. 1, 2.4988–2.4998.
⑤—Exc. No. 5, .0005–.0021; No. 5 .0015–.0031.
⑥—Diesel engine.
⑦—Buick built engine.

ENGINE TIGHTENING SPECIFICATIONS★

★ Torque specifications are for clean and lightly lubricated threads only. Dry or dirty threads produce increased friction which prevents accurate measurement of tightness.

Year & Engine/V.I.N.	Spark Plugs Ft. Lbs.	Cylinder Head Bolts Ft. Lbs.	Intake Manifold Ft. Lbs.	Exhaust Manifold Ft. Lbs.	Rocker Arm Shaft Bracket Ft. Lbs.	Rocker Arm Cover Ft. Lbs.	Connecting Rod Cap Bolts Ft. Lbs.	Main Bearing Cap Bolts Ft. Lbs.	Flex Plate to Crankshaft Ft. Lbs.	Vibration Damper or Pulley Ft. Lbs.
1977–79 V8-425/S,T	25	95⑤	30	③	70⑥	30①	40	90	75	310
1977–80 V8-350/R,B	25	130⑤	40⑤	25⑦	25⑥	7	42	②	60	310
1978–83 V8-350/N④	—	130⑤	40⑤	25	25⑥	3	42	120	60	200–310

Continued

ENGINE TIGHTENING SPECIFICATIONS★—Continued

★ Torque specifications are for clean and lightly lubricated threads only. Dry or dirty threads produce increased friction which prevents accurate measurement of tightness.

Year & Engine/V.I.N.	Spark Plugs Ft. Lbs.	Cylinder Head Bolts Ft. Lbs.	Intake Manifold Ft. Lbs.	Exhaust Manifold Ft. Lbs.	Rocker Arm Shaft Bracket Ft. Lbs.	Rocker Arm Cover Ft. Lbs.	Connecting Rod Cap Bolts Ft. Lbs.	Main Bearing Cap Bolts Ft. Lbs.	Flex Plate to Crankshaft Ft. Lbs.	Vibration Damper or Pulley Ft. Lbs.
1980–82 V6-252/4⑧	15	80	45	25	30	4	40	100	60	225
1980–81 V8-368/6,9	25	95	30	③	⑥⑪	71①	40	90	75	17
1982–83 V8-250/8	10	⑨	⑩	20	20⑥	50①	20	85	35	20

①—Inch pounds. Retorque after engine has been run.
②—Exc. No. 5, 80 ft. lbs.; No. 5, 120 ft. lbs.
③—Long screws, 35 ft. lbs. Short screw, 12 ft. lbs.
④—Diesel engine.
⑤—Clean and dip entire bolt in engine oil before tightening.
⑥—Rocker arm pivot bolt to head.
⑦—1979 with lock tabs, 30 ft. lbs.
⑧—Buick built engine.
⑨—Torque bolts to 45 ft. lbs., then retorque to 90 ft. lbs.
⑩—Refer to text for procedure.
⑪—70 ft. lbs. on 1980 models; 22 ft. lbs. on 1981 models.

ALTERNATOR & REGULATOR SPECIFICATIONS

Year	Model	Alternator					Regulator						
		Rated Hot Output Amps.	Field Current 12 Volts @ 80° F.	Output @ 14 Volts		Model	Field Relay			Voltage Regulator		
				2000 R.P.M. Amps.	5000 R.P.M. Amps.		Air Gap In.	Point Gap In.	Closing Voltage	Air Gap In.	Point Gap In.	Voltage @ 125 F.
1977–79	1101023	80	4.0–4.5	—	—	Integral	—	—	—	—	—	—
	1101033	80	4.0–4.5	—	—	Integral	—	—	—	—	—	—
	1102380	63	4.0–4.5	—	—	Integral	—	—	—	—	—	—
1980–81	1101046	80	4.0–4.5	—	—	Integral	—	—	—	—	—	—
	1102921	63	4.0–4.5	—	—	Integral	—	—	—	—	—	—
	—	70	4.0–4.5	—	—	Integral	—	—	—	—	—	—
1980–83	1101091	100	4.0–4.5	—	—	Integral	—	—	—	—	—	—
1982–83	1101046	80	—	—	—	Integral	—	—	—	—	—	—
	1101050	100	—	—	—	Integral	—	—	—	—	—	—

WHEEL ALIGNMENT SPECIFICATIONS

Year	Model	Caster Angle, Degrees		Camber Angle, Degrees				Toe-In. Inch	Toe-Out on Turns, Deg.	
		Limits	Desired	Limits		Desired			Outer Wheel	Inner Wheel
				Left	Right	Left	Right			
1977–78	Eldorado	−1/2 to +1/2	Zero	−3/8 to +3/8	−3/8 to +3/8	Zero	Zero	−1/16 to +1/16	—	—
	Seville	+1 1/2 to +2 1/2	+2	−3/8 to +3/8	−3/8 to +3/8	Zero	Zero	0 to +1/8	—	—
	Others	+2 1/2 to +3 1/2	+3	+1/8 to +7/8	+1/8 to +7/8	+1/2	+1/2	−1/16 to +1/16	—	—
1979	Eldorado	+2 to 3	+2 1/2	−1/2 to +1/2	−1/2 to +1/2	Zero	Zero	−1/16 to +1/16	—	—
	Seville	+1 1/2 to +2 1/2	+2	−3/8 to +3/8	−3/8 to +3/8	Zero	Zero	0 to +1/8	—	—
	Others	+2 1/2 to +3 1/2	+3	+1/8 to +7/8	+1/8 to +7/8	+1/2	+1/2	−1/16 to +1/16	—	—
1980–83	Eldorado & Seville	+2 to 3	+2 1/2	−1/2 to +1/2	−1/2 to +1/2	Zero	Zero	−1/16 to +1/16	—	—
	Others	+2 1/2 to +3 1/2	+3	+.1 to +.9	+.1 to +.9	+1/2	+1/2	1/8	—	—

CADILLAC—Exc. Cimarron

STARTING MOTOR SPECIFICATIONS

Year	Engine/V.I.N.	Starter Number	Brush Spring Tension Oz①	Free Speed Test			Resistance Test①	
				Amps.②	Volts	R.P.M.	Amps.	Volts
1977–78	V8-350/R,B③⑧	1108765	35	65–95	9	7000–10500	—	—
	V8-425/S,T④	1109038	35	65–95	9	7000–10500	—	—
	V8-425/S,T⑤	1109039	35	65–95	9	7000–10500	—	—
1979	V8-350/B③⑧	1109072	—	—	—	—	—	—
	V8-350/B⑤⑧	1998205	—	—	—	—	—	—
	V8-350/N③⑤⑥	1109214	—	—	—	—	—	—
	V8-425/S⑦	1109062	—	65–95	9	7000–10500	—	—
	V8-425/T⑧	1109063	—	—	—	—	—	—
1980	V8-350/N④⑥	1109216	—	65–95	9	9500–13000	—	—
	V8-350/N③⑤⑥	1109218	—	—	—	—	—	—
	V8-350/8③⑤⑧	1998205	—	—	—	—	—	—
	V8-368/5④⑦	1109062	—	65–95	9	7000–10500	—	—
	V8-368/T③⑤⑧	1998205	—	—	—	—	—	—
1981	V6-252/4⑦	1109062	—	65–95	9	7000–10500	—	—
	V8-350/N⑥	1109216	—	65–95	9	9500–13000	—	—
	V8-368/T⑧	1109062	—	65–95	9	7000–10500	—	—
1982	V8-250/8⑧	1109531	—	—	—	—	—	—
	V6-252/4⑦	1109062	—	65–95	9	7000–10500	—	—
	V8-350/N⑥	1109216	—	65–95	9	9500–13000	—	—
1983	V8-250/8④⑧	1109531	—	—	—	—	—	—
	V8-250/8③⑤⑧	1998233	—	—	—	—	—	—
	V8-350/N④⑥	1109216	—	65–95	9	9500–13000	—	—
	V8-350/N③⑤⑥	1109495	—	—	—	—	—	—

①—Minimum.
②—Includes solenoid.
③—Seville.
④—Exc. Eldorado & Seville.
⑤—Eldorado
⑥—Diesel engine.
⑦—4 Bbl.
⑧—Fuel Injected.

COOLING SYSTEM & CAPACITY DATA

Year	Model or Engine/V.I.N.	Cooling Capacity, Qts.		Radiator Cap Relief Pressure, Lbs.	Thermo. Opening Temp.	Fuel Tank Gals.	Engine Oil Refill Qts.①	Transmission Oil			Rear Axle Oil Pints
		Less A/C	With A/C					3 Speed Pints	4 Speed Pints	Auto. Trans. Qts.②	
1977	Eldorado	—	25.8	15	195	27½	5	—	—	⑥	4⑧
	Seville	—	17.25	15	195	21	4	—	—	⑤	4¼
	Others	—	20.8	15	195	24½	4	—	—	⑤	4¼
1978	Eldorado	—	24.3	15	195	27½	5	—	—	⑥	4⑧
	Seville Exc. Diesel	—	17.25	15	180	21	4	—	—	⑤	4¼
	Seville Diesel	—	18.9	15	195	21	7⑭	—	—	⑪	4¼
	Others	—	19.8	15	195	24	4	—	—	⑤	4¼
1979	Eldorado V8-350 E.F.I./B	—	14.75⑨	15	180	19.6⑬	4	—	—	⑩	3⅛⑧
	Eldorado V8-350 Diesel/N	—	18.5	15	195	19.6	7⑭	—	—	⑩	3⅛⑧
	Seville V8-350 E.F.I./B	—	17.25	15	180	21	4	—	—	⑫	4¼
	Seville V8-350 Diesel/N	—	20	15	195	21	7⑭	—	—	⑪	4¼
	Others V8-425/S,T	—	20.8	15	195	25	4	—	—	⑫	4¼
	Others V8-350 Diesel/N	—	23.8	15	195	27	7⑭	—	—	⑪	4¼

Continued

COOLING SYSTEM & CAPACITY DATA—Continued

Year	Model or Engine/V.I.N.	Cooling Capacity, Qts.		Radiator Cap Relief Pressure, Lbs.	Thermo. Opening Temp.	Fuel Tank Gals.	Engine Oil Refill Qts. ①	Transmission Oil			Rear Axle Oil Pints
		Less A/C	With A/C					3 Speed Pints	4 Speed Pints	Auto. Trans. Qts. ②	
1980	Eldorado V8-350 E.F.I./8	—	15.2	15	178	20.6	4	—	—	⑩	3⅕⑧
	Eldorado V8-368 D.E.F.I./9	—	22.4	15	178	20.6	5	—	—	⑩	3⅕⑧
	Eldorado V8-350 Diesel/N	—	18.5	15	195	23	7⑭	—	—	⑩	3⅕⑧
	Seville V8-350 E.F.I./8	—	15.2	15	178	20.6	4	—	—	⑩	3⅕⑧
	Seville V8-368 D.E.F.I./9	—	22.4	15	178	20.6	5	—	—	⑩	3⅕⑧
	Seville V8-350 Diesel/N	—	18.5	15	195	23	7⑭	—	—	⑩	3⅕⑧
	Others V6-252/4	—	13	15	195	25	4	—	—	4③	4¼
	Others V8-368/6	—	21.4	15	195	20.7	4	—	—	4③	4¼
	Others V8-350 Diesel/N	—	23.7	15	195	26	7⑭	—	—	⑪	4¼
1981	Eldorado V6-252/4	—	13.1	15	195	21.1	4	—	—	⑩	3⅕⑧
	Eldorado V8-368 D.E.F.I./9	—	22.4	15	178	20.3	4	—	—	⑩	3⅕⑧
	Eldorado V8-350 Diesel/N	—	18.4	15	195	22.8	7⑮	—	—	⑩	3⅕⑧
	Seville V6-252/4	—	13.1	15	195	21.1	4	—	—	⑩	3⅕⑧
	Seville V8-368 D.E.F.I./9	—	22.4	15	178	20.3	4	—	—	⑩	3⅕⑧
	Seville V8-350 Diesel/N	—	18.4	15	195	22.8	7⑮	—	—	⑩	3⅕⑧
	Others V6-252/4	—	18.2	15	195	25	4	—	—	⑰	4¼
	Others V8-368/9	—	21.4	15	195	25	4	—	—	⑰	4¼
	Others V8-350 Diesel/N	—	23.7	15	195	27	7⑮	—	—	⑰	4¼
1982	Eldorado V6-252/4	—	13.1	15	195	21.1	4	—	—	⑦	3⅕⑧
	Seville V6-252/4	—	13.1	15	195	21.1	4	—	—	⑦	3⅕⑧
	Others V6-252/4	—	18.2	15	195	25	4	—	—	⑯	4¼
	Eldorado V8-250/8	—	11.8	15	195	20.3	5④	—	—	⑦	3⅕⑧
	Seville V8-250/8	—	11.8	15	195	20.3	5④	—	—	⑦	3⅕⑧
	Others V8-250/8	—	10.8	15	195	25	4④	—	—	⑯	4¼
	Eldorado V8-350 Diesel/N	—	18.4	15	195	22.8	7⑮	—	—	⑦	3⅕⑧
	Seville V8-350 Diesel/N	—	18.4	15	195	22.8	7⑮	—	—	⑦	3⅕⑧
	Others V8-350 Diesel/N	—	23.7	15	195	27	7⑮	—	—	⑯	4¼
1983	Eldorado V8-250/8	—	10.9	15	195	20.3	5④	—	—	⑥	3⅕⑧
	Seville V8-250/8	—	10.9	15	195	20.3	5④	—	—	⑥	3⅕⑧
	Others V8-250/8	—	11.0	15	195	24.5	4④	—	—	⑱	4¼
	Eldorado Diesel/N	—	18.4	15	195	22.8	7⑮	—	—	⑥	3⅕⑧
	Seville Diesel/N	—	18.4	15	195	22.8	7⑮	—	—	⑥	3⅕⑧
	Others Diesel/N	—	23.7	15	195	26	7⑮	—	—	⑱	4¼

①—Add one quart with filter change.
②—Approximate. Make final check with dipstick.
③—Oil pan only.
④—Includes filter.
⑤—Oil pan 4 qts. Total capacity 12½ qts.
⑥—Oil pan 5 qts. Total capacity 13 qts.
⑦—Oil pan 5 qts. Total capacity 11¾ qts.
⑧—Front drive axle.

⑨—Heavy duty cooling system, 15½ qts.
⑩—Oil pan 5 qts. Total capacity 12 qts.
⑪—Oil pan 3 qts. Total capacity 9 qts.
⑫—Oil pan 4½ qts. Total capacity 12½ qts.
⑬—Early models, 19.6 gals.; late models, 18.1 gals.
⑭—Includes filter. Recommended diesel engine oil—1978, use oil designated SE/CD; 1979–80, use oil designated SE/CC.

⑮—Includes oil filter. Recommended diesel engine oil—use oil designated SF/CD, SF/CC or SE/CC on all except 1982–83 models or SF/CD, SF/CC on 1982–83 models.
⑯—Oil pan 3½ qts. Total capacity 11 qts.
⑰—THM 200C—oil pan 3½ qts., total capacity 11 qts.; THM 350 & 350C—oil pan 3.15 qts., total capacity 10 qts.; THM 400—oil pan 3 qts., total capacity 10 qts.
⑱—Oil pan, 5 qts. Total capacity, 11 qts.

BRAKE SPECIFICATIONS

Year	Model	Brake Drum Inside Diameter	Wheel Cylinder Bore Diameter			Master Cylinder Bore Diameter		
			Disc Brake	Front Drum Brake	Rear Drum Brake	Disc Brakes	Drum Brakes	Power Brakes
1977–78	Brougham	—	2¹⁵⁄₁₆	—	2½①	1⅛	—	1⅛
	DeVille	11	2¹⁵⁄₁₆	—	1	1⅛	—	1⅛
	Eldorado	—	2¹⁵⁄₁₆	—	2½①	1⅛	—	1⅛
	Fleetwood	12	2¹⁵⁄₁₆	—	¹⁵⁄₁₆	1⅛	—	1⅛
	Seville	—	2¹⁵⁄₁₆	—	2½①	1⅛	—	1⅛
1979	Seville	—	2¹⁵⁄₁₆	—	2½①	1⅛	—	1⅛
	Eldorado	—	2½	—	2⅛①	1	—	1
	Brougham	—	2¹⁵⁄₁₆	—	2½①	1⅛	—	1⅛
	DeVille	11	2¹⁵⁄₁₆	—	1	1⅛	—	1⅛
	Fleetwood	12	2¹⁵⁄₁₆	—	¹⁵⁄₁₆	1⅛	—	1⅛
1980–83	Seville	—	2½	—	2⅛①	1	—	1
	Eldorado	—	2½	—	2⅛①	1	—	1
	Brougham	11	2¹⁵⁄₁₆	—	1	1⅛	—	1⅛
	DeVille	11	2¹⁵⁄₁₆	—	1	1⅛	—	1⅛

①—Rear disc brake.

Electrical Section

STARTER, REPLACE

1979–83

1. Disconnect battery ground cable (two ground cables on diesel engines).
2. Raise and support front of vehicle.
3. Remove starter braces, shields, brackets and clips that may interfere with starter removal.
4. Remove starter attaching bolts, then lower starter.
5. Disconnect wiring harness from starter and remove starter.
6. Reverse procedure to install.

1977–78

1. Disconnect battery ground cable at battery.
2. On Eldorado, disconnect starter harness at connector at right rear of engine.
3. Raise front end of car.
4. On all except Eldorado models, disconnect battery lead at starter solenoid and disconnect neutral switch wire and coil feed wire at starter solenoid terminals.
5. On Eldorado, remove spring clip securing wire to solenoid housing.
6. On Seville, remove crossover pipe.
7. Remove screw and nut securing support bracket to starter and crankcase.
8. Unfasten starter motor from crankcase and remove starter by pulling it forward, then toward RH front wheel and up over steering linkage toward rear of car.
9. Reverse procedure to install.

IGNITION LOCK, REPLACE

1979–83

1. Remove steering wheel as described under Horn Sounder and Steering Wheel.
2. Remove turn signal switch as described under Turn Signal Switch, Replace, then remove buzzer switch.
3. Place ignition switch in Run position, then remove lock cylinder retaining screw and lock cylinder.
4. To install, rotate lock cylinder to stop while holding housing, Fig. 1. Align cylinder key with keyway in housing, then push lock cylinder assembly into housing until fully seated.
5. Install lock cylinder retaining screw. Torque screw to 40 in. lbs. for standard columns. On adjustable columns, torque retaining screw to 22 in. lbs.
6. Install buzzer switch, turn signal switch and steering wheel.

1977–78

1. Follow procedure to remove the turn signal switch as described further on.
2. Turn ignition switch to the "On" or "Run"

Fig. 1 Ignition lock removal. 1979–83 models

Fig. 2 Lock cylinder removal, 1977–78 models

Fig. 3   Ignition switch, 1977—83

Fig. 4   Mechanical neutral switch system with Tilt-Telescope column. 1977—83

Fig. 5   Mechanical neutral start system with standard column. 1977—83 models

position.

3. Insert a small screwdriver into slot next to the switch mounting screw boss, Fig. 2. Gently tap on screw-driver until screw-driver breaks through thin wall casting. Depress lock cylinder retaining tab with screw-driver and remove cylinder.
4. To install lock, hold lock cylinder sleeve and rotate key clockwise against stop. Making sure that buzzer switch drive tang is below outside diameter of lock cylinder, insert cylinder into cover bore with key on cylinder sleeve aligned with keyway in housing until cylinder touches lock sector shaft.

NOTE: Insert a 1/16 inch drill shank between lock cylinder knob and column housing to avoid assembling lock cylinder too far into steering column.

5. While maintaining a light inward force, rotate lock cylinder counter-clockwise until drive section of cylinder mates with sector drive shaft. Push in until snap ring on lock snaps into groove in housing.
6. Check for freedom of operation of lock cylinder.

IGNITION SWITCH, REPLACE
1977—83

1. Disconnect battery cable and position ignition key in "Lock".
2. Remove steering column lower cover.
3. Loosen two upper column support nuts and allow column to drop as far as possi-

ble without removing the nuts.

NOTE: Do not remove nuts as column may bend under its own weight.

4. Disconnect switch connector and remove switch, Fig. 3.
5. When reassembling, make sure the ignition key is in the "Lock" position. Assemble switch on actuator rod. Hold rod stationary and move switch towards bottom of column then back off one detent on standard steering column models. On models with tilt column, move switch toward upper end of column and back off one detent.

LIGHT SWITCH, REPLACE
1979—83 Eldorado & 1980—83 Seville

1. Disconnect battery ground cable.
2. Remove instrument cluster trim panel.
3. Remove two screws attaching switch to cluster carrier, then pull switch rearward to remove.
4. Reverse procedure to install.

1977—83 Except Eldorado & Seville

1. Disconnect battery ground cable.
2. Remove left hand instrument panel insert.
3. Remove three screws attaching light switch to instrument panel.
4. On vehicles equipped with Cruise Control and Twilight Sentinel, remove two screws retaining Cruise Control switch to instrument panel.

5. Slide Cruise Control switch forward to remove headlamp switch.
6. Disconnect electrical connector from headlamp switch, then if used, disconnect Guidematic connector from under instrument panel.
7. Remove switch.
8. Reverse procedure to install.

1977—79 Seville

1. Disconnect battery ground cable.
2. Remove lower left instrument panel assembly.
3. Pull knob to "ON" position, depress button on bottom of switch and remove knob and shaft assembly.
4. Remove headlamp case to lower instrument panel attaching screws.
5. Remove sleeve attaching headlamp switch to case.
6. On vehicles without Guide-Matic and Twilight Sentinel remove sleeve retaining escutcheon, washer and lens to backplate.
7. On vehicles equipped with Guide-Matic and Twilight Sentinel, remove Guide-Matic knob, wave washer and Twilight Sentinel lever by pulling outward. Remove lens, then spanner nut and potentiometer from backplate.
8. Reverse procedure to install.

1977—78 Eldorado

1. Disconnect battery ground cable.
2. Remove steering column lower cover.
3. Disconnect headlamp electrical connector and lower bulb.
4. Pull knob to "ON" position, depress spring loaded button and remove knob and shaft, escutcheon and washer.
5. Remove case to instrument support screw.

Fig. 6   Mechanical neutral start system in Park position

Fig. 7   Compressing lock plate & removing snap ring

Fig. 8   Taping turn signal connector & wiring

Fig. 9   Instrument cluster. 1977-79 Seville

Fig. 10   Instrument panel cluster. 1977-78 Eldorado

6. Lower switch assembly, disconnect upper bulb and remove switch.
7. Reverse procedure to install.

STOP LIGHT SWITCH

1977-83

The stoplight is retained to the brake pedal bracket. To adjust, pull the brake pedal fully up to its stop. This action automatically adjusts the switch.

NEUTRAL START SWITCH

1977-83 Models

Actuation of the ignition switch is prevented by a mechanical lockout system, Figs. 4 and 5, which prevents the lock cylinder from rotating when the selector lever is out of Park or Neutral. When the selector lever is in Park or Neutral, the slots in the bowl plate and the finger on the actuator rod align allowing the finger to pass through the bowl plate in turn actuating the ignition switch, Fig. 6. If the selector lever is in any position other than Park or Neutral, the finger contacts the bowl plate when the lock cylinder is rotated, thereby preventing full travel of the lock cylinder.

NOTE: On all models incorporating an electric neutral start switch, this switch plus the back-up light switch and parking brake vacuum release valve are combined into one unit. This unit is mounted on the steering column under the instrument panel.

TURN SIGNAL SWITCH, REPLACE

1977-83

Standard column
1. Disconnect battery cable and remove steering wheel.

2. Remove lock plate cover screws and cover.
3. With a suitable compressor, compress lock plate and spring and remove snap ring from shaft, Fig. 7.
4. Remove lock plate, cancelling cam, preload spring and thrust washer.
5. Remove steering column lower cover and the signal lever.
6. On car equipped with cruise control proceed as follows:
   a. Disconnect cruise control wire from harness.
   b. Remove harness protector from cruise control.
   c. Wrap wire around turn signal lever until lever is disconnected. Do not remove wire from column.
7. On all models remove bolts at upper support.
8. Remove four screws securing upper mounting bracket to column and remove bracket.
9. Disconnect turn signal harness and remove wires from plastic protector. Wrap a piece of tape around connector and harness to facilitate removal, Fig. 8.
10. Remove screw securing turn signal switch to column and pull switch out.
11. Reverse procedure to install.

Tilt & Telescope Wheel
1. Disconnect battery cable.
2. Remove steering wheel and slide rubber sleeve from steering shaft.
3. Remove plastic retainer from C-ring.
4. With a suitable compressor, thread bolt into steering shaft lock hole.
5. Compress preload spring and remove C-ring, Fig. 7.
6. Remove compressor and remove lock plate, horn contact carrier and preload spring.
7. Remove steering lower cover and the signal lever.
8. On cars equipped with cruise control proceed as follows:
   a. Disconnect cruise control wire from harness.
   b. Remove harness protector from cruise control.
   c. Wrap wire around turn signal lever until lever is disconnected. Do not

remove wire from column.
9. On all models remove bolts at upper support.
10. Remove four screws securing upper mounting bracket to column and remove bracket.
11. Disconnect turn signal harness and remove wires from plastic protector. Wrap a piece of tape around connector and harness to facilitate removal, Fig. 8.
12. Remove screw securing turn signal switch to column and pull switch out.
13. Reverse procedure to install.

HORN SOUNDER & STEERING WHEEL, REPLACE

1977-83

1. Disconnect battery ground cable.
2. Remove three screws from back of spokes and lift pad assembly from wheel.
3. On tilt and telescope wheels remove three screws securing lever and knob assembly to flange and screw assembly. Unscrew flange and screw assembly from steering shaft and remove. Remove lever and knob assembly.
4. On standard wheels, scribe an alignment mark on wheel hub in line with slash mark on steering shaft to be used upon installation.
5. Loosen steering shaft nut, apply a suitable puller to loosen wheel; then remove puller, nut and wheel.
6. Remove three screws securing three contact wires to wheel.
7. Reverse procedure to install.

INSTRUMENT CLUSTER, REPLACE

CAUTION: On vehicles equipped with an Air Cushion Restraint system, turn ignition switch to "Lock," disconnect battery ground cable and tape end, thereby deactivating system.

Fig. 11 Instrument cluster. 1977-83 Except Eldorado & Seville

Labels in figure:
LOWER INSTRUMENT PANEL ASSEMBLY
SPEEDOMETER CLUSTER
VIEW Ⓐ
SHIFT INDICATOR CABLE
WINDSHIELD WIPER SWITCH
HEADLAMP SWITCH
CRUISE CONTROL SWITCH
LOWER STEERING COLUMN COVER
STEERING COLUMN GASKET
Ⓜ ALL FASTENERS ARE METRIC
LEFT INSTRUMENT PANEL INSERT (CLUSTER BEZEL)

1979-83 Eldorado & 1980-83 Seville

1. Disconnect battery ground cable.
2. Remove instrument cluster trim panel.
3. Remove headlamp and windshield wiper switches.
4. Unlock headlamp, windshield wiper and cruise control wire connectors from cluster carrier.
5. Disconnect speedometer cable and instrument cluster wiring.
6. Remove instrument cluster attaching screws and remove cluster assembly.
7. Reverse procedure to install.

1977-79 Seville

1. Disconnect battery ground cable.
2. Remove steering column lower cover, 4 screws attaching cluster bezel to instrument panel, then press bezel downward, rotate top outward and carefully remove bezel.
3. Position shift lever in "Park" and remove screw attaching indicator cable to steering column.
4. Remove two screws securing top of cluster to instrument panel support and two screws securing speedometer cable retainer to cluster, Fig. 9.

NOTE: Do not remove speedometer cable retainer.

5. Pull cluster outward to disengage speedometer cable, then rotate cluster downward and disconnect wire connector. Remove cluster.
6. Reverse procedure to install.

1977-83 Except Seville & 1979-83 Eldorado

1. Disconnect battery ground cable.
2. Remove cluster bezel, then with shift lever in "Park" remove screw securing shift indicator cable to steering column.
3. Remove four screws securing cluster to instrument horizontal support, Figs. 10 and 11.

NOTE: Do not remove the 2 outboard screws which retain speedometer cable mounting.

4. On 1977-78 except Eldorado models, remove screw located directly above steering column, retaining cluster to speedometer mounting plate.
5. Disengage speedometer cable at neck by pulling cluster straight out and depressing retaining spring.

NOTE: To remove cluster, place shift lever in low range and on cars with tilt wheel, place wheel in lowest position.

6. Rotate cluster downward, disconnect printed circuit connector and remove cluster.
7. Reverse procedure to install.

RADIO, REPLACE

NOTE: When installing radio, be sure to adjust antenna trimmer for peak performance.

1979-83 Eldorado & 1980-83 Seville

1. Disconnect battery ground cable.
2. Remove center applique retaining screws, radio knobs, and hex nuts, then remove center applique.
3. Remove rear window defogger switch.
4. Remove radio mounting screws, then pull radio rearward. Disconnect electrical connectors and antenna lead from radio, then remove radio.
5. Reverse procedure to install.

1977-83 Except Eldorado & Seville

1. Remove center instrument panel insert.
2. Remove the four screws retaining radio to lower instrument panel.
3. Disconnect electrical connectors and antenna leads(s) and remove radio.

1977-79 Seville

1. Remove E.F.I. Electronic Control Unit as described in "Electronic Fuel Injection Section".
2. Remove screw attaching A/C outlet to heater case.
3. Disconnect antenna lead, then remove nut securing radio to rear mounting bracket.
4. Remove control knobs, anti-rattle springs, washers and nuts.

NOTE: On models with tape player, control knobs are retained by a 5/64" allen head screw.

5. Disconnect wiring harness and remove radio.
6. Reverse procedure to install.

1977-78 Eldorado

1. Disconnect battery ground cable.
2. Remove ash tray, radio knobs, washers, control rings and nuts.
3. Remove radio to lower support brace nut from rear and rotate brace to the right.
4. Disconnect wires, antenna lead and the dial bulb from radio.
5. Lower left hand side of radio and remove radio through the ash tray opening.
6. Reverse procedure to install.

W/S WIPER MOTOR
1977-83

1. Raise hood and remove cowl screen. On 1980-83 Eldorado and Seville, remove cowl panel prior to removing cowl screen.
2. Loosen transmission drive link to crank arm attaching nuts.

Fig. 12 Heater core. 1979–83 Eldorado & 1980–83 Seville

Fig. 13 Blower motor. 1977–83 (Typical)

3. Remove transmission drive link from motor crank arm.
4. Disconnect motor electrical connectors and hoses.
5. Remove motor attaching screws, then remove motor while guiding crank arm through hole.
6. Reverse procedure to install.

NOTE: Check to ensure wiper motor is in Park position before assembling crank arm to transmission drive link.

W/S WIPER TRANSMISSION

1977–83

1. Raise hood and remove cowl vent screen. On Seville it is first necessary to remove cowl panel.
2. On 1977–78 models except Eldorado and 1979–83 all models remove left and right wiper arm and blade assemblies. On 1977–78 Eldorado models remove wiper arm and blade from transmission to be removed.
3. Loosen attaching nuts securing transmission drive link to motor crank arm.

NOTE: On 1977–78 Eldorado models if only left side is to be removed, it will not be necessary to loosen nuts securing right drive link to motor crank arm.

4. Disconnect transmission drive link from crank arm.
5. Remove attaching screws securing transmission to body.
6. Remove transmission and linkage assembly through plenum chamber opening.

W/S WIPER SWITCH

1979–83 Eldorado & 1980–83 Seville

1. Disconnect battery ground cable.
2. Remove instrument cluster trim panel.
3. Remove two screws attaching switch to cluster carrier, then pull switch rearward to remove.
4. Reverse procedure to install.

Except 1979–83 Eldorado & 1980–83 Seville

1. Disconnect battery ground cable.
2. Remove left hand climate control outlet grille.
3. Remove screw securing switch to instrument panel.
4. Pull control switch and electrical connector out and disconnect from panel.

HEATER CORE, REPLACE

After draining radiator and disconnecting heater hoses and battery ground cable proceed as follows:

1979–83 Eldorado & 1980–83 Seville

1. Plug heater core outlets to prevent spillage when removing heater core.
2. Remove instrument panel sound absorbers, then lower steering column.
3. Remove instrument cluster trim panel and instrument cluster as described under Instrument Cluster, Replace.
4. Remove radio front speakers.
5. Remove screws attaching manifold to heater case.
6. Remove instrument panel upper and lower attaching screws, then disconnect parkbrake release cable.
7. Disconnect instrument panel wiring harness from dash wiring assembly.
8. Disconnect right hand remote control mirror cable from instrument panel pad.
9. Disconnect speedometer cable from clip and temperature control cable from heater case.
10. Disconnect radio and A/C wiring, vacuum lines and all necessary wiring to remove instrument panel. If equipped with pulse wipers, remove wiper switch, and then disconnect wire connector from instrument cluster carrier and separate pulse wiper jumper harness from wiper switch wire connector.
11. Remove instrument panel and wiring harness assembly.
12. Remove four screws retaining defroster nozzle to cowl and one screw at heater case, then remove defroster nozzle.
13. Disconnect vacuum hoses to programmer and vacuum actuators.
14. Disconnect wire connector from programmer.
15. From engine side of dash, remove four nuts retaining heater case to cowl, Fig. 12.

16. From passenger compartment side of dash, remove one screw retaining heater case to cowl, and remove heater case.
17. Remove four screws securing heater core to case and remove heater core.
18. Reverse procedure to install.

1977–83 Except Eldorado & Seville

1. Disconnect electrical connectors from blower motor, blower resistors and thermostatic cycling switch.
2. Remove right hand windshield washer nozzle and remove right hand air inlet screen from plenum and cover plate at center of plenum opening.
3. Remove screws retaining thermostatic cycling switch and position switch aside.
4. Remove the 16 fasteners retaining cover and remove cover.
5. Remove one screw and retainer holding heater core to frame at top.
6. Place temperature door in the max. heat position and reach through temperature housing and push lower forward corner of heater core away from housing, then rotate core parallel to housing. This will cause core to snap out of lower clamp. Remove heater core from temperature housing.
7. Reverse procedure to install.

1977–79 Seville

1. Remove right hand wheel housing.
2. Plug heater core tubes to prevent spilling coolant into vehicle when core is removed.
3. Remove instrument panel right hand insert and applique.
4. Remove fuel injection control unit.
5. Remove radio, glove box door and glove box.
6. Remove A/C programmer.
7. Remove right hand lower instrument panel.
8. Remove screws retaining A/C distributor to heater case and remove distributor.
9. Remove clips retaining vacuum harness to heater case and disconnect vacuum hoses at heater mode door, bulkhead grommet and defroster actuator. Position vacuum harness out of way.
10. Disconnect hose from in-car sensor aspirator.
11. From under hood, remove three nuts retaining heater case to cowl, then from inside vehicle, remove two screws retaining heater case to cowl and move heater

assembly from cowl.
12. Disconnect vacuum hose from A/C mode door actuator and remove heater assembly.

CAUTION: Heater core pipes are very long. Use care when removing heater assembly.

---

13. Remove rubber seal from around heater core pipes, then remove screw and clip from beneath seal.
14. Remove screws from opposite side of core and remove core.
15. Reverse procedure to install.

1977–78 Eldorado

1. Plug heater core tubes to prevent spilling coolant into vehicle when core is removed.
2. Remove instrument panel pad.
3. Remove center A/C outlet support and connector from position between cowl and horizontal support.
4. Remove left A/C outlet hose from A/C distributor, then remove center support and braces.
5. Remove A/C distributor and defroster nozzle.
6. On vehicles without Air Cushion, remove glove compartment.
7. Disconnect vacuum and electrical connectors from programmer.
8. Disconnect vacuum hoses from recirc. door actuator, defroster door actuator, mode door actuators and position hoses out of way.

9. Disconnect aspirator hose from in-car sensor.
10. Remove three nuts and one screw retaining heater case to cowl at engine side of cowl.
11. Remove heater case from under instrument panel.
12. Remove seal from around core tubes and remove screw and clip from beneath seal.
13. Remove two screws and clip from opposite side of core and remove core from case.
14. Reverse procedure to install.

BLOWER MOTOR, REPLACE

1979–80 Eldorado, 1980 Seville & 1981–83 All Models

1. Disconnect battery ground cable.
2. Disconnect wire connector and cooling hose.
3. Remove five blower motor attaching screws and remove blower motor.
4. Reverse procedure to install.

1977–80 Except 1979–80 Eldorado & 1980 Seville

1. Disconnect battery ground cable.
2. Remove cooling hose from nipple and blower.
3. Disconnect electrical connector at lead to motor.
4. Unfasten and remove motor, Fig. 13.
5. Reverse procedure to install.

SPEED CONTROL, ADJUST

Bead Chain Adjustment

On 1977–83 Eldorado, install the bead chain with second ball on the inboard slot of the throttle plate clip. This will provide the proper adjustment.

On 1977–83 Seville models, install bead chain to throttle plate clip, and adjust chain in clip to provide a minimum of sag without holding the throttle open. Inboard to outboard slot on the clip will provide a 1/2 ball adjustment.

On 1977–83 models except Eldorado and Seville, a control cable is used in place of the bead chain. With cable installed in throttle bracket and throttle lever, pull power unit end of cable as far as it will go. If one of four holes in power unit tab is aligned with cable pin, connect pin to tab with retainer. If tab does not align, move cable away from tab until the next closest hole in tab aligns with cable pin and connect pin to tab with retainer.

Brake Release Switch Adjustment, 1977–83

With brake pedal depressed, push cruise control/stoplight switch fully into retainer and pull brake pedal fully back to rest position. Switch will back out of retainer and adjust automatically.

Vacuum Dump Valve Adjustment

With brake pedal depressed, push vacuum valve switch all the way into the retaining clip. Pull the brake pedal to the stop to automatically adjust the valve.

Engine Section

See Buick Exc. Skyhawk, 1980–83 Skylark & 1982–83 Century Chapter for Service Procedures on V6-252 Engine
See Oldsmobile Chapter for Service Procedures on V8-350 Diesel Engine

1981 V8-368 MODULATED DISPLACEMENT ENGINE

Description

The 1981 V8-368 engine is of a modulated displacement design which deactivates select cylinders to reduce engine displacement from eight cylinders to six cylinders to four cylinders as necessary. Reducing the number of operating cylinders is accomplished through the use of valve selectors, Fig. 1. At low power requirements, the valve selectors deactivate both intake and exhaust valves on two or four cylinders. For full power output, normal valve operation is restored. In each of the deactivated cylinders, the piston continues to travel, but the intake and exhaust valves are closed. By closing both valves, the cylinders are not allowed to cool and there is a smooth flow of power when the valves are reactivated and the cylinders return to power operation.

Since this engine does not supply adequate vacuum, a belt-driven vacuum pump, Fig. 1A,

Fig. 1 Modulated displacement engine valve selector operation. 1981 V8-368

Fig. 1A Vacuum pump installation. 1981 V8-368 modulated displacement engine

Fig. 1C Front engine mounts. 1980-82 models with V6-252 except Eldorado

Fig. 1B Engine & transmission mounts. 1982-83 models with V8-250 engine

is installed. The vacuum pump supplies vacuum for proper operation of the various vacuum operated accessories.

System Components

Certain engine operating conditions are monitored by the sensors used in the Digital Electronic Fuel Injection System's (DEFI) Electronic Control Module (ECM). This information includes engine speed, coolant temperature, throttle position and intake manifold absolute pressure. The ECM processes the input data and, based on data and programming, determines the number of operating cylinders required. The ECM then energizes the electrical solenoids in the valve selectors. Each selector controls both the intake and exhaust valve on one cylinder. Valve selectors are installed on cylinders 1, 4, 6 and 7. In the 6 cylinder mode of operation, cylinders 1 and 4 are deactivated. In the 4 cylinder mode of operation, cylinders 6 and 7 are also deactivated. Other engine system components that have been changed or modified to accommodate the Modulated Displacement engine are the ECM, rocker arm covers, rocker arm supports on modulated cylinders and the necessary wiring harnesses. Also, due to the decreased engine vacuum levels during the 6 and 4 cylinder modes of operation, an auxiliary vacuum pump is used to allow normal operation of vacuum operated systems. A belt driven vacuum pump attached to the power steering pump is used.

System Operation

The operating principle of the valve selectors is to control the pivot point of the rocker arm assembly, and by so doing cause the rocker arm to open the valve or allow the valve to remain closed while the remainder of the valve train operates normally. During active operation, the rocker arm pivots near the center of the rocker arm fulcrum point. As the cam lobe reaches its high point the valve is opened, allowing the air/fuel mixture to enter the cylinder. When the valve selector is activated and the engine is operating in either the 4 or 6 cylinder mode, and the cam lobe is on its highest point, the valve will not open because the rocker arm does not pivot at the center of its fulcrum point. The selector will shift the rocker arm pivot point and allow the rocker arm to slide up and down its mounting stud. This shifts the fulcrum point to the tip of the now stationary valve. With the valve held closed by its spring, the cylinder is inactive. The valve selectors are mounted on the intake and exhaust valve rocker arms above the rocker arm fulcrums. When the solenoid is not energized, view A, Fig. 1A, the selector body is prevented from moving upward by contact between the body projections and the blocking plate above it. The rocker arm pivots near its center, the valves operate normally and the cylinder is active. When the selector is energized, view B, Fig. 1A, the blocking plate is rotated by the solenoid to align the windows in the blocking plate with the body projections. As the rocker arm is lifted by the push rod, the rocker arm and body ride up the stud since the body is no longer restrained by the blocking plate. The rocker arm now pivots at the tip of the valve and the valve remains closed. The body is spring loaded downward

by an internal spring. This spring provides valve train action and normal hydraulic lifter function when the valve train is deactivated by providing tension in the valve body and maintaining zero valve lash. The solenoid force is less than that required to overcome blocking plate/body friction when the valve is lifted. This prevents deactivation of the valve while it is lifted, which would cause abrupt valve seating. The valve selector, if defective, must be replaced as an assembly.

ENGINE MOUNTS, REPLACE

1982-83 V8-250

Engine Mount, Replace
1. Open hood, then remove screws securing strut support rod and position rods aside.
2. Position upper radiator shroud so that it will not be damaged when engine is raised.
3. Raise and support vehicle, then remove engine mount through bolt.
4. Raise engine slightly using suitable jack until engine mount bracket is free from mount.
5. Remove nuts securing engine mount, then remove engine mount.

Transmission Mount, Replace
1. Raise and support vehicle.
2. Remove transmission mount to extension housing bolts.
3. Remove bolts securing crossmember to frame, Fig. 1B.
4. Support transmission with suitable jack, then remove transmission mount to frame strut.
5. Remove crossmember, then remove mount from crossmember.
6. Reverse procedure to install.

1980-82 V6-252

Removal
1. Remove front engine mount to cylinder block bolts, Figs. 1C and 1D.
2. Raise and support vehicle.
3. Using a suitable lifting device, support engine weight at front edge of oil pan.
4. Remove rear engine mount to cylinder

Fig. 1D Front engine mounts. 1981–82 Eldorado V6-252

block bolts.
5. Raise engine slightly and remove engine mount through-bolts.
6. Remove mount.

Installation
1. Install rear engine mount to cylinder block bolts and torque to 55 ft. lbs.
2. Lower engine until mounts rest on crossmember bracket.
3. Install and tighten engine mount through-bolts.
4. Lower vehicle. Install front engine mount bolts and torque to 55 ft. lbs.

1980–81 Eldorado & Seville V8-368

Refer to Fig. 1E when replacing engine mounts.

1977–83 V8 Exc. Eldorado & Seville

1. Open hood.
2. Remove two screws on each side securing radiator cover to strut support rods. Loosen one screw on each side and position support rods aside.
3. Remove two screws securing upper radiator shroud to radiator cover and one screw securing upper radiator hose bracket to shroud. Drill out the nine rivets securing upper shroud to lower shroud and remove the upper shroud.
4. Raise and support vehicle.
5. Remove through bolt from mount being replaced, Fig. 1F.
6. Loosen the through bolt on the mount on the opposite side.
7. Using a suitable jack under the oil pan, raise engine until the bracket is free from the engine mount. Remove three flanged locking nuts and bolts, then the engine mount.
8. Reverse procedure to install.

Fig. 1F Front engine mounts.
1977–83 V8 Exc. Eldorado & Seville

Fig. 1E Front engine mounts. 1980–81 Eldorado & Seville V8-368

1977–79 Seville

1. Remove fan shroud, then the wheel housing struts from both sides.
2. Raise vehicle, then remove crossover pipe and engine mount through bolts.
3. Support vehicle, raise engine until support can be removed from engine block.
4. Working through opening between lower control arm and frame, remove bolts attaching engine mount to frame and the mount, Fig. 2.
5. Reverse procedure to install.

1977–80 Eldorado & 1980 Seville Except V8-250 & 368

Left Front Mount
1. Remove radiator cover and disconnect battery ground cable.
2. Raise car and remove nut and washer from mount stud.
3. Remove capscrew securing transmission cooler lines to final drive bracket.
4. Remove screw securing top of steering gear flex coupling shroud to frame.
5. Remove nut from large through bolt securing top of engine mount and top of final drive bracket to engine.
6. Remove nut from lower engine mount through bolt.

NOTE: Attach box end wrench to nut, then use pry bar between wrench and engine.

7. Remove remaining screw securing flex coupling shroud to frame and remove shroud.
8. Remove cross bar bolt, nut and washers securing bottom of final drive bracket to final drive. Remove bracket by tipping back and to left of car.
9. Using block of wood and jack stand, lift engine from frame at crankshaft pulley to relieve load on engine mount bolts and remove bolts from mount.
10. Loosen, but do not remove, nut and wash-

er from right engine mount stud.
11. Raise engine enough to remove mount, Figs. 3 and 4. Work mount down and forward between fuel pump and frame.

Right Front Mount
1. Remove radiator cover.
2. Remove nut and washer securing left engine mount to frame.
3. Raise car and remove nut and washer securing right mount to frame.
4. Reach between right mount and oil pump to attach open end wrench to nut on lower bolt securing mount to engine. Holding this wrench in place, remove lower mounting bolt from rear, using ratchet, U-joint socket and 18″ extension.

Fig. 2 Front engine mounts. 1977–79 Seville

CADILLAC—Exc. Cimarron

Fig. 3 Front engine mounts. 1979–80 Eldorado & 1980 Seville V8-350

Fig. 4 Front engine mounts. 1977–78 Eldorado

5. Work end wrench up between oil pump and crankshaft pulley and position wrench in a straight vertical position to engage nut on upper mounting bolt. Holding wrench in place, use same tools as in Step 4 to remove upper mounting bolt.

NOTE: If nut is impossible to engage, an alternative is to first perform the following Step, then use a 5″ extension and a 9/16″ crowfoot adapter and engage tool on nut by slipping between oil pump and A.I.R. pump.

6. Place jackstand under crankshaft pulley and using wood blocks to avoid damage to pulley, either raise engine or lower chassis to remove mount.

CAUTION: When separating engine and chassis, observe relative position of frme rail and right drive axle tri-pot housing. Interference between these parts requires removal of right drive axle before mount can be removed. Furthermore, if tri-pot housing does clear the frame, vertical movement is limited by presence of fuel lines. Do not allow tri-pot housing to contact fuel lines.

7. Work mount free and pull rearward over tri-pot housing to remove, Figs. 3 and 4.
8. Reverse procedure to install.

ENGINE, REPLACE

1982–83 V8-250

1. Disconnect battery ground cable and drain cooling system.
2. Remove screws securing strut support rods and position rods aside.
3. Remove radiator shroud to radiator support screws. Remove staples securing upper and lower fan shrouds.
4. Remove radiator cover from radiator support.
5. Remove power steering reservoir from upper fan shroud, then position reservoir aside and remove fan shroud.
6. Mark hood hinge outlines on hood, then remove hood.
7. Remove air cleaner and duct assembly.
8. Disconnect upper radiator hose from thermostat housing.
9. Disconnect following electrical connectors:
   a. Coolant temperature sensor.
   b. Engine metal temperature switch.
   c. MAT sensor.
   d. Idle speed control motor.
   e. Throttle position sensor.
   f. EGR solenoid.
   g. AIR management valve.
   h. Oxygen sensor.
   i. Ignition timing connector.
   j. Distributor and A/C compressor.
   k. Alternator, cruise control servo and right side cylinder head ground wires.
10. Disconnect wiring harness support clips and position harness aside.
11. Disconnect brake vacuum hose from pipe, throttle linkage, and vapor canister hose.
12. Remove clutch fan assembly, then disconnect lower radiator hose.
13. Remove A/C compresor mounting bolts and position compressor aside with all lines attached.
14. Disconnect coolant reservoir hose and remove water nipple from rear of intake manifold.
15. Disconnect fuel inlet and return lines.
16. On Brougham and DeVille models, raise and support vehicle, then proceed as follows:
   a. Disconnect oil cooler lines from filter adapter, then remove filter adapter.
   b. Remove strut rods connecting engine mounts to flywheel cover.
   c. Remove flywheel cover.
   d. Remove six engine to transmission screws, then remove motor mount through bolts.
   e. Remove screws securing flywheel to converter.
   f. Disconnect starter motor electrical connectors, then disconnect exhaust pipes from exhaust manifold.
   g. Lower vehicle to ground, then support transmission with suitable jack.
   h. Attach suitable lifting equipment to engine lift brackets, then raise engine slowly and position forward to disengage from transmission.
   i. Remove engine from vehicle.
   j. Reverse procedure to install.
17. On Eldorado and Seville models, raise and support vehicle, then proceed as follows:
   a. Disconnect oil cooler lines from junction at right hand side of engine compartment.
   b. Remove six engine to transaxle screws, then remove nuts securing engine mount brackets to transmission.
   c. Remove flywheel cover and screws securing flywheel to converter.
   d. Disconnect starter motor electrical connectors, then disconnect exhaust pipes from exhaust manifold.
   e. Lower vehicle, then support transaxle with suitable jack.
   f. Attach suitable lifting equipment to engine lift brackets, then raise engine slowly and pull forward to disengage from transmission.
   g. Remove engine from vehicle.
   h. Reverse procedure to install.

1980–82 V6-252, Except Eldorado & Seville

Removal
1. Mark hood hinge and hinge bracket for installation alignment, then remove hood.
2. Remove battery ground cable.
3. Drain engine coolant, remove air cleaner, then disconnect A/C compressor ground wire from mounting bracket.
4. Disconnect compressor clutch connector.
5. Remove compressor from mounting bracket and position out of the way.
6. Remove fan, pulley and belts.
7. Disconnect radiator and heater hoses and position aside, then remove radiator and fan shroud.
8. Remove power steering pump from bracket and position aside.
9. Disconnect and plug fuel pump hose.
10. Disconnect vacuum feed hose from carburetor, then the vacuum modulator and power brake vacuum hoses from engine.
11. Disconnect the three evaporative canister to carburetor hoses.
12. Disconnect throttle and TV cable from carburetor.
13. Disconnect Cruise Control servo cable at mounting bracket, if equipped.
14. Disconnect all sending unit switch connections from engine. Remove alternator, then disconnect engine wiring harness at engine.
15. Raise and support vehicle, then disconnect engine wiring harness at starter and remove starter.
16. Disconnect exhaust pipes from exhaust manifold.
17. Remove lower flywheel cover, then mark flywheel and converter for reassembly alignment. Remove converter to flywheel bolts.
18. Remove engine to transmission bolts and engine mount through-bolts.
19. Lower vehicle and support transmission. Using a suitable lifting device, raise engine. Ensure wiring harness, vacuum hoses and other parts are clear of engine before removal.
20. Lift engine just enough to clear engine mounts, then lift transmission support

1-122

evenly and alternately until engine is separated from transmission and can be removed.

Installation

1. Lower engine into vehicle, engaging transmission. Align flywheel and converter marks, then install and torque flywheel bolts to 35 ft. lbs.
2. Install and tighten engine mount through-bolts and nuts.
3. Raise and support vehicle, then install transmission to engine bolts and torque to 35 ft. lbs.
4. Install starter, then install flywheel cover. Connect starter electrical leads.
5. Connect exhaust pipes to exhaust manifolds.
6. Lower vehicle, then connect engine wiring harness, throttle cable, vacuum and water hoses, emission control line from canister to air cleaner and the transmission cooler line clip to exhaust manifold stud.
7. Connect battery ground cable to A/C compressor bracket.
8. Connect fuel line to fuel pump.
9. Install power steering pump into bracket. Adjust power steering belt tension.
10. Install fan shroud and radiator assembly. Attach radiator hoses and transmission cooler lines.
11. Install pulley, fan and belts. Adjust belt tension.
12. Install A/C compressor into bracket and connect wiring.
13. Install alternator to bracket and connect wiring.
14. Install air cleaner.
15. Install engine coolant; ensure proper level is attained after engine reaches operating temperature.
16. Connect negative battery cable to battery.
17. Install hood, aligning marks made at removal.

1979–81 Eldorado & 1980–81 Seville Exc. V8-250

1. Mark hood hinge location on hood, then remove hood.
2. Disconnect battery cables and remove battery from vehicle.
3. Remove battery ground cable ground screw from right hand fender.
4. Drain cooling system, then remove air cleaner assembly.
5. Relieve fuel pressure from E.F.I. lines by loosely installing valve depressor J-5420 on pressure fitting. Position shop towels or a suitable container under fitting, then slowly tighten valve depressor until pressure is relieved.
6. Raise vehicle and remove crossover pipe from vehicle.
7. Disconnect shift linkage from transmission.
8. Remove clamp and disconnect fuel hose from fuel pipe.
9. Remove left and right drive axle to output shaft attaching screws.
10. Remove nuts from left and right hand engine mounts and nut and washer from left and right hand transmission mounts.
11. Remove two fan shroud lower attaching screws and disconnect lower radiator hose from radiator, then lower vehicle.
12. Disconnect upper radiator hose and transmission cooler lines from radiator, then remove radiator upper cover and slide radiator out of vehicle.
13. Remove clutch fan and radiator shroud.
14. Disconnect power steering hoses at steering gear and cap hoses and fittings.

15. Remove clamp and disconnect fuel return hose from presure regulator fuel return pipe.
16. Disconnect M.A.P. hose at throttle body, then pull hose out of tie straps and position aside.
17. If equipped with cruise control, disconnect vacuum hose from power unit, then pull hose out of tie strap and position on top of cowl.
18. Disconnect canister hose, vacuum supply hose and throttle cable from throttle body and position out of way.
19. Disconnect heater hoses at water valve and water pump.
20. Disconnect power brake unit vacuum hose.
21. Disconnect speedometer cable from transmission.
22. Disconnect engine wiring harness from bulkhead connector, E.S.S. connector from distributor, heater wire from water valve, wiring from wiper motor and washer bottle and ground strap from cowl.
23. Remove coolant reservoir and disconnect wiring from A/C compressor clutch.
24. Remove A/C compressor and A.I.R. pump drive belts.
25. Remove compressor to mounting bracket attaching bolts and position compressor on right hand fender skirt. Use care not to damage refrigerant hoses.
26. Install a suitable engine lifting fixture.
27. Carefully raise engine and pull forward until transmission clears front of dash.
28. Remove engine, transmission and drive as an assembly.
29. Reverse procedure to install.

1977–79 Seville

1. Disconnect battery ground cable.
2. Drain cooling system and remove air cleaner.
3. Remove hood and wheel housing struts from both sides.

NOTE: Scribe outline of hinge on underside of hood before removing to aid alignment at installation.

4. Remove fan shroud and disconnect power brake vacuum hose at steel line.
5. Disconnect wiring harness left side branch at fuel injectors, coolant sensor, oil pressure switch, HEI feed, heater turn-on switch, speed sensor and generator. Position harness aside.
6. Remove heater hose at rear of intake manifold.
7. Remove radiator hoses.
8. Remove fan and clutch assembly.
9. Remove distributor cap and secondary wiring.
10. Disconnect wiring harness right side branch at fuel injectors, throttle switch, EGR solenoid, fast idle valve, air temperature sensor, A/C compressor, MAP sensor, economy lite hose and two compressor ground wires.
11. Disconnect throttle linkage and position aside, remove vapor canister hose from throttle body.
12. Remove fuel inlet line from fuel rail.

NOTE: Use backup wrench on fuel rail to prevent damage to fitting. Ensure fuel pressure is relieved before loosening fitting.

13. Disconnect power steering hoses at steering gear and cap hoses and connections.

14. Disconnect fuel return line from pressure regulator outlet.
15. Remove compressor from engine and position aside.

NOTE: Do not disconnect refrigerant hoses from compressor.

16. Raise vehicle and remove exhaust pipe from right bank manifold.
17. Remove torque converter cover, then remove starter.
18. Remove clip securing transmission oil cooler lines to oil pan.
19. Remove bolts securing flex plate to converter.
20. Remove engine mount through bolts, then the crossover pipe.
21. Remove engine to transmission attaching bolts.
22. Remove screws attaching heater water valve to evaporator and position valve aside.
23. Support transmission, then raise engine off mounts and reposition transmission mount. Raise engine, then pull forward to disengage transmission and remove engine.
24. Reverse procedure to install.

1977–78 Eldorado

1. Disconnect battery ground cable.
2. Scribe hood hinge locations and remove hood.
3. Drain cooling system.
4. Remove air cleaner, inlet duct, vacuum hoses and hot air ducts.
5. Disconnect upper radiator hose from thermostat housing and remove at cradle.
6. Remove radiator cover.
7. Remove fan assembly.
8. Disconnect alternator wiring, right bank spark plug wires and heater turn-on switch wiring and position harness aside.
9. Disconnect water control valve hose at rear of cylinder block.
10. Disconnect starter motor wiring harness at multiple connector.
11. Remove power steering pump and position aside with hoses attached.
12. Remove all drive belts.
13. Remove A/C compressor mounts and position aside with refrigerant hoses attached.
14. Disconnect throttle and Cruise Control linkage from carburetor or throttle body and bracket, then position cables aside.
15. Disconnect wiring on left branch of engine harness and position harness aside.
16. On vehicles equipped with Electronic Fuel Injection, disconnect manifold harness and position aside.
17. On all models, disconnect vacuum lines from carburetor or throttle body and position aside.
18. Remove left exhaust manifold flange nuts.
19. Remove transmission cooler line bracket screw, then the filler pipe nut from exhaust manifold.
20. Remove upper screw securing steering gear flex coupling shroud to frame.
21. Raise and support vehicle.
22. Remove remaining screw securing steering gear flex coupling shroud to frame.
23. Remove bolt and nut securing final drive bracket to engine mount.
24. Disconnect fuel pump fuel lines and plug lines and pump ports.
25. Remove lower radiator hose.

26. Remove right exhaust manifold flange nuts.
27. Remove starter motor and position aside with wiring attached.
28. Remove flywheel inspection cover.
29. Remove converter to flywheel retaining screws.
30. Remove the two lower transmission to engine screws.
31. Remove right output shaft screws.
32. Remove two output shaft bracket to cylinder block screws and one screw securing bracket to final drive.
33. Loosen right shock absorber mounting nut and position shock absorber outboard.
34. Move drive axle rearward as far as possible and remove output shaft.
35. Lower vehicle.
36. Remove four screws securing transmission to engine, two screws at the top and two screws at the left side.
37. Attach suitable engine lifting equipment to engine.
38. Support transmission with a suitable jack.
39. Remove engine from vehicle.
40. Reverse procedure to install.

1977-81 Brougham & DeVille Except V8-250

1. Disconnect battery ground cable.
2. Drain cooling system.
3. Remove self-tapping screw and washer securing each wheelhouse strut to radiator cover and position struts aside.
4. Remove two screws securing top radiator shroud to cradle and one screw securing upper radiator hose to shroud. Drill out nine rivets securing upper shroud to lower shroud. Remove two screws securing radiator cover to cradle and the cover.
5. On all models, scribe hood hinge locations and remove hood.
6. Remove air cleaner and inlet duct.
7. Disconnect upper radiator hose from thermostat housing.
8. Disconnect wiring at the following locations: coolant temperature sender, ignition coil or H.E.I. distributor, downshift switch, engine metal temperature switch, anti-dieseling solenoid, oil pressure switch, heater turn-on switch and A/C compressor.
9. On vehicles equipped with Electronic Fuel Injection, disconnect EFI wiring harness and position aside.
10. On all models, bend back clips on rocker cover and position harness aside.
11. Disconnect brake hose from brake pipe.
12. Remove Cruise Control servo and disconnect bead chain at carburetor.
13. Disconnect throttle linkage from carburetor and position aside.
14. Disconnect vapor canister hose.
15. Disconnect power steering pump and position aside with hoses attached.
16. Remove fan and spacer.
17. Remove right side spark plug wires and position aside.
18. Remove A/C compressor and position aside with refrigerant line attached.
19. Disconnect alternator wiring and bend back clips securing harness to right valve cover and position harness aside.
20. Disconnect PCV vacuum line and the automatic level control vacuum line, if equipped.
21. Disconnect modulator line from carburetor.

22. Remove hot water valve hose from rear of right cylinder head.
23. Remove two nuts securing each cowl to wheelhouse tie strut to wheelhousing. Loosen nuts securing each strut to cowl and swing the struts outboard.
24. Remove two top screws securing engine to transmission.
25. Raise and support vehicle.
26. Remove nut and washer securing each engine mount to frame.
27. Remove starter motor.
28. Remove flywheel inspection cover.
29. Remove screws securing converter to flywheel.
30. Support the exhaust system and disconnect exhaust pipes from exhaust manifolds.
31. Disconnect fuel line and vapor return line from fuel pump.
32. Support transmission with a suitable jack. Remove remaining engine to transmission bolts.
33. Attach suitable engine lifting equipment to engine.
34. Remove engine from vehicle.
35. Reverse procedure to install.

INTAKE MANIFOLD, REPLACE

With E.F.I.

V8-250

1. Drain coolant from radiator, then disconnect radiator hose from thermostat housing.
2. Disconnect electrical connectors from coolant sensor, MAT sensor, throttle position sensor, distributor, ISC motor and fuel injectors.
3. Disconnect heater hoses from manifold.
4. Disconnect fuel lines from throttle body and remove distributor.
5. Remove both rocker arm covers.
6. Remove rocker arm support and rocker arms as an assembly.
7. Remove bolts securing A/C compressor, then position compressor aside with all hoses and lines attached.
8. Remove vacuum harness connectors from rear of manifold.
9. Remove intake manifold bolts and lower thermostat housing to front cover bolts.

NOTE: Engine lift brackets must be bent or positioned aside for intake manifold removal.

10. Remove intake manifold by lifting straight up off dowels.
11. Reverse procedure to install. Refer to Fig. 4A for intake manifold bolt tightening sequence, bolt length and torque procedure.

V8-350

1. Disconnect battery ground cable and drain cooling system.
2. Remove air cleaner and crankcase filter.
3. Disconnect throttle and Cruise Control linkage from throttle body. Remove cable from bracket and position aside.

4. Disconnect coolant temperature tell-tale switch, H.E.I. lead wire, speed sensor connector and injector valve wiring.
5. Disconnect EGR solenoid leads, throttle position switch, fast idle valve, air temperature sensor connector and MAP sensor hose.
6. Disconnect the two ground wires from A/C compressor bracket.
7. Disconnect the two vacuum hoses from throttle body to TVS switch.
8. Disconnect vacuum hoses and power brake pipe from rear of throttle body.
9. Disconnect fuel line from fuel rail.
10. Remove PCV valve from rocker cover.
11. Disconnect spark plug leads and position aside.
12. Disconnect upper radiator hose, by-pass hose and the heater hose, located at the rear of the manifold.
13. Remove A/C compressor and position aside with refrigerant hoses attached.
14. Remove fuel return hose from pressure regulator.
15. On 1978-82 models, remove oil pressure switch and oil fill tube.
16. Remove intake manifold bolts and the intake manifold.
17. Reverse procedure to install. Torque intake manifold bolts in sequence, Fig. 5, to 40 ft. lbs.

V8-368 & 425

1. Disconnect battery ground cable and remove air cleaner and crankcase filter.
2. Disconnect throttle cable and cruise control linkage, if equipped, from throttle body. Remove cable from bracket and position aside.
3. Working on engine left side, disconnect coolant temperature tell-tale switch wire, HEI lead wire, speed sensor connector, downshift switch and injector wires. Disconnect harness from fuel rail brackets and position aside.
4. Disconnect two vacuum hoses from throttle body to TVS switch.
5. Disconnect vacuum hoses and power brake pipe from throttle body.

NOTE: Use a back-up wrench when removing power brake pipe to prevent damage to fitting.

6. Disconnect fuel line from fuel rail.

NOTE: Use a back-up wrench on fuel rail to prevent damage to fitting.

7. Working on engine right side, disconnect injector wires, EGR solenoid leads, air temperature sensor connector and MAP sensor hose. Disconnect harness from fuel rail brackets and position aside.
8. Remove PCV valve from rocker cover and position aside.
9. Remove spark plug leads and distributor cap.
10. Remove front fuel rail.
11. Position A/C compressor aside, do not disconnect refrigerant lines.
12. Remove fuel return hose from pressure regulator.
13. Remove manifold bolts and lift manifold from engine. Do not pry or lift manifold by the fuel rails or the mounting brackets.
14. Reverse procedure to install. Torque manifold bolts to 30 ft. lbs.

BOLT TIGHTENING SEQUENCE

1 TIGHTEN BOLTS 1, 2, 3, & 4 IN SEQUENCE TO 15.0-20.0 N·m (11-15 FT-LBS)

2 TIGHTEN BOLTS 5 THRU 16 IN SEQUENCE TO 24.5-30.0 N·m (18-22 FT-LBS).

3 RETIGHTEN ALL BOLTS IN SEQUENCE TO 24.5-30.0 N·m (18-22 FT-LBS).

↑ FRONT OF ENGINE

POSITION	BOLT
1	MEDIUM
2	MEDIUM
3	MEDIUM
4	MEDIUM
5	SHORT
6	SHORT
7	SHORT
8	SHORT
9	SHORT
10	SHORT
11	SHORT
12	MEDIUM
13	MEDIUM
14	SHORT
15	LONG
16	MEDIUM

Fig. 4A Intake manifold bolt tightening sequence. V8-250

Fig. 5 Intake manifold tightening sequence. V8-350

Less E.F.I.

Except V6-252

1. Disconnect battery ground cable and remove air cleaner.
2. Disconnect throttle linkage and Cruise Control linkage, if equipped.
3. Disconnect coil wires at H.E.I. connector, then remove distributor cap and disconnect right hand spark plug wires at spark plugs and place aside.
4. Disconnect wire connectors from temperature sender, down shift switch and anti-dieseling solenoid.
5. Remove coil, anti-dieseling solenoid and solenoid bracket.
6. Disconnect vacuum lines from carburetor, remove Cruise Control servo top mounting bolt and position brake hose aside, if equipped.
7. Disconnect wiring connector from A/C compressor, if equipped.
8. Disconnect fuel line at carburetor and remove vacuum lines from intake manifold.
9. Loosen power steering mounting bolts and pivot pump toward engine. Remove A/C compressor drive belt, then the screws attaching compressor rear mounting to engine and the screws attaching compressor mounting flange to front mounting bracket. Position compressor aside.
10. Remove PCV valve from rocker cover.
11. Remove manifold to cylinder head bolts, intake manifold, manifold shield and gaskets.

12. Reverse procedure to install.

V6-252

1. Disconnect battery ground cable, then drain cooling system.
2. Remove air cleaner.
3. Disconnect the following:
   a. Upper radiator hose and heater hose at manifold.
   b. Accelerator linkage at carburetor, linkage bracket at manifold and cruise control chain if equipped.
   c. Booster vacuum pipe at manifold.
   d. Fuel line at carburetor.
   e. Transmission vacuum modulator line.
   f. Idle stop solenoid wire, if equipped.
   g. Distributor wires and temperature sending unit wire.
   h. Vacuum hoses from, distributor TVS and EFE valve pipe, from carburetor to vacuum manifold.
   i. Fuel economy and load leveler hose, if equipped.
   j. Coolant by-pass hose at manifold.
4. Remove distributor cap and rotor to gain access to left intake manifold torx head bolt. Use Tool J-24394 or equivalent to remove torx head bolt.
5. Remove accelerator linkage springs.
6. Remove compressor upper bracket, if equipped.
7. Remove intake manifold.
8. Reverse procedure to install.

CYLINDER HEAD, REPLACE

V8-250

NOTE: Some V8-250 engine blocks may exhibit casting porosity, indicated by oil leakage around the threads of cylinder head bolts. This leakage is caused by porosity between a pressurized oil passage and the threaded bolt hole. This condition occurs between an oil gallery and holes #11, 12, 13, 14, 17, 18, 19 or 20, Fig. 6. An internal oil leak will occur around these bolts and will rarely be detected. However, when this condition is experienced at bolt holes #1, 2, 3, 4, 5, 6, 7, 8, 9, 10, 15, or 16, Fig. 6, an external oil leak may result. To provide a permanent repair for this condition, remove the bolt and clean both the bolt and hole with a suitable cleaner. With compressed air, blow out the bolt hole and apply a suitable two-part epoxy to the lower 5 or 6 threads of

the bolt. Install the bolt and torque to 90 ft. lbs.

1. Remove valve covers, then remove intake manifold as described under "Intake Manifold, Replace".
2. On right hand side cylinder head removal, remove alternator and AIR pump.
3. For left hand side cylinder head removal, remove vacuum pump and bracket. Remove bolts and position power steering pump aside.
4. Remove exhaust manifold from cylinder head, then remove bolt securing AIR pipe to cylinder head.
5. Remove cylinder head bolts, then remove cylinder head.
6. Reverse procedure to install. refer to Fig. 6A for cylinder head bolt tightening sequence.

V8-350

1. Drain cooling system and remove intake manifold as described under "Intake Manifold Replace".
2. Remove exhaust manifolds.
3. Remove rocker cover, rocker arm bolts, pivots, rocker arms and push rods.

NOTE: Note location of rocker arms and pivots to ensure installation in original position.

4. Remove cylinder head bolts and the cylinder head.
5. When installing cylinder head it is impor-

Fig. 6 Cylinder head bolt hole locations. V8-250

INBOARD
OUTBOARD

Fig. 6A Cylinder head bolt tightening sequence. V8-250

Fig. 7 Location and length of cylinder head bolts. V8-350

Bolt Location	Length
A (Bolt)	2.96 (Short)
B (Bolt)	4.16 (Long)
C (Bolt/Stud Head)	2.96 (Short)
D (Bolt/Stud Head)	4.16 (Long)
E (Bolt-Special)*	4.16 (Long)*

* This special bolt has an extra thick hex head which is drilled and tapped to accept the temperature switch.

tant that cylinder head bolts are installed in the correct position, refer to Fig. 7. Torque cylinder head bolts in sequence, Fig. 7A. Torque intake manifold bolts in sequence shown in Fig. 5.

V8-368 & 425

NOTE: Engine rocker arm covers on 1980–81 V8-368 engines are made of a nylon material and are sealed to the cylinder head with RTV sealer. Use caution when removing covers. Do not pry the cover off. If cover removal is difficult, use a rubber mallet and tap gently in an upward direction on lower surface and only at ribbed areas of the cover. When installing covers, clean off all old sealant thoroughly, including sealing groove in cover face. Apply a new bead of sealer, P/N 1051435 or equivalent and torque attaching screws to 30 inch pounds.

1. Drain coolant from radiator.
2. Remove intake manifold.
3. Disconnect ground strap at rear of cylinder heads from cowl where used.
4. Disconnect wiring connector for high engine temperature warning system from sending unit at rear of left cylinder head.
5. Remove alternator if working on right cylinder head, or partially remove power steering pump if working on left cylinder head.
6. Remove A.I.R. manifold from both cylinder heads if equipped.
7. Disconnect wiring harness from cylinder head and and position out of the way.
8. Remove exhaust manifold from cylinder head.

NOTE: On early production V8-368 D.E.F.I. engine, with non-locking bolts and lock tabs, exhaust manifold leaks may be corrected by replacing lock tabs and bolts with prevailing torque bolts. The prevailing torque bolts should be torqued to 15 ft. lbs. Later production V8-368 D.E.F.I. engines are equipped with prevailing torque bolts.

Fig. 7A Cylinder head tightening sequence. V8-350

9. Remove rocker arm cover.
10. Remove rocker arm asemblies and lift out push rods.
11. Remove cylinder head bolts, remove head.
12. After carefully removing all gasket material from mating surfaces of head and block, position new gasket over dowels and install cylinder head in reverse order of removal, being sure to install the bolts as indicated in Fig. 8.

NOTE: When installing cylinder head bolts no torque sequence is required, start at center and work from side to side outwards and towards the ends.

VALVE ARRANGEMENT

Front to Rear

V6-252	E-I-I-E-I-E
V8-368, 425	
Left	E-I-E-I-E-I-E-I
Right	I-E-I-E-I-E-I-E
V8-250, 350	I-E-I-E-E-I-E-I

VALVE LIFT SPECS

Engine	Year	Intake	Exhaust
V8-350	1977–80	.400	.400
V8-350①	1978–83	.375	.376
V8-368, 425	1977–80	.457	.473
V6-252②	1980–82	.357	.366
V8-250	1982–83	.384	.396

①—Diesel engine. Refer to Oldsmobile Chapter for service procedures on this engine.
②—Refer to Buick Chapter for service procedures.

Bolt Location	Length
A (Bolt)	4.36" (Medium)
B (Bolt)	4.77" (Long)
C (Bolt)	3.02" (Short)
D (Bolt/stud)	4.77" (Long)

Fig. 8 Location and length of cylinder head screws. V8-368 & 425

VALVE TIMING

Intake Opens Before TDC

Engine	Year	Degrees
V6-252②	1980–82	16
V8-250	1982–83	37
V8-350	1977–80	22
V8-350①	1978–83	16
V8-368	1980–81	11
V8-425	1977–80	21

①—Diesel engine. Refer to Oldsmobile Chapter for service procedures on this engine.
②—Refer to Buick Chapter for service procedures.

ROCKER ARMS, REPLACE

V8-250

1. Remove valve cover.
2. Remove nuts from stud headed cylinder head bolts, then remove valve train support with rocker arms and pivots as an assembly, Fig. 8A.

Fig. 8A Rocker arm assembly exploded view. V8-250

Fig. 9 Rocker arm components disassembled. V8-350

Fig. 9A Rocker arm assembly. V8-368 modulated
displacement engine.

NOTE: Pivot assemblies may be damaged unless rocker arms and pivots are removed as an assembly.

3. Position rocker arm support in suitable vise and remove rocker arms and pivots.
4. Install rocker arms and pivots into valve train support and tighten pivot bolts.
5. Position valve train support over mounting studs and snug tighten retaining nuts.
6. Check push rods for correct positioning, then tighten nuts alternately and evenly.

V8-350

1. Remove rocker cover, rocker arm bolts, pivot and rocker arms.

NOTE: Remove each set as a unit.

2. Position rocker arms on cylinder head, apply lubricant 1050169 or equivalent to wear points on pivot, then install pivot.
3. Install rocker arm bolts, tighten alternately, torque to 25 ft. lbs., Fig. 9.

1981 V8-368

On V8-368 modulated displacement engines, refer to Fig. 9A for rocker arm replacement.

1977–80 V8-425 & 1980 V8-368

When disassembling the rocker arm assembly, be sure to keep the supports and rocker arms in order so they can be installed in the exact same position.

Install rocker arms on supports and place supports in retainers as shown in Fig. 10.

Place capscrews through the reinforcements, supports and retainers and position assemblies on cylinder head. Make sure that push rods are properly seated in the lifter seats and in the rocker arms. Lubricate rocker arm bearing surfaces before assembling in order to prevent wear. Torque rocker arm support bolts to 70 ft. lbs.

On occasion an engine will be manufactured with an oversize valve and valve guide bore. A number stamped on the inboard side of the head will indicate which valve and valve guide bore are oversize. The number 10 would indicate that a .010 inch oversize valve is installed in the adjacent valve guide bore.

V8-250, 368, 425

Check valve stem to valve guide clearance, clearance should be no more than .005 inch. Service valves are available in standard (.343 inch) and .003, .006 and .013 inch oversizes. If clearance is found to be excessive, valve guide should be reamed out to next oversize using appropriate reamer, and a corresponding oversize valve installed. On some engines, valves with a .003 inch oversize diameter and .003 inch oversize valve guides are installed at the factory. Engines so fitted will be identified by a "3" stamped on the cylinder head gasket surface inline with the oversize valve.

Fig. 10 Rocker arm components

VALVE GUIDES

V8-350

Valve stem to guide clearance should be .001-.003 inch. Service valves are available in standard (.343 inch) and .003, .005, .010, .013 inch oversizes. If stem to guide clearance is excessive, ream valve guide bore to the next oversize using appropriate reamer. Install proper oversize valve and valve seal. Valve seals can be identified as follows:

Intake
  Std.-.005 O.S. . . . . . . Gray Colored
  .010-.013 O.S. . . . . . Orange Colored
Exhaust
  Std.-.005 O.S. . . . . . . Ivory Colored
  .010-.013 O.S. . . . . . . Blue Colored

Fig. 11 Hydraulic valve lifter

Front Cover Attaching Bolts (5/16")
Torque To 22 ft. lbs.

Self Tapping Water Pump Attaching Screws. Use Oil On Installation. Torque To 13 ft. lbs.

Torque To 35 ft. lb

Fig. 12 Engine front cover attaching screws V8-350

HYDRAULIC VALVE LIFTERS, REPLACE

The valve lifters may be lifted out of their bores after removing the rocker arms, push rods and intake manifold. Adjustable pliers with taped jaws may be used to remove lifters that are stuck due to varnish, carbon, etc. Fig. 11 illustrates the type of lifter used.

TIMING CASE COVER, REPLACE

V8-250

1. Disconnect battery ground cable and drain cooling system.
2. On Brougham and DeVille models, position support rods aside.
3. Disconnect wiring harness from upper fan shroud clamps.
4. Remove power steering pump reservoir from upper fan shroud, then remove upper fan shroud.
5. Remove clutch fan, then loosen alternator and AIR pump mounting bolts and remove drive belts.

Fig. 15 Timing gear locating marks. V8-350

Key	No.	Size	Torque
V8-368			
A	4	3/8—16 × 1-3/8	22 ft. lbs.
C	3	5/16—18 × 1-1/4	10 ft. lbs.
D	1	5/16—18 × 5/8	10 ft. lbs.
E	2	3/8—16 × 5/8	22 ft. lbs.
V8-425			
A	4	3/8—16 × 1-3/8	25 ft. lbs.
C	3	5/16—18 × 1-1/4	15 ft. lbs.
D	1	5/16—18 × 5/8	15 ft. lbs.
E	2	3/8—16 × 5/8	25 ft. lbs.

Fig. 13 Engine front cover attaching screws. V8-368, 425

6. Loosen power steering pump retaining bolts and remove vacuum pump drive belts.
7. Remove A/C compressor mounting bolts, then remove drive belt and position compressor aside with all hoses and lines attached.
8. Remove alternator and support bracket, then disconnect coolant reservoir hose at water pump.
9. Disconnect hoses from water pump.
10. Remove water pump and crankshaft pulleys.
11. Remove A/C compressor bracket from engine.
12. Remove timing mark tab from front cover, then remove crankshaft vibration damper.
13. Remove bolts securing front cover to cylinder block, then remove cover, water pump and lower thermostat housing as an assembly.
14. Reverse procedure to install. Coat oil pan front lip with suitable sealer.

V8-350

1. Drain cooling system, disconnect radiator hoses, heater hose and bypass hose.
2. Remove radiator upper support and radiator.
3. Remove belts, fan, fan pulley, crankshaft pulley and harmonic balancer.
4. Remove oil pan, front cover attaching bolts, front cover and water pump.
5. Reverse procedure to install, refer to Fig. 12.

V8-368, 425

1. Remove harmonic balancer.
2. Loosen starter sufficiently to gain access

DOWEL HOLES IN CAMSHAFT AND SPROCKET MUST LINE UP

TIMING MARKS

Fig. 14 Timing gear locating marks. V8-368, 425

to oil pan screws and lower front of oil pan until it clears front studs.
3. Drain radiator and remove lower hose from water pump.
4. Remove the 10 screws securing front cover to the cylinder block and remove cover with water pump as an assembly.
5. Reverse removal procedure, to install, referring to Fig. 13

TIMING CASE COVER OIL SEAL, REPLACE

V8-250

1. Remove crankshaft pulley and vibration damper.
2. Remove front cover oil seal using tools J-1859-03 and J-23129 or equivalents.
3. Lubricate new seal with engine oil, then install using tool J-29662 or equivalent.
4. Install vibration damper and crankshaft pulley.

V8-350

1. Remove drive belts, crankshaft pulley and harmonic balancer.
2. Using tool J-1859-03 or a suitable puller, remove front cover oil seal.
3. Apply sealer to outside diameter of seal.
4. Position seal on front cover, then using tools No. J-25264 and J-21150, drive seal into place.
5. Install harmonic balancer and crankshaft pulley, install and adjust drive belts.

DOWEL

KEYWAY

WHEN PROPERLY TIMED, MARKS WILL LINE UP AS SHOWN.

NOTE: ENGINE IS ON THE #1 FIRING STROKE IN THIS POSITION.

Fig. 15A Timing gear location marks. V8-250

NOTCH TOWARD
FRONT OF ENGINE

Fig. 16   Piston & rod assembly. V8-250

LETTER "F"

SPIT HOLE

RIGHT BANK
NOS. 2, 4, 6, 8

LEFT BANK
NOS. 1, 3, 5, 7

Fig. 16A   Piston & rod assembly. V8-350

REAR

REAR

LEFT BANK
NOS. 2, 4, 6, 8

RIGHT BANK
NOS. 1, 3, 5, 7

Fig. 17   Piston & rod assembly. V8-368, 425

V8-368, 425, 500

1. Remove vibration damper.
2. With a thin blade screw driver or similar tool, pry out front cover oil seal.
3. Lubricate new seal and fill cavity with wheel bearing grease. Position seal on end of crankshaft with garter spring side toward engine.
4. Using a suitable installer, drive seal into cover until it bottoms against cover.

TIMING CHAIN, REPLACE

Except V8-368 Modulated Displacement

1. Remove engine front cover as outlined above.
2. Remove two capscrews and washers that hold sprocket to camshaft.
3. Remove camshaft sprocket with chain.
4. Remove crankshaft sprocket, if necessary.
5. To install, reverse removal procedure, being sure to line up the timing marks as shown in Figs. 14, 15 and 15A.

V8-368 Modulated Displacement

1. Remove engine front cover as described previously.
2. Remove distributor, oil pump and crankshaft oil slinger.
3. Remove fuel pump and fuel pump eccentric from camshaft.
4. Remove screws securing camshaft sprocket to camshaft.
5. Remove camshaft sprocket and chain as an assembly.
6. Reverse procedure to install.

CAMSHAFT, REPLACE

V8-250

1. Remove timing chain as described previously.
2. Remove valve lifters as described under "Valve Lifters, Replace".
3. Remove radiator, then remove camshaft from engine. Use caution not to damage camshaft bearings when removing camshaft.
4. Reverse procedure to install.

V8-350

1. Disconnect battery, then remove air cleaner.
2. Drain cooling system and remove radiator, four bolts attaching A/C condenser to radiator and position condenser aside.

MEASURE PISTON 3/16" BELOW CROSS SLOT- PERPENDICULAR TO PISTON PIN

CROSS SLOT

Fig. 18   Measuring piston diameter

3. Remove crankshaft pulley and balancer, then the front cover.
4. Remove A/C compressor from engine and position aside.

NOTE: Do not disconnect refrigerant hoses from compressor.

---

5. Remove intake manifold as described under "Intake Manifold Replace".
6. Remove rocker covers, rocker arms, push rods and lifters.

NOTE: Note position of rocker arms, pivots, push rods and lifers to ensure installation in original position.

---

7. Remove camshaft.
8. Reverse procedure to install.

V8-368, 425

1. Remove engine front cover.
2. Remove distributor and oil pump.
3. Remove oil slinger from crankshaft.
4. Remove fuel pump and fuel pump eccentric.
5. Unfasten and remove camshaft sprocket with chain attached.
6. Remove valve lifters as previously outlined.
7. Remove radiator.
8. Carefully slide camshaft forward until it is out of engine.

9. Reverse procedure to install.

PISTONS & RODS ASSEMBLE

On all engines, assemble and install the piston and rod assemblies as shown in Figs. 16, 16A and 17.

Measure connecting rod side clearance using a suitable feeler gauge. Clearances should be .008–.020 inch on Cadillac built engines, .006–.020 inch on Oldsmobile built engines and .006–.023 inch on Buick built engines.

PISTONS

V8-250

When measuring piston diameter, place micrometer 3/16 inch below cross slot or 3/8 inch below oil ring groove, Fig. 18. Cylinder liner diameter is measured by placing a micrometer two inches down from top of liner and perpendicular to cylinder centerline. The difference between the two readings should be .0010–.0018 inch. Cylinder bore out-of-round should not exceed .0008 inch and piston bore taper should not exceed .0005–.002 inch. If any reading is not as specified, piston and cylinder liner assembly must be replaced. No attempt should be made to rebore or hone cylinder liners. Refer to "Cylinder Liner, Replace" for procedure.

V8-350

Measure pistons for size, Fig. 18. Measure cylinder bore, piston to cylinder bore clearance should be .00075–.00175 inch. Measure piston for taper, the largest reading must be at the bottom of the skirt. Allowable taper is .000–.0001 inch.

Cylinder and piston sizes are indicated by a letter stamped on the cylinder gasket surface of the block. The letters that denote cylinder and piston sizes are listed in Fig. 19.

V8-368, 425

Pistons should be measured for size as shown in Fig. 18. Cylinders should be measured 1 1/8" from the top, crosswise to the cylinder block. The clearance should be .0006–.0014 for V8-368, 425 engines in this position at room temperature (70°F). Subtract .0001" from measurement for every 6° above 70°.

Letter	Cylinder Size (Diameter in inches)	Piston Size (Diameter in inches)
A	4.0560-4.0565	4.05475-4.05525
B	4.0565-4.0570	4.05525-4.05575
C	4.0570-4.0575	4.05575-4.05625
D	4.0575-4.0580	4.05625-4.05675
J	4.0660-4.0665	4.06475-4.06525
K	4.0665-4.0670	4.06525-4.06575
L	4.0670-4.0675	4.06575-4.06625
M	4.0675-4.0680	4.06625-4.06675

Fig. 19   Cylinder and piston sizes. V8-350

LETTER	CYLINDER SIZE (DIAMETER IN INCHES)	PISTON SIZE (DIAMETER IN INCHES)
A	3.8000 - 3.8004	3.7990 - 3.7994
B	3.8004 - 3.8008	3.7994 - 3.7998
C	3.8008 - 38012	3.7998 - 3.8002
D	3.8012 - 3.8016	3.8002 - 3.8006
E	3.8016 - 3.8020	3.8006 - 3.8010

Fig. 20   Cylinder & piston sizes. V8-368

Letter	Cylinder Size (Diameter in Inches)	Piston Size (Diameter in Inches)
A	4.0820-4.0824	4.0810-4.0814
B	4.0824-4.0828	4.0814-4.0818
C	4.0828-4.0832	4.0818-4.0822
D	4.0832-4.0836	4.0822-4.0826
E	4.0836-4.0840	4.0826-4.0830
AA	4.0920-4.0924	4.0910-4.0914
BB	4.0924-4.0928	4.0914-4.0918
CC	4.0928-4.0932	4.0918-4.0922
DD	4.0932-4.0936	4.0922-4.0926
EE	4.0936-4.0940	4.0926-4.0930

Fig. 21   Cylinder & piston sizes. V8-425

On V8-368, 425 engines an identification letter is stamped on the cylinder head face of cylinder block located directly below cylinder bore. The letters are in groups of two for adjacent cylinders (such as "A" "B") midway between the two cylinders. This letter denotes the cylinder size as shown in Figs. 20 and 21. The table indicates piston sizes to match corresponding bore sizes. This makes it possible to maintain the proper clearance between block and piston.

If double letters (such a "AA" "BB") appear, it indicates that the cylinder has been bored .010" over the diameter indicated by the single letter in the chart.

Cylinder bores must not be reconditioned to more than .0100 inch oversize, as pistons are not available over this range.

PISTON RINGS

NOTE: On 1979–80 V8-350 engines except diesel, when measuring compression ring gap clearance, refer to Fig. 22 for piston ring identification. For Muskegon and Perfect Circle piston rings, ring gap should be .013 to .023 in. For Sealed Power piston rings, ring gap should be .010 to .020 in.

Replacement rings are available on all except V8-250 engines in standard size and .010 inch oversize. On V8-250 engine, replacement rings are available in standard size only. If piston ring clearance is excessive on this engine, new piston and cylinder liner must be installed. Refer to "Cylinder Liner, Replace".

PISTON PINS

V8-350

Piston pin to piston clearance should be

.0003–.0005 inch. If clearance is more than .0005 inch, a new piston pin should be installed. Piston pin to connecting rod is a press fit and clearance should be .0008–.0018 inch tight fit.

V8-250, 368, 425

Piston pins are a matched fit with the piston and are not available separately. Piston pins are pressed in the connecting rods and will not become loose enough to cause a knock or tapping until after very high mileages. In such cases a new piston and pin assembly should be installed.

CYLINDER LINER, REPLACE

V8-250

NOTE: The cylinder heads, pistons, connecting rods, bearings and crankshaft must be removed from engine before replacing cylinder liners.

1. If original liners, Fig. 22A, are to be reinstalled, mark position of liner in cylinder block and keep piston with original liner for reference during installation.
2. Use tool J-29775 or equivalent to remove liners from cylinder block. Discard O ring from bottom of cylinder liner.
3. Check cylinder liner and block mating surfaces to ensure they are free of nicks and burrs.
4. If original liners are to be installed into original block, it is not necessary to gauge their height. Install new O ring seal onto liner, align reference marks made during removal, then install liner into block using tool J-29775 or equivalent.

5. If new liner and piston assembly is to be installed, or if original block experienced overheating, then cylinder liner height must be gauged.
6. Position new liner into block without O ring.
7. Position gauge J-29776 or equivalent onto cylinder liner. Check to ensure that spring loaded guide pins fit into liner with machined pads resting on edge of liner and dial indicator contacting block deck face. Apply moderate pressure to gauge until dial indicator stops moving.
8. Record this reading. If reading is on + side of dial indicator, cylinder liner is higher than block face by indicated amount. If reading is on − side, cylinder liner is below block face.
9. Repeat steps 7 and 8 at two other locations. Take average of three readings as actual liner height.
10. Specified liner height is .01–.08 mm above block deck face. If specified height cannot be obtained, replace liner with new one. Liners may be rotated in block to obtain specified height.
11. If liner height is satisfactory, then liner-to-liner height must be checked. Install adjacent liners into cylinder block without O ring. Using gauge J-29766 or equivalent, measure height between liners while second liner is held firmly in place, Fig. 22B. Liner-to-liner height should be ±.05 mm. Mark liners in this position.
12. When installing liners into block, check to ensure that liners are installed in marked position. Install O ring onto liner, then install liner into block using tool J-29775 or equivalent.

MAIN & ROD BEARINGS

V8-350

Main bearing clearance should not exceed .0035 inch. If clearance is more than .0035

TOP & SECOND

PERFECT CIRCLE

TOP & SECOND

SEALED POWER

TOP & SECOND

MUSKEGON

Fig. 22   Piston ring identification. 1979–80 V8-350 gasoline engine

Fig. 22A   Cylinder liner assembly. V8-250

Fig. 22B Measuring liner to liner height. V8-250

NO.LETTER·STD
LETTER 'A' - .0005
LETTER 'B' - .0010
LETTER 'C' - .0015

Fig. 23 Main bearing identification. V8-350

J-25285

After Correctly Positioning Seal, Rotate Tool Slightly And Cut Off Each End Of Seal Flush With Block

Fig. 24 Rear main bearing oil seal installation. V8-350

inch replace both bearing shells. Main bearings are available in undersizes, Fig. 23.

Rod bearing clearance should not exceed .0035 inch. If clearance is more than .0035 inch replace both bearing shells and recheck clearance.

V8-250, 368, 425

Main and rod bearings are supplied by Cadillac in standard sizes only.

CRANKSHAFT OIL SEAL, REPLACE

V8-350

To replace upper rear main bearing seal, the crankshaft must be removed. After removing crankshaft use tool No. J-25285 to install seal, Fig. 24.

Lower rear main bearing seal can be installed with crankshaft in place and engine in vehicle. Remove oil pan, then the rear main bearing cap. Remove bearing and seal from cap. Position new seal in groove in bearing cap. Using tool J-25285, hammer seal into groove. Rotate tool slightly, then cut seal ends flush with bearing cap surface. Pack seal end fibers away from edges, using a screw driver. Install bearing in cap, then install cap, lubricate bolt threads and torque to 120 ft. lbs. Install oil pan and lower flywheel cover.

V8-250, 368, 425

Rear main bearing installation tool can be made from shim stock or a metal banding strap using dimensions in Fig. 25.

The two seal halves are identical and can be used in either the lower or upper location. However, both seal halves are pre-lubricated with a film of wax for break-in. Do not remove or damage this film.

To install the lower half of the seal into the bearing cap, slide either end of seal into position at one end of bearing cap and place tool on seal land at other end of bearing. Make sure seal is positioned over bearing ridge and lip of seal is facing forward (car position).

Hold thumb over end of seal that is flush with split line to prevent it from slipping upward, and push seal into seated position by applying pressure to the other end. Make sure seal is pressed down firmly and is flush on each side to avoid possibility of a leak at seal split line. Avoid pressing on lip as damage to sealing edge could result.

To install upper half of seal in cylinder block (with crankshaft in car), position "shoehorn" tool on land of block, Fig. 26. Start seal into groove in block with lip facing forward and rotate seal into position. Do not press on lip or sealing edge may be damaged. Both ends of seal must be flush at seal split line to avoid leaks. If necessary, Lubriplate or its equivalent may be used to facilitate installation of both upper and lower seal halves. Do not use silicone or a leak may result.

OIL PAN, REPLACE

NOTE: Some 1981 V8 engines might exhibit an oil leak at the second oil pan bolt from front of the engine, on the left hand side. The hole for the bolt in the block may have been drilled through into the crankcase. A leak can be corrected by removing and cleaning the bolt and hole. Coat the bolt with a suitable sealer and reinstall.

1982–83 V8-250 Except Eldorado & Seville

1. Disconnect battery ground cable, then raise and support vehicle.
2. Drain engine oil and remove oil filter.
3. Remove flywheel cover and support struts.
4. Disconnect exhaust pipe from manifold and remove catalytic converter bracket bolt.
5. Remove oil pan nuts and bolts, then lower exhaust pipe and remove oil pan from vehicle.
6. Reverse procedure to install. Use suitable RTV sealer in sufficient quantities when

installing pan. Torque pan attaching bolts and nuts to 11 ft. lbs.

1982–83 V8-250 Eldorado & Seville

1. Raise and support vehicle and drain engine oil. Remove oil filter.
2. Remove flywheel cover, then remove final drive assembly.
3. Disconnect exhaust pipe from manifold, then remove front suspension stone shield.
4. Remove bolts securing engine mount to frame crossmember.
5. Remove oil pan bolts and nuts, then lower exhaust pipe and remove oil pan from vehicle.
6. Reverse procedure to install. Use suitable RTV sealer in sufficient quantities when installing pan. Torque pan attaching bolts to 11 ft. lbs.

1980–82 V6-252 Except 1982 Eldorado & Seville

Removal
1. Raise and support vehicle. Drain oil.
2. Remove flywheel cover.
3. Remove exhaust crossover pipe.
4. Remove oil pan attaching bolts and the oil pan.

Installation
1. Reverse procedure to install. Ensure oil pan and cylinder block mating surfaces are clean.

NOTE: 1981–82 V6-252 engines use RTV silicone sealer in place of a cork gasket for oil pan to crankcase sealing. If replace-

Fig. 25 Main bearing oil seal tool. V8-250, 368, 425

SHOEHORN INSTALLER

REAR MAIN SEAL

Fig. 26 Installing rear main bearing oil seal. V8-368, 425

CADILLAC—Exc. Cimarron

Engine oiling system. V8-350

Engine oiling system. V8-368, 425, 500

ment of the oil pan or gasket is necessary, either RTV sealer or a cork gasket may be used for reassembly. If RTV sealer is used, the pan rail and block mating surfaces should be thoroughly cleaned and a 1/4 inch bead of sealant applied evenly to the pan rail. Use caution to avoid any breaks or gaps in the sealer during application.

2. Torque oil pan bolts to 14 ft. lbs.
3. Torque flywheel cover bolts to 4 ft. lbs.
4. Lower vehicle and add oil.

1982 V6-252 Eldorado & Seville

1. Disconnect battery ground cable.
2. Remove one final drive to transmission bolt.
3. Install engine support and hoist car, then install jack stands and lower hoist.
4. Disconnect idler arm bracket at frame.
5. Lock steering wheel in full left position.
6. Disconnect drive axles from output shafts and disconnect battery cable bracket from output shaft support, then disconnect shaft support from engine block.
7. Remove remaining final drive to transmission bolts and place transmission jack under final drive.
8. Remove final drive cover and final drive unit.
9. Remove splash shield, then disconnect starter wires and remove starter.
10. Remove flywheel cover and drain oil pan.
11. Remove oil pan attaching bolts and remove oil pan.
12. Reverse procedure to install. Apply suitable RTV sealer when installing pan.

1977–82 Except Eldorado & Seville

1. Disconnect battery ground cable.
2. Remove two screws on each side securing radiator cover to strut rods, support rods and loosen two screws at strut. Position support rods aside.

3. Remove two screws securing upper radiator shroud to radiator and one screw securing upper radiator hose clamp to shroud.
4. Drill out the six rivets securing the upper shroud to the lower shroud and remove shroud.
5. Loosen drive belts and remove crankshaft pulleys.
6. Raise vehicle and drain oil pan.
7. Remove exhaust "Y" pipe at exhaust manifold and converter.
8. Remove through bolts from engine mounts.
9. Remove starter motor.
10. Remove transmission lower cover.
11. Using a suitable jack, raise engine to gain clearance for oil pan removal.
12. Remove nuts and screws securing oil pan to cylinder block.
13. Reverse procedure to install.

1977–80 V8-350 Seville

1. Remove wheel housing struts from both fenders.
2. Remove fan shroud.
3. Remove front motor mount through bolts, disconnect crossover pipe at manifold.
4. Remove starter, then remove converter cover.
5. Remove oil pan attaching bolts, raise engine until pan can be removed.
6. Reverse procedure to install.

1977–78 Eldorado

To remove the oil pan it is necessary to remove the engine as described previously.

1979–80 Eldorado V8-350

1. Remove final drive assembly with output shafts attached. Refer to "Final Drive" section for procedure.
2. Disconnect starter motor electrical connectors, then remove starter.
3. Drain oil from crankcase, then remove oil

pan attaching screws and the oil pan.
4. Reverse procedure to install.

OIL PUMP, REPLACE

1982–83 V8-250

1. Remove oil pan as described previously.
2. Remove bolts securing oil pump to engine, then remove pump.
3. Reverse procedure to install.

V8-350

1. Remove oil pan, then remove pump to rear main bearing attaching screws, remove pump.

V8-368, 425, 500

1. Raise car and remove oil filter.
2. Remove five screws securing pump to engine. *The screw nearest the pressure regulator should be removed last, allowing the pump to come down with the screw.*
3. Remove pump drive shaft.
4. Reverse procedure to install, being sure to pack the pump with petrolatum.

OIL PUMP, SERVICE

V8-250

1. Remove screws securing pump cover to housing.
2. Remove drive shaft, drive gear and driven gear from pump housing.
3. Remove oil pressure regulator valve and spring from bore in housing assembly. Inspect oil pressure regulator for nicks and burrs.
4. Check for free length of 2.57 inches on regulator spring. Check that spring can be compressed to 1.46 inches under 9.3–10.5 lbs. load.
5. Inspect drive gear and driven gear for nicks and burrs.

Fig. 27 Water pump attaching screws. V8-368, 425

Key	No.	Size	Torque
C	[2]	5/16-18 × 1-1/2	22 foot/lbs.
D	[1]	5/16-18 × 2-1/2	22 foot/lbs.
E	[4]	1/4-20 × 1-1/4	13 foot/lbs.
G	[1]	5/16-18 × 1-1/2 [Stud On Head]	22 foot/lbs.

Fig. 28 Water pump attaching screws. V8-350

KEY	NO.	SIZE	TORQUE N·M	TORQUE FT. LBS.
A	4	M10 X 1.50 X 45	40	30
B	1	M8 X 1.25 X 35	20	15
C	3	M6 X 1.0 (NUT)	7	5
D	1	(1620262)	10	7
E	1	M10 X 1.50 (NUT)	40	30
F	1	M10 X 1.50 X 50 (STUD HEAD)	40	30

Fig. 29 Water pump attaching screws. V8-250

6. Inspect pump housing for excessive wear.
7. Check pump cover interior surface for scoring. Check pump housing cover surface for wear.
8. Check drive shaft for damage and wear.
9. To assemble, install pump drive gear over drive shaft so that retaining ring is inside gear. Position drive gear over pump housing shaft closest to pressure regulator bore.
10. Position driven gear over remaining shaft in pump housing, meshing driven gear with drive gear.
11. Install oil pressure regulator spring and valve in bore of housing.
12. install pump cover over drive shaft and install retaining screws. Torque to 5 ft. lbs.

V8-350

1. Remove oil pump as described previously.
2. Remove oil pump driveshaft extension.

NOTE: Do not attempt to remove washers from drive shaft extension. The drive shaft extension and washers must be serviced as an assembly if washers are not 1 11/32 inch from end of shaft.

3. Remove cotter pin, spring and pressure regulator valve.

NOTE: Place finger over pressure regulator bore before removing cotter pin, as the spring is under pressure.

4. Remove oil pump cover screws, then remove cover and washer.
5. Remove drive gear and idler gear from pump housing.
6. Check gears for scoring or other damage. If damaged, install new gears.
7. Check pressure regulator valve, valve spring and bore for damage. Check valve to bore clearance which should be .0025-.0050 inch.
8. Install gears and shaft in pump body and check gear end clearance by placing a straight edge over the gears and measure the clearance between the straight edge and gasket surface. The end clearance

should be .0015-.0025 inch. If end clearance is near the excessive clearance, check for scores in the cover that would bring the clearance over the specified limit.
9. Reverse procedure to assemble.

V8-368, 425

1. Remove oil pump as described previously.
2. Slide drive shaft, drive gear and driven gear out of pump housing.
3. Using a 5/16 inch hex head wrench, remove plug from pump housing assembly and remove oil pressure regulator valve and spring from bore in housing assembly.
4. Inspect oil pressure regulator valve for nicks and burrs that might cause a leak or binding condition in bore of pump housing.
5. Check free length of regulator valve spring. It should be about 2.57 inches to 2.69 inches. A force of 9.3 to 10.5 pounds should be required to compress spring to a length of 1.46 inches.
6. Inspect drive gear and driven gear for nicks and burrs.
7. Inspect pump housing for wear and score marks.
8. Check pump mating surfaces on engine block for wear and score marks.
9. Reverse procedure to assemble.

BELT TENSION DATA

	New Lbs.	Used Lbs.
1977-80		
All	110-140	60-120
1981-82 Brougham & DeVille, Exc. V8-250		
Air Conditioning	168	67
A.I.R. Pump	78	45
Generator	145	90
Power Steering	168	67

	New Lbs.	Used Lbs.
1981-82 Eldorado & Seville, Exc. V8-250		
Air Conditioning	168	67
A.I.R. Pump	78	45
Generator	145	90
Power Steering	145	67
1982-83 V8-250		
Air Conditioning/Steering Pump	202	90
A.I.R. Pump	180	67
Generator	147	56
Vacuum Pump	49	25

WATER PUMP, REPLACE

1977-80

1. Disconnect battery ground cable, then drain cooling system.
2. On DeVille models, remove two screws, one from each side at radiator end of support rods. Loosen screws at strut end of support rods and move support rods aside.
3. Remove screws from upper fan shroud and remove screw securing upper radiator hose brace.
4. Drill out seven rivets securing upper fan shroud to lower fan shroud, then remove upper shroud.
5. Remove fan assembly.
6. Loosen generator mounting screws and remove drive belt.
7. Loosen power steering pump mounting screws and remove power steering pump belt.
8. Remove water pump pulley from shaft.
9. Disconnect water inlet hose from water pump.
10. Disconnect fuel line at carburetor inlet and fuel pump. Remove fuel line.
11. Loosen screws securing crankshaft pulley to hub approximately half way and move pulley out slightly.
12. Remove screws securing water pump to engine front cover, then remove pump, Figs. 27 and 28. Discard gasket and clean gasket surfaces.
13. Remove studs from pump flange, if equipped.
14. Reverse procedure to install.

1981–83

1. Disconnect battery ground cable, then drain cooling system.
2. On DeVille models, remove two screws, one from each side at radiator end of support rods. Loosen screws at strut end of support rods and move support rods aside.
3. Remove screws from upper fan shroud, then remove wiring harness from upper fan shroud clamps.
4. Remove screws securing power steering pump reservoir to upper fan shroud, then remove reservoir.
5. Remove staples securing upper fan shroud to lower shroud and remove upper shroud.
6. Remove fan assembly.
7. Loosen generator mounting screws and remove drive belt.
8. Loosen A.I.R. pump mounting screws and remove drive belt.
9. Remove lower power steering pump mounting bolt and loosen the remaining bolt. Remove the vacuum pump drive belt.
10. Loosen A/C compressor mounting bolts and remove drive belt.
11. Remove air conditioning compressor from engine mounting brackets and position aside. Do not remove high and low pressure lines from compressor.
12. Remove generator and support bracket from engine.
13. Loosen clamp and disconnect coolant reservoir to water pump hose at pump.
14. Loosen clamps and disconnect water pump inlet and outlet hoses at pump.
15. Remove water pump and crankshaft pulleys.
16. Remove A/C compressor bracket at water pump.
17. Remove timing mark tab from front cover.
18. Remove screws and nuts securing water pump, Fig. 29, to engine front cover and remove pump. Discard gasket and clean gasket surfaces.
19. Reverse procedure to install.

FUEL PUMP, REPLACE

With Fuel Injection

1980–83 Eldorado & Seville

NOTE: The fuel pump on these models can be replaced separately from the sending unit.

1. Remove fuel pump and sender assembly as described in "In Tank Fuel Pump" removal procedure.
2. Remove filter screen from pump.
3. Cut off rubber coupler and remove fuel pump from bracket.
4. Disconnect electrical wiring from pump.
5. Lubricate fuel tube and fuel pump outlet tube with vaseline. Slide new rubber coupler onto fuel tube.
6. Connect wiring to fuel pump. Then install new rubber isolator and pump onto mounting bracket. Align fuel pump outlet with fuel tube and slide rubber coupler into position.

NOTE: Support pump bracket to prevent it from bending during coupler installation.

7. Position new in-tank filter in same position as old filter.
8. Reverse procedure to install.

Except 1980–83 Eldorado & Seville
1. Remove fuel inlet and outlet hoses.
2. Pull back rubber boot and remove nuts from electrical terminals, then the electrical leads.
3. Remove fuel pump to mounting bracket screws, then the fuel pump assembly.
4. Reverse procedure to install. Torque fuel pump mounting screws to 25 inch lbs. Connect 14 dark green wire to the positive terminal and the 14 black wire to the negative terminal.

In-Tank Fuel Pump
1. Remove fuel tank.
2. Remove fuel gauge tank unit locknuts and the fuel pump feed wires to tank unit.
3. Using tool J-24187, disengage lock ring from fuel tank. Remove tool and lift gauge-pump unit from tank.
4. Reverse procedure to install.

1977–82 Less Fuel Injection

1. Raise car and disconnect fuel line at pump and plug line.
2. Disconnect fuel pipe to fuel filter at pump.
3. Remove mounting screw on upper pump flange.
4. Remove nut from mounting stud at lower pump flange.
5. Tipping pump upward, pull pump straight out from engine and remove.
6. Reverse procedure to install.

Rear Axle, Propeller Shaft & Brakes

For 1979–83 Eldorado & 1980–83 Seville front wheel drive axle service procedures refer to Main Index

REAR AXLE

1979–83 Eldorado & 1980–83 Seville

The spindle and wheel bearing is a unitized assembly which eliminates the need for periodic maintenance and adjustments. The spindle and wheel bearing assembly is bolted to the rear suspension control arm, Fig. 1.

Wheel Bearing Inspection
1. Raise and support rear of vehicle, then remove wheel and tire assembly.
2. Free disc brake shoes from disc or remove calipers, then reinstall two wheel nuts to secure disc to bearing.
3. Mount dial indicator as shown in Fig. 1A, then grasp rotor and check inward and outward movement of spindle assembly. Movement should be less than .020 in.
4. Remove dial indicator and rotate spindle by hand to check for roughness or grinding within the spindle.
5. Replace spindle and bearing assembly if out of specifications or roughness or grinding is present.

Spindle & Bearing Assembly, Replace
1. Raise vehicle and remove wheel and tire assembly.
2. Remove brake caliper assembly.
3. Mark wheel stud and corresponding place on rotor for use during installation, then

remove rotor.
4. Remove four nuts and bolts attaching spindle and bearing assembly to control arm, Fig. 1.
5. Reverse procedure to install. Torque spindle to lower control arm attaching bolts to 34 ft. lbs.

1977–78 Eldorado

On these axles the rear wheel spindles are a press fit and bolted to the rear axle, Fig. 2. As shown, tapered roller bearings are used in the rear wheels. These bearings do not require regularly scheduled repacking. When major brake service work is to be performed, however, it is recommended that the bearings be cleaned and repacked.

Fig. 1 Rear wheel spindle disassembled. 1979–83 Eldorado & 1980–83 Seville

Fig. 1A   Checking wheel bearing for looseness. 1979–83 Eldorado & 1980–83 Seville

Fig. 2   Rear wheel spindle disassembled. 1977–78 Eldorado

Wheel Bearing Adjustment

Adjustment of the rear wheel bearings should be made while revolving the wheel at least three times the speed of the nut rotation when taking torque readings.

1. Check to make sure that hub is completely seated on wheel spindle.
2. While rotating wheel, tighten spindle nut to 30 ft-lbs. Make certain all parts are properly seated and that threads are free.
3. Back nut off ½ turn, then retighten nut to 2 ft. lbs. and install cotter pin.
4. If cotter pin cannot be installed in either of the two holes in the spindle, with the nut at 2 ft. lbs., back nut off until cotter pin can be installed.
5. The rear hub must be rotated at least three revolutions during tightening of spindle nut. The final adjustment to be 2 ft. lbs. to provide .004″ bearing end play.
6. Peen end of cotter pin snug against side of nut. If it can be moved with a finger, vibration may cause it to wear and break.

Wheel Spindle, Replace

1. Raise and support rear of vehicle.
2. Remove tire and wheel assembly.
3. Remove rear brake drum or caliper and disc assembly.
4. Remove dust cap, cotter pin, spindle nut, washer and outer cone and roller bearing assembly.
5. Carefully pull hub off spindle.
6. On vehicles with rear drum brakes:
   a. If equipped with Track Master, loosen sensor mounting screw, and pull sensor downward, part way out of installed position. This will avoid possible damage to sensor when hub is reinstalled.
   b. Disconnect brake line from brake cylinder, then remove backing plate retaining nuts and position backing plate out of the way.

CAUTION: Do not allow backing plate to hang unsupported, as parking brake cable or sensor wiring harness can be damaged.

7. On vehicles with rear disc brakes, remove the four nuts retaining spindle to axle

housing.
8. Install one axle housing to spindle nut just far enough to engage threads, then using a slide hammer puller, pull spindle from axle housing.
9. Remove the remaining nut and bolt and remove spindle.

NOTE: If spindle threads were damaged during removal, use a ¾″-20 thread chaser to repair threads.

10. To install, use a slide hammer puller and drive spindle into axle until spindle is fully seated.
11. Install a new gasket on wheel spindle.
12. On vehicles with rear drum brakes, reinstall backing plate and torque retaining nuts to 40 ft. lbs., then reconnect brake line and torque fitting to 14 ft. lbs.
13. On vehicles with rear disc brakes, install spindle to axle housing retaining nuts and bolts and torque nuts to 40 ft. lbs.
14. Install hub, outer cone and roller bearing assembly, washer and nut. Adjust rear bearing as described previously.
15. On vehicles with Track Master, adjust sensor as described under "Anti-Skid Brake Systems" located elsewhere in this manual.
16. Install brake drum or disc and caliper assembly.
17. If brake line was disconnected, bleed brake system.

Rear Axle, Replace

1. Raise and support vehicle with jack stands placed underneath frame side rails.
2. Using a suitable jack, support weight of axle by raising it about ⅜ inch.
3. Remove brake drums or disc and caliper assembly.
4. Remove hubs.
5. If equipped with Track Master, disconnect wiring connectors from sensor harness and brake pipe and position harness out of the way.
6. On vehicles with rear drum brakes, disconnect brake lines at wheel cylinders and remove the four brake backing plate nuts.

CAUTION: Do not allow backing plate to hang unsupported, as parking brake cable can be damaged.

7. Disconnect rubber brake hose and plug

hose to minimize fluid leakage.
8. Disconnect overtravel link from bracket and deflate shock absorbers.
9. On vehicles with rear drum brakes, remove screw retaining rear brake pipe distributor to axle and disconnect brake pipes from the four retaining clips.
10. Disconnect shock absorbers at lower mounts, then raise axle to relieve tension on upper control arms and remove bolt and nut retaining each upper control arm to axle brackets.

CAUTION: Stand clear of axle assembly before performing next step, as springs can snap from their seats, resulting in personal injury or damage.

11. Carefully lower axle assembly until spring tension is relieved, then remove springs.
12. Remove bolt and nut retaining each lower control arm to axle brackets.

NOTE: It may be necessary to rotate axle slightly to remove bolts.

13. Remove rubber bumpers from top of axle housing, then lower axle assembly and remove from vehicle.
14. Reverse procedure to install.
15. Torque upper control arm bolts at frame end to 145 ft. lbs. and at axle end to 110 ft. lbs. Torque lower control arm bolts to 145 ft. lbs. Torque shock absorber lower mounting nuts to 50 ft. lbs. Torque spindle or brake backing retaining nuts to 40 ft. lbs.
16. On vehicles with Track Master, adjust sensor as described under "Anti-Skid Brake Systems" located elsewhere in this manual.

1977–83 Exc. Eldorado & 1980–83 Seville

In this axle, Fig. 3, the rear axle housing and differential carrier are cast into an integral assembly. The drive pinion assembly is mounted in two opposed tapered roller bearings. The pinion bearings are preloaded by a spacer behind the front bearing. The pinion is positioned by a washer between the head of the pinion and the rear bearing.

The differential is supported in the carrier by two tapered roller side bearings. These bearings are preloaded by spacers located

Fig. 3 Rear axle assembly. 1977–83 Exc. Eldorado (Typical)

between the bearings and carrier housing. The differential assembly is positioned for proper ring gear and pinion backlash by varying these spacers. The differential case houses two side gears in mesh with two pinions mounted on a pinion shaft which is held in place by a lock pin. The side gears and pinions are backed by thrust washers.

Rear Axle, Replace 1977–83 Exc. Eldorado & Seville

1. Raise vehicle and support rear axle and frame.
2. Disconnect overtravel lever from link, if equipped.
3. Remove shock absorbers from lower mount.
4. Place jack under front differential to relieve tension on lower control arm.
5. Remove upper and lower control arms as outlined under "Control Arms and Bushings, Replace" procedure in Rear Suspension Secion.
6. Remove propeller shaft and support with wire.
7. Remove brake hose at differential housing and plug.

CAUTION: If axle is allowed to wind up as it is lowered, springs may snap from their seats and could cause injury or damage.

Use extreme caution to prevent wind-up condition.

8. Lower axle shaft and remove springs from vehicle.
9. Reverse procedure to install.

Rear Axle, Replace 1977–79 Seville

1. Remove rear springs as outlined under "Leaf Spring, Replace" procedure in Rear Suspension Secion.
2. Remove clip securing brake hose to underbody and disconnect hose from brake line.

3. Remove stabilizer bar.
4. Mark propeller shaft flange and pinion flange to insure installation in original position. Then, disconnect prop shaft from pinion flange and secure with wire to underbody.
5. Lower axle and remove from vehicle.
6. Reverse procedure to install.

Differential, Remove

1. Raise vehicle and support so axle can be raised and lowered.
2. Disconnect leveling control lever from link and hold lever down until shock absorbers are deflated.
3. Remove shock absorber lower mounting bolts and position shock aside.
4. Mark propeller shaft flange and pinion flange to ensure installation in original position. Remove attaching screws and position propeller shaft aside.
5. Remove stabilizer bar link nuts, retainer and bushings.
6. Remove nut from parking brake equalizer, then disconnect cables at connectors.
7. Remove clips securing brake tubing to axle, then lower axle slightly.
8. Position drain pan under axle, loosen rear cover bolts and allow axle to drain, then remove cover.
9. Remove wheel and brake drum.
10. Remove differential cross shaft through bolt, then the shaft. Push in on axle shafts, then remove "C" locks and pull axle shafts out about 1 inch.
11. Install cross shaft and bolt, then remove side bearing cap and bearing.

NOTE: Mark bearing caps to ensure installation in original position

12. Remove one ring gear attaching bolt, position tools, Fig. 4, and pull differential case from housing until side shims can be removed, then remove differential.

NOTE: Mark shims to ensure installation in original position.

13. Reverse procedure to install.

Axle Shaft, Replace

1. Raise vehicle and remove wheel and brake drum.
2. Place drain pan under differential and remove cover.
3. Remove differential cross shaft.
4. Push axle shaft toward center of vehicle and remove "C" lock from butt end of axle shaft.
5. Remove axle shaft from housing.
6. Reverse procedure to install.

Bearing Replace

1. Remove axle shaft.
2. Position tool J-22813-01 on bearing, attach slide hammer J-2619, then remove bearing and seal.
3. Lubricate bearing and seal with bearing lubricant.
4. Position bearing on tool J-23765 and drive bearing in until tool bottoms against tube.

NOTE: Bearing should be .550″ from end of axle tube.

5. Using suitable tool, tap seal in until flush with axle tube.

Fig. 4 Removing differential. 1977–83 Exc. Eldorado & 1980–83 Seville

PROPELLER SHAFT, REPLACE

Service Note

If drive line shudder, roughness, vibration or rumble is experienced, it may be due to misalignment of the propeller shaft assembly. To make this check, however, a special Propeller Shaft Alignment Gauge Set. No. J-8905 must be used. Inasmuch as this equipment is not likely to be found in general repair shops, it is recommended that a Cadillac dealer having this equipment do the work.

1. Raise vehicle on hoist with transmission in neutral.

NOTE: Mark propeller shaft relationship to axle pinion flange to maintain balance.

2. Remove propeller shaft flange retaining bolts.

CAUTION: Do not allow propeller shaft to be supported by front or center universal joint, as damage to universal joint may result. Rear of propeller shaft must be supported to underbody of vehicle.

3. Pull propeller shaft forward to clear pinion flange and support rear end of shaft.

NOTE: Place a suitable container under transmission, to catch any fluid which may leak when slip joint is removed.

4. On two piece type propeller shafts, remove the two center bearing supports to frame bolts and nuts.
5. Slide propeller shaft rearward until slip yoke comes off transmission output shaft.

NOTE: Place a protective device such as a cardboard shipping cover, over yoke. This will prevent damage to yoke when shaft is removed.

6. Remove shaft and install a spare yoke

into transmission extension housing to prevent loss of oil.
7. Reverse procedure to install. Torque flange attaching bolts to 70 ft. lbs.
8. Check transmission oil.

1977–78 ELDORADO DRIVE AXLES

General Description

Each drive axle, Fig. 5, consists of an axle shaft, with a ball type constant velocity joint at the outboard end and a tri-pot type at the inboard end. The torsional damper on the right hand shaft is not serviceable and must be replaced as a unit.

The inboard joint is not only flexible to operate at various angles, but can also move in and out as required by suspension movement.

Right Drive Axle

1. Disconnect battery ground cable and remove wheel and the wheel disc.

NOTE: If drive axle is to be removed, remove cotter pin and loosen but do not remove spindle nut.

2. Raise vehicle so front vehicle weight is supported at lower control arms.
3. Loosen right front shock absorber lower mounting nut, then, using a screwdriver, pry shock absorber at the mount inner sleeve until it contacts nut.

NOTE: Do not remove shock absorber from lower mount since lower control arm may drop.

4. Place a short piece of rubber hose on both lower control arm torsion bar connectors.
5. Remove screws and lockwashers securing right drive axle to output shaft.
6. Position inboard end of axle rearward toward starter to provide access to output shaft.
7. Remove output shaft support strut to final drive housing screw, then the two screws securing right output shaft support to the engine.
8. Slide output shaft outboard to disengage splines, then move inboard end of the assembly forward and downward until clear of vehicle.
9. Using a block of wood and a hammer, strike end of drive axle to unseat axle at hub.

NOTE: Loosen spindle nut just enough to allow axle to unseat.

10. Rotate axle inboard and forward, guiding axle over front cross-member and from under vehicle.
11. Reverse procedure to install.

Left Drive Axle

1. Raise and support vehicle with jack stands underneath frame side rails.
2. Remove wheel and tire and drive axle spindle nut.
3. Remove the six drive axle to output shaft screws and lockwashers.

Fig. 5 Eldorado drive axle, exploded. 1977-78

NOTE: Discard the six screws and lock-washers. Use new ones during reassembly.

4. Loosen shock absorber upper bolt, then remove the ball joint cotter pin and nut and remove brake hose clip from joint stud.
5. Using a hammer, strike, knuckle in area of ball joint. Lift up on upper arm and remove joint stud from steering knuckle.

CAUTION: Use care to avoid damaging brake hose.

6. Remove brake hose bracket from frame, then carefully tip disc and knuckle assembly out at upper end to extent of brake hose.

CAUTION: To prevent damaging the brake hose, wire the assembly to upper control arm so that brake hose does not support weight of knuckle assembly.

7. Rotate inner end of drive axle toward front of vehicle, then guide drive axle out of knuckle and remove drive axle.
8. Remove output shaft retaining bolt.

NOTE: To prevent output shaft from rotating, install two screws in output shaft flange.

9. Remove output shaft by pulling straight out.

CAUTION: Use care when removing out-

Fig. 6 Removing outer joint from axle

Fig. 7 Removing and installing inner snap ring

Fig. 8 Removing balls from outer joint

Fig. 9   Removing cage and inner race

Fig. 10   Removing inner race from cage

Fig. 11   Installing new seal clamp

ut shaft to avoid damaging oil seal.

10. Reverse procedure to install.

Outer Constant Velocity Joint

1. Remove inner and outer seal clamps by cutting with a chisel and slide seal down axle shaft to gain access to joint.
2. Wipe excess grease from joint and spread snap ring and slide joint off spline, Fig. 6.
3. Remove inner race snap ring, Fig. 7.
4. Hold constant velocity joint in one hand then tilt cage and inner race so that one ball can be removed, Fig. 8. Continue until all balls have been removed.

NOTE: It may be necessary to tap the outer cage to rotate it.

5. Turn cage 90° with slot in cage aligned with short land on outer race and lift cage out of race, Fig. 9.
6. Turn short land of inner race 90° in line with hole in cage. Lift land on inner race up through hole in cage, then turn up and out to separate, Fig. 10.
7. Reverse procedure to install, using new seal clamps, Fig. 11. Cut off excess strap.

Inner Constant Velocity Joint

1. Remove small seal clamp bank by cutting it with a chisel.
2. Remove large end of seal from joint hous-

ing by prying up crimped edge on seal adapter. Drive seal adapter and seal off of joint housing with hammer and chisel, Fig. 12.

NOTE: Use care when removing seal adapter not to damage it or the seal.

3. Slide seal and adapter down axle shaft until joint is exposed.

NOTE: Do not allow spider leg balls to fall off by accident as adapter is moved.

4. Remove spider leg balls.
5. Remove spider outer snap ring, Fig. 13.
6. Tap spider assembly from shaft.
7. Reverse procedure to install, being sure to stake seal adapter to joint housing, Fig. 14.

Right Hand Output Shaft

1. Disconnect negative battery cable.
2. Raise car and install a short length of rubber hose on lower control arm torsion bar connector, Fig. 15.
3. Remove six drive axle-to-output shaft bolts and lock washers.
4. Remove output shaft support mounting bolts.
5. Rotate inboard end of drive axle rearward.
6. Pull output shaft out until it clears final drive then lower splined end and remove from car.
7. Reverse procedure to install.

Right Hand Output Shaft Bearing, Replace

1. Remove output shaft as described above.
2. Remove three output shaft bearing retainer-to-support bolts.
3. Using two fabricated steel plates and four $3/8 \times 24$ bolts five inches long illustrated in Fig. 16, tighten bolts alternately to press out bearing.
4. Reverse procedure to install.

Left Hand Output Shaft

1. Remove left drive axle.
2. Remove output shaft retaining bolt and pull shaft out of final drive.
3. Reverse procedure to install.

Final Drive, Replace

The final drive unit is not serviced but is replaced as a unit.
1. Disconnect negative battery cable.
2. Remove approximately one gallon of fluid from transmission then remove transmission filler tube and plug tube hole.
3. Remove bolts "A" and "B" and nut "H", Fig. 17.
4. Remove bolt securing transmission oil cooler lines to final drive.
5. Remove nut from large through bolt, final drive support bracket to final drive.
6. Disconnect left front engine mount support bracket from engine. And final drive support bracket from left front engine mount support.
7. Remove right output shaft as outlined above.
8. Remove six left output shaft-to-drive axle bolts and lock washers.
9. Loosen final drive cover screws and drain fluid, then remove cover.
10. Compress left hand inner constant velocity joint and secure drive axle to frame with a piece of wire to provide clearance.
11. Disconnect left tie strut from crossmember and loosen strut to side rail bolt. Then rotate strut outboard until clear of final drive.
12. Remove final drive support bracket.
13. Remove remaining final drive-to-transmission bolts and nut "G".
14. Disengage final drive splines from transmission.

NOTE: To avoid damage to seals, final

Fig. 12   Removing seal adapter

Fig. 13   Removing spider snap ring

Fig. 14   Installing seal adapter on joint housing

Fig. 15   Rubber hose location

Fig. 16   Removing right hand output shaft support and bearing

drive unit should be supported by a suitable jack and proper alignment must be maintained throughout removal.

15. Remove final drive unit from underside of car by sliding unit toward front of car, permitting ring gear to rotate up over steering linkage and work unit free from car.

16. Reverse procedure to install, being very careful to maintain proper final drive-to-transmission alignment to prevent seal damage.

DRUM BRAKE ADJUSTMENTS

Self-Adjusting Brakes

These brakes, Fig. 18, have self-adjusting shoe mechanisms that assure correct lining-to-drum clearances at all times. The automatic adjusters operate only when the brakes are applied as the car is moving rearward.

Although the brakes are self-adjusting, an initial adjustment is necessary after the brake shoes have been relined or replaced, or when the length of the star wheel adjuster has been changed during some other service operation.

Frequent usage of an automatic transmission forward range to halt reverse vehicle motion may prevent the automatic adjusters from functioning, thereby inducing low pedal heights. Should low pedal heights be encountered, it is recommended that numerous forward and reverse stops be made with a moderate pedal effort until satisfactory pedal height is obtained.

NOTE: If a low pedal height condition cannot be corrected by making numerous reverse stops (provided the hydraulic system is free of air) it indicates that the self-adjusting mechanism is not functioning. Therefore, it will be necessary to remove the brake drum, clean, free up and lubricate the adjusting mechanism. Then adjust the brakes, being sure the parking brake is fully released.

The recommended method of adjusting the brakes is by using the Drum-to-Brake Shoe Clearance Gauge to check the diameter of the brake drum inner surface, Fig. 19. Turn the tool to the opposite side and fit over the brake shoes by turning the star wheel until the gauge just slides over the linings, Fig. 20. Rotate the gauge around the brake shoe lining surface to assure proper clearance.

PARKING BRAKE, ADJUST

1977–83 W/Rear Disc Brakes

1. Lubricate parking brake cables at equalizer and underbody rub points. Check all cables for freedom of operation.
2. Fully release parking brake and raise vehicle.
3. Hold cable stud from turning and tighten equalizer nut until cable slack is removed and levers are against stops on caliper housing. If levers are off stops, loosen cable until levers return to stop.
4. Operate parking brake several times to check adjustment. When properly adjusted, the parking brake pedal should move 6¼–7¼ inches on 1977–78 Seville, 5¼–6¾ inches on 1977–83 all except Seville and 1980–83 Eldorado, 4–5½ inches on 1979–83 Eldorado and 1980–83 Seville and 6¾–7¾ inches on 1979 Seville.

Fig. 17   Final drive attachment

Fig. 18 Rear drum brake. Except 1977–78 Eldorado

Fig. 19 Measuring brake drum inner diameter

Fig. 20 Checking brake shoe lining clearance

1977–83 W/Rear Drum Brakes

1. With service brakes properly adjusted, lubricate parking brake linkage at equalizer and cable stud with heat-resistant lubricant, and check for free movement of cables.
2. Depress parking brake pedal about 1½" on 1977–83 models except Seville from full released position.
3. Raise rear wheels off floor.
4. Hold brake cable and stud from turning and tighten equalizer nut until a slight drag is felt on either wheel (going forward). After each turn of equalizer nut, check to see if either wheel begins to drag.
5. Release parking brake. No brake drag should be felt at either rear wheel. Operate several times to check adjustment.

VACUUM RELEASE PARKING BRAKE

1977–83

The foot-operated parking brake is mounted on the cowl to the left of the steering column. It incorporates a vacuum release, Fig. 21, operated by a vacuum diaphragm that is connected to the parking brake mechanism. When the transmission selector is moved into any Drive position, a vacuum valve in the neutral safety switch opens, allowing diaphragm to be actuated by engine vacuum.

The diaphragm is connected by a link to a release mechanism on the parking brake. Vacuum acting on the diaphragm unlocks the parking brake pedal, permitting it to return to the release position by spring action. Any abnormal leaks in the vacuum release system will prevent proper brake release. A manual release is provided and may be used if the automatic release is inoperative or if manual release is desired at any time.

NOTE: Under some conditions, aided by cold weather, the parking brake vacuum release valve (integral with the back-up light switch on steering column) may not release the parking brake automatically. Although when the brake is applied, the "Brake" indicator light will go on, brake can be released manually. If this condition is present the back-up light switch must be replaced.

Testing Vacuum Release

1. If the mechanism is inoperative, first check for damaged or kinked vacuum hoses and for loose hose connections at the diaphragm, vacuum release valve at neutral safety switch, and at engine manifold connection.
2. Check adjustment of neutral safety switch and operation of vacuum release valve.
3. Check diaphragm piston travel by running engine and moving transmission selector lever from drive to neutral. The manual release lever should move up and down as vacuum is applied and released. If no movement is observed, or if movement is slow (more than 1 or 2 seconds to complete the full stroke) diaphragm is leaking and should be replaced.
4. Check brake release with vacuum applied. If diaphragm piston completes full stroke but does not release brake, a malfunction of the pedal assembly is indicated, and the complete parking brake assembly should be replaced.
5. Check operation of parking brake with engine off. Parking brake should remain engaged regardless of transmission selector lever position. If not, replace parking brake assembly.

MASTER CYLINDER, REPLACE

1. Remove brake lines from master cylinder. Plug lines and ports.
2. Remove booster to master cylinder attaching nuts, then remove master cylinder.
3. Reverse procedure to install. On 1977–80 models, torque master cylinder attaching nuts to 20 ft. lbs., 1981 models to 22–30 ft. lbs. and 1982–83 models to 28 ft. lbs. On 1977–78 models, torque brake line to master cylinder nuts to 15 ft. lbs., on 1979–80 models to 20 ft. lbs., on 1981 models to 10–15 ft. lbs. and on 1982–83 models to 18 ft. lbs.

POWER BRAKE UNIT, REPLACE

Service Bulletin

A sign of brake fluid dampness below the master cylinder at the power brake unit or on wheel cylinders at the bottom of the boot, does not necessarily indicate that these cylinders are leaking.

A small amount of fluid leakage at these areas can occur due to the creeping action of a very light film of fluid on the cylinder bores around the seals. This action provides proper seal lubrication. In addition, normal brake heat will produce a slight escape of lubricant from the impregnated, porous-metal wheel cylinder pistons.

Normal dampness at the master cylinder or wheel cylinders is not easily distinguishable from a definite leak. Therefore, this condition must be checked carefully.

If there is sufficient dampness to form a "teardrop" of fluid at the bottom of the master cylinder or on the bottom of the wheel cylin-

Fig. 21 Parking brake linkage. 1977–83 drum brake (typical)

ders at the boot area, the rate of fluid seepage is too high and the cause should be determined and corrected.

Hydro-Boost

1977–83
1. With engine off pump brake pedal several times to empty accumulator of fluid.
2. Remove master cylinder to booster attaching nuts, then move master cylinder away from booster with brakes lines attached.
3. Remove three hydraulic lines from booster, cap all ports and lines to prevent entry of dirt and loss of fluid.
4. Remove retainer and washer securing booster pedal rod to brake pedal arm.
5. Remove four booster to firewall attaching nuts.
6. Loosen booster from firewall and move booster pedal rod inboard until it disconnects from brake arm.
7. Remove spring washer from brake pedal arm and remove booster.

Vacuum Booster

1979–83 Eldorado
1. Disconnect engine wiring harness clips from brake unit.
2. Remove two nuts retaining master cylinder to brake unit, and position master cylinder away from brake unit.

NOTE: Do not disconnect brake lines from master cylinder. Use care not to bend or kink lines.

3. Remove check valve from brake unit.
4. Remove four nuts attaching brake unit to cowl and pedal support bracket.
5. Disconnect brake unit push rod from brake pedal, then remove brake unit from vehicle.

1977–83 Seville
1. Disconnect and cap brake lines, remove wiring harness from combination valve.
2. Remove master cylinder to brake booster attaching nuts, then the master cylinder and combination valve.

3. Disconnect vacuum line from check valve.
4. Remove clip and washer from push rod pin at brake pedal, however, do not remove push rod.
5. Remove twilight sentinel amplifier attaching screws and wiring harness and lower unit, if equipped.
6. Remove brake booster to cowl attaching nuts, slide booster out and disconnect push rod from brake pedal pin.
7. Reverse procedure to install.

1977–83 Exc. Seville & 1979–83 Eldorado
1. Disconnect hydraulic lines from master cylinder on power unit. Cap line fittings to prevent dirt entering system.
2. Disconnect vacuum hose from vacuum check valve on power unit. Remove steering column lower cover.
3. Remove cotter pin and spring spacer that attach power unit push rod to brake pedal relay lever.
4. Unfasten and remove power unit from cowl.

1977–83 Eldorado & 1980–83 Seville Drive Link Belt

LINK BELT SPROCKETS

Removal

After removal of transmission as described elsewhere in this manual, proceed as follows:
1. Remove sprocket housing cover attaching bolts and cover.
2. Remove sprocket bearing retaining snap rings from retaining grooves in support housing located under drive and driven sprockets, Fig. 1.

NOTE: Do not remove the snap rings from beneath the sprockets, leave them in a loose position between the sprockets and the bearing assemblies.

3. Remove drive and driven sprockets, link belt, bearings and shafts simultaneously by alternately pulling upwards on driven support housing, Fig. 2

NOTE: If sprockets and link belt are difficult to remove, place a small piece of masonite, or similar material between the sprocket and a short pry bar. Alternately pry upward under each sprocket. Do not pry on links or aluminum case, Fig. 3.

4. Remove link belt from drive and driven sprockets.

Installation
1. Place link belt around the drive and driven sprockets so that the links engage

the teeth of the sprockets, colored guide link which has etched numerals facing link cover.
2. Simultaneously place link belt, drive and driven sprockets into support housing,

Fig. 1.
3. Using a plastic mallet, gently seat the sprocket bearing assemblies into the support housing.

Fig. 1 Removing or installing retaining rings

Fig. 2   Removing or installing sprockets and link assembly

Fig. 3   Removing tight sprockets

4. Install sprocket assembly to support housing snap rings, Fig. 2.
5. Install new case to cover and plate assembly sprocket housing gasket.

NOTE: One sprocket cover housing attaching bolt is 1/4 inch longer. This bolt must be installed in the tapped hole located directly over the cooler fittings on the transmission case.

6. Install sprocket housing cover and plate assembly and eighteen attaching bolts. Torque bolts to 8 ft. lbs.

Rear Suspension

SHOCK ABSORBER, REPLACE

1977–83

1. If equipped with Automatic Level Control, disconnect air lines from shock absorber fittings.
2. With the rear axle supported properly disconnect shock absorber at upper and lower mountings.

NOTE: Use care not to damage brake hoses or lines when removing shock absorber.

3. Reverse procedure to install.

COIL SPRINGS, REPLACE

1979–83 Eldorado & 1980–83 Seville

1. Raise and support rear of vehicle, then remove wheel and tire assembly.
2. Remove stabilizer bar as described under Stabilizer Bar, Replace.
3. Using a suitable jack support lower control arm.
4. Disconnect automatic level air line at shock absorber. If removing left hand spring from vehicle, disconnect automatic level control link from ball pivot at control arm.
5. Disconnect shock absorber from upper and lower mountings and remove shock absorber.
6. Carefully lower control arm until spring tension is relieved, then remove spring and insulator, Fig. 1.
7. Reverse procedure to install. Locate bottom end of spring between dimples on lower control arm assembly.

1977–83 Except Eldorado & Seville

1. Support vehicle at frame and support rear axle using a suitable jack.
2. Remove shock absorbers.
3. If equipped with Automatic Level Control, remove bolts attaching stabilizer bar to lower control arms and remove stabilizer bar.
4. Remove bolt attaching brake line junction block to rear axle housing, then disconnect brake lines from clips on rear axle housing.
5. If equipped with Automatic Level Control, disconnect link from leveling valve arm.

Fig. 1   1979–83 Eldorado & 1980–83 Seville rear suspension

Fig. 2 1977–83 rear suspension (typical). Except Eldorado & Seville

Fig. 3 Coil spring installation. 1977–83 Except Eldorado & Seville

6. Position a jack stand under nose of differential carrier to relieve tension on lower control arm to axle housing bolts, then remove bolts, Fig. 2.
7. Disconnect drive shaft from pinion flange and support from frame with wire.
8. Remove jack stand from under nose of differential carrier, then remove upper control arm pivot bolts at rear axle housing.
9. Disconnect left hand parking brake cable at equalizer and cable at frame by removing clip.
10. Disconnect parking brake cable from clip at center of rear cross member and cable at "C" connector located at left hand side of frame.
11. Lower axle assembly to a point where springs can be pried out, using care not to stretch brake lines or parking brake cables.

NOTE: When lowering axle and prying out springs, use care to prevent axle assembly from rotating, as springs may snap from seats.

12. Reverse procedure to install. Note spring positions, Fig. 3.

1977–78 Eldorado

1. Support vehicle at frame and support rear axle with a suitable jack.
2. If equipped with Automatic Level Control, disconnect overtravel lever link and place lever in center position.
3. Disconnect shock absorbers from lower mountings and rear brake hose from brake line.
4. On standard cars, disconnect propeller shaft from differential pinion flange.
5. Remove upper control arm rear mount bolt and lift arm from axle bracket, Fig. 4.
6. Lower axle assembly slowly until springs are free.

NOTE: When lowering axle assembly, use care to prevent axle from rotating, as springs may snap from the seats. If necessary, compress springs by hand to remove.

7. Reverse procedure to install. Note spring positions, Fig. 5. Tighten control arm bolt with vehicle at curb height.

LEAF SPRING, REPLACE

1977–79 Seville

1. Raise vehicle on hoist.

Fig. 4 1977–78 Eldorado rear suspension (typical)

Fig. 5 Coil spring installation. 1977–78 Eldorado

2. Using a suitable jack, raise axle until spring tension is relieved, Fig. 6.
3. Disconnect Automatic Level Control overtravel lever from link.
4. Push overtravel lever down to deflate shock absorbers, then remove shock lower mounting nut and bolt and position shock absorber aside.
5. Back off parking brake adjustment at equalizer and remove cable clip from spring front retaining bracket and cable clamps from bottom of spring.
6. Loosen spring front eye to retaining bracket bolt.
7. Remove spring front bracket to underbody attaching screws.
8. Lower axle until bolt can be removed from spring front eye and remove bracket from spring.
9. Remove nuts securing lower spring plate to axle and stabilizer bar brackets.
10. Remove upper and lower spring pads and spring plate, support spring, then remove both nuts from rear shackle.
11. Separate spring and shackle and remove spring.

CONTROL ARMS & BUSHINGS, REPLACE

NOTE: Replace one control arm at a time as axle assembly may slip sideways, making installation difficult.

Upper Control Arms

1977–83 Except Eldorado & Seville
1. Support vehicle at frame and support rear axle using a suitable jack.
2. If vehicle is equipped with Automatic Level Control, remove bolt attaching height control link to right upper control arm. Position overtravel lever in center position.
3. Position a jack stand under differential pinion retainer.
4. Remove both control arm pivot bolts and control arm.
5. Reverse procedure to install. Tighten control arm pivot bolts with vehicle at curb height.

1977–78 Eldorado
1. Perform steps 1 and 2 as outlined under "Coil Springs, Replace" 1977–78 Eldo-

Fig. 7 Upper control arm axle bracket bushing removal, 1977–78 Eldorado

Fig. 6 Rear suspension. 1977–79 Seville

rado. On Eldorado disconnect shock absorbers from lower mountings.
2. Remove control arm front and rear mount bolts.
3. On Eldorado, replace axle bracket bushing as required, Figs. 7 and 8. New bushing is installed with flanged side outboard of bracket.
4. Reverse procedure to install. Tighten control arm bolts with vehicle at curb height.

Lower Control Arms

1979–83 Eldorado & 1980–83 Seville
1. Raise and support rear of vehicle, then remove wheel and tire assembly.
2. Remove stabilizer bar as described under Stabilizer Bar, Replace.
3. Disconnect brake line bracket from control arm, then remove caliper assembly.
4. Mark a wheel stud and a corresponding point on the rotor for alignment, then remove rotor.
5. If left hand control arm is to be removed, disconnect automatic level control link from ball pivot on control arm.
6. Using a suitable jack support control arm.
7. Disconnect air line from shock absorber, then disconnect shock absorber from upper and lower mountings and remove shock absorber.
8. Carefully lower the control arm until spring tension is relieved, then remove spring and insulator.
9. Remove two bolts mounting control arm to frame and remove control arm, Fig. 1.
10. Reverse procedure to install. Torque control arm to frame mounting bolts to 75 ft. lbs.

1977–83 Except Eldorado & Seville
1. Support vehicle at frame and support rear axle using a suitable jack.
2. If equipped with Automatic Level Control, remove two bolts securing stabilizer bar to control arm being removed.

3. Remove front and rear lower control arm nuts.
4. Position a suitable jack under front of differential carrier to relieve tension on lower control arm bolts.
5. Remove front and rear lower control arm bolts and lower control arm.

NOTE: Lower control arm bushings are not serviceable.

6. Reverse procedure to install. Tighten control arm bolts with vehicle at curb height.

1977–78 Eldorado

Follow "Upper Control Arms" 1977–78 Eldorado procedure for replacement of lower control arms.

NOTE: Lower control arm bushings are not serviceable.

Fig. 8 Upper control arm axle bracket bushing installation, 1977–78 Eldorado

STABILIZER BAR, REPLACE

1979–83 Eldorado & 1980–83 Seville

1. Raise and support rear of vehicle.
2. Remove nuts and bolts securing front of stabilizer bar to control arms.
3. Remove inside nut and bolt from each side of stabilizer bar link, then loosen outside nut and bolt on the stabilizer link.
4. Rotate bottom parts of link to one side and slip stabilizer out of bushings.

1977–83 Except Eldorado & Seville

1. Raise and support rear of vehicle.
2. Remove bolts securing stabilizer bar to lower control arms, then remove stabilizer bar from vehicle.

1977–79 Seville

1. Raise and support rear of vehicle.
2. Remove nuts and bolts securing stabilizer bushings and brackets to lower spring plates.
3. Remove nuts from link bolts, then remove washers and grommets.
4. Remove stabilizer bar from vehicle, then remove bushings and brackets from bar.

Front End & Steering Section

FRONT SUSPENSION EXC. ELDORADO & 1980–83 SEVILLE

1977–79 Seville & 1977–83 Brougham & DeVille

The front suspension consist of two upper and lower control arm assemblies, steel coil springs, shock absorbers, stabilizer bar, two integral steering arms, and knuckles, Fig. 1. Ball joints are used at outer ends of upper and lower control arms. The upper ball joints is riveted to the upper control arm. The lower ball joint is pressed into the lower control arm.

A stabilizer bar is mounted in rubber bushings to the front frame side rails and is attached to the lower control arms by means of steel links.

Wheel Alignment

1977–79 Seville & 1977–83 Brougham & DeVille

Caster and camber are adjusted by adding or removing shims from between the upper control arm and frame bracket, Fig. 2. Caster is adjusted by transfering shims from front to rear and rear to front. Transfering shims from front bolt to rear bolt will increase positive caster, from rear bolt to front bolt will increase negative caster.

Camber is adjusted by adding or removing an equal number of shims from the front and rear bolts. To increase positive camber remove an equal amount of shims from front and rear bolts, to increase negative camber add an equal amount of shims to front and rear bolts.

After adjusting caster and camber torque nut to 70–80 ft. lbs. Tighten bolt with the least amount of shims first. After adjusting caster and camber toe-in must be adjusted.

NOTE: The difference in thickness between front and rear shim packs should not exceed .40 inch. If difference is greater than .40 inch check arms, frame and related parts for damage.

TOE-IN, ADJUST

Toe-in can be adjusted by loosening the clamp bolts at each end of each tie rod and turning each tie rod to increase or decrease its length as necessary until proper toe-in is secured and the steering gear is on the high point for straight-ahead driving.

Fig. 1   Front suspension disassembled. 1977–79 Seville & 1977–83 Brougham & DeVille

Wheel Bearings, Adjust

Service Bulletin

Looseness at a front wheel does not necessar-

Fig. 3   Caster and camber adjustment. 1977–79 Seville & 1977–83 Brougham & DeVille

FRONT SUSPENSION BALL JOINT WEAR INDICATOR

WORN — NEW

SINTERED IRON BEARING

WEAR SURFACES

HOUSING SOCKET

.050 INCH

RUBBER PRESSURE RING

WEAR INDICATOR

WHEN BALL JOINT WEAR CAUSES WEAR INDICATOR SHOULDER TO RECEDE WITHIN THE SOCKET HOUSING REPLACEMENT IS REQUIRED

Fig. 3 Ball joint wear indicator. 1977–83 except Eldorado & 1980–83 Seville

Fig. 4 Removing ball joint studs from steering knuckle. 1977–79 Seville & 1977–83 Brougham & DeVille

ily indicate worn bearings or a loose spindle nut, since the tapered roller bearings used on front wheels of all standard Cadillacs should not be preloaded and normally can have up to .004″ end play.

1. While rotating wheel and tire assembly, tighten spindle nut to 15 ft. lbs. for 1977 vehicles and 12 ft. lbs. for 1978–83 vehicles making certain that hub is fully seated on spindle.
2. Back off spindle nut until free, and tighten nut finger tight.
3. Install new cotter pin. If pin cannot be installed, back off nut to next hole and install pin.

NOTE: Cotter pin must be tight after installation, as vibration can break pin.

Wheel Bearings, Replace

1977–83

1. Remove caliper retaining bolts, then slide caliper off disc and using a length of wire, attach caliper to upper control arm.

NOTE: Never allow caliper to hang from brake hose.

2. Remove dust cap, cotter pin, spindle nut, washer and outer bearing assembly.
3. Remove hub and disc assembly, being careful to avoid damage to spindle threads or grease seal.
4. Remove inner bearing grease seal and bearing assembly.

NOTE: Inner and outer bearing cups are press fit in hub and can be driven out from the opposite side using a brass drift. Tap alternately on opposite sides to prevent cocking cup and damaging hub.

Checking Ball Joints For Wear

Upper Ball Joint

1977–79 Seville & 1977–83 Brougham & DeVille
If ball joint has any noticeable lateral movement or can be twisted within its socket using finger pressure, the joint must be replaced.

Lower Ball Joint
1977–83

A wear indicator is built in the ball joint. Remove dirt deposits around service plug and observe position of nipple. Refer to Fig. 3, for wear tolerance.

Upper Ball Joint, Replace

1977–79 Seville, 1977–83 Brougham & DeVille

1. Raise vehicle and remove wheel.

2 x 4

J-9519-10

J-9519-7

Fig. 5 Removing ball joint from lower control arm. 1977–79 Seville & 1977–82 DeVille

2. Remove cotter pin from upper ball joint stud.
3. Remove caliper and position aside.

NOTE: When removing caliper use care not to damage brake tubing or hose. Secure caliper to frame with wire.

4. Loosen stud nut, however, not more than one turn.
5. Using tool No. J-23742, free ball joint stud from steering knuckle, Fig. 4.

NOTE: The lower control arm must be supported so spring can not force arm down.

6. Remove upper ball joint stud nut, allow steering knuckle to swing out of way and place block of wood between frame and upper control arm.
7. To remove rivets securing ball joint to upper control arm, grind rivet heads off, then, using a punch, drive rivets out.

NOTE: Use care not to damage ball joint seat or upper control arm when removing rivets.

8. Position ball joint on upper control arm, install bolts through bottom of control arm, install and torque nuts to 25 ft. lbs.
9. Remove block of wood from between frame and upper control arm, position upper ball stud to steering knuckle, install and torque nut to 60 ft. lbs. Install cotter pin.

NOTE: If cotter pin hole is not aligned do not back nut off. Nut may be torqued to a maximum of 100 ft. lbs. (1/6 additional turn) to align cotter pin hole.

10. Install caliper, lubricate ball joint and install wheel.
11. Check wheel alignment.

Lower Ball Joint, Replace

1977–79 Seville, 1977–83 Brougham & DeVille

1. Raise vehicle and remove wheel.
2. Remove cotter pin from lower ball joint stud and loosen nut one turn.
3. Using tool No. J-23742, free ball joint

Fig. 6 Removing and installing front spring. 1977–79 Seville & 1977–83 Brougham & DeVille

stud from steering knuckle, Fig. 4.

NOTE: Lower control arm must be supported so spring cannot force arm down.

4. Remove lower stud nut and pull upward and outward on bottom of brake disc to free ball joint stud from steering knuckle.
5. Lift upper control arm up with steering knuckle and hub attached and place a block of wood between frame and upper control arm.

NOTE: It may be necessary to remove tie rod from steering knuckle.

6. Using tools J-9519-10 and J-9519-7, remove ball joint from lower control arm, Fig. 5.
7. Install ball joint in lower control arm using tools J-9519-9 and J-9519-10.

NOTE: Position bleed vent in ball joint rubber boot to face inward and the stud cotter pin hole to face forward.

8. Remove block of wood from between frame and upper control arm, then install lower ball joint stud in steering knuckle. Install and torque nut to 80 ft. lbs. and install cotter pin.

NOTE: If cotter pin hole is not aligned do not back nut off. Nut may be torqued to a maximum of 125 ft. lbs. (1/6 additional turn) to align cotter pin holes.

9. Lubricate ball joint and install tie rod; if removed. Torque tie rod nut to 35 ft. lbs. and install cotter pin.
10. Install wheel and check wheel alignment.

Shock Absorber, Replace

The shock absorbers are removed through the bottom of the lower control arm after unfastening it at the top and bottom.

To install, place the retainer and rubber grommet on the upper stem and fully extend the shock absorber rod. Insert the shock absorber up into the coil spring and guide the

Fig. 7 Front suspension disassembled. 1979–83 Eldorado & 1980–83 Seville

stem through the tower in the crossmember. Then place the lower end in position on the lower control arm. Install bolts and torque to 22 ft. lbs. on all except Seville or 19 ft. lbs. on Seville. On all models, install shock stud retaining nut and tighten to end of threads on stud (about 1 1/8 inch).

Coil Spring, Replace

1977–79 Seville & 1977–83 Brougham & DeVille

1. Raise vehicle on hoist, remove shock absorber lower mounting bolts and push shock through control arm up into spring.
2. Support vehicle so control arms hang free and disconnect stabilizer bar from lower control arm.
3. Secure tool No. J-23028-01 to a suitable jack, position tool so lower control arm is supported by inner bushings, Fig. 6.
4. Raise jack to relieve spring tension from lower control arm pivot and install a safety chain around spring and through lower control arm.
5. Remove bolt from rear of lower control arm, then remove other bolt and slowly lower control arm until all spring tension is relieved.
6. Remove safety chain, spring and spring insulator.
7. Reverse procedure to install.

NOTE: When installing spring, bottom coil must cover all or part of one inspection hole on the lower control arm. The other inspection hole must be fully or partially uncovered.

ELDORADO & 1980–83 SEVILLE FRONT SUSPENSION

The front suspension consists of two upper and two lower control arms, a stabilizer bar, shock absorbers and a right and left torsion bar, Figs. 7 and 8. Torsion bars are used instead of the conventional coil springs. The front end of the torsion bar is attached to the lower control arm. The rear of the torsion bar is mounted into an adjustable arm in the torsion bar crossmember. The standing height of the car is controlled by this adjustment.

Standing Height, Adjust

The standing height must be checked and adjusted if necessary before checking and adjusting front wheel alignment. The standing height is controlled by the adjustment setting of the torsion bar adjusting bolt, Figs. 7 and 8. Clockwise rotation of the bolt increases standing height: counterclockwise rotation decreases standing height.

To check vehicle height, measure from lower edge of front shock absorber dust tube (A) to centerline of lower attachment (B), Fig. 9. This dimension between (A) and (B) should be 8 3/16–8 7/16 inch on 1977–78 vehicles and 5 1/2–6" on 1979–83 vehicles.

Wheel Alignment, Adjust

1979–83 Eldorado & 1980–83 Seville

Caster

Record camber reading, then hold front cam bolt and loosen nut, Fig. 10. Turn front cam bolt to obtain 1/4 of the desired caster change. At front cam bolt a positive camber change produces a positive caster change and a nega-

Fig. 8   Front suspension disassembled. 1977–78 Eldorado

Fig. 9   Checking standing height
1977–83 Eldorado & 1980–83 Seville

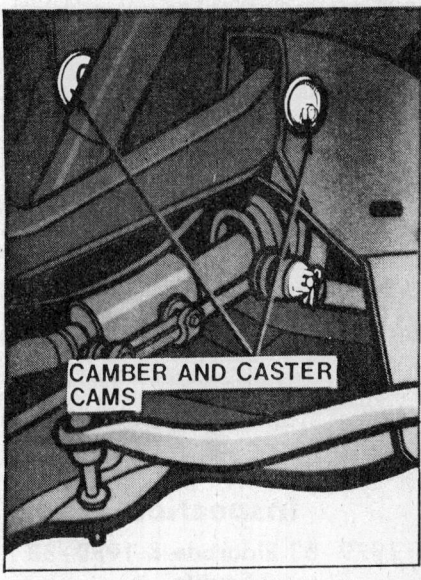

Fig. 10   Caster-camber cam locations.
1977–83 Eldorado & 1980–83 Seville

tive camber change produces a negative caster change. Hold cam bolt in position and tighten nut. Loosen rear cam bolt nut and rotate cam bolt to return camber to setting recorded previously, Fig. 10. When adjustment has been completed hold rear cam bolt and torque nut to 80 ft. lbs.

Camber

While holding cam bolt in position, loosen cam bolt nut, Fig. 10. Rotate cam bolt to obtain a change in camber equal to ½ the needed correction. Hold cam bolt in position and tighten cam bolt nut. To obtain the remaining ½ of needed correction apply the above procedue to the other cam bolt.

1977–78 Eldorado

Caster and camber can be adjusted from under hood or under car. If under hood method is used, adjustments must be rechecked due to the change in weight distribution. After checking vehicle standing height adjust caster and camber as follows:

1. Loosen front and rear adjusting cam nuts, Fig. 10.
2. Rotate front cam to correct for ½ of incorrect camber reading.
3. Rotate rear cam to bring camber reading to 0°.
4. Tighten front and rear cam nuts, then check caster.

NOTE: If caster is within specifications, procede to step 7.

5. If caster is to be adjusted, loosen front and rear cam nuts.
6. Rotate front cam bolt so that camber will change ¼ of desired caster change.

NOTE: A change of 1° in camber reading will change caster reading about 2°. To correct for excessive negative caster rotate front cam bolt to increase positive camber. To correct for excessive positive caster rotate front cam bolt to increase

negative camber.

7. Set camber to specifications by rotating rear cam bolt.
8. Torque front and rear cam nuts to 95 ft. lbs.

NOTE: When tightening cam nuts ensure cam bolt does not move, any movement of cam bolt will affect wheel alignment.

Toe-In, Adjust

Toe-in is adjusted by turning the tie rod adjusting tubes at outer ends of each tie rod after loosening clamp bolts. Readings should be taken only when front wheels are straight ahead and steering gear is on its high spot.

Fig. 11 Sealed wheel bearing assembly. 1979–83 Eldorado & 1980–83 Seville

1979–83 Eldorado & 1980–83 Seville

1. Loosen clamp bolts at each end of tie rod adjusting sleeve.
2. Turn tie rod adjusting sleeve to obtain the proper toe-in adjustment.
3. After completing adjustment, check to ensure that the number of threads at each end of sleeve are equal and tie rod end housings and clamps are properly positioned. Torque clamp bolt to 15 ft. lbs.

1977–78 Eldorado

1. Center steering wheel, raise car and check wheel run-out.
2. Loosen tie rod adjuster nuts and adjust tie rods to obtain the specified toe-in.
3. Tighten tie rod adjuster nuts to 20–22 ft-lbs.
4. Position adjuster clamps so that opening of clamps are facing up. Interference with front suspension components could occur while turning if clamps are facing down.

Wheel Bearing Inspection

1979–83 Eldorado & 1980–83 Seville

The front wheel bearing is a sealed unit bearing. The bearing can not be adjusted or repacked. There are darkened areas on the bearing assembly. These darkened areas are from a heat treatment process and do not indicate need for bearing replacement, Fig. 11.

To check wheel bearing assembly for looseness, free brake pads from disc or remove calipers. Install two lug nuts to secure disc to bearing. Mount dial indicator as shown in Fig. 12, then rock disc and note indicator reading. If looseness exceeds .005 in. replace hub and bearing assembly.

Wheel Bearing & Steering Knuckle, Replace

1977–83 Eldorado & 1980–83 Seville

1. Raise and support vehicle under lower control arms.
2. Remove drive axle nut and washer and remove wheel and tire assembly.

3. Remove brake hose clip from ball joint and replace nut, then remove brake caliper off disc, and using a length of wire support caliper on suspension.

NOTE: Do not allow caliper to hang from brake hose as this could cause damage and premature failure of hose.

4. Mark hub and disc assembly for alignment during assembly and remove disc, then strike steering knuckle in area of upper ball joint until upper ball joint is loose.

CAUTION: Use extreme care to prevent striking and damaging brake hose or ball joint seal.

5. Place a short length of rubber hose over lower control arm torsion bar connector to avoid damage to inboard tri-pot joint seal when hub and knuckle are removed.
6. Using appropriate puller, disconnect tie rod end, upper and lower ball joints and remove steering knuckle and hub assembly, Figs. 13 and 14.

Checking Ball Joints For Wear

1. Raise car and position jack stands under lower control arms as near as possible to each ball joint.
2. Clamp vise grips on end of drive axle and position a dial indicator so that dial indicator ball rests on vise grip, Fig. 15.
3. Place a pry bar between lower control arm and outer race and pry down on bar. Reading must not exceed 1/8".

Upper Ball Joint, Replace

1979–83 Eldorado & 1980–83 Seville

1. Raise vehicle and support under lower control arms.
2. Remove wheel and tire assembly.
3. Remove cotter pin and nut from upper ball joint stud, then disconnect brake hose clip from stud.
4. Using a hammer and brass drift, disengage ball joint stud from steering knuckle.
5. Place a block of wood between control arm and frame, then drill rivets with a 1/8 in. drill bit 1/4 in. deep from top side of control arm.
6. Drill rivet heads off using a 1/2 inch drill bit. Do not drill into control arm.
7. Using a hammer and punch, drive rivets out and remove ball joint.
8. Install ball joint into control arm and torque nuts and bolts 8 ft. lbs.

1977–78 Eldorado

1. Remove upper control arm and grind head off three rivets. Using a hammer and punch, drive out rivets.
2. Install new ball joint, securing it in place with three bolts and nuts contained in the kit.
3. Install upper control arm and lubricate ball joint fitting until grease escapes between seal and steering knuckle, Fig. 16.

Fig. 12 Checking wheel bearing for looseness. 1979–83 Eldorado & 1980–83 Seville

Lower Ball Joint, Replace

1979–83 Eldorado & 1980–83 Seville

1. Remove knuckle.
2. Using 1/8 in. drill bit, drill center of rivets 1/4 in. deep, then using 1/2 in. drill bit, drill deep enough to remove rivet heads.
3. Using a hammer and punch, drive rivets out and remove ball joint.
4. Install service ball joint into control arm and torque bolts 8 ft. lbs.

1977–78 Eldorado

1. Remove lower control arm and cut off two rivet heads from sides of control arm. Grind off head of rivet at bottom of control arm, then drive rivet out of arm.
2. Install service ball joint, securing it to control arm with bolts and nuts contained in kit.

Torsion Bar, Replace

1977–78 Eldorado

Removal

1. Support vehicle so front suspension hangs at full rebound position.
2. Remove adjusting bolts from torsion bar adjuster nuts.
3. Install tool J-22517-01 on torsion bar crossmember, Fig. 17. It may be necessary to pry the crossmember downward to install the tool "U"-bolt.
4. Tighten tool center bolt until torsion bar adjusting arm is raised enough to permit removal of adjuster nut, then remove nut.
5. Loosen tool center bolt until clear of adjusting arm.
6. Repeat steps 3 through 5 on other end of crossmember.
7. Remove parking brake cable from guide at right side of vehicle.
8. Remove torsion bar crossmember bolts, nuts, shim and retainer from both ends of crossmember. Move crossmember as far as possible toward the side opposite torsion bar being removed. One end of crossmember should be clear of frame.

9. Lower end of crossmember and drive rearward until torsion bar is free from crossmember.

NOTE: Use caution not to damage parking brake cable when lowering crossmember. It may be necessary to loosen parking brake cable at equalizer to provide additional slack.

10. Remove torsion bar from lower control arm connector.

NOTE: It is possible to remove both torsion bars at one time, however, installation is easier with one torsion mounted at all times.

Inspection
1. Check torsion bar for nicks, scratches or dents. If any of these conditions exist the torsion bar must be replaced.

Installation
1. Lubricate approximately three inches of each end of torsion bar with suitable lubricant, P/N 9985092 or equivalent.
2. Install torsion bar into lower control arm connector.

NOTE: Torsion bars are stamped with letters "R" for right hand and "L" for left hand. The stamped end of torsion bar is installed in lower control chamber.

3. Position torsion bar adjusting arm in crossmember, hold arm in place and slide torsion bar rearward until seated in adjusting arm.

NOTE: The tape on torsion bar, located near lower control arm connector, should be fully visible but within ¼ inch of connector.

4. Position crossmember on frame and install shim between crossmember and frame on each side. Install retainer over crossmember insulator.
5. Ensure torsion bar adjusting arms are properly positioned and install and torque crossmember nuts and bolts to 120 inch lbs.

Fig. 13 Wheel bearing & steering knuckle assembly. 1979–83 Eldorado & 1980–83 Seville

Fig. 14 Wheel bearing & steering knuckle assembly. 1977–78 Eldorado

6. Install parking brake cable through guide on vehicle right side and adjust cable if loosened.
7. Install tool J-22517 or J-22517-01 and tighten tool center bolt until torsion bar adjusting arm is raised enough to install adjuster nut and install nut. Remove tool.
8. Lubricate threads on new torsion bar adjusting bolts and install bolts into adjuster nuts.
9. Check vehicle standing height and wheel alignment. Adjust if necessary.

1979–83 Eldorado & 1980–83 Seville

1. Raise and support vehicle, then remove

Fig. 15 Checking ball joints for wear. 1977–83 Eldorado & 1980–83 Seville

Fig. 16 Repacking upper ball joint. 1977–78 Eldorado

Fig. 17 Torsion bar removal tool installation 1977–78 Eldorado

Fig. 18 Torsion bar removal. 1979–83 Eldorado & 1980–83 Seville

parts as shown in Fig. 18.
2. Remove torsion bar adjusting screw as shown in Fig. 18.

NOTE: Count number of turns when removing screw. When installing, turn screw in the same number of turns to return vehicle to proper height.

3. Slide torsion bar forward in lower control arm until torsion bar clears support, then pull down on bar and remove from control arm.
4. Reverse procedure to install.

POWER STEERING GEAR, REPLACE

1. Disconnect pressure and return lines from gear and plug all lines and openings.
2. Remove stone shield, if equipped. On Eldorado and 1980–83 Seville, remove plastic retainers from frame coupling shield, then remove shield.
3. Remove nuts and bolts from flex coupling, then raise and support vehicle.
4. Remove pitman arm nut, then remove pitman arm from pitman arm shaft on all except Eldorado and 1980–83 Seville and from intermediate shaft on Eldorado and 1980–83 Seville.
5. On all except Eldorado and 1980–83 Seville, remove steering gear to frame retaining bolts, then remove gear. On Eldorado and 1980–83 Seville, remove steering gear to frame bolts, then remove gear by positioning forward and downward. Remove nut from pitman shaft, then remove pitman arm from shaft.

POWER STEERING PUMP, REPLACE

1977–80

Except Seville

1. Disconnect pressure and return lines from pump and filter inlet.
2. Remove nut securing pump mounting bracket to cylinder head stud.
3. Remove adjusting screw securing mounting bracket to front of cylinder block.
4. Remove drive belts from pulley.
5. Remove bottom pivot screw and steering pump with bracket and filter attached.
6. Reverse procedure to install.

Seville

1. Remove alternator and alternator adjusting bracket.
2. Disconnect pressure and return lines at pump.
3. Loosen pump adjusting bolt, pivot bolt and pivot nut. Remove belt from pulley.
4. Remove nuts and spacer securing pump mounting bracket to water pump and timing chain cover.
5. Remove bracket connecting bolt, then remove pump and bracket as an assembly.

1981–83

V6-252

1. Disconnect pressure and return lines from pump.
2. Loosen adjusting screws on front and rear bracket, then remove drive belt.
3. Remove adjusting screws securing front of mounting bracket.
4. Remove adjusting nut securing pump to rear mounting bracket.
5. Remove pivot screw, then remove steering pump and bracket as an assembly.
6. Reverse procedure to install.

V8-250

1. Loosen A/C mounting bracket and vacuum pump bracket, then remove belts from pulley.
2. Disconnect pressure and return lines from pump and plug all openings.
3. Remove two bolts holding pump to engine block through access holes in pulley, then remove pump.
4. Reverse procedure to install.

V8-350

1. Remove cruise control servo as necessary, if equipped.
2. Loosen generator adjusting bolt, then remove alternator belt. Pivot alternator aside with wiring attached.
3. Remove alternator adjusting bracket, then disconnect pressure and return hoses from pump.
4. Loosen pump adjusting bolt, pivot bolt and pivot nut. Remove belt from pulley.
5. Remove nuts and spacer securing pump mounting bracket to water pump and timing chain cover. Remove bracket connecting bolt, then remove steering pump and bracket as an assembly.
6. Reverse procedure to install.

V8-368

1. Disconnect pressure and return lines from steering pump.
2. Loosen vacuum pump adjusting screw, then remove drive belt.
3. Remove nut securing pump mounting bracket to cylinder head stud.
4. Remove adjusting screw and nuts securing mounting bracket.
5. Remove drive belts from pulley.
6. Remove nut and bolt securing vacuum pump brace, then remove brace.
7. Remove pivot bolt, then remove pump and bracket as an assembly.
8. Reverse procedure to install.

CAMARO · CHEVROLET
CORVETTE · MALIBU
MONTE CARLO · NOVA

INDEX OF SERVICE OPERATIONS

NOTE: Refer to the back of this manual for vehicle manufacturer's special service tool suppliers.

SERIAL NUMBER LOCATION

Plate on left front door pillar or top of left side instrument panel

ENGINE NUMBER LOCATION

Buick built engines have the distributor located at the front of the engine. On 1979–83 models, the engine production code is located on front of right hand valve cover and top of left hand valve cover. On 1978 models, the engine production code is located on the right front of block.

On Chevrolet built 6-250 engines, the code is located on the cylinder block next to the distributor. Chevrolet built V8 engines have the distributor located at the rear of the engine with clockwise rotor rotation. On 1979–83 engines, the engine production code is located front of right hand valve cover. On 1977–78 V8 engines, the code is stamped on the right hand side of engine.

Pontiac built 4-151 engine, stamped on engine flange at left rear of engine above drive end of starter motor.

ENGINE IDENTIFICATION CODE

Engines are identified in the following table by the code letter or letters immediately following the engine serial number.

ENGINE V.I.N. CODE

On 1977–80 vehicles, the fifth digit in the V.I.N. denotes engine code. On 1981–83 vehicles, the eighth digit in the V.I.N. denotes engine code.

CAMARO

CODE		V.I.N. CODE	YEAR	CODE		V.I.N. CODE	YEAR	CODE		V.I.N. CODE	YEAR
CCD	6-250	D	1977	DRL	8-350	L	1979	X3H	4-151③	2	1982
CCF	6-250	D	1977	DRY	8-350	L	1979	X5A	4-151③	2	1982
CCW	6-250	D	1977	DTM	8-305	G	1979	X5F	4-151③	2	1982
CKH	6-250	D	1977	C8B	8-305	G	1979	X5H	4-151③	2	1982
CKM	8-350	L	1977	C8C	8-350	L	1979	CBT	V6-173	1	1982
CKR	8-350	L	1977	CRA	V6-229	K	1980	CBU	V6-173	1	1982
CKS	8-350	L	1977	CRC	V6-229	K	1980	CBW	V6-173	1	1982
CPA	8-305	U	1977	OM	V6-231①	A	1980	CBX	V6-173	1	1982
CPC	8-305	U	1977	ON	V6-231①	A	1980	CBZ	V6-173	1	1982
CPY	8-305	U	1977	C8X	8-267	J	1980	CJB	V6-173	1	1982
C2K	8-305	U	1977	CPD	8-267	J	1980	CKA	V6-173	1	1982
C2L	8-305	U	1977	D9B	8-305	H	1980	CKB	V6-173	1	1982
C8Y	6-250	D	1977	CEJ	8-305	H	1980	C7A	V6-173	1	1982
CCC	6-250	D	1977	CEL	8-305	H	1980	C7B	V6-173	1	1982
CCH	6-250	D	1978	CEM	8-305	H	1980	C7C	V6-173	1	1982
CCJ	6-250	D	1978	CET	8-305	H	1980	C7D	V6-173	1	1982
CCK	6-250	D	1978	CML	8-305	H	1980	CFA	V8-305	H	1982
C3Y	6-250	D	1978	CHA	8-350	L	1980	CFB	V8-305	H	1982
CTH	8-305	U	1978	CEU	8-350	L	1980	CFC	V8-305	H	1982
CTJ	8-305	U	1978	DAH	V6-229	K	1981	CFD	V8-305	H	1982
CTK	8-305	U	1978	DAJ	V6-229	K	1981	CFF	V8-305	H	1982
C3N	8-305	U	1978	RA	V6-231①	A	1981	CFH	V8-305	H	1982
CHF	8-350	L	1978	DFH	V8-267	J	1981	CFR	V8-305	H	1982
CHJ	8-350	L	1978	D8H	V8-267	J	1981	CFT	V8-305	H	1982
CHL	8-350	L	1978	DHJ	V8-305	H	1981	CFW	V8-305	H	1982
CHR	8-350	L	1978	DHK	V8-305	H	1981	CFY	V8-305	H	1982
CHS	8-350	L	1978	D6D	V8-305	H	1981	CFZ	V8-305	H	1982
CHT	8-350	L	1978	DHZ	V8-305	H	1981	CRA	V8-305	H	1982
CHU	8-350	L	1978	DKB	V8-305	H	1981	C2R	V8-305	H	1982
C3T	8-350	L	1978	DMA	V8-350	L	1981	C2S	V8-305	H	1982
DKA	6-250	D	1979	D5A	V8-350	L	1981	C2T	V8-305	H	1982
DKB	6-250	D	1979	D5B	V8-350	L	1981	C2U	V8-305	H	1982
DKD	6-250	D	1979	5A	4-151③	9	1982	C2W	V8-305	H	1982
DNH	8-305	G	1979	5F	4-151③	9	1982	C2X	V8-305	H	1982
DNK	8-305	G	1979	5H	4-151③	9	1982	CFJ	V8-305	7	1982
DRC	8-350	L	1979	X3A	4-151③	2	1982	CFK	V8-305	7	1982
DRD	8-350	L	1979	X3C	4-151③	2	1982	CFM	V8-305	7	1982
DRF	8-350	L	1979	X3F	4-151③	2	1982	CFN	V8-305	7	1982
DRH	8-350	L	1979								

CHEVROLET

CODE		V.I.N. CODE	YEAR	CODE		V.I.N. CODE	YEAR	CODE		V.I.N. CODE	YEAR
CCC	6-250	D	1977	CUD	8-350	L	1977	CHH	8-350	L	1978
CCF	6-250	D	1977	CCA	6-250	D	1977	CHJ	8-350	L	1978
CCR	6-250	D	1977	CJA	6-250	D	1977	CHK	8-350	L	1978
CCS	6-250	D	1977	CJB	6-250	D	1977	CHL	8-350	L	1978
CKA	8-350	L	1977	CJF	6-250	D	1977	CHM	8-350	L	1978
CKB	8-350	L	1977	CCH	6-250	D	1978	CNT	8-350	L	1978
CKC	8-350	L	1977	CCK	6-250	D	1978	DCA	6-250	D	1979
CLL	8-350	L	1977	CCL	6-250	D	1978	DCB	6-250	D	1979
CMM	8-350	L	1977	CCM	6-250	D	1978	DCC	6-250	D	1979
CPM	8-305	U	1977	CEJ	8-305	U	1978	DCD	6-250	D	1979
CPR	8-305	U	1977	CEK	8-305	U	1978	DKB	6-250	D	1979
CUB	8-350	L	1977	CTL	8-305	U	1978	DKC	6-250	D	1979
CUC	8-350	L	1977	CHF	8-350	L	1978	DKD	6-250	D	1979

Continued

CHEVROLET—Continued

CODE		V.I.N. CODE	YEAR	CODE		V.I.N. CODE	YEAR	CODE		V.I.N. CODE	YEAR
DKF	6-250	D	1979	D8D	V8-267	J	1981	C4U	V8-267	J	1982
DNL	8-305	G	1979	D8F	V8-267	J	1981	C4W	V8-267	J	1982
DNM	8-305	G	1979	DHD	V8-305	H	1981	CFA	V8-305	H	1982
DNR	8-305	G	1979	DHF	V8-305	H	1981	CFB	V8-305	H	1982
DRA	8-350	L	1979	DHH	V8-305	H	1981	CFC	V8-305	H	1982
DRB	8-350	L	1979	DHR	V8-305	H	1981	CFD	V8-305	H	1982
DRH	8-350	L	1979	DHS	V8-305	H	1981	CFF	V8-305	H	1982
DRJ	8-350	L	1979	DHT	V8-305	H	1981	CFH	V8-305	H	1982
DRK	8-350	L	1979	D6B	V8-305	H	1981	CFR	V8-305	H	1982
DRL	8-350	L	1979	D6C	V8-305	H	1981	CFT	V8-305	H	1982
DRY	8-350	L	1979	DMD	V8-350	L	1981	CFW	V8-305	H	1982
DRZ	8-350	L	1979	VKH	V8-350②	N	1981	CFY	V8-305	H	1982
DTY	V8-305	G	1979	VKJ	V8-350②	N	1981	CFZ	V8-305	H	1982
DTZ	V8-305	G	1979	VKK	V8-350②	N	1981	CRA	V8-305	H	1982
DXA	V8-305	G	1979	VKN	V8-350②	N	1981	C2R	V8-305	H	1982
DUB	8-350	L	1979	VKP	V8-350②	N	1981	C2S	V8-305	H	1982
DUC	8-350	L	1979	CCA	V6-229	K	1982	C2T	V8-305	H	1982
DUD	8-350	L	1979	CCC	V6-229	K	1982	C2U	V8-305	H	1982
CLC	V6-229	K	1980	CCF	V6-229	K	1982	C2W	V8-305	H	1982
ES	V6-231①	A	1980	CCH	V6-229	K	1982	C2X	V8-305	H	1982
ET	V6-231①	A	1980	CCK	V6-229	K	1982	VAB	V8-350②	N	1982
CPC	8-267	J	1980	CCM	V6-229	K	1982	VAC	V8-350②	N	1982
CPH	8-267	J	1980	CCN	V6-229	K	1982	VAD	V8-350②	N	1982
CED	8-305	H	1980	CCR	V6-229	K	1982	VAK	V8-350②	N	1982
CEH	8-305	H	1980	CCS	V6-229	K	1982	VAL	V8-350②	N	1982
CMH	8-305	H	1980	MA	V6-231①	A	1982	VAM	V8-350②	N	1982
CMJ	8-305	H	1980	MC	V6-231①	A	1982	VAN	V8-350②	N	1982
CMR	8-305	H	1980	MG	V6-231①	A	1982	VAP	V8-350②	N	1982
CMS	8-305	H	1980	MK	V6-231①	A	1982	VAS	V8-350②	N	1982
CMT	8-305	H	1980	ML	V6-231①	A	1982	VAU	V8-350②	N	1982
CHC	8-350	L	1980	MM	V6-231①	A	1982	VAW	V8-350②	N	1982
VBS	8-350 Diesel②	N	1980	CDB	V8-267	J	1982	VAX	V8-350②	N	1982
VBT	8-350 Diesel②	N	1980	CDC	V8-267	J	1982	VAY	V8-350②	N	1982
DAD	V6-229	K	1981	CDD	V8-267	J	1982	VAZ	V8-350②	N	1982
NL	V6-231①	A	1981	CDJ	V8-267	J	1982	VBA	V8-350②	N	1982
RL	V6-231①	A	1981	C4N	V8-267	J	1982	VBL	V8-350②	N	1982
RK	V6-231①	A	1981	C4R	V8-267	J	1982	VBP	V8-350②	N	1982
DFD	V8-267	J	1981	C4S	V8-267	J	1982	VBW	V8-350②	N	1982
DFF	V8-267	J	1981	C4T	V8-267	J	1982	VB4	V8-350②	N	1982

MALIBU & MONTE CARLO

CODE		V.I.N. CODE	YEAR	CODE		V.I.N. CODE	YEAR	CODE		V.I.N. CODE	YEAR
CCC	6-250	D	1977	SJ	V6-231①	A	1979	CRC	V6-229	K	1980
CCD	6-250	D	1977	SO	V6-231①	A	1979	ED	V6-231①	A	1980
CCF	6-250	D	1977	DHA	V6-200	M	1979	EF	V6-231①	A	1980
CKH	8-350	L	1977	DHB	V6-200	M	1979	EG	V6-231①	A	1980
CKJ	8-350	L	1977	DHC	V6-200	M	1979	EH	V6-231①	3	1980
CKK	8-350	L	1977	DMA	8-267	J	1979	OP	V6-231①	A	1980
CKM	8-350	L	1977	DMB	8-267	J	1979	OR	V6-231①	A	1980
CKR	8-350	L	1977	DMC	8-267	J	1979	CPA	8-267	J	1980
CPY	8-305	U	1977	DMD	8-267	J	1979	CPB	8-267	J	1980
EA	6-231①	A	1978	DMF	8-267	J	1979	CEA	8-305	H	1980
OH	6-231①	A	1978	DMH	8-267	J	1979	CEC	8-305	H	1980
OK	6-231①	A	1978	DNS	8-305	H	1979	CER	8-305	H	1980
CWA	6-250	D	1978	DNT	8-305	H	1979	CMC	8-305	H	1980
CWB	6-250	D	1978	DNU	8-305	H	1979	CMD	8-305	H	1980
CWC	6-250	D	1978	DNW	8-305	H	1979	CMF	8-305	H	1980
CWD	6-250	D	1978	DNX	8-305	H	1979	CMM	8-305	H	1980
CER	8-305	U	1978	DNY	8-305	H	1979	CHB	8-350	L	1980
CPZ	8-305	U	1978	DRX	8-350	L	1979	DAA	V6-229	K	1981
CRU	8-305	U	1978	DTA	8-305	H	1979	DAB	V6-229	K	1981
CRW	8-305	U	1978	DTB	8-305	H	1979	DAC	V6-229	K	1981
CRX	8-305	U	1978	DTF	8-305	H	1979	D7A	V6-229	K	1981
CRY	8-305	U	1978	DTH	8-305	H	1979	D7B	V6-229	K	1981
CRZ	8-305	U	1978	DTJ	8-305	H	1979	DAK	V6-229	K	1981
CMA	8-350	U	1978	DTS	8-305	H	1979	NB	V6-231①	A	1981
CMB	8-350	L	1978	DTU	8-305	H	1979	NE	V6-231①	3	1981
CMC	8-350	L	1978	DTW	8-305	H	1979	RO	V6-231①	3	1981
CMD	8-350	L	1978	DTX	8-305	H	1979	DFA	V8-267	J	1981
NJ	V6-231①	A	1979	DUF	8-350	L	1979	DFB	V8-267	J	1981
RA	V6-231①	A	1979	DUH	8-350	L	1979	DFC	V8-267	J	1981
RB	V6-231①	A	1979	DUJ	8-350	L	1979	D8A	V8-267	J	1981
RJ	V6-231①	A	1979	CLA	V6-229	K	1980	D8B	V8-267	J	1981
RM	V6-231①	A	1979	CLB	V6-229	K	1980	D8C	V8-267	J	1981

Continued

MALIBU & MONTE CARLO—Continued

CODE		V.I.N. CODE	YEAR	CODE		V.I.N. CODE	YEAR	CODE		V.I.N. CODE	YEAR
DHA	V8-305	H	1981	MG	V6-231①	A	1982	CFB	V8-305	H	1982
DHB	V8-305	H	1981	MK	V6-231①	A	1982	CFC	V8-305	H	1982
DHC	V8-305	H	1981	ML	V6-231①	A	1982	CFD	V8-305	H	1982
DHM	V8-305	H	1981	MM	V6-231①	A	1982	CFF	V8-305	H	1982
DHN	V8-305	H	1981	UAA	V6-262②	V	1982	CFH	V8-305	H	1982
D6A	V8-305	H	1981	UAD	V6-262②	V	1982	CFR	V8-305	H	1982
DMC	V8-350	L	1981	UAJ	V6-262②	V	1982	CFT	V8-305	H	1982
CCA	V6-229	K	1982	CDB	V8-267	J	1982	CFW	V8-305	H	1982
CCC	V6-229	K	1982	CDC	V8-267	J	1982	CFY	V8-305	H	1982
CCF	V6-229	K	1982	CDD	V8-267	J	1982	CFZ	V8-305	H	1982
CCH	V6-229	K	1982	CDJ	V8-267	J	1982	CRA	V8-305	H	1982
CCK	V6-229	K	1982	C4N	V8-267	J	1982	C2R	V8-305	H	1982
CCM	V6-229	K	1982	C4R	V8-267	J	1982	C2S	V8-305	H	1982
CCN	V6-229	K	1982	C4S	V8-267	J	1982	C2T	V8-305	H	1982
CCR	V6-229	K	1982	C4T	V8-267	J	1982	C2U	V8-305	H	1982
CCS	V6-229	K	1982	C4U	V8-267	J	1982	C2W	V8-305	H	1982
MA	V6-231①	A	1982	C4W	V8-267	J	1982	C2X	V8-305	H	1982
MC	V6-231①	A	1982	CFA	V8-305	H	1982				

CHEVY NOVA

CODE		V.I.N. CODE	YEAR	CODE		V.I.N. CODE	YEAR	CODE		V.I.N. CODE	YEAR
CCD	6-250	D	1977	C2D	6-250	D	1977	CHJ	8-350	L	1978
CCF	6-250	D	1977	C2K	8-305	U	1977	CHL	8-350	L	1978
CCT	6-250	D	1977	C2L	8-305	U	1977	DKA	6-250	D	1979
CCU	6-250	D	1977	C8Y	6-250	D	1977	DKB	6-250	D	1979
CCW	6-250	D	1977	CCH	6-250	D	1978	DKD	6-250	D	1979
CKH	8-350	L	1977	CCK	6-250	D	1978	DNF	8-305	G	1979
CKM	8-350	L	1977	CCJ	6-250	D	1978	DNJ	8-305	G	1979
CKR	8-350	L	1977	C2D	6-250	D	1978	DNK	8-305	G	1979
CKS	8-350	L	1977	CTH	8-305	U	1978	DRJ	8-350	L	1979
CPA	8-305	U	1977	CTJ	8-305	U	1978	DRY	8-350	L	1979
CPC	8-305	U	1977	CTK	8-305	U	1978	DTM	8-305	G	1979
CPY	8-305	U	1977	C2K	8-305	U	1978	C8D	8-305	G	1979

CORVETTE

CODE		V.I.N. CODE	YEAR	CODE		V.I.N. CODE	YEAR	CODE		V.I.N. CODE	YEAR
CKZ	8-350	L	1977	CLR	8-350	L	1978	ZCA	8-305	4	1980
CLA	8-350	L	1977	CLS	8-350	L	1978	ZAK	8-350	8	1980
CLB	8-350	L	1977	CMR	8-350	H	1978	ZBC	8-350	6	1980
CLC	8-350	L	1977	CMS	8-350	H	1978	ZAM	8-350	8	1980
CLD	8-350	X	1977	ZAA	8-350	8	1979	ZBD	8-350	6	1980
CLF	8-350	X	1977	ZAB	8-350	8	1979	ZDA	V8-350	6	1981
CLH	8-350	L	1977	ZAC	8-350	8	1979	ZDB	V8-350	6	1981
CHD	8-350	L	1977	ZAD	8-350	8	1979	ZBA	V8-350	6	1982
CKD	8-350	L	1977	ZAF	8-350	8	1979	ZBC	V8-350	6	1982
CHW	8-350	L	1978	ZBA	8-350	4	1979	ZFN	V8-350	6	1982
CLM	8-350	L	1978	ZBB	8-350	4	1979				

①—Buick built engine.　②—Oldsmobile built engine.　③—Pontiac built engine.

GRILLE IDENTIFICATION

1977 Nova

1977 Nova Concours

1977 Malibu Classic

Continued

1977 Monte Carlo

1977 Impala

1977 Caprice & Estate Wagon

1977–78 Corvette

1978 Camaro

1978 Camaro Z28

1978 Caprice & Estate Wagon

1978 Chevy Nova

1978 Impala

1978 Malibu

1978 Malibu Classic

1978–79 Monte Carlo

1979 Corvette

1979 Chevy Nova

1979 Caprice

1979 Camaro

1979 Camaro Z28

1979 Malibu

GRILLE IDENTIFICATION—Continued

1980 Malibu Classic

1980 Caprice Classic

1980 Impala

1980 Monte Carlo

1980–81 Camaro Sport Coupe

1980–81 Camaro Berlinetta

1980–81 Camaro Z28

1980–82 Corvette

1981 Malibu

1981 Monte Carlo

1981–82 Caprice

1982 Malibu

1982 Monte Carlo

1982–83 Camaro Exc. Z28

1982–83 Camaro Z28

1983 Malibu

1983 Monte Carlo

GENERAL ENGINE SPECIFICATIONS

Year	Engine CID①/Liter	Engine V.I.N. Code ②	Carburetor	Bore and Stroke	Compression Ratio	Net Brake H.P. @ R.P.M.③	Maximum Torque Ft. Lbs. @ R.P.M.	Normal Oil Pressure Pounds
1977	6-250, 4.1L	D	1ME, 1 Bbl. ④	3.875 × 3.53	8.25	110 @ 3800	195 @ 1600	36–41
	V8-305, 5.0L	U	2GC, 2 Bbl.④	3.736 × 3.48	8.5	145 @ 3800	245 @ 2400	32–40
	V8-350, 5.7L	L	M4MC, 4 Bbl.④	4.00 × 3.48	8.5	170 @ 3800	270 @ 2400	32–40
	V8-350, 5.7L	L	M4MC, 4 Bbl.④	4.00 × 3.48	8.5	180 @ 4000	270 @ 2400	32–40
	V8-350, 5.7L	X	M4MC, 4 Bbl.④	4.00 × 3.48	9.0	210 @ 5200	255 @ 3600	32–40
1978	V6-200, 3.3L	M	M2ME, 2 Bbl.④	3.50 × 3.48	8.2	95 @ 3800	160 @ 2000	34–39
	V6-231, 3.8L⑤	A	2GE, 2 Bbl.④	3.80 × 3.40	8.0	103 @ 3800	180 @ 2000	37
	6-250, 4.1L	D	1 ME, 1 Bbl.④	3.875 × 3.53	8.2	90 @ 3600	180 @ 1600	36–41
	6-250, 4.1L	D	1ME, 1 Bbl.④	3.875 × 3.53	8.2	110 @ 3800	195 @ 1600	36–41
	V8-305, 5.0L	U	2GC, 2 Bbl.④	3.736 × 3.48	8.5	135 @ 3800	240 @ 2000	45
	V8-305, 5.0L	U	2GC, 2 Bbl.④	3.736 × 3.48	8.5	145 @ 3800	245 @ 2000	45
	V8-350, 5.7L	L	M4MC, 4 Bbl.④	4.00 × 3.48	8.2	160 @ 3800	260 @ 2400	32–40
	V8-350, 5.7L	L	M4MC, 4 Bbl.④	4.00 × 3.48	8.2	170 @ 3800	270 @ 2400	32–40
	V8-350, 5.7L	L	M4MC, 4 Bbl.④	4.00 × 3.48	8.2	175 @ 3800	265 @ 2400	32–40
	V8-350, 5.7L	L	M4MC, 4 Bbl.④	4.00 × 3.48	8.2	185 @ 4000	280 @ 2400	32–40
1979	V6-200, 3.3L	M	M2ME, 2 Bbl.④	3.50 × 3.48	8.2	95 @ 3800	160 @ 2000	45
	V6-231, 3.8L③	A	M2ME, 2 Bbl.④	3.80 × 3.40	8.0	115 @ 3800	190 @ 2000	37
	6-250, 4.1L	D	1ME, 1 Bbl.④	3.876 × 3.53	8.1	90 @ 3600	175 @ 1600	40
	6-250, 4.1L	D	1ME, 1 Bbl.④	3.876 × 3.53	8.0	115 @ 3800	200 @ 1600	40
	V8-267, 4.4L	J	M2MC, 2 Bbl.④	3.50 × 3.48	8.2	125 @ 3800	215 @ 2400	45
	V8-305, 5.0L	G	M2MC, 2 Bbl.④	3.736 × 3.48	8.4	125 @ 3200	235 @ 2000	45
	V8-305, 5.0L	G	M2MC, 2 Bbl.④	3.736 × 3.48	8.4	130 @ 3200	245 @ 2000	45
	V8-305, 5.0L	H	M4MC, 4 Bbl.④	3.736 × 3.48	8.4	155 @ 4000	225 @ 2400	45
	V8-305, 5.0L	H	M4MC, 4 Bbl.④	3.736 × 3.48	8.4	160 @ 4000	235 @ 2000	45
	V8-350, 5.7L	L	M4MC, 4 Bbl.④	4.00 × 3.48	8.2	165 @ 3800	260 @ 2400	45
	V8-350, 5.7L	L	M4MC, 4 Bbl.④	4.00 × 3.48	8.2	170 @ 4000	265 @ 2400	45
	V8-350, 5.7L	L	M4MC, 4 Bbl.④	4.00 × 3.48	8.2	170 @ 3800	270 @ 2400	45
	V8-350, 5.7L	L	M4MC, 4 Bbl.④	4.00 × 3.48	8.2	175 @ 4000	270 @ 2400	45
	V8-350, 5.7L	L	M4MC, 4 Bbl.④	4.00 × 3.48	8.9	195 @ 4000	280 @ 2400	45
	V8-350, 5.7L	L	M4MC, 4 Bbl.④	4.00 × 3.48	8.2	195 @ 4000	285 @ 3200	45
	V8-350, 5.7L	L	M4MC, 4 Bbl.④	4.00 × 3.48	8.9	225 @ 5200	270 @ 3600	45
1980	V6-229, 3.8L	K	M2ME, 2 Bbl.④	3.736 × 3.48	8.6	115 @ 4000	175 @ 2000	45
	V6-231, 3.8L⑤	A	M2ME, 2 Bbl.⑥④	3.80 × 3.40	8.0	110 @ 3800	190 @ 1600	45
	V6-231, 3.8L⑤⑦	3	M4ME, 4 Bbl.④⑧	3.80 × 3.40	8.0	170 @ 4000	265 @ 2400	37
	V8-267, 4.4L	J	M2ME, 2 Bbl.④	3.50 × 3.48	8.5	120 @ 3600	215 @ 2000	45
	V8-305, 5.0L	8	M4ME, 4 Bbl.④⑧	3.736 × 3.48	8.6	155 @ 4000	240 @ 1600	45
	V8-305⑫	H	M4ME④	3.736 × 3.48	8.5	180 @ 4200	255 @ 2000	45
	V8-350, 5.7L⑬	L	M4ME, 4 Bbl.④	4.00 × 3.48	8.5	190 @ 4200	280 @ 2400	45
	V8-350, 5.7L⑫	6	M4ME, 4 Bbl.④	4.00 × 3.48	9.0	230 @ 5200	275 @ 3600	45
	V8-350, 5.7L⑫	8	M4ME, 4 Bbl.④	4.00 × 3.48	8.5	190 @ 4400	280 @ 2400	45
	V8-350, 5.7L⑨⑩	N	Fuel Injected	4.057 × 3.385	22.5	105 @ 3200	205 @ 1600	30–45
1981	V6-229, 3.8L⑪	K	E2ME, 2 Bbl.④	3.736 × 3.48	8.6	110 @ 4200	170 @ 2000	45
	V6-231, 3.8L⑤	A	E2ME, 2 Bbl.④	3.80 × 3.40	8.0	110 @ 3800	190 @ 1600	45
	V6-231, 3.8L⑤⑦	3	E4ME, 4 Bbl.④	3.80 × 3.40	8.0	170 @ 4000	275 @ 2400	45
	V8-267, 4.4L⑪	J	E2ME, 2 Bbl.④	3.50 × 3.48	8.3	115 @ 4000	200 @ 2400	45
	V8-305, 5.0L	H	E4ME, 4 Bbl.④	3.736 × 3.48	8.6	150 @ 3800	240 @ 2400	45
	V8-305⑬	H	M4ME④	3.736 × 3.48	8.6	165 @ 4000	180 @ 4200	45
	V8-350, 5.7L	L	E4ME, 4 Bbl.④	4.00 × 3.48	8.2	175 @ 4000	275 @ 2400	45
	V8-350, 5.7L⑫	6	E4ME, 4 Bbl.④	4.00 × 3.48	8.2	190 @ 4200	280 @ 1600	45
	V8-350, 5.7L⑨⑩	N	Fuel Injection	4.057 × 3.385	22.5	105 @ 3200	200 @ 1600	45
1982	4-151, 2.5L⑭	2	Fuel Injection	4.00 × 3.00	8.2	90 @ 4000	132 @ 2800	37.5
	V6-173, 2.8L	1	E2SE, 2 Bbl.④	3.50 × 2.99	8.5	102 @ 4800	142 @ 2400	50–65
	V6-229, 3.8L⑪	K	E2ME, 2 Bbl.④	3.736 × 3.480	8.6	110 @ 4200	170 @ 2000	50–65

Continued

GENERAL ENGINE SPECIFICATIONS—Continued

Year	Engine CID①/Liter	V.I.N. Code ②	Carburetor	Bore and Stroke	Compression Ratio	Net Brake H.P. @ R.P.M.③	Maximum Torque Ft. Lbs. @ R.P.M.	Normal Oil Pressure Pounds
	V6-231, 3.8L⑤	A	E2ME, 2 Bbl.④	3.80 × 3.40	8.0	110 @ 3800	190 @ 1600	50–65
	V6-262, 4.3L⑨⑩	V	Fuel Injection	4.057 × 3.385	22.5	85 @ 3600	165 @ 1600	30–45
	V8-267, 4.4L⑪	J	E2ME, 2 Bbl.④	3.50 × 3.48	8.3	115 @ 4000	205 @ 2400	45
	V8-305, 5.0L	H	E4ME, 4 Bbl.④	3.736 × 3.480	8.6	145 @ 4000	240 @ 2000	50–65
	V8-305, 5.0L	7	Fuel Injection	3.736 × 3.480	9.5	165 @ 4200	240 @ 2400	50–65
	V8-350, 5.7L	6	Fuel Injection	4.00 × 3.48	9.0	200 @ 4200	285 @ 2800	45
	V8-350, 5.7L⑨⑩	N	Fuel Injection	4.057 × 3.385	22.5	105 @ 3200	200 @ 1600	30–45
1983	4-151, 2.5L⑭	2	Fuel Injection	4.00 × 3.00	8.2	92 @ 4000	134 @ 2800	37.5
	V6-173, 2.8L	1	E2SE, 2 Bbl.④	3.50 × 2.99	8.5	107 @ 4800	145 @ 2100	50–65
	V6-229, 3.8L	K	E2ME, 2 Bbl.④	3.736 × 3.480	8.6	110 @ 4200	170 @ 2000	50–65
	V6-231, 3.8L⑤	A	E2ME, 2 Bbl.④	3.80 × 3.40	8.0	110 @ 3800	190 @ 1600	45
	V6-262, 4.3L⑨⑩	V	Fuel Injection	4.057 × 3.385	21.6	85 @ 3600	165 @ 1600	30–45
	V8-305, 5.0L	H	E4ME, 4 Bbl.④	3.736 × 3.480	8.6	150 @ 3800	240 @ 2400	50–65
	V8-305, 5.0L	7	Fuel Injection	3.736 × 3.480	9.5	175 @ 4200	250 @ 2800	45
	V8-350, 5.7L⑨⑩	N	Fuel Injection	4.057 × 3.385	21.6	105 @ 3200	200 @ 1600	30–45

①—C.I.D.—Cubic inch displacement.
②—V.I.N.—On 1977–80 vehicles, the fifth digit in the V.I.N. denotes engine code. On 1981–83 vehicles, the 8th digit in the V.I.N. denotes engine code.
③—Ratings are net—As installed in the vehicle.
④—Rochester.
⑤—For service procedures on this engine, see Buick chapter.
⑥—Calif. V6-231 with Electronic Fuel Control E2ME.
⑦—Turbocharged.
⑧—Calif. V8 with Electronic Fuel Control, E4ME.
⑨—For service procedures on this engine, see Oldsmobile chapter.
⑩—Diesel.
⑪—Exc. Calif.
⑫—Corvette.
⑬—Camaro Z28.
⑭—For service procedures on this engine, refer to Pontiac chapter.

TUNE UP SPECIFICATIONS

The following specifications are published from the latest information available. This data should be used only in the absence of a decal affixed in the engine compartment.

★ When using a timing light, disconnect vacuum hose or tube at distributor and plug opening in hose or tube so idle speed will not be affected.

● When checking compression, lowest cylinder must be within 70 percent of highest.

▲ Before removing wires from distributor cap, determine location of the No. 1 wire in cap, as distributor position may have been altered from that shown at the end of this chart.

Spark plug types shown in this chart are recommendations of the original vehicle manufacturer and not MOTOR.

Check local sources for other spark plug manufacturers listings.

Year & Engine/V.I.N.	Spark Plug Type	Gap	Firing Order Fig. ▲	Man. Trans.	Auto. Trans.	Mark Fig.	Man. Trans.	Auto. Trans.	Man. Trans.	Auto. Trans.	Fuel Pump Pressure
				Ignition Timing BTDC①★			Curb Idle Speed②		Fast Idle Speed		

CAMARO 1977

Year & Engine/V.I.N.	Type	Gap	Firing Order Fig.	Man. Trans.	Auto. Trans.	Mark Fig.	Man. Trans.	Auto. Trans.	Man. Trans.	Auto. Trans.	Fuel Pump Pressure
6-250/D Exc. Calif. & High Alt.	R46TS	.035	H	6°	8°	B	⑥	⑦	2000	2000	4–5
6-250/D Calif.	R46TS	.035	H	—	⑧	B	—	⑦	—	1800	4–5
6-250/D High Alt.	R46TS	.035	H	—	10°	B	—	425/600D	—	2000	4–5
V8-305/U Exc. Calif.	R45TS	.045	C	8°	8°	B	600/700	500/650D	—	—	7½–9
V8-305/U Calif.	R45TS	.045	C	—	6°	B	—	500/650D	—	—	7½–9
V8-350/L Exc. High Alt.	R45TS	.045	C	8°	8°	B	700	500/650D	1300⑤	1600⑤	7½–9
V8-350/L High Alt.	R45TS	.045	C	—	8°	B	—	600/650D	—	1600⑤	7½–9

Continued

TUNE UP SPECIFICATIONS—Continued

The following specifications are published from the latest information available. This
data should be used only in the absence of a decal affixed in the engine compartment.

★ When using a timing light, disconnect vacuum hose or tube at distributor and plug opening in hose or tube so idle speed will not be affected.

● When checking compression, lowest cylinder must be within 70 percent of highest.

▲ Before removing wires from distributor cap, determine location of the No. 1 wire in cap, as distributor position may have been altered from that shown at the end of this chart.

Spark plug types shown in this chart are recommendations of the original vehicle manufacturer and not MOTOR.

Check local sources for other spark plug manufacturers listings.

Year & Engine/V.I.N.	Spark Plug Type	Gap	Ignition Timing BTDC①★ Firing Order Fig. ▲	Man. Trans.	Auto. Trans.	Mark Fig.	Curb Idle Speed② Man. Trans.	Auto. Trans.	Fast Idle Speed Man. Trans.	Auto. Trans.	Fuel Pump Pressure
CAMARO—Continued											
1978											
6-250/D Exc. Calif.	R46TS	.035	H	6°	10°	B	425/800	425/550D	2000	2100	4–5
6-250/D Calif.	R46TS	.035	H	—	6°	B	—	400/600D	—	2000	4–5
V8-305/U Exc. Calif.	R45TS	.045	C	4°	4°	B	600	500D	—	—	7½–9
V8-305/U Calif.	R45TS	.045	C	—	8°	B	—	500/600D	—	—	7½–9
V8-350/L Exc. Calif. & High Alt.	R45TS	.045	C	6°	6°	B	700	500/600D	1300	1600	7½–9
V8-350/L Calif.	R45TS	.045	C	—	8°	B	—	500/600D	—	1600	7½–9
V8-350/L High Alt.	R45TS	.045	C	—	⑨	B	—	500/650D	—	1600	7½–9
1979											
6-250/D Exc. Calif.	R46TS	.035	H	12°	8°	B	800	675D	1800	2000	4–5
6-250/D Calif.	R46TS	.035	H	—	6°	B	—	600D	—	2000	4–5
V8-305/G Exc. Calif.	R45TS	.045	C	4°	4°	G	600/700	500/600D	1300	1600	7½–9
V8-305/G Calif.	R45TS	.045	C	—	4°	G	—	600/650D	—	1950	7½–9
V8-350/G Exc. Calif. & High Alt.	R45TS	.045	C	6°	6°	G	700	500/600D	1300	1600	7½–9
V8-350/L Calif.	R45TS	.045	C	—	8°	G	—	500/600D	—	1600	7½–9
V8-350/L High Alt.	R45TS	.045	C	—	8°	G	—	600/650D	—	1750	7½–9
1980											
V6-229/K	R45TS	.045	F	8°	12°	G	700/800	600/675D	1300	1750	4½–6
V6-231/A	R45TSX	.060	D	—	15°	E⑪	—	600D	—	2200	4¼–5¾
V8-267/J	R45TS	.045	C	—	4°	④	—	500/600D	—	1850	7½–9
V8-305/H Exc. Calif.	R45TS	.045	C	4°	4°	④	700	500/600D	1500	1850	7½–9
V8-305/H Calif. Exc. Z28	R45TS	.045	C	—	4°	④	—	550/650D	—	2200	7½–9
V8-305/H Calif. Z28	R45TS	.045	C	—	—	④	—	550/650D	—	—	7½–9
V8-350/L	R45TS	.045	C	6°	6°	④	700	500/600D	1500	1850	7½–9
1981											
V6-229/K	R45TS	.045	F	6°	6°	G	③	③	2200	2200	4½–6
V6-231/A	R45TS8	.080	D	—	15°	E⑪	—	③	—	1800	3 Min.
V8-267/J	R45TS	.045	C	—	6°	A	—	500	—	2200	4½–6
V8-305/H	R45TS	.045	C	6°	6°	A	700/800	500/600D	2200	2200	7½–9
V8-350/L	R45TS	.045	C	—	6°	A	—	500/600D	—	2200	7½–9
1982											
4-151 E.F.I./2	R44TSX	.060	I	8°⑳	8°⑳	J	⑲	⑲	⑲	⑲	—
V6-173/1	R43TS	.045	K	10°	10°	L	850㉑	600D㉒	2600	2500	6–7½
V8-305/H	R45TS	.045	C	6°	6°	A	700/800	500/600D	7800	2200	7½–9
V8-305 E.F.I./7	R45TS	.045	C	—	6°㉓	A	—	⑲	—	⑲	7½–9

CHEVROLET—Camaro, Chevrolet, Corvette, Malibu, Monte Carlo & Nova

TUNE UP SPECIFICATIONS—Continued

The following specifications are published from the latest information available. This data should be used only in the absence of a decal affixed in the engine compartment.

★ When using a timing light, disconnect vacuum hose or tube at distributor and plug opening in hose or tube so idle speed will not be affected.

● When checking compression, lowest cylinder must be within 70 percent of highest.

▲ Before removing wires from distributor cap, determine location of the No. 1 wire in cap, as distributor position may have been altered from that shown at the end of this chart.

Spark plug types shown in this chart are recommendations of the original vehicle manufacturer and not MOTOR. Check local sources for other spark plug manufacturers listings.

Year & Engine/V.I.N.	Spark Plug Type	Gap	Firing Order Fig. ▲	Ign. Timing Man. Trans.	Ign. Timing Auto. Trans.	Mark Fig.	Curb Idle Man. Trans.	Curb Idle Auto. Trans.	Fast Idle Man. Trans.	Fast Idle Auto. Trans.	Fuel Pump Pressure
CAMARO—Continued											
1983											
4-151 E.F.I./2	R44TSX	.060	I	—	—	J	㉔	650D	—	—	—
V6-173/1	R43CTS	.045	K	—	—	L	—	—	—	—	6–7½
V8-305/H	R45TS	.045	C	—	—	A	—	—	—	—	7½–9
V8-305 E.F.I./7	R45TS	.045	C	—	—	A	—	—	—	—	—
MALIBU & MONTE CARLO											
1977											
6-250/D Exc. Calif. & High Alt.	R46TS	.035	H	6°	8°	B	⑥	⑦	2000	2000	4–5
6-250/D Calif.	R46TS	.035	H	—	6°	B	—	425/550D	—	1800	4–5
6-250/D High Alt.	R46TS	.035	H	—	10°	B	—	425/600D	—	2000	4–5
V8-305/U	R45TS	.045	C	—	8°	B	—	500/650D	—	—	7½–9
V8-350/L Exc. High Alt.	R45TS	.045	C	—	8°	B	—	500/650D	—	1600⑤	7½–9
V8-350/L High Alt.	R45TS	.045	C	—	8°	B	—	500/650D	—	1600⑤	7½–9
1978											
V6-200/M	R45TS	.045	F	8°	8°	G	700	600D	1300	1600	4½–6
V6-231/A	R46TSX	.060	D	15°	15°	E⑪	600/800	600/670D	—	—	3 Min.
V8-305/U Exc. Calif. & High Alt.	R45TS	.045	C	4°	4°	G	600	500D	—	—	7½–9
V8-305/U Calif.	R45TS	.045	C	—	6°	G	—	500/600	—	—	7½–9
V8-305/U High Alt.	R45TS	.045	C	—	8°	G	—	600/700D	—	—	7½–9
V8-350/L Exc. Calif. & High Alt.	R45TS	.045	C	—	6°	G	—	500/600D	—	1600	7½–9
V8-350/L Calif.	R45TS	.045	C	—	8°	G	—	500/600D	—	1600	7½–9
V8-350/L High Alt.	R45TS	.045	C	—	8°	G	—	500/650D	—	1600	7½–9
1979											
V6-200/M	R45TS	.045	F	8°	12°	G	700/800	600/700D	1300	1600	4½–6
V6-231/A Exc. Calif. & High Alt.	R45TSX	.060	D	—	15°	E⑪	—	⑫	—	2200	3 Min.
V6-231/A Calif. & High Alt.	R45TSX	.060	D	—	15°	E⑪	—	600D	—	2200	3 Min.
V8-267/J	R45TS	.045	C	4°	8°	G	600/700	500/600D	1300	1600	7½–9
V8-305/H Exc. High Alt.	R45TS	.045	C	4°	4°	G	700	500/600D	1300	1600	7½–9
V8-305/H High Alt.	R45TS	.045	C	—	8°	G	—	600/650D	—	1750	7½–9
V8-350/L	R45TS	.045	C	—	8°	G	—	600/650	—	1750	7½–9
1980											
V6-229/K	R45TS	.045	F	8°	12°	G	700/800	600/675D	1300	1750	4½–6
V6-231/A Exc. Calif.⑳	R45TSX	.060	D	—	15°	E⑪	—	560/670D	—	2200	4¼–5¾

Continued

1-162

TUNE UP SPECIFICATIONS—Continued

The following specifications are published from the latest information available. This data should be used only in the absence of a decal affixed in the engine compartment.

★ When using a timing light, disconnect vacuum hose or tube at distributor and plug opening in hose or tube so idle speed will not be affected.

● When checking compression, lowest cylinder must be within 70 percent of highest.

▲ Before removing wires from distributor cap, determine location of the No. 1 wire in cap, as distributor position may have been altered from that shown at the end of this chart.

☞ Spark plug types shown in this chart are recommendations of the original vehicle manufacturer and not MOTOR.

Check local sources for other spark plug manufacturers listings.

Year & Engine/V.I.N.	Spark Plug Type ☞	Gap	Firing Order Fig. ▲	Ignition Timing BTDC ① ★ Man. Trans.	Auto. Trans.	Mark Fig.	Curb Idle Speed ② Man. Trans.	Auto. Trans.	Fast Idle Speed Man. Trans.	Auto. Trans.	Fuel Pump Pressure
MALIBU & MONTE CARLO—Continued											
1980											
V6-231/A Calif. ⑬	R45TSX	.060	D	—	15°	E ⑪	—	600D	—	2200	4¼–5¾
V6-231/3 Exc. Calif. ⑭	R45TS	.040	D	—	15°	E ⑪	—	550D	—	2200	5
V6-231/3 Calif. ⑭	R45TS	.040	D	—	15°	E ⑪	—	600D	—	2200	5
V8-267/J	R45TS	.045	C	—	4°	④	—	500/600D	—	1850	7½–9
V8-305/H Exc. Calif.	R45TS	.045	C	4°	4°	④	700	500/600D	1500	1850	7½–9
V8-305/H Calif.	R45TS	.045	C	—	4°	④	—	550/650D	—	2200	7½–9
1981											
V6-229/K	R45TS	.045	F	6°	6°	G	③	③	2200	2200	4½–6
V6-231/A ⑳	R45TS8	.080	D	—	15°	E ⑪	—	③	—	1800	3 Min.
V6-231/3 ㉑	R45TS	.040	D	—	15°	E ⑪	—	650D	—	2200	5
V8-267/J	R45TS	.045	C	—	6°	A	—	500/600D	—	2200	7½–9
V8-305/H	R45TS	.045	C	6°	6°	A	700/800	500/600D	2200	2200	7½–9
V8-350/L	R45TS	.045	C	—	6°	A	—	500/600D	—	2200	7½–9
1982											
V6-229/K	R45TS	.045	F	—	TDC	G	—	③	—	2200	4½–6
V6-231/A	R45TS8	.080	D	—	15°	E ⑪	—	③	—	1800	3 Min.
V6-262 Diesel/V Exc. High Alt.	—	—	—	—	7° ㉕ ㉖ ㉗	—	—	650D	—	725D	—
V6-262 Diesel/V High Alt.	—	—	—	—	7° ㉕ ㉖ ㉘	—	—	650D	—	725D	—
V8-267/J	R45TS	.045	C	—	2°	A	—	500/600D	—	2200	7½–9
V8-305/H	R45TS	.045	C	—	6°	A	—	500/600D	—	2200	7½–9
V8-350 Diesel/N Exc. High Alt.	—	—	—	—	4° ㉕ ㉖ ㉙	—	—	600D	—	750D	—
V8-350 Diesel/N High Alt.	—	—	—	—	4° ㉕ ㉖ ㉚	—	—	600D	—	750D	—
1983											
V6-229/K	R45TS	.045	F	—	—	G	—	—	—	—	4½–6
V6-231/A	R45TS8	.080	D	—	15°	E ⑪	—	③	—	2200	4¼–5¾
V6-262 Diesel/V	—	—	—	—	—	—	—	—	—	—	—
V8-305/H	R45TS	.045	C	—	—	A	—	—	—	—	7½–9
V8-350 Diesel/N	—	—	—	—	㉕ ㉜	—	—	600D	—	750D	—
CHEVY NOVA											
1977											
6-250/D Exc. Calif. & High Alt.	R46TS	.035	H	6°	8°	B	⑥	⑦	2000	2000	4–5
6-250/D Calif.	R46TS	.035	H	—	6°	B	—	⑦	—	1800	4–5
6-250/D High Alt.	R46TS	.035	H	—	10°	B	—	425/600D	—	2000	4–5
V8-305/U Exc. Calif.	R45TS	.045	C	8°	8°	B	600/700	500/650D	—	—	7½–9
V8-305/U Calif.	R45TS	.045	C	—	6°	B	—	500/650D	—	—	7½–9

TUNE UP SPECIFICATIONS—Continued

The following specifications are published from the latest information available. This data should be used only in the absence of a decal affixed in the engine compartment.

★ When using a timing light, disconnect vacuum hose or tube at distributor and plug opening in hose or tube so idle speed will not be affected.

● When checking compression, lowest cylinder must be within 70 percent of highest.

▲ Before removing wires from distributor cap, determine location of the No. 1 wire in cap, as distributor position may have been altered from that shown at the end of this chart.

Spark plug types shown in this chart are recommendations of the original vehicle manufacturer and not MOTOR.

Check local sources for other spark plug manufacturers listings.

Year & Engine/V.I.N.	Spark Plug Type	Gap	Firing Order Fig. ▲	Ignition Timing BTDC① ★ Man. Trans.	Auto. Trans.	Mark Fig.	Curb Idle Speed② Man. Trans.	Auto. Trans.	Fast Idle Speed Man. Trans.	Auto. Trans.	Fuel Pump Pressure
CHEVY NOVA—Continued											
1977											
V8-350/L Exc. High Alt.	R45TS	.045	C	8°	8°	B	700	500/650D	1300⑤	1600⑤	7½-9
V8-350/L High Alt.	R45TS	.045	C	—	8°	B	—	600/650D	—	1600⑤	7½-9
1978											
6-250/D Exc. Calif.	R46TS	.035	H	6°	10°⑮	B	425/800	425/550D	2000	2100	4-5
6-250/D Calif.	R46TS	.035	H	—	6°	B	—	400/600D	—	2000	4-5
V8-305/U Exc. Calif.	R45TS	.045	C	4°	4°	G	600	500D	—	—	7½-9
V8-305/U Calif.	R45TS	.045	C	—	6°	G	—	500/600D	—	—	7½-9
V8-350/L	R45TS	.045	C	—	8°	G	—	⑯	—	1600	7½-9
1979											
6-250/D Exc. Calif.	R46TS	.035	H	12°	8°	B	800	675D	1800	2000	4-5
6-250/D Calif.	R46TS	.035	H	—	6°	B	—	600D	—	2000	4-5
V8-305/G Exc. Calif.	R45TS	.045	C	4°	4°	G	600/700	500/600D	1300	1600	7½-9
V8-305/G Calif.	R45TS	.045	C	—	4°	G	—	600/650D	—	1950	7½-9
V8-350/L Calif.	R45TS	.045	C	—	8°	G	—	500/600D	—	1600	7½-9
V8-350/L High Alt.	R45TS	.045	C	—	8°	G	—	600/650D	—	1750	7½-9
CHEVROLET											
1977											
6-250/D Exc. Calif. & High Alt.	R46TS	.035	H		8°	B	⑦			2000	4-5
6-250/D Calif.	R46TS	.035	H		6°	B	⑦			1800	4-5
6-250/D High Alt.	R46TS	.035	H		10°	B		425/600D		2000	4-5
V8-305/U Exc. Calif.	R45TS	.045	C		8°			500/650D			7½-9
V8-305/U Calif.	R45TS	.045	C		6°			500/650D			7½-9
V8-350/L Exc. High Alt.	R45TS	.045	C		8°			500/650D		1600⑤	7½-9
V8-350/L High Alt.	R45TS	.045	C		8°			600/650D		1600⑤	7½-9
1978											
6-250/D Exc. Calif.	R46TS	.035	H	—	⑰	B	—	425/550D	—	2100	4-5
6-250/D Calif.	R46TS	.035	H	—	6°	B	—	400/600D	—	2000	4-5
V8-305/U Exc. Calif.	R45TS	.045	C	—	4°	G	—	500D	—	—	7½-9
V8-305/U Calif.	R45TS	.045	C	—	6°	G	—	500/600D	—	—	7½-9
V8-350/L Exc. Calif. & High Alt.	R45TS	.045	C	—	6°	G	—	500/600D	—	1600	7½-9
V8-350/L Calif.	R45TS	.045	C	—	8°	G	—	500/600D	—	1600	7½-9
V8-350/L High Alt.	R45TS	.045	C	—	8°	G	—	500/650D	—	1600	7½-9
1979											
6-250/D Exc. Calif.	R46TS	.035	H	—	8°	B	—	675D	—	2000	4-5
6-250/D Calif.	R46TS	.035	H	—	6°	B	—	600D	—	2000	4-5
V8-305/G Exc. Calif.	R45TS	.045	C	—	4°	G	—	500/600D	—	1600	7½-9
V8-305/G Calif.	R45TS	.045	C	—	4°	G	—	600/650D	—	1950	7½-9

Continued

TUNE UP SPECIFICATIONS—Continued

The following specifications are published from the latest information available. This
data should be used only in the absence of a decal affixed in the engine compartment.

★ When using a timing light, disconnect vacuum hose or tube at distributor and plug opening in hose or tube so idle speed will not be affected.

● When checking compression, lowest cylinder must be within 70 percent of highest.

▲ Before removing wires from distributor cap, determine location of the No. 1 wire in cap, as distributor position may have been altered from that shown at the end of this chart.

Spark plug types shown in this chart are recommendations of the original vehicle manufacturer and not MOTOR.
Check local sources for other spark plug manufacturers listings.

Year & Engine/V.I.N.	Spark Plug Type	Gap	Firing Order Fig. ▲	Ignition Timing BTDC① ★ Man. Trans.	Auto. Trans.	Mark Fig.	Curb Idle Speed② Man. Trans.	Auto. Trans.	Fast Idle Speed Man. Trans.	Auto. Trans.	Fuel Pump Pressure
CHEVROLET—Continued											
1979											
V8-350/L Exc. Calif. & High Alt.	R45TS	.045	C	—	6°	G	—	500/600D	—	1600	7½–9
V8-350/L Calif.	R45TS	.045	C	—	8°	G	—	600/650D	—	1750	7½–9
V8-350/L High Alt.	R45TS	.045	C	—	8°	G	—	500/600D	—	1600	7½–9
1980											
V6-229/K	R45TS	.045	F	—	12°	G	—	600/675D	—	1750	4½–6
V6-231/A	R45TSX	.060	D	—	15°	E⑪	—	600D	—	2200	4¼–5¾
V8-267/J	R46TS	.035	C	—	6°	④	—	500/600D	—	1850	7½–9
V8-305/H Exc. Calif.	R45TS	.045	C	—	4°	④	—	500/600D	—	1850	7½–9
V8-305/H Calif.	R45TS	.045	C	—	4°	④	—	550/650D	—	2200	7½–9
V8-350/L	R45TS	.045	C	—	6°	④	—	500/600D	—	1850	7½–9
V8-350 Diesel/N Exc. High Alt.	—	—	—	—	4½°㉕㉖㉛	—	—	600/750D	—	750D	—
V8-350 Diesel/N High Alt.	—	—	—	—	5½°㉕㉖㉛	—	—	600/750D	—	750D	—
1981											
V6-229/K	R45TS	.045	F	—	6°	G	—	㉒	—	2200	4½–6
V6-231/A	R45TS8	.080	D	—	15°	E⑪	—	㉒	—	1800	3 Min.
V8-267/J	R45TS	.045	C	—	6°	A	—	500/600D	—	2200	7½–9
V8-305/H	R45TS	.045	C	—	6°	A	—	500/600D	—	2200	7½–9
V8-350/L	R45TS	.045	C	—	6°	A	—	500/600D	—	2200	7½–9
V8-350 Diesel/N Exc. High Alt.	—	—	—	—	4°㉕㉖㉛	—	—	600/750D	—	750D	—
V8-350 Diesel/N High Alt.	—	—	—	—	5°㉕㉖㉛	—	—	600/750D	—	750D	—
1982											
V6-229/K	R45TS	.045	F	—	TDC	G	—	③	—	2200	4½–6
V6-231/A	R45TS8	.080	D	—	15°	E⑪	—	③	—	1800	3 Min.
V8-267/J	R45TS	.045	C	—	2°	A	—	500/700D	—	2200	7½–9
V8-305/H	R45TS	.045	C	—	6°	A	—	500/600D	—	2200	7½–9
V8-350 Diesel/N Less High Alt. Package	—	—	—	—	4°㉕㉖㉙	—	—	600D	—	750D	7½–9
V8-350 Diesel/N With High Alt. Package	—	—	—	—	4°㉕㉖㉚	—	—	600D	—	750D	7½–9
1983											
V6-229/K	R45TS	.045	F	—	—	G	Man.	Auto.	Man.	—	4½–6
V6-231/A	R45TS8	.080	D	—	15°	E⑪	—	③	—	2000	4½–5
V8-305/H	R45TS	.045	C	—	—	A	—	—	—	—	7½–9
V8-350 Diesel/N	—	—	—	—	㉕㉜	—	—	600D	—	750D	—
CORVETTE											
1977											
V8-350/L Exc. High Alt. & High Perf.	R45TS	.045	C	8°	8°	B	700	500/650D	1300⑤	1600⑤	7½–9
V8-350/L High Alt. Exc. High Perf.	R45TS	.045	C	—	8°	B	—	600/650D	—	1600⑤	7½–9
V8-350/X High Perf.	R45TS	.045	C	12°	12°	B	800	700/800D	1300⑤	1600⑤	7½–9

Continued

TUNE UP SPECIFICATIONS—Continued

The following specifications are published from the latest information available. This data should be used only in the absence of a decal affixed in the engine compartment.

★ When using a timing light, disconnect vacuum hose or tube at distributor and plug opening in hose or tube so idle speed will not be affected.

● When checking compression, lowest cylinder must be within 70 percent of highest.

▲ Before removing wires from distributor cap, determine location of the No. 1 wire in cap, as distributor position may have been altered from that shown at the end of this chart.

Spark plug types shown in this chart are recommendations of the original vehicle manufacturer and not MOTOR.

Check local sources for other spark plug manufacturers listings.

Year & Engine/V.I.N.	Spark Plug Type	Gap	Firing Order Fig. ▲	Ignition Timing BTDC① ★ Man. Trans.	Auto. Trans.	Mark Fig.	Curb Idle Speed② Man. Trans.	Auto. Trans.	Fast Idle Speed Man. Trans.	Auto. Trans.	Fuel Pump Pressure
CORVETTE—Continued											
1978											
V8-350/L Exc. Calif. & High Perf.	R45TS	.045	C	6°	6°	B	700	⑲	1300	1600	7½–9
V8-350/L Calif. Exc. High Perf.	R45TS	.045	C	—	8°	B	—	500/600D	—	1600	7½–9
V8-350/H High Perf.	R45TS	.045	C	12°	12°	B	900	700/800D	1600	1600	7½–9
1979											
V8-350/8 Exc. High Alt. & High Perf.	R45TS	.045	C	6°	6°	B	700	500/600D	1300	1600	7½–9
V8-350/8 High Alt. & High Perf.	R45TS	.045	C	—	8°	B	—	600/650D	—	1750	7½–9
V8-350/4 High Perf.	R45TS	.045	C	12°	12°	B	900	700/800D	1300	1600	7½–9
1980											
V8-305/H	R45TS	.045	C	—	4°	④	—	650D	—	—	7½–9
V8-350/8 Exc. High Alt. & High Perf.	R45TS	.045	C	6°	6°	B	700	500/600D	1300	1600	7½–9
V8-350/8 High Alt. & High Perf.	R45TS	.045	C	—	8°	B	—	600/650D	—	1750	7½–9
V8-350/6 High Perf.	R45TS	.045	C	12°	12°	B	900	500/600D	1300	1600	7½–9
1981											
V8-350/6	R45TS	.045	C	6°	6°	B	700/800	500/600D	2200	2200	7½–9
1982											
V8-350/6	R45TS	.045	C	—	6°㉒	A	—	⑲	—	⑲	—

①—BTDC—Before top dead center.
②—Idle speed on man. trans. vehicles is adjusted in Neutral and on auto. trans. equipped vehicles is adjusted in Drive unless otherwise specified. Where two idle speeds are listed, the higher speed is with A/C or idle solenoid energized.
③—Equipped with idle speed control motor.
④—Early models, Fig. G; late models, Fig. A.
⑤—With cam follower tang on high step of fast idle cam, EGR vacuum hose disconnected & plugged & A/C off.
⑥—Less A/C, 425/750 RPM; with A/C, 425/800 RPM.
⑦—Less A/C, 425/550D RPM; with A/C, 425/600D RPM.
⑧—Except distributor No. 1110725, 6° BTDC; distributor No. 1110725, 8° BTDC.
⑨—Except engine code CHU, 8° BTDC; engine code CHU, 6° BTDC.
⑩—Injection timing to 800 RPM.

⑪—The harmonic balancer on these engines has two timing marks. The timing mark measuring 1/16 in. is used when setting timing with a hand held timing light. The mark measuring 1/8 in. is used when setting timing with magnetic timing equipment.
⑫—Less idle solenoid, 500D RPM; with idle solenoid, 560/670D RPM.
⑬—Except turbocharged engine.
⑭—Turbocharged engine.
⑮—Nova 4 dr. sedan with A/C, set at 8° BTDC.
⑯—Except high altitude, 500/600D RPM; high altitude, 500/650D RPM.
⑰—Less A/C, 10° BTDC; with A/C, 8° BTDC.
⑱—Except high altitude, 500/600D RPM; high altitude, 600/650D RPM.
⑲—Automatically controlled by Electronic Fuel Injection.
⑳—Ground diagnostic terminal for base timing.

㉑—1100N with A/C.
㉒—700D with A/C.
㉓—Disconnect single near HEI distributor.
㉔—Less A/C, 850 RPM; with A/C, 900 RPM.
㉕—Using diesel timing meter J-33075.
㉖—ATDC—After top dead center.
㉗—Injection timing at 1300 RPM. When operating at altitudes above 4000 ft., set at 8° ATDC.
㉘—Injection timing at 1300 RPM. When operating at altitudes below 4000 ft., set at 6° ATDC.
㉙—Injection timing at 1250 RPM. When operating at altitudes above 4000 ft., set at 5° ATDC.
㉚—Injection timing at 1250 RPM. When operating at altitudes below 4000 ft., set at 3° ATDC.
㉛—Injection timing at 1200 RPM.
㉜—Injection timing, 4° ATDC at 1250 RPM.

Continued

TUNE UP NOTES—Continued

Fig. A

"0" is TDC
Marks 2° Increments

Fig. B

FIRING ORDER
1·8·4·3·6·5·7·2

SCREW

SCREWS

SCREW

Fig. C

FIRING ORDER
1·6·5·4·3·2

SCREW

SCREWS

SCREW

Fig. D

TIMING MARK FOR HAND HELD TIMING LIGHT

MAGNETIC PICK-UP FOR MAGNETIC PICK-UP TUBE

15

Fig. E

FIRING ORDER—
1·6·5·4·3·2

Fig. F

BEFORE AFTER

Fig. G

SCREWS

FIRING ORDER
1 5 3 6 2 4

FRONT

SCREWS

Fig. H

FIRING ORDER
1·3·4·2

SCREW

SCREW

Fig. I

BEFORE AFTER

Fig. J

FIRING ORDER 1·2·3·4·5·6

SCREWS (4)

Fig. K

B   A

16 12 8 4 0 4

Fig. L

CHEVROLET—Camaro, Chevrolet, Corvette, Malibu, Monte Carlo & Nova

DISTRIBUTOR SPECIFICATIONS

★Note: If unit is checked on vehicle, double the RPM and degrees to get crankshaft figures.

| Distributor Part No. ① | Advance Starts | Centrifugal Advance Degrees @ RPM of Distributor | | | Full Advance | Vacuum Advance | |
		Intermediate Advance				Inches of Vacuum to Start Plunger	Max. Adv. Dist. Deg. @ Vacuum
1977							
1103239	—	—	—	—	—	—	—
1103244	—	—	—	—	—	—	—
1103246	—	—	—	—	—	—	—
1103248	—	—	—	—	—	—	—
1103256	—	—	—	—	—	—	—
1110678	0 @ 500	3½ @ 800	—	—	10 @ 2050	4	12 @ 15
1110681	0 @ 500	3½ @ 800	—	—	10 @ 2100	4	7½ @ 12
1978							
1103281	0 @ 500	5 @ 850	—	—	10 @ 1900	—	—
1103282	0 @ 500	5 @ 850	—	—	10 @ 1900	4	10 @ 10
1103285	0 @ 600	6 @ 1000	—	—	11 @ 2200	4	5 @ 8
1103286	0 @ 550	6 @ 800	8 @ 1200	—	11 @ 2300	—	—
1103291	0 @ 600	6½ @ 800	—	—	8 @ 1000	—	—
1103337	0 @ 550	6 @ 800	—	—	8 @ 1200	4	12 @ 10
1103353	0 @ 550	6 @ 800	—	—	8 @ 1200	4	10 @ 10
1110695	0–3 @ 1000	—	—	—	6–9 @ 1800	7	12 @ 13
1110696	0 @ 500	5 @ 850	—	—	10 @ 1900	3	8 @ 6½
1110697	0 @ 500	5 @ 850	—	—	10 @ 1900	3	8 @ 6½
1110715	0 @ 500	3½ @ 800	—	—	10 @ 2100	4	12 @ 15
1110716	0 @ 500	3½ @ 800	—	—	10 @ 2100	4	7½ @ 12
1110718	0 @ 500	3½ @ 800	—	—	10 @ 2100	4	9 @ 12
1110731	0–2 @ 1000	—	—	—	6–9 @ 1800	4	8 @ 9
1979							
1103281	0 @ 500	5 @ 850	—	—	10 @ 1900	4	9 @ 12
1103282	0 @ 500	5 @ 850	—	—	10 @ 1900	4	10 @ 11
1103285	0 @ 600	6 @ 1000	—	—	11 @ 2100	4	5 @ 8
1103291	0 @ 600	6½ @ 800	—	—	8 @ 1000	4	5 @ 8
1103337	0 @ 550	6 @ 800	8 @ 1200	—	11 @ 2300	4	12 @ 11
1103353	0 @ 550	6 @ 800	8 @ 1200	—	11 @ 2300	4	10 @ 10
1103368	0 @ 500	5 @ 850	—	—	10 @ 1900	4	10 @ 11
1103370	0 @ 650	—	—	—	8 @ 2100	3	12 @ 10
1103371	0 @ 500	4 @ 850	—	—	11 @ 2200	3	12 @ 10
1103379	0 @ 500	5 @ 850	—	—	10 @ 1900	3	10 @ 8½
1110696	0 @ 500	5 @ 850	—	—	10 @ 1900	2	8 @ 7½
1110716	0 @ 500	3½ @ 800	—	—	10 @ 2100	4	7½ @ 12
1110748	0 @ 500	3½ @ 800	—	—	10 @ 2100	4	10 @ 11
1110766	0–2 @ 1000	—	—	—	8½ @ 1800	4	12 @ 12
1110767	0–2 @ 1000	—	—	—	8½ @ 1800	3	10 @ 12
1980							
1103282	0 @ 500	5 @ 850	—	—	10 @ 1900	4	10 @ 11
1103337	0 @ 550	6 @ 800	8 @ 1200	—	11 @ 2300	4	12 @ 11
1103353	0 @ 550	6 @ 800	8 @ 1200	—	11 @ 2300	4	10 @ 10
1103368	0 @ 500	5 @ 850	—	—	10 @ 1900	4	5 @ 8
1103370	0 @ 650	—	—	—	8 @ 2100	3	12 @ 10
1103371	0 @ 500	4 @ 850	—	—	11 @ 2200	3	12 @ 10
1103379	0 @ 500	5 @ 850	—	—	10 @ 1900	3	10 @ 8.5
1110696	0 @ 500	5 @ 850	—	—	10 @ 1900	2	8 @ 7.5
1110716	0 @ 500	3½ @ 800	—	—	10 @ 2100	4	7½ @ 12
1110756	0 @ 700	2 @ 850	—	—	7 @ 1900	2	12 @ 10
1110766	0 @ 1000	—	—	—	6½–8½ @ 1800	4	12 @ 12
1110767	0 @ 2000	—	—	—	6½–8½ @ 1800	4	10 @ 12

Continued

DISTRIBUTOR SPECIFICATIONS—Continued

★Note: If unit is checked on vehicle, double the RPM and degrees to get crankshaft figures.

| Distributor Part No.① | Centrifugal Advance Degrees @ RPM of Distributor | | | | Vacuum Advance | |
	Advance Starts	Intermediate Advance		Full Advance	Inches of Vacuum to Start Plunger	Max. Adv. Dist. Deg. @ Vacuum
1981						
1103434	—	—	—	—	—	—
1103443	—	—	—	—	—	—
1110754	—	—	—	—	—	—
1111386	—	—	—	—	—	—
1982						
1103494	—	—	—	—	—	—
1110597	—	—	—	—	—	—
1983						
1103460	—	—	—	—	—	—
1103519	—	—	—	—	—	—
1103539	—	—	—	—	—	—
1110584	—	—	—	—	—	—

①—Stamped on distributor housing cover.

BRAKE SPECIFICATIONS

| Year | Model | Brake Drum Inside Diameter | Wheel Cylinder Bore Diameter | | | Master Cylinder Bore Diameter | | |
			Disc Brake	Front Drum Brake	Rear Drum Brake	Disc Brakes	Drum Brakes	Power Brakes
1977	Camaro	9 1/2	2 15/16	—	15/16	15/16	—	1 1/8
	Chevelle & Monte Carlo	11	2 15/16	—	15/16	15/16	—	1 1/8
	Nova	9 1/2	2 15/16	—	15/16	15/16	—	1 1/8
	Chevrolet	9 1/2⑤	2 15/16	—	7/8①	1 1/8①	—	1 1/8
	Corvette	—	③	—	—	1 1/8	—	1 1/8
1978	Camaro	9 1/2	2 15/16	—	15/16	15/16	—	1 1/8
	Malibu	9 1/2	2 1/2	—	3/4	15/16	—	1 1/8
	Monte Carlo	9 1/2	2 1/2	—	3/4	15/16	—	1 1/8
	Nova	9 1/2	2 15/16	—	15/16	15/16	—	1 1/8
	Chevrolet	9 1/2⑤	2 15/16	—	7/8①	1 1/8	—	1 1/8
	Corvette	—	③	—	—	1 1/8	—	1 1/8
1979	Camaro	9 1/2	2 15/16	—	15/16	15/16	—	1 1/8
	Malibu	9 1/2	2 1/2	—	3/4	15/16	—	1 1/8
	Monte Carlo	9 1/2	2 1/2	—	3/4	15/16	—	1 1/8
	Nova	9 1/2	2 15/16	—	15/16	1	—	1 1/8
	Chevrolet	9 1/2⑤	2 15/16	—	7/8①	1 1/8	—	1 1/8
	Corvette	—	③	—	—	1 1/8	—	1 1/8
1980–81	Camaro	9 1/2	2 15/16	—	15/16	1 1/8⑥	—	1 1/8
	Malibu & Monte Carlo	9 1/2	2 1/2	—	3/4	15/16	—	15/16
	Chevrolet	9 1/2⑤	2 15/16	—	7/8①	1 1/8	—	1 1/8
	Corvette	—	③	—	—	1 1/8	—	1 1/8
1982	Camaro	9 1/2	⑦	—	3/4	15/16⑧	—	15/16⑧
	Malibu & Monte Carlo	9 1/2	2 1/2	—	3/4	1 1/8	—	1 1/8
	Chevrolet	9 1/2⑤	2 15/16	—	②④	1 1/8	—	1 1/8
	Corvette	—	③	—	—	1 1/8	—	1 1/8
1983	Camaro	9 1/2	2 1/2	—	3/4	15/16⑧	—	15/16⑧
	Malibu & Monte Carlo	9 1/2	2 1/2	—	3/4	1 1/8	—	1 1/8
	Chevrolet	9 1/2⑤	2 15/16	—	②④	1 1/8	—	1 1/8

①—Sta. Wagon 15/16".
②—7/8" or 15/16".
③—Front 1 7/8"; Rear 1 3/8".
④—Sta. Wag. 1".
⑤—Sta. Wagon 11".
⑥—1980 V6 models less power brakes, 1".
⑦—Front 2 1/2"; Rear 1 57/64".
⑧—With four wheel disc brakes, 1".

PISTONS, PINS, RINGS, CRANKSHAFT & BEARINGS

Year	Engine Model/V.I.N. Code	Piston Clearance	Ring End Gap① Comp.②	Ring End Gap① Oil②	Wristpin Diameter	Rod Bearings Shaft Diameter	Rod Bearings Bearing Clearance	Main Bearings Shaft Diameter	Main Bearings Bearing Clearance	Thrust on Bear. No.	Shaft End Play
1982–83	4-151/F⑭	.0017–.0041	.010	.015	.9400	2.0000	.0005–.0026	2.3000	.0005–.0022	5	.0035–.0085
1982–83	V6-173/1	.0016–.0027	.010	.020	.9054	1.9983–1.9993	.0014–.0035	2.4936–2.4946	.0017–.0029	3	.002–.007
1978–79	V6-200/M	.0007–.0017	.010	.015	.9272	2.0986–2.0998	.0013–.0035	③	④	4	.002–.006
1980–83	V6-229/K	.0007–.0017	.010	.015	.9272	2.0986–2.0998	.0013–.0035	③	④	4	.002–.006
1978	V6-231/A⑨	.0008–.0020	.010	.015	.9392	2.2487–2.2495	.0005–.0026	2.4995	.0004–.0015	2	.004–.008
1979	V6-231/A⑨	.0008–.0020	.013	.015	.9392	2.2487–2.2495	.0005–.0026	2.4995	.0004–.0015	2	.003–.009
1980–83	V6-231/A⑨	.0008–.0020	.013	.015	.9392	2.2487–2.2495	.0005–.0026	2.4995	.0003–.0018	2	.003–.009
1977	6-250/D	.0010–.0020	.010	.015	.9272	1.9928–2.000	.0007–.0027	2.2983–2.2993	.0003–.0029	7	.002–.006
1978–79	6-250/D	.0010–.0020	.010	.015	.9272	1.998–2.000	.0010–.0026	2.2979–2.2994	⑩	7	.002–.006
1982–83	V6-262/V⑤⑪	.0030–.0040	.015	.015	1.0952	2.3742–2.3750	.0003–.0025	2.9993–3.0003	⑫	3	.0035–.0135
1979–82	V8-267/J	.0007–.0017	.010	.015	.9272	2.0986–2.0998	.0013–.0035	③	④	5	.002–.006
1977	8-305/U	.0007–.0017	.010	.015	.9272	2.099–2.100	.0013–.0035	③	④	5	.002–.006
1978–83	8-305⑬	.0007–.0017	.010	.015	.9272	2.0986–2.0998	.0013–.0035	③	④	5	.002–.006
1977	8-350/L⑥	.0007–.0017	.010	.015	.9272	2.099–2.100	.0013–.0035	③	④	5	.002–.006
	8-350/L⑦	.0046–.0056	.010	.015	.9272	2.099–2.100	.0013–.0035	③	④	5	.002–.006
1978–80	8-350/L⑥	.0007–.0017	.010	.015	.9272	2.0986–2.0998	.0013–.0035	③	④	5	.002–.006
	8-350/L⑦	.0046–.0056	.010	.015	.9272	2.0986–2.0998	.0013–.0035	③	④	5	.002–.006
1981	V8-350/L⑥	.0007–.0017	.015	.020	.9272	2.099–2.100	.0013–.0035	③	④	5	.002–.007
	V8-350/L⑦	.0046–.0056	.010	.015	.9272	2.0986–2.0998	.0013–.0035	③	④	5	.002–.006
	V8-350/6⑦	.0025–.0035	.010	.015	.9272	2.0988–2.0998	.0013–.0035	③	④	5	.002–.006
1980–83	8-350/N⑤⑪	.0050–.0060	.015	.015	1.0951	2.1238–2.1248	.0005–.0026	2.9993–3.0003	⑧	3	.0035–.0135

①—Fit rings tapered bores to the clearance listed in tightest portion of ring travel.
②—Clearances specified are minimum gaps.
③—Front: 2.4484–2.4493; intermediate: 2.4481–2.4490; rear: 2.4479–2.4488.
④—Front: .0008–.0020; intermediate: .0011–.0023; rear: .0017–.0032.
⑤—Refer to Oldsmobile Chapter for service procedures on this engine.
⑥—Except Corvette High Performance engine.
⑦—Corvette High Performance engine.
⑧—No. 1, 2, 3, 4: .0005–.0021; No. 5: .0015–.0031.
⑨—Refer to Buick Chapter for service procedures on this engine.
⑩—Nos. 1–6; .0010–.0024. Nos. 7; .0016–.0035.
⑪—Diesel engine.
⑫—No. 1, 2, 3: .0005–.0021; No. 4: .0020–.0034.
⑬—For V.I.N. code, refer to the "General Engine Specifications" at the beginning of the chapter.
⑭—Refer to the Pontiac chapter for service procedures on this engine.

REAR AXLE SPECIFICATIONS

Year	Model	Carrier Type	Ring Gear & Pinion Backlash Method	Ring Gear & Pinion Backlash Adjustment	Pinion Bearing Preload Method	Pinion Bearing Preload New Bearings Inch-Lbs.	Pinion Bearing Preload Used Bearings Inch-Lbs.	Differential Bearing Preload Method	Differential Bearing Preload New Bearings Inch-Lbs.	Differential Bearing Preload Used Bearings Inch-Lbs.
1977–79	Corvette	Integral	Shims	.005–.008	Spacer	20–25①	5–10①	Shims	—	—
1977–79	Exc. Corvette	Integral	Shims	.005–.008	Spacer	15–30①	5–10①	Shims	—	—
1980–83	Exc. Corvette	Integral	Shims	.005–.008	Spacer	15–30①	10–15①	Shims	—	—
1980–82	Corvette	Integral	Shims	.005–.009	Shims	15–35①	—	Shims	—	—

①—Use inch-pound torque wrench on pinion shaft nut.
②—Total preload measured with torque wrench at pinion flange nut with new seal installed.

VALVE SPECIFICATIONS

Year	Engine Model/V.I.N.	Valve Lash Int.	Valve Lash Exh.	Valve Angles Seat	Valve Angles Face	Valve Spring Installed Height	Valve Spring Pressure Lbs. @ In.	Stem Clearance Intake	Stem Clearance Exhaust	Stem Diameter Intake	Stem Diameter Exhaust
1977	6-250/D	3/4 Turn [5]		46	45	$1\frac{21}{32}$	175 @ 1.26	.0010–.0027	.0010–.0027	.3410–.3417	.3410–.3417
	8-305/U	3/4 Turn [5]		46	45	[2]	[1]	.0010–.0027	.0010–.0027	.3410–.3417	.3410–.3417
	8-350/L	3/4 Turn [5]		46	45	[2]	[1]	.0010–.0027	.0010–.0027	.3410–.3417	.3410–.3417
1978	V6-200/M	1 Turn [5]		46	45	$1\frac{23}{32}$	200 @ 1.25	.0010–.0027	.0010–.0027	.3410–.3417	.3410–.3417
	V6-231/A [4]	Hydraulic [3]		45	45	1.727	168 @ 1.327	.0015–.0032	.0015–.0032	.3402–.3412	.3405–.3412
	6-250/D	1 Turn [5]		46	45	$1\frac{21}{32}$	175 @ 1.26	.0010–.0027	.0010–.0027	.3410–.3417	.3410–.3417
	V8-305/U	1 Turn [5]		46	45	$1\frac{23}{32}$	200 @ 1.25	.0010–.0027	.0010–.0027	.3410–.3417	.3410–.3417
	V8-350/L [7]	1 Turn [5]		46	45	$1\frac{23}{32}$	200 @ 1.25	.0010–.0027	.0010–.0027	.3410–.3417	.3410–.3417
	V8-350/L [6]	1 Turn [5]		46	45	[2]	[1]	.0010–.0027	.0010–.0027	.3410–.3417	.3410–.3417
1979	V6-200/M	1 Turn [5]		46	45	$1\frac{23}{32}$	200 @ 1.25	.0010–.0027	.0010–.0027	.3410–.3417	.3410–.3417
	V6-231/A [4]	Hydraulic [3]		45	45	1.727	168 @ 1.327	.0015–.0032	.0015–.0032	.3402–.3412	.3405–.3412
	6-250/D	1 Turn [5]		46	45	$1\frac{21}{32}$	175 @ 1.26	.0010–.0027	.0015–.0032	.3410–.3417	.3410–.3417
	V8-267/J	1 Turn [5]		46	45	$1\frac{23}{32}$	200 @ 1.25	.0010–.0027	.0010–.0027	.3410–.3417	.3410–.3417
	V8-305/G	1 Turn [5]		46	45	$1\frac{23}{32}$	200 @ 1.25	.0010–.0027	.0010–.0027	.3410–.3417	.3410–.3417
	V8-350/L [7]	1 Turn [5]		46	45	$1\frac{23}{32}$	200 @ 1.25	.0010–.0027	.0010–.0027	.3410–.3417	.3410–.3417
	V8-350/L [6]	1 Turn [5]		46	45	[2]	[1]	.0010–.0027	.0010–.0027	.3410–.3417	.3410–.3417
1980	V6-229/K	1 Turn [5]		46	45	$1\frac{23}{32}$	200 @ 1.25	.0010–.0027	.0010–.0027	.3410–.3417	.3410–.3417
	V6-231/A [4]	Hydraulic [3]		45	45	1.727	182 @ 1.34	.0015–.0035	.0015–.0032	.3402–.3412	.3405–.3412
	V8-267/J	1 Turn [5]		46	45	$1\frac{23}{32}$	200 @ 1.25	.0010–.0027	.0010–.0027	.3410–.3417	.3410–.3417
	V8-305/H	1 Turn [5]		46	45	$1\frac{23}{32}$	200 @ 1.25	.0010–.0027	.0010–.0027	.3410–.3417	.3410–.3417
	V8-350/L [7]	1 Turn [5]		46	45	$1\frac{23}{32}$	200 @ 1.25	.0010–.0027	.0010–.0027	.3410–.3417	.3410–.3412
	V8-350/L [6]	1 Turn [5]		46	45	[2]	[1]	.0010–.0027	.0010–.0027	.3410–.3417	.3410–.3412
	V8-350 Diesel/N [8]	Hydraulic [3]		[9]	[10]	1.67	151 @ 1.30	.0010–.0027	.0015–.0032	.3425–.3432	.3420–.3427
1981	V6-229/K	1 Turn [5]		46	45	1.70	175 @ 1.25	.0010–.0027	.0010–.0027	.3410–.3417	.3410–.3417
	V6-231/A [4]	Hydraulic [3]		45	45	1.727	182 @ 1.34	.0015–.0035	.0015–.0032	.3402–.3412	.3405–.3412
	V8-267/J	1 Turn [5]		46	45	1.70	175 @ 1.25	.0010–.0027	.0010–.0027	.3410–.3417	.3410–.3417
	V8-305/H	1 Turn [5]		46	45	1.70	175 @ 1.25	.0010–.0027	.0010–.0027	.3410–.3417	.3410–.3417
	V8-350/L [7]	1 Turn [5]		46	45	1.70	[11]	.0010–.0027	.0010–.0027	.3410–.3417	.3410–.3417
	V8-350/L [6]	1 Turn [5]		46	45	[2]	[1]	.0010–.0027	.0010–.0027	.3410–.3417	.3410–.3417
	V8-350 Diesel/N [8]	Hydraulic [3]		[9]	[10]	1.67	155 @ 1.30	.0010–.0027	.0015–.0032	.3425–.3432	.3420–.3427
1982	V6-231/A [4]	Hydraulic [3]		45	45	1.727	220 @ 1.34	.0015–.0035	.0015–.0032	.3401–.3412	.3405–.3412
	V8-267/J	1 Turn [5]		46	45	$1\frac{23}{32}$	200 @ 1.25	.0010–.0027	.0010–.0027	.3410–.3417	.3410–.3417
	V8-350/6 [6]	1 Turn [5]		46	45	[2]	[1]	.0010–.0027	.0010–.0027	.3410–.3417	.3410–.3417
1982–83	4-151/F [12]	Hydraulic [3]		46	45	1.66	151 @ 1.254	.0010–.0027	.0010–.0027	.3418–.3425	.3418–.3425
	V6-173/1	1½ Turn [5]		46	45	1.57	195 @ 1.1811	.0010–.0026	.0010–.0026	.3410–.3420	.3410–.3420
	V6-229/K	1 Turn [5]		46	45	$1\frac{23}{32}$	200 @ 1.25	.0010–.0027	.0010–.0027	.3410–.3417	.3410–.3417
	V6-262 Diesel/V [8]	Hydraulic [3]		[9]	[10]	1.67	210 @ 1.22	.0010–.0027	.0015–.0032	.3425–.3432	.3420–.3427
	V8-305/H	1 Turn [5]		46	45	$1\frac{23}{32}$	200 @ 1.25	.0010–.0027	.0010–.0027	.3410–.3417	.3410–.3417
	V8-350 Diesel/N [8]	Hydraulic [3]		[9]	[10]	1.67	210 @ 1.22	.0010–.0027	.0015–.0032	.3425–.3432	.3420–.3427
1983	V6-231/A [4]	Hydraulic [3]		45	44	—	[13]	.0015–.0035	.0015–.0032	.3401–.3412	.3405–.3412

[1]—Intake 200 @ 1.25; Exhaust 200 @ 1.16.
[2]—Intake, $1\frac{23}{32}$. Exhaust $1\frac{19}{32}$.
[3]—No Adjustment.
[4]—Refer to Buick Chapter for service procedures on this engine.
[5]—Turn rocker arm stud nut until all lash is eliminated, then tighten nut the additional turn listed.
[6]—Corvette.
[7]—Except Corvette.
[8]—Refer to Oldsmobile Chapter for service procedures on this engine.
[9]—Intake, 45°; Exhaust, 31°.
[10]—Intake, 44°; Exhaust, 30°.
[11]—Intake, 184 @ 1.70; Exhaust, 190 @ 1.16.
[12]—Refer to Pontiac chapter for service procedures.
[13]—Intake, 164 @ 1.34"; exhaust, 182 @ 1.34".

ENGINE TIGHTENING SPECIFICATIONS

★Torque specifications are for clean and lightly lubricated threads only. Dry or dirty threads produce increased friction which prevents accurate measurement of tightness.

Year	Engine Model/V.I.N.	Spark Plugs Ft. Lbs.	Cylinder Head Bolts Ft. Lbs.	Intake Manifold Ft. Lbs.	Exhaust Manifold Ft. Lbs.	Rocker Arm Stud Ft. Lbs.	Rocker Arm Cover Ft. Lbs.	Connecting Rod Cap Bolts Ft. Lbs.	Main Bearing Cap Bolts Ft. Lbs.	Flywheel to Crankshaft Ft. Lbs.	Vibration Damper or Pulley Ft. Lbs.
1982–83	4-151/F [19]	7-15	85	29	44	20	6	32	70	44	160
1982–83	V6-173/1	7-15	70	23	25	46	8	37	69	50	75

Continued

ENGINE TIGHTENING SPECIFICATIONS—Continued

★Torque specifications are for clean and lightly lubricated threads only. Dry or dirty threads produce increased friction which prevents accurate measurement of tightness.

Year	Engine Model/V.I.N.	Spark Plugs Ft. Lbs.	Cylinder Head Bolts Ft. Lbs.	Intake Manifold Ft. Lbs.	Exhaust Manifold Ft. Lbs.	Rocker Arm Stud Ft. Lbs.	Rocker Arm Cover Ft. Lbs.	Connecting Rod Cap Bolts Ft. Lbs.	Main Bearing Cap Bolts Ft. Lbs.	Flywheel to Crankshaft Ft. Lbs.	Vibration Damper or Pulley Ft. Lbs.
1978–79	V6-200/M	⑨	65	30	20	—	45③	45	70	60	60
1980–83	V6-229/K	22	65	30	20	—	45③	45	70	60	60
1978–83	V6-231/A⑩	15	80	45	25	30④	4	40	100	60	225
1982–83	V6-262/V⑭⑮	—	⑯⑰	41⑯	29	28⑦	—	42	107	48	160–350
1977–79	6-250/D	15	95⑧	⑥	30	—	45③	35	65	60	60
1979–82	8-267/J	22	65	30	20	—	45③	45	70	60	60
1977–83	8-305⑱	②	65	30	20	—	45③	45	70	60	60
1977	8-350/L	②	65	30	20①	50	45③	45	70⑤	60	60
1978–79	V8-350/L⑪	22	65	30	20①	—	45③	45	80⑬	60	60
1980–81	V8-350/L⑪	22	65	30	20①	—	45③	45	70	60	60
1978–82	V8-350⑫⑱	②	65	30	20①	50	45③	45	70	60	60
1980–83	V8-350/N⑭⑮	—	130⑯	40⑯	25	28⑦	—	42	120	60	200–310

①—Inside bolts 30 ft. lbs.
②—1977–78, 15 ft. lbs. 1979–83, 22 ft. lbs.
③—Inch lbs.
④—Rocker arm shaft to cylinder head bolts.
⑤—Outer bolts on engines with 4 bolt caps 65 ft. lbs.
⑥—Integral Intake Manifold.
⑦—Rocker arm pivot bolt.
⑧—Left hand front head bolt 85 ft. lbs.
⑨—1978, 20 ft. lbs.; 1979, 22 ft. lbs.

⑩—Refer to Buick Chapter for service procedures on this engine.
⑪—Except Corvette.
⑫—Corvette.
⑬—Outer bolts on engines with 4 bolt caps 70 ft. lbs.
⑭—Diesel engine.
⑮—Refer to Oldsmobile Section for service procedures on this engine.
⑯—Clean & dip bolt in engine oil before

tightening to obtain correct torque reading.
⑰—Bolts 5, 6, 11, 12, 13 & 14, 59 ft. lbs.; All others, 142 ft. lbs.
⑱—For V.I.N. code, refer to the "General Engine Specifications" at the beginning of the chapter.
⑲—Refer to Pontiac chapter for service procedures.

ALTERNATOR & REGULATOR SPECIFICATIONS

Year	Model	Alternator				Regulator						
		Rated Hot Output Amps.	Field Current 12 Volts @ 80° F.	Output @ 14 Volts 2000 R.P.M. Amps.	5000 R.P.M. Amps.	Model	Field Relay Air Gap In.	Point Gap In.	Closing Voltage	Voltage Regulator Air Gap In.	Point Gap In.	Voltage @ 125°F.
1977–79	1102394	37	4–4.5	—	33	Integral	—	—	—	—	—	—
	1102474	61	4–4.5	—	57	Integral	—	—	—	—	—	—
	1102478	55	4–4.5	—	51	Integral	—	—	—	—	—	—
	1102479	55	4–4.5	—	51	Integral	—	—	—	—	—	—
	1102480	61	4–4.5	—	57	Integral	—	—	—	—	—	—
	1102484	42	4–4.5	—	38	Integral	—	—	—	—	—	—
	1102486	61	4–4.5	—	57	Integral	—	—	—	—	—	—
	1102491	37	4–4.5	—	33	Integral	—	—	—	—	—	—
1980	1101044	70	4–4.5	—	—	Integral	—	—	—	—	—	—
	1101066	70	4–4.5	—	—	Integral	—	—	—	—	—	—
	1101071	70	4–4.5	—	—	Integral	—	—	—	—	—	—
	1102474	61	4–4.5	—	57	Integral	—	—	—	—	—	—
	1102484	42	4–4.5	—	38	Integral	—	—	—	—	—	—
	1103043	42	4–4.5	—	—	Integral	—	—	—	—	—	—
	1103044	63	4–4.5	—	—	Integral	—	—	—	—	—	—
	1103085	55	4–4.5	—	—	Integral	—	—	—	—	—	—
	1103088	55	4–4.5	—	—	Integral	—	—	—	—	—	—
	1103091	63	4–4.5	—	—	Integral	—	—	—	—	—	—
	1103092	55	4–4.5	—	—	Integral	—	—	—	—	—	—
	1103100	55	4–4.5	—	—	Integral	—	—	—	—	—	—
	1103102	63	4–4.5	—	—	Integral	—	—	—	—	—	—
	1103118	37	4–4.5	—	—	Integral	—	—	—	—	—	—
	1103122	63	4–4.5	—	—	Integral	—	—	—	—	—	—
	1103161	37	4–4.5	—	—	Integral	—	—	—	—	—	—
	1103162	37	4–4.5	—	—	Integral	—	—	—	—	—	—

Continued

ALTERNATOR & REGULATOR SPECIFICATIONS—Continued

Year	Alternator					Regulator							
				Output @ 14 Volts			Field Relay			Voltage Regulator			
	Model	Rated Hot Output Amps.	Field Current 12 Volts @ 80° F.	2000 R.P.M. Amps.	5000 R.P.M. Amps.	Model	Air Gap In.	Point Gap In.	Closing Voltage	Air Gap In.	Point Gap In.	Voltage @ 125°F.
1981	1101044	70	4–4.5	—	—	Integral	—	—	—	—	—	—
	1101066	70	4–4.5	—	—	Integral	—	—	—	—	—	—
	1101071	70	4–4.5	—	—	Integral	—	—	—	—	—	—
	1103043	42	4–4.5	—	—	Integral	—	—	—	—	—	—
	1103044	63	4–4.5	—	—	Integral	—	—	—	—	—	—
	1103085	55	—	—	—	Integral	—	—	—	—	—	—
	1103088	55	4–4.5	—	—	Integral	—	—	—	—	—	—
	1103091	63	4–4.5	—	—	Integral	—	—	—	—	—	—
	1103092	55	4–4.5	—	—	Integral	—	—	—	—	—	—
	1103100	55	4–4.5	—	—	Integral	—	—	—	—	—	—
	1103102	63	4–4.5	—	—	Integral	—	—	—	—	—	—
	1103103	63	4–4.5	—	—	Integral	—	—	—	—	—	—
	1103118	37	4–4.5	—	—	Integral	—	—	—	—	—	—
	1103122	—	4–4.5	—	—	Integral	—	—	—	—	—	—
	1103161	37	4–4.5	—	—	Integral	—	—	—	—	—	—
	1103162	37	4–4.5	—	—	Integral	—	—	—	—	—	—
	1103169	63	4–4.5	—	—	Integral	—	—	—	—	—	—
1982	1100110	42	—	—	—	Integral	—	—	—	—	—	—
	1100179	42	—	—	—	Integral	—	—	—	—	—	—
	1100187	70	—	—	—	Integral	—	—	—	—	—	—
	1100199	63	—	—	—	Integral	—	—	—	—	—	—
	1101044	70	4–4.5	—	—	Integral	—	—	—	—	—	—
	1101045	85	—	—	—	Integral	—	—	—	—	—	—
	1101066	70	4–4.5	—	—	Integral	—	—	—	—	—	—
	1101071	70	—	—	—	Integral	—	—	—	—	—	—
	1101075	70	4–4.5	—	—	Integral	—	—	—	—	—	—
	1101088	70	—	—	—	Integral	—	—	—	—	—	—
	1101443	85	—	—	—	Integral	—	—	—	—	—	—
	1101449	70	—	—	—	Integral	—	—	—	—	—	—
	1103043	42	4–4.5	—	—	Integral	—	—	—	—	—	—
	1103044	63	4–4.5	—	—	Integral	—	—	—	—	—	—
	1103085	55	4–4.5	—	—	Integral	—	—	—	—	—	—
	1103088	55	4–4.5	—	—	Integral	—	—	—	—	—	—
	1103091	63	4–4.5	—	—	Integral	—	—	—	—	—	—
	1103092	55	4–4.5	—	—	Integral	—	—	—	—	—	—
	1103100	55	4–4.5	—	—	Integral	—	—	—	—	—	—
	1103102	63	4–4.5	—	—	Integral	—	—	—	—	—	—
	1103118	37	4–4.5	—	—	Integral	—	—	—	—	—	—
	1103122	—	4–4.5	—	—	Integral	—	—	—	—	—	—
	1103161	37	4–4.5	—	—	Integral	—	—	—	—	—	—
	1103162	37	4–4.5	—	—	Integral	—	—	—	—	—	—
	1103169	63	4–4.5	—	—	Integral	—	—	—	—	—	—
	1103187	42	—	—	—	Integral	—	—	—	—	—	—
	1103197	63	—	—	—	Integral	—	—	—	—	—	—
1983	All	37	4–4.5	—	—	Integral	—	—	—	—	—	—
	All	42	4–4.5	—	—	Integral	—	—	—	—	—	—
	All	55	4–4.5	—	—	Integral	—	—	—	—	—	—
	All	63	4–4.5	—	—	Integral	—	—	—	—	—	—
	All	78	4–4.5	—	—	Integral	—	—	—	—	—	—

CHEVROLET — Camaro, Chevrolet, Corvette, Malibu, Monte Carlo & Nova

STARTING MOTOR SPECIFICATIONS

Year	Model/V.I.N.	Starter Number	Brush Spring Tension Oz.①	Free Speed Test			Resistance Test②	
				Amps.	Volts	R.P.M.	Amps.	Volts
1977–78	6-250/D	1108774	—	50–80③	9	5500–10500	—	—
	V8-305/U⑥	1109056	—	50–80③	9	5500–10500	—	—
	V8-305/U⑦	1108799	—	50–80③	9	5500–10500	—	—
	V8-350/L⑦	1109059	—	65–95③	9	7500–10500	—	—
	V8-350/L⑥	1109052	—	65–95③	9	7500–10500	—	—
1978	V6-200/M	1109524	—	—	—	—	—	—
	V6-231/A	1108797	—	—	—	—	—	—
1979	V6-200/M	1109056	—	50–80③	9	7500–11400	—	—
	V6-231/A	1109061	—	60–85③	9	6800–10300	—	—
	6-250/D	1108774	—	60–88③	9	6500–10100	—	—
	V8-267/J	1109524	—	45–70③	9	7000–11900	—	—
	V8-305/G⑤	1108774	—	60–88③	9	6500–10100	—	—
	V8-305/G⑩	1109056	—	50–80③	9	7500–11400	—	—
	V8-350/L⑥	1109052	—	65–95③	9	7500–10500	—	—
	V8-350/L⑦	1109059	—	65–95③	9	7500–10500	—	—
1980	V6-229/K	1109524	—	50–80③	10.6	7500–11400	—	—
	V6-231/A	1109061	—	65–95③	10.6	7500–10500	—	—
	V8-267/J⑪	1109524	—	50–80③	10.6	7500–11400	—	—
	V8-267/J⑧	1109064	—	60–85③	9	6800–10300	—	—
	V8-305/H⑨	1109524	—	50–80③	10.6	7500–11400	—	—
	V8-305/H⑥⑧	1109064	—	60–85③	9	6800–10300	—	—
	V8-305/H⑦⑧	1109067, 074	—	—	—	—	—	—
	V8-305/H④	1998217	—	—	—	—	—	—
	V8-350⑮④⑥	1109052	—	65–95③	9	7500–10500	—	—
	V8-350⑮④⑦	1109059	—	65–95③	9	7500–10500	—	—
	V8-350/L⑥	1109067	—	—	—	—	—	—
	V8-350/L⑦	1109065	—	65–95③	9	7500–10500	—	—
1980–81	V8-350 Diesel/N	1109213	—	—	—	—	—	—
1981	V6-229/K	1109524	—	—	—	—	—	—
	V6-231/A⑩	1109061	—	—	—	—	—	—
	V8-267/J⑤, V8-305/L⑥	1109064	—	—	—	—	—	—
	V8-267/J⑩	1109524	—	—	—	—	—	—
	V8-305/L⑦⑧	1109074	—	—	—	—	—	—
	V8-350/L⑧	1109065	—	—	—	—	—	—
1982	4-151/F⑯	1109533	—	45–70	9	7000–11900	—	—
	V6-173/1	1109535	—	45–70	9	7000–11900	—	—
	V6-229/K⑫	1109524	—	—	—	—	—	—
	V6-229/K⑬	1109534	—	—	—	—	—	—
	V6-231/A	1109524	—	—	—	—	—	—
	V6-262/V, V8-350/N⑰	1998552	—	—	—	—	—	—
	V8-267/J⑫, V8-305/H⑫	1109064	—	—	—	—	—	—
	V8-267/J⑬	1109534	—	—	—	—	—	—
	V8-305/H⑬	1109534	—	45–70	9	7000–11900	—	—
	V8-350/6④	1998241	—	70–110	9	6500–10700	—	—
1983	4-151/F⑯	1109556	—	55–85	10	6000–12000	—	—
	V6-173/1	1998236	—	60–85	10	6800–10300	—	—
	V6-229/K, V6-231/A	1998236	—	60–85	10	6800–10300	—	—
	V6-262/V, V8-350/N⑰	1998554	—	160–240	10	4400–6300②	—	—
	V8-305/H, V8-350/7	1100534	—	45–70	10	7000–11900	—	—

①—Minimum.
②—Pinion speed.
③—Includes solenoid.
④—Corvette.
⑤—Exc. Malibu & Malibu Classic.
⑥—With auto. trans.
⑦—With manual trans.
⑧—Camaro.
⑨—Except Camaro & Corvette.
⑩—Malibu & Malibu Classic.
⑪—Except Camaro.
⑫—Malibu & Monte Carlo.
⑬—Exc. Malibu & Monte Carlo.
⑭—Exc. Corvette.
⑮—1980 V.I.N. code is 8 or 6 (high performance).
⑯—Refer to Pontiac chapter for service procedures.
⑰—Diesel Engine.

WHEEL ALIGNMENT SPECIFICATIONS

Year	Model	Caster Angle, Degrees		Camber Angle, Degrees					Toe-In. Inch	Toe-Out on Turns, Deg.①	
		Limits	Desired	Limits		Desired				Outer Wheel	Inner Wheel
				Left	Right	Left	Right				
CAMARO											
1977	All	+1/2 to +1 1/2	+1	+1/2 to +1 1/2	+1/2 to +1 1/2	+1	+1		0 to 1/8	—	—
1978–81	All	+1/2 to +1 1/2	+1	+1/2 to +1 1/2	+1/2 to +1 1/2	+1	+1		1/16 to 3/16	—	—
1982–83	All	+2 1/2 to +3 1/2	+3	+1/2 to +1 1/2	+1/2 to +1 1/2	+1	+1		⑤	—	—
CHEVELLE, MALIBU & MONTE CARLO											
1977	Chevelle③	+1/2 to +1 1/2	+1	+1/2 to +1 1/2	0 to +1	+1	+1/2		0 to 1/8	—	—
	Chevelle④	②	①	+1/2 to +1 1/2	0 to +1	+1	+1/2		0 to 1/8	—	—
	Monte Carlo	+4 1/2 to +5 1/2	+5	+1/2 to +1 1/2	0 to +1	+1	+1/2		0 to 1/8	—	—
1978–83	All③	+1/2 to +1 1/2	+1	0 to +1	0 to +1	+1/2	+1/2		1/16 to 3/16	—	—
	All④	+2 1/2 to +3 1/2	+3	0 to +1	0 to +1	+1/2	+1/2		1/16 to 3/16	—	—
CHEVY NOVA											
1977	All③	−1 1/2 to −1/2	−1	+.3 to +1.3	+.3 to +1.3	+.8	+.8		0 to 1/8	—	—
	All④	+1/2 to +1 1/2	+1	+.3 to +1.3	+.3 to +1.3	+.8	+.8		0 to 1/8	—	—
1978–79	All③	−1 1/2 to −1/2	−1	+.3 to +1.3	+.3 to +1.3	+.8	+.8		1/16 to 3/16	—	—
	All④	+1/2 to +1 1/2	+1	+.3 to +1.3	+.3 to +1.3	+.8	+.8		1/16 to 3/16	—	—
CHEVROLET											
1977	All	+2 1/2 to +3 1/2	+3	+.3 to +1.3	+.3 to +1.3	+.8	+.8		+1/16 to 1/8	—	—
1978–83	All	+2 1/2 to +3 1/2	+3	+.3 to +1.3	+.3 to +1.3	+.8	+.8		1/16 to 3/16	—	—
CORVETTE											
1977–78	Front Whl. Align.	+2 to +2 1/2	+2 1/4	+1/4 to +1 1/4	+1/4 to +1 1/4	+3/4	+3/4		3/16 to 5/16	—	—
	Rear Whl. Align.	—	—	+5/8 to +1 1/8	+5/8 to +1 1/8	+7/8	+7/8		−1/32 to +1/32	—	—
1979	Front Whl. Align.	+2 to +2 1/2	+2 1/4	+1/4 to +1 1/4	+1/4 to +1 1/4	+3/4	+3/4		3/16 to 5/16	—	—
	Rear Whl. Align.	—	—	−1 to 0	−1 to 0	−1/2	−1/2		1/16 to 1/8	—	—
1980	Front Whl. Align.	+2 to +2 1/2	+2 1/4	+1/4 to +1 1/4	+1/4 to +1 1/4	+3/4	+3/4		3/16 to 5/16	—	—
	Rear Whl. Align.	—	—	+.2 to +1.2	+.2 to +1.2	+.7	+.7		−1/16 to +1/16	—	—
1981–82	Front Whl. Align.	+1 3/4 to +2 3/4	+2 1/4	+1/4 to +1 1/4	+1/4 to +1 1/4	+3/4	+3/4		3/16 to 5/16	—	—
	Rear Whl. Align.	—	—	−1/2 to +1/2	−1/2 to +1/2	Zero	Zero		0 to 1/8	—	—

①—Equipped with radial tires, +2°; equipped with bias belted tires, +1°.
②—Equipped with radial tires, +1 1/2° to +2 1/2°;
③—Manual steering.
equipped with bias belted tires, +1/2° to 1 1/2°.
④—Power steering.
⑤—Z-28, +.15°; except Z-28, +.2°.

COOLING SYSTEM & CAPACITY DATA

Year	Model or Engine/V.I.N.	Cooling Capacity, Qts.		Radiator Cap Relief Pressure, Lbs.	Thermo. Opening Temp.	Fuel Tank Gals.	Engine Oil Refill Qts. ①	Transmission Oil			Rear Axle Oil Pints
		Less A/C	With A/C					3 Speed Pints	4 Speed Pints	Auto. Trans. Qts. ②	
CAMARO											
1977	6-250/D	14.6	14.7	15	195	21	4	3	—	⑤	4 1/4
	V8-305/U	17.2	17.9	15	195	21	4	3	—	⑤	4 1/4
	V8-350/L	17.3	18.0	15	195	21	4	—	3	⑤	4 1/4
1978	6-250/M	15	16	15	195	21	4	—	—	⑪	4 1/4
	V8-305/U	17.5	18.5	15	195	21	4	—	3	⑪	4 1/4
	V8-350/L	17.5	18.5	15	195	21	4	—	3	⑪	4 1/4
1979	6-250/D	14.5	14.5	15	195	21	4	3	—	⑪	4 1/4
	V8-305/G	17⑬	18	15	195	21	4	—	3	⑪	4 1/4
	V8-350/L	17⑬	18	15	195	21	4	—	3	⑪	4 1/4
1980	V6-229/K	14.5	14.5	15	195	21	4⑯	3	—	⑳	4 1/4
	V6-231/A	12	12	15	195	21	4	—	—	⑳	4 1/4
	V8-267/J	15	15	15	195	21	4	—	—	⑳	4 1/4
	V8-305/H	15	15	15	195	21	4	—	3	⑳	4 1/4
	V8-350/L	16	16	15	195	21	4	—	3	⑳	4 1/4

Continued

COOLING SYSTEM & CAPACITY DATA—Continued

Year	Model or Engine/V.I.N.	Cooling Capacity, Qts. Less A/C	With A/C	Radiator Cap Relief Pressure, Lbs.	Thermo. Opening Temp.	Fuel Tank Gals.	Engine Oil Refill Qts. ①	Transmission Oil 3 Speed Pints	4 Speed Pints	Auto. Trans. Qts. ②	Rear Axle Oil Pints
CAMARO—Continued											
1981	V6-229/K	14½	14½	15	195	20.8	4⑯	3½	—	⑪	③
	V6-231/A	12	12	15	195	20.8	4	—	—	⑪	③
	V8-267/J	15	15	15	195	20.8	4	—	—	⑪	③
	V8-305/H	15	15	15	195	20.8	4	—	3½	⑪	③
	V8-350/L	16	16	15	195	20.8	4	—	—	⑪	③
1982	4-151/F㉖	12½	12¾	15	195	16	3⑯	—	3½	⑪	3½
	V6-173/I	12½	12½	15	195	16	4⑯	—	3½	⑪	3½
	V8-305/H,7	15	15	15	195	16	4	—	3½	⑪	3½
1983	4-151/F㉖	8.8	9.1	15	195	16	3⑯	—	3½	㉗	3½
	V6-173/I	12½	12½	15	195	16	4⑯	—	3½	㉗	3½
	V8-305/H	15	15	15	195	16	4	—	3½	㉗	3½
	V8-305 E.F.I./7	15	15	15	195	16	4	—	3½	㉗	3½
MALIBU & MONTE CARLO											
1977	6-250/D	15	17	15	195	22	4	3	—	⑤	4
	V8-305/U	17½	18½	15	195	22	4	—	—	⑤	4
	V8-350/L	17½	18½	15	195	22	4	—	—	⑤	4
1978	V6-200/M	15	17	15	195	17.5	4	3	3	⑪	3¼
	V6-231/A	15	17	15	195	17.5	4	3	3	⑪	3¼
	V8-305/U	18	20	15	195	17.5	4	—	3	⑪	3¼
	V8-350/L	18	20	15	195	17.5	4	—	—	⑪	3¼
1979	V6-200/M	18.5	18.5	15	195	18.1	4	3	—	⑪	3¼
	V6-231/A	15.5	15.5	15	195	18.1	4	—	—	⑪	3¼
	V8-267/J	21	21	15	195	18.1	4	—	—	⑪	3¼
	V8-305/G	19	19	15	195	18.1	4	—	3	⑪	3¼
	V8-350/L	19.5	19.5	15	195	18.1	4	—	3	⑪	③
1980	V6-229/K	18.5	18.5	15	195	18.1	4⑯	3	—	⑳	③
	V6-231/A	15.5	15.5	15	195	18.1	4	—	—	⑳	③
	V8-267/J	21.0	21.0	15	195	18.1	4	—	—	⑳	③
	V8-305/H	19.0	19.0	15	195	18.1	4	—	3	⑳	③
1981	V6-229/K	18½	18½	15	195	18.1	4⑯	3½	—	⑪	③
	V6-231/A	15½	15½	15	195	18.1	4	—	—	⑪	③
	V8-267/J	21	21	15	195	18.1	4	—	—	⑪	③
	V8-305/H	19	19	15	195	18.1	4	—	3½	⑪	③
1982	V6-229/K	18½	18½	15	195	18.1	4⑯	—	—	⑪	③
	V6-231/A	15½	15½	15	195	18.1	4⑯	—	—	⑪	③
	V8-267/J	21	21	15	195	18.1	4	—	—	⑪	③
	V8-305/H	19	19	15	195	18.1	4	—	—	⑪	③
1983	V6-229/K	18½	18½	15	195	18.1	4⑯	—	—	⑪	3½
	V6-231/A	15½	15½	15	195	18.1	4⑯	—	—	⑪	3½
	V6-262/V⑱	14.5	15.3	15	195	19.8	6⑫	—	—	⑪	3½
	V8-305/H	19	19	15	195	18.1	4	—	—	⑪	3½
	V8-350/N⑱	18.4	18.4	15	195	19.8	7⑫	—	—	⑪	3½
CHEVY NOVA											
1977	6-250/D	14	15	15	195	21	4	3	—	⑨	⑩
	V8-305/U	17	18	15	195	21	4	3	—	⑨	⑩
	V8-350/L	17	18	15	195	21	4	—	3	⑨	⑩
1978–79	6-250/D	14	15	15	195	21	4	3	—	⑪	⑩
	V8-305㉑	16	17	15	195	21	4	—	3	⑪	⑩
	V8-350/L	16	17	15	195	21	4	—	—	⑪	⑩

Continued

COOLING SYSTEM & CAPACITY DATA—Continued

Year	Model or Engine/V.I.N.	Cooling Capacity, Qts.		Radiator Cap Relief Pressure, Lbs.	Thermo. Opening Temp.	Fuel Tank Gals.	Engine Oil Refill Qts. ①	Transmission Oil			Rear Axle Oil Pints
		Less A/C	With A/C					3 Speed Pints	4 Speed Pints	Auto. Trans. Qts. ②	
CHEVROLET											
1977	6-250/D	15	16	15	195	21⑮	—	—	—	4⑧	⑩
	V8-305/U	18	20	15	195	21⑮	4	—	—	4⑧	⑩
	V8-350/L	18	20	15	195	21⑮	4	—	—	4⑧	⑩
1978–79	6-250/D	14	15	15	195	21⑮	4	—	—	⑪	⑩
	V8-305㉑	16½⑬	17½	15	195	21⑮	4	—	—	⑪	⑩
	V8-350/L	16½⑬	17½	15	195	21⑮	4	—	—	⑪	⑩
1980	V6-229/K	14.25	14.25	15	195	25⑮	4⑯	—	—	⑳	③
	V6-231/A	11.75	11.75	15	195	25⑮	4	—	—	⑳	③
	V8-267/J	⑰	⑰	15	195	25⑮	4	—	—	⑳	③
	V8-305/H	15.5	15.5	15	195	25⑮	4	—	—	⑳	③
	V8-350/L	16.25	16.25	15	195	25⑮	4	—	—	⑳	③
	V8-350/N⑱	18.3	18	15	195	25⑮	7④	—	—	⑳	③
1981	V6-229/K	14¼	14¼	15	195	25⑮	4⑯	—	—	⑪	③
	V6-231/A	11¾	11¾	15	195	25⑮	4⑯	—	—	⑪	③
	V8-267/J	⑰	⑰	15	195	25⑮	4	—	—	⑪	③
	V8-305/H	15½	15½	15	195	25⑮	4	—	—	⑪	③
	V8-350/N⑱	18.3	18	15	195	25⑮	7④	—	—	⑪	③
1982	V6-229/K	14¼	14¼	15	195	25⑮	4⑯	—	—	⑪	③
	V6-231/A	11¾	11¾	15	195	25⑮	4⑯	—	—	⑪	③
	V8-267/J	⑰	⑰	15	195	25⑮	4	—	—	⑪	③
	V8-305/H	15½	15½	15	195	25⑮	4	—	—	⑪	③
	V8-350/N⑱	18.3	18.3	15	195	27⑲	7⑫	—	—	⑪	③
1983	V6-229/K	14¼	14¼	15	195	25⑮	4⑯	—	—	⑪	③
	V6-231/A	11¾	11¾	15	195	25⑮	4⑯	—	—	⑪	③
	V8-305/H	15½	15½	15	195	25⑮	4	—	—	⑪	③
	V8-350/N⑱	18.3	18.3	15	195	25⑮	4	—	—	⑪	③
CORVETTE											
1977	V8-350㉒	21	21	15	195	17	4	—	3	⑥	3¾
1978	V8-350㉓	21	21	15	195	23.7	4	—	3	10	3¾
1979	V8-350㉔	21	21⑭	15	195	24	4	—	3	⑦	3¾
1980	V8-305/H	17½	18½	15	195	20	3¼	—	—	⑦	3¾
	V8-350㉕	17½	18½	15	195	20	3¼	—	3½	⑦	3¾
1981	V8-350/6	21	22	15	195	23.7	4	—	3.4	4⑧	3¾
1982	V8-350/6	21	21	15	195	23.7	4	—	3	10	4

① —Add one quart with filter change.
② —Approximate. Make final check with dipstick.
③ —7½" ring gear, 3½ pts.; 8½" ring gear, 4¼ pts.; 8¾" ring gear, 5.4 pts.
④ —Includes filter. Use recommended diesel engine oil, designated SF/CC, SF/CD or SE/CC.
⑤ —THM 200, 250 & 350 total capacity 10 qts. THM 400 total capacity 11 qts.
⑥ —THM 350, 10 qts.; THM 400, 11 qts.
⑦ —Oil pan only, 3 qts. Total capacity, 10 qts.
⑧ —Oil pan only.
⑨ —Refill capacities: THM 200, 8¼ qts. THM 350, 6¾ qts.
⑩ —3¼ pts. for 7½" ring gear. 4 pts. for 8½" and 8¾" ring gears.

⑪ —THM 200 oil pan only, 3½ qts. Total capacity, 5 qts., CBC 350 oil pan only, 3 qts. Total capacity, 10 qts.
⑫ —Includes filter. Use recommended diesel engine oil, designated SF/CC or SF/CD.
⑬ —With heavy duty cooling system, add 1 qt.
⑭ —With auto. trans., add 1 qt.
⑮ —Sta. Wag., 22 gals.
⑯ —With or without filter change.
⑰ —Exc. Sta. Wag. Standard cooling, 16.75 qts.; Sta. Wag. with standard cooling, 15.5 qts.
⑱ —Diesel.
⑲ —With filter change. Use recommended diesel engine oil, designated SE/CC.
⑳ —THM 200, oil pan only 3½ qts., total capacity 5 qts. THM 250, oil pan 4 qts., total capacity 10¾ qts. THM 350, oil pan only 3

qts., total capacity 10 qts.
㉑ —1978 V.I.N. code is V, 1979 V.I.N. code is G.
㉒ —1977 V.I.N. code is L or X (high performance).
㉓ —1978 V.I.N. code is L or H (high performance).
㉔ —1979 V.I.N. code is 8 or 4 (high performance).
㉕ —1980 V.I.N. code is 8 or 6 (high performance).
㉖ —Refer to Pontiac chapter for service procedures.
㉗ —THM 200C, oil pan only, 3½ qts.; total capacity, 5 qts.; THM 700-4R, oil pan only, 4.45 qts.; total capacity, 11½ qts.

Electrical Section

STARTER, REPLACE

NOTE: Make certain that if any shims are removed, replace them properly.

1980–83 V8-350 Diesel

1. Disconnect battery ground cable.
2. Noting position of wires, disconnect starter wiring.
3. Remove upper support attaching bolt.
4. Remove flywheel housing cover (4 screws).
5. Remove starter (2 bolts).

NOTE: If equipped with dual exhaust, the left-hand exhaust pipe may have to be disconnected to provide clearance.

6. Reverse procedure to install. If shims were removed, they must be installed in their original location.

Exc. 1980–83 V8-350 Diesel

1. Disconnect ground cable at battery.
2. Raise vehicle to working height.
3. Disconnect all wires at solenoid.

NOTE: Reinstall terminal nuts as each wire is disconnected as thread size is different but may be mixed and stripped.

4. Loosen starter front bracket (nut on V8 and bolt on Sixes) then remove two mounting bolts.

NOTE: On V8 engines using solenoid heat shield, remove front bracket upper bolt and detach bracket from starter.

5. Remove front bracket bolt or nut and rotate bracket clear of work area. Then lower starter from vehicle by lowering front end first (hold starter against bell housing and sort of roll end-over-end).
6. Reverse removal procedure to install and torque mount bolts to 25–35 ft. lbs. On Corvette, apply a suitable sealing compound around starter where it enters engine splash shield.

IGNITION LOCK, REPLACE

1979–83

1. Remove steering wheel as described under Horn Sounder and Steering Wheel.
2. Remove turn signal switch as described under Turn Signal Switch, Replace, then remove buzzer switch.
3. Place ignition switch in "Run" position, then remove lock cylinder retaining screw and lock cylinder.
4. To install, rotate lock cylinder to stop while holding housing, Fig. 1. Align cylinder key with keyway in housing, then push lock cylinder assembly into housing until fully seated.
5. Install lock cylinder retaining screw. Torque screw to 40 in. lbs. for standard columns. On adjustable columns, torque retaining screw to 22 in. lbs.
6. Install buzzer switch, turn signal switch and steering wheel.

1977–78

1. Follow the procedure to remove the turn signal switch as described further on.
2. The lock cylinder should be removed in the "Run" position only.

NOTE: On all models except Corvette, do not remove buzzer switch since damage to the lock cylinder will result.

3. Place a thin tool (small screwdriver or knife blade) into the slot, Fig. 2, next to the switch mounting screw boss (right hand slot) and depress spring latch at bottom of slot which releases lock. Remove lock.

IGNITION SWITCH, REPLACE

1977–83

The ignition switch is mounted on top of the mast jacket inside the brake pedal support and is actuated by a rod and rack assembly.
1. Disconnect battery cable.
2. Disconnect and lower steering column.

NOTE: It may be necessary, on some models, to remove the upper column mounting bracket if it hinders servicing of switch.

CAUTION: Use extreme care when lowering steering column to prevent damage to column assembly. Only lower steering column a sufficient distance to perform ignition switch service.

3. On 1977–82 models, the switch should be in the "Off" unlocked position before removal, Fig. 3. If the lock cylinder was removed, pull actuator rod to the full downward position. Remove ignition switch retaining screws and the ignition switch.
4. Reverse procedure to install. On 1977–82 models, place gear shift lever in neutral position and install ignition switch in "Off" unlocked position, Fig. 3.

LIGHT SWITCH, REPLACE

1978–83 Malibu & Monte Carlo

1. Disconnect battery ground cable.
2. Remove instrument panel bezel.
3. Pull switch knob to "On" position.
4. Remove three screws attaching windshield wiper/light switch mounting plate to cluster and pull assembly rearward.
5. Depress shaft retainer button on switch and pull knob and shaft assembly from switch.
6. Remove ferrule nut and switch assembly from mounting plate.
7. Reverse procedure to install.

Fig. 1   Ignition lock. 1979–83 models

Fig. 2   Ignition lock removal. 1977–78 models

1978–82 Corvette

1. Disconnect battery ground cable.
2. Remove left air distribution duct.
3. Remove instrument cluster to instrument panel attaching screws and pull cluster rearward.
4. Disconnect speedometer cable and electrical connectors and remove cluster.
5. Remove two instrument panel to left door pillar attaching screws and pull left side of instrument panel slightly rearward.
6. Depress light switch shaft retainer button and pull out knob and shaft assembly from switch. Remove the switch retaining bezel.
7. Disconnect vacuum hoses from switch and the electrical connector.
8. Remove light switch from vehicle.
9. Reverse procedure to install.

1977–83 Chevrolet

1. Disconnect battery ground cable.
2. Pull switch knob to "On" position and reach up under instrument panel and depress switch shaft retainer, then pull knob and shaft assembly from switch.
3. Remove windshield wiper switch.
4. Remove light switch ferrule nut and remove switch from panel.
5. Disconnect electrical connector from switch and remove switch from vehicle.
6. Reverse procedure to install.

1977 Chevelle & Monte Carlo

1. Disconnect battery ground cable.
2. Remove instrument panel pad.
3. Remove left radio speaker to one side.
4. Pull headlamp control knob to "ON" position and while standing outside vehicle on left side, reach in and behind instrument panel and depress switch shaft retainer and pull knob and shaft assembly out.
5. Remove ferrule nut and switch from panel.

1977 Corvette

1. Disconnect battery cable.
2. Remove screws securing mast jacket trim covers and remove covers.
3. Remove left side console forward trim panel.
4. Lower steering column.
5. Remove screws securing left instrument panel to door opening, top of dash and left side of center instrument panel.

Fig. 3 Ignition switch assembly.

6. Pull cluster down and tip forward for access.
7. Depress switch shaft retainer and remove the knob and shaft assembly. Remove switch retaining bezel.
8. Disconnect vacuum hoses from switch, tagging them for assembly. Pry the connector from the switch and remove the switch.

1977–81 Camaro

1. Disconnect battery ground cable.
2. Remove steering column lower cover.
3. Reach up under cluster and depress lighting switch shaft retainer while pulling gently on shaft.
4. Remove nut securing switch to carrier.
5. Remove cluster carrier screws and tilt right side of cluster out.
6. Unplug connector and remove switch.

1982–83 Camaro

1. Disconnect battery ground cable.
2. On models equipped with A/C, remove left instrument panel sound insulator.
3. Reach up under instrument panel and depress switch shaft retainer, then remove knob and shaft assembly.
4. Remove switch retaining nut, then disconnect wiring connector and remove switch.
5. Reverse procedure to install.

1977–79 Nova

1. Disconnect battery ground cable.
2. Pull switch knob to "ON" position.

3. Reach up under instrument panel and depress switch shaft retainer, then remove knob and shaft assembly.
4. Remove ferrule nut and switch from panel.
5. Disconnect multi-contact connector from light switch.
6. Reverse procedure to install.

STOP LIGHT SWITCH, REPLACE

1977–83 Except Corvette

NOTE: On 1982–83 Camaro, remove hush panel.

1. Disconnect wiring connector at switch.
2. Remove retaining nut, if so equipped, and unscrew switch from bracket.
3. To install: Depress brake pedal and push new switch into clip until shoulder bottoms out.
4. Plug connector onto switch and check operation. Electrical contact should be made when pedal is depressed 3/8 to 5/8 from fully released position.

1977–82 Corvette

1. Disconnect wiring connector at switch.
2. Remove retaining nut and unscrew switch from bracket.
3. Upon installation, check for proper operation. Electrical contact should be made when pedal is depressed 1/4 to 5/8. Switch bracket has a slotted screw hole for adjustment.

CLUTCH START SWITCH, REPLACE

1982–83 Camaro

1. Disconnect wire connector at switch.
2. Remove retaining nut, if so equipped and unscrew switch from bracket.
3. To install; depress brake pedal, then insert and push switch into clip until shoulder bottoms out.
4. Plug connector on switch and check for proper operation.

1977–82 Corvette

1. Disconnect wiring connector from switch.
2. Remove retainer from pins or link on clutch pedal arm.
3. Remove retaining screw and switch.

Fig. 4 Mechanical neutral start system. 1977–83 Chevrolet & 1978–83 Malibu & Monte Carlo with standard column

Fig. 5 Mechanical neutral start system. 1977–83 Chevrolet & 1978–83 Malibu & Monte Carlo with tilt column

Fig. 6 Mechanical neutral start system in Park position. 1977–83 Chevrolet & 1978–83 Malibu & Monte Carlo

Fig. 7 Removing lock plate retaining ring

1977–83 Except Corvette & 1982 Camaro

1. Disconnect wiring connector from switch.
2. Compress switch actuating shaft retainer and remove shaft with switch attached from switch bracket.

NEUTRAL SAFETY SWITCH, REPLACE

1977–83 Chevrolet & 1978–83 Malibu & Monte Carlo

Actuation of the ignition switch is prevented by a mechanical lockout system, Figs. 4 and 5, which prevents the lock cylinder from rotating when the selector lever is out of Park or Neutral. When the selector lever is in Park or Neutral, the slots in the bowl plate and the finger on the actuator rod align allowing the finger to pass through the bowl plate in turn actuating the ignition switch, Fig. 6. If the selector lever is in any position other than Park or Neutral, the finger contacts the bowl plate when the lock cylinder is rotated, thereby preventing full travel of the lock cylinder.

1977–83 All Except 1977–83 Chevrolet, 1978 Malibu & Monte Carlo & 1982–83 Camaro

Column Shift & 1977–83 Floor Shift Exc. Corvette & 1982–83 Camaro

1. Disconnect wiring connector at switch terminals.
2. Unfasten and remove switch from mast jacket.
3. To install: position shift lever against

"Park" gate on models with floor shift, or "Neutral" gate on models with column shift, by rotating lower lever counter-clockwise as viewed from drivers seat.
4. Assemble switch to column by inserting actuating tang in shifter tube slot.
5. Tighten screws, connect wiring connector and move selector lever out of "Park" on models with floor shift or "Neutral" on models with column shift to shear pin which is part of new switch.

1977–82 Corvette

1. Disconnect shift control lever arm from transmission control rod.
2. Remove shift control knob.
3. Remove trim plate.
4. Remove control assembly from seal and disconnect switch wiring.
5. Remove switch from control assembly.
6. To install, position gearshift in Drive position, align hole in contact support with hole in switch and insert a pin (3/32") to hold support in place.
7. Place contact support drive slot over drive tang and tighten switch mounting screws.
8. Connect wiring harness to switch wiring.
9. Install trim plate control knob and connect shift lever arm to transmission control rod.

1982 Camaro

1. Remove floor console cover, then disconnect electrical connectors from switch.
2. Place shift lever in "Neutral" position of detent plate, then remove switch attaching screws and switch.
3. To install, ensure that the shift lever is in "Neutral", then position switch on shift lever making sure pin on shaft is in slot of switch.
4. Install attaching screws and torque to 16 inch lbs.
5. Move shift lever out of "Neutral" to shear pin which is part of new switch.
6. Reconnect electrical connectors to switch, then apply parking brake and start engine. Check backup lights and seat belt warning system for proper operation and ensure that engine will start only in "Park" or "Neutral".
7. Turn ignition off and install floor console.

TURN SIGNAL SWITCH, REPLACE

1977–83

1. Disconnect battery cable, then remove steering wheel and column to instrument panel trim cover.
2. Remove cover from shaft. *The cover retaining screws need not be completely removed from the cover.*
3. Using a suitable tool, compress lock plate (horn contact carrier on tilt models) and remove snap ring ("C" ring on tilt models), Fig. 7.

NOTE: On 1977–83 models remove lock plate cover with a suitable screwdriver. On 1977–82 Corvette models with tilt-telescopic column, place a 5/16 inch nut under each leg of puller.

Fig. 8 Taping turn signal connector and wires. 1977–83

4. Remove lock plate, cancelling cam, upper bearing preload spring, thrust washer and signal lever.
5. Push hazard warning knob in and unscrew knob.
6. Pull connector from bracket and wrap upper part of connector with tape to prevent snagging the wires during removal. On Tilt models, position shifter housing in "Low" position. Remove harness cover.
7. Remove retaining screws and remove switch, Figs. 8 and 9.
8. Reverse procedure to install.

COLUMN-MOUNTED DIMMER SWITCH, REPLACE

1977–83 Chevrolet; 1978–82 Corvette; 1978–83 Malibu, Monte Carlo & 1982–83 Camaro

1. Disconnect battery ground cable.
2. Remove instrument panel lower trim and on models with A/C, remove A/C duct extension at column.
3. Disconnect shift indicator from column and remove toe-plate cover screws.
4. Remove two nuts from instrument panel support bracket studs and lower steering column, resting steering wheel on front seat.
5. Remove dimmer switch retaining screws and the switch. Tape actuator rod to column and separate switch from rod.

Fig. 9 Removing turn signal switch. 1977–83

Fig. 10 Steering wheel and horn attachment. 1977–83 standard wheel. (Typical)

Fig. 11 Instrument cluster bezel removal (Typical). 1978–83 Malibu & Monte Carlo

Fig. 12 Instrument cluster removal (Typical). 1978–83 Malibu & Monte Carlo

6. Reverse procedure to install. To adjust switch, depress dimmer switch slightly and install a 3/32 inch twist drill to lock the switch to the body. Force switch upward to remove lash between switch and pivot. Torque switch retaining screw to 35 inch lbs. and remove tape from actuator rod. Remove twist drill and check for proper operation.

HORN SOUNDER & STEERING WHEEL, REPLACE

1977–83 Cushioned Rim Wheel

1. Disconnect battery ground cable.
2. Pry off horn button cap.
3. Remove three spacer screws, spacer, plate and belleville spring.
4. Remove steering wheel nut, washer and snap ring.
5. Using a suitable puller, remove steering wheel.
6. Reverse procedure to install.

1977–83 Standard Wheel

1. Disconnect battery ground cable.
2. Remove attaching screws on underside of the steering wheel, Fig. 10.
3. Lift steering wheel shroud and pull horn wires from cancelling cam tower.
4. Remove steering wheel nut, washer and snap ring.
5. Using a suitable puller, remove steering wheel.
6. Reverse procedure to install.

1977–82 Corvette

1. Disconnect battery ground cable.
2. Remove horn button cap.
3. Remove shim, if used, then the screw securing the center star screw and the star screw and lever.
4. Remove snap ring and nut from shaft.
5. Using a suitable puller, remove steering wheel assembly.
6. To disassemble the steering wheel assembly, remove three screws securing wheel and separate, then remove four screws retaining extension to wheel and separate.
7. Reverse procedure to install.

INSTRUMENT CLUSTER, REPLACE

NOTE: On some 1980 models, a yellow flag with the word "emissions" will rotate into the odometer window at 30,000 mile intervals indicating either a catalyst or oxygen sensor change is required. After performing the required maintenance, the emissions flag can be reset after removing the instrument cluster lens. Using a pointed tool inserted at an angle to engage flag wheel detents, rotate flag wheel downward. When flag wheel is reset, the alignment mark will be in center of odometer window.

1978–81 Malibu Standard Cluster

1. Disconnect battery ground cable.
2. Remove clock set stem knob, if equipped.
3. Remove instrument bezel retaining screws, Fig. 11.
4. Pull bezel from panel slightly and disconnect rear defogger switch, if equipped.
5. Remove bezel, Fig. 11.
6. Remove two screws at transmission selector indicator and lower indicator assembly to disconnect cable.
7. Remove three screws at windshield wiper/light switch mounting plate and pull assembly rearward for access to lower left cluster attaching bolt and nut.
8. Remove nuts attaching cluster to instrument panel.
9. Pull cluster rearward and disconnect the speedometer cable and all wiring and cables.
10. Remove cluster from vehicle, Fig. 13.
11. Reverse procedure to install.

1978–81 Malibu Optional Cluster & 1978–82 Monte Carlo & 1982–83 Malibu

1. Disconnect battery ground cable.
2. Remove radio knobs and clock set stem knob.
3. Remove instrument bezel retaining screws, Fig. 11.
4. Pull bezel rearward slightly and disconnect the rear defogger switch and remote control mirror control, if equipped.
5. Remove bezel, Fig. 11.
6. Remove speedometer retaining screws, pull speedometer from cluster slightly, disconnect speedometer cable and remove speedometer.

Fig. 13 Instrument cluster. 1977–83 Chevrolet

7. Remove fuel gauge or tachometer retaining screws, disconnect electrical connectors and remove fuel gauge or tachometer.
8. Remove clock or voltmeter retaining screws, disconnect electrical connectors and remove clock or voltmeter.
9. Disconnect transmission shift indicator cable from steering column.
10. Disconnect all wiring connectors and remove cluster case, Fig. 12.
11. Reverse procedure to install.

1977–83 Chevrolet

1. Disconnect battery ground cable.
2. Remove four steering column lower cover screws and the cover.
3. If equipped with automatic transmission, disconnect shift indicator cable from steering column.
4. Remove two steering column to instrument panel screws and lower steering column.

CAUTION: Use extreme care when lowering steering to prevent damage to column assembly.

5. Remove six screws and the three snap-in fasteners from perimeter of instrument cluster lens, Fig. 13.
6. Remove two screws from upper surface of grey sheet metal trim plate.
7. Remove two stud nuts from lower corner of cluster.
8. Disconnect speedometer cable and pull cluster from instrument panel.
9. Disconnect electrical connectors from cluster and remove from vehicle.
10. Reverse procedure to install.

1977 Chevelle & Monte Carlo

1. Disconnect battery ground cable.
2. Remove radio knobs and clock stem set knob, if equipped.
3. Remove instrument bezel retaining screws, Figs. 14 and 15.
4. Pull bezel out to disconnect tail gate release or rear defogger switch, if equipped.
5. Remove instrument bezel.
6. Reverse procedure to install.

1982–83 Camaro

1. Disconnect battery ground cable.
2. Remove instrument cluster bezel, Fig. 16A.
3. Remove 6 cluster retaining screws, then pull cluster back and disconnect speedometer cable and electrical connectors.
4. Reverse procedure to install.

1977–81 Camaro

1. Disconnect battery ground cable.
2. Remove 6 screws securing trim cover beneath steering column. Two of these screws are located above the ash tray.
3. Remove headlamp switch retaining nut.
4. From behind panel, disconnect cigar lighter and unscrew retainer. Note grounding ring.
5. From under lower edge of cluster, remove screw on either side of column, Fig. 16.
6. Remove 4 screws visible on front of carrier.
7. Remove screw retaining ground wire for wiper switch. Screw is fastened under top left corner of switch.

Fig. 14 Instrument cluster. 1977 Chevelle with standard cluster

Fig. 15 Instrument cluster. 1977 Chevelle with optional cluster & Monte Carlo

Fig. 16   Instrument cluster. 1977–81 Camaro

Fig. 16A   Instrument cluster. 1982–83 Camaro

8. Carefully tilt carrier out of access to the connectors on headlamp and wiper switches.
9. Remove lens screws then cluster screws.
10. Disconnect shift indicator from steering column.
11. Disconnect speedometer cable and tilt cluster forward and remove remaining connectors.
12. Lift cluster out.
13. Reverse procedure to install.

1977–79 Nova

1. Disconnect battery ground cable.
2. Lower steering column and apply protective covering to mast jacket to protect paint.
3. Remove three screws above front of heater control securing it to instrument cluster, Fig. 17.
4. Remove radio control knobs, washers, bezel nuts and front support at lower edge of cluster. This will allow radio to remain in panel.
5. Remove screws at top, bottom and sides of cluster securing it to panel.
6. Tilt console forward and reach behind to disconnect speedometer cable and all other connections and lift instrument panel out of carrier after removing screws.
7. Reverse procedure to install.

1977–82 Corvette

Left Hand Side 1978–82
1. Disconnect battery ground cable.
2. Remove left air distribution duct.
3. Remove lens to bezel attaching screws and the lens.
4. Remove cluster to instrument panel attaching screws.
5. Pull cluster rearward slightly, then disconnect speedometer cable and electrical connectors.
6. Remove cluster from vehicle.
7. Reverse procedure to install.

Left Hand Side 1977
1. Disconnect battery ground cable.
2. Lower steering column.
3. Remove screws and washers securing left instrument panel to door opening, top of dash and left side of center instrument panel, Fig. 18.
4. Unclip and remove floor console trim panel.
5. Pull cluster slightly forward to obtain clearance for removal of speedometer cable housing nut, tachometer cable hous-

ing nut, headlamp and ignition switch connectors and panel illuminating lamps.
6. Reverse procedure to install.

Center Cluster 1977–82 Models
1. Disconnect battery ground cable.
2. Remove console tunnel side panels.
3. Remove radio knobs.
4. Remove two screws securing console trim plate to instrument cluster.
5. Remove rear window defogger switch, if equipped, from console trim plate.
6. Remove five screws from upper perimeter of instrument cluster.
7. Pull instrument cluster outward slightly and disconnect electrical connectors.
8. Remove cluster from vehicle.
9. Reverse procedure to install.

FRONT W/S WIPER MOTOR

1977–83 Except Corvette

1. Raise hood and remove cowl screen or grille.
2. Disconnect wiring and washer hoses.
3. Reaching through cowl opening, loosen transmission drive link attaching nuts to motor crankarm.
4. Disconnect drive link from motor crankarm.
5. Remove motor attaching screws.

Fig. 17   Instrument cluster (Typical). 1977–79 Chevy Nova

Fig. 18   Instrument panel. 1977 Corvette

6. Remove motor while guiding crankarm through hole.
7. Reverse procedure to install.

1977—82 Corvette

1. Make sure wiper motor is in "Park" position.
2. Disconnect washer hoses and electrical connectors from assembly.
3. Remove the air intake screen.
4. Remove the nut which retains the crank arm to the motor.
5. Remove the ignition shield and distributor cap to gain access to the motor retaining screws or nuts.

NOTE: *Remove left bank spark plug wires from the cap and mark both cap and wires for aid in reinstallation.*

6. Remove three motor retaining screws or nuts and remove motor.

CAUTION: Wiper motor must be in the "Park" position prior to installation on the cowl. Do not install a motor that was dropped or hung by the drive link.

REAR WIPER MOTOR, REPLACE

1982—83 Camaro

1. Remove wiper blade using tool No. J-8966 or equivalent.
2. Remove nut and spacer from wiper motor shaft, then raise lid and remove lift window trim panel.
3. Disconnect wire connectors from motor, then remove rivets securing motor support to trim panel and remove assembly from vehicle.
4. Remove motor attaching screws and motor.
5. Reverse procedure to install.

FRONT W/S WIPER TRANSMISSION, REPLACE

1977—80 W/Rectangular Motor

1. Remove wiper arms and blades.
2. Raise hood and remove cowl vent screen or grille.
3. Disconnect wiring from motor.
4. Loosen, but do not remove, transmission drive link to motor crankarm attaching nuts and disconnect drive link from crankarm.
5. Remove right and left transmission to body attaching screws and guide transmission and linkage through cowl opening.

NOTE: When installing, motor must be in "Park" position.

6. Reverse procedure to install.

1977—83 W/Round Motor

1. Raise hood and remove cowl vent screen.
2. On Chevelle, Monte Carlo, Camaro and 1977—80 Chevrolet models, remove right and left wiper arm and blades.
3. Loosen, do not remove, attaching nuts securing drive link to motor crankarm.
4. Disconnect transmission drive link from motor crankarm.
5. On Chevelle, Monte Carlo, Camaro and 1977—80 Chevrolet models, remove right and left transmission to body screws.
6. Remove transmission and linkage through cowl opening.

NOTE: When installing, motor must be in "Park" position.

7. Reverse procedure to install.

1977—82 Corvette

1. Make sure motor is in "Park" position.
2. Disconnect battery ground cable.
3. Open hood and remove chamber screen.
4. Loosen nuts retaining ball sockets to crankarm and detach drive rod from crankarm.
5. Remove transmission nuts, then lift rod assemblies from chamber.
6. Remove transmission linkage from chamber.
7. Reverse procedure to install.

REAR W/S WIPER TRANSMISSION, REPLACE

1982—83 Camaro

1. Remove three mounting grommets from transmission housing cover and cover.
2. Remove drive link retainer, then disengage drive link from cam drive pin and position so that cam retainer is accessible.

NOTE: When reassembling drive link to cam, a new retainer must be used.

3. Remove cam retainer and washer, then cam from shaft.

NOTE: During assembly, if cam does not seat fully when pushed onto drive shaft, rotate cam 180 degrees.

4. Drill out three rivets attaching housing to wiper gearbox, and remove transmission.
5. Reverse procedure to install.

NOTE: A service kit is available for installation of the transmission. The kit includes screw, nuts and washers to replace the rivets.

W/S WIPER SWITCH, REPLACE

1978—82 Corvette

1. Disconnect battery ground cable.
2. Remove left air distribution duct.
3. Remove instrument cluster attaching screws and pull cluster rearward.
4. Disconnect speedometer cable and all electrical connectors, then remove cluster.
5. Remove two instrument panel to left door pillar attaching screws and pull left side of instrument panel rearward for access.

6. Remove wiper switch to mounting plate screws, disconnect electrical connector and remove switch.
7. Reverse procedure to install.

1978—83 Malibu & Monte Carlo

1. Disconnect battery ground cable.
2. Remove instrument panel bezel.
3. Remove screws securing wiper switch mounting plate to cluster and pull assembly rearward.
4. Disconnect electrical connector and remove wiper switch.
5. Reverse procedure to install.

1978—83 Chevrolet

1. Disconnect battery ground cable.
2. Remove screws securing control shroud on instrument panel. (One screw is hidden above headlight switch shaft and one is hidden above cigarette lighter knob.)
3. Lift off shroud and remove remaining screws.
4. Unplug wiper switch and remove.
5. Reverse procedure to install.

1977 Corvette

1. Disconnect battery ground cable.
2. Remove steering wheel, turn signal switch and ignition lock as outlined previously.
3. Remove tilt release lever.
4. Remove three turn signal housing attaching screws, then remove housing while guiding the w/s wiper switch wire connector up through column shroud.
5. Turn housing over, then remove 7/16 in. pivot bolt and lift switch from housing.
6. Reverse procedure to install.

1977—79 Nova

1. Disconnect battery ground cable.
2. Disconnect wire connector from rear of wiper switch.
3. Remove three attaching screws from rear of switch.
4. Lift switch out from rear of instrument panel.
5. Reverse procedure to install.

1977 Chevrolet

1. Disconnect battery ground cable.
2. Pull light switch to "On" position and reach under instrument panel and depress shaft release button, then pull shaft from switch.
3. With a suitable tool, pry out wiper switch assembly and disconnect electrical connector.
4. Remove switch from vehicle.
5. Reverse procedure to install.

1977 Chevelle & Monte Carlo

1. Disconnect battery ground cable.
2. Remove instrument cluster.
3. Pull electric connector off rear of wiper switch.
4. Remove screws from front of switch and lift switch out front of panel.
5. Reverse procedure to install.

1977—81 Camaro

1. Disconnect battery ground cable.
2. Remove trim plate and A/C outlet from below steering column if so equipped.
3. Remove light switch.

1 Remove ignition and dimmer switch
2 Remove parts as shown

INSTALL
1 Assemble rack so that first rack tooth engages between first and second tooth of sector
2 Install parts as shown
3 Install ignition and dimmer switch. Refer to step 5

Housing without bearing retainer and bushing has spun-in bearing. If repair is necessary, complete housing assembly replacement is necessary

Fig. 18A Windshield wiper switch remove, except tilt column. 1982–83 Camaro

4. Remove 6 screws securing instrument carrier. Two of these are behind the cluster on either side of steering column.

NOTE: Cigar lighter grounding ring may have to be removed with lighter housing to gain access to left side of carrier.

5. Disconnect wiper switch wiring.
6. Tilting carrier forward, reach behind and remove 3 switch retaining screws and lift out switch.
7. Reverse procedure to install.

1982–83 Camaro

1. Refer to Figs. 18A and 18B for wiper switch replacement.

RADIO, REPLACE

NOTE: When installing radio, be sure to adjust antenna trimmer for peak reception. Also, be sure to connect speaker before applying power to radio.

1978–83 Malibu & Monte Carlo

1. Disconnect battery ground cable.
2. Remove control knobs from control shafts.
3. Remove trim plate attaching screws and trim plate.
4. Disconnect antenna lead and wire connector from radio.
5. Remove stud nut at right side of bracket attachment.
6. Remove control shaft nuts and washers.
7. Remove instrument panel bracket screws and bracket.
8. Remove radio through opening in instrument panel.
9. Reverse procedure to install.

1977–83 Chevrolet

1. Disconnect battery ground cable.
2. Remove control knobs from control shafts.
3. Remove three radio trim plate attaching screws.
4. Remove two screws and bottom nut attaching radio bracket to instrument panel.

REMOVE
1 Remove parts as shown

INSTALL
1 Install parts as shown

Fig. 18B Windshield wiper switch remove, tilt column. 1982–83 Camaro

5. Disconnect antenna lead and wire connector from radio.
6. Remove radio with mounting bracket attached from instrument panel.
7. Remove bracket from radio.
8. Reverse procedure to install.

1977–82 Corvette

1. Disconnect battery ground cable.
2. Remove control knobs from control shafts.
3. Remove instrument cluster as described under Instrument Cluster, Replace.
4. Remove screw attaching radio mounting bracket to reinforcement on floor pan.
5. Pull radio outward and disconnect antenna lead and wire connector from rear of radio.
6. Remove mounting bracket from radio.
7. Reverse procedure to install.

1977 Chevelle & Monte Carlo

1. Disconnect battery ground cable.
2. On A/C vehicles, remove left lap cooler duct.
3. Pull off radio knobs and bezels.
4. Remove control shaft nuts and washers.
5. Disconnect antenna, speaker and power wires.
6. Remove radio to support bracket stud nut.
7. Push radio forward until shafts clear instrument panel and then lower from car.
8. Reverse procedure to install.

1977–83 Camaro & 1977–79 Nova

1. Disconnect battery ground cable.
2. Pull off radio control knobs and bezels.
3. Remove control shaft nuts and washers.
4. Remove screws or nuts from radio brackets.

Fig. 19 Blower motor & heater core. 1978–83 Malibu & Monte Carlo Less A/C

SCREW ATTACHING SEQUENCE AS FOLLOWS. ①② THEN CLOCKWISE FROM ② AROUND MODULE

BLOWER MOTOR
D&C COOLING TUBE
D&C ELECTRICAL CONNECTORS
R&R MOTOR SCREWS
R&R IMPELLER

APPLY SEALER TO TOP AND SIDES ONLY
EXTEND COVERAGE BELOW LOWER
SCREW ON BOTH VERTICAL FLANGES.

VIEW A

EVAPORATOR CORE
* D-E-C A/C SYSTEM
D&C MODULE RUBBER SEAL
R&R MODULE SCREEN
R&R R.H. W/SHLD. WIPER ARM
R&R DIAG. CONN., HI-BLOWER RELAY, THERM. SWITCH MNTG.
D&C AIR ELECTRICAL CONNECTORS AT MODULE TOP
R&R MODULE TOP COVER
R&R ACCUMULATOR BRACKET SCREWS
D&C REFRIGERANT LINES AT ACCUMULATOR & LIQUID LINE
R&R CORE
APPLY NEW SEALING MATERIAL

SEAL
PULL OFF

MODULE LEAF SCREEN
R&R SCREWS

A/C MODULE
D&C NEG. BATTERY CABLE
* D-E-C A/C SYSTEM
R&R HOOD
R&R R.H. W/SHLD. WIPER ARM
R&R MODULE LEAF, SCREEN, SEAL, TOP COVER/BLOWER MOTOR AS ASM.
R&R EVAPORATOR CORE
R&R HEATER CORE
R&R GLOVE BOX
D&C TEMP. CABLE AT MODULE
R&R A/C DUCTWORK & HEATER DISTRIBUTOR OUTLET
R&R A/C CONTROL (LEAVING HARNESSES, CABLES, ETC. ATTACHED TO MODULE)
D&C COMPRESSOR & PRESSURE CUT-OUT SWITCH WIRING
R&R VACUUM RESERVE TANK
R&R ACCUMULATOR BRACKET
R&R MODULE TO COWL SCREWS
TRANSFER PARTS
APPLY NEW STRIP – CAULK
TYPE SEALING MATERIAL

HEATER CORE
** D-R RADIATOR COOLANT
D&C HOSES AT CORE PIPES
R&R RET. BRACKET & GROUND STRAP
D&C MODULE RUBBER SEAL
R&R MODULE SCREEN
R&R R.H. W/SHIELD. WIPER ARM
R&R DIAG. CONN., HI-BLOWER RELAY, THERM. SWITCH MNTG. SCREWS
D&C ALL ELECTRICAL CONNECTORS AT MODULE TOP
R&R MODULE TOP COVER
R&R CORE
APPLY NEW SEALING MATERIAL

**DRAIN AND REPLACE

*DISCHARGE-EVACUATE-CHARGE A/C SYSTEM–ALWAYS TAPE ALL OPEN REFRIGERANT LINES AND USE NEW O-RINGS DIPPED IN CLEAN, 525 VISCOSITY REFRIGERANT OIL.

Fig. 20 Blower motor & heater core. 1978–83 Malibu & Monte Carlo with A/C

5. Push radio forward until shafts clear instrument panel and lower unit enough to remove electrical connections.
6. Disconnect antenna, speaker and power leads and remove radio.
7. Reverse procedure to install.

1982–83 Camaro

1. Disconnect battery ground cable.
2. Remove three console bezel and four radio to console attaching screws.
3. Pull radio outward and disconnect electrical connector, then remove radio.
4. Reverse procedure to install.

BLOWER MOTOR, REPLACE

1977–83 Malibu & Monte Carlo, 1977–83 Chevrolet & 1978–81 Camaro

1. Disconnect battery ground cable.
2. Disconnect blower motor lead wire. On models with A/C, disconnect cooling tube.

3. Remove blower motor to case attaching screws, then remove blower motor, Figs. 19 through 23.
4. Reverse procedure to install.

1982–83 Camaro

1. Disconnect battery ground cable.
2. Disconnect blower motor and resistor wires.
3. On models equipped with A/C, disconnect cooling tube.
4. Remove blower motor retaining screws and motor/cage assembly from case.
5. While holding blower motor cage, remove cage retaining screw and slide cage from motor shaft.
6. Reverse procedure to install.

1980–82 Corvette

1. Disconnect battery ground cable.
2. Remove A/C compressor mounting bolts and position compressor aside with refrigerant lines attached.
3. Remove air cleaner from front and right side inlet ducts, then position air cleaner out of way.
4. Remove engine coolant recovery bottle.

5. Disconnect hose and electrical connections from blower motor.
6. Remove blower motor mounting flange attaching screws, then remove blower with impeller from vehicle.

1977–79 Corvette

1. Disconnect battery ground cable.
2. Remove radiator supply tank, if so equipped.
3. Disconnect blower motor wires.
4. Remove blower motor to case mounting screws and remove motor, Fig. 23.
5. Reverse procedure to install.

1977 Camaro & 1977–79 Nova

1. Disconnect battery ground cable.
2. Disconnect blower lead and remove all hoses and wires connected to fender skirt then raise vehicle.
3. On all except Nova, remove all fender skirt retaining bolts except those retaining skirt to radiator support. On Nova, remove the eight rearmost fender skirt to fender retaining screws.

Fig. 21 Blower motor & heater core. 1977–83 Chevrolet less A/C

Fig. 22 Blower motor & core. 1977–83 Chevrolet with A/C

4. Pull out and down on fender skirt and wedge a 2 × 4 inch block of wood between skirt and fender to allow room for blower motor removal.
5. Remove blower to case retaining screws and remove blower assembly. Gently pry flange, since sealer will act as an adhesive, Fig. 23.

NOTE: On Nova, remove blower retaining nut and separate wheel and motor before removing through fender and skirt.

6. Reverse procedure to install.

HEATER CORE, REPLACE

Less Air Cond.

1982–83 Camaro
1. Disconnect battery ground cable and drain cooling system.
2. Remove right lower hush panel and instrument panel trim panel.
3. On models equipped with V8-305 fuel injected engine, remove ESC module.
4. Remove lower right instrument panel carrier to cowl screw.
5. Remove heater case cover attaching screws and cover.

NOTE: To gain access to the upper left screw, position a long 3/8 inch socket extension through the opening exposed by removal of the trim panel. Carefully lift lower right corner of instrument panel to align socket extension.

Fig. 23 Blower motor (Typical). Except 1977–83 Chevrolet & 1978–83 Chevelle & Monte Carlo

6. Remove support plate and baffle screws, then heater core, support plate and baffle from case.

1978–83 Malibu & Monte Carlo
1. Disconnect battery ground cable and drain cooling system.
2. Disconnect heater hoses from heater core. Plug core outlets to prevent coolant spillage.
3. Disconnect wire connectors, then remove front module cover attaching screws and cover.
4. Remove heater core from module, Fig. 19.
5. Reverse procedure to install.

1977–83 Chevrolet
1. Disconnect battery ground cable and drain cooling system.
2. Disconnect heater hoses from heater core. Plug core outlets to prevent coolant spillage.
3. Remove attaching screws from around perimeter of heater core cover on engine side of dash panel.
4. Pull heater core cover from dash panel mounting.
5. Remove heater core from module assembly, Fig. 21.
6. Reverse procedure to install.

1977–83 Exc. 1977–83 Chevrolet & 1978–83 Malibu & Monte Carlo & 1982–83 Camaro
1. Disconnect battery ground cable.
2. Drain radiator, disconnect heater hoses at core and plug openings to prevent spillage of water.
3. Remove nuts from air distributor duct studs on engine side of firewall, Figs. 24 through 27.
4. On 1977 Chevelle and Monte Carlo, remove distributor duct retaining screw.
5. On Nova, remove glove box and door and drill out lower right hand distributor stud with a 1/4" drill.
6. On Camaro, remove glove box, radio, and defroster duct to distributor duct screw.
7. On Corvette, remove right instrument panel pad, right hand dash braces, center dash console duct and floor outlet duct, radio and center dash console.
8. On all models, pull distributor duct from firewall being careful not to bend cable.
9. On Camaro, disconnect cable and resistor wires and remove distributor and core.

10. On all other models, remove core assembly from duct.
11. Reverse procedure to install.

With Air Cond.

1982–83 Camaro
For removal procedure, refer to "Heater Core, Replace" less air conditioning.

1978–83 Malibu & Monte Carlo
1. Disconnect battery ground cable and drain cooling system.
2. Disconnect heater hoses at heater core.
3. Remove retaining bracket and ground strap.
4. Remove module rubber seal and module screen, Fig. 20.
5. Remove right hand w/s wiper arm.
6. Remove high blower relay and thermostatic switch mounting screws.
7. Disconnect wire connector at top of module, then remove module top cover.
8. Remove heater core from module.
9. Reverse procedure to install.

1977–83 Chevrolet
1. Disconnect battery ground cable and drain cooling system.
2. Disconnect heater hoses at heater core. Cap core outlets to prevent coolant spillage.
3. Remove diagnosis connector to upper case attaching screws.
4. Disconnect wire connectors from blower motor, resistor, blower relay and thermostatic switch.
5. Remove wiring harness retainer from blower case shroud.

Fig. 24 Heater core. 1977 Chevelle & Monte Carlo (Typical)

Fig. 25 Heater core. 1977–79 Chevy Nova (Typical)

Fig. 26 Heater core. 1977–81 Camaro (Typical)

Fig. 27 Heater core. 1977–82 Corvette (Typical)

6. Remove module screen to cowl attaching screws and remove screen.
7. Remove upper case to lower case attaching screws.

NOTE: Two screws are located inside air intake area at case separation point.

8. Disconnect wire connector from thermostatic switch, then remove screws attaching switch to evaporator case. Carefully remove insulation and loosen two clamps enough to pull formed end of switch capillary tube from under clamps attaching tube to evaporator inlet pipe for installation.
9. Remove evaporator inlet pipe support bracket to case attaching screws and remove bracket.
10. Remove heater-evaporator core case cover, using care not to damage sealer.
11. Remove heater core to case attaching screws at top of heater core, then remove heater core, Fig. 22.

NOTE: The heater core is held in position at bottom by a spring clip. Pull up firmly on heater core to disengage from clip. When installing, position core base in alignment with clip before lowering core into case. Upper retaining bracket will line up with hole at top of core when core is properly seated.

12. Reverse procedure to install.

1977 Chevelle & Monte Carlo
1. Disconnect battery ground cable and drain radiator.
2. Disconnect heater hoses from core and plug hoses and core openings.
3. Remove distributor case stud nuts projecting through firewall, Fig. 24. On 1977, remove resistor assembly and the

last stud nut through its opening.
4. Remove glove box door and glove box.
5. On all models, remove right hand lap cooler and kick pad cover.
6. On all models, disconnect center duct hoses and remove center duct to selector duct screws, then remove center duct.
7. Remove floor distributor duct.
8. Remove lower right hand distributor duct to dash panel screw.
9. On all models, remove air selector retaining screws, then lower selector assembly. Disconnect all wiring, vacuum lines and cables.
10. On all models, remove core and housing from selector assembly, then core from housing.
11. Reverse procedure to install.

1977–79 Nova
1. Disconnect battery ground cable and drain radiator.
2. Disconnect heater hoses and plug hoses and core openings to prevent coolant spillage.
3. Remove accessible stud nut from air selector duct, Fig. 25.
4. Remove right hand fender skirt to fender and skirt reinforcing screws. Lower skirt to wheel and remove remaining stud nut.
5. Remove glove box door, glove box and right hand kick pad recirculating air valve.
6. Remove center and floor ducts. Remove screws securing selector duct halves together, then separate.
7. Remove selector duct right half to firewall screws and remove duct.
8. Disconnect all wiring and cables. Scribe location of temperature camming plate on selector duct and remove plate and core.
9. Reverse procedure to install.

1977–81 Camaro
1. Disconnect battery ground cable.
2. Drain radiator and disconnect heater hoses from core. Plug openings to prevent spillage of coolant.

3. Remove nuts from distributor studs on engine side of firewall, Fig. 26.
4. Remove glove box and radio.
5. Remove defroster duct to distributor duct screw. With radio removed, the defroster duct can be pulled rearward to gain clearance for distributor duct removal.
6. Carefully pull distributor from firewall and disconnect wiring and cables. Remove duct and core from vehicle.
7. Reverse procedure to install.

1981–82 Corvette
1. Disconnect battery ground cable and drain radiator.
2. Disconnect heater hoses from core and plug hoses and core openings.
3. Remove heater case retaining nut from top of blower case.
4. Remove glove box.
5. Remove console side panels retaining screw and swing both sides out.
6. Remove center gauge cluster assembly and radio.
7. Remove right windshield pillar trim panel.
8. Remove right side dash panel retaining screws and pull panel rearward to release upper retaining clip.
9. Remove right side vent, main vent distribution, and lower heater deflector ducts.
10. Remove heater-defroster distribution duct assembly, then disconnect temperature cable and vacuum hose from heater housing.
11. Remove heater housing assembly from vehicle and heater core from housing.
12. Reverse procedure to install.

1977–80 Corvette
1. Disconnect battery ground cable. Drain radiator and disconnect heater hoses from core. Plug openings to prevent spillage of coolant.

Fig. 28 Servo unit rod adjustment

Fig. 29 Release switches and brackets (Typical). 1977–83

2. Remove nuts from engine side distributor duct, Fig. 27.
3. Remove right hand dash pad and center instrument cluster. Remove dash braces.
4. Disconnect right dash outlet duct from center duct. Remove screws attaching center duct to selector duct and remove center duct.
5. Remove screws attaching selector duct to firewall and pull selector rearward and to the right. Disconnect cables and wiring.
6. Remove selector duct from car. Remove temperature door camming plate from duct and remove core and housing.
7. Reverse procedure to install.

SPEED CONTROLS

1977—83 Cruise Master

Servo Unit Adjustment

Adjust the bead chain cable or rod so that it is as tight as possible without holding the throttle open when the carburetor is set at its lowest idle throttle position. The cable is adjusted by turning the hex portion of servo. The bead chain or cable is adjusted so there is 1/16 inch of lost motion in servo cable. The rod is adjusted by turning link onto rod. With rod hooked through tab, on power unit, turn link onto rod until dimension in Fig. 28 is obtained, then install link and retainer. This adjustment should be made with ignition off and fast idle cam in off position with throttle completely closed.

When connecting the bead chain or cable (engine stopped) manually set the fast idle cam at its lowest step and connect the chain so that it does not hold the idle screw off the cam. If the chain needs to be cut, cut it three beads beyond the bead that pulls the linkage.

Regulator Unit Adjustment

To remove any difference between engagement and cruising speed, one adjustment is possible. However, no adjustment should be made until the following items have been checked or serviced.
1. Bead chain or cable properly adjusted.
2. All hoses in good condition, properly attached, not leaking, pinched or cracked.
3. Regulator air filter cleaned and properly oiled.
4. Electric and vacuum switches properly adjusted.

Engagement—Cruising Speed Zeroing

If the cruising speed is lower than the engagement speed, loosen the orifice tube locknut and turn the tube outward; if higher turn the tube inward. Each 1/4 turn will alter the engagement-cruising speed difference one mph. Tighten locknut after adjustment and check the system operation at 50 mph.

Brake Release Switch

The electric brake switch is actuated when the brake pedal is depressed .38–.64 inch, Fig. 29. The vacuum release switch is actuated when brake pedal is moved 5/16 inch on all units.

Gasoline Engine Section

Refer to Pontiac Chapter for service procedures on 4-151 engines.
Refer to Buick Chapter for service procedures on V6-231 engines & turbocharger service.

ENGINE MOUNTS, REPLACE

1982—83 V6-173

1. Disconnect battery ground cable.
2. Remove upper half of fan shroud.
3. Raise and support vehicle.
4. Remove engine mount through bolt, then raise front of engine to release weight from mount.
5. Remove mount to engine bolts and mount.

NOTE: Raise engine only enough to provide sufficient clearance for mount removal. Check for interference between rear of engine and cowl panel which could result in distributor damage.

6. Reverse procedure to install.

1978—79 V6-200

1. Remove mount retaining bolt from below frame mounting bracket, Fig. 1.
2. Raise front of engine and remove mount to engine bolts and remove mount.

NOTE: Right hand mount may be removed by loosening through bolt. It is not necessary to remove it. Raise engine only enough to provide sufficient clearance for mount removal. Check for interference between rear of engine and cowl panel.

3. Reverse procedure to install.

1977—79 6-250

1. Remove nut, washer and engine mount through-bolt.
2. Raise engine to release weight from mount.
3. Remove bracket-to-mount bolt, then remove mount.
4. Install new mount on bracket.
5. Lower engine, install through-bolt and tighten all mount bolts, Figs. 2, 3 and 4.

1977—83 All V-8 & 1980—83 V6-229

1. Remove mount retaining bolt from below frame mounting bracket, Figs. 5 and 6.
2. Raise front of engine and remove mount to engine bolts and mount. On models equipped with V6-229 engine, the right hand mount may be removed by loosening the through bolt.

NOTE: Raise engine only enough to provide sufficient clearance for mount removal. Check for interference between rear of engine and cowl panel which could result in distributor damage.

3. Reverse procedure to install.

ENGINE, REPLACE

NOTE: V8 engines are equipped with two strap type lifting rings, one at the right front, the other at the left rear of the engine. Use of

Fig. 1 Engine mounts (Typical). V6-200

Fig. 2 Engine mounts (Typical). Chevelle, Chevrolet Malibu & Monte Carlo 6-250

Fig. 3 Engine mounts (Typical). 1977—79 Nova 6-250

Fig. 4 Engine mounts (Typical). 1977-79 Camaro 6-250

these rings eliminates the need to remove the rocker arm covers to install lifting adapters.

1982-83 Camaro

1. Disconnect battery ground cable.
2. Scribe hood hinge locations and remove hood.
3. Remove air cleaner and drain cooling system.
4. Remove radiator hoses, coolant recovery hose, upper fan shroud and transmission cooler lines.
5. Remove radiator, fan assembly and heater hoses.
6. Disconnect accelerator linkage, and on models equipped with cruise control, cruise control detent cable.
7. Remove vacuum brake booster line, then the distributor cap.
8. Remove any remaining hoses and wires interfering with engine removal.
9. Remove power steering pump and position aside.
10. Raise and support vehicle.
11. Remove exhaust pipes from manifold.
12. Remove dust cover and catalytic converter attaching bolts, then disconnect starter wires.
13. Remove bell housing bolts and engine mount through bolts.
14. Disconnect fuel lines from fuel pump.
15. Lower vehicle.
16. Support transmission with a suitable jack.
17. Remove A.I.R./Converter pipes bracket.
18. Remove engine assembly from vehicle, including wire from bracket at rear left of engine.
19. Reverse procedure to install.

1977-83 Exc. 1982-83 Camaro

1. Disconnect battery ground cable.
2. Scribe hood hinge locations and remove hood.
3. Remove air cleaner.
4. Drain cooling system.
5. Disconnect radiator and heater hoses,

Fig. 5 Engine mounts. 1977-83 V8 Except Corvette (typical)

then remove radiator and shroud.
6. Disconnect wiring at following locations: starter solenoid, alternator, temperature switch, oil pressure switch and on 1977-79 vehicles, ignition coil, or, on 1980-82 models, distributor.
7. Disconnect accelerator linkage, fuel line from tank to pump, hoses from vapor storage canister and vacuum line to power brake unit at manifold.
8. Remove power steering pump and position aside with hoses attached.
9. Raise and support vehicle.
10. Drain oil pan.
11. Disconnect exhaust pipe(s) at manifold and catalytic converter bracket from rear transmission mount.
12. Remove starter.
13. Remove flywheel splash shield or converter housing cover.
14. On models equipped with automatic transmission, remove converter to flywheel attaching bolts.
15. On all models, remove engine mount through bolts.
16. Remove bell housing bolts.

Fig. 6 Engine mounts. 1977-82 Corvette (typical)

17. Lower vehicle.
18. Support transmission with a suitable jack.
19. Attach suitable engine lifting equipment to engine and raise engine slightly.
20. Remove engine mount to engine brackets.
21. Remove engine assembly from vehicle.
22. Reverse procedure to install.

CYLINDER HEAD, REPLACE

V6-173

1. Remove intake manifold.
2. Raise and support vehicle.
3. Disconnect exhaust pipe from manifold, then drain engine block.
4. If left hand cylinder head is to be removed, remove dipstick tube attachment.
5. Lower vehicle.
6. Loosen rocker arms until push rods can be

Fig. 7 Cylinder head tightening sequence. V6-200

Fig. 7A Cylinder head tightening sequence. V6-173

ALL BOLTS 30 LB. FT.

STUDS

Fig. 8 Intake manifold tightening sequence. V6-200

Fig. 9 Cylinder head tightening sequence. 6-250

Fig. 10 Cylinder head tightening sequence. Small V8 engines

Fig. 11 Intake manifold tightening sequence. Small V8 engines

Fig. 8A Intake manifold tightening sequence. V6-173

removed.
7. If right hand cylinder head is to be removed, remove alternator bracket.
8. Remove cylinder head bolts and cylinder head.
9. Reverse procedure to install. Coat cylinder head bolts with sealer. Torque cylinder bolts in sequence shown in Fig. 7A and intake manifold bolts in sequence shown in Fig. 8A.

V6-200, 229 & All V8s

1. Drain cooling system and engine block.
2. Remove intake and exhaust manifolds.
3. Remove alternator lower mounting bolt and position alternator aside.
4. If equipped with A/C, remove compressor and forward mounting bracket and position aside.
5. Remove rocker arm cover, rocker arms and push rods.

NOTE: Keep rocker arm, rocker arm balls and push rods in order so they can be installed in the same position.

6. On all 1981–83 models, except Corvette, remove diverter valve.
7. Remove cylinder head bolts and cylinder head.
8. Reverse procedure to install. Tighten cylinder head and intake manifold bolts in sequence shown in Figs. 7 and 8 and 10 & 11.

1977–79 6-250

Exc. Integral Intake Manifold
1. Drain cooling system and remove air cleaner.
2. Disconnect choke rod, accelerator pedal rod at bellcrank on manifold, and fuel and vacuum lines at carburetor.
3. Disconnect exhaust pipe at manifold flange, then unfasten and remove manifolds and carburetor as an assembly.
4. Remove fuel and vacuum line retaining clip from water outlet and disconnect wire harness from temperature sending unit and coil, leaving harness clear of clips on rocker arm cover.
5. Disconnect radiator hose at water outlet housing and battery ground strap at cylinder head.
6. Remove spark plugs and coil.
7. Remove rocker arm cover. Back off rocker arm nuts, pivot rocker arms to clear push rods and lift out push rods.
8. Unfasten and remove cylinder head.
9. Reverse procedure to install and tighten head bolts in the sequence shown in Fig. 9.

With Integral Intake Manifold
1. Disconnect battery ground cable and remove air cleaner.
2. Remove power steering pump and A.I.R. pump brackets, if equipped.
3. Raise vehicle and disconnect exhaust pipe at manifold and converter bracket at transmission mount. If equipped with manifold converter, disconnect exhaust pipe from converter and remove converter.
4. Lower vehicle and remove rear heat shield and accelerator cable bracket.
5. Remove exhaust manifold attaching bolts and exhaust manifold.
6. Remove rocker arm covers, rocker arms and push rods.

NOTE: Keep rocker arms, rocker arm balls and push rod in order so they can be installed in the same position.

7. Drain cooling system and engine block.
8. Remove fuel and vacuum line from retaining clip at water outlet, then disconnect wires at temperature sending unit.
9. Disconnect air injection hose at check valve, if equipped.
10. Disconnect radiator hose at water outlet housing and battery ground cable at cylinder head.
11. Remove cylinder attaching bolts and cylinder head.
12. Reverse procedure to install. Tighten cylinder head bolts in sequence shown in Fig. 9.

VALVES, ADJUST

NOTE: After the engine has been thoroughly warmed up the valves may be adjusted with the engine shut off as follows: With engine in position to fire No. 1 cylinder the following valves may be adjusted: V6-173, Exhaust 1-2-3, intake 1-5-6. V6-200 and 229, Exhaust 1-5-6, intake 1-2-3. 6-250, Exhaust 1-3-5, intake 1-2-4. V8's, Exhaust 1-3-4-8, intake 1-2-5-7. Then crank the engine one more complete revolution which will bring No. 4 cylinder on V6-173, V6-200 and 229, engine and No. 6 cylinder on 6-250 and V8 engines, to the firing position at which time the following valves may be adjusted: V6-173, Exhaust 4-5-6, intake 2-3-4. V6-200 and 229, Exhaust 2-3-4, intake 4-5-6. 6-250, Exhaust 2-4-6, intake 3-5-6. V8's, Exhaust 2-5-6-7, intake 3-4-6-8.

Fig. 12 Removing valve rocker arm stud

Fig. 13 Installing valve rocker arm stud

Fig. 14   Hydraulic valve lifter

Fig. 15   Timing gear oil nozzle removal. 6-250

CENTERING TOOL MUST BE INSTALLED AS SHOWN BEFORE TIGHTENING TIMING COVER TO CENTER SEAL SURFACE AROUND C/S.

J-23042 TIMING COVER SEAL ALIGNER AND INSTALLER

Fig. 16   Installing timing case cover. 6-250

The following procedure, performed with the engine running should be done only in case readjustment is required.

1. After engine has been warmed up to operating temperature, remove valve cover and install a new valve cover gasket.
2. With engine running at idle speed, back off valve rocker arm nut until rocker arm starts to clatter.
3. Turn rocker arm nut down slowly until the clatter just stops. This is the zero lash position.
4. Turn nut down 1/4 additional turn and pause 10 seconds until engine runs smoothly. Repeat additional 1/4 turns, pausing 10 seconds each time, until nut has been turned down the number of turns listed in the *Valve Specifications Chart* from the zero lash position.

NOTE: This preload adjustment must be done slowly to allow the lifter to adjust itself to prevent the possibility of interference between the intake valve head and top of piston, which might result in internal damage and/or bent push rods. Noisy lifters should be replaced.

ROCKER ARM STUDS, REPLACE

Rocker arm studs that have damaged threads may be replaced with standard studs. If studs are loose in the head, oversize studs (.003" or .013") may be installed after reaming the holes with a proper size reamer.

1. Remove the old stud by placing a suitable spacer, Fig. 12, over stud. Install nut and flat washer and remove stud by turning nut.
2. Ream hole for oversize stud.
3. Coat press-fit area of stud with rear axle lube. Then install new stud, Fig. 13. If tool shown is used, it should bottom on the head.

VALVE ARRANGEMENT

Front to Rear

6-250	E-I-I-E-I-I-E-E-I-I-E
Small V8	E-I-I-E-I-I-E-I-E

VALVE LIFT SPECS

Engine	Year	Intake	Exhaust
4-151⑧	1982	.4060	.4060
V6-173	1982	.3490	.3930
V6-200	1978–79	.3730	.4100
V6-229	1980–82	.3730	.4100
V6-231①②	1981–82	.3730	.3660
V6-231①②	1979–80	.3570	.3660
	1978	.3830	.3660
V6-231①③	1980–82	.3410	.3660
6-250	1977–79	.3880	.4051
V6-262⑥⑦	1982	.3750	.3750
V8-267	1980–82	.3570	.3900
	1979	.3730	.3900
V8-305	1980–82	.3570	.3900
	1977–79	.3727	.4100
V8-305⑨	1982	.3900	.4100
V8-350④	1977–81	.3900	.4100
V8-350⑤	1977–80	.4500	.4600
	1982	.4100	.4230
V8-350⑥⑦	1980–82	.3750	.3760

①—Refer to Buick Chapter for service procedures on this engine.
②—Except turbocharged engine.
③—Turbocharged engine.
④—Except Corvette high performance engine.
⑤—Corvette high performance engine.
⑥—Diesel engine.
⑦—Refer to Oldsmobile Chapter for service procedures on this engine.
⑧—Refer to Pontiac Chapter for service procedures on this engine.
⑨—Fuel injected engine.

VALVE TIMING

Intake Opens Before TDC

Engine	Year	Degrees
4-151⑥	1982	33
V6-173	1982	25
V6-200	1978–79	34
V6-229	1980–82	42
V6-231①	1979–82	16
	1978	17
6-250	1977–79	16
V6-262④⑤	1982	16
V8-267	1981–82	44
V8-267	1979–80	28
V8-305⑦	1982	38
V8-305	1981–82	44
V8-305	1977–80	28
V8-350	1981	38
V8-350②	1977–80	28
V8-350③	1977–80	52
	1982	32
V8-350④⑤	1980–82	16

①—Refer to Buick Chapter for service procedures on this engine.
②—Except Corvette high performance engine.
③—Corvette high performance engine.
④—Diesel engine.
⑤—Refer to Oldsmobile Chapter for service procedures on this engine.
⑥—Refer to Pontiac Chapter for service procedures on this engine.
⑦—Fuel injected engine.

PUSH RODS

On engines that use push rods with a hardened insert at one end, the hardened end is identified by a color stripe and should always be installed toward the rocker arm during assembly.

Service Bulletin

On 6-250 engines with air conditioning, it is not necessary to remove the distributor wires, etc. to replace the valve push rod cover and/or gasket.

1. Remove coil and bracket from block.
2. Remove distributor hold-down clamp.
3. Lift distributor up for clearance (do not disengage from cam gear), then remove push rod cover.
4. Use new gasket and reverse procedure to install.

VALVE GUIDES

On all engines valves operate in guide holes bored in the head. If clearance becomes excessive, use the next oversize valve and ream the bore to fit. Valves with oversize stems are available in .003, .015 and .030 inch.

HYDRAULIC LIFTERS, REPLACE

Valve lifters may be lifted from their bores after removing rocker arms and push rods.

Fig. 17   Removing camshaft gear from camshaft. 6-250

Fig. 18   Checking camshaft end play which should be .001 to .005. 6-250

Fig. 19   Timing gear locating marks. 6-250 engines

Adjustable pliers with taped jaws may be used to remove lifters that are stuck due to varnish, carbon, etc. Fig. 14 illustrates the type of lifter used.

TIMING CASE COVER, REPLACE

NOTE: On all engines the cover oil seal may be replaced without taking off the timing gear cover. After removing the vibration damper, pry out the old seal with a screwdriver. Install the new seal with the lip or open end toward inside of cover and drive it into position.

V6-173

1. Remove water pump, then, on vehicles equipped with A/C, remove compressor and mounting bracket and position aside.
2. Remove vibration damper, then disconnect lower radiator hose from cover and heater hose from water pump.
3. Remove cover retaining bolts and cover.
4. Thoroughly clean sealing surfaces of front cover and engine block, then apply a continuous thin bead of anaerobic sealant #1052357 or equivalent to front cover sealing surface.
5. Install front cover and water pump on engine, then install retaining bolts and nut and torque to specifications.

NOTE: Final torquing of bolts must be completed within five minutes of installing the cover.

6. Reconnect hoses and install vibration damper.
7. Install A/C compressor and mounting bracket.
8. Service cooling system as required.

6-250

1. To remove cover, remove radiator.
2. Remove vibration damper.

3. Remove the two oil pan to front cover attaching screws.
4. Remove front cover to cylinder block attaching screws.
5. Pull cover slightly forward; then, using a sharp knife, cut oil pan front seal flush with cylinder block at both sides of cover.
6. Remove cover and attached portion of oil pan front seal.
7. Pry oil seal out of cover with a large screwdriver. Install new seal with open side of seal inside of cover and drive or press seal into place.
8. If oil nozzle is to be replaced, remove it with pliers as shown in Fig. 15. Drive new nozzle in place, using a suitable light plastic or rubber hammer.
9. Clean gasket surfaces.
10. Cut tabs from new oil pan front seal, then install seal on cover, pressing tips into cover holes.
11. Install a suitable centering tool over end of crankshaft.
12. Coat gasket with light grease and stick it in position on cover.
13. Apply a 1/8 inch bead of RTV sealer at joint of oil pan and cover.
14. Install cover over centering tool, Fig. 16, and install cover screws, tightening them to 6 to 8 ft. lbs. *It is important that the centering tool be used to align the cover so the vibration damper installation will not damage the seal and position seal evenly around damper hub surface.*

V6 & V8 Engines Exc. V6-173

1. Remove vibration damper and water pump.
2. Remove cover retaining screws and cover.
3. Clean gasket surface of block and timing case cover.
4. Remove any excess oil pan gasket material that may be protruding at the oil pan to engine block junction.
5. Apply a thin bead of RTV #1052366 sealer or equivalent to the joint formed at oil pan and block.
6. Coat new gasket with sealer and position it on cover, then install cover to oil pan seal on cover and coat bottom of seal with engine oil.
7. Position cover on engine and loosely install the upper bolts.
8. Tighten screws alternately and evenly while pressing downward on cover so that dowels are aligned with holes in cover. Do

not force cover over dowels as cover can be distorted.
9. Install remaining cover screws, vibration damper and water pump.

TIMING GEARS, REPLACE

6-250

When necessary to install a new camshaft gear, the camshaft will have to be removed as the gear is a pressed fit on the shaft. The camshaft is held in position by a thrust plate which is fastened to the crankcase by two capscrews which are accessible through two holes in the gear web.

Use an arbor press to remove the gear and when doing so, a suitable sleeve, Fig. 17, should be employed to support the gear properly on its steel hub.

Before installing a new gear, assemble a new thrust plate on the shaft and press the gear on just far enough so that the thrust plate has practically no clearance, yet is free to turn. The correct clearance is from .001" to .005", Fig. 18.

The crankshaft gear can be removed by utilizing the two tapped holes in conjunction with a gear puller.

When the timing gears are installed, be sure the punch-marks on both gears are in mesh, Fig. 19. Backlash between the gears should be from .004" to .006", Fig. 20. Check the run-out of the gears, and if the camshaft gear run-out exceeds .004" or the crank gear run-out is in excess of .003", remove the gear (or gears) and examine for burrs, dirt or some other fault which may cause the run-out. If these conditions are not the cause, replace the gear (or gears).

TIMING CHAIN, REPLACE

V6 & V8 Engines

1. Remove timing chain cover as outlined previously.
2. Remove crankshaft oil slinger.
3. Crank engine until timing marks on sprockets are in alignment, Fig. 21.
4. Remove three camshaft-to-sprocket bolts.
5. Remove camshaft sprocket and timing chain together. Sprocket is a light press fit on camshaft for approximately 1/8". If sprocket does not come off easily, a light blow with a plastic hammer on the lower edge of the sprocket should dislodge it.
6. If crankshaft sprocket is to be replaced, remove it with a suitable gear puller. Install new sprocket, aligning key and keyway.

Fig. 20 Checking timing gear backlash with dial indicator. Lash should be .004 to .006". 6-250

Fig. 21 Timing gear locating marks. V6 & V8 engines

Fig. 22 Piston & rod assembly. 6-250 engine

7. Install chain on camshaft sprocket. Hold sprocket verticle with chain hanging below and shift around to align the timing marks on sprockets.
8. Align dowel in camshaft with dowel hole in sprocket and install sprocket on camshaft. *Do not attempt to drive sprocket on camshaft as welch plug at rear of engine can be dislodged.*
9. Draw sprocket onto camshaft, using the three mounting bolts. Tighten to 20 ft. lb. torque.
10. Lubricate timing chain and install cover.

CAMSHAFT

6-250 Engines

It is recommended that the engine be removed from the vehicle for camshaft removal. Remove valve train components, engine front cover, fuel pump and distributor. Remove camshaft thrust plate screws and pull camshaft from cylinder block.

V6 & V8 Engines

1. Remove valve lifters and engine front cover.
2. Remove grille.
3. On all models, remove fuel pump and the push rod.
4. Remove timing chain as outlined previously.
5. On all except V6-173, install two 5/16-18×4 bolts in camshaft bolt holes, then remove camshaft.
6. Reverse procedure to install.

PISTONS & RODS, ASSEMBLE

1977-82

Assemble pistons to connecting rods as shown in Figs. 22 to 25A.

Upon installation, measure the connecting rod side clearance using a suitable feeler gauge. Clearance should be as follows:

Engine	Year	Clearance
V6-173	1982	.006–.017
V6-200	1978–79	.006–.014
V6-229	1980–82	.006–.014
6-250	1977–79	.007–.016
V8-267	1980–82	.006–.014
V8-305	1977–78	.008–.014
	1979–82	.006–.014
V8-350	1977–78	.008–.014
V8-350①	1979–82	.006–.014
V8-350②	1979–82	.008–.014

①—Except Corvette high performance engine.
②—Corvette high performance engine.

Fig. 23 Piston & rod assembly. V8-267, 305, & 350

PISTONS, PINS & RINGS

Pistons are available in standard and oversizes of .001 and .030 inch on all except V6-200 and .030 inch on V6-200.

Piston rings are available in standard and oversizes of .030 inch.

MAIN & ROD BEARINGS

Connecting rod bearings are available in standard and undersizes of .001, .002, .010 and .020 inch.

Main bearings are available in standard and undersizes of .001, .002, .009, .010 and .020 inch.

NOTE: 6-250 Engines

The rear main bearing journal has no oil hole drilling. To remove the upper bearing half (bearing half with oil hole) proceed as follows after cap is removed:

1. Use a small drift punch and hammer to start the bearing rotating out of the block.
2. Use a pair of pliers (tape jaws) to hold the bearing thrust surface to the oil slinger and rotate the crankshaft to pull the bearing out.
3. To install, start the bearing (side not notched) into side of block by hand, then use pliers as before to turn bearing half into place.
4. The last 1/4 inch movement may be done by holding just the slinger with the pliers or tap in place with a drift punch.

CRANKSHAFT REAR OIL SEAL, REPLACE

Exc. V6-173

NOTE: These engines are equipped with helix type rear seal. A seal starting tool, Fig. 26, must be used to prevent the upper seal half from coming into contact with the sharp edge of the block.

Fig. 24 Piston & rod assembly. V8-350 high perf.

Fig. 25 Piston & rod assembly. V6-200, 229

Fig. 25A Piston & rod assembly. V6-173

When necessary to correct an oil leak due to a defective seal, always replace the upper and lower seal halves as a unit, Fig. 27. *When installing either half, lubricate the lip portion only with engine oil, keeping oil off the parting line surface as this is treated with glue. Always clean crankshaft surface before installing a new seal.*

1. To replace the lower seal, remove seal from groove in bearing cap, using a small screwdriver to pry it out.
2. Insert new seal and roll it in place with finger and thumb.
3. To replace the upper seal (with engine in car) use a small hammer and tap a brass pin punch on one end of the seal until it protrudes far enough to be removed with pliers.
4. Position tip of tool, Fig. 26, between crankshaft and seal seat in cylinder block.
5. Position seal between crankshaft and tip of tool with seal bead contacting tip of tool. Ensure oil seal lip is facing toward front of engine.
6. Roll seal around crankshaft, using tool as a "Shoehorn" to protect seal bead from sharp corner of seal seat surface in cylinder block.

NOTE: Tool must remain in position until seal is properly seated with both ends flush with block.

Fig. 26 Fabricated seal starting tool for helix type seal

7. Remove tool, using care not to dislodge seal.
8. Install new seal into bearing cap with tool as outlined previously.
9. Install bearing cap with sealant applied to the cap to case interface. Do not apply sealant to seal ends. Torque rear main bearing cap bolts to specifications as listed in the "Engine Tightening Specification Chart".

V6-173

1. Remove oil pan and oil pump as described further on.
2. Remove rear main bearing cap.
3. Using tool No. J-29114-2, gently drive upper seal into groove approximately 1/4 in.
4. Repeat step 3 for other end of seal.
5. Measure the amount that was driven in on one side and add 1/16 in. Using a suitable cutting tool, cut this length from the oil rear main bearing cap lower seal using the main bearing cap as a guide. Repeat this step for the other end of seal.
6. Place piece of cut seal into groove of seal installer tool guide No. J-29114-1 and install tool guide onto engine block.
7. Using seal packing tool No. J29114-2, drive piece of seal into block. Drive seal in until packing tool contacts machined stop.
8. Remove tool guide and repeat steps 6 and 7 for other end of seal.
9. Install new seal in bearing cap.
10. Install rear main bearing cap. Apply a thin film of sealant No. 1052357 or equivalent to rear main bearing cap and case interface. Use care not to allow sealant to contact crankshaft journal or main bearing.

OIL PAN, REPLACE

1982–83 Camaro V6-173 & V8-305

1. Disconnect battery ground cable, then remove fan shroud.
2. Raise and support vehicle, then drain crankcase.
3. Remove A.I.R. pipe and hanger bolts from catalytic converter.

4. Remove starter motor attaching bolts and position starter motor aside.
5. Remove engine mount through bolts, then raise engine.
6. Remove oil pan attaching bolts and oil pan.

NOTE: If oil pan removal is hampered by the forward crankshaft throw and/or counterweight extending downward, turn crankshaft as needed to put throw in a horizontal position.

7. Reverse procedure to install. Apply a 1/8 inch wide bead of RTV sealant #1052366 or equivalent on oil pan sealing flange.

NOTE: If M6 x 1.0 bolts are used, torque to 8 ft. lbs. If M8 x 1.25 bolts are used, torque to 18 ft. lbs.

1980–82 V6-229

1. Disconnect battery ground cable, then remove upper half of fan shroud.
2. On 1981–83 models equipped with cruise control, remove cruise control servo bracket.
3. Raise vehicle and drain crankcase.
4. Disconnect exhaust crossover pipe from exhaust manifold.
5. Remove torque converter cover, if equipped.

Fig. 27 Crankshaft and rear oil seal (typical)

Fig. 28 Oil pump exploded view. 6-250 engine

6. Remove starter motor attaching bolts and position starter motor aside.
7. Remove left hand engine mount through bolt, then lossen right hand engine mount through bolt.
8. Raise engine and reinstall through bolt. Do not tighten through bolt.
9. Remove oil pan attaching bolts and remove oil pan.
10. Reverse procedure to install. Torque oil pan attaching bolts to 80 inch lbs. Torque engine mount attaching bolts to 50 ft. lbs.

1978—83 V8 Exc. Corvette & 1982—83 Camaro

1. Disconnect battery ground cable.
2. Remove air cleaner and snorkle.
3. Remove upper half of fan shroud.

NOTE: On 1978–80 Camaro and 1978–79 Nova equipped with heavy duty cooling system, and all 1981–83 except Chevrolet, remove fan shroud since it is of one piece construction.

4. On 1978–79 Malibu and Monte Carlo, remove engine oil dipstick and tube.
5. On 1978–79 Chevrolet, remove vacuum reservoir, if equipped.
6. On 1978–80 Camaro and 1978–79 Nova, remove distributor cap and position aside.
7. On 1981–83 models equipped with cruise control, remove cruise control servo bracket.
8. On all models, raise and support vehicle, then drain oil pan.

Engine oiling system. 6-250

9. Disconnect exhaust crossover pipe at exhaust manifold and catalytic converter.
10. Remove flywheel cover or torque converter cover.

NOTE: If equipped with manual transmission, remove starter motor before the flywheel cover.

---

11 Support engine with a suitable jack and remove engine mount through bolts.
12. Remove oil pan bolts and lower oil pan. Check that the forward crankshaft throw and/or counterweight is not extending downward as to block removal of oil pan. Rotate crankshaft as necessary to position crankshaft to permit pan removal.
13. Raise engine and install engine mount through bolts.
14. Remove oil pan.
15. Reverse procedure to install. Torque oil pan bolts to 80 inch lbs.

1977—79 6-250

1. Disconnect battery ground cable.
2. Raise vehicle on hoist, then drain engine oil.
3. Remove starter, then remove flywheel housing cover, or torque converter housing cover.
4. Remove engine mount through bolts, then raise engine, reinstall through bolts to engine mounts and lower the engine.
5. Remove oil pan bolts and oil pan.
6. Reverse procedure to install.

1978—79 V6-200 & 1977 V8 Exc. Corvette

1. Disconnect battery ground cable.
2. Remove oil dipstick and tube.
3. Remove exhaust crossover pipe.
4. If equipped with automatic transmission, remove converter housing cover.
5. Remove starter bolt and inboard brace, then swing starter aside.
6. Remove oil pan retaining bolts and oil pan.
7. Reverse procedure to install.

1977—82 Corvette

1. Disconnect battery ground cable.
2. Raise and support vehicle, then drain oil pan.
3. Remove engine oil dipstick and tube.
4. Disconnect idler arm and lower steering linkage.
5. Remove flywheel splash shield.
6. On 1977–80 models, disconnect exhaust pipe from exhaust manifold and catalytic converter.
7. Remove oil pan bolts and oil pan.
8. Reverse procedure to install. Torque oil pan bolts to 80 inch lbs.

OIL PUMP,

Oil Pump, Replace

1. Remove oil pan as described previously.
2. On 6-250 engines, remove the two flange mounting bolts, pickup pipe bolt and then remove pump.
3. On all except 6-250 engines, remove pump to rear main bearing cap bolt and remove pump and extension shaft.
4. Reverse procedure to install. Make sure that installed position of oil pump screen is with bottom edge parallel to oil pan rails on all except 6-250 engines.

Fig. 29 Oil pump exploded view. V6-200 and V8 engines

Oil Pump Service

1. Remove oil pump as described previously.
2. Remove pump cover screws and pump cover. On 6-250 engine oil pump, remove gasket, Figs. 28 & 29.
3. Mark gear teeth so they can be reassembled with same teeth indexing, then remove drive gear, idler gear and shaft.
4. Remove pressure regulator valve retaining pin, pressure regulator valve and related parts.
5. If pickup screen and pipe require replacement, mount pump in a soft-jawed vise and extract pipe from pump.
6. Wash all parts in cleaning solvent and dry with compressed air.
7. Inspect pump body and cover for cracks and excessive wear.
8. Inspect pump gears for damage or excessive wear.
9. Check drive gear shaft for looseness in pump body.
10. Inspect inside of pump cover for wear that would allow oil to leak past the ends of the gears.
11. Inspect pickup screen and pipe assembly for damage to screen, pipe or relief grommet.
12. Check pressure regulator valve for fit in pump housing.
13. Reverse procedure to assemble. Turn drive shaft by hand to check for smooth operation.

NOTE: The pump gears and body are not serviced separately. If the pump gears or body are damaged or worn, the pump assembly should be replaced. Also, if the pick-up screen and pump assembly was removed, it should be replaced with a new one as loss of the press fit condition could result in an air leak and loss of oil pressure.

Engine oiling system. V8 engines

BELT TENSION DATA

	New Lbs.	Used Lbs.
1977–83		
Air Condition	135–145	95
Air Pump		
Fan and Power Steering	120–130	75

WATER PUMP, REPLACE

1. Disconnect battery ground cable and drain cooling system.
2. Remove fan shroud or upper radiator support, as applicable, then remove accessory drive belts.
3. Remove fan and pulley from water pump hub.
4. Remove upper and lower alternator brackets. On 1982-83 Camaro, remove air brace and bracket.
5. If equipped with power steering, remove power steering lower bracket from water pump and position aside.
6. Remove radiator lower hose and heater hose from water pump.
7. Remove water pump attaching bolts and pump.

NOTE: On 6-250 engines, pull pump straight out of block first to prevent damage to the impeller.

8. Reverse procedure to install.

FUEL PUMP, REPLACE

1. Disconnect fuel lines from pump.
2. Disconnect vapor return line, if so equipped.
3. Remove fuel pump attaching bolts and pump.
4. Reverse procedure to install.

Diesel Engine Section

Refer to the Oldsmobile Chapter for service procedures on the 1980–83 V8-350 and 1982–83 V6-262 Diesel engines.

Clutch & Transmission Section

CLUTCH PEDAL, ADJUST

1977–83 Except Corvette

1. Disconnect return spring at clutch fork.
2. Rotate clutch lever and shaft assembly until pedal is against rubber bumper on dash brace.
3. Push outer end of clutch fork rearward until throwout bearing lightly contacts pressure plate fingers.
4. Install push rod in gauge hole and increase length until all lash is removed, Fig. 1.

NOTE: On 1977 Chevelle, it may be necessary to move rubber bumper rearward to obtain additional clutch pedal travel.

5. Remove swivel or rod from gauge hole and insert into lower hole on lever. Install retainer and tighten lock nut being careful not to change rod length.
6. Reinstall return spring and check pedal free travel:
   1982-83 Camaro, 27/32 to 1 11/64 inch.
   1978-81 Malibu & Monte Carlo, 43/64 to 1 17/64 inch.
   1977-81 Camaro & Nova, 55/64 to 1 29/64 inch.
   1977 Chevelle & Monte Carlo, 45/64 to 1 5/16.

1978–82 Corvette

1. Rotate clutch lever and shaft assembly until clutch pedal is firmly against rubber bumper on dash brace.
2. Install swivel "C", Fig. 2, in hole in clutch lever and shaft assembly.
3. Install retainer.
4. With nuts "A" and "B", Fig. 2, loose on rod "D", apply approximately 5 lbs. load in direction of arrow "E" until bearing lightly contacts belleville spring fingers.
5. Tighten lock nut "B", Fig. 2, toward swivel "C" until dimension "X" is .37–.43 inch.
6. Tighten nut "A", Fig. 2, to lock swivel "C" against nut "B".
7. Clutch pedal free play should be 1–1½ inch.

1977 Corvette

1. Disconnect return spring between toe pan brace and cross shaft lever, Fig. 3.
2. Rotate clutch lever and shaft assembly until pedal is against dash brace rubber bumper.
3. Install swivel (C) into clutch lever hole and install retainer.
4. Loosen nuts (A) and (B), then apply a 5 pound load in direction of arrow (F) until bearing lightly contacts plate fingers.
5. Rotate nut (B) toward swivel until dimension "X" is approximately 3/8 to 7/16 inch, then tighten nut (A) to lock swivel against nut (B).
6. Reinstall return spring and adjust clutch pedal free travel which should be 1 to 1½ inch.

CLUTCH, REPLACE

1977–83

1. Support engine and remove transmission as outlined further on.
2. Disconnect clutch fork push rod and spring.

Fig. 2 Clutch pedal adjust. 1978-81 Corvette

Fig. 1 Clutch pedal adjust. Except Corvette

Fig. 3 Clutch pedal adjust. 1977 Corvette

Fig. 4 Three-speed column shift linkage adjustment. 1977–81 Chevrolet, Nova, Chevelle & Camaro (typical)

Fig. 5 Three-speed floor shift linkage adjustment. 1978–81 Malibu & Monte Carlo (typical)

3. Remove flywheel housing.
4. Slide clutch fork from ball stud and remove fork from dust boot.

NOTE: Look for "X" mark on flywheel and on clutch cover. If "X" mark is not evident, prick punch marks on flywheel and clutch cover for indexing purposes during installation.

---

5. Loosen clutch-to-flywheel attaching bolts evenly one turn at a time until spring pressure is released. Then remove bolts and clutch assembly.
6. Reverse procedure to install.

MANUAL TRANSMISSION, REPLACE

NOTE: It may be necessary to remove the catalytic converter and its support bracket to facilitate transmission removal.

1982–83 Camaro

1. Raise and support vehicle, then drain transmission fluid.
2. Remove torque arm and propeller shaft.
3. Disconnect speedometer cable and all electrical connectors at transmission, then remove exhaust brace.
4. Remove shifter support attaching bolts from transmission and disconnect shift linkage from shifter.
5. Support transmission with a suitable jack, then remove crossmember and transmission mount attaching bolts and the crossmember and mount.
6. Remove transmission attaching bolts and the transmission.
7. Reverse procedure to install.

1977–81 Exc. Corvette

1. Disconnect battery ground cable.
2. Remove shift lever knob and, on four speed models, the spring and "T" handle.
3. Raise and support vehicle.
4. Disconnect speedometer cable and TCS wiring at transmission.
5. Remove propeller shaft.

6. Remove transmission mount to crossmember bolts and the crossmember to frame bolts.
7. Remove shift lever attaching bolts and shift levers from transmission. Disconnect back drive rod at bell housing crank on floor shift models.
8. On floor shift models, remove bolts attaching shift control assembly to support on transmission. Carefully pull unit downward until shift lever clears rubber boot and remove assembly from vehicle.
9. On all models, remove transmission to clutch housing upper retaining bolts and install guide pins in holes and remove the lower retaining bolts.
10. Slide transmission rearward until clutch drive gear clears the clutch assembly and remove transmission from vehicle.
11. Reverse procedure to install.

1977–81 Corvette

1. Disconnect battery ground cable.
2. Remove shifter ball spring and "T" handle.
3. Remove console trim plate.
4. Raise and support vehicle.
5. Remove right and left exhaust pipes from vehicle.
6. Disconnect propeller shaft from transmission slip yoke. Lower the propeller shaft and remove slip yoke from transmission.
7. Remove transmission rear mount to rear mount bracket.
8. With a suitable jack, raise engine slightly to lift transmission off rear mount bracket.
9. Remove bolts retaining transmission linkage mounting bracket to frame.
10. Disconnect shifter rods from levers at transmission cover.
11. Remove bolts attaching shift control to mounting bracket, then the mounting bracket. Remove shifter mechanism with rods and levers attached.
12. Remove shift levers from transmission and disconnect the speedometer cable and TCS switch wiring.
13. Remove transmission mount bracket to crossmember bolts, then the mount bracket. Remove bolts retaining rear mount cushion and exhaust pipe yoke.
14. Remove transmission to clutch housing bolts and the lower left extension bolt.
15. Pull transmission rearward until clear of

clutch housing, rotating transmission clockwise while pulling rearward. To allow clearance for transmission removal, slowly lower rear of engine until tachometer drive cable at distributor clears horizontal ledge across front of dash.
16. Remove transmission from vehicle.
17. Reverse procedure to install.

THREE SPEED SHIFT LINKAGE, ADJUST

1977–81

Column Shift

1. Place shift lever in "Reverse" position and ignition switch in "Lock".
2. Raise vehicle on a hoist.
3. Loosen shift control rod swivel lock nuts. Pull down slightly on 1/R rod attached to column lever to remove any slack and then tighten clevis lock nut at transmission lever, Fig. 4.
4. Unlock ignition switch and shift column lever to "Neutral". Position column lower levers in "Neutral", align gauge holes in levers and insert gauge pin.
5. Support rod and swivel to prevent movement and tighten 2/3 shift control rod lock nut.
6. Remove alignment tool from column lower levers and check operation. Then place column lever in "Reverse" and check interlock control.

Floor Shift

1. Place ignition switch in "Off" position and raise vehicle.
2. Loosen lock nuts at shift rod swivels, Figs. 5 and 6. The rods should pass freely through the swivels.
3. Place transmission shift levers in neutral position.
4. Move shift control lever into the neutral detent position, align control assembly levers and insert locating pin into lever alignment slot.
5. Tighten lock nuts at shift rod swivels and remove locating pin.
6. Place transmission control lever in reverse position and the ignition switch in "Lock" position. Loosen lock nut at back-

Fig. 6 Three-speed floor shift linkage. 1977–81 except 1978–81 Malibu & Monte Carlo (typical)

Fig. 7 Four-speed linkage. 1977–82 except Corvette, 1978–81 Malibu & Monte Carlo (typical)

NOTE: TRANS LEVERS AND SHIFTER LEVERS MUST BE IN NEUTRAL POSITION AT TIME OF ASSEMBLY OF RODS .250/.249 GAGE PIN MUST FIT FREELY THROUGH LEVERS (IN NEUTRAL POSITION).

Fig. 8 Four-speed shift linkage adjustment. 1978–81 Malibu & Monte Carlo

drive control rod swivel, then pull rod downward slightly to remove slack in the column mechanism, then tighten the lock nut.
7. Check interlock control. The ignition switch should move freely to and from the "Lock" position.
8. Check transmission shift operation and if satisfactory, lower vehicle.

FOUR SPEED SHIFT LINKAGE, ADJUST

1982 Camaro

1. Place levers (L), (M) and (N) in neutral position, Fig. 6A. To obtain neutral posi-

tion, move levers counter-clockwise to forward detent, then clockwise one detent.
2. Move lever (F) to neutral position. Align holes of levers (E), (H) and (J) with notch in lever and bracket assembly, then insert Gauge J-33195 or equivalent to secure levers in neutral position.
3. Attach rod (C) to lever (N) with washer (A) and retainer (B).
4. Loosely assemble nuts (R) and (T) and swivel (S) on rod (C).
5. Insert swivel (S) into lever (E), then attach washer (Q) and secure with retainer (P). Apply a load on lever (N) in direction of arrow (Z). At the same time, finger tighten nuts (T) and (R) against swivel, then torque nuts to 25 ft. lbs.
6. Repeat steps 3, 4 and 5 for rod (D) and levers (J) and (M).
7. Repeat steps 3, 4 and 5 for rod (K) and levers (H) and (L).
8. Remove gauge and check that centerlines of shift levers are aligned to provide free crossover motion.

1977–81

Exc. Corvette
The procedure, Figs. 7 and 8, is the same as that for Three Speed transmissions described previously.

1978–81 Corvette
1. Place levers (K), (M), and (P) in neutral position, Fig. 9. To obtain neutral position, move levers counter-clockwise to forward detent, then clockwise one detent.
2. Move lever (E) to neutral position. Align levers (C), (D) and (F) with notch in lever and bracket assembly, then insert a suitable tool to secure levers in neutral position.
3. Attach rod (N) to lever (C) with retainer (G).
4. Loosen assembly nuts (Q) and (S) and swivel (R) on rod (N).
5. Insert swivel (R) into lever (P), attach washer (B) and secure retaining (A). Apply a load on lever (P) in direction of arrow (Z). Tighten nut (S) against swivel, then nut (Q) against swivel.
6. Repeat steps 3, 4 and 5 for rod (J) and levers (F) and (K).
7. Repeat steps 3, 4 and 5 for rod (L) and levers (D) and (M).

Fig. 6A Four-speed shift linkage adjustment. 1982–83 Camaro

Fig. 9 Four-speed shift linkage adjustment. 1978–81 Corvette

Fig. 10 Four-Speed linkage. 1977 Corvette (Typical)

8. Remove alignment tool from levers. The centerlines of shift levers must be aligned to provide free crossover motion.
9. Check for proper operation. Be sure all cables have adequate clearance around control rods.

1977 Corvette
1. Place ignition switch in "Lock" position and raise vehicle.
2. Loosen swivel and clevis lock nuts from both shift rods, Fig. 10. The rods should pass freely through the swivels. Disconnect backdrive cable from column lock tube lever.
3. Place shift control lever in neutral position and insert a locking pin, .644 inch diameter, in notch of lever and bracket assembly.
4. Place transmission levers in neutral position.
5. Hold reverse rod and lever rearward against locating pin, tighten rear lock nut against swivel and tighten the front lock nut.
6. Hold 1st–2nd rod against locating pin and adjust clevis so clevis pin passes freely through clevis and lever. Tighten lock nut against clevis and install washer and lock pin.
7. Hold 3rd–4th rod and lever rearward against locating pin and adjust swivel so swivel pin freely passes through lever. Tighten forward nut against lever, then the rear nut. Remove locating pin.
8. Check for proper operation.

9. Loosen two nuts at steering column to dash panel bracket.
10. Place transmission shift lever in reverse and the ignition switch in "Lock" position, if not previously done.
11. Rotate lock tube lever counter-clockwise to remove any free play. Reposition cable bracket until cable eye passes over retaining pin on lever.
12. Hold the bracket in position and have an assistant tighten the steering column to dash panel bracket retaining nuts.
13. Install cotter pin and washer retaining backdrive cable to lever pin.
14. Check interlock. The ignition switch must move freely to and from "Lock" position with transmission shift lever in reverse.
15. Lower vehicle.

Rear Axle, Propeller Shaft & Brakes

FLANGE
DEFLECTOR
OIL SEAL
BEARING
BEARING SPACER
DRIVE PINION
BEARING
SHIM
PINION
THRUST WASHERS
DIFFERENTIAL CARRIER
DIFFERENTIAL CASE
SHIM
AXLE SHAFT
BEARING CAP
SIDE GEAR
COVER
RING GEAR
PINION SHAFT
SHAFT LOCK BOLT
"C" LOCK
BEARING
GASKET

Fig. 1   Rear axle. 1977–83 Chevrolet, Chevelle, Malibu, Monte Carlo, Nova & Camaro. "C" Type

FLANGE
SEAL
FRONT BEARING
REAR BEARING
SHIM
DRIVE PINION
DIFFERENTIAL PINION
SIDE GEAR BEARING
BEARING SHIM
YOKE BEARING
RING GEAR
SEAL
SIDE GEAR YOKE
DIFFERENTIAL PINION SHAFT
DIFFERENTIAL CASE
CARRIER CASE

Fig. 2   Rear axle. 1977–82 Corvette

REAR AXLE

Figs. 1 and 2 illustrate the rear axle assemblies used. When necessary to overhaul any of these units, refer to the *Rear Axle Specifications* table in this chapter.

1977–82 Corvette

NOTE: These models are equipped with Positraction differentials.

In this axle, the drive pinion is mounted in two tapered roller bearings that are preloaded by a spacer. The pinion is positioned by a shim located between the head of the drive pinion and the rear pinion bearing. The front bearing is held in place by a large washer and a locking pinion nut.

The differential is supported in the carrier by two tapered roller side bearings.

The differential side bearings are preloaded by shims between the bearings and carrier housing, Fig. 2. The differential assembly is positioned for proper ring gear and pinion backlash by varying the position and thickness of these shims.

The ring gear is bolted to the case. The case houses two side gears in mesh with two pinions mounted on a pinion shaft which is held in place by a lock screw. The side gears are backed by thrust washers.

The differential side gears drive two splined yokes which are retained by snap rings located on the yoke splined end. The yokes are supported on caged needle bearings pressed into the carrier, adjacent to the differential bearings. A lip seal, pressed into the carrier outboard of the bearing, prevents oil leakage and dirt entry.

REMOVE & REPLACE

1980–82 Corvette
1. Raise vehicle and remove spare tire.
2. Remove spare tire cover by removing support hooks attached to carrier cover.
3. Remove exhaust system, then position jack stands under front control arms to support vehicle.
4. Remove heat shield.
5. Using a suitable jack and C-clamp, raise spring to relieve tension, then disconnect spring from spindle support.
6. Remove rear spring cover plate.
7. Place alignment marks on cam bolt for reassembly, then remove cam bolt from bracket.
8. Remove bolts attaching strut bracket to carrier, then lower strut rods by pushing outward on wheel and tire assembly.
9. Mark propeller shaft and pinion flange, then disconnect propeller shaft
10. Remove differential carrier to frame crossmember mount bolt, Fig. 2A.
11. Position jack stand under carrier, then remove carrier to body attaching bolts, Fig. 2A.
12. Lower differential to gain access to cover bolts.
13. Drain differential and remove cover.
14. Disconnect drive shaft at spindle at companion flange.
15. Lower and remove differential assembly.
16. Remove drive shafts from side yokes.
17. Reverse procedure to install.

1977–79 Corvette

It is not necessary to remove the rear axle assembly for any normal repairs. The axle shafts and carrier assembly can easily be removed from the vehicle, leaving the rear axle housing in place.

1. Raise and support vehicle.
2. Remove exhaust system components located behind front crossmember for clearance.
3. Disconnect driveshaft at carrier yokes.
4. Remove carrier front mounting bracket bolt.
5. Remove propeller shaft.
6. Disconnect strut rod bracket from carrier and lower bracket with strut rods attached.
7. Loosen the four spring to carrier bolts.
8. Remove eight carrier cover bolts, allowing lubricant to drain from carrier.
9. Position drive yokes in a position to facilitate carrier removal.
10. Remove carrier from vehicle.
11. Reverse procedure to install.

1977–83 Exc. Corvette

In these rear axles, Fig. 1, the rear axle housing and differential carrier are cast into an integral assembly. The drive pinion assembly is mounted in two opposed tapered roller bearings. The pinion bearings are preloaded by a spacer behind the front bearing. The pinion is positioned by a washer between the head of the pinion and the rear bearing.

The differential is supported in the carrier by two tapered roller side bearings. These bearings are preloaded by spacers located between the bearings and carrier housing. The differential assembly is positioned for proper ring gear and pinion backlash by varying these spacers. The differential case houses two side gears in mesh with two pinions mounted on a pinion shaft which is held in place by a lock pin. The side gears and pinions are backed by thrust washers.

Remove & Replace

Construction of the axle assembly is such that service operations may be performed with the housing installed in the vehicle or with the housing removed and installed in a holding fixture. The following procedure is necessary only when the housing requires replacement.

1. Raise and support vehicle, then support rear axle with a suitable jack.
2. Disconnect shock absorbers from lower

Fig. 2A Differential carrier front support mounting. 1980–82 Corvette

mountings.
3. Remove propeller shaft.
4. Disconnect upper control arms from axle housing attachments, if equipped with coil springs.
5. Disconnect brake line from axle housing junction block and the parking brake cable.
6. Disconnect lower control arms from axle housing attachments, if equipped with coil springs.
7. On models equipped with coil springs, lower axle slowly until springs can be moved. Roll axle assembly out from under vehicle.
8. On models equipped with leaf springs, remove leaf springs as outlined under "Leaf Springs & Bushings, Replace" in Rear Suspension Section. Roll axle assembly out from under vehicle.
9. Reverse procedure to install.

AXLE SHAFT, REPLACE

1977–83 C, G, K, M, & P Type

1. Raise vehicle and remove wheel and brake drum.
2. Drain lube from carrier and remove cover.
3. Remove differential pinion shaft lock screw and remove differential pinion shaft.
4. Pull flanged end of axle shaft toward cen-

ter of vehicle and remove "C" lock from button end of shaft.
5. Remove axle shaft from housing, being careful not to damage seal.
6. Reverse foregoing procedure to install the axle shaft.

1977–79 "B" & "O" Type

1. Raise vehicle and remove wheel and brake drum.
2. Remove bolts attaching axle shaft retainer plate to backing plate.
3. Using a slide hammer/puller, the axle shaft can now be removed.

NOTE: You may find the wheel bearing will come out in pieces as you remove the shaft. The inner race with bearing and one retainer plate will come out with the shaft. The outer race and inner retainer plate will remain in the axle housing. These pieces can easily be removed. Even though the bearing is not in one piece it is no indication that the bearing has failed.

1977–82 Corvette

1. Raise and support vehicle.
2. Disconnect inboard driveshaft trunnion from side gear yoke.
3. On 1982 models, remove plastic splash shields attaching screws and the shields.
4. On 1977–79 models, bend bolt lock tabs downward.
5. Remove bolts securing shaft flange to spindle drive flange.
6. Scribe a mark on the camber adjusting cam and mounting bracket for alignment during assembly.
7. Loosen camber adjusting nut and rotate cam so the high point of the cam faces inboard. This pushes the control arm outboard providing spindle-driveshaft clearance.
8. Remove driveshaft by withdrawing outboard end first.
9. Reverse procedure to install.

CORVETTE REAR SPINDLE

1. Referring to Fig. 3, raise vehicle and remove wheel and tire.
2. Apply parking brake to prevent spindle from turning and remove cotter pin and nut from spindle.
3. Release parking brake and remove drive spindle flange from splined end of spindle.

Fig. 3 Corvette rear wheel spindle (typical)

Fig. 4 Corvette rear wheel spindle removal (typical)

WHEEL CYLINDER LINKS
SECONDARY SHOE & LINING
SHOE GUIDE
PARKING BRAKE STRUT
STRUT SPRING
ADJUSTER LEVER
ACTUATING LINK
WHEEL CYLINDER SCREWS
BACKING PLATE
HOLD DOWN PINS
PARKING BRAKE LEVER
WHEEL CYLINDER
PRIMARY SHOE AND LINING
HOLD DOWN SPRING
ADJUSTING SCREW SPRING
ADJUSTING SCREW
LEVER RETURN SPRINGS
HOLD DOWN SPRING & CUP
BRAKE SHOE RETURN SPRING

Fig. 5   Rear drum brake (Typical)

Fig. 6   Adjusting parking brake shoes. 1977–82 Corvette

4. Remove brake caliper and disc.
5. Using the puller, Fig. 4, remove spindle.

NOTE: When using puller tool J-22602, ensure puller plate is positioned vertically in the torque control arm before applying pressure to the puller screw.

6. When spindle is removed, the outer bearing will remain on the spindle. The inner bearing, tubular spacer, end play shim and both outer races will remain in the spindle support.
7. Reverse procedure to install.

PROPELLER SHAFT

1977–83

These models use a one-piece propeller shaft.

BRAKE ADJUSTMENTS

1977–83 Self-Adjusting Brakes

These brakes, Fig. 5, have self-adjusting shoe mechanisms that assure correct lining-to-drum clearances at all times. The automatic adjusters operate only when the brakes are applied as the car is moving rearward or when the car comes to an uphill stop.

Although the brakes are self-adjusting, an initial adjustment is necessary after the brake shoes have been relined or replaced, or when the length of the adjusting screw has been changed during some other service operation.

Frequent usage of an automatic transmission forward range to halt reverse vehicle motion may prevent the automatic adjusters from functioning, thereby inducing low pedal heights. Should low pedal heights be encountered, it is recommended that numerous forward and reverse stops be made until satisfactory pedal height is obtained.

NOTE: If a low pedal condition cannot be corrected by making numerous reverse stops

(provided the hydraulic system is free of air) it indicates that the self-adjusting mechanism is not functioning. Therefore it will be necessary to remove the brake drum, clean, free up and lubricate the adjusting mechanism. Then adjust the brakes, being sure the parking brake is fully released.

Adjustment

1. Using a suitable punch, knock out lanced area in backing plate or drum. If drum is installed on vehicle when this is done, remove drum and clean brake compartment of all metal.

NOTE: When adjustment is completed, a new hole cover must be installed in the backing plate.

2. Using Tool J-6166 or equivalent, turn brake adjusting screw to expand brake shoes at each wheel until wheel can just be turned by hand. Drag should be equal on all wheels.
3. On all except 1982 Camaro, back off adjusting screw at each wheel 30 notches.
4. On 1982 Camaro, back off screw 12 notches.
5. If shoe still drags slightly on drum, back off adjusting screw an additional one or two notches.
6. When adjusting screw has been backed off approximately 12 notches, brakes should be free of drag. Heavy drag at this point indicates tight parking brake cables.
7. Install adjusting hole cover in brake backing plate.
8. Check parking brake for proper adjustment.

PARKING BRAKE, ADJUST

1977–82 Except Corvette & 1982 Camaro With Rear Disc Brakes

1. Jack up both rear wheels.

2. Apply parking brake exactly two ratchet clicks on Camaro, Nova, 1978–83 Malibu and Monte Carlo and 1982–83 Chevrolet, three clicks on 1977 Chevelle and Monte Carlo, or one click on 1977–81 Chevrolet.
3. Tighten adjusting nut until left rear wheel can just be rotated rearward but is locked when forward rotation is attempted.
4. Release parking brake and check to ensure that rear wheels rotate freely in either direction with no brake drag.

1982–83 Camaro With Rear Disc Brakes

1. Lubricate parking brake cables at underbody rub points and at equalizer hooks and ensure free movement of all cables.
2. With parking brake fully released, jack up both rear wheels.
3. Remove slack from cable by holding brake cable stud and tightening equalizer nut.

NOTE: After tightening nut, check that caliper levers are against stops on caliper housing. If not, loosen cable until levers return to stops.

4. Actuate parking brake several times to check adjustment.

1977–82 Corvette

1. With car on lift or jack stands, remove wheel. (On optional knock-off wheels, the adapter bracket must be removed to gain access to the hole in the hat section of the disc.)
2. Turn disc until the adjusting screw can be seen through hole in disc.
3. Insert a screwdriver through hole in disc and tighten adjusting screw by moving your hand away from the floor on both the left and right sides, Fig. 6.
4. Tighten until disc will not move, then back off 6 to 8 notches.
5. Apply emergency brake two notches from inside of car.
6. Tighten brake cables at equalizer to produce a light drag with wheels mounted.
7. Fully released parking brake handle and rotate rear wheels. No drag should be evident with handle released.

MASTER CYLINDER, REPLACE

1977–83

1. Disconnect brake pipes from master cyl-

inder. Plug lines and master cylinder ports to prevent entry of foreign material.
2. Disconnect brake pedal from master cylinder push rod, if equipped with manual brakes.
3. Remove master cylinder attaching nuts and the master cylinder.
4. Reverse procedure to install.

POWER BRAKE UNIT

1980–83 Hydro-Boost

NOTE: Pump brake pedal several times with engine off to deplete accumulator of fluid.

1. Remove two nuts attaching master cylinder to booster, then move master cylinder away from booster with brake lines attached.
2. Remove three hydraulic lines from boost-

er. Plug and cap all lines and outlets.
3. Remove retainer and washer securing booster push rod to brake pedal arm.
4. Remove four nuts attaching booster unit to dash panel.
5. From engine compartment, loosen booster from dash panel and move booster push rod inboard until it disconnects from brake pedal arm. Remove spring washer from brake pedal arm.
6. Remove booster unit from vehicle.
7. Reverse procedure to install. To purge system, disconnect feed wire from injection pump. Fill power steering pump reservoir, then crank engine for several seconds and recheck power steering pump fluid level. Connect injection pump feed wire and start engine, then cycle steering wheel from stop to stop twice and stop engine. Discharge accumulator by depressing brake pedal several times, then check fluid level. Start engine, then turn steering wheel from stop to stop and turn engine off. Check fluid level and add fluid as necessary. If foaming occurs, stop engine and wait for approximately one hour

for foam to dissipate, then recheck fluid level.

1977–83 Except Hydro-Boost

1. Remove vacuum hose from check valve and master cylinder retaining nuts.
2. Pull master cylinder forward so it clears mounting studs and move to one side. Support cylinder to avoid stress on hydraulic lines.
3. Remove power unit to dash nuts. On 1977 Chevelle and Monte Carlo, remove brake line clip from power unit.
4. Remove brake pedal push rod retainer and disconnect push rod from pin.

NOTE: On 1977 Chevelle and Monte Carlo, push brake pedal to floor. This pushes power unit away from dash, providing clearance to remove push rod.

5. Remove power unit from vehicle.
6. Reverse procedure to install.

Rear Suspension

SHOCK ABSORBER, REPLACE

1977–83 All

1. If equipped with Superlift shock absorbers, disconnect air lines from shock absorber fittings.
2. With rear axle properly supported, disconnect shock absorber from upper and lower mountings, Figs. 1, 2, 3 and 3A.
3. Reverse procedure to install.

COIL SPRINGS, REPLACE

1977–82 Chevrolet, Chevelle, Malibu & Monte Carlo

1. Support vehicle at frame and rear axle.
2. Disconnect shock absorbers at lower mountings.
3. Disconnect upper control arms from axle housing.
4. If equipped with a stabilizer bar, disconnect bar from either right or left hand side of control arm.
5. If necessary on 1977 models, disconnect brake line at junction block on axle hous-

ing. On all models, remove brake hose support bolt and support without disconnecting the brake lines.
6. Lower axle until it reaches end of its travel and using a suitable tool, pry lower pigtail over retainer on axle bracket. Remove spring and insulator.
7. Reverse procedure to install. Springs must be installed with an insulator between upper seat and spring and positioned properly, Fig. 4.

1982–83 Camaro

1. Raise and support vehicle and support rear axle with a suitable adjustable jack.
2. Remove track bar mounting bolt from axle and loosen track bar bolt at body brace.
3. Disconnect rear brake hose clip at underbody, then disconnect shock absorbers at lower mountings.
4. On models equipped with 4-151 engine, remove propeller shaft.
5. Lower rear axle and remove springs and insulators.
6. Reverse procedure to install.

LEAF SPRINGS & BUSHINGS, REPLACE

1977–81 Camaro & 1977–79 Nova

1. Support vehicle at frame and rear axle, removing tension from spring.
2. Disconnect shock absorber from lower mounting.
3. Loosen spring front mount bolt.
4. Remove spring front mounting bracket attaching screws, lower axle and remove bracket.
5. Disconnect parking brake cable from spring plate bracket.
6. Remove spring plate by removing axle bracket nuts on single leaf models and the "U" bolts on multi-leaf models.

7. Support spring, remove front mount bolt and disassemble rear shackle.
8. Replace rear shackle and spring eye bushings as necessary, Figs. 5 and 6.
9. Reverse procedure to install.

1977–82 Corvette

1. Support vehicle at frame and remove rear wheels.
2. Install a "C" clamp approximately 9 inches from end of spring.
3. Place a suitable jack under spring, Fig. 7, and place a wooden block between "C" clamp and jack pad.
4. Raise jack until load is off spring link, then remove cotter pin, link nut and spring cushion, Figs. 8 and 8A. Lower jack, removing tension from spring.
5. Repeat steps 2, 3 and 4 on opposite side of spring.
6. Remove bolts from spring center clamp plate, then remove clamp plate.
7. Remove spring from vehicle.
8. Reverse procedure to install.

LEAF SPRING SERVICE

NOTE: The spring leaves are not serviced separately, however, the spring leaf inserts may be replaced.

Fig. 1   Rear suspension. 1978–83 Chevrolet, Malibu & Monte Carlo (typical)

Fig. 2   Rear suspension. 1977–81 Camaro, 1977–79 Nova (typical)

Fig. 3 Rear suspension (typical). 1977–82 Corvette

NOTE Spring must be positioned with end of coil towards rear of chassis within limits shown.

PARALLEL TO ℄ OF VEHICLE

FWD

90°

5°

15°

FRAME

Fig. 4 Coil spring installation. 1977–83 all models

1. Clamp spring in a vise and remove spring clips.
2. File peened end of center bolt to permit nut removal, remove nut and open vise slowly, allowing spring to expand.
3. Replace spring leaves or leaf inserts.
4. On Corvette, to replace main leaf cushion retainers, chisel flared portion until retainer can be removed from leaf. Install new retainers and flare over with a hammer.

5. On all models use a drift to align center bolt holes, compress spring in vise and install new center bolt and nut. Peen end of bolt to retain nut.
6. Align springs and bend spring clips into position.

NOTE: Overtightening of spring clips will cause spring binding.

J·21058·15   J·21978·1
J·21058·8
J·22553·1

Fig. 5 Leaf spring bushings removal. 1977–81 Camaro. 1977–79 Nova

1. RAIL
2. JOUNCE BUMPER
3. SPRING INSULATOR ASM.
4. COIL SPRING
5. OPTIONAL STABILIZER BAR
6. LOWER CONTROL ARM
7. UNDERBODY
8. TORQUE ARM
9. PROP SHAFT
10. DAMPER ASM. WITH 4 CYC. ENGINE
11. SHOCK ABSORBER
12. TRACK BAR
13. TRACK BAR BRACE

WITH RR DISC BRAKES

Fig. 3A Rear suspension. 1982–83 Camaro

J·21058·15 J·22553·2   J·21058·8
J·22553·1

Fig. 6 Leaf spring bushing installation. 1977–81 Camaro, 1977–79 Nova

Wood Block   Spring Link

"C" Clamp   Position Jack So That Jack Pad Rests Against Wood Block

Fig. 7 Supporting leaf spring. 1977–82 Corvette

Fig. 8 Transverse spring mounting. 1977–82 Corvette

Fig. 10 Control arms front all & lower control arm rear bushings installation. 1977–83 Chevrolet

Fig. 11 Upper control arm front & all lower control arm bushing. 1977–83 Malibu & Monte Carlo removal. Also upper control arm rear bushing removal. 1977–83 Chevrolet

Fig. 8A Rear suspension. 1981–82 Corvette

Upper Control Arms

1977–83 Chevrolet, Chevelle Malibu & Monte Carlo

1. Support vehicle at frame and rear axle with a suitable jack.
2. Remove control arm front and rear mounting bolts.
3. Replace bushings as necessary.
4. Reverse procedure to install. Control arm bolts must be tightened with vehicle at curb height.

Lower Control Arms

1977–83 Chevrolet, Chevelle Malibu & Monte Carlo & 1982–83 Camaro

Follow "Upper Control Arms" 1977–82 procedure for replacement of lower control arms.

NOTE: When replacing bushings, use suitable tools as shown in Figs. 9, 10 and 11.

CONTROL ARMS & BUSHINGS, REPLACE

NOTE: On Monte Carlo & 119″ wheelbase station wagons, if both upper or lower control arms are to be removed at the same time, remove coil springs as outlined previously.

NOTE: When replacing bushings, use suitable tools as shown in Figs. 9 through 13.

STABILIZER BAR, REPLACE

1977–83 Chevrolet, Malibu & Monte Carlo

1. Support vehicle at rear axle.
2. Remove bolts securing stabilizer bar to

Fig. 12 Upper control arm rear bushing removal. 1977–83 Malibu & Monte Carlo

lower control arms, Fig. 14.
3. Reverse procedure to install. Use spacer shims, if needed, placed equally on each side of stabilizer bar. Tighten attaching bolts with vehicle at curb height.

1977–81 Camaro & 1977–79 Nova

1. Support vehicle at rear axle.
2. Disconnect stabilizer bar from spring plate brackets, Fig. 15.

Fig. 9 Control arms front all & lower control arm rear bushing removal. 1977–83 Chevrolet (Typical)

Fig. 13 Upper control arm rear bushing installation. 1977–83 Malibu & Monte Carlo

Fig. 14 Stabilizer bar installation. 1977–83 Chevrolet, Malibu & Monte Carlo (Typical)

Fig. 15 Stabilizer bar installation. 1977–81 Camaro & 1977–79 Nova (Typical)

INSTALL FLANGE OF BUSHING ON WHEEL SIDE OF LINK

Fig. 16 Stabilizer bar installation. 1977–82 Corvette

3. Disconnect stabilizer bar from body brackets.
4. Reverse procedure to install. Tighten attaching bolts with vehicle at curb height.

1977–82 Corvette

1. Disconnect stabilizer bar from torque control arms and remove stabilizer bar frame brackets, Fig. 16.
2. Replace bushings as necessary, Fig. 16.
3. Reverse procedure to install.

1	BODY BRACKET
2	78 NM (58 FT. LB.)
3	BODY BRACE BRACKET
4	TRACK BAR
5	BODY BRACKET
6	TRACK BAR BRACE
7	125 NM (93 FT. LB.)
8	47 NM (34 FT. LB.)
9	SPRING SEAT

VIEW A

FRT

FRT

Fig. 16A Torque bar and torque brace replacement. 1982–83 Camaro

Fig. 17 Indexing camber cam & bracket. 1977–82 Corvette

TRACK BAR & BRACE, REPLACE

1982–83 Camaro

1. Raise vehicle and support rear axle at curb height.
2. Remove track bar mounting bolt and nut from rear axle and from body bracket, then remove track bar, Fig. 16A.
3. Remove heat shield attaching screws from track bar brace.
4. Remove three track bar brace to body brace screws.
5. Remove nut and bolt from body bracket, then remove track bar brace.
6. Reverse procedure to install.

STRUT ROD, REPLACE

1977–82 Corvette

1. Support vehicle at frame.
2. Disconnect shock frame from lower mounting.

3. Remove cotter pin and nut from strut rod shaft. Pull shaft toward front of vehicle and remove from bracket.
4. Mark position of camber adjusting cam to ensure proper installation, Fig. 17 and loosen camber bolt nut.
5. Remove bolts securing strut rod bracket to carrier.
6. Remove camber bolt and nut, pull strut rod out of bracket and remove bushing caps.
7. Replace bushings as necessary, Fig. 18.
8. Reverse procedure to install.

TORQUE CONTROL ARMS & BUSHINGS, REPLACE

1977–82 Corvette

1. Perform steps 1 thru 4 as outlined under "Leaf Spring Replace" 1977–82 Corvette procedure.
2. If equipped with a stabilizer shaft, disconnect shaft at torque arms.

Fig. 18 Strut rod bushing. 1977–82 Corvette replacement

Fig. 19 Torque control arm installation 1977–82 Corvette

Fig. 20 Torque control arm bushing removal. 1977–82 Corvette

1. Disconnect shock absorber at lower mounting.
4. Disconnect and lower strut rod shaft.
5. Disconnect axle drive shaft from spindle flange by removing attaching bolts.

NOTE: It may be necessary to force torque arm outboard providing clearance to lower axle drive shaft.

6. Disconnect brake line from caliper and from torque arm. Disconnect parking brake cable.
7. Remove torque arm forward mounting bolt and toe-in shims, Fig. 19, and pull torque arm out of frame attachment.
8. Replace bushings if necessary as described under "Torque Control Arm Bushing Service."
9. Reverse procedure to install.

Torque Control Arm Bushing Service

1. Using an ¹¹⁄₁₆ inch twist drill, drill out flared end of bushing retainer, remove retainer plate and retainer from bushing.
2. Spread bushing with a chisel, Fig. 20, and tap bushing from arm.

NOTE: If bushing is rusted in torque arm, torque arm may spread during bushing removal. Install a "C" clamp torque arm, preventing torque arm spreading.

3. Oil steel portion of new bushing and press bushing into arm, Fig. 21.
4. Place retainer plate over flared portion of bushing retainer and insert retainer into bushing.
5. Make a flaring tool back-up plate, Fig. 22, with ½ inch bolt holes.
6. Place back-up plate on flared end of bushing retainer and assemble tool to plate, Fig. 23, with ½ × 5 inch bolts. Center threaded hole in tool # J-8111-23 over unflared end of bushing retainer. Also center chamfered retainer plate over retainer tube.

Fig. 21 Torque control arm bushing installation. 1977–82 Corvette

7. Lubricate end of tool # J-8880-5 and thread screw into tool, flaring retainer.

CROSSMEMBER & ISOLATION MOUNT, REPLACE

1977–79 Corvette

1. Remove leaf spring as outlined under "Leaf Spring Replace" 1977–82 Corvette procedure.
2. Remove differential carrier and cover as outlined in "Rear Axle, Propeller Shaft & Brakes" section 1977–82 Corvette procedure.
3. Support crossmember and remove bolts securing isolation mounts to frame and lower the crossmember.

Fig. 23 Flaring torque control arm bushing retainer 1977–82 Corvette

4. To replace isolation mount, straighten isolation mount tabs and using a suitable ram, press on outer steel shell or inner steel insert, removing mount from crossmember. Install new mount into position, compress outer sleeve, press mount into crossmember and bend over locking tabs, Fig. 24.
5. Reverse procedure to install crossmember.

REAR WHEEL ALIGNMENT

1977–82 Corvette

Rear wheel camber and toe-out should be inspected and corrected if rear tires show unusual wear.

Camber, Adjust

Wheel camber is obtained by adjusting the eccentric cam and bolt assembly located at the inboard mounting of the strut rod, Fig. 3. Place rear wheels on alignment machine and determine camber angle.

To adjust, loosen camber bolt nut and rotate cam and bolt assembly until the camber angle is within specifications listed in the front of this chapter.

Toe-In, Adjust

Rear wheel toe-in is adjusted by inserting slotted shims of varying thickness inside the frame side member on both sides of the torque control arm pivot bushing. Shims are available in thicknesses of ¹⁄₆₄", ¹⁄₃₂", ⅛" and ¼".

To adjust, loosen torque arm pivot bolts until shims are free enough to remove. Position torque arm assembly until toe-in is within specifications listed in the front of this chapter. Shim gap toward vehicle centerline between end of control arm bushing and frame side inner wall.

Fig. 22 Flaring tool back-up plate dimension

Fig. 24 Crossmember isolation mount replacement. 1977–79 Corvette

Front Suspension & Steering Section

Fig. 1   Front suspension. Exc. 1982–83 Camaro (Typical)

Fig. 2   Exploded view of front suspension. 1982–83 Camaro

FRONT SUSPENSION

All front suspension systems are basically similar, being of the S.L.A. (short-long arm) type with independent coil springs riding on the lower control arms. Ball joints connect the upper and lower control arms to the steering knuckles, Fig. 1, except on 1982–83 Camaro, Fig. 2.

WHEEL ALIGNMENT

NOTE: Before adjusting caster and camber angles after complaint of excessive tire wear or poor handling, the front bumper should be raised and quickly released to allow car to return to its normal height.

1977–83 All Exc. 1982–83 Camaro

Caster and camber adjustments are made by means of shims between the upper control arm inner support shaft and the support bracket attached to the frame. Shims may be added, subtracted or transferred to change the readings as follows:

Caster, Adjust

Transfer shims from front to rear or rear to front. The transfer of one shim to the front bolt from the rear bolt will decrease positive caster. On shim (1/32") transferred from the rear bolt to the front bolt will change caster about 1/2 degree.

Camber, Adjust

Change shims at both the front and rear of the shaft. Adding an equal number of shims at both front and rear of the support shaft will decrease positive camber. One shim (1/32") at each location will move camber approximately 1/5 degree on 1977–81 Camaro, Chevelle and Nova, on Chevrolet and Corvette the change will be about 1/6 degree.

1982–83 Camaro

Caster and camber adjustments are made by moving the position of the upper strut mount assembly. To make adjustment, re-move dust cap and fender bolt and attach tool J-29724 to original fender bolt, Fig. 3. Tighten the turnbuckle and loosen the three strut mount attaching nuts.

Adjust camber by rotating the turnbuckle to move mount assembly inward or outward. Move mount inboard to decrease camber, or outboard to increase camber.

Adjust caster by lightly tapping the mount assembly foward or rearward. Move mount foward to decrease caster, or rearward to increase caster.

When adjustments are completed, torque the three strut mount attaching nuts to 20 ft. lbs.

TOE-IN, ADJUST

Toe-in can be adjusted by loosening the clamp bolts at each end of each tie rod and turning each tie rod to increase or decrease its length as necessary until proper toe-in is secured and the steering gear is on the high point for straight-ahead driving.

WHEEL BEARINGS, ADJUST

1977–83

1. While rotating wheel forward, torque spindle nut to 12 ft. lbs.
2. Back off nut until "just loose" then hand tighten nut and back it off again until either hole in spindle lines up with hole in nut.

Fig. 3   Adjusting camber and caster. 1982–83 Camaro

NOTE: Do not back off nut more than 1/2 flat.

3. Install new cotter pin. With wheel bearing properly adjusted, there will be .001–.005 inch end play.

WHEEL BEARINGS, REPLACE

Disc Brakes

1. Raise car and remove front wheels.
2. Remove bolts holding brake caliper to its mounting and insert a fabricated block (1 1/16 × 1 1/16 × 2 inches in length) between the brake pads as the caliper is being removed. Once removed, the caliper can be wired or secured in some manner away from the disc.
3. Remove spindle nut and hub and disc assembly. Grease retainer and inner wheel bearing can now be removed.
4. Reverse procedure to install.

CHECKING BALL JOINTS FOR WEAR

Upper Ball Joint

1. Raise front of vehicle with jacks placed between the coil spring pocket and ball joint of lower control arm.
2. Shake top of wheel in and out. Observe steering knuckle for any movement relative to the control arm.
3. Replace upper ball joint if looseness is indicated.

Lower Ball Joint

Raise car and support lower control arm so spring is compressed in the same manner as if the wheels were on the ground and check axial (up and down) play at ball joint. If play exceeds 1/16", replace the joint.

Another indication of lower ball joint excessive wear is when difficulty is experienced when lubricating the joint. If the liner has worn to the point where the lubrication grooves in the liner have been worn away, then abnormal pressure is required to force

Fig. 4 Lower ball joint wear indicator.
1977–83 Exc. Corvette & 1982–83 Camaro

Fig. 5 Removing upper & lower ball
joint stud from knuckle.

lubricant through the joint. Should this condition be evident, replace both lower ball joints.

NOTE: All models except Corvette have a wear indicator built into the lower ball joint, Fig. 4.

UPPER BALL JOINT, REPLACE

1977–82 All, Exc. 1982 Camaro

NOTE: On 1980–82 models except 1982 Camaro, tool No. J-29193 must be used to seat ball joint stud on steering knuckle. Torque tool to 40 ft. lbs., then remove tool and install and torque stud nut to 60 ft. lbs.

1. Support weight of vehicle at outer end of lower control arm.
2. Remove wheel assembly.
3. Remove nut from upper ball joint stud.
4. Remove stud from knuckle, Fig. 5.
5. Cut off ball rivets with a chisel.
6. Enlarge ball stud attaching holes in control arm (if necessary) to accept the bolts

included in the ball joint replacement kit.
7. Install and tighten new ball joint. Tighten to the following torques: 1977–82 Corvette, 50 ft. lbs., 1977–79 all except Corvette, 60 ft. lbs., 1980–83 all except Corvette and 1982–83 Camaro, 65 ft. lbs. The nut may be tightened up to 1/16 additional turn to line up cotter pin hole.
8. Reassemble ball joint to steering knuckle.

NOTE: On 1978–82 Malibu and Monte Carlo, the cotter pin must be installed from the rear, Fig. 6.

LOWER BALL JOINT, REPLACE

NOTE: On 1980–82 models except 1982 Camaro, tool No. J-29194 must be used to seat ball joint stud on steering knuckle. Torque tool to 40 ft. lbs., then remove tool and tighten stud nut to 80 ft. lbs.

1. Support vehicle at frame and lower control arm with suitable jacks.

Fig. 6 Ball joint cotter pin installation.
1978–83 Malibu & Monte Carlo

2. Remove wheel and, if equipped with disc brakes, caliper assembly.
3. Loosen ball joint stud nut not more than one turn and, using a suitable tool, Fig. 5, press ball stud free of steering knuckle, then remove stud nut.
4. Lower the jack from under the control arm.
5. With a suitable tool, replace lower ball joint.
6. Reverse procedure to install. Tighten nut to the following torques: 1977 Chevrolet, 93 ft. lbs., 1977–79 except Corvette and 1977 Chevrolet, 83 ft. lbs., 1980–83 all except Corvette, 90 ft. lbs., 1977–82 Corvette, 80 ft. lbs. The nut may be tightened up to an additional 1/16 turn to line up cotter pin hole.

NOTE: On 1978–82 Malibu and Monte Carlo, the cotter pin must be installed from the rear, Fig. 6.

SHOCK ABSORBER, REPLACE

1977–82 All, Exc. 1982 Camaro

1. Hold shock upper stem from turning with a suitable wrench and remove nut and grommet.
2. Unfasten lower shock pivot from lower control arm and pull shock and mounting out through bottom of spring housing.
3. Reverse removal procedure to install. Tighten the upper retaining nut to the following torques: 1977–82 Corvette, 90 inch lbs., 1977–79 all except Corvette, 90 inch lbs., 1980–83 all except Corvette and 1982–83 Camaro, 8 ft. lbs. Tighten the lower retaining nut to the following torques: 1977–82 Corvette, 150 inch lbs., 1977–82 all except Corvette and 1982–83 Camaro, 20 ft. lbs.

STRUT, REPLACE

1982–83 Camaro

1. Raise and support vehicle.
2. Remove wheel and support lower control arm with a suitable jack.
3. Remove brake hose bracket and two strut to knuckle bolts.
4. Remove upper mounting assembly cover.
5. Remove nut from upper end of strut, then the strut and shield.

Fig. 7 Supporting coil spring. 1977–83 All

Fig. 8 Power steering control valve and adapter assembly. 1977–82 Corvette

6. Reverse procedure to install. Tighten strut to knuckle bolts to 195 ft. lbs., and strut to upper mount nut to 50 ft. lbs.

COIL SPRING, REPLACE

1977–82 All, Exc. 1982–83 Camaro

1. Disconnect shock absorber from lower mounting, push shock absorber through hole in lower control arm and compress into spring.
2. Support vehicle by frame so control arms hang free.
3. Install a safety chain through spring and lower control arm.
4. Install tool J-23028 onto a suitable jack and position jack so control arm is supported by bushings seated in grooves of tool, Fig. 7.
5. Remove stabilizer to lower control arm attachment.
6. Raise jack to relieve tension on control arm bolts and remove bolts.
7. Lower jack until tension is removed from spring, remove chain and spring from vehicle.
8. Reverse procedure to install. Install pivot bolts (front bolt first) and nuts and torque to the following specifications: 1977 all except Corvette, 100 ft. lbs., 1978–79 Camaro, Malibu, Monte Carlo and Nova, 62 ft. lbs., 1978–79 Chevrolet, 92 ft. lbs., 1980–83 Malibu and Monte Carlo, 65 ft. lbs., 1980–83 Chevrolet and 1980–81 Camaro, 90 ft. lbs. Torque stabilizer bar link nuts to the following specifications: 1977–82 all except Corvette and 1982–83 Camaro, 13 ft. lbs., 1977–82 Corvette, 18 ft. lbs.

1982–83 Camaro

1. Raise and support vehicle and remove wheel.
2. Remove stabilizer link and bushings from lower control arm.
3. Remove pivot bolt nuts, leaving the bolts installed.
4. Install tool J-23028 onto a suitable jack and position so that tool supports bushings, Fig. 7.
5. Raise jack to relieve tension on pivot bolts and remove bolts.
6. Carefully lower jack until tension is removed from spring and remove spring from vehicle.
7. Reverse procedure to install. Torque pivot bolt nuts to 65 ft. lbs. and stabilizer link nut to 20 ft. lbs.

CAUTION: The spring force under compression is very great. Exercise every safety pre-

caution when performing this operation to see that individuals and materials subject to damage are removed from the path of the spring when the control arm is being lowered. Also, the compressed spring should be relaxed immediately after lowering the control arm to reduce the time of exposure to the great compressive force.

STEERING GEAR, REPLACE

1977–83 All Models

NOTE: On models where shield is installed, remove shield from coupling.

1. Remove nuts, washers and bolts at steering coupling.
2. Remove pitman arm nut and washer from sector shaft and mark relation of arm position to shaft.
3. Use a suitable puller to remove pitman arm.
4. Unfasten gear from frame and remove assembly.
5. Reverse procedure to install. Torque the steering gear to frame attaching bolts to 30 ft. lbs. on 1977–82 Corvette, 70 ft. lbs. on all 1977–81 except Corvette, or 80 ft. lbs. on all 1982–83 except Corvette. Torque coupling flange bolts to 30 ft. lbs. on all models. Torque coupling flange nuts to 20 ft. lbs. on all except 1977–78 Nova. On 1977–78 Nova, torque to 18 ft. lbs. Torque sector shaft to pitman arm nut to 185 ft. lbs. on all 1977–83 except 1980–81 Camaro, Chevrolet, Malibu and Monte Carlo. On these models, torque to 180 ft. lbs.

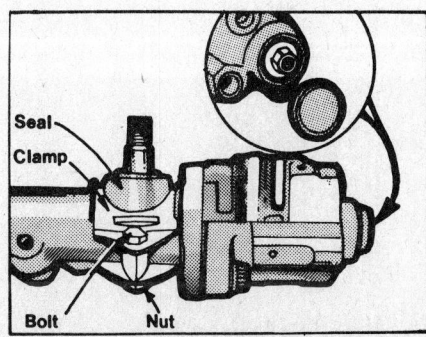

Fig. 9 Power steering control valve ball stud seal replacement. 1977–82 Corvette

INTEGRAL POWER STEERING, REPLACE

1977–82 Exc. Corvette

To remove gear assembly, disconnect pressure and return hoses from gear housing and cap both hoses and steering gear outlets to prevent foreign material from entering system, then follow procedure as outlined under *Steering Gear, Replace.*

LINKAGE TYPE POWER STEERING

1977–82 Corvette

Power steering equipment consists of a recirculating ball type steering gear and linkage to which a hydraulic power mechanism has been added as part of the steering linkage. The hydraulic mechanism furnishes additional power to *assist* the manual operation so that the turning effort at the steering wheel is greatly reduced. The hydraulic mechanism consists of three basic units: a hydraulic pump and reservoir, a control valve, and a power cylinder.

Control Valve, Adjust
1. Disconnect cylinder rod from frame bracket.
2. With car on a hoist, start the engine. One of the following two conditions will exist:
   a. If piston rod remains retracted, turn the adjusting nut clockwise until the rod begins to move out. Then turn the nut counterclockwise until the rod just begins to move in. Now turn the nut clockwise to exactly one half the rotation needed to change the direction of shaft movement.
   b. If the rod extends upon starting the pump, move the nut counter-clockwise until the rod begins to retract, then clockwise until the rod begins to move out again. Now turn the rod to exactly one half the rotation needed to change the direction of shaft movement.

NOTE: *Do not turn the nut back and forth more than is absolutely necessary to balance the valve.*

3. Restart engine. Front wheels should not turn from center if valve has been properly balanced.

Power Cylinder Repairs

Removal
1. Disconnect two hydraulic lines at power cylinder.

2. Unfasten power cylinder rod from brace at frame.
3. Unfasten power cylinder from relay rod bracket.
4. Remove power cylinder from car.

Inspection

1. Inspect seals for leaks around cylinder rod and if leaks are present, replace seals as follows:
2. Use a hook tool to remove retaining ring. Remove wiper ring, back-up washer, back-up ring and seal. *Piston rod seal should not be removed unless there are signs of leakage along the piston shaft at shaft seal.*
3. Examine brass fitting hose connection seats for cracks or damage and replace if necessary.
4. For service other than seat or seal replacement, replace the power cylinder.

Installation

1. Install power cylinder on car by reversing removal procedure. Torque the frame bracket to rod nut to 23 ft lbs. and the relay rod bracket nut to 45 ft. lbs. Additional torque may be applied to align castellation with hole in stud, not to exceed 30 ft. lbs. on frame bracket to rod nut and 50 ft. lbs. on relay rod bracket nut.
2. Reconnect two hoses, fill system with fluid and bleed system as outlined below.

Filling & Bleeding System

1. Fill reservoir to proper level with Automatic Transmission Fluid and let fluid remain undisturbed for about two minutes.
2. Raise front wheels off floor.
3. Run engine at idle for two minutes.
4. Increase engine speed to about 1500 rpm.
5. Turn wheels from one extreme to the other, lightly contacting stops.
6. Lower wheels to floor and turn wheels right and left.
7. Recheck for leaks.
8. Check oil level and refill as required. Pump pressure should be 870 lbs.

Control Valve Repairs

Replace, Fig. 8

1. Loosen relay rod-to-control valve clamp.
2. Disconnect hose connections at control valve.
3. Disconnect control valve from pitman arm.
4. Unscrew control valve from relay rod.
5. Remove control valve from car.
6. Reverse procedure to install. Torque relay rod clamp bolt to 25 ft. lbs. Torque pitman arm nut to 45 ft. lbs. plus additional torque required to align castellation with hole in stud not to exceed 50 ft. lbs.

Ball Stud Seal, Replace

In servicing the control valve, refer to Fig. 8. To replace the ball stud seal, refer to Fig. 9 and proceed as follows:

1. Remove pitman arm with a suitable puller.
2. Remove clamp by removing nut, bolt and spacer. If crimped type clamp is used, straighten clamp end and pull clamp and seal off end of stud.
3. Install new seal and clamp over stud so lips on seal mate with clamp. (A nut and bolt attachment type clamp replaces the crimped type for service, Fig. 8).
4. Center the ball stud, seal and clamp in opening in adapter housing, then install spacer, bolt and nut.

POWER STEERING PUMP, REPLACE

1977–82

1. Disconnect hoses at power steering pump, then plug pump parts and hoses.
2. Loosen pump adjusting bolt and remove pump drive belt.
3. Remove pump to support bracket attaching bolts and the pump.
4. Reverse procedure to install. Torque attaching bolts to the following specifications: 1977–82 Corvette, 25 ft. lbs., 1977–78 with V8 engine, all except Corvette, 25 ft. lbs., 1977–78 with six cylinder engine, all except Corvette, 18 ft. lbs., 1979–83 all except Corvette, 35 ft. lbs.

1982-83 CHEVROLET CAVALIER
BUICK SKYHAWK · CADILLAC CIMARRON
OLDSMOBILE FIRENZA · PONTIAC 2000

INDEX OF SERVICE OPERATIONS

NOTE: Refer to the back of this manual for vehicle manufacturer's special service tool suppliers.

VEHICLE IDENTIFICATION NUMBER LOCATION

On top of instrument panel, left front.

ENGINE NUMBER LOCATION

On pad on left front of engine block below cylinder head.

ENGINE IDENTIFICATION CODE

Year	Engine	V.I.N. Code	Engine Code	Year	Engine	V.I.N. Code	Engine Code	Year	Engine	V.I.N. Code	Engine Code
1982	4-112①	G	CXA, CXC, CXD		4-112①	G	CYX, CYY, CYZ		4-112②	O	UHJ, UHK, UHL
	4-112①	G	CYA, CYB, CYC		4-112①	G	CZF, CZJ, CZK		4-112②	O	UHP, UHS, UHT
	4-112①	G	CYD, CYF, CYH		4-112①	G	CZY, CZZ		4-112②	O	UHY, UHZ
	4-112①	G	CYJ, CYK, CYM		4-112①	G	C8A, C8B, C8C		4-122	B	CSA, CSB, CSC
	4-112①	G	CYN, CYR, CYS		4-112①	G	C8D, C8F, C8H			①—Overhead valve engine.		
	4-112①	G	CYT, CYU, CYW		4-112①	G	C8J, C8K, C8M			②—Overhead cam engine.		

GRILLE IDENTIFICATION

1982 Cadillac Cimarron

**1982–83 Buick Skyhawk
Exc. "T" Type**

**1982–83 Chevrolet Cavalier
Except Hatchback**

**1982–83 Chevrolet Cavalier
Hatchback**

1982–83 Olds Firenza

1982–83 Pontiac 2000

1983 Buick "T" Type

1983 Cadillac Cimarron

GENERAL ENGINE SPECIFICATIONS

Year	Engine CID①/Liter	Engine V.I.N. Code②	Carburetor	Bore and Stroke	Compression Ratio	Net H.P. @ R.P.M.③	Maximum Torque Ft. Lbs. @ R.P.M.	Normal Oil Pressure Pounds
1982	4-112/1.8L⑤	G	E2SE, 2 Bbl.④	3.50 × 2.90	9.0	85 @ 5100	100 @ 2800	45
	4-112/1.8L⑥	O	E.F.I.⑦	3.33 × 3.12	9.0	84 @ 5200	102 @ 2800	45
	4-122/2.0L	B	E2SE, 2 Bbl.④	3.50 × 3.14	9.0	90 @ 5100	111 @ 2700	—
1983	4-112/1.8L⑥	O	E.F.I.⑦	3.33 × 3.12	9.0	84 @ 5200	102 @ 2800	45
	4-122/2.0L	P	E.F.I.⑦	3.50 × 3.15	9.3	86 @ 4900	110 @ 3000	63–77

①—CID—cubic inch displacement.
②—On 1982–83 vehicles the eighth digit denotes engine code.
③—Ratings are net as installed in vehicle.
④—Rochester.
⑤—Overhead valve engine.
⑥—Overhead cam engine.
⑦—Electronic Fuel Injection.

TUNE UP SPECIFICATIONS

The following specifications are published from the latest information available. This data should be used only in the absence of a decal affixed in the engine compartment.

★ When using a timing light, disconnect vacuum hose or tube at distributor and plug opening in hose or tube so idle speed will not be affected.

● When checking compression, lowest cylinder must be within 70 percent of highest.

▲ Before removing wires from distributor cap, determine location of the No. 1 wire in cap, as distributor position may have been altered from that shown at the end of this chart.

☞ Spark plug types shown in this chart are recommendations of the original vehicle manufacturer and not MOTOR.

Check local sources for other spark plug manufacturers listings.

Year & Engine/V.I.N.	Spark Plug Type ☞	Spark Plug Gap	Ignition Timing BTDC①★ Firing Order Fig. ▲	Ignition Timing BTDC①★ Man. Trans.	Ignition Timing BTDC①★ Auto. Trans.	Ignition Timing BTDC①★ Mark Fig.	Curb Idle Speed② Man. Trans.	Curb Idle Speed② Auto. Trans.	Fast Idle Speed Man. Trans.	Fast Idle Speed Auto. Trans.	Fuel Pump Pressure
1982											
4-112/G 2 Barrel③	④	.035	A	12°⑤	12°⑤	B⑥	⑦	⑦	2400	2300	4½⑧
4-112 E.F.I./O⑨	R42XLS6	.060	C	—	8°⑩	D	—	800D⑪	—	⑪	—
4-122/B	④	.035	A	—	12°	B⑥	—	⑦	—	2300	4½⑧
1983											
4-112 E.F.I./O⑨	R42XLS6	.060	C	—	8°	D	—	⑪	—	⑪	—
4-122/P	R42CTS	.035	A	TDC	TDC	B⑥	⑪	⑪	⑪	⑪	—

①—BTDC—Before top dead center.
②—Idle speed on man. trans. vehicles is adjusted in Neutral & on auto. trans. equipped vehicles is adjusted in Drive unless otherwise specified.
③—Overhead valve engine.
④—Original equipment spark plugs, R42TS or R42CTS. When replacing spark plugs, use R42CTS.
⑤—Disconnect 4 terminal Electronic Spark Timing (EST) wire connector to place system in ignition timing bypass mode. Connect a suitable inductive pickup timing light to ignition coil high tension lead near distributor. The pulley notch will appear to move slightly as each cylinder is fired during the ignition timing check. This slight pulley notch movement should be centered at the proper timing degree mark on the timing tab, see note 6. After completing adjustment, reconnect EST wire connector.
⑥—The crankshaft pulley has two ignition timing notches located 180° apart. The notch for No. 1 cylinder is scribed across the three pulley sheave surfaces, while the second notch is scribed across the center sheave only.
⑦—Idle speeds are controlled by the idle speed control motor.
⑧—Minimum.
⑨—Overhead cam engine.
⑩—Ground diagnostic connector located under dash panel. The check engine light should begin flashing. Check average timing of cylinder Nos. 1 & 4. After completing adjustment, remove ground from diagnostic connector.
⑪—Idle speed is controlled by the idle air control assembly.

Fig. A

Fig. B

Continued

TUNE UP NOTES—Continued

Fig. C

Fig. D

DISTRIBUTOR SPECIFICATIONS

Distributor Ident. No.①	Centrifugal Advanced Degrees @ RPM of Distributor				Vacuum Advance	
	Advance Starts	Intermediate Advance			Full Advance	Inches of Vacuum to Start Plunger	Max. Adv. Dist. Deg. @ Vacuum
1982						
1103440②	—	—	—	—	—	—	—
1103500②	—	—	—	—	—	—	—
1103575②	—	—	—	—	—	—	—
1110599②	—	—	—	—	—	—	—
1983						
1103455②	—	—	—	—	—	—	—
1103515②	—	—	—	—	—	—	—

①—Stamped on distributor housing plate.   ②—Electronic Spark Timing.

ALTERNATOR & REGULATOR SPECIFICATIONS

Year	Alternator					Regulator						
	Model	Rated Hot Output Amps.	Field Current 12 Volts @ 80°F	Output @ 14 Volts		Model	Field Relay			Voltage Regulator		
				2000 R.P.M. Amps.	5000 R.P.M. Amps.		Air Gap In.	Point Gap In.	Closing Voltage	Air Gap In.	Point Gap In.	Voltage @ 125°F
1982	1100169①	63	4–4.5	—	—	Integral	—	—	—	—	—	—
	1100220①	63	4–4.5	—	—	Integral	—	—	—	—	—	—
	1101438②	70	4–4.5	—	—	Integral	—	—	—	—	—	—
1983	1100258③	78	—	—	—	Integral	—	—	—	—	—	—
	1100288③	78	—	—	—	Integral	—	—	—	—	—	—
	1100289③	78	—	—	—	Integral	—	—	—	—	—	—
	1100290③	55	—	—	—	Integral	—	—	—	—	—	—
	1100291③	55	—	—	—	Integral	—	—	—	—	—	—

Continued

ALTERNATOR & REGULATOR SPECIFICATIONS—Continued

Year	Alternator					Regulator							
				Output @ 14 Volts			Field Relay			Voltage Regulator			
	Model	Rated Hot Output Amps.	Field Current 12 Volts @ 80°F	2000 R.P.M. Amps.	5000 R.P.M. Amps.	Model	Air Gap In.	Point Gap In.	Closing Voltage	Air Gap In.	Point Gap In.	Voltage @ 125°F
	1105091③	63	—	—	—	Integral	—	—	—	—	—	—
	1105092③	63	—	—	—	Integral	—	—	—	—	—	—
	1105249②	85	—	—	—	Integral	—	—	—	—	—	—
	1105331②	85	—	—	—	Integral	—	—	—	—	—	—
	1105335③	63	—	—	—	Integral	—	—	—	—	—	—

①—10 SI. ②—15 SI. ③—12 SI.

STARTING MOTOR SPECIFICATIONS

Year	Engine/V.I.N.	Starter Ident. No.	Brush Spring Tension Oz.①	Free Speed Test			Resistance Test	
				Amps.	Volts	R.P.M.	Amps.	Volts
1982	4-112/G③	1109537	—	45–75②	9	6500–9700	—	—
	4-112/O④	—	—	55–85②	9	6000–12000	—	—
	4-122/B	1109562	—	45–70②	9	7000–11900	—	—
1983	4-112/O④	1109551	—	55–85②	10	6000–12000	—	—
	4-122/P	1109562	—	50–75②	10	6000–11900	—	—

①—Minimum.
②—Includes solenoid.
③—Overhead valve engine.
④—Overhead cam engine.

VALVE SPECIFICATIONS

Year	Engine/V.I.N.	Valve Lash		Valve Angles		Valve Spring Installed Height	Valve Spring Pressure Lbs. @ In.	Stem Clearance		Stem Diameter	
		Int.	Exh.	Seat	Face			Intake	Exhaust	Intake	Exhaust
1982	4-112/G②	1½ Turn①		46	45	1.598	182 @ 1.33	.0011–.0026	.0014–.0031	.3139–.3144	.3129–.3136
1982-83	4-112/O③	Hydraulic④		45	46	—	—	.0006–.0016	.0012–.0024	—	—
	4-122/B,P	1½ Turn①		46	45	1.598	182 @ 1.33	.0011–.0026	.0014–.0031	.3139–.3144	.3129–.3136

①—Turn rocker arm adjusting nut until all lash is eliminated, then tighten nut an additional one and one-half turn to center plunger.
②—Overhead valve engine.
③—Overhead cam engine.
④—Hydraulic valve compensator, no adjustment.

PISTONS, PINS, RINGS, CRANKSHAFT & BEARINGS

Year	Engine Model/V.I.N.	Piston Clearance	Ring Gap①		Wristpin Diameter ②	Rod Bearings		Main Bearings			
			Comp.	Oil		Shaft Diameter	Bearing Clearance	Shaft Diameter	Bearing Clearance	Thrust on Bear. No.	Shaft End Play
1982	4-112/G③	.0008–.0018	.010	—	.9054	1.9983–1.9993	.0010–.0031	④	⑤	4	.002–.007
1982-83	4-112/O⑥	.0007⑧	.012	.016		1.9280–1.9286	.0007–.0024	⑦	.0006–.0016	3	.002–.012
	4-122/B,P	.0008–.0018	.010	—	.9054	1.9983–1.9993	.0010–.0031	④	⑤	4	.002–.007

①—Fit rings in tapered bores for clearance given in tightest portion of ring travel. Clearances specified are minimum gaps.
②—Minimum diameter.
③—Overhead valve engine.
④—Nos. 1, 2, 3, 4, 2.4945–2.4954 inch; No. 5, 2.4937–2.4946 inch.
⑤—Nos. 1, 2, 3, 4, .0006–.0018 inch; No. 5, .0014–.0026 inch.
⑥—Overhead cam engine.
⑦—Brown color code, 2.2830–2.2832 inch; green color code, 2.2828–2.2830 inch.
⑧—Maximum.

ENGINE TIGHTENING SPECIFICATIONS ★

★ Torque specifications are for clean and lightly lubricated threads only. Dry or dirty threads produce increased friction which prevents accurate measurement of tightness.

Year	Engine Model/V.I.N.	Spark Plugs Ft. Lbs.	Cylinder Head Bolts Ft. Lbs.	Intake Manifold Ft. Lbs.	Exhaust Manifold Ft. Lbs.	Rocker Arm Stud Ft. Lbs.	Rocker Arm Cover Ft. Lbs.	Connecting Rod Cap Bolts Ft. Lbs.	Main Bearing Cap Bolts Ft. Lbs.	Flywheel to Crankshaft Ft. Lbs.	Vibration Damper or Pulley Ft. Lbs.
1982	4-112/G①	7–15	65–75	20–25	22–28	43–49	6–9	34–40	63–74	45–55	66–84
1982–83	4-112/O②	—	③	16	19	—	5	39	57	45	20
	4-122/B,P	7–15	65–75	20–25	22–28	43–49	6–9	34–40	63–74	45–55	66–84

①—Overhead valve engine.
②—Overhead cam engine.
③—Torque cylinder head & camshaft carrier bolts to 18 ft. lbs., then tighten bolts an additional 180° in 60° increments. Start engine & allow to reach operating temperature, then tighten bolts an additional 30° to 50°.

BRAKE SPECIFICATIONS

Year	Model	Brake Drum Inside Diameter	Wheel Cylinder Bore Diameter			Master Cylinder Bore Diameter		
			Front Disc Brake	Front Drum Brake	Rear Drum Brake	With Disc Brakes	With Drum Brakes	With Power Brakes
1982	All	7.87	2.24	—	.630	.866	—	.866
1983	All	7.87	2.24	—	.630①	.866	—	.866

①—Sta. wag., .690 inch.

WHEEL ALIGNMENT SPECIFICATIONS

Year	Model	Caster Angle, Degrees		Camber Angle Degrees				Toe-Out Inch	Toe-Out on Turns, Deg.	
		Limits	Desired	Limits		Desired			Outer Wheel	Inner Wheel
				Left	Right	Left	Right			
1982	All	—	—	+.1 to +1.1	+.1 to +1.1	+.6	+.6	①	—	—
1983	All	+.7 to +2.7	+1.7	+.2 to +1.2	+.2 to +1.2	+.7	+.7	②	—	—

①—.25° toe-out.   ②—.13° toe-out.

COOLING SYSTEM & CAPACITY DATA

Year	Model or Engine/V.I.N.	Cooling Capacity, Qts.		Radiator Cap Relief Pressure, Lbs.	Thermo. Opening Temp.	Fuel Tank Gals.	Engine Oil Refill Qts.	Transaxle Oil	
		Less A/C	With A/C					Manual Transaxle Pts.	Auto. Transaxle Qts. ①
1982	Cavalier 4-112/G	9.0	9.3	15	195	14	4②	6	③
	Cimarron 4-112/G	—	8.28	15	195	14	4②	6	③
	Firenza 4-112/G	8.0	8.0	15	195	14	4②	6	③
	J2000 4-112/G	8.3	8.3	15	195	14	4②	6	③
	Skyhawk 4-112/G	—	—	15	195	14	4②	6	③
	Firenza 4-112/O	7.8	7.9	15	195	14	3②	6	③
	J2000 4-112/O			15	195	14	3②	6	③
	Skyhawk 4-112/O			15	195	14	3②	6	③
	Firenza 4-122/B			15	195	14	4②	6	③
	Skyhawk 4-122/B			15	195	14	4②	6	③

Continued

COOLING SYSTEM & CAPACITY DATA—Continued

Year	Model or Engine/V.I.N.	Cooling Capacity, Qts.		Radiator Cap Relief Pressure, Lbs.	Thermo. Opening Temp.	Fuel Tank Gals.	Engine Oil Refill Qts.	Transaxle Oil	
		Less A/C	With A/C					Manual Transaxle Pts.	Auto. Transaxle Qts. ①
1983	Cavalier 4-112/O	7.8	7.8	15	195	13.6	3②	5.4	③
	Firenza 4-112/O	8.0	8.0	15	195	13.6	3②	5.4	③
	2000 4-112/O	7.8	7.9	15	195	13.6	3②	⑤	③
	Skyhawk 4-112/O	7.8	7.8	15	195	13.6	3②	5.4	③
	Cavalier 4-122/P	9.6	9.7	15	195	13.6	4②	5.4	③
	Cimarron 4-122/P	④	④	15	195	13.6	4②	5.4	③
	Firenza 4-122/P	8.0	8.0	15	195	13.6	4②	5.4	③
	2000 4-122/P	7.8	7.9	15	195	13.6	4②	⑤	③
	Skyhawk 4-122/P	9.7	9.75	15	195	13.6	4②	5.4	③

①—Approximate, make final check with dip-stick.
②—With or without filter change.
③—Oil pan only, 4 qts. After overhaul, less torque converter drain, 6 qts.; with torque converter drain, 9 qts.
④—Man. trans., 8.7 qts.; auto. trans., 9.3 qts.
⑤—4 spd., 5.9 pts.; 5 spd., 5.3 pts.

Electrical Section

STARTER, REPLACE

Except 4-112 Overhead Cam Engine

1. Disconnect battery ground cable.
2. Raise and support front of vehicle.
3. Disconnect solenoid wires and battery cable at starter.
4. Remove rear engine mount support bracket, then the A/C compressor support rod (if equipped).
5. Remove starter to engine mounting bolts and lower starter. Note position of shims if used.
6. Reverse procedure to install.

4-112 Overhead Cam Engine

1. Disconnect battery ground cable, then remove air cleaner.
2. Remove lower starter to engine mounting bolt.
3. Remove rear starter brace attaching bolt from engine block and nut from starter, then remove brace.

4. Disconnect battery positive cable and solenoid leads from starter motor.
5. Remove upper starter motor to engine block mounting bolt, then raise and support front of vehicle.
6. Disconnect speedometer cable.
7. While pushing upward on shift cable, lower armature end of starter motor down between stabilizer and engine, then remove starter motor.

NOTE: It may be necessary to pry engine block forward to provide clearance for starter motor removal.

8. Reverse procedure to install.

IGNITION LOCK, REPLACE

1. Remove steering wheel as outlined under "Steering Wheel, Replace" procedure.
2. Remove turn signal switch as outlined under "Turn Signal Switch, Replace" pro-

cedure.
3. Remove buzzer switch.
4. Turn lock cylinder to "Run" position, then remove the lock cylinder retaining screw and lock cylinder, Fig. 1.
5. To install, rotate lock cylinder to stop while holding housing. Align cylinder key with keyway in housing, then push cylinder into housing until fully seated.
6. Install lock cylinder retaining screw.
7. Install buzzer switch, turn signal switch and steering wheel.

IGNITION & DIMMER SWITCHES, REPLACE

1. Remove steering wheel as outlined under "Steering Wheel, Replace" procedure, then the turn signal switch and lock cylinder as previously described.
2. Refer to Figs. 2 and 3 to remove ignition and dimmer switches.
3. When installing dimmer switch, depress switch slightly and install a 3/32 drill into switch. Force switch upward to remove lash and tighten retaining screw.

Fig. 1 Lock cylinder removal

Fig. 2 Ignition & dimmer switch removal. Models less tilt column

Fig. 3 Ignition & dimmer switch removal. Models with tilt column

W/S WIPER SWITCH, REPLACE

1. Remove turn signal switch as outlined under "Turn Signal Switch, Replace" procedure.
2. Refer to Figs. 4 and 5 for wiper switch replacement.

PULSE W/S WIPER MODULE, REPLACE

1982–83 Cavalier, Cimarron & 2000

1. Disconnect battery ground cable.
2. Remove headlamp switch knob by depressing retaining clip behind knob and pulling knob from shaft.
3. Remove left hand trimplate attaching screws and the trimplate.
4. Remove screws retaining module to adapter assembly.
5. Disconnect wire connectors from module.
6. Remove module from instrument panel.
7. Reverse procedure to install.

Fig. 4 W/S wiper switch removal. Models less tilt column

Fig. 5 W/S wiper switch removal. Models with tilt column

1982-83 Firenza & Skyhawk

1. Disconnect battery ground cable.
2. Remove six screws attaching steering column trim cover to instrument panel and two screws attaching cover to left hand instrument panel insulator, then remove trim cover.
3. Disengage retaining clip and remove pulse wiper module from cover.
4. Remove screw attaching module ground wire to instrument panel lower brace, then disconnect wire connector and remove module.
5. Reverse procedure to install.

REAR WINDOW DEFROSTER OR WASHER/WIPER SWITCH, REPLACE

1. Disconnect battery ground cable.
2. Remove lower trimplate and disconnect switch wiring connector.
3. Depress switch retaining tabs and remove switch from dash.
4. Reverse procedure to install.

STOPLIGHT SWITCH, ADJUST

Insert stoplight switch into tubular clip until switch body seats fully into clip. Pull brake pedal rearward against internal pedal stop. The switch will be properly positioned in the tubular clip automatically.

NOTE: Rotate switch 1/2 turn counterclockwise to be sure that switch does not hold brake pedal down after adjustment.

BACKUP LIGHT/NEUTRAL START SWITCH, REPLACE

NOTE: On vehicles equipped with automatic transmission, the neutral start and backup light switches are combined into one unit and must be replaced as an assembly.

Man. Trans.
1. Disconnect battery ground cable.
2. Apply parking brake and block wheels, then place gear shift lever in Neutral position.
3. Remove front ash tray, then remove two console attaching screws through ash tray opening.
4. Remove retaining screw, then remove gear shift knob.
5. On 1982-83 Cavalier, Cimarron and J2000, proceed as follows:
   a. Remove one console attaching screw located under parking brake handle.
   b. Toward rear of console, remove one screw from each side retaining console to rear bracket.
6. On 1982-83 Firenza and Skyhawk, proceed as follows:
   a. Pull upward on front of console trim cover, then lift cover from console and

disconnect wire connector.
   b. Remove three screws attaching console to front mounting bracket.
   c. Remove rear ash tray, then remove screw attaching console to rear mounting bracket.
7. On all models, remove console assembly.

NOTE: On models equipped with arm rest, it may be necessary to remove arm rest assembly to provide clearance for console removal.

8. Disconnect wire connector from backup light switch.
9. Remove retaining clip, then remove backup light switch from side of shifter.
10. Reverse procedure to install.

Auto. Trans.
1. Disconnect battery ground cable.
2. Apply parking brake and block wheels, then place gear shift lever in Neutral position.
3. Remove front ash tray, then remove two console attaching screws through ash tray opening.
4. Carefully pry button from center of shift lever knob, then remove snap ring retaining knob.
5. Pull front of console trim cover upward, then lift trim cover from console and disconnect wire connector.
6. Remove three screws attaching front of console to mounting bracket.
7. Remove rear ash tray, then remove screw attaching console to rear support.
8. Remove console assembly.

Fig. 6 Compressing lock plate

Fig. 7 Instrument cluster. 1982–83 Cavalier, Cimarron & 2000

NOTE: On models equipped with arm rest, it may be necessary to remove arm rest assembly to provide clearance for console removal.

9. Disconnect wire connector from Neutral Safety/Backup light switch.
10. Remove screws attaching switch to shifter lever, then remove switch.
11. If the same switch is to be reinstalled, proceed as follows:
    a. Place shift lever in Neutral position.
    b. Position switch to shift lever and loosely install attaching screws.
    c. Rotate switch on shifter to align adjustment hole with carrier tang, then insert a 2.34 mm diameter pin into hole to a depth of 5 mm.
    d. Torque switch attaching screws to 20 inch lbs., then remove gauge pin.
12. If a new replacement switch is to be installed, proceed as follows:
    a. Position shift lever in the Neutral position.
    b. Insert switch carrier tang into hole on shift lever, then install switch and torque attaching screws to 20 inch lbs.

NOTE: Replacement switches are held in the Neutral position by an internal plastic pin.

    c. Move shift lever out of Neutral position to shear switch internal plastic pin.
13. Install console and connect battery ground cable.
14. Check to ensure that vehicle will not start in any shift lever position except Neutral and Park.

CLUTCH START SWITCH, REPLACE

1. Remove lower left hush panel.
2. Disconnect wiring connector from switch.
3. Disconnect switch link from pedal, then remove switch retaining screw and switch.
4. Reverse procedure to install.

TURN SIGNAL SWITCH, REPLACE

1. Disconnect battery ground cable.
2. Remove steering wheel as outlined under "Steering Wheel, Replace" procedure.

3. Using a suitable screwdriver, pry cover from housing.
4. Using lock plate compressing tool J-23653-4, compress lock plate and pry snap ring from groove on steering shaft, Fig. 6. Slowly release compressing tool, then remove tool and lock plate from shaft.
5. Slide canceling cam and bearing preload spring from steering shaft.
6. Remove turn signal (multi-function) lever.
7. Remove hazard warning knob retaining screw, button, spring and knob.
8. Remove actuator arm screw and actuator arm.
9. Remove switch retaining screws and pull switch upward from column, guiding wire harness through column.
10. Reverse procedure to install.

STEERING WHEEL, REPLACE

1. Disconnect battery ground cable.
2. Remove steering wheel center pad.
3. Remove steering wheel retaining nut and retainer.
4. Scribe alignment marks on steering wheel and shaft to aid installation.
5. Using tool J-1859-03 or equivalent, remove steering wheel from shaft.
6. Reverse procedure to install.

INSTRUMENT CLUSTER, REPLACE

1982–83 Cavalier, Cimarron & 2000

1. Disconnect battery ground cable.
2. Remove six screws attaching instrument panel trimplate to instrument panel.
3. Pull top of trimplate outward and remove trimplate from instrument panel.
4. Remove four screws securing instrument cluster to instrument panel, Fig. 7.
5. Remove screws attaching steering column cover to instrument panel, then the lower column cover.
6. Remove two steering column retaining bolts and lower steering column to floor.
7. Pull instrument cluster out slightly and disconnect speedometer cable.
8. On automatic transmission equipped vehicles, disconnect vehicle speed sensor (VSS) connector from rear of cluster.
9. Remove cluster and disconnect instrument panel harness connector from printed circuit located at rear of cluster.
10. Reverse procedure to install.

1982–83 Firenza & Skyhawk

1. Disconnect battery ground cable.
2. Remove six screws attaching steering column trim cover to instrument panel and two screws attaching trim cover to left hand instrument panel trim cover, then remove trim cover.
3. Remove screw attaching right end of left hand trim cover to instrument panel, then pull trim cover rearward to disengage retaining clips and remove cover.
4. Remove screw attaching left end of right hand trim cover to instrument panel, then remove two screws from center trim cover and four screws from front of glove compartment. Pull right hand trim cover rearward to disengage retaining clips, then disconnect wire connectors and remove trim cover.
5. Remove seven screws attaching cluster trim cover to instrument cluster pad, then remove trim cover.
6. Remove five screws attaching bezel and lens to instrument cluster carrier, then remove bezel and lens.
7. Loosen two upper steering column mounting bolts, then lower steering column slightly to provide clearance for cluster removal.
8. Remove four screws attaching cluster housing to cluster carrier, then pull housing slightly outward and disconnect speedometer cable and remove cluster housing, Fig. 7A.
9. Reverse procedure to install.

HEADLIGHT SWITCH, REPLACE

1982–83 Cavalier, Cimarron & 2000

1. Disconnect battery ground cable.
2. Remove headlight switch knob by pulling knob to full "ON" position, depressing retaining clip behind knob and pulling knob from shaft.
3. Gently pry left hand side trimplate out of instrument panel.
4. Remove switch retaining nut, rotate and tilt switch forward and pull switch instrument panel.
5. Disconnect wiring connector and remove switch.
6. Reverse procedure to install.

1982–83 Firenza & Skyhawk

1. Disconnect battery ground cable.
2. Remove six screws attaching steering column lower cover to instrument panel,

1. INSTRUMENT PANEL   3. CLUSTER HOUSING   5. I.P. HARNESS   7. L.H. CLUSTER LEAD
2. CLUSTER CARRIER   4. SCREW   6. RETAINER   8. R.H. CLUSTER LEAD

Fig. 7A   Instrument cluster. 1982—83 Firenza & Skyhawk

then remove lower cover.
3. Remove one screw attaching right end of left hand trim cover to instrument panel, then pull cover rearward to detach retaining clips.
4. Remove four screws attaching headlamp switch to instrument panel, then pull switch rearward and disconnect wire connector.
5. Reverse procedure to install.

RADIO, REPLACE

1982—83 Cavalier, Cimarron & 2000

1. Disconnect battery ground cable.
2. Loosen six instrument panel trimplate to instrument panel attaching screws and remove trimplate.

NOTE: Determine whether right side of radio is retained with nut or rubber stud.

3. On vehicles equipped with radio side retainer nut:
   a. Without A/C, remove right lower hush panel then loosen side retainer nut. Disconnect wire and antenna connections and remove radio from instrument panel.
   b. With A/C, remove right lower hush panel, A/C duct and A/C control head, then loosen side retainer nut. Disconnect wiring and antenna connections and remove radio from instrument panel.
4. On vehicles equipped with radio side retainer rubber stud, remove two radio bracket to instrument panel attaching screws, then pull radio forward and disconnect wiring and antenna connections. Remove radio from instrument panel.
5. Reverse procedures to install.

1982—83 Firenza & Skyhawk

1. Disconnect battery ground cable.
2. Remove six screws attaching steering column trim cover to instrument panel, then lower trim cover.
3. Remove screw attaching left end of right hand trim cover to instrument panel.
4. Remove two screws from under center trim cover and four screws from front of

1	HEATER CASE AIR INLET ASM.
2	STUD DASH PANEL
3	LOCATING STUDS DASH PANEL
4	HEATER CORE
5	HEATER MODULE ASM.
6	MODULE COVER

FRT

VIEW A

Fig. 8   Heater core & blower motor. (Typical) Models less A/C

glove compartment, then pull trim cover rearward to disengage retaining clips and disconnect wire connectors.

5. Remove four screws attaching upper and lower radio mounting brackets to instrument panel.
6. Pull radio out just enough to disconnect wire connector and antenna lead, then remove radio.
7. Reverse procedure to install.

W/S WIPER MOTOR, REPLACE

1. Disconnect battery ground cable.
2. Remove wiper arms from transmission spindle shafts.
3. Remove shroud top vent grille panel and screen.
4. Loosen, but do not remove, transmission drive link to motor crank arm attaching nuts, then pull drive link out of motor crank arm.
5. Disconnect wiper motor electrical connections and remove wiper motor attaching bolts.
6. Rotate wiper motor upward and outward, and remove from vehicle.
7. Reverse procedure to install.

W/S WIPER TRANSMISSION ASSEMBLY, REPLACE

1. Remove wiper arms from transmission spindle shafts.
2. Remove shroud top vent grille panel and screen.

3. Loosen, but do not remove, transmission drive link to motor crank arm attaching nuts then pull drive link from motor crankarm.
4. Remove transmission to cowl panel attaching screws and the transmission assembly.
5. Reverse procedure to install.

BLOWER MOTOR, REPLACE

1. Disconnect battery ground cable.
2. Disconnect blower motor electrical connections.
3. Remove plastic water shield from right side of cowl.
4. Remove blower motor retaining screws and blower motor.
5. Reverse procedure to install.

HEATER CORE, REPLACE

Less Air Conditioning

1. Disconnect battery ground cable and drain cooling system.
2. Disconnect heater hoses from heater core.
3. Remove heater outlet deflector.
4. Remove heater core module cover retaining screws and module cover, Fig. 8.
5. Remove heater core retaining straps and heater core.
6. Reverse procedure to install.

With Air Conditioning

1. Disconnect battery ground cable and

drain cooling system.
2. Raise and support vehicle and disconnect drain tube from heater and evaporator assembly.
3. Lower vehicle and remove right and left hush panels, steering column trim cover and glovebox.
4. Remove heater duct retaining screw and heater duct.
5. Remove heater core cover attaching screws, then gently pull cover rearward and out of vehicle, Fig. 9.

CAUTION: When removing heater core assembly, pull assembly straight toward interior of vehicle until plastic drain tube clears cowl. If assembly is tilted in any direction before tube clears cowl, the drain tube may break.

6. Remove heater core retaining clamps and heater core from case.
7. Reverse procedure to install.

CRUISE CONTROL

Release Switches

Automatic Transmission

Both the electrical and vacuum release switches are located at the brake pedal. To adjust, depress brake pedal and insert switch fully into tubular clip. Pull pedal rearward until clicking sounds are no longer audible. The switch is now automatically adjusted.

Manual Transmission

On manual transmission equipped vehicles, the electrical release switch is located at the

1	HEATER & EVAPORATOR
2	DRAIN TUBE
3	BLOWER ASSEMBLY

NOTICE: WHEN REMOVING THE HEATER & EVAPORATOR ASSEMBLY, PULL ASSEMBLY STRAIGHT TOWARD INTERIOR OF CAR UNTIL PLASTIC DRAIN TUBE CLEARS COWL. IF ASSEMBLY IS TILTED IN ANY DIRECTION BEFORE THE TUBE CLEARS THE COWL, THE TUBE MAY BREAK.

Fig. 9 Heater core & blower motor. (Typical) Models with A/C clutch pedal, while the vacuum release switch is found at the brake pedal. Adjustment procedures for these switches are the same as for those under automatic transmission equipped vehicles.

Servo, Adjust

With engine off and carburetor in slow idle position, connect cable swivel to third ball on servo chain. Adjust cable nuts until chain has a slight amount of slack, then tighten lock nut securely.

Cruise Speed, Adjust

The cruise speed adjustment can be set as follows:
1. If cruise speed is lower than engagement speed, loosen orifice tube locknut and turn orifice tube counterclockwise.
2. If cruise speed is higher than engagement speed, loosen orifice tube locknut and turn orifice tube clockwise.

NOTE: Each 1/4 turn of orifice tube will change cruise speed approximately one mile per hour. Tighten locknut after adjustment is completed.

Fig. 10 Aspirated assisted vacuum system schematic

ASPIRATOR ASSISTED VACUUM SYSTEM

The aspirator assisted vacuum system supplements engine vacuum when engine vacuum is low. The system, Fig. 10, consists of an aspirator, 3-port check valve, 2-port check valve and related components such as the air pump and air management valve. The air for the aspirator is tapped off the air line that connects the air pump to the air management valve. Aspirator vacuum and manifold vacuum (after passing through the 2-port check valve) supply the two upper ports of the 3-port check valve. The lower of the 3-port check valve supplies air to the cruise control transducer. The aspirator assisted vacuum system operates as follows:
a. Under normal vacuum conditions, air is bled into the system from the transducer resume valve to the lower "T" of the 3-port check valve, then to the 2-port check valve and finally into the intake manifold, Fig. 10.
b. Also during normal operation, as the air pump is pumping air into the air management valve, a small amount of air is diverted through the aspirator to the atmosphere. As air passes through the aspirator, a venturi action inside the aspirator

assembly develops a vacuum. This vacuum is used to provide the vacuum assist needed under high cruise conditions.
c. Should manifold vacuum fall below aspirator vacuum, the 2-port check valve is designed to close while the 3-port check valve is designed to open. Opening of the 3-port check valve exposes the higher vacuum at the aspirator, providing the needed vacuum for proper cruise operation.

To check the aspirator system for correct operation, note the following information:
a. Ensure all hoses and connections are secure and check valves are correctly installed.

NOTE: The check valves are arrowhead shaped in the direction of air flow.

b. Connect a suitable vacuum gauge to the aspirator output at point A, Fig. 10.
c. Start and operate engine at 2500 RPM.

NOTE: Engine should be thoroughly warmed up to ensure that the computer command control system (CCC) is operating in closed loop.

d. Check vacuum gauge. A minimum of 6

inches should be indicated. If vacuum reading is not within specified amount, clean aspirator using a suitable solvent and recheck. Also check air pump for air output. If there is no air output from the air pump, check air pump for damage. If air pump is not damaged, proceed to step e.
e. Disconnect vacuum gauge at port A, Fig. 10. Disconnect and plug 2-port check valve at port B. Blow air into the resume valve hose at port C. Air should flow through and exit at port A.
f. Remove plug from 2-port check valve at port B and plug hose at port A. Blow air into cruise resume valve at port C. Air should flow and exit at port B.

NOTE: Steps e & f determine if the hoses and check valves are operating in one direction. To check for operation in the opposite direction, proceed to step g.

g. Blow air into hose at port A while port B is plugged, then into port B while hose at port A is plugged.

NOTE: No air should exist at port C in either case.

4-112 & 122 Overhead Valve
Engine Section

ENGINE MOUNTS, REPLACE

Front Engine Mount

1. Disconnect battery ground cable.
2. Remove engine mount nuts, then raise and support vehicle.
3. Remove inner fender shield attaching bolts, then the shield.
4. Support engine and remove and discard engine mount attaching bolts, Fig. 1.
5. Remove engine mount from vehicle.

CAUTION: Whenever engine mount is removed, alignment bolt M6X1X65 must be used during installation to prevent power train misalignment.

6. Reverse procedure to install, using new engine mount bolts. Remove alignment bolt and torque engine mount to side frame bolts to 35–45 ft. lbs. Torque all other nuts and bolts to 25–35 ft. lbs.

NOTE: If excessive effort is required to remove alignment bolt, loosen transaxle adjusting bolts to align powertrain components.

Rear Engine Mount

1. Disconnect battery ground cable.
2. Raise and support vehicle.
3. If equipped with manual transaxle, remove oil filter.
4. Support engine and remove engine mount nuts, Fig. 2.
5. Remove and discard engine mount to engine attaching bolts.
6. Remove engine mount from vehicle.
7. Reverse procedure to install. Check oil level and torque nuts to 15–20 ft. lbs. and bolts to 25–35 ft. lbs.

ENGINE, REPLACE

1. Disconnect battery ground cable, then drain cooling system.
2. Remove air cleaner.
3. Remove power steering pump, if

Engine Oiling System

Fig. 1 Engine front mount

Fig. 2 Engine rear mount

FRONT OF ENGINE →

CYLINDER HEAD BOLT TIGHTENING SEQUENCE

Fig. 3 Cylinder head bolt tightening sequence

CYLINDER HEAD, REPLACE

NOTE: The cylinder head, carburetor TBI (Throttle Body Injection) unit and the intake and exhaust manifolds are removed as an assembly.

1. Disconnect battery ground cable, drain cooling system and remove air cleaner.
2. Raise and support vehicle, then remove exhaust manifold shield.
3. Disconnect exhaust pipe at exhaust manifold and heater hose at intake manifold.
4. Lower vehicle, then remove engine lift bracket and distributor.
5. Disconnect vacuum manifold from alternator bracket.
6. Disconnect and tag all vacuum lines that will interfere with cylinder head removal, then disconnect AIR pipe at exhaust check valve.
7. Disconnect accelerator linkage at carburetor or TBI unit, then remove accelerator linkage bracket bolt and the bracket.
8. Disconnect all electrical wires that will interfere with cylinder head removal, then remove upper radiator hose from cylinder head.
9. Remove dipstick tube bracket bolt and the hot water tube bracket.
10. Remove idler pulley assembly and AIR/power steering belt.
11. Remove power steering pump, if equipped, and position aside.
12. Remove AIR bracket to intake manifold bolt.
13. On power steering equipped vehicles, remove AIR pump pulley, AIR pump through bolt and power steering pump adjusting bracket.
14. Loosen AIR bracket lower bolt and rotate bracket aside.
15. Disconnect fuel line from carburetor or TBI unit.
16. Remove alternator and position aside. Do not remove wires.
17. Remove alternator upper support bracket and brace.
18. Remove rocker arm cover and rocker arms, then the push rods.
19. Remove cylinder head bolts and the cylinder head assembly.
20. Reverse procedure to install. Coat cylinder head and cylinder head bolts with sealer and install bolts finger tight. Torque cylinder head bolts to specification in sequence shown in Fig. 3.

ROCKER ARM STUDS

Rocker arm studs that have stress cracks or damaged threads can be replaced. If threads in cylinder head are damaged or stripped, the head can be retapped and a helical type insert added. When installing a new rocker arm stud, torque stud to 43–49 ft. lbs.

VALVES, ADJUST

1. Crank engine until mark on crankshaft pulley is aligned with TDC mark on timing tab. Check to ensure engine is in the No. 1 cylinder firing position by placing fingers on No. 1 cylinder rocker arms as mark on pulley comes near TDC mark on

equipped, and position aside.
4. Disconnect window washer bottle and position aside.
5. If equipped with A/C, remove A/C relay bracket at bulkhead.
6. Disconnect bulkhead wire harness connections.
7. If equipped with cruise control, disconnect servo bracket and position aside.
8. Disconnect and tag all vacuum hoses and electrical wires that will interfere with engine removal.
9. Remove master cylinder attaching nuts, disconnect master cylinder from vacuum booster and position aside.
10. Disconnect heater hose at engine hot water pipe, then remove upper radiator hose.
11. Remove fan assembly, horn and carburetor or TBI unit linkage.
12. Raise and support vehicle, then disconnect fuel line at fuel pump and heater hose at intake manifold. Remove lower radiator hose.
13. If equipped with A/C, remove A/C support brace retaining bolts and the support brace.
14. Remove exhaust manifold shield, starter to engine retaining bolts and starter.
15. Disconnect exhaust pipe from exhaust manifold.
16. Remove front tires, then disconnect front stabilizer bar from lower control arms.
17. Separate ball joints from steering knuckles using tool J-29330, or equivalent.
18. Disengage, then remove drive axles from transaxle.
19. Remove transaxle strut to transaxle bracket attaching bolts, then disconnect

strut at bracket and crossmember.
20. If equipped with A/C, remove inner fender shield attaching bolts and inner fender shield.
21. If equipped with A/C, remove A/C compressor drive belt, then disconnect A/C compressor from mounting bracket and position compressor aside. Do not disconnect hoses from compressor.
22. Remove rear engine mount attaching nuts and plate.
23. If equipped with automatic transaxle, remove oil filter.
24. Disconnect speedometer cable at transaxle or, if equipped with cruise control, at transducer.
25. Lower vehicle and, if equipped with automatic transaxle, disconnect oil coolant lines at transaxle.
26. Remove front engine mount nuts.
27. Disconnect clutch, shift and/or detent cables from transaxle.
28. Install suitable lifting device, then remove transaxle mount attaching bolts, transaxle mount and bracket.
29. Remove engine and transaxle as an assembly.
30. Install engine/transaxle assembly using engine mount alignment bolt M6X1X65 to ensure proper power train alignment.
31. Lower engine/transaxle assembly into vehicle then install transaxle mount and bracket, using new bolts, Fig. 1.
32. Tighten transaxle mount and front engine mount nuts.
33. Remove engine/transaxle assembly lifting device and raise vehicle.
34. Reverse procedures to complete installation.

1. Air Cleaner	9. A.I.R. Pump	17. Cylinder Head
2. Carburetor	10. Rocker Arm	18. Generator Bracket
3. Coil and Coil Wire	11. Push Rod	19. Generator
4. Fuel Line	12. Push Rod Guide	20. Valves
5. E.F.E. Grid	13. E.G.R. Valve	21. Lifter
6. Rocker Arm Cover	14. Thermostat Outlet	22. Exhaust Manifold
7. Intake Manifold & Gasket	15. Thermostat and Gasket	23. Cylinder Head Gasket
8. A.I.R. Mounting Bracket	16. Adapter	24. A.I.R. Pipes

Cylinder head assembly & components. 1982 4-112 & 122

1. Air Cleaner
2. TBI Unit
3. Coil and Coil Wire
4. Fuel Line
5. E.F.E. Grid
6. Rocker Arm Cover
7. Intake Manifold & Gasket
8. A.I.R. Mounting Bracket
9. A.I.R. Pump
10. Rocker Arm
11. Push Rod
12. Push Rod Guide
13. E.G.R. Valve
14. Thermostat Outlet
15. Thermostat
16. Adapter
17. Cylinder Head
18. Generator Bracket
19. Generator
20. Valves
21. Lifter
22. Exhaust Manifold
23. Cylinder Head Gasket
24. A.I.R. Pipes

Cylinder head assembly & related components. 1983 4-122

1. Distributor Assembly
2. Oil Filter
3. Fuel Pump
4. Dipstick
5. Cam Sprocket
6. Thrust Plate
7. Camshaft and Bearings
8. Cylinder Block
9. Engine Lift Hook
10. Water Pump Pulley
11. Water Pump
12. Water Inlet
13. Dampener
14. Tensioner
15. Piston Rings
16. Piston
17. Starter
18. Accessory Drive Pulley
19. Hub
20. Seal

21. Front Cover
22. Timing Chain
23. Cranksprocket
24. Connecting Rod Bearings
25. Connecting Rod Bearing Cap
26. Main Bearings
27. Crankshaft

28. Main Thrust Bearing
29. Rope Seal
30. Main Bearing Caps
31. Flywheel and Flex Plate
32. Oil Pump
33. Oil Pan
34. Seal

Cylinder block assembly & components

PULLEY

TIMING NOTCH

NOTE: PULLEY CONTAINS TWO SETS OF NOTCHES 180° APART. USE NOTCH CUT ACROSS ENTIRE LENGTH OF PULLEY FOR #1 TDC.

Fig. 4 Aligning crankshaft pulley timing marks

NOTE: AT TIME OF INSTALLATION, FLANGES MUST BE FREE OF OIL. A 2.0-3.0 BEAD OF SEALANT MUST BE APPLIED TO FLANGES AND SEALANT MUST BE WET TO TOUCH WHEN BOLTS ARE TORQUED.

ROCKER ARM COVER

BALL
ROCKER ARM
PUSH ROD
PUSH ROD RETAINER
ROCKER ARM STUD

Fig. 5 Rocker arms & rocker arm cover

timing tab. If valves are not moving, the engine is in the No. 1 firing position. If valves move as pulley nears TDC mark on timing tab, engine is in No. 4 cylinder firing position and should be rotated one revolution to reach the No. 1 cylinder firing position.

NOTE: The crankshaft pulley contains two sets of marks 180° apart. Use those marks which cut across entire length of pulley to find No. 1 cylinder firing position, Fig. 4.

2. With engine in No. 1 cylinder firing position, adjust the following valves: Exhaust: 1, 3; Intake: 1, 2. To adjust valves, back off adjusting nut until lash is felt at push rod, then tighten adjusting nut until all lash is removed, Fig. 5. This can be determined by rotating the push rod while tightening the adjusting nut. When all lash has been eliminated, the push rod will no longer rotate, Fig. 6. Turn the adjusting nut the additional number of turns listed in the Valve Specifications Chart.
3. Crank engine one full revolution until mark on crankshaft pulley and TDC mark are again aligned. This is the No. 4 cylinder firing position. With engine in this position, the following valves can be adjusted: Exhaust 2, 4; Intake 3, 4.
4. Install rocker arm cover, then start engine and check timing and idle speed.

VALVE GUIDES

Valve guides are an integral part of the cylinder head and are not removable. If valve stem clearance becomes excessive, the valve guide should be reamed to the next oversize and the appropriate oversize valves installed. Valves are available in .003, .006, and .012 inch oversizes.

VALVE LIFTERS, REPLACE

1. Remove rocker arm cover attaching bolts and rocker arm cover.
2. Loosen rocker arm stud nut and rotate rocker arm so that pushrod can be removed. Remove pushrod.
3. Using tool J-29834, remove valve lifter from lifter bore, Fig. 7.

VALVE ARRANGEMENT

Front to Rear

4-112 & 122 . . . . E-I-I-E-E-I-I-E

VALVE LIFT SPECS.

Engine	Year	Intake	Exhaust
4-112 & 122	1982	.393	.393

VALVE TIMING

Intake Opens Before TDC

Year	Engine	Degrees
1982	4-112 & 122	32

Fig. 6 Valve adjustment

1. Lifter Body
2. Push Rod Seat
3. Metering Valve
4. Check Ball
5. Check Ball Retainer
6. Push Rod Seat Retainer
7. Plunger
8. Check Ball Spring
9. Plunger Spring

Fig. 7 Sectional view of hydraulic valve lifter

Fig. 8 Removing crankshaft pulley & hub

4. Coat base of new lifter with "Molykote", or equivalent, and install lifter into lifter bore.
5. Reverse procedure to install and adjust valves as outlined under "VALVES, ADJUST" procedure.

ENGINE FRONT COVER, REPLACE

1. Disconnect battery ground cable.
2. Remove accessory drive belts, then raise and support vehicle.
3. Remove right front wheel and tire.
4. Remove right inner fender splash shield attaching bolts and the shield.
5. Remove A/C drive belt, if equipped.
6. Remove crankshaft pulley retaining bolts and crankshaft pulley, Fig. 8.
7. Using tool J-24420, remove crankshaft hub from crankshaft.
8. Remove engine front cover retaining bolts and front cover.
9. Clean sealing surface of front cover and engine block. Apply a 2 mm bead of RTV sealant to front cover sealing surface.
10. Position front cover to engine block. Using centering tool J-23042, install front retaining bolts and torque bolts to 6–9 ft. lbs. Remove centering tool, Fig. 9.
11. Reverse procedure to install.

TIMING CHAIN, REPLACE

1. Remove engine front cover as previously described.
2. Place No. 1 cylinder at TDC and align timing marks on crankshaft and camshaft sprockets, Fig. 10.
3. On 1982 models, remove timing chain upper attaching bolts, then loosen nut as far as possible without removing. On 1983 models, remove timing chain tensioner as described under Timing Chain Tensioner, Replace.
4. Remove camshaft sprocket retaining bolt. Tap lower edge of sprocket with plastic

mallet and remove sprocket and timing chain.
5. If crankshaft sprocket is to be replaced, remove sprocket using a suitable puller.
6. To install crankshaft sprocket, align keyway on sprocket with key on crankshaft.
7. Align timing marks, Fig. 10, and install timing chain on sprockets.
8. Align dowel on camshaft with dowel hole on camshaft sprocket, then install sprocket to camshaft, using retaining bolt to draw sprocket fully to camshaft. Torque bolt to 66–85 ft. lbs.
9. Lubricate timing chain with engine oil, then install timing chain tensioner.
10. Install engine front cover as outlined previously.

TIMING CHAIN TENSIONER, REPLACE

1982 4-112 & 122

1. Remove engine front cover as described under Engine Front Cover, Replace.
2. Remove attaching bolt (1), Fig. 11, and lower nut.

NOTE: Use a suitable tool, such as a loop of wire, to prevent nut from falling into oil pan.

3. Remove timing chain tensioner.

Fig. 9 Installing front cover

Fig. 10   Valve timing marks

Fig. 11   Timing chain tensioner. 1982
4-112 & 4-122

Fig. 12   Compressing timing chain tensioner
spring. 1983 4-122

4. Position timing chain tensioner to engine.
5. Using a suitable tool, such as a wire loop around nut, position nut on stud.
6. Install bolt (1), Fig. 11, finger tight.
7. Torque nut to 15 to 22 ft. lbs. and bolt to 13 to 18 ft. lbs.

1983 4-122

1. Remove engine front cover as described under Engine Front Cover, Replace.
2. Remove tensioner attaching bolts, then remove tensioner.
3. Position tangs of tool No. J33875 under

tensioner sliding blocks, then pull tool to compress tensioner spring.
4. While compressing tensioner spring, insert a cotter pin or other suitable tool into hole (A), Fig. 12, to hold spring in the compressed position, then remove tool No. J33875.
5. Position tensioner to engine, then install attaching bolts and remove cotter pin holding tensioner spring in the compressed position.

CAMSHAFT, REPLACE

1. Remove engine from vehicle as previously described.
2. Remove valve lifters and engine front cover as described previously.
3. Mark position of rotor to distributor body, then remove distributor from engine.
4. Remove fuel pump and fuel pump push rod from engine block.
5. Remove timing chain and camshaft sprocket as previously described.
6. Remove camshaft thrust plate to engine block retaining bolts and the thrust plate, Fig. 10.
7. Remove camshaft from engine block.
8. Reverse removal procedure to install. When installing camshaft, align crankshaft and camshaft sprocket timing marks, Fig. 10.

PISTON & ROD ASSEMBLE

Install piston to rod with notch and hole on piston facing toward front of engine and rod bearing tang slot opposite camshaft, Fig. 13.

Fig. 13   Piston & rod assembly

Fig. 14 Removing oil pan & pump

1. PICK UP TUBE AND SCREEN.
2. PUMP COVER.
3. DRIVE GEAR AND SHAFT.
4. IDLER GEAR.
5. PUMP BODY.
6. PRESSURE REGULATOR SPRING.
7. PRESSURE REGULATOR VALVE.
8. RETAINING PIN.
9. GASKET.
10. ATTACHING BOLTS.

Fig. 15 Sectional view of oil pump assembly

Upon installation, measure the connecting rod side clearance using a suitable feeler gauge. Measurement taken should be as follows:

Engine	Year	Clearance in Inch
4-112	1982	.004–.024
4-122	1982–83	.004–.024

PISTONS, PINS, & RODS

Pistons and rings are available in standard and oversizes of .020 and .040 inch. Oversize piston pins are not available due to the press fit design.

MAIN & ROD BEARINGS

NOTE: When removing No. 1 main bearing cap, it will be necessary to remove the timing chain tensioner, refer to Timing Chain Tensioner, Replace.

Main bearings are available in standard size and undersizes of .0013 inch, and connecting rod bearings are available in standard size and undersizes of .0010 inch.

OIL PAN, REPLACE

1. Disconnect battery ground cable, then remove exhaust pipe shield.
2. Raise and support front of vehicle, then drain crankcase.
3. Disconnect exhaust pipe at exhaust manifold.
4. Detach A/C compressor brace at starter motor and A/C compressor bracket.
5. Remove flywheel cover and starter motor bracket, then remove starter motor and position aside.
6. Remove A/C compressor mounting bracket.
7. Remove four right hand suspension support bolts, then lower suspension support slightly to provide clearance for oil pan removal.
8. On models equipped with auto. transaxle, remove oil filter adapter.
9. Remove oil pan attaching bolts and oil pan.
10. Reverse procedure to install. Before installing oil pan, apply a thin coat of RTV sealer to both ends of oil pan rear seal, then seat seal firmly into rear main bearing cap. Do not allow sealer to extend beyond oil pan rear seal tabs. Apply a continuous 2 mm bead of RTV sealer along oil pan side rails in line with bolt holes, circling inward around each bolt hole location. Also apply RTV sealer to oil pan surface which contacts engine front cover. This bead of sealer must meet the bead at each oil pan side rail. Do not apply any RTV sealer to oil pan rear seal mating surface. Carefully install oil pan and torque attaching bolts alternately and evenly to 6 to 9 ft. lbs., then to a final torque of 13 to 18 ft. lbs. Torque attaching bolts while RTV sealer is still wet to touch.

OIL PUMP SERVICE

Removal

1. Drain crankcase, then remove oil pan as previously described.
2. Remove pump to rear main bearing attaching bolt, then remove pump, extension shaft and retainer, Fig. 14.

Disassemble

1. Remove four pump cover to body attaching bolts, then remove cover, idler and drive gears and shaft, Fig. 15.

NOTE: Place align mark on oil pump drive and idler gear teeth so they can be installed in the same position.

---

2. Remove pressure regulator valve retaining pin, spring and the valve from pump body.

Inspection

Inspect pump components and should any of the following conditions exist, the oil pump assembly should be replaced.
1. Inspect pump body, gears and cover for cracks or excessive wear.
2. Check drive gear shaft for looseness in housing.
3. Check inside of pump cover for wear that would allow oil to leak past ends of gears.
4. Check oil pickup screen assembly for damage to screen or pickup tube.
5. Check pressure regulator valve for fit in pump body.

Assemble

1. Install a replacement pickup screen and tube assembly, if removed. Position pump in a soft jawed vise, then apply sealer to end of tube and tap into position using tool No. J8369 and a plastic hammer. Use care not to damage inlet screen and tube assembly when installing on pump housing.

Fig. 16   Replacing crankshaft rear main bearing oil seal

Fig. 17   Replacing water pump assembly

2. Place pressure regulator valve, spring and retaining pin into pump body, then install drive gear and shaft.
3. Install idler gear into pump body, then the pump cover gasket. Fig. 15.
4. Install pump cover and cover retaining bolts, then torque bolts to 6–9 ft. lbs.

Installation

1. Align oil pump extension shaft to distributor drive gear socket and pump housing with dowels on cap, then install shaft retainer and pump assembly.
2. Install oil pump assembly retaining bolt to rear main bearing cap and torque bolt to 26–35 ft. lbs.
3. Install oil pan as previously described.

REAR MAIN BEARING OIL SEAL, REPAIR

1. Remove oil pan and oil pump as previously described.
2. Remove rear main bearing cap.
3. Using packing tool J-29114-2, gently drive upper seal into groove approximately 1/4 inch, Fig. 16.
4. Repeat step 3 for other end of seal.
5. Measure the amount that was driven in on one side and add 1/8 inch. Using a suitable cutting tool, cut this length from the rear main bearing cap seal using the rear main bearing cap as a guide. Repeat this step for the other end of seal.
6. Place piece of cut seal onto groove of seal installer guide tool J-29114-1 and install

guide tool to cylinder block.
7. Using packing tool J-29114-2, drive piece of seal into block until packing tool contacts machined stop on guide tool, Fig. 16.
8. Remove guide tool and repeat steps 6 and 7 for other end of seal.
9. Install new seal in bearing cap and cut seal ends flush with bearing cap sealing surface.
10. Place a piece of plastigage on rear main journal, install bearing cap and torque bolts to 70 ft. lbs.
11. Remove rear main bearing cap and check bearing clearance. If not within specifications, check for seal end fraying. Adjust as necessary.
12. Apply a 2 mm bead of sealant 1052357 or equivalent to rear main bearing cap and crankcase mating surfaces. Install cap, making sure sealant does not contact crankshaft journal or main bearing. Torque main bearing cap bolts to 70 ft. lbs.

WATER PUMP, REPLACE

1. Disconnect battery ground cable and drain cooling system.
2. Remove accessory drive belts.
3. Remove alternator to alternator bracket retaining bolts and position alternator aside.
4. Remove water pump pulley to water pump attaching bolts, then the pulley from water pump.
5. Remove four water pump to block attach-

ing bolts and the water pump, Fig. 17.
6. Clean sealing surfaces of pump and engine block and place a 1/8 inch bead of sealant 1052289, or equivalent, to sealing surfaces. Install pump. Coat threaded area of pump bolts with sealant 1052080, install torque bolts to 13–18 ft. lbs.
7. Reverse removal procedures to complete installation.

BELT TENSION DATA

	New Lbs.	Used Lbs.
Air Cond.	168②	90①
Alternator	145②	70①
Power Steer.	145②	70①
Air Pump	145②	70①

①—Minimum
②—Maximum

FUEL PUMP, REPLACE

1. Disconnect battery ground cable.
2. Raise and support vehicle.
3. Disconnect inlet hose and outlet pipe from fuel pump.
4. Remove two fuel pump retaining nuts and rotate pump upward to clear studs in block. Remove fuel pump from vehicle.
5. Clean block to pump mating surface and install new gasket over studs in block.
6. Install pump and pump retaining nuts and torque nuts to 15–22 ft. lbs.
7. Reverse procedure to complete installation.

ENGINE MOUNTS, REPLACE

Front Engine Mount

1. Disconnect battery ground cable.
2. Remove engine mount nuts, then raise and support vehicle.
3. Remove inner fender shield attaching bolts, then the shield.
4. Support engine and remove and discard engine mount attaching bolts, Figs. 1 and 2.
5. Remove engine mount from vehicle.

CAUTION: Whenever engine mount is removed, alignment bolt M6X1X65 must be used during installation to prevent power train misalignment.

6. Reverse procedure to install, using new engine mount bolts. Remove alignment bolt.

NOTE: If excessive effort is required to remove alignment bolt, loosen transaxle adjusting bolts to align powertrain components.

Rear Engine Mount

1. Disconnect battery ground cable.
2. Raise and support vehicle.
3. If equipped with manual transaxle, remove oil filter.
4. Support engine and remove engine mount nuts, Fig. 3.
5. Remove and discard engine mount to engine attaching bolts.
6. Remove engine mount from vehicle.
7. Reverse procedure to install.

ENGINE, REPLACE

1. Disconnect battery ground cable, then drain cooling system.
2. Remove air cleaner, then disconnect engine electrical harness connector at bulkhead and electrical connector at brake cylinder.
3. Disconnect throttle cable from bracket and E.F.I. assembly.
4. Disconnect vacuum hoses from E.F.I. assembly, then disconnect power steering high pressure hose at cut-off switch.
5. Disconnect vacuum hoses at map sensor and canister, then disconnect air conditioning relay cluster switches.
6. Disconnect power steering return hose at power steering pump.
7. Disconnect ECM electrical connectors, then pull harness through bulkhead and position harness over engine.
8. Disconnect upper and lower radiator hoses from engine, then disconnect wire connector at temperature switch on thermostat housing.
9. Disconnect transmission shift cable at transmission, then raise and support vehicle.
10. Disconnect speedometer cable at transmission and bracket.
11. Disconnect exhaust pipe at exhaust manifold and remove exhaust pipe from converter.

1	TORQUE 50 N·m (38 LB. FT.)
2	ENGINE MOUNTING BRACKET
3	ALIGNMENT BOLT MUST BE REMOVED AFTER ENGINE INSTALLATION
4	TORQUE 7 N·m (5 LB. FT.)
5	TORQUE 31 N·m (23 LB. FT.)
6	TORQUE 27 N·m (20 LB. FT.)

VIEW A

Fig. 1 Front engine mounts

1	TORQUE 31 N·m (23 LB. FT.)
2	TORQUE 50 N·m (38 LB. FT.)

RIGHT HAND FRONT W/O A.C.

RIGHT HAND FRONT W/A.C.

Fig. 2 Right hand front engine mount brackets

1	TORQUE 54 N·m (40 LB. FT.)

RIGHT REAR W/O P/S

RIGHT REAR W/PWR. STEER.

Fig. 3 Right hand rear engine mount brackets

Disassembled view of engine

Engine oiling system. 4-112 overhead cam engine

Fig. 4 Cylinder head & camshaft carrier bolt loosening sequence

Fig. 5 Cylinder head & camshaft carrier bolt tightening sequence

12. Remove heater hoses from heater core, fuel lines at flex hoses and transmission cooler lines at flex hoses.
13. Remove front wheels, right hand spoiler section and splash shield.
14. Remove and support right and left brake calipers.
15. Using tool No. J-24319-1 or equivalent, remove right and left tie rod ends.
16. Disconnect electrical connectors at A/C compressor, then remove A/C compressor and mounting brackets. Using a piece of wire, support compressor in wheel opening.
17. Remove six front suspension support attachment bolts.
18. Lower vehicle and support front end by placing jack stands under core support.
19. Using a suitable hoist, position front post of hoist to rear of cowl.
20. Using a suitable piece of wood (4" × 4" × 6'), position onto front post of hoist.
21. Raise vehicle slightly and remove jack stands from front end.
22. Position a suitable dolly under engine and transaxle assembly.
23. Position three pieces of wood (4" × 4" × 12") under engine and transaxle assembly only, allowing support rails to hang free.
24. Slightly lower vehicle onto dolly and remove two rear transaxle mount attaching bolts.
25. Remove three left front engine mount attaching bolts and two engine support to body attaching bolts behind right hand inner axle U-joint.
26. Remove one bolt and nut from right hand chassis side rail to engine mount bracket.
27. Remove six strut attaching nuts, then raise vehicle, allowing engine, transaxle and suspension assemblies to rest onto dolly.
28. Remove engine and transaxle as an assembly.
29. Position engine and transaxle assembly into vehicle.
30. Loosely install transaxle and left front mounts to side rail bolts.
31. To prevent powertrain misalignment, install bolt No. M6X1X65 into left front mount.
32. Torque transaxle mount bolts to 42 ft. lbs.

and left front mount bolts to 18 ft. lbs.
33. Install right rear mount to body bolts and torque to 38 ft. lbs.
34. Position a suitable jack under control arms and raise struts into position, then install retaining nuts.
35. Raise vehicle, then using suitable lifting equipment, raise control arms and install tie rod ends.
36. Reverse procedure to complete installation.

CYLINDER HEAD, REPLACE

1. Disconnect battery ground cable, remove air cleaner and drain cooling system.
2. Remove alternator and pivot bracket from camshaft carrier housing.
3. Remove power steering pump and bracket and position aside.
4. Disconnect ignition coil electrical connectors, then remove coil.
5. Disconnect spark plug wires from distributor cap.
6. Remove throttle cable from bracket on intake manifold.
7. Disconnect accelerator cable, downshift cable and throttle valve cable from E.F.I. assembly.
8. Disconnect ECM connectors from E.F.I. assembly.
9. Disconnect vacuum brake hose from filter, then disconnect inlet and return fuel lines from flex joints.
10. Remove water pump bypass hose from intake manifold and water pump.
11. Disconnect ECM harness connectors and heater hose from intake manifold.
12. Disconnect exhaust pipe from exhaust manifold and breather hose from camshaft carrier.
13. Disconnect upper radiator hose, then disconnect engine electrical harness and wires from thermostat housing.
14. Remove timing cover and timing probe holder.
15. Loosen water pump bolts and remove timing belt.
16. Loosen camshaft carrier and cylinder head bolts a little at a time in sequence shown in Fig. 4.

NOTE: Camshaft carrier and cylinder head bolts should only be removed when engine is cold.

17. Remove camshaft carrier assembly.
18. Remove cylinder head, intake manifold and exhaust manifold as an assembly.
19. Remove all carbon deposits from combustion chambers and valve ports. Check cylinder head for cracks in the exhaust ports and combustion chambers. Remove water jacket plugs and clean, if necessary.
20. Reverse procedure to install. Torque cylinder head bolts a time at a time in sequence shown in Fig. 5 to 18 ft. lbs. Tighten each bolt in the proper sequence an additional 180° in 60° increments.
21. After installation is completed (with the exception of brackets that install onto carrier), start engine and let engine idle until thermostat opens. Turn engine off and torque all bolts an additional 30 to 50° in the proper sequence.

ROCKER ARM & HYDRAULIC VALVE LASH COMPENSATORS, REPLACE

1. Disconnect battery ground cable.
2. Remove camshaft carrier cover.
3. Using tool No. J-33302 or equivalent, Fig. 6, compress valve springs and remove rocker arms. Place rocker arms in a suitable rack so they can be installed in the same location.
4. Remove hydraulic lash compensators and place them in a rack so they can be installed in the same location.
5. Reverse procedure to install.

NOTE: No adjustment of valve lash is re-

Fig. 6 Using tool No. 33302 to compress valve spring

☐1 TENSION GAGE J-26486
☐2 ADJUSTMENT TOOL J-33039

Fig. 7 Timing belt tension adjustment

Fig. 8 Camshaft sprocket removal

quired. The preload of the hydraulic valve lash compensator is automatic and servicing of the compensator requires only care and cleanliness be exercised in the handling of these components.

VALVE SPRING & VALVE STEM OIL SEAL, REPLACE

Removal

1. Disconnect battery ground cable.
2. Remove rocker arms and spark plugs.
3. Install air line adapter tool No. J-23590 or equivalent, into spark plug port and apply compressed air to hold valves in place.
4. Using tool No. J-33302 or equivalent, Fig. 6, compress valve spring and remove rocker guides, valve locks, caps and valve spring.
5. Remove valve stem oil seal.

Installation

1. Using clean engine oil, lubricate valve stem and install new valve stem oil seal over valve stem and seat onto valve guide.
2. Position valve spring and cap over valve stem. Using tool No. J-33302 or equivalent, compress valve spring and install valve locks.
3. Install rocker guides and rocker arms, then remove tool J-33302.
4. Remove air line adapter tool and install spark plugs.
5. Install camshaft carrier cover. Torque bolts to 5 ft. lbs.

VALVE SEAT SERVICE

Using a suitable dial indicator measure valve seat concentricity. Valve seat should be concentric to within .002 inch of total indicator reading. Ensure valve guide bores are free from carbon or dirt to allow proper seating of the pilot in the valve guide. When reconditioning the valve seats, use a 45° stone to rough the valve seat and another stone with the same angle to finish the valve seat. Narrow down the valve seats to the proper width, .051–.055 inch for intake valves and .067–.071 for exhaust valves.

VALVE GUIDES

Valve guides are an integral part of the cylinder head. If valve stem to guide clearance is excessive, the guide should be reamed to the next oversize and the appropriate oversize valve installed. Valves are available in standard size and oversize of .010 inch (.25 mm).

CRANKSHAFT PULLEY

Removal

1. Disconnect battery ground cable.
2. Loosen alternator and power steering bracket bolt, then remove drive belt.
3. Remove inner fender splash shield, then remove crankshaft pulley bolts and pulley.

Installation

1. Position pulley onto crankshaft sprocket. Using a suitable sealer, coat threads of pulley bolts and install onto pulley. Torque bolts to 15 ft. lbs.
2. Install splash shield.
3. Install alternator and power steering belt, then connect battery ground cable.

TIMING BELT, REPLACE

1. Disconnect battery ground cable.
2. Remove timing belt front cover, then rotate crankshaft until timing mark on crankshaft pulley aligns with 10° BTDC mark on indicator tab. The mark on the camshaft sprocket must align with mark on camshaft carrier.
3. Remove crankshaft pulley as previously described.
4. Remove timing probe holder.
5. Loosen water pump bolts, then rotate water pump to loosen and remove timing belt.
6. Reverse procedure to install. Note the following information:
   a. Ensure mark on camshaft sprocket aligns with mark on camshaft carrier. The timing mark on the crankshaft pulley should align with the 10° BTDC mark on the indicator tab.
   b. Using tool No. J-33039 or equivalent, Fig. 7, rotate water pump clockwise

until all slack is removed from timing belt. Install tool No. J-26486 or equivalent, Fig. 1, between water pump and camshaft sprockets so pointer is midway between sprockets.

7. To adjust timing belt tension, refer to Fig. 7 and note the following information:

Belt Size . . . . .748 inch

Initial Adjustment	
New Belt	74 ft. lbs.
Used Belt	59 ft. lbs.

Checking Valve	
New Belt	59–88 ft. lbs.
Used Belt	44–74 ft. lbs.

NOTE: These values are for a cold engine.

a. If timing belt tension is incorrect, loosen and using tool No. J-33039 or equivalent, rotate water pump until proper tension is obtained.
b. Torque water pump bolts to 19 ft. lbs. Ensure water pump does not shift when torquing bolts.

TIMING BELT REAR COVER, REPLACE

1. Disconnect battery ground cable.
2. Remove timing belt as described under "TIMING BELT, REPLACE".
3. Remove timing belt rear cover bolts and cover.
4. Reverse procedure to install. Torque cover bolts to 19 ft. lbs.

CAMSHAFT CARRIER COVER, REPLACE

1. Remove air cleaner and disconnect breather hoses.
2. Remove cover bolts and cover.
3. Reverse procedure to install. Torque camshaft carrier cover bolts to 5 ft. lbs.

CAMSHAFT SPROCKET, REPLACE

1. Disconnect battery ground cable.
2. Remove timing belt front cover and align mark on camshaft sprocket with mark on camshaft carrier cover.
3. Remove timing probe holder.
4. Loosen water pump bolts and remove timing belt from camshaft sprocket.

Fig. 9 Crankshaft front oil seal installation

ARROW TOWARD FRONT OF ENGINE

NUMBERED SIDE OF ROD TOWARD INTAKE MANIFOLD SIDE OF ENGINE

Fig. 10 Piston & rod assembly

Fig. 11 Rear main bearing oil seal installation

5. Remove camshaft carrier cover.
6. Using a suitable tool, secure camshaft and remove camshaft sprocket bolt, washer and sprocket, Fig. 8.
7. Reverse procedure to install. Torque camshaft sprocket bolt to 34 ft. lbs, timing probe holder to 19 ft. lbs and camshaft carrier cover bolts to 5 ft. lbs.

CAMSHAFT

Removal

1. Disconnect battery ground cable.
2. Remove camshaft carrier cover.
3. Using tool No. J-33302 or equivalent, Fig. 6, compress valve springs and remove rocker arms.
4. Remove timing belt front cover and timing belt as described under "TIMING BELT, REPLACE".
5. Remove camshaft sprocket as described under "CAMSHAFT SPROCKET, REPLACE".
6. Disconnect spark plug wires from spark plugs, then remove distributor from engine.
7. Remove camshaft thrust plate from rear of camshaft carrier.
8. Slide camshaft rearward and remove camshaft from carrier.

Installation

1. Using tool No. J-33085 or equivalent, install new front oil seal onto camshaft carrier.
2. Position camshaft into carrier.

NOTE: Ensure not to damage front oil seal when installing camshaft.

3. Install camshaft thrust plate and bolts. Torque bolts to 70 inch lbs.
4. Check camshaft end play. End play should be within .016 to .064 inch.
5. Install distributor, camshaft sprocket, timing belt and timing belt front cover.
6. Using tool No. J-33302 or equivalent, Fig. 6, compress valve springs and install rocker arms.
7. Install camshaft carrier cover. Torque bolts to 5 ft. lbs.

CRANKSHAFT SPROCKET, REPLACE

1. Disconnect battery ground cable.
2. Remove timing belt as described under "TIMING BELT, REPLACE".
3. Remove crankshaft sprocket bolt, washer and sprocket.
4. Reverse procedure to install. Refer to step 7 under "TIMING BELT, REPLACE" and adjust belt tension. Torque crankshaft sprocket bolt to 115 ft. lbs.

CRANKSHAFT FRONT OIL SEAL, REPLACE

1. Disconnect battery ground cable.
2. Remove crankshaft sprocket as described under "CRANKSHAFT SPROCKET, REPLACE".
3. Remove key and rear thrust washer from end of crankshaft.
4. Using a suitable tool, remove crankshaft front oil seal.
5. During installation of crankshaft front oil seal, position tool No. J-33083 or equivalent, Fig. 9, onto crankshaft. Lubricate front oil seal lip and install onto crankshaft.
6. Reverse procedure to complete installation.

PISTON & ROD ASSEMBLE

Assemble piston to rod, with arrow on piston facing toward front of engine and numbered side toward intake manifold side of engine, Fig. 10. Upon installation, measure connecting rod side clearance using a suitable feeler gauge. Side clearance should be .0027 to .0095 inch.

PISTONS, PINS & RINGS

Pistons and rings are available in standard size and oversize of .020 inch (.5 mm). Piston pins are available in standard size only.

MAIN & ROD BEARINGS

Main and rod bearings are available in standard sizes and undersizes of .010 inch (.25 mm) and .020 inch (.5 mm).

REAR MAIN BEARING OIL SEAL, REPLACE

1. Remove engine from vehicle as described under "ENGINE, REPLACE".

2. On vehicles equipped with automatic transaxle, remove flywheel dust cover and flex plate to torque converter bolts.
3. Remove bell housing bolts and separate engine from transaxle assembly.
4. On vehicles equipped with automatic transaxle, remove flex plate.
5. On vehicles equipped with manual transaxle, remove pressure plate, clutch disc and flywheel.
6. Using a suitable tool, remove rear main bearing oil seal.
7. Reverse procedure to install. During installation of seal, position seal over seal pilot tool No. J-33004 or equivalent, Fig. 11. Using clean engine oil, lubricate new rear oil seal and position onto crankshaft by turning starter bolts on tool No. J-33004 in rotational sequence until rear oil seal bottoms in engine block.

OIL PAN, REPLACE

1. Disconnect battery ground cable.
2. Raise and support vehicle.
3. Remove right front wheel and right hand splash shield.
4. Remove lower A/C bracket strut rod bolt and swing aside.
5. Remove flywheel dust cover.
6. Disconnect exhaust pipe from exhaust manifold.
7. Drain engine oil, remove oil pan bolts and oil pan.
8. Reverse procedure to install. Using a suitable sealer, coat threads of oil pan bolts. Torque bolts to 4 ft. lbs.

OIL PUMP SCREEN & PICK-UP TUBE, REPLACE

1. Disconnect battery ground cable.
2. Remove oil pan as described under "OIL PAN, REPLACE".
3. Remove pick-up tube support bolts, pick-up tube to oil pump bolts, pick-up tube and "O" ring.
4. Reverse procedure to install. Torque pick-up tube to oil pump bolts to 5 ft. lbs. Torque pick-up tube support bolts to 5 ft. lbs.

OIL PUMP

Removal

1. Disconnect battery ground cable.
2. Remove crankshaft sprocket and timing belt rear cover.
3. Disconnect engine oil pressure switch electrical connector from the switch.
4. Remove oil pan and oil filter.
5. Remove pick-up tube to engine block bolts, pick-up tube and oil pump.

Fig. 12 Disassembled view of oil pump

Disassemble

1. Remove five screws and rear cover from oil pump, Fig. 12.
2. Remove gears, plug, pressure regulator valve plunger and spring.
3. If necessary, remove pick-up tube and "O" ring from oil pump body.

Inspection

NOTE: After disassembling the oil pump, thoroughly clean all oil pump components and check them for excessive wear and damage.

1. Using a suitable straight edge and feeler gauge, Fig. 13, check oil pump clearances.
2. Check clearances for the following oil pump components:
   a. Clearance between idler gear and oil pump body should be .004–.007 inch.
   b. Clearance between drive gear and oil pump body should be .014–.018 inch.
   c. Clearance between gears and oil pump cover should be .002–.004 inch.
3. If clearances obtained are not within specified limits, replace worn or damaged oil pump components.

Assemble

1. Install valve plunger and spring.
2. Using a suitable sealer, coat threads of pressure regulator valve plunger plug and install. Torque plug to 15 ft. lbs.
3. Install oil pump gears into oil pump body.

Installation

1. Install gasket and oil pump onto engine. Torque oil pump bolts to 5 ft. lbs.
2. Install pick-up tube and bolts. Torque bolts to 5 ft. lbs.
3. Install oil pan and oil filter.
4. Connect engine oil pressure switch electrical connector to switch.
5. Install timing belt rear covers and crankshaft sprocket.

WATER PUMP, REPLACE

1. Disconnect battery ground cable.
2. Remove hose from water pump.
3. Remove water pump bolts, water pump, and "O" ring.
4. Reverse procedure to install.

ELECTRIC FUEL PUMP, REPLACE

1. Depressurize fuel system as follows:
   a. Remove fuel pump fuse from fuse panel.
   b. Start engine and operate until fuel supply remaining in fuel lines is consumed. Engage starter for approximately 3 seconds to ensure fuel pres-

Fig. 13 Checking drive gear to oil pump housing clearance

sure has been relieved.
   c. With ignition switch in the "OFF" position, install fuel pump fuse.

NOTE: Unless this procedure is followed before servicing fuel system, fuel spray could occur.

2. Disconnect battery ground cable.
3. Raise and support vehicle.
4. Remove fuel tank.
5. Remove fuel meter pump assembly by turning cam lock ring counterclockwise.
6. Remove fuel meter pump assembly from fuel tank and fuel pump from fuel meter.
7. Pull fuel pump upward into fuel hose while pulling outward away from bottom support.

NOTE: Do not damage rubber insulator and strainer during fuel pump removal.

8. After fuel pump assembly is clear of bottom support, pull pump assembly out of rubber connector and from vehicle.
9. Reverse procedure to install.

Clutch & Transaxle Section

CLUTCH PEDAL, ADJUST

The clutch is automatically adjusted by a self-adjusting mechanism, Fig. 1, mounted to the clutch pedal and bracket assembly. The clutch cable is a fixed length and cannot be shortened or lengthened, however, the position of the cable can be changed by adjusting the position of the detent in relation to the clutch pedal. This is accomplished by pulling the clutch pedal upward to the rubber bumper. This action forces the pawl against the stop and causes the pawl to be out of mesh with the detent teeth, allowing the cable to play out until the detent spring load is balanced against the load applied by the release bearing.

Inspection

1. With engine running and parking brake applied, depress clutch pedal to approximately ½ inch from floor mat.
2. Move shift lever between "First" and "Reverse" gears several times. If no gear clashing occurs when shifting into "Reverse", the clutch is releasing fully.
3. If the shifting in Step 2 is not smooth, the clutch is not releasing fully and the linkage should be inspected.
4. Check clutch pedal bushings for sticking or excessive wear.
5. Have an assistant depress the clutch pedal to the floor and observe clutch fork lever travel at transaxle. The end of the clutch fork lever should have a total travel of approximately 1.5 to 1.7 inches.
6. To check the self-adjusting mechanism,

depress the clutch pedal and observe if the pawl firmly engages the teeth of the detent.

CLUTCH, REPLACE

1. Remove transaxle as outlined under "MANUAL TRANSAXLE, REPLACE" procedure.
2. Mark position of pressure plate to flywheel to aid reassembly.
3. Gradually loosen pressure plate to flywheel attaching bolts until spring tension is relieved.
4. Support pressure plate and remove attaching bolts, pressure plate and driven disc, Fig. 2.
5. Clean pressure plate and flywheel mounting surfaces. Inspect bearing retainer outer surface of the transaxle.

6. Place pressure plate and driven disc in position and support with tool No. J-29074, Fig. 3.

NOTE: The driven disc is installed with the damper springs offset toward the transaxle. Stamped letters found on the driven disc identify the "Flywheel Side".

7. Install and gradually torque the pressure plate to flywheel attaching bolts to 15 ft. lbs. Remove support tool.
8. Lubricate the release bearing outside diameter groove and inside diameter recess.
9. Install transaxle.

MANUAL TRANSAXLE SHIFT CABLE, ADJUST

4 Speed Manual Transaxle

Shift Cable Adjustment
1. Disconnect battery ground cable.
2. Place shift lever into first gear position, then loosen shift cable nuts at levers (D) and (F), Fig. 4.
3. Remove console trim plate, then slide shift lever boot upward on shift lever.
4. Remove console assembly.
5. With shift lever in the first gear position and held against stop, insert a suitable yoke type clip to hold lever in position, Fig. 4.
6. Insert a 5/32 inch drill bit into alignment hole on side of shifter assembly, Fig. 4.
7. Rotate lever (D), Fig. 4, in direction of arrow while tightening cable retaining nut.
8. Tighten cable retaining nut at lever (F), Fig. 4.
9. Remove drill bit and yoke clip, then install console and connect battery ground cable.
10. Check shift lever for proper operation and readjust as necessary.

Shifter Shaft Washer Selection

When shift cables are properly adjusted, but improper first and second gear shifts are encountered, it may be necessary to check the shifter shaft selective thrust washer. This washer helps position the shifter shaft for proper shifter operation. Proceed as follows to determine the correct selective thrust washer thickness:

Fig. 1 Clutch self-adjusting mechanism

1. Remove reverse inhibitor fitting, spring and washer from end housing, then position shifter shaft into second gear.
2. Measure distance from end of housing to shifter shaft shoulder, dimension A, Fig. 5.
3. Apply a load of 9 to 13 lbs. to opposite end of shifter shaft, then measure distance from end of housing to shifter shaft shoulder, dimension B, Fig. 5.
4. Subtract measurement obtained in step 2 from measurement obtained in step 3, which will equal the thickness of the selective thrust washer to be installed, dimension C, Fig. 5. When selecting a thrust washer, refer to Fig. 5A.

5 Speed Manual Transaxle

1. Disconnect battery ground cable.
2. Place shift lever in third gear position, then remove lock pin (H), Fig. 6, and reinstall with tapered end of pin facing downward to lock transaxle in third gear.
3. Loosen shift cable retaining nuts at levers (G) and (F), Fig. 6.
4. Remove console trim plate and pull shifter boot upward on shift lever.
5. Remove console assembly from vehicle.
6. Insert a 5/32 inch drill bit into align hole on side of shifter assembly, Fig. 6.
7. Align shifter lever slot with slot in shifter plate, then insert a 13/16 inch drill bit.
8. Tighten nuts at levers (G) and (F), Fig. 6,

then remove drill bits from alignment holes.
9. Remove lock pin (H), Fig. 6, and reinstall with tapered end facing upward.
10. Install console assembly and connect battery ground cable.
11. Check shifter for proper operation and readjust as necessary.

MANUAL TRANSAXLE, REPLACE

4 Speed Manual Transaxle

1. Disconnect battery ground cable.
2. Install engine support fixture so that one end is supported on cowl tray over the wiper motor and the other end rests on the radiator support. Connect fixture hook to engine lift ring and raise engine to relieve weight from engine mounts, Fig. 7.

CAUTION: The engine support fixture must be positioned in the center of the cowl and the attaching parts properly torqued before supporting engine. This fixture is not intended to support entire weight of engine and transaxle. Personal injury may result from improper use of support fixture.

Fig. 2 Clutch assembly

Fig. 3 Aligning clutch disc & pressure plate

Fig. 4 Four speed manual transaxle shift cable adjustment

Fig. 5 Four speed manual transaxle shifter shaft selective washer measurement

3. Remove heater hose clamp at transaxle mount bracket, then disconnect horn wires and remove horn assembly.

NOTE: Whenever the transaxle mount is removed, alignment bolt M6X1X65 must be installed in right front engine mount to prevent powertrain misalignment.

4. Remove transaxle mount attaching bolts. Discard mount to sideframe attaching bolts.
5. Disconnect clutch cable at clutch release lever, then remove transaxle mount bracket attaching bolts and nuts.
6. Disconnect shift cables and remove retaining clips at transaxle.
7. Disconnect ground cable at transaxle mounting stud, then remove air management valve attaching bolts to provide clearance for removal of upper right hand transaxle to engine attaching bolt. Remove four upper transaxle to engine mounting bolts.

Dimension "C" Fig. 5 Inch (mm)	Ident. Color & No. of Stripes	Shim Part No.
.0708 (1.8)	3 White	14008235
.0827 (2.1)	1 Orange	476709
.0945 (2.4)	2 Orange	476710
.1063 (2.7)	3 Orange	476711
.1181 (3.0)	1 Blue	476712
.1299 (3.3)	2 Blue	476713
.1417 (3.6)	3 Blue	476714
.1535 (3.9)	1 White	476715
.1654	2 White	476716

Fig. 5A Shifter shaft selective thrust washer identification chart. Four manual transaxle

Fig. 6 Five speed manual transaxle shift cable adjustment

Fig. 7 Engine support fixture installation

8. Raise and support vehicle, then remove left front wheel.
9. Remove left front inner splash shield retaining screws and the splash shield.
10. Remove transaxle strut to transaxle bracket and crossmember attaching bolts and remove strut from vehicle.
11. Remove transaxle strut bracket attaching bolts and the strut bracket.
12. Remove clutch housing cover attaching bolts, then disconnect speedometer cable at transaxle.
13. Disconnect stabilizer bar at the left suspension support and control arm.
14. Using tool J-29330, separate left ball joint from steering knuckle.
15. Remove left suspension support to chassis attaching bolts, then remove the support and lower control arm as an assembly.
16. Install boot protectors at drive axles, then disengage both drive axles at transaxle. Remove left drive axle from transaxle housing bore.
17. Attach the transaxle case to a suitable jack, then remove two lower transaxle to engine mounting bolts.
18. Slide transaxle away from engine, lower jack and guide right drive axle from transaxle housing bore. Remove transaxle from vehicle.
19. Reverse removal procedure to install.

NOTE: When installing transaxle, guide the right drive axle into transaxle bore as transaxle is being raised. The right drive axle cannot be installed after the transaxle is connected to engine.

5 Speed Manual Transaxle

1. Disconnect battery ground cable.
2. Support engine using engine holding fixture J22825-1. Position holding fixture so that one end is supported by the cowl tray and the other end is resting on the radiator support, Fig. 7. Attach holding fixture hook to engine lifting bracket and raise engine just enough to relieve weight from engine mounts.

NOTE: The engine holding fixture must be located in center of cowl and fixture attachments properly torqued before supporting engine. This support is not designed to support the entire weight of the engine and transaxle assembly.

3. Remove transaxle mount attaching bolts.

NOTE: When removing transaxle mount, alignment bolt M6X1X65 must be installed in right front engine mount to ensure proper powertrain alignment.

4. Disconnect clutch cable at clutch fork, then remove transaxle mount bracket retaining bolts and nuts.
5. Disconnect shift cables and remove retaining clips at transaxle.
6. Disconnect ground cables at transaxle mounting stud, then remove air management valve attaching bolts to provide clearance for upper right hand transaxle to engine attaching bolt.
7. Raise and support front of vehicle, then drain transaxle fluid.
8. Remove left hand front wheel and tire assembly, then remove front inner splash shield.
9. Remove transaxle strut and strut bracket.
10. Remove clutch cover attaching bolts, then disconnect speedometer cable at transaxle.
11. Disconnect stabilizer bar at left hand suspension support and control arm.
12. Detach ball joint from steering knuckle.
13. Remove left hand front suspension support attaching bolts, then remove support and control arm as an assembly.
14. Install boot protectors, then disengage drive axle shafts at transaxle using tool Nos. J28468, J29794 and a suitable screwdriver. Remove left hand drive axle shaft from transaxle.
15. Secure transaxle to a suitable transaxle jack, then remove transaxle to engine attaching bolts.
16. Remove transaxle by sliding toward drivers side of vehicle (away from engine), then carefully lower jack while guiding right hand drive axle shaft out of transaxle.
17. Reverse procedure to install. When installing transaxle, carefully guide right hand drive axle shaft into transaxle bore as transaxle is being raised. The right hand drive axle shaft cannot be installed once the transaxle has been connected to the engine.

Rear Axle, Rear Suspension & Brakes Section

DESCRIPTION

The rear suspension, Fig. 1, is a semi-independent type suspension consisting of an axle assembly with trailing arms and twisting cross beam, coil springs and double action shock absorbers. A stabilizer bar is available and is attached to the inside of the axle beam and to the lower end of the control arms. A single unit hub and bearing assembly is bolted to each end of the axle assembly. The hub and bearing assembly is a sealed, non-serviceable unit and must be replaced as an assembly.

REAR AXLE, REPLACE

1. Raise vehicle and support vehicle. Support rear suspension with suitable jack.
2. Disconnect stabilizer bar at axle assembly, if equipped, Fig. 2.
3. Remove rear wheel assembly and brake drum. Do not hammer on brake drum since damage to bearings may result.
4. Remove shock absorber to lower mounting bracket attaching bolts, then disconnect shock absorbers from axle assembly, Fig. 2.
5. Disconnect parking brake cable and brake lines at axle brackets.
6. Carefully lower rear axle assembly and remove coil springs and insulators.
7. Remove control arm to underbody bracket bolts, then lower the axle assembly and remove from vehicle.

8. Remove hub to rear axle attaching bolts, then the hubs, bearings and backing plates from rear axle assembly.
9. Reverse procedure to install and bleed brake system.

HUB & BEARING ASSEMBLY, REPLACE

1. Raise and support vehicle, then remove wheel and tire assembly and brake drum.

NOTE: Do not hammer brake drum since damage to bearing may result.

2. Remove four hub/bearing assembly to rear axle attaching bolts, then the hub/bearing assembly from axle.

NOTE: The upper rear hub attaching bolt may not clear brake shoe when removing hub and bearing assembly. Partially remove hub and bearing assembly prior to removing this bolt.

3. Reverse procedure to install. Torque hub to axle attaching bolts to 37 ft. lbs.

CAUTION: Use care not to drop hub/bearing assembly since damage to bearing may result.

SHOCK ABSORBER, REPLACE

1. Open deck lid, then remove trim cover and shock absorber upper retaining nut.
2. Raise rear of vehicle and support rear axle using a suitable jack.
3. Remove shock absorber lower attaching bolt, then disconnect shock absorber from mounting bracket, Fig. 2. Remove shock absorber from vehicle.

1	CONTROL ARM BUSHING
2	AXLE ASSEMBLY
3	SPRING INSULATOR
4	SHOCK ABSORBER

FRONT

Fig. 1 Rear suspension

1	17 N·m 13 FT. LB.	4	SPACER MUST CONTACT BRACE WHEN SPACER & PARTS ARE INSTALLED.	5	UNDERBODY	
2	14 N·m 10 FT. LB.			6	SHOCK STUD	
3	BRACE			7	SHOCK	
				8	AXLE ASSEMBLY	

VIEW B
SHOCK TO AXLE R.H. SHOWN

FRONT

B

Fig. 2 Stabilizer bar & shock absorber removal

FRONT OF CAR
17 N·m (13 FT-LBS)
WASHER
INSULATOR
ROD GUIDE SLEEVE
INSULATOR (BLACK)
UNDERBODY
SHOCK ROD
UNDERBODY

NUT
WASHER
WASHER P.O.A. INSULATOR ASSEMBLY
ROD GUIDE SLEEVE
UNDERBODY
INSULATOR
WASHER P.O.A. INSULATOR ASSEMBLY
SHOCK ABSORBER

Fig. 2A Rear shock absorber upper attachment components. 1982 Cimarron

4. Reverse procedure to install. Torque lower attaching bolt to 41 ft. lbs. and upper attaching nut to 13 ft. lbs.

NOTE: When installing upper shock absorber attachment components on 1982–83 Cimarron models, refer to Fig. 2A, for proper installation order.

COIL SPRING, REPLACE

1. Raise and support rear of vehicle. Support rear axle using a suitable jack.
2. Remove wheel and tire assemblies.
3. Remove brake line bracket attaching bolts from frame, Fig. 2, and allow brake lines to hang freely.
4. Remove shock absorber to lower mounting bracket bolts, then disconnect shock absorbers from axle assembly.

CAUTION: Do not suspend rear axle by brake hoses since damage to hoses may result.

5. Carefully lower rear axle assembly and remove springs and insulators.
6. Reverse procedure to install. Position ends of upper coil in seat of body and within limits shown in Fig. 3.

CONTROL ARM BUSHING, REPLACE

1. Raise rear of vehicle and support rear axle under front side of spring seat using a suitable jack.
2. Remove wheel and tire assembly.
3. If right hand side bushing is to be replaced, disconnect brake line bracket from body. If left hand side bushing is to be replaced, disconnect brake line bracket from frame and parking brake cable at hook guide.
4. Remove control arm to mounting bracket attaching nut, bolt and washer, then allow control arm to rotate downward.
5. The bushing can now be replaced using tools shown in Figs. 4 and 5. When installing bushing, the arrow on the installer must align with arrow on the receiver, Fig. 4.
6. Reverse procedure to complete installation.

NOTE: The control arm attaching bolt must be torqued after vehicle is lowered to floor and is

VIEW A

1	CENTER BRAKE PIPE	5	SPRING INSULATOR
2	BRAKE HOSE	6	SPRING
3	BRAKE PIPE BRACKET	7	COMPRESSION BUMPER
4	UNDERBODY	8	AXLE ASM.
		9	15mm MAX. (.594")
		10	SPRING
		11	SPRING STOP PART OF SPRING SEAT.

FRONT

VIEW A (BOTH SPRINGS)

Fig. 3 Coil spring installation

1	PLATE—J29376-7	3	NUT—J-21474-18
2	REMOVER—J-29376-6	4	RECEIVER—J-29376-1

Fig. 4 Control bushing removal

1	RECEIVER J29376-1	3	NUT J-21474-18	5	BUSHING MUST BE INDEXED IN INSTALLER, AND INSTALLER ARROW MUST ALIGN WITH ARROW ON RECEIVER FOR PROPER BUSHING INSTALLATION.
2	PLATE J29376-7	4	INSTALLER J29376-4		

Fig. 5 Control arm bushing installation

Fig. 7 Measuring brake drum inside diameter

Fig. 6 Exploded view of rear drum brake

Fig. 8 Adjusting brake shoe clearance

in its standing height position. Torque attaching bolt to 67 ft. lbs.

DRUM BRAKE ADJUSTMENTS

The rear drum brakes, Fig. 6, have self-adjusting shoe mechanisms that assure correct lining-to-drum clearances at all times. The automatic adjusters operate only when the brakes are applied as the vehicle is moving rearward.

Although the brakes are self-adjusting, an initial adjustment is necessary after the brake shoes have been replaced, or when the length of the star wheel adjuster has been changed during some other service operation.

Adjustment

1. Raise and support vehicle, then remove rear wheels and brake drums.
2. Check to make sure that parking brake cable linkage and levers on secondary brake shoe are in "free" position.
3. Using tool J-21177, measure brake drum inside diameter, Fig. 7.
4. Turn brake adjusting screw to expand shoes to diameter obtained on outside caliper portion of tool J-21177, Fig. 8.
5. Adjust parking brake.

NOTE: Whenever rear drum brakes are serviced, the parking brake linkage cable at the equalizer must always be readjusted to prevent possible damage to brake shoes.

6. Install brake drums, wheels and tires and lower vehicle to floor.
7. Drive vehicle alternately forward and backward, applying brakes moderately, to obtain satisfactory pedal height.

PARKING BRAKE, ADJUST

1. Lift parking brake lever five ratchet clicks, then raise and support rear of vehicle.
2. Tighten adjusting nut until right rear wheel can be rotated backward, but is locked when forward rotation is attempted.
3. Release parking brake lever. Both wheels should rotate freely with no brake drag.

MASTER CYLINDER, REPLACE

1. Disconnect electrical connector and four brake lines at master cylinder.
2. Remove two master cylinder to brake booster attaching nuts, then the master cylinder from vehicle.
3. Reverse procedure to install. Bleed brake system.

POWER BRAKE UNIT, REPLACE

1. Remove master cylinder as previously described.
2. Disconnect power brake unit pushrod at brake pedal.
3. Disconnect vacuum hose from vacuum check valve. Plug vacuum hose to prevent entry of dirt.
4. Remove four power brake unit to dash panel attaching nuts, then the power brake unit from vehicle.
5. Reverse procedure to install. Torque attaching bolts to 22–33 ft. lbs.

Front Suspension & Steering Section

Refer to the Main Index for drive axle service

DESCRIPTION

The front suspension, Fig. 1, on these vehicles is of the MacPherson strut design. The lower control arms pivot from the lower side rails through rubber bushings. The upper end of the strut is isolated by a rubber mount incorporating a non-serviceable bearing for wheel turning. The tie rods connect to the steering arm on the strut, below the spring seat. The lower end of the steering knuckle pivots on a ball stud which is retained to the lower control arm by rivets and is secured to the steering knuckle with a nut and cotter pin. The sealed wheel bearings are integral with the hub and are serviced as an assembly.

WHEEL ALIGNMENT

NOTE: Toe setting is the only adjustment normally required. However, in special circumstances, such as damage due to road hazard or collision, camber may be adjusted by modifying the strut assembly.

Camber Adjustment

1. Secure bottom of strut assembly in a suitable vise.
2. Enlarge bottom holes in outer flanges with a round file until holes in outer flanges match slots in inner flanges, Fig. 2.
3. Connect strut to steering knuckle and install bolts finger tight.
4. Grasp top of tire firmly, then move tire inboard or outboard until correct camber reading is obtained. Tighten retaining bolts enough to secure camber setting.
5. Remove wheel and tire and torque strut to steering knuckle retaining bolts to 140 ft. lbs.

Toe-Out

Toe-Out is controlled by tie rod position. Adjustment is made by loosening the clamp bolts at the steering knuckle end of the tie rods and rotating the rods to obtain proper toe setting. After correct toe setting is obtained, torque clamp bolts to 14 ft. lbs.

WHEEL BEARING, REPLACE

Removal

1. Loosen hub nut with vehicle on ground.

Fig. 1 Front suspension

Fig. 2 Modifying strut bracket to adjust camber

Fig. 3 Front hub & wheel bearing assembly

Fig. 4 Front hub & bearing assembly removal

Fig. 5 Hub nut installation

2. Raise and support vehicle, then remove front wheel.
3. Install drive axle protective boot cover J-28712.
4. Remove hub nut.
5. Remove brake caliper from support and suspend caliper from flame with a length of wire. Do not suspend caliper by brake hose.
6. Remove three hub and bearing attaching bolts. If the old bearing is being reinstalled, mark attaching bolts and corresponding holes for reinstallation, Fig. 3.
7. Using tool J-28733 or equivalent, remove bearing from steering knuckle, Fig. 4.

NOTE: If excessive corrosion is present, ensure that bearing is loose in the knuckle before using puller tool.

8. If installing new bearing, replace steering knuckle seal.

NOTE: Do not move drive axle until hub nut is installed and torqued to specifications.

Installation

1. Clean and inspect bearing mating surfaces and steering knuckle bore for dirt, nicks and burrs.
2. If installing new steering knuckle seal, apply grease to seal and knuckle bore, then press seal into steering knuckle.
3. Push bearing onto axle shaft and install two hub to steering knuckle attaching bolts. Install a longer bolt into third

BOLT MUST BE INSTALLED IN DIRECTION SHOWN

Fig. 6 Assembling lower ball joint to lower control arm

mounting hole and through hub cutout. Install hub to axle retaining nut and torque to 70 ft. lbs., Fig. 5.
4. Remove long bolt and replace with original bolt. Torque hub to steering knuckle attaching bolts to 63 ft. lbs.
5. Install brake caliper and wheel assembly.
6. Lower vehicle and torque hub to axle nut to 185 ft. lbs.

LOWER BALL JOINT, REPLACE

1. Raise and support vehicle, then remove

wheel and tire.
2. Locate center of rivet body and mark with a center punch.
3. Using a 1/8 inch drill, drill pilot holes completely through the rivets. Using a 1/2 inch drill, drill final holes through rivets to ensure fitting of new ball joint.
4. Remove ball joint stud retaining nut, then, using tool J-29330, separate ball joint from steering knuckle. Remove ball joint from lower control arm.
5. Assemble new ball joint to lower control arm with bolts provided in service package, Fig. 6. Torque bolts to 50 ft. lbs.
6. Insert ball joint stud into steering knuckle and torque nut to 55 ft. lbs.
7. Install wheel and tire, check toe setting and adjust as required.

LOWER CONTROL ARM & BUSHING, REPLACE

1. Raise and support vehicle, then remove wheel and tire.
2. Disconnect stabilizer bar at lower control arm and control arm support.
3. Using tool J-29330, separate ball joint from steering knuckle.
4. Remove control arm support to chassis retaining bolts and remove control arm support and control arm as an assembly.
5. Separate control arm from support, then using tools shown in Fig. 7, remove bushings from control arm.

CONTROL ARM

J 29792-1

J 29797-2

SUPPORT PLATE

TO REMOVE, INSERT J 29792-1 INTO BUSHING, SUPPORT CONTROL ARM ON J 29792-2, AND PRESS AS SHOWN.

CONTROL ARM

J 29792-2

J 29792-3

SUPPORT PLATE

TO INSTALL, SUPPORT CONTROL ARM ON J 29792-3, PLACE BUSHING INTO J 29792-2, AND PRESS BUSING INTO CONTROL ARM USING J 29792-1. LUBRICATE BUSHING.

Fig. 7 Replacing lower control arm bushing

1. LOOSELY INSTALL CENTER BOLT INTO HOLE (A).
2. LOOSELY INSTALL TIE BAR BOLT INTO OUTBOARD HOLE (B).
3. INSTALL BOTH REAR BOLTS INTO HOLES (C) TORQUE REAR BOLTS.
4. INSTALL BOLT INTO CENTER HOLE(D), THEN TORQUE.
5. TORQUE BOLT IN HOLE (A).
6. INSTALL BOLT INTO FRONT HOLE (E), THEN TORQUE.
7. TORQUE BOLT IN HOLE (B).

Fig. 8   Replacing lower control arm

Fig. 9   Stabilizer bar installation

Fig. 10   Installing strut assembly

6. Lubricate new bushings and install into control arm using tools shown in Fig. 7.
7. Attach lower control arm to control arm support and torque pivot bolts to 67 ft. lbs.
8. Install control arm support to chassis, using attaching bolt tightening sequence shown in Fig. 8. Torque bolts to 63 ft. lbs.
9. Reverse procedure to complete installation. Check toe setting and adjust as required.

STEERING KNUCKLE, REPLACE

1. Raise and support vehicle, then remove wheel and tire.
2. Remove front hub and bearing as outlined under "WHEEL BEARING, REPLACE" procedure.
3. Using tool J-29330, separate ball joint from steering knuckle.
4. Remove strut to steering knuckle attaching bolts, then disconnect strut from steering knuckle.
5. Assemble strut to new steering knuckle and install attaching bolts finger tight.

6. Insert ball joint stud into steering knuckle and torque stud nut to 55 ft. lbs.
7. Torque strut to steering knuckle attaching bolts to 140 ft. lbs.
8. Reverse removal procedure to complete installation.

STABILIZER BAR & BUSHINGS, REPLACE

1. Raise and support vehicle, allowing control arms to hang freely.
2. Remove left front wheel and tire.
3. Disconnect stabilizer bar at control arms and control arm supports.
4. Remove rear and center control arm support bolts, lower support assembly and remove stabilizer bar through left side of vehicle.
5. Install stabilizer bar bushing with slit facing toward front of vehicle, Fig. 9.
6. Holding stabilizer bar approximately 2¼ inches above support assembly, torque stabilizer bar to control arm support attaching bolts to 20 ft. lbs, Fig. 9.
7. Install stabilizer bar to lower control arm and torque attaching bolts to 15 ft. lbs, Fig. 9.

STRUT ASSEMBLY, REPLACE

1. Raise hood and remove strut protective cap and three strut to body attaching nuts.
2. Raise and support vehicle, allowing suspension to hang freely.
3. Remove wheel and tire, then install drive axle protective cover, J-28712.
4. Using tool J-24319, disconnect tie rod from strut assembly.
5. Remove strut to steering knuckle attaching bolts, then remove strut from vehicle.
6. Reverse procedure to install. Position flats of strut mounting bolts as shown in Fig. 10. Torque all nuts and bolts to specifications.

STRUT ASSEMBLY SERVICE

Disassembly

1. Clamp strut compressor tool J-26584 in a suitable vise.
2. Place strut assembly in compressor tool and install bottom adapter J-26584-86, making sure that adapter captures strut and locating pins are fully engaged, Fig. 11.
3. Rotate strut assembly to align top mounting assembly lip with strut compressor support notch.
4. Insert J-26584-88 top adapters between top mounting assembly and top spring seat. Position top adapters so that split line is perpendicular to spring compressor, Fig. 11.

INSTALL TOP ADAPTERS WITH SPLIT LINE IN THIS POSITION.

SUPPORT

ADAPTERS J26584-88

DIRECTION OF

STRUT FLANGE

ADAPTER J26584-86

Fig. 11 Removing damper & coil spring from strut

5. Rotate compressor forcing screw clockwise until top support flange contacts top adapters. Continue rotating forcing screws until strut spring is compressed approximately ½ inch.

CAUTION: Do not bottom the spring or strut damper rod.

LONG EXTENSION AND SOCKET TO FIT HEX ON DAMPER SHAFT

DAMPER SHAFT

Fig. 14 Aligning strut assembly

CUT LINE GROOVE

STEERING ARM

VISE

PIPE CUTTER

Fig. 12 Strut reservoir tube removal

6. Remove damper top nut, then remove strut mounting assembly from damper shaft.
7. Rotate forcing screw counterclockwise to relieve spring tension, then remove spring from strut assembly.

Strut Cartridge Replacement

1. Clamp strut assembly firmly in a suitable vise. Do not overtighten.
2. Install pipe cutter at cut line groove located at top of strut damper. Cut around groove until reservoir tube is cut completely through, Fig. 12.
3. Remove and discard end cap, cylinder and piston rod assembly.

90 N·m (68 FT. LBS.)

STRUT MOUNTING ASSEMBLY

SPRING SEAT

₵ OF SPINDLE

FLAT ₵

SPRING SEAT MUST BE INSTALLED WITH FLAT 10° FORWARD OF CENTERLINE OF STRUT ASM SPINDLE.

SPRING INSULATOR

BUMPER

SHIELD

SPRING

FRT

STRUT

Fig. 13 Strut coil spring & upper mounting installation

4. Place flaring cup tool, provided in service package, onto open end of reservoir tube and strike with hammer until cup flat outer surface rests on reservoir tube.
5. Install strut carriage into reservoir tube and align grooves on cartridge base with pads at bottom of reservoir tube.
6. Using tool J-29778, torque cartridge retaining hex nut to 140–170 ft. lbs.

Assembly

1. Perform Steps 1 & 2 as outlined in the "Disassembly" procedure.
2. Rotate strut assembly until mounting flange is facing outward, opposite compressor forcing screw.
3. Position spring on strut, making sure spring is properly seated on bottom

RH MOUNTING CLAMP

INSTALL THIRD

LH MOUNTING CLAMP

INSTALL FIRST

INSTALL FOURTH

INSTALL SECOND

50 N·m (35 FT. LBS.) AFTER REACHING TORQUE REQUIRED, NUT MUST ALWAYS BE TIGHTENED (UP TO 1/6 TURN) FURTHER. NEVER BACK OFF TO INSERT COTTER PIN.

PULL SEAL OVER END OF COLUMN BUSHING UNTIL SEAL LOCKS INTO PLACE

COLUMN

COLUMN BUSHING

SEAL ASSEMBLY

FLEXIBLE COUPLING

STUD

USE DOUBLE NUT TO TORQUE STUD

* STUDS ARE REUSABLE UP TO THREE TIMES.

DISCONNECT TIE ROD

TIE ROD

J-24319-01

STRUT

Fig. 15 Power rack & pinion steering gear removal

spring plate, Fig. 13.
4. Install strut spring seat assembly and J26584-88 top adapters over strut spring.
5. Turn compressor forcing screw until compressor top support contacts top adapters.
6. Install a long extension and socket onto hex on damper shaft to align components during installation, Fig. 14.
7. Compress spring until approximately 1½″ of damper shaft extends through spring plate.
8. Remove extension and socket, then position top mounting assembly over damper shaft and install retaining nut. Torque retaining nut to 68 ft. lbs.
9. Turn forcing screw counterclockwise and remove strut assembly from compressor.

MANUAL STEERING GEAR, REPLACE

1. Disconnect battery ground cable.
2. Remove left hand sound insulator.
3. From under instrument panel, pull downward on steering column seal, then remove upper pinch bolt from flexible coupling.
4. Remove air cleaner, then remove windshield washer reservoir attaching screws and position reservoir aside.
5. Raise and support front of vehicle, then remove both front wheel and tire assemblies.
6. Disconnect tie rods from struts using tool No. J24319-01, then lower vehicle.
7. Remove steering gear mounting clamps, Fig. 15.
8. Move steering gear assembly slightly forward, then remove lower pinch bolt from flexible coupling and detach coupling from steering gear stub shaft.
9. Remove dash panel seal from steering gear.
10. Raise and support front of vehicle, then remove splash shield from left inner fender.
11. Place left hand knuckle and hub assembly in the full left turn position, then remove steering gear through access hole in left hand inner fender.
12. Reverse procedure to install. If steering gear mounting clamp studs have backed out during removal, install double nuts on stud and torque stud to 15 ft. lbs. Torque coupling to stub shaft pinch bolt to 29 ft. lbs. and coupling to steering col-

Fig. 16 Power steering pump removal

umn shaft pinch bolt to 30 ft. lbs. Torque steering gear mounting clamp attaching nuts to 28 ft. lbs. Torque tie rod to strut attaching nuts to 35 ft. lbs. The tie rod to strut attaching nuts can be tightened up to an additional ⅙ turn to allow installation of cotter pin.

POWER STEERING GEAR, REPLACE

1. Disconnect battery ground cable.
2. Remove left hand sound insulator.
3. From under instrument panel, pull downward on steering column seal, then remove upper pinch bolt from flexible coupling.
4. Remove air cleaner, then remove windshield washer reservoir attaching screws and position reservoir aside.
5. Disconnect pressure line from steering gear and remove screw attaching line bracket to cowl.

6. Raise and support front of vehicle, then remove both front wheel and tire assemblies.
7. Disconnect tie rods from struts using tool No. J24319-01, then lower vehicle.
8. Remove steering gear mounting clamps, Fig. 15.
9. Move steering gear slightly forward, then disconnect return line from gear and drain power steering fluid.
10. Remove lower pinch bolt from flexible coupling, then detach coupling from steering gear stub shaft and remove dash seal.
11. Raise and support front of vehicle, then remove splash shield from left inner fender.
12. Place steering knuckle and hub assembly into the full left turn position, then remove steering gear through access hole in left hand inner fender.
13. Reverse procedure to install. If steering gear mounting clamps have backed out during removal, install double nuts on stud and torque to 15 ft. lbs. Torque coupling to stub shaft pinch bolt to 37 ft. lbs. and coupling to steering column shaft pinch bolts to 30 ft. lbs. Torque steering gear mounting clamp attaching nuts to 28 ft. lbs. Torque pressure and return line fittings to 20 ft. lbs. Torque tie rod to strut attaching nuts to 35 ft. lbs. The tie rod to strut attaching nuts can be tightened up to an additional ⅙ turn to allow installation of cotter pin.

POWER STEERING PUMP, REPLACE

1. Remove air cleaner assembly.
2. Disconnect reservoir to pump hose and pressure line from pump.
3. Remove clip attaching pressure line to pump.
4. Loosen pump pivot and adjusting bolts, then remove pump drive belt.
5. Remove three pump to bracket attaching bolts, Fig. 16.

NOTE: On some models, the pump may be attached to bracket by special bolts. To remove these special bolts, use tool No. T-45 or equivalent.

6. Remove pump from mounting bracket.
7. Reverse procedure to install.

CHEVROLET VEGA • PONTIAC ASTRE

INDEX OF SERVICE OPERATIONS

NOTE: Refer to the back of this manual for vehicle manufacturer's special service tool suppliers.

VEHICLE IDENTIFICATION NUMBER LOCATION

On top of instrument panel, left front.

ENGINE NUMBER LOCATION

4-140, On pad at right side of cylinder block below No. 3 spark plug at cylinder head parting line.
4-151, On distributor mounting pad.

ENGINE IDENTIFICATION CODE

Engines are identified in the following table by the code letter or letters immediately following the engine serial number.

Year	Engine	V.I.N. Code①	Engine Code Prefix	Year	Engine	V.I.N. Code①	Engine Code Prefix	Year	Engine	V.I.N. Code①	Engine Code Prefix
1977	4-140	B	CAA	1977	4-140	B	CBS	1977	4-140	B	CBZ
	4-140	B	CAB		4-140	B	CBT		4-151	V	WC
	4-140	B	CAC		4-140	B	CBU		4-151	V	WD
	4-140	B	CAY		4-140	B	CBV		4-151	V	YL
	4-140	B	CAZ		4-140	B	CBW		4-151	V	YM
	4-140	B	CBK		4-140	B	CBX		4-151	V	ZH
	4-140	B	CBL		4-140	B	CBY		4-151	V	ZJ

①—The fifth digit of the V.I.N. denotes the engine code.

GRILLE IDENTIFICATION

1977 Astre

1977 Vega

GENERAL ENGINE SPECIFICATIONS

Year	Engine CID①/Liter	Engine V.I.N. Code②	Carburetor	Bore and Stroke	Compression Ratio	Net H.P. @ R.P.M.③	Maximum Torque Ft. Lbs. @ R.P.M.	Normal Oil Pressure Pounds
1977	4-140, 2.3L	B	5210C, 2 Bbl④	3.500 × 3.625	8.00	84 @ 4400	117 @ 2400	36—45
	4-151, 2.5L	V	5210C, 2 Bbl④	4.00 × 3.00	8.25	88 @ 4400	128 @ 2400	36—41

①—CID—cubic inch displacement.
②—The fifth digit in the V.I.N denotes engine code.
③—Ratings Net—as installed in the vehicle.
④—Holley.

DISTRIBUTOR SPECIFICATIONS

★ If unit is checked on vehicle double the RPM and degrees to get crankshaft figures.

Distributor Part No.①	Centrifugal Advance Degrees @ RPM of Distributor				Vacuum Advance		Distributor Retard
	Advance Starts	Intermediate Advance		Full Advance	Inches of Vacuum To Start Plunger	Max. Adv. Dist. Deg. @ Vacuum	Max. Ret. Dist. Deg. @ Vacuum
1977							
1103229②	0 @ 600	3 @ 800	—	10 @ 2200	3½	10 @ 12	—
1103230②	0 @ 600	3 @ 800	—	10 @ 2200	3½	10 @ 9	—
1103231②	0 @ 600	—	—	10 @ 2200	3½	10 @ 12	—

Continued

DISTRIBUTOR SPECIFICATIONS—Continued

★ If unit is checked on vehicle double the RPM and degrees to get crankshaft figures.

| Distributor Part No.① | Centrifugal Advance Degrees @ RPM of Distributor | | | | | Vacuum Advance | | Distributor Retard |
	Advance Starts	Intermediate Advance			Full Advance	Inches of Vacuum To Start Plunger	Max. Adv. Dist. Deg. @ Vacuum	Max. Ret. Dist. Deg. @ Vacuum
1977—Continued								
1103263②	0 @ 600	—	—	—	10 @ 2200	3½	10 @ 9	—
1103303②	0 @ 600	—	—	—	10 @ 2200	9	10 @ 16	—
1110538②	0 @ 425	4 @ 600	—	—	8½ @ 1000	5	12 @ 10	—
1110539②	0 @ 425	4 @ 600	—	—	8½ @ 1000	5	12 @ 10	—

①—Located on distributor housing plate.
②—High Energy Ignition.

TUNE UP SPECIFICATIONS

The following specifications are published from the latest information available. This data should be used only in the absence of a decal affixed in the engine compartment.

★ When using a timing light, disconnect vacuum hose or tube at distributor and plug opening in hose or tube so idle speed will not be affected.

● When checking compression, lowest cylinder must be within 80 percent of highest.

▲ Before removing wires from distributor cap, determine location of the No. 1 wire in cap, as distributor position may have been altered from that shown at the end of this chart.

Spark plug types shown in this chart are recommendations of the original vehicle manufacturer and not MOTOR.

Check local sources for other spark plug manufacturers listings.

| Year & Engine | Spark Plug | | Ignition Timing BTDC★① | | | | Curb Idle Speed② | | Fast Idle Speed | | Fuel Pump Pressure |
	Type	Gap Inch	Firing Order Fig. ▲	Man. Trans.	Auto. Trans.	Mark Fig.	Man. Trans.	Auto. Trans.	Man. Trans.	Auto. Trans.	
1977											
4-140 Exc. Calif. & Hi. Alt.	R43TS	.035	A	TDC	2°	B	700/1250	650/850	2500	2500	3–4½
4-140 Calif.	R43TS	.035	A	2°ATDC	TDC	B	800/1250	650/850	2500	2500	3–4½
4-140 Hi. Alt.	R43TS	.035	A	TDC	2°	B	800/1250	700/850	2500	2500	3–4½
4-151 Less A/C	R43TSX	.060	C	③	③	D	500/1000	500/650	2200	2400	3–4½
4-151 With A/C	R43TSX	.060	C	③	③	D	500/1200	650/850	2200	2400	3–4½

①—BTDC—Before top dead center.
②—Idle speed on manual trans. vehicles is adjusted in Neutral and on auto. trans. equipped vehicles is adjusted in Drive unless otherwise specified. Where two idle speeds are listed, the higher speed is with the A/C or idle solenoid energized.
③—Exc. Calif., 14° BTDC; Calif., 12° BTDC.

Continued

TUNE UP NOTES—Continued

Fig. A

Fig. B

Fig. C

Fig. D

Fig. E

Fig. F

STARTING MOTOR SPECIFICATIONS

Year	Model	Starter Number	Brush Spring Tension Oz.①	Free Speed Test			Resistance Test	
				Amps.	Volts	R.P.M.	Amps.	Volts
1977	4-140 Std. Trans.	1108771	—	50–75②	9	6500–10000	—	—
	4-140 Auto. Trans.	1108772	—	50–75②	9	6500–10000	—	—
	4-151	1109412	—	50–75②	9	6500–10500	—	—

①—Minimum.　　　②—Includes solenoid.

ALTERNATOR & REGULATOR SPECIFICATIONS

Year	Model	Alternator		Cold Output @ 14 Volts		Regulator	Field Relay			Voltage Regulator		
		Rated Hot Output Amps.	Field Current 12 Volts @ 80 F.	2000 R.P.M. Amps.	5000 R.P.M. Amps.	Model	Air Gap In.	Point Gap In.	Closing Voltage	Air Gap In.	Point Gap In.	Voltage @ 125° F.
1977	1102851	55	4–4.5	—	51	Integral	—	—	—	—	—	—
	1102858	37	4–4.5	—	33	Integral	—	—	—	—	—	—
	1102891	55	4–4.5	—	51	Integral	—	—	—	—	—	—
	1102893	63	4–4.5	—	60	Integral	—	—	—	—	—	—

VALVE SPECIFICATIONS

Year	Engine Model	Valve Lash		Valve Angles		Valve Spring Installed Height	Valve Spring Pressure Lbs. @ In.	Stem Clearance		Stem Diameter	
		Int.	Exh.	Seat	Face			Intake	Exhaust	Intake	Exhaust
1977	4-140	Hydraulic①		46	45	1.75	190 @ 1.31	.001–.0027	.001–.0027	.3410–.3417	.3410–.3417
	4-151	Hydraulic①		46	45	1.69	82 @ 1.66	.001–.0027	②	.3400	.3400

①—No adjustment.　　　②—Top, .0010–.0027"; bottom, .0020–.0037".

CHEVROLET VEGA • PONTIAC ASTRE

ENGINE TIGHTENING SPECIFICATIONS★

★Torque specifications are for clean and lightly lubricated threads only. Dry or dirty threads produce increased friction which prevents accurate measurement of tightness.

Year	Engine Model	Spark Plugs Ft. Lbs.	Cylinder Head Bolts Ft. Lbs.	Intake Manifold Ft. Lbs.	Exhaust Manifold Ft. Lbs.	Rocker Arm Stud Ft. Lbs.	Cam Cover Ft. Lbs.	Connecting Rod Cap Bolts Ft. Lbs.	Main Bearing Cap Bolts Ft. Lbs.	Flywheel to Crankshaft Ft. Lbs.	Vibration Damper or Pulley Ft. Lbs.
1977	4-140	15	60	30	30	—	35①	35	65	60	80
	4-151	15	95	②	②	60	③	30	65	55	160

①—Inch pounds.
②—Intake to exhaust manifold, 40 ft. lbs. Manifold to cylinder head nut, 30 ft. lbs. Manifold to cylinder head bolt, 40 ft. lbs.
③—Rocker arm cover, 85 inch lbs.

PISTONS, PINS, RINGS, CRANKSHAFT & BEARINGS

Year	Engine Model	Piston Clearance	Ring End Gap①		Wristpin Diameter	Rod Bearings		Main Bearings		Thrust on Bear. No.	Shaft End Play
			Comp.	Oil		Shaft Diameter	Bearing Clearance	Shaft Diameter	Bearing Clearance		
1977	4-140	.0018–.0028	②	.010	.9272	1.999–2.000	.0007–.0027	2.2983–2.2993	.0003–.0029	4	.002–.008
	4-151	.0025–.0033	.010	.010	.9400	2.000	.0005–.0026	2.2983–2.2993	.0002–.0022	5	.0015–.0085

①—Fit rings in tapered bores for clearance listed in tightest portion of ring travel.
②—Top ring .015; lower ring .009.

WHEEL ALIGNMENT SPECIFICATIONS

Year	Model	Caster Angle, Degrees		Camber Angle, Degrees				Toe-In. Inch	Toe-Out on Turns, Deg.	
		Limits	Desired	Limits		Desired			Outer Wheel	Inner Wheel
				Left	Right	Left	Right			
1977	All	−.3 to −1.3	−.8	−.3 to +.7	−.3 to +.7	+.2	+.2	①	—	—

①—0 to ⅛ inch toe-out.

BRAKE SPECIFICATIONS

Year	Model	Brake Drum Inside Diameter	Wheel Cylinder Bore Diameter			Master Cylinder Bore Diameter		
			Disc Brake	Front Drum Brake	Rear Drum Brake	Disc Brakes	Drum Brakes	Power Brakes
1977	All	9½	1⅞	—	11/16	¾	—	¾

COOLING SYSTEM & CAPACITY DATA

Year	Model or Engine	Cooling Capacity, Qts.		Radiator Cap Relief Pressure, Lbs.		Thermo. Opening Temp.	Fuel Tank Gals.	Engine Oil Refill Qts. ①	Transmission Oil				Rear Axle Oil Pints
		With Heater	With A/C	With A/C	No A/C				3 Speed Pints	4 Speed Pints	5 Speed Pints	Auto. Trans. Qts. ②	
1977	4-140⑤	8.8	8.8	15	15	195	16	3½⑥	—	2.4	3.5	④	2.8
	4-140③	8	8	15	15	195	16	3½⑥	—	3	3	④	2¾
	4-151	11.2	11.2	15	15	195	16	3	—	2.4	3.5	④	2¾

①—Add 1 quart with filter change.
②—Approximate; make final check with dipstick.
③—Vega.
④—Turbo Hydra-Matic 200, refill 3 qts., total capacity 9.6 qts. Turbo Hydra-Matic 250, refill 2½ qts., total capacity 10 qts.
⑤—Astre.
⑥—Add ½ quart with filter change.

Year	Model	Carrier Type	Ring Gear & Pinion Backlash		Pinion Bearing Preload			Differential Bearing Preload		
			Method	Adjustment	Method	New Bearings Inch-Lbs.	Used Bearings Inch-Lbs.	Method	New Bearings Inch-Lbs.	Used Bearings Inch-Lbs.
1977	All	Integral	Shims	.005–.008	Spacer	10–25	8–12	Shims	—	—

Electrical Section

STARTER, REPLACE

NOTE: The following procedure may vary slightly depending on model and series of vehicle.

1. Disconnect battery ground cable at battery.
2. Disconnect all wires at solenoid terminals.

NOTE: Reinstall the nuts on the terminals as each wire is removed as thread size is different and if mixed, stripping of threads may occur.

3. Loosen starter front bracket then remove two mount bolts, Fig. 1.
4. Remove front bracket bolt and rotate bracket clear of work area then lower starter from vehicle by lowering front end first.
5. Reverse procedure to install.

IGNITION LOCK, REPLACE

1. Remove the turn signal switch as described further on.
2. The lock cylinder should be removed in the "Run" position only. Removal in any other position will damage the buzzer switch.
3. Insert a small screw driver or similar tool into the turn signal housing slot, Fig. 2. Keeping the tool to the right side of the slot, break the housing flash loose, and at the same time depress the spring latch at the lower end of the lock cylinder. With the latch depressed, the lock cylinder can be removed from the housing.

IGNITION SWITCH, REPLACE

The ignition switch is mounted on the top of the steering column jacket near the front of the dash. It is located inside the channel section of the brake pedal support and is completely inaccessible without first lowering the steering colunn.

1. Lower the steering column and be sure it is properly supported before proceeding.
2. The switch should be positioned in Lock position before removing, Fig. 3.

3. Unfasten and remove the switch, detaching it from the actuating rod.
4. When installing, make sure the lock and the switch are in the Lock position. Then install the activating rod into the switch and fasten the switch.

LIGHT SWITCH, REPLACE

1. Disconnect ground cable at battery.
2. Pull headlamp switch knob to "ON" position.
3. Reach under instrument panel and depress switch shaft retainer button while pulling on the switch control shaft knob.
4. With a large bladed screwdriver, remove the light switch ferrule nut from front of instrument panel, Fig. 4.
5. Disconnect the multi-contact connector from side of switch and remove switch.

STOP LIGHT SWITCH

1. Reach under right side of instrument panel at brake pedal support and release wiring harness connector at switch.
2. Pull switch from mounting bracket.
3. When installing switch, adjust by bringing brake pedal to normal position. Electrical contact should be made when pedal is depressed as shown in Fig. 5. To adjust, the switch may be rotated or pulled in the clip.

CLUTCH START SWITCH

NOTE: The clutch pedal must be fully depressed and the ignition switch in START position for the vehicle to start.

Fig. 1   Starter motor installation

Fig. 2   Ignition lock removal

SWITCH IN LOCK POSITION

Fig. 3   Ignition switch assembly

Fig. 4   Light switch replacement

Fig. 5 Stop light switch replacement

The clutch switch assembly mounts with two tangs to the clutch pedal brace switch pivot bracket and the clutch pedal arm, Fig. 6.

1. Under the instrument panel on the clutch pedal support remove the multi-contact connector from switch.
2. Compress switch assembly actuating shaft barb retainer and push out of clutch pedal.
3. Compress switch assembly pivot bracket barb and lift off switch.
4. When installing new switch, no adjustments are necessary as the switch is self aligning.

NEUTRAL SAFETY SWITCH, REPLACE

1. Remove screws securing floor console, Fig. 7.
2. Disconnect electrical plugs on backup contacts and neutral start contacts of switch assembly.
3. Place shift lever in Neutral.

4. Remove two screws securing shift indicator plate.
5. Remove two screws securing shift lever curved cover.
6. Remove two screws securing switch to lever assembly.

NOTE: Screws are hidden beneath lever cover.

7. Tilt switch to right while lifting switch out of lever hole.
8. When installing switch, make sure it is in Neutral position. When switch is installed, shifting out of Neutral will shear the switch plastic locating pin.

TURN SIGNAL SWITCH, REPLACE

1. Remove steering wheel with suitable puller.
2. Place screw driver blade into cover slot, pry up and out to free cover from lock plate.
3. Place Lock Plate Compressing Tool J-23653, Fig. 8, on end of steering shaft and compress the lock plate as far as possible using the shaft nut as shown. Pry the round wire snap ring out of the shaft groove and discard the ring. Remove tool and lift lock plate off end of shaft.
4. Slide the singal cancelling cam, upper bearing preload spring and thrust washer off the end of shaft.
5. Remove turn signal lever screw and remove the lever.
6. Push hazard warning knob in and unscrew the knob.
7. Wrap upper part of connector with tape, Fig. 9, to prevent snagging of wires during switch removal.
8. Remove three screws on switch and pull switch straight up through housing.

HORN SOUNDER & STEERING WHEEL

1. Disconnect battery ground cable.

Fig. 6 Clutch operated neutral start switch

2. On regular production steering wheel models, remove the two screws securing the steering wheel shroud from beneath the wheel and remove the shroud. On GT or optional wheel models, pry off horn button cap.
3. Remove steering wheel nut and use a suitable puller to remove the steering wheel.

NOTE: Remove snap ring before steering wheel nut.

INSTRUMENT CLUSTER

Standard Cluster

The instrument cluster bezel is retained by

Fig. 8 Removing lock plate retaining ring

Fig. 7 Neutral safety switch installation (Typical)

Fig. 9 Taping turn signal connector and wires

nine screws, Fig. 10. After removal of bezel, remove cluster lens-light shield combination (2 screws at top of lens and 2 screws at bottom of light shield). The lens tips out at the top and then lifts off. Instruments are then easily removed.

GT Cluster

The cluster bezel is retained by six screws, Fig. 11. After removal of bezel, remove the lens light shield (6 screws). Then lift lens and light shield straight out. Instruments are then accessible for replacement.

W/S WIPER MOTOR

1. Raise hood.
2. Reaching through cowl opening, loosen the two transmission drive link attaching nuts to motor crankarm.
3. Remove transmission drive link from motor crankarm.
4. Disconnect wiring and unfasten motor and remove.

W/S WIPER SWITCH

1. Beneath instrument panel, unplug the headlamp switch multi-connector for clearance to wiper switch screw.
2. Unplug connector on bottom of wiper switch.
3. On all models, remove two mounting screws from switch and lower switch from instrument panel.

RADIO, REPLACE

NOTE: When installing radio, be sure to adjust antenna trimmer for peak performance.

1. Remove battery ground cable.
2. Remove knobs, controls, washers and nuts from radio bushings.
3. Disconnect antenna lead, power connector and speaker connectors from rear of radio.
4. Remove two screws securing radio mounting bracket to instrument panel lower reinforcement and lift out radio.

HEATER CORE, REPLACE

Without Air Conditioning

1. Disconnect battery ground cable.
2. Disconnect blower motor lead wire.
3. Place a pan under vehicle and disconnect heater hoses at core connections and secure ends of hoses in a raised position.
4. Remove the coil bracket to dash panel stud nut and move coil out of way.
5. Remove the blower inlet to dash panel screws and nuts and remove the blower inlet, blower motor and wheel as an assembly.
6. Remove the core retainer strap screws and remove the core.
7. When replacing core, be sure the blower inlet sealer is intact.

With Air Conditioning

1. Disconnect battery ground cable.
2. Position a pan under heater core tubes, then disconnect heater hoses and secure

Fig. 10 Instrument panel. Standard cluster

Fig. 11 Instrument panel. GT cluster

in a raised position. Cap core tubes to prevent coolant spillage during removal.
3. From engine side of dash panel remove nuts from selector duct studs, Fig. 12.
4. Remove glove box and door as an assembly.
5. Remove right hand outlet to instrument panel attaching screws, then remove outlet and flexible hose.
6. Remove intermediate duct to left hand outlet.
7. Remove steering column to toe pan plastic retainer, insulation and attaching screws.
8. Remove steering column to dash panel attaching nuts, then lower column and support on driver's seat.

NOTE: Place protective tape over steering column to prevent damage to finish when lowering instrument cluster assembly.

9. Remove instrument panel bezel, then remove ash tray and retainer.
10. Remove A/C control to instrument panel attaching screws.
11. Disconnect wire connector and antenna lead from radio.
12. Remove instrument cluster to dash panel

attaching screws and allow cluster assembly to rest on steering column.
13. Disconnect speedometer cable, then push A/C control forward and allow control to rest on floor, using care not kink cable.
14. Remove center duct to selector duct attaching screws and duct to upper instrument panel retainer.
15. Slide center duct to left to clear lower instrument panel to cluster tab, then slide to right to remove.
16. Remove defroster duct to selector duct attaching screws.
17. Remove remaining selector duct to dash panel attaching screws, then pull duct rearward and disconnect all electrical leads and vacuum lines.
18. Disconnect temperature door cable and remove selector duct assembly.

NOTE: Ensure all electrical leads and vacuum lines are disconnected before removing duct assembly.

19. Pry off or punch out temperature door bell crank, then remove temperature door, Fig. 13.
20. Remove backing plate attaching screws and temperature door cable retainer.

Fig. 12 Air distribution ducts and outlets on air conditioned models

Fig. 13 Removing temperature door bell crank on air conditioned vehicles

VIEW A

Fig. 14 Blower motor (Typical)

21. Remove heater core and backing plate as an assembly.
22. Remove core straps, then remove heater core.

BLOWER MOTOR, REPLACE

1. Disconnect the battery ground cable.

2. On all models, disconnect blower motor lead wire.
3. Scribe the blower motor flange to case position.
4. Remove the blower to case attaching screws and remove the blower wheel and motor assembly, Fig. 14. Pry the flange gently if the sealer acts as an adhesive.
5. Remove the blower motor wheel retaining nut and separate the motor and wheel.
6. To install, reverse steps 1 thru 5, lining

up the scribe marks on the motor flange which were made at removal.

NOTE: Assemble the blower wheel to the motor with the open end of the blower away from the motor. Replace sealer at the motor flange if necessary.

4-140 Engine Section

CHECKING ENGINE MOUNTS

Raise engine to remove weight from mounts leaving a slight tension in the rubber. Observe both mounts while raising engine. Check for the following and replace if:
a. Hard rubber surface is covered with heat check cracks.
b. Rubber is separated from metal plate of mount.
c. Rubber is split through center.

If there is relative movement between a metal plate of the mount and its attaching points lower the engine on the mounts and tighten the screws or nuts attaching the mounts to the engine, frame, or bracket.

ENGINE MOUNTS, REPLACE
Front

1. Raise vehicle on hoist and support front of engine to take weight off front mounts.

2. If only one mount is being replaced, remove the mount-to-engine bracket nut on the mount not being replaced, Fig. 1.
3. Remove the stud nut and two bolts securing mount to housing support.
4. Remove the three stud nuts securing the bracket to the engine. On the right side remove the starter brace at starter and on air conditioned equipped vehicles, remove the compressor rear lower brace at the compressor.
5. Raise front of engine to provide maximum clearance without imposing stress on other engine components.
6. Remove mount and bracket as a unit and separate by removing stud nut.

Rear

CAUTION: The rear mount serves to locate the power train fore and aft and side to side; therefore mark relationship of rear mount to transmission support cross member to ensure proper alignment when new mount is installed.

1. Remove crossmember-to-mount bolts, Figs. 2 and 3.
2. Raise transmission at extension housing to release weight from mount.
3. Remove mount-to-transmission bolts, then remove mount.

ENGINE, REPLACE

1. Remove hood.
2. Disconnect battery positive cable at battery and negative cable at engine block (except on air conditioned vehicle).
3. Drain cooling system and disconnect hoses at radiator. Disconnect heater hoses at water pump and at heater inlet (bottom hose).
4. Disconnect emission system hoses: PCV at cam cover; cannister vacuum hose at carburetor; PCV vacuum at inlet manifold and bowl vent at carburetor.
5. Remove radiator panel or shroud and remove radiator, fan and spacer.
6. Remove air cleaner, disconnecting vent tube at base of cleaner.

7. Disconnect electrical leads at: Delcotron, ignition coil, starter solenoid, oil pressure switch, engine temperature switch, transmission controlled spark switch at transmission, transmission controlled spark solenoid and engine ground strap at cowl.
8. Disconnect: Automatic transmission throttle valve linkage at manifold mounted bellcrank, fuel line at rubber hose to rear of carburetor, transmission vacuum modulator and air conditioning vacuum line at inlet manifold, accelerator cable at manifold bellcrank.
9. On air conditioned cars, disconnect compressor at front support, rear support, rear lower bracket and remove drive belt from compressor.
10. Move compressor slightly forward and allow front of compressor to rest on frame forward brace, then secure rear of compressor to engine compartment so it is out of way.
11. Disconnect power steering pump, if equipped, and position it out of way.
12. Raise car on hoist and disconnect exhaust pipe at manifold.
13. Remove engine flywheel dust cover or converter underpan.
14. On automatic transmission cars, remove converter-to-flywheel retaining bolts and nuts and install converter safety strap.
15. Remove converter housing or flywheel housing-to-engine retaining bolts.
16. Loosen engine front mount retaining bolts at frame attachment and lower vehicle.
17. Install floor jack under transmission.
18. Install suitable engine lifting equipment and raise engine slightly to take weight from engine mounts and remove engine front mount retaining bolts.
19. Remove engine and pull forward to clear transmission while slowly lifting engine from car.

CYLINDER HEAD, REPLACE

1. Remove engine front cover and camshaft cover as outlined further on.
2. Remove timing belt and camshaft sprocket.
3. Remove intake and exhaust manifolds.
4. Disconnect hose at thermostat housing.

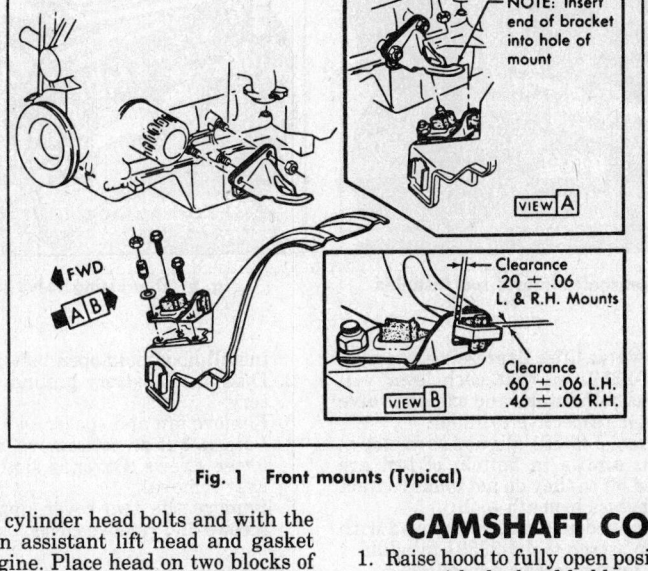

Fig. 1   Front mounts (Typical)

5. Remove cylinder head bolts and with the aid of an assistant lift head and gasket from engine. Place head on two blocks of wood to prevent damage to valves.
6. Reverse procedure to install and tighten head bolts in sequence shown in Fig. 4.

NOTE: Cylinder head bolts are of different lengths. Install the longer bolts adjacent to intake manifold.

VALVES, ADJUST

These engines use hydraulic valve lifters which require no lash adjustment. Also, these lifters are not interchangeable with the previous type valve lifters since the cylinder head has been re-designed to facilitate the use of the new type lifters.

VALVE ARRANGEMENT

Front to Rear

4-140 . . . . I-E-I-E-I-E-I-E

CAMSHAFT COVER

1. Raise hood to fully open position and support with the hood hold-open link.
2. Disconnect battery negative cable at battery.
3. Remove air cleaner wing nut. Disconnect ventilation tube at camshaft cover or at air cleaner; then remove air cleaner.
4. Remove PCV valve from grommet at front of cover.
5. Remove cover-to-cylinder head screws and withdraw cover from head.

CAMSHAFT, REPLACE

1. Remove hood from vehicle.
2. Drain engine coolant.
3. Remove engine front cover, refer to "Engine Front Cover" procedure.
4. Remove timing belt as outlined in "Timing Belt and Water Pump" procedure.
5. Remove camshaft sprocket as outlined in "Camshaft Sprocket" procedure.
6. Remove cam retainer and seal assembly.
7. Remove camshaft cover as outlined in "Camshaft Cover" procedure.
8. Disconnect fuel line at carburetor.
9. Remove Pulse A.I.R. tubing.
10. Remove EGR thermal vacuum switch.
11. Remove distributor.
12. Raise vehicle on a hoist, disconnect engine from the mounts at body attachment. Raise front of engine and install wood blocks, approximately 1–1½ inches thick, between engine mounts and body.
13. Lower vehicle.
14. Install camshaft removal tool as shown in Fig. 5 to cylinder head as follows:
    a. Position tool J-23591 to cylinder head so that attaching holes align with cam cover lower attaching holes.

NOTE: Ensure all foreign material is removed from cylinder head so that tool J-23591 seats properly.

AUTOMATIC TRANSMISSION

Fig. 2   Rear mount. Automatic trans.

SYNCHROMESH TRANSMISSION

Fig. 3   Rear mount. Synchromesh trans.

Fig. 4   Cylinder head tightening sequence

Fig. 5 Camshaft removal tool installed

Fig. 6 Depressing valve tappets

Fig. 7 Sprocket alignment marks

b. Align valve lifter depressing levers on tool J-23591 so that each lever will depress both intake and exhaust valve for their respective cylinder.

c. With tool J-23591 aligned as in step b, ensure screws in bottom of tool are backed off so they do not make contact with bosses beneath tool.

d. Install hardened screws supplied with tool, to attach tool J-23591 to cylinder head; torque screws securely.

e. Turn screws in bottom of tool downward until they just seat against corresponding bosses on the cylinder head.

f. Apply a suitable heavy lubricant to ball end of lever depressing screws and tightening screws of the valve lifters.

NOTE: Set engine timing mark to 12 o'clock before depressing valves. Use a torque wrench on pivot arm screws, Fig. 6. Do not exceed 12 ft. lbs. of torque to depress valves.

15. Camshaft can be removed by sliding it forward until it clears the cylinder head.

16. Reverse procedure to install.

CAMSHAFT BEARINGS

After removal of the camshaft as described previously, the bearings can be removed without removing the camshaft end plug.

NOTE: Install bearings from rear to front. Align oil holes in the rear three bearings with oil holes in bearing bore. Position oil holes in the first two bearings at 11 o'clock with oil groove in front bearing facing forward.

CAM LOBE LIFT SPECS.

| All | 1977 | .4000 | .4150 |

VALVE TIMING

Intake Open Before TDC

| All | 1977 | 34 |

VALVE GUIDES

On all engines, valves operate in guide holes bored in the cylinder head. If clearance becomes excessive, use the next oversize valve and ream the bore to fit. Valves with oversize stems are available in .003, .015 and .030″.

ENGINE FRONT COVER

1. Raise hood to fully open position and

install hood hold-open bolt.

2. Disconnect battery ground cable at battery.

3. Remove fan and spacer.

4. Loosen, but do not remove, the two cover lower screws. Cover is slotted to permit easy removal.

5. Remove the two cover upper retaining screws and remove cover.

TIMING BELT & WATER PUMP

1. Remove engine front cover as previously described.

2. Remove accessory drive pulley or damper.

3. Drain coolant and loosen water pump bolts to relieve tension on belt.

4. Remove timing belt lower cover, then remove belt from sprockets.

5. Remove water pump bolts and lift off pump after removing hoses.

CAMSHAFT SPROCKET

After removal of timing belt, the camshaft sprocket can be removed as follows:

1. Align one hole in sprocket with bolt head behind sprocket, then using a socket on bolt head to prevent cam from turning, remove sprocket retaining bolt and withdraw sprocket from camshaft.

2. When installing, be sure timing marks are aligned as in Fig. 7.

NOTE: A simplified method is provided for checking camshaft and crankshaft alignment. Proper alignment is assured by making sure hole in left rear of the timing belt upper cover is in line with the corresponding hole in the camshaft sprocket with engine at TDC compression stroke. Check alignment by inserting a pencil or other similar tool through the hole in cover. If alignment is correct, tool will also enter small hole in cam gear, Fig. 8.

CRANKSHAFT SPROCKET

1. Remove engine front cover, accessory drive pulley, timing belt and timing belt lower cover.

2. Install suitable puller to crankshaft sprocket and remove sprocket.

OIL PUMP (CRANKCASE FRONT COVER) SEAL

1. Remove engine front cover, accessory

drive pulley, timing belt and timing belt lower cover and crankshaft sprocket.

2. Pry old seal from front cover being careful not to damage seal housing or seal lip contact surfaces.

3. Coat seal with light engine oil and apply an approved sealing compound to outside diameter of seal.

4. Position seal, closed end outward, onto crankshaft. Then install seal into bore using tool J-23624, Fig. 9.

PISTONS & RODS, ASSEMBLE

The "F" on the front of the piston must face the front of the engine when the piston and road assembly is installed in its proper cylinder, Fig. 10.

Upon installation, the recommended connecting rod side clearance should be .0085–.0135 inch.

Piston Oversizes

Oversize pistons are available in oversizes of .010 and .020 inch.

MAIN & ROD BEARINGS

Undersizes

Bearings are available in .001, .002, .010 and .020″ undersizes.

NOTE: If for any reason main bearing caps are replaced, shimming may be necessary. Laminated shims for each cap are available for service. Shim requirements will be determined by bearing clearance.

OIL PAN

1. Raise vehicle on a hoist and drain engine

Fig. 8   Checking sprocket alignment

Fig. 9   Installing crankshaft front seal

"F" TOWARD FRONT OF ENGINE

NUMBERED SIDE OF ROD

Fig. 10   Piston and rod assembly

Fig. 11   Removing oil pan baffle

Fig. 12   Oil pump pressure regulator

Fig. 13   Checking driven gear-to-housing clearance

7. Remove pick up screen to baffle support bolts, then remove support from baffle.
8. Remove bolt securing oil pan drain back tube to baffle. Then rotate baffle 90 degrees towards left side of car and remove baffle from pick up screen, Fig. 11.

OIL PUMP (CRANKCASE FRONT COVER)

1. Remove engine front cover, accessory drive pulley, timing belt, timing belt lower cover and crankshaft sprocket.
2. Raise vehicle on a hoist and remove oil pan and baffle.
3. Remove bolts and stud securing oil pump to cylinder case.

Inspection

1. Clean gasket surfaces, then wash parts in approved solvent and blow out all passages.
2. Check pressure regulator for free operation, Fig. 12.
3. Inspect pump gears for nicks, broken

oil.
2. Support front of engine so weight is off front mounts, and remove frame crossmember and both front crossmember braces.
3. Disconnect idler arm at frame side rail.

NOTE: On air conditioned vehicles, disconnect idler arm at relay rod.

4. Mark relationship of steering linkage pitman arm to steering gear pitman shaft and remove pitman arm.

NOTE: Do not rotate steering gear pitman shaft while arm is disconnected as this

will change steering wheel alignment.

5. Remove flywheel cover or converter underpan.
6. Remove oil pan to cylinder case screws, tap pan lightly to break sealing bond and remove oil pan.

Fig. 14   Checking drive gear-to-crescent clearance

Fig. 15   Checking driven gear-to-crescent clearance

Fig. 16   Checking gear end clearance

Fig. 17 Tensioning adapter locating hole

Fig. 18 Adjusting timing belt

parts and other damage.

4. Check clearance between outside diameter of driven gear and pump. Clearance should be .0038–.0068″, Fig. 13.
5. Check clearance between outside diameter of drive gear and crescent. Clearance should be .0023–.0093″, Fig. 14.
6. Check clearance between inside diameter of driven gear and pump crescent. Clearance should be .0068–.0148″, Fig. 15.
7. Check gear end clearance. It should be .0009–.0023″, Fig. 16.

NOTE: The pump gears and body are not serviced separately. If pump gears or body are worn, replacement of the entire oil pump assembly is necessary.

WATER PUMP, REPLACE

1. Raise hood to fully open position and install hold-open bolt.
2. Disconnect battery ground cable at battery.
3. Remove engine fan and spacer.
4. Loosen, but do not remove, the two cover lower screws. Cover is slotted to permit easy removal.
5. Remove the two cover upper retaining screws and remove cover.
6. Drain coolant and loosen water pump bolts to relieve tension in timing belt.
7. Remove radiator lower hose and heater hose at water pump.
8. Unfasten and remove water pump.

TIMING BELT TENSION, ADJUST

1. Drain coolant at engine block and remove fan and extension.
2. Remove engine front cover.
3. Remove water pump retaining bolts, clean gasket surfaces on block and pump. Install new gasket and loosely install water pump bolts.

NOTE: Apply an approved anti-seize compound to the water pump bolts before installation.

Fig. 19 Removing fuel pump and gauge unit

Fig. 20 Engine lubrication system

4. Position tool J-23564 in gauge hole adjacent to left side of pump, Fig. 17.
5. Apply 15 ft. lbs. of torque to water pump as shown in Fig. 18. Tighten water pump bolts while maintaining torque on side of pump.
6. Reinstall front cover, fan, extension and fill cooling system.

FUEL PUMP, REPLACE

Removal
1. Disconnect battery ground cable.
2. Disconnect meter and pump wires at rear wiring harness connector.
3. Raise vehicle on hoist and drain fuel tank.
4. Disconnect fuel line hose at gauge unit pick up line.
5. Disconnect tank vent lines to vapor separator.
6. Remove gauge ground wire screw at underbody floorpan.
7. Remove tank straps bolts and lower tank carefully.
8. Unscrew retaining ring using spanner wrench J-24187, Fig. 19, and remove pump-tank unit assembly.

Replacement
1. Remove flat wire conductor from plastic clip on fuel tube.
2. Squeeze clamp and pull pump straight back about 1/2 inch.
3. Remove two nuts and lockwashers and conductor wires from pump terminals.
4. Squeeze clamp and pull pump straight back to remove it from tank unit. Take care to prevent bending of circular support bracket.
5. Slide replacement pump through circular support bracket until it rests against rubber coupling. Make sure pump has rubber isolator and saran strainer attached.
6. Attach two conductor wires to pump terminals using lockwashers and nuts being certain flat conductor is attached to terminal located on side away from float arm.
7. Squeeze clamp and push pump into rubber coupling.
8. Replace flat wire conductor in plastic clip on fuel pick up tube.
9. Install unit into tank and replace fuel tank.

BELT TENSION DATA

1977	New Lbs.	Used Lbs.
Air Condition	135–145	95
A.I.R. Pump	120–130	75
Generator	120–130	75
Power Steering	120–130	75
Timing Belt	100–140	—

4-151 Engine Section

Refer to the "Monza, Skyhawk, Starfire & Sunbird" chapter for service procedures on this engine.

Clutch & Transmission Section

CLUTCH PEDAL, ADJUST

Initial adjustment after clutch and/or cable replacement is made at two points, at the ball stud and the lower end of the cable.
1. Ball stud adjustment is made before attaching the cable as follows: using gauge J-23644, place it so flat end is against the front face of the clutch housing and the hooked end is located at the point of cable attachment on the fork, Fig. 1.
2. Turn ball stud inward until clutch release bearing lightly contacts the clutch spring levers, then install the lock nut and tighten being careful not to change the adjustment. Remove the gauge by pulling outward at the housing end.
3. To adjust the cable, place it through the hole in the fork and pull it until the clutch pedal is firmly against the rubber bumper.
4. Push the clutch fork forward until the throwout bearing lightly contacts the clutch spring levers, then screw the lock pin on the cable until it bottoms out on the fork. Turn an 1/4 additional clockwise revolution, set pin into groove in the fork and attach return spring. This procedure will produce .90″ lash at the pedal.
   Adjustment for normal clutch wear is accomplished by loosening the lock nut and by turning the clutch fork ball stud counterclockwise until .90″ of free play is obtained at the pedal.

CLUTCH REPLACE

1. Remove transmission.
2. Remove clutch fork cover then disconnect clutch return spring and control cable from clutch fork.
3. Remove flywheel housing lower cover and flywheel housing, Fig.2.
4. Remove release bearing from the clutch fork and sleeve by sliding lever off ball stud and against spring force. If ball stud is to be replaced, remove cap, lock nut and stud from housing.
5. Make sure alignment marks on clutch assembly and flywheel are distinguishable.
6. Loosen clutch cover to flywheel bolts one turn at a time until spring pressure is released, to avoid bending the clutch cover flange.
7. Support the pressure plate and cover assembly while removing bolts and clutch assembly.

NOTE: Do not disassemble the clutch cover, spring and pressure plate for repairs. If defective replace complete assembly.

8. Reverse procedure to install making sure to index alignment marks.
9. After installing crossmember, loosely install retaining bolts, then the crossmember to transmission mount bolts. Tighten all retaining bolts to specifications and remove the engine support.

CAUTION: Check position of engine in front mounts and realign as necessary.

LINKAGE ADJUST

3 & 4 Speed Exc. 70mm (Brazil)

1. Place ignition switch in "Off" position.
2. Raise vehicle and loosen shift rod nuts at swivels.
3. Position shift levers in neutral.
4. Place shift control in neutral position, align control levers and install gauge pin into levers and brackets.
5. On 3 speed models, tighten 1st-Rev. shift rod nut against swivel, then tighten 2-3 shift rod nut against swivel, torque nuts to 120 in. lbs.
6. On 4 speed models, tighten 1-2 shift rod nut against swivel, then tighten 3-4 shift rod nut against swivel, torque nuts to 120 in. lbs.
7. On 4 speed models, torque reverse shift rod nut to 120 in. lbs.
8. On all models, remove gauge pin and check linkage for operation.

Fig. 1 Clutch adjusting gauge in place

Fig. 2 Clutch & housing

TRANSMISSION, REPLACE

3 & 4 Speed Exc. 70mm (Brazil)

1. Raise vehicle on a hoist and drain lubricant.
2. On 1976–77 models, remove torque arm, referring to the "Rear Suspension" section. On all models, remove the propeller shaft.
3. Disconnect speedo cable, TCS switch and back-up lamp switch.
4. Disconnect transmission control rod and lever assemblies from shifter shafts. Tie rods up out of way.
5. Remove crossmember to transmission mount bolts.
6. Support engine with an appropriate jack stand and remove crossmember to frame bolts and remove crossmember.
7. Remove transmission to clutch housing upper retaining bolts and install guide pins in holes.
8. Remove lower bolts, then slide transmission rearward and remove from vehicle.

NOTE: Inspect throwout bearing support gasket located beneath lip of support. If necessary, replace gasket before installing transmission.

4 Speed 70mm (Brazil)

1. Push shift lever boot down and loosen lock nut, remove upper portion of shift lever.
2. Remove console, retainer and boot, then remove shift control from extension housing.
3. Raise vehicle and drain lubricant.
4. Remove torque arm, referring to the "Rear Suspension" section.
5. Remove propeller shaft, then disconnect speedometer cable and back-up light switch.
6. Disconnect clutch return spring and cable at fork.
7. Remove transmission to crossmember bolts.
8. Remove converter bracket and damper, if equipped.
9. Remove crossmember to frame bolts, support transmission, then remove crossmember.
10. Remove clutch housing to engine attaching bolts, slide transmission and clutch housing rearward and remove from vehicle.

5 Speed Unit

1. Remove boot retainer, then slide boot up on control lever.
2. Remove foam insulator, then remove four control lever attaching bolts and control lever.
3. Raise vehicle and remove propeller shaft.
4. Remove damper assembly, converter bracket and torque arm bracket.
5. Disconnect speedometer cable and back-up light switch wire connector.
6. Support transmission using a suitable jack.
7. Remove transmission support, then remove transmission to clutch housing attaching bolts and slide exhaust bracket forward.
8. Slide transmission rearward and remove from vehicle.

Rear Axle, Propeller Shaft & Brakes

REAR AXLE

Description

The rear axle, Fig. 1, is a semi-floating type consisting of a cast carrier and large bosses on each end into which two welded steel tubes are fitted. The carrier contains an overhung hypoid pinion and ring gear. The differential is a two pinion arrangement.

The overhung hypoid drive pinion is supported by two preloaded tapered roller bearings. The pinion shaft is sealed by means of a molded, spring loaded, rubber seal. The seal is mounted on the pinion shaft flange which is splined and bolts to the hypoid pinion shaft.

The ring gear is bolted to a one piece differential case and is supported by two preloaded tapered roller bearings.

Replace

1. Support vehicle at frame and using a suitable jack support axle housing.
2. Remove wheels, brake drums and axle shafts.
3. Disconnect brake lines from axle tube clips and remove bolt securing brake line junction block to rear axle housing.

NOTE: Do not disconnect brake lines from wheel cylinders or junction block.

4. Remove brake backing plates and secure backing plates to frame.
5. Remove parking brake cable adjusting nuts at equalizer, pull center cable rearward and disconnect two rear cables from body connectors.
6. Disconnect rear brake hose at floor pan and cap ends of hose and line.
7. Disconnect shock absorber from rear axle.
8. Disconnect track rod, then slowly lower axle until all spring tension is relieved and pry springs from axle housing pads.
9. Disconnect propeller shaft and torque arm and position aside.

NOTE: Support axle at companion flange

to prevent housing from rotating.

10. Remove lower control arm attaching bolts from axle housing.
11. Remove support at companion flange, then the axle assembly.
12. Reverse procedure to install.

AXLE SHAFT, REPLACE

1. Raise vehicle on a hoist and remove wheel and tire assembly and brake drum.
2. Drain lubricant from axle by removing carrier cover.
3. Unscrew pinion shaft lock screw and remove pinion shaft, Fig. 2.
4. Push flanged end of axle shaft toward center of car and remove "C" lock from button end of shaft.
5. Remove axle shaft from housing being careful not to damage seal.

Oil Seal &/or Bearing Replacement

1. If replacing seal only, remove the seal by using the button end of axle shaft. Insert the button end of shaft behind the steel case of the seal and pry seal out of bore being careful not to damage housing.
2. If replacing bearings, insert tool J-22813 into bore so tool head grasps behind bearing, Fig. 3. Slide washer against seal, or bearing, and turn nut against washer. Attach slide hammer J-2619 and remove bearing.
3. Pack cavity between seal lips with a high melting point wheel bearing lubricant. Position seal on tool J-21491 and position seal in axle housing bore, tap seal in bore just below end of housing, Fig. 4.

PROPELLER SHAFT, REPLACE

1. Raise vehicle on a hoist.
2. Remove torque arm bolts at rear axle, then referring to the "Rear Suspension" section, loosen attaching bolt at transmission and swing arm away.
3. On all models mark relationship of shaft to companion flange and disconnect the rear universal joint by removing trunnion bearing "U" bolts. Tape bearing cups to trunnion to prevent dropping and loss of bearing rollers, Fig. 5.
4. Withdraw propeller shaft front yoke from transmission.
5. When installing, be sure to align marks made in removal to prevent driveline vibration.

Fig. 1   Rear axle cross section

Fig. 2   Differential pinon shaft removal

Fig. 3   Removing wheel bearing and seal

Fig. 4   Installation seal and wheel bearing

Fig. 5   Propeller shaft cross section

Fig. 6 Self-adjusting brakes

Fig. 7 Drum knock out provision.

BRAKE ADJUSTMENTS

These brakes, Fig. 6, have self-adjusting shoe mechanisms that assure correct lining-to-drum clearances at all times. The automatic adjusters operate only when the brakes are applied as the car is moving rearward.

Although the brakes are self-adjusting, an initial adjustment is necessary after the brake shoes have been relined or replaced, or when the length of the adjusting screw has been changed during some other service operation.

Frequent usage of an automatic transmission forward range to halt reverse vehicle motion may prevent the automatic adjusters from functioning, thereby inducing low pedal heights. Should low pedal heights be encountered, it is recommended that numerous forward and reverse stops be made until satisfactory pedal height is obtained.

NOTE: If a low pedal condition cannot be corrected by making numerous reverse stops (provided the hydraulic system is free of air) it indicates that the self-adjusting mechanism is not functioning. Therefore it will be necessary to remove the brake drum, clean, free up and lubricate the adjusting mechanism. Then adjust the brakes, being sure the parking brake is fully released.

Adjustment

A lanced "knock out" area, Fig. 7, is provided in the web of the brake drum for servicing purposes in the event retracting of the brake shoes is required in order to remove the drum.

1. With brake drum off, disengage the actuator from the star wheel and rotate the star wheel by spinning or turning with a screwdriver.
2. Using the brake drum as an adjustment fixture, turn the star wheel until the drum slides over the brake shoes with a slide drag.
3. Turn the star wheel 1¼ turns to retract the brake shoes. This will allow sufficient lining-to-drum clearance so final adjustment may be made.
4. Install drum and wheel.

NOTE: If lanced area in brake drum was knocked out, be sure all metal has been removed from brake compartment. Install new hole cover in drum to prevent contamination of brakes. Make certain that drums are installed in the same position as when removed with the drum locating tang in line with the locating hole in the wheel hub.

5. Make final adjustment by driving and stopping in forward and reverse until satisfactory pedal height is obtained.

NOTE: The recommended method of adjusting the brakes is by using a Drum-to-Brake Shoe Clearance Gauge to check the diameter of the brake drum inner surface. Turn the tool to the opposite side and fit over the brake shoes by turning the star wheel until the gauge just slides over the linings. Rotate the gauge around the brake shoe lining surface to assure proper clearance.

PARKING BRAKE, ADJUST

1. Raise and support vehicle.
2. Apply parking brake one notch from fully released position and raise hoist.
3. Loosen equalizer check nut and tighten the adjusting nut until a slight drag is felt when rear wheels are rotated.
4. Tighten check nut securely.
5. Release parking brake and rotate rear wheels. No drag should be present.

MASTER CYLINDER, REPLACE

1. Disconnect cylinder push rod from brake pedal.
2. Disconnect brake lines from two outlets on cylinder and cover ends of lines to prevent entry of dirt.
3. Unfasten and remove cylinder from dash.

POWER BRAKE UNIT

1. Remove the vacuum hose from check valve and then remove the master cylinder retaining nuts.
2. Remove the bolt securing the brake pipe distributor and switch assembly to fender skirt.
3. Pull master cylinder forward until it just clears mounting studs and move aside. Support cylinder to avoid stress on hydraulic lines.
4. Remove power unit to dash nuts.
5. Remove brake pedal pushrod retainer and disconnect push rod from pin.
6. Remove power unit from vehicle.

Rear Suspension

Fig. 1   Rear suspension (Typical)

DESCRIPTION

This rear suspension system does not use upper control arms, instead, it uses a torque arm mounted rigidly to the differential housing at the rear and to the transmission through a rubber bushing or insulator at the front. This torque arm prevents axle housing rotation caused by starting and stopping. Along with the torque arm a track rod is used to connect the axle housing to the body to control side sway and a rear stabilizer shaft is used for improved handling, Fig. 1.

SHOCK ABSORBER, REPLACE

1. With the rear axle supported properly disconnect shock absorber from upper and lower mounting, Fig. 1.

NOTE: Use a wrench to hold lower mounting stud from turning.

2. Reverse procedure to install.

COIL SPRING, REPLACE

1. Support vehicle at frame and rear axle with a suitable jack.
2. Disconnect shock absorbers from lower mountings.
3. Lower rear axle until springs can be removed.

NOTE: Do not stretch or damage brake hoses.

4. Reverse procedure to install.

CONTROL ARMS & BUSHINGS, REPLACE

NOTE: Replace control arms one at a time to prevent axle misalignment, making installation difficult.

Lower Control Arms

1. Support vehicle at rear axle.
2. Disconnect stabilizer bar, if used, from lower arms.
3. Remove control arm front and rear mount bolts.
4. Replace bushings as necessary.
5. Reverse procedure to install. Control arm bolts must be tightened with vehicle at curb height.

Fig. 2   Stabilizer bar installation

STABILIZER BAR, REPLACE

1. Remove bolts securing stabilizer bar to lower control arms, Fig. 2.
2. Reverse procedure to install.

TRACK ROD, REMOVAL

1. Raise vehicle and support axle assembly.
2. Remove bolts at underbody end of rod.
3. Remove bolts at axle bracket and remove track rod, Figs. 3 and 4.
4. Reverse removal procedure to install and torque bolts to specifications.

TORQUE ARM, REPLACE

1. Raise vehicle by axle assembly and support underbody with jackstands.
2. Disconnect mounting bracket from transmission, then remove through bolt and separate bracket from torque arm.
3. Remove bolts attaching torque arm to rear axle housing, then remove torque arm, Figs. 4 thru 6.
4. To replace bushing, use an arbor press and tool J-25317-2 as a receiver and press bushing out of arm, then position new bushing in torque arm with bushing sleeve aligned with the length of the torque arm. Press bushing into place using tool J-25317-1 over bushing to properly locate bushing in arm.
5. Reverse removal procedure to install and torque nuts and bolts to specifications.

Fig. 3 Track rod installation. 1977 models

Fig. 4 Torque arm installation. Manual transmission models with 4-140 (Typical)

Fig. 5 Torque arm installation. Models equipped with 4-151 (Typical)

Fig. 6 Torque arm installation

Front Suspension & Steering Section

FRONT SUSPENSION

The front suspension, Fig. 1, is of the A frame type with short and long control arms. The upper control arm is bolted to the front end sheet metal at each inner pivot point. Rubber bushings are used for mounting.

The lower control arms attach to the front end sheet metal with cam type bolts through rubber bushings. The cam bolts adjust caster and camber.

The upper ball joint is riveted in the upper arm and the lower ball joint is pressed into the lower arm.

Coil springs are mounted between the lower control arms and the shock absorber tower.

WHEEL ALIGNMENT

Caster

Caster angle is adjusted by loosening the rear lower control arm pivot nut and rotating the cam until proper setting is reached, Fig. 2.

NOTE: This eccentric cam action will tend to move the lower control arm fore or aft thereby varying the caster. Hold the cam bolt while tightening the nut.

Camber

Camber angle is adjusted by loosening the front lower control arm pivot nut and rotating the cam until setting is reached, Fig. 2.

NOTE: This eccentric cam action will move the lower arm in or out thereby varying the setting. Hold the cam bolt head while tightening the nut.

TOE-IN, ADJUST

1. Loosen clamp bolt nut at each end of each tie rod and rotate the sleeve until proper toe-in is reached.
2. Position tie rod ball stud assembly straight on a center line through their attaching points.
3. Tighten clamp nuts.

WHEEL BEARINGS, ADJUST

1. With wheel raised, remove hub cap, dust cap and cotter pin from end of spindle.
2. While rotating wheel, tighten spindle nut to 12 ft. lbs.
3. Backoff adjusting nut to the just loose position, then retighten nut hand tight.
4. Loosen until either hole in spindle is aligned with slot in nut, then install cotter pin.

5. Spin wheel to check that it rolls freely and then lock the cotter pin.

NOTE: Wheel bearings should have zero preload and the allowable end play is .001–.005 inch.

WHEEL BEARINGS, REPLACE

1. Raise vehicle on a hoist and remove the wheel and tire assembly.
2. Remove the brake caliper from the disc by removing the mounting pins and stamped nuts, Fig. 3.
3. Remove hub grease cap, cotter pin, spindle nut and washer and remove hub and bearings.
4. Remove inner bearing by prying out the grease seal.

CHECKING BALL JOINTS FOR WEAR

Upper Ball Joint

The upper ball joint is checked for wear by checking the torque required to rotate the ball joint stud in the assembly. This is done after first dislodging the ball joint from the steering

Fig. 1   Front suspension (Typical)

Fig. 2   Caster and camber adjustment

knuckle.
1. Install the stud nut to the ball stud in the seat.
2. Check the torque required to turn the ball stud.

NOTE: Specified rotating torque for a new joint is 1 to 4 ft. lbs. If readings are excessively high or low replace joint.

Lower Ball Joint

NOTE: All vehicles use lower ball joints incorporating wear indicators, Fig. 4.

The lower ball joint is checked for wear by checking to be sure torque is present. After dislodging ball joint from steering knuckle perform the following:
1. Install the stud nut to the ball stud.
2. Check the torque required to turn the ball stud in the seat.

NOTE: Some torque is required, if zero torque is observed, sufficient wear has taken place for replacement of the ball joint.

UPPER BALL JOINT, REPLACE

1. Raise vehicle on a hoist and remove wheel and tire assembly.

2. Support lower control arm with a floor jack.
3. Remove upper ball stud nut and remove ball stud from knuckle, Fig. 5.
4. Remove control arm pivot bolts and remove control arm.
5. Grind off rivets securing ball joint to arm.
6. Install new ball joint using bolts and nuts supplied in kit.

LOWER BALL JOINT, REPLACE

1. Place vehicle on hoist and support lower control arm at outer end on a jack.
2. Free lower ball stud from knuckle, Fig. 5.
3. Using tool shown in Fig. 6, press ball joint out of control arm.
4. Position new ball joint so that grease bleed vent in rubber boot is facing inboard.
5. Install tool shown in Fig. 7 and press new joint into arm.
6. Install lube fitting in joint and install stud into steering knuckle.

Fig. 3   Removing caliper mounting pins

Fig. 4   Lower ball joint wear indicator

Fig. 5 Removing upper & lower ball joint stud from knuckle

Fig. 6 Removing lower ball joint

Fig. 7 Installing lower ball joint

Fig. 8 Front shock absorber mountings

Fig. 9 Removing front coil spring

SHOCK ABSORBER, REPLACE

1. Hold shock absorber stem and remove the nut, upper retainer and rubber grommet, Fig. 8.
2. Raise vehicle on a hoist.
3. Remove bolts from lower end of shock absorber and lower the shock from the vehicle

COIL SPRING, REPLACE

1. With shock absorber removed and stabilizer bar removed, raise the vehicle and place jackstands under front braces.
2. Remove the wheel and tire assembly.
3. Place a floor jack under the lower arm and support the arm. Use a block of wood between the control arm and the jack, Fig. 9.
4. Remove the lower ball stud from the knuckle.
5. Remove the tie rod end from the knuckle.
6. Lower the control arm by slowly lowering the jack until the spring can be removed.

MANUAL STEERING GEAR, REPLACE

1. Remove the pot joint coupling clamp bolt at the steering gear wormshaft.

2. Remove "K" brace.
3. Remove pitman arm nut and washer from pitman shaft and mark relation of arm position to shaft.
4. Remove pitman arm with suitable puller.
5. Remove bolts securing gear to frame and remove gear assembly.

POWER STEERING GEAR, REPLACE

1. Remove battery from vehicle to provide access to steering gear.
2. Remove clamp securing intermediate shaft to steering shaft.
3. Disconnect both hydraulic lines from steering gear and allow to drain. Position lines out of way to provide clearance for gear removal.
4. Raise vehicle and remove clamps at stabilizer bar.
5. Remove left front crossmember.
6. Remove pitman shaft nut, then using tool No. J-6632, remove pitman arm from pitman shaft.
7. Remove three steering mounting bolts and lock washers.
8. Lift steering gear and remove pitman arm, then position gear to provide clearance for removal.
9. Remove steering gear and intermediate shaft as an assembly, the steering gear spacer is also removed.
10. Remove plastic shield.
11. Remove pot joint clamp and separate steering gear from pot joint.
12. Remove pot joint from intermediate shaft.

POWER STEERING PUMP, REPLACE

Removal

1. Disconnect hoses at pump or steering gear.
2. Cap or plug all open ports and hoses.
3. Loosen pump adjusting bolt and remove pump belt.

NOTE: It may be necessary to remove other belts vbefore gaining access to pump belt.

4. Remove pump assembly to mounting bracket bolts and remove pump assembly.

Installation

1. Position pump assembly to mounting bracket and install mounting bolts loosely.
2. Connect and tighten power steering hoses to steering gear or pump.
3. Fill reservoir. Bleed pump by turning pulley counter-clockwise until air bubbles cease to appear.
4. Tighten mounting bracket to pump assembly bolts securely.
5. Install pump belt and tighten according to specs given in belt tension chart.
6. Tighten adjusting bolt.
7. Bleed system as follows:
   a. Start engine and run for about two seconds. Add oil if necessary.
   b. Raise and support front end and increase engine speed to approximately 1500 rpm.
   c. Turn wheels right and left, lightly contacting the wheel stops.
   d. Add oil if necessary.
   e. Lower vehicle and repeat procedure.
   f. Check oil level and refill as required.

1977–80 CHEV. MONZA
BUICK SKYHAWK • OLDS STARFIRE
PONT. SUNBIRD

INDEX OF SERVICE OPERATIONS

NOTE: Refer to the back of this manual for vehicle manufacturer's special service tool suppliers.

VEHICLE IDENTIFICATION LOCATION

On top of instrument panel, left front.

ENGINE NUMBER LOCATION

4-140 Cyl: On pad at right side of cylinder block, above starter.

4-151 Exc. Crossflow Engine: On pad at right front side by distributor shaft hole.

4-151 Crossflow Engine: On pad at left front corner of engine above water pump.

V6 & V8: On pad at front right hand side of cylinder block.

ENGINE IDENTIFICATION CODE

4-140 & Chevrolet V8 engines are identified by the code letters immediately following the engine number. 4-151 engines are identified by the code letters on the pad. V6 engines are identified by the code letters immediately preceding the engine number.

Monza

Year/Engine	V.I.N. Code[5]	Engine Code
1977		
4-140	B	CAY, CAZ, CBK, CBL
4-140	B	CBS, CBT, CBU, CBW
4-140	B	CBX, CBY, CBZ
V8-305	U	CPK, CPL, CPU, CPX
V8-305	U	CRC, CRD
1978		
4-151	V	WB, WD, WH
4-151	V	XL, XN
4-151	V	AC, AD
4-151	V	ZA, ZB, ZC, ZD, ZF
4-151	V	ZH, ZJ, ZK, ZL, ZN
V6-196	C	PC, PD
V6-231	—	OC, OD, OE, OF
V8-305	U	CTA, CTB, CTC, CTD, CTF
1979		
4-151	I, V	AB, AC, AD, AF, AM
4-151	I, V	WD, WJ, XJ, XK
4-151	I, V	ZA, ZB, ZP, ZR
V6-196	C	FC, FD
V6-231A	A	NA, NB, NC, NF
V8-305	G	DNA, DNB, DNC, DND
V8-305	G	DTK, DTL
1980		
4-151	V	A7, A9
4-151	V	XC, XD
4-151	V	WD, WJ
4-151	V	XC, XD
V6-231	A	EX, EY, EZ
V6-231	A	OA, OB, OC

Skyhawk

Year/Engine	V.I.N. Code[5]	Engine Code
1977		
V6-231	C	SA, SB, SD
V6-231	C	SO, SX, SY
1978		
V6-231	A, G, 2	OA, OB, OC
V6-231	A, G, 2	OD, OE, OF
V6-231	A, G, 2	OG
1979		
V6-231	A, C, 2	NA, NB, NC
V6-231	A, C, 2	N3, NG, NH
V6-231	A, C, 2	NM
1980		
V6-231	A	EL, EN, EX, EY, EZ
V6-231	A	OA, OB, OC

Starfire

Year/Engine	V.I.N. Code[5]	Engine Code
1977		
4-140 Std. Tr.①	B	CAY, CBS
4-140 Std. Tr.②	B	CAZ, CBL
4-140 Auto. Tr.①	B	CBT
4-140 Auto. Tr.②	B	CBL

Starfire—cont'd.

Year/Engine	V.I.N. Code[5]	Engine Code
4-140 Std. Tr.③	B	CBS
4-140 Auto. Tr.③	B	CBT
V6-231 Std. Tr.①	C	SA
V6-231 Std. Tr.②	C	SB
V6-231 Auto. Tr.①	C	SD, SW
V6-231 Auto. Tr.②	C	SE, SY
V6-231 Auto. Tr.③	C	SF
V6-231 Std. Tr.①	C	FH
V6-231 Std. Tr.②	C	FO
V6-231 Auto. Tr.①	C	FI
V6-231 Auto. Tr.②	C	FJ
V6-231	C	SQ, SR
V8-305 Auto. Trans.①	U	CRL
V8-305 Auto. Trans.②	U	CRM, CRS
V8-305 Auto. Trans.③	U	CRT
V8-305	U	CPX, CPY
1978		
4-151 Auto. Trans.①	V	XL, XN
4-151 Man. Trans.①	V	WB, WD, WH
4-151 Auto. Trans.②	1	ZK, ZJ
V6-231 Man. Trans.②	A	OA
V6-231 Auto. Trans.①	A	ED, OB
V6-231 Man. Trans.②	A	OD
V6-231 Man. Trans.②	A	OE
V6-231 Man. Trans.②	A	OF
V6-231 Auto. Trans.③	A	OC
V6-231	A	OH
V8-305 Man. Trans.①	U	CTA
V8-305 Auto. Trans.②	U	CTB
V8-305 Auto. Trans.①	U	CTF
V8-305 Auto. Trans.③	U	CTD
1979		
4-151 Auto. Trans.④	V	XJ, XK
4-151 Man. Trans.④	V	WJ, WM
4-151 Auto. Trans.②	1	ZP, ZR
4-151 Man. Trans.①	1	AF, AH
V6-231 Auto. Trans.④	A	NB, NM
V6-231 Auto. Trans.①	AL	NH
V6-231 Man. Trans.④	A	NA
V6-231 Man. Trans.②	A	NC
V6-231 Auto. Trans.③	A	NE
V6-231 Auto. Trans.③	A	SM, SS
V8-305 Auto. Trans.④	G	DTL
V8-305 Man. Trans.④	G	DTK
V8-305 Auto. Trans.②	G	DND
1980		
4-151 Auto. Trans.①	V	XC, XD
4-151 Man. Trans.①	V	WD, WJ
4-151 Auto. Trans.①	V	ZA, ZB
4-151 Man. Trans.①	V	A7, A9
V6-231 Auto. Trans.①	A	EZ, OA
V6-231 Man. Trans.①	A	EX
V6-231 Auto. Trans.②	A	OB, OC
V6-231 Auto. Trans.②	A	EY

Sunbird

Year/Engine	V.I.N. Code[5]	Engine Code
1977		
4-140 Std. Tr.①	B	CAY, CBS, CBZ
4-140 Std. Tr.②	B	CAZ, CBK, CBV
4-140 Std. Tr.③	B	CBS, CBZ
4-140 Auto. Tr.①③	B	CBT
4-140	B	CAK, CBL, CBU
4-140	B	CBW, CBX, CBY

Sunbird—cont'd.

Year/Engine	V.I.N. Code[5]	Engine Code
4-151 Std. Tr.①	V	WC, WD
4-151 Auto. Tr.①	VV	YL, YM
4-151 Auto. Tr.②	V	ZH, ZJ
4-151	V	ZD, ZF, ZN, ZP
V6-231 Std. Tr.①	C	SA
V6-231 Std. Tr.②	C	SB
V6-231 Auto. Tr.①	C	SD
V6-231 Auto. Tr.②	C	SY
V6-231 Auto. Tr.②	C	SX
V6-231	C	SO
1978		
4-151 Man. Trans.①	V, 1	WB, WD, WH
4-151 Auto. Trans.①	V, 1	XN, XL
4-151 Auto. Trans.②	V, 1	ZJ, ZK
4-151	V, 1	AC, AD
4-151	V, 1	ZA, ZB, ZC, ZD
4-151	V, 1	ZH, ZF, ZL, ZN
V6-231 Auto. Trans.①	A	ED
V6-231 Man. Trans.①	A	OA
V6-231 Auto. Trans.②	A	EK, EL, EE, OE, EG
V6-231 Man. Trans.②	A	OD
V6-231 Auto. Trans.③	A	OC
V6-231 Man. Trans.②	A	OF
V6-231	A	OE, OB
1979		
4-151 Man. Trans.②	V, 1	AF, AH
4-151 Man. Trans.④	V, 1	WJ, WM
4-151 Auto. Trans.④	V, 1	XJ, XK
4-151 Auto. Trans.②	V, 1	ZP, ZR
V6-231 Man. Trans.④	A	NA, NG, RA
V6-231 Man. Trans.②	A	NC
V6-231 Auto. Trans.④	A	NK, NL, NM
V6-231 Auto. Trans.②	A	RG, RH, RW, RY
V8-305 Auto. Trans.②	G	DND
V8-305 Auto. Trans.④	G	DNJ, DTL
V8-305 Man. Trans.④	G	DTK, DTM
4-151 Auto. Trans.①	V, 1	XC, XD
4-151 Man. Trans.①	V, 1	WD, WJ
4-151 Auto. Trans.①	V, 1	ZA, ZB
4-151 Man. Trans.②	V, 1	A7, A9
V6-231 Auto. Trans.①	A	EB, EC, EO, EP
V6-231 Auto. Trans.①	A	EZ, OA, OK, OL
V6-231 Man. Trans.①	A	EA, EJ, OX
V6-231 Auto. Trans.②	A	EF, EG, ES, ET
V6-231 Auto. Trans.②	A	OB, OC, OM, ON
V6-231 Man. Trans.①	A	EY
1980		
4-151	V	A7, A9
4-151	V	WD, WJ
4-151	V	XC, XD
4-151	V	ZA, ZB
V6-231	A	EX, EY, EZ
V6-231	A	OA, OB, OC

①—Except California.
②—California.
③—High altitude.
④—Exc. High altitude & Calif.
⑤—Fifth digit of the V.I.N. denotes the engine code.

GRILLE IDENTIFICATION

1977 Towne Coupe with Sport Option

1977–78 Oldsmobile Starfire

1977 Chevrolet Monza Towne Coupe Less Sport Option

1977–78 Buick Skyhawk

1978 Pontiac Sunbird

1977 Pontiac Sunbird

1977 Pontiac Formula Sunbird

1979–80 Buick Skyhawk

1978–80 Chevrolet Monza

**1978–79 Chevrolet Monza 2+2
1980 Chevrolet Monza Spyder**

1979 Pontiac Sunbird Sport Safari

1979 Oldsmobile Starfire

1979 Pontiac Sunbird Coupe & Hatchback

1980 Oldsmobile Starfire

1980 Pontiac Sunbird

GENERAL ENGINE SPECIFICATIONS

Year	Engine CID①/Liter	Engine V.I.N. Code②	Carburetor	Bore and Stroke	Compression Ratio	Net H.P. @ R.P.M.③	Maximum Torque Lbs. Ft. @ R.P.M.	Normal Oil Pressure Pounds
1977	4-140, 2.3L	B	5210C, 2Bbl⑤	3.501 × 3.625	8.0	84 @ 4400	117 @ 2400	36–45
	4-151, 2.5L	V	5210C, 2Bbl⑤	4.00 × 3.00	8.3	87 @ 4400	128 @ 2400	36–41
	V6-231, 3.8L	C	2GC, 2Bbl④	3.80 × 3.40	8.0	105 @ 3200	185 @ 2000	37
	V8-305, 5.0L	U	2GC, 2Bbl④	3.736 × 3.48	8.5	145 @ 3800	245 @ 2400	32–40
1978	4-151, 2.5L	V	5210C, 2Bbl⑤⑥	4.00 × 3.00	8.3	85 @ 4400	123 @ 2800	36–41
	V6-196, 3.2L	C	2GE, 2Bbl④	3.50 × 3.40	8.0	86 @ 3600	160 @ 2000	37
	V6-231, 3.8L	A	2GE, 2Bbl④	3.80 × 3.40	8.0	103 @ 3800	180 @ 2000	37
	V8-305, 5.0L	U	2GC, 2Bbl④	3.736 × 3.48	8.5	135 @ 3800	240 @ 2000	32–40
	V8-305, 5.0L	G	2GC, 2Bbl④	3.736 × 3.48	8.5	145 @ 3800	245 @ 2400	32–40
1979	4-151, 2.5L	V	2SE, 2Bbl④	4.00 × 3.00	8.3	85 @ 4400	123 @ 2800	36–41
	4-151, 2.5L	9	6510, 2Bbl⑤	4.00 × 3.00	8.3	90 @ 4400	128 @ 2400	36–41
	V6-196, 3.2L	C	M2ME, 2Bbl④	3.50 × 3.40	8.0	105 @ 4000	160 @ 2000	37
	V6-231, 3.8L	A	M2ME, 2Bbl④	3.80 × 3.40	8.0	115 @ 3800	190 @ 2000	37
	V8-305, 5.0L	G	M2MC, 2Bbl④	3.736 × 3.48	8.4	130 @ 3200	245 @ 2000	32–40
1980	4-151, 2.5L	9	2SE, 2Bbl④	4.00 × 3.00	8.2	90 @ 4000	134 @ 2400	36–41
	4-151, 2.5L	5	E2SE, 2Bbl④	4.00 × 3.00	8.2	90 @ 4000	130 @ 2400	36–41
	V6-231, 3.8L	A	M2ME, 2Bbl④	3.80 × 3.40	8.0	115 @ 3800	188 @ 2000	37

①—CID—cubic inch displacement.
②—The fifth digit in the V.I.N. denotes engine code.
③—Ratings are net—As installed in vehicle.
④—Rochester.
⑤—Holley.
⑥—Calif. only.

WHEEL ALIGNMENT SPECIFICATIONS

Year	Model	Caster Angle, Degrees Limits	Caster Angle, Degrees Desired	Camber Angle, Degrees Limits Left	Camber Angle, Degrees Limits Right	Camber Angle, Degrees Desired Left	Camber Angle, Degrees Desired Right	Toe-In. Inch	Toe-Out on Turns, Deg.① Outer Wheel	Toe-Out on Turns, Deg.① Inner Wheel
1977	All	−1¼ to −¼	−¾	−¼ to +¾	−¼ to +¾	+¼	+¼	0 to ⅛②	—	—
1978–79	All	−1.3 to −.3	−.8	−.3 to +.7	−.3 to +.7	+.2	+.2	0 to ⅛②	—	—
1980	Monza	−1.3 to −.3	−.8	−.6 to +1	−.6 to +1	+.4	+.4	−⅖ to +1/20	—	—
	Skyhawk	−.8 to −.7	−.75	−.3 to −.2	−.3 to −.2	+¼	+¼	0 to ⅛	—	—
	Starfire③	0 to −2	−1	0 to +1½	0 to +1½	+¾	+¾	1/16	—	—
	Starfire④	0 to +2	+1	0 to +1½	0 to +1½	+¾	+¾	1/16	—	—
	Sunbird	−¼ to −1¼	−¾	−¾ to +¼	−¾ to +¼	+¼	+¼	1/16②	—	—

①—Incorrect toe out when other adjustments are correct indicates bent steering arms.
②—Toe-out.
③—Manual steer.
④—Power steer.

TUNE UP SPECIFICATIONS

The following specifications are published from the latest information available. This
data should be used only in the absence of a decal affixed in the engine compartment.

★ When using a timing light, disconnect vacuum hose or tube at distributor and plug opening in hose or tube so idle speed will not be affected.

● When checking compression, lowest cylinder must be within 80 percent of highest.

▲ Before removing wires from distributor cap, determine location of No. 1 wire in cap, as distributor position may have been altered from that shown at the end of this chart.

☞ Spark plug types shown in this chart are recommendations of the original vehicle manufacturer and not MOTOR. Check local sources for other spark plug manufacturers listings.

Year & Engine	Spark Plug Type ☞	Gap	Firing Order Fig. ▲	Ignition Timing BTDC①★ Man. Trans.	Auto. Trans.	Mark Fig.	Curb Idle Speed② Man. Trans.	Auto. Trans.	Fast Idle Speed Man. Trans.	Auto. Trans.	Fuel Pump Pressure
1977											
4-140 Exc. Calif. & High Alt.	R43TS	.035	A	TDC	2°	B	700/1250	650/850D	2500③	2500③	3–4½
4-140 Calif.	R43TS	.035	A	⑧	TDC	B	800/1250	650/850D	2500③	2500③	3–4½
4-140 High Alt.	R43TS	.035	A	TDC	2°	B	800/1250	700/850D	2500③	2500③	3–4½
4-151 Exc. Calif.	R44TSX	.060	E	14⑨	14°	F	⑩	⑪	2200③	2400③	4–5½
4-151 Calif.	R44TSX	.060	E	—	12°	F	—	⑪	—	2400③	4–5½
V6-231⑫	⑬	⑬	G	12°	12°	H⑭	600/800	600D	—	—	3–4½
V6-231⑮	R46TSX	.060	I	—	15°	J⑭	—	600/670D	—	—	3–4½
V8-305 Exc. Calif. & High Alt.	R45TS	.045	C	8°	8°	D	600/700	500/700D	—	—	7½–9
V8-305 Calif.	R45TS	.045	C	—	6°	D	—	500/700D	—	—	7½–9
V8-305 High Alt.	R45TS	.045	C	—	⑯	D	—	600/700D	—	—	7½–9
1978											
4-151 Exc. Calif.	R43TSX	.060	E	14°⑨	12°⑨	F	⑰	⑪	2200③	2200③	4–5½
4-151 Calif.	R43TSX	.060	E	—	14°⑨	F	—	⑪	—	2400③	4–5½
V6-196	R46TSX	.060	I	15°	15°	J⑭	600/800	600D	—	—	3–4½
V6-231	R46TSX	.060	I	15°	15°	J⑭	600/800	600/670D	—	—	3–4½
V8-305 Exc. Calif. & High Alt.	R45TS	.045	C	4°	4°	D	600	500D	—	—	7½–9
V8-305 Calif.	R45TS	.045	C	—	6°	D	—	500D	—	—	7½–9
V8-305 High Alt.	R45TS	.045	C	—	8°	D	—	600D	—	—	7½–9
1979											
4-151 Exc. Calif.	R43TSX	.060	E	12°	12°	F	④	⑪	2200	2400	4–5½
4-151 Calif.	R43TSX	.060	E	14°⑨	14°⑨	F	⑦	⑪	2000	2400	4–5½
V6-196	⑤	.060	I	15°	15°	J⑭	600/800	550/670D	2200	2200	3–4½
V6-231	⑤	.060	I	15°	15°	J⑭	600/800	⑥	2200	2200	3–4½
V8-305 Exc. Calif.	R45TS	.045	C	4°	4°	D	600	500/600D	1300	1600	7½–9
V8-305 Calif.	R45TS	.045	C	—	2°	D	—	600/650D	—	1600	7½–9
1980											
4-151 Exc. Calif.	R44TSX	.060	E	12°	12°	F	1000	650D	—	—	6½–8
4-151 Calif.	R44TSX	.060	E	14°	14°	F	1000	650D	—	—	6½–8
V6-231	⑤	.060	I	15°	15°	J⑭	800	600D	—	—	3–4½

Continued

TUNE UP NOTES

①—BTDC—Before top dead center.
②—Idle speed on man. trans. vehicles is adjusted in Neutral & on auto. trans. equipped vehicles is adjusted in Drive unless otherwise specified. Where two idle speeds are listed, the higher speed is with the A/C or idle solenoid energized.
③—On high step of fast idle cam with A/C off.
④—Less A/C, 500/900 RPM; with A/C, 900/1250 RPM.
⑤—R45TSX or R46TSX.
⑥—Less idle solenoid, 600D RPM; with idle solenoid, 550/670D RPM.
⑦—These engines use two different harmonic

balancers. The harmonic balancer used on late models has two timing marks. The mark measuring 1/16 inch is used when setting timing with a conventional timing light. The mark measuring 1/8 inch is used when setting timing with magnetic timing equipment.
⑧—2°ATDC, after top dead center.
⑨—At 1000 RPM.
⑩—Less A/C, 500/1000 RPM; with A/C, 500/1200 RPM.
⑪—Less A/C, 500/650D RPM; with A/C, 650/850D RPM.
⑫—Except even fire engine.

⑬—On early models, use R46TS gapped at .040"; on late models, use R46TSX gapped at .060".
⑭—The harmonic balancer on these engines has two timing marks. The mark measuring 1/16 inch is used when setting timing with a conventional timing light. The mark measuring 1/8 inch is used when setting timing with magnetic timing equipment.
⑮—Even fire engine.
⑯—Except engine code CPU, 8°BTDC; engine code CPU, 6°BTDC.
⑰—Less A/C, 500/1000 RPM; with A/C, 900/1200 RPM.

Fig. A

Fig. B

Fig. C

Fig. D

Fig. E

Fig. F

Fig. G

Fig. H

Fig. I

Fig. J

DISTRIBUTOR SPECIFICATIONS

★ If unit is checked on vehicle double the RPM and degrees to get crankshaft figures.

| Distributor Part No.① | Centrifugal Advance Degrees @ RPM of Distributor | | | | | Vacuum Advance | | Distributor Retard |
	Advance Starts	Intermediate Advance			Full Advance	Inches if Vacuum To Start Plunger	Max. Adv. Dist. Deg. @ Vacuum	Max. Ret. Dist. Deg. @ Vacuum
1977								
1103229	0 @ 600	3 @ 800	—	—	10 @ 2200	3½	10 @ 12	—
1103230	0 @ 600	3 @ 800	—	—	10 @ 2200	3½	10 @ 9	—
1103231	0 @ 600	—	—	—	10 @ 2200	3½	10 @ 12	—
1103239	—	—	—	—	—	—	—	—
1103244	—	—	—	—	—	—	—	—
1103252	—	—	—	—	—	—	—	—
1110538	0 @ 425	4 @ 600	—	—	8½ @ 1000	5	12 @ 10	—
1110539	0 @ 425	4 @ 600	—	—	8½ @ 1000	5	12 @ 10	—
1110677	0–2.2 @ 760	8.9–11 @ 1800	—	—	11 @ 2500	6	12¾ @ 20	—
1110686	0–2.15 @ 890	3.15–5.5 @ 1300	8.8–11 @ 1800	—	11 @ 2500	6	4¾ @ 20	—
1978								
1103281	0 @ 500	5 @ 850	—	—	10 @ 1900	4	9 @ 12	—
1103282	0 @ 500	5 @ 850	—	—	10 @ 1900	4	10 @ 10	—
1103312	0 @ 600	—	—	—	10 @ 2200	5	8 @ 11	—
1103328	0 @ 600	—	—	—	10 @ 2200	3½	10 @ 9③	—
1103329	0 @ 600	—	—	—	10 @ 2200	3½	10 @ 12	—
1103365	0 @ 600	—	—	—	10 @ 2200	5	8 @ 11	—
1110695	0–3 @ 1000	—	—	—	9 @ 1800	3–6	12 @ 13④	—
1110731	0–2 @ 1000	—	—	—	7½ @ 1800	4–6	8 @ 9	—
1110732	0–2 @ 1000	—	—	—	7½ @ 1800	4–6	7 @ 13	—
1979								
1103281	1 @ 575	5 @ 850	—	—	10 @ 1900	4	10 @ 13	—
1103285	1 @ 675	6 @ 1000	—	—	11 @ 2100	4	12 @ 7	—
1103365	0 @ 1000	—	—	—	10 @ 2350	5	11 @ 11½	—
1103379	1 @ 575	5 @ 850	—	—	10 @ 1900	2½	11 @ 8½	—
1110677	0 @ 638	—	—	—	10 @ 1800	5	12 @ 9½	—
1110695	0 @ 840	—	—	—	7½ @ 1800	4	12 @ 11	—
1110726	0 @ 600	5 @ 1200	—	—	9 @ 2000	3½	10½ @ 8	—
1110757	0 @ 600	5 @ 1200	—	—	9 @ 2000	3½	10½ @ 8	—
1110766	1 @ 975	—	—	—	7½ @ 1800	4	12½ @ 11½	—
1110767	1 @ 975	—	—	—	7½ @ 1800	3½	10½ @ 12½	—
1110768	1 @ 625	3 @ 1200	—	—	7½ @ 1800	3½	10½ @ 12½	—
1110770	1 @ 975	—	—	—	7½ @ 1800	3	10½ @ 9½	—
1980								
1110554	0 @ 840	—	—	—	7½ @ 1800	3	12 @ 11.9	—
1110555	0 @ 425	3 @ 1200	—	—	7½ @ 1800	4	12 @ 11	—
1110558	0 @ 500	4½ @ 1200	—	—	7 @ 2000	3	7½ @ 5	—
1110559	0 @ 600	4½ @ 1200	—	—	7 @ 2000	3	7½ @ 5	—
1110560	0 @ 500	3½ @ 1000	—	—	7 @ 2325	4	10 @ 10	—

①—Located on distributor housing plate.
②—Monza, 12 @ 12; Sunbird, 10 @ 14.
③—Manual trans., 10° @ 12″.
④—High altitude, 8° @ 9″.

MONZA • (1977–80) SKYHAWK • STARFIRE • SUNBIRD

STARTING MOTOR SPECIFICATIONS

Year	Model	Starter Number	Brush Spring Tension Oz.①	Free Speed Test			Resistance Test	
				Amps.	Volts	R.P.M.①	Amps.	Volts
1977	4-140 Std. Trans.	1108771	35	50–75②	9	6500–10000	—	—
	4-140 Auto. Trans.	1108772	35	50–75②	9	6500–10000	—	—
	4-151	1109412	—	—	—	—	—	—
	V6-231	1108797	35	50–80②	9	5500–10500	—	—
	V8-305	1108790	35	55–80②	9	3500–6000	—	—
1978–79	4-151	1109521	35	45–75②	9	6500–9700	—	—
	4-151	1108771	35	50–75②	9	6500–10000	—	—
	4-151	1108772	35	50–75②	9	6500–10000	—	—
	V6-196	1108797	35	55–80②	9	5500–10500	—	—
	V6-231	1108797	35	55–80②	9	5500–10500	—	—
	V6-231	1109061	35	60–85②	9	6800–10300	—	—
	V8-305	1108415	35	35–75②	9	6000–9000	—	—
	V8-305	1108790	35	55–80②	9	3500–6000	—	—
	V8-305	1109064	35	60–85②	9	6800–10300	—	—
	V8-305	1109524	35	45–70②	9	7000–11900	—	—
1979	V8-305	1109062	35	65–95②	9	7500–10500	—	—
1980	4-151	1109521	35	45–75②	9	6500–9700	—	—
	V6-231	1109061	35	60–85②	9	6800–10300	—	—

①—Minimum.
②—Includes solenoid.

ALTERNATOR & REGULATOR SPECIFICATIONS

Year	Model	Rated Hot Output Amps.	Field Current 12 Volts @ 80° F.	Cold Output @ 14 Volts		Model	Field Relay			Voltage Regulator		
				2000 R.P.M. Amps.	5000 R.P.M. Amps.		Air Gap In.	Point Gap In.	Closing Voltage	Air Gap In.	Point Gap In.	Voltage @ 125° F.
1977	1102881	37	4–4.5	—	33	Integral	—	—	—	—	—	13.6–14.2
	1102854	63	4–4.5	—	60	Integral	—	—	—	—	—	—
1977–78	1102394	37	4–4.5	—	33	Integral	—	—	—	—	—	13.8–14.8②
	1102479	55	4–4.5	—	51	Integral	—	—	—	—	—	13.6–14.2
	1102495	55	4–4.5	—	55①	Integral	—	—	—	—	—	13.6–14.2
	1102858	37	4–4.5	—	33	Integral	—	—	—	—	—	13.6–14.8②
1978	1102394	37	4–4.5	—	33	Integral	—	—	—	—	—	—
	1102478	55	4–4.5	—	51	Integral	—	—	—	—	—	13.6–14.2
	1102479	55	4–4.5	—	51	Integral	—	—	—	—	—	—
	1102495	55	—	—	—	Integral	—	—	—	—	—	—
	1102844	63	4–4.5	—	60	Integral	—	—	—	—	—	13.6–14.2
	1102851	55	4–4.5	—	51	Integral	—	—	—	—	—	—
	1102854	63	4–4.5	—	60	Integral	—	—	—	—	—	13.6–14.2
	1102858	37	4–4.5	—	33	Integral	—	—	—	—	—	—
	1102891	55	4–4.5	—	51	Integral	—	—	—	—	—	—
	1102893	63	4–4.5	—	60	Integral	—	—	—	—	—	—
	1102910	63	4–4.5	—	60	Integral	—	—	—	—	—	13.6–14.2
	1102911	55	4–4.5	—	51	Integral	—	—	—	—	—	13.6–14.2
	1102913	61	4–4.5	—	57	Integral	—	—	—	—	—	13.6–14.2
1979	1102394	37	4–4.5	—	33	Integral	—	—	—	—	—	13.8–14.8
	1102478	55	4–4.5	—	51	Integral	—	—	—	—	—	13.8–14.8
	1102479	55	4–4.5	—	51	Integral	—	—	—	—	—	13.8–14.8
	1102495	55	4–4.5	—	51	Integral	—	—	—	—	—	13.8–14.8
	1102844	63	4–4.5	—	—	Integral	—	—	—	—	—	13.8–14.8

Continued

ALTERNATOR & REGULATOR SPECIFICATIONS—Continued

Year		Alternator					Regulator						
				Cold Output @ 14 Volts			Field Relay			Voltage Regulator			
	Model	Rated Hot Output Amps.	Field Current 12 Volts @ 80° F.	2000 R.P.M. Amps.	5000 R.P.M. Amps.	Model	Air Gap In.	Point Gap In.	Closing Voltage	Air Gap In.	Point Gap In.	Voltage @ 125° F.
	1102854	63	4–4.5	—	—	Integral	—	—	—	—	—	13.8–14.8
	1102881	37	4–4.5	—	33	Integral	—	—	—	—	—	13.8–14.8
	1102910	63	4–4.5	—	—	Integral	—	—	—	—	—	13.8–14.8
	1102911	55	4–4.5	—	51	Integral	—	—	—	—	—	13.8–14.8
	1103033	37	4–4.5	—	33	Integral	—	—	—	—	—	13.8–14.8
	1103059	63	4–4.5	—	—	Integral	—	—	—	—	—	13.8–14.8
1980	1103084	55	—	—	—	Integral	—	—	—	—	—	14.7
	1103085	55	—	—	—	Integral	—	—	—	—	—	14.7
	1103086	63	—	—	—	Integral	—	—	—	—	—	14.7
	1103100	55	—	—	—	Integral	—	—	—	—	—	13.9–14.5
	1103101	37	—	—	—	Integral	—	—	—	—	—	13.9–14.5
	1103102	63	—	—	—	Integral	—	—	—	—	—	13.9–14.5
	1103118	37	—	—	—	Integral	—	—	—	—	—	14.7
	1103120	63	—	—	—	Integral	—	—	—	—	—	14.7
	1103121	63	—	—	—	Integral	—	—	—	—	—	14.7

①—At 5500 RPM.
②—At 85°F.

VALVE SPECIFICATIONS

Year	Engine Model	Valve Lash		Valve Angles		Valve Spring Installed Height	Valve Spring Pressure Lbs. @ In.	Stem Clearance		Stem Diameter	
		Int.	Exh.	Seat	Face			Intake	Exhaust	Intake	Exhaust
1977	4-140	Hydraulic④	Hydraulic④	46	45	1.746	190 @ 1.31	.0010–.0027	.0010–.0027	.3410–.3417	.3410–.3417
	4-151	Hydraulic④	Hydraulic④	46	45	1.69	82 @ 1.66	.0017–.0030	.0017–.0030	.340	.340
	V6-231	Hydraulic④	Hydraulic④	45	45	1.727	168 @ 1.327	.0015–.0032	.0015–.0032	.3402–.3412	.3405–.3412
	V8-305	¾ Turn③		46	45	②	⑤	.0010–.0027	.0010–.0027	.3410–.3417	.3410–.3417
1978	4-151	Hydraulic④	Hydraulic④	46	45	1.69	176 @ 1.254	.0010–.0027	.0010–.0027	.340	.340
	V6-196	Hydraulic④	Hydraulic④	45	45	1.727	168 @ 1.327	.0015–.0035	.0015–.0032	.3402–.3412	.3405–.3412
	V6-231	Hydraulic④	Hydraulic④	45	45	1.727	168 @ 1.327	.0015–.0035	.0015–.0032	.3402–.3412	.3405–.3412
	V8-305	1 Turn③		46	45	②	⑤	.0010–.0027	.0010–.0027	.3410–.3417	.3410–.3417
1979	4-151	Hydraulic④	Hydraulic④	46	45	1.66	151 @ 1.254	.0010–.0027	.0010–.0027	.3418–.3425	.3418–.3425
	V6-196	Hydraulic④	Hydraulic④	45	45	1.727	168 @ 1.34	.0015–.0035	.0015–.0032	.3402–.3412	.3405–.3412
	V6-231	Hydraulic④	Hydraulic④	45	45	1.727	①	.0015–.0035	.0015–.0032	.3402–.3412	.3405–.3412
	V8-305	1 Turn③		46	45	②	⑥	.0010–.0027	.0010–.0027	.3410–.3417	.3410–.3417
1980	4-151	Hydraulic④	Hydraulic④	46	45	1.66	176 @ 1.254	.0010–.0027	.0010–.0027	.3418–.3425	.3418–.3425
	V6-231	Hydraulic④	Hydraulic④	45	45	1.727	①	.0015–.0035	.0015–.0032	.3402–.3412	.3405–.3412

①—Intake 164 @ 1.34, Exhaust 182 @ 1.34.
②—Intake 1.70, Exhaust 1.61.
③—Turn rocker arm stud nut until all lash is eliminated, then tighten nut the additional turn listed.
④—No adjustment.
⑤—Intake 200 @ 1.25; Exhaust 200 @ 1.16.
⑥—Intake, 180 @ 1.25; exhaust 190 @ 1.16.

PISTONS, PINS, RINGS, CRANKSHAFT & BEARINGS

Year	Engine Model	Piston Clearance	Ring End Gap①		Wrist-pin-Diameter	Rod Bearings		Main Bearings		Thrust on Bear. No.	Shaft End Play
			Comp.	Oil		Shaft Diameter	Bearing Clearance	Shaft Diameter	Bearing Clearance		
1977	4-140	.0018–.0028	②	.010	.9272	1.999–2.000	.0007–.0027	2.3004	.0003–.0029	4	.002–.008
	4-151	.0025–.0033	.010	.010	.9272	1.999–2.000	.0006–.0026	2.2983–2.2993	.0003–.0022	5	.0015–.0085

PISTONS, PINS, RINGS, CRANKSHAFT & BEARINGS—Continued

| Year | Engine Model | Piston Clearance | Ring End Gap① | | Wrist-pin-Diameter | Rod Bearings | | Main Bearings | | | |
			Comp.	Oil		Shaft Diameter	Bearing Clearance	Shaft Diameter	Bearing Clearance	Thrust on Bear. No.	Shaft End Play
	V6-231	.0008–.0020	.013	.015	.9393	1.9991–2.000	.0005–.0026	2.4995	.0004–.0015	2	.004–.008
	V8-305	.0007–.0027	.010	.015	.9272	2.099–2.100	.0013–.0035	2.4502	③	5	.002–.007
1978	4-151	.0025–.0033	.010	.010	.9400	2.000	.0005–.0026	2.2983–2.2993	.0002–.0022	5	.0015–.0085
	V6-196	.0008–.0020	.010	.015	.9393	2.2487–2.2495	.0005–.0026	2.4995	.0004–.0017	2	.0004–.0008
	V6-231	.0008–.0020	.010	.015	.9393	2.2487–2.2495	.0005–.0026	2.4995	.0003–.0017	2	.003–.009
	V8-305	.0007–.0027	.010	.015	.9272	2.099–2.100	.0013–.0035	④	③	5	.002–.006
1979	4-151	.0025–.0033	②	.015	.940	2.000	.0005–.0026	2.300	.0005–.0022	5	.0035–.0085
	V6-196	.0008–.0020	.010	.010	.9393	2.2487–2.2495	.0005–.0026	2.4995	.0003–.0018	2	.003–.009
	V6-231	.0008–.0020	.013	.015	.9393	2.2487–2.2495	.0005–.0026	2.4995	.0003–.0018	2	.003–.009
	V8-305	.0007–.0017	.010	.015	.9272	2.099–2.100	.0013–.0035	④	③	5	.002–.006
1980	4-151	.0025–.0033	.010	.015	.940	2.000	.0005–.0026	2.300	.0005–.0022	5	.0035–.0085
	V6-231	.0008–.0020	.013	.015	.9393	2.2487–2.2495	.0005–.0026	2.4995	.0003–.0018	2	.003–.009

①—Fit rings in tapered bore for clearance listed in tightest portion of ring travel.
②—#1—.015", #2—.009".
③—#1—.0008—.0020, #2, 3 & 4—.0011—.0023, #5—.0017–.0032.
④—#1—2.4484–2.4493, #2, 3 & 4— 2.4481–2.4490, #5—2.4479–2.4488.

BRAKE SPECIFICATIONS

| Year | Model | Brake Drum Inside Diameter | Wheel Cylinder Bore Diameter | | | Master Cylinder Bore Diameter | | |
			Disc Brake	Front Drum Brake	Rear Drum Brake	Disc Brakes	Drum Brakes	Power Brakes
1977	All	9½	2½	—	①	②	—	②
1978–79	All	③	2½	—	11/16	7/8	—	7/8
1980	All	9½	2½	—	11/16	7/8	—	7/8

①—Exc. Sunbird, ¾"; Sunbird, 11/16".
②—Exc. Sunbird, & 1977 Monza, ¾"; Sunbird & 1977 Monza 7/8".
③—Exc. Monza, 97/8"; Monza 9½".

ENGINE TIGHTENING SPECIFICATIONS★

★ Torque specifications are for clean and lightly lubricated threads only. Dry or dirty threads produce increased friction which prevents accurate measurement of tightness.

Year	Engine Model	Spark Plugs Ft. Lbs.	Cylinder Head Bolts Ft. Lbs.	Intake Manifold Ft. Lbs.	Exhaust Manifold Ft. Lbs.	Rocker Arm Stud Ft. Lbs.	Cam Cover Ft. Lbs.①	Connecting Rod Cap Bolts Ft. Lbs.	Main Bearing Cap Bolts Ft. Lbs.	Flywheel to Crankshaft Ft. Lbs.	Vibration Damper or Pulley Ft. Lbs.
1977	4-140	20	60	30	30	—	80②	35	65	65	80
	V6-231	20	80	45	25	30③	4	40	⑥	60	175
	V8-262, 305, 350	15	65	30	20④	—	45②	45	70	60	60
1977	4-151	15	95	⑤	⑤	—	—	32	65	55	160
1978	4-151	15	95	⑤	⑤	20	85②	30	65	55	160
1978–79	V6-196	20	80	45	25	30③	4	40	100	60	225
	V6-231	20	80	45	25	30③	4	40	100	60	225
	V8-305	22	65	30	20④	—	⑦	45	80	60	60
1979–80	4-151	15	90	29	44	75	6	32	70	⑧	200
1980	V6-231	20	80	45	25	30③	4	40	100	60	225

①—Rocker arm cover ft. lbs.
②—In. lbs.
③—Rocker arm shaft to cylinder head.
④—Inside bolts 30 ft. lbs.
⑤—Bolts, 40; Nuts, 30.
⑥—1976, 115 ft. lbs.; 1977, 100 ft. lbs.
⑦—1978, 45 in. lbs.; 1979, 50 in. lbs.
⑧—1979, 50 ft. lbs.; 1980, 44 ft. lbs.

COOLING SYSTEM & CAPACITY DATA

Year	Model or Engine	Cooling Capacity, Qts.		Radiator Cap Relief Pressure, Lbs.	Thermo. Opening Temp.	Fuel Tank Gals.	Engine Oil Refill Qts. ①	Transmission Oil				Rear Axle Oil Pints
		Less A/C	With A/C					3 Speed Pints	4 Speed Pints	5 Speed Pints	Auto. Trans. Quts. ②	
1977	4-140	8	8	15	195	18½	3	—	2.4	3½	④	3.5
	4-151	12	12	15	195	18½	3	—	2.4	3½	④	3.5
	V6-231	⑦	⑦	15	195	18½	4	—	2.4	3½	④	⑥
	V8-305	18	18	15	195	18½	4	—	2.4	3½	④	2.8
1978–79	4-151	10.7	10.7	15	195	⑤	3	—	3	3½	④	3½③
	V6-196	12	12	15	195	⑤	4	—	3	3½	④	3½③
	V6-231	12	12	15	195	⑤	4	—	3	3½	④	3½③
	V8-305	16.6	18.0	15	195	⑤	4	—	3	3½	④	3½③
1980	Monza 4-151	11¾	11¾	15	195	18½	3⑧	—	3.4	—	⑨	3½
	Starfire 4-151	11	11.5	15	195	18½	3⑧	—	3.12	—	⑨	3½
	Sunbird 4-151	10.9	—	15	195	18½	3⑧	—	3	—	⑨	3½
	Monza V6-231	12	12	15	195	18½	4	—	3.4	—	⑩	3½
	Skyhawk V6-231	12.35	12.72	15	195	18½	4	—	—	—	⑩	3½
	Starfire V6-231	12	12.5	15	195	18½	4	—	3.12	—	⑩	3½
	Sunbird V6-231	12.3	12.3	15	195	18½	4	—	3	—	⑩	3½

①—Add 1 qt. with filter change.
②—Approximate. Make final check with dip stick.
③—3¾ qts. on Skyhawk.
④—Refill 3 qts., total capacity 10 qts.
⑤—Exc. Sunbird Station Wagon, Monza "S" Coupe & Station Wagon 18½; Sunbird Station Wagon 16; Monza "S" Coupe & Station Wagon 15.
⑥—Skyhawk; 2.8. Sunbird; 3.5.
⑦—Exc. Sunbird, 12 qts.; Sunbird 13 qts.
⑧—With or without filter change.
⑨—T.H.M. 200, refill, 3½ qts.; total capacity, 9½ qts.
⑩—T.H.M. 350, refill, 3¼ qts.; total capacity, 12¼ qts.

REAR AXLE SPECIFICATIONS

Year	Model	Carrier Type	Ring Gear & Pinion Backlash		Pinion Bearing Preload			Differential Bearing Preload		
			Method	Adjustment	Method	New Bearings Inch-Lbs.	Used Bearings Inch-Lbs.	Method	New Bearings Inch-Lbs.	Used Bearings Inch-Lbs.
1977–80	Monza	Integral	Shim	.005–.008	Spacer	10–25	8–12	Shim	—	—
	Skyhawk	Integral	Shim	.006–.008	Spacer	10–25	8–12	Shim	35–40	20–25
	Starfire	Integral	Shim	.005–.009	Spacer	10–25	8–12	Shim	—	—
	Sunbird	Integral	Shim	.006–.008	Spacer	10–25	8–12	Shim	35–40	20–25

Electrical Section

STARTER, REPLACE

Exc. V6-196, 231

1. Disconnect battery ground cable and disconnect all wires at solenoid terminals.

NOTE: Reinstall the nuts on the terminals as each wire is removed, as thread size is different and if mixed, stripping of threads may occur.

2. Loosen starter front bracket and remove the two mounting bolts.
3. Remove from bracket bolt or nut and rotate brace clear of work area, then remove starter from vehicle by lowering front end of starter first.
4. Reverse procedure to install.

V6-196, 231

1. Disconnect battery ground cable.
2. On models with manual transmission loosen engine crossmember attaching bolts.
3. On models with automatic transmission, remove crossover pipe and flywheel inspection cover.
4. On all models, remove starter attaching bolts, then lower starter and disconnect wiring.

NOTE: On models with manual transmission, it may be necessary to pull down on engine crossmember to gain clearance when removing starter assembly.

5. Reverse procedure to install.

IGNITION LOCK, REPLACE

Late 1978 & 1979–80

1. Remove steering wheel as described un-

Fig. 1   Ignition lock removal. Late 1978 & 1979–80

Fig. 1A   Ignition lock removal 1977 & early 1978

der Horn Sounder and Steering Wheel.
2. Remove turn signal switch as described under Turn Signal Switch, Replace, then remove buzzer switch.
3. Place ignition switch in Run position, then remove lock cylinder retaining screw and lock cylinder.
4. To install, rotate lock cylinder to stop while holding housing, Fig. 1. Align cylinder key with keyway in housing, then push lock cylinder assembly into housing until fully seated.
5. Install lock cylinder retaining screw. Torque screw to 40 in. lbs. for standard columns. On adjustable columns, torque retaining screw to 22 in. lbs.
6. Install buzzer switch, turn signal switch and steering wheel.

1977 & Early 1978

1. Remove steering wheel as described under "Horn Sounder & Steering Wheel" procedure.
2. On 1978 Coupe, S Coupe and station wagon models, remove turn signal switch as described under "Turn Signal Switch, Replace" procedure.
3. On all models except 1978 Coupe, S Coupe and station wagon, pull directional switch rearward far enough to slip it over end of shaft. Do not pull harness out of column.
4. With ignition switch in "Run" position, insert a small screwdriver or similar tool into turn signal housing slot, Fig. 1A. Keeping tool to right side of slot, break housing flash loose and at same time

depress spring latch at lower end of lock cylinder.
5. Remove lock cylinder from housing.

IGNITION SWITCH, REPLACE

Exc. 1978–79 Station Wagon

1. Disconnect battery ground cable.
2. Remove left A/C outlet duct.
3. Remove steering column to support retaining nuts and allow column to lower.
4. Disconnect connector from switch, then remove switch retaining screws and remove switch.
5. Reverse procedure to install with ignition switch in "lock" position, Fig. 2.

1978–79 Station Wagon

The ignition switch is mounted on the top of the steering column jacket near the front of the dash. It is located inside the channel section of the brake pedal support and is completely inaccessible without first lowering the steering column.
1. Lower the steering column and be sure it is properly supported before proceeding.
2. The switch should be positioned in Lock position before removing, Fig. 2.

3. Unfasten and remove the switch, detaching it from the actuating rod.
4. When installing, make sure the lock and the switch are in the Lock position. Then install the activating rod into the switch and fasten the switch.

NEUTRAL SAFETY SWITCH, REPLACE

Exc. 1978–79 Station Wagon

1. Disconnect battery ground cable.
2. Remove console cover.
3. Disconnect connector from switch, then remove switch retaining screws and remove switch.
4. Reverse procedure to install and make certain that switch is correctly adjusted.

1978–79 Station Wagon

1. Remove screws securing floor console, Fig. 3.
2. Disconnect electrical plugs on backup contacts and neutral start contacts of switch assembly.
3. Place shift lever in Neutral.
4. Remove two screws securing shift indicator plate.
5. Remove two screws securing shift lever curved cover.
6. Remove two screws securing switch to lever assembly.

Fig. 2   Ignition switch assembly

Fig. 3   Neutral safety switch installation. 1978–79 Station Wagon

Fig. 4   Light switch replacement. 1978–79 Station Wagon

Fig. 5 Compressing lock plate and removing retaining ring

Fig. 6 Taping turn signal connector and wires

Fig. 7 Removing turn signal switch

NOTE: Screws are hidden beneath lever cover.

7. Tilt switch to right as you lift switch out of lever hole.
8. When installing switch, make sure it is in Neutral position. When switch is installed shifting out of Neutral will shear the switch plastic locating pin.

LIGHT SWITCH, REPLACE

Exc. 1978–79 Station Wagon

1. Disconnect battery ground cable.
2. Remove left A/C duct if equipped.
3. Reaching under instrument panel, release and pull switch knob and shaft assembly out of switch.
4. Remove switch bezel retaining nut, then

disconnect switch connector and remove switch.
5. Reverse procedure to install.

1978–79 Station Wagon

1. Disconnect ground cable at battery.
2. Pull headlamp switch knob to "ON" position.
3. Reach under instrument panel and depress switch shaft retainer button while pulling on the switch control shaft knob.
4. With a large bladed screwdriver, remove the light switch ferrule nut from front of instrument panel, Fig. 4.
5. Disconnect the multi-contact connector from side of switch and remove switch.

STOP LIGHT SWITCH, REPLACE

1. Reach under right side of instrument panel at brake pedal support and disconnect wiring harness connector at switch.
2. Pull switch from mounting bracket.
3. When installing switch, adjust by bring-

ing brake pedal to normal position. Electrical contact should be make when pedal is depressed 3/8 to 5/8 inch. To adjust, the switch may be rotated or pulled in the clip.

CLUTCH START SWITCH, REPLACE

NOTE: The clutch pedal must be fully depressed and the ignition switch in START position for the vehicle to start.

The clutch switch assembly mounts with two tangs to the clutch pedal brace switch pivot bracket and the clutch pedal arm.
1. Under the instrument panel on the clutch pedal support, remove the multi-contact connector from switch.
2. Compress switch assembly actuating shaft barb retainer and push out of clutch pedal.
3. Compress switch assembly pivot bracket barb and lift off switch.
4. When installing new switch, no adjustments are necessary as the switch is self aligning.

TURN SIGNAL SWITCH, REPLACE

1. Remove steering wheel with suitable puller.
2. Remove three cover screws and lift cover off the shaft.

NOTE: These screws have plastic retainers on the back of the cover so it is not necessary to completely remove these screws.

3. Place Lock Plate Compressing Tool J23653, Fig. 5, on end of steering shaft and compress the lock plate as far as possible using the shaft nut as shown. Pry the round wire shap ring out of the shaft grove and discard the ring. Remove tool and lift lock plate and cover off end of shaft.
4. Slide the signal cancelling cam, upper bearing preload spring and thrust washer off the end of the shaft.
5. Remove turn signal lever screw and remove the lever.
6. Push hazard warning knot in and unscrew the knob.

Fig. 8 Air distribution ducts and outlets on air conditioned models. 1978–79 Station Wagon

Fig. 9 Removing temperature door bell crank on air conditioned vehicles. 1978—79 Station Wagon

Fig. 10 Instrument panel pad. Except Station Wagon

7. Wrap upper part of connector with tape, Fig. 6, to prevent snagging of wires during switch removal.
8. Remove three screws on switch and pull switch straight up through housing, Fig. 7.

HORN SOUNDER & STEERING WHEEL, REPLACE

1. Disconnect battery ground cable.
2. On regular production steering wheel models, remove the two screws securing the steering wheel shroud from beneath the wheel and remove the shroud. On optional wheels models, pry off horn button cap.
3. Remove steering wheel nut and use a suitable puller to remove the steering wheel.

RADIO, REPLACE

1. Disconnect battery ground cable.
2. Remove radio control knobs and bezels, then the shaft nuts and washers.
3. Disconnect antenna lead from radio rear and remove screws securing radio to instrument panel reinforcement.
4. Lower radio from instrument panel and disconnect electrical connectors from radio.
5. Remove mounts from radio.
6. Reverse procedure to install.

HEATER CORE, REPLACE

Exc. 1978—79 Station Wagon

Less Air Conditioning
1. Disconnect battery ground cable and disconnect blower motor electrical lead.
2. Place a pan under vehicle, then disconnect heater hoses from core and secure hoses in a raised position.
3. Remove blower inlet to dash panel screws and nuts, then remove blower inlet and blower motor and wheel assembly.
4. Remove core retaining strap screws and remove core.
5. Reverse procedure to install making certain that blower inlet sealer is intact, replace as necessary.

1977—80 With Air Conditioning

NOTE: The heater core can be removed without purging the A/C refrigerant system or removing he evaporator case half of the assembly by using the following procedure.

1. Disconnect battery ground cable.
2. Remove floor outlet duct, then remove glove box and door as an assembly.
3. Remove left and right hand dash outlets using a suitable tool.
4. Remove instrument panel pad.
5. Disconnect vacuum hoses at valves on left end of heater and evaporator unit.
6. Remove insulation tray located below instrument cluster, then loosen console and slide console rearward.
7. Remove instrument panel to dash attaching screws. Place a protective covering over steering column, then lower instrument panel to steering column. Disconnect speedometer cable, radio leads and control head connectors.
8. Remove right hand instrument panel and lap cooler as an assembly.
9. Remove modular duct to heater and evaporator case screw, then remove duct assembly.
10. Disconnect temperature door cable and wiring harness.
11. Disconnect heater hoses from heater core. Plug core tubes to prevent spillage when removing heater core.
12. Remove three heater case stud nuts lo-

cated in engine compartment.
13. Remove heater core case to evaporator core case attaching screws.
14. Drive on studs to break case loose from dash panel.
15. Remove heater core case assembly.
16. Remove heater core to case attaching screws, then remove heater core.

1978—79 Station Wagon

Less Air Conditioning
1. Disconnect battery ground cable.
2. Disconnect blower motor lead wire.
3. Place a pan under vehicle and disconnect heater hoses at core connections and secure ends of hoses in a raised position.
4. Remove the coil bracket to dash panel stud nut and move coil out of way.
5. Remove the blower inlet to dash panel screws and nuts and remove the blower inlet, blower motor and wheel as an assembly.
6. Remove the core retainer strap screws and remove the core.
7. When replacing core, be sure the blower inlet sealer is intact.

With Air Conditioning
1. Disconnect battery ground cable.
2. Position a pan under heater core tubes, then disconnect heater hoses and secure in a raised position. Cap core tubes to prevent coolant spillage during removal.
3. From engine side of dash panel remove nuts from selector duct studs, Fig. 8.

Fig. 11 Standard instrument panel cluster. 1978—79 Station Wagon

4. Remove glove box and door as an assembly.
5. Remove right hand outlet to instrument panel attaching screws, then remove outlet and flexible hose.
6. Remove intermediate duct to left hand outlet.
7. Remove steering column to toe pan plastic retainer, insulation and attaching screws.
8. Remove steering column to dash panel attaching nuts, then lower column and support on driver's seat.

NOTE: Place protective tape over steering column to prevent damage to finish when lowering instrument cluster assembly.

9. Remove instrument panel bezel, then remove ash tray and retainer.
10. Remove A/C control to instrument panel attaching screws.
11. Disconnect wire connector and antenna lead from radio.
12. Remove instrument cluster to dash panel attaching screws and allow cluster assembly to rest on steering column.
13. Disconnect speedometer cable, then push A/C control forward and allow control to rest on floor, using care not to kink cable.
14. Remove center duct to selector duct attaching screws and duct to upper instrument panel retainer.
15. Slide center duct to left to clear lower instrument panel to cluster tab, then slide to right to remove.
16. Remove defroster duct to selector duct attaching screws.
17. Remove remaining selector duct to dash panel attaching screws, then pull duct rearward and disconnect all electrical leads and vacuum lines.
18. Disconnect temperature door cable and remove selector duct assembly.

NOTE: Ensure all electrical leads and vacuum lines are disconnected before removing duct assembly.

19. Pry off or punch out temperature door bell crank, then remove temperature door Fig. 9.
20. Remove backing plate attaching screws and temperature door cable retainer.
21. Remove heater core and backing plate as an assembly.
22. Remove core straps, then remove heater core.

BLOWER MOTOR, REPLACE

1. Disconnect battery ground cable and disconnect blower motor electrical leads. On some models, it may be necessary to remove coolant recovery tank attaching screws and position tank aside. Do not disconnect hoses from tank.
2. Scribe blower motor flange to case position.
3. Remove blower motor retaining screws and remove blower motor and wheel assembly. Pry flange gently, if sealer acts as an adhesive.
4. Reverse removal procedure to install, aligning scribe marks made during removal.

Fig. 12 Optional instrument panel cluster. 1978—79 Coupe, S Coupe & Station Wagon

INSTRUMENT PANEL PAD, REPLACE

Exc. Station Wagon

1. Remove eleven screws from around edge of pad, Fig. 10.
2. On models equipped with A/C, disconnect left hand duct.
3. Pry upward on pad to disengage clips located rear of pad, then remove pad assembly.

1978—79 Station Wagon

1. Remove clock stem knob, then remove instrument cluster bezel, Figs. 11 and 12.
2. Remove one screw at lower left edge of pad and three screws located along lower right hand side of pad.
3. Sharply rap lower right edge of pad upward to disengage retaining clips at top right of pad, then remove pad assembly.

INSTRUMENT CLUSTER, REPLACE

1978—79 Station Wagon

Standard Cluster
The instrument cluster bezel is retained by nine screws, Fig. 11. After removal of bezel, remove cluster lens-light shield combination (2 screws at top of lens and 2 screws at bottom of light shield). The lens tips out at the top and then lifts off. Instruments are then easily removed.

GT Cluster
The cluster bezel is retained by six screws, Fig. 12. After removal of bezel, remove the lens light shield (6 screws). Then lift lens and light shield straight out. Instruments are then accessible for replacement.

Exc. Station Wagon

Standard Cluster
Remove four screws securing bezel and lens to instrument panel. Remove bezel and lens. Instruments are then accessible for replacement.

GT Cluster
Disconnect battery ground cable. Remove knob from clock stem, then remove six screws attaching cluster bezel to instrument panel. Remove six lens and light shield attaching screws, then remove lens and light shield. Instruments are then accessible for replacement.

W/S WIPER SWITCH, REPLACE

Exc. Station Wagon

1. Disconnect battery ground cable.
2. Remove screws securing light shield to wiper switch and position light shield aside.

NOTE: The light shield retaining screws also retain the upper portions of the wiper switch to the mounting bosses.

3. Remove lower switch mounting screw, lower switch from panel and disconnect electrical connector, then remove switch.
4. Reverse procedure to install.

1978—79 Station Wagon

1. Beneath instrument panel, unplug the headlamp switch multi-connector for clearance to wiper switch screw.
2. Unplug connector on bottom of wiper switch.
3. Remove two mounting screws from switch and lower switch from instrument panel.

W/S WIPER MOTOR, REPLACE

1. Raise hood, remove cowl screen.
2. Reaching through cowl opening, loosen the two transmission drive link attaching nuts to motor crankarm.
3. Remove transmission drive link from motor crankarm.
4. Disconnect wiring and unfasten motor and remove.

Engine Section

ENGINE MOUNTS, REPLACE

4-140

1. Raise vehicle on hoist and support front of engine to take weight off front mounts.
2. If only one mount is being replaced, remove the mount-to-engine bracket nut on the mount not being replaced.
3. Remove the stud nut and two bolts securing mount to housing support.
4. Remove the three stud nuts securing the bracket to the engine. On the right side remove the starter brace at starter and on air conditioned equipped vehicles, remove the compressor rear lower brace at the compressor.
5. Raise front of engine to provide maximum clearance without imposing stress on other engine components.
6. Reverse procedure to install.

4-151

1. Remove bracket to engine bolts and the chassis to engine mount attaching nut, Fig. 1.
2. Raise engine to release weight from mount.
3. Remove mount and separate from engine bracket.
4. Reverse procedure to install.

V6-196, 231

1. Raise car and provide frame support at front of car.
2. Support weight of engine at forward edge of pan.
3. Remove mount to engine block bolts. Raise engine slightly and remove mount to mount bracket bolt and nut. Remove mount.
4. Reverse above procedure to install and torque to specifications as shown in Fig. 2.

V8-305

1. Remove lower mount bolts from frame bracket, Fig. 3, and raise engine to relieve weight from mount.
2. Remove mount from engine.
3. Install new mount on engine, lower engine and install lower mount bolts to frame bracket.

ENGINE, REPLACE

4-140 & V8-305

1. Scribe relationship between hood hinges and the hood, then remove hood from hinges.
2. Disconnect battery positive cable at battery and negative cable at engine block (except on air conditioned vehicles).
3. Drain cooling system and disconnect hoses at radiator. Disconnect heater hoses at water pump and at heater inlet (bottom hose).
4. Disconnect emission system hoses: PCV at cam cover; cannister vacuum hose at carburetor; PCV vacuum at inlet manifold and bowl vent at carburetor.
5. Remove radiator panel or shroud and remove radiator, fan and spacer.
6. Remove air cleaner, disconnecting vent tube at base of cleaner.
7. Disconnect electrical leads at: Delcotron, ignition coil, starter solenoid, oil pressure switch, engine temperature switch, transmission controlled spark switch at transmission, transmission controlled spark solenoid and engine ground strap at cowl.
8. Disconnect: Fuel line at rubber hose to rear of carburetor, transmission vacuum modulator and air conditioning vacuum line at inlet manifold, accelerator cable at manifold bellcrank.
9. On air conditioned cars, disconnect compressor at front support, rear support, rear lower bracket and remove drive belt from compressor.
10. Move compressor slightly forward and allow front of compressor to rest on frame forward brace, then secure rear of compressor to engine compartment so it is out of way.
11. Disconnect power steering pump, if equipped, and position it out of way.
12. Raise car on a hoist and disconnect exhaust pipe at manifold.
13. Remove engine flywheel dust cover or converter underpan.
14. On automatic transmission cars, remove converter-to-flywheel retaining bolts and nuts and install coverter safety strap.
15. Remove converter housing or flywheel housing-to-engine retaining bolts.
16. Loosen engine front mount retaining bolts at frame attachment and lower vehicle.
17. Install floor jack under transmission.
18. Install suitable engine lifting equipment and raise engine slightly to take weight from engine mounts and remove engine front mount retaining bolts.
19. Remove engine and pull forward to clear transmission while slowly lifting engine from car.

4-151

1. Disconnect battery cables and drain cooling system.
2. Scribe relationship between hood hinges and the hood, then remove hood from hinges.
3. Disconnect distributor, starter and alternator wiring, engine to body ground strap, oil pressure and engine temperature sender wires, and all external vacuum hoses.
4. Remove air cleaner.
5. Remove radiator shroud assembly and fan, then disconnect coolant hoses from engine.
6. Disconnect accelerator linkage.

Fig. 1 Engine mounts. 4-151

Fig. 2 Engine mounts. V6-196, 231

Fig. 3   Engine mounts, V8-305, 350

Fig. 4   Cylinder head tightening sequence. 4-140

Fig. 5   Cylinder head tightening sequence. 4-151

7. If equipped with power steering or A/C, remove pump or compressor from mounting brackets and position aside. Do not disconnect hoses or lines.
8. Disconnect fuel lines.
9. Raise vehicle and drain oil pan.
10. Disconnect exhaust pipe from manifold.
11. If equipped with automatic transmission, remove converter cover and the converter retaining bolts, then slide converter rearward.
12. If equipped with manual transmission, disconnect clutch linkage and remove clutch cross shaft.
13. On all models, remove four lower bell housing bolts.
14. Disconnect transmission filler tube support and the starter wiring harness.
15. Remove front engine mount bolts.
16. Lower vehicle and, using a suitable jack and block of wood, support transmission.
17. Install suitable engine lifting equipment and support engine.
18. Remove the two remaining bell housing bolts.
19. Raise transmission slightly.
20. Move engine forward to separate from transmission, tilt front of engine upward and remove from vehicle.

V6-196, 231

NOTE: On models with manual transmission, engine and transmission are removed as an assembly.

1. Scribe alignment marks at hood hinge and hinge bracket, then remove hood.

2. Disconnect battery ground cable, then drain cooling system.
3. Remove air cleaner.
4. On models equipped with A/C, disconnect compressor ground wire and wire connector, then remove compressor mounting bracket bolts and position compressor aside.
5. Remove drive belts, fan and pulley.
6. Disconnect radiator and heater hoses from engine and position out of way.
7. Remove fan shroud assembly.
8. Remove power steering pump bracket bolts and position pump aside, if equipped.
9. Disconnect fuel pump hoses and install plugs.
10. Disconnect battery ground cable from engine.
11. Disconnect vacuum hose from carburetor to manifold and vacuum hoses to vacuum modulator and power brake unit, if equipped.
12. Disconnect throttle cable from carburetor.
13. Disconnect wire connectors from alternator, oil and coolant sending units.
14. Disconnect engine to body ground straps at engine.
15. Raise vehicle and disconnect starter cables and cable shields, if equipped.
16. Disconnect exhaust pipe from exhaust manifold.
17. Remove lower flywheel cover.
18. On models with automatic transmission, remove flywheel to converter attaching bolts. Mark converter and flywheel so they can be installed in the same position. Remove transmission to engine attaching bolts.
19. On models with manual transmission, disconnect driveshaft, shift linkage, clutch equalizer shaft and transmission.
20. Remove motor mount through bolts and cruise control bracket, if equipped, then lower vehicle.
21. On models with automatic transmission, support transmission.
22. Attach a suitable lifting device to engine and raise engine so that mounting through bolts can be removed. Ensure all wiring harness, vacuum lines and other components are clear before removing engine from vehicle.
23. On models with automatic transmission, raise engine clear of mounts and raise transmission support accordingly and alternately until transmission can be disengaged from engine. On all models carefully raise engine and remove from vehicle.

CYLINDER HEADS, REPLACE

Some cylinder head gaskets are coated with a special lacquer to provide a good seal once the parts have warmed up. Do not use any additional sealer on such gaskets. If the gasket does not have this lacquer coating, apply suitable sealer to both sides.

4-140

1. Remove engine front cover and camshaft cover as outlined further on.
2. Remove timing belt and camshaft sprocket.
3. Remove intake and exhaust manifolds.
4. Disconnect hose at thermostat housing.
5. Remove cylinder head bolts and with the aid of an assistant lift head and gasket from engine. Place head on two blocks of wood to prevent damage to valves.
6. Reverse procedure to install and tighten head bolts in sequence shown in Fig. 4.

4-151

1979–80 Cross Flow Engine
1. Drain cooling system and remove air cleaner.
2. Remove alternator, power steering pump and A/C compressor brackets from cylinder head and engine block.
3. Remove intake and exhaust manifolds.
4. Disconnect all electrical connectors from cylinder head.

Fig. 6   Intake manifold tightening sequence. 1977–80 4-151 except cross flow engine

Fig. 7   Intake manifold tightening sequence. 1979–80 4-151 cross flow engine

Fig. 8 Cylinder head tightening sequence. V6-196, 231

Fig. 9 Intake manifold tightening sequence. V6-196, 231

Fig. 10 Cylinder head tightening sequence. V8-305

Fig. 11 Intake manifold tightening sequence. V8-305

5. Disconnect ignition wire from spark plugs, then remove spark plugs.
6. Disconnect fuel line at rear engine lifting bracket.
7. Remove rocker arm cover and back off rocker arm nuts. Pivot rocker arm and remove push rods.
8. Remove cylinder head attaching bolts, cylinder head and gasket.
9. Reverse procedure to install. Torque cylinder head bolt in sequence shown in Fig. 5 and intake manifold bolts in sequence shown, Fig. 7.

1977–80 Except Cross Flow Engine

1. Disconnect battery ground cable.
2. Drain cooling system and remove air cleaner.
3. Disconnect accelerator cable from bellcrank at manifold, then the fuel and vacuum lines at carburetor.
4. Remove intake and exhaust manifolds.
5. Remove alternator to cylinder head bracket bolts.

NOTE: If equipped with power steering or A/C, remove right side front bracket to facilitate cylinder head removal.

6. Disconnect wiring harness from temperature sender and remove from clips on rocker arm cover.
7. Disconnect coolant hoses at water outlet housing and the ground strap at cylinder head.
8. Remove spark plugs and rocker arm cover. Loosen rocker arm nuts, pivot rocker arms aside and remove push rods.
9. Remove cylinder head bolts and the cylinder head.
10. Reverse procedure to install. Torque cylinder head and intake manifold bolts in sequence shown in Figs. 5 and 6.

V6-196, 231

1. Drain coolant and disconnect battery.
2. Remove intake manifold.
3. When removing right cylinder head, remove Delcotron and/or A/C compressor with mounting bracket and move out of the way. *Do not disconnect hoses from A/C compressor.*
4. When removing left cylinder head, remove oil dipstick, power steering pump and move out of the way with hoses attached.
5. Disconnect exhaust manifold from head to be removed.
6. Remove rocker arm shaft and lift out push rods.
7. Remove cylinder head.
8. Reverse procedure to install. Torque cylinder head and intake manifold bolts in sequence shown in Figs. 8 and 9.

V8-305

1. Remove intake and exhaust manifolds.
2. Remove rocker arm covers.
3. Remove rocker arm nuts, rocker arm balls and rocker arms.

NOTE: Rocker arms, rocker arm balls and push rods must be installed in the original position.

4. Drain coolant from cylinder block, then remove cylinder head bolts and cylinder head.
5. Reverse procedure to install. Torque cylinder head and intake manifold bolts on sequence shown in Figs. 10 and 11.

ROCKER ARMS, REPLACE

V6-196, 231

A nylon retainer is used to retain the rocker arms. Break them below their heads with a chisel, Fig. 12, or pry out with channel locks. Production rocker arms can be installed in any sequence since the arms are identical, however, replacement arms are identified with a stamping right (R) and left (L).

ROCKER ARM STUDS, REPLACE

4-151

Rocker arm studs that are cracked or have damaged heads, can be removed from the cylinder head using a deep socket. Install and torque replacement rocker arm stud to 60 ft. lbs. on 1977–80 except cross flow engine and 75 ft. lbs. on 1979–80 cross flow engine.

V8-305

Rocker arm studs that have damaged threads may be replaced with standard studs. If studs are loose in the head, oversize studs (.003″ or .013″) may be installed after reaming

Fig. 12 Removing nylon rocker arm retainer. V6-196, 231

Fig. 13 Removing rocker arm stud. V8-305

Fig. 14 Installing rocker arm stud. V8-305

Fig.15 Hydraulic valve lifter. 4-151, V6-196, 231 and V8-305

VALVE GUIDES

Valve guides are an integral part of the cylinder head and are not removable. If valve stem clearance is excessive, the valve guide should be reamed to the next oversize and the appropriate oversize valves installed. Valves are available in .003, .015 and .030 inch oversize for the 4-140 and V8-305, .003 and .005 for the 4-151 and .010 and .006 inch for the V6-196, 231.

VALVE LIFTERS, REPLACE

4-151, V6-196, 231 & V8-305

Failure of an hydraulic valve lifter is generally caused by an inadequate oil supply or dirt. An air leak at the intake side of the oil pump or too much oil in the engine will cause air bubbles in the oil supply to the lifters, causing them to collapse. This is a probable cause of trouble if several lifters fail to function, but air in the oil is an unlikely cause of failure of a single unit.

On 4-151 engines, valve lifters may be lifted out of their bores after loosening and rotating rocker arm for clearance and removing push rod and push rod cover. On V6 and V8 models, valve lifters may be lifted out of their bores after removing the rocker arms, push rods and intake manifold. Adjustable pliers with taped jaws may be used to remove lifters that are stuck due to varnish, carbon, etc. Fig. 15 illustrates the type of lifter used.

---

the holes with a proper size reamer.

1. Remove old stud by placing a suitable spacer, Fig. 13 over stud. Install nut and flat washer and remove stud by turning nut.
2. Ream hole for oversize stud.
3. Coat press-fit area of stud with rear axle lube. Then install new stud, Fig. 14. If tool J-6880 shown is used, it should bottom on the head.

VALVES, ADJUST

4-140

These engines use hydraulic valve lifters are used and no valve lash adjustment is required. These lifters are not interchangeable with the type previously used since the cylinder head has been re-designed to facilitate installation of the new type lifter.

V8-305

NOTE: *After the engine has been thoroughly warmed up the valves may be adjusted with the engine shut off as follows: With engine in position to fire No. 1 cylinder the followng valves may be adjusted: Exhaust 1-3-4-8, intake 1-2-5-7. Then crank the engine one more complete revolution which will bring No. 6 cylinder to the firing position at which time the following valves may be adjusted: Exhaust 2-5-6-7, intake 3-4-6-8.*

The following procedure, performed with the engine running should be done only in case readjustment is required.

1. After engine has been warmed up to operating temperature, remove valve cover and install a new valve cover gasket on cylinder head to prevent oil from running out.
2. With engine running at idle speed, back off valve rocker arm nut until rocker arm starts to clatter.
3. Turn rocker arm nut down slowly until the clatter just stops. This is the zero lash position.
4. Turn nut down ¼ additional turn and pause 10 seconds until engine runs smoothly. Repeat additional ¼ turns, pausing 10 seconds each time, until nut has been turned down the number of turns listed in the *Valve Specifications*

Chart from the zero-lash position.

NOTE: This preload adjustment must be done slowly to allow the lifter to adjust itself to prevent the possibility of interference between the intake valve head and top of piston, which might result in internal damage and/or bent push rods. Noisy lifters should be replaced.

VALVE ARRANGEMENT

Front to Rear

4-140	I-E-I-E-I-E-I-E
4-151	E-I-I-E-E-I-I-E
V6-196, 231	E-I-E-I-I-E
V8-305	E-I-I-E-E-I-I-E

CAM LOBE LIFT SPECS.

	Year	Intake	Exhaust
4-140	1977	.4000	.4150

VALVE LIFT SPECS.

Engine	Year	Intake	Exhaust
4-151	1977–80	.406	.406
V6-196	1978	.323	.366
V6-196	1979	.341	.366
V6-231	1977–78	.3830	.3660
V6-231	1979–80	.3570	.3660
V8-305	1977–79	.3727	.4100

VALVE TIMING

Intake Opens Before TDC

Engine	Year	Degrees
4-140	1977	34
4-151	1977–80	33
V6-196	1978	18
V6-196	1979	16
V6-231	1977–78	17
V6-231	1979–80	16
V8-305	1977–79	28

CAMSHAFT COVER, REPLACE

4-140

1. Raise hood to fully open position and install bolt through the hood hold-open link.
2. Disconnect battery negative cable at battery.
3. Remove air cleaner wing nut. Disconnect ventilation tube at camshaft cover or at air cleaner; then remove air cleaner.
4. Remove PCV valve from grommet at front of cover.
5. Remove cover-to-cylinder head screws and withdraw cover from head.

ENGINE FRONT COVER, REPLACE

4-140

1. Raise hood to fully open position and install hood hold-open bolt.
2. Disconnect battery ground cable at battery.
3. Remove fan and spacer.
4. Loosen, but do not remove, the two cover lower screws. Cover is slotted to permit easy removal.
5. Remove the two cover upper retaining screws and remove cover.

Fig. 16 Valve timing marks aligned for correct valve timing. V6-196, 231

Fig. 17 Valve timing marks aligned for correct valve timing. V8-305, 350

Fig. 18 Valve timing marks aligned for correct valve timing. 4-151

4-151

1. Disconnect battery ground cable.
2. Remove torsional damper and the two oil pan to front cover screws, then front cover bolts.
3. Pull cover forward slightly and cut oil pan front seal flush with cylinder block at both sides of cover.
4. Remove front cover.

V6-196, 231

1. Drain cooling system and remove radiator.
2. Remove fan, pulleys and belts.
3. Remove crankshaft pulley and reinforcement.
4. If equipped with power steering, remove any pump bracket bolts attached to timing chain cover and loosen and remove any other bolts necessary that will allow pump and brackets to be moved out of the way.
5. Remove fuel pump.
6. Remove Delcotron and brackets.
7. Remove distributor cap and pull spark plug wire retainers off brackets on rocker arm cover. Swing distributor cap with wires attached out of the way.
8. Remove distributor. *If chain and sprockets are not to be disturbed, note position of distributor rotor for installation in the same position.*
9. Loosen and slide clamp on thermostat bypass hose rearward.
10. Remove bolts attaching chain cover to block.
11. Remove two oil pan-to-chain cover bolts and remove cover.
12. If seal replacement is required, drive seal from cover using a suitable punch.
13. Position packing around opening with ends of packing facing upward. Drive shedder into position using a suitable punch and stake in three locations.
14. Rotate a hammer handle around packing until balancer hub can be inserted through opening.

V8-305

1. Drain cooling system.
2. Remove alternator and A.I.R. pump, if necessary.
3. Remove fan, fan shroud and radiator.
4. Remove crankshaft damper.
5. Remove front cover attaching bolts and front cover.
6. If seal replacement is required, pry seal

from cover using a screw driver.
7. Position seal so open end faces toward inside of cover.
8. Drive seal into position using tool No. J-23042.

TIMING CHAIN, REPLACE

V6-196, 231 & V8-305

1. Remove timing chain cover.
2. Turn crankshaft so that sprockets are aligned as shown in Figs. 16 and 17.
3. Remove oil slinger.
4. On V6-196, 231, remove camshaft distributor drive gear and fuel pump eccentric, then using two large screwdrivers, alternately pry camshaft sprocket and crankshaft sprocket until camshaft is free. Remove camshaft sprocket and chain, then slide crankshaft sprocket off crankshaft.
5. On V8-305 remove three camshaft to sprocket bolts, then remove camshaft sprocket and timing chain together. Sprocket is a light press fit on camshaft, if sprocket does not come off easily, a light blow with a plastic hammer should dislodge it. If crankshaft sprocket is to be replaced, remove it with a suitable puller.
6. To install, assemble chain on sprockets with timing marks aligned as shown in Figs. 16 and 17.
7. Complete installation in reverse order of removal.

TIMING GEARS

4-151 Engine

When necessary to install a new camshaft gear, the camshaft will have to be removed as the gear is a pressed fit on the camshaft. The camshaft is held in place by a thrust plate which is retained to the engine by two capscrews which are accessible through the two holes in the gear web.

To remove gear, use an arbor press and a suitable sleeve to properly support gear on its steel hub.

Before installing gear, assemble thrust plate and gear spacer ring, then press gear onto shaft until it bottoms against spacer ring. The thrust plate end clearance should be .0015–.0050 inch. If clearance is less than .0015 inch, the spacer ring should be replaced. If clearance is greater than .0050 inch, the thrust plate should be replaced.

The crankshaft gear can be removed using a puller and two bolts in the tapped holes of the gear.

When installing timing gears, make sure that the marks on the gears are properly aligned, Fig. 18.

NOTE: The valve timing marks, Fig. 18, does not indicate TDC, compression stroke for No. 1 cylinder for use during distributor installation. When installing the distributor, rotate engine until No. 1 cylinder is on compression stroke and the camshaft timing mark is 180° from the valve timing position shown in Fig. 18.

CAMSHAFT, REPLACE

4-140

1. Remove hood.
2. Remove camshaft timing sprocket.
3. Remove timing belt upper cover and cam retainer and seal assembly.
4. Remove camshaft cover.
5. Disconnect fuel line at carburetor and remove idle solenoid from bracket.
6. Remove carburetor choke coil, cover and rod assembly.
7. Remove distributor.
8. Raise vehicle on a hoist, disconnect engine front mounts at body attachment, raise front of engine and install wood blocks, about 1½″ thick, between engine mounts and body. Lower vehicle.
9. Install camshaft removal tool as shown in Fig. 19, to cylinder head as follows:
   a. Position tool to cylinder head so attaching holes align with cam cover lower attaching holes.
   b. Align tappet depressing levers on tool so each lever will depress both intake and exhaust valve for their respective cylinder. Lever should fit squarely in notches adjacent to valve tappets.
   c. With tool aligned, make sure screws in bottom of tool are backed off so they do not make contact with bosses beneath tool.
   d. Install hardened screws supplied with tool, to attach tool to head. Torque screws securely.
   e. Turn screws in bottom of tool downward until they just seat against corresponding bosses on head.
   f. Apply a heavy body lubricant to ball end of lever depressing screws and proceed to tighten screws to depress

Fig. 19   Camshaft removal tool installed. 4-140

Fig. 20   Depressing valve tappets. 4-140

tappets, Fig. 20.

NOTE: Use a torque wrench to tighten screws the final few turns. About 10 ft. lbs. is required to depress tappets.

10. At this point the camshaft can be removed by sliding it forward from the head.

4-151

1979-80 Cross Flow Engine

1. Disconnect battery ground cable, then drain crankcase and cooling system.
2. Remove radiator, fan, water pump pulley and grille assembly.
3. Remove rocker arm cover, then loosen, remove rocker arm stud nuts and pivot rocker arms so that push rod can be removed.
4. Remove push rod cover, then remove push rods and valve lifters.
5. Remove oil pump driveshaft and gear assembly.
6. Remove front pulley hub and timing gear cover, then remove spark plugs.
7. Remove two camshaft thrust plate screws through holes in camshaft gear.
8. Pull camshaft and gear assembly from block. Use care not to damage camshaft bearings.

1977-80 Except Cross Flow Engine

1. Disconnect battery ground cable.
2. Drain oil pan and cooling system.
3. Remove fan, water pump pulley, radiator and the grille.
4. Remove distributor, fuel pump and spark plugs.
5. Remove valve train components.
6. Remove engine front cover.
7. Remove two camshaft thrust plate screws.
8. Remove camshaft and gear assembly from engine. Use care not to damage camshaft bearing surfaces.

V6-196, 231 & V8-305

NOTE: If engine is in the car, the radiator, grille and A/C components will have to be removed. If engine is out of car, proceed as

follows:

1. To remove camshaft, remove rocker arm assemblies, push rods and valve lifters.
2. Remove timing chain and sprockets.
3. On V8-305 engines install two 5/16" (18×4") bolts in camshaft bolt holes.
4. On all engines, slide camshaft out of engine using care not to damage the bearing surfaces.

TIMING BELT, REPLACE
4-140

1. Remove engine front cover as previously described.

Fig. 21   Sprocket alignment marks. 4-140

2. Remove accessory drive pulley or damper.
3. Drain coolant and loosen water pump bolts to relieve tension on belt.
4. Remove timing belt lower cover, then remove belt from sprockets.

CAMSHAFT SPROCKET, REPLACE
4-140

After removal of timing belt, the camshaft sprocket can be removed as follows:

1. Align one hole in sprocket with bolt head behind sprocket, then using a socket on bolt head to prevent cam from turning, remove sprocket retaining bolt and withdraw sprocket from camshaft.
2. When installing, be sure timing marks are aligned as in Fig. 21.

NOTE: A simplified method is provided for checking camshaft and crankshaft alignment. Proper alignment is assured by making sure hole in left rear of the timing belt upper cover is in line with the corresponding hole in the camshaft sprocket. Check alignment by inserting a pencil or other similar tool through hole in cover. If alignment is correct, the tool will enter small hole in cam gear, Fig. 22.

CRANKSHAFT SPROCKET, REPLACE
4-140

1. Remove engine front cover, accessory drive pulley, timing belt and timing belt lower cover.
2. Install suitable puller to crankshaft sprocket and remove sprocket.

OIL PUMP (CRANKCASE FRONT COVER) SEAL, REPLACE
4-140

1. Remove engine front cover, accessory

Fig. 22   Checking sprocket alignment. 4-140

Fig. 23   Installing crankcase front oil seal. 4-140

drive pulley, timing belt and timing belt lower cover and crankshaft sprocket.

2. Pry old seal from front cover being careful not to damage seal housing or seal lip contact surfaces.

3. Coat seal with light engine oil and apply an approved sealing compound to outside diameter of seal.

4. Position seal, closed end outward, onto crankshaft. Then install seal into bore using tool J-23624, Fig. 23.

PISTONS & RODS, ASSEMBLE

When installing connecting rod to crankshaft check side clearance. On all engines except V8-305 side clearance should be between .006–.022 inch, on V8-305 clearance should be between .006–.017 inch.

4-140

The "F" on the front of the piston must face the front of the engine when the piston and rod assembly is installed in its proper cylinder, Fig. 24.

4-151

Assemble piston to rod with the notch on piston facing toward front of engine and the raised notch side of rod at bearing end facing toward rear of engine, Fig. 25.

V6-196, 231 & V8-305

Rods and pistons should be assembled and installed as shown in Figs. 26 and 27.

PISTONS, PINS & RINGS

4-140

Pistons and rings are avilable in standard sizes and oversizes of .010, .020 and .030 inch.

4-151

Pistons and rings are available in standard

Fig. 24   Piston and rod assembly. 4-140

Fig. 25   Piston and rod assembly. 4-151

Fig. 26   Piston and rod assembly. V6-196, 231

Fig. 27 Piston and rod assembly. V8-305

Fig. 28 Removing oil pan baffle. 4-140

sizes and oversizes of .010 and .030 inch. Piston pins are avilable in oversizes of .001 and .003 inch.

V6-196, 231 & V8-305

Pistons are available in standard sizes and oversizes of .001, .005, .010, .020 and .030 inch for the V6-196, 231 & .001, .020 and .030 for the V8-305.

Rings are furnished in standard sizes and oversizes of .010, .020 and .030 inch for the V6-196, 231 and .020 and .030 for the V8-305.

Piston pins are furnished in standard sizes and oversizes of .003 and .005 inch for the V6-196, 231.

MAIN & ROD BEARINGS

Main and rod bearings are available in standard sizes and undersizes of .001, .002, .020 and .030 inch for the 4-140, .001, .002 and .010 inch for the 4-151, .001, .002, .003 and .010 inch for the V6-196, 231 and .001, .002, .009, .010 and .020 inch for the V8-305.

NOTE: If for any reason the bearing caps are replaced on the 4-140, shimming may be necessary. Laminated shims for each cap are available for service. Shim requirements will be determined by bearing clearance.

OIL PAN, REPLACE

4-140

1. Raise vehicle on a hoist and drain engine oil.
2. Support front of engine so weight is off front mounts, and remove frame crossmember and both front crossmember braces.
3. Disconnect idler arm at frame side rail.

NOTE: On air conditioned vehicles, disconnect idler arm at relay rod.

4. Mark relationship of steering linkage pitman arm to steering gear pitman shaft and remove pitman arm.

NOTE: Do not rotate steering gear pitman shaft while arm is disconnected as this will change steering wheel alignment.

5. Remove flywheel cover or converter underpan.
6. Remove oil pan to cylinder case screws, tap pan lightly to brake sealing bond and remove oil pan.
7. Remove pick up screen to baffle support bolts, then remove support from baffle.
8. Remove bolt securing oil pan drain back tube to baffle. Then rotate baffle 90 degrees towards left side of car and remove baffle from pick up screen, Fig. 28.

4-151

1. Disconnect battery ground cable.
2. Raise vehicle and drain oil pan.
3. Remove rear section of frame crossmember.
4. Disconnect exhaust pipe from manifold and loosen hanger bracket.
5. Remove starter and position aside.
6. Remove flywheel housing inspection cover.
7. Disconnect steering linkage at steering gear and idler arm support.
8. Remove oil pan bolts and the oil pan.

V6-196, 231

1. Support vehicle on hoist and drain oil.
2. Remove transmission dust cover and exhaust crossover pipe.
3. Remove oil pan bolts and allow pan to drop.
4. Reverse removal procedure to install.

V8-305

1. Disconnect battery ground cable.
2. Raise vehicle, drain oil pan and disconnect crossover pipe.
3. Remove underpan and splash shield from converter housing.
4. On 1976 models, support engine, then remove crossmember and braces.

NOTE: Scribe reference marks on each side of brace to ensure crossmember installation in original position.

5. On 1976 models, disconnect idler arm at frame side rail.
6. On all models, remove starter, then the oil pan.

OIL PUMP, REPLACE

4-140

1. Remove engine front cover, accessory drive pulley, timing belt, timing belt lower cover and crankshaft sprocket.
2. Raise vehicle on a hoist and remove oil pan and baffle.
3. Remove bolts and stud securing oil pump to cylinder case.

Inspection
1. Clean gasket surfaces, then wash parts in approved solvent and blow out all passages.
2. Check pressure regulator for free operation, Fig. 29.
3. Inspect pump gears for nicks, broken parts and other damage.
4. Check clearance between outside diameter, of driven gear and pump. Clearance should be .0038–.0068″, Fig. 30.
5. Check clearance between outside diameter of drive gear and crescent. Clearance should be .0023–.0093″, Fig. 31.
6. Check clearance between inside diameter of driven gear and pump crescent. Clearance should be .0068–.0148″, Fig. 32.
7. Check gear end clearance. It should be .0009–.0023″, Fig. 33.

NOTE: The pump gears and body are not serviced separately. If pump gears or body are worn, replacement of the entire oil pump is necessary.

Fig. 29   Oil pump pressure regulator. 4-140

Fig. 30   Checking driven gear to housing clearance. 4-140

Fig. 31   Checking drive gear to crescent clearance. 4-140

Fig. 32   Checking driven gear to crescent clearance. 4-140

Fig. 33   Checking gear end clearance. 4-140

4-151

1. Remove oil pan as outlined previously.
2. Remove two flange mounting bolts and nut from main bearing cap bolt, then the oil pump and screen assembly.
3. Should any of the following conditions be found, it is advisable to replace the pump assembly:
   a. Inspect pump body for cracks or wear.
   b. Inspect gears for wear or damage.
   c. Check shaft for looseness in housing.
   d. Check inside of cover for wear that would permit oil to leak past ends of gear.
   e. Check oil pick-up screen for damage.
   f. Check pressure regulator valve plunger for proper fit in body.

V6-196, 231

1. To remove pump, take off oil filter.
2. Disconnect wire from oil pressure indicator switch in filter by-pass valve cap (if so equipped).
3. Remove screws attaching oil pump cover to timing chain cover. Remove cover and

slide out pump gears. Replace any parts not serviceable.
4. Remove oil pressure relief valve cap, spring and valve, Fig. 34. Remove oil filter by-pass valve cap, spring and valve. Replace any parts of valve not serviceable.
5. Check relief valve in its bore in cover. Valve should have no more clearance than an easy slip fit. If any perceptible side shake can be felt, the valve and/or cover should be replaced.
6. The filter by-pass valve should be flat and free of nicks and scratches.

Assembly & Installation

1. Lubricate and install pressure relief valve and spring in bore of pump cover. Install cap and gasket. Torque cap to 30–35 lbs.
2. Install filter by-pass valve flat in its seat in cover. Install spring, cap and gasket. Torque cap to 30–35 ft-lbs.
3. Install pump gears and shaft in pump body section of timing chain cover to check gear end clearance. Check clearance as shown in Fig. 35. If clearance is less than .0018″ check timing chain cover for evidence of wear.
4. If gear end clearance is satisfactory, remove gears and pack gear pocket *full* of vaseline, not Chassis lube.

5. Reinstall gears so vaseline is forced into every cavity of gear pocket and between teeth of gears. *Unless pump is packed with vaseline, it may not prime itself when engine is started.*
6. Install cover and tighten screws alternately and evenly. Final tightening is 10–15 ft-lbs. torque. Install filter on nipple.

V8-305

After removing the oil pan, remove pump from rear main bearing cap. Disconnect pump

Fig. 34   Oil pump cover and pressure relief valve. V6-196, 231

Fig. 35   Checking oil pump gear end clearance. V6-196, 231

Engine oiling system. 4-140

Engine oiling system. V8-305

BY-PASS AT 10 LBS. PER SQ. IN.

shaft from extension by removing clip from collar. Remove pump cover and take out idler gear, drive gear and shaft.

Should any of the following conditions be found it is advisable to replace the pump assembly.

1. Inspect pump body for cracks or wear.
2. Inspect gears for wear or damage.
3. Check shaft for looseness in housing.
4. Check inside of cover for wear that would permit oil to leak past the ends of gear.
5. Check oil pick-up screen for damage to screen, by-pass valve or body.
6. Check for oil in air chamber.

CRANKSHAFT REAR OIL SEAL, REPLACE

When necessary to correct an oil leak due to a defective seal, always replace the upper and lower halves as a unit. *When installing either half, lubricate the lip portion only with engine oil, keeping oil off the parting line surface as this is treated with glue. Always clean crankshaft surface before installing a new seal. Be careful of seal retainer tang while inserting a new seal so that it doesn't cut the seal.*

4-151

1979–80 Cross Flow Engine
The rear main bearing oil seal is a one piece unit and is replaced without removing the oil pan or crankshaft.

1. Remove transmission, flywheel housing and flywheel.
2. Using a suitable screwdriver, remove rear main bearing oil seal. Use care not to scratch crankshaft.
3. Lubricate inside and outside diameters of replacement seal with engine oil. Install seal by hand onto rear crankshaft flange with helical lip side facing toward engine. Ensure seal is firmly and evenly seated.
4. Install flywheel, flywheel housing and transmission.

1977–80 Except Cross Flow Engine
The rear main bearing oil seal can be

VALVE LIFTER OIL GALLERIES

MAIN OIL GALLERY

OIL PICKUP SCREEN AND HOUSING

OIL PUMP

OIL FILTER

Engine oiling system (typical). V6-196, 231

replaced without removing the crankshaft.

1. Remove oil pan and rear main bearing cap.
2. To replace the lower seal, remove seal from groove in bearing cap, using a small screwdriver to pry it out.
3. Insert new seal and roll it in place with finger and thumb.

.004 SHIM STOCK

1/2

11/64

Fig. 36 Fabricated seal starting tool for helix type seal. V8-305

4. To replace the upper seal (with engine in car) use a small hammer and tap a brass pin punch on one end of the seal until it protrudes far enough to be removed with pliers.
5. Insert the new seal, gradually pushing with a hammer handle until seal is rolled into place.
6. Install bearing cap with new seal and tighten bearing cap bolts.

V8-305

NOTE: V8-305 engines are equipped with helix type rear seal. A seal starting tool, Fig. 36, must be used to prevent the upper seal half from coming into contact with the sharp edge of the block. Place the tip of the tool into the seal channel and "shoehorn" the seal into the upper seal channel.

GAGE HOLE

Fig. 37 Tensioning adaptor locating hole

J-23654

Fig. 38 Adjusting timing belt

1. To replace the lower seal, remove seal from groove in bearing cap, using a small screwdriver to pry it out.
2. Insert new seal and roll it in place with finger and thumb.
3. To replace the upper seal (with engine in car) use a small hammer and tap a brass pin punch on one end of the seal until it protrudes far enough to be removed with pliers.
4. Position tip of tool, Fig. 36, between crankshaft and seal seat in cylinder block.
5. Position seal between crankshaft and tip of tool with seal bead contacting tip of tool. Ensure oil seal lip is facing toward front of engine.
6. Roll seal around crankshaft, using tool as a "Shoehorn" to protect seal bead from sharp corner of seal seat surface in cylinder block.

NOTE: Tool must remain in position until seal is properly seated with both ends flush with block.

7. Remove tool, using care not to dislodge seal.
8. Install new seal into bearing cap with tool as outlined previously.
9. Install bearing cap with sealant applied to the cap to case interface. Do not apply sealant to seal ends. Torque rear main bearing cap bolts to specifications as listed in the "Engine Tightening Specification Chart".

CRANKSHAFT REAR OIL SEAL REPAIR,

V6-196, 231

Since the braided fabric seal used on these engines can be replaced only when the crank-

shaft is removed, the following repair procedure is recommended.

1. Remove oil pan and bearing cap.
2. Drive end of old seal gently into groove, using a suitable tool, until packed tight. This may vary between 1/4 and 3/4 inch depending on amount of pack required.
3. Repeat previous step for other end of seal.
4. Measure and note amount that seal was driven up on one side. Using the old seal removed from bearing cap, cut a length of seal the amount previously noted plus 1/16 inch.
5. Repeat previous step for other side of seal.
6. Pack cut lengths of seal into appropriate side of seal groove. A guide tool, J-21526-1, and packing tool, J-21526-2, may be used since these tools have been machined to provide a built-in stop.
7. Install new seal in bearing cap.

TIMING BELT TENSION, ADJUST

4-140

1. Drain coolant at engine block and remove fan and extension.
2. Remove engine front cover.
3. Remove water pump retaining bolts, clean gasket surfaces on block and pump. Install new gasket and loosely install water pump bolts.

NOTE: Apply an approved anti-seize compound to the water pump bolts before installation.

4. Position tool J-23564 in gauge hole adjacent to left side of pump, Fig. 37.
5. Apply 15 ft. lbs. of torque to water pump as shown in Fig. 38. Tighten water pump bolts while maintaining torque on side of

pump.
6. Reinstall front cover, fan, extension and fill cooling system.

BELT TENSION DATA

	New lbs.	Used lbs.
Alternator		
4-140	120–130	75
4-151		
1977	110–140	70
1978–79	120–130	75
1980		
5/16 in.	80	50
3/8 in. exc. cogged belt	140	70
3/8 in. cogged belt	—	60
15/32 in.	165	90
V6-196, 231		
1977–78	120–140	75
1979	146	67
1980		
5/16 in.	80	50
3/8 in. exc. cogged belt	140	70
3/8 in. cogged belt	—	60
15/32 in.	165	90
V8-305	120–130	75
Air Conditioning		
4-140	135–145	95
4-151		
1977	110–140	70
1978–79	120–130	75
1980		
5/16 in.	80	50
3/8 in. exc. cogged belt	140	70
3/8 in. cogged belt	—	60
15/32 in.	165	90
V6-196, 231		
1977–78	145–165	90
1979	168	90
1980		
5/16 in.	80	50
3/8 in. exc. cogged belt	140	70

	New lbs.	Used lbs.
³/₈ in. cogged belt	—	60
¹⁵/₃₂ in.	165	90
V8-305	135–145	95
Air Pump		
4-140	120–130	75
V6-196, 231		
1977–78	60–80	60
1979	79	45
1980		
⁵/₁₆ in.	80	50
³/₈ in. exc. cogged belt	140	70
³/₈ in. cogged belt	—	60
¹⁵/₃₂ in.	165	90
V8-305	120–130	75
Power Steering		
4-140	120–130	75
4-151		
1977	110–140	70
1978–79	120–130	75
1980		
⁵/₁₆ in.	80	50
³/₈ in. exc. cogged belt	140	70
³/₈ in. cogged belt	—	60
¹⁵/₃₂ in.	165	90
V6-196, 231		
1977–78	145–165	90
1979	168	90
1980		
⁵/₁₆ in.	80	50
³/₈ in. exc. cogged belt	140	70
³/₈ in. cogged belt	—	60
¹⁵/₃₂ in.	165	90
V8-305	120–130	75
Timing belt		
4-140	100–140	

WATER PUMP, REPLACE

4-140

1. Raise hood to fully open position and install hold-open bolt.
2. Disconnect battery ground cable at battery.
3. Remove engine fan and spacer.
4. Loosen, but do not remove, the two cover lower screws. Cover is slotted to permit easy removal.
5. Remove the two cover upper retaining screws and remove cover.
6. Drain coolant and loosen water pump bolts to relieve tension in timing belt.

Fig. 39   Removing fuel pump and gauge unit

7. Remove radiator lower hose and heater hose at water pump.
8. Remove water pump bolts and water pump.

4-151, V6-196, 231 & V8-305

1. Drain cooling system and loosen fan pulley bolts.
2. On V8-262, 305 engines, remove alternator and A.I.R. pump, if necessary.
3. On all engines, disconnect radiator and heater hoses from water pump.
4. Remove fan and pulley, then remove water pump.

FUEL PUMP, REPLACE

4-151

NOTE: Before installing the pump, it is good practice to crank the engine so that the nose of the camshaft eccentric is out of the way of the fuel pump rocker arm when the pump is installed. In this way there will be the least amount of tension on the rocker arm, thereby easing the installation of the pump.

1. Disconnect fuel line from pump.
2. Remove pump attaching bolts and pump.
3. Remove all gasket material from the pump and block gasket surfaces. Apply sealer to both sides of new gasket.
4. Position gasket on pump flange and hold pump in position against its mounting surface. Make sure rocker arm is riding on camshaft eccentric.
5. Press pump tight against its mounting. Install retaining screws and tighten them alternately.
6. Connect fuel lines. Then operate engine and check for leaks.

Except 4-151

Removal
1. Disconnect battery ground cable.
2. Disconnect meter and pump wires at rear wiring harness connector.
3. Raise vehicle on hoist and drain fuel tank.
4. Disconnect fuel line hose at gauge unit pick up line.
5. Disconnect tank vent lines to vapor separator.
6. Remove gauge ground wire screw at underbody floorpan.
7. Remove tank straps bolts and lower tank carefully.
8. Unscrew retaining ring using spanner wrench J-22554, Fig. 39, and remove pump-tank unit assembly.

Installation
1. Remove flat wire conductor from plastic lip on fuel tube.
2. Squeeze clamp and pull pump straight back about ½ inch.
3. Remove two nuts and lockwasher and conductor wires from pump terminals.
4. Squeeze clamp and pull pump straight back to remove it from tank unit. Take care to prevent bending of circular support bracket.
5. Slide replacement pump through circular support bracket until it rests against rubber coupling. Make sure pump has rubber isolator and saran strainer attached.
6. Attach two conductor wires to pump terminals using lockwashers and nuts being certain flat conductor is attached to terminal located on side away from float arm.
7. Squeeze clamp and push pump into rubber coupling.
8. Replace flat wire conductor in plastic clip on fuel pick up tube.
9. Install unit into tank and replace fuel tank.

Clutch & Transmission Section

Fig. 1 Ball stud adjustment

CLUTCH PEDAL, ADJUST

Ball Stud Adjustment

1. Before attaching clutch cable, place gauge J-23644 with flat end against face of clutch housing and locate hooked end of gauge at point of cable attachment for fork, Fig. 1.
2. Turn ball stud inward until clutch release bearing contacts clutch spring fingers.
3. Install lock nut and torque to 25 ft. lbs., use care not to change ball stud adjustment.
4. Install ball stud cap, then remove gauge by pulling outward at housing end.

Clutch Cable Adjustment

NOTE: Ball stud adjustment must be correct before adjusting clutch cable.

1. With return spring disconnected, place cable through hole in clutch fork, Fig. 2.

Fig. 2 Clutch cable adjustment

2. Pull cable until clutch pedal is firmly against clutch pedal stop.
3. Push clutch fork forward until release bearing contacts clutch spring fingers.
4. Tighten adjusting pin on cable until it contacts fork surface.
5. Rotate cable pin an additional 1/4 turn clockwise and position pin into groove on fork.
6. Attach return spring, then cycle clutch pedal approximately 3 times. Lash at clutch pedal should be .65 to 1.15 in. for 1978–80 Skyhawk, 1977–80 Monza and Sunbird, 5/8 to 1 1/8 in. for 1977 Skyhawk and 11/16 to 1 1/8 in. for 1977–80 Starfire.

CLUTCH, REPLACE

1. Remove transmission.
2. Remove clutch fork cover then disconnect clutch return spring and control cable from clutch fork.
3. Remove flywheel housing lower cover and flywheel housing.
4. Remove release bearing from the clutch fork and sleeve by sliding lever off ball stud and against spring pressure. If ball stud is to be replaced, remove cap, lock nut and stud from housing.
5. Make sure alignment marks on clutch assembly and flywheel are distinguishable.
6. Loosen clutch cover to flywheel bolts one turn at a time until spring pressure is released to avoid bending clutch cover flange, Fig. 3.
7. Support the pressure plate and cover assembly while removing bolts and clutch assembly.

NOTE: Do not diassemble the clutch cover, spring and pressure plate for repairs. If defective, replace complete assembly.

8. Reverse procedure to install making sure to index alignment marks.
9. After installing crossmember, loosely install retaining bolts, then the crossmember to transmission mount bolts. Tighten all bolts to specifications and remove the engine support.

CAUTION: Check position of engine in front mounts and realign as necessary.

Fig. 3 Clutch & components (typical)

FOUR SPEED
TRANSMISSION, REPLACE

1977-80

1. Raise vehicle on a hoist and drain lubricant.
2. Place shift lever in neutral, then disconnect transmission control rod and lever assemblies from shifter shafts. Tie rods up and out of way.
3. Remove propeller shaft and torque arm bracket.
4. Remove catalytic converter bracket from transmission and disconnect exhaust pipe and converter.
5. Disconnect speedometer cable, TCS switch and back-up lamp switch.
6. Remove crossmember to transmission mount bolts.
7. Support engine with an appropriate jack stand and remove crossmember to frame bolts and remove crossmember.
8. Remove transmission to clutch housing upper retaining bolts and install guide pins in holes.
9. Remove lower bolts, then slide transmission rearward and remove from vehicle.

NOTE: Inspect throwout bearing support gasket located beneath lip of support. If necessary, replace gasket before installing transmission.

LINKAGE, ADJUST

1977-80 4 Speed Except 70mm (Brazil)
1. Place ignition switch in off position.
2. Raise vehicle, then loosen lock nuts at swivels on shift rods, Fig. 4. Rods should pass freely through swivels.
3. Place transmission shift levers in neutral position.
4. Place shift control lever in neutral posi-

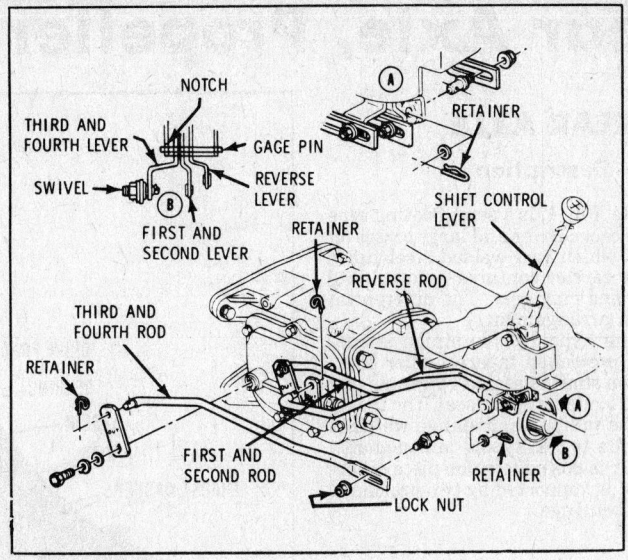

Fig. 4   Shift linkage adjustment.
4 speed transmission

tion, then align control levers and install gauge pin into levers and bracket.
5. Tighten 1st-2nd shift rod nut against swivel, then tighten 3rd-4th shift rod nut against swivel. Torque nuts to 120 in. lbs.
6. Torque reverse shift rod control nut to 120 in. lbs.
7. Remove gauge pin from shifter assembly and check linkage adjustment.

FIVE SPEED
TRANS., REPLACE

1. Remove shifter assembly and raise vehi-

cle.
2. Remove propeller shaft and torque arm bracket, then disconnect speedometer cable from transmission.
3. Remove crossmember to transmission bolts and the catalytic converter support bracket.
4. Support engine and remove crossmember.
5. Remove transmission to clutch housing upper retaining bolts and install guide pins.
6. Remove lower transmission to clutch housing bolts, slide transmission rearward and lower from vehicle.
7. Remove back-up lamp switch and fill plug, then drain transmission.

Rear Axle, Propeller Shaft & Brakes

REAR AXLE

Description

The rear axle, Fig. 1, is a semi-floating type consisting of a cast carrier and large bosses on each end into which two welded steel tubes are fitted. The carrier contains an overhung hypoid pinion and ring gear. The differential is a two pinion arrangement.

The overhung hypoid drive pinion is supported by two preloaded tapered roller bearings. The pinion shaft is sealed by means of a molded, spring loaded, rubber seal. Flange is mounted on the pinion shaft flange which is splined and bolts to the hypoid pinion shaft.

The ring gear is bolted to a one piece differential case and is supported by two preloaded tapered roller bearings.

Removal

1. Support vehicle at frame and using a suitable jack support axle housing.
2. Remove wheels, brake drums and axle shafts.
3. Disconnect brake lines from axle tube clips and remove bolt securing brake line junction block to rear axle housing.

NOTE: Do not disconnect brake lines from wheel cylinders or junction block.

4. Remove brake backing plates and secure backing plates to frame.
5. Remove parking brake cable adjusting nuts at equalizer, pull center cable rearward and disconnect two rear cables from body connectors.
6. Disconnect rear brake hose at floor pan and cap ends of hose and line.
7. Disconnect shock absorber from rear axle.
8. Disconnect track rod, then slowly lower axle until all spring tension is relieved and pry springs from axle housing pads.
9. Disconnect propeller shaft and torque arm and position aside.

NOTE: Support axle at companion flange to prevent housing from rotating.

10. Remove lower control arm attaching bolts from axle housing.
11. Remove support at companion flange, then the axle assembly.

Fig. 1 Rear axle cross section

AXLE SHAFT, REPLACE

1. Raise vehicle on a hoist and remove wheel and tire assembly and brake drum.
2. Drain lubricant from axle by removing carrier cover.
3. Unscrew pinion shaft lock screw and remove pinion shaft, Fig. 2.
4. Push flanged end of axle shaft toward center of car and remove "C" lock from button end of shaft.
5. Remove axle shaft from housing being careful not to damage seal.

Oil Seal &/ or Bearing Replacement

1. If replacing seal only, remove the seal by using the button end of axle shaft. Insert the button end of shaft behind the steel case of the seal and pry seal out of bore being careful not to damage housing.
2. If replacing bearings, insert tool J-22813 into bore so tool head grasps behind bearing, Fig. 3. Slide washer against seal, or bearing, and turn nut against washer. Attach slide hammer J-2619 and remove bearing.
3. Pack cavity between seal lips with a high melting point wheel bearing lubricant. Position seal on tool J-21491 and position seal in axle housing bore, tap seal in bore just below end of housing, Fig. 4.

Fig. 2 Differential pinion shaft removal

Fig. 3 Removing wheel bearing and seal

Fig. 4 Installing seal and wheel bearing

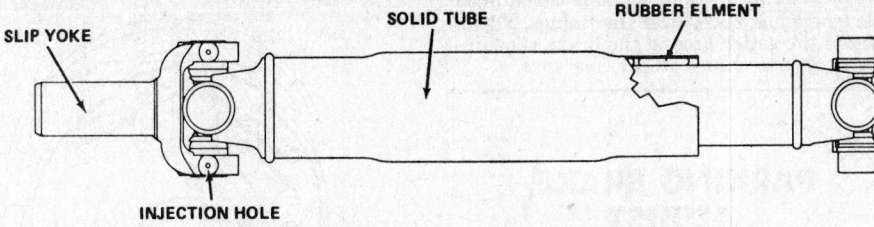

SLIP YOKE — SOLID TUBE — RUBBER ELMENT —

INJECTION HOLE

Fig. 5 Propeller shaft cross section (typical)

NOTE: If a low pedal condition cannot be corrected by making numerous reverse stops (provided the hydraulic system is free of air) it indicates that the self-adjusting mechanism is not functioning. Therefore it will be necessary to remove the brake drum, clean, free up and lubricate the adjusting mechanism. Then adjust the brakes, being sure the parking brake is fully released.

PROPELLER SHAFT

The propeller shaft used is made up of concentric steel tubes with rubber elements between, Fig. 5.

Propeller Shaft, Replace

1. Raise vehicle on a hoist.
2. Disconnect torque arm at rear axle, then referring to the "Rear Suspension" section, loosen attaching bolt at transmission and swing torque arm away from shaft. Mark relationship of shaft to companion flange and disconnect the rear universal joint by removing trunnion bearing "U" bolts. Tape bearing cups to trunnion to prevent dropping and loss of bearing rollers.
3. Withdraw propeller shaft front yoke from transmission.
4. When installing, be sure to align marks made in removal to prevent driveline vibration.

BRAKE ADJUSTMENTS

These rear wheel brakes, Fig. 6, have self-adjusting shoe mechanisms that assure correct lining-to-drum clearances at all times. The automatic adjusters operate only when the brakes are applied as the car is moving rearward.

Although the brakes are self-adjusting, an initial adjustment is necessary after the brake shoes have been relined or replaced, or when the length of the adjusting screw has been changed during some other service operation.

Frequent usage of an automatic transmission forward range to halt reverse vehicle motion may prevent the automatic adjusters from functioning, thereby inducing low pedal heights. Should low pedal heights be encountered, it is recommended that numerous forward and reverse stops be made until satisfactory pedal height is obtained.

Adjustment

A lanced "knock out" area is provided in the web of the brake drum for servicing purposes in the event retracting of the brake shoes is required in order to remove the drum.

1. With brake drum off, disengage the actuator from the star wheel and rotate the star wheel by spinning or turning with a screwdriver.
2. Using the brake drum as an adjustment fixture, turn the star wheel until the drum slides over the brake shoes with a slide drag.
3. Turn the star wheel 1¼ turns to retract the brake shoes. This will allow sufficient lining-to-drum clearance so final adjustment may be made.
4. Install drum and wheel.

NOTE: *If lanced area in brake drum was knocked out, be sure all metal has been removed from brake compartment. Install new hole cover in drum to prevent contamination of brakes. Make certain that drums are installed in the same position as when removed with the drum locating*

WHEEL CYLINDER LINKS — WHEEL CYLINDER SCREWS —
SECONDARY SHOE & LINING — BACKING PLATE —
SHOE GUIDE —
PARKING BRAKE STRUT —
STRUT SPRING —
ADJUSTER LEVER —
ACTUATING LINK —

HOLD DOWN PINS —
HOLD DOWN SPRING & CUP —
PARKING BRAKE LEVER —
WHEEL CYLINDER —
PRIMARY SHOE AND LINING —
HOLD DOWN SPRING —
ADJUSTING SCREW SPRING —
ADJUSTING SCREW —
LEVER RETURN SPRINGS —
BRAKE SHOE RETURN SPRING —

Fig. 6 Rear brake disassembled, passenger side

Fig. 7 Measuring brake drum inner diameter

tang in line with the locating hole in the wheel hub.

5. Make final adjustment by driving and stopping in forward and reverse until satisfactory pedal height is obtained.

NOTE: The recommended method of adjusting the brakes is by using the Drum-to-Brake Shoe Clearance Gauge to check the diameter of the brake drum inner surface, Fig. 7. Turn the tool to the opposite side and fit over the

brake shoes by turning the star wheel until the gauge just slides over the linings, Fig. 8. Rotate the gauge around the brake shoe lining surface to assure proper clearance.

PARKING BRAKE, ADJUST

1. Raise vehicle and remove propeller shaft.
2. Apply parking brake one notch from fully released position and raise hoist.
3. Loosen equalizer check nut and tighten the adjusting nut until a slight drag is felt when rear wheels are rotated.

NOTE: It may be necessary to remove drive shaft to gain access to parking brake equalizer.

4. Tighten check nut securely.
5. Release parking brake and rotate rear wheels. No drag should be present.

MASTER CYLINDER, REPLACE

1. Disconnect cylinder push rod from brake pedal.
2. Disconnect brake lines from two outlets on cylinder and cover ends of lines to prevent entry of dirt.
3. Unfasten and remove cylinder from brake booster.

Fig. 8 Checking brake shoe lining clearance

POWER BRAKE UNIT, REPLACE

1. Remove the vacuum hose from check valve and then remove the master cylinder retaining nuts.
2. Remove the bolt securing the brake pipe distributor and switch assembly to fender skirt.
3. Pull master cylinder forward until it just clears mounting studs and move aside. Support cylinder to avoid stress on hydraulic lines.
4. Remove power unit to dash nuts.
5. Remove brake pedal pushrod retainer and disconnect push rod from pin.
6. Remove power unit from vehicle.

Rear Suspension

DESCRIPTION

This rear suspension system does not use upper control arms, instead, it uses a torque arm mounted rigidly to the differential housing at the rear and to the transmission through a rubber bushing at the front. This torque arm prevents axle housing rotation caused by starting and stopping. Along with the torque arm a track rod is used to connect the axle housing to the body to control side sway and a rear stabilizer shaft is used for improved handling, Fig. 1.

SHOCK ABSORBER, REPLACE

1. With the rear axle supported properly disconnect shock absorber from upper and lower mounting, Fig. 1.

NOTE: Use a wrench to hold lower mounting stud from turning.

2. Reverse procedure to install.

COIL SPRING, REPLACE

1. Support vehicle at frame and rear axle with a suitable jack.
2. Disconnect shock absorbers from lower mountings.
3. Lower rear axle until springs can be

removed.
4. Reverse procedure to install.

STABILIZER BAR, REPLACE

1. Remove bolts securing stabilizer bar to lower control arms. Fig. 2.
2. Reverse procedure to install and torque bolts to specifications.

TRACK ROD, REPLACE

1. Raise vehicle and support axle assembly.
2. Remove bolts at underbody end of rod, Figs. 2 and 3.
3. Remove bolts at axle bracket and remove track rod.
4. Reverse removal procedure to install and torque bolts to specifications.

TIE-ROD

TORQUE ARM

STABILIZER SHAFT

LOWER CONTROL ARM

Fig. 1 Rear suspension.

Fig. 2   1977–80 stabilizer bar removal.

Fig. 3   Track rod removal. 1977–78

Fig. 4   Torque arm removal. Manual transmission. Except models w/4-151 engine

Fig. 5   Torque arm removal. Automatic transmission. Except models w/4-151 engine

Fig. 6 Torque arm removal. 1977–80 models w/4-151 engine (typical)

TORQUE ARM, REPLACE

1. Raise vehicle by axle assembly and support underbody with jackstands.
2. Lower axle assembly slightly and remove torque arm to differential bolts.
3. Disconnect mounting bracket from transmission and then remove through bolt from bracket and remove torque arm, Figs. 4 and 5.

NOTE: On 1977–80 models with 4-151 engine, refer to Fig. 6 for torque arm to transmission removal and installation.

4. To replace bushing, use an arbor press and tool J-25317-2 as a receiver and press bushing out of arm, then position new bushing in torque arm with bushing sleeve aligned with the length of the torque arm. Press bushing into place using tool J-25317-1 over bushing to properly locate bushing in arm.
5. Reverse removal procedure to install and torque nuts and bolts to specifications.

LOWER CONTROL ARM, REPLACE

1. Raise and support vehicle at rear axle.

Fig. 7 Lower control arm

2. Disconnect stabilizer bar from lower control arms.
3. Remove control arm front and rear mount bolts and remove control arm, Fig. 7.
4. Reverse removal procedure to install and torque bolts to specifications.

Front End & Steering Section

FRONT SUSPENSION

The front suspension, Fig. 1, is of the A frame type with short and long control arms. The upper control arm is bolted to the front end sheet metal at each inner pivot point. Rubber bushings are used for mounting.

The lower control arms attach to the front end sheet metal with cam type bolts through rubber bushings. The cam bolts adjust caster and camber.

The upper ball joint is riveted in the upper arm and the lower ball joint is pressed into the lower arm.

Coil springs are mounted between the lower control arms and the shock absorber tower.

WHEEL ALIGNMENT

Caster

Caster angle is adjusted by loosening the rear lower control arm pivot nut and rotating the cam until proper setting is reached, Fig. 2.

NOTE: This eccentric cam action will tend to move the lower control arm fore or aft thereby varying the caster. Hold the cam bolt while tightening the nut.

Camber

Camber angle is adjusted by loosening the front lower control arm pivot nut and rotating the cam until setting is reached, Fig. 2.

NOTE: This eccentric cam action will move the lower arm in or out thereby varying the setting. Hold the cam bolt head while tightening the nut.

TOE-IN, ADJUST

1. Loosen clamp bolt nut at each end of each tie rod and rotate the sleeve until proper toe-in is reached.
2. Position tie rod ball stud assembly straight on a center line through their attaching points.
3. Position clamp as shown in Fig. 3 and tighten clamp nuts.

WHEEL BEARINGS, ADJUST

1977–80 Monza, Skyhawk, Sunbird & 1978–80 Starfire

1. While rotating wheel, tighten spindle nut

Fig. 2 Caster and camber adjustment

to 12 ft. lbs.
2. Backoff adjusting nut to the just loose position, then retighten nut hand tight.
3. Loosen until either hole in spindle is aligned with slot in nut, then install cotter pin.
4. Spin wheel to check that it rolls freely and then lock the cotter pin.

NOTE: Wheel bearings should have zero pre-load and the allowable end play is .001–.005 inch.

1977 Starfire

1. While rotating wheel, torque spindle nut to 30 ft. lbs.
2. Back off nut 1/2 turn.
3. Tighten spindle nut finger tight and insert cotter pin. If cotter pin cannot be installed, back off nut not more than 1/24 turn to align slot and pin hole.
4. With bearings properly adjusted, end play should be .001–.008 inch.

WHEEL BEARINGS, REPLACE

1. Raise vehicle on a hoist and remove the wheel and tire assembly.
2. Remove the brake caliper from the disc by removing the mounting pins and stamped nuts, Figs. 4 & 5.
3. Remove hub grease cap, cotter pin, spindle nut and washer and remove hub and bearings.
4. Remove inner bearing by prying out the grease seal.

UPPER CONTROL ARM

TORQUE WITH CONTROL ARMS AT CURB HEIGHT.

NUT 65 ft. lbs.

WASHER

BOLT

BOLT

CAM ASSY.

LOWER CONTROL ARM

CAMBER ADJUSTMENT MUST BE MADE BEFORE CASTER ADJUSTMENT.

CAM

LOCK WASHER

NUT 140 ft. lbs.

CAM ASSY.

CAP

CAP

BUSHING

LOWER CONTROL ARM

Fig. 1   Front suspension (typical)

CHECKING BALL JOINTS FOR WEAR

Upper Ball Joint

The upper ball joint is checked for wear by checking the torque required to rotate the ball joint stud in the assembly. This is done after first dislodging the ball joint from the steering knuckle.

1. Install the stud nut to the ball stud in the seat.
2. Check the torque required to turn the ball stud.

NOTE: Specified torque for a new joint is 2 to 4 ft. lbs. rotating torque. If readings are excessively high or low, replace the joint.

Lower Ball Joint

The lower ball joints incorporate wear indicators for visual inspection, Fig. 6.

UPPER BALL JOINT, REPLACE

1. Raise vehicle on hoist and support lower control arm with a suitable jack stand.

NOTE: Floor jack or stand must remain under control arm spring seat during removal and installation to retain spring and control arm in position. Since the

weight of the vehicle is used to relieve spring tension to the upper control arm, the floor stands must be positioned between the spring seats and ball joints of the lower control arms for maximum leverage.

ADJUSTER TUBE

SLOT IN ADJUSTER TUBE

CLAMP

DO NOT LOCATE ADJUSTER TUBE SLOT IN THIS AREA

Fig. 3   Adjuster sleeve and clamp location

2. Remove wheel, then loosen upper ball joint from steering knuckle as follows:
   a. Remove cotter pin from upper ball joint stud and clean threads.
   b. Remove upper ball joint nut and install tool J-8806, Fig. 7.
   c. Apply pressure on stud by expanding tool until stud breaks loose.
   d. Remove tool and upper ball joint nut, then pull stud free from knuckle. Support knuckle assembly to prevent weight of assembly from damaging brake hose.
3. With control arm in raised position, drill four rivets 1/4 inch deep using a 1/8 inch diameter drill bit. Using 1/2 inch diameter drill bit, drill off rivet heads.
4. Using a suitable punch, punch out rivets then remove ball joint.
5. Using four bolts and nuts provided in kit install new ball joint, torque to 8 ft. lbs. Torque upper ball joint nut to 65 ft. lbs.

LOWER BALL JOINT, REPLACE

1. Raise vehicle and support with suitable stands positioned under frame.
2. Remove tire and wheel assembly.
3. Place floor jack under control arm spring seat.

NOTE: Floor jack must remain under control arm spring seat during removal and

Fig. 4 Removing caliper retaining stamped nuts

Fig. 5 Removing caliper mounting pins

installation to retain spring and control arm in position.

4. To disconnect the lower control arm ball joint from steering knuckle proceed as follows:
   a. Remove cotter pin from ball joint stud and remove stud nut.
   b. Break ball joint loose from knuckle using tool J-8806, Fig. 7A.
5. After stud breaks loose guide lower control arm out of opening in splash shield with a putty knife or other suitable tool.
6. Block knuckle assembly out of the way by placing a wooden block between frame and upper control arm.
7. Remove ball joint seal by prying off retainer with a screwdriver or driving off with a chisel.
8. Remove grease fitting and install tools, Fig. 8, and remove lower ball joint from lower control arm.

NOTE: When installing new ball joint

Fig. 6 Lower ball joint wear indicator

position the grease fitting so it faces inboard.

9. Reverse procedure to install, Fig. 9. Torque ball joint stud nut to 60 ft. lbs.

SHOCK ABSORBER, REPLACE

1. Hold shock absorber stem and remove the nut, upper retainer and rubber grommet, Fig. 10.
2. Raise vehicle on a hoist.
3. Remove bolts from lower end of shock absorber and lower the shock from the vehicle.

COIL SPRING, REPLACE

Exc. Starfire

1. With shock absorber removed and stabilizer bar removed, raise the vehicle and place jackstands under front braces.
2. Remove the wheel and tire assembly.
3. Place a floor jack under the lower arm and support the arm. Use a block of wood between the control arm and the jack, Fig. 11.
4. Remove the lower ball stud from the knuckle.

Fig. 7 Removing upper ball joint from steering knuckle

Fig. 7A Removing lower ball joint from steering knuckle

Fig. 8 Removing lower ball joint

Fig. 9   Installing lower ball joint

5. Remove the tie rod end from the knuckle.
6. Lower the control arm by slowly lowering the jack until the spring can be removed.
7. Reverse procedure to install. Torque steering knuckle stud nut to 60 ft. lbs. and install cotter pin.

NOTE: Do not back off nut to insert cotter pin. Advance nut to the next slot that lines up with the hole in the stud.

Starfire

1. Place transmission in Neutral.
2. Disconnect shock absorber from upper mounting.
3. Raise vehicle, support at frame and remove wheel.
4. Remove stabilizer link nut, grommets, washers and bolt.
5. Remove shock absorber.
6. Install lower plate BT-7522, Fig. 12, with pivot ball seat facing downward into spring coils. Rotate plate to fully seat it in lower control arm spring seat.
7. Install upper plate BT-7522, Fig. 12, with pivot ball seat facing upward into spring coils. Insert ball nut BT-7408-4 through spring coils and onto upper plate.
8. Install rod BT-7408-5 through shock absorber opening in lower control arm and through the lower and upper plates. Depress lock pin on shaft and thread shaft into upper ball nut BT-7408-4. Ensure lock pin is fully extended above ball nut upper surface.
9. With ball nut tang engaged in upper plate slot, rotate upper plate until it contacts upper spring seat.

Fig. 11   Removing front coil spring. Exc. Starfire

10. Install lower pivot ball, thrust bearing and nut on rod, then rotate nut until coil spring is compressed to be free in the seat.
11. Mark location of lower control arm pivot bolt cams and remove the pivot bolts. Move control arm forward and remove coil spring.
12. Reverse procedure to install.

MANUAL STEERING GEAR, REPLACE

1. Remove the pot joint coupling clamp bolt at the steering gear wormshaft.
2. Remove pitman arm nut and washer from pitman shaft and mark relation of arm position to shaft.
3. Remove pitman arm with suitable puller.
4. Remove bolts securing gear to frame and remove gear assembly.

POWER STEERING GEAR, REPLACE

Exc. 1978—79 Station Wagon

Replacement procedures for removing the gear assembly are the same as for the manual type gear with the following additions:
1. Remove left front crossmember brace.
2. Disconnect both pressure and return hoses from the gear housing and cap both hoses and steering gear outlets to prevent entry of dirt.

1978—79 Station Wagon

1. If necessary, remove battery to gain access to steering gear.
2. Remove clamp securing intermediate shaft to steering shaft.
3. Disconnect both hydraulic lines from steering gear and allow to drain. Position lines out of way to provide clearance for gear removal.
4. Raise vehicle and remove clamps at stabilizer bar.
5. Remove left front crossmember.
6. Remove pitman shaft nut, then using tool No. J-6632, remove pitman arm from pitman shaft.
7. Remove three steering mounting bolts and lock washers.
8. Lift steering gear and remove pitman arm, then position gear to provide clearance for removal.
9. Remove steering gear and intermediate shaft as an assembly, the steering gear spacer is also removed.
10. Remove plastic shield.
11. Remove pot joint clamp and separate steering gear from pot joint.
12. Remove pot joint from intermediate shaft.

POWER STEERING PUMP, REPLACE

Removal

1. Disconnect hoses at pump or steering gear. Plug hose ends and ports to prevent fluid loss and entrance of dirt.
2. Loosen pump attaching bolts and remove drive belt. On some models with air conditioning, it will be necessary to remove the compressor belt first.
3. Remove attaching bolts and the pump from vehicle.

Fig. 10   Front shock absorber mountings

Installation

1. Position pump assembly on mounting brackets and loosely install attaching bolts.
2. Connect and tighten the hoses at the pump and steering gear.
3. Fill the reservoir. Bleed the pump by turning the pulley backwards (counterclockwise as viewed from the front) until air bubbles cease to appear.
4. Reinstall the pump belt over the pulley. Adjust to proper tension given in the belt tension chart and tighten the attaching bolts. Reinstall the compressor belt, if removed.
5. Bleed the system.
   a. Start the engine and run for a few seconds. Add fluid if necessary. Repeat this procedure until the fluid level remains constant after running the engine.
   b. Raise the front wheels off the ground and support the vehicle.
   c. Run engine at high idle (approximately 1500 rpm) and turn the wheels right and left, lightly contacting the wheel stops.
   d. Lower vehicle and turn the wheels right and left on the ground. Check the fluid level and fill as required.
   e. If fluid is extremely foamy, allow vehicle to stand a few minutes and repeat bleeding procedure.

Fig. 12   Coil spring replacement tool. Starfire

1980—83
CHEVROLET CITATION · BUICK SKYLARK
OLDSMOBILE OMEGA · PONTIAC
PHOENIX

INDEX OF SERVICE OPERATIONS

NOTE: Refer to the back of this manual for vehicle manufacturer's special service tool suppliers.

SERIAL NUMBER LOCATION

On top of instrument panel, left front.

ENGINE NUMBER LOCATION

On 4-151 engine, the engine code stamping is located on pad at left front of cylinder block below cylinder head. On V6-173, the engine code label is located at front and rear of left rocker arm cover.

ENGINE V.I.N. CODE

On 1980 vehicles, the fifth digit in the V.I.N. denotes engine code. On 1981-83 vehicles, the eighth digit in the V.I.N. denotes engine code.

ENGINE IDENTIFICATION CODE

4-151 engine are identified by code letters on pad. V6-173 are identified by code letters immediately following the engine number.

Year	Engine	V.I.N. Code	Code
1980	4-151①②	5	WA, WB
	4-151①③	5	XA, XB
	4-151②④	5	AC, AU
	4-151③④	5	Z4, Z6, Z9

Year	Engine	V.I.N. Code	Code
	V6-173①②	7	CNF, CNH
	V6-173①③	7	CNJ, CNK
	V6-173②④	7	CNL, CNM
	V6-173③④	7	CNR, CNS
	V6-173	7	DDB, DCZ
1981	4-151③	5	WAN, WAO
	4-151③	5	WAL, WAM
	V6-173③	X	DBB, DBD
	V6-173②	X	DBA, DBC
	V6-173③	X	DBN, DBS
	V6-173③	Z	DJD, DJF
	V6-173③	Z	DBU, DBX
1982	4-151②	R	3L, 3M

Year	Engine	V.I.N. Code	Code
	4-151③	R	3P, 3S
	V6-173①②	X	CAY, CBC
	V6-173③	X	CBJ, CBK
	V6-173①②	X	CBT, CBE
	V6-173①③	X	CBU, CBX
	V6-173②④	X	CBA, CBF
	V6-173①②	Z	CJJ
	V6-173③	Z	CJK, CJS
	V6-173②④	Z	CJM

① —Except Calif.
② —Man. trans.
③ —Auto. trans.
④ —California.

GRILLE IDENTIFICATION

1980 Buick Skylark

1980 Buick Skylark Sport Coupe

1980 Chevrolet Citation

1980 Oldsmobile Omega

1980 Pontiac Phoenix

1981 Buick Skylark

1981 Buick Skylark Sport Coupe

1981-82 Chevrolet Citation "X-11"
1983 Chevrolet Citation

1981-83 Oldsmobile Omega "ES"

1981 Pontiac Phoenix

1981-82 Chevrolet Citation Exc. "X-11"

1982 Oldsmobile Omega Exc. "ES"

Continued

GRILLE IDENTIFICATION—Continued

1982-83 Buick Skylark
Exc. "T" Type

1983 Buick Skylark "T" Type

1983 Oldsmobile Omega
Exc. "ES"

1983 Pontiac Phoenix

GENERAL ENGINE SPECIFICATIONS

Year	Engine CID①/Liter	V.I.N. Code②	Carburetor	Bore and Stroke	Compression Ratio	Net H.P. @ R.P.M.③	Maximum Torque Lbs. Ft. @ R.P.M.	Normal Oil Pressure Pounds
1980	4-151, 2.5L	5	2SE, 2 Bbl.④⑤	4.0 × 3.0	8.3	90 @ 4000	134 @ 2400	36—41
	V6-173, 2.8L	7	2SE, 2 Bbl.④⑤	3.5 × 3.0	8.6	115 @ 4800	150 @ 2000	30—45
1981	4-151, 2.5L	5	2 Bbl.④	4 × 3	8.2	84 @ 3600	125 @ 2400	30—45
	V6-173, 2.8L	X	2 Bbl.④	3.50 × 3.0	8.5	110 @ 4800	145 @ 2400	30—45
	V6-173, 2.8L	Z	2 Bbl.④	3.50 × 3.0	8.9	135 @ 5400	142 @ 2400	30—45
1982-83	4-151, 2.5L	R	T.B.I.	4.0 × 3.0	8.2	90 @ 4000	134 @ 2400	37.5
	V6-173, 2.8L	X	E2SE, 2 Bbl.④	3.5 × 3.0	8.5	112 @ 5100	148 @ 2400	50—65
	V6-173, 2.8L H.O.	Z	E2SE, 2 Bbl.④	3.5 × 3.0	8.9	135 @ 5400	142 @ 2400	50—65

①—CID—cubic inch displacement.
②—On 1980 vehicles the fifth digit in the VIN denotes engine code. On 1981-82 vehicles the eighth digit denotes engine code.
③—Ratings are net—as installed in vehicle.
④—Rochester.
⑤—Model E2SE used on vehicles equipped with C-4 system.
⑥—Throttle body injection.

TUNE UP SPECIFICATIONS

The following specifications are published from the latest information available. This data should be used only in the absence of a decal affixed in the engine compartment.

★ When using a timing light, disconnect vacuum hose or tube at distributor and plug opening in hose or tube so idle speed will not be affected.

● When checking compression, lowest cylinder must be within 70 percent of highest.

▲ Before removing wires from distributor cap, determine location of the No. 1 wire in cap, as distributor position may have been altered from that shown at the end of this chart.

☞ Spark plug types shown in this chart are recommendations of the original vehicle manufacturer and not MOTOR.
Check local sources for other spark plug manufacturers listings.

Year & Engine/V.I.N.	Spark Plug Type ☞	Gap	Ignition Timing BTDC①★ Firing Order Fig. ▲	Man. Trans.	Auto. Trans.	Mark Fig.	Curb Idle Speed② Man. Trans.	Auto. Trans.	Fast Idle Speed Man. Trans.	Auto. Trans.	Fuel Pump Pressure
1980											
4-151/5 Exc. Calif.	R43TSX	.060	A	10°	10°	B	1000/1300	650/900D	2200	2600	6½—8
4-151/5 Calif.	R43TSX	.060	A	10°	10°	B	1000/1200	650/900D	2200	2600	6½—8
V6-173/7 Exc. Calif.	R44TS	.045	C	2°	6°	D	750/1200	③	1900	2000	6—7½
V6-173/7 Calif.	R44TS	.045	C	6°	10°	D	750	④	2000	2000	6—7½
1981											
4-151/5	R44TSX	.060	E	4°	4°	B	800/1000	550/675D	2600	2600	6½—8
V6-173/X⑤	R43TS⑥	.045	C	6°	10°	D	850/1100	600/850D	⑦	2600	6—7½
V6-173/Z H.O.⑧	R43TS⑥	.045	C	—	10°	D	—	650/850D	—	2400	6—7½
1982											
4-151/R	R44TSX	.060	E	8°⑨⑩	8°⑨⑩	B	⑪	⑪	⑪	⑪	—
V6-173/X Exc. H.O.	R43TS⑥	.045	C	10°	10°	D	800/1050	600/800D	⑦	2600	6—7½
V6-173/Z H.O.⑧	R42TS	.045	C	6°	10°	D	850/1100	750/900D	2600	2800	6—7½

Continued

TUNE UP SPECIFICATIONS—Continued

The following specifications are published from the latest information available. This data should be used only in the absence of a decal affixed in the engine compartment.

★ When using a timing light, disconnect vacuum hose or tube at distributor and plug opening in hose or tube so idle speed will not be affected.

● When checking compression, lowest cylinder must be within 70 percent of highest.

▲ Before removing wires from distributor cap, determine location of the No. 1 wire in cap, as distributor position may have been altered from that shown at the end of this chart.

🔌 Spark plug types shown in this chart are recommendations of the original vehicle manufacturer and not MOTOR. Check local sources for other spark plug manufacturers listings.

Year & Engine/V.I.N.	Spark Plug Type 🔌	Gap	Ignition Timing BTDC① ★ Firing Order Fig. ▲	Man. Trans.	Auto. Trans.	Mark Fig.	Curb Idle Speed② Man. Trans.	Auto. Trans.	Fast Idle Speed Man. Trans.	Auto. Trans.	Fuel Pump Pressure
1983											
4-151/R	R44TSX	.060	E	8°	8°	B	⑪	⑪	⑪	⑪	—
V6-173/X Exc. H.O.	R43CTS	.045	C	10°	10°	D	775	600D	2500N	2500N	6-7½
V6-173/Z H.O.⑧	R42CTS	.045	C	10°	10°	D	800	725D	2600N	2700N	6-7½

① BTDC—Before top dead center.
② Idle speed on man. trans. vehicles is adjusted in Neutral & on auto. trans. equipped vehicles is adjusted in Drive unless otherwise specified. Where two idle speeds are listed, the higher speed is with the A/C or idle solenoid energized.
③ Less A/C, 700D RPM; with A/C, 700/850D RPM.
④ Less A/C, 700D RPM; with A/C, 700/800D RPM.
⑤ Except Citation X-11 models
⑥ R42TS recommended for heavy duty operation.
⑦ Models less A/C, 2400 RPM; models with A/C 2600 RPM.
⑧ High output engine.
⑨ At 1050 RPM.
⑩ Ground diagnostic connector located under dash. The check engine light should flash on and off when in diagnostic mode. Check average ignition timing of cylinder Nos. 1 and 4, and reset as necessary. After completing ignition timing check, remove ground from diagnostic connector and ensure that check engine light is off.
⑪ Idle speed controlled by an electronic control module.

Fig. A

Fig. B

Fig. C

Fig. D

Fig. E

DISTRIBUTOR SPECIFICATIONS

★If unit is checked on the vehicle, double the RPM and degrees to get crankshaft figures.

Distributor Ident. No.①	Centrifugal Advanced Degrees @ RPM of Distributor					Vacuum Advance	
	Advance Starts	Intermediate Advance			Full Advance	Inches of Vacuum to Start Plunger	Max. Adv. Dist. Deg. @ Vacuum
1980							
1103361	0–2¼ @ 550	5¾–8 @ 1100	—	—	12 @ 2400	3½	5¾ @ 20
1103362	0–2¼ @ 550	8¼–10½ @ 1250	—	—	14 @ 2400	3½	5¾ @ 20
1110782	0–2 @ 525	1¼–4½ @ 650	—	—	11½ @ 2000	3½	10½ @ 8
1110783	0–1½ @ 700	2–4½ @ 850	—	—	11½ @ 2000	4	10 @ 10½
1110786	0–1½ @ 525	1¼–3½ @ 650	—	—	11½ @ 2000	3½	10½ @ 9
1110787	0 @ 525	3½ @ 850	—	—	10½ @ 2000	3½	10 @ 9
1981							
1110567	—	—	—	—	—	—	—
1110579	—	—	—	—	—	—	—
1982							
1110593	—	—	—	—	—	—	—
1110597	—	—	—	—	—	—	—
1983							
1103519	—	—	—	—	—	—	—

①—Stamped on distributor housing plate.

ALTERNATOR & REGULATOR SPECIFICATIONS

Year	Alternator					Regulator							
	Model	Rated Hot Output Amps.	Field Current 12 Volts @ 80°F	Ouput @ 14 Volts		Model	Field Relay			Voltage Regulator			
				2000 R.P.M. Amps.	5000 R.P.M. Amps.		Air Gap In.	Point Gap In.	Closing Voltage	Air Gap In.	Point Gap In.	Voltage @ 125°F	
1980	1103043	42	—	—	—	Integral	—	—	—	—	—	14.7	
	1103078	42	—	—	—	Integral	—	—	—	—	—	14.7	
	—	63	—	—	—	Integral	—	—	—	—	—	—	
	—	70	—	—	—	Integral	—	—	—	—	—	—	
1981–82	11100115	42	—	—	—	Integral	—	—	—	—	—	—	
	1103187	42	—	—	—	Integral	—	—	—	—	—	—	
	1103197	63	—	—	—	Integral	—	—	—	—	—	—	
	1101067	70	—	—	—	Integral	—	—	—	—	—	—	
1983	—	42	—	—	—	Integral	—	—	—	—	—	—	
	—	63	—	—	—	Integral	—	—	—	—	—	—	
	—	70	—	—	—	Integral	—	—	—	—	—	—	
	—	78	—	—	—	Integral	—	—	—	—	—	—	

STARTING MOTOR SPECIFICATIONS

Year	Engine/V.I.N.	Starter Ident. No.	Brush Spring Tension Oz.	Free Speed Test			Resistance Test	
				Amps.	Volts	R.P.M.	Amps.	Volts
1980	4-151/5, V6-173/7	1109526	—	45–70①	9	7000–11900	—	—
1981	4-151/5, V6-173/X,Z	1109530	—	—	—	—	—	—
1982	4-151/R, V6-173/X,Z	1109533	—	—	—	—	—	—
1983	4-151/R, V6-173/X,Z	1103519	—	—	—	—	—	—

①—Includes solenoid.

VALVE SPECIFICATIONS

Year	Engine/V.I.N.	Valve Lash Int.	Valve Lash Exh.	Valve Angles Seat	Valve Angles Face	Valve Spring Installed Height	Valve Spring Pressure Lbs. @ In.	Stem Clearance Intake	Stem Clearance Exhaust	Stem Diameter Intake	Stem Diameter Exhaust
1980	4-151/5	Hydraulic①		46	45	1.69	151 @ 1.254	.0010–.0027	.0010–.0027	.3418–.3425	.3418–.3425
	V6-173/7	1½ Turn②		46	45	1.57	195 @ 1.181	.0010–.0027	.0010–.0027	.3409–.3417	.3409–.3417
1981	4-151/5	Hydraulic①		46	45	1.69	151 @ 1.254	.0010–.0027	.0010–.0027	.3418–.3425	.3418–.3425
	V6-173/X,Z	1½ Turn②		46	45	1.57	195 @ 1.181	.0010–.0027	.0010–.0027	.3410–.3417	.3410–.3417
1982–83	4-151/R	Hydraulic①		46	45	1.69	151 @ 1.254	.0010–.0027	.0010–.0027	.3418–.3425	.3418–.3425
	V6-173/X,Z	1½ Turn②		46	45	1.57	195 @ 1.181	.0010–.0027	.0010–.0027	.3410–.3417	.3410–.3417

①—No adjustment.

②—Turn rocker arm stud nut until all lash is eliminated, then tighten nut the additional turn listed.

PISTONS, PINS, RINGS, CRANKSHAFT & BEARINGS

Year	Engine Model/V.I.N.	Piston Clearance	Ring Gap① Comp.	Ring Gap① Oil	Wristpin Diameter	Rod Bearings Shaft Diameter	Rod Bearings Bearing Clearance	Main Bearings Shaft Diameter	Main Bearings Bearing Clearance	Thrust on Bear. No.	Shaft End Play
1980	4-151/5	.0017–.0041	②	.015	.9400	2.000	.0005–.0026	2.300	.0005–.0022	5	.0035–.0085
	V6-173/7	.0017–.0027	.010	.020	.9054	1.9983–1.9994	.0014–.0035	2.4937–2.4946	.0017–.0030	3	.002–.006
1981	4-151/5	.0017–.0041	.010	.015	.927	2.000	.0005–.0026	2.300	.0002–.0022	5	.0035–.0085
	V6-173/X,Z	.0018–.0028	.010	.020	.905	2.000	.0005–.0020	2.494	.0005–.0015	3	.0020–.0079
1982–83	4-151/R	.0017–.0041	.010	.015	.927	2.000	.0005–.0026	2.300	.0002–.0022	5	.0035–.0085
	V6-173/X,Z	.0018–.0028	.010	.020	.905	2.000	.0005–.0020	2.494	.0005–.0015	3	.0020–.0079

①—Fit rings in tapered bores for clearance given in tightest portion of ring travel. Clearances specified are minimum gaps.

②—Upper, .015"; lower, .009".

ENGINE TIGHTENING SPECIFICATIONS★

★ Torque specifications are for clean and lightly lubricated threads only. Dry or dirty threads produce increased friction which prevents accurate measurement of tightness.

Year	Engine Model/V.I.N.	Spark Plugs Ft. Lbs.	Cylinder Head Bolts Ft. Lbs.	Intake Manifold Ft. Lbs.	Exhaust Manifold Ft. Lbs.	Rocker Arm Stud Ft. Lbs.	Rocker Arm Cover Ft. Lbs.	Connecting Rod Cap Bolts Ft. Lbs.	Main Bearing Cap Bolts Ft. Lbs.	Flywheel to Crankshaft Ft. Lbs.	Vibration Damper or Pulley Ft. Lbs.
1980	4-151/5	7–15	75	29	44	75①	6	32	70	44	200
	V6-173/7	7–15	65–75	20–25	22–28	43–49	6–9	34–40	63–74	45–55	66–84
1981	4-151/5	7–15	75	29	44	20②	6	32	70	44	200
	V6-173/X,Z	7–15	65–75	20–25	22–28	43–49	6–9	34–40	63–74	45–55	66–84
1982	4-151/R	7–15	85③	29	44	20②	6	32	70	44	200
	V6-173/X,Z	7–15	65–75	20–25	22–28	43–49	6–9	34–40	63–74	45–55	66–84
1983	4-151/R	7–15	85③	29	44	20②	6	32	70	44	200
	V6-173/X,Z	7–15	65–75	20–25	22–28	43–49	6–9	34–40	63–74	45–55	66–84

①—Rocker arm nut, 20 ft. lbs.　②—Rocker arm bolt.　③—Requires thread sealer.

BRAKE SPECIFICATIONS

Year	Model	Brake Drum Inside Diameter	Wheel Cylinder Bore Diameter Front Disc Brake	Wheel Cylinder Bore Diameter Front Drum Brake	Wheel Cylinder Bore Diameter Rear Drum Brake	Master Cylinder Bore Diameter With Disc Brakes	Master Cylinder Bore Diameter With Drum Brakes	Master Cylinder Bore Diameter With Power Brakes
1980–81	All	7.874	2.24	—	.689	.874	—	.874
1982–83	All	7.87	2.94	—	.67	.87	—	.87

WHEEL ALIGNMENT SPECIFICATIONS

| Year | Model | Caster Angle, Degrees | | Camber Angle Degrees | | | | Toe-In Inch | Toe-Out on Turns, Deg. | |
| | | Limits | Desired | Limits | | Desired | | | Outer Wheel | Inner Wheel |
				Left	Right	Left	Right			
1980–81	All	−2° to +2°②	0°	+½° to +1½°	+½° to +1½°	+1°	+1°	①	—	—
1982–83	All	0° to +4°②	+2°	−.50° to +.50°	−1° to +1°	0	0	③	—	—

①—2.5 mm. ②—Left & right side should be equal with 2°. ③—−.1" to +.1".

COOLING SYSTEM & CAPACITY DATA

| Year | Model or Engine/V.I.N. | Cooling Capacity, Qts. | | Radiator Cap Relief Pressure, Lbs. | Thermo. Opening Temp. | Fuel Tank Gals. | Engine Oil Refill Qts. | Transaxle Oil | |
		Less A/C	With A/C					Manual Transaxle Pts.	Auto. Transaxle Qts. ①
1980	Citation 4-151/5	9½	9¾	15	195	14	3②	6	③
	Omega 4-151/5	8½	8¾	15	195	14	3②	6	③
	Phoenix 4-151/5	8.3④	8.6④	15	195	14	3②	6	③
	Skylark 4-151/5	8.3⑤	8.6⑤	15	195	14	3②	6	③
	Citation V6-173/7	11½	11¾	15	195	15	4②	6	③
	Omega V6-173/7	10¼⑥	10¾⑥	15	195	14	4②	6	③
	Phoenix V6-173/7⑦	10.2⑧	10.6⑧	15	195	14	4②	6	③
	Phoenix V6-173/7⑨	10.5⑧	10.8	15	195	14	4②	6	③
	Skylark V6-173/7	10.2⑧	10.6⑧	15	195	14	4②	6	③
1981	Citation 4-151/5	—	—	15	195	14	3②	6	③
	Omega 4-151/5	8½	8¾	15	195	14	3②	6	③
	Phoenix 4-151/5	8.3	8.6	15	195	14	3②	6	③
	Skylark 4-151/5	8.3	8.5	15	195	14	3②	6	③
	Citation V6-173/X,Z	—	—	15	195	14	4②	6	③
	Omega V6-173/X,Z	10.6	10.7	15	195	14	4②	6	③
	Phoenix V6-173/X,Z	10.2	10.6	15	195	14	4②	6	③
	Skylark V6-173/X,Z	10.3	10.7	15	195	14	4②	6	③
1982	Citation 4-151/R	9.8	9.8	15	195	14	3②	6	5⑩
	Omega 4-151/R	—	—	15	195	14	3②	6	5⑩
	Phoenix 4-151/R	8.3	8.6	15	195	14	3②	6	5⑩
	Skylark 4-151/R	9.5	9.8	15	195	14	3②	6	5⑩
	Citation V6-173/X,Z	10.66	11.07	15	195	14	4②	6	5⑩
	Omega V6-173/X,Z	—	—	15	195	14	4②	6	5⑩
	Phoenix V6-173/X,Z	10.2	10.6	15	195	14	4②	6	5⑩
	Skylark V6-173/X,Z	11.45	11.84	15	195	14	4②	6	5⑩
1983	Citation 4-151/R	9½	9¾	15	195	14	3②	6	5⑩
	Omega 4-151/R	9.5	9.8	15	195	14	3②	6	5⑩
	Phoenix 4-151/R	9½	9¾	15	195	14	3②	6	5⑩
	Skylark 4-151/R	9.5	9.7	15	195	14	3②	6	5⑩
	Citation V6-173/X,Z	11½	11¾	15	195	14	4②	6	5⑩
	Omega V6-173/X,Z	10.0	10.7	15	195	14	4②	6	5⑩
	Phoenix V6-173/X,Z	11½	11¾	15	195	14	4②	6	5⑩
	Skylark V6-173/X,Z	11.4	11.8	15	195	14	4②	6	5⑩

①—Approximate make final check with dipstick.
②—With or without filter change.
③—Oil pan capacity, 4 qts.; total capacity, 6 qts.
④—With heavy duty cooling system, man. trans. 8.7 qts., auto. trans., 9.3 qts.
⑤—With heavy duty cooling system, 8.7 qts.
⑥—With heavy duty cooling system, 11 qts.
⑦—Exc. Calif.
⑧—Heavy duty cooling system, 10.8 qts.
⑨—California.
⑩—Total Capacity.

Electrical Section

STARTER, REPLACE

1. Disconnect battery ground cable.
2. Raise and support vehicle.
3. Remove the starter to engine brace.
4. Remove starter mounting bolts and lower starter. Note position of shims, if used.
5. Disconnect solenoid wires and the battery cable.
6. Remove starter from vehicle.
7. Reverse procedure to install.

IGNITION LOCK, REPLACE

1. Remove steering wheel as outlined under "Steering Wheel, Replace" procedure.
2. Remove turn signal switch as outlined under "Turn Signal Switch, Replace" procedure.
3. Remove the buzzer switch.
4. Turn lock cylinder to "Run" position, then remove the lock cylinder retaining screw

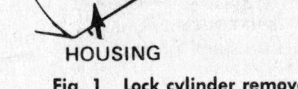

Fig. 1 Lock cylinder removal

and the lock cylinder, Fig. 1.

5. To install, rotate lock cylinder to the stop while holding housing. Align cylinder key with keyway in housing, then push lock cylinder into housing until fully seated.
6. Install lock cylinder retaining screw.
7. Install buzzer switch, turn signal switch and steering wheel.

IGNITION & DIMMER SWITCHES, REPLACE

1. Remove turn signal switch as outlined under "Turn Signal Switch, Replace" procedure.
2. Refer to Figs. 2 and 3 to remove ignition and dimmer switches.
3. When installing dimmer switch, depress switch slightly to install a 3/32 inch twist drill. Force switch upward to remove lash and tighten retaining screw.

REMOVE

1. Remove parts as shown.

INSTALL

1. Install parts as shown.
2. Position rod in slider hole and install ignition switch. Install lower stud and tighten to 3.9 N•m (35 in. lbs.)
3. Install dimmer switch and depress switch slightly to insert 3/32" drill. Force switch up to remove lash, then tighten screw, and nut to 3.9 N•m (35 in. lbs.).
4. Place shifter in neutral and install shift lever.

INSTALL IGNITION SWITCH

Fig. 2 Ignition & dimmer switch removal & installation. Except tilt column

REMOVE

1. Remove parts as shown.

INSTALL

1. Install parts as shown.
2. Position rod in slider hole and install ignition switch. Install lower stud and tighten to 3.9 N•m (35 in. lbs.).
3. Install dimmer switch and depress switch slightly to insert 3/32" drill. Force switch up to remove lash, then tighten screw, and nut to 3.9 N•m (35 in. lbs.).
4. Place shifter in neutral and install shift lever.

Fig. 3   Ignition & dimmer switch removal & installation. Tilt column

W/S WIPER SWITCH, REPLACE

1. Remove turn signal switch as outlined under "Turn Signal Switch, Replace" procedure.
2. Refer to Figs. 4 and 5 for wiper switch replacement.

PULSE W/S WIPER SWITCH, REPLACE

Citation

1. Disconnect battery ground cable.

2. Remove radio knobs and nuts and the clock knob.
3. Remove instrument cluster bezel to instrument panel carrier retaining screws and pull bezel rearward.
4. Depress headlamp switch shaft retaining button and pull knob and shaft assembly from switch.
5. Disconnect accessory switch wiring connectors.
6. Remove instrument cluster bezel.
7. Remove controller knob and ferrule nut attaching controller to bezel.
8. Disconnect wiring connector at steering column.
9. Remove switch instrument panel.

10. Reverse procedure to install.

Omega

1. Disconnect battery ground cable.
2. Remove headlamp switch knob by depressing retaining clip behind knob and pulling knob from shaft.
3. Remove left hand trim cover attaching screws and the trim cover.
4. Remove two screws retaining controller switch to adapter assembly.
5. Disconnect wiring connector at steering column.
6. Remove switch from instrument panel.
7. Reverse procedure to install.

Fig. 4 Windshield wiper switch removal & installation. Except tilt column

Phoenix

1. Disconnect battery ground cable.
2. Remove the switch knob and the four screws securing the trim plate.
3. Pull trim plate rearward and rotate for clearance for switch.
4. Remove light guide and the switch retaining screws.
5. Remove screws securing steering column trim cover to instrument panel and the trim cover.
6. Disconnect switch harness connector.
7. Cut both ends of pulse wiring harness as close to the steering column as possible. Remove the switch end and wiring harness end.
8. Install new switch in instrument panel and make electrical connection at instrument panel wiring harness. Route the new controller wiring under steering column and secure wiring so as not to fall in the driver's foot area.

Tighten nut until tool slightly depresses lock plate

Fig. 6 Compressing lock plate

9. Reverse Steps 1 through 5 to complete installation.

Skylark

1. Disconnect battery ground cable.
2. Remove the knobs from the following: W/S wiper switch, rear window defogger switch and radio.
3. Remove headlamp switch knob by depressing retaining clip behind knob and pulling knob from shaft.
4. Remove radio retaining nuts.
5. Remove three screws at bottom of instrument panel trim plate.
6. Place transmission shift lever in "Low" and remove instrument panel trim plate.
7. Remove switch retaining screws.
8. Pull switch rearward and cut the five wire harness at rear of switch.
9. Feed new wiring harness through switch cavity and pull through bottom of instrument panel.
10. Connect wiring harness between column mounted switch and related junction block.
11. Reverse Steps 1 through 7 to complete installation.

STOPLAMP SWITCH, ADJUST

Insert switch into tubular clip until the switch body seats on the tube clip. Pull the brake pedal rearward against internal pedal stop. The switch will be properly positioned in the tubular clip.

NEUTRAL SAFETY SWITCH

These vehicles do not use a neutral safety switch. To prevent starting the vehicle while in gear, a mechanical block on the transmission gear selector prevents starting the engine when the transmission is in any gear other than Park or Neutral.

TURN SIGNAL SWITCH, REPLACE

1. Disconnect battery ground cable.
2. Remove steering wheel as outlined under "Steering Wheel, Replace" procedure.
3. Using a screwdriver, pry cover from housing.
4. Using lock plate compressing tool J-23653, compress lock plate and pry snap ring from groove on shaft, Fig. 6. Slowly release lock plate compressing tool, remove tool and lock plate from shaft end.
5. Slide canceling cam and upper bearing preload spring from end of shaft.
6. Remove turn signal (multi-function) lever.
7. Remove hazard warning knob retaining screw, button, spring and knob.
8. Remove pivot arm.
9. Wrap upper part of electrical connector with tape to prevent snagging of wires during switch removal.
10. Remove switch retaining screws and pull switch up from column, guiding wire harness through column.
11. Reverse procedure to install.

Fig. 5 Windshield wiper switch removal & installation. Tilt column

STEERING WHEEL, REPLACE

1. Disconnect battery ground cable.
2. Remove horn button or pad.
3. Remove retainer and steering wheel retaining nut.
4. Remove steering wheel with a suitable puller (tool No. J-1859-03 or BT-61-9).
5. Reverse procedure to install.

HEADLAMP SWITCH, REPLACE

Citation

1. Disconnect battery ground cable.
2. Pull switch knob to full "On" position.
3. Remove instrument panel bezel to panel carrier attaching screws.
4. Remove radio knobs and nuts and the clock knob.

Fig. 7 Instrument cluster trim cover. 1980-82 Citation

Fig. 8 Instrument cluster. 1980–82 Citation

PULL CONNECTOR OUT, TURN CLOCKWISE
AND PUSH THROUGH HOLE IN ADAPTER
ASSEMBLY TO REMOVE
USE SAME PROCEDURE FOR L. H. CONNECTOR

Fig. 9 Instrument cluster. 1980–83 Omega

5. Pull bezel rearward and depress headlamp switch shaft retaining button and pull knob and shaft assembly from switch.
6. Disconnect accessory switch wiring connectors.
7. Remove instrument cluster bezel.
8. Remove switch ferrule nut and push switch forward out from mounting hole.
9. Lift switch up and out through opening above switch mounting, then disconnect electrical connector.
10. Remove switch from instrument panel.
11. Reverse procedure to install.

Omega

1. Disconnect battery ground cable.
2. Remove headlamp switch knob by depressing retaining clip behind knob and pulling knob from shaft.
3. Remove left hand trim cover attaching screws and the trim cover.
4. Remove switch attaching screws and pull switch from panel.

NOTE: The switch plugs directly into a terminal plug in the switch mounting cavity.

5. Reverse procedure to install.

Phoenix

1. Disconnect battery ground cable.
2. Remove steering column trim cover attaching screws and the trim cover.
3. Pull headlamp switch to full "On" position, depress knob release button on switch and remove rod and knob assembly.
4. Remove left hand trim plate attaching screws and the trim plate.
5. Remove switch escutcheon, disconnect electrical connector from switch and remove switch from instrument panel.
6. Reverse procedure to install.

Skylark

1. Disconnect battery ground cable.
2. Remove headlamp switch knob by depressing retaining clip behind knob and pulling knob from shaft.
3. Remove escutcheon from switch and shaft.

4. Remove the knobs from the following: W/S wiper switch, rear window defogger switch and radio.
5. Remove radio retaining nuts.
6. Remove three screws from bottom of instrument panel trim plate.
7. Place transmission shift lever in "Low", then remove instrument panel trim plate.
8. Remove headlamp switch retaining screws and pull switch from panel.

NOTE: The switch plugs directly into a terminal plug in the switch mounting cavity.

9. Reverse procedure to install.

INSTRUMENT CLUSTER, REPLACE

Citation

1. Disconnect battery ground cable.
2. Remove radio knobs and nuts and the clock knob.
3. Remove instrument cluster bezel to panel carrier attaching screws, then pull bezel rearward for access, Fig. 7.
4. Depress headlamp switch shaft retaining

button and pull knob and shaft assembly from switch.
5. Pull bezel rearward and disconnect accessory switch wiring connectors.
6. Remove instrument cluster bezel.
7. Remove four screws securing cluster assembly to instrument panel pad.
8. Disconnect shift indicator cable from steering column shift bowl.
9. Pull cluster rearward and disconnect speedometer cable and electrical connectors.
10. Remove instrument cluster from vehicle, Fig. 8.
11. Reverse procedure to install.

Omega

1. Disconnect battery ground cable.
2. Remove the 2 screws attaching assembly line communication link connector bracket to steering column trim cover if so equipped. Remove the 2 screws attaching steering column trim cover to instrument panel and remove trim cover.
3. Mark location of shift indicator clip on steering column shift bowl for proper reassembly. Remove shift indicator clip. Remove the 2 bolts holding steering column to support and lower steering column, resting steering wheel on front seat.

Fig. 10 Instrument cluster. 1980–82 Phoenix

Fig. 11   Instrument cluster trim cover. 1980–82 Skylark

Fig. 12   Instrument cluster. 1980–82 Skylark

4. Remove four screws attaching center instrument panel trim cover to instrument panel pad.
5. Pull trim cover rearward and disconnect accessory switch wiring and remote control mirror cable, if equipped. Remove trim cover.
6. Remove four screws attaching instrument cluster assembly to instrument panel pad.
7. Disconnect shift indicator cable from steering column shift bowl.
8. Pull cluster rearward and disconnect speedometer cable and electrical connections.
9. Remove instrument cluster from vehicle, Fig. 9.
10. Reverse procedure to install.

Phoenix

1. Disconnect battery ground cable.
2. Remove four speedometer cluster trim plate attaching screws and the trim plate.
3. Remove steering column trim cover attaching screws and the trim cover.
4. Remove speedometer cluster attaching screws.
5. Disconnect shift indicator detent cable, marking the cable location on steering column shift bowl.
6. Disconnect speedometer cable and pull cluster from panel.
7. Disconnect wiring harness from cluster and remove cluster from vehicle, Fig. 10.
8. Reverse procedure to install.

Skylark

1. Disconnect battery ground cable.
2. Disconnect speedometer cable at cruise control transducer, if equipped, or at upper and lower cable connections.
3. Remove trip meter reset knob retaining screw and pull knob from meter.
4. Remove knobs from the following: W/S wiper switch, rear window defogger switch and radio.
5. Remove headlamp switch knob by depressing retaining clip behind knob and pulling knob from shaft. Remove switch escutcheon.

6. Remove radio retaining nuts.
7. Remove three screws from bottom of instrument panel trim plate, Fig. 11.
8. Place transmission shift lever in "Low" and remove instrument panel trim plate.
9. Remove four instrument cluster lens plate screws and the lens plate.
10. Remove four instrument cluster cover plate screws and the cover plate.
11. Disconnect shift indicator spring below speedometer and slide indicator needle toward the right side and out from cluster housing.
12. Pull instrument cluster rearward and disconnect speedometer cable and electrical connections.
13. Remove instrument cluster from vehicle, Fig. 12.
14. Reverse procedure to install.

RADIO, REPLACE

Citation

1. Disconnect battery ground cable.
2. Remove radio knob and nuts and the clock knob.
3. Remove instrument cluster bezel to panel carrier attaching screws, then pull bezel rearward.
4. Depress headlamp switch shaft retaining button and pull knob and shaft assembly from switch.
5. Pull bezel rearward and disconnect accessory switch wiring connectors.
6. Remove instrument cluster bezel.
7. Remove two screws securing radio bracket to instrument panel.
8. Pull radio rearward while twisting slightly toward left side and disconnect electrical connections. Remove lamp socket.
9. Remove radio from instrument panel.
10. Reverse procedure to install.

Omega

1. Disconnect battery ground cable.
2. Remove radio knobs.
3. Pull out glove box switches and disconnect the wiring connectors.

4. Remove two screws securing glove box stop arm to door.
5. Remove two screws from instrument panel molding and pull molding rearward to remove. Note that the molding is retained by five clips.
6. Remove ash tray assembly, then the lamp and socket assembly from lamp housing.
7. Pull radio and ash tray retainer out from panel and disconnect all electrical connections.
8. Remove radio from panel.
9. Reverse procedure to install.

Phoenix

1. Disconnect battery ground cable.
2. Remove eight screws attaching center instrument panel trim plate and the trim plate.
3. Remove two radio attaching screws and pull radio from panel, then disconnect all electrical connectors from radio. Remove radio from panel.
4. Remove radio knobs and separate face plate from radio.
5. Reverse procedure to install.

Skylark

1. Disconnect battery ground cable.
2. Remove the knobs from the following: W/S wiper switch, rear window defogger switch and radio.
3. Remove headlamp switch knob by depressing retaining clip behind knob and pulling knob from shaft. Remove the switch escutcheon.
4. Remove radio retaining nuts.
5. Remove three screws at bottom of instrument panel trim plate.
6. Place transmission shift lever in "Low" and remove instrument panel trim plate.
7. Remove radio mounting plate screws.
8. Disconnect all electrical connection from radio.
9. Pull radio out through instrument panel opening.
10. Reverse procedure to install.

W/S WIPER MOTOR, REPLACE

1. Remove wiper arms as outlined previously.
2. Remove the lower windshield reveal molding, front cowl panel and cowl screen. Disconnect washer hose.

NOTE: Prior to removing the front cowl screen, mask the corners of the hood to prevent damage to paint.

3. Loosen but do not remove transmission drive link to motor crank arm attaching nuts. Then, disconnect drive link from motor crank arm.
4. Disconnect wiper motor electrical connections.
5. Remove wiper motor attaching bolts.
6. On models equipped with A/C, support motor assembly and remove motor crank arm. Use a suitable pair of locking pliers and wrench, remove crank arm nut and the crank arm.
7. On all models, rotate motor assembly upward and outward to remove.
8. Reverse procedure to install.

W/S WIPER TRANSMISSION, REPLACE

1. Remove lower windshield reveal molding, wiper arms and front cowl panel.
2. Loosen but do not remove drive link to motor crank arm attaching nuts.
3. Remove transmission to cowl panel attaching screws and the transmission.
4. Reverse procedure to install.

BLOWER MOTOR, REPLACE

1. Disconnect battery ground cable.
2. Disconnect blower motor electrical connections.
3. Remove blower motor attaching screws and the blower motor, Fig. 13.
4. Reverse procedure to install.

HEATER CORE, REPLACE

Less Air Conditioning

1. Disconnect battery ground cable and drain cooling system.
2. Disconnect the heater hoses from heater core.
3. Remove radio noise supression strap.
4. Remove heater core cover retaining screws and the cover, Fig. 13.
5. Remove heater core from vehicle.
6. Reverse procedure to install.

With Air Conditioning

1. Disconnect battery ground cable and drain cooling system.
2. Disconnect heater hoses from heater core.
3. Remove right side hush panel and open the glove box.
4. Remove heater duct retaining screw and the duct.
5. Remove instrument panel support bracket.
6. Remove heater case side cover retaining screws and the cover.
7. Remove heater core retaining clamps and the inlet and outlet tube support clamps.

Fig. 13   Heater core & blower motor, less A/C

8. Remove heater core from case.
9. Reverse procedure to install.

CRUISE CONTROL, ADJUST

Brake Release Switches

Electrical & Vacuum Switches
Push the switch fully into the retaining clip, then pull the brake pedal upward to adjust switch position. The electrical switch should break the electrical circuit when the brake pedal is depressed approximately .23–.51 inch.

Servo, Adjust

Models With Rod
Install the pin retainer to provide minimum slack with carburetor in slow idle position.

Models With Bead Chain
Assemble the chain into swivel and install retainer so that slack in the chain is not greater than one-half the diameter of the ball stud with the engine at operating temperature and the idle solenoid de-energized.

Cruise Speed, Adjust

The cruise speed adjustment can be set as follows:
1. If car cruises below engagement speed, screw orifice tube on transducer outward.
2. If car cruises above engagement speed, screw orifice tube inward.

NOTE: Each 1/4 turn of the orifice tube will change cruise speed about one mile per hour. Snug up lock nut after each adjustment.

ENGINE MOUNTS, REPLACE

4-151

1. Raise and support front of vehicle, then remove chassis to mount attaching nuts, Figs. 1 and 1A.
2. On models equipped with A/C, remove forward torque rod attaching bolts at radiator support panel.
3. Raise engine slightly using a suitable engine lifting device. Raise engine only enough to provide clearance for mount removal.
4. Remove two upper mount to engine support bracket attaching nuts and remove engine mount.
5. Reverse procedure to install.

V6-173

1. Remove mount retaining nuts from below cradle mounting bracket.
2. Raise engine and remove mount to engine attaching nuts, then remove mount, Figs. 2 and 2A. Raise engine only enough to provide clearance for mount removal.
3. Reverse procedure to install, then lower engine into position. Install retaining nuts and torque to 35 ft. lbs.

NOTE: After engine mount is properly installed, check both transaxle mounts for proper alignment. If window "A" is not properly located, Fig. 3, loosen mount to cradle retaining nuts and allow mount to reposition itself. If transaxle mount is allowed to remain out of position, damage to drive train components may result. Torque retaining nuts to 18 ft. lbs.

Fig. 1 Engine mounts. 1980-81 4-151

ENGINE, REPLACE

4-151

1. Disconnect battery ground cable.
2. Drain cooling system, then remove air cleaner.
3. Disconnect distributor, starter, alternator, oil pressure and engine temperature sender wiring and all other electrical connections that will interfere with engine removal. Also disconnect engine to body ground cable.
4. Disconnect and tag all vacuum hose connections that will interfere with engine removal.
5. Disconnect throttle and transaxle linkage at carburetor, then remove upper radiator hose.
6. On models equipped with A/C, remove A/C compressor from mounting bracket and position aside. Do not disconnect hoses.
7. Remove front engine strut assembly.
8. Disconnect heater hose at intake manifold.
9. Remove transaxle to engine attaching bolts, leaving the upper two bolts in place.
10. Remove front mount to cradle bracket attaching nuts.
11. Remove forward exhaust pipe, then remove flywheel inspection cover and starter motor.
12. On models equipped with automatic transmission, remove torque converter to flywheel attaching bolts.
13. Remove power steering pump and bracket and position aside, if equipped.
14. Remove heater hose and lower radiator hose.
15. Remove two rear transaxle support bracket bolts.
16. Disconnect fuel line at fuel pump.
17. Using a suitable jack and a block of wood placed under the transaxle, raise engine and transaxle until engine front mount studs clear cradle bracket.
18. Using suitable engine lifting equipment, put tension on engine, then remove the two remaining transaxle bolts.
19. Slide engine forward and lift engine from vehicle.
20. Install engine using suitable engine lifting equipment. Align engine with transaxle bell housing.

NOTE: Do not completely lower engine into chassis while jack is supporting transaxle.

21. With engine lifting equipment supporting engine, install two upper bell housing to engine attaching bolts.
22. Remove jack supporting transaxle, then lower engine onto chassis mounts and remove engine lifting equipment.
23. Raise and support front of vehicle, then install front mount to chassis attaching nuts.
24. To complete installation, reverse procedure following steps 1 through 16.

1980-81 V6-173

Manual Transaxle

1. Disconnect battery cables from battery, then remove air cleaner.
2. Drain cooling system, then disconnect and tag all vacuum hoses that will interfere with engine removal.
3. Disconnect throttle linkage from carburetor.
4. Disconnect engine wiring harness connector.
5. Disconnect radiator hoses from radiator and heater hoses from engine.
6. Remove power steering pump and bracket from engine, if equipped.
7. Disconnect clutch cable from transaxle and shift linkage from transaxle shift levers. Remove cables from transaxle bosses.
8. Disconnect speedometer cable from transaxle, then lower vehicle.
9. Install engine support fixture J-22825 between cowl and radiator support, locate support hook into engine rear lifting eye, Fig. 4. Raise engine until weight is relieved from mount assemblies.
10. Remove all but one transaxle to engine attaching bolts.
11. Unlock steering column and raise vehicle.
12. Remove stabilizer bar to lower control arm attaching nuts.
13. Remove side and crossmember plate to side and crossmember assembly attaching bolts and remove plate assembly on lefthand side. Loosen plate bolts on right side.
14. Remove crossover pipe, then remove front, rear and side powertrain mount to cradle attaching bolts.
15. Remove left front wheel and tire assembly.
16. Remove front crossmember to right side member attaching bolts.
17. Using tool No. J-28468, pull both driveshafts from transaxle assembly.
18. Remove lefthand side cradle to body mount attaching bolts.
19. Swing side and crossmember assembly to left and secure to fender well.
20. Lower left side of engine by loosening engine support fixture J-22825, then position a suitable jack under transaxle.

Fig. 1A Engine mounts. 1982-83 4-151

21. Remove the one remaining transaxle to engine attaching bolt, then separate transaxle from engine and lower transaxle from vehicle.
22. Install suitable engine lifting equipment.
23. If equipped with A/C, remove A/C compressor from mounting bracket and position aside. Do not disconnect hoses.
24. Disconnect forward strut bracket from radiator support and position out of way.
25. Raise engine and remove from vehicle.
26. Reverse procedure to install.

Automatic Transaxle

1. Disconnect battery ground cable and remove air cleaner.
2. Drain cooling system, then disconnect all vacuum hoses that will interfere with engine removal.
3. Disconnect detent cable and throttle cable from carburetor.
4. Disconnect engine wiring harness connector and engine to body ground strap at engine forward strut.
5. Disconnect radiator hoses from radiator and heater hoses from engine.
6. Remove power steering pump and bracket from engine and position aside.
7. Raise vehicle and remove crossover pipe.
8. Disconnect fuel lines at hose connects on right hand side of engine.
9. Remove engine front mount to cradle attaching nuts.
10. Disconnect battery cables from starter motor and transaxle case.
11. Remove torque converter housing cover and disconnect torque converter from flex plate.
12. Remove transaxle to engine block support bracket bolts.
13. Lower vehicle and support transaxle by positioning a suitable jack under transaxle rear extension.
14. Remove engine strut bracket from radiator support and position out of way.
15. Remove transaxle to engine retaining bolts. Note location of ground stud.
16. If equipped with A/C, remove A/C compressor from mounting bracket and position aside.
17. Install suitable engine lifting equipment, then raise engine and remove from vehicle.
18. Reverse procedure to install.

1982-83 V6-173

1. Disconnect battery cables from battery and remove air cleaner.
2. Drain cooling system.
3. Remove engine strut bracket from radiator support and swing rearward.
4. Remove AIR pump and bracket, then remove A/C compressor from mounting bracket and place aside, if so equipped.
5. Disconnect vacuum hosing to all non-engine mounted components.
6. Disconnect accelerator cable and detent cable if so equipped.
7. Disconnect engine harness from ECM and pull connector through front of dash.
8. Disconnect engine harness from junction block at left side of dash panel.
9. Disconnect radiator and heater hoses from engine.
10. Remove power steering pump and bracket assembly from engine, if so equipped.
11. Disconnect fuel lines rubber hose connections at left side of engine compartment.
12. Raise vehicle, remove engine front mount-to-cradle and mount-to-engine bracket retaining nuts at right side of

vehicle.
13. Disconnect battery cables from starter motor and transaxle case and remove starter.
14. Remove transaxle inspection cover and on automatic transaxle models, disconnect torque converter flex plate.
15. Remove crankshaft lower pulley and remove all bolts.
16. Disconnect exhaust pipe.
17. Remove lower transaxle-to-engine bolt, located at back side of engine.
18. Disconnect power steering cut-off switch, if so equipped.
19. Remove exhaust cross over pipe, then lower vehicle.
20. Remove remaining transaxle-to-engine bolts. Make note of ground stud location.
21. Place a support under transaxle rear extension. Install suitable lifting device and remove engine.
22. Reverse procedure to install.

FRONT ENGINE MOUNT

Fig. 2 Engine mounts. 1980—81 V6-173

CYLINDER HEAD, REPLACE

4-151

1. Raise and support front of vehicle, then drain cooling system and disconnect exhaust pipe from exhaust manifold.
2. Lower vehicle and remove oil dipstick tube and air cleaner.
3. Disconnect wire connectors and vacuum hoses from carburetor.
4. Remove EGR valve base plate from intake manifold.
5. Disconnect heater hose from intake manifold, then remove AIR system discharge tube attaching bolt from intake manifold.
6. Remove ignition coil lower attaching bolt, then disconnect wiring from coil.
7. Disconnect all wiring from cylinder head

FRONT ENGINE MOUNT

DRAIN HOLE MUST POINT REARWARD.

VIEW A

MOUNT BRACKET

FRT

RADIATOR SUPPORT

FWD

STRUT

STRUT BRACKET

BRACKET LE2

WITH A/C

FRT

ENGINE STRUT

FRT

Fig. 2A Engine mounts. 1982—83 V6-173

ALLOW WINDOW ('A') TO CENTER IN INTERLOCK ('B') BEFORE TORQUING RETAINING NUTS

'A'

'A'

'B'

'B'

REAR MOUNT

FRONT MOUNT

Fig. 3 Transaxle mount alignment. V6-173

and intake manifold, then remove engine upper support attaching bolt from engine strut.

8. Remove A/C compressor and position aside with refrigerant lines attached.
9. Remove alternator drive belt, then remove AIR pump bracket bolt from engine block.
10. Disconnect throttle and throttle valve cables from carburetor and intake manifold.
11. Disconnect upper radiator hose from cylinder head, then disconnect AIR hose from tube assembly.
12. Remove rocker arm cover, then remove rocker arms and push rods.
13. Remove cylinder head attaching bolts, then lift cylinder head and intake and exhaust manifolds as an assembly from cylinder block.
14. Reverse procedure to install. Coat heads and threads of cylinder bolts with a suitable sealing compound, then install bolts finger tight. Tighten cylinder head bolts in sequence shown in Figs. 5 and 5A. Tighten intake manifold bolts in sequence shown in Fig. 6, if necessary.

V6-173

1. Remove intake manifold, then disconnect exhaust pipe from exhaust manifold.
2. If left hand cylinder head is to be removed, remove alternator bracket and stud, heat stove pipe, P.A.I.R. pipe and dipstick tube pipe bracket from cylinder head.
3. Loosen rocker arm stud nuts until push rods can be removed.
4. Remove cylinder head attaching bolts, then remove cylinder head.
5. Reverse procedure to install. Coat cylinder head bolt threads with sealer and install bolts finger tight. Torque cylinder bolts in sequence shown in Fig. 7 and intake manifold bolts in sequence shown in Fig. 8.

ROCKER ARM STUDS

4-151

Rocker arm studs that are cracked or have damaged threads can be removed from the cylinder head using a deep well socket. Install and torque new rocker arm stud to 75 ft. lbs.

V6-173

Rocker arm studs that are cracked or have damaged threads can be replaced. If threads in cylinder head are damaged or stripped, the head can be retapped and a helical type insert added. When installing a new rocker arm stud, torque stud to 43 to 49 ft. lbs.

VALVES, ADJUST

V6-173

1. Crank engine until mark on torsional damper is aligned with TDC mark on timing tab. Check to ensure engine is in the No. 1 cylinder firing position by placing fingers on No. 1 cylinder rocker arms as mark on damper comes near TDC mark

Fig. 4 Engine support fixture

Fig. 5 Cylinder head tightening sequence. 1980 4-151

Fig. 5A Cylinder head bolt tightening sequence. 1981—83 4-151

on timing tab. If valves are not moving, the engine is in the No. 1 firing position. If valves move as damper mark nears TDC mark on timing tab, engine is in the No. 4 cylinder firing position and should be rotated one revolution to reach the No. 1 cylinder firing position.

2. With engine in the No. 1 cylinder firing position, adjust the following valves: Exhaust- 1, 2, 3; Intake- 1, 5, 6. To adjust valves, back off adjusting nut until lash is felt at push rod, then tighten adjusting nut until all lash is removed. This can be determined by rotating the push rod while tightening the adjusting nut. When all lash has been eliminated, turn adjusting nut the additional number of turns listed in the Valve Specifications.

3. Crank engine one revolution until mark on torsional damper and TDC mark are again aligned. This is the No. 4 cylinder firing position. With engine in this position, the following valve can be adjusted: Exhaust- 4, 5 & 6; Intake- 2, 3 & 4.

4. Install rocker arm covers, then start engine and check timing and idle speed.

VALVE ARRANGEMENT

Front to Rear

4-151	I-E-I-E-E-I-E-I
V6-173 Right	E-I-E-I-I-E
V6-173 Left	E-I-I-E-I-E

Fig. 6 Intake manifold tightening sequence. 4-151

VALVE LIFT SPECS.

Engine	Year	Intake	Exhaust
4-151	1980	.406	.406
	1981—83	.398	.398
V6-173	1980—83	.347	.394
V6-173 H.O.	1981	.393	.410
	1982—83	.394	.410

VALVE TIMING

Intake Opens Before TDC

Engine	Year	Degrees
4-151	1980—83	33
V6-173	1980—83	25
V6-173 H.O.	1981—83	31

VALVE GUIDES

Valve guides are an integral part of the cylinder head and are not removable. If valve stem clearance becomes excessive, the valve guide should be reamed to the next oversize and the appropriate oversize valves installed. Valves are available in .003 and .005 inch oversizes for 4-151 engine and .0035, .0155 and .0305 inch for V6-173 engines.

VALVE LIFTERS

NOTE: Some V6-173 engines will be equipped with both standard and .25 mm. oversize valve lifters. The cylinder case will be marked

Fig. 7 Cylinder head tightening sequence. V6-173

where the oversize valve lifters are installed with a daub of white paint and .25 mm. O.S. will be stamped on the valve lifter boss, Fig. 9.

Failure of a hydraulic valve lifter, Fig. 10, is generally caused by an inadequate oil supply or dirt. An air leak at the intake side of the oil pump or too much oil in the engine will cause air bubbles in the oil supply to the lifters causing them to collapse. This is a probable cause of trouble if several lifters fail to function, but air in oil is an unlikely cause of failure of a single unit.

On 4-151 engines, valve lifters can be removed after removing rocker arm cover, intake manifold and push rod cover. Loosen rocker arm stud nut and rotate rocker arm so that push rod can be removed, then remove valve lifter. It may be necessary to use tool No. J-3049 to facilitate lifter removal.

On V6-173 engines, valve lifters can be removed after removing rocker arm covers, intake manifold, rocker stud nuts, rocker arm balls, rocker arms and push rods.

Fig. 8 Intake manifold tightening sequence. V6-173

Fig. 9 Oversize valve lifter marking. V6-173

Fig. 10 Hydraulic valve lifter components

ENGINE FRONT COVER, REPLACE

4-151

1. Remove drive belts, then remove right front inner fender splash shield.
2. Remove crankshaft pulley attaching bolt, then remove pulley and hub from shaft.
3. Remove alternator lower bracket.
4. Remove front engine mount to cradle nuts, then install suitable engine lifting equipment and raise engine.
5. Remove engine mount bracket to cylinder block bolts, then remove mount and bracket as an assembly.
6. Remove oil pan to front cover attaching screws. Pull front cover slightly forward to permit cutting of oil pan front seal.
7. Using a suitable cutting tool, cut oil pan front seal flush with cylinder block at both sides of cover.
8. Remove front cover and attached portion of oil pan front seal, then remove front cover gasket.
9. Clean gasket surfaces on cylinder block and front cover.
10. Cut tabs from a new oil pan front seal using a suitable cutting tool, then install seal to front cover, pressing tabs into holes provided on front cover.
11. Coat front cover gasket with gasket sealer, then position gasket on front cover.
12. Apply a ⅛ inch bead of RTV sealer to joint formed at oil pan and cylinder block.
13. Install centering tool No. J-23042 into front cover seal bore. It is important that the centering tool be used to align front cover, otherwise damage to seal may result when hub is installed.
14. Install front cover to block, then install and partially tighten the two oil pan to front cover screws.
15. Install front cover to cylinder block attaching screws. Torque all cover attaching screws to 90 inch lbs., then remove centering tool J-23042.
16. Install front mount bracket assembly and alternator lower mounting bracket.
17. Lower engine and remove engine lifting equipment.
18. Install lower mount to cradle nuts, crankshaft pulley and hub, right front fender inner splash shield and drive belts.

NOTE: Apply Drylock No. 299 or equivalent to threaded area of crankshaft pulley to hub bolts before installing bolts.

V6-173

1. Disconnect battery ground cable, then drain cooling system and remove drive belts.
2. Remove water pump as described under Water Pump, Replace, Fig. 11.
3. If equipped with A/C, remove compressor from mounting bracket and position compressor aside, then remove mounting bracket.
4. Raise vehicle and remove inner fender splash shield.
5. Remove accessory drive pulley, then remove damper retaining bolt.
6. Using tool No. J-23523, remove damper.
7. Disconnect lower radiator hose from front cover.
8. Remove front cover retaining bolts, then remove front cover, Fig. 11.
9. Reverse procedure to install. Clean sealing surfaces on front cover and engine block. Apply a ³/₃₂ in. diameter bead of sealant No. 1052357 or equivalent to front cover sealing surface.

TIMING GEARS

4-151 Engine

When necessary to install a new camshaft gear, the camshaft will have to be removed as the gear is a pressed fit on the camshaft. The camshaft is held in place by a thrust plate which is retained to the engine by two capscrews which are accessible through the two holes in the gear web.

To remove gear, use an arbor press and a suitable sleeve to properly support gear on its steel hub.

Before installing gear, assemble thrust plate and gear spacer ring, then press gear onto shaft until it bottoms against spacer ring. The thrust plate end clearance should be .0015–.0050 inch. If clearance is less than .0015 inch, the spacer ring should be replaced. If clearance is greater than .0050 inch, the thrust plate should be replaced.

The crankshaft gear can be removed using a puller and two bolts in the tapped holes of the gear.

When installing timing gears, make sure that the marks on the gears are properly aligned, Fig. 12.

NOTE: The valve timing marks, Fig. 12, does not indicate TDC, compression stroke for No. 1 cylinder for use during distributor installation. When installing the distributor, rotate engine until No. 1 cylinder is on compression stroke and the camshaft timing mark is 180° from the valve timing position shown in Fig. 12.

TIMING CHAIN, REPLACE

V6-173

1. Remove front cover as described under Front Cover, Replace.
2. Place No. 1 piston at top dead center with marks on camshaft and crankshaft sprockets aligned, Fig. 13.
3. Remove camshaft sprocket bolts, then remove sprocket and timing chain. If sprocket does not come off easily, tap lower edge of sprocket with a plastic mallet.

Fig. 11 Engine front cover & water pump. V6-173

TIMING MARKS

Fig. 12 Valve timing marks. 4-151

4. If crankshaft sprocket is to be replaced, remove sprocket using a suitable puller. Install new sprocket, aligning key and keyway.
5. Install timing chain on camshaft sprocket. Hold sprocket vertically with chain hanging down and align marks on camshaft and crankshaft sprockets.
6. Align dowel pin hole in sprocket with dowl pin on camshaft, then install sprocket on camshaft.
7. Using camshaft sprocket attaching bolts, draw sprocket on camshaft. Torque bolts to 15 to 20 ft. lbs.
8. Lubricate timing chain with engine oil, then install front cover as outlined previously.

CAMSHAFT, REPLACE

4-151

1. Remove engine from vehicle as described under Engine, Replace.
2. Remove rocker arm cover, then loosen rocker arm stud nuts and pivot rocker arms clear of push rods.
3. Remove distributor and fuel pump.
4. Remove push rod cover, push rods and valve lifters.
5. Remove alternator, alternator lower mounting bracket and engine front mount bracket assembly.
6. Remove oil pump driveshaft and gear assembly.
7. Remove front pulley hub and front cover assembly.
8. Working through holes in camshaft sprocket, remove two camshaft thrust plate retaining screws.
9. Pull camshaft and gear assembly from engine block. Use care not to damage camshaft bearings.
10. Reverse procedure to install. When installing camshaft, align crankshaft and camshaft valve timing marks on gear teeth, Fig. 12.

Fig. 13 Valve timing marks. V6-173

NOTE: The valve timing marks, Fig. 12, does not indicate TDC compression stroke for No. 1 cylinder for use during distributor installation. When installing the distributor, rotate engine until No. 1 cylinder is on compression stroke and the camshaft timing mark is 180 degrees from valve timing position shown in Fig. 12.

V6-173

1. Remove engine from vehicle as described under "Engine, Replace."
2. Remove valve lifters and engine front cover as described previously.
3. Remove fuel pump and push rod.
4. Remove timing chain and sprocket as described under Timing Chain, Replace.
5. Withdraw camshaft from engine, using care not to damage camshaft bearings.
6. Reverse procedure to install. When installing timing chain, align valve timing marks as shown in Fig. 13.

NOTE: The valve timing marks, Fig. 13, does not indicate TDC compression stroke for No. 1 cylinder for use during distributor installation. When installing the distributor, rotate engine until No. 1 cylinder is on compression stroke and the camshaft timing mark is 180 degrees from valve timing position shown in Fig. 13.

PISTONS & RODS, ASSEMBLE

4-151

Assemble piston to rod with notch on piston facing toward front of engine and the raised notch side of rod at bearing end facing toward rear of engine, Fig. 14.
Upon installation, measure the connecting rod side clearance using a suitable feeler gauge. Clearance should be .006 to .022 inch.

V6-173

Assemble pistons to connecting rods as shown in Fig. 15.

Upon installation, measure the connecting rod side clearance using a suitable feeler gauge. Clearance should be .006 to .017 inch.

PISTONS, PINS & RINGS

4-151

Pistons and rings are available in standard and oversizes of .010, .020 and .030 inch. Piston pins are available in oversizes of .001 and .003 inch.

V6-173

Pistons and rings are available in standard size and oversizes of .05 and 1 mm.

MAIN & ROD BEARINGS

Main and rod bearings are available in standard size and undersizes of .001, .002 and .010 inch for the 4-151 engine. Main bearings are available in standard size and undersizes of .013 and .026 mm and connecting rod bearings are available in standard size and undersizes of .016 and .032 mm. for the V6-173 engine.

OIL PAN, REPLACE

4-151

1. Raise vehicle and drain crankcase.
2. Remove engine front mount to cradle attaching nuts.
3. Disconnect exhaust pipe at manifold and rear transaxle mount.
4. Remove starter motor and flywheel housing cover.
5. Remove alternator upper mounting bracket.
6. Install a suitable engine lifting device and raise engine.
7. Remove lower alternator mounting bracket and engine support bracket.
8. Remove oil pan attaching bolts and oil pan.
9. Clean engine block and oil pan gasket surfaces.

Fig. 14 Piston & rod assembly. 4-151

Fig. 15 Piston & rod assembly. V6-173

10. Reverse procedure to install. Apply a 1/8 in. by 1/4 in. long bead of RTV sealer at split lines of front and side oil pan gaskets. Also apply a small amount of RTV sealer in depressions where rear oil pan gasket engages engine block.

NOTE: When installing oil pan attaching bolts, the bolts attaching the oil pan to the front cover should be installed last. These bolts are installed at an angle and the bolt holes will only be aligned after the other oil pan bolts have been installed.

V6-173

1. Disconnect battery ground cable, then raise vehicle and drain crankcase.
2. Disconnect crossover pipe from exhaust manifold, if necessary.
3. Remove flywheel housing cover, then remove starter motor.
4. On models equipped with manual transaxle, remove engine mounting bracket to engine mount attaching nuts, then raise engine approximately 18 mm.
5. Remove oil pan attaching bolts and oil pan.
6. Reverse procedure to install. Apply a 1/8 in. bead of RTV sealer to oil pan sealing flange.

OIL PUMP SERVICE

4-151

Removal
1. Drain crankcase, then remove oil pan as described under "Oil Pan, Replace."
2. Remove two oil pump mounting bolts and nuts from main cap bolt and remove oil pump and screen as an assembly.

Disassemble
1. Remove four pump cover to body attaching screws, then remove cover, idler and drive gears and shaft, Fig. 16.
2. Remove pin, retainer, spring and pressure regulator valve.

Inspection
Inspect pump components and should any of the following conditions be found, the oil pump assembly should be replaced.
a. Inspect pump body for cracks and excessive wear.

Fig. 17 Oil pump disassembled. V6-173

Fig. 16 Oil pump disassembled. 4-151

b. Inspect oil pump gears for damage, cracks or excessive wear.
c. Check shaft for looseness in housing.
d. Check cover for wear that would allow oil to leak past ends of gears.
e. Check oil pick screen for damage to screen or relief grommet. Also remove any debris from screen surface.
f. Check pressure regulator valve for fit in body.

Assemble
1. Place drive gear and shaft in pump body, then install idler gear with smooth side of gear facing pump cover, Fig. 16.
2. Install and torque pump cover attaching screws to 105 inch lbs. Check to ensure that pump rotates freely.
3. Install pressure regulator valve, spring, retainer and pin.

Installation
1. Align oil pump shaft with tang on oil pump drive shaft, then install pump on block, positioning pump flange over oil pump drive shaft lower bushing.
2. Install oil pump mounting bolts and torque bolts to 20 ft. lbs., then install oil pan as described under Oil Pan, Replace.

Fig. 18 Positioning tool J-29176 against timing cover boss. V6-173

V6-173

Removal
1. Remove oil pan as described under Oil Pan, Replace.
2. Remove pump to rear main bearing cap bolt and remove pump and extension shaft.

Disassembly
1. Remove pump cover attaching bolts and pump cover, Fig. 17.
2. Mark drive and idler gear teeth so they can be installed in the same position, then remove idler and drive gear and shaft from pump body.
3. Remove pin, spring and pressure regulator valve from pump cover.
4. If pick-up tube and screen assembly are to be replaced, mount pump cover in a soft jawed vise and remove pick-up tube from cover. Do not remove screen from pick-up tube, these components are serviced as an assembly.

Inspection
1. Inspect pump body and cover for excessive wear and cracks.
2. Inspect pump gear for damage or excessive wear. If pump gears are damaged or worn, the entire pump assembly must be replaced.
3. Check drive gear shaft for looseness in pump body.
4. Inspect pump cover for wear that would allow oil to leak past gear teeth.
5. Inspect pick-up tube and screen assembly for damage.
6. Check pressure regulator valve for fit in pump cover.

Assembly
1. If pick-up tube and screen were removed, apply sealer to end of pick-up tube, then mount pump cover in a soft jawed vise and using tool No. J-8369, tap pick-up tube into position using a plastic mallet.

NOTE: Whenever the pick-up tube and screen assembly has been removed, a new pick-up tube and screen assembly should be installed. Use care when installing pick-up tube and screen assembly so that tube does not twist, shear or collapse. Loss of a press fit condition could result in an air leak and a loss of oil pressure.

2. Install pressure regulator valve, spring and pin, Fig. 17.

Fig. 19 Applying sealer to water pump mating surfaces. V6-173

3. Install drive gear and shaft in pump body.
4. Align marks made during disassembly, then install idler gear.
5. Install pump cover gasket, cover and attaching bolts. Torque bolts to 6 to 9 ft. lbs.
6. Rotate pump drive shaft by hand and check pump for smooth operation.

Installation
1. Assemble pump and extension shaft with retainer to rear main bearing cap, aligning top end of hexagon extension shaft with hexagon socket on lower end of distributor shaft.
2. Install pump to rear main bearing cap bolt.
3. Install oil pan as described under Oil Pan, Replace.

CRANKSHAFT REAR OIL SEAL, REPLACE
4-151

NOTE: The rear main oil seal is a one piece unit and is replaced without removing the oil pan or crankshaft.

1. Remove transaxle and flywheel.
2. Using a suitable screwdriver, remove rear main bearing oil seal. Use care not to scratch crankshaft.
3. Lubricate inside and outside diameters of replacement seal with engine oil. Install seal by hand onto rear crankshaft flange with helical lip side facing toward engine. Ensure seal is firmly and evenly seated.
4. Install flywheel and transaxle.

REAR MAIN BEARING OIL SEAL REPAIR
V6-173

1. Remove oil pan and oil pump as described previously.
2. Remove rear main bearing cap.
3. Using tool No. J-29114-2, gently drive upper seal into groove approximately 1/4 in.
4. Repeat step 3 for other end of seal.
5. Measure the amount that was driven in on one side and add 1/16 in. Using a suitable cutting tool, cut this length from the oil rear main bearing cap lower seal using the main bearing cap as a guide. Repeat this step for the other end of seal.
6. Place piece of cut seal into groove of seal installer tool guide No. J-29114-1 and install tool guide onto engine block.

7. Using seal packing tool No. J29114-2, drive piece of seal into block. Drive seal in until packing tool contacts machined stop.
8. Remove tool guide and repeat steps 6 and 7 for other end of seal.
9. Install new seal in bearing cap.
10. Install rear main bearing cap. Apply a thin film of sealant No. 1052357 or equivalent to rear main bearing cap and case interface. Use care not to allow sealant to contact crankshaft journal or main bearing.

BELT TENSION DATA

	New Lbs.	Used Lbs.
Air Cond.		
4-151	135–165	65①
V6-173	145	65–80
Alternator		
4-151	120–150	55①
V6-173	145	65–80
Power Steer.		
4-151	120–150	55①
V6-173	135	65–80

①—Minimum.

WATER PUMP, REPLACE
4-151

Removal
1. Disconnect battery negative cable.
2. Remove accessory drive belts.
3. Using tool J 25034, remove pulley.
4. Remove water pump attaching bolts and remove pump.

Installation
1. With sealing surfaces cleaned, place a 1/8 inch bead of sealant, part number 1052289 or equivalent, on water pump sealing surface.
2. With sealing surfaces still wet, install pump and attaching bolts. Coat threaded area of bolts with part number 1052080 sealer or equivalent and torque bolts to 6 ft. lbs.
3. Using tool J-25033, install pulley on pump.
4. Install accessory drive belts and adjust to specifications.
5. Connect battery negative cable.

V6-173
1. Disconnect battery ground cable, then drain cooling system.
2. Disconnect heater hose at water pump, then remove drive belts and water pump pulley.

3. Using the existing tapped hole in the cylinder head, install tool No. J-29167 and torque mounting bolt to 10 ft. lbs., Fig. 18.
4. Remove water pump attaching bolts, then remove pump assembly from engine.
5. Clean mating surfaces of water pump and cylinder block, then apply a bead of sealant 1052375 or equivalent to water pump mating surface, Fig. 19.
6. Apply sealant 1052080 or equivalent to pump attaching bolt threads, then install water pump assembly. Torque M6x1.0 bolts to 8 ft. lbs., M8x1.25 bolts to 16 ft. lbs. and M10x1.5 bolts to 25 ft. lbs.
7. Remove tool J-29176, then install water pump pulley and drive belts and connect heater hose to pump.
8. Fill cooling system and connect battery ground cable, then start engine and check for leaks.

FUEL PUMP, REPLACE

1. Disconnect battery ground cable, then raise and support vehicle.
2. On V6-173 models, remove shields and oil filter.
3. On all models, disconnect fuel inlet hose from pump, then disconnect vapor return hose if equipped.
4. Loosen fuel line at carburetor, then disconnect fuel outlet line from fuel pump.
5. Remove two fuel pump attaching bolts, then remove fuel pump.
6. Position fuel pump and gasket on block, then install attaching bolts. Tighten fuel pump attaching bolts evenly and alternately.

NOTE: Before installing fuel pump, it is a good practice to crank the engine so that the fuel pump eccentric is out of the way of the fuel pump rocker arm when pump is installed. In this way there will be less tension on the rocker arm, thereby easing installation of pump.

7. Connect fuel outlet line to fuel pump. If difficulty is encountered in starting fitting, disconnect upper end of fuel line from carburetor and connect fuel line to fuel pump, then tighten fittings at carburetor and fuel pump.
8. Install fuel inlet hose and vapor return hose, if equipped.
9. On V6-173 models, install oil filter and shields, then check oil level.
10. On all models, lower vehicle and connect battery ground cable. Start engine and check for leaks.

Clutch & Transaxle Section

CLUTCH PEDAL, ADJUST

The clutch is automatically adjusted by a self-adjusting mechanism, Fig. 1, mounted to the clutch pedal and bracket assembly. The cable is a fixed length cable and cannot be shortened or lengthened, however, the position of the cable can be changed by adjusting the position of the quadrant in relation to the clutch pedal. The self-adjusting mechanism monitors clutch cable tension and adjusts the quadrant position, changing the effective cable length.

Inspection

1. With engine running and service and parking brakes applied, depress clutch pedal to approximately ½ inch from floor mat.
2. Move shift lever between "First" and "Reverse" gears several times. If no clashing of the gears occur when going into "Reverse", the clutch is releasing fully.
3. If the shifting in Step 2 is not smooth, the clutch is not releasing fully and the linkage should be inspected and corrected as necessary.
4. Check clutch pedal bushings for sticking or excessive wear.
5. Have an assistant depress the clutch pedal to the floor and observe clutch fork lever travel at transaxle. The end of the clutch fork lever should have a total travel of approximately 1.6–1.8 inches.
6. To check the self-adjusting mechanism, proceed as follows:
   a. Depress the clutch pedal and observe if the pawl firmly engages the teeth of the quadrant.
   b. Release the clutch pedal and observe if the pawl is lifted off the quadrant teeth by the stop on the bracket.

CLUTCH, REPLACE

1. Remove transaxle as outlined under "Manual Transaxle, Replace" procedure.
2. Mark position of pressure plate to flywheel to aid reassembly.
3. Gradually loosen pressure plate attaching bolts until spring pressure is relieved.
4. Support pressure plate and remove mounting bolts, pressure plate and driven disc, Fig. 2.

5. Clean pressure and flywheel mounting surfaces. Inspect bearing retainer outer surface of transaxle.
6. Place driven disc in relative installed position and support with a dummy shaft.

NOTE: The driven disc is installed with the damper springs offset toward the transaxle. Stamped letters found on the driven disc identify the "Flywheel Side."

---

7. Install and gradually tighten the pressure plate to flywheel bolts. Remove dummy shaft.
8. Lubricate the release bearing outside diameter groove and the inside diameter recess.
9. Install transaxle.

MANUAL TRANSAXLE SHIFT CABLE, ADJUST

1. Remove shifter boot and retainer.
2. Install two 5/32 inch diameter pins or No. 22 twist drills into the alignment holes in the control assembly.
3. Connect the two shift cables to the control assembly using the studs and pin retainers. The cables must be routed properly and operate freely.
4. Place transaxle into "First" gear by pushing the rail selector shaft inward (Downward) just to the point of resistance of the inhibitor spring. Then, rotate shift lever fully counter-clockwise.
5. Install stud with cable "A" attached, Fig. 3, into slotted area in shift lever "F".
6. Install stud with cable "B" attached, Fig. 3, into slotted area of select lever "D" while gently pulling on lever "D" to remove lash.
7. Remove the two pins or twist drills from control assembly.
8. Check for proper operation. If "Hang-up" is encountered when shifting in the 1–2 gear range and the shift cables are ad-

justed properly, it may be necessary to change the shifter shaft selective washer. Perform the following procedure to obtain correct washer thickness:
   a. Remove reverse inhibitor fitting spring and washer from end of housing.
   b. Place shifter shaft in "Second" gear.
   c. Measure dimension "A", Fig. 4, which is distance between end of housing and the shoulder just behind end of shaft.
   d. Apply a 9–13 pound load on opposite end of shaft, then measure dimension "B", Fig. 4, which is distance between end of housing and end of shifter shaft major diameter.
   e. Subtract dimension "B" from dimension "A" to obtain dimension "C".
   f. Refer to the following chart to obtain correct thickness shim:

Dimension "C" Inch	Shim Part No.
.07–.09	14008235
.09–.10	476709
.10–.11	476710
.11–.12	476711
.12–.13	476712
.13–.15	476713
.15–.16	476714
.16–.17	476715
.17–.18	476716

MANUAL TRANSAXLE, REPLACE

1980–81

1. Disconnect battery ground cable from transaxle case and secure to upper radiator hose.
2. If equipped, remove transaxle strut bracket bolts at transaxle on left side of vehicle.
3. Remove the upper four engine to transaxle bolts and the bolt toward the rear of the vehicle near the cowl, Fig. 5. This bolt is installed from the engine side.
4. Loosen but do not remove the engine to

Fig. 1 Clutch self-adjusting mechanism

Fig. 2 Clutch assembly

Fig. 3 Manual transaxle shift cable adjustment

Fig. 4 Manual transaxle shifter shaft selective washer measurement

Fig. 5 Transaxle to engine attachment

Fig. 6 Engine support tool installation

transaxle bolt near the starter at front of vehicle.

5. Disconnect speedometer cable from transaxle. If equipped with Cruise Control, remove transaxle speedometer cable at cruise control transducer.
6. Remove retaining clip and washer from transaxle shift linkage at transaxle.
7. Remove clips securing shift cable to mounting bosses on transaxle case.
8. Install engine support fixture, Fig. 6, so that one end is supported on cowl tray over wiper motor and the other end rests on the radiator support. Connect fixture hook to engine lift ring and raise engine to relieve weight from engine mounts.

CAUTION: The engine support fixture must be positioned in the center of the cowl and the attaching parts properly torqued before supporting engine. This fixture is not intended to support entire weight of engine and transaxle. Personal injury could result from improper use of the support fixture.

9. Unlock steering column and raise and support vehicle.
10. Drain fluid from transaxle case.
11. Remove two nuts securing stabilizer bar

Fig. 7 Cradle attachments

to vehicle left side lower control arm, Fig. 7.

12. Remove four bolts securing vehicle left side stabilizer bar retaining plate to cradle, Fig. 7.
13. Loosen four bolts securing stabilizer bracket on vehicle right side, Fig. 7.
14. If necessary, disconnect and remove exhaust pipe.
15. Pull stabilizer bar downward on vehicle left side.
16. Remove four nuts and disconnect the front and rear transaxle mounts at cradle, Fig. 7.
17. Remove two rear center crossmember bolts, Fig. 7.
18. Remove three front cradle attaching bolts at vehicle right side, Fig. 7. The nuts are accessible by pulling back the splash shield next to the frame rail.
19. If equipped, remove top bolt from lower front transaxle damper "Shock Absorber".
20. Remove left front wheel.
21. Remove the front cradle to body attaching bolts on left side of vehicle, then the rear cradle to body attaching bolts, Fig. 7.
22. Using tool J-28468 or equivalent, pull left side driveshaft from transaxle assembly. The right side driveshaft may be disconnected from the case. When the transaxle assembly is removed, the right side driveshaft may be swung aside. Use the boot protector when disconnecting the driveshafts.
23. Swing the partial cradle toward the vehicle left side and secure outboard of the fender well.
24. Remove the flywheel and starter shield bolts and the shields.
25. If equipped, remove two transaxle extension bolts from engine to transaxle bracket.
26. Securely attach the transaxle case to a suitable jack.
27. Remove the last transaxle to engine bolt.
28. Remove transaxle by sliding toward vehicle left side, away from engine. Lower transaxle from vehicle.
29. Reverse procedure to install and note the following:
    a. When installing the transaxle, position the right side drive axle shaft into its bore as transaxle is being installed. The right hand driveshaft cannot be readily installed after the transaxle is attached to the engine.

Fig. 8 Transaxle to engine attachment

b. After the transaxle is attached to the engine, swing the cradle into position and immediately install the cradle to body bolts. When swinging the cradle into the installed position, guide the left side driveshaft into the case bore.

1982–83

1. Disconnect battery ground cable from transaxle case and attach to upper radiator hose with wire or tape.
2. Remove two transaxle strut bracket bolts at transaxle, on left side of engine compartment, if so equipped.
3. Remove exhaust crossover pipe, if equipped.
4. Remove top four engine to transaxle bolts and one to rear of vehicle near cowl. The bolt nearer cowl is installed from engine side, Fig. 8.
5. Loosen but do not remove transaxle bolt near starter, at front of vehicle.
6. Disconnect speedometer cable at transaxle. On vehicles equipped with cruise control, remove transaxle speedometer cable at cruise control transducer.
6. Remove retaining clip and washer from transaxle shift linkage at transaxle.
7. Remove clips securing shift cables to mounting bosses on transaxle case.
8. Disconnect clutch cable. Install engine support fixture.
9. Remove left hand side and crossmember assembly using following procedures:
    a. Rotate steering wheel so that intermediate shaft to steering gear stub shaft attaching bolt is in up position and remove bolt.
    b. Raise vehicle.
    c. Position jack under engine to act as a support during removal and installation.
    d. Remove left front tire and wheel assembly.
    e. Remove power steering pressure and return line brackets.
    f. Disconnect drive line vibration absorber and disconnect front stabilizer bar from left hand lower control arm.
    g. Disconnect left lower ball joint at knuckle then remove both front stabilizer bar reinforcement.
    h. Using a ½ inch drill bit, drill through spot weld located between rear holes of left hand front stabilizer bar mounting.
    i. Disconnect engine and transaxle mounts from cradle.
    j. Remove side to crossmember bolts also bolts from left side body mounts.
    k. Remove left side and front crossmember assembly. It may be necessary to pull or gently pry crossmember loose.
10. Drain fluid from transaxle.
11. Install drive axle boot seal protectors. Disconnect drive axles from transaxle then swing left side drive axle outward from transaxle. Right side drive axle can be removed as transaxle is being removed from vehicle.
12. Remove flywheel and starter shield bolts. Remove shields.
13. Securely attach transaxle case to jack for removal.
14. Remove last transaxle to engine bolt.
15. Remove transaxle by sliding to left side, away from engine. Carefully lower jack, and move transaxle to bench.
16. Reverse procedure to install and note the following:
    a. When installing the transaxle, position the right side drive axle shaft into its bore as transaxle is being installed. The right hand driveshaft cannot be readily installed after the transaxle is attached to the engine.
    b. After the transaxle is attached to the engine, swing the cradle into position and immediately install the cradle to body bolts. When swinging the cradle into the installed position, guide the left side driveshaft into the case bore.

Rear Axle, Rear Suspension & Brakes

DESCRIPTION

The rear suspension. Fig. 1, consists of a rear axle assembly, control arms, coil springs, shock absorbers and a track bar. The rear axle is trailing arm type design. A stabilizer bar is welded to the inside of the axle housing and is an integral part of the axle assembly. A single unit hub and bearing assembly is bolted to each end of the axle assembly. The hub and bearing assembly is a sealed unit and must be replaced as an assembly.

REAR AXLE, REPLACE

1. Raise rear of vehicle and support rear axle using a suitable jack.
2. Remove rear wheel assembly and brake drum. Do not hammer on brake drum since damage to bearings may result.
3. Disconnect parking brake cable at equalizer, then remove brake line brackets from frame.
4. Disconnect shock absorber from lower mountings on axle housing.
5. Remove track bar attaching nut and bolt and disconnect track bar from axle housing.

NOTE: Do not suspend rear axle by brake hoses, otherwise damage to hoses may result.

6. Carefully lower rear axle assembly and remove coil spring and insulators.
7. Disconnect brake lines from control arm attachments.
8. Remove parking brake cable from rear axle attachments.
9. Remove hub attaching bolts, then the hub and bearing assembly and position backing plate out of way.
10. Remove control arm bracket to underbody attaching bolts, then lower axle assembly and remove from vehicle.
11. Reverse procedure to install. If control arm brackets were removed from control arms, torque attaching nuts to 34 ft. lbs. The control arm brackets must be at a 45 degree angle as shown in Fig. 2. Torque control arm to underbody attaching bolts to 20 ft. lbs. Torque track bar attaching nut to 33 ft. lbs.

Fig. 1   Rear axle and suspension

Fig. 2   Control arm bracket installation

HUB & BEARING ASSEMBLY, REPLACE

1. Raise and support rear of vehicle, then remove wheel and tire assembly and brake drum.

NOTE: Do not hammer on brake drum since damage to bearing may result.

2. Remove four hub and bearing assembly to rear axle attaching bolts, then the hub and bearing assembly from axle.
3. Reverse procedure to install. Torque hub and bearing assembly to rear axle attaching bolts to 35 ft. lbs.

NOTE: Use care not to drop hub and bearing assembly since damage to bearing may result.

COIL SPRING, REPLACE

1. Raise rear of vehicle and support rear axle using a suitable jack.
2. Remove right and left brake line bracket attaching bolts from frame and allow brake lines to hang freely.
3. Remove track bar attaching nut and bolt, then disconnect track bar from axle housing.
4. Disconnect shock absorbers at lower mountings.

NOTE: Do not suspend rear axle by brake hoses since damage to hoses may result.

5. Carefully lower rear axle assembly and remove springs and insulators.
6. Reverse procedure to install, Fig. 3.

CONTROL ARM BUSHING, REPLACE

1. Raise rear of vehicle and support rear axle under front side of spring seat using a suitable jack.
2. If right hand side bushing is to be replaced, disconnect parking brake cable from equalizer.
3. Remove parking brake cables from bracket attachment and position out of way.
4. Disconnect brake line bracket from frame.

Fig. 3   Coil spring & insulator installation

5. Disconnect shock absorber from lower mounting, then pull spring out of way.
6. Remove four control arm to underbody attaching bolts and allow control arm to rotate downward.
7. Remove nut and bolt from bracket attachment and remove bracket.
8. The bushing can now be replaced using tools shown in Figs. 4 and 5. When installing bushing, press bushing in until end of bushing is aligned with scribed line on tool J-28685-2, Fig. 5.
9. Reverse procedure to install control arm. Install bracket to control arm as shown in Fig. 2.

TRACK BAR, REPLACE

1. Raise rear of vehicle and support rear axle using a suitable jack.
2. Remove nut and bolt attaching track bar at axle housing and underbody and remove track bar, Fig. 6.

3. Reverse procedure to install, Fig. 6. Open side of track bar must face rear of vehicle. Also nut must be at rear of attachments at both axle and underbody attachments. Torque attaching nut at axle bracket to 33 ft. lbs. Torque attaching nut at underbody reinforcement to 34 ft. lbs.

SHOCK ABSORBER, REPLACE

1. Open deck lid and remove trim cover, then remove shock absorber upper attaching nut.
2. Raise rear of vehicle and support rear axle using a suitable jack.
3. Disconnect shock absorber at lower attachment and remove shock absorber from vehicle.
4. Reverse procedure to install. Torque shock absorber lower attaching nut to 34

Fig. 4 Control arm bushing removal

ft. lbs. Torque shock absorber upper attaching nut to 7 ft. lbs.

DRUM BRAKE ADJUSTMENTS

These brakes, Fig. 7, have self adjusting shoe mechanisms that assure correct lining-to-drum clearances at all times. The automatic adjusters operate only when the brakes are applied as the car is moving rearward.

Although the brakes are self-adjusting, an initial adjustment is necessary after the brake shoes have been relined or replaced, or when the length of the star wheel adjuster has been changed during some other service operation.

Frequent usage of an automatic transmission forward range to halt reverse vehicle motion may prevent the automatic adjusters from functioning, thereby inducing low pedal heights. Should low pedal heights be encountered, it is recommended that numerous forward and reverse stops be made until satisfactory pedal height is obtained.

NOTE: If a low pedal height condition cannot be corrected by making numerous reverse stops (provided the hydraulic system is free of air) it indicates that the self-adjusting mechanism is not functioning. Therefore, it will be necessary to remove the brake drum, clean, free up and lubricate the adjusting mechanism. Then adjust the brakes as follows, being sure the parking brake is fully released.

Adjustment

A lanced "knock out" area is provided in the web of the brake drum for servicing purposes on some models. When adjustment is required on models that do not have a lanced area on the brake drum, carefully drill a 1/2 in. hole into the round flat area on the backing plate opposite the parking brake cable. If lanced area of brake drum has been knocked out or if a hole was drilled in backing plate, ensure that all metal particles are removed from the brake compartment.

1. Turn brake adjusting screw to expand shoes until wheel can just be turned by hand.
2. Using a suitable tool to hold actuator from adjuster, back off adjuster 30 notches. If shoes still drag, back off one or two additional notches.

NOTE: Brakes should be free of drag when adjuster has been backed off approximately 12 notches. Heavy drag at this point indicates tight parking brake cables.

3. Install adjusting hole cover on brake drum or backing plate.
4. Check parking brake adjustment.

PARKING BRAKE, ADJUST

Need for parking brake adjustment is indicated if the service brake operates with sufficient pedal reserve, but the parking brake pedal travel is less than 9 ratchet clicks or more than 16 ratchet clicks.

1. Depress parking brake pedal three ratchet clicks, then raise and support rear of vehicle.
2. Check to ensure that equalizer nut groove is sufficiently lubricated with grease, then tighten adjusting nut until right rear wheel can just be rotated rearward, but is locked when forward rotation is attempted.
3. Release parking brake lever. Both wheels should rotate freely in either direction with no brake drag.

Fig. 5 Control arm bushing installation

MASTER CYLINDER, REPLACE

1. Disconnect master cylinder push rod from brake pedal.
2. Disconnect wire connector at brake warning pressure switch.
3. Disconnect brake lines from master cylinder, then remove two master cylinder mounting nuts and remove master cylinder.
4. Reverse procedure to install, then bleed brake system.

POWER BRAKE UNIT, REPLACE

1. Disconnect brake unit push rod from brake pedal.
2. Remove two master cylinder to power brake unit mounting nuts, then position master cylinder away from brake unit with brake lines attached.

NOTE: Use care not to bend or kink brake lines.

3. Disconnect vacuum hose from vacuum check valve. Plug vacuum hose to prevent entry of dirt.
4. Remove power brake unit to dash panel attaching nuts, then remove brake unit.
5. Reverse procedures to install.

Fig. 6 Track bar installation

Fig. 7 Disassembled view of rear drum brake

Front Suspension & Steering Section

Refer to the Main Index for drive axle service.

DESCRIPTION

The front suspension, Fig. 1, on these vehicles is a MacPhereson strut design. The lower control arms pivot from the engine cradle. This engine cradle has isolation mounts to the body and conventional rubber bushings are used for the lower control arm pivots. The upper end of the strut is isolated by a rubber mount incorporating a bearing for wheel turning. The lower end of the steering knuckle pivots on a ball stud which is retained in the lower control arm with rivets and is clamped to the steering knuckle. Sealed wheel bearings are used and are bolted to the steering knuckle.

Fig. 1 Front suspension

WHEEL ALIGNMENT

NOTE: Camber and toe-in are the only adjustments that can be performed on these vehicles.

Camber

The camber angle is adjusted by loosening the strut cam bolt and the through bolt and rotating the cam bolt to move the upper portion of the steering knuckle inboard or outboard. When correct camber angle is obtained, torque cam and through bolts to 140 ft. lbs.

NOTE: When performing this adjustment, the top through bolt must be loosened to prevent damage to the outer cam guide.

Toe-In

Toe-in is controlled by tie-rod position. Adjustment is made by loosening the nuts at the steering knuckle end of the tie-rods and rotating the rods to obtain proper toe-in setting. When adjusting toe-in, the tie-rod boot clamps must be removed. After correct toe-in setting is obtained, torque tie-rod nuts to 45 ft. lbs.

WHEEL BEARING, REPLACE

Removal

1. Loosen hub nut with vehicle on ground.
2. Raise and support vehicle and remove front wheel.
3. Install drive axle boot cover, tool J-28712.
4. Remove and discard hub nut.
5. Remove brake caliper from support and suspend caliper from frame with a length of wire. Do not suspend caliper by the brake hose.
6. Remove three hub and bearing attaching bolts. If the old bearing is being re-installed, mark attaching bolts and holes for re-installation, Fig. 2.
7. Using tool J-28733 or equivalent, remove bearing, Fig. 3.

NOTE: If excessive corrosion is present, ensure that the bearing is loose in the knuckle before using puller tool.

8. If installing new bearing, replace steering knuckle seal.

Installation

1. Clean and inspect bearing mating surfaces and steering knuckle bore for dirt, nicks and burrs.
2. If installing steering knuckle seal, use tool J-28671 or equivalent to install seal, Fig. 4. Apply grease to seal and knuckle bore.
3. Push bearing onto axle shaft.
4. Tighten hub nut to fully seat bearing.
5. Install bearing attaching bolts and torque to 63 ft. lbs, Fig. 2.
6. Install caliper assembly and the wheel.
7. Lower vehicle and torque hub nut to 225 ft. lbs.

LOWER BALL JOINT, REPLACE

For removal and installation procedures, refer to Fig. 5.

LOWER CONTROL ARM & BUSHINGS, REPLACE

For removal and installation procedures, refer to Fig. 6.

STEERING KNUCKLE, REPLACE

For removal and installation procedures, refer to Fig. 7.

STABILIZER BAR & BUSHINGS, REPLACE

For removal and installation procedures, refer to Fig. 8.

Fig. 2 Front wheel bearing assembly & seal

Fig. 3 Removing front wheel bearing assembly

Fig. 4 Installing front wheel bearing seal

Fig. 5 Lower ball joint removal & installation

Fig. 6 Lower control arm & bushing removal & installation

REMOVE

1. Refer to front wheel bearing removal.
2. Mark cam bolt.
3. Remove parts as shown.

INSTALL

1. Install knuckle to ball joint.
2. Loosely install knuckle to strut.
3. Refer to front wheel bearing installation.
4. Place jackstand under hub and rotor assembly and lower hoist to load control arm. Then place cam in position as noted and tighten nuts.
5. Install parts as shown.

KNUCKLE

MARK CAM BEFORE REMOVING BOLTS

BOLT SHOULD EASILY GO IN PLACE. IF NOT, CHECK STUD ALIGNMENT

190 N•m (140 FT. LBS.)

CAM BOLT

STRUT

54 N•m (40 FT. LBS.)

KNUCKLE

TIE ROD

CONTROL ARM

60 N•m (45 FT. LBS.)

J-6627 or BT-7101

REMOVE TIE ROD END

J-22269-01

27mm or 1-1/8" SOCKET

TIE ROD END

INSTALL TIE ROD END

Fig. 7   Steering knuckle removal & installation

Do not remove studs from control arm.

LOWER CONTROL ARM

BUSHING

CROSSMEMBER

End of stabilizer should be equal distance from bushing on both sides.

45 N•m (35 FT. LBS.)

CROSSMEMBER

BRACKET

BUSHING

FRONT STABILIZER

PLATE

55 N•m (40 FT. LBS.)

STRUT ASSEMBLY, REPLACE

For removal and installation procedures, refer to Fig. 9.

STRUT ASSEMBLY SERVICE

Disassembly

1. Clamp strut compressor, tool J-26584, in a suitable vise.
2. Open hinged front section of tool J-26584-4 bottom adapter, Fig. 10.
3. Place strut assembly into bottom adapter of compressor and close front section of adapter, ensuring that adapter is closed and the locating pin is fully engaged.
4. Rotate strut assembly to align top mounting assembly lip with strut compressor support notch.
5. Insert J-26584-40 top adapters between the top mounting assembly and top spring seat.

6. Rotate compressor forcing screw clockwise until top support flange contacts the J-26584-40 top adapters. Continue rotating forcing screw, compressing the strut spring approximately 1½ inch or four complete turns.

CAUTION: Do not bottom the spring or strut damper rod.

7. Remove the top nut from strut damper shaft and the top mounting assembly.
8. Rotate compressor forcing screw counterclockwise to relieve spring tension and remove spring from strut assembly, Fig. 11.

Assembly

1. Perform Steps 1 through 3 as outlined in the "Disassembly" procedure.
2. Rotate strut assembly until mounting flange is facing outward, opposite compressor forcing screw.
3. Place spring on strut, ensuring the spring

EXHAUST PIPE

20 N•m (15 FT. LBS.)

SEAL

FRONT PIPE

Fig. 8   Stabilizer bar & bushing removal & installation

INSTALL DRIVE AXLE COVER

J-28712

24 N•m (18 FT. LBS.)

190 N•m (140 FT. LBS.)

FWD

Fig. 9 Strut assembly removal & installation

REMOVE

1. Hoist car and remove wheel.
2. Remove brake line clip bolt.
3. Remove parts as shown.

   Do not allow strut assembly to contact axle boot; install tool as shown.

MARK CAM BEFORE REMOVING BOLTS

INSTALL

1. Install parts as shown.
2. Place jack stand under hub and rotor assembly. Lower hoist and place cam in position as noted in removal.
3. Raise hoist.
4. Install brake line clip.
5. Remove axle cover.
6. Install wheel and lower car.

   A front end alignment is necessary if the strut damper assembly is replaced.

SUPPORT

ADAPTORS J-26584-30

HINGE BOTTOM ADAPTOR J-26584-4

DIRECTION OF STRUT FLANGE

DISASSEMBLE STRUT

Fig. 10 Strut damper & coil spring removal

90 N•m (68 FT. LBS.)

STRUT MOUNTING ASSEMBLY

1.4 N•m (12 IN. LBS.)

SPRING SEAT

SHIELD

STRUT BUMPER

SPRING

SPRING INSULATOR

ABSORBER AND STRUT ASSEMBLY

Fig. 11 Strut assembly components

is properly seated on the bottom spring plate, Fig. 11.

4. Place strut spring seat assembly on top of spring.
5. Place both J-26584-40 top adapters over spring seat assembly.
6. Rotate compressor forcing screw until the compressor top support just contacts the top adapters. Do not compress the spring.
7. Install tool J-26584-27 strut alignment rod through top spring seat and thread the rod onto damper shaft hand tight, Fig. 12.
8. Rotate compressor forcing screw clockwise until approximately 1½ inches of the damper shaft can be pulled upward through the top spring plate with the alignment rod.

CAUTION: Do not compress spring until bottomed.

9. Remove alignment rod, place top mounting assembly over damper shaft and install nut. Torque nut to 68 ft. lbs.
10. Rotate compressor forcing screw counterclockwise and remove strut assembly from compressor.

ALIGNMENT ROD J-26584-27

DAMPER SHAFT

ASSEMBLE STRUT

Fig. 12 Installing strut alignment rod

STEERING COLUMN

SEAL ASSEMBLY

STEERING KNUCKLE

HEAT SHIELD

BUSHING

SHAFT ASSEMBLY

PIN

SLEEVE

62 N·m (45 FT. LBS.)

40 N·m (30 FT. LBS.)

95 N·m (70 FT. LBS.)

CROSS MEMBER

J-6627 or BT-7101

REMOVE TIE ROD END

Fig. 13   Steering gear Replacement. 1982–83

STEERING GEAR, REPLACE

1982-83

Removal

1. On models equipped with power steering, disconnect and cap hydraulic lines at steering gear.
2. Pull intermediate shaft seal upward, then remove intermediate shaft to steering gear stub shaft pinch bolt, Fig. 13.
3. Raise and support vehicle, then remove both front wheel and tire assemblies.
4. Using tool J6627 or equivalent, disconnect tie rod ends from steering knuckles.
5. Remove AIR pipe bracket to crossmember attaching bolt, if equipped.
6. Remove two rear frame cradle mounting bolts and lower rear of cradle 4 to 5 inches.

CAUTION: Do not lower cradle more than specified, as damage to engine components may result.

7. Remove steering gear heat shield from crossmember.

8. Remove steering gear assembly mounting bolts, then the steering gear assembly through the left wheel opening.

Installation

1. Place steering gear assembly into mounts on crossmember, then install and torque mounting bolts to 70 ft. lbs.
2. Install heat shield.
3. Raise frame cradle and install mounting bolts. Torque bolts to specification.
4. Install AIR pipe bracket to crossmember, then connect tie rod ends to steering knuckles. Torque ball studs to 30 ft. lbs.
5. Install wheel and tire assemblies and lower vehicle.
6. Connect intermediate shaft to steering gear stub shaft, install pinch bolt and torque to 45 ft. lbs.
7. Check and adjust toe-in as required.

1980-81

Removal

1. On models equipped with power steering, remove line clip to bracket attaching bolt, then disconnect and cap pressure and return lines at steering gear.

2. On all models, remove bolt attaching speedometer cable retainer clip to transmission, then position cable aside to provide clearance for gear removal.
3. Remove upper left hand steering gear housing bracket nut, then raise and support front of vehicle at body.
4. Remove both wheel and tire assemblies.
5. Remove cotter pins and nuts from both tie rod ends, then disconnect tie rod ends from steering knuckles using tool No. J-6627 or BT-7101, Fig. 14.
6. Remove A.I.R. hose shield.
7. Remove rear frame cradle mounting bolts, then lower rear of frame cradle approximately 3 to 4 inches.
8. Remove remaining steering gear housing bracket nuts, then remove reinforcement and brackets.
9. Disconnect intermediate shaft from steering gear stub shaft, then remove steering gear through left wheel opening, Fig. 14.

Installation

1. Install supports, then position steering gear in vehicle.
2. Connect intermediate shaft to steering

IF STUDS BACK OUT OF WELD NUTS IN COWL, DOUBLE NUT, INSTALL AND TORQUE THE STUD TO 44 N·m (32 ft. lbs.) BEFORE INSTALLING SUPPORTS AND GEAR.

BOOT

INTERMEDIATE SHAFT

SCREW DRIVER

SUPPORT

63 N·m (45 FT. LBS.)

BE SURE TO INSTALL SUPPORTS AS SHOWN

BRACKET

32 N·m (24 FT. LBS.)

J-6627 or BT-7101

REMOVE TIE ROD END

STEERING KNUCKLE

47 N·m (35 ft. lbs.) AFTER REACHING TORQUE REQUIRED, NUT MUST ALWAYS BE TIGHTENED (UP TO 1/16 TURN) FURTHER, NEVER BACK OFF, TO INSERT COTTER PIN.

Fig. 14 Steering gear replacement. 1980–81

BRACKET

50 N·m (35 FT. LBS.)

SPACER

BRACKET

SPACER

PUMP ASSEMBLY

PULLEY

PIN

25 N·m (19 FT. LBS.)

38 N·m (28 FT. LBS.)

Fig. 15 Power steering pump replacement. 4-151

gear stub shaft, then torque clamp bolt to 45 ft. lbs.

3. Install steering gear housing brackets, reinforcement and attaching nuts. Torque right hand upper and lower and left hand lower bracket nuts to 24 ft. lbs.
4. Raise frame cradle, then install and torque rear mounting bolts to 80 ft lbs.
5. Install A.I.R. hose shield, then connect tie rod ends to steering knuckles. Torque tie rod end nuts to 40 ft. lbs. on 1980 models, 35 ft. lbs. on 1981 models, then install cotter pins. If cotter pins cannot be inserted, tighten nut up to an additional 1/16 turn to align cotter pin holes.
6. Install wheel and tire assemblies, then lower vehicle.
7. Torque upper left hand steering gear housing bracket bolt to 24 ft. lbs.
8. Install speedometer cable retainer clip.
9. On models with power steering, connect pressure and return lines to steering gear, then install line clip. Check power steering fluid level and bleed system.
10. On all models, check and adjust toe-in as necessary.

POWER STEERING PUMP, REPLACE

4-151
1. Raise and support vehicle, then remove radiator hose clamp bolt.
2. Disconnect and cap hydraulic lines at power steering pump.
3. Remove power steering pump to rear bracket attaching nut.
4. Remove front pump bracket to engine and front pump bracket to rear pump bracket attaching bolts, Fig. 15.
5. Remove pump and bracket assembly from

Fig. 16   Power steering pump replacement. V6-173

vehicle.
6. Reverse procedure to install.

6-173
1. Disconnect battery ground cable.
2. Disconnect electrical connector at blower motor, then remove blower motor from vehicle.
3. Disconnect heater hose from water pump

and hydraulic lines from power steering pump. Cap lines to avoid fluid leakage.
4. Remove rear pump bracket to engine bracket attaching nut and front pump bracket to cylinder head attaching bolts, Fig. 16.
5. Remove pump and bracket assembly from vehicle.
6. Reverse procedure to install.

1982–83 CHEVROLET CELEBRITY · BUICK CENTURY · OLDSMOBILE CUTLASS CIERA · PONTIAC 6000

> Refer to the 1980–83 Citation, Omega, Phoenix and Skylark Chapter for service procedures not covered in this chapter.

INDEX OF SERVICE OPERATIONS

NOTE: Refer to the back of this manual for vehicle manufacturer's special service tool suppliers.

VEHICLE IDENTIFICATION NUMBER LOCATION

On top of instrument panel, left front.

ENGINE NUMBER LOCATION

On 4-151, V6-173 & V6-181 engines, the engine code stamping is located on vertical pad on engine to transmission mounting flange located on forward side of block. On V6-262 diesel engines, the engine code stamping is located on vertical pad located on right side of engine front cover.

ENGINE V.I.N. CODE

The eighth digit of the seventeen digit V.I.N. code denotes engine code.

ENGINE IDENTIFICATION CODES

Year	Engine	V.I.N. Code	Code
1982	4-151①	R	3M, 3S, 3J
	4-151①	R	3K, 3L, 3P
	V6-173②	X	CAY, CAZ, CBA
	V6-173②	X	CBC, CBD, CBF
	V6-173②	X	CBH, CBJ, CBK
	V6-173②	X	CMC, CMF, CMH

Year	Engine	V.I.N. Code	Code
	V6-173②	X	CMJ, CMM, CMS
	V6-173②	X	C7N, C7R, C7S
	V6-173②	X	C7T, C7U, C7W
	V6-173②	X	D2A, D2B, D2C
	V6-173②	X	D2D, D2F, D2H
	V6-181③	E	EA, EB

Year	Engine	V.I.N. Code	Code
	V6-262④	T	UAC, UAH, UAL

①—Pontiac built engine.
②—Chevrolet built engine.
③—Buick built engine.
④—Oldsmobile built diesel engine.

GRILL IDENTIFICATION

1982—83 Buick Century Exc. "T" Type

1982—83 Chevrolet Celebrity

1982—83 Olds. Cutlass Ciera Exc. Brougham, ES & LS

1982—83 Olds. Cutlass Ciera Brougham & LS

1982—83 Pontiac Phoenix Exc. "STE"

1983 Buick Century "T" Type

1983 Pontiac Phoenix "STE"

GENERAL ENGINE SPECIFICATIONS

Year	Engine CID① /Liter	Engine V.I.N. Code②	Carburetor	Bore and Stroke	Compression Ratio	Net H.P. @ R.P.M.③	Maximum Torque Ft. Lbs. @ R.P.M.	Normal Oil Pressure Pounds
1982–83	4-151, 2.5L	R	T.B.I	4.00 × 3.00	8.2	90 @ 4000	132 @ 2800	36–41
	V6-173, 2.8L	X	E2SE, 2 Bbl④	3.50 × 2.99	8.5	112 @ 5100⑥	145 @ 2400	50–65
	V6-181, 3.0L	E	E2ME, 2 Bbl④	3.80 × 2.66	8.45	110 @ 4800	145 @ 2600	37
	V6-262, 4.3L⑤	T	Fuel Injection	4.05 × 3.385	21.6	85 @ 3600	165 @ 1600	30–45

①—CID—cubic inch displacement.
②—The eighth digit denotes engine code.
③—Ratings are net—as installed in vehicle.
④—Rochester.
⑤—Diesel engine.
⑥—High output engine, 135 @ 5400.

TUNE UP SPECIFICATIONS

The following specifications are published from the latest information available. This data should be used only in the absence of a decal affixed in the engine compartment.

★ When using a timing light, disconnect vacuum hose or tube at distributor and plug opening in hose or tube so idle speed will not be affected.

● When checking compression, lowest cylinder must be within 70 percent of highest.

▲ Before removing wires from distributor cap, determine location of the No. 1 wire in cap, as distributor position may have been altered from that shown at the end of this chart.

👉 Spark plug types shown in this chart are recommendations of the original vehicle manufacturer and not MOTOR.

Check local sources for other spark plug manufacturers listings.

Year & Engine/V.I.N.	Spark Plug Type 👉	Spark Plug Gap	Ignition Timing BTDC① ★ Firing Order Fig. ▲	Ignition Timing Man. Trans.	Ignition Timing Auto. Trans.	Mark Fig.	Curb Idle Speed② Man. Trans.	Curb Idle Speed② Auto Trans.	Fast Idle Speed Man. Trans.	Fast Idle Speed Auto. Trans.	Fuel Pump Pressure
1982											
4-151/R	R44TXS	.060	A	8°③⑦	8°③⑦	B	⑩	⑩	⑩	⑩	9–13
V6-173/X	R43TS	.045	C	10°④	10°⑤	D	800N	600D	2400/2600N	2600N	6–7½
V6-181/E	R44TS8	.080	E	—	15°	F	—	⑩	—	2300P	6–7½
V6-262/T	—	—	—	—	5°⑥⑧⑨	—	—	650D	—	725D	5½–6½
1983											
4-151/R	R44TXS	.060	A	8°⑪	8°⑫	B	⑩	⑩	⑩	⑩	
V6-173/X	R43CTS	.045	C	10°⑬	10°⑤	D	775N	600D	2500N	2500N	6–7½
V6-181/E	R44TS8	.080	E	—	15°⑭	F	—	⑩	—	2300P	5½–6½
V6-262/T	—	—	—	—	—	—	—	—	—	—	—

①—BTDC—Before top dead center.
②—Where two idle speeds are listed, the first is for vehicles with A/C.
③—At 1050N RPM.
④—At 800N RPM.
⑤—At 600D RPM.
⑥—At 1300P RPM.
⑦—Ground diagnostic connector located under dash. The check engine light should flash on & off when in diagnostic mode. Check average ignition timing of cylinder Nos. 1 & 4, reset as necessary. After completing ignition timing check, remove ground from diagnostic connector & ensure that check engine light is off.
⑧—ATDC—After top dead center.
⑨—Using diesel engine timing meter J-23375.
⑩—Idle speed controlled by electronic control module.
⑪—At 850N RPM.
⑫—At 750N RPM.
⑬—At 775N RPM.
⑭—At slow idle.

FIRING ORDER 1-3-4-2
FRONT OF ENGINE
SCREW
SCREW
FRONT OF CAR

Fig. A

BEFORE AFTER

Fig. B

FIRING ORDER 1-2-3-4-5-6
FRONT OF ENGINE
SCREWS (4)
FRONT OF CAR

Fig. C

Continued

TUNE UP—Continued

Fig. D

FRONT OF ENGINE

SCREWS

SCREWS

FIRING ORDER
1 - 6 - 5 - 4 - 3 - 2

FRONT OF VEHICLE

Fig. E

Fig. F

DISTRIBUTOR SPECIFICATIONS

★If unit is checked on the vehicle, double the RPM and degrees to get crankshaft figures.

Distributor Ident. No.①	Centrifugal Advanced Degrees @ RPM of Distributor			Vacuum Advance	
	Advance Starts	Intermediate Advance	Full Advance	Inches of Vacuum to Start Plunger	Max. Adv. Dist. Deg. @ Vacuum
1982					
1110593	—	—	—	—	—
1110597	—	—	—	—	—
1103470	—	—	—	—	—
1983					
1103519	—	—	—	—	—

①—Stamped on distributor housing plate.

ENGINE TIGHTENING SPECIFICATIONS★

★Torque specifications are for clean and lightly lubricated threads only. Dry or dirty threads produce increased friction which prevents accurate measurement of tightness.

Year	Engine Model/ V.I.N.	Spark Plugs Ft. Lbs.	Cylinder Head Bolts Ft. Lbs.	Intake Manifold Ft. Lbs.	Exhaust Manifold Ft. Lbs.	Rocker Arm Stud Ft. Lbs.	Rocker Arm Cover Ft. Lbs.	Connecting Rod Cap Bolts Ft. Lbs.	Main Bearing Cap Bolts Ft. Lbs.	Flywheel to Crankshaft Ft. Lbs.	Vibration Damper or Pulley Ft. Lbs.
1982-83	4-151/R	7-15	85	29	44	20	6	32	70	44	200
	V6-173/X	7-15	65-75	20-25	22-28	43-49	6-9	34-40	63-74	45-55	66-84
	V6-181/E	15	80	45	25	30③	4	40	100	60	225
	V6-262/T②	—	①	41	29	④	—	42	105	76	160-350

①—See text for procedure.
②—Diesel engine.
③—Rocker arm shaft.
④—Rocker arm stud, 11 ft. lbs.; rocker arm nut, 28 ft. lbs.

BRAKE SPECIFICATIONS

Year	Model	Brake Drum Inside Diameter	Wheel Cylinder Bore Diameter			Master Cylinder Bore Diameter		
			Front Disc Brake	Front Drum Brake	Rear Drum Brake	With Disc Brakes	With Drum Brakes	With Power Brakes
1982-83	All	7.87	2.24	—	.689	.874	—	.874

WHEEL ALIGNMENT SPECIFICATIONS

Year	Model	Caster Angle, Degrees		Camber Angle, Degrees				Toe-In Inch	Toe-Out on Turns Deg.	
		Limits	Desired	Limits		Desired			Outer Wheel	Inner Wheel
				Left	Right	Left	Right			
1982-83	All	0—+4°	+2°	−½° to +½°	−½° to +½°	0°	0°	0	—	—

ALTERNATOR & REGULATOR SPECIFICATIONS

| Year | Model | Alternator | | | | | Regulator | | | | | | |
| | | Rated Hot Output Amps. | Field Current 12 Volts @ 80°F | Output @ 14 Volts | | Model | Field Relay | | | Voltage Regulator | | |
				2000 R.P.M. Amps.	5000 R.P.M. Amps.		Air Gap In.	Point Gap In.	Closing Voltage	Air Gap In.	Point Gap In.	Voltage @ 125°F
1982	1100113	63	—	—	—	Integral	—	—	—	—	—	—
	1100164	55	—	—	—	Integral	—	—	—	—	—	—
	1100166	63	—	—	—	Integral	—	—	—	—	—	—
	1100174	55	—	—	—	Integral	—	—	—	—	—	—
	1100192	85	—	—	—	Integral	—	—	—	—	—	—
	1100193	85	—	—	—	Integral	—	—	—	—	—	—
	1100196	63	—	—	—	Integral	—	—	—	—	—	—
	1101037	70	—	—	—	Integral	—	—	—	—	—	—
	1101039	70	—	—	—	Integral	—	—	—	—	—	—
	1101044	70	—	—	—	Integral	—	—	—	—	—	—
	1101067	70	—	—	—	Integral	—	—	—	—	—	—
	1101084	85	—	—	—	Integral	—	—	—	—	—	—
	1101086	85	—	—	—	Integral	—	—	—	—	—	—
	1101448	80	—	—	—	Integral	—	—	—	—	—	—
	1103197	63	—	—	—	Integral	—	—	—	—	—	—

STARTING MOTOR SPECIFICATIONS

| Year | Engine/V.I.N. | Starter Ident. No. | Brush Spring Tension Oz.① | Free Speed Test | | | Resistance Test | |
				Amps.	Volts	R.P.M.	Amps.	Volts
1982	4-151, V6-173, V6-181③	1109530	—	85②	9	6800–10300	—	—
	V6-262 Diesel/T	1998553	—	160–220	9	4000–5500	—	—
	V6-262 Diesel/T	22515863	—	125–170	9	3200–4100	—	—

①—Minimum.
②—Maximum.

③—For V.I.N. code, Refer to the "General Engine Specifications" at the beginning of chapter.

PISTONS, PINS, RINGS, CRANKSHAFT & BEARINGS

| Year | Engine Model/V.I.N. | Piston Clearance | Ring Gap ① | | Wristpin Diameter | Rod Bearings | | Main Bearings | | | Shaft End Play |
			Comp.	Oil		Shaft Diameter	Bearing Clearance	Shaft Diameter	Bearing Clearance	Thrust on Bear. No.	
1982	4-151/R	③	.010	.015	.940	2.000	.0005–.0026	2.300	.0005–.0022	5	.0035–.0085
	V6-173/X	.0017–.0027	.010	.020	.9053	2.000	.0014–.0036	2.490	.0017–.0030	3	.002–.007
	V6-181/E	.0008–.0020	.013	.015	.9392	2.2491	.0005–.0026	2.4995	.0003–.0018	3	.003–.009
	V6-262/T②	.003–.004	.015	.015	1.0958	2.250	.0003–.0025	2.999	.0005–.0021	3	.0035–.0135
1983	4-151/R	④	.010	.020	.940	2.000	.0005–.0026	2.300	.0005–.0022	5	.0035–.0085
	V6-173/X	.0017–.0027	.010	.020	.9053	2.000	.0014–.0037	2.490	.0017–.0030	3	.002–.007
	V6-181/E	⑤	.010	.015	.9392	2.2491	.0005–.0026	2.4995	.0003–.0018	3	.003–.009
	V6-262/T②	.0035–.0045	⑥	.015	1.0950	2.250	.0005–.0025	2.9998	⑦	3	.0035–.0135

①—Fit rings in tapered bores for clearances given in tightest portion of ring travel. Clearances specified are minimum gaps.
②—Diesel engine.
③—Top of bore, .0025–.0033 inch; bottom of bore, .0017–.0041 inch.
④—Top of bore, .0025–.003 inch; bottom of bore, .0015–.004 inch.
⑤—Top of bore, .001–.002 inch; bottom of bore, .0015–.0035 inch.
⑥—Top compression ring, .019 inch; lower compression ring, .013 inch.
⑦—Nos. 1 thru 4, .0021–.005 inch; No. 5, .002–.0034 inch.

VALVE SPECIFICATIONS

Year	Engine/V.I.N.	Valve Lash Int.	Valve Lash Exh.	Valve Angles Seat	Valve Angles Face	Valve Spring Installed Height	Valve Spring Pressure Lbs. @ In.	Stem Clearance Intake	Stem Clearance Exhaust	Stem Diameter Intake	Stem Diameter Exhaust
1982-83	4-151/R	Hydraulic①		46	45	1.66	151 @ 1.254	.0010–.0027	.0010–.0032	.3418–.3425	.3418–.3425
	V6-173/X	1½ Turns②		46	45	1.57	195 @ 1.180	.0010–.0027	.0010–.0027	.3410–.3417	.3410–.3417
	V6-181/E	Hydraulic①		45	45	1.727	220 @ 1.340	.0015–.0035	.0015–.0032	.3401–.3412	.3405–.3412
	V6-262 Diesel/T	Hydraulic①		③	④	1.67	210 @ 1.220	.0010–.0027	.0015–.0032	.3425–.3432	.3420–.3427

①—No adjustment.
②—Turn rocker arm stud nut until all lash is eliminated, then tighten nut the additional turns listed.
③—Intake, 45°; Exhaust, 31°.
④—Intake, 44°; Exhaust, 30°.

COOLING SYSTEM & CAPACITY DATA

Year	Model & Engine/V.I.N.	Cooling Capacity Qts. Less A/C	Cooling Capacity Qts. With A/C	Radiator Cap Relief Pressure, Lbs.	Thermo. Opening Temp.	Fuel Tank Gals.	Engine Oil Refill Qts.	Transaxle Oil Manual Trans. Pts.	Transaxle Oil Auto. Transaxle Qts.①
1982	4-151/R	9.4	9.7	15	195	16	3②	6	5
	V6-173/X	11.4	11.7	15	195	16	4②	6	5
	V6-181/E	13.5	14.25	15	195	16	4③	6	5
	V6-262/T⑤	13.2	13.7	15	195	16	6④	6	5
1983	4-151/R	9.4⑥	9.7⑥	15	195	16	3②	6	⑦
	V6-173/X	11.9⑧	12.4⑧	15	195	16	4②	6	⑦
	V6-181/E	13.5⑨	14.4	15	195	16	4③	6	⑦
	V6-262/T⑤	13⑩	13.9	16–18.5	195	16	6④	6	⑦

①—Approximate, make final check with dipstick.
②—With or without filter change.
③—Add 1 qt. with filter change.
④—Includes filter. Use recommended diesel engine oil, designated SF/CC or SF/CD.
⑤—Diesel Engine.
⑥—W/heavy duty cooling system, 12 qts.
⑦—Oil pan only, 4 qts.; total capacity, 6 qts.
⑧—W/heavy duty cooling system, 12.7 qts.
⑨—W/heavy duty cooling system, 14 qts.
⑩—W/heavy duty cooling system, 13.9 qts.

Electrical Section

Refer to the 1980–83 Citation, Omega, Phoenix and Skylark, "Electrical Section" for service procedures not covered in this section.

STARTER, REPLACE

Except V6-262 Diesel

1. Disconnect battery ground cable.
2. Raise and support vehicle.
3. From beneath vehicle, remove two starter motor to engine bolts and lower starter. On 4-151 engine remove nut securing starter bracket to rear of starter.
4. Disconnect solenoid wires and battery cable then, remove starter.
5. Reverse procedure to install.

V6-262 Diesel

1. Disconnect battery ground cable. On engines with heavy duty option there will be two batteries. Install a suitable engine holding device.
2. Raise and support vehicle. Remove left and center engine mount stud nuts, then 2 front cradle mount bolts and lower cradle. Remove flywheel cover.
3. Remove starter lower shield nut and starter flex shield for removal accessibility.
4. Disconnect wires from starter noting position of wires for installation.
5. Remove starter attaching bolts, then remove starter.

W/S WIPER SWITCH, REPLACE

1. Remove turn signal switch as outlined under "Turn Signal Switch, Replace" procedure.
2. Refer to Figs. 1 and 2 for wiper switch replacement.

HEADLAMP SWITCH, REPLACE

Celebrity

1. Disconnect battery ground cable.
2. Remove headlamp switch knob.
3. Remove instrument cluster trim cover.

REMOVE

1. Remove ignition and dimmer switch.
2. Remove parts as shown.
3. For KEY RELEASE refer below.

INSTALL

1. For KEY RELEASE refer below.
2. Assemble rack so that first rack tooth engages between first and second tooth of sector.
3. Install parts as shown.
4. Install ignition and dimmer switch.

WASHER — HOUSING — PIVOT AND SWITCH ASSY. — BEARING — PIVOT PIN — BOWL — CAP SCREW — SCREW — PIN — SECTOR — BUSHING — HORN CONTACT — RETAINER — GATE

Punch

REMOVE AND INSTALL SECTOR

Punch

INSTALL BEARING

WAVE WASHER — LEVER — SPRING

KEY RELEASE COLUMN

INSTALL LEVER AND RETURN SPRING

KEY RELEASE COLUMN

Fig. 1 Housing and wiper switch removal & installation. Standard steering column

SCREW — COVER — ACTUATOR — SHIELD — SPRING — PIVOT AND SWITCH ASSEMBLY — PIVOT PIN — CAP — TILT LEVER

PUNCH

PIVOT PIN

REMOVE AND INSTALL PIVOT ASSEMBLY

Fig. 2 Cover and wiper switch removal & installation. Tilt steering column

4. Remove screws attaching headlamp switch mounting plate to instrument cluster carrier.
5. Disconnect headlamp switch connector.
6. Remove headlamp switch from mounting plate.
7. Reverse procedure to install.

Century

1. Disconnect battery ground cable.
2. Remove instrument cluster trim cover.
3. Remove left side instrument cluster switch trim panel by removing three screws and gently rocking panel out.
4. Remove the headlamp rocker switch or rheostat by removing three screws and pulling switch assembly straight out (one screw is common to both switch assemblies).
5. Reverse procedure to install.

Cutlass Ciera

1. Remove left hand trim pad.
2. Remove three screws attaching switch to instrument panel.
3. Pull switch rearward to remove.
4. Reverse procedure to install.

6000

1. Disconnect battery ground cable.
2. Remove steering column trim cover, headlight rod and knob assembly.
3. Remove left trim plate.
4. Remove three screws attaching switch and bracket assembly to instrument panel, disconnect electrical connector and remove switch/bracket assembly.
5. Loosen bezel and remove switch from bracket.
6. Reverse procedure to install.

INSTRUMENT CLUSTER, REPLACE

Celebrity, Fig. 3

1. Disconnect battery ground cable.
2. Remove headlamp switch knob, then remove ten screws attaching trim plate to carrier and remove trim plate, Fig. 4.
3. Remove three screws at underside of trim pad, then remove upper screw at right of trim pad opening and two screws at right end of trim pad. Remove trim pad, Fig. 5.
4. Remove six cluster lens to carrier attaching screws.
5. Tilt cluster rearward slightly and disconnect all electrical connectors and speedometer cable. Remove cluster.
6. Reverse procedure to install.

Century

1. Disconnect battery ground cable.
2. Disconnect speedometer cable at cruise control transducer (if equipped). If not equipped with cruise control, disconnect cable at upper and lower cable connections.
3. Remove nine screws retaining trim plate to cluster, then put gear shift lever in low and gently pull on trim plate to remove.
4. Remove shift indicator cable clip from shift bowl.
5. Remove lap vent trim cover by removing two attaching screws.
6. Lower steering column by removing front two retaining bolts.

Fig. 3   Instrument cluster. 1982–83 Celebrity

7. Pull instrument cluster outward three inches, and disconnect speedometer cable from cluster by pushing retaining clip toward cluster and pulling cable away from speedometer.
8. Pull cluster out remainder of the way, then remove one screw retaining electrical connector, Fig. 6.
9. Reverse procedure to install.

Cutlass Ciera

1. Carefully insert a clean putty knife blade between the trim panel and left trim pad, then gently pry trim panel outward. Using same procedure, remove center trim cover.
2. Remove three screws in steering column trim collar and remove collar, then remove ash tray.
3. Remove six screws attaching trim pad to instrument panel, Fig. 7. Remove trim pad.
4. Remove 8 screws attaching cluster trim cover to instrument panel, then remove cover.
5. Disconnect speedometer cable at transmission or cruise control transducer (if equipped).
6. Remove steering column trim cover.
7. Disconnect shift indicator clip from steering column shift bowl.
8. Remove 4 screws attaching cluster assembly to instrument panel.
9. Pull assembly out far enough to reach behind cluster and disconnect speedometer cable.
10. Remove cluster assembly.
11. Reverse procedure to install.

6000

1. Remove headlight rod knob assembly.
2. Using thin, flat tool carefully pry left side trim plate away from instrument panel.
3. Remove six screws attaching instrument cluster to instrument panel carrier.
4. Remove instrument panel cluster.
5. Reverse procedure to install.

RADIO, REPLACE

Century

1. Disconnect battery ground cable.
2. Remove instrument panel trim plate.
3. Remove right side instrument panel switch trim panel by removing three screws and gently rocking panel out.
4. Remove four radio assembly attaching screws.
5. Disconnect antenna cable, power and speaker electrical connections.
6. Pull radio outward through instrument panel carrier housing.
7. Reverse procedure to install.

Except Century

1. Disconnect battery ground cable.
2. Remove instrument panel trim plate, except Cutlass Ciera, on Cutlass Ciera left side trim pad.
3. Remove three screws at radio bracket, except Cutlass Ciera, on Cutlass Ciera four screws.
4. Pull radio rearward and disconnect elec-

CLUSTER TRIM PAD

Fig. 4   Trim plate removal. 1982–83 Celebrity

Fig. 5 Trim pad removal. 1982-83 Celebrity

trical connectors and antenna lead.
5. Remove radio.
6. Reverse procedure to install.

W/S WIPER MOTOR, REPLACE

1. Raise hood, then remove right and left wiper arm and blade assemblies.
2. Remove shroud grille to body attaching screws, then shroud grille.
3. Loosen, but do not remove nuts securing transmission drive link to motor crank arm, then disconnect drive link.
4. Disconnect wiring connectors and washer hoses.
5. Remove 3 screws attaching wiper motor to firewall.
6. Remove motor while guiding crank arm through hole.
7. Reverse procedure to install. Motor must be in "Park" position before assembling transmission drive link to crank arm. Torque transmission drive link to 53–75 in. lbs.

W/S WIPER TRANSMISSION, REPLACE

1. Raise hood, then remove right and left wiper arm and blade assemblies.
2. Remove shroud grille to body attaching screws, then shroud grille.
3. Loosen, but do not remove nuts securing transmission drive link to motor crank arm, then disconnect drive link, Fig. 8.
4. Remove 6 screws attaching wiper transmission to body, Fig. 8.
5. Carefully guide transmission assembly through access hole in upper shroud panel to remove.
6. Reverse procedure to install. Torque transmission drive link nuts to 53–75 in. lbs.

HEATER CORE, REPLACE

Less A/C

1. Drain cooling system.
2. Remove heater inlet and outlet hoses.

3. Remove radio noise supression strap.
4. Remove cover retaining screws and cover.
5. Remove heater core.
6. Reverse procedure to install.

With A/C

1. Drain cooling system.
2. On all except diesel engine models, disconnect heater inlet and outlet hoses. On diesel engine models, raise vehicle and disconnect heater inlet and outlet hoses, then lower vehicle.
3. On diesel engine models, remove instrument panel lower sound absorber. On all models, working inside vehicle, remove the heater ducts, then the heater case side cover.
4. Remove heater lower outlet.
5. Remove 2 housing cover to air valve housing clips, then the housing cover.
6. Remove heater core retaining straps, core tubing retainers, then the core.
7. Reverse procedure to install.

Fig. 6 Instrument cluster removal. 1982-83 Century

Fig. 7 Trim pad removal. 1982-83 Cutlass Ciera

Fig. 8 Windshield wiper transmission removal (typical)

4-151 Engine Section

Refer to 1980–83 Citation, Omega, Phoenix and Skylark "ENGINE SECTION" for service procedures on this engine.

V6-173 Engine Section

Refer to 1980–83 Citation, Omega, Phoenix and Skylark "ENGINE SECTION" for service procedures on this engine.

V6-181 Engine Section

ENGINE MOUNTS, REPLACE

1. Raise and support front of vehicle.
2. Attach suitable engine lifting fixture to engine.
3. Remove mount to engine mount bracket nuts. Raise engine slightly and remove mount to frame nuts. Remove mount, Fig. 1.
4. Reverse procedure to install.

ENGINE, REPLACE

1. Disconnect battery cables from battery and remove air cleaner.
2. Drain cooling system.
3. Disconnect vacuum hosing to all non-engine mounted components.
4. Disconnect detent cable from carburetor lever.
5. Disconnect accelerator linkage.
6. Disconnect engine harness connector.
7. Disconnect radiator hoses from radiator and heater hose from engine.
8. Remove power steering pump and bracket assembly from engine, if equipped.
9. Disconnect fuel lines at rubber hose connections.
10. Raise vehicle and disconnect exhaust pipe at manifold.
11. Remove engine front mount to cradle retaining nuts, located at right side of vehicle.
12. Disconnect battery cables from starter motor and transaxle case.
13. Remove flex plate cover, then disconnect torque converter form flex plate.

Fig. 1 Engine mount removal

14. Remove transaxle case to cylinder case support bracket bolts, Fig. 2.
15. Lower vehicle. Place a support under transaxle rear extension.
16. Disconnect ground strap from engine at engine forward strut. Remove engine strut bracket from radiator support and swing rearward.
17. Remove transaxle to cylinder case retaining bolts. Make note of ground stud location.
18. If equipped with A/C, remove compressor and lay aside.
19. Using a suitable lifting device, remove engine.
20. Reverse procedure to install.

CYLINDER HEAD, REPLACE

1. Disconnect battery ground cable.
2. Remove intake manifold, then loosen and remove belts.

3. If left cylinder head is to be removed, remove dipstick, also remove air and vacuum pumps with mounting bracket if equipped, and position aside with hoses attached.
4. If right cylinder head is to be removed, remove alternator, also disconnect power steering gear pump and brackets attaching to cylinder head.
5. Disconnect wires from spark plugs, then remove spark plug wire clips from rocker arm cover studs.
6. Remove exhaust manifold bolts from head being removed.
7. With air hose and cloths, clean dirt off cylinder head and adjacent area.
8. Remove rocker arm cover, then rocker arm and shaft assembly from cylinder head. Lift out push rods, keeping them in order to ensure proper installation.
9. Loosen all cylinder head bolts, then remove bolts and lift off cylinder head.
10. Reverse procedure to install. Torque cylinder head bolts in sequence shown in Fig. 3 to specifications.

ROCKER ARMS

A nylon retainer is used to retain the rocker arm. Break them below their heads with a chisel, Fig. 4, or pry out with channel locks. Production rocker arms can be installed in any sequence since the arms are identical.

Fig. 2 Transaxle to engine case support bracket removal

Fig. 3 Cylinder head bolt tightening sequence

Rocker Arm Retainers

Fig. 4 Removing nylon retainer

Fig. 5 Service rocker arm identification

Fig. 6 Service rocker arm installation

Fig. 7 Exploded view of hydraulic valve lifter

Replacement rocker arms for all engines are identified with a stamping, right (R) and left (L), Fig. 5 and must be installed as shown in Fig. 6.

To install rocker arms, position arm on rocker shaft, centering it over the ¼ inch hole in the rocker shaft. Then, install new rocker arm retainers in the holes using a ½ inch drift to seat them.

VALVE ARRANGEMENT

Front to Rear

V6-181 . . . . E-I-I-E-I-E

VALVE LIFT SPEC.

Engine V6-181	Year 1982–83	Intake	Exhaust
		—	—

VALVE TIMING

Engine V6-181	Year 1982–83	Degrees
		—

VALVE GUIDES

The valve guides are an integral part of the cylinder head and cannot be replaced.

If valve stem clearance is excessive, the valve guide must be reamed and an oversize valve installed. On 1982–83 V6-181 engine, valves are available in oversize of .010 inch.

Fig. 8 Engine front cover removal & installation

VALVE LIFTERS

Failure of an hydraulic valve lifter, Fig. 7, is generally caused by dirt or an inadequate oil supply. An air leak at the intake side of the oil pump or too much oil in the engine will cause air bubbles in the oil supply to the lifters, causing them to collapse. This is a probable cause of trouble if several lifters fail to function, but air in the oil is an unlikely cause of failure of a single unit.

The valve lifters may be lifted out of their bores after removing the rocker arms, push rods and intake manifold. Adjustable pliers with taped jaws may be used to remove lifters that are stuck due to varnish, carbon, etc. Fig. 7 illustrates the type of lifter used.

ENGINE FRONT COVER, REPLACE

1. Drain engine coolant.
2. Disconnect upper and lower radiator hoses and heater return hose at water pump.
3. Remove water pump pulley and belts.
4. Remove alternator bracket and alternator.
5. Remove distributor. If timing chain and sprockets are not going to be disturbed, note position of distributor rotor for reinstallation in same position.
6. Remove balancer bolt and washer, then remove balancer assembly.
7. Remove bolts attaching engine front cover to cylinder block, Fig. 8, also remove two oil pan to engine front cover bolts.
8. Remove engine front cover assembly and gasket, Fig. 8.
9. Reverse procedure to install.

NOTE: Prior to reinstalling the engine front cover, remove the oil pump cover and pack the space around the oil pump drive gears completely full of petroleum jelly. Failure to do this may result in the pump losing its prime, causing a "dry" engine start.

When reinstalling engine front cover bolts, apply a suitable sealer to the threads to prevent leakage.

TIMING CHAIN, REPLACE

1. With front cover removed, as outlined in "ENGINE FRONT COVER, REPLACE", temporarily install balancer bolt and washer in end of crankshaft. Turn crankshaft so timing marks on sprockets are as close together as possible. Remove balancer bolt and washer using a sharp blow on wrench handle, so bolt can be removed

without changing position of sprockets.
2. Remove crankshaft oil slinger and camshaft sprocket bolts.
3. Using two large screwdrivers, alternately pry off sprockets and chain.
4. Thoroughly clean all parts that are to be reused.
5. Assemble timing chain on sprockets and slide sprockets and chain assembly onto camshaft and crankshaft with timing marks aligned as shown in Fig. 9.
6. Install sprocket bolts and torque to 20 ft. lbs.
7. Install oil slinger, camshaft thrust button and engine front cover.

CAMSHAFT, REPLACE

1. Remove engine as outlined in "ENGINE, REPLACE".
2. Remove intake manifold.
3. Remove rocker arm covers.
4. Remove rocker arm and shaft assemblies, push rods and valve lifters.
5. Remove timing chain cover.
6. Align timing marks of camshaft and crankshaft sprocket. This avoids burring of camshaft journals by crankshaft during removal. Remove timing chain and sprocket.

Fig. 9 Valve timing marks

Fig. 10 Piston and rod assembly

7. Slide camshaft forward out of bearing bores, using care so as not to damage bearing surfaces.
8. Reverse procedure to install. When installing camshaft, align crankshaft and camshaft timing marks as shown in Fig. 9.

PISTON & ROD, ASSEMBLE

Rods and pistons should be assembled and installed as shown in Fig. 10.

Measure connecting rod side clearance using a suitable feeler gauge. Clearance should be .0005–.0026 inch.

PISTONS, PINS & RINGS

Pistons are available in standard sizes and oversizes of .010 and .030 inch. Rings are available in standard sizes and oversizes of .010 and .030 inch. Piston pins are supplied with piston and available only in standard sizes.

MAIN & ROD BEARINGS

Main bearings are available in standard sizes and undersizes of .001 and .002 inch. Rod bearings are available in standard sizes and in undersize of .008.

Fig. 13 Checking length and diameter of pump gear

Fig. 11 Oil pump cover and relief valve and spring installation

OIL PAN, REPLACE

1. Disconnect battery ground cable.
2. Raise and support vehicle.
3. Drain oil and remove flywheel cover.
4. Remove oil pan.
5. Reverse procedure to install. Apply RTV sealer to oil pan flange and torque oil pan bolts to 10 ft. lbs.

OIL PUMP SERVICE

Removal & Inspection

1. Remove oil filter.
2. Remove screws attaching oil pump cover assembly to timing chain cover. Remove cover assembly and slide out oil pump gears.
3. Wash off gears and inspect for wear or scoring. Replace any gears not found serviceable.
4. Remove oil pressure relief valve cap, spring and valve, Fig. 11. Oil filter bypass valve and spring are staked in place and should not be removed.
5. Wash parts thoroughly, inspect relief valve for wear or scoring. Check relief valve spring to see that it is not worn on its side or collapsed. Replace any relief valve spring that is questionable.
6. Check relief valve in its bore in cover. The valve should have no more clearance than an easy slip fit. If any excessive clearance can be felt, valve and/or cover should be replaced.
7. Check relief by-pass valve for cracks, or warping. Valve should be free of nicks or scratches.

Assembly & Installation

1. Lubricate and install pressure relief valve and spring in bore of oil pump cover, Fig. 11.
2. Install cap and gasket. Torque cap to 35 ft. lbs.
3. Install oil pump gears and shaft in oil pump body section of timing chain cover to check gear end clearance and side clearance.
4. Check oil pump end clearance by placing a straight edge over gears and measure clearance between straight edge and gasket surface, Fig. 12. Clearance should be between .002 and .006 inch. If clearance is less than .002 inch, measure gears and pocket to determine which is out of specification, Fig. 13 and 14.
5. Check oil pump side clearance. Clearance should be between .002 and .005 inch. If clearance is greater than .0050 inch, measure gears and pocket to determine which is out of specification, Figs. 13 and 14.
6. Check oil pump cover flatness by placing a straight edge across cover face, using feeler gauge between straight edge and

Fig. 12 Checking oil pump gear end clearance

pump cover. If clearance is .001 or more pump cover must be replaced.
7. If gear clearance and oil pump cover is flat and side clearance is satisfactory remove gears and pack gear pocket full of petroleum jelly.

NOTE: Never use chassis lube when reinstalling oil pump gears.

8. Reinstall gears so petroleum jelly fills entire gear pocket and between teeth of gears. Place gasket in position.

NOTE: Unless the pump is packed with petroleum jelly it may fail to prime itself when engine is started and damage to engine may result.

9. Install cover assembly screws. To ensure proper seal of gasket, torque screws alternately and evenly to 10 ft. lbs.
10. Install filter on nipple.

REAR MAIN BEARING OIL SEAL REPAIR

1. Remove oil pan and oil pump as described previously.
2. Remove rear main bearing cap.
3. Using tool No. J-29114-2, gently drive upper seal into groove approximately 1/4 in.
4. Repeat step 3 for other end of seal.

Fig. 14 Checking depth and diameter of gear pocket

30 N·m
(22 FT. LB.)

10 N·m
(7 FT. LBS.) ←FRT

Fig. 15 Water pump removal & installation

5. Measure the amount that was driven in on one side and add 1/16 in. Using a suitable cutting tool, cut this length from the oil rear main bearing cap lower seal using the main bearing cap as a guide. Repeat this step for the other end of seal.
6. Place piece of cut seal into groove of seal installer tool guide No. J-29114-1 and install tool guide onto engine block.
7. Using seal packing tool No. J29114-2, drive piece of seal into block. Drive seal in until packing tool contacts machined stop.
8. Remove tool guide and repeat steps 6 and 7 for other end of seal.
9. Install new seal in bearing cap.
10. Install rear main bearing cap. Apply a thin film of sealant No. 1052357 or equivalent to rear main bearing cap and case interface. Use care not to allow sealant to contact crankshaft journal or main bearing.

ELECTRIC FUEL PUMP, REPLACE

1. Drain fuel tank.
2. Disconnect tank unit wire from connector in rear compartment.
3. Remove ground wire retaining screw from under body.
4. Disconnect hoses from tank unit.
5. Support fuel tank and disconnect the two fuel tank retaining straps.
6. Remove fuel tank from vehicle.
7. Remove fuel gage retaining cam, using tool J-24187, or other suitable tool.
8. Remove tank unit from tank.
9. Electric fuel pump can be unbolted from tank sending unit after sending unit has been removed.
10. Reverse procedure to install.

WATER PUMP, REPLACE

1. Disconnect battery ground cable.
2. Remove accessory drive belts.
3. Remove water pump attaching bolts, Fig. 15.
4. Remove engine support strut.
5. Place jack under front crossmember and raise jack until vehicle just starts to raise.
6. Remove front two body mount bolts, (#1 and #3), Fig. 16, also remove lower cushions and retainers.
7. Thread body mount bolts with retainers a minimum of three turns into cage nuts so bolts restrain cradle movement.
8. Release floor jack slowly until crossmember contacts body mount bolt retainers. As jack is being lowered watch and correct any interference with hose, lines,

MOUNT #3   MOUNT #4

MOUNT #2

MOUNT #1

Fig. 16 Removing front body mounts

pipes and cables.

NOTE: Do not lower the cradle without it being restrained as possible damage can occur to the body and underhood items.

9. Remove water pump from engine.
10. Reverse procedure to install.

BELT TENSION DATA

	New Lbs.	Used Lbs.
Air Cond. V6-181	145	65–80
Alternator V6-181	145	65–80
Power Steer. V6-181	135	65–80

V6-262 Diesel Engine Section

ENGINE, REPLACE

1. Drain cooling system. Remove serpentine drive belt, also remove vacuum pump drive belt, if equipped with A/C.
2. Remove air cleaner and install a suitable cover.
3. Disconnect battery ground cable at battery (on vehicles equipped with heavy duty system there will be two batteries), ground wires at inner fender and engine ground strap.
4. Raise vehicle. Remove flywheel cover.
5. Remove flywheel to torque converter attaching bolts.
6. Disconnect exhaust pipe from rear exhaust manifold.
7. Remove engine to transaxle brace.
8. Remove engine mount to cradle retaining nuts and washers.
9. Disconnect leads to starter motor, No. 2 cylinder glow plug and battery ground cable at transaxle to engine bolt.
10. Disconnect lower oil cooler hose and plug openings.
11. Remove accessible power steering pump bracket fasteners and lower vehicle.
12. Remove remaining power steering pump bracket/brace.
13. Remove heater outlet pipe.

14. Disconnect all remaining glow plug leads at glow plugs.
15. Disconnect all other leads at engine, disconnect engine harness at cowl connector and body mounted relays and position engine harness aside.
16. If equipped with A/C, disconnect compressor with brackets and lines attached and position aside.
17. Disconnect fuel and vacuum hoses, plug all fuel line openings.
18. Disconnect throttle and T.V. cables at injection pump and cable bracket. Position cables aside.
19. Disconnect upper oil cooler hose and plug openings. Remove exhaust crossover pipe heat shield.
20. Disconnect and position aside transaxle filler tube.
21. Remove exhaust crossover pipe.
22. Remove engine mounting strut and strut brackets.
23. Install a suitable engine lifting device.

NOTE: When installing lifting chains to cylinder heads, ensure that washers are used under the chains and bolt heads and the bolts are torqued to 20 ft. lbs.

24. Position a suitable support under trans-

axle rear extension. As engine is being removed it may be necessary to raise support. Remove engine to transaxle bolts, then engine.
25. Reverse procedure to install.

NOTE: Before installing the flex plate to converter bolts, ensure the weld nuts on the converter are flush with the flex plate and converter rotates freely by hand in this position. Hand start the three bolts and finger tighten, then torque converter bolts to 35 ft. lbs. This ensures proper alignment of converter.

INTAKE MANIFOLD, REPLACE

Removal

1. Disconnect battery(s) ground cable(s), then remove air cleaner.
2. Drain radiator coolant, then disconnect upper radiator hose from water outlet, and heater hoses from intake manifold.
3. Remove fuel injection pump. Refer to "Injection Pump, Replace".

Fig. 1 Intake manifold drain tube removal & installation

Fig. 2 Removal & installation of intermediate adapter, pump adapter & seal

Fig. 3 Intake manifold installation

4. Disconnect wiring from engine accessories.
5. If equipped with cruise control, remove servo.
6. If equipped with A/C, remove compressor and braces. Position aside.
7. Remove alternator assembly.
8. Disconnect engine mounting strut.
9. Remove fuel lines, filter and brackets. Plug all openings.
10. Disconnect glow plug controller and sending units wire connectors.
11. Disconnect heat shield from exhaust pipe crossover.
12. Using a suitable back-up wrench, remove left (forward) injection lines and plug all openings.
13. Disconnect T.V. and throttle cables from bracket.
14. Remove intake manifold drain tube, Fig. 1.
15. Remove injection pump intermediate adapter, pump adapter and seal, Fig. 2.
16. Remove intake manifold.

Installation

1. Thoroughly clean machined surfaces of cylinder head and intake manifold, ensuring neither surface becomes gouged or scratched. Clean all bolts and bolt holes.
2. Using a suitable sealer, coat both sides of the manifold to head sealing gasket surface, and place in position, Fig. 3.
3. Install end seals, ensure ends are positioned under cylinder heads. Apply RTV sealer to each end of seal, Fig. 3.

NOTE: The end seals and mating surfaces must be dry to prevent gasket slippage.

4. Carefully position intake manifold on engine.
5. Lubricate intake manifold bolts entire length with lubricant 1052080 or equivalent.
6. Install bolts. Torque to specifications following sequence shown in Fig. 4, to 15 ft. lbs. Then retorque to specifications.
7. Reverse steps 1 through 15 of removal procedure to complete installation.

CYLINDER HEAD, REPLACE

1. Remove intake manifold and valve cover.
2. Remove or loosen any accessory bracket or pipe that interferes with removal of cylinder head.
3. Disconnect glow plug wiring and block heater lead (if equipped).
4. Remove ground strap from right cylinder head.
5. Remove rocker arm nuts, pivots, rocker arms and push rods. Scribe mark on pivots and separate so they may be easily identified and replaced in their original location.
6. Disconnect exhaust crossover pipe from exhaust manifold on side being removed and loosen it on opposite side.
7. Remove pipe plugs covering upper cylinder head bolts, Fig. 5.
8. Remove engine block drain plug, from side that is to be worked on.
9. Remove cylinder head bolts and cylinder head. If necessary to remove pre-chamber, remove glow plug and nozzle, then tap out with a small blunt 1/8 inch drift. Do not use tapered drift.

10. Reverse procedure to install. Refer to Fig. 6 for correct torque sequence. Torque cylinder head bolts except bolts 5, 6, 11, 12, 13 and 14 to 142 ft. lbs. Torque bolts 5, 6, 11, 12, 13 and 14 to 59 ft. lbs.

NOTE: The head gaskets used on this engine are composition type, and not to be used with a sealer of any kind. Any sealer applied may result in head gasket leakage.

ROCKER ARMS

NOTE: This engine uses valve rotators, Fig. 7. The rotator operates on a sprag clutch principle utilizing the collapsing action of a coil spring to give rotation to the rotor body which turns the valve.

1. Remove valve cover.
2. Remove flanged bolts, rocker arm pivot and rocker arms, Fig. 7.
3. When installing rocker arm assemblies, lubricate wear surfaces with suitable lubricant. Torque flanged bolts to 28 ft. lbs.

Fig. 4 Intake manifold torquing sequence

Fig. 5 Cylinder head pipe plug removal

Fig. 6 Cylinder head bolt tightening sequence

Fig. 7 Exploded view of cylinder head

Fig. 8 Inspecting valve stem for rotator malfunction

Fig. 9 Measuring valve stem height

VALVE ROTATORS

The rotator operates on a Sprag clutch principle utilizing the collapsing action of coil spring to give rotation to the rotor body which turns the valve, Fig. 7.

To check rotator action, draw a line across rotator body and down the collar. Operate engine at 1500 rpm, rotator body should move around collar. Rotator action can be in either direction. Replace rotator if no movement is noted.

When servicing valves, valve stem tips should be checked for improper wear pattern which could indicate a defective valve rotator, Fig. 8.

VALVE LIFT SPECS.

Engine	Year	Intake	Exhaust
V6-262 Diesel	1982-83	.375	.375

VALVE ARRANGEMENT

V6-262 Diesel .... I-E-E-I-E-I

VALVE TIMING

Intake Opens Before TDC

Engine	Year	Degrees
V6-262 Diesel	1982-83	16

VALVES

Whenever a new valve is installed or after grinding valves, it is necessary to measure the valve stem height with the special tool as shown in Fig. 9.

There should be at least .015 inch clearance between the gauge and end of valve stem. If clearance is less than .015 inch, remove valve and grind end of valve stem as required.

Check valve rotator height, Fig. 10. If valve stem end is less than .005 inch above rotator, the valve is too short and a new valve must be installed.

VALVE GUIDES

Valve stem guides are not replaceable, due to being cast in place. If valve guide bores are worn excessively, they can be reamed oversize.

If a standard valve guide bore is being reamed, use a .003″ or .005″ oversize reamer. For the .010″ oversize valve guide bore, use a .013″ oversize reamer. If too large a reamer is used and the spiraling is removed, it is possible that the valve will not receive the proper lubrication

NOTE: Occasionally a valve guide will be oversize as manufactured. These are marked on the cylinder head. If no markings are present, the guide bores are standard. If oversize markings are present, any valve replacement will require an oversize valve. Service valves are available in standard diameters as well as .003″, .005″, .010″ and .013″ oversize.

VALVE LIFTER, REPLACE

NOTE: Some engines have both standard and .010 inch oversize valve lifters. The .010 inch oversize valve lifters are etched with a "0" on the side of the lifter. Also, the cylinder block will be marked if an oversize lifter is used, Fig. 11.

1. Remove intake manifold as outlined previously.
2. Remove valve covers, rocker arm assemblies and push rods. Note location of valve train components so they can be installed in original position.
3. Remove hydraulic lifter retainer bolts, then retainer, Fig. 12.
4. Remove valve lifters, then disassemble, Fig. 13.
5. If plunger and body appear satisfactory, blow off air to remove all particles of dirt. Install the plunger in the body without other parts and check for free movement. A simple test is to be sure that the plunger will drop of its own weight in the body, Fig. 13.
6. Reverse procedure to install.

NOTE: Plungers are not interchangeable as they are selectively fitted to the bodies at the factory.

FRONT OIL SEAL, REPLACE

1. Disconnect battery ground cables.

Fig. 10 Measuring valve rotator height

Fig. 11 Oversize valve lifter marking

Fig. 12 Hydraulic roller lifter retainer and guide

Fig. 13 Exploded view of hydraulic roller lifter

Fig. 14 Front oil seal removal

Fig. 15 Front oil seal installation

2. Remove accessory drive belts.
3. Remove crankshaft pulley and harmonic balancer.
4. Using tool BT-6406, remove front oil seal, Fig. 14.
5. Apply suitable sealant to outside diameter of new oil seal.
6. Using tool J-29659, install new oil seal, Fig. 15.
7. Install harmonic balancer and crankshaft pulley.
8. Install and tension accessory drive belts.

ENGINE FRONT COVER, REPLACE

1. Disconnect battery ground cables.
2. Drain cooling system and disconnect lower radiator and heater hoses.
3. Remove drive belts, crankshaft pulley, harmonic balancer and accessory brackets.
4. Remove timing indicator.
5. Remove front cover attaching bolts, then the front cover. Also, remove the dowel pins. It may be necessary to grind a flat on the dowel pin to provide a rough surface for gripping.
6. Grind a chamber on one end of each dowel pin, Fig. 16.
7. Cut excess material from front end of oil pan gasket on each side of cylinder block.
8. Trim approximately 1/8 inch from each end of new front pan seal, Fig. 17.
9. Install new front cover gasket and apply suitable sealer to gasket around coolant holes.
10. Apply RTV sealer to mating surfaces of cylinder block, oil pan and front cover.
11. Place front cover on cylinder block and press downward to compress seal. Rotate cover right and left and guide oil pan seal into cavity with a small screwdriver.
12. Apply engine oil to bolts.
13. Install two bolts finger tight to retain cover.
14. Install the two dowel pins, chamfered end first.
15. Install timing indicator and remaining bolts. Torque bolts as shown in Fig. 18.
16. Install harmonic balancer and crankshaft pulley.
17. Install accessory brackets.
18. Install drive belts.
19. Connect lower radiator and heater hoses.
20. Connect ground cables to batteries.

TIMING CHAIN & GEARS, REPLACE

1. Remove front cover as outlined previously. Loosen rocker arm pivot bolts evenly so that some lash is present between rocker arms and valves.
2. Remove oil slinger, cam gear, crank gear and timing chain.
3. Install key in crankshaft, if removed.
4. Install cam gear, crank gear and timing chain with timing marks aligned, Fig. 19.
5. Install oil slinger.
6. Install front cover.

Fig 16 Dowel pin chamfer

Fig. 17 Trimming oil pan seal

1. CAMSHAFT
2. CRANKSHAFT
3. CAMSHAFT SPROCKET KEY
4. INJECTION PUMP DRIVE GEAR
5. CRANKSHAFT SPROCKET KEY
6. FRONT CAMSHAFT BEARING RETAINER
7. 65 N·m (48 FT. LBS.)
8. CRANKSHAFT SPROCKET
9. TIMING CHAIN
10. CAMSHAFT SPROCKET
11. WASHER
12. 87 N·m (64 FT. LBS.)
13. SLINGER
14. GASKET
15. FRONT COVER
16. 55 N·m (41 FT. LBS.)
17. 28 N·m (21 FT. LBS.)
18. PROBE HOLDER (RPM COUNTER)
19. CRANKSHAFT BALANCER
20. WASHER
21. 217-475 N·m (160 - 350 FT. LBS.)
22. PULLEY ASSEMBLY
23. 40 N·m (30 FT. LBS.)
24. COVER

Fig. 18 Engine front cover installation

Fig. 19   Valve timing marks

Fig. 20   Fuel injection pump driven gear removal and installation

Fig. 21   Main bearing identification

CAMSHAFT & INJECTION PUMP DRIVE & DRIVEN GEARS, REPLACE

1. Remove engine assembly as previously outlined.
2. Remove intake manifold and gasket.
3. Remove oil pump drive assembly.
4. Remove front cover, then rotate crankshaft so that timing marks are in alignment.
5. Remove all rocker arms, pivots, push rods, and lifters. Note valve train component location for proper location upon installation.
6. Remove bolt securing camshaft sprocket, then remove both cam and crank sprocket. If crank sprocket is tight on shaft, remove with a suitable puller.
7. Remove bolts retaining front camshaft bearing retainer, then remove retainer.
8. Remove cam sprocket key.
9. Remove injection pump drive gear.
10. Remove intake manifold, intermediate pump adapter and pump adapter. Remove snap ring, selective washer, driven gear and spring, Fig. 20.
11. Install a long bolt into camshaft to act as a handle and carefully slide camshaft out of block.

NOTE: Do not force the camshaft out of the block. Damage to the bearing and or the camshaft can result.

If the bearings are to be replaced, it will be necessary to remove the oil pan before removing the bearings.

12. Reverse procedure to install. Check injection pump driven gear end play. If end play is not .002–.006 inch, replace selective washer, Fig. 20. Selective washers are available from .080 to .115 inch in increments of .003 inch.

PISTON & ROD, ASSEMBLE

The pistons must be installed with the notch in the top facing the front of the engine.

Measure the connecting rod side clearance using a suitable feeler gauge. Clearance should be .008–.021 inch.

Fig. 22   Packing upper rear main bearing seal

Fig. 23   Trimming upper rear main bearing seal

24 N·m
(18 FT. LBS.)

WASHER

Fig. 24   Oil pump removal

DRIVE SHAFT EXTENSION

PUMP BODY

IDLER GEAR

OIL INTAKE

VALVE   RETAINING PIN

SPRING

DRIVE GEAR   GASKET

GASKET

COVER

Fig. 25   Oil pump disassembled

1

2

1 J-29785 REMOVAL

2 J-29786 INSTALL UNTIL FLUSH

Fig. 26   Water pump pully removal & installation

PISTON, RINGS & PINS

Pistons are available in standard sizes and .010 oversizes. Rings are available in standard and oversizes of .010 and .030.

MAIN & ROD BEARINGS

Main bearings are available in standard sizes and undersizes of .0005, .0010 and .0015 inch. The amount of undersize and part number is stamped on the bearing shell, Fig. 21.

Rod bearings are available in standard sizes and an undersize of .010 inch.

REAR CRANKSHAFT SEAL SERVICE

Since the braided fabric seal used on these engines can be replaced only when the crankshaft is removed, the following repair procedure is recommended.
1. Remove oil pan and bearing cap.
2. Drive end of old seal gently into groove, using a suitable tool, until packed tight. This may vary between 1/4 and 3/4 inch depending on amount of pack required.
3. Repeat previous step for other end of seal.
4. Measure and note amount that seal was driven up on one side. Using the old seal removed from bearing cap, cut a length of seal the amount previously noted plus 1/16 inch.
5. Repeat previous step for other side of seal.
6. Pack cut lengths of seal into appropriate side of seal groove. A packing tool, BT-6433, Fig. 22, may be used since the tool has been machined to provide a built-in stop. Use tool BT-6436 to trim the seal flush with block, Fig. 23.
7. Install new seal in lower bearing cap.

OIL PAN, REPLACE

1. Install suitable engine lifting fixture.
2. Raise vehicle but keep rear slightly lower than front.
3. Install suitable supports at front of body at forward lift points.
4. Drain engine oil.
5. Remove left side steering gear to cradle bolt, then loosen right side steering gear to cradle bolt.
6. Remove front stabilizer bar.
7. Using 1/2 inch drill bit, drill through spot weld located between rear holes at left hand front stabilizer bar mounting.
8. Remove engine and transaxle to cradle mount nuts.
9. Disconnect left lower ball joint from knuckle.
10. Position suitable support and block of wood under transaxle oil pan, then raise transaxle until mount stud clears cradle.
11. Remove bolts securing front crossmember to right side of cradle.
12. Remove left side body mount bolts.
13. Remove left side and front crossmember assembly, then lower rear crossmember below left side by careful use of a pry bar.
14. Remove flywheel cover, starter assembly and engine mount bracket.
15. Remove oil pan attaching bolts and oil pan.
16. Reverse procedure to install.

OIL PUMP, REPLACE & SERVICE

Replacement

1. Remove oil pan as outlined previously.
2. Remove oil pump to rear main bearing cap attaching bolts, Fig. 24.
3. Remove oil pump and drive shaft extension.
4. Reverse procedure to install. Torque attaching bolts to 22 ft. lbs.

Service

Disassembly

1. Remove oil pump drive shaft extension, Fig. 25. Do not attempt to remove washers from drive shaft extension. The drive shaft extension and washers are serviced as an assembly.
2. Remove cotter pin, spring and pressure regulator valve, Fig. 25.

NOTE: Apply pressure on pressure regulator bore before removing cotter pin since the spring is under pressure.

---

3. Remove oil pump cover attaching screws, then oil pump cover and gasket.
4. Remove drive gear and idler gear from pump body.

Inspection

1. Check gears for scoring or other damage, replace if necessary.
2. Proper end clearance is .0005–.0075 inch.
3. Check pressure regulator valve, valve spring and bore for damage. Proper bore to valve clearance is .0025–.0050 inch.

4. Check extension shaft ends for wear.

Assembly

1. Install gears and shaft in oil pump body.
2. Check gear end clearance by placing a straight edge over the gears and measure the clearance between the straight edge and gasket surface. If end clearance is excessive, check for scores in cover that would bring the clearance over specified limits.
3. Install cover and torque attaching screws to 7 ft. lbs.
4. Install pressure regulator valve, closed end first, into bore, then the valve spring and cotter pin.

WATER PUMP, REPLACE

1. Disconnect battery ground cable.
2. Drain radiator.
3. Disconnect heater return hose at water pump, then remove bolt retaining heater water return pipe to intake manifold and position aside.
4. Remove vacuum pump drive belt, if equipped with A/C.
5. Remove serpentine drive belt.
6. Remove alternator. Then, remove A/C compressor or vacuum pump brackets (if equipped).
7. Remove water pump attaching bolts and water pump assembly.
8. Remove water pump pulley, Fig. 26.
9. Reverse procedure to install.

FUEL PUMP, REPLACE

1. Ensure ignition switch is in "off" position.
2. Remove air cleaner and disconnect 12

Fig. 27 Roosa-Master pump fuel flow schematic

Fig. 28 CAV pump fuel flow schematic

volt lead wire from pump.
3. Use 3/4 inch wrench to support the inlet fitting firmly, then with 5/8 inch wrench disconnect inlet tube and plug openings.
4. Repeat step three to disconnect outlet fitting. Place a suitable rag under pump outlet side to collect fuel since this line is slightly pressurized.

NOTE: Do not overtwist pump outlet fitting; otherwise cover crimp may be loosened.

5. Remove pump mounting bracket nut and pump.
6. Remove dust plugs from openings on new pump, then install pump and bracket assembly on engine. Torque pump mounting bracket nut to 18 ft. lbs. Torque inlet and outlet fuel line fittings to 19 ft. lbs.

NOTE: In some instances, it may be necessary to adjust pump location by loosening the bracket screw and turning the pump to get the exact alignment between pump fittings and fuel lines. Be sure to torque bracket screw after the adjustment.

7. After pump is installed, disconnect fuel line at fuel filter and turn ignition switch "On" in order to prime and bleed lines. Use a suitable container to catch fuel. If pump runs with a clicking sound or there

are air bubbles in fuel, check for leaks in line. Check all connections to see that they are dry and that no fuel is leaking. When clicking sound disappears, tighten fuel line at filter.

BELT TENSION DATA

NOTE: This engine is equipped with a serpentine drive belt that is self adjusting

DIESEL FUEL INJECTION PUMP, DESCRIPTION

The 1982 V6-262 diesel engine may be equipped with one of two fuel injection pumps, the Roosa-Master or the CAV pump.

The pump is mounted on top of the engine. It is gear driven off the camshaft and turns at camshaft speed. It is a high pressure rotary pump that injects a metered amount of fuel to each cylinder at the proper time. The six high pressure delivery pipes from the pump to the injection nozzle in each cylinder are the same length to prevent any difference in timing, cylinder-to-cylinder. The fuel injection pump provides the required timing advance under all operating conditions. Engine RPM is controlled by a rotary fuel metering valve. Pushing down on the accelerator pedal moves the throttle cable to open the metering valve and allow more fuel to be delivered. The injection

pump also has a low pressure transfer pump to deliver fuel from the fuel line to the high pressure pump.

The fuel filter is located between the electric fuel pump and the injection pump.

The fuel tank is at the rear of the vehicle, connected by fuel pipes and hoses to the fuel pump. Excess fuel returns from the fuel injection pump to the fuel tank through pipes and hoses.

The fuel flow schematics, Figs. 27 and 28, show the major components and their relationships and also provides a means of determining the differences in the two systems.

INJECTION PUMP TIMING

NOTE: Alignment of timing marks may be used in situations where timing meter J-33075 is not available. However for optimum engine operation, the timing should be adjusted with the meter. For adjustment of timing marks use following procedure.

1. The mark on the injection pump adapter must be aligned with the mark on the injection pump flange.
2. To adjust:
   a. Loosen the injection pump retaining nuts with tool J-25304.
   b. Align the mark on the injection pump flange with the mark on the injection

Fig. 29 Roosa-Master pump pressure tap plug location

Fig. 30 CAV pump torque screw location

1. FAST IDLE SOLENOID.
2. HOUSING PRESSURE COLD ADVANCE SOLENOID.
3. FUEL SHUT OFF (SHUT DOWN) SOLENOID.
4. TORQUE CONVERTER CLUTCH SWITCH (PART OF VACUUM REGULATOR VALVE).

Fig. 31 Roosa Master pump solenoids and connectors location

Fig. 32 CAV pump solenoids and connectors location

Fig. 33 Air crossover removal & installation

Fig. 34 Offset on fuel injection pump

pump adapter.
c. Torque injection pump retaining nuts to 35 ft. lbs.

FUEL INJECTION PUMP HOUSING FUEL PRESSURE CHECK

1. Remove air crossover and install screen covers J-29657 or other suitable covers.
2. Remove pressure tap plug on Roosa-Master pump, or torque screw on CAV pump, Figs. 29 and 30. If equipped with torque screw, to avoid disturbing adjustment add a second nut to lock nut, then back out screw with nuts attached.
3. Attach low pressure gage to adapters.
4. Connect magnetic pick-up tachometer.
5. With gear shift lever in park position and parking brake on, check pressure with engine running at 1000 RPM. Pressure should be between 8–12 psi with no more than 2 psi fluctuation.
6. If pressure is at 0, check operation of housing pressure cold advance as follows:
   a. Remove electrical connector from housing pressure cold advance terminal, Figs. 31 and 32. If pressure remains at 0, remove injection pump cover and check operation of advance solenoid. If it is binding, repair or replace parts as necessary.
   b. If pressure is as specified with housing cold pressure advance electrical connector disconnected, check operation of temperature switch located in cylinder head bolt.
7. If pressure is not within specifications, replace fuel return line connector assembly.
8. Remove tachometer, pressure gauge and adapter.
9. Install a new pressure tap plug seal on pressure tap plug and install plug into pump housing.
10. Remove screened covers and install air crossover.

INJECTION PUMP, REPLACE

Removal

1. Remove air cleaner assembly.
2. Remove crankcase ventilation filter and pipes from valve cover and air crossover.
3. Remove air crossover, Fig. 33, and install

suitable intake screen covers.
4. Remove fuel lines, filter and fuel pump as an assembly. Plug all openings.
5. Remove throttle and T.V. cables from intake manifold brackets and position aside.
6. Disconnect fuel return line from injection pump.
7. Disconnect injection line clamps that are closest to the pump.
8. Disconnect injection lines from pump and plug all openings. Then carefully reposition lines to gain enough clearance to remove pump.
9. Remove two bolts retaining injection pump.
10. Remove pump and discard pump to adapter "O"-ring.

Installation

1. Position No. 1 cylinder at firing position by aligning mark on balance with zero mark on indicator located at front of engine.
2. Align offset tang on pump drive shaft with pump driven gear, Fig. 34.
3. Install new pump to adapter "O"-ring, then install pump.
4. If a new intermediate adapter is installed, set injection pump at center of slots in pump mounting flange. If original intermediate adapter is being used, align pump timing mark with mark on intermediate adapter. Install two bolts and washers retaining pump and torque bolts to 35 ft. lbs.
5. Reverse steps 1 through 8 of removal

Fig. 35 Roosa-Master pump right side view

procedure for remainder of installation. If necessary adjust T.V. cable, pump timing, vacuum regulator valve or idle speed.

INJECTION NOZZLES, REPLACE

1. Remove fuel lines, using a backup wrench on upper injection nozzle hex.
2. Plug nozzle and lines to prevent damage or contamination. Then remove nozzles by applying torque to largest nozzle hex.
3. When working on rear bank, it may be necessary to perform following procedures:
   a. Remove engine support strut.
   b. Place a floor jack under front crossmember of cradle and raise jack until it just starts to raise vehicle.
   c. Remove front two body mount bolts with lower cushions and retainers. Remove cushions from bolts.
   d. Thread body mount bolts with retainers a minimum of three turns into cage nuts so that the bolts restrain cradle movement.
   e. Release floor jack slowly until crossmember contacts body mount bolt retainers. As jack is being lowered watch and correct any interference with hose, lines, pipes and cables.

NOTE: Do not lower cradle without it being restrained as possible damage may occur to the body and underhood items.

4. Remove copper nozzle gasket from cylinder head if gasket did not remain on nozzle.
5. Reverse procedure to install. Apply suitable lubricant to nozzle threads, then torque nozzles to 25 ft. lbs. When tightening nozzle, torque must be applied to largest nozzle hex. Torque fuel line to 25 ft. lbs. using a backup wrench on upper injection nozzle hex.

NOTE: Failure to apply the correct lubricant can cause engine damage. Use lubricant No. 9985462 or equivalent.

VACUUM REGULATOR VALVE, REPLACE

1. Note location of valve vacuum hoses, then disconnect vacuum hoses.
2. Remove two valve attaching bolts, then valve.
3. Reverse procedure to install.

Fig. 36 Installation of tool J-29601 on injection pump. Roosa-Master pump

Fig. 37 Roosa-Master pump with cover removed

Fig. 38 Installation of pump cover. Roosa-Master pump

ROOSA-MASTER PUMP ON VEHICLE SERVICE

Throttle Shaft Seal, Replace

1. Disconnect battery ground cable.
2. Remove air cleaner and air crossover, Fig. 33, then install air screens J-29657.
3. Disconnect injection pump fuel solenoid, housing pressure cold advance wires and fuel return pipe, Fig. 35.
4. Remove throttle rod, vacuum regulator valve, return spring and throttle cable bracket.
5. Place tool J-29601 over throttle shaft and pin, then position spring clip of tool over throttle shaft advance cam and tighten wing nut. Without loosening wing nut, pull tool off shaft. This will provide proper alignment during reassembly, Fig. 36.
6. Drive pin from throttle shaft and remove shaft advance cam and fiber washer. Remove any burrs from shaft which may have resulted from pin removal.
7. Clean injection pump cover, upper portion of pump, throttle shaft and guide stud area. Position several shop cloths in engine valley area to absorb fuel.
8. Remove injection pump cover screws, then cover.

CAUTION: Use care to avoid any foreign matter from entering pump when cover is removed. If any object or foreign matter enter pump, it must be removed before engine is started as injection pump damage or engine damage may occur.

9. Note position of metering valve spring before removal as its position must be duplicated exactly during reassembly, Fig. 37.
10. Remove guide stud and washer, noting parts before removal.
11. Rotate min-max governor assembly up for clearance then remove it, Fig. 37. If idle governor spring becomes disengaged from throttle block, it must be reinstalled with tightly wound coils toward throttle block.
12. Remove throttle shaft assembly and inspect shaft for unusual wear or damage, replace if necessary. It may be necessary to loosen nuts at injection pump mounting flange and rotate pump slightly to allow throttle shaft to clear intake manifold.
13. Inspect throttle shaft bushings in pump housing for damage or unusual wear. If replacement of bushings is necessary, it must be performed by a qualified repair facility.
14. Remove throttle shaft seals. Do not cut

seals to remove, as any nicks in the seal seat will cause leakage.
15. Install new shaft seals, lubricated with chassis grease. Use care to avoid cutting seals on sharp edges of shaft.
16. Carefully slide throttle shaft into pump to point where min-max governor assembly will slide back onto throttle shaft, Fig. 37.
17. Rotate min-max governor assembly downward, then hold in position and slide throttle shaft and governor into position.
18. Install new fiber washer, throttle shaft advance cam (do not tighten screw at this time) and a new throttle shaft drive pin, Fig. 35.
19. Align throttle shaft advance cam so tool J-20601 can be installed over throttle shaft, pins in slots and spring clip over advance cam.
20. Insert a .005 inch feeler gauge between cam and fiber washer, then tighten cam screw and remove tool J-29601.
21. Install guide stud with new washer, assuring that upper extension of metering valve spring slides on top of guide stud. Torque guide studs to 85 inch lbs.

CAUTION: Over torquing may strip the aluminum threads in the housing.

22. Hold throttle in idle position and install new pump cover seal. Making sure that screws are not in cover, position cover above ¼ inch forward toward shaft end and about ⅛ inch above pump, Fig. 38. More cover rearward and downward into position, using care to avoid cutting seal, then reinstall cover screws. Each screw must have a flat washer and internal lock washer, with flat washer against pump cover. Torque screws to 37 inch lbs. and install vacuum regulator.
23. Reconnect both battery ground cables, then turn ignition switch to run position and touch pink solenoid wire to solenoid. A clicking noise should be heard as the wire is connected and disconnected. If not, the linkage may be jammed in the wide open position and the engine must not be started. Proceed to step 24. If clicking is heard, connect pump solenoid and housing pressure cold advance wires and proceed to step 25.
24. Remove cover, then ground solenoid lead (opposite hot lead) and connect pink wire. With ignition switch in run position, the solenoid in the cover should move the linkage. If not, the solenoid must be replaced. Minimum voltage across solenoid terminals must be 12 volts. Reinstall cover and repeat step 23.
25. Install throttle cable bracket, throttle

rod, throttle cable and return springs. Make sure timing marks on pump and adapter are aligned and make sure nuts retaining pump are tight. Install fuel return pipe.
26. Start engine and check for fuel leaks.

NOTE: Rough idle may be due to air in the pump. Allow sufficient time for air to purge by allowing engine to idle. It may be necessary to turn engine off to allow air bubbles to rise to top of pump where they will be purged.

27. Adjust Vacuum Regulator Valve, then remove intake manifold screens and install air crossover and air cleaner, Fig. 33.

Pump Cover Seal And/Or Guide Stud, Replace

1. Disconnect battery ground cable.
2. Remove air cleaner and air crossover, Fig. 33, and install air screen J-29657.
3. Disconnect injection pump fuel solenoid, housing pressure cold advance wires and fuel return pipe.
4. Clean injection pump cover, upper portion of pump and guide stud area. Position shop cloths to absorb fuel.
5. Remove injection pump cover screws, then cover.

CAUTION: Use care to avoid any foreign matter from entering pump when cover is removed. If any object or foreign matter enter pump, it must be removed before starting engine as injection pump damage or engine damage may occur.

6. Note position of metering valve spring before removal as its position must be duplicated exactly during reassembly, Fig. 37.
7. Remove guide stud and washer, noting location of parts before removal.
8. Refer to steps 21 thru 27 under "Throttle Shaft Seal, Replace" procedure for reassembly of "Pump Cover Seal And/Or Guide Stud".

Solenoids, Replace

1. Remove pump cover.
2. Remove terminal contact nuts, then remove solenoid from cover noting position of any insulating washers.
3. Place solenoid in cover ensuring that shut-off solenoid linkage is free. Also, check that housing pressure cold advance solenoid plunger is centered so that it will contact fitting check ball, Fig. 31.

4. Place insulator washers on terminal studs and install terminal nuts. Torque nuts to 10–15 inch lbs. and replace pump cover.

CAV PUMP ON VEHICLE SERVICE

End Plate Access Plug Or Stop Plug Washer, Replace

1. Remove air cleaner and install cover J-26996-1 or equivalent.
2. Clean any dirt from area.
3. Remove stop plug and/or end plate plug and discard washers.
4. Reverse procedure to install. Torque stop plug to 80 inch lbs. and end plate to 43 ft. lbs.

Fuel Inlet Connection Washer, Replace

1. Remove air cleaner and install cover J-26996-1 or equivalent.
2. Clean any dirt from area.
3. Remove fuel inlet pipe, Fig. 39.
4. Remove inlet connection and discard washer.
5. Reverse procedure to install. Using new washer, install inlet to pump and torque to 33 ft. lbs.

Governor Control Cover Gasket, Replace, Fig. 40

1. Remove air crossover, Fig. 33, and install cover J-29657.
2. Clean any dirt from injection pump cover and upper area of pump.
3. Place several rags in engine valley to catch spilled fuel.
4. Remove fuel return pipe.
5. Remove control cover screws and cover, discarding washers and gasket.

NOTE: Extreme care must be exercised to keep foreign material out of the pump when the cover is off. If any objects are dropped into the pump, they must be

Fig. 39   CAV pump fuel inlet pipe removal

removed before the engine is started or injection pump or engine damage may occur.

---

6. Reverse procedure to install. Torque screws to 25 inch lbs.

Housing Pressure Cold Advance Solenoid, Replace, Fig. 40

1. Remove governor control cover, see "Governor Control Cover Gasket, Replace".
2. Remove solenoid terminal nut, spring filter, insulating washers and solenoid. Discard gasket.
3. Reverse procedure to install. Torque terminal nut to 20 in. lbs. and ensure solenoid is centered in cover.

Stop Solenoid, Replace, Fig. 40

1. Remove air cleaner and install cover J-26996-1.
2. Clean dirt from area around solenoid.
3. Remove electrical lead.
4. Remove solenoid and "O"-ring. Discard "O"-ring.
5. Reverse procedure to install. Torque solenoid to 130 inch lbs.

Throttle Shaft Seal, Replace

1. Remove air crossover and install cover J-29657 or equivalent.

---

2. Disconnect fuel return pipe, then remove governor control cover screws and cover.
3. Remove fast idle solenoid and vacuum regulator valve.
4. Disconnect throttle cable and T.V. cable.
5. Disconnect throttle return spring.
6. Install tool J-29601 or equivalent over throttle shaft with slots of tool engaging vacuum regulator valve lock pin. Place spring clip of tool over throttle shaft advance cam and tighten wing nut. Without loosening wing nut, pull tool off of shaft.
7. Remove lock pin from throttle shaft, Fig. 41.
8. Remove rollpin from pump housing and remove governor support rod.
9. Tilt governor carrier assembly by lifting end nearest drive end of pump and remove carrier from pump housing.
10. Remove clamping screw from light load cam, then remove cam.
11. Remove E clip from throttle shaft, then remove throttle shaft from pump.
12. Remove and discard O rings.
13. Check throttle shaft assembly and governor housing bores for damage and wear and replace as necessary.
14. Lubricate shaft and O rings with oil and assemble larger O rings onto shaft.
15. Install throttle shaft into housing until thrust washers can be installed onto shaft in original positions. Install smaller O ring onto shaft.
16. Assemble light load advance cam onto shaft and install but do not tighten clamping screw.
17. Install E clip into throttle shaft recess. If new throttle shaft is installed, shaft end play must be checked and adjusted by selective fitting of thrust washers. Throttle shaft end play should be .006–.012 inch.
18. Install new pin onto head of shaft. Align throttle shaft advance cam until tool J-29601 or equivalent can be installed over throttle shaft. Tighten cam screw, then remove tool J-29601.
19. Rotate throttle lever forwards to the drive end of pump. Install governor carrier assembly onto pump housing and engage lug on underside of throttle block with cut away notch in throttle shaft.
20. Lubricate governor support rod and new O ring, then install O ring onto support

1. Rubber "O" ring
2. Back leakage connection
3. Elbow connection
4. Governor control cover
5. Joint (Gasket)
6. Spring filter
7. Cold advance solenoid
8. Backing washer
9. Rubber "O" ring
10. Insulating washer
11. Plain washer
12. Nut
13. Locknut
14. Tang drive hub
15. Snap ring
16. Rubber "O" ring
17. Shakeproof washer
18. Screw - dome headed
19. Inspection cover
20. Rubber sealing joint (Gasket)
21. Stop solenoid
22. Throttle lever
23. Shakeproof washer
24. Hexagon socket screw

Fig. 40   Exploded view of CAV pump

1. Rubber "O" ring
2. Idling adjuster screw
3. Thrust washer
4. "E" type circlip
5. Thrust washer
6. Rubber "O" ring
7. Clamp screw
8. Light load advance cam
9. Pin
10. Locknut and rubber "O" ring
11. Torque screw
12. Throttle shaft
13. Maximum speed adjustment screw (Do not adjust)

Fig. 41   Throttle shaft and seals. CAV pump

1. Rubber "O" ring
2. Governor support rod
3. Locking pin
4. Sleeve
5. Throttle lever
6. Idling screw and spring
7. Governor carrier assembly
8. Idle spring
9. Governor arm
10. Throttle block
11. Throttle shaft

Fig. 42   Governor assembly. CAV pump

21. Insert plain end of rod through rear of governor housing and into carrier assembly sleeve.
22. Install support rod into housing and install new locking pin, Fig. 42.
23. Install governor cover and fuel return pipe.
24. Install throttle return springs and connect throttle cable.
25. Connect TV detent cable.
26. Install vacuum regulator valve and fast idle solenoid.
27. Start engine and check for leaks. Install air crossover and air cleaner.

Clutch & Transaxle Section

> Refer to the 1980–83 Citation, Omega, Phoenix and Skylark, "CLUTCH & TRANSAXLE SECTION" for service procedures not covered in this section.

Rear Axle, Rear Suspension & Brakes

> Refer to the 1980–83 Citation, Omega, Phoenix and Skylark, "REAR AXLE, REAR SUSPENSION & BRAKES" section for service procedures not covered in this section.

Front Suspension & Steering Section

> Refer to the 1980–83 Citation, Omega, Phoenix and Skylark, "FRONT SUSPENSION & STEERING SECTION" for service procedures not covered in this section

POWER STEERING PUMP, REPLACE

V6-262 Diesel, Fig. 1

1. Remove drive belt, then drain power steering fluid from power steering pump reservoir.
2. Raise and support vehicle and disconnect pressure and return lines from power steering pump.
3. Working through access holes in pump pulley, remove three bolts from front of pump.
4. Remove two nuts holding lower brace to engine and remove bracket.
5. Remove pump and pulley assembly from vehicle.
6. Reverse procedure to install.

Fig. 1 Power steering pump removal & installation. V6-262 Diesel

CHEVROLET CHEVETTE • PONTIAC 1000

CAUTION

This vehicle contains many parts dimensioned in the metric system. Most fasteners are metric and many are very close in dimension to familiar customary measurements in the inch system. However, it is important to note that, during any vehicle maintenance procedures, replacement fasteners must have the same measurements as those removed, whether metric or customary. Mismatched or incorrect fasteners can result in vehicle damage or malfunction or possible personal injury. Therefore, fasteners removed from the vehicle should be saved for re-use or care should be taken to select a replacement that matches the original.

INDEX OF SERVICE OPERATIONS

NOTE: Refer to the back of this manual for vehicle manufacturer's special service tool suppliers.

CHEVROLET CHEVETTE • PONTIAC 1000

1-371

VEHICLE IDENTIFICATION NUMBER LOCATION

On top of instrument panel, left front.

ENGINE NUMBER LOCATION

On pad at right side of cylinder block, below No. 1 spark plug.

ENGINE V.I.N. CODE

On 1977–80 vehicles, the fifth digit in the V.I.N. denotes engine code. On 1981–83 vehicles, the eighth digit in the V.I.N. denotes engine code.

ENGINE IDENTIFICATION CODE

Engines are identified in the following table by the code letter or letters immediately following the engine serial number.

Year	Engine	V.I.N. Code	Code	Year	Engine	V.I.N. Code	Code	Year	Engine	V.I.N. Code	Code
1977	4-85	I	CDS, CVA, CVB	1979	4-97	E	DBA, DBB, DBC		4-97	9	DCD, DCF, DCH
	4-97	E	CNA, CNB, CNC		4-97	E	DBD, DBF, DBH		4-97	9	DCJ, DCU, DCW
	4-97	E	CND, CNF, CNH		4-97	E	DBJ, DBK, DBL		4-97	9	DCX, DCY, DCZ
	4-97	E	CNR, CNS, CNT		4-97	E	DBM, DBR, DBS		4-110	D	
	4-97	E	CNU		4-97	E	DBT, DBU, DBW	1982	4-97	C	CHA, C2A, CHW
	4-97	E	CYC, CYD, CYF		4-97	E	DBX, DBY, DBZ		4-97	C	CUF, CHD, C2B
	4-97	E	CYH, CYY, CYZ		4-97	O	DSA, DSB		4-97	C	CHX, CUH, CHF
1978	4-97	E	CYA, CYB, CYJ	1980	4-97	9	CKA, CKB, CKC		4-97	C	C2C, CUA, CUJ
	4-97	E	CYK, CYL, CYM		4-97	9	CKD, CKF, CKH		4-97	C	CHK, C2D, CUB
	4-97	E	CYR, CYS, CYT		4-97	9	CKJ, CKK,		4-97	C	CUK, CHN, CHT
	4-97	E	CYU, CYW, CYX		4-97	O	CKL, CKM, CKR, CKS		4-97	C	CUD
	4-97	J	ZTT, ZTU, ZTW	1981	4-97	9	DCA, DCB, DCC		4-110	D	
	4-97	J	ZTX								

GRILLE IDENTIFICATION

1977 Chevette

1978 Chevette

1979–80 Chevette

1981 T1000

1981–83 Chevette

1982–83 T1000

GENERAL ENGINE SPECIFICATIONS

Year	Engine CID①/Liter	VIN Code	Carburetor	Bore and Stroke	Compression Ratio	Net H.P. @ R.P.M.②	Maximum Torque Lbs. Ft. @ R.P.M.	Normal Oil Pressure Pounds
1977	4-85, 1.4 Liter⑨	I③	IME, 1 Bbl④	3.228 × 2.606 82.0 × 66.2 mm.	8.5 —	52 @ 5300 —	67 @ 3400 97 Joules @ 3400	36–46 —
	4-97, 1.6 Liter⑤	E③	IME, 1 Bbl④	3.228 × 2.980 82.0 × 75.7 mm.	8.5 —	60 @ 5300 —	77 @ 3200 104 Joules @ 3200	36–46 —
1978	4-97, 1.6 Liter⑤	E③	IME, 1 Bbl④	3.228 × 2.980 82.0 × 75.7 mm.	8.5 —	63 @ 4800 —	82 @ 3200 —	34–42 —
	4-97, 1.6 Liter⑤⑥	J③	IME, 1 Bbl④	3.228 × 2.980 82.0 × 75.7 mm.	8.5 —	68 @ 5000 —	84 @ 3200 —	34–42 —
1979	4-97, 1.6 Liter⑤	E③	5210C, 2 Bbl⑦	3.228 × 2.980 82.0 × 75.3 mm.	8.5 —	70 @ 5200 —	82 @ 2400 —	55 —
	4-97, 1.6 Liter⑤⑥	O③	5210C, 2 Bbl⑦	3.228 × 2.980 82.0 × 75.7 mm.	8.5 —	74 @ 5200 —	88 @ 2800 —	55 —
1980	4-97, 1.6 Liter⑤	9③	6510C, 2 Bbl⑦	3.228 × 2.980 82.0 × 75.7 mm.	8.5 —	70 @ 5200 —	82 @ 2400 —	55 —
	4-97, 1.6 Liter⑤⑥	O③	5210C, 2 Bbl⑦	3.228 × 2.980 82.0 × 75.7 mm.	8.6 —	74 @ 5200 —	88 @ 2800 —	55 —

Continued

GENERAL ENGINE SPECIFICATIONS—Continued

Year	Engine CID①/Liter	VIN Code	Carburetor	Bore and Stroke	Com-pression Ratio	Net H.P. @ R.P.M.②	Maximum Torque Lbs. Ft. @ R.P.M.	Normal Oil Pressure Pounds
1981	4-97, 1.6 Liter⑤	9⑧	5210C, 2 Bbl⑦	3.228 × 2.980 82.0 × 75.7 mm.	8.6	70 @ 5200	82 @ 2400	55
	4-110, 1.8 Liter⑩	D⑧	Fuel Injection	3.310 × 3.230 84.0 × 82.0 mm.	22.1	51 @ 5000	72 @ 2000	64
1982	4-97, 1.6 Liter⑤	C⑧	6510C, 2Bbl.⑦	3.228 × 2.980 82.0 × 75.7 mm.	9.2	65 @ 5200	80 @ 3200	55
	4-110, 1.8 Liter⑩	D⑧	Fuel Injection	3.310 × 3.230 84.0 × 82.0 mm.	22.1	51 @ 5000	72 @ 2000	64
1983	4-97, 1.6 Liter⑤	C⑧	2 Bbl⑦	3.228 × 2.980 82.0 × 75.7 mm.	9.2	—	—	57
	4-110, 1.8 Liter⑩	D⑧	Fuel Injection	3.310 × 3.230 84.0 × 82.0 mm.	22	—	—	64

①—CID—Cubic inch displacement.
②—Ratings are net as installed in vehicle.
③—Fifth digit in the VIN denotes engine code.
④—Rochester
⑤—1600 cc engine.
⑥—High output engine.
⑦—Holley.
⑧—Eighth digit in the VIN denotes engine code.
⑨—1400 cc engine.
⑩—Diesel engine

TUNE UP SPECIFICATIONS

The following specifications are published from the latest information available. This data should be used only in the absence of a decal affixed in the engine compartment.

★ When using a timing light, disconnect vacuum hose or tube at distributor and plug opening in hose or tube so idle speed will not be affected.

● When checking compression, lowest cylinder must be within 70 percent of highest.

▲ Before removing wires from distributor cap, determine location of the No. 1 wire in cap, as distributor position may have been altered from that shown at the end of this chart.

Spark plug types shown in this chart are recommendations of the original vehicle manufacturer and not MOTOR.

Check local sources for other spark plug manufacturers listings.

Year & Engine/V.I.N.	Spark Plug Type	Gap	Firing Order Fig. ▲	Man. Trans.	Auto. Trans.	Mark Fig.	Man. Trans.	Auto. Trans.	Man. Trans.	Auto. Trans.	Fuel Pump Pressure
1977											
4-85/I	R43TS	.035	A	12°	12°	B	600/800	600/800D	2300④	2400④	5–6½
4-97.6/E, Exc. Calif. & High Alt.	R43TS	.035	A	8°	8°	B	600/800	⑦	2300④	2400④	5–6½
4-97.6/E, Calif. & High Alt.	R43TS	.035	A	8°	8°	B	800	⑦	—	2400④	5–6½
1978											
4-97.6 Exc. Calif. & High Alt.⑭	R43TS	.035	A	8°	8°	B	600/800	⑦⑧	④⑨	2400④	5–6½
4-97.6 Calif. & High Alt.⑭	R43TS	.035	A	8°	8°	B	800	⑦⑧	—	2400④	5–6½
1979											
4-97.6/E, Exc. Calif.	R42TS	.035	A	12°	18°	③	800/1150	750/1150	2500⑤	2500⑤	2½–6½
4-97.6/E, Calif.⑩	R42TS	.035	A	12°	16°	③	800/1150	750/1150	2500⑤	2500⑤	2½–6½
4-97.6/O, Calif.⑪	R42TS	.035	A	12°	12°	③	800/1150	750/1150	2500⑤	2500⑤	2½–6½
1980											
4-97.6 Exc. Calif.⑮	R42TS	.035	A	12°	18°	C	800/1150	750/1150	2500	2500	2½–6½
4-97.6 Calif.⑮	R42TS	.035	A	12°	18°	C	800/1150	800/1150	2600	2500	2½–6½
1981											
4-97.6/9	R42TS	.035	A	18°	18°	C	800/1150⑥	700D⑫	2500	2500	2½–6½
4-110 Diesel/D	—	—	—	18°⑬	18°⑬	—	625	725D	950	950	—
1982											
4-97.6/C	R42TS	.035	A	4°	4°	C	700	700D	2500	2500	2½–6½
4-110 Diesel/D	—	—	—	18°⑬	18°⑬	—	625	725D	950	950	—
1983											
4-97.6/C	R42TS	.035	A	—	—	C	800⑯	700D	—	—	5–6½
4-110 Diesel/D											

Ignition Timing BTDC①★ columns: Man. Trans., Auto. Trans., Mark Fig. — Curb Idle Speed② columns: Man. Trans., Auto. Trans. — Fast Idle Speed columns: Man. Trans., Auto. Trans.

Continued

TUNE UP NOTES—Continued

①—BTDC—Before top dead center.
②—Idle speed on man. trans. vehicles is adjusted in Neutral & on auto. trans. equipped vehicles is adjusted in Drive unless otherwise specified. Where two idle speeds are listed, the higher speed is with the A/C or idle solenoid energized.
③—Early production, Fig. B; late production, Fig. C.
④—With stop screw on high step of fast idle cam & A/C off.

⑤—With stop screw on high step of fast idle cam, EGR vacuum line disconnected & plugged & A/C off.
⑥—Models with carburetor No. 14023777, set at 700 RPM.
⑦—Less A/C, 600/800D RPM; with A/C, 800/950D RPM.
⑧—With A/C on, compressor clutch wires disconnected.
⑨—Except high output engine, 2300 RPM; high output engine, 2400 RPM.

⑩—Exc. high output engine.
⑪—High output engine.
⑫—With solenoid energized, 1400 RPM with transmission in Park.
⑬—Injection timing static.
⑭—On 4-97.6 C.I.D. engine, V.I.N. code is E; 4-97.6 H.O. engine, V.I.N. code is J.
⑮—On 4-97.6 C.I.D. engine, V.I.N. code is 9; 4-97.6 H.O. engine, V.I.N. code is O.
⑯—700 RPM with 3.36:1 axle.

FIRING ORDER: 1·3·4·2

Fig. A

Fig. B

Fig. C

VALVE SPECIFICATIONS

Year	Engine/ V.I.N.	Valve Lash Int.	Valve Lash Exh.	Valve Angles Seat	Valve Angles Face	Valve Spring Installed Height	Valve Spring Pressure Lbs. @ In.	Stem Clearance Intake	Stem Clearance Exhaust	Stem Diameter Intake	Stem Diameter Exhaust
1977–79	All	Hydraulic		①	②	1.26 32 mm.	173 @ .886 770N @ 22.5 mm.	.0006–.0017 .015–.045 mm.	.0014–.0025 .035–.065 mm.	.3138–.3144 7.970–7.986 mm.	.3130–.3136 7.950–7.965 mm.
1980–81	4-97.6/9	Hydraulic		45	46	1.26 32 mm.	173 @ .886 770N @ 22.5 mm.	.0006–.0017 .015–.045 mm.	.0014–.0025 .035–.065 mm.	.3138–.3144 7.970–7.986 mm.	.3130–.3136 7.950–7.965 mm.
1981–83	4-110/ D③	.010④ .25 mm.	.014④ .35 mm.	45	45	⑤	⑥	.0015–.0028 .039–.071 mm.	.0018–.0030 .045–.077 mm.	.3128–.3124 7.946–7.961 mm.	.3126–.3132 7.940–7.955 mm.
1982–83	4-97.6/ C	Hydraulic		45	46	1.30 33.1 mm.	170 @ .917 756N @ 23.3 mm.	.0006–.0017 .015–.045 mm.	.0014–.0025 .035–.65 mm.	.3138–.3144 7.970–7.986 mm.	.3130–.3136 7.950–7.965 mm.

①—46° on 1977 models; 45° on 1978–79 models
②—45° on 1977 models; 46° on 1978–79 models
③—Diesel Engine
④—Hot or Cold
⑤—Free length, inner 1.783 inch; outer 1.846 inch.
⑥—Inner, 19–22 lbs. @ 1.516 inch; outer, 32–37 lbs. @ 1.614 inch.

CHEVROLET CHEVETTE • PONTIAC 1000

DISTRIBUTOR SPECIFICATIONS

★ Note: If unit is checked on vehicle, double the RPM and degrees to get crankshaft figures.

Distributor Part No.①	Advance Starts	Centrifugal Advance Degrees @ RPM of Distributor Intermediate Advance			Full Advance	Inches of Vacuum to Start Plunger	Max. Adv. Dist. Deg. @ Vacuum
1977							
1110687	0 @ 600	4 @ 1200	—	—	12 @ 2400	4② (14kPa③)	13 @ 12② (41 kPa③)
1110693	0 @ 600	4 @ 1200	—	—	12 @ 2400	4② (14 kPa③)	17 @ 18② (27 kPa③)
1110702	0 @ 600	4 @ 1200	—	—	12 @ 2400	4② (14 kPa③)	15 @ 12② (41 kPa③)
1110703	0 @ 600	4 @ 1200	—	—	12 @ 2850	4② (14 kPa③)	15 @ 12② (41 kPa③)
1978							
1110705	0 @ 600	4 @ 1000	—	—	10 @ 2400	4② (14 kPa③)	15 @ 12② (41 kPa③)
1110707	0 @ 600	4 @ 1000	—	—	10 @ 2400	4② (14 kPa③)	7 @ 8② (27 kPa③)
1110712	0 @ 600	4 @ 1000	—	—	10 @ 2400	4② (14 kPa③)	13 @ 12② (41 kPa③)
1110713④	0 @ 600	4 @ 1000	—	—	11 @ 2625	4② (14 kPa③)	15 @ 12② (41 kPa③)
1979							
1110740	0 @ 760	1.5 @ 1100	—	—	8 @ 1625	4	15 @ 10②
1110741	0 @ 760	1 @ 850	1.5 @ 1100	—	8 @ 2625	4	7 @ 8②
1110742	0 @ 600	4 @ 1000	—	—	10 @ 2400	5	8 @ 11.5②
1110743	0 @ 600	4 @ 1000	—	—	12 @ 2850	4	15 @ 10②
1110744	0 @ 600	4 @ 1000	—	—	10 @ 2400	4	15 @ 10②
1110759	0 @ 600	4 @ 1000	—	—	12 @ 2850	4	9 @ 7.5②
1110760	0 @ 760	1 @ 850	1.5 @ 1100	—	8 @ 2625	5	8 @ 11.5②
1110778	0 @ 600	4 @ 1000	—	—	12 @ 2850	5	12 @ 12②
1980							
1110788	—	—	—	—	—	—	—
1110789	—	—	—	—	—	—	—
1110792	—	—	—	—	—	—	—
1110793	—	—	—	—	—	—	—
1110794	0 @ 760	1.5 @ 1100	—	—	8 @ 2625	2.9	10 @ 5.9②
1110795	0 @ 600	4 @ 1000	—	—	12 @ 2850	2.9	12.5 @ 7.4②
1981							
1110580	—	—	—	—	—	—	—
1982							
1103440	—	—	—	—	—	—	—
1103501	—	—	—	—	—	—	—
1110575	—	—	—	—	—	—	—
1110585	—	—	—	—	—	—	—
1983							
1103506	—	—	—	—	—	—	—

①—Stamped on distributor housing.
②—Inches Hg.
③—kPa—kilopascals.
④—High output engine.

WHEEL ALIGNMENT SPECIFICATIONS

Year	Model	Caster Angle, Degrees Limits	Caster Angle, Degrees Desired	Camber Angle, Degrees Limits Left	Camber Angle, Degrees Limits Right	Camber Angle, Degrees Desired Left	Camber Angle, Degrees Desired Right	Toe-In. Inch	Toe-Out on Turns, Deg. Outer Wheel	Toe-Out on Turns, Deg. Inner Wheel
1977–81	All	+3½° to 5½°	+4½°	−.2° to +.6°	−.2° to +.6°	+.2°	+.2°	①	—	—
1982	All	+4° to +6°	+5°	−.2° to +.6°	−.2° to +.6°	+.2°	+.2°	②	—	—
1983	All	+3° to +7°	+5°	−.5° to +.9°	−.5° to +.9°	+.2°	+.2°	③	—	—

①—1977 & 1981, 1/64 to 7/64 inch (.5 to 2.5 mm);
　　1978–80, 1/8 to 9/64 inch (1.3 to 3.7 mm).
②—+.06° ± .04° (+1.5 mm ± 1.0 mm)
③—−.02° to +.14° (−.5 mm to +3.5 mm)

PISTONS, PINS, RINGS, CRANKSHAFT & BEARINGS

Year	Engine/ V.I.N.	Piston Clearance Top of Skirt	Ring End Gap①		Wrist- pin Diameter	Rod Bearings		Main Bearings		Thrust on Bear. No.	Shaft End Play
			Comp.	Oil		Shaft Diameter	Bearing Clearance	Shaft Diameter	Bearing Clearance		
1977–80	All	.0008–.0016 .020–.040 mm	.009 .229 mm	.015 .381 mm	.9052 22.992 mm	1.8093– 1.8103 45.958– 45.984 mm	.0014–.0031 .036– .078 mm	2.0078–2.0088 51.0– 51.024 mm	②	5	.004–.008 .100– .202 mm
1981–83	4-97④	.0007–.0015 .020–.040 mm	.009 .229 mm	.015 .381 mm	.9052 22.992 mm	1.8093–1.8103 45.958– 45.984 mm	.0013–.0060 .033–.052 mm	2.0078–2.0088 51.0–51.024 mm	②	5	.004–.008 .100– .202 mm
1981–83	4-110/D ③	.0060–.0070 .143–.167 mm	.012 .300 mm	.012 .300 mm	.9842 24.998 mm	1.925–1.926 48.895– 48.920 mm	.0016–.0032 .040–.081 mm	2.201–2.202 55.905–55.930 mm	.0015–.0031 .039–.080 mm	3	.002–.009 .06–24 mm

①—Fit ring in tapered bore for clearance listed in tightest portion of ring travel.
②—No. 1, 2, 3 & 4, .0006–.0018 (.014–046 mm); No. 5, .0009–.0026 (.024–.066 mm)
③—Diesel Engine
④—For V.I.N. code, refer to the "General Engine Specifications" at the front of the chapter.

REAR AXLE SPECIFICATIONS

Year	Model	Carrier Type	Ring Gear & Pinion Backlash		Pinion Bearing Preload			Differential Bearing Preload		
			Method	Adjustment	Method	New Bearings Inch-Lbs.	Used Bearings Inch-Lbs.	Method	New Bearings Inch-Lbs.	Used Bearings Inch-Lbs.
1977–79	All	Integral	Shims	—	Spacer	15–25 1.7–2.82 N-m	5–10 .056–1.13 N-m	Shims	—	—
1980–81	All	Integral	Shims	—	Spacer	15–25 1.7–2.82 N-m	5–10 .056–1.13 N-m	Shims	—	—
1982–83	All	Integral	Shims	—	Spacer	①	5–10 .056–1.13 mm	Shims	—	—

①—With NDH bearings, 10–20 inch lbs; with Timken bearings, 5–15 inch lbs.

ALTERNATOR & REGULATOR SPECIFICATIONS

Year	Alternator					Regulator							
				Output @ 14 Volts			Field Relay			Voltage Regulator		
	Model	Rated Hot Output Amps.	Field Current 12 Volts @ 80° F.	2000 R.P.M. Amps.	5000 R.P.M. Amps.	Model	Air Gap In.	Point Gap In.	Closing Voltage	Air Gap In.	Point Gap In.	Voltage @ 125° F.
1977	1102845	32	4.0–4.5	—	31	Integral	—	—	—	—	—	13.8–14.8①
	1102846	55	4.0–4.5	—	51	Integral	—	—	—	—	—	—
1978–80	1102845	32	4.0–4.5	—	31	Integral	—	—	—	—	—	13.8–14.8①
1980	1103080	32	—	—	—	Integral	—	—	—	—	—	13.8–14.8①
1981–82	1100138②	42	—	—	—	Integral	—	—	—	—	—	—
	LR155-12B③	55	—	—	—	Integral	—	—	—	—	—	—

①—At 85° F.
②—Exc. diesel engine
③—Diesel engine

STARTING MOTOR SPECIFICATIONS

Year	Model	Starter Number	Brush Spring Tension Oz①	Free Speed Test			Resistance Test	
				Amps.	Volts	R.P.M.①	Amps.	Volts
1977	All	1109414	—	50–75②	9	6500	—	—
1978	All	1110941	—	—	—	—	—	—
1979–80	All	1109522	—	—	—	—	—	—
1981–83	4-97/③	1109532	—	—	—	—	—	—
	4-110 Diesel/D	94238758	—	—	—	—	—	—

①—Minimum.
②—Includes solenoid.
③—For V.I.N. code, refer to the "General Engine Specifications" at the beginning of the chapter.

ENGINE TIGHTENING SPECIFICATIONS

★ Torque specifications are for clean and lightly lubricated threads only. Dry or dirty threads produce increased friction which prevents accurate measurement of tightness.

Year	Engine/ V.I.N.	Spark Plugs Ft. Lbs.	Camshaft Carrier Bolts Ft. Lbs.	Intake Manifold Ft. Lbs.	Exhaust Manifold Ft. Lbs.	Camshaft Sprocket Bolt Ft. Lbs.	Cam Cover In. Lbs.	Connecting Rod Cap Bolts Ft. Lbs.	Main Bearing Cap Bolts Ft. Lbs.	Flywheel to Crankshaft Ft. Lbs.	Vibration Damper or Pulley Ft. Lbs.
1977–78	All	15 20.3 N-m	75 102 N-m	16 22 N-m	①	75 102 N-m	14 1.6 N-m	37 50N-m	46 63 N-m	46 63 N-m	75 102 N-m
1979	All	18.4 25 N-m	71 97 N-m	16 22 N-m	①	75 102 N-m	14 1.6 N-m	37 50 N-m	46 63 N-m	46 63 N-m	75 102 N-m
1980–82	4-97⑧	18.4 25 N-m	75 100 N-m	15 20 N-m	①	75 100 N-m	14 1.6 N-m	40 54 N-m	50 68 N-m	50 68 N-m	75 100 N-m
1981	4-110/D②	③	28 40 N-m	15 20 N-m	47 64 N-m	⑤	65 88 N-m	75 100 N-m	40⑥ 54 N-m	110 149 N-m
1982	4-110/D②	③	⑦	30	—	45	⑤	65	65–72	40⑥	110

①—Center bolts, 15 ft. lbs. (22 Newton-meters); end legs, 22 ft. lbs. (30 Newton-meters).
②—Diesel engine
③—Glow Plugs—54 ft. lbs., 73 N-m

④—Cylinder head bolts—105 ft. lbs., 142 N-m
⑤—Rocker arm cover—7 ft. lbs., 10 N-m
⑥—Apply loctite to threads, do not lubricate bolts

⑦—Cylinder head bolts; new, 83–98 ft. lbs.; used, 90–105 ft. lbs.
⑧—For V.I.N. code, refer to the "General Engine Specifications" at the beginning of the chapter.

COOLING SYSTEM & CAPACITY DATA

Year	Model or Engine/ V.I.N.	Cooling Capacity, Qts. Less A/C	Cooling Capacity, Qts. With A/C	Radiator Cap Relief Pressure, Lbs.	Thermo. Opening Temp.	Fuel Tank Gals.	Engine Oil Refill Qts.	Transmission Oil 3 Speed Pints	Transmission Oil 4 Speed Pints	Transmission Oil Auto. Trans. Qts. ①	Rear Axle Oils Pints
1977	All	8½ 8 ltr.	9 8.5 ltr.	15	190	13 49.2 ltr.	4 3.8 ltr.	—	3 1.5 ltr.	⑤	2 .9 ltr.
1978	All	8.5 8 ltr.	9.0 8.5 ltr.	15	190	12.5 47.3 ltr.	4 3.8 ltr.	—	3 1.5 ltr.	5 4.6 ltr.	2 .92 ltr.
1979	All	9 8.5 ltr.	9.25 8.8 ltr.	15	190	12.5 47.3 ltr.	4 3.8 ltr.	—	3 1.5 ltr.	5 4.6 ltr.	1.75 .83 ltr.
1980	All	9 8.5 ltr.	9.25 8.8 ltr.	15	190	12.5 47.3 ltr.	4 3.8 ltr.	—	3.4 1.6 ltr.	③	1.75 .83 ltr.
1981	All	9 8.5 ltr.	9.25 8.8 ltr.	15	190	12.5 47.3 ltr.	4 3.8 ltr.	—	3.4 1.6 ltr.	③	1.75 .83 ltr.
1981–82	4-110/D④	9 8.5 ltr.	—	15	180	12.5 47.3 ltr.	6⑤ 5.8 ltr.	—	3.25 1.5 ltr.	⑥	1.75 .81 ltr.
1982	4-97/C	9 8.5 ltr.	9.25 8.6 ltr.	15	190	12.5 47.3 ltr.	4⑤ 3.8 ltr.	—	⑦	②	1.75 .81 ltr.
1983	4-97/C	9 8.5 ltr.	9.25 8.6 ltr.	15	190	12.5 47.3 ltr.	4⑤ 3.8 ltr.	—	3.4 1.6 ltr.	⑥	1.75 .81 ltr.
	4-110/D④	9 8.5 ltr.	—	15	180	12.5 47.3 ltr.	6⑤ 5.8 ltr.	—	3.3 1.55 ltr.	⑥	1.75 .81 ltr.

①—Approximate. Make final check with dipstick.
②—After overhaul, 4.9 qts.; oil pan only, 3 qts.

③—Drain and refill, 3 qts. (2.7 ltrs.)
④—Diesel engine.
⑤—Includes filter.
⑥—After overhaul, 5 qts.; oil pan only, 3.5

qts.
⑦—4 sp. manual trans., 3.5 pts; 5 sp. manual trans., 4 pts.

BRAKE SPECIFICATIONS

Year	Model	Brake Drum Inside Diameter	Wheel Cylinder Bore Diameter Disc Brake	Wheel Cylinder Bore Diameter Front Drum Brake	Wheel Cylinder Bore Diameter Rear Drum Brake	Master Cylinder Bore Diameter Disc Brakes	Master Cylinder Bore Diameter Drum Brakes	Master Cylinder Bore Diameter Power Brakes
1977–80	All	7.88 200 mm	1⅞ 47.62 mm	—	¾ 19 mm	¾ 19 mm	—	¾ 19 mm
1981–82	All	7.87 200 mm	1⅞ 47.62 mm	—	0.69 17.5 mm	¾ 19 mm	—	¾ 19 mm
1983	All	7.87 200 mm	2.05 52 mm	—	0.69 17.5 mm	0.87 22 mm	—	0.87 22 mm

Fig. 1 Starter removal & installation. 1981–83
Diesel engine models

Fig. 1A Ignition lock removal & installation. 1979–83

STARTER REPLACE

Diesel Engine

Refer to Fig. 1 for starter removal and installation.

Gasoline Engine

1980–83 Less Power Brakes
1. Disconnect battery ground cable, then remove air cleaner.
2. Disconnect fuel line at carburetor and position aside.
3. Disconnect vacuum hoses at carburetor.
4. Remove splash shield from distributor coil and position aside.
5. Remove upper and lower starter retaining bolts.
6. Disconnect electrical leads from starter and position starter aside for access.
7. Remove master cylinder mounting nuts to gain access for removing starter. It will be necessary to move the master cylinder aside to remove the starter.
8. Remove starter.
9. Reverse procedure to install.

1980–83 With Power Brakes
1. Disconnect battery ground cable, then remove air cleaner.
2. Disconnect fuel line at carburetor and position aside.
3. Remove splash shield from distributor coil and position aside.
4. Remove upper starter retaining bolt.

NOTE: To remove the upper starter retaining bolt on models equipped with A/C, use a 15mm short socket with short extension, universal 12 inch extension and a ratchet or speed handle. Access to the bolt is gained through the intake manifold 3rd and 4th runners. After completely loosening the bolt, remove it with a magnet.

5. Remove steering column cover screws and cover.

6. Remove steering column upper mounting nuts and toe pan screw.
7. Raise and support front of vehicle.
8. Remove steering shaft from steering coupling. Lower vehicle and move steering column from inside vehicle for access to starter.
9. Disconnect electrical leads from starter.
10. Remove lower starter retaining bolt and remove starter.
11. Reverse procedure to install.

1977–79 Less A/C
1. Disconnect battery ground cable and remove air cleaner.
2. Remove distributor cap and position aside.
3. Remove the fuel line from fuel pump and carburetor.
4. Disconnect electrical connectors from ignition coil, remove coil bracket retaining screws and the coil and bracket assembly.
5. Disconnect vacuum hose from vacuum advance unit and the electrical connector from the oil pressure sender, then remove the sender.

Fig. 2 Ignition lock removal. 1977–78

6. Disconnect electrical leads from starter and remove the brace screw from bottom of starter housing.
7. Remove starter retaining screws and the starter from vehicle.
8. Reverse procedure to install.

1977–79 With A/C
1. Disconnect battery ground cable and remove air cleaner.
2. Remove starter upper retaining screw.
3. Remove steering column lever cover attaching screws.
4. Remove mast jacket lower bracket screw and the steering column upper mounting bracket.
5. Disconnect the four electrical connectors from steering column, then raise vehicle.
6. Disconnect steering column flexible coupling and position aside.
7. Disconnect electrical leads from starter and remove brace screw from bottom of starter.
8. Remove starter lower mounting screw.
9. With a suitable jack, raise engine approximately 1/2 inch to provide clearance for starter removal.
10. Lower starter and remove from vehicle.
11. Reverse procedure to install.

IGNITION LOCK, REPLACE

1979–83

1. Remove steering wheel as described under Horn Sounder and Steering Wheel.
2. Remove turn signal switch as described under Turn Signal Switch, Replace, then remove buzzer switch.
3. Place ignition switch in Run position, then remove lock cylinder retaining screw and lock cylinder.
4. To install, rotate lock cylinder to stop while holding housing, Fig. 1A. Align cylinder key with keyway in housing, then push lock cylinder assembly into housing until fully seated.
5. Install lock cylinder retaining screw. Torque screw to 40 in. lbs. for standard columns. On adjustable columns, torque retaining screw to 22 in. lbs.

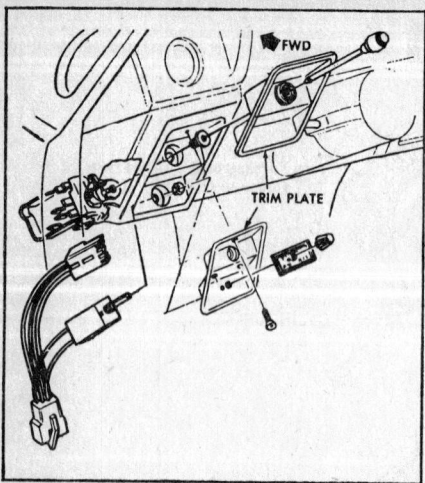

Fig. 3   Light switch replacement

Fig. 4   Clutch start switch replacement

Fig. 5   Neutral start switch replacement

6. Install buzzer switch, turn signal switch and steering wheel.

1977–78

1. Remove steering wheel as outlined under "Horn Sounder & Steering Wheel".
2. Remove turn signal switch as outlined under "Turn Signal Switch, Replace".

NOTE: Do not remove buzzer switch or damage to lock cylinder may result.

3. With ignition lock in run position, insert a small screw driver or similar tool into turn signal housing slot, Fig. 2. Keep tool to right side of housing slot and depress retainer at bottom of slot.
4. Remove lock cylinder from housing.

LIGHT SWITCH, REPLACE

1. Disconnect battery ground cable.
2. Pull headlamp switch knob to "ON" position, Fig. 3.
3. Reach under instrument panel and depress switch shaft retainer button while pulling on the switch control shaft knob.
4. With a large bladed screwdriver, remove the light switch ferrule nut from front of instrument panel.

5. Disconnect the multi-contact connector from side of switch and remove switch.
6. Reverse procedure to install.

STOP LIGHT SWITCH, REPLACE

1. Reach under right side of instrument panel at brake pedal support and release wiring harness connector at switch.
2. Pull switch from mounting bracket.
3. When installing switch, adjust by bringing brake pedal to normal position. Electrical contact should be made when pedal is depressed .53 inch (13.5 mm). To adjust, the switch may be rotated or pulled in the clip.

CLUTCH START SWITCH, REPLACE

NOTE: The clutch pedal must be fully depressed and the ignition switch in START position for the vehicle to start.

The clutch switch assembly mounts with two tangs to the clutch pedal brace switch pivot bracket and the clutch pedal arm, Fig. 4.
1. Under the instrument panel on the clutch pedal support remove the multi-contact connector from switch.

2. Compress switch assembly actuating shaft barb retainer and push out of clutch pedal.
3. Compress switch assembly pivot bracket barb and lift off switch.
4. When installing new switch, no adjustments are necessary as the switch is self aligning.

NEUTRAL SAFETY SWITCH, REPLACE

1. Remove floor console cover.
2. Disconnect electrical plugs on backup contacts, seat belt warning contacts and neutral start contacts of switch assembly, Fig. 5.
3. Place shift lever in Neutral.
4. Remove two screws securing switch to lever assembly.
5. When installing switch, make sure it is in Neutral position. When switch is installed, shifting out of Neutral will shear the switch plastic locating pin.

A/C COMPRESSOR CUT-OUT SWITCH

Vehicles equipped with automatic transmission and air conditioning utilize a full throttle A/C compressor cut-out switch, Fig. 6, which de-energizes the A-C compressor clutch

Fig. 6   A/C compressor cut-out switch

Fig. 8   Compressing lock plate and removing retaining ring

Fig. 9   Removing pivot arm

Key No.	Part Name
1	NUT, HEXAGON JAM
2	COVER ASSEMBLY, SHAFT LOCK
3	RING, RETAINING
4	LOCK, STEERING SHAFT
5	CAM ASSEMBLY, TURN SIGNAL CANCELLING
6	SPRING, UPPER BEARING
7	SCREW, PAN HEAD CROSS RECESS
8	SCREW, FLAT HEAD CROSS RECESS
9	SCREW, ROUND HEAD CROSS RECESS
10	ARM, PIVOT
11	SPACER, TURN SIGNAL SCREW
12	SWITCH ASSEMBLY, TURN SIGNAL
13	SWITCH ASEMBLY, PIVOT &
14	SCREW HEX WASHER HEAD TAPPING
15	WASHER, THRUST
16	SWITCH ASSEMBLY, BUZZER

Key No.	Part Name
17	CLIP, BUZZER SWITCH RETAINING
18	HOUSING, STEERING COLUMN
19	BEARING ASSEMBLY
20	RETAINER, BEARING
21	SECTOR, SWITCH ACTUATOR
22	SPRING, RACK PRELOAD
23	RACK, SWITCH ACTUATOR
24	BOLT ASSEMBLY, SPRING &
25	WASHER, SPRING THRUST
26	WASHER, WAVE
27	LEVER, KEY RELEASE

Key No.	Part Name
28	SPRING, LOCK INHIBITER
29	HOUSING ASSEMBLY, SHROUD &
30	SCREW, PAN HEAD CROSS RECESS
31	ROD, SWITCH ACTUATOR

Key No.	Part Name
32	ROD, DIMMER SWITCH ACTUATOR
33	SWITCH ASSEMBLY, DIMMER
34	SWITCH ASSEMBLY, IGNITION
35	SCREW, WASHER HEAD
36	JACKET ASSEMBLY, STEERING COLUMN
37	SEAL, STEERING SHAFT
38	BUSHING, STEERING COLUMN JACKET
39	SHAFT ASSEMBLY, STEERING
40	RETAINER

Service Kits
201 — BOLT ASSEMBLY, SPRING &
202 — HOUSING ASSEMBLY, BEARING, SHAFT, SECTOR &
203 — SECTOR SERVICE UNIT, IGNITION SWITCH ACTUATOR
204 — SHAFT REPAIR KIT, INJECTION STEERING

Fig. 7 Steering column, disassembled

during full throttle acceleration. A pressure sensitive switch, located in the transmission, overrides the cut-out switch when the transmission is in third gear during full throttle acceleration.

TURN SIGNAL SWITCH, REPLACE

1. Remove steering wheel as described under "Horn Sounder & Steering Wheel" procedure.
2. Using a screw driver pry up and out to free cover from lock, Fig. 7.
3. Position lock plate compressing tool No. J-23653 on end of steering shaft and compress lock plate, Fig. 8.
4. Pry snap ring out of groove and discard, then remove tool J-23653 and lift lock plate off end of shaft.
5. Slide canceling cam, upper bearing preload spring and thrust washer off end of shaft.
6. Rotate multi-function lever to off position, then pull lever straight out to disengage.
7. Depress hazard warning knob and unscrew knob.
8. Remove two screws, pivot arm and spacer, Fig. 9.
9. Wrap upper part of connector with tape to prevent snagging of wires during switch removal, Fig. 10.
10. Remove three switch attaching screws and pull switch straight up guiding wires through column housing.

HORN SOUNDER & STEERING WHEEL, REPLACE

1. Disconnect battery ground cable.
2. Pry off horn button cap and retainer.
3. Remove steering wheel nut retainer and nut.

NOTE: Do not over expand retainer.

4. Using a suitable puller remove steering wheel.

Fig. 10 Taping turn signal switch and wires

W/S WIPER, DIMMER OR IGNITION SWITCHES

Removal

1. Disconnect battery ground cable.
2. Remove steering column mounting bracket and unsnap switch connector from jacket.
3. Remove steering wheel.
4. Remove lock plate cover with a suitable screwdriver, Fig. 7.
5. Remove ring and lock plate. Use caution to prevent shaft from sliding out bottom of column. Slide upper bearing preload spring and turn signal cancelling cam off upper steering shaft, then the thrust washer off shaft.
6. Rotate turn signal lever-W/S switch assembly counter-clockwise to stop (Off position) and pull straight out to disengage.
7. Remove two screws, pivot arm and spacer, Fig. 9. Note that pivot arm retains spacer.
8. Lower steering column, then remove turn signal switch mounting screws and the switch.
9. Pull actuator rod to the stop to place ignition switch in "Off-Unlock". Remove upper attaching screw, releasing dimmer switch and actuator. The switches may now be removed, Figs. 11 and 12.
10. Remove remaining ignition switch retaining screw and the ignition switch.

Fig. 11 Ignition switch

Installation

1. Assemble windshield wiper switch and pivot assembly onto housing.
2. Assemble buzzer switch and lock cylinder, then turn lock cylinder clockwise to stop and then counter-clockwise to other stop (OFF-UNLOCK) position. Position ignition switch, Fig. 13, then move slider to extreme left (ACC) and slide back two positions to the right to OFF-UNLOCK position. Install actuator rod into slider and install the bottom screw only, to retain the ignition switch. Do not move switch out of detent.
3. Install washer, spring and cancelling cam on steering shaft. Position cancelling cam lobes in relation to signal switch springs and assemble shaft lock and install new retaining ring, Fig. 7.
4. Install cover and snap ring, then install multi-function switch lever. Align lever pin with switch slot and push lever until it seats.
5. Install pinched end of dimmer switch actuator rod into dimmer switch, then install other end of rod into pivot switch. Install but do not tighten upper ignition switch screw. Depress dimmer switch and insert a 3/32 inch drill to lock switch body, Fig. 13.
6. Move dimmer switch up, removing lash between both switches and rod, then install and tighten upper ignition switch screw. Remove drill and check dimmer switch for proper operation.
7. Snap electrical connector into place and raise steering column, then install mounting nuts and torque to 22 ft. lbs. (30 Nm) and install steering wheel.

INSTRUMENT CLUSTER, REPLACE

1. Disconnect battery ground cable.
2. Remove clock stem knob.
3. Remove cluster bezel and lens retaining screws, then the bezel and lens, Fig. 14.
4. Remove instrument cluster to instrument panel retaining nuts and pull cluster toward vehicle rear.
5. Disconnect all electrical connectors and speedometer cable from cluster, then remove cluster.
6. Reverse procedure to install.

RADIO, REPLACE

1. Disconnect battery ground cable.
2. Remove mounting stud nut from bottom of radio, and the control knobs from shafts.
3. Remove screws from center trim panel and pull panel and radio toward the rear of the vehicle.
4. Disconnect all electrical connectors from radio.
5. Remove radio retaining nuts from radio control shafts.
6. Remove radio from vehicle.
7. Reverse procedure to install.

HEATER CORE, REPLACE

1. Disconnect battery ground cable and drain cooling system.
2. Disconnect heater hoses from core and plug openings in core.
3. Remove heater core housing to dash panel attaching screws, then the housing.
4. Remove core from housing.

BLOWER MOTOR, REPLACE

1. Disconnect battery ground cable.
2. Disconnect blower lead wire.
3. Remove blower motor to case attaching screws then the blower and wheel as an assembly.

NOTE: Scribe mark on blower motor and case so motor is installed in original position.

4. Remove nut and separate motor from wheel.
5. Reverse procedure to install.

NOTE: At assembly position open end of blower wheel away from blower motor. Replace sealer at blower motor flange if necessary.

W/S WIPER MOTOR, REPLACE

1. Reach under instrument panel above steering column and loosen transmission drive link to motor crank arm attaching nuts.
2. Disengage transmission drive link from motor crank arm.

Fig. 12 Dimmer & ignition switch replacement

3. Raise hood and disconnect electrical connectors.
4. Remove motor attaching bolts.
5. Remove motor while guiding crank arm through hole.
6. To install, align sealing gasket to base of motor assembly and reverse remaining removal procedure.

NOTE: If the wiper motor to dash panel sealing gasket is damaged during removal, it should be replaced to prevent possible water leaks.

W/S WIPER TRANSMISSION, REPLACE

1. Remove instrument panel pad and cluster housing.
2. On models with A/C, remove left A/C duct attaching screws and position duct aside.
3. On all models, remove left side air duct.
4. Remove speedometer cable shield and left side instrument brace.
5. From under instrument panel, loosen transmission drive link to motor crank arm attaching nuts and disengage drive link.
6. Remove wiper arms and blades, then remove transmission to dash panel attaching bolts.
7. Move transmission assembly to left, then while rotating assembly, work out through instrument panel access hole at right upper center of instrument panel.

NOTE: When installing, ensure motor is in park position.

Fig. 14 Instrument cluster

Fig. 13 Dimmer switch alignment

Gasoline Engine Section

ENGINE MOUNT, REPLACE

Front

1. Remove heater assembly and position on top of engine.
2. Remove radiator upper support.
3. Remove engine mount nuts and the restraint cable.
4. Raise vehicle, install engine lifting device and raise engine to relieve weight from mounts.
5. Remove mount to engine bracket, then using tool J-25510, remove mount.

Rear

1. Raise vehicle and remove crossmember to mount bolts.
2. Raise transmission at extension housing to relieve weight from mount.
3. Remove mount to transmission bolts and the mount.

ENGINE, REPLACE

1. Remove hood.
2. Disconnect battery cables and remove clips securing battery cable to right side frame rail.
3. Drain cooling system and disconnect radiator and heater hoses.
4. Disconnect engine wiring harness.
5. Remove radiator upper support, radiator and fan.
6. Remove air cleaner.
7. Disconnect fuel line at rubber hose located along left side frame rail.
8. Disconnect accelerator and automatic transmission throttle valve linkage, if equipped.
9. Remove A/C compressor from mounting bracket and position aside, if equipped.
10. Raise vehicle and disconnect exhaust pipe at manifold.
11. Remove flywheel dust cover.
12. On models with automatic transmission, remove converter to flywheel bolts.
13. Remove converter housing to engine bolts on automatic transmission models or flywheel housing to engine bolt on manual transmission models, then lower vehicle.
14. Support transmission using a suitable jack.
15. Remove safety straps from engine mounts, then remove engine mount bolts.
16. Install engine lifting device, raise engine

slowly, pull engine forward to clear transmission and remove engine from vehicle.

INTAKE MANIFOLD, REPLACE

1. Disconnect battery ground cable and drain cooling system.
2. Remove air cleaner and disconnect upper radiator hose and heater hoses from intake manifold.
3. Remove EGR valve.
4. Disconnect fuel line, wiring, vacuum hoses and linkage from carburetor.
5. If equipped with A/C, perform the following:
   a. Remove radiator upper support, alternator and A/C drive belts.
   b. Remove fan, pulley and timing belt cover.
   c. Position A/C compressor aside.
   d. Raise vehicle and remove the lower A/C compressor bracket.
   e. Lower vehicle and remove the upper A/C compressor bracket.
6. On all models, remove ignition coil and position aside.
7. Remove intake manifold attaching bolts and the intake manifold.
8. Reverse procedure to install.

CYLINDER HEAD, REPLACE

1. Remove timing belt.
2. Drain cooling system, remove upper radiator hose and heater hose at intake manifold.
3. Remove air cleaner, then remove accelerator support bracket.
4. Disconnect spark plug wires.
5. Disconnect wiring harnesses at idle solenoid, choke, temperature sending switch and alternator.
6. Raise vehicle and disconnect exhaust pipe at manifold.
7. Lower vehicle and remove bolt retaining dipstick bracket to manifold.
8. Disconnect fuel line at carburetor.
9. Remove coil bracket bolts and position coil aside.
10. Remove camshaft covers, then remove camshaft cover to housing attaching studs.
11. Remove rocker arms, guides and lash adjusters.

NOTE: Rocker arms, guides and lash adjusters must be installed in original location during assembly.

12. Remove camshaft carrier from cylinder head.

NOTE: It may be necessary to use a wedge to separate camshaft carrier from cylinder head.

13. Remove cylinder head and manifold as an assembly.
14. Reverse procedure to install, tighten cylinder bolts in the sequence, Fig. 1.

HYDRAULIC VALVE LIFTERS

Failure of an hydraulic valve lifter is generally caused by an inadequate oil supply or dirt. An air leak at the intake side of the oil pump or too much oil in the engine will cause air bubbles in the oil supply to the lifters, causing them to collapse. This is a probable cause of trouble if several lifters fail to function, but air in the oil is an unlikely cause of failure of a single unit.

ROCKER ARMS, REPLACE

1. Remove camshaft covers.
2. On 1980–83 models, remove carburetor.
3. Using tool J-25477, depress valve spring and remove rocker arm, guide and lash adjuster, Fig. 2.

NOTE: Rocker arms, guides and lash adjusters must be installed in the same location during assembly.

VALVE GUIDES

Valve guides are an integral part of the cylinder head. If stem to guide clearance is excessive, the guide should be reamed to the next oversize and the appropriate oversize valve installed. Valves are available in standard size and oversizes of .003 in. (.075mm), .006 in. (.150mm), and .012 in. (.300mm).

CAMSHAFT COVER, REPLACE

1. Raise hood to fully open position.
2. Disconnect battery ground cable.
3. Remove air cleaner, PCV valve, air cleaner snorkle and heat tube assembly.
4. Remove spark plug wires from retainer on camshaft cover.
5. Remove accelerator cable support and position aside.
6. Remove nut and gasket from stud and the camshaft cover.

Fig. 1   Cylinder tighening sequence

Fig. 2   Depressing valve spring

Fig. 3   Aligning camshaft sprocket

CAMSHAFT SPROCKET, REPLACE

1. Remove drive belts, then the fan and pulley.
2. Remove timing belt front cover.
3. Loosen idler pulley and remove timing belt from camshaft sprocket.
4. Remove camshaft sprocket bolt and washer, remove camshaft sprocket.

CAMSHAFT, REPLACE

1. Remove camshaft sprocket as described under "Camshaft Sprocket" procedure.
2. Remove rocker arms.
3. Remove heater assembly and position aside.
4. Remove camshaft carrier rear cover.
5. Remove camshaft thrust plate bolts, slide camshaft rearward and remove thrust plate.
6. Raise engine, then carefully slide camshaft from carrier.

CAM LOBE LIFT SPECS.

Year	Intake	Exhaust
All 1977	.232 (5.893mm)	.232 (5.893mm)
All 1978–83	.2407 (6.1163mm)	.2407 (6.1163mm)

Fig. 5   Timing belt idler arm and pulley

VALVE TIMING

Intake Open Before TDC

Engine	Year	Degrees
All	1976	32
All	1977	29
Exc. Hi Output	1978–83	28
Hi Output	1978–80	31

TIMING BELT FRONT COVER, REPLACE

Upper Cover

1. Raise hood and disconnect battery ground cable.
2. Remove fan.
3. Remove upper cover retaining screw and the upper cover.

Lower Cover

1. Remove crankshaft pulley.
2. Remove upper front cover.
3. Remove lower cover attaching nut and the lower cover.

UPPER REAR TIMING BELT COVER, REPLACE

1. Remove timing belt front cover, timing belt and camshaft sprocket.
2. Remove three upper rear timing belt cover to camshaft carrier attaching screws.
3. Inspect camshaft seal and replace, if necessary.

TIMING BELT, REPLACE

1. Remove timing belt front upper and lower covers and crankshaft pulley.
2. Loosen idler pulley bolt and remove timing belt from camshaft and crankshaft sprockets.
3. Position timing belt over crankshaft sprocket, then install crankshaft pulley.
4. Position crankshaft at TDC number 1 cylinder.
5. Align timing mark on camshaft sprocket with hole in upper rear cover, Fig. 3.
6. Install timing belt on crankshaft and camshaft sprockets, then adjust belt tension.

TIMING BELT TENSION, ADJUST

1. Remove fan, drive belt, pulley and upper timing belt cover.
2. Rotate crankshaft at least one revolution and position No. 1 piston at top dead center.
3. Install belt tension gauge, Tool J-26486, Fig. 4, on timing belt midway between the cam sprocket and idler pulley. Ensure the gauge center finger engages in a notch on the belt.
4. Correct belt tension is 70 ft. lbs. To adjust, loosen idler pulley attaching bolt, Fig. 5. Then, using a 1/4 inch allen wrench, rotate the pulley counterclockwise on the attaching bolt until correct belt tension is obtained and torque attaching bolt to 13–18 ft. lbs. (18–24 N-m).

Fig. 4   Adjusting timing belt tension

5. Remove gauge and install upper timing belt cover, pulley, drive belt and fan.

CRANKSHAFT SPROCKET, REPLACE

1. Remove timing belt front cover, crankshaft pulley and timing belt.
2. Remove crankshaft sprocket.

PISTON & ROD ASSEMBLE

Assemble pistons and rods as indicated in Fig. 6. Measure connecting rod side clearance with a feeler gauge. Side clearance should be .004–.012 inch.

Fig. 6   Piston and rod assembly

Fig. 7 Installing engine lifting device to facilitate oil pan removal

Fig. 8 Fabricating crankcase front cover to oil pan seal

Fig. 9 Installing crankcase front cover

PISTONS, & RINGS

Pistons and rings are available in standard size, .001 and .030 in. (.750mm) oversize.

MAIN & ROD BEARINGS

Main bearings are available in standard size and undersizes of .001 in. (.026mm), .002 in. (.050mm), .010 in. (.250mm) and .020 in. (.500mm).

Rod bearings are available in standard size and undersizes of .001 in. (.026mm), .010 in. (.250mm) and .020 in. (.500mm).

OIL PAN, REPLACE

1977

1. Remove heater housing from dash and position on top of engine.
2. Remove motor mount nuts, then pull back motor mount restraint cables.
3. Remove radiator upper support, on models with A/C remove upper fan shroud.
4. Remove flywheel splash shield.
5. On models with manual transmission, remove rack and pinion to front crossmember attaching bolts and position aside.
6. On all models, loosen converter to exhaust pipe clamp bolts.
7. Remove oil pan bolts.
8. Install engine lifting device and raise engine until oil pan can be removed, Fig. 7.

1978 All & 1979–83 Less Turbo Hydra-Matic 200 Automatic Transmission

NOTE: This procedure applies only to 1978–83 models equipped with manual transmission or Turbo Hydra-Matic 180 automatic transmission. The Turbo Hydra-Matic 180 automatic transmission is equipped with a full converter housing, while the Turbo Hydra-Matic 200 automatic transmission has a partial converter housing and splash shield.

1. Disconnect battery ground cable, then drain cooling system.
2. Remove upper radiator support. On models equipped with A/C, remove upper half of fan shroud.

3. On models equipped with automatic transmission, disconnect transmission oil cooler lines from radiator.
4. On all models, disconnect radiator hoses, then remove radiator from vehicle.
5. If equipped with A/C, remove condenser to radiator support attaching nuts and position on top of engine.
6. Remove heater core housing and position on top of engine.
7. Remove engine mount retaining nuts and clips.
8. Raise and support front of vehicle, then drain crankcase.
9. Disconnect exhaust pipe at exhaust manifold, then remove body to crossmember braces.
10. Remove rack and pinion steering gear unit from cross member and steering shaft, then pull unit down and out of way.
11. Remove stabilizer bar from body.
12. Install a suitable engine lifting device and raise engine sufficiently to permit oil pan removal.
13. Remove oil pan attaching screws, then pull pan down and remove oil pump pickup tube and screen assembly.
14. Remove oil pan through from of vehicle.
15. Reverse procedure to install. When installing oil pump pick-up tube and screen assembly, use a new seal. Torque oil pan attaching screws to 55 inch lbs.

1979–83 With Turbo Hydra-Matic 200 Automatic Transmission

NOTE: This procedure applies only to 1979–83 models equipped with Turbo Hydra-Matic 200 automatic transmission. The Turbo Hydra-Matic 200 automatic transmission is equipped with a partial converter housing and splash shield, while the Turbo Hydra-Matic 180 automatic transmission has a full converter housing.

1. Disconnect battery ground cable, then remove air cleaner.
2. Remove heater housing assembly from front of dash panel and position on top of engine.
3. Pull back on motor mount wire restraints and remove mount nuts.
4. Remove radiator upper support or fan shroud, as necessary.
5. Raise and support front of vehicle, then drain crankcase.

6. Remove converter housing splash shield.
7. Remove rack and pinion steering gear unit from front crossmember.
8. Loosen catalytic converter to rear exhaust pipe clamp bolts.
9. Install a suitable engine lifting device and raise engine sufficiently to permit oil pan removal.
10. Remove oil pan attaching screws, then remove oil pan.
11. Reverse procedure to install. Torque oil pan attaching screws to 55 inch lbs.

OIL PUMP, REPLACE

1. Remove coil bracket attaching bolts and position coil aside.
2. Remove fuel pump and push rod.
3. Remove distributor.
4. Remove oil pan.
5. Remove oil pump screen and pipe assembly.
6. Remove oil pump.
7. Reverse procedure to install.

CRANKSHAFT REAR OIL SEAL, REPLACE

1. Disconnect battery ground cable.
2. Remove transmission, as described under "TRANSMISSION, REPLACE".
3. Remove flywheel.
4. Remove rack and pinion bracket bolts.
5. Remove left side strut assembly.
6. Disconnect flex coupling and pull steering gear down.
7. Drain engine oil and remove oil pan.
8. Remove oil pump suction pipe and screen.
9. Remove rear main cap and oil seal.
10. Install new seal in case, then reverse procedure to install. Apply RTV sealer or equivalent in vertical grooves until excess exits slots adjacent to rear seal, and also apply a bead of RTV sealer to the oil pan.

CRANKCASE FRONT COVER, REPLACE

1. Remove timing belt upper and lower front covers, crankshaft pulley, timing belt and crankshaft sprocket.

2. Remove three crankcase front cover to oil pan attaching bolts, then the crankcase cover to engine attaching bolts.
3. Remove crankcase front cover, cover gasket and front portion of oil pan gasket.

NOTE: To fabricate a replacement crankcase front cover to oil pan gasket, position crankcase cover over a new oil pan gasket as shown in Fig. 8. When installing gasket apply sealer to cut off portion of gasket.

4. Inspect crankshaft oil seal, replace if necessary.
5. Install crankcase front cover using tool J-26434, Fig. 9.

BELT TENSION DATA

	New Lbs.	Used Lbs.
1977-83		
A/C Compressor	135-145	90-100
Timing Belt		
15 mm	55	—
19 mm	70	—
All other belts	120-130	70-80

FUEL PUMP, REPLACE

1979-83

1. Disconnect battery ground cable.
2. Remove distributor cap.
3. Remove spark plug wire retaining clips.
4. Remove coil wire and coil assembly.
5. Remove air cleaner assembly.
6. Disconnect fuel pump inlet and outlet hoses.
7. Remove fuel pump and gasket.
8. Reverse procedure to install.

1977-78

1. Raise vehicle and remove ignition coil.
2. Remove A/C compressor rear bracket, if equipped.
3. Remove fuel pump attaching bolts and fuel pump.
4. Reverse procedure to install.

WATER PUMP, REPLACE

1. Position No. 1 cylinder at top dead center.

NOTE: When No. 1 cylinder is at top dead center, a 1/8 in. drill rod may be inserted through the hole in the rear timing belt cover into the hole located on camshaft sprocket.

2. Disconnect battery ground cable, then drain cooling system.
3. Loosen alternator and A/C drive belts, then remove crankshaft pulley.
4. On models equipped with A/C, remove upper portion of fan shroud, if equipped.
5. On models less A/C, remove radiator upper mounting panel, if equipped.
6. On all models, remove engine fan.
7. Remove timing belt cover attaching bolts and nuts, then remove timing belt cover.
8. Loosen idler pulley mounting bolts and allow pulley to rotate clockwise.
9. Remove timing belt from camshaft and crankshaft pulleys.
10. Disconnect lower radiator hose and heater hose from water pump.
11. Remove water pump to cylinder block attaching bolts, then remove water pump.
12. Reverse procedure to install. Before installing timing belt cover, adjust timing belt tension as described under "Timing Belt Tension Adjust."

Diesel Engine Section

DIESEL ENGINE TROUBLESHOOTING

Hard Starting

1. Check fuel level, replenish if necessary.
2. Check notched line on injection pump flange, reset timing as necessary.
3. Check to ensure fuel is reaching injection nozzles. If fuel is reaching injectors:
   a. Check connections of fuse, glow plugs, Q.S.S.I. controller and glow plug relays.
   b. Check fuel spray pattern, and ensure injection starting pressure is 1707 p.s.i.
   c. Check to ensure valve clearances are satisfactory. Refer to specifications.
   d. Check compression pressure in each cylinder. Standard value should be 441 psi.
   e. Check to ensure proper installation of timing belt and camshaft.
   If fuel is not reaching injectors:
   a. Check for air in fuel filter.
   b. Check if air is being drawn into fuel line through leakage in the pipe joints.
   c. Check operation of fuel cut out solenoid.
   d. Check fuel filter for restrictions.
   e. Check fuel pipes for restrictions.
   f. Check delivery valve for possible sticking.
4. Replace or readjust setting of injection pump.

Engine Idling Rough

1. Check if idle speed is within specifications.
2. Check to ensure accelerator control cable is not binding or twisting.
3. Check accelerator lever setting for looseness.

4. Check for air or water in fuel filter.
5. Check for proper alignment on injection pump flange.
6. Check engine mounting for cracks or looseness.
7. Check fuel spray pattern, and ensure injection starting pressure is 1707 p.s.i.
8. Check to ensure intake clearances are satisfactory. Refer to specifications.
9. Check compression pressure in each cylinder. Standard value should be 441 p.s.i.
10. Check to ensure proper installation of timing belt and camshaft.
11. Check delivery valve for sticking.
12. Replace or readjust setting of injection pump.

Engine Lacks Power

1. Check air cleaner for restrictions.
2. Check to ensure accelerator control cable is not binding or twisting.
3. Check seals on full load adjustment bolt and maximum speed stop bolt.
4. Check to ensure accelerator control lever is in full contact with maximum speed stop bolt.
5. Check exhaust system for restrictions.
6. Check for air in fuel filter.
7. Check notched line on injection pump flange, repair as necessary.
8. Check engine mounting for cracks or looseness.
9. Check fuel spray pattern, and ensure injection starting pressure is 1707 p.s.i.
10. Check to ensure valve clearances are satisfactory. Refer to specifications.
11. Check compression pressure in each cylinder. Standard value should be 441 p.s.i.
12. Check to ensure proper installation of timing belt and camshaft.
13. Check delivery valve for sticking.
14. Replace or readjust setting of injection pump.

Engine Overheating

1. Check coolant level in radiator.
2. Check condition of coolant for contamination, ratio of anti-freeze to water, and leakage of oil into coolant.
3. Check for leakage in hoses, and clamps.
4. Check water pump and thermostat housing for leakage.
5. Check for damaged cylinder head gasket.
6. Check fan belt tension. Deflection of fan belt should be no more than .4 inch.
7. Check operation of fan clutch.
8. Check for proper operation of radiator cap.
9. Check thermostat operation. Thermostat opening temperature is 180° F.
10. Check injection timing.
11. Check condition of water pump impeller.
12. Check to ensure proper level of engine oil.
13. Replace or readjust setting of injection pump.

Engine Knocking

1. Check if engine has been thoroughly warmed up.
2. Check injection timing.
3. Check fuel spray pattern, and ensure injection starting pressure is 1707 p.s.i.
4. Check compression pressure in each cylinder. Standard value should be 441 p.s.i.
5. Check to ensure proper quality of fuel.
6. Replace or readjust setting of injection pump.

Noise Indicating Abnormal Leakage

1. Check exhaust system for loose connections or leakage.

CONTROLLER

Position to which connector terminal is connected

1. Starter switch (ON position)
2. Sensing resistor
3. Thermo switch
4. Starter switch (ST position)
5. Sensing resistor
6. Glow plug relay No. 1
7. Ground
8. Glow indicator lamp
9. Not used

Fig. 1   Controller wiring connections

2. Check to ensure proper installation of nozzles and glow plugs.
3. Check for damaged cylinder head gasket.
4. Check to ensure valve clearances are satisfactory. Refer to specifications.
5. Check compression pressure in each cylinder. Standard value should be 441 p.s.i.

Continuous Noise

1. Check fan belt tension. Deflection of fan belt should be no more than .4 inch.
2. Check to ensure cooling fan is secure.
3. Check water pump bearing for wear and damage.
4. Check operation of generator and vacuum pump.
5. Check to ensure valve clearances are satisfactory. Refer to specifications.

Slapping Noise

1. Check valve retainers for damage.
2. Check to ensure valve clearances are satisfactory. Refer to specifications.
3. Check rocker arms for damage.
4. Check camshaft for seizure.
5. Check to ensure flywheel bolts are secure.
6. Check crankshaft and thrust bearing for wear and damage.
7. Check main bearing oil clearances.
8. Check connecting rod bearing and bushing oil clearances.
9. Check to ensure clearance between pistons and cylinder walls is satisfactory. Refer to specifications.

Excessive Oil Consumption

1. If oil is leaking:
   a. Check engine oil level.
   b. Check to ensure drain plug is secure.
   c. Check oil pipes for leakage.
   d. Check cooler seat gasket, oil filter and oil seal retainer for leakage.
   e. Check cylinder head cover, oil pan and oil pump gaskets for leakage.
   f. Check cylinder head gasket for leakage.
   g. Check oil seals for leakage.
   h. Check function of P.C.V.
   i. Check to ensure flywheel bolts are secure.
2. If oil is burning:
   a. Check to ensure quality of oil.
   b. Check valve stem oil seals.
   c. Check valve guides and valve stems for wear and damage.
   d. Check for damaged cylinder head gasket.

e. Check to ensure proper setting of piston rings.
   f. Check piston rings for wear and damage.
   g. Check cylinder walls for wear and damage.

Excessive Fuel Consumption

1. Check air cleaner for restrictions.
2. Check fuel lead adjustment bolt seal for leakage.
3. Check fuel pipes for leakage.
4. Check exhaust system for restrictions.
5. Check if idle speed is within specifications.
6. Check to ensure proper quality of fuel.
7. Check injection timing.
8. Check fuel spray pattern, and ensure injection starting pressure is 1707 p.s.i.
9. Check to ensure valve clearances are satisfactory. Refer to specifications.
10. Check compression pressure in each cylinder. Standard valve should be 441 p.s.i.
11. Check delivery valve for sticking.
12. Replace or readjust setting of injection pump.

DIESEL ENGINE ELECTRICAL TROUBLESHOOTING

NOTE: In a normally operating quick start system, when coolant temperature is below 122° F. and the key is in the "On" position, the glow plug indicator turns on for about 3.5 seconds and No. 1 Relay turns on for a few seconds.

Relay No. 1 And Glow Indicator Are Both Inoperative

1. Starter circuit fuse is burnt out or fusible link wire is open.
2. Starter wire circuit is open or not properly connected.
3. Controller defective or not properly connected.
4. Starter switch is inoperative.

Relay No. 1 Inoperative

1. Relay No. 1 is open.
2. Relay coil in relay No. 1 is open.
3. Controller to No. 1 relay circuitry is open or not properly connected.
4. Grounding circuit for No. 1 relay is open or not properly connected.

5. Controller is inoperative.
6. Circuit from controller to signal feed wire of sensing resistor is open or not properly connected.
7. Terminals of sensing resistor are not connected.
8. Main terminal of No. 1 relay not connected.
9. Main contact open in No. 1 relay.
10. Terminals in quick preheat circuit not connected.
11. Engine harness ground not properly connected.
12. Quick preheating wiring not properly connected or circuit open.

Glow Indicator Light Inoperative

1. Controller damaged.
2. Indicator circuit not properly connected or open.
3. Light bulb burnt out.

Relay No. 1 Turns Off Within 2 Seconds

1. Controller damaged.
2. One or more glow plugs defective.
3. Wiring at connector poorly connected.

Relay No. 1 Will Not Turn Off After A Few Seconds

1. Controller damaged.

Relay No. 1 Operates When Coolant Temperature Is Above 122° F.

1. Thermostat switch is inoperative.
2. Short in circuit.

NOTE: In a normally operating quick start system, when coolant temperature is below 122° F. and, the key held in the "Start" position, the glow plug indicator and the No. 2 relay will remain on until key is moved to "On" position.

Relay No. 2 And Glow Indicator Inoperative

1. Starter switch "R" circuit not properly connected or open.

Relay No. 2 Inoperative

1. Relay No. 2 terminals not connected.
2. Circuit between R terminal and No. 2 relay not properly connected or open.
3. No. 2 relay coil is open.

Glow Indicator Light Inoperative

1. Controller damaged.

NOTE: In a normally operating quick start system, when coolant temperature is above 122° F. and the key is in the "On" position the glow plug indicator light will turn on for about 0.3 seconds.

Glow Plug Light Remains On For 3.5 Seconds And Causes Relay No. 1 To Turn On

1. Thermo-switch circuit not properly con-

Fig. 2   Dropping resistor test connections

Fig. 3   Testing glow plug

Fig. 4   Glow plug relay test connections

nected or open.
2. Thermostat switch is inoperative.

DIESEL ENGINE ELECTRICAL DIAGNOSIS & TESTING

Controller

Controller in this system has four functions. As engine coolant temperature changes, it controls the glow plug relay. For determining glow plug heating requirements, it monitors differences between sensing resistance and glow plug resistance. It controls rapid preheat circuit to 1,908° F. of glow plug temperature and, during pre-heat cycle, controls glow plug pre-heat indicator lamp (3.5 sec.). Refer to Fig. 1 for wiring connections.

Dropping Resistor

During stabilized heating, this fixed value resistor is used to lower voltage of glow plugs. Check dropping resistor by performing continuity check across the terminals. Replace resistor if no continuity is found. Refer to Fig. 2.

Glow Plugs

The glow plugs used in this system are the fast warm up type. Check glow plugs by performing continuity test across plug terminals and body. If no continuity is found, heater wire is damaged and glow plug should be replaced. Refer to Fig. 3.

Glow Plug Relay

This relay is main relay for stabilized heating circuit and rapid pre-heat cycle. Check glow relay by performing continuity test

across terminals C and D while battery voltage is applied to terminals A and B. If no continuity is found, replace glow plug relay. Refer to Fig. 4.

Glow Plug Relay 2

During starting, this relay is used to provide stabilized heating. To check this relay, use same procedure as for glow plug relay 1.

Fusible Links

These two in-line fusible links are used to protect the glow plug electrical wiring. To check fusible links, perform continuity check across terminals. If no continuity is found, fusible link should be replaced. Refer to Fig. 5.

Sensing Resistor

Used in series with the glow plugs, this shunt type sensing resistor causes a small voltage drop which is monitored by the controller.

Thermo Switch

This thermo switch is used to provide a ground circuit to controller circuitry when engine temperature is above 122° F. To check thermo switch, perform continuity check across terminal and body while end of thermal switch is submerged in water. Gradually bring temperature of water to 122° F. Replace thermal switch if continuity is not found at this temperature. Refer to Fig. 6.

ENGINE, REPLACE

1. Remove hood.
2. Disconnect battery ground cable and drain cooling system.

3. Disconnect radiator hoses and remove radiator.
4. Disconnect engine wiring harnesses.
5. Remove air cleaner.
6. Disconnect accelerator and automatic transmission throttle valve linkage, if equipped.
7. Disconnect fuel lines and heater hoses.
8. Remove A/C compressor from mounting bracket and position aside, if equipped.
9. Remove power steering pump and bracket and position aside, if equipped.
10. Disconnect vacuum hose to master cylinder.
11. Remove engine mount nuts.
12. Raise vehicle and disconnect exhaust pipe at manifold.
13. Remove engine strut (shock type).
14. Remove flywheel dust cover.
15. On models with automatic transmission, remove converter to flywheel bolts.
16. Remove transmission rear crossmember to body bolts and bellhousing bolts.
17. Reinstall crossmember bolts.
18. Lower vehicle.
19. Remove oil filter.
20. Install engine lifting device, raise and remove engine.
21. Reverse procedure to install.

CYLINDER HEAD, REPLACE

1. Disconnect battery ground cable and drain cooling system.
2. Remove cam cover.
3. Remove timing belt. It will not be necessary to remove lower cover and damper.

Fig. 5   Fusible link test connections

Fig. 6   Testing thermo switch

Fig. 7   Cylinder head tightening sequence

Fig. 8   Removing valve guides

Fig. 9   Installing valve guides

Fig. 10   Timing mark locations on damper pulley

4. Remove camshaft.
5. Remove glow plug resistor wires and injector lines.
6. Remove fuel return line hose.
7. Raise vehicle and disconnect exhaust pipe at manifold.
8. Lower vehicle and remove oil feed pipe at rear of cylinder head.
9. Disconnect upper radiator hose.
10. Remove cylinder head bolts. Remove cylinder head and gasket.
11. Reverse procedure to install, tighten cylinder head bolts in sequence shown in Fig. 7.

VALVE TIMING

Intake Opens Before TDC

Engine	Year	Degrees
4-110.8	1981–83	32°

VALVES, ADJUST

1. Remove cam cover.
2. Inspect the rocker arm shaft bracket bolts for looseness, retorque as necessary.
3. Bring No. 1 cylinder to TDC on compression stroke.
4. Adjust valve clearances of cylinder No. 1, intake valve of No. 2 and exhaust valve of No. 3. Turn crankshaft one full revolution to bring cylinder No. 4 TDC on compression stroke. Adjust clearances of cylinder No. 4, exhaust valve of No. 2 and intake valve of No. 3.
5. Reinstall cam cover.

VALVE GUIDE, REPLACE

1. Using tool No. J-26512 drive out the valve guide from the lower face of the cylinder head, Fig. 8.
2. Apply engine oil to outer circumference of valve guide, using tool No. J-26512 drive the guide into position from the upper face of the cylinder head, Fig. 9.

NOTE: Always replace valve guide and valve as a set.

TIMING BELT, REPLACE

1. Disconnect battery ground cable.
2. Remove undercover and drain coolant.
3. Remove fan shroud, alternator belt, cooling fan and water pump pulley.
4. Remove ten bolts securing upper dust cover, remove dust cover.
5. Remove bypass hose.
6. Bring cylinder No. 1 to TDC, Fig 10, ensure that setting mark on injection pump pulley is in alignment with front plate, then fix the pulley with 8 mm 1.25 pitch bolt, Fig. 11 and Fig. 12.
7. Remove cam cover and loosen valve adjustment screws so rocker arms are in a free state. Fix the camshaft by installing fixing plate, tool No. J-29761 into the slit in rear end of the camshaft, Fig. 13.
8. Remove crankshaft damper pulley, lower dust cover and timing belt holder, Fig. 14.

NOTE: Under no circumstances should the crankshaft be disturbed from TDC.

9. Remove tension pulley spring then loosen tension pulley and plate bolts, remove timing belt.
10. Remove camshaft pulley bolt, using a suitable puller remove camshaft pulley, then reinstall pulley and bolt. Tighten bolt just enough to allow the pulley to be turned smoothly by hand.
11. Install new timing belt using sequence shown in Fig. 15. Ensure that belt cogs are properly installed in pulleys. Do not disturb crankshaft setting.
12. Concentrate belt looseness on tension pulley, depress tension pulley with finger and install tension spring. Semi-tighten bolts in numerical sequence 1 and 2 to prevent movement of tension pulley, Fig. 16.
13. Tighten camshaft pulley bolt.
14. Remove injection pump pulley lock bolt and camshaft fixing plate.
15. Install crankshaft damper pulley, ensure No. 1 cylinder is at TDC.
16. Ensure injection pump pulley mark is in alignment with mark on plate and fixing plate should fit smoothly into the rear slit of the camshaft. Remove plate.
17. Loosen tensioner plate bolts and pulley. Concentrate looseness of belt on tensioner, then tighten the bolts in numerical sequence 1, 2, and 3. Fig. 17. Torque bolts 1 and 2, 11 to 18 ft. lbs. Bolt 3, 47 to 61 ft. lbs.

Fig. 11   Injection pump pulley alignment

Fig. 12   Fixing injection pump pulley with lock bolt

Fig. 13   Fixing camshaft in place with tool No. J-29761

Fig. 14   Timing belt holder

Fig. 15   Timing belt installation sequence

Fig. 16   Semi-tightening sequence of tension pulley

18. Using a belt tension gauge, check tension between camshaft pulley and injection pump pulley. Tension should be 47 to 64 lbs.
19. Remove crankshaft damper and install timing belt holder.
20. Adjust valves. Refer to "Valves, Adjust" for procedure.
21. Reverse steps 1 through 8 to reassemble.

INJECTION TIMING, ADJUST

1. Check that alignment mark on injection pump flange is aligned with alignment mark on front plate.
2. Bring cylinder No. 1 to TDC on compression stroke by turning crankshaft until timing mark on pulley aligns with pointer, Fig. 10.

NOTE: The damper pulley has eleven notched lines as shown in Fig. 10. Four lines on one side, seven elsewhere. The four lines are intended for service use while the other seven are for factory use only.

3. Remove upper dust cover, ensure the injection pump belt is properly tensioned and the timing marks are aligned. See "Timing Belt, Replace".
4. Remove the cam cover and rear plug, ensure that the fixing plate fits smoothly into the camshaft rear slit, then remove the fixing plate. See "Timing Belt,

Replace".
5. Disconnect the injection pipe from the injection pump, remove distributor head screw and gasket, install static timing gauge J-29763, Fig. 18. Set the lift approximately .040 inch (1 mm) from the plunger.
6. Bring No. 1 piston to a point 45–60 degrees BTDC by turning the crankshaft, set dial indicator to zero. Turn crankshaft slightly in both directions, ensuring gauge indication is stable.
7. Turn crankshaft in normal direction of rotation until the 18 degree mark on the damper is aligned with the timing pointer, Fig. 10. Note reading of dial indicator, if reading is not .020 inch (.5 mm), hold crankshaft at 18 degrees and loosen the two nuts on injection pump flange, Fig. 19. Move pump until reading on dial indicator is .020 inch (.5 mm), then tighten nuts.

INJECTION PUMP, REPLACE

1. Remove timing belt. See "Timing Belt, Replace".
2. To prevent rotation of injection pump pulley during disassembly, thread a 8 mm 1.25 pitch bolt through the pulley into the housing, Fig. 12.
3. Remove injection pump pulley bolt.
4. Remove bolt installed in step two, then using a suitable puller remove injection pump pulley.
5. Disconnect fuel cut solenoid valve switch

wiring and tachometer pick up sensor wiring at connector.
6. Disconnect accelerator cable from pump lever. If equipped with automatic transmission, remove throttle valve control cable.
7. Disconnect vacuum hose from fast idle actuator.
8. Disconnect fuel hoses from injection pump.
9. Remove six screws attaching injection pipe clips and remove.
10. Remove injection pipes.
11. Remove injection pump rear bracket then control lever spring.
12. Remove attaching nuts and pump with fast idle device installed.
13. Install injection pump with fast idle device installed by aligning notched line on pump flange with the line on the front plate.
14. Install rear bracket bolts following sequence in Fig. 20.
15. Install the injection pump pulley by aligning it with key groove, torque nut to 43 to 50 ft. lbs. Hold pulley from rotating by installing a bolt as described in step 2.
16. Refer to "Timing Belt, Replace" for reassembly procedures.

ROCKER ARM SHAFT ASSEMBLY, REPLACE

1. Remove cam cover.
2. Remove rocker arm shaft bracket bolts and nuts, then remove rocker arm shaft and rocker arm assembly.

Fig. 17   Torquing tension pulley bolt sequence

Fig. 18   Static timing gauge, J-29763 installed

Fig. 19   Injection pump flange nuts

Fig. 20 Injection pump rear bracket tightening sequence

Fig. 21 Rocker arm bracket bolt tightening sequence

Fig. 22 Piston & connecting rod assembly

3. Prior to installation, apply a generous amount of engine oil to the rocker arm shaft, rocker arms and valve stem end caps.
4. Install rocker arm shaft assembly and tighten bolts in sequence as shown in Fig. 21.
5. Adjust valves. Refer to "Valves, Adjust" for procedure.

CAMSHAFT, REPLACE

1. Remove cam cover.
2. Remove timing belt as described in "Timing Belt, Replace".
3. Remove camshaft gear as described in "Timing Belt, Replace".
4. Remove rocker arm shaft assembly as described in "Rocker Arm Shaft Assembly, Replace".
5. Remove bolts attaching front head plate and remove.
6. Remove the camshaft bearing cap bolts, then remove bearing caps with cap side bearing.
7. Remove camshaft oil seal followed by the camshaft.
8. Install camshaft oil seal, camshaft and rocker arm shaft assembly. Loosen rocker arm adjustment screws so the rocker arms are in a free state. Reverse procedure from step five to reinstall.

CRANKSHAFT FRONT OIL SEAL, REPLACE

1. Remove timing belt. Refer to "Timing Belt, Replace".

2. Remove crankshaft hub center bolt and washer.
3. Using a suitable puller, remove hub from crankshaft.
4. Using puller No. J-29752, remove crankshaft timing belt pulley.
5. Pry out front oil seal using a suitable screwdriver.
6. Apply clean engine oil to inner and outer surfaces of new seal, using a suitable seal installer, install the oil seal.
7. Postion crankshaft timing belt pulley flange into seal, align pulley groove with crankshaft key. Drive pulley onto crankshaft using installer tool No. J-26587.
8. Align crankshaft hub keyway with crankshaft key, install center bolt. Torque to 98 to 119 ft. lbs.
9. Reinstall timing belt. Refer to "Timing Belt, Replace".

CRANKSHAFT REAR OIL SEAL, REPLACE

1. Remove the clutch pressure plate assembly.
2. Remove the six flywheel attaching bolts, then the flywheel.
3. Using a suitable screwdriver, pry out the rear seal.
4. Apply clean engine oil to all sides of new seal.
5. Install the oil seal in the oil seal retainer using tool No. J-29818.
6. Position flywheel on crankshaft hub. Using new bolts, apply loctite to threads and install flywheel. Torque bolts 36 to 43 ft. lbs.
7. Reverse procedure to install remaining parts.

PISTON & CONNECTING ROD

Install the piston on the connecting rod, so that the combustion chamber on piston head is on the same side with the cylinder mark side (side with bearing stopper) of the connecting rod big end. The front of the piston should be on same side as the "Isuzu" mark on the connecting rod, Fig. 22. Pistons are available in oversizes of .010 and .030 in.

Check connecting rod side clearance with a feeler gauge. Clearance should be .003–.024 inch.

OIL PAN, REPLACE

1. Remove engine assembly. Refer to "Engine, Replace" for procedure.
2. Remove fourteen bolts and four nuts attaching oil pan and remove.
3. Discard old gasket, clean mounting surfaces. Install new gasket using a suitable sealing compound on oil pan, and install.
4. Torque bolts 4 to 6 ft. lbs.

OIL PUMP, REPLACE

1. Remove timing belt. Refer to "Timing Belt, Replace".

Fig. 23 Removing oil pump

Fig. 24 Oil pump, disassembled

Fig. 25 Oil cooler assembly

2. Remove four allen bolts securing oil pump, remove oil pump and pulley as an assembly, see Fig. 23.
3. Refer to "Oil Pump, Inspection & Service".
4. Prior to installation apply a generous amount of clean engine oil to vane, install with taper side towards the cylinder body.
5. Install new pump O-ring, lubricate with motor oil and install in the housing groove. Lubricate oil pump rotor and install pump body together with pulley.
6. Reverse procedure to install.

OIL PUMP, INSPECTION & SERVICE

Disassembly, Fig. 24.

1. Inspect all parts for any signs of abnormal wear, or damage.

2. Measure outside diameter of pulley flange. Diameter should be 1.1–1.1035 inch (27.94–28.03 mm).
3. Using a straightedge and feeler gauge, check clearance between vane and cylinder body in direction of thrust. Clearance should be .0011–.0027 inch (.03–.07 mm).
4. Check clearance between vane and cylinder body. Clearance should be .0094–.0141 inch (.24–.36 mm).
5. Check clearance between vane and rotor. Clearance should be .0051–.0059 (.13–.15).
6. Reassemble as shown in Fig. 24.

OIL COOLER, REPLACE

1. Disconnect battery ground cable.

2. Remove oil cooler drain plug, allow cooler to drain.
3. Remove rubber hoses.
4. Remove two joint bolts securing cooler, Fig. 25.
5. Install new joint bolt gaskets and install cooler.
6. Reverse steps 1 to 3 to install.

WATER PUMP, REPLACE

1. Disconnect battery ground cable.
2. Drain cooling system.
3. Remove four nuts securing cooling fan and pulley assembly and remove. Remove fan belt.
4. Remove crankshaft damper pulley.
5. Remove front engine dust covers.
6. Remove by-pass hose.
7. Remove five water pump attaching bolts and remove pump.
8. Reverse procedure to install.

Clutch & Transmission Section

CLUTCH, ADJUST

Initial Ball Stud Adjustment

1. Place gage, J-23644 for 1977 models, J-28449 for 1978–83 models, with flat end against clutch housing front face and the hooked end positioned in the bottom depression of the clutch fork, Fig. 1.
2. Turn ball inward until clutch release bearing contacts clutch spring.
3. Install and torque lock nut to 25 ft. lbs. (33 N-m).
4. Remove gage.

Clutch Cable Attachment & Adjustment

Late 1977 & 1978–83
1. Install clutch cable through hole in clutch fork and seat, then install return spring.
2. From engine compartment, pull cable until clutch pedal is firmly against pedal stop and hold in position, Fig. 2.
3. Install snap ring in first fully visble groove in cable from sleeve, then release cable.
4. Clutch pedal lash should be .58 to 1.08 in. (15–27 mm), if not, adjust clutch pedal as described under Clutch Pedal Adjustment.

Early 1977
1. Install cable through clutch fork hole and pull until clutch pedal firmly contacts bumper. Hold cable in position.
2. Push clutch fork forward until throwout bearing contacts clutch spring fingers. Then, thread nut on cable until bottomed against spherical surface of clutch fork.
3. To adjust clutch pedal free play, follow either of the two methods outlined below Fig. 3.
4. Attach return spring.
5. Clutch pedal free travel should be .812 inch (20.6mm).

Method 1—Place a .171 inch (4.35 mm) shim stock against surface D of nut B. Thread locknut onto cable until it contacts shim stock. Remove shim stock and back off nut B until it contacts lock nut. Torque lock nut to 4 ft. lbs. (6 N-m).

Method 2—Rotate nut B 4.35 turns counter-clockwise. Thread lock nut on cable until it contacts nut B. Torque lock nut to 4 ft. lbs. (6 N-m).

Fig. 1   Ball stud adjustment

Fig. 2   Clutch cable adjustment. Late 1977 & 1978–83

Clutch Pedal Adjustment

Later 1977 & 1978–83
1. If clutch pedal lash is insufficient, remove snap ring from cable and allow cable to move into dash by one cable notch, then reinstall snap ring, Fig. 2.
2. If clutch pedal lash is excessive, remove snap ring from cable, and pull cable out of dash by one cable notch, then reinstall snap ring, Fig. 2.
3. Check to ensure clutch pedal lash is .58 to 1.08 in. (15–27 mm).

Early 1977
1. Loosen cable ball stud lock nut, located on the clutch housing right side.
2. Adjust ball stud to obtain .812 inch (20.6mm) clutch pedal free travel.
3. Torque lock nut to 25 ft. lbs. (33 N-m).
4. Check adjustment.

CLUTCH, REPLACE
1. Raise vehicle and remove transmission as outlined under "Manual Transmission, Replace" procedure.
2. Remove release bearing from the clutch fork and sleeve by sliding lever off ball stud and against spring force. If ball stud is to be replaced, remove cap, lock nut and stud from housing.
3. Make sure alignment marks on clutch assembly and flywheel are distinguishable.

Fig. 3 Clutch cable adjustment. Early 1977

4. Loosen clutch cover to flywheel bolts one turn at a time until spring pressure is released, to avoid bending the clutch cover flange.
5. Support the pressure plate and cover assembly while removing bolts and clutch assembly.

NOTE: Do not disassemble the clutch cover, spring and pressure plate for repairs. If defective replace complete assembly.

6. Reverse procedure to install making sure to index alignment marks.

CAUTION: Check position of engine in front mounts and realign as necessary.

MANUAL TRANSMISSION, REPLACE
1. Remove shifter assembly.
2. Raise vehicle and drain transmission lubricant.
3. Remove propeller shaft.
4. Disconnect speedometer cable and the back-up lamp switch.
5. Disconnect return spring and clutch cable from clutch fork.
6. Remove transmission to crossmember bolts.
7. Remove exhaust manifold nuts and the catalytic converter to transmission bracket bolts.
8. Remove crossmember to frame bolts, then the crossmember from vehicle.
9. Remove dust cover.
10. Remove clutch housing to engine retaining bolts, slide transmission rearward and remove from vehicle.
11. Reverse procedure to install.

Rear Axle, Propeller Shaft & Brakes

REAR AXLE

Description

The rear axle, Fig. 1, is a semi-floating type consisting of a cast carrier and large bosses on each end into which two welded steel tubes are fitted. The carrier contains an overhung hypoid pinion and ring gear. The differential is a two pinion arrangment.

The overhung hypoid drive pinion, is supported by two preloaded tapered roller bearings. The pinion shaft is sealed by means of a molded, spring loaded, rubber seal. The seal is mounted on the pinion shaft flange which is splined and bolts to the hypoid pinion shaft.

The ring gear is bolted to a one piece differential case and is supported by two preloaded tapered roller bearings.

A rear axle extension housing is bolted to the axle housing and is attached to the underbody by a center bearing support. An extension shaft inside the housing is splined to the drive pinion at the rear end and to the companion flange at the forward end.

Removal

1. Raise vehicle on a hoist.
2. Place adjustable lifting device under axle.
3. Disconnect rear shock absorbers from axle and remove propeller shaft and extension housing, Fig. 2.
4. Remove both rear wheels.
5. Retract shoes and remove right and left brake drums, Fig. 3.
6. Disconnect brake lines from clips on axle tubes.

Fig. 1 Rear axle cross section

Fig. 2 Rear axle assembly

Fig. 3 Retracting brake shoes

Fig. 4 Rear drum brake

7. Disconnect track and stabilizer bars from axle tube.
8. Remove differential cover and drain lubricant.
9. Unscrew differential lock screw, remove pinion shaft and axle shaft "C" locks. Reinstall pinion shaft and tighten lock screw to retain differential gears.
10. Remove both axle shafts.
11. Remove brake backing plate retaining nuts and remove backing plates, with shoes and brake lines attached, and wire to frame.
12. Remove right and left lower control arm pivot bolts at axle.
13. Lower axle assembly slowly until coil spring tension is released, then remove axle.

AXLE SHAFT, REPLACE

1. Raise vehicle on a hoist and remove wheel and tire assembly and brake drum.
2. Drain lubricant from axle by removing carrier cover.
3. Unscrew pinion shaft lock screw and remove pinion shaft.
4. Push flanged end of axle shaft toward center of car and remove "C" lock from button end of shaft.
5. Remove axle shaft from housing being careful not to damage seal.

Oil Seal &/or Bearing Replacement

1. If replacing seal only, remove the seal by using the button end of axle shaft. Insert the button end of shaft behind the steel case of the seal and pry seal out of bore being careful not to damage housing.
2. If replacing bearings, insert tool J-25593 into bore so tool head grasps behind bearing. Slide washer against seal, or bearing, and turn nut against washer. Attach slide hammer J-2619 and remove bearing.
3. Lubricate bearing with rear axle lubricant, then install bearing into housing bore with tool J-25594 and slide hammer J-8092. Make sure tool contacts end of axle housing to insure proper bearing depth.
4. Pack cavity between seal lips with a high melting point wheel bearing lubricant. Position seal on tool J-22922 and position seal in axle housing bore, tap seal in bore until flush with end of axle housing.

REAR AXLE EXTENSION

Replace

1. Raise vehicle and support rear axle.
2. Disconnect propeller shaft from the rear

yoke and remove from transmission, Fig. 2.
3. Support front end of rear axle carrier housing. Ensure the rear axle extension is also supported.
4. Disconnect center support bracket from underbody and the extension housing flange from axle housing.
5. Remove axle extension housing from vehicle. Pry extension housing from axle housing with a suitable screwdriver, if necessary.
6. Reverse procedure to install.

Service

1. Remove bolt securing extension housing to center support bracket.
2. Mount companion flange in a vise and loosen lock nut.
3. Drive splined companion flange off shaft by tapping on lock nut end of shaft.
4. Remove lock nut, companion flange and thrust washer, then pull shaft from housing. If centering bearing, located in the rubber cushion, remains on extension shaft, drive off shaft with a suitable drift.
5. Note position of bearing in rubber cushion and the cusion in center support. Then, using a suitable screwdriver, separate rubber cushion from center support bracket and remove bearing from cushion.
6. Clean, inspect and replace components, if necessary.
7. Install rubber cushion into center support bracket and place center support assembly over extension housing.
8. Press bearing onto extension shaft and insert shaft into housing through rubber cushion. Install thrust washer with circular cavity facing toward bearing, then the companion flange, using the lock nut to press flange onto shaft splines.
9. Install bolts retaining bracket to housing.

PROPELLER SHAFT, REPLACE

1. Raise vehicle on a hoist. Mark relationship of shaft to companion flange and disconnect the rear universal joint by removing trunnion bearing "U" bolts. Tape bearing cups to trunnion to prevent dropping and loss of bearing rollers.
2. Withdraw propeller shaft front yoke from transmission.
3. When installing, be sure to align marks made in removal to prevent driveline vibration.

BRAKE ADJUSTMENTS

Disc brakes are used on front wheels and drum brakes are use on rear wheels. Rear brake adjustment is automatic. Adjustment takes place whenever brakes are applied. An adjuster is attached to each brake shoe by means of a pin, Fig. 4. This pin is smaller than the slot in the brake shoe. When brakes are applied and brake shoes move outward the automatic adjuster follows. When brakes are released the brake shoe moves inward until it contacts the automatic adjuster pin. The space between adjuster pin and slot in brake shoe provides shoe to drum clearance.

NOTE: If manual adjustment or shoe retraction is necessary refer to Fig. 3.

PARKING BRAKE, ADJUST

1. Raise vehicle.
2. Apply parking brake three notches from fully released position.
3. Tighten equalizer adjusting nut until a light drag is felt when rear wheels are rotated in a forward direction.
4. Release parking brake and rotate rear wheels. No drag should be felt.

MASTER CYLINDER, REPLACE

1. Disconnect push rod from brake pedal and remove push rod boot.
2. Remove air cleaner.
3. Disconnect brake lines from master cylinder. Cap ends of lines to prevent entry of dirt.
4. Remove master cylinder to dash attaching nuts and the master cylinder.

POWER BRAKE UNIT, REPLACE

1. Remove air cleaner, then disconnect vacuum hose from check valve.
2. Remove master cylinder brace rod.

3. Remove remaining master cylinder to brake unit attaching nuts, then pull master forward until it clears brake unit mounting studs. Carefully move master cylinder aside with brake lines attached.

NOTE: Support master cylinder to avoid stress on brake lines. Move master cylinder only enough to provide clearance for brake unit removal.

4. Remove nuts attaching brake unit to dash panel.
5. Remove push rod to pedal retainer and slide push rod off pedal pin.
6. Remove power brake unit from vehicle.

Rear Suspension Section

DESCRIPTION

This suspension system, Fig. 1, incorporates two tubular lower control arms, a straight track rod, two shock absorbers, two coil springs and a stabilizer bar.

SHOCK ABSORBER, REPLACE

1. Raise vehicle and support rear axle with a suitable jack.
2. Disconnect shock absorber from upper and lower mounting.
3. Reverse procedure to install.

COIL SPRING, REPLACE

1. Raise vehicle and support rear axle with a suitable jack.
2. Disconnect both shock absorbers from lower brackets.
3. Disconnect rear axle extension bracket.

NOTE: Ensure axle is properly supported before disconnecting extension bracket.

4. Slowly lower axle until springs and insulators can be removed.

NOTE: When lower axle ensure that brake hoses do not stretch or become damaged.

5. Reverse procedure to install.

TRACK ROD, REPLACE

1. Raise vehicle and support rear axle with a suitable jack.
2. Disconnect stabilizer bar, if equipped, Fig. 2.
3. Remove control arm front and rear attaching bolts and control arm, Fig. 3.
4. Remove attaching bolts and track rod.
5. Reverse procedure to install.

NOTE: Vehicle must be at curb height when tightening pivot bolts.

LOWER CONTROL ARMS, REPLACE

1. Raise vehicle and support rear axle.
2. Disconnect stabilizer bar, if equipped, Fig. 2.
3. Disconnect the front and rear control arm attaching bolts and remove control arm from vehicle, Fig. 3.

NOTE: Replace one control arm at a time to prevent axle from rolling or slipping sideways.

4. Reverse procedure to install.

STABILIZER BAR, REPLACE

1. Raise vehicle and support rear axle.
2. Disconnect stabilizer bar from underbody and axle tube connections, Fig. 2, then remove stabilizer bar from vehicle.
3. Reverse procedure to install.

Fig. 1   Rear suspension

Fig. 2   Stabilizer bar installation

Fig. 3   Track rod and lower control arm

Front Suspension & Steering Section

DESCRIPTION

This front suspension system, Fig. 1, uses long and short control arms with coil springs mounted between the lower control arms and front suspension crossmember.

WHEEL ALIGNMENT

Caster
Caster angle is adjusted by rearranging washers located at both ends of the upper control arm, Fig. 2. A kit consisting of two washers, one of 3 mm thickness and one of 9mm thickness, must be used when adjusting caster angle.

Fig. 1   Front suspension

Camber
Camber is adjusted by removing the upper ball joint, rotating it ½ turn and reinstalling it with flat of upper flange on inboard side of control arm, Fig. 3. This will increase positive camber by approximately 1°.

TOE-IN ADJUST

To adjust toe-in, loosen tie rod jam nuts at tie rod ends and loosen clamp at rubber bellows. Turn each tie rod to increase or decrease its length until proper toe-in is obtained. Torque jam nut to 50 ft. lbs.

Fig. 2 Caster adjustment

NOTE: TO INCREASE CAMBER, DISCONNECT UPPER BALL JOINT, ROTATE 180° TO POSITION "FLAT" OF FLANGE INBOARD, THEN RECONNECT BALLJOINT.

Fig. 3 Camber adjustment

Fig. 4 Separating ball joint studs from steering knuckle

WHEEL BEARINGS, ADJUST

1. While rotating wheel in the forward direction, torque spindle nut to 12 ft. lbs.
2. Back spindle nut off to the just loose position.
3. Hand tighten spindle nut, then loosen until cotter holes are aligned, install cotter pin.

NOTE: Do not loosen nut more than 1/2 flat to align cotter pin holes.

---

4. With bearings properly adjusted, end play must be .001–.005 inch.

WHEEL BEARINGS, REPLACE

1. Raise vehicle, remove wheel and tire assembly.
2. Remove two caliper mounting bracket to steering knuckle attaching bolts, remove caliper.
3. Remove hub dust cap, cotter pin, spindle nut, washer, outer wheel bearing and hub.
4. Pry out grease seal, then remove inner bearing from hub.

SHOCK ABSORBER, REPLACE

1. Hold upper stem of shock absorber, and remove nut, retainer and grommet.
2. Raise vehicle and remove lower shock absorber retaining bolts.
3. Lower shock absorber from vehicle.
4. Reverse procedure to install. Torque shock absorber lower retaining bolts to 35–50 ft. lbs. and the upper retaining nut to 60–120 in. lbs.

BALL JOINTS, REPLACE

Upper Ball Joint

1. Raise vehicle and remove wheel and tire assembly.
2. Support lower control arm using a suitable jack.
3. Loosen upper ball joint stud nut, however, do not remove nut.

4. Position tool J-26407 with cupped end over lower ball joint stud and turn threaded end of tool until upper ball joint stud is free of steering knuckle, Fig. 4.
5. Remove tool, then the upper stud nut.

NOTE: Discard the stud nut. The stud nut is of special design and must be replaced whenever removed or loosened.

---

6. Remove two nuts securing ball joint to upper control arm and the ball joint.

NOTE: Inspect tapered hole in steering knuckle. If out of round or damaged, the knuckle must be replaced.

---

7. Install ball joint on upper control arm and torque bolts to 29 ft. lbs.
8. Position upper ball joint stud on steering knuckle, then install a standard nut to draw ball joint into position on knuckle. Torque standard nut to 35 ft. lbs., then remove standard nut. Install special nut for final assembly and torque to 29–36 ft. lbs.
9. Install wheel and tire assembly and lower vehicle.

Lower Ball Joint

1. Raise vehicle and remove wheel and tire assembly.
2. Support lower control arm using a suitable jack.
3. Loosen lower ball joint stud nut, however, do not remove nut.
4. Position tool J-26407 with cupped end of tool over upper ball joint stud and turn threaded end of tool until lower ball joint stud is free of steering knuckle, Fig. 4.
5. Remove tool, then the lower ball joint stud nut.

NOTE: Discard the stud nut. The stud nut is of special design and must be replaced whenever removed or loosened.

---

6. Remove ball joint from lower control arm.

NOTE: Inspect tapered hole in steering knuckle, if out of round or damaged, the knuckle must be replaced.

---

7. Insert ball joint through lower control arm and into steering knuckle.
8. Install a standard nut to draw ball joint

into position on knuckle. Torque standard nut to 35 ft. lbs., then remove standard nut. Install special nut for final assembly and torque to 41–54 ft. lbs.
9. Install wheel and tire assembly and lower vehicle.

COIL SPRING, REPLACE

1. Support vehicle by frame, remove wheel and tire assembly.
2. Disconnect stabilizer bar from lower control arm and tie rod from steering knuckle.
3. Support lower control arm using a suitable jack.
4. Loosen lower ball joint stud nut, then use tool J-26407 to free stud from steering knuckle, position knuckle and hub out of way. Remove stud nut.

NOTE: Discard stud nut. The stud nut is of special design and must be replaced whenever removed or loosened.

---

5. Loosen lower control arm pivot bolts.
6. Install a safety chain around spring and through lower control arm.
7. Slowly lower control arm until spring is extended as far as possible, then use pry bar to carefully lift spring over lower control arm spring seat.

LOWER CONTROL ARM, REPLACE

1. Remove coil spring as described in "Coil Spring, Replace".
2. Remove control arm pivot bolts, and then remove arm.
3. Reverse procedure to install. Torque lower control arm pivot bolts to 49 ft. lbs.

UPPER CONTROL ARM, REPLACE

1. Support vehicle by frame, remove tire and wheel assembly.
2. Position jack to support lower control arm.
3. Disconnect upper ball joint as described in "Ball Joints, Replace".
4. Remove upper control arm pivot bolts, then remove control arm from vehicle.
5. Reverse procedure to install. Torque upper control arm pivot bolts to 47 ft. lbs.

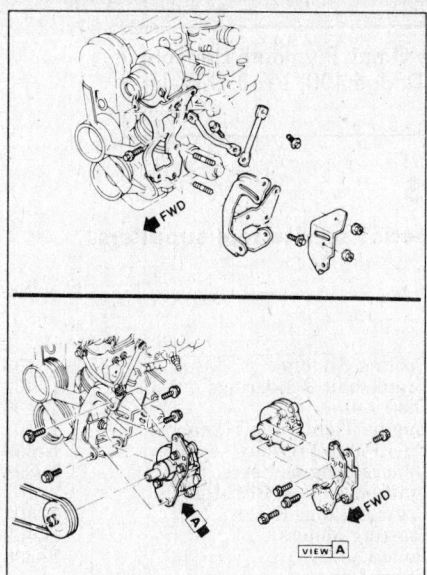

Fig. 5 Power steering pump installation (Typical)

Fig. 6 Power steering reservoir installation

Fig. 7 Power steering hoses installation

STEERING GEAR, REPLACE

1. Raise vehicle and remove bolts and shield.
2. Remove tie rod cotter pins and nuts from tie rod ends and separate tie rods from steering knuckles.
3. Remove flexible coupling pinch bolt.

4. Remove steering gear clamp bolts, then the steering gear assembly from vehicle.
5. Reverse procedure to install. Torque steering knuckle to tie rod nut to 30 ft. lbs., flex coupling pinch bolt to 30 ft. lbs. and steering gear clamp bolt to 14 ft. lbs.

POWER STEERING GEAR, REPLACE

1981–83

The procedure for power steering gear replacement is identical to manual type gear replacement. In addition, it is necessary to disconnect and connect the two hydraulic lines at the steering gear.

POWER STEERING PUMP, REPLACE

1981–83

1. Remove pump adjusting bolt.
2. Remove lower brace to pump bracket attaching bolt.
3. Remove crossmember to frame support brace, then disconnect hydraulic lines at pump.
4. Remove rear pump adjusting bracket, then the front pivot bolt.
5. Remove front pump bracket to engine attaching bolt, then the pump and bracket.
6. Reverse procedure to install.

NOTE: Refer to Figs. 6 and 7 for installation of power steering reservoir and hoses.

NOTE: The following models are covered in this chapter: 1978—83 Dodge Omni, Plymouth Horizon; 1981—83 Dodge Aries & Plymouth Reliant; 1982—83 Chrysler LeBaron & Dodge 400; 1983 Chrysler E Class, Dodge Charger, 600 & Plymouth Turismo.

INDEX OF SERVICE OPERATIONS

NOTE: Refer to the back of this manual for vehicle manufacturer's special service tool suppliers.

GRILLE IDENTIFICATION

1978–80 Omni (4 Door)

1978–80 Horizon (4 Door)

1979–80 Omni 024 (2 Door)

1979–81 Horizon TC3 (2 Door)

1981 Omni (4 Door)

1981 Horizon (4 Door)

1981–82 Omni 024 (2 Door)

1981–82 Reliant

1981–83 Aries

1982 Horizon TC3 (2 Door)

1982–83 400

1982–83 Horizon (4 Door)

1982–83 LeBaron

1982–83 Omni (4 Door)

1983 Charger 2.2

1983 Diplomat

1983 E Class

1983 Reliant

1983 600

1983 Turismo

GENERAL ENGINE SPECIFICATIONS

Year	Engine CID①/Liter	Engine VIN Code②	Carburetor	Bore and Stroke Inch (Millimeters)	Compression Ratio	Net H.P. @ R.P.M.③	Maximum Torque Ft. Lbs. @ R.P.M.	Normal Oil Pressure Pounds @ 2000 RPM
1978	4-105, 1.7L④⑥	A	5220, 2 Bbl.⑦	3.13 × 3.40 (79.5 × 86.4)	8.2	70 @ 5600	85 @ 3200	60–90
	4-105, 1.7L⑤⑥	A	5220, 2 Bbl.⑦	3.13 × 3.40 (79.5 × 86.4)	8.2	75 @ 5600	90 @ 3200	60–90
1979	4-105, 1.7L④⑥	A	5220, 2 Bbl.⑦	3.13 × 3.40 (79.5 × 86.4)	8.2	65 @ 5200	85 @ 2800	60–90
	4-105, 1.7L⑤⑥	A	5220, 2 Bbl.⑦	3.13 × 3.40 (79.5 × 86.4)	8.2	70 @ 5200	85 @ 2800	60–90
1980	4-105, 1.7L④⑥	A	1005222 Bbl.⑦	3.13 × 3.40 (79.5 × 86.4)	8.2	65 @ 5200	85 @ 2400	60–90
	4-105, 1.7L⑤⑥	A	5220, 2 Bbl.⑦	3.13 × 3.40 (79.5 × 86.4)	8.2	65 @ 5200	85 @ 2400	60–90
1981	4-105, 1.7L⑥	A	6520, 2 Bbl.⑦	3.13 × 3.40 (79.5 × 86.4)	8.2	63 @ 5200	83 @ 2400	60–90
	4-135, 2.2L⑧	B	6520, 2 Bbl.⑦	3.44 × 3.62 (87.5 × 92)	8.5	84 @ 4800	111 @ 2500	50
	4-156, 2.6L⑨	D	Mikuni, 2 Bbl.	3.59 × 3.86 (91.1 × 98)	8.2	92 @ 4800	131 @ 2500	57
1982	4-105, 1.7L⑥	A	6520, 2 Bbl.⑦	3.13 × 3.40 (79.5 × 86.4)	8.2	63 @ 4800	83 @ 2400	60–90
	4-135, 2.2L⑧	B	6520, 2 Bbl.⑦	3.44 × 3.62 (87.5 × 92)	8.5	84 @ 4800	111 @ 2400	50
	4-156, 2.6L⑨	D	Mikuni, 2 Bbl.	3.59 × 3.86 (91.1 × 98)	8.2	92 @ 4500	131 @ 2500	57
1983	4-105, 1.7L⑥	B	6520, 2 Bbl.⑦	3.13 × 3.40 (79.5 × 86.4)	8.2	63 @ 4800	83 @ 2400	60–90
	4-135, 2.2L⑧	C	6520, 2 Bbl.⑦	3.44 × 3.62 (87.5 × 92.0)	9.0	94 @ 5200	117 @ 3200⑩	50
	4-156, 2.6L⑨	G	Mikuni, 2 Bbl.	3.59 × 3.86 (91.1 × 98.0)	8.2	93 @ 4500	131 @ 2500	57

①—CID—cubic inch displacement.
②—On 1978–80 models, the 5th digit of the V.I.N. denotes engine code. On 1981–83 models, the 8th digit of the V.I.N. denotes engine code.
③—Ratings are net—as installed in vehicle.
④—Calif. & high altitude.
⑤—Exc. Calif. & high altitude.
⑥—1700 cc.
⑦—Holley.
⑧—2200 cc.
⑨—2600 cc.
⑩—On Dodge 600 & Chrysler E Class with T.B.I. 120 @ 3200.

TUNE UP SPECIFICATIONS

The following specifications are published from the latest information available. This data should be used only in the absence of a decal affixed in the engine compartment.

▲Before removing wires from distributor cap, determine location of the No. 1 wire in cap, as distributor position may have been altered from that shown at the end of this chart.

●When checking compression, lowest cylinder must be within 25 PSI of the highest.

☞ Spark plug types shown in this chart are recommendations of the original vehicle manufacturer and not MOTOR.

Check local sources for other spark plug manufacturers listings.

Year & Engine/VIN Code	Spark Plug Type ☞	Spark Plug Gap	Ignition Timing BTDC① ★ Firing Order Fig. ▲	Ignition Timing BTDC① ★ Man. Trans.	Ignition Timing BTDC① ★ Auto. Trans.	Ignition Timing BTDC① ★ Mark Fig.	Curb Idle Speed Man. Trans.	Curb Idle Speed Auto. Trans.	Fast Idle Speed Man. Trans.	Fast Idle Speed Auto. Trans.	Fuel Pump Pressure
1978											
4-105/A Man. Trans.	RN12Y⑤	.035	A	15°	—	B	900	—	1100⑥	—	4–6
4-105/A Auto. Trans.	RN12Y⑤	.035	A	—	15°	C	—	900N	—	1100⑥	4–6
1979											
4-105/A Man. Trans.	RN12Y⑤	.035	A	15°	—	B	900	—	1400⑥	—	4–6
4-105/A Auto. Trans.	RN12Y⑤	.035	A	—	15°	C	—	900N	—	1700⑥	4–6
1980											
4-105/A Man. Trans.③	RN12Y⑤	.035	A	12°	—	B	900	—	1400⑦	—	4–6
4-105/A Man. Trans.④	RN12Y⑤	.035	A	10°	—	B	900	—	1400⑦	—	4–6

Continued

TUNE UP SPECIFICATIONS—Continued

The following specifications are published from the latest information available. This data should be used only in the absence of a decal affixed in the engine compartment.

▲Before removing wires from distributor cap, determine location of the No. 1 wire in cap, as distributor position may have been altered from that shown at the end of this chart.

●When checking compression, lowest cylinder must be within 25 PSI of the highest.

🖐 Spark plug types shown in this chart are recommendations of the original vehicle manufacturer and not MOTOR. Check local sources for other spark plug manufacturers listings.

Year & Engine/VIN Code	Spark Plug		Ignition Timing BTDC①★				Curb Idle Speed		Fast Idle Speed		Fuel Pump Pressure
	Type 🖐	Gap	Firing Order Fig. ▲	Man. Trans.	Auto. Trans.	Mark Fig.	Man. Trans.	Auto. Trans.	Man. Trans.	Auto. Trans.	
1980—Continued											
4-105/A Auto. Trans.③	RN12Y⑤	.035	A	—	12°	C	—	900N	—	1700⑦	4–6
4-105/A Auto. Trans.④	RN12Y⑤	.035	A	—	10°	C	—	900N	—	1700⑦	4–6
1981											
4-105/A Man. Trans.	65PR4⑧	.048	A	12°	—	B	900	—	1400⑨	—	4½–6
4-105/A Auto. Trans.	65PR4⑧	.048	A	—	10°	C	—	900N	—	1400⑨	4½–6
4-135/B Man. Trans.③	65PR⑧	.035	D	10°	—	E	900	—	1100⑨	—	4½–6
4-135/B Auto. Trans.③	65PR⑧	.035	D	—	10°	C	—	900N	—	1500⑩	4½–6
4-135/B Man. Trans.④	65PR⑧	.035	D	10°	—	E	900	—	1100⑨	—	4½–6
4-135/B Auto. Trans.④	65PR⑧	.035	D	—	10°	C	—	900N	—	1600⑩	4½–6
4-156/D	65PR⑧	.041	F	—	7°	G	—	800N⑪	—	—	4½–6
1982											
4-105/A Man. Trans.	⑬	.035	A	20°⑫	—	B	850	—	1400	—	4½–6
4-105/A Auto. Trans.	⑬	.035	A	—	12°	C	—	900N	—	1400	4½–6
4-135/B Man. Trans.	⑬	.035	D	12°	—	E	850	—	1300	—	4½–6
4-135/B Auto. Trans.	⑬	.035	D	—	12°	C	—	900N	—	1600	4½–6
4-156/D	⑬	.041	F	—	7°	G	—	800N⑪	—	—	4½–6
1983											
4-105/B	⑬	.035	A	20°⑫	—	B	850	—	1400	—	4½–6
4-135/C Man. Trans.	⑬	.035	D	⑭	—	E	850	—	1300	—	4½–6
4-135/C Auto. Trans.	⑬	.035	D	—	⑭	C	—	900N	—	1600	4½–6
4-156/G	⑬	.041	F	—	7°	G	—	800N⑪	—	—	4½–6

① —BTDC—Before top dead center.
② —N:Neutral.
③ —Exc. California.
④ —California.
⑤ —Champion.
⑥ —On lowest step of fast idle cam, w/radiator fan operating, EGR disconnected & plugged, idle stop switch grounded & A/C off.
⑦ —On lowest step of fast idle cam, w/radiator fan operating, EGR & dist. vacuum advance disconnected & plugged & A/C off.
⑧ —Mopar.
⑨ —On 3rd step of fast idle cam (next to lowest), w/radiator fan operating, carb. switch

grounded & EGR disconnected & plugged.
⑩ —On 3rd step of fast idle cam (next to lowest), w/radiator fan operating, carb. switch grounded, EGR disconnected & plugged & green duty cycle solenoid wire disconnected.
⑪ —If mileage on vehicle is less than 300 mi., set at 750 RPM.
⑫ —If an adjustable timing light is not available and a standard timing light is to be used, bring No. 1 cylinder to compression stroke, then align flywheel timing mark with the 16° BTDC mark on flywheel housing. Using a piece of chalk, draw a line on the flywheel at

the 12° BTDC mark, then start engine and check ignition timing. The chalk mark on the flywheel should be aligned with the 16° BTDC mark on the flywheel housing, if not adjust ignition timing as necessary.
⑬ —On early model 1982 vehicles, use spark plug Mopar 65PR. Late model 1982 & 1983 models are equipped with production spark plugs RN12YC, which when serviced should be replaced by spark plug Champion RN12Y or Mopar 65PR.
⑭ —Exc. high altitude 10° BTDC; High altitude 6° BTDC.

Fig. A

Fig. B

Fig. C

Continued

TUNE UP NOTES—Continued

Fig. D

Fig. E

Fig. F

Fig. G

DISTRIBUTOR SPECIFICATIONS

★Note: If unit is checked on vehicle, double the RPM and degrees to get crankshaft figures.

Distributor Part No.①	Centrifugal Advance Degrees @ RPM of Distributor			Vacuum Advance	
	Advance Starts	Intermediate Advance	Full Advance	Start Dist. Degrees @ Inches of Vacuum	Maximum Dist. Degrees
1978–79					
5206275④	—	—	—	—	—
1980					
5206935②	.2 @ 600	1.5–3.5 @ 650	3.7–5.7 @ 2500	.8–2.5 @ 7"	11.5
5206925②	0 @ 575	6 @ 800	11 @ 2800	2 @ 11"	12.5
5206945③④	—	—	—	—	—
1981–83					
4243694	0 @ 600	6 @ 1400	10 @ 3000	0 @ 5.1	7.5
4243707	0 @ 600	6 @ 1400	10 @ 3000	0 @ 3.1	10
5206945	—	—	—	—	—
5206975	—	—	—	—	—

①—Stamped on distributor housing
②—Exc. Calif.
③—Calif.
④—Electronic spark control (Lean Burn) system.

VALVE SPECIFICATIONS

Year	Model/ VIN	Valve Lash Int. in. (MM)	Valve Lash Exh. in. (MM)	Valve Angles Seat	Valve Angles Face	Valve Spring Installed Height Inch (Millimeters)	Valve Spring Pressure Lbs. @ In.	Stem Clearance Intake Inch (Millimeters) ①	Stem Clearance Exhaust Inch (Millimeters) ①	Stem Diameter Intake Inch (Millimeters)	Stem Diameter Exhaust Inch (Millimeters)
1978–80	4–105/A (1700 cc)	.008C (.20C)	.016C (.30C)	45°	45°	③	④	.020 (.5)	.027 (.7)	.314 (7.97)	.313 (7.95)
1981–83	4–105/A (1700 cc)	.010H (.25H)	.018H (.45H)	45°	45°	③	④	.020 (.5)	.027 (.7)	.314 (7.97)	.313 (7.95)
	4–135/⑤ (2200 cc)	Hydraulic		45°	45°	1.65 (41.9)	175 @ 1.22	.0009–.0026 (.022–.065)	.0028–.0044 (.070–.113)	.312–.313 (7.935–7.953)	.311–.312 (7.906–7.924)
	4–156/⑤ (2600 cc)	.006H② (.15H)	.010H (.25H)	43°	45°	1.59 (40.4)	61 @ 1.59	.0012–.0024 (.03–.06)	.0020–.0035 (.05–.09)	.300 (8)	.300 (8)

①—Refer to text.
②—Jet valve clearance, .006H.
③—Inner valve spring, 1.13 inch (28.6 mm); outer valve spring, 1.28 inch (32.6 mm).
④—Inner valve spring, 48 @ .720; outer valve spring, 100 @ .878.
⑤—For V.I.N. code, refer to the "General Engine Specifications" at the front of the chapter.
⑥—On 1981–82 stem clearance is .0028–.0044 (.070–.113) & on 1983 stem clearance is .0030–.0047 (.076–.119).

ENGINE TIGHTENING SPECIFICATIONS★

★Torque specifications are for clean and lightly lubricated threads only. Dry or dirty threads produce increased friction which prevents accurate measurement of tightness.

Year	Engine Model/ VIN	Spark Plugs Ft. Lbs.	Cylinder Head Bolts Ft. Lbs.	Intake Manifold Inch Lbs.	Exhaust Manifold Inch Lbs.	Camshaft Cover Inch Lbs.	Connecting Rod Cap Bolts Ft. Lbs.	Main Bearing Cap Bolts Ft. Lbs.	Flywheel to Crankshaft Ft. Lbs.	Crankshaft Pulley Ft. Lbs.
1978–80	4–105/A 1700 cc	20	60①	200②	150	48	35	47	52	58
1981–83	4–105/④ 1700 cc	20	60①	200②	200	48	35	47	⑤	58
	4–135/④ 2200 cc	26	45①	200	200	105	40①	30①	65	20.8
	4–156/④ 2600 cc	18.3	③	150	150	53	34	58	100	87

①—Turn torque wrench an additional 90 degrees after the specified torque has been achieved.
②—Intake to exhaust manifold inboard nut, 150 inch lbs. Intake to exhaust manifold outboard nut, 200 inch lbs.
③—Cold engine, 69 ft. lbs.; warm engine, 76 ft. lbs.
④—For V.I.N code, refer to the "General Engine Specifications" at the front of the chapter.
⑤—Man. trans., 60 ft. lbs.; auto. trans., 40 ft. lbs.

BRAKE SPECIFICATIONS

Year	Model	Brake Drum Inside Diameter Inch (Millimeter)	Wheel Cylinder Bore Diameter Disc Brake Inch (Millimeter)	Wheel Cylinder Bore Diameter Rear Drum Brake Inch (Millimeter)	Master Cylinder Bore Diameter Inch (Millimeter)
1978–80	All	7.87 (200)	1.89 (48)	5/8 (15.9)	.877 (22.27)
1981–83	Aries & Reliant	7.87 (200)	2.130 (54)	5/8 (15.9)	.875 (22.23)
	Horizon & Omni	7.87 (200)	1.894 (48.11)	5/8 (15.9)	.875 (22.23)
1982–83	LeBaron & 400	7.87 (200)	2.130 (54)	5/8 (15.9)	7/8 (22.23)
1983	Charger & Turismo	7.87 (200)	1.894 (48.11)	5/8 (15.9)	.875 (22.23)
	E Class & 600	8.66 (220)	2.130 (54)	5/8 (15.9)	7/8 (22.23)

PISTONS, PINS, RINGS, CRANKSHAFT & BEARINGS

Year	Engine Model/ VIN	Piston Clearance Top of Skirt Inch (Millimeter)	Ring End Gap① Comp. Inch (Milli-meter)	Ring End Gap① Oil Inch (Milli-meter)	Wristpin Diameter Inch (Millimeter)	Rod Bearings Shaft Diameter Inch (Millimeter)	Rod Bearings Bearing Clearance Inch (Millimeter)	Main Bearings Shaft Diameter Inch (Millimeter)	Main Bearings Bearing Clearance Inch (Millimeter)	Thrust on Bear. No.	Shaft End Play Inch (Millimeter)
1978–80	4-105/A 1700 cc	.0004–.0015 (.011–.039)	.012 (.3)	.012 (.3)	.866 (21.997–22.001)	1.81 (46)	.0004–.0025 (.010–.064)	2.12 (54)	.0008–.0030 (.020–.080)	3	.003–.007 (.07–.18)
1981	4-105/A 1700 cc	.0004–.0015 (.011–.039)	.012 (.3)	.016 (.41)	.866 (21.997–22.001)	1.8087–1.8094 (45.94–45.96)	.0011–.0034 (.028–.088)	2.1236–2.1244 (53.94–53.96)	.0008–.0030 (.020–.080)	3	.003–.007 (.07–.18)
	4-135/B 2200 cc	.0005–.0015 (.013–.038)	.011 (.28)	.015 (.38)	.9008 (22.88)	1.968–1.969 (49.987–50.013)	.0004–.0026 (.011–.067)	2.362–2.363 (59.987–60.013)	.0004–.0026 (.011–.067)	3	.002–.007 (.05–.18)
	4-156/D 2600 cc	.0010–.0020 (.02–.04)	.010 (.25)	.0078 (.2)	.866 (22)	2.0866 (53)	.0008–.0028 (.02–.07)	2.3622 (60)	.0008–.0028 (.02–.07)	3	.002–.007 (.05–.18)
1982–83	4-105/A 1700 cc	.0004–.0015 (.011–.039)	.012 (.3)	.016 (.41)	.866 (21.997–22.001)	1.8087–1.8094 (45.94–45.96)	.0011–.0034 (.028–.088)	2.1236–2.1244 (53.94–53.96)	.0008–.0030 (.020–.080)	3	.003–.007 (.07–.18)
	4-135/② 2200 cc	.0005–.0015 (.013–.038)	.011 (.28)	.015 (.38)	.9008 (22.88)	1.968–1.969 (49.987–50.013)	.0008–.0034 (.019–.087)	2.362–2.363 (59.987–60.013)	.0003–.0031 (.007–.080)	3	.002–.007 (.05–.18)
	4-156/② 2600 cc	.0010–.0020 (.02–.04)	.010 (.25)	.0078 (.2)	.866 (22)	2.0866 (53)	.0008–.0028 (.02–.07)	2.3622 (60)	.0008–.0028 (.02–.07)	3	.002–.007 (.05–.18)

①—Minimum.

②—For V.I.N. code, refer to the "General Engine Specifications" at the front of the chapter.

ALTERNATOR & REGULATOR SPECIFICATIONS

Year	Alternator Part Number	Alternator Rated Hot Output Amps.	Alternator Field Current 12 Volts @ 80° F.	Alternator Output @ 15 Volts 1250 R.P.M.	Regulator Part Number	Field Relay Air Gap In.	Field Relay Point Gap In.	Field Relay Closing Voltage	Voltage Regulator Air Gap In.	Voltage Regulator Point Gap In.	Voltage Regulator Voltage @ 80° F.
1978–81	Yellow①	60	5	57	4091050	—	—	—	—	—	13.9–14.6
	Brown①	65	5	62	—	—	—	—	—	—	13.9–14.6
1981–83	A4T25191②	75	—	63–70③	Integral	—	—	—	—	—	14.1–14.7④
1982–83	Yellow①	60	5.5	45	4111990	—	—	—	—	—	13.9–14.6
	Brown①	78	5.5	56	4111990	—	—	—	—	—	13.9–14.6

①—Chrysler alternator.　②—Mitsubishi alternator.　③—At 13.5 volts & 1000 RPM.　④—At 68° F.

STARTING MOTOR SPECIFICATIONS

Year	Engine/VIN	Model	Ident. Number	Brush Spring Tension Oz.	Free Speed Test Amps.①	Free Speed Test Volts	Free Speed Test R.P.M.②
1978–80	4-105/A (1700 cc)③	Bosch	5206260	—	47	11	6600
	4-105/A (1700 cc)③	Nippondenso	5206270	—	47	11	6600
1978–83	4-105 (1700 cc)④⑤	Bosch	5206255	—	47	11	6600
	4-105 (1700 cc)④⑤	Nippondenso	5206265	—	47	11	6600
1981	4-105/A (1700 cc)③	Bosch	5213080	—	47	11	6600
	4-105/A (1700 cc)③	Nippondenso	5213085	—	47	11	6600
	4-135/B (2200 cc)	Bosch	5213045	—	47	11	6600
	4-135/B (2200 cc)	Nippondenso	5213190	—	47	11	6600
1981–83	4-156/D (2600 cc)	Nippondenso	5213235	—	85	11	3700
1982–83	4-105 (1700 cc)③⑤	Bosch	5213395	—	47	11	6600
	4-105 (1700 cc)③⑤	Nippondenso	5213295	—	47	11	6600
	4-135 (2200 cc)③⑤	Bosch	5213045	—	47	11	6600
	4-135 (2200 cc)④⑤	Bosch	5213395	—	47	11	6600
	4-135 (2200 cc)⑤	Nippondenso	5213645	—	47	11	6600

①—Maximum current draw.　③—Automatic Transmission.　⑤—For V.I.N. code, refer to the "General Engine
②—Minimum speed.　④—Manual Transmission.　　Specifications" at the front of the chapter.

WHEEL ALIGNMENT SPECIFICATIONS

Year	Model	Caster Angle, Degrees		Camber Angle, Degrees				Toe In. Inch	Toe Out on Turns, Deg.	
		Limits	Desired	Limits		Desired			Outer Wheel	Inner Wheel
				Left	Right	Left	Right			
1978–80	Horizon & Omni①	—	—	−1/4 to +3/4	−1/4 to +3/4	+5/16	+5/16	②	—	—
	Horizon & Omni①	—	—	−1 1/2 to −1/2	−1 1/2 to −1/2	−1	−1	④	—	—
1981	Aries & Reliant①	—	—	−1/4 to +3/4	−1/4 to +3/4	+5/16	+5/16	⑤	—	—
	Aries & Reliant③	—	—	−1 to 0	−1 to 0	−1/2	−1/2	⑥	—	—
	Horizon & Omni①	—	—	−1/4 to +3/4	−1/4 to +3/4	+5/16	+5/16	⑤	—	—
	Horizon & Omni③	—	—	−1 1/2 to −1/2	−1 1/2 to −1/2	−1	−1	④	—	—
1982–83	Aries & Reliant①	—	—	−1/4 to +3/4	−1/4 to +3/4	+5/16	+5/16	⑤	—	—
	Aries & Reliant③	—	—	−1 to 0	−1 to 0	−1/2	−1/2	⑥	—	—
	Horizon & Omni①	—	—	−1/4 to +3/4	−1/4 to +3/4	+5/16	+5/16	⑤	—	—
	Horizon & Omni③	—	—	−1/4 to −1 1/4	−1/4 to −1 1/4	−3/4	−3/4	④	—	—
	LeBaron & 400①	—	—	−1/4 to +3/4	−1/4 to +3/4	+5/16	+5/16	⑤	—	—
	LeBaron & 400③	—	—	−1 to 0	−1 to 0	−1/2	−1/2	⑥	—	—
1983	Charger & Turismo①	—	—	−1/4 to +3/4	−1/4 to +3/4	+5/16	+5/16	⑤	—	—
	Charger & Turismo③	—	—	−1/4 to −1 1/4	−1/4 to −1 1/4	−3/4	−3/4	④	—	—
	E Class & 600①	—	—	−1/4 to +3/4	−1/4 to +3/4	+5/16	+5/16	⑤	—	—
	E Class & 600③	—	—	−1 to 0	−1 to 0	−1/2	−1/2	⑥	—	—

①—Front wheel alignment.
②—5/32" out to 1/8" in. (.3 out to .2° in).
③—Rear wheel alignment.
④—5/32" out to 11/32" in (.3° out to .7° in).
⑤—7/32" out to 1/8" in (.4° out to .2° in).
⑥—3/16" out to 3/16" in (.38° out to .38° in).

COOLING SYSTEM & CAPACITY DATA

Year	Model or Engine/VIN	Cooling Capacity		Radiator Cap Relief Pressure, Lbs.	Thermo. Opening Temp. Degrees F. (Centigrade)	Fuel Tank Gals. (Litres)	Engine Oil Refill Qts. (Litres)	Transmission Oil		Final Drive Pints (Litres) ②
		Less A/C Qts. (Litres)	With A/C Qts. (Litres)					4 Speed Pints (Litres)	Auto. Trans. Qts. (Litres) ①	
1978	All	6.5 (6.2)	6.5 (6.2)	16	195 (90.6)	13 (49)	4④ (3.8)	2.8 (1.25)	7.3③ (6.9)	2.4 (1.1)
1979–80	All	6.0 (5.7)	6.0 (5.7)	16	195 (90.6)	13 (49)	4④ (3.8)	2.8 (1.25)	7.3③ (6.9)	2.4 (1.1)
1981–82	4-105/A (1.7L)	6 (5.7)	6 (5.7)	16	195 (90.6)	13 (49)	4④ (3.8)	3 (1.4)	7.3⑤ (6.9)	2.4 (1.1)
	4-135/B (2.2L)	7 (6.6)	7 (6.6)	16	195 (90.6)	13 (49)	4④ (3.8)	4 (1.8)	7.5⑤ (7.1)	2.4 (1.1)
	4-156/D (2.6L)	8.5 (8.1)	8.5 (8.1)	16	195 (88)	13 (49)	5⑥ (5)	4 (1.8)	8.5⑤ (8.1)	2.4 (1.1)
1983	4-105 (1.7L)/B	6 (5.7)	6 (5.7)	16	195 (90.6)	13 (49)	4④ (3.8)	3 (1.4)	8.4⑦ (7.9)	2.4 (1.1)
	4-135 (2.2L)/C	9 (8.5)	9 (8.5)	16	195 (90.6)	13 (49)	4④ (3.8)	4 (1.8)	8.9⑦ (8.4)	2.4 (1.1)
	4-156 (2.6L)/G	9 (8.5)	9 (8.5)	16	195 (88)	13 (49)	4④ (3.8)	4 (1.8)	8.9⑦ (8.4)	2.4 (1.1)

①—Approximate. Make final check with dipstick.
②—Automatic trans. only.
③—Drain & refill, 2.5 qts.
④—With or without filter change.
⑤—Drain & refill, 3 qts.
⑥—Includes 1/2 qt. for filter change.
⑦—Drain & refill, 4 qts.

Electrical Section

STARTER, REPLACE

1981–83 4-105 & 135

1. Disconnect battery ground cable.
2. Remove starter to flywheel housing and rear bracket to engine or transaxle attaching bolts.
3. On models equipped with 4-135 engine, loosen air pump tube at exhaust manifold, then position tube bracket away from starter motor.
4. If equipped, remove heat shield clamp and heat shield.
5. Disconnect starter cable at starter motor and solenoid leads at solenoid, then remove starter motor.
6. Reverse procedure to install.

1978–80 4-105 & 1981–83 4-156

1. Disconnect battery ground cable.
2. Disconnect starter cable at starter.
3. Disconnect solenoid lead wire from solenoid.
4. Remove starter attaching bolts and the starter.
5. Reverse procedure to install.

IGNITION LOCK, REPLACE

1981–83 Aries, Reliant; 1982–83 LeBaron, 400; 1983 E Class & 600

Models Less Tilt Column

1. Disconnect battery ground cable.
2. Remove turn signal switch as described under Turn Signal Switch, Replace.
3. Disconnect horn and ignition key lamp ground wires, then remove ignition key lamp attaching screw and lamp.
4. Remove four screws attaching upper bearing housing to lock housing, then remove snap ring from upper end of steering shaft and remove upper bearing housing.
5. Remove lock plate spring and lock plate from steering shaft.
6. Position lock cylinder in Lock position and remove ignition key.
7. Remove key waring buzzer attaching screws, then remove buzzer.
8. Remove two screws attaching ignition switch to steering column, then remove switch by rotating switch 90° and sliding from rod.

9. Remove two screws attaching dimmer switch, then disengage dimmer switch from actuator rod.
10. Remove two bellcrank attaching screws, then slide bellcrank up into lock housing until it can be disconnected from ignition switch actuator rod.
11. With lock cylinder in Lock position, insert a small diameter screwdriver into lock cylinder release holes and push inward until spring loaded lock cylinder retainers release, Fig. 1.
12. Grasp lock cylinder and pull from lock housing bore.
13. Reverse procedure to install. The lock cylinder and ignition switch must be in the Lock position.

Models W/Tilt Column

1. Disconnect battery ground cable.
2. Remove turn signal switch as described under Turn Signal Switch, Replace.
3. Remove ignition key lamp.
4. Position ignition lock cylinder in the Lock position, then remove ignition key.
5. Insert a thin screwdriver into lock cylinder release slot and depress spring latch which release lock cylinder, then grasp lock cylinder and remove from column, Fig. 2.
6. Reverse procedure to install.

1978–83 Horizon, Omni; 1983 Charger & Turismo

1. Remove steering wheel, column covers and turn signal switch.
2. With a hack saw blade, cut the upper 1/4 inch from the retainer pin boss, Fig. 3.
3. Using a suitable drift, drive roll pin from housing and remove lock cylinder.
4. Insert new cylinder into housing, ensuring that it engages the lug or ignition switch driver.
5. Install roll pin.
6. Check for proper operation.

IGNITION SWITCH, REPLACE

1981–83 Aries, Reliant; 1982–83 LeBaron, 400; 1983 E Class & 600

1. Disconnect battery ground cable.
2. Remove under panel sound deadener.
3. Disconnect speed control switch.
4. Remove two screws attaching switch to column.
5. Rotate switch 90° and pull-up to disen-

gage from ignition switch rod, Fig. 4.
6. Reverse procedure to install. When installing new switch push up gently on switch to take up slack in rod system.

1978–83 Horizon, Omni; 1983 Charger & Turismo

1. Disconnect battery ground cable.
2. Remove connector from ignition switch.
3. Place ignition lock in "Lock" position and remove key.
4. Remove the two ignition switch mounting screws and permit the switch and push rod to drop below the column jacket, Fig. 5.
5. Rotate the switch 90° for removal of switch from push rod.
6. Position ignition switch in "Lock" position, the second detent from the top of the switch.
7. Place switch at right angle to column and insert push rod.
8. Align switch on bracket and loosely install screws.
9. With a light rearward load on the switch, tighten attaching screws.
10. Connect ignition switch wiring connector and battery ground cable.
11. Check for proper operation.

LIGHT SWITCH, REPLACE

1981–83 Aries, Reliant; 1982–83 LeBaron, 400; 1983 E Class & 600

1. Disconnect battery ground cable, then place gearshift lever in "1" position.
2. Remove left upper and lower instrument cluster bezel attaching screws, then detach bezel from five retaining clips and remove bezel.
3. Remove three screws attaching headlamp switch retainer plate to instrument panel.
4. Pull headlamp switch and retainer plate rearward and disconnect wire connector, then depress button on switch and remove switch knob and stem.
5. Remove switch retainer plate escutcheon, then remove nut attaching switch to plate.
6. Reverse procedure to install.

1978–83 Horizon, Omni; 1983 Charger & Turismo

1. Disconnect battery ground cable.
2. Reach under instrument panel and depress light switch knob release button, then pull light switch knob and shaft from switch.
3. Remove four bezel attaching screws and the bezel.

Fig. 1 Ignition lock cylinder removal.
1981–83 Aries, Reliant; 1982–83 LeBaron, 400; 1983 E Class & 600 less tilt column

Fig. 2 Ignition lock cylinder removal.
1981–83 Aries, Reliant; 1982–83 LeBaron, 400; 1983 E Class & 600 W/tilt column

Fig. 3 Key cylinder roll pin removal.
1978–83 Horizon, Omni; 1983 Charger & Turismo

Fig. 4 Ignition switch replacement. 1981–83 Aries, Reliant; 1982–83 LeBaron, 400; 1983 E Class & 600

4. Remove switch attaching screws and disconnect electrical connector from switch, Fig. 6.
5. Remove switch from panel.
6. Reverse procedure to install.

DIMMER SWITCH, REPLACE

1981–83 Aries, Reliant; 1982–83 LeBaron, 400; 1983 E Class & 600

1. Disconnect battery ground cable, then disconnect electrical connector from switch.
2. Remove two screws attaching switch to column, Fig. 7.
3. Reverse procedure to install. During installation, push gently up on switch to take up rod slack.

1978–83 Horizon, Omni; 1983 Charger & Turismo

1. Disconnect battery ground cable, then disconnect connector from switch.
2. Remove the two switch mounting screws and disengage switch from push rod, Fig. 8.
3. To install switch, firmly seat push rod into switch, then compress switch until two .093 inch drill shanks can be inserted into alignment holes. Position upper end of push rod in pocket of wash/wipe switch.

NOTE: This can be done by feel, or if nec-

Fig. 8 Dimmer switch installation. 1978–83 Horizon, Omni; 1983 Charger & Turismo

Fig. 5 Ignition switch replacement. 1978–83 Horizon, Omni; 1983 Charger & Turismo

Fig. 7 Dimmer switch replacement. 1981–83 Aries, Reliant; 1982–83 LeBaron, 400; 1983 E Class & 600

essary, by removing lower column cover.

4. Apply a light rearward pressure on switch, then install screws and remove drills.

NOTE: The switch should click when lever is lifted, and again as lever returns, just before it reaches its stop in the down position.

5. Reconnect wiring connector to switch and connect battery ground cable.

TURN SIGNAL SWITCH, REPLACE

1981–83 Aries, Reliant; 1982–83 LeBaron, 400; 1983 E Class & 600

1. Disconnect battery ground cable.
2. Remove horn button and switch and steering wheel nut, then remove steering wheel using a suitable puller.

Fig. 9 Compressing lock plate cylinder. 1981–83 Aries, Reliant; 1982–83 LeBaron, 400; 1983 E Class & 600

Fig. 6 Light switch replacement. 1978–83 Horizon, Omni; 1983 Charger & Turismo

3. Remove instrument panel lower bezel and steering column cover.
4. On models with tilt steering column, remove transmission gearshift indicator, then remove two nuts attaching steering column to lower panel. Remove four attaching bolts, then remove bracket from column.
5. On models less tilt column, position gearshift lever into its full clockwise position. On models with tilt column, place gearshift lever to its midway position.
6. On models with tilt column, carefully remove plastic cover from lock plate, then depress lock plate with tool No. C-4156 and remove snap ring, Fig. 9. Remove lock plate, canceling cam and upper bearing spring from steering shaft.
7. Remove turn signal lever attaching screws, then remove lever. On models with speed control allow lever to hang from column.
8. Remove turn signal switch and upper bearing attaching screws, then carefully remove turn signal switch, while guiding wire up through column opening, Fig. 10.
9. Reverse procedure to install.

1978–83 Horizon, Omni; 1983 Charger & Turismo

Removal
1. Disconnect battery ground cable.
2. Remove horn button or horn pad, three screws and the horn switch.
3. Remove steering wheel nut and the steering wheel with a suitable puller.
4. Remove four screws from the lower steering column cover and the cover.
5. Remove screw securing washer-wiper switch and position switch aside.
6. Disconnect turn signal and hazard warning wiring connector, disengage wiring harness from support bracket and remove

Fig. 10 Turn signal switch replacement. 1981–83 Aries, Reliant; 1982–83 LeBaron, 400; 1983 E Class & 600

vinyl tape securing key in buzzer wires to turn signal harness.

7. Remove three turn signal switch retainer screws, Fig. 11.
8. Remove turn signal and hazard warning switch while guiding wiring harness out from column.

Installation

1. Guide wiring harness downward through column until the switch is properly seated.
2. Install switch retainer and the three screws.
3. Snap plastic harness retainer into support bracket, connect harness connector and tape key in buzzer wires to harness.
4. Install washer-wiper switch and retaining screw.
5. Install lower steering column cover.
6. Install steering wheel, horn switch and horn button.
7. Connect battery ground cable.

INSTRUMENT CLUSTER, REPLACE

1981–83 Aries, Reliant; 1982–83 LeBaron, 400; 1983 E Class & 600

1. Disconnect battery ground cable.
2. Remove cluster and upper right bezels, Fig. 12.

Fig. 11 Turn signal switch replacement. 1978–83 Horizon, Omni; 1983 Charger & Turismo

3. Remove rear panel top mounting screws. Then lift rearward edge of panel top cover and remove two screws attaching upper cluster housing to base panel.
4. Remove two screws attaching cluster housing to base panel from lower cluster. Then lift rearward edge of panel top cover and slide cluster housing rearward.
5. Disconnect left and right side wiring harness.
6. Disconnect speedometer cable, then remove cluster housing.

7. Reverse procedure to install.

1978–83 Horizon, Omni; 1983 Charger & Turismo

1. Disconnect battery ground cable.
2. Remove two make-lens assembly lower attaching spring pins by pulling rearward with suitable pliers.
3. Pull mask-lens rearward, lower slightly and remove from cluster.
4. Disconnect speedometer cable.
5. Remove two speedometer attaching screws and the speedometer.
6. Disengage two wiring harness connectors. On Rallye cluster disconnect three harness connectors.
7. Remove two cluster attaching screws, Fig. 13. On Rallye cluster remove four screws.
8. Remove cluster upper attaching spring pins and pull cluster from panel.
9. Disconnect clock wiring, if equipped.
10. Remove cluster from vehicle.
11. Reverse procedure to install.

WIPER SWITCH, REPLACE

1981–83 Aries, Reliant; 1982–83 LeBaron, 400; 1983 E Class & 600

1. Disconnect battery ground cable, then remove steering wheel assembly.

Fig. 12 Instrument cluster (Typical). 1981–83 Aries, Reliant; 1982–83 LeBaron, 400; 1983 E Class & 600

Fig. 13   Instrument panel (Typical). 1978–83 Omni, Horizon; 1983 Charger & Turismo

Fig. 14   W/S wiper switch removal.
1981–83 Aries, Reliant; 1982–83 LeBaron,
400; 1983 E Class & 600

3. Remove pivot shaft chromed nut and ring from pivot shaft.
4. Remove two wiper motor mounting screws.
5. Disconnect wiper motor wiring harness from motor pigtail wire.
6. Remove wiper motor from vehicle.
7. Reverse procedure to install.

2. On models equipped with intermittent wiper system, remove two screws attaching turn signal lever cover to lock housing and remove turn signal lever cover.
3. Remove screw attaching W/S wiper switch attaching screw and remove switch, Fig. 14.
4. Reverse procedure to install.

1978–83 Horizon, Omni; 1983 Charger & Turismo

1. Disconnect battery ground cable.
2. Disconnect wiper switch and turn signal switch wiring harness connectors.
3. Remove lower column cover.
4. Remove horn button.
5. Place ignition lock in "Off" position and turn steering wheel so the access hole in hub area is at 9 o'clock position.
6. With a suitable screwdriver, loosen turn signal lever screw through access hole.
7. Disengage dimmer push rod from wiper switch.
8. Unsnap wiring clip and remove wiper switch.
9. Reverse procedure to install.

WINDSHIELD WIPER MOTOR, REPLACE

Front

1981–83 Aries, Reliant; 1982–83 LeBaron, 400; 1983 E Class & 600
1. Disconnect battery ground cable.
2. Remove wiper arm and blade assemblies, then remove wiper arm pivot attaching screws.
3. Remove wiper motor cover, then disconnect wire connector from motor.
4. Remove cowl screen, then remove three wiper motor mounting nuts.

5. Push pivots downward into plenum chamber, then pull motor outward to clear mounting stud. Move wiper motor toward driver's side of vehicle as far as possible and pull right hand pivot and link assembly through opening, then move motor toward passenger side of vehicle and remove wiper motor, and left hand pivot and link assembly.
6. Remove nut from end of motor shaft and remove motor crank.
7. Reverse procedure to install.

1978–83 Horizon, Omni; 1983 Charger & Turismo
1. Remove wiper arm assemblies.
2. Remove the nuts from the left and right pivots.
3. Remove wiper motor plastic cover.
4. Disconnect wiper motor wiring harness.
5. Remove three bolts from wiper motor mounting bracket.
6. Disengage the pivots from cowl top mounting positions.
7. Remove wiper motor, cranks, pivots and drive link assembly from cowl plenum chamber.
8. Remove wiper motor from drive crank linkage.
9. Reverse procedure to install.

Rear

1981–83 Aries, Reliant; 1982–83 LeBaron & 400
1. Disconnect battery ground cable.
2. Remove wiper arm and blade assembly.
3. Remove wiper motor cover, then disconnect wire connector from motor.
4. Remove four screws attaching wiper motor bracket to liftgate, then remove wiper motor.
5. Reverse procedure to install.

1978–83 Horizon, Omni; 1983 Charger & Turismo
1. Remove wiper motor plastic cover.
2. Remove arm and blade assembly.

RADIO, REPLACE

1981–83 Aries, Reliant; 1982–83 LeBaron, 400; 1983 E Class & 600

1. Disconnect battery ground cable, then remove center bezel.
2. On vehicles equipped with mono-speaker, remove speaker, then disconnect from radio.
3. Remove two screws attaching radio to base panel, then pull radio through front face of base panel.
4. Disconnect wiring harness, antenna lead and ground strap.
5. Reverse procedure to install.

1978–83 Horizon, Omni; 1983 Charger & Turismo

1. Disconnect battery ground cable.
2. Remove seven bezel attaching screws and open the glove box.
3. Remove bezel, guiding the right end around glove box.
4. Remove radio mounting screws.
5. Pull radio from panel and disconnect wiring, ground strap and antenna lead from radio.
6. Remove radio from vehicle.
7. Reverse procedure to install.

HEATER CORE, REPLACE

Less A/C

1981–83 Aries, Reliant; 1982–83 LeBaron, 400; 1983 E Class & 600
1. Disconnect battery ground cable, then drain cooling system.
2. Disconnect wire connector from blower motor, then disconnect control cable from mode door.
3. Disconnect heater hoses from heater core, then cap heater core tube openings to prevent coolant spillage.
4. Remove glove box, then remove nut attaching hanger bracket to heater assembly through glove box opening.

Fig. 15   Heater assembly. 1981–83 Aries, Reliant; 1982–83 LeBaron, 400; 1983 E Class & 600 less air conditioning

Fig. 17   Heater assembly. 1981–83 Aries, Reliant; 1982–83 LeBaron, 400; 1983 E Class & 600 with air conditioning

5. From engine compartment of dash panel, remove two nuts attaching heater assembly.
6. Carefully slide heater assembly out from under instrument panel, Fig. 15.
7. Remove insulation from around heater core tubes, then remove upper core mounting screw.
8. Using a screwdriver, pry retainer tabs from outer edges of heater housing cover, then remove cover.
9. Remove lower heater core to housing attaching screws, then slide heater core from housing.
10. Reverse procedure to install.

1978–83 Horizon, Omni; 1983 Charger & Turismo
1. Disconnect battery ground cable and drain cooling system.
2. Remove center outside air floor vent housing.
3. Remove ash tray.
4. Remove two screws retaining defroster duct adapter to heater unit.

NOTE: The left hand screw is accessible through the ash tray housing access hole.

5. Remove the adapter and push the flexible connector upward and position aside.
6. Disconnect temperature control cable.
7. Remove glove box and door assembly.
8. Disconnect blower motor wiring connector.
9. Disconnect heater hoses and plug heater core tube openings.
10. Remove two nuts retaining heater unit to dash panel, Fig. 16.
11. Remove screw attaching heater brace bracket to instrument panel.
12. Remove heater unit support strap nut. Disconnect strap from plenum stud and lower heater unit from panel.
13. Disconnect mode control cable and remove heater unit from vehicle.
14. Remove left heater outlet duct.

15. Remove four screws from blower motor mounting plate, then the blower motor from heater unit.
16. Remove defroster duct adapter.
17. Remove outside air and defroster door cover.
18. Remove screw from center of defroster door, then the door, screw and screw retaining plate.
19. Remove defroster door control rod from heater unit.
20. Remove heater core cover.
21. Slide heater core from heater unit.
22. Reverse procedure to install.

With A/C

1981–83 Aries, Reliant; 1982–83 LeBaron, 400; 1983 E Class & 600
1. Disconnect battery ground cable, then drain cooling system.
2. Discharge refrigerant system, then disconnect heater hoses at heater core and cap heater core tubes to prevent coolant spillage.
3. Disconnect vacuum hoses at intake manifold and water valve.
4. Remove two screws attaching heater control bezel to instrument panel, then remove bezel.
5. Remove two screws attaching A/C and heater control to instrument panel, then remove control.
6. Remove right hand scuff plate and cowl trim panels, then remove glove box.
7. If equipped, remove console, then remove forward console mounting bracket.
8. Remove two center duct retaining screws from bottom of lower panel, then disconnect center duct to right hand duct retaining tabs through glove box opening.
9. Disconnect over column duct, then slide center duct downward from instrument panel.
10. Remove defroster duct from under panel, then disconnect condensation drain tube from engine side of dash panel.
11. Disconnect wire connectors and control cables from A/C and heater housing.
12. Remove right hand cowl to plenum brace, then pull carpet rearward from under unit.
13. Remove A/C and heater housing hanger bracket attaching screw, then remove four nut attaching unit to dash panel from engine compartment.
14. Pull unit rearward so that mounting studs clear dash panel, then carefully remove unit from under instrument panel.
15. Remove nut from mode door actuator arm, then remove two retaining clips from front edge of cover.
16. Remove two attaching screws, then remove mode door actuator from housing.
17. Remove fifteen cover to housing attach-

Fig. 16   Heater assembly. 1978–83 Horizon, Omni; 1983 Charger & Turismo less air conditioning

ASSEMBLY TO PLENUM MOUNTING BRACE

EVAPORATOR HEATER ASSEMBLY

EVAPORATOR HEATER ASSEMBLY TO CENTER DISTRIBUTION DUCT SEAL

PANEL SUPPORT BRACKET

CONDENSATE DRAIN TUBE

A/C UNIT DRAIN TUBE RETAINER

DASH PANEL

VIEW IN DIRECTION OF ARROW Z

Fig. 18 Heater assembly. 1978-83 Horizon, Omni; 1983 Charger & Turismo with air conditioning

BLOWER MOTOR ASSEMBLY

Fig. 19 Blower motor replacement. 1978-83 Horizon, Omni; 1983 Charger & Turismo less air conditioning

BLOWER ASSEMBLY

Fig. 20 Blower motor replacement. With air conditioning

ing screws, then remove cover and lift out mode door, Fig. 9.

18. Remove screw from heater core retaining bracket, then remove heater core.

19. Reverse procedure to install.

1978-83 Horizon, Omni; 1983 Charger & Turismo

1. Disconnect ground cable, drain radiator and discharge refrigerant system.
2. Disconnect temperature door cable from evaporator heater assembly.
3. Remove glove box.
4. Disconnect vacuum harness from control panel and the blower motor feed wire and anti-diesel relay wires.
5. Remove right hand bezel.
6. Remove central air duct cover from central air distribution duct.
7. Remove three screws retaining central air distribution duct, then the duct.
8. Remove defroster duct adapter.
9. Remove "H" valve and disconnect heater hoses. Plug heater core tube openings.
10. Remove condensate drain tube from evaporator heater unit.
11. Disconnect vacuum lines at intake manifold and water valve.
12. Remove evaporator heater unit to dash panel retaining nuts, Fig. 18.
13. Remove panel support bracket.
14. Remove right side cowl lower bracket.
15. Remove instrument panel pivot bracket screw from right side.
16. Remove screws securing lower instrument panel at steering column.
17. Pull back carpet from under evaporator heater assembly as far as possible.
18. Remove nut from A/C to plenum mounting brace and blower motor ground cable.
19. Support unit and remove brace from stud.
20. Lift evaporator heater unit and pull rearward to clear dash panel and liner. Also, the lower instrument panel will have to

be pulled rearward to provide adequate clearance for unit removal. Slowly lower the evaporator heater unit, slide rearward and remove from vehicle.

21. Remove 1/4-20 nut from mode door actuator arm on top cover and two retaining clips from front edge of cover.
22. Remove mode door actuator attaching screws and the actuator.
23. Remove fifteen screws securing cover to evaporator heater assembly and the cover.
24. Remove mode door from unit.
25. Remove screw from heater core tube retaining bracket, then the heater core from evaporator heater assembly.
26. Reverse procedure to install.

BLOWER MOTOR, REPLACE

Less A/C

1981-83 Aries, Reliant; 1982-83 LeBaron, 400; 1983 E Class & 600

1. Perform steps 1 through 14 as described under Heater Core, Replace.
2. Remove blower motor to heater housing attaching screws, then remove blower motor.
3. Remove clamp retaining blower motor wheel to shaft, then remove two nuts attaching retainer plate to blower motor and remove plate.
4. Reverse procedure to install.

1978-83 Horizon, Omni; 1983 Charger & Turismo

1. Disconnect battery ground cable.
2. Disconnect blower motor wiring connector.
3. Remove left heater outlet duct.
4. Remove four screws retaining blower motor mounting plate to heater unit.
5. Remove blower motor assembly, Fig. 19.
6. Reverse procedure to install.

With A/C

1. Disconnect battery ground cable.
2. Remove three screws securing glove box to instrument panel and the glove box.
3. Disconnect blower motor feed and ground wires. Remove wires from retaining clip on recirculating housing.
4. Disconnect blower motor vent tube from A/C unit.
5. Loosen recirculation door actuator from bracket and remove actuator from housing. Do not disconnect vacuum lines.
6. Remove seven screws securing recirculating housing to A/C unit, then the housing.
7. Remove three blower motor mounting flange nuts and the blower motor, Fig. 20.
8. Reverse procedure to install.

SPEED CONTROL

Lock-in Screw Adjustment, Fig. 21

Lock-in accuracy will be affected by poor engine performance (need for tune-up), loaded gross weight of car (trailering), improper slack in control cable. After the foregoing items have been considered and the speed sags or drops more than 2 to 3 mph when the speed control is activated, the lock-in adjusting screw should be turned counter-clockwise approximately 1/4 turn per one mph correction required.

If a speed increase of more than 2 to 3 mph occurs, the lock-in adjusting screw should be turned clockwise 1/4 turn per one mph correction required.

CAUTION: This adjustment must not exceed two turns in either direction or damage to the unit may occur.

Fig. 21 Speed control lock-in screw adjustment

Throttle Cable Adjustment, Fig. 22

Optimum servo performance is obtained with a given amount of free play in the throttle control cable. To obtain proper free play, insert a 1/16″ diameter pin between forward end of slot in cable end of carburetor linkage pin (hair pin clip removed from linkage pin). With choke in full open position and carbure-

tor at curb idle, pull cable back toward dash panel without moving carburetor linkage until all free play is removed. Tighten cable clamp bolt to 45 inch-pounds, remove 1/16″ pin and install hair pin clip.

Brake Switch Adjustment

1981–83 Aries, Reliant; 1982–83 LeBaron, 400; 1983 E Class & 600

Position stop light switch to retaining bracket, then with brake pedal depressed, push switch forward into retaining bracket until it is fully seated. Slowly release brake pedal and allow pedal striker to rachet switch rearward in bracket to the correct position. No further adjustment is necessary.

1980–83 Horizon, Omni; 1983 Charger & Turismo
1. Loosen switch bracket.
2. Insert .130 spacer gauge between brake push rod and switch with pedal in free position.
3. Push switch bracket assembly toward

Fig. 22 Speed control servo throttle cable adjustment

brake push rod until plunger is fully depressed and switch contacts spacer.
4. Tighten bracket bolt to 75 in-lbs. and remove spacer.

4-105 Engine Section

Fig. 1 Engine mount. Front

Fig. 2 Engine mount. Right side, 1978–80

Fig. 2A Engine mount. Left side, 1978–80

Fig. 3 Engine mount. Right side, 1981–83

Fig. 3A Engine mount. Left side, 1981–83

Fig. 3B Correct positioning of extended tip screws

Fig. 4 Cylinder head tightening sequence

ENGINE MOUNTS

NOTE: When positioning the engine on 1981–83 models, check driveshaft length as outlined in the "Front Suspension & Steering Section" under "Driveshaft Length, Adjust." The engine mounts incorporate slotted bolt holes to permit side-to-side positioning of the engine thereby affecting the length of the driveshaft. Failure to properly position engine may result in extensive damage to the engine.

Refer to Figs. 1 through 3 when replacing the engine mounts.

NOTE: The left engine mount is attached with two types of mounting screws. Two of the three are of the pilot type with extended tips. Extended tip screws must be installed in the proper position, Fig. 3B. Damage to the shift cover or difficult shifting may occur if the screws are incorrectly installed.

ENGINE, REPLACE

Manual Trans.

NOTE: The engine and transmission are removed as an assembly.

1. Disconnect battery cables and drain cooling system.
2. Scribe hood hinge locations and remove hood.
3. Remove radiator hoses, then the radiator and shroud assembly.
4. Remove air cleaner.
5. Remove A/C compressor mounting bolts and position compressor aside, if equipped.
6. Disconnect all wiring, hoses, lines and cables from engine.
7. Remove air diverter valve and lines from air pump.
8. Remove alternator belt and alternator.
9. Disconnect clutch and speedometer cables.
10. Raise and support vehicle.
11. Disconnect drive shafts from transmission and secure aside with wire.
12. Disconnect exhaust pipe from manifold.
13. Remove air pump hoses and lines, then the air pump belt and the air pump.
14. Disconnect transmission linkage.
15. Lower vehicle.
16. Attach suitable engine lifting equipment to engine.
17. Raise engine slightly and remove front engine mount bolt.
18. Remove right and left engine mount bolts.

CAMSHAFT BEARING CAPS

5 N•m (48 IN. LB.)

COVER GASKET REPLACE IF DAMAGED

ALWAYS REPLACE

19 N•m (168 IN. LB.)

CAMSHAFT

VALVE ADJUSTING DISC

CAM FOLLOWER BEFORE INSTALLING CHECK FOR WEAR AND CHECK CAMSHAFT END PLAY

VALVE SPRINGS

VALVE SPRING SEAT, LOWER

VALVE STEM SEAL

VALVE GUIDE

CYLINDER HEAD BOLT

OIL SEAL

CYLINDER HEAD

CYLINDER HEAD GASKET

VALVES

Fig. 5 Cylinder head assembly

19. Remove engine and transmission assembly from vehicle.
20. Reverse procedure to install.

Auto. Trans.

NOTE: The engine is removed without the transmission.

1. Disconnect battery cables and drain cooling system.
2. Scribe hood hinge locations and remove hood.
3. Remove radiator hoses and the air cleaner.
4. Remove A/C compressor mounting bolts and position compressor aside, if equipped.
5. Disconnect all wiring, hoses, lines and cables from engine.
6. Remove air diverter valve and lines from air pump, if equipped.
7. Remove alternator belt and the alternator.
8. Remove upper bellhousing bolts.
9. Raise and support vehicle and remove front wheels.
10. Remove left and right splash shields.
11. Remove power steering pump belt and pump mounting bolts. Position pump aside.
12. Remove water pump and crankshaft pulleys.
13. Remove front engine mounting bolt.
14. Remove transmission inspection cover, then the flex plate bolts.
15. Remove starter motor.
16. Remove lower bellhousing bolts.
17. Lower vehicle and support transmission with a suitable jack.
18. Attach suitable engine lifting equipment to engine.
19. Remove engine oil filter and the right engine mount.
20. Lift and remove engine from vehicle.
21. Reverse procedure to install.

Fig. 6 Checking valve clearance

Fig. 7 Valve adjusting disc replacement

Fig. 8 Camshaft bearing cap identification

Fig. 9 Piston markings

CYLINDER HEAD, REPLACE

1. Drain cooling system and perform Steps 1 through 18 as outlined under "Timing Belt, Replace" procedure.
2. Remove intake and exhaust manifolds from cylinder head.
3. Disconnect all wiring, hoses and cables attached to cylinder head.
4. Remove cam cover bolts and the cam cover.
5. Loosen cylinder head attaching bolts in reverse sequence found in Fig. 4.
6. Remove cylinder head from engine, Fig. 5.
7. Reverse procedure to install. Insert bolts No. 8 and 10 first, to center the cylinder head on engine block. Torque bolts to specifications in sequence, Fig. 4. To properly tension the timing belt, perform Steps 19 through 23 as outlined under "Timing Belt, Replace" procedure.

VALVE ARRANGEMENT

Front to Rear

4-105 . . . . E-I-E-I-I-E-I-E

VALVE LIFT SPECS.

Engine	Year	Intake	Exhaust
4-105	1978–83	.406	.406

VALVE TIMING

Intake Opens Before TDC

Engine	Year	Degrees
4-105	1978	23
	1979–83	14

VALVES, ADJUST

1. Using a feeler gauge, check valve clearance, Fig. 6. The cylinder head should be moderately warm, coolant temperature 95° F. Check clearances on all valves following the firing order, 1-3-4-2.
2. If valve clearance is greater than specified, remove valve adjusting disc and insert a thicker disc to obtain proper clearance.
3. If valve clearance is less than specified, remove valve adjusting disc and insert a thinner disc to obtain proper clearance.

Fig. 10 Connecting rod assemblies

Fig. 11 Crankshaft assembly

NOTE

ALL PARTS SHOWN IN THIS ILLUSTRATION CAN BE REMOVED AND INSTALLED WITH ENGINE IN CAR.

TIMING BELT SPROCKET ON CAMSHAFT DO NOT REMOVE WHEN REPLACING TIMING BELT, DRIVE OR ADJUSTING VALVE TIMING

79 N·m (58 ft lb)

TENSIONER FOR TIMING BELT CHECK FOR FREE MOVEMENT

TIMING BELT CHECK FOR WEAR/ADJUSTING INSTALLING: REMOVE WATER PUMP PULLEY

V-BELT CHECK FOR WEAR ADJUSTING TENSION

43 N·m (32 ft lb)

24 N·m (18 ft lb)

OIL SEAL FOR INTERMEDIATE SHAFT

CRANKSHAFT PULLEY NOTE POSITION WHEN INSTALLING DRIVE BELT

OIL SEAL FOR CRANKSHAFT

79 N·m (58 ft lb)

79 N·m (58 ft lb)

TIMING BELT SPROCKET ON INTERMEDIATE SHAFT

TIMING BELT SPROCKET ON CRANKSHAFT

27 N·m (20 ft lb) REMOVE ONLY WHEN SEPARATING V-BELT PULLEY FROM DRIVE BELT SPROCKET

14 N·m (10 ft lb)

Fig. 12   Timing belt & sprockets installation

Fig. 13   Aligning timing marks on crankshaft & intermediate shaft sprockets

assemblies. One uses a stud and nut to retain the bearing cap and the other uses a bolt to retain the bearing cap, Fig. 10.

PISTONS, RINGS & PINS

Pistons are available in standard sizes and oversizes of 0.25, 0.50 and 1.0 mm.

Rings are available in standard sizes and oversizes of 0.25, 0.50 and 1.0 mm.

MAIN & ROD BEARINGS

Main bearings are available in standard sizes and undersizes of 0.25, 0.50 and 0.75 mm. Refer to Fig. 11 for bearing installation.

Rod bearings are available in standard sizes and undersizes of 0.25, 0.50 and 0.75 mm.

TIMING BELT, REPLACE

1. Disconnect battery ground cable.
2. Remove A/C compressor adjusting strap screws and the drive belt, if equipped. Remove screws from compressor mount and stabilizer brackets, then position compressor aside. Remove compressor bracket from alternator and the compressor mount bracket.
3. Loosen alternator adjusting strap and remove drive belt.
4. Remove alternator mount bolts and position alternator aside.
5. Remove alternator and compressor mounting bracket from retainer bracket.
6. Loosen power steering pump drive belt, if equipped.
7. Raise and support vehicle.
8. Remove inner fender shield.
9. Remove air compressor, water pump and air pump drive belts, if equipped.
10. Remove idler pulley assembly.
11. Remove crankshaft pulley, Fig. 12, and power steering belt, if equipped.
12. Remove lower plastic timing belt cover.
13. Lower vehicle and support engine with a suitable jack.
14. Remove right engine mounting bolt and raise engine slightly.
15. Loosen timing belt tensioner and remove timing belt.
16. Rotate crankshaft and intermediate sprockets until markings are aligned on sprockets, Fig. 13.

4. To replace valve adjusting disc, depress cam follower with tool L-4417 or equivalent and remove with a narrow screwdriver, Fig. 7, and a magnet. Install new disc and recheck clearance.
5. Valve adjusting discs are available in thicknesses of 3.00 mm to 4.25 mm in increments of .05 mm.

VALVE GUIDES

The valve guides may be removed by pressing out from the combustion chamber side. Coat the new valve guide with oil and press into cold cylinder head until the shoulder is seated. The replacement valve guides have a shoulder. Do not exert a pressure greater than one ton after the valve guide shoulder is seated since the shoulder may break. Ream valve guide to .315–.316 inch.

CAMSHAFT, REPLACE

1. Remove timing belt as outlined under "Timing Belt, Replace".

2. Remove camshaft sprocket.
3. Remove bearing caps 5, 1 and 3, Fig. 8.
4. Diagonally loosen and remove bearing caps 2 and 4, Fig. 8.
5. Remove camshaft from cylinder head.
6. Lubricate bearing shells, journals and contact faces of bearing caps.
7. Install caps in proper order, observing off center bearing position.
8. Reverse Steps 1 through 5 to complete installation.

PISTON & ROD ASSEMBLY

When installing the piston and connecting rod assembly the arrow on top of the piston must face toward the front of engine, Fig. 9, and the forged mark on the connecting rod must face toward the intermediate shaft, Fig. 10.

Connecting rod clearance should be .015 inch maximum.

NOTE: There are two types of connecting rod

Fig. 14 Aligning camshaft sprocket with cylinder head cover

Fig. 15 Timing belt tensioner tool installation

Fig. 16 Front engine oil seals removal

17. Rotate camshaft sprocket until marking on sprocket is aligned with cylinder head cover, Fig. 14.
18. Install timing belt.
19. Remove spark plug and rotate engine to place No. 1 cylinder at Top Dead Center, compression stroke.
20. Install belt tension tool L-4502 horizontally on large hex of timing belt tensioner pulley, Fig. 15, then loosen tensioner lock nut.
21. Reset tension tool, if necessary, to be within 15 degrees of the horizontal.
22. Rotate engine clockwise two crankshaft revolutions, then tighten tensioner lock nut.
23. Remove tension tool and reverse Steps 1 through 14 to assemble.

FRONT ENGINE OIL SEAL SERVICE

Refer to Figs. 16 and 17 to replace the crankshaft, intermediate shaft or camshaft seal.

REAR CRANKSHAFT OIL SEAL SERVICE

1. Using a suitable screwdriver, pry oil seal out. Use caution not to nick or damage crankshaft flange seal surface.
2. Place tool L-4455-1 over crankshaft, Fig. 18.
3. Place replacement oil seal over tool and tap seal into position with a mallet.

OIL PUMP, REPLACE

Removal

1. Remove oil pan and gasket.
2. Remove oil pump mounting screws, then the oil pump from engine block, Fig. 19.

Installation

1. Install oil pump with shaft in bore until pump mounting face contacts engine block. It may be necessary to rotate pump body to engage pump shaft tongue in distributor shaft groove.
2. Install oil pump mounting screws.
3. Install oil pan gasket and oil pan.

OIL PUMP SERVICE

Disassembly

1. Lightly clamp oil pump in a vise with shaft facing downward.
2. Remove two screws from cover.
3. Push shaft upward and remove shaft and drive gear assembly.
4. Pry deflector plate from assembly and remove strainer.

NOTE: The relief valve is staked in place and is not serviceable.

Inspection

1. Check end play, Fig. 20. End play should be .001–.006 inch.
2. Check gear backlash, Fig. 21. Backlash should be .002–.008 inch. If not, replace pump gears.
3. Check cover for flatness with a .002 inch feeler gauge, Fig. 22.
4. Use compressed air to check relief valve for proper movement, Fig. 23.

Assembly

1. Lightly lubricate all parts.
2. Install driven gear and the drive gear/shaft assembly.
3. Place cover on pump body and install cover screws.
4. Rotate shaft in each direction. If any binding is detected, disassemble pump and inspect for nicks on gears and/or foreign material.

FUEL PUMP, REPLACE

1. Disconnect fuel lines from fuel pump.
2. Remove fuel pump mounting bolts.
3. Remove fuel pump from vehicle.
4. Reverse procedure to install.

WATER PUMP, REPLACE

1. Disconnect battery ground cable.
2. Drain cooling system.
3. Disconnect radiator hoses and bypass hose from water pump.
4. Remove A/C compressor from mounting brackets and position aside with refrigerant lines attached, if equipped.
5. Remove alternator.
6. Disconnect diverter valve hose at valve, then remove the rear air pump bracket and front air pump bracket, if equipped.
7. Remove alternator bracket from water pump.
8. Remove timing belt cover bolt and two top water pump attaching bolts.
9. Remove water pump from vehicle.
10. Reverse procedure to install.

BELT TENSION DATA

		New	Used
1978–80	Air Cond.	55	40
	Air Pump	65	45
	Alternator	75	55
	Power Steer.	40	25
1981–83	Air Cond.	90	45
	Air Pump	70	40
	Alternator	65	40
	Power Steer.	80	50

Fig. 17 Front engine oil seals installation

Fig. 18 Rear crankshaft oil seal installation

OIL DIPSTICK

OIL PRESSURE AND
CHOKE HEAT SWITCH
10 N•m (84 IN. LB.)

19 N•m (168 IN. LB.)

20 N•m (180 IN. LB.)

OIL FILTER
NOTE
TIGHTEN ¾ TO 1 TURN
AFTER GASKET CONTACTS BASE.

ENGINE OIL FILLING CAPACITIES:
WITH OIL FILTER CHANGE OR
WITHOUT OIL FILTER CHANGE

4.0 LITRES (4.0 QUARTS)
(3 IMP. QTS.)

OIL PUMP DRIVE GEAR
AND SHAFT ASSEMBLY

OIL PUMP DRIVEN GEAR

10 N•m (84 IN. LB.)

19 N•m (168 IN. LB.)

STRAINER

OIL DEFLECTOR PLATE
PRY OFF WITH SCREWDRIVER

OIL PAN GASKET
ALWAYS REPLACE

OIL PAN BOLT

30 N•m (22 IN. LB.)

Fig. 19 Engine lubrication system

Fig. 20 Checking oil pump end play

Fig. 21 Checking oil pump gear backlash

Fig. 22 Checking oil pump cover for flatness

Fig. 23 Checking oil pump relief valve with
compressed air

ENGINE MOUNTS

NOTE: When positioning the engine on 1981–83 models, check driveshaft length as outlined in the "Front Suspension & Steering Section" under "Driveshaft Length, Adjust." The engine mounts incorporate slotted bolt holes to permit side-to-side positioning of the engine thereby affecting the length of the driveshaft. Failure to properly position engine may result in extensive damage to the engine.

Refer to Figs. 1 through 1C when replacing the engine mounts.

NOTE: The left engine mount is attached with two types of mounting screws. Two of the three are of the pilot type with extended tips. Extended tip screws must be installed in the proper position, Fig. 1D. Damage to the shift cover or difficult shifting may occur if the screws are incorrectly installed.

ENGINE, REPLACE

1. Disconnect battery ground cable.
2. Scribe alignment marks on hood and hood hinge, then remove hood.
3. Drain cooling system, then disconnect radiator hoses at radiator and engine.
4. Remove radiator and fan shroud, then remove air cleaner.
5. Remove A/C compressor from mounting bracket and position aside with hoses attached, if equipped.
6. Remove power steering pump from mounting bracket and position aside with hoses attached, if equipped.
7. Drain crankcase and remove oil filter.
8. Disconnect wire connectors at alternator, carburetor and engine.
9. Disconnect fuel line, heater hose and accelerator cable.
10. Remove alternator from mounting bracket and position aside.
11. On models equipped with manual transmission, disconnect clutch cable, then remove transmission lower cover.
12. On all models, disconnect exhaust pipe from exhaust manifold, then remove starter motor.
13. On models equipped with automatic transmission, remove transmission case lower cover and place alignment marks on flex plate and torque converter, then remove converter to flex plate attaching screws. Attach a C-clamp to front lower portion of converter housing to retain torque converter in housing when engine is being removed.
14. On all models, install a suitable transmission holding fixture and attach a suitable engine lifting device.
15. Remove right hand inner splash shield, then disconnect ground strap.
16. Remove right hand engine mount to insulator through bolt.
17. Remove transmission case to engine block attaching bolts.
18. Remove front engine mount to bracket bolt, then carefully lift engine from vehicle.
19. Reverse procedure to install.

TIMING SPROCKETS & OIL SEALS

Alternator Belt Removal

1. Disconnect battery ground cable.
2. Loosen alternator locking screw, then loosen adjusting screw and remove belt.
3. Reverse procedure to install.

Alternator & Compressor Mounting Bracket, Fig. 2

1. Remove power steering pump locking screw, Fig. 2A.
2. Remove pivot bolt and nut, then remove drive belt.
3. Reverse procedure to install.

Power Steering Pump Mounting Bracket

1. Remove power steering pump from bracket, then remove bracket from engine, Fig. 2A.
2. Reverse procedure to install.

Fig. 1 Engine mount. Right side

Fig. 1A Front engine mount

Fig. 1B Engine mount. Left side Automatic Transaxle

Fig. 1C Engine mount. Left side Manual Transaxle

Fig. 1D Correct positioning of extended tip screws

TORQUE		
A	54 N•m	40 FT. LBS.
B	41 N•m	30 FT. LBS.
C	23 N•m	200 IN. LBS.

Fig. 2. Alternator & compressor mounting bracket, replacement

TORQUES		
A	54 N•m	40 FT. LBS.
B	41 N•m	30 FT. LBS.

Fig. 2A Power steering pump & mounting bracket, replacement

Fig. 3 Timing belt cover removal

Fig. 4 Crankshaft, intermediate shaft & camshaft oil seal removal

Fig. 5 Crankshaft, intermediate shaft & camshaft oil seal installation

Fig. 6 Aligning crankshaft & intermediate shaft timing marks

Crankshaft Pulley & Water Pump Pulley

1. Remove screws retaining water pump pulley to pump shaft.
2. Remove bolts retaining crankshaft pulley.
3. Raise and support front of vehicle, then remove right inner splash shield and remove crankshaft pulley.
4. Reverse procedure to install

Timing Belt Cover

1. Remove nuts securing cover to cylinder head, Fig. 3.
2. Remove screws securing cover to cylinder head, then remove both halves of timing belt cover.
3. Position a suitable jack under engine, then remove right hand engine mount bolt and raise engine slightly.
4. Loosen timing belt tensioner, then remove timing belt.
5. Reverse procedure to install.

Crankshaft Sprocket

1. With timing belt removed from engine, remove the crankshaft sprocket bolt.
2. Remove crankshaft sprocket using a suitable puller.

Crankshaft, Intermediate Shaft & Camshaft Oil Seal Service

Refer to Figs. 4 and 5 for removal and installation of crankshaft, intermediate shaft or camshaft seals.

NOTE: On late model 1981 2.2L engines, the camshaft oil seals were changed from steel backed to uni-directional rubber backed type seals. This change made necessary an increase in the cylinder rear seal bore to prevent accidental mixing of the uni-directional front and rear seals.

The replacement seal for early built 2.2L engines will also be rubber backed with arrows indicating the direction of rotation and location in the head marked on the seal. The seals must be installed as indicated.

Crankshaft & Intermediate Shaft Timing

1. Rotate crankshaft and intermediate shaft until markings on sprockets are aligned, Fig. 6.

Camshaft Timing

1. Rotate camshaft until arrows on hub are aligned with No. 1 camshaft cap to cylinder head line, Fig. 7. Small hole must be located along vertical center line.
2. Install timing belt. Refer to "Adjusting Drive Belt Tension" described elsewhere for proper drive belt adjustment.

Fig. 7   Aligning camshaft timing marks

Fig. 8   Camshaft & intermediate shaft sprocket replacement

Fig. 9   Adjusting drive belt tension

3. Rotate crankshaft two full revolutions and recheck timing.

NOTE: Do not allow oil or solvents to contact the timing belt since they will deteriorate the rubber and cause tooth skippage.

Camshaft & Intermediate Shaft Removal & Installation

Refer to Fig. 8 for removal and installation of camshaft and intermediate shaft sprocket.

Adjusting Drive Belt Tension

1. Remove spark plugs then rotate crankshaft to TDC position.
2. Using a suitable tool, loosen tensioner lock nut, Fig. 9.
3. Reset belt tension so that belt tensioning tool axis is within 15° of horizontal.
4. Rotate crankshaft two revolutions in clockwise direction and position at TDC, then tighten tensioner lock nut.

INTAKE & EXHAUST MANIFOLD

1. Disconnect battery ground cable and drain coolant system.
2. Remove air cleaner and disconnect all vacuum and fuel lines and electrical connectors from carburetor.
3. Disconnect throttle linkage, then remove power steering pump drive belt.
4. Disconnect power brake vacuum hose from manifold, if equipped.
5. Disconnect hoses from water crossover, then raise and support vehicle and disconnect exhaust pipe from exhaust manifold.
6. Remove power steering pump and position aside, then remove intake manifold support bracket.

Fig. 10   Valve spring, replace

7. Remove EGR tube, then the intake manifold retaining screws.
8. Lower vehicle and remove intake manifold.

NOTE: When the screws are removed from the intake manifold water cover for any reason, the two center screws must be resealed when reinstalled or water and/or vacuum leaks could result. The correct method for resealing the bolts is as follows: Clean the threads in the manifold and on the bolts. Apply a suitable thread sealant, then install the screws and torque to 105 inch lbs.

9. Remove exhaust manifold retaining nuts, then the exhaust manifold.
10. Reverse procedure to install.

CYLINDER HEAD & VALVE ASSEMBLY

Removing & Installing Valve Springs

Cylinder Head Off Engine
1. Using suitable tool to hold valves in head, compress valve spring enough to remove and install valve bead locks, Fig. 10.

Cylinder Head On Engine
1. Rotate crankshaft until piston is at TDC on compression stroke.
2. Apply 90–100 psi. of compressed air into spark plug hole of valve being removed.
3. Using suitable tool, compress valve spring enough to remove valve stem locks.
4. Remove valve spring and spring seat.
5. Remove valve seal.

Cylinder Head Bolt Tightening Sequence

1. Referring to bolt tightening sequence, Fig. 11, tighten cylinder head bolts in three steps as follows:
   a. Torque bolts to 30 ft. lbs.
   b. Torque bolts to 45 ft. lbs.
   c. Advance each bolt an additional ¼ turn (90 degrees).

Camshaft Bearing Caps

1. With caps removed from engine, check oil holes for obstructions.
2. With caps aligned in proper sequence, ensure arrow on caps 1, 2, 3 and 4 point toward timing belt, Fig. 12.

Fig. 11   Cylinder head bolt tightening sequence

Fig. 12   Camshaft bearing cap installation

Fig. 13   Piston & connecting rod assembly

Fig. 14 Oil pump replacement

Fig. 15 Measuring oil pump end play

OUTER ROTOR

Fig. 16 Measuring oil pump outer rotor thickness

3. Apply suitable sealant to No. 5 bearing cap.
4. Install caps before installing camshaft seals, then torque cap bolts to 160 inch lbs.

VALVE LIFT SPECS.

Engine	Year	Intake	Exhaust
4-135	1981–83	.430	.430

VALVE TIMING

Intake Opens Before TDC

Engine	Year	Degrees
4-135	1981–83	12

PISTON & ROD ASSEMBLY

When installing the piston and rod assembly, indentation on top of piston must face towards timing belt side of engine, Fig. 13. The oil hole on the connecting rod must face timing belt side of engine and be on the same side as the indented mark on the piston.

Connecting rod clearance should be .005–.013 inch.

ENGINE LUBRICATION SYSTEM

Oil Pump Assembly

1. With oil pan removed, remove screw securing oil pump to cylinder block, Fig. 14.
2. Reverse procedure to install. Torque oil pump attaching screws to 200 inch lbs.

NOTE: The oil pump must fully seat on the cylinder block before the mounting bolts are tightened. Check for proper seating by rotating the pump body on the block. The pump body should move a few degrees in both directions with no further movement into the block. If not, the mating surfaces should be cleaned of any foreign material preventing proper seating, otherwise damage to the oil pump, pump driveshaft and gear, or distributor drive may result.

Oil Pump Service

1. Measure the following oil pump clearances:
   a. End play, Fig. 15. End play should be .001–.006 in.
   b. Outer rotor thickness, Fig. 16. Thickness should be .825 in. minimum. Install outer rotor with chamfered edge in pump body.
   c. Clearance between rotors, Fig. 17,

should be .010 in. maximum.
   d. Outer rotor clearance, Fig. 18. Clearance should be .014 in. maximum.
   e. Oil pump cover, Fig. 19. Clearance should be .015 in. maximum.
   f. Oil pressure relief valve spring length should be 1.95 in.

WATER PUMP, REPLACE

1. Disconnect battery ground cable.
2. Drain cooling system, and remove upper radiator hose.
3. Remove A/C compressor from mounting brackets and position aside with refrigerant lines attached, if equipped.
4. Remove alternator.
5. Disconnect lower radiator hose, bypass hose and four water pump to engine attaching screws, then remove water pump.
6. Reverse procedure to install.

BELT TENSION DATA

1981–83		New	Used
	Air Cond.	40	30
	Air Pump	45	35
	Alternator	110	80
	Power Steer.	75	55

FEELER GAUGE   INNER ROTOR

OUTER ROTOR

Fig. 17 Measuring clearance between oil pump rotors

FEELER GAUGE   OUTER ROTOR

Fig. 18 Measuring oil pump outer rotor clearance

STRAIGHT EDGE

FEELER GAUGE   COVER

Fig. 19 Measuring oil pump cover clearance

ENGINE MOUNTS

NOTE: When positioning the engine on 1981–83 models, check driveshaft length as outlined in the "Front Suspension & Steering Section" under "Driveshaft Length, Adjust." The engine mounts incorporate slotted bolt holes to permit side-to-side positioning of the engine thereby affecting the length of the driveshaft. Failure to properly position engine may result in extensive damage to the engine.

Refer to Figs. 1 through 1B when replacing the engine mounts.

NOTE: The left engine mount is attached with two types of mounting screws. Two of the three are of the pilot type with extended tips. Extended tip screws must be installed in the proper position, Fig. 1C. Damage to the shift cover or difficult shifting may occur if the screws are incorrectly installed.

ENGINE, REPLACE

1. Disconnect battery ground cable.
2. Scribe alignment marks on hood and hood hinge, then remove hood.
3. Drain cooling system, then disconnect radiator hoses at radiator and engine.
4. Remove radiator and fan shroud, then remove air cleaner.
5. Remove A/C compressor from mounting bracket and position aside with hoses attached, if equipped.
6. Remove power steering pump from mounting bracket and position aside with hoses attached, if equipped.
7. Drain crankcase and remove oil filter.
8. Disconnect wire connectors at alternator, carburetor and engine.
9. Disconnect fuel line, heater hose and accelerator cable.
10. Remove alternator from mounting bracket and position aside.
11. On models equipped with manual transmission, disconnect clutch cable, then remove transmission lower cover.
12. On all models, disconnect exhaust pipe from exhaust manifold, then remove starter motor.
13. On models equipped with automatic transmission, remove transmission case lower cover and place alignment marks on flex plate and torque converter, then remove converter to flex plate attaching screws. Attach a C-clamp to front lower portion of converter housing to retain torque converter in housing when engine is being removed.
14. On all models, install a suitable transmission holding fixture and attach a suitable engine lifting device.
15. Remove right hand inner splash shield, then disconnect ground strap.
16. Remove right hand engine mount to insulator through bolt.
17. Remove transmission case to engine block attaching bolts.
18. Remove front engine mount to bracket bolt, then carefully lift engine from vehicle.
19. Reverse procedure to install.

TIMING GEARS & OIL SEALS

Timing Chain Case Cover

1. Disconnect battery ground cable.
2. Remove alternator locking screw, then loosen jam nut and adjusting screw. Remove drive belt.
3. Remove distributor retaining nut, then remove distributor from cylinder head and position aside.
4. Remove front and rear A/C compressor to bracket attaching screws, then remove A/C compressor and position aside.
5. Remove power steering pump pivot and lock screws, then remove drive belt.
6. Remove power steering pump mounting screw and nut, then position power steering pump aside.
7. Remove power steering pump bracket to engine attaching screws, then remove bracket.

8. Raise vehicle and remove right inner splash shield.
9. Drain crankcase, then remove crankshaft drive pulley.
10. Lower vehicle and position a suitable jack under engine.
11. Remove engine mount to frame side rail through bolt, then remove engine oil dipstick.
12. Remove air cleaner assembly.
13. Disconnect battery ground cable, then the spark plug wires.
14. Disconnect vacuum hoses from cylinder head cover.
15. Remove cylinder head cover screws, then the cylinder head cover.
16. Remove oil pan attaching screws, then remove oil pan.
17. Remove timing indicator plate from timing chain case cover.
18. Remove engine mounting plate from timing chain case cover.
19. Remove cylinder head cover as previously described.
20. Remove two front cylinder head screws. Do not disturb any other cylinder head bolts.
21. Refer to Fig. 2 and remove remaining screws securing chain case cover to engine.

Ⓐ	54 N•m (40 FT. LBS.)
Ⓑ	28 N•m (250 IN. LBS.)
Ⓒ	95 N•m (70 FT. LBS.)
Ⓓ	15 N•m (130 IN. LBS.)

Fig. 1 Engine mount. Right side

Ⓐ	54 N•m (40 FT. LBS.)
Ⓑ	61 N•m (45 FT. LBS.)

Fig. 1B Engine mount. Left side

Ⓐ	54 N•m (40 FT. LBS.)
Ⓑ	68 N•m (50 FT. LBS.)
Ⓒ	75 N•m (55 FT. LBS.)

Fig. 1A Front engine mount

Fig. 1C Correct positioning of extended tip screws

Fig. 2 Chain case cover removal

Fig. 2A Silent shaft drive chain, replace

Fig. 3 Camshaft drive chain, replace

Fig. 4 Camshaft timing mark alignment

Fig. 5 Timing chain installation

Fig. 6 Silent Shaft chain adjustment & installation with engine removed

Silent Shaft Drive Chain

1. Remove chain case cover as previously described.
2. Remove sprocket screws, then the drive chain, crankshaft sprocket and silent shaft sprocket, Fig. 2A.

Camshaft Drive Chain

1. Remove chain case cover as previously described.
2. Remove camshaft sprocket holder, then the left and right timing chain guides, Fig. 3.
3. Depress tensioner to remove drive chain.
4. Remove crankshaft and camshaft sprockets.

Camshaft Installation

1. With camshaft bearing caps installed, rotate camshaft until timing marks are aligned as shown in Fig. 4.

Timing Chain Installation

1. Install sprocket holder, then left and right chain guides, Fig. 5.
2. Rotate crankshaft until No. 1 piston is at TDC on compression stroke.
3. Install tensioner spring assembly onto oil pump body, Fig. 3.
4. Install timing chain on camshaft sprocket

and crankshaft sprocket. Ensure timing marks are aligned, Fig. 5. Timing marks on sprockets are punch marks on the teeth while timing marks on chain are plated links.
5. Align crankshaft sprocket to the crankshaft keyway and slide into place. Align camshaft sprocket dowel hole to camshaft dowel hole.
6. Install dowel pin, then the distributor drive gear. Install sprocket screw onto camshaft and torque to 40 ft. lbs.

Silent Shaft Chain Installation & Adjustment

1. Install silent shaft chain drive pulley onto crankshaft.
2. Install silent shaft chain onto oil pump sprocket and silent shaft sprocket, Fig. 4.
3. Ensure timing marks are aligned. Timing marks on the sprockets are punch marks on the teeth, while timing marks on the chain are plated links.
4. Align crankshaft sprocket plated link with punch mark on sprocket.
5. Position chain on crankshaft sprocket, then install oil pump sprocket and silent shaft sprockets on their respective shafts.
6. Install oil pump and silent shaft sprocket screws and torque to 25 ft. lbs.
7. Install three chain guides. Snug tighten retaining bolts.
8. Refer to Fig. 6 and adjust silent shaft chain tension as follows:

a. Tighten chain guide "A" mounting screws.
b. Tighten chain guide "B" mounting screws.
c. Shake oil pump and silent shaft sprockets to collect slack at point "P".
d. Adjust position of chain guide "B" so that when the chain is pulled in direction of arrow "F", clearance between chain guide "B" and chain links will be .4–.14 in. Tighten chain guide "B" mounting screws.
9. Install new gasket on chain case, coat gasket with suitable sealant, then install chain case to block and torque attaching screws to 156 in. lbs.

Tension Adjustment With Engine Installed

1. Remove cover over access hole in chain case cover, Fig. 7.
2. Loosen bolt "B", Fig. 7.
3. Apply pressure by hand on boss indicated in Fig. 7, then torque bolt "B" to 160 in. lbs.

Fig. 7 Silent Shaft chain adjustment with engine installed

Fig. 8 Rear oil seal, replace

Fig. 9 Main bearing cap installation

Fig. 10 Oil pump & Silent Shaft, removal

Fig. 11 Piston ring installation

Fig. 12 Installing oil ring side rail.

CRANKSHAFT, BEARINGS & SILENT SHAFT

Rear Oil Seal, Replace

1. Remove screws attaching crankshaft rear oil seal retainer, then the retainer, Fig. 8.
2. Remove separator from retainer, then the oil seal.
3. Install new seal into retainer, then the separator. Ensure oil hole is positioned at separator bottom.

Main Bearing Caps

1. Install main bearing caps in sequence and ensure arrows on caps are pointed in direction of timing chain, Fig. 9.

Oil Pump & Silent Shaft

1. Refer to Fig. 10 and remove silent shaft screw, then the silent shaft.
2. Remove oil pump to cylinder block screw, then the oil pump.

Fig. 13 Piston ring end gap location

PISTONS & RODS

Refer to Fig. 11 for correct piston ring installation and note the following groove clearances:
1. No. 1 upper: .0024–.0039 in. (.06–.10 mm). wear limit: .004 in. (.1 mm).
2. No. 2 intermediate: .0008–.0024 in. (.02–.06 mm). Wear limit: .004 in. (.1 mm).
3. Oil ring upper: .010–.018 in. (.25–.45 mm). Wear limit: .039 in. (.1 mm).
4. Oil ring intermediate: .010–.018 in. (.25–.45 mm). Wear limit: .039 in. (.1 mm).
5. Oil ring side rail: .008–.035 in. (.2–.4 mm) Wear limit: .059 in. (.15 mm). Connecting rod side clearance should be .004–.010 inch.

Installing Piston Ring Side Rail

1. Place one end of side rail between piston ring groove and spacer expander, Fig. 12.
2. Hold end of ring firmly and press downward on portion to be installed until side rail is in position. Do not use a piston ring expander.
3. Install upper side rail first, then the lower side rail.

Fig. 14 Cylinder head bolt removal sequence

Piston Ring End Gap Location

1. Position piston ring end gaps as shown in Fig. 13.
2. Position oil ring expander gap at least 45° from side rail gaps but not on piston pin center line or in thrust direction.

CYLINDER HEAD & VALVE ASSEMBLY

Cylinder Head Bolt Removal & Installation

1. Refer to Fig. 14 for cylinder head bolt removal sequence.
2. Refering to bolt tightening sequence, Fig. 15, tighten cylinder head bolts in three steps as follows:
   a. Torque all bolts except No. 11 to 35 ft. lbs.
   b. Torque all bolts except No. 11 to 69 ft. lbs. on a cold engine or 75 ft. lbs. on a hot engine.
   c. Torque cylinder head to chain case cover bolts (No. 11) to 156 in. lbs.

Fig. 15 Cylinder head bolt tightening sequence

Fig. 16 Camshaft bearing cap installation

Fig. 17 Rocker arm shaft assembly

Camshaft Bearing Cap

1. Align camshaft bearing caps with arrows pointing toward timing chain, Fig. 16. Install caps in numerical order.

Rocker Arm Shaft Assembly

1. Refer to Fig. 18 and install bolts into front bearing caps.
2. Install wave washers, rocker arms, bearing caps and springs in order shown, Fig. 17.
3. Place rocker shaft assembly into position, then rotate camshaft until dowel pin hole is at vertical centerline, Fig. 4.
4. Tighten camshaft bearing cap bolts in the following order:
   a. No. 3 cap bolts to 85 inch. lbs.
   b. No. 2 cap bolts to 85 inch. lbs.
   c. No. 4 cap bolts to 85 inch. lbs.
   d. Front cap bolts to 85 inch. lbs.
   e. Rear cap bolts to 85 inch. lbs.
5. Repeat step 4, increasing torque to 175 inch lbs.

Installed Valve Spring Height

1. Measure installed height of valve spring between spring seat and spring retainer, Fig. 18. Installed height should be 1.590 in. If height is greater than 1.629 in., replace spring.

Valve Clearance Adjustment

NOTE: Check hot torque on cylinder head bolts before performing valve adjustments.

1. With engine at operating temperature, position piston at TDC on compression stroke.
2. Loosen valve adjuster lock nut, then adjust valve clearance by rotating ad-

justing screw while measuring with a feeler gauge, Fig. 19.
3. Valve clearance should be as follows: Intake—.006 in; Exhaust—.010 in.
4. Tighten lock nut securely while holding adjusting screw with screwdriver.

Jet Valve Service

1. Install jet valve assembly into cylinder head.
2. Using suitable socket, torque jet valve to 168 inch lbs.

NOTE: Ensure that socket wrench is not tilted with respect to centerline of jet valve as damage to the valve stem may result. Check hot torque on cylinder head bolts before performing jet valve adjustments.

Fig. 18 Measuring installed valve spring height

3. With engine at operating temperature, position piston at TDC of compression stroke.
4. Loosen jet valve adjuster lock nut, Fig. 20.
5. Proper valve clearance is obtained by rotating adjusting screw while measuring clearance with feeler gauge.
6. Valve clearance should be .006 in.
7. Tighten lock nut securely while holding adjusting screw with screwdriver.

Intake Manifold, Replace

1. Disconnect battery ground cable and drain coolant system.
2. Disconnect hose between water pump and intake manifold.
3. Disconnect carburetor air horn and position aside.
4. Disconnect carburetor and intake manifold vacuum hoses, throttle linkage, and fuel line.
5. Remove fuel filter and fuel pump and position aside.
6. Remove mounting nuts and washers securing intake manifold, then the intake manifold.

VALVE LIFT SPECS.

Engine	Year	Intake	Exhaust
4-156	1981–83	.410	.410

Fig. 19 Adjusting valve clearance

Fig. 20 Adjusting jet valve clearance

Fig. 21 Oil pump gear alignment

1-423

CHRYSLER CORP.—Front Wheel Drive

VALVE TIMING

Intake Opens Before TDC

Engine 4-156	Year 1981–83	Degrees 25

ENGINE LUBRICATION SYSTEM

Oil Pump Clearances

Refer to Fig. 10 and measure the following clearances:
1. Drive gear to body—.0043–.0059 in.
(.11–.15 mm).
2. Driven gear to bearing—.0008–.0020 in. (.02–.05 mm).
3. Driven gear end play—.0024–.0047 in. (.06–.12 mm).
4. Drive gear end play—.0016–.0028 in. (.04–.07 mm).
5. Drive gear to body clearance—.0043–.0059 in. (.11–.15 in).
6. Drive gear to bearing—.0008–.0020 in (.02–.05 mm).
7. Relief valve spring length—1.850 in. (47 mm).
8. Relief valve spring load—9.5 lbs. at 1.575 in. (40 mm).

Refer to Fig. 21 and align mating marks of drive and driven gears, then prime pump with clean oil and install onto engine.

WATER PUMP, REPLACE

1. Disconnect battery ground cable.
2. Drain cooling system.
3. Disconnect radiator hose, bypass hose, and heater hose from water pump.
4. Remove drive pulley shield.
5. Remove locking screw and pivot screws.
6. Remove drive belt and remove water pump from engine.
7. Reverse procedure to install.

BELT TENSION DATA

1981–83	New	Used
Power Steer.	110	75
Exc. Power Steer.	120	80

Clutch & Transaxle Section

CLUTCH, ADJUST

1981–83 Models W/ 4-135

The clutch release cable, Fig. 1, on these models cannot be adjusted. When the cable is properly routed, the spring between the clutch pedal and positioner adjuster will hold the clutch cable in the proper position. An adjuster pivot is used to hold release cable in place to ensure complete clutch release when the clutch pedal is depressed.

1978–83 Models W/ 4-105 Engine

1. Pull upward on clutch cable at housing attachment, Fig. 2.
2. Rotate sleeve downward until sleeve snugly contacts grommet.
3. Rotate sleeve so end of sleeve seats into rectangular groove in grommet.
4. Check for proper operation.

CLUTCH, REPLACE

1981–83 Models W/ 4-135 Engine

1. Remove transmission as outlined under "Manual Transaxle, Replace" procedure.
2. Mark relationship between clutch cover and flywheel for reference during reassembly, then insert suitable clutch disc aligning tool through clutch hub.
3. Gradually loosen clutch cover attaching bolts, then remove pressure plate and cover assembly and disc from flywheel.
4. Remove clutch release shaft and slide release bearing assembly off input shaft seal retainer. Remove fork from release bearing thrust plate.
5. Reverse procedure to install. Align reference marks made during reassembly. Using clutch disc alignment tool, install disc, plate and cover to flywheel and torque bolts to 21 ft. lbs.

1978–83 Models W/ 4-105 Engine

Removal
1. Remove transmission as outlined under "Manual Transaxle, Replace" procedure.
2. Gradually loosen and remove bolts attaching flywheel to pressure plate.
3. Remove flywheel and clutch disc, Fig. 3.
4. Remove retaining ring and release plate.

Fig. 1 Clutch cable routing. 1981–83 models w/ 4-135 engine

Fig. 2 Clutch pedal free play adjustment. 1978–83 models w/ 4-105 engine

Fig. 3 Clutch assembly. 1978-83 models w/ 4-105 engine

Fig. 4 Centering clutch disc. 1978-83 models w/ 4-105 engine

Fig. 5 Lock pin removal & installation. 1981-83 models w/ 4-135 engine

Fig. 6 Adjusting rod-type gear shift linkage. 1981-83 models w/4-135 engine

5. Mark position of pressure plate on crankshaft.
6. Gradually loosen and remove bolts attaching pressure plate to flywheel.
7. Remove spacer and pressure plate.

Installation

1. Thoroughly clean surfaces of flywheel and pressure plate with fine sandpaper or crocus cloth. Also, ensure that all oil or grease has been removed.
2. Align marks on pressure plate and crankshaft and install pressure plate and spacer on crankshaft. Install and torque attaching bolts to 55 ft. lbs. (75 Nm).
3. Install release plate and retaining ring.
4. Using tool L-4533 to center clutch disc, Fig. 4, install disc and flywheel onto pressure plate. Ensure the drilled mark on flywheel is at the top so the two dowels in the flywheel align the proper holes in the pressure plate.

5. Install and torque flywheel to pressure plate attaching bolts to 15 ft. lbs. (20 Nm).
6. Remove centering tool.
7. Install transaxle and adjust clutch.
8. Check for proper operation.

GEARSHIFT LINKAGE, ADJUST

1981-83 Models W/ 4-135 Engine

Rod Linkage

1. Remove lock pin from transaxle selector shaft housing (Fig. 5).
2. Reverse lock pin so long end is facing downward, and insert pin into same threaded hole while pushing selector shaft into selector housing.
3. Raise and support vehicle then loosen clamp bolt that secures gearshift tube to gearshift rod.
4. Check that gearshift connector slides and rotates freely in gearshift tube.
5. Position shifter mechanism connector assembly so that isolator is spaced .050 inch away from upstanding flange, while rib on isolator is aligned fore and aft with hole in blocker bracket. Hold connector isolator in this position and torque clamp bolt on gearshift tube to 170 inch lbs. No significant force should be placed on linkage during this procedure, Fig. 6.
6. Lower vehicle, remove lock pin from selector shaft housing and reinstall lock pin in reversed position. Torque pin to 105 in. lbs.
7. Check for proper operation.

LET.	TORQUE	
	N•M	IN. LBS.
Ⓐ	28	250
Ⓑ	8	70
Ⓒ	7	60
Ⓓ	3	30

Fig. 7 Cable operated gearshift linkage

Fig. 8 Cable adjusting pins

Fig. 9 Adjusting selector cable

Fig. 10 Adjusting crossover cable

Cable Linkage, Fig. 7

1. Remove lock pin from transaxle selector shaft housing, Fig. 5.
2. Reverse lock pin so long end is down and insert lock pin into same threaded hole while pushing selector shaft in 1–2 neutral position.
3. Remove gearshift knob, retaining nut, and pull-up ring.
4. Remove console attaching screws.
5. Make two cable adjusting pins as shown in Fig. 8.
6. Adjust selector cable and torque adjusting screw as shown in Fig. 9.

NOTE: The selector cable adjusting screw must be torqued properly.

7. Adjust crossover cable and torque adjusting screw as shown in Fig. 10.

NOTE: The crossover cable adjusting screw must be torqued properly.

8. Remove lock pin from selector shaft housing and reinstall lock pin so long end is up in selector shaft housing, Fig. 5.
9. Check for proper operation and reinstall console, pull-up ring, retaining nut, and gearshift knob.

1978–83 Models W/ 4-105 Engine

1. Place shift lever in neutral at 3–4 position.
2. Loosen shift tube clamp.

Fig. 11 Aligning slider & block bracket marks. 1978–83 models w/ 4-105 engine

3. Align tab on slider with hole in blocker bracket, Fig. 11.
4. Install a 1/2 inch spacer, Fig. 12, to set gearshift unit lock-out.

NOTE: If the blocker bracket has a 5/8 stamp imprint at the forward vertical face of the reinforcement strap, Fig. 13, it indicates that a 5/8 inch spacer must be used in place of the 1/2 inch spacer.

5. Tighten shift tube clamp and remove spacer.
6. Check for proper operation.

MANUAL TRANSAXLE, REPLACE

1981–83 Models W/ 4-135 Engine

1. Disconnect battery ground cable.
2. Raise and support vehicle and install suitable engine support fixture.
3. Disconnect gearshift linkage and clutch cable from transaxle.
4. Remove front wheel and tire assemblies.
5. Remove left front splash shield, then the impact bracket from transaxle if so equipped.
6. Refer to "Driveshafts, Replace" to disconnect driveshafts.
7. Support transaxle and remove upper clutch housing bolts.
8. Remove left engine mount from transaxle noting location of bolts.
9. Remove anti-rotational link, Fig. 14.
10. Remove engine to transaxle toward left side of vehicle until mainshaft clears clutch and lower and remove transaxle.
12. Reverse procedure to install. When installing left engine mount, refer to "Engine mounts" section.

1978–83 Models W/ 4-105 Engine

1. Remove engine timing access hole plug, then rotate engine to align drilled mark on flywheel with pointer on clutch housing on 1978 early production models only.
2. Disconnect battery ground cable.
3. Disconnect shift linkage rods, starter wiring and backup lamp switch wiring.

Fig. 12 Installing spacer. 1978–83 models w/ 4-105 engine

Fig. 13 Revised gearshift blocker bracket. 1978–83 models w/ 4-105 engine

Fig. 14 Removing anti-rotational link

4. Remove starter and disconnect clutch cable.
5. Remove bolt attaching speedometer adapter to transaxle.
6. With speedometer cable housing connected, pull adapter and pinion from transaxle.

7. Raise and support vehicle. Also, support engine with suitable equipment.
8. Disconnect right hand drive shaft and position aside.
9. Remove left hand drive shaft.
10. Remove left splash shield.
11. Drain transaxle fluid.
12. Remove bolts from left engine mount.

13. Remove transaxle to engine attaching nuts and bolts.
14. Slide transaxle toward left side of vehicle until mainshaft clears clutch.
15. Lower and remove transaxle from vehicle.
16. Reverse procedure to install.

Rear Axle, Rear Suspension & Brakes Section

REAR AXLE, REPLACE

1981–83 Aries & Reliant, 1982–83 LeBaron & 400, 1983 E Class & 600

1. Raise and support vehicle, support rear axle, and remove rear wheels.
2. Disconnect parking brake cable at connector and cable housing at floor pan bracket, Fig. 1.
3. Disconnect shock absorbers and track bar at rear axle. Support track bar end.
4. Lower axle until spring and isolator assemblies, Fig. 2, come free and can be removed.
5. Support pivot ends of trailing arms and remove pivot bracket bolts. Lower and remove axle from vehicle.
6. Reverse procedure to install. Torque brake tube assembly to hose fitting to 140 inch lbs. Torque other components as shown in Fig. 2.

Fig. 1 Parking brake cable & brake tube assemblies. 1981–83 Aries & Reliant; 1982–83 LeBaron & 400; 1983 E Class & 600

1978–83 Horizon & Omni & 1983 Charger & Turismo

1. Raise and support vehicle.
2. Remove wheels.

3. Removing brake fitting and retaining clips securing flexible brake line.
4. Remove parking brake cable adjusting connection nut.
5. Release parking brake cables from bracket by slipping ball-end of cables through brake connectors.
6. Pull parking brake cable through bracket.
7. Remove brake drums.
8. Remove brake assembly and spindle retaining bolts.
9. Position spindle aside using a piece of wire.
10. Support axle and suspension with a suitable jack.
11. Remove shock absorber mounting bolts.
12. Remove trailing arm to hanger bracket mounting bolt.
13. Lower rear axle from vehicle.
14. Reverse procedure to install.

SHOCK ABSORBER & COIL SPRING, REPLACE

1981–83 Aries & Reliant; 1982–83 LeBaron & 400; 1983 E Class & 600

Removal
1. Raise and support vehicle.
2. Support axle assembly and remove both lower shock absorber attaching bolts.
3. Lower axle assembly until spring and spring upper isolater can be removed, Fig. 2.

Installation
1. Position jounce bumper to rail, install and torque attaching screws to 70 in. lbs. (7Nm).
2. Install isolator over jounce bumper and install spring.
3. Raise axle and loosely assemble both shock absorber to axle screws. Remove axle support and lower vehicle.
4. With suspension supporting vehicle, torque shock absorber attaching screws to 40 ft. lbs. (54 Nm.).

1978–83 Horizon & Omni; 1983 Charger & Turismo

Replacement
1. Remove upper shock absorber mounting protective cap, located inside vehicle at upper rear wheel well area.

NOTE: On 024, TC3, Charger and Turismo models, it is necessary to remove the lower rear quarter trim panel for access.

2. Remove upper shock absorber mounting nut, isolator retainer and upper isolator, Fig. 3.

TORQUE		
Ⓐ	54 N·m	40 FT. LBS.
Ⓑ	108 N·m	80 FT. LBS.
Ⓒ	61 N·m	45 FT. LBS.
Ⓓ	8 N·m	70 IN. LBS.

Fig. 2 Rear axle & suspension assembly. 1981–83 Aries & Reliant; 1982–83 LeBaron & 400; 1983 E Class & 600

LET	TORQUE	
A	20 FT LBS	27 N·m
B	40 FT LBS	54 N·m
C	45 FT LBS	61 N·m
D	80 FT LBS	108 N·m

Fig. 4   Retracting coil spring

Fig. 3   Rear axle & suspension assembly. 1978–83 Horizon & Omni; 1983 Charger & Turismo

3. Raise and support vehicle.
4. Remove shock absorber lower mounting bolt.
5. Remove shock absorber and coil spring assembly from vehicle.
6. Reverse procedure to install.

Service

1. Install coil spring retractors, tool L-4514, on coil spring and support in a vise, Fig. 4. Grip 4 or 5 coils of the spring in the retractors. Also, do not extend retractors more than 9¼ inches.
2. Tighten retractors evenly until spring pressure is released from upper spring seat.
3. Hold flat end of push rod and loosen retaining nut.

CAUTION: Ensure that spring is properly compressed before loosening retaining nut since personal injury may result.

4. Remove lower isolator, push rod sleeve and upper spring seat.
5. Remove shock absorber from coil spring.
6. Remove jounce bumper and dust shield from push rod, Fig. 5.
7. Remove lower spring seat. Fig. 5.
8. Reverse procedure to assemble.

REAR WHEEL ALIGNMENT

Due to the design of the rear suspension and the incorporation of stub axles or wheel spindles, it is possible to adjust the camber and toe of the rear wheels on these vehicles. Adjustment is controlled by adding shims approximately .010 inch thick between the spindle mounting surface and spindle mounting plate. The amount of adjustment is approximately 0° 18′ per shim. Refer to Figs. 6 through 9 for proper placement of the shims.

REAR WHEEL BEARING, ADJUST

1. Torque adjusting nut to 270 inch lbs. (30 Nm) while rotating wheel.
2. Stop wheel and loosen adjusting nut.
3. Tighten adjusting nut finger tight. End play should be .001–.003 inch.
4. Install castle lock with slots aligned with cotter pin hole.
5. Install cotter pin and grease cap.

Fig. 5   Jounce bumper, dust shield & lower spring seat replacement

SERVICE BRAKES, ADJUST

Since the rear brakes on these vehicles are not self-adjusting, periodic adjustment is required as follows:
1. Raise and support vehicle.
2. Remove adjusting hole covers from brake supports.
3. Release parking brake and back off cable adjustment to slacken cable.
4. Insert a narrow screwdriver into adjusting nut hole. Move screwdriver handle downward on left side or upward on right side until wheels are locked, Fig. 11.

Fig. 6   Shim installation for toe-out

Fig. 7   Shim installation for toe-in

Fig. 8   Shim installation for positive camber

Fig. 9   Shim installation for negative camber

Fig. 10   Wheel bearing assembly

Fig. 11   Adjusting service brakes

5. Back off nut 10 clicks.
6. Adjust parking brake.

PARKING BRAKE, ADJUST

1. Raise and support vehicle.
2. Release parking brake and back off adjustment to slacken cable.
3. Tighten cable adjusting nut until a slight drag is obtained while rotating wheels.
4. Loosen cable adjusting nut until the wheels rotate freely, then an additional two turns.
5. Apply and release parking brake to check for proper operation. The rear wheels should rotate without dragging.

MASTER CYLINDER, REPLACE

Manual Brakes

1. Disconnect and plug brake tubes from master cylinder. Cap master cylinder ports.
2. Disconnect stop lamp switch mounting bracket from beneath instrument panel.
3. Pull brake pedal rearward to disengage push rod from master cylinder.

NOTE: Pulling the brake pedal rearward will destroy the grommet. Install a new grommet when installing the push rod.

4. Remove master cylinder attaching nuts.
5. Remove master cylinder from vehicle.
6. Reverse procedure to install.

Power Brakes

1. Disconnect and plug brake tubes from master cylinder. Cap master cylinder ports.
2. Remove master cylinder attaching nuts.
3. Remove master cylinder from power brake unit.
4. Reverse procedure to install.

POWER BRAKE UNIT, REPLACE

1. Remove master cylinder attaching nuts, slide master cylinder from mounting studs and support on fender shield. Do not disconnect brake tubes from master cylinder.
2. Disconnect vacuum hose from power brake unit.
3. From beneath instrument panel, install a suitable screwdriver between the center tang on retainer clip and the brake pedal pin. Rotate the screwdriver so the retainer center tang will pass over brake pedal pin. Pull retainer clip from pin.
4. Remove power brake unit attaching nuts and the power brake unit from vehicle.
5. Reverse procedure to install.

Front Suspension & Steering Section

DESCRIPTION

These vehicles use a MacPherson type front suspension with the vertical shock absorber struts attached to the upper fender reinforcement and the steering knuckle, Fig. 1. The lower control arms are attached inboard to a crossmember and outboard to the steering knuckle through a ball joint to provide lower steering knuckle position. During steering maneuvers, the strut and steering knuckle rotate as an assembly.

The drive shafts are attached inboard to the transaxle output drive flanges and outboard to the driven wheel hub.

WHEEL ALIGNMENT

Caster

The caster angle on these vehicles cannot be adjusted.

Camber

To adjust camber, loosen the cam and through bolts, Fig. 2. Rotate the upper cam bolt to move the top of the wheel in or out to achieve the specified camber angle. Torque cam bolts to 45 ft. lbs., then advance bolts an additional 1/4 turn (90 degrees).

Toe-In

To adjust toe-in, center the steering wheel and hold in position with a suitable tool. Loosen the tie rod lock nuts and rotate the rod, Fig. 3, to adjust toe-in to specifications. Use care not to twist the steering gear rubber boots. Torque the tie rod lock nuts to 55 ft. lbs. (75 Nm). Adjust position of steering gear rubber boots. Remove steering wheel holding tool.

STRUT DAMPER ASSEMBLY, REPLACE

Removal

1. Raise and support vehicle, then remove front wheels.
2. Mark position of camber adjusting cam, then remove the camber adjusting bolt and through bolt and the brake hose to damper bracket retaining screw, Fig. 4.
3. Remove strut damper to fender shield mounting nut and washer assemblies.
4. Remove strut damper from vehicle.

Installation

1. Position strut assembly into fender reinforcement, then install retaining nuts and washers and torque to 20 ft. lbs.
2. Position steering knuckle and washer plate to strut, then install upper cam and lower through bolts.
3. Install brake hose retainer on damper, then index cam bolt to alignment mark made during removal.
4. Position a 4 inch or larger C-clamp on steering knuckle and strut, Fig. 4A, then tighten clamp just enough to eliminate any looseness between strut and knuckle. Check alignment of marks made during removal, then tighten bolts to 45 ft. lbs. plus an additional 1/4 turn beyond the specified torque.
5. Remove C-clamp, then install wheel and tire assembly.

STRUT
DAMPER

DRIVE SHAFTS

LOWER CONTROL ARM

STEERING KNUCKLE

Fig. 1   Front suspension

LOOSEN BOLTS

ADJUST CAMBER

TIGHTEN
BOLTS TO
115 N•m
(85 FOOT
POUNDS)

Fig. 2   Camber adjustment

COIL SPRING, REPLACE

1. Remove strut damper assembly as outlined previously.
2. Using a suitable tool, compress coil spring.
3. Remove strut rod nut while holding strut rod to prevent rotation.
4. Remove the mount assembly, Fig. 5.
5. Remove coil spring from strut damper.
6. Inspect mount assembly for deterioration of rubber isolator, retainers for cracks and distortion and bearings for binding.
7. Install the bumper dust shield assembly.
8. Install spring and seat, upper spring retainer, bearing and spacer, mount assembly and the rebound bumper, retainer and rod nut upper.

NOTE: Position the spring retainer alignment notch parallel to the damper lower attaching brackets.

9. Torque strut rod nut to 60 ft. lbs. (81 Nm). Do not release spring compressor before torquing nut.
10. Remove spring compressor.

BALL JOINTS

The lower control arm ball joints operate with no free play. On early 1978 models, the ball joints are riveted to the lower control arm. On these models the ball joint and lower control arm are replaced as an assembly. On late 1978 and 1979–80 models, the ball joints are bolted to the lower control arm. On these models, the ball joint can be replaced without replacing the entire lower control arm. When installing ball joint to lower control arm, tighten attaching bolt to 60 ft. lbs. On

1981–83 models, the ball joint is pressed into the lower control arm. On these models, the ball joint can be pressed from the lower control arm using a 1 1/16 inch deep socket and tool No. C-4699-2. When pressing ball joint into lower control arm, use tool Nos. C-4699-1 and C-4699-2. Install ball joint seal using a 1 1/2 socket and tool No. C-4699-2.

NOTE: On some models the ball joint is welded to the lower control arm. On these models the ball joint and lower control arm must be replaced as an assembly.

Checking Ball Joints

1981–83
With weight of vehicle resting on wheel and tire assembly, attempt to move grease fitting with fingers, Fig. 6. Do not use a tool or added force to attempt to move grease fitting. If grease fitting moves freely, then ball joint is worn and should be replaced.

1978–80
1. Raise and support vehicle.
2. With suspension in full rebound position, attach a dial indicator to lower control arm with the plunger resting against steering knuckle leg, Fig. 6A.
3. Place a pry bar on top of the ball joint housing to lower control arm bolt with tip of bar under the steering knuckle leg.
4. With the pry bar, raise and lower the steering knuckle to measure the axial travel.
5. If measurement is .050 inch or greater, the ball joint should be replaced.

LOWER CONTROL ARM, REPLACE

Removal

1. Raise and support vehicle.
2. Remove the front inner pivot through bolt, the rear stub strut nut, retainer and bushing and the ball joint to steering knuckle clamp bolt, Fig. 7.
3. Separate the ball joint from the steering knuckle by prying between the ball stud retainer and the lower control arm.

NOTE: Pulling the steering knuckle

LOOSEN NUT TO ADJUST
RE-TIGHTEN TO 75 N•m (55 FOOT POUNDS)

ADJUST TOE

RE-ADJUST
BOOTS

Fig. 3   Toe-in adjustment

Front Wheel Drive—CHRYSLER CORP.

TORQUE 27 N•m (20 FOOT POUNDS)

TORQUE 13 N•m (10 FOOT POUNDS)

CAM BOLT

MARK CAM LOCATION
BEFORE REMOVING BOLTS

ADJUST CAMBER
AND TOE WHEN
REPLACING
SHOCK ABSORBER

WASHER PLATE

TORQUE NUTS TO
61 N•m (45 FT. LBS.)
PLUS ¼ TURN

Fig. 4 Strut damper replacement

CAM
BOLT

MARK

Fig. 4A Strut damper installation

3. Install front pivot bolt and loosely assemble nut, Figs. 7 and 7A.
4. Install stub strut bushing and retainer and loosely assemble nut.
5. Place sway bar bracket stud through control arm and install retainer and nut. Torque nut to 70 ft. lbs. (94 Nm) on 1978–80 vehicles and 22 ft. lbs. (30 Nm) on 1981–83 vehicles.
6. Install ball joint stud into steering knuckle, then the clamp bolt. Torque bolt to 50 ft. lbs. (67 Nm).
7. Lower vehicle and with suspension support vehicle torque front pivot bolt to 105 ft. lbs. (142 Nm) and the stub strut nut to 70 ft. lbs. (94 Nm).

STEERING KNUCKLE, REPLACE

Removal

1. On 1979–83 models, remove cotter pin and nut lock.
2. Loosen hub nut with brakes applied, Figs. 8, 9 and 9A.

NOTE: The nub and driveshaft are splined together through the knuckle (Bearing) and retained by the hub nut.

3. Raise and support vehicle, then remove front wheel.
4. Remove hub nut. Ensure that the splined driveshaft is free to separate from spline in hub during knuckle removal. A pulling force on the shaft can separate the inner C/V joint. Tap lightly with a brass drift, if required.

"Out" from vehicle after releasing from ball joint can separate inner C/V joint.

4. Remove sway bar to control arm nut and reinforcement and rotate control arm over sway bar. Remove rear stub strut bushing, sleeve and retainer.

Installation

1. Install retainer, bushing and sleeve on stub strut.
2. Position control arm over sway bar and install rear stub strut and front pivot into crossmember.

ROD NUT — 81 N•m (60 FOOT POUNDS)
RETAINER (REBOUND STOP)
BUMPER (REBOUND)
MOUNTING TOWER
RETAINER
ISOLATOR — MOUNT ASSEMBLY (STRUT DAMPER)
RETAINER
SPACER
BEARING
RETAINER (SPRING)
SPACER (IF EQUIPPED)
BUMPER
DUST SHIELD

COIL POSITION

Fig. 5 Strut damper assembly

Fig. 6 Checking ball joint for wear. 1981–83

Fig. 6A Checking lower ball joint. 1978-80

5. Disconnect the tie rod end from steering arm with a suitable puller.
6. Disconnect brake hose retainer from strut damper.
7. Remove clamp bolt securing ball joint stud into steering knuckle and brake caliper adapter screw and washer assemblies.
8. Support caliper with a piece of wire. Do not hang by brake hose.
9. Remove rotor.
10. Mark position of camber cam upper adjusting bolt and loosen both bolts.
11. Support steering knuckle and remove cam adjusting and through bolts. Move upper knuckle "Leg" from strut damper bracket and lift knuckle from ball joint stud.

NOTE: Support driveshaft during knuckle removal. Do not permit driveshaft to hang after separating steering knuckle from vehicle.

Installation

1. Place steering knuckle on lower ball joint stud and the driveshaft through hub.
2. Position upper "Leg" of knuckle into strut damper bracket and install cam and through bolts. Place cam in original position. Place a 4 inch or larger C-clamp on strut and steering knuckle, then tighten clamp just enough to eliminate looseness between knuckle and strut. Check to ensure that cam alignment marks made during remove are aligned, then tighten bolts to 45 ft. lbs. plus an additional ¼ turn beyond specified torque and remove C-clamp.
3. Install and torque ball joint to steering knuckle clamp bolt to 50 ft. lbs. (68 Nm).
4. Install tie rod end into steering arm and torque nut to 25 ft. lbs. (33 Nm) on 1978 models and 35 ft. lbs. (47 Nm) on 1979-83 models. Install cotter pin.
5. Install rotor.
6. Install caliper over rotor and position adapter to steering knuckle. Install adapter to knuckle bolts and torque to 85 ft. lbs. (115 Nm).
7. Attach brake hose retainer to strut damper and torque screw to 10 ft. lbs. (13 Nm).
8. On 1978 models:
   a. Install washer and new hub nut after cleaning chips from thread lock groove. Do not reuse hub nuts.
   b. With brakes applied, torque hub nut to 200 ft. lbs. (271 Nm).

Fig. 7 Lower control arm assembly. 1978-80

c. Stake the hub nut as shown in Fig. 10.
9. On 1979-83 models:
   a. Install and hub nut.
   b. With brakes applied, torque hub nut to 180 ft. lbs. (245 Nm).
   c. Install nut lock and new cotter pin, Fig. 9A.

HUB & BEARING, REPLACE

NOTE: If 1978-80 Horizon and Omni models show premature wheel bearing failures, an improperly grounded engine may be the

Fig. 7A Lower control assembly. 1981-83

Fig. 8   Steering knuckle assembly. 1978

CAM BOLT
115 N•m (85 FOOT POUNDS)

STRUT DAMPER
(REFERENCE)

ADAPTOR SCREW AND WASHER
115 N•m (85 FOOT POUNDS)

DRIVE SHAFT

BRAKE CALIPER

BEARING

STEERING LINKAGE
33 N•m (25 FOOT POUNDS)

SHIELD

SCREW
26 N•m
(20 FOOT POUNDS)

RETAINER

CLAMP BOLT
67 N•m (50 FOOT POUNDS)

HUB
WASHER

LOWER CONTROL ARM
(REFERENCE)

KNUCKLE

HUB NUT
271 N•m (200 FOOT POUNDS)
AND STAKE

Fig. 9   Steering knuckle assembly. 1979–81

CAM BOLT
122 N•m (90 FOOT POUNDS)

STRUT DAMPER
(REFERENCE)

ADAPTOR SCREW AND WASHER
115 N•m (85 FOOT POUNDS)

DRIVE SHAFT

BRAKE CALIPER

BEARING

SCREW
26 N•m
(20 FOOT POUNDS)

SHIELD

STEERING LINKAGE
47 N•m (35 FOOT POUNDS)

HUB

RETAINER

WASHER

CLAMP BOLT
67 N•m (50 FOOT POUNDS)

COTTER
PIN

LOWER CONTROL ARM
(REFERENCE)

KNUCKLE

NUT LOCK

WHEEL BOLT

HUB NUT
245 N•m (180 FOOT POUNDS)

Fig. 9A   Steering knuckle assembly. 1982–83

CAM BOLT NUT
61 N•m (45 FOOT POUNDS) PLUS ¼ TURN

STRUT DAMPER
(REFERENCE)

ADAPTOR SCREW AND WASHER
115 N•m (85 FOOT POUNDS)

WEAR SLEEVE

SEAL

BRAKE CALIPER

DRIVE SHAFT

WASHER
PLATE

SCREW
26 N•m
(20 FOOT POUNDS)

BEARING

STEERING LINKAGE
47 N•m (35 FOOT POUNDS)

HUB

RETAINER

WASHER

CLAMP BOLT
67 N•m (50 FOOT POUNDS)

COTTER
PIN

GASKET

KNUCKLE

NUT LOCK

WHEEL BOLT

LOWER CONTROL ARM
(REFERENCE)

HUB NUT
245 N•m (180 FOOT POUNDS)

cause. When this problem is encountered, a high pitch whining noise will be emitted from the bearing and the bearing outer race and bearing balls will appear black due to arcing across the race. Also a wear pattern will be indicated on the outer surface of the bearing race. Check for the following proper ground conditions: battery ground cable to transmission mounting bolt, battery ground cable to body ground, braided strap from right hand motor mount to frame side rail and braided strap from right rear of engine to firewall. If all ground cables and straps are properly installed, check for a broken or separated battery ground cable or body ground cable and replace as necessary. After correcting the improper engine ground condition, replace wheel bearing and race.

Removal

1. Remove steering knuckle as outlined previously.
2. Remove hub with a suitable puller or tool L-4539, Fig. 11.

NOTE: The bearing inner races will separate and the outer race will remain in the hub.

3. Remove bearing outer race from hub with a suitable puller, Fig. 12.
4. Remove brake dust shield and bearing retainer.
5. Remove bearing from knuckle with a suitable press and socket, Fig. 13.

Installation

1. Press new bearing into knuckle with a suitable press and installer tool, Fig. 14.
2. Install brake dust shield and bearing retainer. Torque retaining screws to 20 ft. lbs. (27 Nm).
3. Press hub into bearing with a suitable press and socket, Fig. 15.
4. Install steering knuckle as outlined previously.

SERVICE NOTE

A new front wheel bearing seal is available for 1978–80 Omni and Horizon that replaces the original slinger assembly. The new seal assembly should be installed in place of the original slinger any time a bearing or outer CV joint is serviced. The sealing surface must be thoroughly cleaned. The seal and knuckle contact surfaces must be packed with Mopar Multi Mileage Grease or equivalent.

SWAY BAR, REPLACE

Removal, Figs. 15A & 15B

1. Raise and support front of vehicle.
2. On 1978–81 models, remove end bushing to control arm nut and reinforcement plate. On 1982–83 models, remove nuts, bolts and retainer at control arm.
3. On 1978–81 models, remove sway bar to crossmember linkage (nut, retainer and insulators at top of crossmember). Bushing are permanently installed on sway bars. On 1982–83 models, remove bolts at crossmember clamps, then remove clamps.
4. Remove sway bar.

Fig. 11 Hub removal

Fig. 10   Staking hub nut. 1978

Fig. 12   Removing outboard inner race

NOTE: On 1978–81 models it may be necessary to disassemble the intermediate linkage.

Installation

NOTE: The 1982–83 front wheel drive vehicles have a linkless sway bar in the front suspension. The new sway bar is nearly symmetric looking and it is possible to install the sway bar improperly in the vehicle when it is removed for service. Always mark the sway bar prior to removal to assure proper installation. Sway bars used for production and service replacement are marked on the left (driver side) by a daub or stripe of paint.

1. On 1978–1981 models, loosely assemble intermediate links and straps to sway bar, and sleeve, retainer and isolators to links. On 1982–83 models, position crossmember bushings on bar with curved surface up and split to front of vehicle. Set upper clamps onto crossmember bushings, lift bar assembly into crossmember and install lower clamps and bolts.

2. On 1978–81 models, position link ends through crossmember and install upper isolators, retainers and nut. On 1982–83 models, position retainers at control arms, then insert bolts and install nuts.
3. With lower control arms raised to design height, tighten bolts, Figs. 15A and 15B.

DRIVESHAFTS, REPLACE

1978–82 Models W/ 4-105 Engine & Manual Transaxle

Removal
1. Remove hub nut as outlined under "Steering Knuckle, Replace" procedure.
2. Remove clamp bolt securing ball joint stud into steering knuckle.
3. Separate ball joint stud from steering knuckle.

4. Separate outer C/V joint splined shaft from hub while moving knuckle/hub assembly away from C/V joint, Fig. 16 and 16A.

NOTE: The separated outer joint and shaft must be supported during inner joint separation from transaxle drive flange. Secure assembly to control arm during next step. Also, the grease slonger must not be bent or damaged during service procedures. Do not attempt to remove, repair or replace.

5. Using a suitable tool or tool L-4550, remove six 8mm allen head screws at-

Fig. 13   Removing bearing from knuckle

Fig. 14   Installing bearing into knuckle

Fig. 15   Installing hub into knuckle

Fig. 15A Sway bar assembly. 1978–81

Fig. 15B Sway bar assembly. 1982–83

taching inner C/V joint to transaxle drive flange. Clean foreign material from C/V joint and drive flange.

NOTE: On 1979–83 models, remove plastic caps installed over allen head screws.

6. Release outer assembly from control arm.
7. To remove driveshaft assembly, hold both inner and outer housings parallel and rotate outer assembly downward and the inner assembly upward at drive flange.
8. Remove driveshaft from vehicle.

Installation
1. If lubricant was lost during handling, fill

C/V joint housing with lubricant, P/N 4131389 or equivalent.
2. Clean grease from joint housing, face, screw holes and transaxle drive flange prior to installation.
3. Support assembly vertically with inner housing upward.

NOTE: Do not move inner joint in or out during reassembly to drive flange since this movement can force the lubricant from the joint.

4. Position inner housing to drive flange and rotate assembly upward. Locate inner housing in drive flange. Support the outer end of driveshaft, Fig. 13. Do not permit assembly to hang.

5. Secure inner C/V joint to drive flange with new allen head screws. Then, using tool L-4550 or equivalent, torque the six screws to 440 inch lbs. (50 Nm). On 1979–83 models, install plastic caps over allen head screws.

NOTE: Failure to properly torque screws may result in failure during vehicle operation.

6. Push knuckle/hub assembly out and install splined outer C/V joint shaft into hub.
7. Install knuckle assembly on ball joint stud. Install and torque clamp bolt to 50 ft. lbs. (68 Nm).
8. On 1978 models, install and torque hub nut to 200 ft. lbs. (271 Nm). Stake hub nut as shown in Fig. 8.
9. On 1979–82 models, install washer and hub nut. Torque nut to 180 ft. lbs. (245 Nm). Install nut lock and cotter pin.
10. If, after attaching driveshaft assembly in the vehicle the inboard boot appears collapsed or deformed, vent the inner boot by inserting a round tipped, small diameter rod between the boot and shaft. As venting occurs, the boot will return to the normal shape.

NOTE: After installation of driveshaft, check the driveshaft length as outlined in "Driveshaft Length, Adjust."

Except 1978–83 Models W/ 4–105 Engine & Manual Transaxle

Removal

NOTE: On 1978–81 and early 1982 models, the inboard C/V joints have stub shafts splined into the differential side gears and are retained with circlips, Figs. 16 and 16A. The circlip "Tangs" are located on a machined surface on the inner end of the stub shafts and are removed and installed with the shaft. On late 1982 & 1983 models, the driveshafts are spring loaded and are retained to the side gears by constant spring pressure provided by the spring contained in the C/V joints, Fig. 16B.

1. On 1978–81 and early 1982 models, drain transaxle differential unit and remove cover.
2. If removing the right hand driveshaft, the speedometer pinion must be removed prior to driveshaft removal, Fig. 17.
3. On 1978–81 and early 1982 models, rotate driveshaft to expose circlip tangs, Fig. 18. Using needle nose pliers, compress circlip tangs while prying shaft into side gear splined cavity, Fig. 19. The circlip will be compressed in the cavity with the shaft.
4. Remove clamp bolt securing ball joint clamp bolt to steering knuckle. Then, separate ball joint stud from steering knuckle. Do not damage ball joint or C/V joint boots.
5. Separate outer C/V joint splined shaft from hub by holding C/V housing while moving knuckle/hub assembly away from C/V joint.

NOTE: Do not damage slinger on outer C/V joint. Do not attempt to remove, repair or replace.

Fig. 16 Driveshaft assemblies. 1978—80

Fig. 16B Drive shaft assembly.
Late 1982 & 1983 except models w/ 4-105
engine & manual transaxle

Fig. 16A Driveshaft assemblies. 1981 & early 1982

Fig. 17 Speed pinion replacement.
Except 1978—83 models w/4-105 engine &
manual transaxle

6. Support assembly at C/V joint housings and remove by pulling outward on the inner C/V joint housing. Do not pull on the shaft.

NOTE: If removing left hand driveshaft assembly, the removal may be aided by inserting a screwdriver blade between the differential pinion shaft and carefully prying against the end face of stub.

7. Remove driveshaft assembly from vehicle.

Installation

NOTE: Install new circlips on inner joint shaft before installation, Fig. 20.

1. On 1978—81 and early 1982 units, ensure tang on circlips are aligned with flattened end of shaft before inserting shaft into transaxle. If not, this can cause jamming or component damage.
2. Hold inner joint assembly at housing while aligning and guiding the inner joint spline into transaxle.
3. While holding the inner joint housing, quickly thrust the shaft into the differential. This will complete the lock-up of the driveshaft to the axle side gear.

NOTE: On 1978—81 and early 1982 models, inspect circlip positioning in side gears to verify lock-up.

4. Push knuckle/hub assembly out and install splined outer C/V joint shaft into hub.

Fig. 18 Circlips exposed. 1978—81 & early 1982 models less 4-105 engine & manual transaxle

Fig. 19 Compressing circlip. 1978–81 & early 1982 models less 4-105 engine & manual transaxle

5. Install knuckle assembly on ball joint stud.
6. Install and torque clamp bolt to 50 ft. lbs. (68 Nm).
7. Install speedometer pinion, Fig. 17.
8. On 1978–81 and early 1982 models, apply a 1/16 inch bead of silicone sealant, part number 4026070, to differential cover sealing surface and mating surface of transaxle case after both have been properly cleaned and inspected.
9. On 1978–81 and early 1982 models, install differential cover and torque retaining screws to 250 inch lbs. (28 Nm).
10. Fill differential to bottom of filler plug hole with Dexron automatic transmission fluid.
11. On 1978 models, install and torque hub nut to 200 ft. lbs. (271 Nm). Stake nut as shown in Fig. 10.
12. On 1979–82 models, install washer and hub nut. Torque hub nut to 180 ft. lbs. (245 Nm). Install nut lock and cotter pin.
13. If, after attaching driveshaft assembly in vehicle the inboard boot appears collapsed or deformed, vent the inner boot by inserting a round tipped, small diameter rod between the boot and shaft. As venting occurs, the boot will return to the normal shape.

NOTE: After installation of driveshaft, check the driveshaft length as outlined in "Driveshaft Length, Adjust."

Fig. 20 Circlip installation. 1978–81 & early 1982 models less 4-105 engine & manual transaxle

Fig. 20A Right side driveshaft length

Fig. 20B Measuring clearance between bushing and support bracket

Fig. 21 Driveshaft components. 1981–83

Fig. 21A   Removing 3 ball tripod housing. 1981–83 inner C/V joint

DRIVESHAFT LENGTH, ADJUST

1981–83

If the vertical bolts on both engine mounts have been loosened, or the vehicle has experienced front structural damage, driveshaft length must be checked.

The engine mounts incorporate slotted bolt holes to permit side-to-side positioning of the engine, thereby affecting the length of the driveshaft. To check driveshaft length proceed as follows:

NOTE: Measuring of the right driveshaft (passenger side) will indicate proper positioning of both sides.

1. Position the vehicle so that the weight of the body is on all four wheels.
2. Using a tape measure or other suitable measuring device, measure direct distance from inner edge of outboard boot to inner edge of inboard boot, Fig. 20A.
3. If measurement matches length shown in Fig. 20A, no further action is required. If measurement is not within given range, engine position must be corrected as follows:
   a. Remove load on engine motor mounts by carefully supporting engine and transmission assembly with a floor jack.
   b. Loosen right and left engine mount vertical fasteners and front engine mount bracket to front crossmember bolts.

NOTE: The right and left engine mount rubber bushings should be positioned to provide approximately .06–.14 inch clearance between the bushing and the supporting bracket, Fig. 20B. When bracket movement is required, it will be necessary to obtain proper bushing to bracket clearance as well as proper driveshaft length.

   c. Pry engine right or left as required to achieve proper driveshaft assembly

length. A total of .47 inch is available for driveshaft length adjustment. Insert 3mm thick spacers adjacent to isolator snubber on each side. These spacers must be in place when engine mount fasteners are tightened, Fig. 20B.
   d. Torque right and left engine mount vertical bolts to 250 inch lbs. and torque front engine mount bolts to 40 ft. lbs.

INNER CONSTANT VELOCITY JOINT SERVICE

1981–83

Disassemble, Fig. 21
1. Remove clamp and boot from joint and discard.
2. On Citroen units, separate tripod from housing by slightly deforming retaining ring at three locations, Fig. 21A. If necessary, cut retaining ring from housing and install replacement retaining ring with inner flange rolled, then stake into machined groove with a suitable punch.

NOTE: When removing tripod from housing, secure rollers. After tripod has been removed, secure assembly with tape.

3. On 1981 and early 1982 G.K.N. non-spring loaded units, slide tripod from housing, Fig. 21A. On late 1982–83 G.K.N. spring loaded units, bend tabs on joint cover using needle nose pliers, then remove tripod from housing.
4. Remove snap ring from end of shaft, then remove tripod using brass punch.

Inspection

Remove grease from assembly and inspect bearing race and tripod components for wear and damage and replace as necessary. On late 1982 spring loaded joints inspect spring, spring cup and sperical end of connecting shaft for wear and damage and replace as necessary.

NOTE: Components of spring loaded and non-

spring loaded inner C/V joints cannot be interchanged.

Assemble
1. Slide small end of boot over shaft. On Tubular type shafts, align boot lip with mark on shaft outer diameter. On solid type shafts, position small end of boot in groove on shaft.
2. Place rubber clamp over groove on boot.
3. Install tripod on shaft with non-chamfered face of tripod body facing shaft retainer groove.
4. Lock tripod assembly on shaft by installing retaining ring in shaft groove.
5. Distribute two packets of special grease provided with boot and clamp kit in boot.
6. On 1981–83 models with 4-105 engine and manual transaxle, install joint housing over tripod, then position large end of boot in groove in housing. Add two additional packets of grease after boot has been secured to housing.
7. On 1981 and early 1982 models less 4-105 engine with manual transaxle, distribute one packet of grease in housing before positioning housing over tripod. On Citroen units, reform retainer ring. On all units, secure boot to housing with boot clamp.
8. On late 1982 & 1983 models less 4-105 engine and manual transaxle, distribute one packet of grease in housing, then position spring with spring cup attached to exposed end, into spring pocket. Place a small amount of grease on spring cup, then position housing over tripod. On Citroen units, reform retainer ring. On G.K.N. units, bend retaining tabs. On all units, position boot over boot groove in housing, then install clamp.

NOTE: When installing housing, check to insure that spring remains in pocket and centered in housing. Also ensure that spring cup contacts spherical end of connecting shaft.

1978–80

Disassembly, Figs. 21 & 22A
1. Cut the metal clamps from the boot and discard boot.

Fig. 22 Driveshaft components. 1979—80

2. Remove grease from inside of joint housing and 3-ball and trunion assembly, Fig. 23.
3. Remove retaining rings from shaft-end groove, then the tripod with a brass drift, Fig. 24.

Inspection

Inspect the joint housing ball raceway and tripod components for excessive wear. Replace if necessary.

Assembly, Figs. 22 & 22A

1. To install new boot, slide small rubber clamp onto shaft, then the small end of boot over the shaft.

NOTE: On tubular shafts, position the boot lip face in line with the mark on the shaft outside diameter. On solid shafts, position the small boot end in the machined groove.

---

2. Clamp the small boot end by placing the rubber clamp over the boot groove.

3. Install the tripod on the shaft with the non-chamfered face of the tripod body facing the shaft retainer groove.
4. Install the retaining ring in the groove to lock the tripod assembly on the shaft.
5. Distribute two packets of grease in the boot. The packets of proper lubricant are provided in the boot joint kits.
6. On manual driveshafts, install the joint housing over the tripod and position the large end of boot in the groove on the housing. Two additional packets of grease are to be added after the boot is secured to the housing.
7. On automatic driveshafts, position housing over tripod and position boot over housing groove. One additional packet of grease is to be added after securing boot to housing.
8. On all driveshafts, install large metal clamp on boot, ensuring that the boot is properly located on the shaft and is not twisted.
9. Install the clamp tags in the slots and tighten clamp by hand.
10. Clamp bridge with tool C-4124 and squeeze to complete tightening the clamp.

Do not cut through the clamp bridge and/or damage the boot.

11. On manual driveshafts, distribute two additional packets of grease in the joint housing. First push forward gently on the housing to provide space to accommodate volume of grease required.

OUTER CONSTANT VELOCITY JOINT SERVICE

Disassembly

Figs. 21, 22 22A, 25 & 25A

1. Cut boot clamps from boot and discard boot and clamps.
2. Clean grease from joint.
3. Support shaft in a soft jawed vise, support the outer joint and tap with a mallet to dislodge joint from internal circlip installed in a groove at the outer end of the shaft, Fig. 26. Do not remove slinger from housing.
4. Remove circlip from shaft groove and discard, Fig. 27.
5. Unless the shaft requires replacement, do not remove the heavy lock ring from the shaft, Fig. 27.
6. If the constant velocity joint was operating satisfactorily and the grease does not appear contaminated, proceed to "Assembly" procedure, Step 7.
7. If the constant velocity joint is noisy or badly worn, replace entire unit. The repair kit will include boot, clamps, circlip and lubricant. Clean and inspect the joint outlined in the following steps.
8. Clean surplus grease and mark relative position of inner cross, cage and housing with a dab of paint.
9. Hold joint vertically in a soft jawed vise.
10. Press downward on one side of the inner race to tilt cage and remove ball from opposite side, Fig. 28. If joint is tight, use a hammer and a brass drift to tap inner race. Do not strike the cage. Repeat this step until all six balls are removed. A screwdriver may be used to pry the balls loose.
11. Tilt the cage assembly vertically and position the two opposing, elongated cage windows in area between ball grooves. Remove cage and inner race assembly by pulling upward from the housing, Fig. 29.
12. Rotate inner cross 90 degrees to cage and align one of the race spherical lands with an elongated cage window. Raise land into cage window and remove inner race by swinging outward, Fig. 30.

Inspection

1. Check housing ball races for excessive wear.
2. Check splined shaft and nut threads for damage.
3. Inspect the balls for pitting, cracks, scouring and wear. Dulling of the surface is normal.
4. Inspect cage for excessive wear on inner and outer spherical surfaces, heavy brinelling of cage, window cracks and chipping.
5. Inspect inner race (Cross) for excessive wear or scouring of ball races.
6. If any of the defects listed in Steps 1 through 5, are found, replace the C/V assembly as a unit.

NOTE: Polished areas in races (Cross and

Fig. 23 Removing 3-ball tripod, housing & shaft assembly. 1978–80 inner C/V joints

Fig. 24 Remove snap ring & tripod. Inner C/V joints

Fig. 25 Outer C/V joint disassembled. 1981–83

housing) and on cage spheres are normal and does not indicate a need for joint replacement unless they are suspected of causing noise and vibration.

Assembly

1981–83 Units, Figs. 21 & 25

1. If removed, position wear sleeve on joint housing, then tap sleeve onto housing using tool No. C-4698.
2. Lightly oil components, then align marks made during disassembly.
3. Align one of the inner race lands with elongated window of cage, then insert race into cage and pivot 90°.
4. Align elongated cage windows with housing land, then pivot cage 90°. The curved side of the elongated cage windows and inner race counterbore should face outward from joint.
5. Lubricate ball races with one packet of grease from kit.
6. Tilt cage and inner race assembly and insert balls.
7. With shaft supported in a soft jawed vise, install boot. On G.K.N. units, slip small clamp over spacer ring and shaft.
8. Slide small end of boot over spacer ring and shaft, then position boot end in machined groove.

NOTE: On Citroen units, position vent sleeve under boot at clamp area.

9. Install snap ring on shaft. When installing use care not to overexpand snap ring.

10. Position joint housing on shaft, then engage by tapping sharply with a soft faced mallet.
11. Check to ensure that snap ring is properly seated, by attempting to pull joint from shaft.
12. Locate large end of boot over housing.
13. On G.K.N. units, secure boot clamps using tool No. C-4124. On Citroen units, secure boot clamps using tool C-4653.

NOTE: G.K.N. units use steel clamps, while Citroen units use a strap type clamp.

1978–80 Units, Figs. 22, 22A & 25A

1. Lightly lubricate all components before assembling joint.
2. Align parts according to paint markings.
3. Insert one inner race (Cross) lands into an elongated cage window and feed race into cage. Pivot cross 90 degrees to complete cage assembly.
4. Align opposite elongated cage windows with housing land and insert cage assembly into housing. Pivot cage 90 degrees to complete installation.

NOTE: When properly assembled, the curved side of the elongated cage windows and the inner cross counterbore should face outward from the joint, Fig. 31.

5. Apply lubricant to ball races between all sides of ball grooves.

6. Insert balls into raceway by tilting cage and inner race assembly. Ensure that locking ring is seated in the groove.
7. To install new boot, slide small metal clamp over lock ring and shaft.
8. Slide end of boot over lock ring and shaft, then position in machined groove.
9. Place small metal clamp over boot groove. Locate clamp tags in slots and hand tighten. Clamp bridge with tool C-4124 and squeeze to complete tightening.
10. Insert new circlip in shaft groove. Do not expand or twist circlip during assembly.
11. Position tool L-4538 on shaft splines with the tapered end outboard and compress circlip, Fig. 32. Ensure that sufficient spline area is left ahead of the tool to provide entry of outer joint onto shaft, Fig. 33.
12. Place outer joint on splined end, engage splines and rap with a mallet, allowing tool to slide along with the joint.
13. Remove tool and check that circlip is properly seated by attempting to pull joint from shaft.
14. Place large end of boot over joint housing, ensuring that boot is not twisted.
15. Place large metal clamp over boot and locate clamp tags in slots, hand tightening the clamp.
16. Clamp bridge with tool L-4124 and squeeze to complete tightening. Do not cut through clamp bridge and/or damage boot.

RACK & PINION STEERING GEAR, REPLACE

NOTE: These vehicles are equipped with manual steering gears supplied by two different manufacturers, Burman and Cam Gears. The

Fig. 25A Outer C/V joint disassembled. 1978–80

Fig. 26 Removing joint from shaft. Outer C/V joints

Fig. 27 Circlip removal. Outer C/V joints

Fig. 28 Ball removal. Outer C/V joints

Fig. 29 Cage & cross assembly removal. Outer C/V joints

Fig. 30 Removing cross from cage. Outer C/V joints

replacement rubber boots for these gears are not interchangeable.

The Burman gear can be identified by the name "Burman" cast on the housing and is visible from under the hood.

The Cam Gear steering gear has no identification markings.

1. Raise and support vehicle, then remove front wheels.
2. Remove tie rod ends with a suitable puller.
3. Remove splash shields and boot seal shields.
4. Drive out lower roll pin attaching pinion shaft to lower universal joint.
5. On power steering units, disconnect hoses from steering gear.

6. On all models, remove bolts attaching steering gear to front suspension crossmember. Loosen crossmember from vehicle frame.
7. Remove steering gear from left side of vehicle.
8. Reverse procedure to install.

POWER STEERING PUMP, REPLACE

4-105 & 135 Engines

1. Remove power steering pump drive belt adjusting bolt and nut, then remove nut attaching pump end hose bracket, if equipped.
2. Raise and support vehicle, then remove nut attaching pump pressure hose locating bracket to crossmember.
3. Disconnect pressure hose from steering gear and allow fluid to drain into a suitable container.

4. Remove drive belt splash shield, then disconnect both pressure and return hoses at power steering pump. Cap hoses and fitting to prevent entry of dirt.
5. Remove lower stud nut and pivot bolt from power steering pump, then lower vehicle.
6. Remove drive belt pulley from pump, then move pump rearward to clear mounting bracket and remove adjusting bracket.
7. Rotate pump so that pulley faces rear of vehicle, then lift pump assembly from vehicle.
8. Reverse procedure to install.

4-156 Engine

1. Disconnect pressure and return lines from pump. Cap all lines and fittings.
2. Remove belt adjustment and pivot bolts, then remove drive belt from pulley.
3. Remove power steering pump and mounting bracket as an assembly from vehicle.
4. Reverse procedure to install.

Fig. 31 Cage & cross assembly. Outer C/V joints

Fig. 32 Compressing circlip. Outer C/V joints

Fig. 33 Positioning joint into shaft splined. Outer C/V joints

CHRYSLER CORP.
REAR WHEEL DRIVE

NOTE: This chapter includes service procedures for all models except 1978–83 Dodge Omni & Horizon; 1981–83 Dodge Aries & Plymouth Reliant; 1982–83 Chrysler LeBaron & Dodge 400; 1983 Chrysler E Class, Dodge Charger, 600 & Plymouth Turismo.

INDEX OF SERVICE OPERATIONS

NOTE: Refer to the back of this manual for vehicle manufacturer's special service tool suppliers.

Rear Wheel Drive—CHRYSLER CORP.

VEHICLE NUMBER LOCATION

1977—83: On plate attached to dash pad and visible through windshield.

ENGINE NUMBER LOCATION

1977—83 Six: Right front of block below cylinder head.

1977—83 318, 360: Left front of block below cylinder head.

1977—80 V8-400: Upper right front of cylinder block.

1977—78 V8-440: Top of block left bank next to front tappet rail.

ENGINE IDENTIFICATION CODE

1977—83 engines are identified by the cubic inch displacement found within the engine number stamped on the pad.

CHRYSLER & IMPERIAL GRILLE IDENTIFICATION

1977 New Yorker

1977 Cordoba

1977–78 LeBaron
1978 Town & Country

1978 Cordoba

1978 New Yorker

1979 Cordoba

1979 300 Limited Edition

1979 LeBaron & Town & Country

1979–80 Newport

1979–80 New Yorker

1980 Cordoba

1980 LeBaron

1981 LeBaron

1981–83 Cordoba

1981 Newport

1981 New Yorker

1981–83 Imperial

CHRYSLER & IMPERIAL GRILLE IDENTIFICATION—Continued

1981 "300" & 1982 Cordoba LS

1982-83 New Yorker

DODGE GRILLE IDENTIFICATION

1977 Aspen

1977 Aspen R/T

1977-78 Monaco

1977 Charger Daytona

1977-78 Charger SE

1977-78 Diplomat

1978-79 Aspen

1978-79 Magnum

1979 Diplomat

1980 Aspen

1980-82 Diplomat

1980-83 Mirada

1979-81 St. Regis

PLYMOUTH GRILLE IDENTIFICATION

1977 Volaré & Road Runner

1977–78 Fury

1977 Gran Fury

1978 Volaré & Road Runner

1979 Volaré & Road Runner

1980 Volaré

1980–81 Gran Fury

1982–83 Gran Fury

GENERAL ENGINE SPECIFICATIONS

Year	Engine CID①/Liter	Engine V.I.N. Code②	Carburetor	Bore and Stroke	Com-pression Ratio	Net H.P. @ R.P.M.③	Maximum Torque Ft. Lbs. @ R.P.M.	Normal Oil Pressure Pounds
CHRYSLER & IMPERIAL								
1977	V8-318, 5.2L④	G	BBD, 2 Bbl.⑤	3.91 × 3.31	8.6	135 @ 3600	235 @ 1600	30–80
	V8-318, 5.2L	G	BBD, 2 Bbl.⑤	3.91 × 3.31	8.6	145 @ 4000	245 @ 1600	30–80
	V8-360, 5.9L⑥	K	2245, 2 Bbl.⑦	4.00 × 3.58	8.4	155 @ 3600	275 @ 2000	30–80
	V8-360, 5.9L④	J	TQ, 4 Bbl.⑤	4.00 × 3.58	8.4	170 @ 4000	270 @ 1600	30–80
	V8-400, 6.6L	N	TQ, 4 Bbl.⑤	4.34 × 3.38	8.2	190 @ 3600	305 @ 3200	30–80
	V8-440, 7.2L	T	TQ, 4 Bbl.⑤	4.32 × 3.75	8.2	185 @ 3600	310 @ 2400	30–80
1978	6-225, 3.7L	C	1945, 1 Bbl.⑦	3.40 × 4.12	8.4	100 @ 3600	170 @ 1600	30–70
	6-225, 3.7L	D	BBD, 2 Bbl.⑤	3.40 × 4.12	8.4	110 @ 3600	180 @ 2000	30–70
	V8-318, 5.2L⑨⑲	G	BBD, 2 Bbl.⑤	3.91 × 3.31	8.5	140 @ 4000	245 @ 1600	30–80
	V8-318, 5.2L⑩	G	2280, 2 Bbl.⑦	3.91 × 3.31	8.5	145 @ 4000	245 @ 1600	30–80
	V8-318, 5.2L⑧⑨	H	TQ, 4 Bbl.⑤	3.91 × 3.31	8.5	155 @ 4000	245 @ 1600	30–80
	V8-360, 5.9L⑲	K	2245, 2 Bbl.⑦	4.00 × 3.58	8.4	155 @ 3600	270 @ 2400	30–80
	V8-360, 5.9L⑧	J	TQ, 4 Bbl.⑤	4.00 × 3.58	8.4	170 @ 4000	270 @ 1600	30–80
	V8-400, 6.6L	N	TQ, 4 Bbl.⑤	4.34 × 3.38	8.2	190 @ 3600	305 @ 3200	30–80
	V8-440, 7.2L	T	TQ, 4 Bbl.⑤	4.32 × 3.75	8.2	185 @ 3600	310 @ 2400	30–80
1979	6-225, 3.7L	C	1945, 1 Bbl.⑦	3.40 × 4.12	8.4	100 @ 3600	165 @ 1600	30–70
	6-225, 3.7L	D	BBD, 2 Bbl.⑤	3.40 × 4.12	8.4	110 @ 2000	180 @ 2000	30–70
	V8-318, 5.2L⑥	G	2280, 2 Bbl.⑦	3.91 × 3.31	8.5	135 @ 4000	250 @ 1600	30–80
	V8-318, 5.2L④	H	TQ, 4 Bbl.⑤	3.91 × 3.31	8.5	155 @ 4000	245 @ 1600	30–80
	V8-360, 5.9L⑲	K	2245, 2 Bbl.⑦	4.00 × 3.58	8.4	150 @ 3600	265 @ 2400	30–80
	V8-360, 5.9L⑧	J	TQ, 4 Bbl.⑤	4.00 × 3.58	8.4	170 @ 4000	270 @ 1600	30–80
	V8-360, 5.9L	L	TQ, 4 Bbl.⑤	4.00 × 3.58	8.0	195 @ 4000	280 @ 2400	30–80
1980	6-225, 3.7L	C	1945, 1 Bbl.⑦	3.40 × 4.12	8.4	90 @ 3600	160 @ 1600	30–70
	V8-318, 5.2L	G	BBD, 2 Bbl.⑤	3.91 × 3.31	8.5	120 @ 3600	245 @ 1600	30–80

Continued

GENERAL ENGINE SPECIFICATIONS—Continued

Year	Engine CID①/Liter	V.I.N. Code②	Carburetor	Bore and Stroke	Com-pression Ratio	Net H.P. @ R.P.M.③	Maximum Torque Ft. Lbs. @ R.P.M.	Normal Oil Pressure Pounds
CHRYSLER & IMPERIAL—Continued								
	V8-318, 5.2L	H	TQ, 4 Bbl.⑤	3.91 × 3.31	8.5	155 @ 4000	240 @ 2000	30–80
	V8-360, 5.9L	K	BBD, 2 Bbl.⑤	4.00 × 3.58	8.4	130 @ 3200	—	30–80
	V8-360, 5.9L⑪	L	TQ, 4 Bbl.⑤	4.00 × 3.58	8.0	185 @ 4000	275 @ 2000	30–80
1981	6-225, 3.7L⑥	E	1945, 1 Bbl.⑦	3.40 × 4.12	8.4	85 @ 3600	165 @ 1600	30–70
	6-225, 3.7L④	E	6145, 1 Bbl.⑦	3.40 × 4.12	8.4	85 @ 3600	165 @ 1600	30–70
	V8-318, 5.2L⑥	K	BBD, 2 Bbl.⑤	3.91 × 3.31	8.6	130 @ 4000	230 @ 2000	30–80
	V8-318, 5.2L④	M	TQ, 4 Bbl.⑤	3.91 × 3.31	8.6	165 @ 4000	240 @ 2000	30–80
	V8-318, 5.2L	J	E.F.I.⑱	3.91 × 3.31	8.4	140 @ 4000	240 @ 2000	30–80
1982	6-225, 3.7L⑥	E	1945, 1 Bbl.⑦	3.40 × 4.12	8.4	90 @ 3600	160 @ 1600	30–70
	6-225, 3.7L④	E	6145, 1 Bbl.⑦	3.40 × 4.12	8.4	90 @ 3600	160 @ 1600	30–70
	V8-318, 5.2L⑥	K	BBD, 2 Bbl.⑤	3.91 × 3.31	8.5	130 @ 4000	230 @ 2000	30–80
	V8-318, 5.2L④	M	TQ, 4 Bbl.⑤	3.91 × 3.31	8.5	165 @ 4000	240 @ 2000	30–80
	V8-318, 5.2L	J	E.F.I.⑱	3.91 × 3.31	8.5	140 @ 4000	245 @ 2000	30–80
1983	6-225, 3.7L	E	6145, 1 Bbl.⑦	3.40 × 4.12	8.4	90 @ 3600	165 @ 1600	30–70
	V8-318, 5.2L	K	BBD, 2 Bbl.⑤	3.91 × 3.31	8.5	130 @ 4000	230 @ 1600	30–80
	V8-318, 5.2L	J	E.F.I.⑱	3.91 × 3.31	8.5	140 @ 4000	245 @ 2000	30–80
DODGE								
1977	6-225, 3.7L④	C	1945, 1 Bbl.⑦	3.40 × 4.12	8.4	90 @ 3600	170 @ 1600	30–70
	6-225, 3.7L⑥	C	1945, 1 Bbl.⑦	3.40 × 4.12	8.4	100 @ 3600	170 @ 1600	30–70
	6-225, 3.7L	D	BBD 2 Bbl.⑤	3.40 × 4.12	8.4	110 @ 3600	180 @ 2000	30–70
	V8-318, 5.2L④	G	BBD, 2 Bbl.⑤	3.91 × 3.31	8.6	135 @ 3600	235 @ 1600	30–80
	V8-318, 5.2L	G	BBD, 2 Bbl.⑤	3.91 × 3.31	8.6	145 @ 4000	245 @ 1600	30–80
	V8-360, 5.9L⑥	K	2245, 2 Bbl.⑦	4.00 × 3.58	8.4	155 @ 3600	275 @ 2000	30–80
	V8-360, 5.9L④	J	TQ, 4 Bbl.⑤	4.00 × 3.58	8.4	170 @ 4000	270 @ 1600	30–80
	V8-360, 5.9L⑫	L	TQ, 4 Bbl.⑤	4.00 × 3.58	8.0	175 @ 4000	275 @ 2000	30–80
	V8-400, 6.6L	N	TQ, 4 Bbl.⑤	4.34 × 3.38	8.2	190 @ 3600	305 @ 3200	30–80
	V8-440, 7.2L⑧	T	TQ, 4 Bbl.⑤	4.32 × 3.75	8.2	185 @ 3600	310 @ 2400	30–80
	V8-440, 7.2L⑲	T	TQ, 4 Bbl.⑤	4.32 × 3.75	8.2	195 @ 3600	320 @ 2000	30–80
	V8-440, 7.2L④⑫	U	TQ, 4 Bbl.⑤	4.32 × 3.75	7.8	230 @ 4000	330 @ 3200	30–80
	V8-440, 7.2L⑥⑫	U	TQ, 4 Bbl.⑤	4.32 × 3.75	7.8	245 @ 4000	350 @ 3200	30–80
1978	6-225, 3.7L⑬	C	1945, 1 Bbl.⑦	3.40 × 4.12	8.4	90 @ 3600	160 @ 1600	30–70
	6-225, 3.7L⑥	C	1945, 1 Bbl.⑦	3.40 × 4.12	8.4	100 @ 3600	170 @ 1600	30–70
	6-225, 3.7	D	BBD, 2 Bbl.⑤	3.40 × 4.12	8.4	110 @ 3600	180 @ 2000	30–70
	V8-318, 5.2L	G	BBD, 2 Bbl.⑤	3.91 × 3.31	8.5	140 @ 4000	245 @ 1600	Normal–80
	V8-318, 5.2L④	H	TQ, 4 Bbl.⑤	3.91 × 3.31	8.5	155 @ 4000	245 @ 1600	30–80
	V8-360, 5.9L	K	2245, 2 Bbl.⑦	4.00 × 3.58	8.4	155 @ 3600	270 @ 2400	30–80
	V8-360, 5.9L⑧⑮	J	TQ, 4 Bbl.⑤	4.00 × 3.58	8.0	160 @ 3600	265 @ 1600	30–80
	V8-360, 5.9L⑧⑭	L	TQ, 4 Bbl.⑤	4.00 × 3.58	8.4	170 @ 4000	270 @ 1600	30–80
	V8-360, 5.9L⑮⑲	L	TQ, 4 Bbl.⑤	4.00 × 3.58	8.0	175 @ 4000	260 @ 2400	30–80
	V8-400, 6.6L	N	TQ, 4 Bbl.⑤	4.34 × 3.38	8.2	190 @ 3600	305 @ 3200	30–80
1979	6-225, 3.7L④	C	1945, 1 Bbl.⑦	3.40 × 4.12	8.4	90 @ 3600	170 @ 1600	30–70
	6-225, 3.7L⑥	C	1945, 1 Bbl.⑦	3.40 × 4.12	8.4	100 @ 3600	160 @ 1600	30–70
	6-225, 3.7L⑥	D	BBD, 2 Bbl.⑤	3.40 × 4.12	8.4	110 @ 3600	180 @ 2000	30–70
	V8-318, 5.2L⑥	G	2280, 2 Bbl.⑦	3.91 × 3.31	8.5	135 @ 4000	250 @ 1600	30–80
	V8-318, 5.2L④	H	TQ, 4 Bbl.⑤	3.91 × 3.31	8.5	155 @ 4000	245 @ 1600	30–80
	V8-360, 5.9L⑥	K	2245, 2 Bbl.⑦	4.00 × 3.58	8.4	150 @ 3600	265 @ 2400	30–80
	V8-360, 5.9L④	J	TQ, 4 Bbl.⑤	4.00 × 3.58	8.4	170 @ 4000	270 @ 1600	30–80
	V8-360, 5.9L④	L	TQ, 4 Bbl.⑤	4.00 × 3.58	8.0	190 @ 3600	275 @ 1600	30–80
	V8-360, 5.9L⑥	L	TQ, 4 Bbl.⑤	4.00 × 3.58	8.0	195 @ 4000	280 @ 2400	30–80

Continued

GENERAL ENGINE SPECIFICATIONS—Continued

Year	Engine CID①/Liter	V.I.N. Code②	Carburetor	Bore and Stroke	Compression Ratio	Net H.P. @ R.P.M.③	Maximum Torque Ft. Lbs. @ R.P.M.	Normal Oil Pressure Pounds
DODGE—Continued								
1980	6-225, 3.7L	C	1945, 1 Bbl.⑦	3.40 × 4.12	8.4	90 @ 3600	160 @ 1600	30–70
	V8-318, 5.2L	G	BBD, 2 Bbl.⑤	3.91 × 3.31	8.5	120 @ 3600	245 @ 1600	30–80
	V8-318, 5.2L	H	TQ, 4 Bbl.⑤	3.91 × 3.31	8.5	155 @ 4000	240 @ 2000	30–80
	V8-360, 5.9L	K	BBD, 2 Bbl.⑤	4.00 × 3.58	8.4	130 @ 3200	—	30–80
	V8-360, 5.9L	L	TQ, 4 Bbl.⑤	4.00 × 3.58	8.4	185 @ 4000	275 @ 2000	30–80
	V8-360, 5.9L⑪	L	TQ, 4 Bbl.⑤	4.00 × 3.58	8.0	185 @ 4000	275 @ 2000	30–80
1981	6-225, 3.7L⑥	E	1945, 1 Bbl.⑦	3.40 × 4.12	8.4	85 @ 3600	83 @ 2400	35–65
	6-225, 3.7L④	E	6145, 1 Bbl.⑦	3.40 × 4.12	8.4	85 @ 3600	165 @ 1600	30–70
	V8-318, 5.2L⑥	K	BBD, 2 Bbl.⑤	3.91 × 3.31	8.6	130 @ 4000	230 @ 2000	35–65
	V8-318, 5.2L	M	TQ, 4 Bbl.⑤	3.91 × 3.31	8.6	165 @ 4000	240 @ 2000	35–65
1982	6-225, 3.7L⑥	E	1945, 1 Bbl.⑦	3.40 × 4.12	8.4	90 @ 3600	160 @ 1600	30–70
	6-225, 3.7L④	E	6145, 1 Bbl.⑦	3.40 × 4.12	8.4	90 @ 3600	160 @ 1600	30–70
	V8-318, 5.2L⑥	K	BBD, 2 Bbl.⑤	3.91 × 3.31	8.5	130 @ 4000	230 @ 2000	30–80
	V8-318, 5.2L④	M	TQ, 4 Bbl.⑤	3.91 × 3.31	8.5	165 @ 4000	240 @ 2000	30–80
1983	6-225, 3.7L	E	6145, 1 Bbl.⑦	3.40 × 4.12	8.4	90 @ 3600	165 @ 1600	30–70
	V8-318, 5.2L	K	BBD, 2 Bbl.⑤	3.91 × 3.31	8.5	130 @ 4000	230 @ 1600	30–70
PLYMOUTH								
1977	6-225, 3.7L④	C	1945, 1 Bbl.⑦	3.40 × 4.12	8.4	90 @ 3600	170 @ 1600	30–70
	6-225, 3.7L⑥	C	1945, 1 Bbl.⑦	3.40 × 4.12	8.4	100 @ 3600	170 @ 1600	30–70
	6-225, 3.7L	D	BBD, 2 Bbl.⑤	3.40 × 4.12	8.4	110 @ 3600	180 @ 2000	30–70
	V8-318, 5.2L④	G	2245, 2 Bbl.⑦	3.91 × 3.31	8.6	135 @ 3600	235 @ 1600	30–80
	V8-318, 5.2L⑥	G	2245, 2 Bbl.⑦	3.91 × 3.31	8.6	145 @ 4000	245 @ 1600	30–80
	V8-360, 5.9L	K	2245, 2 Bbl.⑦	4.00 × 3.58	8.4	155 @ 3600	275 @ 2000	30–80
	V8-360, 5.9L	J	TQ, 4 Bbl.⑤	4.00 × 3.58	8.4	170 @ 4000	270 @ 1600	30–80
	V8-360, 5.9L⑫	L	TQ, 4 Bbl.⑤	4.00 × 3.58	8.0	175 @ 4000	275 @ 2000	30–80
	V8-400, 6.6L	N	TQ, 4 Bbl.⑤	4.34 × 3.38	8.2	190 @ 3600	305 @ 3200	30–80
	V8-440, 7.2L⑧	T	TQ, 4 Bbl.⑤	4.32 × 3.75	8.2	185 @ 3600	310 @ 2400	30–80
	V8-440, 7.2L⑲	T	TQ, 4 Bbl.⑤	4.32 × 3.75	8.2	195 @ 3600	320 @ 2000	30–80
	V8-440, 7.2L④⑫	U	TQ, 4 Bbl.⑤	4.32 × 3.75	7.8	230 @ 4000	330 @ 3200	30–80
	V8-440, 7.2L⑥⑫	U	TQ, 4 Bbl.⑤	4.32 × 3.75	7.8	245 @ 4000	350 @ 3200	30–80
1978	6-225, 3.7L⑬	C	1945, 1 Bbl.⑦	3.40 × 4.12	8.4	90 @ 3600	160 @ 1600	30–70
	6-225, 3.7L	C	1945, 1 Bbl.⑦	3.40 × 4.12	8.4	100 @ 3600	170 @ 1600	30–70
	6-225, 3.7L	D	BBD, 2 Bbl.⑤	3.40 × 4.12	8.4	110 @ 3600	180 @ 2000	30–70
	V8-318, 5.2L⑥⑯	G	BBD, 2 Bbl.⑤	3.91 × 3.31	8.5	140 @ 4000	245 @ 1600	30–80
	V8-318, 5.2L⑥⑰	G	BBD, 2 Bbl.⑤	3.91 × 3.31	8.5	145 @ 4000	245 @ 1600	30–80
	V8-318, 5.2L⑧	H	TQ, 4 Bbl.⑤	3.91 × 3.31	8.5	155 @ 4000	245 @ 1600	30–80
	V8-360, 5.9L	K	2245, 2 Bbl.⑦	4.00 × 3.58	8.4	155 @ 3600	270 @ 2400	30–80
	V8-360, 5.9L	L	TQ, 4 Bbl.⑤	4.00 × 3.58	8.4	175 @ 4000	260 @ 2400	30–80
	V8-400, 6.0L	N	TQ, 4 Bbl.⑤	4.34 × 3.38	8.2	190 @ 3600	305 @ 3200	30–80
1979	6-225, 3.7L	C	1945, 1 Bbl.⑦	3.40 × 4.12	8.4	100 @ 3600	165 @ 1600	30–70
	6-225, 3.7L⑥	C	BBD, 2 Bbl.⑤	3.40 × 4.12	8.4	110 @ 3600	180 @ 2000	30–70
	V8-318, 5.2L⑥	G	2280, 2 Bbl.⑦	3.91 × 3.31	8.5	135 @ 4000	250 @ 1600	30–80
	V8-318, 5.2L④	H	TQ, 4 Bbl.⑤	3.91 × 3.31	8.5	155 @ 4000	245 @ 1600	30–80
	V8-360, 5.9L	J	TQ, 4 Bbl.⑤	4.00 × 3.58	8.0	195 @ 4000	280 @ 2400	30–80
1980	6-225, 3.7L	C	1945, 1 Bbl.⑦	3.40 × 4.12	8.4	90 @ 3600	160 @ 1600	30–70
	V8-318, 5.2L	G	BBD, 2 Bbl.⑤	3.91 × 3.31	8.5	120 @ 3600	245 @ 1600	30–80
	V8-318, 5.2L	H	TQ, 4 Bbl.⑤	3.91 × 3.31	8.5	155 @ 4000	240 @ 2000	30–80
	V8-360, 5.9L	K	BBD, 2 Bbl.⑤	4.00 × 3.58	8.4	130 @ 3200	—	30–80
	V8-360, 5.9L	L	TQ, 4 Bbl.⑤	4.00 × 3.58	8.4	185 @ 4000	275 @ 2000	30–80
1981	6-225, 3.7L⑥	E	1945, 1 Bbl.⑦	3.40 × 4.12	8.4	85 @ 3600	165 @ 1600	30–70
	6-225, 3.7L④	E	6145, 1 Bbl.⑦	3.40 × 4.12	8.4	85 @ 3600	165 @ 1600	30–70
	V8-318, 5.2L⑥	K	BBD, 2 Bbl.⑤	3.91 × 3.31	8.6	130 @ 4000	230 @ 2000	35–65
	V8-318, 5.2L	M	TQ, 4 Bbl.⑤	3.91 × 3.31	8.6	165 @ 4000	240 @ 2000	35–65

Continued

GENERAL ENGINE SPECIFICATIONS—Continued

Year	Engine CID①/Liter	V.I.N. Code②	Carburetor	Bore and Stroke	Compression Ratio	Net H.P. @ R.P.M.③	Maximum Torque Ft. Lbs. @ R.P.M.	Normal Oil Pressure Pounds
PLYMOUTH—Continued								
1982	6-225, 3.7L⑥	E	1945, 1 Bbl.⑦	3.40 × 4.12	8.4	90 @ 3600	160 @ 1600	30–70
	6-225, 3.7L④	E	6145, 1 Bbl.⑦	3.40 × 4.12	8.4	90 @ 3600	160 @ 1600	30–70
	V8-318, 5.2L⑥	K	BBD, 2 Bbl.⑤	3.91 × 3.31	8.5	130 @ 4000	230 @ 2000	30–80
	V8-318, 5.2L④	M	TQ, 4 Bbl.⑤	3.91 × 3.31	8.5	165 @ 4000	240 @ 2000	30–80
1983	6-225, 3.7L	E	6145, 1 Bbl.⑦	3.40 × 4.12	8.4	90 @ 3600	165 @ 1600	30–70
	V8-318, 5.2L	K	BBD, 2 Bbl.⑤	3.91 × 3.31	8.5	130 @ 4000	230 @ 1600	30–80

①—CID—Cubic Inch Displacement.
②—On 1977–80 vehicles, the fifth digit in the VIN denotes engine code. On 1981–83 vehicles, the eighth digit in the VIN denotes the engine code.
③—Ratings are net—as installed in vehicle.
④—California.
⑤—Carter.
⑥—Exc. California.
⑦—Holley.
⑧—California & high altitude.
⑨—LeBaron.
⑩—Cordoba.
⑪—With dual exhaust.
⑫—High performance.
⑬—High altitude.
⑭—Exc. Aspen Coupe & Sedan.
⑮—Aspen Coupe & Sedan.
⑯—Fury.
⑰—Volare.
⑱—Electronic Fuel Injection.
⑲—Except Calif. & high altitude.

TUNE UP SPECIFICATIONS

The following specifications are published from the latest information available. This data should be used only in the absence of a decal affixed in the engine compartment.

★ When using a timing light, disconnect vacuum hose or tube at distributor and plug opening in hose or tube so idle speed will not be affected.

● When checking compression, lowest cylinder must be within 80 percent of highest.

▲ Before removing wires from distributor cap, determine location of the No. 1 wire in cap, as distributor position may have been altered from that shown at the end of this chart.

☞ Spark plug types shown in this chart are recommendations of the original vehicle manufacturer and not MOTOR.

Check local sources for other spark plug manufacturers listings.

Year & Engine/V.I.N.	Spark Plug Type ☞	Gap	Firing Order Fig. ▲	Ignition Timing BTDC① ★ Man. Trans.	Auto. Trans.	Mark Fig.	Curb Idle Speed Man. Trans.	Auto. Trans.②	Fast Idle Speed Man. Trans.	Auto. Trans.	Fuel Pump Pressure
CHRYSLER & IMPERIAL											
1977											
V8-318/G Exc. Calif. & High Alt.⑬	RN12Y④	.035	H	—	8°	B	—	700N	—	1400⑦	5–7
V8-318/G Calif. & High Alt.⑬	RN12Y④	.035	H	—	TDC	B	—	850N	—	1500⑦	5–7
V8-318/G Exc. Calif.⑭	RN12Y④	.035	H	—	6°	B	—	700N	—	1300⑦	5–7
V8-318/G Calif.⑭	RN12Y④	.035	H	—	8°	B	—	750N	—	1500⑦	5–7
V8-360/K 2 Barrel	RN12Y④	.035	H	—	10°	B	—	700N	—	1700⑦	5–7
V8-360/J 4 Barrel⑬	RN12Y④	.035	H	—	6°	B	—	750N	—	1700⑦	5–7
V8-360/J 4 Barrel⑭	RN12Y④	.035	H	—	10°	B	—	750N	—	1500⑦	5–7
V8-400/N⑭	④⑮	.035	J	—	10°	F	—	750N	—	1400⑦	5–7
V8-440/T⑬	RJ13Y④	.035	J	—	8°	D	—	750N	—	1200⑦	5–7
V8-440/T Exc. Calif. & High Alt.⑭	RJ13Y④	.035	J	—	12°	D	—	750N	—	1400⑦	5–7
V8-440/T Calif. & High Alt.⑭	RJ13Y④	.035	J	—	8°	D	—	750N	—	1600⑦	5–7
1978											
6-225/C,D Exc. Calif. & High Alt.	RBL16Y④	.035	G	12°	12°	K	750	750N	1500	1600⑦	3½–5
6-225/C Calif. & High Alt.	RBL16Y④	.035	G	—	8°	K	—	750N	—	⑦⑯	3½–5
V8-318/G 2 Barrel	RN12Y④	.035	H	16°	16°	C	700	750N	1400	⑦⑰	5–7
V8-318/H 4 Barrel	RN12Y④	.035	H	—	10°	C	—	750N	—	1600⑦	5–7
V8-360/K 2 Barrel	RN12Y④	.035	H	—	20°	C	—	750N	—	1600⑦	5–7

Continued

TUNE UP SPECIFICATIONS—Continued

The following specifications are published from the latest information available. This
data should be used only in the absence of a decal affixed in the engine compartment.

★ When using a timing light, disconnect vacuum hose or tube at distributor and plug opening in hose or tube so idle speed will not be affected.

● When checking compression, lowest cylinder must be within 80 percent of highest.

▲ Before removing wires from distributor cap, determine location of the No. 1 wire in cap, as distributor position may have been altered from that shown at
the end of this chart.

☞ Spark plug types shown in this chart are recommendations of the original vehicle manufacturer and not MOTOR.

Check local sources for other spark plug manufacturers listings.

Year & Engine/V.I.N.	Spark Plug Type ☞	Gap	Firing Order Fig. ▲	Ignition Timing BTDC① ★ Man. Trans.	Auto. Trans.	Mark Fig.	Curb Idle Speed Man. Trans.	Auto. Trans.②	Fast Idle Speed Man. Trans.	Auto. Trans.	Fuel Pump Pressure
CHRYSLER & IMPERIAL 1978—Continued											
V8-360/J 4 Barrel Exc. Calif. ⑭⑱	RN12Y④	.035	H	—	16°	C	—	750N	—	1500⑦	5–7
V8-360/J 4 Barrel Calif. ⑩⑬	RN12Y④	.035	H	—	12°	C	—	750N	—	1500⑦	5–7
V8-400/N	④⑳	.035	J	—	㉑	E	—	750N	—	1500⑦	5–7
V8-440/T Exc. Calif. & High Alt.	OJ13Y④	.035	J	—	㉒	C	—	750N	—	1400⑦	5–7
V8-440/T Calif. & High Alt.	OJ13Y④	.035	J	—	8°	C	—	750N	—	1600⑦	5–7
1979											
6-225/C 1 Barrel Exc. Calif.	RBL16Y④	.035	G	12°	12°	K	675	675N	1400⑦	1600⑦	3½–5
6-225/C 1 Barrel Calif.	RBL16Y④	.035	G	—	8°	K	—	750N	—	1500⑦	3½–5
6-225/D 2 Barrel	RBL16Y④	.035	G	—	12°	K	—	725N	—	1600⑦	3½–5
V8-318/G 2 Barrel	RN12Y④	.035	H	—	16°	C	—	730N	—	1600⑦	5–7
V8-318/H 4 Barrel⑱	RN12Y④	.035	H	—	16°	C	—	750N	—	1600⑦	5–7
V8-318/H 4 Barrel⑩	RN12Y④	.035	H	—	16°	C	—	850N	—	1600⑦	5–7
V8-360/K 2 Barrel	RN12Y④	.035	H	—	12°	C	—	750N	—	1600⑦	5–7
V8-360/J 4 Barrel	RN12Y④	.035	H	—	16°	C	—	750N	—	1600⑦	5–7
1980											
6-225/C Exc. Calif.	RBL16Y④	.035	G	—	12°	K	—	725N	—	1600⑦	3½–5
6-225/C Calif.	RBL16Y④	.035	G	—	12°	K	—	750N	—	—	3½–5
V8-318/G 2 Barrel	RN12Y④	.035	H	—	12°	C	—	700N	—	1500⑦	5–7
V8-318/H 4 Barrel	RN12Y④	.035	H	—	16°	C	—	700N	—	—	5–7
V8-360/K 2 Barrel	RN12Y④	.035	H	—	12°	C	—	700N	—	1500⑦	5–7
V8-360/L 4 Barrel	RN12Y④	.035	H	—	16°	C	—	750N	—	—	5–7
1981											
6-225/E Exc. Calif.	560PR4⑥	.048	G	—	12°	K	—	650N	—	1600	4–5½
6-225/E Calif.	560PR4⑥	.048	G	—	16°	K	—	750N	—	2000	4–5½
V8-318/K, M Less E.F.I.	65PR4③⑥	.048③	H	—	16°	C	—	700N	—	1400	5¾–7¼
V8-318/J E.F.I.	68ER⑥	.035	H	—	12°	C	—	580N	—	—	7½–11½ ⑨
1982											
6-225/E Exc. Calif.	560PR⑥	.035	G	—	12°	K	—	625N	—	1600	4–5½
6-225/E Calif.	560PR⑥	.035	G	—	12°	K	—	725N	—	1950	4–5½
V8-318/K 2 Barrel	65PR⑥	.035	H	—	16°	C	—	600N	—	1400	5¾–7¼
V8-318/M 4 Barrel	65PR⑥	.035	H	—	16°	C	—	650N	—	1400	5¾–7¼
V8-318/J E.F.I.	68ER⑥	.035	H	—	12°	C	—	580N	—	—	7½–11½ ⑨
1983											
6-225/E	RBL16Y④	.035	G	—	16°	K	—	750N	—	2000	4–5½
V8-318/K Less E.F.I.	RN12YC④⑤	.035	H	—	16°	C	—	700N	—	1400	5¾–7½
V8-318/J E.F.I.	RN12YC④⑤	.035	H	—	12°	C	—	580D	—	—	7½–11½ ⑨

Continued

TUNE UP SPECIFICATIONS—Continued

The following specifications are published from the latest information available. This data should be used only in the absence of a decal affixed in the engine compartment.

★ When using a timing light, disconnect vacuum hose or tube at distributor and plug opening in hose or tube so idle speed will not be affected.

● When checking compression, lowest cylinder must be within 80 percent of highest.

▲ Before removing wires from distributor cap, determine location of the No. 1 wire in cap, as distributor position may have been altered from that shown at the end of this chart.

☞ Spark plug types shown in this chart are recommendations of the original vehicle manufacturer and not MOTOR.

Check local sources for other spark plug manufacturers listings.

Year & Engine/V.I.N.	Spark Plug Type ☞	Gap	Firing Order Fig. ▲	Ignition Timing BTDC① ★ Man. Trans.	Auto. Trans.	Mark Fig.	Curb Idle Speed Man. Trans.	Auto. Trans.②	Fast Idle Speed Man. Trans.	Auto. Trans.	Fuel Pump Pressure
DODGE											
1977											
6-225/C 1 Barrel ⑧	RBL15Y④	.035	G	12°	12°	A	700	700N	1700⑦	1700⑦	3½–5
6-225/C 1 Barrel Exc. Calif.⑱⑳	RBL15Y④	.035	G	6°	2°	A	700	700N	1400⑦	1700⑦	3½–5
6-225/C 1 Barrel Calif.⑩⑳	RBL15Y④	.035	G	8°	8°	A	750	750N	1600⑦	1700⑦	3½–5
6-225/D 2 Barrel Exc. Calif.	RBL15Y④	.035	G	12°	12°	A	750	750N	1500⑦	1600⑦	3½–5
6-225/D 2 Barrel Calif.	RBL15Y④	.035	G	4°	4°	A	850	850N	1600⑦	1700⑦	3½–5
V8-318/G Exc. Calif. & High Alt.⑬	RN12Y④	.035	H	8°	8°	B	700	700N	1400⑦	1400⑦	5–7
V8-318/G Calif. & High Alt.⑬	RN12Y④	.035	H	—	TDC	B	—	850N	—	1500⑦	5–7
V8-318/G Exc. Calif.⑭	RN12Y④	.035	H	—	6°	B	—	700N	—	1300⑦	5–7
V8-318/G Calif.⑭	RN12Y④	.035	H	—	8°	B	—	750N	—	1500⑦	5–7
V8-360/K 2 Barrel	RN12Y④	.035	H	—	10°	B	—	700N	—	1700⑦	5–7
V8-360/J,L 4 Barrel⑬	RN12Y④	.035	H	—	6°	B	—	750N	—	1700⑦	5–7
V8-360/J,L 4 Barrel⑭	RN12Y④	.035	H	—	10°	B	—	750N	—	1500⑦	5–7
V8-400/N⑭	④⑮	.035	J	—	10°	F	—	750N	—	1400⑦	5–7
V8-440/T⑬	RJ13Y④	.035	J	—	8°	D	—	750N	—	1200⑦	5–7
V8-440/T Exc. Calif. & High Alt.⑭	RJ13Y④	.035	J	—	12°	D	—	750N	—	1400⑦	5–7
V8-440/T Calif. & High Alt.⑭	RJ13Y④	.035	J	—	8°	D	—	750N	—	1200⑦	5–7
V8-440/U High Perf.⑭	RJ11Y④	.035	J	—	8°	D	—	750N	—	1600⑦	6–7½
1978											
6-225/C 1 Barrel Exc. Calif.⑱	RBL16Y④	.035	G	12°	12°	K	700	700N	1400⑦	1600⑦	3½–5
6-225/C 1 Barrel Calif.⑩	RBL16Y④	.035	G	—	8°	K	—	750N	—	⑦⑯	3½–5
6-225/D 2 Barrel	RBL16Y④	.035	G	12°	12°	K	750	750N	1500⑦	1600⑦	3½–5
V8-318/G 2 Barrel	RN12Y④	.035	H	—	16°	C	—	750N	—	⑦⑰	5–7
V8-318/H 4 Barrel⑱	RN12Y④	.035	H	—	10°	C	—	750N	—	1600⑦	5–7
V8-318/H 4 Barrel⑩	RN12Y④	.035	H	—	16°	C	—	850N	—	1600⑦	5–7
V8-360/K 2 Barrel	RN12Y④	.035	H	—	20°	C	—	750N	—	1600⑦	5–7
V8-360/J,L 4 Barrel Exc. Calif.⑭⑱	RN12Y④	.035	H	—	16°	C	—	750N	—	1500⑦	5–7
V8-360/J,L 4 Barrel Calif.⑩⑬	RN12Y④	.035	H	—	⑲	C	—	750N	—	1500⑦	5–7
V8-400/N	④⑳	.035	J	—	㉑	E	—	750N	—	1500⑦	5–7

Continued

TUNE UP SPECIFICATIONS—Continued

The following specifications are published from the latest information available. This
data should be used only in the absence of a decal affixed in the engine compartment.

★ When using a timing light, disconnect vacuum hose or tube at distributor and plug opening in hose or tube so idle speed will not be affected.

● When checking compression, lowest cylinder must be within 80 percent of highest.

▲ Before removing wires from distributor cap, determine location of the No. 1 wire in cap, as distributor position may have been altered from that shown at the end of this chart.

☞ Spark plug types shown in this chart are recommendations of the original vehicle manufacturer and not MOTOR.

Check local sources for other spark plug manufacturers listings.

Year & Engine/V.I.N.	Spark Plug Type ☞	Gap	Firing Order Fig. ▲	Ignition Timing BTDC① ★ Man. Trans.	Auto. Trans.	Mark Fig.	Curb Idle Speed Man. Trans.	Auto. Trans.②	Fast Idle Speed Man. Trans.	Auto. Trans.	Fuel Pump Pressure
DODGE—Continued											
1979											
6-225/C 1 Barrel Exc. Calif.	RBL16Y④	.035	G	12°	12°	K	675	675N	1400⑦	1600⑦	3½–5
6-225/C 1 Barrel Calif.	RBL16Y④	.035	G	—	8°	K	—	750N	—	1500⑦	3½–5
6-225/D 2 Barrel	RBL16Y④	.035	G	—	12°	K	—	725N	—	1600⑦	3½–5
V8-318/G 2 Barrel	RN12Y④	.035	H	—	16°	C	—	730N	—	1600⑦	5–7
V8-318/H 4 Barrel	RN12Y④	.035	H	—	16°	C	—	750N	—	1600⑦	5–7
V8-360/K 2 Barrel	RN12Y④	.035	H	—	12°	C	—	750N	—	1600⑦	5–7
V8-360/J,L 4 Barrel	RN12Y④	.035	H	—	16°	C	—	750N	—	1600⑦	5–7
1980											
6-225/C Exc. Calif.	RBL16Y④	.035	G	12°	12°	K	725	725N	—	1600⑦	3½–5
6-225/C Calif.	RBL16Y④	.035	G	—	12°	K	—	750N	—	—	3½–5
V8-318/G 2 Barrel	RN12Y④	.035	H	—	12°	C	—	700N	—	1500⑦	5–7
V8-318/H 4 Barrel	RN12Y④	.035	H	—	16°	C	—	700N	—	—	5–7
V8-360/K 2 Barrel	RN12Y④	.035	H	—	12°	C	—	700N	—	1500⑦	5–7
V8-360/L 4 Barrel	RN12Y④	.035	H	—	16°	C	—	750N	—	—	5–7
1981											
6-225/E Exc. Calif.	560PR4⑥	.048	G	—	12°	K	—	650N	—	1600	4–5½
6-225/E Calif.	560PR4⑥	.048	G	—	16°	K	—	750N	—	2000	4–5½
V8-318/K,M	65PR4③⑥	.048③	H	—	16°	C	—	700N	—	1400	5¾–7¼
1982											
6-225/E Exc. Calif.	560PR⑥	.035	G	—	12°	K	—	625N	—	1600	4–5½
6-225/E Calif.	560PR⑥	.035	G	—	12°	K	—	725N	—	1950	4–5½
V8-318/K 2 Barrel	65PR⑥	.035	H	—	16°	C	—	600N	—	1400	5¾–7¼
V8-318/M 4 Barrel	65PR⑥	.035	H	—	16°	C	—	650N	—	1400	5¾–7¼
1983											
6-225/E	RBL16Y④	.035	G	—	16°	K	—	750N	—	2000	4–5½
V8-318/K	RN12YC④⑤	.035	H	—	16°	C	—	700N	—	1400	5¾–7½
PLYMOUTH											
1977											
6-225/C 1 Barrel ⑫	RBL15Y④	.035	G	12°	12°	A	700	700N	1700⑦	1700⑦	3½–5
6-225/C 1 Barrel Exc. Calif. ⑱㉓	RBL15Y④	.035	G	6°	2°	A	700	700N	1400⑦	1700⑦	3½–5
6-225/C 1 Barrel Calif. ⑩㉓	RBL15Y④	.035	G	8°	8°	A	750	750N	1600⑦	1700⑦	3½–5
6-225/D 2 Barrel Exc. Calif.	RBL15Y④	.035	G	12°	12°	A	750	750N	1500⑦	1600⑦	3½–5
6-225/D 2 Barrel Calif.	RBL15Y④	.035	G	4°	4°	A	850	850N	1600⑦	1700⑦	3½–5
V8-318/G Exc. Calif. & High Alt.	RN12Y④	.035	H	8°	8°	B	700	700N	1400⑦	1400⑦	5–7

Continued

CHRYSLER CORP.—Rear Wheel Drive

TUNE UP SPECIFICATIONS—Continued

The following specifications are published from the latest information available. This data should be used only in the absence of a decal affixed in the engine compartment.

★ When using a timing light, disconnect vacuum hose or tube at distributor and plug opening in hose or tube so idle speed will not be affected.

● When checking compression, lowest cylinder must be within 80 percent of highest.

▲ Before removing wires from distributor cap, determine location of the No. 1 wire in cap, as distributor position may have been altered from that shown at the end of this chart.

☞ Spark plug types shown in this chart are recommendations of the original vehicle manufacturer and not MOTOR.

Check local sources for other spark plug manufacturers listings.

Year & Engine/V.I.N.	Spark Plug Type ☞	Gap	Firing Order Fig. ▲	Ignition Timing BTDC① ★ Man. Trans.	Auto. Trans.	Mark Fig.	Curb Idle Speed Man. Trans.	Auto. Trans.②	Fast Idle Speed Man. Trans.	Auto. Trans.	Fuel Pump Pressure
PLYMOUTH—Continued											
1977											
V8-318/G Calif. & High Alt.	RN12Y④	.035	H	—	TDC	B	—	850N	—	1500⑦	5–7
V8-360/J 2 Barrel	RN12Y④	.035	H	—	10°	B	—	700N	—	1700⑦	5–7
V8-360/J,L 4 Barrel⑬	RN12Y④	.035	H	—	6°	B	—	750N	—	1700⑦	5–7
V8-360/J,L 4 Barrel⑭	RN12Y④	.035	H	—	10°	B	—	750N	—	1500⑦	5–7
V8-400/N⑭	④⑮	.035	J	—	10°	F	—	750N	—	1400⑦	5–7
V8-440⑬	RJ13Y④	.035	J	—	8°	D	—	750N	—	1200⑦	5–6
V8-440/T Exc. Calif. & High Alt.⑭	RJ13Y④	.035	J	—	12°	D	—	750N	—	1400⑦	5–7
V8-440/T Calif. & High Alt.⑭	RJ13Y④	.035	J	—	8°	D	—	750N	—	1200⑦	5–7
V8-440/U High Perf.⑭	RJ11Y④	.035	J	—	8°	D	—	750N	—	1600⑦	6–7½
1978											
6-225/C 1 Barrel Exc. Calif.⑱	RBL16Y④	.035	G	12°	12°	K	700	700N	1400⑦	1600⑦	3½–5
6-225/C 1 Barrel Calif.⑩	RBL16Y④	.035	G	—	8°	K	—	750N	—	⑦⑯	3½–5
6-225/D 2 Barrel	RBL16Y④	.035	G	12°	12°	K	750	750N	1500⑦	1600⑦	3½–5
V8-318/G 2 Barrel	RN12Y④	.035	H	—	16°	C	—	750N	—	⑦⑰	5–7
V8-318/H 4 Barrel	RN12Y④	.035	H	—	10°	C	—	750N	—	1600⑦	5–7
V8-360/K 2 Barrel	RN12Y④	.035	H	—	20°	C	—	750N	—	1600⑦	5–7
V8-360/L 4 Barrel Exc. Calif.⑭⑱	RN12Y④	.035	H	—	16°	C	—	750N	—	1500⑦	5–7
V8-360/L 4 Barrel Calif.⑩⑬	RN12Y④	.035	H	—	⑲	C	—	750N	—	1500⑦	5–7
V8-400/N⑭	④⑳	.035	J	—	㉑	E	—	750N	—	1500⑦	5–7
1979											
6-225/C 1 Barrel Exc. Calif.	RBL16Y④	.035	G	12°	12°	K	675	675N	1400⑦	1600⑦	3½–5
6-225/C 1 Barrel Calif.	RBL16Y④	.035	G	—	8°	K	—	750N	—	1500⑦	3½–5
6-225/D 2 Barrel	RBL16Y④	.035	G	—	12°	K	—	725N	—	1600⑦	3½–5
V8-318/G 2 Barrel	RN12Y④	.035	H	—	16°	C	—	730N	—	1600⑦	5–7
V8-318/H 4 Barrel⑱	RN12Y④	.035	H	—	16°	C	—	750N	—	1600⑦	5–7
V8-318/H 4 Barrel⑩	RN12Y④	.035	H	—	16°	C	—	850N	—	1600⑦	5–7
V8-360/K 2 Barrel	RN12Y④	.035	H	—	12°	C	—	750N	—	1600⑦	5–7
V8-360/J 4 Barrel	RN12Y④	.035	H	—	16°	C	—	750N	—	1600⑦	5–7

Continued

TUNE UP SPECIFICATIONS—Continued

The following specifications are published from the latest information available. This
data should be used only in the absence of a decal affixed in the engine compartment.

★ When using a timing light, disconnect vacuum hose or tube at distributor and plug opening in hose or tube so idle speed will not be affected.

● When checking compression, lowest cylinder must be within 80 percent of highest.

▲ Before removing wires from distributor cap, determine location of the No. 1 wire in cap, as distributor position may have been altered from that shown at the end of this chart.

☞ Spark plug types shown in this chart are recommendations of the original vehicle manufacturer and not MOTOR.

Check local sources for other spark plug manufacturers listings.

Year & Engine/V.I.N.	Spark Plug Type ☞	Gap	Ignition Timing BTDC① ★ Firing Order Fig. ▲	Man. Trans.	Auto. Trans.	Mark Fig.	Curb Idle Speed Man. Trans.	Auto. Trans.②	Fast Idle Speed Man. Trans.	Auto. Trans.	Fuel Pump Pressure
PLYMOUTH—Continued											
1980											
6-225/C Exc. Calif.	RBL16Y④	.035	G	12°	12°	K	725	725N	—	1600⑦	3½–5
6-225/C Calif.	RBL16Y④	.035	G	—	12°	K	—	750N	—	—	3½–5
V8-318/G 2 Barrel	RN12Y④	.035	H	—	12°	C	—	700N	—	1500⑦	5–7
V8-318/H 4 Barrel	RN12Y④	.035	H	—	16°	C	—	700N	—	—	5–7
V8-360/K 2 Barrel	RN12Y④	.035	H	—	12°	C	—	700N	—	1500⑦	5–7
V8-360/L 4 Barrel	RN12Y④	.035	H	—	16°	C	—	750N	—	—	5–7
1981											
6-225/E Exc. Calif.	560PR4⑥	.048	G	—	12°	K	—	650N	—	1600	4–5½
6-255/E Calif.	560PR4⑥	.048	G	—	16°	K	—	750N	—	2000	4–5½
V8-318/K,M	65PR4③⑥	.048③	H	—	16°	C	—	700N	—	1400	5¾–7¼
1982											
6-225/E Exc. Calif.	560PR⑥	.035	G	—	12°	K	—	625N	—	1600	4–5½
6-255/E Calif.	560PR⑥	.035	G	—	12°	K	—	725N	—	1950	4–5½
V8-318/K 2 Barrel	65PR⑥	.035	H	—	16°	C	—	600N	—	1400	5¾–7¼
V8-318/M 4 Barrel	65PR⑥	.035	H	—	16°	C	—	650N	—	1400	5¾–7¼
1983											
6-225/E	RBL16Y④	.035	G	—	16°	K	—	750N	—	2000	4–5½
V8-318/K	RN12YC④⑤	.035	G	—	16°	C	—	700N	—	1400	5¾–7½

①—BTDC—Before top dead center.

②—N: Neutral. D: Drive.

③—If poor driveability condition is encountered during engine warmup on 1981 V8-318 2 Barrel engines built prior to Feb. 1, 1981, the spark plugs should be removed & regapped to .035 inch. These engines are equipped with spark plug type 65PR4 gapped at .048 inch. When replacing spark plugs, type 65PR gapped at .035 inch should be used.

④—Champion.

⑤—Original equipment spark plug. When replacing spark plugs use RN12Y.

⑥—Mopar.

⑦—With stop screw on second highest step of fast idle cam.

⑧—Aspen.

⑨—In tank electric fuel pump.

⑩—High altitude.

⑪—Carburetor No. 9109S, 1400 RPM; carburetor No. 9112S, 1200 RPM.

⑫—Volare.

⑬—Except Electronic Lean Burn engines.

⑭—Electronic Lean Burn engines.

⑮—Except high perform, engine, RJ13Y; high perf. engine, RJ11Y.

⑯—Except high altitude, 1500 RPM; high altitude, 1700 RPM.

⑰—Except high altitude, 1600 RPM; high altitude, 1700 RPM.

⑱—Except high altitude.

⑲—Distributor No. 3874115, 6° BTDC; distributor No. 3874858, 8° BTDC.

⑳—Except high perf., OJ13Y; high perf., OJ11Y.

㉑—Engine code E-64, 4500 lbs. vehicle curb weight, 24° BTDC; all other 20° BTDC.

㉒—Monaco.

㉓—Fury.

㉔—Except high perf., 5–7 psi.; high perf., 6–7½ psi.

Fig. A

Fig. B

Fig. C

Fig. D

Fig. E

Continued

TUNE UP NOTES—Continued

Fig. F

Fig. G

Fig. H

Fig. J

Fig. K

DISTRIBUTOR SPECIFICATIONS

★ Note: If unit is checked on vehicle, double the RPM and degrees to get crankshaft figures.

Distributor Part No.①	Centrifugal Advance Degrees @ RPM of Distributor					Vacuum Advance		Distributor Retard
	Advance Starts	Intermediate Advance			Full Advance	Inches of Vacuum to Start Plunger	Max. Adv. Dist. Deg. @ Vacuum	Max. Retard Dist. Deg. @ Vacuum
CHRYSLER & IMPERIAL								
1977								
3874115	1.3–3.1 @ 600	5.8–7.5 @ 800	—	—	12 @ 2000	7	12 @ 12.5	—
3874173	1.3–3.1 @ 600	3.5–5.5 @ 700	—	—	10 @ 2000	8	11 @ 14	—
3874858	1.4–3.4 @ 600	6–8 @ 800	—	—	8.5 @ 2400	7	12.5 @ 12.5	—
3874909	.2–2.2 @ 600	1.5–3.5 @ 650	—	—	9.6 @ 2300	8	12 @ 13.5	—
3874913	1.7–4.1 @ 600	4.8–7 @ 700	—	—	13.6 @ 2350	8	12 @ 13.5	—
3874917	.6–2 @ 500	3.7–5.4 @ 700	—	—	10 @ 2000	7	12.5 @ 12.5	—
4091015②	—	—	—	—	—	—	—	—
4091017②	—	—	—	—	—	—	—	—
4091019②	—	—	—	—	—	—	—	—
4091140②	—	—	—	—	—	—	—	—
1978								
3874115	1.3–3.1 @ 600	5.8–7.5 @ 800	—	—	12 @ 2000	7	12 @ 12.5	—
3874173	1.3–3.1 @ 600	3.5–5.5 @ 700	—	—	10 @ 2000	8	11 @ 14.0	—
3874858	1.4–3.4 @ 600	6–8 @ 800	—	—	8.5 @ 2400	7	12.5 @ 12.5	—
3874876	.2–2.2 @ 600	1.5–3.5 @ 650	—	—	5.7 @ 2500	7	9.8 @ 11.5	—

Continued

DISTRIBUTOR SPECIFICATIONS—Continued

★ Note: If unit is checked on vehicle, double the RPM and degrees to get crankshaft figures.

Distributor Part No.①	Centrifugal Advance Degrees @ RPM of Distributor					Vacuum Advance		Distributor Retard
	Advance Starts	Intermediate Advance			Full Advance	Inches of Vacuum to Start Plunger	Max. Adv. Dist. Deg. @ Vacuum	Max. Retard Dist. Deg. @ Vacuum
CHRYSLER & IMPERIAL—Continued								
1978—Continued								
3874929	1.4–3.4 @ 600	5.6–7.6 @ 800	—	—	11.7 @ 2300	7	9.8 @ 11.5	—
4091101	1–1.2 @ 600	1.7–3.7 @ 800	—	—	5.8–7.8 @ 2060	9	9.5 @ 12.5	—
4091140②	—	—	—	—	—	—	—	—
4091709②	—	—	—	—	—	—	—	—
4091711②	—	—	—	—	—	—	—	—
1979								
3874876	.2–2.2 @ 600	1.5–3.5 @ 650	—	—	3.7–5.7 @ 2500	7	9.8 @ 11.5	—
4091101	1.0–1.2 @ 600	1.7–3.7 @ 800	—	—	5.8–7.8 @ 2060	9	9.5 @ 12.5	—
4091140②	—	—	—	—	—	—	—	—
1980								
3874876	.2 @ 600	1.5–3.5 @ 650	—	—	5.7 @ 2500	7	9.8 @ 11.5	—
4091490②	—	—	—	—	—	—	—	—
4111501	1.5 @ 700	1.5–3.5 @ 900	—	—	10 @ 2200	6	12 @ 15	—
4111784②	—	—	—	—	—	—	—	—
1981								
4091140②	—	—	—	—	—	—	—	—
4145717	.2–2.2 @ 600	1.5–3.5 @ 650	—	—	5.7 @ 2500	7	12 @ 15	—
4145751②	—	—	—	—	—	—	—	—
4145753②	—	—	—	—	—	—	—	—
4145848	.2–2.2 @ 600	1.5–3.5 @ 650	—	—	5.7 @ 2500	7	12 @ 15	—
1982								
4145954	0–1.6 @ 600	0–2 @ 900	—	—	4.5 @ 2500	4	12 @ 11	—
1982–83								
4091140②	—	—	—	—	—	—	—	—
4145751②	—	—	—	—	—	—	—	—
4145753②	—	—	—	—	—	—	—	—

①—Stamped on distributor housing.
②—Electronic Spark Control distributor cannot be checked on vehicle.

DODGE & PLYMOUTH
1977

Distributor Part No.①	Advance Starts	Intermediate Advance			Full Advance	Inches of Vacuum to Start Plunger	Max. Adv. Dist. Deg. @ Vacuum	Max. Retard Dist. Deg. @ Vacuum
3874115	1.3–3.1 @ 600	5.8–7.5 @ 800	—	—	12 @ 2000	7	12 @ 12.5	—
3874173	1.3–3.1 @ 600	3.5–5.5 @ 700	—	—	10 @ 2000	8	11 @ 14	—
3874714	.3–2.4 @ 500	4.2–6.2 @ 650	—	—	8.9 @ 2500	7	9.8 @ 11.5	—
3874858	1.4–3.4 @ 600	6–8 @ 800	—	—	8.5 @ 2400	7	12.5 @ 12.5	—
3874876	.2–2.2 @ 600	1.5–3.5 @ 650	—	—	5.7 @ 2500	7	9.8 @ 11.5	—
3874909	.2–2.2 @ 600	1.5–3.5 @ 650	—	—	9.6 @ 2300	8	12 @ 13.5	—
3874913	1.7–4.1 @ 600	4.8–7.0 @ 700	—	—	13.6 @ 2350	8	12 @ 13.5	—
3874917	.6–2 @ 500	3.7–5.4 @ 700	—	—	10 @ 2000	7	12.5 @ 12.5	—
3874929	1.4–3.4 @ 600	5.6–7.6 @ 800	—	—	11.7 @ 2300	7	9.8 @ 11.5	—
4091015②	—	—	—	—	—	—	—	—
4091017②	—	—	—	—	—	—	—	—
4091019②	—	—	—	—	—	—	—	—
4091039	.2–2.2 @ 600	1.5–3.5 @ 650	—	—	5.7 @ 2500	7	9.8 @ 11.5	—
4091101	1.0–1.2 @ 600	1.7–3.7 @ 800	—	—	7.8 @ 2060	9	9.5 @ 12.5	—
4091140②	—	—	—	—	—	—	—	—

Continued

DISTRIBUTOR SPECIFICATIONS—Continued

★ Note: If unit is checked on vehicle, double the RPM and degrees to get crankshaft figures.

Distributor Part No.①	Centrifugal Advance Degrees @ RPM of Distributor					Vacuum Advance		Distributor Retard
	Advance Starts	Intermediate Advance			Full Advance	Inches of Vacuum to Start Plunger	Max. Adv. Dist. Deg. @ Vacuum	Max. Retard Dist. Deg. @ Vacuum
DODGE & PLYMOUTH—Continued								
1978								
3874115	1.3–3.1 @ 600	5.8–7.5 @ 800	—	—	12 @ 2000	7	12 @ 12.5	—
3874173	1.3–3.1 @ 600	3.5–5.5 @ 700	—	—	10 @ 2000	8	11 @ 14.0	—
3874858	1.4–3.4 @ 600	6–8 @ 800	—	—	8.5 @ 2400	7	12.5 @ 12.5	—
3874876	.2–2.2 @ 600	1.5–3.5 @ 650	—	—	5.7 @ 2500	7	9.8 @ 11.5	—
4091101	1–1.2 @ 600	1.7–3.7 @ 800	—	—	5.8–7.8 @ 2060	9	9.5 @ 12.5	—
4091140②	—	—	—	—	—	—	—	—
4091709②	—	—	—	—	—	—	—	—
4091711②	—	—	—	—	—	—	—	—
1979								
3874876	.2–2.2 @ 600	1.5–3.5 @ 650	—	—	3.7–5.7 @ 2500	7	9.8 @ 11.5	—
4091101	1–1.2 @ 600	1.7–3.7 @ 800	—	—	5.8–7.8 @ 2060	9	9.5 @ 12.5	—
4091140②	—	—	—	—	—	—	—	—
1980								
3874876	.2 @ 600	1.5–3.5 @ 650	—	—	5.7 @ 2500	7	9.8 @ 11.5	—
4091490②	—	—	—	—	—	—	—	—
4111501	0 @ 675	1.5–3.5 @ 900	—	—	10 @ 2200	6	12 @ 15	—
4111784②	—	—	—	—	—	—	—	—
1981								
4145717	.2–2.2 @ 600	1.5–3.5 @ 650	—	—	5.7 @ 2500	7	12 @ 15	—
4145751②	—	—	—	—	—	—	—	—
4145753②	—	—	—	—	—	—	—	—
4145848	.2–2.2 @ 600	1.5–3.5 @ 650	—	—	5.7 @ 2500	7	12 @ 15	—
1982								
4145954	0–1.6 @ 600	0–2 @ 900	—	—	4.5 @ 2500	4	12 @ 11	—
1982–83								
4145751②	—	—	—	—	—	—	—	—
4145753②	—	—	—	—	—	—	—	—

①—Stamped on distributor housing.
②—Electronic Spark Control system distributor, cannot be checked on vehicle.

Rear Wheel Drive—CHRYSLER CORP.

VALVE SPECIFICATIONS

Year	Engine/V.I.N.	Valve Lash Int.	Valve Lash Exh.	Valve Angles Seat	Valve Angles Face	Valve Spring Installed Height	Valve Spring Pressure Lbs. @ In.	Stem Clearance Intake	Stem Clearance Exhaust	Stem Diameter Intake	Stem Diameter Exhaust
CHRYSLER & IMPERIAL											
1977	V8-318/G	Hydraulic①		45	②	1¹¹/₁₆	177 @ 1⁵/₁₆	.001–.003	.002–.004	.372–.373	.371–.372
	V8-360/K,J	Hydraulic①		45	②	1²¹/₃₂	193 @ 1¼	.001–.003	.002–.004	.372–.373	.371–.372
	V8-400/N, 440/T	Hydraulic①		45	45	1⁵⁵/₆₄	200 @ 1⁷/₁₆	.0011–.0028	④	.3723–.3730	⑥
1978	6-225/C,D	.010H	0.20H	45	②	1²¹/₃₂	144 @ 1⁵/₁₆	.001–.003	.002–.004	.372–.373	.371–.372
	V8-318/G,H	Hydraulic①		45	②	1²¹/₃₂	177 @ 1⁵/₁₆	.001–.003	.002–.004	.372–.373	.371–.372
	V8-360/K,J	Hydraulic①		45	②	1²¹/₃₂	177 @ 1⁵/₁₆	.001–.003	.002–.004	.372–.373	.371–.372
	V8-360/L③	Hydraulic①		45	②	1²¹/₃₂	193 @ 1¼	.0015–.0035	.0025–.0045	.3715–.3725	.3705–.3715
	V8-400/N, 440/T	Hydraulic①		45	45	1⁵⁵/₆₄	200 @ 1⁷/₁₆	.0011–.0028	④	.3723–.3730	⑥
1979–80	6-225/C,D	.010H	.020H	45	②	1¹¹/₁₆	144 @ 1⁵/₁₆	.001–.003	.002–.004	.372–.373	.371–.372
	V8-318/G,H	Hydraulic①		45	45	1¹¹/₁₆	177 @ 1⁵/₁₆	.001–.003	.002–.004	.372–.373	.371–.372
	V8-360/K,J	Hydraulic①		45	45	1¹¹/₁₆	177 @ 1⁵/₁₆	.001–.003	.002–.004	.372–.373	.371–.372
	V8-360/L③	Hydraulic①		45	45	1²¹/₃₂	193 @ 1¼	.0015–.0035	.0025–.0045	.3715–.3725	.3705–.3715
1981–83	6-225/E	Hydraulic①		45	②	1¹¹/₁₆	144 @ 1⁵/₁₆	.001–.003	.002–.004	.372–.373	.371–.372
	V8-318/K,M⑩	Hydraulic①		45–45½	44½–45	1¹¹/₁₆	177 @ 1⁵/₁₆	.001–.003	.002–.004	.372–.373	.371–.372
	V8-318/J⑧	Hydraulic①		45–45½	44½–45	1²¹/₃₂	193 @ 1¼	.0015–.0035	.0025–.0045	.3715–.3725	.3705–.3715
DODGE & PLYMOUTH											
1977	6-225/C,D	.010H	.020H	45	②	1¹¹/₁₆	144 @ 1⁵/₁₆	.001–.003	.002–.004	.372–.373	.371–.372
	V8-318/G	Hydraulic①		45	②	1¹¹/₁₆	177 @ 1⁵/₁₆	.001–.003	.002–.004	.372–.373	.371–.372
	V8-360/K,J	Hydraulic①		45	②	1²¹/₃₂	193 @ 1¼	.001–.003	.002–.004	.372–.373	.371–.372
	V8-360/L③	Hydraulic①		45	②	1²¹/₃₂	193 @ 1¼	.0015–.0035	.0025–.0045	.3715–.3725	.3705–.3715
	V8-400/N, 440/T	Hydraulic①		45	45	1⁵⁵/₆₄	200 @ 1⁷/₁₆	.0011–.0028	④	.3723–.373	⑥
	V8-400/N, 440/U③	Hydraulic①		45	45	1⁵⁵/₆₄	246 @ 1²³/₆₄	.0016–.0033	⑤	.3718–.3725	⑦
1978	6-225/C,D⑨	.010H	.020H	45	②	1²¹/₃₂	144 @ 1⁵/₁₆	.001–.003	.002–.004	.372–.373	.371–.372
	V8-318/G,H	Hydraulic①		45	②	1²¹/₃₂	177 @ 1⁵/₁₆	.001–.003	.002–.004	.372–.373	.371–.372
	V8-360/K,J	Hydraulic①		45	②	1²¹/₃₂	177 @ 1⁵/₁₆	.001–.003	.002–.004	.372–.373	.371–.372
	V8-360/L③	Hydraulic①		45	②	1²¹/₃₂	193 @ 1¼	.0015–.0035	.0025–.0045	.3715–.3725	.3705–.3715
	V8-400/N, 440/T	Hydraulic①		45	45	1⁵⁵/₆₄	200 @ 1⁷/₁₆	.0011–.0028	④	.3723–.3730	⑥
	V8-400/N, 440/U③	Hydraulic①		45	45	1⁵⁵/₆₄	246 @ 1²³/₆₄	.0016–.0033	⑤	.3718–.3725	⑦
1979–80	6-225/C,D	.010H	.020H	45	②	1¹¹/₁₆	144 @ 1⁵/₁₆	.001–.003	.002–.004	.372–.373	.371–.372
	V8-318/G,H	Hydraulic①		45	45	1¹¹/₁₆	177 @ 1⁵/₁₆	.001–.003	.002–.004	.372–.373	.371–.372
	V8-360/K,J	Hydraulic①		45	45	1¹¹/₁₆	177 @ 1⁵/₁₆	.001–.003	.002–.004	.372–.373	.371–.372
	V8-360/L③	Hydraulic①		45	45	1²¹/₃₂	193 @ 1¼	.0015–.0035	.0025–.0045	.3715–.3725	.3705–.3715
1981–83	6-225/E	Hydraulic①		45	②	1¹¹/₁₆	144 @ 1⁵/₁₆	.001–.003	.002–.004	.372–.373	.371–.372
	V8-318/K,M	Hydraulic①		45–45½	44½–45	1¹¹/₁₆	177 @ 1⁵/₁₆	.001–.003	.002–.004	.372–.373	.371–.372

①—No adjustment.
②—Intake 45°, exhaust 43°.
③—High Performance.
④—Hot end .0021–.0038, Cold end .0011–.0028.
⑤—Hot end .0026–.0043, Cold end .0016–.0033.
⑥—Hot end 3713–.372, Cold end .3723–.373.
⑦—Hot end .3708–.3715, Cold end .3718–.3725.
⑧—With Electronic Fuel Injection.
⑨—Some Aspen & Volaré models w/6-225 2 bar. carb. will be equipped w/hydraulic lifters which cannot be adjusted.
⑩—Less Electronic Fuel Injection.

PISTONS, PINS, RINGS, CRANKSHAFT & BEARINGS

Year	Engine/V.I.N.	Piston Clearance Top of Skirt	Ring End Gap① Comp.	Oil	Wristpin Diameter	Rod Bearings Shaft Diameter	Bearing Clearance	Main Bearings Shaft Diameter	Bearing Clearance	Thrust on Bear. No.	Shaft End Play
CHRYSLER & IMPERIAL											
1977	V8-318/G	.0005–.0015	.010	.015	.9842	2.124–2.125	.0005–.0025	2.4995–2.5005	.0005–.0020	3	.002–.009
	V8-360/J,K	.0005–.0015	.010	.015	.9842	2.124–2.125	.0005–.0025	2.4995–2.5005	.0005–.0020	3	.002–.009
	V8-400/N	.0003–.0013	.013	.015	1.0936	2.375–2.376	.0005–.0025	2.6245–2.6255	.0005–.0020	3	.002–.009
	V8-440/T	.0003–.0013	.013	.015	1.0936	2.375–2.376	.0005–.0025	2.7495–2.7505	.0005–.0020	3	.002–.009
1978	6-225/C,D	.0005–.0015	.010	.015	.9008	2.1865–2.1875	.0005–.0025	2.7495–2.7505	.0005–.0020	3	.002–.009
	V8-318/G,H	.0005–.0015	.010	.015	.9842	2.1240–2.1250	.0005–.0025	2.4995–2.5005	.0005–.0020	3	.002–.009
	V8-360/J,K	④	.010	.015	.9842	2.1240–2.1250	.0005–.0025	2.8095–2.8105	.0005–.0020	3	.002–.009
	V8-400/N	.0003–.0013	.013	.015	1.0936	2.375–2.376	③	2.6245–2.6255	.0005–.0020	3	.002–.009
	V8-440/T	.0003–.0013	.013	.015	1.0936	2.375–2.376	③	2.7495–2.7505	.0005–.0020	3	.002–.009
1979	6-225/C,D	.0005–.0015	.010	.015	.9008	2.1865–2.1875	.0005–.0025	2.7495–2.7505	.0005–.0020	3	.002–.009
	V8-318/G,H	.0005–.0015	.010	.015	.9842	2.1240–2.1250	.0005–.0025	2.4995–2.5005	.0005–.0020	3	.002–.009
	V8-360/J,K,L	④	.010	.015	.9842	2.1240–2.1250	.0005–.0025	2.8095–2.8105	.0005–.0020	3	.002–.009
1980	6-225/C	.0005–.0015	.010	.015	.9008	2.1865–2.1875	.0005–.0025	2.7495–2.7505	.0005–.0020	3	.002–.009
	V8-318/G,H	.0005–.0015	.010	.015	.9842	2.1240–2.1250	.0005–.0025	2.4995–2.5005	②	3	.002–.009
	V8-360/J,K,L	④	.010	.015	.9842	2.1240–2.1250	.0005–.0025	2.8095–2.8105	②	3	.002–.009
1981–83	6-225/E	.0005–.0015	.010	.015	.9008	2.1865–2.1875	.0010–.0025	2.7495–2.7505	.0010–.0025	3	.0035–.0095
	V8-318/J,K,M	.0005–.0015	.010	.015	.9842	2.124–2.125	.0005–.0025	2.4995–2.5005	②	3	.002–.009
DODGE & PLYMOUTH											
1977	6-225/C,D	.0005–.0015	.010	.015	.9008	2.1865–2.1875	.0005–.0025	2.7495–2.7505	.0005–.0020	3	.002–.009
	V8-318/G	.0005–.0015	.010	.015	.9842	2.124–2.125	.0005–.0025	2.4995–2.5005	.0005–.0020	3	.002–.009
	V8-360/J,K,L	.0005–.0015	.010	.015	.9842	2.125–2.125	.0005–.0025	2.4995–2.5005	.0005–.0020	3	.002–.009
	V8-400/N	.0003–.0013	.013	.015	1.0936	2.375–2.376	.0005–.0025	2.6245–2.6255	.0005–.0020	3	.002–.009
	V8-440/T,U	.0003–.0013	.013	.015	1.0936	2.375–2.376	.0005–.0025	2.7495–2.7505	.0005–.0020	3	.002–.009
1978	6-225/C,D	.0005–.0015	.010	.015	.9008	2.1865–2.1875	.0005–.0025	2.7495–2.7505	.0005–.0020	3	.002–.009
	V8-318/G,H	.0005–.0015	.010	.015	.9842	2.1240–2.1250	.0005–.0025	2.4995–2.5005	.0005–.0020	3	.002–.009
	V8-360/J,K,L	④	.010	.015	.9842	2.1240–2.1250	.0005–.0025	2.8095–2.8105	.0005–.0020	3	.002–.009
	V8-400/N	.0003–.0013	.013	.015	1.0936	2.375–2.376	③	2.6245–2.6255	.0005–.0020	3	.002–.009
	V8-440/T	.0003–.0013	.013	.015	1.0936	2.375–2.376	③	2.7495–2.7505	.0005–.0020	3	.002–.009
1979	6-225/C,D	.0005–.0015	.010	.015	.9008	2.1865–2.1875	.0005–.0025	2.7495–2.7505	.0005–.0020	3	.002–.009
	V8-318/G,H	.0005–.0015	.010	.015	.9842	2.1240–2.1250	.0005–.0025	2.4995–2.5005	.0005–.0020	3	.002–.009
	V8-360/J,K,L	④	.010	.015	.9842	2.1240–2.1250	.0005–.0025	2.8095–2.8105	.0005–.0020	3	.002–.009
1980	6-225/C	.0005–.0015	.010	.015	.9008	2.1865–2.1875	.0005–.0025	2.7495–2.7505	.0005–.0020	3	.002–.009
	V8-318/G,H	.0005–.0015	.010	.015	.9842	2.1240–2.1250	.0005–.0025	2.4995–2.5005	②	3	.002–.009
	V8-360/J,K,L	④	.010	.015	.9842	2.1240–2.1250	.0005–.0025	2.8095–2.8105	②	3	.002–.009
1981–83	6-225/E	.0005–.0015	.010	.015	.9008	2.1865–2.1875	.0010–.0025	2.7495–2.7505	.0010–.0025	3	.0035–.0095
	V8-318/K,M	.0005–.0015	.010	.015	.9842	2.124–2.125	.0005–.0025	2.4995–2.5005	②	3	.002–.009

①—Fit rings in tapered bores for clearance listed in tightest portion of ring travel.
②—No. 1, .0005–.0015"; No. 2, 3, 4 & 5, .0005–.0020".
③—Exc. High perf. engine, .0005"–.0025"; High perf. engine, .0005"–.0030".
④—With 2 bbl. carb., .0005"–.0015"; With 4 bbl. carb., .001"–.002".

ALTERNATOR & REGULATOR SPECIFICATIONS

Year	Unit Number	Ground Polarity	Field Coil Draw Amperes	Current Output			Operating Voltage			Voltage Regulator Point Gap	Regulator Armature Air Gap
				Engine R.P.M.	Amperes	Volts	Engine R.P.M.	Volts	Voltage @ 80°F ①		
1977–80	Bronze Tag	Negative	4.5–6.5②	1250	40⑤	15	1250	15	13.9–14.6	—	—
	Natural Tag	Negative	4.5–6.5②	1250	47⑤	15	1250	15	13.9–14.6	—	—
1977–81	Yellow Tag③	Negative	4.5–6.5②	1250	57⑤	15	1250	15	13.9–14.6	—	—
	Brown Tag	Negative	4.5–6.5②	1250	62⑤	15	1250	15	13.9–14.6	—	—
	Yellow Tag④	Negative	4.75–6.0②	900	72⑤	13	900	13	13.9–14.6	—	—
1978–80	Violet Tag	Negative	4.5–6.5②	1250	40⑤	15	1250	15	13.9–14.6	—	—
1982–83	Yellow Tag③	Negative	4.5–6.5②	1250	47⑤	15	1250	15	13.9–14.6	—	—
	Brown Tag	Negative	4.5–6.5②	1250	58⑤	15	1250	15	13.9–14.6	—	—
	Yellow Tag⑥	Negative	4.75–6.0②	900	97⑤	13	900	13	13.9–14.6	—	—

①—For each 10 degree rise in temperature subtract .04 volt. Temperature is checked with thermometer two inches from installed voltage regulator cover.
②—Current draw at 12 volts while turning rotor shaft by hand.
③—60 amp rating.
④—100 amp rating.
⑤—Minimum output.
⑥—114 amp rating.

STARTING MOTOR SPECIFICATIONS

Year	Part No.	Rotation ①	Brush Spring Tension, Ounces	No Load Test			Torque Test		
				Amperes	Volts	R.P.M.	Amperes	Volts	Torque, Ft. Lbs.
1977–79	3755250	Clockwise	32–36	90	11	5700	475–550	4	—
	3755900	Clockwise	32–36	90	11	3700	475–550	4	—
1980	4111855	—	32–36	90	11	5700	475–550	4	—
1980–83	4111860	—	32–36	90	11	5700	475–550	4	—

①—Viewed from drive end.

ENGINE TIGHTENING SPECIFICATIONS★

★ Torque specifications are for clean and lightly lubricated threads only. Dry or dirty threads produce increased friction which prevents accurate measurement of tightness.

Year	Engine/V.I.N	Spark Plugs Ft. Lbs.	Cylinder Head Bolts Ft. Lbs.	Intake Manifold Ft. Lbs.	Exhaust Manifold Ft. Lbs.	Rocker Arm Shaft Bracket Ft. Lbs.	Rocker Arm Cover In. Lbs.	Connecting Rod Cap Bolts Ft. Lbs.	Main Bearing Cap Bolts Ft. Lbs.	Flywheel to Crankshaft Ft. Lbs.	Vibration Damper to Crankshaft Ft. Lbs.
1977	6-225/C,D	10	70	240①	120①	24	40	45	85	55	②
	V8-318/G, 360/J,K,L	30	95	45	20	200①	40	45	85	55	100
	V8-400, 440	30	70	45	40	24	40	45	85	55	135
1978	6-225/C,D	10	70	④	120①	24	40	45	85	55	②
	V8-318/G,H, 360/J,K,L	30	105	45	③	200①	40	45	85	55	100
	V8-400/N, 440/T	30	70	45	30	25	40	45	85	55	135
1979–80	6-225/C,D	10	70	④	120①	24	40	45	85	55	②
1979	V8-318/G,H, 360/J,K,L	30	⑤	45	③	200①	40	45	85	55	100
1980	V8-318/G,H, 360/J,K,L	30	95	40	③	200①	40	45	85	55	100
1981–83	6-225/E	10	70	④	120①	24	80	45	85	55	②
	V8-318/J,K,M	30	95	45	③	200①	80	45	85	55	100

①—Inch pounds.
②—Press fit.
③—Screw, 20 ft. lbs.; Nut, 15 ft. lbs.
④—Intake to exhaust manifold stud nut 240 in. lbs., Intake to exhaust manifold bolts 200 in. lbs.
⑤—V8-360, 105 ft. lbs. Some V8-318 engine blocks have cylinder head bolt holes drilled through the block into the water jacket. Insert a screwdriver into block head bolt holes. If it goes in at least 2 inches, head bolt must be sealed with suitable sealer and torqued to 95 ft. lbs.; all other V8-318 head bolts, 105 ft. lbs.

WHEEL ALIGNMENT SPECIFICATIONS

NOTE: See that riding height is correct before checking wheel alignment

Year	Model	Caster Angle, Degrees		Camber Angle, Degrees				Toe In. Inch	Toe Out on Turns, Deg.	
		Limits	Desired	Limits		Desired			Outer Wheel	Inner Wheel
				Left	Right	Left	Right			
CHRYSLER & IMPERIAL										
1977–78	Chrysler	−1/2 to +2	+3/4	0 to +1	−1/4 to +3/4	+1/2	+1/4	1/8	18.3	20
1977–79	Cordoba	−1/2 to +2	+3/4	0 to +1	−1/4 to +3/4	+1/2	+1/4	1/8	18	20
	LeBaron	+1 1/2 to +3 3/4	+2 1/2	0 to +1	−1/4 to +3/4	+1/2	+1/4	1/8	18	20
1979	Chrysler	−1/2 to +2	+3/4	0 to +1	−1/4 to +3/4	+1/2	+1/4	1/8	18	20
1980–81	Cordoba, LeBaron	+1 1/4 to +3 3/4	+2 1/2	−1/4 to +1 1/4	−1/4 to +1 1/4	+1/2	+1/2	1/16 to 3/16	18	20
	Newport, New Yorker	−1/4 to +2 1/4	+1	−1/4 to +1 1/4	−1/4 to +1 1/4	+1/2	+1/2	1/16 to 3/16	18	20
1981	Imperial	+1 1/4 to +3 3/4	+2 1/2	−1/4 to +1 1/4	−1/4 to +1 1/4	+1/2	+1/2	1/16 to 3/16	18	20
1982–83	All	+1 1/4 to +3 3/4	+2 1/2	−1/4 to +1 1/4	−1/4 to +1 1/4	+1/2	+1/2	1/16 to 3/16	18	20
DODGE										
1977	Man. Steer.②	−1 3/4 to +3/4	−1/2	0 to +1	−1/4 to +3/4	+1/2	+1/4	1/16 to 1/4	①	20
	Power Steer.②	−1/2 to +2	+3/4	0 to +1	−1/4 to +3/4	+1/2	+1/4	1/16 to 1/4	①	20
	Aspen	+1 1/2 to +3 3/4	+2 1/2	0 to +1	−1/4 to +3/4	+1/2	+1/2	1/16 to 1/4	18.0	20
	Diplomat	+1 1/2 to +3 3/4	+2 1/2	0 to +1	−1/4 to +3/4	+1/2	+1/4	1/8	18.0	20
1978–79	Man. Steer.②	−1 3/4 to +3/4	−1/2	0 to +1	−1/4 to +3/4	+1/2	+1/4	1/8	18.0	20
	Power Steer.②	−1/2 to +2	+3/4	0 to +1	−1/4 to +3/4	+1/2	+1/4	1/8	18.0	20
	Aspen	+1 1/2 to +3 3/4	+2 1/2	0 to +1	−1/4 to +3/4	+1/2	+1/4	1/8	18.0	20
	Diplomat	+1 1/2 to +3 3/4	+2 1/2	0 to +1	−1/4 to +3/4	+1/2	+1/4	1/8	18.0	20
1980–81	Aspen, Diplomat & Mirada	+1 1/4 to +3 3/4	+2 1/2	−1/4 to +1 1/4	−1/4 to +1 1/4	+1/2	+1/2	1/16 to 3/16	18	20
	St. Regis	−1/4 to +2 1/4	+1	−1/4 to +1 1/4	−1/4 to +1 1/4	+1/2	+1/2	1/16 to 3/16	18	20
1982–83	All	+1 1/4 to +3 3/4	+2 1/2	−1/4 to +1 1/4	−1/4 to +1 1/4	+1/2	+1/2	1/16 to 3/16	18.	20

①—Charger SE & Monaco, 18°; Royal Monaco, 18.3°. ②—Except Aspen & Diplomat.

Year	Model	Caster Angle, Degrees		Camber Angle, Degrees				Toe In. Inch	Toe Out on Turns, Deg.	
PLYMOUTH										
1977	Man. Steer.②	−1 3/4 to +3/4	−1/2	0 to +1	−1/4 to +3/4	+1/2	+1/4	1/16 to 1/4	①	20
	Power Steer.②	−1/2 to +2	+3/4	0 to +1	−1/4 to +3/4	+1/2	+1/4	1/16 to 1/4	①	20
	Volaré	+1 1/2 to +3 3/4	+2 1/2	0 to +1	−1/4 to +3/4	+1/2	+1/2	1/16 to 1/4	18.0	20
1978	Man. Steer.②	−1 3/4 to +3/4	−1/2	0 to +1	−1/4 to +3/4	+1/2	+1/4	1/8	18.0	20
	Power. Steer.②	−1/2 to +2	+3/4	0 to +1	−1/4 to +3/4	+1/2	+1/4	1/8	18.0	20
	Volaré	+1 1/2 to 3 3/4	+2 1/2	0 to +1	−1/4 to +3/4	+1/2	+1/4	1/8	18.0	20
1979	Volaré	+1 1/2 to +3 3/4	+2 1/2	0 to +1	−1/4 to +3/4	+1/2	+1/4	1/8	18.0	20
1980	Gran Fury	−1/4 to +2 1/4	+1	−1/4 to +1 1/4	−1/4 to +1 1/4	+1/2	+1/2	1/16 to 3/16	18	20
	Volaré	+1 1/4 to +3 3/4	+2 1/2	−1/4 to +1 1/4	−1/4 to +1 1/4	+1/2	+1/2	1/16 to 3/16	18	20
1981	Gran Fury	−1/4 to +2 1/4	+1	−1/4 to +1 1/4	−1/4 to +1 1/4	+1/2	+1/2	1/16 to 3/16	18	20
1982–83	All	+1 1/4 to +3 3/4	+2 1/2	−1/4 to +1 1/4	−1/4 to +1 1/4	+1/2	+1/2	1/16 to 3/16	18	20

①—Fury, 18.8°. ②—Except Volaré.

BRAKE SPECIFICATIONS

Year	Model	Brake Drum Inside Diameter	Wheel Cylinder Bore Diameter			Master Cylinder Bore Diameter		
			Disc Brake	Front Drum Brake	Rear Drum Brake	Disc Brake	Drum Brake	Power Brake
CHRYSLER & IMPERIAL								
1977	Chrysler	11	3.1	—	15/16	1.03	—	1.03
	Cordoba	11	2¾	—	15/16	1.03	—	1.03
	LeBaron	10	2.755	—	15/16	1.03	—	1.03
1978	Chrysler	11	3.102	—	15/16	1.03	—	1.03
	Cordoba	③	2.755	—	15/16	1.03	—	1.03
	LeBaron	10	2.755	—	15/16	1.03	—	1.03
1979	Chrysler	③	2.755	—	15/16	1.03	—	1.03
	Cordoba	③	2.755	—	15/16	1.03	—	1.03
	LeBaron	10	2.755	—	15/16	1.03	—	1.03
1980	Chrysler, Cordoba	②	2.755	—	15/16	1.03	—	1.03
	LeBaron	10	2.755	—	15/16	1.03	—	1.03
1981	Chrysler, Cordoba	10④	2.755	—	15/16	1.03	—	1.03
	Imperial	10	2.755	—	15/16	1.03	—	1.03
	LeBaron	10①④	2.755	—	15/16	1.03	—	1.03
1982–83	Chrysler	10①④	2.755	—	15/16	1.03	—	1.03
	Cordoba & Imperial	10	2.755	—	15/16	1.03	—	1.03
DODGE								
1977	Aspen	10①	2¾	—	15/16	1.03	—	1.03
	Charger	11	2¾	—	15/16	1.03	—	1.03
	Monaco	11	2¾	—	15/16	1.03	—	1.03
	Royal Monaco	11	3.1	—	15/16	1.03	—	1.03
	Diplomat	10	2.755	—	15/16	1.03	—	1.03
1978	Aspen	②	2.755	—	15/16	1.03	—	1.03
	Charger	③	2.755	—	15/16	1.03	—	1.03
	Diplomat	10	2.755	—	15/16	1.03	—	1.03
	Monaco	②③	2.755	—	15/16	1.03	—	1.03
1979	Aspen	②	2.755	—	15/16	1.03	—	1.03
	Diplomat	10	2.755	—	15/16	1.03	—	1.03
	Magnum XE	③	2.755	—	15/16	1.03	—	1.03
	St. Regis	③	2.755	—	15/16	1.03	—	1.03
1980	Aspen, Diplomat	②	2.755	—	15/16	1.03	—	1.03
	Mirada, St. Regis	②	2.755	—	15/16	1.03	—	1.03
1981	Diplomat	10①④	2.755	—	15/16	1.03	—	1.03
	Mirada	10④	2.755	—	15/16	1.03	—	1.03
	St. Regis	10④	2.755	—	15/16	1.03	—	1.03
1982–83	Diplomat	10①④	2.755	—	15/16	1.03	—	1.03
	Mirada	10	2.755	—	15/16	1.03	—	1.03
PLYMOUTH								
1977	Volaré	10①	2¾	—	15/16	1.03	—	1.03
	Fury	11	2¾	—	15/16	1.03	—	1.03
	Gran Fury	11	3.1	—	15/16	1.03	—	1.03
1978	Fury	②③	2.755	—	15/16	1.03	—	1.03
	Volaré	②	2.755	—	15/16	1.03	—	1.03
1979	Volaré	②	2.755	—	15/16	1.03	—	1.03
1980	Gran Fury	②	2.755	—	15/16	1.03	—	1.03
	Volaré	②	2.755	—	15/16	1.03	—	1.03
1981	Gran Fury	10④	2.755	—	15/16	1.03	—	1.03
1982–83	Gran Fury	10①④	2.755	—	15/16	1.03	—	1.03

①—Wagon 11".
②—Exc. Taxi & police, 10"; taxi & police 11".
③—Exc. 9¼" axle, 10"; 9¼" axle, 11".
④—Heavy duty 11".

COOLING SYSTEM & CAPACITY DATA

Year	Model or Engine/V.I.N.	Cooling Capacity, Qts, Less A/C	With A/C	Radiator Cap Relief Pressure, Lbs.	Thermo. Opening Temp.	Fuel Tank Gals.	Engine Oil Refill Qts. ①	3 Speed Pints	4 Speed Pints	Auto. Trans. Qts. ②	Rear Axle Oil Pints
CHRYSLER											
1977	V8-318/G	16½	18	16	195	⑤	4	—	—	8½	4½
	V8-360/JK	16	16	16	195	⑤	4	—	—	8½③	4½
	V8-400/N	16½	16½	16	195	⑤	4	—	—	8¼	4¼
	V8-440/T	16	16	16	195	⑤	4	—	—	8¼	4½
1978	6-225/C,D	12	14	16	195	19½	4	—	—	8½	2
	V8-318/G,H	16	17½	16	195	⑪	4	—	—	8½	4½
	V8-360/J,K	16	16	16	195	⑪	4	—	—	8¼	4½
	V8-400/N	16½	16½	16	195	⑪	4	—	—	8¼	4½
	V8-440/T	16½	16½	16	195	⑪	4	—	—	8¼	4½
1979	6-225/C,D	11.5	⑯	16	195	⑫	4	—	7	8½	⑮
	V8-318/G,H	15	⑧	16	195	⑭	4	—	7	8½	⑮
	V8-360/J,K,L	⑨	⑨	16	195	⑭	4	—	7	8½	⑮
1980	LeBaron 6-225/C	11½	12½	16	195	18	4	—	—	8.15	④
	LeBaron V8-318/G,H	15	15½	16	195	18	4	—	—	8.15	④
	Cordoba 6-225/C	11½	12½	16	195	21	4	—	—	8.15	4½
	Cordoba V8-318/G,H	15	15½	16	195	21	4	—	—	8.15	4½
	Cordoba V8-360/K,L	14	14	16	195	21	4	—	—	8.15	4½
	Newport, New Yorker 6-225/C	11½	14½	16	195	21	4	—	—	8.15	4½
	Newport, New Yorker V8-318/G,H	15	17½	16	195	21	4	—	—	8.15	4½
	Newport, New Yorker V8-360/K,L	16	16	16	195	21	4	—	—	8.15	4½
1981	LeBaron 6-225/E	11½	12½	16	195	18	4	—	—	8.15	⑥
	LeBaron V8-318/K,M	15	15½	16	195	18	4	—	—	8.15	⑥
	Cordoba 6-225/E	11½	14½	16	195	18	4	—	—	8.15	⑥
	Cordoba V8-318/K,M	15	17½	16	195	18	4	—	—	8.15	⑥
	Newport, New Yorker 6-225/E	11½	14½	16	195	21	4	—	—	8.15	⑥
	Newport, New Yorker V8-318/K,M	15	17½	16	195	21	4	—	—	8.15	⑥
1982–83	Cordoba 6-225/E	11½	15	16	195	18	4	—	—	8½	⑥
	Cordoba V8-318/K,M	15	15½	16	195	18	4	—	—	8½	⑥
	New Yorker 6-225/E	11½	12½	16	195	18	4	—	—	8½	⑥
	New Yorker V8-318/K,M	15	15½	16	195	T8	4	—	—	8½	⑥
IMPERIAL											
1981	All	15	17.5	16	195	18	4	—	—	8.15	4.4
1982–83	All	15½	16½	16	195	18	4	—	—	8½	4.4
DODGE											
1977	Aspen 6-225/C,D	12	14	16	195	18⑦	4	4¾	7	8½	2
	Aspen 8-318/G	16	17½	16	195	20	4	4¾	7	8½	4½
	Aspen 8-360/J,K,L	16	17½	16	195	20	4	—	—	8½	4½
	Charger 8-318/G	16½	18	16	195	25½	4	—	—	8½	4½
	Charger 8-360/J,K,L	16	16	16	195	25½	4	—	—	8½③	4½
	Charger 8-400/N	16½	16½	16	195	25½	4	—	—	8¼	4½
	Monaco 6-225/C,D	13	14½	16	195	25½⑦	4	4¾	—	8½	4½
	Monaco 8-318/G	16½	18	16	195	25½⑦	4	4¾	—	8½	4½
	Monaco 8-360/J,K,L	16	16	16	195	25½⑦	4	—	—	8½③	4½
	Monaco 8-400/N	16½	16½	16	195	25½⑦	4	—	—	8¼	4½
	Monaco 8-440/T,U	16	16	16	195	20½	4	—	—	8½	4½

Continued

COOLING SYSTEM & CAPACITY DATA—Continued

Year	Model or Engine/V.I.N.	Cooling Capacity, Qts, Less A/C	Cooling Capacity, Qts, With A/C	Radiator Cap Relief Pressure, Lbs.	Thermo. Opening Temp.	Fuel Tank Gals.	Engine Oil Refill Qts. ①	Transmission Oil 3 Speed Pints	Transmission Oil 4 Speed Pints	Transmission Oil Auto. Trans. Qts. ②	Rear Axle Oil Pints
DODGE—Continued											
	Royal Monaco 8-318/G	17½	17½	16	195	20½	4	—	—	8½③	4½
	Royal Monaco 8-360/J,K,L	16	16	16	195	26½⑬	4	—	—	8½③	4½
	Royal Monaco 8-400/N	16½	16½	16	195	26½⑬	4	—	—	8½③	4½
	Royal Monaco 8-440K/T,U	16	16	16	195	20½	4	—	—	8½③	4½
1978	Diplomat	16	17½	16	195	19½	4	—	—	8½	4½
	Aspen 6-225/C,D	12	14	16	195	⑩	4	4¾	7	8½	2
	Aspen V8-318/G,H	16	17½	16	195	⑩	4	4¾	7	8½	2
	Aspen V8-360/J,K,L	16	16	16	195	⑩	4	4¾	7	8½	4½
	Charger V8-318/G,H	16½	18	16	195	25½	4	—	—	8½	4½
	Charger V8-360/J,K,L	16	16	16	195	25½	4	—	—	8¼	4½
	Charger V8-400/N	16½	16½	16	195	25½	4	—	—	8¼	4½
	Diplomat 6-225/C,D	12	14	16	195	19½	4	—	7	8½	2
	Diplomat V8-318/G,H	16	17½	16	195	19½	4	—	7	8½	2
	Diplomat V8-360/J,K,L	16	16	16	195	19½	4	—	7	8½	4½
	Monaco 6-225/C,D	13	14½	16	195	20½	4	4¾	—	8½	4½
	Monaco V8-318/G,H	16½	18	16	195	25½⑦	4	4¾	—	8½	4½
	Monaco V8-360/J,K,L	16	16	16	195	25½⑦	4	4¾	—	8½	4½
	Monaco V8-400/N	16½	16½	16	195	25½⑦	4	4¾	—	8¼	4½
1979	Aspen 6-225/C,D	11.5	12.5	16	195	⑩	4	4.8	7	8½	④
	Aspen V8-318/G,H	15	16.5	16	195	19.5	4	4.8	7	8½	④
	Aspen V8-360/J,K,L	15	15	16	195	19.5	4	4.8	7	8½	④
	Diplomat 6-225/C,D	12.5	12.5	16	195	⑩	4	—	7	8½	④
	Diplomat V8-318/G,H	15	16.5	16	195	19.5	4	—	7	8½	④
	Diplomat V8-360/J,K,L	15	15	16	195	19.5	4	—	7	8½	④
	Magnum XE V8-318/G,H	15	17.5	16	195	21	4	—	—	8½	4.5
	Magnum XE V8-360J,K,L	16	16	16	195	21	4	—	—	8½	4.5
	St. Regis 6-225/C,D	11.5	14.5	16	195	21	4	—	—	8½	4.5
	St. Regis V8-318/G,H	15	17.5	16	195	21	4	—	—	8½	4.5
	St. Regis V8-360/J,K,L	16	16	16	195	21	4	—	—	8½	4.5
1980	Aspen, Diplomat 6-225/C	11½	12½	16	195	18	4	4¾	—	8.15	④
	Aspen, Diplomat V8-318/G,H	15	15½	16	195	18	4	—	—	8.15	④
	Aspen V8-360/K,L	14	14	16	195	18	4	—	—	8.15	④
	Mirada 6-225/C	11½	12½	16	195	21	4	—	—	8.15	4½
	Mirada V8-318/G,H	15	15½	16	195	21	4	—	—	8.15	4½
	Mirada V8-360/K,L	14	14	16	195	21	4	—	—	8.15	4½
	St. Regis 6-225/C	11½	14½	16	195	21	4	—	—	8.15	4½
	St. Regis V8-318/G,H	15	17½	16	195	21	4	—	—	8.15	4½
	St. Regis V8-360/K,L	16	16	16	195	21	4	—	—	8.15	4½
1981	All 6-225/E	11.5	⑰	16	195	⑱	4	—	—	8.15	⑥

Continued

COOLING SYSTEM & CAPACITY DATA—Continued

Year	Model or Engine/V.I.N.	Cooling Capacity, Qts, Less A/C	Cooling Capacity, Qts, With A/C	Radiator Cap Relief Pressure, Lbs.	Thermo. Opening Temp.	Fuel Tank Gals.	Engine Oil Refill Qts. ①	Transmission Oil 3 Speed Pints	Transmission Oil 4 Speed Pints	Transmission Oil Auto. Trans. Qts. ②	Rear Axle Oil Pints
DODGE—Continued											
	All V8-318/KM	15	⑲	16	195	⑱	4	—	—	8.15	⑥
1982–83	Diplomat 6-225/E	11½	⑳	16	195	18	4	—	—	8½	⑥
	Diplomat V8-318/K,M	15	15½	16	195	18	4	—	—	8½	⑥
	Mirada 6-225/E	11½	12½	16	195	18	4	—	—	8½	⑥
	Mirada V8-318/K,M	15	15½	16	195	18	4	—	—	8½	⑥
PLYMOUTH											
1977	Fury 6-225/C,D	13	14½	16	195	25½⑦	4	4¾	—	8½	4½
	Fury 8-318/G	16½	18	16	195	25½⑦	4	4¾	—	8½	4½
	Fury 8-360/J,K,L	16	16	16	195	25½⑦	4	—	—	8½	4½
	Fury 8-400/N	16½	16½	16	195	25½⑦	4	—	—	8¼	4½
	Fury 8-440/T,U	16	16	16	195	20½	4	—	—	8½	4½
	Gran Fury 8-318/G	17½	17½	16	195	20½	4	—	—	8½③	4½
	Gran Fury 8-360/J,K,L	16	16	16	195	26½⑬	4	—	—	8½③	4½
	Gran Fury 8-400/N	16½	16½	16	195	26½⑬	4	—	—	8½③	4½
	Gran Fury 8-440/T,U	16	16	16	195	26½⑬	4	—	—	8½③	4½
1978	Fury 6-225/C,D	13	14½	16	195	25½⑦	4	4¾	—	8½	4½
	Fury V8-318/G,H	16½	18	16	195	25½⑦	4	4¾	—	8½	4½
	Fury V8-360/J,K,L	16	16	16	195	25½⑦	4	4¾	—	8½	4½
	Fury V8-400/N	16½	16½	16	195	25½⑦	4	4¾	—	8¼	4½
1980	Gran Fury 6-225/C	11½	14½	16	195	21	4	—	—	8.15	4½
	Gran Fury V8-318/G,H	15	17½	16	195	21	4	—	—	8.15	4½
	Gran Fury V8-360/K,L	16	16	16	195	21	4	—	—	8.15	4½
1981	Gran Fury 6-225/E	11½	14½	16	195	21	4	—	—	8.15	⑥
	Gran Fury V8-318/K,M	15	17½	16	195	21	4	—	—	8.15	⑥
1982–83	Gran Fury 6-225/E	11½	12½	16	195	18	4	—	—	8½	⑥
	Gran Fury V8-318/K,M	15	15½	16	195	18	4	—	—	8½	⑥
VOLARÉ											
1977	Volaré 6-225/C,D	12	14	16	195	18⑦	4	4¾	7	8½	2
	Volaré 8-318/G	16	17½	16	195	20	4	4¾	7	8½	4½
	Volaré 8-360/J,K,L	16	17½	16	195	20	4	—	—	8½	4½
1978	Volaré 6-225/C,D	12	14	16	195	⑩	4	4¾	7	8½	2
	Volaré V8-318/G,H	16	17½	16	195	⑩	4	4¾	7	8½	2
	Volaré V8-360/J,K,L	16	16	16	195	⑩	4	4¾	7	8½	4½
1979	Volaré 6-255/C,D	12.5	12.5	16	195	⑩	4	4.8	7	8½	④
	Volaré V8-318/G,H	15	16.5	16	195	19.5	4	—	—	8½	④
	Volaré V8-360/J,K,L	15	15	16	195	19.5	4	—	—	8½	④
1980	Volaré 6-225/C	11½	12½	16	195	18	4	4¾	—	8.15	④
	Volaré V8-318/G,H	15	15½	16	195	18	4	—	—	8.15	④
	Volaré V8-360/K,L	14	14	16	195	18	4	—	—	8.15	④

① —Add 1 qt. with filter change.
② —Approximate. Make final check with dipstick.
③ —With A-727 transmission (heavy duty), 8¼ qts.
④ —With 7¼ inch ring gear, 2 pts.; 8¼ inch ring gear, 4½ pts.
⑤ —Cordoba 25½ gals.; Chrysler 26½ gals.; Wagon 24 gals.
⑥ —With 7¼" ring gear, 2½ pts.; with 8¼" ring gear, 4.4 pts.; with 9¼" ring gear, 4½ pts.
⑦ —Wagons, 20 gals.
⑧ —Exc. LeBaron, 17.5 qts.; LeBaron, 16.5 qts.
⑨ —Exc. LeBaron, 16 qts.; LeBaron, 15 qts.
⑩ —6 cyl. exc. Station Wag. 18 gal.; 8 cyl. & Station Wag., 19½ gals.
⑪ —LeBaron, 19½ gals.; Cordoba, 25½ gals.; Chrysler, 26½ gal.
⑫ —Exc. LeBaron, 21 gal.; LeBaron exc. Wag. 18 gal.; LeBaron Wagon, 19½ gals.
⑬ —Wagons, 24 gals.
⑭ —Exc. LeBaron, 21 gals.; LeBaron, 19.5 gals.
⑮ —Exc. LeBaron, 4½ pts.; LeBaron, 7¼ inch ring gear, 2 pts.; 8¼ & 9¼ inch ring gear, 4½ pts.
⑯ —Exc. LeBaron, 14.5 qts.; LeBaron, 12.5 qts.
⑰ —Except Diplomat, 14½ qts.; Diplomat, 12½ qts.
⑱ —Diplomat & Mirada, 18 gals.; St. Regis, 21 gals.
⑲ —Except Diplomat, 17½ qts.; Diplomat, 15½ qts.
⑳ —1982, 15 qts.; 1983, 12½ qts.

REAR AXLE SPECIFICATIONS

Year	Model	Carrier Type	Ring Gear & Pinion Backlash		Pinion Bearing Preload			Differential Bearing Preload		
			Method	Adjustment	Method	New Bearings Inch-Lbs.	Used Bearings Inch-Lbs.	Method	New Bearings Inch-Lbs.	Used Bearings Inch-Lbs.
1977–83	8¼"⑤	Integral	②	.006–.008	①	20–35④	10–25④	②	③	③
	9¼"⑤	Integral	②	.006–.008	①	20–35④	10–25④	②	③	③
	7¼"	Integral	②	.004–.006	①	15–25	—	②	③	③

①—Collapsible spacer.
②—Threaded adjusters.
③—Preload is correct when ring gear and pinion

backlash is properly adjusted.
④—Adjust by turning pinion shaft nut with an inch-pound torque wrench with seal re-

moved.
⑤—"C" lock type.

Electrical Section

STARTER, REPLACE

1. Disconnect ground cable at battery.
2. Remove cable at starter.
3. Disconnect wires at solenoid.
4. Remove one stud nut and one bolt attaching starter motor to flywheel housing.
5. Slide transmission oil cooler bracket off stud (if so equipped).
6. Remove starter motor and removeable seal.
7. Reverse above procedure to install.

NOTE: When tightening attaching bolt and nut be sure to hold starter away from engine to insure proper alignment.

CLUTCH SWITCH

1977–80

A clutch switch is used which necessitates depressing the clutch pedal before the engine can be started.

IGNITION SWITCH & LOCK, REPLACE

1977–83

1. Disconnect battery ground cable and remove turn signal switch as outlined elsewhere in this chapter.
2. Remove ignition key lamp assembly retaining screw and the assembly.
3. Remove snap ring from upper end of steering shaft.
4. Remove bearing housing to lock housing retaining screws, then the bearing housing from shaft.
5. Remove bearing lower snap ring from shaft.
6. Pry sleeve from steering shaft lock plate hub, then, using a suitable punch, drive lock plate groove pin from lock plate.

NOTE: Drive pin from end without grooves.

7. Remove lock plate from shaft, then the shaft through lower end of column.
8. Remove shift indicator pointer screw, if equipped.
9. Remove buzzer switch retaining screw and the switch.

10. Remove lock lever guide plate retaining screws and the guide plate.
11. Place lock cylinder in the "Lock" position and remove key. With a suitable tool, depress spring loaded lock retainer and pull lock cylinder from housing bore, Fig. 1.
12. Remove ignition switch retaining screws and the ignition switch.
13. Reverse procedure to install.

IGNITION SWITCH, ADJUST

1979–83 Except Cordoba, Mirada & 1979–80 Magnum

1. Disconnect battery ground cable.
2. Place transmission in Park and ignition lock in the lock position.
3. If switch was not removed from column, loosen two mounting bolts and insert a lock pin into hole on switch marked lock. If switch was removed from column, pin switch in the lock position, then place switch into rod and rotate 90 degrees over mounting holes. Loosely install mounting bolts. Replacement switches are supplied with locking pins.
4. Apply light upward pressure to align rod and switch and hold switch in this position while tightening retaining bolts. Remove locking pin.
5. Remove lock pin from switch.
6. Reverse procedure to install.

Fig. 1 Lock cylinder removal. 1977–83

COLUMN MOUNTED DIMMER SWITCH, ADJUST

1979–81 Newport, New Yorker & St. Regis; 1980–81 Gran Fury; 1980–83 Cordoba & Mirada; 1981–83 Imperial

1. Loosen two switch mounting screws, then depress switch plunger slightly and insert locking pin.
2. Apply light upward pressure to remove free play between switch and rod.
3. While holding switch with slight upward pressure tighten the two mounting screws.
4. Remove locking pin and check switch for proper operation.

LIGHT SWITCH, REPLACE

1979–81 Newport, New Yorker & St. Regis; 1980–81 Gran Fury; 1980–83 Cordoba & Mirada; 1981–83 Imperial

1. If equipped, remove intermittent wipe and power antenna module assembly.
2. Disconnect battery ground cable.
3. Depress switch stem release button and pull knob and stem from switch.
4. Using a small screwdriver, snap out switch trim bezel, then remove mounting nut.
5. Pull switch from cluster and disconnect wire connector.
6. Reverse procedure to install.

1977–80 Aspen, Volaré, 1977–81 LeBaron, 1977–83 Diplomat & 1982–83 Gran Fury & New Yorker

1. Disconnect battery ground cable.
2. Remove cluster bezel.
3. Remove switch mounting plate attaching screws and pull switch and plate assembly outward.
4. Depress headlight switch stem, then depress release button and pull knob and stem from switch.

5. Remove switch mounting nut, then disconnect electrical connector and remove switch.
6. Reverse procedure to install.

1977–78 Fury, 1977–79 Charger, Cordoba, 1977–78 Monaco & 1978–79 Magnum

1. Disconnect battery ground cable and fusible link.
2. Remove instrument cluster upper bezel and escutcheon mounting screw.
3. Remove switch mounting plate to cluster housing screws, pull switch from housing and disconnect electrical connector.
4. Depress release button on rear of switch and pull knob and stem from switch.
5. Remove switch escutcheon and mounting nut.
6. Reverse procedure to install.

1977–78 Chrysler Newport & New Yorker

1. Disconnect battery ground cable.
2. Remove headlight switch lens.
3. Remove headlight switch to mounting plate retaining nut.
4. Remove switch.
5. Reverse procedure to install.

1977 Gran Fury & Royal Monaco

1. Disconnect battery ground cable.
2. Remove instrument cluster bezel.
3. Remove windshield wiper switch mounting screws and headlight switch mounting screws.
4. Pull switch outwards and disconnect electrical leads, then pull switch to the "ON" position and depress release button on side of switch. Remove knob and stem from switch.
5. Remove escutcheon and mounting plate retaining nut and remove switch.
6. Reverse procedure to install.

STOP LIGHT SWITCH, REPLACE

1977–83

1. Disconnect battery ground cable.
2. Disconnect wiring from switch and remove switch from brake pedal bracket.
3. Reverse procedure to install.

NEUTRAL SAFETY & BACK-UP SWITCH, REPLACE

1977–83

1. Unscrew switch from transmission case, allowing fluid to drain into a container, Fig. 2.
2. Move shift lever to "Park" and then to "Neutral" positions and inspect to see that switch operating lever is centered in switch opening in case.
3. Screw switch into transmission case and torque to 24 ft. lbs.

Fig. 2 Neutral safety switch.

4. Add fluid to proper level.
5. Check to see that switch operates only in "Park" and "Neutral".

HORN SOUNDER & STEERING WHEEL, REPLACE

1977–83

1. Disconnect ground cable at battery.
2. On steering wheels with center horn button, remove button by pulling outwards. On steering wheels with pressure sensitive switch pad, remove mounting screws from underside of wheel, then disconnect horn wire when removing pad.
3. On models with center horn button, disconnect horn switch wire and remove switch and ring.
4. On all models, remove steering wheel nut and use a suitable puller to remove steering wheel.

CAUTION: Do not bump or hammer on steering shaft to remove wheel as damage to shaft may result.

---

5. Reverse procedure to install.

TURN SIGNAL SWITCH, REPLACE

1981–83

1. Disconnect battery ground cable.
2. Remove steering wheel as described under "Steering Wheel, Replace".
3. On models equipped with tilt column, remove lock plate cover and lock plate.
4. On all models, remove lower instrument panel bezel.
5. On 1981 LeBaron, 1981–83 Diplomat and 1982–83 Gran Fury and New Yorker models equipped with tilt column, remove gear shift indicator, then remove two nuts attaching steering column to lower instrument panel reinforcement. Remove steering column to lower panel reinforcement mounting bracket from steering column.
6. On all models, unsnap four plastic retainers and remove wiring through steering column.
7. Disconnect light blue wire connector, then remove turn signal lever attaching screw and allow lever assembly to hang loosely from column.

8. Remove turn signal/hazard warning switch attaching screws, then pull switch from steering column, while carefully guiding wires up through column opening.
9. Reverse procedure to install.

1977–80

1. Disconnect battery ground cable and remove steering wheel.
2. Remove steering column cover. On Charger, Cordoba, Coronet, Fury, Magnum and 1977–78 Monaco, it is necessary to remove the lower instrument panel bezel.
3. On models with tilt column proceed as follows:
   a. On all models except Charger, Cordoba, Coronet, Fury, Magnum and 1977–78 Monaco, remove gearshift indicator.
   b. On all models, remove steering column to lower panel reinforcement nuts.
   c. Remove mounting bracket attaching bolts and the mounting bracket from steering column.
   d. Remove wiring trough screws and the wiring trough.
4. On all models except models with Tilt columns, unsnap retainer clips attaching wiring trough to steering column and remove wiring trough.
5. Position shift lever at the full clockwise position except on Tilt columns. On Tilt columns, position shift lever at the midpoint.
6. Disconnect turn signal switch wiring harness connector.
7. Remove turn signal lever attaching screw and the lever.

NOTE: On models equipped with speed control, it is not necessary to remove lever but allow lever to hang.

---

8. Remove hazard warning switch and upper bearing retainer mounting screws.
9. Carefully pull switch from column, guiding wires through column opening.
10. Reverse procedure to install.

INSTRUMENT CLUSTER, REPLACE

1981–83 Imperial

1. Disconnect battery ground cable.
2. Remove cigar lighter and ash tray from instrument panel.
3. Remove instrument panel cluster overlay attaching screws, then remove overlay.
4. Remove lower instrument panel cluster bezel attaching screws, then remove bezel.
5. Remove instrument cluster bezel attaching screws and bezel, then remove plastic pins retaining cluster mask to cluster and remove mask.
6. Remove instrument cluster to panel attaching screws, then pull cluster forward and disconnect wire connectors from cluster.
7. Remove cluster assembly.
8. Reverse procedure to install.

Fig. 2A Electronic instrument cluster. 1981–83 Imperial

(Labels in figure: INSTRUMENT PANEL, MAP LAMP, CLAMP, BEZEL, SCREW, SPACER, SHELL, LAMP, SCREW, LIGHTER ELEMENT, DIFFUSER, ASH TRAY HOUSING, SCREW, ASH TRAY, HOOD AND BRAKE RELEASE HOUSING, ELECTRONIC CLUSTER, HEADLAMP SWITCH, RETAINING NUT, BEZEL, KNOB AND SHAFT, BEZEL AND LENS)

1979–81 Newport, New Yorker & St. Regis, 1980–81 Gran Fury & 1980–83 Cordoba & Mirada

1. Disconnect battery ground cable.
2. Remove five hood and brake release bezel screws, then the bezel.
3. Remove four accessory switch bezel screws, then the bezel.
4. Pull gearshift pointer cable from steering column.
5. Remove the lower left and right hand bezels and the gearshift pointer cable.
6. Remove three steering column toe plate bolts at firewall, then the nuts and washers attaching steering column bracket to instrument panel steering column support bracket. Lower the steering column, allowing steering wheel to rest on seat.
7. Disconnect speedometer cable and the right hand mirror control cable.
8. Remove five screws securing instrument cluster to panel, Fig. 3.
9. Roll cluster downward and disconnect headlamp switch electrical connector and instrument cluster wiring.
10. Remove instrument cluster from vehicle.
11. Reverse procedure to install.

1977–81 LeBaron & 1977–83 Diplomat & 1982–83 Gran Fury & New Yorker

1. Disconnect battery ground cable.
2. Remove lower panel assembly.

Fig. 3 Instrument cluster removal. 1979–81 Newport, New Yorker & St. Regis & 1980–81 Gran Fury & 1980–83 Cordoba & Mirada

(Labels in figure: INSTRUMENT PANEL, MOUNTING SCREW, CLUSTER ASSEMBLY)

3. Remove left lower reinforcement by removing two screws located at left end.
4. Remove gear shift indicator.
5. Remove steering column toe plate mounting bolts and upper steering column mounting nuts, then lower steering column.
6. Disconnect speedometer cable.
7. Remove two mounting screws and detach fuse block from mid reinforcement.
8. Remove one screw attaching radio to mid reinforcement.
9. Remove four upper and four lower cluster mounting screws, Fig. 4.
10. Pull cluster out from instrument panel and disconnect wire connectors, control cables and vacuum harness, then remove cluster assembly.
11. Reverse procedure to install.

1977–80 Aspen & Volaré

1. Disconnect battery ground cable.
2. Remove steering column cover and instrument panel end cap.
3. Remove lower left reinforcement and remove gearshift indicator.
4. Remove steering column toe plate bolts, then remove the two upper mounting nuts and lower steering column.

Fig. 4 Instrument cluster. (Typical) 1977—81 LeBaron, 1977—83 Diplomat & 1982—83 Gran Fury & New Yorker

Fig. 5   Instrument cluster. 1977—80 Aspen & Volaré

5. Remove left side cowl mouldings, then disconnect speedometer cable.
6. Remove two mounting screws, then detach fuse block from mid reinforcement.
7. Remove 1 screw attaching radio to mid-reinforcement, 4 screws at bottom of cluster and 3 screws at top of cluster, Fig. 5.
8. Pull cluster from panel, then disconnect all electrical connectors, control cables and vacuum hoses and remove cluster.
9. Reverse procedure to install.

1977—78 Fury, 1977—79 Charger, Cordoba, 1977—78 Monaco & 1978—79 Magnum

1. Disconnect battery ground cable.
2. Remove trim pad, radio and heater or A/C controls, Fig. 6.
3. Remove cluster housing reinforcement bracket.

4. Disconnect speedo cable, all electrical connectors and three wiring through clips from cluster.
5. Remove upper cluster bezel and instrument panel and cap.
6. Remove steering column to support bracket nuts.
7. Remove cluster housing to instrument panel retaining screws, then remove cluster.
8. Reverse procedure to install.

1977 Gran Fury, Royal Monaco & 1977—78 Chrysler Newport & New Yorker

1. Disconnect battery ground cable.
2. Remove instrument panel upper cover, then working through top of panel, disconnect speedometer cable and printed circuit multiple connector.
3. Remove instrument cluster bezel, Figs. 7 & 8.
4. On Chrysler, remove gear selector and warning lamp bezel.
5. On all models disconnect instrument cluster lens and cluster housing from carrier.
6. Pull cluster out and disconnect two illumination and warning light modules.
7. Disconnect remaining electrical leads and remove cluster assembly.
8. Reverse procedure to install.

Fig. 6   Instrument cluster. 1977—78 Fury, 1977—79 Charger, Cordoba, 1977—78 Monaco & 1978—79 Magnum

INSTRUMENT CLUSTER BEZEL (IMPERIAL)

GEAR SELECTOR AND WARNING LAMP BEZEL (IMPERIAL)

SCREW

ASH TRAY

FINISH PLATE

BEZEL

ELEMENT

SHELL

CLIP

CLAMP

REAR WINDOW DEFOGGER SWITCH

KNOB

RADIO

SCREW

BRACKET

GEAR SELECTOR AND WARNING LAMP BEZEL (CHRYSLER)

AIR OUTLET COVER*

TAILGATE WINDOW SWITCH

INSTRUMENT CLUSTER BEZEL (CHRYSLER)

TAILGATE UNLOCK SWITCH

WINDSHIELD WIPER AND WASHER SWITCH

SWITCH MOUNTING BRACKET

CLUSTER HOUSING

KNOB TRIP ODOMETER

CLOCK

LENS

SEAL

HEADLIGHT SWITCH ASSEMBLY

SENSOR (ATC ONLY)

CLUSTER HOUSING

VIEW IN DIRECTION OF ARROW A

*LEFT AIR CONDITIONER AIR OUTLET, IF SO EQUIPPED

Fig. 7 Instrument cluster. 1977–78 Chrysler Newport & New Yorker

Fig. 8 Instrument cluster. 1977 Gran Fury & Royal Monaco

NUT
BEZEL
VIEW IN DIRECTION OF ARROW A
COVER USED WITHOUT CLOCK
KNOBS
SCREW
REAR WINDOW DEFOGGER SWITCH
INSTRUMENT CLUSTER BEZEL
RETAINER CLIP
ASH TRAY PH139
BEZEL
NUT
SCREW
NUT
RADIO
BRACKET
SCREW
SWITCH LIGHT
PIN
SUB BEZEL
BEZEL
NUT
CLUSTER LENS
SCREW
LIGHTER LIGHT
SPRING NUT
MOUNTING PLATE
ELEMENT
SCREW
SHELL AND CLAMP
SCREW
TAILGATE DOOR UNLOCK SWITCH
TAILGATE WINDOW LIFT SWITCH
SCREW
SCREW
COVER*
SCREW
CLOCK
SCREW
SWITCH LIGHT
SCREW
WINDSHIELD WIPER AND WASHER SWITCH
OIL AND TEMPERATURE GAUGE (IF SO EQUIPPED)
SCREW
CLUSTER HOUSING
HEADLIGHT SWITCH
MOUNTING PLATE
RETAINER
ESCUTCHEON
SCREW
KNOB AND STEM

* LEFT AIR CONDITIONER AIR OUTLET, IF SO EQUIPPED

VACUUM LINES TO WATER VALVE AND MANIFOLD VACUUM TEE

HEATER ASSEMBLY TO PLENUM MOUNTING BRACE

BLOWER MOTOR ASSEMBLY

CENTER DISTRIBUTION DUCT

HEATER DISTRIBUTION HOUSING

VIEW IN DIRECTION OF ARROW X

Fig. 9 Heater core & blower motor assembly (less A/C). 1979 Magnum, 1979–81 Newport, New Yorker, St. Regis & Cordoba & 1980–81 Gran Fury & Mirada

HEATER ASSEMBLY MOUNTING BRACE

VACUUM ACTUATOR

CENTER DISTRIBUTION DUCT

BLOWER MOTOR ASSEMBLY

HEATER DISTRIBUTION HOUSING

Fig. 9A Heater core & blower motor assembly (less A/C). 1982–83 All models

W/S WIPER MOTOR, REPLACE

1977–83

1. Disconnect battery ground cable.
2. Remove wiper arm and blades.
3. Remove cowl screen.
4. Remove drive crank arm retaining nut and drive crank. Disconnect wiring to motor.
5. Unfasten and remove wiper motor.
6. Reverse procedure to install.

W/S WIPER TRANSMISSION REPLACE

1977–83

1. Disconnect the battery ground cable.
2. On all models except Aspen & Volaré, remove top plastic screen. On Aspen and Volaré, disconnect washer hose to gain access to drive crank.
3. On all models, remove the arm and blade assemblies.
4. Remove the drive crank from the wiper motor by removing the attaching nut.
5. On all models except Aspen, Diplomat, LeBaron, Volaré and 1982–83 Gran Fury and New Yorker, remove six pivot mounting screws.
6. On Aspen, Diplomat, LeBaron, Volaré and 1982–83 Gran Fury and New Yorker, remove pivot mounting nut and washer.
7. Reverse procedure to install.

W/S WIPER SWITCH, REPLACE

1979–81 Newport, New Yorker & St. Regis; 1980–81 Gran Fury; 1980–83 Cordoba & Mirada; 1981–83 Imperial; 1982–83 Diplomat, Gran Fury & New Yorker

Refer to "1977–83 procedure for turn signal switch removal.

1977–80 Aspen, Volaré, 1977–81 LeBaron & Diplomat

1. Disconnect battery ground cable.
2. Remove instrument cluster bezel.
3. Remove switch module assembly attaching screws, then pull assembly out and let hang in order to gain access to switch.
4. Remove switch knob from stem, then remove switch mounting screws.
5. Disconnect switch wire connector and remove switch.
6. Reverse procedure to install.

1977 Aspen, Volaré, Diplomat & LeBaron

1. Disconnect battery ground cable.
2. Remove cluster bezel.
3. Remove switch mounting plate attaching screws and pull switch and plate assembly outward.
4. Pull knob off switch and remove switch retaining nut.
5. Disconnect electrical connector and remove switch.
6. Reverse procedure to install.

1977–79 Charger, Cordoba & Fury, 1977–78 Monaco & 1978–79 Magnum

1. Disconnect battery ground cable.
2. Remove instrument cluster upper bezel and the switch escutcheon mounting screw.
3. Remove switch to cluster housing retaining screws and pull headlamp switch to the "On" position.
4. Slide escutcheon on shaft toward rear of vehicle and rotate upward, thereby gaining clearance for switch removal.
5. Pull switch from cluster housing, disconnect electrical connector and remove switch.
6. Reverse procedure to install.

1977 Gran Fury, Royal Monaco, 1977–78 Chrysler Newport & New Yorker

1. Disconnect battery ground cable.
2. Remove instrument cluster bezel.

3. Remove switch mounting screws.
4. Disconnect electrical connector and remove switch from bezel.
5. Reverse procedure to install.

RADIO, REPLACE

NOTE: When installing radio, be sure to adjust antenna trimmer for peak performance.

1979–81 Newport, New Yorker & St. Regis; 1980–81 Gran Fury; 1980–83 Cordoba & Mirada; 1981–83 Imperial

1. Disconnect battery ground cable.
2. Remove center bezel, then remove radio to panel attaching screws.
3. Pull radio from instrument panel, then disconnect antenna and electrical leads.
4. Reverse procedure to install.

1977–80 Aspen, Volaré, 1977–81 LeBaron, 1977–83 Diplomat & 1982–83 Gran Fury & New Yorker

1. Disconnect battery ground cable.
2. Remove instrument cluster bezel, then the radio mounting screws.
3. Pull radio from panel and disconnect all wiring, then remove radio from vehicle.
4. Reverse procedure to install.

1977–78 Fury, 1977–79 Charger, Cordoba, 1977–78 Monaco & 1978–79 Magnum

1. Disconnect battery ground cable.
2. Remove instrument cluster lower bezel.
3. From under panel, disconnect electrical leads and support bracket from radio.
4. From front of panel, remove radio attaching screws and remove radio from front of panel.
5. Reverse procedure to install.

1977 Gran Fury, Royal Monaco, 1977–78 Chrysler Newport & New Yorker

1. Disconnect battery ground cable.
2. Remove bezel. On Fury and Monaco, also remove sub bezel.
3. Remove lamp assembly from radio (monaural only).

Fig. 10A Heater core & blower motor assembly (with A/C). 1982–83 All models

Fig. 10 Heater core & blower motor assembly (with A/C). 1979 Magnum, 1979–81 Newport, New Yorker, St. Regis & Cordoba & 1980–81 Gran Fury, Mirada & 1981 Imperial

7. On all models, remove glove box, ash tray and housing, right hand lap cooler duct, lower right hand trim panel or bezel, and the right hand cowl trim pad.
8. Disconnect blower motor electrical connections.
9. Disconnect temperature control cable from heater housing, then remove heater distribution housing, Figs. 9 and 9A.
10. Support heater housing and remove the heater housing to plenum mounting brace. Pull housing rearward and move toward right side to remove.
11. Remove heater housing top cover, then the heater core retaining screw.
12. Lift heater core from housing.
13. Reverse procedure to install.

With Air Conditioning
1. Disconnect battery ground cable and drain cooling system.
2. Discharge air conditioning refrigerant system.
3. Disconnect heater hoses from heater core.
4. Remove "H" valve and cap refrigerant lines. Remove condensate drain tube.
5. Disconnect vacuum lines from engine compartment and push grommet and vacuum lines through dash panel.

NOTE: On manual air conditioning systems, the vacuum lines are connected to the manifold vacuum tee and water valve. On semi-automatic air conditioning systems, the vacuum lines are connected to the vacuum reservoir and water valve.

6. Remove four nuts attaching evaporator heater assembly to dash panel.
7. Move front seat rearward and remove console, if equipped.
8. On models except Cordoba, Imperial, Magnum and Mirada, remove air conditioning switch control from dash panel and disconnect vacuum harness from harness extension.
9. On all models, remove ash tray and housing and the glove box assembly.
10. Disconnect right hand lap cooler tube from lap cooler and remove the right hand trim panel or bezel.
11. Remove right hand cowl trim pad and disconnect blower motor electrical connections.
12. On Cordoba, Imperial, Magnum and Mirada, disconnect vacuum harness from harness extension, then remove heater distribution duct.

4. Remove radio to panel retaining screws and instrument panel upper cover.
5. Working through top of panel, disconnect antenna lead and remove radio mounting bracket nut.
6. On monaural radio, disconnect speaker lead from speaker. On stereo radio, disconnect speaker lead from radio.
7. Pull radio out from panel and disconnect electrical lead.
8. Reverse procedure to install.

HEATER CORE, REPLACE

Before attempting to remove a heater core, disconnect the battery ground cable, drain the radiator and remove inlet and outlet hoses from heater assembly in engine compartment.

1979 Magnum; 1979–81 Newport, New Yorker & St. Regis; 1979–83 Cordoba; 1980–81 Gran Fury; 1980–83 Mirada; 1981–83 Imperial

Less Air Conditioning
1. Disconnect battery ground cable and drain cooling system.
2. Disconnect heater hoses from heater core.
3. Disconnect vacuum hoses from water valve and manifold tee, then push hoses and grommet through dash panel.
4. Remove four nuts securing heater assembly to dash panel.
5. Move front seat rearward and remove console, if equipped.
6. On models except Cordoba, Imperial, Magnum and Mirada, remove heater control and disconnect vacuum harness from extension harness.

Fig. 11 Heater core & blower motor. 1977–78 less air conditioning (Typical)

13. On all models, disconnect temperature control cable from evaporator heater housing.
14. On models except Cordoba, Imperial, Magnum and Mirada, remove heater distribution housing and the center distribution duct.
15. On all models, remove the hi/lo door actuator, Figs. 10 and 10A.
16. On models with semi-automatic air conditioning system, remove vacuum servo actuator from housing and the in-car air hose from compensator.
17. On all models, support housing and remove brace between housing and plenum. Then, pull housing rearward and move toward right aide to remove.
18. Remove housing top cover and the heater core retaining screw.
19. Lift heater core from housing.
20. Reverse procedure to install.

1977–80 Aspen, Volaré, 1977–81 LeBaron, 1977–83 Diplomat & 1982–83 Gran Fury & New Yorker

Less Air Conditioning
1. Disconnect battery ground cable and drain cooling system.
2. Disconnect and plug heater hoses from dash panel.
3. Remove heater core tube dash panel seals and retainer.
4. Remove instrument cluster bezel assembly, upper cover, steering column cover, right intermediate side cowl trim panel and the lower instrument panel.
5. Remove instrument panel center to lower reinforcement.
6. Remove right vent control cable from unit.
7. Disconnect temperature and mode door control cables from unit, then the blower motor resistor block wiring.
8. Remove heater assembly mounting nuts in engine compartment.
9. Remove heater support to plenum bracket and pull heater unit from dash panel.
10. Separate heater housing by removing retainer clips.
11. Remove heater core tube support clamp and slide heater core from housing.
12. Reverse procedure to install.

With Air Conditioning
1. Disconnect battery ground cable and drain cooling system.
2. Discharge refrigerant system.
3. Remove air cleaner, then disconnect heater hoses from heater core. Install plugs in heater core tubes to prevent coolant from spilling when removing unit.
4. Remove "H" valve, then cap refrigerant lines to prevent dirt and moisture from entering.
5. Remove instrument cluster bezel assembly.
6. Remove instrument panel upper cover, steering column cover and right intermediate side cowl trim panel.
7. Remove lower instrument panel.
8. Remove instrument center to lower reinforcement.
9. Remove floor console, if equipped.
10. Remove right center air distribution duct.
11. Disconnect locking tab on defroster distribution duct.
12. Disconnect temperature control cable from evaporator housing.
13. Disconnect blower motor resistor block wire connector.

14. Disconnect vacuum lines from water valve and vacuum source tee.
15. Remove wiring from evaporator housing and vacuum lines from inlet air housing, then disconnect vacuum harness coupling.
16. Remove drain tube from engine compartment.
17. Remove nuts from evaporator housing mounting studs on engine side of dash panel.
18. Remove hanger strap from plenum stud above evaporator housing, then tilt evaporator housing back to clear dash panel and remove housing from vehicle.
19. Remove blend air door lever from shaft.
20. Remove top cover screws and the cover.
21. Remove heater core from housing.
22. Reverse procedure to install.

1977–78 Fury, Charger, Cordoba, Monaco & 1978 Magnum

Less Air Conditioning
1. Disconnect fusible link and drain coolant.
2. Disconnect heater hoses from core tubes and plug tubes to prevent coolant from spilling into interior of vehicle.
3. Remove nuts from around blower motor and one from center of dash panel, then remove lower instrument panel bezel, glove box and door.
4. Disconnect antenna lead from radio, then remove screw from housing to plenum support rod on right side of housing above outside air opening.
5. Disconnect air door control cables and wire from blower motor resistor.
6. Tip heater assembly down and out from under instrument panel.
7. Remove screws retaining front cover to heater assembly, then cut rubber seal in two places where front cover separates cover from housing.
8. Remove core tube retaining screw located behind housing and between core tubes.
9. Remove sponge rubber gaskets from core tubes and remove heater core from housing.
10. Reverse procedure to install.

With Air Conditioning
1. Disconnect fusible link and drain coolant.
2. Disconnect heater hoses from core tubes and plug tubes to prevent coolant from spilling into interior of vehicle.
3. Discharge A/C refrigerant and disconnect line from H-valve and cover tubing sealing plate. Remove expansion valve from evaporator and cover evaporator sealing plate and both sealing surfaces of expansion valve.
4. Disconnect blower motor wires and remove blower motor cooling tube.
5. Remove glove box, ash tray and housing bezel, right lap cooler, right side cowl panel and air distribution duct.
6. Remove A/C mode door vacuum actuator from bracket and shift actuator forward on top of unit.
7. Disconnect connector from seat belt interlock control module and disconnect wires from blower motor resistor.
8. Disconnect antenna lead from radio and remove radio.
9. Remove housing retaining nuts through

engine compartment, then remove rubber drain tube.
10. Remove support bracket from rear of unit to plenum.
11. Pull unit back so that tubes clear dash panel, then rotate so that right end of unit comes out first from under the instrument panel.
12. Carefully remove plenum air seal, then disconnect vacuum hose from inlet air door actuator.
13. On 1977-78 models, remove 18 clamps holding front and rear covers separate housings.
14. On all models, carefully lift left half of housing seal from rear cover. Do not remove entire seal as the lower portion is a water seal.
15. Remove two retaining screws from mounting plate and one from between heater core tubes and lift heater core from housing.
16. Reverse procedure to install.

1977 Gran Fury, Royal Monaco, 1977–78 Chrysler Newport & New Yorker

Less Air Conditioning
1. Disconnect battery ground cable and drain radiator.
2. Disconnect heater hoses and plug hose fittings on heater core.
3. Move front seat rearward and remove instrument panel lower cover. Unplug antenna lead from radio and disconnect upper level vent vacuum line.
4. Disconnect the upper level vent from heater housing and the mounting bracket from dash, then swing duct back.
5. Disconnect electrical connectors from blower motor resistor and control cable from clip and crank.
6. Disconnect support bracket and swing bracket out of way.
7. From engine compartment, remove five retaining nuts from studs.
8. Roll or tip housing out from under instrument panel and disconnect control cable from clip and the blend air door crank.
9. Remove core tube locating screw from between core tubes, remove housing retaining nuts, separate housing and remove core.
10. Reverse procedure to install.

With Air Conditioning
1. Discharge refrigerant system.
2. Disconnect fusible link, drain cooling system, remove air cleaner and disconnect heater hoses at heater core. Install plugs in heater core tubes to prevent coolant spillage when removing heater core.
3. Remove "H" valve, then cap refrigerant lines to prevent entry of dirt and moisture.
4. Move front seat rearward to provide room to remove unit.
5. Remove lap cooler and instrument panel lower cover.
6. Remove A/C distribution duct.
7. Disconnect antenna lead from radio and wires and vacuum lines from unit.
8. Remove drain tube. On models with ATC, disconnect wire connectors and vacuum connector from servo, amplifier and master and compressor switches. Disconnect aspirator tube.
9. On all models, remove temperature control cable from clip on unit.
10. Remove retaining nut from support bracket.

DEFROSTER DUCT

REAR HOUSING

EXISTING STUD
IN PLENUM
PANEL

INLET AIR DOOR
HOUSING ASSEMBLY

FRONT HOUSING

REAR HOUSING

HEAT/DEFROST
DOOR ACTUATOR

TO PUSH BUTTON
EXTENSION ASSEMBLY

A/C DOOR ACTUATOR

INLET AIR DOOR
ACTUATOR

SUPPORT BRACKET

BLOWER MOTOR
RESISTOR BLOCK

INLET AIR DOOR
HOUSING ASSEMBLY

ENGINE SIDE HOUSING

Fig. 12 Heater core & blower motor. 1977–78 with air conditioning (Typical)

Fig. 13 Speed Control lock-in screw adjustment. 1977-83

Fig. 14 Speed Control servo cable throttle adjustment. 1977-83

11. From engine side of dash panel, remove retaining nuts from studs.
12. Tilt housing and remove from under instrument panel.
13. Remove mode door and blend air door levers.
14. Remove attaching screws and lift off top cover.
15. Remove four heater core retaining screws and three screws from core tube seal, then lift heater core from housing.
16. Reverse procedure to install.

BLOWER MOTOR, REPLACE

1982-83 Diplomat, Gran Fury & New Yorker

NOTE: The blower motor is accessible from under right side of instrument panel.

Less A/C
1. Disconnect battery ground cable.
2. Disconnect blower motor ground and feed wires.
3. Remove blower motor to heater housing attaching screws, then remove blower motor, Fig. 9A.
4. Reverse procedure to install.

With A/C
1. Disconnect battery ground cable.
2. Disconnect blower motor feed wire, then remove blower motor housing to recirculation housing attaching nuts and separate blower motor housing from upper housing, Fig. 10A.
3. Remove blower motor plate attaching screws, then remove wire grommet, mounting plate and blower motor and wheel as an assembly.
4. Reverse procedure to install.

1979 Magnum; 1979-81 Newport, New Yorker & St. Regis; 1979-83 Cordoba; 1980-81 Gran Fury; 1980-83 Mirada & 1981-83 Imperial

NOTE: The blower motor is accessible from under right side of instrument panel.

1. Disconnect battery ground cable.
2. Remove glove box assembly.

3. Disconnect blower motor electrical connections.
4. Remove heater housing or evaporator-heater housing to plenum brace.
5. Remove blower motor mounting screws and the blower motor, Figs. 9, 9A, 10, and 10A.
6. Reverse procedure to install.

1977-80 Aspen, Volaré, 1977-81 LeBaron & Diplomat

Less Air Conditioning
1. Remove heater assembly and heater core as outlined under "Heater Core, Replace".
2. Remove blower motor vent tube.
3. Remove blower motor mounting nuts and the blower motor.
4. Reverse procedure to install.

With Air Conditioning

NOTE: All service to the blower motor is performed under the right side of the instrument panel.

1. Disconnect battery ground cable and the blower motor feed wire.
2. Remove blower motor mounting nuts from bottom of recirculation housing.
3. Separate upper and lower blower motor housing, then remove blower motor mounting plate screws.
4. Remove wire grommet, mounting plate and blower motor.
5. Reverse procedure to install.

1977 Gran Fury & Royal Monaco, 1977-78 Chrysler Newport & New Yorker

The blower motor is mounted to the engine side housing under the right front fender between the inner fender shield and the fender, Figs. 11 and 12. The inner fender shield must be removed to service the blower motor.

1977-78 Charger, Fury, Cordoba, Monaco; 1978 Magnum

Less Air Conditioning
The heater assembly must be removed to service the blower motor. See procedure for

Heater Core Removal to remove assembly, then proceed to *Remove Blower Motor* as follows:
1. Disconnect blower motor lead from resistor block. Disconnect the ground wire from the mounting plate.
2. Remove six screws and retaining clips holding blower motor mounting plate to housing. Separate the blower motor and mounting plate from the housing, Fig. 12.
3. Remove the blower wheel from the motor shaft.
4. Remove the two retaining nuts and separate the motor from the mounting plate. Remove the motor, Fig. 11.
5. Reverse procedure to install.

With Air Conditioning

NOTE: All service to the blower motor is made from the engine compartment side.

1. Disconnect battery ground cable. Disconnect the feed wire at the connector and the ground wire. Remove the air tube.
2. Remove three screws located on the outer surface of the mounting plate.
3. Remove the mounting plate and blower motor as an assembly, Fig. 12.

SPEED CONTROLS, ADJUST

Lock-in Screw Adjustment, Fig. 13
Lock-in accuracy will be affected by poor engine performance (need for tune-up), loaded gross weight of car (trailering), improper slack in control cable. After the foregoing items have been considered and the speed sags or drops more than 2 to 3 mph when the speed control is activated, the lock-in adjusting screw should be turned counter-clockwise approximately 1/4 turn per one mph correction required.

If a speed increase of more than 2 to 3 mph occurs, the lock-in adjusting screw should be turned clockwise 1/4 turn per one mph correction required.

CAUTION: This adjustment must not exceed

two turns in either direction or damage to the unit may occur.

Throttle Cable Adjustment, Fig. 14

Optimum servo performance is obtained with a given amount of free play in the throttle control cable. To obtain proper free play, insert a 1/16″ diameter pin between forward end of slot in cable end of carburetor linkage pin (hair pin clip removed from linkage pin). With choke in full open position and carbure-tor at curb idle, pull cable back toward dash panel without moving carburetor linkage until all free play is removed. Tighten cable clamp bolt to 45 inch-pounds, remove 1/16″ pin and install hair pin clip.

Brake Switch Adjustment

1. Loosen switch bracket.
2. Insert proper spacer gauge between brake push rod and switch with pedal in free position. On 1977–78 models, the spacer must be .120 in. for 1977–78 full size models and .140 in. for 1977–78 inter-mediates. On all 1979 models a .140 inch spacer is used. On 1980–81 Gran Fury, Newport, New Yorker and St. Regis models, a .150 inch spacer is used. On 1980–81 models except Gran Fury, Newport, New Yorker and St. Regis and all 1982–83 models, a .130 inch spacer is used.
3. Push switch bracket assembly toward brake push rod until plunger is fully depressed and switch contacts spacer.
4. Tighten bracket bolt to 75 in-lbs. and remove spacer.

Engine Section

ENGINE MOUNTS, REPLACE

1. Disconnect throttle linkage at transmission and at carburetor.
2. Raise hood and position fan to clear radiator hose and radiator top tank.
3. Remove torque nuts from insulator studs.
4. Raise engine just enough to remove front engine mount.
5. Reverse above to install.

ENGINE, REPLACE

All V8 Engines

1. Scribe a line on hinge brackets on hood to assure proper adjustments when installing. Then remove hood.
2. Remove battery, drain cooling system, remove all hoses, fan shroud, disconnect oil cooler lines and remove radiator.
3. On models with A/C, remove compressor from mounting bracket and position on right fender.

NOTE: Do not tilt compressor when removed from mounting bracket. Before installing compressor turn pulley several revolutions by hand to ensure all oil is back in compressor oil sump.

4. On all models, remove distributor cap, vacuum lines and wiring.
5. Remove carburetor, linkage, starter wires and oil pressure wire.
6. Disconnect power steering hoses, if equipped.
7. Remove starter, alternator, charcoal canister and horns.
8. Disconnect exhaust pipe at manifold.
9. On vehicles with automatic transmission:
   a. Mark converter and drive plate to aid in installation.
   b. Remove torque converter drive plate bolts.
   c. Install a C-clamp on bottom front of torque converter, to assure that converter remains properly positioned in transmission housing.
   d. Remove converter housing to engine bolts.
   e. Support transmission in its normal position to assure ease of installation.
10. On vehicles with manual transmission, remove transmission.
11. Attach engine lifting fixture.
12. Remove engine front mounting bolts, then raise and work engine out of chassis.
13. Reverse procedure to install.

6-225

1. Scribe hood hinge outlines on hood and remove hood.
2. Drain cooling system and remove battery and carburetor air cleaner.
3. Disconnect transmission cooler lines at radiator (if equipped).
4. Remove radiator and hoses.
5. On models with A/C, remove compressor from mounting bracket and position on right fender.

NOTE: Do not tilt compressor when removed from mounting bracket. Before installing compressor turn pulley several revolutions by hand to ensure all oil is back in compressor sump.

6. On all models, remove closed ventilation system and evaporative control system from cylinder head cover.
7. Disconnect fuel lines, vacuum lines, carburetor linkage and wiring to engine.
8. Disconnect power steering hoses, if equipped.
9. Remove starter, alternator and horns.
10. Disconnect exhaust pipe at manifold.
11. Remove converter cover plate.
12. On manual transmission equipped vehicles disconnect propeller shaft, tie out of the way and disconnect wires and linkage at transmission.
13. On manual transmission equipped vehicles attach engine support fixture, re-move engine rear crossmember and remove transmission.
14. On automatic transmission equipped vehicles disconnect torque converter drive plate from engine. Mark converter and drive plate to aid in installation. Support transmission in its normal position in relation to the vehicle, to insure ease of installation.
15. Attach lifting fixture to cylinder head and attach chain hoist.
16. Remove engine support and front engine mounting bolts and lift engine from chassis.
17. Reverse procedure to install.

CYLINDER HEAD, REPLACE

6-225

1. Drain cooling system.
2. Remove carburetor air cleaner and fuel line.
3. Disconnect accelerator linkage.
4. Remove vacuum control tube at carburetor and distributor.
5. Disconnect spark plug wires, heater hose and clamp holding by-pass hose.
6. Disconnect heat indicator sending unit wire.

NOTE: On models equipped with air pump, disconnect diverter valve vacuum line from intake manifold and remove air tubes from cylinder head.

7. Disconnect exhaust pipe at manifold.
8. On 1977 models, remove intake and exhaust manifold and carburetor as a unit.
9. On all models, remove closed vent system and rocker arm cover.
10. Remove rocker shaft assembly and push rods.

NOTE: During disassembly note location of push rods so they can be installed in the same position.

11. On 1977 models, remove cylinder head bolts and lift off cylinder head. On 1978–83 models, remove cylinder head bolts, then remove cylinder head and intake and exhaust manifold as an assembly.

Fig. 1   Cylinder head tightening sequence. 6-225

Fig. 2 Intake manifold tightening sequence. V8-318, 360

Fig. 3 Cylinder head tightening sequence. V8-318, 360

Fig. 4 Cylinder head tightening sequence. V8-400, 440

Fig. 3A Cylinder head bolt hole identification. Some 1979 and all 1980—83 Chrysler Corp. V8-318 engines.

12. Install the head in the reverse order of removal, and tighten the bolts in the sequence shown in Fig. 1.
13. *When installing the manifolds, loosen the three bolts holding the intake and exhaust manifolds together. This is required to maintain proper alignment.* Install intake and exhaust manifolds with cup side of the conical washers against the manifolds.

V8-318, 360

NOTE: The intake manifold attaching bolts on some engines are tilted upward about 30 degrees at an angle to the manifold-to-cylinder head gasket face. The purpose of this design is to provide more effective sealing at the cylinder block end gaskets. If the intake manifold is removed the installation should be such that the bolt tightening is done evenly and in the sequence shown in Fig. 2.

With gaskets in place start all bolts, leaving them loose. Run bolts 1 through 4 down so the heads just touch manifold. Then tighten these four bolts to 25 foot-pounds torque. After checking to see that gaskets are properly seated at all surfaces, tighten remaining bolts to 25 foot-pounds. Finally tighten all bolts in the sequence shown to specifications.

1. Drain cooling system and disconnect battery ground cable.
2. Remove alternator, carburetor air cleaner and fuel line. Disconnect accelerator linkage.
3. Remove vacuum advance hose and distributor cap and wires.
4. Disconnect coil wires, heat indicator wire, heater and by-pass hoses.
5. Remove closed ventilation system and rocker arm covers.
6. Remove intake manifold, coil and carburetor as an assembly.
7. Remove exhaust manifolds.
8. Remove rocker arm and shaft assemblies. Remove push rods.

NOTE: During disassembly note location of push rods so they can be installed in the same position.

9. Remove head bolts and cylinder heads.
10. Reverse procedure to install heads and tighten bolts in sequence, Fig. 3.

Service Note

Some 1979 and all 1980—83 V8-318 engines have cylinder head bolt holes drilled through the block into the water jacket in certain locations, Fig. 3A. On 1979 models, this type cylinder block is identified by engine numbers beginning with 9M3180702 or 4104230-318. If engine number cannot be determined, refer to Fig. 3A and insert a screwdriver into the head bolt holes. If the screwdriver can be inserted at least two inches into a hole, that hole is open to the water jacket. Cylinder head bolts in these locations must have sealer 4057989 or equivalent applied to the threads to prevent engine coolant leakage. Ensure old sealer is cleaned from the threads before applying new sealer. Cylinder head bolt torque on these engines has been reduced to 95 ft. lbs.

V8-400, 440

1. Drain cooling system, remove air cleaner, fuel line from pump and carburetor, distributor vacuum tube and alternator.

NOTE: On models equipped with high mount air pump, disconnect diverter

Fig. 5 Intake manifold tightening sequence. V8-400 & 440

valve vacuum line from intake manifold and air pump line from exhaust manifolds.

2. Disconnect throttle linkage at carburetor, distributor cap, coil wires, heat indicator sending unit wire and heater hoses at engine.
3. Remove spark plugs and cables, and closed vent system.
4. Remove intake manifold, carburetor and coil as an assembly.
5. Remove exhaust manifolds.
6. Remove cylinder head covers and spark plug cable support brackets.
7. Remove rocker shaft assemblies. *Do not remove bolts from end brackets.*
8. Remove push rods and valve lifter chamber cover.

NOTE: During disassembly note location of push rods so they can be installed in the same position.

9. Remove attaching bolts and lift off heads.
10. Reverse the foregoing procedure to install the heads. Tighten bolts in the sequence shown in Fig. 4. Tighten intake manifold bolts in sequence shown in Fig. 5.

VALVES, ADJUST

6-225

NOTE: Some 1978 Aspen and Volare models

Fig. 6 Rocker arm and shaft assembly. 6-225

with 6-225 2 bar. carb. engines will be equipped with hydraulic lifters which can not be adjusted.

Before the final valve lash adjustment is made, operate the engine for 5 minutes at a fast idle to stabilize engine temperatures.

Before starting the adjustment procedure, make two chalk marks on the vibration damper. Space the marks approximately 120° apart (1/3 of circumference) so that with the timing mark the damper is divided into three equal parts. Adjust the valves for No. 1 cylinder. Repeat the procedure for the remaining valves, turning the crankshaft 1/3 turn in the direction of normal rotation while adjusting the valves in the firing order sequence of 153624.

VALVE ARRANGEMENT

Front to Rear

8-318, 360	E-I-I-E-E-I-I-E
8-400, 440	E-I-I-E-E-I-I-E
6-225	E-I-E-I-E-I-E-I-E-I-E

VALVE LIFT SPECS.

Engine	Year	Intake	Exhaust
6-225	1977-80	.406	.414
	1981-83	.378	.378
8-318	1977	.373	.399
	1978-83	.373	.400
8-360	1977-80	.410	.410
8-400	1977②	.434	.464
	1977①	.434	.430
	1978 All	.434	.430
8-440	1977①	.434	.430
	1977-78②	.449	.464

①—Exc. Hi. Perf.
②—Hi. Perf.

VALVE TIMING SPECS.

Intake Opens Before TDC

Engine	Year	Degrees
6-225	1977-80	16
	1981-83	6
8-318	1977-83	10
8-360	1977-80	18
8-400	1977 All	20
	1978 All	18
8-440	1977 All	20
	1978 Exc. Hi. Perf.	18
	1978 Hi. Perf.	21

ROCKER ARMS, REPLACE

6-225

1. Remove closed ventilation and evaporation control systems.
2. Remove rocker arm cover.
3. Remove rocker shaft bolts and retainers.
4. Lift off rocker arms and shaft.

Inspection

Clean all parts with a suitable solvent. Be sure the inside of the shaft is clean and the oil holes are open. The drilled oil hole in the bore of the rocker arm must be open to the trough and valve end of the arms. The trough also feeds oil to the adjusting screw and push rod.

The shaft should be free from excessive wear in arm contact areas. The shaft should be smooth in retainer contact areas. The adjusting screws in the rocker arms should have a uniform round end. The drag torque should be smooth and uniform. The retainers should be smooth and undamaged in the shaft contact area.

Assemble and Install

1. Referring to Fig. 6, note position of oil hole on forward end of shaft which denotes the upper side of shaft. Rocker arms must be put on the shaft with the adjusting screw to the right side of the engine. Place one of the small retainers on the one long bolt and install the bolt in the rear hole in the shaft from the top side.
2. Install one rocker arm and one spacer; then two rocker arms and a spacer. Continue in same sequence until all rocker arms and spacers are on the shaft.
3. Place a bolt and small retainer in front

hole in shaft.
4. Place a bolt and the one *wide* retainer through the center hole in the shaft with six rocker arms on each side of center.
5. Install remaining bolts and retainers.
6. Locate the assembly on the cylinder head and position rocker arm adjusting screws in push rods.
7. Tighten bolts finger tight, bringing retainers in contact with the shaft *between* rocker arms.
8. Tighten bolts to specified torque.
9. After running engine to normal operating temperature, adjust valve lash to specifications.
10. Complete the job by installing the remaining parts removed.

V8-318, 360

To provide correct lubrication for the rocker arms on these engines, the rocker shafts have a small notch machined at one end and these notches must always face inward toward the center of the engine when installed. In other words, the notched end must be toward the rear of the engine on the right bank, and to the front of the engine on the left bank.

Rocker arms must be correctly positioned on the shaft prior to installation on cylinder head, Fig. 7.

It is also important when installing the rocker shaft assembly on the cylinder head to position the short retainers at each end and in the center, and to place long retainers in the two remaining positions.

V8-400, 440

1. Install rocker shafts so that the 3/16" diameter rocker arm lubrication holes point downward into rocker arm, and so that the 15 degree angle of these holes point outward toward valve end of rocker arm, Fig. 8. The 15 degree angle is determined from the center line of the bolt holes through the shaft which are used to attach the shaft assembly to the cylinder head.
2. On all engines, install rocker arms and shaft assembly, making sure to install long stamped steel retainers in No. 2 and 4 positions.

NOTE: Use extreme care in tightening the bolts so that valve lifters have time to bleed down to their operating length. Bulged lifter bodies, bent push rods and permanent noisy operation may result if lifters are forced down too rapidly.

3. Installation should be as shown in Fig. 7.

Fig. 7 Rocker arm and shaft assembly installed. 8-318, 360, 400, 440

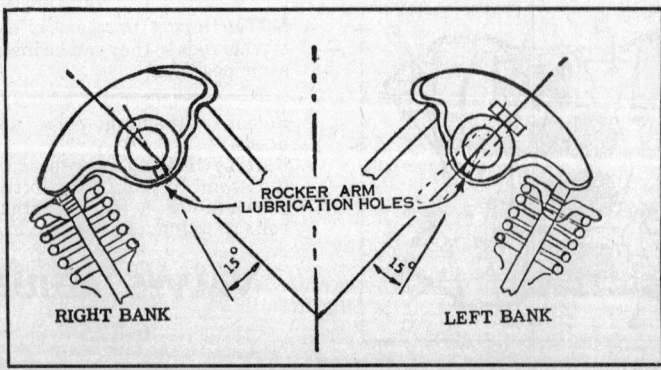

Fig. 8 Rocker arm shaft installation. V8-400, 440

Fig. 9   Removing valve lifter

VALVE GUIDES

Valves operate in guide holes bored directly in the cylinder head. When valve stem-to-guide clearance becomes excessive, valves with oversize stems of .005, .015 and .030 inch are available for service replacement. When necessary to install valves with oversize stems the valve bores should be reamed to provide the proper operating clearance.

VALVE LIFTERS, REPLACE

1977–83 6-225 & 1980–83 V8-318

After taking off rocker arm and shaft assembly, lift out push rods. The valve lifters may then be removed with a suitably long magnet rod. If the lifters cannot be removed with the magnet rod, a special tool (C-4129) may be used, Fig. 9. Insert the tool through the push rod opening in the cylinder head and into lifter. Turn the handle to expand the tool in the lifter, then with a twisting motion remove the lifter from its bore.

1978–79 V8-318, 360

1. Drain cooling system and remove air cleaner.
2. Remove valve covers, rocker shaft assemblies and push rods.

NOTE: Keep push rods in order so they can be installed in the same position.

3. Remove upper radiator hose, heater hose and bypass hose from intake manifold.
4. Remove distributor and intake manifold assembly, then remove lifters.

NOTE: Keep lifters in order so they can be installed in the same position.

5. Reverse procedure to install.

Fig. 11   Valve timing marks aligned for correct valve timing. All Sixes

1977 V8-318, 360 & 1977–78 V8-400, 440

Chrysler Tool is available for this operation. To remove the lifter, insert the tool in the lifter body. (This portion of the tool can be used to remove lifters without a varnish build-up around the bottom of the body.) Lift the lifter out of the bore, Fig. 10. If they are struck proceed as follows:

Slide the puller portion of the tool through the cylinder head push rod holes and seat it firmly in the top of the lifter. Insert the puller pin through the body and tool shaft in the holes provided, Fig. 9. Grasp the tool handle and pull the lifter out of the bore as shown.

TIMING CHAIN COVER, REPLACE

6-225

1. To remove cover, drain cooling system and remove radiator and fan.
2. Remove vibration damper with a puller.
3. Loosen oil pan bolts to allow clearance and remove chain case cover.
4. Reverse above procedure to install cover.

V8-400, 440

1. Drain cooling system.
2. Remove radiator, fan and belt.
3. Remove power steering pump and alternator attaching bolts and position pump and alternator aside.
4. If equipped with A/C, position compressor aside.
5. Remove water pump and housing as an assembly.
6. Remove crankshaft bolt and pulley from vibration damper and remove damper with a puller.
7. Remove key from crankshaft.
8. Remove chain case cover and gasket, *Use extreme caution to avoid damaging the oil pan gasket; if damaged it will be necessary to remove the oil pan in order to install a new pan gasket.*
9. Reverse procedure to install.

V8-318, 360

1. Remove radiator, fan and belt.
2. Remove water pump and housing as a unit.
3. Remove power steering pump, if necessary.
4. Remove crankshaft pulley.
5. Remove key from crankshaft.
6. Remove fuel pump.
7. Loosen oil pan bolts and remove front bolt at each side.
8. Remove chain case cover and gasket, *using extreme caution to avoid damaging oil pan gasket otherwise oil pan will have to be removed. It is normal to find particles of neoprene collected between crankshaft seal retainer and oil slinger.*
9. Reverse procedure to install.

TIMING CHAIN, REPLACE

6-225

1. After removing chain case cover as outlined above, take off camshaft sprocket attaching bolt.
2. Remove chain with camshaft sprocket.

Fig. 10   Hydraulic valve lifter

3. Clean all parts and dry with compressed air.
4. Inspect timing chain for broken or damaged links. Inspect sprockets for cracks and chipped, worn or damaged teeth.

Installation

1. Turn crankshaft so sprocket timing mark is toward and directly in line with centerline of camshaft.
2. Temporarily install camshaft sprocket. Rotate camshaft to position sprocket timing mark toward and directly in line with centerline of crankshaft; then remove camshaft sprocket.
3. Place chain on crankshaft sprocket and position camshaft sprocket in chain so sprocket can be installed with timing marks aligned without moving camshaft, Fig. 11.
4. Install parts removed in reverse order of removal.

V8 Engines

To install chain and sprockets, lay both the camshaft and crankshaft sprockets on the bench. Position the sprockets so that the timing marks are next to each other. Place the chain on both sprockets, then push the gears apart as far as the chain will permit. Use a straightedge to form a line through the exact centers of both gears. The timing marks must be on this line, Fig. 12.

Slide the chain with both sprockets on the camshaft and crankshaft at the same time; then recheck the alignment.

NOTE: On V8 engines, use tool No. C-3509 to prevent camshaft from contacting welch plug in rear of engine block. Remove distributor

Fig. 12   Valve timing marks aligned for correct valve timing. All V8s

Fig. 13 Camshaft and related parts. 6-225

and oil pump-distributor drive gear. Position tool against rear side of cam gear and attach tool with distributor retainer plate bolt.

CAMSHAFT & BEARINGS, REPLACE

6-225

The camshaft is supported by four precision type, steel backed, babbitt-lined bearings. Rearward thrust is taken by the rear face of the sprocket hub contacting the front of the engine block.

The camshaft, Fig. 13, can be removed after removing the grille, radiator and timing chain. To remove the camshaft bearings, the engine must be removed from the vehicle.

1. Remove valve lifters, oil pump, fuel pump and distributor.
2. Install a long bolt into front of camshaft to aid removal. Remove camshaft using care not to damage bearings.
3. Remove welch plug back of rear camshaft bearing.
4. Remove bearings with suitable puller equipment.
5. Install new bearings, being sure the oil holes in bearings line up with the corresponding oil holes in the crankcase.

NOTE: Install No. 1 camshaft bearing 3/32 in. inward from front face of cylinder block.

6. Apply sealer to welch plug and plug bore, then install plug at rear of camshaft.

V8 Engines

To remove the camshaft, remove all valve lifters, timing chain and sprockets. Remove distributor and oil pump-distributor drive gear. Remove fuel pump and see that push rod has moved away from eccentric drive cam. On V8-318 & 360 engine, remove thrust plate, 1977–83 engines incorporate a timing chain oil tab, before removing, note position of tab so it can be installed in the same manner. On all engines withdraw camshaft from engine, using care to see that camshaft lobes do not damage the camshaft bearings.

If camshaft bearings are to be replaced, it is recommended that the engine be removed from the chassis and the crankshaft taken out in order that any chips or foreign material may be removed from the oil passages.

NOTE: On V8-400 & 440 engines, install No. 1 camshaft bearing 1/32 in. inward from front face of cylinder block.

Apply sealer to welch plug and plug bore, then install plug at rear of camshaft.

PISTON & ROD, ASSEMBLE

6-225

Piston and rod assemblies must be installed as shown in Figs. 14 and 15.

V8 Engines

When installing piston and rod assemblies in the cylinders, the compression ring gaps should be diametrically opposite one another and not in line with the oil ring gap. The oil ring expander gap should be toward the outside of the "V" of the engine. The oil ring gap should be turned toward the inside of the engine "V".

Immerse the piston head and rings in clean engine oil and, with a suitable piston ring compressor, insert the piston and rod assembly into the bore. Tap the piston down into the bore, using the handle of a hammer.

Assemble the pistons to the rods as shown in Fig. 16.

PISTONS, PINS & RINGS

Pistons are available in standard sizes and the following oversizes: 1977 .005, .020; 1978–83 .020.

Pins are available in the following oversizes: V8-318 & 360, .003, .008 inch. Not furnished on all other engines.

Rings are available in the following oversizes: std. to .009, .020–.029, .040–.049 inch.

MAIN & ROD BEARINGS

Main bearings are furnished in standard sizes and the following undersizes: .001, .002, .003, .010, .012".

Rod bearings are furnished in standard sizes and the following undersizes: .001, .002, .003, .010, .012".

V8-400 and 440 use either forged or cast

Fig. 14 Piston and rod assembly. 1977 6-225, engines

crankshafts. These engines require that a matching torque converter, short block, damper and connecting rods be used.

If replacement of the crankshaft, torque converter, crankshaft damper or short engine is required, it is important that matching parts are used otherwise severe engine vibration will result, (Consult Chrysler Parts Dept.).

The cast crankshaft engine can be easily identified since it has the letter "E" stamped on the engine numbering pad following the built date.

Also, V8-440 engines built starting January 1976, will have external balance weights at the front damper and torque converter and a clock face will appear on the number 1 counterweight of the cast crankshaft.

6-225 engines built after June 1, 1976 may be equipped with either a cast or forged

Fig. 16 Piston and rod assembly, V8 engines

Fig. 15 Piston and rod assembly. 1978–83 6-225

Fig. 17 Lower oil seal & retainer. 6-225

ADD SEALER

SEALS

360 ENGINE BEARING CAP

318 ENGINE BEARING CAP

Fig. 18 Rear main bearing caps. V8-318 & 360

crankshaft. The following parts are not interchangeable between cast and forged crankshaft engines, crankshaft, crankshaft bearings, connecting rods and bearings and cylinder block. On models equipped with manual transmission, cast crankshaft engine vibration damper is not interchangeable with forged crankshaft engine and requires that a crankshaft screw and washer be used and torqued to 135 ft. lbs. On models equipped with automatic transmission, vibration damper and torque converter are interchangeable between cast and forged crankshaft engines.

CRANKSHAFT REAR OIL SEAL, REPLACE

6-225

Replacement seals are of two piece rubber type composition which make possible the replacement of upper rear seal without removing crankshaft. Both halves must be used. After removing oil pan, rear main bearing cap and seal retainer, pry lower rope seal from retainer with small screwdriver. Screw a special tool into upper rope seal and carefully pull to remove seal while rotating crankshaft. Wipe crankshaft surface clean, then oil lightly before installing new upper seal. After oiling seal lip, hold seal with paint stripe to rear tightly against crankshaft with thumb. Carefully slide seal into groove in block making sure sharp edge does not shave or nick seal. Crankshaft may be rotated to ease seal into groove but sealing lip must not be damaged. Install other half of seal into lower seal retainer again with paint stripe to rear, then install rear main bearing cap and torque to specifications. Before installing seal retainer, apply a small amount of gasket sealer to mating surface of retainer but not on seal ends or seal lip, Fig. 17. Install retainer and torque to 30 ft. lbs.

V8-318 & 360

Replacement of rear main bearing oil seals is similar to procedure given above for 6 cylinder engines. A seal retainer is not found on these engines; lower half of seal is installed into groove in rear main bearing cap.

The 318 engine has capseals in addition to lower seal secured by rear main bearing cap. Cap seal with yellow paint is installed, narrow sealing edge up, into right side with bearing cap in engine position. Cap seals must be flush with shoulder of bearing cap to prevent oil leakage.

The 360 engine requires sealer to be applied adjacent to rear main bearing oil seal as cap seals are not used, Fig. 18. After applying sealer, quickly assemble rear main bearing cap to block and torque to specifications.

V8-400, 440

Replacement seals are of two piece rubber type composition which make possible the replacement of upper rear seal without removing crankshaft. Both halves must be used. After removing oil pan, seal retainer and rear main bearing cap, pry lower rope seal and side seals from lower seal retainer with small screwdriver. Thoroughly clean seal retainer grooves. Screw a special tool into upper rope seal and carefully pull to remove seal while rotating crankshaft. Wipe crankshaft surface clean, then oil lightly before installing new upper seal. After oiling seal lip, hold seal with paint stripe to rear tightly against crankshaft with thumb. Carefully slide seal into groove in block making sure sharp edge does not shave or nick seal. Crankshaft may be rotated to ease seal into groove but sealing lip must not be damaged. Install other half of seal with paint stripe to rear into seal retainer. Install rear main bearing cap and torque to specifications. The side seals used with the rear seal retainer should be installed in the retainer and then into the engine as quickly as possible. These seals are made from a material that expands rapidly when oiled. Apply sealer to mating face of seal retainer but not to side seals or main bearing seal ends, then oil side seals with mineral spirits or diesel fuel. Install seals in seal retainer grooves then quickly install retainer and torque to 30 ft. lbs. Failure to pre-oil seals will result in an oil leak.

OIL PAN, REPLACE

CAUTION: *Engine oil pan bolts on V8-440 engines are 13/16" long with the exception of two bolts at the rear center of the oil pan. The two rear center bolts are 9/16" long and thread into the aluminum seal retainer. Do not use longer bolts than 9/16" at this location as they will bottom in the aluminum seal retainer and, if forced in may strip the threads and damage the seal retainer, causing an oil leak.*

6-225

1. Drain radiator, disconnect battery ground cable and radiator hoses and remove oil dipstick.
2. Remove shroud attaching screws, separate shroud from radiator and position rearward on engine.
3. Raise vehicle and drain oil pan.
4. Remove engine to transmission support bracket.
5. Disconnect exhaust pipe, then torque converter inspection shield.
6. Remove center link from steering arm and idler arm ball joints.
7. Support front of engine with a jack stand placed under the right front corner of oil pan.
8. Remove engine front mount bolts. Raise engine approx. 1½ to 2".
9. Remove oil pan attaching screws, rotate engine crankshaft to clear counterweights and remove oil pan.
10. Reverse procedure to install.

V8-400, 440

1. Disconnect battery ground cable and drain crankcase.
2. Raise car on hoist and disconnect steering linkage from idler arm and pitman arm.
3. Remove outlet vent pipe and disconnect exhaust pipe branches from manifolds.
4. Remove clamp attaching exhaust pipe to extension and remove exhaust pipe.
5. Remove converter dust shield.
6. Remove oil pan bolts and turn flywheel until counterweight and connecting rods at the front end of crankshaft are at their highest position to provide clearance, and lower the pan. Turn the pan to clear oil screen and suction pipe.
7. On some models, it may be necessary to release motor mounts and raise engine approximately 1½ to 2 inches.
8. Reverse procedure to install.

V8-318, 360

1977 Royal Monaco, Gran Fury; 1977–78 Charger, Fury & Monaco; 1977–79 Cordoba; 1979 Magnum; 1979–81 Newport, New Yorker & St. Regis

1. Disconnect battery ground cable and remove oil level dipstick.
2. Raise vehicle and drain crankcase, then remove engine to torque converter left housing strut.
3. Remove steering idler arm ball joints from center link.
4. Disconnect exhaust pipes from exhaust manifolds.

Fig. 19 Oil pump. 6-225

Fig. 20 Oil pump. V8-318 & 360

5. Remove oil pan attaching bolts.
6. Position a suitable jack under transmission remove rear engine mount to transmission extension attaching bolts.
7. Raise transmission until rear of oil pan can be lowered to clear transmission.
8. Reverse procedure to install.

1977–80 Aspen & Volaré; 1977–81 LeBaron; 1977–83 Diplomat; 1978 Chrysler; 1980–83 Cordoba & Mirada; 1981–83 Imperial; 1982–83 Gran Fury & New Yorker

1. Disconnect battery ground cable and remove engine oil level dipstick.
2. Raise vehicle and drain crankcase.
3. Remove exhaust crossover pipe, then disconnect and lower center link.
4. Remove starter and starter mounting stud.
5. Remove torque converter inspection cover.
6. Remove oil pan attaching bolts and oil pan.
7. Reverse procedure to install.

1977–80 V8-360 4 Bar. Carb.

1. Disconnect battery ground cable and remove oil dipstick.
2. Remove fan shroud attaching bolts and place shroud over fan.
3. Raise vehicle and disconnect steering linkage center link.
4. Remove oil pan bolts.
5. Raise transmission slightly with a suitable jack and remove rear engine mount to transmission bolts.
6. Lower rear of oil pan until clear of transmission.
7. Lower transmission and loosely install the rear engine mount bolts.
8. Loosen front engine mounts from frame.
9. Raise engine with a suitable jack approximately one inch and remove oil pan.
10. Reverse procedure to install.

OIL PUMP, REPLACE

Six Cylinder

1. Drain radiator and disconnect upper and lower hoses.
2. Remove fan shroud (if equipped).
3. Raise vehicle on a hoist, support front of engine with a jack stand place under right front corner of engine oil pan. *Do not support engine at crankshaft pulley or vibration damper.*

4. Remove front engine mounts.
5. Raise engine 1½ to 2 inches.
6. Remove oil filter, pump attaching bolts and remove pump assembly.
7. Reverse procedure to install.

V8 Engines

SERVICE BULLETIN

1978–80 V8-318, 360 Low Oil Pressure: An incorrectly installed oil line plug, part number 3462871, may cause low or dropping oil pressure. To check plug for proper position:

1. Remove oil pressure sending unit from rear of cylinder block.
2. Insert a ⅛ inch wire into sensing unit hole to measure distance between plug and top of machined surface of oil pressure sending unit hole.
3. The distance should be 7½ to 7 11/16 inches.
4. If measurement is less than 7½ inches, use a suitable dowel drift to drive plug into proper position.
5. If measurement is greater than 7 11/16 inches, remove oil pan and the No. 5 main bearing cap. Drive plug upward to properly position.

On 318, 360 engines, remove oil pump from rear main bearing cap.

On V8-400 and 440 engines, unfasten oil pump from engine and remove pump and filter assembly from bottom of engine.

Fig. 21 Oil pump. V8-400 & 440

OIL PUMP SERVICE
6-225

To disassemble, remove the pump cover seal ring, Fig. 19. Press off the drive gear, supporting the gear to keep load off aluminum body. Remove rotor and shaft and lift out outer pump rotor. Remove oil pressure relief valve plug and lift out spring and plunger. Remove oil pressure sending unit.

Inspection

1. The rotor contact area and the bores for the shaft and valve in the pump body should be smooth, free from scratches, scoring or excessive wear.
2. The pump cover should be smooth, flat and free from scoring or ridges. Lay a straightedge across the cover. If a .0015″ feeler gauge can be inserted under the straightedge, the cover should be replaced.
3. All surfaces of the outer rotor should be smooth and uniform, free from ridges, scratches or uneven wear. Discard a rotor less than .649 inch thick for 1977–80 or .825 inch thick for 1981–83 and/or less than 2.469 inch in diameter.
4. The inner rotor and shaft assembly should be smooth, free from scoring and uneven wear. Discard rotors less than .649 inch thick for 1977–80 or .825 inch thick for 1981–83.
5. Place outer rotor in pump body and measure clearance between rotor and body. Discard pump body if clearance is more than .014″.
6. Install inner rotor and shaft in pump body. Shaft should turn freely but without side play. If clearance between rotor teeth is more than .010 inch, replace both rotors.
7. Measure rotor end clearance. If feeler gauge of more than .004 inch can be inserted between straightedge and rotors, install a new pump body.
8. The oil pressure relief valve should be smooth, free from scratches or scoring, and should be a free fit in its bore.
9. The relief valve spring has a free length of 2¼ inches and should test between 22.3 and 23.3. pounds when compressed to 1 19/32 inch. If not, replace the spring.

Assemble and Install

1. With pump rotors in body, press drive gear on shaft, flush with end of shaft.
2. Install seal ring in groove in body and install cover. Tighten bolts to 95 inch lbs. Test pump for free turning.

Engine oiling system. 6-225

5. Mating surface of the pump cover should be smooth. If scratched or grooved, replace the pump.
6. Lay a straight edge across the cover. If a .0015 inch feeler gauge can be inserted between the cover and the straight edge, replace the pump.
7. Measure thickness and diameter of outer rotor. If rotor thickness is .825 inch or less on V8-318 engines, or .943 inch or less on V8-360 engines or if the diameter of the rotor is 2.429 inches or less, replace the outer rotor.
8. If the inner rotor is .825 inch or less on V8-318 engines, or .943 inch or less on V8-360 engines, replace the inner rotor and shaft assembly.
9. Install the outer rotor into the housing. Press rotor to one side with the fingers and measure the clearance between the rotor and body with a feeler gauge. If the measurement is .014 inch or greater, replace the pump.
10. Place the inner rotor and shaft into the pump. If clearance between the rotors is .010 inch or greater, replace the shaft and both rotors.
11. Place a straightedge across the face of the pump between bolt holes. If a feeler gauge of .004 inch or greater can be inserted, replace the pump.
12. Check the oil pump relief valve plunger for scoring and free operation in the bore. Small marks may be removed with 400-grit sand paper.
13. The relief valve spring should have a free length of 2-1/32 to 2-3/64 inch and should test between 16.2 and 17.2 pounds when compressed to 1-11/32 inch. If not, replace the spring.

V8-318, 360

After removing the pump from the engine, it should be disassembled, cleaned and inspected for wear, Fig. 20.

1. To remove the relief valve, remove the cotter pin and drill a 1/8 inch hole into the relief valve retainer cap and install a self-threading sheet metal screw.
2. Clamp screw into vise and tap on housing lightly with a soft hammer to remove the retaining cap, then remove the relief valve spring and valve.
3. Remove the oil pump cover and discard the oil seal ring.
4. Remove pump rotor, shaft and lift out outer rotor.

V8-400, 440

After removing the pump from the engine it should be disassembled, cleaned and inspected for wear, Fig. 21.

1. The mating surface of the filter base (oil pump cover) should be smooth. Replace the filter base if scratched or grooved.
2. Lay a straightedge on the filter base surface. If a .0015 inch feeler gauge can be inserted between the pump cover and straightedge, replace the filter base.
3. If the outer rotor thickness is .943 inch or less and diameter 2.469 inches or less, replace shaft and both rotors.
4. If inner rotor length is .943 inch or less, replace both rotors and shaft.
5. Install outer rotor into pump body, press to one side with fingers and measure clearance between pump body and rotor. If measurement is .014 inch or greater, replace the pump body.
6. Install inner rotor into pump body and place a straightedge across the face between two bolt holes. If a feeler gauge of .004 inch or greater can be inserted between the rotors and the straightedge, replace the pump body.
7. If the tip clearance between the rotors is .010 inch or greater, replace shaft and both rotors.
8. The relief valve spring has a free length of 2 1/4 inches and should test between 22.3 and 23.3 pounds when compressed to 1 19/32 inch. If not, replace the spring.
9. Check the oil pump relief valve plunger for scoring and free operation in its bore. Small marks may be removed with 400-grit sand paper.

3. Install oil pressure relief valve spring. Use new washer (gasket) and tighten plug securely.
4. If pump shaft turns freely, remove pump cover and outer rotor before installation of pump on engine.
5. Install oil pressure sending unit and tighten to 60 inch lbs. (5 ft. lbs.)
6. Using a new gasket, install pump on engine and tighten bolts to 200 inch lbs. (16 ft. lbs.)
7. Install oil filter reservoir on pump. Install filter element and tighten cover nuts to 25 ft. lbs.
8. Connect oil pressure sending unit wire.
9. Complete the installation by reversing steps as given under Oil Pump, Replace.

Engine oiling system, 1977 V8-318, 360

BELT TENSION DATA

	New①	Used①
1977–83 All	120	70

①—Belt tension in lbs.

Engine Oiling System, 1978–83 V8-318 & 360

WATER PUMP, REPLACE

CAUTION: When it becomes necessary to remove a fan clutch of the silicone type, the assembly must be supported in the vertical position to prevent leaks of silicone fluid from the clutch mechanism. This loss of fluid will render the fan clutch inoperative.

6-225

1. Drain cooling system, then remove battery, upper and lower radiator hoses and fan shroud.
2. Remove all drive belts, then remove fan attaching bolts, fan, spacer and pulley.
3. Remove A/C compressor and air pump bracket to water pump attaching bolts, then position compressor and air pump aside. Keep compressor in upright position.
4. Disconnect by-pass and heater hoses from water pump.
5. Remove water pump attaching bolts and remove pump assembly.
6. Reverse procedure to install.

V8-318, 360

1. Drain cooling system and disconnect battery ground cable.
2. Remove all drive belts, then remove radiator shroud and position over fan.
3. Remove fan assembly, pulley and fan shroud.

4. Remove alternator adjusting strap and mounting bolts and position alternator aside.
5. Remove A/C compressor with mounting brackets and position aside, if equipped. Keep compressor in upright position.
6. Remove power steering pump mounting bolts and position pump aside, if equipped.
7. Remove air pump and mounting brackets, if equipped. Disconnect air hose at pump fittings.
8. Disconnect by-pass and heater hoses at water pump.
9. Disconnect lower radiator hose from pump.
10. Remove remaining water pump attaching bolts and remove pump assembly.
11. Reverse procedure to install.

V8-400, 440

1. Drain cooling system and disconnect battery ground cable.

Engine oiling system. V8-400, 440 engines

2. Remove upper radiator hose and fan shroud. Position shroud back on engine.
3. Remove all drive belts, then remove fan attaching bolts, fan, spacer and pulley.
4. Remove water pump attaching bolts and remove pump assembly.
5. Reverse procedure to install.

SERVICE BULLETIN

CORE HOLE PLUG SIZES: When replacing a cup-type core hole plug in an engine, the size of the hole in the cylinder head, water jacket or rear bearing bore for the camshaft should be checked. At these locations a 1/16" oversize hole is sometimes bored in production and an oversize core plug installed.

Core plugs 1/16" oversize are available for replacement should they be required at these locations.

FUEL PUMP, REPLACE

SERVICE NOTE

Before installing the pump, it is good practice to crank the engine so that the nose of the camshaft eccentric is out of the way of the fuel pump rocker arm when the pump is installed. In this way there will be the least amount of tension on the rocker arm, thereby easing the

installation of the pump.

1. Disconnect fuel lines from fuel pump.
2. Remove fuel pump attaching bolts and fuel pump.
3. Remove all gasket material from the pump and block gasket surfaces. Apply sealer to both sides of new gasket.
4. Position gasket on pump flange and hold pump in position against its mounting surface. Make sure rocker arm is riding on camshaft eccentric.
5. Press pump tight against its mounting. Install retaining screws and tighten them alternately.
6. Connect fuel lines. Then operate engine and check for leaks.

Clutch & Transmission Section

CLUTCH PEDAL, ADJUST

1. Inspect condition of clutch pedal rubber stop, if stop is damaged install a new one.
2. Where necessary, disconnect interlock clutch rod at transmission end.
3. Adjust linkage by turning self-locking adjusting nut to provide 5/32" free movement at outer end of fork. This movement will provide the prescribed one-inch free play at pedal.
4. Assemble interlock clutch rod (if used) to transmission pawl.

CLUTCH, REPLACE

Removal

1. Remove transmission and clutch housing pan.
2. Remove return spring from clutch release fork and clutch housing or torque shaft lever.
3. Remove spring washer securing fork rod to torque shaft lever and remove rod from

torque shaft and release fork.
4. Remove clutch release bearing assembly, release fork and boot from clutch housing.
5. Mark clutch cover and flywheel so that they may be assembled in their original position to maintain balance.
6. Loosen clutch cover retaining screws one or two turns at a time in succession until cover is loose and remove screws.
7. Remove clutch assembly and disc from clutch housing using care to avoid contaminating the friction surfaces.

Installation

1. Lubricate pilot bushing in crankshaft with Multi-Purpose Grease number 2932524 or equivalent.
2. Clean surfaces of flywheel and pressure plate, making certain no oil or grease remains on these parts.
3. Hold cover plate and disc in place and insert a special clutch aligning tool or a spare clutch shaft through the hub of the disc and into the crankshaft pilot bearing.

Fig. 1 Gearshift lever adjustment. 1977–80 three speed transmission

Fig. 2 Gearshift linkage adjustment. 1977–80 three speed floor shift transmission

4. Bolt clutch cover loosely to flywheel, being sure marks previously made are lined up.
5. To avoid distortion of clutch cover, tighten cover bolts a few turns each in progression until all are tight. The final tightening should be 200 inch lbs.

THREE SPEED TRANSMISSION, REPLACE

1. Disconnect shift rods from transmission levers.

   NOTE: If shift rods are retained by plastic grommets, disconnect the shift levers from the transmission to avoid replacing the grommets.

2. Drain lubricant from transmission and disconnect propeller shaft.
3. Disconnect speedometer cable and backup light switch connector.
4. If necessary, disconnect exhaust pipes from exhaust manifolds.
5. Raise engine slightly using a suitable support fixture or jack and disconnect extension housing from center crossmember.
6. Support transmission with a suitable jack and remove center crossmember.
7. Remove transmission to clutch housing retaining bolts, then slide transmission rearward until input shaft clears clutch disc and remove transmission.
8. Reverse procedure to install.

FOUR SPEED & OVERDRIVE TRANSMISSION, REPLACE

1. Remove console and shift components.
2. Drain fluid from transmission.
3. Disconnect propeller shaft at rear universal joint and carefully pull yoke out of extension housing. *Be careful not to*

Fig. 3 Gearshift linkage adjustment. 1977–79 four speed transmission

scratch or nick ground surface on sliding spline yoke during removal and installation of shaft.
4. Disconnect speedometer cable and stop light switch leads.
5. Disconnect left-hand exhaust pipe (dual exhaust) from manifold.
6. Disconnect parking cable where necessary.
7. Support rear of engine with a jack.
8. Raise engine slightly and disconnect extension housing from removable center crossmember.
9. Support transmission with a suitable jack and remove center crossmember.
10. Remove transmission-to-clutch housing bolts.
11. Slide transmission rearward and out of vehicle.
12. Reverse procedure to install.

SHIFT LINKAGE, ADJUST THREE SPEED TRANS.

Column Shift

1. Loosen both shift rod swivels.
2. With transmission shift levers in neutral (middle detent), move shift lever to align locating slots in bottom of steering column shift housing and bearing housing. Install suitable tool in slot to maintain alignment.
3. Place screwdriver or other suitable tool

between crossover blade and 2nd-3rd lever at steering column so that both lever pins are engaged by crossover blade, Fig. 1.
4. Torque both shift rod swivel bolts to 125 inch lbs.
5. Remove gearshift housing locating tool and remove tool from crossover blade at steering column.
6. Shift through all gears to check adjustment and crossover smoothness. Check for operation of steering column lock in reverse and other gear positions. If properly adjusted, ignition should lock in reverse position only without having to force shift lever.

Floor Shift

1. Place shift lever in neutral position and disconnect shift rods from levers.
2. Fabricate alignment tool from 1/16 in. thick sheet metal as shown in Fig. 2.
3. Insert alignment tool into slots in levers and frame to hold levers in neutral position, Fig. 2.
4. Place transmission levers in neutral position and adjust shift rod swivels so that rods will install freely into levers.
5. Secure rods with washers and clips, then remove alignment tool and check shifter operation.

SHIFT LINKAGE, ADJUST FOUR SPEED TRANS.

1977–79

1. Install floor shift lever aligning tool, Fig. 3, to hold levers in neutral position. Crossover alignment tool shown in Fig. 3, will have to be fabricated.
2. With all rods disconnected from transmission shift levers, place levers in neutral position.
3. Starting with 1-2 shift rod, rotate shift rods until ends of rods enter shift levers. It may be necessary to remove clip at shifter end to rotate rods.
4. Replace washers and clips, then remove aligning tool and check shifting action.

Rear Axle, Propeller Shaft & Brakes

NOTE: Figs. 1, 1A and 2 illustrate the various rear axle assemblies used on these cars. When necessary to overhaul any of these units, refer to the *Rear Axle Specifications* table in this chapter.

INTEGRAL TYPE REAR AXLE

NOTE: The following changes have been made in the design of the 7 1/4 inch rear axle during the 1982 model year for all models except Imperial.

1. The inboard ends of the 8 1/4 inch axle shaft tubes are swadged down in size and pressed into the 7 1/4 inch carrier, Fig. 1A.

2. The 7 1/4 inch axle shafts ball bearings are replaced with the 8 1/4 inch axle shaft roller bearings.
3. The axle shafts are retained with the standard 8 1/4 inch axle "C" lock washer, Fig. 1A.
4. The 7 1/4 inch differential side gears now have a counterbore to incorporate the "C" lock washers. These side gears can be used on the early design 7 1/4 inch axles, but the early design side gears cannot be used on the later design 7 1/4 inch axle.
5. The late design carrier has two cast holes to allow lube to flow into the tubes to lubricate the axle shaft roller bearings, Fig. 1A.

Servicing the late design 7 1/4 inch rear axle is the same as the early design 7 1/4 inch differential, except for the axle shaft and axle shaft bearing. When replacing axle shaft or axle shaft bearing refer to "Axle Shaft, Replace

(Fig. 2 Type)" for service procedures.

Two types of integral carrier axles are used. In both types, the drive pinion is mounted in two opposing tapered roller bearings which are preloaded by a spacer positioned between them.

In the unit shown in Fig. 1, the differential is supported by two tapered roller side bearings. These bearings are preloaded by spacers located between the bearings and carrier housing. The differential assembly is positioned for ring and pinion backlash by varying these spacers.

Axle shafts in this unit are held in place by retainers at the outer ends of the shafts. These retainers are bolted through the brake backing plates to the rear axle tubes.

In the unit shown in Fig. 2, the differential is also supported by two tapered roller bear-

Fig. 1 Integral rear axle (typical). 1977—83

ings. A threaded differential bearing adjuster is located in each bearing pedestal cap to eliminate differential side play, adjust and maintain ring and pinion backlash and provide a means of obtaining differential bearing preload.

Axles are retained by means of a "C" washer which is installed into a groove in the inner end of the axle shaft inside the differential unit.

On both these units, a removable stamped steel cover, bolted to the rear of the carrier, permits inspection and service of the differential without removal of the complete axle assembly from the vehicle.

NOTE: 7¼ and 8¼ in. axle differentials have balanced side and pinion gears. Any attempt to mix these side or pinion gears with previously manufactured ones will result in lock up or excessive differential backlash. Side and pinion gears must be replaced as a set.

"C" WASHER LOCK

CAST LUBE HOLES (2)

Fig. 1A Late design 7¼ inch "C" lock type rear axle. 1982—83

REAR AXLE, REPLACE

1. Raise rear of vehicle and position safety stands at front of rear springs.
2. Remove rear wheels, then disconnect brake lines at wheel cylinders. Cap brake line fittings to prevent loss of fluid.
3. Disconnect parking brake cables.
4. Mark drive shaft and pinion flanges for reassembly, then remove drive shaft.
5. Disconnect shock absorbers from spring plate studs, then loosen rear spring U-bolt nuts and remove U-bolts.
6. Remove axle assembly from vehicle.

Axle Shaft, Replace (Fig. 1 Type)

1. With wheel removed, remove clips holding brake drum on wheel studs and remove drum.
2. Disconnect brake lines at wheel cylinders.
3. Using access hole in axle flange, remove retainer nuts from end of housing.
4. Remove axle shaft and brake assembly, using a slide hammer-type puller.
5. Remove brake assembly from axle shaft with care to avoid damaging shaft in seal contact area.
6. Remove oil seal from axle housing.
7. *Remove axle shaft bearings only when necessary. Removal of bearings makes them unfit for further use.*
8. *Axle shaft end play is pre-set and not adjustable. End play is accomplished by the amount of end play built into the bearings. The two axle housing brake support plate gaskets on each side are used for sealing purposes only. Always replace the gaskets once they have been removed.*
9. Press bearing and collar on shaft firmly against shoulders on shaft.
10. Install new oil seal in housing.
11. Install brake assembly on axle housing and carefully slide axle shaft through oil seal and into side gear splines.
12. Tap end of axle shaft lightly to position axle shaft bearing into bearing bore and attach retainer plate to housing.
13. Install brake drums and wheels.

Fig. 2 Integral "C" washer type rear axle (typical). 1977—83

Fig. 3 Location of "C" washer locks

Fig. 4 Left rear brake (10—11 inch). 1977—83

Axle Shaft, Replace (Fig. 2 Type)

1. With wheel and brake drum removed, or caliper and rotor assembly removed, loosen differential housing cover and drain lubricant. Remove cover.
2. Turn differential case to make pinion shaft lock screw accessible and remove lock screw and shaft.
3. Push axle shaft inward toward center of car and remove "C" washer from groove in axle shaft, Fig. 3.
4. Remove axle shaft from housing, being careful not to damage the axle bearing, which will remain in the housing.
5. The axle bearing and/or seal can now be removed if necessary.
6. Reverse procedure to install.

PROPELLER SHAFT, REPLACE

1. Remove both rear universal joint roller and bushing assembly clamps from pinion yoke. Do not disturb retaining strap holding roller assemblies on cross.
2. Lower front of vehicle slightly to prevent loss of transmission oil and pull drive shaft out as an assembly.
3. To install, carefully slide yoke into splines on transmission output shaft.
4. Align rear of propeller shaft with pinion yoke and position roller and bushing assemblies into seats of pinion yoke.
5. Install bushing clamps and tighten clamp bolts to 170 inch lbs.

BRAKE ADJUSTMENTS

1977—83 Self Adjusting Brakes

These brakes, Fig. 4, have self-adjusting shoe mechanisms that assure correct lining-to-drum clearances at all times. The automatic adjusters operate only when the brakes are applied as the car is moving rearward.

Although the brakes are self-adjusting, an initial adjustment is necessary when the brake shoes have been relined or replaced, or when the length of the star wheel adjuster has been changed during some other service operation.

Frequent usage of an automatic transmission forward range to halt reverse vehicle motion may prevent the automatic adjusters from functioning, thereby inducing low pedal heights. Should low pedal heights be encountered, it is recommended that numerous forward and reverse stops be made until satisfactory pedal height is obtained.

SERVICE NOTE

If a low pedal height condition cannot be corrected by making numerous reverse stops (provided the hydraulic system is free of air) it indicates that the self-adjusting mechanism is not functioning. Therefore, it will be necessary to remove the drum, clean, free up and lubricate the adjusting mechanism. Then adjust the brakes, being sure the parking brake is fully released.

Adjustment

1. Each backing plate has two adjusting hole covers; remove the rear cover and turn the adjusting screw upward with a screwdriver or other suitable tool to expand the shoes until a slight drag is felt when the drum is rotated.
2. While holding the adjusting lever out of engagement with the adjusting screw, Fig. 5, back off the adjusting screw until wheel rotates freely with no drag.
3. Install wheel and adjusting hole cover. Adjust brakes on remaining wheels in the same manner.
4. If pedal height is not satisfactory, drive the vehicle and make sufficient reverse stops until proper pedal height is obtained.

PARKING BRAKE, ADJUST

1. Release parking brake lever and loosen cable adjusting nut to be sure cable is slack.
2. With rear wheel brakes properly adjusted tighten cable adjusting nut until a slight drag is felt when the rear wheels are rotated. Then loosen the cable adjusting nut until both rear wheels can be rotated freely.
3. To complete the operation, back off an additional two turns of the cable adjusting nut.
4. Apply and release parking brake several times to be sure rear wheels are not dragging when cable is in released position.

VACUUM RELEASE PARKING BRAKE

The parking brake is pedal applied and released by a vacuum chamber. When the engine is started and vacuum is developed, energy is then available to release the parking brake. This is controlled by the transmission shift linkage. When the transmission is in "Neutral", vacuum is cut off from the release chamber and there is no action of the parking brake pedal.

When the transmission is shifted into a drive gear (forward or reverse), the vacuum control valve is opened, actuating the vacuum release chamber mounted on the parking brake assembly.

NOTE: *In the event of engine failure and no vacuum, the brake may be released by a manual release lever mounted on the left side of the parking brake pedal assembly. This assembly prevents the vehicle from being driven with the parking brake in the applied position.*

Testing Vacuum Release

1. If the mechanism is inoperative, first check for damaged or kinked vacuum hoses and for loose hose connections at the vacuum chamber, vacuum release valve at neutral safety switch, and at engine manifold connection.

Fig. 5 Releasing brake lever with screwdriver while adjusting star wheel

2. Check adjustment of neutral safety switch and operation of vacuum release valve.
3. Check vacuum chamber piston travel by running engine and shifting transmission selector from drive to neutral. The manual release lever should move up and down as vacuum is applied and released. If no movement is observed or if movement is slow (more than 1 or 2 seconds to complete full stroke), the vacuum chamber is leaking and should be replaced.
4. Check brake release with vacuum applied. If vacuum chamber piston completes full stroke but does not release brake, a malfunction of the pedal assembly is indicated.
5. Check operation of parking brake with engine off. Parking brake should remain engaged regardless of transmission selector position.

Parking Brake Vacuum Valve, Replace

1. With engine off, place shift lever in drive, remove vacuum hoses and retaining screws and remove valve from steering column.
2. To install, move actuating arm on valve against spring to extreme position or until locating holes line up and install a #42 drill in hole, Fig. 6.
3. Place shift lever in park and install valve but do not tighten screws. Rotate valve clockwise until actuating arm contacts

tab in steering column then tighten screws.
4. Remove drill and install vacuum hoses making sure that hose from engine manifold is attached to center fitting on valve.
5. Start engine and check that parking brake can be set in neutral and park and will release in reverse and drive positions.

BRAKE MASTER CYLINDER, REPLACE

Exc. 1978–83 With Aluminum Master Cylinder

1. Disconnect brake lines from master cylinder. Install plugs in outlets to prevent fluid leakage.
2. Remove nuts that attach master cylinder to cowl panel or power brake unit.
3. Disconnect pedal push rod (manual brakes) from brake pedal.
4. Slide master cylinder straight out from cowl panel and/or power brake unit.
5. Reverse procedure to install.

1978–83 With Aluminum Master Cylinder

Manual Brakes
1. Disconnect brake lines from master cylinder. Install plugs in outlets to prevent fluid leakage.
2. From under instrument panel, disconnect stop lamp switch mounting bracket and position aside.
3. Grasp brake pedal and pull backward to disengage push rod from master cylinder piston.

NOTE: This will require a pull of about 50 pounds. Also, the retention grommet will be destroyed.

4. Remove master cylinder to cowl retaining nuts and remove master cylinder by pulling straight out.

CAUTION: Make sure to remove all traces of old grommet from push rod groove and master cylinder piston.

Fig. 6 Parking brake vacuum release valve. 1977–78 (typical)

5. Reverse procedure to install. Install new grommet on push rod, then lubricate grommet with water and align push rod with master cylinder piston. Using brake pedal, apply pressure to fully seat push rod into piston.

Power Brakes
1. Disconnect primary and secondary brake tubes from master cylinder, then cap lines and master cylinder fitting.
2. Remove nuts attaching master cylinder to power brake unit, then slide master cylinder from power brake unit.
3. Reverse procedure to install.

POWER BRAKE UNIT, REPLACE

1977–83

1. Remove master cylinder retaining nuts, then carefully slide out master cylinder from power brake and allow it to rest on fender shield.
2. Disconnect vacuum hose from power brake.
3. From under instrument panel, disconnect push rod from brake pedal. On linkage type power brake unit, also remove lower pivot retaining bolt.
4. Remove power brake retaining nuts and remove power brake unit.
5. Reverse procedure to install.

Rear Suspension

SHOCK ABSORBER, REPLACE

To replace shock absorber, support rear axle properly and disconnect shock absorber at upper and lower mountings.

LEAF SPRINGS & BUSHINGS, REPLACE

1. Support rear axle, relieving tension from spring.

   NOTE: 1977–78 Full Size Models are equipped with preloaded "tension" type springs and a spring stretcher (C-4211) must be used during spring removal.

2. Disconnect shock absorber from lower mounting.
3. Remove "U" bolts and spring plate, Figs. 1 and 2, or lower spring seat isolator retainer and isolator, Figs. 1 and 2.
4. Remove spring front hanger to body mount bracket nuts, Fig. 3.
5. Remove rear shackle bolts, lower spring, thus pulling spring front hanger bolts out of holes.
6. Remove front hanger and rear shackle from spring. To replace pivot bushings, refer to Fig. 4. Bushing replacement is accomplished in one operation.
7. Reverse procedure to install.

Leaf Spring Service

To replace interliners, remove spring alignment clips and on all models except Imperial, discard alignment clips. Separate spring leaves with a screwdriver or other suitable tool and remove interliners. Thoroughly clean spring surfaces before installation of new interliners.

To replace zinc interleaves, clamp spring in a vise and remove center bolt. Open vise carefully, allowing spring to expand. Interleaves can now be serviced. Install a drift through spring center bolt holes and clamp spring in a vise. Remove drift and install center bolt.

SWAY BAR, REPLACE

1. Remove nuts, retainers and rubber insulators from sway bar upper links, Figs. 5 and 6.
2. Disconnect sway bar brackets from frame.
3. Remove link from support assembly and replace insulators. Reverse procedure to install.

Fig. 1   Rear spring isolator. 1977 All & 1978 Chrysler

TOOL C-4219

Fig. 4   Spring pivot bushing replacement

Fig. 2   Rear spring isolator. 1978 except Chrysler & 1979–83 All

Fig 3   Rear spring (typical)

Fig. 5   Sway bar installation. 1977–80 Aspen, Volare, 1977–81 LeBaron, 1977–83 Diplomat, 1980–83 Cordoba, Mirada, 1981–83 Imperial & 1982–83 Gran Fury & New Yorker

Fig. 6   Sway bar installation. Except 1977–80 Aspen, Volare, 1977–81 LeBaron, 1977–83 Diplomat, 1980–83 Cordoba, Mirada, 1981–83 Imperial & 1982–83 Gran Fury & New Yorker

Front Suspension & Steering Section

FRONT SUSPENSION

Models with Transverse Torsion Bar Front Suspension

This front suspension, Fig. 1, incorporates two transverse torsion bars which react on the outboard end of the lower control arms. The torsion bars are anchored in the front crossmember opposite the affected wheel. The torsion bars are mounted parallel to the front crossmember through a "Pivot Cushion Bushing", attached to the crossmember, and turns and extends rearward to the lower control arm. The torsion bar ends are provided with an isolated bushing, bolted to the lower control arm and sway bar, which acts as the lower control arm strut.

Riding height is controlled by the torsion bar adjusting bolts on the anchor end of the torsion bar. The right torsion bar is adjusted from the left side and the left torsion bar is adjusted from the right side.

The torsion bar assembly incorporates the "Pivot Cushion Bushing" and "Bushing to Lower Control Arm". The lower control arm inner ends are bolted to the crossmember and pivots through bushings.

Caster and camber settings are made by loosening the upper control arm pivot bar bolt nuts and adjusting as necessary.

Models with Longitudinal Torsion Bar Front Suspension

This suspension, Figs. 2 and 3, consists of two torsion bar springs (right and left), two sets of upper and lower control arms, four ball joints and two struts.

The front ends of the torsion bar springs engage the lower control arms at the inner pivot points. The rear end of the torsion bars engage adjustable anchor and cam assemblies that are supported by brackets welded to the frame side rails and a removable crossmember.

The upper control arms are mounted on removable brackets that are bolted to the frame side rails. The lower control arms are attached to the frame front crossmember by a pivot shaft and bushing assembly. The pivot shafts are mounted in replaceable rubber bushings.

The steering knuckles are connected to the upper and lower control arms by means of ball joints. To prevent the possibility of fore and aft movement of the lower control arms, a strut is attached to the front crossmember and to the lower control arm.

1977–78 Chrysler Exc. Cordoba, 1977 Gran Fury, Royal Monaco

This suspension has new lower control arms with pressed in ball joints and more serviceable struts. Caster and camber settings are made by loosening the upper control arm pivot bar bolt nuts and adjusting as necessary.

1977–78 Charger, Fury & Monaco; 1977–79 Cordoba; 1978–79 Magnum; 1979–81 Newport, New Yorker & St. Regis; 1980–81 Gran Fury

This suspension has a rubber mounted crossmember, a torsion bar crossmember, more serviceable struts and a lower control arm with pressed in ball joints. Caster and camber settings are made by loosening the upper control arm pivot bar bolt nuts and adjusting as necessary.

WHEEL ALIGNMENT

NOTE: Front suspension height must be checked and corrected as necessary before performing wheel alignment.

1. Remove all foreign material from exposed threads of cam adjusting bolt nuts or pivot bar adjusting bolt nuts.
2. Record initial camber and caster readings before loosening cam bolt nuts or pivot bar bolt nuts.
3. On vehicles using cam bolts, the camber and caster is adjusted by loosening the cam bolt nuts and turning the cam bolts as necessary until the desired setting is obtained. On vehicles using pivot bars, tool C-4576 is required to adjust caster and camber. When performing adjustments, the camber settings should be held as close as possible to the "desired" setting, and the caster setting should be held as nearly equal as possible on both wheels.

SERVICE NOTE:

There may be cases when the vehicle may not have sufficient positive camber adjustment. Upper control arm plate spacers are available that will allow more positive camber adjustment, if required. If this condition is encountered, use spacer 1-4014352 for front suspension upper control arm front pivot support and spacer 1-4014353 for the rear pivot support. To install spacers, proceed as follows:

1. Loosen but do not remove caster/camber adjustment nut.
2. Raise vehicle and remove wheel and tire assembly.
3. Loosen but do not remove shock absorber upper mounting nut.
4. Remove two support plate bolts at front end of plate, then loosen two rear bolts enough to slide front spacer between support plate and frame.
5. Align holes in spacer with holes in support plate and frame.
6. Insert two front bolts and start threads. Do not tighten.
7. Repeat steps 4 through 6 for rear spacer.
8. Torque the four support plate bolts to 65 ft. lbs. and the shock absorber upper nut to 25 ft. lbs.
9. Lower vehicle and adjust alignment on side that spacers were installed.

Fig. 1   Transverse torsion bar front suspension.

Fig. 2   Upper control arm & steering knuckle (Typical).

Fig. 3 Longitudinal torsion bar & lower control arm (Typical).

Fig. 4 Checking lower ball joint for wear

TOE-IN, ADJUST

1977–83

With the front wheels in straight ahead position, loosen the clamps at each end of both adjusting tubes. Adjust toe-in by turning the tie rod sleeve which will "center" the steering wheel spokes. If the steering wheel was centered, make the toe-in adjustment by turning both sleeves an equal amount. Position the clamps so they are on the bottom and tighten bolts to 15 ft. lbs.

WHEEL BEARINGS, ADJUST

1. Tighten adjusting nut to 20–25 ft. lbs. while rotating wheel.
2. On 1977–80 models, back off adjusting nut to completely release bearing. On 1981–83 models, back off adjusting nut 1/4 turn.
3. Finger tighten adjusting nut while rotating wheel, then align nut lock with cotter pin slot and install cotter pin.
4. The resulting adjustment should be .0001–.003 end play.

WHEEL BEARINGS, REPLACE

(Disc Brakes)

1. Raise car and remove front wheels.
2. Remove grease cap, cotter pin, lock nut and bearing adjusting nut.
3. Remove bolts that attach caliper to steering knuckle.
4. Slowly slide caliper up and away from disc and support caliper on steering knuckle arm.

NOTE: Do not allow caliper to hang by brake hose.

5. Remove thrust washer and outer bearing cone. Remove hub and disc assembly. Grease retainer and inner bearing can now be removed.
6. Reverse procedure to install.

CHECKING BALL JOINTS FOR WEAR

Upper Ball Joint

1. Position a suitable jack under lower control arm and raise wheel and tire assembly clear of floor, then remove wheel cover and wheel bearing dust cover and cotter pin.
2. Tighten wheel bearing adjusting nut just enough to remove all play between hub, bearings and spindle.
3. Lower jack positioned under lower control arm to allow tire to lightly contact floor.
4. Grasp top of tire and move wheel and tire assembly inward and outward. While moving tire inward and outward, check for movement at ball joints between steering knuckle and upper control arm.
5. If any lateral movement is present, the upper ball joint should be replaced.
6. After completing upper ball joint check, readjust wheel bearing as described under "Wheel Bearings, Adjust".

Lower Ball Joint

NOTE: If loose ball joints are suspected, first make sure the front wheel bearings are properly adjusted and that the control arms are tight.

1. Raise front of vehicle and place jack stands underneath each lower control arm as far out as possible.

NOTE: The upper control arms must not contact the rubber rebound bumpers.

2. With weight of vehicle on lower control arms, attach dial indicator onto lower control arm, Fig. 4.
3. Place dial indicator plunger tip against ball joint housing and zero dial indicator.
4. Using a pry bar under the center of the tire, raise and lower the tire and measure the axial travel of the ball joint housing with respect to the ball joint. If the axial travel is .030 inch or more than specified, the ball joint should be replaced.

BALL JOINTS, REPLACE

Upper Ball Joint

1. Place ignition switch in the "Off" position.
2. Using a suitable jack raise front of vehicle and position a jack stand under lower control arm as close to wheel and tire assembly as possible. Check to ensure that jack stand is not in contact with brake splash shield. Also check to ensure that rubber rebound bumper is not in contact with frame.

NOTE: The torsion bar will remain in the loaded position.

3. Remove wheel and tire assembly.
4. Remove cotter pin and nut from lower ball joint stud. Position tool No. C3564-A over lower ball joint stud, allowing tool to rest on knuckle arm, then set tool securely against upper ball joint stud.
5. Tighten tool to apply pressure against upper ball joint stud, then strike knuckle with hammer to loosen stud.
6. Remove tool, then detach upper ball joint from knuckle.

NOTE: Support knuckle and brake assembly to prevent damage to lower ball joint and brake hoses.

7. Remove upper ball joint from upper control arm, using tool No. C3561 for 1977 Gran Fury, Royal Monaco and 1977–78 Newport and New Yorker. On all models except 1977 Gran Fury, Royal Monaco and 1977–78 Newport and New Yorker, use tool No. C3560 to remove ball joint from upper control arm.
8. Reverse procedure to install. Thread upper ball joint into control arm as far as possible by hand. On 1977 Gran Fury, Royal Monaco and 1977–78 Newport and New Yorker, torque upper ball joint into control to 150 ft. lbs. using tool No. C3561. On all models except 1977 Gran Fury, Royal Monaco and 1977–78 Newport and New Yorker, torque upper ball joint into control arm to 125 ft. lbs. using tool No. C3560. Torque upper and lower ball joint stud nuts to 135 ft. lbs. on 1977 Gran Fury, Royal Monaco and Newport and New Yorker, 100 ft. lbs. on all models except 1977 Gran Fury, Royal Monaco and 1977–78 Newport and New Yorker. After tightening lower ball joint stud nut, install cotter pin.

NOTE: Ball joint seals should be replaced whenever they have been removed.

Fig. 5 Measuring front suspension height. 1981 Newport, New Yorker & St. Regis

Fig. 6 Measuring front suspension height. 1981 LeBaron, 1981–83 Cordoba, Diplomat, Imperial, Mirada & 1982–83 Gran Fury & New Yorker

Lower Ball Joint

1. Place ignition switch in the "Off" position.
2. Raise vehicle and support so front suspension is in the full rebound position. Position jack stands under front frame for additional support.
3. Remove wheel and tire assembly, then remove disc brake caliper and support with wire hook to prevent brake hose from becoming damaged.
4. Remove disc brake hub and rotor assembly and splash shield, then disconnect shock absorber at lower mounting.
5. Release load on torsion bar by rotating adjusting bolt counter-clockwise.
6. Remove upper and lower ball joint stud nuts and cotter pin, then position tool No. C3564-A over upper ball joint stud so that tool is resting on steering knuckle.
7. Rotate threaded portion of tool to lock it against lower ball joint stud. Tighten tool to place pressure on lower ball joint stud, then strike steering knuckle with a hammer to loosen stud. Remove tool and disconnect lower ball joint.
8. Use tool No. C4212 to press ball joint from lower control arm.
9. Position replacement ball joint on lower control arm, then press into control arm using tool No. C4212.
10. Install seal over lower ball joint. On 1977 Gran Fury, Royal Monaco and 1977–78 Newport and New Yorker, use tool No. C4034 to press retainer portion of seal until it is locked in position. On all models except 1977 Gran Fury, Royal Monaco and 1977–78 Newport and New Yorker, use tool No. C4039 to press retainer portion of seal until it is locked in position.
11. Position lower ball joint to steering knuckle, then install upper and lower stud nuts and torque to 135 ft. lbs. on 1977 Gran Fury, Royal Monaco and 1977–78 Newport and New Yorker, 100 ft. lbs. on all models except 1977 Gran Fury, Royal Monaco and 1977–78 Newport and New Yorker. After tightening stud nuts, install cotter pin.
12. Place tension on torsion bar by rotating adjusting bolt clockwise.
13. Install disc brake assembly and wheel and tire assembly, then adjust front wheel bearing as described under "Wheel Bearings, Adjust".
14. Lubricate ball joint, then lower vehicle and adjust vehicle riding height.

TORSION BAR, REPLACE

1977–80 Aspen, Volaré, 1977–81 LeBaron, 1977–83 Diplomat, 1980–83 Cordoba, Imperial, Mirada & 1982–83 Gran Fury & New Yorker

Removal

1. Raise vehicle and support so front suspension is in full rebound position.
2. Rotate anchor adjusting bolts located in frame crossmember, counter-clockwise to release load on both torsion bars. Then, remove anchor adjusting bolt from torsion bar to be removed.
3. Raise lower control arms until 2⅞ inch clearance is obtained between crossmember ledge at jounce bumper and the torsion bar end bushing and support lower arms at this height.

NOTE: This procedure will align the sway bar and the lower control arm attaching points for disassembly and component realignment and attachment during assembly.

4. Remove sway bar to control arm attaching bolt and retainers, then the two bolts securing torsion bar end bushing to lower control arm.
5. Remove two bolts securing torsion bar pivot cushion bushing to crossmember, then the torsion bar and anchor assembly from crossmember.
6. Separate anchor from torsion bar.

Inspection

1. Inspect seal for damage and replace, if necessary.
2. Inspect bushing to lower control arm and pivot cushion bushing. Inspect seals on cushion bushing for cuts, tears or severe deterioration that may allow moisture to enter under cushion. If corrosion is evident, replace torsion bar assembly.
3. Inspect torsion bars for paint damage and touch up, if necessary.
4. Clean anchor hex openings and torsion bar hex ends.
5. Inspect torsion bar adjusting bolt and swivel for damage or corrosion and replace, if necessary.

Installation

1. Slide balloon seal over torsion bar end with cupped end facing toward hex.
2. Lubricate torsion bar hex end with lubricant, P/N 2525035, and install hex end into anchor bracket. With the torsion bar in horizontal position, the anchor bracket ears should be positioned nearly straight upward. Position swivel into anchor bracket ears.
3. Install torsion bar anchor bracket assembly into crossmember anchor retainer, then the anchor adjusting bolt and bearing.
4. Install two bolt and washer assemblies securing pivot cushion bushing to crossmember. Leave assemblies loose enough to install friction plates.
5. With lower control arms supported as outlined in step 3 under "Removal", install the two bolt and nut assemblies securing torsion bar bushing to lower control arm and torque nuts to 70 ft. lbs.
6. Ensure that torsion bar anchor bracket is fully seated in crossmember. Then install friction plates between crossmember and pivot cushion bushing with open end of slot to rear and bottomed out on mounting bolt. Tighten cushion bushing bolts to 85 ft. lbs. Place balloon seal over anchor bracket.
7. Install new bolt through sway bar, retainer cushions and sleeve and attach to lower control arm end bushing, then torque bolt to 50 ft. lbs.
8. Rotate anchor adjusting bolt clockwise to load torsion bar.
9. Lower vehicle and adjust riding height.

Except 1977–80 Aspen, Volaré, 1977–81 LeBaron, 1977–83 Diplomat, 1980–83 Cordoba, Imperial, Mirada & 1982–83 Gran Fury & New Yorker

The torsion bars are not interchangeable side for side. The bars are marked either right or left by an "R" or an "L" stamped on one end of the bar. The general procedure for replacing a torsion bar is as follows:

Removal

1. Remove upper control arm rebound bumper.

2. If vehicle is to be raised on a hoist, make sure it is lifted on the body only so suspension is in full rebound position (no load).
3. Release all load from torsion bar by turning anchor adjusting bolt counterclockwise.
4. Slide rear anchor balloon seal off of rear anchor and remove lock ring from anchor.
5. Remove torsion bar, by sliding bar out through rear of rear anchor. Use care not to damage balloon seal when it is removed from torsion bar.

NOTE: On some models, it may be necessary to remove transmission torque shaft to provide clearance.

Inspection

1. Inspect balloon seal for damage and replace if necessary.
2. Inspect torsion bar for scores or nicks. Dress down all scratches and nicks to remove sharp edges, then paint repaired areas with a rust preventive.
3. Remove all foreign material from hex openings in anchors and from hex ends of torsion bars.
4. Inspect adjusting bolt and swivel and replace if there is any sign of corrosion or other damage. Lubricate for easy operation.

Installation

1. Insert torsion bar through rear anchor.
2. Slide balloon seal over torsion bar with cupped end toward rear of bar.
3. Coat both ends of torsion bar with a long mileage lubricant.
4. Slide torsion bar in hex opening of lower control arm.
5. Install lock ring, making sure it is seated in groove.
6. Pack annular opening in rear anchor completely full of a long mileage lubricant.
7. Position lip of balloon seal in groove of anchor.
8. Turn adjusting bolt clockwise to place a load on torsion bar.
9. Lower vehicle to floor and adjust front suspension height.
10. Install upper control arm rebound bumper.

SWAY BAR, REPLACE

1977–80 Aspen & Volare; 1977–81 Diplomat & LeBaron; 1980–81 Cordoba & Mirada; 1981 Imperial & 1982–83 All Models

1. Raise vehicle and support front of vehicle

NOTE: Sway bar to lower control arm attaching points are aligned only when lower control arms are at design height. If frame contact or twin post hoist is used, release load on torsion bar by turning adjuster bolts counter-clockwise, then raise lower control arms until clearance between crossmember ledge and torsion bar to lower control arm bushing is 27⁄8 inches. Support lower control arms with jack stand during sway bar removal and installation.

2. With lower control arms properly supported, remove sway bar to torsion bar

Fig. 7   Measuring front suspension height. 1977–80 models

bushing attaching bolts, retainers, cushions and sleeves.
3. Remove retainer assembly strap bolts and retainer straps, then remove sway bar.
4. Reverse procedure to install. Inspect cushions and bushings for excessive wear or deterioration and replace as necessary.

1977 Gran Fury & Royal Monaco; 1977–78 Chrysler Station Wagon

1. Place ignition switch in off or unlocked position.
2. Raise vehicle on suitable hoist to place front suspension in rebound position.
3. Turn front wheel to extreme right or left.
4. Remove upper bolts, retainers and insulators from both sides of bar. Link sleeve will remain in position as secured through lower control arm.
5. Remove two screws and washers securing retainers to bar bushings at frame and remove retainers.
6. Remove bar by moving in direction that wheels are turned until opposite end clears lower control arm strut, lower that end below strut and move in opposite directions until other end clears strut, then move bar clear of frame in direction wheels are turned.
7. Reverse procedure to install. Inspect cushions and bushing for excessive wear or deterioration and replace as necessary.

Except 1977 Gran Fury & Royal Monaco; 1977–78 Chrysler Station Wagon; 1977–80 Aspen & Volare; Diplomat & LeBaron; 1980–81 Cordoba & Mirada; 1981 Imperial & 1982–83 All Models

1. Place ignition switch in off or unlocked position.
2. Raise vehicle on hoist to place front suspension in rebound position.
3. Remove wheel cover and wheel and tire assembly.
4. Remove nut and bolt on each end of bar attaching sway bar to strut clamp. Remove nut and bolt from both sway bar link straps to free sway bar from links.
5. Remove sway bar by pulling unit out through frame crossmember openings in

direction of area where wheel has been removed.
6. Reverse procedure to install. Inspect cushions and bushing for excessive wear or deterioration and replace as necessary.

RIDING HEIGHT, ADJUST

Before taking measurements, grasp the bumpers at the center (rear bumper first) and jounce the car up and down several times. Jounce the car at the front bumper the same number of times and release the bumper at the same point in the cycle each time.

1981–83 Models

1. On 1981 Newport, New Yorker and St. Regis models, the height is measured from the bottom of the frame side rail, between radiator yoke and forward edge of crossmember, to ground, Fig. 5.
2. On 1981 LeBaron, 1981–83 Cordoba, Diplomat, Imperial, Mirada and 1982–83 Gran Fury and New Yorker, the height is measured from the head of the front suspension front crossmember insulator bolt to ground, Fig. 6.
3. If necessary, turn torsion bar adjusting bolt clockwise to increase height and counterclockwise to decrease height.
4. After completing adjustment, jounce vehicle and recheck riding height. Both sides must be measured even though only one side may have been adjusted. Front vehicle height should not vary more than 1⁄4 inch from the specified riding height. Riding height should also be within 1⁄4 inch side to side.

1977–80 Models

1. On 1977–80 models except Aspen, Volaré and Diplomat and LeBaron, measure distance from a point 1 inch forward of rear face of torsion bar anchor to the floor (Measurement A), Fig. 7. The distance should be as listed below.
2. On 1977–80 Aspen, Volaré and Diplomat and LeBaron, measure distance from lowest point of lower control arm inner pivot bushing to the floor, Fig. 7. The distance should be as listed below.
3. Measure the other side in the same manner.
4. Adjust by turning the torsion bar anchor adjusting nut *clockwise to increase* the height and *counterclockwise to decrease* the height. The difference from side-to-side should not exceed 1⁄8 inch.
5. After adjusting, jounce the car and recheck the measurements on both sides, even if only one side may have been adjusted.

Chrysler & Imperial

1977–78	Newport, New Yorker	10-1⁄8"
1977–79	Cordoba	10-3⁄4"
1977–80	LeBaron	10-1⁄4"
1979–80	Newport, New Yorker	10-3⁄4"
1980	Cordoba	10-1⁄4"
1981	Newport, New Yorker	163⁄4"
1981–83	Cordoba, LeBaron	121⁄2"
1981–83	Imperial	121⁄2"
1982–83	Newport, New Yorker	121⁄2"

Dodge

1977–79	Charger, Magnum	10-3⁄4"
	Dart	10-15⁄16"
	Monaco	10-1⁄8"
1977–80	Aspen	10-1⁄4"

1977	Royal Monaco	10-1/8"
1977–78	Monaco Exc. Sta. Wag.	10-3/4"
	Monaco Sta. Wag.	11-1/4"
1977–80	Diplomat	10-1/4"
1979–80	St. Regis	10-3/4"
1980	Mirada	10-1/4"
1981	St. Regis	16-3/4"
1981–83	Diplomat, Mirada	12-1/2"

Plymouth

1977	Gran Fury	10-1/8"
1977–78	Fury Exc. Sta. Wag.	10-3/4"
	Fury Sta. Wag.	11-1/4"
1977–80	Volare	10-1/4"
1980–80	Gran Fury	10-3/4"
1981	Gran Fury	16-3/4"
1982–83	Gran Fury	12-1/2"

MANUAL STEERING GEAR, REPLACE

CAUTION: To avoid damage to the energy absorbing steering column, it is recommended that the steering column be completely detached from floor and instrument panel before steering gear is removed.

1. Use a suitable puller to remove steering arm from under vehicle.
2. Remove gear to frame retaining bolts and remove gear.
3. Reverse procedure to install.

POWER STEERING GEAR, REPLACE

1. Disconnect battery ground cable.
2. Remove steering column.
3. Disconnect fluid hoses from steering gear and support free ends above pump to avoid loss of fluid. Plug fittings on gear.
4. Disconnect steering arm from gear with suitable puller.
5. Remove gear to frame retaining bolts or nuts and remove gear.
6. Reverse procedure to install.

POWER STEERING PUMP, REPLACE

1. Loosen power steering pump mounting and locking bolts, then remove drive belt.
2. Disconnect pressure and return lines at power steering pump.
3. Remove pump mounting bolts, then remove pump and mounting bracket.
4. Reverse procedure to install.

FORD & MERCURY
Full Size Models

NOTE: This chapter includes service procedures for the 1977–82 LTD, Marquis & 1983 LTD Crown Victoria & Grand Marquis.

For service procedures on the 1983 LTD & Marquis models, refer to the "Ford & Mercury—Compact Intermediate Models Chapter."

Refer to the back of this manual for vehicle manufacturer's special service tool suppliers.

INDEX OF SERVICE OPERATIONS

ENGINE & SERIAL NUMBER LOCATION

Plate On Left Front Door Pillar

GRILLE IDENTIFICATION

1977–78 Ford "LTD" & Custom

1977–78 Ford "LTD" Landau

1977–78 Mercury

1979–82 Mercury Marquis

1979–82 LTD

1979–82 Ford LTD Landau & Country Squire

1983 Ford LTD Crown Victoria & Country Squire

GENERAL ENGINE SPECIFICATIONS

Year	Engine CID①/Liter	V.I.N. Code②	Carburetor	Bore and Stroke	Compression Ratio	Net H.P. @ R.P.M.③	Maximum Torque Ft. Lbs. @ R.P.M.	Normal Oil Pressure Pounds
FORD								
1977	V8-302, 5.0L	F	2150, 2 Bbl.⑤	4.00 × 3.00	8.4	—	—	40–65
	V8-351M, 5.8L④⑥	Q	2150, 2 Bbl.⑤	4.00 × 3.50	8.0	161 @ 3600	285 @ 1800	50–75
	V8-351W, 5.8L⑥⑦	H	2150, 2 Bbl.⑤	4.00 × 3.50	8.3	149 @ 3200	291 @ 1600	40–65
	V8-400, 6.6L⑥	S	2150, 2 Bbl.⑤	4.00 × 4.00	8.0	173 @ 3800	326 @ 1600	50–75
	V8-400, 6.6L⑧	S	2150, 2 Bbl.⑤	4.00 × 4.00	8.0	168 @ 3800	323 @ 1600	50–75
	V8-460, 7.5L	A	4350, 4 Bbl.⑤	4.36 × 3.85	8.0	197 @ 4000	353 @ 2000	35–65
1978	V8-302, 5.0L	F	2150, 2 Bbl.⑤	4.00 × 3.00	8.4	134 @ 3400	248 @ 1600	40–65
	V8-351M, 5.8L④	Q	2150, 2 Bbl.⑤	4.00 × 3.50	8.3	145 @ 3400	273 @ 1800	50–75
	V8-351W, 5.8L⑦	H	2150, 2 Bbl.⑤	4.00 × 3.50	8.0	144 @ 3200	277 @ 1600	40–65
	V8-400, 6.6L	S	2150, 2 Bbl.⑤	4.00 × 4.00	8.0	160 @ 3800	314 @ 1800	50–75
	V8-460, 7.5L⑨	A	4350, 4 Bbl.⑤	4.36 × 3.85	8.0	—	—	40–65
	V8-460, 7.5L⑩	A	4350, 4 Bbl.⑤	4.36 × 3.85	8.0	202 @ 4000	348 @ 2000	40–65
1979	V8-302, 5.0L⑥	F	2700VV, 2 Bbl.⑤	4.00 × 3.00	8.4	129 @ 3600	223 @ 2600	40–65
	V8-302, 5.0L⑧	F	2700VV, 2 Bbl.⑤	4.00 × 3.00	8.4	130 @ 3600	226 @ 2200	40–65
	V8-351W, 5.8L⑥⑦	H	7200VV, 2 Bbl.⑤	4.00 × 3.50	8.3	142 @ 3200	286 @ 1400	40–65
	V8-351W, 5.8L⑦⑧	H	2150, 2 Bbl.⑤	4.00 × 3.50	8.3	138 @ 3200	260 @ 2200	40–65
1980	V8-302, 5.0L	F	2700VV, 2 Bbl.⑤	4.00 × 3.00	8.4	130 @ 3600	230 @ 1600	40–60
	V8-351W, 5.8L⑦	G	7200VV, 2 Bbl.⑤	4.00 × 3.50	8.3	140 @ 3400	265 @ 2000	40–60
	V8-351W, 5.8L H.O.⑦⑪	G	7200VV, 2 Bbl.⑤	4.00 × 3.50	8.3	—	—	40–60

Continued

FORD & MERCURY—Full Size Models

GENERAL ENGINE SPECIFICATIONS—Continued

Year	Engine CID①/Liter	V.I.N. Code②	Carburetor	Bore and Stroke	Compression Ratio	Net H.P. @ R.P.M.③	Maximum Torque Ft. Lbs. @ R.P.M.	Normal Oil Pressure Pounds
FORD—Continued								
1981	V8-255, 4.2L	D	7200VV, 2 Bbl.⑤	3.68 × 3.00	8.2	120 @ 3400	205 @ 2600	40–60
	V8-302, 5.0L⑧	F	7200VV, 2 Bbl.⑤	4.00 × 3.00	8.4	130 @ 3400	230 @ 2200	40–60
	V8-302, 5.0L⑥	F	7200VV, 2 Bbl.⑤	4.00 × 3.00	8.4	130 @ 3400	235 @ 1800	40–60
	V8-351W, 5.8L⑦	G	7200VV, 2 Bbl.⑤	4.00 × 3.50	8.3	145 @ 3200	270 @ 1800	40–60
	V8-351W, 5.8L H.O.⑦⑪	G	7200VV, 2 Bbl.⑤	4.00 × 3.50	8.3	165 @ 3600	285 @ 2200	40–60
1982	V8-255, 4.2L	D	7200VV, 2 Bbl.⑤	3.68 × 3.00	8.2	122 @ 3400	209 @ 2400	40–60
	V8-302, 5.0L	F	7200VV, 2 Bbl.⑤	4.00 × 3.00	8.4	132 @ 3400	236 @ 1800	40–60
1983	V8-302, 5.0L	F	E.F.I.⑫	4.00 × 3.00	—	—	—	40–60
MERCURY								
1977	V8-400, 6.6L⑥	S	2150, 2 Bbl.⑤	4.00 × 4.00	8.0	173 @ 3800	326 @ 1600	50–75
	V8-400, 6.6L⑧	S	2150, 2 Bbl.⑤	4.00 × 4.00	8.0	168 @ 3800	323 @ 1600	50–75
	V8-460, 7.5L	A	4350, 4 Bbl.⑤	4.36 × 3.85	8.0	197 @ 4000	353 @ 2000	35–65
1978	V8-351M, 5.8L④	Q	2150, 2 Bbl.⑤	4.00 × 3.50	8.0	145 @ 3400	273 @ 1800	50–75
	V8-400, 6.6L	S	2150, 2 Bbl.⑤	4.00 × 4.00	8.0	160 @ 3800	314 @ 1800	45–75
	V8-460, 7.5L⑨	A	4350, 4 Bbl.⑤	4.36 × 3.85	8.0	—	—	35–65
	V8-460, 7.5L⑩	A	4350, 4 Bbl.⑤	4.36 × 3.85	8.0	202 @ 4000	348 @ 2000	35–65
1979	V8-302, 5.0L⑥	F	2700VV, 2 Bbl.⑤	4.00 × 3.00	8.4	129 @ 3600	223 @ 2600	40–65
	V8-302, 5.0L⑧	F	2700VV, 2 Bbl.⑤	4.00 × 3.00	8.4	130 @ 3600	226 @ 2200	40–65
	V8-351W, 5.8L⑦	H	7200VV, 2 Bbl.⑤	4.00 × 3.50	8.3	138 @ 3200	260 @ 2200	40–65
1980	V8-302, 5.0L	F	2700VV, 2 Bbl.⑤	4.00 × 3.00	8.4	130 @ 3600	230 @ 1600	40–60
	V8-351W, 5.8L⑦	G	7200VV, 2 Bbl.⑤	4.00 × 3.50	8.3	140 @ 3400	265 @ 2000	40–60
	V8-351W, 5.8L H.O.⑦⑪	G	7200VV, 2 Bbl.⑤	4.00 × 3.50	8.3	—	—	40–60
1981	V8-255, 4.2L	D	7200VV, 2 Bbl.⑤	3.68 × 3.00	8.2	120 @ 3400	205 @ 2600	40–60
	V8-302, 5.0L⑧	F	7200VV, 2 Bbl.⑤	4.00 × 3.00	8.4	130 @ 3400	230 @ 2200	40–60
	V8-302, 5.0L⑥	F	7200VV, 2 Bbl.⑤	4.00 × 3.00	8.4	130 @ 3400	235 @ 1800	40–60
	V8-351W, 5.8L⑦	G	7200VV, 2 Bbl.⑤	4.00 × 3.50	8.3	145 @ 3200	270 @ 1800	40–60
	V8-351W, 5.8L H.O.⑦⑪	G	7200VV, 2 Bbl.⑤	4.00 × 3.50	8.3	165 @ 3600	285 @ 2200	40–60
1982	V8-255, 4.2L	D	7200VV, 2 Bbl.⑤	3.68 × 3.00	8.2	122 @ 3400	209 @ 2400	40–60
	V8-302, 5.0L	F	7200VV, 2 Bbl.⑤	4.00 × 3.00	8.4	132 @ 3400	236 @ 1800	40–60
1983	V8-302, 5.0L	F	E.F.I.⑫	4.00 × 3.00	—	—	—	40–60

①—C.I.D.—cubic inch displacement.
②—On 1977–80 models the fifth digit of V.I.N. denotes engine code. On 1980–83 models, the eighth digit of V.I.N. denotes engine code.
③—Ratings are net—as installed in vehicle.
④—Modified engine.
⑤—Motorcraft.
⑥—Exc. Calif.
⑦—Windsor engine.
⑧—Calif. only.
⑨—Police Interceptor.
⑩—Exc. Police Interceptor.
⑪—High Output engine.
⑫—E.F.I.—electronic fuel injection.

Full Size Models—FORD & MERCURY

TUNE UP SPECIFICATIONS

The following specifications are published from the latest information available. This data should be used only in the absence of a decal affixed in the engine compartment.

★ When using a timing light, disconnect vacuum hose or tube at distributor and plug opening in tube or hose so idle speed will not be affected.

● When checking compression, lowest cylinder must be within 75% of the highest.

▲ Before removing wires from distributor cap, determine location of the No. 1 wire in cap, as distributor position may have been altered from that shown at the end of this chart.

☞ Spark plug types shown in this chart are recommendations of the original vehicle manufacturer and not MOTOR.
Check local sources for other spark plug manufacturers listings.

Year & Engine/V.I.N.	Spark Plug Type ☞	Gap	Ignition Timing BTDC [1] ★ Firing Order Fig. ▲	Man. Trans.	Auto. Trans.	Mark Fig.	Curb Idle Speed [2] Man. Trans.	Auto. Trans.	Fast Idle Speed Man. Trans.	Auto. Trans.	Fuel Pump Pressure
1977											
V8-302/F	ARF-52	.050	A	—	8°	C	—	650D	—	2000[5]	6–8
V8-351W/H [6]	ARF-52	.050	B	—	4°	C	—	625D	—	2100[5]	6–8
V8-351M/Q [3][7][8]	ARF-52	.050	B	—	10°	C	—	650D	—	1350[4]	6–8
V8-351M/Q [3][7][9]	ARF-52	.050	B	—	9°	C	—	650D	—	1350[4]	6–8
V8-351M/Q [3][7][10]	ASF-52	.050	B	—	8°	C	—	500/600D	—	1350[4]	6–8
V8-400/S Exc. Calif. [7][11]	ARF-52	.050	B	—	8°	C	—	[12]	—	1350[4]	6–8
V8-400/S Exc. Calif. [7][13]	ARF-52	.050	B	—	12°	C	—	600D	—	1350[4]	6–8
V8-400/S Exc. Calif. [7][14]	ARF-52	.050	B	—	10°	C	—	600D	—	1350[4]	6–8
V8-400/S Exc. Calif. [7][15]	ARF-52	.050	B	—	6°	C	—	600D	—	1350[4]	6–8
V8-400/S Calif.	ARF-52-6	.060	B	—	6°	C	—	500/600D	—	1350[4]	6–8
V8-460/A Exc. High Alt. [7][16]	ARF-52	.050	A	—	16°	C	—	525/650D	—	1350[4]	5.7–6.7
V8-460/A Exc. High Alt. [7][17]	ARF-52	.050	A	—	10°	C	—	[18]	—	1350[4]	5.7–6.7
V8-460/A High Alt.	ARF-52	.050	A	—	18°	C	—	500/600D	—	1350[4]	5.7–6.7
1978											
V8-302/F	ARF-52	.050	A	—	14°	C	—	500/600D	—	2100[5]	6–8
V8-351W/H [6]	ARF-52	.050	B	—	14°	C	—	600/675D[19]	—	2100[5]	6–8
V8-351M/Q [3][7][20]	ASF-52	.050	B	—	9°	C	—	600/675D[19]	—	1350[4]	6–8
V8-351M/Q [3][7][21]	ASF-52	.050	B	—	12°	C	—	600/675D[19]	—	1350[4]	6–8
V8-400/S Exc. Calif. & High Alt.	ASF-52	.050	B	—	13°	C	—	575/650D[19]	—	1350[4]	6–8
V8-400/S Calif.	ASF-52	.050	B	—	16°	C	—	600/650D[19]	—	1350[4]	6–8
V8-400/S High Alt.	ASF-52	.050	B	—	8°	C	—	650D	—	2100[5]	6–8
V8-460/A [7][22]	ARF-52	.050	A	—	16°	C	—	580/650D[19]	—	1350[4]	5.7–7.7
V8-460/A [7][23]	ARF-52	.050	A	—	10°	C	—	580/650D[19]	—	1350[4]	5.7–7.7
1979											
V8-302/F Exc. Calif. [7][24]	[25]	.050	A	—	8°	C	—	600/675D[19]	—	2100[5]	6–8
V8-302/F Exc. Calif. [7][26]	[25]	.050	A	—	6°	C	—	550/625D[19]	—	1750[5]	6–8
V8-302/F Calif. [7][27]	[28]	.060	A	—	12°	C	—	600/675D[19]	—	1800[5]	6–8
V8-302/F Calif. [7][29]	[28]	.060	A	—	6°	C	—	550/625D[19]	—	1800[5]	6–8
V8-351W/H Exc. Calif. [6][30][31]	[25]	.050	B	—	15°	C	—	600/650D[19]	—	2100[5]	6–8
V8-351W/H Exc. Calif. [6][30][32]	[25]	.050	B	—	10°	C	—	600/650D[19]	—	2200[5]	6–8
V8-351W/H Exc. Calif. [6][33]	[25]	.050	[34]	—	[35]	C	—	550/640D[19]	—	2000[5]	6–8
V8-351W/H Calif. [6][33]	[25]	.050	[34]	—	[35]	C	—	620D	—	2100[5]	6–8
1980											
V8-302/F Sedan Exc. Calif. [7][30][38][39]	ASF-52	.050	A	—	6°	C	—	500D	—	1850[4]	6–8
V8-302/F Sedan Exc. Calif. [7][30][38][40]	ASF-52	.050	A	—	8°	C	—	500D	—	1850[4]	6–8
V8-302/F Sta. Wag. Exc. Calif. [30][38]	ASF-52	.050	A	—	6°	C	—	500D	—	[4][7][41]	6–8
V8-302/F Calif. & High Alt. [33]	ASF-52	.050	[36]	—	[35]	C	—	500/650D	—	2000[37]	6–8
V8-351W/G Exc. High Output [6][33]	ASF-52	.050	[34]	—	[35]	C	—	550/640D	—	1650[37]	6–8
V8-351W/G High Output [6][33]	ASF-42	.044	[34]	—	[35]	C	—	550/700D	—	1500[37]	6–8

TUNE UP SPECIFICATIONS—Continued

The following specifications are published from the latest information available. This data should be used only in the absence of a decal affixed in the engine compartment.

★ When using a timing light, disconnect vacuum hose or tube at distributor and plug opening in tube or hose so idle speed will not be affected.

● When checking compression, lowest cylinder must be within 75% of the highest.

▲ Before removing wires from distributor cap, determine location of the No. 1 wire in cap, as distributor position may have been altered from that shown at the end of this chart.

☞ Spark plug types shown in this chart are recommendations of the original vehicle manufacturer and not MOTOR.

Check local sources for other spark plug manufacturers listings.

Year & Engine/V.I.N.	Spark Plug Type ☞	Gap	Ignition Timing BTDC① ★ Firing Order Fig. ▲	Man. Trans.	Auto. Trans.	Mark Fig.	Curb Idle Speed② Man. Trans.	Auto. Trans.	Fast Idle Speed Man. Trans.	Auto. Trans.	Fuel Pump Pressure
1981											
V8-255/D Exc. Calif.	ASF-52	.050	A	—	7°	C	—	500/650D	—	1800④	6–8
V8-255/D Calif.	ASF-52	.050	A	—	5°	C	—	500/650D	—	1800④	6–8
V8-302/F	ASF-52	.050	A	—	8°	C	—	500D	—	1800④	6–8
V8-351W/G⑥㉝	ASF-52	.050	㉞	—		C	—	550/640D	—	1650㊲	6–8
1982											
V8-255/D	ASF-52	.050	A	—	7°	C	—	500/650D	—	1800④	6–8
V8-302/F Exc. High Alt.	ASF-52	.050	A	—	8°	C	—	500D	—	1800④	6–8
V8-302/F High Alt.	ASF-52	.050	A	—	14°	C	—	500D	—	1800④	6–8
1983											
V8-302 E.F.I./F	ASF-52	.050	A	—	—	C	—	—	—	—	—

①—B.T.D.C.—Before top dead center.
②—Idle speed on manual trans. vehicles is adjusted in Neutral & on auto. trans. equipped vehicles is adjusted in Drive unless otherwise specified. Where two idle speeds are listed, the higher speed is with the A/C or throttle solenoid energized. On models equipped with vacuum release brake, whenever adjusting ignition timing or idle speed, vacuum line to brake release mechanism must be disconnected & plugged to prevent parking brake from releasing when selector lever is moved to Drive.
③—Modified engine.
④—On kickdown step of cam.
⑤—On high step of fast idle cam.
⑥—Windsor engine.
⑦—Refer to engine calibration code on engine identification label located at rear of left valve cover. The calibration code is located on the label after the engine code number and preceded by the letter C and the revision code is located below the calibration code and is preceded by the letter R.
⑧—Calibration code 7-14B-R1.
⑨—Calibration codes 7-14B-R10 & 7-14C-R11.
⑩—Calibration code 7-34B-R0.
⑪—Calibration codes 7-17B-R1 & 7-37A-R0.
⑫—Calibration code 7-17B-R1, 600D RPM;

7-37A-R0, 500/650D RPM.
⑬—Calibration code 7-17B-R15.
⑭—Calibration code 7-17B-R16.
⑮—Calibration codes 7-17C-R1 & 7-17C-R11.
⑯—Calibration codes 7-19A-R1 & 7-19A-R17.
⑰—Calibration codes 7-19A-R2 & 7-19A-R3.
⑱—Calibration codes 7-19A-R2, 525/650D RPM; 7-19A-R3, 550/650D RPM.
⑲—With throttle solenoid energized. Higher idle speed is with A/C on, compressor clutch de-energized, if equipped.
⑳—Calibration code 8-14B-R0.
㉑—Calibration codes 8-14B-R13 & 8-14B-R22.
㉒—Calibration code 8-19A-R1.
㉓—Calibration codes 8-19C-R11 & 8-19C-R14.
㉔—Calibration codes 9-11B-R0, 9-11C-R1A, 9-11C-R1N & 9-11J-R0.
㉕—ASF-52 or ARF-52.
㉖—Calibration codes 9-11E-R1 & 9-11F-R1.

㉗—Calibration codes 9-11N-R0, 9-11R-R0, 9-11S-R0 & 9-11V.
㉘—ASF-52-6 or ARF-52-6.
㉙—Calibration code 9-11Q-R0.
㉚—Models less Electronic Engine Control (EEC) System.
㉛—Models less variable venturi carburetor.
㉜—Models with variable venturi carburetor.
㉝—Models with Electronic Engine Control (EEC) System.
㉞—Firing order, 1-3-7-2-6-5-4-8. Cylinder numbering (front to rear): Right bank 1-2-3-4, left bank 5-6-7-8. Refer to Fig. D for spark plug wire connections at distributor.
㉟—Engine cranking reference timing 10° BTDC. Ignition timing is not adjustable.
㊱—Firing order, 1-5-4-2-6-3-7-8. Cylinder numbering (front to rear): Right bank 1-2-3-4, left bank 5-6-7-8. Refer to Fig. D for spark plug wire connections at distributor.
㊲—On 2nd highest step of fast idle cam.
㊳—Except high altitude.
㊴—Calibration codes, 0-13A-R0, R11, R14 & 0-13F-R11.
㊵—Calibration codes, 0-13D-R0, R10, & R11.
㊶—Except calibration code 0-13A-R11, 1850 RPM; calibration code 0-13A-R11, 1700 RPM.

Fig. A

FIRING ORDER 1-3-7-2-6-5-4-8

Fig. B

Fig. C

SPARK PLUG CONNECTIONS 5.8/6.6L (351/400 CID) V-8

SPARK PLUG CONNECTIONS 5.0L (302 CID) V-8

Fig. D

STARTING MOTOR SPECIFICATIONS

Year	Model/V.I.N.	Ident. No.	Rotation	Brush Spring Tension Ounces	No Load Test			Torque Test		
					Amperes	Volts	R.P.M.	Amperes	Volts	Torque Ft. Lbs.
1977	V8-351M/Q	D5AF-EA	C	80	80	12	—	670	—	15.5
	V8-400/S	D6OF-AA	C	80	80	12	—	670	—	15.5
	V8-460/A	D6AF-AA	C	40	70	12	—	—	—	—
1978	V8-302/F	D8OF-AA	C	80	80	12	—	670	5.0	15.5
	V8-351M/Q	D8AF-AA	C	80	80	12	—	670	5.0	15.5
	V8-351W/H	D8OF-AA	C	80	80	12	—	670	5.0	15.5
	V8-400/S	D8AF-AA	C	80	80	12	—	670	5.0	15.5
	V8-460/A	D8AF-BA	C	80	80	12	—	670	5.0	15.5
1979	V8-302/F	D8OF-AA	C	80	80	12	—	670	5.0	15.5
	V8-351W/H	D8OF-AA	C	80	80	12	—	670	5.0	15.5
1980–81	V8-255/D, 302/F	D8OF-AA	C	40–80	85	12	—	670	5.0	15.5
	V8-351W/G	D8OF-AA	C	40–80	85	12	—	670	5.0	15.5
1982	V8-255/D, 302/F	E1AF-BA	C	40–80	85	12	—	670	5.0	15.5
1983	V8-302/F	—	C	40–80	85	12	—	670	5.0	15.5

ALTERNATOR & REGULATOR SPECIFICATIONS

Year	Make or Model ①	Current Rating		Field Current @ 75°F.		Voltage Regulator				Field Relay	
		Amperes	Volts	Amperes	Volts	Part No. (10316)	Voltage @ 75°F.	Contact Gap	Armature Air Gap	Armature Air Gap	Closing Voltage @ 75°F.
1977	Orange②	40	15	2.9	12	D4AF-AA	13.5–15.3	—	—	—	2.5–4
	Green②	60	15	2.9	12	D4AF-AA	13.5–15.3	—	—	—	2.5–4
	All③	70	15	2.9	12	D4TF-AA	13.5–15.3	—	—	—	2.5–4
	All③	90	15	2.9	12	D4TF-AA	13.5–15.3	—	—	—	2.5–4
1978	Orange②	40	15	2.9	12	D4AF-AA	13.5–15.3	—	—	—	—
	Green②	60	15	2.9	12	D4AF-AA	13.5–15.3	—	—	—	—
	Green②④	60	15	4.0	12	D8BF-AA⑤	—	—	—	—	—
	Black③	70	15	2.9	12	D4TF-AA	13.5–15.3	—	—	—	—
	Red③	90	15	2.9	12	D4TF-AA	13.5–15.3	—	—	—	—
	Red③④	90	15	4.0	12	D8BF-AA⑤	—	—	—	—	—
1979	Orange②④	40	15	4.0	12	D8BF-AA⑤	13.8–14.6	—	—	—	—
	Black②④	65	15	4.0	12	D8BF-AA⑤	13.8–14.6	—	—	—	—
	Green②④	60	15	4.0	12	D8BF-AA⑤	13.8–14.6	—	—	—	—
	Black③④	70	15	4.0	12	D8BF-AA⑤	13.8–14.6	—	—	—	—
	Red③④	90	15	4.0	12	D8BF-AA⑤	13.8–14.6	—	—	—	—
1980–81	Orange②④	40	15	4.0	12	D9BF-AB⑤	13.8–14.6	—	—	—	—
	Black②④	65	15	4.0	12	D9BF-AB⑤	13.8–14.6	—	—	—	—
	Green②④	60	15	4.0	12	D9BF-AB⑤	13.8–14.6	—	—	—	—
	Black③④	70	15	4.0	12	D9BF-AB⑤	13.8–14.6	—	—	—	—
	Red③④	100	15	4.0	12	D9BF-AB⑤	13.8–14.6	—	—	—	—
1982	Orange②④	40	15	4.0	12	E1AF-BA⑤	13.8–14.6	—	—	—	—
	Black②④	65	15	4.0	12	E1AF-BA⑤	13.8–14.6	—	—	—	—
	Green②④	60	15	4.0	12	E1AF-BA⑤	13.8–14.6	—	—	—	—
	Black③④	70	15	4.0	12	E1AF-BA⑤	13.8–14.6	—	—	—	—
	Red③④	100	15	4.0	12	E1AF-BA⑤	13.8–14.6	—	—	—	—
1983	Orange②④	40	15	4.25	12	E2AF-AA	—	—	—	—	—
	Black②④	65	15	4.25	12	E2AF-AA	—	—	—	—	—
	Green②④	60	15	4.25	12	E2AF-AA	—	—	—	—	—
	Black③④	70	15	4.25	12	E2AF-AA	—	—	—	—	—
	Red③④	100	15	4.25	12	E2AF-AA	—	—	—	—	—

①—Stamp color code.
②—Rear terminal alternator.
③—Side terminal alternator.
④—Solid state alternator.
⑤—Electronic voltage regulator. These units are color coded black for systems w/warning indicator lamp & blue for systems w/ammeter.

FORD & MERCURY—Full Size Models

REAR AXLE SPECIFICATIONS

Year	Carrier Type	Ring Gear & Pinion Backlash Inch	Nominal Pinion Locating Shim, Inch	Pinion Bearing Preload				Differential Bearing Preload	Pinion Nut Torque Ft.-Lbs.①
				New Bearings With Seal Inch-Lbs.	Used Bearings With Seal Inch-Lbs.	New Bearings Less Seal Inch-Lbs.	Used Bearings Less Seal Inch-Lbs.		
1977–78	Integral	.008–.012	.030	17–27	8–14	—	—	.008–.012⑤	140
	Removable	.008–.012	.015	17–27④	8–14	—	—	.008–.012③	②
1979	Integral	.008–.012	.030	17–27	8–14	—	—	.008–.012	140
	Removable	.008–.012	.015	17–27	8–14	—	—	.008–.012	170①
1980	Integral	.008–.015	.030	17–27	8–14	—	—	.008–.012	140
1981–83	Integral	.008–.015	.030	16–29	8–14	—	—	.016⑥	⑦

①—If torque cannot be obtained, install new spacer.
②—Collapsible spacer 170 ft. lbs.; solid spacer 200 ft. lbs.
③—Case spread with new bearings; with used bearings .005–.008".
④—Solid spacer 13–33 inch-lbs.
⑤—Case spread with new bearing; with used bearings .006–.010".
⑥—Differential case spread.
⑦—With 7.5 inch ring gear, 170 ft.-lbs.; with 8.5 inch ring gear, 140 ft.-lbs.

DISTRIBUTOR SPECIFICATIONS

★Note: If unit is checked on vehicle, double the RPM and degrees to get crankshaft figures.

Distributor Part No.①	Centrifugal Advance Degrees @ RPM of Distributor					Vacuum Advance		Distributor Retard
	Advance Starts	Intermediate Advance			Full Advance	Inches of Vacuum to Start Plunger	Max. Adv. Dist. Deg. @ Vacuum	Max. Retard Dist. Deg. @ Vacuum
1977								
D6AE-AA	0–2 @ 500	4–6 @ 700	—	—	14 @ 2500	3	15¼ @ 11½	—
D6VE-CA	0–1 @ 450	7½–9½ @ 725	—	—	14 @ 2500	3½	13¼ @ 15	—
D7AE-BA	0–1 @ 425	2¾–4¾ @ 625	—	—	13½ @ 2250	3½	15¼ @ 12	—
D7AE-CA	0–1 @ 700	3½–6 @ 1600	—	—	10¾ @ 2500	3	15¼ @ 11	—
D7AE-DA	0–1 @ 450	3¾–5¾ @ 675	—	—	14 @ 2500	3.2	15¼ @ 14.5	—
D7DE-CA	0–1 @ 450	4¾–6¾ @ 700	—	—	15½ @ 2500	3	15¼ @ 11	—
D70E-CA	0–1 @ 450	2¾–4¾ @ 575	—	—	16 @ 2500	3½	15¼ @ 14.5	—
1978								
D8AE-CA	0 @ 1100	3.5–6 @ 1600	—	—	9.5 @ 2500	3	17.5 @ 14	—
D8AE-GA	0 @ 450	3.5–5.5 @ 700	—	—	8.25 @ 2500	5.5	15.25 @ 16.5	—
1979–80								
D9AE-AAA	0–2.75 @ 500	.9–2.9 @ 530	—	—	10.6–13.25 @ 2500	2.3	12.75–15.25 @ 25	—
D9AE-ABA	0–2 @ 580	4.25–6.25 @ 950	—	—	9.25–12.25 @ 2500	2.8	6.75–9.25 @ 25	2–4 @ 9.3
D9AE-DA	②	—	—	—	—	—	—	—
D9AE-TA	0–3 @ 490	2.9–4.9 @ 600	—	—	10–13 @ 2500	2.2	12.75–15.25 @ 25	—
D9AE-ZA	0–3 @ 500	4.9–6.9 @ 660	—	—	12.25–14.75 @ 2500	1.8	14.75–17.25 @ 25	—
D9SE-AA	0–2 @ 500	2–4 @ 600	—	—	3.6–6.1 @ 2500	2.8	14.75–17.25 @ 25	—
D94E-AA	②	—	—	—	—	—	—	—
1981								
D9AE-DA	—	—	—	—	—	—	—	—
E1AE-EA	—	—	—	—	—	—	—	—
E1AE-JA	—	—	—	—	—	—	—	—
E1AE-KA	—	—	—	—	—	—	—	—
E1SE-BA	—	—	—	—	—	—	—	—
1982								
E1SE-BA	—	9.5–12 @ 1250	—	—	—	—	—	—
E2AE-FA	—	9.5–12 @ 1250	—	—	—	—	—	—
E1AE-KA	—	7–9 @ 1250	—	—	—	—	—	—

①—Basic part No. 12127.
②—EEC system distributor.

VALVE SPECIFICATIONS

Year	Engine Model/V.I.N.	Valve Lash Int.	Valve Lash Exh.	Valve Angles Seat	Valve Angles Face	Valve Spring Installed Height	Valve Spring Pressure Lbs. @ In.	Stem Clearance Intake	Stem Clearance Exhaust	Stem Diameter Intake	Stem Diameter Exhaust
1977	V8-302/F	.096–.168④		45	44	⑦	⑨	.0010–.0027	.0015–.0032	.3416–.3423	.3411–.3418
	V8-351W/H③	.096–.168④		45	44	⑧	⑩	.0010–.0027	.0015–.0032	.3416–.3423	.3411–.3418
	V8-351M/Q②	.125–.175④		45	44	1 53/64	226 @ 1.39	.0010–.0027	.0015–.0032	.3416–.3423	.3411–.3418
	V8-400/S	.125–.175④		45	44	1 53/64	226 @ 1.39	.0010–.0027	.0015–.0032	.3416–.3423	.3411–.3418
	V8-460/A	.100–.150④		45	44	1 13/16	229 @ 1.33⑪	.0010–.0027	.0010–.0027	.3416–.3423	.3416–.3423
1978	V8-302/F	.071–.193④		45	44	⑦	⑨	.0010–.0027	.0015–.0037	.3416–.3423	.3411–.3418
	V8-351M/Q②	.100–.200④		45	44	1 13/16	226 @ 1.39	.0010–.0027	.0015–.0037	.3416–.3423	.3411–.3418
	V8-351W/H③	.071–.193④		45	44	①	⑤	.0010–.0027	.0015–.0037	.3416–.3423	.3411–.3418
	V8-400/S	.100–.200④		45	44	1 13/16	226 @ 1.39	.0010–.0027	.0015–.0037	.3416–.3423	.3411–.3418
	V8-460/A	.075–.175④		45	44	1 13/16	229 @ 1.33	.0010–.0027	.0010–.0027	.3416–.3423	.3416–.3423
1979	V8-302/F	.096–.165④		45	44	⑦	⑤	.0010–.0027	.0015–.0032	.3416–.3423	.3411–.3418
	V8-351W/H③	.123–.173④		45	44	⑥	⑫	.0010–.0027	.0015–.0032	.3416–.3423	.3411–.3418
1980	V8-302/F	.096–.163		45	44	⑧	⑬	.0010–.0027	.0015–.0032	.3416–.3423	.3411–.3418
	V8-351W/G③	.096–.163④		45	44	⑧	⑬	.0010–.0027	.0015–.0032	.3416–.3423	.3411–.3418
1980–81	V8-351W H.O./G③⑮	.096–.146④		45	44	⑧	⑯	.0010–.0027	.0015–.0032	.3416–.3423	.3411–.3418
1981	V8-351W/G③	.096–.146④		45	44	⑧	⑬	.0010–.0027	.0015–.0032	.3416–.3423	.3411–.3418
	V8-255, 302⑱	.096–.146④		45	44	⑭	⑬	.0010–.0027	.0015–.0032	.3416–.3423	.3411–.3418
1982	V8-255/D, 302/F	.096–.146④		45	44	⑭	⑰	.0010–.0027	.0015–.0032	.3416–.3423	.3411–.3418
1983	V8-302/F	.096–.146④		45	44	⑭	⑱	.0010–.0027	.0015–.0032	.3416–.3423	.3411–.3418

①—Intake, 1 51/64; exhaust, 1 39/64.
②—Modified engine.
③—Windsor engine.
④—Clearance specified is obtainable at valve stem tip with lifter collapsed. See "Valves, Adjust" text.
⑤—Intake, 200 @ 1.34; exhaust, 200 @ 1.20.
⑥—Intake, 1 25/32; exhaust 1 11/16.
⑦—Intake, 1 11/16; exhaust, 1 39/64.
⑧—Intake, 1 25/32; exhaust, 1 39/64.
⑨—Intake, 200 @ 1.31; exhaust, 200 @ 1.20.
⑩—Intake, 200 @ exhaust, 200 @ 1.20.
⑪—Police, 315 @ 1.32.
⑫—Intake, 226 @ 1.39; exhaust, 200 @ 1.20.
⑬—Intake, 205 @ 1.36; exhaust, 200 @ 1.20.
⑭—Intake, 1 11/16; exhaust, 1 19/32.
⑮—High output engine.
⑯—Intake, 204 @ 1.33; exhaust, 205 @ 1.15.
⑰—Intake, 205 @ 1.36; exhaust, 205 @ 1.15.
⑱—Intake, 205 @ 1.36; exhaust, 205 @ 1.05.

BRAKE SPECIFICATIONS

Year	Model	Brake Drum Inside Diameter	Wheel Cylinder Bore Diameter Front Disc Brake	Wheel Cylinder Bore Diameter Front Drum Brake	Wheel Cylinder Bore Diameter Rear Brake	Master Cylinder Bore Diameter With Disc Brakes	Master Cylinder Bore Diameter With Drum Brakes	Master Cylinder Bore Diameter With Power Brakes
1977–78	All①	11.03	3.10	—	1.00	1.00	—	1.00
	All②	—	3.10	—	2.6	1.00	—	1.00
1979	①③	10.00	2.88	—	.875	1.00	—	1.00
	①④	11.03	2.88	—	.9375	1.00	—	1.00
	All②	—	2.88	—	2.6	1.00	—	1.00
1980–83	All③	10.00	2.88	—	.9375	1.00	—	1.00
	All④	11.03	2.88	—	.9375	1.00	—	1.00

①—Except 4 wheel disc brakes.
②—With 4 wheel disc brakes.
③—Sedan except police, taxi & trailer tow.
④—Station wagon, police, taxi & trailer tow.

PISTONS, PINS, RINGS, CRANKSHAFT & BEARINGS

Year	Engine Model/V.I.N.	Piston Clearance	Ring End Gap① Comp.	Ring End Gap① Oil	Wristpin Diameter	Rod Bearings Shaft Diameter	Rod Bearings Bearing Clearance	Main Bearings Shaft Diameter	Main Bearings Bearing Clearance	Thrust on Bear. No.	Shaft End Play
1977	V8-302/F	.0018–.0026	.010	.015	.9122	2.1228–2.1236	.0008–.0015	2.2482–2.2490	②	3	.004–.008
	V8-351W/H③	.0018–.0026	.010	.015	.9122	2.3103–2.3111	.0008–.0015	2.9994–3.0002	.0008–.0015	3	.004–.008
	V8-351M/Q⑤	.0014–.0022	.010	.015	.9752	2.3103–2.3111	.0008–.0015	2.9994–3.0002	.0008–.0015	3	.004–.008
	V8-400/S	.0014–.0022	.010	.015	.9752	2.3103–2.3111	.0008–.0015	2.9994–3.0002	.0008–.0015	3	.004–.008
	V8-460/A	.0014–.0022	.010	.015	1.0401	2.4992–2.5000	.0008–.0015	2.9994–3.0002	.0008–.0015	3	.004–.008
	V8-460/A④	.0022–.0032	.010	.015	1.0401	2.4992–2.5000	.0008–.0015	2.9994–3.0002	.0008–.0015	3	.004–.008

Continued

PISTONS, PINS, RINGS, CRANKSHAFT & BEARINGS—Continued

Year	Engine Model/V.I.N.	Piston Clearance	Ring End Gap①		Wristpin Diameter	Rod Bearings		Main Bearings			
			Comp.	Oil		Shaft Diameter	Bearing Clearance	Shaft Diameter	Bearing Clearance	Thrust on Bear. No.	Shaft End Play
1978	V8-302/F	.0018–.0026	.010	.015	.9122	2.1228–2.1236	.0008–.0015	2.2482–2.2490	②	3	.004–.008
	V8-351W/H③	.0018–.0026	.010	.015	.9122	2.3103–2.3111	.0008–.0015	2.9994–3.0002	.0008–.0015	3	.004–.008
	V8-351M/Q⑤	.0014–.0022	.010	.015	.9752	2.3103–2.3111	.0008–.0015	2.9994–3.0002	.0008–.0015	3	.004–.008
	V8-400/S	.0014–.0022	.010	.015	.9752	2.3103–2.3111	.0008–.0015	2.9994–3.0002	.0008–.0015	3	.004–.008
	V8-460/A	.0014–.0022	.010	.015	1.0401	2.4992–2.5000	.0008–.0015	2.9994–3.0002	.0008–.0015	3	.004–.008
1979	V8-302/F	.0018–.0026	.010	.015	.9122	2.1228–2.1236	.0008–.0015	2.2482–2.2490	②	3	.004–.008
	V8-351W/H③	.0018–.0026	.010	.015	.9122	2.3103–2.3111	.0008–.0015	2.9994–3.0002	.0008–.0015	3	.004–.008
1980	V8-302/F	.0018–.0026	.010	.015	.9122	2.1228–2.1236	.0008–.0026	2.2486	②	3	.004–.008
	V8-351W/G③	.0018–.0026	.010	.015	.9122	2.1228–2.1236	.0008–.0026	2.9998	.0008–.0015	3	.004–.008
1981	V8-255/D	.0014–.0024	.010	.015	.9122	2.1228–2.1236	.0008–.0024	2.2482–2.2490	②	3	.004–.008
	V8-302/F	.0018–.0026	.010	.015	.9122	2.1228–2.1236	.0008–.0024	2.2482–2.2490	②	3	.004–.008
	V8-351W/ G③	.0018–.0026	.010	.015	.9122	2.3103–2.3111	.0007–.0025	2.9994–3.0002	.0008–.0015	3	.004–.008
1982	V8-255/D	.0014–.0024	.010	.015	.9122	2.1228–2.1236	.0008–.0015	2.2482–2.2490	⑥	3	.004–.008
1982–83	V8-302/F	.0018–.0026	.010	.015	.9122	2.1228–2.1236	.0008–.0015	2.2482–2.2490	⑥	3	.004–.008

①—Fit rings in tapered bores for clearance listed in tightest portion of ring travel.
②—No. 1, .0001–.0015; all others, .0004–.0015.
③—Windsor engine.
④—Police.
⑤—Modified engine.
⑥—No. 1, .0004–.0025; all others, .0004–.0015.

WHEEL ALIGNMENT SPECIFICATIONS

Year	Model	Caster Angle, Degrees		Camber Angle, Degrees				Toe-In. Inch	Toe-Out on Turns, Deg.	
		Limits	Desired	Limits		Desired			Outer Wheel	Inner Wheel
				Left	Right	Left	Right			
1977–78	All	+1¼ to +2¾	+2	−¼ to +1¼	−½ to +1	+½	+½	3/16	18.72	20
1979–82	All	+2¼ to +3¾	+3	−¼ to +1¼	−¼ to +1¼	+½	+½	3/16①	18.51	20
1983	All	+2¼ to +4	+3	−¼ to +1¼	−¼ to +1¼	+½	+½	1/16	18.51	20

①—1980–82, 1/16 inch.

ENGINE TIGHTENING SPECIFICATIONS★

★ Torque specifications are for clean and lightly lubricated threads only. Dry or dirty threads produce increased friction which prevents accurate measurement of tightness.

Year	Engine Model/V.I.N.	Spark Plugs Ft. Lbs.	Cylinder Head Bolts Ft. Lbs.	Intake Manifold Ft. Lbs.	Exhaust Manifold Ft. Lbs.	Rocker Arm Stud Nut or Bolt Ft. Lbs.	Rocker Arm Cover Ft. Lbs.	Connecting Rod Cap Bolts Ft. Lbs.	Main Bearing Cap Bolts Ft. Lbs.	Flywheel to Crank-shaft Ft. Lbs.	Vibration Damper or Pulley Ft. Lbs.
1977–80	V8-302/F	10–15	65–72	23–25	18–24	④	3–5	19–24	60–70	75–85	70–90
	V8-351W/H,G①	10–15	105–112	23–25	18–24	④	3–5	40–45	95–105	75–85	70–90
	V8-351M/Q②	10–15	95–105	③	18–24	18–25	3–5	40–45	95–105	75–85	70–90
	V8-400/S	10–15	95–105	③	18–24	18–25	3–5	40–45	95–105	75–85	70–90
	V8-460/A	10–15	130–140	22–32	28–33	18–25	5–6	40–45	95–105	75–85	70–90
1981	V8-351W/G①	10–15	105–112	23–25	18–24	18–25	3–5	40–45	95–105	75–85	70–90
1981–82	V8-255/D	10–15	65–72	18–20	18–24	18–25	3–5	19–24	60–70	75–85	70–90
1981–83	V8-302/F	10–15	65–72	23–25	18–24	18–25	3–5	19–24	60–70	75–85	70–90

①—Windsor engine.
②—Modified engine.
③—1977–78: 5/16″ bolts 19–25 ft. lbs., 3/8″ bolts 22–32 ft. lbs.
④—1977 & early 1978 rocker arm stud nut, 17–23 ft. lbs.; late 1978 & 1979–80 fulcrum bolt to cylinder head, 18–25 ft. lbs.

COOLING SYSTEM & CAPACITY DATA

Year	Model or Engine/V.I.N.	Cooling Capacity, Qts.		Radiator Cap Relief Pressure, Lbs.	Thermo. Opening Temp.	Fuel Tank Gals.	Engine Oil Refill Qts. ①	Transmission Oil		Auto. Trans. Qts. ②	Rear Axle Oil Pints
		Less A/C	With A/C					3 Speed Pints	4 Speed Pints		
FORD											
1977	V8-351/Q⑩	17.1	17.5	13–19	191	24.2④	4	—	—	⑬	⑤
	V8-400/S	17.1	17.2	13–19	191	24.2④	4	—	—	⑬	⑤
	V8-460/A⑦	18.5	18.5	13–19	191	24.2④	4	—	—	⑬	⑤
	V8-460/A③	19.0	19.0	13–19	191	24.2④	6	—	—	⑬	⑤
1978	V8-302/F	14.7	15.2	14–18	191	24.2⑭	4	—	—	10	⑥
	V8-351/H⑨	15.9	16.3	14–18	191	24.2⑭	4	—	—	11	⑥
	V8-351/Q⑩	17.0	17.0	14–18	191	24.2⑭	4	—	—	11	⑥
	V8-400/S	17.0	17.0	14–18	191	24.2⑭	4	—	—	11	⑥
	V8-460/A③	19.7	19.7	14–18	191	24.2⑭	6	—	—	12½	⑥
	V8-460/A⑦	18.6	18.6	14–18	191	24.2⑭	4	—	—	12½	⑥
1979	V8-302/F	13.3⑧	13.8⑧	16	196	19⑯	4	—	—	11.8	⑰
	V8-351W/H⑨	14.6⑪	15.2⑪	16	196	19⑯	4	—	—	11.0	⑰
1980	V8-302/F	13	13.3	16	196	19⑯	4⑫	—	—	⑳	⑲
	V8-351W/G⑨	13.9	14	16	196	19⑯	4⑫	—	—	⑱	⑲
1981	V8-255/D	13.8	13.8	16	191	20	4⑫	—	—	12	⑲
	V8-302/F	13	13.4	16	196	20	4⑫	—	—	12	⑲
	V8-351W/G⑨	13.8	13.8⑮	16	196	20	4⑫	—	—	12	⑲
1982	V8-255/D	14.7	15	16	191	20	4⑫	—	—	12	3¾
	V8-302/F	13	13.4	16	196	20	4⑫	—	—	12	3¾
1983	V8-302/F	13	13.4	16	191	20	4⑫	—	—	12	3¾
MERCURY											
1977	V8-400/S	17.1	17.2	13–19	191	24.2⑥	4	—	—	⑬	⑤
	V8-460/A	18.5	18.5	13–19	191	24.2④	4	—	—	⑬	⑤
	V8-460/A	19.0	19.0	13–19	191	24.2④	6	—	—	⑬	⑤
1978	V8-351/H⑨	16.3	16.3	14–18	191	24.2⑭	4	—	—	⑬	⑥
	V8-400/S	17.0	17.5	14–18	191	24.2⑭	4	—	—	11	⑥
	V8-460/A③	19.7	19.7	14–18	191	24.2⑭	6	—	—	12½	⑥
	V8-460/A⑦	18.6	18.6	14–18	191	24.2⑭	4	—	—	12½	⑥
1979	V8-302/F	13.3⑧	13.8⑧	16	196	19⑯	4	—	—	11.8	⑰
	V8-351W/H⑨	14.6⑪	15.2⑪	16	196	19⑯	4	—	—	11.0	⑰
1980	V8-302/F	13	13.3	16	196	19⑯	4⑫	—	—	⑳	⑲
	V8-351W/G⑨	13.9	14	16	196	19⑯	4⑫	—	—	⑱	⑲
1981	V8-255/D	13.8	13.8	16	191	20	4⑫	—	—	12	⑲
	V8-302/F	13	13.4	16	196	20	4⑫	—	—	12	⑲
	V8-351W/G⑨	13.8	13.8⑮	16	196	20	4⑫	—	—	12	⑲
1982	V8-255/D	14.7	15	16	191	20	4⑫	—	—	12	3¾
	V8-302/F	13	13.4	16	196	20	4⑫	—	—	12	3¾
1983	V8-302/F	13	13.4	16	191	20	4⑫	—	—	12	3¾

①—Add one quart with filter change.
②—Approximate. Make final check with dipstick.
③—Police models.
④—Station wagons 21 gals. Add 8 gals. with auxiliary tank.
⑤—WER axles 4 pts.; all others 5 pts.
⑥—Exc. models with 460 engine, locking or optional axles, 4 pts.; Models with 460 engine, locking or optional axles, 5 pts.
⑦—Exc. police models.
⑧—Police, 14.2 qts.
⑨—Windsor engine.
⑩—Modified engine.
⑪—Police, Trailer tow, 15.6 qts.
⑫—When changing engine oil on these models, both drain plugs must be removed to fully drain crankcase. One drain plug is located at the front of the oil pan, while the other drain plug is located at rear left side of the oil pan.
⑬—FMX 11 qts., C6 12¼ qts. C4, 10¼ qts.
⑭—Station wagons, 21 gals.
⑮—Trailer tow, 15 qts.
⑯—Station wagon, 20 gal.
⑰—Axle code WGZ, 4 pts.; Axle code WGY, 3.5 pts.
⑱—C4, 10 qts.; FMX, 11 qts.; F10D Overdrive auto. trans., 12 qts.
⑲—7½" ring gear, 3½ pts.; 8½" ring gear, 4 pts.
⑳—C4, 10 qts.; FMX, 11 qts.; C6, 11.8 qts.; Overdrive auto. trans., 12 qts.

STARTER, REPLACE

SERVICE BULLETIN

STARTER PROBLEMS: If the starter is noisy or if it locks up, before condemning the starter, loosen the three mounting bolts enough to hand fit the starter properly into the pilot plate. Then tighten the mounting bolts, starting with the top bolt.

1977–83 Ford & Mercury

1. Disconnect battery ground cable, then disconnect starter cable at starter terminal.
2. Remove mounting bolts and starter.

NOTE: On some models, it may be necessary to turn the wheels right or left to remove starter.

3. Reverse procedure to install and torque bolts to 15–20 ft. lbs.

IGNITION LOCK, REPLACE

1979–83

1. Disconnect battery ground cable.
2. Remove steering column trim shroud.
3. Disconnect key warning switch electrical connector.
4. Turn ignition lock to "On" position.
5. Using a 1/8" pin or punch located in the 4 o'clock hole and 1 1/4 inch from outer edge of lock cylinder housing, depress retaining pin while pulling the lock cylinder from housing.
6. Turn lock cylinder to "On" position and insert cylinder into housing. Ensure that the lock cylinder is fully seated and aligned into the interlocking washer before turning key to "Off" position. This will permit the retaining pin to extend into the lock cylinder housing hole.

7. Rotate key to check for proper mechanical operation.
8. Connect key warning switch electrical connector.
9. Connect battery ground cable.
10. Check for proper operation.

1977–78

1. Disconnect battery ground cable.
2. *Units with Fixed Steering Columns:* Remove steering wheel and trim pad. Insert a wire pin in the hole located inside the column halfway down the lock cylinder housing, Fig. 1, *Units with Tilt Steering Columns:* Insert wire pin in the hole located on the outside of the flange casting next to the emergency flasher button, Fig. 1.
3. Place the gear shift lever in "Park" position, and turn the lock cylinder with the ignition key to "Run" position.
4. Depress the wire pin while pulling up on the lock cylinder to remove. Remove the wire pin.
5. To install insert the lock cylinder into housing in the flange casting, and turn the key to "Off" position. Be certain that the cylinder is fully inserted before turning to the "Off" position. This action will extend the cylinder retaining pin into the cylinder housing.
6. Turn the key to check for correct operation in all positions.
7. Install the steering wheel and trim pad on fixed column units.
8. Connect the battery ground cable.

IGNITION SWITCH, REPLACE

1979–83

1. Disconnect battery ground cable.
2. Remove upper column shroud.
3. Disconnect ignition switch electrical connector.
4. With a 1/8 inch twist drill, drill out the switch retaining bolt heads. Then, remove the bolts with a "Easy Out" or

equivalent.
5. Disengage ignition switch from actuator and remove from vehicle, Fig. 2.
6. On 1979–81 models, adjust ignition switch to "Lock" position. On 1982–83 models, adjust ignition switch to "Run" position. Insert a .050 inch drill or equivalent through the switch housing and into the carrier to prevent movement.

NOTE: A replacement ignition switch includes an installed adjusting pin.

7. On 1979–81 models, rotate ignition key to "Lock" position. On 1982–83 models, place lock cylinder in the "Run" position, which is approximately 90° from the "Lock" position.
8. Install ignition switch on actuator pin.
9. Install switch break-off head mounting bolts and tighten until the bolt heads shear.
10. Remove adjusting pin or drill.
11. Connect ignition switch electrical connector.
12. Connect battery ground cable and check for proper operation.
13. Install column shroud.

1977–78

1. Disconnect battery cable.
2. Remove steering column shroud and lower steering column from brake support bracket.
3. Disconnect switch wiring and remove two switch retaining nuts. Disconnect switch from actuator and remove switch, Fig. 3.
4. Move shift lever to Park position. Place ignition key in Lock position and remove the key.

NOTE: New replacement switches are pinned in the Lock position by a plastic shipping pin inserted in a locking hole in the switch. For an existing switch, pull plunger out as far as it will go then back one detent to Lock position and insert a 3/32 drill in locking hole to retain switch in Lock position.

Fig. 1 Ignition Lock. 1977–83

Fig. 2 Ignition switch. 1979–83

ACTUATING ROD

LOCKING TABS

Fig. 3   Ignition switch. 1977-78 All

KNOB RELEASE
BUTTON

Fig. 4   Light switch. Ford and
Mercury. Typical

HEADLIGHT KNOB
AND SHAFT ASSEMBLY

INSERT HOOKED
TOOL INTO KNOB SLOT
TO DEPRESS SPRING;
THEN PULL OFF SHAFT.

Fig. 5   Light switch knob removal

5. With locking pin in place, install switch on steering column, determine mid position of actuator lash and tighten retaining bolts.
6. Remove locking pin.

LIGHT SWITCH, REPLACE

1979-83

1. Disconnect battery ground cable.
2. From instrument panel, depress light switch knob and shaft retainer button on side of switch and, while holding button in, pull knob and shaft assembly from switch, Fig. 4.
3. Unscrew trim bezel and remove lock nut.
4. From under instrument panel, pull switch from panel while tilting downward, disconnect electrical connector and remove switch.
5. Reverse procedure to install.

1977-78

1. Disconnect battery ground cable.
2. Remove wiper switch knob.
3. On 1977-78 models, remove shaft knob by inserting hooked wire, Fig. 5, into knob slot and depressing spring.
4. With headlight switch "On" on all models, depress release button on switch housing and remove knob and shaft, Fig. 4.
5. On all models remove bezel nut from light switch, then remove lower finish panel.
6. Remove three mounting plate screws.
7. Disconnect electrical connector. If equipped with concealed headlamps, disconnect vacuum hoses from switch and remove switch.
8. Reverse procedure to install.

STOP LIGHT SWITCH, REPLACE

1977-83

1. Referring to Fig. 6, disconnect wires at connector.
2. Remove hairpin retainer and slide switch, push rod and nylon washers and bushing away from pedal, and remove switch.
3. Position the new switch, push rod, bushing and washers on brake pedal pin and secure with hairpin retainer.
4. Connect wires at connector and install wires in retaining clip.

TO FRONT
OF VEHICLE

SWITCH
ASSEMBLY-13480

PART OF WIRING
ASSEMBLY

BRAKE PEDAL

CONNECTOR
LOCKING MECHANISM

NYLON WASHER-2B129

STOP LIGHT SWITCH
ASSEMBLY-13480

BRAKE PEDAL

HAIRPIN
RETAINER

PUSH ROD THRU
DASH PANEL TO
MASTER CYLINDER

NYLON
WASHER-2B129

PART OF WIRING ASSEMBLY

CONNECTOR
LOCKING
MECHANISM ON
SWITCH WITH
SIDE TERMINALS

DIMPLE

FLANGE

NOTE: BUSHING FLANGE
TO BE ASSEMBLED ON
OPPOSITE SIDE OF PUSH
ROD FROM DIMPLE
IN SWITCH FRAME

Fig. 6   Mechanical stop light switch.
1977-83 Ford & Mercury

Fig. 7 Instrument cluster. 1977-78 Ford & Mercury

TURN SIGNAL SWITCH, REPLACE

1979-83

1. Disconnect battery ground cable.
2. On models with tilt column, unsnap extension shroud, located below steering wheel, from retaining clip. On all models, remove five attaching screws, then remove steering column trim shroud.
3. Remove turn signal switch lever by grasping lever and using a pulling twisting motion of the hand, while pulling lever straight out of switch.
4. Peel foam sight shield from switch, then disconnect two turn signal switch wire connectors.
5. Remove two screws attaching turn signal switch to lock cylinder housing, then disengage switch from housing.
6. Reverse procedure to install.

1977-78

1. Remove retaining screw from underside of steering wheel spoke and lift off the pad horn switch/trim cover and medallion as an assembly.
2. Disconnect horn switch wires from terminals.
3. Remove steering wheel retaining nut and remove steering wheel with a suitable puller.

4. Remove turn signal switch lever by unscrewing it from column.
5. Remove shroud from steering column.
6. Disconnect column wiring connector plug and remove screws that secure switch to column.
7. On tilt column models, remove wires and terminals from column wiring plug.

NOTE: *Record the color code and position of each wire before removing it from plug. A hole provided in the flange casting on fixed column models makes it unnecessary to separate wires from plug. The plug with wires installed can be guided through the hole.*

8. Remove plastic cover sleeve from wiring harness and remove the switch from top of column. On vehicles equipped with speed control, transfer the ground brush located in the turn signal cancelling cam to the new switch assembly.
9. Reverse procedure to install.

NEUTRAL SAFETY SWITCH

1977-83

Column Shift

The neutral safety switch has been eliminated and is replaced by a series of steps

designed into the steering column selector lever hub casting.

HORN SOUNDER, REPLACE

1979-83

Refer to "TURN SIGNAL SWITCH, RE-PLACE" for horn switch replacement.

1977-78
Rim-Blow Type

The rubber insert and copper strip assembly is not replaceable on vehicles with speed control. If a new insert assembly is required the entire steering wheel must be replaced.

1. Remove the pad from the steering wheel (three screws).
2. Remove medallion from the pad.
3. After removing the steering wheel nut the wheel can be removed from the shaft with a wheel puller.
4. Reverse procedure to install.

Except Rim-Blow Type

1. Disconnect battery ground cable.
2. Remove steering column pad (2 screws).
3. Push down and turn horn ring and remove ring and spring.
4. Reverse procedure to install.

Fig. 8 Plenum assembly removal (Typical). 1979–83

Fig. 9 Heater core removal (Typical). 1979–83

INSTRUMENT CLUSTER, REPLACE

1979–83

1. Disconnect battery ground cable.
2. Disconnect speedometer cable.
3. Remove instrument cluster trim cover attaching screws and the trim cover.
4. Remove the two lower steering column cover attaching screws and the cover.
5. Remove steering column shroud lower half.
6. Remove screws securing transmission indicator column bracket to steering column. Detach cable loop from pin on shift lever and remove bracket from column.
7. Remove four instrument cluster attaching screws.
8. Disconnect cluster feed plug and remove cluster assembly from vehicle.
9. Reverse procedure to install.

1977–78

1. Disconnect the battery ground cable.
2. Remove two steering column cover screws and remove the cover.
3. Remove two instrument cluster trim cover attaching screws and remove cover, Fig. 7.
4. Reach behind the cluster and disconnect the cluster feed plug from its receptacle.
5. Disconnect the speedometer cable.
6. Remove steering column cover shroud, then remove the screw attaching the transmission indicator cable to the steering column.
7. Remove the four cluster attaching screws and remove the cluster assembly.
8. Reverse procedure to install.

W/S WIPER MOTOR, REPLACE

1979–83

1. Disconnect battery ground cable.

2. On 1979 and 1982–83 models, disconnect right side washer nozzle hose and remove right side wiper arm and blade assembly from pivot shaft.
3. Remove wiper motor and linkage cover.
4. Disconnect linkage drive arm from the motor output arm crankpin by removing retaining clip.
5. Disconnect the wiring connectors from the motor.
6. Remove three bolts retaining the motor to the dash panel extension and the motor.
7. Reverse procedure to install.

1977–78

1. Disconnect battery ground cable.
2. Remove wiper arm and blade assemblies from pivot shafts.
3. Remove left cowl screen (four screws) for access.
4. Disconnect linkage drive arm from the motor output crankpin by removing retaining clip.
5. From engine side of dash, remove two wire connectors from motor.
6. Remove three bolts that retain motor to dash and remove motor. If output arm catches on dash during removal, hand-turn the arm clockwise so it will clear opening in the dash. Before installing motor, be sure output arm is in park position.
7. Reverse procedure to install.

W/S WIPER SWITCH, REPLACE

1979–83

1. Disconnect battery ground cable.
2. Remove the steering column cover screws and separate the two halves.

3. Remove wiper switch retaining screws, disconnect wiring connector and remove switch.
4. Reverse procedure to install.

1977–78

1. Disconnect battery ground cable.
2. Remove wiper and headlight switch knobs.
3. Remove headlight switch bezel, trim panel retaining screw and trim panel.
4. Remove wiper switch retaining screws, pull switch rearward, disconnect connector and remove switch.
5. Reverse procedure to install.

W/S WIPER TRANSMISSION, REPLACE

1979–83

1. Disconnect battery ground cable.
2. Remove wiper arm and blade assemblies from the pivot shafts. Remove rear hood seal.
3. Remove wiper motor and linkage cover for access to linkage.
4. Disconnect the linkage drive arm from the motor crank pin by removing the retaining clip.
5. Remove the six bolts retaining the left and right pivot shafts to the cowl, and remove the complete linkage assembly.
6. Reverse procedure to install.

1977–78

1. Disconnect battery and remove wiper arm and blade assemblies from pivot shafts.
2. Remove cowl screens for access to linkage.
3. Disconnect the left linkage arm from the drive arm by removing the clip.

SEE VIEW A

1/2"

1-5/8"

DRILL DIMPLE

DRILL 1" DIA HOLE TANGENT TO CENTERLINE OF THE BEAD, AT DRILL DIMPLE WHICH IS LOCATED 1/2" FROM CENTERLINE OF BEAD

ACCESS HOLE BEAD ON RIGHT FENDER APRON

DRILL DIMPLE

CUT ALONG DOTTED LINE ON CENTERLINE OF BEAD AND REMOVE

VIEW B

VIEW A

FENDER APRON

357903-S8 SCREW (8 REQ'D)

COVER PLATE

SECTION A-A

APPLY ROPE SEALER ALONG INSIDE EDGE OF COVER

A

A

APPLY ROPE SEALER ALONG INSIDE EDGE OF COVER

357903-S8 SCREW (8 REQ'D)

DRILL EIGHT (8) 1/8" HOLES IN APRON USING COVER AS TEMPLATE

COVER PLATE

VIEW D

VIEW C

Fig. 10 Blower motor access. 1977–78 Ford & Mercury

4. Remove the three bolts retaining the left pivot shaft assembly to the cowl.
5. Remove the left arm and pivot shaft assembly through the cowl opening.
6. Disconnect linkage drive arm from motor crankpin by removing the clip.
7. Remove three bolts that connect drive arm pivot shaft assembly to the cowl and remove the pivot shaft drive arm and right arm as an assembly.
8. Reverse procedure to install.

RADIO, REPLACE

NOTE: When installing radio, be sure to adjust antenna trimmer for peak performance.

1979-83

NOTE: For an all-electronic radio, perform stem 6 first.

1. Disconnect battery ground cable.
2. Remove radio knobs and screws attaching the bezel to instrument panel.
3. Remove the radio mounting plate attaching screws.
4. Pull radio to disengage it from the lower rear support bracket.
5. Disconnect radio wiring and remove radio.
6. Remove the radio to mounting plate retaining nuts and washers and remove the mounting plate.
7. Remove the rear upper support retaining nut and remove the support.
8. Reverse procedure to install. Perform step 6 first if equipped with all-electronic radio.

1977-78

1. Disconnect battery ground cable.
2. Remove radio knobs and instrument panel bezel.
3. Remove mounting plate retaining screws and pull radio disengaging it from rear bracket.
4. Disconnect antenna and electrical wires and remove radio.
5. Reverse procedure to install.

HEATER CORE, REPLACE

1979-83

1. Disconnect battery ground cable, then drain cooling system.
2. Disconnect heater hoses from heater core. Plug heater hoses and core fittings to prevent coolant spillage.
3. Remove bolt located below w/s wiper motor, attaching left end of plenum to dash panel.
4. Remove nut attaching upper left hand corner of evaporator or heater case to dash panel.
5. Disconnect vacuum control system supply hose from vacuum source, then push grommet and hose into pasenger compartment.
6. Remove glove box, then loosen right hand door sill plate and remove side cowl trim panel.
7. Remove bolt attaching right hand side of instrument panel to side cowl.

8. Remove instrument panel pad as follows:
   a. Remove two screws from each defroster nozzle opening in pad.
   b. From front lower edge of panel pad, remove five attaching screws.
   c. From each end of pad, remove one attaching screw.
   d. On Ford models, remove screw from lower end of pad through glove box door opening.
   e. Lift pad assembly from instrument panel.
9. On models less ATC, disconnect temperature control cable from plenum bracket and blend air door crank.
10. On models equipped with ATC, disconnect temperature control cable and vacuum harness connector from ATC sensor. Disconnect ATC sensor tube from sensor and evaporator case connector, then disconnect wire connector from EV relay.
11. Remove push clip attaching center duct bracket to plenum, then rotate bracket upward and to the right.
12. Disconnect vacuum harness at vacuum connector near floor air distribution duct.
13. Disconnect the white vacuum hose from the outside recirculating air door vacuum motor.
14. Remove two screws from rear side of floor air distribution duct to plenum, Fig. 8. To remove the right hand screw, it may be necessary to remove the two screws attaching the lower panel door vacuum motor to the mounting bracket.
15. Remove push fastener attaching floor air distribution duct to left end of plenum, then remove floor air distribution duct.
16. Remove two nuts located along lower flange of plenum.
17. Carefully move plenum rearward, so that heater core tubes and plenum case upper stud clear openings in dash panel, then remove plenum from vehicle by rotating upper portion of the plenum forward, down and out from under instrument panel. It may be necessary to carefully pull the lower edge of the instrument panel rearward while the plenum is being removed from behind the instrument panel.
18. Remove retaining screws from heater core cover, then the cover from the plenum assembly, Fig. 9.
19. Remove retaining screw from heater core inlet and outlet tube bracket.
20. Pull heater core and seal assembly from plenum assembly.
21. Reverse procedure to install.

1977-78 with Air Cond.

1. Drain cooling system.
2. Disconnect heater hoses from core tubes.
3. Remove heater core cover plate and gasket.
4. Pull heater core and mounting gasket up out of case.
5. Remove core mounting gasket. Remove heater core.
6. Reverse procedure to install.

1977-78 less Air Cond.

1. Drain cooling system and disconnect heater hoses from the core.
2. Remove the core cover and gasket and remove the heater core.
3. Reverse procedure to install.

BLOWER MOTOR, REPLACE

1979-83

1. Disconnect battery ground cable.
2. Disconnect blower motor ground wire and the engine ground wire and position wiring aside.
3. Disconnect blower motor lead connector from wiring harness hard shell connector.
4. Remove blower motor cooling tube from blower motor.
5. Remove blower motor retaining screws.
6. Rotate blower motor slightly to the right so the bottom edge of the mounting plate follows the contour of the wheelwell splash panel. Then, lift blower motor up and out of housing assembly.
7. Reverse procedure to install.

1977-78

NOTE: The blower motor is located in the right side of the case to the right of the hood hinge under the right front fender. It is necessary to cut an opening in the right front fender apron to gain access to the blower motor assembly.

1. Disconnect the blower motor lead wire (orange) at the rear of the right hood hinge.
2. Remove the ground wire (black) from the upper cowl.
3. Remove the right front tire and wheel assembly.
4. Locate and cut opening in fender apron, Fig. 10. Care must be taken to avoid damage to the heater case by drill push-through or over-travel.
5. Remove the four blower motor mounting screws and disconnect the cooler tube from the motor.
6. Carefully move the motor and wheel assembly forward out of the heater case through the access hole.
7. A replacement cover plate is available from Ford, part no. #18A475.
8. Reverse procedure to install.

SPEED CONTROLS
1979-83

Actuator Cable Adjustment
1. Deactivate the throttle positioner.
2. Set carburetor at hot idle.
3. Pull the actuator cable to remove slack.
4. While maintaining light tension on the actuator cable, insert the cable retaining clip.

Vacuum Dump Valve
The vacuum dump valve is mounted on a moveable mounting bracket. The valve should be adjusted so that it is closed when the brake pedal is not depressed and opens when the brake pedal is depressed.

1977-78

Adjust bead chain to obtain .06-.25" actuator arm free travel when engine is at hot idle. The adjustment should be made to take as much slack as possible out of the chain without restricting the carburetor lever from returning to idle.

On vehicles with a solenoid anti-diesel valve, perform adjustment with ignition switch in the "On" position.

Engine Section

Fig. 1 Engine mount (typical). 1977-78 V8-302, 351W

ENGINE MOUNTS, REPLACE

CAUTION: Whenever self-locking mounting bolts and nuts are removed, they must be replaced with new self-locking bolts and nuts.

1977-83 V8-255, 302, 351W

1. Remove the nut and through bolt attaching the insulator to the support bracket, Figs. 1 and 2.
2. Raise the engine slightly with a jack and a wood block placed under the oil pan.
3. Remove the engine insulator assembly to cylinder block attaching bolts. Remove the engine insulator assembly and the heat shield, if so equipped.
4. Reverse procedure to install.

1977-78 V8-351M, 400

1. Remove the fan shroud attaching bolts. Remove the transmission oil cooler lines

Fig. 3 Engine mount. 1977-78 V8-351 M, 400

Fig. 2 Engine mounts. 1979-83 V8-255, 302 & 351W

from the retaining bracket on the block.
2. Remove the through bolt and lock nut attaching the insulator support bracket, Fig. 3. Remove the bolt and nut on the opposite mount to prevent distortion of the insulator.
3. Raise the engine slightly with a jack and a wood block placed under the oil pan.
4. Remove the engine insulator assembly to cylinder block attaching bolts and lockwashers.
5. Remove the engine insulator assembly and heat shield, if equipped.
6. Reverse procedure to install.

1977-78 V8-460

1. Block rear wheels and set parking brake. Raise front of vehicle with floor jack and install safety stands.
2. Position jack under the front area of the oil pan. Place a wood block between the jack and oil pan. Raise the jack just enough to support the engine.
3. Remove the nut through bolt that attaches the front support insulator to the lower support bracket, Fig. 4.
4. Remove the bolts attaching the support insulator and heat shield to the cylinder block. Replace the insulator on one side before proceding to the other insulator.
5. Reverse procedure to install.

ENGINE, REPLACE

NOTE: Because of engine compartment tolerances, the engine should not be removed and installed with the transmission attached.

1979-83

1. Disconnect battery and alternator ground cables.
2. Drain cooling system and oil pan.
3. Remove hood.
4. Remove air cleaner and intake duct assembly.
5. Disconnect radiator hoses from engine.
6. Disconnect transmission oil cooler lines from radiator.

7. Remove fan shroud attaching bolts, then the radiator, fan, spacer, pulley and shroud.
8. Remove alternator mounting bolts and position alternator aside.
9. Disconnect oil pressure sending unit electrical connector.
10. Disconnect fuel tank line at fuel pump and plug line.
11. Disconnect accelerator cable from carburetor.
12. Disconnect throttle valve vacuum line from intake manifold.
13. Disconnect manual shift rod and retracting spring at shift rod stud.
14. Disconnect transmission filler tube bracket from engine block.
15. Isolate and remove A/C compressor from vehicle, if equipped.
16. Disconnect power steering pump bracket from cylinder head and water pump and position aside, if equipped.
17. Disconnect power brake vacuum line

Fig. 4 Engine mount (typical). 1977-78 V8-460

Fig. 5 Cylinder head tightening sequence. V8 engines

from intake manifold, if equipped.
18. Disconnect heater hoses from engine.
19. Disconnect coolant temperature sending unit electrical connector.
20. Remove upper converter housing to engine attaching bolts.
21. Disconnect ignition coil and distributor wiring. Remove harness from left hand rocker arm cover and position aside. Disconnect ground strap from engine block.
22. Raise and support front of vehicle.
23. Disconnect starter motor wiring and remove starter motor.
24. Disconnect exhaust pipes from manifold.
25. Disconnect engine mounts from frame brackets.
26. Disconnect secondary air line to catalytic converter, if equipped.
27. Disconnect transmission oil cooler lines from retainer.
28. Remove converter housing inspection cover.
29. Disconnect converter from flywheel. Secure converter in housing.
30. Remove remaining converter housing to engine bolts.
31. Lower vehicle and support transmission. Attach suitable engine lifting equipment to engine.
32. Raise engine slight and pull forward to disengage from transmission.
33. Remove engine from vehicle.
34. Reverse procedure to install.

1977–78

1. Disconnect battery ground cable, drain cooling system and crankcase and remove hood and air cleaner assembly.
2. Disconnect or remove all Thermactor components that may interfere with engine removal.
3. Disconnect hoses and oil cooler lines from radiator, then remove radiator, fan shroud and fan.
4. Remove all drive belts.
5. Disconnect power steering pump and alternator and position units out of the way.
6. If equipped with air conditioning, isolate and remove compressor.
7. Disconnect all hoses, lines and wiring from engine. Make certain to remove ground wires from block and right cylinder head.
8. Disconnect fuel line from pump and plug line.
9. Disconnect accelerator cable or linkage, then disconnect downshift linkage (if used).
10. Raise and properly support vehicle, then disconnect exhaust system from engine and remove starter. On six cylinder engines, remove transmission oil filler tube bracket.
11. Remove engine front support through bolts.
12. If equipped with automatic transmission, remove converter cover, converter to flywheel bolts, and downshift rod.
13. If equipped with manual transmission,

Fig. 6 Intake manifold tightening sequence. V8-225, 302, 351W

remove clutch linkage from engine block.
14. Remove the four lower engine to clutch housing or converter housing bolts, then lower vehicle and remove the two upper engine to clutch housing or converter housing bolts.
15. Position jack under transmission, then using a suitable hoist, carefully remove engine from vehicle.
16. Reverse procedure to install.

CYLINDER HEAD, REPLACE

Tighten cylinder head bolts a little at a time in three steps in the sequence shown in Fig. 5. Final tightening should be to the torque specifications listed in the *Engine Tightening* table. After bolts have been tightened to specifications, *they should not be disturbed.*

1979–83 V8-255, 302 & 351W

1. Disconnect battery ground cable.
2. Remove intake manifold and carburetor as an assembly.
3. Remove rocker arm cover.
4. If left cylinder head is being removed, isolate and remove A/C compressor, if equipped.
5. Remove EGR cooler, if equipped with V8-351W and EEC system.
6. If left cylinder head is being removed, disconnect power steering pump bracket from cylinder head and engine block and position assembly aside. Remove Thermactor crossover tube from rear of cylinder heads.
7. Remove ignition coil, alternator mounting bracket bolt and spacer.
8. Loosen rocker arm stud nuts or bolts so that rocker arms can be rotated to the side.

Fig. 7 Applying RTV sealer for intake manifold installation. V8-255

9. Remove push rods, keeping them in sequence so they may be returned to their original locations. Remove exhaust valve stem caps.
10. Disconnect exhaust pipes from exhaust manifold.
11. Unfasten and remove cylinder head.
12. Reverse removal procedure to install the head. Tighten cylinder head down in the sequence shown in Fig. 5. When installing intake manifold refer to Fig. 6 for bolt tightening sequence.

NOTE: On V8-255 engines, when installing intake manifold, a 1/8 in. bead of RTV sealer should be applied at mating surfaces of intake manifold, cylinder head and cylinder block, Fig. 7. After intake manifold seals and gaskets have been positioned, apply a 1/16 in. bead of RTV sealer to the outer end of each intake manifold seal for the entire width of the seal, Fig. 7.

1977–78 V8-302, 351, 400

1. Remove intake manifold and carburetor as an assembly. Remove EGR cooler if equipped.
2. Disconnect battery ground cable at cylinder head.
3. Remove rocker arm cover.
4. On air conditioned cars, remove compressor.
5. On car with power steering, disconnect pump bracket from left cylinder head and remove drive belt. Wire power steering pump out of the way and in position that will prevent oil from draining out.

NOTE: If left cylinder head is being removed on an engine equipped with Thermactor Exhaust Emission Control System, disconnect hose from air manifold on left head. If a right head is to be removed, remove air pump and bracket and disconnect hose on right head.

6. Remove generator or alternator.
7. Disconnect exhaust manifold at exhaust pipes.
8. Loosen rocker arm stud nuts or bolts so that rocker arms can be rotated to the side.
9. Remove push rods, keeping them in sequence so they may be returned to their original locations.
10. Unfasten and remove cylinder head.
11. Reverse removal procedure to install the

FORD & MERCURY—Full Size Models

Fig. 8 Intake manifold tightening sequence. V8-351M, 400

head. Tighten cylinder head down in the sequence shown in Fig. 5. When installing intake manifold refer to Figs. 6, 7 and 8 for bolt tightening sequence.

1977–78 V8-460

1. Remove intake manifold and carburetor as an assembly.
2. Disconnect muffler inlet pipe at exhaust manifold.
3. Loosen air conditioner compressor belt if so equipped.
4. Loosen alternator retaining bolts and remove bolt retaining alternator bracket to right head.
5. If air conditioned, isolate compressor at service valves and hoses from compressor. Remove nuts retaining compressor bracket to water pump. Remove bolts retaining compressor to upper mounting bracket and lay compressor out of way. Remove compressor upper bracket from head.
6. If not air conditioned, remove bolts retaining power steering reservoir bracket to left head and position reservoir out of way.
7. Remove rocker arm covers and rocker arms. Remove push rods in sequence so they can be installed in their positions.
8. Remove head retaining bolts and lift head with exhaust manifold.

NOTE: If necessary to break gasket seal, pry at forward corners of cylinder heads against casting bosses provided on cylinder block. Avoid damaging machine surfaces on head and gasket.

9. Install cylinder heads in reverse order of removal and torque bolts in sequence shown in Fig. 5. When installing intake manifold refer to Fig. 9 for bolt tightening sequence.

Fig. 11 Inspection of rocker arm stud nut. 1977 & early 1978 V8-302, 351W

Fig. 9 Intake manifold tightening sequence. V8-460

VALVE ARRANGEMENT
Front to Rear

Right . . . . I-E-I-E-I-E-I-E
Left . . . . E-I-E-I-E-I-E-I

VALVE LIFT SPECS.

Engine	Year	Intake	Exhaust
V8-255	1982	.375	.375
V8-302	1977–79	.382	.398
	1980–83	.375	.391
V8-351	1977–78②	.406	.406
	1978–79①	.419	.419
	1980–81①	.411	.411
V8-351 H.O.	1980–81①③	.442	.450
V8-400	1977	.427	.433
	1978	.428	.432
V8-460	1977–78	.437	.481

①—Windsor engine.
②—Modified engine.
③—High output engine.

VALVE TIMING
Intake Opens Before TDC

Engine	Year	Degrees
V8-255	1981–82	16
V8-302	1977–83	16
V8-351	1977–78②	19½
	1978–80①	23
V8-400	1977–78	17
V8-460	1977–78	8

①—Windsor engine.
②—Modified engine.

Fig. 12 Rocker arm. Late 1978 & 1979–83 V8-255, 302 & 351W

Fig. 10 Valve rocker arm parts. 1977 & early 1978 V8-302, 351W

VALVES, ADJUST

To eliminate the need of adjusting valve lash, a positive stop rocker arm stud and nut is used on 1977 and early 1978 V8-302 and 351W engines, Fig. 10, and a positive stop fulcrum bolt and seat is used on V8-351M, 400 and 460 and late 1978 and 1979–83 V8-255, 302 and 351W engines, Figs. 12 and 16.

It is very important that the correct push rod be used and all components be installed and torqued as follows:

1. Position the piston of the cylinder being worked on at TDC of its compression stroke.
2. On 1977 and early 1978 V8-302 and 351W engines, lubricate and install rocker arm and fulcrum seat on the stud. Thread nut onto the stud until it contracts the shoulder and torque to 17–23 ft. lbs.

NOTE: Each rocker arm stud nut should be inspected when adjusting valve clearance, Fig. 11.

3. On V8-351M, 400, 460 and late 1978 and 1979–83 V8-255, 302 and 351W engines, install rocker arm, fulcrum seat and oil deflector. Install fulcrum bolt and torque to 18–25 ft. lbs.
A .060″ shorter push rod or a .060″ longer

Fig. 13 Checking valve clearance on models with hydraulic lifters

Fig. 14 Rocker arm stud removal. 1977 & early 1978 V8-302, 351W

Fig. 15 Positive stop type rocker arm stud installation. 1977 & early 1978 V8-302, 351W

Fig. 16 Rocker arm and related parts. V8-351M, 400, 460

rod are available for service to provide a means of compensating for dimensional changes in the valve mechanism. Valve stem-to-rocker arm clearance should be as listed in the *Valve Specifications* table, with the hydraulic lifter completely collapsed, Fig. 13. Repeated valve grind jobs will decrease this clearance to the point that if not compensated for the lifters will cease to function.

When checking valve clearance, if the clearance is less than the minimum, the .060″ shorter push rod should be used. If clearance is more than the maximum, the .060″ longer push rod should be used. (See *Valve Specifications* table.) To check valve clearance, proceed as follows:

V8-255, 302, 351W, 351M, 400 & 460
1. Mark crankshaft pulley at three locations, with number 1 location at TDC timing mark (end of compression stroke), number 2 location one half turn (180°) clockwise from TDC and number 3 location three quarter turn clockwise (270°) from number 2 location.
2. Turn the crankshaft to the number 1 location and check the clearance on the following valves:
   V8-255, 302 & 460
No. 1 Intake	No. 1 Exhaust
No. 7 Intake	No. 5 Exhaust
No. 8 Intake	No. 4 Exhaust
V8-351W, 351M & 400
No. 1 Intake	No. 1 Exhaust
No. 4 Intake	No. 3 Exhaust
No. 8 Intake	No. 7 Exhaust
3. Turn the crankshaft to the number 2 location and check the clearance on the following valves:
V8-255, 302 & 460
No. 5 Intake	No. 2 Exhaust
No. 4 Intake	No. 6 Exhaust
V8-351W, 351M & 400
No. 3 Intake	No. 2 Exhaust
No. 7 Intake	No. 6 Exhaust
4. Turn the crankshaft to the number 3 location and check the clearance on the following valves:
V8-255, 302 & 460
No. 2 Intake	No. 7 Exhaust
No. 3 Intake	No. 3 Exhaust
No. 6 Intake	No. 8 Exhaust
V8-351W, 351M & 400
No. 2 Intake	No. 4 Exhaust
No. 5 Intake	No. 5 Exhaust
No. 6 Intake	No. 8 Exhaust

VALVE GUIDES

Valve guides in these engines are an integral part of the head and, therefore, cannot be removed. For service, guides can be reamed oversize to accommodate one of three service valves with oversize stems (.003″, .015″ and .030″).

Check the valve stem clearance of each valve (after cleaning) in its respective valve guide. If the clearance exceeds the service limits of .0055″, ream the valve guides to accommodate the next oversize diameter valve.

ROCKER ARM & STUD SERVICE

1977 & Early 1978 V8-302 & 351W

If necessary to replace a rocker arm stud, a kit is available which contains a stud remover, Fig. 14, a stud installer, Fig. 15, and two reamers, one .006″ and the other .015″. For .010″ oversize studs, use reamer No. T66P-6A527-B.

Rocker arm studs that are broken or have damaged threads may be replaced with standard studs. Loose studs in the head may be replaced with .006″, .010″ or .015″ oversize studs which are available for service.

When going from a standard size stud to a .010 or .015″ oversize stud, always use a .006″ reamer before finish reaming with a .010 or .015″ reamer.

If a stud is broken off flush with the stud boss, use an easy-out to remove the broken stud, following the instructions of the tool manufacturer.

ROCKER ARMS

Late 1978 & 1979–83 V8-255, 302, 351W

These engines use a bolt and fulcrum at-

Fig. 17 Hydraulic valve lifter disassembled (typical)

Fig. 18 Timing marks aligned for correct valve timing. V8s

Fig. 19 Camshaft and related parts. All-V8

tachment, Fig. 12. To remove, remove attaching bolt, then the fulcrum, rocker arm and fulcrum guide, if the other rocker arm is being removed.

1977 & Early 1978 V8-302, 351W

A positive stop rocker arm stud and nut eliminates the need for adjusting valve lash, Fig. 10.

Installation

1. Position the piston of the cylinder to be worked on at TDC compression stroke.
2. Locate stud properly with tool T69P-6049D. Make sure tool bottoms on the head.
3. Lubricate rocker arm components and place rocker arm and fulcrum on the stud.
4. Thread nut onto the stud until it contacts the shoulder then tighten nut to 18–22 ft-lbs.

V8-351M, 400, 460

The rocker arm is supported by a fulcrum bolt which fits through the fulcrum seat and threads into the cylinder head. To disassemble, remove the bolt, oil deflector, fulcrum seat and rocker arm, Fig. 16.

VALVE LIFTERS, REPLACE

NOTE: The internal parts of each hydraulic valve lifter assembly are a matched set. If these are mixed, improper valve operation may result. Therefore, disassemble, inspect and test each assembly separately to prevent mixing the parts.

Fig. 17 illustrates the type of hydraulic lifter used. See the *Trouble Shooting Chapter* under the heading *Engine Noises* for causes of hydraulic valve lifter noise.

1. Remove intake manifold and related parts.
2. Remove rocker arm covers.
3. Loosen rocker arm stud nuts or bolts and rotate rocker arms to the side.
4. Lift out push rods, keeping them in sequence in a rack so they may be installed in their original location.
5. Using a magnet rod, remove valve lifters and place them in sequence in a rack so they may be stalled in their original location.
6. Reverse procedure to install.

TIMING CASE COVER, REPLACE

NOTE: To replace the seal in the timing gear cover, it is necessary to remove the cover as outlined below.

V8-255, 302, 351, 400

1. Drain cooling system and oil pan.
2. Disconnect lower radiator hose from water pump.
3. Disconnect heater hose from water pump and slide water pump bypass hose clamp toward pump.
4. Unfasten and position alternator and bracket out of way.
5. If equipped with power steering or air conditioning, remove the drive belts.
6. Remove the fan, spacer, pulley and drive belt.
7. Remove crankshaft pulley and vibration damper.

NOTE: If equipped with EEC II system, disconnect crankshaft position sensor electrical connector.

8. Disconnect fuel pump outlet line from pump and remove pump retaining bolts and lay pump to one side with flex line attached.
9. Remove oil dipstick and the oil pan to front cover attaching bolts.
10. Unfasten and remove the front cover and water pump as an assembly.
11. Reverse procedure to install.

V8-460

1. Drain cooling system and crankcase.
2. Remove bolts attaching fan to water pump and remove screws attaching radiator shroud to radiator.
3. Remove fan assembly and radiator shroud.
4. Disconnect radiator hoses at engine and cooler lines at radiator and remove radiator upper support and radiator assembly.
5. Loosen alternator and air pump, then remove drive belt with water pump pulley.
6. If air conditioned, loosen idler pulley and remove compressor support.

7. Remove vibration damper from crankshaft.
8. Disconnect power steering lines at pump and unfasten and remove the pump.
9. Loosen bypass hose at pump and disconnect heater return tube at pump.
10. Disconnect and plug fuel inlet line at pump and disconnect fuel outlet line from pump. Unfasten and remove fuel pump.
11. Unfasten and remove cylinder front cover.
12. Reverse procedure to install.

TIMING CHAIN, REPLACE

V8-255, 302, 351, 400

After removing the cover as outlined above, crank the engine until the timing marks are aligned as shown in Fig. 18. Remove camshaft sprocket retaining bolt, washer and fuel pump eccentric and, on 1981–83 models with electronic fuel injection, remove spacer. Slide both sprockets and chain forward and remove them as an assembly.

Reverse procedure to install the chain and sprockets, being sure the timing marks are aligned.

V8-460

1. To remove the chain, first take off the front cover as outlined previously.
2. Crank engine until timing marks on camshaft sprocket is adjacent to timing mark on crankshaft sprocket, Fig. 18.
3. Remove camshaft sprocket cap screw and fuel pump eccentric.
4. Slide both sprockets and chain forward and remove as an assembly.
5. Reverse procedure to install the chain, being sure to align the timing marks as shown, Fig. 18.

CAMSHAFT, REPLACE

V8-255, 302, 351, 400 & 460

NOTE: It may be necessary to remove or reposition radiator, A/C compressor and grille components to provide adequate clearance.

1. To remove camshaft, remove cylinder front cover and timing chain.
2. Remove distributor cap and spark plug wires, then remove distributor.
3. Disconnect automatic transmission oil cooler lines from radiator and remove radiator.

Fig. 20 Piston and rod assembly. All V8 engines

4. Remove intake manifold and carburetor as an assembly.
5. Remove rocker arm covers.
6. Loosen rocker arm stud nuts or bolts and rotate rocker arms to one side.
7. Remove push rods, keeping them in sequence in a rack so they may be installed in their original location.
8. Using a magnet, remove valve lifters and place them in a rack in sequence so they may be installed in their original location.
9. Remove camshaft thrust plate, Fig. 19 and carefully pull camshaft from engine, using care to avoid damaging camshaft bearings.
10. Reverse procedure to install.

CAMSHAFT BEARINGS

When necessary to replace camshaft bearings, the engine will have to be removed from the vehicle and the plug at the rear of the cylinder block will have to be removed in order to utilize the special camshaft bearing removing and installing tools required to do this job. If properly installed, camshaft bearings require no reaming—nor should this type bearing be reamed or altered in any manner in an attempt to fit bearings.

PISTON & ROD, ASSEMBLE

Assemble the pistons to the rods so the notch or arrow faces toward the front of engine and the numbered side of rod faces away from center of engine, Fig. 20. After installation, check side clearance between connecting rods at each crankshaft journal. Clearance should be .010–.020 in.

PISTONS, PINS & RINGS

Pistons and rings are available in standard sizes and oversizes of .003, .020, .030 and .040 inch.
Oversize piston pins of .001 and .002" are available.

MAIN & ROD BEARINGS

Main and rod bearings are available in standard sizes and the following undersizes: V8-255, 302, 351, 400, 460: .001, .002, .010, .020, .030, .040".

Fig. 21 Split-lip rear crankshaft seal installation on V8-255, 302, 351, 400, 460

CRANKSHAFT OIL SEAL, REPLACE

V8-255, 302, 351, 400, 460

A rubber split-lip rear crankshaft oil seal is available for service. This seal can be installed without removal of the crankshaft and also eliminates the necessity of seal installation tools.
1. Remove oil pan.
2. Remove rear main bearing cap.
3. Loosen remaining bearing caps, allowing crankshaft to drop down about 1/32".
4. Remove old seals from both cylinder block and rear main bearing cap. Use a brass rod to drift upper half of seal from cylinder block groove. Rotate crankshaft while drifting to facilitate removal.
5. Carefully clean seal groove in block with a brush and solvent. Also clean seal groove in bearing cap. Remove the oil seal retaining pin from the bearing cap if so equipped. *The pin is not used with the split-lip seal.*
6. Dip seal halves in clean engine oil.
7. Carefully install upper seal half in its groove with undercut side of seal toward front of engine, Fig. 21, by rotating it on shaft journal of crankshaft until approximately 3/8" protrudes below the parting surface. *Be sure no rubber has been shaved from outside diameter of seal by bottom edge of groove.*
8. Retighten main bearing caps and torque to specifications.
9. Install lower seal in main bearing cap with undercut side of seal toward front of engine, and allow seal to protrude about 3/8" above parting surface to mate with upper seal upon cap installation.
10. Apply suitable sealer to parting faces of cap and block. Install cap and torque to specifications.

Fig. 22 Crankshaft rear oil seals

NOTE: If difficulty is encountered in installing the upper half of the seal in position, lightly lap (sandpaper) the side of the seal opposite the lip side using a medium grit paper. After sanding, the seal must be washed in solvent, then dipped in clean engine oil prior to installation.

SERVICE BULLETIN

A revised crankshaft rear oil seal has been released for service. This new seal may be received when ordering an oil pan gasket kit and is installed in the same manner as described previously, Fig. 22.

OIL PAN, REPLACE

1979–83 V8-255, 302 & 351W

1. Disconnect battery ground cable and remove air cleaner assembly.
2. Disconnect accelerator cable and kickdown rod from carburetor.
3. Remove accelerator mounting bracket bolts and bracket.
4. Remove fan shroud attaching screws and position shroud over fan.
5. Disconnect wiper motor electrical connector and remove wiper motor.
6. Disconnect windshield washer hose.
7. Remove wiper motor mounting cover.
8. Remove oil level dipstick, then the dipstick tube retaining bolt from exhaust manifold.
9. If equipped with EGR cooler, remove Thermactor air dump tube retaining clamp, then the Thermactor crossover tube at rear of engine.
10. On all models, raise and support vehicle.
11. Drain oil pan.
12. On vehicles equipped with EEC, remove filler tube from transmission oil pan and drain transmission, then remove starter motor.
13. Disconnect fuel tank fuel line at fuel pump and plug line.
14. Disconnect exhaust pipes from manifolds.
15. If equipped with EGR cooler, remove

Fig. 23 Oil pump. V8-255, 302, 351W & 460

Fig. 24 Oil pump assembly. V8-351M & 400

Engine oiling system (typical)

crossmember.
24. With a suitable jack, raise engine as far as possible.
25. Place a block of wood between each engine mount and chassis bracket. When engine is secured in this position, remove jack.
26. Remove oil pan attaching bolts and lower the oil pan.
27. Remove oil pick-up tube bolts and lower tube in oil pan.
28. Remove oil pan from vehicle.
29. Reverse procedure to install.

1977–78 V8-302, 351, 400

1. Drain oil pan and remove dip stick.
2. Remove fan shroud bolts and place shroud over fan.
3. On V8-351M, 400 engines, remove starter.
4. On all engines, remove engine front mount to chassis bolts, raise engine and install wood blocks between mounts and chassis, then lower engine onto the wood blocks.
5. On V8-302, 351W engines, disconnect stabilizer bar from lower control arms and position stabilizer bar and control arms to permit oil pan removal. Also, on all models with automatic transmission, position oil cooler lines aside for pan removal.
6. Remove oil pan bolts and oil pan.
7. Reverse procedure to install.

V8-460

1. Drain oil pan, then remove starter.
2. Disconnect sway bar and pull forward on struts.
3. Remove fan shroud bolts, place shroud on fan and remove oil filter.

NOTE: *To allow clearance for removal of oil pan, remove the front engine mount nuts. Then position floor jack under front*

exhaust gas sensor from exhaust manifold, then the Thermactor secondary air tube to converter housing clamps.
16. On all models, remove dipstick tube from oil pan.
17. Loosen rear engine mount attaching nuts.
18. Remove engine mount through bolts.
19. Remove shift crossover bolts at transmission.
20. If equipped with EGR cooler, disconnect exhaust pipes from catalytic converter outlet, then the catalytic converter secondary air tube and inlet pipes to exhaust manifold.
21. On all models, disconnect transmission kickdown rod.
22. Remove torque converter housing cover.
23. Remove brake line retainer from front

leading edge of oil pan (use wood block between pan and jack). Raise engine about 1¼" and insert a 1" block of wood between insulators and frame crossmember. Then remove floor jack.

4. Remove oil pan screws and lower pan to crossmember.
5. Crank engine to obtain necessary clearance between crankshaft counterweight and rear of oil pan. Then remove pan.
6. Reverse procedure to install.

OIL PUMP, REPLACE

1. Remove oil pan as described under Oil Pan, Replace.
2. On V8-255, 302 and 351W engine, remove oil inlet pickup tube and screen assembly.
3. On all engines, remove oil pump attaching bolts and remove oil pump and intermediate drive shaft.
4. Reverse procedure to install. Prime oil pump with engine oil before installing. Position intermediate drive shaft into distributor sprocket. With intermediate drive shaft firmly seated, the stop on the shaft should contact crankcase surface. Remove shaft and adjust as necessary. Position pump with intermediate drive shaft insert to cylinder block, then install and torque attaching bolts to 22 to 32 ft. lbs.

NOTE: Do not force oil pump into position on cylinder block. If pump drive shaft is misaligned with distributor shaft, rotate drive shaft to a new position.

OIL PUMP, SERVICE

Figs. 23 & 24

1. With all parts clean and dry, check the inside of the pump housing and the outer race and rotor for damage or excessive wear.
2. Check the mating surface of the pump cover for wear. If this surface is worn, scored or grooved, replace the cover.

3. Measure the clearance between the outer race and housing. This clearance should be .001–.013 inch.
4. With the rotor assembly installed in the housing, place a straight edge over the rotor assembly and housing. Measure the clearance between the straight edge and the rotor and outer race. Maximum recommended limits is .004". *The outer race, shaft and rotor are furnished only as an assembly.*
5. Check the drive shaft-to-housing bearing clearance by measuring the O.D. of the shaft and the I.D. of the housing bearing. The recommended clearance limits are .0015–.0030".
6. Inspect the relief valve spring for a collapsed or worn condition.
7. Check the relief valve piston for scores and free operation in the bore. The specified piston clearance is .0015–.0030".

BELT TENSION DATA

		New Lbs.	Used Lbs.
1977–80 Exc. 1/4"		140	110
1/4" inch		65	50
1980	Ribbed belt		
	w/o tensioner	155	150
	Ribbed belt		
	with tensioner	130	130

		New Lbs.	Used Lbs.
1981	1/4" V Belt	65	50
	All other V Belts	140	105
	V Ribbed Belts		
	4K①	110	100
	5K②	125	120
	5K③	108	108
	6K④	165	150
	6K⑤	113	113
1982–83	1/4" V Belt	65	50
	All other V Belts	140	105
	V Ribbed Belt		
	4K Exc. Air Pump①	130	120
	4K Air Pump①	110	105
	5K②	150	135
	6K⑤	113	110
	6K⑥	160	145

①—4 grooves.
②—5 grooves fixed.
③—5 grooves with absorber.
④—6 grooves with absorber.
⑤—6 grooves with tensioner.
⑥—6 grooves fixed.

WATER PUMP, REPLACE

All V8's

1. Drain cooling system, then remove carburetor air inlet tube.
2. On models equipped with a fan shroud, remove shroud attaching bolts and place shroud over fan and spacer. Remove fan and spacer from water pump shaft, then remove fan shroud.
3. Remove alternator drive belt, A/C drive belt and idler pulley bracket, if so equipped. Remove power steering drive belt and power steering pump, if so equipped. Remove all brackets from water pump, then remove water pump.
4. Disconnect radiator lower hose and heater hose at water pump.
5. Remove drive belt, fan, spacer or fan drive clutch and pulley.
6. Reverse procedure to install.

FUEL PUMP, REPLACE

1. Disconnect fuel lines from fuel pump.
2. Remove pump retaining bolts and remove pump.
3. Remove all gasket material from the pump and block gasket surfaces. Apply sealer to both sides of new gasket.
4. Position gasket on pump flange and hold pump in position against its mounting surface. Make sure rocker arm is riding on camshaft eccentric.
5. Press pump tight against its mounting. Install retaining screws and tighten them alternately.
6. Connect fuel lines. Then operate engine and check for leaks.

Rear Axle, Propeller Shaft & Brakes

REAR AXLES

Figs. 1 and 2 illustrate the rear axle assemblies used on these cars. When necessary to overhaul either of these units, refer to the *Rear Axle Specifications* table in this chapter.

Integral Carrier Type

The gear set consists of a ring gear and an overhung drive pinion which is supported by two opposed tapered roller bearings, Fig. 1. The differential case is a one-piece design with openings allowing assembly of the internal parts and lubricant flow. The differential pinion shaft is retained with a threaded bolt (lock) assembled to the case.

The roller type wheel bearings have no inner race, and the rollers directly contact the bearing journals of the axle shafts. The axle shafts do not use an inner and outer bearing retainer. Rather, they are held in the axle by means of C-locks, Fig. 3. These C-locks also fit into a machined recess in the differential side gears within the differential case. There is no retainer bolt access hole in the axle shaft flange.

Rear Axle, Replace

1. Raise rear of vehicle and remove wheel and tire assembly.
2. Remove brake drums.
3. Mark drive shaft and pinion flange for reassembly, then disconnect drive shaft at pinion flange and remove drive shaft from transmission extension housing. Install seal replacer tool in extension housing to prevent leakage.
4. Disconnect vent hose from rear vent tube, then all the hydraulic brake lines from axle housing retaining clips and wheel cylinders.

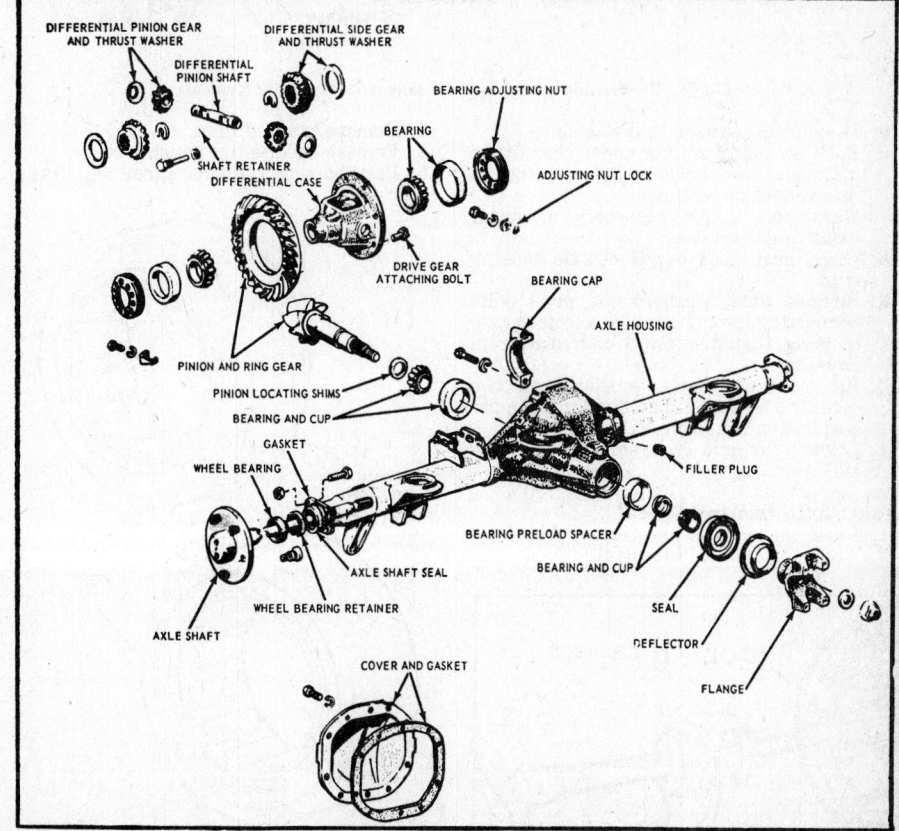

Fig. 1 Integral type rear axle assembly (typical)

Fig. 3 Axle shaft C locks 1977–83 Ford integral type axle

Fig. 2 Removable carrier type of rear axle assembly (typical)

member and lower hoist to allow axle to lower as far as possible.
6. Working through differential case opening, remove pinion shaft lock bolt and pinion shaft.
7. Push axle shaft(s) inward toward center of axle housing and remove C-lock(s) from housing, Fig. 3.
8. Remove axle shaft, using extreme care to avoid contact of shaft seal lip with any portion of axle shaft except seal journal.
9. Use a hook-type puller to remove seal and bearing, Fig. 4.

NOTE: On 1977–79 models, two types of bearings are used, one requires a snug press fit in the axle housing flanges and the other has a ground race and a loose fit is acceptable, Fig. 5. Therefore, when removing bearings, if a loose fit is encountered it does not indicate excessive wear or damage.

10. Reverse procedure to install, using suitable driving tools, Fig. 6, to install seal and bearing. New seals are pre-packed with lubricant and do not require oil soaking before installation. Torque bearing retainer nuts to 20–40 ft. lbs.

Removable Carrier Type

In these axles, Fig. 2, the drive pinion is straddle-mounted by two opposed tapered roller bearings which support the pinion shaft in front of the drive pinion gear, and straight roller bearing that supports the pinion shaft at the rear of the pinion gear. The drive pinion is assembled in a pinion retainer that is bolted to the differential carrier. The tapered roller

5. Disconnect parking brake cable.
6. Position safety stands under rear frame members, then lower axle far enough to relieve spring tension.
7. Disconnect shock absorbers at lower mounting brackets.
8. Disconnect track bar from axle housing stud.
9. Remove nuts, washers and pivot bolts connecting lower suspension arms to axle housing, then disconnect both arms from housing.
10. Remove nuts, bolts, washers and two eccentric washers, then disconnect upper suspension arm from axle housing.
11. Lower rear axle and remove from vehicle.

Axle Shaft, Bearing & Seal
1. Raise car on hoist and remove wheels.
2. Drain differential lubricant.

3. Remove brake drums.
4. Remove differential housing cover.
5. Position safety stands under rear frame

TORRINGTON (SNUG FIT)

BOWER (LOOSE FIT)

TOOL 1177 OR T73L-1177-C

TOOL- 1175-AC

Fig. 4 Using hook-type tool to remove oil seal

Fig. 5 Axle shaft bearing identification. 1977–79 models w/integral type axle

Fig. 6 Using special driver to install oil seal

Fig. 7 Removing axle shaft with slide hammer-type puller

bearings are preloaded by a collapsible spacer between the bearings. The pinion is positioned by a shim or shims located between the drive pinion retainer and the differential carrier.

The differential is supported in the carrier by two tapered roller side bearings. These bearings are preloaded by two threaded ring nuts or sleeves between the bearings and pedestals. The differential assembly is positioned for proper ring gear and pinion backlash by varying the adjustment of these ring nuts. The differential case houses two side gears in mesh with two pinions mounted on a pinion shaft which is held in place by a pin. The side gears and pinions are backed by thrust washers. With high performance engines, an optional rear axle having a four-pinion differential is also used.

The axle shafts are of unequal length, the left shaft being shorter than the right. The axle shafts are mounted on sealed ball bearings or tapered roller bearings which are pressed on the shafts.

SERVICE BULLETIN

All Ford Built Rear Axles: Recent manufacturing changes have eliminated the need for marking rear axle drive pinions for individual variations from nominal shim thicknesses. In the past, these pinion markings, with the aid of a shim selection table, were used as a guide to select correct shim thicknesses when a gear set or carrier assembly replacement was performed.

With the elimination of pinion markings, use of the shim selection table is no longer possible and the methods outlined below must be used.

1. Measure the thickness of the original pinion depth shim removed from the axle. Use the same thickness upon installation of the replacement carrier or drive pinion. If any further shim change is necessary, it will be indicated in the tooth pattern check.
2. If the original shim is lost, substitute a nominal shim for the original and use the tooth pattern check to determine if further shim changes are required.

Rear Axle, Replace

1. Raise rear of vehicle and remove wheel and tire assembly.
2. On models equipped with rear drum brakes, remove brake drums.
3. On models equipped with rear disc brakes, remove calipers from anchor plates, then remove two retaining nuts and slide rotors off axle shafts.

NOTE: Secure calipers to frame with

wire.

4. Make marks on drive shaft yoke and pinion flange for reassembly, then disconnect drive shaft at rear axle U-joint and remove drive shaft from transmission extension housing. Install seal replacer tool in extension housing to prevent leakage.
5. Disconnect anti-skid sensor, if equipped.
6. Position safety stands under frame rear members, then support axle housing using a suitable jack.
7. Disconnect brake hydraulic lines from axle housing retaining clips.
8. Disconnect vent tube from rear housing.
9. Disconnect shock absorbers from lower mounting brackets.
10. Disconnect track bar from mounting stud on rear axle housing bracket.

NOTE: The axle housing mounting bracket has two holes, the track bar should be attached to the lower hole.

11. Lower rear axle housing until coil springs are released, then remove springs and insulators.
12. Disconnect suspension lower arms from axle housing, then disconnect suspension upper arms from housing.
13. Lower axle housing and remove from vehicle.

Axle Shaft, Bearing & Seal

1. Remove rear wheel assembly, then the brake drum or caliper and rotor assembly.
2. Remove axle shaft retainer nuts and bolts.
3. Pull axle shaft assembly from housing. It may be necessary to use a suitable slide hammer type puller, Fig. 7.
4. To replace wheel bearing on models equipped with tapered roller bearings:
   a. Drill a 1/4 inch hole in inner bearing retainer approximately 3/4 of the thickness of the bearing retainer deep.

NOTE: Do not drill completely through the bearing retainer since damage to the axle shaft may result.

   b. Place a cold chisel across the drilled hole and strike with a hammer to break retainer, then discard retainer, Fig. 8.
   c. Using suitable press and plates, press bearing from axle shaft. Do not apply heat since the heat will weaken the axle shaft bearing journal area.
   d. Install lubricated seal and bearing on axle shaft, ensuring the cup rib ring faces toward the axle flange.

NOTE: The lubricated seal of the bearing assembly used with drum brake installations is of a different length than the seal used on disc brake installations and are not interchangeable. For identification, the seal used on drum brake installations has a grey color outer rim and on disc brake installations, the seal has a black oxide appearance.

   e. Press new bearing into place, then the bearing retainer firmly against the bearing.
   f. Remove old bearing cup from axle

Fig. 8 Splitting bearing inner retainer for bearing removal

housing with a suitable puller. Place new bearing cup on bearing and apply lubricant to outside diameter of seal and bearing cup and install in axle housing.

5. To replace wheel bearing on models equipped with ball bearings:
   a. Remove oil seal from axle housing, Fig. 4.
   b. Loosen bearing inner retainer by striking retainer ring in several places with a cold chisel and slide off shaft, Fig. 8.

NOTE: On some models, it may be necessary to drill a 1/4 inch hole in inner bearing retainer approximately 3/4 of the thickness of the bearing retainer deep before using the cold chisel.

   c. Using suitable press and plates, press bearing from shaft. Do not heat axle shaft since the heat will damage the shaft.
   d. Install outer retainer on shaft and press bearing into place. Press inner retainer onto shaft until firmly seated against bearing.
   e. Install oil seal into axle housing, Fig. 6.
6. On all units, slide axle shaft assembly into housing, engaging axle shaft splines in the side gear.
7. Install and torque axle shaft retainer nuts and bolts to 50–75 ft. lbs. on 1977 models, 50–70 ft. lbs. on 1978 models.

PROPELLER SHAFT, REPLACE

1. Mark the relationship of the driveshaft to pinion flange, then disconnect rear U-joint or companion flange from drive pinion flange.
2. Pull drive shaft toward rear of car until front U-joint yoke clears transmission extension housing and output shaft.
3. Install a suitable tool, such as a seal driver, in seal to prevent lube from leaking from transmission.
4. Before installing, check U-joints for freedom of movement. If a bind has resulted from misalignment after overhauling the U-joints, tap the ears of the drive shaft sharply to relieve the bind.
5. If rubber seal installed on end of transmission extension housing is damaged, install a new seal.
6. Lubricate yoke spline with special spline

Fig. 9 Brake adjustment gauge

lubricant. *This spline is sealed so that transmission fluid does not "wash" away spline lubricant.*

7. Install yoke on transmission output shaft.
8. Align marks on driveshaft and pinion flange, then install U-bolts and nuts which attach U-joint to pinion flange. Tighten U-bolts evenly to prevent binding U-joint bearings.

BRAKE ADJUSTMENTS

1. Use the brake shoe adjustment gauge shown in Fig. 9 to obtain the drum inside diameter as shown. Tighten the adjusting knob on the gauge to hold this setting.
2. Place the opposite side of the gauge over the brake shoes and adjust the shoes by turning the adjuster screw until the gauge just slides over the linings. Rotate the gauge around the lining surface to assure proper lining diameter adjustment and clearance.
3. Install brake drum and wheel. Final adjustment is accomplished by making several firm reverse stops, using the brake pedal.

Self-Adjusting Brakes

These brakes, Fig. 10, have self-adjusting shoe mechanisms that assure correct lining-

Fig. 11 Backing off brake adjustment by disengaging adjusting lever with screwdriver

Fig. 10 Rear drum type brakes

to-drum clearances at all times. The automatic adjusters operate only when the brakes are applied as the car is moving rearward.

Although the brakes are self-adjusting, an initial adjustment is necessary after the brake shoes have been relined or replaced, or when the length of the star wheel adjuster has been changed during some other service operation.

Frequent usage of an automatic transmission forward range to halt reverse vehicle motion may prevent the automatic adjusters from functioning, thereby inducing low pedal heights. Should low pedal heights be encountered, it is recommended that numerous forward and reverse stops be performed with a firm pedal effort until satisfactory pedal height is obtained.

NOTE: If a low pedal height condition cannot be corrected by making numerous reverse stops (provided the hydraulic system is free of air), it indicates that the self-adjusting mechanism is not functioning. Therefore, it will be necessary to remove the brake drums, clean, free up and lubricate the adjusting mechanism. Then adjust the brakes, being sure the parking brake is fully released.

Initial Adjustment

1. Remove adjusting hole cover from brake backing plate and, from the backing plate side, turn the adjusting screw upward with a screwdriver or other suitable tool to expand the shoes until a slight drag is felt when the drums are rotated.
2. Remove the drum.
3. While holding the adjusting lever out of engagement with the adjusting screw, Fig. 11, back off the adjusting screw about one full turn with the fingers.

NOTE: *If finger movement will not turn the screw, free it up. If this is not done, the adjusting lever will not turn the screw during vehicle operation. Lubricate the screw with oil and coat with wheel bearing grease. Any other adjustment procedure may cause damage to the adjusting screw with consequent self-adjuster problems.*

4. Install wheel and drum, and adjusting hole cover. Adjust brakes on remaining wheels in the same manner.
5. If pedal height is not satisfactory, drive

the vehicle and make sufficient reverse stops with a firm pedal effort until proper pedal height is obtained.

PARKING BRAKE, ADJUST

Check parking brake cables when brakes are fully released. If cables are loose, adjust as follows:

1977–83 Rear Drum Brakes

1. Make sure parking brake is released.
2. Place transmission in neutral and raise the vehicle.
3. Tighten the adjusting nut against the cable equalizer to cause rear brakes to drag.
4. Then loosen the adjusting nut until the rear wheels are fully released. There should be no drag.
5. Lower vehicle and check operation.

1977–78 Rear Disc Brakes

1. Fully release parking brake, then place transmission in neutral and support vehicle at rear axle.
2. Tighten adjuster nut until levers on calipers just begin to move, then loosen adjuster nut until levers just return to stop position.
3. Apply and release parking brake. Check

Fig. 12 Connections for automatic parking brake release. Typical

levers on caliper to determine if they are fully returned by attempting to pull lever rearward. If lever moves, the adjustment is too tight and must be readjusted.

VACUUM RELEASE PARKING BRAKE

The vacuum power unit will release the parking brakes automatically when the shift lever is moved into any drive position with the engine running. The brakes will not release automatically, however, when the shift lever is in neutral or park position with the engine running, or in any position with the engine off.

The power unit piston rod is attached to the release lever. Since the release lever pivots against the pawl, a slight movement of the release lever will disengage the pawl from the ratchet, allowing the brakes to release. The release lever pivots on a rivet pin in the pedal mount.

As shown in Fig. 12, hoses connect the power unit and the engine manifold to a vacuum release valve in the transmission neutral safety switch. Moving the transmission selector lever into any drive position with the engine running will open the release valve to connect engine manifold vacuum to one side of the actuating piston in the power unit. The pressure differential thus created will cause the piston and link to pull the release lever.

MASTER CYLINDER, REPLACE

1. Disconnect brake lines from master cylinder.
2. Remove nuts retaining master cylinder to brake booster.
3. Remove master cylinder.
4. Reverse procedure to install.

HYDRO-BOOST BRAKE BOOSTER, REPLACE

1. Working from inside of car under instrument panel, disconnect booster push rod link from brake pedal. To do this, proceed as follows:
2. Disconnect stop light switch wires at connector. Remove hairpin retainer. Slide switch off brake pedal pin just far enough for switch outer hole to clear pin. Then lift switch straight upward from pin. Slide master cylinder push rod and nylon washers and bushing off brake pedal pin.
3. Open hood and disconnect brake line at master cylinder outlet fitting.
4. Disconnect the pressure, steering gear and return lines, then plug lines and ports.
5. Remove Hydro-Boost to dash panel nuts and remove assembly from panel, sliding push rod link from engine side of dash panel.
6. Reverse procedure to install. To purge

system, disconnect coil wire so that engine will not start. Fill power steering pump reservoir, then while engaging starter, pump brake pedal. Do not cycle steering wheel until all residual air has been purged from the hydro boost unit. Check fluid level, then connect coil wire and start engine. Apply brakes with a pumping action and cycle steering wheel, then check system for leaks.

POWER BRAKE UNIT, REPLACE

1. Working from inside of car under instrument panel, disconnect booster push rod link from pedal. To do this, proceed as follows:
2. Disconnect stop light switch wires at connector. Remove hairpin retainer. Slide switch off brake pedal pin just far enough for switch outer hole to clear pin. Then lift switch straight upward from pin. Slide master cylinder push rod and nylon washers and bushing off brake pedal pin.
3. Open hood and disconnect brake line at master cylinder outlet fitting.
4. Disconnect vacuum hose from booster unit. If equipped with automatic transmission disconnect transmission vacuum unit hose.
5. Remove four attaching nuts and remove booster and bracket from dash panel, slide push rod link out from engine side of dash panel. Remove four spacers.
6. Remove push rod link boot from dash panel.
7. Reverse procedure to install.

Rear Suspension

Fig. 1 Rear suspension (typical). 1977–78

SHOCK ABSORBER, REPLACE

1. With the rear axle supported properly disconnect shock absorber at upper mounting and compress it to clear hole in spring seat.
2. Disconnect shock absorber from stud on axle bracket.
3. Reverse procedure to install.

COIL SPRING, REPLACE

1. Raise rear of vehicle and support at frame. Support rear axle with a suitable jack.
2. Disconnect shock absorbers at lower mountings.
3. Disconnect brake line from rear brake hose and remove hose to bracket clip.
4. Lower axle to remove springs.

NOTE: On some models, it may be necessary to disconnect the right hand parking brake cable from right hand upper arm retainer before lowering axle.

5. Reverse procedure to install. Install an insulator between upper and lower seats and the spring on 1977–78 models and between upper seat and spring on 1979–83 models.

Fig. 2 Rear suspension. 1979-83

CONTROL ARMS, REPLACE

NOTE: Control arms must be replaced in pairs.

1. Raise rear of vehicle and support at frame. Support axle with a suitable jack.
2. On 1977-78 models, disconnect track bar from frame mounting bracket.
3. On 1979-83 models, remove stabilizer bar.
4. Lower axle and install a second jack under differential pinion nose.
5. Disconnect control arm from axle bracket. On upper arms, disconnect arm from crossmember and on lower arms, disconnect arm from frame attachment bracket.
6. Reverse procedure to install.

TRACK BAR, REPLACE

1977-78
1. Remove cover from track bar axle attachment and disconnect track bar from mounting stud, Fig. 1.
2. Disconnect track bar from frame side rail.
3. Reverse procedure to install.

STABILIZER BAR, REPLACE

1979-83
1. Raise and support vehicle at frame side rails.
2. Support rear axle with a suitable jack and position axle so the shock absorbers are fully extended.
3. Remove bolts, nuts and spacers attaching stabilizer bar to lower arms, Fig. 2.
4. Remove stabilizer bar from vehicle.
5. Reverse procedure to install.

Front Suspension & Steering Section

FRONT SUSPENSION

1979-83

Referring to Fig. 1, note that the lower control arms pivot on two bolts and bushings attached to the crossmember. Previous models used only one bolt and bushing to attach the lower control arm to the suspension crossmember.

1977-78

Referring to Fig. 2, note that the lower control arm pivots on a bolt in the front crossmember. The struts, which are connected between the lower control arms and frame crossmember, prevent the control arms from moving forward and backward.

WHEEL ALIGNMENT

SERVICE BULLETIN

WHEEL BALANCING DIFFERS: On cars with disc brakes, dynamic balancing of the wheel-and-tire assembly on the car should not be attempted without first pulling back the shoe and lining assemblies from the rotor. If this is not done, brake drag may burn out the motor on the wheel spinner.

The drag can be eliminated by removing the wheel, taking out the two bolts holding the caliper splash shield, and detaching the shield. Then push the pistons into their cylinder bores by applying steady pressure on the shoes on each side of the rotor for at least a minute. If necessary, use waterpump pliers to apply the pressure.

After the pistons have been retracted, reinstall the splash shield and wheel. The wheel-and-tire assembly can then be dynamically balanced in the usual way. After the balancing job has been completed, be sure to pump the brake pedal several times until the shoes are seated and a firm brake pedal is obtained.

1977-83

Caster and camber can be adjusted by loosening the bolts that attach the upper suspension arm to the shaft at the frame side rail, and moving the arm assembly in or out in the elongated bolt holes, Figs. 3 and 3A. Since any movement of the arm affects both caster and camber, both factors should be balanced against one another when making the adjustment.

Fig. 1 Front suspension. 1979-83

Fig. 2 Front suspension. 1977—78

Fig. 3 Adjusting caster & camber. 1977—78

Fig. 3A Adjusting caster & camber. 1979—83

NOTE: On 1977–78 models, use alignment tool T69P-3000A, Fig. 3. On 1979–83 models, use alignment tool T79P-3000A, Fig. 3A. Install the tool with the pins in the frame holes and the hooks over the upper arm inner shaft. Tighten the hook nuts snug before loosening the upper arm inner shaft attaching bolts.

Caster, Adjust
1. Tighten the tool front hook nut or loosen the rear hook nut as required to increase caster to the desired angle.
2. To decrease caster, tighten the rear hook nut or loosen the front hook nut as required.

NOTE: The caster angle can be checked without tightening the inner shaft retaining bolts.

3. Check the camber angle to be sure it did not change during the caster adjustment and adjust if necessary.
4. Torque the upper arm inner shaft retaining bolts to 120–140 ft. lbs. and remove tool.

Camber, Adjust
1. Loosen both inner shaft retaining bolts.
2. Tighten or loosen the hook nuts as necessary to increase or decrease camber.
3. Recheck caster and readjust if necessary.
4. Torque upper arm inner shaft retaining bolts to 120–140 ft. lbs.

TOE-IN, ADJUST

Position the front wheels in their straight-ahead position. Then turn both tie rod adjusting sleeves an equal amount until the desired toe-in setting is obtained. Torque tie rod sleeve clamp bolt to 20–22 ft. lbs.

WHEEL BEARINGS, ADJUST

1. With wheel rotating, tighten adjusting nut to 17–25 ft. lbs.
2. Back off adjusting nut ½ turn and retighten nut to 10–15 inch lbs.
3. Place nut lock on nut so that castellations on lock are aligned with cotter pin hole in spindle and install cotter pin.
4. Check front wheel rotation, if it rotates noisily or roughly, clean, inspect or replace wheel bearings as necessary.

WHEEL BEARINGS, REPLACE

(Disc Brakes)

1. Raise car and remove front wheels.
2. Remove caliper mounting bolts.

NOTE: It is not necessary to disconnect the brake lines for this operation.

3. Slide caliper off of disc, inserting a spacer between the shoes to hold them in their bores after the caliper is removed. Position caliper assembly out of the way.

NOTE: Do not allow caliper to hang by brake hose.

4. Remove hub and disc assembly. Grease retainer and inner bearing can now be removed.
5. Reverse procedure to install.

Fig. 4 Measuring lower ball joint radial play, which should not exceed ¼"

Fig. 5 Lower ball joint wear indicators. 1979—83

CHECKING BALL JOINTS FOR WEAR

Upper Ball Joint

1. Raise car on floor jacks placed beneath lower control arms.
2. Grasp lower edge of tire and move wheel in and out.
3. As wheel is being moved in and out, observe upper end of spindle and upper arm.
4. Any movement between upper end of spindle and upper arm indicates ball joint wear and loss of preload. If any such movement is observed, replace upper ball joint.

NOTE: During the foregoing check, the lower ball joint will be unloaded and may move. Disregard all such movement of the lower ball joint. Also, do not mistake loose wheel bearings for a worn ball joint.

Lower Ball Joint

1977–78
1. Raise car on jacks placed under lower control arms as shown in Fig. 4. This will unload ball joints.
2. Adjust wheel bearings.
3. Attach a dial indicator to lower control arm and position so that its plunger rests against the inner side of the wheel rim adjacent to the lower ball joint.
4. Grasp tire at top and bottom and slowly move it in and out as shown in Fig. 4.
5. If reading on dial indicator exceeds ¼″, replace lower ball joint.

1979–83
These models are equipped with lower ball joint wear indicators, Fig. 5. To check ball joint for wear, support vehicle in normal driving position with both ball joints loaded. Observe the checking surface of the ball joint. If the checking surface is inside the cover, Fig. 5, replace the ball joint.

SHOCK ABSORBER, REPLACE

1. Remove nut, washer and bushing from shock absorber upper end.
2. Raise vehicle and install safety stands.
3. Remove two thread-cutting screws from lower end of shock absorber, then remove shock absorber.
4. Reverse procedure to install.

NOTE: If threads in lower arm become damaged, re-use original thread-cutting screws along with 5/16-18 locknuts.

COIL SPRING, REPLACE

1979–83

1. Raise and support vehicle.
2. Remove wheel.
3. Disconnect stabilizer bar link from lower control arm.
4. Remove shock absorber.

Fig. 6   Replacing coil spring. 1977–78

5. Remove steering center link from pitman arm.
6. Compress coil spring with a suitable spring compressor, tool D-78P-5310-A or equivalent.
7. Remove two lower control arm pivot bolts and disengage arm from crossmember.
8. Remove spring from vehicle.
9. Reverse procedure to install. Torque stabilizer bar to lower control arm nuts to 9–12 ft. lbs. Torque lower control arm to crossmember bolts to 120–140 ft. lbs.

1977–78

1. Raise vehicle and support front end of frame with jack stands.
2. Disconnect shock absorber from lower arm, collapse shock absorber into the spring and place a jack under the lower arm for support, Fig. 6.
3. Remove strut and rebound bumper bolts and disconnect lower end of sway bar stud from lower arm.
4. Remove the nut and bolt retaining the inner end of the lower arm to the crossmember.
5. Carefully lower jack to relieve spring pressure on lower arm, then remove the spring.
6. Reverse procedure to install.

BALL JOINTS, REPLACE

NOTE: Ford Motor Company recommends that new ball joints should not be installed on used control arms and that the control arm be replaced if ball joint replacement is required. However, aftermarket ball joint repair kits which do not require control arm replacement, are available and can be installed using the following procedure.

The ball joints are riveted to the upper and lower control arms. The ball joints can be replaced on the car by removing the rivets and retaining the new ball joint to the control arm with the attaching bolts, nuts and washers furnished with the ball joint kit.

When removing a ball joint, use a suitable pressing tool to force the ball joint out of the spindle.

POWER STEERING GEAR, REPLACE

1977–83

1. Remove stone shield, if equipped.
2. Disconnect pressure and return lines from steering gear. Plug lines and ports in gear to prevent entry of dirt.
3. Remove two bolts that secure flex coupling to steering gear and to column.
4. Raise car and remove sector shaft nut.
5. Use a puller to remove pitman arm.
6. Support steering gear, then remove attaching bolts.
7. Work steering gear free of flex coupling and remove it from car.
8. Reverse procedure to install.

POWER STEERING PUMP, REPLACE

1978–83 Models

1. Disconnect power steering pump return line and allow power steering pump fluid to drain into a suitable container.
2. Disconnect power steering pump pressure hose from pump fitting.
3. On 1978–79 models, remove power steering pump mounting bracket attaching bolts, then disconnect drive belt from pulley and remove pump, pulley and mounting bracket as an assembly.
4. On 1980–83 models, disconnect drive belt from power steering pump pulley, remove pulley, then remove pump.
5. Reverse procedure to install. Torque pump to mounting bracket bolts to 30–45 ft. lbs.

NOTE: On Ford model C11 power steering pump, torque pressure hose to pump fitting to 10–15 ft. lbs. End play on this fitting is normal and does not indicate a loose fitting.

1977 Models

Ford/TRW Pump
1. Disconnect power steering pump return line and allow power steering fluid to drain into a suitable container.
2. Disconnect pressure line from power steering pump.
3. Remove bolts from front of pump and nut at rear of pump attaching pump to mounting bracket, then disconnect drive belt from pulley and remove pump.
4. Reverse procedure to install. Torque pump to mounting bracket nut to 20–30 ft. lbs. and mounting bracket to pump bolts to 30–45 ft. lbs.

Saginaw Pump
1. Disconnect pressure and return lines from power steering pump, then cap lines and fittings.
2. Loosen power steering pump adjusting bracket nut, then remove bolts attaching power steering pump mounting bracket to A/C compressor mounting bracket, if equipped.
3. Disconnect drive belt from pulley, then remove power steering pump and bracket as an assembly.
4. Reverse procedure to install. Torque pump to mounting bracket nuts to 30–45 ft. lbs.

FORD & MERCURY
Compact & Intermediate Models

> **NOTE:** The 1977–83 Ford Mustang, Pinto, Mercury Bobcat and 1979–83 Capri are located elsewhere in this manual. Refer to the back of this manual for vehicle manufacturer's special service tool suppliers.

INDEX OF SERVICE OPERATIONS

ENGINE & SERIAL NUMBER LOCATION:

Vehicle warranty plate on rear face of left front door.

GRILLE IDENTIFICATION

1977 Comet

1977 Granada

1977 Maverick

1977 Monarch

1977 LTD II

1977 Thunderbird

1977-79 Cougar

1977-79 Cougar XR-7

1978 Fairmont
European Sport Option (ESO)

1978 Thunderbird

1978-79 LTD II

1978-80 Granada

1978-80 Monarch

1978-81 Fairmont

1978-81 Fairmont Futura

1978-81 Zephyr

1979 Thunderbird

1980 Cougar

GRILLE IDENTIFICATION—Continued

1980 Thunderbird

1981 Cougar & 1982 Cougar Sta. Wag.

1981 Granada

1981–82 Thunderbird

1982 Cougar Exc. Sta. Wag.

1982 Granada

1982–83 Fairmont

1983 Cougar

1983 Ford LTD

1983 Mercury Marquis

1983 Thunderbird

GENERAL ENGINE SPECIFICATIONS

Year	Engine CID①/Liter	V.I.N. Code②	Carburetor	Bore and Stroke	Com-pression Ratio	Net H.P. @ R.P.M.③	Maximum Torque Ft. Lbs. @ R.P.M.	Normal Oil Pressure Pounds
1977	6-200, 3.3L④⑦	T	YFA, 1 Bbl.⑥	3.68 × 3.13	8.5	96 @ 4400	151 @ 2000	30–50
	6-200, 3.3L④⑤	T	YFA, 1 Bbl.⑥	3.68 × 3.13	8.5	97 @ 4400	153 @ 2000	30–50
	6-250, 4.1L⑤⑧	L	YFA, 1 Bbl.⑥	3.68 × 3.91	8.1	86 @ 3000	185 @ 1800	40–60
	6-250, 4.1L④⑤	L	YFA, 1 Bbl.⑥	3.68 × 3.91	8.1	98 @ 3600	190 @ 1400	40–60
	6-250, 4.1L④⑦	L	YFA, 1 Bbl.⑥	3.68 × 3.91	8.1	98 @ 3400	182 @ 1800	40–60
	V8-302, 5.0L⑤⑧	F	2700VV, 2 Bbl.⑪	4.00 × 3.00	8.1	122 @ 3400	222 @ 1400	40–65
	V8-302, 5.0L④⑦⑨	F	2150, 2 Bbl.⑪	4.00 × 3.00	8.4	122 @ 3200	237 @ 1600	40–65
	V8-302, 5.0L⑯⑰⑮	F	2150, 2 Bbl.⑪	4.00 × 3.00	8.4	130 @ 3400	243 @ 1800	40–65
	V8-302, 5.0L④⑤⑨	F	2150, 2 Bbl.⑪	4.00 × 3.00	8.4	134 @ 3600	245 @ 1600	40–65
	V8-302, 5.0L④⑤⑩	F	2150, 2 Bbl.⑪	4.00 × 3.00	8.4	137 @ 3600	245 @ 1600	40–65
	V8-351W, 5.8L④⑤⑨⑬	H	2150, 2 Bbl.⑪	4.00 × 3.50	8.3	135 @ 3200	275 @ 1600	40–65
	V8-351W, 5.8L④⑤⑬⑰⑮	H	2150, 2 Bbl.⑪	4.00 × 3.50	8.3	149 @ 3200	291 @ 1600	40–65
	V8-351M, 5.8L④⑤⑭⑰⑮	H	2150, 2 Bbl.⑪	4.00 × 3.50	8.0	161 @ 3600	285 @ 1800	50–75
	V8-351M, 5.8L⑤⑧⑭⑰⑮	H	2150, 2 Bbl.⑪	4.00 × 3.50	8.0	161 @ 3600	286 @ 1800	50–75
	V8-400, 6.6L④⑤⑰⑮	S	2150, 2 Bbl.⑪	4.00 × 4.00	8.0	173 @ 3800	326 @ 1600	50–75
	V8-400, 6.6L⑤⑧⑰⑮	S	2150, 2 Bbl.⑪	4.00 × 4.00	8.0	168 @ 3800	323 @ 1600	50–75

Continued

GENERAL ENGINE SPECIFICATIONS—Continued

Year	Engine CID①/Liter	V.I.N. Code②	Carburetor	Bore and Stroke	Compression Ratio	Net H.P. @ R.P.M.③	Maximum Torque Lbs. Ft. @ R.P.M.	Normal Oil Pressure Pounds
1978	4-140, 2.3L	Y	5200, 2 Bbl.①	3.781 × 3.126	9.0	88 @ 4800	118 @ 2800	50
	6-200, 3.3L	T	YFA, 1 Bbl.⑥⑱	3.68 × 3.13	8.5	85 @ 3600	250 @ 1600	30—50
	6-250, 4.1L	L	YFA, 1 Bbl.⑥	3.68 × 3.91	8.5	97 @ 3200	210 @ 1400	40—60
	V8-302, 5.0L⑧⑨⑲	F	2700VV, 2 Bbl.⑪	4.00 × 3.00	8.1	133 @ 3600	243 @ 1600	40—60
	V8-302, 5.0L④⑰	F	2150, 2 Bbl.⑪	4.00 × 3.00	8.4	134 @ 3400	248 @ 1600	40—60
	V8-302, 5.0L④⑨⑲⑮	F	2150, 2 Bbl.⑪	4.00 × 3.00	8.4	139 @ 3600	250 @ 1600	40—60
	V8-351, 5.8L⑬	H	2150, 2 Bbl.⑪	4.00 × 3.50	8.3	144 @ 3200	277 @ 1600	40—60
	V8-351, 5.8L⑭	H	2150, 2 Bbl.⑪	4.00 × 3.50	8.0	152 @ 3600	278 @ 1800	50—75
	V8-400, 6.6L	S	2150, 2 Bbl.⑪	4.00 × 4.00	8.0	166 @ 3800	319 @ 1800	50—75
1979	4-140, 2.3L	Y	5200, 2 Bbl.⑪	3.781 × 3.126	9.0	88 @ 4800	118 @ 2800	40—60
	6-200, 3.3L	T	YFA, 1 Bbl.⑥⑱	3.68 × 3.13	8.5	85 @ 3600	154 @ 1600	30—50
	6-250, 4.1L	L	YFA, 1 Bbl.⑥	3.68 × 3.91	8.6	97 @ 3200	210 @ 1400	40—60
	V8-302, 5.0L④⑰⑮	F	2150, 2 Bbl.⑪	4.00 × 3.00	8.4	133 @ 3400	245 @ 1600	40—65
	V8-302, 5.0L④⑨	F	2150, 2 Bbl.⑪	4.00 × 3.00	8.4	137 @ 3600	243 @ 2000	40—65
	V8-302, 5.0L⑧⑨	F	2700VV, 2 Bbl.⑪	4.00 × 3.00	8.4	138 @ 3800	239 @ 2200	40—65
	V8-302, 5.0L④⑲	F	2150, 2 Bbl.⑪	4.00 × 3.00	8.4	140 @ 3600	250 @ 1800	40—65
	V8-302, 5.0L⑧⑲	F	2700VV, 2 Bbl.⑪	4.00 × 3.00	8.4	143 @ 3600	243 @ 2200	40—65
	V8-351W, 5.8L④⑬⑯	H	2150, 2 Bbl.⑪	4.00 × 3.50	8.3	135 @ 3200	286 @ 1400	40—65
	V8-351W, 5.8L⑧⑬⑰	H	2150, 2 Bbl.⑪	4.00 × 3.50	8.0	149 @ 3800	258 @ 2200	50—75
	V8-351M, 5.8L④⑭⑰	H	2150, 2 Bbl.⑪	4.00 × 3.50	8.0	151 @ 3600	270 @ 2200	50—75
1980	4-140, 2.3L④⑳	A	5200, 2 Bbl.⑪	3.781 × 3.126	9.0	88 @ 4600	119 @ 2600	40—60
	4-140, 2.3L⑧⑳	A	6500, 2 Bbl.⑫	3.781 × 3.126	9.0	89 @ 4800	122 @ 2600	40—60
	4-140, 2.3L④㉑	A	5200, 2 Bbl.⑫	3.781 × 3.126	9.0	—	—	40—60
	4-140, 2.3L⑧㉑	A	6500, 2 Bbl.⑫	3.781 × 3.126	9.0	—	—	40—60
	6-200, 3.3L④	B	1946, 1 Bbl.⑫	3.68 × 3.13	8.6	91 @ 3800	160 @ 1600	30—50
	6-200, 3.3L⑧	B	1946C, 1 Bbl.⑫	3.68 × 3.13	8.6	—	—	30—50
	6-250, 4.1L④⑨	C	YFA, 1 Bbl.⑥	3.68 × 3.91	8.6	90 @ 3200	194 @ 1660	40—60
	V8-255, 4.2L⑲	D	2150, 2 Bbl.⑪	3.68 × 3.00	8.8	119 @ 3800	194 @ 2200	40—60
	V8-255, 4.2L⑯⑮	D	2150, 2 Bbl.⑪	3.68 × 3.00	8.8	115 @ 3800	191 @ 2000	40—60
	V8-255, 4.2L⑧⑨	D	2150, 2 Bbl.⑪	3.68 × 3.00	8.8	117 @ 3800	193 @ 2000	40—60
	V8-302, 5.0L⑨	F	2150, 2 Bbl.⑪	4.00 × 3.00	8.4	134 @ 3600	232 @ 1600	40—60
	V8-302, 5.0L④⑯⑮	F	2150, 2 Bbl.⑪	4.00 × 3.00	8.4	131 @ 3600	231 @ 1600	40—60
	V8-302, 5.0L⑧⑯⑮	F	2150, 2 Bbl.⑪	4.00 × 3.00	8.4	132 @ 3600	232 @ 1400	40—60
1981	4-140, 2.3L	A	6500, 2 Bbl.⑫	3.781 × 3.126	9.0	88 @ 4600	118 @ 2600	40—60
	6-200, 3.3L	B	1946, 1 Bbl.⑫	3.68 × 3.13	8.6	88 @ 3800	154 @ 1400	30—50
	V8-255, 4.2L④	D	2150, 2 Bbl.⑪	3.68 × 3.00	8.2	115 @ 3400	195 @ 2200	40—60
	V8-255, 4.2L⑧	D	7200VV, 2 Bbl.⑪	3.68 × 3.00	8.2	120 @ 3400	205 @ 2600	40—60
	V8-302, 5.0L④	F	2150, 2 Bbl.⑪	4.00 × 3.00	8.4	130 @ 3400	235 @ 1600	40—60
	V8-302, 5.0L⑧	F	7200VV, 2 Bbl.⑪	4.00 × 3.00	8.4	130 @ 3400	235 @ 1800	40—60
1982	4-140, 2.3L	A	6500, 2 Bbl.⑫	3.781 × 3.126	9.0	86 @ 4600	117 @ 2600	40—60
	6-200, 3.3L	B	1946, 1 Bbl.⑫	3.68 × 3.13	8.6	87 @ 3800	154 @ 1400	30—50
	V6-232, 3.8L④	3	2150, 2 Bbl.⑪	3.81 × 3.39	8.8	112 @ 4000	175 @ 2600	54—59
	V6-232, 3.8L⑧	3	7200VV, 2 Bbl.⑪	3.81 × 3.39	8.8	118 @ 4000	186 @ 2600	54—59
	V8-255, 4.2L④	D	2150, 2 Bbl.⑪	3.68 × 3.00	8.2	122 @ 3400	209 @ 2400	40—60
	V8-255, 4.2L⑧	D	7200VV, 2 Bbl.⑪	3.68 × 3.00	—	—	—	40—60
1983	4-140	A	YFA, 1 Bbl.⑥	3.78 × 3.12	—	—	—	50
	6-200	X	1946, 1 Bbl.⑫	3.68 × 3.12	—	—	—	50
	V6-232	3	2150, 2 Bbl.⑪	3.8 × 3.4	—	—	—	40—60

Continued

GENERAL ENGINE SPECIFICATION NOTES—Continued

①—CID—cubic inch displacement.
②—On 1977-80 models, the fifth digit of the V.I.N. denotes engine code. On 1981-83 models, the eighth digit of the V.I.N. denotes engine code.
③—Ratings are NET—as installed on vehicle.
④—Except California.
⑤—With auto. trans.
⑥—Carter.

⑦—With manual trans.
⑧—California.
⑨—Granada & Monarch.
⑩—Comet & Maverick.
⑪—Motorcraft.
⑫—Holley.
⑬—Windsor engine.
⑭—Modified engine.
⑮—Thunderbird.

⑯—Cougar XR-7.
⑰—LTD II & Cougar.
⑱—Fairmont & Zephyr with auto. trans., Holley 1946.
⑲—Fairmont & Zephyr.
⑳—Non-Turbocharged.
㉑—Turbocharged.

TUNE UP SPECIFICATIONS

The following specifications are published from the latest information available. This data should be used only in the absence of a decal affixed in the engine compartment.

★ When using a timing light, disconnect vacuum hose or tube at distributor and plug opening in hose or tube so idle speed will not be affected.

● When checking compression, lowest cylinder must be within 75% of the highest.

▲ Before removing wires from distributor cap, determine location of the No. 1 wire in cap, as distributor position may have been altered from that shown at the end of this chart.

Spark plug types shown in this chart are recommendations of the original vehicle manufacturer and not MOTOR.

☞ Check local sources for other spark plug manufacturers listings.

Year & Engine/V.I.N.	Spark Plug Type ☞	Gap	Firing Order Fig. ▲	Ignition Timing BTDC① ★ Man. Trans.	Auto. Trans.	Mark Fig.	Curb Idle Speed② Man. Trans.	Auto. Trans.	Fast Idle Speed Man. Trans.	Auto. Trans.	Fuel Pump Pressure
1977											
6-200/T	BRF-82	.050	F	6°	6°	C	800	650D	1700③	1700③	5—7
6-250/L Exc. Calif.⑫⑬	BRF-82	.050	F	4°	6°	A	⑭	⑮	1700③	1700③	5—7
6-250/L Exc. Calif.⑧⑫⑯	BRF-82	.050	F	TDC	—	A	800	—	1700③	—	5—7
6-250/L Calif.	BRF-82	.050	F	—	8°	A	—	500/600D	—	2100③	5—7
V8-302/F Exc. Calif. & High Alt.⑦	ARF-52	.050	G	—	6°	B	—	700D	—	2100④	6—8
V8-302/F Exc. Calif. & High Alt.⑧	ARF-52	.050	G	6°	2°	B	800	650D	2100④	2100④	6—8
V8-302/F Exc. Calif. & High Alt.⑰	ARF-52	.050	G	—	2°	B	—	500/600D	—	2100④	6—8
V8-302/F Calif.⑦	ARF-52-6	.060	G	—	12°	B	—	500/600D	—	1900④	6—8
V8-302/F High Alt.⑫⑱	ARF-52-6	.060	G	—	12°	B	—	500/600D	—	1900④	6—8
V8-302/F High Alt.⑫⑲	ARF-52	.050	G	—	12°	B	—	500/650D	—	④⑳	6—8
V8-351W/H⑤⑧	ARF-52	.050	H	—	4°	B	—	625D	—	2100④	6—8
V8-351W/H⑤⑫⑰㉑	ARF-52	.050	H	—	14°	B	—	550/625D	—	2100④	6—8
V8-351W/H⑤⑫⑰㉒	ARF-52	.050	H	—	4°	B	—	625D	—	2100④	6—8
V8-351M/H Exc. Calif.⑥⑫⑰㉓	ARF-52	.050	H	—	10°	B	—	650D	—	1350③	6—8
V8-351M/H Exc. Calif.⑥⑫⑰㉔	ARF-52	.050	H	—	9°	B	—	650D	—	1350③	6—8
V8-351M/H Exc. Calif.⑥⑫⑰㉕	ASF-52	.050	H	—	8°	B	—	500/650D	—	1350③	6—8
V8-351M/H Calif.⑥⑫⑰㉖	ARF-52-6	.060	H	—	8°	B	—	500/600D	—	1350③	6—8
V8-351M/H Calif.⑥⑫⑰㉗	ARF-52-6	.060	H	—	6°	B	—	500/600D	—	1350③	6—8
V8-400/S Exc. Calif.⑫⑰㉘	ARF-52	.050	H	—	8°	B	—	600D	—	1350③	6—8
V8-400/S Exc. Calif.⑫⑰㉙	ARF-52	.050	H	—	12°	B	—	600D	—	1350③	6—8

Continued

TUNE UP SPECIFICATIONS—Continued

The following specifications are published from the latest information available. This data should be used only in the absence of a decal affixed in the engine compartment.

★ When using a timing light, disconnect vacuum hose or tube at distributor and plug opening in hose or tube so idle speed will not be affected.

● When checking compression, lowest cylinder must be within 75% of the highest.

▲ Before removing wires from distributor cap, determine location of the No. 1 wire in cap, as distributor position may have been altered from that shown at the end of this chart.

☞ Spark plug types shown in this chart are recommendations of the original vehicle manufacturer and not MOTOR.

Check local sources for other spark plug manufacturers listings.

Year & Engine/V.I.N.	Spark Plug Type ☞	Gap	Ignition Timing BTDC① ★ Firing Order Fig. ▲	Man. Trans.	Auto. Trans.	Mark Fig.	Curb Idle Speed② Man. Trans.	Auto. Trans.	Fast Idle Speed Man. Trans.	Auto. Trans.	Fuel Pump Pressure
1977—Continued											
V8-400/S Exc. Calif.⑫⑰㉚	ARF-52	.050	H	—	10°	B	—	600D	—	1350③	6–8
V8-400/S Exc. Calif.⑫⑰㉛	ARF-52	.050	H	—	6°	B	—	600D	—	1350③	6–8
V8-400/S Exc. Calif.⑫⑰㉜	ARF-52	.050	H	—	8°	B	—	500/650D	—	1350③	6–8
V8-400/S Calif.⑰	ARF-52-6	.060	H	—	6°	B	—	500/600D	—	1350③	6–8
1978											
4-140/Y	AWSF-42	.034	D	6°	20°	E	850	800D	1600③	2000④	5–7㉝
6-200/T Exc. Calif. & High Alt.	BSF-82	.050	F	10°	10°	C	800	650D	1700③	1700③	5–7
6-200/T Calif.	BSF-82	.050	F	—	6°	C	—	650D	—	1700③	5–7
6-200/T High Alt.⑫㉞	BSF-82	.050	F	—	12°	C	—	650D	—	1700③	5–7
6-200/T High Alt.⑫㉟	BSF-82	.050	F	—	10°	C	—	650D	—	1700③	5–7
6-250/L Exc. Calif.	BSF-82	.050	F	4°	14°	A	800	600/700D㊱	1700③	1700③	5–7
6-250/L Calif.	BSF-82	.050	F	—	6°	A	—	600/700D㊱	—	2000③	5–7
V8-302/F Exc. Calif. & High Alt.㊲	ARF-52	.050	G	—	6°	B	—	600/675D㊱	—	④⑫㊳	6–8
V8-302/F Exc. Calif. & High Alt.⑧	ARF-52	.050	G	—	2°	B	—	600/675D㊱	—	2100④	6–8
V8-302/F Exc. Calif. & High Alt.⑰	ARF-52	.050	G	—	14°	B	—	600D	—	2100④	6–8
V8-302/F Calif.	ARF-52-6	.060	G	—	12°	B	—	600D	—	1800④	6–8
V8-302/F High Alt.	ARF-52	.050	G	—	14°	B	—	650/725D㊱	—	2000④	6–8
V8-351W/H⑤	ARF-52	.050	H	—	14°	B	—	600/675D㊱	—	2100④	6–8
V8-351M/H Exc. Calif. & High Alt.⑥⑫㊴	ASF-52	.050	H	—	8°	B	—	650D	—	1350③	6–8
V8-351M/H Exc. Calif. & High Alt.⑥⑫㊵	ASF-52	.050	H	—	14°	B	—	㊱㊶	—	1350③	6–8
V8-351M/H Exc. Calif. & High Alt.⑥⑫㊷	ASF-52	.050	H	—	12°	B	—	600/675D㊱	—	1350③	6–8
V8-351M/H Exc. Calif. & High Alt.⑥⑫㊸	ASF-52	.050	H	—	9°	B	—	600/675D㊱	—	1350③	6–8
V8-351M/H Calif.	ASF-52	.050	H	—	16°	B	—	600/650D㊱	—	2300④	6–8
V8-351M/H High Alt.	ASF-52	.050	H	—	12°	B	—	650D	—	2200④	6–8
V8-400/S Exc. Calif. & High Alt.⑫㊹	ASF-52	.050	H	—	13°	B	—	575/650D㊱	—	1350③	6–8
V8-400/S Exc. Calif. & High Alt.⑫㊺	ASF-52	.050	H	—	14°	B	—	600/675D㊱	—	1350③	6–8
V8-400/S Calif.	ASF-52	.050	H	—	14°	B	—	600/675D	—	2300④	6–8
V8-400/S High Alt.	ASF-52	.050	H	—	8°	B	—	650D	—	2100④	6–8

Continued

FORD & MERCURY—Compact & Intermediate Models

TUNE UP SPECIFICATIONS—Continued

The following specifications are published from the latest information available. This data should be used only in the absence of a decal affixed in the engine compartment.

★ When using a timing light, disconnect vacuum hose or tube at distributor and plug opening in hose or tube so idle speed will not be affected.

● When checking compression, lowest cylinder must be within 75% of the highest.

▲ Before removing wires from distributor cap, determine location of the No. 1 wire in cap, as distributor position may have been altered from that shown at the end of this chart.

Spark plug types shown in this chart are recommendations of the original vehicle manufacturer and not MOTOR.

Check local sources for other spark plug manufacturers listings.

Year & Engine/V.I.N.	Spark Plug Type	Gap	Firing Order Fig. ▲	Ign. Man. Trans.	Ign. Auto. Trans.	Mark Fig.	Curb Man. Trans.	Curb Auto. Trans.	Fast Man. Trans.	Fast Auto. Trans.	Fuel Pump Pressure
1979											
4-140/Y Exc. Calif.	AWSF-42	.034	D	6°	20°	E	850/1300(36)	600/800	(3)(12)(51)	2000(3)	5-7(33)
4-140/Y Calif.	AWSF-42	.034	D	6°	17°	E	850	600/750	1800(3)	1800(3)	5-7(33)
6-200/T Exc. Calif.	(52)	.050	F	8°	10°	C	700/850(36)	650D	1600(3)	1700(3)	5-7
6-200/T Calif.	(52)	.050	F	—	6°	C	—	600/650D	—	2150(3)	5-7
6-250/L Exc. Calif.	(52)	.050	F	—	10°	A	—	600/700D	—	1700(3)	5-7
6-250/L Calif.	(52)	.050	F	—	6°	A	—	600/700D	—	2300(3)	5-7
V8-302/F Exc. Calif.	(46)	.050	G	12°	8°	B	800/850(36)	600/675D	2300(3)	2100(4)	6-8
V8-302/F Calif.	(53)	.060	G	—	12°	B	—	600/675D	—	1800(4)	6-8
V8-351W/H Exc. Calif.(5)(12)(49)	(46)	.050	H	—	15°	B	—	600/675D	—	2100(4)	6-8
V8-351W/H Exc. Calif.(5)(12)(50)	(46)	.050	H	—	10°	B	—	600/650D	—	2200(4)	6-8
V8-351M/H Exc. Calif.(6)	(46)	.050	H	—	12°	B	—	600/650D	—	2200(4)	6-8
V8-351M/H Calif.(6)	(46)	.050	H	—	14°	B	—	600/650D	—	2300(4)	6-8
1980											
4-140/A Exc. Calif.(12)(47)(55)(56)	AWSF-42	.034	D	—	20°	E	—	800D	—	2000(3)	5-7(33)
4-140/A Exc. Calif.(12)(47)(55)(57)	AWSF-42	.034	D	—	17°	E	—	800D	—	2000(3)	5-7(33)
4-140/A Exc. Calif.(47)(58)	AWSF-42	.034	D	6°	6°	E	850	750D	1800(3)	2000(3)	5-7(33)
4-140/A Calif.(47)	AWSF-42	.034	D	6°	12°	E	850	750D	2000(3)	2000(3)	5-7(33)
4-140/A(48)	AWSF-32	.034	D	6°	10°	E	—	800D	—	(3)(12)(59)	5-7(33)
6-200/B Exc. Calif.(12)(37)(55)(60)	BSF-82	.050	F	—	7°	C	—	550/700D	—	2000(3)	5-7
6-200/B Exc. Calif.(12)(37)(55)(61)	BSF-82	.050	F	—	10°	C	—	550/700D	—	2000(3)	5-7
6-200/B Exc. Calif.(37)(58)	BSF-82	.050	F	(12)(62)	10°	C	700	550/700D	1600(3)	2000(3)	5-7
6-200/B Exc. Calif.(58)(63)	BSF-82	.050	F	—	10°	C	—	625/700D	—	2000(3)	5-7
6-250/C(55)	BSF-82	.050	F	8°	—	A	600	—	1700(3)	—	5-7
6-250/C(58)	BSF-82	.050	F	4°	10°	A	700/800	550/650D	1700(3)	1700(3)	5-7
V8-255/D Exc. Calif. & High Alt.(64)	ASF-42	.050	G	—	6°	B	—	(12)(65)	—	(4)(12)(66)	6-8
V8-255/D Calif.(8)	ASF-42	.050	G	—	6°	B	—	500/650D	—	1800(4)	6-8
V8-255/D Calif.(64)	ASF-42	.050	G	—	6°	B	—	(12)(67)	—	2000(4)	6-8
V8-255/D High Alt.(37)	ASF-42	.050	G	—	6°	B	—	500/650D	—	2000(4)	6-8
V8-302/F Exc. Calif. & High Alt.(8)	ASF-52	.050	G	—	8°	B	—	(12)(68)	—	2100(4)	6-8
V8-302/F Exc. Calif. & High Alt.(12)(63)(69)	ASF-52	.050	G	—	8°	B	—	(12)(70)	—	2000(4)	6-8
V8-302/F Exc. Calif. & High Alt.(12)(63)(71)	ASF-52	.050	G	—	10°	B	—	500/650D	—	2000(4)	6-8

Continued

TUNE UP SPECIFICATIONS—Continued

The following specifications are published from the latest information available. This data should be used only in the absence of a decal affixed in the engine compartment.

★ When using a timing light, disconnect vacuum hose or tube at distributor and plug opening in hose or tube so idle speed will not be affected.

● When checking compression, lowest cylinder must be within 75% of the highest.

▲ Before removing wires from distributor cap, determine location of the No. 1 wire in cap, as distributor position may have been altered from that shown at the end of this chart.

Spark plug types shown in this chart are recommendations of the original vehicle manufacturer and not MOTOR.

Check local sources for other spark plug manufacturers listings.

Year & Engine/V.I.N.	Spark Plug Type ☞	Spark Plug Gap	Ignition Timing BTDC① ★ Firing Order Fig. ▲	Ignition Timing BTDC① ★ Man. Trans.	Ignition Timing BTDC① ★ Auto. Trans.	Ignition Timing BTDC① ★ Mark Fig.	Curb Idle Speed② Man. Trans.	Curb Idle Speed② Auto. Trans.	Fast Idle Speed Man. Trans.	Fast Idle Speed Auto. Trans.	Fuel Pump Pressure
1980—Continued											
V8-302/F Calif.⑧	ASF-52	.050	G	—	6°	B	—	500/650D	—	2100④	6–8
V8-302/F Calif. ⑫㉢㉜	ASF-52	.050	G	—	10°	B	—	500/650D	—	2000④	6–8
V8-302/F Calif. ⑫㉣㉝	ASF-52	.050	G	—	6°	B	—	⑫㉞	—	2100④	6–8
V8-302/F High Alt.⑧	ASF-52	.050	G	—	8°	B	—	500/650D	—	2000④	6–8
V8-302/F High Alt.㉢	ASF-52	.050	G	—	8°	B	—	⑫㉟	—	2000④	6–8
1981											
4-140/A	AWSF-42	.034	D	6°	12°	E	850⑨	750D㊆	2000③	2300③	5–7㉝
6-200/B⑩⑫	BSF-92	.050	F	—	10°	C	—	600D	—	2000③	5–7㉝
6-200/B⑪⑫	BSF-92	.050	F	—	12°	C	—	600D	—	2000③	5–7㉝
V8-255/D Exc. Calif. ㊄	ASF-52	.050	G	—	10°	B	—	500D	—	1600③	6–8
V8-255/D Exc. Calif.㊆	ASF-52	.050	G	—	10°	B	—	500D	—	1700③	6–8
V8-255/D Calif. ㊄	ASF-52	.050	G	—	8°	B	—	500/650D	—	1500③	6–8
V8-255/D Calif.㊆	ASF-52	.050	G	—	12°	B	—	500/650D	—	1500③	6–8
V8-302/F Exc. Calif.	ASF-52	.050	G	—	10°	B	—	500D	—	1600③	6–8
V8-302/F Calif.	ASF-52	.050	G	—	8°	B	—	500/675D	—	1600③	6–8
1982											
4-140/A Exc. Calif.	AWSF-42	.034	D	6°	12°	E	850	800D	1800③	2000③	5–7㉝
4-140/A Calif.	AWSF-42	.034	D	4°	12°	E	850	800D	1600③	1800③	5–7㉝
6-200/B Exc. High Alt.	BSF-92	.050	F	—	10°	C	—	450/600D	—	2000③	5–7㉝
6-200/B High Alt.	BSF-92	.050	F	—	12°	C	—	450/600D	—	2000③	5–7㉝
V6-232/3 Exc. Calif. & High Alt.	AGSP-52	.044	I	—	㊍	J	—	550/650D	—	2200④	6–8
V6-232/3 Calif.	AGSP-52	.044	I	—	12°	J	—	550/650D	—	1200③	6–8
V6-232/3 High Alt.	AGSP-52	.044	I	—	12°	J	—	550/650D	—	2100③	6–8
V8-255/D Exc. High Alt.	ASF-52	.050	G	—	8°	B	—	500/650D	—	1500③	6–8
V8-255/D High Alt.	ASF-52	.050	G	—	14°	B	—	500/650D	—	1700③	6–8
1983											
4-140/A	AWSF-44	.044	D	—	—	E	850	800D	—	—	5.5–6.5
6-200/X	BSF-92	.050	F	—	—	C	—	550	—	—	6–8
V6-232/3	AWSF-52	.044	I	—	—	J	—	㊐	—	—	6–8

①—B.T.D.C.—Before top dead center.
②—Idle speed on manual trans. vehicles is adjusted in Neutral & on auto. trans. equipped vehicles is adjusted in Drive unless otherwise specified. Where two idle speeds are listed, the higher speed is with the A/C or throttle solenoid energized. On models equipped with vacuum release brake, whenever adjusting ignition timing or idle speed, vacuum line to brake release mechanism must be disconnected & plugged to prevent parking brake from releasing when selector lever is moved to Drive.
③—On kickdown step of cam.
④—On high step of fast idle cam.
⑤—Windsor engine.
⑥—Modified engine.
⑦—Comet & Maverick.
⑧—Granada & Monarch.
⑨—If mileage on vehicle is less than 100 mi., set idle at 100 RPM less than specified.
⑩—Calibration code 1-12B-R0.
⑪—Calibration code 1-12B-R10.
⑫—Refer to engine calibration code on engine identification label, located at rear of left valve cover on V6 & V8 engines, on front of valve cover on in line 4 & 6 cyl. engines. The calibration code is located on the label after the engine code number is preceded by the letter C and the revision code is located below the calibration code and is preceded by the letter R.

TUNE UP NOTES—Continued

⑬—Calibration codes, man. trans. 7-8A-R2, 7-8A-R3 & 7-8A-R10; auto. trans. 7-29A-R1, 7-29A-R3 & 7-29A-R15.
⑭—Calibration code 7-8A-R2, 850 RPM; 6-8A-R3 & 7-8A-410, 800 RPM.
⑮—Calibration codes 7-29A-R1 & 7-29A-R3, 600D RPM; 7-29A-R15, less A/C 600D RPM, with A/C 700D RPM.
⑯—Calibration code 7-8A-R12.
⑰—LTD II, Cougar & Thunderbird.
⑱—Calibration codes, Comet & Maverick 7-11Z-R0; Granada & Monarch, 7-11Y-R2.
⑲—Calibration codes, 7-11Z-R4 & 7-11Z-R6; Granada & Monarch, 7-11Y-R4 & 7-11Y-R6.
⑳—Except calibration code 7-11Z-R4, 2000 RPM; calibration code 7-11Z-R4, 2100 RPM.
㉑—Calibration code 7-32B-R1.
㉒—Calibration codes 7-32B-R10 & 7-32B-R12.
㉓—Calibration codes 7-14A-R1 & 7-14B-R1.
㉔—Calibration codes 7-14A-R10, 7-14B-R10 & 7-14C-R11.
㉕—Calibration codes 7-34A-R0 & 7-34B-R0.
㉖—Calibration codes 7-14N-R0 & 7-14N-R12.
㉗—Calibration codes 7-14N-R13 & 7-14N-R17.
㉘—Calibration code 7-17B-R1.
㉙—Calibration code 7-17B-R15.
㉚—Calibration code 7-17B-R16.
㉛—Calibration code 7-17C-R1.
㉜—Calibration codes 7-37A-R0 & 7-37A-R1.
㉝—With pump to fuel tank return line pinched off & a new fuel filter installed.
㉞—Calibration code 8-7Z-R0.
㉟—Calibration code 8-7Z-R2.
㊱—With throttle solenoid energized. Higher idle speed is with A/C on & compressor clutch de-energized, if equipped.

㊲—Fairmont & Zephyr.
㊳—Calibration code 8-31B-R0, 1900 RPM; 8-11M-R0 & 8-11M-R16, 2100 RPM.
㊴—Calibration code 8-14H-R0.
㊵—Calibration codes 8-14A-R12 & 8-34A-R0.
㊶—Calibration code 8-14A-R12, 600/675D RPM; 8-34A-R0, 600/650D RPM.
㊷—Calibration code 8-14A-R22.
㊸—Calibration code 8-14A-R0.
㊹—Calibration codes 8-17A-R0 & 8-17C-R0.
㊺—Calibration code 8-37A-R0.
㊻—ASF-52 or ARF-52.
㊼—Except turbocharged engine.
㊽—Turbocharged engine.
㊾—Calibration code, 9-12E-R0.
㊿—Calibration code, 9-12G-R0.
51—Calibration codes 9-2A-R0 & 9-2B-R0 1800 RPM; calibration codes 9-2C-R0 & 9-2D-R0, 1600 RPM.
52—BSF-82 or BRF-82.
53—ASF-52-6 or ARF-52-6.
54—Models less Automatic Overdrive Transmission
55—Models less Thermactor pump.
56—Calibration code 9-21B-R10.
57—Calibration codes 0-21A-R0 & 0-21B-R0.
58—Models w/Thermactor pump.
59—Calibration codes 0-1H-R10, R11, R15 & 0-1S-R0, R10 & R11, 2000 RPM; calibration codes 0-1H-R19, R20 & 0-1S-R15, 2150 RPM.
60—Calibration code 0-27A-R3.
61—Calibration code 0-27A-R10.
62—Calibration code 0-6A-R0, 10° BTDC; calibration code, 0-6B-R1, 12° BTDC.
63—Cougar XR-7 & Thunderbird.

64—Cougar, Fairmont, Thunderbird & Zephyr.
65—Calibration codes 0-16C-R0 & R15, 500/650D; calibration code 0-16C-R13, 550/700D; calibration code 0-16C-R18, 550/625D; calibration code 0-16C-R19, 500/625D.
66—Except calibration code 0-16C-R0, 1800 RPM; calibration code 0-16C-R0, 2000 RPM.
67—Calibration code 0-16S-R14, 500/650D RPM; calibration code 0-16S-R17, 500/625D RPM.
68—Calibration code 9-11C-R1, 600/675D RPM; calibration code 0-11D-R0, 500/650D RPM.
69—Calibration codes 0-11A-R0 & R10.
70—Calibration code 0-11A-R0, 500/650D RPM; calibration code 0-11A-R10, 500/625D RPM.
71—Calibration code 0-11B-R0.
72—Calibration codes 0-11P-R12 & R13.
73—Calibration codes 0-11N-R0, R10, R11 & R13.
74—Calibration codes 0-11N-R0 & R10, 500/650D RPM; calibration codes 0-11N-R11 & R13, 500/625D RPM.
75—Calibration code 0-11W-R0, 500/700D RPM; calibration code 0-11W-R10, 550/625D RPM.
76—If mileage on vehicle is less than 100 mi., set idle at 50 RPM less than specified.
77—Models with Automatic Overdrive Transmission.
78—Cougar & Granada, 10°BTDC; Cougar XR-7 & Thunderbird, 12°BTDC.
79—Exc. Calif., 700D; Calif., 650D; A/C blower on, A/C compressor off.

Fig. A

Fig. B

Fig. C

FIRING ORDER 1-3-4-2

Fig. D

Fig. E

FIRING ORDER 1-5-3-6-2-4

Fig. F

TUNE UP NOTES—Continued

Fig. G

Fig. H

Fig. I

Fig. J

DISTRIBUTOR SPECIFICATIONS

★Note: If unit is checked on vehicle, double the RPM and degrees to get crankshaft figures.

Distributor Ident. No. ①	Centrifugal Advance Degrees @ RPM of Distributor					Vacuum Advance		Distributor Retard
	Advance Starts	Intermediate Advance			Full Advance	Inches of Vacuum to Start Plunger	Max. Adv. Dist. Deg. @ Vacuum	Max. Retard Dist. Deg. @ Vacuum
1977								
D5DE-AFA	$-3/4$ to $+1\frac{1}{4}$ @ 500	$3-5\frac{1}{4}$ @ 700	—	—	$6\frac{1}{2}$ @ 1000	5	$13\frac{1}{4}$ @ 15	—
D6DE-JA	$1-4$ @ 500	$5-7\frac{1}{4}$ @ 700	—	—	$9\frac{1}{2}$ @ 1000	5	$13\frac{1}{4}$ @ 15	—
D6AE-AA	$0-2$ @ 500	$4-6$ @ 700	$7\frac{3}{4}-9\frac{1}{2}$ @ 1500	—	14 @ 2500	3	$13\frac{3}{4}$ @ $11\frac{1}{2}$	—
D7AE-BA	$0-1$ @ 425	$2\frac{3}{4}-4\frac{3}{4}$ @ 625	—	—	$13\frac{1}{2}$ @ 2250	3.5	$15\frac{1}{4}$ @ 12	—
D7AE-CA	$0-1$ @ 700	$3\frac{1}{2}-6$ @ 1600	—	—	$10\frac{3}{4}$ @ 2500	3	$15\frac{1}{2}$ @ 11	—
D7AE-DA	$0-1$ @ 450	$3\frac{3}{4}-5\frac{3}{4}$ @ 675	—	—	14 @ 2500	3.2	$15\frac{1}{2}$ @ $14\frac{1}{2}$	—
D7BE-CA	—	—	—	—	—	—	—	—
D7BE-DA	$0-1$ @ 500	$1\frac{3}{4}-3\frac{3}{4}$ @ 600	—	—	$8\frac{1}{2}$ @ 2500	3	$11\frac{1}{4}$ @ 11	—
D7BE-EA	$0-1$ @ 550	$4\frac{3}{4}-6\frac{3}{4}$ @ 625	—	—	$13\frac{3}{4}$ @ 2450	3	$11\frac{1}{4}$ @ $13\frac{1}{2}$	—
D7BE-FA	$0-1$ @ 500	$1-3$ @ 575	—	—	$8\frac{1}{4}$ @ 2500	3.1	$7\frac{1}{4}$ @ $6\frac{1}{2}$	—
D7DE-CA	$0-1$ @ 450	$4\frac{3}{4}-6\frac{3}{4}$ @ 700	—	—	$15\frac{1}{2}$ @ 2500	3	$15\frac{1}{4}$ @ 11	—
D7DE-DA	—	—	—	—	—	—	—	—
D7DE-FA	$0-1$ @ 425	$2\frac{1}{2}-4\frac{1}{2}$ @ 575	—	—	$13\frac{3}{4}$ @ 2500	3	$15\frac{1}{4}$ @ $13\frac{1}{2}$	—
D7DE-GA	$0-1$ @ 525	$2\frac{1}{4}-4\frac{1}{4}$ @ 700	—	—	$7\frac{1}{4}$ @ 2500	3	$13\frac{1}{4}$ @ 13	—
D7OE-CA	$0-1$ @ 450	$2\frac{3}{4}-4\frac{3}{4}$ @ 575	—	—	16 @ 2500	3.5	$15\frac{1}{4}$ @ $14\frac{1}{2}$	—
D7ZE-BA	$0-1$ @ 425	$6-8$ @ 650	—	—	16 @ 2500	3.5	$13\frac{1}{4}$ @ 15.2	—
1978								
D7AE-UA	$0-1$ @ 650	$0-2$ @ 700	—	—	$10\frac{1}{2}$ @ 2500	4	$13\frac{1}{2}$ @ 15	—

Continued

DISTRIBUTOR SPECIFICATIONS—Continued

★Note: If unit is checked on vehicle, double the RPM and degrees to get crankshaft figures.

| Distributor Ident. No.① | Centrifugal Advance Degrees @ RPM of Distributor | | | | | Vacuum Advance | | Distributor Retard |
	Advance Starts	Intermediate Advance			Full Advance	Inches of Vacuum to Start Plunger	Max. Adv. Dist. Deg. @ Vacuum	Max. Retard Dist. Deg. @ Vacuum
1978—Continued								
D7BE-GA	0–1 @ 500	2–2¾ @ 600	—	—	8¾ @ 2500	3	7¼ @ 7	—
D7DE-AA	0–1 @ 500	1¾–4 @ 750	—	—	12½ @ 2500	3	13¼ @ 14	—
D7DE-CA	0–1 @ 450	5–8 @ 700	—	—	15¼ @ 2500	3	15¼ @ 11½	—
D7EE-CA	0–1 @ 800	1–3½ @ 1500	—	—	7½ @ 2500	2.3	13¾ @ 15¾	—
D7EE-DA	0–1 @ 510	3¾–5¾ @ 725	—	—	14 @ 2500	1.75	13¼ @ 12.4	—
D7EE-EA	0–1 @ 525	3.6–5.6 @ 725	—	—	14 @ 2500	2	13¼ @ 15¾	—
D8AE-BA	0–1 @ 450	4–6 @ 700	—	—	14 @ 2500	4.5	17¼ @ 14½	—
D8AE-CA	0–1 @ 1100	3½–6 @ 1600	—	—	9½ @ 2500	3	12½ @ 14	—
D8AE-GA	0–1 @ 450	3½–5½ @ 700	—	—	8¼ @ 2500	5.5	15¼ @ 16½	—
D8AE-HA	0–1 @ 450	4–6 @ 700	—	—	14 @ 2500	3.25	17¼ @ 13½	—
D8AE-JA	0–1 @ 700	2¾–6½ @ 1500	—	—	10½ @ 2400	3.25	15½ @ 13	—
D8AE-LA	0–1 @ 775	3½–5½ @ 1350	—	—	9¼ @ 2500	3.75	17¼ @ 14½	—
D8BE-CA	0–1 @ 1000	—	—	—	4¾ @ 2500	3	11¼ @ 11½	—
D8BE-EA	0–1 @ 550	2¾–4¾ @ 1100	—	—	9½ @ 2500	4.5	11¼ @ 12½	—
D8BE-FA	0–1 @ 500	1½–3½ @ 600	—	—	9½ @ 2500	3.5	11¼ @ 13½	—
D8BE-JA	0–1 @ 550	5½–7½ @ 1050	—	—	10½ @ 2500	3.5	9¼ @ 13	—
D8DE-CA	0–1 @ 1000	1–3 @ 600	—	—	4¾ @ 2500	3	11¼ @ 11½	—
D8DE-EA	0–1 @ 450	3–5 @ 600	—	—	12¼ @ 2500	2	13¼ @ 10.8	—
D8ZE-CA	0–1 @ 575	6–7¾ @ 1200	—	—	11½ @ 2500	2.5	12¼ @ 15.7	—
1979								
D7AE-UA	0–2 @ 730	—	—	—	10¼ @ 2500	2.3	13¼ @ 25	—
D7DE-AA	0–1 @ 525	1¾–4 @ 750	—	—	12½ @ 2500	3	15¼ @ 11	—
D7EE-CA	0–1 @ 800	1–3½ @ 1500	—	—	7½ @ 2500	2.3	13¼ @ 15¾	—
D7EE-DA	0–1 @ 510	3¾–5¾ @ 725	—	—	14 @ 2500	1.75	13¼ @ 12.4	—
D7EE-EA	0–1 @ 525	3.6–5.6 @ 725	—	—	14 @ 2500	2	13¼ @ 15¾	—
D7EE-HA	0–2½ @ 1200	—	—	—	7½ @ 2500	2.3	13¼ @ 15¾	—
D8BE-EA	0–1 @ 550	2¾–4¾ @ 1100	—	—	9½ @ 2500	4.5	11¼ @ 12½	—
D8BE-JA	0–1 @ 550	5½–7½ @ 1050	—	—	10½ @ 2500	3.5	9¼ @ 13	—
D8DE-CA	0–1 @ 475	1–3 @ 600	—	—	9 @ 2500	2	13¼ @ 10.8	—
D8DE-EA	0–1 @ 450	3–5 @ 600	—	—	12¼ @ 2500	3	13¼ @ 14	—
D8OE-AA	0–2¾ @ 500	6–7 @ 725	—	—	16.3 @ 2500	2	15¼ @ 25	—
D9AE-PA	0–3¾ @ 550	1¾–4⅛ @ 610	—	—	7⅛ @ 2500	2	17¼ @ 25	—
D9BE-CA	0–1 @ 700	4 @ 1100	—	—	7½ @ 2500	4	12 @ 14	—
D9DE-CA	0–1 @ 1000	1–3 @ 600	—	—	6½ @ 2500	3	11¼ @ 11½	—
D9SE-AA	0–2 @ 500	2–4 @ 600	—	—	6¼ @ 2500	2.8	17¼ @ 25	—
D9TE-BA	0–1 @ 550	2¾–4¾ @ 1100	—	—	9½ @ 2500	4.5	11¼ @ 15¾	—
D9ZE-CA	0–3 @ 500	2¾–4⅞ @ 590	—	—	12¾ @ 2500	2.8	17¾ @ 15½	—
D97E-CA	0–1 @ 450	3–5 @ 600	—	—	13 @ 2500	4	8½ @ 13	—
1980								
D8BE-EA	1 @ 550	5 @ 1100	—	—	8 @ 2500	4.5	9½ @ 12.5	—
D8BE-JA	1 @ 550	7½ @ 1050	—	—	10½ @ 2500	3.5	9¼ @ 13	—
D9BE-DA	1 @ 675	4½ @ 925	—	—	9½ @ 2500	4.5	11¼ @ 13.5	—
D9DE-CA	1 @ 1000	3 @ 600	—	—	6½ @ 2500	4	11¼ @ 11.5	—
D9ZE-CA	3 @ 500	5 @ 590	—	—	13¾ @ 2500	4.8	17¼ @ 13.2	—
D94E-AA	—	—	—	—	—	—	—	—
EOEE-BA	2½ @ 610	3 @ 650	—	—	13 @ 2500	4	9¼ @ 25	—
EOEE-CA	2½ @ 580	5¾ @ 740	—	—	14 @ 2500	4½	13¼ @ 25	—
EOEE-DA	3½ @ 600	5¾ @ 730	—	—	14 @ 2500	5	13¼ @ 25	—
EOEE-FA	2½ @ 1140	—	—	—	8 @ 2500	5	9¼ @ 25	—
EOSE-CA	2 @ 635	5 @ 840	—	—	13 @ 2500	5	13¼ @ 25	—
EOZE-AA	2 @ 635	5 @ 840	—	—	12 @ 2500	5	8½ @ 25	—

Continued

DISTRIBUTOR SPECIFICATIONS—Continued

★ Note: If unit is checked on vehicle, double the RPM and degrees to get crankshaft figures.

Distributor Ident. No.①	Centrifugal Advance Degrees @ RPM of Distributor				Vacuum Advance		Distributor Retard
	Advance Starts	Intermediate Advance		Full Advance	Inches of Vacuum to Start Plunger	Max. Adv. Dist. Deg. @ Vacuum	Max. Retard Dist. Deg. @ Vacuum
1980—Continued							
E0ZE-BA	1¾ @ 540	5 @ 760	—	11¼ @ 2500	4	11¼ @ 25	—
E0ZE-EA	2½ @ 540	5 @ 675	—	8 @ 2500	5	13 @ 25	—
1981							
D8BE-EA	—	3–5½ @ 1250	—	—	—	—	—
E0BE-BA	—	—	—	—	—	—	—
E0EE-BA	—	2½–6½ @ 1250	—	—	—	—	—
E0EE-DA	—	6–8½ @ 1250	—	—	—	—	—
E1BE-BA	—	—	—	—	—	—	—
E1BE-DA	—	—	—	—	—	—	—
E1SE-CA	—	—	—	—	—	—	—
E1SE-DA	—	—	—	—	—	—	—
E1SE-FA	—	—	—	—	—	—	—
1982							
E0EE-CA③	—	8.5–11 @ 1250	—	—	—	—	—
E0EE-CA④	—	7.5–10 @ 1250	—	—	—	—	—
E0EE-DA	—	8–11.5 @ 1250	—	—	—	—	—
E0EE-BA	—	9.5–12.5 @ 1250	—	—	—	—	—
E2BE-CA	—	8–11.5 @ 1250	—	—	—	—	—
E1BE-EA	—	9.5–11.5 @ 1250	—	—	—	—	—
E2DE-AA	—	5–7.5 @ 1250	—	—	—	—	—
E2SE-DA	—	8.5–11 @ 1250	—	—	—	—	—
E2SE-BA	—	9.5–11.5 @ 1250	—	—	—	—	—
E2SE-CA	—	11–13.5 @ 1250	—	—	—	—	—
E2SE-AA⑤	—	7–9.5 @ 1250	—	—	—	—	—
E1BE-DA	—	10–12.5 @ 1250	—	—	—	—	—
E2SE-AA⑥	—	10–12.5 @ 1250	—	—	—	—	—
1983							
E3ZE-DA	—	—	—	—	—	—	—
E2SE-CA	—	—	—	—	—	—	—

①—Basic Ident. No. 12127.
②—EEC System distributor.
③—Models w/5-speed transmission.
④—Models w/4-speed transmission.
⑤—Exc. Calif.
⑥—California.

STARTING MOTOR SPECIFICATIONS

Year	Engine/ V.I.N.	Ident. No.	Brush Spring Tension, Ounces	No Load Test			Torque Test		
				Amperes	Volts	R.P.M.	Amperes	Volts	Torque Ft. Lbs.
1977	6-200/T	D6BF-AA, BA	80	80	12	—	670	5	15.5
	6-250, V8-302, 351/①⑤	D6OF-AA	80	80	12	—	670	5	15.5
	V8-351/H①	D6DF-AA	80	80	12	—	670	5	15.5
	V8-351/H②	D5AF-EA	80	80	12	—	670	5	15.5
	V8-400/S	D6OF-AA	80	80	12	—	670	5	15.5
1978	4-140/Y③	D8BF-AA	40	70	12	—	460	5	9
	4-140/Y④	D8EF-AA	40	70	12	—	460	5	9
	6-200/T③	D8BF-AA	80	80	12	—	670	5	15.5

Continued

STARTING MOTOR SPECIFICATIONS—Continued

Year	Engine/ V.I.N.	Ident. No.	Brush Spring Tension, Ounces	No Load Test			Torque Test		
				Amperes	Volts	R.P.M.	Amperes	Volts	Torque Ft. Lbs.
	6-200/T④	D8BF-CA	80	80	12	—	670	5	15.5
	6-250/L	D8OF-AA	80	80	12	—	670	5	15.5
	V8-302/F	D8OF-AA	80	80	12	—	670	5	15.5
	V8-351/H①	D8OF-AA	80	80	12	—	670	5	15.5
	V8-351/H②	D8AF-AA	80	80	12	—	670	5	15.5
	V8-400/S	D8AF-AA	80	80	12	—	670	5	15.5
1979	V8-351/H①	D8OF-AA	80	80	12	—	670	5	15.5
	V8-351/H②	D8AF-AA	80	80	12	—	670	5	15.5
	4-140/Y	D8EF-AA	40	70	12	—	460	5	9
	6-200/T③	D8BF-AA	80	80	12	—	670	5	15.5
	6-200/T④	D8BF-CA	80	80	12	—	670	5	15.5
	6-250/L	D8OF-AA	80	80	12	—	670	5	15.5
	V8-255, 302/⑤	D8OF-AA	80	80	12	—	670	5	15.5
1980	4-140/A	D8EF-AA	80	80	12	—	460	5	9
	6-200/B③	D8BF-AA	40–80	85	12	—	670	5	15.5
	6-200/B④	D8BF-CA	40–80	85	12	—	670	5	15.5
	6-250/C	D8OF-AA	40–80	85	12	—	670	5	15.5
	V8-255, 302/⑤	D8OF-AA	40–80	85	12	—	670	5	15.5
1981	4-140/A	E1ZF-AA	80	80	12	—	460	5	9
	6-200/B	E1BF-BA	40–80	85	12	—	670	5	15.5
	V8-255, 302/⑤	E1AF-BA	40–80	85	12	—	670	5	15.5
1982	4-140/A	E2BF-AA	80	80	12	—	460	5	9
	6-200/B	E1AF-BA	40–80	85	12	—	670	5	15.5
	V6-232/3	E25F-AA	40–80	85	12	—	670	5	15.5
	V8-255/D	E1AF-BA	40–80	85	12	—	670	5	15.5
1983	4-140/A	—	80	80	12	—	500	5	9.5
	6-200/X	—	80	85	12	—	670	5	15.5
	V6-232/3	—	80	85	12	—	670	5	15.5

①—Windsor engine.
②—Modified engine.

③—Manual trans.
④—Auto. trans.

⑤—For V.I.N. code, refer to the "General Engine Specifications" at the beginning of the chapter.

ALTERNATOR & REGULATOR SPECIFICATIONS

Year	Color Code Stamp	Current Rating①		Field Current @ 75°F.		Voltage Regulator				Field Relay	
		Amperes	Volts	Amperes	Volts	Model No. (10316)	Voltage @ 75°F.	Contact Gap	Armature Air Gap	Armature Air Gap	Closing Voltage @ 75°F.
1977	Orange③⑦	40	15	2.9	12	D4AF-AA	13.5–15.3	④	④	④	2.5–4.0
	Green③⑦	60	15	2.9	12	D4AF-AA	13.5–15.3	④	④	④	2.5–4.0
	All⑧	70	15	2.9	12	D4TF-AA	13.5–15.3	④	④	④	2.5–4.0
	All⑧	90	15	2.9	12	D4TF-AA	13.5–15.3	④	④	④	2.5–4.0
1978	Orange③⑦	40	15	2.9	12	D4AF-AA	13.5–14.3	④	④	④	—
	Green③⑦	60	15	2.9	12	D4AF-AA	13.5–14.3	④	④	④	—
	Green③⑤⑦	60	15	4.0	12	D8BF-AA⑥	13.8–14.6	④	④	④	—
	Black③⑧	70	15	2.9	12	D4TF-AA	13.5–14.3	④	④	④	—
	Red③⑧	90	15	2.9	12	D4TF-AA	13.5–14.3	④	④	④	—
	Red③⑤⑧	90	15	4.0	12	D8BF-AA⑥	13.8–14.6	④	④	④	—
1979	Orange③⑤⑦	40	15	4.0	12	D8BF-AA⑥	13.8–14.6	④	④	④	—
	Green③⑤⑦	60	15	4.0	12	D8BF-AA⑥	13.8–14.6	④	④	④	—
	Black③⑤⑦	65	15	4.0	12	D8BF-AA⑥	13.8–14.6	④	④	④	—
	Black③⑤⑧	70	15	4.0	12	D8BF-AA⑥	13.8–14.6	④	④	④	—
	Red③⑤⑧	100	15	4.0	12	D8BF-AA⑥	13.8–14.6	④	④	④	—
1980–81	Orange③⑤⑦	40	15	4.0	12	D9BF-AB⑥	13.8–14.6	④	④	④	—

Continued

ALTERNATOR & REGULATOR SPECIFICATIONS—Continued

Year	Color Code Stamp	Current Rating①		Field Current @ 75°F.		Voltage Regulator				Field Relay	
		Amperes	Volts	Amperes	Volts	Model No. (10316)	Voltage @ 75°F.	Contact Gap	Armature Air Gap	Armature Air Gap	Closing Voltage @ 75°F.
	Green③⑤⑦	60	15	4.0	12	D9BF-AB⑥	13.8–14.6	④	④	④	—
	Black③⑤⑦	65	15	4.0	12	D9BF-AB⑥	13.8–14.6	④	④	④	—
	Black③⑤⑧	70	15	4.0	12	D9BF-AB⑥	13.8–14.6	④	④	④	—
	Red③⑤⑧	100	15	4.0	12	D9BF-AB⑥	13.8–14.6	④	④	④	—
1982	Orange③⑤⑦	40	15	4.0	12	E1AF-AA⑥	13.8–14.6	④	④	④	—
	Green③⑤⑦	60	15	4.0	12	E1AF-AA⑥	13.8–14.6	④	④	④	—
	Black③⑤⑦	65	15	4.0	12	E1AF-AA⑥	13.8–14.6	④	④	④	—
	Black③⑤⑧	70	15	4.0	12	E1AF-AA⑥	13.8–14.6	④	④	④	—
	Red③⑤⑧	100	15	4.0	12	E1AF-AA⑥	13.8–14.6	④	④	④	—
1983	Orange③⑤⑦	40	15	4.25	12	—	—	—	—	—	—
	Black③⑤⑦	65	15	4.25	12	—	—	—	—	—	—
	Green③⑤⑦	60	15	4.25	12	—	—	—	—	—	—
	Black③⑤⑧	70	15	4.25	12	—	—	—	—	—	—
	Red③⑤⑧	100	15	4.25	12	—	—	—	—	—	—

①—Current rating stamped on housing.
②—Voltage regulation stamped on cover.
③—Stamp color.
④—Not adjustable.
⑤—Solid state alternator.
⑥—Electronic voltage regulator. These units are color coded black for systems w/warning indicator lamp & blue for systems w/ammeter.
⑦—Rear terminal alternator.
⑧—Side terminal alternator.

VALVE SPECIFICATIONS

Year	Engine/V.I.N.	Valve Lash		Valve Angles		Valve Spring Installed Height	Valve Spring Pressure Lbs. @ In.	Stem Clearance		Stem Diameter, Standard	
		Int.	Exh.	Seat	Face			Intake	Exhaust	Intake	Exhaust
1977	6-200/T	.110–.160④		45	44	1³⁷⁄₆₄	⑱	.0008–.0025	.0010–.0027	.3100–.3107	.3098–.3105
	6-250/L	.096–.184④		45	44	1³⁷⁄₆₄	⑲	.0008–.0025	.0010–.0027	.3100–.3107	.3098–.3105
	V8-302/F	.096–.168④		45	44	⑨	⑮	.0010–.0027	.0015–.0032	.3416–.3423	.3411–.3418
	V8-351/H⑧	.096–.168④		45	44	⑦	⑫	.0010–.0027	.0015–.0032	.3416–.3423	.3411–.3418
	V8-351/H⑤, 400/S	.125–.175④		45	44	1⁵³⁄₆₄	226 @ 1.39	.0010–.0027	.0015–.0032	.3416–.3423	.3411–.3418
1978	4-140/Y	.040–.050⑥		45	44	1⁹⁄₁₆	189 @ 1.16	.0010–.0027	.0015–.0032	.3416–.3423	.3411–.3418
	6-200/T	.110–.160④		45	44	1³⁷⁄₆₄	150 @ 1.22	.0008–.0025	.0010–.0027	.3100–.3107	.3098–.3105
	6-250/L	.096–.184④		45	44	1³⁷⁄₆₄	150 @ 1.22	.0008–.0025	.0010–.0027	.3100–.3107	.3098–.3105
	V8-302/F①	.096–.168④		45	44	⑭	⑮	.0010–.0027	.0015–.0032	.3416–.3423	.3411–.3418
	V8-302/F②	③④		45	44	⑭	⑮	.0010–.0027	.0015–.0032	.3416–.3423	.3411–.3418
	V8-351/H①⑧	.096–.168④		45	44	⑦	⑫	.0010–.0027	.0015–.0032	.3416–.3423	.3411–.3418
	V8-351/H②⑧	.142④		45	44	⑦	⑫	.0010–.0027	.0015–.0032	.3416–.3423	.3411–.3418
	V8-351/H	.125–.175④		45	44	1⁵³⁄₆₄	226 @ 1.39	.0010–.0027	.0015–.0032	.3416–.3423	.3411–.3418
	V8-400/S	.125–.175④		45	44	1⁵³⁄₆₄	226 @ 1.39	.0010–.0027	.0015–.0032	.3416–.3423	.3411–.3418
1979	4-140/Y	.040–.050⑥		45	44	1⁹⁄₁₆	187 @ 1.16	.0010–.0027	.0015–.0032	.3416–.3423	.3411–.3416
	6-200/T	.110–.160④		45	44	1³⁷⁄₆₄	150 @ 1.22	.0008–.0025	.0010–.0027	.3100–.3107	.3098–.3105
	6-250/L	.096–.184④		45	44	1³⁷⁄₆₄	150 @ 1.22	.0008–.0025	.0010–.0027	.3100–.3107	.3098–.3105
	V8-302/F	.096–.165④		45	44	⑨	⑩	.0010–.0027	.0015–.0032	.3416–.3423	.3411–.3418
	V8-351/H⑧	.123–.173④		45	44	⑪	⑰	.0010–.0027	.0015–.0032	.3416–.3423	.3411–.3418
	V8-351/H⑤	.125–.175④		45	44	1⁵³⁄₆₄	226 @ 1.39	.0010–.0027	.0015–.0032	.3416–.3423	.3411–.3418
1980	4-140/A	.040–.050⑥		45	44	1⁹⁄₁₆	167 @ 1.16	.0010–.0027	.0015–.0032	.3416–.3423	.3411–.3418
	6-200/B	.110–.184④		45	44	1³⁷⁄₆₄	150 @ 1.22	.0008–.0025	.0010–.0027	.3100–.3107	.3098–.3105
	6-250/C	.096–.160④		45	44	1³⁷⁄₆₄	150 @ 1.22	.0008–.0025	.0010–.0027	.3100–.3107	.3098–.3105
	V8-255/D	.071–.193④		45	44	⑨	⑩	.0010–.0027	.0015–.0032	.3416–.3423	.3411–.3418
	V8-302/F	.071–.193④		45	44	⑨	⑬	.0010–.0027	.0015–.0032	.3416–.3423	.3411–.3418
1981	4-140/A	.040–.050⑥		45	44	1⁹⁄₁₆	167 @ 1.16	.0010–.0027	.0015–.0032	.3416–.3423	.3411–.3418
	6-200/B	.110–.160④		45	44	1³⁷⁄₆₄	150 @ 1.22	.0008–.0025	.0010–.0027	.3100–.3107	.3098–.3105
	V8-255/D	.096–.146④		45	44	⑨	⑭	.0010–.0027	.0015–.0032	.3416–.3423	.3411–.3418
	V8-302/F	.096–.146④		45	44	⑨	⑭	.0010–.0027	.0015–.0032	.3416–.3423	.3411–.3418
1982	4-140/A	.040–.050⑥		45	44	1⁹⁄₁₆	167 @ 1.16	.0010–.0027	.0015–.0032	.3416–.3423	.3411–.3418

Continued

VALVE SPECIFICATIONS—Continued

Year	Engine/V.I.N.	Valve Lash Int.	Valve Lash Exh.	Valve Angles Seat	Valve Angles Face	Valve Spring Installed Height	Valve Spring Pressure Lbs. @ In.	Stem Clearance Intake	Stem Clearance Exhaust	Stem Diameter, Standard Intake	Stem Diameter, Standard Exhaust
	6-200/B	.110–.184④		45	44	1 19/32	150 @ 1.22	.0008–.0025	.0010–.0027	.3100–.3107	.3098–.3105
	V6-232/3	.088–.189④		45	44	1 47/64	215 @ 1.79	.0010–.0027	.0015–.0032	.3416–.3423	.3411–.3418
	V8-255/D	.096–.146④		45	44	⑨	⑯	.0010–.0027	.0015–.0032	.3416–.3423	.3411–.3418
1983	4-140/A	.040–.050⑥		45	44	1 9/16	167 @ 1.16	.0010–.0027	.0015–.0032	.3416–.3423	.3411–.3418
	6-200/X	.110–.184④		45	44	1 19/32	150 @ 1.22	.0008–.0025	.0010–.0027	.3100–.3107	.3098–.3105
	V6-232/3	.088–.189④		45	44	1 47/64	215 @ 1.79	.0010–.0027	.0015–.0032	.3416–.3423	.3411–.3418

①—Early 1978 engines.
②—Late 1978 engines.
③—Exc. Calif., .121; Calif., .142.
④—Clearance is obtained at valve stem tip with hydraulic lifter collapsed. If clearance is less than the minimum install an undersize push rod; if clearance is greater than the maximum install on oversize push rod.
⑤—Modified engine.
⑥—Measured at cam with hydraulic lifter completely collapsed.
⑦—Intake, 1 51/64; Exhaust, 1 39/64.
⑧—Windsor engine.
⑨—Intake, 1 11/16 in.; exhaust, 1 19/32 in.
⑩—Intake, 201 @ 1.36; exhaust, 200 @ 1.20.
⑪—Intake, 1 25/32 in.; exhaust, 1 19/32 in.
⑫—Intake, 200 @ 1.34; exhaust, 200 @ 1.20.
⑬—Intake, 204 @ 1.36; exhaust, 200 @ 1.20.
⑭—Intake, 205 @ 1.36; exhaust, 200 @ 1.20.
⑮—Intake, 200 @ 1.31, exhaust 200 @ 1.20.
⑯—Intake, 205 @ 1.36; exhaust, 205 @ 1.15.
⑰—Intake, 226 @ 1.39; exhaust, 200 @ 1.20.
⑱—Intake, 156 @ 1.20; exhaust, 148 @ 1.23.
⑲—Intake, 156 @ 1.20; exhaust, 154 @ 1.20.

PISTONS, PINS, RINGS, CRANKSHAFT & BEARINGS

Year	Engine/V.I.N.	Piston Clearance	Ring End Gap① Comp.	Ring End Gap① Oil	Wristpin Diameter	Rod Bearings Shaft Diameter	Rod Bearings Bearing Clearance	Main Bearings Shaft Diameter	Main Bearings Bearing Clearance	Thrust on Bear. No.	Shaft End Play
1977	6-200/T	.0013–.0021	.008	.015	.9121	2.1232–2.1240	.0008–.0015	2.2482–2.2490	.0008–.0015	5	.004–.008
	6-250/L	.0013–.0021	.008	.015	.9121	2.1232–2.1240	.0008–.0015	2.3982–2.3990	.0008–.0015	5	.004–.008
	V8-302/F	.0018–.0026	.010	.015	.9121	2.1228–2.1236	.0008–.0015	2.2482–2.2490	⑤	3	.004–.008
	V8-351/H②	.0018–.0026	.010	.015	.9121	2.3103–2.3111	.0008–.0015	2.9994–3.0002	.0008–.0015	3	.004–.008
	V8-351/H⑥	.0014–.0022	.010	.015	.9752	2.3103–2.3111	.0008–.0015	2.9994–3.0002	.0008–.0015	3	.004–.008
	V8-400/S	.0014–.0022	.010	.015	.9752	2.3103–2.3111	.0008–.0015	2.9994–3.0002	.0008–.0015	3	.004–.008
1978	4-140/Y	.0014–.0022	.010	.015	.9120	2.0464–2.0472	.0008–.0015	2.3986	.0008–.0015	5	.004–.008
	6-200/T	.0013–.0021	.008	.015	.9121	2.1232–2.1240	.0008–.0015	2.2486	.0008–.0015	5	.004–.008
	6-250/L	.0013–.0021	.008	.015	.9121	2.1232–2.1240	.0008–.0015	2.3986	.0008–.0015	5	.004–.008
	V8-302/F	.0018–.0026	.010	.015	.9121	2.1228–2.1236	.0008–.0015	2.2486	⑤	3	.004–.008
	V8-351M/H②	.0014–.0022	.010	.015	.9752	2.3103–2.3111	.0008–.0015	2.9998	.0008–.0015	3	.004–.008
	V8-351W/H⑥	.0018–.0026	.010	.015	.9122	2.3103–2.3111	.0008–.0015	2.9998	.0008–.0015	3	.004–.008
	V8-400/S	.0014–.0022	.010	.015	.9752	2.3103–2.3111	.0008–.0015	2.9998	.0008–.0015	3	.004–.008
1979	4-140/Y	.0014–.0022	.010	.015	.9121	2.0464–2.0472	.0008–.0015	2.3982–2.3990	.0008–.0015	3	.004–.008
	6-200/T	.0013–.0021	.008	.015	.9121	2.1232–2.1240	.0008–.0015	2.2482–2.2490	.0008–.0015	5	.004–.008
	6-250/L	.0013–.0021	.008	.015	.9121	2.1232–2.1240	.0008–.0015	2.3982–2.3990	.0008–.0015	5	.004–.008
	V8-302/F	.0018–.0026	.010	.015	.9121	2.1228–2.1236	.0008–.0015	2.2482–2.2490	⑧	3	.004–.008
	V8-351W/H②	.0018–.0026	.010	.015	.9121	2.3103–2.3111	.0008–.0015	2.9994–3.0002	.0008–.0015	3	.004–.008
	V8-351M/H⑥	.0003–.0005	.010	.015	.9752	2.3103–2.3111	.0008–.0015	2.9994–3.0002	.0008–.0015	3	.004–.008
1980	4-140/A④	.0014–.0022	.010	.015	.9121	2.0462–2.0472	.0008–.0015	2.3982–2.3990	.0008–.0015	3	.004–.008
	4-140/A⑦	.0034–.0042	.010	.015	.9121	2.0462–2.0472	.0008–.0015	2.3982–2.3990	.0008–.0015	3	.004–.008
	6-200/B	.0013–.0021	.008	.015	.9121	2.1232–2.1240	.0008–.0015	2.2482–2.2490	.0008–.0015	5	.004–.008
	6-250/C	.0013–.0021	.008	.015	.9121	2.1232–2.1240	.0008–.0015	2.3982–2.3990	.0008–.0015	5	.004–.008
	V8-255/D	.0018–.0026	.010	.015	.9121	2.1228–2.1236	.0008–.0015	2.2482–2.2490	⑧	3	.004–.008
	V8-302/F	.0018–.0026	.010	.015	.9121	2.1228–2.1236	.0008–.0015	2.2482–2.2490	⑧	3	.004–.008
1981	4-140/A	.0014–.0022	.010	.015	.9121	2.0462–2.0472	.0008–.0015	2.3982–2.3990	.0008–.0015	3	.004–.008
	6-200/B	.0013–.0021	.008	.015	.9121	2.1232–2.1240	.0008–.0015	2.2482–2.2490	.0008–.0015	5	.004–.008
	V8-255/D	.004–.0024	.010	.015	.9121	2.1228–2.1236	.0008–.0015	2.2482–2.2490	⑧	3	.004–.008
	V8-302/F	.0018–.0026	.010	.015	.9121	2.1228–2.1236	.0008–.0015	2.2482–2.2490	⑧	3	.004–.008
1982	4-140/A	.0014–.0022	.010	.015	.9121	2.0465–2.0472	.0008–.0015	2.3982–2.3990	.0008–.0015	3	.004–.008
	6-200/B	.0013–.0021	.008	.015	.9121	2.1232–2.1240	.0008–.0015	2.2482–2.2490	.0008–.0015	5	.004–.008
	V6-232/3	.0014–.0022	.010	.015	.9121	2.3103–2.3111	.0010–.0014	2.5190–2.5198	.0010–.0014	3	.004–.008
	V8-255/D	.0014–.0024	.010	.015	.9121	2.1228–2.1236	.0008–.0015	2.2482–2.2490	③	3	.004–.008

Continued

PISTONS, PINS, RINGS, CRANKSHAFT & BEARINGS—Continued

Year	Engine/V.I.N.	Piston Clearance	Ring End Gap① Comp.	Ring End Gap① Oil	Wristpin Diameter	Rod Bearings Shaft Diameter	Rod Bearings Bearing Clearance	Main Bearings Shaft Diameter	Main Bearings Bearing Clearance	Thrust on Bear. No.	Shaft End Play
1983	4-140/A	.0014–.0022	.010	.015	.9121	2.0465–2.0472	.0008–.0015	2.399–2.3982	.0008–.0015	5	.004–.008
	6-200/X	.0013–.0021	.008	.015	.9121	2.1232–2.1240	.0008–.0015	2.2482–2.2490	.0008–.0015	3	.004–.008
	V6-232/3	.0014–.0022	.010	.015	.9121	2.3103–2.3111	.0010–.0014	2.5190–2.5198	.0010–.0014	3	.004–.008

①—Fit rings in tapered bores for clearance listed in tightest portion of ring travel.
②—Windsor engine.
③—No. 1, .0004–.0025; No. 2, 3, 4, 5, .004–.0015.
④—Non-Turbocharged.
⑤—No. 1: .0005–.0015; No. 2, 3, 4, 5: .0005–.0015.
⑥—Modified engine.
⑦—Turbocharged.
⑧—No. 1: .0001–.0015; No. 2, 3, 4, 5: .0004–.0015.

ENGINE TIGHTENING SPECIFICATIONS★

★ Torque specifications are for clean and lightly lubricated threads only. Dry or dirty threads produce increased friction which prevents accurate measurement of tightness.

Year	Engine/V.I.N.	Spark Plugs Ft. Lbs.	Cylinder Head Bolts Ft. Lbs.	Intake Manifold Ft. Lbs.	Exhaust Manifold Ft. Lbs.	Rocker Arm Shaft Bracket Ft. Lbs.	Rocker Arm Cover Ft. Lbs.	Connecting Rod Cap Bolts Ft. Lbs.	Main Bearing Cap Bolts Ft. Lbs.	Flywheel to Crankshaft Ft. Lbs.	Vibration Damper or Pulley Ft. Lbs.
1977–78	4-140/Y	5–10	80–90	14–21	16–23	—	4–7	30–36	80–90	54–65	100–120
	6-200/T, 250/L	10–15	70–75	—	18–24	30–35	3–5	21–26	60–70	75–85	85–100
	V8-302/F	10–15	65–72	23–25	18–24	⑤	3–5	19–24	60–70	75–85	70–90
	V8-351W/H③	10–15	105–112	23–25	18–24	⑤	3–5	40–45	95–105	75–85	70–90
	V8-351M/H①	10–15	95–105	④	18–24	18–25⑥	3–5	40–45	95–105	75–85	70–90
	V8-400/S	10–15	95–105	④	18–24	18–25⑥	3–5	40–45	95–105	75–85	70–90
1979	4-140/Y	5–10	80–90	14–21	16–23	—	5–8	30–36	80–90	56–64	100–120
	6-200/T	10–15	70–75	—	18–24	30–35	3–5	21–26	60–70	75–85	85–100
	6-250/L	10–15	70–75	—	18–24	30–35	3–5	21–26	60–70	75–85	85–100
	V8-302/F	10–15	65–72	23–25	18–24	18–25⑥	3–5	19–24	60–70	75–85	70–90
	V8-351W/H③	10–15	105–112	23–25	18–24	18–25⑥	3–5	40–45	95–105	75–85	70–90
	V8-351M/H①	10–15	95–105	④	18–24	18–25⑥	3–5	40–45	95–105	75–85	70–90
1980	4-140/A	5–10	80–90	⑦	16–23	—	6–8	30–36	80–90	56–64	100–120
	6-200/B	10–15	70–75	—	18–24	30–35	3–5	21–26	60–70	75–85	85–100
	6-250/C	10–15	70–75	—	18–24	30–35	3–5	21–26	60–70	75–85	85–100
	V8-255/D	10–15	65–72	23–25	18–24	18–25⑥	3–5	19–24	60–70	75–85	70–90
	V8-302/F	10–15	65–72	23–25	18–24	18–25⑥	3–5	19–24	60–70	75–85	70–90
1981	4-140/A	5–10	80–90	14–21	16–23	—	6–8	30–36	80–90	56–64	100–120
	6-200/B	10–15	70–75	—	18–24	30–35	3–5	21–26	60–70	75–85	85–100
	V8-255/D	10–15	65–72	18–20	18–24	18–25⑥	3–5	19–24	60–70	75–85	70–90
	V8-302/F	10–15	65–72	23–25	18–24	18–25⑥	3–5	19–24	60–70	75–85	70–90
1982	4-140/A	5–10	80–90	14–21	16–23	—	5–8	30–36	80–90	56–64	100–120
	6-200/B	10–15	70–75	—	18–24	30–35	3–5	21–26	60–70	75–85	85–100
	V6-232/3	17–22	⑧	18.4	15–22	18.4–25.8	36–61②	31–36	65–81	54–64	93–121
	V8-255/D	10–15	65–72	18–20	18–24	18–25⑥	3–5	19–24	60–70	75–85	70–90
1983	4-140/A	5–10	80–90	14–21	16–23	—	5–8	30–36	80–90	56–64	100–120
	6-200/X	10–15	70–75	—	18–24	30–35	3–5	21–26	60–70	75–85	85–100
	V6-232/3	17–22	⑧	18.4	15–22	18.4–25.8	36–61②	31–36	65–81	54–64	93–121

①—Modified engine.
②—Inch lbs.
③—Windsor engine.
④—5/16" bolts, 19–25 ft. lbs.; 3/8" bolts, 22–32 ft. lbs.
⑤—1977 & early 1978 rocker arm stud nut, 17–23 ft. lbs.; late 1978 fulcrum bolt to cylinder head, 18–25 ft. lbs.
⑥—Fulcrum bolt to cylinder head.
⑦—Except turbocharged engine, 14–21 ft. lbs;
turbocharged engine, 13–18 ft. lbs.
⑧—Tighten in 4 steps: 1, 47 ft. lbs.; 2, 55 ft. lbs.; 3, 63 ft. lbs.; 4, 74 ft. lbs. Back off all bolts 2–3 turns, retorque in 4 steps.

WHEEL ALIGNMENT SPECIFICATIONS

Year	Model	Caster Angle, Degrees		Camber Angle, Degrees				Toe-In. Inch	Toe-Out on Turns, Deg	
		Limits	Desired	Limits		Desired			Outer Wheel	Inner Wheel
				Left	Right	Left	Right			
1977	Comet	−1¼ to +¼	−½	−½ to +1	−½ to +1	+¼	+¼	⅛	18.36①	20
	Cougar	+3¼ to +4¾	+4	−¼ to +1¼	−½ to +1	+½	+¼	⅛	18.06	20
	Granada	−1¼ to +¼	−½	−½ to +1	−½ to +1	+¼	+¼	⅛	18.43②	20
	Maverick	−1¼ to +¼	−½	−½ to +1	−½ to +1	+¼	+¼	⅛	18.36①	20
	Monarch	−1¼ to +¼	−½	−½ to +1	−½ to +1	+¼	+¼	⅛	18.43②	20
	LTD II	+3¼ to +4¾	+4	−¼ to +1¼	−½ to +1	+½	+¼	⅛	18.06	20
	Thunderbird	+3¼ to +4¾	+4	−¼ to +1¼	−½ to +1	+½	+¼	⅛	18.06	20
1978–79	Cougar	+3¼ to +4¾	+4	−¼ to +1¼	−½ to +1	+½	+¼	⅛	18.06	20
	Fairmont	+1⅛ to +1⅝	+⅞	−⅜ to +1⅛	−⅜ to +1⅛	+⅜	+⅜	5/16	19.74	20
	Granada	−1¼ to +¼	−½	−½ to +1	−½ to +1	+¼	+¼	⅛	18.43②	20
	LTD II	+3¼ to +4¾	+4	−¼ to +1¼	−½ to +1	+½	+¼	⅛	18.06	20
	Monarch	−1¼ to +¼	−½	−½ to +1	−½ to +1	+¼	+¼	⅛	18.43②	20
	Thunderbird	+3¼ to +4¾	+4	−¼ to +1¼	−½ to +1	+½	+¼	⅛	18.06	20
	Zephyr	+1⅛ to +1⅝	+⅞	−⅜ to +1⅛	−⅜ to +1⅛	+⅜	+⅜	5/16	19.74	20
1980	Cougar XR-7	+1⅛ to +1⅞	+1	−½ to +1¼	−½ to +1¼	+⅜	+⅜	3/16	19.84	20
	Fairmont, Sedan	+1⅛ to +1⅞	+1	−5/16 to +1 3/16	−5/16 to +1 3/16	+7/16	+7/16	3/16	19.74	20
	Fairmont, Sta. Wag.	−⅛ to +1⅝	+¾	−¼ to +1¼	−¼ to +1¼	+½	+½	3/16	19.74	20
	Granada	−1¼ to +¼	−½	−½ to +1	−½ to +1	+¼	+¼	⅛	18.43②	20
	Monarch	−1¼ to +¼	−½	−½ to +1	−½ to +1	+¼	+¼	⅛	18.43②	20
	Thunderbird	+1⅛ to +1⅞	+1	−½ to +1¼	−½ to +1¼	+⅜	+⅜	3/16	19.84	20
	Zephyr, Sedan	+1⅛ to +1⅞	+1	−5/16 to +1 3/16	−5/16 to +1 3/16	+7/16	+7/16	3/16	19.74	20
	Zephyr, Sta. Wag.	−⅛ to +1⅝	+¾	−¼ to +1¼	−¼ to +1¼	+½	+½	3/16	19.74	20
1981	Cougar	+1⅛ to +1⅞	+1	−5/16 to +1 3/16	−5/16 to +1 3/16	+7/16	+7/16	3/16	19.84	20
	Cougar XR-7	+1⅛ to +1⅞	+1	−½ to +1¼	−½ to +1¼	+⅜	+⅜	3/16	19.77	20
	Fairmont, Sedan	+1⅛ to +1⅞	+1	−5/16 to +1 3/16	−5/16 to +1 3/16	+7/16	+7/16	3/16	19.84	20
	Fairmont, Sta. Wag.	−⅛ to +1⅝	+¾	−¼ to +1¼	−¼ to +1¼	+½	+½	3/16	19.84	20
	Granada	+1⅛ to +1⅞	+1	−5/16 to +1 3/16	−5/16 to +1 3/16	+7/16	+7/16	3/16	19.84	20
	Thunderbird	+1⅛ to +1⅞	+1	−½ to +1¼	−½ to +1¼	+⅜	+⅜	3/16	19.77	20
	Zephyr, Sedan	+1⅛ to +1⅞	+1	−5/16 to +1 3/16	−5/16 to +1 3/16	+7/16	+7/16	3/16	19.84	20
	Zephyr, Sta. Wag.	−⅛ to +1⅝	+¾	−¼ to +1¼	−¼ to +1¼	+½	+½	3/16	19.84	20
1982	Cougar Sedan	+1⅛ to +1⅞	+1	−5/16 to +1 3/16	−5/16 to +1 3/16	+7/16	+7/16	3/16	19.84	20
	Cougar Sta. Wag.	+1⅛ to +1⅝	+¾	−¼ to +1¼	−¼ to +1¼	+½	+½	3/16	19.84	20
	Cougar XR-7	+1⅛ to +1⅞	+1	−½ to +1¼	−½ to +1¼	+⅜	+⅜	3/16	19.73	20
	Fairmont	+1⅛ to +1⅞	+1	−5/16 to +1 3/16	−5/16 to +1 3/16	+7/16	+7/16	3/16	19.84	20
	Granada Sedan	+1⅛ to +1⅞	+1	−5/16 to +1 3/16	−5/16 to +1 3/16	+7/16	+7/16	3/16	19.84	20
	Granada Sta. Wag.	−⅛ to +1⅝	+¾	−¼ to +1¼	−¼ to +1¼	+½	+½	3/16	19.84	20
	Thunderbird	+1⅛ to +1⅞	+1	−½ to +1¼	−½ to +1¼	+⅜	+⅜	3/16	19.73	20
	Zephyr	+1⅛ to +1⅞	+1	−5/16 to +1 3/16	−5/16 to +1 3/16	+7/16	+7/16	3/16	19.84	20
1983	Cougar	+½ to +2	+1¼	−½ to +1	+¼ to +1	+¼	+¼	3/16	19.73	20
	Fairmont	+1⅛ to +2⅛	+1⅛	−5/16 to +1 3/16	−5/16 to +1 3/16	+7/16	+7/16	3/16	19.84	20
	LTD Sedan	+1⅛ to +2⅛	+1⅛	−5/16 to +1 3/16	−5/16 to +1 3/16	+7/16	+7/16	3/16	19.84	20
	LTD Sta. Wagon	−⅛ to +1⅞	+⅞	−¼ to +1¼	−¼ to +1¼	+¼	+¼	3/16	19.84	20
	Marquis Sedan	+1⅛ to +2⅛	+1⅛	−5/16 to +1 3/16	−5/16 to +1 3/16	+7/16	+7/16	3/16	19.84	20
	Marquis Sta. Wagon	−⅛ to +1⅞	+⅞	−¼ to +1¼	−¼ to +1¼	+½	+½	3/16	19.84	20
	Thunderbird	+½ to +2	+1¼	−½ to +1	+¼ to +1	+¼	+¼	3/16	19.73	20
	Zephyr	+1⅛ to +2⅛	+1⅛	−5/16 to +1 3/16	−5/16 to +1 3/16	+7/16	+7/16	3/16	19.84	20

①—Power steering 18.13°.　②—Power steering 18.20°.

COOLING SYSTEM & CAPACITY DATA

Year	Model or Engine/V.I.N.	Cooling Capacity Qts.		Radiator Cap Relief Pressure, Lbs.	Thermo. Opening Temp.	Fuel Tank Gals.	Engine Oil Refill Qts. [1]	Transmission Oil			Rear Axle Oil Pints
		Less A/C	With A/C					3 Speed Pints	4 Speed Pints	Auto. Trans. Qts. [2]	
1977	6-200/T[3]	8.7	8.7	13	191	19.2	4	3½	—	7¼	4½
	6-200/T[4]	9.9	9.9	16	191	19.2	4	3½	5	8¼	[13]
	6-250/L[3]	9.6	9.6	13	191	19.2	4	3½	—	8¼	4½
	6-250/L[4]	10.5	10.7	16	191	19.2	4	—	5	8¼	[13]
	V8-302/F[3]	13.5	14.1	13	191	19.2	4	3½	—	10¼	4½
	V8-302/F[4]	14.4	14.6	16	191	19.2	4	—	—	8¼	[13]
	V8-302/F[14]	14.8	15.1	16	191	[7]	4	—	—	10¼	5
	V8-351W/H[4][5]	15.7	16.7	16	191	19.2	4	—	—	10¼	[13]
	V8-351W/H[5][14]	15.9	16.2	16	191	[7]	4	—	—	[8]	5
	V8-351M/H[9][14]	17.1	17.1	16	191	[7]	4	—	—	[8]	5
	V8-400/S[14]	17.1	17.1	16	191	[7]	4	—	—	[10]	5
1978	4-140/Y[15]	8.7	9.1	[16]	191	16	4	—	2.8	8	3.5
	6-200/T[15]	8.7	8.9	[16]	191	16	4	3½	—	[17]	3.5
	6-250/L[4]	10.5	10.6	16	191	18	4	—	5	8¼	[18]
	V8-302/F[15]	13.5	14.1	[16]	191	16	4[32]	—	—	10	3½
	V8-302/F[4]	14.2	14.3	16	191	18	4	—	5	8¼	[18]
	V8-302/F[14]	14.3	14.6	16	191	21	4	—	—	10¼	5
	V8-351W/H[5][14]	15.4	15.7	16	191	21	4	—	—	[8]	5
	V8-351M/H[9][14]	16.5	16.5	16	191	21	4	—	—	[8]	5
	V8-400/S[14]	16.5	16.5	16	191	21	4	—	—	[8]	5
1979	4-140/Y[15]	8.6	10.3	[16]	191	16	4	—	2.8	8	3½
	6-200/T[15]	9	9	16	191	16	4	—	4½	[19]	3½
	6-250/L[4]	[20]	[21]	16	191	18	4	—	4½	[22]	4½
	V8-302/F[15]	13.9	14	16	195	16	4	—	4½	10	3½
	V8-302/F[4]	14.2	14.3	16	195	18	4	—	4½	10	4½
	V8-302/F[14]	14.3	14.6	16	195	21[23]	4	—	—	10	5
	V8-351W/H[5][14]	15.4	15.7	16	195	21[23]	4	—	—	[24]	5
	V8-351M/H[9][14]	16.5	16.5	16	195	21[23]	4	—	—	[24]	5
1980	4-140/A[25]	8.6	9	[16]	191	14	4	—	2.8	6.7	[27]
	4-140/A[26]	9.2	9.2	[16]	191	12.7	4½	—	3.5	—	[27]
	6-200/B	8.1	8.1	16	196	14	4	—	4½	[30]	[27]
	6-250/C	10.6	10.8	16	196	18	4	—	4½	[34]	[35]
	V8-255/D[15]	13.4	13.5	16	196	14	4[32]	—	—	10	[27]
	V8-255/D[4]	14.6	14.7	16	196	18	4	—	—	9.6	[35]
	V8-255/D[29]	13.2	13.3	16	196	17½	4[32]	—	—	10.1	5
	V8-302/F[4]	14.2	14.3	16	196	18	4	—	—	9.6	[35]
	V8-302/F[39]	12.7	12.8	16	196	17½	4[32]	—	—	[31]	5
1981	4-140/A[15]	8.6	9.2	[16]	191	14	4	—	2.8	[36]	[27]
	4-140/A[33]	8.6	9.2	[16]	191	14	4	—	4.5	6.8	3½
	6-200/B[15]	8.4	8.5	16	196	16	4	—	—	[37]	[27]
	6-200/B[33]	8.4	8.5	16	196	16	4	—	—	[37]	3½
	6-200/B[29]	8.4	8.5	16	196	17½	4	—	—	7.7	3½
	V8-255/D[15]	14.8	15.2	16	191	16	4[32]	—	—	9.6	[27]
	V8-255/D[33]	14.8	15.2	16	196	16	4[32]	—	—	9.6	3½
	V8-255/D[29]	14.9	15	16	191	18	4[32]	—	—	[31]	3½
	V8-302/F[29]	13.2	13.4	16	196	18	4[32]	—	—	12	3½
1982	4-140/A[15][33]	8.6	9.4	[16]	191	16[6]	4	—	2.8	8	3½
	6-200/B[15]	8.4	8.5	16	196	16[6]	4	—	—	[11]	3½
	6-200/B[33]	10.7	10.8	16	196	16[6]	4	—	—	[11]	3½
	6-200/B[29]	8.4	8.5	16	196	21	4	—	—	[11]	3½
	V6-232/3[33]	8.4	8.5	16	196	16[6]	4	—	—	12	3½
	V6-232/3[29]	10.7	10.8	16	196	21	4	—	—	12	3½
	V8-255/D[29]	14.9	15	16	191	21	4	—	—	12	3½

Continued

FORD & MERCURY—Compact & Intermediate Models

COOLING SYSTEM & CAPACITY DATA—Continued

Year	Model or Engine/V.I.N.	Cooling Capacity Qts.		Radiator Cap Relief Pressure, Lbs.	Thermo. Opening Temp.	Fuel Tank Gals.	Engine Oil Refill Qts. ①	Transmission Oil			Rear Axle Oil Pints
		Less A/C	With A/C					3 Speed Pints	4 Speed Pints	Auto. Trans. Qts. ②	
1983	4-140/A	8.6	9.4	⑯	191	16	4	—	2.8	8	㊱
	6-200/X	8.4	8.5	16	191	16	4	—	—	11	㊱
	V6-232/3	10.7	10.8	16	197	㊲	4	—	—	㊳	㊱

①—Add 1 qt. with filter change.
②—Approximate. Make final check with dipstick.
③—Comet & Maverick.
④—Granada & Monarch.
⑤—Windsor engine.
⑥—With option extended range fuel tank, 20 gals.
⑦—Except sta. wag., 26½ gals.; sta. wag., 21¼ gals.
⑧—C4, 10¼ qts.; FMX, 11 qts.; C6, 12¼ qts.
⑨—Modified engine
⑩—FMX, 11 qts.; C6, 12¼ qts.
⑪—C3, 8 qts.; C5, 11 qts.
⑫—C3, 8 qts.; C4, w/10¼ in. torque converter, 7.2 qts.; C4 w/12 in. torque converter, 9.6 qts.
⑬—Models w/8 in. ring gear, 4½ pts.; models w/8.7" ring gear, 4 pts.; models w/4 wheel disc. brakes, 5 pts.
⑭—Cougar, LTD II & Thunderbird.
⑮—Fairmont & Zephyr.
⑯—Less A/C, 13 psi.; with A/C 16 psi.
⑰—C3, 8 qts.; C4, 6.7 qts.
⑱—Models w/2.47 rear axle ratio, 4 pts.; models w/3.00 rear axle ratio, 4½ pts.; models w/4 wheel disc brakes, 5 pts.
⑲—C3, 8 qts.; C4, 7½ qts.
⑳—Except Calif. 10.5 qts.; California, 10.7 qts.
㉑—Man. trans. 10.6 qts.; auto. trans. 10.8 qts.
㉒—C4, 8¼ qts.; Jatco, 8½ qts.
㉓—W/optional fuel tank, 27.5 gals.
㉔—C4, 10 qts.; FMX, 11 qts.
㉕—Non-turbocharged engine.
㉖—Turbocharged engine.
㉗—With 7.5 inch ring gear, 3.5 pts.; with 6.75 ring gear, 2.5 pts.
㉘—C3, 8 qts.; C4, 6.8 qts.
㉙—Cougar XR-7 & Thunderbird.
㉚—C3, 8 qts; C4, 7.1 qts.
㉛—C4, 10.1 qts; F10D auto. overdrive trans., 12 qts.
㉜—Dual sump oil pan. Remove both drain plugs to fully drain oil. One drain plug located at front of oil pan. Second drain plug located at left side of oil pan.
㉝—Cougar & Granada.
㉞—Jatco, 8.6 qts.; C4, 9.6 qts.
㉟—8 inch ring gear, 4.5 pts.; 9 inch ring gear, 5 pts.
㊱—Standard, 3¼ pts.; Traction-Lok, 3½ pts.
㊲—LTD & Marquis, 16 gal.; Thunderbird & Cougar, 21 gal.
㊳—Automatic 3 speed, 11 qts.; automatic 4 speed, 12 qts.

BRAKE SPECIFICATIONS

Year	Model	Brake Drum Inside Diameter	Wheel Cylinder Bore Diameter			Master Cylinder Bore Diameter		
			Front Disc Brake	Front Drum Brake	Rear Brake	With Disc Brakes	With Drum Brakes	With Power Brakes
1977	Maverick & Comet	10.00	2.600	—	.938	.938	—	.938
	Granada & Monarch	10.00	2.600	—	②	.938	—	③
	Cougar, LTD II & Thunderbird	11.03	3.100	—	④	1.00	—	1.00
1978–79	Cougar, LTD II & Thunderbird	11.03	3.10	—	.9375	1.00	—	1.00
	Fairmont & Zephyr	⑤	2.36	—	.8125	.875	—	.875
	Granada & Monarch	10.00	2.60	—	②	③	—	③
1980	Cougar XR-7 & Thunderbird	9.00	2.36	—	.8125	.875	—	.875
	Fairmont & Zephyr	⑤	2.36	—	.8125	.875	—	.875
	Granada & Monarch	10.00	2.60	—	②	③	—	③
1981	Cougar & Granada	⑥	2.36	—	.8125	.875	—	.875
	Cougar XR-7 & Thunderbird	9.00	2.36	—	.8125	.875	—	.875
	Fairmont & Zephyr	⑤	2.36	—	.8125	.875	—	.875
1982	Cougar & Granada	⑤	2.36	—	.8125	.827	—	.827
	Cougar XR-7 & Thunderbird	①	2.36	—	.8125	.827	—	.827
	Fairmont & Zephyr	9	2.36	—	.8125	.827	—	.827
1983	Cougar & Thunderbird	9	2.36	—	.75	.827	—	.827
	Fairmont	9	2.36	—	.813	.827	—	.827
	LTD, Marquis & Zephyr	⑤	2.36	—	.813	.827	—	.827

①—With 6 cyl. engine 9"; with V8 engine 10".
②—Drum .938"; Disc 2.1".
③—Power rear drum .938"; Power rear disc 1.00".
④—Except Station Wagon—.938"; Station Wagon—1.00".
⑤—Exc. sta. wag. 9"; Sta. wag. 10".
⑥—Models with 4 or 6 cyl. engine, 9"; models with V8 engine, 10".

REAR AXLE SPECIFICATIONS

Year	Ring Gear Diameter	Carrier Type	Ring Gear & Pinion Backlash Inch	Nominal Pinion Locating Shim, Inch	Pinion Bearing Preload				Differential Bearing Preload	Pinion Nut Torque Ft.-Lbs.①
					New Bearings With Seal Inch-Lbs.	Used Bearings With Seal Inch-Lbs.	New Bearings Less Seal Inch-Lbs.	Used Bearings Less Seal Inch-Lbs.		
1977–78	8.7" WER③	Integral	.008–.012	.030	17–27	8–14	—	—	.008–.012②	140
1977–79	8"	Removal	.008–.012	.022	17–27	8–14	—	—	.008–.012⑥	170
	9"	Removal	.008–.012	.015	17–27④	8–14	—	—	.008–.012⑥	⑤
1978–79	7½" WGX③	Integral	.008–.012	.030	17–27	8–14	—	—	.016⑦	140
1979	6¾"	Integral	.008–.012	.030	17–27	6–12	—	—	.016⑦	140
1980	6¾"	Integral	.008–.012	.030	17–27	6–12	—	—	.016⑦	140
	7½" WGX③	Integral	.008–.012	.030	16–29	8–14	—	—	.016⑦	170
	9"	Removal	.008–.015	.030	17–27	8–14	—	—	.008–.012⑦	170
1981	6¾" WGG③	Integral	.008–.015	.030	16–29	8–14	—	—	.016⑦	140
1981–83	7½" WGX, WGZ③	Integral	.008–.015	—	16–29	8–14	—	—	.016⑦	170

① —If torque cannot be obtained, install new spacer.
② —Case spread with new bearings. With used bearings .006–.010".
③ —Indentification tag prefix.
④ —Solid spacer 13–33 inch-lbs.
⑤ —With collapsible spacer 170 ft. lbs., with solid spacer 200 ft. lbs.
⑥ —Case spread with new bearings. With used bearings .005–.008".
⑦ —Case spread across differential.

Electrical Section

STARTER, REPLACE

1978–83 Fairmont, Zephyr, 1981–82 Cougar, Granada & 1983 LTD & Marquis 4-140

1. Disconnect battery ground cable.
2. Raise vehicle on hoist.
3. Remove starter shield.
4. Disconnect starter cable from motor.
5. Remove starter attaching bolts and remove starter.

1980–82 Cougar XR-7, 1980–83 Thunderbird & 1983 Cougar V6-232, V8-255 & 302

1. Disconnect battery ground cable.
2. Raise vehicle and remove cross brace.
3. Remove starter motor attaching bolts, then lower starter motor and disconnect starter cable.
4. Reverse procedure to install.

1978–83 Fairmont, Zephyr, 1981–82 Cougar & Granada 6-200

1. Disconnect battery ground cable, then remove upper starter attaching bolt.
2. Remove exhaust heat shield, then disconnect starter cable from starter motor.
3. Raise vehicle and remove wishbone brace.
4. Remove lower starter mounting bolts, then remove starter motor.
5. Reverse procedure to install.

1978–83 Fairmont, Zephyr & 1981–82 Cougar & Granada V6-232, V8-255 & 302

1. Disconnect battery ground cable.
2. Raise vehicle and remove wishbone brace.
3. Remove starter motor attaching bolts and remove starter assembly.
4. Disconnect starter cable from starter motor.
5. Reverse procedure to install.

1977–80 Granada & Monarch V8-302

1. Disconnect battery ground cable.
2. Disconnect starter cable from starter.
3. Remove engine mount through bolt and nut.
4. Remove two bolts retaining insulator to block and remove insulator.
5. Position a suitable jack under engine and raise engine.
6. Remove starter attaching bolts and starter.

1977–79 Cougar, LTD II & Thunderbird, 1977 Comet & Maverick

1. Disconnect battery ground cable.
2. Raise vehicle and disconnect starter cable at starter.
3. Remove starter attaching bolts and starter.
4. Reverse procedure to install.

NOTE: On engines equipped with a solenoid actuated starter, turn wheel to full right and remove the idler arm to frame bolts. On some models, it may be necessary to turn wheels aside to aid starter removal.

FIXED STEERING COLUMN
LOCK CYLINDER HOUSING
LOCK CYLINDER
PIN HOLE FOR CYLINDER RELEASE
LOCK
ACC.
OFF
RUN
START
LOCK CYLINDER OPERATING PATTERN

TILT STEERING COLUMN
LOCK CYLINDER
LOCK CYLINDER HOUSING
EMERGENCY FLASHER BUTTON

Fig. 1 Ignition lock

Fig. 2 Ignition switch. 1978—83 Fairmont, Zephyr, 1980—82 Cougar XR-7, 1980—83 Thunderbird, 1981—82 Cougar, Granada & 1983 Cougar, LTD & Marquis

NOISY STARTER OR STARTER LOCKUP: If either of these situations occur, loosen the three mounting bolts enough to hand fit the starter properly into pilot plate. Then tighten starter mounting bolts, starting with top bolt. Starter should not be replaced until it has been proven noisy after proper alignment has been established by the above method.

IGNITION LOCK, REPLACE

1. Disconnect the battery ground cable.
2. *Units With Fixed Steering Columns:* Remove steering wheel and trim pad. Insert a wire pin into the hole inside the column halfway down the lock cylinder housing, Fig. 1. *Units with Tilt Steering Columns:* Insert wire pin in the hole located on the outside of the flange casting next to the emergency flasher button, Fig. 1.
3. Place the gear shift lever in "Park" (with automatic trans) or "Reverse" (with manual trans) position, and turn the lock cylinder with the ignition key to "Run" position.
4. Depress the wire pin while pulling up on the lock cylinder to remove. Remove the wire pin.
5. To install insert the lock cylinder into housing in the flange casting, and turn the key to "Off" position. Be certain that the cylinder is fully inserted before turning to the "Off" position. This action will expend the cylinder retaining pin into the cylinder housing.
6. Turn the key to check for correct operation in all positions.
7. Install the steering wheel and trim pad on fixed column units.
8. Connect the battery ground cable.

Fig. 3 Ignition switch installation 1977 Comet & Maverick

Fig. 4 Ignition switch installation. 1977—79 Cougar, LTD II & Thunderbird & 1977—80 Granada & Monarch

Fig. 5 Light switch knob removal. 1977–80 Granada, LTD II & Monarch

Fig. 7 Mechanical stop light switch.

Fig. 6 Light switches. (Typical)

IGNITION SWITCH, REPLACE

1978–83 Fairmont & Zephyr; 1980–82 Cougar XR-7, 1980–83 Thunderbird; 1981–82 Granada; 1981–83 Cougar; 1983 LTD & Marquis

1. Disconnect battery ground cable, then remove steering column trim shroud by removing four screws.
2. Disconnect ignition switch wire connector.
3. Drill out bolts that attach switch to lock cylinder housing using a 1/8 in. drill. Remove the two bolts using an easy-out or equivalent.
4. Disengage ignition switch from actuator pin, Fig. 2.
5. On 1978–81 models, adjust switch by sliding carrier to "Lock" position and inserting a drill bit through switch housing and into carrier. On 1978–79 models, insert a 7/16 inch drill bit. On 1980–81 models, insert a .050 inch drill bit.
6. On 1982 models, adjust switch by sliding carrier to "Run" position and inserting a 1/8 inch drill bit through housing and into carrier.
7. On 1978–81 models, rotate ignition key to "Lock" position, then install switch on actuator pin.
8. On 1982 models, rotate ignition key to the run position, which is approximately 90° from Lock position, then install ignition switch on actuator pin.
9. Install new switch to lock cylinder housing break away bolts and torque bolt until heads break away.

10. Remove drill bit from switch housing, then connect switch wire connector.
11. Connect battery ground cable and check switch for proper operation, then install steering column trim shroud.

Except 1978–83 Fairmont & Zephyr; 1980–82 Cougar XR-7, 1980–83 Thunderbird; 1981–82 Granada; 1981–83 Cougar; 1983 LTD & Marquis

1. On 1977–79 Cougar, LTD II and Thunderbird models, remove instrument cluster as described under Instrument Cluster, Replace.
2. On all models, remove steering column shroud and lower steering column from brake support bracket.
3. Disconnect battery cable.
4. Disconnect switch wiring and remove two switch retaining nuts. Disconnect switch from actuator and remove switch, Figs. 3 and 4.
5. Move shift lever to "Park" position on automatic transmissions and Reverse on standard transmission units. Place ignition key in "Lock" position and remove the key.

NOTE: New replacement switches are pinned in the "Lock" position by a plastic shipping pin inserted in a locking hole in the switch. For an existing switch, pull plunger out as far as it will go then back one detent to "Lock" position and insert a 3/32" drill in locking hole to retain switch in Lock position.

6. With locking pin in place, install switch on steering column, determine mid position of actuator lash and tighten retaining bolts.
7. Remove locking pin.

LIGHT SWITCH, REPLACE

1. Disconnect battery ground cable.
2. On 1977–80 Granada, LTD II and Mon-

arch models, to remove light switch knob, bend a discarded bowden cable into shape shown in Fig. 5. Insert hooked end of cable into knob slot to depress spring, then pull knob from shaft.
3. On all other models, remove control knob and shaft assembly, by placing knob in full "On" position, then pressing knob release button on switch and pulling out knob and shaft, Fig. 6. To gain access to the release button on Comet, Fairmont, Maverick and Zephyr models with air conditioning it may be necessary to first disconnect the left A/C duct.
4. On all models, remove bezel nut. Disconnect multiple plug connector, vacuum hoses if vehicle is equipped with headlight doors and remove switch.
5. Reverse procedure to install. On 1977–80 Granada, LTD II and Monarch models, align triangular holes in knob and shaft, then press knob onto shaft until knob bottoms. On all other models, install knob and shaft by inserting shaft into the switch until a distinct click is heard. In some instances it may be necessary to rotate the shaft slightly until it engages the switch carrier.

STOP LIGHT SWITCH, REPLACE

1. Disconnect battery ground cable and disconnect wires at switch connector.

NOTE: On 1977–80 Granada and Monarch models with vacuum power brake units, loosen brake booster nut 1/4 turn, thereby eliminating binding during removal.

2. Remove hairpin retainer and slide stop light switch, push rod, nylon washers and bushings away from brake pedal, and remove switch, Fig. 7.
3. Reverse procedure to install and on 1977–80 Granada and Monarch models, torque brake booster retaining nuts to 13-25 ft. lbs.

ATTACHING SCREWS

NEUTRAL START SWITCH & HARNESS ASSEMBLY

SWITCH ADJUSTMENT
D1ZA-7A247-
LOOSEN ENGINE SHIFT HAND SELECTOR INTO (←→) HOLD USING FORWARD
NEUTRAL START SWITCH REARWARD (←→) TO END OF TRAVEL. FORWARD
LIGHT PRESSURE, TIGHTEN SCREWS, CHECK LINKAGE ADJ.

NEUTRAL ALIGNMENT MARK

NEUTRAL POSITION

ACTUATOR LEVER

Fig. 8   Neutral safety switch. 1977–79 Cougar & LTD II with console

GAUGE PIN (NO. 43 DRILL)

NEUTRAL START SWITCH

31/64"

GAUGE PIN

THREE HOLE

Fig. 9   Neutral safety switch. Transmission mounted

NEUTRAL SAFETY SWITCH, REPLACE

1977–79 Cougar, LTD II & Thunderbird Console

Removal & Adjustment, Fig. 8.
1. Place selector lever in neutral.
2. Raise vehicle and remove nut that secures shift rod to transmission manual lever.
3. Lower vehicle and remove selector level handle and dial housing.
4. Disconnect dial light and neutral start switch wires at dash panel.

NOTE: On models with FMX transmission, disconnect seat belt warning circuit connector.

5. Remove selector lever and housing assembly.
6. Remove pointer back up shield attaching screws and remove shield.
7. Remove neutral start switch to selector lever housing attaching screws.
8. Push neutral start switch harness plug inward and remove switch and harness assembly.
9. Position switch and harness assembly on selector lever housing, then install but do not tighten attaching screws.

NOTE: Before installing switch and harness assembly, ensure selector lever is against neutral detent stop and actuator lever is properly aligned in neutral position.

10. Place selector lever in "Park" position and hold against forward stop.
11. Move neutral start switch rearward to end of its travel, then while holding switch in rearward position tighten attaching screws.

12. Install pointer back up shield, then position selector lever and housing assembly on console and install attaching bolts.
13. Connect dial indicator, neutral start switch and seat belt warning circuit (if equipped) wire connectors.
14. Install dial housing and shift lever handle, then place selector lever in "Drive" position.
15. Raise vehicle and install shift rod on transmission manual lever.
16. Check shift linkage adjustment, then lower vehicle and check operation of neutral start switch.

1977 Comet & Maverick; 1977–80 Monarch; 1977–82 Granada; 1978–83 Fairmont & Zephyr; 1980–82 Cougar XR-7; 1980–83 Thunderbird; 1981–83 Cougar; 1983 LTD & Marquis

Transmission Mounted Switch, Fig. 9
1. Remove downshift linkage rod from transmission downshift lever.
2. Apply penetrating oil to downshift lever shaft and nut; then remove downshift outer lever.
3. Remove switch attaching bolts.
4. Disconnect multiple wire connector and remove switch from transmission.
5. Install new switch.
6. With transmission manual lever in neutral, rotate switch and install gauge pin (#43 drill) into gauge pin holes.

NOTE: The shank end of the drill must be inserted $^{31}/_{64}$ in. ($^{15}/_{32}$ in., 1983 models) into each of the gauge pin holes.

7. Tighten switch attaching bolts and remove gauge pin.
8. Complete the installation in reverse order of removal.

TURN SIGNAL SWITCH, REPLACE

1978–83 Fairmont & Zephyr; 1980–82 Cougar XR-7; 1980–83 Thunderbird; 1981–82 Granada; 1981–83 Cougar; 1983 LTD & Marquis

1. Disconnect battery ground cable.
2. Remove four steering column trim shroud attaching screws, then remove trim shroud.
3. Remove turn signal switch lever by grasping the lever and by using a pulling and twisting motion of the hand while pulling the lever straight out from the switch.
4. Peel back foam shield from turn signal switch, then disconnect two wire connectors from switch.
5. Remove two screws attaching turn signal switch to lock cylinder housing, then disengage switch from housing.
6. Reverse procedure to install.

Except 1978–83 Fairmont & Zephyr; 1980–82 Cougar XR-7; 1980–83 Thunderbird; 1981–82 Granada; 1980–83 Cougar; 1983 LTD & Marquis

1. Remove retaining screw from underside of steering wheel spokes and lift off pad horn switch/trim cover and medallion as an assembly.
2. Disconnect horn switch wires from terminals.
3. Remove steering wheel retaining nut and remove steering wheel with suitable puller.
4. Remove turn signal switch lever by unscrewing it from steering column.
5. Remove shroud from under steering column.
6. Disconnect steering column wiring connector plugs and remove screws that secure switch to column.
7. On tilt column, remove wires and terminals from column plug. *NOTE: Record color code and position of wires before removing. A hole provided in the flange casting on fixed columns makes it unnecessary to separate wires from plug as the plug with wires can be guided through hole.*
8. Remove plastic cover sleeve from wiring harness and remove switch from top of column.

Fig. 10   Instrument cluster 1977–80 Granada & Monarch (Typical)

Labels on figure: Gage Retaining Nuts; Left Turn Indicator; Speedometer Attaching Screws; Right Turn Indicator; Mask And Lens Assembly; Mask And Lens Assembly Attaching Screws (5); Cluster Back Plate; Cluster Illumination Lights; High-Beam Indicator; Engine Warning Light; Alternator Warning Light; Brake Warning Light; Fasten Belts Warning Lights; Fuel Economy Indicator (Optional); Speedometer; Transmission Selector Indicator Cover (All Except Steering Column Mounted Automatic Transmission); Fuel Gage

HORN SOUNDER, REPLACE

NOTE: On 1978–83 Fairmont, Zephyr, 1980–82 Cougar XR-7, 1980–83 Thunderbird, 1981–82 Granada, 1981–83 Cougar and 1983 LTD & Marquis models, the horn sounder is located on the turn signal, headlight dimmer and horn lever. Refer to Turn Signal Switch Replace, when replacing lever.

The horn button used on some models may be removed by twisting the button counterclockwise. The horn switch on some models is part of the trim cover assembly and if defective, the trim cover must be replaced. The horn sounder on rim-blow steering wheels equipped with speed control cannot be replaced and if defective, the steering wheel assembly must be replaced. On rim-blow steering wheels without speed control, the horn sounder (plastic strip and copper insert) may be replaced using the following procedure:

1. Remove trim pad and disconnect lead wires.
2. Remove plastic cover and lift out horn insert on inner diameter of steering wheel.
3. Reverse procedure to install.

STEERING WHEEL, REPLACE

1. Disconnect battery ground cable.
2. Remove steering wheel trim pad, horn button or ring.
3. Disconnect horn and speed control wiring, if equipped.
4. Remove steering wheel nut.
5. Mark relationship between steering shaft and steering wheel hub for proper reinstallation.
6. Remove steering wheel with a suitable puller.
7. Reverse procedure to install.

INSTRUMENT CLUSTER, REPLACE

1980–82 Cougar XR-7, 1980–83 Thunderbird & 1983 Cougar, LTD & Marquis

STANDARD CLUSTER

1981–82 Models
1. Disconnect battery ground cable.
2. Disconnect speedometer cable, then remove instrument panel trim cover and steering column shroud.
3. Remove screw attaching transmission shift lever indicator cable bracket to steering column, then detach cable loop from pin on shift cane lever and remove plastic clamp from around steering column.
4. Remove four instrument cluster retaining screws, then disconnect cluster feed plug and remove instrument cluster.
5. Reverse procedure to install.

1980 Models
1. Disconnect battery ground cable.
2. Disconnect speedometer cable.
3. Remove steering column shroud and instrument cluster trim cover.
4. Remove six instrument cluster lens and mask attaching screws, then remove lens and mask.
5. Remove four instrument cluster attaching screws.
6. Disconnect cluster feed plug from printed circuit connector, then remove cluster assembly.
7. Reverse procedure to install.

ELECTRONIC CLUSTER
1. Disconnect battery ground cable.
2. Remove four instrument panel lower trim cover attaching screws, then remove trim cover.
3. Remove steering column shroud.
4. Remove six instrument cluster trim panel attaching screws, then remove trim panel.

5. Remove four instrument cluster to instrument panel attaching screws.
6. Remove screw attaching transmission selector lever indicator cable bracket to steering column, then detach cable loop from pin on steering column.
7. Carefully pull cluster assembly away from instrument panel.
8. Disconnect speedometer cable and cluster feed plug and ground wire from cluster back plate, then remove cluster assembly.
9. Reverse procedure to install.

1978–83 Fairmont, Zephyr & 1981–82 Cougar & Granada

1. Disconnect battery ground cable.
2. Remove steering column shroud.
3. Remove instrument cluster trim cover.
4. Remove screw retaining PRND21 control cable clamp to steering column. Then, disconnect the cable from pin on steering column. Remove plastic clamp from steering column.
5. Remove two upper and two lower screws retaining instrument cluster to instrument panel.
6. Pull cluster from instrument panel and disconnect speedometer cable.
7. Disconnect electrical connectors from instrument cluster.
8. Remove instrument cluster from vehicle.
9. Reverse procedure to install.

1977–80 Granada & Monarch

1. Disconnect battery ground cable.
2. Remove lower cluster cover from below steering column.
3. Remove steering column shroud.
4. On all models, remove headlamp switch knob and shaft assembly and bezel.
5. Remove four cluster finish panel attaching screws.
6. Using a right angle screwdriver, pry along edges of finish panel, thereby removing studs from retainers and remove finish panel.
7. Disconnect automatic transmission indicator cable and speedometer cable.
8. Remove four screws retaining cluster to instrument panel, then pull cluster out and disconnect feed plug from printed circuit, Fig. 10.
9. Disconnect wires from fuel gauge if equipped with low fuel warning light and remove cluster.
10. Reverse procedure to install

1977–79 Cougar XR7, LTD II & Thunderbird

1. Disconnect battery ground cable.
2. Remove upper and lower retaining screws from cluster trim cover and remove the cover, Figs. 11 and 12.
3. On 1977–79 models with standard cluster, remove clock or cover to cluster attaching screw and clock or cover to instrument panel retaining screw.
4. On all models, remove two upper and two lower screws retaining cluster to the panel.
5. Pull cluster away from panel and disconnect speedo cable.
6. Disconnect cluster feed plug from receptacle in printed circuit.
7. If equipped, remove Park, Belts and Fuel Economy lights from receptacles.

8. On Cougar, LTD II and Thunderbird models, disconnect overlay harness connector.
9. Remove cluster.
10. Reverse procedure to install.

1977 Comet & Maverick

1. Disconnect battery ground cable.
2. From under instrument panel, disconnect speedometer cable.
3. Remove two retaining screws at the top of the cluster and swing it down from the panel, Fig. 13.
4. Disconnect electrical connections and remove cluster.
5. Reverse procedure to install.

W/S WIPER MOTOR, REPLACE

1980–82 Cougar XR-7; 1980–83 Thunderbird; 1981–82 Granada; 1981–83 Cougar, Fairmont & Zephyr; 1983 LTD & Marquis

1. Disconnect battery ground cable.
2. On Cougar XR-7 and Thunderbird, 1983 Cougar models, remove right hand wiper arm and blade assembly. On Fairmont, Granada, Zephyr and 1981–82 Cougar models, remove both wiper arm and blade assemblies.
3. Remove cowl grille attaching screws, then remove cowl grille.
4. Remove clip, then disconnect linkage drive arm from motor crankpin.
5. Disconnect wire connector from wiper motor, then remove wiper motor attaching bolts and lift motor from cowl opening.

1978–80 Fairmont & Zephyr & 1980 Cougar

1. Disconnect battery ground cable.
2. Remove left hand wiper arm from pivot shaft and place on cowl grille.
3. Remove cowl grille attaching screws, then raise left hand corner of cowl grille to gain access to linkage drive arm.
4. Disconnect linkage arm from motor output arm pin by removing retaining clip.
5. Disconnect wiper motor wire connector.
6. Remove wiper motor to cowl attaching bolts, then remove wiper motor.

1978–81 Fairmont, Zephyr, 1982 Cougar, Granada & 1983 LTD & Marquis Sta. Wag. Liftgate Wiper Motor

1. Disconnect battery ground cable.
2. Remove wiper arm and blade assembly.
3. Remove pivot shaft attaching nut and spacers.
4. Remove license plate housing attaching screws, then disconnect lamp wire connector and remove housing.
5. Disconnect wiper motor wire connector.
6. Remove linkage arm lock clip, then pry off arm and remove linkage.
7. Remove wiper motor and bracket attaching bolts, then remove motor and bracket.

1978–80 Granada & Monarch

1. Disconnect battery ground cable.
2. Remove instrument panel pad.

Fig. 11 Instrument cluster. 1977–79 Cougar, LTD II & Thunderbird with performance cluster

3. Remove speaker mounting bracket, then disconnect wire connector and remove speaker.
4. Remove defroster nozzle and air distribution duct.
5. Remove wiper motor to cowl attaching bolts, then remove wiper motor.

1977 Comet, Maverick, Granada & Monarch

1. Disconnect battery ground cable.
2. On all models, remove evaporator case center distribution duct assembly.
3. Working over top of brake support assembly, remove wiper motor pivot clip and disconnect linkage from motor arm.
4. Remove wiper motor attaching bolts and wiper motor.

NOTE: Some Granada and Monarch models may have an additional instrument panel brace which must be detached from the floor pan and swung to one side to provide access to wiper motor attaching bolts.

1977–79 Cougar, Thunderbird & LTD II

1. Disconnect battery ground cable.
2. Remove wiper arm and blade assembly.

Fig. 12 Instrument cluster. 1977–79 Cougar, LTD II & Thunderbird with standard cluster

Fig. 13 Instrument cluster. 1977 Comet & Maverick

3. Remove left cowl screen, then remove retaining clip and disconnect drive arm from motor crankpin.
4. Disconnect wire connectors from motor, then remove attaching bolts and motor.

NOTE: If output arm catches on dash during removal, handturn arm clockwise so it will clear. Before installing ensure output arm is in "park" position.

W/S WIPER, TRANSMISSION REPLACE

1979–83 Fairmont & Zephyr; 1980–82 Cougar XR-7; 1980–83 Thunderbird; 1981–82 Granada; 1981–83 Cougar; 1983 LTD & Marquis

1. Disconnect battery ground cable, then remove wiper arm and blade assemblies.

2. Remove cowl grille attaching screws, then remove cowl grille.
3. Remove clip, then disconnect linkage drive arm from wiper motor crankpin.
4. On Fairmont, Granada, Zephyr and 1981–82 Cougar models, remove four bolts attaching left and right pivot shafts to cowl, then remove linkage assembly.
5. On Cougar XR-7, Thunderbird and 1983 Cougar models, remove two bolts attaching right pivot shaft to cowl, then remove nut, washer and spacer from left pivot shaft, then remove linkage assembly.

1978 Fairmont & Zephyr

1. Disconnect battery ground cable.
2. Remove wiper arms and blade assemblies from pivot shafts, then remove cowl grille attaching screws.
3. If left pivot shaft assembly is to be removed, disconnect linkage drive arm from right drive arm by removing retaining clip.
4. If right pivot shaft assembly is to be

removed, disconnect linkage drive arm from motor and left drive arm by removing retaining clips.
5. Remove pivot shaft retaining screws, then remove linkage and pivot shaft assemblies.

1977–79 Cougar, LTD II & Thunderbird

1. Disconnect battery ground cable.
2. Remove wiper arm and blade assemblies.
3. Remove cowl screen. Screen snaps into cowl and the arm stop is integral with the screen.
4. Disconnect linkage drive arm from motor by removing retaining clip.
5. Remove pivot shaft retaining bolts and remove linkage and pivot shaft assemblies.

1977 Comet, Maverick & 1977–80 Granada & Monarch

Left Side:
1. Remove instrument cluster.
2. Remove wiper arm and blade.
3. Working through cluster opening, disconnect both pivot shaft links from motor drive arm by removing retaining clip.
4. Remove three pivot shaft assembly retaining bolts and remove assembly through cluster opening.
5. Reverse procedure to install.

Right Side:
1. Disconnect battery ground cable and remove wiper blade and arm.
2. On air conditioned units, remove right duct assembly.
3. From under the instrument panel, disconnect first left then right pivot shaft link from motor drive arm.
4. Reaching between utility shelf and instrument panel, remove pivot shaft retaining bolts and lower assembly out from under panel.
5. Reverse procedure to install.

W/S WIPER SWITCH, REPLACE

1977–79 Except Comet, Fairmont, Granada, Maverick, Monarch & Zephyr

1. Disconnect battery ground cable.
2. Remove wiper switch knob, bezel nut and bezel. The wiper switch knob is removed in the same manner as the headlight switch knob, Fig. 5.
3. Pull out switch from under panel and disconnect plug connector from switch.
4. Reverse procedure to install.

1979–83 Fairmont & Zephyr; 1980–82 Cougar XR-7; 1980–83 Thunderbird; 1981–82 Granada; 1981–83 Cougar; 1983 LTD & Marquis

1. Disconnect battery ground cable.
2. Remove four steering column shroud attaching screws, then grasp top and bottom of shroud and separate.

FORD & MERCURY—Compact & Intermediate Models

3. Using a screwdriver, disconnect wire connector from wiper switch.
4. Remove two wiper switch attaching screws, then remove switch.
5. Reverse procedure to install.

1978–81 Fairmont, Zephyr, 1982 Cougar, Granada & 1983 LTD & Marquis Sta. Wag. Liftgate Wiper Motor

1. Disconnect battery ground cable.
2. Remove wiper switch knob, then remove two bezel retaining screws.
3. Pull switch retainer away from instrument panel.
4. Remove wiper switch retaining nut, then separate switch from retainer.
5. Disconnect wire connector from wiper switch, then remove switch.
6. Reverse procedure to install.

1977–80 Granada, Monarch Column Mounted Switch

1. Disconnect battery ground cable.
2. Disconnect turn signal and wiper/washer switch wire connector.
3. Remove lower instrument panel shield.
4. Remove two screws and separate steering column cover halves.
5. Pull wire cover from bottom on column and remove cover.
6. With a screwdriver, disengage wiring shield tang and pry shield to remove.
7. Remove screw securing turn signal and windshield wiper/washer switch assembly to column, then remove the assembly.
8. Reverse procedure to install.

1977 Comet, & Maverick

1. Disconnect battery ground cable and remove switch knob.
2. On units without air conditioning, remove bezel nut and pull switch through panel. On air conditioned units, remove instrument cluster.
3. Disconnect wiring and remove switch.
4. Reverse procedure to install.

RADIO, REPLACE

NOTE: When installing radio, be sure to adjust antenna trimmer for peak performance.

1980–82 Cougar XR-7, 1980–83 Thunderbird & 1983 Cougar, LTD & Marquis

1. Disconnect battery ground cable.
2. Remove radio knobs, then remove instrument panel center trim panel.
3. Remove radio mounting plate attaching screws.
4. Pull radio to disengage from lower rear support bracket, then disconnect power antenna, speaker leads and floor switch lead, if equipped and remove radio.
5. Reverse procedure to install.

1978–83 Fairmont, Zephyr & 1981–82 Cougar & Granada

1. Disconnect battery ground cable.
2. Disconnect power lead, speaker leads and antenna lead from radio.
3. Remove control knobs, discs, control knob shaft nuts and washers.
4. Remove ash tray and bracket.
5. Remove radio rear support attaching nut.
6. Remove instrument panel lower reinforcement.
7. Remove heater or A/C floor ducts.
8. Remove radio from bezel and rear support, then lower radio from instrument panel.
9. Reverse procedure to install.

1977–80 Granada & Monarch

1. Disconnect battery ground cable.
2. Remove headlamp switch.
3. Remove knobs from heater and A/C control, windshield wiper switch and radio.
4. Remove instrument panel applique.
5. Disconnect antenna lead.
6. Remove radio bezel to instrument panel screws, then pull radio and bezel out to disconnect remaining electrical leads and remove radio from panel.
7. Remove rear support bracket and bezel from radio.
8. Reverse procedure to install.

1977–79 Thunderbird

1. Disconnect battery ground cable.
2. Pull radio knobs off shafts.
3. Remove nut from radio control shafts.
4. Remove radio rear support attaching screw at instrument panel.
5. Disconnect power and speaker wires at connectors.
6. Disconnect antenna lead and remove radio.
7. Reverse procedure to install.

1977 Comet, Maverick

1. Disconnect battery ground cable.
2. Disconnect power lead, speaker lead and antenna lead from radio.
3. Remove radio knobs, discs, control shaft nuts and washers.
4. Remove radio rear support attaching nut.
5. Remove radio from bezel and from rear support.
6. Reverse procedure to install.

1977–79 Cougar & LTD II

1. Disconnect battery ground cable.
2. Pull off radio control knobs.
3. Remove radio support to instrument panel attaching screw.
4. Remove bezel nuts from radio control shafts, then lower radio and disconnect speaker, power and antenna wire from radio.
5. Reverse procedure to install.

HEATER CORE, REPLACE

1980–82 Cougar XR-7, 1980–83 Thunderbird & 1983 Cougar, LTD & Marquis

1. Disconnect battery ground cable.

2. Remove steering column cover assembly, then remove left and right finish panels, Fig. 14.
3. Remove two screws from sides of instrument panel pad and retainer assembly.
4. Remove pad and retainer assembly and upper finish panel.
5. Remove steering column attaching bolts, then carefully lower steering column just enough to allow access to transmission gear selector lever cable assembly. Reach between steering column and instrument panel, then carefully lift selector lever cable from lever and remove cable clamp from steering column tube.
6. Lower steering column and allow to rest on front seat.
7. Remove screw attaching instrument panel to brake pedal support through steering column opening.
8. Disconnect termperature door cable from door and heater/evaporator cable bracket.
9. Disconnect vacuum hose connectors at evaporator housing.
10. Disconnect blower motor resistor wire from resistor on heater/evaporator case and blower motor feed wire at inline connector.
11. Support instrument panel, then remove three screws attaching top of instrument panel to cowl.
12. Remove one screw attaching each end of instrument panel to cowl side panels, then remove two screws attaching instrument panel to floor.
13. Move instrument panel rearward and disconnect speedometer cable and any wires that will prevent instrument panel from being placed on front seat.

NOTE: Use care when removing instrument panel to prevent damage to panel or steering column surfaces.

14. Drain cooling system, then disconnect heater hoses from heater core. Plug heater core tubes to prevent coolant spillage.
15. From engine compartment, remove two nuts attaching heater/evaporator case to dash panel.
16. From passenger compartment, remove bolts attaching heater/evaporator case and air inlet duct support brackets to cowl top panel.
17. Remove one nut attaching bracket at left side of heater/evaporator case to dash panel, then remove one nut retaining bracket below case to dash panel.
18. Carefully pull case away from dash panel to gain access to heater core cover attaching bolts.
19. Remove five heater core cover attaching bolts, then remove cover.
20. Remove heater core and seals from case, then remove seals from heater core tubes, Figs. 15 and 16.
21. Reverse procedure to install.

1978–83 Fairmont, Zephyr & 1981–82 Cougar & Granada

Less Air Conditioning
1. Disconnect battery ground cable and drain cooling system.
2. Disconnect heater hoses from heater core and seal the core tubes.
3. Remove glove box liner.
4. Remove instrument panel to cowl brace retaining screws and brace.
5. Place temperature control lever in the warm position.

Fig. 14 Instrument panel trim panels (Typical). 1980–82 Cougar XR-7, Thunderbird & 1983 LTD & Marquis

ACCESS COVER
-18N277-

DOOR SHAFT
-19B752-

SEAL -18C676-

SEAL
-18A597-

HEATER CORE
-18476-

DOOR SHAFT
-18A293-

VACUUM MOTOR
-18A318-

RESTRICTOR
DOOR
-19A555-

UPPER CASE
-19A626-

SEAL
-19B588-

HEAT-DEFROST
DOOR
-19B749-

SEAL
-19A672-

DOOR SHAFT
-19D846-

TEMPERATURE BLEND
DOOR
-19D843-

VACUUM
MOTOR
18A318-

BAFFLE
19A999-

CLIP
19A779-

SEAL
-19B739-

BLOWER RESISTOR
-19A706-

DRAIN
19874-

LOWER CASE
-19C831-

Fig. 15 Heater core less air conditioning. 1980–82 Cougar XR-7, 1980–83 Thunderbird & 1983 Cougar, LTD & Marquis

FRONT CASE HALF – 18A532

OUTSIDE AIR INLET DUCT – 19408

RETENTION CLIP (10) 19A779

HEATER CORE SUPPORT BRACKET – 18A441

HEAT-DEFROST SEPARATOR PLATE – 18C296

BLOWER MOTOR 18527

HEAT-DEFROST DOOR – 18A574

BLOWER WHEEL 18504

TEMPERATURE BLEND DOOR – 18B545

CLAMP 384260-S

HEATER CORE AND SEAL 18B539

REAR CASE HALF – 18A332

CASE ASSEMBLY SCREW (5)

RESISTOR ASSEMBLY 18591

HEATER CORE COVER 18B300

Fig. 15A   1978–83 Fairmont, Zephyr, 1981–82 Cougar & Granada

6. Remove heater core cover retaining screws and the cover, Figs. 15 and 15A.
7. From engine compartment, remove heater case assembly mounting stud nuts.
8. Push heater core tubes and seal toward passenger compartment to loosen heater core from case assembly.
9. Remove heater core through glove box opening.
10. Reverse procedure to install.

With Air Conditioning

1. Disconnect battery ground cable.
2. Remove screws attaching instrument cluster trim panel to instrument panel pad.
3. Remove instrument panel pad to instrument panel screws at each defroster opening.
4. Remove instrument panel pad edge to

instrument panel screws, and pad.
5. Remove steering column lower cover to instrument panel screws then the cover.
6. Remove two nuts and bracket securing steering column to instrument panel and brake pedal support. Support steering column on front seat.
7. Remove instrument panel to brake pedal support screw at steering column opening.
8. Remove screw attaching lower brace to lower edge of instrument panel below radio.
9. Remove screw attaching the brace to lower edge of instrument panel.
10. Disconnect temperature control cable from blend door and evaporator case bracket.
11. Disconnect vacuum hose connectors from evaporator case.
12. Disconnect blower resistor wire connector

from resistor on evaporator housing, then the blower motor feed wire at in-line connector.
13. Support instrument panel and, with an angle Phillips screwdriver, remove three screws attaching top of instrument panel to the cowl.
14. Remove screws attaching instrument panel to cowl side panels.
15. Move instrument panel rearward and disconnect speedometer cable and any wiring that will not permit the instrument panel to be positioned on the front seat.
16. Drain cooling system.
17. Disconnect heater hoses from heater core and seal core tubes.
18. From engine compartment, remove nuts retaining evaporator case to dash panel.
19. From passenger compartment, remove screws attaching evaporator case support bracket and air inlet duct support bracket

Fig. 16 Heater core with air conditioning. 1978–83 Fairmont, Zephyr, 1980–82 Cougar XR-7, 1980–83 Thunderbird, 1981–82 Granada, 1981–83 Cougar & 1983 LTD & Marquis

BLOWER MOTOR AND
WHEEL ASSEMBLY

ALIGNMENT
DIMPLES

HEATER CASE
ASSEMBLY

ALIGNMENT
HOLES

SELF-TAPPING SCREW –42127-S8
#10-12 x 1/2 HEX. WASHER HD.
4 REQUIRED

GROMMET

CORE ASSEMBLY

CORE COVER
PLATE

POLYURETHANE
MOUNTING PADS

SELF-TAPPING SCREW –42127-S8
#10-12 x 1/2 HEX. WASHER HD.
4 REQUIRED

Fig. 17   Heater core & blower motor less air conditioning. 1977–80 Granada & Monarch; 1977–79 Cougar, LTD II & Thunderbird

NOTE: Use extreme care when pulling back on instrument panel to avoid cracking plastic panel. Also, there is very little clearance between plenum and wiper motor assembly.

10. Using tab molded into rear heater core seal, pull heater core to left, then as rear surface of heater core clears evaporator case, pull core rearward and downward to clear instrument panel.
11. Reverse procedure to install, making certain that heater core tube to dash panel seal is in place between evaporator case and dash panel.

1977–79 Cougar, LTD II & Thunderbird

Less Air Conditioning
1. Disconnect battery ground cable and drain cooling system.
2. Disconnect heater hoses from heater core and plug core openings.
3. Remove heater assembly to dash retaining nuts.
4. Disconnect electrical wiring from door crank arms.
5. Disconnect electrical wiring from resistor and blower motor.
6. Remove glove box.
7. Remove right air duct control to instrument panel retaining nuts and bolts and the screws securing the right air duct, then remove the duct.
8. Remove heater assembly from vehicle.
9. Remove heater core cover pad and slide heater core from case, Fig. 17.

With Air Conditioning: 1977–79 Cougar, LTD II & Thunderbird
1. Disconnect battery ground cable and drain cooling system.
2. Disconnect heater hoses from heater core and plug core openings.
3. Remove heater core cover plate retaining screws and the plate.
4. Press downward on heater core and tip toward front of vehicle to release the heater core seal from housing Fig. 19.
5. Lift heater core from case and remove from vehicle.

1977 Comet & Maverick

Less Air Conditioning
1. Disconnect battery ground cable and drain engine cooling system.
2. Disconnect blower motor ground wire from fender apron at engine side of dash.
3. Disconnect heater hoses at engine block.
4. Remove heater assembly to dash panel mounting nuts.
5. Remove glove compartment and on all models remove right cowl trim panel.
6. Remove cable retaining clips and the push nuts at door crank arms. Disconnect control cables from crank arms.
7. Remove defroster air duct from left side of heater assembly.
8. Disconnect motor lead from resistor assembly on bottom of heater.
9. Remove heater case to instrument panel support bracket mounting screw.
10. Pull heater hoses through dash panel and disconnect hoses from heater core.

---

to cowl top panel.
20. Remove one nut retaining bracket at left end of evaporator case to dash panel and one nut retaining bracket beneath the case to dash panel.
21. Pull evaporator case assembly from dash panel.
22. Remove screws attaching heater core access cover from evaporator case, Fig. 16.
23. Remove heater core from evaporator case.
24. Reverse procedure to install.

1977–80 Granada & Monarch

Less Air Conditioning
1. Drain cooling system and disconnect heater hoses from heater core.
2. Remove glove box and the right and floor air distribution ducts.
3. Disconnect heater control cables and wiring harness from resistor assembly. Remove right vent cable bracket from instrument panel.
4. Remove vent duct to upper cowl mounting bolt.
5. Remove heater case to dash panel nuts, then the heater case and vent duct assembly.
6. Remove core cover and seal, then slide core from case, Fig. 17.

With Air Conditioning
1. Disconnect battery ground cable and drain coolant system, then disconnect heater hoses from core at engine side of dash panel.

NOTE: Easier access may be obtained by first disconnecting suction hose and moving it out of the way.

2. Remove heat distribution duct from instrument panel, seat belt interlock module and glove box liner, then loosen right door sill scuff plate and remove right cowl side from trim panel.
3. Loosen instrument panel to right cowl side bolt and remove instrument panel brace bolt at lower rail under glove box.
4. Remove tunnel to cowl brace, located to left of evaporator plenum assembly, if equipped.
5. Remove defroster nozzle by removing instrument panel crash pad, removing radio speaker or panel cowl brace, removing four nozzle to cowl bracket screws and lifting defroster nozzle upward through crash panel, Fig. 18.
6. Disconnect vacuum hoses from A/C-Defrost and A/C-Heat door motors and remove vacuum harness to plenum clip screw, then remove the two A/C-Heat mounting nuts and swing door rearward on crankarm.
7. Remove two plenum to left mounting bracket screws and remove the two screws and three clips securing plenum to evaporator case.
8. Swing bottom of plenum away from evaporator case and disengage S-clip on forward flange of plenum, then raise plenum to clear tabs on top of evaporator case.
9. Move plenum to left as far as possible (about 4 inches), pulling rearward on instrument panel to gain clearance.

EVAPORATOR CASE (UPPER)

MANIFOLD PLATE

EVAPORATOR CORE TUBE SEAL

PLENUM ASSEMBLY

HEATER CORE

CASE CLAMP (UPPER)

CASE CLAMP (LOWER)

HEATER CORE TUBE SEAL

DRAIN TUBE

2 REQ'D

3 REQ'D

SEAL

EVAPORATOR CORE

AIR INLET DUCT

EVAPORATOR CASE (LOWER)

Fig. 18 Heater core. 1977–80 Granada & Monarch with air conditioning

HEATER CORE COVER

ATTACHING SCREW 4 REQUIRED

POWER VENT ONLY

HEATER CORE AND SEAL

USE EXPANDING TOOL TO REMOVE CLIPS

HEATER CORE ASSEMBLY

Fig. 19 Heater core with air conditioning 1977–79 Cougar, LTD II & Thunderbird

Fig. 20 Heater core less air conditioning. 1977 Comet & Maverick

Fig. 21   Blower motor. 1978—83 Fairmont, Zephyr w/Air conditioning, 1980—82 Cougar XR-7, 1980—83 Thunderbird, 1981—82 Granada w/Air conditioning, 1981—83 Cougar & 1983 LTD & Marquis

11. Separate halves of heater and remove core, Fig. 20.

With Air Conditioning: 1977 Comet & Maverick
1. Disconnect battery ground cable and remove air cleaner.
2. Drain cooling system, then discharge refrigerant from A/C system.
3. Disconnect evaporator core tubes from expansion valve and heater hose from heater core.

NOTE: Place tape over evaporator core tubes and expansion valve fittings. Install plugs in heater hoses and core outlets to prevent coolant spillage.

4. Remove three A/C assembly to dash panel attaching nuts.
5. Remove lower instrument extension.
6. Remove radio.
7. On all models, disconnect right and left A/C register air duct assemblies from plenum chamber.
8. Remove floor distribution duct from blower housing.
9. On all models, disconnect vacuum lines from actuators and water valve
10. Remove any tape or clips retaining vacuum switch and control cable from door crank arm. Remove any vacuum lines to unit, then disconnect wires from A/C thermostat and resistor.
11. On 1977 models, disconnect blower motor wire connector and vacuum source line at connector and remove blower motor.
12. On all models, remove evaporator housing to cowl upper support attaching

screw, then move assembly rearward to clear mounting studs.
13. Pull drain tube from floor pan, then lower evaporator assembly and remove from vehicle.
14. Remove clips and separate housing halves.
15. Remove water valve vacuum switch and blend air door shaft, door and door frame from lower half of housing.
16. Lift heater core out of lower housing.

BLOWER MOTOR, REPLACE

1978—83 Fairmont, Zephyr Less Air Conditioning

1. Disconnect battery ground cable.
2. Remove screw securing right register duct mounting bracket to lower edge of instrument panel.
3. Remove screws securing ventilator control cable lever assembly to lower edge of instrument panel.
4. Remove glove box liner.
5. Remove plastic rivets securing grille to ventilator floor outlet, then the grille from the bottom of the ventilator assembly.
6. Remove right register duct and register assembly.
7. Remove screws securing ventilator assembly to blower housing portion of the heater case assembly.
8. Slide ventilator assembly toward the right, then downward to remove from under instrument panel.

9. Remove push nut from door crank arm.
10. Remove control cable housing retaining screw, then control cable assembly from ventilator assembly.
11. Disconnect blower lead wire from resistor assembly, push through hole in case.
12. Remove right side cowl trim panel and the ground terminal lug retaining screw.
13. Remove blower motor retaining screws and the blower motor.
14. Reverse procedure to install.

1978—83 Fairmont, Zephyr With Air Conditioning, 1980—82 Cougar XR-7, 1980—83 Thunderbird, 1981—82 Granada, 1981—83 Cougar & 1983 LTD & Marquis

1. Disconnect battery ground cable.
2. Remove glove box and disconnect vacuum hose from outside—recirc air door motor.
3. Remove instrument panel lower right to side attaching bolt.
4. Remove screw attaching support brace to top of air inlet duct.
5. Disconnect blower motor lead wire.
6. Remove nut securing blower motor housing lower bracket to evaporator case.
7. Remove side cowl trim panel and the blower ground wire screw.
8. Remove screw securing top of air inlet duct to evaporator case.
9. Move air inlet duct and blower housing assembly downward from evaporator case, Fig. 21.
10. Remove blower motor mounting plate screws and the blower motor.

NOTE: Do not remove mounting plate from motor.

11. Reverse procedure to install.

1977–80 Granada & Monarch

Less Air Conditioning

Remove heater case as outlined in the "1977–80 Granada & Monarch" procedure under "Heater Core, Removal," then remove screws securing blower motor to case, Fig. 17.

With Air Conditioning

1. Disconnect battery ground cable.
2. Loosen right door sill scuff plate and remove right cowl side trim panel, then remove right lower instrument panel to cowl side bolt.
3. Remove cowl to loosen instrument panel brace bolt, then disconnect wiring harness connectors from blower motor and remove cooling tube from motor.
4. Remove the four blower motor attaching screws and remove blower motor from scroll by pulling on lower edge of instrument panel to gain clearance.

NOTE: Use extreme care when pulling back on instrument panel to avoid cracking plastic panel.

5. Reverse procedure to install.

1977–79 Cougar, Thunderbird & LTD II

Less Air Conditioning

1. Follow the procedure to remove the heater core as described previously.
2. Remove the heater assembly from the vehicle, and place it on a bench.
3. Remove the four mounting screws and remove the blower motor and wheel assembly from the blower, Fig. 17.
4. Reverse procedure to install.

With Air Conditioning: 1977–79 Cougar, LTD II & Thunderbird

1. Remove instrument panel pad, glove box and side cowl trim panel.
2. Remove instrument panel attachment on right side.
3. Remove one nut attaching blower motor housing to engine side of dash panel.
4. Remove one nut attaching blower motor to passenger compartment side of dash panel.
5. Remove one blower housing mounting bracket and cowl top inner screw.
6. Disconnect vacuum line from outside-recirculating air door vacuum motor.
7. Disconnect blower motor lead wire from connector and blower motor ground wire.
8. Remove blower housing assembly.
9. Remove blower motor and wheel as an assembly from blower housing.

1977 Comet & Maverick

Less Air Conditioning

1. Remove the heater core as described previously.
2. Disconnect the blower motor lead wire (orange) from the resistor.
3. Remove the four blower motor mounting plate nuts and remove the motor and

Fig. 22   Servo assembly & throttle linkage (typical)

Labels in figure: VACUUM HOSE TO VACUUM RESERVOIR; SUPPLY VACUUM CHECK VALVE; SERVO ASSEMBLY (THROTTLE ACTUATOR); BALL CHAIN RETAINING PIN; ACTUATOR VACUUM LINE; UPPER SPEEDOMETER CABLE; ACTUATOR BRACKET; BLUE CONNECTOR; RED CONNECTOR; SPEED SENSOR; BEAD CHAIN ADJUSTER ASSEMBLY; LOWER SPEEDOMETER CABLE; BEAD CHAIN ADJUST TO MAINTAIN .06 TO .250 SERVO ARM FREE TRAVEL WITH ENGINE ON HOT IDLE

wheel assembly from the heater assembly.

With Air Conditioning

The blower housing has to be removed to gain access to the blower motor.

1. On 1977 models, remove lower instrument panel extension.
2. On all models, remove radio.
3. On all models, remove the floor air distribution duct from the bottom of the blower housing. Remove the blower housing mounting stud nut and lock plate.
4. Rotate the blower housing to unlock the slotted tabs on the blower housing from their lock pins on the evaporator housing. There are two tabs and two pins. Disconnect the red and yellow hoses at the vacuum motor on the blower housing. Disconnect the resistor and ground wires, and remove the blower housing.
5. On all models, remove seven clips and separate blower motor housing halves.
6. Remove three blower motor mounting plate retaining nuts, and remove the motor and wheel assembly from the housing.
7. When installing be sure that the A/C Heat-Door is positioned properly before clipping the right and left housings together.

SPEED CONTROLS

Except 1979–83 Fairmont, Zephyr, 1980–82 Cougar XR-7, 1980–83 Thunderbird, 1981–82 Granada & 1981–83 Cougar

Adjust bead chain to obtain .06–.25" actua-

tor arm free travel when engine is at hot idle. The adjustment should be made to take as much slack as possible out of the chain without restricting the carburetor lever from returning to idle, Fig. 22.

On vehicles with a solenoid anti-diesel valve, perfom adjustment with ignition switch in the "ON" position.

1979–83 Fairmont, Zephyr, 1980–82 Cougar XR-7, 1980–83 Thunderbird, 1981–82 Granada, 1981–83 Cougar & 1983 LTD & Marquis

Bead Chain Adjustment

This adjustment should be made to remove as much slack as possible from the chain without restricting the carburetor lever from returning to the idle speed position. On vehicles equipped with a solenoid throttle positioner, the adjustment should be performed with the throttle positioner disengaged.

Vacuum Dump Valve

The vacuum dump valve is mounted on a moveable mounting bracket. The valve should be adjusted so that it is closed when the brake pedal is not depressed and opens when the brake pedal is depressed.

Actuator Cable Adjustment

1. Deactivate the throttle positioner.
2. Set carburetor at hot idle.
3. Pull the actuator cable to remove slack.
4. While maintaining light tension on the actuator cable, insert the cable retaining clip.

Engine Section

> **NOTE:** Refer to "FORD MUSTANG & PINTO ● MERCURY BOBCAT & CAPRI" Section for service on the 2300 cc (4-140) engine & Turbocharged engine.

ENGINE MOUNTS

Caution: Whenever self-locking mounting bolts and nuts are removed, they must be replaced with new self-locking bolts and nuts.

1978–83 Fairmont, Zephyr, 1980–82 Thunderbird, Cougar XR-7, 1981–82 Cougar, Granada & 1983 LTD & Marquis 6-200

1. Remove fan shroud screws.
2. Support engine with suitable jack and wooden block.
3. On LTD and Marquis models, remove engine damper lower bolt and No. 2 crossmember bracket, Fig. 1A.
4. On all models, remove nut and washer assemblies from insulators at No. 2 crossmember.
5. Raise engine with jack until insulator studs clear crossmember.
6. Disconnect bracket from engine and remove engine mount.
7. Reverse procedure to install. Torque fasteners according to Figs. 1 and 1A.

1977–80 Granada, Monarch & 1977 Comet & Maverick 6-200 & 250

1. Remove the insulator to support bracket retaining nuts, Fig. 1B.

2. Using a wood block placed under the oil pan, raise the engine enough to clear the insulator.
3. Remove the retaining screws and nuts from the insulator(s). Remove the insulator(s).
4. Reverse procedure to install.

1982–83 V6-232

1. Support engine using a suitable jack and wooden block placed under oil pan.
2. Remove nut and washer attaching mount to chassis, then raise engine slightly, Fig. 2.
3. Remove bolts attaching engine mount and bracket to engine, then remove mount.
4. Reverse procedure to install.

1981 Cougar & Granada V8-255

1. Remove fan shroud attaching screws, then position shroud over fan.
2. Using a suitable jack with a wooden block placed under oil pan, support engine.
3. Remove nut and through bolt attaching insulator to support bracket, Fig. 3.
4. Raise engine slightly, then remove insulator and bracket assembly to cylinder block attaching bolts.
5. Remove insulator assembly and heat shield, if equipped.
6. Reverse procedure to install.

1980–82 Cougar XR-7 & Thunderbird V8-255 & 302

1. Remove fan shroud attaching screws.
2. Using a suitable jack with a wooden block placed under oil pan, support engine.
3. Remove nut and through bolt attaching insulator to frame crossmember.
4. Raise engine slightly, then remove insulator and heat shield, if equipped, Fig. 3.
5. Reverse procedure to install.

1978–81 Fairmont & Zephyr V8-255 & 302

1. Remove fan shroud attaching screws.
2. Remove nuts attaching insulators to lower bracket, Fig. 3.
3. Raise engine slightly using a block of wood placed under the oil pan and a suitable jack.
4. Remove bolts attaching insulator to engine block.
5. Remove insulator assembly.
6. Reverse procedure to install.

1977 Comet, Maverick, 1977–80 Granada & Monarch V8-255, 302, 351W

1. Using a block of wood and jack placed under oil pan, support engine.
2. Remove through bolt attaching motor

Fig. 1 Engine mounts. 1983 LTD & Marquis 6-200

Fig. 1A Engine mounts. 1978–83 Fairmont, Zephyr, 1980–82 Cougar, XR-7, Thunderbird & 1981–82 Granada 6-200

mount to crossmember, Figs. 4 and 5.
3. Remove engine mount to engine attaching bolts.
4. Raise engine slightly and remove engine mount and heat shield (if used).
5. Reverse procedure to install.

1977–79 V8-302 & 351W Except Comet, Fairmont, Granada, Maverick, Monarch & Zephyr

1. Remove fan shroud attaching screws.

2. Support engine using a block of wood placed under the oil pan and a suitable jack.
3. Remove nut and through bolt attaching insulator to frame crossmember, Fig. 6.
4. Raise engine slightly and remove insulator and heat shield, if equipped.
5. Reverse procedure to install.

1977–79 V8-351M & 400

1. Remove fan shroud attaching bolts.
2. Remove through bolt and nut attaching insulator to insulator support bracket,

Fig. 4   Engine mounts. 1977 Comet & Maverick V8

Fig. 1B   Engine mounts. 1977 Comet & Maverick, 1977–80 Granada & Monarch 6-200, 250

Fig. 3   Engine mounts (typical). 1978–81 Fairmont, Zephyr, 1980–82 Cougar XR-7, Thunderbird & 1981 Cougar & Granada V8-255, 302

Fig. 5   Engine mounts. 1977–80 Granada & Monarch V8-255, 302, 351W

GRANADA/COUGAR

REAR SUPPORT

THUNDERBIRD/XR-7

NO. 3 CROSSMEMBER

NO. 2 CROSSMEMBER

ENGINE DAMPER

FRONT SUPPORT (LEFT)

INTAKE MANIFOLD ATTACHING STUD/BOLT

FRONT SUPPORT (RIGHT)

Fig. 2 Engine mount. 1982 V6-232

Fig. 7

3. Raise engine slightly using a block of wood placed under the oil pan and a suitable jack.
4. Remove insulator assembly to engine block attaching bolts and lock washers.
5. Remove insulator and heat shield, if equipped.
6. Reverse procedure to install.

ENGINE, REPLACE

6-200 & 250

1. Remove battery ground cable.
2. Remove hood assembly.
3. Drain cooling system and oil pan.
4. Disconnect crankcase ventilation hose and remove air cleaner.
5. Disconnect canister purge hose from P.C.V. valve.
6. Disconnect radiator and heater hoses and remove all drive belts.
7. If equipped with automatic transmission, disconnect transmission oil cooler lines from radiator.
8. On all models, remove radiator, then the fan, spacer and pulley.
9. Disconnect alternator and starter wiring, then the accelerator cable from carburetor.
10. If equipped with Thermactor system, remove or disconnect components that may interfere with engine replacement.
11. If equipped with A/C, remove compressor from mounting bracket and position aside with refrigerant line attached.
12. On all models, disconnect and plug fuel pump inlet line.
13. Disconnect ignition coil wires, then the oil pressure and water temperature wiring from sending units.
14. Remove starter motor.
15. If equipped with manual transmission, disconnect clutch retracting spring, then the clutch equalizer shaft and arm bracket from underbody rail. Remove arm bracket and equalizer shaft.
16. On all models, raise vehicle and remove flywheel or converter housing upper attaching bolts.
17. Disconnect exhaust pipe from manifold. Loosen exhaust pipe clamp and slide off support bracket on engine.
18. Disconnect front engine mounts from underbody bracket.
19. Remove flywheel or converter housing cover.
20. If equipped with manual transmission, remove flywheel housing lower attaching bolts.
21. If equipped with automatic transmission, remove converter to flywheel bolts, then the converter housing lower attaching bolts.
22. On all models, lower vehicle and support transmission and flywheel or converter housing with a suitable jack.
23. Attach suitable lifting equipment to engine and remove engine from vehicle.
24. Reverse procedure to install.

V6-232

1. Disconnect battery ground cable, then drain cooling system and crankcase.
2. Mark position of hood hinges, then remove hood.
3. Remove air cleaner, air inlet duct and heat tube.
4. Remove fan shroud and fan assembly, then loosen accessory drive belt idler and

Fig. 6   Engine mounts, 1977–79 V8-302 351W exc. Comet, Fairmont, Granada, Maverick, Monarch & Zephyr

remove drive belt and water pump pulley.
5. Disconnect upper and lower radiator hoses at radiator.
6. Disconnect Thermactor hose at air tube check valve, then remove air tube valve bracket attaching bolt at rear of right hand cylinder head.
7. Remove secondary wire from ignition coil.
8. Remove bolts attaching power steering pump mounting bracket, then remove pump and bracket assembly and position aside with hoses attached, if equipped.
9. On models with A/C, remove compressor mounting bracket attaching bolts, then remove compressor and mounting bracket assembly and secure to right hand shock absorber tower with refrigerant lines attached.
10. Remove alternator and position aside.
11. Disconnect heater hoses from water pump and heater tube.
12. On models equipped with speed control, disconnect servo chain at carburetor, then remove servo bracket attaching bolts and servo.
13. Disconnect all necessary vacuum hoses and wiring connectors.
14. Remove engine ground strap to dash panel attaching screw.
15. Disconnect transmission downshift linkage, throttle cable from carburetor, then remove throttle cable bracket attaching bolts.
16. Disconnect fuel line and PCV valve hose from carburetor.
17. Remove carburetor assembly from intake manifold. On models equipped with 7200 VV two barrel carburetor, remove spark knock intensity sensor and adapter assembly which is located between carburetor and thermostat housing.
18. With EGR spacer and phenolic gasket in position, install engine lifting plate T75T-6000-A or suitable over carburetor mounting studs, then install nuts.
19. Raise vehicle and disconnect fuel inlet hose from fuel pump. Cap fuel hose to prevent entry of dirt.
20. Remove inspection cover from torque converter housing, then remove nuts attaching flex plate to torque converter.

Fig. 7   Engine mounts, 1977–79 V8-400 & V8-351M

21. Remove starter motor.
22. Remove transmission cooler line retaining clips, then disconnect exhaust pipe from exhaust manifold.
23. Remove four lower engine to transmission attaching bolts, then lower vehicle.
24. Remove engine mount to crossmember attaching nuts.
25. Lower vehicle and position a suitable transmission jack under transmission. Raise jack just enough to support weight of transmission.
26. Remove two upper engine to transmission attaching bolts, then place a 1/4 inch piece of plywood or other suitable material between engine and radiator to prevent damage to radiator.
27. Carefully raise engine slightly, then pull away transmission and lift from vehicle.

V8-255, 302 & 351W

1. Remove battery ground cable.
2. Remove hood.
3. Drain cooling system and oil pan.
4. Remove air cleaner and intake duct assembly.
5. Disconnect radiator and heater hoses, then remove all drive belts.
6. If equipped with automatic transmission, disconnect transmission oil cooler lines from radiator.
7. On all models, remove fan shroud attaching bolts, then the radiator, fan, spacer, pulley and shroud.
8. Remove alternator mounting bolts and position alternator aside with wiring attached.
9. Disconnect oil pressure and water temperature wiring from sending units, then the accelerator cable from carburetor.
10. Disconnect and plug fuel pump inlet line.
11. If equipped with automatic transmission, disconnect throttle valve vacuum line from intake manifold. Disconnect manual shift rod and the retracting spring at shift rod stud. Disconnect transmission filler tube bracket from engine block.
12. If equipped with Thermactor system, remove or disconnect components that may interfere with engine replacement.
13. If equipped with A/C, isolate and remove compressor.
14. If equipped with power steering, disconnect pump bracket from cylinder head and position assembly aside.
15. If equipped with power brakes, disconnect brake vacuum line from intake manifold.
16. On all models, remove flywheel or converter housing upper attaching bolts.
17. Disconnect ignition coil wiring.

Fig. 8 Cylinder head tightening sequence. 1977 6-200 & 250

Fig. 8A Cylinder head tightening sequence. 1978–83 6-200 & 250

Fig. 9 Cylinder head tightening sequence. 1982–83 V6-232

18. Remove wiring harness from left side rocker arm cover and position aside. Disconnect ground strap from engine block.
19. Raise front of vehicle. Disconnect starter wiring, then remove starter motor.
20. Disconnect exhaust pipes from manifolds.
21. Disconnect engine mounts from brackets on frame.
22. If equipped with manual transmission, remove bolts attaching clutch equalizer bar to frame rail, then the equalizer from engine block. Remove remaining flywheel housing to engine bolts.
23. If equipped with automatic transmission, disconnect transmission oil cooler lines from retainer and remove converter housing inspection cover. Remove converter to flywheel bolts and secure converter in housing. Remove remaining converter housing to engine bolts.
24. On all models, lower vehicle and support transmission with a suitable jack.
25. Attach suitable engine lifting equipment to engine.
26. Lift engine slightly and pull forward to disengage from transmission, then remove engine from vehicle.
27. Reverse procedure to install.

V8-351M & 400

1. Remove battery ground cable.
2. Drain cooling system and oil pan.
3. Remove hood.
4. Remove air cleaner and air intake duct.
5. Disconnect radiator and heater hoses, then remove all drive belts.
6. If equipped with automatic transmission, disconnect transmission oil cooler lines from radiator.
7. On all models, remove fan shroud attaching bolts, then the radiator, fan, spacer, pulley and shroud.
8. Remove power steering pump brackets and position pump aside with lines attached.
9. If equipped with Thermactor system, remove or disconnect components that may interfere with engine replacement.
10. If equipped with A/C, isolate and remove compressor.
11. On all models, remove alternator bracket mounting bolts and position alternator aside with wiring attached. Disconnect alternator ground wire from engine block.
12. Remove wires from engine block and right hand cylinder head.
13. Disconnect and plug fuel pump inlet line.
14. Disconnect vacuum lines at rear of intake manifold. Disconnect vacuum control valve hoses and wiring, if equipped.

15. Disconnect accelerator cable or linkage from carburetor, then the transmission downshift linkage, if equipped.
16. Disconnect engine wiring harness from ignition coil, water temperature sending unit and oil pressure sending unit. Remove wiring harness from hold down clips.
17. Raise and support vehicle.
18. Disconnect exhaust pipes from exhaust manifolds and remove the heat control valve, if equipped, or the manifold to pipe spacer.
19. Disconnect starter motor wiring and remove starter motor.
20. Remove engine front support through bolts and the starter motor cable clamp from right front engine support.
21. If equipped with automatic transmission, remove converter inspection cover, then the converter to flywheel bolts. Remove downshift rod, then the four lower converter housing to engine bolts and the adapter plate to converter housing bolt.
22. If equipped with manual transmission, disconnect clutch linkage from engine block and remove the four lower flywheel housing bolts.
23. On all models, lower the vehicle and remove the two upper converter housing or flywheel housing bolts.
24. Attach suitable engine lifting equipment to engine and support transmission with a suitable jack.
25. Raise engine slightly and pull forward to disengage from transmission, then remove engine from vehicle.
26. Reverse procedure to install.

CYLINDER HEAD, REPLACE

Tighten cylinder head bolts a little at a time in three steps in the sequence shown in the illustrations. Final tightening should be to the torque specifications listed in the *Engine Tightening* table. After tightening the bolts to specifications, *they should not be disturbed*.

6-200 & 250

1. Drain cooling system and remove air cleaner.
2. Disconnect exhaust pipe from manifold and pull it down.
3. Disconnect accelerator cable and transmission downshift rod from carburetor.
4. Disconnect fuel inlet line at fuel filter hose, and distributor vacuum line at carburetor.
5. Disconnect coolant lines at carburetor spacer, if equipped. Remove radiator upper hose at outlet housing.

6. Disconnect distributor vacuum line at distributor. Disconnect carburetor fuel inlet line at fuel pump. Remove lines as an assembly.
7. Disconnect spark plug wires at plugs and temperature sending unit wire at sending unit.
8. Remove crankcase ventilation system. Remove hoses from Thermactor system as necessary for accessability.
9. Remove valve rocker arm cover.
10. Remove rocker arm shaft assembly.
11. Remove valve push rods.
12. Remove remaining cylinder head bolts and lift off head.
13. Reverse procedure to install. Torque cylinder head according to sequence shown in Figs. 8 and 8A in three steps: step 1, 50–55 ft. lbs.; step 2, 60–65 ft. lbs.; step 3, 70–75 ft. lbs.

V6-232

1. Disconnect battery ground cable, then drain cooling system.
2. Remove air cleaner, air intake duct and heat tube.
3. Loosen accessory drive belt idler and remove drive belt.
4. If left cylinder head is to be removed, proceed as follows:
   a. Remove oil filler cap.
   b. If equipped with power steering, remove pump bracket attaching bolts, then remove pump and bracket assembly and position pump aside with hoses attached.
   c. If equipped with A/C, remove compressor bracket attaching bolts, then position compressor and bracket assembly aside with refrigerant lines attached.
5. If right cylinder head is to be removed, proceed as follows:
   a. Remove Thermactor diverter valve and hose assembly.
   b. Remove accessory drive belt idler, then remove alternator.
   c. Remove Thermactor pump pulley, then remove Thermactor pump.
   d. Remove alternator mounting bracket.

NOTE: On models equipped with Tripminder, the fuel supply line from the fuel pump to the fuel sensor will have to be disconnected to gain access to the upper alternator bracket bolt.

   e. Remove PCV valve.
6. Remove intake manifold and exhaust manifolds.
7. Remove rocker arm cover attaching screws, then loosen cover by using a putty knife under cover flange and remove cover. Do not use excess force when loosening rocker arm cover as cover may become damaged.
8. Loosen rocker arm fulcrum bolt enough to allow rocker arms to be rotated to one side, then remove push rods.

Fig. 10 Intake manifold tightening sequence. 1982–83 V6-232

NOTE: Tag push rods so they can be installed in the same position.

9. Remove cylinder head attaching bolts, then remove cylinder head and gasket.
10. Reverse procedure to install. Apply a thin coating of pipe sealant D8AZ-19558-A or equivalent to the shorter cylinder head bolts which are installed on the exhaust manifold side of the cylinder head. Do not apply pipe sealant to long bolts which are installed on the intake manifold side of the cylinder head. Tighten cylinder head bolts in four steps to torque listed under Engine Tightening Specifications using sequence shown in Fig. 9. Step 1, 47 ft. lbs.; step 2, 55 ft. lbs.; step 3, 63 ft. lbs.; step 4, 74 ft. lbs. Loosen cylinder bolts approximately 2 to 3 turns, then retighten bolts in four steps to specified torque in sequence, Fig. 9. When installing intake manifold, tighten mounting bolts to torque specified under Engine Tightening Specifications in sequence shown in Fig. 10 in three steps: step 1, 5 ft. lbs.; step 2, 10 ft. lbs.; step 3, 18 ft. lbs.

Fig. 13 Intake manifold tightening sequence V8-255, 302 & V8-351W

Fig. 11 Applying RTV sealer for intake manifold installation. 1980–82 V8-255, 302 & 1982–83 V6-232

NOTE: Before installing intake manifold, apply a 1/8 inch bead of silicone rubber sealer D6AZ-19562-B or equivalent at mating surfaces of intake manifold, cylinder heads and cylinder block, Fig. 11. Also apply a 1/8 inch bead of sealer to the outer end of each intake manifold seal for the full width of the seal.

V8-255, 302, 351, 400

1. Remove intake manifold and carburetor as an assembly.
2. Disconnect battery ground cable at cylinder head.
3. If left head is being removed, remove A/C compressor (if equipped). Also remove and wire power steering pump out of the way. If equipped with Thermactor System, disconnect hose from air manifold on left cylinder head.
4. If right head is to be removed, remove alternator mounting bracket bolt and spacer, ground wire and air cleaner inlet duct.
5. If right head is to be removed on an engine with Thermactor System, remove air pump from bracket. Disconnect hose from air manifold.
6. Disconnect exhaust manifolds at exhaust pipes.
7. Remove rocker arm covers. If equipped with Thermactor System, remove check valve from air manifold.
8. On 1977 and early 1978 V8-302 and 351W engines, loosen rocker arm stud nut so that rocker arms can be rotated to one side. On V8-351M, 400 and late 1978 and 1979–82 V8-255, 302 and 351W, remove fulcrum bolts, oil deflector (if used), fulcrum and rocker arms. On all engines, remove push rods. Keep push rods and rocker arm components in order so they may be installed in original position.
9. Remove head bolts and lift head off block.
10. Reverse procedure to install. Torque cylinder head bolts in sequence shown in Fig. 12, and torque intake manifold bolts in sequence shown in Figs. 13 and 14.

NOTE: On 1980–82 V8-255, 302 engines, be-

Fig. 12 Cylinder head tightening. V8 engines

fore installing intake manifold, apply a 1/8 in. bead of silicone rubber sealer D6AZ-19563-A or B or equivalent at mating surfaces of intake manifold, cylinder heads and cylinder block, Fig. 11. Also apply a 1/16 in. bead of sealer to the outer end of each intake manifold seal for the full width of the seal.

VALVE ARRANGEMENT

Front to Rear

4-140	E-I-E-I-E-I-E-I
6-200, 250	E-I-I-E-I-E-E-I-E-I-I-E
V6-232 Right	I-E-I-E-I-E
V6-232 Left	E-I-E-I-E-I
V8-255, 302 Right	I-E-I-E-I-E-I-E
V8-255, 302 Left	E-I-E-I-E-I-E-I
V8-351, 400 Right	I-E-I-E-I-E-I-E
V8-351, 400 Left	E-I-E-I-E-I-E-I

VALVE LIFT SPECS

Engine	Year	Intake	Exhaust
4-140	1978–83	.3997	.3997
6-200	1977–83	.372	.372
6-250	1977–80	.372	.372
V6-232	1982–83	.415	.417
V8-255	1980–82	.3753	.3753
V8-302	1976–77	.3823	.3884
	1978–79	.3823	.3980
	1980–81	.3753	.3909
V8-351W①	1977–79	.4186	.4186
V8-351M②	1977–79	.4065	.4065
V8-400	1977–78	.428	.4325

①—Windsor engine.
②—Modified engine.

Fig. 14 Intake manifold tightening sequence V8-351M, 400

Fig. 15 Compressing lifter to check valve clearance. V8 engines (typical of 6 cylinder engines)

Fig. 16 Rocker arm assembly. 1977 & early 1978 V8-302, 351W

Fig. 17 Rocker arm stud nut. 1977 & early 1978 V8-302, 351W

VALVE TIMING

Intake Opens Before TDC

Engine	Year	Degrees
4-140	1978–82	22
6-200	1977–82	20
6-250	1977–80	18
V6-232	1982	13
V8-255	1980–82	16
V8-302	1977–81	16
V8-351②	1977–79	23
V8-351①	1977–79	19.5
V8-400	1977–78	17

①—Modified.
②—Windsor engine.

VALVES, ADJUST

6-200 & 250

A .060 inch longer or a .060 inch shorter push rod is available to compensate for dimensional changes in the valve train. If clearance is less than the minimum, the .060 inch shorter push rod should be used. If clearance is more than the maximum, the .060 inch longer push rod should be used.

The procedure used to check the valve clearance is to rotate the crankshaft with an auxiliary starter switch until the No. 1 piston is near TDC at the end of the compression stroke, and then compress the valve lifter using tool 6513-K or equivalent, Fig. 15. At this point the following valves can be checked:

No. 1 Intake	No. 3 Exhaust
No. 1 Exhaust	No. 4 Intake
No. 2 Intake	No. 5 Exhaust

After the clearance of these valves have been checked, rotate the crankshaft until the No. 6 piston is on TDC at the end of its compression stroke (1 revolution of the crankshaft), and then compress the valve lifter using tool 6513-K or equivalent, Fig. 15, and check the following valves:

No. 2 Exhaust	No. 5 Intake
No. 3 Intake	No. 6 Intake
No. 4 Exhaust	No. 6 Exhaust

V6-232

A .060 inch longer or a .060 inch shorter push rod is available to compensate for dimensional changes in the valve train. If clearance is less than specified, the .060 inch shorter push rod should be used. If clearance is more than the maximum specified, the .060 inch longer push rod should be used.

Using an auxiliary starter switch crankshaft until No. 1 cylinder is at TDC compression stroke, then compress valve lifter using tool T82C-6500-A or equivalent, Fig. 15. At this point, the following valves can be checked:

No. 1 Intake	No. 3 Intake
No. 1 Exhaust	No. 4 Exhaust
No. 2 Exhaust	No. 6 Intake

After clearance on these valves has been checked, rotate crankshaft until No. 5 cylinder is at TDC compression stroke (1 revolution of crankshaft), and then compress valve lifter using tool No. T82C-6500-A or equivalent, Fig. 15, and check the following valves:

No. 2 Intake	No. 5 Intake
No. 3 Exhaust	No. 5 Exhaust
No. 4 Intake	No. 6 Exhaust

Fig. 18 Rocker arm assembly. V6-232 & Late 1978 & 1979–82 V8-255, 302, 351W

V8 Engines

For these engines, a .060″ longer or a .060″ shorter push rod is available to provide a means of compensating for dimensional changes in the valve train and rocker arm. If the clearance is less than the minimum, the .060″ shorter push rod should be used. If clearance is more than the maximum the .060″ longer push rod should be used.

1977 and early 1978 V8-302 and 351W engines use a positive stop rocker arm stud and nut, Fig. 16. Before checking valve lash, check condition of stud nut, Fig. 17. Torque stud nut to 18–22 ft. lbs.

Late 1978 and 1979–82 V8-255, 302 and 351W engines use a bolt and fulcrum attachment, Fig. 18.

To check valve clearance, proceed as follows:

1. Mark crankshaft pulley at three locations with number 1 location at TDC timing mark (end of compression stroke), number 2 location one half turn (180°) clockwise from TDC and number 3 location three quarter turn clockwise (270°) from TDC.

2. Turn the crankshaft to the number 1 location, then compress valve lifter using tool T71P-6513-A or equivalent, Fig. 15, and check the clearance on the following valves:

   V8-255, 302

No. 1 Intake	No. 1 Exhaust
No. 7 Intake	No. 5 Exhaust
No. 8 Intake	No. 4 Exhaust

   V8-351, 400

No. 1 Intake	No. 1 Exhaust
No. 4 Intake	No. 3 Exhaust
No. 8 Intake	No. 7 Exhaust

3. Turn the crankshaft to the number 2 location, then compress valve lifter using tool T71P-6513-A or equivalent, Fig. 15, and check the clearance on the following valves:

   V8-255, 302

No. 4 Intake	No. 2 Exhaust
No. 5 Intake	No. 6 Exhaust

   V8-351, 400

No. 3 Intake	No. 2 Exhaust
No. 7 Intake	No. 6 Exhaust

4. Turn the crankshaft to the number 3 location, then compress valve lifter using tool T71P-6513-A or equivalent, Fig. 15, and check the clearance on the following valves:

   V8-255, 302

No. 2 Intake	No. 3 Exhaust
No. 3 Intake	No. 7 Exhaust
No. 6 Intake	No. 8 Exhaust

   V8-351, 400

No. 2 Intake	No. 4 Exhaust
No. 5 Intake	No. 5 Exhaust
No. 6 Intake	No. 8 Exhaust

   adjust valve lash.

Fig. 19 Rocker arm stud removal 1977 & early 1978 V8-302 & 351W

ROCKER ARM STUD, REPLACE

1977 & Early 1978 V8-302 & 351W

If it is necessary to replace a rocker arm stud, a rocker arm stud kit is available and contains a stud remover, Fig. 19, a stud installer, Fig. 20, and two reamers, one .006 in. and the other .015 in. If a .010 in. oversize stud is to be installed, use reamer T66P-6A527-B.

Rocker arm studs that have been broken or have damaged threads, may be replaced with standard size studs. Loose studs in the cylinder head may be replaced with .006, .010 or .015 in. oversize studs. Standard and oversize studs can be identified by measuring the stud diameter within 1⅛ in. from pilot end of stud. The diameter of the rocker arm studs is as follows: standard .3714 to .3721 in.; .006 in. oversize, .3774 to .3781 in., 010 in. oversize, .3814 to .3821 in.; .015 in. oversize stud, .3864 to .3871 in.

When replacing a standard size stud with a .010 or .015 in. oversize stud, always use a .006 in. reamer before finishing with a .010 or .015 in. oversize reamer.

If a stud is broken off flush with the stud boss, use an easy-out to remove the broken stud, following the instructions of the tool manufacturer.

Installation

1. Position the piston of the cylinder being worked on at TDC compression stroke.
2. Locate stud properly with tool T69P-6049D, Fig. 20. Make sure tool bottoms on the head.
3. Lubricate rocker arm components and place rocker arm and fulcrum on the stud.
4. Thread nut onto the stud until it contacts the shoulder, then tighten nut to 18–22 ft lbs.

VALVE GUIDES

Valve guides consist of holes bored in the cylinder head. For service the guide holes can be reamed oversize to accommodate valves with oversize stems of .003, .015 and .030 inch from 1977–79 engine, .015 and .030 inch for 1980–82 engines.

ROCKER ARM SERVICE

6-200 & 250

Disassemble

1. To disassemble, remove pin and spring washer from each end of rocker shaft, Fig. 21.
2. Slide rocker arms, springs and supports off the shaft, being sure to identify location of parts for reassembly.
3. If it is necessary to remove the plugs from the shaft ends, drill or pierce the plug on one end. Then use a steel rod to knock out the plug on the opposite end. Working from the open end, knock out the remaining plug.

Assemble

1. Lubricate all parts with engine oil. Apply Lubriplate to the rocker arm pads.
2. If plugs were removed from shaft ends, use a blunt tool or large diameter pin punch and install a plug (cup side out) in each end of shaft.
3. Install spring washer and pin on one end of shaft.
4. Install rocker arms, supports and springs in order shown in Fig. 21. *Be sure oil holes in shaft are facing downward.*
5. Complete the assembly by installing remaining spring washer and pin.

V6-232

These engines use stamped steel rocker arms retained by a fulcrum seat which bolts directly to the cylinder head and guides the

Fig. 20 Positive stop type rocker arm stud installation. 1977 & early 1978 V8-302 & 351W

rocker arm. Torque fulcrum bolts in two steps as follows: For each valve rotate crankshaft until tappet rests on heel (base circle) of camshaft lobe and torque fulcrum bolt to 5–11 ft. lbs. After initial torquing all fulcrum bolts, final torque to 19–25 ft. lbs. Final torque may be done with camshaft in any position.

V8-255, 351M, 400 & Late 1978 & 1979–81 V8-302, 351W

These engines use stamped steel rocker arms retained by a fulcrum seat, Figs. 18 and 22. The fulcrum seat bolts directly to the cylinder head and guides the rocker arm.

VALVE LIFTERS, REPLACE

6-200 & 250

When necessary to replace valve lifters, remove cylinder head and related parts as outlined previously. Then, using a magnet rod, Fig. 23, remove and install one lifter at a time to be sure they are placed in their original bores.

When installing, apply Lubriplate to each lifter foot and coat the remainder of lifter with oil before installation.

V6-232, V8-255, 302, 351 & 400

1. Remove intake manifold.
2. Remove rocker arm covers. On engines with stud mounted rocker arms, loosen stud nuts and rotate rocker arms to one side. On other engines, remove fulcrum bolt, fulcrum, rocker arm and fulcrum guide (if used).
3. Remove push rods in sequence so they can be installed in their original bores.
4. Using a magnet rod, Fig. 22, remove the lifters and place them in a numbered rack so they can be installed in their original bores. *If the lifters are stuck in their bores by excessive varnish, etc., it may be necessary to use a plier-type tool to remove them. Rotate the lifter back and forth to loosen it from the gum or varnish.*

Fig. 21 Rocker arm shaft assembly. 6-200 & 250

Fig. 22 Rocker arm assembly. V8-351M & 400

5. The internal parts of each lifter are matched sets. Do not intermix parts. Keep the assemblies intact until they are to be cleaned, Fig. 24.

TIMING CASE COVER, REPLACE

NOTE: To replace the seal in the timing gear cover, it is necessary to remove the cover as outlined below.

6-200 & 250

Removal

1. Disconnect battery ground cable.
2. Drain cooling system and oil pan.
3. Disconnect radiator hoses from engine, then the transmission oil cooler lines from radiator, if equipped.
4. Remove radiator, then the drive belt, fan and pulley.
5. If equipped with A/C, remove condenser attaching bolts and position condenser forward with refrigerant lines attached.

Fig. 24 Hydraulic valve lifter

Remove compressor drive belt.

6. On all models, remove accessory drive pulley and the crankshaft damper with a suitable puller.
7. On 6-200 engines, remove front cover attaching screws from cover and oil pan. Pry cover from cylinder block slightly and cut oil pan gasket flush with front face of cylinder block.
8. On 6-250 engines, remove oil pan, then the front cover.
9. On all models, clean mating surfaces of cylinder block and front cover.

Installation

1. Apply oil resistant sealer to new front cover gasket and position gasket on front cover. Apply sealer to exposed area of gasket.
2. On 6-200 engines, apply sealer to gasket surface of oil pan. Cut and position the required portions of a new gasket on oil pan. Apply sealer to exposed areas of gasket, including the corners where contact is made with the front cover gasket.
3. On all models, install front cover.
4. Lubricate hub of crankshaft damper with Lubriplate or equivalent, then install damper. Torque attaching bolt to specifications.
5. On 6-250 engines, install oil pan.
6. On all models, install accessory drive pulley.
7. Reverse "Removal" steps 1 through 5 to complete installation.

V6-232

1. Disconnect battery ground cable, then drain cooling system.
2. Remove air cleaner and air intake duct.
3. Remove fan shroud attaching screws and fan and fan clutch attaching bolts, then remove fan and clutch assembly and shroud.
4. Loosen accessory drive belt idler, then remove drive belt and water pump pulley.
5. On models equipped with power steering, remove pump bracket attaching bolts, then position pump aside with hoses attached.
6. On models equipped with A/C, remove compressor front support bracket.
7. Disconnect coolant bypass hose and heater hose at water pump and upper radiator hose at thermostat housing.
8. Disconnect ignition coil secondary wire from distributor cap, then remove distributor cap with ignition wires attached.
9. With No. 1 cylinder at TDC compression stroke, mark position of rotor to distributor housing and position of distributor housing to front cover.
10. Remove distributor hold down clamp, then lift distributor from front cover.
11. On models equipped with Tripminder, remove fuel flow meter support bracket. Do not remove flow meter or disconnect fuel lines.
12. Raise and support front of vehicle, then remove crankshaft pulley using a suitable puller.
13. Remove fuel pump shield, then disconnect fuel pump to carburetor fuel line at fuel pump.
14. Remove fuel pump attaching bolts and position aside with fuel hose attached.
15. Remove oil filter, then disconnect lower radiator hose from water pump.
16. Remove oil pan as described under Oil Pan, Replace.
17. Lower vehicle and remove from cover attaching bolts, Fig. 25.

Fig. 23 Removing valve lifter with magnetic rod

NOTE: One of the front cover attaching bolts is located behind the oil filter adapter. Also tag bolts as they are removed so that they can be installed at the same location.

18. Remove ignition timing indicator, then remove front cover and water pump as an assembly.
19. Remove camshaft thrust button and spring from camshaft.
20. Reverse procedure to install. Before installing front cover attaching bolts at location 10, Fig. 25, coat threads of bolt with pipe sealant D8AZ-19558-A or equivalent. Also lubricate camshaft thrust button with polyethylene grease before installing. Torque front cover attaching bolts to 15 to 22 ft. lbs.

NOTE: If a replacement front cover is to be installed, the water pump, oil pump, oil filter adapter and intermediate shaft must be removed from the front cover to be replaced and reinstalled on the replacement front cover. Also it may be necessary to rotate crankshaft 180° from the No. 1 cylinder TDC location to position fuel pump eccentric for fuel pump installation. When installing distributor, No. 1 cylinder must be at TDC position and marks made during removal must be aligned.

V8 Engines

1. To remove cover, drain cooling system and crankcase. Remove air cleaner and disconnect battery ground cable.
2. Remove water hose as necessary.
3. Remove generator support bolt at water pump, and loosen generator mounting bolts.

Fig. 25 Front cover attaching bolt locations. 1982-83 V6-232

Fig. 26 Timing marks aligned for correct valve timing. 6-200 & 250

Fig. 27 Timing marks aligned for correct valve timing. 1982–83 V6-232

Fig. 28 Timing marks aligned for correct valve timing. V8 engines

4. Remove fan, spacer and pulley.
5. Remove power steering drive belt (if equipped). If air conditioned, remove compressor drive belt.
6. Remove crankshaft pulley and adapter.
7. Remove fuel pump and lay it to one side with flexible fuel line attached.
8. Remove oil level dipstick tube bracket and oil filler tube bracket.
9. Remove oil pan-to-front cover bolts.
10. Remove cover and water pump as an assembly.
11. Drive out cover seal with a pin punch. Clean out recess in cover.
12. Coat a new seal with grease and drive seal in until it is fully seated in recess. Check seal after installation to be sure spring is properly positioned in seal.
13. Reverse removal procedure to install cover.

TIMING CHAIN

After removing the cover as outlined above, remove the crankshaft front oil slinger. Crank the engine until the timing marks are aligned as shown in Figs. 26, 27 and 28. Remove camshaft sprocket retaining bolt(s) and washer. Slide both sprockets and chain forward and remove them as an assembly.

Reverse the order of the foregoing procedure to install the chain and sprockets, being sure the timing marks are aligned.

CAMSHAFT, REPLACE

6-200 & 250

1. Remove air cleaner, then drain cooling system and crankcase.

2. Remove radiator and grille.
3. If equipped with air conditioning, remove condensor retaining bolts and position condensor aside.

NOTE: Do not disconnect refrigerant lines.

---

4. Disconnect accelerator spring, accelerator cable and distributor vacuum line from carburetor.
5. Remove fuel line and distributor vacuum line.
6. Disconnect engine temperature sensor wire, then remove distributor, fuel pump and oil filter.
7. Remove cylinder head and lifters.
8. Remove damper and oil level dipstick.
9. On vehicles with 6-250 engines, remove oil pan and oil pump.
10. Remove front cover, timing chain and sprockets.
11. Remove camshaft thrust plate, then the camshaft by pulling toward front of engine, Fig. 29.

CAUTION: Use care to avoid damaging camshaft bearings.

---

12. Reverse procedure to install.

V6 & V8 Engines

1. Drain cooling system and remove radiator and grille.
2. If equipped with air conditioning:
   a. On 255, 302 and 351W engines, remove condensor retaining bolts and position condensor aside without disconnecting refrigerant lines.
   b. On V6-232, 351M and 400 engines, purge refrigerant from system and remove condensor.
3. Remove front cover, timing chain and sprockets.
4. Remove intake manifold.
5. Remove push rods and lifters.

NOTE: On 400 engines, make sure that number one cylinder is at top dead center position.

---

6. Remove thrust plate, then carefully remove camshaft by pulling toward front of engine, Fig. 30.

CAUTION: Use care to avoid damaging camshaft bearings.

---

7. Reverse procedure to install.

Fig. 29 Camshaft and related parts. 6-200 & 250

Fig. 30 Camshaft and related parts. V8 engines

Fig. 31   Piston & rod assembly. 6-200 & 250 engines

Fig. 32   Piston & rod assembly. 1982 V6-232

Fig. 33   Piston & rod assembly. V8s

PISTON & ROD ASSEMBLY

When installed, piston and rod assembly should have the notch or arrow in piston head toward front of engine with connecting rod numbers positioned as shown in Figs. 31, 32 and 33. Check side clearance between connecting rods at each crankshaft journal. Clearance should be .0035–.0105 for 4-140, 6-200 and 6-250 engines, .0047–.0114 for V6-232 engine, and .010–.020 for V8-302, V8-351M, V8-351W and V8-400 engines.

PISTONS, PINS & RINGS

Pistons are available in standard sizes and

Fig. 34   Split-lip crankshaft rear seal installation

oversizes of .003, .020, .030 and .040 in. Piston rings are available in standard sizes and oversizes of .020, .030 and .040 in. Piston pins are available in standard size and oversizes of .001 and .002 in.

MAIN & ROD BEARINGS

Main and rod bearings are available in standard sizes and undersizes of .001, .002, .010, .020 and .030 in.

CRANKSHAFT REAR OIL SEAL, REPLACE

Split Lip Type

1. Remove oil pan.
2. Remove rear bearing cap.
3. Loosen remaining bearing caps, allowing crankshaft to drop down about 1/32".
4. Remove old seals from both cylinder block and rear main bearing cap. Use a brass rod to drift upper half of seal from cylinder block groove. Rotate crankshaft while drifting to facilitate removal.
5. Carefully clean seal groove in block with a brush and solvent. Also clean seal groove in bearing cap. Remove the oil seal retaining pin from the bearing cap if so equipped. *The pin is not used with the split-lip seal.*
6. Dip seal halves in clean engine oil.
7. Carefully install upper seal half in its groove with undercut side of seal toward front of engine, Fig. 34, by rotating it on shaft journal of crankshaft until approximately 3/8" protrudes below the parting surface. *Be sure no rubber has been shaved from outside diameter of seal by bottom edge of groove.*
8. Retighten main bearing caps and torque to specifications.
9. Install lower seal in main bearing cap with undercut side of seal toward front of engine, and allow seal to protrude about 3/8" above parting surface to mate with upper seal upon cap installation.
10. Apply suitable sealer to parting faces of cap and block. Install cap and torque to specifications.

NOTE: If difficulty is encountered in installing the upper half of the seal in position, lightly lap (sandpaper) the side of the seal

opposite the lip side using a medium grit paper. After sanding, the seal must be washed in solvent, then dipped in clean engine oil prior to installation.

SERVICE BULLETIN

A new crankshaft rear oil seal has been released for service. This new seal may be received when ordering an oil pan gasket kit and is installed in the same manner as described above, Fig. 35.

OIL PAN, REPLACE

1977 Comet & Maverick 6-200

1. Drain crankcase, then remove oil level dipstick and flywheel housing cover.
2. Remove oil pan and gasket.
3. Reverse procedure to install.

Fig. 35   Crankshaft oil seals

1978–83 Fairmont, Zephyr, 1980–82 Cougar XR-7, Thunderbird & 1981–82 Cougar & Granada 6-200 & 250

1. If equipped with automatic transmission, disconnect transmission oil cooler lines at radiator.
2. On all models, remove radiator top support, then the oil level dipstick.
3. Raise and support vehicle, and drain oil pan.
4. Remove nuts and bolts attaching sway bar to chassis and allow sway bar to hang downward.
5. Remove "K" brace.
6. Lower rack and pinion steering gear.
7. Remove starter motor.
8. Remove nuts attaching engine mounts to support brackets.
9. Loosen rear insulator to crossmember attaching bolts.
10. Slightly raise engine and place a 1¼ inch spacer between engine support insulator and chassis bracket.

NOTE: Loosen fan shroud attaching screws to prevent damage to fan when raising engine.

11. Support and raise transmission slightly with a suitable jack.
12. Remove oil pan attaching bolts and lower oil pan to crossmember.
13. Remove oil pump intermediate driveshaft, pick-up tube and screen assembly and allow components to drop into oil pan.
14. Position transmission oil cooler lines aside, if equipped, and remove oil pan from vehicle. It may be necessary to rotate crankshaft.
15. Reverse procedure to install.

1977–80 Granada & Monarch 6-250

1. On automatic transmission vehicles, disconnect transmission oil cooler lines at radiator.
2. Remove both radiator top support bolts, then raise vehicle and drain crankcase.
3. Remove the four bolts and nuts retaining sway bar to chassis and allow bar to hang down.
4. Remove starter motor, then remove both engine mount retaining nuts to support brackets.
5. Loosen but do not remove both rear mount insulator to crossmember bolts.
6. Raise front of engine and place 1¼ inch wooden blocks between engine mount and chassis bracket.
7. Lower engine and raise transmission slightly, then remove oil pan bolts and lower oil pan to crossmember.
8. Position crankshaft rear throw in the up position, then position transmission oil cooler lines aside and remove oil pan.
9. Reverse procedure to install.

1982–83 Cougar, Cougar XR-7, Granada & Thunderbird V6-232

1. Disconnect battery ground cable, then remove air cleaner and air intake duct.
2. Remove fan shroud attaching screws and position shroud over fan, then remove engine oil dipstick.
3. Remove vacuum solenoid from dash panel

and position on engine with vacuum hoses attached.
4. Raise and support front of vehicle, then remove exhaust pipe to exhaust manifold attaching nuts.
5. Drain crankcase, then remove oil filter.
6. Remove shift linkage bracket to converter housing attaching bolts.
7. Disconnect transmission oil cooler lines at radiator. Remove four converter cover attaching bolts, then remove converter cover.
8. Remove bolts attaching engine damper to No. 2 crossmember.
9. Disconnect steering gear at flex coupling, then remove steering gear to main crossmember attaching bolts and allow steering gear to rest on frame.
10. Remove nuts and bolts attaching from engine mounts to chassis, then raise engine approximately 2 to 3 inches and insert wooden block between engine mounts and frame.

NOTE: On some models, it may be necessary to raise engine as much as 5 inches to provide clearance for oil pan removal. On these models, transmission fluid dipstick tube may contact Thermactor air tube. If contact occurs, lower engine and remove dipstick and air tube.

11. Remove oil pan attaching bolts, then lower oil pan to crossmember.
12. Remove oil pump pickup tube attaching bolts and pickup tube bracket attaching nut, then lower pickup tube into oil pan.
13. Remove oil pan through front of vehicle, then remove oil pan gaskets and seals.
14. Reverse procedure to install. Using a small screwdriver, work tabs of oil pan seal into gap between rear main bearing cap and cylinder block, then with tabs positioned, work seal into groove on rear main bearing cap. Apply a ⅛ inch bead of silicone sealer D6AZ-19562-B or equivalent where front cover and cylinder block join and where rear main bearing cap and cylinder block join. Apply a ⅛ inch bead along oil pan rail surface of cylinder block and a ¼ inch bead along front cover to oil pan surface.

1980–82 Cougar XR-7 & Thunderbird V8-255 & 302

1. Disconnect battery ground cable.
2. Remove fan shroud attaching screws and position shroud over fan, then remove dipstick and tube assembly.
3. Raise vehicle and drain crankcase.
4. Disconnect steering flex coupling, then remove two bolts attaching steering gear to main crossmember and let steering gear rest on frame away from oil pan.
5. Unclip and position splash pan away from ends of stabilizer.
6. Remove brackets attaching stabilizer bar to frame, then pull bar downward.
7. Remove transmission shift linkage bracket from frame rail.
8. Remove engine mount attaching bolts, then disconnect and plug transmission oil cooler lines.
9. Disconnect exhaust pipe at exhaust manifolds.
10. Loosen transmission mount nuts, then position a suitable jack under engine and raise engine until engine mount bolts clear frame mounts and pry engine as far

forward as it will slide on the transmission mounts.
11. Position two wooden blocks between engine mounts and frame.
12. Remove oil pan attaching bolts, then lower oil pan to frame.
13. Remove oil pump attaching bolts and inlet tube attaching nut, then lower oil pump assembly into oil pan.
14. Remove oil pan. When removing, pull pan forward of stabilizer bar and steering gear flex coupling.

NOTE: It may be necessary to rotate the crankshaft so that oil pan will clear crankshaft counterweights.

15. Reverse procedure to install.

1978–81 Fairmont, Zephyr & 1981 Cougar & Granada V8-255 & 302

1. Remove fan shroud attaching bolts and position shroud over fan.
2. Raise and support vehicle, then drain oil pan.
3. Remove two bolts attaching steering gear to main crossmember and let steering gear rest on frame away from oil pan.
4. Remove engine mount attaching bolts.
5. Raise engine with a suitable jack and place wood blocks between engine mounts and frame.
6. Remove rear "K" braces.
7. Remove oil pan attaching bolts and lower oil pan to frame.
8. Remove oil pump attaching bolts and the inlet tube attaching nut, then lower pump into oil pan.
9. Remove oil pan, rotating crankshaft as necessary to provide clearance for oil pan.
10. Reverse procedure to install.

1977 Comet & Maverick & 1977–80 Granada & Monarch V8-302

1. Raise and support vehicle, then drain oil pan.
2. Remove stabilizer bar from chassis.
3. Remove engine front support through bolts, then the supports. If equipped, remove bolt and nut securing power steering lines to rear side of lower arm.
4. Remove idler arm bracket retaining bolts and pull linkage downward and aside.
5. Remove oil pan attaching bolts and the oil pan.
6. Reverse procedure to install.

1977–79 Cougar, LTD II & Thunderbird V8-302, 351 & 400

1. Remove oil level dipstick, then remove fan shroud retaining screws and position shroud over fan.
2. Raise vehicle and drain crankcase.
3. On 351M and 400 engines, remove starter.
4. Remove stabilizer retaining bolts and lower sway bar.
5. Remove engine mount through bolts, then raise engine and insert wooden blocks between engine mounts and brackets.

Engine oiling system. V8-255, 302, 351, 400

Engine oiling system. 6-200 & 250

OIL PUMP, REPLACE

6-200 & 250

1. Remove oil pan and related parts as directed above.
2. Unfasten and remove pump, gasket and intermediate drive shaft.
3. Prime pump by filling either the inlet or outlet port with engine oil. Rotate pump shaft to distribute oil within pump body.
4. Position intermediate drive shaft into distributor socket.
5. Position new gasket on pump housing. Insert intermediate drive shaft into oil pump.
6. Install pump and shaft as an assembly.
7. Install oil pan.

V6-232

On these engines, the oil pump is contained within the front cover, Fig. 36.

V8-255, 302, 351, 400

1. Remove oil pan as outlined above.
2. Remove pump inlet tube and screen.
3. Remove pump retaining bolts and remove pump, gasket and intermediate shaft.
4. To install, position intermediate drive shaft into distributor socket. With shaft seated in socket, stop on shaft should touch roof of crankcase. Remove shaft and position stop as necessary.

6. If equipped with automatic transmission, position oil cooler lines aside.
7. Remove oil pan retaining bolts and oil pan.
8. Reverse procedure to install.

5. With new gasket on pump housing and stop properly positioned, insert intermediate shaft into oil pump. Install pump and shaft as a unit. *Do not force pump into position if it will not seat readily. The drive shaft hex may be misaligned with distributor shaft. To align, rotate shaft into new position.*
4. Prime pump by filling either inlet or outlet port with engine oil. Rotate pump shaft to distribute oil within pump body.
5. Position new gasket on pump housing.
6. Insert intermediate drive shaft into oil pump.
7. Install pump and shaft as a unit.
8. Complete installation in reverse order of removal.

OIL PUMP, REPAIRS

V8-255, 302, 351, 400 & All Sixes

Referring to Figs. 36 thru 39, disassemble pump. To remove the oil pressure relief valve, insert a self-threading sheet metal screw of the proper diameter into the oil pressure relief valve chamber cap and pull cap out of chamber. Remove spring and plunger.

The inner rotor and shaft and the outer race are serviced as an assembly. One part should not be replaced without replacing the other.

BELT TENSION DATA

	New	Used
1977-81		
Exc. 1/4" Belts.	140	105
1/4" Belts.	65	50

Fig. 36 Oil pump assembly. V6-232

Fig. 37 Oil pump assembly. 6-200 & 250

Fig. 38 Oil pump assembly. V8-255, 302, 351W

Fig. 39 Oil pump assembly. V8-351M & 400

	New	Used
1981		
V Ribbed Belts		
4K①	105	100
5K②	125	120
5K③	108	108
6K②	155	150
6K④	113	113
1982–83		
Except ¼"	140	105
¼"		
Except Air Pump	65	50
Air Pump	110	105
Ribbed Belt		
4 Rib		
Except Air Pump	130	115
Air Pump	110	105
5 Rib	150	135
6 Rib		
V6	175	145
V8	113	110

① —4 groves.
② —5 grooves fixed.
③ —W/ absorber.
④ —W/ tensioner.

WATER PUMP, REPLACE

6-200 & 250

1. Drain cooling system, then remove Thermactor pump, power steering and A/C drive belts, if equipped.
2. Disconnect lower radiator hose, then remove fan belt, fan and drive clutch and water pump pulley.
3. Disconnect heater hose at water pump.
4. Remove water pump attaching bolts, then remove water pump.
5. Reverse procedure to install.

V6-232

1. Drain cooling system, then remove air cleaner and air intake duct.
2. Remove fan shroud attaching screws and fan and fan clutch attaching bolts, then remove fan and fan clutch and shroud.
3. Loosen accessory drive belt idler, then remove drive belt and water pump pulley.
4. On models equipped with power steering, remove pump mounting bracket attaching bolts, position pump aside with hoses attached.
5. On models equipped with A/C, remove compressor front support bracket.
6. Disconnect lower radiator hose, coolant bypass hose and heat hose from water pump.
7. On models equipped with Tripminder, remove fuel flow sensor support bracket. Do not disconnect fuel lines.
8. Remove water pump attaching bolts, then remove water pump.
9. Reverse procedure to install.

V8-255, 302 & 351W

1. Drain cooling system, then on models equipped with a fan shroud, remove fan shroud attaching bolts and position shroud over fan.
2. Remove fan, spacer and fan shroud.
3. Remove A/C compressor drive belt and idler pulley bracket, if equipped.
4. Remove alternator drive belt, then remove power steering drive belt and pump, if equipped.
5. Remove all accessory brackets attached to water pump, then remove water pump pulley.
6. Disconnect lower radiator hose, heater hose and bypass hose from water pump.
7. Remove water pump to front cover attaching bolts, then remove water pump.
8. Reverse procedure to install.

V8-351M & 400

1. Disconnect battery ground cable, then drain cooling system.
2. Remove air inlet tube and fan shroud attaching bolts, then position shroud rearward.
3. Remove fan and spacer from water pump shaft.
4. Remove A/C compressor drive belt lower idler pulley and compressor mount to water pump bracket, if equipped.
5. Remove alternator and power steering drive belts, if equipped.
6. Remove water pump pulley.
7. Remove alternator bracket from water pump and position out of way.
8. Disconnect lower radiator hose, heater hose and bypass hose from water pump.
9. Remove water pump attaching bolts, then remove water pump.
10. Reverse procedure to install.

FUEL PUMP, REPLACE

1. Disconnect fuel lines from pump.
2. Remove pump attaching bolts and pump.
3. Remove all gasket material from pump and block gasket surfaces. Apply sealer to both sides of new gasket.
4. Position gasket on pump flange and hold pump in position against its mounting surface. Make sure rocker arm is riding on camshaft eccentric.
5. Press pump tight against its mounting. Install retaining screws and tighten them alternately.
6. Connect fuel lines. Then operate engine and check for leaks.

NOTE: Before installing the pump, it is good practice to crank the engine so that the nose of the camshaft eccentric is out of the way of the fuel pump rocker arm when the pump is installed. In this way there will be the least amount of tension on the rocker arm, thereby easing installation of the pump.

Clutch & Transmission Section

CLUTCH PEDAL, ADJUST

1981—83 Fairmont, Zephyr, 1981—82 Cougar, Granada & 1983 LTD & Marquis

These models incorporate a self adjusting clutch mechanism. The adjust mechanism consists of a spring loaded rachet quadrant attached to the clutch cable. To accomplish this adjustment, grasp clutch pedal and pull upward, then slowly depress clutch pedal. If a click is heard during the procedure, an adjustment was necessary and has been accomplished. This procedure should be performed at least every 5000 miles.

1978—80 Fairmont & Zephyr

1978 4-140
1. From under vehicle, remove release lever return spring and dust shield.
2. Loosen clutch cable lock nut and adjusting nut at release lever.
3. Move release lever forward until free play is eliminated and hold lever in this position for adjustment.
4. Insert a .30 in. spacer against release lever cable spacer, then tighten adjusting nut against spacer finger tight.
5. Tighten lock nut against adjusting nut, using care not to disturb adjustment. Torque lock nut to 5 to 8 ft. lbs. Cycle clutch pedal several times, then recheck free play. Free play at clutch pedal should be approximately 1½ in.
6. Install dust shield and return spring.

1978 6-200
1. Pull clutch toward front of vehicle until adjusting nut can be rotated. Rotate adjusting away from rubber insulator approximately .30 in. Do not rotate nylon nut until it is free of rubber insulator. If necessary, to free adjusting nut from dash insulator it may be necessary to remove clutch pedal bumper stop from clutch pedal. The clutch pedal bumper stop must be reinstalled before adjusting clutch pedal free play.
2. Release cable, then pull cable until free play at release lever is eliminated.
3. Rotate adjusting nut until it contacts rubber insulator, then index tabs into next notch. Free play at clutch pedal should be approximately 1½ in. Cycle clutch pedal several times and recheck free play.

1979—80 4-140 & V8-302
1. Remove dust shield, then loosen clutch cable locknut.
2. Turn adjusting nut as necessary to obtain a total clutch pedal stroke of 5.3 inches on models with 4-140 engines, and 6.5 inches on models with V8-302 engines.

NOTE: Turning adjusting nut clockwise will raise pedal and counterclockwise will lower pedal.

3. Tighten locknut against adjusting nut using care not to disturb the adjustment. Apply and release the clutch pedal several times and recheck pedal height.

4. On 1979 models, when clutch pedal is properly adjusted, the clutch pedal can be raised 2.7 inches on models with 4-140 engines, and 1.5 inches on models with V8-302 engines.

NOTE: This negative free play is normal and is required to provide for clutch facing wear.

5. Install dust shield.

1979—80 6-200
1. Pull cable toward front of vehicle until adjusting nut can be rotated. Do not rotate nylon adjusting nut until it is free of rubber insulator. To release nut from rubber insulator, it may be necessary to block the clutch release forward so the clutch is partially disengaged.
2. Rotate nut clockwise until 5.3 inches of clutch pedal stroke can be obtained when the nut has been reinstalled in the rubber insulator. Cycle the clutch pedal several times and recheck the adjustment. On 1979 models, when properly adjusted clutch pedal can be raised 2.7 inches.

NOTE: This negative free play is normal and is required to provide for clutch facing wear.

Except 1978—83 Fairmont, Zephyr, 1981—82 Cougar, Granada & 1983 LTD & Marquis

1. Disconnect clutch return spring from release lever.
2. On 1977—80 models remove locking pin, then on all models loosen adjusting nut.
3. Move release lever rearward until release bearing lightly contacts clutch pressure plate release fingers.
4. Slide rod until it seats in release lever pocket.
5. Insert proper feeler gauge (see below) between adjusting nut and swivel sleeve, then tighten adjusting nut finger tight against feeler gauge.
   1977 Comet & Maverick .136″
   1977—80 Granada & Monarch .136″
6. On 1977—80 models, rotate rod slightly to align flat with pin hole in adjusting nut, then install locking pin and remove feeler gauge.
7. On all models, connect return spring to release lever.
8. Depress clutch pedal a minimum of five times, then recheck free play setting with the feeler gauge. Check free travel of pedal which should be ⅞ to 1⅛ inch.

CLUTCH, REPLACE

1978—83 Fairmont, Zephyr, 1981—82 Cougar, Granada & 1983 LTD & Marquis

NOTE: On 1981—83 models lift clutch pedal

upward to disengage clutch cable self adjuster pawl and quadrant. Push quadrant forward, then detach cable from quadrant and allow quadrant to swing rearward slowly.

4-140
1. Raise vehicle and remove release lever spring and dust shield.
2. Loosen clutch cable lock nut and adjusting nut, then disconnect clutch cable from release lever.
3. Remove retaining clip, then remove clutch cable from clutch housing.
4. Remove starter motor.
5. Remove bolts attaching engine rear plate to lower front portion of fly-wheel housing.
6. Remove transmission and flywheel housing as described under Transmission, Replace.
7. Remove clutch release lever from housing by pulling lever through opening in housing until retainer spring is disengaged from pivot.
8. Remove pressure plate cover attaching bolts.

NOTE: Loosen bolts evenly to relieve spring tension without distorting cover. Mark cover and flywheel so that pressure plate can be installed in the same position.

9. Remove pressure plate and clutch disc from flywheel.
10. Reverse procedure to install. Adjust clutch pedal as described under Clutch Pedal, Adjust.

6-200 & V8-302
1. Raise vehicle, then remove transmission as described under Transmission, Replace.
2. Remove dust shield and loosen clutch cable adjusting nut, then disengage clutch cable from release lever.
3. Disengage clutch cable from flywheel housing.
4. Remove starter.
5. Remove bolts attaching engine rear plate to front lower portion of flywheel housing.
6. Remove bolts attaching housing to cylinder block.
7. Move housing back just far enough to clear pressure plate and remove housing.
8. Remove clutch release lever from housing by pulling lever through housing opening until retainer spring is disengaged from pivot.
9. Remove pressure plate cover attaching bolts.

NOTE: Loosen bolts evenly to relieve spring tension without distorting cover. Mark cover and flywheel so that pressure plate can be installed in the same position.

10. Remove pressure plate and clutch disc from flywheel.
11. Reverse procedure to install. Adjust clutch pedal as described under Clutch Pedal, Adjust.

Except 1978–83 Fairmont, Zephyr, 1981–82 Cougar, Granada & 1983 LTD & Marquis

1. Remove transmission as described under Transmission, Replace.
2. Disconnect clutch release lever retaining spring.
3. Loosen clutch adjusting rod nuts and remove adjusting rod.
4. Remove starter motor.
5. Remove engine rear plate to lower flywheel housing attaching bolts.
6. Remove flywheel housing to engine attaching bolts and clutch equalizer bar pivot bracket, if equipped.
7. Move flywheel housing back just far enough to clear pressure plate and remove housing.

NOTE: Use care not to disturb clutch linkage.

---

8. Pull clutch release lever through opening in housing until retainer spring is disengaged from pivot.
9. Remove pressure plate cover attaching bolts.

NOTE: Loosen bolts evenly to relieve spring tension without distorting cover. Mark cover and flywheel so that pressure plate can be installed in the same position.

---

10. Remove pressure plate and clutch disc from flywheel.
11. Reverse removal procedure to install the clutch and adjust the pedal as outlned in Clutch Pedal, Adjust.

THREE SPEED TRANS. REPLACE

1977–78

1. Raise and support vehicle on a hoist or safety stands.
2. Disconnect electrical connectors from transmission.
3. Mark drive shaft so that it may be installed in the same position, then disconnect it from rear U joint and remove it from output shaft.

NOTE: Plug extension housing to prevent loss of lubricant.

---

4. Disconnect speedometer cable and shift linkages from transmission.
5. Support transmission with suitable jack and remove engine rear support nuts. Remove the crossmember and rear support insulator.
6. Support engine and remove transmission.

NOTE: Do not depress clutch pedal with transmission removed.

Fig. 1 Shift lever boot removal. 1978–83 Fairmont, Zephyr, 1981–82 Cougar, Granada & 1983 LTD & Marquis

FOUR SPEED OVERDRIVE TRANSMISSION, REPLACE

1979–80 Fairmont, Granada, Monarch & Zephyr

1. Raise vehicle and mark drive shaft so it can be installed in the same position, then disconnect driveshaft at rear U-joint flange. Slide driveshaft from transmission output shaft, then install an extension housing seal installation tool into extension housing opening to prevent lubricant spillage.
2. Disconnect speedometer cable from extension housing.
3. Remove shifter tower to turret assembly attaching screws, then remove shift tower.
4. Support engine using a suitable jack, then remove extension housing to engine rear support attaching bolts.
5. Raise rear of engine slightly to relieve weight from crossmember, then remove crossmember to frame side support attaching bolts and remove crossmember.
6. Support transmission using a suitable jack, then remove bolts attaching transmission to flywheel housing.
7. Move transmission rearward until input shaft clears flywheel, then lower transmission from vehicle. It may be necessary to lower engine slightly to obtain clearance for transmission removal.
8. Reverse procedure to install.

1977–78 Granada & Monarch

1. Disconnect battery ground cable.
2. Remove shift lever boot bezel and the four shift lever boot to floor attaching screws. Lift boot upward.
3. Remove two bolts attaching shift lever to shift control, then the shift lever and boot.
4. From beneath vehicle, disconnect shift rods from shift control levers.
5. Disconnect back-up lamp switch electrical connector and remove switch from retainer by pulling and twisting the switch in both directions.

NOTE: Do not use pliers or other tools since damage to the switch may result.

---

6. Remove shift control assembly to extension housing attaching bolts, then the shift control assembly.
7. Raise vehicle and remove propeller shaft.
8. Disconnect speedometer cable from extension housing.
9. Support engine with a suitable jack and remove extension housing to engine rear support attaching bolts.
10. Support transmission with a suitable jack and release weight from crossmember. Remove bolts attaching crossmember to frame side supports and the crossmember.
11. Remove transmission to flywheel housing bolts.
12. Move transmission rearward and lower from vehicle.
13. Reverse procedure to install. Adjust shift linkage as outlined under "Gearshift Linkage".

FOUR SPEED TRANS., REPLACE

1978–83 Fairmont, Zephyr, 1981–82 Cougar, Granada & 1983 LTD & Marquis

1. Remove coin tray, then remove four screws attaching boot to floor pan and pull boot up on shift lever. Remove three lever attaching screws, then remove shift lever and boot assembly, Figs. 1 and 2.
2. From under hood, remove flywheel housing to engine block upper attaching bolts or nuts.
3. Raise and support vehicle.
4. Mark driveshaft so that it can be installed in the same position, then remove driveshaft and install a plug in transmission extension housing to prevent lubricant leakage.
5. Remove clutch release lever dust cover, then disconnect clutch cable from release lever.
6. Remove starter motor.

N800003-S101
3 REQ'D.
24-33 N·m
(17-25 LB-FT)

7C404
18-24 N·m
(13-18 LB-FT)

7K387 ASSEMBLY

56705-S2
4 REQ'D.
4-9 N·m
(3-7 LB-FT)

7B118 ASSEMBLY

7K327 ASSEMBLY
ADJUST KNOB FOR CORRECT
SHIFT PATTERN POSITIONING
BEFORE TIGHTENING.

45263-S101
4 REQ'D.

Fig. 2 Shift lever installation. 1978–83 Fairmont, Zephyr, 1981–82 Cougar, Granada & 1983 LTD & Marquis

1st & 2nd SHIFT ROD

REVERSE SHIFT ROD

BACK-UP LAMP SWITCH

3rd/OVERDRIVE SHIFT ROD

Fig. 3 Four speed overdrive gear shift linkage. 1977–78 Granada & Monarch

7. Remove speedometer cable attaching screw, then lift cable from extension housing.
8. Support rear of engine using a suitable jack, then remove bolts attaching crossmember to body.
9. Remove bolts attaching crossmember to extension housing and remove crossmember.
10. Lower engine as required to permit removal of bolts attaching flywheel housing to engine. Slide transmission rearward from engine and lower from vehicle.

NOTE: It may be necessary to slide mounting bracket forward from catalytic converter heat shield to provide clearance to move transmission rearward for removal.

11. Remove cover attaching bolts and drain lubricant.
12. Remove flywheel housing to transmission attaching bolts, then remove flywheel housing.
13. Reverse procedure to install.

GEARSHIFT LINKAGE, ADJUST

NOTE: *If the transmission shifts hard or will not engage, the gearshift levers may need adjusting at the cross-over. Move the shift lever through all positions to see that the cross-over operation is smooth. If not, adjust as follows:*

1977 3 Speed Column Shift

1. Place selector lever in Neutral position.
2. Loosen two gear shift rod adjusting nuts at transmission.
3. Check to ensure that transmission gear shift levers are in the Neutral position.
4. Fabricate an alignment pin from a piece of 3/16 in. drill rod bent into an L shape.
5. Insert alignment pin through 1st/reverse and 2nd/3rd gear shift levers and both holes in lower casting, then tighten two gear shift rod adjusting nuts.
6. Remove alignment pin, then start engine and check linkage for proper operation.

1977–78 3 Speed Floor Shift

NOTE: Floor shift linkages incorporate a transmission lock rod. This rod must be adjusted AFTER the shift linkage has been adjusted. With shift lever in Neutral and lock rod adjustment nut loose, align hole in steering column socket casting with alignment mark and insert a .180″ dia. rod. The casting must not rotate with the rod in this position.

1. Connect shift rods to transmission levers.
2. Ensure transmission is in neutral.
3. Insert alignment pin through hole in boot and into shift control assembly alignment hole.
4. Install slotted ends of shift rods over flats of studs in shift control assembly, then install and torque lock nuts.
5. Remove alignment pin.

1977–78 4 Speed Overdrive

1. Attach shift rods to transmission levers, Fig. 3.
2. Shift reverse lever (middle) clockwise to place transmission in reverse.
3. Insert alignment pin through hole in boot and into shift control assembly alignment hole.
4. Attach slotted ends of 1-2 and 3-overdrive shift rods over flats of studs on shift control assembly. Install lock nuts and torque to 10 to 20 ft. lbs.
5. Shift transmission to neutral and attach reverse lever. Torque lock nut to 10 to 20 ft. lbs.
6. Remove alignment pin.

Rear Axle, Propeller Shaft & Brakes

Fig. 1 Disassembled view of Ford WER integral carrier type rear axle assembly

Fig. 1A Disassembled view of Ford WGF & WGG (6¾″ Ring Gear) integral carrier type rear axle assembly

REAR AXLES

Ford WER Integral Carrier, Fig. 1

The gear set consists of a ring gear and an overhung drive pinion which is supported by two opposed tapered roller bearings. The differential case is a one-piece design with openings allowing assembly of the internal parts and lubricant flow. The differential pinion shaft is retained with a threaded bolt (lock) assembled to the case.

The roller type wheel bearings have no inner race, and the rollers directly contact the bearing journals of the axle shafts. The axle shafts do not use an inner and outer bearing retainer. Rather, they are held in the axle by means of C-locks, Fig. 4. These C-locks also fit into a machined recess in the differential side gears within the differential case. There is no retainer bolt access hole in the axle shaft flange.

Ford WGF & WGG (6¾″ Ring Gear) Integral Carrier, Fig. 1A

This rear axle is an integral design hypoid with the centerline of the pinion set below the centerline of the ring gear. The semi-floating axle shafts are retained in the housing by ball bearings and bearing retainers at axle ends.

The differential is mounted on two opposed tapered roller bearings which are retained in the housing by removable caps. Differential bearing preload and drive gear backlash is adjusted by nuts located behind each differential bearing cup.

The drive pinion assembly is mounted on two opposed tapered roller bearings. Pinion bearing preload is adjusted by a collapsible spacer on the pinion shaft. Pinion and ring gear tooth contact is adjusted by shims between the rear bearing cone and pinion gear.

Ford WGX & WGZ Integral Carrier, Fig. 2

The gear set consist of a ring gear and an overhung drive pinion which is supported by two opposed tapered roller bearings. Pinion bearing preload is maintained by a collapsible spacer on the pinion shaft and adjusted by the pinion nut. The differential case is a one piece design with two openings to allow assembly of internal components and lubricant flow. The pinion shaft is retained with a threaded bolt assembled to the case. The differential case is mounted in the carrier between two opposed tapered roller bearings. The bearings are retained in the carrier by removable bearing caps. Differential bearing preload and ring gear backlash are adjusted by the use of shims located between the differential bearing cups and the carrier housing. Axle shafts are held in the housing by C-locks positioned in a slot on the axle shaft splined end, Fig. 4.

Removable Carrier Type

In these axles, Fig. 3, the drive pinion is straddle-mounted by two opposed tapered roller bearings which support the pinion shaft in front of the drive pinion gear, and a straight roller bearing that supports the pinion shaft at the rear of the pinion gear. The drive pinion is assembled in a pinion retainer that is bolted to the differential carrier. The tapered roller bearings are preloaded by a collapsible spacer between the bearings. The pinion is positioned by a shim or shims located between the drive pinion retainer and the differential carrier.

The differential is supported in the carrier by two tapered roller side bearings. These bearings are preloaded by two threaded ring nuts or sleeves between the bearings and the pedestals. The differential assembly is positioned for proper ring gear and pinion backlash by varying the adjustment of these ring nuts. The differential case houses two side gears in mesh with two pinions mounted on a pinion shaft which are held in place by a pin. The side gears and pinions are backed by thrust washers.

The axle shafts are of unequal length, the left shaft being shorter than the right. The axle shafts are mounted in sealed ball bearings which are pressed on the shafts.

Rear Axle, Replace

Leaf Spring Suspension
1. Raise vehicle and support at rear frame members.
2. Drain lubricant from axle.
3. Mark drive shaft and pinion flanges for reassembly, then disconnect drive shaft at rear axle U-joint and remove drive shaft from transmission extension housing. Install seal replacer tool in extension housing to prevent leakage.
4. Disconnect shock absorbers at lower mountings.
5. Remove rear wheels and brake drums, then disconnect brake lines at wheel cylinders.
6. Disconnect vent hose from vent tube, then remove vent tube from brake junction and axle housing.
7. Remove clips retaining brake lines to axle housing.
8. Support rear axle housing using a suitable jack, remove U-bolts and plates.
9. Lower rear axle and remove vehicle.
10. Reverse procedure to install.

Coil Spring Suspension
1. Raise rear of vehicle support at frame members and rear axle, then remove wheel and tire assembly.
2. Remove brake drums and disconnect brake lines at wheel cylinders.
3. Make marks on drive shaft yoke and pinion flange for reassembly, then disconnect drive shaft at rear axle U-joint and remove drive shaft from transmission extension housing. Install seal replacer tool in extension housing to prevent leakage.
4. Position a drain pan under differential carrier, then remove carrier attaching bolts and allow differential to drain.
5. Disconnect stabilizer bar, if equipped.
6. Disconnect shock absorbers from lower mountings.
7. Remove brake lines from retaining clips on rear axle housing, then remove brake line junction block retaining screw.
8. Position a suitable jack under axle housing to prevent housing from tilting when removing control arms.
9. Disconnect lower control arms from axle housing and position control arms downward.
10. Disconnect upper control arms from axle housing and position control arms upward.
11. Disconnect air vent line.
12. Lower axle slightly and remove coil springs and insulators.

Fig. 2 Disassemble view of Ford WGX & WGZ integral carrier type rear axle assembly

13. Lower axle housing and remove from vehicle.

Axle Shaft, Replace

Removable Carrier Type
1. Remove wheel assembly.
2. Remove brake drum or rotor and caliper assembly.
3. Working through hole provided in axle shaft flange, Fig. 5, remove nuts that secure wheel bearing retainer.
4. Pull axle shaft out of housing. If bearing is a tight fit in axle housing use a slide hammer-type puller, Fig. 6. Remove brake backing plate and secure to frame rail with wire.
5. If the axle shaft bearing is to be replaced, loosen the inner retainer by nicking it deeply with a chisel in several places, Fig. 7. The bearing will then slide off easily.
6. Press bearing from axle shaft.
7. Inspect machined surface of axle shaft and housing for rough spots that would affect sealing action of the oil seal. Carefully remove any burrs or rough spots.
8. Press new bearing on shaft until it seats firmly against shoulder on shaft.
9. Press inner bearing retainer on shaft until it seats firmly against bearing.
10. If oil seal is to be replaced, use a hook-

type tool to pull it out of housing, Fig. 8. Wipe a small amount of oil resistant sealer on outer edge of seal before it is installed, Fig. 9.

Installation
1. Place a new gasket on each side of brake carrier plate and slide axle shaft into housing.
2. Start the splines into the differential side gear and push the shaft in until bearing bottoms in housing.
3. Install retainer. On 1977 Comet, Granada, Maverick, Monarch and all 1978-80 models, torque retaining nuts to 20 to 40 ft. lbs. On 1977 models except Comet, Granada, Maverick and Monarch, torque retaining nuts to 35 to 55 ft. lbs.
4. Install brake drum or caliper and rotor and wheel assembly.

Ford WER Integral Carrier Type
1. Raise car on hoist and remove wheels.
2. Drain differential lubricant.
3. Remove brake drums.
4. Remove differential housing cover.
5. Position safety stands under rear frame member and lower hoist to allow axle to lower as far as possible.
6. Working through differential case opening, remove pinion shaft lock bolt and pinion shaft.

Fig. 3   Rear axle assembly with removable carrier

Fig. 4   Axle shaft C-lock. WER, WGX & WGZ integral type rear axle

Fig. 5   Removing nuts from wheel bearing retainer

7. Push axle shaft(s) inward toward center of axle housing and remove C-lock(s) from housing, Fig. 4.
8. Remove axle shaft, using extreme care to avoid contact of shaft seal lip with any portion of axle shaft except seal journal.
9. Use a hook-type puller to remove seal and bearing, Fig. 8.

NOTE: Two types of bearings are used, Fig. 8A. One requires a light press fit in the housing flange, while on the other, a loose fit is acceptable. Therefore, if a loose fitting bearing is encountered, it does not indicate excessive wear or damage

10. Reverse procedure to install, using suitable driving tools, Fig. 9, to install seal and bearing. New seals are prepacked with lubricant and do not require oil soaking before installation.

Ford WGF & WGG Integral Carrier Type

1. Remove wheel and tire assembly, then remove nuts attaching brake drum to axle shaft flange and remove brake drum.
2. Working through opening in axle shaft flange, remove nuts securing axle shaft bearing retainer, Fig. 5.

3. Using a suitable puller, pull axle shaft from housing, Fig. 6.
4. Remove brake backing plate and attach to frame side rail with a piece of wire.
5. If rear wheel bearing is to be replaced, loosen inner retainer ring by nicking it deeply in several places with a chisel, Fig. 7, then slide retainer from axle shaft.
6. Press bearing from axle shaft using tool No. T71P-4621-B.
7. Using a hook type puller, remove oil seal from axle housing, Fig. 8.
8. Position bearing retainer and bearing on axle shaft, then using tool No. T62F-4621-A, press bearing onto shaft until firmly seated against shoulder.
9. Using bearing installation tool, press inner retainer onto shaft until retainer is firmly seated against bearing.

Fig. 6   Removing axle shaft with slide hammer-type puller

Fig. 7   Splitting bearing inner retainer for bearing removal

Fig. 8   Using hook-type tool to remove oil seal

Fig. 8A Axle shaft bearing identification. WER, WGX & WGZ integral type rear axle

10. Wipe all lubricant from oil seal area of axle housing, then install oil seal using tool No. T79P-1177-A, Fig. 9.
11. Install gasket on housing flange, then install brake backing plate.
12. Carefully slide axle shaft into housing using care not to damage oil seal, then install bearing retainer attaching nuts and torque to 20 to 40 ft. lbs.
13. Install brake drum and retaining nuts, then install wheel and tire assembly.

Ford WGX & WGZ Integral Carrier Type
1. Raise and support rear of vehicle.
2. Remove wheel and tire assembly and brake drum.
3. Remove rear axle housing cover and drain lubricant.
4. Remove diferential pinion lock screw and differential pinion shaft.
5. Push axle shafts inward and remove C-locks, Fig. 4.
6. Remove axle shaft from housing using care not to damage oil seal.
7. Remove bearing and seal as an assembly using a suitable slide hammer, Fig. 8, if necessary.

NOTE: Two types of bearing are used, Fig. 8A. One requires a light press fit in the housing flange, while on the other a loose fit is acceptable. Therefore, if a loose fitting bearing is encountered, it does not indicate excessive wear or damage.

8. Lubricate bearing with rear axle lubricant and install bearing into housing bore using tool No. T78P-1225-A.
9. Install axle shaft seal into housing using tool No. T78P-1177-A, Fig. 9.
10. Reverse procedure to install axle shaft.

PROPELLER SHAFT, REPLACE

1. Disconnect rear U-joint from drive pinion flange.
2. Pull drive shaft toward rear of car until

Fig. 9 Using special driver to install oil seal

front U-joint yoke clears transmission extension housing and output shaft.
3. Install a suitable tool, such as a seal driver, in seal to prevent lube from leaking from transmission.
4. Before installing, check U-joints for freedom of movement. If a bind has resulted from misalignment after overhauling the U-joints, tap the ears of the drive shaft sharply to relieve the bind.
5. If rubber seal installed on end of transmission extension housing is damaged, install a new seal.
6. On a manual shift transmission, lubricate yoke spline with conventional transmission grease. On an automatic transmission, lubricate yoke spline with special spline grease. *This spline is sealed so that transmission fluid does not "wash" away spline lubricant.*
7. Install yoke on transmission output shaft.
8. Install U-bolts and nuts which attach U-joint to pinion flange. Tighten U-bolts evenly to prevent binding U-joint bearings.

BRAKE ADJUSTMENTS

SERVICE BULLETIN

REVISED BRAKE ADJUSTMENT PROCEDURE: Some models use a new front and rear brake backing plate which omits the adjusting slot for manual brake adjustment. The backing plates have a partially stamped knock-out slot for use ONLY when the brake drums cannot be removed in a normal manner. The open slot is then covered with a rubber plug as used in the past to prevent contamination of the brakes.

When servicing a vehicle requiring a brake adjustment, the metal knock-out plugs should NOT be removed. Rather the drums should be removed and brakes inspected for a malfunction.

Although the brakes are self-adjusting, an initial adjustment will be necessary after a brake repair, such as relining or replacement. The initial adjustment can be obtained by the new procedure which follows:
1. Use the brake shoe adjustment gauge shown in Fig. 10 to obtain the drum inside diameter as shown. Tighten the adjusting knob on the gauge to hold this setting.
2. Place the opposite side of the gauge over the brake shoes and adjust the shoes by turning the adjuster screw until the

Fig. 10 Revised brake adjustment

gauge just slides over the linings. Rotate the gauge around the lining surface to assure proper lining diameter adjustment and clearance.
3. Install brake drum and wheel. Final adjustment is accomplished by making several firm reverse stops, using the brake pedal.

Self-Adjusting Brakes

These brakes, Fig. 11 have self-adjusting shoe mechanisms that assure correct lining-to-drum clearances at all times. The automatic adjusters operate only when the brakes are applied as the car is moving rearward.

Although the brakes are self-adjusting, an initial adjustment is necessary after the brake shoes have been relined or replaced, or when the length of the star wheel adjuster has been changed during some other service operation.

Frequent usage of an automatic transmission forward range to halt reverse vehicle motion may prevent the automatic adjusters from functioning, thereby inducing low pedal heights. Should low pedal heights be encountered, it is recommended that numerous forward and reverse stops be made until satisfactory pedal height is obtained.

NOTE: If a low pedal condition cannot be corrected by making numerous reverse stops (provided the hydraulic system is free of air) it indicates that the self-adjusting mechanism is not functioning. Therefore, it will be necessary to remove the brake drum, clean, free up and lubricate the adjusting mechanism. Then adjust the brake, being sure the parking brake is fully released.

PARKING BRAKE, ADJUST

1977–83 All

Rear Drum Brakes
1. Make sure parking brake is released.
2. Place transmission in neutral and raise the vehicle.
3. Tighten the adjusting nut against the cable equalizer to cause rear brakes to drag.
4. Then loosen the adjusting nut until the rear wheels are fully released. There should be no drag.
5. Lower vehicle and check operation.

Fig. 11 Rear drum brake mechanism

Rear Disc Brakes

1. Fully release parking brake, then place transmission in neutral and support vehicle at rear axle.
2. Tighten adjuster nut until levers on calipers just start to move, then loosen the nut just enough to obtain full travel to the off position.

NOTE: If brake cables are replaced in any system having a foot-actuated control assembly, stroke parking brake control with about 100 pounds pedal effort, then repeat adjustment.

3. The lever is in the off position when a ¼ inch diameter pin can be freely inserted past the side of the lever into the ¼ inch diameter holes in the cast iron housing.
4. Apply and release the parking brake, then apply and release the service brake pedal with moderate force. Check parking brake levers on calipers to determine if they are fully returned to the off position.

NOTE: If the ¼ inch pin cannot be freely inserted, the adjustment is too tight. Repeat adjustment procedure. Also, if levers do not return to off position, parking and service brake function will be affected as the vehicle is driven.

Vacuum Release Unit

The vacuum power unit will release the parking brake automatically when the transmission selector lever is moved into any driving position with the engine running. The brakes will not release automatically, however, when the selector lever is in neutral or park position with the engine running, or in any other position with the engine off.

The lower end of the release handle extends out for alternate manual release in the event of vacuum power failure or for optional manual release at any time.

MASTER CYLINDER, REPLACE

1977–82 Less Power Brakes

1. Working from inside vehicle below instrument panel, disconnect master cylinder push rod from brake pedal.
2. Disconnect stop light switch wires, remove hairpin retainer and slide stop light switch off brake pedal pin just far enough to clear end of pin. Then lift switch straight upward from pin.
3. Slide master cylinder push rod with nylon washers and bushings from brake pedal pin.
4. Remove brake tubes from outlet ports of master cylinder.
5. Remove lock nuts that secure master cylinder to dash panel and lift cylinder forward and upward from vehicle.
6. Reverse procedure to install.

1977–83 Power Brakes

1. Disconnect brake lines from master cylinder.
2. Remove nuts retaining master cylinder to brake booster.
3. Remove master cylinder.

POWER BRAKE UNIT, REPLACE

1977–83 Except Hydro-Boost

1. Working under instrument panel, disconnect stop light switch wires at connector.

2. Remove hairpin type retainer. Slide stop light switch off brake pedal pin just far enough for the switch outer hole to clear the pin, then lower switch away from pin.
3. Slide booster push rod link and nylon washers and bushing off brake pedal pin.
4. On 1978–83 Fairmont, Zephyr, 1980–82 Cougar XR-7, 1980–83 Thunderbird, 1981–82 Cougar, Granada and 1983 LTD and Marquis, remove air cleaner. On models with 4-140 engine, disconnect accelerator cable from carburetor, then remove screw that secures accelerator cable to shaft bracket and remove cable from bracket. Remove two screws that secure accelerator shaft bracket to manifold and rotate bracket toward engine.
5. On 1977 Comet and Maverick with 6-250 engine, remove air cleaner and disconnect accelerator cable from carburetor.
6. On all 1977 Comet and Maverick models, remove fender to cowl brace.
7. On 1977–79 Cougar, LTD II, and Thunderbird models, equipped with speed control, remove left cowl screen, then remove servo mounting bracket attaching nuts and position servo cable.
8. On all models, disconnect brake line from master cylinder.
9. Disconnect vacuum hose from booster at check valve.
10. Unfasten and remove booster and bracket assembly from dash panel, sliding push rod link out from engine side of dash panel.

1977–80 Hydro-Boost

1. Disconnect stoplight switch wires at connector and remove hairpin retainer, then slide stoplight switch off brake pedal pin far enough for switch outer hole to clear pin and remove pin from switch.
2. Slide hydro-boost push rod and nylon washers and bushing off brake pedal pin.
3. Remove master cylinder and position to one side without disturbing hydraulic lines.

NOTE: It is not necessary to disconnect brake lines, but care should be taken not to deform lines.

4. Disconnect pressure, steering gear and return lines from booster, then plug lines and ports in hydro-boost to prevent entry of dirt.
5. Remove hydro-boost retaining nuts, and remove assembly sliding push rod link from engine side of dash panel.
6. Reverse procedure to install. To purge system, disconnect coil wire so that engine will not start. Fill power steering pump reservoir, then while engaging starter, pump brake pedal. Do not cycle steering wheel until all residual air has been purged from the hydro boost unit. Check fluid level, then connect coil wire and start engine. Apply brakes with a pumping action and cycle steering wheel, then check system for leaks.

Rear Suspension

SHOCK ABSORBER, REPLACE

1978–83 Fairmont & Zephyr; 1980–82 Cougar XR-7; 1980–83 Thunderbird; 1981–82 Granada; 1981–83 Cougar; 1983 LTD & Marquis

1. On sedans, open trunk to gain access to upper shock absorber attachment. On station wagons, remove side panel trim covers.
2. Remove rubber cap from shock absorber stud.
3. On all models, remove shock absorber attaching nut, washer and insulator.
4. Raise vehicle and support rear axle.
5. Compress shock absorber to clear hole in upper shock absorber tower.
6. On 1978–83 Fairmont, Zephyr and 1981–82 Cougar and Granada models, remove nut and washer from shock absorber lower mounting stud, then remove shock absorber. On 1980–82 Cougar XR-7 and 1980–83 Thunderbird models, remove shock absorber protective cover, then remove shock absorber to lower mounting bracket bolt.
7. Reverse procedure to install. On all models, torque upper shock mount to 25 ft. lbs. On 1978–80 Fairmont and Zephyr, torque bottom bolt to 55 ft. lbs. On 1981–83 Fairmont and Zephyr and 1981–82 Cougar and Granada, torque bottom bolt to 65 ft. lbs. On 1980–81 Cougar XR-7 and Thunderbird, torque lower bolt to 70 ft. lbs.; 1982 Cougar XR-7 and Thunderbird, 60–65 ft. lbs.; 1983 Cougar and Thunderbird, 45–59 ft. lbs. On 1983 LTD and Marquis, torque bottom bolt to 55–70 ft. lbs.

Except 1978–83 Fairmont & Zephyr; 1980–82 Cougar XR-7; 1980–83 Thunderbird; 1981–82 Granada; 1981–83 Cougar; 1983 LTD & Marquis

1. Raise and properly support vehicle.
2. Disconnect shock absorber from its lower and upper mounting, then remove shock absorber.
3. Reverse procedure to install.

LEAF SPRINGS & BUSHINGS, REPLACE

1977 Comet & Maverick & 1977–80 Granada & Monarch

1. Raise rear of vehicle and support at frame. Support axle with a suitable jack.
2. Disconnect shock absorbers from lower mountings.

3. Lower jack and remove spring plate "U" bolts and spring plate, Fig. 1.
4. Raise axle to remove weight from spring and disassemble rear shackle.
5. Remove spring front mount bolt.
6. Replace spring front eye bushings as necessary, Figs. 2 and 3.
7. Reverse procedure to install.

STABILIZER BAR, REPLACE

1978–83 Fairmont & Zephyr; 1980–82 Cougar XR-7; 1980–83 Thunderbird; 1981–82 Granada; 1981–83 Cougar; 1983 LTD & Marquis

1. Raise and support rear of vehicle.
2. Remove four bolts attaching stabilizer bar to lower control arms.
3. Remove stabilizer bar from vehicle.

Fig. 1   Leaf spring suspension (typical)

Fig. 2   Spring front bushing removal

Fig. 3   Spring front bushing installation

Fig. 4 Stabilizer bar installation
1977—79 Cougar, LTD II & Thunderbird

1977—79 Cougar, LTD II & Thunderbird

1. Remove bolts securing stabilizer bar to rear link assemblies on both sides, Fig. 4.
2. Remove nuts securing mounting bracket to lower mounting clamp and remove bar.
3. Reverse procedure to install.

COIL SPRING, REPLACE

1978—83 Fairmont & Zephyr; 1980—82 Cougar XR-7; 1980—83 Thunderbird; 1981—82 Granada; 1981—83 Cougar; 1983 LTD & Marquis

1. Remove stabilizer bar as described under Stabilizer Bar, Replace, if equipped.
2. Position a suitable jack under rear axle, then raise vehicle and support body at rear body crossmember.
3. Lower axle until shock absorbers are fully entended.

NOTE: Support axle with jack stands or a suitable jack.

4. Position a suitable jack under lower control arm pivot bolt and remove nut and bolt. Carefully and slowly lower the control arm until all spring tension is relieved.
5. Remove coil spring and insulators from vehicle, Fig. 5.

1977—79 Cougar, LTD II & Thunderbird

1. Raise rear of vehicle and support at frame. Support axle with a suitable jack.
2. Disconnect shock absorbers from lower mountings.
3. Lower axle to remove springs.
4. Reverse procedure to install. Install an insulator between upper and lower seats and spring.

CONTROL ARMS, REPLACE

NOTE: Upper and lower control arms must be replaced in pairs.

1978—83 Fairmont & Zephyr; 1980—82 Cougar XR-7; 1980—83 Thunderbird; 1981—82 Granada; 1981—83 Cougar; 1983 LTD & Marquis

Upper Arm
1. Raise vehicle and support body at rear body crossmember.
2. Remove upper arm pivot bolt and nut, Fig. 5.
3. Remove front pivot bolt and nut, then remove upper arm from vehicle.

Lower Arm
1. Remove stabilizer bar as described under Stabilizer Bar, Replace, if equipped.
2. Position a suitable jack under rear axle, then raise vehicle and support body at rear body crossmember.
3. Lower axle until shock absorbers are fully extended.

NOTE: Support axle with jack stands or a suitable jack.

4. Position a suitable jack under lower control arm rear pivot bolt and remove nut bolt, Fig. 5. Carefully and slowly lower the control arm until all spring tension is relieved, then remove coil spring and insulators.

Fig. 5 Rear suspension (typical). 1978—83 Fairmont, Zephyr; 1980—82 Cougar XR-7, 1980—83 Thunderbird, 1981—82 Granada, 1981—83 Cougar & 1983 LTD & Marquis

5. Remove lower control arm front pivot bolt and nut, then remove lower control arm assembly.

1977–79 Cougar, LTD II & Thunderbird

Upper Arm

1. Raise vehicle and support at frame side rails.
2. Lower axle and support axle under differential nose as well as under axle.
3. Remove nut and bolt attaching upper arm to axle housing, then disconnect arm from housing, Fig. 6.
4. Remove nut and bolt attaching upper arm to crossmember, then remove control arm from vehicle.

Lower Arm

1. Raise vehicle and support at frame side rails.
2. Lower axle until all spring tension is relieved.
3. Support axle under differential pinion nose as well as under axle.

Fig. 6 Rear suspension, 1977–79 Cougar, LTD II & Thunderbird

4. Remove lower control arm pivot bolt and nut from axle bracket, then disconnect arm from bracket, Fig. 6.
5. Remove pivot bolt and nut from frame bracket, then remove lower control arm from vehicle.

Front Suspension & Steering Section

FRONT SUSPENSION

1978–83 Fairmont & Zephyr; 1980–82 Cougar XR-7; 1980–83 Thunderbird; 1981–82 Granada; 1981–83 Cougar; 1983 LTD & Marquis

This suspension, Fig. 1, is a modified McPherson strut design, which uses shock struts and coil springs. The springs are mounted between the lower control arm and a spring pocket in the crossmember.

1977–79 Cougar, LTD II & Thunderbird

The front suspension, Fig 2, has the coil spring mounted on the lower arm.

1977 Comet & Maverick & 1977–80 Granada & Monarch

Referring to Fig. 3, each front wheel rotates on a spindle. The upper and lower ends of the spindle are attached to ball joints that are mounted to an upper and lower control arm. The upper arm pivots on a bushing and shaft assembly that is bolted to the underbody. The lower arm pivots on a bolt that is located in an underbody bracket.

A coil spring seats between the upper arm and the top of the spring housing. A double-acting shock absorber is bolted to the arm and the top of the spring housing.

Struts, which are connected between the lower control arms and the underbody, prevent the arms from moving fore and aft.

WHEEL ALIGNMENT

1978–83 Fairmont & Zephyr; 1980–82 Cougar XR-7; 1980–83 Thunderbird; 1981–82 Granada; 1981–83 Cougar; 1983 LTD & Marquis

Caster & Camber

The caster and camber angles of this suspension are factory pre-set and cannot be adjusted in the field.

1977 Comet & Maverick & 1977–80 Granada & Monarch

As shown in Fig. 4, caster is controlled by the front suspension strut. To obtain positive caster, loosen the strut rear nut and tighten the strut front nut against the bushing. To obtain negative caster, loosen the strut front nut and tighten the strut rear nut against the bushing. Torque strut to underbody nut to 70–80 ft. lbs.

Camber is controlled by the eccentric cam located at the lower arm attachment to the side rail. To adjust camber, loosen the camber adjustment bolt nut at the rear of the body bracket. Spread the body bracket at the camber adjustment bolt area just enough to permit lateral travel of the arm when the adjustment bolt is turned. Rotate the bolt and eccentric clockwise from the high position to increase camber or counterclockwise to decrease it. Torque lower arm to underbody bolt to 85–100 ft. lbs.

1977–79 Cougar, LTD II & Thunderbird

Caster and camber can be adjusted by loosening the bolts that attach the upper suspension arm to the shaft at the frame side rail, and moving the arm assembly in or out in the elongated bolt holes, Fig. 5. Since any movement of the arm affects both caster and cam-

ber, both factors should be balanced against one another when making the adjustment.

Install the tool with the pins in the frame holes and the hooks over the upper arm inner shaft. Tighten the hook nuts snug before loosening the upper arm inner shaft attaching bolts, Fig. 5.

Caster, Adjust

1. Tighten the tool front hook nut or loosen the rear hook nut as required to increase caster to the desired angle.
2. To decrease caster, tighten the rear hook nut or loosen the front hook nut as required.

NOTE: The caster angle can be checked without tightening the inner shaft retaining bolts.

---

3. Check the camber angle to be sure it did not change during the caster adjustment and adjust if necessary.
4. Torque the upper arm inner shaft retaining bolts to 120–140 ft. lbs. and remove tool.

Camber, Adjust

1. Install tool as previously outlined.
2. Loosen both inner shaft retaining bolts.
3. Tighten or loosen the hook nuts as necessary to increase or decrease camber.
4. Recheck caster angle. Torque upper arm inner shaft retaining bolts to 120–140 ft. lbs.

TOE-IN, ADJUST

1978–83 Fairmont & Zephyr; 1980–82 Cougar XR-7; 1980–83 Thunderbird; 1981–82 Granada; 1981–83 Cougar; 1983 LTD & Marquis

1. Check to see that steering shaft and steering wheel marks are in alignment and in

380335-S

38391
2 REQ'D.

N620483-S2
6 REQ'D.
68-102 N·M (50-75 FT. LB.)

N800237-S100
4 REQ'D.
203-298 N·M (150-220 FT. LB.)

N605919-S2
6 REQ'D.
47-88 N·M (35-50 FT. LB.)

N620467-S7
2 REQ'D.
8-16 N·M (6-12 FT. LB.)

APRON REF.

5415
2 REQ'D.

N800235-S100
4 REQ'D.

N800202-S2
4 REQ'D.
19-35 N·M (14-26 FT. LB.)

N800236-S100
4 REQ'D.
163-244 N·M (120-180 FT. LB.)

N800241-S
2 REQ'D.

5482

5D485 L.H.
5C495 R.H.

18A084
2 REQ'D.

5310
2 REQ'D.

5486
2 REQ'D.

N800234-S100
4 REQ'D.

5414
2 REQ'D.

N088201-S2
2 REQ'D.

12045-S
2 REQ'D.

3106 L.H.
3105 R.H.

381612-S100 REF.
2 REQ'D.
108-163 N·M (80-120 FT. LB.)

VIEW Z

3051 L.H.
3042 R.H.

KC-55490-A
8 REQ'D.

37110-S2
8 REQ'D.

VIEW Z

N800200-S2
2 REQ'D.

Fig. 1   Front suspension (typical). 1978–83 Fairmont & Zephyr, 1980–82 Cougar XR-7, 1980–83 Thunderbird, 1981–82 Granada, 1981–83 Cougar & 1983 LTD & Marquis

STABILIZER BAR

BOLT MUST BE INSTALLED FROM TOP OF STABILIZER BAR (HEAD UP)

INNER SHAFT

BALL JOINT
3263

BUSHING
3068

UPPER ARM
3082

SPRING INSULATOR
5415

INSULATOR CLAMP
5486

SPRING
5310

SPINDLE
3105 - 6

STRUT
3468

ABSORBER
18124

SPACER

BUSHING

BALL JOINT
3395

LOWER ARM
3078 - 9

Fig. 2   Front suspension (typical). 1977–79 Cougar, LTD II & Thunderbird

the top position.
2. Loosen clamp screw on the tie rod bellows and free the seal on the rod to prevent twisting of the bellows, Fig. 6
3. Place opened end wrench on flats of tie rod socket to prevent socket from turning, then loosen tie rod jam nuts.
4. Use suitable pliers to turn the tie rod inner end to correct the adjustment to specifications. Do not use pliers on tie rod threads. Turning to reduce number of threads showing will increase toe-in. Turning in the opposite direction will reduce toe-in.
5. Torque tie rod jam nuts to 35–50 ft. lbs.

1978–83 Fairmont & Zephyr; 1980–82 Cougar XR-7; 1980–83 Thunderbird; 1981–82 Granada; 1981–83 Cougar; 1983 LTD & Marquis

Check the steering wheel spoke position when the front wheels are in the straight-ahead position. If the spokes are not in the normal position, they can be adjusted while toe-in is being adjusted
1. Loosen clamp bolts on each tie rod end sleeve.
2. Adjust toe-in. If steering wheel spokes are in their normal position, lengthen or shorten both rods equally to obtain correct toe-in. If spokes are not in normal position, make necessary rod adjustments to obtain correct toe-in and steering wheel spoke alignment.

Fig. 3 Front suspension (typical). 1977 Comet & Maverick & 1977–80 Granada & Monarch

Fig. 4 Caster and camber adjustments. 1977 Comet & Maverick & 1977–80 Granada & Monarch

WHEEL BEARINGS, ADJUST

1. With wheel rotating, tighten adjusting nut to 17–25 ft. lbs.
2. Back off adjusting nut ½ turn and re-tighten nut to 10–15 inch lbs.
3. Place nut lock on nut so that castellations on lock are aligned with cotter pin hole in spindle and install cotter pin, Fig 7.
4. Check front wheel rotation, if it rotates noisily or rough, clean, inspect or replace wheel bearings as necessary.

WHEEL BEARINGS, REPLACE

(Disc Brakes)

1. Raise car and remove front wheels.
2. Remove caliper mounting bolts.

NOTE: It is not necessary to disconnect the brake lines for this operation.

3. Slide caliper off of disc, inserting a clean spacer between the shoes to hold them in their bores after the caliper is removed. Position caliper out of the way.

NOTE: Do not allow caliper to hang by brake hose.

4. Remove hub and disc assembly. Grease retainer and inner bearing can now be removed.

CHECKING BALL JOINTS FOR WEAR

Upper Ball Joint

1977–80 Granada & Monarch
1. Raise car on frame contact hoist or by

floor jacks placed beneath underbody until wheel falls to full down position.
2. Grasp the lower edge of tire and move the wheel in and out.
3. While the wheel is being moved observe any movement between the upper end of the spindle and upper arm. If any movement is observed replace the ball joint.

1977–79 Cougar, LTD II & Thunderbird
1. Raise vehicle and place floor jacks beneath lower control arms.
2. Grasp the lower edge of tire and move the wheel in and out.
3. While the wheel is being moved observe any movement between the upper end of the spindle and upper arm. If any movement is observed replace the ball joint.

1977 Comet & Maverick
1. Raise car on frame contact hoist or by floor jacks placed beneath underbody until wheel falls to full down position as

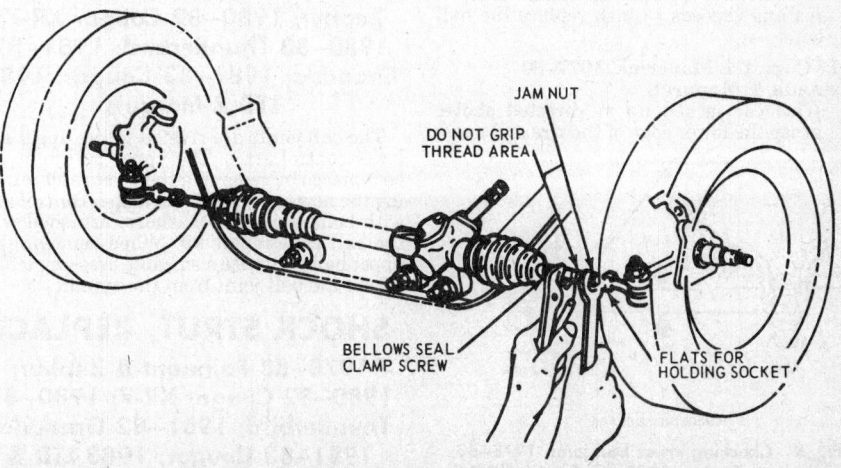

Fig. 5 Caster and Camber adjustment. 1977–79 Cougar, LTD II & Thunderbird

Fig. 6 Toe-in adjustment. 1978–83 Fairmont, Zephyr, 1980–82 Cougar XR-7, 1980–83 Thunderbird, 1981–82 Granada, 1981–83 Cougar & 1983 LTD & Marquis

WITH DRUM AND WHEEL ROTATING, TORQUE THE ADJUSTING NUT

INSTALL LOCK ON NUT SO THAT CASTELLATIONS ARE ALIGNED WITH COTTER PIN HOLE.

BACK OFF NUT AND NUT LOCK ONE CASTELLATION INSTALL COTTER PIN.

Fig. 7 Front wheel bearing adjustment

Fig. 8 Measuring upper ball joint for radial play. 1977 Comet & Maverick

shown in Fig. 8. This will unload upper ball joint.

2. With front wheel bearings properly adjusted, attach a dial indicator to the upper control arm and position the indicator so that its plunger rests against the inner side of the wheel rim adjacent to the upper arm ball joint.
3. Grasp tire at top and bottom and slowly move it in and out, Fig. 6. Reading on dial will indicate the amount of radial play. If reading exceeds ¼", replace the upper ball joint.

Lower Ball Joint

1978–83 Fairmont & Zephyr; 1980–82 Cougar XR-7; 1980–83 Thunderbird; 1981–82 Granada; 1981–83 Cougar; 1983 LTD & Marquis

1. Support vehicle in normal driving position with both ball joints loaded.
2. Clean area around grease fitting and checking surface.

NOTE: The checking surface is the round boss into which the grease fitting is installed.

3. The checking surface should project outside the cover, Fig. 9. If surface is inside cover replace lower arm assembly.

1977–79 Cougar, LTD II & Thunderbird

1. Raise vehicle and place floor jacks under the lower control arms, Fig. 10.
2. Adjust wheel bearings and place a dial indicator to the lower arm and position the indicator so that the plunger rests against the inner side of the wheel rim adjacent to the lower ball joint.
3. Grasp tire at top and bottom and move it slowly in and out. Reading on dial will indicate the amount of radial play. If reading exceeds ¼ inch replace the ball joint.

1977 Comet & Maverick, 1977–80 Granada & Monarch

1. With car jacked up as directed above, grasp the lower edge of the tire and move

BALL JOINT COVER

NEW **WORN**

CHECKING SURFACE

Fig. 9 Checking lower ball joint. 1978–83 Fairmont, Zephyr, 1980–82 Cougar XR-7, 1980–83 Thunderbird, 1981–82 Granada, 1981–83 Cougar & 1983 LTD & Marquis

it in and out.

2. As wheel is being moved in and out, observe lower end of spindle and lower arm.
3. Any movement between lower end of spindle and lower arm indicates ball joint wear and loss of preload. If such movement is observed, replace lower arm and/or ball joint.

NOTE: During the foregoing check, the ball joints will be unloaded and may move. Therefore disregard any movement of the upper ball joint when checking the lower ball joint and any movement of the lower ball joint when checking the upper ball joint. Also, do not mistake loose wheel bearings for a worn ball joint.

BALL JOINTS, REPLACE

NOTE: Ford Motor Company recommends that new ball joints should not be installed on used control arms and that the control arm be replaced if ball joint replacement is required. However, aftermarket ball joint repair kits which do not require control arm replacement, are available and can be installed using the following procedure.

1978–83 Fairmont & Zephyr; 1980–82 Cougar XR-7; 1980–83 Thunderbird; 1981–82 Granada; 1981–83 Cougar; 1983 LTD & Marquis

These ball joints are not serviceable. If they require replacement, the control arm and ball joint must be replaced as an assembly.

Except 1978–83 Fairmont & Zephyr; 1980–82 Cougar XR-7; 1980–83 Thunderbird; 1981–82 Granada; 1981–83 Cougar; 1983 LTD & Marquis

The ball joints are riveted to the upper and lower control arms. The upper ball joint can be replaced by removing the rivets and retaining the new ball joint to the upper control arm with bolts, nuts and washers furnished with the ball joint repair kit. When removing an upper ball joint, use a suitable pressing tool to loosen the ball joint from the spindle.

SHOCK STRUT, REPLACE

1978–83 Fairmont & Zephyr; 1980–82 Cougar XR-7; 1980–83 Thunderbird; 1981–82 Granada; 1981–83 Cougar; 1983 LTD & Marquis

1. Place ignition switch in the Unlocked

position so that front wheels are free to move.

2. From engine compartment, remove one strut to upper mounting nut. Use a screwdriver in rod slot to hold rod stationary when removing nut.
3. Raise front of vehicle by lower control arms, then place safety stands under frame jack pads located rearward of wheels.
4. Remove wheel and tire assembly, then remove brake caliper, rotor assembly and dust shield.
5. Remove two nuts and bolts attaching lower strut to spindle.

NOTE: Gas pressurized struts (1983 Cougar, LTD, Marquis, and Thunderbird) must be held firmly during removal of the last spindle-to-strut bolt since gas pressure will cause strut to extend fully when bolt is removed.

6. Lift strut upward from spindle to compress rod, then pull downward and remove strut.
7. Reverse procedure to install. Torque upper mount attaching nut to 60 to 75 ft. lbs. Remove suspension load from lower control arm by lowering front of vehicle, then torque lower mounting nuts to 150 to 180 ft. lbs.

MAXIMUM TOLERANCE

Fig. 10 Measuring lower ball joint for radial play. 1977–79 Cougar, LTD II & Thunderbird

SHOCK ABSORBER, REPLACE

1977 Comet & Maverick & 1977–80 Granada & Monarch

1. Raise hood and remove upper mounting bracket-to-spring tower retaining nuts.
2. Raise front of car and place safety stands under lower control arms.
3. Remove shock absorber lower retaining nuts and washers.
4. Lift shock absorber from spring tower.
5. Reverse procedure to install. Torque shock absorber upper attachment bolts to 10–16 ft. lbs., shock absorber upper bracket to body nuts to 32–48 ft. lbs. and shock absorber to spring seat to 8–12 ft. lbs.

1977–79 Cougar, LTD II & Thunderbird

1. Remove upper mounting nut, washer and bushing from shock absorber.
2. Raise vehicle and install safety stands.
3. Remove the shock absorber lower retaining screws and remove shock absorber. Torque shock absorber upper attachment bolts to 22–30 ft. lbs. and shock absorber to lower arm to 12–18 ft. lbs.

COIL SPRING, REPLACE

1978–83 Fairmont & Zephyr; 1980–82 Cougar XR-7; 1980–83 Thunderbird; 1981–82 Granada; 1981–83 Cougar; 1983 LTD & Marquis

1. Raise front of vehicle and position safety stands under jack pads located rearward of wheels, then remove wheel and tire assembly.
2. Disconnect stabilizer bar link from lower control arm.
3. Remove steering gear attaching bolts, then position gear out of way.
4. Using tool 3290-C or equivalent, disconnect tie rod from spindle.
5. Using spring compressor D78P-5310-A or equivalent, compress spring until it is free from lower seat.
6. Remove two lower control arm pivot bolts and disengage control arm from frame, then remove spring from seat. If a replacement spring is to be installed, measure compressed length of spring being removed to assist in compressing and installing the replacement spring.
7. Reverse procedure to install. When installing spring, locate lower end of coil between two holes in lower control arm spring pocket. On 1978–81 models, torque control arm pivot bolt nuts to 200–220 ft. lbs., stabilizer bar link nut to 9 to 12 ft. lbs. and steering gear to crossmember attaching bolts to 90 to 100 ft. lbs. On 1982 models, torque lower control arm pivot nuts to 215 to 260 ft. lbs., stabilizer bar to lower control arm nut 6 to 12 ft. lbs. and steering gear to crossmember bolts to 90 to 100 ft. lbs. On 1983 models, torque control arm pivot nuts to 150–180 ft. lbs., stabilizer bar link nut to 6–12 ft. lbs., steering gear to crossmember nuts to 90–100 ft. lbs., and tie rod end to 35 ft. lbs.

Fig. 11   Removing or installing front spring. 1977–79 Cougar, LTD II & Thunderbird

1977 Comet & Maverick & 1977–80 Granada & Monarch

1. Remove shock absorber and upper mounting bracket as an assembly.
2. Raise car on hoist and install safety stands.
3. Remove wheel, hub and drum or caliper and rotor.
4. Install a suitable spring compressor and compress spring.
5. Remove two upper-arm-to-spring tower retaining nuts and swing upper arm outward from spring.
6. Release spring compressor. Then remove spring.
7. Reverse procedure to install. Torque upper arm and inner shaft to body nuts to 85–100 ft. lbs.

1977–79 Cougar, LTD II & Thunderbird

1. Raise vehicle and support front end of frame with jack stands.
2. Disconnect shock absorber from lower arm and place a jack under the lower arm for support, Fig. 11.
3. Remove strut and rebound bumper bolts and disconnect lower end of sway bar stud from lower arm.
4. Remove the nut and bolt that retains the inner end of the lower arm to the crossmember.
5. Carefully lower jack relieving spring pressure on the lower arm, then remove the spring.
6. Reverse procedure to install. Spring should be positioned on lower arm so that end is no more than 1/2 inch from depression in lower arm. Torque strut to lower arm bolts to 80–115 ft. lbs., stabilizer bar to lower arm to 9–12 ft. lbs. and lower arm inner pivot nut to 95–110 ft. lbs.

STABILIZER BAR &/OR INSULATOR

1978–83 Fairmont & Zephyr; 1980–82 Cougar XR-7; 1980–83 Thunderbird; 1981–82 Granada; 1981–83 Cougar; 1983 LTD & Marquis

1. Raise vehicle and place jack stands under lower control arms.
2. Disconnect stabilizer bar from links, then remove stabilizer insulator retaining clamps and remove stabilizer.
3. To remove insulator, cut insulators and plastic sleeves from stabilizer bar. Before installing new insulators, coat the necessary parts of the stabilizer with grease, then install the insulators and sleeves.
4. Reverse procedure to install stabilizer bar. Install new stabilizer link bolts with heads facing down and torque to 9–12 ft. lbs. on 1978–81 models, 6 to 12 ft. lbs. on 1982–83 models. Using new bolts, install stabilizer insulator retaining clamps and torque to 20 to 26 ft. lbs. on 1978 models, 14 to 16 ft. lbs. on 1979–80 models, 25 to 30 ft. lbs. on 1981 models, 20 to 25 ft. lbs. on 1982–83 models.

POWER STEERING GEAR, REPLACE

Integral Power Rack & Pinion

1. Disconnect battery ground cable.
2. Remove bolt retaining flexible coupling to input shaft.
3. Turn ignition key "ON" and raise vehicle.
4. Remove the two tie rod end retaining nuts, then separate studs from spindle arms, using a suitable tool.
5. Support gear and remove attaching bolts, then lower gear enough to gain access to pressure and return lines, and remove bolt attaching the hose bracket to the gear.
6. Disconnect pressure and return lines and remove steering gear. Plug lines and ports to prevent entry of dirt.
7. Reverse procedure to install. Torque pressure and return line fittings to 10–15 ft. lbs., gear housing to crossmember mounting bolt to 80–100 ft. lbs., steering flex coupling bolt to 20–30 ft. lbs. and tie rod end to spindle arm nut to 35–47 ft. lbs.

NOTE: On some models, hoses can swivel when torqued properly. Do not over tighten.

Integral Power Steering Gear

1. Disconnect pressure and return lines from gear and plug openings to prevent entry of dirt.
2. Remove two bolts that secure flex coupling to gear and column.
3. Raise vehicle and remove pitman arm with suitable puller.
4. If vehicle is equipped with synchromesh transmission, remove clutch release retracting spring to provide clearance to remove gear.
5. Support gear and remove three gear attaching bolts.

Fig. 12   Power steering pump installation. Typical

MANUAL STEERING GEAR, REPLACE

Rack & Pinion

1. Disconnect battery ground cable, turn ignition "On" and raise vehicle.
2. Remove tie rod end retaining nuts and using ball joint separator, separate tie rod ends from spindle arms.
3. Remove pinion shaft to flexible coupling bolt and the bolts securing steering gear to crossmember.
4. Turn front wheels, then remove steering gear from left side of vehicle.
5. Reverse procedure to install. Torque connecting rod end to spindle arm nut to 35–47 ft. lbs. on 1977–80 models and 41–61 ft. lbs. on 1981–83 models. Torque flex coupling to 20–37 ft. lbs. and torque steering gear to crossmember bolts to 80–100 ft. lbs. on 1977–80 models and 90–100 ft. lbs. on 1981–83 models.

Except Rack and Pinion

1. Remove flex coupling bolts.
2. Remove pitman arm nut and remove arm from shaft using a puller.
3. With manual transmission it may be necessary to disconnect the clutch linkage and on V8 models it may be necessary to lower the exhaust system.
4. Unfasten and remove steering gear.
5. Reverse procedure to install. Torque steering gear to side rail bolts to 50–60 ft. lbs. and pitman arm to sector shaft nut to 200–225 ft. lbs.

CONTROL VALVE, REPLACE

Non-Integral Power Steering

1. Disconnect fluid fittings at control valve and drain fluid from lines by turning wheels to left and right.
2. Loosen clamp at right-hand end of sleeve. Remove roll pin from steering arm-to-idler arm rod through slot in sleeve.
3. Using tool 3290-C, remove ball stud from sector shaft arm.

NOTE: The use of any other tool may result in damage to the control valve assembly.

4. Turn wheels fully to left and unthread control valve from idler arm rod.
5. Reverse procedure to install. Measure distance between center of left spindle connect-rod hole in idler arm to edge of control valve. Distance must be 2.55–2.65 inches. Torque valve sleeve clamp nut to 13–17 ft. lbs., ball stud nut to 35–47 ft. lbs., worm screw hose clamp to 30–60 in. lbs., return line to control valve to 16–25 ft. lbs., pressure line to control valve to 15–19 ft. lbs. and pressure and return lines to power cylinder to 15–19 ft. lbs. Connect short control valve to power cylinder hose to valve port "C" and other hose to valve port "A".

POWER STEERING PUMP, REPLACE

1977–83 Models Exc. 1977 Models with TRW Pump

1. Disconnect return hose from power steering pump and allow fluid to drain into a suitable container.
2. Remove pressure hose from power steering pump fitting.
3. On models less fixed pump, remove mounting bracket attaching bolts, then disconnect drive belt from pulley and remove pump.
4. On models with fixed pump, remove drive belt from pulley, then remove pulley and lift pump from engine compartment.
5. Reverse procedure to install. Refer to Fig. 12 for torque specifications.

1977 Models with TRW Pump

1. Disconnect return hose from power steering pump and allow fluid to drain into a suitable container.
2. Disconnect pressure hose from pump, then remove front mounting bracket to pump attaching bolts. On models with V8 engine also remove nut attaching pump to rear of mounting bracket.
3. Disconnect drive belt from pulley, then remove pump from engine compartment.
4. Reverse procedure to install. Torque pump bracket front bolt to 30–45 ft. lbs., pump to bracket rear nut to 20–30 ft. lbs., pressure hose to pump nut to 28–37 ft. lbs. except on 302 cu. inch engines which are torqued to 25–34 ft. lbs. and return hose to pump to 12–24 inch lbs.

FORD ESCORT & EXP · MERCURY LN7 & LYNX

INDEX OF SERVICE OPERATIONS

NOTE: Refer to the back of this manual for vehicle manufacturer's special service tool suppliers.

ENGINE IDENTIFICATION

Engine code is eighth digit in serial number
(VIN) located on left side dash.

GRILLE IDENTIFICATION

1981 Escort

1981 Lynx

1982 Escort; 1983 Escort GL & Sta. Wag.

1982-83 EXP

1982-83 LN7

1982 Lynx

1983 Escort GT

1983 Lynx RS

1983 Lynx GS & Sta. Wag.

GENERAL ENGINE SPECIFICATIONS

Year	Engine CID①/Liter	VIN Code②	Carburetor	Bore and Stroke	Compression Ratio	Net H.P. @ R.P.M.③	Maximum Torque Ft. Lbs. @ R.P.M.	Normal Oil Pressure Pounds
1981	97.6, 1.6 L	2	740, 2 Bbl.④	3.15 × 3.13	8.8	65 @ 5200	85 @ 3000	40
1982	97.6, 1.6 L	2	740, 2 Bbl.④	3.15 × 3.13	8.8	70 @ 4600	89 @ 3000	30—50
1983	97.6, 1.6 L	2	740, 2 Bbl.④	3.15 × 3.13	8.8	—	—	—
	97.6, 1.6 L	2	EFI	3.15 × 3.13	9.5	—	—	—
	97.6, 1.6 L H.O.	2	740, 2 Bbl.④	3.15 × 3.13	—	—	—	—

①—CID—Cubic inch displacement.

②—The eighth digit in the VIN denotes engine code.

③—Ratings are net—as installed in vehicle.

④—Motorcraft.

TUNE UP SPECIFICATIONS

The following specifications are published from the latest information available. This
data should be used only in the absence of a decal affixed in the engine compartment.

★ When using a timing light, disconnect vacuum hose or tube at distributor and plug opening in hose or tube so idle speed will not be affected.
● When checking compression, lowest cylinder must be within 75 percent of highest.
▲ Before removing wires from distributor cap, determine location of the No. 1 wire in cap, as distributor position may have been altered from that shown at
the end of this chart.

☞ Spark plug types shown in this chart are recommendations of the original vehicle manufacturer and not MOTOR.

Check local sources for other spark plug manufacturers listings.

Year & Engine/V.I.N.	Spark Plug			Ignition Timing BTDC① ★			Curb Idle Speed		Fast Idle Speed		Fuel Pump Pressure
	Type ☞	Gap	Firing Order Fig. ▲	Man. Trans.	Auto. Trans.	Mark Fig.	Man. Trans.	Auto. Trans.②	Man. Trans.	Auto. Trans.	
1981											
4-97.6 (1.6L)/2 Exc. Calif.	AGSP-32	.044	A	10°⑦	10°⑦	B	900③⑧	750D④	2400⑤⑨	2400⑤	4–6⑥
4-97.6 (1.6L)/2 Calif.	AGSP-32	.044	A	10°⑦	6°⑦	B	900③⑧	750D④	2400⑤⑨	2400⑤	4–6⑥
1982											
4-97.6/2 Exc. Calif.⑩⑪⑫	AWSF-32	.044	A	—	12°⑦	B	—	800D③	—	2400⑤	4½–6½⑥
4-96.6/2 Exc. Calif. & High Alt.⑪⑬⑭	AWSF-32	.044	A	—	10°⑦	B	—	750D⑮	—	2400⑤	4½–6½⑥
4-97.6/2 Exc. High Alt.⑩⑪⑯	⑰	.044	A	6°⑦	—	B	800⑮	—	2400⑤	—	4½–6½⑥
4-97.6/2 Exc. High Alt.⑪⑬⑱	AWSF-32	.044	A	14°⑦	—	B	800⑮	—	2400⑤	—	4½–6½⑥
4-97.6/2 Exc. High Alt.⑪⑬⑲⑳	AWSF-32	.044	A	14°⑦	—	B	650/1300	—	2200⑤	—	4½–6½⑥
4-97.6/2 Exc. High Alt.⑪⑬㉑	AWSF-32	.044	A	12°⑦	—	B	800⑮	—	2400⑤	—	4½–6½⑥
4-97.6/2 Exc. High Alt.⑪⑬㉒	AWSF-32	.044	A	10°⑦	—	B	800⑮	—	2400⑤	—	4½–6½⑥
4-97.6/2 Calif.⑩⑪㉓	AWSF-32	.044	A	—	12°⑦	B	—	800D③	—	2400⑤	4½–6½⑥
4-97.6/2 Calif.⑩⑪㉔	AWSF-32	.044	A	—	8°⑦	B	—	800D③	—	2400⑤	4½–6½⑥
4-97.6/2 Calif.⑪⑬㉕	AWSF-32	.044	A	—	8°⑦	B	—	750D⑮	—	2400⑤	4½–6½⑥
4-97.6/2 Calif.⑪⑬㉖	AWSF-32	.044	A	—	10°⑦	B	—	750D⑮	—	2400⑤	4½–6½⑥
4-97.6/2 High Alt.⑩⑪㉗	AWSF-32	.044	A	8°⑦	—	B	800⑯	—	2400⑤	—	4½–6½⑥
4-97.6/2 High Alt.⑪⑬㉘	AWSF-32	.044	A	10°⑦	10°⑦	B	800⑯	750D⑮	2400⑤	2400⑤	4½–6½⑥
4-97.6 H.O./2㉙	AWSF-32	.044	A	10°⑦	10°⑦	B	—	750D⑮	—	2200⑤	4½–6½⑥

①—BTDC—Before top dead center.
②—D: Drive.
③—With A/C on, 1700 RPM, if equipped.
④—With A/C on, 1850 RPM, if equipped.
⑤—On kick down step of cam.
⑥—With pump to tank return pinched off.
⑦—At 800 RPM.
⑧—If mileage on vehicle is less than 100 mi., set at 750 RPM.
⑨—If mileage on vehicle is less than 100 mi., set at 2200 RPM.
⑩—Early production EXP & LN7.
⑪—Refer to engine calibration code on engine identification label, located at front of engine timing belt cover. The calibration code is located on the label below the engine sequence number (ESN) & is preceded by the letter C. The revision code is located next to the calibration code & is preceded by the letter R.
⑫—Calibration code 1-4E-R0.
⑬—Escort, Lynx & late production EXP & LN7.
⑭—Calibration code 2-4C-R0.
⑮—With A/C on, 1500N RPM, if equipped.
⑯—Calibration codes 1-3S-R0 & 1-3S-R11.
⑰—Calibration code 1-3S-R0, use AGSP-32; code 1-3S-R11, use AWSF-32.
⑱—Calibration codes 2-3A-R10 & 2-3C-R0.
⑲—Calibration codes 2-3D-R0, R1, R14 & R15.
⑳—Models less A/C & power steering.
㉑—Calibration code 2-3E-R0.
㉒—Calibration code 2-3G-R0.
㉓—Calibration code 1-4S-R0.
㉔—Calibration code 1-4S-R10.
㉕—Calibration code 2-4Q-R0.
㉖—Calibration code 2-4Q-R10.
㉗—Calibration code 1-3Y-R10.
㉘—Calibration code, man. trans. 2-3X-R0; auto. trans., 2-4X-R0.
㉙—High output engine.

FIRING ORDER 1·3·4·2
FRONT OF CAR ↓

Fig. A

16 8 0

Fig. B

DISTRIBUTOR SPECIFICATIONS
★If unit is checked on vehicle, double the RPM and degrees to get crankshaft figures.

Distributor Part No.	Centrifugal Advance Degrees @ RPM of Distributor				Vacuum Advance			Distributor Retard
	Advance Starts	Intermediate Advance		Full Advance	Inches of Vacuum to start Plunger	Max. Adv. Dist. Deg. @ Vacuum		Max. Ret. Dist. Deg. @ Vacuum
1981								
E1EE-AB, AC, AE①②	—	—	9½–12 @ 1250	—	—	—	—	—
E1EE-AB, AC, AE①③	—	—	7½–10 @ 1250	—	—	—	—	—
E1EE-JA, JB②④	—	—	9½–12 @ 1250	—	—	—	—	—
E1EE-JA, JB③④	—	—	7½–10 @ 1250	—	—	—	—	—
1982								
E1EE-AB, AC, AE, AF①⑤	—	—	7½–10 @ 1250	—	—	—	—	—
E1EE-AB, AC, AE, AF①⑥	—	—	8½–11 @ 1250	—	—	—	—	—
E1EE-KA, KB②④⑤	—	—	7½–10 @ 1250	—	—	—	—	—
E1EE-KA, KB③④	—	—	5½–8 @ 1250	—	—	—	—	—
E2EE-EA, GA②④⑤	—	—	10–12 @ 1250	—	—	—	—	—
E2EE-EA, GA③④	—	—	9–11 @ 1250	—	—	—	—	—
E2EE-EA, GA④⑥	—	—	10–12 @ 1250	—	—	—	—	—
E2EE-FA①②⑤	—	—	10½–13 @ 1250	—	—	—	—	—
E2EE-FA①⑤	—	—	⑦	—	—	—	—	—
E2EE-FA⑥	—	—	10½–13 @ 1250	—	—	—	—	—
E2EE-LA	—	—	8½–11 @ 1250	—	—	—	—	—

①—Man. Trans.
②—Except Calif.
③—Calif.
④—Auto Trans.
⑤—Except high altitude.
⑥—High altitude.
⑦—Calibration code 2-3C-R0. 10½–13 @ 1250; Calibration code, 2-3E-R0, 9½–12 @ 1250; Calibration code, 2-3G-R1, 8½–11 @ 1250.

STARTING MOTOR SPECIFICATIONS

Year	Engine Model/V.I.N.	Ident. No.①	Brush Spring Tension, Ounces	No Load Test			Torque Test		
				Amperes	Volts	R.P.M.	Amperes	Volts	Torque Ft. Lbs.
1981	4-97.6 (1.6L)/2	E1EF-AB	80	80	—	—	500	—	—
1982	4-97.6 (1.6L)/2	E1EF-AD	80	80	—	—	500	—	—
1983	4-97.6 (1.6L)/2	—	80	80	—	—	500	—	—

①—Basic ident. No., 11001.

ALTERNATOR & REGULATOR SPECIFICATIONS

Year	Ident. Stamp Color	Current Rating		Field Current @ 75°F.		Voltage Regulator				Field Relay	
		Amperes	Volts	Amperes	Volts	Ident. No.①	Voltage @ 75°F	Contact Gap	Armature Air Gap	Armature Air Gap	Closing Voltage @ 75°F.
1981	Orange	40	15	4	12	D9BF-AB	13.8–14.6	—	—	—	—
	Green	60	15	4	12	D9BF-AB	13.8–14.6	—	—	—	—
	Black	65	15	4	12	D9BF-AB	13.8–14.6	—	—	—	—
1982–83	Orange	40	15	4	12	②	13.8–14.6	—	—	—	—
	Green	60	15	4	12	②	13.8–14.6	—	—	—	—
	Black	65	15	4	12	②	13.8–14.6	—	—	—	—

①—Basic ident. No., 10316.
②—1982 Escort & Lynx, E1AF-AA; 1982 EXP & LN7, E1TF-AA; 1983 Escort & Lynx, E2AF-AA; 1983 EXP & LN7, E2TF-AA.

VALVE SPECIFICATIONS

Year	Engine	Valve Lash		Valve Angles		Valve Spring Installed Height	Valve Spring Pressure Lbs. @ In.	Stem Clearance		Stem Diameter	
		Int.	Exh.	Seat	Face			Intake	Exhaust	Intake	Exhaust
1981	4-97.6 (1.6L)/2	.059–.194①		45	44	1.46	180 @ 1.09	.0008–.0027	.0015–.0032	.316	.315
1982	4-97.6 (1.6L)/2	.059–.194①		45	44	1.46	180 @ 1.09	.0008–.0027	.0018–.0037	.316	.315
1983	4-97.6 (1.6L)/2	.059–.194①		45	45.6	1.46	200 @ 1.09	.0008–.0027	.0018–.0037	.316	.315
	4-97.6 (1.6L)/2 E.F.I. & H.O.	.059–.194①		45	45.6	1.46	206 @ 1.09	.0008–.0027	.0018–.0037	.316	.315

①—With hydraulic valve lash adjuster completely collapsed.

PISTONS, PINS, RINGS, CRANKSHAFT & BEARINGS

| Year | Engine/VIN | Piston Clearance | Ring End Gap[1] | | Wrist pin Diameter | Rod Bearings | | Main Bearings | | | Shaft End Play |
			Comp.	Oil		Shaft Diameter	Bearing Clearance	Shaft Diameter	Bearing Clearance	Thrust on Bear. No.	
1981–83	4-97.6, 1.6L/2	.0008–.0016	.012	.016	.8119–.8124	1.885–1.886	.0008–.0015	2.2826–2.2834	.0008–.0015	3	.004–.008

[1]—Fit rings in tapered bores for clearance listed in tightest portion of ring travel.

ENGINE TIGHTENING SPECIFICATIONS

Year	Engine/VIN	Spark Plugs Ft. Lbs.	Cylinder Head Bolts Ft. Lbs.	Intake Manifold Ft. Lbs.	Exhaust Manifold Ft. Lbs.	Rocker Arm Shaft Bracket Ft. Lbs.	Rocker Arm Cover Ft. Lbs.	Connecting Rod Cap Bolts Ft. Lbs.	Main Bearing Cap Bolts Ft. Lbs.	Flywheel to Crank-shaft Ft. Lbs.	Vibration Damper or Pulley Ft. Lbs.
1981–82	4-97.6 (1.6L)/2	17–23	44[1]	12–15	15–20	7–11[2]	6–8	19–25	67–80	59–69	74–90
1983	4-97.6 (1.6L)/2	8–15	44[1]	12–15	15–20	7–11[2]	6–8	19–25	67–80	54–64	74–90

[1]—Then tighten bolts an additional 1/2 turn in 1/4 turn increments after specified torque has been obtained.
[2]—Rocker arm stud to cylinder head.

BRAKE SPECIFICATIONS

| Year | Model | Brake Drum Inside Diameter | Wheel Cylinder Bore Diameter | | | Master Cylinder Bore Diameter | | |
			Front Disc Brakes	Front Drum Brakes	Rear Brakes	With Disc Brakes	With Drum Brakes	With Power Brakes
1981	All	[1]	2.125	—	.811	.828	—	.828
1982–83	Escort & Lynx	8	2.125	—	.811	.828	—	.828
	EXP & LN7	7.1	2.125	—	.811	.828	—	.828

[1]—Hatchback, 7.1"; Liftgate, 8.0".

WHEEL ALIGNMENT SPECIFICATIONS

| Year | Model | Caster Angle, Degrees | | Camber Angle, Degrees | | | | Toe-In Inch | Toe-Out on Turns, Deg. | |
| | | Limits | Desired | Limits | | Desired | | | Outer Wheel | Inner Wheel |
				Left	Right	Left	Right			
1981	Front	+.55 to +2.05	+1.3	+1.4 to +2.9	+.95 to +2.45	+2.15	+1.7	[1]	[2]	20
	Rear	—	—	−1.45 to +.25	−1.45 to +.25	−.6	−.6	0–.36	—	—
1982–83	Front	+.55 to +2.05	+1.3	+1.4 to +2.9	+.95 to +2.45	+2.15	+1.7	[1]	[3]	20
	Rear	—	—	−1.45 to +.25	−1.45 to +.25	−.6	−.6	.09	—	—

[1]—Toe out, .10 inch.   [2]—Left wheel, 19.97°; right wheel, 17.04°.   [3]—Left wheel, 20°; right wheel, 17°.

COOLING SYSTEM & CAPACITY DATA

| Year | Model or Engine/VIN | Cooling Capacity, Qts. | | Radiator Cap Relief Pressure, Lbs. | Thermo. Opening Temp. | Fuel Tank Gals. | Engine Refill Qts.[1] | Transaxle Oil | |
		Less A/C	With A/C					4 & 5 Speed Pints	Auto Trans. Qts.[1]
1981	4-97.6 (1.6L)/2	6.3	6.4	16	191	[2]	4[3]	5	9.8
1982	4-97.6 (1.6L)/2	8	8	16	191	11.3	4[3]	5	9.8
1983	4-97.6 (1.6L)/2	6.7	8	16	191	11.3	4[3]	[4]	8.3

[1]—Approximate. Make final check with dipstick.   [2]—Models w/man. trans., 9 gals.; models w/auto. trans., 10 gals.; models w/extended range option, 11.3 gals.   [3]—Includes filter.   [4]—4 speed trans., 5 pints; 5 speed trans., 6.1 pints.

Electrical Section

STARTER, REPLACE

1. Disconnect battery ground cable and raise and support vehicle. Disconnect starter cable from starter motor terminal.
2. On vehicles equipped with manual transmission, remove three nuts attaching roll restrictor brace to transmission-side starter studs and remove brace.
3. Remove two bolts ataching starter rear support bracket. Remove retaining nut from rear of starter stud bolt, then remove bracket.
4. Remove three starter mounting nuts or bolts and the starter.
5. Reverse procedure to install.

IGNITION SWITCH, REPLACE

1982–83

1. Disconnect battery ground cable, then remove five steering column shroud attaching screws.
2. Remove two bolts and two nuts attaching steering column to column bracket, then lower steering column assembly to seat and remove column shrouds.
3. Disconnect ignition switch wire connector, then rotate ignition switch lock cylinder to the Run position.
4. Using a ⅛ inch drill bit, drill out shear bolts retaining ignition switch to lock cylinder housing.
5. Remove the two shear bolts using an easy out.
6. Detach ignition switch from actuator pin, then remove switch.
7. Check to ensure that ignition switch actuator pin slot and ignition switch lock cylinder are in the Run position.

NOTE: Replacement ignition switches are set in the Run position. The Run position on the ignition switch lock cylinder is located approximately 90° from the lock position.

8. Position ignition switch on actuator pin. It may be necessary to move switch slightly to align switch to column mounting bolt holes.
9. Install and tighten shear bolts until heads break-off.
10. Connect wire connector to ignition switch, then connect battery ground cable and check ignition switch for proper operation.

SWITCH ACTUATOR

Fig. 1   Ignition switch. 1982–83

11. Position upper shroud on column, then raise steering column and install column mounting bracket to instrument panel attaching bolts. Torque bolts to 15 to 25 ft. lbs.
12. Position lower shroud on column and install attaching bolts.

1981

1. Disconnect battery ground cable.
2. Remove steering column upper and lower trim shroud. It may be necessary to loosen four steering column attaching nuts to facilitate shroud removal.
3. Disconnect ignition switch electrical connector, Fig. 1A.
4. Using a ⅛ in. drill, drill out the break-off head bolts attaching the switch to the lock cylinder.
5. Remove two switch retaining bolts using an easy out, then disengage the ignition switch from the actuator pin.
6. Adjust ignition switch by sliding carrier to the switch lock position, then insert a 1/16 in. drill bit through switch housing and into carrier.

NOTE: A replacement switch assembly includes an adjusting pin already installed.

7. Rotate lock cylinder to lock position and install switch onto actuator pin. Then install new break-off head bolts. Hand tighten the bolts.
8. Locate ignition switch upward on steering column until all travel in screw slots is used.
9. Hold switch in this position and tighten break off head bolts until heads break off.

Fig. 1A   Ignition switch removal. 1981

Fig. 2   Turn signal switch removal

Fig. 3   Stop light switch

Fig. 4 Instrument cluster removal

Fig. 5 Windshield wiper motor

Remove adjustment drill bit, connect electrical connector, then install upper and lower trim shroud.

TURN SIGNAL SWITCH, REPLACE

1981—83

1. Disconnect battery ground cable, then remove the upper and lower trim shroud.
2. Grasp switch lever. Using a pulling and twisting motion, pull lever straight out from switch, Fig. 2.
3. Pull back switch cover from switch, then disconnect two switch electrical connectors.
4. Remove screws securing switch to lock cylinder housing, then the switch.
5. Reverse procedure to install.

STOPLIGHT LIGHT SWITCH, REPLACE

1981—83

1. Disconnect battery ground cable.
2. Disconnect electrical connector from switch.

NOTE: On vehicles equipped with standard brakes, the locking tab must be lifted before electrical connector can be removed.

3. On vehicles equipped with standard brakes, remove retainer, then slide the switch, push rod, white nylon washer and bushing away from pedal. Remove switch

from vehicle, Fig. 3.
4. On vehicles equipped with power brakes, remove retainer and outer white nylon washer from pedal pin. Slide switch off brake pedal pin far enough so that outer side of plate of switch clears pin. Remove switch, Fig. 3.

STEERING WHEEL, REPLACE

1. Disconnect battery ground cable.
2. Remove steering hub cover assembly, then the steering wheel attaching nut. Discard nut.
3. Remove steering wheel from steering shaft using tool T67L3600A. Do not use a knock-off type steering wheel puller or strike end of steering column with a hammer since damage to steering column bearings will result.
4. Reverse procedure to install. Use a new wheel nut and torque to 13–20 ft. lbs.

INSTRUMENT CLUSTER, REPLACE

1981—83

1. Disconnect battery ground cable.
2. Remove steering column lower cover, then the four cluster opening finish panel retaining screws and the finish panel.
3. Remove two upper and two lower screws retaining instrument panel.
4. From under instrument panel, disconnect speedometer cable, then pull cluster away from instrument panel, Fig. 4. Disconnect cluster electrical connector.
5. Reverse procedure to install.

Auxiliary Cluster, Replace

EXP & LN7

1. Disconnect battery ground cable, then pull trim cover at bottom edge and slide out of tabs at top edge.
2. Remove three cluster to console attaching screws, then pull cluster outward and disconnect wire connector.
3. Remove cluster from console.
4. Reverse procedure to install.

Graphic Warning Display, Replace

Escort & Lynx

1. Disconnect battery ground cable, then remove console finish panel by prying at bottom edge to disengage retainers.
2. Remove three module to console attaching screws, then pull module outward and disconnect wire connector.
3. Remove module from console.
4. Reverse procedure to install.

HORN SOUNDER, REPLACE

NOTE: On these models, the horn sounder is located on the turn signal, headlight dimmer and horn lever. Refer to Turn Signal Switch, Replace when replacing lever.

HEADLAMP SWITCH, REPLACE

1981—83

1. Disconnect battery ground cable, then on vehicles without A/C, the left hand air vent control cable from the instrument panel.
2. Remove screws securing fuse panel bracket and position fuse panel to the side.
3. Place headlamp switch in the "On" position and depress the headlamp knob and shaft retainer button on headlamp switch. Remove knob and shaft assembly.
4. Remove headlamp switch bezel and disconnect electrical connector, then remove switch.
5. Reverse procedure to install

FORD ESCORT & EXP • MERCURY LN7 & LYNX

Fig. 6 Windshield wiper linkage, removal

RADIO, REPLACE

1981–83

1. Disconnect battery ground cable.
2. Remove A/C floor duct, if equipped.
3. Disconnect power, speaker and antenna leads from radio.
4. Remove knobs, discs, control shaft, nuts and washers from radio.
5. Remove ash tray and bracket, then the radio.
6. Remove radio rear support attaching nut.
7. Reverse procedure to install.

W/S WIPER SWITCH

1981–83

NOTE: The switch handle is an integral part of the switch and cannot be removed separately.

1. Disconnect battery ground cable.
2. Remove upper steering column trim shroud, then disconnect electrical connector.
3. Pull back shield, then remove two screws securing switch. Remove switch.
4. Reverse procedure to install.

W/S WIPER MOTOR, REPLACE

1981–83

1. Disconnect battery ground cable.
2. Lift passenger side water shield cover

Fig. 7 Heater core removal, less air conditioning

Fig. 8 Heater core removal, with air conditioning

Fig. 9 Vent assembly removal

Fig. 10 Blower motor removal. Less air conditioning

Fig. 11 Speed control actuator cable assembly

from cowl, then disconnect motor electrical connector.
3. Remove linkage retaining clip from motor arm, then the three bolts attaching motor to mounting bracket, Fig. 5.
4. Disconnect operating arm from motor, then separate motor from mounting bracket and remove from vehicle.
5. Reverse procedure to install.

W/S WIPER TRANSMISSION, REPLACE

1981—83

1. Remove wiper arm and blade assemblies from pivot shaft.
2. Disconnect battery ground cable.
3. Disconnect linkage drive arm from motor crank pin, then remove nut from each pivot shaft.
4. Remove linkage and pivots from cowl chamber, Fig. 6.
5. Reverse procedure to install.

HEATER CORE, REPLACE

Less Air Conditioning
1. Disconnect battery ground cable and drain cooling system.
2. Disconnect heater hoses from heater core and plug all open lines and fittings to prevent spillage.
3. Remove glove box and liner and move temperature lever to warm position.
4. Remove heater core cover, then working from engine compartment, loosen two nuts attaching heater case assembly to dash panel.
5. Push heater core toward passenger compartment, then pull heater core through blove box opening and remove from vehicle, Fig. 7.
6. Reverse procedure to install.

With Air Conditioning
1. Disconnect battery ground cable and drain cooling system.

2. Disconnect heater hoses from heater core and plug all lines and fittings.
3. Remove floor duct from plenum.
4. Remove screws attaching heater core cover to plenum, then the cover and heater core, Fig. 8.
5. Reverse procedure to install.

BLOWER MOTOR, REPLACE

Less Air Conditioning
1. Disconnect battery ground cable.
2. Remove screws securing right ventilator control cable to instrument panel.
3. Remove screw securing right register duct to lower right edge of instrument panel.
4. Remove glove box and hinge bar from instrument panel.
5. Pull right register duct from installed position between air inlet duct and right register opening, Fig. 9.
6. Remove ventilator grille from bottom of ventilator assembly, then screws securing right ventilator assembly to blower housing.
7. Remove hub clamp spring from blower wheel hub, Fig. 10.
8. Pull blower wheel from blower shaft, then remove three blower motor flange attaching screws.
9. Pull blower motor from housing, disconnect electrical connector, then remove motor from vehicle.
10. Reverse procedure to install.

With Air Conditioning
1. Disconnect battery ground cable.
2. Remove glove box door and instrument panel lower reinforcement from instrument panel.
3. Disconnect blower motor electrical connector, then remove blower motor and mounting plate from evaporator housing.
4. Rotate motor until mounting plate flats clear edge of glove box opening, then remove motor.

5. Remove hub clamp wheel spring from blower wheel hub and remove blower wheel from motor shaft.
6. Reverse procedure to install.

SPEED CONTROLS

1981—83

Actuator Cable Adjustment
1. Remove cable retaining clip, then disengage throttle positioner.
2. Place carburetor throttle lever at the curb idle speed position.
3. Pull on actuator cable end tube to remove slack from cable, Fig. 11.
4. While maintaining light tension on actuator cable, insert cable retaining clip.

Vacuum Dump Valve Adjustment
1. Firmly depress brake pedal and hold in position.
2. Pull inward on dump valve until collar contacts retaining clip.
3. Position a .050 to .100 inch shim between pedal and dump valve button.
4. Pull brake pedal rearward to its normal position and allow dump valve to rachet into retaining clip.

Clutch Switch Adjustment

NOTE: This adjustment should be performed on models with manual transmission, when speed control will not engage.

1. Position and support clutch pedal in the full upward position against pedal stop.
2. Loosen switch attaching screw and slide switch forward toward clutch pedal, until clearance between switch plunger cap and switch housing is .030 inch, then tighten attaching screw.
3. Remove support holding clutch pedal in the full upward position and check speed control for proper operation. Ensure that speed control disengages when clutch pedal is depressed.

Engine Section

ENGINE MOUNTS

Refer to Fig. 1 when replacing the engine mounts.

ENGINE, REPLACE

1. Disconnect battery ground cable, then mark location of hinges and remove hood.
2. Remove air cleaner, fresh air intake tube and hot air tube.
3. Drain cooling system, then disconnect secondary coil wire from distributor.
4. Remove alternator and thermactor pump.
5. Disconnect A/C compressor clutch wire from compressor.
6. On models with automatic transaxle, disconnect upper and lower oil cooler lines at radiator, then remove transmission oil cooler line clips.
7. Disconnect upper and lower radiator

hoses.
8. Disconnect heater hoses from engine.
9. Disconnect wire connector from electric cooling fan and remove fan motor and shroud assembly, then remove radiator.
10. Remove power steering pump filler tube and cap pump opening to prevent fluid spillage, if equipped.
11. Disconnect all necessary vacuum hose and electrical connections.
12. Disconnect fuel supply and return hoses at metal connector to engine.
13. On models with automatic transaxle, disconnect throttle kickdown linkage.
14. Disconnect vacuum hose at power brake booster, if equipped.
15. Disconnect hose to thermactor valve, then disconnect accelerator cable at carburetor and bracket.
16. Disconnect fuel evaporation hose at metal tube located on left hand fender.
17. Loosen upper power steering pump pivot bolt, then remove upper pump to adjusting bracket attaching bolts, if equipped.
18. Remove upper rear thermactor pump bracket bolt, then install lifting eye.

19. Remove upper A/C compressor to mounting bracket attaching bolts, then remove clip retaining A/C compressor inlet line to exhaust manifold.
20. Raise and support vehicle, then loosen power steering pump lower adjusting bolt and remove drive belt. Remove power steering pump to lower bracket attaching bolts, then remove pump from bracket by passing pulley through adjusting bracket opening. Secure power steering pump against dash panel.
21. Remove heater supply and return tube clamps.
22. Remove starter motor ground cable and engine ground strap, then remove knee brace located at front of starter motor.
23. On models with manual transaxle, remove roll restrictor.
24. Remove starter motor and knee brace rear section, then disconnect exhaust pipe at inlet connector.
25. On models with automatic transaxle, remove converter cover and bracket. On models with manual transaxle, remove lower flywheel cover and brackets.

N606089-S2
88-95 Nm
(65-70 LB. FT.)

N620482-S2
3 REQ'D.
34-40 Nm
(25-30 LB. FT.)

N605802-S2
3 REQD.
41-47 Nm
(30-35 LB. FT.)

N606088-S2

68031

6F010

N801355-S2
3 REQ'D.

TRANS. ASSY.

6031

N620483-S2

6B032 ASSY.

N801312-S2
6 REQ'D.

MEMBER FRT.
CROSS

6B021

5L482 ASSY. R.H.
5L483 ASSY. L.H.

N605786-S2
4 REQ'D.
27-34 Nm
(20-25 LB. FT.)

N801711-S2
88-95 Nm
(65-70 LB. FT.)

N805576-S2
6 REQD.
61-70 Nm
(45-50 LB. FT.)

VIEW Z
FOR MAN. TRANS.

N620483-S2
88-95 Nm
(65-70 LB. FT.)

6F012 ASSY.

N620483-S2
88-95 Nm
(65-70 LB. FT.)

N800199-S2
109-115 Nm
(80-85 LB. FT.)

6A023

N620482-S2
61-70 Nm
45-50 LB. FT.

N801560-S2
81-88 Nm
(60-65 LB. FT.)

ACCESSORY
DRIVE BOLTS

ENGINE MOUNT
NO. 3A

VIEW X

N605800
48-54 Nm
(35-40 LB. FT.)

6B049 ASSY.

N620483-S2
88-95 Nm
(65-70 LB. FT.)

VIEW X

VIEW Y

N606087-S2

6A025

TRANS.

ENGINE MOUNT
NO. 4

N606071-S2
2 REQD.
41-47 Nm
(30-35 LB. FT.)

N606065-S2
41-47 Nm
(30-35 LB. FT.)

N801641-S36
88-95 Nm
(65-70 LB. FT.)

VIEW Y
FOR MAN. TRANS.

6031

TRANS. ASSY.

N606091-S2
88-95 Nm
(65-70 LB. FT.)

6B032 ASSY.

N801711-S2
2 REQD.
88-95 Nm
(65-70 LB. FT.)

VIEW Z
FOR AUTO. TRANS.
SAME AS MAN. TRANS.
EXCEPT AS SHOWN

ENGINE MOUNT
NO. 1

VIEW Z

N606087-S2

6B049 ASSY.

N620483-S2
88-95 Nm
(65-70 LB. FT.)

6A025

SHIFT LINKAGE BRKT.

620484-S2
2 REQ'D.

TRANS.

N801315-S100
2 REQD.
129-135 Nm
(95-100 LB. FT.)

N801641-S36
88-95 Nm
(65-70 LB. FT.)

VIEW Y
FOR AUTO. TRANS.

Fig. 1 Engine mounts

26. Using tool No. T81P-6312-A, remove crankshaft pulley.
27. On models with automatic transaxle, remove converter to flywheel attaching nuts, then remove lower converter housing to engine attaching bolts.
28. On models with manual transaxle, remove lower clutch housing to engine attaching bolts.
29. Remove coolant by pass hose from intake manifold, then remove lower No. 3-A engine mount bolt and nut from under insulator, Fig. 1.
30. Remove A/C compressor lower bracket bolt, if equipped.
31. Lower vehicle and attach a suitable lifting device to engine. Attach lifting device to engine using a 10mm bolt to exhaust side of cylinder head at the transaxle end and at lifting eye of thermacter pump bracket. A stabilizer chain may also be attached to alternator bracket bolt.
32. Remove engine mount No. 3-A through bolt, then remove engine mount, Fig. 1.
33. Remove A/C compressor bracket, if equipped.
34. On models with manual transaxle, remove timing belt cover.
35. Position a suitable transmission jack under transaxle.
36. On models with automatic transaxle, remove upper converter housing to engine attaching bolts. On models with manual transaxle, remove upper clutch housing to engine attaching bolts.
37. Remove engine from vehicle.

NOTE: On models with automatic transaxle, check to ensure that torque converter studs are from flywheel before removing engine.

CYLINDER HEAD, REPLACE

1. Disconnect battery ground cable and drain coolant system.
2. Disconnect heater hose from intake manifold and radiator upper hose from cylinder head.

FRONT OF VEHICLE ↓

Fig. 2 Cylinder head bolt tightening sequence

3. Disconnect cooling fan switch electrical connector.
4. Remove air cleaner assembly and PCV hose.
5. Disconnect all necessary vacuum hoses, then remove rocker arm cover.
6. Remove all accessory drive belts, then the crankshaft pulley.
7. Remove timing belt cover and bring No. 1 cylinder to TDC on compression stroke.
8. Remove distributor cap and spark plug wires as an assembly.
9. Loosen both belt tensioner attaching bolts using tool T81P-6254A or equivalent.
10. Position belt tensioner as far left as possible, then remove timing belt. Refer to "Timing Belt, Replace" for procedure. Discard used belt.
11. Disconnect EGR tube from EGR valve, then the PVS hose connectors using tool T81P-8564A or equivalent.
12. Disconnect choke cap electrical connector, fuel supply and return lines, accelerator cable and, if equipped, speed control cable.
13. Disconnect altitude compensator, if equipped, from dash panel and position on heater/A/C air intake.
14. Disconnect alternator air intake tube and alternator electrical connectors. Remove alternator and bracket.
15. On vehicles equipped with power steering, remove thermactor pump drive belt, thermactor pump and mounting bracket.

Fig. 3 Timing belt cover removal

Fig. 4 Piston & rod assembly

No. 2 intake & No. 3 exhaust.
Rotate crankshaft 180° clockwise from above position and check the following valves:
No. 2 intake & No. 3 exhaust.
No. 4 intake & No. 4 exhaust.

VALVE GUIDES

Valve guide reamers are available in over-sizes of .003, .015 and .030 in. When reaming a valve guide to an oversize, use the reamer in sequence from the smallest oversize first, to the next largest, etc. Always reface the valve seat after the valve guide has been reamed and use a suitable tool to remove the corner that forms on the inner diameter of the top of the valve guide.

CAMSHAFT, REPLACE

1. Disconnect battery ground cable and remove air cleaner assembly.
2. Disconnect PCV hose and remove accessory drive belts.
3. Remove crankshaft pulley, then the timing belt cover, Fig. 3.
4. Remove valve cover, then rotate engine until No. 1 piston is on TDC of compression stroke.
5. Remove rocker arm hex flange nuts, fulcrums and rocker arms.
6. Remove fulcrum washers, then the tappets.
7. Remove crankshaft sprocket, then the timing belt. Refer to "Timing Belt, Replace" for procedure. Discard the belt.
8. Remove camshaft sprocket, key and distributor assembly.
9. Loosen both timing belt tensioner attaching bolts using tool T81P-6254A or equivalent.
10. Remove camshaft thrust plate, then the fuel pump.
11. Remove ignition coil and bracket.
12. Remove camshaft from back of head towards transaxle.
13. Reverse procedure to install. Lubricate camshaft with suitable oil before installing. Check camshaft seal for damage and wear.

16. Raise and support vehicle, then disconnect exhaust pipe from exhaust manifold.
17. Lower vehicle, then remove cylinder head bolts and washers. Discard the bolts.
18. Remove cylinder head with intake and exhaust manifolds attached.

NOTE: Do not place cylinder head on flat surface as damage to the spark plugs or gasket surfaces may result.

19. Reverse procedure to install. Torque cylinder head bolts in sequence shown in Fig. 2. After torquing all bolts to specifications, refer to "Timing Belt, Replace" for belt tensioning data.

NOTE: Before installing cylinder head, the crankshaft must be rotated to position No. 1 piston at 90 degrees before top dead center. To position the piston, rotate crankshaft until pulley keyway is at the nine o'clock position. To time the valve train to this piston position, rotate camshaft until keyway is at the six o'clock position. The camshaft and crankshaft must not be rotated from this position until after the timing belt and gears have been installed.

VALVE ARRANGEMENT

Front to Rear

1.6 L .... I-E-I-E-I-E-I-E

VALVE LIFT SPECS

Engine	Year	Intake	Exhaust
1.6 L	1981–83	.377	.377
1.6 L, E.F.I. & H.O.	1983	.396	.396

VALVE TIMING

Intake Opens Before TDC

Engine	Year	Degrees
1.6 L	1981	16
1.6 L	1982	20

VALVES, ADJUST

The 1.6 L engines are equipped with overhead camshafts and hydraulic lash adjusters. Valve stem to rocker arm clearance is measured with the tappet completely collapsed. Perform the following procedure when measuring valve tappet clearance:

1. Rotate engine until No. 1 piston is on TDC of compression stroke.
2. Position suitable hydraulic lifter compressor tool onto rocker arm and slowly apply pressure to bleed tappet. Continue applying pressure until lifter plunger bottoms. Hold tappet in this position and check clearance between rocker arm and valve stem tip with feeler gauge. Collapsed tappet gap should be .059–.194 in. (1.50–4.33 mm). If clearance is less than specified, check for worn or damaged fulcrums, tappets or camshaft lobes.
3. With No. 1 piston on TDC of compression stroke, check the following valves:
No. 1 intake & No. 1 exhaust.

CAMSHAFT POINTER MUST BE ALIGNED WITH THE TIMING MARK.

TURN THE CRANKSHAFT UNTIL KEYWAY IS AT 12 O'CLOCK.

Fig. 5 Aligning camshaft to cylinder head timing marks

PRESSURE IS RELIEVED FROM THE BELT

PRY THE TENSIONER AWAY FROM THE BELT AND TIGHTEN ONE OF THE ATTACHING BOLTS

Fig. 6 Relieving timing belt tension

TIMING BELT - INSTALLED VIEW

BELT TENSIONER PULLEY

TENSIONER SPRING

Fig. 7 Timing belt installed

PISTON & ROD ASSEMBLE

Assemble the piston to the rod with arrow facing front of engine and numbered side of rod facing exhaust manifold side of engine, Fig. 4. Check side clearance between connecting rods at each connecting rod crankshaft journal. Clearance should be .004–.011 in.

PISTONS, RINGS & PINS

Standard size pistons and rings are color coded red or blue and oversize pistons and rings have .004 OS stamped on their dome. Piston to bore clearance should be .0008–.0016 in. (.020–.040 mm). Measure cylinder bore and select a piston to ensure proper clearance. When the piston to bore clearance is in the lower 1/3 of the specified range, a red piston should be used; in the middle 1/3 range a blue piston should be used and in the upper 1/3 range a .004 OS piston should be used. Piston pins are not available in oversize.

MAIN & ROD BEARINGS

Main and rod bearings are available in standard size and undersizes of .001 and .002 in.

TIMING BELT, REPLACE

NOTE: If the timing belt tension is released or the belt removed, a new belt must be installed.

1. Disconnect battery ground cable and re-

NOTE: WHEN THE CRANKSHAFT KEYWAY IS AT THE 12 O'CLOCK POSITION, NUMBER ONE PISTON IS AT TDC. WHEN THE KEYWAY IS AT THE 9 O'CLOCK POSITION, NUMBER ONE PISTON IS 90° BEFORE TDC.

move accessory drive belts.
2. Remove timing belt cover, Fig. 3.

NOTE: Align timing mark on camshaft sprocket with timing mark on cylinder head, Fig. 5.

3. Install timing belt cover and insure that timing mark on crankshaft pulley aligns with TDC mark on front cover. Remove timing belt cover.

INSTALL THE CAMSHAFT SEAL USING SEAL INSTALLER T81P-6292-A

Fig. 8 Camshaft front oil seal installation

INSTALL THE CRANKSHAFT SEAL USING SEAL INSTALLER T81P-6700-A

Fig. 9 Crankshaft front oil seal installation

TIGHTEN THE ATTACHING BOLTS TO 80-94 N·m (59-69 LB-FT)

Fig. 10   Rear cover plate, removal

4. Loosen both timing belt tensioner attaching bolts using tool T81P-6254A or equivalent.
5. Position belt tensioner away from belt as far as possible, then tighten one of the tensioner attaching bolts, Fig. 6.
6. Remove crankshaft pulley, then the timing belt. Discard timing belt.
7. Install timing belt over gears in counterclockwise direction starting at crankshaft. Ensure belt span between crankshaft and camshaft is kept tight as belt is installed over remaining gears, Fig. 7.
8. Loosen belt tensioner attaching bolts and allow tensioner to locate against belt.
9. Tighten one tensioner attaching bolt using tool T81P-6254A or equivalent.
10. Install crankshaft pulley, drive plate and pulley attaching bolt.
11. Hold crankshaft pulley stationary using tool YA-826 or equivalent and torque pulley attaching bolt to 74–90 ft. lbs. (100–121 Nm).
12. Rotate crankshaft two complete revolutions and check that cam sprocket pointer is aligned with TDC mark.
13. Loosen belt tensioner attaching bolt tightened in step 9, 1/4 to 1/2 turn maximum.
14. Secure crankshaft so it cannot rotate, then torque camshaft sprocket counterclockwise to 44–48 ft. lbs. (60–65 Nm). While maintaining this torque, tighten tensioner attaching bolts.

NOTE: Do not apply torque to camshaft sprocket attaching bolt. Apply torque to the hex on the sprocket.

15. Remove crankshaft pulley and install timing belt cover.
16. Install accessory drive belts and connect battery ground cable.

TIGHTEN THE INTAKE MANIFOLD ATTACHING NUTS TO 16-17 N·m (12-13 LB·FT)

TIGHTEN THE NUTS IN TWO PROGRESSIVE STEPS IN THE SEQUENCE SHOWN

Fig. 11   Intake manifold bolt tightening sequence

FRONT ENGINE OIL SEAL SERVICE

1. Remove timing belt as described under "Timing Belt, Replace".
2. Remove camshaft sprocket or crankshaft pulley as necessary.
3. Remove appropriate seal, Figs. 8 and 9.
4. Reverse procedure to install.

REAR CRANKSHAFT OIL SEAL SERVICE

1. Remove engine as described under "Engine, Replace".
2. Remove rear cover plate, Fig. 10, then the flywheel.
3. Using suitable tool, pierce seal metal casing.
4. Insert sheet metal screw into hole until screw forces seal out of retainer.
5. Reverse procedure to install using suit-

ATTACHING BOLT (6) TIGHTEN TO 8-11 N·m (6-8 LB-FT)

SUPPORT BRACE

GASKET

OIL PUMP

PICK-UP TUBE

BRACE ATTACHING BOLT TIGHTEN TO 14-17 N·m (10-13 LB-FT)

Fig. 13   Oil pump removal

DRAIN PLUG

TIGHTEN THE ATTACHING BOLTS USING THE SEQUENCE INSIDE THE DIAGRAM RETIGHTEN THE ATTACHING BOLTS USING THE SEQUENCE OUTSIDE THE DIAGRAM

Fig. 12   Oil pan bolt tightening sequence

able seal installation tool to install seal.

INTAKE MANIFOLD, REPLACE

1. Disconnect battery ground cable and drain coolant system.
2. Disconnect heater hose from intake manifold and remove air cleaner assembly.
3. Disconnect vacuum hoses as necessary, then the electrical connectors from idle fuel solenoid, bowl vent and choke.
4. Remove EGR supply tube.
5. Raise and support vehicle, then disconnect PVS hose using tool T81P-8564A or equivalent.
6. Remove intake manifold nuts Nos. 2, 3, and 6, Fig. 11, then lower vehicle.
7. Disconnect fuel line at fuel filter and return line at carburetor.
8. Disconnect accelerator cable and, if equipped, speed control cable.
9. On vehicles equipped with automatic transmission, disconnect throttle valve linkage at carburetor, then remove cable bracket attaching bolts.
10. On vehicles equipped with power steering, remove thermactor pump drive belt, thermactor pump, mounting bracket and by-pass hose.
11. Remove fuel pump, then three remaining manifold attaching nuts. Remove intake manifold.

NOTE: Do not place manifold on flat surface as damage to gasket surfaces may result.

12. Reverse procedure to install. Tighten intake manifold stud nuts in sequence shown in Fig. 11 to torque listed in Engine Tightening Specifications.

OIL PAN, REPLACE

1. Disconnect battery ground cable, then raise and support vehicle.
2. Drain engine oil, then disconnect starter electrical connectors.
3. Remove knee brace, then the starter.
4. Remove transaxle knee braces, then the oil pan retaining bolts. Remove the oil pan and discard gaskets.

Fig. 14 Oil pump

5. Reverse procedure to install using suitable sealant on all pan gaskets. Refer to Fig. 12 for oil pan bolt tightening sequence.

OIL PUMP, REPLACE

1. Perform steps 1 thru 4 as described under "Timing Belt, Replace".
2. Remove timing belt from camshaft and crankshaft pulleys and water pump gear.
3. Raise and support vehicle, then drain engine oil.
4. Remove crankshaft pulley, then the timing belt. Discard timing belt.
5. Remove crankshaft drive plate assembly, then the crankshaft pulley and gear.
6. Disconnect starter electrical connectors, then remove knee brace from engine.
7. Remove starter, then the rear section of knee brace. Remove transmission inspection plate.
8. Remove oil pan retaining bolts, then the oil pan.
9. Remove oil pick up tube brace to cylinder block bolt.
10. Remove oil pump attaching bolts, oil pump and gaskets, Fig. 13.
11. Reverse procedure to install using suitable sealant on all pan gaskets.

OIL PUMP SERVICE

Refer to Fig. 14 and measure the following clearances:

a. Outer race to housing: .0027–.0055 in. (.069–.140 mm).
b. Outer race and rotor to cover: .001–.0025 in. (.040–.66 mm.).
c. Relief valve to bore: .007–.0031 in. (.02–.08 mm).

FUEL PUMP, REPLACE

1. Loosen fuel supply attaching nut at fuel pump outlet and the fuel pump mounting bolts.
2. Manually rotate engine until pump push rod is positioned on low side of cam.
3. Disconnect fuel lines from fuel pump.
4. Remove pump mounting bolts, then the pump and gasket.
5. Reverse procedure to install.

WATER PUMP, REPLACE

1. Disconnect battery ground cable and drain coolant system.
2. Remove accessory drive belts, then the engine front timing cover.
3. Position No. 1 cylinder at TDC, then loosen both belt tensioner attaching bolts.
4. Secure tensioner as far left as possible, then remove timing belt. Discard timing belt.
5. Remove camshaft sprocket, then the rearward front timing cover stud.
6. Disconnect heater return tube hose connection at water pump inlet tube.
7. Remove water pump inlet tube fasteners, then the tube and gasket.
8. Remove water pump to cylinder block bolts, then the water pump.
9. Reverse procedure to install. Refer to "Timing Belt, Replace" for proper belt tensioning procedures.

BELT TENSION DATA

		New	Used
1981	1/4 inch	50–80	40–60
	4 ribbed	90–120	90–110
	5 ribbed	110–140	110–130
1982–83	1/4 inch	50–80	40–60
	Air Pump		
	4 ribbed	90–130	90–120
	All Others		
	4 ribbed	110–150	100–130
	5 ribbed	130–170	120–150

Clutch & Transaxle Section

CLUTCH, ADJUST

The cable operated clutch control system, Fig. 1, is self adjusting and periodic adjustments are not required. If the clutch cable is replaced for any reason, an initial adjustment is performed by pulling the clutch pedal to its full upward position.

CLUTCH, REPLACE

1. Remove transmission as described under "Manual Transaxle, Replace" procedure.
2. Loosen pressure plate cover attaching bolts evenly to avoid distorting cover. If same pressure plate and cover are to be installed, mark cover and flywheel so pressure plate can be installed in original position.
3. Remove pressure plate and clutch disc from flywheel, Fig. 2.
4. Position clutch disc and pressure plate onto flywheel with flatter side of clutch disc facing toward flywheel.
5. Ensure three dowel pins on flywheel are aligned with dowel pins on pressure plate.
6. Snug tighten cover attaching bolts, then align clutch disc using tool T81P-7550A or equivalent. Torque bolts to 12–24 ft. lbs. (17–32 N.m.).
7. Remove alignment tool, then install transaxle and perform initial clutch adjustment.

GEARSHIFT LINKAGE, ADJUST, FIG. 3

Adjustment of the external gearshift link-age is not necessary and no provision is made for adjustment.

MANUAL TRANSAXLE, REPLACE

4 Speed

1. Disconnect battery ground cable and drain transaxle fluid.
2. Disconnect clutch cable from transaxle case.
3. Raise and support vehicle, then remove bolt securing brake hose routing clip to suspension strut bracket at both front wheels.
4. Remove lower control arm ball joint to steering knuckle bolt, then separate lower control arm from knuckle.

NOTE: Do not reuse nut and bolt. Plastic shield located behind rotor contains a molded pocket which accepts the lower control arm ball joint. When separating control arm from knuckle, clearance for ball joint may be obtained by bending shield backward towards rotor. Failure to provide clearance for the ball joint may result in damage to the shield.

Fig. 1 Clutch linkage

✱ USE ESE-M2C101-C (SAE 10W-30)

● USE ESA-M1C75-B (CIAZ-19590-B)

Fig. 2 Clutch assembly

DISASSEMBLED VIEW

FRONT OF VEHICLE

1. KNOB – GEAR SHIFT LEVER
2. NUT – SHIFT KNOB LOCKING
3. UPPER BOOT ASSEMBLY – GEAR SHIFT LEVER
4. SCREW – TAPPING (4 REQUIRED)
5. LOWER BOOT ASSEMBLY – GEAR SHIFT LEVER
6. BOOT RETAINER ASSEMBLY – GEAR SHIFT LEVER
7. BOLT – BOOT RETAINER (4 REQUIRED)
8. NUT – SPRING (4 REQUIRED)
9. LEVER ASSEMBLY – GEARSHIFT
10. BOLT – TAPPING (4 REQUIRED)
11. SCREW – TAPPING (4 REQUIRED)
12. SUPPORT ASSEMBLY (SHIFT STABILIZER BAR)
13. BUSHING – GEAR SHIFT STABILIZER BAR

14. SLEEVE – GEAR SHIFT ROD
15. SCREW – TAPPING (2 REQUIRED)
16. COVER – CONTROL SELECTOR
17. BUSHING – ANTI TIZZ
18. HOUSING – CONTROL SELECTOR
19. ASSEMBLY – SHIFT ROD AND CLEVIS
20. ASSEMBLY – CLAMP
21. CLAMP – GEAR SHIFT LEVER (2 REQUIRED)
22. NUT – CLAMP ASSEMBLY
23. RETAINING SPRING – GEAR SHIFT TUBE
24. BOLT -- STABILIZER BAR ATTACHING
25. WASHER – FLAT (2 REQUIRED)
26. ASSEMBLY – NUT/WASHER (4 REQUIRED)

Fig. 3   Gearshift linkage

5. Remove right side inner constant velocity joint from transaxle, then wire halfshaft to underbody in level position to prevent damage to the assembly.
6. Repeat step 5 for removal of left side inner constant velocity joint. If joint cannot be pried from transaxle, insert tool T81P-4026A or equivalent through right hand side of case and tap out joint.
7. Disconnect front stabilizer bar at both lower control arms and discard nuts, then remove two front stabilizer bar brackets and the stabilizer bar.
8. Disconnect speedometer cable and back-up lamp switch electrical connector.
9. Remove three nuts from starter mounting studs which secure roll restrictor bracket. Remove engine roll restrictor and starter stud bolts.
10. Remove stiffener brace attaching bolts from lower portion of clutch housing, and the shift mechanism crossover spring.
11. Remove shift mechanism stabilizer bar to transaxle attaching bolt, and the shift mechanism to shift shaft attaching bolt. Remove shift mechanism from shift shaft.
12. Position suitable jack under transaxle, then loosen nut on rear mounting stud.

13. Remove three attaching bolts from rear mount, then three attaching bolts from front mount.
14. Lower jack until transaxle assembly clears rear mount. Support engine with suitable jack positioned under oil pan while transaxle is lowered.
15. Remove four engine to transaxle attaching bolts, then the transaxle from vehicle.
16. Reverse procedure to install.

5 Speed

1. Disconnect battery ground cable and drain transaxle fluid.
2. Wedge a seven inch wood block under clutch pedal.
3. Disconnect clutch cable from clutch release shaft assembly, then remove the clutch cable casing from rib on top surface of transaxle case.
4. Remove two top transaxle to engine mounting bolts.
5. Remove top bolt that secures air management valve bracket to transaxle.
6. Raise vehicle on hoist, then remove lower control arm ball joint to steering knuckle attaching nut and bolt. Discard nut and

bolt and repeat procedure on opposite side.
7. Pry lower control arm from knuckle on both sides of vehicle using suitable pry bar. Use care not to damage or cut ball joint.
8. Pry left inboard CV joint assembly from transaxle using suitable pry bar.

NOTE: Lubricant will drain from the seal at this time. Install two shipping plugs T81P-1177-B or equivalent.

9. Remove inboard CV joint from transaxle. Repeat procedure on other side.

NOTE: If the CV joint assembly cannot be pried from the transaxle, insert tool T81P-4026-A or other suitable tool through the left side and tap the joint out. Tool can be used from either side of the transaxle.

10. Wire left & right half shaft assemblies in level position.
11. Using a small screwdriver, remove back-up lamp switch connector from transaxle backlamp switch.
12. Remove engine roll restrictor bracket by removing three nuts from starter mounting studs.
13. Remove three heater pipe bracket attaching screws, then remove engine roll restrictor.
14. Remove three starter stud bolts and remove starter.
15. Disconnect shift mechanism from shaft.
16. Disconnect and remove control selector indicator switch arm from shift shaft.
17. Remove shift mechanism stabilizer bar to transaxle attaching bolt, then remove control selector indicator switch and bracket.
18. Remove speedometer cable from transaxle.
19. Remove two stiffener brace attaching bolts from lower position of clutch housing.
20. Position a transmission jack under transaxle.
21. Remove two rear mount and air management valve to transaxle securing bolts, then remove three bolts attaching front mount to transaxle.
22. Lower transaxle support jack until transaxle clears rear mount and support engine with suitable jack.

NOTE: Use a suitable piece of wood between the jack and engine or damage may occur to the oil pan.

23. Remove remaining four engine-to-transaxle attaching bolts.
24. Remove transaxle from rear face of the engine and lower it from vehicle.

NOTE: The transaxle case casting may have sharp edges. Wear protective gloves when handling the transaxle assembly.

25. Reverse procedure to install. Torque the following as specified, engine-to-transaxle bolts 26–31 ft. lbs., front transaxle mount bolts 25–35 ft. lbs., rear transaxle mount bolts 40–51 ft. lbs., starter stud bolts 30–40 ft. lbs., starter nuts 25–30 ft. lbs.

Rear Suspension & Brakes Section

DESCRIPTION

These vehicles use a modified MacPherson strut independent rear suspension, Fig. 1. Each side consists of a shock strut, lower control arm, tie rod, spindle and a coil spring mounted between the lower control arm and body crossmember side rail.

SHOCK STRUT, REPLACE

1. Raise and support vehicle.
2. Remove rear compartment access panels. On four-door models, remove quarter trim panel.
3. Loosen top shock strut attaching nut, then remove wheel assembly.
4. Remove clip retaining brake hose to rear shock and position hose aside.
5. Loosen but do not remove two nuts and bolts securing shock strut to spindle.
6. Remove top mounting nut, washer and rubber insulator, Fig. 2.
7. Remove two bottom mounting bolts, then the shock strut from the vehicle.
8. Reverse procedure to install.

LOWER CONTROL ARM, REPLACE

1. Raise and support vehicle, then remove wheel assembly.
2. Place a suitable jack under lower control arm between spring and spindle mounting.

NOTE: Rear suspension should be at full rebound and the shock strut fully extended.

3. Remove control arm to body mounting nuts, then the control arm to spindle mounting nuts. Do not remove bolts.

Fig. 1   Rear suspension, exploded view

FRONT OF VEHICLE

NOTE: ALL BOLTS MUST BE INSTALLED IN DIRECTION SHOWN

4. Remove spindle end mounting bolt, then slowly lower jack until spring and spring insulator can be removed.
5. Remove bolts from body mountings, then the control arm from vehicle.
6. Reverse procedure to install.

TIE ROD, REPLACE

1. Raise and support vehicle.
2. Scribe a reference mark on tie rod front bracket at bolt head centerline for use during reassembly.
3. Remove nut, washer and insulators attaching tie rod to spindle.
4. Remove nut and bolt attaching tie rod to body bracket, then the tie rod.

NOTE: It may be necessary to pry front bracket sheet metal apart slightly to remove tie rod from body.

5. Place a new dished washer over tie rod end with flange toward middle of rod, Fig. 3.
6. Install tie rod through spindle bushings and place eye of rod into body bracket. Secure rod to bracket using a new nut and bolt. Do not tighten.
7. Place another dished washer over end of rod with flange toward end of rod, then install a new nut and torque to 65–75 ft. lbs.
8. Using suitable jack, raise lower control arm to curb height.
9. Align center of bolt head with reference mark on body bracket, then torque tie rod front bolt to 90–100 ft. lbs. This bolt must be installed with head inboard on vehicle.
10. Lower vehicle to ground.

SPINDLE, REPLACE

1. Raise and support vehicle.

2. Remove wheel assembly, then the brake drum and wheel bearings.
3. Remove brake backing plate assembly, then the tie rod retaining nut and dished washer.
4. Remove two nuts and bolts securing strut to spindle.
5. Remove nut and bolt securing lower control arm to spindle, then the spindle.
6. Reverse procedure to install.

COIL SPRING, REPLACE

1. Raise and support vehicle. Support lower control arm with suitable jack.
2. Remove tire and wheel assembly.
3. Remove nut, bolt and washer securing lower control arm to spindle.
4. Lower control arm until spring can be removed.
5. Reverse procedure to install. A new spring insulator must be used when replacing the spring.

Fig. 2   Shock absorber strut upper mounting components

N801309-S100 NUT

18A182 UPPER MOUNTING

18A002 REINFORCEMENT (PART OF QUARTER PANEL)

18A183 LOWER MOUNTING

18080 SHOCK ABSORBER (STRUT)

5K570 JOUNCE BUMPER

Fig. 3   Tie rod installation

BUSHINGS 5K897

WASHER WITH SMALL I.D. N801335

TIE ROD 5K848

WASHER WITH LARGE I.D. N801336

SPINDLE 4A013

NOTE: WASHERS N801336 AND N801335 MUST BE INSTALLED IN THIS POSITION WITH DISH AWAY FROM BUSHINGS

Fig. 4 Rear brake assembly. Models w/7 inch brake drum dia.

Fig. 5 Rear brake assembly. Models w/8 inch brake drum dia.

BRAKE ADJUSTMENTS

Although the brakes are self-adjusting, Figs. 4 and 5, an initial adjustment will be necessary after a brake repair. The initial adjustment can be obtained as follows:

1. On 7 in. brakes, pivot adjuster quadrant until it meshes with knurled pin and is in third or fourth notch of the outboard end of the quadrant, Fig. 6.
2. On 8 in. brakes, determine inside diameter of drum brake surface using brake shoe gauge tool D81L-1103-A or equivalent, Fig. 6. Adjust brake shoe diameter to fit gauge. Hold automatic adjusting lever out of engagement while rotating adjusting screw and ensure that screw rotates freely.
3. Install drum and wheel assembly, then adjust wheel bearings as described in Fig. 7.
4. Complete adjustment by applying brakes several times, then check brake operation by making several stops from varying speeds.

NOTE: If brake drum cannot be removed for brake servicing, remove rubber plug from backing plate inspection hole. On 7 in. brakes,

insert a suitable tool into the hole until it contacts adjuster assembly pivot. Apply pressure sideways on the pivot point allowing adjuster quadrant to ratchet and release the brake adjustment. On 8 in. brakes remove the brake line to axle retention bracket. This will allow sufficient room for insertion of a suitable tool to disengage adjusting lever and back off the adjusting screw.

PARKING BRAKE, ADJUST

1. Pump brake pedal three times before making adjustment.
2. Place transmission in neutral, then raise and support vehicle.
3. Position parking brake control assembly in 12th notch position (two notches from full application). Tighten adjusting nut until rear wheel brakes drag slightly with control assembly fully released. Repeat procedure as necessary to ensure proper adjustment.
4. Reposition control assembly in 12th notch, then loosen adjusting nut enough to eliminate rear brake drag with the control assembly fully released.

5. Lower vehicle and check operation of parking brake.

MASTER CYLINDER, REPLACE

Less Power Brakes

1. Disconnect battery ground cable.
2. Disconnect stoplamp switch electrical connector and remove switch retainer.
3. Slide stoplamp switch off pedal pin far enough to clear end of pin, then remove switch from pin.
4. From inside engine compartment loosen two master cylinder attaching nuts, then slide master cylinder push rod, nylon washers and bushings from brake pedal pin.
5. Disconnect brake lines from master cylinder, then remove nuts securing master cylinder to dash panel. List cylinder forward and upward and remove from vehicle.
6. Reverse procedure to install.

With Power Brakes

1. Disconnect battery ground cable, then the

Fig. 6 Parking brake adjustment

Fig. 7 Rear wheel bearing, assembly

brake lines from master cylinder.

2. Remove nuts attaching master cylinder to brake booster assembly and remove master cylinder.

3. Reverse procedure to install.

POWER BRAKE UNIT, REPLACE

1. Remove master cylinder as described under Master Cylinder, Replace, Power Brakes.

2. From inside passenger compartment, disconnect stoplamp switch electrical connector.

3. Remove pushrod retainer and outer nylon washer from pedal pin, then slide switch along brake pedal far enough for outer hole to clear pin. Slide switch upward and remove.

4. Remove booster to dash panel attaching nuts, then slide booster pushrod and pushrod bushing from brake pedal pin.

5. From inside engine compartment, disconnect manifold vacuum hose from booster check valve.

6. Move booster forward until booster studs clear dash panel, then remove booster.

7. Reverse procedure to install.

REAR WHEEL BEARING, ADJUST

1. Raise and support vehicle, then remove dust cover from hub.

2. Remove cotter pin and nut retainer.

3. Torque adjusting nut, Fig. 7, to 17–25 ft. lbs. (23–24 Nm) while rotating drum assembly.

4. Back off adjusting nut 1/2 turn, then retighten adjusting nut to 10 to 15 inch lbs. Position adjusting nut retainer over nut so that slots are aligned with cotter pin hole, then install cotter pin.

5. Install dust cover and lower vehicle to ground.

Front Suspension & Steering Section

DESCRIPTION

These vehicles use a MacPherson type front suspension with the vertical shock absorber struts attached to the upper fender reinforcements and the steering knuckle, Fig. 1. The lower control arms are attached inboard to a crossmember and outboard to the steering knuckle through a ball joint to provide lower steering knuckle position.

WHEEL ALIGNMENT

Caster & Camber

Caster and camber angles are preset at the factory and cannot be adjusted.

Toe-In

To adjust toe-in, lock steering wheel in the straight ahead position using suitable steering wheel holder. Remove small outer clamp from steering boot to prevent boot from twisting during adjustment procedure. Loosen tie rod adjusting nuts, then adjust left and right tie rods until each wheel has 1/2 the desired total toe specification. Tighten tie rod adjusting nuts, replace steering gear rubber boots and tighten clamp. Remove steering wheel holding tool.

STRUT ASSEMBLY, REPLACE

1. Raise and support vehicle, then remove tire and wheel assembly.

2. Remove brake hose retaining bracket from strut.

3. Place suitable jack under lower control arm and raise strut as far as possible without raising vehicle.

4. Install spring compressor tool T81P-5310A and compress spring until gap between coils is 1/8 in., Fig. 2.

NOTE: Spring must be compressed before strut is removed to insure that no excessive force is applied to the constant velocity universal joints.

5. Remove steering knuckle-to-strut pinch bolt, then loosen two top mount to apron nuts.

6. Lower jack from control arm, then using a large screwdriver, spread knuckle-to-strut pinch joint.

7. Place block of wood 2×4×7½ in. against knuckle shoulder. Using suitable pry bar between wood block and lower spring seat, separate strut from knuckle, Fig. 3.

8. Remove two top mounting nuts, then the strut, spring and top mount assembly from vehicle.

9. Install 18 mm deep socket onto strut shaft nut. Insert 6 mm allen wrench into shaft end, then clamp mount into vise, Fig. 4.

10. Remove top shaft mounting nut from shaft while holding allen wrench with pliers.

NOTE: Do not clamp directly on strut with vise as damage to strut may result.

11. Remove strut top mount components and spring.

NOTE: If only strut or top mount is to be

Fig. 1 Front suspension

Fig. 2 Installing coil spring compressor

Fig. 3 Separating shock absorber strut from knuckle

serviced, do not remove spring compressor tool from spring.

12. Reverse procedure to install. Refer to Fig. 5 for proper installation sequence of top mount components. Torque strut shaft nut to 48—62 ft. lbs., install new steering knuckle pinch nut and torque to 66—81 ft. lbs. and torque two top mount attaching nuts to 22—29 ft. lbs.

CHECKING BALL JOINTS

1. Raise and support vehicle.
2. With suspension in full rebound position, grasp lower edge of tire and move wheel in and out, Fig. 6.
3. Observe lower end of knuckle and lower control arm as wheel is being moved in and out. Any movement between lower end of knuckle and lower arm indicates excessive ball joint wear.
4. If any movement is observed, install a new lower control arm assembly. The lower ball joint and control arm are serviced as an assembly only. Refer to Lower Control Arm, Replace in this section.

NOTE: AS WHEEL IS BEING MOVED IN AND OUT, OBSERVE THE LOWER END OF THE KNUCKLE AND THE LOWER CONTROL ARM. ANY MOVEMENT BETWEEN LOWER END OF THE KNUCKLE AND THE LOWER ARM INDICATES ABNORMAL BALL JOINT WEAR

Fig. 6 Checking lower ball joint

Fig. 4 Removing shock absorber strut top mounting nut

LOWER CONTROL ARM, REPLACE

1. Raise and support vehicle.
2. Remove nut from stabilizer bar, then the large dished washer.
3. Remove lower control arm inner pivot bolt and nut.
4. Remove lower control arm ball joint pinch bolt, then using a screwdriver, separate the control arm from the steering knuckle and remove from vehicle.

NOTE: Ensure steering column is in unlocked position. Do not use a hammer to separate ball joint from knuckle.

5. Reverse procedure to install. Torque pinch bolt and nut to 37—44 ft. lbs., torque lower control arm inner pivot nut and bolt to 44—55 ft. lbs. and torque stabilizer bar nut to 80—115 ft. lbs.

STEERING KNUCKLE, REPLACE

1. Raise and support vehicle, then remove wheel assembly.
2. Remove cotter pin from tie rod end stud, then the slotted nut.
3. Using tool 3290C and adapter T81P3504W, remove tie rod end from knuckle.
4. Remove brake caliper, then the hub from the driveshaft.
5. Remove pinch bolt and nut securing lower arm to steering knuckle, then using a screwdriver, separate lower arm from knuckle.

NOTE: Ensure steering column is in un-

PRY BAR
DO NOT ALLOW THE PRY BAR TO DAMAGE THE BALL JOINT BOOT

CONTROL ARM BALL JOINT

NOTE: EXERCISE CARE NOT TO DAMAGE OR CUT BALL JOINT BOOT. PRY BAR MUST NOT CONTACT LOWER ARM.

Fig. 7 Separating ball joint from steering knuckle

BEARING AND SEAL ASSY. MUST BE SEATED INTO THE SPRING SEAT

1 DUST CAP 18A179
2 NUT AND WASHER N801442
3 UPPER MOUNT 18183
4 THRUST PLATE 3K048
5 BEARING AND SEAL 3B155
6 SPRING SEAT 5A324
7 NUT N801310-S100 (2)
8 SPRING INSULATOR 5415
9 SPRING 5310
10 JOUNCE BUMPER, FRONT 18A085
11 SHOCK ABSORBER STRUT 18045

Fig. 5 Installation of shock absorber strut top mounting components

locked position. Do not use a hammer to separate ball joint from knuckle.

6. Remove shock absorber strut to steering knuckle pinch bolt, then using a screwdriver, slightly open knuckle to strut pinch joint.
7. Remove steering knuckle from shock absorber strut, Fig. 3, then from the vehicle.
8. Reverse procedure to install. Torque steering knuckle to shock strut assembly pinch bolt to 66—81 ft. lbs., torque lower control arm to steering knuckle pinch bolt to 37—44 ft. lbs. and install new slotted nut then torque to 23—35 ft. lbs.

STABILIZER BAR, REPLACE

1. Raise and support vehicle.
2. Remove stabilizer insulator mounting bracket bolts.
3. Remove stabilizer bar to control arm attaching bolts, then the stabilizer bar assembly.
4. Remove worn insulators from stabilizer bar.

DIFFERENTIAL HOUSING

CV JOINT ASSEMBLY

PRY BAR

EXHAUST PIPE

Fig. 8 Removing halfshaft from differential housing

Fig. 9 Separating outer constant velocity joint from hub

Fig. 10 Installing inner constant velocity joint into differential side gear

Fig. 11 Hub nut staking tool fabrication

5. Reverse procedure to install. Torque stabilizer bar to control arm attaching bolt to 80–115 ft. lbs. and torque stabilizer insulator mounting bracket bolts to 60–70 ft. lbs.

STEERING GEAR, REPLACE

Manual Steering

1. Disconnect battery ground cable, then turn ignition switch to "On" position.
2. Remove access panel from dash below steering column.
3. Remove intermediate shaft bolts at gear input shaft and at steering column shaft.
4. Using a wide blade screwdriver, spread slots enough to loosen intermediate shaft at both ends.
5. Turn steering wheel fully left to allow clearance for tie rod removal.
6. Remove tie rod ends from steering knuckles using tool 3290C and adapter T81P3504W. Turn right wheel to full left position.
7. Remove left tie rod end from tie rod, then on vehicles equipped with automatic transmission disconnect speedometer cable at transmission.
8. Disconnect secondary air tube at check valve, then exhaust pipes from exhaust manifold.
9. Remove exhaust hanger bracket from below steering gear. Wire exhaust system aside.
10. Remove gear mounting brackets and insulators, then separate gear from intermediate shaft while simultaneously pulling upward on shaft from inside vehicle.

NOTE: Right and left hand brackets and insulators are not interchangeable.

11. Rotate gear forward and downward to clear input shaft.
12. Ensure input shaft is in full left turn position, then remove gear through right side apron opening until left tie rod clears shift linkage.
13. Lower left side of gear and remove gear from vehicle.
14. Reverse procedure to install. Ensure input shaft is at full left turn stop and right wheel assembly is in full left turn position. Use caution not to damage steering gear bellows.

Power Steering

1. Disconnect battery ground cable, then turn ignition switch to "On" position.
2. Remove access panel from dash below steering column.
3. Remove four screws from dash panel steering column boot, then slide boot along intermediate shaft.
4. Remove intermediate shaft bolts at gear input shaft and from steering column shaft.
5. Using wide blade screwdriver, spread slot wide enough to loosen intermediate shaft at both ends.
6. Turn steering wheel to full left stop to facilitate gear removal.
7. On all vehicles except 1.6 L. engine and manual transmission without air conditioning, remove pressure switch electrical connector, then the switch.
8. On vehicles equipped with air conditioning, secure liquid line above dash opening.
9. Disconnect secondary air tube at check valve, then the exhaust pipes from exhaust manifold. Secure exhaust system to the side.
10. Remove exhaust hanger brackets from below steering gear and from side apron.
11. Disconnect pressure and return lines from intermediate connector and drain fluid.
12. Remove tie rod ends from steering knuckles using tool 3290C and adapter T81P3504W. Turn right wheel to full turn position.
13. On vehicles equipped with manual transmission, remove left tie rod end from tie rod.
14. On vehicles equipped with automatic transmission, disconnect speedometer cable from transmission.
15. On vehicles equipped with automatic transmission, disconnect shift cable assembly from transmission.
16. Remove screws securing heater water tube to brace below oil pan.
17. Remove nut from lower bolt securing engine mounting bracket to transmission housing. Tap bolt out as far as possible.
18. Remove gear mounting brackets and insulators.
19. Remove gear from intermediate shaft by pushing upward on shaft with bar while pulling gear downward.
20. Rotate gear downward and forward to clear input shaft.
21. Ensure input shaft is in full left turn position, then move gear through right side apron opening until left tie rod clears opening. Use caution to avoid damaging bellows.
22. Lower left side of gear and remove gear from vehicle.
23. Reverse procedure to install.

POWER STEERING PUMP, REPLACE

1. Remove air cleaner, thermactor pump drive belt and thermactor pump.
2. Remove power steering reservoir filler extension. Cover opening to prevent entry of dirt.
3. From underneath vehicle, loosen one power steering pump adjusting bolt and remove one pump to mounting bracket bolt, then disconnect return hose.
4. Form engine compartment, loosen one power steering pump adjusting bolt, then loosen pivot and remove drive belts.
5. Remove the remaining two power steering pump to bracket retaining bolts, then remove pump from bracket by passing pulley through adjusting bracket opening.
6. Disconnect pressure hose from power steering pump, then remove pump.
7. Reverse procedure to install.

DRIVESHAFTS, REPLACE

NOTE: If removing both right and left side halfshafts, plugs T81P-1177B or equivalent must be installed. Failure to do so may result in dislocation of differential side gears, necessitating transaxle disassembly to re-align the gears. Also, halfshaft removal and installation procedures are the same for manual and automatic transaxles except for the following: due to automatic transaxle case configuration the right side halfshaft assembly must be removed first. Tool T81P-4026A or equivalent is then inserted into transaxle to remove left side inner constant velocity joint assembly from transaxle. If only the left side halfshaft is to be removed from the vehicle, remove right side halfshaft assembly from the transaxle case only and secure to underside of vehicle, then remove left side halfshaft assembly. The hub nut and lower control arm to steering knuckle attaching bolt and nut must be discarded after removal and new nuts and bolts installed.

1. Loosen hub nut without unstaking. Use of a chisel or similar tool to unstake nut may damage spindle threads.
2. Raise and support vehicle and remove wheel assemblies.
3. Remove bolt attaching brake hose routing clip to suspension strut.
4. Remove nut from ball joint to steering knuckle attaching bolt, then drive bolt from knuckle using suitable punch and hammer.
5. Separate ball joint from steering knuckle using pry bar, Fig. 7.

NOTE: Lower ball joints fit into a pocket

Fig. 13 Separating constant velocity joint from shaft

Fig. 14 Stub shaft stop ring

Fig. 15 Assembling constant velocity joints onto halfshafts

LEGEND:

1. OUTER BEARING RACE AND STUB SHAFT ASSEMBLY	11. STOP RING
2. BEARING CAGE	12. CIRCLIP
3. BALL BEARINGS (6)	13. BOOT CLAMP (SMALL)
4. INNER BEARING RACE	14. BOOT
5. BOOT CLAMP (LARGE)	15. BOOT CLAMP (LARGE)
6. BOOT	16. BEARING RETAINER
7. BOOT CLAMP (SMALL)	17. BEARING CAGE
8. CIRCLIP	18. BALL BEARINGS (6)
9. STOP RING	19. INNER BEARING RACE
10. INTERCONNECTING SHAFT	20. OUTER BEARING RACE AND STUB SHAFT ASSEMBLY
	21. CIRCLIP
	22. DUST DEFLECTOR

Fig. 12 Halfshaft assemblies

formed in the plastic disc brake shield. The shield must be positioned away from the ball joint while removing ball joint from steering knuckle.

---

6. Remove halfshaft from differential housing using suitable pry bar. Use caution not to damage dust deflector located between shaft and case, Fig. 8.

NOTE: Use caution not to damage differential oil seal, constant velocity joint boot or constant velocity joint dust deflector.

7. Separate outer constant velocity joint from hub using puller T81P-1104C or equivalent, Fig. 9, and adapters T81P-1104B and T81P-1104A or equivalent.

NOTE: Do not use a hammer to separate outboard constant velocity joint stub shaft from hub as damage to internal components may result.

8. Reverse procedure to install. Install new

circlip on inboard constant velocity joint stub shaft. Align splines of inboard constant velocity joint stub shaft with splines in differential. Push joint into differential until circlip seats in side gear, Fig. 10. Torque hub nut to 180-200 ft. lbs. (244-271 Nm) and stake nut, Fig. 11.

CONSTANT VELOCITY JOINT SERVICE, FIG. 12

Removal

NOTE: Service is the same for both inner and outer constant velocity joints.

1. Place halfshaft in suitable vice. Use caution not to damage boot or clamp.
2. Cut large boot clamp and remove from boot, then position boot upward on shaft. If boot only is being replaced due to damage, check joint grease for contamination. If joints were operating satisfactorily and grease is not contaminated, add grease and install new boot. If grease is contaminated, joint must be completely disassembled.

3. Separate constant velocity joint from shaft using tool T81P-3514A or equivalent, Fig. 13. If necessary, boot may be removed from shaft by cutting remaining clamp and removing boot.
4. Remove circlip from end of shaft and discard. Inspect stop ring for damage and replace as necessary, Fig. 14.

Installation

1. Inspect splines at each end of shaft for damage and wear. Inner constant velocity joint must be installed onto longer splines, Fig. 15.
2. Ensure stop ring is in proper position, then install new circlip into groove nearest end of shaft.

Fig. 16 Installing constant velocity joint clamp

Fig. 18 Outer constant velocity joint bearing cage configuration

Fig. 17 Halfshaft assembled length

Fig. 19 Removing outer constant velocity joint bearings

8. Ensure boot is seated in groove, then refer to step 3 for clamp installation.

Disassembly & Assembly

Outer Joint

Fig. 20 Removing bearing cage and inner race assembly from outer constant velocity joint

NOTE: Two different bearing cages are used on the outer joints. One type contains four equal sized windows and two elongated windows while the other type contains six windows of equal size, Fig. 18.

1. Position stub shaft in suitable vise with bearing facing upward.
2. Press downward on inner race until bearing can be removed, Fig. 19. Remove all six bearings in this manner.
3. Pivot bearing cage and inner race assembly into position shown in Fig. 20. Align cage windows with outer race lands while pivoting cage, Fig. 21, then remove from outer race.
4. To separate inner race from cage, determine cage design and proceed as follows: on cages with six equal windows rotate inner race upward and remove from cage. On cages with two elongated windows,

3. Install joint boot until it seats in its groove, then install clamp. Tighten clamp securely but do not damage boot or cut clamp bridge, Fig. 16.
4. Position boot upward towards end of shaft, then position constant velocity joint onto shaft and tap into position using plastic mallet. Joint is fully seated when circlip locks in groove cut into joint bearing inner race. Check for proper seating by trying to pull joint from shaft.
5. Lubricate joints with lubricant packs supplied with service kit. On outer joint, fill boot with 2/3 packet and pack joint with 1 1/3 packet of lubricant. On inner joint, fill boot with one packet and pack joint with one packet of lubricant. Use lubricant D8RZ-19590A or equivalent only.
6. Position boot over joint, then pry end of boot upward to release any trapped air.
7. Position joint inward or outward as necessary to adjust halfshaft to length shown in Fig. 17.

pivot inner race until it is in position shown in Fig. 20, then align one inner race band with one elongated window and position race through the window. Rotate inner race upward and remove from cage, Fig. 22.
5. Reverse procedure to assemble. Refer to Fig. 23 for ball groove and window alignment and proper counterbore positioning.

Inner Joint, Fig. 24

1. Remove circlip from end of joint stub shaft, then using suitable cutters, cut and remove ball retainer, Fig. 25. Discard retainer since a new retainer is not required for assembly.
2. Gently tap joint on work surface until assembly can be removed by hand, Fig. 26.
3. Remove bearings from cage by prying with a dulled screwdriver. Use caution not to damage or scratch any components, Fig. 27.
4. Rotate inner race to align lands with cage windows, then remove race from bearing cage through wider end of cage, Fig. 28.
5. Reverse procedure to assemble.

Fig. 21 Aligning inner cage and bearing race

Fig. 22 Removing inner race from bearing cage

Fig. 23 Counterbore positioning and ball groove & window alignment

Fig. 24   Inner constant velocity joint assembly

Fig. 25   Removing inner constant velocity joint outer ball retainer

Fig. 26   Removing inner constant velocity joint inner race and bearing assembly

Fig. 27   Removing bearings from cage

Fig. 28   Removing inner race from bearing cage

FORD MUSTANG & PINTO
MERCURY BOBCAT & CAPRI
INDEX OF SERVICE OPERATIONS

NOTE: Refer to the back of this manual for vehicle manufacturer's special service tool suppliers.

Page No.   Page No.   Page No.

ENGINE & SERIAL NUMBER LOCATION:

Vehicle warranty plate on rear face of left front door.

GRILLE IDENTIFICATION

1977–78 Mercury Bobcat

1977 Mustang II Cobra

1977 Pinto

1977 Pinto Wagon With Cruising Option

1977–78 Mustang

1978 Mustang II Cobra

1978 Pinto

1979–80 Bobcat

1979–81 Capri

1979–82 Mustang

1979–80 Pinto

1981 Mustang Cobra

1982 Capri

1982 Mustang GT

1983 Capri

1983 Mustang

GENERAL ENGINE SPECIFICATIONS

Year	Engine CID/Liter①	V.I.N. Code②	Carburetor	Bore and Stroke	Compression Ratio	Net H.P. @ R.P.M.③	Maximum Torque Ft. Lbs. @ R.P.M.	Normal Oil Pressure Pounds
1977	4-140, 2.3L⑭	Y	5200, 2 Bbl.⑥	3.781 × 3.126	9.0	89 @ 4800	120 @ 3000	40—60
	4-140, 2.3L⑮	Y	5200, 2 Bbl.⑥	3.781 × 3.126	9.0	⑯	119 @ 3000	40—60
	V6-171, 2.8L⑰	Z	2150, 2 Bbl.⑥	3.66 × 2.70	8.7	90 @ 4200	139 @ 2600	40—55
	V6-171, 2.8L⑱	Z	2150, 2 Bbl.⑥	3.66 × 2.70	8.7	90 @ 4000	139 @ 2600	40—55
	V6-171, 2.8L⑲	Z	2150, 2 Bbl.⑥	3.66 × 2.70	8.7	88 @ 4000	138 @ 2600	40—55
	V6-171, 2.8L⑳	Z	2150, 2 Bbl.⑥	3.66 × 2.70	8.7	93 @ 4200	140 @ 2600	40—55
	V8-302, 5.0L㉑	F	2150, 2 Bbl.⑥	4.00 × 3.00	8.4	129 @ 3400	242 @ 2000	40—60
	V8-302, 5.0L㉒	F	2150, 2 Bbl.⑥	4.00 × 3.00	8.1	132 @ 3600	228 @ 1600	40—60
	V8-302, 5.0L⑤	F	2150, 2 Bbl.⑥	4.00 × 3.00	8.4	139 @ 3600	247 @ 1800	40—60
1978	4-140, 2.3L	Y	5200, 2 Bbl.⑥	3.781 × 3.126	9.0	88 @ 4800	118 @ 2800	50
	V6-171, 2.8L	Z	2150, 2 Bbl.⑥	3.66 × 2.70	8.7	90 @ 4200	143 @ 2200	40—55
	V8-302, 5.0L	F	2150, 2 Bbl.⑥	4.00 × 3.00	8.4	⑦	⑨	40—60
1979	4-140, 2.3L⑪	Y	5200, 2 Bbl.⑥	3.781 × 3.126	9.0	88 @ 4800	118 @ 2800	40—60
	4-140, 2.3L⑫	W	6500, 2 Bbl.④	3.781 × 3.126	9.0	—	—	40—60
	V6-171, 2.8L	Z	2700VV, 2 Bbl.⑥	3.66 × 2.70	8.7	102 @ 4400	138 @ 3200	40—60
	6-200, 3.3L⑤	T	1946, 1 Bbl.④	3.68 × 3.13	8.5	85 @ 3600	154 @ 1600	30—50
	V8-302, 5.0L	F	⑩	4.00 × 3.00	8.4	140 @ 3600	250 @ 1800	40—65
1980	4-140, 2.3L⑪	A	5200, 2 Bbl.⑥	3.781 × 3.126	9.0	—	—	50
	4-140, 2.3L⑫	A	6500, 2 Bbl.④	3.781 × 3.126	9.0	—	—	55
	6-200, 3.3L	T	1946, 1 Bbl.④	3.68 × 3.126	8.5	—	—	30—50
	V8-255, 4.2L	D	2150, 2 Bbl.⑥	3.68 × 3.00	8.8	131 @ 2600	—	40—60
1981	4-140, 2.3L⑪	A	5200, 2 Bbl.⑥⑬	3.781 × 3.126	9.0	88 @ 4600	118 @ 2600	40—60
	4-140, 2.3L㉑	A	5200, 2 Bbl.⑥⑬	3.781 × 3.126	9.0	—	—	40—60
	6-200, 3.3L	T	1946, 1 Bbl.④	3.68 × 3.13	8.6	94 @ 4000	158 @ 1400	30—50
	V8-255, 4.2L⑮	D	2150, 2 Bbl.⑥	3.68 × 3.00	8.2	120 @ 3400	205 @ 2600	40—60
	V8-255, 4.2L⑭	D	7200VV, 2 Bbl.⑥	3.68 × 3.00	8.2	115 @ 3400	195 @ 2200	40—60
1982	4-140, 2.3L	A	5200, 2 Bbl.⑥⑬	3.781 × 3.126	—	—	—	40—60
	6-200, 3.3L	T	1946, 1 Bbl.④	3.68 × 3.13	—	—	—	40—60
	V8-255, 4.2L⑭	D	2150, 2 Bbl.⑥	3.68 × 3.00	—	—	—	30—50
	V8-255, 4.2L⑮	D	7200VV, 2 Bbl.⑥	3.68 × 3.00	—	—	—	40—60
	V8-302, 5.0L H.O.	F	2150A, 2 Bbl.⑥	4.00 × 3.00	8.4	160 @ 4200	247 @ 2400	40—60
1983	4-140, 2.3L	A	YFA, 1 Bbl.	3.78 × 3.12	—	—	—	40—60
	V6-232, 3.8L	3	2150, 2 Bbl.⑥	3.8 × 3.4	—	—	—	40—60
	V8-302 H.O., 5.0L	F	4180, 4 Bbl.④	4.0 × 3.0	—	174 @ 4200	244 @ 2400	40—60

① —CID—cubic inch displacement.
② —On 1977–80 vehicles the fifth digit in the VIN denotes engine code. On 1981–83 vehicles the eighth digit denotes engine code.
③ —Net rating—as installed on vehicle.
④ —Holley.
⑤ —Auto. trans. exc. Calif.
⑥ —Motorcraft.
⑦ —Exc. Calif. 139 @ 3600; Calif. 133 @ 3600.
⑧ —Auto. trans. Calif. only.
⑨ —Exc. Calif. 250 @ 1600; Calif. 243 @ 1600.
⑩ —Calif. Motorcraft 2700VV; exc. Calif. Ford 2150.
⑪ —Non-Turbocharged.
⑫ —Turbocharged.
⑬ —Some vehicles equipped with model 6500 Feedback Carburetor.
⑭ —Exc. Calif.
⑮ —Calif. only.
⑯ —Sedan 88 @ 4800. Station Wagon 85 @ 4800.
⑰ —Station Wagons, exc. Calif.
⑱ —Sedans, Calif. only.
⑲ —Station Wagons, Calif. only.
⑳ —Sedans, exc. Calif.
㉑ —Man. trans. exc. Calif.

TUNE UP SPECIFICATIONS

The following specifications are published from the latest information available. This data should be used only in the absence of a decal affixed in the engine compartment.

★ When using a timing light, disconnect vacuum hose or tube at distributor and plug opening in hose or tube so idle speed will not be affected.

● When checking compression, lowest cylinder must be within 75 percent of highest.

▲ Before removing wires from distributor cap, determine location of the No. 1 wire in cap, as distributor position may have been altered from that shown at the end of this chart.

Spark plug types shown in this chart are recommendations of the original vehicle manufacturer and not MOTOR. Check local sources for other spark plug manufacturers listings.

Year & Engine/V.I.N.	Spark Plug Type	Gap	Firing Order Fig. ▲	Ignition Timing BTDC① ★ Man. Trans.	Auto. Trans.	Mark Fig.	Curb Idle Speed② Man. Trans.	Auto. Trans.	Fast Idle Speed Man. Trans.	Auto. Trans.	Fuel Pump Pressure
1977											
4-140, 2300 cc/Y Exc. Calif. High Alt.	AWRF-42	.034	G	6°	20°	E	850	600/800D	③⑦⑧	2000③	5–7④
4-140, 2300 cc/Y Calif.	AWRF-42	.034	G	6°	20°	E	⑦⑨	600/750D	1800③	1800③	5–7④
4-140, 2300 cc/Y High Alt.	AWRF-42	.034	G	6°	20°	E	550/850	⑦⑩	1800③	③⑦⑪	5–7④
V6-171, 2800 cc/Z Exc. Calif.⑦⑫	AWRF-42	.034	H	10°	—	F	850	—	1700③	—	3.5–6
V6-171, 2800 cc/Z Exc. Calif.⑦⑬	AWSF-42	.034	H	12°	12°	F	850	700/750D	1700③	1600③	3.5–6
V6-171, 2800 cc/Z Calif.	AWRF-42	.034	H	—	6°	F	—	600/750D	—	1800⑤	3.5–6
V8-302/F Exc. Calif. & High Alt.	ARF-52	.050	D	8°	4°	C	850	700D	2000⑤	2100⑤	6–8
V8-302/F Calif.	ARF-52-6	.060	D	—	12°	C	—	500/700D	—	1900⑤	6–8
V8-302/F High Alt.⑦⑭	ARF-52-6	.060	D	—	12°	C	—	500/700D	—	1900⑤	6–8
V8-302/F High Alt.⑦⑮	ARF-52	.050	D	—	12°	C	—	500/650D	—	2000⑤	6–8
1978											
4-140, 2300 cc/Y Exc. Calif. & High Alt.⑦⑯	AWSF-42	.034	G	6°	20°	E	⑰	800D	1600③	2000③	5–7④
4-140, 2300 cc/Y Exc. Calif. & High Alt.⑦⑱	AWSF-42	.034	G	6°	20°	E	850	600/800D	1800③	2000③	5–7④
4-140, 2300 cc/Y Calif.⑦⑲	AWSF-42	.034	G	6°	20°	E	⑳	750D	1800③	1800③	5–7④
4-140, 2300 cc/Y Calif.⑦㉑	AWSF-42	.034	G	6°	17°	E	850	750D	1850③	1850③	5–7④
4-140, 2300 cc/Y High Alt.	AWSF-42	.034	G	6°	20°	E	550/850	550/800D	1800③	2000③	5–7④
V6-171, 2800 cc/Z Exc. Calif.	AWSF-42	.034	H	10°	12°	F	700/850	650/750D㉒	1700③	1600③	3–6
V6-171, 2800 cc/Z Calif.	AWSF-42	.034	H	10°	6°	F	600/800	750D	1600⑤	1750⑤	3–6
V8-302/F Exc. Calif. & High Alt.	ARF-52	.050	D	10°	4°	C	⑦㉒㉓	⑦㉒㉔	2000⑤	2100⑤	6–8
V8-302/F Calif.	ARF-52-6	.060	D	—	10°	C	—	700D	—	1900⑤	6–8
V8-302/F High Alt.	ARF-52	.050	D	—	14°	C	—	650/725D㉒	—	2000⑤	6–8
1979											
4-140, 2300 cc/Y Exc. Calif.㉕	AWSF-42	.034	G	6°	20°	E	850/1300㉒	600/800D	③⑦㉙	2000③	5–7④
4-140, 2300 cc/Y Calif.㉕	AWSF-42	.034	G	6°	17°	E	850	600/750D	③㉚	③㉚	5–7④
4-140, 2300 cc/W㉖	AWSF-32	.034	G	2°	—	E	900/1300㉒	—	③㉛	—	5–7④

Continued

TUNE UP SPECIFICATIONS—Continued

The following specifications are published from the latest information available. This data should be used only in the absence of a decal affixed in the engine compartment.

★ When using a timing light, disconnect vacuum hose or tube at distributor and plug opening in hose or tube so idle speed will not be affected.

● When checking compression, lowest cylinder must be within 75 percent of highest.

▲ Before removing wires from distributor cap, determine location of the No. 1 wire in cap, as distributor position may have been altered from that shown at the end of this chart.

Spark plug types shown in this chart are recommendations of the original vehicle manufacturer and not MOTOR. Check local sources for other spark plug manufacturers listings.

Year & Engine/V.I.N.	Spark Plug Type 👆	Gap	Firing Order Fig. ▲	Ignition Timing BTDC①★ Man. Trans.	Auto. Trans.	Mark Fig.	Curb Idle Speed② Man. Trans.	Auto. Trans.	Fast Idle Speed Man. Trans.	Auto. Trans.	Fuel Pump Pressure
1979—Continued											
V6-171, 2800 cc/Z Exc. Calif.	AWSF-42	.034	H	10°	⑦�34	F	850	650/750D	1300③	1600③	3—6
V6-171, 2800 cc/Z Calif.	AWSF-42	.034	H	—	6°	F	—	700D	—	1750⑤	3—6
6-200/T Exc. Calif.	BSF-82	.050	A	8°	10°	B	700/850㉒	650D	1600③	1700③	5—7
6-200/T Calif.	BSF-82	.050	A	—	6°	B	—	600/650D	—	2150③	5—7
V8-302/F Exc. Calif.	㉗	.050	D	12°	8°	C	800/875㉒	600/675D	2300⑤	2100⑤	6—8
V8-302/F Calif.	㉘	.060	D	—	12°	C	—	600/675D	—	1800⑤	6—8
1980											
4-140, 2300 cc/A Exc. Calif. ⑦㉕㉟㊲	AWSF-42	.034	G	—	20°	E	—	600/800D	—	2000③	5—7④
4-140, 2300 cc/A Exc. Calif. ⑦㉕㉟㊳	AWSF-42	.034	G	—	17°	E	—	650/800D	—	2000③	5—7④
4-140, 2300 cc/A Exc. Calif. ㉕㊱	AWSF-42	.034	G	6°	6°	E	850	750D	2000③	1800③	5—7④
4-140, 2300 cc/A Calif. ㉕	AWSF-42	.034	G	6°	12°	E	850	750D	2000③	2000③	5—7④
4-140, 2300 cc/A Exc. Calif. ㉖	AWSF-42	.034	G	6°	10°	E	850	650/800D	1800③	③⑦㊴	④㊵
4-140, 2300 cc/A Calif. ㉖	AWSF-42	.034	G	2°	10°	E	900	650/800D	1800③	③⑦㊶	④㊵
6-200/T Exc. Calif. ㉟	BSF-82	.050	A	—	⑦㊷	B	—	550/700D	—	2000③	5—7
6-200/T Exc. Calif. ㊱	BSF-82	.050	A	⑦㊸	10°	B	700/900	550/700D	1600③	2000③	5—7
6-200/T Calif.	BSF-82	.050	A	—	⑦㊹	B	—	600/700D	—	2300③	5—7
V8-255/D Exc. Calif. ⑦㊺㊻	ASF-42	.050	D	—	6°	C	—	500D	—	2000⑤	6—8
V8-255/D Exc. Calif. ⑦㊺㉜	ASF-42	.050	D	—	6°	C	—	550D	—	1800⑤	6—8
V8-255/D Calif.	ASF-42	.050	D	—	6°	C	—	550D	—	1800⑤	6—8
V8-255/D High Alt.	ASF-42	.050	D	—	6°	C	—	500D	—	2000⑤	6—8
1981											
4-140/A	AWSF-42	.034	G	6°	12°	E	850㉝	750D	2000③	2300③	5—7④
6-200/T	BSF-92	.050	A	8°	⑦㊼	B	700	600D	1800③	2000③	5—7
V8-255/D Exc. Calif.	ASF-52	.050	D	—	10°	C	—	500/650D	—	1600③	6—8
V8-255/D Calif.	ASF-52	.050	D	—	8°	C	—	500/650D	—	1500③	6—8
1982											
4-140/A Exc. Calif. ㉕	AWSF-42	.034	G	6°	12°	E	850	800D	1800③	2000③	5—7④
4-140/A Calif. ㉕	AWSF-42	.034	G	4°	12°	E	850	800D	1600③	1800③	5—7④

Continued

TUNE UP SPECIFICATIONS—Continued

The following specifications are published from the latest information available. This data should be used only in the absence of a decal affixed in the engine compartment.

★ When using a timing light, disconnect vacuum hose or tube at distributor and plug opening in hose or tube so idle speed will not be affected.

● When checking compression, lowest cylinder must be within 75 percent of highest.

▲ Before removing wires from distributor cap, determine location of the No. 1 wire in cap, as distributor position may have been altered from that shown at the end of this chart.

☞ Spark plug types shown in this chart are recommendations of the original vehicle manufacturer and not MOTOR. Check local sources for other spark plug manufacturers listings.

Year & Engine/V.I.N.	Spark Plug Type ☞	Gap	Ignition Timing BTDC①★ Firing Order Fig. ▲	Man. Trans.	Auto. Trans.	Mark Fig.	Curb Idle Speed② Man. Trans.	Auto. Trans.	Fast Idle Speed Man. Trans.	Auto. Trans.	Fuel Pump Pressure
1982—Continued											
6-200/T	BSF-92	.050	A	—	⑥	B	—	450/600D	—	2000③	5—7
V8-255/D Exc. High Alt.	ASF-52	.050	D	—	8°	C	—	500/700D	—	1500③	6—8
V8-255/D High Alt.	ASF-52	.050	D	—	14°	C	—	500/700D	—	1600③	6—8
V8-302 H.O./F Exc. Calif.	ASF-42	.044	I	—	—	C	700	—	—	—	6—8
V8-302 H.O./F Calif.	ASF-42	.044	I	—	—	C	700	—	—	—	6—8
1983											
4-140/A	AWSF-44	.044	G	—	—	E	—	—	—	—	5½—6½
V6-232/3	AWSF-52	.044	J	—	—	K	—	—	—	—	6—8
V8-302 H.O./F	ASF-42	.044	I	—	—	C	—	—	—	—	6½—8

①—B.T.D.C.—Before top dead center.
②—Idle speed on manual trans. vehicles is adjusted in Neutral & on auto. trans. equipped vehicles is adjusted in Drive unless otherwise specified. Where two idle speeds are listed, the higher speed is with the A/C or throttle solenoid energized.
③—On kickdown step of cam.
④—With pump to fuel tank line pinched off & a new fuel filter installed.
⑤—On high step of fast idle cam.
⑥—Except calibration code 1-12B-R10, 10° BTDC; calibration code, 1-12B-R10, 12° BTDC.
⑦—Refer to engine calibration code on engine identification label located at rear of left valve cover on V6 & V8 engines, on front of valve cover on inline 4 & 6 cyl. engines. The calibration code is located on the label after the engine codes number & is preceded by the letter C & the revision code is located below the calibration code is preceded by the letter R.
⑧—Except calibration code 7-2B-R16, 1600 RPM; calibration code 7-2B-R16, 1800 RPM.
⑨—Except calibration code 7-2N-R1, 800/850 RPM; calibration code 7-2N-R1, 650/850 RPM.
⑩—Calibration code 7-1X-RO, 550/750D RPM; 7-1X-R10, 550/800D RPM.
⑪—Calibration code 7-1X-RO, 1800 RPM; 7-1X-R10, 2000 RPM.
⑫—Calibration code 7-3A-R2.
⑬—Calibration codes, man. trans. 7-3A-R10; auto. trans., 7-4A-R2.
⑭—Calibration code 7-11X-R2.
⑮—Calibration codes 7-11X-R4 & 7-11X-R6.
⑯—Calibration codes, man. trans. 8-2A-RO & 8-2A-R10; auto. trans. 8-1A-RO & 8-1B-R10.
⑰—Calibration code 8-2A-RO, 850 RPM; 8-2A-R10, 900 RPM.
⑱—Calibration codes, man. trans., 8-2B-RO auto trans., 8-21B-RO & 8-21B-R11.
⑲—Calibration codes, man. trans., 8-2N-RO & 8-2N-R11; auto. trans. 8-1N-RO.
⑳—Calibration code 8-2N-RO, 650/900 RPM, 8-2N-R11, 600/850 RPM.
㉑—Calibration codes, man. trans. 8-2P-RO & 8-2T-RO; auto. trans., 8-1R-R1.
㉒—With throttle solenoid energized. Higher idle speed is with A/C on & compressor clutch de-energized, if equipped.
㉓—Calibration code 8-10A-RO, 900/975 RPM; 8-10A-R10, 800/875 RPM.
㉔—Calibration code 8-31A-RO, 700/775D RPM; 8-31A-R10, 700/825 RPM.
㉕—Except turbocharged engine.
㉖—Turbocharged engine
㉗—ASF-52 or ARF-52.
㉘—ASF-52-6 or ARF-52-6.
㉙—Calibration codes 9-2A-RO & 9-2B-RO, 1800 RPM; calibration codes 9-2C-RO & 9-2D-RO, 1600 RPM.
㉚—Except Bobcat & Pinto, 1800 RPM; Bobcat & Pinto, 1850 RPM.
㉛—Except Calif., 1800 RPM; California, 1850 RPM.
㉜—Calibration code 0-16A-R12.
㉝—If mileage on vehicle is less than 100 mi., set idle speed 100 RPM less than specified.
㉞—Calibration code 9-4A-RO, 9° BTDC; calibration codes 9-4A-R10A & 9-4A-R10N, 6° BTDC.
㉟—Models less Thermactor air pump.
㊱—Models with Thermactor air pump.
㊲—Calibration code, 9-21B-R10.
㊳—Calibration codes, 0-21A-RO & 0-21B-RO & R10.
㊴—Except calibration code 0-1H-R20, 2000 RPM; calibration code 0-1H-R20, 2150 RPM.
㊵—Manual trans., 5—7 psi.; auto. trans. models use an electric fuel pump.
㊶—Except calibration code 0-1S-R15, 2000 RPM; calibration code 0-1S-R15, 2150 RPM.
㊷—Calibration code 0-27A-R3, 7° BTDC; calibration code 0-27A-R10, 10° BTDC.
㊸—Calibration code 0-6A-RO, 10° BTDC; calibration code 0-6A-R1, 12° BTDC.
㊹—Except calibration code 0-7P-R11, 10° BTDC; calibration code 0-7P-R11, 7° BTDC.
㊺—Except high altitude.
㊻—Calibration code 0-16A-RO.
㊼—Except calibration code 1-12B-R10, 10° BTDC; calibration code 1-12B-R10, 12° BTDC.

TUNE UP NOTES—Continued

Fig. A

Fig. B

Fig. D

Fig. E

Fig. C

Fig. G

Fig. H

Fig. I

Fig. J

Fig. K

DISTRIBUTOR SPECIFICATIONS

★ If unit is checked on vehicle double the RPM and degrees to get crankshaft figures.

Distributor Part No.	Centrifugal Advance Degrees @ RPM of Distributor				Vacuum Advance		Distributor Retard
	Advance Starts	Intermediate Advance		Full Advance	Inches of Vacuum To Start Plunger	Max. Adv. Dist. Deg. @ Vacuum	Max. Ret. Dist. Deg. @ Vacuum
1977							
D7EE-CA	0–1 @ 800	1–3.5 @ 1500	—	7.5 @ 2500	2.3	13¼ @ 15.75	—
D7EE-DA	0–1 @ 510	3.75–5.75 @ 725	—	14 @ 2500	1.75	13¼ @ 12.4	—
D7EE-EA	0–1 @ 525	3.6–5.6 @ 725	—	14 @ 2500	2	13¼ @ 15.75	—
D7EE-GA	0–1 @ 525	3.75–5.75 @ 740	—	14 @ 2500	2.25	13¼ @ 15.75	—
D7EE-HA	0–1 @ 775	1.75–3.7 @ 1500	—	7.5 @ 2500	2	13¼ @ 15.75	—
D7OE-GA	0–1 @ 425	6–8 @ 650	—	16 @ 2500	3	13¼ @ 16	—
D7ZE-BA	0–1 @ 425	6–8 @ 650	—	16 @ 2500	3.5	13¼ @ 15.2	—
D7ZE-CA	0–1 @ 575	6.25–8.25 @ 1250	—	12 @ 2500	2.2	15¼ @ 16	—
77TF-AA	0–1 @ 625	5–7.5 @ 1000	—	10.5 @ 2100	4	10 @ 12	—
77TF-CA	0–1 @ 600	5–7.5 @ 1000	—	10.5 @ 2100	3.5	7 @ 8.5	—
77TF-DA	0–1 @ 600	5–7.5 @ 900	—	10.5 @ 2100	4.5	7 @ 10	—
1978							
D7DE-AA	0–1 @ 550	—	1¾–4 @ 750	12½ @ 2500	3	15¼ @ 11	—
D7DE-JA	0–1 @ 550	—	3½–5½ @ 650	10¾ @ 2500	3	13¼ @ 16	—
D7EE-CA	0–1 @ 800	—	1–3½ @ 1500	7½ @ 2500	2.3	13¼ @ 15.75	—
D7EE-DA	0–1 @ 510	—	3¾–5¾ @ 725	14 @ 2500	1.75	13¼ @ 12.4	—
D7EE-EA	0–1 @ 525	—	3⅝–5⅝ @ 725	14 @ 2500	2	13¼ @ 15.75	—
77TF-AA	0–1 @ 625	—	5–7½ @ 1000	10½ @ 2100	4	10 @ 12	—
77TF-CA	0–1 @ 600	—	5–7½ @ 900	10½ @ 2100	4.5	7 @ 10	—
77TF-HA	0–1 @ 600	—	5–7 @ 900	12 @ 2100	4.5	7 @ 10	—
D8ZE-BA	0–1 @ 425	—	6–8 @ 650	16 @ 2500	3.5	13¼ @ 14	—
D8ZE-CA	0–1 @ 575	—	6–7¾ @ 1200	11½ @ 2500	2.5	12¼ @ 15.7	—
1979							
77TF-CA	0–1 @ 600	5–7.5 @ 900	—	8–10.5 @ 2100	4.5	5–7 @ 10	—
79TF-FA	0–1 @ 600	4–7 @ 1000	—	10–12 @ 2100	4.5	2–4 @ 10	—
D7EE-CA	0–2.12 @ 1237	—	—	5–7.5 @ 2500	2.3	10.75–13.25 @ 15.75	—
D7EE-DA	0–2.25 @ 530	3.75–5.75 @ 725	—	11.5–14 @ 2500	1.75	10.75–13.26 @ 12.4	—
D7EE-EA	0–3 @ 500	3.25–5.5 @ 700	—	11.25–14 @ 2500	2	10.75–13.25 @ 15.75	—
D8DE-EA	0–1 @ 450	3–5 @ 600	—	9.25–12.25 @ 2500	2.5	10.75–13.25 @ 14.3	—
D9BE-CA	0–1 @ 575	2.75–4.75 @ 1050	—	6–8.75 @ 2500	2	10.75–13.25 @ 15.3	—
D9BE-DA	0–1 @ 550	2.75–4.75 @ 1100	—	7–9.5 @ 2500	4.5	8.75–11.25 @ 12.5	—
D9ZE-EA	0–2.5 @ 487	4.5–6.5 @ 662	—	10.5–13 @ 2500	1.8	10.75–13.25 @ 16.2	—
D9ZE-FA	0–2.5 @ 487	4.5–6.5 @ 662	—	10.5–13 @ 2500	1.8	8.75–11.25 @ 14.8	—
D9ZE-CA	0–1 @ 450	3–5 @ 600	—	9.5–12.25 @ 2500	2.8	14.75–17.25 @ 15.3	—
1980							
D8BE-EA	2 @ 760	2.7–4.75 @ 1100	—	6.7–9.5 @ 2500	2.4	8.75–11.25 @ 25	—
D94E-AA	—	—	—	—	—	—	—
D9BE-CA	—	—	—	—	—	—	—
D9BE-DA	2 @ 630	2.5–4.5 @ 925	—	5.9–9.75 @ 2500	1.8	8.75–11.25 @ 25	—
D9ZE-CA	—	—	—	—	—	—	—

Continued

DISTRIBUTOR SPECIFICATIONS—Continued

★ If unit is checked on vehicle double the RPM and degrees to get crankshaft figures.

Distributor Part No.	Centrifugal Advance Degrees @ RPM of Distributor					Vacuum Advance		Distributor Retard
	Advance Starts	Intermediate Advance			Full Advance	Inches of Vacuum To Start Plunger	Max. Adv. Dist. Deg. @ Vacuum	Max. Ret. Dist. Deg. @ Vacuum
1980—Continued								
EOEE-BA	2.4 @ 610	1.1–3.1 @ 650	—	—	10.2–13.1 @ 2500	2	6.75–9.25 @ 25	—
EOEE-CA	2.5 @ 580	3.75–5.75 @ 740	—	—	11.3–14 @ 2500	1.7	10.75–13.25 @ 25	—
EOEE-DA	3.2 @ 600	3.75–5.7 @ 730	—	—	11.6–14 @ 2500	2.1	10.75–13.25 @ 25	—
EOEE-EA	3.1 @ 500	4.3–6.75 @ 660	—	—	11.1–13.75 @ 2500	2	6.75–9.25 @ 25	—
EOEE-FA	2.6 @ 1140	—	—	—	5.1–7.9 @ 2500	2	6.75–9.25 @ 25	—
EOSE-CA	2 @ 635	2.8–4.6 @ 840	—	—	9.1–11.75 @ 2500	2.1	10.75–13.25 @ 25	—
EOZE-AA	3.3 @ 500	3–5.1 @ 620	—	—	9.9–12.7 @ 2500	2.3	10.75–13.25 @ 25	—
EOZE-BA	1.75 @ 540	2.95 @ 760	—	—	8.6–11.3 @ 2500	1.7	8.75–11.25 @ 25	—
EOZE-DA	—	—	—	—	—	—	—	—
EOZE-GA	3 @ 500	4.6–7.6 @ 650	—	—	10.6–13.4 @ 2500	2.2	10.75–13.25 @ 25	—
EOZE-HA	2.75 @ 500	.75–2.75 @ 535	—	—	6.6–9.3 @ 2500	2.2	6.75–9.25 @ 25	—
1981								
D8BE-EA	—	3–5.5 @ 1250	—	—	—	—	—	—
D9BE-DA	—	3–5.5 @ 1250	—	—	—	—	—	—
EOEE-BA	—	3.5–6.5 @ 1250	—	—	—	—	—	—
EOEE-DA	—	6–8.5 @ 1250	—	—	—	—	—	—
E1BE-BA	—	—	—	—	—	—	—	—
E1SE-CA	—	—	—	—	—	—	—	—
E1SE-EA	—	—	—	—	—	—	—	—
1982								
EOEE-CA	—	8.5–11 @ 1250	—	—	—	—	—	—
EOEE-CA①	—	7.5–10 @ 1250	—	—	—	—	—	—
EOEE-DA	—	8–11 @ 1250	—	—	—	—	—	—
EOEE-BA	—	9.5–12.5 @ 1250	—	—	—	—	—	—
E2BE-CA	—	8–10.5 @ 1250	—	—	—	—	—	—
E1BE-EA	—	9.5–11.5 @ 1250	—	—	—	—	—	—
E2BE-BA	—	7–9.5 @ 1250	—	—	—	—	—	—
E2SE-AA	—	10–12.5 @ 1250	—	—	—	—	—	—
E2ZE-DA	—	11–13 @ 1250	—	—	—	—	—	—
1983								
E3ZE-DA	—	—	—	—	—	—	—	—
E3ZE-EA	—	—	—	—	—	—	—	—
E2SE-CA	—	—	—	—	—	—	—	—

①—Manual transmission.

STARTING MOTOR SPECIFICATIONS

Year	Engine Model/V.I.N.	Ident. No.	Brush Spring Tension, Ounces	No Load Test			Torque Test		
				Amperes	Volts	R.P.M.	Amperes	Volts	Torque Ft. Lbs.
1977	4-140/Y	D6EF-BA	40 Min.	70	—	—	460	5	9.0
	V6-171/Z	D6EF-AA	40 Min.	70	—	—	460	5	9.0
	V8-302/F	D6OF-AA	80 Min.	80	—	—	670	5	15.5
1978–79	4-140/Y	D8EF-AA	40 Min.	70	—	—	460	5	9.0
	V6-171/Z	D8ZF-AA	40 Min.	70	—	—	460	5	9.0
	V8-302/F	D8OF-AA	80 Min.	80	—	—	670	5	15.5
1979	6-200/T	D8BF-CA	80 Min.	80	—	—	670	5	15.5
1980	4-140/A	D8EF-AA	40 Min.	80	—	—	460	5	9.0
	6-200/T①	D8DF-AA	80 Min.	85	—	—	670	5	15.5
	6-200/T②	D8BF-CA	80 Min.	85	—	—	670	5	15.5
	V8-255/D	D8OF-AA	80 Min.	85	—	—	670	5	15.5
1981	4-140/A	E1ZF-AA	80 Min.	80	—	—	460	5	9.0
	4-140/A	E1ZF-AB	80 Min.	80	—	—	460	5	9.0
	4-140/A	E2BF-AA	80 Min.	80	—	—	460	5	9.0
	6-200/T①	E1BF-AA	40–80	85	—	—	670	5	15.5
	6-200/T②	E1BF-BA	40–80	85	—	—	670	5	15.5
	6-200/T②	E1AF-BA	40–80	85	—	—	670	5	15.5
	V8-255/D	E1AF-BA	40–80	85	—	—	670	5	15.5
1982	4-140/A	E2BF-AA	80 Min.	80	—	—	460	5	9.0
	6-200/T①	E1BF-AA	40–80	85	—	—	670	5	15.5
	6-200/T②	E1AF-BA	40–80	85	—	—	670	5	15.5
	V8-255/D	E1AF-BA	40–80	85	—	—	670	5	15.5
	V8-302/F	E1AF-BA	40–80	85	—	—	670	5	15.5

①—Manual transmission   ②—Automatic transmission

BRAKE SPECIFICATIONS

Year	Model	Brake Drum Inside Diameter	Wheel Cylinder Bore Diameter			Master Cylinder Bore Diameter		
			Front Disc Brakes	Front Drum Brakes	Rear Brakes	With Disc Brakes	With Drum Brakes	With Power Brakes
1976–79	Capri, Mustang, Pinto & Bobcat	9.0	2.6	—	.875	.938	—	.938
1980	Bobcat & Pinto	9.0	2.6	—	.875	.938	—	.938
	Capri & Mustang	9.0	2.36	—	.875	.875	—	.75
1981–83	Capri & Mustang	9.0	2.36	—	.75	.875	—	.875

REAR AXLE SPECIFICATIONS

Year	Ring Gear Diameter	Carrier Type	Ring Gear & Pinion Backlash Inch	Nominal Pinion Locating Shim, Inch	Pinion Bearing Preload				Differential Bearing Preload	Pinion Nut Torque Ft. Lbs.
					New Bearings With Seal Inch-Lbs.	Used Bearings With Seal Inch-Lbs.	New Bearings Less Seal Inch-Lbs.	Used Bearings Less Seal Inch-Lbs.		
1977–78	6¾" WGF②	Integral	.008–.012	.022	17–27	6–12	—	—	.004–.008①	140
1977–79	8"	Removable	.008–.012	.022	17–27	8–14	—	—	.004–.008①	170
1979	6¾" WGF, WGG②	Integral	.008–.012	.030	17–27	6–12	—	—	.016③	140
1979–80	7½" WGX, WGZ②	Integral	.008–.012	.030	17–27	8–14	—	—	.016③	140
1980	8, 9"	Removable	.008–.012	④	17–27	8–14	—	—	.005–.008①	170
1980	6¾" WGF, WGG②	Integral	.008–.015	.030	17–27	6–12	—	—	.016③	140
1981–83	7½" WGX	Integral	.008–.015	.030	16–29	8–14	—	—	.016③	170
	6¾" WGG②	Integral	.008–.015	.030	16–29	8–14	—	—	.016③	140

①—Case spread with new bearings; with used bearings, .003–.005".   ②—Identification tag code.   ③—Case spread.   ④—8 inch ring gear, .022"; 9 inch ring gear, .015".

ALTERNATOR & REGULATOR SPECIFICATIONS

Year	Make or Model	Current Rating Amperes	Volts	Field Current @ 75°F. Amperes	Volts	Voltage Regulator Make or Model	Voltage @ 75°F.	Contact Gap	Armature Air Gap	Field Relay Armature Air Gap	Closing Voltage @ 75°F.
1977	Orange①④	40	15	2.9	12	D4AF-AA	13.5–15.3	—	—	—	2.5–4.0
	Green①④	60	15	2.9	12	D4AF-AA	13.5–15.3	—	—	—	2.5–4.0
	All⑤	70	15	2.9	12	D4TF-AA	13.5–15.3	—	—	—	2.5–4.0
	All⑤	90	15	2.9	12	D4TF-AA	13.5–15.3	—	—	—	2.5–4.0
1978	Orange①④	40	15	2.9	12	D4AF-AA	13.5–15.3	—	—	—	—
	Green①④	60	15	2.9	12	D4AF-AA	13.5–15.3	—	—	—	—
	Green①④⑥	60	15	4.0	12	D8VF-AA⑦	13.8–14.6	—	—	—	—
	Black①⑤	70	15	2.9	12	D4AF-AA	13.5–15.3	—	—	—	—
	Red①⑤	90	15	2.9	12	D4AF-AA	13.5–15.3	—	—	—	—
	Red①⑤⑥	90	15	4.0	12	D8VF-AA⑦	13.8–14.6	—	—	—	—
1979	Orange①④⑥	40	15	4.0	12	D8VF-AA②⑦	13.8–14.6	—	—	—	—
	Green①④⑥	60	15	4.0	12	D8VF-AA②⑦	13.8–14.6	—	—	—	—
	Black①④⑥	65	15	4.0	12	D8VF-AA②⑦	13.8–14.6	—	—	—	—
	Black①⑤⑥	70	15	4.0	12	D8VF-AA②⑦	13.8–14.6	—	—	—	—
	Red①⑤⑥	100	15	4.0	12	D8VF-AA⑦	13.8–14.6	—	—	—	—
1980	Orange①④⑥	40	15	4.0	12	D9VF-AB③⑦	13.8–14.6	—	—	—	—
	Green①④⑥	60	15	4.0	12	D9VF-AB③⑦	13.8–14.6	—	—	—	—
	Black①④⑥	65	15	4.0	12	D9VF-AB③⑦	13.8–14.6	—	—	—	—
	Black①⑤⑥	70	15	4.0	12	D9VF-AB③⑦	13.8–14.6	—	—	—	—
1981	Orange①④⑥	40	15	4.0	12	—	13.8–14.6	—	—	—	—
	Green①④⑥	60	15	4.0	12	—	13.8–14.6	—	—	—	—
	Black①④⑥	65	15	4.0	12	—	13.8–14.6	—	—	—	—
	Black①⑤⑥	70	15	4.0	12	—	13.8–14.6	—	—	—	—
	Red①⑤⑥	100	15	4.0	12	—	13.8–14.6	—	—	—	—
1982–83	Orange①④⑥	40	15	4.0	12	—	13.8–14.6	—	—	—	—
	Green①④⑥	60	15	4.0	12	—	13.8–14.6	—	—	—	—
	Black①④⑥	65	15	4.0	12	—	13.8–14.6	—	—	—	—
	Black①⑤⑥	70	15	4.0	12	—	13.8–14.6	—	—	—	—
	Red①⑤⑥	90	15	4.0	12	—	13.8–14.6	—	—	—	—

①—Color of identification tag.
②—Pinto & Bobcat use D8BF-AA.
③—Pinto & Bobcat use D9BF-AB.
④—Rear terminal alternator.
⑤—Side terminal alternator.
⑥—Solid state alternator.
⑦—Electronic voltage regulator. These units are color coded black for systems w/warning indicator lamp & blue for system w/ammeter.

WHEEL ALIGNMENT SPECIFICATIONS

Year	Model	Caster Angle, Degrees Limits	Desired	Camber Angle, Degrees Limits Left	Right	Desired Left	Right	Toe-In, Inch	Toe-Out on Turns, Deg. Outer Wheel	Inner Wheel
1977–78	Mustang	+1/8 to +15/8	+7/8	−1/4 to +11/4	−1/4 to +11/4	+1/2	+1/2	1/8	18.84	20
1977–79	Bobcat & Pinto①	+1/4 to +13/4	+1	−1/4 to +11/4	−1/4 to +11/4	+1/2	+1/2	1/8	18.84	20
	Bobcat & Pinto②	−1/2 to +1	+1/4	−1/4 to +11/4	−1/4 to +11/4	+1/2	+1/2	1/8	18.84	20
1979	Capri & Mustang	+1/4 to +13/4	+1	−1/2 to +1	−1/2 to +1	+1/4	+1/4	5/16	19.74	20
1980	Bobcat & Pinto①	+1/4 to +13/4	+1	−1/4 to +11/4	−1/4 to +11/4	+1/2	+1/2	1/8	18.84	20
	Bobcat & Pinto②	−3/4 to +11/4	+1/4	−1/4 to +11/4	−1/4 to +11/4	+1/2	+1/2	1/8	18.84	20
1980–81	Capri & Mustang	+1/4 to +13/4	+1	−1/2 to +1	−1/2 to +1	+1/4	+1/4	3/16	19.84	20
1982	Capri & Mustang	+3/8 to +17/8	+11/8	−1/2 to +1	−1/2 to +1	+1/4	+1/4	3/16	19.84	20
1983	Capri & Mustang	−3/8 to +21/8	+11/4	−1/2 to +1	−1/2 to +1	+1/4	+1/4	3/16	—	—

①—Exc. sta. wag.　　　②—Sta. wag.

PISTONS, PINS, RINGS, CRANKSHAFT & BEARINGS

Year	Engine/ V.I.N.	Piston Clearance	Ring End Gap① Comp.	Oil	Wristpin Diameter	Rod Bearings Shaft Diameter	Bearing Clearance	Main Bearings Shaft Diameter	Bearing Clearance	Thrust on Bear. No.	Shaft End Play
1977–78	4-140/Y	.0014–.0022	.010	.015	.9121	2.0464–2.0472	.0008–.0015	2.3982–2.3990	.0008–.0015	3	.004–.008
	V6-171/Z	.0011–.0019	.015	.015	.9448	2.1252–2.1260	.0006–.0015	2.2433–2.2441	.0008–.0015	3	.004–.008
	V8-302/F	.0018–.0026	.010	.015	.9121	2.1228–2.1236	.0008–.0015	2.2482–2.2490	⑤	3	.004–.008
1979	4-140/W,Y	.0014–.0022	.010	.015	.9121	2.0464–2.0472	.0008–.0015	2.3982–2.3990	.0008–.0015	3	.004–.008
	V6-171/Z	.0011–.0019	.015	.015	.9448	2.1252–2.1260	.0006–.0016	2.2433–2.2441	.0008–.0015	3	.004–.008
	6-200/T③	.0013–.0021	.008	.015	.9121	2.1232–2.1240	.0008–.0015	2.2482–2.2490	.0008–.0015	3	.004–.008
	V8-302/F	.0018–.0026	.010	.015	.9121	2.1228–2.1236	.0008–.0015	2.2482–2.2490	②	3	.004–.008
1980	4-140/A⑥	.0014–.0022	.010	.015	.9121	2.0462–2.0472	.0008–.0015	2.3982–2.3990	.0008–.0015	3	.004–.008
	4-140/A④	.0034–.0042	.010	.015	.9121	2.0462–2.0472	.0008–.0015	2.3982–2.3990	.0008–.0015	3	.004–.008
	6-200/T③	.0013–.0021	.008	.015	.9121	2.1232–2.1240	.0008–.0015	2.2482–2.2490	.0008–.0015	3	.004–.008
	V8-255/D③	.0018–.0026	.010	.015	.9121	2.1328–2.1236	.0008–.0015	2.2482–2.2490	②	3	.004–.008
1981	4-140/A⑥	.0014–.0022	.010	.015	.9121	2.0462–2.0472	.0008–.0015	2.3982–2.3990	.0008–.0015	3	.004–.008
	4-140/A④	.0034–.0042	.010	.015	.9121	2.0462–2.0472	.0008–.0015	2.3982–2.3990	.0008–.0015	3	.004–.008
	6-200/T③	.0013–.0021	.008	.015	.9121	2.1232–2.1240	.0008–.0015	2.2482–2.2490	.0008–.0015	3	.004–.008
	V8-255/D③	.0014–.0024	.010	.015	.9121	2.1328–2.1236	.0008–.0015	2.2482–2.2490	②	3	.004–.008
1982	4-140/A	.0014–.0022	.010	.015	.9121	2.0465–2.0472	.0008–.0015	2.3982–2.3990	.0008–.0015	3	.004–.008
	6-200/T③	.0013–.0021	.008	.015	.9121	2.1232–2.1240	.0008–.0015	2.2482–2.2490	.0008–.0015	3	.004–.008
	V8-255/D③	.0014–.0024	.010	.015	.9121	2.1228–2.1236	.0008–.0015	2.2482–2.2490	⑦	3	.004–.008
	V8-302 H.O./F③	.0018–.0026	.010	.015	.9121	2.1228–2.1236	.0008–.0015	2.2482–2.2490	⑦	3	.004–.008
1983	4-140/A	.0014–.0022	.010	.015	.9118	2.1720–2.1728	.0008–.0015	2.3982–2.399	.0008–.0015	3	.004–.008
	V6-232/3	.0014–.0022	.010	.015	.9119	2.4266–2.4274	.0001–.0014	2.5190–2.5198	.0001–.0014	3	.004–.008
	V8-302 H.O./F	.0018–.0026	.010	.015	.9119	2.2390–2.2398	.0008–.0015	2.2482–2.2490	⑦	3	.004–.008

①—Fit rings in tapered bores for clearance listed in tightest portion of ring travel.
②—No. 1, .0001–.0015; others, .0004–.0015.
③—Refer to the Ford & Mercury—Compact & Intermediate chapter for service procedures on this engine.
④—Turbocharged engine.
⑤—No. 1, .0001–.0015"; others, .0005–.0015.
⑥—Except turbocharged engine.
⑦—No. 1, .0004–.0025; others, .0004–.0015.

ENGINE TIGHTENING SPECIFICATIONS

★ Torque specifications are for clean and lightly lubricated threads only. Dry or dirty threads produce increased friction which prevents accurate measurement of tightness.

Year	Engine/V.I.N.	Spark Plugs Ft. Lbs.	Cylinder Head Bolts Ft. Lbs.	Intake Manifold Ft. Lbs.	Exhaust Manifold Ft. Lbs.	Rocker Arm Shaft Bracket Ft. Lbs.	Rocker Arm Cover Ft. Lbs.	Connecting Rod Cap Bolts Ft. Lbs.	Main Bearing Cap Bolts Ft. Lbs.	Flywheel to Crankshaft Ft. Lbs.	Vibration Damper or Pulley Ft. Lbs.
1977–78	4-140/Y	5–10	80–90	14–21	16–23	—	4–7	30–36	80–90	54–64	100–120
	V6-171/Z	10–15	65–80	②	20–30	43–49	3–5	21–25	65–75	47–51	92–103
	V8-302/F①	10–15	65–72	23–25	18–24	③	3–5	19–24	60–70	75–85	70–90
1979	4-140/W,Y	5–10	80–90	14–21	16–23	—	6–8	30–36	80–90	54–64	100–120
	V6-171/Z	10–15	65–80	②	20–30	43–49	3–5	21–25	65–75	47–51	92–103
	6-200/T①	10–15	70–75	—	18–24	30–35	3–5	21–26	60–70	75–85	85–100
	V8-302/F①	10–15	65–72	23–25	18–24	18–25④	3–5	19–24	60–70	75–85	70–90
1980–81	4-140/A	5–10	80–90	14–21	16–23	—	6–8	30–36	80–90	56–64	100–120
	4-140/A	5–10	80–90	13–18	16–23	—	6–8	30–36	80–90	56–64	100–120
	6-200/T①	10–15	70–75	—	18–24	30–35	3–5	21–26	60–70	75–85	85–100
	V8-255/D①	10–15	65–72	⑤	18–24	18–25④	3–5	19–24	60–70	75–85	70–90
1982	4-140/A	5–10	80–90	14–21	16–23	—	5–8	30–36	80–90	56–64	100–120
	6-200/T	10–15	70–75	—	18–24	30–35	3–5	21–26	60–70	75–85	85–100
	V8-255/D①	10–15	65–72	18–20	18–24	18–25④	3–5	19–24	60–70	75–85	70–90
	V8-302 H.O./F①	10–15	65–72	23–25	18–24	18–25④	3–5	19–24	60–70	75–85	70–90
1983	4-140/A	5–10	80–90	14–21	16–23	—	5–8	30–36	80–90	56–64	100–120
	V6-232/3	17–22	⑥	18	—	18–25④	3–5	31–36	65–81	54–64	93–121
	V8-302 H.O./F	10–15	65–72	23–25	18–24	18–25④	3–5	19–24	60–70	75–85	70–90

ENGINE TIGHTENING SPECIFICATIONS—Continued

①—Refer to the Ford & Mercury—Compact & Intermediate Chapter for service procedures.
②—Bolt & nut, 15–18 ft. lbs.; stud, 10–12 ft. lbs.
③—1977 & early 1978 rocker arm stud nut, 17–23 ft. lbs.; late 1978 fulcrum bolt to cylinder head, 18–25 ft. lbs.
④—Rocker fulcrum bolt to cylinder head.
⑤—1980, 23–25 ft. lbs.; 1981, 18–20 ft. lbs.
⑥—Tighten in (4) steps: (1) 47 ft. lbs., (2) 55 ft. lbs., (3) 63 ft. lbs., (4) 74 ft. lbs., then back off all bolts 2–3 revolutions and repeat steps 1 through 4.

VALVE SPECIFICATIONS

Year	Engine/V.I.N.	Valve Lash Int.	Valve Lash Exh.	Valve Angles Seat	Valve Angles Face	Valve Spring Installed Height	Valve Spring Pressure Lbs. @ In.	Stem Clearance Intake	Stem Clearance Exhaust	Stem Diameter, Standard Intake	Stem Diameter, Standard Exhaust
1977	4-140/Y	.040–.050②		45	44	1.560	189 @ 1.16	.0010–.0027	.0015–.0032	.3416–.3423	.3411–.3418
	V6-171/Z	.014C	.016C	45	44	1.593	144 @ 1.222	.0008–.0025	.0018–.0035	.3159–.3167	.3149–.3156
	V8-302/F⑤	.096–.168⑥		45	44	③	④	.0010–.0027	.0015–.0032	.3416–.3423	.3411–.3418
1978	4-140/Y	.040–.050②		45	44	1.560	189 @ 1.16	.0010–.0027	.0015–.0032	.3416–.3423	.3411–.3418
	V6-171/Z	.014C	.016C	45	44	1.593	144 @ 1.222	.0008–.0025	.0018–.0035	.3159–.3167	.3149–.3156
	V8-302/F⑤⑦	.096–.168⑥		45	44	③	④	.0010–.0027	.0015–.0032	.3416–.3423	.3411–.3418
	V8-302/F⑤⑧	⑥⑨		45	44	③	④	.0010–.0027	.0015–.0032	.3416–.3423	.3411–.3418
1979	4-140/W, Y	.040–.050②		45	44	1.56	187 @ 1.16	.0010–.0027	.0015–.0032	.3416–.3423	.3411–.3418
	V6-171/Z	.014C	.016C	45	44	1.593	144 @ 1.222	.0008–.0025	.0018–.0035	.3159–.3167	.3149–.3156
	6-200/T⑤	.110–.160⑥		45	44	1$^{17/32}$	150 @ 1.22	.0008–.0025	.0010–.0027	.310–.3107	.3098–.3105
	V8-302/F⑤	.096–.165⑥		45	44	③	①	.0010–.0027	.0015–.0032	.3416–.3423	.3411–.3418
1980	4-140/A	.040–.050②		45	44	1.56	167 @ 1.16	.0010–.0027	.0015–.0032	.3416–.3423	.3411–.3418
	6-200/T⑤	.110–.184⑥		45	44	1.578	150 @ 1.22	.0008–.0025	.0010–.0027	.3100–.3107	.3098–.3105
	V8-255/D⑤	.123–.173⑥		45	44	③	①	.0010–.0027	.0015–.0032	.3416–.3423	.3411–.3418
1981	4-140/A	.040–.050②		45	44	1.56	167 @ 1.16	.0010–.0027	.0015–.0032	.3416–.3423	.3411–.3418
	6-200/T⑤	.110–.184⑥		45	44	1.58	150 @ 1.22	.0008–.0025	.0010–.0027	.3100–.3107	.3098–.3105
	V8-255/D⑤	.096–.146⑥		45	44	③	⑩	.0010–.0027	.0015–.0032	.3416–.3423	.3411–.3418
1982	4-140/A	.040–.050②		45	44	1.56	167 @ 1.16	.0010–.0027	.0015–.0032	.3416–.3423	.3411–.3418
	6-200/T⑤	.110–.184⑥		45	44	1.58	150 @ 1.22	.0008–.0025	.0010–.0027	.3100–.3107	.3098–.3105
	V8-255/D⑤	.096–.146⑥		45	44	③	⑪	.0010–.0027	.0015–.0032	.3416–.3423	.3411–.3418
	V8-302 H.O./F⑤	.096–.146⑥		45	44	③	⑪	.0010–.0027	.0015–.0032	.3416–.3423	.3411–.3418
1983	4-140/A	.040–.050②		45	44	1.56	167 @ 1.16	.0010–.0027	.0015–.0032	.3416–.3423	.3411–.3418
	V6-232/3⑤	.088–.189⑥		45	44	1.74	215 @ 1.79	.0010–.0027	.0015–.0032	.3416–.3423	.3411–.3418
	V8-302 H.O./F⑤	.123–.146⑥		45	44	⑫	⑬	.0010–.0027	.0015–.0032	.3416–.3423	.3411–.3418

①—Intake, 201 @ 1.36; exhaust, 200 @ 1.20.
②—Measured at cam with hydraulic valve lash adjuster completely collapsed.
③—Intake, 1 11/16; exhaust, 1 19/32.
④—Intake 200 @ 1.31; exhaust 200 @ 1.20.
⑤—Refer to the Ford & Mercury—Compact & Intermediate Chapter for service procedures on this engine.
⑥—Clearance is obtained at valve stem tip with hydraulic lifter collapsed. If clearance is less than the minimum install an undersize push rod; if clearance is greater than the maximum install an oversize push rod.
⑦—Early 1978 engines. On these engines a stud & nut are used to retain rocker arm to cylinder head.
⑧—Late 1978 engines. On these engines a fulcrum bolt is used to retain rocker arm to cylinder head.
⑨—Except Calif., .121; California, .142.
⑩—Intake, 205 @ 1.36; exhaust, 200 @ 1.20.
⑪—Intake, 205 @ 1.36; exhaust, 205 @ 1.15.
⑫—Intake, 1 25/32; exhaust, 1 39/64.
⑬—Intake, 205 @ 1.33; exhaust, 205 @ 1.05.

COOLING SYSTEM & CAPACITY DATA

Year	Model or Engine/V.I.N.	Cooling Capacity, Qts. Less A/C	Cooling Capacity, Qts. With A/C	Radiator Cap Relief Pressure, Lbs.	Thermo. Opening Temp.	Fuel Tank Gals.	Engine Oil Refill Qts. ①	Transmission Oil 3 Speed Pints	Transmission Oil 4 & 5 Speed Pints	Auto. Trans. Qts. ②	Rear Axle Oil Pints
1977	4-140/Y	⑨	9.1	13	191	⑫	4	—	⑤	⑥	⑦
	V6-171/Z	⑩	9.2	13	191	④	4½⑧	—	⑤	⑥	⑦
	V8-302/F	16.3	16.3	13	191	16.5	4	—	⑤	⑥	4
1978	4-140/Y⑬	8.6	9.0	13	191	⑯	4	—	2.8	⑰	⑱
	4-140/Y⑭	8.8	9.1	13	191	13	4	—	3.5	⑰	⑱
	V6-171/Z⑬	8.5	9.2	13	191	⑯	4½⑧	—	2.8	⑰	⑱
	V6-171/Z⑭	⑮	9.0	13	191	13	4½⑧	—	3.5	⑰	⑱
	V8-302/F	14.6	14.6	13	191	16.5	4	—	3.5	7	⑱

Continued

COOLING SYSTEM & CAPACITY DATA—Continued

Year	Model or Engine/V.I.N.	Cooling Capacity, Qts.		Radiator Cap Relief Pressure, Lbs.	Thermo. Opening Temp.	Fuel Tank Gals.	Engine Oil Refill Qts. ①	Transmission Oil			Rear Axle Oil Pints
		Less A/C	With A/C					3 Speed Pints	4 & 5 Speed Pints	Auto. Trans. Qts. ②	
1979	4-140/Y⑬	8.6	9.0	13	191	㉒	4	—	2.8	⑰	2.5
	4-140/Y⑲⑳	8.8	9.1	13	191	11.5	4⑧	—	2.8	⑰	2.5
	4-140/W⑲㉑	8.8	10.2	13	191	12.2	4⑧	—	4.5	⑰	3.5
	V6-171/Z⑬	8.5	9.1	13	195	㉒	4½⑧	—	2.8	⑰	4.5
	V6-171/Z⑲	8.6	9.1	16	195	12.2	4½⑧	—	4.5	⑰	3.5
	6-200/T	9.0	9.0	16	191	16	4	—	—	⑭	3.5
	V8-302/F	14	14.6	16	195	12.2	4㉖	—	4.5	③	3.5
1980	4-140/A⑬	8.6	8.9	13	191	㉒	4	—	2.8	㉔	㉓
	4-140/A⑲⑳	8.6	9	㉗	191	11.5	4	—	㉘	6.7	㉓
	4-140/A⑲㉑	9.2	9.2	16	191	12.5㉕	4½	—	㉙	6.7	㉓
	6-200/T⑲	8.1	8.1	16	191	12.5	4	—	4.5	⑰	㉓
	V8-255/D⑲	13.4	13.5	16	196	12.5	4㉖	—	—	10	㉓
1981	4-140/A⑲⑳	8.6	9	㉗	191	12.5	4	—	㉘	㉔	㉚
	4-140/A⑲㉑	9.4	9.4	16	191	12.5	4½	—	㉙	㉔	㉚
	6-200/T⑲	8.4	8.4	16	196	12.5	4	—	4.5	㉛	㉚
	V8-255/D⑲	14.7	15	16	191	12.5	4㉖	—	—	9.6	㉚
1982	4-140/A⑲	8.6	9.4	㉗	191	15.4	4	—	㉘	8	㉚
	6-200/T⑲	8.4	8.4	16	196	15.4	4	—	—	⑪	㉚
	V8-255/D⑲	14.7	15	16	191	15.4	4	—	—	11	㉚
	V8-302 H.O./F⑲	13.1	13.4	16	196	15.4	4	—	4.5	—	㉚
1983	4-140/A	10.2	10.2	㉗	191	15.4	4	—	2.8	8	㉜
	V6-232/3	—	—	16	196	15.4	4	—	—	11	㉜
	V8-302/F	13.1	13.4	16	196	15.4	4	—	4.5	—	3.5

①—Add 1 qt. with filter change unless otherwise noted.

②—Approximate. Make final check with dipstick.

③—C3 trans., 8 qts.; C4 trans., 10 qts.

④—Exc. Sta. Wag., 13 gals.; Sta. Wag. 14 gals. Add 3½ gals. with auxiliary fuel tank.

⑤—Bobcat & Pinto, 2.8 pts.; Mustang, 3½ pts.

⑥—C3 trans., 8 qts.; C4 trans., 7¼ qts.

⑦—With 6¾″ ring gear Bobcat & Pinto, 2.2 pts.; Mustang, 3 pts.; units with 8 inch ring gear, 4 pts.

⑧—Add ½ qt. with filter change.

⑨—Bobcat & Pinto, 8.7 qts.; Mustang, 8.5 qts.

⑩—Bobcat & Pinto, 8.5 qts.; Mustang w/man. trans., 8.3 qts.; Mustang w/auto. trans., 8.8 qts.

⑪—C3, 8 qts.; C5, 11 qts.

⑫—Bobcat Calif. 11.7 gals.; Exc. Sta. Wag., 13 gals.; Sta. Wag., 14 gals. Add 3½ gals. with auxiliary fuel tank.

⑬—Bobcat & Pinto.

⑭—Mustang.

⑮—Man. trans., 8.3 qts.; Auto. trans., 8.8 qts.

⑯—Exc. Sta. Wag., 13 gals.; Sta. Wag., 14 gals.

⑰—C3 trans., 8 qts.; C4 trans., 7 qts.

⑱—6¾″ axle—Pinto & Bobcat 2.2 pts., Mustang, 3 pts., 8″ axle 4 pts.

⑲—Capri & Mustang.

⑳—Non-turbocharged.

㉑—Turbocharged.

㉒—Exc. Sta. Wag. & Calif. auto. trans. sedan, 13 gals.; Calif. auto. trans. sedan, 11.7 gals.; Sta. Wag., 14 gals.

㉓—6¾ inch axle, 2.5; 7½ inch axle, 3.5; 8 inch axle, 4.5.

㉔—C3, 8 qts.; C4, 6.7 qts.

㉕—Automatic transmission, 11.9 gal.

㉖—Dual sump oil. When draining oil, it is necessary to remove both drain plugs. One drain plug is located at front of oil pan. The second plug is located on left side of oil pan.

㉗—Less A/C, 13 psi.; with A/C, 16 psi.

㉘—4 spd. man. trans., 2.8 pts.; 5 spd. overdrive man. trans., 3.7 pts.

㉙—4 spd. man. trans., 3.5 pts.; 5 spd. overdrive man. trans., 3.7 pts.

㉚—6¾″ ring gear axle, 2.5 pts.; 7½″ ring gear axle, 3.5 pts.

㉛—C3, 8 qts.; C4 w/10¼ in. torque converter, 7.2 qts.; C4 w/12 in. torque converter, 9.6 qts.

㉜—Standard rear axle, 3.25 pts.; traction-lok rear axle, 3.55 pts.

Electrical Section

STARTER, REPLACE

1979–83 Capri & Mustang

4-140

1. Disconnect battery ground cable, then raise and support front of vehicle.
2. Remove starter motor heat shield, then disconnect cable from starter motor.
3. Remove starter motor attaching bolts, then remove starter motor.
4. Reverse procedure to install.

6-200

1. Disconnect battery ground cable, then raise and support front of vehicle.
2. Remove upper starter motor mounting bolt, then remove starter heat shield by loosening lower starter mounting bolt and removing nut from stud.
3. Disconnect starter cable from starter motor, then remove starter motor lower mounting bolt and remove starter motor.

4. Reverse procedure to install.

V6-171 & V8-255 & 302

1. Disconnect battery ground cable, then raise and support front of vehicle.
2. On models with V8 engine, remove wishbone brace.
3. Remove starter motor attaching bolts, then lower starter motor and disconnect starter cable.
4. Reverse procedure to install.

Fig. 1 Ignition lock

1977–78 Mustang & 1977–80 Bobcat & Pinto

1. Disconnect battery ground cable.
2. Raise vehicle and remove four bolts from crossmember under bell housing.
3. Remove flex coupling clamping screw from steering gear, then the three bolts attaching steering gear to crossmember.
4. Disconnect steering gear from flex coupling and pull gear down to gain access to starter.
5. Disconnect starter cable and remove three attaching bolts and starter.
6. Reverse procedure to install.

IGNITION LOCK

1977–83

1. Disconnect battery ground cable.
2. Remove the steering wheel trim pad and the steering wheel. Insert a wire pin in the hole located inside the column halfway down the lock cylinder housing, Fig. 1.
3. Place the gear shift lever in *PARK* (with auto. trans) or *REVERSE* (with manual trans) turn the lock cylinder with the ignition key to *RUN* position.
4. Depress the wire while pulling up on the lock cylinder to remove. Remove the wire pin.
5. To install insert the lock cylinder into the housing in the flange casting, and turn the key to *OFF* position. This action will extend the cylinder retaining pin into the cylinder housing.
6. Turn the key to check for correct operation in all positions.
7. Install the steering wheel and trim pad. Reconnect the battery ground cable.

IGNITION SWITCH, REPLACE

1982–83 Capri & Mustang

Removal
1. Disconnect battery ground cable.
2. Remove steering column trim shroud.

NOTE: For tilt column only, remove upper extension shroud.

3. Disconnect electrical connector from switch, Fig. 2
4. Rotate ignition key to On (Run) position.
5. Using a 1/8" twist drill, drill out the bolt heads securing the bolts using an "Easy Out" or equivalent.
6. Disengage switch from the actuator pin.

Installation
1. Adjust switch by sliding the carrier to the switch On (Run) position.
2. Check to ensure that the ignition key lock cylinder is in the On (Run) position by rotating the key lock cylinder approximately 90 degrees from the Lock position.
3. Install switch onto the actuator pin.
4. Secure the switch with new break-off head bolts. Tighten bolts until heads shear.
5. Connect electrical connector to switch.
6. Install steering column trim shroud.

NOTE: For tilt column only, install upper extension shroud.

7. Connect battery ground cable.
8. Check for proper operation.

1979–81 Capri & Mustang

Removal
1. Disconnect battery ground cable.
2. Rotate ignition key to "Lock" position.
3. Remove steering column trim shroud.
4. Using a 1/8 inch twist drill, drill out the bolt heads securing the switch to the lock cylinder. Then, remove the bolts using an "Easy Out" or equivalent, Fig. 2.
5. Disengage the actuator rod from switch.
6. Disconnect electrical connector from switch.
7. Remove switch from vehicle.

Installation
1. With ignition key in "Lock" position, place switch on actuator rod.
2. Secure the switch with two new "Break-

Fig. 2 Ignition switch. 1979–83 Capri & Mustang

Off Head" bolts. Tighten the bolts until the heads shear.
3. Remove the locking pin from new switch, if installed.
4. Connect switch electrical connector.
5. Connect battery ground cable.
6. Check for proper operation.

Exc. 1979–83 Capri & Mustang

1. Remove shrouding from steering column and detach and lower steering column from brake support bracket.
2. Disconnect battery ground cable.
3. Disconnect switch wiring at plug, Fig. 3.
4. Remove two nuts that retain switch to column.
5. Lift switch vertically upward to disengage actuator rod from switch.
6. To install switch, both the locking mechanism at top of column and the switch must be in LOCK position for correct adjustment.
7. Move shift lever into PARK (with automatic transmission) or REVERSE (with manual transmission), turn the key to LOCK position and remove the key.

Fig. 3 Ignition switch installation. 1977–80 Bobcat & Pinto & 1977–78 Mustang

Fig. 5 Neutral safety switch adjustment. C4 units

Fig. 4 Stoplight switch installation

Installation

1. Install switch on transmission and replace attaching bolts.
2. With transmission manual lever in neutral, rotate switch and install gauge pin (No. 43 drill) into gauge pin hole, Fig. 5.
3. Tighten switch attaching bolts and remove gauge pin.
4. Install outer downshift lever and attaching nut.
5. Install downshift linkage rod to downshift lever.
6. Install switch wire connector and check operation of switch. The engine should start only with lever in NEUTRAL or PARK.

TURN SIGNAL SWITCH, REPLACE

1979—83 Capri & Mustang

1. Disconnect battery ground cable.
2. On models with tilt column, remove upper extension shroud by unsnapping shroud retaining clips at the 9 o'clock position.
3. Remove five attaching screws, then separate and remove two trim shroud halves.
4. Grasp turn signal switch lever by grasping and using a twisting pulling motion while pulling lever outward.
5. Peel back foam shield from turn signal switch, then disconnect two turn signal switch electrical connectors.
6. Remove two screws attaching turn signal switch to lock housing, then disengage switch from housing and remove.
7. Reverse procedure to install.

1977—78 Mustang & 1977—80 Bobcat & Pinto

1. Disconnect battery ground cable.
2. Remove steering wheel.
3. Unscrew turn signal switch lever from column.
4. Remove shroud from under steering column.
5. Disconnect steering column wiring connector plugs from bracket.
6. Remove turn signal switch attaching screws.
7. Remove plastic cover sleeve from wiring harness.
8. Pull switch and wiring up from steering columns.
9. Reverse procedure to install.

NOTE: *New switches, when received, are already pinned in LOCK position by a plastic shipping pin inserted in a locking hole on top of switch.*

---

8. Position the hole in the end of switch plunger to the hole in the actuator and install the connecting pin.
9. Position switch on column and install retaining nuts, but do not tighten them.
10. Move switch up and down along column to locate the mid-position of rod lash and then tighten nuts.
11. Remove the plastic or substitute locking pin, connect battery and check switch for proper start in PARK or NEUTRAL.

LIGHT SWITCH, REPLACE

1977—83 Mustang, 1980 Bobcat & Pinto, 1979—83 Capri

1. Disconnect battery ground cable.
2. Depress shaft release button by inserting a screwdriver through hole in underside of instrument panel, then remove knob and shaft.
3. Remove bezel nut, lower switch, disconnect electrical connector and remove switch.

1977—79 Bobcat & Pinto

1. Disconnect battery ground cable.

2. Remove instrument cluster as described further on.
3. Remove headlight switch knob and shaft assembly and retaining nut.
4. Disconnect connector plug from switch and remove switch from cluster opening.
5. Reverse procedure to install.

STOP LIGHT SWITCH, REPLACE

1. Disconnect wires at connector.
2. Remove hairpin retainer, slide switch, push rod and nylon washers and bushing away from the pedal and remove the switch, Fig. 4.
3. Reverse procedure to install.

NEUTRAL SAFETY, SWITCH, REPLACE

C4 Units

Removal

1. Remove downshift linkage rod from transmission downshift lever.
2. Remove downshift outer lever retaining nut and lever.
3. Remove two switch attaching bolts.
4. Disconnect wire connector and remove switch.

Fig. 6   Instrument cluster (Typical) 1979—83 Capri & Mustang

HORN SOUNDER, REPLACE

1979—83 Capri & Mustang

1. Disconnect battery ground cable, then remove steering column cover attaching screws and steering column cover.
2. With wire connectors exposed, carefully lift connector retaining tabs and disconnect connectors.
3. Remove switch attaching screws and the switch.
4. Reverse procedure to install.

1977—78 Mustang & 1977—80 Bobcat & Pinto

The horn sounder can be removed by depressing it and turning counter-clockwise or by removing retaining screws from under steering wheel spokes.

INSTRUMENT CLUSTER, REPLACE

1979—83 Capri & Mustang

1. Disconnect battery ground cable.
2. Remove three upper retaining screws from instrument cluster trim cover, then the trim cover.
3. Remove two upper and two lower screws retaining instrument cluster to instrument panel.
4. Pull cluster from panel slightly and disconnect speedometer cable and the print-ed circuit electrical connectors.
5. Remove instrument clusters from instrument panel, Fig. 6.
6. Reverse procedure to install.

1977—80 Bobcat & Pinto

Main Cluster

1. Remove two screws attaching upper half to lower half of steering column shroud, then remove lower half shroud.
2. Loosen forward steering column attaching nuts one or two turns.
3. Loosen rearward steering column attaching nuts 3/8 to 1/2 inch.
4. Disconnect wire connectors at printed circuit board and tachometer.
5. Disconnect speedometer cable.
6. Remove four cluster attaching screws and pull cluster out along angle of steering column, Fig. 7.

Auxiliary Cluster

1. Remove main cluster as described above.
2. Remove two screws attaching auxiliary cluster to instrument panel.
3. Remove auxiliary cluster mask from front of instrument panel.
4. Disconnect wire connector from printed circuit board, then remove auxiliary cluster through access provided by removal of main instrument cluster.

1977—78 Mustang

1. Disconnect battery ground cable.
2. On all models, remove instrument cluster trim cover.
3. Disconnect speedometer cable by pressing on flat section of quick disconnect.
4. Remove cluster retaining screws, pull cluster from instrument panel, disconnect electrical connectors, then remove cluster, Fig. 8.

**Fig. 7   Instrument-cluster removal (Typical).
1977—80 Bobcat & Pinto**

Fig. 8 Instrument cluster (Typical). 1977–78 Mustang

W/S WIPER MOTOR, REPLACE

1981–83

1. Disconnect battery ground cable, then remove right hand wiper arm and blade assembly.
2. Remove cowl grille, then remove clip and disconnect linkage drive arm from motor crank pin.
3. Disconnect wiper motor wire connector, then remove three motor attaching screws and pull motor through opening.
4. Reverse procedure to install.

1977–80

1. Loosen two nuts and disconnect wiper pivot shaft and link from the motor drive arm ball, on Bobcat and Pinto models. A link retaining clip is used on Capri & Mustang models.
2. Remove three motor attaching screws and lower motor away from under the left side of the instrument panel.
3. Disconnect wiper motor wires and remove motor.

W/S WIPER TRANSMISSION, REPLACE

1981–83 Capri & Mustang

1. Disconnect battery ground cable, then

remove right wiper arm and blade assembly from pivot shaft.
2. Remove cowl grille, then remove clip and disconnect linkage drive arm from wiper motor crank pin.
3. Remove two screws retaining right hand pivot shaft to cowl and large nut and spacer from left pivot shaft, then remove linkage assembly.
4. Reverse procedure to install.

1979–80 Capri & Mustang

1. Remove wiper motor and linkage cover for access to linkage.
2. Disconnect linkage drive arm from motor crank pin by removing the clip.
3. Remove bolts retaining right pivot shaft and the nut retaining left pivot shaft.
4. Remove assembly from vehicle.
5. Reverse procedure to install.

1979–80 Bobcat & Pinto

1. Disconnect battery ground cable, then remove wiper arms and blades from pivot shafts.
2. Remove heater control cover from instrument panel to floor brace, then remove brace.
3. Remove glove box and door, trim panel located below glove box, floor heat distribution duct and center register.
4. Remove two wiring loom retainer attaching screws and pull wiring loom down and out of way.
5. Remove A/C defroster air distribution

duct.
6. Loosen two nuts retaining wiper pivot shaft and link assembly to motor drive arm ball, then remove screws attaching both pivots.
7. Remove pivot shaft and link assembly from under left side of instrument panel.
8. Reverse procedure to install. Apply a 3/16 in. bead of sealer around each screw and main pivot stem before installing gasket.

1977–78 Bobcat, Mustang & Pinto

NOTE: On Bobcat & Pinto models equipped with air conditioning, remove blower motor to gain access to wiper transmission as described further on in this chapter.

1. Remove wiper arms and blades from pivot shafts.
2. Loosen two nuts retaining wiper pivot shaft and link assembly to the motor drive arm ball.
3. Remove three screws attaching each pivot shaft and remove assembly from under left side of instrument panel.

W/S WIPER SWITCH, REPLACE

1979–83 Capri & Mustang

1. Disconnect battery ground cable.

2. Remove steering column shroud attaching screws and the shroud.
3. Disconnect electrical connector from wiper switch.
4. Remove wiper switch attaching screws and the switch.
5. Reverse procedure to install.

1977–78 Mustang

Dash Mounted Switch
1. Disconnect battery ground cable.
2. Remove switch knob and bezel nut, pull switch from panel, disconnect electrical connector and remove switch.

Column Mounted Switch
1. Disconnect battery ground cable.
2. Disconnect turn signal and wiper/washer switch wiring connector.
3. Remove lower instrument panel shield.
4. Pull wiring cover from bottom on column and remove cover.
5. With a screwdriver, disengage wiring shield tang and pry shield to remove.
6. Remove screw securing turn signal and wiper/washer switch assembly to column, then remove the assembly.

1977–80 Bobcat & Pinto

1. Remove instrument cluster as outlined previously.
2. Insert a thin bladed screwdriver into the slot in the switch knob and depress the spring. Then pull the knob from the switch shaft.
3. Remove wiper switch bezel nut. Then unplug wires and remove switch.

RADIO, REPLACE

NOTE: When installing radio, be sure to adjust antenna trimmer for peak performance.

1979–83 Capri & Mustang

1. Disconnect battery ground cable.
2. Disconnect all electrical leads from radio.
3. Remove control knobs, discs, control shaft nuts and washers.
4. Remove ash tray and bracket.
5. Remove radio rear support attaching nut.
6. Remove instrument panel lower reinforcement.
7. Remove A/C or heater floor ducts.
8. Remove radio from bezel and rear support, then lower from instrument panel.
9. Reverse procedure to install.

1977–78 Mustang

1. Disconnect battery ground cable.
2. Remove radio knobs, discs, shaft nuts and washers. Remove ash tray.
3. Remove radio rear support to instrument panel nut.
4. Lower radio, disconnect wiring and remove radio.

1977–80 Bobcat & Pinto

1. Disconnect battery ground cable.
2. Remove instrument panel trim brace cover.
3. Remove rear support to radio attaching

Fig. 9   Heater core replacement. 1979–83 Capri & Mustang less A/C

bolt.
4. Remove four screws attaching the bezel to the instrument panel opening.
5. Pull radio out from instrument panel and disconnect speaker, power and antenna wires and remove radio.

HEATER CORE, REPLACE

Less Air Conditioning

1979–83 Capri & Mustang
1. Drain cooling system and disconnect battery ground cable.
2. Disconnect heater hoses from heater core and plug core openings.
3. Remove glove box liner.
4. Remove instrument panel to cowl brace retaining screws and the brace.
5. Move temperature control lever to warm position.
6. Remove the four heater core cover retaining screws, then the cover through the glove box opening.
7. Remove heater core assembly mounting stud nuts from engine compartment.
8. Push core tubes and seal toward passenger compartment to loosen core from case assembly.
9. Remove heater core from case through the glove box opening, Fig. 9.
10. Reverse procedure to install.

Exc. 1979–83 Capri & Mustang
1. Drain coolant and disconnect battery.
2. Disconnect blower motor ground wire at

engine side of dash.
3. Disconnect heater hoses at engine block.
4. Remove four heater assembly-to-dash mounting nuts from the engine side of the dash.
5. Remove the glove box.
6. Disconnect control cables from heater. Remove mounting bracket clips and disconnect cables from door crank arms.
7. Remove radio as outlined previously.
8. Working inside car, remove snap rivet that attaches the forward side of the defroster air duct to the plenum chamber. Move the air duct back into the defroster nozzle to disengage it from the tabs on the plenum chamber. Now, tilt the forward edge of the duct up and forward to disengage it from the nozzle and remove it from the left side of the heater assembly.
9. Remove heater case-to-instrument panel support bracket mounting screw and remove the heater case. At the same time, pull the two heater hoses in through the dash panel. Then disconnect the hoses from the heater core in the case.
10. Remove compression gasket from cowl air inlet.
11. Remove eleven clips from around the front and rear case flanges and separate the front and rear halves of the case, Fig. 10.
12. Lift heater core from front half of case.

With Air Conditioning

1979–83 Capri & Mustang
1. Disconnect battery ground cable.

Fig. 10 Heater core removal 1977–78 Mustang & 1977–80 Bobcat & Pinto less A/C

Labels in figure:
- HEATER CASE ASSY. FRONT
- COMPRESSION GASKET
- HEATER CORE
- HEATER CASE ASSY. REAR
- Screw Driver / PRY DOWN TO REMOVE CLIP / VIEW A
- Screw Driver / PRY CLIP DOWN TO INSTALL / VIEW B
- L 1516-A

2. Remove screws securing the left side of instrument panel pad retaining tabs to the instrument panel, in the upper right and left corners of the instrument panel cluster area.
3. Remove screws securing the right side of instrument panel pad retaining tabs to instrument panel, located in the two openings at the top edge of the right instrument panel trim applique, above the glove box.
4. Remove screws securing leading edge of instrument panel pad to defroster openings. Use a magnetic or locking tang type phillips screwdriver. Do not let screws drop into defroster openings since plenum door damage may result.
5. Raise the overhanging edge of the instrument panel pad to clear retaining tabs and pull pad rearward to remove from top of instrument panel.
6. Remove screws attaching steering column opening lower cover to instrument panel, then the cover.
7. Remove steering column trim shrouds.
8. Remove nuts securing steering column to brake pedal support and lower steering column for access to gearshift selector lever and cable assembly.
9. Reach between steering column and instrument panel and lift selector lever cable off selector lever. Then, remove cable clamp from steering column tube.
10. Rest steering column of front seat.
11. Remove screws attaching instrument panel to brake pedal support at steering column opening.
12. Remove screw attaching lower brace to lower edge of instrument panel, below the radio.
13. Remove screw attaching brace to lower edge of instrument panel.
14. Disconnect temperature control cable from temperature blend door and evaporator case bracket.

15. Disconnect seven-port vacuum hose connectors at evaporator case.
16. Disconnect blower resistor wire connector from resistor and the blower motor feed wire at in-line connector near the blower resistor wire connector.
17. Support instrument panel and remove three screws securing top of instrument panel to the cowl.
18. Remove screw at each side of instrument panel securing instrument panel to cowl side panels.
19. Move instrument panel rearward and disconnect speedometer cable and any wiring that will not permit the panel to lay on the front seal.
21. Drain cooling system.
22. Disconnect heater hoses from heater core tubes. Plug heater core tubes.
23. Remove two nuts securing evaporator case to dash panel from engine compartment.
24. From the passenger compartment, remove screws attaching the evaporator case support bracket and air inlet duct support bracket to cowl top panel.
25. Remove one nut retaining the bracket at left end of evaporator case to the dash panel and the one nut securing the bracket below the case to the dash panel.
26. Pull evaporator case assembly from dash panel to gain access to the screws retaining heater core access cover to the evaporator case.
27. Remove five heater core access cover attaching screws and the access cover.
28. Remove heater core and seals from evaporator case.
29. Remove the two seals from the heater core tubes.
30. Reverse procedure to install.

1977–78 Mustang
1. Disconnect battery ground cable and remove the battery.

2. Drain cooling system and discharge A/C refrigerant system.
3. Remove instrument panel pad.
4. Remove radio speaker assembly.
5. Remove both "A" pillar mouldings.
6. Remove both side kick panel pad assemblies.
7. Remove the lower steering column cover.
8. Remove the steering column to cowl panel shake brace.
9. Remove accelerator pedal assembly and disconnect the two cables.
10. Remove the bottom bolt retaining center shake brace to instrument panel assembly.
11. Disconnect antenna lead from radio.
12. Disconnect the five connectors at the left cowl panel.
13. Disconnect electrical connector from wiper switch.
14. Disconnect the five connectors from the right cowl panel.
15. Disconnect electrical connector from dimmer switch assembly.
16. Disconnect the heater blower motor resistor.
17. Disconnect temperature control cable.
18. Remove the two evaporator to upper cowl bracket screws.
19. Disconnect the main wiring harness in the engine compartment and push the connectors into the passenger compartment.
20. Disconnect the three remaining connectors and push the connectors into the passenger compartment.
21. Disconnect the turn signal switch assembly.
22. Lower the steering column.
23. Disconnect electrical connectors from ignition switch.
24. Disconnect electrical connector from stop light switch assembly.
25. Remove instrument panel to steering column center support bracket.
26. Remove instrument panel retaining bolts and the instrument panel.
27. Disconnect heater hoses from heater core.
28. Remove the two screws attaching evaporator manifold plate to expansion valve body.
29. Separate expansion valve body and STV housing manifold from evaporator manifold plate.
30. Remove four nuts retaining evaporator to dash panel and the evaporator assembly.
31. Remove the eight upper to lower case attaching screws.
32. Remove rubber seal from heater core tubes.
33. Remove upper half from evaporator case.
34. Remove air deflector mounting screw on lower case to left of heater core, then the air deflector and heater core.
35. Reverse procedure to install.

1977–80 Bobcat & Pinto
1. Disconnect battery ground cable, drain radiator and discharge refrigerant from A/C system.
2. Remove refrigerant lines and the front half of refrigerant manifold.

NOTE: Remove manifold mounting stud to ensure clearance for removal of evaporator case.

3. Disconnect heater hoses from core tubes

and remove condensation drain hose in engine compartment.

4. Remove glove box.
5. Disconnect vacuum hoses from evaporator case and temperature control cable from blend door crank arm.
6. Remove heat distribution duct.
7. Remove staples retaining fold down door on plenum, Fig. 11. Bend fold down door from locating tabs on plenum and remove adapter duct.

NOTE: During installation, position fold down door between locating tabs and tape in place with two pieces of black tape, Fig. 11.

8. Remove blower motor and wheel from blower scroll.
9. Install a 1/4-20 hex washer head screw in mounting tab of inlet duct to upper cowl bracket, holding inlet duct in place.

NOTE: Leave screw in position during installation of case assembly.

10. Remove inlet duct to evaporator case screws.

NOTE: One upper case to inlet duct screw is located under outside-recirc. motor mounting bracket.

11. Remove evaporator to cowl bracket screws and the evaporator to dash panel nuts in engine compartment. Rotate evaporator down and away from instrument panel and remove from under panel.
12. Remove upper to lower case screws and rubber seal from heater core tubes.
13. Remove upper half of evaporator case and move rubber seal on evaporator core forward and pull evaporator core from lower case.
14. Remove heater core upper straps, air deflector mounting screw, then remove air deflector and heater core.

BLOWER MOTOR, REPLACE

Less Air Conditioning

1979–83 Capri & Mustang
1. Disconnect battery ground cable.
2. Remove right ventilator assembly.
3. Disconnect blower lead wire connector from spade terminal of resistor assembly and push back through hole in case.
4. Remove right side trim panel for access to blower ground terminal lug, then remove the ground terminal lug retaining screw.
5. Remove blower motor flange retaining screws from inside the blower housing.
6. Remove blower motor from housing.
7. Reverse procedure to install.

Exc. 1979–83 Capri & Mustang
1. Follow procedure to remove the heater core as described previously.
2. Disconnect the blower motor lead wire (orange) from the resistor.
3. Remove the four blower mounting plate nuts and remove the motor and wheel assembly, Fig. 12.
4. Reverse procedure to install.

Fig. 11 A/C defrost air distribution duct fold down door. 1977–80 Bobcat & Pinto

With Air Conditioning

1979–83 Capri & Mustang
1. Disconnect battery ground cable.
2. Remove glove box and disconnect hose from outside-recirculation door vacuum motor.
3. Remove instrument panel lower right to side cowl attaching bolt.
4. Remove screw attaching support brace to top of air inlet duct.
5. Disconnect blower motor feed wire at connector.
6. Remove nut retaining blower housing lower support bracket to evaporator case.
7. Remove side cowl trim panel.
8. Remove blower motor ground wire screw.
9. Remove screw attaching top of air inlet duct to evaporator case.
10. Pull air inlet duct and blower housing assembly downward and away from evaporator case.
11. Remove four blower motor mounting plate screws, then the blower motor assembly from blower housing.
12. Reverse procedure to install.

Exc. 1979–83 Capri & Mustang
1. Remove glove box.
2. Remove four screws retaining blower mo-

Fig. 12 Blower motor. (Typical)

tor and wheel to blower scroll.
3. Remove blower motor and wheel assembly.

NOTE: On 1977–80 models, it may be necessary to remove bolt securing instrument panel to right side cowl and pull instrument panel rearward to provide clearance for blower motor removal.

SPEED CONTROL
1977–83

Bead Chain Adjustment

Adjust bead chain to obtain a taut chain with the engine at hot idle. The adjustment should be made as to remove as much slack as possible from the bead chain without restricting the carburetor lever from returning to idle. On vehicles equipped with a solenoid throttle positioner, perform adjustment with throttle positioner deactivated.

Actuator Cable Adjustment
1. Deactivate the throttle positioner.
2. Set carburetor at hot idle.
3. Pull the actuator cable to remove slack.
4. While maintaining light tension on the actuator cable, insert the cable retaining clip.

Vacuum Dump Valve

The vacuum dump valve is mounted on a moveable mounting bracket. The valve should be adjusted so that it is closed when the brake pedal is not depressed and opens when the brake pedal is depressed.

2300 cc Engine Section

NOTE: This U.S. built engine is designed to metric specifications and therefore metric tooling will be required.

ENGINE MOUNTS, REPLACE

1979–83 Capri & Mustang

1. Support engine using a wood block and jack placed under the engine.
2. Remove fan shroud, if necessary.
3. Remove screw attaching fuel pump shield to left hand support bracket, if so equipped.
4. Remove nut and washer assemblies at-

taching both insulators to the crossmember, Fig. 1.
5. Raise engine sufficiently to clear the insulator studs from the crossmember.
6. Remove bolts attaching insulator and bracket assembly from engine and remove insulator and bracket assembly.
7. Reverse procedure to install. Torque insulator and bracket assembly to 33–45 ft. lbs. Torque crossmember nut assemblies onto insulator studs to 70–100 ft. lbs.

1977–80 Bobcat & Pinto
1977–78 Mustang

1. Remove fan shroud screws and support engine with a suitable jack and place a piece of wood under oil pan.
2. Remove insulator to support bracket through bolt, Figs. 1A and 2.

3. Remove support bracket mounting bolts, raise engine slightly, then remove support bracket.
4. Remove insulator to engine block bolts and insulator.
5. Reverse procedure to install.

ENGINE, REPLACE

1. Raise hood and secure in vertical position.
2. Drain coolant from radiator and oil from crankcase.
3. Remove air cleaner and exhaust manifold shroud.
4. Disconnect battery ground cable.
5. Remove radiator hoses and remove radiator and fan.
6. Disconnect heater hoses from water pump

Fig. 1 Engine mounts. 1979–83 Capri & Mustang

Fig. 1A Engine mount installation. 1977–78 Mustang

Fig. 2 Engine mount installation (typical). 1977–80 Bobcat & Pinto

and carburetor choke fitting.

7. Disconnect wires from alternator and starter and disconnect accelerator cable from carburetor. On A/C vehicles, remove compressor from bracket and position it out of way with lines attached.
8. Disconnect flex fuel line from tank line and plug tank line.
9. Disconnect primary wire at coil and disconnect oil pressure and temperature sending unit wires at sending units.
10. Remove starter and raise vehicle to remove the flywheel or converter housing upper attaching bolts.
11. Disconnect inlet pipe at exhaust manifold. Disconnect engine mounts at underbody bracket and remove flywheel or converter housing cover.
12. On vehicle with manual shift, remove flywheel housing lower attaching bolts.
13. On vehicle with automatic transmission, disconnect converter from flywheel and remove converter housing lower attaching bolts.
14. Lower vehicle and support transmission and flywheel or converter housing with a jack.
15. Attach engine lifting hooks to brackets and carefully lift engine out of engine compartment.

CYLINDER HEAD, REPLACE

1. Drain cooling system and remove air cleaner and rocker arm cover.
2. Remove intake and exhaust manifolds and carburetor.
3. Remove timing case cover and drive belt.
4. Remove water outlet elbow from head.
5. Remove cylinder head bolts, then remove cylinder head.

NOTE: The cylinder head retaining bolts have 12 point heads.

6. Reverse procedure to install. Torque cylinder head bolts in sequence shown in Fig. 3 and intake manifold bolts in sequence shown in Fig. 4.

NOTE: When installing cylinder head, position camshaft at 5 o'clock position, Fig. 3, allowing minimal protrusion of the valves from the cylinder head.

VALVE ARRANGEMENT

Front to Rear

2300 cc Engine . . . . E-I-E-I-E-I-E-I

VALVE LIFT SPECS.

Engine	Year	Intake	Exhaust
2300 cc	1977–83	.3997	.3997

VALVE TIMING

Intake Opens Before TDC

Engine	Year	Degrees
2300 cc	1977–83	22

VALVES, ADJUST

The valve lash on this engine cannot be adjusted due to the use of hydraulic valve lash adjusters, Fig. 5. However, the valve train can be checked for wear as follows:

1. Crank engine to position camshaft with flat section of lobe facing rocker arm of valve being checked.
2. Remove rocker arm retaining spring.

NOTE: Late models do not incorporate the retaining spring.

Fig. 3 Cylinder head installation. 2300 cc engine

Fig. 4 Intake manifold tightening sequence. 2300 cc engine

Fig. 5 Valve train installation. 2300 cc engine

T74P-6565-B

CAM ON BASE CIRCLE

FEELER GAUGE

Fig. 6 Checking valve clearance. 2300 cc engine

3. Collapse lash adjuster with tool T74P-6565B and insert correct size feeler gauge between rocker arm and camshaft lobe, Fig. 6. If clearance is not as listed in the "Valve Specifications" chart in front of this chapter, remove rocker arm and check for wear and replace as necessary. If rocker arm is found satisfactory, check valve spring assembled height and adjust as needed. If valve spring assembled height is within specifications listed in the front of this chapter, remove lash adjuster and clean or replace as necessary.

VALVE GUIDES

Valve guides consist of holes bored in the cylinder head. For service the guides can be reamed oversize to accommodate valves with oversize stems of .003, .015 and .030 inch.

ROCKER ARM SERVICE

1. Remove rocker arm cover.
2. Rotate camshaft until flat section of lobe faces rocker arm being removed.
3. With tool T74P-6565B, collapse lash adjuster and, if necessary, valve spring and slide rocker arm over lash adjuster.
4. Reverse procedure to install.

NOTE: Before rotating camshaft, ensure that lash adjuster is collapsed to prevent valve train damage.

LASH ADJUSTER, REPLACE

The hydraulic valve lash adjusters can be

removed after rocker arm removal. There are two types of lash adjusters available, Type 1, being the standard lash adjuster, Fig. 7, and Type II, having a .020 inch oversize outside diameter, Fig. 8.

FRONT ENGINE SEALS, REPLACE

To gain access to the front engine seals, remove the timing belt cover and proceed as follows:

Crankshaft Oil Seal
1. Without removing cylinder front cover, remove crankshaft sprocket with tool T74P-6306A, Fig. 9.
2. Remove crankshaft oil seal with tool T74P-6700B, Fig. 10.
3. Install a new crankshaft oil seal with tool T74P-6150A, Fig. 11.
4. Install crankshaft sprocket with recess facing engine block, Fig. 12.

RETAINING RING
FOLLOWER ARM FULCRUM
PLUNGER
PLUNGER RETURN SPRING
BODY

Fig. 7 Valve lash adjuster, Type I. 2300 cc engine

RETAINING RING
FOLLOWER ARM FULCRUM
METERING PLATE
PLUNGER
PLUNGER RETURN SPRING
BODY

Fig. 8 Valve lash adjuster, Type II. 2300 cc engine

TOOL-T74P-6306-A

Fig. 9 Crankshaft sprocket removal. 2300 cc engine

Fig. 10   Crankshaft front oil seal removal. 2300 cc engine

Fig. 11   Engine front seals installation. 2300 cc engine

Fig. 12   Crankshaft sprocket installation. 2300 cc engine

Fig. 13   Camshaft & auxiliary shaft sprockets removal. 2300 cc engine

Camshaft & Auxiliary Shaft Oil Seals

1. Remove camshaft or auxiliary shaft sprocket with tool T74P-6256A, Fig. 13.
2. Remove oil seal with tool T74P-6700B, Fig. 14.
3. Install a new oil seal with tool T74P-6150A, Fig. 11.
4. Install camshaft or auxiliary shaft sprocket with tool T74P-6256A with center arbor removed.

TIMING BELT

1. Position crankshaft at TDC, No. 1 cylinder compression stroke.
2. Remove timing belt cover, loosen belt tensioner, and remove belt from sprockets, Fig. 15. Tighten tensioner bolt, holding tensioner in position.

NOTE: Do not rotate crankshaft or camshaft after belt is removed. Rotating either component will result in improper valve timing.

3. To install belt, ensure timing marks are aligned, Fig. 16, and place belt over sprockets.
4. Loosen tensioner bolt, allowing tensioner to move against belt.
5. Rotate crankshaft two complete turns, removing slack from belt. Torque tensioner adjustment and pivot bolts and check alignment of timing marks, Fig. 16.
6. Install timing belt cover.

CAMSHAFT, REPLACE

1. Remove rocker arm cover and rocker arms.
2. Remove timing belt cover, camshaft sprocket bolt and washer, then slide sprocket and belt guide off camshaft.
3. Remove camshaft retaining plate from rear of head, then remove camshaft from front of head.

PISTON & ROD, ASSEMBLE

Assemble the rod to the piston with the arrow on top of piston facing front of engine, Fig. 17.

Check side clearance between connecting rods at each connecting rod crankshaft journal. Clearance should be .0035–.0105 in.

PISTONS, PINS & RINGS

Oversize pistons are available in oversizes of .003″, .020″, .030″ and .040″. Oversize rings are available in .020″, .030″ and .040″ oversizes. Oversize pins are not available.

MAIN & ROD BEARINGS

Undersize main bearings are available in .002″, .020″, .030″ and .040″ undersizes. Undersize rod bearings are available in undersizes of .002″, .010″, .020″, .030″ and .040″.

The crankshaft and main bearings are installed with arrows on main bearing caps facing front of engine, Fig. 18. Install PCV baffle between bearing journals No. 3 and 4.

CRANKSHAFT OIL SEAL

1. Remove oil pan.
2. Remove rear main bearing cap.
3. Loosen remaining bearing caps, allowing crankshaft to drop down about 1/32″.
4. Install a sheet metal screw into seal and pull screw to remove seal.
5. Carefully clean seal groove in block with a brush and solvent. Also clean seal groove in bearing cap.
6. Dip seal halves in clean engine oil.
7. Carefully install upper seal half in its groove with locating tab toward rear of engine, Fig. 19, by rotating it on shaft journal of crankshaft until approximately

3/8″ protrudes below the parting surface. *Be sure no rubber has been shaved from outside diameter of seal by bottom edge of groove.*

8. Retighten main bearing caps and torque to specifications.
9. Install lower seal in main bearing cap with undercut side of seal toward front of engine, and allow seal to protrude about

Fig. 14 Camshaft & auxiliary shaft seals removal. 2300 cc engine

Fig. 16 Valve timing marks. 2300 cc engine

Fig. 15 Drive belt & sprockets installation. 2300 cc engine

3/8″ above parting surface to mate with upper seal upon cap installation.

10. Apply suitable sealer to parting faces of cap and block. Install cap and torque to specifications.

NOTE: If difficulty is encountered in installing the upper half of the seal in position, lightly lap (sandpaper) the side of the seal opposite the lip side using a medium grit paper. After sanding, the seal must be washed in solvent, then dipped in clean engine oil prior to installation.

OIL PAN, REPLACE
1980–83

1. Disconnect battery ground cable.
2. Remove fan shroud, then raise and sup-

port vehicle.

NOTE: If equipped with an electric fan, disconnect power lead to fan motor. Remove fan and shroud assembly.

3. Drain crankcase.
4. Remove right and left engine support nuts and bolts, then using a jack and wooden block, raise engine as far as possible. Place wooden blocks between mounts and chassis brackets, then lower jack and remove it.
5. Remove shake brace, then remove sway bar retaining bolts and lower the sway bar.
6. Remove starter motor, then remove steering gear retaining bolts and lower the steering gear.
7. Remove oil pan retaining bolts and oil pan.

NOTE: Crank engine to position number 4 piston up so rear of oil pan clears crankshaft throw.

8. Reverse procedure to install.

1977–79

1. Drain crankcase and remove oil dipstick and flywheel inspection cover.
2. Disconnect steering cable from rack and pinion, then rack and pinion from crossmember and move forward to provide clearance.
3. Unfasten and remove oil pan. To install oil pan, refer to Fig. 20.

OIL PUMP, REPLACE

The oil pump, Fig. 21, can be removed after oil pan removal, Fig. 22.

ARROW POINTING TOWARD
FRONT OF ENGINE

BOSS

NUMBER ON LEFT SIDE OF ROD

Fig. 17 Piston & rod. 2300 cc engine

OIL PUMP REPAIRS

1. Remove end plate and withdraw O ring from groove in body.
2. Check clearance between lobes of inner and outer rotors. This should not exceed .006″. Rotors are supplied only in a matched pair.
3. Check clearance between outer rotor and the housing, Fig. 23. This should not exceed .010″.
4. Place a straightedge across face of pump body, Fig. 24. Clearance between face of rotors and straightedge should not exceed .005″.
5. If necessary to replace rotor or drive shaft, remove outer rotor and then drive out retaining pin securing the skew gear to drive shaft and pull off the gear.
6. Withdraw inner rotor and drive shaft.

BELT TENSION DATA

	New Lbs.	Used Lbs.
1977–80 Exc. ¼ inch	140	110
¼ inch	65	50
1980		
Ribbed Belt w/o Tensioner	155	150
Ribbed Belt w/ Tensioner	130	130
1981		
Except ¼″	140	110
¼″	65	40
V Ribbed Belt		
4K	105	100
5K ①	125	120
5K ②	108	108
6K ①	155	150
6K ②	113	113
1982–83		
Except ¼″	140	105
¼″	65	50
V Ribbed Belt		
4 Rib		
Except Air Pump	130	115
Air Pump	110	105
5 Rib	150	135
6 Rib ①	160	145
6 Rib ②	113	110

①—W/ tensioner.
②—W/ absorber.

OIL PRIOR TO ASSEMBLY

6325-CAP REAR

ARROWS TO FRONT OF ENGINE AS SHOWN

OIL-AFTER INSTALLATION IN BLOCK

6334-CAP FRONT INTMDT.

6333-BEARING

OIL-CRANKSHAFT JOURNALS AND THRUST FACES-AFTER INSTALLATION TO BLOCK

6329-CAP FRONT

6327-CAP REAR INTMDT.

KEY

6330-CAP CENTER

FRONT OF ENGINE

6303-CRANKSHAFT

NOTE:
—CAPS MUST BE SEATED PRIOR TO BOLT RUNDOWN
—DO NOT ALLOW CRANKSHAFT TO ROTATE BEARINGS
—TORQUE ALL MAIN BEARING CAP BOLTS TO SPECIFICATION

REAR FACES OF THRUST BEARINGS MUST BE FLUSH, PRIOR TO FINAL TORQUE OF BOLTS

CAP REF

N 3 JOURNAL (THRUST BEARING)

THRUST BEARING LOWER-6A339

THRUST BEARING UPPER-6337

PRESS PINS TO BOTTOM-3 PLACES— PRIOR TO CRANKSHAFT INSTALLATION

6333-BEARING

BLOCK REF

JOURNAL N 3

FRONT OF ENGINE

APPLY OIL-TO UPPER BEARING THRUST FACES IN BLOCK

JOURNAL N 4

6333-BEARING

SECTION A

VIEW FOR PCV BAFFLE INSTALLATION

Fig. 18 Crankshaft & main bearing installation. 2300 cc engine

WATER PUMP, REPLACE

1. Drain cooling system and disconnect hoses from pump.
2. Loosen alternator and remove drive belt.
3. Remove fan, spacer and pulley.
4. Remove water pump attaching bolts and water pump after removing drive belt cover.

FUEL PUMP, REPLACE

1. Disconnect fuel lines from pump.
2. Remove fuel pump attaching bolts and fuel pump.

Engine oiling system. 2300 cc engine

Fig. 19 Crankshaft rear oil seal installation. 2300 cc engine

SEALER NOTE: CLEAN THE AREA WHERE SEALER IS TO BE APPLIED BEFORE INSTALLING THE SEALS. USE FORD SPOT REMOVER B7A-19521-A OR EQUIVALENT. AFTER THE SEALS ARE IN PLACE, APPLY A 1/16 INCH BEAD OF C3AZ-19562-A OR -B SEALER AS SHOWN. SEALER MUST NOT CONTACT SEALS.

1. APPLY GASKET ADHESIVE EVENLY TO OIL PAN FLANGE AND TO PAN SIDE GASKETS. ALLOW ADHESIVE TO DRY PAST WET STAGE, THEN INSTALL GASKETS TO OIL PAN.
2. APPLY SEALER TO JOINT OF BLOCK AND FRONT COVER. INSTALL SEALS TO FRONT COVER AND REAR BEARING CAP AND PRESS SEAL TABS FIRMLY INTO BLOCK. BE SURE TO INSTALL THE REAR SEAL BEFORE THE REAR MAIN BEARING CAP SEALER HAS CURED.
3. POSITION 2 GUIDE PINS AND INSTALL THE OIL PAN. SECURE THE PAN WITH THE FOUR M8 BOLTS SHOWN ABOVE.
4. REMOVE THE GUIDE PINS AND INSTALL AND TORQUE THE EIGHTEEN M6 BOLTS, BEGINNING AT HOLE A AND WORKING CLOCKWISE AROUND THE PAN.

Fig. 20 Oil pan installation. 2300 cc engine

Fig. 21 Oil pump. 2300 cc engine

SCREW AND WASHER

6600-OIL PUMP

6A618-SHAFT ASSY
OIL PUMP INTERMEDIATE

Fig. 22   Oil pump installation.
2300 cc engine

Feeler Gauge

Fig. 23   Checking outer rotor to housing
clearance. 2300 cc engine

Straight Edge

Feeler Gauge

Fig. 24   Checking rotor end play.
2300 cc engine

2800 cc V6 Engine Section

ENGINE MOUNTS, REPLACE

1. Remove fan shroud screws and support engine with a suitable jack and a block of wood under the oil pan.
2. On all models except 1979 Capri and Mustang remove insulator to insulator support bracket through bolt, support bracket to frame bolts, raise engine slightly, then remove support bracket, Figs. 1 & 2.
3. On 1979 Capri and Mustang, remove nuts and washer attaching the insulator to the No. 2 crossmember pedestals. Lift engine slightly to disengage insulator stud from cross member, Fig. 1.
4. Remove bolt attaching fuel pump shield to left hand engine bracket, if equipped.
5. Remove insulator assembly to engine block bolts, then remove insulator and heat shield.

Fig. 1   Engine mounts (typical). 1977–79 Capri & Mustang

ENGINE, REPLACE

1. Disconnect battery cables and remove hood.
2. Remove air cleaner and intake duct.
3. Drain cooling system, disconnect radiator hoses from radiator, then remove radiator. Disconnect heater hoses from engine block and water pump.

NOTE: Remove fan shroud and position shroud over fan before removing radiator.

4. Remove alternator and bracket.
5. Disconnect ground wires from engine block.
6. Disconnect fuel tank line from fuel pump and plug line.
7. Disconnect all linkage from engine and wires from ignition coil.

NOTE: If equipped with Thermactor system, remove or disconnect system components interfering with engine removal.

8. Raise vehicle and place on jack stands.
9. Disconnect exhaust pipes from exhaust manifold and remove starter.
10. Remove engine front support through bolts or attaching nuts.
11. On vehicles equipped with automatic transmission, disconnect converter from flywheel, remove downshift rod, then remove converter housing to engine bolts and adapter plate to converter housing bolt.
12. On vehicles equipped with manual transmission, remove clutch linkage and bell housing to engine bolts.
13. On all models, lower vehicle and attach a suitable lifting sling to brackets on exhaust manifold.
14. Support transmission with a suitable jack, raise engine slightly and pull from transmission, then lift engine from engine compartment.

CYLINDER HEAD, REPLACE

1. Disconnect battery ground cable, disconnect linkage and drain coolant.
2. Remove distributor, coolant hoses, rocker arm covers, fuel line and filter, carburetor and intake manifold.
3. Remove rocker arm shaft, oil baffles and push rods.
4. Remove exhaust manifold.
5. Remove cylinder head bolts and cylinder head.
6. Reverse procedure to install. Torque cylinder head bolts in sequence shown in Fig. 3, and intake manifold bolts in sequence shown in Fig. 4.

VALVE ARRANGEMENT

Front to Rear

2800 cc engine—
Right . . . . I-E-I-E-E-I
Left . . . . I-E-E-I-E-I

Fig. 3   Cylinder head tightening sequence. 2800 cc engine

VALVE LIFT SPECS.

Engine	Year	Intake	Exhaust
2800 cc	1977–79	.3730	.3730

VALVE TIMING

Intake Opens Before TDC

Engine	Year	Degrees
2800 cc	1977–79	20

VALVES, ADJUST

Cold Setting

1977–79
1. Remove all necessary components to allow removal of valve covers, then remove valve covers.
2. Slowly crank engine until intake valve for number 5 cylinder just starts to open. The camshaft is now correctly positioned to adjust valves on number 1 cylinder.
3. Refer to "Valves Specifications" chart, then using a feeler gauge of the specified clearance, adjust number 1 cylinder intake valve so that feeler gauge has a light to moderate drag, and a feeler gauge .001 inch greater is very tight, Fig. 5.

NOTE: Do not use a step-type "go/no-go" gauge. Also, when checking valve lash, insert gauge between rocker arm and front or rear of valve tip and move

Fig. 2 Engine mounts (typical). 1977–79 Bobcat & Pinto

gauge toward opposite edge with a rearward or forward motion parallel to the crankshaft centerline. Inserting gauge at outboard edge, and moving inward toward carburetor, will produce an erroneous "feel" and result in excessively tight valves.

4. Using the same procedure as in step 3, adjust the number 1 cylinder intake valve using a feeler gauge of the specified clearance.
5. Adjust the remaining valves in sequence of firing order (1-4-2-5-3-6), by positioning the camshaft according to the following chart:

	With Intake Valve Just Opening for Cyl. No.					
	5	3	6	1	4	2
Adjust Both Valves For Cyl. No.	1	4	2	5	3	6

VALVE GUIDES

Valve guides consist of holes bored in the cylinder head. For service the guides can be reamed oversize to accomodate valves with oversize stems of .003, .015 and .030.".

ROCKER ARM SERVICE

1. Disconnect throttle rod from carburetor and remove rocker arm cover.
2. Remove rocker arm shaft stand bolts, rocker arm shaft assembly and oil baffle, Fig. 6.
3. Remove cotter pin and spring washer from ends of rocker shaft and slide rocker arms, springs and shaft supports off shaft, marking components for proper reassembly, Fig. 7.

4. Remove plugs from shaft ends by drilling a hole in one plug, insert a long rod through drilled plug and knock the opposite plug from shaft. Remove the drilled plug in same manner.
5. With a blunt tool, install plugs in end of rocker shafts with cup side out.
6. Install spring washer and cotter pin on one end of shaft and install components in proper sequence as marked during disassembly.

NOTE: Oil holes in rocker shaft must face downward during installation.

VALVE LIFTERS, REPLACE

Remove cylinder head as outlined previously and using a magnet, remove lifters from their bores.

Fig. 4 Intake manifold tightening sequence. 2800 cc engine

Fig. 5 Adjusting valve lash. 2800 cc engine

Fig. 6 Rocker arm replacement.
2800 cc engine

Fig. 7 Rocker arm shaft assembly. 2800 cc engine

TIMING CASE COVER

1. Remove oil pan as described further on.
2. Drain coolant and remove radiator, then remove any other components as necessary to obtain clearance.
3. If equipped, disconnect A/C compressor and bracket and place aside.
4. Remove alternator, Thermactor pump, drive belts, fan, water pump, hoses and harmonic balancer or pulley.
5. Remove cover retaining bolts and remove cover.

CRANKSHAFT FRONT OIL SEAL

The crankshaft front oil seal may be serviced without removing the cylinder front cover as follows:
1. Drain coolant and remove radiator, crankshaft pulley and water pump drive belt.
2. Pull oil seal from front cover, Fig. 8.
3. Install new oil seal with tool T72C-6150, Fig. 9.
4. Install crankshaft pulley, water pump drive belt, radiator, then refill cooling system.

TIMING GEARS

1. Drain, then remove radiator and oil pan.

2. Remove cylinder front cover and water pump.
3. Align timing marks, Fig. 10.
4. Using a suitable gear puller, remove crankshaft gear and key.
5. Remove camshaft gear with a suitable gear puller.

NOTE: Do not rotate crankshaft or camshaft with gears removed as rotation of either component can result in improper valve timing.

---

6. Install key in camshaft, then press camshaft gear onto camshaft.
7. Install key in crankshaft, then press crankshaft gear onto crankshaft with tool T72C-6150, Fig. 11, and make sure timing marks are aligned, Fig. 10.
8. Install cylinder front cover, water pump, radiator and oil pan.
9. Refill cooling system and oil pan. Start engine and adjust ignition timing, if necessary.

CAMSHAFT, REPLACE

1. Drain coolant, then remove radiator, fan, water pump pulley and belt.
2. Remove distributor, alternator, Thermactor pump, fuel line, filter, carburetor and intake manifold.
3. Remove rocker arm covers, rocker arm assemblies, pushrods and lifters. Identify pushrods and lifters so they can be reinstalled in their original location.
4. Remove oil pan as described further on.
5. Remove timing case cover as described previously.
6. Remove camshaft gear retaining bolt and

slide gear off shaft and remove camshaft thrust plate.
7. Carefully remove camshaft from engine using care to avoid damage to camshaft bearings Fig. 12.

PISTON & ROD ASSEMBLY

Assemble the piston to the rod with the notches facing front of engine and the numbered side of the rod toward left side of engine, Fig. 13.

PISTONS, PINS & RINGS

Oversize pistons and rings are available in .020″ and .040″ oversizes. Oversize pins are not available.

CRANKSHAFT REAR OIL SEAL

1. Remove transmission assembly.
2. On automatic transmission vehicles, remove flywheel.
3. On manual transmission vehicles, remove clutch assembly, flywheel, clutch housing and rear plate.
4. Punch two holes on opposite sides of seal just above bearing cap to cylinder block split line and install a sheet metal screw

Fig. 8 Removing crankshaft front oil seal. 2800 cc engine

Fig. 9 Installing crankshaft front oil seal. 2800 cc engine

Fig. 10 Valve timing marks. 2800 cc engine

Fig. 11   Crankshaft gear installation. 2800 cc engine

Fig. 12   Camshaft components. 2800 cc engine

in each hole. Using two large screwdrivers, pry evenly on both screws to remove seal, Fig. 14.

NOTE: Use care to avoid damaging the crankshaft oil seal surface.

5. Install new seal with tool T72C-6165, Fig. 15.

Fig. 13   Piston & rod. 2800 cc engine

OIL PAN, REPLACE

1979 Capri & Mustang

1. Disconnect battery ground cable.
2. Remove fan shroud attaching screws and position shroud over fan.
3. Raise and support vehicle, then drain oil pan.
4. Remove two bolts attaching steering gear to main crossmember and rest steering gear on frame away from oil pan.
5. Remove engine mount attaching nuts.
6. Raise engine with a suitable jack and place wood blocks between the engine mounts and the frame.
7. Remove rear "K" braces.
8. Remove oil pan attaching bolts and lower oil pan to frame.
9. Remove oil pump attaching bolts and lower oil pump into oil pan.
10. Remove oil pan. It may be necessary to rotate crankshaft to provide adequate clearance.
11. Reverse procedure to install.

Exc. 1979 Capri & Mustang

1. Disconnect battery ground cable.
2. Remove oil level dipstick.
3. Drain cooling system and disconnect upper and lower radiator hoses.
4. Remove fan shroud attaching bolts and place shroud over fan.
5. Raise vehicle and drain crankcase, then remove splash shield and starter.
6. If equipped with automatic transmission, disconnect cooler lines at radiator.

7. Disconnect steering gear and power steering hoses (if equipped) and position gear aside, then disconnect sway bar and rotate to allow clearance.
8. Remove engine front support nuts, then raise engine and place wood blocks between engine front supports and chassis.
9. Remove converter or clutch housing cover.
10. Remove oil pan bolts and oil pan.

OIL PUMP, REPLACE

The oil pump, Fig. 16, can be removed after oil pan removal.

OIL PUMP REPAIRS

1. Remove end plate and withdraw O ring from groove in body.
2. Check clearance between lobes of inner and outer rotors. This should not exceed .006″. Rotors are supplied only in a matched pair.
3. Check clearance between outer rotor and the housing, Fig. 17. This should not exceed .010 inch.
4. Place a straightedge across face of pump body, Fig. 18. Clearance between face of rotors and straightedge should not exceed .005 inch.
5. If necessary to replace rotor or drive shaft, remove outer rotor and then drive out retaining pin securing the skew gear to drive shaft and pull off the gear.
6. Withdraw inner rotor and drive shaft.

Fig. 14   Removing crankshaft rear oil seal. 2800 cc engine

Fig. 15   Installing crankshaft rear oil seal. 2800 cc engine

Fig. 16   Oil pump. 2800 cc engine

Engine oiling system. 2800 cc engine

Fig. 17   Checking outer rotor to housing clearance. 2800 cc engine

Fig. 18   Checking rotor end play. 2800 cc engine

BELT TENSION DATA

	New Ft. Lbs.	Used Ft. Lbs.
1977–79 Exc. 1/4 inch	140	110
1/4 inch	65	50

WATER PUMP, REPLACE

1. Drain coolant and disconnect heater hose and lower radiator hose from pump.
2. Loosen alternator and remove drive belt.
3. Remove fan and pulley.
4. Remove water pump mounting bolts, water pump, water inlet housing and thermostat.

FUEL PUMP, REPLACE

1. Disconnect fuel lines from pump.
2. Remove fuel pump attaching bolts and fuel pump.

6-200 Engine Section

Refer to the Ford & Mercury—Compact & Intermediate chapter for service procedures on this engine not included in this section.

Oil Pan, Replace

1. If equipped with automatic transmission, disconnect transmission oil cooler lines from radiator, then remove the radiator top support.
2. Remove dipstick, then raise and support vehicle and drain crankcase.
3. Remove the four bolts and nuts retaining sway bar to chassis and allow sway bar to hang down.
4. Remove K-brace, then lower the rack and pinion steering gear.
5. Remove starter motor, then remove the two engine mounts to support bracket nuts and loosen the two rear insulator to crossmember retaining bolts.
6. Raise engine and place a 1¼ inch wooden block between each engine support insulator and chassis bracket, then lower engine onto wood blocks.
7. Using floor jack, raise transmission slightly, then remove the oil pan retaining bolts and lower oil pan onto crossmember.
8. Position transmission oil cooler lines aside and remove oil pan. If necessary, rotate engine so crankshaft throws clear oil pan rail.
9. Reverse procedure to install.

V6-232 Engine Section

Refer to Ford & Mercury—Compact & Intermediate Chapter for service procedures on this engine.

V8 Engine Section

NOTE: Refer to the Ford & Mercury—Compact & Intermediate chapter for service procedures on this engine not included in this section.

ENGINE MOUNTS, REPLACE

1979–83 Capri & Mustang

1. Remove fan shroud attaching screws.
2. Remove nuts attaching insulators to lower bracket, Fig. 1.
3. Raise engine with a suitable jack and a block of wood placed under oil pan.
4. Remove insulator to engine block attaching bolts.
5. Remove insulator from vehicle.
6. Reverse procedure to install.

1977–78 Mustang

1. Remove fan shroud screws and support engine with a suitable jack and a block of wood under the oil pan.
2. Remove insulator to frame through bolt, Fig. 2.

Fig. 1 Engine mount. 1979–83 Capri & Mustang

Fig. 3 Serpentine drive belt

3. Remove insulator to engine block attaching bolts.
4. Raise engine slightly, then remove insulator and heat shield, if equipped.
5. Reverse procedure to install.

VALVES, ADJUST

The firing order of the 1982–83 V8-302 H.O. engine is 1-3-7-2-6-5-4-8, while the firing order for the 1977–79 V8-302 and 1980–82 V8-255 engines is 1-5-4-2-6-3-7-8. Therefore when adjusting valves on the 1982–83 V8-302 H.O. engine, refer to the procedure for the V8-351 engine in the "Ford & Mercury—Compact & Intermediate" chapter.

OIL PAN, REPLACE

1979–83

1. Disconnect battery cables.
2. Remove fan shroud retaining bolts and position fan shroud over fan.
3. Raise and support vehicle, then drain crankcase.

NOTE: Some oil pans have dual oil sumps. Make sure to remove both drain plugs to thoroughly drain oil.

4. Remove the two bolts retaining steering gear to main crossmember and allow steering gear to rest on frame away from oil pan.
5. Remove engine mount retaining bolts, then raise engine and place a 2 x 4 inch wooden block between each engine mount and vehicle frame.
6. Remove rear K-braces
7. Remove oil pan retaining bolts and lower oil pan onto frame.
8. Remove oil pump retaining bolts and the inlet tube retaining nut from No. 3 main bearing cap stud. Lower the oil pump assembly into the oil pan.
9. Remove oil pan. If necessary, rotate engine so that crankshaft throws clear oil pan rail.
10. Reverse procedure to install.

1977–78

1. Disconnect battery cables.
2. Remove fan shroud retaining bolts and position fan shroud over fan.
3. Raise and support vehicle, then drain crankcase.
4. Remove the four crossmember retaining bolts and remove crossmember.
5. Remove retaining bolt from flex joint to release steering pinion shaft. Remove the 3 nuts and bolts retaining steering gear to crossmember. Remove the 4 bolts retaining sway bar to chassis and move sway bar down.
6. Remove starter motor.
7. Remove oil pan retaining bolts and oil pan.
8. Reverse procedure to install.

SERPENTINE DRIVE BELT

Some engines are equipped with a serpentine drive belt, Fig. 3, to drive the accessories in place of the usual arrangement. This "V" ribbed belt drives the fan/water pump, alternator, secondary air pump, optional A/C com-

Fig. 2 Engine mounts. 1977–78 Mustang

pressor and optional power steering pump.

The tensioner arm should be checked to ensure that the top edge of the arm is located between the two index marks scribed on the circumference next to the slot of the tensioner housing, Fig. 4. If the tensioner arm is not properly aligned, the drive belt and pulleys should be inspected for wear and binding. If the drive belt and pulleys are satisfactory, the tensioner must be replaced as outlined in the following procedure.

Drive belt & Tensioner, Replace

1. Insert a 16 inch pry bar or equivalent in the slot of the tensioner bracket, and using the tensioner housing as a fulcrum, push the pry bar downward to force the tensioner pulley upward, relieving tension on belt, Fig. 3.
2. Remove drive belt.

Fig. 4 Serpentine drive belt tensioner alignment marks

3. Remove bolt securing tensioner assembly to alternator bracket.
4. Remove tensioner assembly.
5. Position tensioner assembly so the tang, located on the rear of the assembly, is placed to fit in the hole or slot in alternator bracket.
6. Install the tensioner assembly bolt through the hole in the alternator bracket and torque bolt to 55-80 ft. lbs.
7. Install drive belt by inserting the pry bar as outlined in Step 1. Refer to decal located on top of the windshield washer/coolant expansion reservoir for proper belt routing.
8. Remove pry bar.
9. The drive belt is automatically tensioned when the tensioner arm is located between the two index marks, Fig. 4.

Turbocharger Section

DESCRIPTION

The turbocharger Fig. 1 is an exhaust driven device which compresses the air fuel mixture that is used to increase engine power on a demand basis, allowing a smaller more economical engine to be used. An optional turbocharger is available on 1979–81 Capri and Mustang that are equipped with the 4-140 (2300 cc) engine.

A turbine in the exhaust gas flow is connected through a shaft, to the impeller (compressor) near the carburetor, Fig. 2. During normal, steady operation, the turbine does not rotate with sufficient speed to boost pressure to compress the air-fuel mixture. As the speed increases the mixture is compressed allowing the denser mixture to enter the combustion chambers, in turn developing more engine power during the combustion cycle.

The intake manifold pressure (boost) is controlled by a wastegate valve which is used to bypass a portion of the exhaust gasses around the turbine at a predetermined point in the cycle, limiting the boost pressure. The wastegate starts to open when the turbocharger boost pressure reaches approximately 5 PSI and routes a sufficient portion of the exhaust gasses around the turbine to limit maximum boost to 5½ PSI.

A green light on the instrument panel indicates that the turbocharger is in a safe boost condition. A red light and buzzer is used to indicate a malfunction or if boost pressure rises above 5½ PSI. If the oil temperature exceeds a predetermined level, just the warning light will flash.

The high cylinder temperature created by boosted combustion can result in detonation, therefore, two spark retardation points have been designed into the electronic ignition system.

At approximately 1 PSI of boost pressure, a switch in the intake manifold, Fig. 3, sends an electrical signal to the ignition module which electronically retards the ignition timing six degrees. At 4 PSI of boost pressure, another manifold switch sends a signal and timing is retarded an additional six degrees.

LUBRICATION

Turbochargers are lubricated from the engine oil system. These turbochargers operate at speeds up to 120,000 RPM which makes the

The COMPRESSOR is a centrifugal, radial outflow type. It comprises a cast compressor wheel, backplate assembly, and specially-designed housing that encloses the wheel and directs the air/fuel mixture through the compressor.

The CENTER HOUSING supports the compressor and turbine wheel shaft in bearings which contain oil holes for directing lubrication to the bearing bores and shaft journals.

The OUTLET ELBOW ASSEMBLY contains the WASTEGATE ASSEMBLY, or bypass valve, which allows a portion of the exhaust gas to bypass the turbine wheel so boost pressure can be controlled.

The ACTUATOR is a spring-loaded diaphragm device that senses the outlet pressure of the compressor.

The TURBINE is a centripetal, radial inflow type. It comprises a cast turbine wheel, wheel shroud, and specially-designed housing that encloses the wheel and directs the exhaust gas through the turbine.

Fig. 1 Turbocharger assembly 1979–81 4-140 (2300) engine Capri & Mustang

lubrication of the bearings which support the shaft important for cooling as well as friction.

The oil enters the turbocharger through an inlet fitting in the center housing. This inlet fitting directs oil to the center housing bearings, the oil then drains from the turbocharger through a return hole in the center housing. When changing oil and filter on a turbocharged engine disconnect the ignition switch connector from the distributor then crank engine several times until the oil light goes out. Reconnect the ignition wire to the distributor. This procedure will aid in the filling of the oil system before starting engine.

NOTE: Engine oil on turbocharged engines must be changed every 3000 miles since turbocharger bearing damage may occur from oil contamination.

DIAGNOSIS, TESTING & TROUBLE SHOOTING

Prior to performing any diagnostic or testing procedure check all vacuum hoses and wiring for proper routing and connections, carburetor linkage for damage or any problems which may occur in a non-turbocharged engine.

CAUTION: A turbocharged engine has exhaust pipes located high in the engine compartment. Care must be taken to avoid accidental contact with hot exhaust pipes, since personal injury may occur.

Detonation With Turbo Light On

1. Improper grade of fuel being used.
2. Engine overheating.
3. Turbocharger wastegate actuator lines loose or split.
4. Improper operation of turbocharger boost pressure control system.
5. Improper operation of pressure activated spark retard system.
6. Leaking turbocharger compressor oil seal.
7. Improper operation of spark control system or spark delay valve.
8. Partially or fully clogged PCV valve system.
9. Defective or improperly adjusted carburetor.
10. Defective fuel pump or restriction in fuel system.
11. Defective or improperly adjusted distributor.
12. Low cylinder compression in one or more cylinders.
13. Contaminated fuel supply.
14. Defective thermostat or restriction in cooling system.

⇨ EXH. TO TURBO
➤ EXH. FROM TURBO
➧ ATMOSPHERIC AIR
⫸ PRESSURIZED AIR

Fig. 2 Turbocharger air flow

Engine Lacks Power Or Emits Black Exhaust Smoke

1. Partial or completely clogged air cleaner.
2. Loose compressor to intake manifold connections.
3. Vacuum leak at intake manifold.
4. Exhaust leak at engine exhaust manifold.
5. Leakage at turbocharger mounting flange.
6. Turbocharger rotating assembly binding or dragging.
7. Restrictions in compressor-to-intake manifold duct.
8. Restrictions in engine exhaust system.
9. Restriction in engine intake manifold.
10. Defective or improperly adjust carburetor.
11. Defective fuel pump or clogged fuel lines.
12. Transmission not shifting properly.
13. Defective distributor spark control.
14. Turbocharger wastegate not operating properly.

Excessive Oil Consumption Or Emits Blue Exhaust Smoke

1. Leaking or clogged turbocharger oil supply and drain lines or fittings.
2. Clogged air cleaner, fuel system, or evaporative control system.
3. Clogged PCV valve system.
4. Defective or improperly adjusted carburetor or defective fuel pump.
5. Leaking vacuum lines or intake manifold.
6. EGR system not working properly.
7. Defective thermofactor system.
8. Cylinder compression low in one or more cylinders.
9. Leaking turbocharger compressor or turbine oil seals.
10. Check valve train for proper operation.

Wastegate Boost Pressure (In-Vehicle Test)

1. Check that the wastegate actuator rod is attached to wastegate arm with retaining clip, Fig. 5.
2. Remove vacuum lines from the the diaphragm.
3. Install an external vacuum source to vacuum side of diaphragm, Fig. 5. Apply 25 inches vacuum and hold. If vacuum drops below 18.0 after 60 sec. replace diaphragm.
4. Install an external pressure source to the pressure side of diaphragm, Fig. 5. Apply 5 psi pressure and hold. If pressure drops below 2 psi after 60 seconds, replace diaphragm.
5. Using a dial indicator to measure wastegate actuator rod travel, Fig. 5, apply pressure until the dial indicator shows 0.015 inch linear displacement. Pressure should be about 6.8 psi. If pressure is not as specified, check wastegate activating diaphragm. If wastegate activating arm stays closed, replace diaphragm.
6. Release pressure, remove test equipment and reconnect vacuum lines to diaphragm.
7. Remove actuator rod clip. Remove rod from wastegate arm. Check to see if arm rotates a minimum of 40°. If it does not

INTAKE MANIFOLD is redesigned.

OIL SUPPLY and RETURN lines are new.

TURBOCHARGER is an exhaust driven device which compresses the air/fuel mixture.

EGR TUBE and VALVE are new.

NEW INTAKE and EXHAUST VALVES and CYLINDER HEAD GASKET handle increased loads, stresses, and temperatures.

CROSSOVER PIPE moves exhaust gas from one side of the engine to the other, and DOWN PIPE connects the exhaust system to the turbocharger.

UPGRADED RADIATOR enhances engine cooling.

TURBO BOOST/OVERBOOST AND ENGINE OIL OVERTEMPERATURE WARNING SYSTEM is new.

FORGED PISTONS increase durability. The pin offset is decreased, and the second land width and bore clearance increased. The TOP RING is ductile iron, and the LOWER COMPRESSION RING is chromed.

OIL CAPACITY is increased by 1/2 quart.

ELECTRONIC PRESSURE RETARD SYSTEM retards spark to eliminate possibility of detonation.

MAIN BEARINGS AND ROD BEARINGS have increased load capacity.

The OIL PUMP has a stiffer relief valve spring to maintain normal oil pressure.

Fig. 3 Turbocharger system

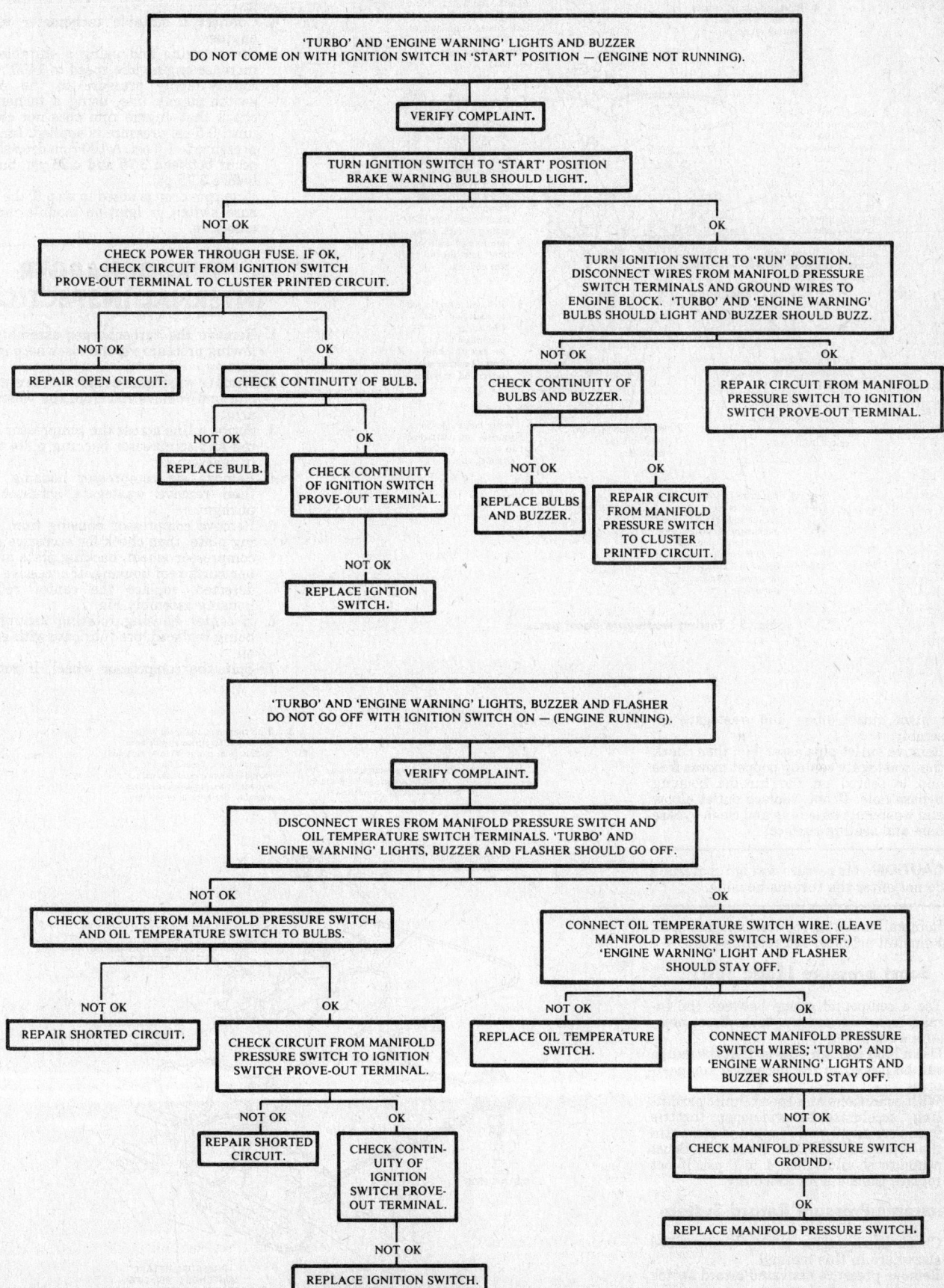

Fig. 4   Turbocharger boost/overboost warning system diagnosis

6. Release pressure, remove test equipment, and reinstall system components.

5. Install a dial indicator to measure wastegate actuator rod travel. Very slowly apply pressure until the dial indicator shows 0.015 inch linear displacement. Pressure should be 6.8 ±0.5 psi. If pressure is not as specified, check wastegate activating diaphragm. If wastegate actuator arm stays closed, replace diaphragm.

4. Install an external pressure source to pressure side of diaphragm. Apply 5 psi pressure and trap. If pressure drops below 2 psi after 60 seconds, replace diaphragm.

3. Install an external vacuum source to vacuum side of diaphragm. Apply 25 inches Hg vacuum and trap. If vacuum drops below 18.0 inches after 60 seconds, replace diaphragm.

2. Remove the vacuum lines from the diaphragm.

7. Remove actuator rod clip. Remove rod from wastegate arm. Check if arm rotates a minimum of 40°. If not, replace outlet elbow and wastegate assembly.

8. Remove outlet pipe assembly. Check that wastegate sealing poppet moves free on the pintle and is seating on the turbine housing bypass hole. If not, replace outlet elbow and wastegate assembly and/or clean bypass hole and sealing surface. Make sure foreign materials don't enter the turbine housing.

9. Reinstall actuator rod to wastegate arm. (Pressurize diaphragm to 6 psi for ease of installation.) Reinstall actuator rod retaining clip.

1. Verify that wastegate actuator rod is attached to wastegate arm with retaining clip.

Fig. 5 Testing wastegate boost pressure

3. Remove distributor vacuum line and plug it.
4. Connect a suitable tachometer to the engine.
5. Start engine and using a suitable tool increase engine idle speed to 1400 rpm.
6. Slowly apply pressure to the retard switch supply line, using a tachometer check that engine rpm does not change until 0.5 psi pressure is applied. Increase pressure to 1.0 psi. A 100 rpm drop should occur between 3.75 and 4.25 psi, but not before 3.75 psi.
7. If no rpm drop is noted in step 6, the pressure switch or ignition module may be defective.

TURBOCHARGER INTERNAL INSPECTION

1. Remove the turbocharger assembly following procedure found elsewhere in this section.
2. Remove wastegate actuator rod retaining clip and remove rod from the wastegate arm.
3. Scribe a line across the compressor housing and compressor backing plate to aid in reassembly.
4. Remove six compressor housing bolts, then remove wastegate actuator diaphragm.
5. Remove compressor housing from backing plate, then check for excessive oil on compressor wheel, backing plate and inner surface of housing. If excessive oil is detected, replace the center rotating housing assembly Fig. 7.
6. If center housing rotating assembly is being replaced, pre-lubricate with engine oil.
7. Spin the compressor wheel. If rotating

replace outlet elbow and wastegate assembly.

8. Remove outlet pipe assembly, then check that wastegate sealing poppet moves free and is seated on the turbine housing bypass hole. If not, replace outlet elbow and wastegate assembly and clean bypass hole and sealing surface.

CAUTION: Make sure foreign materials do not enter the turbine housing.

9. Reinstall actuator rod to wastegate arm. Reinstall actuator rod retaining clip.

Boost pressure (Road Test)

1. Tee a compound gauge between the intake manifold and the turbo boost pressure switch, Fig. 6.
2. Use a long enough hose so that the gauge can be placed in the passenger compartment.
3. With conditions and speed limits permitting, accelerate at wide-open throttle from zero to 40 to 50 mph and maintain the top speed for 2 to 3 seconds. Boost pressure should reach 4 to 6 psi. If not replace the actuator assembly.

Electronic Pressure Retard System

1. Check basic engine timing as described elsewhere in this manual.
2. Remove pressure activated retard switch assembly supply line, cap the open line and install an external pressure source to the pressure switch assembly.

1 Tee a compound gauge between the intake manifold and the turbo boost pressure switch.

2 Use a long enough hose so that the gauge can be placed in the passenger compartment.

3 With conditions and speed limits permitting, accelerate at wide-open throttle from zero to 40 to 50 mph and maintain the top speed for 2 to 3 seconds. Boost pressure should reach 4 to 6 psi. If not, replace the actuator assembly. See Page 30 of this book.

TO NO. 4 RUNNER (INTAKE) DISCRETE PORT

INTAKE MANIFOLD (RUNNER) — PRESSURE AT BOOST

DSI II DISTRIBUTOR

DUAL-MODE IGNITION TIMING MODULE

PRESSURE RETARD SWITCHES (1 PSI, 1 PSI— REDUNDANT SWITCH, 4 PSI)

Fig. 6 Compound gauge hook-up for boost pressure road test

Fig. 7 Compressor housing turbine housing and center housing rotating assembly

an accurate measurement has been made. If the bearing radial clearance is less then 0.003 inch or greater then 0.006 inch, replace the turbocharger center rotating housing assembly.

NOTE: Continued operation of a turbocharger having excessive bearing radial clearance will result in severe damage to the compressor and turbine wheels and the housings.

11. Turbocharger bearing axial clearance
   (a) If not already done, remove five bolts connecting the turbine outlet elbow assembly and remove the elbow.
   (b) Attach a dial indicator (Tool 4201-C) to the center housing so that the indicator plunger extends through the oil outlet port and contacts the shaft, Fig. 9.
   (c) Manually push the turbine wheel assembly as far away from the dial indicator tip as possible.
   (d) Set the dial indicator to zero while holding the turbine wheel away from the tip of the plunger.
   (e) Manually push the turbine wheel assembly toward the dial indicator tip as far as possible.
   (f) Repeat step 3 and check that the dial indicator returns to zero.
   (g) Repeat steps 3, 4, 5, and 6 to make sure an accurate measurement has been made. If the bearing axial clearance is less than 0.001 inch or greater than 0.003 inch, replace the turbocharger center rotating housing assembly.

assembly binds or drags, replace the center housing rotating assembly.
8. Check turbine wheel for binding, blade cracking or bending, and excessive sludge build up. If any of these conditions exist, replace the turbocharger center rotating housing.
9. To check the turbocharger bearing clearances, remove turbine housing from center housing rotating assembly, and measure clearances.
10. Turbocharger bearing radial clearance
   (a) Remove two bolts connecting the turbine oil outlet fitting to the center housing and remove the fitting Fig. 7. Attach a dial indicator (Tool 4201-C) to the center housing so that the indicator plunger (Tool T79L-4201-A) extends through the oil outlet port and contacts the shaft Fig. 8.
   (b) Manually apply pressure equally and simultaneously to both the compressor and the turbine wheels to move the shaft away from the dial indicator plunger as far as possible.
   (c) Set the dial indicator to zero while holding the shaft away from the plunger tip.
   (d) Manually apply pressure equally and simultaneously to both the compressor and turbine wheels to move the shaft towards the dial indicator plunger as far as possible. Note the maximum reading on dial indicator.
   (e) Manually apply pressure equally and simultaneously to both the compressor and turbine wheels as required to move the turbine wheel assembly shaft away from the dial indicator as far as possible. The dial indicator should return to zero.
   (f) Repeat steps 2, 3, 4, and 5 to make sure

1 Remove turbocharger assembly from engine
2 Remove wastegate actuator rod retaining clip and remove rod from wastegate arm.
3 Remove 2 bolts connecting the turbine oil outlet fitting to the center housing and remove the fitting.
4 Attach a dial indicator (Tool 4201-C) to the center housing so that the indicator plunger (Tool T79L-4201-A) extends through the oil outlet port and contacts the shaft.

8 Repeat step 5 and note that the dial indicator returns to zero.
9 Repeat steps 5, 6, 7, and 8 to make sure an accurate measurement has been made. If the bearing radial clearance is less than 0.003 inch or greater than 0.006 inch, replace the turbocharger center rotating housing assembly.

Fig. 8 Checking turbocharger bearing radial clearance

NOTE: Continued operation of a turbocharger having excessive bearing axial clearance will result in severe damage to the compressor and turbine wheels and housings.

TURBOCHARGER SERVICE

Before performing turbocharger service, note the following general precautions:

1. Clean area around turbocharger assembly with non-caustic solution before removal of assembly. Cover openings of engine assembly connections to prevent entry of foreign material while turbocharger is off engine.
2. When removing turbocharger assembly, do not bend, nick or in any way damage the compressor or turbine wheel blades. Any damage may result in rotating assembly imbalance, and failure of center housing, compressor, and/or turbine housings.
3. Before disconnecting the center housing from either the compressor or the turbine housing, scribe location of components for assembly in original position.

Wastegate Actuator Assembly, Replace

1. Disconnect two vacuum hoses from actuator.
2. Remove clip attaching actuator rod to wastegate arm.
3. Remove two bolts attaching actuator diaphragm assembly to compressor housing.
4. Reverse procedure to install.

Outlet Elbow & Wastegate Assembly, Replace

1. Raise vehicle.
2. Loosen turbocharger exhaust pipe at catalytic converter.
3. Lower vehicle.
4. Disconnect turbocharger down pipe at outlet elbow and wastegate assembly.
5. Remove clip attaching actuator rod to wastegate linkage.
6. Remove five bolts attaching outlet and wastegate elbow assembly.
7. Reverse procedure to install.

Turbine Outlet Elbow Assembly, Replace

1. Disconnect turbocharger exhaust outlet pipe from elbow assembly.
2. Remove turbocharger heat shield.
3. Raise vehicle.
4. Disconnect turbocharger exhaust crossover pipe from the catalytic converter.
5. Lower car.
6. Remove clip attaching wastegate linkage to actuator rod.
7. Remove five bolts attaching outlet elbow to turbine housing.

---

1 Remove turbocharger assembly from engine

2 Remove wastegate actuator rod retaining clip and remove rod from the wastegate arm.

3 Remove 5 bolts connecting the turbine outlet elbow assembly and remove the elbow.

NOTE: One bolt is located inside the elbow housing.

4 Attach a dial indicator (Tool 4201-C) to the center housing so that the indicator plunger extends through the oil outlet port and contacts the shaft, as illustrated.

TURBINE WHEEL

5 Manually push the turbine wheel assembly as far away from the dial indicator tip as possible.

6 Set the dial indicator to 0 while holding the turbine wheel away from the plunger tip.

DIAL INDICATOR

7 Manually push the turbine wheel assembly toward the dial indicator tip as far as possible.

8 Repeat step 5 and note that the dial indicator returns to zero.

9 Repeat steps 5, 6, 7, and 8 to make sure an accurate measurement has been made. If the bearing axial clearance is less than 0.001 inch or greater than 0.003 inch, replace the turbocharger center rotating housing assembly.

Fig. 9   Checking turbocharger bearing axial clearance

NOTE: One bolt is located inside the outlet elbow.

8. Reverse procedure to install.

Turbocharger Assembly, Replace

1. Remove air cleaner.
2. Remove turbocharger heat shield.
3. Raise vehicle.
4. Remove exhaust outlet pipe and exhaust down pipe.
5. Lower vehicle.
6. Remove boost control tube and oil supply line.
7. Remove throttle bracket.
8. Remove rear wastegate actuator vacuum line.
9. Remove EGR tube and dipstick tube.
10. Remove necessary vacuum hoses.
11. Remove four bolts attaching turbocharger to intake manifold.
12. Remove four bolts from turbocharger rear brace and remove turbocharger from engine.
13. Reverse procedure to install, replacing the three O-rings and greasing the compressor outlet O-ring.

Compressor Housing, Replace

1. Remove turbocharger assembly from engine as outlined previously in this section.
2. Remove wastegate actuator rod retaining clip and remove rod from the wastegate arm.
3. Scribe a line across the compressor housing and center rotating housing assembly to aid in reassembly.
4. Remove six compressor housing bolts, wastegate activating diaphragm and compressor housing from the backing plate.
5. Reverse procedure to install.

Turbine Housing, Replace

1. Remove turbocharger assembly from engine as outlined previously in this section.
2. Remove wastegate actuator rod retaining clip and remove rod from wastegate arm.
3. Scribe a line across the turbine housing and center housing to aid in reassembly.
4. Remove six turbine housing bolts, then remove turbine housing from the center housing.
5. Reverse procedure to install.

Clutch & Transmission Section

CLUTCH PEDAL, ADJUST

1981—83 Capri & Mustang

These models incorporate a self adjusting clutch mechanism. The adjust mechanism consists of a spring loaded rachet quadrant attached to the clutch cable. To accomplish this adjustment, grasp clutch pedal and pull upward, then slowly depress clutch pedal. If a click is heard during the procedure, an adjustment was necessary and has been accomplished. This procedure should be performed at least every 5000 miles.

1979—80 Capri & Mustang

NOTE: These models do not require a free play adjustment. A clutch pedal height adjustment will be required instead.

1. From under vehicle remove dust shield.
2. Loosen clutch cable lock nut. Turn adjusting nut clockwise to raise clutch pedal and counter clockwise to lower clutch pedal. The total clutch pedal stroke should be 5.3 in. for 4-140 engine and 6.5 in. for V8-302 engine.
3. Torque lock nut to 5 to 8 ft. lbs., using care not to disturb adjustment.
4. Cycle clutch pedal several times, then recheck pedal height.
5. When clutch system is properly adjusted the clutch pedal can be raised approximately 2.7 in. on 4-140 engines and 1.5 in. for V8-302 engines, before contacting the clutch pedal stop.

1977—78 Mustang

1. Remove cable retaining clip at dash panel and remove cable retaining screw from fender apron.
2. Pull cable toward front of vehicle until nut can be rotated. Rotate nut from adjustment sleeve about 1/4 inch.
3. Release cable to neutralize the linkage and pull cable until free movement of release lever is eliminated.
4. Rotate adjusting nut toward adjustment sleeve until contact is made, then index into the next notch.

5. Install cable retaining clip, cable retaining bracket and retaining screw.

1977—80 Bobcat & Pinto

1. Loosen clutch cable lock nut at flywheel housing.
2. Pull cable toward front of vehicle so the nylon adjuster nut tabs are clear of the housing boss, then rotate nut toward vehicle front approximately 1/4 inch.
3. Release the cable, neutralizing the system, and pull cable forward again so release lever free movement is eliminated.
4. Rotate the adjusting nut until contact is made between index tab face and the housing, then index the tabs to engage the nearest housing groove.
5. Torque lock nut to 15 ft. lbs.

CLUTCH, REPLACE

1977—80 Bobcat & Pinto

1. Remove shift lever by removing knob and boot, then compress rubber spring and remove retaining snap ring. Bend shift lever lock tabs up and remove plastic dome nut from extension housing.
2. Raise vehicle on a hoist.
3. Disconnect drive shaft from U joint flange and slide drive shaft off transmission output shaft. Insert tool over output shaft to prevent loss of lubricant.
4. Disconnect speedometer cable and back-up light switch wire connector from extension housing.
5. Disconnect lower end of clutch cable at release lever.
6. Remove starter motor.
7. Remove bolts securing engine rear plate to front lower part of flywheel housing.
8. Support rear of engine using a suitable jack, then remove bolt attaching engine rear support. Also remove crossmember attaching bolts and remove the crossmember.
9. Remove bolts attaching flywheel housing to engine block.
10. Move transmission and flywheel housing assembly rearward until housing clears

the clutch pressure plate. Lower transmission and remove.
11. Unfasten and remove the pressure plate, marking same to assure correct assembly.

1977—78 Mustang & 1979—83 Capri & Mustang

NOTE: On 1981—83 Capri and Mustang, lift clutch pedal upward to disengage clutch cable self adjuster pawl and quadrant. Push quadrant forward, then detach cable from quadrant and allow quadrant to slowly swing rearward.

1. Loosen clutch cable adjusting nut to allow slack in cable.
2. Position gear shift lever in neutral, then remove the three lever attaching screws and remove lever.
3. Remove driveshaft then cover extension housing to prevent lubricant leakage.
4. Disconnect electrical leads and speedometer cable from transmission.
5. Support rear of engine and remove crossmember, then lower engine as necessary and remove transmission attaching bolts and transmission.
6. Disconnect clutch release cable from lever and flywheel housing.
7. Disconnect starter cable and remove starter motor.
8. On models with V6 engine, remove number 2A crossmember. This crossmember is located behind the number 2 crossmember which supports the engine.
9. On all models, remove flywheel housing.
10. Evenly loosen and remove pressure plate attaching screws to prevent distortion of pressure plate. If pressure plate is to be reused, mark pressure plate and flywheel to assure correct assembly.

4 & 5 SPEED TRANS., REPLACE

The transmission is removed as described under "Clutch Replace".

Rear Axle, Propeller Shaft & Brakes

REAR AXLE

Integral Type

This rear axle, Fig. 1, is an integral design hypoid with the centerline of the pinion set below the centerline of the ring gear. The semi-floating axle shafts are retained in the housing by ball bearings and bearing retainers at axle ends.

The differential is mounted on two opposed tapered roller bearings which are retained in the housing by removable caps. Differential bearing preload and drive gear backlash is adjusted by nuts located behind each differential bearing cup.

The drive pinion assembly is mounted on two opposed tapered roller bearings. Pinion bearing preload is adjusted by a collapsible spacer on the pinion shaft. Pinion and ring gear tooth contact is adjusted by shims between the rear bearing cone and pinion gear.

Removable Carrier Type

In these axles, Fig. 2, the drive pinion is straddle-mounted by two opposed tapered roller bearings which support the pinion shaft in front of the drive pinion gear, and a straight roller bearing that supports the pinion shaft at the rear of the pinion gear. The drive pinion is assembled in a pinion retainer that is bolted to the differential carrier. The tapered roller bearings are preloaded by a collapsible spacer between the bearings. The pinion is positioned by a shim or shims located between the drive pinion retainer and the differential carrier.

The differential is supported in the carrier by two tapered roller side bearings. These bearings are preloaded by two threaded ring nuts or sleeves between the bearings and the pedestals. The differential assembly is positioned for proper ring gear and pinion back-

lash by varying the adjustment of these ring nuts. The differential case houses two side gears in mesh with two pinions mounted on a pinion shaft which is held in place by a pin. The side gears and pinions are backed by thrust washers.

The axle shafts are of unequal length, the left shaft being shorter than the right. The axle shafts are mounted in sealed ball bearings which are pressed on the shafts.

Rear Axle, Replace

1. Raise vehicle and support at rear frame members.
2. Drain lubricant from axle.
3. Mark drive shaft and pinion flanges for reassembly, then disconnect drive shaft at rear axle U-joint and remove drive

Fig. 1 Disassembled integral rear axle (typical)

shaft from transmission extension housing. Install seal replacer tool in extension housing to prevent leakage.

4. Disconnect shock absorbers at lower mountings.
5. Remove rear wheels and brake drums, then disconnect brake lines at wheel cylinders.
6. Disconnect vent hose from vent tube, then remove vent tube from brake junction and axle housing.
7. Remove clips retaining brake lines to axle housing.
8. Support rear axle housing using a suitable jack.
9. On models with coil springs, disconnect upper control arms from mountings on axle housing, then carefully lower axle assembly until spring tension is relieved and remove coil springs. Disconnect lower control arms from axle housing.
10. On models with leaf springs, remove U-bolts and plates.
11. Lower rear axle and remove vehicle.
12. Reverse procedure to install.

AXLE SHAFT, BEARING & OIL SEAL

Integral Type

1. Remove wheel and tire from brake drum.
2. Remove Tinnerman nuts that secure brake drum to axle flange and remove brake drum.
3. Working through hole in each axle flange, remove nuts that secure wheel bearing retainer plate. Then pull the axle shaft assembly out of the housing being careful not to cut or rough up the seal.

NOTE: *The brake backing plate must not be dislodged. Replace one nut to hold the plate in place after shaft is removed.*

4. If wheel bearing is to be replaced, loosen inner retainer ring by nicking it deeply with a chisel in several places. It will then slide off.
5. Remove bearing from shaft.

Removable Carrier Type

1. Remove wheel assembly.
2. Remove brake drum from flange.
3. Working through hole provided in axle shaft flange, remove nuts that secure wheel bearing retainer.
4. Pull axle shaft out of housing. If bearing is a tight fit in axle housing use a slide hammer-type puller.
5. Remove brake backing plate.
6. If the axle shaft bearing is to be replaced, loosen the inner retainer by nicking it deeply with a chisel in several places. The bearing will then slide off easily.
7. Press bearing from axle shaft.
8. Inspect machined surface of axle shaft and housing for rough spots that would affect sealing action of the oil seal. Carefully remove any burrs or rough spots.
9. Press new inner bearing retainer on shaft until it seats firmly against shoulder on shaft.
10. Press inner bearing retainer on shaft until it seats firmly against bearing.
11. If oil seal is to be replaced, use a hook-type tool to pull it out of housing. Wipe a small amount of oil resistant sealer on

outer edge of seal before it is installed.

Installation

1. Place a new gasket on each side of brake carrier plate and slide axle shaft into housing. Start the splines into the differential side gear and push the shaft in until bearing bottoms in housing.
2. Install retainer and tighten nuts to 20–40 ft. lbs.
3. Install brake drum and wheel.

PROPELLER SHAFT

1. To maintain balance, mark relationship of rear drive shaft yoke and the drive pinion flange of the axle if alignment marks are not visible.
2. Disconnect rear U-joint from companion flange, Fig. 3. Wrap tape around loose bearing caps to prevent them from falling off spider. Pull drive shaft toward rear of car until slip yoke clears transmission extension housing and the seal. Install tool in extension housing to prevent lubricant leakage.

BRAKE ADJUSTMENTS

The hydraulic drum brakes, Fig. 4, are self-adjusting and require a manual adjustment only after brake shoes have been replaced. The adjustment is made as follows:

1. Using tool HRE 8650, Fig. 5, determine inside diameter of brake drum.
2. Reverse tool and adjust brake shoes to fit the gauge. Hold automatic adjusting lever out of engagement while rotating adjusting screw, to prevent burring slots in screw.

Fig. 2 Disassembled rear axle with removable carrier (typical)

Fig. 3 Drive shaft and universal joints disassembled

Fig. 5 Brake adjustment

Fig. 6 Parking brake adjustment

PARKING BRAKE, ADJUST

1. Release parking brake.
2. Place transmission in Neutral and raise vehicle until rear wheels clear floor.
3. Tighten adjusting nut on equalizer rod at the control, Fig. 6, to cause the rear wheel brakes to drag.
4. Loosen adjusting nut until rear brakes are just free.

MASTER CYLINDER, REPLACE

Exc. Power Brakes

1. Disconnect stoplight switch wires at connector. Remove spring retainer and slide stop light switch off brake pedal pin just far enough to clear end of pin, then lift switch straight upward from the pin.
2. Slide master cylinder push rod and nylon washers and bushings off brake pedal pin.
3. Remove brake tubes from master cylinder ports.
4. Unfasten and remove master cylinder by lifting forward and upward from vehicle.

Power Brakes

Disconnect brake tubes from master cylinder, then remove attaching nuts and slide master cylinder forward and upward from vehicle.

POWER BRAKE UNIT, REPLACE

1. Remove stoplight switch and slide booster push rod, bushing and inner nylon washer from brake pedal pin.
2. Remove air cleaner.
3. On all except Capri and Mustang with

Fig. 4 Self-adjusting rear brake assembly.

with V8 engine, disconnect accelerator cable from carburetor. Remove screws securing accelerator cable bracket to engine and rotate bracket toward engine. On models with 4-140 engine, disconnect inlet hose of choke water cover and position aside.
4. On Bobcat and Pinto, disconnect vacuum hoses from solenoid on fender apron, then remove the solenoid.
5. On 1976–78 Mustang with 4-140 or V6-171 engines, disconnect vacuum hose from EGR vacuum reservoir.
6. On all models, disconnect vacuum hose from power brake unit.
7. Disconnect hydraulic lines from master cylinder and cap open lines and ports.
8. Remove master cylinder.
9. From inside vehicle, remove power brake unit to dash panel attaching nuts.
10. From engine compartment, pull power brake unit forward until push rod clears panel, raise front of unit and remove from vehicle.

Rear Suspension

SHOCK ABSORBER, REPLACE

1979–83 Capri & Mustang

NOTE: On hatchback models, the upper shock absorber upper mounting is accessible from the luggage compartment. On hatchback and fastback models, remove side panel trim covers to gain access to the upper shock absorber mounting.

1. Disconnect shock absorber from upper mounting.
2. Raise vehicle and support rear axle.
3. Compress shock absorber to clear hole in upper shock absorber tower.
4. Disconnect shock absorber from lower mounting and remove shock absorber from vehicle.

1977–78 Mustang & 1977–80 Bobcat & Pinto

1. With rear axle supported properly disconnect shock absorber from lower mounting.
2. Remove bolts securing upper mounting bracket to underbody.
3. Remove bracket from shock absorber.
4. Reverse procedure to install.

LEAF SPRINGS & BUSHINGS, REPLACE

1977–78 Mustang & 1977–80 Bobcat & Pinto

1. Raise rear of vehicle and support at frame. Support axle with a suitable jack.

2. Disconnect shock absorbers from lower mountings.
3. Lower jack and remove spring plate "U" bolts and spring plate, Fig. 1.
4. Raise axle to remove weight from spring and disassemble rear shackle.
5. Remove spring front mount bolt.
6. Replace spring front eye bushing as necessary, Figs. 2 and 3.
7. Reverse procedure to install.

COIL SPRING, REPLACE

1979–83 Capri & Mustang

1. Raise rear of vehicle and support at rear body crossmember.
2. Remove stabilizer bar, if equipped.
3. Lower axle housing until shock absorbers are fully extended.

er control arm pivot bolt to 70 to 100 ft. lbs. on 1979–80 models, 90 to 100 ft. lbs. on 1981–83 models with suspension at curb height.

CONTROL ARMS & BUSHINGS, REPLACE

1979–83 Capri & Mustang

Upper Control Arm
1. Raise rear of vehicle and support at rear body crossmember.
2. Remove upper control arm rear and front pivot bolts, then remove control arm.
3. If control arm axle bracket bushings are to be replaced, refer to Figs. 5 and 6.
4. Position upper control arm into side rail bracket, then install front pivot bolt. Do not tighten bolt at this time.
5. Raise rear axle until upper control arm rear pivot bolt hole is aligned with hole in axle housing, then install rear pivot bolt. Do not tighten bolt at this time.
6. Position suspension at curb height, then torque control arm pivot bolts to 70 to 100 ft. lbs.

Lower Control Arms
1. Remove coil spring as described under Coil Spring, Replace.
2. Remove lower control arm front pivot bolt and nut, then remove control arm.
3. Reverse procedure to install. Torque front and rear pivot bolts to 70 to 100 ft. lbs. with suspension at curb height.

STABILIZER BAR, REPLACE

1979–83 Capri & Mustang

1. Raise and support rear of vehicle.
2. Remove four bolts attaching stabilizer bar to brackets on lower control arms.
3. Remove stabilizer bar from vehicle.

Fig. 1 Leaf spring rear suspension. 1977–78 Mustang & 1977–80 Bobcat & Pinto

NOTE: The axle housing must be supported with a suitable jack.

4. Position a suitable jack under lower control arm rear pivot bolt to support control arm, then remove pivot bolt.
5. Carefully lower the lower control arm until spring tension is relieved, then remove coil spring and insulator.
6. Reverse procedure to install. Torque low-

Fig. 4 Coil spring rear suspension. 1979–83 Capri & Mustang

Fig. 2 Spring, front bushing removal. 1977–78 Mustang & 1977–80 Bobcat & Pinto

Fig. 3 Spring, front bushing installation. 1977–78 Mustang & 1977–80 Bobcat & Pinto

Fig. 5 Upper control arm axle bracket bushing removal. 1979–83 Capri & Mustang

Fig. 6 Upper control arm axle bracket bushing installation. 1979–83 Capri & Mustang

Front Suspension & Steering Section

FRONT SUSPENSION

1979–83 Capri & Mustang

The front suspension is of the modified McPherson strut design, which uses shock struts and coil springs. The springs are mounted between the lower control and a spring pocket in the crossmember.

1977–78 Mustang & 1977–80 Bobcat & Pinto

The upper and lower ends of the spindle are attached to upper and lower ball joints which are mounted in upper and lower arms. The upper arm pivots on a bushing and shaft assembly which is bolted to the frame. The lower arm pivots on a bolt in the front crossmember, Fig. 2.

WHEEL ALIGNMENT

1979–83 Capri & Mustang

Caster & Camber
The caster and camber angles of this suspension are factory pre-set and can not be adjusted.

1977–78 Mustang & 1977–80 Bobcat & Pinto

Caster and Camber
1. Working inside front wheel housing, install special tool, one at each end of the upper arm inner shaft. Turn the special tool bolts inward until the bolt ends contact the body metal, Fig. 3.
2. Loosen the two upper arm inner shaft-to-body bolts. The upper shaft will move inboard until stopped by the tool bolt ends solidly contacting the body metal.
3. Turn the special tool bolts inward or outward until caster and camber are within specifications. Tightening these bolts on the special tool forces the arm outward; while loosening the bolts on the tools permits the arm and inner shaft to move inboard due to weight force.
4. When properly adjusted, torque shaft-to-body bolts to 95–120 ft. lbs., then remove the special tools.

TOE-IN, ADJUST

1. Check to see that steering shaft and steering wheel marks are in alignment and in the top position.
2. Loosen clamp screw on the tie rod bellows and free the seal on the rod to prevent twisting of the bellows, Fig. 4.
3. Loosen tie rod jam nut.
4. Use suitable pliers to turn the tie rod inner end to correct the adjustment to specifications. Do not use pliers on tie rod threads. Turning to reduce number of threads showing will increase toe-in. Turning in the opposite direction will reduce toe-in. On 1977–81 models, torque tie rod jam nuts to 35–50 ft. lbs. On 1982–83 models, torque to 43–50 ft. lbs.

WHEEL BEARINGS, ADJUST

1. Raise vehicle until wheel and tire clear

380335-S

38391
2 REQ'D.

N800237-S100
4 REQ'D.
150-220 FT-LBS (203-298 N·m)

N620483-S2
6 REQ'D.
50-75 FT-LBS (68-102 N·m)

N605919-S2
6 REQ'D.
35-50 FT-LBS (47-88 N·m)

N620467-S7
2 REQ'D.
6-12 FT-LBS (8-16 N·m)

APRON REF.

5415
2 REQ'D.

N800235-S100
4 REQ'D.

N800202-S2
4 REQ'D.
14-26 FT-LBS (19-35 N·m)

N800236-S100
4 REQ'D.
120-180 FT-LBS (163-244 N·m)

N800241-S
2 REQ'D.

5D485 L.H.
5C495 R.H.

18A084
2 REQ'D.

5310
2 REQ'D.

5482

5486
2 REQ'D.

N800234-S100
4 REQ'D.

5414
2 REQ'D.

N088201-S2
2 REQ'D.

12045-S
2 REQ'D.

3106 L.H.
3105 R.H.

VIEW Z

381612-S100 REF.
2 REQ'D.
80-120 FT-LBS (108-163 N·m)

3051 L.H.
3042 R.H.

KC-55490-A
8 REQ'D.

37110-S2
8 REQ'D.

VIEW Z

N800200-S2
2 REQ'D.

Fig. 1 Front suspension assembly. 1979–83 Capri & Mustang

floor.
2. Remove wheel cover and dust cap from hub.
3. Remove cotter pin and lock nut.
4. While rotating wheel assembly, torque the adjusting nut to 17–25 ft. lbs. to seat the bearings.
5. Back off the adjusting nut one half turn. Retighten the nut to 10–15 in. lbs. with a torque wrench or finger tight.
6. Locate the nut lock on the adjusting nut so the castellations on the lock are aligned with the cotter pin hole in the spindle.
7. Install new cotter pin and replace dust cap and wheel cover.

WHEEL BEARINGS, REPLACE

(Disc Brakes)
1979–83 Capri & Mustang

1. Raise vehicle and remove front wheels.
2. Remove caliper mounting bolts.

NOTE: It is not necessary to disconnect the brake lines for this operation.

3. Slide caliper off of disc, inserting a clean spacer between the shoes to hold them in their bores after the caliper is removed. Position caliper out of the way.

NOTE: Do not allow caliper to hang by

brake hose.

4. Remove hub and disc assembly. Grease retainer and inner bearing can now be removed.
5. Reverse procedure to install.

1977–78 Mustang & 1977–80 Bobcat & Pinto

1. Raise car and remove front wheels.
2. Use a 3/4" wrench to loosen the large bolt at top of caliper assembly and washer at the front of the caliper. Loosen it until it can be turned with the fingers.
3. Remove the smaller bolt at bottom of caliper with a 5/8" wrench.
4. Insert a strong piece of wire carefully through the upper opening in the caliper and fasten it. Position the free end of the wire over the suspension upper arm.
5. When removing caliper from disc the brake pads must be held apart. Do this by inserting a piece of wood or cardboard. While holding the caliper, remove the large bolt in front. Now carefully slide the caliper back and slightly upward to remove it. While doing this, insert the wood or cardboard between the brake pads.
6. Carefully move caliper back to suspension upper arm and fasten loose end of wire so caliper will not drop.
7. Dust cap can now be removed from hub. Remove nut lock, etc. and rock disc to ease out washer and outer bearing. Disc can now be removed to service grease seal

or inner bearing.

CHECKING BALL JOINTS FOR WEAR

Upper Ball Joint
1977–78 Mustang & 1977–80 Bobcat & Pinto

1. Raise car and place floor jacks beneath lower arms.
2. Grasp lower edge of tire and move wheel in and out.
3. As the wheel is being moved, notice any movement between the upper end of the spindle and the upper arm. If movement is present, replace the ball joint.

Lower Ball Joint
1979–83 Capri & Mustang

Support vehicle in normal driving position with both ball joints loaded. Clean area around grease fitting and checking surface. The checking surface is the round boss into which the grease fitting is installed. The checking surface should project outside the ball joint cover, Fig. 5. If checking surface is inside the cover replace the lower control arm assembly.

1977–78 Mustang & 1977–80 Bobcat & Pinto

1. Raise vehicle and place jacks under lower arms as shown in Fig. 6.
2. Be sure wheel bearings are properly ad-

Fig. 2 Front suspension assembly (typical). 1977–78 Mustang & 1977–80 Bobcat & Pinto

Fig. 3 Caster and camber adjustment. 1977–78 Mustang & 1977–80 Bobcat & Pinto

justed.
3. Attach a dial indicator to lower arm and position indicator so that plunger rests against inner side of wheel rim near lower ball joint.
4. Grasp tire at top and bottom and slowly move tire in and out. If the reading exceeds .250", replace the joint.

SHOCK STRUT, REPLACE

1979–83 Capri & Mustang

1. Place ignition switch in the unlocked position.
2. From engine compartment, remove upper shock absorber mounting nut.
3. Raise front of vehicle and support lower control arms. Position safety stands under frame jacking pads located rearward of wheels.
4. Remove wheel and tire assembly.
5. Remove caliper, rotor and dust shield.
6. Remove two bolts attaching shock absorber to spindle.
7. Lift strut upward from spindle to compress rod, then pull downward and remove shock absorber.
8. Reverse procedure to install. Torque upper mounting nut to 60 to 75 ft. lbs. Torque lower mounting nuts to 150 to 180 ft. lbs.

SHOCK ABSORBER, REPLACE

1977–78 Mustang & 1977–80 Bobcat & Pinto

1. Disconnect upper end of the shock.
2. Raise vehicle and install safety stands.
3. Disconnect lower end of shock. It may be necessary to use a pry bar to free "T" shaped end of the shock from the lower end.
4. Reverse procedure to install. Torque shock absorber to lower arm nut to 70 ft. lbs. and shock absorber upper attachment to 26 ft. lbs.

COIL SPRING, REPLACE

1979–83 Capri & Mustang

1. Raise front of vehicle and place safety stands under jack pads located rearward of wheels, then remove wheel and tire assembly.
2. Disconnect stabilizer bar link from lower control arm.
3. Remove steering gear attaching bolts and position gear out of way.
4. Using tool 3290-C, disconnect tie rod from spindle.
5. Install spring compressor D78P-5310-A and compress coil spring until it is free of the spring seat.

Fig. 4 Toe-in adjustment (typical)

Fig. 5 Checking lower ball joint for wear. 1979–83 Capri & Mustang

MAXIMUM TOLERANCE

Fig. 6   Measuring lower ball joint play

Fig. 7   Steering gear installation (typical)

NOTE: Ensure spring compressor is properly installed before compressing spring. Also ensure spring is sufficiently compressed to permit removal of lower control arm pivot bolts.

6. Remove two lower control arm pivot bolts, then disengage lower control arm and remove spring assembly, Fig. 1.

NOTE: Measure compressed length of spring and amount of curvature to aid in compressing and installing spring.

7. Reverse procedure to install. Ensure lower spring end is positioned between two holes in lower control arm spring pocket. Torque stabilizer bar to lower arm to 9 ft. lbs., steering gear to No. 2 crossmember to 95 ft. lbs. and tie rod to spindle to 40 ft. lbs.

1977–78 Mustang & 1977–80 Bobcat & Pinto

1. Raise vehicle and support front end with safety stands.
2. Place a jack under lower arm to support it.
3. Disconnect lower end of shock.
4. Remove bolts that attach strut to lower arm.
5. Remove nut that retains shock to crossmember and remove the shock.
6. Remove nut and bolt that secures inner end of lower arm to crossmember.
7. Carefully lower jack to relieve pressure from spring and remove spring.
8. Reverse procedure to install. Torque shock to lower arm nut to 70 ft. lbs., strut to lower arm bolts to 40–60 ft. lbs., shock to crossmember nut to 22–30 ft. lbs. and lower arm to crossmember to 40–60 ft. lbs.

BALL JOINTS, REPLACE

1979–83 Capri & Mustang

On these models, the lower ball joint and lower control arm must be replaced as an assembly.

1977–78 Mustang & 1977–80 Bobcat & Pinto

NOTE: Ford Motor Company recommends

that new ball joints should not be installed on used control arms and that the control arm be replaced if ball joint replacement is required. However, aftermarket ball joint repair kits which do not require control arm replacement, are available and can be installed using the following procedure.

The ball joints are riveted to the control arms. The ball joints can be replaced on the car by removing the rivets and replacing them with new attaching bolts, nuts and washers furnished with the kit.

When removing a ball joint, use a suitable pressing tool to force the ball joint out of the spindle.

STEERING GEAR, REPLACE

1979–83 Capri & Mustang

1. Disconnect battery ground cable.
2. Remove bolt attaching flexible coupling to input shaft.
3. Place ignition switch in the On position, then raise and support front of vehicle.
4. Remove cotter pins and nuts from tie rod ends, then using a suitable tool separate tie rods from spindle arms, Fig. 7.
5. Support steering gear, then remove two nuts, bolts and washers attaching steering gear to crossmember. On power steering gears, lower gear slightly and disconnect pressure and return lines. Cap lines and fittings to prevent entry of dirt.
6. Remove steering gear from vehicle.
7. Reverse procedure to install. Torque flexible coupling to input shaft bolt to 20–30 ft. lbs., tie rod to spindle arm nuts to 35–47 ft. lbs. and steering gear to crossmember bolts to 80–100 ft. lbs. Torque pressure line fitting at gear housing to 10–15 ft. lbs.

1977–78 Mustang, 1977–80 Bobcat & Pinto

Manual Steering Gear
1. Disconnect battery ground cable, turn ignition "On" and raise vehicle.
2. Remove tie rod end retaining nuts and using ball joint separator (tool 329OC), separate tie rod ends from spindle arms, Fig. 7.
3. Remove pinion shaft to flexible coupling bolt and the bolts securing steering gear to crossmember.

NOTE: On 1977–78 Mustang, the number 2A crossmember, located behind the front crossmember, must be removed to permit steering gear removal.

4. Turn front wheels, then remove steering gear from left side of vehicle.

Power Steering Gear
1. Disconnect battery ground cable.
2. Remove bolt retaining flexible coupling to input shaft.
3. Turn ignition key "On" and raise vehicle.
4. Remove the two tie rod end retaining nuts, then separate studs from spindle arms, using a suitable tool.
5. On Mustang models, remove the number 2A crossmember located behind the front crossmember to allow removal of steering gear retaining bolts.
6. Support gear and remove attaching bolts, then lower gear enough to gain access to pressure and return lines, and remove bolt attaching the hose bracket to the gear.
7. Disconnect pressure and return lines and remove steering gear. Plug lines and ports to prevent entry of dirt.

POWER STEERING PUMP, REPLACE

1978–83

1. Disconnect return hose from power steering pump reservoir and allow fluid to drain into a suitable container.
2. Disconnect pressure hose from power steering pump fitting, then remove pump mounting bracket and disconnect drive belt from pulley.
3. On 2.3L, 3.8L and 5.0L which incorporate a fixed pump system, remove the belt from the pulley, and remove the pulley.
4. On all models, remove power steering pump.
5. Reverse procedure to install. Torque pump to mounting bracket bolts to 30–45 ft. lbs. and pressure hose to pump tube nut to 12–15 ft. lbs.

NOTE: End play of pressure hose to pump fitting is normal and does not indicate a loose fitting. Do not overtorque.

1977

1. Disconnect return line from power steering pump reservoir, and allow fluid to drain into a suitable container.
2. Disconnect pressure line from power steering pump.
3. Remove bolts attaching pump to front of mounting bracket. On 8 cylinder models, also remove nut attaching pump to rear of bracket.
4. Disconnect drive belt from pulley, then remove power steering pump.
5. Reverse procedure to install. Torque pressure hose to pump nut to 32 ft. lbs., pump to bracket front bolts to 30–45 ft. lbs., pump to bracket rear nut to 20–30 ft. lbs. and return hose to pump clamp to 12–24 in. lbs.

LINCOLN

INDEX OF SERVICE OPERATIONS

NOTE: Refer to the back of this manual for vehicle manufacturer's special service tool suppliers.

SERIAL & ENGINE NUMBER LOCATION

Vehicle Warranty Plate on Left Front Door Pillar

GRILLE IDENTIFICATION

1977–79 Continental

1977–79 Mark V

1977–80 Versailles

1980 Continental

1980–82 Mark VI

1980–82 Mark VI
w/Auxiliary Lamps

1981 Continental &
1982 Lincoln Town Car

1982–83 Lincoln Continental

1983 Mark VI

GENERAL ENGINE SPECIFICATIONS

Year	Engine C.I.D./Liter[1]	V.I.N. CODE[2]	Carburetor	Bore and Stroke	Compression Ratio	Net H.P. @ R.P.M.[3]	Maximum Torque Ft. Lbs. @ R.P.M.	Normal Oil Pressure Pounds
1977	V8-302, 5.0L	F	2150, 2 Bbl.[4]	4.00 × 3.00	8.1	122 @ 3400	222 @ 1400	40–60
	V8-351W, 5.8L	H	2150, 2 Bbl.[4]	4.00 × 3.50	8.1	135 @ 3200	275 @ 1600	45–65
	V8-400, 6.6L[5]	S	2150, 2 Bbl.[4]	4.00 × 4.00	8.0	179 @ 4000	329 @ 1600	45–75
	V8-400, 6.6L[6]	S	2150, 2 Bbl.[4]	4.00 × 4.00	8.0	181 @ 4000	331 @ 1600	45–75
	V8-460, 7.5L	A	4350, 4 Bbl.[4]	4.362 × 3.850	8.0	208 @ 4000	356 @ 2000	35–65
1978	V8-302, 5.0L	F	2150, 2 Bbl.[4]	4.00 × 3.00	8.1	133 @ 3600	243 @ 1600	40–60
	V8-400, 6.6L	S	2150, 2 Bbl.[4]	4.00 × 4.00	8.0	166 @ 3800	319 @ 1800	50–75
	V8-460, 7.5L	A	4350, 4 Bbl.[4]	4.362 × 3.850	8.0	210 @ 4200	357 @ 2200	35–65
1979	V8-302, 5.0L[5]	F	2150, 2 Bbl.[4]	4.00 × 3.00	8.4	130 @ 3600	237 @ 1600	40–65
	V8-302, 5.0L[6]	F	2150, 2 Bbl.[4]	4.00 × 3.00	8.4	133 @ 3600	236 @ 1400	40–65
	V8-400, 6.6L	S	2150, 2 Bbl.[4]	4.00 × 4.00	8.0	159 @ 3400	315 @ 1800	50–75
1980	V8-302, 5.0L	F	2150, 2 Bbl.[4]	4.00 × 3.00	8.4	132 @ 3600	232 @ 1400	40–60
	V8-302, 5.0L	F	[7]	4.00 × 3.00	8.4	129 @ 3600	231 @ 2000	40–60
	V8-351W, 5.8L	G	7200VV, 2 Bbl.[4]	4.00 × 3.50	8.3	140 @ 3400	265 @ 2000	40–60
1981	V8-302, 5.0L	F	[7]	4.00 × 3.00	8.4	130 @ 3400	230 @ 2000	40–60
1982	V6-232, 3.8L[5]	3	2150, 2 Bbl.[4]	3.81 × 3.39	8.8	112 @ 4000	175 @ 2600	54–59
	V6-232, 3.8L[6]	3	7200VV, 2 Bbl.[4]	3.81 × 3.39	8.8	118 @ 4000	186 @ 2600	54–59

GENERAL ENGINE SPECIFICATIONS—Continued

Year	Engine C.I.D./Liter①	Engine V.I.N. CODE②	Carburetor	Bore and Stroke	Compression Ratio	Net H.P. @ R.P.M.③	Maximum Torque Ft. Lbs. @ R.P.M.	Normal Oil Pressure Pounds
	V8-302, 5.0L⑤	F	2150, 2 Bbl.④	4.00 × 3.00	8.4	—		40–60
	V8-302, 5.0L⑥	F	7200VV, 2 Bbl.④	4.00 × 3.00	8.4	131 @ 3400	229 @ 1200	40–60
	V8-302, 5.0L	F	⑦	4.00 × 3.00	8.4	134 @ 3400	232 @ 3200	40–60
1983	V8-302, 5.0L	F	⑦	4.00 × 3.00	—	—	—	40–60

①—C.I.D.—cubic inch displacement.
②—On 1977–80 vehicles the fifth digit in the VIN denotes engine code. On 1981–83 vehicles the eighth digit denotes engine code.
③—Ratings are net—as installed in vehicle.
④—Motorcraft.
⑤—Exc. Calif.
⑥—Calif.
⑦—Electronic Fuel Injection.

TUNE UP SPECIFICATIONS

The following specifications are published from the latest information available. This data should be used only in the absence of a decal affixed in the engine compartment.

★ When using a timing light, disconnect vacuum hose or tube at distributor and plug opening in hose or tube so idle speed will not be affected.

● When checking compression, lowest cylinder must be within 75 percent of highest.

▲ Before removing wires from distributor cap, determine location of No. 1 wire in cap, as distributor position may have been altered from that shown at the end of this chart.

☞ Spark plug types shown in this chart are recommendations of the original vehicle manufacturer and not MOTOR.

Check local sources for other spark plug manufacturers listings.

Year & Engine/V.I.N.	Spark Plug Type ☞	Spark Plug Gap	Firing Order Fig. ▲	Ignition Timing BTDC①★ Man. Trans.	Ignition Timing BTDC①★ Auto. Trans.	Mark Fig.	Curb Idle Speed② Man. Trans.	Curb Idle Speed② Auto. Trans.	Fast Idle Speed Man. Trans.	Fast Idle Speed Auto. Trans.	Fuel Pump Pressure
1977											
V8-302/F Calif.	ARF-52	.050	D	—	12°	B	—	700D	—	—	6–8
V8-302/F High Alt.	ARF-52	.050	D	—	12°	B	—	500/650D	—	2000④	6–8
V8-351W/H⑤	ARF-52	.050	E	—	4°	B	—	625D	—	2100④	6–8
V8-400/S Calif.	ARF-52-6	.060	E	—	6°	B	—	500/600D	—	1350③	6–8
V8-460/A Exc. Calif. & High Alt.⑥⑦	ARF-52	.050	D	—	16°	B	—	525/650D	—	1350③	5.7–7.7
V8-460/A Exc. Calif. & High Alt.⑥⑧	ARF-52	.050	D	—	10°	B	—	⑨	—	1350③	5.7–7.7
V8-460/A High Alt.	ARF-52	.050	D	—	18°	B	—	500/600D	—	1350③	5.7–7.7
1978											
V8-302/F⑩	ARF-52	.050	⑪	—	30°⑫	B	—	625D	—	1900④	6–8
V8-400/S Exc. Calif. & High Alt.	ASF-52	.050	E	—	13°	B	—	575/650D⑬	—	1350③	6–8
V8-400/S Calif.	ASF-52	.050	E	—	16°	B	—	600/650D⑬	—	2300④	6–8
V8-400/S High Alt.	ASF-52	.050	E	—	8°	B	—	650D	—	2100④	6–8
V8-460/A Exc. Calif. & High Alt.⑥⑭	ARF-52	.050	D	—	16°	B	—	580/650D⑬	—	1350③	5.7–7.7
V8-460/A Exc. Calif. & High Alt.⑥⑮	ARF-52	.050	D	—	10°	B	—	580/650D⑬	—	1350③	5.7–7.7
1979											
V8-302/F Exc. Calif.⑩	⑯	.050	⑪	—	30°⑫	B	—	625D	—	1900④	6–8
V8-302/F Calif.⑩	⑯	.050	⑪	—	15°⑫	B	—	625D	—	2100④	6–8
V8-400/S Exc. Calif.	⑯	.050	E	—	14°	B	—	600/675D	—	2200④	6–8
V8-400/S Calif.⑥⑱	⑲	.060	E	—	14°	B	—	600/650D	—	2200④	6–8
V8-400/S Calif.⑥⑳	⑯	.050	E	—	16°	B	—	600/650D	—	2300④	6–8

Continued

TUNE UP SPECIFICATIONS—Continued

The following specifications are published from the latest information available. This data should be used only in the absence of a decal affixed in the engine compartment.

★ When using a timing light, disconnect vacuum hose or tube at distributor and plug opening in hose or tube so idle speed will not be affected.

● When checking compression, lowest cylinder must be within 75 percent of highest.

▲ Before removing wires from distributor cap, determine location of No. 1 wire in cap, as distributor position may have been altered from that shown at the end of this chart.

🖑 Spark plug types shown in this chart are recommendations of the original vehicle manufacturer and not MOTOR.

Check local sources for other spark plug manufacturers listings.

Year & Engine/V.I.N.	Spark Plug Type 🖑	Gap	Ignition Timing BTDC①★ Firing Order Fig. ▲	Man. Trans.	Auto. Trans.	Mark Fig.	Curb Idle Speed② Man. Trans.	Auto. Trans.	Fast Idle Speed Man. Trans.	Auto. Trans.	Fuel Pump Pressure
1980											
V8-302/F Versailles Exc. High Alt.	ASF-52	.050	⑪	—	6°	B	—	550D	—	④⑦㉒	6–8
V8-302/F Versailles High Alt.	ASF-52	.050	⑪	—	8°	B	—	550D	—	2100④	6–8
V8-302/F E.F.I. Exc. Versailles	ASF-52	.050	⑪	—	⑰	B	—	550D	—	2100㉓	—
V8-351W/G⑤⑩	ASF-52	.050	⑪	—	—	B	—	550/640D	—	1650㉑	6–8
1981											
V8-302/F E.F.I. Exc. Calif.	ASF-52	.050	⑪	—	⑰	B	—	550D	—	2200㉑	—
V8-302/F E.F.I. Calif.	ASF-52	.050	⑪	—	⑰	B	—	550D	—	2150㉑	—
1982											
V6-232/3 Exc. Calif.	AGSP-52	.044	A	—	12°	F	—	550/650D	—	2200④	6–8
V6-232/3 Calif.	AGSP-52	.044	A	—	12°	F	—	550/650D	—	2200③	6–8
V8-302/F Exc. Calif.	ASF-52	.050	D	—	12°	B	—	550D	—	1700③	6–8
V8-302/F High Alt.	ASF-52	.050	D	—	12°	B	—	550D	—	1700③	6–8
V8-302/F Calif.	ASF-52	.050	⑪	—	—	B	—	550D	—	—	6–8
V8-302/F E.F.I. Exc. Calif.	ASF-52	.050	⑪	—	⑰	B	—	550D	—	2200㉓	—
V8-302/F E.F.I. Calif.	ASF-52	.050	⑪	—	⑰	B	—	550D	—	2150㉓	—
1983											
V8-302/F E.F.I.	ASF-52	.050	⑪	—	⑰	B	—	—	—	—	—

①—B.T.D.C.—Before top dead center.
②—Idle speed on manual trans. vehicles is adjusted in Neutral & on auto. trans. equipped vehicles is adjusted in Drive unless otherwise specified. Where two idle speeds are listed, the higher speed is with the A/C or throttle solenoid energized. On models equipped with vacuum release brake, whenever adjusting ignition timing or idle speed, vacuum line to brake release mechanism must be disconnected & plugged to prevent parking brake from releasing when selector is moved to Drive.
③—On kickdown step of cam.
④—On high step of fast cam.
⑤—Windsor engine.
⑥—Refer to engine calibration code on engine

identification label, located at rear of left valve cover. The calibration code is located on the label after the engine code number and is preceded by the letter C and the revision code is located below the calibration code and is preceded by the letter R.
⑦—Calibration codes 7-19A-R1 & 7-19A-R17.
⑧—Calibration codes 7-19A-R2 & 7-19A-R3.
⑨—Calibration code 7-19A-R2, 525/650D RPM 7-19A-R3, 550/650D RPM.
⑩—Models equipped with Electronic Engine Control (EEC) System.
⑪—Firing order for V8-302, 1-5-4-2-6-3-7-8. Firing order for V8-351W, 1-3-7-2-6-5-4-8. Cylinder numbering (front to rear): Right bank 1-2-3-4, left bank 5-6-7-8. Refer to Fig. C for spark plug wire connections at distributor.

⑫—At 625 RPM. Ignition timing is not adjustable.
⑬—With throttle solenoid energized. Higher idle speed is with A/C on, compressor clutch de-energized, if equipped.
⑭—Calibration code 8-19A-R1.
⑮—Calibration codes 8-19B-R11 & 8-19B-R14
⑯—ASF-52 or ARF-52.
⑰—Ignition timing is not adjustable.
⑱—Calibration code 9-17P-R0A.
⑲—ASF-52 or ARF-52-6.
⑳—Calibration code 9-17Q-R0.
㉑—On 2nd highest step of fast idle cam.
㉒—Calibration code 0-11E-R0, 2100 RPM; calibration code 0-11E-R13, 2200 RPM.
㉓—On 1st step of idle cam.

TUNE UP NOTES—Continued

FIRING ORDER · 1 · 4 · 2 · 5 · 3 · 6

Fig. A

Fig. B

Fig. C

FIRING ORDER 1-5-4-2-6-3-7-8

Fig. D

FIRING ORDER 1-3-7-2-6-5-4-8

Fig. E

Fig. F

VALVE SPECIFICATIONS

Year	Engine Model/V.I.N.	Valve Lash ① Int.	Valve Lash ① Exh.	Valve Angles Seat	Valve Angles Face	Valve Spring Installed Height	Valve Spring Pressure Lbs. @ In.	Stem Clearance Intake	Stem Clearance Exhaust	Stem Diameter Intake	Stem Diameter Exhaust
1977	V8-302/F	.096–.168		45	44	③	⑤	.0010–.0027	.0015–.0032	.3416–.3423	.3411–.3418
	V8-351W/H	.096–.168		45	44	④	⑤	.0010–.0027	.0015–.0032	.3416–.3423	.3411–.3418
	V8-400/S	.100–.200		45	44	1¹³⁄₁₆	226 @ 1.39	.0010–.0027	.0015–.0032	.3416–.3423	.3411–.3418
	V8-460/A	.075–.175		45	44	1¹³⁄₁₆	②	.0010–.0027	.0010–.0027	.3416–.3423	.3416–.3423
1978–79	V8-302/F	.096–.168		45	44	③	⑤	.0010–.0027	.0015–.0032	.3416–.3423	.3411–.3418
	V8-400/S	.125–.175		45	44	1⁵³⁄₆₄	226 @ 1.39	.0010–.0027	.0015–.0032	.3416–.3423	.3411–.3418
	V8-460/A	.100–.150		45	44	1¹³⁄₁₆	229 @ 1.33	.0010–.0027	.0010–.0027	.3416–.3423	.3416–.3423
1980	V8-302/F	.096–.163		45	44	③	⑥	.001–.0027	.0015–.0032	.3416–.3423	.3411–.3418
	V8-351W/G	.096–.163		45	44	④	⑥	.001–.0027	.0015–.0032	.3416–.3423	.3411–.3418
1981	V8-302/F	.096–.146		45	44	③	⑥	.001–.0027	.0015–.0032	.3416–.3423	.3411–.3418
1982	V6-232/3	.088–.189		45	44	1¾	215 @ 1.40	.001–.0027	.0015–.0032	.3416–.3423	.3411–.3418
	V8-302/F	.096–.146		45	44	③	⑦	.001–.0027	.0015–.0032	.3416–.3423	.3411–.3418
1983	V8-302/F	.096–.146		45	44	⑧	⑨	.001–.0027	.0015–.0032	.3416–.3423	.3411–.3418

①—Clearance is obtained at valve stem tip with hydraulic lifter collapsed. If clearance is less than minimum, install an undersize push rod; if clearance is greater than maximum, install an oversize push rod.

②—Intake, 229 @ 1.33; exhaust, 253 @ 1.33.
③—Intake, 1¹¹⁄₁₆; exhaust, 1¹⁹⁄₃₂.
④—Intake, 1⁵¹⁄₆₄; exhaust, 1³⁹⁄₆₄.
⑤—Intake, 190–210 @ 1.31; exhaust, 190–210 @ 1.20.

⑥—Intake, 204 @ 1.36; exhaust, 200 @ 1.20.
⑦—Intake, 186–214 @ 1.36; exhaust, 195–215 @ 1.15.
⑧—Intake, 1⁴³⁄₆₄–1⁴⁵⁄₆₄; exhaust, 1³⁷⁄₆₄–1³⁹⁄₆₄.
⑨—Intake, 196–214 @ 1.36; exhaust, 195–215 @ 1.05.

DISTRIBUTOR SPECIFICATIONS

★ Note: If unit is checked on vehicle, double the RPM and degrees to get crankshaft figures.

Distributor Ident. No.①	Centrifugal Advance Degrees @ RPM of Distributor				Vacuum Advance		Distributor Retard
	Advance Starts	Intermediate Advance		Full Advance	Inches of Vacuum to Start Plunger	Max. Adv. Dist. Deg. @ Vacuum	Max. Retard Dist. Deg. @ Vacuum
1977							
D6AE-AA	0–2 @ 500	4–6 @ 700	7¼–9½ @ 1500	14 @ 2500	3	15¼ @ 11½	—
D6VE-CA	0–1 @ 450	7½–9½ @ 725	—	14 @ 2500	3.5	13¼ @ 15	—
D7AE-DA	0–1 @ 450	3¾–5¾ @ 675	—	14 @ 2500	3.2	15¼ @ 14½	—
D7DE-FA	−1 to +1½ @ 450	1¾–4½ @ 550	—	13¾ @ 2500	4.5	15¼ @ 12½	—
D7DE-GA	0–1 @ 525	2¼–4¼ @ 700	—	7¼ @ 2500	3	13½ @ 16	—
D7DE-HA	−1 to +½ @ 550	2–4 @ 750	—	6½ @ 2500	5	12½ @ 15	—
1978							
D7DE-AA	−1 to +½ @ 500	2¾–5 @ 1000	—	12½ @ 2500	3	15½ @ 16	—
D8DE-EA	0–3 @ 500	4–6½ @ 1000	—	12¼ @ 2500	3	13¼ @ 16	—
1979							
D9AE-YA	0–2 @ 630	2.25–4.25 @ 775	—	9.75–12.6 @ 2500	2	14.75–17.25 @ 25	—
D9AE-ACA	0–2 @ 725	—	—	7.5–10.25 @ 2500	2.4	6.9–9.25 @ 25	—
D8OE-AA	0–2.75 @ 500	6–7 @ 725	—	13.65–16.3 @ 2500	2	12.75–15.25 @ 25	—
D8DE-AA②	—	—	—	—	—	—	—
1980							
D94E-AA②	—	—	—	—	—	—	—
D94E-DA②	—	—	—	—	—	—	—
E0SE-CA	0–2 @ 635	2.8–4.6 @ 840	—	9.6–12.2 @ 2500	—	11.25–18.32 @ 25	—
E02E-EA	0–2.6 @ 540	3.5–5.5 @ 675	—	4.8–7.5 @ 2500	2.4	11.25–18.32 @ 25	—
1981							
D9AE-AA②	—	—	—	—	—	—	—
1982							
E2SE-BA③	—	9.5–11.5 @ 1250	—	—	—	—	—
E2SE-DA③	—	8.5–11 @ 1250	—	—	—	—	—
1983							
E3VE-AA②	—	—	—	—	—	—	—

①—Basic part No. 12127.　　②—EEC system distributor.　　③—V6-232, 3.8L engine.

REAR AXLE SPECIFICATIONS

Year	Model	Carrier Type	Ring Gear & Pinion Backlash Inch	Nominal Pinion Locating Shim, Inch	Pinion Bearing Preload				Differential Bearing Preload	Pinion Nut Torque Ft.-Lbs.
					New Bearings With Seal Inch-Lbs.	Used Bearings With Seal Inch-Lbs.	New Bearings Less Seal Inch-Lbs.	Used Bearings Less Seal Inch-Lbs.		
1977–80	All	Removable	.008–.012	④	17–27①	8–14①	—	—	②	③
1980–83	All	Integral	.008–.015	.030	16–29	8–14	—	—	.016	⑤

①—Bearing set with collapsible spacer; with solid spacer 13–33 inch-lbs.
②—Case spread with new bearings, 1975–80, .008–.012 inch; with used bearings, .005–.008 inch.
③—With collapsible spacer 170 ft. lbs., with solid spacer 200 ft. lbs.
④—With 8 inch ring gear, .022 inch; with 9 inch ring gear, .015 inch.
⑤—With 7.5 inch ring gear, 170 ft. lbs., with 8.5 inch ring gear 140 ft. lbs.

LINCOLN

STARTING MOTOR SPECIFICATIONS

Year	Car Model/V.I.N.	Ident. No.	Brush Spring Tension, Ounces	No Load Test			Torque Test		
				Amperes	Volts	R.P.M.	Amperes	Volts	Torque Ft. Lbs.
1977	V8-302/F, 351W/H	D8OF-AA	80	80	12	—	670	5.0	15½
	V8-400/S	D5AF-EA	80	80	12	—	670	5.0	15½
	V8-460/A	D6AF-AA	40	70	12	—	—	—	—
1978–79	V8-302	D8OF-AA	80	80	12	—	670	5.0	15½
	V8-400/S	D8AF-AA	80	80	12	—	670	5.0	15½
	V8-460/A	D8AF-AA	80	80	12	—	670	5.0	15.5
1980	V8-302/F	D8OF-AA	40–80	85	12	—	670	5.0	15.5
	V8-351W/G	D8OF-AA	40–80	85	12	—	670	5.0	15.5
1981	V8-302/F	E1AF-BA	40–80	85	12	—	670	5.0	15.5
1982	V6-232/3	E25F-AA	40–80	85	12	—	670	5.0	15.5
	V8-302/F	E1AF-BA	40–80	85	12	—	670	5.0	15.5

ALTERNATOR & REGULATOR SPECIFICATIONS

Year	Ident. No.①	Current Rating②		Field Current @ 75°F.		Voltage Regulator				Field Relay	
		Amperes	Volts	Amperes	Volts	Ident. No. ③⑥	Voltage @ 75°F.	Contact Gap	Armature Air Gap	Armature Air Gap	Closing Voltage @ 75°F.
1977	Orange④⑨	40	15	2.9	12	D4AF-AA	13.5–15.3	—	—	—	
	Green④⑨	60	15	2.9	12	D4AF-AA	13.5–15.3	—	—	—	
	70 All⑤	70	15	2.9	12	D4AF-AA	13.5–15.3	—	—	—	
	90 All⑤	90	15	2.9	12	D4TF-AA	13.5–15.3	—	—	—	
1978	Orange④⑨	40	15	2.9	12	D4AF-AA	13.5–15.3	—	—	—	
	Green④⑨	60	15	2.9	12	D4AF-AA	13.5–15.3	—	—	—	
	Green④⑦⑨	60	15	4.0	12	D8BF-AA⑧	14.0–14.4	—	—	—	
	Black④⑤	70	15	2.9	12	D4AF-AA	13.5–15.3	—	—	—	
	Red④⑤	90	15	2.9	12	D4TF-AA	13.5–15.3	—	—	—	
	Red④⑤⑦	90	15	4.0	12	D8BF-AA⑧	14.0–14.4	—	—	—	
1979	Orange④⑨	40	15	4.0	12	D8BF-AA⑧	13.8–14.6	—	—	—	
	Black④⑨	65	15	4.0	12	D8BF-AA⑧	14.0–14.4	—	—	—	
	Green④⑨	60	15	4.0	12	D8BF-AA⑧	13.8–14.6	—	—	—	
	Black④⑤	70	15	4.0	12	D8BF-AA⑧	14.0–14.4	—	—	—	
	Red④⑤	100	15	4.0	12	D8BF-AA⑧	14.0–14.4	—	—	—	
1980–81	Orange⑦⑨	40	15	4.0	12	D9BF-AB⑧	13.8–14.6	—	—	—	
	Black⑦⑨	65	15	4.0	12	D9BF-AB⑧	13.8–14.6	—	—	—	
	Green⑦⑨	60	15	4.0	12	D9BF-AB⑧	13.8–14.6	—	—	—	
	Black⑤⑦	70	15	4.0	12	D9BF-AB⑧	13.8–14.6	—	—	—	
	Red⑤⑦	100	15	4.0	12	D9BF-AB⑧	13.8–14.6	—	—	—	
1982	Orange⑦⑨	40	15	4.0	12	E1AF-AA⑧	13.8–14.6	—	—	—	
	Black⑦⑨	65	15	4.0	12	E1AF-AA⑧	13.8–14.6	—	—	—	
	Green⑦⑨	60	15	4.0	12	E1AF-AA⑧	13.8–14.6	—	—	—	
	Black⑤⑦	70	15	4.0	12	E1AF-AA⑧	13.8–14.6	—	—	—	
	Red⑤⑦	100	15	4.0	12	E1AF-AA⑧	13.8–14.6	—	—	—	
1983	Orange⑦⑨	40	15	4.25	12	E1ZF-FA	—	—	—	—	
	Black⑦⑨	65	15	4.25	12	E1ZF-FA	—	—	—	—	
	Green⑦⑨	60	15	4.25	12	E1ZF-FA	—	—	—	—	
	Black⑤⑦	70	15	4.25	12	E1ZF-FA	—	—	—	—	
	Red⑤⑦	100	15	4.25	12	E1ZF-ZA	—	—	—	—	

①—Basic No. 10300.
②—Stamped on housing.
③—Stamped on cover.
④—Stamp color code.
⑤—Side terminal alternator.
⑥—Basic No. 10316.
⑦—Solid state alternator.
⑧—Electronic voltage regulator. These units are color coded black for system w/warning indicator lamp & blue for systems w/ammeter.
⑨—Rear terminal alternator.

PISTONS, PINS, RINGS, CRANKSHAFT & BEARINGS

Year	Model/VIN	Piston Clearance	Ring End Gap① Comp.	Ring End Gap① Oil	Wristpin Diameter	Rod Bearings Shaft Diameter	Rod Bearings Bearing Clearance	Main Bearings Shaft Diameter	Main Bearings Bearing Clearance	Thrust on Bear. No.	Shaft End Play
1977–80	V8-351W④	.0018–.0026	.010	.015	.9121	2.3103–2.3111	.0008–.0015	2.9994–3.0002	.0008–.0015	3	.004–.008
1977–78	V8-460/A	.0014–.0022	.010	.015	1.040	2.4992–2.500	.0008–.0015	2.9994–3.0002	.0008–.0015	3	.004–.008
1977–81	V8-302/F	.0018–.0026	.010	.015	.9121	2.1228–2.1236	.0008–.0015	2.2482–2.2490	③	3	.004–.008
1977–79	V8-400/S	.0014–.0022	.010	.015	.9751	2.3103–2.3111	.0008–.0015	2.9994–3.0002	.0008–.0015	3	.004–.008
1982	V6-232/3	.0014–.0022	.010	.015	.9121	2.3103–2.3111	.001–.0014	2.5198–2.5190	.001–.0014	3	.004–.008
1982–83	V8-302/F	.0018–.0026	.010	.015	.9121	2.1228–2.1236	.0008–.0015	2.2482–2.2490	②	3	.004–.008

①—Fit rings in tapered bores for clearance listed in tightest portion of ring travel.
②—#1 .0004–.0025; others, .0004–.0015.
③—#1 .0001–.0015; others, .0005–.0015.
④—1977–79, H; 1980, G.

ENGINE TIGHTENING SPECIFICATIONS★

★ Torque specifications are for clean and lightly lubricated threads only. Dry or dirty threads produce increased friction which prevents accurate measurement of tightness.

Year	Model/V.I.N.	Spark Plugs Ft. Lbs.	Cylinder Head Bolts Ft. Lbs.	Intake Manifold Ft. Lbs.	Exhaust Manifold Ft. Lbs.	Rocker Arm Shaft Bracket Ft. Lbs.	Rocker Arm Cover Ft. Lbs.	Connecting Rod Cap Bolts Ft. Lbs.	Main Bearing Cap Bolts Ft. Lbs.	Flywheel to Crankshaft Ft. Lbs.	Vibration Damper or Pulley Ft. Lbs.
1977–78	V8-460/A	10–15	130–140	22–32	28–33	18–25①	5–6	40–45	95–105	75–85	70–90
1977–80	V8-351W⑧	10–15	105–112	23–25	18–24	③	3–5	40–45	95–105	75–85	70–90
	V8-400/S	10–15	95–105	②	18–24	18–25①	3–5	40–45	95–105	75–85	70–90
1977–83	V8-302/F	10–15	65–72	23–25	18–24	③	3–5	19–24	60–70	75–85	70–90
1982	V6-232/3	17–23	④	⑤	15–22	⑥	⑦	31–36	65–81	54–64	93–121

①—Rocker arm fulcrum bolt to cyl. head; or rocker arm stud nut.
②—5/16" bolts, 19–25 ft. lbs.; 3/8" bolts, 22–32 ft. lbs.
③—1977 & Early 1978 rocker arm stud nut, 17–23 ft. lbs.; Late 1978 & 1979–82, rocker arm fulcrum bolt to cylinder head, 18–25 ft. lbs.
④—Tighten bolts in 4 steps; #1, 47 ft. lbs.; #2, 55 ft. lbs.; #3, 63 ft. lbs.; #4, 74 ft. lbs.; then back off all bolts 2–3 turns and repeat sequence.
⑤—Tighten bolts in three steps; #1, 5.1 ft. lbs.; #2, 10.3 ft. lbs.; #3, 18.4 ft. lbs.
⑥—Rocker arm fulcrum bolt to cylinder head, tighten bolts in two steps; #1, 5.1–11.0 ft. lbs.; #2, 18.4–25.8 ft. lbs.
⑦—36–61 in. lbs.
⑧—1977–79, H; 1980, G.

BRAKE SPECIFICATIONS

Year	Model	Brake Drum Inside Diameter	Wheel Cylinder Bore Diameter Front Disc Brakes	Wheel Cylinder Bore Diameter Front Drum Brakes	Wheel Cylinder Bore Diameter Rear Brakes	Master Cylinder Bore Diameter With Disc Brakes	Master Cylinder Bore Diameter With Drum Brakes	Master Cylinder Bore Diameter With Power Brakes
1977	Lincoln	11.030	3.100	—	1.000②	1.00①	—	1.00①
	Mark V	③	3.100	—	2.6	1 1/8	—	1 1/8
	Versailles	③	2.6	—	2.125	1.00	—	1.00
1978–79	Lincoln	11.030	3.1	—	1.000②	1.00①	—	1.00①
	Mark V	③	3.1	—	2.6	1.125	—	1.125
	Versailles	③	2.6	—	2.1	1.00	—	1.00
1980	Lincoln	④	2.88	—	.9375	1.00	—	1.00
	Mark VI	④	2.88	—	.9375	1.00	—	1.00
	Versailles	③	2.6	—	2.125	1.00	—	1.00
1981	Lincoln & Mark VI	10.00	2.88	—	.9375	1.00	—	1.00
1982–83	Town Car	10.00	2.88	—	.9375	1.00	—	1.00
	Mark VI	10.00	2.88	—	.9375	1.00	—	1.00
	Continental	③	2.38	—	2.1	1.125	—	1.125

①—With 4 wheel disc brakes, 1 1/8".
②—On models with 4 wheel disc brakes, 2.6".
③—4 wheel disc brakes.
④—V8-302, 10 inches; V8-351W, 11.03 inches.

LINCOLN

COOLING SYSTEM & CAPACITY DATA

Year	Model or Engine	Cooling Capacity, Qts. Less A/C	Cooling Capacity, Qts. With A/C	Radiator Cap Relief Pressure, Lbs.	Thermo. Opening Temp.	Fuel Tank Gals.	Engine Oil Refill Qts. ①	Transmission Oil 3 Speed Pints	Transmission Oil 4 Speed Pints	Transmission Oil Auto. Trans. Qts. ②	Rear Axle Oil Pints
1977	Lincoln	⑥	⑥	16	191	24.2⑦	4	—	—	⑤	5
	Mark V	⑨	⑨	16	191	24.2⑦	4	—	—	⑤	5
	Versailles	⑧	⑧	16	191	19.2	4	—	—	10	5
1978	Lincoln	⑩	⑩	16	191	24.2	4	—	—	12½	5
	Mark V	③	③	16	191	25	4	—	—	12½	5
	Versailles	14.3	14.3	16	191	19.2	4	—	—	10¼	5
1979	Lincoln	—	16.9	16	196	24.2	4	—	—	11.8	5
	Mark V	—	16.9	16	196	25	4	—	—	11.8	5
	Versailles	—	14.3	16	196	19.2	4	—	—	10	5
1980	Lincoln	—	13.4	16	196	18⑫	4⑪	—	—	12	⑬
	Mark VI	—	13.4	16	196	18⑫	4⑪	—	—	12	⑬
	Versailles	—	13.4	16	196	19.2	4	—	—	9.6	5
1981	Lincoln & Mark VI	—	13.4	16	195	18	4	—	—	12	4
1982–83	Town Car	—	13.4	16	195	18	4⑪	—	—	12.0	3¾
	Mark VI	—	13.4	16	195	18	4⑪	—	—	12.0	3¾
	Continental	—	④	16	195	⑭	4⑮	—	—	12.0	3.25

①—Add one quart with filter change.
②—Approximate. Make final check with dipstick.
③—V8-400, 16.9 qts.; V8-460, 18.9 qts.
④—V8-302, 13.4 qts.; V6-232, 11.1 qts.
⑤—FMX, 11 qts.; C6, 12.2 qts.
⑥—V8-400, 17.1 qts.; V8-460, 18.5 qts.
⑦—Calif. V8-400, 20.0 gal.
⑧—V8-302, 14.6 qts.; V8-351, 15.7 qts.
⑨—V8-400, 17.5 qts.; V8-460, 19.4 qts.
⑩—V8-400, 16.9 qts.; V8-460, 18.7 qts.
⑪—Dual sump oil pan. When draining oil, it is necessary to remove both drain plugs. One drain plug is located at front of oil pan. The second drain plug is located on left side of oil pan.
⑫—V8-351W, 20 gal.
⑬—7.5 inch axle, 3.5 pts; 8.5 inch axle, 4 pts.
⑭—V8-302, 22.6 gals; V6-232, 20 gals.
⑮—For V8-302 engines, refer to note ⑪.

WHEEL ALIGNMENT SPECIFICATIONS

Year	Model	Caster Angle, Degrees Limits	Caster Angle, Degrees Desired	Camber Angle, Degrees Limits Left	Camber Angle, Degrees Limits Right	Camber Angle, Degrees Desired Left	Camber Angle, Degrees Desired Right	Toe In. Inch	Toe Out on Turns, Deg.① Outer Wheel	Toe Out on Turns, Deg.① Inner Wheel
1977	Versailles	−1¼ to +¼	−½	−½ to +1	−½ to +1	+¼	+¼	1/8	②	20
	Lincoln	+1¼ to +2¾	+2	−¼ to +1¼	−½ to +1	+½	+¼	1/8	18.16	20
	Mark V	+1¼ to +2¾	+2	−¼ to +1¼	−½ to +1	+½	+¼	3/16	18.09	20
1978–79	Lincoln	+1¼ to +2¾	+2	−¼ to +1¼	−½ to +1	+½	+¼	1/8	18.16	20
	Mark V	+3¼ to +4¾	+4	−¼ to +1¼	−½ to +1	+½	+¼	3/16	18.09	20
	Versailles	−1¼ to +¼	−½	−½ to +1	−½ to +1	+¼	+¼	1/8	②	20
1980	Versailles	−1¼ to +¼	−½	−½ to +1	−½ to +1	+¼	+¼	1/8	②	20
1980–81	Lincoln	+2¼ to +3¾	+3	−¼ to +1¼	−¼ to +1¼	+½	+½	1/16	18.51	20
	Mark VI	+2¼ to +3¾	+3	−¼ to +1¼	−¼ to +1¼	+½	+½	1/16	18.51	20
1982	Town Car	+2¼ to +3¾	+3	−¼ to +1¼	−¼ to +1¼	+½	+½	1/16	18.51	20
	Mark VI	+2¼ to +3¾	+3	−¼ to +1¼	−¼ to +1¼	+½	+½	1/16	18.51	20
	Continental	+1⅛ to +1⅞	+1	−½ to +1¼	−½ to +1¼	+⅜	+⅜	3/16	19.13	20
1983	Town Car	+2¼ to +4	+3	−¼ to +1¼	−¼ to +1¼	+½	+½	1/16	18.51	20
	Mark VI	+2¼ to +4	+3	−¼ to +1¼	−¼ to +1¼	+½	+½	1/16	18.51	20
	Continental	+⅜ to +2⅛	+1¼	−½ to +1¼	−½ to +1¼	+⅜	+⅜	1/8	19.13	20

①—Incorrect toe-out, when other adjustments are correct, indicates bent steering arms.
②—With power steering; 18.20 & Without 18.43.

Electrical Section

STARTER, REPLACE

1977–80 Versailles

1. Disconnect battery ground cable, then raise vehicle on a hoist.
2. Disconnect starter cable at starter terminal.
3. Remove through bolt and nut attaching motor mount insulator to mounting bracket.
4. Using a suitable jack raise engine.
5. Remove starter mounting bolts, then remove starter.
6. Reverse procedure to install.

1979–83 Except Versailles

1. Disconnect battery ground cable, then raise and support vehicle.
2. Disconnect starter cable at starter terminal, then remove starter mounting bolts.
3. Remove starter. On some models, it may be necessary to turn wheels to the left or right to gain clearance for removal.
4. Reverse procedure to install. Torque starter cable to starter motor bolt to 70–110 inch lbs.

1977–78 Except Versailles

1. Disconnect battery ground cable and support vehicle on hoist.
2. Disconnect cable and wires from solenoid.
3. On Mark V models, loosen the two front brace retaining bolts, then remove all other brace retaining bolts and allow brace to hang.
4. Turn wheels fully to the right and remove the two bolts attaching the steering idler arm to the frame.
5. Remove starter attaching bolts and remove starter.
6. Reverse procedure to install.

IGNITION LOCK, REPLACE

1980–83 Except Versailles

1. Disconnect battery ground cable.
2. On models with tilt wheel, remove upper column extension shroud by unsnapping from retaining clip at 9 o'clock position.
3. Remove steering column trim shroud.
4. Disconnect key warning switch electrical connector.
5. Turn ignition lock to "On" position.
6. Using a 1/8" pin or punch located in the 4 o'clock hole and 1 1/4 inch from outer edge of lock cylinder housing, depress retaining pin while pulling the lock cylinder from housing.
7. Turn lock cylinder to "On" position and insert cylinder into housing. Ensure that the lock cylinder is fully seated and aligned into the interlocking washer before turning key to "Off" position. This will permit the retaining pin to extend into the lock cylinder housing hole.
8. Rotate key to check for proper mechanical operation.
9. Connect key warning switch electrical connector.
10. Connect battery ground cable.
11. Check for proper operation.

1977–79 All & 1980 Versailles

1. Disconnect the battery ground cable.
2. **Units With Fixed Steering Columns:** Remove the steering wheel trim pad and steering wheel. Insert a wire pin in the hole located inside the column halfway down the lock cylinder housing, Fig. 1.
Units With Tilt Steering Columns: Insert wire pin in the hole located on the outside of the flange casting next to the emergency flasher button, Fig. 1.
3. Place the gear shift lever in *Park* position, and turn the lock cylinder with the ignition key to the *Run* position.
4. Depress the wire pin while pulling up on the lock cylinder to remove. Remove the wire pin.
5. To install insert the lock cylinder into the housing in the flange casting, and turn the key to the *Off* position. Be certain that the cylinder is fully inserted before turning to the *Off* position. This action will extend the cylinder retaining pin into the cylinder housing.
6. Turn the key to check for correct operation in all positions.
7. Install the steering wheel and trim pad on fixed column units.
8. Connect the battery ground cable.

IGNITION SWITCH, REPLACE

1982–83

1. Disconnect battery ground cable.
2. For tilt wheel only, remove upper column extension shroud by unsnapping from retaining clip at 9 o'clock position.
3. Remove steering column trim shrouds.
4. Disconnect ignition switch electrical connector. Turn the lock cylinder to the "On" position.
5. With a 1/8 inch drill, drill out the switch retaining bolt heads. Then, remove the bolts with an "Easy Out" or equivalent.
6. Disengage ignition switch from actuator and remove from vehicle, Fig. 2.
7. Adjust ignition switch by sliding the carrier to the switch "On" position.

NOTE: A replacement ignition switch will be pre-set in the "On" position.

Fig. 1 Ignition lock cylinder

Fig. 2 Ignition switch installation. 1980–81 Continental & Mark VI

8. Ensure the lock cylinder is in approximately the "On" position and install the ignition switch onto the actuator pin.
9. Install switch break-off head mounting bolts and tighten until heads shear.
10. Reconnect switch electrical connector and battery ground cable. Check the ignition switch for proper operation in all switch positions. Be sure the column is locked in the lock position.
11. Reinstall shrouds.

1980–81 Continental & Mark VI

1. Disconnect battery ground cable.
2. Remove upper column shroud.
3. Disconnect ignition switch electrical connector.
4. With a ⅛ inch diameter twist drill, drill out the switch retaining bolt heads. Then, remove the bolts with a "Easy Out" or equivalent.
5. Disengage ignition switch from actuator and remove from vehicle, Fig. 2.
6. Adjust ignition switch by sliding the carrier to the switch "Lock" position. Insert a .050 inch drill or equivalent through the switch housing and into the carrier to prevent movement.

NOTE: A replacement ignition switch includes an installed adjusting pin.

7. Rotate ignition key to "Lock" positon.
8. Install ignition switch on actuator pin.
9. Install switch break-off head mounting bolts and tighten until the bolt heads shear.
10. Remove adjusting pin or drill.
11. Connect ignition switch electrical connector.
12. Connect battery ground cable and check for proper operation.
13. Install column shroud.

1977–79 Mark V & 1977–80 Versailles

1. Disconnect battery ground cable.
2. On 1977–79 Mark V, remove instrument cluster as described under "Instrument Cluster, Replace".
3. Remove steering column shroud, then detach and lower steering column from brake support bracket.
4. Disconnect switch wiring, then remove two nuts retaining switch to steering column, Fig. 3.
5. Lift switch vertically upward to disengage actuator rod, then remove switch.
6. When installing ignition switch, both locking mechanism at top of column and ignition switch must be in Lock position for correct adjustment. To hold mechanical parts in column in Lock position, move shift lever to Park, then turn key to Lock position and remove key.

NOTE: New replacement switches are pinned in Lock position by a metal pin inserted in locking hole located on side of switch. For existing switch, move switch carrier using a .010 in. diameter rod to lock detent. Insert a ⁵⁄₆₄ in. drill bit into lock hole on side of switch to hold switch in Lock position.

Fig. 3 Ignition switch installation. Except Continental & Mark VI

7. Connect switch plunger to actuator rod.
8. Position switch on column and install retaining nuts, but do not tighten.
9. Move switch up and down along column to locate mid-position of rod lash, then tighten switch retaining nuts.
10. Remove locking pin, then connect battery ground cable and check switch for proper operation.
11. Attaching steering column to brake support and install steering column shroud.
12. On 1977–79 Mark V models, install instrument cluster.

Fig. 4 Ignition switch installation. 1977–79 Continental

Fig. 5   Light switch. 1977–83 (typical)

1977–79 Continental

1. Disconnect battery ground cable.
2. On 1978–79 models, remove instrument cluster as described under Instrument Cluster, Replace.
3. On all models remove shrouding from steering column and detach and lower steering column from brake support bracket.
4. Disconnect switch wiring at multiple plug, Figs. 3 and 4.
5. Remove two nuts that retain switch to column.
6. Detach switch plunger from actuator rod and remove the switch.
7. Move shift lever to Park position. Place ignition key in Lock position and remove the key.

NOTE: New replacement switches are pinned in the Lock position by a plastic shipping pin inserted in a locking hole in the switch. For an existing switch, pull plunger out as far as it will go then back one detent to Lock position and insert a 3/32" drill in locking hole to retain switch in Lock position.

8. With locking pin in place, install switch on steering column, determine mid position of actuator lash and tighten retaining bolts.
9. Remove locking pin.
10. Attach steering column to brake support and install shrouding.
11. On 1978–79 models, install instrument cluster.

LIGHT SWITCH, REPLACE

1982–83 Continental

1. Disconnect battery ground cable.
2. Remove steering column trim shrouds.
3. Unsnap the instrument panel cluster lower moulding to expose five screws along bottom of cluster lens and remove.
4. Remove the left hand lower pad retaining screws and carefully tilt the pad out from under the cluster lens.
5. Disconnect the headlamp switch wiring connectors.
6. Insert a hooked tool into headlight switch knob slot and remove spring tension on knob, then pull off.
7. Remove switch retaining nut and lens.
8. Remove second nut and screw retaining the switch to lower pad and remove.
9. Reverse procedure to install.

1982–83 Mark VI & Town Car

1. Disconnect battery ground cable.
2. Insert a hooked tool into headlight switch

knob slot and remove spring tension on knob, then pull off.
3. Remove steering column lower shroud and lower left hand instrument panel trim bezel.
4. Remove five headlight switch mounting bracket retaining screws.
5. Carefully pull switch and bracket from instrument panel and disconnect switch wiring.
6. On Mark VI models, mark and remove vacuum hoses from switch distributor valve.
7. Remove locknut and screw retaining switch to switch bracket.
8. Reverse procedure to install.

1980–81 Continental & Mark VI

1. Disconnect battery ground cable.
2. From instrument panel, depress light switch knob and shaft retainer button on side of switch and, while holding button in, pull knob and shaft assembly from switch, Fig. 5.
3. Unscrew trim bezel and remove lock nut.
4. From under instrument panel, pull switch from panel while tilting downward, disconnect electrical connector and remove switch.
5. Reverse procedure to install.

1977 Mark IV & 1977–79 Mark V

1. Disconnect battery ground cable.
2. Remove instrument cluster trim panel.
3. Remove the headlight switch mounting plate.
4. Remove bezel nut and disconnect multiple connector.
5. Remove vacuum lines, if so equipped.
6. Remove the switch.
7. Reverse procedure to install.

1977–79 Continental & 1977–80 Versailles

1. Disconnect battery ground cable.
2. Remove control knob and shaft by pressing knob release button and pulling it out of switch housing, Fig. 5.
3. Remove bezel nut and lower switch assembly.
4. Disconnect multiple plug and vacuum hoses at switch body and remove switch.

Fig. 6   Stop light switch 1977–83

5. Reverse procedure to install.

STOP LIGHT SWITCH, REPLACE

1977–83

1. Disconnect wires at switch connector.
2. Remove hairpin retainer, slide switch, push rod and nylon washers and bushing away from brake pedal, and remove switch, Fig. 6.

NOTE: On 1977–80 Versailles models, loosen brake booster nuts at pedal support approximately 1/4 inch so booster is free to move to eliminate binding during switch removal.

3. Reverse above procedure to install.

NEUTRAL SAFETY SWITCH, REPLACE

1982–83 Continental

1. Place shift lever in low position.
2. Raise and support vehicle. Place a suitable jack under transmission.
3. Disconnect throttle valve linkage rod and manual shift linkage from transmission.
4. Position a drain pan under the rear of the extension housing and remove propeller shaft.
5. Disconnect muffler inlet pipe from the catalytic converter and on Continental models, disconnect the converter inlet flange from the Y pipe and remove the converter.
6. Using the jack, raise the transmission enough to remove the weight from the rear engine mount.
7. On Continental models, remove the rear engine mount to crossmember nuts, then remove one crossmember to frame bolt and swing the crossmember out of the way. On Mark VI and Town Car models, remove the rear engine mount then remove rear crossmember from the vehicle.
8. Lower transmission enough to gain access to neutral safety switch.
9. Disconnect switch wiring connector by

lifting the harness straight up, without side to side motion.

10. Using tool T74P-77247-A or equivalent remove the switch and O-ring. Discard the O-ring.

11. Reverse procedure to install making note of the following; always install a new O-ring on the neutral safety switch. Do not over tighten the switch, torque to 7–8 ft. lbs. only, and if any self-locking nuts and bolts were removed they must be replaced with the new self-locking nuts and bolts.

1977–80 Versailles W/Floor Shift

Transmission Mounted Switch, Fig. 7

1. Remove downshift linkage rod from transmission downshift lever.
2. Apply penetrating oil to downshift lever shaft and nut; then remove downshift outer lever.
3. Remove switch attaching bolts.
4. Disconnect multiple wire connector and remove switch from transmission.
5. Install new switch.
6. With transmission manual lever in neutral, rotate switch and install gauge pin (#43 drill) into gauge pin holes.
7. Tighten switch attaching bolts and remove gauge pin.
8. Complete the installation in reverse order of removal.

1977–81 Except Versailles W/Floor Shift

The neutral safety switch has been eliminated and is replaced by a series of steps designed into the steering column selector lever hub casting.

TURN SIGNAL SWITCH, REPLACE

1980–83 All

1. Disconnect battery ground cable.
2. On models with tilt wheels, remove upper column extension shroud by unsnapping from retaining clip at 9 o'clock position.
3. Remove steering column cover attaching screws and the cover.
4. Carefully lift wiring connector plug retainer tabs and disconnect the plugs from switch.
5. Remove switch retaining screws and lift up switch assembly.
6. Reverse procedure to install.

Fig. 7 Neutral safety switch. 1977–80 Versailles

1977–79

1. Remove retaining screw from underside of steering wheel spoke and lift off the pad horn switch/trim cover and medallion as an assembly.
2. Disconnect horn switch wires from terminals.
3. Remove steering wheel retaining nut and remove steering wheel using suitable puller.
4. Remove turn signal switch lever by unscrewing it from steering column.
5. Remove shroud from under steering column.
6. Disconnect steering column wiring connector plugs and remove the screws that secure switch assembly to the column.
7. On vehicles with tilt column, remove wires and terminals from steering column wiring connector plug.

NOTE: *Record the color code and location of each wire before removing it from connector. A hole provided in the flange on fixed columns makes it unnecessary to separate the wires from the connector plug. The plug with wires installed can be guided through the hole.*

---

8. Remove the plastic cover sleeve from the wiring harness and remove the switch and wires from the top of the column.

NOTE: On models with speed control, transfer the ground brush located in the turn signal switch cancelling cam to the new switch assembly.

9. Reverse procedure to install.

HORN SOUNDER & STEERING WHEEL, REPLACE

1980–83 Except Versailles

Refer to "TURN SIGNAL SWITCH, REPLACE" for horn switch replacement.

1977–79 All & 1980 Versailles

1. Disconnect battery ground cable.
2. Remove screws from behind wheel spoke holding crash pad to wheel. Lift pad and disconnect horn wires. Disconnect speed control wires if used and remove pad.
3. Remove steering wheel nut. Install a suitable puller and remove steering wheel.
4. Reverse procedure to install.

INSTRUMENT CLUSTER, REPLACE

1982–83 Continental

1. Disconnect battery ground cable.
2. Remove steering column shroud.
3. Snap off instrument panel mouldings.
4. Remove seventeen instrument panel assembly to instrument panel and instrument panel pad retaining screws, then remove trim assembly, Fig. 7A.
5. Disconnect PRND3L cable from steering column.
6. Remove four cluster retaining screws from instrument panel and move cluster away from instrument panel.
7. Disconnect wiring harness connector and remove cluster.
8. Reverse procedure to install.

1980–81 Continental & Mark VI; 1982–83 Mark VI & Town Car

Less Electronic Cluster
1. Disconnect battery ground cable.
2. Disconnect speedometer cable, then remove trim cover screws and remove trim cover.

Fig. 7B Instrument cluster. 1980–81 Continental & Mark VI, 1982–83 Mark VI & Town Car

Fig. 8 Instrument cluster. 1978–79 Continental

Fig. 7A Electronic instrument panel. 1982–83 Continental

3. Remove lower steering column cover screws and remove cover.
4. Remove PRND21 bracket retaining screw, then disconnect cable loop and bracket pin from steering column. Also remove the column bracket from column.
5. Remove cluster retaining screws, then disconnect electrical feed plug from connector and remove cluster, Fig. 7B.

With Electronic Cluster
1. Disconnect battery ground cable.
2. Remove steering column cover, lower instrument panel trim cover, keyboard trim panel and panel on left of column.
3. Remove the ten instrument cluster trim cover retaining screws, then remove trim cover.
4. Remove the four screws retaining instrument cluster to instrument panel and pull cluster forward. Disconnect both electrical plugs and ground wire from their receptacles, then disconnect speedometer cable by pressing on flat surface of plastic connector.
5. Remove PRND31 cable bracket retaining screw, then disconnect cable loop and bracket pin from steering column.
6. Remove plastic clamp from around steering column, then remove cluster, Fig. 7B.
7. Reverse procedure to install.

1978–79 Continental

1. Disconnect battery ground cable.
2. Remove two steering column lower cover screws and remove lower cover.
3. Remove two instrument cluster trim cover attaching screws and remove trim cover.
4. Disconnect the cluster feed plug from behind the cluster.
5. Disconnect the speedometer cable. Unsnap and remove the steering column shroud cover. Unhook the shift indicator cable from the tab in the shroud retainer.

Fig. 9 Instrument cluster. 1977–80 Versailles

Fig. 10 Instrument panel lower pad removal (typical). 1977 Continental

6. Remove screw attaching shift indicator cable bracket to the steering column. Disconnect cable loop from the pin on the steering column.
7. Remove the four cluster attaching screws and remove cluster assembly, Fig. 8.
8. Reverse procedure to install.

1977–80 Versailles

1. Disconnect battery ground cable.
2. Remove screws securing lower cluster applique beneath steering column.
3. Remove steering column shroud.
4. Remove headlamp switch knob and shaft assembly, then the switch bezel.
5. Remove four screws from cluster front cover.
6. Using a right angle screwdriver, pry along edges of finish panel, thereby removing studs from retainers and remove finish panel.
7. Pull front cover slightly outward at top, then rearward at bottom to disengage cover to panel retainers.
8. Remove cluster front cover.
9. Remove screw attaching transmission indicator cable bracket to steering column and detach cable loop from pin on column.
10. Disconnect speedometer cable connector.
11. Remove four screws securing cluster to instrument panel.
12. Pull cluster from instrument panel and disconnect electrical connectors, Fig. 9.
13. Remove cluster from vehicle.
14. Reverse procedure to install.

1977 Continental

1. Disconnect battery ground cable.
2. Remove steering column trim shroud, then remove instrument panel lower pad as follows Fig. 10.
   a. From behind panel, remove the two nuts retaining right end of panel to instrument panel.

b. From bottom edge, remove the five pad to instrument cluster screws.
   c. Remove the three left hand end finish panel retaining screws, then swing pad assembly outward to disengage tabs at top of cluster and remove pad assembly.
3. Disconnect lower instrument cluster electrical connector from printed circuit.
4. Remove PRND21 control cable to steering column screw.
5. Remove instrument cluster retaining screws, pull cluster from panel and disconnect electrical connector.
6. Remove instrument cluster, Fig. 11.
7. Reverse procedure to install.

1977–79 Mark V

1. Disconnect battery ground cable.
2. Remove three screws attaching upper access cover to instrument panel pad.
3. Remove one screw retaining lower cluster applique cover below steering column.
4. Squeeze lower half of steering column shroud together and separate lower half from upper.
5. Remove upper half of shroud from column.
6. Remove one screw attaching PRNDL control cable to steering column.
7. Remove heated backlite control knob.
8. Reach under panel and depress the button on side of headlight switch while withdrawing switch control knob and shaft. Remove headlight switch bezel.
9. Reach under panel and disconnect speedometer cable.
10. Remove wiper/washer control knob.
11. Remove threaded wiper/washer bezel.
12. Remove cigar lighter from its receptacle.
13. Remove four screws retaining cluster front cover. Remove one screw attaching shift indicator cable bracket to steering column and disconnect cable with transmission selector in PARK position.

14. Insert a right angle standard tip screwdriver along edges of finish panel withdrawing studs in sequence gradually around periphery of panel.
15. Remove two screws from cluster light baffle at cluster top.
16. Remove five screws retaining cluster to instrument panel.
17. Pull cluster away from panel and disconnect printed circuit feed plug.
18. Tilt cluster out, bottom first, and move cluster toward center of vehicle, Fig. 12.
19. Reverse procedure to install.

W/S WIPER MOTOR, REPLACE

1982–83 Continental

1. Disconnect battery ground cable.
2. Remove right hand side wiper and blade assembly.
3. Remove cowl top grille retaining screws and remove grille.
4. Disconnect linkage drive arm from the motor output arm crankpin by removing retainer clip.
5. Disconnect electrical connector and remove three motor attaching screws.
6. Pull the motor from the opening.
7. Reverse procedure to install.

1980–81 Continental & Mark VI; 1982–83 Mark VI & Town Car

1. Disconnect battery ground cable.
2. Disconnect right side washer nozzle hose clip and remove right side wiper arm and blade assembly from pivot shaft.
3. Remove wiper motor linkage cover.
4. Disconnect linkage drive arm from the motor output arm crankpin by removing retainer clip.
5. Disconnect the wiring connectors from the motor.

DISASSEMBLED VIEW

ASSEMBLED VIEW

Fig. 11 Instrument cluster (typical). 1977 Continental

6. Remove three bolts retaining the motor to the dash panel extension and the motor.
7. Reverse procedure to install.

1978–80 Versailles

1. Disconnect battery ground cable.
2. Remove eight instrument panel pad attaching screws, then remove pad.
3. Remove speaker mounting bracket, then disconnect wire connector and remove speaker.
4. Remove defroster nozzle and air distribution duct. Remove interlock module from bracket and disconnect multiple connector.
5. Remove wiper bracket to cowl attaching bolts and drive arm clip, then remove wiper motor.
6. Reverse procedure to install.

1977 Versailles

1. Disconnect battery ground cable.
2. Remove accelerator pedal and instrument panel to floor brace.

3. Remove drive arm clips and disconnect rod from drive arm.
4. Disconnect electrical connector and manual linkage.
5. Remove wiper motor retaining screws, then remove motor and bracket assembly.
6. Reverse procedure to install.

1977–79 Exc. Versailles

1. Disconnect battery ground cable.
2. Remove wiper arm and blade assemblies.
3. Remove left cowl screen for access through cowl opening.
4. Disconnect linkage drive arm from motor output arm crankpin by removing the retaining clip.
5. From engine side of dash, disconnect wire connectors from motor.
6. Remove bolts that retain motor to dash and remove the motor. If the output arm catches on dash during removal, hand-turn the arm clockwise so it will clear the opening in dash.

NOTE: *Before installing motor be sure the output arm is in the Park position.*

7. Reverse procedure to install.

W/S WIPER TRANSMISSION, REPLACE

1982–83 Continental

1. Disconnect battery ground cable.
2. Remove right hand side wiper arm and blade assembly.
3. Remove cowl top grille retaining screws and remove grille.
4. Disconnect linkage drive arm from the motor output arm crankpin by removing retainer clip.
5. Remove the right side pivot shaft retaining screws then, remove the large nut and spacer from the left side pivot shaft.
6. Remove linkage.
7. Reverse procedure to install.

1980–81 Continental & Mark VI; 1982–83 Mark VI & Town Car

1. Disconnect battery ground cable.
2. Remove wiper arm and blade assemblies from the pivot shafts.
3. Remove wiper motor and linkage cover for access to linkage.
4. Disconnect the linkage drive arm from the motor crank pin by removing the retaining clip.
5. Remove the six bolts retaining the left and right pivot shafts to the cowl, and remove the complete linkage assembly.
6. Reverse procedure to install.

1977–80 Versailles

Left Side:
1. Remove instrument cluster.
2. Remove wiper arm and blade.
3. Working through cluster opening, disconnect both pivot shaft links from motor drive arm by removing retaining clip.
4. Remove three pivot shaft assembly retaining bolts and remove assembly through cluster opening.
5. Reverse procedure to install.

Right Side:
1. Disconnect battery ground cable and remove wiper blade and wiper arm.
2. If air conditioned, remove right duct assembly by unclipping duct from right connector and sliding left end out of plenum chamber. Lower duct assembly out from under instrument panel.
3. From under the instrument panel, disconnect first left then right pivot shaft link from motor drive arm.
4. Reaching between utility shelf and instrument panel, remove pivot shaft retaining bolts and lower assembly out from under panel.
5. Reverse procedure to install.

1977–79 Mark V

1. Disconnect battery ground cable and remove wiper arm and blades.
2. Remove cowl top (left and center) retaining screws.
3. Disconnect linkage drive arm from the motor by removing retaining clip.
4. Remove pivot shaft retaining bolts and remove linkage and pivot shaft.

NOTE: When installing pivot shaft as-

Fig. 12 Instrument cluster (Typical). 1977–79 Mark IV & V

semblies, be sure to force the linkage connecting clip into the locked position.

5. Reverse procedure to install.

1977–79 Continental

1. Disconnect battery ground cable.
2. Remove wiper arm and blade assemblies.
3. Remove left and center cowl screens for access to linkage.
4. Disconnect left linkage arm from the drive arm by removing the clip.
5. Remove three bolts retaining left pivot shaft assembly to the cowl and remove the left arm and pivot shaft assembly through cowl opening.
6. Disconnect linkage drive arm from motor crankpin by removing the clip.
7. Remove three bolts that connect the drive arm pivot assembly to the cowl and remove the pivot shaft drive arm and right arm as an assembly.
8. Reverse procedure to install.

W/S WIPER SWITCH, REPLACE

1980–83 All

1. Disconnect battery ground cable.

2. Remove the steering column cover screws and separate the two halves.
3. Remove wiper switch retaining screws, disconnect wiring connector and remove switch.
4. Reverse procedure to install.

1977–80 Versailles

NOTE: The wiper/washer switch is an integral part of the turn signal arm and cannot be replaced separately.

1. Disconnect battery ground cable.
2. Disconnect wiper/washer and turn signal electrical connector from under instrument panel.
3. Remove lower instrument panel shield retaining screws and shield.
4. Remove steering column cover screws and separate cover halves.
5. Remove wiring cover by pulling it, then remove wiring shield by prying out.
6. Using an internal bit screwdriver, remove wiper/washer and turn signal arm assembly.
7. Reverse procedure to install.

1977–79 Mark V

1. Disconnect battery ground cable.
2. Remove instrument cluster finish panel.

3. Remove switch mounting plate and disconnect cigar lighter and wiper switch wires.
4. Remove switch bezel nut and remove switch.
5. Reverse procedure to install.

1977–79 Continental

1. Disconnect battery ground cable.
2. Pull the knob and remove retaining nut and gasket from switch shaft.
3. Lower switch from behind instrument panel and disconnect the multiple connector.
4. Reverse procedure to install.

RADIO, REPLACE

NOTE: When installing radio, be sure to adjust antenna trimmer for peak performance.

1982–83 Continental

1. Disconnect battery ground cable.
2. Remove center instrument panel trim panel.
3. Remove four radio and mounting bracket to instrument panel retaining screws.

VACUUM HOSE TO VACUUM RESERVOIR

SUPPLY VACUUM CHECK VALVE

SERVO ASSEMBLY (THROTTLE ACTUATOR)

BALL CHAIN RETAINING PIN

ACTUATOR VACUUM LINE

UPPER SPEEDOMETER CABLE

ACTUATOR BRACKET

BEAD CHAIN ADJUSTER ASSEMBLY

BLUE CONNECTOR

RED CONNECTOR

BEAD CHAIN ADJUST TO MAINTAIN .06 TO .250 SERVO ARM FREE TRAVEL WITH ENGINE ON HOT IDLE

SPEED SENSOR

LOWER SPEEDOMETER CABLE

Fig. 13 Servo assembly & throttle linkage installation. 1977–83 (typical)

4. Push radio towards the front of vehicle and raise back end slightly so rear support bracket clears clip in instrument panel and carefully pull out radio.
5. Disconnect radio wiring and remove radio.
6. Remove rear support bracket.
7. Reverse procedure to install.

1980–81 Continental & Mark VI, 1982–83 Mark VI & Town Car

1. Disconnect battery ground able.
2. Remove radio plate to instrument panel retaining screws.
3. Pull radio rearward until the rear support bracket is clear of instrument panel.
4. Disconnect radio wiring and antenna lead. Remove radio.
5. Remove screws securing front bracket to radio and remove, remove rear support bracket.
6. Reverse procedure to install.

1978–79 Continental

1. Disconnect battery ground cable.
2. Remove the radio knobs and the screws attaching bezel to instrument panel.
3. Remove radio mounting plate attaching screws and pull radio to disengage it from lower rear support bracket.
4. Disconnect electrical leads and remove the radio.
5. Remove mounting plate and rear support from radio.
6. Reverse procedure to install.

1977–80 Versailles

1. Disconnect battery ground cable.
2. Remove headlamp switch.
3. Remove knobs from heater and A/C control, windshield wiper switch and radio.
4. Remove instrument panel applique.
5. Remove radio bezel to instrument panel

screws, then pull radio and bezel out to disconnect antenna lead and electrical leads, then remove radio from panel.
6. Remove rear support bracket and bezel from radio.
7. Reverse procedure to install.

1977–79 Mark V

1. Disconnect battery ground cable.
2. Pull radio knobs and discs from shafts.
3. Remove twilight sentinel amplifier.
4. Remove air conditioning duct located under radio.
5. Remove radio rear support to panel screw, disconnect radio electrical leads and remove radio.
6. Reverse procedure to install.

1977 Continental

1. Disconnect battery ground cable.
2. Remove radio knobs and discs, then map light assembly.
3. Remove steering column shroud, ash tray door pad and instrument cluster panel pad.
4. Remove center register applique, then disconnect cigar lighter and glove box light switch electrical connectors.
5. Remove radio bracket to instrument panel tab nut and radio mounting bracket to instrument panel screws.
6. Pull radio out, disconnect wiring and remove radio.
7. Reverse procedure to install.

SPEED CONTROLS, ADJUST

1977–83

Adjust bead chain cable to obtain desired free travel with engine warm and carburetor at idle position. Desired free travel is 1/8–1/4 inch, Fig. 13. The adjustment should be made to take as much slack as possible out of the

bead chain without restricting the carburetor lever from returning to idle. On vehicles with solenoid anti-diesel valve, perform the adjustment with the ignition switch in the ON position.

HEATER CORE, REPLACE

1982–83 Continental

1. Disconnect battery ground cable.
2. Remove steering column cover assembly, then remove left and right finish panels, Fig. 6A.
3. Remove two screws from sides of instrument panel pad and retainer assembly.
4. Remove pad and retainer assembly and upper finish panel.
5. Remove steering column attaching bolts, then carefully lower steering column just enough to allow access to transmission gear selector lever cable assembly. Reach between steering column and instrument panel, then carefully lift selector lever cable from lever and remove cable clamp from steering column tube.
6. Lower steering column and allow to rest on front seat.
7. Remove screw attaching instrument panel to brake pedal support through steering column opening.
8. Disconnect temperature door cable from door and heater/evaporator cable bracket.
9. Disconnect vacuum hose connectors at evaporator housing.
10. Disconnect blower motor resistor wire from resistor on heater/evaporator case and blower motor feed wire at inline connector.
11. Support instrument panel, then remove three screws attaching top of instrument panel to cowl.
12. Remove one screw attaching each end of instrument panel to cowl side panels, then remove two screws attaching instrument panel to floor.
13. Move instrument panel rearward and disconnect speedometer cable and any wires that will prevent instrument panel from being placed on front seat.

NOTE: Use care when removing instrument panel to prevent damage to panel or steering column surfaces.

---

14. Drain cooling system, then disconnect heater hoses from heater core. Plug heater core tubes to prevent coolant spillage.
15. Discharge A/C system, then remove high and low side pressure hoses. Cap the hose openings to prevent entry of dirt or moisture.
16. From engine compartment, remove two nuts attaching heater/evaporator case to dash panel.
17. From passenger compartment, remove bolts attaching heater/evaporator case and air inlet duct support brackets to cowl top panel.
18. Remove one nut attaching bracket at left side of heater/evaporator case to dash panel, then remove one nut retaining bracket below case to dash panel.
19. Carefully pull case away from dash panel to gain access to heater core cover attaching bolts.
20. Remove five heater core cover attaching bolts, then remove cover
21. Remove heater core and seals from case, then remove seals from heater core tubes.
22. Reverse procedure to install.

SCREW
N610958-S2

NUT
45332-S2

RECIRCULATING
DUCT ASSEMBLY
19C590

SCREEN
018A14

SCREW
56956-S2

PLENUM CHAMBER
19740

SCREW
386877-S36

SCREW
56956-S2

NUT
45335-S38

NUT
55734-S2

WIRING
ASSEMBLY

NUT
45332-S2

EVAPORATOR ASSEMBLY
19850

Fig. 14 Plenum & air inlet duct assembly. 1980–81 Continental & Mark VI, 1982–83 Mark VI & Town Car

1980–81 Continental & Mark VI; 1982–83 Mark VI & Town Car Figs. 14 & 15

1. Disconnect battery ground cable.
2. Disconnect heater hoses from core. Plug hoses and heater core tubes to prevent coolant loss during core removal.
3. Remove one bolt located below the windshield wiper motor retaining left end of plenum to dash panel.
4. Remove one nut retaining the upper left corner of evaporator case to dash panel.
5. Disconnect vacuum supply hose from vacuum source, then push grommet and hose into passenger compartment.
6. Remove glove compartment, then loosen right door sill plate and remove right side cowl trim panel.
7. Remove bolt retaining lower right end of insturment panel to side cowl, then remove instrument panel pad as follows:
   a. Remove screws retaining instrument panel pad to instrument panel at each defroster opening.
   b. Remove the one screw retaining each outboard end of pad to instrument panel.
   c. Remove the five screws retaining lower edge of instrument panel pad, then pull instrument panel pad rearward and remove it.
8. Disconnect temperature control cable housing from bracket at top of plenum, then disconnect cable from temperature blend door crank arm.
9. Remove push clip retaining the center register duct bracket to the plenum and rotate bracket to the right.
10. Disconnect vacuum jumper harness at multiple vacuum connector near the floor air distribution duct, then disconnect white vacuum hose from the outside-recirculating door vacuum motor.
11. Remove screws retaining the passenger

side of floor air distribution duct to the plenum. It may be necessary to remove the two screws retaining the partial (lower) panel door vacuum motor to mounting bracket to gain access to right screw.
12. Remove the plastic push fastener retain-

SCREW
(5 REQUIRED)
42141-S2

COVER
–18N276–

HEATER CORE AND
SEAL ASSEMBLY
–18476–

SEAL
–18658–

PLENUM
ASSEMBLY

GASKET SEAL
–18B623–

Fig. 15 Heater core removal. 1980–81 Continental & Mark VI, 1982–83 Mark VI & Town Car

ing floor air distribution duct to left end of planeum and remove floor air distribution duct.
13. Remove nuts from the two studs along lower edge of plenum.
14. Carefully move plenum rearward to allow heater core tubes and stud at top of plenum to clear holes in dash panel. Remove plenum by rotating top of plenum forward, down and out from under instrument panel. Carefully pull lower edge of instrument panel rearward as necessary while rolling the plenum from behind the instrument panel.
15. Remove the four retaining screws from heater core cover and remove cover from plenum.
16. Remove heater core retaining screw then pull core and seal assembly from plenum assembly.
17. Reverse procedure to install.

1977–80 Versailles

1. Disconnect battery ground cable and drain cooling system.
2. Disconnect hoses from heater core. Plug heater core tubes to prevent coolant leakage.
3. Remove washer nut from plenum assembly mounting stud on engine side of dash panel.
4. Remove floor duct, seat belt interlock module and bracket, glove box liner and shields.
5. Loosen right door sill scuff plate, right A-pillar trim cover and right cowl side trim panel.
6. Loosen instrument panel to right cowl side bolt and remove instrument panel brace at lower rail below glove box opening.
7. If used, remove tunnel to cowl brace located on left side of plenum assembly.
8. Disconnect vacuum hoses from A/C-Defrost and Heat/Defrost door motors.

Remove screw from clip retaining vacuum harness to plenum.

9. Remove the two Heat/Defrost door motor mounting nuts and swing motor rearward on door crankarm.
10. Remove the two screws retaining plenum to left mounting bracket, then remove the two screws and three clips retaining plenum to evaporator case.
11. Swing bottom of plenum away from evaporator case to disengage S-clip on forward flange of plenum, then raise plenum to clear tabs on top of evaporator case.
12. Move plenum to left while pulling instrument rearward to gain clearance. Use care to avoid cracking plastic.

NOTE: There is very little clearance between plenum and wiper motor assembly.

13. Pull heater core to the left, then as rear surface of heater core clears evaporator case, pull core rearward and downward to clear instrument panel.
14. Reverse procedure to install. Before installing core, make sure that heater core tube to dash panel seal is in place.

1977–79 Continental

1. Drain radiator and disconnect heater hoses from core.
2. On 1978–79 models, remove engine vacuum distribution connector, located on dash panel above heater core cover plate to provide clearance. Also remove electrical harness ground terminal located on dash panel above heater core plate.
3. On all models, remove heater core cover and gasket, then lift heater core and lower mounting gasket from evaporator housing, Fig. 16.
4. Reverse procedure to install.

1977–78 Mark V

1. Drain radiator and disconnect heater hoses from core.
2. Remove glove box, then heater air outlet register from plenum assembly by disengaging the snap clips.
3. Disconnect temperature control cable from blend door crank arm.
4. Remove vacuum hoses from high-low door motor, panel-defrost door motor and the in-line tee connector to temperature by-pass door motor.
5. Disconnect resistor wiring and remove plenum case flange screws, then remove plenum case rear half.
6. Reverse procedure to install.

BLOWER MOTOR, REPLACE

1982–83 Continental

1. Disconnect battery ground cable.
2. Remove glove box and shield, then dis-

```
SCREW (7 REQUIRED)
COVER
COVER GASKET
5/8" INLET
HEATER CORE
EVAPORATOR
CASE ASSEMBLY
3/4" OUTLET
CORE MOUNTING
GASKET - LOWER
HEATER CORE RETENTION
SPRING CLIP
```

Fig. 16 Heater core removal. 1977–79 Continental

connect vacuum hose from outside-recirculating air door vacuum motor.
3. Remove instrument panel lower right to side cowl attaching bolt then, remove screw attaching support brace to top of air inlet duct.
4. Disconnect blower motor power lead at wire connector.
5. Remove blower motor housing lower support bracket to heater/evaporator attaching nut.
6. Remove side cowl trim panel.
7. Remove ashtray receptacle, then remove two screws securing instrument panel to transmission tunnel inside ashtray opening.
8. Remove screw attaching top of air inlet duct to heater/evaporator case.
9. Remove air inlet duct and blower housing assembly down and away from the evaporator case.
10. Remove assembly from vehicle, then remove four blower motor mounting plate screws and remove blower motor from housing.
11. Reverse procedure to install.

1980–81 Continental & Mark VI; 1982–83 Mark VI & Town Car

1. Disconnect battery ground cable.
2. Disconnect blower motor lead from wiring harness, then remove blower motor cooling tube from blower motor.
3. Remove the four blower motor retaining screws.
4. Rotate motor and wheel assembly slightly to the right so that bottom edge of mounting plate follows contour of wheel well splash panel, then lift the motor and wheel assembly up and out of housing.
5. Reverse procedure to install.

1977–80 Versailles

1. Disconnect battery ground cable.
2. Remove glove box.
3. Loosen right door sill scuff plate, right A-pillar trim cover and remove right cowl side trim panel.
4. Remove right lower instrument panel to cowl side bolt.
5. Remove cowl to lower instrument panel brace bolt.
6. Disconnect electrical connector from motor.
7. Remove blower motor assembly retaining screws and then blower motor. Pull rearward on lower edge of instrument panel to gain clearance.

NOTE: Do not remove mounting plate from blower motor, as the plate location is critical and should not be changed.

8. Reverse procedure to install.

1977–78 Mark V

1. Remove glove box, recirculating air register and duct assembly.
2. Remove blower lower housing to dash screws.
3. Disconnect vacuum hose from outside-recirculating air door motor and remove motor from blower lower housing, leaving motor actuator connected to door crank arm.
4. Disconnect blower motor wiring and remove blower motor housing flange screws.
5. Separate upper and lower blower housing and remove lower housing and motor from under instrument panel.
6. Remove blower motor from lower housing.
7. Reverse procedure to install.

1977–79 Continental

1. Remove the hood.
2. Remove the right hood hinge and right fender inner support brace as an assembly.
3. Disconnect the blower motor air cooling tube from the motor.
4. Disconnect the motor lead wire from the harness and the ground wire from the dash panel.
5. Disconnect the rear section of the right front fender apron from the fender around the wheel opening (7 screws) and remove the two lower fender-to-cowl mounting screws.
6. Separate the fender apron from the fender wheel opening so that the apron can be pushed downward away from the blower motor.
7. Remove the four blower motor mounting plate screws. Move the motor and wheel forward out of the blower scroll and remove the assembly through the opening while applying pressure to the fender apron to enlarge the opening.
8. Reverse procedure to install.

Engine Section

ENGINE MOUNTS, REPLACE

CAUTION: Whenever self-locking mounting bolts and nuts are removed, they must be replaced with new self-locking bolts and nuts.

1980–83 Continental, Mark VI & 1982–83 Town Car

1. Remove the nut and through bolt attaching the insulator to the support bracket, Figs. 1, 1A and 1B.
2. Raise the engine slightly with a jack and a wood block placed under the oil pan.
3. Remove the engine insulator assembly to cylinder block attaching bolts. Remove the engine insulator assembly and the heat shield, if so equipped.
4. Reverse procedure to install.

1977–80 Versailles

1. On 1979–80 models, disconnect fan shroud from radiator and set shroud back on the fan. On all models, support engine using a jack and block of wood placed under oil pan.

2. Remove through bolt attaching insulator to insulator support bracket, Fig. 2.
3. Raise engine slightly and remove insulator and support bracket to engine attaching bolts.
4. Remove insulator and support bracket assembly.
5. Reverse procedure to install.

1977–79 Continental V8-400 & 1978 Continental V8-460

1. On Continental V8-400 models, discon-

nect transmission oil cooler lines from retaining bracket on block. On all models, remove fan shroud attaching bolts.
2. Remove through bolt attaching insulator to support bracket or crossmember, Figs. 3 and 3A.
3. Raise engine slightly using a jack and block of wood placed under oil pan.
4. Remove insulator to engine attaching bolts.
5. Remove insulator and heat shield, if equipped.
6. Reverse procedure to install.

1977 Continental V8-460

1. Block the rear wheels and set the parking brake. Raise front of vehicle and install safety stands.
2. Remove the bolts that attach the support bracket to the cylinder block, Fig. 3.
3. Place a block of wood between a jack and the front edge of the oil pan. Raise the engine high enough to provide clearance to remove the support and not damage the radiator.
4. Remove the through bolts from the support insulator. Lift the insulator from the number 2 crossmember.
5. Remove the bracket-to-insulator attach-

Fig. 1A Engine mounts. 1982 Continental V8-302

Fig. 1B Engine mounts. 1980–81 Continental, 1980–83 Mark VI & 1982–83 Town Car V8-302, 351W

Fig. 2 Engine mounts. 1977–80 Versailles

Fig. 3 Engine mounts. 1977–79 Continental V8-400

Fig. 3A Engine mounts. 1977–78 Continental V8-460

Fig. 4 Engine mounts. 1977–79 Mark V V8-460

REAR SUPPORT

NO. 3 CROSSMEMBER

NO. 2 CROSSMEMBER

FRONT SUPPORT (RIGHT)

FRONT SUPPORT (LEFT)

Fig. 1 Engine mounts. 1982 Continental V6-232

Fig. 5 Engine Mount. 1977–78 Mark V V8-460

UPPER BRACKET 6043 ASSEMBLY
HEAT SHIELD
6D037 ASSEMBLY L.H.
6D036 R.H.
35–60 FT. LB.
SUPPORT INSULATOR
6B032 ASSEMBLY L.H.
6038 R.H.
20–34 FT. LB.
30–45 FT. LB.
THROUGH BOLT
DIRECTION OF BOLT
OPTIONAL
#2 CROSSMEMBER

ing bolt and separate the units.
6. Reverse procedure to install.

1977–79 Mark V

1. Remove the fan shroud attaching screws and support the engine using a jack and a block of wood under the oil pan.
2. Remove the through bolt and nut attaching the insulator to the frame crossmember, Figs. 4 and 5.
3. Remove the insulator to upper bracket attaching nuts.
4. Raise the engine enough to remove the insulator and heat shield if so equipped.
5. If required, the upper bracket can now be removed by removal of the three screws holding the bracket to the cylinder block.
6. Reverse procedure to install.

ENGINE, REPLACE

1982 Continental V6-232

1. Disconnect battery ground cable, then drain cooling system and crankcase.
2. Mark position of hood hinges, then remove hood.
3. Remove air cleaner, air inlet duct and heat tube.
4. Remove fan shroud and fan assembly, then loosen accessory drive belt idler and remove drive belt and water pump pulley.
5. Disconnect upper and lower radiator hoses at radiator.
6. Disconnect Thermactor hose at air tube check valve, then remove air tube valve bracket attaching bolt at rear of right hand cylinder head.
7. Remove secondary wire from ignition coil.
8. Remove bolts attaching power steering pump mounting bracket, then remove pump and bracket assembly and position aside with hoses attached if equipped.
9. On models with A/C, remove compressor mounting bracket attaching bolts, then remove compressor and mounting bracket assembly and secure to right hand shock absorber tower with refrigerant lines attached.

Fig. 6 Cylinder head tightening sequence. V6-232

10. Remove alternator and position aside.
11. Disconnect heater hoses from water pump and heater tube.
12. On models equipped with speed control, disconnect servo chain at carburetor, then remove servo bracket attaching bolts and servo.
13. Disconnect all necessary vacuum hoses and wiring connectors.
14. Remove engine ground strap to dash panel attaching screw.
15. Disconnect transmission downshift linkage, throttle cable from carburetor, then remove throttle cable bracket attaching bolts.
16. Disconnect fuel line and PCV valve hose from carburetor.
17. Remove carburetor assembly from intake manifold. On models equipped with 7200 VV two barel carburetor, remove spark knock intensity sensor and adapter assembly which is located between carburetor and thermostat housing.
18. With EGR spacer and phenolic gasket in position, install engine lifting plate T75T-6000-A or equivalent over carburetor mounting studs, then install nuts.
19. Raise vehicle and disconnect fuel inlet hose from fuel pump. Cap fuel hose to prevent entry of dirt.
20. Remove inspection cover from torque converter housing, then remove nuts attaching flex plate to torque converter.
21. Remove starter motor.
22. Remove transmission cooler line retaining clips, then disconnect exhaust pipe from exhaust manifold.
23. Remove four lower engine to transmission attaching bolts, then lower vehicle.
24. Remove engine mount to crossmember attaching nuts.
25. Lower vehicle and position a suitable transmission jack under transmission. Raise jack just enough to support weight of transmission.
26. Remove two upper engine to transmission attaching bolts, then place a 1/4 inch piece of plywood or other suitable material between engine and radiator to prevent damage to radiator.
27. Carefully raise engine slightly, then pull away from transmission and lift from vehicle.
28. Reverse procedure to install. Torque fasteners according to numbers in Fig. 1: 1, 35–50 ft. lbs.; 2, 50–70 ft. lbs.; 3, 35–60 ft. lbs.; 4, 35–60 ft. lbs.; 5, 70–90 ft. lbs.; 6, 35–50 ft. lbs.; 7, 70–90 ft. lbs.

1977–80 Versailles, 1980–83 Continental & Mark VI & 1982–83 Town Car V8-302, 351W

NOTE: On models equipped with Thermactor system, remove or disconnect components that will interfere with engine removal or installation.

Fig. 6A Intake manifold tightening sequence. V6-232

1. Drain cooling system and crankcase.
2. Remove hood, then disconnect battery and alternator ground cables from cylinder block.
3. Remove air cleaner and duct assembly.
4. Disconnect upper and lower radiator hoses from engine block and transmission oil cooler lines from radiator.
5. Remove bolts attaching fan shroud to radiator.
6. Remove radiator, fan, spacer, pulley and fan shroud.
7. Remove alternator mounting bolts and position alternator aside.
8. Disconnect oil pressure sending unit wire connector and fuel line at fuel pump. Plug fuel tank line.
9. Disconnect accelerator cable from carburetor and throttle valve vacuum line at intake manifold.
10. Disconnect transmission manual shift rod, then disconnect retracting spring at shift rod stud.
11. Disconnect transmission oil filler tube bracket from engine block.
12. On models equipped with A/C, isolate and remove compressor.
13. Remove power steering pump bracket from cylinder head and position pump aside. Position pump so that fluid will not drain from reservoir.
14. Disconnect heater hoses from water pump and intake manifold and temperature sending unit wire connector.
15. Remove converter housing to engine upper attaching bolts.
16. Disconnect primary wire connector from ignition coil, then remove wiring harness from left rocker arm cover and position out of way. Disconnect ground strap from block.
17. Raise front of vehicle and remove starter.
18. Disconnect exhaust pipes from exhaust manifold, then remove engine support insulators from brackets on frame.
19. Disconnect transmission oil cooler lines from retainer and remove converter housing inspection cover.
20. Disconnect flywheel from converter, secure converter to converter housing.
21. Remove remaining converter housing to engine attaching bolts, then lower vehicle and support transmission using a suitable jack.
22. Attach engine lifting device to lifting brackets on intake manifold, then raise engine slightly and disconnect from transmission.
23. Carefully lift engine from engine compartment.
24. Reverse procedure to install.

1977–79 Except Versailles

NOTE: Because of engine compartment toler-

Fig. 7 Cylinder head tightening, V8 Engines

ances, the engine should not be removed and installed with the transmission attached.

1. Disconnect battery ground cable, drain cooling system and crankcase and remove hood and air cleaner assembly.
2. Disconnect or remove all Thermactor components that may interfere with engine removal.
3. Disconnect hoses and oil cooler lines from radiator, then remove radiator, fan shroud and fan.
4. Remove all drive belts.
5. Disconnect power steering pump and alternator and position units out of the way.
6. If equipped with air conditioning, isolate and remove compressor.
7. Disconnect all hoses, lines and wiring from engine. Make certain to remove ground wires from block and right cylinder head.
8. Disconnect fuel line from pump and plug line.
9. Disconnect speed control at carburetor, if equipped.
10. Disconnect engine wiring harness.
11. Disconnect accelerator cable or linkage, then disconnect downshift linkage (if used).
12. Raise and properly support vehicle, then disconnect exhaust system from engine and remove starter.
13. Remove engine front support through bolts.
14. Remove converter cover, converter to flywheel bolts, and downshift rod.
15. Remove the four lower engine to clutch housing or converter housing bolts, then lower vehicle and remove the two upper engine to clutch housing or converter housing bolts.
16. Position jack under transmission, then using a suitable hoist, carefully remove engine from vehicle.
17. Reverse procedure to install.

CYLINDER HEAD, REPLACE

NOTES Before installing cylinder head, wipe off engine block gasket surface and be certain no foreign material has fallen into cylinder bores, bolt holes or in the valve lifter area. It is good practice to clean out bolt holes with compressed air.

Some cylinder head gaskets are coated with a special lacquer to provide a good seal once the parts have warmed up. Do not use any additional sealer on such gaskets. If the gasket does not have this lacquer coating, apply suitable sealer to both sides.

Tighten cylinder head bolts a little at a time in three steps in the sequence shown in the illustrations. Final tightening should be to the torque specifications listed in the *Engine Tightening* table. After the bolts have been torqued to specifications, *they should not be disturbed.*

V6-232

1. Disconnect battery ground cable, then drain cooling system.
2. Remove air cleaner, air intake duct and heat tube.
3. Loosen accessory drive belt idler and remove drive belt.
4. If left cylinder head is to be removed, proceed as follows:
   a. Remove oil filler cap.
   b. If equipped with power steering, remove pump bracket attaching bolts, then remove pump and bracket assembly and position pump aside with hoses attached.
   c. If equipped with A/C, remove compressor bracket attaching bolts, then position compressor and bracket assembly aside with refrigerant lines attached.
5. If right cylinder head is to be removed, proceed as follows:
   a. Remove Thermactor diverter valve and hose assembly.
   b. Remove accessory drive belt idler, then remove alternator.
   c. Remove Thermactor pump pulley, then remove Thermactor pump.
   d. Remove alternator mounting bracket.

NOTE: On models equipped with Tripminder, then fuel supply line from the fuel pump to the fuel sensor will have to be disconnected to gain access to the upper alternator bracket bolt.

   e. Remove PCV valve.
6. Remove intake manifold, and exhaust manifolds.
7. Remove rocker arm cover and attaching screws, then loosen cover by using a putty knife under cover flange and remove cover. Do not use excess force when loosening rocker arm cover as cover may become damaged.
8. Loosen rocker fulcrum bolt enough to allow rocker arms to be rotated to one side, then remove push rods.

NOTE: Tag push rods so they can be installed in the same position.

9. Remove cylinder head attaching bolts, then remove cylinder head and gasket.
10. Reverse procedure to install. Apply a thin coating of pipe sealant D8AZ-19558-A or equivalent to the shorter cylinder head bolts which are installed on the exhaust manifold side of the cylinder head. Do not apply pipe sealant to long bolts which are installed on the intake manifold side of the cylinder head. Tighten cylinder head bolts in four steps to torque listed under Engine Tightening Specifications using sequence shown in Fig. 6. Loosen cylinder bolts approximately 2 to 3 turns, then retighten bolts in four steps to specified torque in sequence, Fig. 6. When installing intake manifold, tighten mounting bolts to torque specified under Engine Tightening Specifications in sequence shown in Fig. 6A.

NOTE: Before installing intake manifold, apply a 1/8 inch bead of silicone rubber sealer D6AZ-19562-B or equivalent at mating surfaces of intake manifold, cylinder heads and

Fig. 7A Intake manifold tightening sequence. V8-302 & 351W

cylinder block. Also apply a 1/8 inch bead of sealer to the outer end of each intake manifold seal for the full width of the seal.

V8-302, 351W & 400

1. Remove intake manifold and carburetor as an assembly.
2. Disconnect battery ground cable at cylinder head.
3. If left head is being removed, remove A/C compressor (if equipped). Also remove and wire power steering pump out of the way. If equipped with Thermactor System, disconnect hose from air manifold on left cylinder head.
4. If right head is to be removed, remove alternator mounting bracket bolt and spacer, ground wire and air cleaner inlet duct.
5. If right head is to be removed on an engine with Thermactor System, remove air pump from bracket. Disconnect hose from air manifold.
6. Disconnect exhaust manifolds at exhaust pipes.
7. Remove rocker arm covers. If equipped with Thermactor System, remove check valve from air manifold.
8. On 1977 V8-302, 351W and early 1978 V8-302 engines, loosen rocker arm stud nuts so that rocker arms can be rotated to one side. On V8-400 and late 1978 and 1979–83 V8-302 and 351W engines, remove fulcrum bolts, oil deflectors (if used), fulcrums and rocker arms. On all engines, remove push rods. Keep rocker arms and push rods in order so they can be installed in the same position.
9. Remove head bolts and lift head off block.
10. Reverse procedure to install. Torque cylinder head bolts in sequence shown in Fig. 6, and torque intake manifold bolts in sequence shown in Figs. 7 and 8.

Fig. 8 Intake manifold tightening sequence. V8-400

V8-460

1. Remove intake manifold and carburetor as an assembly.
2. Disconnect muffler inlet pipe at exhaust manifold.
3. Loosen air conditioner compressor belt if so equipped.
4. Loosen alternator retaining bolts and remove bolt retaining alternator bracket to right head.
5. If air conditioned, purge system of refrigerent, then remove nuts retaining compressor bracket to water pump. Remove bolts retaining compressor to upper mounting bracket and lay compressor out of way. Remove compressor upper bracket from head.
6. If not air conditioned, remove bolts retaining power steering reservoir bracket to left head and position reservoir out of way.
7. Remove rocker arm covers and rocker arms. Remove push rods in sequence so they can be installed in their positions.
8. Remove head retaining bolts and lift head with exhaust manifold.

NOTE: If necessary to break gasket seal, pry at forward corners of cylinder heads against casting bosses provided on cylinder block. Avoid damaging machined surfaces on head and block.

9. Reverse procedure to install. Torque cylinder head bolts in sequence shown in

Fig. 9 Intake manifold tightening sequence. V8-460

Fig. 6, and torque intake manifold bolts in sequence shown in Fig. 9.

NOTE: *The cylinder head gaskets are marked "Top" or "Front" stamped near the front end of the gasket. The gasket is properly installed when the word is at the forward end of the engine and water passage holes line up. This results in the sealing beads on the right head gasket being inverted with respect to the left head gasket.*

VALVES, ADJUST

V6-232

A .060 inch longer or a .060 inch shorter push rod is available to compensate for dimensional changes in the valve train. If clearance is less than specified, the .060 inch shorter push rod should be used. If clearance is more than the maximum specified, the .060 inch longer push rod should be used.

Fig. 10 Rocker arm assembly. 1977 & early 1978 V8-302 & 351W

Using an auxiliary starter switch crankshaft until No. 1 cylinder is at TDC compression stroke, then compress valve lifter using tool T82C-6500-A or equivalent, Fig. 14. At this point, the following valves can be checked:

No. 1 Intake	No. 3 Intake
No. 1 Exhaust	No. 4 Exhaust
No. 2 Exhaust	No. 6 Intake

After clearance on these valves has been checked, rotate crankshaft until No. 5 cylinder is at TDC compression stroke (1 revolution of crankshaft), and then compress valve lifter using tool No. T82C-6500-A or equivalent, Fig. 14, and check the following valves:

No. 2 Intake	No. 5 Intake
No. 3 Exhaust	No. 5 Exhaust
No. 4 Intake	No. 6 Exhaust

V8-302, 351, 400 & 460

To eliminate the need of adjusting valve lash, a positive stop rocker arm stud and nut is used on 1977 and early 1978 V8-302 and 351W engines, Fig. 10, and a positive stop fulcrum bolt and seat is used on V8-400 and 460 and late 1978 and 1979–83 V8-302 and 351W engines, Figs. 11 and 12.

It is very important that the correct push rod be used and all components be installed and torqued as follows:

1. Position the piston of the cylinder being worked on at TDC of its compression stroke.
2. On 1977 and early 1978 V8-302 and 351 engines, lubricate and install rocker arm and fulcrum seat on the stud. Thread nut

Fig. 11 Rocker arm & related parts. V8-400, 460

Fig. 12 Rocker arm & related parts. V6-232 & Late 1978 & 1979–83 V8-302 & 351W

Fig. 13 Inspection or rocker arm stud nut. 1977 & early 1978 V8-302, 351W

Fig. 14   Compressing lifter to check valve clearance

Fig. 15   Rocker arm stud removal. 1977 & early 1978 V8-302 & 351W

Fig. 16   Positive stop type rocker arm stud installation. 1977 & early 1978 V8-302 & 351W

onto the stud until it contracts the shoulder and torque to 17–23 ft. lbs.

NOTE: Each rocker arm stud nut should be inspected when adjusting valve clearance, Fig. 13.

3. On V8-400, 460 and late 1978 and 1979–83 V8-302 and 351W engines, install rocker arm, fulcrum seat and oil deflector. Install fulcrum bolt and torque to 18–25 ft. lbs.

A .060″ shorter push rod or a .060″ longer rod are available for service to provide a means of compensating for dimensional changes in the valve mechanism. Valve stem-to-rocker arm clearance should be as listed in the *Valve Specifications* table, with the hydraulic lifter completely collapsed, Fig. 14. Repeated valve grind jobs will decrease this clearance to the point that if not compensated for the lifters will cease to function.

When checking valve clearance, if the clearance is less than the minimum, the .060″ shorter push rod should be used. If clearance is more than the maximum, the .060″ longer push rod should be used. (See *Valve Specifications* table.) To check valve clearance, proceed as follows:

V8-302 & 351, 400 & 460
1. Mark crankshaft pulley at three locations, with number 1 location at TDC timing mark (end of compression stroke), number 2 location one half turn (180°) clockwise from TDC and number 3 location three quarter turn clockwise (270°) from number 2 location.
2. Turn the crankshaft to the number 1 location and check the clearance on the following valves:
   V8-302 & 460

No. 1 Intake	No. 1 Exhaust
No. 7 Intake	No. 5 Exhaust
No. 8 Intake	No. 4 Exhaust

   V8-351 & 400

No. 1 Intake	No. 1 Exhaust
No. 4 Intake	No. 3 Exhaust
No. 8 Intake	No. 7 Exhaust

3. Turn the crankshaft to the number 2 location and check the clearance on the following valves:
   V8-302 & 460

   | No. 5 Intake | No. 2 Exhaust |
   | No. 4 Intake | No. 6 Exhaust |

   V8-351 & 400

   | No. 3 Intake | No. 2 Exhaust |
   | No. 7 Intake | No. 6 Exhaust |

4. Turn the crankshaft to the number 3 location and check the clearance on the following valves:
   V8-302 & 460

No. 2 Intake	No. 7 Exhaust
No. 3 Intake	No. 3 Exhaust
No. 6 Intake	No. 8 Exhaust

   V8-351 & 400

No. 2 Intake	No. 4 Exhaust
No. 5 Intake	No. 5 Exhaust
No. 6 Intake	No. 8 Exhaust

VALVE ARRANGEMENT

Front to Rear

V6 Engine Right Bank	I-E-I-E-I-E
V6 Engine Left Bank	E-I-E-I-E-I
V8 Engine Right Bank	I-E-I-E-I-E-I-E
V8 Engine Left Bank	E-I-E-I-E-I-E-I

VALVE LIFT SPECS.

Engine	Year	Intake	Exhaust
V6-232	1982	.415	.417
V8-302	1977	.416	.434
	1978–79	.382	.398
	1980–83	.375	.390
V8-351W	1977	.416	.416
	1980	.411	.411
V8-400	1977–79	.428	.432
V8-460	1977–78	.437	.481

VALVE TIMING

Intake Opens Before TDC

Engine	Year	Degrees
V6-232	1982	13
V8-302①	1977–82	16
V8-302②	1980–81	17
V8-302②	1982	16
V8-351W	1977 & 80	23
V8-400	1977–79	17
V8-460	1977–78	8

①—Less EFI.
②—With EFI.

ROCKER ARM STUDS, REPLACE

1977 & Early 1978 V8-302, 351W

If necessary to replace a rocker arm stud, a rocker arm stud kit is available and contains a stud remover, Fig. 15, a stud installer, Fig. 16, and two reamers, one .006″ and the other .015″. For .010″ oversize studs, use reamer T66P-6A527-B.

Rocker arm studs that are broken or have damaged threads may be replaced with standard studs. Loose studs in the head may be replaced with .006″, .010″ or .015″ oversize studs which are available for service.

When going from a standard size stud to a .015″ oversize stud, always use a .006″ reamer before finishing reaming with a .015″ reamer.

If a stud is broken off flush with the stud boss, use an easy-out to remove the broken stud, following the instructions of the tool manufacturer.

Installation
1. Position the piston of the cylinder to be worked on at TDC compression stroke.
2. Locate stud properly with tool T69P-6049D. Make sure tool bottoms on the head.
3. Lubricate rocker arm components and place rocker arm and fulcrum on the stud.
4. Thread nut onto the stud until it contacts the shoulder then tighten nut to 17–23 ft-lbs.

V6-232, V8-400, 460 & Late 1978 & 1979–83 V8-302 & 351W

The rocker arm is supported by a fulcrum bolt which fits through the fulcrum seat and threads into the cylinder head. To disassemble, remove the bolt, oil deflector, fulcrum seat and rocker arm, Figs. 11 and 12.

VALVE GUIDES

Valve guides in these engines are an integral part of the head and, therefore, cannot be removed. For service, guides can be reamed oversize to accommodate one of three service valves with oversize stems (.003″, .015″ and .030″).

Check the valve stem clearance of each valve (after cleaning) in its respective valve guide. If the clearance exceeds the service limits of .0055″, ream the valve guides to accommodate the next oversize diameter valve.

Fig. 17 Hydraulic valve lifter disassembled (typical)

Fig. 17A Front cover attaching bolt location. V6-232

HYDRAULIC VALVE LIFTERS, REPLACE

NOTE: The internal parts of each hydraulic valve lifter assembly are a matched set. If these are mixed, improper valve operation may result. Therefore, disassemble, inspect and test each assembly separately to prevent mixing the parts.

Fig. 17, illustrates the type of hydraulic lifter used. See the *Trouble Shooting Chapter* under the heading *Engine Noises* for causes of hydraulic valve lifter noise. To replace valve lifters, proceed as follows:

1. Remove intake manifold and related parts.
2. Remove rocker arm covers.
3. Loosen rocker arm stud nuts or bolts and rotate rocker arms to the side.
4. Lift out push rods, keeping them in sequence in a rack so they may be installed in their original location.
5. Using a magnet rod, remove valve lifters and place them in sequence in a rack so they may be installed in their original location.
6. Reverse procedure to install.

TIMING CASE COVER, REPLACE

NOTE: If necessary to replace the cover oil seal the cover must first be removed.

V6-232

1. Disconnect battery ground cable and drain cooling.
2. Remove air cleaner and air duct assembly.
3. Remove fan shoud attaching, then remove fan and clutch assembly and fan shroud.
4. Loosen accessory drive belt idler, then remove drive belt and water pump pulley.
5. On models equipped with power steering, remove pump bracket attaching bolts, then position pump and bracket assembly aside with hoses attached.
6. If equipped with A/C, remove compressor front support bracket.
7. Disconnect by-pass hose, heater hoses and upper radiator hose from engine.
8. Position No. 1 cylinder at TDC compression stroke, then disconnect coil wire from distributor cap. Remove distributor cap and mark position of rotor to distributor body and distributor body to front cover. Remove distributor hold down clamp, then remove distributor.
9. On models equipped with Tripminder, remove fuel flow meter support bracket.
10. Raise vehicle and support, then remove crankshaft damper using a suitable puller.
11. Remove fuel pump shield, then remove fuel pump attaching bolts and position pump aside with fuel hose attached.
12. Remove oil filter, then disconnect lower radiator hose at water pump.
13. Remove oil pan as described under Oil Pan, Replace.
14. Lower vehicle, then remove front cover attaching bolts, Fig. 17A.

NOTE: One of the front cover attaching bolts is located behind the oil filter adapter.

15. Remove ignition timing indicator, then remove front cover and water pump as an assembly.
16. Reverse procedure to install. Coat threads of bolt located at position 10, Fig. 17A, with a suitable sealer before installing. Torque front cover attaching bolts to 15 to 22 ft. lbs.

NOTE: Lubricate camshaft thrust button with Polyethylene grease before installing front cover. Also ensure that thrust button and spring are properly seated.

V8-302, 351W

1. Drain cooling system and crankcase.
2. Remove fan shroud attaching bolts and position shroud over engine fan.
3. Remove engine fan, spacer and shroud.
4. Remove drive belts and A/C idler pulley bracket.
5. Remove power steering pump and position aside.
6. Remove all accessory brackets attached

to water pump, then remove water pump pulley.
7. Disconnect lower radiator hose, heater hose and by-pass hose from water pump.
8. Remove crankshaft pulley from vibration damper.
9. Remove damper attaching screw and washer, then using a suitable puller, remove damper.
10. Disconnect fuel pump outlet line, then remove fuel pump attaching bolts and position pump aside.
11. Remove oil level dip stick.
12. Remove oil pan to front cover attaching bolts.
13. Remove front cover to engine block attaching bolts, then remove front cover and water pump as an assembly.

NOTE: Use a thin blade knife to cut oil pan gasket flush with cylinder block face prior to separating front cover from cylinder block.

14. Reverse procedure to install.

V8-400

1. Drain cooling system and disconnect battery ground cable.
2. Remove fan shroud attaching bolts then position shroud rearward.
3. Remove drive belts and A/C lower idler pulley.
4. Remove compressor mount to water pump bracket, if equipped.
5. Remove water pump pulley.
6. Remove alternator and power steering pump brackets from water pump and position aside.
7. Disconnect lower radiator hose and heater hose from water pump.
8. Remove crankshaft pulley and vibration damper attaching screw, then using a suitable puller, remove damper.
9. Remove timing pointer.
10. Remove front cover and water pump to engine block attaching bolts, then remove front cover and water pump as an assembly.
11. Reverse procedure to install.

V8-460

1. Drain cooling system and crankcase.
2. Remove engine fan and radiator shroud.
3. Disconnect upper and lower radiator hoses and transmission oil cooler lines from radiator.
4. Remove radiator upper support and radiator.
5. Remove drive belts and water pump pulley.
6. Remove A/C compressor support, if equipped.

Fig. 18 Valve timing marks. V6-232

the chain, being sure to align the timing marks as shown in Fig. 18.

CAMSHAFT, REPLACE

If it is necessary to replace the camshaft only it may be accomplished without removing the engine from the chassis. But if the camshaft bearings are to be replaced the engine will have to be removed. To remove the camshaft, proceed as follows:

1980—82 V8-302, 351W & 1982 V6-232 Except Versailles

NOTE: It may be necessary to remove or reposition radiator, A/C compressor and grille components to provide adequate clearance.

1. To remove camshaft, remove front cover and timing chain.
2. Remove distributor cap and spark plug wires, then remove distributor.
3. Disconnect automatic transmission oil cooler lines from radiator and remove radiator.
4. Remove intake manifold and carburetor as an assembly.
5. Remove rocker arm covers.
6. Loosen rocker arm fulcrum or bolts and rotate rocker arms to one side.
7. Remove push rods, keeping them in sequence in a rack so they may be installed in their original location.
8. Using a magnet, remove valve lifters and place them in a rack in sequence so they may be installed in their original location.
9. Remove camshaft thrust plate, and carefully pull camshaft from engine, using care to avoid damaging camshaft bearings.
10. Reverse procedure to install.

NOTE: Prior to installation of the camshaft, lubricate push rods and camshaft lobes with lubricant part No. D9AZ-19579-C or equivalent on V6-232 engines and D0AZ-19584-A or equivalent for V8-302 & 351W engines. Using engine oil SF, lubricate valve tappets & bores.

V8-302, 351W Versailles

1. Remove hood latch assembly, then disconnect A/C ambient temperature sensor

Fig. 18A Valve timing marks. V8 Engines

wire connector and remove hood latch support brackets.
2. Remove condenser to radiator support attaching bolts, then remove fender to radiator support braces at each side of engine compartment.
3. Remove air dam and gasket located between radiator support and grille opening panel.
4. Carefully lift condenser upward until clearance is obtained to remove camshaft.
5. Remove cylinder front cover and timing chain as outlined previously.
6. Remove intake manifold and carburetor as an assembly.
7. Remove rocker covers. Loosen rocker arm stud nuts or fulcrum bolts and rotate rocker arms to the side.
8. Remove push rods and valve lifters in sequence so they can be installed in the same position.
9. Remove camshaft thrust plate, then carefully remove camshaft from engine, Fig. 19.

NOTE: When removing camshaft, use care not to damage camshaft bearings.

10. Reverse procedure to install.

V8-400

1. Drain cooling system, then disconnect upper and lower radiator hose and transmission oil cooler lines from radiator.
2. If equipped with A/C, remove condenser.
3. Remove front cover and timing chain as outlined previously.
4. Remove fuel pump.
5. Remove intake manifold and carburetor as an assembly.
6. Remove rocker covers, then loosen fulcrum bolts and rotate rocker arms to the side.
7. Remove push rods and valve lifters in sequence so they can be installed in the same position.
8. Position No. 1 piston at TDC, then remove thrust plate and withdraw camshaft from engine, Fig. 19.

NOTE: When removing camshaft, use care not to damage camshaft bearings.

9. Reverse procedure to install.

7. Remove crankshaft pulley and vibration damper attaching screw, then remove damper using a suitable puller.
8. Remove woodruff key from crankshaft.
9. Loosen by-pass hose at water pump, then disconnect heater return hose from water pump.
10. Remove fuel pump.
11. Remove front cover to cylinder block attaching bolts, then remove front cover and water pump assembly.

NOTE: Using a thin blade knife, cut oil pan seal flush with cylinder block face prior to separating front cover from cylinder block.

12. Reverse procedure to install.

TIMING CHAIN, REPLACE

1. To remove the chain, first take off the timing chain cover as outlined previously.
2. Crank the engine until the timing mark on the camshaft sprocket is adjacent to the timing mark on the crankshaft sprocket, Figs. 18 & 18A.
3. Remove cap screws, lock plate and fuel pump eccentric from front of camshaft.
4. Place a screwdriver behind the camshaft sprocket and carefully pry the sprocket and chain off the camshaft.
5. Reverse the foregoing procedure to install

Fig. 19 Camshaft & related parts (typical). V8 engines

Fig. 20 Piston & rod assembly. V6-232

V8-460

1. Drain crankcase and cooling system.
2. Remove timing cover, chain and sprockets as outlined previously.
3. Remove intake manifold and carburetor as an assembly.
4. Remove rocker arm covers. Back off rocker arm bolts, turn rocker arms sideways and remove push rods in sequence.
5. Remove valve lifters.
6. If air conditioned, unbolt and lay condenser on left fender. Secure in this position.
7. Remove grille.
8. Remove camshaft thrust plate bolts and carefully remove camshaft from front of engine, Fig. 19.
9. Reverse procedure to install.

PISTON & ROD, ASSEMBLE

If the old pistons are serviceable, make certain that they are installed on the rods from which they were removed. The assembly must be assembled as shown in Figs. 20 and 20A.

Check side clearance between connecting rods and crankshaft journal. Clearance should be .010–.020 inch for all engines except V6-232. V6-232 clearance should be .0047–.0114 inch.

PISTONS, RINGS & PINS

Pistons are available in oversizes of .003, .020, .030 and .040".

Piston pins are available in oversizes of .001 and .002".

Rings are available in oversizes of .020, .030 and .040".

MAIN & ROD BEARINGS

Main and rod bearings are available in standard size and undersizes of .001, .002, .010, 020, .030 and .040".

CRANKSHAFT OIL SEAL, REPLACE

1. Remove oil pan and oil pump, if necessary.
2. Remove rear bearing cap, Fig. 21.
3. Loosen remaining bearing caps, allowing crankshaft to drop down about 1/32".
4. Remove old seals from both cylinder block and rear main bearing cap. Use a brass rod to drift upper half of seal from cylinder block groove. Rotate crankshaft while drifting to facilitate removal.
5. Carefully clean seal groove in block with a brush and solvent. Also clean seal groove in bearing cap. Remove the oil seal retaining pin from the bearing cap if so equipped. *The pin is not used with the split-lip seal.*
6. Dip seal halves in clean engine oil.
7. Carefully install upper seal half in its groove with undercut side of seal toward front of engine, Fig. 22, by rotating it on shaft journal of crankshaft until approximately 3/8" protrudes below the parting surface. *Be sure no rubber has been shaved from outside diameter or seal by bottom edge of groove.*
8. Retighten main bearing caps and torque to specifications.
9. Install lower seal in main bearing cap with undercut side of seal toward front of engine, and allow seal to protrude about 3/8" above parting surface to mate with upper seal upon cap installation.
10. Apply suitable sealer to parting faces of cap and block. Install cap and torque to specifications.

NOTE: If difficulty is encountered in installing the upper half of the seal in position, lightly lap (sandpaper) the side of the seal opposite the lip side using a medium grit paper. After sanding, the seal must be washed in solvent,

Fig. 20A Piston & rod assembly. V8 Engines

then dipped in clean engine oil prior to installation.

OIL PAN, REPLACE

1982 Continental V6-232

1. Disconnect battery ground cable, then remove air cleaner and air intake duct.
2. Remove fan shroud attaching screws and position shroud over fan, then remove engine oil dipstick.
3. Remove vacuum solenoid from dash panel and position on engine with vacuum hoses attached.
4. Raise and support front of vehicle, then remove exhaust pipe to exhaust manifold

Engine lubrication (typical). V8 engine

Fig. 21 Crankshaft and related parts. V8 Engines

Fig. 22 Rear crankshaft seal installation

join and where rear main bearing cap and cylinder block join. Apply a ⅛ inch bead along oil pan rail surface of cylinder block and a ¼ inch bead along front cover to oil pan surface.

NOTE: When using silicone sealant, assembly must occur within 15 minutes after sealant application. After this time, the sealer may start to set, and its sealing effectiveness may be reduced.

1980—83 Continental, Mark VI & 1982—83 Town Car V8-302, 351W

1. Disconnect battery ground cable and remove air cleaner assembly.
2. Disconnect accelerator cable and kickdown rod from carburetor.
3. Remove accelerator mounting bracket bolts and bracket.
4. Remove fan shroud attaching screws and position shroud over fan.
5. Disconnect wiper motor electrical connector and remove wiper motor.
6. Disconnect windshield washer hose.
7. Remove wiper motor mounting cover.
8. Remove oil level dipstick, then the dipstick tube retaining bolt from exhaust manifold.
9. If equipped with EGR cooler, remove Thermactor air dump tube retaining clamp, then the Thermactor crossover tube at rear of engine.
10. Raise and support vehicle, then drain engine oil.
11. On models equipped with EEC, remove transmission filler tube from oil pan and drain transmission fluid, then remove starter.
12. Disconnect fuel tank fuel line at fuel pump and plug line.
13. Disconnect exhaust pipes from manifolds.
14. If equipped with EGR cooler, remove exhaust gas sensor from exhaust manifold, then the Thermactor secondary air tube to converter housing clamps.
15. On all models, remove dipstick tube from oil pan.
16. Loosen rear engine mount attaching nuts.
17. Remove engine mount through bolts.
18. Remove shift crossover bolts at transmission.
19. If equipped with EGR cooler, disconnect exhaust pipes from catalytic converter outlet, then the catalytic converter secondary air tube and inlet pipes to exhaust manifold.
20. On all models, disconnect transmission kickdown rod.
21. Remove torque converter housing cover.
22. Remove brake line retainer from front crossmember.
23. With a suitable jack, raise engine as far as possible.
24. Place a block of wood between each engine mount and chassis bracket. When engine is secured in this position, remove jack.
25. Remove oil pan attaching bolts and lower the oil pan.
26. Remove oil pick-up tube bolts and lower tube in oil pan.
27. Remove oil pan from vehicle.
28. Reverse procedure to install.

1977—80 Versailles

1. Disconnect battery ground cable.
2. Remove two fan shroud attaching screws

attaching nuts.
5. Drain crankcase, then remove oil filter.
6. Remove shift linkage bracket to converter housing attaching bolts.
7. Disconnect transmission oil cooler lines at radiator. Remove four converter cover attaching bolts, then remove converter cover.
8. Remove bolts attaching engine damper to No. 2 crossmember.
9. Disconnect steering gear at flex coupling, then remove steering gear to main crossmember attaching bolts and allow steering gear to rest on frame.
10. Remove nuts and bolts attaching from engine mounts to chassis, then raise engine approximately 2 to 3 inches and insert wooden block between engine mounts and frame.

NOTE: On some models, it may be necessary to raise engine as much as 5 inches

to provide clearance for oil pan removal. On these models, transmission fluid dipstick tube may contact Thermactor air tube. If contact occurs, lower engine and remove dipstick and air tube.

11. Remove oil pan attaching bolts, then lower oil pan to crossmember.
12. Remove oil pump pickup tube attaching bolts and pickup tube bracket attaching nut, then lower pickup tube into oil pan.
13. Remove oil pan through front of vehicle, then remove oil pan gaskets and seals.
14. Reverse procedure to install. Using a small screwdriver, work tabs of oil pan seal into gap between rear main bearing cap and cylinder block, then with tabs positioned, work seal into groove on rear main bearing cap. Apply a ⅛ inch bead of silicone sealer D6AZ-19562-B or equivalent where front cover and cylinder block

Fig. 23 Oil pump assembly. V6-232

Fig. 23A Oil pump assembly.
V8-302, 351W & 460

and loosen shroud to prevent damage when raising engine.

3. Raise vehicle and drain crankcase.
4. Remove stabilizer bar from chassis.
5. Remove right and left engine mount through bolts.
6. Loosen transmission oil cooler lines and move aside.
7. Raise engine and position 2 × 4 in. wooden blocks under engine mounts.
8. Remove oil pan attaching bolts and oil pan.

NOTE: It will be necessary to rotate the crankshaft during removal so that rear crankshaft throw is in horizontal position to clear rear oil pan flange.

9. Reverse procedure to install.

1978-79—Continental & Mark V

1. Disconnect battery ground cable. Also disconnect transmission oil cooler lines from radiator and position aside.
2. Remove fresh air intake duct and radiator shroud attaching bolts, then position radiator shroud over fan.
3. Raise vehicle and drain crankcase.
4. On Mark V models, remove "X" brace located below oil pan.
5. On all models, remove end attachments of front stabilizer bar and rotate ends of bar downward to raise center of bar.
6. Support engine using a suitable jack, then remove engine support through bolts.
7. Raise engine and position wooden blocks 3 in. high between each engine support bracket and frame, then lower engine.
8. Remove oil pan attaching bolts, then lower pan to crossmember.
9. On models equipped with V8-400 engines, loosen oil pump and inlet tube and allow assembly to drop into the oil pan.
10. On all models, position rear crankshaft throw horizontally, then remove oil pan.

1977 Continental

1. Disconnect battery ground cable.
2. Disconnect radiator shroud from radiator.

3. Support vehicle on hoist and drain crankcase.
4. Remove starter retaining bolts.
5. Using a floor jack and wooden block under oil pan, raise engine enough to remove weight of engine from supports and remove through bolts from each support.
6. Remove the two forward support bolts from the right support insulator, then loosen the rear support bolt and pivot the insulator upward to gain access to the converter support bolts. Remove converter support bolts and remove bracket from each side of oil pan.
7. Position a 1 inch wooden block under each engine support bracket and remove jack.
8. Remove front stabilizer bar end attachments and rotate ends of bar down to raise center of bar.
9. Remove oil filter.

Fig. 24 Oil pump assembly. V8-400

10. Remove oil pan attaching bolts and remove oil pan.
11. Reverse removal procedure for installation.

1977 Mark IV & V

1. Disconnect battery ground cable.
2. Disconnect transmission oil cooler lines from radiator, then remove radiator shroud attaching bolts and position shroud over fan.
3. Support vehicle on hoist, then drain crankcase and remove oil filter.
4. Remove end attachments of front stabilizer bar and rotate ends of bar down to raise center of bar.
5. Support engine with floor jack and remove engine support through bolts.
6. Remove transmission oil cooler line attaching bolt from engine block and remove starter attaching bolts.
7. Raise engine enough to allow removal of right insulator heat shield, then position a wooden block 3 inches high between each engine support bracket and exhaust manifold. Lower engine allowing blocks to support engine.
8. Remove converter housing to cylinder block support attaching bolts and remove brackets.
9. Remove oil pan attaching bolts and lower pan to crossmember, then move transmission oil cooler lines upward and remove oil pan.
10. Reverse removal procedure for installation.

OIL PUMP, REPLACE

V6-232

On these engines, the oil pump is contained within the front cover, Fig. 23.

V8 Engines

1. Remove oil pan as previously described under "Oil Pan, Replace".
2. Remove the two attaching bolts and remove the oil pump assembly with gasket and drive shaft.
3. Reverse procedure to install.

OIL PUMP, SERVICE

V6-232 Engine

To disassemble, remove oil filter, if necessary, oil pump, cover bolts and cover. Lift oil pump gears from front cover pocket and remove cover gasket. Remove cotter pin from relief valve plug in pump housing. Drill a small hole and insert a self-tapping screw into the plug, then using pliers, remove plug from pump housing. Remove retainer spring and relief valve from pump housing. Using a suitable solvent, thoroughly clean oil pump components. Inspect oil pump as follows:

1. Check oil pump cover gasket surface. Remove any remaining gasket material, burrs and nicks.
2. Position a straightedge across oil pump gears and gasket surface.
3. Using a feeler gauge, measure clearance between straightedge and gasket surface. Clearance should be .002–.005 inch. If clearance is less than .002 inch, proceed to step 4.
4. Using a micrometer, measure oil pump gear thickness. Gear thickness should be .872–.873 inch. If gear is less than .872 inch, replace gear and check reading.
5. Measure front cover gear pocket depth. Depth should be .868–.870 inch. If depth exceeds .870 inch, replace oil pump front cover.
6. Using a feeler gauge, measure side clearance between gear tooth and gear pocket side wall. Clearance should be .002–.005 inch. If clearance exceeds .005 inch, proceed to step 7.
7. Using a micrometer, measure gear diameter. Gear diameter should be 1.664–1.666 inch. If gear diameter is less than 1.664 inch, replace gear and check reading.
8. Measure front cover gear pocket width. Width should be 1.671–1.674 inch. If width is less than 1.671, replace front cover.

V8 Engines

To disassemble, remove the pump cover plate, Figs. 23A and 24, and lift out the rotor and shaft. Remove cotter pin that secures relief valve plug in pump housing. Drill a small hole and insert a self-tapping screw into plug, then using pliers remove plug from pump housing. Then remove the retainer spring and relief valve from the pump housing. Inspect the pump as follows:

1. With all parts clean and dry, check the inside of the pump housing and the outer race and rotor for damage or excessive wear.
2. Check the mating surface of the pump cover for wear. If this surface is worn, scored or grooved, replace the cover.
3. Measure the clearance between the outer race and housing. This clearance should be .001–.013.
4. With the rotor assembly installed in the housing, place a straight edge over the rotor assembly and housing. Measure the clearance between the straight edge and the rotor and outer race. Recommended limits are .0016–.004".
5. Check the drive shaft-to-housing bearing clearance by measuring the O.D. of the shaft and the I.D. of the housing bearing. The recommended clearance limits are .0015–.0030".

6. Inspect the relief valve spring for a collapsed or worn condition.
7. Check the relief valve piston for scores and free operation in the bore. The specified clearance is .0015–.0030 inch.

BELT TENSION DATA

	New	Used
1977–80 ¼ inch	65	50
Exc. ¼ inch	140	110
1981		
Except ¼"	140	110
¼"	65	40
V Ribbed Belt		
4 Rib	105	100
5 Rib①	125	120
5 Rib②	108	108
6 Rib①	155	150
6 Rib②	113	113
1982–83		
Except ¼"	140	105
¼"	65	50
V Ribbed Belt		
4 Rib		
Except Air Pump	130	115
Air Pump	110	105
5 Rib	150	135
6 Rib①	160	145
6 Rib②	113	110

①—W/ tensioner
②—W/ absorber

WATER PUMP, REPLACE

V6-232

1. Drain cooling system, then remove air cleaner and air intake duct.
2. Remove fan shroud attaching screws and fan and fan clutch attaching bolts, then remove fan and fan clutch and shroud.
3. Loosen accessory drive belt idler, then remove drive belt and water pump pulley.
4. On models equipped with power steering, remove pump mounting bracket attaching bolts, position pump aside with hoses attached.
5. On models equipped with A/C, remove compressor front support bracket.
6. Disconnect lower radiator hose, coolant bypass hose and heat hose from water pump.
7. On models equipped with Tripminder, remove fuel flow sensor support bracket. Do not disconnect fuel lines.
8. Remove water pump attaching bolts, then remove water pump.
9. Reverse procedure to install.

V8-302, 351W

1. Drain cooling system, then remove fan shroud attaching bolts and position shroud over fan.
2. Remove fan, spacer and shroud.
3. Remove drive belts, then remove A/C idler pulley bracket.
4. Remove power steering pump and position aside.
5. Remove all accessory brackets which attach to water pump, then remove water pump pulley.
6. Remove lower radiator hose, heater hose and by-pass hose from water pump.
7. Remove water pump to front cover attaching bolts, then remove water pump.
8. Reverse procedure to install.

V8-400

1. Drain cooling system, then disconnect battery ground cable.
2. Remove fan shroud attaching bolts and position shroud rearward.
3. Remove fan and spacer from water pump shaft.
4. Remove drive belts, then remove A/C lower idler pulley.
5. Remove A/C compressor mount from water pump bracket.
6. Remove water pump pulley.
7. Remove alternator and power steering bracket from water pump and position aside.
8. Disconnect lower radiator and heater hose from water pump.
9. Remove water pump attaching bolts and water pump.
10. Reverse procedure to install.

V8-460

1. Drain cooling system and remove fan, fan shroud and drive belts.
2. Disconnect alternator bracket and position out of way.
3. Remove air pump pulley and pivot bolt, then disconnect adjusting bracket at pump. Remove upper bracket bolt and swing bracket out of way.
4. Remove power steering pump attaching bolts and position pump aside.
5. Remove A/C compressor and power steering pump and position aside.

NOTE: Secure compressor to left fender brace.

6. Remove A/C compressor bracket, then disconnect, radiator, heater and bypass hoses from water pump.
7. Remove water pump attaching bolts and water pump.
8. Reverse procedure to install.

FUEL PUMP, REPLACE

1. Disconnect fuel lines from fuel pump.
2. Remove fuel pump attaching bolts and the fuel pump and gasket.
3. Remove all gasket material from the pump and block gasket surfaces. Apply sealer to both sides of new gasket.
4. Position gasket on pump flange and hold pump in position against its mounting surface. Make sure rocker arm is riding on camshaft eccentric.
5. Press pump tight against its mounting. Install retaining screws and tighten them alternately.
6. Connect fuel lines. Then operate engine and check for leaks.

NOTE: Before installing the pump, it is good practice to crank the engine so that the nose of the camshaft eccentric is out of the way of the fuel pump rocker arm when the pump is installed. In this way there will be the least amount of tension on the rocker arm, thereby easing the installation of the pump.

Rear Axle, Propeller Shaft & Brakes

REAR AXLES

Fig. 1 illustrates the rear axle assembly used on these cars. When necessary to overhaul either of these units, refer to the *Rear Axle Specifications* table in this chapter.

1980–83 Integral Carrier

For service procedures on 1980–81 Continental, 1980–83 Mark VI and 1982–83 Town Car 8.5 inch ring gear rear axle, refer to Ford and Mercury Full Size Chapter. For service procedure on 1982–83 Continental 7.5 inch ring gear rear axle, refer to Ford Compact and Intermediate Chapter.

1977–80 Removable Carrier Type

In these axles, Fig. 1, the drive pinion is straddle-mounted by two opposed tapered roller bearings which support the pinion shaft in front of the drive pinion gear, and straight roller bearing that supports the pinion shaft at the rear of the pinion gear. The drive pinion is assembled in a pinion retainer that is bolted to the differential carrier. The tapered roller bearings are preloaded by a collapsible spacer between the bearings. The pinion is positioned by a shim or shims located between the drive pinion retainer and the differential carrier.

The differential is supported in the carrier by two tapered roller side bearings. These bearings are preloaded by two threaded ring nuts or sleeves between the bearings and pedestals. The differential assembly is positioned for proper ring gear and pinion backlash by varying the adjustment of these ring nuts. The differential case houses two side gears in mesh with two pinions mounted on a pinion shaft which is held in place by a pin. The side gears and pinions are backed by thrust washers.

The axle shafts are of unequal length, the left shaft being shorter than the right. The axle shafts are mounted in tapered roller or ball bearings that are pressed on the shafts.

SERVICE BULLETIN

All Ford Built Rear Axles: Recent manufacturing changes have eliminated the need for marking rear axle drive pinions for individual variations from nominal shim thicknesses. In the past, these pinion markings, with the aid of a shim selection table, were used as a guide to select correct shim thicknesses when a gear set or carrier assembly replacement was performed.

With the elimination of pinion markings, use of the shim selection table is no longer possible and the methods outlined below must be used.

1. Measure the thickness of the original pinion depth shim removed from the axle. Use the same thickness upon installation of the replacement carrier or drive pinion. If any further shim change is necessary, it will be indicated in the tooth pattern check.
2. If the original shim is lost, substitute a nominal shim for the original and use the tooth pattern check to determine if further shim changes are required.

REAR AXLE, REPLACE

1980–83 Continental, Mark VI & 1982–83 Town Car

1. Raise vehicle and position safety stands under the rear frame crossmember.

2. Disconnect drive shaft at companion flange and secure it to vehicle using wire.
3. Remove wheels and brake drums. If equipped with rear disc brakes, remove calipers from anchor plates and rotors from shafts.
4. Support axles housing with floor jack.
5. Disconnect brake line from clips that retain line to axle housing, then disconnect vent from rear axle housing.
6. Disconnect shock absorbers from axle housing.
7. Disconnect upper control arms from mountings on axle housing.
8. Lower axle housing assembly until coils springs are released, then remove springs.
9. Disconnect lower control arms from mountings on axle housing, then lower the axle housing and remove it from behicle.
10. Reverse procedure to install.

1977–80 Versailles

1. Raise vehicle and position safety stands under rear frame members.
2. Mark drive shaft yoke and pinion flange for reassembly, then disconnect drive shaft at rear axle U-joint and remove drive shaft from transmission extension housing. Install seal replacer tool in extension housing to prevent leakage.
3. Disconnect shock absorbers from lower mountings.
4. Remove wheel and tire assembly.
5. Remove calipers from anchor plates, then remove two retaining nuts and slide rotors off axle shafts.

NOTE: Secure calipers to frame with wire.

6. Remove vent tube from axle housing.
7. Remove brake lines from axle housing clips.

Fig. 1   Rear axle assembly. 1977–80

Fig. 2   Removing axle shaft with slide hammer-type puller

Fig. 3   Splitting bearing inner retainer for bearing removal

Fig. 4   Using hook-type tool to remove oil seal

Fig. 5   Using special driver to install oil seal

8. Support axle housing using a suitable jack, then remove spring clip nuts and plates.
9. Lower rear axle assembly and remove from vehicle.
10. Reverse procedure to install.

1977–79 Continental

1. Raise rear of vehicle and remove wheel and tire assembly.
2. On models equipped with rear drum brakes, remove brake drums, disconnect brake lines at wheel cylinders.
3. On models equipped with rear disc brakes, remove calipers from anchor plates, then remove two retaining nuts and slide rotors off axle shafts.

NOTE: Secure calipers to frame with wire.

4. Make marks on drive shaft yoke and pinion flange for reassembly, then disconnect drive shaft at rear axle U-joint and remove drive shaft from transmission extension housing. Install seal replacer tool in extension housing to prevent leakage.
5. Position a drain pan under differential carrier, then loosen carrier attaching bolts and allow axle to drain.
6. Disconnect anti-skid sensor wire connector from differential carrier, if equipped.
7. Position safety stands under frame rear members, then support axle housing using a suitable jack.
8. Disconnect brake lines from axle housing retaining clips.
9. Disconnect vent tube from rear housing.
10. Disconnect shock absorbers from lower mounting brackets.
11. Disconnect track bar from mounting stud on rear axle housing bracket.

NOTE: The axle housing mounting bracket has two holes; the track bar should be attached to the upper hole.

12. Lower rear axle housing until coil springs are released, then remove springs and insulators.
13. Disconnect suspension lower arms from axle housing, then disconnect suspension upper arms from housing.

14. Lower axle housing and remove from vehicle.
15. Reverse procedure to install.

1977–79 Mark V

1. Raise rear of vehicle and remove wheel and tire assembly.
2. On models equipped with rear drum brakes, remove brake drums and disconnect brake lines at wheel cylinders.
3. On models equipped with rear disc brakes, remove calipers from anchor plates, then remove two retaining nuts and slide rotors off axle shafts.

NOTE: Secure calipers to frame with wire.

4. Make marks on drive shaft yoke and pinion flange for reassembly, then disconnect drive shaft at rear axle U-joint and remove drive shaft from transmission extension housing. Install seal replacer tool in extension housing to prevent leakage.
5. Position a drain pan under differential carrier, then remove carrier attaching bolts and allow axle to drain.
6. Disconnect anti-skid sensor wire connector from differential carrier, then remove mounting bracket and sensor wiring from axle, if equipped.
7. Disconnect stabilizer, if equipped.
8. Disconnect shock absorber from lower mounting.
9. Remove brake line from retaining clips on rear axle housing, then remove brake line junction block retaining screw.
10. Position a suitable jack under axle housing to prevent housing from tilting when removing control arms.
11. Disconnect lower control arms from axle housing and position them downward.
12. Disconnect upper control arms from axle housing and position them upward.
13. Disconnect air vent line.
14. Lower axle housing slightly and remove coil springs and insulators.
15. Lower axle housing and remove from vehicle.
16. Reverse procedure to install.

AXLE SHAFTS & BEARINGS, REPLACE

1. Remove rear wheel assembly, then the brake drum or caliper and rotor assembly.
2. Remove axle shaft retainer nuts and bolts.
3. Pull axle shaft assembly from housing. It

may be necessary to use a suitable slide hammer type puller, Fig. 2.
4. To replace wheel bearing on models equipped with tapered roller bearings:
   a. Drill a 1/4 inch hole in inner bearing retainer approximately 3/4 of the thickness of the bearing retainer deep.

NOTE: Do not drill completely through the bearing retainer since damage to the axle shaft may result.

   b. Place a cold chisel across the drilled hole and strike with a hammer to break retainer, then discard retainer, Fig. 3.
   c. Using suitable press and plates, press bearing from axle shaft. Do not apply heat since the heat will weaken the axle shaft bearing journal area.
   d. Install lubricated seal and bearing on axle shaft, ensuring the cup rib ring faces toward the axle flange.

NOTE: The lubricated seal of the bearing assembly used with drum brake installations is of a different length than the seal used on disc brake installations and are not interchangeable. For identification, the seal used on drum brake installations has a grey color outer rim and on disc brake installations, the seal has a black oxide appearance.

   e. Press new bearing into place, then the bearing retainer firmly against the bearing.
   f. Remove old bearing cup from axle housing with a suitable puller. Place new bearing cup on bearing and apply lubricant to outside diameter of seal and bearing cup and install in axle housing.
5. To replace wheel bearing on models equipped with ball bearings:
   a. Remove oil seal from axle housing, Fig. 4.
   b. Loosen bearing inner retainer by striking retainer ring in several places with a cold chisel and slide off shaft, Fig. 3.

NOTE: On some models, it may be necessary to drill a 1/4 inch hole in inner bearing retainer approximately 3/4 of

Fig. 6 Rear brake assembly. 1977–83

Fig. 7 Backing off brake adjustment by disengaging adjuster lever with screwdriver

the thickness of the bearing retainer deep before using the cold chisel.

c. Using suitable press and plates, press bearing from shaft. Do not heat axle shaft since the heat will damage the shaft.
d. Install outer retainer on shaft and press bearing into place. Press inner retainer onto shaft until firmly seated against bearing.
e. Install oil seal into axle housing, Fig. 5.
6. On all units, slide axle shaft assembly into housing, engaging axle shaft splines in the side gear.
7. Install and torque axle shaft retainer nuts and bolts to 50–75 ft. lbs. on 1977 Continental, Mark IV and Mark V, 50–70 ft. lbs. on 1978–79 Continental and Mark V. On 1977 Versailles, torque disc brake anchor plate bolts to 90–120 ft. lbs. On 1979 Versailles, torque axle shaft bearing retainer to 50–70 ft. lbs. On 1980 models, torque axle shaft bearing retainer to 20–40 ft. lbs.

PROPELLER SHAFT, REPLACE

To maintain proper drive line balance, mark the drive shaft, universal joints, slip yoke and companion flange before removing the shaft assembly so it can be reinstalled in its original position.
1. On Continental, Town Car and Versailles and 1980–83 Mark VI remove companion flange to drive pinion flange attaching bolts.
2. On Mark V models, disconnect rear U joint from companion flange. Tape loose bearing caps to spider.
3. On all models, pull drive shaft rearward until slip yoke clears transmission extension housing.
4. Reverse procedure to install.

BRAKE ADJUSTMENTS

These brakes, Fig. 6, have self-adjusting shoe mechanisms that assure correct lining-to-drum clearances at all times. The automat-

ic adjusters operate only when the brakes are applied when the car is moving rearward.

Although the brakes are self-adjusting, an initial adjustment is necessary when the brake shoes have been relined or replaced, or when the length of the star wheel adjuster has been changed during some other service operation.

Frequent usage of an automatic transmission forward range to halt reverse vehicle motion may prevent the automatic adjusters from functioning, thereby inducing low pedal heights. Should low pedal heights be encountered, it is recommended that numerous forward and reverse stops be made until satisfactory pedal height is obtained.

NOTE: If a low pedal height condition cannot be corrected by making numerous reverse stops (provided the hydraulic system is free of air) it indicates that the automatic adjusting mechanism is not functioning. Therefore, it will be necessary to remove the brake drum, clean, free up and lubricate the adjusting mechanism. Then adjust the brakes, being sure the parking brake is fully released.

Fig. 8 Brake adjustment with gauge

Adjustment

SERVICE BULLETIN

When servicing a vehicle requiring a brake adjustment, the metal knock-out plugs should NOT be removed. Rather the drums should be removed and brakes inspected for a malfunction.

Although the brakes are self-adjusting, an initial adjustment will be necessary after a brake repair, such as relining or replacement. The initial adjustment can be obtained by the new procedure which follows:

NOTE: If after removing brake drum retaining nuts, the brake drum cannot be removed, pry rubber plug from backing plate. Insert a narrow screwdriver through hole in backing plate and disengage lever from adjusting screw. While holding lever away from adjusting screw, back off adjusting screw using a suitable tool to retract brake shoes, Fig. 7.

1. Use the brake shoe adjustment gauge shown in Fig. 8 to obtain the drum inside diameter as shown. Tighten the adjusting knob on the gauge to hold this setting.
2. Place the opposite side of the gauge over the brake shoes and adjust the shoes by turning the adjuster screw until the gauge just slides over the linings. Rotate the gauge around the lining surface to assure proper lining diameter adjustment and clearance.
3. Install brake drum and wheel. Final adjustment is accomplished by making several firm reverse stops, using the brake pedal.

PARKING BRAKES, ADJUST

Rear Disc Brakes

1. Fully release parking brake, then place transmission in neutral and support vehicle at rear axle.

2. Tighten adjuster nut until levers on calipers just begin to move, then loosen adjuster nut until levers just return to stop position.
3. Apply and release parking brake. Check levers on caliper to determine if they are fully returned by attempting to pull lever rearward. If lever moves, the adjustment is too tight and must be readjusted.

Rear Drum Brakes

1. Make sure the parking brake is fully released.
2. Place transmission in neutral and raise the vehicle.
3. Tighten the adjusting nut against the cable equalizer to cause rear wheel brake drag. Then loosen the adjusting nut until the rear brakes are fully released. There should be no brake drag.
4. Lower the vehicle and check operation.

VACUUM RELEASE UNIT

The vacuum power unit will release the parking brake automatically when the transmission selector lever is moved into any driving position with the engine running. The brakes will not release automatically, however, when the selector lever is in neutral or park position with the engine running, or in any other position with the engine off.

The lower end of the release handle extends out for alternate manual release in the event of vacuum power failure or for optional manual release at any time.

To detect leaks in the vacuum release parking brake lines or to find disconnected or an improperly connected line, listen for a hissing sound along the line routings.

NOTE: Do not apply compressed air to the vacuum system when conducting a leak test. The actuator diaphram in the parking brake vacuum motor may be damaged.

Perform the following to detect leaks in the vacuum release system:
1. Start and operate engine at idle. Position

transmission gear shift lever into Neutral and applying parking brake.
2. Position transmission gear shift lever into Drive and check parking brake sector to insure sector returns to its stop (zero travel position), when the parking brake releases.

NOTE: The parking brake vacuum release does not operate with the transmission in Reverse.

3. If parking brake does not release, disconnect vacuum line from parking brake release vacuum motor and connect a suitable vacuum gauge to the line. A minimum of 10 inches Hg is required to actuate the parking brake vacuum motor. If a minimum reading is obtained, replace parking brake release vacuum line. If a minimum reading is not obtained, replace parking brake vacuum release motor.

MASTER CYLINDER, REPLACE

1. Disconnect brake lines from master cylinder.
2. Remove two nuts attaching master cylinder to power brake unit.
3. Slide master cylinder off mounting studs and remove from vehicle.
4. Reverse procedure to install.

POWER BRAKE UNIT, REPLACE

Except Hydro Boost

1. Disconnect battery ground cable, then remove air cleaner.
2. Disconnect vacuum hose from power brake unit check valve.
3. Disconnect brake lines from master cylinder, then remove two nuts attaching master cylinder to power brake unit and remove master cylinder.

4. Working from under instrument panel, disconnect stop lamp switch wire connector, then remove clip and washer from brake pedal pin. Slide brake lamp switch off brake pedal pin just far enough for outer arm to clear pin, then remove switch. Slide power brake push rod and washer from brake pedal pin.
5. On models equipped with speed control, remove amplifier unit from lower power brake unit mounting stud.
6. Move power brake unit forward until studs clear dash panel, then remove unit.
7. Reverse procedure to install.

Hydro Boost

1. Disconnect stoplight switch wires at connector and remove hairpin retainer, then slide stoplight switch off brake pedal pin far enough for switch outer hole to clear pin and remove pin from switch.
2. Slide hydro-boost push rod and nylon washers and bushing off brake pedal pin.
3. Remove master cylinder and position to one side without disturbing hydraulic lines.

NOTE: It is not necessary to disconnect brake lines, but care should be taken not to deform lines.

4. Disconnect pressure, steering gear and return lines from booster, then plug lines and ports in hydro-boost to prevent entry of dirt.
5. Remove hydro-boost retaining nuts, and remove assembly sliding push rod link from engine side of dash panel.
6. Reverse procedure to install. To purge system, disconnect coil wire so that engine will not start. Fill power steering pump reservoir, then while engaging starter, pump brake pedal. Do not cycle steering wheel until all residual air has been purged from the hydro boost unit. Check fluid level, then connect coil wire and start engine. Apply brakes with a pumping action and cycle steering wheel, then check system for leaks.

Rear Suspension

SHOCK ABSORBER, REPLACE

1982–83 Continental

1. Open trunk to gain access to upper shock absorber attachment.
2. Remove rubber cap if equipped, from shock absorber stud, then remove nut, washer and insulator.
3. Raise vehicle and support rear axle.
4. Remove lower shock absorber protective cover, then remove cross bolt and nut from lower shock absorber mounting bracket.
5. From underneath vehicle, compress shock absorber to clear hole in upper shock tower, then remove shock absorber.

NOTE: The 1982–83 Continental is equipped with gas pressurized shock absorbers which extend unassisted during removal. Do not apply heat or flame to

the shock absorber tube during removal.

6. Reverse procedure to install. While holding shock absorber in position, torque

lower cross bolt to 67.1 ft. lbs. Lower vehicle and install upper mounting nut, washer and insulator and torque nut to 24 to 26 ft. lbs.

Fig. 1 Rear suspension (typical). 1977–80 Versailles

Fig. 2 Spring front bushing removal. 1977–80 Versailles

Fig. 3 Spring front bushing installation. 1977–80 Versailles

Except 1982–83 Continental

1. With the rear axle supported properly disconnect shock absorber at upper mounting and compress it to clear hole.
2. Disconnect shock absorber from lower attachment.
3. Reverse procedure to install.

LEAF SPRINGS & BUSHINGS, REPLACE

1977–80 Versailles

1. Raise rear of vehicle and support at frame. Support axle with a suitable jack.

2. Disconnect shock absorbers from lower mountings.
3. Lower jack and remove spring plate "U" bolts and spring plate, Fig. 1.
4. Raise axle to remove weight from spring and disassemble rear shackle.
5. Remove spring front mount bolt.
6. Replace spring front eye bushings as necessary, Figs. 2 and 3.
7. Reverse procedure to install.

Fig. 4 Rear suspension. 1982–83 Continental

384485-S2
2 REQ'D.

18041
2 REQ'D.

18198
2 REQ'D.

5536
2 REQ'D.

18198
2 REQ'D.

5560
2 REQ'D.

18171
2 REQ'D.

18080
2 REQ'D.

N800414-S100
4 REQ'D.

SEE
VIEW A

4730
2 REQ'D.

N800166-S100
4 REQ'D.

5538 ASSY.
2 REQ'D.

N800414-S100
4 REQ'D.

5500
2 REQ'D.

N800523-S100
4 REQ'D.

N800523-S100
2 REQ'D.

N800169
2 REQ'D.

N800526-S100
2 REQ'D.

N800526-S100

N800523-S100
2 REQ'D.

5A638
2 REQ'D.

N800526-S100
2 REQ'D.

VIEW A

Fig. 5 Rear suspension. 1980—81 Continental, 1980—83 Mark VI & 1982—83 Town Car

COIL SPRINGS, REPLACE

1982—83 Continental

1. Remove stabilizer bar as described under Stabilizer Bar, Replace, if equipped.
2. Position a suitable jack under rear axle, then raise vehicle and support body at rear body crossmember.
3. Lower axle until shock absorbers are fully extended.

NOTE: Support axle with jack stands or a suitable jack.

4. Position a suitable jack under lower control arm pivot bolt and remove nut and bolt. Carefully and slowly lower the control arm until all spring tension is relieved.
5. Remove coil spring and insulators from vehicle, Fig. 4.

LINCOLN

REAR SPRING
5560

SPRING
INSULATORS

UPPER ARM
ADJUSTMENT
BOLT

SHOCK ABSORBER
18125

TRACKING BAR
5A639

BUMPER

LOWER ARM
5A648-9

UPPER ARM
5500

VENT
TUBE

INDENT TOWARD
FRONT OF VEHICLE

LEFT ARM INDENTED
BY 2 NOTCHES IN BUSHING FLANGE

Fig. 6   Rear suspension (typical). 1977–79 Continental

1980–81 Continental, 1980–83 Mark VI & 1982–83 Town Car

1. Raise rear of vehicle and support at frame side sills. Support rear axle with a suitable jack.

LOWER ARM

ECCENTRIC
BUSHING INNER
SLEEVE

UPPER ARM

SHOCK ABSORBER

Fig. 7   Rear suspension (typical). 1977–79 Mark V

2. Disconnect shock absorbers and stabilizer bar from axle housing, Fig. 5.
3. Disconnect right hand parking brake cable from right hand upper arm retainer.
4. Lower the axle housing until coil springs are released.
5. Remove springs and insulators, Fig. 5.

6. Reverse procedure to install.

1977–79 Except Versailles

1. Raise rear of vehicle and support at frame. Support rear axle with a suitable jack.
2. Disconnect shock absorbers at lower mountings.
3. On 1977–79 Lincoln Continental models, disconnect brake hose at rear crossmember and remove hose to bracket clip.
4. Lower axle to remove springs.
5. Reverse procedure to install. On all models except 1977–79 Mark V, install an insulator between each seat and the spring, Fig. 6. On 1977–79 Mark V, an insulator is installed only between upper seat and the spring, Fig. 7.

CONTROL ARMS, REPLACE

1982–83 Continental

Upper Arm

NOTE: Always replace control arms in pairs. Therefore, if one arm requires replacement, replace the same arm on the opposite side of the vehicle.

1. Raise vehicle and support body at rear body crossmember.

2. Remove upper arm pivot bolt and nut, Fig. 5.
3. Remove front pivot bolt and nut, then remove upper arm from vehicle.
4. Reverse procedure to install. Torque upper arm pivot and front pivot bolts to 100 ft. lbs.

Lower Arm

NOTE: Always replace control arms in pairs. Therefore, if one arm requires replacement, replace the same arm on the opposite side of the vehicle.

1. Remove stabilizer bar as described under Stabilizer Bar, Replace, if equipped.
2. Position a suitable jack under rear axle, then raise vehicle and support body at rear body crossmember.
3. Lower axle until shock absorbers are fully extended.

NOTE: Support axle with jack stands or a suitable jack.

4. Position a suitable jack under lower control arm rear pivot bolt and remove nut bolt, Fig. 5. Carefully and slowly lower the control arm until all spring tension is relieved, then remove coil spring and insulators.
5. Remove lower control arm front pivot bolt and nut, then remove lower control arm assembly.

1980–81 Continental, 1980–83 Mark VI & 1982–83 Town Car

NOTE: Always replace control arms in pairs. Therefore, if one arm requires replacement, replace the same arm on the opposite side of vehicle. Also, if both upper and lower control arms are to be removed at the same time, first remove both coil springs.

1. Raise vehicle and support at frame side rails with jack stands.
2. If removing lower control arm, disconnect stabilizer bar from arm.
3. With shock absorbers fully extended, support axle under differential pinion nose and under axle.
4. Remove pivot bolt and nut from frame bracket, then remove control arm, Fig. 5.
5. Reverse procedure to install. Torque pivot bolt and nut to 103–133 ft. lbs.
6. Reverse procedure to install. Torque lower arm front bolt and rear pivot bolts to

Fig. 8   Stabilizer bar installation. 1977–79 Mark V

100 ft. lbs.

1977–79 Except Versailles

NOTE: Upper and lower control arms are replaced in pairs.

1. Raise rear of vehicle and support at frame. Support axle with a suitable jack.
2. On all models except Mark V, disconnect track bar from frame mounting bracket.
3. Lower axle and install a second jack under differential pinion nose.
4. Disconnect control arm from axle bracket. On upper arms, disconnect arm from crossmember and on lower arms, disconnect arm from frame attachment bracket.
5. Reverse procedure to install.

STABILIZER BAR, REPLACE

1982–83 Continental

1. Raise and support rear of vehicle.
2. Remove four stabilizer bar to lower control arm attaching bolts.
3. Remove stabilizer bar from vehicle.
4. Reverse procedure to install. Torque stabilizer bar to lower control arm attaching bolts to 45 to 50 ft. lbs.

1980–81 Continental, 1980–83 Mark VI & 1982–83 Town Car

1. Raise rear of vehicle and support at frame side sills.
2. Lower axle housing until shock absorbers are fully extended.
3. Remove the four bolts, nuts and spacers retaining stabilizer bar lower control arms, then remove stabilizer bar, Fig. 5.
4. Reverse procedure to install. Torque bolts to 70–92 ft. lbs.

1977–79 Mark V

1. Remove bolts securing stabilizer bar to rear link assemblies on both sides, Fig. 8.
2. Remove nuts securing mounting bracket to lower mounting clamp and remove bar.
3. Reverse procedure to install.

TRACK BAR & BUSHINGS, REPLACE

1977–79 Continental

1. Remove cover from track bar axle attachment, then disconnect track bar from mounting stud.
2. Disconnect track bar from frame side rail.
3. Reverse procedure to install.

N620483-S2
6 REQD
81-102 N·m
(60-75 LB-FT)

380335-S

3B391
2 REQD

N800280-S7
8-15 N·m
(6-12 LB-FT)

N800265-S2

FENDER APRON

81-102 N·m
(60-75 LB-FT)

5B482

5482

N800236-S100
203-244 N·m
(150-180 LB-FT)

18A084

5486

N800234-S100

3108 LH
3107 RH

N801923-S2
27-34 N·m
(20-25 LB-FT)

381612-S100
136-163 N·m
(100-120 LB-FT)

72045-S2

N800264-S2

VIEW Y

3051 LH ASSY.
3042 RH ASSY.

5493

NOTE:
LINK BOLT, SPACER, AND
WASHER PART NUMBERS
VARY FOR EACH
VEHICLE LINE.

VIEW Z

5415

N800277-S2

N800799-S100

5310

N800237-S100
292-353 N·m
(215-260 LB-FT)

VIEW X

5414
ASSEMBLE FLUSH TO
1.4" OUT FROM END
OF SPRING

5414
INSULATOR

3051 & 3042

5310

HOLE "A"

HOLE "B"

END OF SPRING MUST CLEAR
HOLE "A" AND COVER HOLE "B"

VIEW Z

VIEW X

Fig. 1 Front suspension. 1982–83 Continental

FRONT SUSPENSION

1982–83 Continental

This suspension, Fig. 1, is a modified McPherson strut design, which uses shock struts and coil springs. The springs are mounted between the lower control arm and a spring pocket in the crossmember.

1977–80 Versailles

Referring to Fig. 2, each front wheel rotates on a spindle. The upper and lower ends of the spindle are attached to ball joints that are mounted to an upper and lower control arm. The upper arm pivots on a bushing and shaft assembly that is bolted to the underbody. The lower arm pivots on a bolt that is located in an underbody bracket.

A coil spring seats between the upper arm and the top of the spring housing. A double-acting shock absorber is bolted to the arm and the top of the spring housing.

Struts, which are connected between lower control arms and the underbody, prevent the arms from moving fore and aft.

Except Versailles & 1982–83 Continental

Referring to Figs. 3 and 4, each wheel rotates on a spindle. The upper and lower ends of the spindle are attached to upper and lower ball joints that are mounted to an upper and lower control arm. The upper control arm pivots on a shaft assembly that is bolted to the frame. The lower control arm pivots on a bolt in the front crossmember. On 1977–79 models, the struts, which are connected between the lower control arms and frame crossmember, prevent the control arms from moving forward or backward.

WHEEL ALIGNMENT

1982–83 Continental

Caster & Camber

The caster and camber angles of this suspension are factory pre-set and cannot be adjusted in the field.

1977–80 Versailles

Caster & Camber

As shown in Fig. 5, caster is controlled by the front suspension strut. To obtain positive caster, loosen the strut rear nut and tighten the strut front nut against the bushing. To obtain negative caster, loosen the strut front nut and tighten the strut rear nut against the bushing.

Camber is controlled by the eccentric cam located at the lower arm attachment to the side rail. To adjust camber, loosen the camber adjustment bolt nut at the rear of the body bracket. Spread the body bracket at the camber adjustment bolt area just enough to permit lateral travel of the arm when the adjustment bolt is turned. Rotate the bolt and eccentric clockwise from the high position to increase camber or counterclockwise to decrease it.

Except Versailles & 1982–83 Continental

Caster and camber can be adjusted by loosening the bolts that attach the upper suspen-

sion arm to the shaft at the frame side rail, and moving the arm assembly in or out in the elongated bolt holes, Figs. 4 and 4A. Since any movement of the arm affects both caster and camber, both factors should be balanced against one another when making the adjustment.

Caster, Adjust

1. To adjust caster, install the adjusting tool as shown in Figs. 6 and 7.
2. Loosen both upper arm inner shaft retaining bolts and move either front or rear of the shaft in or out as necessary to increase or decrease caster angle. Then tighten bolt to retain adjustment.

Camber, Adjust

1. Loosen both upper arm inner retaining bolts and move both front and rear ends of shaft inward or outward as necessary to increase or decrease camber angle.
2. Tighten bolts and recheck caster and readjust if necessary.

TOE-IN, ADJUST

1982–83 Continental

1. Check to see that steering shaft and steering wheel marks are in alignment and in the top position.
2. Loosen clamp screw on the tie rod bellows and free the seal on the rod to prevent twisting of the bellows, Fig. 8.
3. Place opened end wrench on flats of tie rod socket to prevent socket from turning, then loosen tie rod jam nuts.
4. Use suitable pliers to turn the tie rod inner end to correct the adjustment to specifications. Do not use pliers on tie rod threads. Turning to reduce number of threads showing will increase toe-in. Turning in the opposite direction will reduce toe-in.

Exc. 1982–83 Continental

Position the front wheels in their straight-ahead position. Then turn both tie rod adjusting sleeves an equal amount until the desired toe-in setting is obtained.

WHEEL BEARINGS, ADJUST

1. With wheel rotating, tighten adjusting nut to 17–25 ft. lbs.
2. Back off adjusting nut 1/2 turn and re-tighten nut to 10–15 inch lbs.
3. Place nut lock on nut so that castellations on lock are aligned with cotter pin hole in spindle and install cotter pin.
4. Check front wheel rotation, if it rotates noisily or rough, clean, inspect or replace wheel bearings as necessary.

WHEEL BEARINGS, REPLACE

(Disc Brakes)

1. Raise car and remove front wheels.
2. Remove caliper mounting bolts.

NOTE: It is not necessary to disconnect the brake line for this operation.

3. Slide caliper off of the disc, inserting a spacer between the shoes to hold them in their bores after the caliper is removed. Position caliper assembly out of the way.

NOTE: Do not allow caliper to hang by brake hose.

Fig. 2   Front suspension (typical). 1977–80 Versailles

Fig. 3 Front suspension. 1980-81 Continental, 1980-83 Mark VI & 1982-83 Town Car

4. Remove hub and disc. Grease retainer and inner bearing can now be removed.
5. Reverse procedure to install.

CHECKING BALL JOINTS FOR WEAR

Upper Ball Joint

1977-80 Versailles
1. Raise car on frame contact hoist or by floor jacks placed underbody until wheel falls to full down position.
2. Grasp the lower edge of tire and move the wheel in and out.
3. While the wheel is being moved observe any movement between the upper end of the spindle and upper arm. If any movement is observed replace the ball joint.

1977-81 Continental, 1977-83 Mark V & VI & 1982-83 Town Car
1. Raise car on floor jacks placed beneath lower control arms.
2. Grasp lower edge of tire and move wheel in and out.
3. As wheel is being moved in and out, observe upper end of spindle and upper arm.
4. Any movement between upper end of spindle and upper arm indicates ball joint wear and loss of preload. If such movement is observed, replace upper ball joint.

NOTE: During the foregoing check, the lower ball joint will be unloaded and may move. Disregard all such movement of the lower joint. Also, do not mistake loose wheel bearings for a worn ball joint.

Lower Ball Joint

1982-83 Continental
1. Support vehicle in normal driving position with both ball joints loaded.
2. Clean area around grease fitting and checking surface.

NOTE: The checking surface is the round boss into which the grease fitting is installed.

3. The checking surface should project outside the cover, Fig. 9. If surface is inside cover replace lower arm assembly.

1980-81 Continental, 1980-83 Mark VI & 1982-83 Town Car
These models are equipped with lower ball joint wear indicators, Fig. 9 To check ball joint for wear, support vehicle in normal driving position with both ball joints loaded. Observe the checking surface of the ball joint. If the checking surface is inside the cover, Fig. 4B, replace the ball joint.

1977-80 Versailles
1. With car jacked up as directed above, grasp the lower edge of the tire and move it in and out.
2. As wheel is being moved in and out, observe lower end of spindle and lower arm.
3. Any movement between lower end of spindle and lower arm indicates ball joint wear and loss of preload. If such movement is observed, replace lower arm and/or ball joint.

NOTE: During the foregoing check, the ball joints will be unloaded and may move. Therefore disregard any movement of the upper ball joint when checking the lower ball joint and any movement of the lower ball joint when checking the upper ball joint. Also, do not mistake loose wheel bearings for a worn ball joint.

1977-79 Except Versailles
1. Raise car on jacks placed under lower control arms as shown in Fig. 10.
2. With a dial indicator attached to the lower arm, position indicator so that the plunger rests against inner side of wheel rim adjacent to lower ball joint.
3. Grasp tire at top and bottom and slowly move tire in and out. Note reading on dial, which is the radial play. If the reading exceeds 1/4", replace lower ball joint.

BALL JOINTS, REPLACE

1982-83 Continental

These ball joints are not serviceable. If they require replacement, the control arm and ball joint must be replaced as an assembly. Torque ball joint stud nut to 100-120 ft. lbs.

Except 1982-83 Continental

NOTE: Ford Motor Company recommends that new ball joints should not be installed on used control arms and that the control arm be replaced if ball joint replacement is required. However, aftermarket ball joint repair kits

Fig. 4   Front suspension. 1977–79 Except Versailles

Fig. 5   Caster & camber adjustment. 1977–80 Versailles

Fig. 6   Caster and camber adjusting tool. 1977–79 except Versailles

which do not require control arm replacement, are available and can be installed using the following procedure.

When replacing a riveted joint, remove the rivets and retain the new joint in its control arm with the bolts, nuts and washers furnished with the ball joint kit.

Use a suitable pressing tool to force the ball joint from the spindle.

SHOCK STRUT, REPLACE

1982–83 Continental

1. Place ignition switch in the Unlocked position so that front wheels are free to move.

2. From engine compartment, remove one strut to upper mounting nut. Use a screwdriver in rod slot to hold rod stationary when removing nut.
3. Raise front of vehicle by lower control arms, then place safety stands under frame jack pads located rearward of wheels.
4. Remove wheel and tire assembly, then remove brake caliper, rotor assembly and dust shield.
5. Remove two nuts and bolts attaching lower strut to spindle.

NOTE: When removing the second lower strut to spindle nut, hold strut firmly as gas pressure will cause strut to fully extend.

6. Lift strut upward from spindle to compress rod, then pull downward and remove strut.
7. Reverse procedure to install. Torque upper mount attaching nut to 60 to 75 ft. lbs. Remove suspension load from lower control arm by lowering front of vehicle, then torque lower mounting nuts to 150 to 180 ft. lbs.

SHOCK ABSORBER, REPLACE

1977–80 Versailles

1. Raise hood and remove upper mounting bracket-to-spring tower retaining nuts.

Fig. 7   Caster & camber adjusting tools. 1980–81 Continental, 1980–83 Mark VI & 1982–83 Town Car

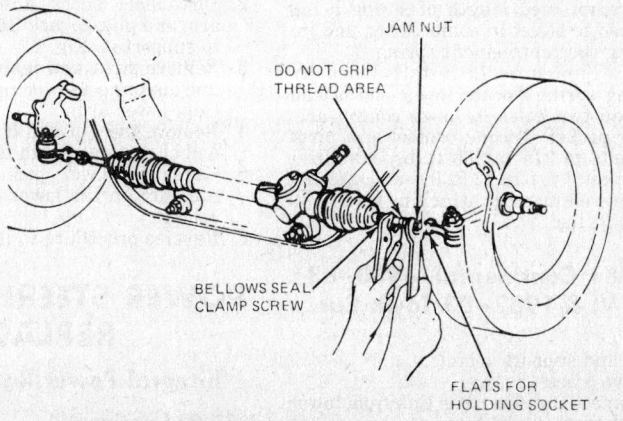

Fig. 8   Toe-in adjustment. 1982–83 Continental

Fig. 9   Lower ball joint wear indicator. 1980–83 Continental, Mark VI & Town Car

2. Raise front of car and place safety stands under lower control arms.
3. Remove shock absorber lower retaining nuts and washers.
4. Lift shock absorber from spring tower.
5. Reverse procedure to install.

1977–81 Continental, 1977–83 Mark V & VI & 1982–83 Town Car

1. Remove nut, washer and bushing from upper end of shock absorber.
2. Raise vehicle and support on stands.
3. Remove screws retaining shock absorber to lower control arm and remove shock absorber.
4. Reverse procedure to install.

COIL SPRING, REPLACE

1982–83 Continental

1. Raise front of vehicle and position safety stands under jack pads located rearward of wheels, then remove wheel and tire assembly.
2. Disconnect stabilizer bar link from lower control arm.
3. Remove steering gear attaching bolts, then position gear out of way.
4. Using tool 3290-C or equivalent, disconnect tie rod from spindle.
5. Using spring compressor D78P-5310-A or equivalent, compress spring until it is free from lower seat.
6. Remove two lower control arm pivot bolts and disengage control arm from frame, then remove spring from seat. If a replacement spring is to be installed, measure compressed length of spring being removed to assist in compressing and installing the replacement spring.
7. Reverse procedure to install. When installing spring, locate lower end of coil between two holes in lower control arm spring pocket. Torque control arm pivot bolt nuts to 215 to 260 ft.lbs., stabilizer bar link nut to 6 to 12 ft. lbs. and steering gear to crossmember attaching bolts to 90 to 100 ft. lbs.

1980–81 Continental, 1980–83 Mark VI & 1982–83 Town Car

1. Raise and support vehicle.
2. Remove wheel.
3. Disconnect stabilizer bar link from lower control arm.
4. Remove shock absorber.

Fig. 10   Checking lower ball joint for wear. 1977–79 Exc. Versailles

5. Remove steering center link from pitman arm.
6. Compress coil spring with a suitable spring compressor, tool D-78P-5310-A or equivalent.
7. Remove two lower control arm pivot bolts and disengage arm from crossmember.
8. Remove spring from vehicle.
9. Reverse procedure to install. Torque pivot bolts to 120–140 ft. lbs.

NOTE: Tail end of spring must be positioned as shown in Fig. 3.

1977–80 Versailles

1. Remove shock absorber and upper mounting bracket as an assembly.
2. Raise car on hoist and install safety stands.
3. Remove wheel, tire, rotor and caliper assembly from spindle.
4. Install a suitable spring compressor and compress spring.
5. Remove two upper-arm-to-spring tower retaining nuts and swing upper arm outward from spring.
6. Release spring compressor, then remove spring.
7. Reverse procedure to install.

1977–79 Except Versailles

1. Raise vehicle and support front end of frame with jack stands.
2. Disconnect shock absorber from lower arm and place a jack under the lower arm to support it, Fig. 11.
3. Remove strut and rebound bumper bolts and disconnect lower end of sway bar stud from lower arm.
4. Remove the nut and bolt retaining inner end of the lower arm to crossmember.
5. Carefully lower jack relieving spring pressure on the lower arm, then remove spring.
6. Reverse procedure to install.

POWER STEERING UNIT, REPLACE

Integral Power Rack & Pinion

1982–83 Continental
1. Disconnect battery ground cable.

Fig. 11   Front spring replacement. Exc. Versailles

2. Remove bolt retaining flexible coupling to input shaft.
3. Turn ignition key "On" and raise vehicle.
4. Remove the tie rod end retaining nuts, then separate studs from spindle arms.
5. Support gear and remove attaching bolts, then lower gear enough to gain access to pressure and return lines, and remove bolt attaching the hose bracket to the gear, and bolts from the crossmember.
6. Disconnect and cap pressure and return lines, then remove steering gear.
7. Reverse procedure to install. Torque pressure and return line fittings to 15–20 ft. lbs. Torque steering gear to crossmember bolts to 80–100 ft. lbs. Torque tie rod ends to spindle arm nuts to 35–47 ft. lbs.

1977–83 Integral Power Steering Gear

Exc. Versailles & 1982–83 Continental
1. Disconnect lines from steering gear and plug lines and ports.
2. Remove the two bolts securing flex coupling to steering gear and to column.
3. Raise vehicle and remove sector shaft nut and pitman arm.

NOTE: Do not damage the seals.

4. Support steering gear and remove three attaching bolts. Remove flex coupling clamp bolt and work steering gear free of coupling, then remove steering gear.
5. Reverse procedure to install.

Control Valve, Replace

Versailles
1. Disconnect fluid fittings at control valve and drain fluid from lines.
2. Loosen clamp at right-hand end of sleeve. Remove roll pin from steering arm-to-idler arm rod through slot in sleeve.
3. Using tool 3290-C, remove ball stud from sector shaft arm.

NOTE: The use of any other tool may

result in damage to the control valve assembly.

---

4. Turn wheels fully to left and unthread control valve from idler arm rod.
5. Reverse procedure to install.

POWER STEERING PUMP, REPLACE

1980–83 Ford C11

Removal
1. Disconnect fluid return hose at reservoir and drain power steering fluid into a container.
2. Remove pressure hose from pump fitting. Do not remove fitting from pump.
3. Disconnect belt from pulley. If necessary, remove pulley from pump installing pulley remover tool T75L-3733-A or equivalent so small diameter threads engage in pump shaft. While holding small hex head, rotate tool nut to remove pulley. Do not apply in and out pressure on pump shaft as this will damage the internal thrust areas.
4. Remove pump.

Installation
1. Place pump in bracket and torque bolts to 30–45 ft. lbs.
2. If pulley was removed, install tool and while holding small hex head, turn tool nut clockwise to install pulley. Pulley must be flush within .010 inch of the end of the pump shaft. Do not apply in and out pressure on shaft. Remove tool.
3. Install pressure hose to pump fitting. Using tube nut wrench torque tube nut to 10–15 ft. lbs. Swivel and/or end play is normal.
4. Connect return hose to pump and tighten clamp. On vehicles with hydro-boost, connect lower return line.
5. On all vehicles, fill reservoir and check system for leaks.

1978–79 Ford C11

1. Disconnect fluid return line at the reservoir and allow fluid to drain into a suitable container.
2. Remove high pressure line from pump fitting.

NOTE: Do not remove the fitting from the pump.

---

3. Remove the pump mounting bracket and belt. Remove pump and bracket from vehicle.
4. Reverse procedure to install.

1977 Ford-TRW

1. Disconnect fluid return line at the reservoir and allow fluid to drain into a suitable container.
2. Disconnect high pressure line from the pump.
3. Remove bolts from the front of the pump and nut at the rear (8 cyl. only) attaching the pump to the pump bracket. Remove the belt and pump.
4. Reverse procedure to install.

1977–79 Saginaw

1. Disconnect the pressure and return lines from the pump and plug them to prevent entry of dirt or the loss of fluid.
2. Loosen the belt tension adjusting bolt.
3. Remove the pump mounting bracket attaching bolts.
4. Remove the pump, mounting bracket and pulley as an assembly.
5. Reverse procedure to install.

INDEX OF SERVICE OPERATIONS

NOTE: Refer to the back of this manual for vehicle manufacturer's special service tool suppliers.

VEHICLE IDENTIFICATION PLATE:

1977–83 on left upper dash.

ENGINE NUMBER LOCATION

Buick built engines have the distributor located at the front of the engine. On 1979–83 models, the engine production code is located on front of right hand valve cover and top of left hand valve cover. On 1977–78 models, the engine production code is located on the right front of block.

Chevrolet built V8 engines have the distributor located at the rear of the engine with clockwise rotor rotation. On 1979–80 V8 engines, the engine production code is located front of right hand valve cover. On 1977–78 V8 engines, the code is stamped on the right hand side of engine.

Oldsmobile built engines have the distributor located at the rear of the engine with counter-clockwise rotor rotation and right side mounted fuel pump. The engine production code is located on the oil filler tube on 1977 thru early 1978 engines or on the left side valve cover on late 1978 & 1979–83 engines.

Pontiac built V8 engines have the distirbutor located at the rear of the engine with counter-clockwise rotor rotation and left side mounted fuel pump. On 1979 V8 engines, the engine production code is located on front of both left and right hand valve covers.

ENGINE IDENTIFICATION CODES

Engine	Engine Code	V.I.N. Code
1977		
V6-231 (11)(22)	RC, RD	A
V6-231 Man. Tr.(4)(11)	SG	C
V6-231 Man. Tr.(2)(11)	SU	C
V6-231 Auto. Tr.(4)(11)	SI	C
V6-231 Auto. Tr.(2)(11)	SK, SL	C
V6-231 Auto. Tr.(3)(11)	SM, SN	C
V8-260 Man. Tr.(4)	OS, OT	F
V8-260 Auto. Tr.(4)	QC, QD, QE, QJ	F
V8-260 Auto. Tr.(2)	QU, QV	F
V8-305 Man. Tr.(4)(6)	CPA	U
V8-305 Auto. Tr.(4)(6)	CPY	U
V8-350 Auto. Tr.(4)(6)	CHY, CUB	L
V8-350 Auto. Tr.(2)(6)	CKR	L
V8-350 Auto. Tr.(2)(6)	CKM	L
V8-350 Auto. Tr.(4)	QK, QL, QN, QO	R
V8-350 Auto. Tr.(4)	QP, QQ	R
V8-350 Auto. Tr.(3)	Q2, Q3	R
V8-350 Auto. Tr.(3)	Q6, Q7, Q8, Q9	R
V8-350 Auto. Tr.(2)	TB, TC, TU, TV	R
V8-350 Auto. Tr.(2)	TN, TO, TX, TY	R
V8-403 Auto. Tr.(4)(15)	UJ, UK, UL, UN	K
V8-403 Auto. Tr.(3)(15)	U2, U3	K
V8-403 Auto. Tr.(2)(15)	VA, VB, VJ, VK	K
V8-403 Auto. Tr.(4)(16)	UE	K
V8-403 Auto. Tr.(3)(16)	U6	K
V8-403 Auto. Tr.(2)(16)	VE	K
1978		
V6-231 Man. Tr.(4)(11)	EA, ET	A
V6-231 Auto. Tr.(4)(11)	EB, EC, EH, OH	A
V6-231 Auto. Tr.(4)(11)	EI, EJ, EM, EN	A
V6-231 Auto. Tr.(3)(11)	EG	A
V6-231 Auto. Tr.(2)(11)	EE, EK, EL, OK	A
V8-260 Auto. Tr.(4)	QJ, QK, QX, QY	F
V8-260 Auto. Tr.(4)	QL, QB, QT, QU	F
V8-260 Auto. Tr.(4)	QD, QE	F
V8-260 Auto. Tr.(3)	Q4, Q5	F
V8-260 Auto. Tr.(2)	TJ, TK, TX, TY	F
V8-305 Man. Tr.(4)(6)(12)	CTH, CRW	U
V8-305 Auto. Tr.(4)(6)(12)	CTJ	U
V8-305 Auto. Tr.(3)(6)(12)	CPZ	U
V8-305 Auto. Tr.(2)(6)(12)	CRY, CRZ	U
V8-305 Auto. Tr.(4)(6)(13)	DAC, AG, AJ, AK	H
V8-305 Auto. Tr.(4)(6)(13)	CAJ, AM, AR	H
V8-305 Auto. Tr.(4)(6)(13)	CPE, AH	H
V8-350 Auto. Tr.(3)(6)	CHL, CMC	L
V8-350 Auto. Tr.(2)(6)	CHJ	L
V8-350 Auto. Tr.(4)	QO, QP, QQ, QS	R
V8-350 Auto. Tr.(3)	Q2, Q3	R
V8-350 Auto. Tr.(2)	TO, TP, TT, TU	R
V8-350 Auto. Tr.(2)	TQ, TS, TV, TW	R
V8-350 Auto. Tr.(5)(18)	QB, QC, QV, QW	N
V8-350 Auto. Tr.(3)	Q6, Q7	N
V8-403 Auto. Tr.(4)(15)	UA, UB, UD, UE	K
V8-403 Auto. Tr.(3)(15)	U2, U3	K
V8-403 Auto. Tr.(2)(15)	VA, VB, VJ, VK	K
V8-403 Auto. Tr.(4)(16)	UC	K
V8-403 Auto. Tr.(3)(16)	U4	K
V8-403 Auto. Tr.(2)(16)	VC	K

Engine	Engine Code	V.I.N. Code
1979		
V6-231 Man. Tr.(4)(11)	NG, RA	A
V6-231 Auto. Tr.(4)(11)	NJ, SJ, RB, SO	A
V6-231 Auto. Tr.(4)(11)	NL, RX, SL, SR	A
V6-231 Auto. Tr.(4)(11)	NK, RC, SK, SP	A
V6-231 Auto. Tr.(3)(11)	RJ	A
V6-231 Auto. Tr.(2)(11)	RG, RW	A
V8-260 Man. Tr.(4)	UC, UD	F
V8-260 Auto. Tr.(4)	UE, UJ, UK, UL	F
V8-260 Auto. Tr.(4)	UN, UO	F
V8-260 Auto. Tr.(3)	U5	F
V8-260 Auto. Tr.(2)	VC	F
V8-260 Man. Tr.(5)(18)	UW, UX, V8, V9	P
V8-260 Auto. Tr.(5)(18)	UP, UQ, V2, V7	P
V8-301 Auto. Tr.(4)(14)	PXP, PYF	Y
V8-305 Auto. Tr.(4)(6)(12)	DTM	G
V8-305 Auto. Tr.(4)(6)(12)	DNJ	G
V8-305 Man. Tr.(4)(6)(13)	DNS	H
V8-305 Auto. Tr.(4)(6)(13)	DNT, DNW, DTX	H
V8-305 Auto. Tr.(3)(6)(13)	DTA	H
V8-305 Auto. Tr.(2)(6)(13)	DNX, DNY	H
V8-350 Auto. Tr.(3)(6)	DRX, DRY	L
V8-350 Auto. Tr.(2)(6)	DRJ	L
V8-350 Auto. Tr.(4)(15)	QO, QN, UT, US	R
V8-350 Auto. Tr.(4)(15)	UU, UV	R
V8-350 Auto. Tr.(3)(15)	U9, TY	R
V8-350 Auto. Tr.(2)(15)	VE, VK	R
V8-350 Auto. Tr.(4)(16)	TW	R
V8-350 Auto. Tr.(3)(16)	TY	R
V8-350 Auto. Tr.(2)(16)	TX	R
V8-350 Auto. Tr.(5)(15)(18)	VO, VN, T2, T3	N
V8-350 Auto. Tr.(5)(15)(18)	QQ, QP, QS, QT	N
V8-350 Auto. Tr.(5)(15)(18)	VO, VN, VQ	N
V8-350 Auto. Tr.(5)(15)(18)	V4, V6	N
V8-350 Auto. Tr.(5)(16)(18)	QU, T6	N
V8-350 Auto. Tr.(3)(16)(18)	QY, U3	N
V8-403 Auto. Tr.(4)	QB	K
V8-403 Auto. Tr.(3)	Q3	K
V8-403 Auto. Tr.(4)	TB	K
1980		
V6-231 Man. Tr.(1)(11)	EA	A
V6-231 Auto. Tr.(1)(11)	EB, EC, EO, EP	A
V6-231 Auto. Tr.(2)(11)	OV, OW	A
V6-231 Auto. Tr.(11)	OX, OY	A
V8-260 Auto. Tr.(1)	QAC, QAD, QAF, QAH	F
V8-260 Auto. Tr.(1)	QBB, QBC, QBD	F
V8-260 Auto. Tr.(1)	QBF, QBH, QBJ	F
V8-305 Auto. Tr.(1)(6)	CEA, CMC, CMD, CMF	H
V8-305 Auto. Tr.(2)(6)	CEC, CMM	H
V8-307 Auto. Tr.(1)(19)	TAA, TAB, TAR, TAS	Y
V8-307 Auto. Tr.(1)(19)	TAT, TAU, TAX, TAW	Y
V8-307 Auto. Tr.(1)(19)	TAJ, TAK, TAY, TAZ	Y
V8-307 Auto. Tr.(1)(20)	TBA, TAM	Y
V8-307 Auto. Tr.(1)(16)	TBB, TAN	Y
V8-350 Auto. Tr.(1)(10)	UAN, UAR	R

Engine	Engine Code	V.I.N. Code
V8-350 Auto. Tr.(1)(19)	UAA, UAB, UAX, UAY	R
V8-350 Auto. Tr.(1)(16)(20)	UAC, UAN, UAZ, UBA	R
V8-350 Auto. Tr.(2)(19)(20)	UAD, UAF	R
V8-350 Auto. Tr.(2)(16)	UAH	R
V8-350 Auto. Tr.(1)(10)(18)	VBP, VBR	N
V8-350 Auto. Tr.(1)(10)(19)(20)	VBM, VBN, VCL, VCM	N
V8-350 Auto. Tr.(1)(18)(19)	VBS, VBT	N
V8-350 Auto. Tr.(1)(16)(18)	VBU	N
V8-350 Auto. Tr.(2)(10)(18)	VCF	N
V8-350 Auto. Tr.(2)(18)(19)(20)	VCD	N
V8-350 Auto. Tr.(2)(16)(18)	VCH	N
1981		
V6-231 Man. Tr.(1)(10)(11)	NA	A
V6-231 Auto. Tr.(1)(10)(11)	NB	A
V6-231 Auto. Tr.(1)(19)(11)	NL	A
V6-231 Auto. Tr.(2)(10)(11)	NF, NT	A
V6-231 Auto. Tr.(2)(19)(11)	NC	A
V6-252 Auto. Tr.(16)(11)		4
V8-260 Auto. Tr.(1)(10)	QKA, QKB, QKH, QKJ	F
V8-260 Auto. Tr.(1)(19)	OKJ, OKH, QKM	F
V8-260 Auto. Tr.(2)(10)	QKC, QKK	F
V8-260 Auto. Tr.(2)(19)	QKN	F
V8-307 Auto. Tr.(1)(10)	TKA, TKB, TKJ, TKU	Y
V8-307 Auto. Tr.(1)(10)(19)(20)	TKL, TLR	Y
V8-307 Auto. Tr.(1)(16)	TKP, TLK	Y
V8-307 Auto. Tr.(2)(10)	TKB	Y
V8-307 Auto. Tr.(2)(10)	TKU	Y
V8-307 Auto. Tr.(1)(19)		Y
V8-350 Auto. Tr.(1)(10)(18)	VKB, VKC, VNJ, VNK	N
V8-350 Auto. Tr.(1)(10)(18)	VLM, VLN, VLP, VNN	N
V8-350 Auto. Tr.(1)(18)(19)	VKH, VKJ, VLL, VLM, VLN, VNN, VNP, VNR, VNT	N
V8-350 Auto. Tr.(1)(18)(21)	VNH, VNK, VNW, VNX	N
V8-350 Auto. Tr.(1)(18)(20)	VKN, VLS, VNX, VNY	N
V8-350 Auto. Tr.(1)(16)(18)	VKU, VNX	N
V8-350 Auto. Tr.(2)(10)(18)	VLY, VNL	N
V8-350 Auto. Tr.(2)(18)(19)(20)(21)	VMJ, VNU	N
V8-350 Auto. Tr.(2)(16)(18)	VMT, VPA	N
1982		
V6-231 Auto. Tr.(1)(10)(23)	MA	A
V6-231 Auto. Tr.(1)(19)	MK	A
V6-231 Auto. Tr.(2)(10)(23)	ML	A
V6-231 Auto. Tr.(2)(19)	MM	A
V6-252 Auto. Tr.(1)(20)	FT	4
V6-252 Auto. Tr.(1)(20)	FV	4
V6-252 Auto. Tr.(2)(20)	FT	4
V6-252 Auto. Tr.(2)(16)	FW	4
V8-260 Auto. Tr.(1)(10)	QAD, QAF	8

Continued

ENGINE IDENTIFICATION CODES—Continued

1982—Continued

Engine	Engine Code	V.I.N. Code
V8-260 Auto.		
Tr. ①⑲㉓	QAA, QAH	8
V8-260 Auto. Tr. ②⑩	QAH	8
V8-260 Auto. Tr. ②⑲㉓	QAC	8
V8-307 Auto. Tr. ①㉓	TAD, TAF	Y
V8-307 Auto.		
Tr. ①⑲⑳㉑	TAA, TAB, TAF, TAK, TAM	Y
V8-307 Auto. Tr. ①⑯	TBB	Y
V8-307 Auto. Tr. ②㉓	TAF	Y
V8-307 Auto.		
Tr. ②⑲⑳㉑	TAB, TAF, TAK, TAM, TMR	Y
V8-307 Auto. Tr. ②⑯	TBB	Y
V6-262 Auto. Tr. ④⑱	UAA, UAD	V
V6-262 Auto. Tr. ②⑱	UAA, UAD	V
V6-262 Auto. Tr. ③⑱	UAJ	V

Engine	Engine Code	V.I.N. Code
V8-350 Auto.		
Tr. ④⑩⑱㉓	VAY, VAZ, VBA, VBB	N
V8-350 Auto.		
Tr. ④⑱⑲	VAB, VAC, VAD	N
V8-350 Auto.		
Tr. ④⑱㉑	VAK, VAL, VAM	N
V8-350 Auto. Tr. ④⑱⑳	VAN, VAP	N
V8-350 Auto. Tr. ④⑯⑱	VAW, VBP	N
V8-350 Auto.		
Tr. ②⑩⑱㉓	VAY, VAZ, VBA, VBB	N
V8-350 Auto. Tr. ②⑱⑲	VAB, VAC, VAD	N
V8-350 Auto. Tr. ②⑱㉑	VAK, VAM	N
V8-350 Auto. Tr. ②⑱⑳	VAN, VAP	N
V8-350 Auto. Tr. ②⑯⑱	VAW	N
V8-350 Auto. Tr. ③⑩⑱㉓	VBC	N
V8-350 Auto. Tr. ③⑱⑲⑳	VAZ	N

Engine	Engine Code	V.I.N. Code
V8-350 Auto. Tr. ③⑱㉑	VAU	N
V8-350 Auto. Tr. ③⑯⑱	VAX	N

①—Except California.
②—California.
③—High altitude.
④—Exc. Calif. & High altitude.
⑤—Exc. high altitude.
⑥—Chevrolet built engine.
⑦—Omega.
⑧—Early production.
⑨—Late production.
⑩—Cutlass.
⑪—Buick built.
⑫—2 barrel carb.
⑬—4 barrel carb.
⑭—Pontiac Built engine.
⑮—Except Toronado.
⑯—Toronado.
⑰—Exc. even fire engine.
⑱—Diesel engine.
⑲—88.
⑳—98.
㉑—Custom Cruiser.
㉒—Even fire engine.
㉓—Cutlass Cruiser.

GRILLE IDENTIFICATION

1977 Omega

1977 Cutlass Supreme

1977 Cutlass "S"

1977 "4-4-2"

1977 Delta 88

1977 98

1977 Toronado

1978 Omega

1978 Cutlass Salon 2 Dr & "4-4-2"

1978 Cutlass Brougham

1978 Cutlass Salon 4 Dr & Cruiser

Continued

GRILLE IDENTIFICATION—Continued

1978 Delta 88 & Cruiser

1978 98

1978 Toronado

1979 Omega Brougham

1979 Cutlass Supreme Brougham

1979 Cutlass Calais & Hurst Olds

1979 Cutlass Salon & "442"

1979 Cutlass Cruiser

1979 Cutlass Salon & Cruiser Brougham

1979 Delta 88 Royale

1979 98 Regency

1979 Custom Cruiser

1979 Toronado Brougham

1980 Omega Brougham

1980 Cutlass Supreme

1980 Cutlass Supreme LS

1980 Cutlass Salon

1980 Cutlass "442"

1980 Delta 88 Royale

1980 98 Regency

1980–82 Toronado

Continued

GRILLE IDENTIFICATION—Continued

1981 Cutlass Supreme

1981 Cutlass Cruiser & Brougham

1981 Cutlass Calais

1981 88 & Custom Cruiser

1981 98 Regency

1982 Cutlass Brougham

1982 Cutlass Supreme

1982 88

1982 98

1982 Cutlass Calais

1982 Toronado

1983 Cutlass Supreme

1983 Cutlass Cruiser

1983 Hurst Olds

1983 88

1983 98

1983 Toronado

GENERAL ENGINE SPECIFICATIONS

Year	Engine CID[1]/Liter	V.I.N. Code[2]	Carburetor	Bore and Stroke	Compression Ratio	Net H.P. @ R.P.M.[3]	Maximum Torque Ft. Lbs. @ R.P.M.	Normal Oil Pressure Pounds
1977	V6-231, 3.8L[9][6]	C	2GC, 2 Bbl.[5]	3.80 × 3.40	8.0	105 @ 3400	185 @ 2000	37
	V6-231[9][16]	A	2GC. 2 Bbl.[5]	3.80 × 3.40	8.0	105 @ 3400	185 @ 2000	37
	V8-260, 4.3L	F	2MC, 2 Bbl.[5]	3.50 × 3.385	8.0	110 @ 3400	205 @ 1600	30–45
	V8-305, 5.0L[4]	U	2GC, 2 Bbl.[5]	3.736 × 3.48	8.5	145 @ 3800	245 @ 2400	32–40
	V8-350, 5.7L	R	M4MC, 4 Bbl.[5]	4.057 × 3.385	8.0	170 @ 3800	275 @ 2000	30–45
	V8-350, 5.7L[10]	R	M4MC, 4 Bbl.[5]	4.057 × 3.385	8.0	170 @ 3800	275 @ 2400	30–45
	V8-350, 5.7L[4][11]	L	M4MC, 4 Bbl.[5]	4.00 × 3.48	8.5	170 @ 3800	270 @ 2400	32–40
	V8-403, 6.6L[7]	K	M4MC, 4 Bbl.[5]	4.351 × 3.385	8.0	185 @ 3600	320 @ 2000	30–45
	V8-403, 6.6L[8]	K	M4MC, 4 Bbl.[5]	4.351 × 3.385	8.0	200 @ 3600	330 @ 2400	30–45
1978	V6-231, 3.8L[9]	A	2GE, 2 Bbl.[5]	3.80 × 3.40	8.0	105 @ 3400	185 @ 2000	37
	V8-260, 4.3L	F	2GC, 2 Bbl.[5]	3.50 × 3.385	7.5	110 @ 2400	205 @ 1800	30–45
	V8-305, 5.0L[4]	U	2GC, 2 Bbl.[5]	3.736 × 3.48	8.5	145 @ 3800	245 @ 2400	32–40
	V8-305, 5.0L[4]	H	M4MC, 4 Bbl.[5]	3.736 × 3.48	8.5	160 @ 4000	235 @ 2400	32–40
	V8-350, 5.7L[4]	L	M4MC, 4 Bbl.[5]	4.00 × 3.48	8.5	160 @ 3800	260 @ 2400	32–40
	V8-350, 5.7L	R	M4MC, 4 Bbl.[5]	4.057 × 3.385	8.0	170 @ 3800	275 @ 2000	30–45
	V8-350, 5.7L[12]	N	Fuel Injection	4.057 × 3.385	22.5	120 @ 3600	220 @ 1600	30–45
	V8-403, 6.6L[7]	K	M4MC, 4 Bbl.[5]	4.351 × 3.385	8.0	185 @ 3600	320 @ 2200	30–45
	V8-403, 6.6L[8]	K	M4MC, 4 Bbl.[5]	4.351 × 3.385	8.0	190 @ 3600	325 @ 2000	30–45
1979	V6-231, 3.8L[9]	A	M2ME, 2 Bbl.[5]	3.80 × 3.40	8.0	115 @ 3800	190 @ 2000	37
	V8-260, 4.3L[12]	P	Fuel Injection	3.50 × 3.385	22.5	90 @ 3600	160 @ 1600	35
	V8-260, 4.3L	F	M2MC, 2 Bbl.[5]	3.50 × 3.385	7.5	105 @ 3600	205 @ 1800	30–45
	V8-301, 4.9L[13]	Y	M2MC, 2 Bbl.[5]	4.00 × 3.00	8.2	135 @ 3800	240 @ 1600	35–40
	V8-305, 5.0L[4]	G	M2MC, 2 Bbl.[5]	3.736 × 3.48	8.5	130 @ 3200	245 @ 2000	32–40
	V8-305, 5.0L[4]	H	M4MC, 4 Bbl.[5]	3.736 × 3.48	8.5	160 @ 4000	235 @ 2400	32–40
	V8-350, 5.7L[4]	L	M4MC, 4 Bbl.[5]	4.00 × 3.48	8.5	160 @ 3600	260 @ 2400	32–40
	V8-350, 5.7L[7]	R	M4MC, 4 Bbl.[5]	4.057 × 3.385	8.0	160 @ 3600	270 @ 2000	35
	V8-350, 5.7L[8]	R	M4MC, 4 Bbl.[5]	4.057 × 3.385	8.0	165 @ 3600	275 @ 2000	35
	V8-350, 5.7L[12]	N	Fuel Injection	4.057 × 3.385	22.5	125 @ 3600	225 @ 1600	30–45
	V8-403, 6.6L	K	M4MC, 4 Bbl.[5]	4.351 × 3.385	7.8	175 @ 3600	310 @ 2000	35
1980	V6-231, 3.8L[9]	A	M2ME, 2 Bbl.[5]	3.80 × 3.40	8.0	110 @ 3800	190 @ 1600	37
	V8-260, 4.3L	F	M2MC, 2 Bbl.[5]	3.50 × 3.385	7.5	—	—	30–45
	V8-305, 5.0L[4][14]	H	M4MC, 4 Bbl.[5]	3.736 × 3.48	8.6	155 @ 4000	240 @ 1600	45
	V8-305, 5.0L[4][15]	H	E4MC, 4 Bbl.[5]	3.736 × 3.48	8.6	155 @ 4000	230 @ 1600	45
	V8-307, 5.0L	Y	M4MC, 4 Bbl.[5]	3.80 × 3.385	7.9	—	—	30–45
	V8-350, 5.7L[12]	N	Fuel Injection	4.057 × 3.385	22.5	—	—	30–45
	V8-350, 5.7L	R	E4MC, 4 Bbl.[5]	4.057 × 3.385	8.0	—	—	30–45
1981	V6-231, 3.8L[9]	A	2ME, 2 Bbl.[5]	3.80 × 3.40	8.0	110 @ 3800	190 @ 1600	30–45
	V8-252, 4.1L[9]	4	M4MC, 4 Bbl.[5]	3.96 × 3.40	8.0	125 @ 4000	205 @ 2000	30–45
	V8-260, 4.3L	F	2MC, 2 Bbl.[5]	3.50 × 3.38	7.5	100 @ 3600	190 @ 1600	30–45
	V8-307, 5.0L	Y	2ME, 2 Bbl.[5]	3.80 × 3.38	8.0	140 @ 3600	240 @ 1600	30–45
	V8-307, 5.0L	Y	M4MC, 4 Bbl.[5]	3.80 × 3.38	8.0	140 @ 3600	240 @ 1600	30–45
	V8-350[12]	N	Fuel Injection	4.05 × 3.38	22.5	105 @ 3200	200 @ 1600	30–45
1982	V6-231, 3.8L[9]	A	E2ME, 2 Bbl.[5]	3.80 × 3.40	8.0	110 @ 3800	190 @ 1600	37
	V6-252, 4.1L[9]	4	E4ME, 4 Bbl.[5]	3.96 × 3.40	8.0	125 @ 4000	205 @ 1600	37
	V6-262, 4.3L[12]	V	Fuel Injection	4.05 × 3.38	21.6	85 @ 3600	165 @ 1600	30–45
	V8-260, 4.3L	8	E2ME, 2 Bbl.[5]	3.50 × 3.38	7.5	100 @ 3600	190 @ 1600	35
	V8-307, 5.0L	Y	E4ME, 4 Bbl.[5]	3.80 × 3.38	8.0	140 @ 3600	240 @ 1600	35
	V8-350, 5.7L[12]	N	Fuel Injection	4.05 × 3.38	22.5	105 @ 3200	200 @ 1600	30–45
1983	V6-231, 3.8L[9]	A	2 Bbl.[5]	3.80 × 3.40	8.0	110 @ 3800	190 @ 1600	37
	V6-252, 4.1L[9]	4	4 Bbl.[5]	3.96 × 3.40	8.0	125 @ 4000	205 @ 2000	37
	V6-262, 4.3L[12]	V	Fuel Injection	4.05 × 3.38	22.5	85 @ 3600	165 @ 1600	30–45
	V8-307, 5.0L[17]	Y	4 Bbl.[5]	3.80 × 3.38	8.0	140 @ 3600	240 @ 1600	30–45
	V8-307, 5.0L[18]	9	E4MC, 4 Bbl.[5]	3.80 × 3.38	—	180	245	30–45
	V8-350, 5.7L[12]	N	Fuel Injection	4.05 × 3.38	22.5	105 @ 3200	200 @ 1600	30–45

Continued

OLDSMOBILE—88, 98, Toronado, 1977–79 Omega, Cutlass Exc. Ciera

GENERAL ENGINE SPECIFICATIONS NOTES

①—CID—cubic inch displacement.
②—On 1977–80 vehicles, the fifth digit in the VIN denotes engine code. On 1981–83 vehicles, the eighth digit in the VIN denotes engine code.
③—All ratings are net—as installed in vehicle.
④—Chevrolet built engine. Distributor located at rear of engine, clockwise rotation.
⑤—Rochester.
⑥—Exc. even fire engine.
⑦—Exc. Toronado.
⑧—Toronado.
⑨—Buick built engine. Distributor located at front of engine.
⑩—Cutlass.
⑪—Omega.
⑫—Diesel.
⑬—Pontiac built engine. Distributor located at rear of engine, clockwise rotation.
⑭—Exc. Calif.
⑮—California.
⑯—Even fire engine.
⑰—Exc. Hurst option.
⑱—Hurst option.

TUNE UP SPECIFICATIONS

The following specifications are published from the latest information available. This data should be used only in the absence of a decal affixed in the engine compartment.

★ When using a timing light, disconnect vacuum hose or tube at distributor and plug opening in hose or tube so idle speed will not be affected.

● When checking compression, lowest cylinder must be within 70 percent of highest.

▲ Before removing wires from distributor cap, determine location of the No. 1 wire in cap, as distributor position may have been altered from that shown at the end of this chart.

Spark plug types in this chart are recommendations of the original vehicle manufacturer and not MOTOR.

Check local sources for other spark plug manufacturers listings.

Year & Engine/VIN	Spark Plug Type	Gap	Firing Order Fig. ▲	Ignition Timing BTDC①★ Man. Trans.	Ignition Timing BTDC①★ Auto. Trans.	Mark Fig.	Curb Idle Speed② Man. Trans.	Curb Idle Speed② Auto. Trans.	Fast Idle Speed Man. Trans.	Fast Idle Speed Auto. Trans.	Fuel Pump Pressure
1977											
V6-231/C⑩⑱	⑲	⑲	I	12°	12°	B⑳	600/800	600/670D㉑	—	—	3 Min.
V6-231/A⑩㊱	R46TSX	.060	A	—	15°	F⑳	—	600/670D㉑	—	—	3 Min.
V8-260/F	R46SZ	.060	J	16°⑤	㉒	G	750	550/650D⑥	900⑦	900⑦	5½–6½
V8-305/F⑭	R45TS	.045	H	8°	8°	C	600	500/650D	—	—	7½–9
V8-350/U, Exc. Calif.⑭㉓	R45TS	.045	H	—	8°	C	—	㉔	—	1600④	7½–9
V8-350/L, Exc. Calif. & High Alt.㉕	R46SZ	.060	J	—	20°⑤	G	—	550/650D⑥	—	900⑦	5½–6½
V8-350/R, Calif.㉕	R46SZ	.060	J	—	㉖	G	—	550/650D⑥	—	1000⑦	5½–6½
V8-350/R, High Alt.㉕	R46SZ	.060	J	—	20°⑤	G	—	600/700D⑥	—	1000⑦	5½–6½
V8-403/K, Exc. Calif. & High Alt.⑬	R46SZ	.060	J	—	㉗	G	—	550/650D⑥	—	900⑦	5½–6½
V8-403/K, Calif. & High Alt.⑬	R46SZ	.060	J	—	20°⑤	G	—	⑥㉘	—	1000⑦	5½–6½
V8-403/K, Toronado	R46SZ	.060	J	—	㉙	G	—	⑥㉚	—	⑦㉛	5½–6½
1978											
V6-231/A⑩	R46TSX	.060	A	15°	15°	F⑳	800	㉜	1850④	1850④	3 Min.
V8-260/F, Exc. Calif. & High Alt.	R46SZ	.060	J	18°⑤	20°⑤	G	650/800⑥	500/650D⑥	750⑦	800⑦	5½–6½
V8-260/F, Calif.	R46SZ	.060	J	—	18°⑤	G	—	500/650D⑥	—	800⑦	5½–6½
V8-260/F, High Alt.	R46SZ	.060	J	—	20°⑤	G	—	550/650D⑥	—	900⑦	5½–6½
V8-305/U, 2 Barrel Exc. Calif.⑭㉝	R45TS	.045	H	4°	4°	E	600/700	500/600D	1600④	1600④	7½–9
V8-305/U, 2 Barrel Calif. & High Alt.⑭	R45TS	.045	H	—	8°	E	—	㉟	—	1600④	7½–9
V8-305/H, 4 Barrel⑭	R45TS	.045	H	—	4°	E	—	500/600D	—	1600④	7½–9
V8-350/R⑭㉓	R45TS	.045	H	—	8°	E	—	㉔	—	1600④	7½–9
V8-350/R, Exc. Calif. & High Alt.㉕	R46SZ	.060	J	—	20°⑤	G	—	550/650D⑥	—	900⑦	5½–6½
V8-350/R, Calif. & High Alt.㉕	R46SZ	.060	J	—	20°⑤	G	—	㉘	—	1000⑦	5½–6½
V8-350 Diesel/N, Exc. High Alt.	—	—	—	4½°㊶㊷㊱	—	—	575/650D⑥	—	—	—	—
V8-350 Diesel/N, High Alt.	—	—	—	5½°㊶㊷㊱	—	—	575/650D⑥	—	—	—	—
V8-403/K, Exc. Calif. & High Alt.⑬	R46SZ	.060	J	—	㊲	G	—	550/650D⑥	—	900⑦	5½–6½
V8-403/K, Calif. & High Alt.⑬	R46SZ	.060	J	—	20°⑤	G	—	㉘	—	1000⑦	5½–6½
V8-403/K, Toronado	R46SZ	.060	J	—	㉙	G	—	⑥㉚	—	⑦㉛	5½–6½

Continued

TUNE UP SPECIFICATIONS—Continued

The following specifications are published from the latest information available. This data should be used only in the absence of a decal affixed in the engine compartment.

★ When using a timing light, disconnect vacuum hose or tube at distributor and plug opening in hose or tube so idle speed will not be affected.

● When checking compression, lowest cylinder must be within 70 percent of highest.

▲ Before removing wires from distributor cap, determine location of the No. 1 wire in cap, as distributor position may have been altered from that shown at the end of this chart.

☞ Spark plug types in this chart are recommendations of the original vehicle manufacturer and not MOTOR.
Check local sources for other spark plug manufacturers listings.

Year & Engine/VIN	Spark Plug Type ☞	Gap	Firing Order Fig. ▲	Ignition Timing BTDC①★ Man. Trans.	Auto. Trans.	Mark Fig.	Curb Idle Speed② Man. Trans.	Auto. Trans.	Fast Idle Speed Man. Trans.	Auto. Trans.	Fuel Pump Pressure
1979											
V6-231/A, Exc. Calif. & High Alt.⑩	R46TSX	.060	A	15°	15°	F⑳	600/800⑥	550/670D⑥	2200	2200	3 Min.
V6-231/A, Calif. & High Alt.⑩	R46TSX	.060	A	—	15°	F⑳	—	600D	—	2200	3 Min.
V8-260/F, Exc. Calif. & High Alt.	R46SZ	.060	J	18°⑤	20°⑤	G	650/800⑥	500/625D⑥	750	800	5½–6½
V8-260/F, Calif.	R46SZ	.060	J	—	18°⑤	G	—	500/625D⑥	—	800	5½–6½
V8-260/F, High Alt.	R46SZ	.060	J	—	20°⑤	G	—	550/650D⑥	—	900	5½–6½
V8-260 Diesel/P, Exc. High Alt	—	—	—	3½°④①④②	4½°④①④②	—	575/695	590/650D	—	—	—
V8-260 Diesel/P, High Alt	—	—	—	4½°④①④②	5½°④①④②	—	575/695	590/650D	—	—	—
V8-301/Y⑮	R46TSX	.060	D	—	12°	L	—	500/650D⑥	—	2000	7–8½
V8-305/G, 2 Barrel⑭	R45TS	.045	H	4°	4°	E	600/700	500/600D⑥	1300	1600	7½–9
V8-305/H, 4 Barrel Exc. High Alt.⑭	R45TS	.045	H	4°	4°	E	700	500/600D⑥	1300	1600	7½–9
V8-305/H, 4 Barrel High Alt.⑭	R45TS	.045	H	—	8°	E	—	600/650D⑥	—	1750	7½–9
V8-350/L, Calif.⑭㉓	R45TS	.045	H	—	8°	E	—	500/600D⑥	—	1600	7½–9
V8-350/L, High Alt.⑭㉓	R45TS	.045	H	—	8°	E	—	600/650D⑥	—	1750	7½–9
V8-350/R Exc. Calif.㉕	R46SZ	.060	J	—	㊳	G	—	550/650D⑥	—	900	5½–6½
V8-350/R Calif.㉕	R46SZ	.060	J	—	20°⑤	G	—	500/600D⑥	—	1000	5½–6½
V8-350 Diesel/N, Exc. High Alt.	—	—	—	—	4½°④①④②�51	—	—	575/650D⑥	—	—	—
V8-350 Diesel/N, High Alt.	—	—	—	—	5½°④①④②�51	—	—	575/650D⑥	—	—	—
V8-403/K, Exc. Calif.	R46SZ	.060	J	—	20°⑤	G	—	550/650D⑥	—	900	5½–6½
V8-403/K, Calif.	R46SZ	.060	J	—	20°⑤	G	—	500/600D⑥	—	1000	5½–6½
1980											
V6-231/A⑧⑩	R45TS	.040	A	15°	15°	F⑳	600/800⑥	550/670D	2200	2000	3 Min.
V8-231/A⑩⑫	R45TSX	.060	A	—	15°	F⑳	—	550/620D	—	2200	3 Min.
V8-260/F	R46SX	.080	J	—	③	G	—	500/625D	—	700D	5½–6½
V8-305/H, Exc. Calif.⑭	R45TS	.045	H	—	4°	㉞	—	500/600D	—	1850	7½–9
V8-305/H, Calif.⑭	R45TS	.045	H	—	4°	㉞	—	550/650D	—	2200	7½–9
V8-307/Y	R46SX	.080	J	—	20°⑤	G	—	500/600D	—	700D	5½–6½
V8-350/R, Exc. Calif.	R46SX	.080	J	—	18°⑤	G	—	500/600D	—	700D	5½–6½
V8-350/R, Calif.	R46SX	.080	J	—	⑨	G	—	550/650D	—	700D	5½–6½
V8-350 Diesel/N, Exc. High Alt.	—	—	—	—	4½°④①④②�51	—	—	600/750D	—	750D	—
V8-350 Diesel/N, High Alt.	—	—	—	—	5½°④①④②�51	—	—	600/750D	—	750D	—
1981											
V6-231/A⑩	R45TS8	.080	A	15°	15°	F⑳	800	㊵	2200	1800	3 Min.
V6-252/4⑩	R45TS8	.080	A	—	15°	F⑳	—	550/690D	—	2200	3 Min.
V8-260/F	R46SX	.080	J	—	㊴	G	—	㊵	—	700D	5½–6½

Continued

TUNE UP SPECIFICATIONS—Continued

The following specifications are published from the latest information available. This data should be used only in the absence of a decal affixed in the engine compartment.

★ When using a timing light, disconnect vacuum hose or tube at distributor and plug opening in hose or tube so idle speed will not be affected.

● When checking compression, lowest cylinder must be within 70 percent of highest.

▲ Before removing wires from distributor cap, determine location of the No. 1 wire in cap, as distributor position may have been altered from that shown at the end of this chart.

Spark plug types in this chart are recommendations of the original vehicle manufacturer and not MOTOR.

Check local sources for other spark plug manufacturers listings.

Year & Engine/VIN	Spark Plug		Ignition Timing BTDC①★				Curb Idle Speed②		Fast Idle Speed		Fuel Pump Pressure
	Type	Gap	Firing Order Fig.▲	Man. Trans.	Auto. Trans.	Mark Fig.	Man. Trans.	Auto. Trans.	Man. Trans.	Auto. Trans.	
1981—Continued											
V8-307/Y, Exc. Calif.	R46SX	.080	J	—	(16)(5)	G	—	(40)	—	650D	5½-6½
V8-307/Y, Calif.	R46SX	.080	J	—	15°(5)	G	—	(40)	—	650D	5½-6½
V8-350 Diesel/N, Exc. High Alt.	—	—	—	—	4°(41)(42)(51)	—	—	600/750D	—	750D	—
V8-350 Diesel/N, High Alt.	—	—	—	—	5°(41)(42)(51)	—	—	600/750D	—	750D	—
1982											
V6-231/A	R45TS8	.080	A	—	15°	F(20)	—	(40)	—	2200	3 Min.
V6-252/4	R45TS8	.080	A	—	15°	F(20)	—	(40)	—	(17)	3 Min.
V6-262 Diesel/N, Exc. High Alt.	—	—	—	—	7°(41)(43)(51)	—	—	650D	—	725D	—
V6-262 Diesel/N, High Alt.	—	—	—	—	7°(41)(44)(51)	—	—	650D	—	725D	—
V8-260/8	R46SX	.080	J	—	20°(5)	G	—	(40)	—	700D	5½-6½
V8-307/Y	R46SX	.080	J	—	20°(5)	G	—	(40)	—	650D	5½-6½
V8-350 Diesel/N, Exc. High Alt.	—	—	—	—	4°(41)(45)(51)	—	—	600D	—	750D	—
V8-350 Diesel/N, High Alt.	—	—	—	—	4°(41)(46)(51)	—	—	600D	—	750D	—
1983											
V6-231/A	R45TS8	—	A	—	15°	F(20)	—	(40)	—	2200	4¼-5¾
V6-252/4	R45TS8	—	A	—	15°	F(20)	—	(40)	—	(50)	4¼-5¾
V6-262 Diesel/V	—	—	—	—	(11)(51)	—	—	660D	—	775D	—
V8-307/Y(47)	R46SX	.080	J	—	20°(5)	G	—	(40)	—	900D	6-7½
V8-307/9(48)	R46SX	.080	J	—	20°(5)	G	—	500D	—	900D	6-7½
V8-350 Diesel/N	—	—	—	—	(49)(51)	—	—	600D	—	750D	—

①—BTDC—Before top dead center.
②—Idle speed on man. trans. vehicles is adjusted in Neutral & on auto. trans. equipped vehicles is adjusted in Drive unless otherwise specified. Where two idle speeds are listed, the higher the speed is with the A/C or idle solenoid energized.
③—88 & Cutlass sta. wag., 20° at 1100 RPM; Cutlass sta. wag., 18° at 1100 RPM.
④—With cam follower or stop screw on high step of fast idle cam, EGR vacuum line disconnected & plugged & A/C off.
⑤—At 1100 RPM.
⑥—Idle speed with solenoid energized is adjusted with A/C on & compressor clutch wires disconnected.
⑦—With stop screw of low step of fast idle cam, EGR disconnected & plugged & A/C off.
⑧—Except Calif. & models w/Computer Controlled Catalytic Converter (C4) System.
⑨—Except Toronado, 18° at 1100 RPM; Toronado, 16° at 1100 RPM.
⑩—Buick built engine.
⑪—Injection timing, 7°ATDC at 1300 RPM.

⑫—California & models w/Computer Controlled Catalytic Converter (C4) system.
⑬—Except Toronado.
⑭—Chevrolet built engine.
⑮—Pontiac built engines.
⑯—Toronado, 15°BTDC. 88, Custom Cruiser & Cutlass Cruiser, except engine codes TMK, TML, TMN & TMS, 15°BTDC; engine codes TMK, TML, TMN & TMS, 18°BTDC.
⑰—Except Toronado Calif. models, 2200 RPM; Toronado California models, 2100 RPM.
⑱—Except even fire engine.
⑲—Early production, R46TS gapped at .040"; late production, R46TSX gapped at .060".
⑳—The harmonic balancer on these engines has two timing marks. The timing mark measuring 1/16 in. is used when setting timing with a hand held timing light. The mark measuring 1/8 in. is used when setting timing with magnetic timing equipment.
㉑—Idle speed with solenoid energized is adjusted with distributor vacuum advance hose disconnected & plugged, A/C on & compressor clutch wires disconnected.
㉒—Except Cutlass, 20°BTDC at 1100 RPM; Cut-

lass 18°BTDC at 1100 RPM.
㉓—Distributor located at rear of engine, rotor rotation clockwise.
㉔—Except high altitude, 500/650D RPM; high altitude, 600/650D RPM.
㉕—Distributor located at rear of engine, rotor rotation counter clockwise.
㉖—Omega & 88 except sta. wag., 18°BTDC at 1100 RPM; Cutlass, 88 sta. wag. & 98, 20°BTDC at 1100 RPM.
㉗—Cutlass except sta. wag., 88 & 98, 20°BTDC at 1100 RPM; Cutlass sta. wag., 22°BTDC at 1100 RPM.
㉘—Except high altitude, 550/650D RPM; high altitude, 600/700D RPM.
㉙—Equipped with Electronic Spark Timing (EST).
㉚—Except Calif. & high altitude, 550/650D RPM; California, 600/650D RPM; high altitude 600/700D RPM.
㉛—Except Calif. & high altitude, 900 RPM; California & high altitude, 1000 RPM.
㉜—Except 88 with A/C, 600D RPM; 88 with A/C, 600/670D RPM see note 21.
㉝—Except high altitude.
㉞—Early models, Fig. E; late models, Fig. K.

Continued

TUNE UP NOTES—Continued

㉟—Except high altitude, 500/650D RPM; high altitude, 600/700D RPM.

㊱—Even fire engine.

㊲—88 except sta. wag. & 98, 18°BTDC at 1100 RPM; 88 sta. wag., 20°BTDC at 1100 RPM.

㊳—Except engine codes QN & QO, 20°BTDC at 1100 RPM; engine codes QN & QO, 18°BTDC at 1100 RPM.

㊴—Cutlass except sta. wag., 20°BTDC at 1100 RPM; Cutlass Cruiser & 88, 18°BTDC at 1100 RPM.

㊵—Idle speed is controlled by the idle speed control (ICS) motor or the idle load compensator (ILC).

㊶—ATDC—After top dead center.

㊷—At 1200 RPM.

㊸—At 1300 RPM. When operating at altitudes above 4000 ft., set at 8°ATDC.

㊹—At 1300 RPM. When operating at altitudes below 4000 ft., set at 6°ATDC.

㊺—At 1250 RPM. When operating at altitudes above 4000 ft., set at 5°ATDC.

㊻—At 1250 RPM. When operating at altitudes below 4000 ft., set at 3°ATDC.

㊼—Except Hurst option.

㊽—Hurst option.

㊾—Injection timing, 4°ATDC at 1250 RPM.

㊿—Except Toronado, 2200 RPM; Toronado, 2100 RPM.

�51—Using diesel timing meter J-33075.

Fig. A

Fig. B

Fig. C

Fig. D

Fig. E

Fig. F

Fig. G

Fig. H

Fig. I

Fig. J

Fig. K

Fig. L

OLDSMOBILE—88, 98, Toronado, 1977–79 Omega, Cutlass Exc. Ciera

DISTRIBUTOR SPECIFICATIONS

★ Note: If unit is checked on vehicle, double the RPM and degrees to get crankshaft figures.

Distributor Part No.①	Centrifugal Advance Degrees @ RPM of Distributor					Vacuum Advance		Distributor Retard
	Advance Starts	Intermediate Advance			Full Advance	Inches of Vacuum to Start Plunger	Max. Adv. Dist. Deg. @ Vacuum	Max. Retard Dist. Deg. @ Vacuum
1977								
1103239	0 @ 600	7½ @ 1350	—	—	10 @ 2100	4	7½ @ 10	—
1103246	0 @ 600	5–7 @ 1000	—	—	12 @ 2100	3	9½ @ 13	—
1103248	0 @ 600	5–7 @ 1000	—	—	12 @ 2100	3	6 @ 9	—
1103259	0 @ 500	—	—	—	9½ @ 2000	6	12 @ 13	—
1103260	0 @ 500	—	—	—	9½ @ 2000	6	12 @ 13	—
1103262	0 @ 455	8½ @ 1188	—	—	13 @ 2233	4	15 @ 11	—
1103264	0 @ 500	—	—	—	6½ @ 1800	5	8 @ 11	—
1103266	0 @ 500	—	—	—	9½ @ 2000	5	8 @ 11	—
1110677	0–2.2 @ 765	8.9–11 @ 1800	—	—	11 @ 2500	6	12¾ @ 20	—
1110686	0–2.2 @ 890	3.2–5.5 @ 1300	—	—	11 @ 2500	6	4¾ @ 20	—
1112990②	—	—	—	—	—	—	—	—
1978								
1103313②	—	—	—	—	—	—	—	—
1103337	0 @ 550	6 @ 800	8 @ 1200	—	11 @ 2300	4	12 @ 10	—
1110731	0–2 @ 1000	—	—	—	9 @ 1800	4	8 @ 9	—
1978–79								
1103281	0 @ 500	5 @ 850	—	—	10 @ 1900	4	9 @ 12	—
1103282	0 @ 500	5 @ 850	—	—	10 @ 1900	4	10 @ 10	—
1103285	0 @ 600	6 @ 1000	—	—	11 @ 2100	4	12 @ 8	—
1103320	0 @ 455	8½ @ 1188	—	—	13 @ 2233	4	15 @ 11	—
1103322	0 @ 300	5½ @ 600	—	—	14½ @ 2000	6	12 @ 13	—
1103323	0 @ 500	—	—	—	9½ @ 2000	5	8 @ 11	—
1103324	0 @ 300	5½ @ 600	—	—	11½ @ 1800	6	12 @ 13	—
1103325	0 @ 500	—	—	—	6½ @ 1800	5	8 @ 11	—
1103342	0–2 @ 1000	—	—	—	9½ @ 2200	5–7	12 @ 13	—
1103346	0 @ 500	—	—	—	9½ @ 2000	6	12 @ 13	—
1103347	0 @ 500	—	—	—	6½ @ 1800	6	12 @ 13	—
1103353	0–1¾ @ 625	2½–3½ @ 850	—	3½–4½ @ 2000	6 @ 2250	3	10 @ 12	—
1103355	0 @ 455	8½ @ 1188	—	—	13 @ 2233	4	15 @ 9	—
1110695	0–3 @ 1000	—	—	—	9 @ 1800	7	12 @ 13	—
1979								
1103259	0 @ 500	—	—	—	10½ @ 2000	4	15 @ 11	—
1103260	0 @ 500	—	—	—	6¾ @ 1600	6	12 @ 13	—
1103262	0 @ 550	—	—	8½ @ 1175	14 @ 2500	4½	15½ @ 20	—
1103264	0 @ 500	—	—	—	8½ @ 1700	5	8 @ 11	—
1103266	0 @ 500	—	—	—	10½ @ 2000	5	8 @ 11	—
1103314	0 @ 413	5 @ 900	—	—	10½ @ 1700	4	12½ @ 12	—
1103368	0 @ 500	5 @ 850	—	—	10 @ 1900	4	5 @ 8	—
1103379	0 @ 500	5 @ 850	—	—	10 @ 1900	3	10 @ 7.5	—
1103396	0 @ 455	8½ @ 1188	—	—	13 @ 2233	5	15 @ 12	—
1110677	0 @ 640	—	—	—	10 @ 1800	5	12 @ 9.5	—
1110683	—	—	—	—	—	—	—	—
1110731	0 @ 950	—	—	7¼ @ 1800	8½ @ 2500	5	12¾ @ 20	—
1110766	0 @ 840	—	—	—	7½ @ 1800	4	12 @ 11	—
1110767	0 @ 840	—	—	—	7½ @ 1800	3	10 @ 12	—
1110768	0 @ 500	2½ @ 800	—	3 @ 1200	7½ @ 1800	3	10 @ 12	—
1110769	0 @ 500	2½ @ 800	—	3 @ 1200	7½ @ 1800	4	12 @ 11	—
1110770	0 @ 840	—	—	—	7½ @ 1800	3	10 @ 9	—
1110779	0 @ 840	—	—	—	7½ @ 1800	3	12 @ 9.5	—

Continued

1–726

DISTRIBUTOR SPECIFICATIONS—Continued

★ Note: If unit is checked on vehicle, double the RPM and degrees to get crankshaft figures.

Distributor Part No.①	Centrifugal Advance Degrees @ RPM of Distributor					Vacuum Advance		Distributor Retard
	Advance Starts	Intermediate Advance			Full Advance	Inches of Vacuum to Start Plunger	Max. Adv. Dist. Deg. @ Vacuum	Max. Retard Dist. Deg. @ Vacuum
1980								
1103384	0 @ 400	4 @ 600	8 @ 1000	—	10 @ 2000	4	7½ @ 12	—
1103386	0 @ 500	5 @ 850	—	—	10 @ 1900	4	8 @ 7.5	—
1103398	0 @ 300	5½ @ 600	—	—	11½ @ 1800	5	15 @ 13.7	—
1103412	0 @ 300	5½ @ 600	—	—	14½ @ 2000	4	15 @ 12.5	—
1103413	0 @ 500	—	—	—	6½ @ 1800	6	15 @ 13.7	—
1103414	0 @ 300	5½ @ 600	—	—	11½ @ 1800	6	12 @ 13	—
1103419	0 @ 300	5½ @ 600	—	—	11½ @ 1800	4	15 @ 11	—
1110552	0 @ 463	2 @ 650	3¼ @ 1250	—	7 @ 1700	3	12 @ 8	—
1110554	0 @ 840	—	—	—	7½ @ 1800	3	12 @ 12	—
1110555	0 @ 500	2½ @ 800	3 @ 1200	—	7½ @ 1800	4	12 @ 11	—
1110784②	—	—	—	—	—	—	—	—
1981								
1103451②	—	—	—	—	—	—	—	—
1103456②	—	—	—	—	—	—	—	—
1103466②	—	—	—	—	—	—	—	—
1110567②	—	—	—	—	—	—	—	—
1110573②	—	—	—	—	—	—	—	—
1110579②	—	—	—	—	—	—	—	—
1111386②	—	—	—	—	—	—	—	—
1982								
1103457②	—	—	—	—	—	—	—	—
1103470②	—	—	—	—	—	—	—	—

①—Stamped on distributor housing plate.   ②—On models with EST, refer to Tune Up Chapter for specifications.

WHEEL ALIGNMENT SPECIFICATIONS

Year	Model	Caster Angle, Degrees		Camber Angle, Degrees				Toe-In. Inch	Toe-Out on Turns, Deg.①	
		Limits	Desired	Limits		Desired			Outer Wheel	Inner Wheel
				Left	Right	Left	Right			
1977	Omega③	−½ to −1½	−1	+¼ to +1¼	+¼ to +1¼	+¾	+¾	0 to ⅛	—	—
	Omega①	+½ to +1½	+1	+¼ to +1¼	+¼ to +1¼	+¾	+¾	0 to ⅛	—	—
	Cutlass②	+1½ to +2½	+2	+½ to +1½	0 to +1	+1	+½	0 to ⅛	—	—
	88, 98	+2½ to +3½	+3	+¼ to +1¼	+¼ to +1¼	+¾	+¾	1/16 to 3/16	—	—
	Toronado②	−½ to +½	0	−¼ to +¾	−¾ to +¼	+¼	−¼	−1/16 to +1/16	—	—
1978	Toronado	−½ to +½	0	−¼ to +¾	−¾ to +¼	+¼	−¼	−1/16 to +1/16	—	—
1978–79	Omega③	−½ to −1½	−1	+¼ to +1¼	+¼ to +1¼	+¾	+¾	+1/16 to +3/16	—	—
	Omega①	+½ to +1½	+1	+¼ to +1¼	+¼ to +1¼	+¾	+¾	+1/16 to +3/16	—	—
1978–83	Cutlass③	+½ to +1½	+1	0 to +1	0 to +1	+½	+½	+1/16 to +3/16	—	—
	Cutlass①	+2½ to +3½	+3	0 to +1	0 to +1	+½	+½	+1/16 to +3/16	—	—
	88, 98	+2½ to +3½	+3	+¼ to +1¼	+¼ to +1¼	+¾	+¾	+1/16 to +3/16	—	—
	Toronado	+2 to +3	+2½	−½ to +½	−½ to +½	0	0	−1/16 to +1/16	—	—

①—Power Steering.
②—Left and right side "camber" should be different at least ¼° and no more than ¾° with the left side having the greater (+) reading.
③—Manual Steering.

ENGINE TIGHTENING SPECIFICATIONS★

★ Torque specifications are for clean and lightly lubricated threads only. Dry or dirty threads produce increased friction which prevents accurate measurement of tightness.

Year	Engine Model/V.I.N.	Spark Plugs Ft. Lbs.	Cylinder Head Bolts Ft. Lbs.	Intake Manifold Ft. Lbs.	Exhaust Manifold Ft. Lbs.	Rocker Arm Shaft Bracket Ft. Lbs.	Rocker Arm Cover Ft. Lbs.	Connecting Rod Cap Bolts Ft. Lbs.	Main Bearing Cap Bolts Ft. Lbs.	Flywheel to Crankshaft Ft. Lbs.	Vibration Damper or Pulley Ft. Lbs.
1977	V6-231[13][16]	20	80	45	25	30	4	40	100	60	175
	V8-260/F	25	85[4]	40	25	25[1]	7	42	80[12]	[7]	310
	V8-305/U[2][8]	15	65	30	20	50[5]	45[6]	45	70	60	60
	V8-350/L[2][8]	15	65	30	20[10]	50[5]	45[6]	45	70	60	60
	V8-350/R	25	130[4]	40[4]	25	25[1]	7	42	80[12]	[7]	310
	V8-403/K	25	130[4]	40[4]	25	25[1]	7	42	80[12]	[7]	310
1978	V6-231/A[13]	25	80	45	25	30	4	40	115	60	175
	V8-260/F	25	85[4]	40[4]	25	25[1]	7	42	80[12]	[14]	200–310
	V8-305[2][17]	15	65	30	20	50[5]	45[6]	45	70	60	60
	V8-350/R[2]	15	65	30	20[10]	50[5]	45[6]	45	70	60	60
	V8-350/R	25	130[4]	40[4]	25	25[1]	7	42	80[12]	[7]	200–310
	V8-350/N[9]	—	130[4]	40[4]	25	25[1]	—	42	120	60	200–310
	V8-403/K	25	130[4]	40[4]	25	25[1]	15[6]	42	80[12]	[7]	200–310
1979	V6-231/A[13]	15	80	45	25	30	4	40	100	60	225
	V8-260/F	25	85[4]	40[4]	25	28[1]	7	42	80[12]	[7]	200–310
	V8-260/P[9]	—	130[4]	40[4]	25	28[1]	—	42	120	[7]	200–310
	V8-301/Y[11]	15	95	35	40	15[5]	6	30	70	95	160
	V8-305[2][17]	22	65	30	20	50[5]	45[6]	45	70	30	60
	V8-350/N[2]	22	65	30	20[10]	50[5]	45[6]	45	70	30	60
	V8-350/R	25	130[4]	40[4]	25	28[1]	7	42	80[12]	[7]	200–310
	V8-350/N[9]	—	130[4]	40[4]	25	28[1]	—	42	120	[7]	200–310
	V8-403/K	25	130[4]	40[4]	25	28[1]	15[6]	42	80[12]	[7]	200–310
1980	V6-231/A[13]	15	80	45	25	30	4	40	100	60	225
	V8-260/F	25	85[4]	40[4]	25	28[1]	—	42	80[12]	60	200–310
	V8-305/H[2]	22	65	30	20	—	45[6]	45	70	60	60
	V8-307/Y	25	130[4]	40[4]	25	28[1]	—	42	70[12]	60	200–310
	V8-350/R	25	130[4]	40[4]	25	28[1]	—	42	80[12]	60	200–310
	V8-350/N[9]	—	130[4]	40[4]	25	28[1]	—	42	120	60	200–310
1981	V6-231/A[13]	15	80	45	25	30	4	40	100	60	225
	V6-252/4[13]	15	80	45	25	30	4	40	100	60	225
	V8-260/F	25	85[4]	40[4]	25	28[1]	—	42	80[12]	60	200–310
	V8-307/Y	25	85[4]	40[4]	25	28[1]	—	42	80[12]	60	200–310
	V8-350/N[9]	—	130[4]	40[4]	25	28[1]	—	42	120	60	200–310
1982–83	V6-231/A[13]	15	80	45	25	30	4	40	100	60	225
	V6-252/4[13]	15	80	45	25	30	4	40	100	60	225
	V6-262/V[9]	—	[3]	41	29	28[1]	—	42	107	48	160–350
	V8-260/8	25	85[4]	40[4]	25	28[1]	—	42	[14]	60[15]	200–310
	V8-307/Y	25	125[4]	40[4]	25	28[1]	—	42	[14]	60[15]	200–310
	V8-350/N[9]	—	130[4]	40[4]	25	28[1]	—	42	120	60	210–300

[1]—Rocker arm pivot bolt to head.
[2]—Chevrolet built engine. Distributor located at rear of engine, clockwise rotation.
[3]—See text for procedure.
[4]—Clean and dip entire bolt in engine oil before tightening.
[5]—Rocker arm stud.
[6]—Inch lbs.
[7]—Auto. trans., 60 ft. lbs.; manual trans, 90 ft. lbs.
[8]—Omega.
[9]—Oldsmobile built diesel engine.
[10]—Inner bolts, 30 ft. lbs.
[11]—Pontiac built engine. Distributor located at rear of engine, clockwise rotation.
[12]—Rear 120 ft. lbs.
[13]—Buick built engine.
[14]—Bearing No. 5, 120 ft. lbs.; all others, 80 ft. lbs.
[15]—With automatic transmission.
[16]—V.I.N. code A, even fire engine; V.I.N. code C, exc. even fire engine.
[17]—V.I.N. code U on 1978 & G on 1979 denotes 2 barrel carb.; V.I.N. code H denotes 4 Bbl. carb.

REAR AXLE SPECIFICATIONS

Year	Model	Carrier Type	Ring Gear & Pinion Backlash		Pinion Bearing Preload			Differential Bearing Preload		
			Method	Adjustment	Method	New Bearings Inch-Lbs.	Used Bearings Inch-Lbs.	Method	New Bearings Inch-Lbs.	Used Bearings Inch-Lbs.
1977–83	Toronado	Removable	Shims	.005–.009	Shims	2–15	2–5	Shims	10–15①	5–7①
1977–83	Others	Integral	Shims	.005–.009	Spacer	24–32	8–12	Shims	②	②
1979–83	Toronado	Removable	Shims	.005–.007	Spacer	22	5	Shims	②	②

①—Over pinion bearing preload.   ②—Slip fit plus .004 inch clearance on each side.

ALTERNATOR & REGULATOR SPECIFICATIONS

Year	Alternator					Regulator						
	Model	Rated Hot Output Amps.	Field Current 12 Volts @ 80° F.	Output @ 14 Volts		Model	Field Relay			Voltage Regulator		
				2000 R.P.M. Amps.	5000 R.P.M. Amps.		Air Gap In.	Point Gap In.	Closing Voltage	Air Gap In.	Point Gap In.	Voltage @ 125° F.
1977–78	1101016	80	—	—	—	Integral	—	—	—	—	—	—
	1101034	80	—	—	—	Integral	—	—	—	—	—	—
	1102394	37	4–4.5	—	33	Integral	—	—	—	—	—	—
	1102479	55	—	—	—	Integral	—	—	—	—	—	—
	1102840	55	—	—	—	Integral	—	—	—	—	—	—
	1102841	42	—	—	—	Integral	—	—	—	—	—	—
	1102842	63	—	—	—	Integral	—	—	—	—	—	—
	1102843	61	4–4.5	—	57	Integral	—	—	—	—	—	—
	1102844	63	—	—	—	Integral	—	—	—	—	—	—
	1102881	37	—	—	—	Integral	—	—	—	—	—	—
	1102913	61	—	—	—	Integral	—	—	—	—	—	—
	1103033	42	—	—	—	Integral	—	—	—	—	—	—
1979	1101016	80	—	—	—	Integral	—	—	—	—	—	—
	1101028	80	—	—	—	Integral	—	—	—	—	—	—
	1101034	80	—	—	—	Integral	—	—	—	—	—	—
	1101043	80	—	—	—	Integral	—	—	—	—	—	13.9–14.5①
	1101048	80	—	—	—	Integral	—	—	—	—	—	—
	1102394	37	4–4.5	—	—	Integral	—	—	—	—	—	13.8–14①
	1102479	55	4–4.5	—	—	Integral	—	—	—	—	—	—
	1102840	55	—	—	—	Integral	—	—	—	—	—	—
	1102841	42	—	—	—	Integral	—	—	—	—	—	—
	1102842	63	—	—	—	Integral	—	—	—	—	—	—
	1102843	61	—	—	—	Integral	—	—	—	—	—	—
	1102844	63	—	—	—	Integral	—	—	—	—	—	—
	1102860	63	—	—	—	Integral	—	—	—	—	—	—
	1102881	37	—	—	—	Integral	—	—	—	—	—	—
	1103033	42	—	—	—	Integral	—	—	—	—	—	—
	1103042	63	—	—	—	Integral	—	—	—	—	—	13.9–14.5①
	1103055	42	—	—	—	Integral	—	—	—	—	—	—
	1103056	63	—	—	—	Integral	—	—	—	—	—	—
	1103076	63	—	—	—	Integral	—	—	—	—	—	—
	1103098	63	—	—	—	Integral	—	—	—	—	—	—
	1103099	63	—	—	—	Integral	—	—	—	—	—	—
1980	1100111	63	—	—	—	Integral	—	—	—	—	—	—
	1100122	63	—	—	—	Integral	—	—	—	—	—	—
	1100124	63	—	—	—	Integral	—	—	—	—	—	—

ALTERNATOR & REGULATOR SPECIFICATIONS—Continued

Year	Alternator			Output @ 14 Volts		Regulator	Field Relay			Voltage Regulator		
	Model	Rated Hot Output Amps.	Field Current 12 Volts @ 80° F.	2000 R.P.M. Amps.	5000 R.P.M. Amps.	Model	Air Gap In.	Point Gap In.	Closing Voltage	Air Gap In.	Point Gap In.	Voltage @ 125° F.
	1101038	70	—	—	—	Integral	—	—	—	—	—	—
	1101044	70	—	—	—	Integral	—	—	—	—	—	—
	1101065	70	—	—	—	Integral	—	—	—	—	—	—
	1101068	70	—	—	—	Integral	—	—	—	—	—	—
	1101071	70	—	—	—	Integral	—	—	—	—	—	—
	1101074	70	—	—	—	Integral	—	—	—	—	—	—
	1103103	63	—	—	—	Integral	—	—	—	—	—	—
	1103104	42	—	—	—	Integral	—	—	—	—	—	—
	1103112	63	—	—	—	Integral	—	—	—	—	—	—
	1103186	63	—	—	—	Integral	—	—	—	—	—	—
	1103186	63	—	—	—	Integral	—	—	—	—	—	—
1980–82	1100110	42	—	—	—	Integral	—	—	—	—	—	—
	1100121	63	—	—	—	Integral	—	—	—	—	—	—
	1103151	63	—	—	—	Integral	—	—	—	—	—	—
1981	1100110	42	—	—	—	Integral	—	—	—	—	—	—
	1100121	63	—	—	—	Integral	—	—	—	—	—	—
	1100156	55	—	—	—	Integral	—	—	—	—	—	—
	1101068	70	—	—	—	Integral	—	—	—	—	—	—
1981–82	1100164	55	—	—	—	Integral	—	—	—	—	—	—
	1101037	70	—	—	—	Integral	—	—	—	—	—	—
	1101045	85	—	—	—	Integral	—	—	—	—	—	—
	1101084	85	—	—	—	Integral	—	—	—	—	—	—
	1101088	70	—	—	—	Integral	—	—	—	—	—	—
1982	1100164	55	—	—	—	Integral	—	—	—	—	—	—
	1100165	63	—	—	—	Integral	—	—	—	—	—	—
	1100190	85	—	—	—	Integral	—	—	—	—	—	—
	1100194	70	—	—	—	Integral	—	—	—	—	—	—
	1100195	85	—	—	—	Integral	—	—	—	—	—	—
	1100198	42	—	—	—	Integral	—	—	—	—	—	—
1983	1100200	78	—	—	—	Integral	—	—	—	—	—	—
	1100230	42	—	—	—	Integral	—	—	—	—	—	—
	1100239	55	—	—	—	Integral	—	—	—	—	—	—
	1100247	63	—	—	—	Integral	—	—	—	—	—	—
	1100260	78	—	—	—	Integral	—	—	—	—	—	—
	1100263	78	—	—	—	Integral	—	—	—	—	—	—
	1100297	42	—	—	—	Integral	—	—	—	—	—	—
	1100298	55	—	—	—	Integral	—	—	—	—	—	—
	1100300	63	—	—	—	Integral	—	—	—	—	—	—
	1101264	78	—	—	—	Integral	—	—	—	—	—	—
	1105022	78	—	—	—	Integral	—	—	—	—	—	—
	1105025	63	—	—	—	Integral	—	—	—	—	—	—
	1105027	63	—	—	—	Integral	—	—	—	—	—	—
	1105029	63	—	—	—	Integral	—	—	—	—	—	—
	1105032	78	—	—	—	Integral	—	—	—	—	—	—
	1105041	78	—	—	—	Integral	—	—	—	—	—	—
	1105042	78	—	—	—	Integral	—	—	—	—	—	—
	1105194	78	—	—	—	Integral	—	—	—	—	—	—
	1105198	85	—	—	—	Integral	—	—	—	—	—	—
	1105250	70	—	—	—	Integral	—	—	—	—	—	—
	1105343	85	—	—	—	Integral	—	—	—	—	—	—

①—At 85° F.

STARTING MOTOR SPECIFICATIONS

Year	Model/V.I.N.	Starter Number	Brush Spring Tension Oz.①	Free Speed Test			Resistance Test②	
				Amps.	Volts	R.P.M.	Amps.	Volts
1977	V6-231⑪	1108797	—	50—80③	9	5500—10000	—	—
	V8-260/F	1108765	—	55—80③	9	3500—6000	—	—
	V8-305/U⑦	1109056	—	50—80③	9	5500—10000	—	—
	V8-305/U⑧	1108779	—	50—80③	9	5500—10000	—	—
	V8-350/L④	1109052	—	55—80③	9	5500—10000	—	—
	V8-350/R⑤	1108765	—	55—80③	9	3500—6000	—	—
	V8-403/K⑥	1108764	—	65—95③	9	7500—10000	—	—
	V8-403/K⑨	1108794	—	65—95③	9	7500—10000	—	—
	V8-403/K⑩	1108795	—	65—95③	9	7500—10000	—	—
1978	V6-231/A	1109061	—	60—85③	9	6800—10300	—	—
	V8-260/F	1109523	—	45—70③	9	7000—11900	—	—
	V8-305⑫④	1109064	—	60—85③	9	6800—10300	—	—
	V8-305⑫⑥	1109524	—	45—70③	9	7000—11900	—	—
	V8-350/L⑦④	1109065	—	65—95③	9	7500—10500	—	—
	V8-350/L⑧④	1109067	—	65—95③	9	7500—10500	—	—
	V8-350/R⑤	1109072	—	65—95③	9	7500—10500	—	—
	V8-350 Diesel/N	1109213	—	40—140③	9	8000—13000	—	—
	V8-403/K⑨	1109072	—	65—95③	9	7500—10500	—	—
	V8-403/K⑩	1109070	—	65—95③	9	7500—10500	—	—
1979	V6-231/A	1109061	—	60—85③	9	6800—10300	—	—
	V8-260/F, V8-301/Y	1109523	—	45—70③	9	7000—11900	—	—
	V8-260 Diesel/P	1109213	—	40—140③	9	8000—13000	—	—
	V8-305⑫⑦	1109064	—	60—85③	9	6800—10300	—	—
	V8-305⑫⑧	1109074	—	60—85③	9	6800—10300	—	—
	V8-350/L④	1109065	—	65—95③	9	7500—10500	—	—
	V8-350/R⑨⑤	1109072	—	65—95③	9	7500—10500	—	—
	V8-350/R⑩⑤	1108759	—	65—95③	9	7500—10500	—	—
	V8-350 Diesel/N	1109213	—	40—140③	9	8000—13000	—	—
	V8-403/K	1109072	—	65—95③	9	7500—10500	—	—
1980	V6-231/A	1109061	—	60—85③	9	7500—10300	—	—
	V8-260/F	1109523	—	45—70③	9	7000—11900	—	—
	V8-265/S	1109523	—	45—70③	9	7000—11900	—	—
	V8-305/H	1109524	—	45—70③	9	7000—11900	—	—
	V8-307/Y⑨	1109523	—	45—70③	9	7000—11900	—	—
	V8-307/Y⑩	1998205	—	65—95③	9	7500—10500	—	—
	V8-350/L⑨	1109072	—	65—95③	9	7500—10500	—	—
	V8-350/L⑩	1998205	—	65—95③	9	7500—10500	—	—
	V8-350 Diesel/N⑨	1109215⑬	—	40—140③	9	8000—13000	—	—
	V8-350 Diesel/N⑨	1109216⑤	—	100—230③	9	8000—14000	—	—
	V8-350 Diesel/N⑩	1109214⑬	—	40—140③	9	8000—13000	—	—
	V8-350 Diesel/N⑩	1109218⑤	—	100—230③	9	8000—14000	—	—
1981	V6-231/A	1109061	—	60—85	9	6800—10300	—	—
	V6-252/4⑨	1998227	—	65—95	9	7500—10500	—	—
	V6-252/4	1998205	—	65—95	9	7500—10500	—	—
	V8-260/F, V8-307/Y⑩	1109523	—	45—70	9	7000—11900	—	—
	V8-307/Y⑥⑨	1998205	—	65—95	9	7500—10500	—	—
	V8-350 Diesel/N⑥⑨	1109216	—	100—230	9	8000—14000	—	—
	V8-350 Diesel/N⑩	1109218	—	100—230	9	8000—14000	—	—
1982	V6-231/A	1998236	—	60—85	9	6800—10300	—	—
	V6-252/4⑨	1998234	—	65—95	9	7500—10500	—	—
	V6-252/4⑩	1998237	—	65—95	9	7500—10500	—	—
	V6-262 Diesel/V	1998552	—	160—220	9	4000—5500	—	—

Continued

STARTING MOTOR SPECIFICATIONS—Continued

Year	Model/V.I.N.	Starter Number	Brush Spring Tension Oz.①	Free Speed Test			Resistance Test②	
				Amps.	Volts	R.P.M.	Amps.	Volts
	V8-260/8	1109544	—	45–70	9	7000–11900	—	—
	V8-307/Y⑥⑨	1109544	—	45–70	9	7000–11900	—	—
	V8-307/Y⑩	1998237	—	65–95	9	7500–10500	—	—
	V8-350 Diesel/N⑥⑨	1998552	—	160–220	9	4000–5500	—	—
	V8-350 Diesel/N⑩	1109495	—	100–230	9	8000–14000	—	—
1983	V6-231/A	1998236	—	60–90	10	6500–10500	—	—
	V6-252/4⑨	1998234	—	70–110	10	6500–10700	—	—
	V6-252/4⑩	1998237	—	70–110	10	6500–10700	—	—
	V6-262 Diesel/V	1998554	—	160–240	10	4400–6300⑬	—	—
	V8-307/Y⑥⑨	1109544	—	50–75	10	6000–11900	—	—
	V8-307/Y⑩	1998237	—	70–110	10	6500–10700	—	—
	V8-350 Diesel/N⑥⑨	1998554	—	160–240	10	4400–6300⑬	—	—
	V8-350 Diesel/N⑩	1109495	—	120–210	10	9000–13400	—	—

①—Minimum.
②—Check capacity of motor by using a 500 ampere meter & a carbon pile rheostat to control voltage. Apply volts listed across motor with armature locked. Current should be as listed.
③—Includes solenoid.
④—Chevrolet built engine. Distributor located at rear of engine, clockwise rotation.
⑤—Oldsmobile built engine. Distributor located at rear of engine, counter-clockwise rotation.
⑥—Cutlass.
⑦—Auto. trans.
⑧—Manual trans.
⑨—88 & 98.
⑩—Toronado.
⑪—V.I.N. code A, even fire engine; V.I.N. code C, exc. even fire engine.
⑫—V.I.N. code U on 1978 models & G on 1979 models denotes 2 Bbl. carb.; V.I.N. code H denotes 4 Bbl. carb.
⑬—Pinion speed.

BRAKE SPECIFICATIONS

Year	Model	Brake Drum Inside Diameter	Wheel Cylinder Bore Diameter			Master Cylinder Bore Diameter		
			Disc Brake	Front Drum Brake	Rear Drum Brake	Disc Brakes	Drum Brakes	Power Brakes
1977	Omega	9½①	2 15/16	—	④	1	—	1 1/8
	Cutlass	11	2½	—	3/4	13/16	—	1 1/8
	Vista Cruiser	11	2 15/16	—	15/16	1 1/8	—	1 1/8
	Custom Cruiser	11	2 15/16	—	15/16	1 1/8	—	1 1/8
	88, 98	11	2 15/16	—	⑤	1 1/8	—	1 1/8
	Toronado	11	2 15/16	—	15/16	1 1/8	—	1 1/8
1978	Omega	9½①	2 15/16	—	7/8	1 1/8	—	1 1/8
	Cutlass	11	2½	—	3/4	7/8	—	15/16
	88	③	2 15/16	—	⑤	1 1/8	—	1 1/8
	98 & Custom Cruiser	11	2 15/16	—	15/16	1 1/8	—	1 1/8
	Toronado	11	2 15/16	—	15/16	1 1/8	—	1 1/8
1979	Omega	9½①	2 15/16	—	④	1	—	1 1/8
	Cutlass	11	2½	—	3/4	7/8	—	15/16
	88	③	2 15/16	—	⑤	1 1/8	—	1 1/8
	98 & Custom Cruiser	11	2 15/16	—	15/16	1 1/8	—	1 1/8
	Toronado	11	2 15/16	—	3/4	15/16	—	15/16
1980–81	Cutlass	9½	2½	—	3/4	7/8	—	7/8
	88	9½	2 15/16	—	7/8	1 1/8	—	1 1/8
	98 & Custom Cruiser	11	2 15/16	—	15/16	1 1/8	—	1 1/8
	Toronado	9½	2 15/16	—	15/16	1	—	1
1982–83	Cutlass	9½	2½	—	3/4	15/16②	—	15/16
	88	9½	2 15/16	—	7/8	1 1/8②	—	1 1/8
	98 & Custom Cruiser	11	2 15/16	—	15/16⑥	1 1/8②	—	1 1/8
	Toronado	9½	2½	—	3/4⑦	1②	—	1

①—With 5 speed trans. 11″.
②—On Cutlass & Toronado models equipped with hydroboost, 1 1/16. On 88 & 98 models equipped with hydro boost, 1 3/16.
③—Except models w/V8-403, 9½″; models w/V8-403, 11″.
④—Exc. 5 speed, 15/16″; 5 speed, 1″.
⑤—88 Exc. 403 7/8″; 88 with 403 & 98, 15/16″.
⑥—Custom Cruiser, 1 inch.
⑦—With rear disc brakes, 2 1/8″.

VALVE SPECIFICATIONS

Year	Model/V.I.N.	Valve Lash		Valve Angles		Valve Spring Installed Height	Valve Spring Pressure Lbs. @ In.	Stem Clearance		Stem Diameter	
		Int.	Exh.	Seat	Face			Intake	Exhaust	Intake	Exhaust
1977	V6-231⑮⑪	Hydraulic⑥		45	45	1.727	⑨	.0015–.0035	.0015–.0032	.3402–.3412	.3405–.3412
	V8-260/F	Hydraulic⑥		②	⑬	1.67	187 @ 1.27	.0010–.0027	.0015–.0032	.3425–.3432	.3420–.3427
	V8-305/U⑧	¾ Turn③		46	45	⑫	200 @ 1.25	.0010–.0027	.0010–.0027	.3410–.3417	.3410–.3417
	V8-350/R	Hydraulic⑥		②	⑬	1.67	187 @ 1.27	.0010–.0027	.0015–.0032	.3425–.3432	.3420–.3427
	V8-350/L⑧	¾ Turn③		46	45	⑫	200 @ 1.25	.0010–.0027	.0010–.0027	.3410–.3417	.3410–.3417
	V8-403/K	Hydraulic⑥		②	⑬	1.67	187 @ 1.27	.0010–.0027	.0015–.0032	.3425–.3432	.3420–.3427
1978	V6-231/A⑪	Hydraulic⑥		45	45	1.727	168 @ 1.33	.0015–.0035	.0015–.0032	.3401–.3412	.3405–.3412
	V8-260/F	Hydraulic⑥		②	⑬	1.670	187 @ 1.27	.0010–.0027	.0015–.0032	.3425–.3432	.3420–.3427
	V8-305⑧⑯	1 Turn③		46	45	1.718	200 @ 1.25	.0010–.0027	.0010–.0027	.3410–.3417	.3410–.3417
	V8-350/R	Hydraulic⑥		②	⑬	1.67	187 @ 1.27	.0010–.0027	.0015–.0032	.3425–.3432	.3420–.3427
	V8-350/L⑧	1 Turn③		46	45	1.718	200 @ 1.25	.0010–.0027	.0010–.0027	.3410–.3417	.3410–.3417
	V8-350/N①	Hydraulic⑥		②	⑬	1.670	151 @ 1.30	.0010–.0027	.0015–.0032	.3425–.3432	.3420–.3427
	V8-403/K	Hydraulic⑥		②	⑬	1.670	187 @ 1.27	.0010–.0027	.0015–.0032	.3425–.3432	.3420–.3427
1979	V6-231/A⑪	Hydraulic⑥		45	45	1.727	168 @ 1.34	.0015–.0035	.0015–.0032	.3402–.3412	.3405–.3412
	V8-260/F	Hydraulic⑥		②	⑬	1.670	187 @ 1.270	.0010–.0027	.0015–.0032	.3425–.3432	.3420–.3427
	V8-260/F①	Hydraulic⑥		②	⑬	1.670	151 @ 1.30	.0010–.0027	.0015–.0032	.3425–.3432	.3420–.3427
	V8-301/Y⑦	Hydraulic⑥		46	45	1.66	166 @ 1.296	.0010–.0027	.0010–.0027	.3418–.3425	.3418–.3425
	V8-305⑧⑯	1 Turn③		46	45	⑤	⑩	.0010–.0027	.0010–.0027	.3410–.3417	.3410–.3417
	V8-350/R	Hydraulic⑥		②	⑬	1.670	187 @ 1.270	.0010–.0027	.0015–.0032	.3425–.3432	.3427–.3420
	V8-350/L⑧	1 Turn③		46	45	⑤	⑩	.0010–.0037	.0010–.0037	.3410–.3417	.3410–.3417
	V8-350/N①	Hydraulic⑥		②	⑬	1.670	151 @ 1.30	.0010–.0027	.0015–.0032	.3425–.3432	.3420–.3427
	V8-403/K	Hydraulic⑥		②	⑬	1.670	187 @ 1.270	.0010–.0027	.0015–.0032	.3425–.3432	.3420–.3427
1980	V6-231/A⑪	Hydraulic⑥		45	45	1.727	168 @ 1.34	.0015–.0035	.0015–.0032	.3402–.3412	.3405–.3412
	V8-260/F	Hydraulic⑥		②	⑬	1.67	187 @ 1.27	.0010–.0027	.0015–.0032	.3425–.3432	.3420–.3427
	V8-305/H⑧	1 Turn③		46	45	1.70	④	.0010–.0027	.0010–.0027	.3410–.3417	.3410–.3417
	V8-307/Y	Hydraulic⑥		②	⑬	1.67	187 @ 1.27	.0010–.0027	.0015–.0032	.3425–.3432	.3420–.3427
	V8-350/R	Hydraulic⑥		②	⑬	1.67	187 @ 1.27	.0010–.0027	.0015–.0032	.3425–.3432	.3420–.3427
	V8-350/N①	Hydraulic⑥		②	⑬	1.67	151 @ 1.30	.0010–.0027	.0015–.0032	.3425–.3432	.3420–.3427
1981	V6-231/A⑪	Hydraulic⑥		45	45	1.727	⑨	.0015–.0035	.0015–.0032	.3401–.3412	.3405–.3412
	V6-252/4⑪	Hydraulic⑥		45	45	1.727	⑨	.0015–.0035	.0015–.0032	.3401–.3412	.3405–.3412
	V8-260/F	Hydraulic⑥		②	⑬	1.67	187 @ 1.27	.0010–.0027	.0015–.0032	.3425–.3432	.3420–.3427
	V8-307/Y	Hydraulic⑥		②	⑬	1.67	187 @ 1.27	.0010–.0027	.0015–.0032	.3425–.3432	.3420–.3427
	V8-350/N①	Hydraulic⑥		②	⑬	1.67	210 @ 1.22	.0010–.0027	.0015–.0032	.3425–.3432	.3420–.3427
1982–83	V6-231/A⑪	Hydraulic⑥		45	45	1.727	⑭	.0015–.0035	.0015–.0032	.3401–.3412	.3405–.3412
	V6-252/4⑪	Hydraulic⑥		45	45	1.727	⑭	.0015–.0035	.0015–.0032	.3401–.3412	.3405–.3412
	V6-262/V①	Hydraulic⑥		②	⑬	2.09	210 @ 1.22	.0010–.0027	.0015–.0032	.3425–.3432	.3420–.3427
	V8-260/8	Hydraulic⑥		②	⑬	1.67	187 @ 1.27	.0010–.0027	.0015–.0032	.3425–.3432	.3420–.3427
	V8-307/Y	Hydraulic⑥		②	⑬	1.67	187 @ 1.27	.0010–.0027	.0015–.0032	.3425–.3432	.3420–.3427
	V8-350/N①	Hydraulic⑥		②	⑬	2.09	210 @ 1.22	.0010–.0027	.0015–.0032	.3425–.3432	.3420–.3427

①—Oldsmobile built diesel engine.
②—Intake 45°, exhaust 31°.
③—Tighten rocker arm adjusting screw to eliminate all push rod end clearance. Then tighten screw the number of turns listed.
④—Intake, 180 @ 1.25; exhaust, 190 @ 1.16.
⑤—Intake, 1.70; Exhaust, 1.61.
⑥—No adjustment.
⑦—Pontiac built engine. Distributor located at rear of engine, clockwise rotation.
⑧—Chevrolet built engine. Distributor located at rear of engine, clockwise rotation.
⑨—Intake, 164 @ 1.34; exhaust, 182 @ 1.34.
⑩—Intake, 200 @ 1.25"; Exhaust 200 @ 1.16".
⑪—Buick built engine.
⑫—Intake, 1²¹⁄₃₂; exhaust, 1¹⁹⁄₃₂.
⑬—Intake 44°, exhaust 30°.
⑭—Intake, 220 @ 1.34; Exhaust 177 @ 1.450.
⑮—V.I.N. code A, even fire engine; V.I.N. code C, exc. even fire engine.
⑯—V.I.N. code U on 1978 models & G on 1979 models denotes 2 Bbl. carb.; V.I.N. code H denotes 4 Bbl. carb.

PISTONS, PINS, RINGS, CRANKSHAFT & BEARINGS

Year	Model/V.I.N.	Piston Clearance	Ring End Gap[1] Comp.	Oil	Wrist-pin Diameter	Rod Bearings Shaft Diameter	Bearing Clearance	Main Bearings Shaft Diameter	Bearing Clearance	Thrust on Bear. No.	Shaft End Play
1977	V6-231[12][17]	.0008–.0020	.010	.015	.9392	2.000	.0005–.0026	2.4995	.0004–.0015	2	.004–.008
	V8-260/F	.0010–.0020	.010	.015	.9805	2.1238–2.1248	.0004–.0033	[3]	[11]	3	.0035–.0135
	V8-305/U[8]	.0025–.0035	.010	.015	.9272	2.199–2.200	.0013–.0035	[13]	[14]	5	.002–.006
	V8-350/L[8]	.0025–.0035	.010	.015	.9272	2.199–2.200	.0013–.0035	[13]	[14]	5	.002–.006
	V8-350/R	.0010–.0020	.010	.015	.9805	2.1238–2.1248	.0004–.0033	[3]	[11]	3	.0035–.0135
	V8-403/K	.0010–.0020	.010	.015	.9805	2.1238–2.1248	.0004–.0033	[3]	[11]	3	.0035–.0135
1978	V6-231/A[12]	.0008–.0020	.010	.015	.9392	2.000	.0005–.0026	2.4995	.0004–.0015	2	.004–.008
	V8-260/F	.0010–.0020	.010	.015	.9805	2.1238–2.1248	.0004–.0033	[3]	[11]	3	.0035–.0135
	V8-305[8][18]	.0007–.0017	.010	.015	.9272	2.0986–2.0998	.0013–.0035	[13]	[14]	5	.002–.006
	V8-350/L[8]	.0007–.0017	.010	.015	.9272	2.0986–2.0998	.0013–.0035	[13]	[14]	5	.002–.006
	V8-350/R	.0010–.0020	.010	.015	.9805	2.1238–2.1248	.0004–.0033	[3]	[11]	3	.0035–.0135
	V8-350/N[6]	.0050–.0060	.015	.0015	1.0951	2.1238–2.1248	.0005–.0026	2.9993–3.0003	[11]	3	.0035–.0135
	V8-403/K	.0010–.0020	.010	.015	.9805	2.1238–2.1248	.0004–.0033	[3]	[11]	3	.0035–.0135
1979	V6-231/A[12]	.0008–.0020	.010	.015	.9392	2.2487–2.2495	.0003–.0018	2.4995	.0005–.0026	2	.004–.008
	V8-260/F	.00075–.00175	[5]	.015	.9805	2.1238–2.1248	.0004–.0033	[3]	[11]	3	.0035–.0135
	V8-260/P[6]	.00050–.00060	[15]	.015	1.0951	2.1238–2.1248	.0005–.0026	2.9993–3.0003	[11]	3	.0035–.0135
	V8-301/Y[7]	.0025–.0033	.010	.015	.9400		.0005–.0025	3.000	.0002–.0020		.003–.009
	V8-305[8][18]	.0007–.0017	.010	.015	.9272	2.0986–2.0998	.0013–.0035	[13]	[14]	5	.002–.006
	V8-350/L[8]	.0007–.0017	.010	.015	.9272	2.0986–2.0998	.0013–.0035	[13]	[14]	5	.002–.006
	V8-350/R	.00075–.00175	[5]	.015	.9805	2.1238–2.1248	.0004–.0033	[3]	[11]	3	.0035–.0135
	V8-350/N[6]	.0050–.0060	.015	.015	1.0951	2.1238–2.1248	.0005–.0026	2.9993–3.0003	[11]	3	.0035–.0135
	V8-403/K	.0005–.0015	[5]	.015	.9805	2.1238–2.1248	.0004–.0033	[3]	[11]	3	.0035–.0135
1980	V6-231/A[12]	.0011–.0023	.013	.015	.9392	2.2487–2.2495	.0004–.0033	2.4995	.0003–.0018	2	.003–.009
	V8-260/F	.00075–.00175	.010	.015	.9805	2.1238–2.1248	.0004–.0033	[2]	[11]	3	.0035–.0135
	V8-305/H[8]	.0007–.0042	[10]	.010	.9272	2.099–2.100	.0013–.0035	[13]	[14]	5	.002–.007
	V8-307/Y	.0005–.0015	.010	.015	.9805	2.1238–2.1248	.0004–.0033	[2]	[11]	3	.0035–.0135
	V8-350/L	.00075–.00175	.010	.015	.9805	2.1238–2.1248	.0005–.0026	[2]	[11]	3	.0035–.0135
	V8-350/N[6]	.0050–.0060	.015	.015	1.0951	2.1238–2.1248	.0005–.0026	3.00	[11]	3	.0035–.0135
1981	V6-231/A, 252/4[12]	.0008–.0020	.013	.015	.9392	2.2487–2.2495	.0005–.0026	2.4995	.0003–.0018	2	.003–.009
	V8-260/F	.00075–.00175	.010	.015	.9805	2.1238–2.1248	.0004–.0033	[16]	[11]	3	.0035–.0135
	V8-307/Y	.00075–.00175	.010	.015	.9805	2.1238–2.1248	.0005–.0026	[16]	[11]	3	.0035–.0135
	V8-350/N[6]	.005–.006	.015	.015	1.0951	2.1238–2.1248	.0005–.0026	3.00	[11]	3	.0035–.0135
1982–83	V6-231/A, 252/4[12]	.0008–.0020	.013	.015	.9392	2.2487–2.2495	.0005–.0026	2.4995	.0003–.0018	2	.003–.009
	V6-262/V[6]	.0035–.0045	[19]	[20]	1.0951	2.2490–2.2510	.0003–.0025	2.9993–3.0003	[4]	3	.0035–.0135
	V8-260/8	.00075–.00175	.010	.015	.9805	2.1238–2.1248	.0004–.0033	[16]	[11]	3	.0035–.0135
	V8-307/Y	.00075–.00175	.010	.015	.9805	2.1238–2.1248	.0004–.0033	[2]	[11]	3	.0035–.0135
	V8-350/N[6]	.003–.004	.015	.015	1.0951	2.1238–2.1248	.0005–.0026	2.9993–3.0003	[9]	3	.0035–.0135

[1]—Fit rings in tapered bores for clearance listed in tightest portion of ring travel.
[2]—No. 2-3-4-5, 2.4985–2.4995; No. 1, 2.4988–2.4998
[3]—No. 1: 2.4988–2.4998; Nos. 2, 3, 4, 5: 2.4985–2.4995.
[4]—Nos. 1, 2 & 3, .0005–.0021; No 4, .0020–.0034.
[5]—Refer to text under "Piston Rings".
[6]—Diesel.
[7]—Pontiac built engine. Distributor located at rear of engine, clockwise rotation.
[8]—Chevrolet built engine. Distributor located at rear of engine, clockwise rotation.
[9]—Nos. 1, 2, 3 & 4, .0005–.0021; No. 5, .0020–.0034.
[10]—Top—.010"; No. 2—.013".
[11]—No. 1, 2, 3, 4: .0005–.0021; No. 5: .0015–.0031.
[12]—Buick built engine.
[13]—No. 1: 2.4484–2.4493; No. 2, 3, 4: 2.4481–2.4490; No. 5: 2.4479–2.4488.
[14]—No. 1: .0008–.0020; No. 2, 3, 4: .0011–.0023; No. 5: .0017–.0032.
[15]—Top—.012"; No. 2—.010".
[16]—No. 2-3-4-5, 2.4990–2.4995; No. 1, 2.4993–2.4998.
[17]—V.I.N. code A, even fire engine; V.I.N. code C, exc. even fire engine.
[18]—V.I.N. code U on 1978 models & G on 1979 models denotes 2 Bbl. carb.; V.I.N. code H denotes 4 Bbl. carb.
[19]—Top—.019"–.027"; No. 2—.013"–.021".
[20]—.015"–.055"

COOLING SYSTEM & CAPACITY DATA

Year	Model or Engine/V.I.N.	Cooling Capacity, Qts. Less A/C	Cooling Capacity, Qts. With A/C	Radiator Cap Relief Pressure, Lbs.	Thermo. Opening Temp.	Fuel Tank Gals.	Engine Oil Refill Qts. ①	Transmission Oil 3 Speed Pints	Transmission Oil 4 Speed Pints	Transmission Oil 5 Speed Pints	Auto. Trans. Qts. ②	Rear Axle Oil Pints
1977	6-231 Omega⑧⑬	12.7	13.7	15	195	21	4	3	—	—	⑭	3½
	6-231 Cutlass⑧⑬	16.9	17.0	15	195	22	4	3	—	—	⑩	4¼
	6-231⑧⑬⑬	11.5	11.4	15	195	⑮⑯	4	—	—	—	⑭	3½
	8-260/F Omega	16.8	17.8	15	195	21	4	—	—	3½	⑭	3½
	8-260/F Cutlass	16.9	17.0	15	195	22	4	—	—	3½	⑭	4¼
	8-260/F⑬	15.5	15.3	15	195	⑮⑯	4	—	—	—	⑭	3½
	8-305/U Omega	—	—	15	195	21	4	3	—	—	⑭	3½
	8-350 Omega⑭	15.6	16.6	15	195	21	4	—	—	—	⑭	3½
	8-350 Cutlass⑭	15.1	15.3	15	195	22	4	—	—	—	⑭	4¼
	8-350⑬⑭	13.8	13.7	15	195	⑮⑯	4	—	—	—	⑭	4¼
	8-403/K Cutlass	16.3	16.4	15	195	22	4	—	—	—	⑭	4¼
	8-403/K⑬	14.9	14.8	15	195	24½⑯	4	—	—	—	⑭	4¼
	8-403/K Toronado	17.2	17.4	15	195	26	5	—	—	—	⑰	4③
1978	V6-231/A Omega⑧	12.75	12.75	15	195	21	4	3.5	—	3.5	⑩	3½
	V6-231/A Cutlass⑧	12	12	15	195	17.5⑳	4	3.5	—	3.5	⑭	4¼
	V6-231/A 88⑧	12.25	12.25	15	195	25.3	4	—	—	—	⑭	㉗
	V8-260/F Cutlass	16.25⑲	16.25⑲	15	195	17.5㉔	4	—	—	3.5	⑭	4¼
	V8-260/F 88	16.25⑳	16.25⑳	15	195	25.3	4	—	—	—	⑭	㉗
	V8-305 Omega㊺	15.75⑲	16.0⑲	15	195	21	4	—	2.5	—	⑩	3½
	V8-305 Cutlass㊺	15.5㉑	15.5㉑	15	195	17.5㉔	4	—	2.5	—	⑭	4¼
	V8-350 Omega㊹	16	16.75	15	195	21	4	—	—	—	⑩	3½
	V8-350 Cutlass㊹	15.5	16.25	15	195	17.5㉔	4	—	—	—	⑭	4¼
	V8-350/N Diesel	18	18	15	195	27.25⑯	7⑦㉖	—	—	—	⑭	㉗
	V8-350⑬㊹	14	15.5	15	195	⑤	4	—	—	—	⑭	㉗
	V8-403/K⑬	15.75	16.5	15	195	25.3⑯	4	—	—	—	⑭	㉗
	V8-403/K Toronado	17.5㉓	17.5㉓	15	195	26	5	—	—	—	⑰	4③
1979	V6-231/A Omega⑧	12.75	12.75	15	195	21	4	3	—	—	⑩	3½
	V6-231/A Cutlass⑧	13.25	13.25	15	195	18.1㉔	4	3	3	—	⑭	4¼
	V6-231/A 88⑧	13.25	13.25	15	195	25	4	—	—	—	⑭	㉗
	V6-260/F Cutlass	16.25⑲	16.25⑲	15	195	18.1㉔	4	—	—	3½	⑭	4¼
	V8-260/F Cutlass㉒	20	20	15	195	19.8	7⑦㉕	—	—	3½	⑭	4¼
	V8-260/F 88	16.25⑳	16.25⑳	15	195	25	4	—	—	—	⑭	㉗
	V8-301/Y 88	20⑪	20⑪	15	195	25	5㉙	—	—	—	⑭	㉗
	V8-305 Omega㊺	15.75⑲	16⑲	15	195	21	4	—	3	—	⑩	3½
	V8-305 Cutlass㊺	15.5㉑	15.5㉑	15	195	18.1㉔	4	—	3	—	⑭	4¼
	V8-350 Omega㊹	16⑲	16⑲	15	195	21	4	—	—	—	⑩	3½
	V8-350 Cutlass⑨㊹	15.5㉑	15.5㉑	15	195	18.1㉔	4	—	—	—	⑭	4¼
	V8-350 Cutlass㉛㊹	14.5㉜	15㉜	15	195	18.1㉔	4	—	—	—	⑭	4¼
	V8-350/N Cutlass㉒	17.5	17.5	15	195	19.8	7⑦㉖	—	—	—	⑭	4¼
	V8-350⑬㊹	14.5㉝	14.5㉝	15	195	㉞	4	—	—	—	⑭	㉗
	V8-350/N⑬㉒	18	18	15	195	27	7⑦㉖	—	—	—	⑭	㉗
	V8-350 Toronado㊹	15㉟	15㉟	15	195	20	4	—	—	—	㊱	3¼③
	V8-350/N Toronado㉒	18.5	18.5	15	195	22.8	7⑦㉖	—	—	—	㊱	3¼③
	V8-403/K⑬	15.75㊲	16.5	15	195	25⑯	4	—	—	—	⑭	㉗
1980	V6-231/A Cutlass⑧	13	13	15	195	18㉔	4	3	—	—	㊲	4½
	V6-231/A 88⑧	13	13	15	195	25	4	—	—	—	㊲	㉗
	V8-260/F Cutlass	16㉕	16㉕	15	195	18㉔	4	—	—	—	㊲	4¼
	V8-305/H Cutlass	15¼㊳	15¼㊳	15	195	18㉔	4	—	—	—	⑫	4¼
	V8-307/Y 88 & 98	15½㊴	15½㊴	15	195	25⑯	4	—	—	—	⑫	㉗
	V8-307/Y Toronado	16¼	16¼	15	195	21	4	—	—	—	㊱	3¼③
	V8-350/R Cutlass	15	15	15	195	18㉔	4	—	—	—	㊲	4¼
	V8-350/R 88 & 98	14½㉟	14½㉟	15	195	25⑯	4	—	—	—	⑫	㉗
	V8-350/R Toronado	15½㉜	15½㉜	15	195	21	4	—	—	—	㊱	3¼③

COOLING SYSTEM & CAPACITY DATA—Continued

Year	Model or Engine/V.I.N.	Cooling Capacity, Qts. Less A/C	Cooling Capacity, Qts. With A/C	Radiator Cap Relief Pressure, Lbs.	Thermo. Opening Temp.	Fuel Tank Gals.	Engine Oil Refill Qts. [1]	3 Speed Pints	4 Speed Pints	5 Speed Pints	Auto. Trans. Qts. [2]	Rear Axle Oil Pints
	V8-350/N Cutlass[22]	17¼	17¼	15	195	19¾[24]	7 [7] [26]	—	—	—	[40]	4¼
	V8-350/N 88 & 98[22]	18¼	18	15	195	27[16]	7 [7] [26]	—	—	—	[37]	[27]
	V8-350/N Toronado[22]	18	18	15	195	23	7 [7] [26]	—	—	—	[36]	3¼[3]
1981	V6-231/A Cutlass[8]	13[41]	13[41]	15	195	18	4	3	—	—	[42]	4¼
	V6-231/A 88[8]	13	13	15	195	25	4	—	—	—	[42]	4¼
	V6-252/4 98	12.8	12.8	15	195	25	4	—	—	—	[18]	4¼
	V6-252/4 Toronado	13.1	13.1	15	195	21	4	—	—	—	[18]	3¼[3]
	V8-260/F Cutlass	15.9[25]	15.5[25]	15	195	18	4	—	—	—	[42]	4¼
	V8-260/F 88	16.5[20]	16.2[20]	15	195	25[16]	4	—	—	—	[42]	4¼
	V8-307/Y Cutlass	14.9[33]	15.6	15	195	18	4	—	—	—	[42]	4¼
	V8-307/Y 88 & Cust. Cruiser	15.6[21]	15.3[21]	15	195	25[16]	4	—	—	—	[30]	4¼
	V8-307/Y 98	16.2	16.2	15	195	25	4	—	—	—	[18]	4¼
	V8-307/Y Toronado	16.5	16.5	15	195	21	4	—	—	—	[28]	3¼[3]
	V8-350/N Cutlass[22]	17.4	17.3	15	195	19¾[4]	7 [7] [26]	—	—	—	[30]	4¼
	V8-350/N 88 & 98[22]	18.3	18	15	195	27[16]	7 [7] [26]	—	—	—	[42]	4¼
	V8-350/N Toronado[22]	18	18	15	195	23	7 [7] [26]	—	—	—	[28]	3¾[3]
1982	V6-231/A Cutlass[8]	13[41]	13[41]	15	195	18	4	—	—	—	[6]	[4]
	V6-231/A 88[8]	13	13	15	195	25[16]	4	—	—	—	[6]	[4]
	V6-252/4 98	12.8	12.8	15	195	25	4	—	—	—	[6]	[4]
	V6-252/4 Toronado	13.1	13.1	15	195	21	4	—	—	—	[6]	3¼[3]
	V6-262/V[22]	14.5	15.3	15	195	19.75	7 [7] [26]	—	—	—	[6]	[4]
	V8-260/8	16.5[20]	16.2[20]	15	195	25[16]	4	—	—	—	[6]	[4]
	V8-307/Y Cutlass	14.9[33]	15.6	15	195	25[16]	4	—	—	—	[6]	[4]
	V8-307/Y 88 & Custom Cruiser	15.6[21]	15.3[21]	15	195	25[16]	4	—	—	—	[6]	[4]
	V8-307/Y 98	16.2	16.2	15	195	25	4	—	—	—	[6]	[4]
	V8-307/Y Toronado	16.5	16.5	15	195	21	4	—	—	—	[6]	3¼[3]
	V8-350/N Cutlass[22]	17.4	17.3	15	195	19.75[24]	7 [7] [26]	—	—	—	[6]	[4]
	V8-350/N 88 & 98[22]	18	18	15	195	26.5[16]	7 [7] [26]	—	—	—	[6]	[4]
	V8-350/N Toronado[22]	18.1	18.1	15	195	22.75	7 [7] [26]	—	—	—	[6]	3¼[3]
1983	V6-231/A Cutlass	13[46]	13[46]	15	195	18	4	—	—	—	[6]	[4]
	V6-231/A 88	13	13	15	195	25[16]	4	—	—	—	[6]	[4]
	V6-252/4 98	12.5	12.5	15	195	25	4	—	—	—	[6]	[4]
	V6-252/4 Toronado	13.25	13.25	15	195	21	4	—	—	—	[6]	3¼[3]
	V6-262/V[22]	13.75	14.25	15	195	19.8[48]	7 [7] [26]	—	—	—	[6]	[4]
	V8-307/Y Cutlass	14.75	15.5	15	195	18	4	—	—	—	[6]	[4]
	V8-307/Y 88	15.5[47]	15.3[47]	15	195	25	4	—	—	—	[6]	[4]
	V8-307/Y 98	15.25[47]	15.25[47]	15	195	25	4	—	—	—	[6]	[4]
	V8-307/Y Toronado	16.25	16.25	15	195	21	4	—	—	—	[6]	3¼[3]
	V8-350/N Cutlass	17.5	17.5	15	195	19.8[48]	7 [7] [26]	—	—	—	[6]	[4]
	V8-350/N 88 & 98	18.25	18	15	195	26	7 [7] [26]	—	—	—	[6]	[4]
	V8-350/N Toronado	18.25	18.25	15	195	22.8	7 [7] [26]	—	—	—	[6]	3¼[3]

[1]—Add one quart with filter change.
[2]—Approximate; make final check with dipstick.
[3]—Final drive
[4]—7.5 inch ring gear, 3.5 pints; 8.5 inch ring gear, 4.25 pints.
[5]—Delta 88 sedan & Calif. coupe, 21 gals.; Custom Cruiser, 22 gals.; all others 25.3 gals.
[6]—THM 200C, oil pan 4⅛ qts.; total capacity, 10½ qts. THM 2004R, oil pan 5 qts.; total capacity, 11 qts. THM 250C & 350C, oil pan 3⅛ qts.; total capacity 10 qts. THM 325-4L, oil pan 5½ qts.; total capacity 13 qts.
[7]—Recommended diesel engine oil—1978, use oil designation SE/CD; 1979–80, use oil designation SE/CC; 1981, use oil designation SF/CC, SF/CD or SE/CC; 1982–83 use oil designation SF/CC or SF/CD.
[8]—Buick built engine.
[9]—Chevrolet built engine. Distributor located at rear of engine, clockwise rotation.
[10]—Oil pan only 3 qts. After overhaul 10 qts.
[11]—Trailer towing, 21 qts.
[12]—T.H.M. 200 & 200C, oil pan 3½ qts.; after overhaul 9½ qts.; T.H.M. 250C, oil pan 4 qts., after overhaul 10 qts.; T.H.M. 350 & 350C, oil pan 3¼ qts., after overhaul 12¼ qts.; T.H.M. 400, oil pan 3 qts., after overhaul 10 qts.
[13]—Full size cars.
[14]—Turbo Hydro-matic 200: Oil pan only, 3 qts.; after overhaul, 9 qts. T.H. 250, 350 & 400: par only, 3 qts.; after overhaul, 10 qts.
[15]—Delta 88 except Calif. V8-350: 21 gals.; Calif. V8-350 & Ninety-Eight models: 24½ gals.
[16]—Custom Cruiser 22 gallons.
[17]—Oil pan only 4 qts. after overhaul 12 qts.

Continued

COOLING SYSTEM & CAPACITY DATA NOTES—Continued

⑱—Oil pan, 3½ qts.; after overhaul, 11¼ qts.
⑲—Heavy duty & trailer towing, 16.75 qts.
⑳—Trailer towing, 17.0 qts.; Heavy duty, 17.25 qts.
㉑—Heavy duty & trailer towing, 16.25 qts.
㉒—Diesel engine.
㉓—Trailer towing, 17.25 qts.
㉔—Cutlass Cruiser, 18.25 gals.
㉕—Heavy duty cooling system & trailer tow, 16½ qts.
㉖—Includes filter.
㉗—Exc. 7.5″ ring gear, 4.25 pts.; 7.5″ ring gear, 3.5 pts.
㉘—Oil pan, 5¼ qts.; after overhaul, 13½ qts.
㉙—With or without filter change.
㉚—T.H.M. 200-4R, oil pan 3½ qts., after overhaul 11¼ qts.; T.H.M. 250C, oil pan 3¼ qts.,

after overhaul 10 qts.
㉛—Oil pan, 4¼ qts., after overhaul 10½ qts.
㉜—Trailer towing, 15.25 qts.
㉝—Heavy duty & trailer towing, 15.5 qts.
㉞—Delta 88 Calif. models & models with power seats, 20.7 gals.; Custom Cruiser, 22 gals.; all other models, 25 gals.
㉟—Heavy duty, 16 qts.; trailer towing 15.5 qts.
㊱—Oil pan, 5 qts.; after overhaul, 12 qts.
㊲—T.H.M. 200 & 200C, oil pan 3½ qts., after overhaul 9½ qts.; T.H.M. 350 & 350C, oil pan 3¼ qts., after overhaul 12¼ qts.
㊳—With heavy duty cooling system, 16 qts.
㊴—High capacity, 16¼ qts., heavy duty trailer tow, 16 qts.

㊵—Oil pan, 3½ qts.; after overhaul, 9½ qts.
㊶—With heavy duty or trailer tow, 13.6 qts.
㊷—T.H.M. 200C, oil pan 4¼ qts., after overhaul 10½ qts.; T.H.M. 250C & 350C, oil pan 3¼ qts., after overhaul 10 qts.
㊸—V.I.N. code A, even fire engine; V.I.N. code C, exc. even fire engine.
㊹—V.I.N. code R, Oldsmobile built engine; V.I.N. code L, Chevrolet built engine.
㊺—V.I.N. code U on 1978 models & G on 1979 models denotes 2 Bbl. carb.; V.I.N. code H denotes 4 Bbl. carb.
㊻—With high capacity, 13.25 qts.
㊼—High capacity cooling, 16.25 qts.; heavy duty trailer tow, 16 qts.
㊽—Cutlass Cruiser, 18 qts.

Electrical Section

IGNITION LOCK, REPLACE

1979–83

1. Remove steering wheel as described under Horn Sounder and Steering Wheel, Replace.
2. Remove turn signal switch as described under Turn Signal Switch. Replace, then remove buzzer switch.
3. Place ignition switch in Run position, then remove lock cylinder retaining screw and lock cylinder.
4. To install, rotate lock cylinder to stop while holding housing, Fig. 1. Align cylinder key with keyway in housing, then push lock cylinder assembly into housing until fully seated.
5. Install lock cylinder retaining screw. Torque screw to 40 in. lbs. for standard columns. On adjustable columns, torque retaining screw to 22 in. lbs.
6. Install buzzer switch, turn signal switch and steering wheel.

1977–78

1. Follow the procedure to remove the turn signal switch as described further on.
2. Position the lock assembly in "Run" position. Insert a long thin screwdriver into the slot as shown in Fig. 2 and pull outward on lock assembly to remove.
3. To install lock, hold lock cylinder sleeve and rotate knob clockwise against stop, then insert cylinder with key on cylinder sleeve aligned with keyway in housing. Push in to abutment of cylinder and sector, then rotate knob counterclockwise, maintaining a light inward push on cylinder until drive section of cylinder mates with drive shaft. Push in until ring snaps into groove and lock cylinder is secured.

STARTER, REPLACE

NOTE: Upon removal of starter, note if any shims are used. If shims are used, they should be reinstalled in their original location during installation.

If starter is noisy during cranking, remove

one .015 inch double shim or add one .015 inch single shim to the outer bolt. If starter makes a high pitched whine after firing, add .015 inch double shims until noise ceases.

1979 V8-260 Diesel W/Man. Trans.

1. Disconnect battery ground cable.
2. Remove fan shroud attaching screws and leave shroud loose.
3. Remove clutch equalizer shaft, if equipped.
4. Support engine with a suitable jack, disconnect engine mounts and raise engine approximately 1½ inches.
5. Disconnect starter wiring.
6. Remove starter attaching bolts and the starter.
7. Reverse procedure to install. If shims were removed, they must be installed in their original location.

1977–83 V6-231 & 252

1. Disconnect battery ground cable, then raise and support vehicle.
2. On vehicles with automatic transmission, disconnect exhaust crossover pipe and

Fig. 1 Ignition lock removal. 1979–83

Fig. 2 Ignition lock removal. 1977–78

Fig. 3 Headlight switch. 1979–83 Toronado

Fig. 4 Headlight switch. 1978–83 Cutlass

disconnect oil cooler lines at transmission, then remove flywheel housing cover.

3. On vehicles with manual transmission, remove front crossmember to body bolts, right and left brace to crossmember bolts, then remove crossmember.
4. Remove starter bolts, then lower the starter, disconnect electrical leads and remove starter.
5. Reverse procedure to install.

1977–83 Exc. Toronado & V8-260 Diesel With Man. Trans.

1. Disconnect battery ground cable, then raise and support vehicle.
2. On all except V8-305 and 350 Chev. built engine:
   a. Remove upper support retaining bolts.
   b. On V8 engines, remove flywheel housing cover.
3. On V8-305 and 350 Chev. built engine, disconnect starter brace, then remove the wire guide retaining bolts.
4. Remove starter retaining bolts, then lower starter, disconnect electrical leads and remove starter.
5. Reverse procedure to install.

1977–83 Toronado

1. Disconnect battery ground cable, then raise and support vehicle.
2. Remove starter attaching bolts and position starter so that starter wiring can be disconnected.
3. Disconnect starter wiring, then lower starter from vehicle.
4. Reverse procedure to install. If shims were removed, they must be installed in their original location.

IGNITION SWITCH, REPLACE

1977–83

1. Disconnect battery ground cable.
2. On models with regular steering column, turn ignition lock to "Off-Unlock" position. On models with tilt and telescope steering column, turn ignition lock to "Accessory" position.
3. Remove cover attaching bolts, loosen toe pan clamp bolts and remove trim cap from lower part of panel.
4. Remove bracket retaining nuts and lower steering column to the seat.
5. Disconnect and remove switch.
6. On models equipped with column mounted dimmer switch, remove two switch attaching screws, then remove switch and disconnect wire connector.
7. Be sure that lock is in same position as when switch was removed then install switch onto actuator and column.
8. Connect wiring and reinstall column. On models with column mounted dimmer switch, install and adjust dimmer switch as described under Column Mounted Dimmer Switch.

LIGHT SWITCH, REPLACE

1979–83 Toronado

1. Disconnect battery ground cable.
2. Remove headlamp switch knob, radio knobs and steering column trim cover.
3. Remove four screws from underside of left hand trim cover, Fig. 3.
4. Remove left hand sound absorber, then carefully pull left hand trim cover from instrument panel.

NOTE: It may be necessary to disconnect

shift indicator cable clip and lower steering column slightly to remove left hand trim cover.

5. Remove two screws attaching switch to instrument cluster carrier, then pull switch rearward to remove.
6. To disconnect wire connector, remove two connector attaching screws, then pry connect at locations shown in Fig. 3.
7. Reverse procedure to install.

1978–83 Cutlass

1. Disconnect battery ground cable.
2. Remove cluster pad assembly.
3. Remove two headlight switch mounting screws, then pull switch away from panel adapter.
4. To disconnect wire connector, pry connector at locations indicated by arrows as shown in Fig. 4. Pull connector out, then slide to left and push forward to remove.
5. Reverse procedure to install. Refer to Fig. 4, to install wire connector.

1977–81 88 & 98

1. Disconnect battery ground cable.
2. Rotate headlight switch so notch on switch faces downward. Bend a 1/8 inch hook on a piece of stiff wire. Use the wire hook in the notch to pull the knob retainer clip and pull knob off shaft.
3. Remove twilight sentinel knob.
4. Position steering column collar upward and remove column lower trim cover.
5. Remove two screws securing trim cover to cluster carrier.
6. Pull trim cover from clips.
7. Remove light switch mounting plate screws.
8. Pull switch through opening and disconnect electrical connector.
9. Remove nut and switch from mounting plate.
10. Reverse procedure to install.

Fig. 5   Brake switch installation. 1977–83

1982–83 88 & 98

1. Disconnect battery ground cable.
2. Remove steering column trim cover, gage cluster and headlamp switch knob.
3. Remove two screws attaching left side trim cover to cluster carrier, then remove trim cover by pulling rearward.
4. Remove two screws attaching mounting plate to cluster carrier.
5. Pull switch and mounting plate rearward and disconnect electrical connector.
6. Remove nut and separate mounting plate from switch.
7. Reverse procedure to install.

1977–78 Toronado

1. Disconnect battery ground cable.
2. Without disconnecting vacuum hoses or electrical connectors, remove heater or air conditioning control.
3. Remove switch escutcheon and pull switch through heater or air conditioning control opening in cluster and disconnect electrical connector.
4. Reverse procedure to install.

1977 Cutlass

Less Air Conditioning
1. Disconnect battery ground cable.
2. Remove steering column trim cover.
3. Pull switch to "On," and push in button on switch rear, then pull switch knob and shaft from switch.
4. Remove switch escutcheon, pull switch from panel and disconnect electrical connector.
5. Reverse procedure to install.

Fig. 7   Back-up light switch adjustment. 1977–79 88 & 98, 1978–79 Cutlass & 1979 Toronado

With Air Conditioning
1. Disconnect battery ground cable.
2. Remove steering column trim cover and disconnect A/C outlet hose.
3. Disconnect parking brake release cable.
4. Remove screws securing left hand control panel and pull control panel from instrument panel.
5. Disconnect switch electrical connector.
6. Pull switch to "On" and push in button on switch rear, then pull switch knob and shaft from switch.
7. Remove switch escutcheon and switch.
8. Reverse procedure to install.

1977–79 Omega

1. Disconnect battery ground cable.
2. Disconnect multiple connector from switch.
3. Pull knob out to headlight "On" position, then depress spring-loaded button on switch body and pull knob out of switch assembly.
4. Remove switch escutcheon.
5. Remove switch from rear of panel.
6. Reverse procedure to install.

STOP LIGHT SWITCH

1977–83

The stop light switch is attached to the brake pedal bracket and is actuated by the brake pedal arm, Fig. 5. When installing the switch, insert switch into tubular clip until switch body seats on tube clip. Pull brake pedal rearward until it contacts brake pedal stop. This moves the switch in the tubular clip providing proper adjustment.

CLUTCH START SWITCH

1977–81

All cars equipped with a manual transmission use a clutch start switch which is mounted on the pedal bracket. The switch closes when the clutch is depressed and completes solenoid connection. When installing switch, no adjustment is necessary.

NEUTRAL START & BACK-UP LIGHT SWITCH, REPLACE

1977 Cutlass, 1977–79 Omega & 1977–78 Toronado

1. Place gear selector in "Neutral" for column shift models, or "Park" for console shift models.
2. Remove screws attaching switch to steering column, then remove switch.
3. Disconnect wiring connectors. Connect wiring connectors to new switch.
4. Position new switch on steering column and loosely install screws.
5. Install .090 inch gauge pin in switch as shown in Fig. 6.
6. Rotate switch until gauge pin aligns with the alignment hole in inner plastic slide.
7. Torque switch attaching screws to 20 inch lbs. and remove gauge pin.

NOTE: Do not overtorque attaching screws.

Fig. 6   Back-up light or neutral start/back-up light switch adjustment

8. Ensure vehicle will start in "Park" or "Neutral" only. If not, repeat procedure.

BACK-UP LIGHT SWITCH, REPLACE

1977–79 88 & 98, 1978–79 Cutlass & 1979 Toronado

1. Place gear selector in "Neutral".
2. Remove screws attaching switch to steering column, then remove switch.
3. Disconnect wiring connectors. Connect wiring connectors to new switch.
4. Position new switch on steering column, aligning the switch carrier tang in the switch tube slot.
5. Install attaching screws and tighten.

NOTE: No adjustment is required. The switch is pinned in the proper position with a plastic shear pin.

6. If adjustment is required:
   a. Place gear selector in "Neutral".
   b. Loosen switch attaching screws.
   c. While rotating switch on column, insert a .096 inch gauge pin in neutral gauge hole a depth of 3/8 inch, Fig. 7.
   d. Tighten attaching screws and remove gauge pin.

Fig. 7A   Back-up light switch installation. 1981 V-8 Toronado & 1982–83 models

Fig. 8 Mechanical neutral start system with standard column. 1977–83 88, 98, 1978–83 Cutlass 1979–83 Toronado

Fig. 9 Mechanical neutral start system with tilt column. 1977–83 88, 98, 1978–83 Cutlass 1979–83 Toronado

Fig. 10 Mechanical neutral start system in Park position. 1977–83 88, 98, 1978–83 Cutlass 1979–83 Toronado

1980–81 Models Exc. 1981 V8 Toronado

1. On 1980 models and 1981 models with column shift, place gear selector in "Neutral". On 1981 models with console shift, place gear selector in "Park".
2. Remove screws attaching switch to steering column, then remove switch.
3. Disconnect wiring connectors. Connect wiring connectors to new switch.
4. Position new switch on steering column and loosely install screws.
5. Install .096 inch gauge pin in switch as shown in Fig. 6.
6. Rotate switch until gauge pin aligns with the alignment hole in inner plastic slide.
7. On 1981 models with console shift, rotate shift bowl clockwise to remove free play, then lightly hold against stop.
8. Tighten attaching screws and remove gauge pin.
9. Ensure vehicle will start in "Park" and "Neutral" only. If not, repeat procedure.

1981 V8 Toronado & 1982–83 Models

1. Place gear selector in "Neutral".
2. Gently rock back-up light switch out of steering column.
3. Disconnect wiring connectors. Connect wiring connectors to new switch.
4. Align switch actuator with hole in shift tube, Fig. 7A.
5. Position connector side of switch into lower jacket cut out.

Fig. 11 Taping turn signal connector and wires

6. Push down front of switch, ensuring switch tangs snap into holes in steering column jacket.
7. Adjust switch by placing gear selector in "Park" position. The switch main housing and housing back should ratchet, providing proper adjustment.

NEUTRAL START SYSTEM
1977–83 88 & 98, 1978–83 Cutlass & 1979–83 Toronado

Actuation of the ignition switch is prevented by a mechanical lockout system, Figs. 8 and 9, which prevents the lock cylinder from rotating when the selector lever is out of Park or Neutral. When the selector lever is in Park or Neutral, the slots in the bowl plate and the finger on the actuator rod align allowing the finger to pass through the bowl plate in turn actuating the ignition switch, Fig. 10. If the selector lever is in any position other than Park or Neutral, the finger contacts the bowl plate when the lock cylinder is rotated, thereby preventing full travel of the lock cylinder.

TURN SIGNAL SWITCH, REPLACE
1977–83 Tilt & Telescope

1. Disconnect battery ground cable and remove steering wheel.
2. Remove instrument panel lower trim panel, then disconnect turn signal harness connector. Remove connector from packet mounting bracket and wrap tape around connector and wires to prevent wires from snagging when removing switch, Fig. 11.
3. Remove four bolts securing column bracket assembly to mast jacket.
4. Disconnect shift indicator.
5. Hold column in position and remove two nuts securing column bracket assembly. Then, remove bracket and turn signal wiring connector. Loosely re-install bracket to hold column in place.
6. Remove rubber bumper and plastic retainer.
7. Using a suitable compressor, Fig. 12, depress lock plate far enough to remove "C" ring from shaft.

NOTE: On Tilt & Telescope, compressor must be positioned on large lips of cancelling cam.

8. Remove lock plate and carrier assembly, then the upper bearing spring.
9. On models less column mounted dimmer switch, place turn signal lever in right turn position and unscrew lever. Lift tilt lever and position in center position.
10. On models with column mounted dimmer switch, remove actuator arm screw and actuator arm, then remove turn signal lever by pulling straight out to disengage.
11. Push in hazard warning knob, then remove screw and hazard warning knob.
12. Remove turn signal switch attaching screws, then pull switch and wiring from top of column.

1977–83 Exc. Tilt & Telescope

1. Disconnect battery ground cable.
2. Remove steering wheel.
3. Remove cover screws and cover.
4. Using suitable compressor, depress lock plate far enough to remove the "C" ring from shaft.
5. Remove lock plate, cancelling cam, spring and signal lever.
6. Depress hazard warning knob then unscrew knob and remove.
7. On models less column mounted dimmer switch, position lever in right turn position and remove three switch attaching screws.
8. On models with column mounted dimmer switch, remove actuator arm screw and actuator arm, then remove turn signal lever by pulling straight out to disengage.

Fig. 12 Compressing lock plate and removing retaining ring

9. Remove panel lower trim cap, disconnect switch harness and remove bolts attaching bracket to column jacket.
10. Disconnect shift indicator if equipped.
11. Remove two nuts holding column in position, remove bracket and wire protector while holding column in position then loosely install bracket to hold column in place.
12. Tape switch wires at connector keeping wires flat, then carefully remove wires and switch.

COLUMN-MOUNTED DIMMER SWITCH, REPLACE

1977—83 88, 98, 1978 Cutlass & 1979—83 Toronado

1. Disconnect battery ground cable.
2. Remove instrument panel lower trim and on models with A/C, remove A/C duct extension at column.
3. Disconnect shift indicator from column and remove toe-plate cover screws.
4. Remove two nuts from instrument panel support bracket studs and lower steering column, resting steering wheel on front seat.
5. Remove dimmer switch retaining screw and the switch. Tape actuator rod to column and separate switch from rod.

NOTE: 1978—83 models, two screws are used to retain dimmer switch to steering column.

6. Reverse procedure to install. To adjust switch, depress dimmer switch slightly and install a $3/32$ inch twist drill to lock the switch to the body. Force switch upward to remove lash between switch and pivot. Torque switch retaining screw to 35 inch lbs. and remove tape from actuator rod. Remove twist drill and check for proper operation.

HORN SOUNDER & STEERING WHEEL, REPLACE

1. Disconnect battery ground cable.
2. For tilt and telescope steering column proceed as follows:
   a. Remove pad assembly retaining screws, disconnect connector and remove pad assembly.
   b. Move locking lever counterclockwise until full release is obtained. Scribe a mark on the plate assembly where the two screws attach plate assembly to locking lever (for ease of installation) and remove the two screws.
   c. Unscrew and remove plate assembly.
3. For standard wheel, pull up on horn cap retainer assembly and disconnect horn contacts.
4. For Deluxe wheel, remove three screws from pad assembly and disconnect connectors.
5. On sport wheel, pull up on and remove emblem and horn contact assembly from wheel.
6. On Wood Grain wheel, carefully pry horn cap assembly from wheel.
7. On all models, remove steering wheel nut

INSTRUMENT PANEL PAD

CLUSTER CARRIER

Fig. 13   Instrument cluster. 1979—83 Toronado

and using a suitable puller, remove steering wheel.

NOTE: Some vehicles have a snap ring on the end of the steering shaft which must be removed before removing steering wheel nut.

8. Reverse procedure to install.

INSTRUMENT CLUSTER, REPLACE

NOTE: On some 1980—83 models, a yellow flag with the word emissions will rotate into the odometer window at 30,000 mile intervals indicating either a catalyst or oxygen sensor change is required. After performing the required maintenance, reset the emissions flag as follows:

a. On Cutlass models, remove cluster pad assembly. On 88, 98 and Toronado, remove left hand trim cover.
b. On all models, remove trip odometer reset knob, if equipped.

c. Remove screws attaching cluster lens to cluster assembly and remove lens.
d. Using a pointed tool inserted at an angle to engage flag wheel detents, rotate flag wheel downward. When flag wheel is reset, the alignment mark will be in center of odometer window.

1979—83 Toronado

1. Disconnect battery ground cable.
2. Remove headlamp switch knob, radio knobs and steering column trim cover.
3. Remove four screws from underside of left hand trim cover.
4. Remove left hand sound absorber, then pull left hand trim cover from instrument panel.

NOTE: It may be necessary to disconnect shift indicator cable clip and lower steering column slightly to remove left hand trim cover.

R. H. INSTRUMENT PANEL MOLDING

INSTRUMENT PANEL ADAPTER

INSTRUMENT PANEL LOWER TRIM COVER

INSTRUMENT CLUSTER BEZEL

INSTRUMENT PANEL CLUSTER PAD

L. H. TRIM COVER

R. H. TRIM COVER

Fig. 14   Instrument panel cluster pad. 1978—83 Cutlass

Fig. 15   Instrument cluster. 1977–83 88 & 98

5. Remove two screws attaching headlamp switch to cluster carrier, then pull switch from carrier.
6. Remove windshield wiper switch, then remove radio from instrument panel.
7. Remove four screws attaching heater-A/C control to cluster. Pull control out of cluster and disconnect wiring, vacuum lines and temperature control cable, then remove control assembly.
8. Unlock headlamp switch, windshield wiper, cruise control and defogger switch connectors from cluster carrier, then disconnect speedometer cable.
9. Remove nine cluster carrier attaching screws, then remove cluster carrier, Fig. 13.

1978–83 Cutlass

1. Disconnect battery ground cable.
2. Remove right hand and left hand trim panels, Fig. 14.
3. Remove the 7 screws retaining cluster pad to panel adapter.
4. Pull panel pad to disengage it from retaining clips and remove pad assembly, Fig. 14.
5. Remove steering column trim cover, then disconnect shift indicator clip from shift bowl.
6. Remove the 4 screws retaining cluster assembly, then disconnect speedometer cable and electrical connectors and remove cluster assembly.
7. Reverse procedure to install.

1977–83 88 & 98

1. Disconnect battery ground cable.
2. Rotate headlight switch so notch on switch faces downward. Bend a 1/8 inch hook on a piece of stiff wire. Use the wire hook in the notch to pull the knob retainer clip and pull knob off shaft.
3. Remove twilight sentinel knob.
4. Position steering column collar upward and remove column lower trim cover.
5. Remove two screws securing trim cover to cluster carrier, Fig. 15.
6. Pull trim cover from clips.
7. Remove radio knobs and cigar lighter.
8. Remove two screws securing to panel, Fig. 15.
9. Pull trim cover from panel clips.
10. Remove radio as outlined under "Radio, Removal."
11. Remove A/C-heater control attaching screws, pull control outward and disconnect control cables and electrical connectors.
12. Remove switches, clock and disconnect ash tray lamp.
13. Remove right hand outside remote mirror control screws.
14. Disconnect shift indicator cable clip.
15. Remove steering column bolts at floor pan and the nuts from the steering column bracket. Then, lower the steering column and rest steering wheel on seat.
16. Disconnect speedometer cable.
17. Remove instrument panel cluster carrier bolts and the two instrument panel screws, Fig. 15.
18. Remove center air duct screws.
19. Pull cluster outward to disconnect electrical connectors.
20. Remove cluster carrier, Fig. 15.

1977–78 Toronado

CAUTION: On vehicles equipped with an Air Cushion Restraint system, turn ignition switch to "Lock," disconnect battery ground cable and tape end, thereby deactivating system.

1. Disconnect battery ground cable.
2. Disconnect electrical connections at flood lamp or map lamp and remove lamp.
3. Carefully pry speakers from clips, disconnect electrical connections and remove speakers.
4. Remove instrument panel pad screws through speaker openings.
5. Remove screws from lower left outside edge of instrument panel pad, instrument cluster above speedometer, lower right hand corner of glove box and glove box top edge.
6. Pull at center edge of instrument panel pad, releasing clips holding instrument panel pad to windshield edge and remove instrument panel pad.
7. Disconnect the right hand instrument panel cover from lower trim panel and remove glove box door.

NOTE: Cover is secured by one screw and five studs pushed through clips mounted in lower panel.

8. If equipped with air conditioning, disconnect upper right hand air hose from duct.
9. On all models, disconnect electrical connectors from clock, trunk release and glove box lamp.
10. Remove the upper trim panel.
11. Disconnect the left hand instrument panel cover, slide steering column cover up the column and pull the left hand

R.H. UPPER TRIM PANEL

CLUSTER ASSY.

Fig. 16   Instrument cluster. 1977–78 Toronado

Fig. 17 Instrument cluster (Typical). 1977-79 Omega

instrument panel cover from lower trim panel.

NOTE: Cover is secured by six studs pushed through clips mounted in lower panel.

12. If equipped with air conditioning, disconnect upper left hand air hose from duct.
13. On all models, disconnect temperature and defroster cables from heater case and remove radio to radio support nut.
14. Remove instrument cluster attaching screws, Fig. 16, pull cluster outward and disconnect speedometer cable.
15. Disconnect electrical connectors from instrument cluster and the vacuum harness from air conditioning or heater control.
16. Disconnect radio electrical connectors, pull fiber optic element from washer fluid indicator lens and remove screw from windshield wiper switch ground.
17. Remove three screws securing wiring harness to lower corners of instrument cluster, then disconnect harness from three retaining clips.
18. Remove instrument cluster assembly.

1977–79 Omega

1. Disconnect battery ground cable.
2. Remove shift indicator needle from shift bowl and lower steering column.

NOTE: Apply protective material to mast jacket to prevent damage to painted surfaces.

3. Remove three screws from front of heater control securing it to cluster.
4. Remove radio knobs, washers, bezel nuts and front support at lower edge of instrument cluster. This allows radio to remain in the panel.
5. Remove screws at top, bottom and side of cluster securing it to instrument panel, Fig. 17.
6. Tilt cluster forward and reach behind to disconnect speedo cable, speed-minder and electrical connectors and lift cluster out of carrier after removing screws.

1977 Cutlass

Speedometer Cluster
1. Disconnect battery ground cable.
2. With automatic transmission column shift, remove lower trim cover (below steering column) then disconnect shift indicator clip on shift bowl.

Fig. 18 Instrument cluster. 1977 Cutlass

3. On all models, lower steering column.
4. Disconnect speedo cable from speedometer.
5. Remove three cluster attaching screws and pull cluster out carefully so shift indicator needle is not damaged. Disconnect wiring connector and remove cluster.

Fuel Gauge & Telltale Assembly
1. Perform steps 1 through 3 as outlined under "Speedometer Cluster" procedure.
2. Remove three assembly attaching screws and pull assembly out of pad, Fig. 18.
3. Disconnect wiring connectors and remove assembly.

W/S WIPER MOTOR, REPLACE
1977–83

1. Raise hood and remove cowl screen or grille.
2. Reach through cowl opening and loosen

transmission drive link attaching nuts to motor crankarm.
3. Disconnect wiring and washer hoses.
4. Disconnect transmission drive link from motor arm.
5. Remove motor attaching screws.
6. Remove motor while guiding crankarm through opening.

W/S WIPER TRANSMISSION, REPLACE
1977–83

Rectangular Motor
1. Remove wiper arms and blades.
2. Raise hood and remove cowl vent screen or grille.
3. Disconnect wiring from motor.
4. Loosen, do not remove, transmission drive link to motor crankarm attaching nuts and disconnect drive link from crankarm.

Fig. 19 W/S wiper switch installation. 1982-83

Fig. 20 Windshield wiper switch. 1979-81 Toronado

Fig. 21 Windshield wiper switch. 1978-81 Cutlass

5. Remove right and left transmission to body attaching screws and guide transmission and linkage out through cowl opening.

Round Motor
1. Raise hood and remove cowl vent screen.
2. On 1977-83 except Toronado, remove right and left wiper arm and blade assemblies. On 1977-83 Toronado, remove arm and blade only from transmission to be removed.
3. Loosen, do not remove, attaching nuts securing transmission drive link to motor crankarm.

NOTE: On 1977-83 Toronado, if only the left transmission is to be removed, it will not be necessary to loosen attaching nuts securing the right transmission drive link to the motor.

4. Disconnect drive link from motor crankarm.
5. On 1977-83 except Toronado, remove right and left transmission to body attaching screws. On 1977-83 Toronado, remove the attaching screws securing only the transmission to be removed.
6. Remove transmission and linkage by guiding it through opening.

W/S WIPER SWITCH, REPLACE

1982-83 All

1. Disconnect battery ground cable.
2. Disconnect electrical connector at base of steering column.
3. Remove steering column wiring harness protector from underside of steering column.
4. Firmly grasp wiper switch lever and pull straight out.
5. To install wiper switch, refer to Fig. 19, for service procedures.

1979-81 Toronado

1. Disconnect battery ground cable.
2. Remove headlamp switch knob, radio knobs and steering column trim cover.

3. Remove four screws from under side of left hand trim cover.
4. Remove left hand sound absorber, then carefully pull left hand trim cover from instrument panel.

NOTE: It may be necessary to disconnect shift indicator cable clip and lower steering column slightly to remove left hand trim cover.

5. Remove two screws attaching switch to cluster, then pull switch rearward to remove, Fig. 20.

1978-81 Cutlass

1. Disconnect battery ground cable.
2. Remove cluster pad assembly.
3. Remove switch retaining screws, then pull switch out to remove, Fig. 21.
4. Reverse procedure to install.

1977-81 88 & 98

1. Disconnect battery ground cable.
2. Rotate headlight switch knob so that notch on back of switch knob is down. Bend a 1/8 in. hook on paper clip wire and use in notch to pull knob retainer clip while pulling knob off shaft.
3. Remove twilight sentinel knob, if equipped.
4. Move steering column collar up and snap out lower trim cover.
5. Remove two trim cover attaching screws, then pull trim cover out of clips.
6. Remove switch mounting plate screws, then pull switch through opening, disconnect wire connector and remove switch.

1977-78 Toronado

1. Disconnect battery ground cable.
2. Remove air conditioning or heater control without disconnecting vacuum harness or electrical connectors.
3. Remove headlamp switch escutcheon and pull headlamp switch through air conditioning or heater control opening without removing electrical connector.
4. Remove windshield wiper switch knob and two switch attaching nuts through air conditioning or heater control open-

ing, then pull switch through opening, disconnect electrical connector and remove switch.

1977 Cutlass

1. Disconnect battery ground cable.
2. Remove steering column trim cover screws and if equipped with air conditioning, disconnect outlet hose.
3. Disconnect parking brake cable.
4. Remove left hand control panel screws, pull control panel from instrument panel and disconnect wiring.
5. Remove electrical connector from wiper switch, wiper switch knob, switch retaining screws and switch.

1977-79 Omega

1. Disconnect battery ground cable.
2. Remove switch electrical connector, switch retaining screws and switch from behind instrument panel.

RADIO, REPLACE

NOTE: When installing radio, be sure to adjust antenna trimmer for peak performance.

1979-83 Toronado

1. Disconnect battery ground cable.
2. Remove headlamp switch knob, radio knobs and steering column trim cover.
3. Remove four screws from underside of left hand trim cover.
4. Remove left hand sound absorber, then pull left hand trim cover from instrument panel.

NOTE: It may be necessary to disconnect shift indicator cable clip and lower steering column slightly to remove left hand trim cover.

5. Remove right hand sound absorber.
6. Remove screw attaching instrument panel wiring harness to radio bracket and screw attaching radio to tie bar. Move tone generator aside, if equipped.
7. Remove four screws attaching radio mounting plate to cluster carrier.

Fig. 22   Heater core. 1979–83 Toronado

Fig. 23   Heater core and blower motor (less air conditioning). 1977–83 88 & 98

8. Disconnect antenna lead and radio wiring.
9. Pull radio and mounting plate rearward to remove.

1978–83 Cutlass

1. Disconnect battery ground cable.
2. Remove instrument panel lower trim cover.
3. Remove the 4 radio mounting plate screws, and the screw from radio support bracket on lower instrument panel tie bar.
4. Pull radio outward, then disconnect antenna and electrical connectors and remove radio.
5. Reverse procedure to install.

1977–83 88 & 98

1. Disconnect battery ground cable.
2. Remove radio knobs, cigar lighter and right hand trim panel cover.
3. Remove radio bracket to lower tie bar screw and the four mounting plate screws.
4. Pull radio out, then disconnect the electrical connectors and antenna lead, and remove radio.
5. Reverse procedure to install.

1977–78 Toronado

1. Disconnect battery ground cable.
2. Disconnect all wiring from radio.
3. Disconnect throttle cable, then remove throttle lever and reinforcement.
4. Remove radio support bracket to tie-bar screw.
5. Remove radio knobs and two nuts securing radio to instrument cluster.
6. Lower radio and remove from behind instrument panel.

1977–79 Omega

1. Disconnect battery cable.
2. Remove ash tray and housing as necessary.
3. Remove knobs, controls, washers, trim plate and nuts from radio.
4. Remove hoses from center A/C distribution duct as necessary.
5. Disconnect all leads to radio.
6. Remove screws or nuts from radio rear mounting bracket and remove radio.

1977 Cutlass

1. Disconnect battery ground cable.
2. Remove four screws from steering column

trim cover and remove cover.
3. Remove knobs from radio by pulling outward on knobs.
4. Remove nuts from front of radio.
5. Remove four screws holding R.H. Control Panel to dash and gently pull panel outward and up.
6. Remove screw from radio support bracket.
7. Remove four screws holding ash tray housing to tie bar and remove housing assembly.
8. Disconnect all leads and remove radio.

HEATER CORE, REPLACE

1979–83 Toronado

1. Disconnect battery ground cable, then drain cooling system.
2. Disconnect heater hoses at heater core, then install plugs in core outlets to prevent spillage.
3. Remove instrument panel sound absorbers, then lower steering column.
4. Remove instrument cluster as described under Instrument Cluster, Replace.
5. Remove radio front speakers.
6. Remove three screws attaching manifold to heater case.
7. Remove four upper and three lower instrument panel attaching screws.
8. Disconnect parking brake release cable.
9. Disconnect instrument wiring harness from dash wiring assembly.
10. Disconnect right hand remote control mirror cable from instrument panel pad.
11. Disconnect speedometer cable from clip and temperate control cable at heater case.
12. Disconnect radio and A/C wiring, vacuum lines and all wiring necessary to remove instrument panel assembly. If equipped with pulse wiper, remove wiper switch and unlock wire connector from cluster carrier, then separate pulse wiper jumper harness from wiper switch wire connector.
13. Remove instrument panel and wiring harness assembly.
14. Remove defroster ducts, then disconnect lines from actuators.
15. Remove blower motor resistor.
16. From engine side of dash panel, remove three heater and A/C case retaining nuts.
17. From passenger compartment, remove

screws and clip retaining heater and A/C case to dash panel.
18. Remove heater and A/C case, then remove heater core from case, Fig. 22.

1977–83 88 & 98

Less A/C
1. Disconnect battery ground cable.
2. Disconnect blower resistor and blower motor wiring.
3. Drain cooling system into a suitable container, then remove heater hoses from heater core.
4. Remove seven screws attaching heater and blower case to plenum case, then remove case.

NOTE: The heater temperature air valve can be removed at this time by disconnecting valve cable and tapping hinge pin down until it clears the upper pivot, then lift valve and hinge pin out of lower pivot, Fig. 23.

---

5. Remove four screws securing heater core shroud, then shroud and core, Fig. 23.
6. Remove core mounting screws and clamps, then separate core from shroud.
7. Reverse procedure to install. Replace sealer as necessary during installation to prevent air and water leaks.

With A/C
1. Disconnect battery ground cable.
2. Disconnect blower resistor and blower motor wiring.
3. Disconnect A/C wiring, then heater core ground strap.
4. Remove thermostatic switch and diagnostic connector (if equipped).
5. Remove right half of hood seal, then seven screws attaching air inlet screen. Remove screen.
6. Remove five bolts attaching case to dash, nine upper to lower case attaching screws around flange and two upper to lower case attaching screws located inside plenum.
7. Remove upper case by lifting straight up, then off, Fig. 24.
8. Remove accumulator bracket, then lift evaporator out of case.
9. Remove heater hoses, then lift heater core out of case.
10. Reverse procedure to install. Replace sealer as necessary during installation to prevent air and water leaks.

Fig. 24 Heater core and blower motor (with air conditioning). 1977–83 88 & 98

Fig. 26 Heater core. 1977–79 Omega (Typical)

Fig. 25 Heater core. 1977–78 Toronado & 1977 Cutlass (Typical)

1977–78 Toronado

1. Disconnect battery ground cable and drain radiator.
2. Disconnect heater hoses and plug hoses and core openings to prevent coolant loss.
3. Remove heater case to dash panel attaching nuts, Fig. 25.
4. Remove instrument panel trim cover and the heater case to cowl bolts.
5. Remove lower air duct.
6. Remove instrument panel pad, then electrical connectors from glovebox light and clock.
7. Remove right hand upper trim panel and on models equipped with A/C, remove manifold from heater case.
8. On all models, remove defroster duct from heater case and disconnect lower dash trim panel.
9. Disconnect temperature and defroster cables, then the vacuum hose from heater case. Remove heater case from dash, then core from case.

Intermediate Models Less A/C

1978–83 Cutlass
1. Disconnect battery ground cable and drain cooling system.
2. Disconnect heater hoses.
3. Disconnect electrical connectors from heater module.
4. Remove module front cover screws.
5. Remove heater core from module.
6. Reverse procedure to install.

1977 Cutlass
1. Disconnect battery ground cable and drain radiator.
2. Disconnect heater hoses and plug hoses and core openings to prevent coolant loss.
3. Remove heater case attaching nuts and screws, disconnect control cables and remove case from dash, then core from case, Fig. 25.

Fig. 27 Blower motor access hole location. 1977–78 Toronado

Fig. 28 Removing blower motor. 1977–78 Toronado

Fig. 29 Sealing blower motor access hole. 1977–78 Toronado

1977-79 Omega
1. Disconnect battery ground cable and drain radiator.
2. Disconnect heater hoses and plug hoses and core openings to prevent coolant loss.
3. Remove heater case retaining nuts from engine side of dash, Fig. 26.
4. Remove glove box and door, then pull heater case from dash.
5. Disconnect blower resistor electrical connector and control cables from case, then remove heater case from dash and core from case.

Intermediate Models With A/C

1978-83 Cutlass
1. Disconnect battery ground cable and drain cooling system.
2. Disconnect heater hoses from core.
3. Remove retention bracket and ground strap.
4. Remove module rubber seal and screen.
5. Remove right hand W/S wiper arm.
6. Remove attaching screws from the diagnostic connector, hi-blower relay and thermostatic switch.
7. Disconnect all electrical connectors from top of module.
8. Remove top cover from module.
9. Remove heater core from module.
10. Reverse procedure to install.

1977 Cutlass
1. Disconnect battery ground cable and drain radiator.
2. Remove glove box and the center A/C manifold.
3. Disconnect vacuum hoses and temperature cable from heater case.
4. Disconnect heater hoses and plug hoses and core openings to prevent coolant loss.
5. Remove heater case to dash panel attaching bolts, then heater case from dash and core from case, Fig. 25.

1977-79 Omega
1. Disconnect battery and drain coolant.
2. Disconnect upper heater hose from core.
3. Remove right front fender skirt bolts and lower skirt to gain access to lower heater hose clamp. Disconnect lower hose and remove lower right hand heater core and case attaching nut.
4. Remove glove box and door.
5. Remove recirculation vacuum diaphragm at right kick panel.
6. Remove heater outlet (at bottom of heater case).
7. Remove cold air distributor duct from heater case.
8. Remove heater case extension screws and separate extension from case.
9. Disconnect cables and wiring and remove case and core assembly, Fig. 26.
10. Separate core from case.

BLOWER MOTOR, REPLACE

1979-83 Toronado

1. Disconnect battery ground cable.
2. Disconnect hi blower relay electrical connectors, then remove relay.
3. Remove screws securing blower motor, then remove blower motor.
4. Reverse procedure to install. Apply continuous bead of suitable sealer to blower motor mounting.

Fig. 30   Blower motor. 1977 Cutlass

1977-83 88 & 98

1. Disconnect battery ground cable.
2. Disconnect blower motor ground and feed wires.
3. Remove six blower motor attaching screws and blower motor, Figs. 23 and 24.

1977-78 Toronado

1. Disconnect battery ground cable.
2. Raise vehicle and remove right front wheel.
3. Referring to Fig. 27, cut along inside of bead.
4. Fold flap over to expose blower motor, Fig. 28.

5. Remove blower motor attaching screws and the blower motor through opening.

NOTE: After blower motor installation, the access hole must be sealed as follows:

a. Drill a hole in flap and install a 5/16 inch self tapping bolt with a large flat washer, Fig. 29.
b. Close flap and drill two holes in inner filler panel and install two 5/16 inch self tapping bolts with large flat washers, Fig. 29.
c. With a suitable sealer, seal edge of flap. Do not use weatherstrip adhesive.

Fig. 31   Blower motor. 1977-79 Omega (Typical)

1977-83 Intermediate Models

1978-83 Cutlass
1. Disconnect battery ground cable.
2. If equipped with air conditioning, disconnect cooling tube from blower motor.
3. On all models, disconnect electrical connector from blower motor.
4. Remove blower motor retaining screws and the blower motor.
5. Reverse procedure to install.

1977 Cutlass, Less A/C
1. Remove the right front fender filler panel.
2. Disconnect the blower motor wiring.
3. Remove the five nuts and two screws securing the inlet assembly to dash.
4. Disengage the inlet assembly from the studs and remove from the car. The blower motor can be removed from the inlet assembly by removing the attaching screws, Fig. 30. The fan is held to the motor shaft by a nut and lock-washer.

1977-79 Omega, Less A/C
1. Disconnect battery and detach hoses from clips on right fender skirt.
2. Raise vehicle on hoist.
3. Remove fender skirt attaching bolts except those retaining the skirt to radiator support.
4. Pull out then down on skirt and place block of wood between skirt and fender to allow clearance for blower motor removal.
5. Disconnect blower motor cooling tube and electrical connections at blower motor.
6. Remove blower motor attaching screws and remove blower motor, Fig. 31. Gently pry motor flange if sealer acts as an adhesive.

1977 Cutlass, with A/C
1. Disconnect battery ground cable and blower motor feed wire.
2. Remove screws securing blower motor to dash, then the blower motor, Fig. 30.
3. Reverse procedure to install.

1977-79 Omega, with A/C
1. Disconnect the battery cable.
2. Remove the fender filler plate attaching bolts and position it forward and inboard.
3. Disconnect the blower feed wire.
4. Remove the blower motor attaching screws and blower motor.

Fig. 32 Centering spring adjustment Except Omega, 1977-83 88 & 98, 1978-83 Cutlass & 1979-83 Toronado

CRUISE CONTROL, ADJUST

System Release Switches, Adjust

Insert switches into tubular clip until the switch seats on clip. Then, pull brake pedal rearward against stop. The switches will be moved in the clip, thereby providing the proper adjustment.

Servo Linkage, Adjust

UNITS WITH SERVO ROD
Except 1978-80 V8-305
With curb idle speed properly adjusted and the carburetor in curb idle position with the engine off, install servo rod retainer in hole that provides clearance between retainer and servo bushing. Some clearance is required, however, do not exceed the width of one hole.

1978-80 V8-305
Screw rod into link with ignition "Off" and fast idle cam off and throttle closed. Hook rod through tab on servo. Adjust length so link assembles over end of stud, then install retainer.

UNITS WITH BEAD CHAIN
Assemble chain to be taut with carburetor in hot idle position and the idle solenoid deenergized. Place chain into swivel cavities which permits chain to have slight slack. Place retainer over swivel and chain assembly. Retainer must be made to rest between balls. Cut off chain flush with side of swivel to

remove excess length. Chain slack should not exceed one half diameter of ball stud, .150 inch, when measured at hot idle position.

UNITS WITH CABLE
Except 1979 V8-301
With throttle closed, ignition and fast idle cam off, adjust cable jam nuts until free play is removed from cable sleeve at carburetor without holding throttle open. Torque jam nuts to 50 in. lbs. Ensure servo boot is over cable washer.

1979 V8-301
1. Set carburetor choke to hot idle position.
2. With cable connected to vacuum servo, pull steel tube of servo as far as it will go and check if one of the cross holes in the steel tube aligns with carburetor lever pin.
3. If one of the cross holes in the steel tube aligns with carburetor lever pin, install the tube, washer and cotter pin.
4. If none of the cross holes in the steel aligns with carburetor lever pin, move tube rearward to align the next closest hole and install cable, washer and cotter pin.

CAUTION: Do not stretch cable to make adjustment, as this will prevent carburetor from returning to normal idle.

Centering Spring, Adjust

Except Omega, 1977-83 88 & 98, 1978-83 Cutlass & 1979-83 Toronado
1. If speed control system holds speed three or more mph higher than selected speed, turn centering spring adjusting screw (C) toward (S) 1/32" or less, Fig. 32.
2. If speed control system holds speed three or more mph below selected speed, turn centering spring adjusting screw (C) toward (F) 1/32" or less. *Do not move adjustment screw (R).*

Engagement-Cruising Speed Zeroing

1977-79 Omega, 1977-83 88 & 98, 1978-83 Cutlass & 1979-83 Toronado
If the cruising speed is lower than the engagement speed, loosen the orifice tube locknut and turn the tube outward; if higher turn the tube inward. Each 1/4 turn will alter the engagement-cruising speed difference one mph. Tighten locknut after adjustment and check the system operation.

Gasoline Engine Section

See Chevrolet Chapter for Service Procedures on V8-305 & 1977–79 V8-350 with distributor at rear of engine, clockwise distributor rotor rotation. See Buick Chapter for Service Procedures on V6-231, V6-252 Engine. See Pontiac Chapter for Service Procedures on 1979 V8-301.

ENGINE MOUNTS

1979–83 Toronado

1. Raise and support vehicle.
2. Remove front splash shield.
3. Remove two screws from engine mount bracket to engine mount on each side, Fig. 1.
4. Place a suitable lifting device under the harmonic balancer and raise engine only enough to remove each mount.
5. Reverse procedure to install.

1977–83 V8 Exc. Toronado

Removal or replacement of a motor mount can be accomplished by supporting the weight of the engine at the area of the mount to be replaced, Figs. 2 thru 4.

1977–78 Toronado

Refer to Fig. 5 to replace engine mounts.

ENGINE, REPLACE

1977–83 V8 Exc. Toronado

1. Mark hood hinge before removing to aid in proper alignment upon reassembly.
2. Drain radiator and disconnect battery.
3. Disconnect radiator hoses, heater hoses, vacuum hoses, power steering pump hoses (if necessary), starter cable at junction block, engine-to-body ground strap, fuel hose from fuel line, wiring and accelerator linkage.
4. Remove fan blade and pulley, coil and upper radiator support.
5. Raise car.
6. Disconnect exhaust pipes at manifolds.
7. Remove torque converter cover and the three bolts securing converter to flywheel.
8. Remove engine mount bolts, then three transmission to engine bolts on right side.
9. Remove starter with wiring attached and position aside.
10. Lower vehicle and support engine with suitable lifting equipment.
11. Support transmission with a suitable jack and remove three left hand transmission to engine bolts.
12. Remove engine from vehicle.

1979–83 Toronado

1. Disconnect battery ground cable and drain cooling system.
2. Remove radiator upper support.
3. Remove air cleaner assembly.

4. Scribe hood hinge locations and remove hood.
5. Disconnect engine ground strap.
6. Disconnect upper and lower radiator hoses from engine.
7. Disconnect transmission oil cooler lines from radiator.
8. Disconnect heater hoses from water pump and water control valve.
9. Remove radiator, fan and the shroud.
10. Disconnect power steering pump bracket from engine and position aside without disconnecting lines.
11. Disconnect A/C compressor bracket from engine and position aside without disconnecting lines.
12. Disconnect fuel lines.
13. Disconnect throttle cable, vacuum hoses and electrical connections.
14. Disconnect left hand exhaust pipe from manifold.
15. On left side of engine, remove through bolt and bracket securing final drive to engine.
16. Raise and support vehicle.
17. Remove flywheel shield.
18. Disconnect right hand exhaust pipe from manifold.
19. Disconnect starter motor wiring and remove starter motor.
20. Remove converter to flywheel bolts. Mark location of converter on flywheel for alignment during installation.
21. Remove splash shield.
22. Remove engine front mounting attaching nuts.
23. Remove two bolts securing right hand

output shaft support brackets. Using a sharp tool, scribe a mark around the washers as far as possible. Use these scribe marks to position bracket upon installation.
24. Remove lower right hand transmission to engine attaching bolts. One bolt retains the modulator line clip.
25. Use a suitable length of chain to retain final drive in vehicle.
26. Lower vehicle and attach suitable engine lifting equipment to engine.
27. Remove the remaining transmission to engine bolts. It may be necessary to raise or lower transmission with a suitable jack to facilitate bolt removal.
28. Raise engine and remove from vehicle.
29. Reverse procedure to install.

1977–78 Toronado

1. Drain radiator and remove hood, marking hinge as a guide for reassembly.
2. If equipped with venturi shroud, unhook strap, remove seal to venturi ring clips and move towards radiator.
3. Remove air cleaner and hot air pipe.
4. Disconnect engine ground strap, upper and lower radiator hoses, transmission oil cooler lines and heater hoses.
5. Remove upper radiator baffle, radiator, fan shroud and venturi components, if equipped.
6. Disconnect power steering pump bracket from engine without disconnecting oil lines. Position pump and bracket assembly aside.

Fig. 1 Front engine mounts. 1979–83 Toronado

Fig. 2 Engine mounts. 1978–83 Cutlass

7. Disconnect A/C compressor bracket from engine without disconnecting refrigerant lines. Position compressor and bracket assembly aside.
8. Disconnect fuel lines at fuel pump, throttle cable, vacuum hoses and electrical connections.
9. Disconnect exhaust pipes from manifolds.
10. Raise vehicle.
11. Loosen upper left hand flywheel cover bolt.
12. Remove starter, then the remaining fly-

wheel cover bolts and pivot cover from upper left hand bolt slot.
13. Mark relationship between converter and flywheel, then remove converter to flywheel bolts.
14. Remove engine front mounting attaching nuts.
15. Remove right hand output shaft support bracket bolts. Mark position of bracket to assist assembly.
16. From vehicle left side, remove final drive to engine through bolt and bracket.
17. Remove lower right hand transmission to

engine attaching bolts.
18. Attach final drive support chain, Fig. 6, and lower vehicle.
19. Install suitable engine lifting equipment and remove remaining engine to transmission bolts.

NOTE: It may be necessary to raise or lower the transmission using a suitable jack with a wood block placed between the jack and transmission.

20. Remove engine from vehicle.
21. Reverse procedure to install.

CYLINDER HEAD, REPLACE

Head gaskets used on these engines are of a special composition material that is not to be used with a sealer.

Prior to installation, clean the head bolts and dip in engine oil. Tighten head bolts in steps and in the sequence shown in Fig. 7. Final torquing should be to the specifications listed in "Engine Tightening Specifications".

V8-260, 307, 350, 403

1. Disconnect battery ground cable.
2. Drain radiator and cylinder block.
3. Remove intake and exhaust manifolds.
4. Remove ground strap from left cylinder head.
5. Remove rocker arm bolts, pivots, rocker arms and push rods. Keep rocker arms, pivots and push rods in order so they can be installed in the same position.
6. Remove cylinder head attaching bolts and remove cylinder head.
7. Reverse procedure to install. Torque cylinder head bolts in sequence shown in Fig. 7 and torque intake manifold bolts in sequence shown in Fig. 8.

VALVE ARRANGEMENT

Front to Rear

V6-231① .... E-I-I-E-I-E
V6-252① .... E-I-I-E-I-E
V8-260, 307, 350③, 403 .... I-E-I-E-E-I-E-I
V8-301④ .... E-I-I-E-E-I-I-E
V8-305, 350② .... E-I-I-E-E-I-I-E

①—Refer to Buick chapter for service procedures.
②—Refer to Chevrolet chapter for service procedures.
③—Oldsmobile engine.
④—Refer to Pontiac chapter for service procedures.

VALVE LIFT SPECS.

Engine	Year	Intake	Exhaust
V6-231②	1977–78	.383	.366
V6-231②	1979–83	.357	.366
V6-252②	1981–83	.357	.366
V8-260	1977–82	.395	.400
V8-301③	1979	.357	.376
V8-305①	1977–79	.3727	.4100
V8-305①	1980	.357	.390
V8-307	1981–83	.400	.400
V8-350	1977–80	.400	.400
V8-350①	1977–80	.390	.410
V8-403	1977–79	.400	.400

①—Refer to Chevrolet chapter for service procedures.
②—Refer to Buick chapter for service procedures.
③—Refer to Pontiac chapter for service procedures.

Fig. 3 Engine mounts. 1978–83 88 & 98

VALVE TIMING

Intake Opens Before TDC

Engine	Year	Degrees
V6-231②	1977-78	17
V6-231②	1979-83	16
V6-252②	1981-83	16
V8-260	1977-82	14
V8-301③	1979	16
V8-305①	1977-80	28
V8-307	1980-83	20
V8-350	1977-80	16
V8-350①	1977-79	28
V8-403	1977-79	16

①—Refer to Chevrolet chapter for service procedures.
②—Refer to Buick chapter for service procedures.
③—Refer to Pontiac chapter for service procedures.

ROCKER ARMS

NOTE: V8 engines use valve rotators, Fig. 9. The rotator operates on a sprag clutch principle utilizing the collapsing action of a coil spring to give rotation to the rotor body which turns the valve.

V8-260, 307, 350, 403

1. Remove valve cover.
2. Remove flanged bolts, rocker arm pivot and rocker arms, Fig. 9.
3. When installing rocker arm assemblies, lubricate wear surfaces with suitable lubricant. Torque flanged bolts to 25 ft. lbs.

VALVE ROTATORS

The rotator operates on a Sprag clutch principle utilizing the collapsing action of coil spring to give rotation to the rotor body which turns the valve, Fig. 9.

To check rotator action, draw a line across rotator body and down the collar. Operate engine at 1500 rpm, rotator body should move around collar. Rotator action can be in either direction. Replace rotator if no movement is noted.

When servicing valves, valve stem tips should be checked for improper wear pattern which could indicate a defective valve rotator, Fig. 10.

VALVES

Whenever a new valve is installed or after grinding valves, it will be necessary to measure valve stem height using the Special Tool shown in Figs. 11 and 12.

On V8-260, 307, 350 and 403 engines, there should be a minimum clearance of .015 inch between gauge surface and the valve stem, Fig. 11.

Check valve rotator height, Fig. 12. If valve stem tip extends less than .005 inch above rotator, replace the valve.

Lacking this tool the only alternative is to lay flat feeler gauges on the retainer and check the distance between the retainer and valve stem tip.

Fig. 4   Engine mounts. 1977 Omega (Typical)

Fig. 5   Front engine mount. 1977-78 Toronado

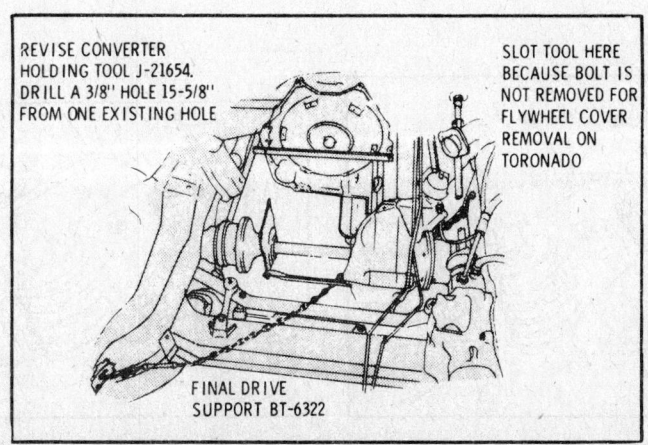

Fig. 6   Final drive supporting tool

Fig. 7 Cylinder head tightening sequence. V8-260, 307, 350, 403

Fig. 8 Intake manifold tightening sequence. V8-260, 307, 350, 403

Fig. 9 Cylinder head exploded. 1977–83 V8

VALVE GUIDES

V8-260, 307, 350, 403

Valve stem guides are not replaceable, due to being cast in place. If valve guide bores are worn excessively, they can be reamed oversize.

If a standard valve guide bore is being reamed, use a .003″ or .005″ oversize reamer. For the .010″ oversize valve guide bore, use a .013″ oversize reamer. If too large a reamer is used and the spiraling is removed, it is possible that the valve will not receive the proper lubrication.

NOTE: Occasionally a valve guide will be oversize as manufactured. These are marked on the cylinder head as shown in Fig. 13. If no markings are present, the guide bores are standard. If oversize markings are present, any valve replacement will require an oversize valve. Service valves are available in standard diameters as well as .003″, .005″, .010″ and .013″ oversize.

Fig. 10 Checking valve stems for rotator malfunction

Fig. 11 Measuring valve stem height. V8-260, 307, 350, 403

Fig. 12 Measuring valve retainer or valve rotator height. V8-260, 307, 350, 403

Fig. 13 Valve guide bore marking. V8-260, 307, 350, 403

VALVE LIFTERS

Valve lifters are available in standard size and an oversize of .010 inch. An "O" is etched on the side of the .010 inch oversize lifter for identification. Also, the cylinder block near the valve lifter bore is marked with an "O". Ensure valve lifters are re-installed in original bores.

Plungers are not interchangeable because they are selectively fitted to the bodies at the factory.

If plunger and body appear satisfactory blow off with air to remove all particles of dirt. Install the plunger in the body without other parts and check for free movement. A simple text is to be sure that the plunger will drop of its own weight in the body, Fig. 14.

Fig. 14 Hydraulic valve lifter (typical)

TIMING CASE COVER, REPLACE

NOTE: When it becomes necessary to replace the cover oil seal, the cover need not be removed.

1977–82 V8-260, 1980–83 307, 1977–80 350 & 1977–79 403

1. Disconnect battery ground cable.
2. Drain cooling system and disconnect radiator hoses and bypass hose.
3. Remove all drive belts, fan and pulley, crankshaft pulley and harmonic balancer, and accessory brackets.
4. Remove timing indicator and water pump.
5. Remove remaining front cover attaching bolts and the front cover. Also, remove the dowel pins. It may be necessary to grind a flat on the dowel pin to provide a rough surface for gripping.
6. Grind a chamfer on one end of each dowel pin.
7. Cut excess material from front end of oil pan gasket on each side of cylinder block.

8. Trim approximately 1/8 inch from each end of new front pan seal.
9. Install new front cover gasket and apply suitable sealer to gasket around coolant holes.
10. Apply RTV sealer to mating surfaces of cylinder block, oil pan and front cover.
11. Place front cover on cylinder block and press downward to compress seal. Rotate cover right and left and guide oil pan seal into cavity with a small screwdriver.
12. Apply engine oil to bolts.
13. Install two bolts finger tight to retain cover.
14. Install the two dowel pins, chamfered end first.
15. Install timing indicator and water pump and torque bolts as shown in Figs. 15 and 16.
16. Install harmonic balancer and crankshaft pulley.
17. Install accessory brackets.
18. Install fan and pulley and drive belts.
19. Connect radiator hoses and bypass hose.
20. Connect battery ground cable.

TIMING CHAIN, REPLACE

V8-260, 307, 350, 403

1. After removing front cover, remove fuel pump eccentric, oil slinger, crankshaft sprocket, chain and camshaft sprocket.
2. Install camshaft sprocket, crankshaft sprocket and timing chain together, aligning timing marks as shown in Fig. 17.
3. Install fuel pump eccentric with flat side rearward, Fig. 18. Then install oil slinger and replace front cover.

CAMSHAFT, REPLACE

V8-260, 307, 350, 403

1. Disconnect battery ground cable and drain radiator.
2. Remove upper radiator baffle and disconnect upper radiator hose from water outlet.
3. Disconnect transmission oil cooler lines at radiator.
4. Remove radiator fan shroud, then the radiator.
5. Disconnect fuel lines from fuel pump.
6. Remove air cleaner and disconnect throttle cable.

7. Remove all drive belts and position alternator, power steering pump and air conditioning compressor aside.
8. Disconnect by-pass hose from water pump and all electrical and vacuum connections from engine.
9. Remove distributor.
10. Raise vehicle and drain oil pan.
11. Remove exhaust cross-over pipe and the starter.
12. Disconnect exhaust pipe from manifold.
13. Install engine support bar.
14. Remove engine mount to bracket bolts, raise engine and remove engine mounts.
15. Remove flywheel cover and engine oil pan.
16. Place wood blocks between exhaust manifolds and cross-member to support engine, then remove engine support bar.
17. Remove crankshaft pulley and balancer, then the engine front cover.
18. Lower vehicle and remove valve covers, intake manifold, rocker arms, push rods and valve lifters.

NOTE: Note position of the valve train components to ensure installation in original location.

Fig. 15 Engine front cover bolts. 1977–78 V8-260, 350, 403

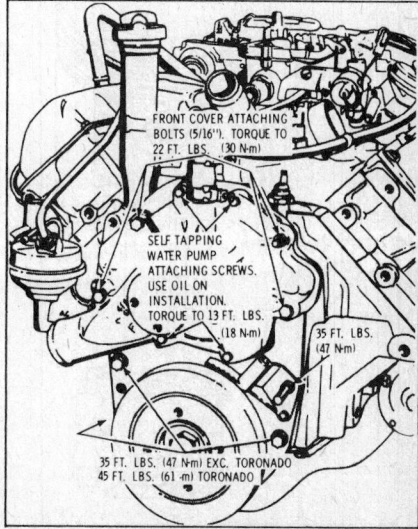

Fig. 16 Engine front cover bolts. 1979–83 V8-260, 307, 350 & 403

**Fig. 17 Timing chain position.
V8-260, 307, 350, 403**

**Fig. 18 Fuel pump eccentric.
V8-260, 307, 350, 403, 455**

**Fig. 19 Assembly of piston to rod.
1977–79 V8-260, 307 & 350**

19. If equipped with A/C, discharge refrigerant and remove condenser.
20. Remove fuel pump eccentric, camshaft sprocket, oil slinger and timing chain.
21. Slide camshaft from front of engine.
22. Reverse procedure to install.

NOTE: *To insure proper camshaft installation, and to provide initial lubrication, it is extremely important that the camshaft be coated with GM Concentrate (Part No. 1051396).*

PISTON & ROD, ASSEMBLE

Lubricate the piston pin hole and piston pin to facilitate installation of pin, then position the connecting rod with its respective piston as shown in Figs. 19, 19A and 20. Measure connecting rod side clearance using a suitable feeler gauge, clearance should be .006–.020 inch.

**NOTCH TOWARD
FRONT OF ENGINE**

**Fig. 19A Assembly of piston to rod.
T980–83 V8-260, 307 & 350**

PISTONS, RINGS & PINS

NOTE: On 1979–83 V8-260, 350 and 403, different types of piston compression rings are used, refer to Fig. 21 for piston ring identification. On V8-260 engines, piston ring end gap should be .009–.019 in. for Sealed Power piston rings and .010–.020 in. for Perfect Circle and Muskegon piston rings. On V8-307 engines, piston ring end gap should be .009–.019 in. for Sealed Power piston rings and .010–.020 in. for TRW piston rings. On V8-350 engines, piston ring end gap should be .010–.020 in. for Sealed Power piston rings and .013–.023 in. for Perfect Circle and Muskegon piston rings. On V8-403 engine, piston ring end gap should be .009–.019 in. for Sealed Power piston rings and .010–.020 in. for Perfect Circle piston rings.

Pistons are available in standard sizes and oversizes of .010 and .030".

Rings are available in standard sizes and oversizes of .010 and .030".

MAIN & ROD BEARINGS

Main bearings are available in standard sizes and undersizes of .0005, .001, .0015, .002, .010 and .020".

Rod bearings are available in standard sizes and undersizes of .001, .002, .005, .010, .012 and .020 inch.

NOTE: Main bearing clearances not within

**Fig. 20 Assembly of piston to rod.
1977–79 V8-403**

	TOP & SECOND
PERFECT CIRCLE	
SEALED POWER	TOP & SECOND
MUSKEGON	TOP & SECOND
TRW	TOP & SECOND

**Fig. 21 Piston compression ring identification.
1979–83 V8-260, 307, 350 & 403**

Amount undersize and part number stamped in the bearing shell

**Fig. 22 Main bearing size location.
V8-260, 307, 350, 403**

Fig. 23   Packing upper rear main bearing oil seal

specifications must be corrected by the use of selective upper and lower shells. Figs. 22 illustrate the undersize identification marking on the bearing tang.

REAR CRANKSHAFT SEAL SERVICE

Since the braided fabric seal used on these engines can be replaced only when the crankshaft is removed, the following repair procedure is recommended.

1. Remove oil pan and bearing cap.
2. Drive end of old seal gently into groove, using a suitable tool, until packed tight. This may vary between 1/4 and 3/4 inch depending on amount of pack required.
3. Repeat previous step for other end of seal.
4. Measure and note amount that seal was driven up on one side. Using the old seal removed from bearing cap, cut a length of seal the amount previously noted plus 1/16 inch.
5. Repeat previous step for other side of seal.
6. Pack cut lengths of seal into appropriate side of seal groove. A packing tool, BT-6433, Fig. 23, may be used since the tool has been machined to provide a built-in stop. Use tool BT-6436 to trim the seal flush with block, Fig. 24.
7. Install new seal in lower bearing cap.

OIL PAN, REPLACE

Exc. Toronado

1. Remove distributor cap and align rotor with No. 1 firing position.
2. Disconnect ground cable, remove dip stick and drain oil pan.
3. Remove upper radiator support and fan shroud attaching screws.
4. Remove flywheel cover and starter.
5. Disconnect exhaust pipes and crossover pipe on single exhaust models.
6. Disconnect engine mounts and raise engine.
7. Remove oil pan bolts and oil pan.
8. Reverse procedure to install. Torque oil pan bolts to 10 ft. lbs.

1980-83 Toronado

1. Disconnect battery ground cable.
2. Raise and support vehicle, then remove three final drive to transmission bolts.
3. Disconnect frame braces, then disconnect idler arm and pitman arm from relay rod.
4. Separate drive axles from output shafts.
5. Remove battery cable bracket from output shaft support.
6. Disconnect output shaft support from engine block.
7. Support transmission with suitable jack, then remove final drive assembly.
8. Remove splash shield and starter motor.
9. Drain engine oil and remove oil pan.
10. Reverse procedure to install.

1979 Toronado

1. Disconnect battery ground cable.
2. Disconnect shroud from upper radiator support.
3. Remove right hand axle cotter pin, retainer and nut.
4. Raise vehicle and remove right wheel.
5. Disconnect right hand tie rod end using tool J-6627 or BT 7101.
6. Disconnect right hand upper ball joint.
7. Remove bolts attaching drive axle to right hand output shaft, then the output shaft.
8. Disconnect starter wiring and remove starter.
9. Remove splash shield.
10. Disconnect pitman arm and idler arm from intermediate rod using tool J-24319-01 or a suitable puller.
11. Drain pan oil.
12. Remove front engine mount to frame nuts.
13. Disconnect shroud from lower radiator support.
14. Using suitable equipment, raise the front of the engine.
15. Remove the right engine mount.
16. Remove oil pan attaching bolts and oil pan.
17. Reverse procedure to install. Torque oil pan attaching bolts to 10 ft. lbs.

1977-78 Toronado

1. Remove engine as outlined previously.
2. Remove dipstick, drain oil and remove mount from front cover.
3. Unfasten and remove oil pan.
4. Apply sealer to both sides of pan gaskets (cork) and install on block.
5. Install front and rear rubber seals.
6. Wipe lube on seal area and install pan. Torque 5/16" bolts to 15 ft-lbs and 1/4" bolts to 10 ft-lbs.
7. Install mount on front cover and install engine.

OIL PUMP REPAIRS

V8-260, 307, 350, 403

1. Remove oil pan and pump baffle. Remove attaching screws and remove pump and drive shaft extension.
2. To service the pump, refer to Fig. 25.
3. To install, insert the drive shaft extension through the opening in the block until the shaft mates into the distributor drive gear. Position pump onto rear main bearing cap and torque the attaching bolts to 35 ft-lbs.
4. Install oil pump baffle and pan.

Fig. 24   Trimming upper rear main bearing oil seal

BELT TENSION DATA

	New Lbs.	Used Lbs.
1981-83		
V6 All		
Air Conditioning	170	90
A.I.R. Pump	80	45
Alternator	145	70
Power Steering	170	90
Vacuum Pump	80	45
V8 All		
Air Conditioning	170	90
A.I.R. Pump	80③	45③
Alternator	160④	80④
Power Steering	170	90
Vacuum Pump	125	55
1979-80		
5/16" Belts	80	50
3/8" Belts①	140	70
3/8" Belts②	140	60
15/32" Belts	165	90
1977-78		
V8 All	110-140	70

①—Except cogged belts
②—Cogged belts
③—3/8" belts; new, 145; used, 70.
④—Cogged belts; new, 145; used, 55.

WATER PUMP, REPLACE

V8-260, 307, 350, 403

1. Drain cooling system and remove heater and lower hoses from pump.
2. Loosen pulley belts and remove fan and pulley. On air conditioned cars, remove clutch fan assembly and pulley.
3. Remove pump from front cover.

FUEL PUMP, REPLACE

1. Disconnect fuel line from fuel pump.
2. Remove fuel pump mounting bolts and the fuel pump.
3. Remove all gasket material from the pump and block gasket surfaces. Apply sealer to both sides of new gasket.
4. Position gasket on pump flange and hold pump in position against its mounting surface. Make sure rocker arm is riding on camshaft eccentric.
5. Press pump tight against its mounting. Install retaining screws and tighten them alternately.
6. Connect fuel lines. Then operate engine and check for leaks.

**Fig. 25 Oil pump disassembled.
V8-260, 307, 350, 403 (Typical)**

Engine lubrication. V8-260, 307, 350, 403 (Typical)

Diesel Engine Section

DIESEL ENGINE SECTION INDEX

DESCRIPTION

Engine Construction

The Oldsmobile four stroke cycle diesel engine is basically the same in construction as the Oldsmobile gasoline engine. The cylinders are numbered 1,3,5,7 on the left bank and 2,4,6,8 on the right bank on 8 cylinder engines or 1, 3 and 5 on the left bank and 2, 4 and 6 on the right bank on 6 cylinder engines. The firing order is 1-8-4-3-6-5-7-2 on 8 cylinder engines or 1-6-5-4-3-2 on 6 cylinder engines. The major differences between the diesel and gasoline versions is in the cylinder heads, combustion chamber, fuel distribution system,

air intake manifold and method of ignition. The cylinder block, crankshaft, main bearings, connecting rods, pistons and pins are of heavy construction due to the high compression ratio required to ignite the diesel fuel. The diesel fuel is ignited when the heat developed in the combustion chamber during the compression stroke reaches a certain temperature.

The valve train operates the same as in the gasoline engine, but are of special design and material for diesel operation. The stainless steel pre-chamber inserts in the cylinder head combustion chambers are serviced separately from the cylinder head. With the cylinder head removed, these pre-chamber inserts can be driven from the cylinder head after remov-

ing the glow plugs or injection nozzles. The glow plugs are threaded into the cylinder head and the injection nozzles are retained by a bolt and clamp. The injection nozzles are spring loaded and calibrated to open at a specified fuel pressure.

Fuel System

The fuel injection pump is mounted on top of the engine and is gear driven by the camshaft and rotates at camshaft speed. This high pressure rotary pump injects a metered amount of fuel to each cylinder at the proper time. Six or eight high pressure fuel delivery pipes from the injection pump to the injection nozzles, Figs. 1 and 1A, are the same length to

Fig. 1   Fuel injection nozzle. 1978–79

Housing Pressure Cold Advance (HPCA)

This feature is used on all 1981–83 engines and advances the injection timing 3° during cold operation. This circuit is actuated by a temperature switch calibrated to open the circuit at 125° F. Below the switching point, housing pressure is decreased from 10 to 0 psi which advances the injection timing 3°. Above the switching point, the switch opens, de-energizing the solenoid and the housing pressure is returned to 10 psi. The fast idle solenoid is energized by the same switch and closes when the temperature falls below 95° F.

Engine Lubrication System

NOTE: On 1978 engines, the recommended diesel engine oil designation is SE/CD. On 1979–80 engines, the recommended diesel

Fig 1A   Fuel injection nozzle. 1980–83

engine oil designation is SE/CC. On 1981 engines, the recommended diesel engine oil is SF/CC, SF/CD or SE/CC. On 1982–83 engines the recommended diesel engine oil is SF/CC or SF/CD.

The diesel engine lubrication system is basically the same as the gasoline engine. The fuel injection pump driven gear is lubricated by oil directed through a passage from the top of the camshaft bearing, Fig. 3. An angled

prevent any difference in timing from cylinder to cylinder. The fuel injection pump provides the required timing advance under all operating conditions. Engine speed is controlled by a rotary fuel metering valve, Figs. 2 and 2A. When the accelerator is depressed, the throttle cable opens the metering valve and allows more fuel to be delivered to the engine. The injection pump also incorporates a low pressure transfer pump to deliver fuel to the fuel line to the high pressure pump, Figs. 2 and 2A.

The fuel filter is located between the mechanical fuel pump and the injection pump on 8 cylinder engines, or between the electric fuel pump and the injection pump on 6 cylinder engines. The diaphragm type mechanical fuel pump used on 8 cylinder engines is mounted on the right hand side of the engine and is driven by a cam on the crankshaft. The electric fuel pump used on 6 cylinder engines is mounted on the engine. The fuel tank at the rear of the vehicle is connected by fuel pipes to the mechanical fuel pump. Excess fuel returns from the fuel injection pump and injection nozzles to the fuel tank through pipes and hoses.

NOTE: Injection nozzles on 1980–83 diesel engines do not use a fuel return line.

"Water in Fuel" System

This system is available on some 1980 and all 1981–83 models. These vehicles have a "Water in Fuel" light mounted in the instrument panel. The "Water in Fuel" light has a bulb check feature and should light for 2 to 2½ seconds when the ignition is turned on. If not, the bulb is burned out or there is an open in the wiring circuit. When there is water in the fuel, the light will come back on and remain on after a 15 to 20 second delay.

A water sensing probe, mounted on the fuel sender, actuates the instrument panel light when it is partially covered with water. About 1 to 2½ gallons of water must be present in the fuel tank to cause the sensor light to activate.

If the "Water in Fuel" lamp goes on while the vehicle is being driven, the fuel system should be checked for water. If the lamp goes on immediately after refueling and before the vehicle is moved, there is a large quantity of water in the tank and should be removed immediately.

The water may be removed from the tank with a pump or by siphoning. The pump or siphon hose should be connected to the quarter inch fuel return hose (the smaller of the two hoses), located under the hood near the fuel pump. Refer to "Purging Water From Fuel Tank" procedure.

Fig. 2   Fuel injection pump circuit, V8 engine

Fig. 2A   Fuel injection pump circuit. V6 engine

1. OIL PICK-UP
2. LIFTER FEED
3. ROCKER ARM VALVE TIP FEED
4. SPLASH LUBE TO TIMING CHAIN FUEL PUMP CAM & DIST. & OIL PUMP DRIVE
5. LEFT MAIN GALLERY FEED
6. CAM BEARING FEED
7. MAIN BEARING FEED
8. ROD BEARING FEED
9. INJECTION PUMP DRIVE BEARING FEED

RIGHT MAIN GALLERY
VACUUM PUMP AND OIL PUMP DRIVE
LEFT MAIN GALLERY
OIL PUMP

Fig. 3 Engine lubricating system. Typical (V6 engine similar)

passage in the shaft portion of the driven gear directs the oil to the rear driven gear bearing. At the front of the right oil gallery, a small orifice sprays oil to lubricate the fuel pump eccentric cam on the crankshaft and timing chain.

Engine Cooling System

The diesel engine cooling system is the same as the gasoline engine except the radiator incorporates two oil coolers. One cooler is used to cool the transmission fluid and the other cooler is used to cool the engine oil.

Engine Electrical System

Eight glow plugs are used to pre-heat the pre-chamber to aid in starting. The type 1 glow plugs are 12 volt heaters and are activated when the ignition switch is turned to the "Run" position. The type 1 system, Figs. 4 and 5, uses steady current applied to 12 volt glow plugs. The type 2 glow plug system, Figs. 16, 17, 18 and 24, uses 6 volt glow plugs with a controlled pulsating current applied to them for starting. The type 2 glow plug system uses an electromechanical controller to control glow plug temperature, preglow time, wait/start lights and after glow time. The 1980 Cutlass Electronic Glow Plug Control System, Fig. 26, uses an electronic module and a control sensor to control glow plug temperature, the glow plug relay and the wait light. On this system a coolant temperature switch controls the fast idle solenoid through a fast idle relay. The 6 volt and 12 volt glow plugs are not interchangeable and can be identified by the wire connector spade. The 6 volt glow plugs have a 5/16 in. wire connector spade, while the 12 volt glow plugs have a 1/4 in. wire connector spade. The glow plugs remain activated for a short time after starting then are automatically turned "Off". Two 12 volt batteries are connected in parallel are required for the higher electical load due to the glow plugs and starter motor. The diesel starter motor is larger than the gasoline engine starter and is designed to crank the engine at least the 100 RPM required for starting. An alternator supplies charging current to both batteries at the same time and there are no switches or relays in the charging circuit.

DIESEL ENGINE ELECTRICAL DIAGNOSIS

Refer to Figs. 4 through 27F for diesel engine electrical diagnosis.

WATER IN FUEL SYSTEM DIAGNOSIS

Water in Fuel Lamp Does Not Go On

If the likelihood of water in the fuel tank exists and the Water In Fuel lamp is off, siphon the fuel tank to check for water by connecting a pump to the fuel return line. If at least 3 gallons of water are siphoned from the tank, proceed as follows:

1. Disconnect Water In Fuel electrical lead at fuel tank and ground the lead. If lamp does not go on, proceed to step 4. If it does, check for at least 8 volts at the electrical lead. If no voltage is present, replace the Water In Tank light bulb.
2. Ground the Water In Tank electrical lead. If lamp does not go on, check for open circuit in wiring, Fig. 27G.
3. Remove fuel level sender and Water in Fuel detector unit from fuel tank.
4. Check connections to "Water In Fuel". If satisfactory, check detector unit as follows:
   a. Remove detector from fuel sender unit, Fig. 27H.
   b. Connect the detector to a bulb and power source as shown in Fig. 27I. The lamp should go on when the detector probe is lowered into the container of water 3/8 inch or less. Make sure water is grounded to negative side of battery.

Water In Fuel Lamp Stays On

Under this condition, siphon the tank to check for water by connecting a pump to the fuel return line. If no water is present, proceed as follows:

1. Disconnect the Water In Fuel electrical lead near the fuel tank. If lamp does not go off, proceed to step 2. If lamp goes off, remove fuel level sender and check detec-

tor as described previously under "Water In Fuel Lamp Does Not Go On".
2. Check for short circuit in wire between the "Water In Fuel" connection at the fuel tank and the dash indicator lamp, Fig. 27G.

ENGINE MOUNTS

Refer to Figs. 28, 28A, 28B, 28C and 28D for engine mount installation.

ENGINE, REPLACE

Exc. Toronado

1. Disconnect ground cable from batteries and drain cooling system.
2. Remove air cleaner.
3. Scribe hood hinge locations and remove hood.
4. Disconnect ground wires at inner fender and the engine ground strap at right cylinder head.
5. Disconnect radiator hoses, oil cooler lines, heater hoses, vacuum hoses, power steering hoses from gear, A/C compressor with brackets and hoses attached, fuel pump hose from fuel pump and the wiring.
6. Remove hairpin clip from bellcrank, on all except 6 cylinder engine.
7. Remove throttle and throttle valve cables from intake manifold brackets and position cables aside.
8. Remove upper radiator support and the radiator on all except 6 cylinder engine.
9. Raise and support vehicle.
10. Disconnect exhaust pipes from exhaust manifold.
11. Remove torque converter cover and the three bolts securing torque converter to flywheel.
12. Remove engine mount bolts or nuts.
13. Remove three engine to transmission bolts on the right side.
14. Disconnect starter wiring and remove starter.
15. Lower vehicle.
16. Attach suitable engine lifting equipment to engine. Support transmission with a suitable jack.
17. Remove the three engine to transmission bolts on the left side.
18. Remove engine from vehicle.
19. Reverse procedure to install.

1979-83 Toronado

1. Disconnect battery ground cable and drain cooling system.
2. Remove radiator upper support.
3. Remove air cleaner assembly.
4. Scribe hood hinge locations and remove hood.
5. Disconnect engine ground strap.
6. Disconnect upper and lower radiator hoses from engine.
7. Disconnect transmission oil cooler lines from radiator.
8. Disconnect heater hoses from water pump and water control valve.
9. Remove radiator, fan and the shroud.
10. Disconnect power steering pump bracket from engine and position aside without disconnecting lines.
11. Disconnect A/C compressor bracket from engine and position aside without disconnecting lines.
12. Disconnect fuel lines.
13. Disconnect throttle cable, vacuum hoses and electrical connections.

DIESEL ENGINE DIAGNOSIS

Condition	Possible Cause	Correction
ENGINE WILL NOT CRANK	1. Loose or corroded battery cables	1. Check connections at battery, engine block and starter solenoid.
	2. Discharged batteries	2. Check charging system.
	3. Starter Inoperative	3. Check starting system.
ENGINE CRANKS SLOWLY— WILL NOT START (Minimum Engine Crank Speed— 100 RPM)	1. Battery cable connections loose or corroded	1. Check connections at battery, engine block and starter.
	2. Batteries undercharged	2. Check charging system.
	3. Wrong engine oil	3. Drain and refill with recommended oil.
ENGINE CRANKS NORMALLY— WILL NOT START	1. Incorrect starting procedure	1. Use recommended starting procedure.
	2. Incorrect or contaminated fuel	2. Flush fuel system and install correct fuel.
	3. No fuel to nozzles	3. Loosen injection line at a nozzle. Do not disconnect. Use care to direct fuel away from sources of ignition. Wipe connection to be sure it is dry. Crank 5 seconds. Fuel should flow from injection line. Tighten connection. If fuel does not flow, check fuel solenoid operation as follows: Connect a 12 volt test lamp from wire at injection pump solenoid to ground. Turn ignition to "ON". Lamp should light. If lamp does not light, check wiring to solenoid.
	4. No fuel to injection pump	4. Remove line at inlet to injection pump fuel filter. Connect hose from line to metal container. Crank engine. If no fuel is discharged, test the fuel supply pump. If the pump is OK, check the injection pump fuel filter and replace if plugged. If filter and inlet line to injection pump are OK, replace injection pump.
	5. Plugged fuel return system	5. Disconnect fuel return line at injection pump and route hose to a metal container. Connect a hose to the injection pump connection and route it to the metal container. Crank the engine; if engine starts and runs, correct restriction in fuel return system.
	6. Pump timing incorrect	6. Make certain that pump timing mark is aligned with mark on adapter.
	7. Glow plug control system inoperative	7. Refer to Diesel Engine Electrical System Diagnosis.
	8. Glow plugs inoperative	8. Refer to Diesel Engine Electrical System Diagnosis.
	9. Internal engine problems	9. Correct as necessary.
	10. No voltage to fuel solenoid	10. Connect a 12 volt test lamp from injection pump solenoid to ground. Turn ignition to "On", lamp should light. If lamp lights, remove test lamp and connect and disconnect solenoid connector and listen for solenoid operation. If solenoid does not operate, remove injection pump for repairs. If lamp does not light, refer to Diesel Engine Electrical System Diagnosis.
	11. Restricted fuel tank filter.	11. Remove fuel tank and check filter.
ENGINE STARTS BUT WILL NOT CONTINUE TO RUN AT IDLE	1. No fuel in tank	1. Install correct fuel in tank.
	2. Incorrect or contaminated fuel	2. Flush fuel system and install correct fuel.
	3. Limited fuel to injection pump	3. Test the fuel supply pump. Replace as necessary.
	4. Fuel solenoid disengaged with ignition switch in the "ON" position	4. Connect a 12 volt test lamp from wire at injection pump solenoid to ground. Turn ignition to "ON". Lamp should light. Turn ignition to "START". Lamp should light. If lamp does not light in both positions, check wiring to solenoid.
	5. Restricted fuel return system	5. Disconnect fuel return line at injection pump and route hose to a metal container. Connect a hose to injection pump connection and route to metal container. Crank engine; if engine starts and runs, correct restriction in fuel return system.

Condition	Possible Cause	Correction
ENGINE STARTS BUT WILL NOT CONTINUE TO RUN AT IDLE (Cont'd)	6. Fast idle solenoid inoperative	6. With engine cold, start car; solenoid should move to support injection pump lever in "fast idle position" for about 5 seconds. If solenoid does not move, refer to Electrical System Diagnosis.
	7. Low idle incorrectly adjusted	7. Adjust idle screw to specification.
	8. Pump timing incorrect	8. Make certain that timing mark, on injection pump, is aligned with mark on adapter.
	9. Glow plug control system malfunction	9. Refer to Diesel Engine Electrical System Diagnosis.
	10. Injection pump malfunction	10. Install replacement pump.
	11. Internal engine problems	11. Correct as necessary.
ENGINE STARTS, IDLES ROUGH, WITHOUT ABNORMAL NOISE OR SMOKE	1. Low idle incorrectly adjusted	1. Adjust idle screw to specification.
	2. Injection line leaks	2. Wipe off injection lines and connections. Run engine and check for leaks. Correct leaks.
	3. Restricted fuel return system	3. Disconnect fuel return line at injection pump and route hose to a metal container. Connect a hose to the injection pump connection and route it to the metal container. Crank the engine; if engine starts and runs, correct restriction in fuel return system.
	4. Incorrect or contaminated fuel	4. Flush fuel system and install correct fuel.
	5. Nozzle(s) inoperative	5. With engine running, loosen injection line fitting at each nozzle in turn. Use care to direct fuel away from sources of ignition. Each nozzle should contribute to rough running. If nozzle is found that does not change idle quality, it should be replaced.
	6. Internal fuel leak at nozzle(s)	6. Disconnect fuel return system from nozzles on one bank at a time. With the engine running, observe the normal fuel seepage at the nozzles. Replace any nozzle with excessive fuel leakage.
	7. Fuel supply pump malfunctions	7. Test the fuel supply pump. Replace if necessary.
	8. Uneven fuel distribution to cylinders	8. Install new or reconditioned nozzles, one at a time, until condition is corrected as indicated by normal idle.
ENGINE STARTS AND IDLES ROUGH WITH EXCESSIVE NOISE AND/OR SMOKE	1. Injection pump timing incorrect	1. Be sure timing mark on injection pump is aligned with mark on adapter.
	2. Nozzle(s) inoperative	2. With engine running, crack injection line at each nozzle, one at a time. Use care to direct fuel away from sources of ignition. Each nozzle should contribute to rough running. If a nozzle is found that does not affect idle quality or changes noise and/or smoke, it should be replaced.
	3. High pressure lines incorrectly installed	3. Check routing of each line. Correct as required.
ENGINE COLD, STARTS AND IDLES ROUGH WITH EXCESSIVE NOISE AND/OR SMOKE, BUT CLEARS UP AFTER WARM-UP	1. Incorrect starting procedure	1. Advise operator on correct procedure. (See owners manual.)
	2. Injection pump timing incorrect	2. Check timing with J-33075 timing meter and reset if needed.
	3. Insufficient engine break-in time	3. Break in engine 2000 miles or more.
	4. Air in system	4. Install a section of clear plastic tubing on the fuel return fitting from the engine. Evidence of bubbles in fuel when cranking or running indicates the presence of an air leak in the suction fuel line.
	5. Inoperative glow plug	5. Replace faulty glow plug.
	6. Nozzle(s) malfunction	6. Remove and clean or replace.
	7. Housing pressure cold advance inoperative	7. Check operation and repair.
ENGINE MISFIRES BUT IDLES CORRECTLY	1. Plugged fuel filter	1. Replace filter.
	2. Incorrect injection pump timing	2. Be sure that timing mark on injection pump and adapter are aligned.
	3. Incorrect or contaminated fuel	3. Flush fuel system and install correct fuel.

Condition	Possible Cause	Correction
ENGINE WILL NOT RETURN TO IDLE	1. External linkage misadjustment or failure	1. Reset linkage or replace as required.
	2. Internal injection pump malfunction	2. Install replacement injection pump.
FUEL LEAKS ON GROUND— NO ENGINE MALFUNCTION	1. Loose or broken fuel line or connection	1. Examine complete fuel system, including tank, supply, injection and return system. Determine source and cause of leak and repair.
	2. Internal injection pump failure	2. Install replacement injection pump.
SIGNIFICANT LOSS OF POWER	1. Incorrect or contaminated fuel	1. Flush fuel system and install correct fuel.
	2. Pinched or otherwise restricted return system	2. Examine system for restriction and correct as required.
	3. Plugged fuel tank vent	3. Remove fuel cap. If "hissing" noise is heard, vent is plugged and should be cleaned.
	4. Restricted supply	4. Examine fuel supply system to determine cause of restriction. Repair as required.
	5. Plugged fuel filter	5. Remove and replace filter.
	6. External compression leaks	6. Check for compression leaks at all nozzles and glow plugs, using "Leak-Tec" or equivalent. If leak is found, tighten nozzle clamp or glow plug. If leak persists at a nozzle, remove it and reinstall with a new carbon stop seal and compression seal.
	7. Plugged nozzle(s)	7. Remove nozzles, check for plugging and have repaired or replaced.
	8. Internal engine problem	8. Correct as necessary.
NOISE—"RAP" FROM ONE OR MORE CYLINDERS	1. Air in fuel system	1. Check for leaks and correct.
	2. Air in high pressure line(s)	2. Crack line at nozzle(s) and bleed air at each cylinder determined to be causing noise. Use care to direct fuel away from sources of ignition and be sure to carefully retighten lines.
	3. Nozzle(s) sticking open or with very low blowoff pressure	3. Replace the nozzle(s) causing the problem.
	4. Internal engine problem	4. Correct as necessary.
NOISE—SIGNIFICANT OVERALL COMBUSTION NOISE INCREASE WITH EXCESSIVE BLACK SMOKE	1. Timing not set to specification	1. Align timing marks on adapter and injection pump.
	2. Internal engine problem	2. Check for presence of oil in the air crossover. If present, determine cause and correct.
	3. Injection pump housing pressure out of specifications.	3. Check housing pressure. If incorrect, replace fuel return line connector assembly.
	4. Internal injection pump problem	4. Replace pump.
NOISE—INTERNAL OR EXTERNAL	1. Fuel supply pump, alternator, water pump, valve train, vacuum pump, bearings etc.	1. Inspect and correct as necessary.
ENGINE OVERHEATS	1. Coolant system leak or oil cooler system leak	1. Check for leaks and correct as required.
	2. Belt failure	2. Replace.
	3. Thermostat malfunction, head gasket failure or internal engine problem	3. Inspect and correct as necessary.
INSTRUMENT PANEL OIL WARNING LAMP "ON" AT IDLE	1. Oil cooler or oil cooler line restricted	1. Remove restriction in cooler or cooler line.
	2. Internal engine problem	2. Correct as necessary.
ODOR OR SMOKE— EXCESSIVE AND NOT PREVIOUSLY COVERED	1. Same as Gasoline Engines	1. Correct as necessary. Refer to Trouble-Shooting Chapter.
ENGINE WILL NOT SHUT OFF WITH KEY	1. Injection pump solenoid does not drop out	1. Refer to electrical diagnosis. If problem is determined to be internal with the injection pump, replace the injection pump.
	2. Injection pump solenoid return spring failed	2. Replace injection pump.

NOTE: With engine at idle, pinch the fuel return line at the injection pump to shut off engine.

1	2	3	4	5	6
IGN. SWITCH -"OFF"-	IGN. SWITCH -"RUN"-	IGN. SWITCH -"RUN"-	IGN. SWITCH -"START"-	IGN. SWITCH -"RUN"-	IGN. SWITCH -"RUN"-
WAIT LAMP - OFF	WAIT LAMP - ON	WAIT LAMP - OFF	WAIT LAMP - OFF	WAIT LAMP - OFF	WAIT LAMP - OFF
START LAMP - OFF	START LAMP - OFF	START LAMP - ON	START LAMP - OFF	START LAMP - OFF	START LAMP - OFF
GLOW PLUGS - OFF	GLOW PLUGS - ON	GLOW PLUGS - ON	GLOW PLUGS - ON	GLOW PLUGS - ON	GLOW PLUGS - OFF
		↓ SEE ✱ 1		↓ SEE ✱ 2 & 3	

✱ 1: If the ignition is left in the "RUN" position 2-5 minutes before turning it to "START", the Glow Plugs and Lamps turn off. This prevents discharging the battery. Turn ignition "OFF" then to "RUN" and wait for Start Lamp. (Voltage to the starter solenoid is also directed to the module and is the signal that the ignition switch was turned to the Start position).

✱ 3: Engine did not start. Ign. switch still in "RUN" position. "GEN" lamp on. Electronic control starts over after 2-4 second delay (step 2). Wait lamp on. Start lamp off, and Glow Plugs on.

CHECK DIESEL AND GAGES FUSES

✱ 2: Engine Running - Generator voltage to turn off the "GEN" lamp is also directed to the module. 9 volts or more indicates the engine is running. Glow plugs remain on the same length of time between No. 5 and 6 as they did between No. 2 and 3.

✱ 4: The extra light bulb is behind the I. P. and located so it cannot be seen. It's purpose is to provide more current to the generator field coil when starting and idling the engine.

✱ 5: Diode prevents generator feedback to fuel solenoid when ignition is turned off. The diode is located behind the instrument cluster and may be serviced separately.

Fig. 4 Diesel engine electrical system. 1978–79 88 & 98 Type 1

1	2	3	4	5	6
IGN. SWITCH -"OFF"-	IGN. SWITCH -"RUN"-	IGN. SWITCH -"RUN"-	IGN. SWITCH -"START"-	IGN. SWITCH -"RUN"-	IGN. SWITCH -"RUN"-
WAIT LAMP - OFF	WAIT LAMP - ON	WAIT LAMP - OFF	WAIT LAMP - OFF	WAIT LAMP - OFF	WAIT LAMP - OFF
START LAMP - OFF	START LAMP - OFF	START LAMP - ON	START LAMP - OFF	START LAMP - OFF	START LAMP - OFF
GLOW PLUGS - OFF	GLOW PLUGS - ON	GLOW PLUGS - ON	GLOW PLUGS - ON	GLOW PLUGS - ON	GLOW PLUGS - OFF
		SEE ✱ 1		SEE ✱ 2 & 3	

✱ 1: If the ignition is left in the "RUN" position 2-5 minutes before turning it to "START", the Glow Plugs and Lamps turn off. This prevents discharging the battery. Turn ignition "OFF" then to "RUN" and wait for Start Lamp. (Voltage to the starter solenoid is also directed to the module and is the signal that the ignition switch was turned to the Start position).

✱ 2: Engine Running - Generator voltage to turn off the "GEN" lamp is also directed to the module. 9 volts or more indicates the engine is running. Glow plugs remain on the same length of time between No. 5 and 6 as they did between No. 2 and 3.

✱ 3: Engine did not start. Ign. switch still in "RUN" position. "GEN" lamp on. Electronic control starts over after 2-4 second delay (step 2). Wait lamp on, Start lamp off, and Glow Plugs on.

✱ 4: The extra light bulb is behind the I. P. and located so it cannot be seen. It s purpose is to provide more current to the generator field coil when starting and idling the engine.

✱ 5: Diode prevents generator feedback to fuel solenoid when ignition is turned off. The diode is located behind the instrument cluster and may be serviced separately.

Fig. 5 Diesel engine electrical system. 1979 Cutlass Type 1

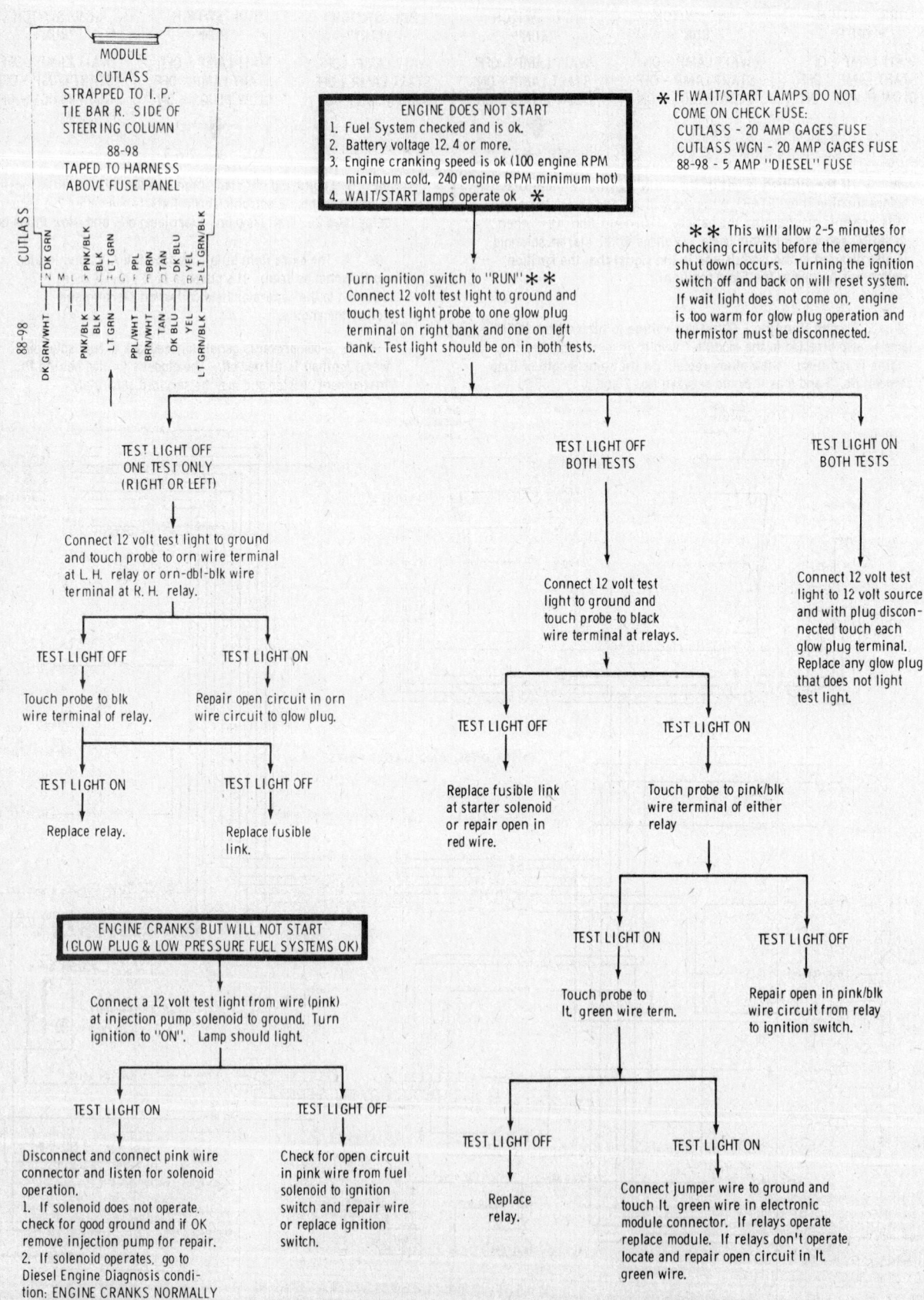

MODULE

CUTLASS
STRAPPED TO I. P.
TIE BAR R. SIDE OF
STEERING COLUMN

88-98
TAPED TO HARNESS
ABOVE FUSE PANEL

CUTLASS

DK GRN
PNK/BLK
BLK
LT GRN
PPL
BRN
TAN
DK BLU
YEL
LT GRN/BLK

88-98

DK GRN/WHT
PNK/BLK
BLK
LT GRN
PPL/WHT
BRN/WHT
TAN
DK BLU
YEL
LT GRN/BLK

ENGINE DOES NOT START
1. Fuel System checked and is ok.
2. Battery voltage 12. 4 or more.
3. Engine cranking speed is ok (100 engine RPM minimum cold, 240 engine RPM minimum hot)
4. WAIT/START lamps operate ok ✱

✱ IF WAIT/START LAMPS DO NOT
COME ON CHECK FUSE:
CUTLASS - 20 AMP GAGES FUSE
CUTLASS WGN - 20 AMP GAGES FUSE
88-98 - 5 AMP "DIESEL" FUSE

✱✱ This will allow 2-5 minutes for checking circuits before the emergency shut down occurs. Turning the ignition switch off and back on will reset system. If wait light does not come on, engine is too warm for glow plug operation and thermistor must be disconnected.

Turn ignition switch to "RUN" ✱✱
Connect 12 volt test light to ground and touch test light probe to one glow plug terminal on right bank and one on left bank. Test light should be on in both tests.

**TEST LIGHT OFF
ONE TEST ONLY
(RIGHT OR LEFT)**

Connect 12 volt test light to ground and touch probe to orn wire terminal at L. H. relay or orn-dbl-blk wire terminal at R. H. relay.

TEST LIGHT OFF

Touch probe to blk wire terminal of relay.

TEST LIGHT ON

Repair open circuit in orn wire circuit to glow plug.

TEST LIGHT ON

Replace relay.

TEST LIGHT OFF

Replace fusible link.

**TEST LIGHT OFF
BOTH TESTS**

Connect 12 volt test light to ground and touch probe to black wire terminal at relays.

TEST LIGHT OFF

Replace fusible link at starter solenoid or repair open in red wire.

TEST LIGHT ON

Touch probe to pink/blk wire terminal of either relay

TEST LIGHT ON

Touch probe to lt. green wire term.

TEST LIGHT OFF

Repair open in pink/blk wire circuit from relay to ignition switch.

TEST LIGHT OFF

Replace relay.

TEST LIGHT ON

Connect jumper wire to ground and touch lt. green wire in electronic module connector. If relays operate replace module. If relays don't operate, locate and repair open circuit in lt. green wire.

**TEST LIGHT ON
BOTH TESTS**

Connect 12 volt test light to 12 volt source and with plug disconnected touch each glow plug terminal. Replace any glow plug that does not light test light.

**ENGINE CRANKS BUT WILL NOT START
(GLOW PLUG & LOW PRESSURE FUEL SYSTEMS OK)**

Connect a 12 volt test light from wire (pink) at injection pump solenoid to ground. Turn ignition to "ON". Lamp should light.

TEST LIGHT ON

Disconnect and connect pink wire connector and listen for solenoid operation.
1. If solenoid does not operate, check for good ground and if OK remove injection pump for repair.
2. If solenoid operates, go to Diesel Engine Diagnosis condition: ENGINE CRANKS NORMALLY WILL NOT START.

TEST LIGHT OFF

Check for open circuit in pink wire from fuel solenoid to ignition switch and repair wire or replace ignition switch.

Fig. 6   Diesel engine electrical diagnosis, part 1 of 5. 1978—79 Type 1

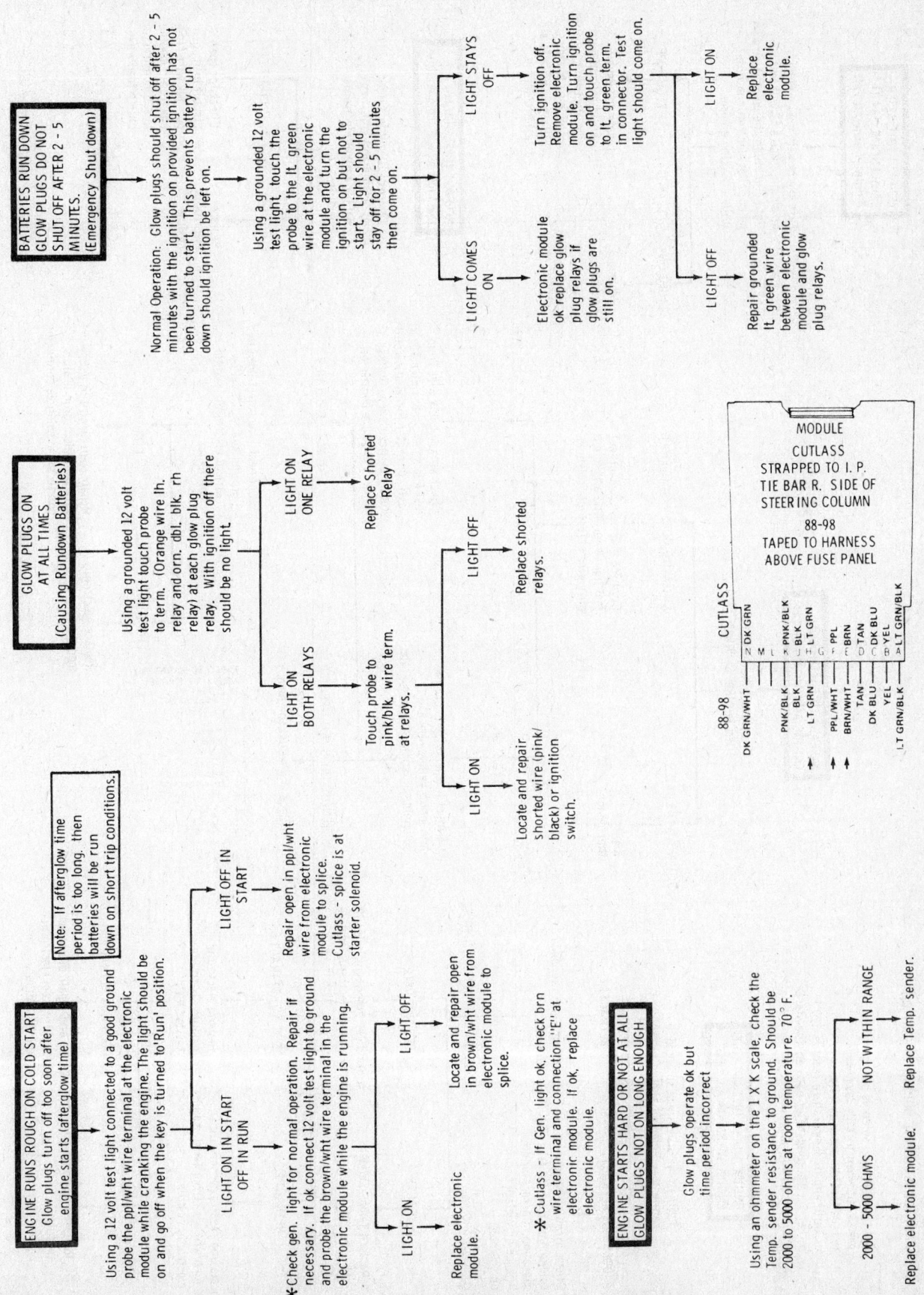

Fig. 7 Diesel engine electrical diagnosis, part 2 of 5. 1978–79 Type 1

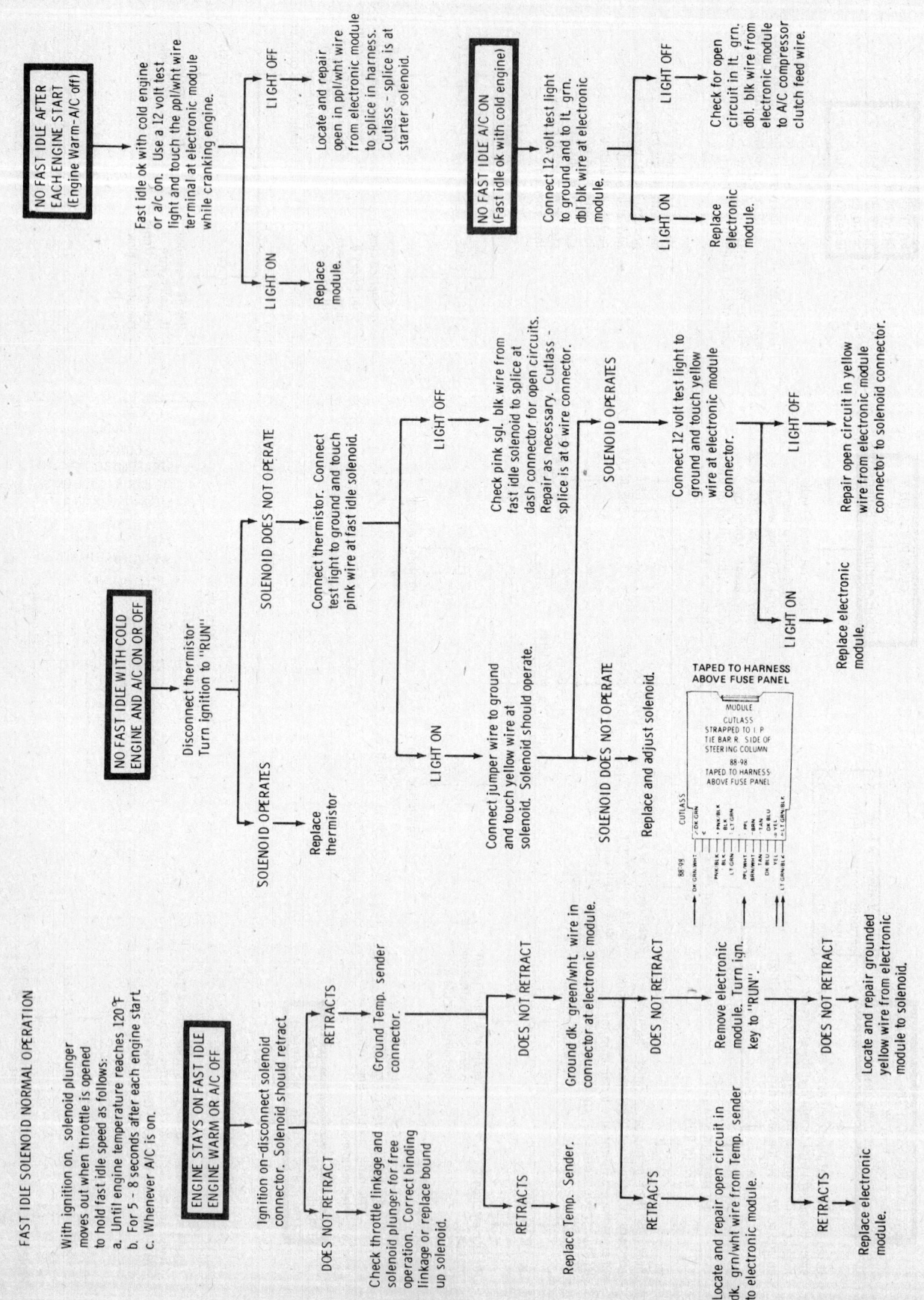

Fig. 8   Diesel engine electrical diagnosis, part 3 of 5. 1978–79 Type 1

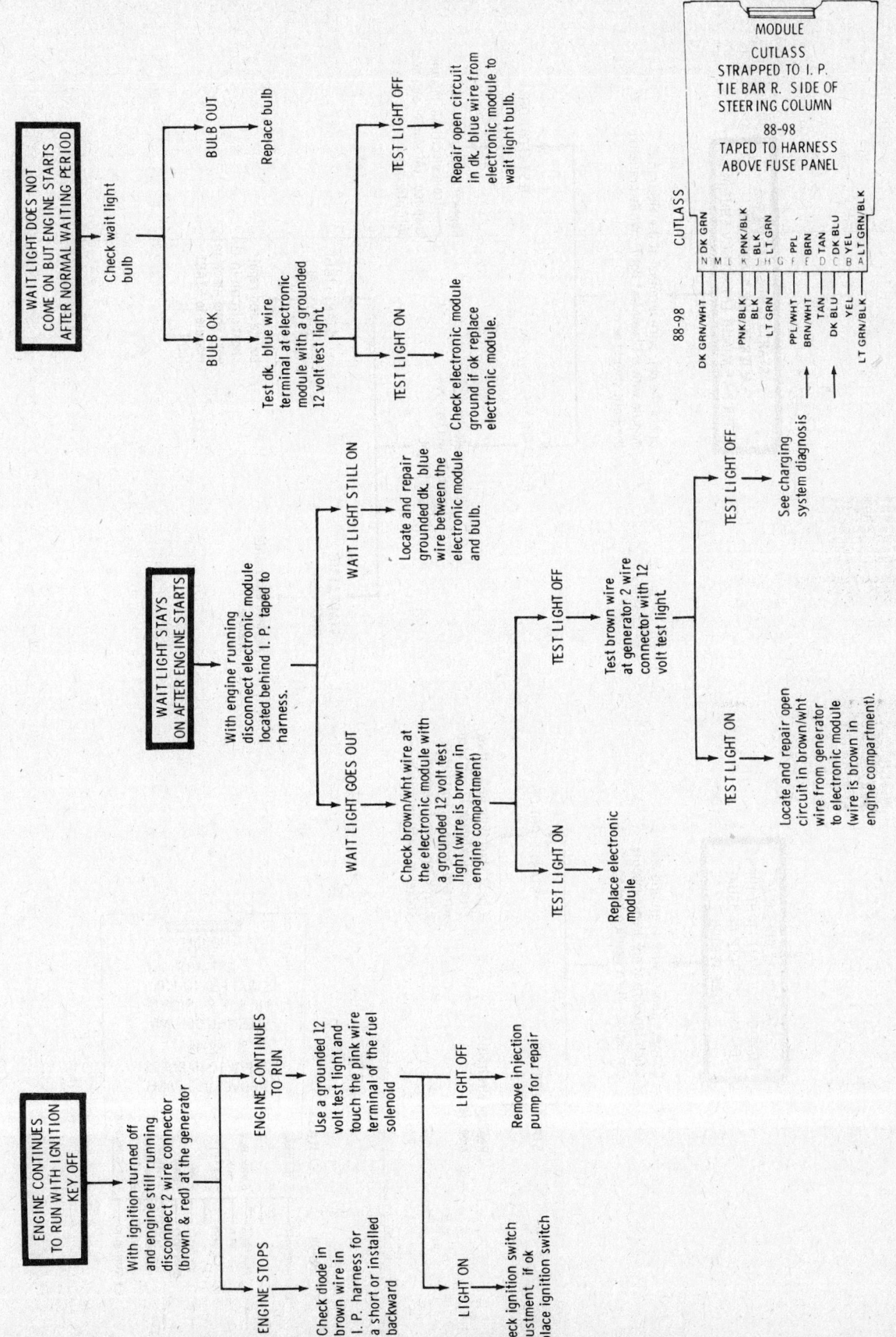

MODULE

CUTLASS
STRAPPED TO I. P.
TIE BAR R. SIDE OF
STEERING COLUMN

88-98
TAPED TO HARNESS
ABOVE FUSE PANEL

CUTLASS

Terminal	Color
N	DK GRN
M	
L	PNK/BLK
K	BLK
J	LT GRN
H	
G	PPL
F	BRN
E	TAN
D	
C	DK BLU
B	YEL
A	LT GRN/BLK

88-98

Color
DK GRN/WHT
PNK/BLK
BLK
LT GRN
PPL/WHT
BRN/WHT
TAN
DK BLU
YEL
LT GRN/BLK

See charging system diagnosis

WAIT LIGHT DOES NOT COME ON BUT ENGINE STARTS AFTER NORMAL WAITING PERIOD

Check wait light bulb

- **BULB OUT** → Replace bulb
- **BULB OK** → Test dk. blue wire terminal at electronic module with a grounded 12 volt test light
  - **TEST LIGHT OFF** → Repair open circuit in dk. blue wire from electronic module to wait light bulb.
  - **TEST LIGHT ON** → Check electronic module ground if ok replace electronic module.

WAIT LIGHT STAYS ON AFTER ENGINE STARTS

With engine running disconnect electronic module located behind I. P. taped to harness.

- **WAIT LIGHT STILL ON** → Locate and repair grounded dk. blue wire between the electronic module and bulb.
- **WAIT LIGHT GOES OUT** → Check brown/wht wire at the electronic module with a grounded 12 volt test light (wire is brown in engine compartment)
  - **TEST LIGHT ON** → Replace electronic module
  - **TEST LIGHT OFF** → Test brown wire at generator 2 wire connector with 12 volt test light.
    - **TEST LIGHT OFF** → See charging system diagnosis
    - **TEST LIGHT ON** → Locate and repair open circuit in brown/wht wire from generator to electronic module (wire is brown in engine compartment).

ENGINE CONTINUES TO RUN WITH IGNITION KEY OFF

With ignition turned off and engine still running disconnect 2 wire connector (brown & red) at the generator

- **ENGINE CONTINUES TO RUN** → Use a grounded 12 volt test light and touch the pink wire terminal of the fuel solenoid
  - **LIGHT OFF** → Remove injection pump for repair
  - **LIGHT ON** → Check ignition switch adjustment, if ok replace ignition switch
- **ENGINE STOPS** → Check diode in brown wire in I. P. harness for a short or installed backward

---

Fig. 9   Diesel engine electrical diagnosis, part 4 of 5. 1978-79 Type 1

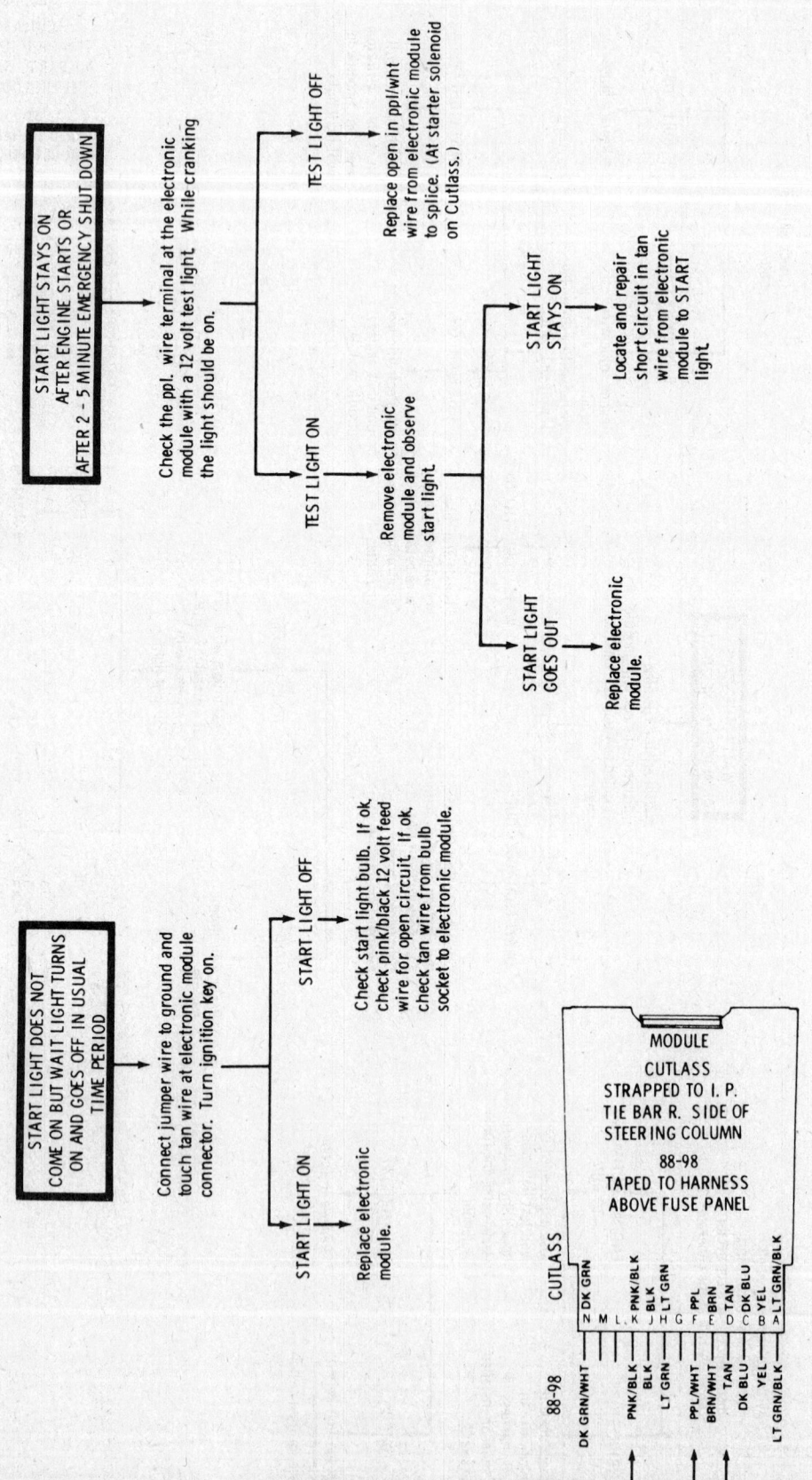

Fig. 10   Diesel engine electrical diagnosis, part 5 of 5. 1978–79 Type 1

1	2	3	4	5	6
IGN. SWITCH -"OFF"-	IGN. SWITCH -"RUN"-	IGN. SWITCH -"RUN"-	IGN. SWITCH -"START"-	IGN. SWITCH -"RUN"-	IGN. SWITCH -"RUN"-
WAIT LAMP - OFF	WAIT LAMP - ON	WAIT LAMP - OFF	WAIT LAMP - OFF	WAIT LAMP - OFF	WAIT LAMP - OFF
START LAMP - OFF	START LAMP - OFF	START LAMP - ON	START LAMP - ON	START LAMP - OFF	START LAMP - OFF
GLOW PLUGS - OFF	GLOW PLUGS - ON	GLOW PLUGS - ON	GLOW PLUGS - ON	GLOW PLUGS - ON	GLOW PLUGS - OFF

ENGINE RUNNING (over columns 5 and 6)

SEE NOTE 1 (under column 3)

SEE NOTE 2 (under column 5)

NOTE 1: If the ignition is left in the "Run" position without starting the engine, the glow plugs will continue to pulse on/off until batteries run down. (About 4 hours when coolant switch is open.)

NOTE 3: Do not manually energize or by-pass the glow plug relay as glow plugs will be damaged instantly.

NOTE 2: Glow plugs will pulse on/off for about 30 seconds after engine starts. Then turn off and remain off as long as engine temperature is above about 120° F (49° C).

NOTE 4: Diodes prevent glow plug operation when the engine is warm (above 120°) the engine is not running and key is in RUN.

IMPORTANT: Do Not use more than a 2–3 candle power test light when making circuit checks.

Fig. 11 Diesel engine electrical system. 1978 Type 2

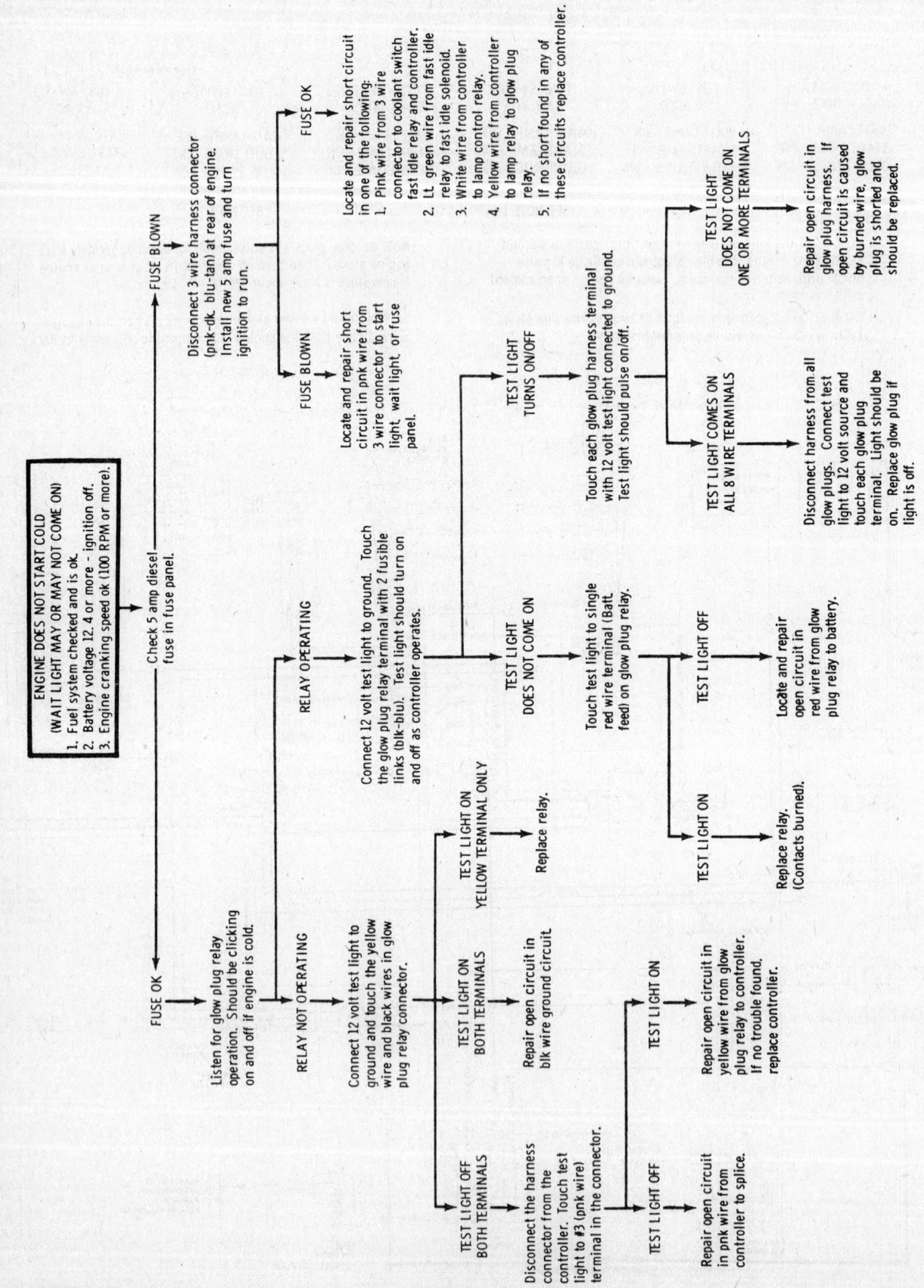

ENGINE DOES NOT START COLD
(WAIT LIGHT MAY OR MAY NOT COME ON)
1. Fuel system checked and is ok.
2. Battery voltage 12.4 or more - ignition off.
3. Engine cranking speed ok (100 RPM or more).

Check 5 amp diesel fuse in fuse panel.

FUSE BLOWN

Disconnect 3 wire harness connector (pnk-dk. blu-tan) at rear of engine. Install new 5 amp fuse and turn ignition to run.

FUSE OK

Locate and repair short circuit in one of the following:
1. Pink wire from 3 wire connector to coolant switch fast idle relay and controller.
2. Lt. green wire from fast idle relay to fast idle solenoid.
3. White wire from controller to lamp control relay.
4. Yellow wire from controller to lamp relay to glow plug relay.
5. If no short found in any of these circuits replace controller.

FUSE BLOWN

Locate and repair short circuit in pnk wire from 3 wire connector to start light, wait light, or fuse panel.

TEST LIGHT TURNS ON/OFF

Touch each glow plug harness terminal with 12 volt test light connected to ground. Test light should pulse on/off.

TEST LIGHT DOES NOT COME ON ONE OR MORE TERMINALS

Repair open circuit in glow plug harness. If open circuit is caused by burned wire, glow plug is shorted and should be replaced.

TEST LIGHT COMES ON ALL 8 WIRE TERMINALS

Disconnect harness from all glow plugs. Connect test light to 12 volt source and touch each glow plug terminal. Light should be on. Replace glow plug if light is off.

FUSE OK

Listen for glow plug relay operation. Should be clicking on and off if engine is cold.

RELAY OPERATING

Connect 12 volt test light to ground. Touch the glow plug relay terminal with 2 fusible links (blk-blu). Test light should turn on and off as controller operates.

TEST LIGHT DOES NOT COME ON

Touch test light to single red wire terminal (Batt feed) on glow plug relay.

TEST LIGHT OFF

Locate and repair open circuit in red wire from glow plug relay to battery.

TEST LIGHT ON

Replace relay. (Contacts burned).

RELAY NOT OPERATING

Connect 12 volt test light to ground and touch the yellow wire and black wires in glow plug relay connector.

TEST LIGHT ON BOTH TERMINALS

Repair open circuit in blk wire ground circuit.

TEST LIGHT ON YELLOW TERMINAL ONLY

Replace relay.

TEST LIGHT OFF BOTH TERMINALS

Disconnect the harness connector from the controller. Touch test light to #3 (pnk wire) terminal in the connector.

TEST LIGHT ON

Repair open circuit in yellow wire from glow plug relay to controller. If no trouble found, replace controller.

TEST LIGHT OFF

Repair open circuit in pnk wire from controller to splice.

Fig. 12   Diesel engine electrical diagnosis, part 1 of 4. 1978 Type 2

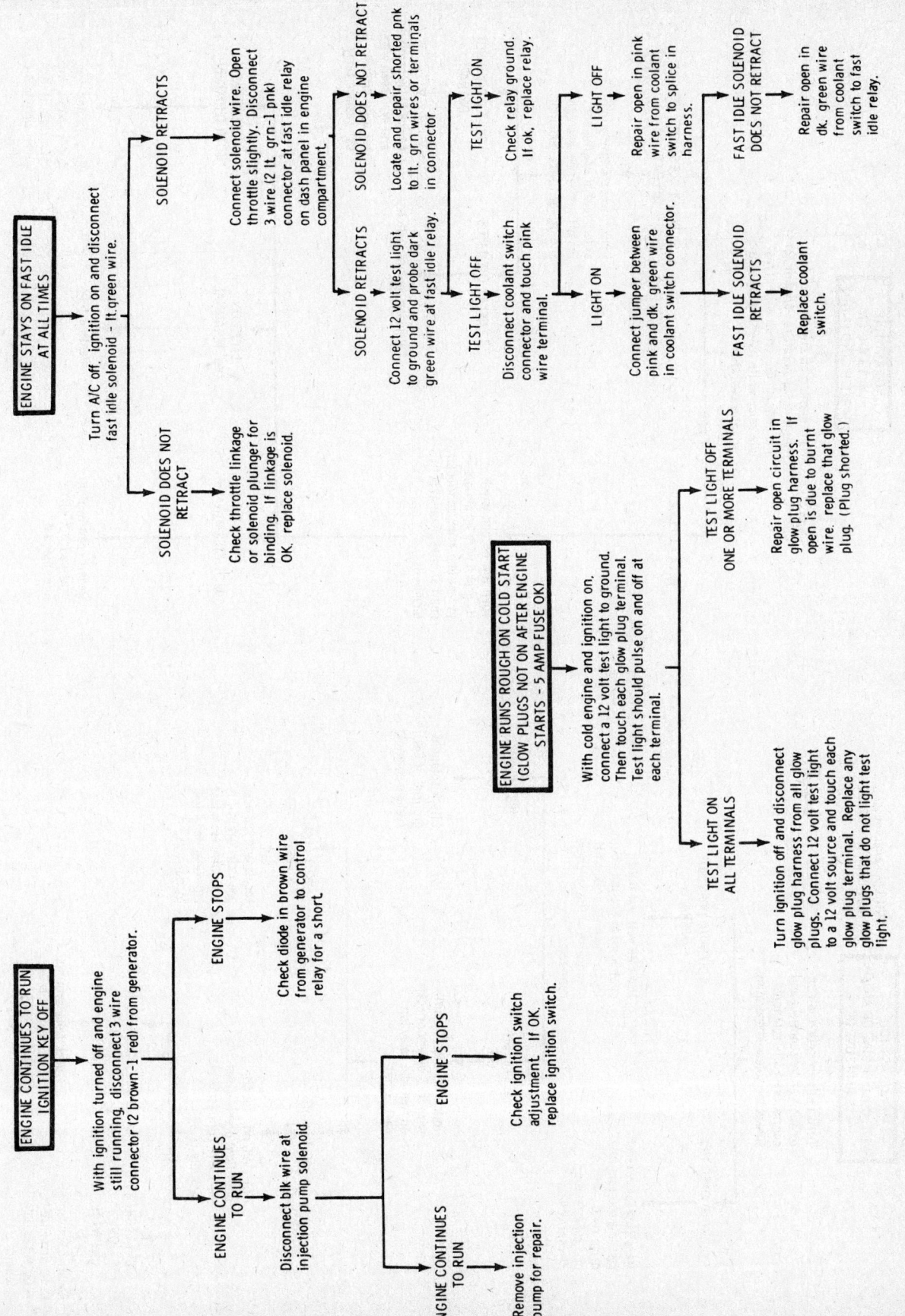

ENGINE STAYS ON FAST IDLE AT ALL TIMES

Turn A/C off, ignition on and disconnect fast idle solenoid - lt.green wire.

SOLENOID RETRACTS

Connect solenoid wire. Open throttle slightly. Disconnect 3 wire (2 lt grn-1 pnk) connector at fast idle relay on dash panel in engine compartment.

SOLENOID DOES NOT RETRACT

Locate and repair shorted pnk to lt. grn wires or terminals in connector.

TEST LIGHT ON

Check relay ground. If ok, replace relay.

LIGHT OFF

Repair open in pink wire from coolant switch to splice in harness.

FAST IDLE SOLENOID DOES NOT RETRACT

Repair open in dk. green wire from coolant switch to fast idle relay.

SOLENOID RETRACTS

Connect 12 volt test light to ground and probe dark green wire at fast idle relay.

TEST LIGHT OFF

Disconnect coolant switch connector and touch pink wire terminal.

LIGHT ON

Connect jumper between pink and dk. green wire in coolant switch connector.

FAST IDLE SOLENOID RETRACTS

Replace coolant switch.

SOLENOID DOES NOT RETRACT

Check throttle linkage or solenoid plunger for binding. If linkage is OK, replace solenoid.

ENGINE RUNS ROUGH ON COLD START (GLOW PLUGS NOT ON AFTER ENGINE STARTS - 5 AMP FUSE OK)

With cold engine and ignition on, connect a 12 volt test light to ground. Then touch each glow plug terminal. Test light should pulse on and off at each terminal.

TEST LIGHT OFF ONE OR MORE TERMINALS

Repair open circuit in glow plug harness. If open is due to burnt wire. replace that glow plug. (Plug shorted.)

TEST LIGHT ON ALL TERMINALS

Turn ignition off and disconnect all glow plug harness from all glow plugs. Connect 12 volt test light to a 12 volt source and touch each glow plug terminal. Replace any glow plugs that do not light test light.

ENGINE CONTINUES TO RUN IGNITION KEY OFF

With ignition turned off and engine still running, disconnect 3 wire connector (2 brown-1 red) from generator.

ENGINE STOPS

Check diode in brown wire from generator to control relay for a short.

ENGINE CONTINUES TO RUN

Disconnect blk wire at injection pump solenoid.

ENGINE STOPS

Check ignition switch adjustment. If OK. replace ignition switch.

ENGINE CONTINUES TO RUN

Remove injection pump for repair.

Fig. 13 Diesel engine electrical diagnosis, part 2 of 4. 1978 Type 2

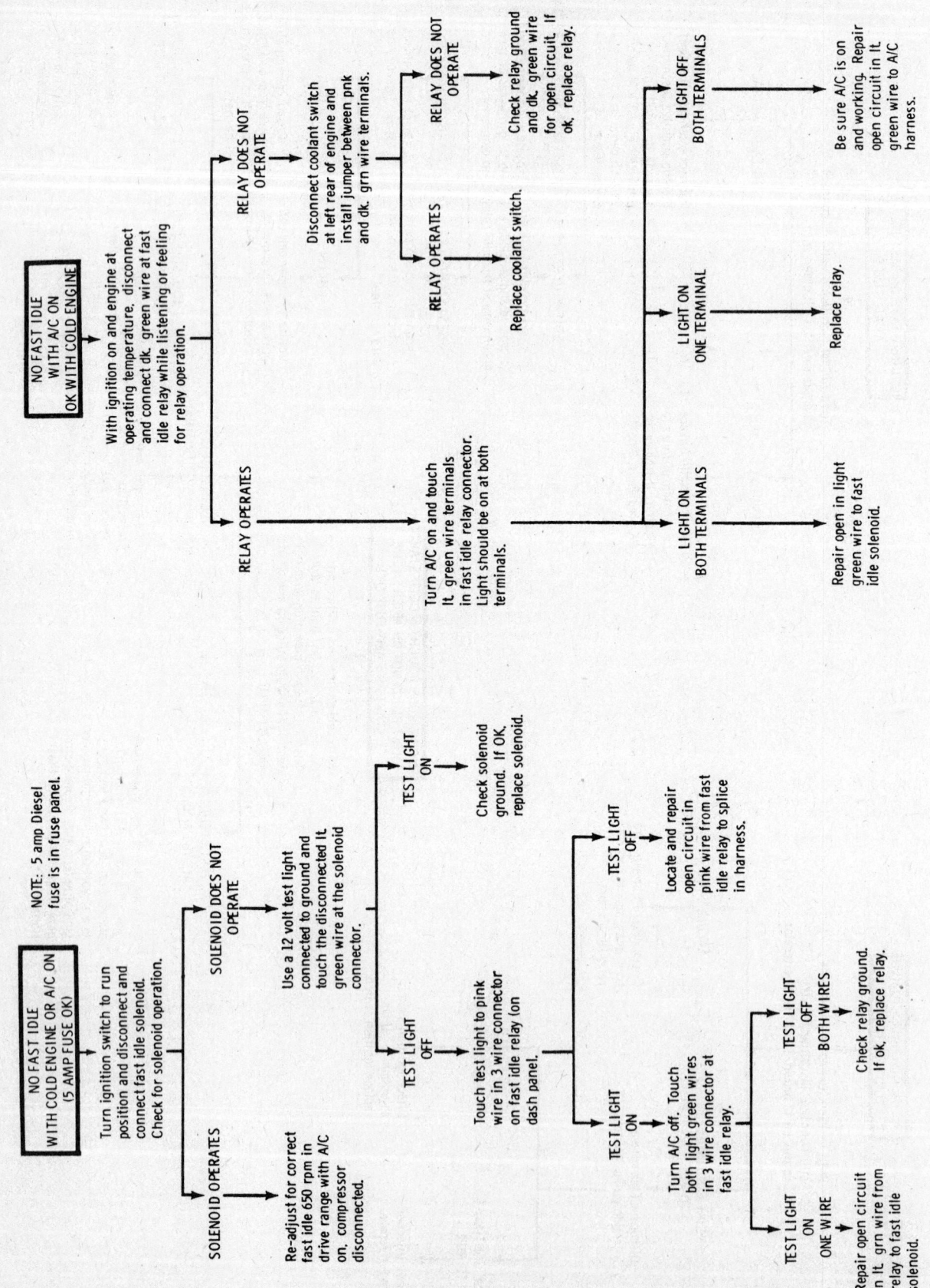

NO FAST IDLE WITH A/C ON OK WITH COLD ENGINE

With ignition on and engine at operating temperature, disconnect and connect dk. green wire at fast idle relay while listening or feeling for relay operation.

RELAY DOES NOT OPERATE → Disconnect coolant switch at left rear of engine and install jumper between pnk and dk. grn wire terminals.

RELAY DOES NOT OPERATE → Check relay ground and dk. green wire for open circuit. If ok, replace relay.

RELAY OPERATES → Replace coolant switch.

RELAY OPERATES → Turn A/C on and touch lt. green wire terminals in fast idle relay connector. Light should be on at both terminals.

LIGHT OFF BOTH TERMINALS → Be sure A/C is on and working. Repair open circuit in lt. green wire to A/C harness.

LIGHT ON ONE TERMINAL → Replace relay.

LIGHT ON BOTH TERMINALS → Repair open in light green wire to fast idle solenoid.

NOTE: 5 amp Diesel fuse is in fuse panel.

NO FAST IDLE WITH COLD ENGINE OR A/C ON (5 AMP FUSE OK)

Turn ignition switch to run position and disconnect and connect fast idle solenoid. Check for solenoid operation.

SOLENOID DOES NOT OPERATE → Use a 12 volt test light connected to ground and touch the disconnected lt. green wire at the solenoid connector.

TEST LIGHT ON → Check solenoid ground. If OK, replace solenoid.

TEST LIGHT OFF → Touch test light to pink wire in 3 wire connector on fast idle relay (on dash panel).

TEST LIGHT OFF → Locate and repair open circuit in pink wire from fast idle relay to splice in harness.

TEST LIGHT ON → Turn A/C off. Touch both light green wires in 3 wire connector at fast idle relay.

TEST LIGHT OFF BOTH WIRES → Check relay ground. If ok, replace relay.

TEST LIGHT ON ONE WIRE → Repair open circuit in lt. grn wire from relay to fast idle solenoid.

SOLENOID OPERATES → Re-adjust for correct fast idle 650 rpm in drive range with A/C on, compressor disconnected.

Fig. 14   Diesel engine electrical diagnosis, part 3 of 4. 1978 Type 2

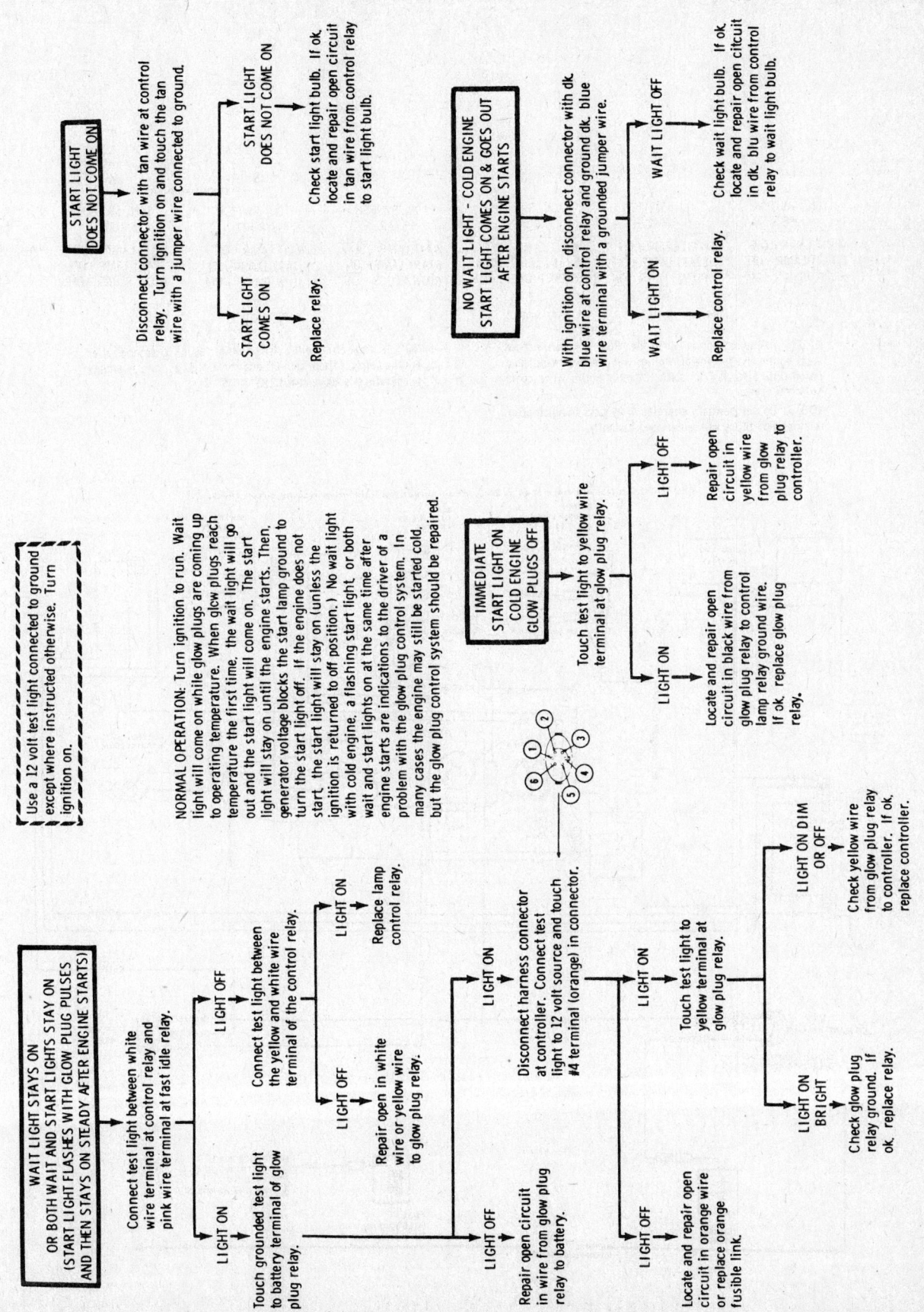

Fig. 15   Diesel engine electrical diagnosis, part 4 of 4. 1978 Type 2

1	2	3		5	6
				ENGINE RUNNING	
IGN. SWITCH "OFF"	IGN. SWITCH "RUN"	IGN. SWITCH "RUN"	IGN. SWITCH "START"	IGN. SWITCH "RUN"	IGN. SWITCH "RUN"
WAIT LAMP - OFF	WAIT LAMP - ON	WAIT LAMP - OFF	WAIT LAMP - OFF	WAIT LAMP - OFF	WAIT LAMP - OFF
START LAMP - OFF	START LAMP - OFF	START LAMP - ON	START LAMP - ON	START LAMP - OFF	START LAMP - OFF
GLOW PLUGS - OFF	GLOW PLUGS - ON	GLOW PLUGS - ON	GLOW PLUGS - ON	GLOW PLUGS - ON	GLOW PLUGS - OFF
		↓		↓	
		SEE NOTE 1		SEE NOTE 2	

NOTE 1: If the ignition is left in the "Run" position without starting the engine, the glow plugs will continue to pulse on/off until batteries run down. (About 4 hours when coolant switch is open.)

NOTE 3: Do not manually energize or by-pass the glow plug relay as glow plugs will be damaged instantly.

NOTE 2: Glow plugs will pulse on/off for about 30 seconds after engine starts. Then turn off and remain off as long as engine temperature is above about 120°F (49°C).

IMPORTANT: Do Not use more than a 2–3 candle power test light when making circuit checks.

Fig. 16 Diesel engine electrical system. 1979 V8-260 Type 2

1	2	3		5	6
				ENGINE RUNNING	
IGN. SWITCH -"OFF"-	IGN. SWITCH -"RUN"-	IGN. SWITCH -"RUN"-	IGN. SWITCH -"START"-	IGN. SWITCH -"RUN"-	IGN. SWITCH -"RUN"-
WAIT LAMP - OFF	WAIT LAMP - ON	WAIT LAMP - OFF	WAIT LAMP - OFF	WAIT LAMP - OFF	WAIT LAMP - OFF
START LAMP - OFF	START LAMP - OFF	START LAMP - ON	START LAMP - ON	START LAMP - OFF	START LAMP - OFF
GLOW PLUGS - OFF	GLOW PLUGS - ON	GLOW PLUGS - ON	GLOW PLUGS - ON	GLOW PLUGS - ON	GLOW PLUGS - OFF
		↓		↓	
		SEE NOTE 1		SEE NOTE 2	

NOTE 1: If the ignition is left in the "Run" position without starting the engine, the glow plugs will continue to pulse on/off until batteries run down. (About 4 hours when coolant switch is open.)

NOTE 3: Do not manually energize or by-pass the glow plug relay as glow plugs will be damaged instantly.

NOTE 2: Glow plugs will pulse on/off for about 30 seconds after engine starts. Then turn off and remain off as long as engine temperature is above about 120° F (49° C).

NOTE 4: Diodes prevent glow plug operation when the engine is warm (above 120°) the engine is not running and key is in RUN.

IMPORTANT: Do Not use more than a 2–3 candle power test light when making circuit checks.

Fig. 17   Diesel engine electrical system, part 1 of 2. 1979 V8-350 Type 2

Fig. 18 Diesel engine electrical system, part 2 of 2. 1979 V8-350 Type 2

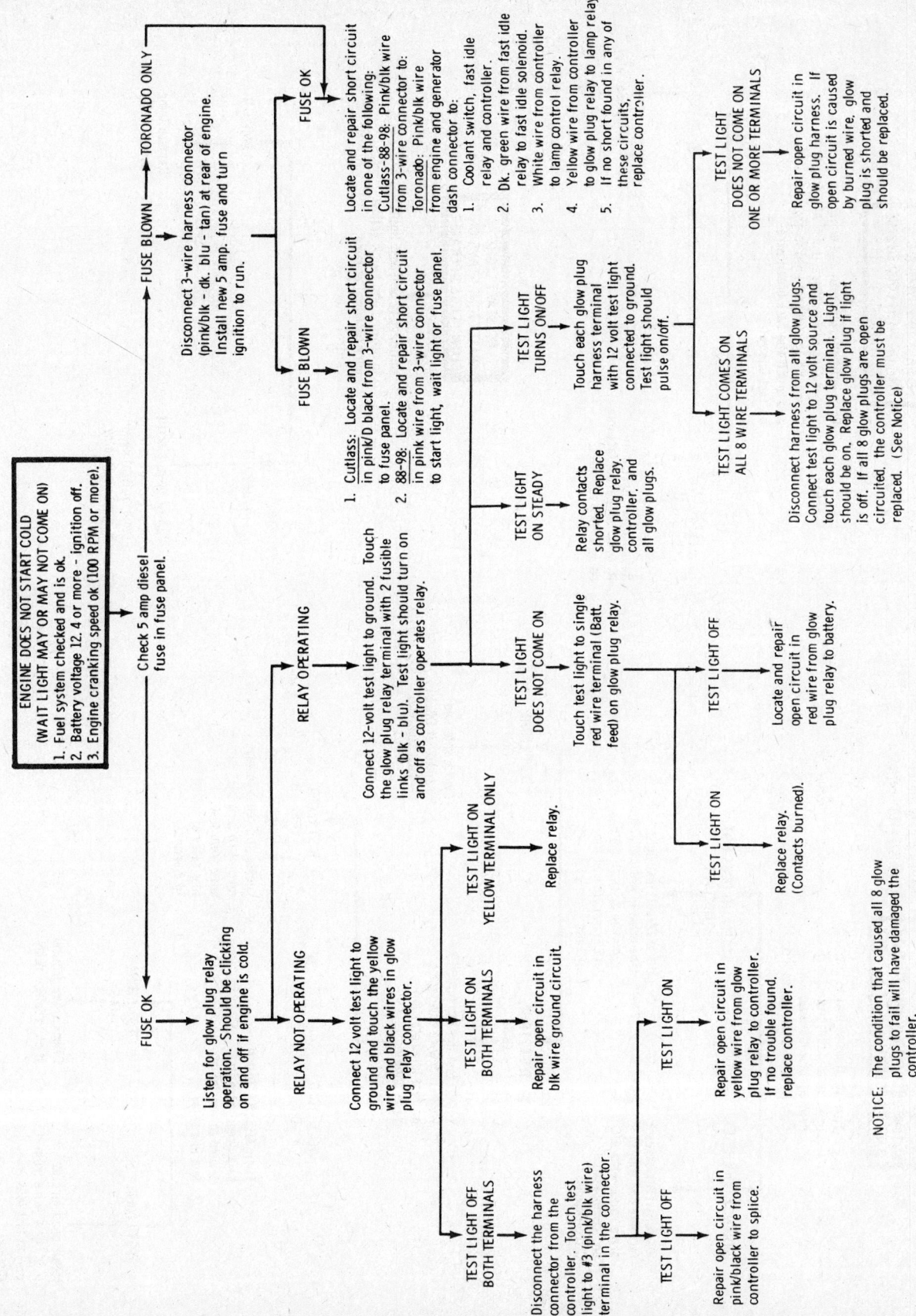

Fig. 19   Diesel engine electrical diagnosis, part 1 of 5. 1979 V8-260 (4.3 litre) & 350 (5.7 litre) Type 2

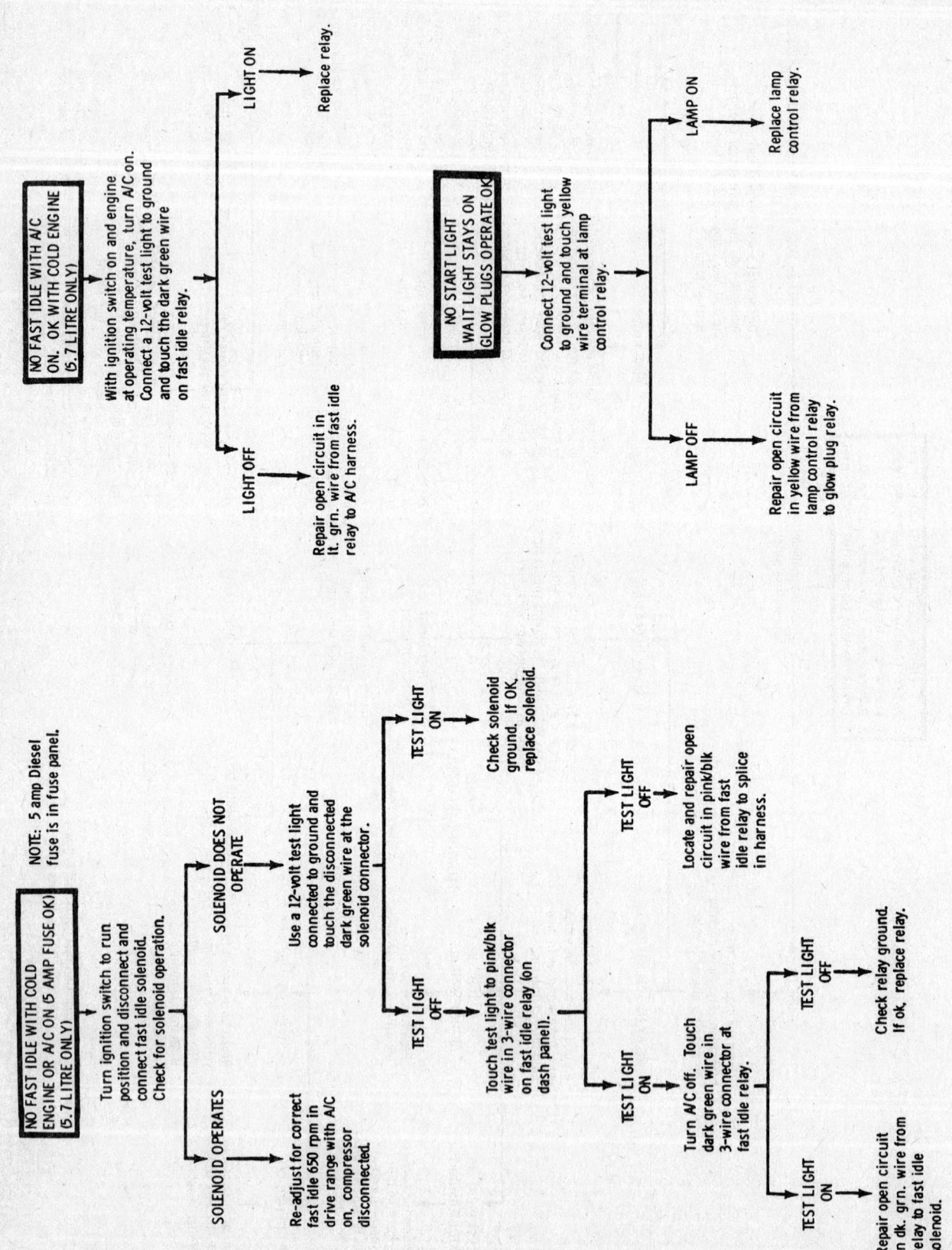

NO FAST IDLE WITH A/C ON. OK WITH COLD ENGINE (5.7 LITRE ONLY)

With ignition switch on and engine at operating temperature, turn A/C on. Connect a 12-volt test light to ground and touch the dark green wire on fast idle relay.

→ LIGHT ON → Replace relay.

→ LIGHT OFF → Repair open circuit in lt. grn. wire from fast idle relay to A/C harness.

NO START LIGHT WAIT LIGHT STAYS ON GLOW PLUGS OPERATE OK

Connect 12-volt test light to ground and touch yellow wire terminal at lamp control relay.

→ LAMP ON → Replace lamp control relay.

→ LAMP OFF → Repair open circuit in yellow wire from lamp control relay to glow plug relay.

NO FAST IDLE WITH COLD ENGINE OR A/C ON (5 AMP FUSE OK) (5.7 LITRE ONLY)

NOTE: 5 amp Diesel fuse is in fuse panel.

Turn ignition switch to run position and disconnect and connect fast idle solenoid. Check for solenoid operation.

→ SOLENOID DOES NOT OPERATE → Use a 12-volt test light connected to ground and touch the disconnected dark green wire at the solenoid connector.

→ TEST LIGHT ON → Check solenoid ground. If OK, replace solenoid.

→ TEST LIGHT OFF → Touch test light to pink/blk wire in 3-wire connector on fast idle relay (on dash panel).

→ TEST LIGHT OFF → Locate and repair open circuit in pink/blk wire from fast idle relay to splice in harness.

→ TEST LIGHT ON → Turn A/C off. Touch dark green wire in 3-wire connector at fast idle relay.

→ TEST LIGHT OFF → Check relay ground. If OK, replace relay.

→ TEST LIGHT ON → Repair open circuit in dk. grn. wire from relay to fast idle solenoid.

→ SOLENOID OPERATES → Re-adjust for correct fast idle 650 rpm in drive range with A/C on, compressor disconnected.

Fig. 20 Diesel engine electrical diagnosis, part 2 of 5. 1979 V8-260 (4.3 litre) & 350 (5.7 litre) Type 2

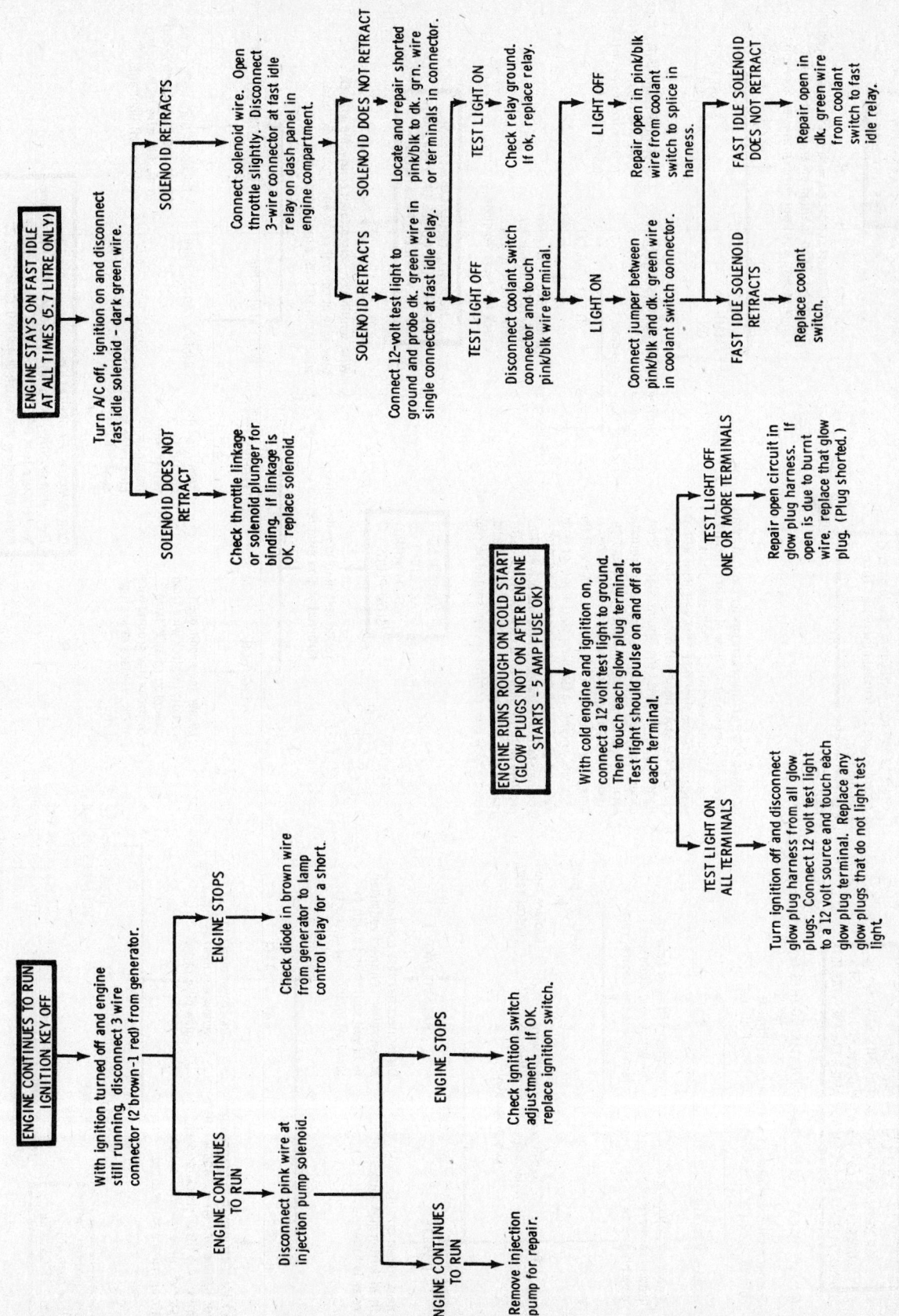

Fig. 21 Diesel engine electrical diagnosis, part 3 of 5. 1979 V8-260 (4.3 litre) & 350 (5.7 litre) Type 2

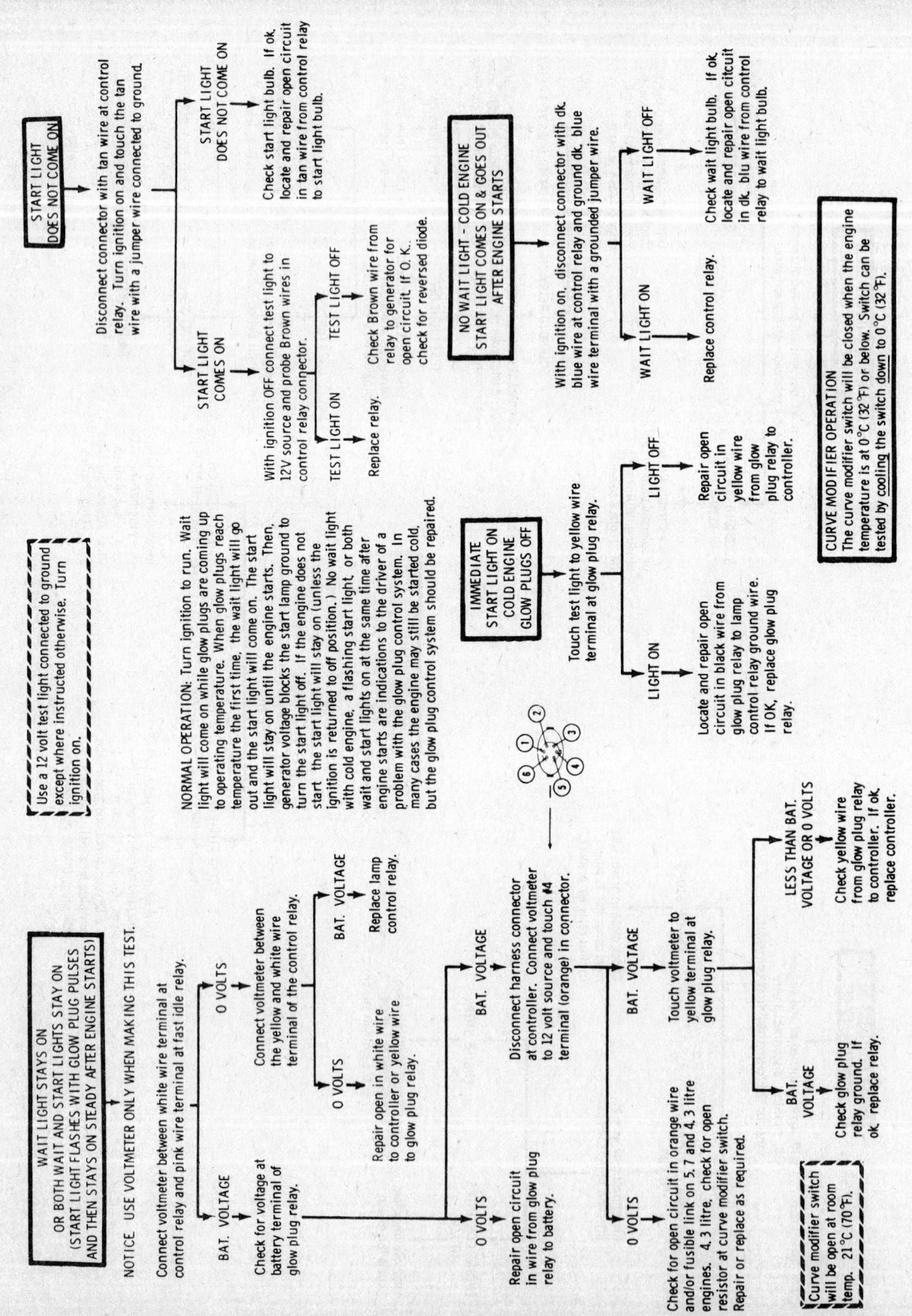

START LIGHT DOES NOT COME ON

Disconnect connector with tan wire at control relay. Turn ignition on and touch the tan wire with a jumper wire connected to ground.

START LIGHT DOES NOT COME ON

Check start light bulb. If ok, locate and repair open circuit in tan wire from control relay to start light bulb.

START LIGHT COMES ON

With ignition OFF connect test light to 12V source and probe Brown wires in control relay connector.

TEST LIGHT OFF

Check Brown wire from relay to generator for open circuit. If O.K. check for reversed diode.

TEST LIGHT ON

Replace relay.

NO WAIT LIGHT - COLD ENGINE START LIGHT COMES ON & GOES OUT AFTER ENGINE STARTS

With ignition on, disconnect connector with dk. blue wire at control relay and ground dk. blue wire terminal with a grounded jumper wire.

WAIT LIGHT OFF

Check wait light bulb. If ok, locate and repair open circuit in dk. blu wire from control relay to wait light bulb.

WAIT LIGHT ON

Replace control relay.

CURVE MODIFIER OPERATION
The curve modifier switch will be closed when the engine temperature is at 0°C (32°F) or below. Switch can be tested by cooling the switch down to 0°C (32°F).

Use a 12 volt test light connected to ground except where instructed otherwise. Turn ignition on.

NOTICE. USE VOLTMETER ONLY WHEN MAKING THIS TEST.

NORMAL OPERATION: Turn ignition to run. Wait light will come on while glow plugs are coming up to operating temperature. When glow plugs reach temperature the first time, the wait light will go out and the start light will come on. The start light will stay on until the engine starts. Then, generator voltage blocks the start lamp ground to turn the start light off. If the engine does not start the start light will stay on (unless the ignition is returned to off position.) No wait light with cold engine, a flashing start light, or both wait and start lights on at the same time after engine starts are indications to the driver of a problem with the glow plug control system. In many cases the engine may still be started cold, but the glow plug control system should be repaired.

IMMEDIATE START LIGHT ON COLD ENGINE GLOW PLUGS OFF

Touch test light to yellow wire terminal at glow plug relay.

LIGHT OFF

Repair open circuit in yellow wire from glow plug relay to controller.

LIGHT ON

Locate and repair open circuit in black wire from glow plug relay to lamp control relay ground wire. If OK, replace glow plug relay.

WAIT LIGHT STAYS ON OR BOTH WAIT AND START LIGHTS STAY ON (START LIGHT FLASHES WITH GLOW PLUG PULSES AND THEN STAYS ON STEADY AFTER ENGINE STARTS)

Connect voltmeter between white wire terminal at control relay and pink wire terminal at fast idle relay.

BAT. VOLTAGE

Check for voltage at battery terminal of glow plug relay.

0 VOLTS

Connect voltmeter between the yellow and white wire terminal of the control relay.

BAT. VOLTAGE

Replace lamp control relay.

0 VOLTS

Repair open in white wire to controller or yellow wire to glow plug relay.

BAT. VOLTAGE

Disconnect harness connector at controller. Connect voltmeter to 12 volt source and touch #4 terminal (orange) in connector.

0 VOLTS

Repair open circuit in wire from glow plug relay to battery.

0 VOLTS

Check for open circuit in orange wire and/or fusible link on 5.7 and 4.3 litre engines. 4.3 litre, check for open resistor at curve modifier switch. Repair or replace as required.

BAT. VOLTAGE

Touch voltmeter to yellow terminal at glow plug relay.

BAT. VOLTAGE

Check glow plug relay ground. If ok. replace relay.

LESS THAN BAT. VOLTAGE OR 0 VOLTS

Check yellow wire from glow plug relay to controller. If ok, replace controller.

Curve modifier switch will be open at room temp. 21°C (70°F).

Fig. 22   Diesel engine electrical diagnosis, part 4 of 5. 1979 V8-260 (4.3 litre) & 350 (5.7 litre) Type 2

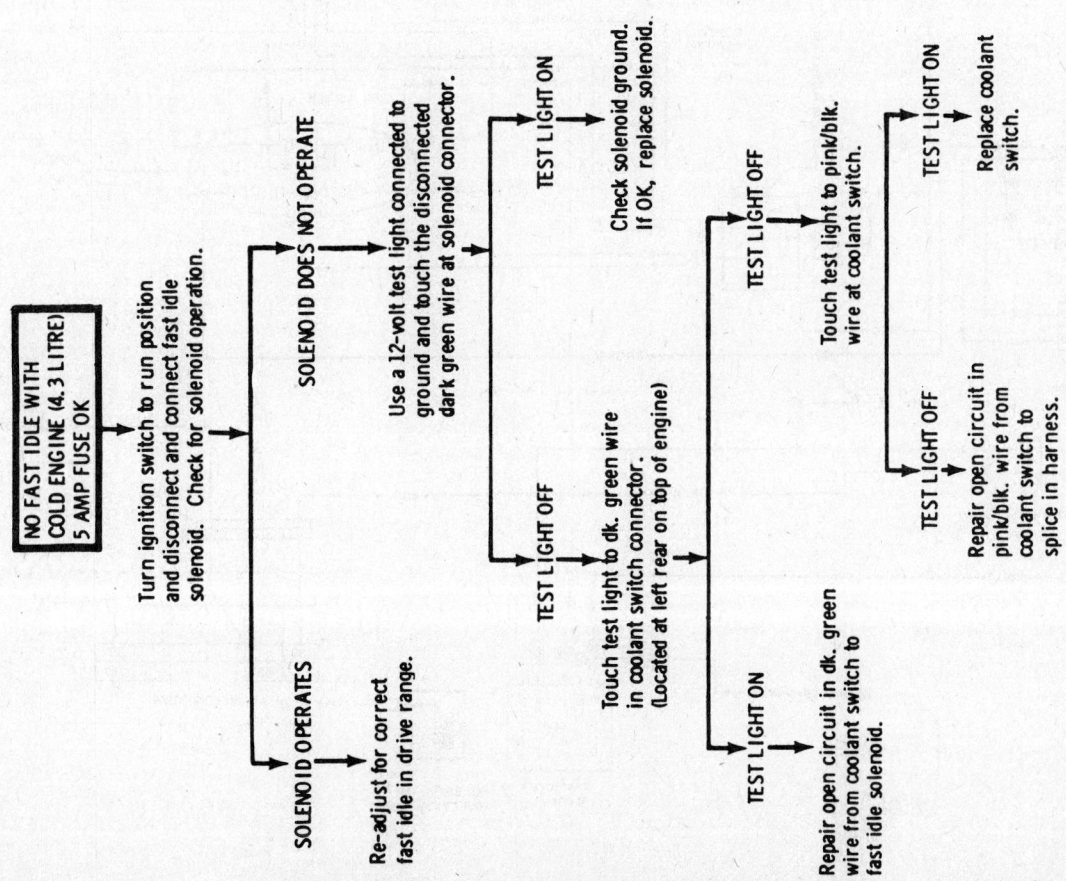

Fig. 23   Diesel engine electrical diagnosis, part 5 of 5. 1979 V8-260 (4.3 litre) Type 2

1	2	3	4	5	6
				⌐ ENGINE RUNNING ⌐	
IGN. SWITCH -"OFF"-	IGN. SWITCH -"RUN"-	IGN. SWITCH -"RUN"-	IGN. SWITCH -"START"-	IGN. SWITCH -"RUN"-	IGN. SWITCH -"RUN"-
WAIT LAMP-OFF	WAIT LAMP-ON	WAIT LAMP-OFF	WAIT LAMP-OFF	WAIT LAMP-OFF	WAIT LAMP-OFF
GLOW PLUGS-OFF	GLOW PLUGS-ON	GLOW PLUGS-ON	GLOW PLUGS-ON	GLOW PLUGS-ON	GLOW PLUGS-OFF

SEE ✱ 1

SEE ✱ 2

✱ 1: If the ignition is left in the "Run" position without starting the engine, the glow plugs will continue to pulse on/off until batteries run down. (About 4 hours when coolant switch is open.)

✱ 3: Do not manually energize or by-pass the glow plug relay as glow plugs will be damaged instantly.

✱ 2: Glow plugs will pulse on/off for about 30 seconds after engine starts. Then turn off and remain off as long as engine temperature is above about 120°F (49°C).

✱ 4: Diodes prevent glow plug operation when the engine is warm (above 120°) the engine is not running and key is in RUN.

IMPORTANT: Do Not use more than a 2-3 candle power test light when making circuit checks.

Fig. 24 Diesel engine electrical system, part 1 of 2. 1980-83 88, 98 & Toronado Type 2

88, 98, Toronado, 1977—79 Omega, Cutlass Exc. Ciera——**OLDSMOBILE**

Fig. 24A   Diesel engine electrical system, part 2 of 2. 1980—83 88, 98 & Toronado Type 2

Fig. 25 Diesel engine electrical diagnosis, part 1 of 4. 1980—83 Type 2

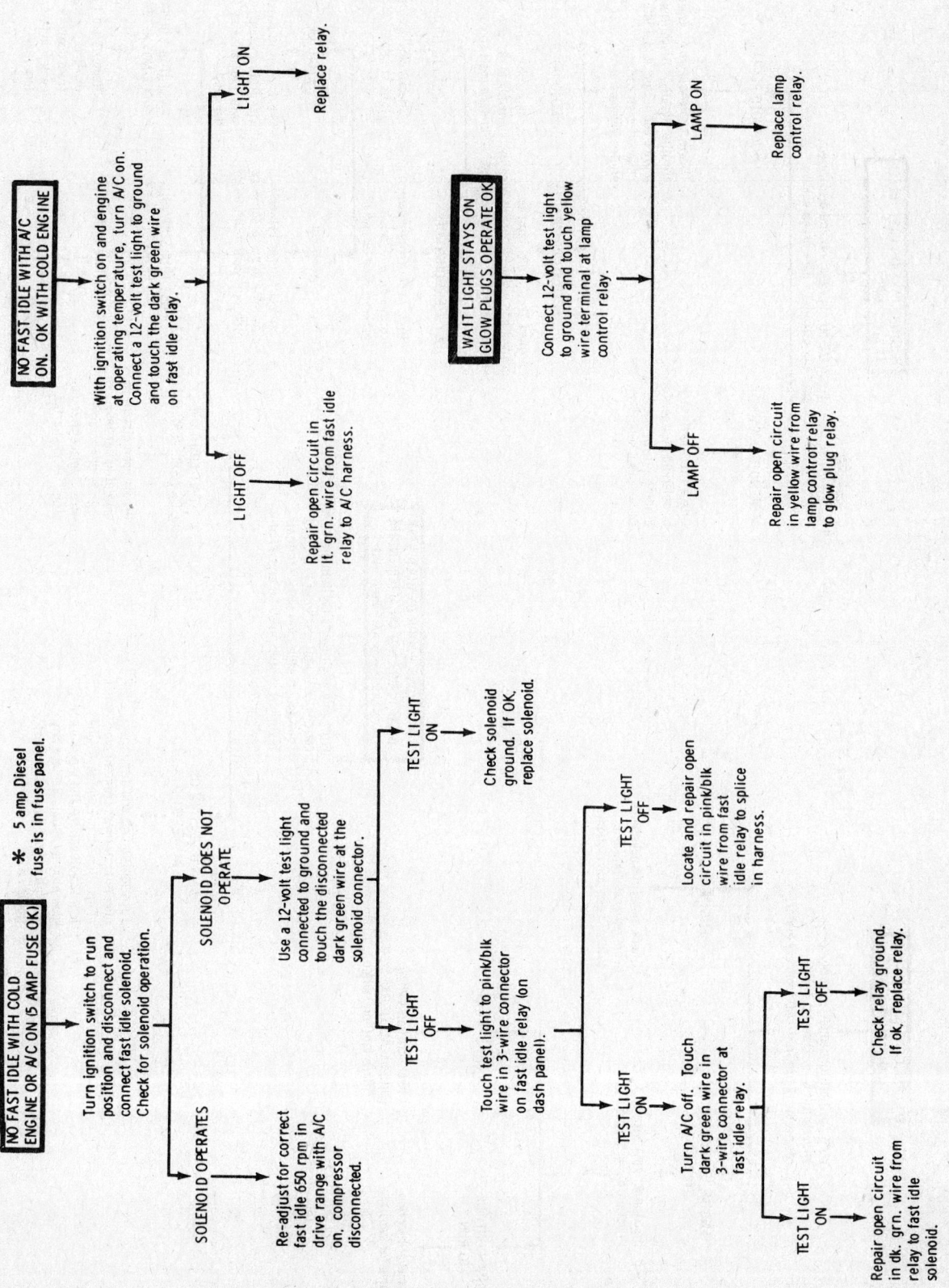

NO FAST IDLE WITH A/C ON. OK WITH COLD ENGINE

With ignition switch on and engine at operating temperature, turn A/C on. Connect a 12-volt test light to ground and touch the dark green wire on fast idle relay.

LIGHT ON → Replace relay.

LIGHT OFF → Repair open circuit in lt. grn. wire from fast idle relay to A/C harness.

WAIT LIGHT STAYS ON GLOW PLUGS OPERATE OK

Connect 12-volt test light to ground and touch yellow wire terminal at lamp control relay.

LAMP ON → Replace lamp control relay.

LAMP OFF → Repair open circuit in yellow wire from lamp control relay to glow plug relay.

* 5 amp Diesel fuse is in fuse panel.

NO FAST IDLE WITH COLD ENGINE OR A/C ON (5 AMP FUSE OK)

Turn ignition switch to run position and disconnect and connect fast idle solenoid. Check for solenoid operation.

SOLENOID DOES NOT OPERATE → Use a 12-volt test light connected to ground and touch the disconnected dark green wire at the solenoid connector.

TEST LIGHT ON → Check solenoid ground. If OK, replace solenoid.

TEST LIGHT OFF → Touch test light to pink/blk wire in 3-wire connector on fast idle relay (on dash panel).

TEST LIGHT OFF → Locate and repair open circuit in pink/blk wire from fast idle relay to splice in harness.

TEST LIGHT ON → Turn A/C off. Touch dark green wire in 3-wire connector at fast idle relay.

TEST LIGHT OFF → Check relay ground. If ok, replace relay.

TEST LIGHT ON → Repair open circuit in dk. grn. wire from relay to fast idle solenoid.

SOLENOID OPERATES → Re-adjust for correct fast idle 650 rpm in drive range with A/C on, compressor disconnected.

Fig. 25A   Diesel engine electrical diagnosis, part 2 of 4. 1980–83 Type 2

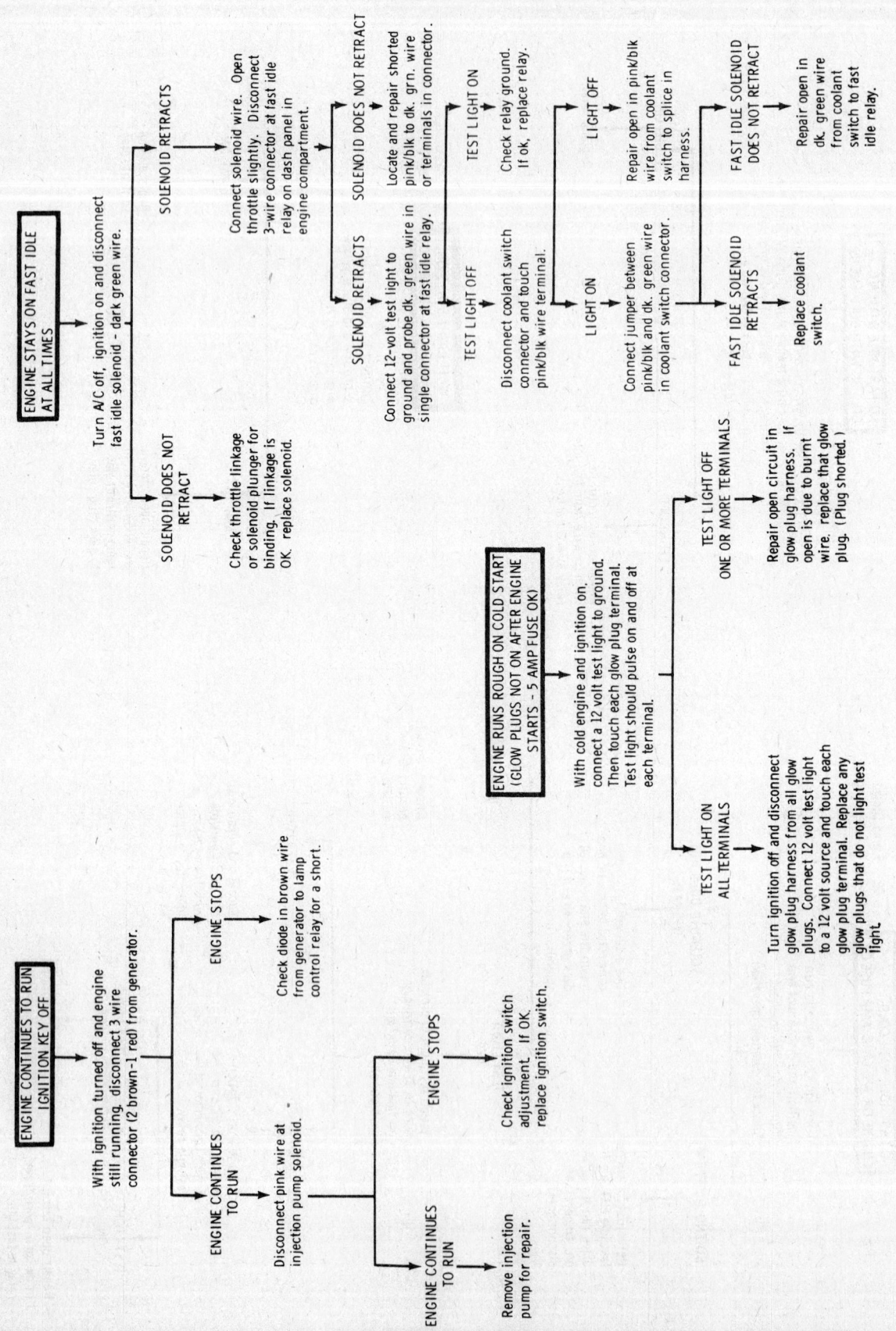

Fig. 25B Diesel engine electrical diagnosis, part 3 of 4. 1980—83 Type 2

NORMAL OPERATION: Turn ignition to run. Wait light will come on while glow plugs are coming up to operating temperature. When glow plugs reach temperature the first time. the wait light will go out to indicate the engine is ready to start. No wait light with cold engine. or a continuous wait light after the engine starts are indications to the driver of a problem with the glow plug control systems. In many cases the engine may still be started cold. but the glow plug system should be repaired.

NO WAIT LIGHT - COLD ENGINE

With ignition on, disconnect connector with dk. blue wire at control relay and ground dk. blue wire terminal with a grounded jumper wire.

→ WAIT LIGHT ON → Replace control relay.

→ WAIT LIGHT OFF → Check wait light bulb. If ok. locate and repair open citcuit in dk. blu wire from control relay to wait light bulb.

Use a 12 volt test light connected to ground except where instructed otherwise. Turn ignition on.

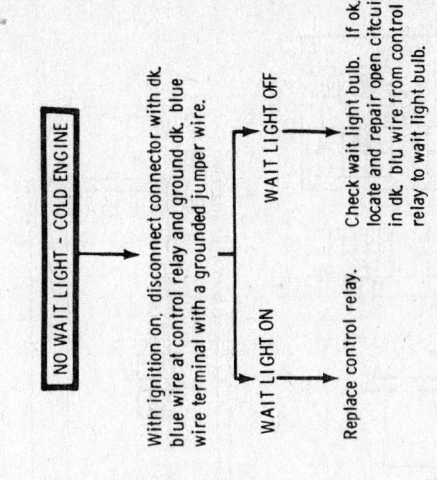

WAIT LIGHT STAYS ON AFTER ENGINE STARTS

NOTICE: USE VOLTMETER ONLY WHEN MAKING THIS TEST.

Connect voltmeter between white wire terminal at control relay and pink wire terminal at fast idle relay.

- 0 VOLTS → Connect voltmeter between the yellow and white wire terminal of the control relay.
  - BAT. VOLTAGE → Replace lamp control relay.
  - 0 VOLTS → Repair open in white wire to controller or yellow wire to glow plug relay.

- BAT. VOLTAGE → Check for voltage at battery terminal of glow plug relay.
  - 0 VOLTS → Repair open circuit in wire from glow plug relay to battery.
  - BAT. VOLTAGE → Disconnect harness connector at controller. Connect voltmeter to 12 volt source and touch #4 terminal (orange) in connector.
    - 0 VOLTS → Check for open circuit in orange wire and/or fusible link. Repair or replace as required.
    - BAT. VOLTAGE → Touch voltmeter to yellow terminal at glow plug relay.
      - BAT. VOLTAGE → Check glow plug relay ground. If ok. replace relay.
      - LESS THAN BAT. VOLTAGE OR 0 VOLTS → Check yellow wire from glow plug relay to controller. If ok. replace controller.

Fig. 25C Diesel engine electrical diagnosis, part 4 of 4. 1980–83 Type 2

Fig. 26 Diesel engine electrical system. 1980-83 Cutlass

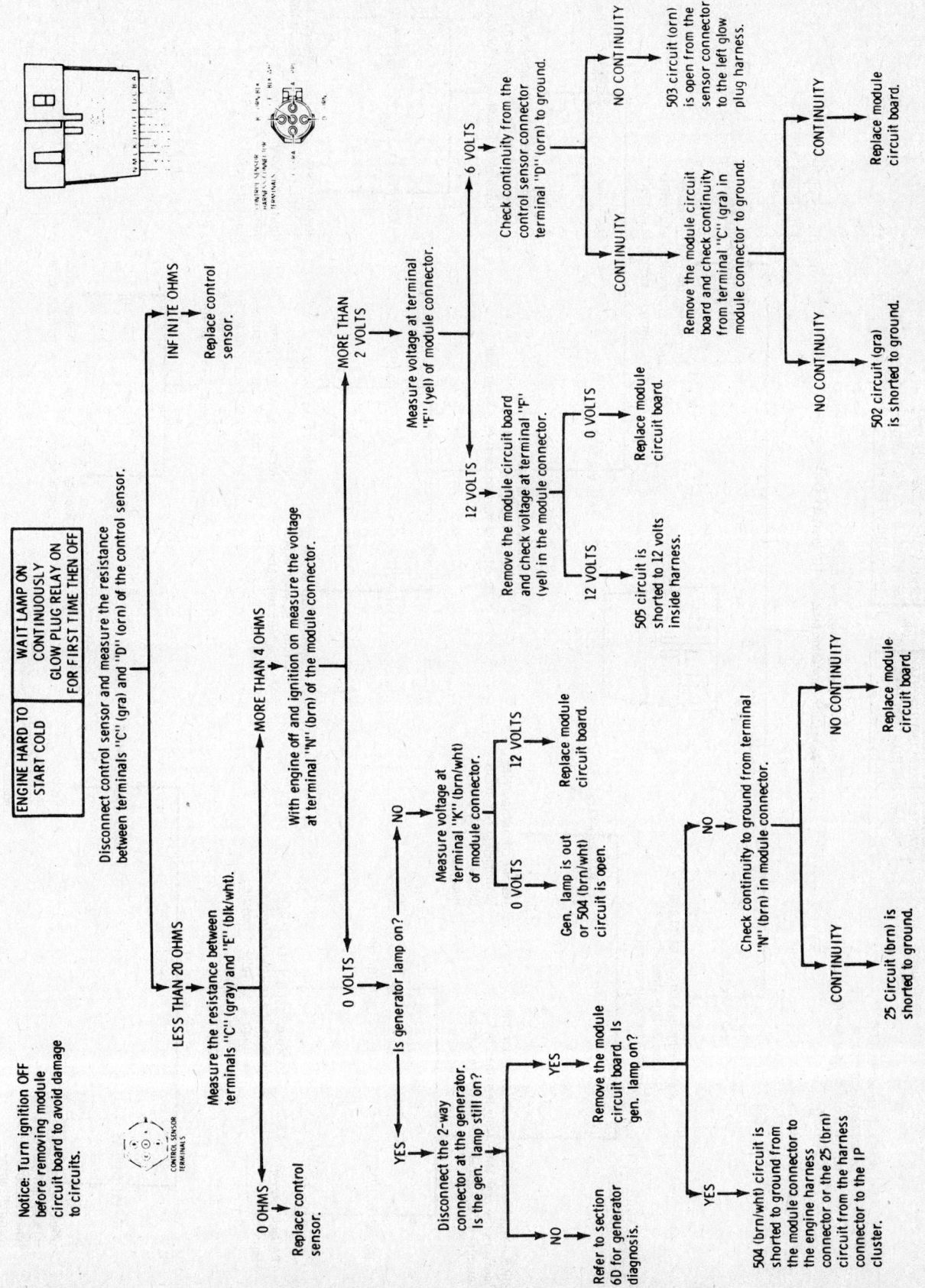

Fig. 27 Diesel engine electrical diagnosis, part 1 of 10. 1980-83 Cutlass

OLDSMOBILE—88, 98, Toronado, 1977—79 Omega, Cutlass Exc. Ciera

Fig. 27A   Diesel engine electrical diagnosis, part 2 of 10. 1980–83 Cutlass Exc. Ciera

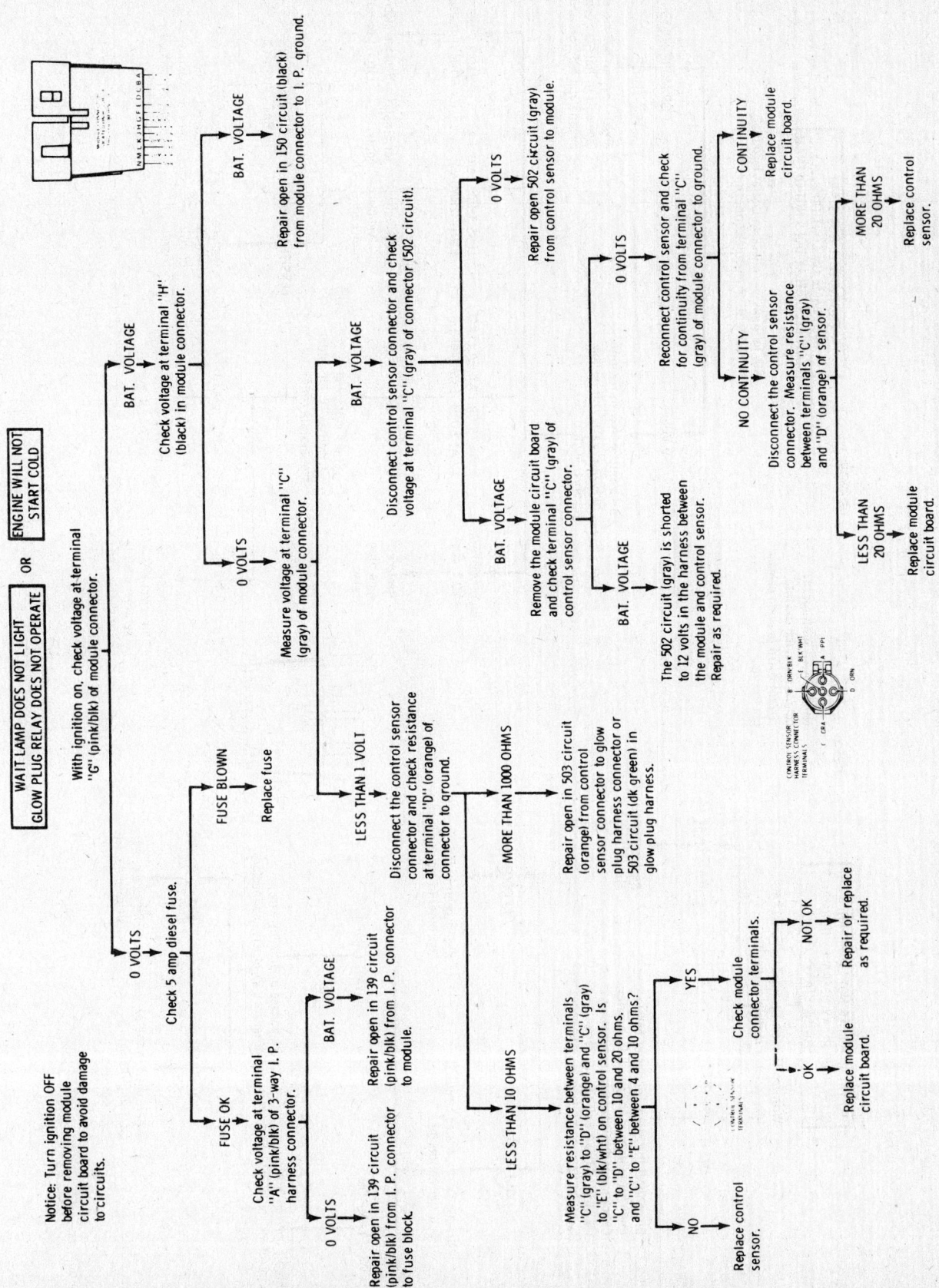

Fig. 27B   Diesel engine electrical diagnosis, part 3 of 10. 1980–83 Cutlass

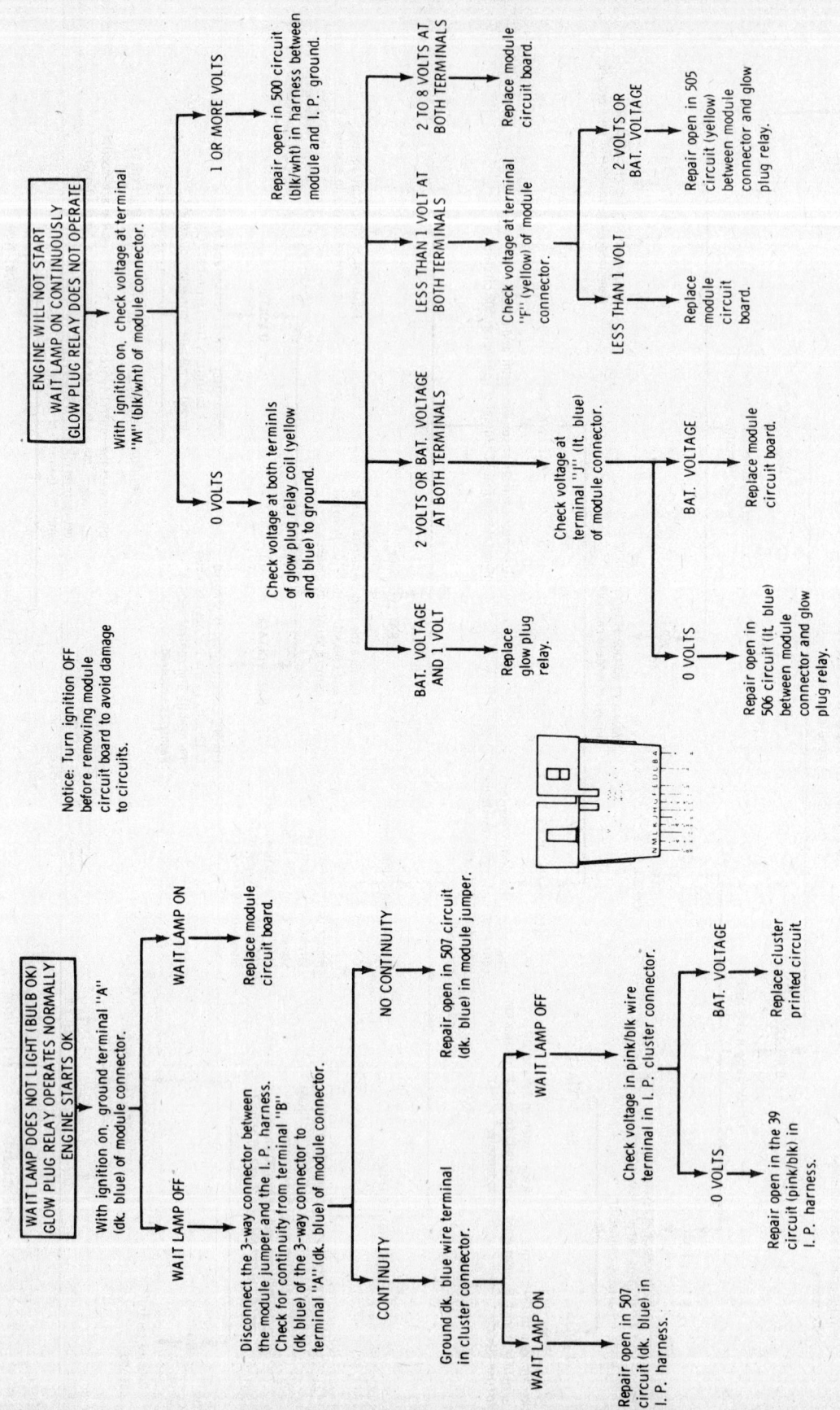

Fig. 27C Diesel engine electrical diagnosis, part 4 of 10. 1980–83 Cutlass

WAIT LAMP ON CONTINUOUSLY GLOW PLUG RELAY OPERATES NORMAL ENGINE STARTS AFTER NORMAL WAIT PERIOD

With ignition on, disconnect the 3-way connector between the module jumper and the I. P. harness.

WAIT LAMP ON → Disconnect the cluster printed circuit connector.

WAIT LAMP ON → Locate and repair short in cluster printed circuit or connector.

WAIT LAMP OFF → Repair short in 507 circuit (dk blue) from 3-way connector to cluster connector.

WAIT LAMP OFF → Reconnect 3-way connector and remove module circuit board.

WAIT LAMP ON → Repair short in 507 circuit (dk blue) between module jumper connector and module connector.

WAIT LAMP OFF → Replace module circuit board.

Notice: Turn ignition OFF before removing module circuit board to avoid damage to circuits.

GENERATOR LAMP DOES NOT OPERATE WAIT LAMP AND GLOW PLUG RELAY OPERATE NORMAL (BULB OK)

Check connections to generator to see if they are properly connected.

NOT CONNECTED → Repair connector.

CONNECTED → With ignition on and engine off, ground terminal "K" (brn/wht) of module connector.

GENERATOR LAMP ON → Ground terminal "N" (brown) of module connector.

GENERATOR LAMP OFF → Repair open in 504 circuit (brn/wht) from module connector to engine harness and/or 25 circuit (brown) to cluster connector.

GENERATOR LAMP OFF → Replace module circuit board.

GENERATOR LAMP ON → Ground the 25 circuit (brown) at the generator connector.

GENERATOR LAMP OFF → Repair open in 25 circuit (brown) from module connector to generator connector.

GENERATOR LAMP ON → Repair generator.

Fig. 27D Diesel engine electrical diagnosis, part 5 of 10. 1980—83 Cutlass

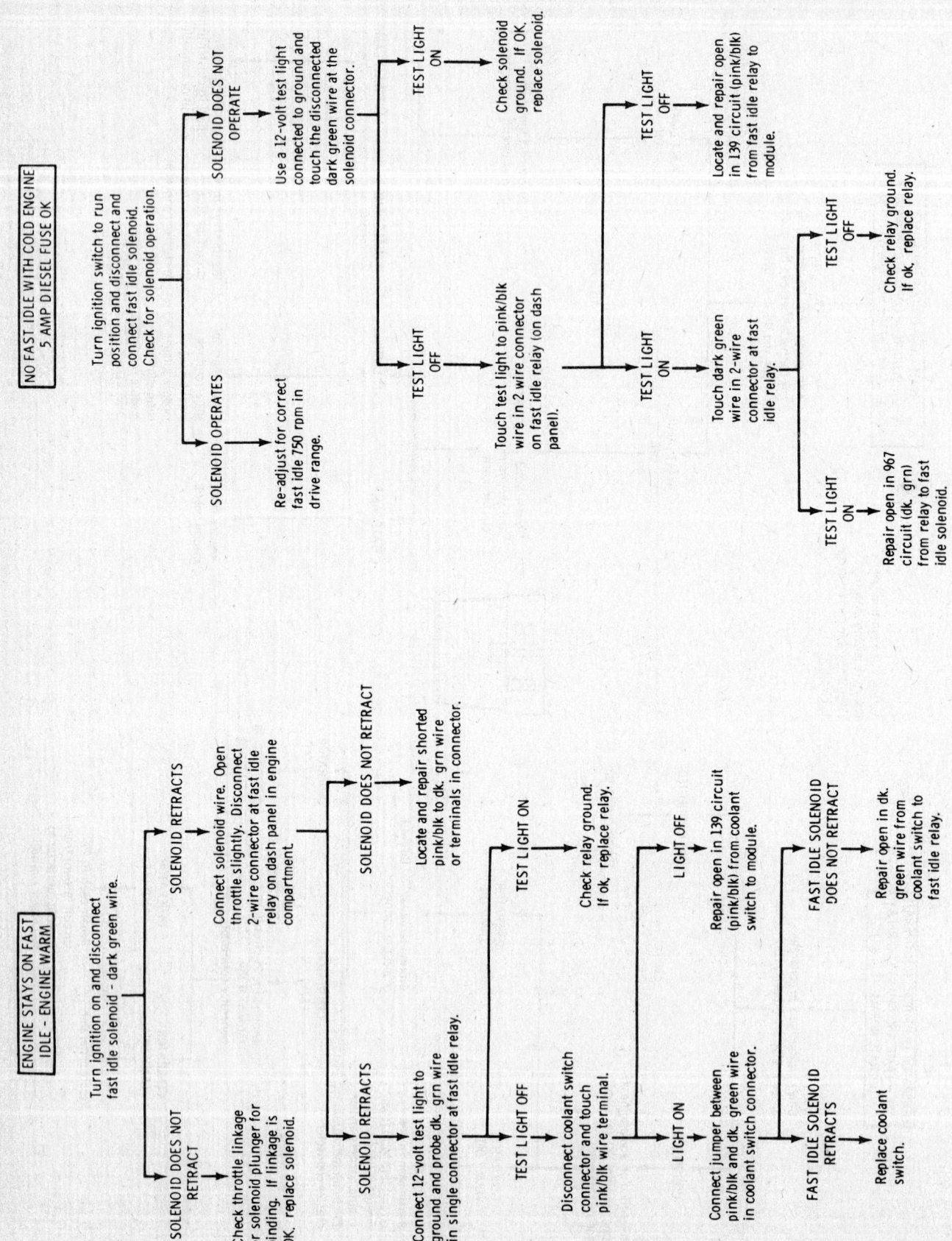

NO FAST IDLE WITH COLD ENGINE 5 AMP DIESEL FUSE OK

Turn ignition switch to run position and disconnect and connect fast idle solenoid. Check for solenoid operation.

SOLENOID DOES NOT OPERATE

Use a 12-volt test light connected to ground and touch the disconnected dark green wire at the solenoid connector.

TEST LIGHT ON

Check solenoid ground. If OK, replace solenoid.

TEST LIGHT OFF

Touch test light to pink/blk wire in 2 wire connector on fast idle relay (on dash panel).

TEST LIGHT OFF

Locate and repair open in 139 circuit (pink/blk) from fast idle relay to module.

TEST LIGHT ON

Touch dark green wire in 2-wire connector at fast idle relay.

TEST LIGHT OFF

Check relay ground. If ok, replace relay.

TEST LIGHT ON

Repair open in 967 circuit (dk. grn) from relay to fast idle solenoid.

SOLENOID OPERATES

Re-adjust for correct fast idle 750 rpm in drive range.

ENGINE STAYS ON FAST IDLE - ENGINE WARM

Turn ignition on and disconnect fast idle solenoid - dark green wire.

SOLENOID RETRACTS

Connect solenoid wire. Open throttle slightly. Disconnect 2-wire connector at fast idle relay on dash panel in engine compartment

SOLENOID DOES NOT RETRACT

Locate and repair shorted pink/blk to dk. grn wire or terminals in connector.

TEST LIGHT ON

Check relay ground. If ok. replace relay.

LIGHT OFF

Repair open in 139 circuit (pink/blk) from coolant switch to module.

FAST IDLE SOLENOID DOES NOT RETRACT

Repair open in dk. green wire from coolant switch to fast idle relay.

SOLENOID DOES NOT RETRACT

Check throttle linkage or solenoid plunger for binding. If linkage is OK. replace solenoid.

SOLENOID RETRACTS

Connect 12-volt test light to ground and probe dk. grn wire in single connector at fast idle relay.

TEST LIGHT OFF

Disconnect coolant switch connector and touch pink/blk wire terminal.

LIGHT ON

Connect jumper between pink/blk and dk. green wire in coolant switch connector.

FAST IDLE SOLENOID RETRACTS

Replace coolant switch.

Fig. 27E   Diesel electrical diagnosis, part 6 of 10. 1980–83 Cutlass with V8 engine

GLOW PLUG RELAY BUZZING

Notice: Turn ignition OFF before removing module circuit board to avoid damage to circuits.

WAIT LAMP AND GLOW PLUG RELAY NORMAL, CAR WON'T START

Disconnect the 3-way connector between control sensor harness and module jumper harness. Check for continuity between terminal "E" (orange) of module connector and terminal "C" (orange) of jumper connector.

Disconnect connector from each glow plug and check continuity to ground from glow plug terminal.

CONTINUITY — NO CONTINUITY

NO CONTINUITY — CONTINUITY

Replace module circuit board.

Repair open in 503 circuit (orange) between module connector and jumper connector.

Replace bad glow plugs.

Measure continuity from glow plug relay output to each glow plug connector.

CONTINUITY — NO CONTINUITY

Check fuel system.

Repair or replace glow plug harness.

Fig. 27F   Diesel engine electrical diagnosis, part 7 of 10. 1980—83 Cutlass with V8 engine

Fig. 27G   Water In Fuel System wiring circuit

Fig. 27H   Water in Fuel System fuel level sender and water detector

Fig. 27I   Checking water detector operation

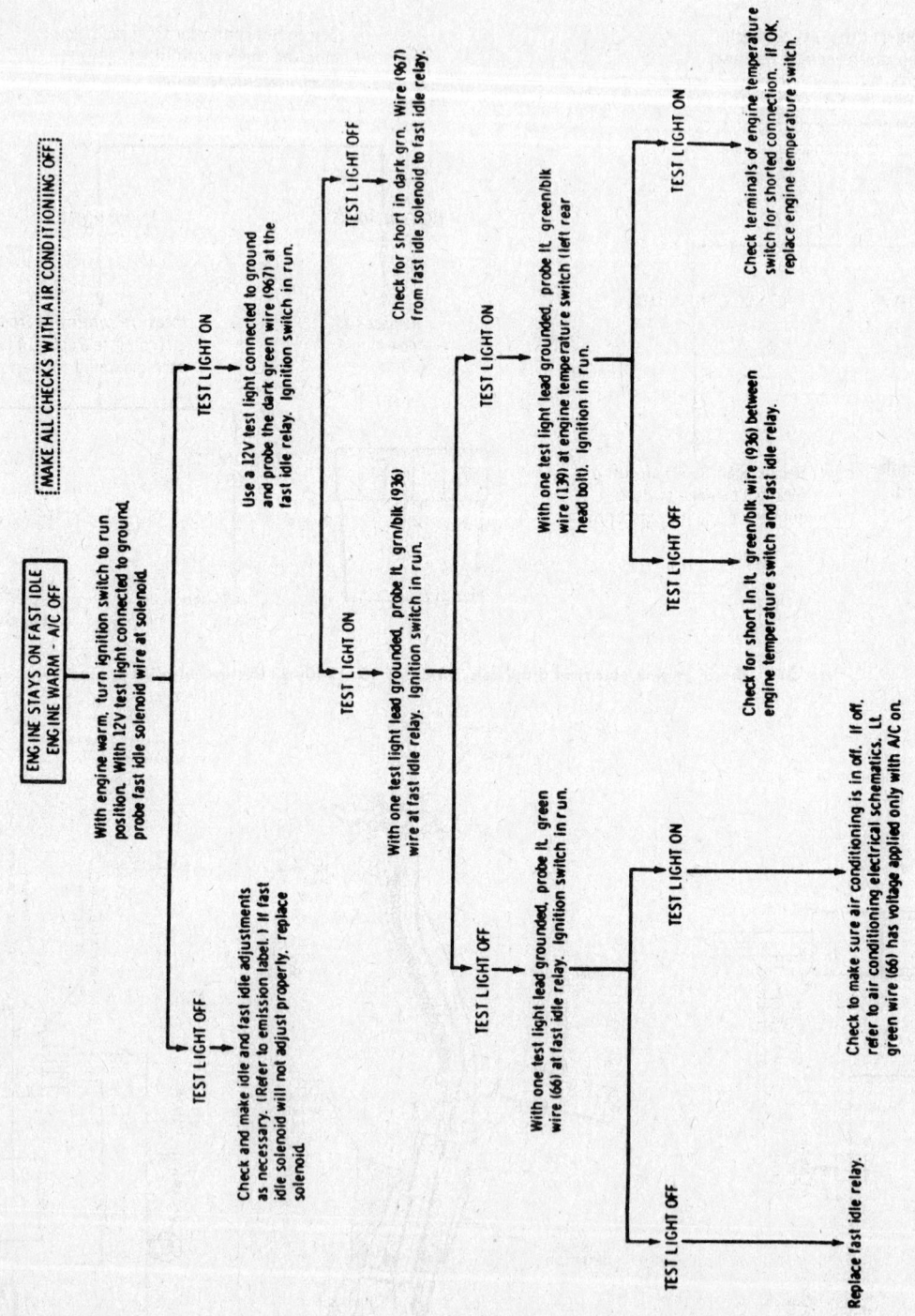

Fig. 27J   Diesel engine electrical diagnosis, part 8 of 10. 1982—83 Cutlass V6 engine

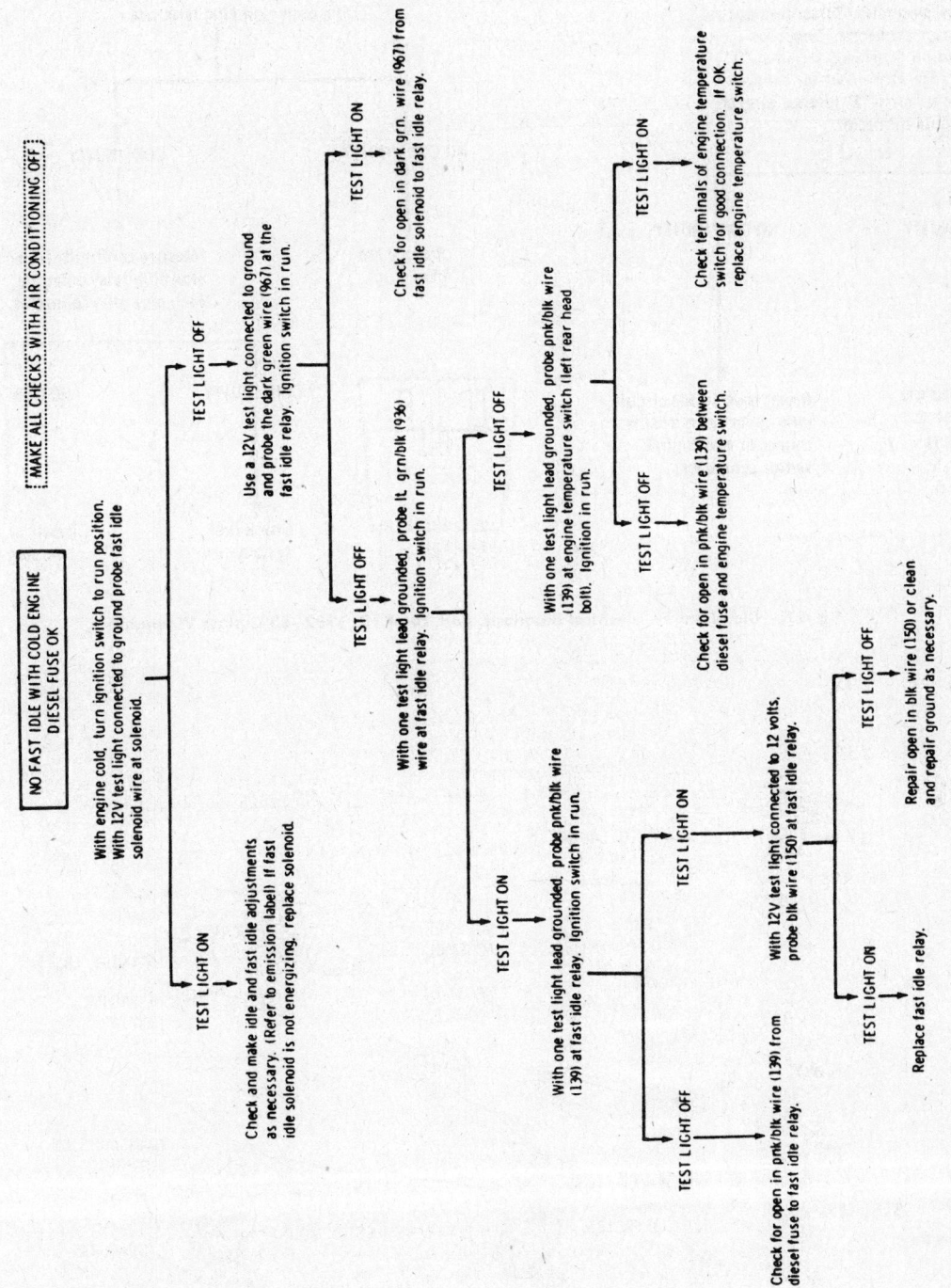

MAKE ALL CHECKS WITH AIR CONDITIONING OFF

NO FAST IDLE WITH COLD ENGINE
DIESEL FUSE OK

With engine cold, turn ignition switch to run position.
With 12V test light connected to ground probe fast idle
solenoid wire at solenoid.

TEST LIGHT ON

Check and make idle and fast idle adjustments
as necessary. (Refer to emission label) If fast
idle solenoid is not energizing, replace solenoid.

TEST LIGHT OFF

Use a 12V test light connected to ground
and probe the dark green wire (967) at the
fast idle relay. Ignition switch in run.

TEST LIGHT ON

Check for open in dark grn. wire (967) from
fast idle solenoid to fast idle relay.

TEST LIGHT OFF

With one test light lead grounded, probe lt. grn/blk (936)
wire at fast idle relay. Ignition switch in run.

TEST LIGHT OFF

With one test light lead grounded, probe pnk/blk wire
(139) at engine temperature switch (left rear head
bolt). Ignition in run.

TEST LIGHT ON

Check terminals of engine temperature
switch for good connection. If OK,
replace engine temperature switch.

TEST LIGHT OFF

Check for open in pnk/blk wire (139) between
diesel fuse and engine temperature switch.

TEST LIGHT ON

With one test light lead grounded, probe pnk/blk wire
(139) at fast idle relay. Ignition switch in run.

TEST LIGHT OFF

Check for open in pnk/blk wire (139) from
diesel fuse to fast idle relay.

TEST LIGHT ON

With 12V test light connected to 12 volts,
probe blk wire (150) at fast idle relay.

TEST LIGHT ON

Repair open in blk wire (150) or clean
and repair ground as necessary.

TEST LIGHT OFF

Replace fast idle relay.

Fig. 27K   Diesel engine electrical diagnosis, part 9 of 10. 1982–83 Cutlass V6 engine

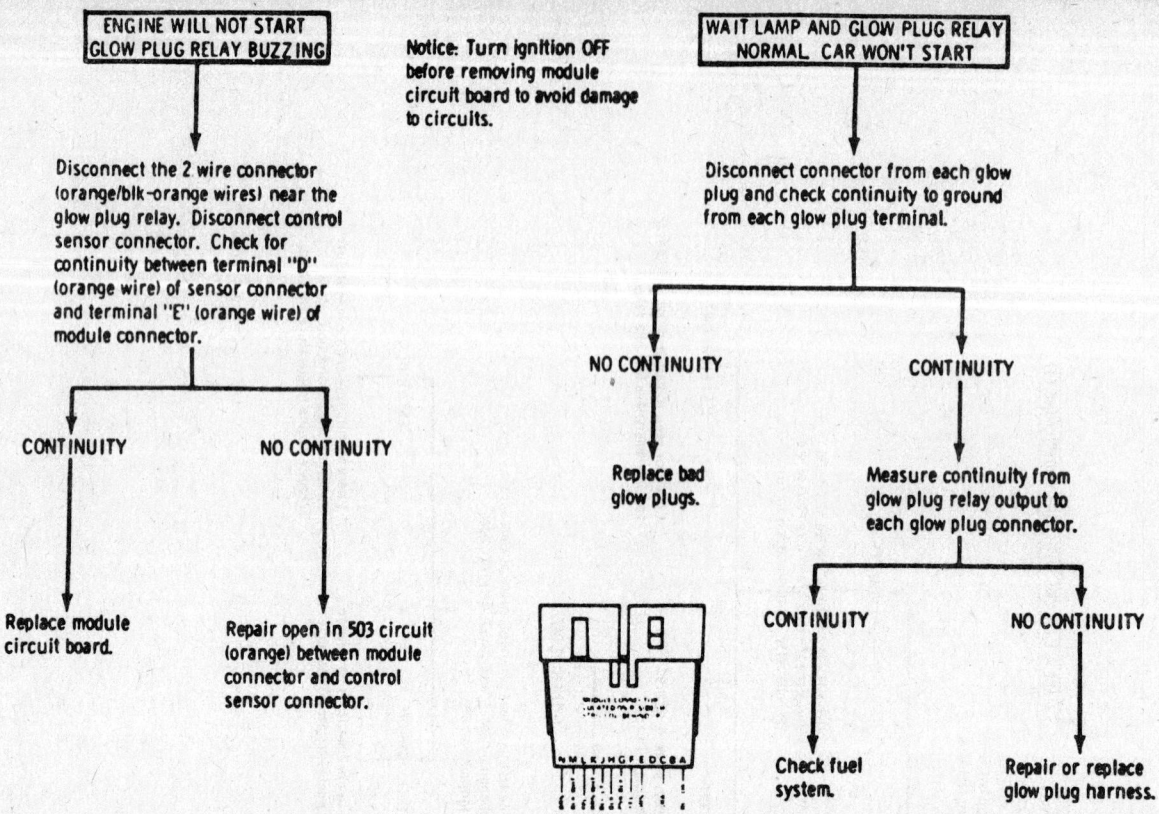

ENGINE WILL NOT START GLOW PLUG RELAY BUZZING

↓

Disconnect the 2 wire connector (orange/blk–orange wires) near the glow plug relay. Disconnect control sensor connector. Check for continuity between terminal "D" (orange wire) of sensor connector and terminal "E" (orange wire) of module connector.

CONTINUITY → Replace module circuit board.

NO CONTINUITY → Repair open in 503 circuit (orange) between module connector and control sensor connector.

Notice: Turn ignition OFF before removing module circuit board to avoid damage to circuits.

WAIT LAMP AND GLOW PLUG RELAY NORMAL. CAR WON'T START

↓

Disconnect connector from each glow plug and check continuity to ground from each glow plug terminal.

NO CONTINUITY → Replace bad glow plugs.

CONTINUITY → Measure continuity from glow plug relay output to each glow plug connector.

CONTINUITY → Check fuel system.

NO CONTINUITY → Repair or replace glow plug harness.

Fig. 27L   Diesel engine electrical diagnosis, part 10 of 10. 1982–83 Cutlass V6 engine

Fig. 28   Diesel engine mounts. 1978 88 & 98

Fig. 28A Diesel engine mount. 1979-83 88 & 98

Fig. 28B Diesel engine mount. 1979-83 Cutlass V8 engine

MOUNTING ASSEMBLY TAB MUST BE INSTALLED INTO SLOT IN RESTRICTOR.

LOCK PLATE

* APPLY 1051343 LOC-TITE #242 OR EQUIVALENT TO THESE BOLTS

R. H. ENGINE MOUNTING BRACKET

61 N·m ✱ (45 FT. LBS.)

RESTRICTOR

47 N·m ✱ (35 FT. LBS.)

STEERING PUMP BRACKET

70 N·m (51 FT. LBS.)

60 N·m (44 FT. LBS.)

L. H. ENGINE MOUNTING BRACKET

61 N·m ✱ (45 FT. LBS.)

ENGINE MOUNTING ASSEMBLY

POSITIONING TAB ON MOUNTING ASSEMBLY MUST BE INSTALLED INTO HOLE/SLOT LOCATED ON FRAME ASSEMBLY

FRAME

100 N·m (74 FT. LBS.)

FRONT OF CAR

ENGINE MOUNTS

Fig. 28C   Diesel engine mount. 1978–83 Toronado

14. Disconnect left hand exhaust pipe from manifold.
15. On left side of engine, remove through bolt and bracket securing final drive to engine.
16. Raise and support vehicle.
17. Remove flywheel shield.
18. Disconnect right hand exhaust pipe from manifold.
19. Disconnect starter motor wiring and remove starter motor.
20. Remove converter to flywheel bolts. Mark location of converter on flywheel for alignment during installation.
21. Remove splash shield.
22. Remove engine front mounting attaching nuts.
23. Remove two bolts securing right hand output shaft support brackets. Using a sharp tool, scribe a mark around the washers as far as possible. Use these scribe marks to position bracket upon installation.
24. Remove lower right hand transmission to engine attaching bolts. One bolt retains

the modulator line clip.
25. Use a suitable length of chain to retain final drive in vehicle.
26. Lower vehicle and attaching suitable engine lifting equipment to engine.
27. Remove the remaining transmission to engine bolts. It may be necessary to raise or lower transmission with a suitable jack to facilitate bolt removal.
28. Raise engine and remove from vehicle.
29. Reverse procedure to install.

INTAKE MANIFOLD, REPLACE

V8 Engine

1. Disconnect ground cables from batteries.
2. Remove air cleaner assembly.
3. Drain cooling system, then disconnect

75 N·m (55 FT. LBS.)

52 N·m 38 FT. LBS.

FRONT MOUNT

BRACKET

WASHER

50 N·m (37 FT. LBS.)

Fig. 28D   Motor mounts. 1982–83 Cutlass V6 engine

BREATHER CAP AND VALVE ASSY.

FLOW CONTROL VALVE

VENT PIPE TO NIPPLE CONNECTOR

VENTILATION PIPE

VENTILATION ELBOW

VENTILATION FILTER ASSEMBLY

Fig. 28E   Crankcase ventilation system. V8 engine

Fig. 29 Air crossover installation. Typical

Fig. 30 Vacuum pump & oil pump drive assembly

Fig. 31 Intake manifold drain tube installation

upper radiator hose and thermostat by-pass hose from water pump outlet. Disconnect heater hose and vacuum hose from water control valve.

4. Remove breather pipes from valve covers and air crossover, Fig. 28E.
5. Remove air crossover and cap intake manifold, Fig. 29.
6. Disconnect throttle rod and return spring. If equipped with Cruise Control, remove servo.
7. Remove hairpin clip from bellcrank and disconnect the cables. Remove throttle and throttle valve cables from intake manifold brackets and position cables aside.
8. Disconnect wiring as necessary.
9. Disconnect or remove alternator and A/C compressor brackets as necessary.
10. Disconnect fuel line from fuel pump and filter and remove fuel filter and bracket.
11. Disconnect lines from injector nozzles and remove injection pump, refer to "Injection Nozzle Replace, Injection Pump & Lines". Cap all open fuel line lines and fittings.
12. Disconnect fuel return line from injection pump.
13. Disconnect vacuum lines at vacuum pump. Remove vacuum pump, if equipped with A/C, or oil pump drive assembly, if less A/C, Fig. 30.
14. Remove intake manifold drain tube, Fig. 31.
15. Remove intake manifold bolts and the intake manifold.
16. Remove adapter seal and injection pump adapter.
17. Reverse procedure to install. Torque intake manifold bolts in sequence, Fig. 32, to specifications.

V6 Engine

1. Disconnect battery ground cable and remove air cleaner.
2. Drain cooling system, then disconnect upper radiator hose and thermostat by-pass hose from water outlet.
3. Disconnect heater inlet hose and on models equipped with air conditioning, the water valve vacuum line.
4. Disconnect crankcase ventilation pipe from air crossover, Fig. 32A. Remove air crossover.
5. Remove fuel pump and plug all open lines and fittings.
6. Remove fuel injection pump as described under "Injection Pump, Replace".
7. Disconnect electrical connectors as necessary.
8. Remove cruise control servo, if equipped.
9. Disconnect fuel lines and position aside. Disconnect vacuum lines as necessary.
10. Remove drain tube, then remove intermediate pump adapter, Fig. 32B.
11. Remove intake manifold bolts and the intake manifold.
12. Reverse procedure to install. Lubricate intake manifold bolts with engine oil before installing, then torque bolts as specified in sequence shown in Fig. 32C. Apply chassis grease to seal area of intake manifold and pump adapter and to inside and outside diameter of seal and seal area of

tool J-28425 or equivalent. Install seal onto tool, then install seal.

CYLINDER HEAD, REPLACE

SERVICE NOTE

New head bolts with increased torque capacity were introduced into production during March 1980 and are now available, Fig. 32D.

When replacing a cylinder head, it is recommended new head bolts be used if they have not already been installed in the engine. When installing later production model head bolts, be sure to clean and oil the threads. Before installation of the cylinder head, ensure bolt holes are tapped deep enough into the block. Blow out any chips or liquid in the bolt holes. Then position cylinder head on cylinder block without the cylinder head gasket. Install bolt and tighten by hand until bolt head contacts the cylinder head. This will indicate that the holes are tapped deep enough into the block, allowing for proper torque. For cylinder head bolt location, part number and size, refer to Fig. 32E.

A new designed head gasket went into production in March 1981, and is available for service replacement. It can be identified by the use of blue print O sealer instead of orange. This gasket is of the slotted and shim design.

No sealer should be used on the gasket during installation. Also the prechamber shield on the cylinder head must be installed towards the cylinder head, Fig. 32F.

1. Remove intake manifold as outlined previously.

Fig. 32 Intake manifold tightening sequence. V8 engine

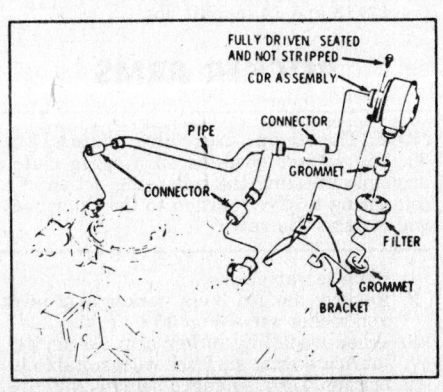

Fig. 32A Crankcase ventilation system. V6 engine

Fig. 32B Removing intermediate pump adapter. V6 engine

Fig. 32C   Intake manifold bolt tightening sequence. V6 engine

→ Identified By Head Markings

Fig. 32D   Cylinder head bolt markings

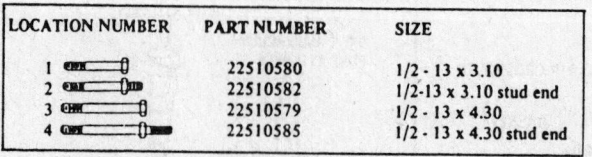

LOCATION NUMBER	PART NUMBER	SIZE
1	22510580	1/2 - 13 x 3.10
2	22510582	1/2-13 x 3.10 stud end
3	22510579	1/2 - 13 x 4.30
4	22510585	1/2 - 13 x 4.30 stud end

Fig. 32E   Cylinder head bolt identification

Fig. 32F   New design cylinder head gasket

Fig. 33   Pre-chamber installation

Fig. 34   Cylinder head tightening sequence. V8 engine

2. Remove valve cover. It may be necessary to remove any interfering accessory brackets.
3. Disconnect glow plug wiring.
4. Remove ground strap from right cylinder head, if removing.
5. Remove rocker arm bolts, pivots, rocker arms and push rod. Note locations of valve train components so they can be installed in original locations.
6. Remove fuel return lines from injection nozzles if equipped.
7. Remove exhaust manifold.
8. Remove engine block drain plug on side of block that cylinder head is being removed.
9. Remove cylinder head bolts and cylinder head. On 1982 V8 diesel remove TCC temperature switch located on exposed right rear cylinder head bolt.

10. If necessary to remove pre-chamber, remove a glow plug or injection nozzle, then tap out pre-chamber with a suitable drift, Fig. 33.
11. Reverse procedure to install. Do not use any sealing compound on cylinder head gasket. On 8 cylinder engines, torque cylinder head bolts in sequence, Fig. 34, to 100 ft. lbs., then to 130 ft. lbs. On 6 cylinder engines, torque cylinder head bolts except bolts 5, 6, 11, 12, 13 and 14, Fig. 34A, to 142 ft. lbs. Torque bolts 5, 6, 11, 12, 13 and 14 to 59 ft. lbs.

ROCKER ARMS

NOTE: This engine uses valve rotators, Fig. 35. The rotator operates on a sprag clutch principle utilizing the collapsing action of a coil spring to give rotation to the rotor body which turns the valve.

1. Remove valve cover.
2. Remove flanged bolts, rocker arm pivot and rocker arms, Fig. 35.
3. When installing rocker arm assemblies, lubricate wear surfaces with suitable lubricant. Torque flanged bolts to 25 ft. lbs. On 8 cylinder engines or 28 ft. lbs. on 6 cylinder engines.

TORQUE ALL BOLTS (EXCEPT 5, 6, 11, 12, 13 & 14) TO 193 N·m (142 FT. LBS.). NUMBERS 5, 6, 11, 12, 13 & 14 TORQUE TO 80 N·m (59 FT. LBS.).

Fig. 34A   Cylinder head bolt tightening sequence. V6 engine

Fig. 35   Cylinder head exploded view

VALVE ROTATORS

The rotator operates on a Sprag clutch principle utilizing the collapsing action of coil spring to give rotation to the rotor body which turns the valve, Fig. 35.

To check rotator action, draw a line across rotator body and down the collar. Operate engine at 1500 rpm, rotator body should move around collar. Rotator action can be in either direction. Replace rotator if no movement is noted.

When servicing valves, valve stem tips should be checked for improper wear pattern which could indicate a defective valve rotator, Fig. 36.

Fig. 36   Checking valve stem for rotator malfunction

VALVE LIFT SPECS.

Engine	Year	Intake	Exhaust
V8-260, 350 Diesel	1978—82	.375	.376
V6-262 Diesel	1982	.375	.375

VALVE ARRANGEMENT

V8-260, 350 Diesel . . . . I-E-I-E-E-I-E-I
V6-262 Diesel . . . . I-E-E-I-E-I

VALVE TIMING

Intake Opens Before TDC

Engine	Year	Degrees
V8-260, 350 Diesel	1978—82	16
V6-262 Diesel	1982	16

VALVES

Whenever a new valve is installed or after grinding valves, it is necessary to measure the valve stem height with the special tool as shown in Fig. 37.

There should be at least .015 inch clearance between the gauge and end of valve stem. If clearance is less than .015 inch, remove valve and grind end of valve stem as required.

Check valve rotator height, Fig. 38. If valve stem end is less than .005 inch above rotator, the valve is too short and a new valve must be installed.

VALVE GUIDES

Valve stem guides are not replaceable, due to being cast in place. If valve guide bores are worn excessively, they can be reamed oversize.

If a standard valve guide bore is being reamed, use a .003″ or .005″ oversize reamer. For the .010″ oversize valve guide bore, use a .013″ oversize reamer. If too large a reamer is used and the spiraling is removed, it is possible that the valve will not receive the proper lubrication.

NOTE: Occasionally a valve guide will be oversize as manufactured. These are marked on the cylinder head as shown in Fig. 39. If no markings are present, the guide bores are standard. If oversize markings are present, any valve replacement will require an oversize valve. Service valves are available in standard diameters as well as .003″, .005″, .010″ and .013″ oversize.

Fig. 37   Measuring valve stem height

Fig. 38   Measuring valve rotator height

VALVE LIFTERS, REPLACE

NOTE: Some engines have both standard and .010 inch oversize valve lifters. The .010 inch oversize valve lifters are etched with a "0" on the side of the lifter. Also, the cylinder block will be marked if an oversize lifter is used, Fig. 40.

1. Remove intake manifold as outlined previously.
2. Remove valve covers, rocker arm assemblies and push rods. Note location of valve train components so they can be installed in original position.
3. On 1981–83 models, remove the hydraulic lifter retainer bolts, Fig. 40A.
4. Remove valve lifters.

Fig. 39 Valve guide bore marking

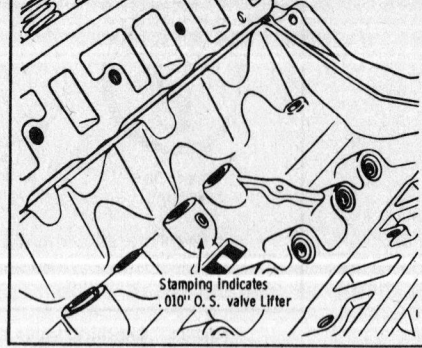

Fig. 40 Oversize valve lifter bore marking

Fig. 40A Hydraulic roller lifter retainer and guide. 1981–83 (Typical)

Fig. 41 Valve lifter exploded view. 1978–80

Fig. 41A Hydraulic roller lifter assembly exploded view. 1981–83

5. Reverse procedure to install.

NOTE: Plungers are not interchangeable because they are selectively fitted to the bodies at the factory.

If plunger and body appear satisfactory blow off with air to remove all particles of dirt. Install the plunger in the body without other parts and check for free movement. A simple test is to be sure that the plunger will drop of its own weight in the body, Figs. 41 and 41A.

FRONT OIL SEAL, REPLACE

1. Disconnect ground cables from batteries.
2. Remove accessory drive belts.
3. Remove crankshaft pulley and harmonic balancer.
4. Using tool BT-6406, remove front oil seal, Fig. 42.
5. Apply suitable sealer to outside diameter of new oil seal.
6. File .020 inch from flange of tool No. J-25264, Fig. 43, to prevent tool from contacting oil slinger before seal is properly seated in front cover.
7. Using tool BT-6611, install new oil seal, Fig. 44.
8. Install harmonic balancer and crankshaft pulley.
9. Install and tension accessory drive belts.

ENGINE FRONT COVER, REPLACE

1. Disconnect ground cables from batteries.
2. Drain cooling system and disconnect radiator hoses and bypass hose.
3. Remove all drive belts, fan and pulley, crankshaft pulley and harmonic balancer, and accessory brackets.
4. Remove timing indicator and water pump.
5. Remove remaining front cover attaching bolts and the front cover. Also, remove the dowel pins. It may be necessary to grind a flat on the dowel pin to provide a rough surface for gripping.
6. Grind a chamfer on one end of each dowel pin, Fig. 45.
7. Cut excess material from front end of oil pan gasket on each side of cylinder block.
8. Trim approximately 1/8 inch from each end of new front pan seal.
9. Install new front cover gasket and apply suitable sealer to gasket around coolant holes.
10. Apply RTV sealer to mating surfaces of cylinder block, oil pan and front cover.
11. Place front cover on cylinder block and press downward to compress seal. Rotate cover right and left and guide oil pan seal into cavity with a small screwdriver.
12. Apply engine oil to bolts.
13. Install two bolts finger tight to retain cover.
14. Install the two dowel pins, chamfered end first.
15. Install timing indicator and water pump and torque bolts as shown in Fig. 46.
16. Install harmonic balancer and crankshaft pulley.
17. Install accessory brackets.
18. Install fan and pulley and drive belts.
19. Connect radiator hoses and bypass hose.
20. Connect ground cables to batteries.

INSTALL SEAL "FLUSH"
BT-6405 OR J-25264
BT-6611 OR J-25288

Fig. 44 Front oil seal installation

FRONT SEAL
BT-6406

Fig. 42 Front oil seal removal

BT-6405 OR J-25264
FILE OFF .020" HERE

Fig. 43 Modifying tool for front oil seal installation

Chamfer

Fig. 45 Dowel pin chamfer

Fig. 46 Engine front cover installation. Typical

Fig. 47 Valve timing marks

TIMING CHAIN & GEARS, REPLACE

1. Remove front cover as outlined previously. On 6 cylinder engines, loosen rocker arm pivot bolts evenly so that some lash is present between rocker arms and valves.
2. Remove oil slinger, cam gear, crank gear and timing chain.
3. Remove fuel pump eccentric from crankshaft.
4. Install key in crankshaft, if removed.
5. Install fuel pump eccentric, if removed.
6. Install cam gear, crank gear and timing chain with timing marks aligned, Fig. 47.

NOTE: With the timing marks aligned in Fig. 47, No. 6 cylinder is in the firing position. To place No. 1 cylinder in the firing position, rotate crankshaft one complete revolution. This will bring the camshaft gear mark to top and No. 1 cylinder will be in the firing position.

7. Install oil slinger.
8. Install front cover.

CAMSHAFT & INJECTION PUMP DRIVE & DRIVEN GEARS, REPLACE

1. Disconnect ground cables from batteries.
2. Drain cooling system.
3. Remove radiator upper baffle.
4. Disconnect upper radiator hose at water outlet and hose support clamp.
5. Disconnect cooler lines at radiator.
6. Remove fan shroud and radiator.
7. Remove intake manifold as outlined previously.
8. Remove engine front cover as outlined previously.
9. Remove valve covers.
10. Remove rocker arm bolts, pivots, rocker arms and push rod. Note valve train component locations to install components in original locations.
11. If equipped with A/C, discharge refrigerant system and remove condenser.
12. On all models, remove timing chain and gears as outlined previously.
13. Position camshaft dowel pin at 3 o'clock position.
14. While holding the camshaft rearward and rocking the injection pump driven gear slide, slide the injection pump drive gear from camshaft.
15. Remove injection pump adapter, snap ring, selective washer, injection pump driven gear and spring, Fig. 48.

NOTE: On some 1980 diesel vehicles, the fuel injection pump shaft spring, Fig. 48, may be missing. The absence of this spring could affect the idle characteristics of the engine. The spring is available as part No. 22502241.

16. Slide camshaft from front of engine.
17. Reverse procedure to install. Check injection pump driven gear end play. If end play is not .002–.006 inch, replace selective washer, Fig. 48. Selective washers are available from .080 to .115 inch in increments of .003 inch.

PISTON & ROD ASSEMBLE

1978-81 V8

Assemble piston to rod and install in cylinder block. On 8 cylinder engines, the piston is installed with the valve depression facing toward the crankshaft. Also, there are two

Fig. 49 Piston & rod installation. 1978-81 V8 engine

Fig. 49A Piston & rod assembly. 1982-83 V6-262 & V8-350

Fig. 48 Fuel injection pump driven gear installation

Fig. 50 Main bearing identification

different pistons used in this engine. In cylinder numbers 1, 2, 3 and 4, the large valve depression faces the front of the engine, Fig. 49. In cylinder numbers 5, 6, 7 and 8 the large valve depression faces the rear of the engine, Fig. 49. The pistons are interchangeable between cylinder numbers 1, 3, 6 and 8 and 2, 4, 5 and 7. Check connecting rod side clearance. Clearance should be .006–.020 inch.

1982–83 V6 & V8

Install piston and rod assembly so that notch at top of piston is facing toward front of engine, Fig. 49A. Check connecting rod side clearance. Clearance should be .006–.020 inch on V8 engines or .008–.021 on V6 engines.

PISTONS, RINGS & PINS

Pistons are available in standard sizes and oversizes of .010 and .030" on 8 cylinder engines or in standard size and oversize of .010 inch on 6 cylinder engines.

Rings are available in standard sizes and oversizes of .010 and .030".

Fig. 52 Trimming upper rear main bearing seal

MAIN & ROD BEARINGS

Main bearings are available in standard sizes and undersizes of .0005, .0010 and .0015 inch. The amount of undersize and part number is stamped on the bearing shell, Fig. 50.

Rod bearings are available in standard sizes and an undersize of .010 inch.

REAR CRANKSHAFT SEAL SERVICE

Since the braided fabric seal used on these engines can be replaced only when the crankshaft is removed, the following repair procedure is recommended.

1. Remove oil pan and bearing cap.
2. Drive end of old seal gently into groove, using a suitable tool, until packed tight. This may vary between 1/4 and 3/4 inch depending on amount of pack required.
3. Repeat previous step for other end of seal.
4. Measure and note amount that seal was driven up on one side. Using the old seal removed from bearing cap, cut a length of seal the amount previously noted plus 1/16 inch.
5. Repeat previous step for other side of seal.
6. Pack cut lengths of seal into appropriate side of seal groove. A packing tool, BT-6433, Fig. 51, may be used since the tool has been machined to provide a built-in stop. Use tool BT-6436 to trim the seal flush with block, Fig. 52.
7. Install new seal in lower bearing cap.

OIL PAN, REPLACE

NOTE: On 1978 engines, the recommended diesel engine oil designation is SE/CD. On 1979–80 engines, the recommended diesel engine oil designation is SE/CC. On 1981 engines, the recommended diesel engine oil is SF/CC, SF/CD and SE/CC. On 1982–83 engines the recommended diesel engine oil is SF/CC or SF/CD.

1978–83 Cutlass, 88, 98

1. Disconnect ground cables from batteries.
2. Remove oil pump drive and vacuum pump, if equipped with A/C, or oil pump drive, if less A/C.
3. Remove oil dipstick.
4. Remove radiator upper support and fan shroud attaching screws.
5. Raise and support vehicle and drain oil pan.
6. Remove flywheel cover.
7. Disconnect exhaust and crossover pipes from exhaust manifold.
8. Remove oil cooler lines at filter base.
9. Disconnect starter wiring and remove starter.
10. Remove engine mounts from engine block, then raise front of engine with suitable equipment.
11. Remove oil pan attaching bolts and the oil pan.
12. Reverse procedure to install. Torque oil pan attaching bolts to 10 ft. lbs.

1979 Toronado

1. Disconnect battery ground cable.
2. Disconnect shroud from upper radiator support.

Fig. 51 Packing upper rear main bearing seal

3. Remove right hand axle cotter pin, retainer and nut.
4. Raise vehicle and remove right wheel.
5. Disconnect right hand tie rod end using tool J-6627 or BT 7101.
6. Disconnect right hand upper ball joint.
7. Remove bolts attaching drive axle to right hand output shaft, then the output shaft.
8. Disconnect starter wiring and remove starter.
9. Remove splash shield.
10. Disconnect pitman arm and idler arm from intermediate rod using tool J-24319-01 or a suitable puller.
11. Drain pan oil.
12. Remove front engine mount to frame nuts.
13. Disconnect shroud from lower radiator support.
14. Using suitable equipment, raise the front of the engine.
15. Remove the right engine mount.
16. Remove oil pan attaching bolts and oil pan.
17. Reverse procedure to install. Torque oil pan attaching bolts to 10 ft. lbs.

1980–83 Toronado

1. Disconnect battery ground cables.
2. Remove three final drive to transmission bolts, then raise and support vehicle.
3. Disconnect frame brace retaining bolts.

Fig. 53 Oil pump installation. Typical

Fig. 54 Oil pump disassembled

Fig. 55 Oil pump driveshaft extension. V8 engines

Fig. 55A Installing fuel line stud & clip assembly

Disconnect idler arm and pitman arm from relay rod.
4. Disconnect drive axles from output shafts.
5. Disconnect battery cable bracket from output shaft support.
6. Disconnect output shaft support from engine block.
7. Position suitable jack under final drive, then remove final drive.
8. Remove splash shield and starter motor.
9. Drain oil, then remove oil pan.

NOTE: To remove oil pan on 1982–83 models, engine must be raised 1–1½ inch using tool No. BT-6501, or equivalent.

10. Reverse procedure to install.

OIL PUMP, REPLACE & SERVICE

Replacement

1. Remove oil pan as outlined previously.
2. Remove oil pump to rear main bearing cap attaching bolts, Fig. 53.
3. Remove oil pump and drive shaft extension.
4. Reverse procedure to install. Torque attaching bolts to 35 ft. lbs.

Service

Disassembly
1. Remove oil pump drive shaft extension, Fig. 54. Do not attempt to remove washers from drive shaft extension. The drive shaft extension and washers is serviced as an assembly.
2. Remove cotter pin, spring and pressure regulator valve.

NOTE: Apply pressure on pressure regulator bore before removing cotter pin since the spring is under pressure.

3. Remove oil pump cover attaching screws and the oil pump cover and gasket.
4. Remove drive gear and idler gear from pump body.

Inspection
1. Check gears for scoring or other damage, replace if necessary.

2. Proper end clearance is .0005–.0075 inch.
3. Check pressure regulator valve, valve spring and bore for damage. Proper bore to valve clearance is .0025–.0050 inch.
4. Check extension shaft ends for wear, Fig. 55.

Assembly
1. Install gears and shaft in oil pump body.
2. Check gear end clearance by placing a straight edge over the gears and measure the clearance between the straight edge and gasket surface. If end clearance is excessive, check for scores in cover that would bring the clearance over specified limits.
3. Install cover and torque attaching screws to 8 ft. lbs.
4. Install pressure regulator valve, closed end first, into bore, then the valve spring and cotter pin.

WATER PUMP, REPLACE

1. Disconnect ground cables from batteries.
2. Drain cooling system.
3. Loosen drive belts and remove fan and pulley assembly.
4. Disconnect all hoses from water pump.
5. Remove water pump attaching screws and the water pump, Fig. 46.
6. Reverse procedure to install.

BELT TENSION DATA

	New Lbs.	Used Lbs.
1982–83③		
3/8"①	160	80
3/8"②	145	55
7/16"	170	90
1979–81		
5/16" Belts	80	50
3/8" Belts①	140	70
3/8" Belts②	140	60
15/32" Belts	165	90
1978		
3/8" Belts	150	70
15/32" Belts	165	90

①—Except cogged belts.
②—Cogged belts.
③—V8 engine only. V6 engine serpentine drive belt is self adjusting.

MECHANICAL FUEL PUMP, REPLACE

SERVICE NOTE

Some diesel engines may exhibit a condition of hard cold starts. If this condition exists, check the fuel pump housing for a crack in the area where the fuel line is connected to the fuel pump, which may allow air to enter the system. The cracked fuel pump housing could be caused by the fuel line vibrating.

To correct this condition, remove the right hand thermostat housing bolt and install stud, part No. 6270979. Disconnect fuel line at the fuel pump and install clip, part No. 343463 onto fuel line as shown in Fig. 55A. Install washer face nut, part No. 10008001. Replace the fuel pump and connect the fuel line.

1. Disconnect fuel lines from pump.
2. Remove fuel pump mounting bolts and the fuel pump.
3. Remove all gasket material from the pump and block gasket surfaces. Apply sealer to both sides of new gasket.
4. Position gasket on pump flange and hold pump in position against its mounting surface. Make sure rocker arm is riding on crankshaft eccentric.
5. Press pump tight against its mounting. Install retaining screws and tighten them alternately.

Fig. 56   Fuel injection pump timing marks. Typical

Fig. 57   Fuel injection pump connections. 1978–80

Fig. 57A   Fuel injection pump connections. 1981–83 V8 engine

Fig. 58   Fuel filter & lines. V8 engine

Fig. 58A   Fuel filter & lines. V6 engine

L. H. SIDE OF ENGINE

R. H. SIDE OF ENGINE

Fig. 59   Fuel return lines. 1978–79

6. Connect fuel lines. Then operate engine and check for leaks.

NOTE: Before installing the pump, it is good practice to crank the engine so that the nose of the crankshaft eccentric is out of the way of the fuel pump rocker arm when the pump is installed. In this way there will be the least amount of tension on the rocker arm, thereby easing the installation of the pump.

INJECTION PUMP TIMING

1. The mark on the injection pump adapter must be aligned with the mark on the injection pump flange, Fig. 56.
2. To adjust:
   a. Loosen the injection pump retaining nuts with tool J-26987.
   b. Align the mark on the injection pump flange with the mark on the injection pump adapter, Fig. 56.
   c. Torque injection pump retaining nuts to 35 ft. lbs.

FUEL INJECTION PUMP HOUSING FUEL PRESSURE CHECK

1. Remove air crossover and install screened covers J-29657 (V6 engines) or J-26996-10 (V8 engines) or equivalent.

Fig. 59A   Fuel return line. 1980–83 V8 engine

Fig. 60 Injection nozzle installation. 1978–79

Fig. 60A Injection nozzle installation. 1980–83

Fig. 61 Offset on fuel injection pump driven gear

Fig. 62 Fuel injection pump adapter installation

Fig. 63 Fuel injection pump adapter seal installation

Fig. 64 Marking fuel injection pump adapter with new timing mark

2. Remove fuel return pressure tap plug, Figs. 57 and 57A and 57B.
3. Install the seal from the pressure tap plug on the pressure tap adapter, tool J-28526, then install the adapter into pump housing.
4. Connect a low pressure gauge to the adapter.
5. Connect pick-up tachometer, tool J-26925, to the engine.
6. Check pressure with engine operating at 1000 RPM in Park. The pressure should be 8–12 PSI with no more than a 2 PSI fluctuation.
7. If pressure reading is zero on 1981–83 models, check operation of housing pressure cold advance as follows:
   a. Disconnect housing cold pressure advance electrical connector.
   b. If pressure reading is still zero, remove injection pump cover and check operation of advance solenoid. Repair or replace as necessary.
   c. If pressure is as specified with housing cold pressure advance electrical connector disconnected, check operation of temperature switch located on cylinder head bolt.
8. If pressure is still low, replace fuel return line connector assembly. If pressure is too high, fuel return system may be restricted. Remove return line at injection pump. Install fitting and short piece of hose to allow return flow to empty into a small container.
9. If pressure is lower than before, correct restriction in fuel line.
10. If pressure is still too high, replace fuel return line connector assembly. If assembly is replaced check injection pump timing and adjust if necessary.
11. If pressure remains too high, remove injection pump for repair.

12. Remove tachometer, pressure gauge and adapter.
13. Install a new pressure tap plug seal on the pressure tap plug and install plug into housing.
14. Remove screened covers and install air crossover.

INJECTION PUMP, REPLACE

Injection Pump & Lines

Removal
1. Disconnect ground cables from batteries.
2. Remove air cleaner.
3. Remove filters and pipes from valve covers and air crossover, Fig. 28E and 32A.
4. Remove air crossover and plug intake manifold, Fig. 29.
5. Disconnect throttle rod and return spring on V8 engines or throttle cable and TV detent cable from pump throttle lever.
6. Remove bellcrank.
7. Remove throttle and throttle valve cables from intake manifold brackets and position cables aside.
8. Remove fuel lines to fuel filter, then the fuel filter, Fig. 58 and 58A.
9. Disconnect fuel line at fuel pump and remove fuel line. If equipped with A/C, remove rear compressor brace.
10. Disconnect fuel return line from injection pump, Fig. 59, 59A and 58A.
11. Slide clamp from fuel return lines at injector nozzles and remove fuel return lines from each bank.
12. Disconnect injection pump lines at injector nozzles, Figs. 60 and 60A. It is nece-

sary to use two wrenches.
13. Remove nuts retaining injection pump with tool No. J-26987.
14. Remove injection pump and cap all lines and fittings.

Installation
1. Align offset tang on pump drive shaft with pump driven gear, Fig. 61, and install injector pump.
2. Loosely install the injector pump retaining nuts and lock washers. Connect fuel lines to injector pump and torque line fittings to 25 ft. lbs., Figs. 60 and 60A.
3. Connect fuel return lines to injector nozzles and injector pump.
4. Align mark on injection pump with line on adapter and torque retaining nuts to 18 ft. lbs. on V8 engines or 35 ft. lbs. on V6 engines.
5. Adjust throttle rod.
6. Install fuel line from fuel pump to fuel filter, Fig. 58 and 58A. If equipped with A/C, install rear compressor brace.
7. Install bellcrank and hairpin clip.
8. Install throttle and throttle valve cables, to intake manifold brackets and attach to bellcrank. Adjust throttle valve cable.
9. Connect throttle rod and return spring on V8 engines or throttle cable and TV cable on V6 engines.
10. Crank engine and check for fuel leaks.
11. Remove plugs from intake manifold and install air crossover, Fig. 29.
12. Install tubes in flow control valve in air crossover and ventilation filters in valve covers, Fig. 28E and 32A.
13. Install air cleaner.

Injection Pump

Removal
1. Disconnect battery ground cable and re-

Fig. 65 Injection nozzle seal installation

Fig. 66 Injection nozzle connections. 1979

Fig. 66A Injection pump right side view. 1981—83. V8 engine

move air cleaner assembly.
2. Remove crankcase ventilation filters and pipes from the valve covers and air crossover.
3. Remove the air crossover, Fig. 29, and install intake manifold screened covers J-26996-10.
4. Disconnect the throttle rod and throttle return spring.
5. Remove bellcrank.
6. Remove throttle and TV detent cables from intake manifold brackets and position cables aside.
7. Remove fuel lines to fuel filter, then the fuel filter, Figs. 58 & 58A.
8. Disconnect fuel line at fuel pump and remove fuel line. If equipped with A/C remove rear compressor brace.
9. Disconnect fuel return line from injection pump, Figs. 59, 59A and 58A.
10. Disconnect the injection line clamps closest to pump.
11. Disconnect the injection lines from pump and cap all openings.
12. Remove three nuts retaining injection pump, using tool No. J-26987.
13. Remove pump and discard the pump to adapter O-ring.

Installation
1. Align offset tang on pump drive shaft with pump driven gear, Fig. 61.
2. Install new pump to adapter O-ring, then install the pump fully seating pump by hand.
3. Align mark on injection pump with line

on adapter and torque retaining nuts to 18 ft. lbs.
4. Remove caps from the openings and connect the injection lines to the pump.
5. Install injection line clamps.
6. Connect the fuel return line.
7. Reconnect the fuel line at the fuel pump. If equipped with A/C, install the rear compressor brace.
8. Install the fuel filter and fuel filter to injection pump line.
9. Install throttle and TV detent cables on intake manifold.
10. Install bellcrank.
11. Install throttle rod and throttle return spring.
12. Remove screened covers from intake manifold, then install air crossover.
13. Install pipes and hoses in the air crossover and ventilation filters in valve covers.
14. Install air cleaner assembly and connect battery ground cable.

INJECTION PUMP ADAPTER, ADAPTER SEAL & NEW TIMING MARK

1. Remove injection pump as outlined previously.
2. Remove injection pump adapter, Fig. 62.
3. Remove seal from injection pump adapter.
4. File mark off injection pump adapter. Do not file mark from injection pump.
5. Position engine to No. 1 cylinder firing position. Align marks on balancer with zero mark on indicator. The injection pump driven gear should be offset to the right when No. 1 cylinder is at top dead

center.
6. Loosely install injection pump adapter.
7. Install seal in injection pump adapter with tool J-28425, Fig. 63.
8. Torque injection pump adapter bolts to 25 ft. lbs.
9. Install timing tool J-26896 into injection pump adapter. Rotate torque wrench counterclockwise to obtain a 50 ft. lbs. reading, then mark injection pump adapter, Fig. 64.
10. Install injection pump as outlined previously.

INJECTION NOZZLE, REPLACE

1981—83

SERVICE NOTE

Injection nozzle body leaks may be corrected by loosening the inlet fitting and retorquing to 45 ft. lbs. on DED type injection nozzles, and 19 ft. lbs. on CAV type injection nozzles. In the event this does not correct the leak, remove the inlet fitting. Using a piece of crocus cloth, press and rotate the end of the inlet fitting against the crocus cloth back and forth about six times. After polishing has been performed, flush inlet fitting using diesel fuel and install fitting onto pump.

1. Remove fuel lines, using a backup wrench on upper injection nozzle hex.

Fig. 66B Installing tool J-29601 on injection pump. 1981—83. V8 engine

Fig. 66C Injection pump with cover removed. 1981—83. V8 engine

Fig. 66D Installing injection pump cover. 1981—83. V8 engine

1. Rubber "O" ring
2. Idling adjuster screw
3. Thrust washer
4. "E" type circlip
5. Thrust washer
6. Rubber "O" ring
7. Clamp screw
8. Light load advance cam
9. Pin
10. Locknut and rubber "O" ring
11. Torque screw
12. Throttle shaft
13. Maximum speed adjustment screw
   (Do not adjust)

Fig. 66E Throttle shaft & seals. V6 engine

1. Rubber "O" ring
2. Governor support rod
3. Locking pin
4. Sleeve
5. Throttle lever
6. Idling screw and spring
7. Governor carrier assembly
8. Idle spring
9. Governor arm
10. Throttle block
11. Throttle shaft

Fig. 66F Governor assembly. V6 engine

2. Remove nozzle by applying torque to largest nozzle hex, Fig. 60A.
3. Cap nozzle and lines to prevent entry of dirt. Also remove copper gasket from cylinder head if gasket did not remain with nozzle.
4. Reverse procedure to install. Torque nozzle to 25 ft. lbs. When tightening nozzle, torque must be applied to largest nozzle hex. Torque fuel line to 25 ft. lbs. using a backup wrench on upper injection nozzle hex.

1978–79

1. Remove fuel line from injector nozzle.
2. Remove fuel line clamps from all nozzles on bank where nozzle is being removed. Remove fuel return line from nozzle being replaced.
3. Remove nozzle hold down clamp and spacer, Fig. 60, then the nozzle with tool J-26952.
4. Cap nozzle inlet line and tip of nozzle.
5. Reverse procedure to install. Install new seals on injection nozzles, Fig. 65. Torque nozzle hold down clamp bolt to 25 ft. lbs.

NOTE: 1979 diesel engines use two different types of connections to attach the high pressure fuel lines to the injection nozzles. Before replacing an injection nozzle or high pressure fuel line, it is necessary to determine which type of connection is used, either the "Flare Type" or "Ferrule Type", Fig. 66. Also, check the replacement part to ensure that the proper connection is used.

TRANSMISSION VACUUM VALVE, REPLACE

1. Note location of the valve vacuum hoses, then disconnect the vacuum hoses.
2. Remove the two valve attaching bolts and the valve.
3. Reverse procedure to install.

THROTTLE SHAFT SEAL, REPLACE

1981–83

V8 Engine
1. Disconnect both battery ground cables.
2. Remove air cleaner and air crossover and install air screens J-26996-2 or J-26996-10.
3. Disconnect injection pump fuel solenoid, housing pressure cold advance wires and fuel return pipe, Fig. 66A.
4. Remove throttle rod, vacuum regulator valve, return spring and throttle cable bracket.
5. Place tool J-29601 over throttle shaft and pin, then position spring clip of tool over throttle shaft advance cam and tighten wing nut. Without loosening wing nut, pull tool off shaft. This will provide proper alignment during reassembly, Fig. 66B.
6. Drive pin from throttle shaft and remove shaft advance cam and fiber washer. Remove any burrs from shaft which may have resulted from pin removal.

7. Clean injection pump cover, upper portion of pump, throttle shaft and guide stud area. Position several shop cloths in engine valley area to absorb fuel.
8. Remove injection pump cover and screws.

CAUTION: Use care to avoid any foreign matter from entering pump when cover is removed. If any object or foreign matter enter pump, it must be removed before engine is started as injection pump damage or engine damage may occur.

9. Note position of metering valve spring before removal as its position must be duplicated exactly during reassembly, Fig. 66C.
10. Remove guide stud and washer, noting parts before removal.
11. Rotate min-max governor assembly up for clearance then remove it, Fig. 66C. If idle governor spring becomes disengaged from throttle block, it must be reinstalled with tightly wound coils toward throttle block.
12. Remove throttle shaft assembly and inspect shaft for unusual wear or damage, replace if necessary. It may be necessary to loosen nuts at injection pump mounting flange and rotate pump slightly to allow throttle shaft to clear intake manifold.
13. Inspect throttle shaft bushings in pump housing for damage or unusual wear. If replacement of bushings is necessary, it must be performed by a qualified repair facility.
14. Remove throttle shaft seals. Do not cut seals to remove, as any nicks in the seal seat will cause leakage.
15. Install new shaft seals, lubricated with chassis grease. Use care to avoid cutting

Fig. 67 Throttle linkage. V8 engine

seals on sharp edges of shaft.

16. Carefully slide throttle shaft into pump to point where min-max governor assembly will slide back onto throttle shaft, Fig. 66C.
17. Rotate min-max governor assembly downward, then hold in position and slide throttle shaft and governor into position.
18. Install new fiber washer, throttle shaft advance cam (do not tighten screw at this time) and a new throttle shaft drive pin, Fig. 66A.
19. Align throttle shaft advance cam so tool J-20601 can be installed over throttle shaft, pins in slots and spring clip over advance cam.
20. Insert a .005 inch feeler gauge between cam and fiber washer, then tighten cam screw and remove tool J-29601.
21. Install guide stud with new washer, assuring that upper extension of metering valve spring slides on top of guide stud. Torque guide studs to 85 inch lbs.

CAUTION: Over torquing may strip the aluminum threads in the housing.

22. Hold throttle in idle position and install new pump cover seal. Making sure that screws are not in cover, position cover

Fig. 69 Transmission vacuum valve adjustment. 1979–82 Turbo Hydra-Matic 350 (Typical)

about 1/4 inch forward toward shaft end and above 1/8 inch above pump, Fig. 66D. Move cover rearward and downward into position, using care to avoid cutting seal, then reinstall cover screws. Each screw must have a flat washer and internal lock washer, with flat washer against pump cover. Torque screws to 37 inch lbs. and install vacuum regulator.

23. Reconnect both battery ground cables, then turn ignition switch to run position and touch pink solenoid wire to solenoid. A clicking noise should be heard as the wire is connected and disconnected. If not, the linkage may be jammed in the wide open position and the engine must not be started. Proceed to step 24. If clicking is heard, connect pump solenoid and housing pressure cold advance wires and proceed to step 25.
24. Remove cover, then ground solenoid lead (opposite hot lead) and connect pink wire. With ignition switch in run position, the solenoid in the cover should move the linkage. If not, the solenoid must be replaced. Minimum voltage across solenoid terminals must be 12 volts. Reinstall cover and repeat step 23.
25. Install throttle cable bracket, throttle rod, throttle cable and return springs. Make sure timing marks on pump and adapter are aligned and make sure nuts retaining pump are tight. Install fuel return pipe.
26. Start engine and check for fuel leaks.

NOTE: Rough idle may be due to air in the pump. Allow sufficient time for air to purge by allowing engine to idle. It may be necessary to turn engine off to allow air bubbles to rise to top of pump where they will be purged.

27. Adjust Transmission Vacuum Valve as described further on, then remove intake manifold screens and install air crossover and air cleaner.

V6 Engine

1. Remove air crossover and install cover J-29657 or equivalent.
2. Disconnect fuel return pipe, Fig. 58A, then remove governor control cover screws and the cover.
3. Remove fast idle solenoid and vacuum regulator valve.
4. Disconnect throttle cable and TC detent cable.
5. Disconnect throttle return spring.
6. Install tool J-29601 or equivalent over throttle shaft with slots of tool engaging vacuum regulator valve lock pin. Place spring clip of tool over throttle shaft advance cam and tighten wing nut. Without loosening wing nut, pull tool off of shaft.
7. Remove lock pin from throttle shaft, Fig. 66E.
8. Remove rollpin from pump housing and remove governor support rod.
9. Tilt governor carrier assembly by lifting end nearest drive end of pump and remove carrier from pump housing.
10. Remove clamping screw from light load cam, then remove cam.
11. Remove E clip from throttle shaft, then remove throttle shaft from pump.
12. Remove and discard 0 rings.
13. Check throttle shaft assembly and governor housing bores for damage and wear and replace as necessary.
14. Lubricate shaft and 0 rings with oil and assemble larger 0 rings onto shaft.

Fig. 68 Throttle valve or detent cable adjustment

15. Install throttle shaft into housing until thrust washers can be installed onto shaft in original positions. Install smaller 0 ring onto shaft.
16. Assemble light load advance cam onto shaft and install but do not tighten clamping screw.
17. Install E clip into throttle shaft recess. If new throttle shaft is installed, shaft end play must be checked and adjusted by selective fitting of thrust washers. Throttle shaft end play should be .006-.012 inch.
18. Install new pin onto head of shaft. Align throttle shaft advance cam until tool J-29601 or equivalent can be installed over throttle shaft. Tighten cam screw, then remove tool J-29601.
19. Rotate throttle lever forwards to the drive end of pump. Install governor carrier assembly onto pump housing and engage lug on underside of throttle block with cut away notch in throttle shaft.
20. Lubricate governor support rod and new 0 ring, then install 0 ring onto support rod using tool J-33096 or equivalent.
21. Insert plain end of rod through rear of governor housing and into carrier assembly sleeve.
22. Install support rod into housing and install new locking pin, Fig. 66F.
23. Install governor cover and fuel return pipe.
24. Install throttle return springs and connect throttle cable.
25. Connect TV detent cable.
26. Install vacuum regulator valve and fast idle solenoid.
27. Start engine and check for leaks. Install air crossover and air cleaner.

Fig. 70 Transmission vacuum valve adjustment. 1978 Turbo-Hydra-Matic 350

PUMP COVER SEAL AND/OR GUIDE STUD, REPLACE

1981-83

1. Disconnect both battery ground cables.
2. Remove air cleaner and air crossover and install air screens J-26996-2 or J-26996-10.
3. Disconnect injection pump fuel solenoid, housing pressure cold advance wires and fuel return pipe.
4. Clean injection pump cover, upper portion of pump and guide stud area. Position shop cloths to absorb fuel.
5. Remove injection pump cover, then remove screws from cover.

CAUTION: Use care to avoid any foreign matter from entering pump when cover is removed. If any object or foreign matter enter pump, it must be removed before starting engine as injection pump damage or engine damage may occur.

---

6. Note position of metering valve spring before removal as its position must be duplicated exactly during reassembly, Fig. 66C.
7. Remove guide stud and washer, noting location of parts before removal.
8. Refer to steps 21 thru 27 under "Throttle Shaft Seal, Replace" procedure for reassembly of "Pump Cover Seal And/Or Guide Stud".

THROTTLE ROD, ADJUST

1. If equipped with Cruise Control, remove clip from Cruise Control rod, then the rod from bellcrank.
2. Remove throttle valve cable from bellcrank, Fig. 67.
3. Loosen the throttle rod locknut and shorten the rod several turns.
4. Rotate the bellcrank to the full throttle stop, then lengthen the throttle rod until the injection pump lever contacts the injection pump full throttle stop. Release the bellcrank.
5. Tighten the throttle rod locknut.
6. Connect the throttle valve cable and Cruise Control rod, if equipped, to bellcrank.

THROTTLE VALVE OR DETENT CABLE, ADJUST

1. Remove throttle rod from bellcrank, Fig. 68.
2. Push snap lock to disengaged position.
3. Rotate bellcrank to full throttle stop position and push in snap lock until flush with cable end fitting. Release bellcrank.
4. Connect the throttle rod.

TRANSMISSION VACUUM VALVE, ADJUST

1979-83

1. Remove air crossover, then install screened covers J26996-2.
2. Remove throttle rod from throttle lever on V8 models or disconnect throttle cable and TV detent cable on V6 models, then loosen transmission vacuum valve injection pump bolts.
3. Install carburetor angle gauge J26701-15 and adapter on injection pump throttle lever, Fig. 69.
4. Rotate throttle lever to the wide open position and set angle gauge to zero degrees.
5. Center bubble in level, then set angle gauge to 49 degrees on 1979 units, 50 degrees on 1980 units, 58 degrees on 1981-83 V8 engines or 49° on V6 engines.
6. Rotate throttle lever so level bubble is centered.
7. Attach a suitable vacuum pump to center port of vacuum valve and install a vacuum gauge to outside port of vacuum valve, then apply 12 inches of vacuum on 1979 units, 18-22 inches of vacuum on 1980-83 units.
8. Rotate vacuum valve clockwise to obtain 8½ to 9 inches of vacuum on 1979 units, 7 to 8 inches of vacuum on 1980 units, 8.6 to 9.2 inches of vacuum on 1981 units and 10.6 inches of vacuum on 1982-83 units, then tighten vacuum valve bolts. Remove vacuum gauge and vacuum pump.
9. Install throttle rod to bellcrank, on V8 models or connect throttle cable and TV detent cable on V6 models, then remove screened covers and install air crossover.

1978

1. Remove throttle rod from bellcrank.
2. Loosen transmission vacuum valve attaching bolts to disengage valve from injection pump shaft.
3. Hold the injection pump lever against injection pump full throttle stop, rotate vacuum valve to full throttle position and insert a .090 inch diameter pin to hold the valve in the full throttle position, Fig. 70.
4. Rotate assembly clockwise until the injection pump shaft lever is contacted, then tighten the valve attaching bolts.
5. Remove pin and release lever.
6. Connect throttle rod.

PURGING WATER FROM FUEL TANK

1980-83 Models With Water In Fuel Detector

On these vehicles, any water in the fuel tank may be purged by siphoning or using a pump. The pump or siphon hose should be connected to the ¼ inch fuel return hose (smaller of the two hoses) under the hood near the fuel pump. Purging should continue until all water is removed from the fuel tank. Also, remove fuel filler cap while purging, and replace cap when completed.

CAUTION: Use all safety precautions while handling the fuel/water mixture.

Clutch & Transmission Section

CLUTCH PEDAL, ADJUST

1977-81

Exc. 1978-81 Cutlass
1. Loosen lower push rod swivel lock nut, Figs. 1 and 2.
2. Disconnect pedal return spring.
3. Rotate clutch lever and shaft assembly until clutch pedal firmly contacts rubber bumper on dash brace.
4. Push outer end of clutch fork rearward until throwout bearing lightly contacts clutch plate.
5. Remove lower push rod swivel retaining clip and install swivel in the gauge (Upper) hole. Reinstall retaining clip.
6. Increase length of push rod until lash is removed.

Fig. 1   Clutch linkage. 1977-79 Omega

7. Install swivel in lower hole of lever and shaft assembly, then install retaining clip.
8. Tighten lock nut against swivel. Do not change rod length.
9. Connect pedal return spring.
10. Free pedal play should be ⅞ to 1½ inch on 1977-79 Omega or ¾ to 1¼ inch on 1977 Cutlass.

1978-81 Cutlass
1. Disconnect clutch return spring.
2. Rotate clutch lever and shaft assembly until clutch pedal firmly contacts rubber bumper on bracket.
3. Push outer end of clutch fork rearward until release bearing lightly contacts clutch plate.
4. Install lower push rod "A", Fig. 3, in

Fig. 2 Clutch linkage. 1977 Cutlass

Fig. 3 Clutch linkage. 1978–81 Cutlass

clutch fork and rod "B", Fig. 3, in gauge (Upper) hole.

5. Increase length of push rod "A" until all lash is removed.
6. Install rod "B" in lower hole of lever and shaft, then the retaining clip.
7. Tighten lock nut "C" against rod "B", Fig. 3. Do not change rod length.
8. Connect return spring.
9. Free pedal play should be 11/16 to 5/8 inch.

CLUTCH, REPLACE
1977–81

1. Remove transmission.
2. Disconnect clutch release spring and clutch rod.
3. Remove clutch release bearing.
4. Remove flywheel housing, leaving starter attached to engine. Release yoke and ball stud will remain in housing.
5. Scribe mark on clutch cover to flywheel for correct assembly.
6. Unfasten and remove clutch cover and disc.

NOTE: Loosen pressure plate bolts alternately, one turn at a time.

7. Reverse removal procedure to install clutch and adjust clutch pedal free play.

THREE SPEED MANUAL TRANS., REPLACE
1977–81

1. On models with floor shift, remove shift lever from shifter assembly.
2. Raise car and remove drive shaft.
3. Disconnect shift rods from shift levers and the TCS switch wiring, if equipped.
4. Support rear of engine.
5. Remove cross support bar-to-rear transmission mount attaching bolts.
6. Remove catalytic converter support bracket.
7. Disconnect parking brake cables from cross support and remove cross support bar.
8. If equipped with dual exhaust it may be necessary to disconnect left-hand exhaust pipe at exhaust manifold to provide clearance.
9. Disconnect speedometer cable.
10. Remove transmission upper attaching bolts and install aligning studs in the bolt holes.
11. Remove lower bolts and remove transmission.
12. Reverse procedure to install.

Fig. 4 Three speed shift linkage (typical)

Fig. 5 Four speed shift linkage. 1978–80

3 SPEED SHIFT LINKAGE, ADJUST

1977—80 Column Shift

1. Place transmission in reverse and raise vehicle.
2. Loosen swivel bolts on shift rods at transmission, ensuring rods are free to move in swivels.
3. Hold 1st-reverse column relay lever in position, push up on shift rod until detent in column is felt, then torque swivel bolt to 20 ft. lbs. on 1978—79 Omega, 26 ft. lbs. on 1977 Omega, 23 ft. lbs. on 1977 Cutlass and 20 ft. lbs. on 1980 Cutlass.
4. Place transmission in Neutral, insert 3/16 inch rod through column relay lever into alignment hole and torque swivel nut to 20 ft. lbs. on 1978—79 Omega, 26 ft. lbs. on 1977 Omega, 23 ft. lbs. on 1977 Cutlass and 20 ft. lbs. on 1980 Cutlass.
5. Lower vehicle and check shift operation.
6. Place transmission in reverse, turn ignition switch to lock position and ensure that the key can be removed, steering wheel will not turn and transmission will not shift out of reverse.
7. Place ignition switch in run position, shift transmission to second gear, ensure that steering wheel will turn and key can not be removed from ignition switch.

1978—81 Floor Shift

1978—81 Cutlass
1. Place ignition switch in "Off" position, then raise vehicle.
2. Remove retainers from shift rods, then place transmission shift levers in neutral.
3. Place control lever in neutral position. Align levers and insert gauge pin into levers and bracket.

4. Loosen nuts on 1st-reverse shift rod and adjust trunion and pin assembly, then tighten nuts.
5. Loosen nuts on 2nd-3rd shift rod and adjust trunion and pin assembly, then tighten nuts.
6. Remove gauge pin, then check linkage for proper operation.

4 SPEED TRANS., REPLACE

1977—80

1. Raise vehicle and drain transmission.
2. Remove propeller shaft.
3. Disconnect speedometer cable and back-up light switch from transmission.
4. Disconnect transmission control rod and lever assemblies from shifter shafts. Position rods aside.
5. Remove crossmember to transmission mount bolts.
6. Remove catalytic converter support bracket.
7. Support engine with a suitable jack and remove crossmember to frame bolts, then the crossmember.
8. Remove transmission to clutch housing upper retaining bolts and install guide pins in holes.
9. Remove the transmission to clutch housing lower retaining bolts, slide transmission rearward and remove from vehicle.
10. Reverse procedure to install.

4 SPEED SHIFT LINKAGE, ADJUST

1977—80

1. Turn ignition switch to "Off" position and raise vehicle.
2. Loosen lock nuts on shift rod swivels, Fig. 5. The rods should pass freely through the swivels.
3. Place transmission shift levers in neutral.
4. Place shift control lever in neutral. Align control levers and install a suitable pin into levers and bracket.
5. Tighten 1st.-2nd. shift rod nut against swivel.
6. Tighten 3rd.-4th. shift rod nut against swivel.
7. Tighten reverse shift control rod nut.
8. Remove pin from control lever assembly and check for proper operation.

5 SPEED TRANS., REPLACE

1977—79

1. Remove Shifter assembly.
2. Raise vehicle and remove propeller-shaft.
3. Disconnect speedometer cable from transmission.
4. Remove crossmember to transmission bolts.
5. Remove catalytic converter support bracket.
6. Support engine and remove crossmember.
7. Remove transmission to clutch housing upper retaining bolts and install guide pins.
8. Remove transmission to clutch housing lower bolts and slide transmission rearward, then remove from vehicle.
9. Remove back-up lamp switch and fill plug. Tilt transmission and drain fluid.
10. Reverse procedure to install.

Toronado Drive Link Belt

For service procedures on Toronado drive link belt or sprockets, refer to the Cadillac chapter, 1977—83 Eldorado & 1980—83 Seville Link Belt section.

Drive Axle, Propeller Shaft & Brakes

For service procedures on 1979—83 Toronado drive axles refer to Main Index
For service procedures on 1977—78 Toronado drive axles, refer to Cadillac chapter, "1977—78 Eldorado drive axles" section.

REAR AXLE
1979—83 Toronado

On these models the hub and wheel bearing is incorporated into one assembly which eliminates the need for wheel bearing adjustment and does not require periodic maintenance.

Wheel Bearing & Spindle, Replace

REAR DISC BRAKES
Removal
1. Raise and support rear of vehicle.
2. Remove tire and wheel assembly.

3. Mark a wheel stud and a corresponding place on the rotor to assist in installation if bearing is not replaced.
4. Disconnect brake line at bracket on control arm.
5. Remove caliper and rotor assembly.
6. Remove four nut and bolts securing the spindle to the control arm and remove bearing assembly Fig. 1.

Installation

NOTE: Before installing bearing, remove all rust and corrosion from bearing mounting surfaces. Lack of a flat surface may result in early bearing failure. A slip fit must exist between the bearing and the control arm assembly.

1. Install rear spindle, shield and plate to lower control arm with four nut and bolt assemblies. Tighten to 32 ft. lbs. Fig. 1.
2. If bearing was not replaced install rotor using reference marks made at time of removal.
3. Install brake caliper assembly.
4. Connect brake line at bracket on control arm, tighten and bleed brake system.

Fig. 1   Wheel bearing and hub assembly removal 1979—83 Toronado

Fig. 3   Rear wheel hub & spindle with True-Track brake. 1977—78

Fig. 2   Rear wheel hub & spindle less True-Track brake. 1977—78

5. Install wheel and tire assembly. Tighten to 100 ft. lbs.
6. Remove support and lower car.

REAR DRUM BRAKES
Removal
1. Raise and support rear of vehicle.
2. Remove tire and wheel assembly.
3. Remove brake drum.
4. Remove four nuts attaching rear wheel bearing assembly to control arm.
5. Remove wheel bearing and four attaching bolts, Fig. 1.

Installation

NOTE: Before installing bearing, remove all rust and corrosion from bearing mounting surfaces. Lack of a flat surface for any reason may result in early bearing failure. A slip fit must exist between the bearing and the control arm assembly.

1. Install four nuts and bolts attaching wheel bearing to rear control arm assembly, Fig. 1.
2. Install brake drum.
3. Install wheel and tire assembly, tighten to 100 ft. lbs.
4. Remove supports and lower car.

1977—78 Toronado

The rear wheel spindles are a press fit and bolted to the rear axle assembly, Figs. 2 and 3. As shown, tapered roller bearings are used in the rear wheels.

Wheel Bearing Adjustment

Adjustment of the rear wheel bearings should be made while revolving the wheel at least three times the speed of the nut rotation when taking torque readings.
1. Check to make sure that hub is completely seated on wheel spindle.
2. While rotating wheel, tighten spindle nut to 25 to 30 ft-lbs. Make certain all parts are properly seated and that threads are free.
3. Back nut off ½ turn, then retighten nut to finger-tight and install cotter pin.
4. If cotter pin cannot be installed in either of the two holes in the spindle, back nut off until cotter pin can be installed.
5. The rear hub must be rotated at least three revolutions during tightening of spindle nut. The final adjustment to be finger-tight to provide .001–.005" bearing end play.
6. Peen end of cotter pin snug against side of nut. If it can be moved with a finger,

vibration may cause it to wear and break.

Wheel Spindle, Replace
Removal
1. Raise and support rear of car and remove hub.
2. Disconnect brake line at wheel cylinder.
3. Unfasten and remove brake backing plate and position out of the way.
4. Remove bolts securing spindle to axle.
5. Use a suitable puller to remove spindle from axle to tube.

Installation
1. Start spindle into axle tube assembly with keyway facing up and install backing plate to spindle attaching bolts. Using a suitable slide hammer, drive spindle into tube while tightening bolts until spindle is fully seated.
2. Remove slide hammer and bolts.
3. Install new gasket on wheel spindle.
4. Install brake backing plate and tighten nuts to 40 ft-lbs.
5. Connect brake line to wheel cylinder, tightening fitting to 14 ft-lbs.
6. Install rear hub.

Rear Axle, Replace

1977—78
1. Raise and support rear of car with jack stands at rear frame pads ahead of rear wheel opening.
2. Remove rear wheels and hubs.
3. Disconnect brake lines at wheel cylinders.
4. Disconnect parking brake cable at equalizer.
5. Disconnect rubber brake hose at underbody connector.
6. Support axle with a suitable jack.
7. If equipped with True Track brakes, disconnect wiring connector from underbody connector.
8. Disconnect shock absorbers from lower mountings.
9. Lower axle and remove coil spring.
10. Remove brake backing plate attaching bolts and position plates aside.
11. Disconnect upper and lower control arms from axle.
12. Lower axle from vehicle.
13. Reverse procedure to install.

Exc. Toronado

Figs. 4 and 5 illustrate the rear axle assemblies used on conventional models. When necessary to overhaul any of these units, refer to the *Rear Axle Specifications* table in this chapter.

Integral Carrier
Type "B" & "O" (Except 7½")

As shown in Fig. 4, the drive pinion is mounted on two tapered roller bearings that are preloaded by two selected spacers. The drive pinion is positioned by shims located between a shoulder on the pinion and the rear bearing. The front bearing is held in place by a large nut.

The differential is supported in the carrier by two tapered roller side bearings. These are preloaded by inserting shims between the bearings and the pedestals. The differential assembly is positioned for ring gear and pinion backlash by varying these shims.

Type C, G, K, M, O (7½") & P

In these rear axles, Fig. 5, the rear axle housing and differential carrier are cast into an integral assembly. The drive pinion assembly is mounted in two opposed tapered roller bearings. The pinion bearings are preloaded by a spacer behind the front bearing. The pinion is positioned by a washer between the head of the pinion and the rear bearing.

The differential is supported in the carrier by two tapered roller side bearings. These bearings are preloaded by spacers located between the bearings and carrier housing. The differential assembly is positioned for proper ring gear and pinion backlash by varying these spacers. The differential case houses two side gears in mesh with two pinions mounted on a pinion shaft which is held in place by a lock pin. The side gears and pinions are backed by thrust washers.

Rear Axle, Replace

Construction of the axle assembly is such that service operations may be performed with the housing installed in the vehicle or with the housing removed and installed in a holding fixture. The following procedure is necessary only when the housing requires replacement.

1977–79 Omega
1. Raise vehicle and support axle using a suitable jack.
2. Disconnect shock absorbers from axle housing.
3. Disconnect properller and support out of way.
4. Remove rear wheel, brake drums and axle shafts.
5. Disconnect brake lines from clips on axle tubes.
6. Remove backing plates and support from frame using wire.
7. Remove lower spring pad brackets, then shift axle to clear springs.
8. Reverse procedure to install.

1977–83 Except Omega
1. Raise car and remove rear wheels, drums and axle shafts.
2. Disconnect brake line from wheel cylinders.
3. Unfasten and support backing plates with wire hooks to frame kickup.
4. Disconnect shock absorbers at housing.
5. Position jack stands under frame rear torque boxes, then disconnect upper control arms and slowly lower axle housing to stands.
6. Remove springs.

7. Remove propeller shaft and support front of axle housing at companion flange to prevent assembly from rotating when the lower control arms are disconnected.
8. Remove lower control arm bolts at axle housing.
9. Remove support at companion flange and lower axle housing.
10. Remove assembly to bench and transfer parts to new axle housing.
11. Reverse procedure to install.

Axle Shaft, Replace

Type C, G, K, M, O (7½") & P
1. Raise vehicle and remove wheel and brake drum.
2. Clean all dirt from area of carrier cover.
3. Drain lubricant from carrier by removing cover.
4. Remove differential pinion shaft lock screw and shaft.

Fig. 4 Integral carrier type rear axle. 1977–83 Type B & O (Except 7½") axle

Fig. 5 Integral carrier type differential. 1977–83 Types C, G, K, M, O (7½") & P axle

CHISEL RETAINER BUT DO NOT MARK SHAFT ON BEARING SURFACE

SHAFT — SEAL — BEARING — RETAINER (OUTER)

Fig. 6 Removing axle shaft bearing retainer

SPIDER AND BEARINGS — STRAP

SPIDER AND BEARINGS — STRAP

SLIP YOKE

Fig. 7 Propeller shaft installation 1977–83 all (Typical)

5. Push flanged end of axle shaft toward center of vehicle and remove "C" lock from button end of shaft.
6. Remove axle shaft from housing, being careful not to damage oil seal.
7. Reverse procedure to install.

Type B & O (Except 7½")
1. Remove wheel and brake drum.
2. Remove axle bearing retainer (4 nuts).

NOTE: On 1977–81 8½ inch axles, new retainers are used and can be identified by a raised area around the axle shaft opening. This raised area provides proper seating of the seal and bearing.

3. Pull axle shaft from housing. If bearing is a tight fit in housing, use a slide hammer-type puller. Do not drag shaft over seal as this may damage seal.
4. Attach one axle bearing retainer nut to hold brake backing plate in position.
5. Before installing axle shaft, examine oil seal. The seals have feathered edges which form a tight seal around the shaft. If these edges are damaged in any way, seal must be replaced. Examine seal surface on shaft; if it is not smooth, dress it down with very fine emery cloth.
6. Reverse removal procedure to install axle shaft, being sure to grease outside of axle bearing, seal surface on axle shaft and bore of axle housing with differential lubricant. Place new gasket and bearing retainer over studs, install nuts and tighten to 40 ft. lbs. on all 1977 models and 35 ft. lbs. on all 1978–83 models.
7. Bearings should be replaced if found to be rough or have greater than .020" end play. Remove bearing only when new bearing is to be installed; once removed it must not be reused.
8. With axle shaft removed from housing, split bearing retainer with a chisel, Fig. 6.
9. Press bearing off shaft.
10. Press new bearing on shaft up against shoulder on shaft.
11. Press retainer on shaft up against bearing.
12. Reverse removal procedure to install axle shaft.

PROPELLER SHAFT

1977–83

The propeller shaft is of one or two piece construction with a single or double U-joint

SECONDARY SHOE AND LINING — RETURN SPRING — ACTUATING LINK — GUIDE — RETURN SPRING — PRIMARY SHOE AND LINING

WHEEL CYLINDER

STRUT — SPRING

ADJUSTER LEVER AND PAWL ASM. — SLEEVE — HOLD DOWN SPRING

SPRING

PIN

LEVER — RETURN SPRING — SOCKET — THRUST WASHER — ADJUSTING SCREW — NUT

Fig. 8 Drum brake assembly exploded. Except 1978–83 Cutlass & 1979–83 Toronado

securing the shaft to the companion flange, Figs. 7 and 8.
1. Mark propeller shaft and companion flange so they can be installed in the same position.
2. On 1977–83 models, remove strap bolts, Fig. 7. Use a piece of tape or wire to hold universal joint bearing caps in place.
3. Lower rear of shaft and slide rearward.
4. Reverse procedure to install. If drive shaft yokes do not have vent holes, lubricate internal splines with engine oil. If drive shaft yokes have vent holes apply lubricant No. 1050169 or equivalent to internal splines prior to installation. Torque strap bolts to 14–16 ft. lbs.

BRAKE ADJUSTMENTS

1977–83

These brakes, Figs. 8, 9 and 10, have self adjusting shoe mechanisms that assure correct lining-to-drum clearances at all times. The automatic adjusters operate only when the brakes are applied as the car is moving rearward.

Although the brakes are self-adjusting, an initial adjustment is necessary after the brake shoes have been relined or replaced, or when the length of the star wheel adjuster has been changed during some other service operation.

Fig. 9   Left rear drum brake exploded. 1978–83 Cutlass   **Fig. 10   Left rear drum brake exploded. 1979–83 Toronado**

Frequent usage of an automatic transmission forward range to halt reverse vehicle motion may prevent the automatic adjusters from functioning, thereby inducing low pedal heights. Should low pedal heights be encountered, it is recommended that numerous forward and reverse stops be made until satisfactory pedal height is obtained.

NOTE: If a low pedal height condition cannot be corrected by making numerous reverse stops (provided the hydraulic system is free of air) it indicates that the self-adjusting mechanism is not functioning. Therefore, it will be necessary to remove the brake drum, clean, free up and lubricate the adjusting mechanism. Then adjust the brakes as follows, being sure the parking brake is fully released.

Adjustment

NOTE: Inasmuch as there is no way to adjust these brakes with the drums installed, the following procedure is mandatory after new linings are installed or if it becomes necessary to change the length of the brake shoe adjusting screw.

1. With brake drums removed, position the caliper shown in Fig. 11 to the inside diameter of the drum and tighten the clamp screw.
2. Next position brake shoe end of the caliper tool over the brake shoes as shown in Fig. 12.
3. Rotate the gauge slightly around the shoes to insure that the gauge contacts the linings at the largest diameter.
4. Adjust brake shoes until the gauge is a snug fit on the linings at the point of largest lining diameter.

NOTE: If it is necessary to back off the brake shoe adjustment, it will be necessary to hold the adjuster lever away from the adjuster screw, Fig. 13.

PARKING BRAKE, ADJUST

1977–83

Depress parking brake pedal 3 clicks on all models except 1977–79 Omega and 1977 88 and 98 and all 1978–83 models. Depress parking brake pedal 2 clicks on 1977 Omega and 6

clicks on 1977 88 and 98 and 2 clicks on all 1978–83 models. Tighten adjusting nut until left rear wheel can just be rotated rearward using both hands and cannot be rotated forward. Release parking brake, rear wheels should turn freely in either direction with no brake drag.

POWER BRAKE UNIT, REPLACE

Hydro-Boost

1978–83

NOTE: Pump brake pedal several times with engine off to deplete accumulator of fluid.

1. Remove two nuts attaching master cylinder to booster, then move master cylinder away from booster with brake lines attached.
2. Remove three hydraulic lines from booster. Plug and cap all lines and outlets.
3. Remove retainer and washer securing booster push rod to brake pedal arm.
4. Remove four nuts attaching booster unit to dash panel.

Fig. 11   Brake shoe gauge measuring inside diameter of brake drum. 1977–83

Fig. 12   Brake shoe gauge measuring outside diameter of brake shoes. 1977–83

Fig. 13   Backing off brake shoe adjustment

5. From engine compartment, loosen booster from dash panel and move booster push rod inboard until it disconnects from brake pedal arm. Remove spring washer from brake pedal arm.
6. Remove booster unit from vehicle.
7. Reverse procedure to install. To purge system, disconnect feed wire from injection pump. Fill power steering pump reservoir, then crank engine for several seconds and recheck power steering pump fluid level. Connect injection pump feed wire and start engine, then cycle steering wheel from stop to stop twice and stop engine. Discharge accumulator by depressing brake pedal several times, then check fluid level. Start engine, then turn steering wheel from stop to stop and turn

engine off. Check fluid level and add fluid as necessary. If foaming occurs, stop engine and wait for approximately one hour for foam to dissipate, then recheck fluid level.

Vacuum Booster

1. Disconnect vacuum hose from vacuum cylinder and cover openings to prevent entrance of dirt.
2. Disconnect pipes from master cylinder outlets and cover openings in master cylinder and end of pipes to prevent entrance of dirt.
3. Disconnect push rod from brake pedal.
4. Unfasten and remove power brake unit.
5. Reverse procedure to install.

BRAKE MASTER CYLINDER, REPLACE

1. Be sure area around master cylinder is clean, then disconnect the hydraulic lines at master cylinder. Plug or tape end of line to prevent entrance of dirt or loss of brake fluid.
2. On Omega models with manual brakes, remove push rod to brake pedal clevis pin.
3. On Cutlass models with manual brakes, remove push rod to brake pedal pin.
4. Remove master cylinder retaining nuts and the master cylinder.
5. Reverse procedure to install.

Rear Suspension

SHOCK ABSORBER, REPLACE

1. With rear axle properly supported, disconnect shock absorber from upper mounting.
2. Disconnect shock absorber from lower mounting.
3. Reverse procedure to install.

LEAF SPRINGS & BUSHINGS, REPLACE
1977–79 Omega

1. Support vehicle at frame and support rear axle, relieving tension from spring.
2. Disconnect shock absorbers from lower mountings and loosen spring front mounting bolt.
3. Remove spring retainer bracket to underbody screws, lower rear axle and remove retainer bracket.
4. Disconnect parking brake cable from spring plate bracket.
5. Remove "U" bolts and spring plate, Fig. 1.
6. Support spring, remove spring front mounting bolt and rear shackle bolts.
7. Replace spring eye bushings and rear shackle frame bushings as necessary, Figs. 2 and 3.
8. Reverse procedure to install.

COIL SPRING, REPLACE
1977–83 Except Omega & Toronado

1. Position a suitable jack under rear axle housing and raise rear of vehicle, then support frame side rails with support stands. Do not lower jack.
2. Disconnect brake line at axle housing.
3. Disconnect upper control arms at axle housing.

Fig. 1 Rear suspension (typical). 1977–79 Omega

4. Disconnect shock absorber at lower mounting, then carefully lower rear axle assembly.

NOTE: Use care not to stretch or kink brake hoses.

5. Remove coil spring from vehicle.

1979–83 Toronado

1. Raise and support rear of vehicle, then remove wheel and tire assembly.
2. Remove stabilizer bar as described under Stabilizer Bar, Replace.
3. Using a suitable jack support lower control arm.
4. Disconnect automatic level air line at shock absorber. If removing left hand spring from vehicle, disconnect automatic level control link from ball pivot at con-

trol arm.
5. Disconnect shock absorber from upper and lower mountings and remove shock absorber.
6. Carefully lower control arm until spring tension is relieved, then remove spring and insulator, Fig. 4.
7. Reverse procedure to install. Locate bottom end of spring between dimples on lower control arm assembly.

1977–78 Toronado

1. Support vehicle at frame.
2. With rear axle properly supported, disconnect shock absorbers from lower mountings, Fig. 5.
3. Carefully lower rear axle and remove springs.

NOTE: It may be necessary to compress springs, using a suitable spring compressor, to facilitate removal.

Fig. 2   Leaf spring bushings removal. 1977–79 Omega

Fig. 3   Leaf spring bushings installation. 1977–79 Omega

Fig. 4   Rear suspension. 1979–83 Toronado

Fig. 5   Rear suspension. 1977–78 Toronado

4. Reverse procedure to install. On 1977–78 models, springs must be properly indexed, Fig. 6.

CONTROL ARMS & BUSHINGS, REPLACE

NOTE: Replace control arms one at a time to prevent axle assembly misalignment, making installation difficult.

Upper Control Arms

Exc. Toronado
1. Support vehicle at frame and rear axle.
2. Remove control arm front and rear mount bolts.
3. Replace axle housing bushing as necessary, Figs. 7 thru 10.
4. On 1978–83 models, replace control arm bushings as necessary, Figs. 11 and 12.
5. Reverse procedure to install. Tighten control arm bolts with vehicle at curb height.

PIGTAIL ON FRAME END OF SPRING MUST POINT TO RIGHT SIDE OF CAR WITHIN LIMITS SHOWN

Fig. 6   Rear coil spring installation. 1977–78 Toronado

Fig. 7   Upper control arm axle bracket bushing removal. 1977 models

Fig. 8   Upper control arm axle bracket bushing installation. 1977 models

Fig. 9   Upper control arm axle bracket bushing removal. 1978—83 models

1977–78 Toronado
1. Support vehicle at frame and rear axle.
2. Remove control arm front and rear mounting bolts.
3. Replace control arm bushings as necessary.

NOTE: When installing upper control arm rear bushing, reverse tool # J-21474-13.

4. Reverse procedure to install. Tighten control arm bolts with vehicle at curb height.

Lower Control Arms
All Exc. Toronado

Follow "Upper Control Arms" procedure for replacement of lower control arms. On 1977 models, control arm bushings are not serviceable. On 1978—83 models, replace control arm bushings as shown in Figs. 11 and 12.

Fig. 10   Upper control arm axle bracket bushing installation. 1978—83 models

1979–83 Toronado
1. Raise and support rear of vehicle, then remove wheel and tire assembly.
2. Remove stabilizer bar as described under Stabilizer Bar, Replace.
3. Disconnect brake line bracket from control arm, then remove caliper assembly.
4. Mark a wheel stud and a corresponding point of the rotor for alignment, then remove rotor.

5. If left hand control arm is to be removed, disconnect automatic level control link from ball pivot on control arm.
6. Using a suitable jack support control arm.
7. Disconnect air line from shock absorber, then disconnect shock absorber from upper and lower mountings and remove shock absorber.
8. Carefully lower the control arm until spring tension is relieved, then remove spring and insulator.
9. Remove two bolts mounting control arm to frame and remove control arm, Fig. 8.
10. Reverse procedure to install.

1977–78 Toronado
Follow "Upper Control Arms" procedure for replacement of lower control arms.

STABILIZER BAR, REPLACE

Exc. 1979–83 Toronado

1. Support vehicle at rear axle.
2. Remove bolts attaching stabilizer bar to the lower control arms, Fig. 13.
3. Reverse procedure to install.

1979–83 Toronado

1. Raise and support rear of vehicle.
2. Remove nuts and bolts securing front of stabilizer bar to control arms.
3. Remove inside nut and bolt from each side of stabilizer bar link, then loosen outside nut and bolt on the stabilizer link.
4. Rotate bottom parts of link to one side and slip stabilizer out of bushings.

Fig. 11   All front & lower control arm rear bushing removal. 1978—83 models

Fig. 12   All front & lower control arm rear bushing installation. 1978—83 models

Fig. 13   Stabilizer bar installation (typical)

Front Suspension & Steering Section

For service procedures on 1977-83 Toronado, refer to Cadillac chapter, "Front Suspension and Steering, Eldorado & 1980-83 Seville" section.

FRONT SUSPENSION

As shown in Figs. 1 and 2, the front suspension is of the conventional "A" frame design with ball joints. Double acting shock absorbers are mounted within the coil springs. Caster and camber are controlled by shims.

WHEEL ALIGNMENT

1977-83

Camber and caster are adjusted by shims placed between the upper pivot shafts and the frame. In order to remove or install shims, *do not remove weight from front wheels.* Loosen pivot shaft-to-frame bolts. To gain access to these bolts, loosen top and rear fasteners on fender filler plate aprons.

To decrease positive caster, add shim at the front bolt. To increase positive caster, remove shim at the front bolt.

To increase camber, remove shims at both front and rear bolt. To decrease camber, add shims at both bolts.

By adding or subtracting an equal amount of shims from both front and rear bolts, camber will change without affecting caster adjustment.

TOE-IN, ADJUST

1977-83

To adjust the toe-in, loosen the clamps at both ends of the adjustable tubes at each tie rod. Then turn the tubes an equal amount until the toe-in is correct. When the tie rods are mounted ahead of the steering knuckle, they must be decreased in length to increase toe-in. When the tie rods are mounted behind the steering knuckle, they must be increased in length to increase toe-in.

NOTE: *The steering knuckle and steering arm "rock" or tilt as front wheel rises and falls. Therefore, it is vitally important to position the bottom face of the tie rod end parallel with the machined surface at the outer end of the steering arm when tie rod length is adjusted. Severe damage and possible failure can result unless this precaution is taken. The tie rod sleeve clamps must be straight down to provide clearance.*

CHECKING BALL JOINTS FOR WEAR

1977-83

If loose ball joints are suspected, first be sure the front wheel bearings are properly adjusted and that the control arms are tight. Then check ball joints for wear as follows:

Referring to Fig. 3, raise wheel with a jack placed under the lower control arm as shown. Then test by moving the wheel up and down to check axial play, and rocking it at the top and bottom to measure radial play.

1977-79 Omega

1. Upper ball joint should be replaced if looseness exceeds .125".

1977-83 Cutlass

1. Upper ball joint should be replaced if looseness exceeds .125".

NOTE: A wear indicator is built into the lower ball joint, Fig. 4.

1977-83 Full Size Cars

1. Upper ball joint should be replaced if looseness exceeds .125".

NOTE: A wear indicator is built into the lower ball joint. Refer to Fig. 4.

Fig. 1   Front suspension. 1977-83 Full Size (Typical)

Fig. 2   Front suspension. 1977-83 Exc. Full Size

Fig. 3   Checking ball joints for wear

Fig. 4 Ball joint wear indicator. 1977–83

Fig. 5 Removing lower ball joint stud from knuckle

Fig. 6 Removing upper ball joint stud from knuckle

BALL JOINTS, REPLACE

On some models the ball joints are riveted to the control arms. All service ball joints, however, are provided with bolt, nut and washer assemblies for replacement purposes.

Some ball joints are pressed into the control arms, in which case they may be pressed out and new ones installed.

LOWER BALL JOINT

1. Raise vehicle and support at frame. Remove wheel.
2. Support lower control arm with a suitable jack.
3. Remove cotter pin and loosen stud nut 2–3 turns. Using tool No. J-8806 or equivalent, break ball joint loose from the knuckle, Fig. 5.
4. Remove stud nut and lower the control arm. Position knuckle assembly aside.
5. Pry ball joint seal retainer from joint and remove seal.
6. Press ball joint from lower control arm with suitable tools.
7. Reverse procedure to install. Torque ball joint stud nut to the following specifications:

Year	Model	Ft. Lbs.
1982–83	All	70
1981	All	90
1980	All	90①
1978–79	All	83 Min.
1977	Cutlass	95
	88 & 98	105

①—Before installing stud nut, tool No. J-29194 must be used to seat the stud on the steering knuckle. Torque tool to 40 ft. lbs., then remove tool and install and torque stud nut.

UPPER BALL JOINT

1. Raise vehicle and support at frame. Remove wheel.
2. Support lower control arm with suitable jack or jack stand.
3. Remove cotter pin and loosen stud nut 2–3 turns. Using tool No. J-8806 or equivalent, break ball joint loose from the knuckle, Fig. 6.
4. Remove stud nut and support knuckle assembly to prevent damage to brake hose.
5. Using a 1/8 inch twist drill, drill the 4 ball joint rivets approximately 1/4 inch. Then drill off rivets heads using a 1/2 inch twist drill.
6. Punch out rivets and remove lower ball joint.
7. Install new ball joint in lower control arm and torque attaching bolts to 8 ft. lbs.
8. Reverse procedure to assemble. Torque ball joint stud nut to the following specifications:

Year	Model	Ft. Lbs.
1982–83	All	50
1981	All	65
1980	All	65①
1978–79	All	60 Min.
1977	All	70

①—Before installing stud nut, tool No. J-29193 must be used to seat the stud on the steering knuckle. Torque tool to 40 ft. lbs., then remove tool and install and torque stud nut.

WHEEL BEARINGS, REPLACE

Disc Brakes

1977–82
1. Raise car and remove front wheels.
2. Remove brake pads and caliper assembly but do not disconnect brake line. Suspend caliper from a wire loop or hook to avoid strain on the brake hose.
3. Remove grease cap, cotter pin and nut. Pull off hub and disc assembly. Grease retainer and inner bearing can now be removed.

WHEEL BEARINGS, ADJUST

1978–83

1. While rotating hub assembly, tighten spindle nut to 12 ft. lbs. to insure bearings are properly seated.
2. Back off nut to the just loose position.
3. Hand tighten spindle nut, then loosen nut until either hole in spindle aligns with slot in nut. Do not back off more than 1/2 flat.
4. Install cotter pin, then measure hub assembly end play. There will be .001 to .005 in. end play when bearings are properly adjusted.

1977

1. While rotating hub assembly, tighten nut

to 30 ft-lbs to insure all parts are properly seated.
2. Back off nut ½ turn.
3. Retighten nut finger tight and install retaining ring or cotter key if possible. If unable to install retaining ring or cotter key, back off nut (not to exceed 1/12 of a turn) until tabs on clip align with serrations in nut.

SHOCK ABSORBER, REPLACE

1977—83

1. Remove upper attaching nut, retainer and grommet from shock absorber.
2. Remove two bolts and washers attaching shock absorber to lower control arm and remove shock absorber.
3. To install, position grommet and retainer over shock and slide shock up through spring and frame. Install and tighten attaching nut and lower cap-screws.

COIL SPRING, REPLACE

IMPORTANT: Left and right coil springs should not be interchanged. Spring part number is stamped on outer side of end coil.

1977—83

1. Place transmission in Neutral.
2. Disconnect shock absorber from upper mounting.
3. Raise vehicle and support at frame. Remove wheel.
4. Disconnect stabilizer bar from lower control arm.
5. Remove shock absorber.
6. Install lower plate BT-7408-1A or 1B, Fig. 7, with pivot ball seat facing downward into spring coils. Rotate plate to fully seat it in lower control arm spring seat.
7. Install upper plate BT-7408-1A or 1B, Fig. 7, with pivot ball seat facing upward into spring coils. Insert ball nut BT-7408-4 through spring coils and onto upper plate.

Fig. 7 Replacing coil spring. 1977—83

8. Install rod BT-7408-5 through shock absorber opening in lower control arm and through the upper and lower plates. Depress lock pin on shaft and thread into upper ball nut BT-7408-4. Ensure lock pin is fully extended above ball nut upper surface.
9. With ball nut tang engaged in slot in upper plate, rotate upper plate until it contacts upper spring seat.
10. Install lower pivot ball, thrust bearing and nut on rod and rotate nut until coil spring is compressed enough to be free in the seat.
11. Remove lower control arm pivot bolts. Move control arm rearward and remove coil spring.
12. Reverse procedure to install.

MANUAL STEERING GEAR, REPLACE

1. Remove two flex coupling flange nuts.

NOTE: On 1977—83 models, remove coupling shield.

2. Hoist and support car with stands under outer ends of lower control arms.
3. Remove nut and use a puller to remove pitman arm.
4. Remove gear-to frame bolts.
5. Position steering linkage out of the way and withdraw gear assembly from under car.
6. Reverse procedure to install unit.

POWER STEERING GEAR, REPLACE

1. Remove coupling flange hub bolt.

NOTE: On 1977—83 models, remove coupling shield.

2. Disconnect hoses from gear and cap gear and hose fittings.
3. Remove pitman arm nut and, using a suitable puller, remove pitman arm.
4. Remove gear-to-frame bolts. Permit lower shaft to slide free of coupling flange, then remove gear with hoses attached.

POWER STEERING PUMP, REPLACE

To replace the power steering pump, loosen pump adjusting bolts and position pump so that drive belt can be removed from pump pulley. Disconnect hydraulic lines from pump and plug all lines and openings to prevent entry of dirt. Remove bolts securing pump or pump and bracket to engine and remove pump from vehicle. It may be necessary, depending on engine and vehicle model, to remove other accessories and components from front of engine to facilitate steering pump removal.

PONTIAC
(Exc. Astre, Sunbird, 1000 & Front Wheel Drive)

INDEX OF SERVICE OPERATIONS

NOTE: Refer to the back of this manual for vehicle manufacturer's special service tool suppliers.

SERIAL NUMBER LOCATION

1977–83: On plate fastened to upper left instrument panel area, visible through windshield.

ENGINE IDENTIFICATION

On Pontiac Built 4-151 engines, the engine code is located on the distributor mounting pad. On 1977–79 V8-301, 350, 400 and 455 engines, the engine code number is located on front of cylinder block below right cylinder head. On 1980–81 V8-265 and 301 engines, the engine code is located on labels attached to front of left and right hand valve covers.

On Buick built 1977 V6-231 engines, the engine code is located on front of block below right cylinder head. On 1978–83 V6-231 and V8-350 engines, the engine code label is located on left hand valve cover.

On Chevrolet Built V6-229, V8-305, and 350 engines, the engine code is located on front of block below right cylinder head.

On Oldsmobile built 1977 V8-350 and 403 engines, the engine code is located on a label attached to the oil filler tube. On 1978–79 V8-403, 1978–81 V8-350 and 1980–83 V8-350 Diesel engines, the engine code is located on a label attached to left hand valve cover.

ENGINE CODES

1977

CODE	TRANS.	V.I.N. Code (18)	ENGINE
WF	(7)	V	4-151(1)
WH	(7)	V	4-151(1)
YR	(6)	V	4-151(1)
YS	(6)(11)	V	4-151(1)
SG	(4)(11)	C	V6-231(1)(13)
SI	(6)(11)	C	V6-231(1)(13)
SJ	(6)(11)	C	V6-231(1)(13)
SK	(6)(11)	C	V6-231(1)(13)
SL	(6)(11)	C	V6-231(1)(13)
SM	(6)(11)	C	V6-231(1)(13)
SN	(6)(11)	C	V6-231(1)(13)
SU	(4)(11)	C	V6-231(1)(13)
RC,RD	(17)	A	V6-231
HK	(6)	Y	V8-301(1)
WB	(5)	Y	V8-301(1)
YH	(6)	Y	V8-301(1)
YW	(6)	Y	V8-301(1)
YX	(6)	Y	V8-301(1)
CPR	(6)	U	V8-305(1)(14)
CRA	(6)	U	V8-305(1)(14)
CKR	(6)	L	V8-350(2)(14)
CKM	(6)	L	V8-350(2)(14)
Q2	(6)	R	V8-350(2)(12)
Q3	(6)	R	V8-350(2)(12)
Q6	(6)	K	V8-350(2)(12)
Q7	(6)	K	V8-350(2)(12)
Q8	(6)	R	V8-350(2)(12)
Q9	(6)	K	V8-350(2)(12)
QP	(6)	K	V8-350(2)(12)
QQ	(6)	K	V8-350(2)(12)
TK	(6)	R	V8-350(2)(12)
TL	(6)	R	V8-350(2)(12)
TN	(6)	R	V8-350(2)(12)
TO	(6)	R	V8-350(2)(12)
TX	(6)	R	V8-350(2)(12)
TY	(6)	R	V8-350(2)(12)
Y9	(6)	P	V8-350(2)
YA	(6)	P	V8-350(2)
YB	(6)	P	V8-350(2)
WA	(5)	Z	V8-400(2)
XA	(6)	Z	V8-400(2)
Y4	(6)	Z	V8-400(2)
Y6	(6)	Z	V8-400(2)
Y7	(6)	Z	V8-400(2)
YC	(6)	Z	V8-400(2)
YD	(6)	Z	V8-400(2)
YU	(6)	Z	V8-400(2)
U2	(6)	K	V8-403(2)(12)
U3	(6)	K	V8-403(2)(12)
UA	(6)	K	V8-403(2)(12)
UB	(6)	K	V8-403(2)(12)
VA	(6)	K	V8-403(2)(12)
VB	(6)	K	V8-403(2)(12)
VJ	(6)	K	V8-403(2)(12)
VK	(6)	K	V8-403(2)(12)

1978

CODE	TRANS.	V.I.N. Code (18)	ENGINE
YB,YC	(6)	V	4-151(1)
EA	(4)	A	V6-231(1)(13)
EC,EE,EI	(6)	A	V6-231(1)(13)

1978—Cont'd

CODE	TRANS.	V.I.N. Code (18)	ENGINE
EJ,EK,EL	(6)	A	V6-231(1)(13)
OE,OH,OK,OR	(6)	A	V6-231(1)(13)
XA,XB,XC	(6)	Y	V8-301(1)
XD,XF	(6)	Y	V8-301(1)
XH,XU,XW	(6)	W	V8-301(2)
CPF	(6)	H	V8-305(2)(14)
CPH,CPZ,CRU	(6)	U	V8-305(1)(14)
CRY,CRZ,CJJ	(6)	U	V8-305(1)(14)
CTH	(4)	U	V8-305(1)(14)
CTK,CTM,CTS	(6)	U	V8-305(1)(14)
CTT,CTU,CTW	(6)	U	V8-305(1)(14)
CTX,CTY,CTZ	(6)	U	V8-305(1)(14)
MA,MB	(6)	X	V8-350(2)(13)
TO,TP,TQ	(6)	R	V8-350(2)(12)
TS,Q2,Q3	(6)	R	V8-350(2)(12)
CHJ,CHL,CMC	(6)	L	V8-350(2)(14)
CHR	(4)	L	V8-350(2)(14)
WC	(4)	Z	V8-400(2)
XJ,XK	(6)	Z	V8-400(2)
X7,X9	(6)	Z	V8-400(2)
Y,YA,YH	(6)	Z	V8-400(2)
YJ,YK	(6)	Z	V8-400(2)
U2,U3	(6)	K	V8-403(2)(12)
U5,U6	(6)	K	V8-403(2)(12)
VA,VB	(6)	K	V8-403(2)(12)
VD,VE	(6)	K	V8-403(2)(12)

1979

CODE	TRANS.	V.I.N. Code (18)	ENGINE
NA,NG	(4)	A	V6-231(1)(10)(13)
NB,NJ,NK	(6)	A	V6-231(1)(10)(13)
NC	(6)	A	V6-231(1)(13)
NE	(6)	A	V6-231(1)(3)(13)
NH	(6)	A	V6-231(1)(8)(13)
NL,NM	(6)	A	V6-231(1)(10)(13)
RA	(6)	A	V6-231(1)(13)
RB,RC,RX	(6)	A	V6-231(1)(10)(13)
RG,RW,RY	(6)	A	V6-231(1)(8)(13)
PWA,PWB	(4)	W	V8-301(2)(10)
PXF,PXH	(6)	Y	V8-301(1)(10)
PXL,PXN,PXS	(6)	W	V8-301(2)(10)
PXP,PXR	(6)	Y	V8-301(1)(10)
PXT,PXU,PXW	(6)	W	V8-301(2)(10)
PX4,PX6	(6)	W	V8-301(2)(10)
PX7,PX9	(6)	Y	V8-301(1)(10)
DND,DNK	(6)	G	V8-305(1)(8)(10)
DNJ,DTL	(6)	G	V8-305(1)(10)(14)
DNX,DNY	(6)	H	V8-305(2)(8)(14)
DTA	(6)	H	V8-305(2)(3)(14)
DTK,DTM	(4)	G	V8-305(1)(10)(14)
SA,SC,SD	(6)	X	V8-350(2)(13)
DNX,DRY	(6)	L	V8-350(2)(3)(8)
DRJ	(6)	L	V8-350(2)(14)
U9	(6)	K	V8-350(2)(3)(12)
VK	(6)	R	V8-350(2)(8)(12)
PWH	(4)	Z	V8-400(2)
Q3	(6)	K	V8-403(2)(3)(12)
TB,TD,TE	(6)	K	V8-403(2)(8)(12)
QB	(6)	K	V8-403(2)(3)(12)
QE,QL,QJ	(6)	K	V8-403(2)(12)

1980

CODE	TRANS.	V.I.N. Code (18)	ENGINE
CLA	(4)	K	V6-229(10)(14)
CLB,CLC	(6)	K	V6-229(10)(14)
EA,EX,OJ	(4)	A	V6-231(10)(13)
EB,EC,EO,EP	(6)	A	V6-231(10)(13)
EZ,OA,OK,OL	(6)	A	V6-231(10)(13)
EF,EG,ES,ET	(6)	A	V6-231(8)(13)
OB,OC,OM,ON	(6)	A	V6-231(8)(13)
XH,XR,X6	(6)	S	V8-265(10)
XT,XW,X3,X9	(6)	W	V8-301(10)
XN,YN,YR	(6)	W	V8-301(10)
YL	(6)	T	V8-301(15)
CEC,CEL,CEM	(6)	H	V8-305(8)(14)
ML,MV	(6)	X	V8-350(10)(13)
UAD,UAF	(6)	R	V8-350(8)(12)
VBN,VBT,VCD, VCP	(6)	N	V8-350(11)(16)

1981

CODE	TRANS.	V.I.N. Code (18)	ENGINE
NA,NZ	(4)	A	V6-231(10)(13)
NB,NL,RA	(6)	A	V6-231(10)(13)
NC,ND,RB	(6)	A	V6-231(8)(13)
RK,RL,RC,RD	(6)	A	V6-231(13)
AU,AW,AZ	(6)	S	V8-265
BA,DB,DC	(6)	S	V8-265
DH,DJ	(6)	S	V8-265
WAV	(6)	S	V8-265
WDB	(6)	S	V8-265
WDH	(6)	S	V8-265(8)
WBD,WBJ	(6)	W	V8-301
WBO	(6)	T	V8-301(15)
DHA,DHB,DHC	(5)(6)	H	V8-305(14)
DHD,DHF,DHH	(5)(6)	H	V8-305(14)
DHJ,DHK,DHU	(5)(6)	H	V8-305(14)
DHZ	(4)	H	V8-305(10)(14)
DHZ	(6)	H	V8-305(8)(14)
DKB,D6A,D6B	(5)(6)	H	V8-305(14)
D6C,D6D	(5)(6)	H	V8-305(14)
TKA,TKB,TKC	(6)	Y	V8-307(10)(12)
TKJ,TKM	(6)	Y	V8-307(10)(12)
TKL,TKR	(6)	Y	V8-307(8)(12)
TKP,TKT,TKU	(6)	Y	V8-307(12)
TKX,TKY,TKZ	(6)	Y	V8-307(12)
TLA,TLB,TLD	(6)	Y	V8-307(12)
TLF,TLH,TLJ	(6)	Y	V8-307(12)
TLK,TLL,TLM,TLN	(6)	Y	V8-307(12)
VKB,VKC,VKH	(6)	N	V8-350(12)(16)
VKJ,VKN,VKR	(6)	N	V8-350(12)(16)
VKU,VKY,VLA	(6)	N	V8-350(12)(16)
VLC,VLD,VLK	(6)	N	V8-350(12)(16)
VLL,VLN,VLP	(6)	N	V8-350(12)(16)
VL8,VLY,VMJ	(6)	N	V8-350(12)(16)
VMT,VMX,VMY	(6)	N	V8-350(12)(16)
VNA,VNB,VNC	(6)	N	V8-350(12)(16)
VND,VNE	(6)	N	V8-350(12)(16)

Continued

CODE	TRANS.	V.I.N. Code ⑱	ENGINE
1982			
X3A,X3C,X3F	④....2		4-151
X3H,X5A,X5F,X5H			
	⑥....2		4-151
CBT,CBU,CBW	⑤⑥....1		V6-173⑭
CBX,CB2,CJB	⑥....1		V6-173⑭
C7A,C7B,C7C,C7D			
	⑥....1		V6-173⑭
MA,MG,MC	⑥....A		V6-231⑬
MK,ML,MM	⑥....A		V6-231⑬
FA,FB,FC	⑥....4		V6-252⑬

CODE	TRANS.	V.I.N. Code ⑱	ENGINE
1982—Cont'd			
FD,FE,FF	⑥....4		V6-252⑬
FG,FH,FJ,FK	⑥....4		V6-252⑬
CFA,CFB,CFC,CFD	⑥....H		V8-305⑭
CFF,CFH,CFR,C2R	⑥....H		V8-305⑭
C2S,C2T,C2U,C2W			
	⑥....H		V8-305⑭
CFT,CFW,CFY,			
CF2,CRA	⑥....H		V8-305⑭
CEJ,CFK,CFM,CFN	⑥....7		V8-305⑭

CODE	TRANS.	V.I.N. Code ⑱	ENGINE
1982—Cont'd			
VAB,VAC,VAD,VAK			
	⑥....N		V8-350⑫⑯
VAL,VAM,VAN,VAP			
	⑥....N		V8-350⑫⑯
VAS,VAU,VAW,			
VAX	⑥....N		V8-350⑫⑯
VAY,VAZ,VBA,VBB			
VBC,VBP,VBU,VBW	⑥....N		V8-350⑫⑯
	⑥....N		V8-350⑫⑯

①—Two barrel carburetor.
②—Four barrel carburetor.
③—Hi Altitude.
④—Manual trans.
⑤—Four speed manual trans.
⑥—Automatic trans.
⑦—Five speed manual trans.
⑧—California.

⑨—One barrel carburetor.
⑩—Exc. California.
⑪—Except even fire engine.
⑫—See Oldsmobile chapter for service procedures.
⑬—See Buick chapter for service procedures.
⑭—See Chevrolet chapter for service procedures.

⑮—Turbocharged engine.
⑯—Diesel.
⑰—Even fire engine.
⑱—On 1977–80 vehicles, the fifth digit in the V.I.N. denotes engine code. On 1981–83 vehicles, the eighth digit in the V.I.N. denotes engine code.

GRILLE IDENTIFICATION

1977 Ventura

1977 LeMans, Sports Cpe, & GT

1977 Grand LeMans

1977 Grand Prix

1977–78 Firebird Trans Am

1977–78 Formula Firebird

1977–79 Phoenix

1978 Bonneville & Grand Safari

1978 Catalina

1977–78 Firebird, Esprit

1977 Catalina

1977 Bonneville & Grand Safari

Continued

GRILLE IDENTIFICATION—Continued

1978–79 Grand Am

1978 Grand LeMans, LeMans Safari

1978 Grand Prix

1979 Grand LeMans, Grand LeMans Safari & Grand Am 4 Dr.

1979 Bonneville Brougham & Safari

1979 Catalina

1979 Grand Prix

1979–80 Firebird Formula

1979–80 Firebird Trans Am

1980 Grand Am

1980 Grand LeMans

1980 Grand Prix

1980 Bonneville & Catalina

1981 Bonneville

1981 LeMans

1981 Grand Prix

1982 Bonneville

1982 Grand Prix

1982–83 Firebird

1983 Bonneville

1983 Grand Prix

GENERAL ENGINE SPECIFICATIONS

Year	Engine CID①/Liter	Engine V.I.N. Code②	Carburetor	Bore and Stroke	Compression Ratio	Net H.P. @ R.P.M.③	Maximum Torque Ft. Lbs. @ R.P.M.	Normal Oil Pressure Pounds
1977	4-151, 2.5L	V	5210C, 2 Bbl.⑨	4.00 × 3.00	8.3	88 @ 4400	128 @ 2400	30—45
	V6-231, 3.8L⑦	C	2GC, 2 Bbl.⑤	3.80 × 3.40	8.0	105 @ 3200	185 @ 2000	37
	V6-231, 3.8L⑦	A	2GE, 2 Bbl.⑤	3.80 × 3.40	8.0	105 @ 3200	185 @ 2000	37
	V8-301, 4.9L	Y	M2MC, 2 Bbl.⑤	4.00 × 3.00	8.2	135 @ 4000	⑩	38—42
	V8-305, 5.0L④	U	2GC, 2 Bbl.⑤	3.736 × 3.48	8.5	145 @ 3800	245 @ 2400	32—40
	V8-350, 5.7L④	L	M4MC, 4 Bbl.⑤	4.00 × 3.48	8.5	170 @ 3800	270 @ 2400	32—40
	V8-350, 5.7L	P	M4MC, 4 Bbl.⑤	3.88 × 3.75	7.6	170 @ 4000	280 @ 1800	55—60
	V8-350, 5.7L⑥	R	M4MC, 4 Bbl.⑤	4.057 × 3.385	8	170 @ 3800	275 @ 2000	37
	V8-400, 6.6L	Z	M4MC, 4 Bbl.⑤	4.12 × 3.75	7.6	180 @ 3600	325 @ 1600	55—60
	V8-400, 6.6L⑪	Z	M4MC, 4 Bbl.⑤	4.12 × 3.75	8.0	200 @ 3600	⑫	55—60
	V8-403, 6.6L⑥	K	M4MC, 4 Bbl.⑤	4.351 × 3.385	8.0	185 @ 3600	320 @ 2200	30—45
1978	4-151, 2.5L	V	5210C, 2 Bbl.⑨	4.00 × 3.00	8.3	85 @ 4400	123 @ 2800	36—41
	V6-231, 3.8L⑦	A	2GC, 2 Bbl.⑤	3.80 × 3.40	8.0	105 @ 3400	185 @ 2000	37
	V8-301, 5.0L	Y	M2MC, 2 Bbl.⑤	4.00 × 3.00	8.2	140 @ 3600	235 @ 2000	35—40
	V8-301, 5.0L	W	M4MC, 4 Bbl.⑤	4.00 × 3.00	8.2	150 @ 4000	240 @ 2000	35—40
	V8-305, 5.0L④⑬	U	2GC, 2 Bbl.⑤	3.736 × 3.48	8.4	135 @ 3800	240 @ 2000	32—40
	V8-305, 5.0L④⑭	H	M4MC, 4 Bbl.⑤	3.736 × 3.48	8.4	145 @ 3800	245 @ 2400	32—40
	V8-350, 5.7L⑦	X	M4MC, 4 Bbl.⑤	3.80 × 3.85	8.0	155 @ 3400	280 @ 1800	—
	V8-350, 5.7L④	L	M4MC, 4 Bbl.⑤	4.00 × 3.48	8.2	160 @ 3800	260 @ 2400	32—40
	V8-350, 5.7L⑥	R	M4MC, 4 Bbl.⑤	4.057 × 3.385	7.9	170 @ 3800	275 @ 2000	30—45
	V8-350, 5.7L④	L	M4MC, 4 Bbl.⑤	4.00 × 3.48	8.2	170 @ 3800	270 @ 2400	32—40
	V8-400, 6.6L	Z	M4MC, 4 Bbl.⑤	4.12 × 3.75	7.7	180 @ 3600	325 @ 1600	35—40
	V8-400, 6.6L⑪	Z	M4MC, 4 Bbl.⑤	4.12 × 3.75	8.1	220 @ 4000	320 @ 2800	55—60
	V8-403, 6.6L⑥	K	M4MC, 4 Bbl.⑤	4.351 × 3.385	7.9	185 @ 3600	320 @ 2000	30—45
1979	V6-231, 3.8L⑦	A	M2ME, 2 Bbl.⑤	3.80 × 3.40	8.0	115 @ 3800	185 @ 2000	37
	V6-231, 3.8L⑦	A	M2ME, 2 Bbl.⑤	3.80 × 3.40	8.0	115 @ 3800	190 @ 2000	37
	V6-231, 3.8L⑦	A	M2ME, 2 Bbl.⑤	3.80 × 3.40	8.0	135 @ 3800	190 @ 2000	37
	V8-301, 4.9L	Y	M2MC, 2 Bbl.⑤	4.00 × 3.00	8.1	130 @ 3200	245 @ 2000	35—40
	V8-301, 4.9L	Y	M2MC, 2 Bbl.⑤	4.00 × 3.00	8.1	135 @ 3800	240 @ 1600	35—40
	V8-301, 4.9L	W	M4MC, 4 Bbl.⑤	4.00 × 3.00	8.1	150 @ 4000	⑮	35—40
	V8-305, 5.0L④	G	M2MC, 2 Bbl.⑤	3.736 × 3.48	8.4	125 @ 3200	245 @ 2000	32—40
	V8-305, 5.0L④	H	M4MC, 4 Bbl.⑤	3.736 × 3.48	8.4	130 @ 3200	245 @ 2000	32—40
	V8-305, 5.0L④	H	M4MC, 4 Bbl.⑤	3.736 × 3.48	8.4	155 @ 4000	225 @ 2400	32—40
	V8-350, 5.7L⑦	X	M4MC, 4 Bbl.⑤	3.80 × 3.85	8.0	155 @ 3400	280 @ 1800	34
	V8-350, 5.7L⑥	R	M4MC, 4 Bbl.⑤	4.057 × 3.385	7.9	160 @ 3600	270 @ 2000	30—45
	V8-350, 5.7L④	L	M4MC, 4 Bbl.⑤	4.00 × 3.48	8.2	165 @ 3800	260 @ 2400	32—40
	V8-400, 6.6L	Z	M4MC, 4 Bbl.⑤	4.12 × 3.75	8.1	220 @ 4000	320 @ 2800	35—40
	V8-403, 6.6L⑥	K	M4MC, 4 Bbl.⑤	4.351 × 3.385	7.9	175 @ 3600	310 @ 2000	30—45
	V8-403, 6.6L⑥	K	M4MC, 4 Bbl.⑤	4.351 × 3.385	7.9	185 @ 3600	315 @ 2000	30—45
1980	V6-229, 3.8L④	K	M2ME, 2 Bbl.⑤	3.376 × 3.48	8.6	115 @ 4000	175 @ 2000	45
	V6-231, 3.8L⑦	A	M2ME, 2 Bbl.⑤	3.80 × 3.40	8.0	115 @ 3800	188 @ 2000	37
	V8-265, 4.3L	S	M2ME, 2 Bbl.⑤	3.75 × 3.00	8.3	120 @ 3600	210 @ 1600	35—40
	V8-301, 4.9L	W	M4ME, 4 Bbl.⑤	4.00 × 3.00	8.2	150 @ 4000	240 @ 2000	35—40
	V8-301, 4.9L⑯	W	M4ME, 4 Bbl.⑤	4.00 × 3.00	8.2	170 @ 4400	240 @ 2200	55—60
	V8-301, 4.9L⑰	T	M4ME, 4 Bbl.⑤	4.00 × 3.00	7.5	205 @ 4000	310 @ 2800	55—60
	V8-305, 5.0L④	H	E4ME, 4 Bbl.⑤	3.736 × 3.48	8.4	150 @ 3800	230 @ 2400	45
	V8-350, 5.7L⑦	X	M4MC, 4 Bbl.⑤	3.80 × 3.85	—	—	—	37
	V8-350, 5.7L⑥	R	E4MC, 4 Bbl.⑤	4.057 × 3.385	—	160 @ 3600	270 @ 2000	30—45
	V8-350, 5.7L⑥⑧	N	Fuel Injection	4.057 × 3.385	22.5	105 @ 3200	205 @ 1600	30—45
1981	V6-231, 3.8L⑥	A	E2ME, 2 Bbl.⑤	4.00 × 3.00	8.0	110 @ 3800	190 @ 1600	35—40
	V8-265, 4.3L	S	E2ME, 2 Bbl.⑤	3.75 × 3.00	8.3	120 @ 4000	205 @ 2000	35—40
	V8-301, 4.9L⑯	W	E4ME, 4 Bbl.⑤	4.00 × 3.00	8.1	135 @ 3600	235 @ 3600	35—40
	V8-301, 4.9L⑰	T	E4ME, 4 Bbl.⑤	4.00 × 3.00	7.5	200 @ 4000	340 @ 2000	55—60

Continued

GENERAL ENGINE SPECIFICATIONS—Continued

Year	Engine CID①/Liter	V.I.N. Code②	Carburetor	Bore and Stroke	Com-pression Ratio	Net H.P. @ R.P.M.③	Maximum Torque Ft. Lbs. @ R.P.M.	Normal Oil Pressure Pounds
1981	V8-305, 5.0L④	H	E4ME, 4 Bbl.⑤	3.736 × 3.48	8.6	145 @ 3800	240 @ 2400	30—45
	V8-307, 5.0L⑥	Y	E4ME, 4 Bbl.⑤	3.80 × 3.385	8.5	145 @ 3800	240 @ 2000	30—45
	V8-350, 5.7L⑥⑧	N	Fuel Injection	4.057 × 3.385	22.5	105 @ 3200	205 @ 1600	37
1982	4-151, 2.5L	2	E.F.I.⑭	4.00 × 3.00	8.2	90 @ 4000	132 @ 2800	36—41
	V6-173, 2.8L④	1	E2SE, 2 Bbl.⑤	3.50 × 3.00	8.5	102 @ 4800	142 @ 2400	50—65
	V6-231, 3.8L⑦	A	E2ME, 2 Bbl.⑤	3.80 × 3.40	8.0	110 @ 3800	190 @ 1600	37
	V6-252, 4.1L⑦	4	E4ME, 4 Bbl.⑤	3.965 × 3.40	8.0	125 @ 3800	210 @ 2000	37
	V8-305, 5.0L④	H	E4ME, 4 Bbl.⑤	3.736 × 3.48	8.6	145 @ 4000	240 @ 2000	50—65
	V8-305, 5.0L④	7	E.F.I.⑭	3.736 × 3.48	9.5	165 @ 4200	240 @ 2400	50—65
	V8-350, 5.7L⑥⑧	N	Fuel Injection	4.057 × 3.385	22.5	105 @ 3200	200 @ 1600	35
1983	4-151, 2.5L	2	E.F.I.⑭	4.00 × 3.00	8.2	92 @ 4000	134 @ 2800	36—41
	V6-173, 2.8L④	1	E2SE, 2 Bbl.⑤	3.50 × 3.00	8.5	107 @ 4800	145 @ 2100	50—65
	V6-173 H.O., 2.8L④	—	E2SE, 2 Bbl.⑤	3.50 × 3.00	8.9	135 @ 5400	145 @ 2400	50—65
	V6-231, 3.8L⑦	A	E2ME, 2 Bbl.⑤	3.80 × 3.40	8.0	110 @ 3800	190 @ 1600	37
	V8-305, 5.0L④	H	E4ME, 4 Bbl.⑤	3.736 × 3.48	8.6	150 @ 4000	240 @ 2400	50—65
	V8-305, 5.0L④	7	E.F.I.⑭	3.736 × 3.48	9.5	175 @ 4200	250 @ 2800	50—65
	V8-350, 5.7L⑥⑧	N	Fuel Injection	4.057 × 3.385	21.6	105 @ 3200	200 @ 1600	30—45

①—CID—Cubic Inch displacement.
②—VIN Code—On 1976–80 vehicles the fifth digit in the VIN denotes engine code. On 1981–82 vehicles the eighth digit in the VIN denotes engine code.
③—Ratings are net—as installed in vehicle.
④—See Chevrolet chapter for service procedures on this engine.
⑤—Rochester.
⑥—See Oldsmobile chapter for service procedures on this engine.
⑦—See Buick chapter for service procedures on this engine.
⑧—Diesel engine.
⑨—Holley.
⑩—Manual trans., 235 @ 2400. Auto. trans., 245 @ 2200.
⑪—High performance Trans Am engine.
⑫—Manual trans., 325 @ 2400; Auto. trans., 325 @ 2200.
⑬—High altitude.
⑭—Electronic Fuel Injection.
⑮—Manual trans., 240 @ 2400; Auto. trans., 240 @ 2200.
⑯—E/C (electronic engine control).
⑰—Turbocharged engine.

TUNE UP SPECIFICATIONS

The following specifications are published from the latest information available. This data should be used only in the absence of a decal affixed in the engine compartment.

★ When using a timing light, disconnect vacuum hose or tube at distributor and plug opening in tube or hose so idle speed will not be affected.

● When checking compression, lowest cylinder must be within 70% of the highest.

▲ Before removing wires from distributor cap, determine location of the No. 1 wire in cap, as distributor position may have been altered from that shown at the end of this chart.

Spark plug types shown in this chart are recommendations of the original vehicle manufacturer and not MOTOR.

Check local sources for other spark plug manufacturers listings.

Year & Engine/V.I.N.	Spark Plug Type	Gap	Firing Order Fig. ▲	Ignition Timing BTDC①★ Man. Trans.	Auto. Trans.	Mark Fig.	Curb Idle Speed② Man. Trans.	Auto. Trans.	Fast Idle Speed Man. Trans.	Auto. Trans.	Fuel Pump Pressure
1977											
4-151/V	R44TSX	.060	F		14°	Q	⑱	⑲	2200⑤	2400⑤	4—5½
V6-231/C⑳	㉑	㉑	G	12°	12°	C㉒	600/800	600D㉓	—	—	4¼—5¾
V6-231/A㉔	R46TSX	.060	D	—	15°	E㉒	—	600/670D㉕	—	—	4¼—5¾
V8-301/Y	R46TSX	.060	O	16°	12°	A	750/850	550/650D	1750	1750	7—8½
V8-305/U	R45TS	.045	P	—	8°	R	—	500/650D	—	—	7½—9
V8-350/P㉖	R45TSX	.060	P	—	16°	H	—	575/650D	—	1800	7½—9
V8-350/L㉗	R45TS	.045	P	—	8°	H	—	㉘	—	1600	7½—9
V8-350/R㉙	R46SZ	.060	M	—	㉚	J	—	㉛	—	1000	5½—6½

TUNE UP SPECIFICATIONS—Continued

The following specifications are published from the latest information available. This data should be used only in the absence of a decal affixed in the engine compartment.

★ When using a timing light, disconnect vacuum hose or tube at distributor and plug opening in tube or hose so idle speed will not be affected.

● When checking compression, lowest cylinder must be within 70% of the highest.

▲ Before removing wires from distributor cap, determine location of the No. 1 wire in cap, as distributor position may have been altered from that shown at the end of this chart.

☞ Spark plug types shown in this chart are recommendations of the original vehicle manufacturer and not MOTOR.

Check local sources for other spark plug manufacturers listings.

Year & Engine/V.I.N.	Spark Plug		Firing Order Fig. ▲	Ignition Timing BTDC① ★			Curb Idle Speed②		Fast Idle Speed		Fuel Pump Pressure
	Type ☞	Gap		Man. Trans.	Auto. Trans.	Mark Fig.	Man. Trans.	Auto. Trans.	Man. Trans.	Auto. Trans.	
1977—Continued											
V8-400/Z	R45TSX	.060	O	18°	㉜	I	775	㉝	1800	1800	7–8½
V8-403/K Exc. Calif. & High Alt.	R46SZ	.060	M	—	22°⑦	J	—	550/650D	—	900	5½–6½
V8-403/K Calif. & High Alt.	R46SZ	.060	M	—	20°⑦	J	—	㉞	—	1000	5½–6½
1978											
4-151/V	R43TSX	.060	F	—	14°⑰	B	—	㊱	—	⑤㊲	4½–5
V6-231/A	R46TSX	.060	D	15°	15°	E㉒	800	㊳	—	—	4½–5.9
V8-301/Y 2 Barrel	R46TSX	.060	O	—	12°	A	—	550/650D	—	2200	7–8½
V8-301/W 4 Barrel	R45TSX	.060	O	—	12°	A	—	550/650D	—	2300	7–8½
V8-305/U Exc. Calif. & High Alt.	R45TS	.045	P	4°	4°	R	600/700	500/600D	1600	1600	7½–9
V8-305/U Calif.	R45TS	.045	P	—	6°	R	—	500/600D	—	1600	7½–9
V8-305/U High Alt.	R45TS	.045	P	—	8°	R	—	600/700D	—	1600	7½–9
V8-350/L㉗	R45TS	.045	P	6°	8°	H	700	⑩	1300	1600	7½–9
V8-350/R㉙	R46SZ	.060	M	—	20°⑦	J	—	550/650D	—	⑪	5½–6½
V8-350/X⑬	R46TSX	.060	N	—	15°	E㉒	—	550D	—	1500	⑭
V8-400/Z	R45TSX	.060	O	16°	㉜	I	775	㉝	1800	1800	7–8½
V8-403/K	R46SZ	.060	M	—	20°⑦	J	—	㉛	—	1000	5½–6½
1979											
V6-231/A	R46TSX	.060	D	15°	15°	E㉒	600/800	㉟	2200	2200	4½–5.9
V8-301/Y 2 Barrel	R46TSX	.060	O	—	12°	A	—	500/650D	—	2000	7–8½
V8-301/W 4 Barrel	R45TSX	.060	O	14°	12°	A	700/800	500/650D	2000	2200	7–8½
V8-305/G 2 Barrel Exc. Calif.	R45TS	.045	P	4°	4°	R	600/700	500/600D	1300	1600	7½–9
V8-305/G 2 Barrel Calif.	R45TS	.045	P	—	4°	R	—	600/650D	—	1950	7½–9
V8-305/H 4 Barrel	R45TS	.045	P	—	4°	R	—	500/600D	—	1600	7½–9
V8-350/L㉗	R45TS	.045	P	—	8°	R	—	⑩	—	1600	7½–9
V8-350/R㉙	R46SZ	.060	M	—	20°⑦	J	—	500/600D	—	1000	5½–6½
V8-350/X⑬	R46TSX	.060	N	—	15°	E㉒	—	550D	—	1550	⑭
V8-400/Z	R45TSX	.060	O	18°	—	I	775	—	1800	—	7–8½
V8-403/K	R46SZ	.060	M	—	20°⑦	J	—	500/600D	—	1000	5½–6½
1980											
V6-229/K	R45TS	.045	D	10°	10°	R	700/750	600/675D	1750	1750	4½–6
V6-231/A Exc. Calif.	R45TS	.040	D	15°	15°	E㉒	600/800	500/670D	2200	2000	3 Min.
V6-231/A Calif.	R45TSX	.060	D	—	15°	E㉒	—	550/620D	—	2200	3 Min.
V8-265/S	R45TSX	.060	O	—	10°	A	—	550/650D	—	2200	7–8½
V8-301/W⑫	R45TSX	.060	O	—	12°	A	—	550/650D	—	2500	7–8½
V8-301/W⑥	R45TSX	.060	O	—	12°	A	—	550D	—	2500	7–8½
V8-301/T⑨	R45TSX	.060	O	—	8°	A	—	600/650D	—	2400	7–8½

Continued

TUNE UP SPECIFICATIONS—Continued

The following specifications are published from the latest information available. This data should be used only in the absence of a decal affixed in the engine compartment.

★ When using a timing light, disconnect vacuum hose or tube at distributor and plug opening in tube or hose so idle speed will not be affected.

● When checking compression, lowest cylinder must be within 70% of the highest.

▲ Before removing wires from distributor cap, determine location of the No. 1 wire in cap, as distributor position may have been altered from that shown at the end of this chart.

Spark plug types shown in this chart are recommendations of the original vehicle manufacturer and not MOTOR.

Check local sources for other spark plug manufacturers listings.

Year & Engine/V.I.N.	Spark Plug Type	Gap	Ignition Timing BTDC①★ Firing Order Fig.▲	Man. Trans.	Auto. Trans.	Mark Fig.	Curb Idle Speed② Man. Trans.	Auto. Trans.	Fast Idle Speed Man. Trans.	Auto. Trans.	Fuel Pump Pressure
1980—Continued											
V8-305/H	R45TS	.045	P	—	4°	④	—	550/650D	—	2200	7½–9
V8-350/X Exc. Calif.⑬	R45TSX	.060	N	—	15°	E㉒	—	550/670D	—	1850	3 Min.
V8-350/R Calif.㉙	R46SX	.080	M	—	18°⑦	J	—	550/650D	—	700	5½–6½
V8-350 Diesel/N	—	—	—	—	③⑩	—	—	575/750D	—	—	—
1981											
V6-231/A	R45TS8	.080	D	15°	15°	E㉒	800	⑯	2200	1800	3 Min.
V8-265/S	R45TSX	.060	O	—	12°	A	—	450D	—	2000	7–8½
V8-301/W Exc. Turbo	R45TSX	.060	O	—	12°	A	—	450D	—	2000	7–8½
V8-301 Turbo/T	R45TSX	.060	O	—	6°	A	—	450D	—	2400	7–8½
V8-305/H	R45TS	.045	P	6°	—	L	800	—	2200	—	7½–9
V8-307/Y	R46SX	.080	M	—	15°⑦	J	—	⑯	—	650D	5½–6½
V8-350 Diesel/N	—	—	—	—	③⑪	—	—	600D	—	750D	—
1982											
4-151 E.F.I./2	R44TSX	.060	K	8°	8°	S	⑯⑫	650D⑯	⑯	⑯	—
V6-173/1	R43CTS	.045	T	10°	10°	U	850	600/700D	2600	2500	6–7½
V6-231/A	R45TS8	.080	D	—	15°	E㉒	—	500D	—	2000	4¼–5¾
V6-252/4	R45TS8	.080	D	—	15°	E㉒	—	500D	—	—	4¼–5¾
V8-305/H	R45TS	.045	P	—	6°	L	—	500/600D	—	2200	7½–9
V8-305 E.F.I./7	R45TS	.045	P	—	6°	L	—	500D	—	1000	—
V8-350 Diesel/N⑬	—	—	—	—	③⑭	—	—	600D	—	750D	—
V8-350 Diesel/N⑮	—	—	—	—	③⑯	—	—	600D	—	750D	—
1983											
4-151 E.F.I./2	R44TSX	.060	K	—	—	S	—	—	—	—	—
V6-173/1	R43CTS	.045	T	—	—	U	—	—	—	—	6–7½
V6-173 H.O.	R42CTS	.045	T	—	—	U	—	—	—	—	6–7½
V6-231/A	R45TS8	.080	D	—	15°	E㉒	—	⑯	—	2200	—
V8-305/H	R45TS	.045	P	—	—	L	—	—	—	—	7½–9
V8-305 E.F.I./7	R45TS	.045	P	—	—	L	—	—	—	—	—
V8-350 Diesel/N	—	—	—	—	③⑧	—	—	600D	—	750D	—

①—BTDC—Before top dead center.
②—Idle speed on man. trans. vehicles is adjusted in Neutral & on auto. trans. equipped vehicles is adjusted in Drive unless otherwise specified. Where two idle speeds are listed, the higher speed is with the A/C or idle solenoid energized.
③—Using Diesel Timing Meter J-33075.
④—Early models, Fig. R; late models, Fig. L.
⑤—On high step of fast idle cam with A/C off.
⑥—E/C (electronic control) engine.
⑦—At 1100 RPM.
⑧—Set at 4° ATDC at 1250 RPM.
⑨—Turbocharged engine.
⑩—Except high altitude, 500/600D RPM; high altitude, 600/650D RPM.
⑪—Except Calif., 900 RPM; California, 1000 RPM.
⑫—Except E/C (electronic control) & turbocharged engines.
⑬—Distributor located at front of engine.
⑭—Less A/C, 5–6½ psi.; with A/C, 5.9–7.4 psi.
⑮—On Grand LeMans & LeMans models, set to 575D RPM.
⑯—Idle speed is controlled by the idle speed control (ICS) motor or the idle load compensator (ILC).
⑰—At 1000 RPM.
⑱—Less A/C, 500/1000 RPM; with A/C, 500/1200 RPM.
⑲—Less A/C, 500/650D RPM; with A/C, 650/850D RPM.
⑳—Except Even-Fire engine.
㉑—R46TS gapped at .040" or R46TSX gapped at .060".
㉒—The harmonic balancer on these engines has two timing marks. The mark measuring 1/16 in. is used when setting timing with a hand held timing light. The mark measuring 1/8 in. is used when setting timing with magnetic timing equipment.
㉓—On Ventura, Phoenix & full size models with A/C, set to 600/670D RPM.
㉔—Even-Fire engine.
㉕—On full size models, idle speed with solenoid energized is set with A/C on.
㉖—Distributor located rear of engine, rotor rotation counter clockwise. Fuel pump located left side of engine.

Continued

TUNE UP NOTES—Continued

㉗—Distributor located rear of engine, rotor rotation clockwise.

㉘—Except high altitude 500/650D RPM; high altitude, 600/650D RPM.

㉙—Distributor located rear of engine, rotor rotation counter clockwise. Fuel located right side of engine.

㉚—Except Firebird, Phoenix & Ventura Calif. models, 20° BTDC at 1100 RPM; Firebird, Phoenix & Ventura California models, 18° BTDC at 1100 RPM.

㉛—Except high altitude, 550/650D RPM; high altitude, 600/700D RPM.

㉜—Except Firebird high performance engine (engine code Y6), 16° BTDC; Firebird high performance engine (engine code Y6), 18° BTDC.

㉝—Except Firebird high performance engine (engine code Y6), 575/650D RPM; Firebird high performance engine (engine code Y6), 600/700D RPM.

㉞—Except high altitude, 550/650D RPM; high altitude, 600/650D RPM.

㉟—Less idle solenoid, 600D RPM; with idle solenoid, 550/670D RPM.

㊱—Less A/C, 500/650D RPM; with A/C, 650/850D RPM.

㊲—Engine code YB, 2200 RPM; engine code YC, 2400 RPM.

㊳—Less idle solenoid, 600D RPM; with idle solenoid, 600/670D RPM.

㊴—Injection timing, 4° ATDC at 1250 RPM.

㊵—Except high altitude, 4½° ATDC at 1200 RPM; high altitude, 5½° ATDC at 1200 RPM.

㊶—Except high altitude, 4° ATDC at 1200 RPM; high altitude, 5° ATDC at 1200 RPM.

㊷—Less A/C, 850 RPM; with A/C, 900 RPM.

㊸—Models less High Altitude Emissions Package.

㊹—At altitudes below 4000 ft., set 4° ATDC at 1250 RPM; at altitudes above 4000 ft., set 5° ATDC at 1250 RPM.

㊺—Models w/ High Altitude Emissions Package.

㊻—At altitudes below 4000 ft., set 3° ATDC at 1250 RPM; at altitudes above 4000 ft., set 4° ATDC at 1250 RPM.

Fig. A

Fig. B

Fig. C

FIRING ORDER 1·6·5·4·3·2

Fig. D

TIMING MARK FOR HAND HELD TIMING LIGHT

MAGNETIC PICK-UP FOR MAGNETIC PICK-UP TUBE

Fig. E

FIRING ORDER 1-3-4-2

Fig. F

FIRING ORDER 1·6·5·4·3·2

Fig. G

"0" is TDC Marks 2° Increments

Fig. H

Fig. I

Fig. J

Continued

TUNE UP NOTES—Continued

Fig. K

Fig. L

Fig. M

Fig. N

Fig. O

Fig. P

Fig. Q

Fig. R

Fig. S

Fig. T

Fig. U

DISTRIBUTOR SPECIFICATIONS

★ Note: If unit is checked on vehicle, double the RPM and degrees to get crankshaft figures.

Distributor Part No.①	Advance Starts	Centrifugal Advance Degrees @ RPM of Distributor			Full Advance	Inches of Vacuum to Start Plunger	Max. Adv. Dist. Deg. @ Vacuum
		Intermediate Advance					
1977							
1103231	0 @ 600	—	—	—	10 @ 2200	3.5	10 @ 12
1103257	0 @ 600	2 @ 700	—	—	8.5 @ 1800	5	10 @ 10
1103259	0 @ 500	—	—	—	9.5 @ 2000	6	12 @ 13
1103260	0 @ 500	—	—	—	6.5 @ 1800	6	12 @ 13
1103263	0 @ 600	—	—	—	10 @ 2200	3.5	10 @ 9
1103264	0 @ 500	—	—	—	6.5 @ 1800	5	8 @ 11
1103266	0 @ 500	—	—	—	9.5 @ 2000	5	8 @ 11
1103269	0 @ 500	4.5 @ 1000	—	—	8.5 @ 2300	5	10 @ 10
1103271	0 @ 500	4 @ 700	—	—	10 @ 2200	5	12.5 @ 11
1103272	0 @ 413	5 @ 900	—	—	10¾ @ 1715	4	12.5 @ 12
1103273	0 @ 500	8.5 @ 1300	—	—	9.5 @ 1800	4	12.5 @ 12
1103276	0 @ 400	2 @ 500	—	—	—	5	10 @ 10
1103278	0 @ 600	2 @ 700	—	—	8 @ 2200	5	10 @ 10
1110677	—	—	—	—	—	—	—
1110686	—	—	—	—	—	—	—
1978							
1103281	0 @ 500	5 @ 850	—	—	10 @ 1900	4	9 @ 12
1103282	0 @ 500	5 @ 850	—	—	10 @ 1900	4	10 @ 10
1103285	0 @ 600	6 @ 1000	—	—	11 @ 2100	4	5 @ 8
1103310	0 @ 500	5.5 @ 1000	—	—	7 @ 2200	4	12.5 @ 12
1103314	0 @ 413	5 @ 900	—	—	10.7 @ 1700	4	12.5 @ 12
1103315	0 @ 500	4 @ 700	—	—	10 @ 2200	5	12.5 @ 11
1103316	0 @ 500	4.5 @ 1000	—	—	8.5 @ 2300	4	12.5 @ 12
1103323	0 @ 500	—	—	—	9.5 @ 2000	5	8 @ 11
1103325	0 @ 500	—	—	—	6.5 @ 1800	5	8 @ 11
1103329	0 @ 600	—	—	—	10 @ 2200	3.5	10 @ 9
1103337	0 @ 550	6 @ 800	—	—	8 @ 1200	4	12 @ 10
1103342	—	2 @ 1000	—	—	9.5 @ 2200	7	12 @ 13
1103343	0 @ 400	2.25 @ 508	—	—	8.25 @ 1820	4	12.5 @ 11
1103346	0 @ 500	—	—	—	9.5 @ 2000	6	12 @ 13
1103347	0 @ 500	—	—	—	6.5 @ 1800	6	12 @ 13
1103359	0 @ 500	4.5 @ 1000	—	—	8.5 @ 2300	5	10 @ 10
1110695	0–3 @ 1000	—	—	—	9 @ 1800	6	12 @ 13
1110731	0–2 @ 1000	—	—	—	9 @ 1800	6	8 @ 9
1979							
1103281	1 @ 575	5 @ 850	—	—	10 @ 1900	4	10 @ 13
1103282	1 @ 600	5 @ 850	—	—	10 @ 1900	3.5	11 @ 11
1103285	1 @ 675	6 @ 1000	—	—	11 @ 2100	4	12 @ 7
1103314	1 @ 525	5 @ 900	—	—	10.5 @ 1725	4	12.5 @ 13
1103315	0 @ 500	3.5 @ 1000	—	—	8.5 @ 2300	6	12.5 @ 12
1103324	2 @ 400	5.5 @ 600	—	—	11.5 @ 1800	6	12.5 @ 12.5
1103325	1 @ 700	—	—	—	6.5 @ 1800	5	8.5 @ 11.5
1103342	1 @ 1100	—	—	—	8.5 @ 2200	6	13 @ 15
1103346	1 @ 650	—	—	—	9.5 @ 2000	6	12.5 @ 13.5
1103353	1.5 @ 600	6 @ 800	8 @ 1200	—	11 @ 2350	3.5	12 @ 11
1103379	1 @ 575	5 @ 850	—	—	10 @ 1900	2.5	11 @ 8.5
1103399	1 @ 575	4 @ 700	—	—	10 @ 2200	4	12.5 @ 13
1103400	1 @ 525	4.5 @ 1000	—	—	8.5 @ 2350	4	12.5 @ 12
1110766	1 @ 975	—	—	—	7.5 @ 1800	4	12.5 @ 11.5

Continued

DISTRIBUTOR SPECIFICATIONS—Continued

★ Note: If unit is checked on vehicle, double the RPM and degrees to get crankshaft figures.

Distributor Part No.①	Centrifugal Advance Degrees @ RPM of Distributor					Vacuum Advance	
	Advance Starts	Intermediate Advance			Full Advance	Inches of Vacuum to Start Plunger	Max. Adv. Dist. Deg. @ Vacuum
1979—Continued							
1110767	1 @ 975	—	—	—	7.5 @ 1800	3.5	10.5 @ 12.5
1110768	1 @ 625	—	—	—	7.5 @ 1800	3.5	10.5 @ 12.5
1110769	1 @ 625	—	—	—	7.5 @ 1800	4	12.5 @ 12.5
1110770	1 @ 975	—	—	—	7.5 @ 3600	3	10.5 @ 9.5
1980							
1103282	1.25 @ 600	5 @ 850	—	—	10 @ 1900	5	10 @ 11
1103407	1 @ 600	8 @ 1000	—	—	11.5 @ 2200	4.5	10 @ 10.5
1103413	0 @ 500	—	—	—	6.5 @ 1800	6	15 @ 13
1103425	1 @ 675	4.5 @ 1000	—	—	9 @ 2300	4.5	10 @ 10.5
1103444	.5 @ 600	8 @ 1000	—	—	12 @ 2200	7.5	9.5 @ 13.5
1103447	1 @ 1100	—	—	—	8.5 @ 2200	7.0	12 @ 14.6
1103450	1 @ 575	—	—	—	9.5 @ 1600	4.5	10 @ 10.5
1110552	1 @ 600	3 @ 1250	—	—	7 @ 1700	3.5	12 @ 8.5
1110554	0 @ 840	—	—	—	7.5 @ 1800	3	12 @ 12
1110555	1 @ 600	3 @ 1200	—	—	7.5 @ 1800	4.5	12 @ 9.5
1110558	1 @ 675	4.5 @ 1200	—	—	7 @ 2000	3.5	8 @ 12
1110559	.25 @ 600	4.5 @ 1200	—	—	7 @ 2000	3.5	8 @ 14
1110560	1 @ 725	3.5 @ 1000	—	—	7 @ 2200	5.0	10.5 @ 10.5
1110752	1 @ 775	4.5 @ 1200	—	—	7 @ 2050	4	8 @ 7.5
1110769	1 @ 600	3 @ 1200	—	—	7.5 @ 1800	4.5	12 @ 9.5
1981							
1103443	—	—	—	—	—	—	—
1103451	—	—	—	—	—	—	—
1103453	—	—	—	—	—	—	—
1103466	—	—	—	—	—	—	—
1110573	—	—	—	—	—	—	—
1111386	—	—	—	—	—	—	—
1982							
1103460	—	—	—	—	—	—	—
1103470	—	—	—	—	—	—	—
1110583	—	—	—	—	—	—	—
1110597	—	—	—	—	—	—	—
1103494	—	—	—	—	—	—	—

①—Stamped on distributor housing plate.　②—On models with EST refer to Tune Up Chapter for Specifications.

BRAKE SPECIFICATIONS

Year	Model	Brake Drum Inside Diameter	Wheel Cylinder Bore Diameter			Master Cylinder Bore Diameter		
			Disc Brake	Front Drum Brake	Rear Drum Brake	Disc Brakes	Drum Brakes	Power Brakes
1977	Firebird & Ventura	9.5	2.9375	—	.938	1	—	1.125
	LeMans	11	2.9375	—	.937	.9375	—	1.125
	Grand Prix	11	2.9375	—	.937	1.125	—	1.125
	Pontiac	11	2.9375	—	②	1.125	—	1.125
1978	Firebird	9.5	2.9375	—	.938	1	—	1.125
	Grand Prix	9.5	2.5	—	.75	.86614	—	.94488
	LeMans	9.5	2.5	—	.75	.86614	—	.94488
	Phoenix	9.5	2.9375	—	.938	1	—	1.125
	Pontiac	11	2.9375	—	.937	1.125	—	1.125

Continued

BRAKE SPECIFICATIONS—Continued

Year	Model	Brake Drum Inside Diameter	Wheel Cylinder Bore Diameter			Master Cylinder Bore Diameter		
			Disc Brake	Front Drum Brake	Rear Drum Brake	Disc Brakes	Drum Brakes	Power Brakes
1979	Firebird	9.5	2.9375	—	.938	1	—	1.125
	Grand Prix	9.5	2.5	—	.75	.86614	—	.94488
	LeMans	9.5	2.5	—	.75	.86614	—	.94488
	Phoenix	9.5	2.9375	—	.938	1	—	1.125
	Pontiac	①	2.9375	—	.937	1.125	—	1.125
1980–81	Firebird	9.5	2.9375	—	.938	1	—	1.125
	Grand Prix	9.5	2.5	—	.75	.86614	—	.94488
	LeMans	9.5	2.5	—	.75	.86614	—	.94488
	Pontiac	①	2.9375	—	.937	1.125	—	1.125
1982–83	Bonneville	①	2.9375	—	.75	1.125	—	1.125
	Firebird	9.5	③	—	.748	④	—	④
	Grand Prix	9.5	2.9375	—	.75	1.125	—	1.125

①—With 4¾ inch bolt circle, 9.5 inches. With 5 inch bolt circle, 11 inches.
②—Exc. Sta. Wag. & V8-403, .875"; Sta. Wag. & V8-403 .9375".
③—Front, 2.5 inch; rear 1.89 inch.
④—Models less 4 wheel disc. brakes, .945 inch; models w/4-wheel disc brakes, 1 inch.

STARTING MOTOR SPECIFICATIONS

Year	Model /V.I.N.	Starter Number	Brush Spring Tension Oz①	Free Speed Test			Resistance Test ②	
				Amps. ①	Volts	R.P.M. ①	Amps. ①	Volts
1977	4-151/V	1109412	35	50–75②	9	6500–10500	—	—
	V6-231/A, C	1108797	35	50–80②	9	5500–10000	—	—
	V8-301/Y	1108758	35	65–95②	9	7500–10500	—	—
	V8-305/V	1109056	35	50–80②	9	5500–10500	—	—
	V8-350/L③	1108796	35	65–95②	9	7500–10000	—	—
	V8-350/R⑥	1108765	35	55–80②	9	3500–6000	—	—
	V8-350/P⑤, 400/Z	1108759	35	65–95②	9	7500–10000	—	—
	V8-403/K	1108794	35	65–95②	9	7500–10000	—	—
1978	4-151/V	1109521	—	45–75②	9	6500–9700	—	—
	V6-231/A	1109061	—	60–85②	9	6800–10300	—	—
	V8-301/W,Y	1109523	—	45–70②	9	7000–11900	—	—
	V8-305/H⑫	1109524	—	45–70②	9	7000–11900	—	—
	V8-305/V⑬⑭	1109064	—	60–85②	9	6800–10300	—	—
	V8-305/V⑬④	1109074	—	60–85②	9	6800–10300	—	—
	V8-350/L③⑭	1109065	—	65–95②	9	7500–10500	—	—
	V8-350/L③④	1109067	—	65–95②	9	7500–10500	—	—
	V8-350/X⑧	1109061	—	60–85②	9	6800–10300	—	—
	V8-350/R⑥, 403/K	1109072	—	65–95②	9	7500–10500	—	—
	V8-400/Z	1108759	—	65–95②	9	7500–10500	—	—
1979	V6-231/A	1109061	—	60–85②	9	6800–10300	—	—
	V8-301/W,Y	1109523	—	45–70②	9	7000–11900	—	—
	V8-305/G⑨	1109064⑪	—	60–85②	9	6800–10300	—	—
	V8-305/H⑩	1109524	—	45–70②	9	7000–11900	—	—
	V8-350/L③	1109065	—	65–95②	9	7500–10500	—	—
	V8-350/X⑧	1109061	—	60–85②	9	6800–10300	—	—
	V8-350/R⑥, 403/K	1109072	—	65–95②	9	7500–10500	—	—
	V8-400/Z	1108759	—	65–95②	9	7500–10500	—	—
1980	V6-229/K	1109524	—	45–70②	9	7000–11900	—	—
	V6-231/A	1109061	—	60–85②	9	6800–10300	—	—
	V8-265/S, 301/T,W	1109523	—	45–70②	9	7000–11900	—	—
	V8-305/H	1109524	—	45–70②	9	7000–11900	—	—
	V8-350/X	1109061	—	60–85②	9	6800–10300	—	—
	V8-350/R⑥	1109072	—	65–95②	9	7500–10500	—	—
	V8-350 Diesel/N	1109213	—	40–140②	9	8000–13000	—	—

Continued

STARTING MOTOR SPECIFICATIONS—Continued

Year	Model/V.I.N.	Starter Number	Brush Spring Tension Oz①	Free Speed Test Amps. ①	Volts	R.P.M.	Resistance Test ② Amps. ①	Volts
1981	V6-231/A	1109061	—	60–85②	9	6800–10300	—	—
	V8-265/S, 301/T,W	1109523	—	45–70②	9	7000–11900	—	—
	V8-305/H⑮	1109524	—	45–70②	9	7000–11900	—	—
	V8-305/H⑦	1109074	—	60–85②	9	6800–10300	—	—
	V8-307/Y	1998205	—	65–95②	9	7500–10500	—	—
	V8-350 Diesel/N	1109216	—	100–230②	9	8000–14000	—	—
1982	4-151/2	1109533	—	45–70②	9	7000–11900	—	—
	V6-173/1	1109535	—	45–70②	9	7000–11900	—	—
	V6-231/A	1998236	—	45–70②	9	7000–11900	—	—
	V6-252/4	1998234	—	60–85②	9	6800–10300	—	—
	V8-305/H,7	⑯	—	60–85②	9	6800–10300	—	—
	V8-350 Diesel/N	1998552	—	160–220②	9	4000–5500	—	—

①—Minimum.
②—Includes solenoid.
③—Distributor located rear of engine, rotor rotation clockwise.
④—Manual trans.
⑤—Distributor located at rear of engine, rotor rotation counter clockwise. Fuel pump located left side of engine.

⑥—Distributor located rear of engine, rotor rotation counter clockwise. Fuel pump located right side of engine.
⑦—Firebird
⑧—Distributor located front of engine.
⑨—Two barrel Carb.
⑩—Four barrel Carb.

⑪—With high output option, 1102844.
⑫—LeMans & Grand Prix.
⑬—Firebird & Phoenix.
⑭—Auto. trans.
⑮—Except Firebird
⑯—Models less 4 spd. man. trans., #1109534; models w/ 4 spd. man. trans., #1998240.

ALTERNATOR & REGULATOR SPECIFICATIONS

Year	Model	Rated Hot Output Amps.	Field Current 12 Volts @ 80°F.	Output @ 14 Volts 2000 R.P.M. Amps.	5000 R.P.M. Amps.	Model	Field Relay Air Gap In.	Point Gap In.	Closing Voltage	Voltage Regulator Air Gap In.	Point Gap In.	Voltage @ 125°F.
1977	1101016	80	4.0–4.9	—	76	Integral	—	—	—	—	—	—
	1102389	42	—	—	—	Integral	—	—	—	—	—	—
	1102394	37	4.0–4.5	—	33	Integral	—	—	—	—	—	—
	1102478	55	—	—	—	Integral	—	—	—	—	—	—
	1102479	55	—	—	—	Integral	—	—	—	—	—	—
	1102485	42	—	—	—	Integral	—	—	—	—	—	—
	1102486	61	4.0–4.5	—	57	Integral	—	—	—	—	—	—
	1102491	37	4.0–4.5	—	33	Integral	—	—	—	—	—	—
	1102840	55	4.0–4.5	—	51	Integral	—	—	—	—	—	—
	1102841	42	—	—	—	Integral	—	—	—	—	—	—
	1102842	63	—	—	—	Integral	—	—	—	—	—	—
	1102843	61	—	—	—	Integral	—	—	—	—	—	—
	1102844	63	—	—	—	Integral	—	—	—	—	—	—
	1102854	63	—	—	—	Integral	—	—	—	—	—	—
	1102881	37	—	—	—	Integral	—	—	—	—	—	—
	1102906	61	—	—	—	Integral	—	—	—	—	—	—
	1102908	63	—	—	—	Integral	—	—	—	—	—	—
	1102909	61	—	—	—	Integral	—	—	—	—	—	—
1978–79	1101016	80	—	—	—	Integral	—	—	—	—	—	—
	1102389	42	—	—	—	Integral	—	—	—	—	—	—
	1102391	61	—	—	—	Integral	—	—	—	—	—	—
	1102392	63	—	—	—	Integral	—	—	—	—	—	—
	1102394	37	4.0–4.5	—	33	Integral	—	—	—	—	—	—
	1102478	55	4.0–4.5	—	51	Integral	—	—	—	—	—	—
	1102479	55	4.0–4.5	—	51	Integral	—	—	—	—	—	—
	1102480	61	4.0–4.5	—	57	Integral	—	—	—	—	—	—
	1102485	42	—	—	—	Integral	—	—	—	—	—	—

ALTERNATOR & REGULATOR SPECIFICATIONS—Continued

Year	Model	Rated Hot Output Amps.	Field Current 12 Volts @ 80°F.	Output @ 14 Volts 2000 R.P.M. Amps.	Output @ 14 Volts 5000 R.P.M. Amps.	Model	Field Relay Air Gap In.	Field Relay Point Gap In.	Field Relay Closing Voltage	Voltage Regulator Air Gap In.	Voltage Regulator Point Gap In.	Voltage Regulator Voltage @ 125°F.
1978–79	1102486	61	4.0–4.5	—	57	Integral	—	—	—	—	—	—
	1102495	37	—	—	—	Integral	—	—	—	—	—	—
	1102841	42	—	—	—	Integral	—	—	—	—	—	—
	1102842	63	—	—	—	Integral	—	—	—	—	—	—
	1102843	61	—	—	—	Integral	—	—	—	—	—	—
	1102844	63	—	—	—	Integral	—	—	—	—	—	—
	1102854	63	—	—	—	Integral	—	—	—	—	—	—
	1102901	61	—	—	—	Integral	—	—	—	—	—	—
	1102909	61	—	—	—	Integral	—	—	—	—	—	—
	1102910	63	—	—	—	Integral	—	—	—	—	—	—
	1102913	61	—	—	—	Integral	—	—	—	—	—	—
	1103033	61	—	—	—	Integral	—	—	—	—	—	—
1979	1101024	80	—	—	—	Integral	—	—	—	—	—	—
	1102860	63	—	—	—	Integral	—	—	—	—	—	—
	1102908	63	—	—	—	Integral	—	—	—	—	—	—
	1103055	42	—	—	—	Integral	—	—	—	—	—	—
	1103056	63	—	—	—	Integral	—	—	—	—	—	—
	1103058	63	—	—	—	Integral	—	—	—	—	—	—
	1103076	63	—	—	—	Integral	—	—	—	—	—	—
1980	1101038	70	—	—	—	Integral	—	—	—	—	—	—
	1103043	42	—	—	—	Integral	—	—	—	—	—	—
	1103103	63	—	—	—	Integral	—	—	—	—	—	—
	1103104	42	—	—	—	Integral	—	—	—	—	—	—
	1103112	63	—	—	—	Integral	—	—	—	—	—	—
1981	1101037	70	—	—	—	Integral	—	—	—	—	—	—
	1101038	70	—	—	—	Integral	—	—	—	—	—	—
	1103088	55	—	—	—	Integral	—	—	—	—	—	—
	1103091	63	—	—	—	Integral	—	—	—	—	—	—
	1103103	63	—	—	—	Integral	—	—	—	—	—	—
1982	1100110	42	—	—	—	Integral	—	—	—	—	—	—
	1100179	42	—	—	—	Integral	—	—	—	—	—	—
	1103187	42	—	—	—	Integral	—	—	—	—	—	—
	1100121	63	—	—	—	Integral	—	—	—	—	—	—
	1103197	63	—	—	—	Integral	—	—	—	—	—	—
	1100199	63	—	—	—	Integral	—	—	—	—	—	—
	1101037	70	—	—	—	Integral	—	—	—	—	—	—
	1101088	70	—	—	—	Integral	—	—	—	—	—	—
	1100187	70	—	—	—	Integral	—	—	—	—	—	—
	1101449	70	—	—	—	Integral	—	—	—	—	—	—
	1101045	85	—	—	—	Integral	—	—	—	—	—	—
	1101443	85	—	—	—	Integral	—	—	—	—	—	—

VALVE SPECIFICATIONS

Year	Model/V.I.N.	Valve Lash Int.	Valve Lash Exh.	Valve Angles Seat	Valve Angles Face	Valve Spring Installed Height	Valve Spring Pressure Lbs. @ In.	Stem Clearance Intake	Stem Clearance Exhaust	Stem Diameter Intake	Stem Diameter Exhaust
1977	4-151/V	Hydraulic⑦		46	45	1.66	176 @ 1.254	.0017–.0030	.0017–.0030	.3400	.3400
	V6-231/C⑥	Hydraulic⑭		45	45	1.727	168 @ 1.327	.0015–.0032	.0015–.0032	.3405–.3412	.3405–3412
	V6-231/A⑥	Hydraulic⑭		45	45	1.727	182 @ 1.340	.0015–.0035	.0015–.0032	.3402–.3412	.3405–3412
	V8-301/Y	Hydraulic⑦		46	45	1.69	170 @ 1.26	.0017–.0020	.0017–.0020	.3400	.3400
	V8-305V①	¾ Turn②		46	45	⑩	⑤	.0010–.0027	.0010–.0027	.3410–.3417	.3410–.3417

Continued

VALVE SPECIFICATIONS

Year	Model/V.I.N.	Valve Lash		Valve Angles		Valve Spring Installed Height	Valve Spring Pressure Lbs. @ In.	Stem Clearance		Stem Diameter	
		Int.	Exh.	Seat	Face			Intake	Exhaust	Intake	Exhaust
1977	V8-350/L①⑱	¾ Turn②		46	45	⑩	⑤	.0010–.0027	.0010–.0027	.3410–.3417	.3410–.3417
	V8-350/R⑰⑬	Hydraulic⑭		⑪	⑫	1.67	187 @ 1.27	.0010–.0027	.0015–.0032	.3425–.3432	.3420–.3427
	V8-350/P⑯	Hydraulic⑦		③	⑧	1.549	131 @ 1.185	.0016–.0033	.0021–.0038	.3412–.3419	.3407–.3414
	V8-400/Z	Hydraulic⑦		③	⑧	1.549	131 @ 1.185	.0016–.0033	.0021–.0038	.3412–.3419	.3407–.3414
	V8-403/K⑰	Hydraulic⑭		⑪	⑫	1.67	187 @ 1.27	.0010–.0027	.0015–.0032	.3425–.3432	.3420–.3427
1978	4-151/V	Hydraulic⑦		46	45	1.66	176 @ 1.254	.0010–.0027	.0010–.0027	.3425–.3418	.3425–.3418
	V6-231/A	Hydraulic⑭		45	45	1.727	182 @ 1.340	.0015–.0035	.0015–.0032	.3402–.3412	.3405–.3412
	V8-301/Y	Hydraulic⑦		46	45	1.66	166 @ 1.296	.0010–.0027	.0010–.0027	.3425–.3418	.3425–.3418
	V8-305/V①	1 Turn②		46	45	1.70	200 @ 1.25	.0010–.0027	.0010–.0027	.3410–.3417	.3410–.3417
	V8-350/L①⑱	1 Turn②		46	45	1.70	200 @ 1.25	.0010–.0027	.0010–.0027	.3410–.3417	.3410–.3417
	V8-350/R⑰⑬	Hydraulic⑭		⑪	⑫	1.67	187 @ 1.270	.0010–.0027	.0015–.0032	.3432–.3425	.3427–.3420
	V8-350/P⑥⑮	Hydraulic⑭		45	45	1.727	175 @ 1.34	.0015–.0035	.0015–.0032	.3720–.3730	.3730–.3723
	V8-400/Z	Hydraulic⑦		③	⑧	1.549	131 @ 1.185	.0016–.0033	.0021–.0038	.3425	.3425
	V8-403/K⑰	Hydraulic⑭		⑪	⑫	1.670	187 @ 1.270	.0010–.0027	.0015–.0032	.3432–.3425	.3427–.3420
1979	V6-231/A	Hydraulic⑭		45	45	1.727	164 @ 1.340	.0015–.0035	.0015–.0032	.3402–.3412	.3405–.3412
	V8-301/W,Y	Hydraulic⑦		46	45	1.66	166 @ 1.296	.0010–.0027	.0010–.0027	.3418–.3425	.3418–.3425
	V8-305/G,H①	Hydraulic⑭		46	45	1.70	200 @ 1.25	.0010–.0027	.0010–.0027	.3410–.3417	.3410–.3417
	V8-350/L①⑱	Hydraulic⑭		46	45	1.70	200 @ 1.25	.0010–.0027	.0010–.0027	.3410–.3417	.3410–.3417
	V8-350/R⑰⑬	Hydraulic⑭		45	46	1.67	187 @ 1.270	.0010–.0027	.0015–.0032	.3425–.3432	.3420–.3427
	V8-350/X⑥⑮	Hydraulic⑭		45	45	1.727	175 @ 1.34	.0015–.0035	.0015–.0032	.3720–.3730	.3730–.3723
	V8-400/Z	Hydraulic⑦		③	⑧	1.549	131 @ 1.185	.0016–.0033	.0021–.0038	.3412–.3419	.3407–.3414
	V8-403/K	Hydraulic⑭		⑪	⑫	1.670	187 @ 1.270	.0010–.0027	.0015–.0032	.3425–.3432	.3420–.3427
1980	V6-229/K①	1 Turn②		46	45	1.70	200 @ 1.25	.0010–.0027	.0010–.0027	.3410–.3417	.3410–.3417
	V6-231/A⑥	Hydraulic⑭		45	45	1.727	182 @ 1.34	.0015–.0035	.0015–.0032	.3401–.3412	.3405–.3412
	V8-265/S	Hydraulic⑦		46	45	1.66	175 @ 1.29	.0010–.0027	.0010–.0027	.3418–.3425	.3418–.3425
	V8-301/T,W	Hydraulic⑦		46	45	1.66	175 @ 1.29	.0010–.0027	.0010–.0027	.3418–.3425	.3418–.3425
	V8-305/L①	1 Turn②		46	45	1.70	200 @ 1.25	.0010–.0027	.0010–.0027	.3410–.3417	.3410–.3417
	V8-350/X⑥⑮	Hydraulic⑭		45	45	1.727	182 @ 1.34	.0015–.0035	.0015–.0032	.3401–.3412	.3405–.3412
	V8-350/R⑰⑬	Hydraulic⑭		⑪	⑫	1.67	187 @ 1.27	.0010–.0027	.0015–.0032	.3425–.3432	.3420–.3427
	V8-350 Diesel/N⑰	Hydraulic⑭		⑪	⑫	1.67	151 @ 1.30	.0010–.0027	.0015–.0032	.3425–.3432	.3420–.3427
1981	V6-231/A⑥	Hydraulic⑭		45	45	1.727	④	.0015–.0035	.0015–.0032	.3401–.3412	.3405–.3412
	V8-265/S	Hydraulic⑦		46	45	1.66	175 @ 1.29	.0010–.0027	.0010–.0027	.3425	.3425
	V8-301/T,W	Hydraulic⑦		46	45	1.66	175 @ 1.29	.0010–.0027	.0010–.0027	.3425	.3425
	V8-305/L①	1 Turn②		46	45	1.70	200 @ 1.25	.0010–.0027	.0010–.0027	.3425–.3432	.3420–.3427
	V8-307/Y⑰	Hydraulic⑭		⑪	⑫	1.67	189 @ 1.27	.0010–.0027	.0015–.0032	.3425–.3432	.3420–.3427
	V8-350 Diesel/N⑰	Hydraulic⑭		⑪	⑫	1.67	210 @ 1.3	.0010–.0027	.0015–.0032	.3425–.3432	.3420–.3427
1982–83	4-151/2	Hydraulic⑭		46	45	1.69	160 @ 1.25	.0010–.0027	.0010–.0027	.3418–.3425	.3418–.3425
	V6-173/1①	1½ Turn②		46	45	1.57	195 @ 1.18	.0010–.0027	.0010–.0027	.3409–.3417	.3409–.3417
	V6-231/A⑥	Hydraulic⑭		45	45	1.727	220 @ 1.34	.0015–.0035	.0015–.0032	.3401–.3412	.3405–.3412
	V6-252/4⑥	Hydraulic⑭		45	44	1.727	④	.0015–.0035	.0015–.0032	.3401–.3412	.3405–.3412
	V8-305/H,7①	1 Turn②		46	45	1.70	200 @ 1.25	.0010–.0027	.0010–.0027	.3425–.3432	.3420–.3427
	V8-350 Diesel/N⑰	Hydraulic⑭		⑪	⑫	1.67	210 @ 1.22	.0010–.0027	.0015–.0032	.3425–.3432	.3420–.3427

①—For service on this engine, see Chevrolet Chapter.
②—Turn rocker arm stud nut until all lash is eliminated, then tighten nut the additional turns listed.
③—Intake 30°, exhaust 45°.
④—Intake 164 ± 5 @ 1.340; Exhaust 182 ± 8 @ 1.340.
⑤—Intake 174–186 @ 1.25; Exhaust 184–196 @ 1.16.
⑥—See Buick chapter for service procedures.
⑦—No adjustment. On V8's, rocker arms are correctly positioned when ball retainer nuts are tightened to 20 ft. lbs.
⑧—Intake 29°, exhaust 44°.
⑩—Intake, 135.1 @ 1.13; Exhaust, 140.8 @ 1.12.
⑪—Intake, 45°; exhaust, 31°.
⑫—Intake, 44°; exhaust, 30°.
⑬—Distributor located at rear of engine, counter clockwise rotor rotation. Fuel pump located right side of engine.
⑭—No adjustment.
⑮—Distributor located at front of engine.
⑯—Distributor located at rear of engine, counter clockwise rotor rotation. Fuel pump located left side of engine.
⑰—See Oldsmobile Chapter for service procedures.
⑱—Distributor located at rear of engine, clockwise rotor rotation.

PISTONS, PINS, RINGS, CRANKSHAFT & BEARINGS

Year	Model/V.I.N.	Piston Skirt Clearance	Ring End Gap① Comp.	Ring End Gap① Oil	Wrist-pin Diameter	Rod Bearings Shaft Diameter	Rod Bearings Bearing Clearance	Main Bearings Shaft Diameter	Main Bearings Bearing Clearance	Thrust on Bear. No.	Shaft End Play
1977	4-151/V	.0025–.0033	.010	.010	.940	2.000	.0005–.0026	2.2983–2.2993	.0002–.0022	5	.0015–.0085
	V6-231/C⑩	.0008–.0020	.010	.015	.93925	1.991–2.000	.0005	2.4995	.0004–.0015	2	.004–.008
	V6-231/A⑩	.0008–.0020	.013	.015	.93925	2.2491	.0005–.0026	2.4995	.0004–.0015	2	.003–.009
	V8-301/Y	.0025–.0033	.010	.035	.927	2.000	.0005–.0025	3.00	.0004–.0020	5	.003–.009
	V8-305/L⑧	.0007–.0017	.010	.015	.9270	2.099–2.100	.0013–.0035	②	④	5	.002–.006
	V8-350/L⑧⑪	.0007–.0017	⑨	.015	.9270	2.099–2.100	.0013–.0035	②	④	5	.002–.006
	V8-350/P⑯	.0025–.0023	.010	.035	.980	2.25	.0005–.0025	3.00	.0004–.0015	5	.003–.009
	V8-350/R⑬⑥	.0005–.0015	.010	.015	.9805	2.1238–2.1248	.0004–.0033	⑮	⑤	3	.0035–.0135
	V8-400/Z	.0025–.0033	.010	.035	.9802	2.25	.0005–.0025	3.00	.0004–.0015	5	.003–.009
	V8-403/K⑬	.0003–.0017	.010	.015	.9805	2.1238–2.1248	.0004–.0033	⑮	⑤	3	.0035–.0135
1978	4-151/V	.0025–.0033	⑨	.015	.940	2.00	.0005–.0026	2.30	.0002–.0022	5	.0035–.0085
	V6-231/A⑩	.0008–.0020	.013	.015	.93925	2.2491	.0005–.0026	2.4995	.0004–.0015	2	.003–.009
	V8-301/W,Y	.0025–.0033	.010	.035	.940	2.25	.0005–.0025	3.00	.0002–.0020	4	.003–.009
	V8-305/H,V⑧	.0007–.0017	.010	.010	.92715	2.009–2.100	.0013–.0035	②	④	5	.002–.006
	V8-350/L⑧⑪	.0007–.0017	⑨	.015	.92715	2.009–2.100	.0013–.0035	②	④	5	.002–.006
	V8-350/X⑩⑦	.008–.0020	.010	.015	.93915	1.991–2.000	.0005–.0026	2.9995	.0004–.0015	3	.003–.009
	V8-350/R⑬⑥	.001–.002	.010	.015	.9805	2.1238–2.1248	.0005–.0026	⑮	⑤	3	.0035–.0135
	V8-400/Z	.0025–.0033	.010	.035	.9802	2.25	.0005–.0025	3.00	.0002–.0017	4	.003–.009
	V8-403/K⑬	.001–.002	.010	.015	.9805	2.1238–2.1248	.0005–.0026	⑮	⑤	3	.0035–.0135
1979	V6-231/A⑩	.0008–.0020	.013	.015	.9392	2.2487–2.2495	.0005–.0026	2.4995	.0003–.0018	2	.003–.009
	V8-301/W,Y	.0025–.0033	.010	.035	.940	2.25	.0005–.0025	3.000	.0002–.0020	4	.003–.009
	V8-305/G,H⑧	.0007–.0017	.010	.015	.9271	2.0986–2.0998	.0013–.0035	②	④	5	.002–.006
	V8-350/L⑧⑪	.0007–.0017	.010	.015	.9271	2.0986–2.0998	.0013–.0035	②	④	5	.002–.006
	V8-350/X⑩⑥	.0008–.0020	.013	.015	.9392	1.991–2.000	.0005–.0026	3.000	.0004–.0015	3	.003–.009
	V8-350/R⑬⑦	.00075–.00175	③	.015	.9805	2.1238–2.1248	.0004–.0033	2.4985–2.4995	⑤	3	.0035–.0135
	V8-400/Z	.0025–.0033	.010	.035	.940	2.25	.0005–.0025	3.000	.0002–.0020	4	.003–.009
	V8-403/K⑬	.0005–.0015	③	.015	.9805	2.1238–2.1248	.0004–.0033	2.4985–2.4995	⑤	3	.0035–.0135
1980	V6-229/K⑧	.0007–.0017	.010	.015	.9271	2.0986–2.0998	.0013–.0035	②	④	4	.002–.006
	V6-231/A⑩	.0008–.0020	.013	.015	.9392	2.2487–2.2495	.0005–.0026	2.4995	.0003–.0018	2	.003–.009
	V8-265/S	.0025–.0033	.010	.010	.927	2.00	.0005–.0026	3.000	.0002–.0018	4	.0035–.0085
	V8-301/W⑫	.0025–.0033	.010	.015	.927	2.25	.0005–.0026	3.000	.0004–.0020	4	.006–.022
	V8-301/T⑭	.0017–.0025	.010	.015	—	2.25	.0005–.0026	3.000	.0004–.0020	4	.006–.022
	V8-305/H⑧	.0007–.0017	.010	.015	.9271	2.0986–2.0998	.0013–.0035	②	④	5	.002–.006
	V8-350/X⑩⑥	.0008–.0020	.013	.015	.9392	1.991–2.000	.0005–.0026	3.000	.0004–.0015	3	.003–.009
	V8-350/R⑬⑦	.00075–.00175	.010	.015	.9805	2.1238–2.1248	.0005–.0026	2.4985–2.4995	⑤	3	.0035–.0135
	V8-350/N⑬	.005–.006	.015	.015	1.0951	2.1238–2.1248	.0005–.0026	2.9993–3.0003	⑤	3	.0035–.0135
1981	V6-231/A⑩	.008–.0020	.013	.015	.9392	2.2487–2.2495	.0005–.0026	2.4995	.0003–.0018	2	.003–.009
	V8-265/S	.0017–.0025	.010	.035	.940	2.00	.0005–.0026	3.00	.0002–.0018	4	.003–.009
	V8-301/T,W	.0017–.0025	.010	.035	.940	2.00	.0005–.0026	3.00	.0002–.0018	4	.003–.009
	V8-305/H⑧	.0007–.0017	.010	.015	.9271	2.090–2.100	.0013–.0035	②	④	5	.002–.007
	V8-307/Y⑬	.0005–.0015	.009	.015	.9805	2.1238–2.1248	.0004–.0033	⑮	⑤	3	.0035–.0135
	V8-350/N⑬	.0005–.0006	.015	.015	1.0951	2.1238–2.1248	.0005–.0026	3.00		⑤	3	.0035–.0135
1982-83	4-151/2	.0025–.0033	.010	.015	.940	2.000	.0005–.0026	2.300	.0005–.0022	5	.0035–.0085
	V6-173/1⑧	.0018–.0028	.020	.020	.905	2.000	.0005–.0026	2.493–2.494	.0005–.0015	3	.0020–.0079
	V6-231/A⑩	.0008–.0020	.013	.015	.9392	2.2487–2.2495	.0005–.0026	2.4995	.0003–.0018	2	.003–.009
	V6-252/4⑩	.0008–.0020	.013	.015	.9392	2.2487–2.2495	.0005–.0026	2.4995	.0003–.0018	2	.003–.009
	V8-305/H,7⑧	.0007–.0017	.010	.015	.9271	2.0986–2.0998	.0018–.0039	②	④	5	.002–.007
	V8-350/N⑬	.005–.006	.015	.015	1.951	2.1238–2.1248	.0005–.0026	2.9993–3.0003	⑤	3	.0035–.0135

①—Fit rings in tapered bores for clearance listed in tightest portion of ring travel.
②—No. 1, 2.4484–2.4493; Nos. 2, 3, 4, 2.4481–2.4490; No. 5, 2.4479–2.4488.
③—Refer to text in Oldsmobile Chapter Engine Section under Piston, Rings & Pins.
④—No. 1, .0008–.0020; Nos. 2, 3, 4, .0011–.0023; No. 5, .0017–.0032.
⑤—No. 1, 2, 3, 4, .0005–.0021; No. 5, .0015–.0031.
⑥—Distributor located at rear of engine, counter clockwise rotor rotation. Fuel pump located right side of engine.
⑦—Distributor located at front of engine.
⑧—For service on this engine, see Chevrolet Chapter.
⑨—No. 1, .013"; No. 2, .010".
⑩—See Buick chapter for service procedures.

Continued

PISTONS PINS, RINGS, CRANKSHAFT & BEARINGS NOTES—Continued

⑪—Distributor located at rear of engine, clockwise rotor rotation.

⑫—Except turbocharged engine.

⑬—See Oldsmobile Chapter for service procedures.

⑭—Turbocharged engine.

⑮—No. 1—2.4988–2.4998; No. 2, 3, 4, 5; 2.4985–2.4995.

⑯—Distributor located at rear of engine, counter

clockwise rotor rotation. Fuel pump located left side of engine.

⑰—No. 1, 2, 3 & 4; .0005–.0021; No. 5, .0020–.0034.

REAR AXLE SPECIFICATIONS

Year	Model	Carrier Type	Ring Gear & Pinion Backlash		Pinion Bearing Preload			Differential Bearing Preload		
			Method	Adjustment	Method	New Bearings Inch-Lbs.	Used Bearings Inch-Lbs.	Method	New Bearings Inch-Lbs.	Used Bearings Inch-Lbs.
1977–83	All	Integral	Shims	.006–.008	①	20–25	10–15	Shims	35–40	20–25

①—Tighten pinion shaft nut with inch-pound torque wrench.

ENGINE TIGHTENING SPECIFICATIONS★

★ Torque specifications are for clean and lightly lubricated threads only. Dry or dirty threads produce increased friction which prevents accurate measurement of thickness.

Year	Model/V.I.N.	Spark Plugs Ft. Lbs.	Cylinder Head Bolts Ft. Lbs.	Intake Manifold Ft. Lbs.	Exhaust Manifold Ft. Lbs.	Rocker Arm Ft. Lbs.	Rocker Arm Cover Ft. Lbs.	Connecting Rod Cap Bolts Ft. Lbs.	Main Bearing Cap Bolts Ft. Lbs.	Flywheel to Crankshaft Ft. Lbs.	Vibration Damper or Pulley Ft. Lbs.
1977	V6-231/C	20	75	45	25	30⑪	5	40	100	55	150
	V6-231/A	15	80	45	25	30⑪	4	40	100	60	225
	V8-301/Y	15	90	35	40	20	7	30	70⑦	95	160
	V8-305/V④	15	65	30	20⑥	—	45⑤	45	70	60	60
	V8-350/L④⑭	15	65	30	20⑥	—	45⑤	45	70	60	60
	V8-350/P⑮	15	95	35	40	20	7	40	100③	95	160
	V8-350/R⑧⑯	25	130	40	25	25	—	42	80③	60	260
	V8-400/Z	15	95	35	40	20	7	40	100③	95	160
	V8-403/K	25	130	40	25	25	—	42	80③	60	260
1977–78	4-151/V	15	95	⑬	⑬	20	85⑤	30	65	55	160
1978–79	V6-231/A⑫	15	80	45	25	30⑪	4	40	100	60	225
	V8-301/W,Y	15	95	35	40	20	6	30	70②	95	160
	V8-305/G,H④	①	65	30	20⑥	—	45⑤	45	70	60	60
	V8-350/L④⑭	①	65	30	20⑥	—	45⑤	45	70	60	60
	V8-350/R⑧⑯	25	130⑨	40⑨	25	25	—	42	80③	⑩	260
	V8-350/X⑫⑰	15	80	45	25	30	4	40	100	60	225
	V8-400/Z	15	95	35	40	20	6	40	100③	95	160
	V8-403/K	25	130⑨	40⑨	25	25	—	42	80③	⑩	260
1980–81	V6-229/K④	22	65	30	20	—	45⑤	45	70	60	60
	V6-231/A⑫	15	80	45	25	30⑪	4	40	100	60	225
	V8-265/S	15	95	35	40	20	6	30	70②	95	160
	V8-301/W⑱	15	95	35	40	20	6	30	70②	95	160
	V8-301/T⑲	20	93	37	40	20	7	28	100②	—	163
	V8-305/H④	22	65	30	20⑥	—	45⑤	45	70	60	60
	V8-350/X⑫⑰	15	80	45	25	30⑪	4	40	100	60	225
	V8-350/R⑧⑯	25	130⑨	40⑨	25	28	—	42	80③	60	200–310
	V8-350 Diesel/N⑧	—	130⑨	40⑨	25	28	—	42	120	60	200–310
1981	V8-307/Y⑧	25	130⑨	40⑨	25	28	—	42	80③	60	200–310
1982–83	4-151/2	15	85	29	44	20	6	32	70	44	160
	V6-173/1④	7–15	65–75	20–25	22–28	43–49	6–9	34–40	63–74	45–55	—
	V6-231/A⑫	15	80	45	25	30⑪	4	40	100	60	225
	V6-252/4⑫	15	80	45	20	30⑪	4	40	100	60	225
	V8-305/H,7④	22	65	30	20⑥	—	4	45	70	60	60
	V8-350 Diesel/N⑧	—	130⑨	40⑨	25	28	—	42	120	60	200–310

Continued

ENGINE TIGHTENING SPECIFICATION NOTES

① —1978, 15; 1979 22.
② —Rear, 100.
③ —Rear 120
④ —For service on this engine, see Chevrolet Chapter.
⑤ —Inch pounds.
⑥ —Inside bolts 30 ft. lbs.
⑦ —Rear, 100 ft. lbs.
⑧ —For service on this engine, see Oldsmobile Chapter.

⑨ —Clean & dip entire bolt in engine oil before tightening.
⑩ —Exc. manual trans. 60 ft. lbs.; manual trans. 90 ft. lbs.
⑪ —Rocker arm shaft to cylinder head.
⑫ —See Buick chapter for service procedures.
⑬ —Intake to exhaust manifold bolts, 40 ft. lbs.; manifold to cylinder head nuts, 30 ft. lbs.; manifold to cylinder head bolts, 40 ft. lbs.
⑭ —Distributor located at rear of engine, clock-

wise rotor rotation.
⑮ —Distributor located at rear of engine, counter clockwise rotor rotation. Fuel pump located left side of engine.
⑯ —Distributor located at rear of engine, counter clockwise rotor rotation. Fuel pump located right side of engine.
⑰ —Distributor located front of engine.
⑱ —Except turbocharged engine.
⑲ —Turbocharged engine.

COOLING SYSTEM & CAPACITY DATA

Year	Model or Engine/V.I.N.	Cooling Capacity, Qts. Less A/C	Cooling Capacity, Qts. With A/C	Radiator Cap Relief Pressure, Lbs.	Thermo. Opening Temp.	Fuel Tank Gals.	Engine Oil Refill Qts. ①	Transmission Oil 3 Speed Pints	Transmission Oil 4 Speed Pints	Transmission Oil 5 Speed Pints	Transmission Oil Auto Trans. Qts. ②	Rear Axle Oil Pints
1977	4-151/V Ventura	12.4	12.4	14–17	195	21	4	3.5	2.4	3.5	3⑮	3½
	V6-231/C Ventura	13.8	13.8	14–17	195	21	4	3.5	2.4	3.5	3⑮	3½
	V6-231/C LeMans	14.5	14.5	14–17	195	22	4	3.5	—	—	4⑧	4.25
	V6-231/C Firebird	13.2	13.2	14–17	195	21	4	3.5	2.5	—	4⑧	4.25
	V6-231/C Pontiac	12.9	12.9	14–17	195	21	4	—	—	—	⑯	⑰
	V8-301/Y Ventura	19.8	20.2㉓	14–17	195	21	5½	3.5	2.4	3.5	3⑱	3½
	V8-301/Y LeMans	20.2	20.8㉓	14–17	195	22	5½	3.5	—	—	⑯	4.25
	V8-301/Y Firebird	19.5	19.5	14–17	195	21	5½	3.5	2.5	—	4⑧	4.25
	V8-301/Y Pontiac	18.6	19.8㉓	14–17	195	21	5½	—	—	—	⑯	⑰
	V8-301/Y Grand Prix	20.5	21.1㉓	14–17	195	25	5½	—	—	—	3¾⑧	4.25
	V8-305/U Ventura	17	18	14–17	195	21	4	3.5	2.4	3.5	3⑱	3½
	V8-350/L,R Ventura	16.6	16.6	14–17	195	21	4	3.5	2.4	3.5	3⑧	3½
	V8-350/P LeMans⑲	21.7	23.9㉓	14–17	195	22	5	3.5	—	—	⑯	4.25
	V8-350/R LeMans⑳	16.7	17.5㉓	14–17	195	22	4	3.5	—	—	⑯	4.25
	V8-350/P Firebird⑲	20.3	23㉓	14–17	195	21	5	3.5	2.5	—	4⑧	4.25
	V8-350/R Firebird⑳	16	18.2㉓	14–17	195	21	4	3.5	2.5	—	4⑧	4.25
	V8-350/P Pontiac⑲	15	16.2㉓	14–17	195	21	5	—	—	—	⑯	⑰
	V8-350/R Pontiac⑳	15	16.2㉓	14–17	195	21	4	—	—	—	⑯	⑰
	V8-350/P Grand Prix⑲	21.9	24.1㉓	14–17	195	25	5	—	—	—	3¾⑧	4.25
	V8-350/R Grand Prix⑳	17	17.8㉓	14–17	195	25	4	—	—	—	3¾⑧	4.25
	V8-400/Z LeMans	21.7	23.9㉓	14–17	195	22	5	3.5	—	—	⑯	4.25
	V8-400/Z Firebird㉑	21.1	22.9	14–17	195	21	5	3.5	2.5	—	4⑧	4.25
	V8-400/Z Firebird㉒	20.4	21.2	14–17	195	21	5	3.5	2.5	—	4⑧	4.25
	V8-400/Z Firebird	—	23㉓	14–17	195	21	5	3.5	2.5	—	4⑧	4.25
	V8-400/Z Pontiac	21.7	23.9㉓	14–17	195	21	5	—	—	—	⑯	⑰
	V8-400/Z Grand Prix	21.9	24.1㉓	14–17	195	25	5	—	—	—	3¾⑧	4.25
	V8-403/K LeMans	17.9	18.7㉓	14–17	195	22	4	3.5	—	—	⑯	4.25
	V8-403/K Firebird	17.1	19.4㉓	14–17	195	21	4	3.5	2.5	—	4⑧	4.25
	V8-403/K Pontiac	16.1	17.3㉓	14–17	195	21	4	—	—	—	⑯	⑰
	V8-403/K Grand Prix	18.2	19.0㉓	14–17	195	25	4	—	—	—	3¾⑧	4.25
1978	4-151/V Phoenix	11.8	11.8	14–17	195	21	3	3.5	2.5	3.5	3⑫	3½
	V6-231/A Phoenix	14.0	14.1	14–17	195	21	4	3.5	2.5	—	3⑫	3½
	V6-231/A LeMans	14.3	14.2	14–17	195	17⑤	4	3.5	2.4	—	3⑫	3½
	V6-231/A Firebird	14.0	14.0	14–17	195	21	4	3.5	2.5	—	3④	4¼
	V6-231/A Grand Prix	14.3	14.2	14–17	195	15	4	3.5	—	—	3⑫	3½
	V6-231/A Pontiac	14.2	14.1	14–17	195	21	4	—	—	—	3⑫	⑰
	V8-301/W,Y LeMans	20.3	20.2	14–17	195	15⑤	5	—	—	—	3⑫	3½
	V8-301/W,Y Grand Prix	20.3	20.2	14–17	195	15	5	—	—	—	3⑫	3½
	V8-301/W,Y Pontiac	20.2	20.1	14–17	195	21	5	—	—	—	3⑫	⑰
	V8-305/H,U Phoenix	16.8	17.0	14–17	195	21	4	—	2.5	—	3⑫	3½
	V8-305/H,U LeMans	17.7	17.4	14–17	195	15⑤	4	—	—	—	3⑫	3½
	V8-305/H,U Firebird	17.2	17.2	14–17	195	21	4	—	3.5	—	3④	4¼
	V8-305/H,U Grand Prix	17.7	17.4	14–17	195	15	4	—	—	—	3⑫	3½

Continued

COOLING SYSTEM & CAPACITY DATA—Continued

Year	Model or Engine/V.I.N.	Cooling Capacity, Qts. Less A/C	Cooling Capacity, Qts. With A/C	Radiator Cap Relief Pressure, Lbs.	Thermo. Opening Temp.	Fuel Tank Gals.	Engine Oil Refill Qts. [1]	3 Speed Pints	4 Speed Pints	5 Speed Pints	Auto Trans. Qts. [2]	Rear Axle Oil Pints
1978	V8-350/L,R Phoenix	17.1	17.8	14—17	195	21	4	—	—	—	3[12]	4¼
	V8-350/L,R LeMans	17.7	18.1	14—17	195	15[5]	4	—	—	—	3[12]	3½
	V8-350/L,R Firebird	17.2	17.2	14—17	195	21	4	—	3.5	—	3[4]	4¼
	V8-350/X Pontiac[6]	16.6	18.5	14—17	195	21	4	—	—	—	3[12]	4¼
	V8-350/L,R Pontiac	16.5	19.1	14—17	195	21[7]	4	—	—	—	3[12]	4¼
	V8-400/Z Firebird	19.7	22.0	14—17	195	21	5	—	2.4	—	3[4]	4¼
	V8-400/Z Pontiac	26.3	20.3	14—17	195	21	5	—	—	—	3[12]	4¼
	V8-403/K Firebird	17.4	18.0	14—17	195	21	4	—	—	—	3[4]	4¼
	V8-403/K Pontiac	17.7	23.0	14—17	195	21	4	—	—	—	3[12]	4¼
1979	V6-231/A Phoenix	14	14	14—17	195	21	4	3.5	3.5	—	3[34]	[17]
	V6-231/A LeMans	14.2	14	14—17	195	18	4	3.5	3.5	—	3[34]	3½
	V6-231/A Firebird	14	14	14—17	195	21	4	3.5	2.5	—	3[34]	4¼
	V6-231/A Grand Prix	14.2	14	14—17	195	18	4	3.5	3.5	—	3[34]	3½
	V6-231/A Pontiac	13.9	13.9	14—17	195	21	4	3.5	2.5	—	3[34]	[31]
	V8-301/W,Y Firebird	[26]	[26]	14—17	195	21	4[33]	3.5	2.5	—	3[34]	4¼
	V8-301/W,Y LeMans	20.3[32]	20.3[32]	14—17	195	18	4[33]	3.5	3.5	—	3[34]	3½
	V8-301/W,Y Grand Prix	20.3[29]	20.3[29]	14—17	195	18	4[33]	3.5	2.5	—	3[34]	4¼
	V8-301/W,Y Pontiac	20.2	20.2	14—17	195	21	4[33]	—	—	—	3[34]	[31]
	V8-305/G,H Phoenix	16.8[11]	17[11]	14—17	195	21	4	3.5	3.5	—	3[34]	[17]
	V8-305/G,H LeMans	17.7[30]	18.3	14—17	195	18	4	3.5	3.5	—	3[34]	3.5
	V8-305/G,H Firebird	17.2[11]	17.8	14—17	195	21	4	3.5	2.5	—	3[34]	4¼
	V8-305/G,H Grand Prix	17.7[30]	18.3	14—17	195	18	4	3.5	3.5	—	3[34]	3½
	V8-350/L,R,X Phoenix	17.1	17.8	14—17	195	21	4	3.5	3.5	—	3[34]	[17]
	V8-350/L,R,X LeMans	17.7[30]	18.3	14—17	195	18	4	3.5	3.5	—	3[34]	3.5
	V8-350/L,R,X Firebird	17.2	17.8	14—17	195	21	4	3.5	2.5	—	3[34]	4¼
	V8-350/L,R,X Pontiac	17	23	14—17	195	21	4	—	—	—	3[34]	[31]
	V8-400/Z Firebird	19.7[24]	20.3[24]	14—17	195	21	5	3.5	2.5	—	3[34]	4¼
	V8-403/K Firebird	17.4[25]	18	14—17	195	21	4	3.5	2.5	—	3[34]	4¼
	V8-403/K Pontiac	17[30]	23[30]	14—17	195	21	4	—	—	—	3[34]	[31]
1980	V6-229/K LeMans	18.5	18.5	15	195	18.1	4	3.5	—	—	[3]	3.5
	V6-231/A LeMans	13.3	13.3	15	195	18.1	4	3.5	—	—	[3]	3.4
	V6-231/A Firebird	14	14	15	195	20.8	4	3.5	—	—	[3]	4¼
	V6-231/A Grand Prix	13.3	13.3	15	195	18.1	4	—	—	—	[3]	3.5
	V6-231/A Pontiac	13.3	13.3	15	195	25[14]	4	—	—	—	[3]	[17]
	V8-265/S LeMans	20.3	20.3	15	195	18.1	4[33]	—	—	—	[3]	3.5
	V8-265/S Firebird	21.6	21.6	15	195	20.8	4[33]	—	—	—	[3]	4¼
	V8-265/S Grand Prix	20.3	20.3	15	195	18.1	4[33]	—	—	—	[3]	3.5
	V8-265/S Pontiac	21.1	21.1	15	195	25[14]	4[33]	—	—	—	[3]	[17]
	V8-301/T LeMans	20.3	20.3	15	195	18.1	4[33]	—	—	—	[3]	3.5
	V8-301/T Firebird	21.6	21.6	15	195	20.8	4[33]	—	—	—	[3]	4¼
	V8-301/T Grand Prix	20.3	20.3	15	195	18.1	4[33]	—	—	—	[3]	3.5
	V8-301/T Pontiac	21.1	21.1	15	195	25[14]	4[33]	—	—	—	[3]	[17]
	V8-305/H LeMans	18.5	18.5	15	195	18.1	4	—	—	—	[3]	3.5
	V8-305/H Firebird	17.3	17.3	15	195	20.8	4	—	—	—	[3]	4¼
	V8-305/H Grand Prix	18.2	18.2	15	195	18.1	4	—	—	—	[3]	3.4
	V8-305/H Pontiac	20.1	20.1	15	195	25[14]	4	—	—	—	[3]	[17]
	V8-350/X Pontiac[19]	14.8	14.8	15	195	25[14]	4	—	—	—	[3]	[17]
	V8-350/R Pontiac[20]	16.4	16.4	15	195	25[14]	5[33]	—	—	—	[3]	[17]
	V8-350 Diesel/N Pontiac	18.2	18.2	15	195	27[14]	7[35]	—	—	—	[3]	[17]
1981	V6-231/A LeMans	13.1	13.1	15	195	18.1	4	3½	—	—	[9]	3.5
	V6-231/A Firebird	13.1	13.1	15	195	20.8	4	3½	—	—	[9]	4.2
	V6-231/A Grand Prix	13.1	13.1	15	195	18.1	4	—	—	—	[10]	3.5
	V6-231/A Pontiac	13.1	13.3	15	195	25	4	—	—	—	[13]	[17]

Continued

COOLING SYSTEM & CAPACITY DATA—Continued

Year	Model or Engine/V.I.N.	Cooling Capacity, Qts. Less A/C	With A/C	Radiator Cap Relief Pressure, Lbs.	Thermo. Opening Temp.	Fuel Tank Gals.	Engine Oil Refill Qts. (1)	3 Speed Pints	4 Speed Pints	5 Speed Pints	Auto Trans. Qts. (2)	Rear Axle Oil Pints
1981	V8-265/S LeMans	20.3	20.3	15	195	18.1	4(33)	—	—	—	(9)	3.5
	V8-265/S Firebird	20.9(36)	20.9(36)	15	195	20.8	4(33)	—	—	—	(9)	4.2
	V8-265/S Grand Prix	20.3	20.3	15	195	18.1	4(33)	—	—	—	(10)	3.5
	V8-265/S Pontiac	19	19	15	195	25	4(33)	—	—	—	(13)	(17)
	V8-301/W LeMans	20.3(27)	21	15	195	18.1	4(33)	—	—	—	(9)	3.5
	V8-301/W Firebird	20.9(36)	20.9(36)	15	195	20.8	4(33)	—	—	—	(9)	4.2
	V8-301/T Firebird	23	23	15	195	20.8	5(33)	—	—	—	(9)	4.2
	V8-305/H Firebird	17.2	17.2	15	195	20.8	4	—	—	—	(9)	4.2
	V8-307/Y Pontiac	15.6(28)	15.3(28)	15	195	25(14)	4	—	—	—	(13)	(17)
	V8-350/N Grand Prix	17	17	15	195	19.8	7(35)	—	—	—	(10)	3.5
	V8-350/N Pontiac	17	17	15	195	27(14)	7(35)	—	—	—	(13)	(17)
1982	4-151/2 Firebird	12.8	13	15	195	16	3(33)	—	3.5	—	(38)	3.5
	V6-173/1 Firebird	12.5	12.5	15	195	16	4(33)	—	3.5	—	(38)	3.5
	V6-231/A Bonneville	13	13	15	195	18	4	—	—	—	(39)	3.5
	V6-231/A Grand Prix	13	13	15	195	18	4	—	—	—	(39)	3.5
	V6-252/4 Bonneville	13	13	15	195	18	4	—	—	—	(39)	3.5
	V6-252/4 Grand Prix	13	13	15	195	18	4	—	—	—	(39)	3.5
	V8-305/H Firebird	15	15	15	195	16	4	—	—	—	(38)	3.5
	V8-305 E.F.I./7 Firebird	15	15	15	195	16	4	—	—	—	(38)	3.5
	V8-350 Diesel/N Bonneville	17.3	17.3	15	195	19.8(5)	7(37)	—	—	—	(39)	3.5
	V8-350 Diesel/N Grand Prix	17.3	17.3	15	195	19.8	7(37)	—	—	—	(39)	3.5
1983	4-151/2 Firebird	12.8	13	15	195	16	3(33)	—	3.5	—	(41)	3.5
	V6-173/1 Firebird	12.5	12.5	15	195	16	4(33)	—	3.5	—	(41)	3.5
	V6-173 H.O. Firebird	12.5	12.5	15	195	16	4(33)	—	3.5	—	(41)	3.5
	V6-231/A Bonneville	13	13	15	195	17.5(5)	4	—	—	—	(40)	3.5
	V6-231/A Grand Prix	13	13	15	195	17.5	4	—	—	—	(40)	3.5
	V8-305/H Bonneville	15.3	15.9	15	195	17.5(5)	4	—	—	—	(40)	3.5
	V8-305/H Firebird	15	15	15	195	16	4	—	—	—	(41)	3.5
	V8-305/H Grand Prix	15.3	15.9	15	195	17.5	4	—	—	—	(40)	3.5
	V8-305 E.F.I./7 Firebird	15	15	15	195	16	4	—	—	—	(41)	3.5
	V8-350 Diesel Bonneville	17.3	17.3	15	195	19.8	7(37)	—	—	—	(40)	3.5
	V8-350 Diesel Grand Prix	17.3	17.3	15	195	19.8	7(37)	—	—	—	(40)	3.5

(1)—Add one quart with filter change.

(2)—Approximate. Make final check with dipstick.

(3)—THM 200—oil pan, 3.5 qts.; after overhaul, 9½ qts. THM 250 & 350—oil pan, 2¾ qts.; after overhaul, 10¼ qts.

(4)—Oil pan only. After overhaul 10 qts.

(5)—Station Wagons, 18 gals.

(6)—Distributor located at front of engine.

(7)—Station Wagons 24 gals.

(8)—Oil pan only. After overhaul 9½ qts.

(9)—T.H.M. 200/C, oil pan 4.15 qts., after overhaul 10.55 qts.; T.H.M. 250/C, oil pan 2¾ qts., after overhaul 10.25 qts.; T.H.M. 350/C, oil pan 3.15 qts., after overhaul 10 qts.; T.H.M. 350/O, oil pan 3.15 qts. after overhaul 11.45 qts.

(10)—T.H.M. 200/C, oil pan 4.25 qts., after overhaul 10.55 qts.; T.H.M. 250/C, oil pan 2.75 qts., after overhaul, 10.25 qts.; T.H.M. 350/C, oil pan 3.15 qts., after overhaul 10 qts.

(11)—With heavy duty cooling system, 17.8 qts.

(12)—Oil pan only. After overhaul; THM 200, 9 qts. THM 350, 10 qts.

(13)—T.H.M. 200/C, oil pan 4.25 qts., after overhaul 10.55 qts.; T.H.M. 250/C, oil pan 2.75 qts., after overhaul 10.25 qts.; T.H.M. 350/C, oil pan 3.15 qts., after overhaul 10 qts.; T.H.M. 200-4R, oil pan 5.05 qts., after overhaul 11 qts.

(14)—Station Wagons 22 gals.

(15)—Oil pan only. After overhaul 6¾ qts.

(16)—THM 200, oil pan only 3 qts.; after overhaul 8¾ qts. THM 350, oil pan only 4 qts.; after overhaul 9.6 qts. THM 400, oil pan only 3¾ qts.; after overhaul 9½ qts.

(17)—7½ inch axle 3½ pints. 8½ & 8¾ inch axle 4¼ pints.

(18)—Oil pan only. After overhaul 8¾ qts.

(19)—With fuel pump located on driver side of engine.

(20)—With fuel pump located on passenger side of engine.

(21)—Manual trans.

(22)—Auto. trans.

(23)—Vehicles equipped with A/C and/or heavy duty cooling system.

(24)—With heavy duty cooling system, 21.7 qts.

(25)—With heavy duty cooling system, 18.1 qts.

(26)—With 2 barrel carb., 19.9 qts. With 4 barrel carb., 20.5 qts. With 2 barrel carb. and heavy duty cooling system, 20.4 qts. With 4 barrel carb. and heavy duty cooling system, 21 qts.

(27)—With heavy duty cooling system, 21 qts.

(28)—With heavy duty cooling system, 16.2 qts.

(29)—With heavy duty cooling system, 20.8 qts.

(30)—With heavy duty cooling system, 18.5 qts.

(31)—Exc. Station Wagon, 3.5 pts.; Station Wagon, 4.25 pts.

(32)—With heavy duty cooling system, 20.8 qts.

(33)—With or without filter change.

(34)—Oil pan only. After overhaul 9 qts.

(35)—Includes filter. Recommended diesel engine oil—on 1980 units, use oil designated SE/CC; on 1981 units, use engine oil designated SF/CC, SF/CD or SE/CC.

(36)—With heavy duty cooling system, 21.6 qts.

(37)—Includes filter. Recommended diesel engine oil—on 1982–83 units, use oil designated SF/CD or SF/CC.

(38)—Oil pan only, 3.5 qts.; after overhaul, 5 qts.

(39)—T.H.M. 250C, oil pan only, 2.75 qts.; after overhaul, 10.25 qts. T.H.M. 350C, oil pan only, 3.15 qts.; after overhaul, 10.15 qts.

(40)—T.H.M. 250C, oil pan only, 2.75 qts.; after overhaul, 10.25 qts. T.H.M. 350C, oil pan only, 3.25 qts.; after overhaul, 10.15 qts.

(41)—T.H.M. 200C, oil pan only, 3½ qts.; after overhaul, 5 qts.; T.H.M. 700-4R, oil pan only, 4.45 qts.; total capacity, 11.5 qts.

WHEEL ALIGNMENT SPECIFICATIONS

Year	Model	Caster Angle, Degrees		Camber Angle, Degrees				Toe-In. Inch	Toe-Out on Turns, Deg.	
		Limits	Desired	Limits		Desired			Outer Wheel	Inner Wheel
				Left	Right	Left	Right			
1977	Ventura②	−1½ to −½	−1	+.3 to +1.3	+.3 to +1.3	+.8	+.8	0 to ⅛	—	—
	Ventura③	+½ to +1½	+1	+.3 to +1.3	+.3 to +1.3	+.8	+.8	0 to ⅛	—	—
	Firebird	+½ to +1½	+1	+½ to +1½	+½ to +1½	+1	+1	0 to ⅛	—	—
	LeMans②	+½ to +1½	+1	+½ to +1½	0 to +1	+1	+½	0 to ⅛	—	—
	LeMans③	①	+2	+½ to +1½	0 to +1	+1	+½	0 to ⅛	—	—
	Grand Prix	+4.5 to +5.5	+5	+½ to +1½	0 to +1	+1	+½	0 to ⅛	—	—
	Pontiac	+2½ to +3½	+3	+.3 to +1.3	+.3 to +1.3	+.8	+.8	⅛ to ¼	—	—
1978	Phoenix②	−1.5 to −.5	−1	+.3 to +1.3	+.3 to +1.3	+.8	+.8	1/16 to 3/16	—	—
	Phoenix③	+.5 to +1.5	+1	+.3 to +1.3	+.3 to +1.3	+.8	+.8	1/16 to 3/16	—	—
	Firebird	+.5 to +1.5	+1	+.5 to +1.5	+.5 to +1.5	+1	+1	1/16 to 3/16	—	—
	Intermediate②	+.5 to +1.5	+1	0 to +1	0 to +1	+.5	+.5	1/16 to 3/16	—	—
	Intermediate③	+2.5 to +3.5	+3	0 to +1	0 to +1	+.5	+.5	1/16 to 3/16	—	—
	Pontiac	+2.5 to +3.5	+3	+.3 to +1.3	+.3 to +1.3	+.8	+.8	1/16 to 3/16	—	—
1979	Phoenix②	−1.5 to −.5	−1	+.3 to +1.3	+.3 to +1.3	+.8	+.8	1/16 to 3/16	—	—
	Phoenix③	+.5 to +1.5	+1	+.3 to +1.3	+.3 to +1.3	+.8	+.8	1/16 to 3/16	—	—
	Firebird	+.5 to +1.5	+1	+.5 to +1.5	+.5 to +1.5	+1	+1	1/16 to 3/16	—	—
	LeMans②	+.5 to +1.5	+1	0 to +1	0 to +1	+.5	+.5	1/16 to 3/16	—	—
	LeMans③	+2.5 to +3.5	+3	0 to +1	0 to +1	+.5	+.5	1/16 to 3/16	—	—
	Grand Prix	+2.5 to +3.5	+3	0 to +1	0 to +1	+.5	+.5	1/16 to 3/16	—	—
	Pontiac	+2.5 to +3.5	+3	.3 to 1.3	.3 to 1.3	+.8	+.8	1/16 to 3/16	—	—
1980	Firebird	+.5 to +1.5	+1	+.5 to +1.5	+.5 to +1.5	+1	+1	1/16 to 3/16	—	—
	LeMans②	+.5 to +1.5	+1	0 to +1	0 to +1	+.5	+.5	1/16 to 3/16	—	—
	LeMans③	+2.5 to +3.5	+3	0 to +1	0 to +1	+.5	+.5	1/16 to 3/16	—	—
	Grand Prix	+2.5 to +3.5	+3	0 to +1	0 to +1	+.5	+.5	1/16 to 3/16	—	—
	Pontiac	+2.5 to +3.5	+3	+.3 to +1.3	+.3 to +1.3	+.8	+.8	1/16 to 3/16	—	—
1981	Firebird	+.5 to +1.5	+1	+.5 to +1.5	+.5 to +1.5	+1	+1	1/16 to 3/16	—	—
	LeMans②	+.5 to +1.5	+1	−.4 to +.6	−.4 to +.6	+.1	+.1	1/16 to 3/16	—	—
	LeMans③	+2.5 to +3.5	+3	−.4 to +.6	−.4 to +.6	+.1	+.1	1/16 to 3/16	—	—
	Grand Prix	+2.5 to +3.5	+3	−.4 to +.6	−.4 to +.6	+.1	+.1	1/16 to 3/16	—	—
	Pontiac	+.5 to +1.5	+1	+.3 to +1.3	+.3 to +1.3	+.8	+.8	1/16 to 3/16	—	—
1982–83	Firebird	+2.5 to +3.5	+3	+½ to +1½	+½ to +1½	+1	+1	⅛ to ¼	—	—
	Grand Prix	+2.5 to +3.5	+3	0 to +1	0 to +1	+.5	+.5	1/16 to 3/16	—	—
	Bonneville	+2.5 to +3.5	+3	0 to +1	0 to +1	+.5	+.5	1/16 to 3/16	—	—

①—Exc. radial tires, +½ to +1½; Radial tires +1½ to +2½.   ②—Manual Steering.   ③—Power steering.

Electrical Section

STARTER, REPLACE

1. Disconnect battery ground cable.
2. Disconnect brace from starter and swing brace forward, then remove heat shields, if used.
3. On 4-151, disconnect wiring from starter, then remove retaining bolts and starter.
4. On all other engines, remove starter retaining bolts, then lower starter, disconnect wiring and remove starter.

NOTE: If any shims are used between starter and engine, make sure that they are reinstalled in the same location and in the same thickness.

5. Reverse procedure to install.

IGNITION LOCK, REPLACE

1979–83

1. Remove steering wheel as described under Horn Sounder and Steering Wheel.
2. Remove turn signal switch as described under Turn Signal Switch, Replace, then remove buzzer switch.
3. Place ignition switch in "Run" position, then, remove lock cylinder retaining screw and lock cylinder.
4. To install, rotate lock cylinder to stop while holding housing, Fig. 1. Align cylinder key with keyway in housing, then push lock cylinder assembly into housing until fully seated.

5. Install lock cylinder retaining screw. Torque screw to 40 in. lbs. for standard columns. On adjustable columns, torque retaining screw to 22 in. lbs.
6. Install buzzer switch, turn signal switch and steering wheel.

1977–78

1. Follow the procedure to remove the turn signal switch as described further on.
2. Remove the lock cylinder in "Run" position by inserting a thin tool (screwdriver or knife blade), Fig. 2, into the slot next to the switch mounting screw boss (right hand slot) and depress spring latch at bottom of slot, which releases lock. Remove lock by pulling out of housing.

NOTE: If this is the first time the lock cylinder is being removed, the slot will be covered by a thin casting "flash" which is easily broken when inserting thin tool.

3. To install, hold lock cylinder sleeve and rotate knob clockwise against stop, then insert cylinder into housing with key on lock cylinder sleeve aligned with keyway in housing. Push into abutment of cylinder and lock sector.
4. Push in until latch snaps into groove and lock cylinder is secured in housing.

IGNITION SWITCH, REPLACE

1. Disconnect battery and loosen toe pan screws.

2. Remove column to instrument panel trim plates.
3. Lower steering column from instrument panel.

NOTE: On some models it may be necessary to remove the upper column mounting bracket if it hinders the servicing of switch.

4. Disconnect switch wires and remove switch.
5. To replace switch move key lock to OFF-LOCK position.
6. Move actuator rod hole in switch to OFF-LOCK position, Fig. 3.
7. Install switch with rod in hole.

LIGHT SWITCH, REPLACE

Except 1982–83 Firebird

1. Remove battery cable, pull knob to "On" position, depress latch button and remove knob and shaft.
2. Remove retaining nut.
3. Remove wire connector and remove switch.
4. Reverse procedure to install.

1982–83 Firebird

1. Remove right and left lower trim plates.
2. Remove instrument panel cluster trim plate.
3. Remove two retaining screws from switch assembly.
4. Depress side tangs and pull switch assembly from instrument panel.
5. Reverse procedure to install.

Fig. 1 Ignition lock replacement. 1979–83 models

Fig. 2 Ignition lock replace. 1977–78

Fig. 3   Ignition switch. 1977–83 (typical)

STOP LIGHT SWITCH, REPLACE

Except 1982–83 Firebird

The stop light switch has a slip fit in the mounting sleeve which permits positive adjustment by pulling the brake pedal up firmly against the stop. The pedal arm forces the switch body to slip in the mounting sleeve bushing to position the switch properly.
1. Disconnect wires from switch and remove switch from bracket.
2. Position switch in bracket and push in to maximum distance. Brake pedal arm moves switch to correct distance on rebound. Check if pedal is in full return position by lifting slightly by hand.
3. Connect switch wires by inserting plug on switch.

1982–83 Firebird

1. Remove left hand side hush panel.
2. Located under instrument panel, disconnect wire connector from switch at brake pedal support.
3. Remove switch from mounting bracket.
4. Depress brake pedal and install new switch into clip, until shoulder on switch bottoms out against clip.
5. If adjustment of the switch is necessary, the switch may be rotated or pulled in the clip. Electrical contact should be made when brake pedal is depressed .053 inch from its fully released position.

NEUTRAL SAFETY SWITCH, REPLACE

Except 1982–83 Firebird

1. Loosen switch retaining screws and place selector lever in "Reverse" on manual transmission models or "Neutral" on automatic transmission models.
2. Rotate switch until alignment hole in outer cover aligns with hole in inner contact carrier. Insert a .089 inch gauge pin into alignment hole on manual transmission models. On 1977–83 models equipped with automatic transmission, insert a .090 in. gauge pin into alignment hole on top of switch. On all models, gauge pin is inserted approximately 3/8 inch.
3. Tighten switch retaining screws and remove gauge pin.

1982–83 Firebird

1. Remove floor console cover.
2. Disconnect wire connectors from backup lamp/neutral start switch.
3. Position gear shift lever into Neutral position.
4. Remove two screws securing neutral starter switch, then remove switch.
5. Ensure gear shift lever is in Neutral position before installing switch.
6. Install new switch in position on gear shift lever. Ensure pin on gear shift lever is in slot of switch. Tighten switch and torque to 14–19 inch lbs.
7. Move gear shift lever out of Neutral position to break plastic shear pin.
8. Connect electrical connectors to switch. Apply parking brake and start vehicle. Ensure vehicle starts only in Park or Neutral positions.
9. Turn ignition off and install floor console cover.

MECHANICAL NEUTRAL START SYSTEM

1977–81 Full Size, 1978–81 Grand Am, Grand Prix & LeMans & 1982–83 Bonneville & Grand Prix

Actuation of the ignition switch is prevented by a mechanical lockout system, Figs. 4 and 5, which prevents the lock cylinder from rotating when the selector lever is out of Park or Neutral. When the selector lever is in Park

Fig. 4   Mechanical neutral start system with standard column. 1977–81 Full size models, 1978–81 Grand Am, Grand Prix and LeMans & 1982–83 Bonneville & Grand Prix

or Neutral, the slots in the bowl plate and the finger on the actuator rod align allowing the finger to pass through the bowl plate in turn actuating the ignition switch, Fig. 6. If the selector lever is in any position other than Park or Neutral, the finger contacts the bowl plate when the lock cylinder is rotated, thereby preventing full travel of the lock cylinder.

CLUTCH START SWITCH

All cars equipped with a manual transmission use a clutch start switch which is mounted on the pedal bracket. The switch closes when the clutch is depressed and completes solenoid connection. When installing switch, no adjustment is necessary.

TURN SIGNAL SWITCH, REPLACE

1977–83

NOTE: *On tilt column, the column must first be lowered from panel.*

1. Remove steering wheel using puller.

CAUTION: *Do not hammer on end of shaft as hammering could collapse shaft or loosen plastic injections which maintain column rigidity.*

Fig. 5   Mechanical neutral start system with tilt column. 1977–81 Full size models, 1978–81 Grand Am, Grand Prix and LeMans & 1982–83 Bonneville & Grand Prix

Fig. 6   Mechanical neutral start system in Park position. 1977–81 Full size models, 1978–81 Grand Am, Grand Prix and LeMans & 1982–83 Bonneville & Grand Prix

Fig. 7   Compressing lock plate and removing retaining ring

Fig. 8   Taping turn signal connector & wires

2. Remove cover by prying out with a screwdriver at slots provided in cover for this purpose.
3. Depress lock plate and pry round wire lock ring out of shaft groove, Fig. 7. Remove lock plate.
4. Slide upper bearing preload spring and turn signal cancelling cam off shaft.
5. Remove turn signal lever.

NOTE: On models with column mounted dimmer switch, remove actuator arm screw and actuator arm before removing turn signal lever.

---

6. Push hazard warning switch in and unscrew knob.
7. Pull turn signal wiring connector out of bracket on jacket and disconnect.
8. Remove three turn signal switch screws.
9. Remove shift indicator cable, if equipped.
10. Lower steering column from instrument panel and remove wire protector, then pull switch straight up with wire protector and remove housing.

NOTE: Place tape around upper part of connector and wires to prevent snagging when switch is being removed, Fig. 8.

COLUMN-MOUNTED DIMMER SWITCH, REPLACE

1977–81 Full Size, 1978–81 Grand Prix & LeMans & 1982–83 Bonneville, Grand Prix & Firebird

1. Disconnect battery ground cable.
2. Remove instrument panel lower trim and on models with A/C, remove A/C duct extension at column.
3. Remove toe-plate cover screws.
4. Remove two nuts from instrument panel support bracket studs and lower steering column, resting steering wheel on front seat.
5. Remove dimmer switch retaining screw(s) and the switch. Tape actuator rod to column and separate switch from rod.
6. Reverse procedure to install. To adjust switch, depress dimmer switch slightly and install a 3/32 inch twist drill to lock the switch to the body. Force switch upward to remove lash between retaining

screws to 35 inch lbs. and remove tape from actuator rod. Remove twist drill and check for proper operation.

HORN SOUNDER & STEERING WHEEL, REPLACE

Except 1982–83 Firebird

1. Disconnect battery ground cable.
2. Remove three screws attaching horn pad assembly to steering wheel.
3. Disconnect horn contact from steering wheel.
4. Remove steering wheel nut retainer and attaching nut.
5. Using steering wheel puller tool No. J-30014-1 or equivalent, remove steering wheel. Note position of steering wheel to shaft.

NOTE: On 1981–83 models, use puller tool No. J-1859-03 or equivalent.

---

6. Reverse procedure to install.

1982–83 Firebird

1. Disconnect battery ground cable.
2. Remove steering wheel shroud screws on underside of steering wheel.
3. Remove steering wheel shroud and horn contact lead assembly from the steering wheel.
4. Remove snap ring and steering wheel nut.
5. Using steering wheel puller tool No. J-2927 or equivalent, remove steering wheel. Note position of steering wheel to shaft.
6. Reverse procedure to install.

INSTRUMENT CLUSTER, REPLACE

1981–83 Models Except 1982–83 Firebird

1. Disconnect battery ground cable.
2. Remove upper and lower instrument panel trim plates, Figs. 9, 12, 13, 14 and 17.
3. Disconnect shift indicator cable from column jacket.

4. Remove two steering column nuts and lower steering column.
5. Remove speaker cover plate and remove two screws securing instrument panel to cowl.
6. Loosen instrument panel pad by removing two outer top screws and three lower screws.
7. Remove fuse panel from firewall.
8. Remove all remaining electrical connections from connectors and speedometer cable from speedometer head.
9. Reverse procedure to install.

1982–83 Firebird

1. Remove right and left lower trim plates, Fig. 19.
2. Remove instrument cluster trim plate.
3. Remove six cluster attachment screws, pull cluster back and disconnect speedometer cable.
4. Disconnect necessary electrical connections.
5. Remove trip odometer and cluster lens.
6. Reverse procedure to install.

1977–80 Models Except 1977 Ventura & 1977–79 Phoenix

1. Disconnect battery ground cable.
2. Remove upper and lower instrument panel trim plates, Figs. 9 thru 13.
3. Remove shift indicator cable.
4. On Firebird, loosen steering column nuts and lower column approximately 1/2 inch.
5. On all models, remove cluster retaining screws, pull cluster outward and disconnect speedometer cable and printed circuit connector, then remove cluster, Figs. 13 thru 17.
6. Reverse procedure to install.

1977 Ventura & 1977–79 Phoenix

1. Disconnect battery ground cable.
2. Remove steering column trim panel, Fig. 18.
3. On 1977–79 models, remove hush panel.
4. Remove three screws retaining heater or A/C control panel to instrument panel carrier.
5. Remove radio control knobs, bezels and nuts.
6. Remove screws at top, bottom and side of carrier securing it to instrument panel pad.

Fig. 9   Instrument panel. 1977–81 Firebird

7. Disconnect shift quadrant indicator cable at shaft bowl (if automatic), remove two steering column to panel nuts.
8. Remove toe plate cover and five tow plate to cowl screws, lower column from panel and protect it with shop towels or tape.
9. Remove ground wire screw from under left side of panel pad above kick pad and disconnect speedo cable from under dash.
10. Tilt carrier and cluster rearward, disconnect printed circuit and cluster ground connectors and rest assembly on top of column.
11. Remove screws from cluster to carrier assembly and remove cluster.
12. Reverse procedure to install.

W/S WIPER MOTOR, REPLACE

1. Raise hood and remove cowl screen or grille.
2. Disconnect wiring and washer hoses.
3. Reaching through opening, loosen transmission drive link to crankarm attaching nuts.
4. Remove drive link from motor crankarm.
5. Remove three motor attaching screws and remove motor while guiding crankarm through opening.
6. Reverse procedure to install.

W/S WIPER TRANSMISSION, REPLACE

With Rectangular Motor
1. Remove wiper arms and blades.
2. Raise hood and remove cowl vent screen or grille.
3. Disconnect wiring from motor.
4. Loosen, but do not remove, transmission drive link to motor crankarm attaching nuts and disconnect drive link from crankarm.
5. Remove right and left transmission to body attaching screws and guide transmission and linkage assembly out through opening.

NOTE: When installing, motor must be in Park position.

With Round Motor
1. Raise hood and remove cowl vent screen.
2. On Intermediates and 1977–81 full size models, remove right and left wiper arm and blade assemblies.
3. Loosen, but do not remove, attaching nuts securing transmission drive link to motor crankarm.
4. Disconnect transmission drive link from motor crankarm.
5. On Intermediate and 1977–81 full size models, remove right and left transmission to body attaching screws.
6. Remove transmission and linkage assembly by guiding it through opening.

NOTE: When installing, motor must be in Park position.

Fig. 10 Instrument panel. 1977 LeMans less optional instrument cluster

W/S WIPER SWITCH, REPLACE

1982–83

1. Remove steering wheel as described under Horn Sounder and Steering Wheel, Replace.
2. Remove turn signal switch as described under Turn Signal Switch, Replace.
3. Remove ignition lock and buzzer as described under Ignition Lock, Replace.

4. Remove and install cover and wiper switch as shown in Fig. 20.
5. Reverse remaining procedure to install.

1977–81 Exc. Phoenix & Ventura

1. Disconnect battery ground cable. Remove upper and lower instrument panel trimplates.
2. Remove switch mounting plate and disconnect connector.
3. Remove switch retaining screws and remove switch.

Fig. 11 Instrument panel. 1977 Grand Am, Grand Prix & LeMans with optional instrument cluster

1977-79 Phoenix & Ventura

1. Disconnect battery ground cable.
2. From under dash, disconnect wiring from switch.
3. Remove screws retaining switch to lower instrument panel and remove switch from panel.

RADIO, REPLACE

NOTE: When installing radio, be sure to adjust antenna trimmer for peak performance.

1978-81 Grand Am, Grand LeMans, Grand Prix, LeMans & 1982-83 Bonneville & Grand Prix

1. Disconnect battery ground cable.
2. Remove upper and lower trim plates.
3. If equipped with console, move shift lever fully rearward.
4. On all models, remove four radio attaching screws from front of radio.
5. Open glove box door and lower by releasing spring clip.
6. Loosen radio rear attaching nut and pull radio outward slightly.
7. Disconnect electrical leads from radio and remove radio from vehicle.
8. Reverse procedure to install.

1977-81 Full Size

1. Disconnect battery ground cable.
2. Remove upper trim plate.
3. Remove radio trim plate by removing the two top screws and ash tray assembly, then disconnect cigar lighter electrical connector and remove the two small screws and large screw retaining ash tray bracket.
4. Remove two screws securing radio.
5. Pull radio from instrument panel opening and disconnect electrical leads from radio.
6. Remove radio from vehicle. Remove bezel nuts from front of radio to remove front trim plate if new radio is installed.
7. Reverse procedure to install.

1977 LeMans

1. Disconnect battery and remove radio knobs and bezels.
2. Remove upper and lower trimplates.
3. Remove radio retaining screws.
4. Remove radio from opening, disconnect connections and antenna lead-in while radio is being pulled out.
5. If new unit is being installed, remove bushing from old unit and install on replacement unit.

1977 Grand Am, Grand Prix & Grand LeMans

1. Disconnect battery ground cable.
2. Remove radio knobs and bezels, then the hex nut from right hand tuning shaft.
3. Remove radio trim plate.
4. Remove radio and radio bracket to instrument panel retaining screws.

Fig. 12   Instrument panel. 1978-81 Grand Am, Grand Prix, LeMans & 1982-83 Bonneville & Grand Prix

NOTE: Radio and bracket must be removed as an assembly.

5. Remove radio and bracket from instrument panel, disconnect wiring harness and antenna lead, then separate bracket from radio.

1977-79 Phoenix & Ventura

1. Disconnect battery ground cable.
2. Remove "hush" panel, if equipped.
3. Remove radio knobs, bezels, nuts and side braces screw and disconnect wiring and antenna.
4. Remove radio from under dash.

1977-83 Firebird

1. Disconnect battery ground cable.
2. Remove glove box and door and right lower A/C duct if equipped.
3. Remove radio knobs and hex nuts and trim plate.
4. Disconnect all leads to radio.
5. Remove radio bracket and radio from passenger side of instrument panel.

HEATER CORE, REPLACE

Without Air Cond.

1982-83 Firebird

1. Disconnect battery ground cable.
2. Drain radiator and remover heater hoses from heater core.
3. Remove right lower hush panel.
4. Remove right lower instrument trim panel.
5. Vehicles equipped with the V8-305 EFI engine, remove ESC module.
6. Remove lower right instrument panel carrier to cowl screw.
7. Remove four heater case cover screws.
8. Remove heater case cover.
9. Remove core support plate and baffle

Fig. 13   Instrument panel and cluster. 1977-81 Full Size

screws.
10. Remove heater core, support plate and baffle from case.
11. Reverse procedure to install.

1978–81 Grand Am, Grand LeMans, Grand Prix, LeMans & 1982–83 Bonneville & Grand Prix
1. Disconnect battery ground cable and drain cooling system.
2. Disconnect heater hoses.
3. Disconnect electrical connectors from heater module.
4. Remove module front cover screws.
5. Remove heater core from module.
6. Reverse procedure to install.

1977–81 Full Size
1. Disconnect battery ground cable.
2. Disconnect hoses from heater core and plug core tubes to prevent spilling coolant.
3. Remove retaining screws from around heater core cover.
4. Remove heater core cover and remove heater core from module, Fig. 21.
5. Reverse procedure to install.

1977–81 Firebird
1. Drain radiator and disconnect heater hoses from core.
2. Remove retaining nuts from core case studs on engine side of dash.
3. Inside car, remove glove box and door on Firebird and heater outlet from case on Firebird.
4. Remove defroster duct retaining screw from heater case and pull entire heater assembly from firewall.
5. Disconnect control cables and wiring and remove assembly.
6. Remove core tube seal and core retaining strips and remove core.

1977–79 Phoenix & Ventura
1. Drain radiator and disconnect heater hoses from core.
2. Disconnect battery ground cable.
3. Remove retaining nuts from core case studs on engine side of dash.
4. Remove glove box and door.
5. On all models, drill out lower right hand heater case stud with 1/4 inch drill from inside vehicle.
6. Pull entire heater core and case assembly from firewall.
7. Disconnect cables and wiring and remove assembly from car.
8. Remove core tube seal and core retaining strips and remove core.

With Air Cond.

1982–83 Bonneville & Grand Prix
1. Disconnect negative battery cable.
2. Discharge air conditioning system and drain cooling system.
3. Remove both windshield wipers and wiper stops.
4. Remove cover windshield molding and leaf screens.
5. Remove lower windshield molding brackets, bolts from upper half of module case, all electrical connections and module cover.
6. Remove heater core clamp bolt and remove heater core.
7. Reverse procedure to install.

Fig. 14   Instrument cluster. 1977–81 Firebird

Fig. 15   Instrument cluster. 1977 LeMans less optional instrument cluster

Fig. 16   Instrument cluster. 1977 Grand Am, Grand Prix & LeMans with optional instrument cluster

1982–83 Firebird

1. Disconnect battery ground cable.
2. Drain radiator and remove heater hoses from heater core.
3. Remove right lower hush panel.
4. Remove right lower instrument trim panel.
5. Vehicles equipped with the V8-305 EFI engine, remove ESC module.
6. Remove lower right instrument panel carrier to cowl screw.
7. Remove four heater case cover screws.
8. Remove heater case cover.
9. Remove core support plate and baffle screws.
10. Remove heater core, support plate and baffle from case.
11. Reverse procedure to install.

1978–81 Grand Am, Grand LeMans, Grand Prix & LeMans

1. Disconnect battery ground cable.
2. Remove right hand windshield wiper arm and blade assembly.
3. Drain cooling system, then disconnect heater hoses at heater core and plug core openings.
4. Remove bracket and ground strap.
5. Remove module cover as follows:
   a. Remove seals and screens, then disconnect wire connector.
   b. Loosen and move up lower windshield reveal moulding, then remove reveal moulding cowl brackets.
   c. Tape a strip of wood below lower edge of windshield over module to prevent damage to windshield.
   d. Remove all cover attaching screws, then cut through sealing material along cowl.
   e. Carefully pry cover off from side, then lift cover away from flange of fender cowl brace.
   f. Remove heater core and seal from module.

1977–81 Full Size

1. Disconnect battery ground cable.
2. Remove right half of hood seal from air inlet screen.
3. Remove air inlet screen.
4. Remove screws securing top of module, then disconnect electrical connectors from electrical components on top of module.
5. Remove thermostatic switch mounting screws from top of module.
6. Remove A/C diagnostic connector mounting screws and position aside.
7. Remove top of module.
8. Disconnect and remove heater core from module, Fig. 22.
9. Reverse procedure to install.

1977 LeMans, Grand Am & Grand Prix

1. Drain radiator and disconnect heater hoses from core.
2. Remove glove box, cold air duct and heater outlet and defroster duct screw.
3. Disconnect heater core case from dash. Remove blower motor resistor to gain access to case upper retaining nut.
4. Move case assembly rearward, freeing case studs from cowl and remove assembly.
5. Disconnect temperature cable and vacuum hoses from case and remove screws securing core inside of case.

1977–81 Firebird

1. Drain radiator.
2. Remove glove box and door.
3. Remove cold air duct (lower right hand duct) and remove left and center lower A/C ducts.

Fig. 17 Instrument cluster. 1978–81 Grand Am, Grand Prix, LeMans, 1982–83 Bonneville & Grand Prix

4. Jack right front area of car and place on safety stand.
5. Remove rocker panel trim on right side and remove screws holding forward portion of rocker panel trim attaching bracket.
6. Remove three lower fender bolts at rear of fender.
7. Remove four fender to skirt bolts at rear of wheel opening.
8. Remove two fender skirt bolts near blower motor area.
9. Pry rear portion of fender out at bottom to gain access to hose clamp on lower core hose and disconnect hose.
10. Disconnect water pump to core hose at core.
11. Remove heater case retaining nuts under hood at dash.
12. Remove two heater case retaining bolts (inside car).
13. Remove console, if equipped. If equipped with tape player, remove console with tape player intact. If equipped with tape player and no console, remove tape player.
14. Disconnect temperature cable at heater case.
15. Remove heater outlet duct.
16. Remove lower defroster duct screw at heater case.
17. Remove right kick panel.
18. Remove heater case and case.
19. Disconnect vacuum hoses from heater case.
20. Remove core from case.

1977–79 Phoenix & Ventura

1. Disconnect battery and drain coolant.
2. Disconnect upper heater hose from core.
3. Remove right front fender skirt bolts and lower skirt to gain access to lower heater hose clamp. Disconnect lower hose and remove lower right hand heater core and case attaching nut.
4. Remove glove box and door.
5. Remove recirculation vacuum diaphragm at right kick panel.
6. Remove heater outlet (at bottom of heater case).

7. Remove cold air distributor duct from heater case.
8. Remove heater case extension screws and separate extension from case.
9. Disconnect cables and wiring and remove case and core assembly.
10. Separate core from case.

BLOWER MOTOR, REPLACE

1978–81 Grand Am, Grand LeMans, Grand Prix, LeMans & 1982–83 Bonneville and Grand Prix

1. Disconnect battery ground cable.
2. If equipped with air conditioning, disconnect cooling tube from blower motor.
3. On all models, disconnect electrical connector from blower motor.
4. Remove blower motor retaining screws and the blower motor.
5. Reverse procedure to install.

1977–81 Full Size Without Air Cond.

1. Disconnect battery ground cable.
2. Disconnect blower motor electrical lead.
3. Remove blower motor retaining screws and remove blower motor, Fig. 21.
4. Reverse procedure to install.

1977–81 Full Size With Air Cond.

1. Disconnect battery ground cable.
2. Remove right half of hood seal from air inlet screen.
3. Remove air inlet screen.
4. Remove screws securing top of module, then disconnect electrical connectors from electrical components on top of module.
5. Remove thermostatic switch mounting screws from top of module.
6. Remove A/C diagnostic connector mounting screws and position aside.
7. Remove top of module.
8. Disconnect and remove blower motor from module, Fig. 22.
9. Reverse procedure to install.

Fig. 18 Instrument panel and cluster. 1977 Ventura & 1977–79 Phoenix

1977–83 Firebird
1. Disconnect battery ground cable.
2. Disconnect wire connector. On models with A/C, disconnect cooling tube.
3. Remove motor attaching screws and nuts, then remove blower motor assembly from case.
4. Reverse procedure to install.

1977 Grand Prix & LeMans
1. Disconnect blower motor feed wire.
2. Remove blower motor retaining screws.
3. Remove blower motor.

1977–79 Phoenix & Ventura
1. Disconnect battery and detach hoses from clips on right fender skirt.
2. Raise vehicle on hoist.
3. Remove fender skirt attaching bolts except those retaining the skirt to radiator support.
4. Pull out then down on skirt and place block of wood between skirt and fender to allow clearance for blower motor removal.
5. Disconnect blower motor cooling tube and electrical connections at blower motor.

6. Remove blower motor attaching screws and remove blower motor. Gently pry motor flange if sealer acts as an adhesive.

SPEED CONTROLS
1977–83 Cruise Control

Brake Release Switches, Adjust
Apply brake pedal and push both switches forward as far as possible. Pull pedal forcibly rearward to adjust switches.

1	TRIM PLATE ASM.-CLUSTER
2	BOLT/SCREW
3	COVER, LOWER R.H.
4	COVER, LOWER L.H.
5	LOWER TRIM PLATE ASM. (LH)
6	LOWER TRIM PLATE ASM. (RH)
7	HEATER ONLY
8	I.P. LOWER REINF.
9	BRACKET
10	CONVENIENCE CENTER MOUNTING BRACKET

VIEW A
(HEATER ONLY)

Fig. 19   Instrument cluster. 1982–83 Firebird

Fig. 20   W/S wiper switch replacement. 1982–83

Fig. 21   Heater core & blower motor (less air conditioning). 1977–83 Full size

Fig. 22   Heater core & blower motor (with air conditioning). 1977–83 Full size

Centering Spring Adjustment Exc. Cruise Master Units

If speed control holds speed three or more mph higher than selected speed, turn centering screw (C) clockwise 1/8 turn or less, Fig. 23.

If speed control holds speed three or more mph below selected speed, turn centering adjustment screw (C) counterclockwise 1/8 turn or less. *Do not move adjustment screw (R).*

Orifice Tube Adjustment, Cruise Master Units

To check engagement speed, engage the system at 55 mph. If vehicle cruises below the engagement speed, loosen the locknut and screw the orifice tube outward. If vehicle cruises above the engagement speed, loosen the locknut and screw the orifice tube inward.

NOTE: Each 1/4 turn of the orifice tube will change the cruise speed about 1 mph. Also, do not remove orifice tube as it cannot be reinstalled once removed.

Bead Chain Adjustment, 1977–83 Buick Built Engines

Assemble chain to be taut with carburetor in hot idle position and the idle solenoid deenergized. Place chain into swivel cavities which permits chain to have slight slack. Place retainer over swivel and chain assembly. Retainer must be made to rest between balls. Cut off chain flush with side of swivel to remove excess length. Chain slack should not exceed one half diameter of ball stud, .150 inch, when measured at hot idle position.

Cable Adjustment, 1977–83 Pontiac Built Engines

1. Set carburetor choke to hot idle position.
2. With cable connected to vacuum servo, pull steel tube of servo as far as it will go and check if one of the cross holes in the steel tube aligns with carburetor lever pin.

Fig. 23   Centering spring adjustment 1977–83 Cruise Control

3. If one of the cross holes in the steel tube aligns with carburetor lever pin, install the tube, washer and cotter pin.
4. If none of the cross holes in the steel aligns with carburetor lever pin, move tube rearward to align the next closest hole and install cable, washer and cotter pin.

CAUTION: Do not stretch cable to make adjustment, as this will prevent carburetor from returning to normal idle.

Cable Adjustment, 1982–83 Chevrolet Built Engines Less Electronic Fuel Injection
1. Assemble cable to cable bracket and throttle lever.

2. Install cable assembly onto servo bracket.
3. Place throttle in fully closed position. Attach servo chain to cable assembly with first two beads of servo chain hanging loose outside cable assembly clip.
4. Adjust cable assembly jam nuts until there is a .03 inch clearance between throttle lever stud pin and end of slot on throttle cable assembly. Torque jam nuts to 35–48 inch lbs. Pull rubber boot over washer on cable.

Cable Adjustment, 1982–83 Chevrolet Built Engines With Electronic Fuel Injection
1. Assemble cable to cable bracket and TBI lever and servo bracket.
2. Place throttle in fully closed position. Attach servo chain to cable assembly with first two beads of servo chain hanging

loosely outside cable assembly clip.
3. Adjust cable jam nuts until cable sleeve at TBI unit is tight but not holding throttle open. Torque jam nuts to 35–48 inch lbs. Pull rubber boot over washer on cable.

Rod Adjustment, 1977–83 Oldsmobile Built Engines
Adjust length of rod to minimum slack with carburetor in hot idle position and the engine static.

Rod Adjustment, 1977–81 Chevrolet Built Engines
Screw rod into link with ignition "Off" and fast idle cam off and throttle closed. Hook rod through tab on servo. Adjust length so link assemblies over end of stud, then install retainer.

Engine Section

For service on V6-231, 252 & 1978–80 V8-350 engines with distributor located at front of engine, see Buick Chapter. For service on V6-173, V6-229, V8-305 & all 1977–80 V8-350 engines with distributor located at rear of engine and fuel pump located on right side of engine, see Chevrolet Chapter.

For service on all V8-307, 350, 350 Diesel & 403 engines with distributor located at rear of engine, fuel pump located on right side of engine and oil filler tube located on engine front cover, see Oldsmobile Chapter.

ENGINE MOUNTS, REPLACE

4-151

1977–78
1. Remove insulator to engine bracket through bolt(s), Fig. 1.
2. Raise engine to release weight off front mounts.
3. Remove insulator and separate from engine bracket.

1982–83
1. Disconnect battery ground cable.
2. Raise and support front of vehicle.
3. Remove mount through bolts on left and right hand side, Fig. 1A.
4. Raise front of engine and remove mount to engine attaching bolts, then remove mounts.
5. Reverse procedure to install.

1977–81 V8-265, 301, 350 & 400

1. Disconnect battery ground cable.
2. Raise engine to release weight off front mounts.
3. Remove bolts fastening engine insulators to engine, Fig. 2.
4. Raise engine just clear of insulator.
5. Remove insulator.

ENGINE, REPLACE

1977–81

1. Disconnect battery cables at battery and drain cooling system.
2. Scribe alignment marks on hood and remove hood from hinges.
3. Disconnect all wiring, ground straps, fuel lines and vacuum hoses from engine.

Fig. 1 Engine mounts. 1977–78 4-151

NOTE: On V8 engines, remove thermal feed switch, located on rear of left cylinder head on all models except Ventura. On Venture models, switch is located on the right cylinder head.

4. Remove air cleaner and upper radiator shield assembly.
5. Disconnect radiator hoses and heater hoses at engine.
6. Remove fan and disconnect accelerator linkage.
7. If equipped with power steering or air

conditioning, remove pump and/or compressor from mountings and set aside. Do not disconnect hoses.
8. On V8, disconnect transmission vacuum modulator line and power brake vacuum line at carburetor and fold back out of way.
9. Raise vehicle on hoist and drain crankcase.
10. Disconnect exhaust pipe from manifold and remove starter.
11. If equipped with automatic transmission, remove converter cover and three converter retaining bolts and slide converter to rear.

12. With manual transmission, disconnect clutch linkage and remove clutch cross shaft.
13. Remove four lower bell housing bolts.
14. Disconnect transmission filler tube support and starter wire harness shield from cylinder head.
15. Remove two front motor mount to frame bracket bolts.
16. Lower vehicle and using a jack and block of wood, support transmission.
17. Support weight of engine with suitable lifting device.
18. Remove two remaining bell housing bolts.
19. Raise transmission slightly.
20. Position engine forward to free it from transmission and remove from car by tilting front of engine up.

1982–83 4-151

1. Disconnect battery ground cable.
2. Drain cooling system.
3. Scribe alignment marks on hood, then remove hood from hinges.
4. Remove A/C compressor, brackets and position aside.
5. Remove upper and lower radiator hoses from engine.
6. Remove fan assembly.
7. On models with auto. trans., remove radiator and shroud assembly. On models with manual transmission, remove upper half of radiator shroud.
8. Disconnect power steering hoses, then remove power steering pump from mounting brackets.
9. Disconnect engine wiring at bulkhead connection.
10. Disconnect inlet and return fuel lines at flex hoses.
11. Remove vacuum brake hose from filter.
12. Disconnect engine to body ground strap from rear of cylinder head.
13. From inside of vehicle, remove right hand hush panel, then disconnect E.C.M. harness from E.C.M. unit.
14. Remove splash shield from right fender and feed E.C.M. harness from inside of vehicle.
15. Disconnect heater hoses from heater core.
16. Disconnect throttle linkage and canister hose from E.F.I. assembly.
17. Raise and support vehicle.
18. Disconnect electrical connectors from transmission.
19. Remove flywheel dust cover.
20. On models equipped with automatic transmission, remove torque converter to flywheel bolts.
21. Remove bell housing to engine bolts.
22. Disconnect exhaust pipe at manifold, then remove exhaust pipe support at bell housing.
23. Disconnect catalytic converter at tail pipe joint, then remove converter and exhaust pipe assembly.
24. Disconnect starter wiring, then remove starter assembly.
25. On models equipped with manual transmission, remove clutch fork return spring.
26. Remove motor mount through bolts.
27. Lower vehicle, then using a suitable jack and block of wood, support transmission.
28. Support weight of engine with suitable lifting device.
29. Remove engine from vehicle. On models equipped with manual transmission, swing engine slightly to the right to remove clutch swing arm from ball.

LEFT HAND VIEW

RIGHT HAND VIEW

Fig. 1A Engine mounts. 1982–83 4-151

Fig. 2 Engine mounts (typical). V8-265, 301, 350 & 400

CYLINDER HEAD, REPLACE

4-151

1. Drain cooling system and remove air cleaner.
2. Disconnect accelerator and fuel and vacuum lines at carburetor.
3. Remove intake and exhaust manifolds.
4. Remove bolts attaching alternator bracket to cylinder head.
5. If equipped with power steering or A/C, remove right side front bracket.
6. Disconnect temperature sending unit wiring harness, battery ground cable and radiator and heater hoses.
7. Disconnect spark plug wires and remove spark plugs.
8. Remove rocker cover, then back off rocker arm nuts.
9. Pivot rocker arms to clear push rods and remove push rods.
10. Remove cylinder head attaching bolts and cylinder head.
11. Reverse procedure to install. Coat cylinder head bolts with sealer. Torque bolts in sequence as shown in Figs. 3 & 4. When installing intake and exhaust manifolds, refer to Figs. 5, 6 and 7 for bolt tightening sequence.

V8-301, 350 & 400

1. Drain cooling system and remove air cleaner.
2. Remove intake manifold, push rod cover and rocker arm cover.

Fig. 3 Cylinder head tightening sequence. 1977–78 4-151

Fig. 4 Cylinder head tightening sequence. 1982–83 4-151

Fig. 5 Manifold tightening sequence. 1977–78 4-151

3. Loosen all rocker arm nuts and move rocker arms off push rods.
4. Remove push rods, keeping them in order so they may be installed in their original locations.
5. Detach exhaust crossover pipe from manifolds.
6. Remove battery ground strap and engine ground strap on left head or engine ground strap.
7. Unfasten and remove head with exhaust manifold attached.

CAUTION: *Use extreme care when handling heads as the rocker arm studs are hardened and may crack if struck.*

NOTE: *If left head is being removed, it will be necessary to raise head off dowel pins, move it forward and maneuver it in order to clear power steering and power brake equipment if so equipped.*

8. Reverse procedure to install. On V8-301, coat cylinder head bolts with sealer.
9. On 1977–82 engines, torque cylinder heads to specifications in sequence shown in Fig. 8.

ROCKER ARM STUDS, REPLACE

With Screw in Studs

1. On V8-301, drain cooling system.
2. Remove rocker arm cover.
3. Remove rocker arm and nut.

4. Using a deep socket, remove rocker stud.
5. Install new stud and tighten to 50 ft. lbs.

NOTE: On V8-301, coat lower rocker arm stud threads with sealer.

6. Install rocker arm and tighten nut to 20 ft. lbs.
7. Install rocker cover using new gasket.

VALVE ARRANGEMENT

Front to Rear

Four Cyl.	E-I-I-E-E-I-I-E
V8s	E-I-I-E-E-I-I-E

VALVE LIFT SPECS.

Year	Engine	Intake	Exhaust
1977	4-151	.406	.406
	V6-231②	.383	.366
	8-301⑤	.377	.377
	8-301⑥	.364	.364
	8-305⑧	.3727	.410
	8-350①③	.400	.400
	8-350④	.364	.364
	8-350⑧⑫	.390	.410
	8-400	.364	.364
	8-403	.400	.400
1978–82	4-151	.406	.406
	V6-231②	.383	.366
1978–79	V8-301	.364	.364
	V8-305	.3727	.410

	V8-350①③	.400	.400
	V8-350⑧⑫	.390	.410
	V8-350②⑨	.323	.339
	V8-400	.364	.364
	V8-403①	.400	.400
1979	V6-231②	.357	.366
1980	V6-229⑫	.373	.410
	V8-350①③	.400	.400
	V8-350②⑨	.357	.366
1980–82	V6-231②	.357	.366
	V8-265	.364	.364
	V8-301⑩	.350	.350
	V8-301⑪	.364	.364
	V8-305⑫	.357	.390
	V8-350①⑦	.376	.376
1981	V8-307①	.400	.400
1982	V6-173⑫	.349	.393
	V6-252②	.358	.366

①—Refer to Oldsmobile Chapter for service procedures.
②—Refer to Buick Chapter for service procedures.
③—Distributor located at rear of engine, counter-clockwise distributor rotor rotation. Fuel pump located at right side of engine.
④—Distributor located at rear of engine, counter-clockwise distributor rotor rotation. Fuel pump located at left side of engine.
⑤—Std. trans.
⑥—Auto. trans.
⑦—Diesel.
⑧—Distributor located at rear of engine, clockwise distributor rotor rotation.
⑨—Distributor located at front of engine.
⑩—Except E/C (Electronic control) engine.
⑪—E/C (Electronic control) engine.
⑫—Refer to Chevrolet Chapter for service procedures.

Fig. 6 Intake manifold tightening sequence. 1982–83 4-151

Fig. 7 Exhaust manifold tightening sequence. 1982–83 4-151

Fig. 8 Cylinder head tightening sequence. V8-301, 350 & 400

Fig. 9 Hydraulic valve lifter

Fig. 10 Front of engine with timing case cover removed. V8 engines

VALVE TIMING

Intake Opens Before TDC

Engine	Year	Degrees
4-151	1977	23
	1978–82	33
V6-229⑮	1980	42
V6-231⑮	1977–82	16
8-265	1980	27
8-265	1981	16
8-301	1977⑤	31
	1977⑥	27
	1978①	27
	1978②	14
	1979①	16
	1979②⑤	27
	1979②⑥	16
	1981⑫	16
	1981⑬	17
8-305⑭	1977–80	28
8-305⑭	1981–82	44
8-307⑧	1981	20
8-350③	1977	29
8-350④⑧	1977–82	16
8-350⑦⑭	1977–79	28
8-350⑨⑮	1978–79	13.5
	1980	16
	1977–78⑤⑩	21
	1977–78⑥⑩	29
	1977–79⑪	16
8-403⑧	1977–79	16

①—2 bar. carb.
②—4 bar. carb.
③—Distributor located at rear of engine, counter clockwise distributor rotor rotation. Fuel pump located at left side of engine.
④—Distributor located at rear of engine, counter clockwise distributor rotor rotation. Fuel pump located at right side of engine.
⑤—Std. trans.
⑥—Auto. trans.
⑦—Distributor located at rear of engine, clockwise distributor rotor rotation.
⑧—Refer to Oldsmobile Chapter for service procedures.
⑨—Distributor located at front of engine.
⑩—Except T/A engine.
⑪—T/A engine.
⑫—Except E/C (Electronic Control) engine.
⑬—E/C (Electronic Control) engine.
⑭—Refer to Chevrolet Chapter for service procedures.
⑮—Refer to Buick Chapter for service procedures.

VALVE GUIDES

Valve guides are cast integral with the cylinder head. Valves with oversize stems are available in .001", .003" and .005" larger than standard.

Oversize reamers are required to enlarge valve guide holes to fit the oversize stems. best results when installing .005" oversize valve stem use a .003" oversize reamer first and then ream to .005" oversize. Always reface the valve and valve seat after reaming valve guide. Valves are marked .001, .003 or .005 with colored ink.

VALVE LIFTERS, REPLACE

1. Remove intake manifold.
2. Remove push rod cover and valve cover.
3. Loosen rocker arm, then rotate rocker arm off push rod and remove push rod.
4. Remove lifter, Fig. 9.

NOTE: If more than one lifter is to be removed, identify lifters and push rods, so they can be reinstalled in their original locations.

5. Reverse procedure to install. Torque rocker arm ball nut to 20 ft. lbs.

TIMING CASE COVER, REPLACE

NOTE: If necessary to replace the cover oil seal it can be accomplished without removing the timing chain cover.

V8s

1. Drain cooling system.
2. Loosen alternator adjusting bolts.
3. Remove fan and accessory drive belts.
4. Remove fan and pulley.
5. Remove water pump.
6. Disconnect radiator hoses.
7. Remove fuel pump.
8. Remove vibration damper.
9. Remove front four oil pan-to-timing chain cover screws.
10. Remove cover attaching screws.
11. Pull cover forward to clear studs and remove.

4-151

1. Disconnect battery ground cable.
2. Remove torsional damper and the two oil pan to front cover screws.
3. Remove front cover retaining screws.
4. Pull cover forward just enough to permit cutting of oil pan front seal, then cut oil

pan front seal flush with cylinder block at both sides and remove front cover.
5. Reverse procedure to install.

TIMING CHAIN, REPLACE

V8 Engines

1. Remove timing chain cover.
2. Remove fuel pump eccentric, bushing and timing chain cover oil seal, Fig. 10.
3. Align timing marks to simplify proper positioning of sprockets during assembly, Fig. 11.

NOTE: The valve timing marks, Fig. 11, does not indicate TDC, compression stroke for No. 1 cylinder for use during distributor installation. When installing the distributor, rotate engine until No. 1 cylinder is on compression stroke and the camshaft timing mark is 180° from the valve timing position shown in Fig. 11.

4. Slide off chain and sprockets.
5. Install new chain and sprockets, making sure timing marks are aligned exactly on a straight line passing through the shaft centers, Fig. 11. Camshaft should extend through sprocket so that hole in fuel pump eccentric will locate on shaft.

Fig. 11 Valve timing marks. V-8 engines

Fig. 12 Camshaft thrust plate screw removal. 4-151

Fig. 13 Camshaft gear removal. 4-151

Fig. 14 Camshaft gear installation & thrust plate clearance check. 4-151

6. Install fuel pump eccentric and bushing, indexing tab on eccentric with keyway cutout in sprocket. Install retainer bolt with washer and tighten securely.
7. Making sure hollow dowels are in place in block, place timing chain cover gasket over studs and dowels.
8. Install cover, making sure O-ring seal is in place.

CAMSHAFT, REPLACE

4-151

1. Disconnect battery ground cable.
2. Drain oil pan and radiator.
3. Remove radiator, fan and water pump pulley.
4. Remove distributor, spark plugs and fuel pump.
5. Remove push rod cover and valve cover, then loosen rocker arms and rotate rocker arms off push rods.
6. Remove push rods and valve lifters.

NOTE: Identify push rods and lifters so they can be reinstalled in their original locations.

---

7. Remove harmonic balancer and timing gear cover.
8. Remove camshaft thrust plate retaining screws, Fig. 12, and carefully pull camshaft out of engine.

NOTE: Use care to avoid damaging camshaft bearings.

---

9. To remove gear, proceed as follows:
   a. Support gear on press using a suitable sleeve, Fig. 13, then press camshaft out of gear using a socket or other suitable tool.

NOTE: Thrust plate must be positioned so that woodruff key in shaft does not damage thrust plate when camshaft is pressed out.

---

   b. To install gear, firmly support camshaft at back of front journal in press using plate adapters.
   c. Place gear spacer ring and thrust plate cover end of shaft and install woodruff key.
   d. Press gear until it bottoms against the gear spacer ring. Check end clearance which should be .0015 to .0050 inch, Fig. 14. If clearance is less than specified, the spacer ring should be replaced. If clearance is greater than specified, the thrust plate should be replaced.
10. Carefully install camshaft making sure that marks are aligned as shown in Fig. 15. Torque thrust plate retaining screws to 75 inch lbs.

NOTE: The valve timing marks shown in Fig. 15 do not indicate TDC compression stroke for No. 1 cylinder for use during distributor installation. Before installing distributor, turn crankshaft one complete revolution to firing position of No. 1 cylinder (TDC compression stroke), then install distributor in its original position and align shaft so that rotor points toward No. 1 cylinder in distributor cap.

---

11. Reverse procedure to install remaining components.

All V8s

The camshaft and camshaft bearings can be replaced with the engine installed in the car or with engine removed and disassembled for overhaul. However, to replace the rear camshaft bearing without removing and completely disassembling the engine, the propeller shaft, transmission and clutch housing must first be removed. The procedure for removing the camshaft is as follows:
1. Drain cooling system and remove air cleaner.
2. Disconnect radiator and heater hoses, distributor vacuum hose and spark plug wires.

Fig. 15 Valve timing marks. 4-151

Engine oiling system. V8s

Fig. 16   Piston & rod assembly. 1977–79 V8-400 & 1977 V8-350. (Oil spurt hole toward camshaft)

Fig. 17   Piston & rod assembly. 4-151, V8-265 & 301 less turbo

Fig. 18   Piston & rod assembly. V8-301 turbo

3. Disconnect carburetor linkage, fuel lines and wire connector from temperature sending unit.
4. Remove hood latch brace.
5. Remove radiator, fan and pulleys.
6. On air conditioned cars, remove alternator and its mounting bracket.
7. Remove crankcase ventilator hose or outlet pipe.
8. Remove distributor.
9. Remove rocker arm covers.
10. Remove intake manifold. *Make certain "O" ring seal between intake manifold and timing chain cover is retained and installed during assembly.*
11. Remove push rod cover.
12. Loosen rocker arm ball retaining nuts so that rocker arms can be disengaged from push rods and turned sideways.
13. Remove push rods and hydraulic lifters, keeping them in proper sequence so that they may be returned to their original locations.
14. Remove vibration damper.
15. Remove fuel pump.
16. Remove timing chain cover.
17. Remove fuel pump eccentric and fuel pump bushing.
18. Remove chain and sprockets.
19. Remove camshaft thrust plate and carefully pull camshaft from engine. *Clearance for camshaft removal is very limited and, in cases where engine mounts are worn excessively, it may be necessary to raise the front of the engine to permit removal.*

Fig. 19   Rear main bearing oil seal tool V8-301, 350, 400

PISTON & ROD, ASSEMBLE

Assemble pistons and rods as indicated in Figs. 16, 17 and 18.

When installing connecting rod and piston assemblies into V8-301 engines, the raised notches at bearing end of each connecting rod must all face toward the rear of the engine. When installing connecting rod and piston assemblies in V8-350 and 400 engines, the raised notches at the bearing end of each connecting rod in the right bank cylinders (2, 4, 6 and 8) must face front of engine. Connecting rods installed in the left bank cylinders (1, 3, 5 and 7) must have all the raised notches facing toward the rear of the engine, Fig. 16.

On all engines, the notch cast in the piston heads must face the front of the engine when the piston and connecting rod assemblies are installed.

Correct piston and connecting rod assembly installation is extremely important as incorrect installation could cause an engine knock.

Upon installation, measure the connecting rod side clearance using a suitable feeler gauge. Measurement obtained should be .006–.022 inch for 4-151, V8-265, 301, 350 and .012–.017 inch for V8-400.

PISTONS, PINS & RINGS

Pistons and rings are available in standard sizes and oversizes of .005, .010, .020 and .030 inch.

Piston pins are available in oversizes of .001 and .003″.

MAIN & ROD BEARINGS

Main bearings are available in standard sizes and undersizes of .001 and .002″.

Rod bearings are available in standard sizes and undersizes of .001 and .002″.

CRANKSHAFT REAR OIL SEAL, REPLACE

V8s

1. Remove oil pan, oil pump and pump drive shaft.
2. Remove oil baffle and cylinder block-to-oil baffle tube.
3. Remove rear main bearing cap.
4. Use tool shown in Fig. 19 made from brass bar stock to pack upper seal as follows:
   a. Insert tool against one end of oil seal in cylinder block and drive seal gently into groove until tool bottoms.
   b. Remove tool and repeat at other end of seal in cylinder block.
5. Clean block and bearing cap parting line thoroughly.
6. Form a new seal in cap.
7. Remove newly formed seal from cap and cut four pieces about 3/8″ long from this seal.
8. Work two 3/8″ pieces into each end of the gaps which have been made at the end of seal in cylinder block. Without cutting off the ends, work these seal pieces in until

Fig. 20   Installing rear main bearing oil seal. V8-265, 301, 350, 400 engines

Fig. 21   Installing oil pan gasket retainers. V8-265, 301, 350 & 400 engines

flush with parting line, being sure that no fibers are protruding over the metal adjacent to the groove.

9. Form another new seal in the cap, Fig. 20.
10. Assemble the cap to the block and torque to specifications.
11. Remove cap and inspect parting line to insure that no seal material has been compressed between the block and cap.
12. Apply a 1/16" bead of sealer from the center of the seal to the external cork groove.
13. Reassemble the cap and torque to specifications.

4-151

1. Remove oil pan and rear main bearing cap.
2. Remove upper half of seal by tapping on one end with a blunt punch until other end of seal protrudes far enough to be removed with pliers. Remove lower half of seal by prying out with a small screwdriver.
3. Install upper half of seal by pushing into plate with lip toward front of engine. Install lower half of seal by pushing with a hammer handle until seal is rolled into place.
4. Torque bearing cap bolts to specifications and install oil pan.

Fig. 23   Rear oil pan gasket positioned in oil pan. V8-265, 301, 350 & 400 engines

OIL PAN, REPLACE

4-151

1. Disconnect battery ground cable and remove engine fan.
2. Raise vehicle and drain oil pan.
3. Disconnect exhaust pipe at manifold and loosen hanger bracket.
4. Remove starter and place aside, then remove flywheel housing inspection cover.
5. Raise engine slightly to remove weight from engine mounts and remove both brackets to engine mount bolts.
6. Remove oil pan bolts, then raise engine to allow oil pan removal and remove oil pan.
7. Reverse procedure to install.

V8-301, 350 & 400 Pontiac Built Engines

1. Disconnect battery ground cable and remove fan.
2. Make sure that all hoses and wiring are properly routed to avoid binding or stretching when engine is raised.
3. On some air conditioned vehicles, it will be necessary to remove A/C compressor from mounting brackets and place aside for clearance.
4. Remove distributors cap, then raise vehicle and drain engine oil.
5. Disconnect exhaust pipes from manifolds, then remove starter and flywheel housing cover.
6. Rotate crankshaft until number on cylinder is at bottom dead center.
7. Remove engine mount through bolts.
8. Remove oil pan bolts, then raise engine just enough to allow oil pan removal and remove oil pan.
9. Reverse procedure to install. Install gasket as shown in Figs. 21, 22 and 23.

OIL PUMP, REPLACE

4-151

Remove oil pan. Remove the two flange mounting bolts and nut and remove pump.

Remove the four cover retaining screws, cover, gears and shaft and regulator parts, Fig. 24.

CAUTION: Do not attempt to remove or disturb oil pick-up tube.

Clean and inspect pump. If any of the following conditions are found, the oil pump should be replaced:
1. Inspect pump body for cracks or wear.
2. Inspect gears for excessive wear or damage.
3. Inspect shaft for looseness in housing.
4. Inspect inside of cover for wear which may permit oil to leak past the ends of the gears.
5. Inspect oil pick-up screen.
To assemble, install drive gear and shaft in housing, then install idler gear with smooth side facing cover. Install cover and screws and torque screws to 105 inch lbs. Make sure that shaft turns freely. Install regulatory valve spring, retainer and pin.
To install pump, align drive shaft with distributor tang, then position pump on engine and install retaining bolts and nut. Torque bolts and nut to 115 inch lbs. on 1977–78 models. On 1982–83 models torque bolts and

Fig. 22   Front oil pan gasket overlapping side gasket, V8-265, 301, 350 & 400 engines

nuts to 22 ft. lbs.

V8 Engines

Remove oil pan. While holding pump in place, remove attaching screws. Lower the pump away from the block with one hand while removing the oil pump drive shaft with the other.

Remove oil screen and pressure regulator parts. Detach cover from pump body and take out gears, Fig. 25.

Examine all parts for damage and assemble. Do not attempt to change oil pressure by varying length of pressure regulator spring.

Position drive shaft in distributor and oil pump drive gear. Place pump in position in the block, indexing the drive shaft with pump drive gear shaft. Install attaching screws with lock washers and tighten securely.

Removal and installation of pump does not affect distributor timing since the oil pump and distributor drive gear are mounted on the distributor shaft.

BELT TENSION DATA

	New Lbs.	Used Lbs.
1977—		
Air Conditioning Exc. 4-151 & V8-305, 350①	135–165	100–105
4-151	110–140	75–80
V8-305, 350①	135–165	80

Fig. 24   Oil pump disassembled. 4-151

BELT TENSION DATA— Cont'd

	New Lbs.	Used Lbs.
1977—Cont'd		
Air Pump		
V6-231	60–80	50–55
V8-305, 350①	120–150	55
V8-350②, 403	110–140	75–80
Alternator		
Exc. V8-305, 350①	110–140	75–80
V8-305, 350①	120–150	55
Power Steering		
V6-231, V8-301, 350③, 400	135–165	100–105
4-151,		
V8-350②, 403	110–140	75–80
V8-305, 350①	120–150	55
1978–81		
Air Conditioning		
Exc. 4-151	135–145	90–100
4-151	120–130	70–80
Air Pump		
Exc. V6-231	120–130	70–80
V6-231	65–75	45–55
Alternator		
All	120–130	70–80
Power Steering		
Exc. 4-151	135–145	90–100
4-151	120–130	70–80
1982		
5/16″ Wide	80	50
3/8″ Wide	140	70
15/32″ Wide	165	90
7/16″ Wide	165	90

①—Distributor located at rear of engine, clockwise distributor rotor rotation.
②—Distributor located at rear of engine, counter clockwise distributor rotor rotation. Fuel pump located at right side of engine.
③—Distributor located at rear of engine, counter clockwise distributor rotor rotation. Fuel pump located at left side of engine.

WATER PUMP, REPLACE

NOTE: Water pump is serviced as an assembly only.

Fig. 25   Oil pump disassembled. V8 Pontiac engines

1. Disconnect battery cable and drain cooling system.
2. Loosen alternator adjusting bolt and remove fan belt.
3. Remove fan and pulley.
4. On 1977–78 V8 engine, remove alternator front bracket.
5. Disconnect radiator and heater hose at pump, then remove water pump retaining bolts and pump.
6. Reverse procedure to install. Torque water pump retaining bolts to 15 ft. lbs. except on 4-151 engines. On 4-151 engines, torque water pump retaining bolts to 18 ft. lbs. on 1977–78 models and 25 ft. lbs. on 1982–83 models.

FUEL PUMP, REPLACE

1. Disconnect fuel lines from pump.
2. Remove pump retaining bolts and pump.

3. Remove all gasket material from the pump and block gasket surfaces. Apply sealer on both sides of new gasket.
4. Position gasket on pump flange and hold pump in position against its mounting surface. Make sure rocker arm is riding on camshaft eccentric.
5. Press pump tight against its mounting. Install retaining screws and tighten them alternately.
6. Connect fuel lines. Then operate engine and check for leaks.

SERVICE NOTE: Before installing the pump, it is good practice to crank the engine so that the nose of the camshaft eccentric is out of the way of the fuel pump rocker arm when the pump is installed. In this way there will be the least amount of tension on the rocker arm, thereby easing the installation of the pump.

Diesel Engine Section

Refer to the Oldsmobile chapter for service procedures on this engine.

Turbocharger Section

DESCRIPTION

The turbocharger, Figs. 1 and 2, is used to increase engine power on demand, while maintaining the capability of good fuel economy.

As engine load increases and the throttle opens, more air-fuel mixture flows into the combustion chambers. As the increased flow is burned, a larger volume of high energy exhaust gasses enters the engine exhaust system and is directed through the turbocharger turbine housing, Fig. 3. Some of the exhaust gas energy is used to increase the speed of the turbine wheel which is connected to the compressor wheel. The increased speed of the compressor wheel compresses the air-fuel mixture from the carburetor and delivers the compressed air-fuel mixture to the intake manifold, Fig. 3. The high pressure in the intake manifold allows a denser charge to enter the combustion chambers, in turn developing more engine power during the combustion cycle.

The intake manifold pressure (Boost) is controlled to a maximum value by an exhaust gas bypass valve (Wastegate), Fig. 3. The wastegate allows a portion of the exhaust gas to bypass the turbine wheel, thereby not increasing turbine speed. The wastegate is operated by a spring loaded diaphragm device sensing the pressure differential across the compressor. When intake manifold pressure reaches a set value above ambient pressure, the wastegate begins to bypass the exhaust gas.

An Electronic Spark Control System is used to retard ignition timing up to 18°–22° to minimize detonation. The power enrichment vacuum regulator (PEVR) is used to control vacuum flow to the carburetor power piston.

NOTE: Engine oil on turbocharged engines must be changed every 3000 miles since turbocharger bearing damage may occur from oil contamination. Before starting engine after changing oil and filter, disconnect ignition switch wire connector (pink wire) from distributor. Crank engine several times, not to exceed 30 seconds for each interval, until oil light goes out, then reconnect ignition switch wire connector to distributor.

DIAGNOSIS & TESTING

Prior to performing any diagnostic or testing procedure check all vacuum hoses and wiring for proper routing and connections, carburetor linkage for freedom of movement, wastegate linkage for damage or any problems which may occur in a non-turbocharged engine.

CAUTION: A turbocharged engine has exhaust pipes located high in the engine compartment. Care must be taken to avoid accidental contact with hot exhaust pipes since personal injury may occur.

Wastegate-Boost Pressure Test

1. Inspect actuator linkage for damage.
2. Check tubing from compressor housing to actuator assembly and the return tubing

WASTE GATE ACTUATOR   CARBURETOR
TURBOCHARGER

ARROWS SHOW DIRECTION OF EXHAUST FLOW

Fig. 1 Turbocharger assembly installation

Fig. 2 Sectional view of turbocharger assembly

from the actuator to the PCV tee.

3. Tee the hand operated vacuum/pressure pump J-23738 into the tubing from the compressor housing to the actuator. At approximately 8.5–9.5 psi. the lever should begin to move and actuate the wastegate. If not, replace actuator assembly and calibrate assembly to open at 9 psi. Use J-23738 or perform "Road Test" as outlined below to measure boost pressure.

Road Test

1. Tee the compound gauge J-28474 into the tubing between compressor housing and actuator assembly with a sufficient length of hose to place the guage in the passenger compartment.
2. With conditions and speed limits permitting, perform a zero to 40–50 mph wide open throttle acceleration and maintain top speed for two to three seconds. Boost pressure should reach 8.5–9.5 psi. If not, replace actuator assembly and, using tool J-23738, calibrate to open at 9 psi.

Power Enrichment Vacuum Regulator (PEVR) Test

1. Inspect PEVR and attaching hoses for deterioration, cracking or other damage and replace as necessary.
2. Tee one hose of manometer J-23951 between yellow stripped input hose and input port. Connect other hose directly to PEVR output port.
3. Start engine and operate at idle speed. There should be no more than 14″ H_2O difference between manometer readings. If difference is greater than 14″ H_2O, replace PEVR.
4. Remove PEVR from intake manifold and install a plug in intake manifold PEVR bore. Connect input and output hoses to PEVR.
5. Tee gauge J-28474 into output hose of PEVR.
6. Start engine and operate at idle speed. The gauge reading from the output port should be 8–10″ Hg.
7. Apply 3 psi. to manifold signal port of PEVR. Vacuum reading from output port should be 1.4–2.6″ Hg. If difficulty is encountered in measuring level of vacuum, apply 5 psi. to manifold signal port of PEVR. There should be no vacuum output from PEVR.
8. If PEVR does not perform as described above, replace PEVR.

TURBOCHARGER INTERNAL INSPECTION

1. Remove the turbocharger assembly but do not separate the center housing rotating assembly from the turbine housing.
2. Manually operate the wastegate linkage and using a small mirror, observe wastegate movement in the elbow assembly. Replace the elbow assembly if the wastegate fails to open or close.
3. Check for loose backplate to center housing rotating assembly bolts and tighten, if necessary.
4. Spin the compressor wheel. If rotating assembly binds or drags, replace the center housing rotating assembly.
5. Inspect center housing rotating assembly for sludge in the oil drain area. Clean, if minor, or replace center housing rotating assembly if excessively sludged or coked.

NORMAL OPERATING MODE

Fig. 3 Turbocharger operating schematic

6. Inspect compressor oil seal for damage or leakage on the compressor wheel side of the backplate. Replace center housing rotating assembly if oil seal damage or leakage is present.
7. If compressor wheel is damaged or severely coked, replace center housing rotating assembly.
8. If center housing rotating assembly is being replaced, pre-lubricate with engine oil.
9. Inspect compressor housing and turbine housing. If either housing is gouged, nicked or distorted, replace if necessary.
10. Remove turbine housing from center housing rotating assembly and check the journal bearing radial clearance and thrust bearing axial clearance as follows:
   a. Journal bearing radial clearance.
   (1) Attach a rack and pinion type dial indicator (Starrett model 656-517 or equivalent with a two inch long, ¾ to 1 inch offset extension rod) to the center housing so the indicator plunger extends through the oil output port and contacts the turbine wheel assembly shaft. If required, a dial indicator mounting adapter can be utilized.
   (2) Manually apply pressure equally and at the same time to both the compressor wheel and turbine wheel as required to move the turbine wheel assembly shaft away from the dial indicator as far as possible.
   (3) Zero the dial indicator.
   (4) Manually apply pressure equally and at the same time to both the compressor and turbine wheels as required to move the turbine wheel assembly shaft toward the dial indicator plunger as far as possible. Note maximum reading on dial indicator.

NOTE: To ensure that the dial indicator reading is the maximum obtainable, roll the wheels slightly in both directions while applying pressure.

   (5) Manually apply pressure equally and at the same time to both the compressor and turbine wheels as required to move the turbine wheel assembly shaft away from the dial indicator as far as possible. The dial indicator should return to zero.

   (6) Repeat steps 2 through 5 as required to ensure the maximum clearance between the center housing bores and the shaft bearing diameters, as indicated by the maximum shaft travel, has been obtained.
   (7) If the maximum bearing radial clearance is less than .003 inch or greater than .006 inch, replace the center housing rotating assembly.

NOTE: Continued operation of a turbocharger having excessive bearing radial clearance will result in severe damage to the compressor and turbine wheels and the housings.

   b. Thrust bearing axial clearance.
   (1) Mount a dial indicator (Starrett model 25-141 or equivalent) at the turbine end of the turbocharger so the dial indicator plunger contacts the end of the turbine wheel assembly.
   (2) Manually move the compressor wheel and turbine wheel assembly in each direction shown on the indicator dial.
   (3) Repeat step 2 to ensure the maximum clearance between the thrust bearing components, as indicated by the maximum turbine wheel assembly travel, has been obtained.
   (4) If the maximum thrust bearing axial clearance is less than .001 inch or greater than .003 inch, replace the center housing rotating assembly.

NOTE: Continued operation of a turbocharger having excessive thrust bearing axial clearance will result in severe damage to the compressor and turbine wheels and the housings.

SERVICE

Before performing turbocharger service, note the following general cautions:

1. Clean area around turbocharger assembly with a non-caustic solution before service. Cover openings of engine assembly connections to prevent entry of foreign material.

2. When removing the assembly, do not bend, nick or in any way damage the compressor or turbine wheel blades. Any damage may result in rotating assembly imbalance, failure of the center housing rotating assembly, and failure of the compressor and/or turbine housing.

3. Before disconnecting center housing rotating assembly from either compressor housing or turbine housing, scribe location of components for assembly in original position.

Wastegate Actuator Assembly, Replace

1. Disconnect two vacuum hoses from actuator.
2. Remove clip from wastegate linkage to actuator rod.
3. Remove two bolts attaching actuator and the actuator.
4. Reverse procedure to install.

Elbow Assembly, Replace

1. Raise and support vehicle, then disconnect turbocharger exhaust outlet pipe and catalytic converter at intermediate pipe.
2. Lower vehicle and disconnect turbocharger exhaust outlet pipe from elbow assembly.
3. Disconnect turbocharger inlet pipe at elbow assembly and loosen at exhaust manifold, then position inlet pipe out of way.
4. Remove wastegate linkage to actuator rod retainer.
5. Disconnect elbow assembly support bracket bolts at elbow and loosen bracket

bolts at intake manifold, then position bracket out of way.
6. Remove bolts attaching elbow assembly to turbine housing, then remove elbow assembly from vehicle.
7. Reverse procedure to install.

Center Housing Rotating Assembly, Replace

1. Remove elbow assembly as described under "Elbow Assembly, Replace".
2. Remove oil feed and return lines from housing.
3. Remove six bolts, three clamps and three lock plates attaching turbine housing to center housing rotating assembly.
4. Reverse procedure to install.

Compressor Housing, Replace

1. Remove elbow assembly and center housing rotating assembly as described previously.
2. Remove air cleaner and EGR valve and heat shield.
3. Remove six bolts attaching compressor housing to plenum.
4. Remove three bolts attaching compressor housing to intake manifold, then remove compressor.
5. Reverse procedure to install.

Turbocharger & Actuator Assembly, Replace

1. Disconnect exhaust inlet and outlet pipes from turbocharger.
2. Remove air cleaner, then disconnect accelerator, cruise control and detent linkages at carburetor and linkage bracket

from plenum.
3. Disconnect fuel line at carburetor and necessary vacuum hoses.
4. Drain approximately three quarts of coolant from cooling system, then disconnect coolant hoses from front and rear of plenum.
5. Disconnect EGR pipe at intake manifold fitting.
6. Remove two bolts attaching turbine housing to bracket on intake manifold, then remove three bolts attaching compressor housing to intake manifold.
7. Remove turbocharger and actuator with carburetor and plenum assembly still attached, from engine. Disconnect vacuum hoses as necessary.
8. Remove six bolts attaching turbocharger and actuator assembly to plenum and carburetor assembly.
9. Remove oil drain from center housing rotating assembly.
10. Reverse procedure to install.

Plenum, Replace

1. Remove turbocharger and actuator assembly as described under "Turbocharger and Actuator Assembly, Replace".
2. Remove throttle bracket and two bolts attaching carburetor to plenum, then remove plenum.
3. Reverse procedure to install.

ECS Detonation Sensor, Replace

1. Squeeze side of metal connector to wire from controller and gently pull straight up to remove. Do not pull on wire.
2. Using a deep socket, remove ECS detonation sensor.
3. Reverse procedure to install.

Clutch & Transmission Section

CLUTCH PEDAL, ADJUST

1. Disconnect return spring from clutch fork.
2. Rotate clutch lever and shaft assembly until clutch pedal is firmly seated against rubber bumper on dash brace.
3. Push outer end of clutch fork rearward until release bearing lightly contacts diaphragm spring fingers.
4. Disconnect lower push rod from lever and shaft assembly and install it in gauge hole.
5. Rotate fork rod finger tight until all lash has been removed from linkage.
6. Remove swivel from gauge hole and install it in hole furthest from lever and shaft assembly. When adjusting a new clutch on 1978–79 Phoenix and Ventura models, if necessary shorten push rod 5/16 inch by turning rod an additional 2½ turns to eliminate clutch interference.
7. Install washers and retainer, then tighten lock nut being careful not to change length of rod.
8. Reconnect return spring and check pedal free travel. Free travel should be 5/8 to 13/8 inch on all except 1978–79 Phoenix and Ventura models. On 1978–79 Phoenix and Ventura models, free travel should be

13/4 to 23/8 inch for a new clutch and 7/8 to 15/16 inch for a used clutch.

NOTE: On 1978–79 Phoenix, when adjusting a used clutch, check for diaphragm finger to clutch disc spring pocket interference when pressing pedal fully to the floor. If interference exists as indicated by a grinding or scraping noise, increase free travel sufficiently to eliminate contact.

CLUTCH, REPLACE

1. Remove transmission as described under "Transmission, Replace."
2. Disconnect clutch fork push rod and spring.
3. Remove flywheel housing from engine.
4. Slide clutch fork from ball stud and remove fork from dust boot.
5. Install a dummy shaft to support clutch assembly during removal.
6. Mark clutch plate and flywheel to ensure reassembly in the same position.
7. Loosen clutch cover to flywheel bolts one turn at a time until spring pressure is relieved, then remove mounting bolts and clutch cover and disc.

THREE-SPEED MANUAL TRANS., REPLACE

1. Disconnect battery ground cable.
2. Raise vehicle and drain lubricant from transmission.
3. Scribe mark on companion flange and drive shaft yoke, then remove drive shaft.
4. Disconnect speedometer cable and back-up light switch wire connector.
5. On models with column shift, disconnect transmission shift levers from transmission shifter shafts. On models with floor shift, it will also be necessary to remove shifter assembly to shifter support bolts and remove shifter assembly from transmission.
6. Remove crossmember to transmission mount bolts and catalytic converter to transmission bracket, if equipped, then remove crossmember to frame bolts.
7. Raise transmission and remove crossmember.
8. Remove transmission to clutch housing upper attaching bolts and install guide pins.
9. Remove transmission to clutch housing lower attaching bolts, then slide transmission straight back on guide pins until

main drive splines are clear of clutch plate and remove transmission from vehicle.

10. Reverse procedure to install.

SHIFT LINKAGE 3 SPEED TRANS., ADJUST

Column Shift

1. Place shift lever in reverse position and ignition switch in Lock position.
2. Raise vehicle and loosen shift control rod swivel lock nuts.
3. Pull down slightly on 1st–reverse control rod attached to column lever to remove slack in column mechanism, then tighten lock nut at transmission.
4. Unlock ignition switch and position shift lever in neutral position. Position column lower levers in neutral, then align gauge holes in levers and insert 3/16 in. gauge pin.

NOTE: Alignment holes are located on lower side of levers.

5. Support rod and swivel to prevent movement of assembly and tighten 2nd–3rd control rod lock nut.
6. Remove alignment tool from column levers and check shifter operation. Place shift lever in reverse and check interlock control.

NOTE: With shift lever in reverse, ignition key must move freely to Lock position. It must not be possible to obtain Lock position in any other selector position than reverse.

Floor Shift

1. Place ignition switch in off position, then raise vehicle.

2. Loosen lock nuts at swivels on shift rods. Rods should pass freely through swivels.
3. Shift shift levers into neutral at transmission.
4. Place shift control lever in neutral detent, then align control assembly levers and insert a 3/16 in. gauge pin into lever alignment slot.
5. Tighten locknuts at shift rod swivels and remove gauge pin.
6. Place shift control lever in reverse position and ignition switch in Lock position. Loosen lock nut at back drive control rod swivel, then pull down on rod slightly to remove slack in column mechanism and tighten clevis jam nut.
7. Check interlock control, ignition key should move freely to and from Lock position.
8. Lower vehicle and check adjustment.

4 SP. TRANS., REPLACE

Follow procedure outlined for three-speed model.

NOTE: For 1982–83 Firebird, torque arm must be removed after step 2 of three speed transmission removal procedure. Refer to "Rear Axle, Propeller Shaft and Brake Section" of this chapter for torque arm removal procedure.

SHIFT LINKAGE 4 SPEED TRANS, ADJUST

1. Place selector lever in neutral.
2. Loosen trunnion nuts on transmission control rod.
3. Place transmission lever and bracket assembly in neutral and install a gauge pin

through hole and slot provided in bracket.
4. Position lever on transmission in neutral.
5. Tighten trunnion nuts and remove gauge pin.
6. Position shift lever in Reverse, set steering column lever in Lock position and lock ignition. Push up on control rod to remove clearance and tighten nut of adjusting swivel.

5 SP. TRANS., REPLACE

1. Disconnect battery ground cable.
2. From inside vehicle, remove screws attaching bezel to tunnel, then remove bezel by slipping over boot and shift lever.
3. With shift lever in neutral, hold boot out of way and remove four bolts attaching shift lever to transmission, then remove shift lever assembly.
4. Raise vehicle and scribe a mark on companion flange and drive shaft yoke, then remove drive shaft.
5. Remove bolts attaching catalytic converter support bracket to transmission.
6. Remove two bolts attaching transmission mount to support.
7. Raise transmission and remove two long end bolts, then remove transmission support.
8. Disconnect speedometer cable and back-up light switch wire connector.
9. Remove transmission to clutch housing upper attaching bolts and install guide pins.
10. Remove transmission to clutch housing lower attaching bolts, then slide transmission back on guide pins until main drive gear splines clear clutch plate and remove transmission from vehicle.

Rear Axle, Propeller Shaft & Brake Section

REAR AXLES

Figs. 1 and 2 illustrate the rear axle assemblies used on 1977–83 conventional models. When necessary to overhaul either of these units, refer to the *Rear Axle Specifications* table in this chapter.

1977–83

In this rear axle, Fig. 1, the rear axle housing and differential carrier are cast into an integral assembly. The drive pinion assembly is mounted in two opposed tapered roller bearings. The pinion bearings are preloaded by a spacer behind the front bearings. The pinion is positioned by a shim between the head of the pinion and the rear bearing.

The differential is supported in the carrier by two tapered roller side bearings. These bearings are preloaded by shims located between the bearings and carrier housing. The differential assembly is positioned for proper ring gear and pinion backlash by varying

these shims. The differential case houses two side gears in mesh with two pinions mounted on a pinion shaft which is held in place by a lock screw. The side gears and pinions are backed by thrust washers.

Rear Axle, Replace

Except 1982–83 Firebird

Construction of the axle assembly is such that service operations may be performed with the housing installed in the vehicle or with the housing removed and installed in a holding fixture. The following procedure is necessary only when the housing requires replacement.

1. Raise car and place a floor jack under center of axle housing so it starts to raise rear axle assembly. Place jack stands solidly under frame members on both sides.
2. Disconnect rear U-joint from drive pinion flange and support propeller shaft out of the way.

3. Remove both axle shafts.
4. Support both brake backing plates out of the way.
5. Disconnect rear brake hose bracket by removing top cover bolt. Remove brake line from housing by bending back tabs.
6. Loosen remaining cover bolts, break loose cover about 1/8 inch and allow lube to drain.
7. Disconnect shock absorbers at axle housing.
8. On models with coil springs:
   a. Disconnect upper control arms at axle housing.
   b. Slowly lower jack until all spring tension is relieved and remove springs.
   c. Disconnect lower control arms and remove axle assembly.
9. On models with leaf springs,
   a. While supporting spring, remove rear shackle from spring.
   b. Lower spring and remove nut and bolt from spring front bushing, remove spring.
   c. Remove axle assembly.

1982–83 Firebird
1. Hoist car and support at frame and under rear axle housing.
2. Disconnect both shock absorbers and remove bolt from left side of track bar to axle.
3. Remove bolt from brake line junction block at axle housing and disconnect brake lines from junction block.
4. Lower rear axle assembly and remove springs.
5. Remove rear wheels and drums and remove rear axle cover and drain lube.
6. Disconnect brake lines from axle housing clips.
7. Remove axle shafts, brake backing plates, lower control arms and torque arm from axle housing.
8. Disconnect drive shaft from rear axle flange and place aside after marking for reinstallation.
9. Remove rear axle housing.
10. Reverse procedure to install.

Axle Shaft, Replace

NOTE: Design allows for axle shaft end play of .018 in. max. on 1977 "B" and "C" axles (except 7½ in.), .002–.020 in. on 1978–79 "B" axles, .022 in. max. on 1977–83 "C", "G", "K" and "O" (7½ in.) and 1978–83 "P" (7½ and 8½ in.) axles and .032 in. max. on 1977–83 "P" (except 7½ and 8½ in.) axles. This end play can be checked with the wheel and brake drum removed by measuring the difference between the end of the housing and the axle shaft flange while moving the axle shaft in and out by hand.

On 1977–83 "C" axles, excessive end play can be compensated for by using selective thickness "C" locks. On all other 1977–83 axles, excessive end play cannot be compensated for by inserting a shim inboard of the bearing in the housing since it ignores the end play of the bearing itself, and may result in improper seating of the gasket or backing plate against the housing. If end play is excessive, the axle shaft and bearing should be removed and the cause of the excessive end play corrected.

Fig. 1   Rear Axle assembly exploded. 1977–83 type "B & O" (Except 7½)

TYPE "B & O" (EXCEPT 7½")
1. To remove, take off wheels and brake drums.
2. Remove nuts holding retainer plates and brake backing plates. Pull retainers clear of bolts and reinstall two lower nuts finger tight to hold backing plate in position.
3. Use a slide hammer-type puller to remove axle shaft, Fig. 3.

Axle Shaft Bearing
1. Press axle shaft bearing off shaft.
2. Press new bearing against shoulder on shaft.

CAUTION: Outer retainer plate which retains bearing in housing must be on axle shaft before bearing is installed. A new outer retainer gasket can be installed after bearing. Use care not to wedge outer retainer between bearing and shoulder of shaft. Do not press bearing and inner retainer on in one operation.

3. Press new inner retainer ring against bearing.

Axle Shaft Seal
1. Insert suitable tongs behind seal and pull straight out to remove seal.
2. Apply sealer to outside diameter of new seal.
3. Position seal over a suitable installer and drive straight into axle housing until tool bottoms on bearing shoulder in housing.

Axle Shaft, Install
1. Apply a coat of wheel bearing grease in bearing recess of housing. Also lightly lubricate the axle shaft with rear axle lube from the sealing surface to about 6" inboard.

Fig. 2   1977–82 type "C", "G", "K", "O" (7½) & "P" differential case

Fig. 3   Removing axle shaft with slide hammer-type puller

2. Install *new* axle housing-to-brake backing plate gasket.
3. Install brake assembly with backing plate in proper position.
4. With a *new* outer retainer gasket in proper position, insert axle shaft until splines engage differential. *Do not allow shaft to drag on seal.*
5. Drive axle shaft into position.
6. Place new outer retainer gasket and retainer over studs and install nuts.
7. Install brake drums and wheels.

TYPE "C", "G", "K", "O" (7½") & "P" AXLE

1. Raise and support car leaving the rear wheels and differential suspended.
2. Remove rear wheels and brake drums.
3. Remove differential cover and drain lubricant.
4. Remove pinion shaft lock bolt and pinion shaft.
5. Push axle shaft inward to permit removal of "C" locks then remove axle shaft.
6. Install axle shaft bearing and seal remover and remove the bearing and seal.

PROPELLER SHAFT, REPLACE

One type of propeller shaft is used on all vehicles. The type being used is a one-piece shaft with two single cardan type U-joints, Fig. 4.

Two methods of retention are used at the rear of the propeller shaft. The first method uses a pair of straps retained by bolts, while the second method uses a set of bolted flanges.

1. Raise and properly support vehicle, then mark relationship of propeller shaft to companion flange in order to insure correct alignment during reassembly.
2. Disconnect rear U-joint by removing strap bolts of flange bolts.

NOTE: If U-joint bearing cups are loose, tape them together to avoid dropping and losing needle rollers.

3. Remove propeller shaft by pulling rearward.

CAUTION: Support propeller shaft during removal. Do not allow propeller shaft to drop or allow universal joints to bend to an extreme angle.

4. Reverse procedure to install, making sure that alignment marks are properly aligned. Torque strap retaining bolts to 15 ft. lbs. Torque flange bolts to 45 ft. lbs.

BRAKE ADJUSTMENTS

1977-83 Self-Adjusting Brakes

These brakes, Figs. 5 and 6 have self-adjusting shoe mechanisms that assure correct lining-to-drum clearances at all times. The automatic adjusters operate only when the brakes are applied as the car is moving rearward.

Although the brakes are self-adjusting, an

Fig. 4 Propeller shaft with single cardan U-joints

Fig. 5 Right rear drum brake (Typical). 1977 Grand Prix, LeMans & Ventura, 1977-79 Phoenix & 1977-81 Bonneville, Catalina & Firebird

Fig. 6 Left rear drum brake (Typical). 1978-81 Grand Am, LeMans, 1978-83 Grand Prix & 1982-83 Bonneville & Firebird

Fig. 7 Backing off adjusting screw

Fig. 8 Measuring brake drum inside diameter

Fig. 9 Checking brake shoe lining clearance

initial adjustment is necessary after the brake shoes have been relined or replaced, or when the length of the star wheel adjuster has been changed during some other service operation.

Frequent usage of an automatic transmission forward range to half reverse vehicle motion may prevent the automatic adjusters from functioning, thereby inducing low pedal heights. Should low pedal heights be encountered, it is recommended that numerous forward and reverse stops be made until satisfactory pedal height is obtained.

If a low pedal height condition cannot be corrected by making numerous reverse stops (provided the hydraulic system is free of air) it indicates that the self-adjusting mechanism is not functioning. Therefore, it will be necessary to remove the drum, clean, free up and lubricate the adjusting mechanism. Then adjust the brakes as follows, being sure the parking brake is fully released.

Adjustment

1. Knock out lanced area from brake backing plate with a suitable punch.

NOTE: If this is done with drum installed on car, drum must be removed and brake area cleaned of all metal particles.

2. Turn brake adjusting screw with tool J6166 or equivalent until brake shoes are expanded to where wheel can just be turned by hand. Amount of effort to turn wheels should be same at all four wheels.
3. Back off adjusting screw 30 notches. Check for brake drag. If brakes still drag back off adjusting screw one or two more notches.

NOTE: Brakes should be free of drag when screw has been backed off approximately 12 notches. Heavy drag at this point indicates tight parking brake cables.

4. Install new adjusting hole cover in brake backing plate cover.
5. Check parking brake adjustment.

NOTE: The recommended method of adjusting the brakes is by using the Drum-to-Brake Shoe Clearance Gauge shown in Fig. 8 to check the diameter of the brake drum inner surface. Turn the tool to the opposite side and fit over the brake shoes by turning the star wheel until the gauge just slides over the linings, Fig. 9. Rotate the gauge around the brake shoe lining surface to assure proper clearance.

PARKING BRAKE, ADJUST

CAUTION: It is very important that parking brake cables are not adjusted too tightly causing brake drag. With automatic brake adjusters, a tight cable causes brake drag and also positions the secondary brake shoe, hence the adjuster lever, so that it continues to adjust to compensate for wear caused by the drag. The result is a cycle of wear and adjustment that can wear out linings very rapidly.

1977–83, Less Rear Disc Brakes

1. Raise and support rear of vehicle.
2. Apply parking brake pedal exactly two ratchet clicks on Firebird, Phoenix and Ventura, three ratchet clicks on Grand Am, Grand Prix, LeMans and 1982 Bonneville, 6 ratchet clicks on 1977–81 full size models.
3. Tighten adjusting nut until left rear wheel can just be rotated rearward but is locked when forward rotation is attempted.
4. Release parking brake and check to ensure that rear wheels rotate freely in either direction with no brake drag.

1982–83 Firebird With Rear Disc Brakes

1. Lubricate parking brake cables at underbody rub points and at equalizer hooks. Check for free movement of all cables.
2. Ensure parking brake hand lever is in fully released position.
3. Raise and support rear of vehicle.
4. Hold brake cable stud from turning and tighten equalizer nut until cable slack is removed.
5. Ensure caliper levers are against stops on caliper housing after tightening equalizer nut.
6. If levers are off the stops, loosen cable until levers return to stops.
7. Operate parking brake lever several times to check adjustment. After cable adjustment is performed, parking brake lever should travel 14 clicks with approximately 150 ± 20 pounds force of handle effort using tool J-28662.
8. Lower vehicle and ensure levers are against caliper stops. If necessary back off parking brake adjuster to keep levers against stops.

POWER BRAKE UNIT, REPLACE

1977–83 All Models

1. Remove vacuum check valve.
2. If brake booster and master cylinder are being removed as an assembly, disconnect hydraulic lines and cover openings in master cylinder and lines to avoid entry of dirt. If only brake booster is to be removed, remove master cylinder retaining nuts and position master cylinder aside.

CAUTION: Be careful not to bend or kink hydraulic lines.

3. Remove clevis pin retainer from brake pedal.
4. Remove brake booster retaining nuts and remove brake booster.
5. Reverse procedure to install.

BRAKE MASTER CYLINDER, REPLACE

1977–83

1. Disconnect brake lines from two outlets on master cylinder and tape end of lines to prevent entrance of dirt.
2. On models less power brakes, disconnect master cylinder push rod from brake pedal.
3. Remove two nuts attaching master cylinder to dash or power brake unit and remove master cylinder from vehicle.

Rear Suspension

SHOCK ABSORBER, REPLACE

NOTE: If vehicle is equipped with Superlift shock absorbers, bleed system air pressure through service valve before disconnecting lines at shock absorber fittings.

1. With rear axle supported properly, disconnect shock absorber from lower mounting nut. Use a wrench to prevent mounting stud rotation.
2. Disconnect shock absorber from upper mounting nut.
3. Reverse procedure to install.

LEAF SPRING & BUSHINGS, REPLACE

1977–81 Firebird & 1977–79 Phoenix & Ventura

1. Raise and support vehicle so that axle can be raised and lowered.
2. Lower axle assembly to relieve tension from spring.
3. Disconnect shock absorber from lower mounting, Fig. 1.
4. Loosen spring eye to bracket retaining bolt.
5. Remove bolts attaching spring retainer bracket to under body.
6. Lower axle assembly to permit access to spring retainer bracket, and remove bracket from spring.
7. Pry parking brake cable out of retainer bracket mounted on anchor plate.
8. Remove lower spring plate to axle bracket retaining nuts.
9. Remove upper and lower cushions and anchor plate.
10. Support spring, then remove lower bolt

from spring rear shackle. Separate shackle and remove spring from vehicle.
11. To replace bushings, refer to Figs. 2 and 3.
12. Reverse procedure to install.

Leaf Spring Service

NOTE: The main leaf may be serviced separately, however, if any of the smaller leaves require replacement, the entire assembly must be replaced.

1. Clamp spring in a vise, remove spring clips and center bolt, then carefully open vise, allowing spring to expand.
2. Replace main leaf and use a drift to align center bolt holes, compress spring in a vise, remove drift and install new center bolt.
3. Align spring leaves and bend spring clips into position.

NOTE: Overtightening spring clips will bind spring action.

COIL SPRING, REPLACE

1977–82 All Exc. Firebird, Phoenix & Ventura

1. Support vehicle at frame rails and support rear axle with a suitable jack.
2. Remove brake line connector block bolt at axle housing.
3. Release brake line from clips on axle housing as necessary.
4. Disconnect upper control arms from axle housing.
5. Disconnect shock absorbers from lower mountings.
6. Lower rear axle. Do not permit the rear

Fig. 1 Leaf spring suspension (typical) 1977 Ventura, 1977–79 Firebird, 1977–79 Phoenix

brake hose to kink or stretch.
7. When the axle has been lowered sufficiently to provide clearance for coil spring removal, remove coil spring.
8. Reverse procedure to install. Ensure that coil springs are properly indexed, Fig. 5.

1982–83 Firebird

1. Raise car on suitable hoist and support rear axle on adjustable type lifting device.
2. Loosen track bar bolt at body brace and remove track bar mounting bolt at axle assembly, Fig. 4A.
3. Disconnect rear brake hose clip at underbody and remove both shock absorber lower attaching nuts.
4. Remove prop shaft from vehicles with four cylinder engines.
5. Lower rear axle and remove coil spring and insulators.
6. Reverse procedure to install.

Fig. 2 Leaf spring front bushing removal

Fig. 3 Leaf spring front bushing installation

SHOCK ABSORBER

15° MAX. (REARWARD)
5° MAX. (FORWARD)

PINION BUMPER

COIL SPRING

BUMPER

UPPER CONTROL ARM

LOWER CONTROL ARM

Fig. 4 Coil spring suspension (typical) Except 1982–83 Firebird

1	RAIL	8	TORQUE ARM
2	JOUNCE BUMPER	9	PROP SHAFT
3	SPRING INSULATOR ASM.	10	DAMPER ASM. WITH 4 CYC. ENGINE
4	COIL SPRING	11	SHOCK ABSORBER
5	OPTIONAL STABILIZER BAR	12	TRACK BAR
6	LOWER CONTROL ARM	13	TRACK BAR BRACE
7	UNDERBODY		

WITH RR DISC BRAKES

Fig. 4A   Coil spring suspension. 1982–83 Firebird

CONTROL ARMS & BUSHINGS, REPLACE

NOTE: Replace control arms one at a time to prevent axle misalignment, making installation difficult.

Upper Control Arms

NOTE: 1982–83 Firebird uses a single torque arm in place of upper control arms. Refer to "Torque Arm, Replace" & Fig. 4A

1. Support vehicle at frame and rear axle.
2. Remove control arm front and rear mounting bolts.

NOTE: On some vehicles, disconnect the shock absorber lower mounting stud to provide clearance. Also, use a suitable jack under the nose of differential housing to aid bolt removal.

FRAME SIDE RAIL (REF.)

FRONT

15° 15°
5° 5°
90° 90°

POSITION SPRING WITH END OF TOP COIL TOWARDS REAR OF CAR WITHIN LIMITS SHOWN

R. H. SIDE OF VEHICLE BOTTOM VIEW

L. H. SIDE OF VEHICLE BOTTOM VIEW

Fig. 5   Indexing coil springs. 1977–81 Full Size and 1977–83 Intermediates

PRESS

J-21465-8

J-23737

J-25317-2

Fig. 6   All front & lower control arm rear bushing removal. 1978–1983 models

J-25317-1

PRESS

J-23737

J-25317-2

Fig. 7   All front & lower control arm rear bushing installation. 1978–83 models

GRIND TOOL OFF AS SHOWN

J-21474-3
J-21474-8   J-21474-4
J-21474-16

THRUST BEARING & WASHER

Fig. 8   Upper control arm rear bushing removal. 1977 models (Typical)

J-21474-3
J-22818
J-21474-13
J-21474-4

THRUST BEARING & WASHER

Fig. 9   Upper control arm rear bushing installation. 1977 models (Typical)

Fig. 10 Upper control arm rear bushing removal. 1978—83 models

Fig. 11 Upper control arm rear bushing installation. 1978—83 models

3. Replace bushings as necessary, Figs. 6 thru 11.

NOTE: On 1977 models, bushings in control arms can only be serviced by replacing control arms.

4. Reverse procedure to install. Tighten control arm bolts with vehicle at curb height.

Lower Control Arms

Follow "Upper Control Arms" procedure for replacement of lower control arms. Lower control arm bushings are serviceable, Figs. 6 & 7.

NOTE: On models equipped with a stabilizer bar, remove stabilizer bar outlined under "Stabilizer Bar & Bushings, Replace" procedure before removing lower control arm mounting bolts.

TORQUE ARM, REPLACE

1. Raise vehicle on suitable hoist and support rear axle assembly with adjustable jack.
2. Loosen track bar bolt at body brace and remove track bar bolt at axle assembly.
3. Disconnect rear brake hose clip at underbody and remove both shock absorber lower attaching nuts.
4. Remove prop shaft from vehicles with four cylinder engine.
5. Lower rear axle and remove coil springs.

NOTE: Coil springs must be removed before removing torque arm to avoid rear axle forward twist which may cause vehicle damage.

6. Remove torque arm rear attaching bolts, front torque arm outer bracket and remove torque arm.
7. Reverse procedure to install. Torque track bar mounting nut at axle to 93 ft. lbs. and torque track bar to body bracket nut to 58 ft. lbs.

STABILIZER BAR & BUSHINGS, REPLACE

Models With Coil Springs

Exc. 1982—83 Firebird
1. With vehicle supported at rear axle, remove bolts attaching stabilizer bar to lower control arms, Fig. 12.
2. Replace bushings as necessary.
3. Reverse procedure to install. Tighten attaching bolts with vehicle at curb.

1982—83 Firebird
Refer to Fig. 14 for removal and installation procedures.

Models With Leaf Springs

1. Raise and support rear of vehicle.
2. Remove clamping bolts to disconnect lower end of each support assembly from stabilizer shaft, Fig. 13.
3. Remove insulator and bracket from below each spring and shock absorber anchor plate.
4. Reverse procedure to install making sure that slit in insulators are positioned toward front of vehicle.

Fig. 12 Stabilizer bar installation. 1977—82 Intermediate Exc. Firebird, Phoenix & Ventura & 1977—81 full size models

Fig. 13 Stabilizer bar installation. 1977 Ventura, 1977—81 Firebird & 1977—79 Phoenix

Fig. 14 Stabilizer bar installation. 1982—83 Firebird

Front Suspension & Steering Section

FRONT SUSPENSION

1977–83,
Exc. 1982–83 Firebird

The front suspension is of the conventional "A" frame design with coil springs and ball joints. The ball joints have a "fixed boot" grease seal for protection against the entry of dirt and water. The steering knuckles and spindles are of integral design and brake cylinders are rigidly attached to the knuckles with the backing plates serving principally as a support for brake shoes and as a protective cover.

On most models, an integral steering knuckle which is a combination steering knuckle, brake caliper support and steering arm is used. On other models, the steering knuckle is of the conventional type with a separate steering arm.

Rubber bushings at the inner ends of the upper control arms pivot on shafts attached to the car frame. Caster and camber adjustments are made with shims at this point, Fig. 1. Direct acting shock absorbers operate within the coil springs.

1982–83 Firebird

The front suspension is designed to allow each wheel to compensate for changes in the road surface level without appreciably affecting the opposite wheel. Each wheel is independently connected to the frame by a steering knuckle, strut assembly, ball joint, and lower control arm. The steering knuckles move in a prescribed three dimensional arc. The front wheels are held in proper relationship to each other by two tie rods which are connected to the steering knuckles and to a relay rod assembly.

Coil springs are mounted between the spring housings on the front crossmember and the lower control arms. The upper portion of each strut assembly extends through the fender well and attaches to the upper mount assembly with a nut, Fig. 2.

The inner ends of the lower control arm have pressed in bushings. Bolts, passing through the bushings, attach the arm to the suspension crossmember. The lower ball joint assembly is a press fit in the arm and attaches to the steering knuckle with a torque prevailing nut.

WHEEL ALIGNMENT

1977–83 All Models,
Exc. 1982–83 Firebird

Caster and camber adjustments are made by placing shims between the upper pivot shafts and frame, Fig. 3. Both adjustments can be made at the same time. In order to remove or install shims, raise car to remove weight from front wheel, then loosen control arm shaft-to-frame bolts.

NOTE: Shim pack thickness should not exceed .40 inch maximum on 1977–83 models. Also, difference between front and rear shim packs should not exceed 3/8 inch maximum.

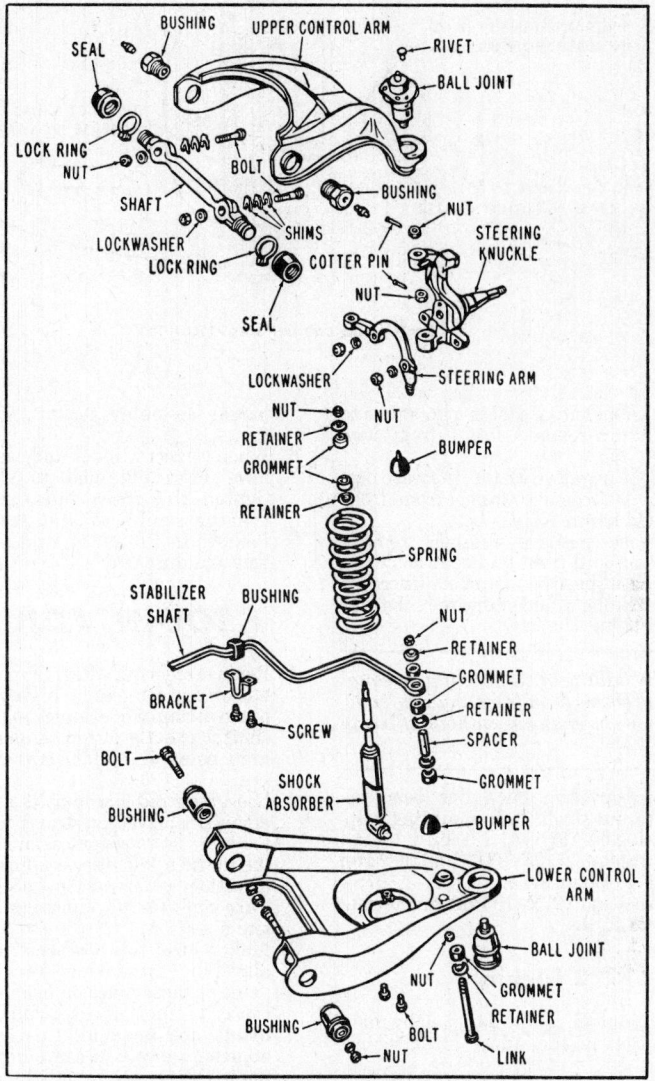

Fig. 1   Disassembled view of front suspension. 1977–83 (typical), Exc. 1982–83 Firebird

Fig. 2   Disassembled view of front suspension. 1982–83 Firebird

Fig. 3   Caster and camber shim location

1. To increase negative caster, add shims to front bolt or remove shims from rear bolt.
2. To decrease negative caster (increase positive caster), remove shims from front bolt or add shims to rear bolt.
3. To increase positive camber, remove shims from both front and rear bolts.
4. To decrease positive camber (increase negative camber), add shims to both front and rear bolts.

NOTE: *By adding or subtracting an equal amount of shims from front and rear bolts, camber will be changed without affecting caster.*

5. After proper shim pack has been installed, torque pivot shaft mounting bolts to 70 ft. lbs on 1978–81 Firebird, Grand Am and LeMans, 1978–83 Grand Prix and 1982–83 Bonneville. On 1978–81 Full-size and 1978–79 Phoenix, torque bolts to 74 ft. lbs.

1982 Firebird

Caster and camber can be adjusted by moving the position of the upper strut mount assembly.
1. Remove dust cap and fender bolt.
2. Attach J-29724, using original fender bolt and tighten the turnbuckle, Fig. 4.
3. Loosen three nuts attaching mount assembly.
4. Adjust camber by rotating the turnbuckle to allow the mount assembly to move inboard or outboard, Fig. 5.
5. Adjust the caster by lightly tapping the

mount assembly forward or rearward, Fig. 6
6. When correct camber and caster readings have been obtained to specifications, tighten the three nuts attaching the mount assembly to 20 ft. lbs.
7. Remove tool J-29724, and install fender bolt and dust cap.

TOE-IN, ADJUST

1. Remove steering wheel trim cover or horn button and set gear on high point by turning steering wheel until mark on end of shaft is exactly at top. This mark locates high point or middle travel of steering gear.
2. Loosen tie rod clamp bolts and turn both adjuster sleeves an equal amount until toe-in is set to specifications. To increase toe-in, turn left tie rod adjuster sleeve in direction of forward rotation of wheels. Turn right tie rod adjuster sleeve in opposite direction.
3. Make sure front wheels are straight ahead by measuring from a reference point at same place on each side of frame center to front of wheel rims. If measurements are unequal, turn both tie rod adjuster sleeves in same direction (so as not to change toe-in) until measurements become equal. Recheck toe-in and readjust as necessary.
4. Torque tie rod clamp bolts to 15 ft. lbs.

NOTE: Open end clamps should be located to a vertical down position. Refer to Figs. 7 and 8.

WHEEL BEARINGS, ADJUST

1. While rotating wheel, torque spindle nut to 12 ft. lbs.
2. Back off spindle nut until just loose, then retighten by hand.
3. Loosen spindle nut until cotter pin can be inserted, however, do not loosen spindle nut more than ½ flat.
4. With bearing properly adjusted, there should be .001–.005 inch end play.

WHEEL BEARINGS, REPLACE

(Disc Brakes)

1. Raise vehicle and remove front wheels.
2. Remove brake hose support to caliper mounting bracket screw.
3. Remove caliper to mounting bracket bolts.

NOTE: Do not place strain on brake hose.

4. Remove spindle nut, and disc and hub assembly. Grease retainer and inner bearing can now be removed.

CHECKING BALL JOINTS FOR WEAR

Except 1982 Firebird

Before checking ball joints for wear, make sure the front wheel bearings are properly adjusted and that the control arms are tight.
Referring to Fig. 9, raise wheel with a jack placed under the lower control at the point shown. Then test by moving the wheel up and down to check axial play, and rocking it at the top and bottom to measure radial play.
1. Upper ball joint should be replaced if there is any noticeable looseness at this joint.
   If the ball joint is the type using a built in rubber pre-load cushion it will be necessary to remove the ball stud from the knuckle. Then replace the ball joint retaining nut on the ball stud. Using a socket and torque wrench, measure

Fig. 4   Installing tool J-29724, for caster and camber adjustment. 1982–83 Firebird

Fig. 5   Camber adjustment. 1982–83 Firebird

Fig. 6   Caster adjustment. 1982–83 Firebird

BOLTS MUST BE INSTALLED IN DIRECTION SHOWN. ROTATE BOTH INNER AND OUTER TIE ROD HOUSINGS REARWARD TO THE LIMIT OF BALL JOINT TRAVEL BEFORE TIGHTENING CLAMPS. WITH THIS SAME REARWARD ROTATION ALL BOLT CENTERLINES MUST BE BETWEEN ANGLES SHOWN AFTER TIGHTENING CLAMPS.

Fig. 7   Tie rod clamp and sleeve positioning. Except 1982–83 Firebird

Fig. 8   Tie rod clamp and sleeve positioning. 1982–83 Firebird

Fig. 9   Checking ball joints for wear

FRONT SUSPENSION BALL JOINT WEAR INDICATOR

WHEN BALL JOINT WEAR CAUSES WEAR INDICATOR SHOULDER TO RECEDE WITHIN THE SOCKET HOUSING REPLACEMENT IS REQUIRED

Fig. 10   Ball joint wear indicator. 1977–83 Exc. 1982–83 Firebird

amount of torque required to turn the ball stud in its socket. If any torque is required, the ball joint is satisfactory. If no torque is required, the ball joint must be replaced.

2. A visual wear indicator is built into the lower ball joint on all models, Fig. 10.

BALL JOINTS, REPLACE

Except 1982–83 Firebird

On all models the upper ball joint is riveted

to the control arm. All service ball joints, however, are provided with bolt, nut and washer assemblies for replacement purposes.

The lower ball joint is pressed into the control arm. They may be pressed out and new joints pressed in.

Upper Ball Joint

1. Raise vehicle and support lower control arm.
2. Remove wheel assembly.
3. Remove upper ball joint stud from steering knuckle, Fig. 11.

4. Drill or chisel rivet heads from ball joint rivets. Then, drive rivets from control arm with a suitable punch.
5. Install new ball joint and torque retaining bolts to 9 ft. lbs.
6. Install ball joint stud into steering knuckle and torque nut to specifications listed below:

Year	Ft. Lbs.
1978–79	64
1980–82	88

7. Install cotter pin.
8. Install wheel assembly and lower vehicle.

Fig. 11 Removing ball joint studs from steering knuckle.

Fig. 12 Removing & installing ball joint. 1982–83 Firebird

Lower Ball Joint

1. Raise vehicle and support lower control arm under spring seats.
2. Remove brake drum and backing plate or caliper.
3. Remove lower ball joint stud from steering knuckle, Fig. 11.
4. With a screwdriver, pry ball joint seal and retainer from ball joint.
5. Press lower ball joint from control arm.
6. Press new ball joint into lower control arm.
7. Install ball joint stud into steering knuckle and torque nut to specifications listed below:

Year	Model	Ft. Lbs.
1978–79	All	83
1980–82	All	88

8. Install cotter pin.
9. Install brake backing plate and drum or caliper, then the wheel assembly.

1982–83 Firebird

1. Raise and support vehicle.
2. Remove tire and wheel assembly.
3. Place a suitable floor jack under control arm spring seat.

CAUTION: Floor jack must remain under control arm spring seat during removal and installation to retain spring and control arm in position.

4. Remove cotter pin and loosen nut. Use tool J-24292A to break ball joint loose from steering knuckle.
5. Remove tool and separate joint from knuckle.
6. Guide lower control arm out of opening in splash shield with a suitable tool.
7. Remove grease fittings, and install special tools as shown in Fig. 12.
8. Reverse procedure to install. Torque ball stud nut to 90 ft. lbs.

SHOCK ABSORBER, REPLACE

Except 1982–83 Firebird

Hold the shock absorber upper stem from turning with a suitable wrench and remove the nut and grommet. Remove the lower shock absorber pivot from the lower control arm and pull the shock absorber and mounting out at the bottom of the spring housing.

To install, reverse the removal procedure. Torque upper retaining nut to 10 ft. lbs. Torque shock absorber lower retaining bolts to 20 ft. lbs.

STRUT, REPLACE

1982–83 Firebird

1. Raise and support vehicle.
2. Remove tire and wheel assembly.
3. Support lower control arm with jackstand.
4. Remove brake hose bracket.
5. Remove two strut-to-knuckle bolts.
6. Remove cover from upper mount assembly.
7. Remove nut from upper end of strut assembly.
8. Remove strut and shield.
9. Reverse procedure to install. Torque nuts to 52 ft. lbs.

COIL SPRING, REPLACE

1977–83, Except 1982–83 Firebird

1. Support vehicle at frame and remove wheel.
2. Disconnect shock absorber from lower control arm and push shock absorber through hole in lower control arm up into spring.
3. Remove stabilizer link nut, link, spacer, grommets and retainer.
4. Support lower control arm with tool J-23028 bolted onto a suitable jack.
5. Install a safety chain through spring and lower control arm, remove the two lower control arm to frame crossmember pivot bolts. Lower jack, allowing spring to expand and remove spring.
6. Reverse procedure to install and torque pivot bolts or nuts to specifications listed below:

Year	Pivot Bolts, Ft. lbs.	Nuts, Ft. lbs.
1977—		
Full Size, Grand Prix & LeMans	90	95
Firebird	—	90
Phoenix & Ventura	—	105
1978–79—		
Phoenix	—	94
1978–81—		
Grand Prix & LeMans	—	70
Full Size	—	124
Firebird	—	90
1982—		
Grand Prix & Bonneville	—	70

1982 Firebird

1. Raise and support vehicle.
2. Remove tire and wheel assembly.
3. Remove stabilizer link and bushings at lower control arm.
4. Remove pivot bolt nuts.

NOTE: Do not remove pivot bolts at this time.

5. Install adapter tool No. J-23028 or equivalent adapter to floor jack and place into position with supporting bushings.
6. Install jackstand under outside frame on opposite side of vehicle.
7. Raise tool No. J-23028 enough to remove both pivot bolts.
8. Lower tool No. J-23028 carefully and remove spring.
9. Remove ball joint from steering knuckle using tool No. J-24292A or equivalent as outlined under "Ball Joint, Replace".
10. Replace bushings in lower control arm.
11. Reverse procedure to install. Torque nut to 70 ft. lbs.

STEERING GEAR, REPLACE

1. Use puller to remove pitman arm from steering gear shaft.
2. Remove flex coupling shield, if equipped, then scribe a mark on worm shaft flange and steering shaft and disconnect lower flange from steering shaft.
3. Unfasten gear housing from frame (3 bolts) and remove from car.

POWER STEERING GEAR, REPLACE

1. Remove flex coupling shield if equipped, then scribe mark on worm shaft flange and steering shaft and disconnect lower flange from steering shaft.
2. Disconnect pressure and return hoses from gear housing.
3. Raise vehicle and disconnect pitman arm from shaft.
4. Remove gear housing to frame bolts and remove steering gear assembly.
5. Reverse procedure to install.

POWER STEERING PUMP, REPLACE

1. Disconnect battery ground cable.
2. Remove power steering pump belt drive, then remove pulley from pump.
3. Disconnect pressure and return line from power steering pump. Cap lines and fittings to prevent entry of dirt.
4. Remove pump and bracket from engine as an assembly, then remove bracket from pump.
5. Reverse procedure to install.

Flasher Locations

Car	1977 TSF	1977 HWF	1978 TSF	1978 HWF	1979 TSF	1979 HWF	1980 TSF	1980 HWF	1981 TSF	1981 HWF	1982 TSF	1982 HWF	1983 TSF	1983 HWF
American Motors	3	⑦	3	②	3	3	12	3	12	3	12	3	12	3
Astre & Vega	5	3	—	—	—	—	—	—	—	—	—	—	—	—
Buick, Regal & 1977–81 Century	4	3	3	3	3	3	3	3	3	3	3	3	3	3
Buick Skylark & 1982–83 Century	10	3	10	3	10	3	6	15	6	15	6	15	6	15
Cadillac Brougham & DeVille	3	3	3	3	3	3	6	3	6	3	6	3	6	3
Cadillac Seville & Eldorado	4⑧	3	4⑧	3	6	3	6	3	6	3	6	3	6	3
Camaro & Firebird	4	3	4	3	4	3	4	3	4	3	4	4	4	4
Capri & Mustang	7	7	7	7	4	4	4	14	4	14	4	14	4	14
Cavalier, Cimarron, 2000 & 1982–83 Skyhawk & Firenza	—	—	—	—	—	—	—	—	—	—	5	3	5	3
Chevelle, Malibu & Monte Carlo	4	3	3	3	3	3	3	3	3	3	3	3	3	3
Chevette & 1000	13	3	13	3	13	3	13	3	13	3	13	3	13	3
Chevrolet Full Size	3	3	3	3	3	3	3	3	3	3	3	3	3	3
Chevrolet Citation & Celebrity	—	—	—	—	—	—	6	15	6	15	6	15	6	15
Chevrolet Nova	10	3	10	3	10	3	—	—	—	—	—	—	—	—
Chrysler, Imperial, LeBaron & E Class	5⑫	3	5⑫	3	7⑫	6⑫	7⑫	6⑫	7⑫	6⑫	3	3	3	3
Comet & Maverick	4	3	—	—	—	—	—	—	—	—	—	—	—	—
Cordoba & Mirada	13	④	14	4	9	3	5	5	5	5	3	3	3	3
Corvette	16	3	16	3	3	3	3	3	3	3	3	3	3	3
Cougar, LTD II & Thunderbird	4	4	4	4	4	4	4	4	4	⑭	4	⑭	4	⑭
Dodge & Plymouth Full Size	5	3	5	3	7	6	7	6	7	6	—	—	—	—
Dodge & Plymouth Intermed.	⑨	3⑩	⑨	3	①	3	3	3	3	3	3	3	3	3
Dodge Aries, 400, 600 & Plymouth Reliant	—	—	—	—	—	—	3	3	3	3	3	3	3	3
Horizon, Omni & 1983 Charger & Turismo	—	—	3	3	3	3	3	3	3	3	3	3	3	3
Escort, EXP, LN7 & Lynx	—	—	—	—	—	—	—	—	4	5	4	5	4	5
Ford & Mercury Full Size	3	4	3	3	3	3	5	5	5	5	5	5	5	5
Fairmont, Zephyr & 1983 LTD & Marquis	—	—	14	11	14	11	4	4	4	14	4	14	4	14
Ford Pinto & Mercury Bobcat	11	11	11	11	6	6	6	6	—	—	—	—	—	—
Granada, Monarch & Versailles	10	4	10	4	10	4	10	4	4	14	4	14	4	14
Grand Am, Grand Prix, LeMans & 1982–83 Bonneville	3⑥	3	3	3	3	3	3	3	3	3	3	3	3	3
Lincoln	10⑤	3	10⑤	3	3③	3	5	5	5	5	5⑮	5⑮	5⑮	5⑮
Monza, Starfire, Sunbird & 1977–80 Skyhawk	12	12	12⑪	4	12⑪	4	12	4	—	—	—	—	—	—
Oldsmobile	3	3	3	3	3	3	3	3	3	3	3	3	3	3
Oldsmobile Cutlass (Exc. Ciera)	4	3	3	3	3	3	3	3	3	3	3	3	3	3
Olds. Omega & Cutlass Ciera	10	3	10	3	10	3	6	15	6	15	6	15	6	15
Oldsmobile Toronado	4	3	4	3	3	3	3	3	3	3	6	3	6	3
Pontiac Full Size, 1977–81	3	3	3	3	3	3	3	3	3	3	—	—	—	—
Pont. Phoenix, Ventura & 6000	10	3	10	3	10	3	6	15	6	15	6	15	6	15

TSF: Turn Signal Flasher.   HWF: Hazard Warning Flasher.

①—Location 9 on Magnum. Location 3 on Aspen, Diplomat & Volaré.
②—Location 3 on Concord & Gremlin. Location 4 on Matador. Location 5 on Pacer.
③—Location 10 on Mark V.
④—On right side of brake pedal support.
⑤—Location 3 on Mark V.
⑥—Location 4 on LeMans.
⑦—Location 6 on Gremlin & Hornet. Location 4 on Matador. Location 5 on Pacer.
⑧—On underside of steering column cover on Eldorado models.
⑨—Location 3 on Aspen, Diplomat & Volaré. Location 13 on Charger, Fury, Magnum & Monaco.
⑩—On right side of brake pedal support on Charger, Fury & Monaco.
⑪—Location 5 on Monza "S" Coupe, Sunbird Coupe & all Sta. Wag.
⑫—Location 3 on LeBaron. Location 5 on Imperial.
⑬—Location 3 on Eldorado.
⑭—Location 14 on Cougar. Location 4 on Cougar XR-7 & Thunderbird.
⑮—Location 4 on Lincoln Continental.

DESCRIPTION

NOTE: 1979, Eldorado, Riviera and Toronado models, two different types of driving axles are used. Early type driving axles can be identified by a groove on the drive axle, while the late type driving axle has no groove, Fig. 1.

The front wheel drive system, Figs. 2 and 3, consists of a final drive unit, left and right hand output shafts and drive axles. On 1979–83 Eldorado, Riviera and Toronado and 1980–83 Seville models, the output shafts are splined to the side gears and are retained by a retaining ring. Each drive axle, Figs. 4 and 5, consists of an axle shaft, with a ball type constant velocity joint at the outboard end and a tri-pot joint at the inboard end. On 1980–83 Citation, Omega, Phoenix and Skylark and 1982–83 Celebrity, Century, Cutlass Ciera and 6000 models, two different types of drive axle design is used. Both designs use the same ball type constant velocity joint at the outboard end. One design uses a ball type constant velocity joint at the inboard end, Fig. 6, the other design uses a tri-pot joint at the inboard end, Fig. 7. Both designs incorporate male splines which lock on the transaxle gears with snap rings, except for the left side inboard joint used with the automatic transaxles. The left side inboard joint used on automatic transaxles models utilizes a female spline which installs over a transaxle stub shaft.

DRIVE AXLE, REPLACE

1980–83 Citation, Omega, Phoenix, Skylark; 1982–83 Celebrity, Century, Cutlass Cierra & 6000

NOTE: On models equipped with tri-pot joints on inboard axles, care must be taken not to over extend joints. When either or both ends are disconnected, over extending the tri-pot joint could result in internal joint separation.

Removal

1. Remove hub nut, then raise and support vehicle and remove wheel and tire assembly.
2. On vehicles equipped with ball type constant velocity inboard joints, Fig. 6, install axle shaft boot seal protector J-28712, Fig. 3, on inboard and outboard seals. On vehicles equipped with tri-pot inboard joints, Fig. 7, install axle boot seal protector J-28712 on outboard seal and J-33162 on inboard seal, Fig. 3.
3. Disconnect brake line clip at strut.
4. Remove disc brake caliper and caliper support.
5. Mark cam bolt to ensure proper camber alignment during installation.
6. Remove bolts attaching steering knuckle to strut.
7. Using tool J-28468 or J-33008 and J-2619-01, Fig. 3, disengage snap rings retaining drive axles.
8. Separate steering knuckle from strut.
9. Carefully pull drive axles from transaxle. On vehicles equipped with tri-pot inboard joints, Fig. 7, do not over extend joints.
10. Using tool J-28733, remove axle shaft from hub and bearing asssembly.

With drive axle assembled, one groove can be seen.

With drive axle assembled, no groove can be seen.

FIRST TYPE   SECOND TYPE

Fig. 1 Drive axle identification. 1979–83 Eldorado, Riviera & Toronado

Fig. 2 Front wheel drive components. 1979–83 Eldorado, Riviera & Toronado; 1980–83 Seville

Fig. 3 Front wheel drive components. 1980–83 Citation, Omega, Phoenix & Skylark; 1982–83 Cavalier, Celebrity, Century, Cimarron, Cutlass Ciera, Firenza, 2000, Skyhawk & 6000

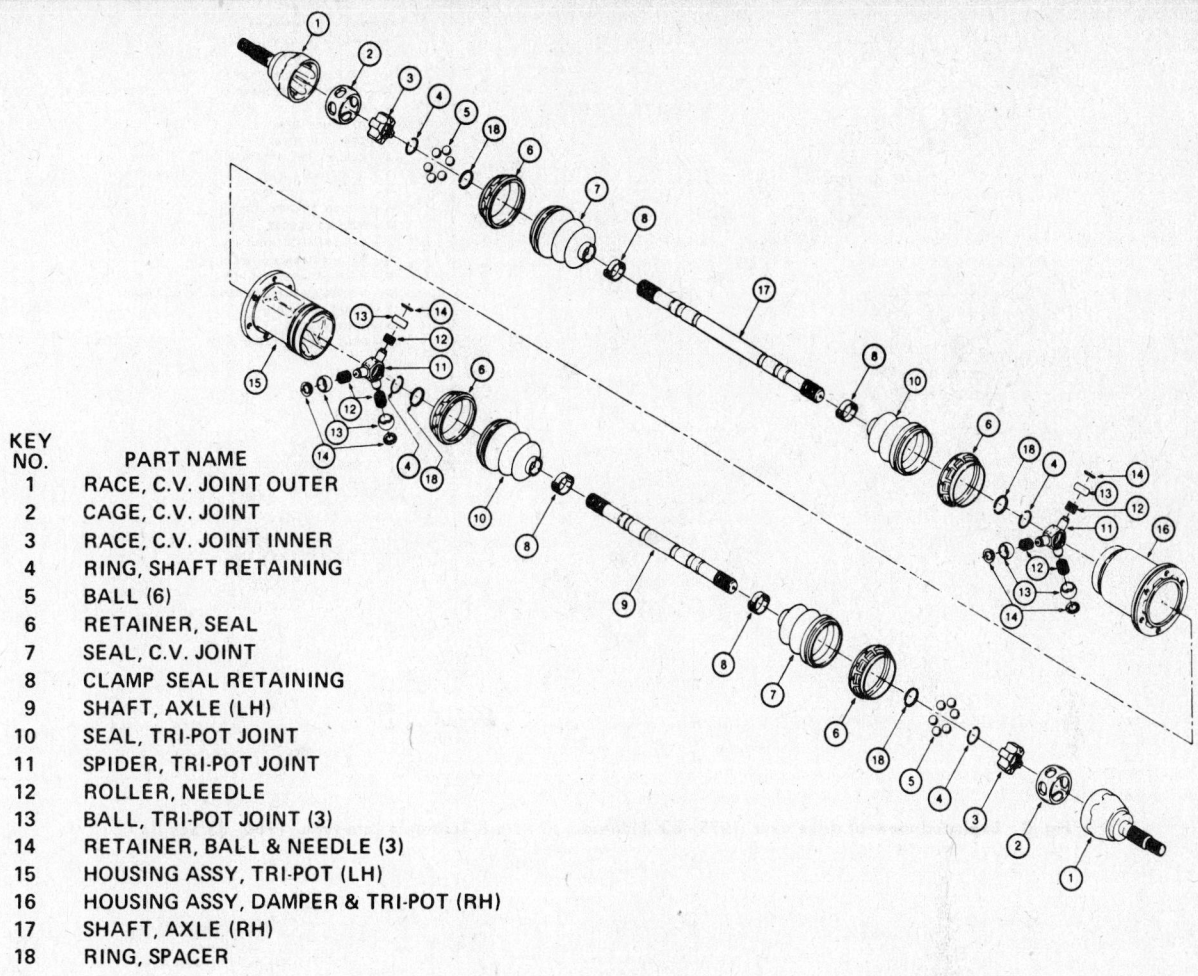

KEY NO.	PART NAME
1	RACE, C.V. JOINT OUTER
2	CAGE, C.V. JOINT
3	RACE, C.V. JOINT INNER
4	RING, SHAFT RETAINING
5	BALL (6)
6	RETAINER, SEAL
7	SEAL, C.V. JOINT
8	CLAMP SEAL RETAINING
9	SHAFT, AXLE (LH)
10	SEAL, TRI-POT JOINT
11	SPIDER, TRI-POT JOINT
12	ROLLER, NEEDLE
13	BALL, TRI-POT JOINT (3)
14	RETAINER, BALL & NEEDLE (3)
15	HOUSING ASSY, TRI-POT (LH)
16	HOUSING ASSY, DAMPER & TRI-POT (RH)
17	SHAFT, AXLE (RH)
18	RING, SPACER

Fig. 4 Exploded view of drive axle. 1979 Eldorado, Riviera & Toronado early type

Installation
1. Loosely install drive axle to steering knuckle and transaxle.
2. Loosely attach steering knuckle to strut bracket.
3. Install disc brake caliper, torque attaching bolts to 30 ft. lbs.
4. Install drive axle to steering knuckle. The drive axle is an interference fit. Install hub nut, when shaft begins to rotate, insert a brass drift in slot on rotor to prevent shaft from turning. It will take approximately 70 ft. lbs. of torque to seat axle shaft.
5. Apply load on hub by lowering vehicle on jack stand. Align cam bolt alignment marks, then torque nut to 140 ft. lbs.
6. Using a screwdriver in groove provided on inner retainer, install axle shaft on transaxle, Fig. 3. Tap on screwdriver until axle shaft is seated in transaxle.
7. Connect brake line clip to strut bracket, then install wheel and tire assembly and lower vehicle.
8. Torque hub nut to 225 ft. lbs.

1982–83 Cavalier, Cimarron, Firenza, 2000 & Skyhawk

NOTE: On models equipped with tri-pot joints on inboard axles, care must be taken not to over extend joints. When either or both ends are disconnected, over extending the tri-pot joint could result in internal joint separa-tion.

Removal
1. Remove hub nut, then raise and support vehicle and remove wheel and tire assembly.
2. On vehicles equipped with ball type constant velocity inboard joints, Fig. 6, install axle shaft boot seal protector J-28712, Fig. 3, on inboard and outboard seals. On vehicles equipped with tri-pot inboard joints, Fig. 7, install axle boot seal protector J-28712 on outboard seal and J-33162 on inboard seal, Fig. 3.
3. Remove disc brake caliper, rotor and caliper support.

NOTE: Prior to beginning next step, it is suggested to mark cam bolt to ensure proper camber alignment during installation.

4. Remove strut to steering knuckle attaching bolts, then seperate steering knuckle from strut bracket.
5. Using tool J-28468 or J-33008 with extension J-29794, remove axle shaft from transaxle, Fig. 3.
6. Using tool J-28733, remove axle shaft from hub and bearing assembly.

Installation
1. Loosely install drive axle to steering knuckle and transaxle.

2. Loosely attach steering knuckle to strut bracket.
3. Remove one hub to steering knuckle attaching bolt and install a longer bolt through hub cutout to prevent hub from turning. Install hub nut and washer and torque to 70 ft. lbs.
4. Remove long bolt and install original hub and bearing to steering knuckle attaching bolt. Torque bolts to 63 ft. lbs.
5. Install disc brake caliper and rotor. Torque caliper attaching bolts to 21–35 ft. lbs.
6. Using a screwdriver in groove provided on inner retainer, install axle shaft into transaxle, Fig. 3. Tap on screwdriver until axle shaft is seated in transaxle.
7. Torque steering knuckle to strut bracket attaching bolts to 140 ft. lbs.
8. Install wheel and tire and lower vehicle.
9. Torque hub nut to 185 ft. lbs.

RIGHT HAND DRIVE AXLE, OUTPUT SHAFT & SEAL, REPLACE

1979–83 Eldorado, Riviera & Toronado; 1980–83 Seville

Removal
1. Disconnect battery ground cable.

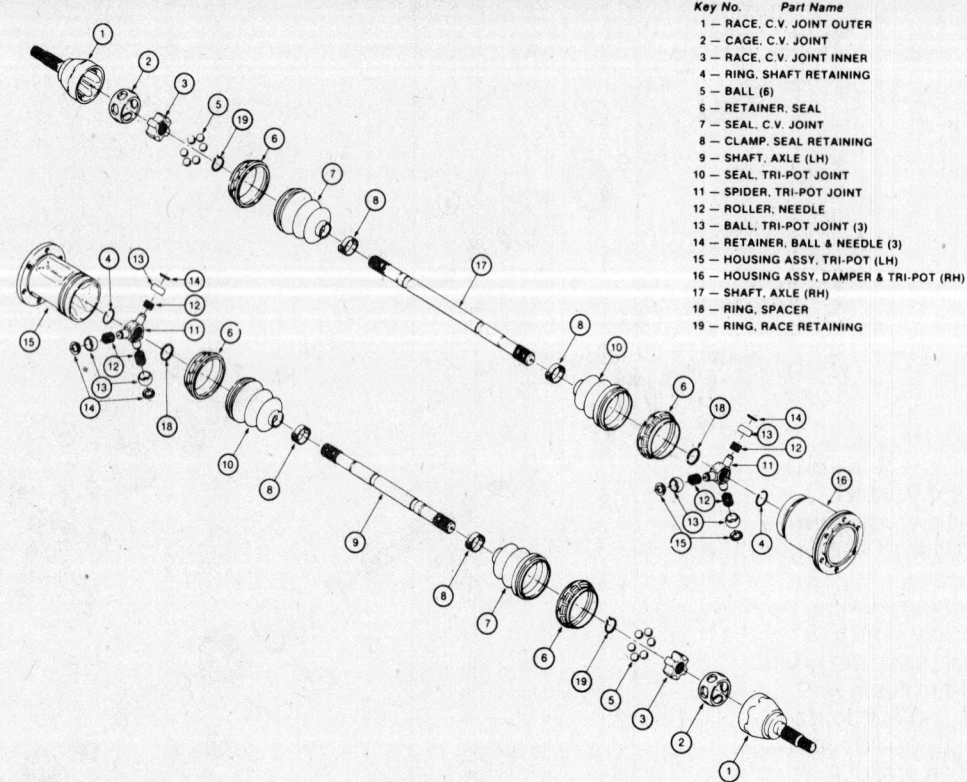

Key No.	Part Name
1 —	RACE, C.V. JOINT OUTER
2 —	CAGE, C.V. JOINT
3 —	RACE, C.V. JOINT INNER
4 —	RING, SHAFT RETAINING
5 —	BALL (6)
6 —	RETAINER, SEAL
7 —	SEAL, C.V. JOINT
8 —	CLAMP, SEAL RETAINING
9 —	SHAFT, AXLE (LH)
10 —	SEAL, TRI-POT JOINT
11 —	SPIDER, TRI-POT JOINT
12 —	ROLLER, NEEDLE
13 —	BALL, TRI-POT JOINT (3)
14 —	RETAINER, BALL & NEEDLE (3)
15 —	HOUSING ASSY, TRI-POT (LH)
16 —	HOUSING ASSY, DAMPER & TRI-POT (RH)
17 —	SHAFT, AXLE (RH)
18 —	RING, SPACER
19 —	RING, RACE RETAINING

Fig. 5   Exploded view of drive axle. 1979-83, Eldorado, Riviera & Toronado late type. 1980-83 Seville

Key No.	Part Name
1 —	RACE, C.V. JOINT OUTER
2 —	CAGE, C.V. JOINT
3 —	RACE, C.V. JOINT INNER
4 —	RING, RACE RETAINING
5 —	BALL (6)
6 —	RETAINER, SEAL
7 —	SEAL, C/V JOINT
8 —	CLAMP, SEAL RETAINING
9 —	SHAFT, AXLE (LH)
10 —	SEAL, D/O JOINT
11 —	RING, BALL RETAINING
12 —	BALL (6)
13 —	RACE, D/O JOINT INNER
14 —	CAGE, D/O JOINT
15 —	RACE, D/O JOINT OUTER
16 —	RING, JOINT RETAINING
17 —	RACE, D/O JOINT OUTER
18 —	SHAFT, AXLE (RH)
19 —	SLINGER

AUTOMATIC TRANSAXLE
(LH SIDE ONLY)

Fig. 6   Exploded view of drive axle with ball type constant velocity inboard joint. 1980-83 Citation, Omega, Phoenix & Skylark;
1982-83 Cavalier, Celebrity, Century Cimarron, Cutlass Ciera, Firenza, 2000, Skyhawk & 6000

1 — RACE, C.V. JOINT OUTER
2 — CAGE, C.V. JOINT
3 — RACE, C.V. JOINT INNER
4 — RING, SHAFT RETAINING
5 — BALL (6)
6 — RETAINER, SEAL
7 — SEAL, C.V. JOINT
8 — CLAMP, SEAL RETAINING
9 — SHAFT, AXLE (LH)
10 — SEAL, TRI-POT JOINT
11 — SPIDER, TRI-POT JOINT
12 — ROLLER, NEEDLE
13 — BALL, TRI-POT JOINT (3)
14 — RING, JOINT RETAINING
15 — HOUSING ASSY, TRI-POT (LH)
16 — HOUSING ASSY, TRI-POT (RH)
17 — SHAFT, AXLE (RH)
18 — RING, SPACER
19 — RING, RACE RETAINING
20 — CLAMP, SEAL RETAINING
21 — RETAINER, NEEDLE
22 — RING, NEEDLE RETAINER

Fig. 7   Exploded view of drive axle with tri-pot inboard joint. 1980—83 Citation, Omega, Phoenix & Skylark; 1982—83 Cavalier, Celebrity, Century, Cimarron, Cutlass Ciera, Firenza, 2000, Skyhawk & 6000

2. Raise front of vehicle and place jack stands under front frame horns.
3. Remove wheel and tire assembly.
4. Remove cotter pin, nut and shield from tie rod pivot, then using puller J-24319, detach tie rod end from steering knuckle.
5. Install drive shaft seal protector J-28712, then remove cotter pin, nut and washer from drive axle, then remove six screws attaching drive axle to output shaft.

NOTE: To prevent axle shaft from rotating when removing nut or attaching screws, insert a drift through opening on top of caliper into corresponding rotor vane.

6. Remove cotter pin and nut from upper ball joint stud nut, then remove brake hose clip from stud and loosely reinstall nut.
7. Using a hammer and brass drift, rap on steering knuckle to free upper ball joint stud. Use care not to damage brake hose or steering knuckle.
8. Remove nut and separate upper ball joint from steering knuckle.
9. Guide drive axle out of steering knuckle and remove from vehicle.

10. Remove two screws attaching battery cable retainer to support and remove two screws attaching output support to engine, then rotate support downward.
11. Remove front nut and bolt from right hand frame brace, then pivot brace outward to provide clearance.
12. Using a plastic mallet, drive on flange end of output shaft until shaft releases from retaining ring, then remove output shaft and support. Use care not to damage output shaft seal surfaces or splines.
13. Using a suitable pry bar, pry output shaft seal out of housing. Pry at two or three different places to avoid cocking seal. Use care not to damage housing.

Installation

1. Using tool No. J-28518, install output shaft seal. Rotate tool to maintain proper alignment when installing seal.
2. Apply wheel bearing grease between lips of seal.
3. Index splines of output shaft with splines of side gear in final drive assembly, then install shaft by tapping on flange end with a soft faced mallet until retaining ring snaps into shaft groove. Ensure shaft is securely locked into position.

NOTE: When installing output shaft, use care not to damage seal.

4. Align output shaft support and engine block attaching screw holes, then install two support attaching screws. Torque screws to 50 ft. lbs.
5. Install two screws attaching battery cable retainer to support.
6. Guide drive axle into position and install splined end axle into steering knuckle.
7. Position upper ball joint stud into steering knuckle, then place brake hose clip on stud and install stud nut. Torque stud nut to 60 ft. lbs., then install cotter pin. The nut may be tightened an additional 1/6 turn to align cotter pin slots.
8. Install six screws attaching output shaft to drive axle. Torque screws to 60 ft. lbs.
9. Install drive axle washer, nut, retainer and cotter pin. Torque nut to 175 ft. lbs. Align cotter pin slot by rotating retainer and bend cotter pin so that retainer is held snugly.
10. Install tie rod pivot on steering knuckle. Torque nut to 44 ft. lbs. The nut may be tightened an additional 1/6 turn to align cotter pin slots.

Fig. 8 Outer constant velocity joint seal removal & installation. 1979 Eldorado, Riviera & Toronado early type

Fig. 9 Outer constant velocity joint seal removal & installation. 1979–83 Eldorado, Riviera, Toronado late type & 1980–83 All models

Fig. 10 Outer constant velocity joint disassembly & assembly. 1979–83 All models

11. Install right hand frame brace bolt and nut. Torque belt to 50 ft. lbs.
12. Install front wheel and tire assembly, then lower vehicle and connect battery ground cable.
13. Check output shaft seal for leakage.

LEFT HAND DRIVE AXLE, OUTPUT SHAFT & SEAL, REPLACE

1979–83 Eldorado, Riviera & Toronado; 1980–83 Seville

Removal
1. Raise front of vehicle and place jack stands under front frame horns.
2. Remove wheel and tire assembly.

3. Remove cotter pin, nut and shield from tie rod pivot, then using puller J-24319, detach tie rod end from steering knuckle.
4. Remove cotter pin, nut and washer from drive axle, then remove six screws attaching drive axle to output shaft.

NOTE: To prevent drive axle from rotating when removing nut or attaching screws, insert a drift through opening on top of caliper into corresponding rotor vane.

5. Remove cotter pin and nut from upper ball joint stud nut, then remove brake hose clip from stud and loosely reinstall nut.
6. Using a hammer and brass drift, rap on steering knuckle to free upper ball joint stud. Use care not to damage brake hose or steering knuckle.

7. Remove nut and separate upper ball joint from steering knuckle.
8. Guide drive axle out of steering knuckle and remove from vehicle.
9. Remove front nut and bolt from left hand frame brace, then pivot brace outward to provide clearance.
10. Using a hammer and brass drift, drive on flange end of output shaft until shaft releases from retaining ring, then remove output shaft.
11. Using a suitable pry bar, pry output shaft seal from housing. Pry at two or three locations to avoid cocking seal. Use care not to damage housing.

Installation
1. Using tool No. J-28518, install output shaft seal. Rotate tool to maintain proper alignment when installing seal.
2. Apply wheel bearing grease between lips of seal.

**Fig. 11 Inner tri-pot seal removal & installation.
1979 Eldorado, Riviera & Toronado early type**

**Fig. 12 Inner tri-pot seal removal & installation.
1979–83 Eldorado, Riviera & Toronado late type.
1980–83 Seville**

3. Index splines of output shaft with splines of side gear in final drive assembly then install shaft by tapping center of flange end with a soft faced mallet until retaining ring snaps into shaft groove. Ensure shaft is securely locked into position.

NOTE: When installing output shaft, use care not to damage seal.

4. Guide drive axle into position and install splined end into steering knuckle.
5. Position upper ball joint stud into steering knuckle, then place brake hose clip on stud and install nut. Torque nut to 60 ft. lbs., then install cotter pin. The nut may be tightened an additional 1/6 turn to align cotter pin slots.
6. Install six screws attaching output shaft to drive axle. Torque screws to 60 ft.

lbs.
7. Install drive axle water nut, retainer and cotter pin. Torque nut to 175 ft. lbs. and bend cotter pin so that retainer is held snugly.
8. Install tie rod pivot on steering knuckle. Torque nut to 44 ft. lbs. The nut may be tightened an additional 1/6 turn to align cotter pin slots.
9. Install left hand frame brace bolt and nut. Torque bolt to 50 ft. lbs.
10. Install wheel and tire assembly, then lower vehicle and check output shaft seal for leakage.

RIGHT HAND OUTPUT SHAFT SUPPORT BEARING, REPLACE

1979–83 Eldorado, Riviera & Toronado; 1980–83 Seville

1. Remove right hand output shaft as described under Right Hand Drive Axle, Output Shaft and Seal, Replace.
2. Remove three screws securing bearing retainer to support.
3. Install tool No. J-22912 between flange end of output shaft and flat area of shaft support, with flat surface of tool against flat area of shaft support. Position assembly on a suitable press and press shaft support, bearing, retainer and slinger from output shaft.
4. Remove bearing from output shaft support.
5. Lubricate output shaft support and bearing, then position bearing into support.
6. Pack bearing with wheel bearing grease, then install retainer and three attaching screws.
7. Place assembled components and slinger on output shaft, then position components and output shaft on a press. Using a standard 1 1/4 in. inside diameter pipe, press bearing and assembled components onto shaft.
8. Check to ensure bearing and support rotate smoothly, then install right hand output shaft.

OUTER CONSTANT VELOCITY JOINT & SEAL, REPLACE

1979–83 Eldorado, Riviera Toronado; 1980–83 Seville, Citation, Omega, Phoenix & Skylark; 1982–83 Cavalier, Celebrity, Century, Cimarron, Cutlass Ciera, Firenza, 2000, Skyhawk & 6000

For removal and installation procedures refer to Figs. 8, 9 and 10.

INNER TRI-POT SEAL, REPLACE

1979–83 Eldorado, Riviera & Toronado; 1980–83 Seville

For removal and installation procedures refer to Figs. 11 and 12.

1980–83 Citation, Omega, Phoenix & Skylark; 1982–83 Cavalier, Celebrity, Century, Cimarron, Cutlass Ciera, Firenza, 2000, Skyhawk & 6000

For removal and installation procedures, refer to Fig. 13.

INNER CONSTANT JOINT & SEAL, REPLACE

1980–83 Citation, Omega, Phoenix & Skylark; 1982–83 Cavalier, Celebrity, Century, Cimarron, Cutlass Ciera, Firenza, 2000, Skyhawk & 6000

For removal and installation procedures, refer to Figs. 14 and 15.

FINAL DRIVE, REPLACE

1980–83 Citation, Omega, Phoenix & Skylark; 1982–83 Cavalier, Celebrity, Century, Cimarron, Cutlass Ciera, Firenza, 2000, Skyhawk & 6000

On these models, the final drive unit is an integral component of the transaxle assembly.

1979–83 Eldorado, Riviera & Toronado; 1980–83 Seville

1. Disconnect battery ground cable.
2. Raise front of vehicle and position jack stands under front frame horns and lower front post.
3. Remove right and left hand frame brace front attaching bolts, then position braces to provide clearance.
4. Position drain pan under final drive cover, then loosen cover and allow lubricant to drain.
5. Remove final drive cover attaching screws, cover and gasket.
6. Remove screws attaching right and left output shafts to drive axles. Separate output shaft flanges from drive axles to permit clearance of final drive assembly with shafts installed.
7. Remove two screws attaching battery cable retainer to right hand output shaft support, then remove two screws securing support to engine. Rotate support downward to provide clearance for removal.
8. Remove final drive to transmission attaching screws that secures rear of final drive shield, then loosen support bracket screw that secure front of shield and remove shield.
9. Remove five remaining final drive to transmission attaching screws.
10. Remove screws attaching final drive support bracket to engine block.
11. Using tool J-24319, disconnect steering linkage intermediate shaft from pitman and idler arms. Push linkage forward to ensure adequate clearance for final drive assembly removal.
12. Slide final drive assembly forward, off transmission splined shaft and remove unit with output shafts attached. Use care not to damage output shaft seal or splines.
13. Reverse procedure to install. Torque final drive to transaxle attaching bolts to 30 ft. lbs., support bracket bolts to 50 ft. lbs. and output shaft to drive shaft attaching bolts to 60 ft. lbs.

Fig. 13 Inner tri-pot seal removal & installation. 1980–83 Citation, Omega, Phoenix & Skylark; 1982–83 Cavalier, Celebrity, Century, Cimarron, Cutlass Ciera, Firenza, 2000, Skyhawk & 6000

Fig. 14 Inner constant velocity joint seal removal & installation. 1980–83 Citation, Omega, Phoenix & Skylark; 1982–83 Cavalier, Celebrity, Century, Cimarron, Cutlass Ciera, Firenza, 2000, Skyhawk & 6000

Fig. 15 Inner constant velocity joint removal & installation. 1980–83 Citation, Omega, Phoenix & Skylark; 1982–83 Cavalier, Celebrity, Century, Cimarron, Cutlass Ciera, Firenza, 2000, Skyhawk & 6000

1983 CARBURETOR ADJUSTMENT SPECIFICATIONS

The following carburetor specifications are the latest additions to the "Carburetor Chapter". Refer to the "Carburetor Chapter," page 2-148 for the location of adjustments.

CARTER BBD ADJUSTMENT SPECIFICATIONS

Year	Carb. Model	Float Level	Pump Travel Inch	Bowl Vent Clearance	Choke Unloader Clearance	Initial Choke Valve Clearance	Choke Vacuum Kick Clearance	Fast Idle Cam Position Clearance	Automatic Choke Setting
CHRYSLER CORP.									
1983	8291S	1/4	.470	—	.280	—	.130	.070	Fixed

HOLLEY 1000, 2000 & 6145 SERIES CARB. ADJUSTMENT SPECIFICATIONS

Year	Carb. Part No.①	Carb. Model	Float Level (Dry)	Fuel Level (Wet)	Pump Setting	Bowl Vent Clearance	Fast Idle Bench	Choke Unloader Clearance	Vacuum Kick Drill Size	Cam Position Drill Size	Choke Setting
CHRYSLER CORP.											
1983	R40042A	6145	②	—	1.615③	—	.090	.250	.150	.090	—

①—Located on tag attached to carburetor or on casting.
②—Flush with top of bowl casting to .050 inch above with bowl inverted.
③—Hole position No. 2.

HOLLEY MODEL 6520 ADJUSTMENT SPECIFICATIONS

Year	Model No.	Float Level	Float Drop	Acc. Pump Hole No.	Choke Vacuum Kick	Choke Setting
1983	R40003A	.480	1.875	3	.070	—
	R40004A	.480	1.875	3	.080	—
	R40005A	.480	1.875	3	.080	—
	R40006A	.480	1.875	3	.080	—
	R40007A	.480	1.875	3	.070	—
	R40008A	.480	1.875	3	.070	—
	R40010A	.480	1.875	3	.080	—
	R40012A	.480	1.875	3	.070	—
	R40014A	.480	1.875	3	.080	—
	R40080A	.480	1.875	2	.045	—
	R40081A	.480	1.875	2	.045	—

MIKUNI CARBURETOR ADJUSTMENT SPECIFICATIONS

Year	Model No.	Float Level	Fast Idle Opening At 68°F	Choke Breaker Opening At 14°F	Unloader Opening At 32°F
1983	4243066	.780	14.5°	.067	.051
	4243306	.780	14.5°	.067	.051
	4243307	.780	14.5°	.067	.051

1983 CARBURETOR ADJUSTMENT SPECIFICATIONS

ROCHESTER 2SE & E2SE ADJUSTMENT SPECIFICATIONS

Year	Carb. Production No.	Float Level	Accel. Pump	Choke Coil Lever	Choke Rod	Vacuum Break Primary	Vacuum Break Secondary	Air Valve Rod	Choke Setting	Unloader	Secondary Lockout
GENERAL MOTORS											
1983	17083356	13/32	—	.085	22°	25°	35°	1°	—	30°	.025
	17083357	13/32	—	.085	22°	25°	35°	1°	—	30°	.025
	17083358	13/32	—	.085	22°	25°	35°	1°	—	30°	.025
	17083359	13/32	—	.085	22°	25°	35°	1°	—	30°	.025
	17083368	13/32	—	.085	22°	25°	35°	1°	—	30°	.025
	17083369	13/32	—	.085	22°	25°	35°	1°	—	30°	.025
	17083370	13/32	—	.085	22°	25°	35°	1°	—	30°	.025
	17083371	13/32	—	.085	22°	25°	35°	1°	—	30°	.025
	17083450	1/4	—	.085	28°	27°	35°	1°	—	45°	.025
	17083451	1/4	—	.085	28°	27°	35°	1°	—	45°	.025
	17083452	1/4	—	.085	28°	27°	35°	1°	—	45°	.025
	17083453	1/4	—	.085	28°	27°	35°	1°	—	45°	.025
	17083454	1/4	—	.085	28°	27°	35°	1°	—	45°	.025
	17083455	1/4	—	.085	28°	27°	35°	1°	—	45°	.025
	17083456	1/4	—	.085	28°	27°	35°	1°	—	45°	.025
	17083458	1/4	—	.085	28°	27°	35°	1°	—	45°	.025
	17083459	1/4	—	.085	28°	27°	35°	1°	—	45°	.025
	17083630	13/32	—	.085	28°	27°	35°	1°	—	45°	.025
	17083631	13/32	—	.085	28°	27°	35°	1°	—	45°	.025
	17083632	13/32	—	.085	28°	27°	35°	1°	—	45°	.025
	17083633	13/32	—	.085	28°	27°	35°	1°	—	45°	.025
	17083634	13/32	—	.085	28°	27°	35°	1°	—	45°	.025
	17083635	13/32	—	.085	28°	27°	35°	1°	—	45°	.025
	17083636	13/32	—	.085	28°	27°	35°	1°	—	45°	.025

ROCHESTER DUAL-JET 2MC, M2MC, M2ME 200, 210 & E2ME ADJUSTMENT SPECIFICATIONS

Year	Carb. Production No.	Float Level	Pump Rod Hole	Pump Rod Adj.	Choke Coil Lever	Choke Rod	Vacuum Break Rich	Vacuum Break Lean	Vacuum Break Front	Vacuum Break Rear	Choke Unloader	Choke Setting
1983	17083190	5/16	—	—	.1206	18°	—	—	28°	24°	32°	—
	17083192	5/16	—	—	.1206	18°	—	—	28°	24°	32°	—
	17083193	5/16	—	—	.1206	18°	—	—	24°	28°	27°	—

ROCHESTER QUADRAJET E4M & M4M SERIES ADJUSTMENT SPECIFICATIONS

Year	Carb. Production No.	Float Level	Pump Rod Hole	Pump Rod Adj.	Fast Idle (Bench) Turns	Choke Coil Lever	Choke Rod	Vacuum Break Front	Vacuum Break Rear	Air-Valve Dash-pot	Choke Setting	Choke Unloader	Air Valve Spring Wind-Up
1983	17082265	3/8	—	—	—	.120	24.5°	26°	26°	.025	—	32°	5/8
	17082266	3/8	—	—	—	.120	24.5°	26°	26°	.025	—	32°	5/8
	17082267	3/8	—	—	—	.120	18°	26°	26°	.025	—	32°	5/8
	17082268	3/8	—	—	—	.120	18°	26°	26°	.025	—	32°	5/8
	17083242	9/32	—	—	—	.120	24.5°	20°	—	.025	—	38°	9/16
	17083244	1/4	—	—	—	.120	24.5°	21°	16°	.025	—	32°	5/8
	17083248	3/8	—	—	—	.120	24.5°	26°	26°	.025	—	32°	5/8
	17083250	7/16	—	—	—	.120	14°	27°	42°	.025	—	35°	1/2
	17083253	7/16	—	—	—	.120	14°	27°	41°	.025	—	35°	1/2
	17083553	7/16	—	—	—	.120	14°	27°	41°	.025	—	35°	1/2

DELCOTRON 12 SI ALTERNATOR SYSTEM

NO. 1 TERMINAL

'R' TERMINAL FOR DIESEL TACHOMETER

NO. 2 TERMINAL

BATTERY TERMINAL

BAT

TEST HOLE

DRIVE END FRAME

SLIP RING END FRAME

BEARING

REGULATOR

BRUSHES

SLIP RINGS

BEARING

SEAL

RECTIFIER BRIDGE

DIODE TRIO

ROTOR

STATOR ASSEMBLY

Fig. 1   Delcotron 12 SI alternator

DESCRIPTION

The Delcotron 12 SI alternator, Fig. 1, can be identified by a plastic cooling fan and smaller end frames when compared to conventional Delcotron SI alternators. It is capable of producing up to 78 amps at full speed, while at idle, 31 amps.

Power to activate the alternator is provided by the brown field wire, Fig. 2. The diode trio is protected by a 10 ohm resistence, provided by the charging system warning light or the choke heater relay if the vehicle is equipped with gauges.

Regulation of the alternator output is controlled by a solid state integral regulator. The regulator components are encased in a solid mold and cannot be adjusted or serviced.

The stator windings are assembled on the inside of a laminated core, which becomes part of the alternator frame. A rectifier bridge containing six diodes is connected to the sta-

tor windings and electrically converts the stator a.c. (alternating current) voltage to d.c. (direct current) voltage, which is then fed to the output terminal. A diode trio connected to the stator windings supplies current to the alternator field. A condensor (or capacitor), mounted in the end frame, protects the rectifier bridge and diode trio from high voltages while suppressing radio noise.

DIAGNOSIS

For diagnosis procedures, refer to "Delcotron SI Alternator Integral Charging System".

DISASSEMBLY, TESTING & REASSEMBLY

Refer to Figs. 3 and 4 for procedures.

BATTERY

INDICATOR LAMP

SWITCH

BAT

R5

R2

R1   D3

D2   TR2   D1

R3   C1   R4   TR1

REGULATOR

DIODE TRIO

FIELD (ROTOR)

STATOR

RECTIFIER BRIDGE

Fig. 2   Delcotron 12 SI alternator wiring schematic

THRU-BOLT LOCATION

NO 1 TERMINAL

'R' TERMINAL FOR DIESEL TACHOMETER

NO 2 TERMINAL

BATTERY TERMINAL

TEST HOLE

THRU BOLTS

1. Make scribe marks on end frames to facilitate reassembly.
2. Remove four thru-bolts and separate drive end frame assembly from rectifier end frame assembly.

TESTING STATOR

(CHECK FOR OPENS)
OHMMETER

OHMMETER (CHECK FOR OPENS)

OHMMETER (CHECK FOR GROUNDS)

5. Check stator for opens with ohmmeter (two checks). If either reading is high (infinite), replace stator.
6. On all series, check stator for grounds. If reading is low, replace stator.

END FRAME VIEW

REGULATOR

INSULATING WASHERS

RESISTOR (USED ON SOME MODELS)

DIODE TRIO

RECTIFIER BRIDGE

CAPACITOR

ATTACHING NUTS

'R' TERMINAL JUMPER FOR DIESEL TACHOMETER

3. Remove three attaching nuts and three regulator attaching screws.
4. Separate stator, diode trio and regulator from end frame. **The regulator cannot be tested on the work bench except with a regulator tester.**

TESTING ROTOR

OHMMETER (CHECK FOR GROUNDS)

OHMMETER CHECK FOR OPENS

7. Check rotor for grounds with ohmmeter. Reading should be very high (infinite). If not, replace rotor.
8. Check rotor for opens. Should read 2.4-3.5 ohms. If not, replace rotor.

Fig. 3 Delcotron 12 SI alternator. Disassembly, testing & reassembly (part 1 of 2)

TESTING TRIO

9. To check diode trio, connect ohmmeter as shown, then reverse lead connections. Should read high and low. If not, replace diode trio.

10. Repeat same test between single connector and each of other connectors.

TESTING RECTIFIER BRIDGE

11. Check rectifier bridge with ohmmeter connected from grounded heat sink to flat metal on terminal, not the stud. Reverse leads. If both readings are the same, replace rectifier bridge.

12. Repeat test between grounded heat sink and other two flat metal clips.

13. Repeat test between insulated heat sink and three flat metal clips, not the stud. To replace bridge, remove attaching screws.

BRUSHES RETAINED IN HOLDER

14. Clean brushes with soft, dry cloth.

15. Put brushes in holder and hold with brush retainer wire.

DRIVE END BEARING

16. Observe stack-up of parts in both illustrations. To remove rotor and drive end bearing, remove shaft nut, washer and pulley, fan and collar. Push rotor from housing.

17. Remove retainer plate inside drive end frame and push bearing out. Clean all parts with soft cloth.

18. Press against outer race to push bearing in. The 12SI uses a sealed bearing -- no lubricant is required. Assemble retainer plate.

19. Press rotor into end frame. Assemble collar, fan, pulley, washer and nut. Torque shaft nut to 54 - 82 N·m (40 - 60 ft. lbs.).

RECTIFIER END BEARING

20. Push slip ring end bearing out from outside toward inside of end frame.

21. Place flat plate over new bearing, press from outside toward inside until bearing is flush with end frame.

22. Assemble brush holder, regulator, resistor, diode trio, rectifier bridge and stator to slip ring end frame.

23. Assemble end frames together with thru-bolts. Remove brush retainer wire.

Fig. 4   Delcotron 12 SI alternator. Disassembly, testing & reassembly (part 2 of 2)

GM ENGINE ELECTRICAL PLUG-IN DIAGNOSIS

1977–83 FULL SIZE MODELS EXCEPT CADILLAC

1977–83 full size models are equipped with two electrical diagnostic connectors, Figs. 1, 2 and 3. The A/C connector is located on top of the A/C module and the engine electrical connector is located on the left fender panel. The following diagnostic procedures require the use of a jumper wire and a voltmeter.

Engine Electrical Diagnosis

Some diagnostic connector wires are spliced into the individual unit feed wire, instead of being connected directly to the connector on the unit. The connector on the unit should be checked before starting a repair. The splice can be checked by connecting a voltmeter to the connector on the unit and the voltage should be the same as at the terminal at the diagnostic connector.

Cranking tests are performed with the engine at any temperature, however, if the engine is extremely hot or cold, the voltage readings obtained will be lower than specified. To determine which of the following problems apply, turn the ignition key to "Start".

a. Poor cranking, or solenoid clicks or chatters.

Fig. 1   Diagnostic connector location. 1977–83 models

b. Solenoid makes no sound, no cranking.

c. Starter runs (spins), engine does not crank.

For all cranking problems, check for a damaged battery, loose or corroded terminals and cables and repair as necessary. If satisfactory, check battery state of charge indicator or specific gravity. If state of charge indicator is "Green" or the specific gravity is 1.200 or more, select condition in the following charts and perform checks with a voltmeter. The parking brakes should be applied with automatic transmission in "Park" and manual transmission in "Neutral", clutch released and the ignition key in the "Start" position. If the state of charge indicator is "Dark" or the specific gravity is less than 1.200, charge battery and recheck condition. Check charging system condition and also for a battery drain.

Fig. 2   Engine electrical wiring circuit. 1977–78 models

GM ENGINE ELECTRICAL PLUG-IN DIAGNOSIS

VOLTMETER CONNECTIONS	VOLTAGE READING	CORRECTION
POOR CRANKING, OR SOLENOID CLICKS OR CHATTERS		
1. 1 and G	9 volts or more	More voltmeter lead from G to engine block, key in "Start". 9 volts or more—Remove starter for repair. Under 9 volts—Check battery ground cable connections at engine block and at battery.
	Under 9 volts	Go to test 2.
2. Bat. Pos. and Bat. Neg. at battery	9.6 volts or more	Go to test 3.
	Under 9.6 volts	Perform battery load test. If OK, remove starter for repair.
3. Bat. Pos. at Battery and 1	.7 volts or more	Check positive cable terminals for clean, tight connections and condition of cable. Check fusible link (solenoid to generator harness).
	Under .7 volts	Check battery ground cable condition and connections.
SOLENOID MAKES NO SOUND—NO CRANKING		
1. 8 and G (Key in Start)	7 volts or more	Remove starter for repair.
	Under 7 volts	Go to test 2.
2. 1 and G	9 volts or more	Go to test 5.
	Under 9 volts	Go to test 3.
3. Bat. Pos. and Bat. Neg. at Battery	9.6 volts or more	Go to test 4.
	Under 9.6 volts	Perform battery load test. If OK, remove starter for repair.
4. Bat. Pos. at Battery and 1	.7 volts or more	Check positive cable terminals for clean, tight connections and condition of cable. Check fusible link (solenoid to generator harness).
	Under .7 volts	Check battery ground cable condition and connections.
5. 9 and G (Key in Start)	7 volts or more	Check purple wire from ignition switch through engine/generator to starter solenoid for open/loose connections.
	Under 7 volts	Go to test 6.
6. 2 and G	7 volts or more	Replace ignition switch.
	Under 7 volts	Check battery wire (red) from ignition switch through engine/generator dash connector to splice for open/loose connection.

VOLTMETER CONNECTIONS	VOLTAGE READING	CORRECTION

STARTER RUNS (SPINS), ENGINE DOES NOT CRANK

Check flywheel gear teeth. If OK, remove starter for repair.

IGNITION MISS OR WILL NOT START (CRANKS OK)

Make a secondary output check (except diesel) using a calibrated spark gap or out-put meter. HEI system should produce at least 25,000 volts (25KV) cranking or engine idling. If not, follow procedure below. If satisfactory, check spark plugs, spark plug cables, distributor cap and rotor.

If car will not start, make voltage checks cranking. If it will start, make checks running. Both cranking and running voltages are given.

VOLTMETER CONNECTIONS	VOLTS CRANKING	VOLTS IDLING
1. 6 and G (Except Diesel)	7 or more	9.6 or more—Check HEI distributor.
	Under 7	Under 9.6—Go to test 2.
2. 4 and G	7 or more	9.6 or more—7 volts or more at HEI battery terminal, check the HEI distributor (fuel solenoid on diesel).
	Under 7	Under 9.6—Go to test 3.
3. 5 and G	7 or more	9.6 or more—Check for open circuit or loose connection in wire from bat. terminal on distributor (fuel solenoid on diesel) through engine dash connector to ignition switch.
	Under 7	Under 9.6—Replace ignition switch.

ALTERNATOR WARNING LIGHT "ON" ENGINE RUNNING

1. Check alternator belt, adjust or replace as needed.
2. Check gauges/trans. fuse, if blown check for short circuit in pink dbl. wht. str. wire from fuse panel to instrument cluster and/or trunk release.
3. Remove 2 wire connector from alternator, if warning light turns off remove alternator for repair. If warning light stays on, check for short circuit in brown wire from alternator connector through engine dash connector to instrument cluster connector (alternator warning, light circuit).

LOW BATTERY, BUT ALTERNATOR LIGHT INDICATES NO PROBLEM

1. Adjust or replace alternator belt as needed.
2. Charge battery.
3. Run engine at 1500 to 2000 RPM for one minute with lights on high beam, heater on high, radio and defogger blower on.

1 and G	Under 12.5 volts	Remove alternator for repair.
	12.5 volts or more	Check for battery drain and driving habits. If no defect is found, make alternator output check.

OVERCHARGING

1. Connect voltmeter to terminal 1 and G. Run engine at 1500 to 2000 RPM until voltmeter reaches maximum, do NOT run engine more than one minute.

1 and G	15.5 or more	Remove alternator for repair.
	Under 15.5 volts	Check for extended driving conditions in hot weather.

Fig. 3 Engine electrical wiring circuit. 1979—83 models

CHEVROLET CHEVETTE

Electrical Diagnosis

This vehicle is equipped with either one or two "Master Electrical Connectors," Fig. 4. One connector is the "Engine Electrical Master Diagnostic Connector" and the other is the "Air Conditioning Electrical Master Diagnostic Connector." These connectors are used to diagnose electrical malfunctions in the air conditioning, charging, cranking and ignition systems.

CAUTION: When performing any of the following tests, ensure transmission is in Neutral on manual transmission models or Park on automatic transmission models. Also, fully apply the parking brake.

Engine Electrical Diagnostic Tests, Fig. 5

NOTE: The following tests are performed with a 14 gauge jumper wire and the ignition switch in the "Off" position.

A/C

ENGINE ELECTRICAL

Fig. 4 ' Master electrical diagnostic connector locations

Starter Does Not Crank Or Cranks Slowly

Test T-1
1. Connect jumper wire between terminal Nos. 1 and 8.
2. If malfunction remains there may be an open wire between terminal No. 8 and the starter solenoid "S" terminal, a faulty connection at the starter solenoid "S" terminal or a poor connection at battery or starter. If the wiring and connections are satisfactory, the starter solenoid may be defective.
3. If starter cranks in step 1, proceed to Test T-2.

Test T-2
1. Connect jumper wire between terminals Nos. 1 and 9.
2. If malfunction remains, the neutral starter switch may be defective or faulty neutral starter switch wiring.
3. If starter cranks in step 1, the ignition switch may be defective or improperly connected.

Engine Cranks But Will Not Start

Test T-3
1. Check for ignition output by removing a spark plug wire, insert an extension into the boot and crank engine while holding the spark plug wire with insulated pliers

Fig. 5   Engine electrical diagnostic test connections

approximately 1/4 inch (6 mm) from engine block.
2. If spark is noted in step 1, the malfunction is not in ignition system (excluding the spark plugs).
3. If no spark occurs in step 1, proceed to Test T-4.

Test T-4
1. Connect jumper wire between terminals Nos. 1 and 4 and crank engine.
2. If engine starts, the ignition switch may be defective or not connected properly.
3. If engine does not start in step 1, proceed to Test T-5.

Test T-5
1. Connect jumper wire between terminal No. 1 and the ignition coil primary feed terminal and crank engine.
2. If engine starts, there is an open wire between test terminal No. 4 and the coil or a faulty coil connection.
3. If engine does not start, the H.E.I. system is malfunctioning.

FUEL ECONOMY & AUTO CARE GUIDE

INTRODUCTION

This chapter has been compiled for the absolute novice in auto care. It will enable you to perform routine chores on your car that will result in dollar savings, greater fuel economy, and provide the satisfaction of knowing that you have had a hand in keeping your car in a safe operating condition. Many of the parts required to perform these chores are available at mass merchandisers and certainly at automotive supply stores. Things such as antifreeze and engine oil can even be found on the shelves of many supermarket food stores. Using this information, you can join the millions of car owners who are doing some of their own car maintenance.

Keep in mind that fuel economy is dependent upon two factors: the vehicle mechanical condition and the driver's technique. Both these factors are controllable by the driver. Make sure that the vehicle is kept in optimum mechanical operating condition. Be alert to changes in power and performance. Change driving habits to achieve maximum fuel economy from the vehicle. This will result in operating a safer vehicle with greater fuel economy.

TUNE-UP
Spark Plug, Replace

Removal

1. Mark all ignition wires since they must be replaced in the same sequence. This can be accomplished in several ways.
   a. Marking tags and attaching them to the ignition wires, according to the engine firing order, front to rear on inline engines, or D1 through D4 on driver's side and P1 through P4 on the passenger side on V8 engines.
   b. Use a white magic marker or nail polish to mark each ignition wire with

FUEL ECONOMY SUGGESTIONS

MECHANICAL

1. Keep engine properly tuned up. An untuned engine will waste fuel and decrease fuel economy.
2. Ensure that front suspension is kept in proper alignment.
3. Check tire inflation. The tires should be inflated to recommended pressures.
4. Keep vehicle properly lubricated. Sufficiently lubricated friction surfaces will enable the vehicle to operate with greater efficiency.
5. Adjust dragging brakes. Make sure that service and parking brakes are properly adjusted to aid in achieving greater fuel economy.
6. Installing radial tires decreases rolling resistance, improving fuel economy.
7. Check condition of cooling system. An engine is most efficient at proper operating temperature.

DRIVER TECHNIQUE

1. Avoid jack rabbit starts. Accelerate gradually where possible.
2. Avoid sudden stops. Try to anticipate stops. Sudden stopping wastes the forward energy of the vehicle and will use more fuel to reach the previous desired speed.
3. Avoid prolonged idling. Also, try to avoid rush hour driving.
4. Make one long trip rather than several short ones.
5. Shift into high gear as soon as possible without damaging the engine or transmission.
6. Keep within speed limits.
7. Don't use brake or clutch pedal as a foot rest.
8. Driving with the air conditioning "On" will decrease fuel economy.
9. If equipped, use speed or cruise control wherever possible.
10. Driving with the windows closed streamlines the vehicle and improves fuel economy.
11. Avoid carrying unnecessary loads in the trunk. Additional weight adversely affects fuel economy.
12. Installing a dash-mounted vacuum gauge and maintaining maximum possible reading (high vacuum) during acceleration and cruise conditions will help in achieving greater fuel economy.
13. Select a grade of fuel that will not produce pre-ignition and detonation, or otherwise damage the engine. Don't buy unnecessary octane.

Typical tool kit necessary to perform the maintenance procedures in this section

Typical engine compartment

1—897

GAP BRIDGED	OIL FOULED	CARBON FOULED
IDENTIFIED BY DEPOSIT BUILD-UP CLOSING GAP BETWEEN ELECTRODES. CAUSED BY OIL OR CARBON FOULING. IF DEPOSITS ARE NOT EXCESSIVE, THE PLUG CAN BE CLEANED.	IDENTIFIED BY WET BLACK DEPOSITS ON THE INSULATOR SHELL BORE ELECTRODES CAUSED BY EXCESSIVE OIL ENTERING COMBUSTION CHAMBER THROUGH WORN RINGS AND PISTONS, EXCESSIVE CLEARANCE BETWEEN VALVE GUIDES AND STEMS, OR WORN OR LOOSE BEARINGS. CAN BE CLEANED IF ENGINE IS NOT REPAIRED, USE A HOTTER PLUG.	IDENTIFIED BY BLACK, DRY FLUFFY CARBON DEPOSITS ON INSULATOR TIPS, EXPOSED SHELL SURFACES AND ELECTRODES. CAUSED BY TOO COLD A PLUG, WEAK IGNITION, DIRTY AIR CLEANER, DEFECTIVE FUEL PUMP, TOO RICH A FUEL MIXTURE, IMPROPERLY OPERATING HEAT RISER OR EXCESSIVE IDLING. CAN BE CLEANED.
WORN	NORMAL	LEAD FOULED
IDENTIFIED BY SEVERELY ERODED OR WORN ELECTRODES. CAUSED BY NORMAL WEAR. SHOULD BE REPLACED	IDENTIFIED BY LIGHT TAN OR GRAY DEPOSITS ON THE FIRING TIP. CAN BE CLEANED.	IDENTIFIED BY DARK GRAY, BLACK, YELLOW OR TAN DEPOSITS OR A FUSED GLAZED COATING ON THE INSULATOR TIP. CAUSED BY HIGHLY LEADED GASOLINE. CAN BE CLEANED.
PRE-IGNITION	OVERHEATING	FUSED SPOT DEPOSIT
IDENTIFIED BY MELTED ELECTRODES AND POSSIBLY BLISTERED INSULATOR. METALLIC DEPOSITS ON INSULATOR INDICATE ENGINE DAMAGE. CAUSED BY WRONG TYPE OF FUEL, INCORRECT IGNITION TIMING OR ADVANCE, TOO HOT A PLUG, BURNT VALVES OR ENGINE OVERHEATING. REPLACE THE PLUG.	IDENTIFIED BY A WHITE OR LIGHT GRAY INSULATOR WITH SMALL BLACK OR GRAY BROWN SPOTS AND WITH BLUISH-BURNT APPEARANCE OF ELECTRODES, CAUSED BY ENGINE OVERHEATING. WRONG TYPE OF FUEL, LOOSE SPARK PLUGS, TOO HOT A PLUG, LOW FUEL PUMP PRESSURE OR INCORRECT IGNITION TIMING. REPLACE THE PLUG.	IDENTIFIED BY MELTED OR SPOTTY DEPOSITS RESEMBLING BUBBLES OR BLISTERS. CAUSED BY SUDDEN ACCELERATION. CAN BE CLEANED.

Fig. 1   Spark plug condition chart

Fig. 2   Distributor cap removal

a white spot. One spot for the first wire, two spots for the second and so on.

2. Remove the spark plug wires from the spark plugs by twisting the boot approximately 1/4-turn, and freeing it from spark plug.
3. Pull wire off by the boot only. Pulling on wires may cause internal breakage.
4. Before loosening plug, blow out loose dirt adjacent to spark plug. If a compressed air supply is not available, you can accomplish this by blowing through a soda straw or a rubber hose.
5. Install the proper size spark plug socket (13/16-inch or 5/8-inch) onto a spark plug. Attach ratchet wrench to socket and turn counterclockwise. Loosen all spark plugs approximately one turn, breaking loose any accumulated carbon adjacent to the spark plugs.

Inspection

Referring to Fig. 1, inspect spark plug and correct any condition causing the abnormal spark plug condition.

Installation

The spark plug should be regapped to the exact specification given by the auto manufacturer. Always use a round wire type gauge. Refer to the "Tune-Up Service" section elsewhere in this book.

Torque spark plug to specifications as listed in the "Engine Tightening Specification" tables in the individual car chapters.

Distributor Cap, Replace

Remove the distributor cap. The distributor cap is retained either by latches, or bale clips, Fig. 2. To remove the first type, depress the latches using a flat screwdriver, then turn the latches one half turn in either direction and lift the cap off the distributor. To remove the second type, insert a flat screwdriver between the bale clip and distributor cap, and pry the clips to disengage them from the cap and lift the cap off the distributor. Inspect condition of cap, Fig. 3, and clean or replace as necessary.

Distributor Rotor, Replace

All distributor rotors except those used on General Motors engines may be removed by simply pulling them upward from the shaft. On General Motors engines, it is necessary to remove the two screws that secures the rotor to the top of the shaft and advance mechanism.

When installing the rotor on all distributors except those used on General Motors V8 engines, align the notch on the shaft with the locating tab inside the open end of the rotor, then slide the rotor onto the shaft. Make sure that the rotor is firmly seated on the shaft.

Rotors used on General Motors engines incorporate two locating dowels on the underside of the rotor. Note that one dowel is square while the other one is round. When installing the rotor, be sure to engage these locating dowels in the proper locating holes, square hole for square dowel and round hole for round dowel. Tighten the retaining screws, however, not too tight since the rotor may crack.

Breaker Points & Condenser, Replace

American Motors 4-121 Engine

1. Remove air cleaner.
2. Remove distributor cap with ignition wires attached and position aside.
3. Remove rotor by pulling upward with even pressure.
4. Remove dust shield.
5. Disconnect breaker point lead from connector.
6. Disconnect primary ignition lead from distributor connector. Remove retaining screw, then the connector and condenser assembly.
7. Install new connector and condenser assembly. Ensure that rubber grommet is properly positioned in square hole of distributor wall. Connect primary ignition lead.
8. Remove point assembly retaining screw.
9. Remove point assembly from plate.
10. Wipe distributor cam clean and inspect.
11. Install replacement points. Ensure that pivot pin is properly seated in pivot hole.
12. Install retaining screw. Do not tighten.
13. Rotate engine in direction of normal rota-

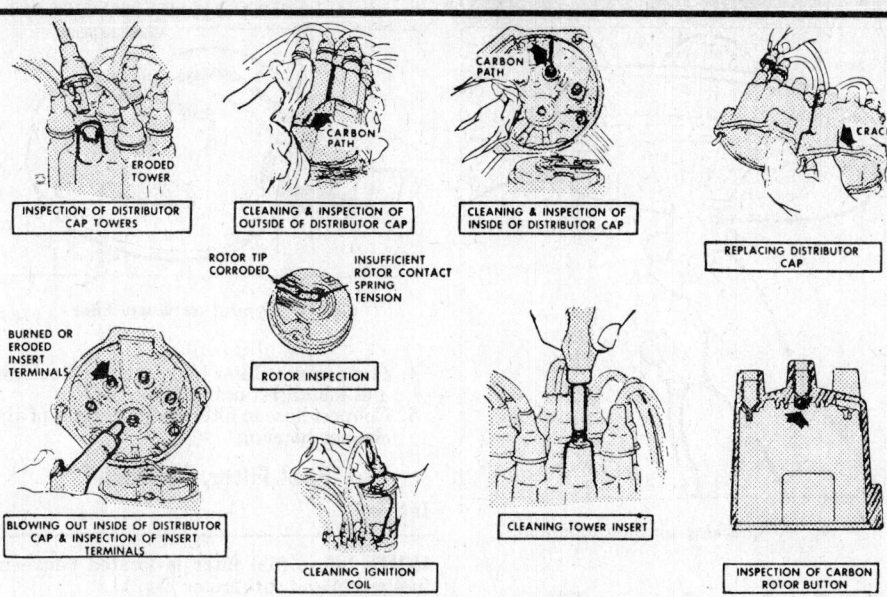

INSPECTION OF DISTRIBUTOR CAP TOWERS

CLEANING & INSPECTION OF OUTSIDE OF DISTRIBUTOR CAP

CLEANING & INSPECTION OF INSIDE OF DISTRIBUTOR CAP

REPLACING DISTRIBUTOR CAP

ROTOR TIP CORRODED

INSUFFICIENT ROTOR CONTACT SPRING TENSION

ROTOR INSPECTION

BURNED OR ERODED INSERT TERMINALS

BLOWING OUT INSIDE OF DISTRIBUTOR CAP & INSPECTION OF INSERT TERMINALS

CLEANING IGNITION COIL

CLEANING TOWER INSERT

INSPECTION OF CARBON ROTOR BUTTON

Fig. 3 Inspecting and cleaning distributor cap

HIGH POINT OF CAM

TAB ON BREAKER PLATE

RUBBING BLOCK

ADJUSTMENT SLOT

Fig. 4 Replacing breaker points. American Motors 4-121

tion until rubbing block is positioned on high point of cam lobe, Fig. 4.

14. Adjust gap to specifications. Refer to "Tune Up Service" chapter. Tighten retaining screw.
15. Apply high temperature distributor cam lubricant to one lobe of cam. A small bead of lubricant is sufficient.
16. Attach point assembly wire lead to connector.
17. Install dust cover and rotor. Be sure rotor seats properly on shaft.
18. Install distributor cap.
19. Install air cleaner.

LUBRICATION, OIL CHANGE, FILTERS & PCV VALVE SERVICE

Engine Oil & Filter Change

NOTE: Engine oil and filter should be changed at intervals recommended by the vehicle manufacturer.

1. Operate engine and allow to reach operating temperature, then turn ignition off.
2. Place drain pan under engine oil pan, then using a suitable wrench remove drain plug, Fig. 5.
3. Allow engine oil to thoroughly drain into pan, then replace drain plug.

NOTE: Do not overtighten drain plug, it can strip the threads in oil pan very easily.

4. If oil filter is to be replaced, position drain pan under filter, then install oil filter wrench and remove filter by turning counter clockwise, Fig. 6.

NOTE: Ensure old oil filter gasket is not on the filter adapter on the engine. Clean adapter before installing new filter.

5. Coat new oil filter gasket with engine oil, then position filter on adapter, Fig. 7. Hand tighten filter until gasket contacts adapter face, then tighten filter one additional turn. Wipe filter and adapter with a clean cloth.

NOTE: Ensure gasket is in position on filter before tightening. Do not use oil filter wrench to tighten filter, hand tighten only.

6. Remove oil filler cap and add quantity of oil specified by manufacturer. Then install filler cap.

NOTE: Only add oil that meets the vehicle manufacturers specifications.

7. Start engine and check to ensure that oil filter and drain plug are not leaking, then turn ignition off.
8. Check oil level to ensure crankcase is full but not overfilled, add oil as necessary.

NOTE: Do not bring oil level above "Full" mark on dipstick; overfilling could result in damage to engine gaskets or seals causing leaks.

Air Filter, Replace

All Exc. General Motors 4-140 Engine
1. Remove wing nut, hex nut or other attaching hardware that secures the air cleaner lid. On some models, the air cleaner lid is also secured by clips on the

Fig. 5 Removing and installing oil pan drain plug (typical)

Fig. 6 Oil filter removal (typical)

Coat Gasket With Engine Oil

Fig. 7 Oil filter installation (typical)

Fig. 8   Replacing air filter (typical)

sides of the housing that must be disengaged, Fig. 8.
2. Remove air cleaner lid from housing assembly and lift out air filter element.

NOTE: To check air filter condition, hold a light behind the element, Fig. 9. If no light can be seen through the element, the filter is excessively dirty and must be replaced.

3. Wipe out housing with a clean rag. Be sure not to allow dirt or other foreign material to enter the carburetor.
4. Install new air filter element, Fig. 8.
5. Install lid onto housing assembly and secure with the attaching hardware previously removed.

General Motors 4-140 Engine

1. Remove bolt or nuts securing air cleaner assembly to carburetor.
2. Pull vent pipe from air cleaner. This is the pipe running between the air cleaner and the cam cover (rocker cover).
3. Remove air cleaner assembly from carburetor and discard.
4. Install new air cleaner assembly and secure with bolt or nuts previously removed.

Fig. 11   Typical location of in-line fuel filter

Fig. 9   Checking air filter condition

Crankcase Emission Filter

American Motors 6 Cyl. & All Ford Motor Co., Fig. 10.

1. Remove top of air cleaner housing.
2. Remove filter pack from filter retainer and clean out retainer.
3. Install new filter in retainer.
4. Install top of air cleaner.

American Motors V8

This filter is located in the sealed oil filler cap. The filter must be cleaned at mileage intervals recommended by the manufacturer by applying light air pressure in reverse direction of normal flow then lightly oil the filter with clean engine oil. If the filter is deteriorated, the oil filler cap must be replaced.

Chrysler Corp.

This filter must be cleaned at mileage intervals recommended by the manufacturer. Disconnect hose from filter and remove filter by pulling it out of the valve cover. Clean filter in kerosene or similar solvent, then lubricate filter by filling it with clean SAE 30 engine oil and inverting it to allow excess oil to drain out. Reinstall filter in valve cover and reconnect hose.

General Motors, All, Fig. 10

1. Remove top of air cleaner housing.
2. Disconnect hose from filter which leads to valve cover.
3. Remove clip which retains filter to air cleaner housing and remove filter.

Fig. 12   Removing fuel hose from fuel filter (typical)

Fig. 10   Typical crankcase filter

4. Position new filter in air cleaner housing and install retaining clip.
5. Connect hose to filter and install top of air cleaner housing.

Fuel Filter, Replace

Inline

NOTE: Inline fuel filter is located between fuel pump and carburetor Fig. 11.

1. Remove air cleaner, if necessary.
2. Loosen fuel hose clamps, then disconnect hoses and remove fuel filter Fig. 12.

NOTE: On some models, fuel filter may be attached to carburetor of fuel line tubing. On these models use suitable wrench to remove filter.

3. Reverse procedure to install, then start engine and check for fuel leaks.

NOTE: Before installing, refer to fuel filter body markings, which indicate the direction in which the fuel filter should be installed.

In-Carburetor

NOTE: The carburetor fuel filter is located in carburetor housing where fuel inlet line is connected to carburetor.

1. Remove air cleaner.
2. Position back up wrench on fuel filter fitting, then using a suitable wrench disconnect fuel inlet line Fig. 13.
3. Remove fuel filter fitting, filter and spring from carburetor.
4. Position spring and filter into carburetor, then install gasket and fitting.

Fig. 13   Disconnecting fuel line

Fig. 14 PCV valve replacement (typical)

NOTE: Position fuel filter in carburetor with open end facing fitting.

5. With back up wrench on fuel filter fitting, carefully connect and tighten fuel inlet line using a suitable wrench Fig. 13.
6. Start engine and check for leaks, then install air cleaner.

PCV Valve, Replace

NOTE: To check PCV valve, remove valve from grommet and shake valve. A metallic clicking noise should be heard, indicating valve is free. If valve does not move freely, it should be replaced. Do not attempt to clean valve.

1. Remove PCV valve from grommet, then disconnect hose, Fig. 14.

NOTE: On American Motors models, PCV valve is located on valve cover on 6 cylinder engine and on intake manifold on V8 engine. On Chrysler Corp. models, valve is located on valve cover. On Ford Motor Co. models, valve is located in PCV valve hose on 2300cc engine, on carburetor spacer on V6 engine, on valve cover on inline 6 cylinder engine and in oil filler cap on V8 engine. On General Motors Corp. models, valve is located on valve cover on 4 cylinder and inline 6 cylinder engines, on intake manifold on V6 engines and on valve cover or intake manifold on V8 engines, depending on model.

2. Install new PCV valve on grommet and connect hose.

NOTE: Ensure valve is properly seated in grommet.

Chassis Lubricating

The first time you do a grease job you will spend much of the time looking for the fittings Figs. 15 and 16.

As you find a fitting, wipe it off with a clean rag. This will help you spot it later and also prevent you from injecting dirt with the grease.

The injection tip of the grease gun should be a catch fit on the fitting nipple. That is, once in place it will not slip off. Slight, straight-on pressure is all that is necessary for the gun tip to engage the fitting. Once that is done, pump the handle. Follow the recommendations below to ensure proper lubrication and also prevent damage to the seals:

American Motors and Ford:
Pump slowly until the rubber boot can be felt or seen to swell slightly.

Chrysler Corp. and General Motors:
Pump slowly until grease starts to flow from bleed holes at the base of the seals, or until the seals start to swell.

NOTE: If the fitting fails to take grease, the lubricant will ooze out between fitting and the top of the gun. Do not just keep pumping, hoping some grease is getting in, or you will have a mess. It is normal for a bit of grease to seep out. But if the fitting is obviously not taking grease, it should be replaced.

Repacking Front Wheel Bearings

1. Remove inner and outer bearings as outlined in car chapters.
2. Clean old lubricant from hub and spindle.
3. Clean inner and outer bearings and bearing races with kerosene.

NOTE: Ensure all of old lubricant is removed before repacking. Allow bearings and races to dry thoroughly. Do not use compressed air to clean bearings.

Fig. 15 Identifying fittings (typical). If vehicle is equipped with plugs, the plugs must be removed and a grease fitting installed prior to lubricating

4. Inspect cones, rollers and races for cracks, nicks and wear and replace as necessary.

NOTE: Bearings and race must be replaced as a unit.

5. Place a small amount of wheel bearing grease in palm of hand, then force grease into large end of roller cage until grease protrudes from small end, Fig. 17.

NOTE: Use only wheel bearing grease that meets the vehicle manufacturers specifications.

6. Lubricate remaining bearings in the same manner, then install and adjust bearings as outlined in car chapter.

NOTE: Apply a light film of grease to lips of grease retainer before installing.

CHECKING & MAINTAINING FLUID LEVELS

NOTE: When checking fluid levels, ensure vehicle is on a level surface. If vehicle is not level, an accurate fluid level reading cannot be obtained.

Fig. 16 Typical fitting locations

Fig. 17 Repacking front wheel bearings

Fig. 18 Replacing thermostat (typical)

Engine Oil Level

1. Warm up engine, then turn ignition off and allow a few minutes for oil to return to crankcase.
2. Remove dipstick and wipe off.
3. Replace dipstick and ensure it is seated in tube.
4. Remove dipstick and inspect to see if oil level is between "Add" and "Full" marks.

NOTE: Add oil only if level is at or below "Add" mark.

5. If oil level is at "Add" mark, one quart of oil will bring level to "Full" mark. If oil level is below "Add" mark, add oil as necessary to bring level between Add & Full marks.

NOTE: Do not bring oil level above "Full" mark, overfilling of crankcase could result in damage to engine gaskets and seals causing leaks. Only add oil that meets the vehicle manufacturers specifications.

6. Replace dipstick.

Battery

1. Remove filler cap and check fluid level in each cell.

NOTE: Keep flame and sparks away from top of battery, otherwise combustible gases present may explode. Do not allow battery electrolyte to contact skin, eyes, fabric or painted surfaces. Flush contacted area with water immediately and thoroughly and seek medical attention if necessary. Wear eye protection when working on or near battery. Do not wear rings or other metal jewelry when working on or near battery.

2. Add water as required to bring fluid level of each cell up to split ring located at bottom of filler well.

NOTE: In areas where water is known to be hard or have a high mineral or alkali

content, distilled water must be used. If water is added during freezing weather, the vehicle should be driven several miles afterwards to mix the water and battery electrolyte.

3. Install filler caps.

Cooling System

NOTE: Add only permanent type anti-freeze that meets the vehicle manufacturers specifications.

CAUTION: Never add large quantities of water into radiator if car has overheated without the engine cooled off or if necessary to service at this time start engine and add water to coolant slowly. This will avoid damage to the engine.

Less Coolant Recovery System

NOTE: Avoid checking coolant level if engine is hot. If coolant level must be checked when engine is hot, muffle radiator cap with a thick cloth, then turn cap counter clockwise until pressure starts to escape. After pressure has been completely relieved, finish removing cap.

1. With engine cold, remove radiator cap and inspect coolant level.
2. Coolant level should be approximately 1 inch below bottom of filler neck.
3. Add solution of 50% water-50% antifreeze as required.
4. Install radiator cap.

With Coolant Recovery System

NOTE: On these type systems do not remove radiator cap to check coolant level.

1. Start engine and allow to reach operating temperature.
2. Visually inspect coolant level in plastic reservoir.
3. On all models except Chrysler Corp. vehicles, coolant level should be between "Full" and "Add" marks or at "Full Hot" mark, depending on reservoir. On Chrysler Corp. vehicles, coolant level should be between the one and two quart marks with engine operating at idle speed.
4. Remove reservoir filler cap and add solution of 50% water-50% antifreeze as required.
5. Install reservoir filler cap.

Brake Master Cylinder Reservoir

1. Clean master cylinder reservoir cover, then using a screw driver unsnap retainer(s) and remove cover.

NOTE: Do not hold cover over vehicle, otherwise brake fluid may damage finish.

2. Brake fluid level should be ¼ inch from top of master cylinder reservoir.

NOTE: If brake fluid level is excessively low, the brake linings should be inspected for wear and brake system checked for leaks. Fluid level in reservoirs servicing

Fig. 19 Checking anti-freeze protection level (typical)

disc brakes will decrease as disc brake pads wear.

3. Add brake fluid as required.

NOTE: Only add brake fluid that meets the vehicle manufacturers specifications. Use only brake fluid that has been in a tightly closed container to prevent contamination from dirt and moisture. Do not allow petroleum base fluids to contaminate brake fluid, otherwise seal damage may result.

4. Install cover and snap retainer into place.

NOTE: Ensure retainer is locked into cover grooves.

Power Steering Pump Reservoir

1. Start engine and allow to reach operating temperature, and turn ignition off.
2. Clean area around filler cap or dipstick, then remove filler cap or dipstick and inspect fluid level.
3. Fluid level should be between "Full" mark and end of dipstick.

NOTE: On models without dipstick, fluid level should be half way up filler neck.

4. Add fluid as necessary, then install filler cap or dipstick.

NOTE: Only add fluid recommended by the vehicle manufacturer.

Fig. 20   Radiator cap (typical)

Automatic Transmission

1. Firmly apply parking brake, then start and run engine for approximately 10 minutes to bring transmission fluid to operating temperature.

NOTE: Do not run engine in unventilated area. Exhaust gases contain carbon monoxide which could be deadly in unventilated areas.

2. With engine running at idle speed, shift selector lever through all positions, then place lever in Neutral on American Motors and Chrysler Corp. vehicles and in Park on Ford Motor Co. and General Motors Corp. vehicles.
3. Clean dipstick cap, then remove dipstick and wipe off.
4. Replace dipstick and ensure it is seated in tube.
5. Remove dipstick and inspect to see if fluid level is between "Add" and "Full" marks.

NOTE: Add fluid only if level is at or below "Add" mark.

6. If fluid level is at "Add" mark, one pint of transmission fluid will bring level to "Full" mark. If fluid level is below "Add" mark, add fluid as necessary to bring level between "Add" and "Full" marks. Transmission fluid is added through the dipstick tube.

NOTE: Do not bring level above "Full" mark, overfilling could result in damage to transmission. Only add automatic transmission fluid of type and specification recommended by the vehicle manufacturer.

7. Replace dipstick and ensure it is seated in tube.

Manual Transmission

1. Set Parking brake and block wheels.
2. Clean area around filler plug, then using a suitable wrench or ratchet remove filler plug.
3. Fluid should be level with bottom of filler plug hole.
4. Add fluid as required, then install filler plug.

NOTE: Only add lubricant recommended by the vehicle manufacturer.

Rear Axle

1. Set parking brake and block wheels.
2. Clean area around filler plug, then using a suitable ratchet remove filler plug.
3. Fluid level should be approximately 1/2 inch below bottom of filler plug hole.
4. Add fluid as required, then install filler plug.

Only add lubricant recommended by the vehicle manufacturer. Do not add conventional axle type lubricant to models equipped with Anti Spin, Controlled, Limited Slip, Positraction, Sure Grip, Traction Lok or Twin Grip axles. A special lubricant must be added to these type axles, refer to vehicle manufacturers recommendations.

COOLING SYSTEM SERVICE

CAUTION: Do not attempt to perform any system servicing when the engine is hot or the

Fig. 21   Radiator cap with pressure release mechanism (typical)

cooling system is pressurized. Even a simple operation such as removing the radiator cap should be avoided since personal injury and loss of coolant may result.

Draining The System

Most cooling systems incorporate a radiator petcock usually located on the engine side of the radiator at either of the lower corners. Some radiator petcocks are located on the side of the radiator. Also, some cooling systems are not equipped with a radiator petcock.
1. Place a suitable container under radiator to catch coolant.
2. On systems equipped with a radiator petcock, turn the tangs (ears) to open the petcock. However, do not apply excessive pressure in either direction since damage to the petcock may result as some petcocks turn clockwise and others counterclockwise to open.
3. On systems not equipped with a radiator petcock, it will be necessary to remove the lower hose from the radiator.
4. Dispose of coolant.

Flushing The System

There are two flushing methods which can be performed without the use of special equipment. One method outlined below requires the use of a garden hose only. The second method requires the use of the garden hose and a "Tee" fitting spliced into one of the heater hoses. The "Tee" fitting and other items and instructions needed to perform this type

Fig. 22   Factory installed coolant recovery system (typical)

Fig. 23   Aftermarket coolant recovery system installation (typical)

Fig. 24   Cleaning hose connections

Fig. 25 Core plug locations (typical)

of flushing are available by aftermarket manufacturers.

1. With cooling system drained, remove thermostat as outlined below:
   a. To locate the thermostat housing on all engines except on Ford V6 engines, follow the upper radiator hose from the radiator to the engine block. On Ford V6 engines, follow the lower radiator hose from the radiator to the engine block. The point at which these hoses connect is the thermostat housing.
   b. The thermostat housing is usually retained by two bolts or nuts. Remove these bolts or nuts and remove the housing.
   c. Lift the thermostat from the mounting flange, Fig. 18, noting the position that it was installed. This is important to avoid reinstalling the thermostat upside down.
   d. Reinstall thermostat housing, however, do not reinstall thermostat. Tighten retaining bolts.
2. Insert garden hose into radiator filler opening, open radiator petcock and turn on water.
3. Start engine and run engine for a few minutes. This should flush out any loose

SMALL CRACKS on the underside can be enlarged for inspection by flexing the belt. Cracks expose the interior to damage and belts can break without warning.

GREASE rots ordinary rubber belts, making the belt sides slick and causing slippage. (V-belts with Neoprene are resistant to grease.)

GLAZED belts with hard surfaces slip causing overheating and low battery voltage, in the case of alternator belts.

ALWAYS CHECK the underside of the belt. Split belts may appear sound from the top, but sides and bottom may be severely split and ready to fail.

Fig. 27 Drive belt inspection

particles in the system.
4. Turn off engine and remove the garden hose.
5. Remove thermostat housing. Thoroughly clean the thermostat housing and engine surfaces of old gasket and sealer. This is necessary to prevent leakage between the housing and engine surfaces.
6. Install new thermostat housing gasket and the thermostat. Make certain that the thermostat is installed exactly in the same position as it was removed.
7. Install thermostat housing and tighten retaining bolts and nuts.
8. Allow radiator to drain.
9. Close radiator petcock, if equipped.
10. Remove coolant overflow tank, if equipped. Thoroughly clean the inside of the tank and reinstall.

Refilling The System

1. Determine the amount of anti-freeze required to achieve a 50/50 solution in the cooling system. Refer to the "Cooling System & Capacity Data" tables in the individual car chapters. Take the total number of quarts listed in the tables and divide by two. This number is the amount of anti-freeze, in quarts, required to achieve the 50/50 solution. This solution will generally provide protection to -35 degrees F. Fig. 19 illustrates a typical anti-freeze hydrometer.
2. Add the amount of anti-freeze to the radiator that was determined in the preceding step. If radiator fills before required amount of anti-freeze is installed, start engine and turn on heater. Add the anti-freeze as the coolant level sinks in the radiator.
3. Continue to run engine with the radiator cap removed until the upper radiator hose becomes hot to the touch.
4. Top up the coolant level in the radiator to the bottom of the filler neck with a 50/50 mixture of anti-freeze and water.
5. If equipped with an overflow tank, add a 50/50 mixture of anti-freeze and water to the cold level as marked on the side of the tank.

Radiator Cap

The radiator filler cap contains a pressure relief valve and a vacuum relief valve, Fig. 20. The pressure relief valve is held against its seat by a spring, which when compressed, allows excessive pressure to be relieved out the radiator overflow. The vacuum valve is also held against its seat by a spring which when compressed opens the valve to relieve the vacuum created when the system cools.

NOTE: Some aftermarket radiator caps incorporate a pressure release mechanism to relieve cooling system pressure before rotating cap, Fig. 21.

The radiator cap should be washed with clean water and pressure checked at regular tune-up intervals. Inspect rubber seal on cap for tears or cracks. If the pressure cap will not hold pressure or does not release at the proper pressure replace the cap.

Coolant Recovery System

The coolant recovery system supplements the standard cooling system in that additional coolant is available from a plastic reservoir, Fig. 22.

Fig. 26 Checking belt tension with a tension gauge

As the coolant is heated it expands within the cooling system and overflows into the plastic reservoir. As the engine cools the coolant contracts and is drawn back into the radiator by vacuum. Thus, the radiator is filled to capacity at all times, resulting in increased cooling efficiency.

Air or vapor entering the system will be forced to the reservoir under the coolant and exits through the reservoir cap.

A special radiator cap is designed to discourage inadvertent removal. The finger grips have been eliminated thereby presenting a round configuration.

Overflow Kit

If your car does not have an overflow reservoir, it is easy enough to retrofit one. Many kits priced at under $5 are available, Fig. 23. A kit should include the following:
1. A clear plastic reservoir with quart markings to indicate fluid level.
2. A replacement radiator cap, with an air sealing gasket in the cap's inside perimeter.
3. Necessary hoses and fittings.

Hose Replacement

The radiator, heater and the coolant bypass hoses are held at each end by a clamp. All clamps but the spring design can be loosened with a screwdriver. To save yourself a long walk after you have removed the hose from your radiator or heater, buy the replacement hose and any necessary clamps before starting the job.

Fig. 28 Pivot bolt and adjusting bolt arrangement

Fig. 29 Adjustment bolt and adjustment slot bolt arrangement

Removal

1. Drain the radiator as outlined previously. Use a clean container, large enough to hold the coolant from your cooling system, to save the coolant for refilling the system after replacing the hose. If you are removing the radiator upper hose or heater hoses, you need only drain the radiator. If you are removing the lower hose, also drain the block as follows: disconnect the lower hose at the radiator. Bend it down and use it as a drain spout.
2. Loosen the clamps at each end of the hose to be removed. You can do this quite easily with a screwdriver. If the clamps are old and corroded, they may be stuck to the hose, loosening the screw may not be enough on some designs, in which case you'll have to pry the clamp a bit.

CAUTION: Be very careful when prying under the clamp. The fittings are extremely fragile and might bend or break if too much force is exerted.

If the hose is held by spring clamps, you may be in for a struggle unless you have spring clamp pliers. There are many types of pliers designed for these clamps, including ordinary slip-joint pliers with recesses cut into the jaws to grip each end of the clamp. To release the clamp you must squeeze the ends together, and if you try to use ordinary pliers, the ends may slip off. The best procedure is to discard the spring type and install a wormdrive band clamp, but if you insist on reusing the one you have, at least invest in a pair of special pliers.

3. Twist the hose back and forth to loosen it from the connector. Slide the hose off the connections. If the hose is stuck, shove in a screwdriver and try to pry loose. If the working angle is poor for the screwdriver, or if the hose is really stuck, cut the hose off the neck with a single-edge razor blade. If the hose being removed is dried and cracked and remnants of it remain on either connection, clean the connection thoroughly with a scraper or putty knife.

Installation

1. With the old hose removed, wire brush the hose connections to remove foreign material, Fig. 24.
2. To ease installation, coat hose neck with a soap solution.
3. Slide the hose in position so that it is completely on the neck at each end, to avoid possibility of kinking and to provide room for proper positioning of the clamp. Except for the wormdrive clamp, which can be opened completely, the clamp must be loosely placed over the

hose prior to fitting its end on the neck.
4. Make sure the clamps are beyond the head and placed in the center of the clamping surface of the connections.
5. Tighten the clamps.
6. Refill the cooling system as outlined in the previous procedure on refilling the cooling system.

Cooling System Leaks

If the coolant level must be adjusted frequently, the cooling system may be leaking either internally or externally. To determine if the system is leaking internally, special equipment must be used such as a pressure tester. To determine if the system is leaking externally, check for leakage in the following locations: radiator and its seams, hoses and their connections, heater core, water pump, coolant temperature sending unit, thermostat housing, hot water choke housing, heater water valve, coolant recovery tank and core plugs, Fig. 25.

DRIVE BELTS

Proper belt tension is important not only to minimize noise and prolong belt life, but also to protect the accessories being driven.

Belts which are adjusted too tight may cause failure to the bearing of the accessory which it drives. Also premature wear and breakage of the belt may result. Belts which are too loose will slip on their pulleys and cause a screeching sound. Loose belts can also cause the battery to go dead, the engine to overheat, hard steering (if equipped with power steering) and air conditioner to malfunction.

Drive Belt Tension Gauge

The use of a belt tension gauge will quickly indicate whether a belt is properly adjusted or not. Low cost tension gauges give spot readings while the more expensive ones give continuous readings as the belt tension is adjusted, Fig. 26.

Drive Belt Inspection

All drive belts should be inspected at regular intervals for uneven wear, cuts, fraying and glazing, Fig. 27.

CAUTION: Engine must be off when checking belts.

Drive Belt Tension Adjustment

1. Run engine until it reaches normal oper-

Fig. 31 Checking belt tension without belt tension gauge.

Fig. 30 Loosening adjusting bolt and pivot bolt

ating temperature, then turn engine off.

CAUTION: Do not attempt to check or adjust any drive belt while engine is running. Turn engine off.

2. Using belt tension gauge following manufacturers instructions, check tension of each belt, one at a time, Fig. 26. Refer to individual vehicle chapter for belt tension specifications.
3. If adjustment is necessary, proceed as follows:
   a. Pivot Bolt and Adjusting Bolt, Figs. 28 and 29. Using a suitable wrench, loosen adjusting bolt and pivot bolt, then using a pry bar, move accessory toward or away from engine until tension gauge reaches specified reading. Make sure to tighten bolts before relieving force applied to pry bar.

CAUTION: Do not pry against power steering housing or air pump housing.

   b. Adjusting Bolt and Adjusting Bolt Slots Fig. 30. Loosen adjusting slot bolts, then loosen or tighten adjusting bolt until tension gauge reaches specified reading. Make sure to tighten adjusting slot bolts.
   c. Idler Pulley Pivot Bolt and Adjusting Bolt. Loosen idler pulley pivot bolt and adjusting bolt, then insert a 1/2 inch flex handle into pulley arm slot and apply force on handle until tension gauge reaches specified reading. Make sure to tighten pivot and adjusting bolt before relieving force on handle.
4. To check tension on a belt without a belt tension gauge, proceed as follows:
   a. Place a straight edge along the belt from pulley to pulley, Fig. 31.
   b. Using a ruler, depress belt at midpoint between pulleys. Measure amount of deflection. For belt with a free span of less than 12 inches between pulleys, amount of deflection should be 1/4 inch. For belts with a free span of more than 12 inches between pulleys, amount of deflection should be 1/2 inch.
   c. Adjust belt tension, if necessary as described previously.
5. Recheck belt tension. Readjust if necessary.

Drive Belt Replacement

To replace a belt, loosen the adjusting bolt and pivot bolt. Move accessory as required to obtain maximum slack on belt. Remove belt by lifting off the pulleys and working it around the fan or other accessories, as neces-

FUEL ECONOMY & AUTO CARE GUIDE

Fig. 32 Tire rotation chart

Fig. 33 Tire tread patterns

sary. Sometimes, on multiple belt arrangements, it will be necessary to remove one or more additional belts in order to remove the defective belt. To install belt, reverse the removal procedure and adjust belt tension as described previously.

NOTE: On accessories which are driven by dual belts, it is advisable to replace both belts even if only one needs replacement.

TIRE CARE

Tire Rotation

The purpose of rotation is to equalize normal tire wear. There is such a thing as normal wear. Nothing lasts indefinitely. By equalizing this wear evenly over the entire tread surface, you extend tire life. Recommended rotation patterns are shown in Fig. 32.

It is wise to provide snow tires with rims of their own, so they do not have to be removed from rims in the late fall. They can be kept on rims of their own during both storage and use. In this way, you will protect tires from the bead damage which becomes a possibility when you break a tire away from a rim.

A studded snow tire should always be mounted on the same wheel of the car year after year. When storing studded snow tires mark tire in chalk with either an R for Right or an L for Left, depending upon which side of the car the tire was mounted.

When storing tires, lay them flat, off the tread, and keep them away from electricity-producing machinery. Laying the tire flat keeps the flat spots from developing over the tread. Electricity-producing machinery creates ozone. Ozone damages rubber.

Tire Maintenance

Tires should be inspected regularly for excessive or abnormal tread wear, fabric breaks, cuts or other damage, Fig. 33. A bulge or bump in the sidewall or tread is reason for iscarding a tire. A bulge indicates that the tread or sidewall has separated from the tire body. The tire is a candidate for an imminent blowout. Look also for small stones or other foreign bodies wedged in the tread. These can be removed by prying them out carefully with a screwdriver.

BATTERY SERVICE

Construction & Operation

To understand why batteries malfunction, some knowledge of batteries is important. Simply stated, the battery is constructed of two unlike materials, a positive plate and a negative plate and a porous separator between the two plates, Fig. 34. This assembly placed in a suitable battery case and filled slightly above the top of the plates with electrolyte (sulphuric acid and distilled water) forms a cell. The 12 volt battery is composed of 6 cells interconnected by plate straps. Note that batteries have varying number of plates per cell, but each cell in any given battery has the same number of plates.

The battery performs the following four basic functions in a vehicle:

1. Supplies electrical energy to the starter motor to crank and start the engine and also to the ignition system while the engine is being started.
2. Supplies electrical energy for accessories such as radio, tape deck, heater and also lights when engine is not running and the ignition switch is in the "OFF" or the "Accessory" position.
3. Supplies additional electrical energy for accessories while the engine is running when the output of the alternator is exceeded by the various accessories.
4. The battery also stabilizes voltage in the electrical system. Satisfactory operation of the ignition system and any other electrical device is impossible with a dam-

aged or weak or even underpowered (low rating) battery.

Sealed Batteries

Sealed batteries, otherwise called "Maintenance Free" or "Freedom" batteries, Fig. 35, are available on some vehicles, and can also be purchased from other sources.

The sealed batteries have unique chemistry and construction methods which provide the following advantages:

Water never needs to be added to the battery.

The battery is completely sealed except for two small vent holes on the side. The vent holes allow what small amount of gases are produced in the battery to escape. The special chemical composition inside the battery reduces the production of gas to an extremely small amount at normal charging voltages.

The battery has a very strong ability to withstand damaging effects of overcharge. Also, the terminals are sealed tightly to minimize leakage. A charge indicator in the cover indicates state of charge.

Compared to a conventional battery whose performance decreases steadily with age, the sealed battery delivers more available power at any time during its life. The battery has a reduced tendency to self-discharge as compared to a conventional battery.

Safety Precautions

CAUTION: Electrolyte solution in the battery is a strong and dangerous acid. It is extremely harmful to eyes, skin and clothing. If acid contacts any part of the body, flush immediately with water for a period not less than 15

Fig. 34 Battery construction

Fig. 35 Typical maintenance free battery

Fig. 36 Battery energy versus falling temperature comparison chart

Fig. 37 Checking specific gravity of electrolyte

minutes. If acid is accidentally swallowed, drink large quantities of milk or water, followed by milk of magnesia, a beaten raw egg or vegetable oil and call physician immediately.

Also when batteries are being charged, highly explosive hydrogen and oxygen gases form in each battery cell. Some of this gas escapes through the vent holes in the plugs on top of battery case and forms an explosive atmosphere surrounding the battery. This explosive gas will remain in and/or around the battery for several hours after the battery has been charged. Sparks or flames can ignite this gas and cause a dangerous battery explosion.

The following precautions must be observed to avoid battery explosion, therefore avoiding personal harm and damage to the vehicle's electrical system.
1. Do not smoke near batteries being charged or which have been recently charged. It is a good practice never to smoke near a battery even though the battery is in the vehicle.
2. Always shield your eyes when working with batteries.
3. Do not disconnect live (working) circuits (lights or accessories operating) at the terminals of batteries since sparking usually occurs at a point where such a circuit is disconnected.
4. When connecting or disconnecting booster leads or cable clamps from battery chargers use extreme caution. Make sure the equipment is disconnected before connecting or disconnecting the booster leads or cable clamps. Poor booster lead connections are a common cause of electrical arcing causing battery explosions.

Causes of Discharged Batteries

There are numerous reasons that could cause a battery to discharge and appear to be defective, therefore the battery should not be condemned as the primary source of electrical and/or starting problems before it has been tested.

The following are some of the common causes that could discharge a good battery.
1. Lights left "ON" or doors not closed properly leaving dome light "ON".
2. Excessive use of accessories with the engine not running.
3. Improper installation of aftermarket accessories.
4. Alternator belt loose or damaged.
5. Dirty battery case causing a self-discharge condition.
6. Loose battery cable terminals.
7. Low alternator output.
8. High resistance in charging circuits caused by other loose electrical connections.

Battery Rating & Capacity

The two most commonly used ratings are the 20 hour rating at 80°F. and the cold cranking load capacity of the battery at 0°F, specified in amps. Batteries are also rated by watts (PWR) Peak Watt Rating which is actually the cold cranking ability of the battery at 0°F.

Yet another battery rating method is the reserve capacity rating in minutes. The purpose of this rating is to determine the length of time a vehicle can be operated with a faulty charging system (malfunctioning alternator or regulator). Batteries are normally marketed by the Ampere-Hour rating which is based on the 20 hour rating. The Ampere-

Hour rating is also normally stamped on the battery case or on a label attached to the battery. A battery capable of furnishing 4 amps for a period of 20 hours is classified as a 80 ampere hour battery (4 amps × 20 hours = 80).

The Ampere-Hour rating should not be confused with the cranking performance of a battery at 0°F. Batteries with the same Ampere-Hour ratings can have various 0°F. cranking capacities. The higher quality battery will have a higher Ampere-Hour rating and a higher cranking capacity rating at 0°F. Note that battery capacity will increase with: 1) larger number of plates per cell 2) larger size of plates 3) larger battery case size allowing for more electrolyte solution.

Selecting A Replacement Battery

Long and troublefree service can be more assured when the capacity or wattage rating of the replacement battery is at least equal to the wattage rating of the battery originally engineered for the application by the manufacturer.

The use of an undersize battery may result in poor performance and early failure. Fig. 36 shows how battery power shrinks while the need for engine cranking power increases with falling temperatures. Sub-zero temperatures reduce capacity of a fully charged battery to 45% of its normal power and at the same time increase cranking load to 3½ times the normal warm weather load.

Hot weather can also place excessive electrical loads on the battery. Difficulty in starting may occur when cranking is attempted shortly after a hot engine has been turned off or stalls. High compression engines can be as difficult to start under such conditions as on the coldest winter day. Consequently, good performance can be obtained only if the battery has ample capacity to cope with these conditions.

A battery of greater capacity should be considered if the electrical load has been increased through the addition of accessories

Watt Rating	5 Amperes	10 Amperes	20 Amperes	30 Amperes	40 Amperes	50 Amperes
Below 2450	10 Hours	5 Hours	2½ Hours	2 Hours		
2450–2950	12 Hours	6 Hours	3 Hours	2 Hours	1½ Hours	
Above 2950	15 Hours	7½ Hours	3¼ Hours	2 Hours	1¾ Hours	1½ Hours

Fig. 38 Battery charging guide

Fig. 39   Cleaning battery terminals

4. Connect one end of the other cable to negative (−) terminal of the good battery.
5. Connect the other end of the cable to engine bolthead or similar good contact spot on the vehicle being started.

CAUTION: Never connect to negative terminal of dead battery.

NOTE: To prevent damage to other electrical components on the vehicle being started, make certain that engine is at idle speed before disconnecting jumper cables.

Fig. 40   Frayed insulation causing short circuit between battery cable and body of vehicle

or if driving conditions are such that the generator cannot keep the battery in a charged condition.

On applications where heavy electrical loads are encountered, a higher output generator that will supply a charge during low speed operation may be required to increase battery life and improve battery performance.

Testing Battery (Specific Gravity)

NOTE: The specific gravity of a sealed battery cannot be checked.

A hydrometer can be used to measure the specific gravity of the electrolyte in each cell. There are several types of hydrometers available, the least expensive consists of a glass tube, a rubber bulb at the end of the tube and several balls within the tube, Fig. 37. To use this type, the specific gravity of the battery must be interpreted by the number of balls which float to the surface of the electrolyte and following the manufacturers instructions.

The hydrometer indicates the concentration of the electrolyte.

Boost Starting A Vehicle With A Discharged Battery

1. Be sure that the ignition key is in the off position and that all accessories and lights are off.
2. Shield eyes. Use goggles or similar eye protection.
3. Connect the booster cables from the positive (+) battery terminal of the discharged battery (vehicle to be started) to the positive (+) battery terminal of the vehicle used as the booster.

Charging The Battery

There are two separate methods of recharging batteries which differ basically in the rate of charge.

Slow Charging Method

Slow charging is the best and only method of completely recharging a battery. This method, when properly applied, may be used safely under all possible conditions of the battery providing the electrolyte is at proper level and the battery is capable of being fully charged. The normal charging rate is 5 amperes.

A fully charged battery is indicated when all cell specific gravities do not increase when checked at three one hour intervals and all cells are gassing freely.

Charge periods of 24 hours or more may be required because of the low charging rate. See charging guide Fig. 38.

Quick Charging Method

In order to get a car back on the road in the least amount of time, it is sometimes necessary to quick charge a battery. The battery cannot be brought up to a full charged condition by the quick charge method. It can be substantially recharged or boosted but, in order to bring it to a fully charged condition, the charging cycle must be finished by charging at a low or normal rate. Some quick chargers have a provision for finishing the charging cycle at a low rate to bring the battery up to a fully charged condition.

CAUTION: Too high a current during quick charging will damage battery plates.

Battery Cable Service

NOTE: At regular intervals, perform a visual inspection of the battery.

This inspection should be performed when any of the underhood maintenance items such as engine oil, transmission fluid or radiator coolant level are checked.

1. Clean any heavy accumulation of dirt or corrosion on the battery terminals and battery tray with a wire brush, Fig. 39. Finish cleaning with a solution of baking soda and water. Diluted ammonia can also be used as a washing agent. Thoroughly flush battery with clean water.

NOTE: Baking soda and ammonia neutralize battery acid. Therefore make sure that these agents are kept out of the battery by keeping the battery caps tightly in place.

2. Check for damaged cable insulation, Fig. 40. Damaged insulation can cause the cable to short out against the body of the vehicle or other accessories. Cables in this condition should be replaced immediately.
3. Check level of electrolyte. If required, add water as described further on.
4. Make sure that battery is securely held in place. A loose or broken bracket can result in battery damage (both internally and externally) from excessive vibration.

Battery Cable, Replace

NOTE: When disconnecting battery cables, first make sure that all accessories are off,

Fig. 41   Removing side type battery terminal

Fig. 42   Removing bolt type terminal

Fig. 43   Removing spread type terminal

Fig. 44 Removing battery terminal using battery terminal puller

Fig. 45 Trico bayonet type wiper blade removal. American Motors & Ford Motor Co.

Fig. 46 Saddle pin type wiper blade removal. American Motors & Ford Motor Co.

disconnect the negative battery cable and then the positive cable. Make sure to reconnect cables in the reverse order of removal.

1. On side terminal batteries, loosen the retaining bolts using a 5/16-inch wrench and disconnect the cable from the battery, Fig. 41.
2. On all other type batteries, loosen the cable retaining bolt using a 1/2-inch or 9/16-inch box wrench, Fig. 42, and lift the cable off the battery posts. Some cables can be removed by squeezing the tabs on the cable terminal using a pair of pliers, Fig. 43, and lifting the cable off the battery posts.
3. If the battery terminals are difficult to remove, use a terminal puller, Fig. 44. Place the legs of the puller underneath the terminal and tighten the puller screw until the terminal is removed.
4. Clean the cable terminals and battery posts using a terminal and post wire brush, Fig. 39.
5. Clean the battery top using a solution of soda and water. Make sure that the battery is thoroughly cleaned and dried. Make sure that you cover the battery caps to avoid entry of the soda and water solution into the battery.
6. To install the cables on a side terminal battery, place the cables onto the battery and tighten the retaining screws using a 5/16-inch wrench.
7. To install the cables on all other types of batteries, place the cables on the battery post and force them all the way down. If the cable is not completely bottomed, spread the cable terminal slightly with a screwdriver, until the terminal is properly positioned.
8. Tighten the terminal bolts using a 1/2-inch or 9/16-inch box wrench.
9. Coat the outside of the terminals with petroleum jelly to prevent corrosion.

Replacing Battery

Careless installation of a new battery can ruin the battery. In removing the old battery, note the location of the positive battery post so the new battery can be installed in the same

position. Always remove the negative (ground) cable first.

Use an open-end wrench to loosen the clamp. If the nut is very tight, use one wrench on the head of the bolt and the other on the nut, to avoid straining and possibly cracking the battery cover. A pair of battery pliers can be used to loosen the nut, but a wrench should always be used on the head of the bolt.

If a cable terminal is corroded to the post, do not try to loosen it by hammering, or by resting a tool on the battery and prying—either method can break the battery container. Use a screw type terminal puller, Fig. 43, or spread the cable terminals slightly with a screwdriver.

Clean any corrosion from the cables, battery case, or hold-downs, and inspect them. Paint any corroded steel parts with acid-proof paint. Make sure that the cable is of the correct size and that its insulation and clamp terminal are in good condition.

Put the new battery in position, making sure it sits level, and tighten the holddowns a little at a time, alternately, to avoid distorting and breaking the battery case. The holddowns should be snug enough to prevent bouncing, but should not be too tight.

NOTE: Before connecting the cables, check the battery terminals to be sure the battery is not reversed.

Clean the battery posts bright with sandpaper or a wire brush.

Don't hammer the terminals down on the posts—the battery case may crack. Spread the terminals slightly if necessary. Connect the starter cable first and the negative (ground) cable last, tightening the terminal bolts after making sure that the cables don't interfere with the vent plugs or rub against the hold-downs.

W/S WIPER BLADE & ELEMENT, REPLACE

American Motors

WIPER BLADE

Except 1977–78 Matador Coupe, 1977–80 Pacer & 1977–82 Liftgate

To remove, press downward on wiper arm to disengage upper stud, then depress tab on blade saddle and pull blade assembly from arm, Fig. 45. To install, slide blade saddle over end of wiper arm until locking stud snaps into place. Check to ensure that wiper blade is securely seated on wiper arm.

1977–78 Matador Coupe, 1977–79 Pacer & 1977–80 Liftgate

To remove, insert a screwdriver or other suitable tool into spring release opening of blade saddle and depress spring clip, then pull

blade assembly from wiper arm, Fig. 46. Install wiper blade assembly by pushing blade saddle on wiper arm pin so that clip engages pin. Check to ensure that wiper blade is securely seated on wiper arm.

1980 Pacer Except Liftgate

NOTE: When removing the pin type plastic wiper blade, grasp ends of wiper blade frame, not wiper blade element, to avoid damaging element.

To remove, grasp both ends of wiper blade frame and reverse contour of blade assembly, then pull blade from wiper arm, Fig. 47. To install, push wiper blade assembly onto wiper arm pin so that frame spring engages pin. Check to ensure that blade assembly is securely seated on wiper arm.

1981–82 Liftgate

To remove, pull upward on blade spring lock, then pull blade assembly from wiper arm pin, Fig. 52. To install, push blade onto wiper arm until spring lock engages pin. Check to ensure wiper blade is securely seated on wiper arm.

WIPER BLADE ELEMENT

1977–79 All Models & 1980–82 Liftgate

To remove, depress wiper element latch lock release tabs and pull element from blade frame retainers, Fig. 48. To install, insert element through each of the retaining tabs and engage latch lock notches with the last retaining tab. Check to ensure that element is engaged with all retainers before installing wiper blade assembly.

1980–82 Except Liftgate

To remove, squeeze wide area of blade element reinforcement and twist slightly to unlock element from blade frame retaining tabs. Pull element from remaining blade frame retaining tabs. To install, insert element through each of the retaining tabs and engage wide portion of element metal reinforcement with last retaining tab. Check to ensure that

Fig. 47 Trico plastic pin type wiper blade removal. American Motors & Ford Motor Co.

Fig. 49 Wiper blade & element removal. Chrysler Corp. 1977–79 types A, B & C & 1980–82 type A except front wheel drive

wiper blade element is engaged with all retaining tabs before installing wiper blade assembly.

Chrysler Corp.

1977–79 Except Front Wheel Drive
1. With wiper switch in the on position, cycle ignition switch on and off to position wiper blades for ease of removal.
2. Raise wiper arm assembly from glass, then actuate wiper blade release mechanism and remove blade from arm, Fig. 49.
3. Three different methods are used to retain wiper blade element to wiper blade. Referring to Fig. 49, replace blade element as follows:
   a. To remove type A wiper blade element, pinch lock on end of element frame, then withdraw element from blade bridge claws. Install wiper element in the same manner, ensuring that wiper blade element is engaged and properly positioned in all wiper blade claws.
   b. To remove type B wiper blade element, lift tab and pinch end bridge to release from center bridge. Slide wiper blade element and end bridge from opposite end bridge. Install wiper blade element in the same manner. After installing, check to ensure that end bridge tab is in the down position to lock element and end bridge to center bridge.
   c. To remove type C wiper blade element, depress button on end bridge to release from center bridge, then withdraw element. When installing wiper blade element, ensure that element is engaged and properly positioned in all bridge claws.
4. Install wiper blade assembly on wiper arm. Check to ensure that blade assembly is securely seated on wiper arm.

1980–82 Except Front Wheel Drive
1. With wiper switch in the on position, cycle ignition switch on and off to position wiper blades for ease of removal.
2. Raise wiper arm from glass.
3. Three different methods are used to retain wiper blades to wiper arms and wiper blade elements to wiper blades. Remove wiper blades and wiper blade elements as follows:
   a. To remove type A wiper blade and element, Fig. 49, pry hinge release slot to remove blade assembly from arm pin. Pinch lock on end of wiper blade element frame and withdraw element from bridge claws.
   b. To remove type B wiper blade and element, Fig. 50, lift release tab on wiper blade using a screwdriver, then remove blade from arm pin. To remove wiper blade element, hold center bridge and move end bridge into a reverse bow, then release element from end claws and slide element out through remaining bridge claws.
   c. To remove type C wiper blade and element, Fig. 51, apply a light reverse pressure to both end bridges to raise internal tension bar out of wiper arm pin lock groove, then remove blade assembly from wiper arm. To remove wiper blade element, pinch lock on end of element frame and withdraw wiper blade element from bridge claws.
4. Install wiper element in the same manner as removed. Ensure that wiper blade element is locked and properly positioned in all bridge claws.
5. Install wiper blade assembly on wiper arm. Check to ensure that blade assembly is securely seated on wiper arm.

1978–82 Front Wheel Drive Except Liftgate
1. With wiper switch in the on position, cycle ignition switch on and off to position wiper blades for ease of removal.
2. Raise wiper arm from glass.
3. On four door models, depress release lever on wiper blade center bridge and slide blade assembly from wiper arm. To remove wiper blade element, lift tab and pinch end bridge to release from center bridge. Slide end bridge from wiper blade element, then remove element from opposite end bridge. After installing wiper blade element, check to ensure that tab on end bridge is in the down position to lock element and end bridge to center bridge.
4. On two door models, lift release tab on wiper blade center bridge pivot, then remove blade assembly from wiper arm. To remove wiper blade element, move wiper blade into a slight reverse bow, then slide element out of bridge claws.
5. When installing blade assembly, check to ensure that wiper blade element is locked and properly positioned in blade frame. Also ensure that blade is securely seated on wiper arm.

1978–82 Front Wheel Drive Liftgate
1. With wiper switch in the on position, cycle ignition switch on and off to position wiper blade for ease of removal.
2. Lift wiper assembly from glass, then depress release lever on blade center bridge and remove blade assembly from

Fig. 48 Wiper blade element removal

Fig. 50 Wiper blade & element removal. Chrysler Corp. 1980–82 type B

Fig. 51 Wiper blade & element removal. Chrysler Corp. 1980–82 type C

wiper arm.

3. Depress release button on end bridge to release from center bridge, then slide wiper blade element and end bridge from opposite end bridge.
4. Engage wiper blade element in all bridge claws.
5. Ensure that all release points are locked with blade assembly.

Ford Motor Co.

1977–78 Except Fairmont & Zephyr & 1979 Granada & Monarch

1. To replace the saddle pin type wiper blade, Fig. 46, proceed as follows:
   a. Insert a screwdriver or other suitable tool into spring release opening in blade saddle.
   b. Depress spring clip and slide blade assembly from wiper arm.
   c. To install, slide blade assembly onto wiper arm until clip engages pin.
2. To replace the bayonet type wiper blade, proceed as follows:
   a. To remove the Anco type blade, press inward on blade saddle tab, then slide blade assembly from wiper arm.
   b. To remove the Trico type blade, Fig. 45, press downward on wiper arm to detach upper stud, then depress tab and slide blade assembly from wiper arm.
   c. To install, slide blade assembly onto arm until locking stud snaps into position.

1978 Fairmont & Zephyr, 1979 Except Granada, Monarch & Versailles & 1980–82 All Models Except 1982 Lincoln Continental

1. With wiper switch in the on position, cycle ignition switch on and off to position wiper blades for ease of removal.
2. To replace Trico wiper blades, Fig. 47, proceed as follows:
   a. With wiper blade assembly resting on windshield, grasp either end of blade

away from windshield, then remove wiper blade from wiper arm.

NOTE: To prevent damage, be sure to grasp wiper blade frame and not end of blade element.

---

   b. To install, push blade assembly onto wiper arm pin until fully seated.
3. To replace Tridon wiper blades, Fig. 52, proceed as follows:
   a. Pull upward on blade spring lock, then pull blade assembly from wiper arm pin.
   b. To install, push blade onto wiper arm pin until spring lock engages pin.

1982 Lincoln Continental
Lift arm assembly and pivot lower end of blade 90° from arm, then remove blade from arm. When installing, both arm prongs must engage into blade slots.

WIPER BLADE ELEMENT

1977–78 Models Except Fairmont & Zephyr & 1979 Granada, Monarch & Versailles

1. To replace Anco type wiper blade element, Fig. 48, proceed as follows:
   a. Depress latch pin and slide wiper blade element from yoke jaws.
   b. To install, slide blade element through blade jaws, then install blade frame into jaw slots. Ensure element engages all yoke jaws.
2. To replace Trico type wiper blade element, Fig. 48, proceed as follows:
   a. Squeeze latch lock and pull wiper blade element from blade frame jaws.
   b. To install wiper blade element, insert element through blade frame jaws. Ensure element is engaged in all blade frame jaws and lock latch is properly seated.

1978 Fairmont & Zephyr, 1979 Except Granada, Monarch & Versailles & 1980–82 All Models

1. To replace Trico wiper blade element,

Fig. 52 Tridon wiper blade removal. American Motors & Ford Motor Co.

proceed as follows:
   a. On wiper blade element, locate wide portion of metal element reinforcement.
   b. Insert a screwdriver between blade frame and wide portion of element reinforcement downward and inward to release element from tab.
   c. Slide wiper blade element from the remaining blade frame jaws.
   d. To install, slide wiper blade element through blade frame jaws, ensuring element is properly locked in all tabs.
2. To replace Tridon wiper blade element, Fig. 53, proceed as follows:
   a. On wiper blade element plastic backing strip, locate a 7/16 in. notch approximately 1 in. from end of element.
   b. Place wiper blade assembly on a firm surface with notched end of plastic backing strip visible, then grasp frame portion of wiper blade and push downward until blade assembly is tightly bowed.
   c. With blade assembly tightly bowed, grasp tip of plastic backing strip and pull upward and twist counter clockwise at the same time to snap backing strip from blade frame tab.
   d. Lift blade assembly from surface and slide backing strip down frame until notch is aligned with next retaining tab, then twist slightly to snap backing strip from tab. Continue this procedure with the remaining blade frame tabs.
   e. Reverse procedure to install. Check to ensure that element backing strip is engaged with all retaining tabs before installing wiper blade on wiper arm.

General Motors

WIPER BLADE

1977–82 Except Astre, Chevette, Monza, Skyhawk, Starfire, Sunbird, T1000 & Vega
On these models, two methods are used to retain the wiper blade to the wiper arm, Fig. 54. To remove the press type release tab blade, depress release tab and separate wiper

Fig. 53 Tridon wiper blade element removal. Ford Motor Co. 1978 Fairmont & Zephyr, 1979 Except Granada, Monarch & Zephyr & 1980–82 All Models

Fig. 54 Wiper blade & element removal. General Motors except Astre, Chevette, Monza Skyhawk, Starfire, Sunbird, T1000 & Vega

Fig. 55 Latch type wiper arm removal

Fig. 56 Wiper arm removal (typical). Chrysler Corp. 1978–82 front wheel drive liftgate & General Motors Models w/rectangular motor

blade from arm. To remove the coil spring retainer blade, insert a screwdriver on top of spring and push downward, then separate blade from wiper arm. To install, push blade onto arm until spring retainer engages in arm pin.

1977 Astre, Vega, 1977-80 Monza, Skyhawk, Starfire, Sunbird & 1977-82 Chevette & T1000

To remove wiper blade assembly, depress blade spring clip and slide blade from wiper arm, Fig. 45. To install, slide wiper blade onto wiper arm until pin on tip of arm engages hole in wiper blade spring clip.

WIPER BLADE ELEMENT

Two different methods are used to retain the element to the wiper blade, Fig. 54. To remove wiper element from the press type release button wiper blade, depress push button and slide element from blade frame. To remove wiper blade element from spring retainer type wiper blade, squeeze retainer clip together and slide element from blade frame. When installing, ensure that element is engaged in all wiper blade frame tabs.

WIPER ARM, REPLACE
American Motors

Except 1977-78 Matador Coupe & 1977-80 Pacer Except Liftgate

The wiper arms are set on the serrated pivot shafts and held securely by spring tension on the arm. To remove, lift arm against spring tension, then using a screwdriver, slide the cap away from the serrated pivot shaft.

1977-78 Matador Coupe & 1977-80 Pacer Except Liftgate

To remove, raise blade end of arm away from windshield, then move slide latch away from pivot shaft, Fig. 55. On left hand side wiper arm, disengage auxiliary arm from pivot pin and remove arm from pivot shaft.

Chrysler Corp.

Except Front Wheel Drive Liftgate

1. Lift wiper arm assembly and pull latch

Fig. 58 Wiper arm removal. Ford Motor Co. 1977-80 Bobcat, Pinto, 1978-81 Fairmont & Zephyr Sta. Wag. liftgate & 1982 Cougar & Granada Sta. Wag. liftgate

from holding position, Fig. 55.
2. Remove arm from pivot with a rocking motion.
3. Reverse procedure to install. Install wiper arm with wiper motor in park position.

Front Wheel Drive Liftgate

Install tool No. C-3982 or equivalent on wiper arm, then lift wiper arm upward and remove from pivot shaft, Fig. 56. When installing wiper arm, wiper motor must be in the park position.

Ford Motor Co.

1977 Comet, Maverick & 1977-78 Mustang

Swing arm and blade assembly away from windshield. While holding assembly in this position, pull arm off shaft using an appropriate tool, Fig. 57. To install, hold arm in the swing out position and push arm onto pivot shaft.

1977-80 Bobcat & Pinto; 1979-81 Fairmont & Zephyr Sta. Wag. Tailgate & 1982 Cougar & Granada Sta. Wag. Tailgate

Swing arm and blade assembly away from glass, this will release spring loaded clip in arm from pivot shaft. Insert a 3/32 in. pin through pin hole to hold clip in the released position, then pull arm from pivot shaft, Fig. 58. Do not remove pin until after wiper arm has been installed on pivot shaft.

Except 1977 Comet & Maverick, 1977-78 Mustang; 1977-80 Bobcat & Pinto; 1978-81 Fairmont & Zephyr Sta. Wag. Tailgate & 1982 Cougar & Granada Sta. Wag. Tailgate

Raise blade end of arm off windshield and move slide latch away from pivot shaft, Fig. 55. This action will unlock the wiper arm from the pivot shaft and hold the blade end of the arm away from the windshield. The wiper arm can now be pulled from the pivot shaft without the aid of any tools. Reverse procedure to install.

General Motors

MODELS W/RECTANGULAR MOTOR

1. Wiper motor must be in "Park" position.
2. Use suitable tool to minimize the possibility of windshield or paint finish damage during arm removal.
3. Remove arm by prying up with tool to disengage arm from serrated transmission shaft, Fig. 56.
4. To install arm to transmission shaft rotate the required distance and direction so that the blades rest in proper position.

MODELS W/ROUND MOTOR

Buick, Chevrolet, Oldsmobile & Pontiac

1. Wiper motor must be in the Park position. On 1979-82 Riviera and Toronado, remove cowl upper panel and screen.
2. Raise hood to gain access to wiper arms.
3. *Corvette only:* Remove the rubber plug from the front of the wiper door actuator then insert a screwdriver, pushing the internal piston rearward to actuate the wiper door open.
4. *On 1977 Intermediate Models and 1977-78 Toronado:* Lift arm off transmission shaft. On left arm, slide articulating arm lock clip, Fig. 59, away from transmission pivot pin and lift arm off pin. *On Full Size and 1978-82 Intermediate Models:* Lift arm and slide latch clip, Fig. 55, out from under wiper arm.
5. Release the wiper arm and lift assembly off transmission shaft.

Fig. 57 Wiper arm removal. Ford Motor Co. 1977 Comet, Maverick & 1977-78 Mustang

6. Reverse procedure to install.

Cadillac

1. Raise hood to gain access to wiper arms. On Seville and 1979-82 Eldorado models, remove front cowl panel and screen.
2. Lift wiper arm and slide latch clip, Fig. 55, out from under wiper arm.
3. Release wiper arm and lift wiper arm assembly off transmission shaft.
4. On 1977-78 Eldorado, at left arm, slide articulating arm lock clip away from transmission pivot pin, Fig. 59, and lift arm off pin.
5. On 1977-78 Eldorado, to install left wiper arm assembly, position the articulating arm over the transmission pivot pin until it locks in place on the pin. Install the left wiper arm assembly to the transmission shaft aligning the keyway to the shaft.
6. On 1977-78 Eldorado, align keyway in right wiper arm assembly to transmission shaft and install arm assembly to shaft.
7. On all models except 1977-79 Seville and 1977-78 Eldorado, align slot in arm and blade assembly to keyway in transmission spindle and position wiper arm on shaft. Lift blade assembly and slide latch clip into place.

NOTE: W/S wiper blade assembly release button or clip must face toward base of arm assembly for proper matching of blade to glass contour.

8. On 1977-79 Seville, position wiper arm assembly on transmission spindle, then lift blade and slide latch clip into place.
9. On all models, release wiper arms and check wiper pattern and park position.

Fig. 59 Wiper articulating arm lock clip. General Motors 1977 intermediate models & 1977-78 Eldorado & Toronado

TROUBLE SHOOTING

INDEX OF SYMPTOMS

INTRODUCTION

STARTING A STALLED ENGINE

When an engine fails to start the chances are that 90 per cent of the cases will involve the ignition system and seldom the fuel system or other miscellaneous reasons. If a systematic procedure is followed the trouble can almost always be found without the use of special equipment.

To begin with, turn on the ignition switch and if the ammeter shows a slight discharge (or if the telltale lamp lights) it indicates that current is flowing. A glance at the gas gauge will indicate whether or not there is fuel in the tank.

Operate the starter and if the engine turns over freely, both the battery and starter are functioning properly. On the other hand, if the starter action is sluggish it may be due to a discharged or defective battery, loose, corroded or dirty battery terminals, mechanical failure in the starter, starter switch or starter drive. If the starter circuit is okay, skip this phase of the discussion and proceed to ignition.

Starter Circuit Checkout

To determine which part of the starter circuit is at fault, turn on the light switch and again operate the starter. Should the lights go out or become dim, the trouble is either in the battery, its connections or cables. A hydrometer test of the battery should indicate better than 1.250 specific gravity, while a voltmeter, placed across the positive and negative posts, should indicate about 12 volts. If either of these tests prove okay, clean and tighten the battery connections and cable terminals or replace any cable which seems doubtful.

If the lights remain bright when the starter is operated, the trouble is between the battery and the starter, or the starter switch is at fault, since it is evident that there is no electrical connection between these points. If these connections are clean and tight, it is safe to assume that the starter or starter switch is defective.

Neutral Safety Switch

If the ammeter shows a slight discharge (or if the telltale lamp lights) when the ignition is turned on, but the system goes dead when the starting circuit is closed, the neutral safety switch may be at fault. To check, bypass the switch with a suitable jumper. If the engine now starts, adjust or replace the switch.

CAUTION: With the safety switch by-passed, the car can be started in any gear. *Be sure the transmission is in neutral or park and the parking brake is applied.*

Primary Ignition Checkout

Let's assume that the battery and starter are doing their job, and that fuel is reaching the carburetor, but the car does not start, then the trouble must be somewhere in the ignition circuit. But first, before starting your diagnosis, it is advisable to give the whole system a visual inspection which might uncover obvious things such as broken or disconnected wires etc.

The best way to start tracing down ignition troubles is to begin with the primary circuit since this is where troubles show up most frequently. First remove the distributor cap and block the points open with a piece of cardboard, then turn on the ignition and with a test bulb or voltmeter check to see if there is current at the terminal on the distributor. If you do not get a reading at this point, the current is cut off somewhere in the connections leading back to the ignition switch or it may be that the condenser has an internal short to the ground. The latter possibility can be eliminated if you can restore current at the distributor terminal by disconnecting the condenser from the distributor plate so that its outside shell is not grounded. With the possibility of a bad condenser out of the way, work toward the ignition switch and test for current at each connection until you get to one where you get a reading. Between this connection and the distributor lies the trouble.

The foregoing steps in checking the primary circuit should include checking the ignition coil resistor for defects or loose connections. As this is done, bear in mind that while the starter cranks the engine, the resistor is by-passed by the starter switch on the American Motors 4-121 engine. This means that while the circuit through the resistor may be satisfactory, a broken connection or high resistance between the starter switch by-pass terminal and the coil would prevent starting. On the other hand, a satisfactory by-pass circuit might start the engine while the engine would stall immediately upon releasing the starter switch if there was a defect in the coil resistance circuit.

If, to begin with, the test equipment shows a current reading at the distributor terminal, it is safe to assume that the trouble is in the unit itself, most likely burned or dirty breaker points. A final positive test for defective breaker points can be made very simply by removing the cardboard from between the points, and positioning the distributor cam by turning the engine to where the points are closed. With the points closed there should be no current at the distributor terminal. If there is current, replace the points.

In an emergency, the points can be cleaned by using the sanded side of a match box, a knife blade, or the sharp edge of a screwdriver to scrape the scale from the contact faces. After cleaning the points, if a gauge is not available to set the gap, a quick adjustment can be made by using four layers of a piece of newspaper. The thickness of the paper is equivalent to about .020", which is the approximate gap setting for most distributors. Of course, at the earliest opportunity, a precise point adjustment should be made.

If the procedure outlined under "Primary Ignition Checkout" does not uncover the trouble then it will be necessary to continue the tests into the secondary ignition circuit.

Secondary Ignition Checkout

First of all, remove the wire from one of the spark plugs, turn on the ignition and operate the starter. While the engine is cranking, hold the terminal of the spark plug wire about 1/4" away from the engine or spark plug base. If the spark is strong and jumps the gap, the trouble is confined to either the spark plugs or lack of fuel. Before going any further, wipe the outside of the plugs to remove any dirt or dampness which would create an easy path for

the current to flow, then try to start the engine again. If it still fails to start, remove one of the spark plugs and if it is wet around the base, it indicates that the fuel system is okay, so it naturally follows that the spark plugs are at fault. Remove all the plugs, clean them and set the gaps. An emergency adjustment of spark plug gaps can be made by folding a piece of newspaper into 6 or 7 layers. When changing the gap, always bend the side (ground) electrode and never the center one as there is danger of breaking the insulation.

Fuel System Checkout

If the spark plug that was removed showed no indication of dampness on its base, check the fuel system. A quick check can be made by simply removing the carburetor air cleaner and looking down into the carburetor. Open and close the throttle manually and if fuel is present in the carburetor, the throttle will operate the accelerating pump, causing it to push gasoline through the pump jet. If it does, check the choke valve. If the engine is cold, the choke valve should be closed. If the choke won't close, the engine can be started by covering the carburetor throat while the engine is cranking, provided, of course, that fuel is reaching the carburetor.

Check the operation of the fuel pump by disconnecting the fuel lines from the pump to the carburetor. Crank the engine and if the pump is working, fuel will pulsate out of the line. If not, either the pump isn't working or the line from the tank to the pump is clogged. Before blaming the pump, however, disconnect the line at the inlet side of the pump which leads to the tank and, while a companion listens at the tank blow through the line. If a gurgling sound is heard back in the tank, the line is open and the trouble is in the pump. Remove the sediment bowl, if so equipped and clean the screen, then replace the bowl and screen, being sure that you have an air-tight fit. If the pump still refuses to function, it should be removed and repaired.

The foregoing discussion will, in most cases, uncover the cause of why an engine won't start. However, if further diagnosis is necessary, the following list will undoubtedly provide the answer.

ENGINE NOISE TESTS

Loose Main Bearing

A loose main bearing is indicated by a powerful but dull thud or knock when the engine is pulling. If all main bearings are loose a noticeable clatter will be audible.

The thud occurs regularly every other revolution. The knock can be confirmed by shorting spark plugs on cylinders adjacent to the bearing. Knock will disappear or be less when plugs are shorted. This test should be made at a fast idle equivalent to 15 mph in high gear. If bearing is not quite loose enough to produce a knock by itself, the bearing may knock if oil is too thin or if there is no oil at the bearing.

Loose Flywheel

A loose flywheel is indicated by a thud or click which is usually irregular. To test, idle the engine at about 20 mph and shut off the ignition. If thud is heard, the flywheel may be loose.

Loose Rod Bearing

A loose rod bearing is indicated by a metallic knock which is usually loudest at about 30 mph with throttle closed. Knock can be reduced or even eliminated by shorting spark plug. If bearing is not loose enough to produce a knock by itself, the bearing may knock if oil is too thin or if there is no oil at the bearing.

Piston Pin

Piston pin, piston and connecting rod noises are difficult to tell apart.

A loose piston pin causes a sharp double knock which is usually heard when engine is idling. Severity of knock should increase when spark plug to this cylinder is short-circuited. However, on some engines the knock becomes more noticable at 25 to 35 mph on the road.

Piston pin rubs against cylinder wall, caused by lock screw being loose or snap ring broken.

Hydraulic Lifters

The malfunctioning of a hydraulic valve lifter is almost always accompanied by a clicking or tapping noise. More or less hydraulic lifter noise may be expected when the engine is cold but if lifters are functioning properly the noise should disappear when the engine warms up.

If all or nearly all lifters are noisy, they may be stuck because of dirty or gummy oil.

If all lifters are noisy, oil pressure to them may be inadequate. Foaming oil may also cause this trouble. If oil foams there will be bubbles on the oil level dipstick. Foaming may be caused by water in the oil or by too high an oil level or by a very low oil level.

If the hydraulic plungers require an initial adjustment, they will be noisy if this adjustment is incorrect.

If one lifter is noisy the cause may be:
1. Plunger too tight in lifter body.
2. Weak or broken plunger spring.
3. Ball valve leaks.
4. Plunger worn.
5. Lock ring (if any) improperly installed or missing.
6. Lack of oil pressure to this plunger.

If ball valve leaks, clean plunger in special solvent such as acetone and reinstall. Too often, plungers are condemned as faulty when all they need is a thorough cleaning.

Gum and dirty oil are the most common causes of hydraulic valve lifter trouble. Engine oil must be free of dirt. Select a standard brand of engine oil and use no other. Mixing up one standard brand with another may cause gummy oil and sticking plungers. Do not use any special oils unless recommended by the car manufacturer and change oil filter or element at recommended intervals.

Loose Engine Mountings

Occasional thud with car in operation. Most likely to be noticed at the moment the throttle is opened or closed.

Excessive Crankshaft End Play

A rather sharp rap which occurs at idling speed but may be heard at higher speeds also. The noise should disappear when clutch is disengaged.

Fuel Pump Noise

Diagnosis of fuel pumps suspected as noisy requires that some form of sounding device be used. Judgment by ear alone is not sufficient, otherwise a fuel pump may be needlessly replaced in attempting to correct noise contributed by some other component. Use of a stethoscope, a long screwdriver, or a sounding rod is recommended to locate the area or component causing the noise. The sounding rod can easily be made from a length of copper tubing 1/4 to 3/8 inch in diameter.

If the noise has been isolated to the fuel pump, remove the pump and run the engine with the fuel remaining in the carburetor bowl. If the noise level does not change, the source of the noise is elsewhere and the original fuel pump should be reinstalled. On models using a fuel pump push rod, check for excessive wear and/or galling of the push rod.

VAPOR LOCK

The term vapor lock means the flow of fuel to the mixing chamber in the carburetor has been stopped (locked) by the formation of vaporized fuel pockets or bubbles caused by overheating the fuel by hot fuel pump, hot fuel lines or hot carburetor.

The more volatile the fuel the greater the tendency for it to vapor lock. Vapor lock is encouraged by high atmospheric temperature, hard driving, defective engine cooling and high altitude.

A mild case of vapor lock will cause missing and hard starting when engine is warm. Somewhat more severe vapor lock will stop the engine which cannot be started again until it has cooled off enough so that any vaporized fuel has condensed to a liquid.

SERVICE NOTE: Some cars have a vapor bypass system. These cars have a special fuel filter which has a metering outlet in the top. Any vapor which forms is bled off and returned to the fuel tank through a separate line alongside the fuel supply line. This system greatly reduces the possibility of vapor lock. However, if vapor lock is suspected examine the bypass valve to see if it is functioning.

PERCOLATION

Percolation means simply that gasoline in the carburetor bowl is boiling over into the intake manifold. This condition is most apt to occur immediately after a hot engine is shut off. Most carburetors have a provision for relieving the vapor pressure of overheated fuel in the carburetor bowl by means of ports. If, however, percolation should take place, the engine may be started by allowing it to cool slightly and then holding the throttle wide open while cranking to clear the intake manifold of excess fuel.

CARBURETOR ICING

The carburetor discharges liquid fuel into the air stream in the form of an atomized spray which evaporates readily. The heat required to evaporate the gasoline is drawn from the entering air, thereby lowering its temperature. The cooler air chills the interior of the carburetor and may cause the moisture in the air to condense into droplets.

Under certain conditions of atmospheric temperature and humidity, the liberated moisture actually collects and freezes on the chilled carburetor surfaces, especially on the throttle plate and surrounding throttle body. When the throttle is almost completely closed for idling, this ice tends to bridge the gap between the throttle plate and throttle body, thereby cutting off the air supply and causing the engine to stall. Opening the throttle for restarting breaks the ice bridge but does not eliminate the possibility of further stalling until the engine and carburetor have warmed up.

For carburetor icing to occur, the outside air must be cool enough so that the refrigerating effect of fuel evaporation in the carburetor bowl will lower the temperatures of the throttle plate and body below both the dew point of moist air and the freezing point of water. The air must also contain sufficient moisture for appreciable condensation of water to occur when it is chilled in the carburetor.

Generally speaking, carburetor icing occurs when winter grade gasoline (more volatile than summer grade) is used and when the atmospheric temperature ranges from 30° to 50° F. at relative humidities in excess of 65%.

Carburetor icing problems can be reduced by the use of anti-icing additives in the fuel. Some fuel refiners use anti-stalling additives in their gasolines which have proved effective in combating carburetor icing.

Another form of carburetor icing has been observed in some engines during high-speed driving on cool, moist days. When certain cars are driven steadily at 60 to 80 mph, the large quantities of cool air passing through the carburetor may result in gradual ice formation within the carburetor's venturi. Since this ice restricts the venturi passage, the resultant increased vacuum in the venturi tends to increase the rate of fuel flow. The fuel-air mixture thus becomes excessively rich, causing loss of power and high fuel consumption.

SPARK KNOCK, PING, DETONATION

All three expressions mean the same thing. It is a sharp metallic knock caused by vibration of the cylinder head and block. The vibration is due to split-second high-pressure waves resulting from almost instantaneous abnormal combustion instead of the slower normal combustion.

The ping may be mild or loud. A mild ping does no harm but a severe ping will reduce power. A very severe ping may shatter spark plugs, break valves or crack pistons.

Pinging is most likely to occur on open throttle at low or moderate engine speed. Pinging is encouraged by:
1. Overheated engine.
2. Low octane fuel.
3. Too high compression.
4. Spark advanced too far.
5. Hot mixture due to hot engine or hot weather.
6. Heavy carbon deposit which increases the compression pressure.

Tendency to ping increases with mixture temperature including high atmospheric temperature; intake manifold heater valve "on" when engine is warm; hot cooling water; hot interior engine surfaces due to sluggish water circulation or water jackets clogged with rust or dirt especially around exhaust valves. Some of these troubles may be confined to one or two cylinders.

If an engine pings objectionably because of too low octane fuel, retard the spark setting but first be sure that the cooling system is in good condition, the mixture not too lean and the combustion chambers free of carbon deposit.

TROUBLE SHOOTING

PRE-IGNITION

Pre-ignition means that the mixture is set on fire before the spark occurs, being ignited by a red hot spot in the combustion chamber such as an incandescent particle of carbon; a thin piece of protruding metal; an overheated spark plug, or a bright red hot exhaust valve. The result is reduction of power and overheating accompanied by pinging. The bright red hot exhaust valve may be due to a leak, to lack of tappet clearance, to valve sticking, or to a weak or broken spring.

Pre-ignition may not be noticed if not severe. Severe pre-ignition results in severe pinging. The most common cause of pre-ignition is a badly overheated engine.

When the engine won't stop when the ignition is shut off, the cause is often due to red hot carbon particles resting on heavy carbon deposit in a very hot engine.

AFTER-BURNING

A subdued put-putting at the exhaust tail pipe may be due to leaky exhaust valves which permit the mixture to finish combustion in the muffler. If exhaust pipe or muffler is red hot, better let it cool, as there is some danger of setting the car on fire. Most likely to occur when mixture is lean.

ENGINE CONTINUES TO RUN AFTER IGNITION IS TURNED OFF

This condition, known as "dieseling," "run on," or "after running," is caused by improper idle speed and/or high temperature. Idle speed and engine temperature are affected by:

Carburetor Adjustment: High idle speed will increase the tendency to diesel because of the inertia of the engine crankshaft and flywheel. Too low an idle speed, particularly with a lean mixture, will result in an increase in engine temperature, especially if the engine is allowed to idle for long periods of time.

Ignition Timing: Because advanced ignition timing causes a corresponding increase in idle speed and retarded timing reduces idle speed, ignition timing influences the tendency to diesel in the same manner as Carburetor Adjustment.

Fuel Mixture: Enriching the idle fuel mixture decreases the tendency to diesel by causing the engine to run cooler.

Fuel Content: High octane fuels tend to reduce dieseling. Increased fuel content of lead alkyl increases the tendency to diesel. Phosphates and nickel fuel additives help prevent dieseling.

Spark Plugs: Plugs of too high a heat range for the engine in question can cause dieseling.

Throttle Plates: If the throttle plates are not properly aligned in the carburetor bore, a resulting leanness in fuel mixture occurs, contributing to dieseling.

Electrical System: Normally, during dieseling, ignition is self-supplied by a "hot spot," self-igniting fuel, etc. However, there is a possibility of the vehicle's electrical system supplying the necessary ignition. When the ignition switch is turned off, a small amount of current can flow from the generator into the primary of the ignition coil through the generator tell-tale light. This is particularly true when the warning light bulb has been changed for one of increased wattage.

NOTE: "Run on" is more prevalent in an engine when the ignition is turned off before the engine is allowed to return to idle. Therefore, it can be reduced by letting the engine return to idle before shutting off the ignition. "Run on" incidence can be reduced on automatic transmission units by turning off the engine when in gear.

A certain amount of "run on" can be expected from any gasoline engine regardless of make, size or configuration. (Diesel engines operate on this principle.) However, if the above suggestions are correctly employed, "Run on" will be reduced to an unnoticeable level.

ENGINE

Condition	Possible Cause	Correction
ENGINE WILL NOT START	1. Weak battery.	1. Test battery specific gravity. Recharge or replace as necessary.
	2. Corroded or loose battery connections.	2. Clean and tighten battery connections. Apply a coat of petroleum to terminals.
	3. Faulty starter.	3. Repair starter motor.
	4. Moisture on ignition wires and distributor cap.	4. Wipe wires and cap clean and dry.
	5. Faulty ignition cables.	5. Replace any cracked or shorted cables.
	6. Open or shorted primary ignition circuit.	6. Trace primary ignition circuit and repair as necessary.
	7. Malfunctioning ignition points or condensor.	7. Replace ignition points & condensor as necessary.
	8. Faulty coil.	8. Test and replace if necessary.
	9. Incorrect spark plug gap.	9. Set gap correctly.
	10. Incorrect ignition timing.	10. Reset timing.
	11. Dirt or water in fuel line or carburetor.	11. Clean lines and carburetor. Replace filter.
	12. Carburetor flooded.	12. Adjust float level—check seats.
	13. Incorrect carburetor float setting.	13. Adjust float level—check seats.
	14. Faulty fuel pump.	14. Install new fuel pump.
	15. Carburetor percolating. No fuel in the carburetor.	15. Measure float level. Adjust bowl vent. Inspect operation of manifold heat control valve.
ENGINE STALLS	1. Idle speed set too low.	1. Adjust carburetor.
	2. Incorrect choke adjustment.	2. Adjust choke.
	3. Idle mixture too lean or too rich.	3. Adjust carburetor.
	4. Incorrect carburetor float setting.	4. Adjust float setting.
	5. Leak in intake manifold.	5. Inspect intake manifold gasket and replace if necessary.
	6. Worn or burned distributor rotor.	6. Install new rotor.
	7. Incorrect ignition wiring.	7. Install correct wiring.
	8. Faulty coil.	8. Test and replace if necessary.
	9. Incorrect tappet lash.	9. Adjust to specifications.
ENGINE LOSS OF POWER	1. Incorrect ignition timing.	1. Reset timing.
	2. Worn or burned distributor rotor.	2. Install new rotor.
	3. Worn distributor shaft.	3. Remove and repair distributor.
	4. Dirty or incorrectly gapped spark plugs.	4. Clean plugs and set gap.
	5. Dirt or water in fuel line, carburetor or filter.	5. Clean lines, carburetor and replace filter.

ENGINE—Continued

Condition	Possible Cause	Correction
ENGINE LOSS OF POWER, continued	6. Incorrect carburetor float setting. 7. Faulty fuel pump. 8. Incorrect valve timing. 9. Blown cylinder head gasket. 10. Low compression. 11. Burned, warped or pitted valves. 12. Plugged or restricted exhaust system. 13. Faulty ignition cables. 14. Faulty coil.	6. Adjust float level. 7. Install new pump. 8. Check and correct valve timing. 9. Install new head gasket. 10. Test compression of each cylinder. 11. Install new valves. 12. Install new parts as necessary. 13. Replace any cracked or shorted cables. 14. Test and replace as necessary.
ENGINE MISSES ON ACCELERATION	1. Dirty, or gap too wide in spark plugs. 2. Incorrect ignition timing. 3. Dirt in carburetor. 4. Acceleration pump in carburetor. 5. Burned, warped or pitted valves. 6. Faulty coil.	1. Clean spark plugs and set gap. 2. Reset timing. 3. Clean carburetor and replace filter. 4. Install new pump. 5. Install new valves. 6. Test and replace if necessary.
ENGINE MISSES AT HIGH SPEED	1. Dirty or gap set too wide in spark plug. 2. Worn distributor shaft. 3. Worn or burned distributor rotor. 4. Faulty coil. 5. Incorrect ignition timing. 6. Dirty jets in carburetor. 7. Dirt or water in fuel line, carburetor or filter.	1. Clean spark plugs and set gap. 2. Remove and repair distributor. 3. Install new rotor. 4. Test and replace if necessary. 5. Reset timing. 6. Clean carburetor, replace filter. 7. Clean lines, carburetor and replace filter.
NOISY VALVES	1. High or low oil level in crankcase. 2. Thin or diluted oil. 3. Low oil pressure. 4. Dirt in valve lifters. 5. Bent push rod. 6. Worn rocker arms. 7. Worn tappets. 8. Worn valve guides. 9. Excessive run-out of valve seats or valve faces. 10. Incorrect tappet lash.	1. Check for correct oil level. 2. Change oil. 3. Check engine oil level. 4. Clean lifters. 5. Install new push rods. 6. Inspect oil supply to rockers. 7. Install new tappets. 8. Ream and install new valves with O/S Stems. 9. Grind valve seats and valves. 10. Adjust to specifications.
CONNECTING ROD NOISE	1. Insufficient oil supply. 2. Low oil pressure. 3. Thin or diluted oil. 4. Excessive bearing clearance. 5. Connecting rod journals out-of-round. 6. Misaligned (bent) connecting rods.	1. Check engine oil level. 2. Check engine oil level. Inspect oil pump relief valve and spring. 3. Change oil to correct viscosity. 4. Measure bearings for correct clearance. 5. Replace crankshaft or regrind journals. 6. Replace bent connecting rods.
MAIN BEARING NOISE	1. Insufficient oil supply. 2. Low oil pressure. 3. Thin or diluted oil. 4. Excessive bearing clearance. 5. Excessive end play. 6. Crankshaft journal worn out-of-round. 7. Loose flywheel or torque converter.	1. Check engine oil level. 2. Check engine oil level. Inspect oil pump relief valve and spring. 3. Change oil to correct viscosity. 4. Measure bearings for correct clearances. 5. Check thrust bearing for wear on flanges. 6. Replace crankshaft or regrind journals. 7. Tighten to correct torque.
OIL PUMPING AT RINGS	1. Worn, scuffed, or broken rings. 2. Carbon in oil ring slot. 3. Rings fitted too tight in grooves.	1. Hone cylinder bores and install new rings. 2. Install new rings. 3. Remove the rings. Check grooves. If groove is not proper width, replace piston.
OIL PRESSURE DROP	1. Low oil level. 2. Faulty oil pressure sending unit. 3. Clogged oil filter. 4. Worn parts in oil pump. 5. Thin or diluted oil. 6. Excessive bearing clearance. 7. Oil pump relief valve stuck. 8. Oil pump suction tube loose, bent or cracked.	1. Check engine oil level. 2. Install new sending unit. 3. Install new oil filter. 4. Replace worn parts or pump. 5. Change oil to correct viscosity. 6. Measure bearings for correct clearance. 7. Remove valve and inspect, clean, and reinstall. 8. Remove oil pan and install new tube if necessary.
NO OIL PRESSURE	1. Low oil level. 2. Oil pressure gauge or sending unit inaccurate.	1. Add oil to correct level. 2. Replace defective unit.

TROUBLE SHOOTING

ENGINE—Continued

Condition	Possible Cause	Correction
NO OIL PRESSURE, continued	3. Oil pump malfunction.	3. Repair oil pump.
	4. Oil pressure relief valve sticking.	4. Remove and inspect oil pressure relief valve assembly.
	5. Oil passages on pressure side of pump obstructed.	5. Inspect oil passages for obstructions.
	6. Oil pickup screen or tube obstructed.	6. Inspect oil pickup for obstructions.
LOW OIL PRESSURE	1. Low oil level.	1. Add oil to correct level.
	2. Oil excessively thin due to dilution, poor quality, or improper grade.	2. Drain and refill crankcase with recommended oil.
	3. Oil pressure relief spring weak or sticking.	3. Remove and inspect oil pressure relief valve assembly.
	4. Oil pickup tube and screen assembly has restriction or air leak.	4. Remove and inspect oil inlet tube and screen assembly. (Fill pickup with lacquer thinner to find leaks.)
	5. Excessive oil pump clearance.	5. Check clearances.
	6. Excessive main, rod, or camshaft bearing clearance.	6. Measure bearing clearances, repair as necessary.
HIGH OIL PRESSURE	1. Improper grade oil.	1. Drain and refill crankcase with correct grade oil.
	2. Oil pressure gauge or sending unit inaccurate.	2. Replace defective unit.
	3. Oil pressure relief valve sticking closed.	3. Remove and inspect oil pressure relief valve assembly.
EXTERNAL OIL LEAK	1. Fuel pump gasket broken or improperly seated.	1. Replace gasket.
	2. Cylinder head cover gasket broken or improperly seated.	2. Replace gasket; check cylinder head cover gasket flange and cylinder head gasket surface for distortion.
	3. Oil filter gasket broken or improperly seated.	3. Replace oil filter.
	4. Oil pan side gasket broken or improperly seated.	4. Replace gasket; check oil pan gasket flange for distortion.
	5. Oil pan front oil seal broken or improperly seated.	5. Replace seal; check timing chain cover and oil pan seal flange for distortion.
	6. Oil pan rear oil seal broken or improperly seated.	6. Replace seal; check oil pan rear oil seal flange; check rear main bearing cap for cracks, plugged oil return channels, or distortion in seal groove.
	7. Timing chain cover oil seal broken or improperly seated.	7. Replace seal.
	8. Oil pan drain plug loose or has stripped threads.	8. Repair as necessary and tighten.
	9. Rear oil gallery plug loose.	9. Use appropriate sealant on gallery plug and tighten.
	10. Rear camshaft plug loose or improperly seated.	10. Seat camshaft plug or replace and seal, as necessary.
EXCESSIVE OIL CONSUMPTION	1. Oil level too high.	1. Lower oil level to specifications.
	2. Oil too thin.	2. Replace with specified oil.
	3. Valve stem oil seals are damaged, missing, or incorrect type.	3. Replace valve stem oil seals.
	4. Valve stems or valve guides worn.	4. Check stem-to-guide clearance and repair as necessary.
	5. Piston rings broken, missing.	5. Replace missing or broken rings.
	6. Piston rings incorrect size.	6. Check ring gap, repair as necessary.
	7. Piston rings sticking or excessively loose in grooves.	7. Check ring side clearance, repair as necessary.
	8. Compression rings installed upside down.	8. Repair as necessary.
	9. Cylinder walls worn, scored, or glazed.	9. Repair as necessary.
	10. Piston ring gaps not properly staggered.	10. Repair as necessary.
	11. Excessive main or connecting rod bearing clearance.	11. Check bearing clearance, repair as necessary.

OIL PRESSURE INDICATOR

LIGHT NOT LIT, IGNITION ON AND ENGINE NOT RUNNING.	1. Bulb burned out.	1. Replace bulb.
	2. Open in light circuit.	2. Locate and correct open.
	3. Defective oil pressure switch.	3. Replace oil pressure switch.

OIL PRESSURE INDICATOR—Continued

Condition	Possible Cause	Correction
LIGHT ON, ENGINE RUNNING ABOVE IDLE SPEED.	1. Grounded wiring between light and switch. 2. Defective oil pressure switch. 3. Low oil pressure.	1. Locate and repair ground. 2. Replace oil pressure switch. 3. Locate cause of low oil pressure and correct.

IGNITION, STARTER & FUEL

Condition	Possible Cause	Correction
NOTHING HAPPENS WHEN START ATTEMPT IS MADE	1. Undercharged or defective battery. 2. Loose battery cables. 3. Burned fusible link in starting circuit. 4. Incorrectly positioned or defective neutral start switch. 5. Loose or defective wiring between neutral start switch and ignition switch. 6. Defective starter motor. 7. Defective starter interlock system.	1. Check condition of battery and recharge or replace as required. 2. Clean and tighten cable connections. 3. Check for burned fusible link. Correct wiring problem. 4. Check neutral start switch adjustment. If O.K., replace switch. 5. Check for loose connections and opens between battery, horn relay, ignition switch, and solenoid "S" terminal. Check battery ground cable. Replace or repair defective item. 6. Repair or replace starter motor. 7. Use emergency button under hood. If car starts, repair circuit in interlock system. If car does not start, check and repair starter circuit.
SOLENOID SWITCH CLICKS BUT STARTER DOES NOT CRANK	1. Undercharged or defective battery. 2. Loose battery cables. 3. Loose or defective wiring at starter. 4. Defective solenoid. 5. "Hot stall" condition. 6. Excessive engine rotational torque caused by mechanical problem within engine. 7. Defective starter motor.	1. Test battery. Recharge or replace battery. 2. Check and tighten battery connections. 3. Tighten connections or repair wiring as required. 4. Replace solenoid. 5. Check engine cooling system. 6. Check engine torque for excessive friction. 7. Repair or replace starter motor.
SLOW CRANKING	1. Vehicle is overheating. 2. Undercharged or defective battery. 3. Loose or defective wiring between battery and engine block. 4. Loose or defective wiring between battery and solenoid "Bat" terminal. 5. Defective starter motor.	1. Check engine cooling system and repair as required. 2. Recharge or replace battery. 3. Repair or replace wiring. 4. Repair or replace wiring. 5. Repair or replace starter.
STARTER SPINS AND/OR MAKES LOUD GRINDING NOISE BUT DOES NOT TURN ENGINE	1. Defective starter motor. 2. Defective ring gear.	1. Repair or replace starter motor. 2. Replace ring gear.
STARTER KEEPS RUNNING AFTER IGNITION SWITCH IS RELEASED—FROM "START" TO "RUN" POSITION	1. Defective ignition switch. 2. Defective solenoid.	1. Replace ignition switch. 2. Replace solenoid.
STARTER ENGAGES ("Clunks") BUT ENGINE DOES NOT CRANK	1. Open circuit in solenoid armature or field coils. 2. Short or ground in field coil or armature.	1. Repair or replace solenoid or starter motor. 2. Repair or replace starter motor.
HARD STARTING (Engine Cranks Normally)	1. Binding linkage, choke valve or choke piston. 2. Restricted choke vacuum and hot air passages. 3. Improper fuel level. 4. Dirty, worn or faulty needle valve and seat. 5. Float sticking. 6. Exhaust manifold heat valve stuck. 7. Faulty fuel pump. 8. Incorrect choke cover adjustment. 9. Inadequate unloader adjustment. 10. Faulty ignition coil. 11. Improper spark plug gap.	1. Repair as necessary. 2. Clean passages. 3. Adjust float level. 4. Repair as necessary. 5. Repair as necessary. 6. Repair as necessary. 7. Replace fuel pump. 8. Adjust choke cover. 9. Adjust unloader. 10. Test and replace as necessary. 11. Adjust gap.

TROUBLE SHOOTING

IGNITION, STARTER & FUEL—Continued

Condition	Possible Cause	Correction
HARD STARTING (Engine Cranks Normally), continued	12. Incorrect initial timing. 13. Incorrect valve timing.	12. Adjust timing. 13. Check valve timing; repair as necessary.
ROUGH IDLE OR STALLING	1. Incorrect curb or fast idle speed. 2. Incorrect initial timing. 3. Improper idle mixture adjustment. 4. Damaged tip on idle mixture screw(s). 5. Improper fast idle cam adjustment. 6. Faulty PCV valve air flow. 7. Exhaust manifold heat valve inoperative. 8. Choke binding. 9. Improper choke setting. 10. Vacuum leak. 11. Improper fuel level. 12. Faulty distributor rotor or cap. 13. Leaking engine valves. 14. Incorrect ignition wiring. 15. Faulty coil. 16. Clogged air bleed or idle passages. 17. Restricted air cleaner. 18. Faulty EGR valve operation if equipped.	1. Adjust curb or fast idle speed. 2. Adjust timing to specifications. 3. Adjust idle mixture. 4. Replace mixture screw(s). 5. Adjust fast idle. 6. Test PCV valve and replace as necessary. 7. Lubricate or replace heat valve as necessary. 8. Locate and eliminate binding condition. 9. Adjust choke. 10. Check manifold vacuum and repair as necessary. 11. Adjust fuel level. 12. Replace rotor or cap. 13. Check cylinder leakdown rate or compression and repair as necessary. 14. Check wiring and correct as necessary. 15. Test coil and replace as necessary. 16. Clean passages. 17. Clean or replace air cleaner. 18. Test EGR system and replace as necessary if equipped.
FAULTY LOW-SPEED OPERATION	1. Clogged idle transfer slots. 2. Restricted idle air bleeds and passages. 3. Restricted air cleaner. 4. Improper fuel level. 5. Faulty spark plugs. 6. Dirty, corroded, or loose secondary circuit connections. 7. Faulty ignition cable. 8. Faulty distributor cap.	1. Clean transfer slots. 2. Clean air bleeds and passages. 3. Clean or replace air cleaner. 4. Adjust fuel level. 5. Clean or replace spark plugs. 6. Clean or tighten secondary circuit connections. 7. Replace ignition cable. 8. Replace cap.
FAULTY ACCELERATION	1. Improper pump stroke. 2. Incorrect ignition timing. 3. Inoperative pump discharge check ball or needle. 4. Worn or damaged pump diaphragm or piston. 5. Leaking main body cover gasket. 6. Engine cold and choke too lean. 7. Faulty spark plug(s). 8. Leaking engine valves. 9. Faulty coil.	1. Adjust pump stroke. 2. Adjust timing. 3. Clean or replace as necessary. 4. Replace diaphragm or piston. 5. Replace gasket. 6. Adjust choke. 7. Clean or replace spark plug(s). 8. Check cylinder leakdown rate or compression, repair as necessary. 9. Test coil and replace as necessary.
FAULTY HIGH-SPEED OPERATION	1. Incorrect ignition timing. 2. Faulty distributor centrifugal advance. 3. Faulty distributor vacuum advance. 4. Low fuel pump volume. 5. Improper spark plug gap. 6. Faulty choke operation. 7. Partially restricted exhaust manifold, exhaust pipe, muffler, or tailpipe. 8. Clogged vacuum passages. 9. Improper size or obstructed main jets. 10. Restricted air cleaner. 11. Faulty distributor rotor or cap. 12. Worn distributor shaft. 13. Faulty coil. 14. Leaking engine valve(s). 15. Faulty valve spring(s). 16. Incorrect valve timing. 17. Intake manifold restricted.	1. Adjust timing. 2. Check centrifugal advance and repair as necessary. 3. Check vacuum advance and repair as necessary. 4. Replace fuel pump. 5. Adjust gap. 6. Adjust choke. 7. Eliminate restriction. 8. Clean passages. 9. Clean or replace as necessary. 10. Clean or replace as necessary. 11. Replace rotor or cap. 12. Replace shaft. 13. Test coil and replace as necessary. 14. Check cylinder leakdown or compression and repair as necessary. 15. Inspect and test valve spring tension and replace as necessary. 16. Check valve timing and repair as necessary. 17. Pass chain through passages.

IGNITION, STARTER & FUEL—Continued

Condition	Possible Cause	Correction
MISFIRE AT ALL SPEEDS	1. Faulty spark plug(s).	1. Clean or replace spark plug(s).
	2. Faulty spark plug cable(s).	2. Replace as necessary.
	3. Faulty distributor cap or rotor.	3. Replace cap or rotor.
	4. Faulty coil.	4. Test coil and replace as necessary.
	5. Primary circuit shorted or open intermittently.	5. Trace primary circuit and repair as necessary.
	6. Leaking engine valve(s).	6. Check cylinder leakdown rate or compression and repair as necessary.
	7. Faulty hydraulic tappet(s).	7. Clean or replace tappet(s).
	8. Faulty valve spring(s).	8. Inspect and test valve spring tension, repair as necessary.
	9. Worn lobes on camshaft.	9. Replace camshaft.
	10. Vacuum leak.	10. Check manifold vacuum and repair as necessary.
	11. Improper carburetor settings.	11. Adjust carburetor.
	12. Fuel pump volume or pressure low.	12. Replace fuel pump.
	13. Blown cylinder head gasket.	13. Replace gasket.
	14. Intake or exhaust manifold passage(s) restricted.	14. Pass chain through passages.
POWER NOT UP TO NORMAL	1. Incorrect ignition timing.	1. Adjust timing.
	2. Faulty distributor rotor.	2. Replace rotor.
	3. Worn distributor shaft.	3. Replace shaft.
	4. Incorrect spark plug gap.	4. Adjust gap.
	5. Faulty fuel pump.	5. Replace fuel pump.
	6. Incorrect valve timing.	6. Check valve timing and repair as necessary.
	7. Faulty coil.	7. Test coil and replace as necessary.
	8. Faulty ignition cables.	8. Test cables and replace as necessary.
	9. Leaking engine valves.	9. Check cylinder leakdown rate or compression and repair as necessary.
	10. Blown cylinder head gasket.	10. Replace gasket.
	11. Leaking piston rings.	11. Check compression and repair as necessary.
INTAKE BACKFIRE	1. Improper ignition timing.	1. Adjust timing.
	2. Faulty accelerator pump discharge.	2. Repair as necessary.
	3. Improper choke operation.	3. Repair as necessary.
	4. Lean fuel mixture.	4. Check float level or manifold vacuum for vacuum leak.
EXHAUST BACKFIRE	1. Vacuum leak.	1. Check manifold vacuum and repair as necessary.
	2. Faulty A.I.R. diverter valve.	2. Test diverter valve and replace as necessary.
	3. Faulty choke operation.	3. Repair as necessary.
	4. Exhaust leak.	4. Locate and eliminate leak.
PING OR SPARK KNOCK	1. Incorrect ignition timing.	1. Adjust timing.
	2. Distributor centrifugal or vacuum advance malfunction.	2. Check advance and repair as necessary.
	3. Excessive combustion chamber deposits.	3. Use combustion chamber cleaner.
	4. Carburetor set too lean.	4. Adjust carburetor.
	5. Vacuum leak.	5. Check manifold vacuum and repair as necessary.
	6. Excessively high compression.	6. Check compression and repair as necessary.
	7. Fuel octane rating excessively low.	7. Try alternate fuel source.
	8. Heat riser stuck in heat on position.	8. Free-up or replace heat riser.
SURGING (Cruising Speeds To Top Speeds)	1. Low fuel level.	1. Adjust fuel level.
	2. Low fuel pump pressure or volume.	2. Replace fuel pump.
	3. Improper PCV valve air flow.	3. Test PCV valve and replace as necessary.
	4. Vacuum leak.	4. Check manifold vacuum and repair as necessary.
	5. Dirt in carburetor.	5. Clean carburetor, replace filter.
	6. Undersize main jets.	6. Replace main jet(s).
	7. Clogged fuel filter screen.	7. Replace fuel filter.
	8. Restricted air cleaner.	8. Clean or replace air cleaner.

TROUBLE SHOOTING

CHARGING SYSTEM

Condition	Possible Cause	Correction
ALTERNATOR FAILS TO CHARGE (No Output or Low Output)	1. Alternator drive belt loose. 2. Regulator base improperly grounded. 3. Worn brushes and/or slip rings. 4. Sticking brushes. 5. Open field circuit. 6. Open charging circuit. 7. Open circuit in stator windings. 8. Open rectifiers.	1. Adjust drive belt to specifications. 2. Connect regulator to a good ground. 3. Install new brushes and/or slip rings. 4. Clean slip rings and brush holders. Install new brushes if necessary. 5. Test all the field circuit connections, and correct as required. 6. Inspect all connections in charging circuit, and correct as required. 7. Remove alternator and disassemble. Test stator windings. Install new stator if necessary. 8. Remove alternator and disassemble. Test the rectifiers. Install new rectifier assemblies if necessary.
LOW, UNSTEADY CHARGING RATE	1. High resistance in body to engine ground lead. 2. Alternator drive belt loose. 3. High resistance at battery terminals. 4. High resistance in charging circuit. 5. Open stator winding.	1. Tighten ground lead connections. Install new ground lead if necessary. 2. Adjust alternator drive belt. 3. Clean and tighten battery terminals. 4. Test charging circuit resistance. Correct as required. 5. Remove and disassemble alternator. Test stator windings. Install new stator if necessary.
LOW OUTPUT AND A LOW BATTERY	1. High resistance in charging circuit. 2. Shorted rectifier. Open rectifier. 3. Grounded stator windings. 4. Faulty voltage regulator.	1. Test charging circuit resistance and correct as required. 2. Perform current output test. Test the rectifiers and install new rectifier heat sink assembly as required. Remove and disassemble the alternator. 3. Remove and disassemble alternator. Test stator windings. Install new stator if necessary. 4. Test voltage regulator. Replace as necessary.
EXCESSIVE CHARGING RATE TO A FULLY CHARGED BATTERY	1. Faulty ignition switch. 2. Faulty voltage regulator.	1. Install new ignition switch. 2. Test voltage regulator. Replace as necessary.
NOISY ALTERNATOR	1. Alternator mounting loose. 2. Worn of frayed drive belt. 3. Worn bearings. 4. Interference between rotor fan and stator leads. 5. Rotor or rotor fan damaged. 6. Open or shorted rectifer. 7. Open or shorted winding in stator.	1. Properly install and tighten alternator mounting. 2. Install a new drive belt and adjust to specifications. 3. Remove and disassemble alternator. Install new bearings as required. 4. Remove and disassemble alternator. Correct interference as required. 5. Remove and disassemble alternator. Install new rotor. 6. Remove and disassemble alternator. Test rectifers. Install new rectifier heat sink assemble as required. 7. Remove and disassemble alternator. Test stator windings. Install new stator if necessary.
EXCESSIVE AMMETER FLUCTUATION	1. High resistance in the alternator and voltage regulator circuit.	1. Clean and tighten all connections as necessary.

CHARGING SYSTEM INDICATOR

Condition	Possible Cause	Correction
LIGHT ON, IGNITION OFF	1. Shorted positive diode.	1. Locate and replace shorted diode.
LIGHT NOT ON, IGNITION ON AND ENGINE NOT RUNNING	1. Bulb burned out. 2. Open in light circuit. 3. Open in field.	1. Replace bulb. 2. Locate and correct open. 3. Replace rotor.
LIGHT ON, ENGINE RUNNING ABOVE IDLE SPEED	1. No generator output. 2. Shorted negative diode. 3. Loose or broken generator belt.	1. Check and correct cause of no output. 2. Locate and replace shorted diode. 3. Tighten or replace and tighten generator belt.

COOLING SYSTEM

Condition	Possible Cause	Correction
HIGH TEMPERATURE INDICATION—OVERHEATING	1. Coolant level low.	1. Replenish coolant level.
	2. Fan belt loose.	2. Adjust fan belt.
	3. Radiator hose(s) collapsed.	3. Replace hose(s).
	4. Radiator blocked to airflow.	4. Remove restriction.
	5. Faulty radiator cap.	5. Replace cap.
	6. Car overloaded.	6. Reduce load.
	7. Ignition timing incorrect.	7. Adjust ignition timing.
	8. Idle speed low.	8. Adjust idle speed.
	9. Air trapped in cooling system.	9. Purge air.
	10. Car in heavy traffic.	10. Operate at fast idle intermittently to cool engine.
	11. Incorrect cooling system component(s) installed.	11. Install proper component(s).
	12. Faulty thermostat.	12. Replace thermostat.
	13. Water pump shaft broken or impeller loose.	13. Replace water pump.
	14. Radiator tubes clogged.	14. Flush radiator.
	15. Cooling system clogged.	15. Flush system.
	16. Casting flash in cooling passages.	16. Repair or replace as necessary. Flash may be visible by removing cooling system components or removing core plugs.
	17. Brakes dragging.	17. Repair brakes.
	18. Excessive engine friction.	18. Repair engine.
	19. Car working beyond cooling system capacity.	19. Install heavy-duty cooling fan and/or radiator.
	20. Antifreeze concentration over 68%.	20. Lower antifreeze content.
	21. Low anti-freeze concentration.	21. Add anti-freeze to provide a minimum 50% concentration.
LOW TEMPERATURE INDICATION—OVERCOOLING	1. Improper fan being used.	1. Install proper fan.
	2. Improper radiator.	2. Install proper radiator.
	3. Thermostat stuck open.	3. Replace thermostat.
	4. Improper fan pulley (too small).	4. Install proper pulley.
COOLANT LOSS—BOILOVER **NOTE:** Immediately after shutdown, the engine enters a period known as heat soak. This is caused because the cooling system is inoperative but engine temperature is still high. If coolant temperature rises above boiling point, it may push some coolant out of the radiator overflow tube. If this does not occur frequently, it is considered normal.	Refer to Overheating Causes in addition to the following:	
	1. Overfilled cooling system.	1. Reduce coolant level to proper specification.
	2. Quick shutdown after hard (hot) run.	2. Allow engine to run at fast idle prior to shutdown.
	3. Air in system resulting in occasional "burping" of coolant.	3. Purge system.
	4. Insufficient antifreeze allowing coolant boiling point to be too low.	4. Add antifreeze to raise boiling point.
	5. Antifreeze deteriorated because of age or contamination.	5. Replace coolant.
	6. Leaks due to loose hose clamps, loose nuts, bolts, drain plugs, faulty hoses, or defective radiator.	6. Pressure test system to locate leak then repair as necessary.
	7. Faulty head gasket.	7. Replace head gasket.
	8. Cracked head, manifold, or block.	8. Replace as necessary.
COOLANT ENTRY INTO CRANKCASE OR CYLINDER	1. Faulty head gasket.	1. Replace head gasket.
	2. Crack in head, manifold or block.	2. Replace as necessary.
COOLANT RECOVERY SYSTEM INOPERATIVE	1. Coolant level low.	1. Replenish coolant.
	2. Leak in system.	2. Pressure test to isolate leak and repair as necessary.
	3. Pressure cap not tight or gasket missing or leaking.	3. Repair as necessary.
	4. Pressure cap defective.	4. Replace cap.
	5. Overflow tube clogged or leaking.	5. Repair as necessary.
	6. Recovery bottle vent plugged.	6. Remove restriction.
NOISE	1. Fan contacting shroud.	1. Reposition shroud and check engine mounts.
	2. Loose water pump impeller.	2. Replace pump.
	3. Dry fan belt.	3. Apply belt dressing or replace belt.
	4. Loose fan belt.	4. Adjust fan belt.
	5. Rough surface on drive pulley.	5. Replace pulley.
	6. Water pump bearing worn.	6. Remove belt to isolate. Replace pump.
NO COOLANT FLOW THROUGH HEATER CORE	1. Plugged return pipe in water pump.	1. Remove obstruction.
	2. Heater hose collapsed or plugged.	2. Remove obstruction or replace hose.
	3. Plugged heater core.	3. Remove obstruction or replace core.
	4. Plugged outlet in thermostat housing.	4. Remove flash or obstruction.
	5. Heater bypass hole in cylinder head plugged.	5. Remove obstruction.

TROUBLE SHOOTING

COOLANT TEMPERATURE INDICATOR

Condition	Possible Cause	Correction
"HOT" INDICATOR; LIGHT NOT LIT WHEN CRANKING ENGINE	1. Bulb burned out. 2. Open in light circuit. 3. Defective ignition switch.	1. Replace bulb. 2. Locate and correct open. 3. Replace ignition switch.
LIGHT ON, ENGINE RUNNING	1. Wiring grounded between light and switch. 2. Defective temperature switch. 3. Defective ignition switch. 4. High coolant temperature.	1. Locate and correct grounded wiring. 2. Replace temperature switch. 3. Replace ignition switch. 4. Locate and correct cause of high coolant temperature.

EXHAUST SYSTEM

Condition	Possible Cause	Correction
LEAKING EXHAUST GASES	1. Leaks at pipe joints. 2. Damaged or improperly installed seals or packing. 3. Loose exhaust pipe heat tube extension connections. 4. Burned or rusted out exhaust pipe heat tube extensions.	1. Tighten U-bolt nuts at leaking joints. 2. Replace seals or packing as necessary. 3. Replace seals or packing as required. Tighten stud nuts or bolts. 4. Replace heat tube extensions as required.
EXHAUST NOISES	1. Leaks at manifold or pipe connections. 2. Burned or blown out muffler. 3. Burned or rusted out exhaust pipe. 4. Exhaust pipe leaking at manifold flange. 5. Exhaust manifold cracked or broken. 6. Leak between manifold and cylinder head.	1. Tighten clamps at leaking connections to specified torque. Replace gasket or packing as required. 2. Replace muffler assembly. 3. Replace exhaust pipe. 4. Tighten attaching bolt nuts. 5. Replace manifold. 6. Tighten manifold to cylinder head stud nuts or bolts.
LOSS OF ENGINE POWER AND/OR INTERNAL RATTLES IN MUFFLER	1. Dislodged turning tubes and or baffles in muffler.	1. Replace muffler.
LOSS OF ENGINE POWER	1. Imploding (inner wall collapse) of exhaust pipe.	1. Replace exhaust pipe.
ENGINE HARD TO WARM UP OR WILL NOT RETURN TO NORMAL IDLE	1. Heat control valve frozen in the open position.	1. Free up manifold heat control using a suitable manifold heat control solvent.
MANIFOLD HEAT CONTROL VALVE NOISE	1. Thermostat broken. 2. Broken, weak or missing anti-rattle spring.	1. Replace thermostat. 2. Replace spring.

CLUTCH & SYNCHRO-MESH TRANSMISSION

Condition	Possible Cause	Correction
CLUTCH CHATTER	1. Worn or damaged disc assembly. 2. Grease or oil on disc facings. 3. Improperly adjusted cover assembly. 4. Broken or loose engine mounts. 5. Misaligned clutch housing.	1. Replace disc assembly. 2. Replace disc assembly and correct cause of contamination. 3. Replace cover assembly. 4. Replace or tighten mounts. 5. Align clutch housing.
CLUTCH SLIPPING	1. Insufficient pedal free play. 2. Burned, worn, or oil soaked facings. 3. Weak or broken pressure springs.	1. Adjust release fork rod. 2. Replace disc assembly and correct cause of contamination. 3. Replace cover assembly.
DIFFICULT GEAR SHIFTING	1. Excessive pedal free play. 2. Excessive deflection in linkage or firewall. 3. Worn or damaged disc assembly. 4. Improperly adjusted cover assembly. 5. Clutch disc splines sticking. 6. Worn or dry pilot bushing. 7. Clutch housing misaligned.	1. Adjust release fork rod. 2. Repair or replace linkage. 3. Replace disc assembly. 4. Replace cover assembly. 5. Remove disc assembly and free up splines or replace disc. 6. Lubricate or replace bushing. 7. Align clutch housing.
CLUTCH NOISY	1. Dry clutch linkage. 2. Worn release bearing. 3. Worn disc assembly.	1. Lubricate where necessary. 2. Replace release bearing. 3. Replace disc assembly.

CLUTCH & SYNCHRO-MESH TRANSMISSION—Continued

Condition	Possible Cause	Correction
CLUTCH NOISY, continued	4. Worn release levers. 5. Worn or dry pilot bushing. 6. Dry contact-pressure plate lugs in cover.	4. Replace cover assembly. 5. Lubricate or replace bushing. 6. Lubricate very lightly.
TRANSMISSION SHIFTS HARD	1. Incorrect clutch adjustment. 2. Clutch linkage binding. 3. Gearshift linkage incorrectly adjusted, bent, or binding. 4. Bind in steering column, or column is misaligned. 5. Incorrect lubricant. 6. Internal bind in transmissions—e.g. shift rails, interlocks, shift forks, synchronizer teeth. 7. Clutch housing misalignment.	1. Adjust clutch pedal free-play. 2. Lubricate or repair linkage as required. 3. Adjust linkage—correct any bind. Replace bent parts. 4. Disconnect shift rods at column. Check for bind/misalignment between tube and jacket by shifting lever into all positions. Correct as required. 5. Drain and refill transmission. 6. Remove transmission and inspect shift mechanism. Repair as required. 7. Check runout at rear face of clutch housing.
GEAR CLASH WHEN SHIFTING FROM ONE FORWARD GEAR TO ANOTHER	1. Incorrect clutch adjustment. 2. Clutch linkage binding. 3. Gear shift linkage incorrectly adjusted, bent, or binding. 4. Clutch housing misalignment. 5. Damaged or worn transmission components: shift forks, synchronizers, shift rails and interlocks. Excessive end play due to worn thrust washers.	1. Adjust clutch. 2. Lubricate or repair linkage as required. 3. Adjust linkage, correct binds, replace bent parts. 4. Check runout at rear face of clutch housing. 5. Inspect components. Repair or replace as required.
TRANSMISSION NOISY	1. Insufficient lubricant. 2. Incorrect lubricant. 3. Clutch housing to engine or transmission to clutch housing bolts loose. 4. Dirt, chips in lubricant. 5. Gearshift linkage incorrectly adjusted, or bent or binding. 6. Clutch housing misalignment. 7. Worn transmission components: front-rear bearings, worn gear teeth, damaged gear teeth or synchronizer components.	1. Check lubricant level and replenish as required. 2. Replace with proper lubricant. 3. Check and correct bolt torque as required. 4. Drain and flush transmission. 5. Adjust linkage, correct binds, replace bent parts. 6. Check runout at rear face of clutch housing. 7. Inspect components and repair as required.
JUMPS OUT OF GEAR	1. Gearshift linkage incorrectly adjusted. 2. Gearshift linkage bent or binding. 3. Clutch housing misaligned. 4. Worn pilot bushing. 5. Worn or damaged clutch shaft roller bearings. 6. Worn, tapered gear teeth; synchronizer parts worn. 7. Shifter forks, shift rails, or detent-interlock parts worn, missing, etc. 8. Excessive end play of output shaft gear train, countershaft gear or reverse idler gear.	1. Adjust linkage. 2. Correct bind, replace bent parts. 3. Check runout at rear face of clutch housing. 4. Replace bushing. 5. Replace bearings. 6. Inspect and replace as required. 7. Inspect and replace as required. 8. Replace thrust washers, and snap rings (output shaft gear train).
WILL NOT SHIFT INTO ONE GEAR—ALL OTHERS OK	1. Gearshift linkage not adjusted correctly. 2. Bent shift rod at transmission. 3. Transmission shifter levers reversed. 4. Worn or damaged shift rails, shift forks, detent-interlock plugs, loose setscrew in shifter fork, worn synchronizer parts.	1. Adjust linkage. 2. Replace rod. 3. Correctly position levers. 4. Inspect and repair or replace parts as required.
LOCKED IN ONE GEAR—CANNOT BE SHIFTED OUT OF THAT GEAR	1. Gearshift linkage binding or bent. 2. Transmission shifter lever attaching nuts loose or levers are worn at shifter fork shaft hole. 3. Shift rails worn or broken, shifter fork bent, setscrew loose, detent-interlock plug missing or worn. 4. Broken gear teeth on countershaft gear, clutch shaft, or reverse idler gear.	1. Correct bind, replace bent components. 2. Tighten nuts, replace worn levers. 3. Inspect and replace worn or damaged parts. 4. Inspect and replace damaged part.

TROUBLE SHOOTING

BRAKES

Condition	Possible Cause	Correction
LOW BRAKE PEDAL (Excessive pedal travel required to apply brake)	1. Excessive clearance between linings and drums caused by inoperative automatic adjusters. 2. Worn brake lining. 3. Bent, distorted brakeshoes. 4. Caliper pistons corroded. 5. Power unit push rod height incorrect.	1. Make 10 to 15 firm forward and reverse brake stops to adjust brakes. If brake pedal does not come up, repair or replace adjuster parts as necessary. 2. Inspect and replace lining if worn beyond minimum thickness specification. 3. Replace brakeshoes in axle sets. 4. Repair or replace calipers. 5. Check height with gauge (only). Replace power unit if push rod height is not within specifications.
LOW BRAKE PEDAL (Pedal may go to floor under steady pressure)	1. Leak in hydraulic system. 2. Air in hydraulic system. 3. Incorrect or non-recommended brake fluid (fluid boils away at below normal temp.).	1. Fill master cylinder to within ¼-inch of rim; have helper apply brakes and check calipers, wheel cylinders combination valve, tubes, hoses and fittings for leaks. Repair or replace parts as necessary. 2. Bleed air from system. Refer to Brake Bleeding. 3. Flush hydraulic system with clean brake fluid. Refill with correct-type fluid.
LOW BRAKE PEDAL (Pedal goes to floor on first application—OK on subsequent applications)	1. Disc brakeshoe (pad) knock back; shoes push caliper piston back into bore. Caused by loose wheel bearings or excessive lateral runout of rotor (rotor wobble). 2. Calipers sticking on mounting surfaces of caliper and anchor. Caused by buildup of dirt, rust, or corrosion on abutment.	1. Adjust wheel bearings and check lateral runout of rotor(s). Refinish rotors if runout is over limits. Replace rotor if refinishing would cause rotor to fall below minimum thickness limit. 2. Clean mounting surfaces and lubricate surfaces with molydisulphide grease or equivalent.
FADING BRAKE PEDAL (Pedal falls away under steady pressure)	1. Leak in hydraulic system. 2. Master cylinder piston cups worn, or master cylinder bore is scored, worn or corroded.	1. Fill master cylinder reservoirs to within ¼-inch of rim; have helper apply brakes, check master cylinder, calipers, wheel cylinders combination valve, tubes, hoses, and fittings for leaks. Repair or replace parts as necessary. 2. Repair or replace master cylinder.
DECREASING BRAKE PEDAL TRAVEL (Pedal travel required to apply brakes decreases, may be accompanied by hard pedal)	1. Caliper or wheel cylinder pistons sticking or seized. 2. Master cylinder compensator ports blocked (preventing fluid return to reservoirs) or pistons sticking or seized in master cylinder bore. 3. Power brake unit binding internally. 4. Incorrect power unit push rod height.	1. Repair or replace calipers, or wheel cylinders. 2. Repair or replace master cylinder. 3. Test unit as follows: a. Raise hood, shift transmission into neutral and start engine. b. Increase engine speed to 1500 RPM, close throttle and fully depress brake pedal. c. Slowly release brake pedal and stop engine. d. Remove vacuum check valve and hose from power unit. Observe for backward movement of brake pedal or power unit-to-brake pedal push rod. e. If pedal or push rod moves backward, power unit has internal bind—replace power brake unit. 4. Adjust push rod height.
SPONGY BRAKE PEDAL (Pedal has abnormally soft, springy, spongy feel when depressed)	1. Air in hydraulic system. 2. Brakeshoes bent or distorted. 3. Brake lining not yet seated to drums and rotors.	1. Bleed brakes. 2. Replace brakeshoes. 3. Burnish brakes.
HARD BRAKE PEDAL (Excessive pedal pressure required to stop car. May be accompanied by brake fade)	1. Loose or leaking power brake unit vacuum hose. 2. Brake lining contaminated by grease or brake fluid. 3. Incorrect or poor quality brake lining. 4. Bent, broken, distorted brakeshoes.	1. Tighten connections or replace leaking hose. 2. Determine cause of contaminations and correct. Replace contaminated brake lining in axle sets. 3. Replace lining in axle sets. 4. Replace brakeshoes and lining.

BRAKES—Continued

Condition	Possible Cause	Correction
HARD BRAKE PEDAL, continued	5. Calipers binding or dragging on anchor. Rear brakeshoes dragging on support plate.	5. Sand or wire brush anchors and caliper mounting surfaces and lubricate surfaces lightly. Clean rust or burrs from rear brake support plate ledges and lubricate ledges. **NOTE:** If ledges are deeply grooved or scored, do not attempt to sand or grind them smooth—replace support plate.
	6. Rear brake drum(s) bell mouthed, flared or barrel shaped (distorted).	6. Replace rear drum(s).
	7. Caliper, wheel cylinder, or master cylinder pistons sticking or seized.	7. Repair or replace parts as necessary.
	8. Power brake unit vacuum check valve malfunction.	8. Test valve as follows: a. Start engine, increase engine speed to 1500 RPM, close throttle and immediately stop engine. b. Wait at least 90 seconds then try brake action. c. If brakes are not vacuum assisted for 2 or more applications, check valve is faulty.
	9. Power brake unit has internal bind or incorrect push rod height (too long).	9. Test unit as follows: a. With engine stopped, apply brakes several times to exhaust all vacuum in system. b. Shift transmission into neutral, depress brake pedal and start engine. c. If pedal falls away under foot pressure and less pressure is required to hold pedal in applied position, power unit vacuum system is working. Test power unit as outlined in item (3) under Decreasing Brake Pedal Travel. If power unit exhibits bind condition, replace power unit. d. If power unit does not exhibit bind condition, disconnect master cylinder and check push rod height with appropriate gauge. If height is not within specifications, replace power unit.
	10. Master cylinder compensator ports (at bottom of reservoirs) blocked by dirt, scale, rust, or have small burrs (blocked ports prevent fluid return to reservoirs).	10. Repair or replace master cylinder. **CAUTION:** Do not attempt to clean blocked ports with wire, pencils, or similar implements.
	11. Brake hoses, tubes, fittings clogged or restricted.	11. Use compressed air to check or unclog parts. Replace any damaged parts.
	12. Brake fluid contaminated with improper fluids (motor oil, transmission fluid, or poor quality brake fluid) causing rubber components to swell and stick in bores.	12. Replace all rubber components and hoses. Flush entire brake system. Refill with recommended brake fluid.
GRABBING BRAKES **(Severe reaction to brake pedal pressure)**	1. Brake lining(s) contaminated by grease or brake fluid.	1. Determine and correct cause of contamination and replace brakeshoes and linings in axle sets.
	2. Parking brake cables incorrectly adjusted or seized.	2. Adjust cables. Free up or replace seized cables.
	3. Power brake unit binding internally or push rod height incorrect.	3. Test unit as outlined in item (3) under Decreasing Brake Pedal Travel. If o.k., check push rod height. If unit has internal bind or incorrect push rod height, replace unit.
	4. Incorrect brake lining or lining loose on brakeshoes.	4. Replace brakeshoes in axle sets.
	5. Brakeshoes bent, cracked, distorted.	5. Replace brakeshoes in axle sets.
	6. Caliper anchor plate bolts loose.	6. Tighten bolts.
	7. Rear brakeshoes binding on support plate ledges.	7. Clean and lubricate ledges. Replace support plate(s) if ledges are deeply grooved. Do not attempt to smooth ledges by grinding.
	8. Rear brake support plates loose.	8. Tighten mounting bolts.
	9. Caliper or wheel cylinder piston sticking or seized.	9. Repair or replace parts as necessary.

BRAKES—Continued

Condition	Possible Cause	Correction
GRABBING BRAKES, continued	10. Master cylinder pistons sticking or seized in bore.	10. Repair or replace master cylinder.
BRAKES GRAB, PULL, OR WON'T HOLD IN WET WEATHER	1. Brake lining water soaked.	1. Drive car with brakes lightly applied to dry out lining. If problem persists after lining has dried, replace brakeshoe lining in axle sets.
	2. Rear brake support plate bent allowing excessive amount of water to enter drum.	2. Replace support plate.
DRAGGING BRAKES (Slow or incomplete release of brakes)	1. Brake pedal binding at pivot.	1. Free up and lubricate.
	2. Power brake unit push rod height incorrect (too high) or unit has internal bind.	2. Replace unit if push rod height is incorrect. If height is o.k., check for internal bind as outlined in item (3) under Decreasing Brake Pedal Travel.
	3. Parking brake cables incorrectly adjusted or seized.	3. Adjust cables. Free up or replace seized cables.
	4. Brakeshoe return springs weak or broken.	4. Replace return springs. Replace brakeshoe if necessary in axle sets.
	5. Automatic adjusters malfunctioning.	5. Repair or replace adjuster parts as required.
	6. Caliper, wheel cylinder or master cylinder pistons sticking or seized.	6. Repair or replace parts as necessary.
	7. Master cylinder compensating ports blocked (fluid does not return to reservoirs).	7. Use compressed air to clear ports. Do not use wire, pencils, or similar objects to open blocked ports.
CAR PULLS TO ONE SIDE WHEN BRAKES ARE APPLIED	1. Incorrect front tire pressure.	1. Inflate to recommended cold (reduced load) inflation pressures.
	2. Incorrect front wheel bearing adjustment or worn—damaged wheel bearings.	2. Adjust wheel bearings. Replace worn, damaged bearings.
	3. Brakeshoe lining on one side contaminated.	3. Determine and correct cause of contamination and replace brakeshoe lining in axle sets.
	4. Brakeshoes on one side bent, distorted, or lining loose on shoe.	4. Replace brakeshoes in axle sets.
	5. Support plate bent or loose on one side.	5. Tighten or replace support plate.
	6. Brake lining not yet seated to drums and rotors.	6. Burnish brakes.
	7. Caliper anchor plate loose on one side.	7. Tighten anchor plate bolts.
	8. Caliper or wheel cylinder piston sticking or seized.	8. Repair or replace caliper or wheel cylinder.
	9. Brakeshoe linings watersoaked.	9. Drive car with brakes lightly applied to dry linings. Replace brakeshoes in axle sets if problem persists.
	10. Loose suspension component attaching or mounting bolts, incorrect front end alignment. Worn suspension parts.	10. Tighten suspension bolts. Replace worn suspension components. Check and correct alignment as necessary.
CHATTER OR SHUDDER WHEN BRAKES ARE APPLIED (Pedal pulsation and roughness may also occur)	1. Front wheel bearings loose.	1. Adjust wheel bearings.
	2. Brakeshoes distorted, bent, contaminated, or worn.	2. Replace brakeshoes in axle sets.
	3. Caliper anchor plate or support plate loose.	3. Tighten mounting bolts.
	4. Excessive thickness variation or lateral rim out of rotor.	4. Refinish or replace rotor.
	5. Rear drum(s) out of round, sharp spots.	5. Refinish or replace drum.
	6. Loose suspension component attaching or mounting bolts, incorrect front end alignment. Worn suspension parts.	6. Tighten suspension bolts. Replace worn suspension components. Check and correct alignment as necessary.
NOISY BRAKES (Squealing, clicking, scraping sound when brakes are applied)	1. Bent, broken, distorted brakeshoes.	1. Replace brakeshoes in axle sets.
	2. Brake lining worn out—shoes contacting drum or rotor.	2. Replace brakeshoes and lining in axle sets. Refinish or replace drums or rotors.
	3. Foreign material imbedded in brake lining.	3. Replace brake lining.
	4. Broken or loose hold-down or return springs.	4. Replace parts as necessary.
	5. Rough or dry drum brake support plate ledges.	5. Lubricate support plate ledges.
	6. Cracked, grooved, or scored rotor(s) or drum(s).	6. Replace rotor(s) or drum(s). Replace brakeshoes and lining in axle sets if necessary.

BRAKES—Continued

Condition	Possible Cause	Correction
PULSATING BRAKE PEDAL	1. Out of round drums or excessive thickness variation or lateral runout in disc brake rotor(s). 2. Bent rear axle shaft.	1. Refinish or replace drums or rotors. 2. Replace axle shaft.

SUSPENSION & STEERING

Condition	Possible Cause	Correction
HARD OR ERRATIC STEERING	1. Incorrect tire pressure. 2. Insufficient or incorrect lubrication. 3. Suspension, steering or linkage parts damaged or misaligned. 4. Improper front wheel alignment. 5. Incorrect steering gear adjustment. 6. Sagging springs.	1. Inflate tires to recommended pressures. 2. Lubricate as required. 3. Repair or replace parts as necessary. 4. Adjust wheel alignment angles. 5. Adjust steering gear. 6. Replace springs.
PLAY OR LOOSENESS IN STEERING	1. Steering wheel loose. 2. Steering linkage or attaching parts loose or worn. 3. Pitman arm loose. 4. Steering gear attaching bolts loose. 5. Loose or worn wheel bearings. 6. Steering gear adjustment incorrect or parts badly worn.	1. Inspect splines and repair as necessary. Tighten steering wheel nut. 2. Tighten, adjust, or replace faulty components. 3. Inspect shaft splines and repair as necessary. Torque attaching nut and stake in place. 4. Tighten bolts. 5. Adjust or replace bearings. 6. Adjust gear or replace defective parts.
WHEEL SHIMMY OR TRAMP	1. Improper tire pressure. 2. Wheels, tires, or brake drums out-of-balance or out-of-round. 3. Inoperative, worn, or loose shock absorbers or mounting parts. 4. Loose or worn steering or suspension parts. 5. Loose or worn wheel bearings. 6. Incorrect steering gear adjustments. 7. Incorrect front wheel alignment.	1. Inflate tires to recommended pressures. 2. Inspect parts and replace unacceptable out-of-round parts. Rebalance parts. 3. Repair or replace shocks or mountings. 4. Tighten or replace as necessary. 5. Adjust or replace bearings. 6. Adjust steering gear. 7. Correct front wheel alignment.
TIRE WEAR	1. Improper tire pressure. 2. Failure to rotate tires. 3. Brakes grabbing. 4. Incorrect front wheel alignment. 5. Broken or damaged steering and suspension parts. 6. Wheel runout. 7. Excessive speed on turns.	1. Inflate tires to recommended pressures. 2. Rotate tires. 3. Adjust or repair brakes. 4. Align incorrect angles. 5. Repair or replace defective parts. 6. Replace faulty wheel. 7. Make driver aware of condition.
CAR LEADS TO ONE SIDE	1. Improper tire pressures. 2. Front tires with uneven tread depth, wear pattern, or different cord design (i.e., one bias ply and one belted tire on front wheels). 3. Incorrect front wheel alignment. 4. Brakes dragging. 5. Faulty power steering gear valve assembly. 6. Pulling due to uneven tire construction.	1. Inflate tires to recommended pressures. 2. Install tires of same cord construction and reasonably even tread depth and wear pattern. 3. Align incorrect angles. 4. Adjust or repair brakes. 5. Replace valve assembly. 6. Replace faulty tire.

HEADLAMPS

Condition	Possible Cause	Correction
ONE HEADLAMP INOPERATIVE OR INTERMITTENT	1. Loose connection. 2. Defective sealed beam.	1. Secure connections to sealed beam including ground. 2. Replace sealed beam.
ONE OR MORE HEADLIGHTS ARE DIM	1. Open ground connection at headlight. 2. Ground wire mislocated in headlight connector (type 2 sealed beam).	1. Repair ground wire connection between sealed beam and body ground. 2. Relocate ground wire in connector.
ONE OR MORE HEADLIGHTS SHORT LIFE	1. Voltage regulator maladjusted.	1. Readjust regulator to specifications.

TROUBLE SHOOTING

Condition	Possible Cause	Correction
ALL HEADLIGHTS INOPERATIVE OR INTERMITTENT	1. Loose connection.	1. Check and secure connections at dimmer switch and light switch.
	2. Defective dimmer switch.	2. Check voltage at dimmer switch with test lamp. If test lamp bulb lights only at switch "Hot" wire terminal, replace dimmer switch.
	3. Open wiring—light switch to dimmer switch.	3. Check wiring with test lamp. If bulb lights at light switch wire terminal, but not at dimmer switch, repair open wire.
	4. Open wiring—light switch to battery.	4. Check "Hot" wire terminal at light switch with test lamp. If lamp does not light, repair open wire circuit to battery (possible open fusible link).
	5. Shorted ground circuit.	5. If, after a few minutes operation, headlights flicker "ON" and "OFF" and/or a thumping noise can be heard from the light switch (circuit breaker opening and closing), repair short to ground in circuit between light switch and headlights. After repairing short, check for headlight flickering after one minute operation. If flickering occurs, the circuit breaker has been damaged and light switch must be replaced.
	6. Defective light switch.	6. Check light switch. Replace light switch, if defective.
UPPER OR LOWER BEAM WILL NOT LIGHT OR INTERMITTENT	1. Open connection or defective dimmer switch.	1. Check dimmer switch terminals with test lamp. If bulb lights at all wire terminals, repair open wiring between dimmer switch and headlights. If bulb will not light at one of these terminals, replace dimmer switch.
	2. Short circuit to ground.	2. Follow diagnosis above (all headlights inoperative or intermittent).

SIDE MARKER LAMPS

Condition	Possible Cause	Correction
ONE LAMP INOPERATIVE	1. Turn signal bulb burnt out (front lamp).	1. Switch turn signals on. If signal bulb does not light, replace bulb.
	2. Side marker bulb burnt out.	2. Replace bulb.
	3. Loose connection or open in wiring.	3. Using test lamp, check "Hot" wire terminal at bulb socket. If test lamp lights, repair open ground circuit. If lamp does not light, repair open "Hot" wire circuit.
FRONT OR REAR LAMPS INOPERATIVE	1. Loose connection or open ground connection.	1. If associated tail or park lamps do not operate, secure all connectors in "Hot" wire circuit. If park and turn lamps operate, repair open ground connections.
	2. Multiple bulbs burnt out.	2. Replace burnt out bulbs.
ALL LAMPS INOPERATIVE	1. Blown fuse.	1. If park and tail lamps do not operate, replace blown fuse. If new fuse blows, check for short to ground between fuse panel and lamps.
	2. Loose connection.	2. Secure connector to light switch.
	3. Open in wiring.	3. Check tail light fuse with test lamp. If test lamp lights, repair open wiring between fuse and light switch. If not, repair open wiring between fuse and battery (possible open fusible link).
	4. Defective light switch.	4. Check light switch. Replace light switch, if defective.

TAIL, PARK AND LICENSE LAMPS

Condition	Possible Cause	Correction
ONE SIDE INOPERATIVE	1. Bulb burnt out. 2. Open ground connection at bulb socket or ground wire terminal.	1. Replace bulb. 2. Jump bulb base socket connection to ground. If lamp lights, repair open ground circuit.
BOTH SIDES INOPERATIVE	1. Tail lamp fuse blown. 2. Loose connection. 3. Open wiring. 4. Multiple bulb burnout. 5. Defective light switch.	1. Replace fuse. If new fuse blows, repair short to ground in "Hot" wire circuit between fuse panel through light switch to lamps. 2. Secure connector at light switch. 3. Using test light, check circuit on both sides of fuse. If lamp does not light on either side, repair open circuit between fuse panel and battery (possible open fusible link). If test lamp lights at light switch terminal, repair open wiring between light switch and lamps. 4. If test lamp lights at lamp socket "Hot" wire terminal, replace bulbs. 5. Check light switch. Replace light switch, if defective.

TURN SIGNAL AND HAZARD WARNING LAMP

TURN SIGNALS INOPERATIVE ONE SIDE	1. Bulb(s) burnt out (flasher cannot be heard). 2. Open wiring or ground connection. 3. Improper bulb or defective turn signal switch. 4. Short to ground (flasher can be heard, no bulbs operate).	1. Turn hazard warning system on. If one or more bulbs are inoperative replace necessary bulbs. 2. Turn hazard warning system on. If one or more bulbs are inoperative, use test lamp and check circuit at lamp socket. If test lamp lights, repair open ground connection. If not, repair open wiring between bulb socket and turn signal switch. 3. Turn hazard warning system on. If all front and rear lamps operate, check for improper bulb. If bulbs are OK, replace defective turn signal switch. 4. Locate and repair short to ground by disconnecting front and rear circuits separately.
TURN SIGNALS INOPERATIVE	1. Blown turn signal fuse. 2. Defective flasher. 3. Loose connection.	1. Turn hazard warning system on. If all lamps operate, replace blown fuse. If new fuse blows, repair short to ground between fuse and lamps. 2. If turn signal fuse is OK and hazard warning system will operate lamps, replace defective turn signal flasher. 3. Secure steering column connector.
HAZARD WARNING LAMPS INOPERATIVE	1. Blown fuse. 2. Defective hazard warning flasher. 3. Open in wiring or defective turn signal switch.	1. Switch turn signals on. If lamps operate, replace fuse if blown. If new fuse blows, repair short to ground. (could be in stop light circuit). 2. If fuse is OK, switch turn signals on. If lamps operate, replace defective hazard flasher. 3. Using test lamp, check hazard switch feed wire in turn signal steering column connector. If lamp does not light on either side of connector, repair open circuit between flasher and connector. If lamp lights only on feed side of connector, clean connector contacts. If lamp lights on both sides of connector, replace defective turn signal switch assembly.

TROUBLE SHOOTING

BACK-UP LAMP

Condition	Possible Cause	Correction
ONE LAMP INOPERATIVE OR INTERMITTENT	1. Loose or burnt out bulb. 2. Loose connection. 3. Open ground connections.	1. Secure or replace bulb. 2. Tighten connectors. 3. Repair bulb ground circuit.
BOTH LAMPS INOPERATIVE OR INTERMITTENT	1. Neutral start or back-up lamp switch maladjusted. 2. Loose connection or open circuit. 3. Blown fuse. 4. Defective neutral start or back-up lamp switch. 5. Defective ignition switch.	1. Readjust or replace bulb. 2. Secure all connectors. If OK, check continuity of circuit from fuse to lamps with test lamp. If lamp does not light on either side of fuse, correct open circuit from battery to fuse. 3. Replace fuse. If new fuse blows, repair short to ground in circuit from fuse through neutral start switch to back-up lamps. 4. Check switch. Replace neutral start or back-up lamp switch, if defective. 5. If test lamp lights at ignition switch battery terminal but not at output terminal, replace ignition switch.
LAMP WILL NOT TURN OFF	1. Neutral start or back-up switch maladjusted. 2. Defective neutral start or back-up lamp switch.	1. Readjust neutral start or back-up lamp switch. 2. Check switch. Replace neutral start or back-up lamp switch, if defective.

STOP LIGHTS

Condition	Possible Cause	Correction
ONE BULB INOPERATIVE	1. Bulb burnt out.	1. Replace bulb.
ONE SIDE INOPERATIVE	1. Loose connection, open wiring or defective bulbs. 2. Defective directional signal switch or canceling cam.	1. Turn on directional signal. If lamp does not operate, check bulbs. If bulbs are OK, secure all connections. If lamp still does not operate, use test lamp and check for open wiring. 2. If lamp will operate by turning directional signal on, the switch is not centering properly during canceling operation. Replace defective cancelling cam or directional signal switch.
ALL INOPERATIVE	1. Blown fuse. 2. Stop-switch maladjusted or defective.	1. Replace fuse. If new fuse blows, repair short to ground in circuit between fuse and lamps. 2. Check stop switch. Adjust or replace stop switch, if required.
WILL NOT TURN OFF	1. Stop switch maladjusted or defective.	1. Readjust switch. If switch still malfunctions, replace.

HORNS

Condition	Possible Cause	Correction
HORNS WILL NOT OPERATE	1. Loose connections in circuit. 2. Defective horn switch. 3. Defective horn relay. 4. Defects within horn.	1. Check and tighten connections. Be sure to check ground straps. 2. Replace defective parts. 3. Replace relay. 4. Replace horn.
HORNS HAVE POOR TONE	1. Low available voltage at horn, or defects within horn.	1. Check battery and charging circuit. Although horn should blow at any voltage above 7.0 volts, a weak or poor tone may occur at operating voltage below 11.0 volts. If horn has weak or poor tone at operating voltage of 11.0 volts or higher, remove horn and replace.
HORNS OPERATE INTERMITTENTLY	1. Loose or intermittent connections in horn relay or horn switch. 2. Defective horn switch.	1. Check and tighten connections. 2. Replace switch.

HORNS—Continued

Condition	Possible Cause	Correction
HORNS OPERATE INTERMITTENTLY, continued	3. Defective relay. 4. Defects within horn.	3. Replace relay. 4. Replace horn.
HORNS BLOW CONSTANTLY	1. Sticking horn relay. 2. Horn relay energized by grounded or shorted wiring. 3. Horn button can be grounded by sticking closed.	1. Replace relay. 2. Check and adjust wiring. 3. Adjust or replace damaged parts.

SPEEDOMETER

Condition	Possible Cause	Correction
SPEEDOMETER NOT OPERATING PROPERLY	1. Noisy speedometer cable. 2. Pointer and odometer inoperative. Inaccurate reading. 3. Kinked cable. 4. Defective speedometer head. 5. Casing connector loose on speedometer case.	1. Loosen over-tightened casing nuts and snap-on at speedometer head. Replace housing and core. Replace broken cable. 2. Check tire size. Check for correct speedometer driven gear. 3. Replace cable. Reroute casing so that bends have no less than 6″ radius. 4. Replace speedometer. 5. Tighten connector.

AIR CONDITIONING

> **NOTE:** This chapter deals only with basic system tests and servicing. For complete air conditioning service details, Motor Air Conditioner & Heater Service Manual is available. It includes unit replacement, servicing, diagnosis and testing, vacuum and wiring diagrams, after-market hang-on units, & truck/trailer refrigeration.

CONTENTS

A/C System Testing

PERFORMANCE TEST

The system should be operated for at least 15 minutes to allow sufficient time for all parts to become completely stabilized. Determine if the system is fully charged by the use of test gauges and sight glass if one is installed on system. Head pressure will read from 180 psi to 220 psi or higher, depending upon ambient temperature and the type unit being tested. The sight glass should be free of bubbles if a glass is used in the system. Low side pressures should read approximately 15 psi to 30 psi, again depending on the ambient temperature and the unit being tested. It is not feasible to give a definite reading for all types of systems used, as the type control and component installation used on a particular system will directly influence the pressure readings on the high and low sides, Fig. 1.

The high side pressure will definitely be affected by the ambient or outside air temperature. A system that is operating normally will indicate a high side gauge reading between 150–170 psi with an 80°F ambient temperature. The same system will register 210–230 psi with an ambient temperature of 100°F. No two systems will register exactly the same, which requires that allowance for variations in head pressures must be considered. Following are the most important normal readings likely to be encountered during the season.

Ambient Temp.	High Side Pressure
80	150–170
90	175–195
95	185–205
100	210–230
105	230–250
110	250–270

Relative Temperature of High and Low Sides

The high side of the system should be uniformly hot to the touch throughout. A difference in temperature will indicate a partial blockage of liquid or gas at this point. The low side of the system should be uni-

AIR CONDITIONING

Evaporator Pressure Gauge Reading	Evaporator Temperature F°	High Pressure Gauge Reading	Ambient Temperature
0	-21°	45	20°
0.6	-20°	55	30°
2.4	-15°	72	40°
4.5	-10°	86	50°
6.8	- 5°	105	60°
9.2	0°	126	70°
11.8	5°	140	75°
14.7	10°	160	80°
17.1	15°	185	90°
21.1	20°	195	95°
22.5	22°	220	100°
23.9	24°	240	105°
25.4	26°	260	110°
26.9	28°	275	115°
28.5	30°	290	120°
37.0	40°	305	125°
46.7	50°	325	130°
57.7	60°		
70.1	70°		
84.1	80°		
99.6	90°		
116.9	100°		
136.0	110°		
157.1	120°		
179.0	130°		

Fig. 1 Pressure-temperature relationship (Typical). Conditions equivalent to 30 mph or 1750 engine rpm

1 — TO SERVICE PORT
2 — TO HOSE
3 — TO COMPRESSOR

VIEW A – FRONT-SEATED

VIEW B – BACK-SEATED

VIEW C – MID POSITIONED

Fig. 2 Service valve positions (Typical). American Motors

formly cool to the touch with no excessive sweating of the suction line or low side service valve. Excessive sweating or frosting of the low side service valve usually indicates an expansion valve is allowing an excessive amount of refrigerant into the evaporator.

Evaporator Output

At this point, provided all other inspection tests have been performed, and components have been found to operate as they should, a rapid cooling down of the interior of the vehicle should result. The use of a thermometer is not necessary to determine evaporator output. Bringing all units to the correct operating specifications will insure that the evaporator performs as intended.

DISCHARGING & EVACUATING SYSTEM

Service Note

On all American Motor models equipped with the York 2 cylinder compressor, 1981 California models equipped with 6-258 engine and Sankyo 5 cylinder rotary compressor and all 1982 models, it is not necessary to discharge refrigerant system for compressor removal. The compressor can be isolated from the system, eliminating need for recharging when performing compressor service or oil level check. Proceed as follows:

Isolating Compressor From System

1. Connect pressure gauge and manifold set, then close both gauge hand valves and crack (mid-position) both service valves, Fig. 2.
2. Start engine and operate air conditioning.
3. Slowly turn suction service valve clockwise toward the front seated position, Fig. 2. When pressure reading drops to zero or less stop engine and finish front-seating suction service valve, then front-seat discharge service valve, Fig. 2.
4. Slowly loosen oil sump filler plug to relieve any internal pressures in the compressor.

NOTE: A face shield should be worn when loosening the oil filler plug.

5. Compressor is now isolated from system, service valve can be removed from compressor. Plug all openings to prevent entry of dirt and moisture.

Purging Compressor of Air

The compressor must be purged of air whenever it has been isolated from the system for oil level check or compressor service.
1. Connect service valve and lines to compressor, then cap service gauge ports on both service valves.
2. Back-seat suction valve to allow refrigerant to enter compressor.

3. Place discharge service valve in mid-position, then loosen discharge service valve gauge port cap to allow refrigerant to force air from compressor.
4. Back-seat discharge service valve and tighten gauge port cap.
5. Remove manifold and gauge set.

Discharging System

1. Connect gauges into system, Figs. 3 and 4, and adjust controls for maximum cooling. *This is necessary when the system has not been operating to return excess oil to the compressor.*
2. Operate engine for 10 to 15 minutes to stabilize the system at 1500–1750 rpm.
3. Adjust engine speed to slow idle, then shut off engine and controls.
4. Open low side hand manifold valve slightly, using a container to catch oil and refrigerant. *Do not discharge the refrigerant near an open flame as a toxic gas (phosgene) can result.*
5. On AMC, Chrysler and Ford full size models, open high side manifold valve slightly. On Ford (except full size) and GM models, allow all refrigerant to discharge through the low side fitting only.

NOTE: Open hand valve(s) only enough to bleed refrigerant from system. Too rapid purging will draw excessive oil from compressor and system.

Fig. 3 Manifold gauge set connections. Chrysler Airtemp RV2 compressor

Fig. 4 Manifold gauge set hose connections (Typical). Except Chrysler Airtemp RV2 compressor

6. On AMC, Chrysler and Ford full size models, close gauge manifold hand valves when refrigerant ceases to bleed from discharge hose and manifold gauges read zero. On Ford (except full size) and GM models, when refrigerant ceases to bleed from the discharge hose on the low side, crack open the high side hand valve to check for any remaining pressure. If pressure does exist, allow high side to discharge slowly. This condition indicates a high side restriction, and it must be diagnosed and corrected before evacuating and charging the system.

Evacuate System with Vacuum Pump

Vacuum pumps suitable for removing air and moisture from A/C systems are commercially available. A specification for system pump-down used here is 28 to 29½" vacuum. This reading can be attained at or near sea level only. For each 1000 feet of altitude this operation is being performed, the reading will be 1" vacuum lower. As an example, at 5000 feet elevation, only 23–24½" of vacuum can be obtained.

CAUTION: The system must be completely discharged before it can be evacuated. Damage to vacuum pump may result if pressurized refrigerant is allowed to enter.

AMC, Chrysler & Ford Full Size Models
1. With gauges connected into system, remove cap from vacuum hose connector. Install center hose from gauge manifold to vacuum pump connector. Mid-position high and low side compressor service valves (if used). Open high and low side gauge manifold hand valves.
2. Operate vacuum pump a minimum of 30 minutes for air and moisture removal. Watch compound gauge that system pumps down into a vacuum. System will reach 28–29½" vacuum in not over 5 minutes. If system does not pump down, check all connections and leak-test if necessary.
3. Close gauge manifold hand valves and shut off vacuum pump.
4. Check ability of system to hold vacuum.

Watch compound gauge to see that gauge does not rise at a faster rate than 1" vacuum every 4 or 5 minutes. If compound gauge rises at too rapid a rate, install partial charge and leak-test. Then evacuate system as outlined above.
5. If system holds vacuum, charge system with refrigerant.

Ford (Except Full Size) & GM Models
1. With hand gauges connected into system, remove cap from vacuum hose connector. Install hand gauge manifold center hose to vacuum pump connector. Open low side gauge manifold hand valve only.
2. Ensure low side gauge is calibrated correctly. It should be reading zero. If not, adjust calibration.
3. Evacuate system with the vacuum pump until the low pressure gauge reads at least 28" of vacuum. Continue evacuating system for an additional 15 minutes for routine system servicing or 20 to 30 minutes, if any parts have been replaced.
4. When system evacuation is complete, close low side gauge manifold hand valve, then turn vacuum pump off.
5. Check ability of system to hold vacuum. Watch low side gauge to see that gauge does not rise at a faster rate than 1" vacuum every 4 to 5 minutes; if low side gauge rises at too rapid a rate, install partial charge and leak test. Evacuate system again.
6. If system holds vacuum, charge system with refrigerant.

Evacuate System Using Charging Station

A vacuum pump is built into the charging station and is constructed to withstand repeated and prolonged use without damage. Complete moisture removal from the system is possible only with a vacuum pump constructed for the purpose.

CAUTION: The system must be completely discharged before it can be evacuated. Damage to the vacuum pump may result if pressurized refrigerant is allowed to enter.

AMC, Chrysler & Ford Full Size Models
1. Connect hose to vacuum pump if system was discharged through charging station.
2. Open high and low side gauge valves of charging station.
3. Connect station into 110-volt current.
4. Engage "Off-On" switch to vacuum pump according to directions of specific station being used.
5. System should pump down into a 28–29½" vacuum in not more than 5 minutes. If system fails to meet this specification, repair as necessary.
6. Operate pump a minimum of 30 minutes to remove all air and moisture.
7. Close high and low side gauge valves. Open switch to turn off pump.
8. Check ability of system to hold vacuum by watching compound gauge to see that it does not rise at a rate higher than 1" of vacuum every 4 or 5 minutes: If rise rate is not within specifications, repair system as necessary. If rise rate is within specifications, charge system with refrigerant.

Ford (Except Full Size Models) & GM Models
1. Connect hose to vacuum pump, if system was discharged through charging station.
2. Open low side gauge hand valve of charging station.
3. Connect station into 110 volt current.
4. Engage "Off-On" switch to vacuum pump according to instructions for specific station being used.
5. Evacuate system with the vacuum pump until the low pressure gauge reads at least 28" of vacuum. Continue evacuating system for an additional 15 minutes for routine system servicing or 20 to 30 minutes, if any parts have been replaced.
6. Close low side gauge hand valve, then turn vacuum pump off.
7. Check ability of system to hold vacuum. Watch low side gauge to see that gauge does not rise at a faster rate than 1" vacuum every 4 to 5 minutes. If low side gauge rises at too rapid a rate, install partial charge and leak test. Then evacuate system again.
8. If system holds vacuum, charge system with refrigerant.

AIR CONDITIONING

CHARGING THE SYSTEM

AMC, Chrysler & Ford Full Size Models

Using 14-Ounce Containers

CAUTION: Do not use 14 ounce cans to charge into high pressure side of system or into a system that is at high temperature. High system pressures could cause charging can to explode.

To prevent waste and to aid in more accurate charging, refrigerant manufacturers package refrigerant in 14-ounce cans. The small containers are advantageous to small shops doing only a limited amount of A/C service work. The small containers are handled in the same manner as the larger drums except care must be taken not to overheat the cans because of the danger of explosion.

1. Install "Fitz-All" valve to container(s). The Fitz-All valve is available for single cans or three cans. Whichever is used, preliminary installation to the can(s) is the same.
2. Close shut-off valve of Fitz-All valve. Pierce can with mechanism which is part of Fitz-All valve.
3. With the system pumped-down, install charging hose to Fitz-All valve. Loosen charging hose at center connector on gauge manifold.
4. Crack Fitz-All shut-off valve to purge air from charging hose. Tighten charging hose connection on gauge manifold and close shut-off valve.
5. Open low side hand valve slowly, allowing refrigerant to enter system. When refrigerant ceases to enter, shut off low side hand valve and start engine. Set engine speed at approximately 1500 rpm and A/C controls at maximum cooling, then open low side hand valve slowly allowing refrigerant to be drawn into the system. Adjust hand valve as necessary so charging pressure does not exceed 50 psig. If necessary, warm refrigerant in a pan of water to aid in the transfer of the charge into the system. Use A/C Data table to determine capacity of system being serviced. If single containers are being used, it will be necessary to replace each as it becomes empty.

NOTE: If it is necessary to warm refrigerant in a pan of water, ensure temperature of water does not exceed 125° F. to prevent bursting of can.

6. Bubbles may appear in sight glass even though system is fully charged. After system is fully charged, test system for leaks and make functional check of system.

Using Charging Station

Most stations contain a charging cylinder into which the exact amount of refrigerant required for the system being serviced may be placed while system pump-down is being per-

formed. The refrigerant charging cylinder contained in the station is heated to the correct temperature to insure proper refrigerant flow to all parts of the system as a gas during the charging operation. Following correct evacuation procedure as to length of time for complete moisture removal, the vacuum pump will so efficiently pump-down the system that opening the correct valves will completely charge the system from the high side, and the use of the compressor in the charging operation will not be required.

1. Prepare charging cyclinder for filling: Open storage drum valve. Close all valves on station. Read storage tank gauge pressure. Rotate dial shroud on charging cylinder to correlate with pressure on gauge. Open cylinder fill valve.
2. Fill charging cylinder: Determine system capacity from A/C Data table. Intermittently open and close pressure relief valve. *When pressure relief valve opens, Freon will enter cylinder and boil. Closing the valve will increase pressure on the Freon, changing it to a liquid to stabilize the refrigerant in the sight glass. Fill to specified level in sight glass and close pressure relief valve.*
3. Charge system: With gauges connected into system, open refrigerant control valve. Open high pressure valve. After full charge has entered system, close refrigerant control valve and high pressure valve. Reseat suction and discharge service valves and remove charging station hoses.
4. Test system for leaks and make functional check of system.

Ford (Exc. Full Size Models) & GM Models

NOTE: The following procedure applies to vehicles which have been discharged, oil level checked and corrected as necessary, and evacuated.

1. With engine running at normal idle speed, set A/C controls to OFF.
2. With refrigerant drums or cans inverted, open valves and allow 1 pound or 1 14 ounce can of liquid refrigerant to enter system through low side service fitting.
3. As soon as 1 pound or 1 14 ounce can of liquid refrigerant enters the system, immediately engage the compressor, by setting the A/C control to NORM and blower speed on HI to draw in the remainder of the recommended refrigerant charge. Refer to specifications.

NOTE: To speed up the charging process, place a fan in front of the condenser so that the additional air flow will maintain the temperature of the condenser below that of the charging cylinder.

4. Close refrigerant source valve and run engine for 30 seconds to clear lines and gauges.

5. With engine running, quickly disconnect the charging hose adapter from the low side fitting.

CAUTION: Disconnect charging hose adapter from low side fitting as quickly as possible to avoid excess loss of refrigerant. Also, never disconnect charging line from adapter, as this will cause a total discharge of the system due to the depressed shrader valve in the service fitting.

6. Replace protective cap on low side fitting and leak check system.
7. Check system for proper system pressures.

LEAK TEST SYSTEM

The propane torch Halide Leak Detector is the most widely used of the detection devices. Therefore, only the procedure for this device will be given. The procedure is the same for any electronic detector, except that the pick-up device registers the presence of refrigerant by a flashing light or high pitched squeal instead of changing the color of the flame. All other steps in preparing the system and leak testing are the same and can be followed as outlined below:

1. Stabilize system at 1500–1750 rpm. If system is empty of refrigerant, it will be necessary to install a partial charge before continuing. With gauges connected into system, adjust A/C controls for maximum cooling. Operate for 10 to 15 minutes, then shut off car engine.
2. Light leak detector. Open valve to a low flame that will not blow itself out. Warm up until copper element turns cherry red. Lower flame until flame tip is even with or slightly below center of element. *For electronic tester, follow preparation procedure as given in operating instructions.*
3. Move leak detector pick-up under hoses, joints, seals, and any possible place for a leak to occur.

NOTE: Freon 12 refrigerant is heavier than air and will move downward. If concentration of refrigerant is located, move pick-up upward to locate leak. Do not inhale fumes produced by burning refrigerant.

4. Watch for color change of flame: Pale blue, no refrigerant; yellow, small amount of refrigerant; purplish-blue, large amount of refrigerant. Repair system as necessary if leaks are located.
5. Check sensitivity of reaction plate: Pass pick-up hose over empty can or crack open refrigerant container; flame should show violent reaction. If no color change, replace reaction plate, following instructions accompanying leak detector. *Too high a flame will result in short life to reaction plate and poor reaction and will soon burn out element.*
6. Charge system if repairs were necessary.

A/C System Servicing

OIL CHARGE

Delco Air & Frigidaire Compressors Models With Cycling Clutch

Oil Charge-Component Replacement

If there are no signs of excessive leakage, add the following amount of oil depending on component to be replaced.

Evaporator . . . . 3 ounces
Condenser . . . . 1 ounce

If accumulator or compressor are to be replaced, drain oil from component to be replaced and measure, then add same amount of new oil to replacement component plus one additional ounce.

CAUTION: On 1981–82 units, if accumulator is replaced, two additional ounces of oil must be added to replace amount captured by desiccant in old accumulator.

NOTE: The radial 4 cylinder compressor does not have an oil sump.

Oil Charge-Leak Condition

On models with axial 6 cylinder compressor, both accumulator and compressor must be removed and oil drained and measured in cases of excessive oil leakage. If oil recovered is 4 ounces or more, add same amount of new refrigerant oil to system. If amount of oil recovered is less than 4 ounces, add 6 ounces of new refrigerant oil to system.

On models with radial 4 cylinder compressor, it will only be necessary to remove and drain and measure oil from accumulator assembly in cases of excessive oil leakage. The radial 4 cylinder compressor does not have an oil sump, therefore it is not necessary to remove compressor in cases of oil leakage. On 1977–80 units, if amount of oil recovered is 2 ounces or more, add same amount of new refrigerant oil to system. If amount of oil recovered is less than 2 ounces, add two ounces of new refrigerant oil to system. On 1981–82 units, if amount of oil recovered is 3 ounces or more, add the same amount of new refrigerant oil to system. If amount recovered is less than 3 ounces, add 3 ounces of new refrigerant oil to system.

NOTE: On 1977–80 units, if accumulator is replaced one additional ounce of oil must be added to replace amount captured by desiccant in old accumulator. On 1981–82 units, if accumulator is replaced two additional ounces of oil must be added to replace amount captured by desiccant in old accumulator.

Models Less Cycling Clutch

RADIAL 4 CYLINDER COMPRESSOR

Component Replacement

When replacing a system component, oil should be added to the system as follows. If compressor is operating, idle engine for 10 minutes with A/C controls set for maximum cooling and high blower prior to discharging system.

Add additional oil as specified if any of components are replaced.

Condenser . . . . 1 ounce
Evaporator . . . . 1 ounce
VIR . . . . 3 ounce
Accumulator . . . . 1 ounce

Compressor Replacement

1. Discharge system and remove compressor from vehicle.
2. Position compressor with shaft end up and allow oil to drain from suction and discharge ports into a container calibrated in ounces.
3. Drain oil from new compressor, then add same amount of new refrigerant oil to new compressor as was drained from original compressor.

NOTE: If system was flushed the total oil capacity must be added to the compressor as specified in the *A/C Data Table*.

4. Install new compressor and charge system.

Component Rupture, Fast Discharge

1. Repair leak and flush system.
2. Remove compressor and drain oil.
3. Add total capacity as specified in A/C *Data Table* of new refrigerant oil to suction port of compressor.
4. Install compressor, charge system and perform leak check.

Slow Leak

1. If refrigerant loss has occurred over an extended period of time, add 3 ounces of refrigerant oil to system.
2. Recharge system.

System Performance Evaluation

When system performance, efficiency and proper oil charge are in doubt, the system should be flushed and the total capacity, as specified in the *A/C Data Table,* of new refrigerant oil be added to the compressor prior to any further checks of the system.

AXIAL 6 CYLINDER COMPRESSOR

Oil Charge

1. Idle engine for 10 minutes at 1250 rpm with system controls set for maximum cooling and high blower speed.
2. Stop engine, discharge system and remove compressor.
3. With compressor in a horizontal position and drain plug down, remove plug and drain oil into a measured container.
4. If 4 ounces or more of oil was drained, add the same amount to the compressor. If less than 4 ounces of oil was drained, add 6 ounces of oil to compressor.

Compressor Replacement

1. Idle engine for 10 minutes at approximately 1250 rpm at maximum cooling and high blower speed to distribute oil in system.
2. Remove compressor from vehicle.

3. Remove plug and allow oil to drain from compressor into a container calibrated in ounces.
4. Drain oil from new compressor.
5. If amount drained from original compressor is more than four ounces, add the same amount of new refrigerant oil to the new compressor plus amount lost during discharge.
6. If amount of oil drained from original compressor is less than 4 ounces, add 6 ounces of new refrigerant oil to the new compressor plus amount lost during discharge.

Component Replacement

Whenever a component of the A/C system is replaced, if not pre-charged by factory, measured quantities of refrigeration oil should be added to the component to assure that the total oil charge in the system is correct before the unit is placed into operation.

The oil is poured directly into the replacement component. If an evaporator is installed, pour oil into the inlet pipe with the pipe held vertically so the oil will drain into the evaporator core. No additional oil is required if valves and hoses are replaced.

Add additional oil as specified if any of the following components are replaced.

Evaporator (front or rear) . . . . 3 ounces
Condenser . . . . 1 ounce
VIR . . . . 1 ounce
Accumulator . . . . 1 ounce
Receiver . . . . 1 ounce

NOTE: If the system is flushed with sufficient quantity of a flushing agent that would remove oil from the system, install the full amount specified in the *A/C Data Table*. On a newly installed system, install the full capacity of oil prior to operation. On systems containing metal particles in the oil, replace or overhaul the compressor, replace the receiver-dehydrator or VIR dessicant and install a high capacity, low pressure drop filter in the liquid line to the filter to protect the expansion valve and new compressor from damage due to foreign particles.

1977–80 Motorcraft Axial 6 Cyl Compressor

Refer to Delco Air and Frigidaire for oil charge procedure.

1980–82 Ford FS6 & Nippondenso 6 Cyl. Compressors

1. If compressor is not seized, operate engine at 1000 to 1500 RPM with A/C on maximum cooling and high blower for approximately 10 minutes.
2. Discharge refrigerant system, then remove compressor from vehicle.
3. Remove drain plug from compressor and pour refrigerant oil into a calibrated container.
4. If oil drained is less than 3 ounces, add 6 ounces of new refrigerant oil to compressor.
5. If oil drained is between 3 and 6 ounces, add the same amount of new refrigerant oil to system.

Fig. 5 Air Temp compressor oil level dipstick fabrication and filler plug location

Fig. 6 Positioning compressor for oil level check. Sankyo compressor

Fig. 7 Positioning front plate for oil level check. Sankyo compressor

Fig. 9 Checking oil level. Sankyo compressor

Fig. 8 (left column)

Fig. 8 Top piston rod as viewed through oil filler port. Sankyo compressor

6. If oil drained is more than 6 ounces, only add six ounces to compressor.

NOTE: Replacement compressors are charged with 10 ounces of refrigerant oil. Before installing a replacement compressor, the oil must be drained and only 6 ounces of oil reinstalled into the replacement compressor. When certain other refrigerant system components are replaced, the oil level must be adjusted to compensate for oil retained in these components. When installing a replacement evaporator core, add 3 ounces of oil to evaporator. When installing a replacement condenser or accumulator, add 1 ounce of oil to the component.

OIL LEVEL CHECK

NOTE: The oil level of these compressors should be checked whenever refrigerant has been lost due to leakage or through normal system servicing.

Chrysler Air Temp Compressors

RV2 Compressor
1. Connect gauge and manifold assembly, Fig. 3, and slowly discharge refrigerant system. Near completion of discharge, flush dipstick with existing freon. This will ensure dipstick is clean and at approximately the same temperature as refrigerant oil in compressor sump.
2. Carefully remove compressor oil sump filler plug, then insert dipstick into hole until it bottoms in sump, Fig. 5.

NOTE: When removing compressor oil sump filler plug a face shield should be worn. Refrigerant dissolved in compressor oil could cause oil to purcolate out through filler plug opening.

3. Remove dipstick and measure oil level, refer to A/C Specification Tables. Add refrigerant oil as necessary to bring oil level within limits.

NOTE: Oil level should be checked only after refrigerant has boiled off and oil surface has stabilized.

4. If any of the following components are to be replaced, it will be necessary to add additional oil to system.
   Evaporator . . . . 2 ounces
   Condenser . . . . 1 ounce
   Filter Drier . . . . 1 ounce
5. On all models, install filler plug, then evacuate and recharge system.

C–171 Compressor
1. Discharge refrigerant from system.
2. On 1979 models, drain and discard oil through drain plug at bottom of compressor. On 1980–82 models, remove compressor from vehicle, then invert compressor and allow oil to drain from suction and discharge ports.
3. On 1979 models, install drain plug and torque to 90–130 inch lbs., then remove suction line and add 5 fluid ounces of clean refrigerant oil through suction port. Then install suction line using a new gasket.
4. On 1980–82 models, add 5 fluid ounces of clean refrigerant oil through suction port, then install compressor and connect suction and discharge lines using new gaskets.
5. Evacuate and recharge system.

NOTE: The C–171 compressor contains 9 to 10 ounces of refrigerant oil. While the A/C system is in operation, the oil is carried through the entire system by the refrigerant. Some of the oil will be retained in the various components of the system. If a replacement evaporator coil is installed, add 2 ounces of refrigerant oil to system. If a replacement condenser coil or filter-drier is installed, add one additional ounce of refrigerant oil to system. This additional oil must be added to compensate for oil removed with the component. Replacement compresssors are charged with 9 to 10 ounces of refrigerant oil, therefore before installing a replacement compressor, approximately 4 ounces of refrigerant oil should be drained from the compressor.

Sankyo 5 Cyl. Rotary Compressor

1979 Chrysler Corp. Models
1. Disconnect and plug vacuum hose from

water valve.
2. With engine at idle speed, operate A/C system for 10 minutes in Max A/C mode, high blower speed and temperature control set at maximum heat.
3. Shut off engine and reconnect water valve vacuum hose, then slowly discharge the A/C system.
4. Loosen compressor mounting bolts and remove belt, then rotate compressor so that oil filler tube is at top dead center position, Fig. 6.
5. Thoroughly clean area around oil filler plug and remove plug.

CAUTION: Use care when removing the filler plug to prevent the dissolved refrigerant in the crankcase oil from percolating out through the filler plug opening. This action will stop as soon as the refrigerant has boiled away. Also, the oil level should be measured only after the refrigerant has boiled away and the oil surface has stabilized.

6. Rotate front plate of clutch hub so that notch in center of lobe is indexed 110° from bottom, Fig. 7. In this position, the ball end of the piston rod aligns with oil filler port, Fig. 8.
7. Looking at front plate with lobe notch at upper left in the 110° position, insert dipstick (tool C-4504) diagonally from upper right to lower left until stop contacts the filler port surface, Fig. 9.

NOTE: Before inserting dipstick, clean and cool the dipstick with refrigerant.

Fig. 10 York compressor oil level dipstick fabrication. Ford Motor Co. models

Fig. 11 York compressor oil level dipstick fabrication. American Motors

8. Remove dipstick and note oil level. The dipstick is marked in eight increments and each increment represents one ounce of oil. Add oil if necessary to bring level within specifications.

1981 American Motors California Models W/ 6–258 Engine & All 1982
When installing a replacement compressor, proceed as follows:
1. Isolate compressor from system, then remove compressor.
2. Remove oil plug from compressor, then drain refrigerant oil into a calibrated container.
3. Drain refrigerant oil from compressor to be installed.
4. Add the same amount of refrigerant oil removed from compressor to be replaced plus 1 ounce to the compressor to be installed.
5. Install drain plug, then install and purge air from compressor.

Tecumseh & York

1. Connect manifold gauge set, Fig. 4, then operate system for approximately 10 minutes or until system pressures stabilize. This will allow oil in the system to return to compressor sump.
2. On American Motors models, isolate compressor as outlined earlier.
3. On Ford Motor Co. models, discharge entire refrigerant system.
4. On all models, slowly loosen compressor oil filler plug to relieve any internal pressures in compressor.

Fig. 12 Tecumseh compressor oil level dipstick fabrication. Ford Motor Co. models

NOTE: A face shield should be worn when loosening or removing oil filler plug.

5. Insert clean dipstick into filler plug hole until it bottoms in sump, Figs. 10, 11 and 12.

NOTE: On York compressors ensure keyway in shaft faces head of compressor before checking oil level.

6. Remove dipstick and measure oil level. Refer to "A/C Data Table" and add refrigerant oil as necessary. Install filler plug and "O" ring.
7. On American Motors models, purge air from compressor.
8. On Ford Motor Co. models, evacuate and recharge system.

AIR CONDITIONING SPECIFICATIONS

Year	Model	Refrigerant Capacity, Lbs.	Refrigeration Oil			Compressor Clutch Air Gap Inch
			Viscosity	Total System Capacity, Ounces	Compressor Oil Level Check, Inches	
AMERICAN MOTORS						
1977	Matador	3	③	7	⑧	—
	Gremlin, Hornet	2	③	7	⑧	—
	Pacer	2 1/8	③	7	⑧	—
1978	AMX, Concord, Gremlin	2	③	7	⑧	—
	Matador	3	③	7	⑧	—
	Pacer	2 1/8	③	7	⑧	—
1979	AMX, Concord, Spirit	2	③	7	⑧	—
	Pacer	2 1/8	③	7	⑧	—
1980	York 2 Cyl. Comp.	⑱	③	7	⑧	—
	Delco Air 4 Cyl. Comp.	⑱	525	6	①	.020–.040
1981	York 2 Cyl. Comp.	2	③	7	⑧	—
	Delco Air 4 Cyl. Comp.	2	525	6	①	.020–.040
	Sankyo 5 Cyl. Comp.	2	500	7–8	①	.016–.031
1982	All	2	500	7–8	①	.016–.031
BUICK—EXC. SKYHAWK, 1980–82 SKYLARK & 1982 CENTURY						
1977–79	Skylark	3 1/2	525	④	①	⑲
	Century & Regal	3 3/4	525	④	①	⑲
	Electra, LeSabre, Riviera	3 3/4	525	④	①	⑲
1980	Century, Regal, Riviera	3 1/2	525	④	①	⑲
	Electra & LeSabre	3 3/4	525	④	①	⑲
1981	Century, Regal, Riviera	3 1/4	525	④	①	⑲
	Electra & LeSabre	3 1/2	525	④	①	⑲
1982	Regal & Riviera	3 1/4	525	6	①	.020–.040
	Electra & LeSabre	3 1/2	525	6	①	.020–.040
CADILLAC—EXC. CIMARRON						
1977–79	All Exc. Seville	⑥	525	⑩	①	⑲
1977–79	Seville	3 1/2	525	10	①	⑲
1980–81	All Models	3 3/4	525	6	①	⑲
1982	All Models	3 1/4	525	6	①	.020–.040
CAMARO, CHEVROLET, MALIBU, MONTE CARLO & NOVA						
1977–79	Nova	3 1/2	525	④	①	⑲
1977–80	Exc. Camaro, Nova	3 3/4	525	④	①	⑲
1977–81	Camaro	3 1/4	525	④	①	⑲
1982 CHEV. CAVALIER, BUICK SKYHAWK, CAD. CIMARRON, OLDS. FIRENZA & PONT. J2000						
1982	All	2 3/4	525	6	①	.020–.040
CHEV. CELEBRITY, BUICK CENTURY, OLDS. CUTLASS CIERA & PONT. 6000						
1982	All Models	2 3/4	525	6	①	.020–.040
CHEVROLET CHEVETTE & PONTIAC T1000						
1977–82	All	2 1/4	525	④	①	⑲
1980–82 CHEVROLET CITATION, BUICK SKYLARK, OLDS OMEGA & PONTIAC PHOENIX						
1980–82	All Models	2 3/4	525	5 1/2–6 1/2	①	.020–.040

Continued

AIR CONDITIONING SPECIFICATIONS—Continued

Year	Model	Refrigerant Capacity, Lbs.	Refrigeration Oil			Compressor Clutch Air Gap Inch
			Viscosity	Total System Capacity, Ounces	Compressor Oil Level Check, Inches	
1977–80 CHEVROLET MONZA, BUICK SKYHAWK, OLDS STARFIRE & PONTIAC SUNBIRD						
1977–80	Monza	$2^{13}/16$	525	④	①	⑲
1977	Skyhawk	3	525	6	①	.020–.040
	Sunbird	$3^1/4$	525	6	①	.020–.040
1977–78	Starfire	$2^1/2$	525	6	①	.020–.040
1978–80	Skyhawk	$2^1/2$	525	6	①	.020–.040
	Sunbird	$2^1/2$	525	6	①	.020–.040
1979–80	Starfire	⑨	525	6	①	.020–.040
CHEVROLET VEGA & PONTIAC ASTRE						
1977	Astre	$2^1/2$	525	$5^1/2$–$6^1/2$	①	.020–.040
	Vega	$2^{13}/16$	525	$5^1/2$–$6^1/2$	①	.020–.040
CHEVROLET CORVETTE						
1977–81	All	3	525	④	①	⑲
CHRYSLER CORP. REAR WHEEL DRIVE						
CHRYSLER						
1977	Newport & New Yorker	$2^3/4$	500	10–12	$2^3/8$ ②	—
	Cordoba & LeBaron	$2^5/8$	500	10–12	$2^3/8$ ②	—
1978–79	All	$2^5/8$	500	⑤	⑰	⑳
1980	Newport & New Yorker	$2^7/8$	500	⑤	⑰	.020–.035
	Cordoba & LeBaron	$2^5/8$	500	⑤	⑰	.020–.035
1981	All	$2^5/8$	500	⑤	⑰	.020–.035
1982	All	$2^5/8$	500	9–10	⑦	.020–.035
DODGE						
1977	Monaco	$2^3/4$	500	10–12	$2^3/8$ ②	—
	Exc. Monaco	$2^5/8$	500	10–12	$2^3/8$ ②	—
1978–79	All	$2^5/8$	500	⑤	⑰	⑳
1980	St. Regis	$2^7/8$	500	⑤	⑰	.020–.035
	Exc. St. Regis	$2^5/8$	500	⑤	⑰	.020–.035
1981	All	$2^5/8$	500	⑤	⑰	.020–.035
1982	All	$2^5/8$	500	9–10	⑦	.020–.035
PLYMOUTH						
1977	Gran Fury	$2^3/4$	500	10–12	$2^3/8$ ②	—
	Fury & Volaré	$2^5/8$	500	10–12	$2^3/8$ ②	—
1978–79	All	$2^5/8$	500	⑤	⑰	⑳
1980	Gran Fury	$2^7/8$	500	⑤	⑰	.020–.035
	Volaré	$2^5/8$	500	⑤	⑰	.020–.035
1981	All	$2^5/8$	500	⑤	⑰	.020–.035
1982	All	$2^5/8$	500	9–10	⑦	.020–.035
CHRYSLER CORP. FRONT WHEEL DRIVE						
1978–79	Horizon & Omni	$2^1/8$	500	7–8	⑪	⑳
1980–81	Horizon & Omni	$2^1/8$	500	⑤	⑦	.020–.035
1981	Aries & Reliant	$2^3/8$	500	⑤	⑦	.020–.035
1982	Horizon & Omni	$2^1/8$	500	9–10	⑦	.020–.035
	Aries, Diplomat Reliant & 400	$2^3/8$	500	9–10	⑦	.020–.035
FORD—FULL SIZE						
1977–79	All	$4^1/4$	525	$10^1/2$	①	.022–.057
1980	All	$3^1/4$	⑫	⑬	①	⑭
1981–82	All	$3^1/4$	500	13	①	.021–.036

AIR CONDITIONING SPECIFICATIONS—Continued

Year	Model	Refrigerant Capacity, Lbs.	Refrigeration Oil			Compressor Clutch Air Gap Inch
			Viscosity	Total Sytem Capacity, Ounces	Compressor Oil Level Check, Inches	

FORD—COMPACT & INTERMEDIATE (EXC. MUSTANG & PINTO)

Year	Model	Refrigerant Capacity, Lbs.	Viscosity	Total Sytem Capacity, Ounces	Compressor Oil Level Check, Inches	Compressor Clutch Air Gap Inch
1977–78	Granada	4¼	525	10½	①	.022–.057
1977–79	York Comp.	⑮	③	10	②⑧	—
	Tecumseh Comp.	⑮	③	11	②⑧	—
1979–80	Granada	4	525	10½	①	.022–.057
1980–81	York Comp.	3½	③	10	②⑧	—
	Tecumseh	3½	③	11	②⑧	—
1982	York Comp.	2½	③	10	②⑧	—
	Tecumseh Comp.	2½	③	11	②⑧	—
	Ford FS-6	2½	500	13	①	.021–.036

FORD ESCORT & EXP; MERCURY LYNX & LN7

Year	Model	Refrigerant Capacity, Lbs.	Viscosity	Total Sytem Capacity, Ounces	Compressor Oil Level Check, Inches	Compressor Clutch Air Gap Inch
1981	Escort & Lynx	2½	500	13	①	.021–.036
1982	All	2½	500	10	①	.021–.036

FORD MUSTANG & MERCURY CAPRI

Year	Model	Refrigerant Capacity, Lbs.	Viscosity	Total Sytem Capacity, Ounces	Compressor Oil Level Check, Inches	Compressor Clutch Air Gap Inch
1977–78	York Comp.	3¼	③	10	②⑧	—
	Tecumseh Comp.	3¼	③	11	②⑧	—
1979–81	York Comp.	3½	③	10	②⑧	—
	Tecumseh Comp.	3½	③	11	②⑧	—
1982	York Comp.	2½	③	10	②⑧	—
	Tecumseh Comp.	2½	③	11	②⑧	—

FORD PINTO & MERCURY BOBCAT

Year	Model	Refrigerant Capacity, Lbs.	Viscosity	Total Sytem Capacity, Ounces	Compressor Oil Level Check, Inches	Compressor Clutch Air Gap Inch
1977–80	York Comp.	2¼	③	10	②⑧	—
	Tecumseh Comp.	2¼	③	11	②⑧	—

LINCOLN CONTINENTAL, MARK V, VI & VERSAILLES

Year	Model	Refrigerant Capacity, Lbs.	Viscosity	Total Sytem Capacity, Ounces	Compressor Oil Level Check, Inches	Compressor Clutch Air Gap Inch
1977–78	Mark V	4½	525	10½	①	.022–.057
	Lincoln	4¼	525	10½	①	.022–.057
1977–78	Versailles	4¼	525	10½	①	.022–.057
1979–80	Exc. Versailles	4¼	⑫	⑬	①	⑭
	Versailles	4	⑫	⑬	①	.022–.057
1981–82	All exc. 1982 Continental	3	500	13	①	.021–.036
1982	Continental	2½	500	13	①	.021–.036

MERCURY—FULL SIZE

Year	Model	Refrigerant Capacity, Lbs.	Viscosity	Total Sytem Capacity, Ounces	Compressor Oil Level Check, Inches	Compressor Clutch Air Gap Inch
1977–79	All	4¼	525	10½	①	.022–.057
1980	All	3¼	⑫	⑬	①	⑭
1981–82	All	3¼	500	13	①	.022–.036

MERCURY—COMPACT & INTERMEDIATE (EXC. BOBCAT & CAPRI)

Year	Model	Refrigerant Capacity, Lbs.	Viscosity	Total Sytem Capacity, Ounces	Compressor Oil Level Check, Inches	Compressor Clutch Air Gap Inch
1977–78	Monarch	4¼	525	10½	①	.022–.057
1977–79	York Comp.	⑯	③	10	②⑧	—
	Tecumseh Comp.	⑯	③	11	②⑧	—
1979–80	Monarch	4	525	10½	①	.022–.057
1980–81	York	3½	③	10	②⑧	—
	Tecumseh	3½	③	11	②⑧	—
1982	York Comp.	2½	③	10	②⑧	—
	Tecumseh	2½	③	11	②⑧	—
	Ford FS-6	2½	500	13	①	.021–.036

Continued

AIR CONDITIONING SPECIFICATIONS—Continued

Year	Model	Refrigerant Capacity, Lbs.	Refrigeration Oil			Compressor Oil Level Check, Inches	Compressor Clutch Air Gap Inch
			Viscosity	Total Sytem Capacity, Ounces	Compressor Oil Level Check, Inches		
OLDSMOBILE—EXC. STARFIRE, 1980–81 OMEGA & 1982 CUTLASS CIERA							
1977–79	Omega	3½	525	④	①	⑲	
1977–80	All exc. Omega	3¾	525	④	①	⑲	
1981	Cutlass	3¼	525	④	①	⑲	
1981	All exc. Cutlass	3½	525	④	①	⑲	
1982	Cutlass	3¼	525	6	①	.020–.040	
1982	All exc. Cutlass	3½	525	6	①	.020–.040	
PONTIAC—EXC. T1000 & FRONT WHEEL DRIVE							
1977	Ventura	3½	525	④	①	⑲	
1977–79	Phoenix	3½	525	④	①	⑲	
1977–79	All exc. Ventura, Phoenix & Firebird	3¾	525	④	①	⑲	
1977–81	Firebird	3¼	525	④	①	⑲	
1980	Gran Prix & LeMans	3¾	525	④	①	⑲	
1980–81	All exc. Gran Prix & LeMans	3½	525	④	①	⑲	
1981	Gran Prix & LeMans	3¼	525	④	①	⑲	
1982	All exc. Firebird	3¼	525	④	①	⑲	
1982	Firebird	3	525	④	①	⑲	

①—Note that "Oil level inches" cannot be checked. Refer to total capacity in ounces. See text for procedure.
②—Dipstick reading with compressor installed.
③—Suniso 5G or Capella E.
④—Axial comp., 10 oz.; radial comp., 6 oz.
⑤—With RV2 compressor, 10–12 ounces. With Sankyo Compressor, 7–8 ounces. With C-171 compressor, 9 ounces.
⑥—With one evaporator, 3¾. With two evaporators, 5.
⑦—Refer to text for C-171 compressor.
⑧—York Comp.—Vertical mount., 7/8–1 1/8; horizontal mount., 13/16–13/16. Tecumseh Comp.—Vertical mount., 7/8–1 3/8; horizontal mount., 7/8–1 5/8.

⑨—With axial compressor, 3 lbs.; with radial compressor, 2½ lbs.
⑩—With one evaporator, 10½. With two evaporators, 13½.
⑪—On Sankyo compressor oil level should be at the third to fourth increment on the dipstick which represents 3 to 4 ounces of oil. Refer to text for procedure. On C-171 compressor, refer to text for procedure.
⑫—Motorcraft compressor, 525 viscosity; Nippondenso compressor, 500 viscosity.
⑬—Motorcraft compressor, 10½ ounces; Nippondenso compressor, 13 ounces.
⑭—Motorcraft compressor, .022–.057"; Nippondenso compressor, .021–.036".

⑮—Maverick, 1 7/8; LTD II & Thunderbird, 4¼; Fairmont, 3½.
⑯—Comet, 1 7/8; Cougar, 4¼; Zephyr, 3½.
⑰—RV2 compressor, 2 3/8 inches. On Sankyo compressors, the oil level should be at the third to fourth increment on the dipstick which represents 3 to 4 ounces of oil. Refer to text for procedure. On C-171 compressor, refer to text.
⑱—AMX, Concord & Spirit, 2; Pacer, 2 1/8.
⑲—R-4 compressor, .020–.040", A-6 compressor, .022–.057".
⑳—RV-2 compressor, non-adjustable; Sankyo compressor, .016–.032"; C-171 compressor, .020–.035".

CHARGING VALVE LOCATIONS

Year & Model	High Press.	Low Press.
AMERICAN MOTORS		
1977–79	Compressor	Compressor
1980–82	①	①
BUICK (EXC. SKYHAWK, 1980–82 SKYLARK & 1982 CENTURY)		
1977–82	⑨	Accumulator
CADILLAC (EXC. CIMARRON)		
1977–79	⑤	Accumulator
1980–82	⑨	Accumulator
CAMARO, CHEVROLET NOVA, MALIBU & MONTE CARLO		
1977–82	⑨	Accumulator
CHEVROLET CAVALIER, BUICK SKYHAWK, CADILLAC CIMARRON, OLDSMOBILE FIRENZA & PONTIAC J-2000		
1982	⑨	Accumulator
1982 CHEVROLET CELEBRITY, BUICK CENTURY, OLDSMOBILE CUTLASS CIERA & PONTIAC 6000		
1982	⑨	Accumulator
CHEVROLET CHEVETTE & PONTIAC T1000		
1977–79	Dis. Pres. Sw.	Accumulator
1980–81	Muffler	Accumulator
1982	⑨	Accumulator

Year & Model	High Press.	Low Press.
1980–82 CHEVROLET CITATION, BUICK SKYLARK, OLDSMOBILE OMEGA & PONTIAC PHOENIX		
1980–82	Muffler	Accumulator
CHEVROLET CORVETTE		
1977	VIR	VIR
1978–82	⑨	Accumulator
CHEVROLET VEGA & PONTIAC ASTRE		
1977	Dis. Pres. Sw.	Accumulator
CHRYSLER		
1977	Compressor	Compressor
1978–82	⑫	Compressor
DODGE (ALL)		
1977	Compressor	Compressor
1978–82	⑫	Compressor
FORD (ALL)		
1977–79⑩	Compressor	Compressor
1977–79⑪	⑤	STV
1980–81⑩	⑭	⑬
1980–81⑪	⑤	Accumulator
1982⑯	⑤	⑥
1982⑰	⑤	Accumulator
LINCOLN CONTINENTAL, MARK IV, V, VI & VERSAILLES		
1977–80④	⑤	⑬
1977–81⑮	⑤	Accumulator
1982⑱	⑤	Accumulator
1982⑲	⑤	⑥

Year & Model	High Press.	Low Press.
MERCURY (ALL)		
1977–79⑩	Compressor	Compressor
1977–79⑪	⑤	STV
1980–81⑩	⑭	⑬
1980–81⑪	⑤	Accumulator
1982⑯	⑤	⑥
1982⑰	⑤	Accumulator
MONZA, SKYHAWK, STARFIRE & SUNBIRD		
1977–79	⑦	⑧
1980	⑨	Accumulator
OLDSMOBILE EXC. STARFIRE, 1980–81 OMEGA & 1982 CUTLASS CIERA & FIRENZA		
1977③	Compressor	VIR
1977–81②	Compressor	Accumulator
1982	⑨	Accumulator
PLYMOUTH (ALL)		
1977	Compressor	Compressor
1978–82	⑫	Compressor
PONTIAC EXC. ASTRE, J-2000, 6000, SUNBIRD, T1000 & 1980–81 PHOENIX		
1977–82	⑨	Accumulator
THUNDERBIRD		
1977–79	Compressor	⑥
1980–81	⑤	⑬
1982	⑤	⑥

①—On models with 6 cylinder engine, the high and low pressure service ports are located on the compressor; On models with 4 cylinder engine, the high and low pressure service ports are located on service valve adapter.
②—Except VIR system.
③—With VIR.
④—Versailles.
⑤—On high pressure line from compressor.

⑥—On low pressure line from compressor.
⑦—4 cyl. eng., on line from condenser; 6 cyl. & 8 cyl. eng., Dis. Press. Switch.
⑧—4 cyl. & 6 cyl. eng. on VIR; 8 cyl. eng., on accumulator.
⑨—High pressure vapor line or muffler.
⑩—2 cyl. compressor.
⑪—6 cyl. compressor.
⑫—With RV2 compressor, on compressor. With

Sankyo or C-171 compressor, on muffler.
⑬—On combination valve.
⑭—On liquid line at combination valve.
⑮—Except Versailles.
⑯—Except full size.
⑰—Full size.
⑱—Except Lincoln Continental
⑲—Lincoln Continental

VARIABLE SPEED FANS

Fig. 1 Typical variable-speed fan installed

The fan drive clutch, Fig. 1, is a fluid coupling containing silicone oil. Fan speed is regulated by the torque-carrying capacity of the silicone oil. The more silicone oil in the coupling the greater the fan speed, and the less silicone oil the slower the fan speed.

Two types of fan drive clutches are in use. On one, Fig. 2, a bi-metallic strip and control piston on the front of the fluid coupling regulates the amount of silicone oil entering the coupling. The bi-metallic strip bows outward with a decrease in surrounding temperature and allows a piston to move outward. The piston opens a valve regulating the flow of silicone oil into the coupling from a reserve chamber. The silicone oil is returned to the reserve chamber through a bleed hole when the valve is closed.

On the other type of fan drive clutch, Fig. 3, a heat-sensitive, bi-metal spring connected to an opening plate brings about a similar result. Both units cause the fan speed to increase with a rise in temperature and to decrease as the temperature goes down.

In some cases a Flex-Fan is used instead of a Fan Drive Clutch. Flexible blades vary the volume of air being drawn through the radiator, automatically increasing the pitch at low engine speeds.

Fan Drive Clutch Test

CAUTION: Do not operate the engine until the fan has been first checked for possible cracks and separations.

Run the engine at a fast idle speed (1000 rpm) until normal operating temperature is reached. This process can be speeded up by blocking off the front of the radiator with cardboard. Regardless of temperatures, the unit must be operated for at least five minutes immediately before being tested.

Stop the engine and, using a glove or a cloth to protect the hand, immediately check the effort required to turn the fan. If considerable effort is required, it can be assumed that the coupling is operating satisfactorily. If very little effort is required to turn the fan, it is an indication that the coupling is not operating properly and should be replaced.

If the clutch fan is the coiled bi-metal spring type, it may be tested while the vehicle is being driven. To check, disconnect the bi-metal spring, Fig. 4, and rotate 90° counter clockwise. This disables the temperature-controlled free-wheeling feature and the clutch performs like a conventional fan. If this cures the overheating condition, replace the clutch fan.

Service Procedure

CAUTION: To prevent silicone fluid from draining into fan drive bearing, do not store or place drive unit on bench with rear of shaft pointing downward.

The removal procedure for either type of fan clutch assembly is generally the same for all cars. Merely unfasten the unit from the water pump and remove the assembly from the car.

The type of unit shown in Fig. 2 may be

Fig. 4 Disconnecting bi-metal spring

partially disassembled for inspection and cleaning. Take off the capscrews that hold the assembly together and separate the fan from the drive clutch. Next remove the metal strip on the front by pushing one end of it toward the fan clutch body so it clears the retaining bracket. Then push the strip to the side so that its opposite end will spring out of place. Now remove the small control piston underneath it.

Check the piston for free movement of the coupling device. If the piston sticks, clean it with emery cloth. If the bi-metal strip is damaged, replace the entire unit. These strips are not interchangeable.

When reassembling, install the control piston so that the projection on the end of it will contact the metal strip. Then install the metal strip with any identification numerals or letters facing the clutch. After reassembly, clean the clutch drive with a cloth soaked in solvent. Avoid dipping the clutch assembly in any type of liquid. Install the assembly in the reverse order of removal.

The coil spring type of fan clutch cannot be disassembled, serviced or repaired. If it does not function properly it must be replaced with a new unit.

Fig. 2 Variable-speed fan with flat bi-metal thermostatic spring

Fig. 3 Variable-speed fan with coiled bi-metal thermostatic spring

ELECTRIC ENGINE COOLING FANS

> **CAUTION:** On models equipped with electric engine cooling fans, the battery ground cable should be disconnected whenever underhood service is performed.

1977–79 MONZA, STARFIRE & 1978–79 SUNBIRD W/V8 ENGINE & A/C

These models are equipped with an auxiliary electric engine cooling fan located in front of the radiator. The fan is thermostatically controlled by a thermostatic switch located at the rear of the right hand cylinder head. When engine temperature reaches approximately 235 degrees F, the thermostatic switch will close and the fan will operate to provide supplemental air flow in addition to that which is supplied by the engine cooling fan.

To replace the fan and motor assembly, disconnect wire connector and ground strap, then remove attaching bolts and fan and motor assembly, Fig. 1.

1979–81 CORVETTE AUXILIARY FAN

Description

Current is supplied to the auxiliary fan motor through a 30 amp. circuit breaker located in the fuse panel. The fan motor is controlled by an engine temperature switch located at the rear of the right hand cylinder head. When engine temperature reaches approximately 238 degrees F, the engine temperature switch will close and the fan motor will operate to provide supplementary air flow in addition to that supplied by the engine cooling fan. When engine temperature decreases to approximately 201 degrees F, the engine temperature switch will open and current will no longer be supplied to the fan motor. The fan motor will only operate when the ignition switch is in the "Run" position.

Fan Motor, Replace

1. Disconnect battery ground cable, then remove fresh air scoop.
2. Remove engine cooling fan, then disconnect fan motor wire connector from vehicle wire connector. Remove retainer securing fan motor wiring to chassis, if equipped.
3. Remove upper fan shroud mounting bolts, then remove fan shroud and auxiliary fan motor as an assembly.
4. Remove nuts attaching auxiliary fan motor to fan shroud, then disconnect wiring from fan motor and remove motor.
5. Reverse prodedure to install.

1978–82 HORIZON, OMNI & 1980–82 ARIES & RELIANT

Description

The fan is controlled by a fan switch which is located on the radiator, Fig. 2. The switch will automatically turn on when coolant temperature reaches 193 to 207 degrees F. On models with A/C, when the A/C system is in operation, the fan motor will operate continually regardless of engine coolant temperature. When the ignition switch is turned off the fan motor will stop operating.

Radiator Fan Switch

The radiator fan switch is located on left hand radiator tank. The switch is normally open and incorporates a bimetal disc which pushes the plunger when coolant temperature reaches approximately 200 degrees F. If the fan motor turns on and off at the appropriate temperature, the switch is operating properly.

To check switch continuity, drain coolant until level is below switch. The switch can be viewed by looking downward through the radiator filler neck. Disconnect electrical connector from switch and remove switch from radiator. Dip switch into an oil bath which has achieved a temperature of 208 degrees F or higher and check switch for continuity using a test lamp or ohmmeter. If continuity is not indicated, replace switch.

Electric Fan Motor

Diagnosis

Disconnect wire connector from fan motor terminal, then connect a 14 gauge jumper wire from battery to fan motor terminal. If fan motor does not operate properly, replace fan motor.

Fan Motor, Replace

1. Disconnect wire connectors from fan motor and fan switch, then drain cooling system.
2. Disconnect upper and lower radiator hoses from radiator. On models equipped with automatic transmission, disconnect fluid cooling hoses from radiator, if necessary.
3. Remove upper fan shroud attaching screws, then lift shroud upward and out of bottom shroud retaining clips, separating shroud from radiator.

> **NOTE:** When removing shroud from radiator, use care not to damage fan or radiator cooling fins.

4. Remove fan motor to shroud attaching screws, then while supporting fan motor and shaft, remove fan motor retaining clip and fan motor.
5. Reverse procedure to install.

Electric Fan Motor Relay

The fan motor relay is used on models equipped with A/C. The relay is located on the

Fig. 1 Auxiliary electric engine cooling fan. 1977–79 Monza, Starfire & 1978–79 Sunbird W/V8 engine & A/C

Fig. 2 Electric engine cooling fan. 1978–82 Horizon, Omni & 1982 Aries & Reliant

left hand shock absorber housing. If radiator fan switch and fan motor test results are satisfactory, but fan motor will not operate the fan motor relay is then suspected. After replacing relay, disconnect wire connector from radiator fan switch and connect a 14 gauge jumper wire between wire connector terminals. Place ignition switch in the Accessory position. Fan motor should operate.

1980—82 CITATION, OMEGA, PHOENIX, SKYLARK & 1982 CAVALIER, CELEBRITY, CENTURY, CIMARRON, CUTLASS CIERA, FIRENZA, J2000 & 6000

Description

The single speed electric cooling fan is used on all models except those equipped with V6 gasoline engines with heavy duty cooling systems and all diesel engines, which use a two-speed electric motor. The fan motor is operated by the cooling fan relay. On single speed models, when coolant temperature exceeds 230 degrees F., the cooling fan temperature switch closes. On two-speed models, when the coolant temperature reaches 226 (diesel 223) degrees F., the low speed cooling fan temperature switch closes, and at 239 (diesel 246) degrees F., the high speed cooling fan temperature switch closes. On all models, when the cooling fan temperature switch closes, it allows current to pass through the choke heater fuse or fuel pump fuse (depending on model) and cooling fan relay coil to ground, thus closing the relay contacts. When the relay contacts are closed, current flows through a fusible link to the fan motor. When coolant temperature falls below a predetermined level, the cooling fan temperature switch opens and current is no longer supplied to the fan motor. On 1980 models and 1982 diesel engined models with A/C, a second switch (diesel engine models use two switches) which senses compressor head pressure to the condensor, is used to activate the fan motor when the A/C compressor is operating. On all other models equipped with A/C, the cooling fan relay is grounded whenever the A/C selector switch is in the Max., Normal or Bi-Level position, causing the cooling fan to operate.

Troubleshooting

1. If fan motor does not operate, check the following:
   a. Check for blown fuse.
   b. Check fusible link.
   c. Disconnect wire connector from engine coolant temperature switch. With ignition "On", ground end of wire. Fan motor should operate.
2. If cooling fan operates whenever the ignition switch is in the Run position, check the following:
   a. Check cooling fan temperature switch, compressor pressure switch, if equipped and other related mechanical components.
   b. Check cooling fan relay.

Fig. 3 Electric engine cooling fan wiring diagram. 1980 Fairmont, Zephyr & 1980—81 Capri & Mustang less A/C

Fan Motor, Replace

1. Disconnect battery ground cable, then disconnect wire connector from fan motor.
2. Detach front lamp wiring harness from fan motor, then remove harness from fan motor frame.
3. Remove fan motor frame to radiator support attaching bolts, then remove fan motor.
4. Reverse procedure to install. Torque fan to radiator support attaching bolts to 85 inch lbs.

1980 FAIRMONT & ZEPHYR & 1980—81 CAPRI & MUSTANG W/4-140 TURBO ENGINE

Description

Two thermal switches are used to activate the cooling fan motor. When engine temperature reaches 221 degrees F, the coolant temperature switch will close, thus activating the normally open coolant relay which supplies current to the fan motor. After engine has been turned off, extreme underhood temperatures may develop, causing fuel vaporization in the carburetor, which could cause a no start or hard starting condition. When carburetor temperature reaches 155 degrees F, the carburetor switch closes providing battery voltage to the fan motor relay which operates the fan motor. When the carburetor temperature switch closes, it also activates a timer which allows the fan motor to operate for a period of approximately 15 to 20 minutes. On models equipped with A/C, the engine cooling fan will operate whenever the compressor clutch is in operation.

Diagnosis, Figs. 3 & 4

Fan Motor Check

Disconnect fan motor wire connector, then connect jumper wires between battery and motor connector terminal with brown yellow wire and motor connector terminal with black wire to ground. If motor fails to operate, replace fan motor. If motor operates, proceed to next test.

Coolant Relay Check

Disconnect delay relay wire connector, then place ignition switch in the On position and connect a jumper wire from coolant temperature switch to ground. If fan motor operates, replace coolant temperature switch. If motor fails to operate, disconnect coolant relay wire connector and check for battery voltage at connector terminals A and B. If battery voltage is not indicated, trace circuit to ignition switch and battery and repair as necessary. If battery voltage is indicated, check for continuity between coolant relay wire connector terminals C and D, with coolant temperature switch connected to ground. If continuity does not exist, repair circuit. If continuity does exist, replace coolant relay.

Delay Relay Check

Disconnect coolant relay wire connector, then place ignition switch in the On position and connect a jumper wire from carburetor temperature switch to ground. If fan motor operates, replace carburetor temperature switch. If fan motor fails to operate, disconnect delay relay wire connector and check for battery voltage at connector terminals E and F. If battery voltage is not indicated, trace circuits and repair as necessary. If battery voltage is indicated, check for continuity between delay relay connector terminals G and H. If continuity does not exist, trace circuit and repair as necessary. If continuity does exist, replace delay relay.

A/C Relay Check

Disconnect A/C compressor clutch lead and connect a jumper wire from battery to compressor clutch. If compressor clutch does not click, replace clutch. If compressor clutch clicks, disconnect coolant and delay relay wire connectors, then disconnect ambient temperature switch wire connector and connect a jumper wire between ambient temperature switch connector terminals. Place ignition switch in the On position and turn on A/C controls. The fan motor should be operating and the compressor clutch should click. If neither occurs, disconnect A/C relay wire connector and check for battery voltage at connector terminals N, J and K. If battery voltage is not indicated, check circuit and repair as necessary. If A/C fuse continues to blow, check for short in circuit, otherwise replace relay. If when jumper wire was connected between ambient switch wire connector terminals only the fan motor operated or only the A/C clutch clicked, or if neither occurred and battery voltage was indicated at A/C relay terminals N, J and K, check for continuity between A/C relay connector terminals L and M. If continuity does not exist, trace circuit and repair as necessary. If continuity does exist, replace A/C relay.

Fan Will Not Stop Operating

With ignition switch and A/C controls in the off position, disconnect A/C relay wire connector, then disconnect coolant relay. If fan stops operating, replace relay that was disconnected at time fan stopped operating. If fan continues to operate, connect a jumper wire from carburetor temperature switch to ground and cycle ignition switch on and off. If fan does not stop operating after approximately 20 minutes, replace delay relay.

Fan Motor, Replace

1. Detach wiring harness retainer from fan shroud, and disconnect fan motor wire connector.
2. Remove four fan shroud and fan motor assembly to radiator attaching screws, then remove shroud and motor assembly.
3. Remove retainer clip from end of fan motor shaft and remove fan blade.
4. Remove three nuts attaching fan motor to shroud, then remove fan motor.
5. Reverse procedure to install.

1981–82 ESCORT & LYNX, 1982 EXP & LN7, 1982 MUSTANG & CAPRI WITH 2.3L ENGINE, 1982 FAIRMONT, ZEPHYR, GRANADA & COUGAR WITH 2.3L ENGINE & A/C, FAIRMONT & ZEPHYR WITH 2.3L ENGINE & FUEL ECONOMY LEADER PACKAGE

Description

The cooling fan is activated by the thermal switch when engine coolant temperature reaches approximately 221 degrees F. The fan will continue to operate until coolant temperature drops to approximately 185 to 193 degrees F, at which time the thermal switch opens, releasing the relay contacts which supply current to the fan motor. On models equipped with A/C, the fan motor will continue to operate whenever the compressor clutch is operating regardless of coolant temperature. On some models, two fuses are used to protect the fan motor and thermal switch. A 16 amp fuse is located in the fan motor relay at the left hand dash panel near the steering column. There is also an 8 amp fuse located in

Fig. 4 Electric engine cooling fan wiring diagram. 1980 Fairmont, Zephyr & 1980–81 Capri & Mustang 4-140 Turbo with A/C

the fuse panel. Cycling of the cooling fan will cause the temperature gauge to read between mid and upper range of the gauge range.

Trouble Shooting

1982 ESCORT, EXP, LN7 & LYNX (1.6L ENGINE) & FAIRMONT & ZEPHYR (2.3L ENGINE) WITH FUEL ECONOMY LEADER PACKAGE, FIG. 5

1. Check cooling fan fusible link. If fusible link is not blown, go to step 2. If blown, repair and retest.
2. Disconnect fan motor electrical connector, then connect a jumper wire from motor ground connection to a known good ground and a jumper wire from battery positive to motor B+ connection. If motor does not run, replace motor. If motor runs, reconnect electrical connector and proceed to step 3.
3. Disconnect coolant temperature switch connector, then connect a jumper wire from connector to ground. If motor runs, check switch ground. If ground is satisfactory, replace coolant temperature switch. If motor does not run, proceed to step 4.

CIRCUIT NUMBER	COLOR
37	Y
197	T/O HASH
228	BR/Y

COLOR CODES

Fig. 5 Electric engine cooling fan wiring diagram. 1982 Escort, EXP, LN7 & Lynx (1.6L engine) & Fairmont & Zephyr (2.3L engine) with Fuel Economy Leader Package

Fig. 6   Electric engine cooling fan wiring diagram. 1982 Escort, EXP, LN7 & Lynx with A/C less power brakes

COLOR CODE

CIRCUIT NO.	COLOR	CIRCUIT NO.	COLOR
37	Y	197	T/O HASH
198	T/Y DOT	175	B/Y DOT
228	B/Y	330	Y/LG
E321	G/W	640	R/YHASH
57	B	347	B/YHASH
354	LG/Y		

NOTE:
CIRCUIT SHOWN IN
NORMAL VEHICLE
RUN MODE, WITH
A/C OFF & COOLANT
TEMP. SWITCH OPEN

Fig. 7   Fan motor terminal identification. 1981–82 Escort, Lynx & 1982 EXP & LN7

Fig. 8   Cooling fan relay wire connector terminal identification. 1982 Escort, EXP, LN7 & Lynx with A/C less power brakes

Fig. 9   A/C relay wire connector terminal identification. 1981–82 Escort, Lynx & 1982 EXP & LN7

4. Using an ohmmeter, check continuity of wire 197 from temperature switch to fan relay. If no continuity exists, check circuit 197 for opens. If continuity exists, connect a jumper wire from coolant temperature switch connector to ground and proceed to step 5.

5. Disconnect fan relay wire connector then, connect a jumper wire from wire terminal 37 to 228. If motor runs, replace fan relay. If motor does not run, check circuit 37 for opens.

1982 ESCORT, EXP, LN7, & LYNX WITH A/C LESS POWER BRAKES, FIG. 6

1. Check cooling fan fusible link. If fusible link is not blown, go to step 2. If blown, repair and retest.

2. Disconnect coolant temperature switch connector, then connect a jumper wire from connector to ground and turn ignition "On." If fan motor does not run, proceed to step 3. If fan motor does run, primary system is operating satisfactorily. If complaint is overheating, replace coolant temperature switch.

3. Reconnnect coolant temperature switch connector. Set A/C controls on maximum and turn ignition "On." If fan motor does not run, proceed to step 4. If fan motor runs, system is satisfactory.

4. Disconnect fan motor electrical connector, then connect a jumper wire from motor ground connection to a known good ground and a jumper wire from battery positive to motor B+ connection, Fig. 7. If motor does not run, replace motor. If motor runs, reconnect electrical connection and proceed to step 5.

5. Disconnect cooling fan relay connector and turn ignition "On." Using a test light, check for voltage at terminals 37 and 354, Fig. 8. If there is no voltage at one or both terminals, service relay feed circuits. If

voltage at both terminals, proceed to step 6.

6. Connect jumper wire between terminals 354 and 228, Fig. 8. If fan motor does not run, repair wiring from relay connector to motor connector. If motor runs, disconnect jumper wire and proceed to step 7.

7. Using an ohmmeter, check continuity of wire 228 from relay connector to coolant temperature switch connector. If no continuity exists, repair wires and/or connectors. If continuity exists, replace cooling fan relay and recheck step 2.

8. Disconnect A/C relay connector. Using an ohmmeter, check continuity of wire 228 from relay to motor. If no continuity exists, repair wires and/or connectors. If continuity exists, proceed to step 9.

9. Reconnect fan motor connector, then disconnect A/C relay connector. Set A/C controls on maximum and turn ignition "On." Using a test light, check for voltage at terminals 37 and 321, Fig. 9. If there is no voltage at one or both terminals, service relay feed circuits or A/C control and recheck step 3. If there is voltage at both terminals, go to step 10.

10. Connect jumper wire to base of relay and connect to known good ground. If fan motor does not run, replace relay and recheck step 3. If fan motor runs, clean relay ground.

1982 ESCORT, EXP, LN7 & LYNX WITH A/C & POWER BRAKES, FIG. 10.

1. Check cooling fan fuse and fusible link. If fuse or fusible link is not blown, proceed to step 2. If fuse or fusible link is blown, repair or replace as necessary and retest.

2. Disconnect coolant temperature switch connector, then connect a jumper wire from connector to ground and turn ignition "On." If fan motor does not run, pro-

ceed to step 5. If fan motor runs, primary system is operating satisfactorily. If complaint is overheating, replace coolant temperature switch.

3. Reconnect coolant temperature switch connector. Set A/C controls on maximum and turn ignition "On." If fan motor does not run, proceed to step 10. If fan motor does run, secondary system is operating satisfactorily, except possibly the coolant temperature switch. If complaint is overheating, proceed to step 4.

4. Using an ohmmeter, check coolant temperature switch body to thermostat housing for continuity. If no continuity exists, tighten switch until continuity exists. Start engine and allow to warm up thoroughly. If fan motor runs, system is satisfactory. If fan motor does not run, replace coolant temperature switch.

5. Disconnect cooling fan motor connector, then connect a jumper wire from motor ground connection to a known good ground and a jumper wire from battery positive to motor B+ connection, Fig. 7. If fan motor does not run, replace motor. If fan motor runs, proceed to step 6.

6. Using an ohmmeter, check fan motor ground. If continuity exists, proceed to step 7. If continuity does not exist, repair ground.

7. Remove jumper wires, then reconnect fan motor connector. Disconnect cooling fan relay connector and switch ignition "On."

Fig. 10 Electric engine cooling fan wiring diagram. 1982 Escort, EXP, LN7 & Lynx with A/C & power brakes

Fig. 11 Cooling fan relay connector terminal identification. 1981 Escort & Lynx, All; 1982 Escort, EXP, LN7 & Lynx with A/C and power brakes

Using a test light, check for voltage at terminals 37 and 354, Fig. 11. If there is no voltage at one or both terminals, repair relay feed circuits. If there is voltage at both terminals, proceed to step 8.

8. Jump terminals 37 to 228 of cooling fan relay connector, Fig. 11. If fan motor does not run, repair wiring from relay connector to fan motor connector. (Check capacitor, if equipped.) If fan motor runs, proceed to step 9.

9. Remove jumper wires. Using an ohmmeter, check continuity of wire 354 from relay connector to coolant temperature switch connector, Fig. 11. If continuity does not exist, repair wires and/or connectors. If continuity does exist, replace cooling fan relay and retest.

10. Disconnect A/C relay connector. Using an ohmmeter, check continuity of wire 228 from relay to motor. If continuity does not exist, repair wires and/or connectors. If continuity does exist, proceed to step 11.

11. Reconnect fan motor connector, then disconnect A/C relay connector. Set A/C controls on maximum and turn ignition "On." Using a test light, check for voltage at terminals 37 and 321, Fig. 9. If there is no voltage at terminal 37, repair relay connector feed circuit. If there is no voltage at terminal 321, proceed to step 13. If there is voltage at both terminals, proceed to step 12.

12. Reconnect A/C relay connector. Connect jumper wire to base of relay to a known good ground. If fan motor does not run, replace relay and retest step 4. If fan motor runs, clean relay ground.

13. Using a test light, test for voltage at circuit 296 of A/C function control harness. If voltage exists, proceed to step 14. If no

voltage exists, repair feed wire from fuse box.

14. Using an ohmmeter, check continuity of terminals 296 to 321 in A/C function control. Continuity should only exist in the following positions: A/C Max., A/C Norm. and Defrost. If continuity is not satisfactory, replace A/C function control. If continuity is satisfactory, proceed to step 15.

15. Using an ohmmeter, check continuity of circuit 321 from A/C function control to A/C relay. If continuity does not exist, repair wiring and/or connectors. If continuity does exist, repeat step 11.

1982 CAPRI & MUSTANG (2.3L ENGINE); 1982 COUGAR, FAIRMONT, GRANADA & ZEPHYR (2.3L ENGINE) WITH A/C, FIG. 12
Fan Motor Inoperative

1. Check cooling fan fuses and fusible link. If fuses or fusible link are not blown, proceed to step 2. If fuses or fusible link are blown, repair or replace as necessary, and retest.

2. Disconnect fan motor electrical connector, then connect a jumper wire from motor ground connection to a known good ground and a jumper wire from battery positive to motor B+ connection. If motor does not run, replace motor. If motor runs, reconnect electrical connector and proceed to step 3.

3. Disconnect coolant temperature switch connector, then connect a jumper wire from connector to ground and turn ignition "On." If fan motor does not run, proceed to step 4. If motor does run, check switch ground, and if satisfactory, replace

coolant temperature switch.

4. Turn ignition "Off," then remove jumper wire installed in step 3. Using an ohmmeter, check continuity of circuit 45 from cooling fan controller terminal #1 to coolant temperature switch. The controller, Fig. 13, is located under instrument panel near steering column. If continuity does not exist, check wire circuit 45 for opens. If continuity does exist, jump coolant temperature switch to ground and proceed to step 5.

5. Without disconnecting wiring connector from controller, Fig. 13, connect battery positive to circuit 68 at controller (terminal #8). If fan motor runs, check ignition feed circuits for opens. If fan motor does not run, remove jumper wire and proceed to step 6.

6. Disconnect cooling fan wiring connector at controller, Fig. 13. Using a jumper wire, connect battery positive current to circuit 228 (terminal #5). If fan motor does not run, check circuit 228 for opens. If motor runs, remove jumper and proceed to step 7.

7. Using a jumper wire, connect circuit 175 to 228 (terminals #2 & 5) at the cooling fan motor controller connector. If motor does not run, check circuit 175 for opens. If motor does run, replace cooling fan controller, then remove jumper wire from temperature switch and reconnect connector.

Fan Motor Operates When Engine Overheats, Does Not Operate With A/C On

1. Set A/C controls selector lever in A/C position and turn ignition "On." If A/C clutch does not engage, proceed to step 2. If A/C clutch does engage, proceed to step 7.

2. Check fuse in fuse panel. If blown, replace. If fuse is not blown, proceed to step 3.

3. Disconnect A/C clutch cycle pressure switch. Use a jumper wire to jump across connector. If A/C clutch does not engage, proceed to step 5. If A/C clutch does engage, proceed to step 4.

4. Check A/C system for low refrigerant charge. If charge is insufficient, leak test, service and charge system. If charge is satisfactory, replace clutch cycling pressure switch.

5. Using a test light, check for voltage on 348 circuit at clutch cycling pressure switch. If there is no voltage, proceed to step 6. If there is voltage, repair open 347 circuit to A/C clutch.

6. Using a test light, test for voltage on 296 and 348 circuits at A/C function selector switch in instrument panel. If there is voltage on 296 but not on 348, replace A/C

Fig. 12 Electric engine cooling fan wiring diagram. 1982 Capri & Mustang (2.3L engine); 1982 Cougar, Fairmont, Granada & Zephyr (2.3L engine) with A/C

COLOR CODES	
CIRCUIT NUMBER	COLOR
687A	GY/Y
68 AND 302	ORG/BR
687	GY/Y
181	BR/O
348	LG/P
347	BK/Y HASH
57	BK
45	Y/R
228	BR/Y
175	BK/Y DOT
297	BK/LG
296	W/P

control assembly. If there is no voltage on 296 circuit, trace circuits 296 and 297 toward ignition switch.

7. Using a test light, check for voltage on 347 circuit (terminal #6) of cooling fan controller, Fig. 13. If there is no voltage, repair open 347 circuit. If voltage does exist, proceed to step 8.

8. Leaving connector attached to controller, ground 57 circuit (terminal #4) of controller. If fan motor runs, repair ground circuit. If fan does not run, replace controller.

1981 ESCORT & LYNX, FIG. 14

1. Check cooling fan fuses located in the fuse panel and fan motor relay. If fuse is not blown, proceed to step 2. If fuse is blown, replace and retest.

2. Disconnect wire connector at coolant temperature switch, then connect a jumper wire between connector terminal and ground and place ignition switch in the Run position. If fan motor operates, proceed to step 3. If fan motor fails to operte, proceed to step 5.

3. If vehicle is equipped with A/C, proceed to step 4. On models less A/C, the system is operating properly and if overheating has occured, replace coolant temperature switch.

Fig. 13 Cooling fan controller terminal identification. 1982 Capri & Mustang (2.3L engine); 1982 Cougar, Fairmont, Granada & Zephyr (2.3L engine) with A/C

4. Connect wire connector to coolant temperature switch, then place A/C control at Max. A/C and ignition switch in Run position. If fan motor operates, system is satisfactory. If fan motor fails to operate, proceed to step 9.

5. Disconnect wire connector at fan motor, then connect a jumper wire between fan motor positive terminal and battery and fan motor negative terminal and ground, Fig. 7. If fan motor operates, proceed to step 6. If fan motor fails to operate, replace fan motor.

6. Disconnect jumper wires and reconnect fan motor wire connector. Disconnect wire connector at fan motor relay, then place ignition switch in the run position and check for voltage at connector terminals 37 and 197, Fig. 11. If no voltage is indicated at one or both terminals, trace circuit and repair as necessary. If voltage is indicated at both circuits, proceed to step 7.

7. Connect a jumper wire between relay wire connector terminals 37 and 228, Fig. 11. If fan motor operates, proceed to step 8. If fan motor fails to operate, trace circuit from wire connector to motor connector and repair as necessary.

8. Disconnect jumper wire from relay wire connector, then check for continuity of circuit 354 from relay wire connector,

Fig. 14 Electric engine cooling fan wiring circuit. 1981 Escort & Lynx

Fig. 11, to coolant temperature switch wire connector. If continuity exists, replace fan relay and perform step 2. If continuity does not exist, check circuit and repair as necessary.

9. Disconnect wire connector at A/C relay and check circuit 228 from relay wire connector, Fig. 11, to fan motor wire connector. If continuity exists, proceed to step 10. If continuity does not exist, trace circuit and repair as necessary.

10. Connect fan motor relay and disconnect wire connect at A/C relay, then place A/C control Max. A/C and ignition switch in Run position. Check for voltage at wire connector terminals 37 and 321, Fig. 9. If voltage is available at both terminals, proceed to step 11. If voltage is not available at one or both terminals, trace circuit and repair as necessary. If problem is not found in circuit, check A/C control and repair as necessary. Proceed to step 4.

11. Connect a jumper wire from A/C relay base to ground. If fan motor operates,

clean relay ground surfaces. If fan motor fails to operate, replace relay and proceed to step 4.

Fan Motor, Replace

1981–82 ESCORT, LYNX & 1982 EXP & LN7

1. Disconnect battery ground cable, then disconnect fan motor wire connector and detach wire loom clip from fan shroud.
2. Remove two nuts attaching fan motor and shroud, then remove fan motor and shroud assembly from vehicle.
3. Remove nut retaining fan blade to fan motor shaft, then remove fan blade.

NOTE: The nut retaining the fan blade to the motor shaft has a left handed thread. The nut should be rotated clockwise to loosen and counter-clockwise to tighten.

4. Remove three nuts and washers attaching fan motor to shroud, then remove fan

motor.
5. Reverse procedure to install. Torque fan motor to fan shroud attaching nuts to 6.6 to 9.6 ft. lbs., fan blade to fan motor retaining nut to 30 to 40 inch lbs. and fan shroud to radiator attaching nuts to 80 to 100 inch lbs.

ALL EXC. 1981–82 ESCORT, LYNX & 1982 EXP & LN7

1. Disconnect battery ground cable, then remove wiring from routing clip.
2. Disconnect fan motor wiring connector.
3. Remove four screws securing mounting bracket and remove fan assembly from vehicle.
4. Remove fan blade retaining clip, then remove fan.
5. Remove nuts securing fan motor to mounting bracket.
6. Reverse procedure to install. Torque fan motor attaching nuts to 70–95 in. lbs., fan shroud to radiator attaching bolts, 70–95 in. lbs.

Fig. 1 Hook-up for testing dash gauge with a spare tank unit

terminals, indicator gauge terminals, or open circuit in wiring harness and printed circuit between components.
5. Connect test lamp or voltmeter ground lead to ground terminal in sending unit wiring harness connector. Light should pulse or meter reading should fluctuate as in step 2. If not, locate open in ground circuit.

NOTE: Do not apply battery voltage to system or ground output terminals of IVR, as damage to system components or wiring circuits may result.

Fig. 2 Conventional type ammeter (typical)

TESTING

Gauge failures are often caused by defective wiring or grounds. The first step in locating trouble should be a thorough inspection of all wiring, terminals and printed circuits. If wiring is secured by clamps, check to see whether the insulation has been severed thereby grounding the wire. In the case of a fuel gauge installation, rust may cause failure by corrosion at the ground connection of the tank unit.

CONSTANT VOLTAGE REGULATOR TYPE (CVR)

The Constant Voltage Regulator (CVR) type indicator is a bimetal-resistance type system consisting of an Instrument Voltage Regulator (IVR), an indicator gauge, and a variable resistance sending unit. Current to the system is applied to the gauge terminals by the IVR, which maintains an average-pulsating value of 5 volts.

The indicator gauge consists of a pointer which is attached to a wire-wound bimetal strip. Current passing through the coil heats the bimetal strip, causing the pointer to move. As more current passes through the coil, heat increases, moving the pointer farther.

The circuit is completed through a sending unit which contains a variable resistor. When resistance is high, less current is allowed to pass through the gauge, and the pointer moves very little. As resistance decreases due to changing conditions in system being monitored, more current passes through gauge coil, causing pointer to move farther.

These procedures apply to Chrysler Corp., Ford, Mercury, and earlier AMC vehicles.

Operational Test

1. Disconnect wiring harness connector at sending unit. Connect a test lamp or voltmeter between terminal in wiring harness connector and ground.
2. With ignition switch in ON position, light should pulse or meter reading should fluctuate.
3. If lamp lights but does not pulse, or if meter reading remains steady, check ground to IVR. If ground is satisfactory, IVR is defective.
4. If lamp fails to light, or if meter reads 0 volts, check for open circuit across IVR

Dash Gauge Test

1. Disconnect battery ground cable and remove gauge from vehicle.
2. Connect ohmmeter between gauge terminals and read coil winding resistance.
3. An upward movement of ohmmeter needle from 10 ohms to 14 ohms is normal, as test current of ohmmeter causes a temperature rise in gauge coil windings.
4. If ohmmeter reads below 10 ohms or above 14 ohms, gauge is defective.

Sending Unit Tests

Fuel Tank Gauge
1. Disconnect wiring harness connector at sending unit and connect ohmmeter between ground terminal and resistor terminal on sending unit.
2. Meter should read 8–86 ohms. If reading shows no continuity (infinite reading), check ground connection to tank gauge.
3. If ground is satisfactory, but reading is not within specification, tank unit is defective.
4. If reading is within specification, remove fuel tank gauge from vehicle and connect ohmmeter between resistor terminal and ground terminal (metal housing on single terminal units).
5. Observe meter while slowly moving float rod between empty and full stops. Meter should read 60–86 ohms at empty stop and 8–12 ohms at full stop. Change in readings should be smooth, without hesitation or jumping.
6. If tank unit fails to operate as outlined, unit is defective.

NOTE: Before installing fuel tank gauge, connect wiring harness connector to gauge and move float rod from empty to full position with ignition key in ON position. If dash gauge reading is incorrect, check IVR and dash gauge. If system tests prove satisfactory, but system still does not operate correctly, check that tank gauge rod is not bent or binding and that float is not damaged, loose or filled with fuel.

Oil & Temperature Sending Units
1. Test dash gauge and IVR as outlined above.
2. If system is satisfactory, start engine and allow it to reach operating temperature.

3. If no reading is indicated on the gauge, check the sending unit-to-gauge wire by removing the wire from the sending unit and momentarily ground this wire to a clean, unpainted portion of the engine.
4. If the gauge still does not indicate, the wire is defective. Repair or replace the wire.
5. If grounding the new or repaired wire causes the dash gauge to indicate, the sending unit is faulty.

VARIABLE VOLTAGE TYPE

The variable voltage type dash gauge consists of two magnetic coils to which battery voltage is applied. The coils act on the gauge pointer and pull in opposite directions. One coil is grounded directly to the chassis, while the other coil is grounded through a variable resistor within the sending unit. Resistance through the sending unit determines current flow through its coil, and therefore pointer position.

When resistance is high in the sending unit, less current is allowed to flow through its coil, causing the gauge pointer to move toward the directly grounded coil. When resistance in the sending unit decreases, more current is allowed to pass through its coil, increasing the magnetic field. The gauge pointer is then attracted toward the coil which is grounded through the sending unit.

These procedures apply to GM and AMC (exc. CVR) vehicles.

System Test

Following is the method of quickly checking the gauge system to determine which component (sender or receiver) of a given system is defective.

System Testing

1. Use a spare gauge tank unit known to be correct.
2. To test whether the dash gauge in question (fuel, oil or temperature) is functioning, disconnect the wire at the gauge which leads to the sending unit.
3. Attach a wire lead from the dash gauge terminal to the terminal of the "test" tank gauge, Fig. 1.
4. Ground the test tank unit to an unpainted portion of the dash panel and move the float arm.

5. If the gauge operates correctly, the sending unit is defective and should be replaced.
6. If the gauge does not operate during this test, the dash gauge is defective and should be replaced.

AMMETERS

The ammeter is an instrument used to indicate current flow into and out of the battery. When electrical accessories in the vehicle draw more current than the alternator can supply, current flows from the battery and the ammeter indicates a discharge (−) condition. When electrical loads of the vehicle are less than alternator output, current is available to charge the battery, and the ammeter indicates a charge (+) condition. If battery is fully charged, the voltage regulator reduces alternator output to meet only immediate vehicle electrical loads. When this happens, ammeter reads zero.

Conventional Ammeter

A conventional ammeter must be connected between the battery and alternator in order to indicate current flow. This type ammeter, Fig. 2, consists of a frame to which a permanent magnet is attached. The frame also supports an armature and pointer assembly. Current in this system flows from the alternator through the ammeter, then to the battery or from the battery through the ammeter into the vehicle electrical system, depending on vehicle operating conditions.

When no current flows through the ammeter, the magnet holds the pointer armature so that the pointer stands at the center of the dial. When current passes in either direction through the ammeter, the resulting magnetic field attracts the armature away from the effect of the permanent magnet, thus giving a reading proportional to the strength of the current flowing.

Trouble Shooting

When the ammeter apparently fails to register correctly, there may be trouble in the wiring which connects the ammeter to the alternator and battery or in the alternator or battery itself.

To check the connections, first tighten the two terminal posts on the back of the ammeter. Then, following each wire from the ammeter, tighten all connections on the ignition switch, battery and alternator. Chafed, burned or broken insulation can be found by following each ammeter wire from end to end.

All wires with chafed, burned or broken insulation should be repaired or replaced. After this is done, and all connections are tightened, connect the battery cable and turn on the ignition switch. The needle should point slightly to the discharge (−) side.

Start the engine and speed it up a little above idling speed. The needle should then move to the charge side (+), and its movement should be smooth.

If the pointer does not behave correctly, the ammeter itself is out of order and a new one should be installed.

Shunt Type Ammeter

American Motors, Ford, 1981–82 Chrysler Corp.

The shunt type ammeter is actually a specially calibrated voltmeter. It is connected to read voltage drop across a resistance wire (shunt) between the battery and alternator.

BAT.
SWITCH IGN.

Fig. 3 Charge indicator lamp wiring. Delco SI type charging system

The shunt is located either in the vehicle wiring or within the ammeter itself.

When voltage is higher at the alternator end of the shunt, the meter indicates a charge (+) condition. When voltage is higher at the battery end of the shunt, the meter indicates a discharge (−) condition. When voltage is equal at both ends of the shunt, the meter reads zero.

Trouble Shooting

Ammeter accuracy can be determined by comparing reading with an ammeter of known accuracy.
1. With engine stopped and ignition switch in RUN position, switch on headlamps and heater fan. Meter should indicate a discharge (−) condition.
2. If ammeter pointer does not move, check ammeter terminals for proper connection and check for open circuit in wiring harness. If connections and wiring harness are satisfactory, ammeter is defective.
3. If ammeter indicates a charge (+) condition, wiring harness connections are reversed at ammeter.

ALTERNATOR INDICATOR LIGHT

Delcotron SI Integral Charging System

This system features an integral solid state regulator mounted inside the alternator slip ring end frame. The alternator indicator lamp is installed in the field wire circuit connected between the ignition "Ign." terminal and alternator No. 1 terminal, Fig. 3. The resistance provided by the alternator warning light circuit is needed to protect the diode trio. The alternator indicator lamp should light when the ignition switch is turned on before engine is started. If lamp does not light, either lamp is burned out or indicator lamp wiring has an open circuit. After engine is started, the indicator lamp should be out at all times. If indicator lamp comes on, alternator belt may be loose, alternator or regulator may be defective, charging circuit may be defective or fuse may be blown.

Motorcraft Alternator

The indicator lamp glows when field relay fails to close. When ignition is in the On position, battery current flows through the charge indicator lamp and a parallel resistor, and through regulator to field, and the lamp comes on. Vehicles with electronic voltage regulator have a 500 ohm resistor. On all others the resistor is 15 ohms. When the alternator builds up enough voltage to close the field relay the charge indicator lamp will go out. Place ignition switch in the Run position with the engine stopped. The lamp should light. If not, the bulb is burned out or indicator lamp has an open circuit.

On vehicles with electro-mechanical or transistorized regulators, an open resistor wire in the alternator charging circuit will usually cause the indicator lamp to remain on until engine speed is increased to approximately 2000 rpm. In some cases the lamp will remain on above 2000 rpm. The charge indicator lamp may be tested using a test light containing a No. 67 or 1155 bulb. Disconnect regulator wire connector from regulator, then place ignition switch in the Run position. Place one test lead on regulator wire connector "l" terminal and other lead on regulator base. Test lamp will light if circuit is in proper working order. If 15 ohm resistor or circuit is open, indicator lamp will operate at full brightness and test lamp will not light.

OIL PRESSURE INDICATOR LIGHT

Many cars utilize a warning light on the instrument panel in place of the conventional dash indicating gauge to warn the driver when the oil pressure is dangerously low. The warning light is wired in series with the ignition switch and the engine unit—which is an oil pressure switch.

The oil pressure switch contains a diaphragm and a set of contacts. When the ignition switch is turned on, the warning light circuit is energized and the circuit is completed through the closed contacts in the pressure switch. When the engine is started, build-up of oil pressure compresses the diaphragm, opening the contacts, thereby breaking the circuit and putting out the light.

Trouble Shooting

NOTE: On some 1978–82 General Motors

FUEL OR TEMPERATURE GAUGE — AMMETER GAUGE — LIGHT EMITTING DIODES

Fig. 4   Gauges Incorporating the L.E.D. system

RELAY — VACUUM SWITCH — HEAD LAMP GROUND — MANIFOLD VACUUM — VACUUM HOSE

Fig. 5   Fuel pacer system. 1977 Charger, Cordoba, Coronet & Fury; 1977 Monaco (Typical)

models, the oil pressure indicator light also serves as the electric choke defect indicator. If Oil or Eng. indicator light does not light, check to ensure electric choke is not disconnected at carburetor. Also check for defect in electric choke heater, blown gauge fuse or defect in lamp or wiring circuit. If indicator light stays on with engine running possible causes are: oil pressure is low, switch to indicator light wiring has an open circuit, oil pressure switch wire connector has disconnected or on some models, gauge or radio fuse has blown.

The oil pressure warning light should go on when the ignition is turned on. If it does not light, disconnect the wire from the engine unit and ground the wire to the frame or cylinder block. Then if the warning light still does not go on with the ignition switch on, replace the bulb.

If the warning light goes on when the wire is grounded to the frame or cylinder block, the engine unit should be checked for being loose or poorly grounded. If the unit is found to be tight and properly grounded, it should be removed and a new one installed. (The presence of sealing compound on the threads of the engine unit will cause a poor ground).

If the warning light remains lit when it normally should be out, replace the engine unit before proceeding further to determine the cause for a low pressure indication.

The warning light sometimes will light up or will flicker when the engine is idling, even though the oil pressure is adequate. However, the light should go out when the engine is speeded up. There is no cause for alarm in such cases; it simply means that the pressure switch is not calibrated precisely correct.

TEMPERATURE INDICATOR LIGHT

Trouble Shooting

If the red light is not lit when the engine is being cranked, check for a burned out bulb, an open in the light circuit, or a defective ignition switch.

If the red light is lit when the engine is running, check the wiring between light and switch for a ground, temperature switch defective, or overheated cooling system.

NOTE: *As a test circuit to check whether the red bulb is functioning properly, a wire which is connected to the ground terminal of the ignition switch is tapped into its circuit. When the ignition is in the "Start" (engine cranking) position, the ground terminal is grounded inside the switch and the red bulb will be lit. When the engine is started and the ignition switch is in the "On" position, the test circuit is opened and the bulb is then controlled by the temperature switch.*

CHRYSLER GAUGE ALERT SYSTEM

L.E.D. (Light Emitting Diode)

The fuel, temperature and ammeter gauges are equipped with a L.E.D. (Light Emitting Diode) mounted in each of the gauge dials, Fig. 4. This diode will illuminate and alert the driver that the system the gauge is monitoring is malfunctioning. The electronic sensor circuit is mounted on the gauge housing. The printed circuit board is permanently attached and is not serviceable. If the L.E.D. is malfunctioning, the gauge and the printed circuit board must be replaced as an assembly.

Operation

Fuel Gauge

When gauge indicator shows approximately 1/8 of a tank of fuel remaining, the L.E.D. will light alerting the driver of a low fuel situation.

Temperature Gauge

When gauge indicator shows engine temperature approximately 240 to 260 degrees F. the L.E.D. will light alerting the driver of an overheat condition.

Ammeter Gauge

This L.E.D. operates independently of the gauge indicator and monitors system voltage. The L.E.D. will alert the driver of three charging system potential malfunctions.

1. A discharging condition, caused by excessive electrical demand on charging system, (engine at idle rpm).
2. A weak or defective battery with ignition

switch in the "ON" position, (before the ignition switch is moved to the "START" position).
3. A weak or defective battery with minimum demand on charging system, while vehicle is being used in stop and go driving (intermittent L.E.D. illumination occurring).

Testing

Fuel and Temperature L.E.D.
Use testor C-3826 for diagnosing systems.

Ammeter L.E.D.

NOTE: Only if battery and charging system are functioning properly can the following test be performed.

Turn ignition switch to the "ON" position and turn on headlights, windshield wipers and stoplights. This will cause excessive demand on charging system activating the L.E.D. immediately or within approximately one minute. If the L.E.D. does not light there is a malfunction in the system. If L.E.D. lights, run engine at approximately 2000 rpm, L.E.D. should stop emitting light, if the L.E.D. continues to emit light there is a malfunction in the system.

NOTE: In all cases of system malfunctions the complete gauge must be replaced.

CHRYSLER FUEL PACER SYSTEM

The Fuel Pacer system, Figs. 5 and 6, incorporates a vacuum switch, relay, vacuum hoses, diodes and the use of the left front fender mounted turn signal indicator lamp. When engine vacuum falls below 4½ inches Hg., electrical contacts in the vacuum switch close, causing the indicator lamp to light, therefore indicating excessive fuel consumption by the engine.

The Fuel Pacer system overrides the blinking action of the fender mounted left turn indicator lamp. However, an inline diode is incorporated in the circuit so the complete turn signal system is not affected. A second in-line diode is placed in the fender mounted indicator lamp feed wire, preventing feedback through the main harness and therefore avoiding some accessories from functioning when the hazard warning flashers are "On", with the ignition switch in the "Accessory" position.

1977 System Tests

Test 1

1. Disconnect vacuum hose from vacuum switch and connect an external vacuum source to the switch.
2. Turn ignition switch to "On" position and observe fender mounted turn indicator lamp. If indicator lamp is lit, the vacuum switch is satisfactory. If not, check the following: defective wiring or connections supplying current through vacuum switch to indicator lamp, burnt indicator bulb or a defective vacuum switch.

Test 2

1. With an external vacuum source connected to the vacuum switch and the ignition switch in the "On" position, apply increasing vacuum to the switch and observe fender mounted indicator lamp.
2. Indicator lamp should turn off at approximately 4½ inches of vacuum. If not, increase vacuum until switch does go out. If lamp goes out, the switch is out of adjustment, requiring readjustment. If lamp does not go out regardless of amount of vacuum applied, the switch is defective, requiring replacement.

Vacuum Switch Adjustment

1977

1. Install a vacuum gauge on the engine.
2. Operate vehicle, noting the vacuum reading at which the indicator lamp glows. This also may be accomplished by carefully loading the engine with the brakes applied.
3. Remove vacuum switch adjusting screw cap.
4. To decrease vacuum setting, turn adjusting screw counter-clockwise. To increase vacuum setting, turn adjusting screw clockwise.
5. Install adjusting screw cap.
6. Operate vehicle or load engine, noting the vacuum reading at which the indicator lamp glows. It may be necessary to readjust switch to obtain desired setting.

BOOST/OVERBOOST WARNING SYSTEM

1979—80 Capri & Mustang, W/Turbocharged 4-140 Engine

Two calibrated pressure switches provide the driver visual indication that turbo boost pressure is satisfactory and visual and audible indication when turbo boost pressure is unsatisfactory. One switch will illuminate the green Turbo lamp located on the instrument panel when turbo boost pressure levels are within satisfactory limits. The second pressure switch will turn off the green Turbo lamp and illuminate the red engine warning lamp and sound the audible buzzer when excessive turbo boost pressure or high engine oil temperatures are encountered. When the red

Fig. 6 Fuel pacer system. 1977 Chrysler, Gran Fury & Royal Monaco (Typical)

engine lamp is constant and buzzer sounds, the turbocharger is in an overboost condition, reduce engine speed immediately until buzzer ceases and warning lamp goes off. When the red engine warning light flashes on and off with no buzzer, this indicates excessive engine oil temperature, reduce engine speed to approximately 2500 RPM. The engine warning lamp should go out within 5 minutes. When the red engine warning lamp flashes on and off and buzzer sounds simultaneously, excessive turbo overboost and/or high engine oil temperatures are occuring, reduce engine speed immediately.

NOTE: Whenever the engine warning lamp has illuminated or the audible buzzer sounds, the vehicle should be inspected as soon as possible to determine the cause.

With ignition switch in start position and engine not operating, the warning lamps should glow and the buzzer should sound to indicate the electrical circuits are operating properly. If warning lamps do not glow or if buzzer does not sound, the boost/overboost electrical system should be checked as soon as possible.

SPEEDOMETERS

The following material covers only that service on speedometers which can be performed by the average service man. Repairs on the units themselves are not included as they require special tools and extreme care when making repairs and adjustments and only an experienced speedometer mechanic should attempt such servicing.

The speedometer has two main parts—the indicator head and the speedometer drive cable. When the speedometer fails to indicate speed or mileage, the cable or housing is probably broken.

Speedometer Cable

Most cables are broken due to lack of lubrication or a sharp bend or kink in the housing.

A cable might break because the speedometer head mechanism binds. If such is the case, the speedometer head should be repaired or replaced before a new cable or housing is installed.

A "jumpy" pointer condition, together with a sort of scraping noise, is due, in most instances, to a dry or kinked speedometer cable. The kinked cable rubs on the housing and winds up, slowing down the pointer. The cable then unwinds and the pointer "jumps".

To check for kinks, remove the cable, lay it on a flat surface and twist one end with the fingers. If it turns over smoothly the cable is not kinked. But if part of the cable flops over as it is twisted, the cable is kinked and should be replaced.

Lubrication

The speedometer cable should be lubricated with special cable lubricant every 10,000 miles.

Fill the ferrule on the upper end of the housing with the cable lubricant. Insert the cable in the housing, starting at the upper end. Turn the cable around carefully while feeding it into the housing. Repeat filling the ferrule except for the last six inches of cable. Too much lubricant at this point may cause the lubricant to work into the indicating hand.

Installing Cable

During installation, if the cable sticks when inserted in the housing and will not go through, the housing is damaged inside or kinked. Be sure to check the housing from one end to the other. Straighten any sharp bends by relocating clamps or elbows. Replace housing if it is badly kinked or broken. Position the cable and housing so that they lead into the head as straight as possible.

Check the new cable for kinks before installing it. Use wide, sweeping, gradual curves when the cable comes out of the transmission and connects to the head so the cable will not be damaged during its installation.

If inspection indicates that the cable and housing are in good condition, yet pointer action is erratic, check the speedometer head for possible binding.

The speedometer drive pinion should also be checked. If the pinion is dry or its teeth are stripped, the speedometer may not register properly.

The transmission mainshaft nut must be tight or the speedometer drive gear may slip on the mainshaft and cause slow speed readings.

ELECTRIC CLOCKS

Regulation of electric clocks used on automobiles is accomplished automatically by merely resetting the time. If the clock is running fast, the action of turning the hands back to correct the time will automatically cause the clock to run slightly slower. If the clock is running slow, the action of turning the hands forward to correct the time will automatically cause the clock to run slightly faster (10 to 15 seconds day).

A lock-out feature prevents the clock regulator mechanism from being reset more than once per wind cycle, regardless of the number of times the time is reset. After the clock rewinds, if the time is then reset, automatic regulation will take place. If a clock varies over 10 minutes per day, it will never adjust sufficiently, and must be repaired or replaced.

Winding Clock When Connecting Battery or Clock Wiring

The clock requires special attention when reconnecting a battery that has been disconnected for any reason, a clock that has been disconnected, or when replacing a blown clock fuse. *It is very important that the initial wind by fully made.* The procedure is as follows:
1. Make sure that all other instruments and lights are turned off.
2. Connect positive cable to battery.
3. Before connecting the negative cable, press the terminal to its post on the battery. Immediately afterward strike the terminal against the battery post to see if there is a spark. If there is a spark, allow the clock to run down until it stops ticking, and repeat as above until there is no spark. Then immediately make the permanent connection before the clock can again run down. The clock will run down in approximately two minutes.
4. Reset clock after all connections have been made. *The foregoing procedure should also be followed when reconnecting the clock after it has been disconnected, or if it has stopped because of a blown fuse. Be sure to disconnect battery before installing a new fuse.*

Trouble Shooting

If clock does not run, check for blown "clock" fuse. If fuse is blown check for short in wiring. If fuse is not blown check for open circuit.

With an electric clock, the most frequent cause of clock fuse blowing is voltage at the clock which will prevent a complete wind and allow clock contacts to remain closed. This may be caused by any of the following: discharged battery, corrosion on contact surface of battery terminals, loose connections at battery terminals, at junction block, at fuse clips, or at terminal connection of clock. Therefore, if in reconnecting battery or clock it is noted that the clock is not ticking, always check for blown fuse, or examine the circuits at the points indicated above to determine and correct the cause.

Fig. 7 Typical vacuum gauge

FIBER OPTIC MONITORING SYSTEM

Fiber optics are non-electric light conductors made up of coated strands which, when exposed to a light source at one end, will reflect the light through their entire length, thereby illuminating a monitoring lens on the instrument panel or fender without the use of a bulb when the exterior lights are turned on.

LOW FUEL WARNING SYSTEM

The switch type consists of an indicator light and a low fuel warning switch located on the instrument panel.

The warning switch contacts are closed by the difference in voltage potential between the fuel gauge terminals. This voltage differential will activate the warning switch when the fuel tank is less than 1/4 full and, in turn, cause the indicator to light.

Trouble Shooting

This system incorporates an indicator light. With ignition switch turned to "ON", the indicator should light. If not, check bulb and all electrical connections. On General Motors switch type, replace warning switch if bulb and connections prove satisfactory. On Ford switch type systems, perform additional tests outlined below.

Improper operation of the warning switch will be indicated when the light remains "ON" when tank is more than 1/4 full. To test system, disconnect connector on warning switch and turn ignition "ON". Starting with the terminal on the end opposite the blank position, connect a jumper wire between the battery positive terminal and connector terminal. The indicator on instrument panel should light. If not, replace warning switch. Skip the next connector terminal and connect a test lamp between the battery positive terminal and connector terminal. The test lamp should light. If not, trace wire from

ignition switch for an open circuit. Test the remaining connector terminals with the test lamp making connections between ground and terminal connectors. If lamp fails to light, trace particular wire for an incomplete circuit.

LOW WASHER FLUID INDICATOR

There are two types of low washer fluid indicating systems used on GM cars. They are the mechanical type and electrically controlled type. The mechanical type consists of a float and rod assembly, sending unit and a fiber optic. The electrically controlled type consists of a float, magnet, contact points and a resistor.

On the mechanical type, the upper end of the rod extends into the sending unit and has colored red and green portions. When the windshield wipers are activated, a lamp bulb in the sending unit lights either the red or green sections of the rod. The colored light is then picked up by the fiber optic and is transmitted through it to the tell tale lens. The lens will show red or green depending upon washer fluid level.

The electrically controlled indicator is activated when the windshield wipers are engaged. A slight amount of current flows from the wiper motor to the washer bottle float unit. This current will either pass through the contact points or the resistor which is in parallel with the points. When the washer fluid level is high, the magnet holds the contact points open. The current will now flow through the resistor where it is reduced so the indicator will not light. When the washer fluid level is low, the float drops and the magnet will separate from the cap assembly allowing the current to pass through the contact points and activate the indicator light.

Trouble Shooting

On the mechanical indicating system, if the tell tale lens fails to glow when the windshield wipers are activated, check lamp bulb in sending unit and see that fiber optic is not broken.

On the electrically controlled system, the first item to check is the indicator bulb. With the windshield wipers "ON", connect a jumper wire between the two terminals on the washer bottle cap. The indicator should then light. If not, replace bulb. If the bulb is found to be satisfactory, remove cap and float assembly from washer bottle. Float should be able to move to the bottom of the stem and the magnet should separate from the cap. If not, replace float and cap assembly.

VACUUM GAUGE

This gauge, Fig. 7, measures intake manifold vacuum. The intake manifold vacuum varies with engine operating conditions, carburetor adjustments, valve timing, ignition timing and general engine condition.

Since the optimum fuel economy is directly proportional to a properly functioning engine, a high vacuum reading on the gauge relates to fuel economy. For this reason the vacuum gauge a "Fuel Economy Indicator." Most gauges have colored sectors the green sector being the "Economy" range and red the "Power" range. Therefore, the vehicle should be operated with gauge registering in the green sector or a high numerical number, Fig. 8, for maximum economy.

LOW COOLANT LEVEL INDICATOR

Some General Motors vehicles use a buzzer or indicator lamp to indicate a low coolant level condition. The buzzer or lamp is activated by a sensor, located in the radiator, when the coolant level becomes one quart or more low.

FUEL USAGE GAUGE

1978–82 Buick & Cadillac

Operation
This system consists of green and amber indicator lights located on the fuel gauge or telltale lamp cluster, a switch mounted on the instrument panel behind the gauges and an interconnecting vacuum hose and tee. The system operates on engine vacuum through a dual contact vacuum sensing switch. When the accelerator is operated slowly and smoothly, engine vacuum remains high and the switch passes current to the green indicator light which indicates economical fuel consumption. When the accelerator pedal is depressed rapidly, vacuum decreases and the switch passes current to the amber indicator light, which indicates high fuel consumption. The amber indicator light will glow when the ignition switch is in the "On" position with the engine stopped.

Functional Test
1. With ignition switch in the "On" position, ground each terminal at the economy switch. Both green and amber indicator lights should glow. If not check for burned out bulbs.
2. With ignition switch in "On" position, amber indicator light should glow. If not, check for loose or disconnected wires at fuel economy switch or for poor ground. If amber indicator light still does not glow replace switch.
3. Start engine and allow to idle, the green indicator light should glow. If not, check for leaking, plugged or kinked vacuum hose between vacuum source and fuel

FUEL TANK PURGE PROCEDURE

Cars which have a "Water in Fuel" light may have the water removed from the fuel tank with a pump or by siphoning. The pump or siphon hose should be hooked up to the 1/4 inch fuel return hose (smaller of the two fuel hoses) above the rear axle or under the hood near the fuel pump. Siphoning should continue until all water is removed from the fuel tank. Use a clear plastic line or observe filter bowl on draining equipment to determine when clear fuel begins to flow. Be sure to remove the cap on fuel tank while using this purge procedure. Replace the cap when finished. The same precautions for handling gasoline should be observed when purging diesel fuel tanks.

Fig. 8 Water in fuel indicator & tank purge procedure. 1981–82 GM with diesel engine

economy switch. Check for loose or disconnected wires at economy switch or poor ground. If green indicator lamp still does not glow, replace switch.

TURBO-POWER INDICATOR

1978–82 Buick V6-231 Turbo-Charged Engine

Century, Regal and Riviera models utilize two lights located in the lower right hand gauge area. The yellow light indicates moderate acceleration and the orange light indicates power or heavy acceleration. When neither light is illuminated, the indication visible is a green paint band signifying economy. LeSabre models utilize three lights located at the bottom of the fuel gauge. On light acceleration or cruising, a green light indicates economy. Moderate acceleration activates a yellow indicator light. The orange light is activated during heavy acceleration.

WATER IN FUEL INDICATOR

1981–82 General Motors With Diesel Engine

The Water In Fuel warning system employs an electronic water detector, mounted inside the fuel tank, on the fuel gauge sending unit. The detector provides a warning when 1–2½ gallons of water are present in the fuel tank by lighting a warning lamp on the instrument panel. The sending unit assembly also contains a provision for siphoning-off water in the tank through the fuel return line, Fig. 8.

The water in fuel lamp will come on for 2–5 seconds each time ignition is switched to RUN position to insure that the lamp is operating. If there is water in the fuel, the warning lamp will come back on after a 15–20 second delay and remain on.

Trouble Shooting
If warning indicator fails to light during bulb check, disconnect wiring harness connector at fuel gauge sending unit, containing a yellow/black stripe wire. With ignition switch in RUN position, connect yellow/black stripe wire to ground, using a suitable jumper wire. If lamp lights, problem is in water detector. If lamp fails to light, check for open circuit between sender and warning lamp, a burned out bulb, or a blown out fuse.

If warning lamp remains on at all times, disconnect wiring harness connector at fuel tank sending unit with ignition switch in RUN position. If warning lamp remains on, check for short circuit to ground between sender and warning lamp. If warning lamp goes out when harness is disconnected, first purge water in fuel tank, Fig. 8, then recheck circuit. If lamp remains on with harness connected to sending unit, water detector is defective.

Electronic gauges and indicator systems differ from conventional gauges in that the signals transmitted from the vehicle sensors are processed by a control module, usually containing a microcomputer or logic chip. While most microcomputer modules are not repairable in the field, many offer self-diagnostic functions to aid in isolating causes for system malfunctions. Common failures are in system sensors and sending units and their related wiring. Since many of the systems operate with very low voltage (often less than 1-volt) signals, care must be taken during repair not to alter the vehicle wiring harness.

CHARGE SYSTEM INDICATOR

1981–82 Chrysler Corp.

Operation

The charge system indicator lamp monitors the complete charging system, under operating conditions, rather than just alternator output. The system consists of an electronic module which plugs into the instrument cluster printed circuit board. A 10-volt diode, in series with a transistor, senses voltage between the cluster feed and ground. At low voltage a small power transistor is turned on, providing a ground to an indicator lamp, which is powered by the ignition feed circuit.

The low voltage indicator lamp comes on when ignition voltage, at the instrument cluster, drops below approximately 11.2 volts. The lamp may come on under heavy electrical loads during engine idling, particularly in cold weather. The lamp should go out when engine speed is increased, or electrical load is decreased.

Trouble Shooting

To test system, first make sure battery is fully charged and charging system is operating properly. With engine stopped and ignition switch in RUN position, connect voltmeter between ground and lower small cavity at ignition feed fuse. Gradually increase electrical load by switching on headlamps and other accessories. Indicator lamp should reach full intensity as meter reading drops below 11.2 volts.

ELECTRONIC DIGITAL CLOCK

1979–82 Ford & Mercury

Operation

This clock features a quartz crystal time base to keep precise time, not varying more than 60 seconds per month. Time, date, or elapsed time are displayed on a four-digit vacuum-fluorescent display. Display is dimmed when headlamps are switched on, but maximum brightness may be obtained by rotating panel lamp dimmer fully clockwise.

When ignition is switched to RUN or ACC position, the clock displays the date for 5 seconds, then automatically displays time. Date may be read at any time by pressing DATE button. Elapsed time is displayed whenever E/T button is pressed, and remains displayed

TO SET TIME:

PULL BUTTON OUT UNTIL IT UNLOCKS.

PUSH RESET SWITCH
1 TO ADVANCE HOURS
2 TO ADVANCE MINUTES

PUSH SAME BUTTON ALL THE WAY UNTIL IT STOPS, THEN RELEASE.

TO SET DATE: (TIME MUST BE SET FIRST)
REPEAT ABOVE WITH DATE BUTTON EXCEPT:
RESET SWITCH
1 ADVANCES MONTH
2 ADVANCES DATE

Fig. 1 Electronic digital clock operation. 1979–82 Ford/Mercury

until button is pressed again. Date and time are on call when elapsed time is being displayed or when ignition is OFF, and will be displayed by pressing DATE or TIME buttons.

Trouble Shooting

Check functions of clock as outlined above. If clock performs as described, but does not register correct time or date, refer to Fig. 1, and set clock. If clock still fails to register correct time, or elapsed time, clock is defective. If clock fails to operate as described, check feed and ground circuits, Fig. 2.

1. With ignition and headlamp switches in OFF position, connect test lamp between cavities 54 and 57 of clock wiring harness connector, Fig. 2. If lamp fails to light, check continuity to ground in circuit 57. If wire has continuity, problem is in dome lamp circuit 54.
2. With ignition ON and headlamps OFF, connect test lamp between cavities 57 and 296 in clock wiring harness connector. If lamp fails to light, problem is in ignition feed circuit 296.
3. With ignition and headlamp switches in ON position, connect test lamp between cavities 57 and 19 in clock wiring harness connector. If test lamp fails to light, problem is in headlamp switch rheostat circuit 19.

Fig. 2 Electronic digital clock wiring diagram (Typical). 1979–82 Ford & Mercury

4. If all circuits are satisfactory, but clock is inoperative, clock is defective.

FUEL DATA PANEL

1982 Cadillac

Operation

The fuel data panel is standard on all 1982 Cadillac models equipped with Digital Fuel Injection (DFI) V-8 engine. The panel includes two buttons to control display of INSTANT/AVERAGE fuel economy or RANGE/FUEL USED functions. A third RESET button is included to reset average functions. Light emitting diodes are used to indicate which function is being displayed on the digital read-out. The RANGE function is not included on models equipped with Electronic Instrument Cluster, as this function is performed by the cluster.

Fuel data is processed by an electronic control module, based on inputs from the speed sensor, fuel gauge sending unit, and fuel injection pulse width. AVERAGE fuel economy is computed by dividing number of miles travelled by amount of fuel used since panel was last reset. FUEL USED is determined from injection pulse width. Since a calibrated amount of fuel is delivered by each injection pulse, the control module is able to calculate the total fuel delivery and determine amount of fuel used since panel was last reset. AVERAGE fuel economy or FUEL USED may be reset by pressing RESET button while function is being displayed; however FUEL USED will automatically reset when value reaches 99.9 gallons.

INSTANT fuel data is present fuel economy at the time display command is given. It is displayed in whole numbers ranging from 0–70 MPG. RANGE is estimated vehicle range in miles, based on fuel remaining and average fuel economy over last 25 miles of operation. Fuel range is displayed to the nearest mile until value falls below approximately 40 miles. At this time, numerical display is replaced by letter "L", to indicate low fuel range.

MILES TO EMPTY SYSTEM

1978–81 Ford Motor Co.

This system indicates the distance to drive on fuel remaining. When over 50 miles of fuel is remaining, the miles to empty indicator will provide a digital read out for a few seconds, of the amount of miles till empty when the button is depressed. The digital readout will remain on if miles to empty is less than 50 miles. The electronic module receives signals from a rheostat in the fuel tank which is separate from the fuel gauge sender unit and a vehicle speed sensor. The system estimates the fuel level and economy and provides a readout of miles to empty. The indicator will read zero before the fuel tank is completely empty.

To avoid unnecessary diagnosis or repairs, the system initially calculates a new miles to empty number using a predetermined fuel economy number when battery has been disconnected or when miles to empty module has been replaced. As the vehicle is driven, the system will calculate fuel economy and adjust miles to empty number accordingly. When refilling fuel tank, place ignition switch in off position to avoid false indications.

GRAPHIC DISPLAY WARNING INDICATOR SYSTEM

1979–82 Ford/Mercury

Operation

This system is equipped with five L.E.D. (light emitting diodes) located on the console, which will indicate running lamp failure, headlamp failure, brake lamp or low w/s washer fluid or fuel level. If a lamp is burned out, the L.E.D. will illuminate, indicating a bulb failure. Application of the emergency flasher or rear turn signal when a turn signal/stop lamp bulb is burned out, will cause the L.E.D. to flash. When w/s washer fluid or fuel is below a predetermined level, the corresponding L.E.D. will illuminate.

Trouble Shooting, Fig. 3

1. Depress graphic indicator button with ignition switch in the ACC or Run position. All of L.E.D. should illuminate, if not check fuse.
2. Check to ensure that indicator module wire connector is properly installed.
3. Visually check vehicle for lamp outage, low w/s washer fluid level and low fuel indicator on instrument panel.
4. If any of the above components are not operating properly, repair inoperative circuit and recheck operation, Figs. 4 through 7.

CONDITION	POSSIBLE SOURCE	ACTION	LOCATION
• Taillamp L.E.D. Illuminated/False Indication	• Bad Bulb • Open Wire	• Replace Bulb • Check Cir. 14/102	• Rear Running Lamps • 14401 Connector to Module
• Headlamp L.E.D. Illuminated or False Indications	• Bad Headlamp Bulb • Non-Halogen Bulb • Open Wire	• Replace Headlamp • Replace with Halogen Bulb • Check Cir. 13 or 108	• Headlamp • 14401 Connector to Module
• Brake Lamp L.E.D. Illuminated or False Indication	• Bad Bulb • Open Wire	• Replace Bulb • Check Cir. 5 and 105, 9 and 104	• Tail lamp • Console
• Low Fuel L.E.D. Illuminated or False Indication	• Low Fuel • Warning Switch (Inoperative)	• Fill Gas Tank • Replace	• Console • Washer Reservoir
• Washer Fluid L.E.D. Illuminated or False Indication	• Low Washer Fluid • Warning Switch (Inoperative)	• Fill Washer Reservoir • Replace	• Under Hood • 14401 Connector to Module
• (Test) No L.E.D.'s Will Illuminate	• No Voltage • Open Wire	• Check Fuse • Check Cir. 296-57D	• Fuse Panel • 14401 Connector to Module
• (Test) One or More L.E.D.'s Will Not Illuminate	• Bad L.E.D.'s	• Replace Indicator	• Console

Fig. 3 Graphic display warning indicator diagnosis chart

TRIP COMPUTER SYSTEM

1979–81 Seville & 1979 Eldorado

The Trip Computer System, consists of three major sections; monitoring section, processing section and display section. The monitoring section consists of sensors located through out the vehicle. The sensors provide information to the microcomputer through a sensor wiring harness on Seville models and instrument panel and engine wiring on Eldorado models. Information from the sensors is supplied to the microcomputer, which analyzes the information. Once the information has been analyzed, the information is then transmitted to the digital display.

With the use of the keyboard, the microcomputer can be programmed to calculate and average miles per gallon, average speed, elapsed time, fuel range, mile remaining to destination and the approximate arrival time at destination. In addition to these functions, the computer can provide time of day, engine Rpm, engine coolant temperature, battery voltage, vehicle speed and fuel level. On 1979 Eldorado models, the digital read out may be converted to the metric equivalent by the conversion switch on the instrument panel.

The fuel gauge will display the letter F if 16 gallons or more of fuel is contained in the fuel tank. When fuel remaining in the fuel tank drops below 16 gallons, the gauge will read the numerical amount of fuel left in the tank.

Fig. 4 Graphic display warning indicator wiring diagram (Typical). 1979–81 Ford & Mercury exc. Escort & Lynx.

Fig. 5 Graphic display warning indicator wiring diagram. 1982 Ford & Mercury exc. Escort & Lynx

Fig. 6 Graphic display warning indicator wiring diagram. Escort & Lynx Base model

Fig. 7 Graphic display warning indicator. Escort & Lynx exc. Base model

The system is designed so that the fuel gauge will read zero before the vehicle runs out of fuel. Two types of in-tank fuel sending units are used with this system. The sending unit used on models equipped with a CB radio have a resistance range of 5 to 95 ohms, while sending units used on models less CB radio have a resistance of 0 to 90 ohms. The digital speedometer will update display reading every ½ second to the nearest one mph up to speeds of 85 mph. The clock and data display will operate as a clock until a keyboard key is depressed. The unit will continue to display the information called for by the keyboard until the ignition switch is cycled off and on or another keyboard key is depressed.

If fuel display shows dashes instead of fuel reading, this indicates that an open circuit exists in the fuel sensing circuit from the micro computer box. The microcomputer is equipped with an Ill light located at the bottom of the computer box. The ill light will be illuminated through a three second initialization period or when clock display is called for with ignition switch in the off position. If ill light is illuminated at any other time, a problem exists in the system or micro computer. Due to the complexity of the microcomputer, a failure in the system external to the computer may indicate that the computer is defective.

Functional Test
1. With ignition switch in the off position, depress clock step and release.
   a. Data display should show time of day, then go out. Other digital displays should remain off.
2. Start engine, then reset trip odometer.
   a. Cluster, data display and fuel gauge should indicate the 8's (speedometer 188), with coolant light and generator light remaining on as long as 8's are displayed. After 8's, coolant and tem-

perature lights disappear, fuel gauge should indicate F, or number of gallons remaining in the fuel tank.
3. Set clock to time of day.
   a. Rotate clock clockwise to advance minutes and counter clockwise to advance hours.
4. Depress keyboard reset key.
   a. Data display will show dashes, then return to clock function.
5. Enter 10 miles by depressing ENT miles and 1 and 0 keys.
   a. Wait for clock function to reappear.
6. Depress DEST key and operate vehicle with rear wheels off the ground or drive vehicle.
   a. 10 should appear on data display.
7. Depress MPG key.
   a. Data display should indicate average mpg. System should first display mileage between 10 and 20, then display should be blank. The second reading should then appear and be between 0 and 30 mpg or zero if not moving.
8. Depress MPG key and note reading, then depress Range key.
   a. Take average mpg shown and multiply by fuel gauge reading, which should equal the range.
9. Depress Speed key.
   a. Data display should be greater than zero.
10. Depress Time key.
    a. Data display should indicate minutes and seconds mode, with seconds advancing.
11. Depress Destination key.
    a. Data display should indicate 10 miles less than the number of miles driven as indicated on trip odometer. If driven more than 10 miles, a negative number should appear.

12. Depress Clock key, then depress Arrive key.
    a. Data display should indicate an arrival time ahead of clock time based on average speed. If vehicle was driven more than 10 miles, dashes will appear.
13. Depress RPM key.
    a. Data display should indicate engine rpm, which will vary with throttle.
14. Depress ENG °F key.
    a. Data display should be between 100 and 220° F.
15. Depress Volts key.
    a. Data display should indicate between 11 and 15 volts with a fully charged battery.
16. Check speed reading on cluster to ensure that readings are valid, not zero when vehicle is moving.
17. Place headlamp switch in the On position, then rotate switch knob.
    a. All displays should or intensify in steps as the rheostat is rotated.
18. After operating vehicle for more than 10 miles, turn ignition switch off, then depress stem of data display and release.
    a. Data display should indicate time of day, then go out. All other displays should remain off.
19. Place ignition switch in the On position
    a. Cluster, data display and fuel gauge should indicate 8's (speedometer 188).
20. After prove out, depress MPG key.
    a. Data display should show average mpg, first reading should be 10 to 20 mpg, then display should go blank, after which zero mph should be indicated.
21. Depress Speed key.
    a. Data display should indicate more

22. Depress Time key.
   a. Data display should indicate hours and minutes.
23. Depress Dest key.
   a. Data display should indicate zero or a negative number, depending on number of miles driven.

TRIP MONITOR SYSTEM

1979–81 Buick

This system consists of a set of computer controlled displays which consists of a fuel display, speedometer display and a data display center. When the ignition switch is placed in the On position, all displays will indicate 8's (speedometer 188) for approximately 3 seconds. This is done to show that all segments of the display are functional. The fuel display will indicate the number of gallons remaining in the fuel tank, when fuel level is between 2 and 19 gallons. When fuel level is below 2 gallons, the fuel display will read E. After one additional gallon of fuel is burned, the E indicated on the fuel display will begin to flash, When fuel level is above 19 gallons, the display will read F. The speedometer display will indicate vehicle speed between 0 and 85 mph. With the ignition switch in the On position, the trip monitor will display fuel range on 1979 models, time of day on 1980 models, after prove out, until a keyboard function is selected. The selected keyboard function will remain on the display until another keyboard key is depressed or the ignition switch is placed in the off position. The trip monitor is equipped with a metric conversion switch which can be used to convert numerical values to the metric system. The digital displays can be dimmed by rotating the headlamp switch knob.

A red indicator light is located at the top of the microcomputer. This light should be illuminated only for one second as the ignition switch is turned off during prove out and when clock stem is depressed with ignition switch off and key removed. If the light is illuminated at any other time, a problem in the trip monitor system wiring, keyboard, cluster assembly or microcomputer is indicated.

The trip monitor system is fused into the A/C and tail lamp circuits. There are also two fuses located on the side of the microcomputer toward the front of the vehicle. Any time the battery has been disconnected, the ignition switch should be cycled on and off until display readouts indicate 8's (188 for speedometer), then ignition switch should be cycled on and off one additional time.

Inspection

1. Check to ensure that metric conversion switch is in the off position, then place ignition switch in the On position. The data and fuel displays should read 8's and speedometer should read 188.
2. Start engine; speedometer should read zero mph, fuel display should indicate number of gallons remaining in fuel tank and data display should indicate fuel

Fig. 8   Tripminder display & keyboard

range on 1979 models, time of day on 1980 models.
3. Depress Clock key on keyboard. Reset clock by depressing clock stem, then rotate clock clockwise to advance minutes, counter clockwise to advance hours. Do not depress and rotate clock may result. With ignition switch in the off position, depress clock stem, time of day should appear and go out. Other displays should remain off.
4. Press reset key twice, data display should show four dashes.
5. Press enter key, data display should read zero.
6. Enter any three digit number within 6 seconds, by depressing the appropriate keys. The data display should indicate the numbers entered for 6 seconds, then change to fuel range on 1979-models, time of day on 1980 models. Do not press any other keys until data display returns to fuel range or time of day.
7. Place headlamp switch in the on position, then rotate switch knob and note that displays dim in steps. The display should return to full brightness when the headlamp switch is placed in the off position.
8. Depress Eng. Temp. key; the data display should read Low if engine is cold or value if engine temperature is between 100 and 258° F. If engine temperature is above 258° F, the display will flash and the instrument panel temperature warning lamp will light.
9. Place metric conversion switch to the on position, the metric light should come on. The fuel reading should change to litres and fuel range and speedometer should change to kilometers. When the metric conversion switch is turned off, the light should go off and the fuel, speedometer, and fuel range readings should return to gallons and miles.
10. Press Trip Time Elapse key; the data display should in minutes and seconds, the amount of time that has elapsed since the clock was reset. Once the display has been shown, turn ignition switch to the off position.
11. Press clock stem in and release. The clock should display the time of day, then go out. Place ignition switch to the On position and press Trip Time Elapse key. The data display should indicate the total elapse time since the clock was reset. This reading should be greater than the value obtained in step 10.
12. Press Dist to Destination key; data display should indicate the number entered in step 6. Press Clock key; if times read-out is accurate, the trip monitor system is functioning properly.

TRIPMINDER SYSTEM

1982 Ford & Mercury

Operation

The Tripminder system consists of a control module and a fuel flow sensor. The control module includes a vacuum fluorescent display, a control keyboard, and a microprocessor control circuit. A vehicle speed signal is supplied to the system by the electronic instrument cluster or from a speed sensor on vehicles with a conventional instrument cluster.

The Tripminder operates with ignition in RUN or ACC position. Each time system ignition is switched to RUN or ACC from OFF position, the display lights in the clock mode. Resetting the clock will be necessary if battery voltage is disconnected from system, or if clock memory is disturbed by voltage surges such as jump starting, electrical storms or high-power radio transmissions.

The four lower control buttons are used to select the desired display, while the three lower buttons are used to reset functions of the display, Fig. 8. TIME, TRIP, and ECON buttons are dual function buttons, which can be pressed a second time to display an alternate function, Fig. 9. On the top row, the "S" button is used to set day, date, and month, as well as time. The "R" button is used to reset displays and the EM button converts display readings from English to Metric units and/or back again.

Trouble Shooting

The Tripminder has a built-in diagnostic capability. Pressing TIME and EM buttons simultaneously will enter Tripminder into this mode. Pressing each button in sequence, Fig. 10, will complete diagnostic check. Any push button malfunction, clock malfunction, or display problems will require replacement of Tripminder module.

FORD ELECTRONIC INSTRUMENT CLUSTER

Except 1982 Lincoln Continental

The electronic instrument cluster, avail-

BUTTON	FIRST PRESS OF BUTTON DISPLAYS	SECOND PRESS OF BUTTON DISPLAYS
TIME	TIME, DAY AND DATE	ELAPSED TIME
TRIP	TRIP ODOMETER	AVERAGE TRIP SPEED
ECON	INSTANTANEOUS FUEL ECONOMY	AVERAGE TRIP FUEL ECONOMY
FUEL	FUEL CONSUMED	FUEL CONSUMED

Fig. 9   Tripminder keyboard function chart

Button	Display	Description
TIME	XX:XX TIME 1	Upper row counting from 00:00 to 99:99
TRIP	.X DIST 2	Upper row displays a number from 0 to 25.5 similar to an odometer.
ECON	FLOW 3	Upper row displays a number from 0 to 250 showing accumulated fuel flow.
FUEL	.0 FUEL 4	Display should not change.
S	X.X DIM 5	Upper row displays a number that varies with IP dimmer.
E M	66:66 NNNNNN	First Press of Button
E M	777.7 ZZZZZZ	Second Press of Button
E M	8888 ++++++	Third Press of Button
E M	NTM 2	Fourth Press of Button
R		System goes back to normal customer operation. (Press S button to avoid getting into the Reset mode for Time, Trip or Econ).

Fig. 10   Tripminder self-diagnostic function chart

Fig. 11 Electronic Instrument Module dimmer circuit. 1982 Lincoln Continental

Fig. 12 Electronic fuel gauge self-check sequence. 1982 Lincoln Continental

Lincoln Continental use a programmable electronic message center which monitors vehicle systems and provides travel data functions. The major difference between electronic and conventional instrument clusters is the manner in which the information is displayed and the calibration of vehicle sensors.

able on 1980–81 Lincoln Continental and 1980–82 Continental Mark VI, Thunderbird and XR-7 models, consists of an electronic bar-type fuel gauge and an electronic digital speedometer. Thunderbird and XR-7 models use a conventional set of warning indicator lights to monitor vehicle and engine conditions, while the Continental Mark VI and

Fig. 13 Electronic fuel gauge wiring circuit with tank calibration shunt. 1982 Lincoln Continental

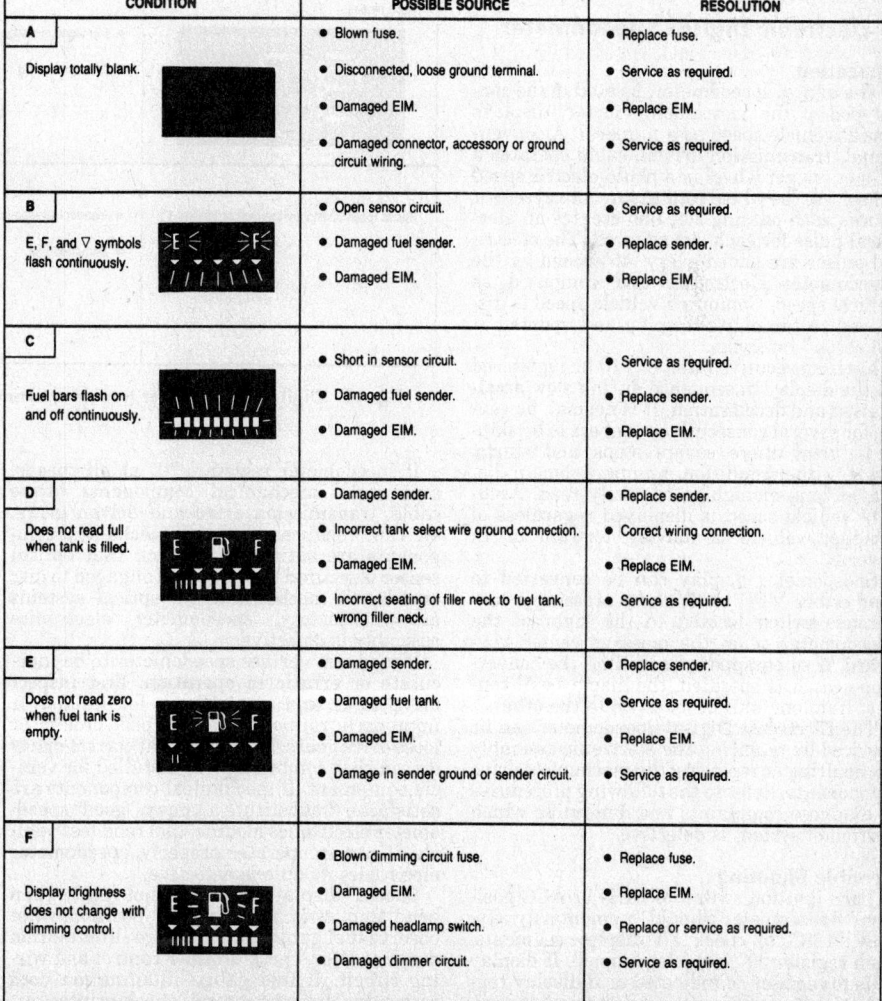

Fig. 14 Electronic fuel gauge trouble shooting chart. 1982 Lincoln Continental

ALL SEGMENTS ON:

ALL SEGMENTS OFF:

MPH OR Km/h

Fig. 15 Digital speedometer self-check sequence. 1982 Lincoln Continental

CONDITION	POSSIBLE SOURCE	RESOLUTION
Display totally blank.	• Blown electronic cluster fuse. • Loose or disconnected cluster ground terminal connection. • Damaged connector, accessory or ground circuit wiring. • Damaged EIM.	• Replace fuse. • Connect or service as required. • Service wiring circuit(s) or connectors as required. • Replace EIM.
Reads 0 MPH (Km/h) when vehicle in motion.	• Unconnected, loose, or broken speed cable. • Damaged EIM. • Damaged odometer.	• Service or replace as required. • Replace EIM. • Replace odometer.
MPH and Km/h symbols flash continuously.	• Optical sensor cable not connected. • Damaged EIM.	• Re-connect cable. • Replace EIM.
Speedometer will not switch between MPH and Km/h modes.	• Damaged EIM. • Damaged message center. • Damaged wiring.	• Replace EIM. • Replace message center. • Service as required.
Speed reads constantly too high or too low.	• Incorrect speedo-transmission gear/tire size. • Damaged EIM.	• Service as required. • Replace EIM.

Fig. 16 Digital speedometer trouble shooting chart. (Part 1 of 2) 1982 Lincoln Continental

The electronic cluster replaces conventional mechanical movement with electronic displays. The vacuum fluorescent type displays are brightly lit for daytime operation. When headlamps or parking lamps are turned on, the display automatically dims for night time driving. Display intensity can then be controlled in the conventional manner by rotating the knob on the headlamp switch.

Operation and trouble shooting information for components of the electronic instrument cluster can be found in the appropriate component section.

Electronic Digital Speedometer

Operation

The digital speedometer, located in the center pod of the instrument cluster, displays actual vehicle speed as a numeral. A conventional, transmission driven, cable operates a 16-slot trigger wheel in a photo-electric speed sensor. As the wheel rotates, an optical sensor counts each passing slot and creates an electrical pulse for each slot counted. The electrical pulses are added every .45 second by the speedometer electronics and computed as vehicle speed. Computed vehicle speed is displayed on the digital display and updated at .45 second intervals.

Each consecutive number will be registered on the display in sequence during slow acceleration and deceleration. It is normal, however, for several consecutive numbers to be skipped during more severe stops and starts. Under either condition, numbers remain displayed long enough to be easily read. Accurate vehicle speed is displayed regardless of whether vehicle is moving forward or in reverse.

Speedometer display can be converted to read either MPH or Km/h by pressing a conversion switch located to the right of the speedometer or on the message center keyboard, if so equipped. Each time the conversion switch is operated, the display will convert from one unit of measure to the other.

The Electronic Digital Speedometer can be serviced by replacing the electronic assembly or repairing or replacing the mechanical drive components. Refer to the following procedures to diagnose complaints and determine which portion of system is defective.

Trouble Shooting

Turn ignition switch to RUN or ACC position. Speedometer should momentarily display "188," to check all display segments, then register "0" (vehicle stopped). If display fails to register as indicated or if display registers broken or other than numerical characters, speedometer electronic assembly is defective.

If speedometer registers "0" at all speeds, first check mechanical components (drive cable, transmission drive and driven gears, etc.) and repair as needed. If mechanical components are satisfactory, check that optical sensor is secured to bridge and engaged to disc encoder. If mechanical and optical systems are satisfactory, speedometer electronics assembly is defective.

If road test verifies speedometer to be inaccurate or erratic in operation, first inspect drive cable and core. Check for kinked or improperly routed cable, chipped, broken or loose drive gears, and check that correct drive/driven gear combination is installed for vehicle equipment. If mechanical components are satisfactory, substitute a known "good" speedometer electronics module, and road test vehicle. If system operates properly, speedometer electronics module is defective.

Should display intensity not dim when headlamp switch is in ON position, first observe fuel gauge. If fuel gauge illumination does not alter, check dimmer control and wiring circuit. If fuel gauge illumination does respond to dimmer control, check printed circuit and speedometer connections. If circuit and connections are satisfactory, speedometer

electronics assembly is defective.

Electronic Fuel Gauge

Operation

The Electronic Fuel Gauge system consists of an electronic module with a vacuum fluorescent display and a specially calibrated fuel tank sending unit. The display consists of four groups of eight bars (segments). Fuel level is indicated by the number of segments brightly lit. Segments above the indicated fuel level are lit to approximately 1/20 the brilliance of indicating segments to provide a reference background.

The display also includes reference marks "F", 1/2, "E" and an international symbol (fuel pump) which are lit at the same brilliance as indicating segments. Empty is indicated when all bar segments are dimmed and the fuel pump symbol flashes. In addition, there is a self-diagnostic feature which warns of an open circuit in the fuel sender circuit. Under this condition, all bar segments are dimmed and the "F", "E", and 1/2 symbols flash continuously.

The electronic fuel gauge sending unit is similar to that of a conventional gauge, but

CONDITION	POSSIBLE SOURCE	RESOLUTION
Display incorrect, segments missing, or display indicates 188 all the time.	• Damaged EIM.	• Replace EIM.
Display brightness does not change with dimming control.	• Blown instrument panel fuse. • Damaged headlamp switch • Damaged EIM. • Damage in dimming circuitry.	• Replace fuse. • Replace switch. • Replace EIM. • Service as required.
Erratic display. Display blinks OFF and ON.	• Damage in electrical power (ACC/GND) circuits. • Damaged EIM.	• Service as required. Intermittent opens or shorts in wiring or poor connector connections/contacts. • Replace EIM.
Speed indication jumps up and down erratically.	• Damaged/bent speedometer cable. • Damaged EIM. • Damaged odometer — opto sensor disc.	• Service or replace as required. • Replace EIM • Service or replace as required.

Fig. 17   Digital speedometer trouble shooting chart. (Part 2 of 2). 1982 Lincoln Continental

ALL SEGMENTS ON THEN FLASHING ISO

FLASHING ISO, THEN ALL SEGMENTS BLANK

CURRENT TEMPERATURE INDICATION

Fig. 18   Electronic temperature gauge self-check sequence. 1982 Lincoln Continental

the electronic gauge sender resistance increases from empty stop to full stop. A conventional gauge sender resistance decreases from empty to full stop. Sender resistance is approximately 5 ohms at empty stop and 205 ohms at full stop.

Trouble Shooting

If fuel gauge fails to operate, check power feed and ground circuits to gauge. If circuits are satisfactory, and fuel sender circuit is satisfactory, display and module must be replaced as an assembly.

If display flashes open circuit warning, disconnect wiring harness connector at sending unit and connect jumper wire between terminals of connector. If gauge stops flashing, problem is in sending unit. If gauge continues to flash, check for open circuit between sending unit and gauge. If circuit is satisfactory, electronic fuel gauge is defective.

NOTE: When ignition is switched to RUN or ACC position, the fuel gauge provides an instantaneous fuel level indication (after prove-out). After this initial reading, the gauge requires several minutes to register changes in fuel level. When it is necessary to read fuel level after filling or draining tank, first turn ignition to OFF, then return switch to RUN or ACC position.

To test fuel gauge sending unit, lower fuel

tank and remove sending unit. Check float rod for free movement, and check that float is not loose, saturated with fuel or otherwise damaged. Connect ohmmeter to terminals on sending unit and operate float rod from empty to full position. At empty stop, meter should read 3–11 ohms; at full stop, meter should read 195–211 ohms. Change in reading while moving float rod should be smooth and progressive, without hesitation or jumping. If sending unit does not perform as outlined, it is defective and should be replaced.

1982 Lincoln Continental

The Electronic Instrument Cluster (EIC) is divided into two sections. An Electronic Information Module (EIM), which consists of a digital speedometer, an electronic fuel gauge, and an electronic temperature gauge, is the main feature of the EIC. A conventional feature section, contained within the main cluster, provides a mechanical odometer, transmission select indicator, and conventional turn signal and high beam indicators. A specially designed Electronic Message Center is included in the instrument panel package to the right of the main instrument cluster.

The EIM is a single service part containing the digital speedometer, electronic fuel gauge, and engine temperature gauge. Within the EIM, the speedometer and both gauges share common electronic circuitry such as power supply, dimming control, and a central micro-

computer. Input/output connections are made by means of a ribbon connector at the rear of the assembly.

The EIM is illuminated and functional when ignition is in RUN or ACC position. Illumination is at maximum intensity when headlamp switch is in OFF position. When headlamps or parking lamps are switched on, the EIM dimming circuit, Fig. 11, is activated, allowing display intensity to be controlled by headlamp switch rheostat. The EIM display is brighter and has greater dimming control than other electronic displays. As a result, when display intensity is adjusted, EIM displays will adjust faster than other displays and EIM display intensity will be lower at full dim position.

Electronic Fuel Gauge

Operation

The fuel gauge section of the EIM is an 11-bar graphic display. Seven large bars indicate approximately 1/8 tank divisions, and four smaller bars in the lower 1/4 of the gauge indicate approximately 1/16 tank divisions. Fuel level is indicated by the number of bars illuminated, and the bars turn off in sequence as fuel in the tank is consumed. Also displayed are "E" and "F" symbols to indicate empty and full positions, an international symbol (fuel pump), and four small triangle symbols which indicate 1/4 tank intervals.

The fuel gauge has two display response modes. After a self-check sequence is completed, the gauge automatically enters the fast response mode. In this mode, the signal from the sending unit is converted into a fuel level indication within a few seconds. As soon as the vehicle is moved, and the first speed signal is received by the EIM, the gauge enters the "normal" response mode. In this mode the sending unit signal is dampened (averaged over time) to prevent false readings due to fuel movement in the tank. Change in fuel level takes several minutes to register on the display in this mode.

When fuel level drops to the point where only two bars are illuminated on the segment display, a low fuel level signal will be displayed. Low fuel is indicated by continuous flashing of the fuel pump symbol. The symbol will continue to flash at one-second intervals until enough fuel has been added to light three or more display bars.

Trouble Shooting

When ignition is switched to RUN or ACC position, the fuel gauge performs a 3-second self-check sequence, Fig. 12, then switches to instant response mode of operation. If an open circuit exists between fuel tank sending unit and EIM, the "E", "F", and ¼ tank symbols will flash at 1-second intervals until problem has been corrected. If a short circuit exists between fuel tank sending unit and EIM, the 11 display bars will flash at 1-second intervals until problem has been corrected.

The fuel tank sending unit is similar to that in conventional type systems, however its resistance ranges from approximately 12 ohms at empty stop to 166 ohms at full stop. The same fuel tank sending unit is used with both 20 and 23 gallon fuel tanks. A tank select wire is included in the wiring harness, Fig. 13, to calibrate gauge for tank being used. Wire is jumped to ground for use with gallon tank.

Diagnosis of electronic fuel gauge complaints is similar to procedure for other electronic systems. Use charts, Fig. 14, to diagnose problems. Any failure to gauge sequence operations or failure of segments or symbols to light will require replacement of EIM assembly.

Digital Speedometer

Operation

The digital electronic speedometer displays vehicle speed numerically up to 85 MPH or 137 Km/h. The speedometer can be switched to read in either MPH or Km/h by pressing a conversion switch button located on the Electronic Message Center keyboard. Each time the button is pressed, speedometer reading will be converted from one unit of measure to the other. The selected unit of measure is indicated on the display to the right of the speed reading. The mode selected will remain locked in unless battery feed to EIM is disconnected, causing case reading to automatically revert to MPH.

Speedometer drive gears and cable are of conventional type, but the cable drives a slotted encoder wheel within the odometer. As slots on rotating encoder wheel pass an optical sensor, the sensor generates an electrical pulse. Pulses are transmitted to the EIM microcomputer which converts the number of pulses to corresponding speed reading.

It is normal for speedometer to display consecutive numbers in sequence during slow acceleration and deceleration, and to skip several consecutive numbers during quick starts and stops. Display information is updated every ½ second, allowing speed reading to be displayed long enough to be read easily. Accurate vehicle speed is displayed regardless of whether vehicle is moving forward or in reverse.

Trouble Shooting

When ignition is switched to RUN or ACC position, the speedometer performs a 3-second self-check sequence, Fig. 15, then reads vehicle speed (usually zero). This sequence verifies that all segments of display are operating in proper order. If optical sensor cable connection is not made or if an open circuit exists in optical sensor diode circuit, the MPH-Km/h indicator will remain flashing at 1-second intervals until problem is corrected.

The first step in diagnosing electronic speedometer complaints is to check mechanical components; drive cable, transmission drive and driven gears, etc. Further diagnosis is similar to procedures for other electronic components. Use charts, Figs. 16 and 17, to locate cause for speedometer complaints. Failure of gauge segments to light or failure to read numerical characters will require replacement of EIM assembly.

Electronic Temperature Gauge

Operation

Engine coolant temperature is displayed on a 9-segment graphic display gauge. Segment

CONDITION	POSSIBLE CAUSE	RESOLUTION
Display totally blank.	• Blown electronic cluster fuse. • Unconnected, loose ground terminal. • Damaged EIM. • Damaged connector, accessory circuit or ground circuit wiring	• Replace fuse. • Service as required. • Replace EIM. • Service as required.
Displays zero bars all the time.	• Open in sensor wiring. • Open temperature sensor. • Damaged EIM.	• Service as required. • Replace sensor. • Replace EIM.
Temperature bars flash on and off continuously.	• Short in sensor wiring. • Short in sensor. • Damaged EIM.	• Service as required. • Replace sensor. • Replace EIM.
Gauge reads cold or hot during normal driving conditions.	• Damaged sensor. • Damaged EIM. • Damaged cooling system. • Damaged wiring.	• Replace sensor. • Replace EIM. • Service as required. • Service as required.
Display erratic. • Blinks ON and OFF intermittently. • Temp. bars flash or display reads zero intermittently.	• Damaged EIM power/ground wiring. • Damaged sensor wiring • Damaged EIM	• Service as required. • Service as required. • Replace EIM.

Fig. 19 Electronic temperature gauge trouble shooting chart. 1982 Lincoln Continental

bars are illuminated in sequence as coolant temperature increases. Also displayed are an international symbol (thermometer), "C" and "H" reference indicators, and a "normal" range indicator. The gauge indicates temperatures within range of 0–260°F.

The temperature gauge will show 0 bars (all segments dark), when coolant temperature is below 0°F. When coolant temperature increases to the point where 8 bars are illuminated, the thermometer symbol will begin to flash. This over-temperature indicator will continue to flash at 1-second intervals until coolant temperature falls below the point where 8 bars are illuminated.

Trouble Shooting

When ignition is switched to RUN or ACC position, temperature gauge performs a 3 second self-check sequence, Fig. 18. This verifies that all segments of the display are in proper working order. If a short circuit exists between the temperature sending unit and EIM, temperature display bars will flash at one-second intervals until problem is corrected. If an open circuit exists in temperature sender circuit, temperature display bars will

not light until problem has been corrected.

The coolant temperature sensor consists of a thermister (temperature-sensitive resistance element) in a brass housing with an integral wiring harness connector. Resistance of sensor is low at higher coolant temperatures, (Approximately 1000 ohms at 260°F.) and increases as coolant temperature decreases to approximately 250,000 ohms at 0°F.

Refer to chart, Fig. 19, to aid in locating malfunctions in temperature gauge sections.

GENERAL MOTORS DIGITAL INSTRUMENT CLUSTER

1981–82 Eldorado & Seville

Operation

The Digital Instrument Cluster is available on Eldorado and Seville models with Digital Fuel Injection (DFI) or diesel engine only. The system consists of three vacuum fluorescent displays, an English/Metric conversion

SYMPTOMS	CHECK THE FOLLOWING	ACTION REQUIRED
CLUSTER DOES NOT OPERATE (NO DISPLAYS LIGHT).	1. INSTRUMENT CLUSTER FUSE. 2. POWER AT CLUSTER CONNECTOR (SEE VOLTAGE AND RESISTANCE). 3. CLUSTER GROUND CONNECTION.	1. DETERMINE CAUSE OF BLOWN FUSE, REPLACE. 2. REPAIR OR REPLACE WIRING HARNESS. 3. REPAIR GROUND CONNECTION.
FUEL DISPLAY SHOWS "--" AT ALL TIMES.	1. TANK UNIT LEAD OPEN OR CONNECTOR/TERMINAL LOOSE (SEE VOLTAGE AND RESISTANCE CHARTS)	1a. REPAIR OPEN WIRE OR REPLACE CONNECTOR/ TERMINAL. 1b. REPAIR OR REPLACE FUEL TANK UNIT.
(ADDITIONAL TEST: WITH IGNITION OFF, SHORT PIN H TO GROUND AT THE CLUSTER CONNECTOR, TURN IGNITION ON AND AFTER SEGMENT CHECK FUEL GAGE SHOULD DISPLAY FLASHING E.)		
FUEL DISPLAY SHOWS "--" PART OF THE TIME.	1. WRONG TANK UNIT INSTALLED. 2. INTERMITTENT OPEN WIRING HARNESS.	1. CHECK PART NUMBER & REPLACE IF NEEDED. 2. REPAIR OR REPLACE WIRING HARNESS.
FUEL DISPLAY SHOWS FLASHING E AT ALL TIMES.	1. TANK UNIT LEAD SHORTED TO GROUND.	1. REPAIR SHORT OR REPLACE HARNESS.
(ADDITIONAL TEST: WITH IGNITION OFF, OPEN PIN H AT THE CLUSTER CONNECTOR, TURN ON IGNITION AND AFTER SEGMENT CHECK FUEL GAGE SHOULD DISPLAY " - ".)		
SPEED DISPLAY SHOWS 0 AT ALL TIMES.	1. CRUISE CONTROL OPERATES CORRECTLY: CHECK FOR SPEED SIGNAL AT CLUSTER CONNECTOR (SEE VOLTAGE AND RESISTANCE CHARTS) 2. CRUISE CONTROL DOES NOT OPERATE: a. CHECK VOLTAGES AT BUFFER AMPLIFIER b. CHECK VOLTAGES AT SPEED SENSOR.	1. REPAIR OR REPLACE WIRING HARNESS (BUFFER AMPLIFIER TO CLUSTER). 2a. REPAIR WIRING HARNESS TO BUFFER AMPLIFIER OR REPLACE BUFFER AMPLIFIER. 2b. REPAIR WIRING HARNESS TO SPEED SENSOR OR REPLACE SPEED SENSOR.
SPEED READS "HIGH" ALL THE TIME. RANGE DISPLAY SHOWS "--" ALL THE TIME.	POSITION OF ENGLISH/ METRIC SWITCHES. 1. OPEN WIRING HARNESS FROM D.F.I. COMPUTOR. 2. PRESENCE OF SERIAL DATA LINE SIGNAL FROM D.F.I.	ADVISE OWNER OF FUNCTIONING OF ENGLISH/ METRIC SWITCH. 1. REPAIR OR REPLACE WIRING HARNESS. 2. REPLACE D.F.I. COMPUTER.*
	(RESETTING THE AVERAGE MPG FUNCTION ON THE MPG HEAD WHEN A LARGE INSTANTANEOUS MPG IS DISPLAYED MAY BE NECESSARY).	
DISPLAYS DO NOT DIM.	1. PARK LIGHT AND PANEL ILLUMINATION FUSES. 2. PARK LIGHT AND/OR PANEL ILLUMINATION VOLTAGES AT CLUSTER CONNECTOR (SEE VOLTAGE AND RESISTANCE CHARTS)	1. DETERMINE CAUSE OF BLOWN FUSE, REPLACE FUSE. 2. REPAIR OR REPLACE WIRING HARNESS.
DISPLAYS DIM AT FULL CLOCKWISE ROTATION OF PANEL ILLUMINATION CONTROL WITH PARK LIGHTS OFF.	OPEN WIRE OR MISSING BULBS (ALL) IN PARK LIGHT CIRCUIT.	REPAIR OR REPLACE WIRE HARNESS, REPLACE BULBS.
ONE OR MORE DIGITS REMAIN IN SEGMENT CHECK, CAN BE DIMMED WITH PARKING LIGHTS ON.		REPLACE CLUSTER.
ONE OR MORE DIGITS OR DISPLAYS DO NOT LIGHT		REPLACE CLUSTER.
*NOTE: OTHER SYSTEMS CONNECT TO THE SERIAL DATA LINK FROM THE D.F.I. COMPUTER (EG., MPG HEAD, ECC). THESE UNITS SHOULD BE CHECKED FOR PROPER OPERATION BEFORE THE D.F.I. COMPUTER IS REPLACED.		

VOLTAGES AT THE INSTRUMENT CLUSTER CONNECTOR WITH THE CONNECTOR PLUGGED INTO THE CIRCUIT BOARD.

SIGNAL	CONNECTOR PIN	VALUE		COMMENTS
PARK LIGHTS	A	0	VOLTS	PARK LIGHTS OFF.
		12	VOLTS	PARK LIGHTS ON, ENGINE NOT RUNNING.
SPEED SENSOR INPUT	C	0 TO 9.6	VOLTS	IGNITION ON, DEPENDS ON POSITION OF SPEEDOMETER FIELD PLATE.
SWITCHED IGNITON	F	0	VOLTS	IGNITION OFF.
		12	VOLTS	IGNITION ON, ENGINE NOT RUNNING.
		14	VOLTS	ENGINE RUNNING.
FUEL TANK	H	0 TO 1.5	VOLTS	DEPENDS ON FUEL IN TANK.
MPG (SERIAL) INPUT	L	2.5 TO 4.0	VOLTS	ENGINE RUNNING, VEHICLE EQUIPPED WITH D.F.I.
PANEL ILLUMINATION	N	0 TO 12	VOLTS	PARK LIGHTS ON, ENGINE NOT RUNNING.
SPEED SENSOR LED INPUT	R	6.8	VOLTS	ENGINE RUNNING, VEHICLE EQUIPPED WITH D.F.I.
GROUND	U	0	VOLTS	

NOTE: ALL THE ABOVE MEASUREMENTS ARE REFERENCED TO GROUND, PIN U, IGNITION OFF UNLESS OTHERWISE STATED.

VOLTAGES OR RESISTANCES AT THE INSTRUMENT CLUSTER CONNECTOR WITH THE CONNECTOR DISCONNECTED.

SIGNAL	CONNECTOR PIN	VALUE		COMMENTS
PARK LIGHTS	A	0	VOLTS	PARK LIGHTS OFF.
		12	VOLTS	PARK LIGHTS ON, ENGINE NOT RUNNING.
SPEED SENSOR INPUT	C	0 TO 9.6	VOLTS	IGNITION ON, DEPENDS ON POSITION OF SPEEDOMETER FIELD PLATE.
SWITCHED IGNITION	F	0	VOLTS	IGNITION OFF
		12	VOLTS	IGNITION ON, ENGINE NOT RUNNING.
		14	VOLTS	ENGINE RUNNING.
FUEL TANK	H	0 TO 90	OHMS	DEPENDS ON FUEL IN TANK.
MPG (SERIAL) INPUT	L	2.5 TO 4.0	VOLTS	ENGINE RUNNING, VEHICLE EQUIPPED WITH D.F.I.
PANEL ILLUMINATION	N	0 TO 12	VOLTS	PARK LIGHTS ON, ENGINE NOT RUNNING.
SPEED SENSOR LED INPUT	R	8	VOLTS	ENGINE RUNNING, VEHICLE EQUIPPED WITH D.F.I.
		0	VOLTS	NO D.F.I.
GROUND	U	0	VOLTS	

NOTE: ALL THE ABOVE MEASUREMENTS ARE REFERENCED TO GROUND, PIN U, IGNITION OFF UNLESS OTHERWISE STATED.

Fig. 20 Digital instrument cluster diagnostic charts. 1981–82 Eldorado & Seville

Fig. 21 Digital instrument cluster wiring diagram. 1981–82 Eldorado & Seville with DFI

Fig. 22 Digital instrument cluster wiring diagram. 1981—82 Eldorado & Seville with diesel engine

switch, and microprocessor circuitry. The system displays vehicle speed, fuel remaining, and fuel range (DFI only) as easy-to-read numerals. Input signals for the system microprocessor are from a specially calibrated fuel tank sending unit, the cruise control speed sensor and a buffer amplifier, and the DFI computer.

Displays are brightly lit for daytime operation. The headlamp switch is incorporated into the system to provide display dimming for night driving. When headlamps or parking lamps are switched on, variable voltage from the headlamp switch rheostat is fed to the system microprocessor. This signal is used to regulate display intensity through the internal circuitry of the microprocessor.

All displays can be set to read in either English or Metric units of measure by operating the conversion switch. An indicator reading MPH or Km/h will be illuminated to the right of the speed display, depending on which unit of measure has been selected. On vehicles equipped with Electronic Climate Control or Fuel Data Panel, the conversion switch also converts their displays. There is no conversion for the odometer, as it is a conventional mechanical type calibrated at the factory to read in miles.

The digital speedometer displays vehicle speed up to 85 MPH or 135 Km/h. Above this speed, the display flashes the highest number displayed. The microprocessor receives the cruise control speed sensor signal from a buffer amplifier. The frequency of this signal is interpreted as vehicle speed by the processor, and displayed as a number by the speedometer.

The fuel gauge displays the letter "F" when fuel tank is within 2 gallons of being full.

When fuel in tank drops below this level, the level is displayed in whole numbers. The letter "E" is displayed when amount of fuel remaining is under 2 gallons and the "E" begins to flash when fuel remaining is less than 1 gallon.

Digital cluster vehicles are equipped with a special fuel tank sending unit which has a variable resistance value of 0–90 ohms, depending on float position. Voltage is applied to the sending unit which allows a voltage signal of 0–1½ volts to be transmitted to the system microprocessor, depending on fuel level in tank. The microprocessor interprets this voltage signal as a specific amount of fuel which is displayed on the fuel gauge.

Fuel range display is available only on vehicles with DFI engine. The instrument cluster microprocessor receives average fuel injection pulse data from the DFI computer and processes it along with fuel remaining data. Fuel range is then computed and displayed on the instrument cluster in miles or kilometers. When fuel range is less than 40 miles, the display shows "--".

Trouble Shooting

When ignition switch is turned to RUN position, a segment check illuminates all segments of all displays for approximately 3 seconds. Each display should show "88", and then display current value (speed, fuel remaining, and range). With headlamp switch in ON position, displays snould dim after segment check. To diagnose malfunctions in system, begin with a road test and operate all display functions. Follow procedures in chart, Fig. 20 and refer to wiring diagrams, Fig. 21 and 22, to locate cause of malfunction.

CHRYSLER CORP. ELECTRONIC INSTRUMENT CLUSTER
1981—82 Imperial
Operation

The electronic instrument cluster allows the operator to monitor important vehicle functions and obtain useful travel information at the touch of a button. The microprocessor controlled system includes an electronic chronometer, odometer, fuel and gear selector display and an electronic digital speedometer. Conventional indicator lamps, controlled by the microprocessor, monitor safety, reminder and engine systems.

Nine buttons located in the instrument panel "brow" are used to operate the cluster. One button allows displays to be converted from U.S. customary to metric or vice versa, one button allows reset of a selected function, and the other buttons are used to call up information from the microcomputer. Two additional buttons below the main panel are used to set time and date on the clock.

Two levels of illumination on the vacuum-fluorescent displays are automatically controlled by a photo-detector mounted on the dashboard. Bright blue-green illumination is provided for daytime operation, while reduced illumination is provided for night driving. During normal night time operation, the display takes 3 seconds to dim. In addition, panel illumination and fluorescent readout illumination can be controlled by the rheostat in the headlamp switch. The photo-detector overrides the dimmer for daytime driving with headlamps on.

**ELECTRONIC INSTRUMENT CLUSTER
GENERAL TROUBLE-SHOOTING PROCEDURE**

ELECTRONIC CLUSTER DIAGNOSTIC CHART

Fig. 23 Electronic instrument cluster trouble shooting charts, 1981—82 Imperial

MPH/Km/H		Miles per hour/Kilometers per hour
1	DTE	Distance to empty fuel tank
2	CK OUT	Warning check out
3	SELECT	Select clock or portion to be set
4	ADV	ADVance clock (only for resetting mode)
5	AV DPG	Average Distance Per Gallon (fuel economy)
6	DIST	Elapsed DIStance
7	E/TIME	Elapsed Time
8	AV SPD	Average vehicle Speed
9	DEST	Distance to DESTination
0	ETA	Estimated Time of day of Arrival
	RESET	Reset Trip Log Functions

NOTE: When activating electrical accessories such as headlamps or power doorlocks while the battery is partially discharged (low voltage condition), the clock display may appear, replacing other messages.

Fig. 24 Electronic message center keyboard function chart. 1980—81 Lincoln Continental, Town Car & Mark VI & 1982 Lincoln Town Car & Mark VI

vehicle travel and sends a signal to the computer. The computer processes this information along with information from the internal time reference base to calculate vehicle speed to within ±4% accuracy.

Signals from a specially designed fuel tank sending unit which monitors fuel level, and from the fuel flow sensor which monitors fuel consumption, are fed to the system computer. The computer processes these signals along with signals from other vehicle sensors and a reference time base, allowing the electronic fuel gauge display to perform several functions. Fuel level, present and trip fuel efficiency, and fuel range can all be obtained from the display.

Fuel supply is displayed both in symbols and numbers. When there is a supply of 14 or more gallons over gauge zero, the display reads FULL. When fuel supply drops below 14 gallons, fuel supply is displayed in numbers, counting down in 1-gallon increments. When 2 gallons or less remain in the supply, LOW FUEL is displayed and flashes at 2-second intervals until supply is exhausted or refilled above the 2-gallon level.

When RANGE button on control panel is pressed, the predicted number of miles that can be driven under existing conditions and fuel remaining will be displayed for 5 seconds. Present fuel economy is displayed by pressing PRESENT button and will remain displayed until button is again pressed. Fuel economy on trips can be determined by pressing the TRIP button on panel. Average fuel efficiency will be displayed on the panel for 5 seconds. To reset TRIP MPG display, press reset button while average fuel economy is being displayed. Display will reset to present fuel economy for 1 minute, then display will flash average fuel efficiency since last reset at 16-second intervals. If present fuel efficiency is not zero, display will not reset to zero.

Transmission gear position will be displayed when driver's seat is occupied or when either door is open. This display is triggered by a steering column switch and the backup lamp switch. A box surrounds the appropriate gear indicator and changes position whenever gear position changes.

Trouble Shooting

The electronic instrument cluster has a self-diagnostic function activated by a switch under the electronic module. This test func-

The electronic chronometer is a digital quartz reference mechanism designed to be accurate to within 120 seconds over a 30-day period. The chronometer is capable of displaying time, date, month, and elapsed time. The elapsed timer will record up to 100 hours of ignition "On" time. The timer stops when ignition is turned off and restarts when ignition is on, unless instructed to reset by operator command. Elapsed time is reset by pushing ET button, then pushing reset button within 5 seconds.

Vehicle and trip distance or kilometers and average speed are available at the touch of a button from the odometer display. Accumulated mileage is displayed whenever the ignition is in the ON position. All information is derived from a distance sensor and an inter-

nal time base. Accumulated mileage stored in the memory is retained, even if the battery is disconnected. The trip monitor records up to 2500 miles of continuous driving, and is activated by pushing TRIP button. To clear and reset trip monitor, RESET button must be pushed within 5 seconds of pushing TRIP button. Average speed is displayed for 5 seconds when AVG. SPD button is pushed. Clearing for reset is accomplished by pushing RESET button while average speed is being displayed.

Vehicle speed is displayed in large numbers by the electronic digital speedometer. Speed display is updated every 1/2 second based on information supplied by the speed sensor, which is located in line with the speedometer cable. The sensor detects each 8 inches of

1. Start Engine
2. Press [2] [CK OUT]

The following sequence will appear on the message center. Follow the first two instructions of turning on headlamps and depressing brake.

| TURN ON HEADLAMPS |
| DEPRESS BRAKE |

| ✓ OK DOOR AJAR |
| ✓ OK TRUNK AJAR |
| ✓ OK CHARGE SYSTEM |
| ✓ OK OIL PRESSURE |
| ✓ OK ENGINE TEMP |
| ✓ OK MILES TO EMPTY |
| ✓ OK WASHER FLUID |
| ✓ OK BRAKE PRESSURE |
✓ OK HEADLAMPS	IF ACTUATED
✓ OK TAILLAMPS	IF ACTUATED
✓ OK BRAKELAMPS	IF ACTUATED

| TURN OFF HEADLAMPS |
| GOES BACK TO PREVIOUS DISPLAY |

These flashing messages will be substituted in the sequence if it requires the drivers attention:

— DOOR AJAR —
— TRUNK AJAR—
— CHARGE SYSTEM —
— OIL PRESSURE —
— ENGINE TEMP —
— MILES TO EMPTY —
—WASHER FLUID —
— BRAKE PRESSURE —
— HEADLAMP OUT —
— TAILLAMP OUT —
— BRAKELAMP OUT —

Fig. 25   Electronic message center system check sequence. 1980–81 Lincoln Continental, Town Car & Mark VI & 1982 Lincoln Town Car & Mark VI

1	CLOCK	Select clock or portion to be set.
2	ALARM	Select alarm or position to be set.
3	E/TIME	Elapsed Time
4	ETA	Estimated Time of Arrival
5	DEST	Distance to Destination
6	DIST	Elapsed Distance
7	AV SPD	Average Speed Since Reset
8	F/ECON	Average Fuel Economy Since Reset/ Instantaneous Fuel Economy
9	DTE	Distance to Empty
0	SET	Day/Date/Alarm Set
	MILES/KM	English/Metric
	Reset	Reset All Functions

Fig. 26   Electronic message center keyboard function chart. 1982 Lincoln Continental

are detected, odometer will read out a failure: FAIL 2 or FAIL 3 and stop test. If no faults are detected, odometer will read out PASS 1, PASS 2, or PASS 3.
4. If there are no detected faults, all display segments will be activated. Cluster will remain in this mode until ignition is turned to the ON position.

FORD ELECTRONIC MESSAGE CENTER

1980—81 Lincoln Continental, Town Car & Mark VI; 1982 Lincoln Town Car & Mark VI

The Electronic Message Center includes a message center display module, a message center control module, special wiring harnesses, and a group of vehicle sensors. The message center is available only on vehicles equipped with the electronic instrument cluster. The electronic clock is the basic display of the message center. It will be displayed every time the system is energized by turning ignition to ON or ACC position. Only a warning message or a keyboard command will override the clock display.

The keyboard, consists of 12 buttons between the heater control and radio, and provides direct access to the message center, allowing the operator to call up a variety of information, Fig. 24. Each time a button is pressed, an audible tone will confirm that the command has been received by the message center control module. Any function called up by pressing a button on the keyboard will remain displayed until the ignition is turned to OFF or another function is called up by the operator. Numbers on the center 10 keys are used as reference for easy location of functions and for entering trip-log data into message center.

A group of sensors continuously monitor important vehicle components and their proper operation. When a failure occurs, the current supplied to the sensor by the control module is routed to ground, completing the circuit. The current flow activates the appropriate electronics within the control module which stores the failure and or transmits failure information to the display module.

The Vehicle System Check-Out system allows the operator to call up present operating conditions of the 11 systems monitored through the vehicle sensors. If a system failure has occurred, the message center control module will indicate the failure when operated in the Check-Out mode, Fig. 25. If no signal has been received by the control module, the system is assumed to be operating properly.

tions when the battery is connected and the door, time delay (ignition key lamp), or seat occupant switch are activated, and the ignition switch and headlamps are off. At conclusion of test, turning ignition to on position will reset cluster for normal operation.

To diagnose and correct reported faults in system, perform complete road test, operate self diagnostic functions and refer to chart, Fig. 23. Make sure all functions operate.

Pre-Road Test Sequence
1. Start engine and record display for fuel remaining, present fuel efficiency (should be zero), speed, accumulated distance, and fuel range.
2. Reset and check average speed, trip efficiency, and trip distance. All should return to zero.

Road Test Sequence
During road test, check for abnormally high or low readings, erratic data, or blanked out displays.
1. Accelerate smoothly to 25 M.P.H. while observing display for erratic operation.
2. Maintain constant, verified speed for 30 seconds, and observe that speedometer

reads correctly. Record average speed.
3. Raise vehicle speed, and observe that display registers change. Record average speed and compare to average taken in step 2. Second reading should be same or higher than reading obtained in step 2.
4. Record present MPG while driving at constant speed for 30 seconds. Check if reading is "reasonable." Accelerate vehicle rapidly, present MPG should drop within 4–8 seconds.
5. At end of road test, before stopping engine, operate all display functions and record readings. Take note of any abnormally high or low readings.

Self Diagnostic Test
1. Remove lower left instrument column bezel and activate test by pressing red button on cluster to right of steering column.
2. A common segment in each digit of the cluster will be activated (flash) simultaneously for two seconds, until all display segments have been tested. Note any inoperative or out of sequence segments.
3. The cluster immediately conducts internal microprocessor checks. If any faults

Button Pressed	Display	Description
1 CLOCK	00:00 TIME 1	Upper row counts from 00.00 to 99:99
2 ALARM	X FLOW 2	X is a number for 0 to 25.5 designating flow from the flow sensor
3 E/TIME	X FUEL 3	X is a number from 0 to 25.5 relating to fuel level in tank
4 ETA	X DIST 4	X is a number from 0 to 25.5 relating to the odometer
5 DEST	X DIM 5	X is a number from 0 to 25.5 varied by the IP dimmer switch
6 DIST	66:66 NNNNNN	Display Test
7 AV	777.7 ZZZZZZ	Display Test
8 F/ECON	8888 + + + + + +	Display Test
9 DTE	777.7 ZZZZZZ	Display Test
0 SET	CTM 2	Level of M.C. & Tone Test
MILES km	66:66 NNNNNN	Display Test
RESET	Clock Display	Exits the Diagnostic Mode. Press to avoid resetting any functions. MILES KM

Fig. 27 Electronic message center self-check sequence. 1982 Lincoln Continental

If a system fails during vehicle operation, the control module sends out a signal to the message center display module along with an electrical pulse to a tone generator. The message center display flashes the appropriate warning message, overriding the clock display, and the tone generator produces a 1-second tone to attract the operator's attention.

Special resistance sections are included in the vehicle warning harness to allow lamp monitor functions. A lamp outage is sensed by measuring voltage drop across these resistance wires. A transistor-diode bridge amplifier monitors these low voltage signals, and provides the display module with the necessary logic level signals. The system monitors brake lamps, tail lamps and low-beam headlamps. A signal is produced when one or more of the lamps is inoperative, or if incorrect bulbs are installed.

1982 Lincoln Continental

The 1982 Lincoln Continental Message Center (MC) is different from the Message Center found on other models. The MC is self-contained with the control module, keyboard, and vacuum-fluorescent display all in one unit and does not display flashing warning messages. Malfunction of buttons, display segments, or logic functions will require replacement of the complete unit.

The clock is the basic display of the Message Center, which is located on the right side of the instrument cluster. When ignition is switched to RUN or ACC position, the unit is switched on and time is displayed. Battery voltage is supplied to the MC at all times in order to provide power for memory circuits. If battery voltage to the unit is interrupted, all stored memory will be lost and the clock will require resetting. This condition will be indicated by a clock display of Monday, January 1, 1:00 A.M., once power has been restored.

The MC keyboard consists of 12 buttons and gives the operator direct access to the Message Center microcomputer. Through the keyboard, a variety of information can be called up, Fig. 26, and the functions and/or displays can be reset. Buttons are illuminated for night time operation whenever headlamp switch is in ON position.

Each time a button is pressed, an audible tone will be generated to signal that the command has been properly received by the Message Center. Any function called up will continue to be displayed until ignition is switched to OFF or another function is called-up. The buttons are numbered from left to right, Fig. 26, and labeled with an abbreviation of their function. Although numbers help in locating specific keys, the numbers are primarily used for entering trip data into the Message Center.

Display illumination is controlled by the microcomputer and the headlamp switch dimming circuit. With headlamp switch in OFF position, display is at maximum intensity for daytime driving. When headlamps or parking lamps are switched on, display automatically dims for night time driving. Display intensity can then be varied by rotating knob on headlamp switch.

In addition to display functions, the MC includes four indicator lamps to warn of low washer fluid or brake, tail or headlamp failure. This system operates when the ignition is in the RUN or ACC position, and turns on appropriately marked warning lamp if one or more lights is inoperative or if washer fluid reservoir is low. Lamp outage is sensed by measuring voltage drop across special resistance wires within vehicle wiring harness. Voltage drop is monitored by a transistor-bridge diode amplifier which in turn energizes indicator lamps.

The Message Center can be programmed into a diagnostic mode of operation by simultaneously pressing 1/CLOCK button and MILES/KM button. The TIME 1 test, Fig. 27, will be displayed first, then other tests can be performed by pressing the appropriate button. Test sequence is not important and can be chosen in any order as many times as desired. To clear diagnostic mode, press RESET and MILES/KM buttons simultaneously to avoid resetting any functions.

STARTING MOTORS & SWITCHES

CONTENTS

Fig. 1 Wiring diagram of a typical starting circuit

STARTER TROUBLE CHECK-OUT

When trouble develops in the starting motor circuit, and the starter cranks the engine slowly or not at all, several preliminary checks can be made to determine whether the trouble lies in the battery, in the starter, in the wiring between them, or elsewhere. Many conditions besides defects in the starter itself can result in poor cranking performance.

To make a quick check of the starter system, turn on the headlights. They should burn with normal brilliance. If they do not, the battery may be run down and it should be checked with a hydrometer.

If the battery is in a charged condition so that lights burn brightly, operate the starting motor. Any one of three things will happen to the lights: (1) They will go out, (2) dim considerably or (3) stay bright without any cranking action taking place.

If Lights Go Out

If the lights go out as the starter switch is closed, it indicates that there is a poor connection between the battery and starting motor. This poor connection will most often be found at the battery terminals. Correction is made by removing the cable clamps from the terminals, cleaning the terminals and clamps, replacing the clamps and tightening them securely. A coating of corrosion inhibitor (vaseline will do) may be applied to the clamps and terminals to retard the formation of corrosion.

If Lights Dim

If the lights dim considerably as the starter switch is closed and the starter operates slowly or not at all, the battery may be run down, or there may be some mechanical condi-

tion in the engine or starting motor that is throwing a heavy burden on the starting motor. This imposes a high discharge rate on the battery which causes noticeable dimming of the lights.

Check the battery with a hydrometer. If it is charged, the trouble probably lies in either the engine or starting motor itself. In the engine, tight bearings or pistons or heavy oil place an added burden on the starting motor. Low temperatures also hamper starting motor performance since it thickens engine oil and makes the engine considerably harder to crank and start. Also, a battery is less efficient at low temperatures.

In the starting motor, a bent armature, loose pole shoe screws or worn bearings, any of which may allow the armature to drag, will reduce cranking performance and increase current draw.

In addition, more serious internal damage is sometimes found. Thrown armature windings or commutator bars, which sometimes occur on over-running clutch drive starting motors, are usually caused by excessive over-running after starting. This is the result of such conditions as the driver keeping the starting switch closed too long after the en-

gine has started, the driver opening the throttle too wide in starting, or improper carburetor fast idle adjustment. Any of these subject the over-running clutch to extra strain so it tends to seize, spinning the armature at high speed with resulting armature damage.

Another cause may be engine backfire during cranking which may result, among other things, from ignition timing being too far advanced.

To avoid such failures, the driver should pause a few seconds after a false start to make sure the engine has come completely to rest before another start is attempted. In addition, the ignition timing should be reset if engine backfiring has caused the trouble.

Lights Stay Bright, No Cranking Action

This condition indicates an open circuit at some point, either in the starter itself, the starter switch or control circuit. The solenoid control circuit can be eliminated momentarily by placing a heavy jumper lead across the

Fig. 2 Checking voltage drop between vehicle frame and grounded battery terminal post

Fig. 3 Checking voltage drop between vehicle frame and starter field frame

Fig. 4 Checking voltage drop between ungrounded battery terminal post and battery terminal on solenoid

COIL & BASE ASSEMBLY MOTOR TERMINAL
RETURN SPRING CONTACT FINGER COVER

SOLENOID CONTROL TERMINAL CONTACT DISC ASSEMBLY BATTERY TERMINAL INSULATOR GASKET

Fig. 5 Solenoid switch, exploded view (Typical)

solenoid main terminals to see if the starter will operate. This connects the starter directly to the battery and, if it operates, it indicates that the control circuit is not functioning normally. The wiring and control units must be checked to locate the trouble, Fig. 1.

If the starter does not operate with the jumper attached, it will probably have to be removed from the engine so it can be examined in detail.

Checking Circuit With Voltmeter

Excessive resistance in the circuit between the battery and starter will reduce cranking performance. The resistance can be checked by using a voltmeter to measure voltage drop in the circuits while the starter is operated. There are three checks to be made:
1. Voltage drop between car frame and grounded battery terminal post (not cable clamp), Fig. 2.
2. Voltage drop between car frame and starting motor field frame, Fig. 3.
3. Voltage drop between insulated battery terminal post and starting motor terminal stud (or the battery terminal stud of the solenoid), Fig. 4.

Each of these should show no more than one-tenth (0.1) volt drop when the starting motor is cranking the engine. Do not use the starter for more than 30 seconds at a time to avoid overheating it.

If excessive voltage drop is found in any of these circuits, make correction by disconnecting the cables, cleaning the connections carefully, and then reconnecting the cables firmly in place. A coating of vaseline on the battery cables and terminal clamps will retard corrosion.

NOTE: On some cars, extra long battery cables may be required due to the location of the battery and starter. This may result in somewhat higher voltage drop than the above recommended 0.1 volt. The only means of

determining the normal voltage drop in such cases is to check several of these vehicles. Then when the voltage drop is well above the normal figure for all cars checked, abnormal resistance will be indicated and correction can be made as already explained.

SOLENOID SWITCHES

The solenoid switch on a cranking motor

not only closes the circuit between the battery and the cranking motor but also shifts the drive pinion into mesh with the engine flywheel ring gear. This is done by means of a linkage between the solenoid switch plunger and the shift lever on the cranking motor.

Fig. 5 shows a solenoid switch used on vehicles with 12-volt systems. Like other solenoid switches, this type is energized by the battery through a separate starting switch. Note, however, that the switch includes an additional small terminal and contact finger. This

CONTROL SWITCH
SOLENOID NEUTRAL SAFETY SWITCH
PLUNGER
CONTACTS
SHIFT LEVER
RETURN SPRING
PINION CLEARANCE
OVERRUNNING CLUTCH CRANKING MOTOR TO BATTERY

Fig. 6 Solenoid switch wiring circuit (Typical)

Fig. 7 A simple tester for use in making continuity and ground tests on armature and field windings

Fig. 8 Checking armature for grounds. If lamp lights armature is grounded and should be replaced

Fig. 9 Measuring commutator runout with dial indicator. Mount shaft in V blocks and rotate commutator. If runout exceeds .003", commutator should be turned in a lathe to make it concentric

Fig. 10 Turning commutator in a lathe. Take light cuts until worn or bad spots are removed. Then remove burrs with No. 00 sandpaper

Fig. 11 Good undercutting should be .002" wider than mica insulation, 1/64" deep and exactly centered so that there are no burrs on the mica. Do not undercut molded commutators

Fig. 12 Checking armature for short circuit. As armature is rotated by hand, steel strip (hacksaw blade) will vibrate if short circuit exists

Fig. 13 Testing field coils for grounds. If a ground is present, lamp will light

noid; a pull-in winding (shown as dashes) and a hold-in winding (shown dotted). Both windings are energized when the external control switch is closed. They produce a magnetic field which pulls the plunger in so that the drive pinion is shifted into mesh, and the main contacts in the solenoid switch are closed to connect the battery directly to the cranking motor. Closing the main switch contacts shorts out the pull-in winding since this winding is connected across the main contacts. The magnetism produced by the hold-in winding is sufficient to hold the plunger in, and shorting out the pull-in winding reduces drain on the battery. When the control switch is opened, it disconnects the hold-in winding from the battery. When the hold-in winding is disconnected from the battery, the shift lever spring withdraws the plunger from the solenoid, opening the solenoid switch contacts and at the same time withdrawing the drive pinion from mesh. Proper operation of the switch depends on maintaining a definite balance between the magnetic strength of the pull-in and hold-in windings.

This balance is established in the design by the size of the wire and the number of turns specified. *An open circuit in the hold-in winding or attempts to crank with a discharged battery will cause the switch to chatter.*

To disassemble the solenoid, remove nuts, washers and insulators from the switch terminal and battery terminal. Remove cover and take out the contact disk assembly.

STARTING MOTOR SERVICE

To obtain full performance data on a starting motor or to determine the cause of abnormal operation, the starting motor should be submitted to a no-load and torque test. These tests are best performed on a starter bench tester with the starter mounted on it.

From a practical standpoint, however, a simple torque test may be made quickly with the starter in the car. Make sure the battery is fully charged and that the starter circuit wires and terminals are in good condition. Then operate the starter to see if the engine turns over normally. If it does not, the torque developed is below standard and the starter should be removed for further checking.

Remove the starter from the engine as outlined in the vehicle chapters, disassemble it as outlined further on and make the tests as suggested in Figs. 8 through 13.

CHRYSLER REDUCTION GEAR STARTER

This reduction gear starting motor, Fig. 14,

terminal has no functional duty in relation to the switch, but is used to complete a special ignition circuit during the cranking cycle only. When the solenoid is in the cranking position, the finger touches the contact disk and provides a direct circuit between the battery and ignition coil.

When reassembling the switch the contact finger should be adjusted to touch the contact disk before the disk makes contact with the main switch terminals. There should be 1/16" to 3/32" clearance between the contact disk and the main terminals when the finger touches.

Fig. 6 is a wiring circuit of a typical solenoid switch. There are two windings in the sole-

has an armature-to-engine crankshaft ratio of 2 to 1 or a 3 1/2 to 1 reduction gear set is built into the motor assembly. The starter utilizes a solenoid shift. The housing of the solenoid is integral with the starter drive end housing.

Disassembly

1. Place gear housing of starter in a vise with soft jaws. *Use vise as a support*

PIN — GEAR HOUSING — CORE — RING — SOLENOID — SOLENOID TERMINAL — SEAL — FORK

SPRING — SOLENOID LEAD — CONTACT AND PLUNGER — RING — SPRING — CLUTCH — RING — SHAFT

BEARING — WASHER — DUST COVER — ACTUATOR — RING — GEAR — WASHER

WASHER — NUT — WASHER — NUT — SCREW AND WASHER

BRUSH HOLDER PLATE — SPRING

SCREW — BRUSH

BATTERY TERMINAL — INSULATOR — SPRING — FIELD FRAME ASSEMBLY — WASHER — ARMATURE — WASHER — ENDHEAD — THROUGH BOLTS

Fig. 14   Chrysler built reduction gear starting motor

fixture only; do not clamp.

2. Remove through bolts and starter end head assembly.
3. Carefully remove armature from gear housing and field frame assembly.
4. Pull field frame assembly from gear housing to expose terminal screw.
5. Support terminal screw with a finger, then remove terminal screw, Fig. 15.
6. Remove field frame assembly.
7. Remove nuts attaching solenoid and brush holder plate assembly to gear housing, then remove the solenoid and brush plate assembly.
8. Remove nut, steel washer and insulating washer from solenoid terminal.
9. Unwind solenoid lead wire from brush terminal, Fig. 16, and remove screws securing solenoid to brush plate, then remove the solenoid from brush plate.

10. Remove nut from battery terminal on brush plate, then the battery terminal.
11. Remove solenoid contact and plunger assembly from solenoid, Fig. 17, then the return spring from the solenoid moving core.
12. Remove dust cover from gear housing, Fig. 18.
13. Release retainer clip positioning driven gear on pinion shaft, Fig. 19.

NOTE: The retainer clip is under tension. Therefore, it is recommended that a cloth be placed over the retainer clip when released, preventing it from springing away.

14. Remove pinion shaft "C" clip, Fig. 20.

15. Push pinion shaft toward rear of housing, Fig. 21, and remove retainer ring and thrust washers, clutch and pinion assembly, with the two shift fork nylon actuators as an assembly, Fig. 22.
16. Remove driven gear and thrust washer.
17. Pull shifting fork forward and remove solenoid moving core, Fig. 23.
18. Remove shifting fork retainer pin, Fig. 24, and remove clutch shifting fork assembly.

Reassembly

NOTE: *The shifter fork consists of two spring steel plates assembled with two rivets, Fig. 25. There should be about 1/16" side movement to insure proper pinion gear engagement. Lubri-*

Fig. 15   Terminal screw replacement

Fig. 16   Unwinding solenoid lead wire

Fig. 17   Solenoid contact & plunger

Fig. 18 Dust cover removal, all (Typical)

Fig. 19 Driven gear snap ring replacement, all (Typical)

Fig. 20 Pinion shaft "C" clip replacement

Fig. 21 Removing pinion shaft

Fig. 22 Clutch assembly replacement (Typical)

Fig. 23 Solenoid core replacement (Typical)

Fig. 24 Shifter fork pin replacement, all (Typical)

Fig. 25 Shifter fork assembly (Typical)

Fig. 26 Shifter fork & clutch assembly (Typical)

cate between plates sparingly with SAE 10 engine oil.

1. Position shift fork in drive housing and install fork retaining pin, Fig. 24. One tip of pin should be straight, *the other tip should be bent at a 15 degree angle away from housing. Fork and pin should operate freely after bending tip of pin.*
2. Install solenoid moving core and engage shifting fork, Fig. 23.
3. Enter pinion shaft in drive housing and install friction washer and driven gear.
4. Install clutch and pinion assembly, Fig. 22, thrust washer, retaining ring, and thrust washer.
5. Complete installation of pinion shaft, engaging fork with clutch actuators, Fig. 26. *Friction washer must be positioned on shoulder of splines of pinion shaft before driven gear is positioned.*
6. Install driven gear snap ring, Fig. 19, then the pinion shaft retaining ring or "C" clip, Fig. 20.
7. Install starter solenoid return spring into movable core bore.

NOTE: Inspect starter solenoid switch contacting washer. If top of washer is burned, disassemble contact switch plunger assembly and reverse the washer.

8. Install solenoid contact plunger assembly

into solenoid, Fig. 17. Ensure contact spring is properly positioned on shaft of solenoid contact plunger assembly.
9. Install battery terminal stud in brush holder.

NOTE: Inspect contacts in brush holder. If contacts are badly burned, replace brush holder with brushes and contacts as an assembly.

10. Position seal on brush holder plate.
11. Install solenoid lead wire through hole in brush holder, Fig. 27, then the solenoid stud, insulating washer, flat washer and nut.
12. Wrap solenoid lead wire around brush terminal post, Fig. 16, and solder with a high temperature resin core solder and resin flux.
13. Install brush holder attaching screws.
14. Install solenoid coil and brush plate assembly into gear housing bore and posi-

Fig. 27   Solenoid to brush holder plate assembly (Typical)

Fig. 28   Solenoid & brush holder installation (Typical)

Fig. 29   Installing brushes & armature thrust washer (Typical)

Fig. 30   Armature installation (Typical)

tion brush plate assembly into starter gear housing, Fig. 28. Then, install and tighten housing attaching nuts.

15. Install brushes with armature thrust washer, Fig. 29. This holds brushes out and facilitates proper armature installation.
16. Install brush terminal screw, Fig. 15.
17. Position field frame on gear housing and install armature into field frame and starter gear housing, Fig. 30, carefully engaging splines of shaft with reduction gear by rotating armature slightly to engage splines.
18. Install thrust washer on armature shaft.
19. Install starter end head assembly, then the through bolts.

DELCO-REMY STARTERS
Except 1978–82 Olds Built Diesel

This type staring motor, Fig. 31, has the solenoid shift lever mechanism and the solenoid plunger enclosed in the drive housing, thus protecting them from exposure to road dirt, icing conditions and splash. They have an extruded field frame and an overrunning clutch type of drive. The overrunning clutch is operated by a solenoid switch mounted to a flange on the drive housing.

Solenoid

The solenoid is attached to the drive end housing by two screws. The angle of the nose of the plunger provides a greater bearing area between the plunger and core tube. A molded push rod, Fig. 32, is assembled in the contact assembly. A shoulder molded on the push rod and a cup that can easily be assembled to the rod and locked into position over two molded bosses holds the contact assembly in place.

To disassemble the cup from the push rod, push in on the metal cup and rotate 1/4 turn so the molded bosses on the rod are in line with openings in the cup; then slide the metal cup off the rod.

To assemble the metal cup on the rod, locate the parts on the rod as shown and align the large openings in the cup with the molded bosses on the rod; then push in on the cup and rotate it 1/4 turn so the small bosses on the rod fall into the keyways of the cup.

Maintenance

Most motors of this type have graphite and oil impregnated bronze bearings which ordinarily require no added lubrication except at times of overhaul when a few drops of light engine oil should be placed on each bearing before reassembly.

Since the motor and brushes cannot be inspected without disassembling the unit, there is no service that can be performed with the unit assembled on the vehicle.

Free Speed Test

With the circuit connected as shown in Fig. 33, use a tachometer to measure armature revolutions per minute. Failure of the motor to perform to specifications may be due to tight or dry bearings, or high resistance connections.

Pinion Clearance

There is no provision for adjusting pinion clearance on this type motor. When the shift lever mechanism is correctly assembled, the pinion clearance should fall within the limits of .010 to .140″. When the clearance is not within these limits, it may indicate excessive wear of the solenoid linkage or shift lever yoke buttons.

Pinion clearance should be checked after the motor has been disassembled and reassembled. To check, disconnect motor field coil connector from solenoid terminal and insulate end. Connect one battery lead to solenoid switch terminal and the other lead to the solenoid frame, Fig. 34. Using a jumper lead connected to the solenoid motor terminal, momentarily flash the lead to the solenoid frame. This will shift the pinion into the cranking position until the battery is disconnected.

After energizing the solenoid with the clutch shifted toward the pinion stop retainer, push the pinion back toward the commutator end as far as possible to take up any slack movement; then check the clearance with feeler gauge, Fig. 35.

Disassembling Motor

NOTE: The 5 MT series starting motor will be used on some 1978–82 models, Fig. 36. On this type starting motor, the field coils and pole shoes are permanently bonded to the motor frame. The frame and field coils must be replaced as an assembly.

Normally the motor should be disassembled only so far as necessary to repair or replace defective parts.

1. Disconnect field coil connectors from sole-

Contact Finger — **Plunger** — **Solenoid** — **Return Spring**

Bushing — **Shift Lever**

Grommet — **Spiral Splines**

Bushing

Brush

Brush Spring — **Insulated Brush Holder**

Grounded Brush Holder — **Armature** — **Field Coil** — **Assist Spring** — **Overrunning Clutch** — **Pinion Stop**

Fig. 31   Delco-Remy starter with enclosed shift lever

noid "motor" terminal.

2. Remove thru bolts.
3. Remove commutator end frame and field frame assembly.
4. Remove armature assembly from drive housing. On some models it may be necessary to remove solenoid and shift lever assembly from the drive housing before removing the armature assembly. *Important: When solenoid is installed, apply sealing compound between field frame and solenoid flange, Fig. 37.*
5. Remove overrunning clutch from armature shaft as follows:
   a) Slide thrust collar off end of armature shaft, Fig. 38.
   b) Slide a standard 1/2" pipe coupling, a 5/8" deep socket or other metal cylinder of suitable size onto shaft so end of coupling or cylinder butts against edge of retainer. Tap end of coupling with

hammer, driving retainer toward armature and off snap ring, Fig. 39.
   c) Remove snap ring from groove in shaft. If snap ring is too badly distorted during removal, use a new one when reassembling the clutch.
   d) Slide retainer, clutch and assist spring from armature shaft.

Reassembling Motor, Figs. 36 & 40

1. Lubricate drive end and splines of armature shaft with lubricant 1960954 or equivalent.
2. Place "assist" spring on drive end of shaft next to armature, with small end against lamination stack.
3. Slide clutch assembly onto armature shaft with pinion outward.
4. Slide retainer onto shaft with cupped surface facing end of shaft.
5. Stand armature on end on wood surface with commutator down. Position snap ring on upper end of shaft and hold in place with a block of wood. Hit wood block with a hammer forcing snap ring over end of shaft, Fig. 41. Slide snap ring into groove, squeezing it to ensure a good fit in groove.
6. Assemble thrust collar on shaft with shoulder next to snap ring.
7. Position retainer and thrust collar next to snap ring. With clutch pressed against assist spring, for clearance next to retainer, use two pairs of pliers at the same time (one pair on either side of shaft) to grip retainer and thrust collar. Then squeeze until snap ring is forced into retainer, Fig. 42.

8. Lubricate drive end housing bushing with lubricant 1960954 or equivalent. Make sure thrust collar is in place against snap ring and retainer; then slide armature and clutch assembly into place in drive housing.
9. Attach solenoid and shift lever assembly to drive housing. Be sure lever buttons are located between sides of clutch collar.
10. Position field frame over armature, *applying sealing compound between frame and solenoid flange* (Fig. 37). Position frame against drive housing, using care to prevent damage to brushes.
11. Lubricate commutator end frame bushing with lubricant 1960954 or equivalent. Make sure leather brake washer is on

Fig. 32   Solenoid contact assembly

Fig. 33   Connections for checking free speed of motor

Fig. 34 Connections for checking pinion clearance

1. FRAME—COMMUTATOR END	10. PLUNGER	19. THRU BOLT
2. BRUSH AND HOLDER PKG.	11. SHIFT LEVER	20. BUSHING—COMMUTATOR END
3. BRUSH	12. PLUNGER RETURN SPRINGER	21. BUSHING—DRIVE END
4. BRUSH HOLDER	13. SHIFT LEVER SHAFT	22. PINION STOP COLLAR
5. HOUSING—DRIVE END	14. LOCK WASHER	23. THRUST COLLAR
6. FRAME AND FIELD ASM.	15. SCREW—BRUSH ATTACHING	24. GROMMET
7. SOLENOID SWITCH	16. SCREW—FIELD LEAD TO SWITCH	25. GROMMET
8. ARMATURE	17. SCREW—SWITCH ATTACHING	26. PLUNGER PIN
9. DRIVE ASM.	18. WASHER—BRAKE	27. PINION STOP RETAINER RING
		28. LEVER SHAFT RETAINING RING

Fig. 36 Disassembled view of Delco-Remy 5MT series starting motor

Fig. 35 Checking pinion clearance

Fig. 38 View of armature and over-running clutch

Fig. 37 Sealing solenoid housing to frame

armature shaft; then slide commutator end frame onto shaft.
12. Install thru bolts and tighten securely.
13. Reconnect field coil connectors to solenoid "motor" terminal.

Olds Built Diesel

1978–81 ALL & 1982 ELDORADO, RIVIERA, SEVILLE & TORONADO

Disassemble
1. Remove screw from field coil connector and solenoid mounting screws, then rotate solenoid 90° and remove solenoid with plunger return spring, Fig. 43.
2. Remove two through bolts, then commutator end frame with washer.
3. Remove end frame assembly from drive gear housing.
4. Remove shift lever pivot bolt.
5. Remove center bearing screws, then remove drive gear housing from armature shaft. Shift lever and plunger assembly, should fall from starter clutch.
6. Remove thrust washer or collar from armature shaft.
7. Position a 5/8 in. deep socket over shaft against retainer, then tap socket to move retainer off snap ring.
8. Remove snap ring from groove in shaft, then remove retainer, clutch assembly, fiber washer and center bearing from armature shaft.
9. Remove roll pin and separate shift lever and plunger.
10. Remove brush pivot pin and brush spring, then replace brushes as necessary.

Assemble
1. Lubricate drive end of armature with

Fig. 39 Removing over-running clutch snap ring retainer

Fig. 40 Disassembled view of Delco-Remy 10MT series starting motor

lubricant 1960954 or equivalent.

2. Install center bearing with bearing facing toward armature winding, then install fiber washer on armature shaft, Fig. 43.
3. Position clutch assembly on armature shaft with pinion facing away from armature.
4. Position retainer on armature shaft with cupped side facing end of shaft.
5. Install snap ring into groove on armature shaft, then install thrust washer.
6. Using two pliers, grip retainer and thrust washer or collar and squeeze until snap ring is forced into retainer and is held securely in groove on armature shaft.
7. Lubricate drive end housing bushing with lubricant 1960954 or equivalent.
8. Engage shift lever yoke with clutch and slide complete assembly into drive gear housing.

9. Install center bearing attaching screws and shift lever pivot bolt.
10. Install solenoid on drive gear housing.
11. Apply sealer No. 1050026 or equivalent to solenoid flange where field frame contacts solenoid.
12. Position field frame against drive gear housing on alignment pin, using care to prevent damage to brushes.
13. Lubricate commutator end frame bushing with lubricant 1960954 or equivalent.
14. Install washer on armature shaft and slide end frame onto shaft, then install and tighten through bolts.
15. Connect field coil connector to solenoid terminal, then check pinion clearance.

1982 EXCEPT ELDORADO, RIVIERA, SEVILLE & TORONADO

Disassemble

1. Remove screw from field coil connector and field frame thru bolts, Fig. 44.
2. Separate field frame and drive gear assemblies, then remove armature and commutator end frame from field frame.
3. Remove solenoid attaching screws and solenoid from drive housing.
4. Remove retaining nut, shift lever shaft and housing thru bolts, then separate drive assembly, drive housing and gear housing.
5. Remove overrunning clutch from drive shaft as follows:
   a. Remove thrust washer from drive shaft.
   b. Slide a 5/8 inch deep socket or a piece of pipe of suitable size over shaft and butt it against retainer. Lightly tap tool to move retainer off snap ring.
   c. Remove snap ring from groove in shaft. If snap ring is too badly distorted, a new one must be used when reassembling the clutch.
   d. Remove retainer and clutch assembly from drive shaft.

Assemble

NOTE: The roller bearings are pre-lubricated and must not be lubricated during assembly of starter motor.

1. Slide clutch assembly onto drive shaft

and position retainer with cupped side toward end of shaft, snap ring and washer.

2. Using two pairs of pliers, force snap ring into retainer and groove, in shaft, Fig. 42.
3. Install plunger and shift lever into drive housing with lever shaft and retaining ring.
4. Place washer over drive shaft on side of gear opposite drive assembly, then lubricate gear teeth with lubricant 1960954, or equivalent.
5. Assemble gear housing with attaching screws and attach solenoid to drive housing.
6. Lubricate bushing in commutator end frame with lubricant 1960954, or equivalent, then slide washer on commutator end of armature shaft.
7. Assemble armature, field frame and commutator end frame to gear housing with thru bolts.
8. Attach field coil connector to solenoid terminal.

V6 DIESEL ALUMINUM STARTER 1982 CELEBRITY, CENTURY, CUTLASS CIERA & 6000

Disassemble

1. Remove nut from field coil connector, solenoid switch mounting screws and solenoid switch, Fig. 45.

Fig. 41 Installing snap ring onto armature shaft

Fig. 42 Installing snap ring into retainer

Fig. 43 Disassembled view of Delco-Remy 25 MT & 27 MT series starting motor. 1978 Olds built diesel, except 1982 Riviera, Seville & Toronado

NOTE: Some starters may have shims between solenoid switch and drive end housing, used to set drive pinion position.

2. Remove thru bolts and brush holder retaining screws.
3. Remove commutator end frame from armature and bearing assembly.
4. Remove field frame assembly and armature from center housing.
5. Bend back each brush spring so that each brush can be backed away from armature approximately 1/4 inch, then release spring to hold brushes in backed out position, Fig. 46.
6. Remove armature from field frame and brush holder.
7. Remove pinion shaft cover on center housing by removing two screws, C-washer and plate, Fig. 47.
8. Remove center housing retaining bolts, center housing and shim thrust washer(s).
9. Remove reduction gear, spring holder and lever springs.
10. Slide a 5/8 inch socket, or piece of pipe of suitable size, over shaft against stopper, then tap tool to move stopper off ring, Fig. 48.
11. Remove ring, stopper and drive pinion. If ring is distorted, a new one must be used on reassembly.
12. Remove pinion shaft and lever assembly, noting direction of levers and lever holders.

Assemble

1. Lubricate bearing surfaces and splines of pinion shaft assembly, nylon lever holders, and both ends of lever with lubricant 2960954, or equivalent.
2. Install lever assembly on overrunning clutch, Fig. 49.

NOTE: If lever is not positioned properly, pinion travel will be incorrect, causing a lock-up in the clutch mechanism.

3. Install pinion shaft and lever assembly into drive end housing.
4. Slide spring, drive pinion and stopper

Fig. 44 Disassembled view of 15MT/GR starting motor. 1982 Eldorado, Riviera, Seville & Toronado with Olds built diesel

ring over pinion shaft with cupped surface of stopper facing end of shaft.
5. Install ring into groove on pinion shaft while forcing drive pinion and stopper down against drive end housing.
6. Force stopper over ring with tool J-22888, Fig. 50.
7. Install the two lever springs and spring holder into drive end housing.
8. Lubricate reduction gear teeth with lubricant 1960954, or equivalent.
9. Install gear and shim thrust washers onto pinion shaft assembly.
10. Assemble center housing to drive end housing, then install and tighten the two attaching bolts.
11. If the drive end housing, pinion shaft, reduction gear, shim washer(s), or center housing were replaced, pinion shaft end play must be checked as follows:
   a. Install plate and C-washer onto end of pinion shaft, then mount drive end housing in a suitable holding fixture.
   b. Insert feeler gauge between C-washer and cover plate, rotate pinion shaft

with a screwdriver and measure end play, Fig. 51. Proper end play is .004–.020 inch.
   c. If end play does not fall within limits, remove plate, C-washer and center bracket, add or remove shim thrust washers as needed, and recheck clearance.
   d. Fill cap one-half full with lubricant 1960954, or equivalent, and install the cap. Install and tighten the two attaching bolts.
12. Install armature, carefully engaging splines of shaft with reduction gear by slightly rotating armature to engage splines.
13. Install field frame and brush holder assembly on center housing.

NOTE: The rubber grommet for the field coil lead must be installed in the locating ribs, Fig. 52.

14. Install brushes by prying back on springs

Fig. 46 Brush holder assembly

Fig. 45 Disassembled view of V6 diesel aluminum starter. 1982 Celebrity, Century, Cutlass Ciera & 6000

Fig. 47 Disassembled view of pinion shaft (overrunning clutch) assembly

to allow brushes to seat against commutator bars.

15. Install commutator end frame onto field frame with alignment marks lined up, Fig. 53.
16. Install and tighten brush holder screws and thru bolts.
17. Install solenoid switch and shims on drive end housing, ensuring that slot in plunger engages with top of lever, then install and tighten the two bolts.
18. Connect field coil connector to solenoid switch terminal.

Pinion Clearance Check
1. Disconnect field coil connector from solenoid terminal and insulate carefully.
2. Connect one 12 volt battery lead to solenoid switch terminal and other lead to starter motor frame.
3. Flash a jumper lead momentarily from solenoid motor terminal to starter motor frame. This will shift pinion into cranking position until battery is disconnected.
4. Push pinion back as far as possible to take up any movement, then check pinion clearance using a feeler gauge. Pinion clearance should be .010–.140 in. On V6 diesel aluminum starter, clearance should be .020–.080 inch. If clearance is not within limits, check for improper installation or worn parts and replace as necessary.

NOTE: On V6 diesel aluminum starter, clearance may be adjusted by adding or removing

Fig. 49 Installing lever assembly on overrunning clutch

Fig. 50 Installing stopper on overrunning clutch

Fig. 48 Removing pinion shaft ring

Fig. 51 Checking pinion shaft end play

Fig. 52 Installing field frame and brush holder assembly

Fig. 53 Installing commutator end frame on field frame

shims located between the switch and front bracket. Adding shims decreases amount of movement. Shims are available in thicknesses of .010 and .020 inch.

FORD MOTORCRAFT STARTER WITH INTEGRAL POSITIVE ENGAGEMENT DRIVE

This type starting motor, Figs. 54 through 57, is a four pole, series parallel unit with a positive engagement drive built into the starter. The drive mechanism is engaged with the flywheel by lever action before the motor is energized.

When the ignition switch is turned on to the start position, the starter relay is energized and supplies current to the motor. The current flows through one field coil and a set of contact points to ground. The magnetic field given off

Fig. 54 Ford Motorcraft positive engagement starting motor. 1977 except V6-2800cc engine

by the field coil pulls the moveable pole, which is part of the lever, downward to its seat. When the pole is pulled down, the lever moves the drive assembly into the engine flywheel, Fig. 58.

When the moveable pole is seated, it functions as a normal field pole and opens the contact points. With the points open, current flows through the starter field coils, energizing the starter. At the same time, current also flows through a holding coil to hold the movable pole in its seated position.

When the ignition switch is released from the start position, the starter relay opens the circuit to the starting motor. This allows the return spring to force the lever back, disengaging the drive from the flywheel and returning the movable pole to its normal position.

1977 Units

Disassemble, Figs. 54 & 55

It may not be necessary to disassemble the starter completely to accomplish repair or replacement of certain parts. Thus, before

Fig. 55 Ford Motorcraft positive engagement starting motor. 1977 V6-2800cc engine

Fig. 56 Ford Motorcraft positive engagement starting motor. 1978–79 V6-2800cc, 1978–82 4-2300cc & 1982 1600cc engines (Typical)

Fig. 57 Ford Motorcraft positive engagement starting motor. 1978–82 except 4-1600cc, 4-2300cc & V6-2800cc engines (Typical)

MOVABLE POLE SEATED BY MAGNETIC ATTRACTION OF ENERGIZED DRIVE COIL

FORKS MOVE DRIVE ASS'Y. INTO ENGAGEMENT

STOP COLLAR LIMITS TRAVEL (RETAINING CLIP)

Fig. 58   Starter drive engaged

Fig. 61   Ford Motorcraft solenoid actuated starter, exploded view

TOOL 10044

Fig. 59   Removing field coil pole shoe screws

disassembling the motor, remove the cover band and starter drive actuating lever cover. Examine brushes to make sure they are free in their holders. Replace brushes if defective or worn beyond their useful limit. Check the tension of each brush spring with a pull scale. Spring tension should not be less than 45 ounces. If disassembly is necessary, proceed as follows:

1. Remove cover band and starter drive actuating lever cover.
2. Remove through bolts, starter drive gear housing, drive gear retaining clip cup and starter drive actuating lever return spring.
3. Remove pivot pin retaining starter gear actuating lever and remove lever and armature.

DISASSEMBLY ORDER

1.	Lead wire	14.	Armature
2.	Bolt	15.	Screw
3.	Solenoid assembly	16.	Bearing retainer
4.	Torsion spring	17.	Pinion assembly
5.	Plunger	18.	Pinion stop retainer
6.	Adjusting plates	19.	Pinion-stop retainer clip
7.	Solenoid	20.	Return spring
8.	Screw	21.	Pinion shaft
9.	Through bolt	22.	Clutch
10.	Rear cover	23.	Dust cover
11.	Motor assembly	24.	Shift lever
12.	Brush holder	25.	Gear case
13.	Yoke		

Fig. 62   Hitachi S13-62A starter

STARTER DRIVE ACTUATING COIL

UPPER GROUND BRUSH

TERMINAL SCREW

FIELD COILS

HOLDING COIL TERMINAL

LOWER GROUND BRUSH

FIELD COIL BRUSHES

Fig. 60   Field coil assembly

4. Remove and discard spring clip retaining starter drive gear to end of armature shaft, and remove starter drive gear.
5. Remove commutator brushes from brush holders and remove brush end plate.
6. Remove two screws retaining ground brushes to frame.
7. On the field coil that operates the drive gear actuating lever, bend tab up on field retainer and remove retainer.
8. Remove field coil retainer screws, Fig. 59. Unsolder field coil leads from terminal screw, and remove pole shoes and coils from frame.
9. Remove starter terminal nut and related parts. Remove any excess solder from terminal slot.

Assemble, Figs. 54 & 55

1. Install starter terminal, insulator, washers and retaining nut in frame, Fig. 60. Be sure to position slot in screw perpendicular to frame end surface.
2. Install field coils and pole pieces. As pole shoe screws are tightened, strike frame several sharp blows with a soft-faced hammer to seat and align pole shoes, then stake the screws.
3. Install solenoid coil retainer and bend tabs to retain tabs to frame.
4. Solder field coils and solenoid wire to starter terminal, using rosin core solder.
5. Check for continuity and grounds in the assembled coils.
6. Position solenoid coil ground terminal over ground screw hole nearest starter terminal.
7. Position ground brushes to starter frame and install retaining screws, Fig. 60.
8. Position starter brush end plate to frame with end plate boss in frame slot.
9. Install drive gear to armature shaft and install a new retaining spring clip.
10. Position fiber thrust washer on commutator end of armature shaft and install armature in frame.
11. Install starter drive actuating lever to frame and starter drive, and install pivot pin.
12. Position actuating lever return spring and drive gear housing to frame and install through bolts. Do not pinch brush leads between brush plate and frame.
13. Install brushes in holders, being sure to center brush springs on brushes.
14. Position drive gear actuating lever cover on starter and install brush cover band.

1978–82 Units

Disassemble, Figs. 56 & 57

1. Remove cover screw, cover, through bolts, starter drive end housing and starter drive plunger lever return spring.
2. Remove plunger lever retaining pin, then remove lever and armature.
3. Remove stop ring retainer from armature shaft, then remove stop ring and starter drive gear assembly.
4. Remove brush end plate and insulator assembly.
5. Remove brushes from brush holder, then remove brush holder. Note position of brush holder to end terminal.
6. Remove two screws retaining ground brushes to frame.
7. Bend up edges of sleeve inserted in frame, then remove sleeve and retainer.
8. Detach field coil ground wire from copper tab on frame.

BRACKET MOUNTING LUG
SOLENOID
1.7L ENGINE A-412 MANUAL TRANSAXLE STARTER
SOLENOID
BRACKET MOUNTING LUG
1.7L ENGINE A-404 AUTOMATIC TRANSAXLE STARTER
SOLENOID
1.7L ENGINE A-460 MANUAL AND 2.2L ENGINE A-460 MANUAL AND A-413 AUTOMATIC TRANSAXLE STARTER
BRACKET MOUNTING LUG

Fig. 63 Bosch starting motors

9. Using tool No. 10044-A, remove three coil retaining screws, Fig. 61. Cut field coil connection at switch post lead and pole shoes and coils from frame.
10. Cut positive brush leads from field coils, as close to field connection as possible.

Assemble, Figs. 56 & 57

1. Position pole pieces and coils in frame, then install retaining screws using tool No. 10044-A, Fig. 61. As pole shoes are tightened, strike frame several times with a soft faced mallet to seat and align pole shoes, then stake screws.
2. Install plunger coil sleeve and retainer, then bend tabs to retain coils to frame.
3. Position grommet on end terminal, then insert terminal and grommet into notch on frame.
4. Solder field coil to starter terminal post strap.

NOTE: Use 300 watt soldering iron and rosin core solder.

5. Check coils for continuity and grounds.
6. Position brushes to starter frame and install retaining screws.
7. Apply a thin coat of Lubriplate 777 or equivalent to armature shaft splines.
8. Install drive gear assembly on armature shaft, then install stop ring and stop ring retainer.
9. Install armature into starter frame.
10. Position starter drive gear plunger to frame and starter drive assembly, then install pivot assembly. Fill end housing bearing bore approximately 1/4 full with grease, then position drive end housing to frame.
11. Install brush holder, then insert brushes into holder and install brush springs.

NOTE: Ensure positive brush leads are properly positioned in slots on brush holder.

12. Install brush end plate. Ensure brush end plate insulator is properly positioned.
13. Install through bolts, then install starter drive plunger lever cover and tighten retaining screw.

FORD MOTORCRAFT SOLENOID ACTUATED STARTER

Description

The solenoid assembly, in this unit, is mounted to a flange on the starter drive housing which encloses the entire shift lever and solenoid plunger mechanism. The solenoid incorporates a pull-in winding and a hold-in winding.

Operation

As the solenoid is energized, it shifts the starting motor pinion into mesh with the engine flywheel ring gear.

At the same time, the solenoid contacts are closed and battery current flows to the motor, turning it and the engine.

After the engine starts, the starter drive is disengaged when the ignition switch is returned from the start position to the run position and the solenoid spring pushes the shift lever back, disengaging the starter drive from the flywheel ring gear.

The starting motor is protected by an overrunning clutch built into the starter drive.

Disassembly, Fig. 61

1. Disconnect the copper strap from the starter terminal of the solenoid, remove the retaining screws and remove solenoid.
2. Loosen retaining screw and slide brush cover band back on frame.
3. Remove commutator brushes from holders. Hold each spring away from the brush with a hook while sliding brush from holder.
4. Remove through bolts and separate end plates and frame.
3. Remove commutator brushes from holders. Hold each spring away from the brush with a hook while sliding brush from holder.
4. Remove through bolts and separate end plates and frame.
5. Remove solenoid plunger and shift fork assembly.
6. Remove armature and drive assembly from frame. Remove drive stop ring and slide drive assembly from shaft. Remove fiber thrust washer from commutator end of shaft.
7. Remove drive stop ring retainer from shaft.

Reassembly, Fig. 61

1. Install drive assembly on shaft and install new stop ring.
2. Install solenoid plunger and shift fork.
3. Place new retainer in drive housing and install armature and drive in housing. Be sure shift lever tangs properly engage drive assembly.
4. Install fiber washer on commutator end of shaft and position frame to drive housing, being sure to index frame and drive housing correctly.
5. Install brush plate assembly being sure to index it properly, install through bolts and tighten to 55–75 inch lbs.
6. Install brushes by pulling each spring away from holder with a hook to allow entry of the brush. Center the brush springs on the brushes. Press insulated brush leads away from all other components to prevent possible shorts.
7. Install rubber gasket and solenoid.

8. Connect copper strap to starter terminal of solenoid.
9. Position cover band and tighten retaining screw.
10. Connect starter to battery and check operation.

HITACHI S13-62A STARTER

Disassembly

1. Disconnect solenoid lead wire.
2. Remove solenoid to starter attaching bolts and remove the solenoid from the shift lever, Fig. 62.
3. Remove the solenoid torsion spring.
4. Remove starter through bolts and separate the rear cover.
5. Using long-nose pliers, remove brushes and brush holder from the armature.
6. Remove the frame and armature together as an assembly from the gear case.
7. Remove two screws from gear drive housing and separate drive housing and solenoid.

Fig. 64 Nippondenso starting motors

Fig. 65 Disconnecting coil wire from solenoid (typical). Bosch units

Fig. 66   Solenoid plunger removal. Bosch units for A-404 auto. transaxle

Fig. 67   "C" washer & bearing washer removal. Bosch units

Fig. 68   Brush plate removal. Bosch units

Fig. 69   Metal plate & rubber gasket removal. Bosch units

Fig. 70   Shift lever bolt removal. Bosch units

Fig. 71   Armature assembly & shift fork. Bosch units for A-404 auto. transaxle

8. Remove two pinions from gear case, then remove the overrunning clutch and retainer.
9. Remove the solenoid return spring.
10. Remove the steel ball from the overrunning clutch.

Assemble

1. Reverse disassembly procedure to assemble, noting the following:
   a. Be sure to install the steel ball and solenoid return spring.
   b. Use caution not to get oil or other contaminants on brushes or armature.
   c. Always replace O-rings with new ones.
   d. Lubricate all necessary parts prior to assembly.

BOSCH & NIPPONDENSO STARTER MOTORS

Dodge Aries, Omni, 400, Plymouth Horizon & Reliant & 1982 Chrysler LeBaron

Description

Bosch units are painted black, while Nippondenso units have an aluminum covered drive side with a yellowish color elsewhere. The starter drive is of the overrunning clutch type with a solenoid switch mounted on the starting motor, Figs. 63 and 64.

Bosch Starter

1.7 L Engine W/A-404 Auto. Transaxle or A-412 Man. Transaxle

1. Disconnect field coil wire from solenoid terminal, Fig. 65.
2. Remove solenoid mounting screws and the solenoid. On automatic transaxle units, remove solenoid plunger from shift fork, Fig. 66.
3. Remove end shield bearing cap, then the

"C" washer and bearing washer, Fig. 67.
4. Remove through bolts and the end shield.
5. Remove both field brushes and the brush plate, Fig. 68.
6. Remove field frame from starter.
7. Remove rubber gasket and metal plate, Fig. 69.
8. Remove clutch lever pivot bolt, Fig. 70.
9. On automatic transaxle units, remove armature assembly and shift lever from drive and housing, Fig. 71.
10. On all models, press stop collar off snap ring, Figs. 72 and 73, and remove snap ring.
11. Remove stop collar and clutch, Fig. 74.
12. On manual transaxle units, remove drive end housing from armature, Fig. 75.
13. Reverse procedure to assemble.

Fig. 72   Pressing stop collar from snap ring. Bosch units except models w/A-412 man. transaxle

Fig. 73   Pressing stop collar from snap ring. Bosch units for A-412 man. transaxle

Fig. 74   Clutch removal (Typical). Bosch units

Fig. 75 Drive end housing removal. Bosch units for A-412 man. transaxle

Fig. 76 Field coil terminal identification. Nippondenso units except 2.6 L engine

Fig. 77 Rubber gasket & metal plate removal. Nippondenso units for A-404 auto. transaxle & A-412 man. transaxle

Fig. 78 Armature shaft lock, washer & spring removal. Nippondenso units for A-404 auto. transaxle & A-412 man. transaxle

Fig. 79 Brush plate removal. Nippondenso units except 2.6 L engine

Fig. 80 Shift lever pivot removal. Nippondenso units for A-404 auto. transaxle & A-412 man. transaxle

1.7 & 2.2 L Engine W/A-413 Auto. Transaxle or A-460 Man. Transaxle

1. Remove nut from solenoid field coil terminal, then remove field coil strap from terminal, Fig. 65.
2. Remove three solenoid attaching screws, then work solenoid from shift fork and remove solenoid.
3. Remove two starter motor end shield bearing cap attaching screws and remove end shield cap, C-washer and bearing washer, Fig. 67.
4. Remove starter motor through bolts, then remove starter motor brush end shield.
5. Remove two starter motor brushes by prying the brush retaining springs back, then remove brush plate, Fig. 68.
6. Slide field frame from armature, then remove armature and clutch assembly from drive end housing.
7. Remove rubber seal and clutch lever bolt from drive end frame, then remove clutch lever.

8. Position armature in a suitable vise, then using a socket, press collar from pinion gear stop snap ring, Fig. 72. Remove snap ring from armature shaft using snap ring pliers.
9. Remove stop collar and clutch assembly from armature shaft, Fig. 73.
10. Reverse procedure to assemble.

Nippondenso Starter

1.7 L Engine W/A-404 Auto. Transaxle or A-412 Man. Transaxle

1. Disconnect field coil wire from solenoid terminal, Fig. 76.
2. Remove solenoid mounting screws and the solenoid.
3. Remove rubber gasket and metal plate, Fig. 77.
4. Remove bearing cover mounting screws and the bearing cover.
5. Remove armature shaft lock, washer, spring and seal, Fig. 78.

6. Remove through bolts and the commutator end frame cover.
7. Remove field brushes and the brush plate, Fig. 79.
8. Remove field frame from starter.
9. Remove shift lever pivot bolt, Fig. 80.
10. Remove armature assembly and shift lever from drive end housing, Fig. 81.
11. Press stop collar off snap ring, Fig. 82.
12. Remove snap ring, stop collar and clutch, Fig. 82.
13. Reverse procedure to assemble.

1.7 L Engine W/A-413 Auto. Transaxle or A-460 Man. Transaxle

1. Remove nut from solenoid field coil terminal, then remove field coil strap, Fig. 76.
2. Remove two nuts attaching solenoid to starter housing, then work solenoid from shift fork and remove solenoid.
3. Remove two attaching screws end shield

Fig. 81 Armature assembly removal. Nippondenso units for A-404 auto. transaxle & A-412 man. transaxle

Fig. 82 Stop collar, snap ring & clutch assembly. Nippondenso units except 2.6 L engine

Fig. 83 C-washer removal. Nippondenso units for A-413 auto. transaxle & A-460 man. transaxle

Fig. 84 Rubber seal removal. Nippondenso units for A-413 auto. transaxle & A-460 man. transaxle

Fig. 85 Armature & clutch assembly removal. Nippondenso units for A-413 auto. transaxle & A-460 man. transaxle

Fig. 86 Clutch shift lever retainer. Nippondenso units for A-413 auto. transaxle & A-460 man. transaxle

Fig. 87 Field coil terminal nut removal. Nippondenso units for 2.6 L engine

Fig. 88 Field brush removal. Nippondenso units for 2.6 L engine

Fig. 89 Separating solenoid from gear and housing. Nippondenso units for 2.6 L engine

bearing cap, then remove end shield cap, C-washer, bearing spring and bearing washer, Fig. 83.
4. Remove two starter motor through bolts, then remove starter motor brush end shield.
5. Pry back on brush spring and remove field brushes, then remove brush plate, Fig. 79.
6. Remove field frame from armature, then remove rubber seal from drive end housing, Fig. 84.
7. Remove armature and clutch assembly from drive end frame, Fig. 85.
8. Remove clutch lever retainer from drive end frame, then remove clutch lever, Fig. 86.
9. Press stop collar from snap ring, then remove snap ring, stop collar and clutch, Fig. 82.
10. Reverse procedure to assemble.

2.6 L Engine
1. Pull rubber boot from field coil terminal,

then remove nut from field coil terminal stud, Fig. 87.
2. Remove field coil lead from field coil terminal stud.
3. Remove two starter motor through bolts, then remove two screws from starter motor end shield.
4. Remove upper left solenoid attaching screw retaining field coil lead retainer, then remove field coil lead retainer.
5. Remove starter motor brush end shield.
6. Pry back on brush retaining springs and remove brushes, then remove brush plate, Fig. 88.
7. Slide armature from field frame, then remove field frame from gear end frame.
8. Remove two gear end frame to solenoid attaching screws, then using a soft faced mallet separate solenoid from end frame, Fig. 89.
9. Remove reduction gear pinion roller retainer from gear end frame, Fig. 90.
10. Remove reduction gear and clutch assembly from gear end frame, Fig. 91.

11. Remove pinion gear from gear end frame, then remove pinion gear rollers.
12. Remove solenoid ball and spring, Fig. 92, then remove two remaining solenoid cover screws from solenoid and remove solenoid cover.
13. Remove solenoid plunger from solenoid housing, Fig. 93.
14. Reverse procedure to assemble.

STARTER DRIVE TROUBLES

Starter drive troubles are easy to diagnose and they usually cannot be confused with ordinary starter difficulties. If the starter does not turn over at all or if it drags, look for trouble in the starter or electrical supply system. Concentrate on the starter drive or ring gear if the starter is noisy, if it turns but does not engage the engine, or if the starter won't disengage after the engine is started. After the starter is removed, the trouble can usually be located quickly.

Fig. 90 Pinion roller retainer removal. Nippondenso units for 2.6 L engine

Fig. 91 Reduction gear & clutch assembly removal. Nippondenso units for 2.6 L engine

Fig. 92 Solenoid ball & spring removal. Nippondenso units for 2.6 L engine

Fig. 93 Solenoid plunger removal. Nippondenso units for 2.6 L engine

Worn or chipped ring gear or starter pinion are the usual causes of noisy operation. Before replacing either or both of these parts try to find out what caused the damage. With the Bendix type drive, incomplete engagement of the pinion with the ring gear is a common cause of tooth damage. The wrong pinion clearance on starter drives of the over-running clutch type leads to poor meshing of the pinion and ring gear and too rapid tooth wear.

A less common cause of noise with either type of drive is a bent starter armature shaft. When this shaft is bent, the pinion gear alternately binds and then only partly meshes with the ring gear. Most manufacturers specify a maximum of .003″ radial run-out on the armature shaft.

When Clutch Drive Fails

The over-running clutch type drive seldom becomes so worn that it fails to engage since it is directly activated by a fork and lever, Fig. 94. The only thing that is likely to happen is that, once engaged, it will not turn the engine because the clutch itself is worn out. A much more frequent difficulty and one that rapidly wears ring gear and teeth is partial engagement. Proper meshing of the pinion is controlled by the end clearance between the pinion gear and the starter housing or pinion stop, if used.

The clearance is set with the starter off the car and with the drive in the engaged position. To check the clearance, supply current to the starter solenoid with the electrical connection between starter and solenoid removed. Supplying current to the solenoid but not the starter will prevent the starter from rotating during the test. Take out all slack by pushing lightly on the starter drive clutch housing

Fig. 94 Overrunning clutch drive. When assembling, make sure curved sides of yoke shoes are toward gear end of clutch. Reversed yoke shoes can cause improper meshing of pinion

while inserting a feeler gauge between pinion and housing or pinion stop, Fig. 95.

On late model cars, the solenoids are completely enclosed in the starter housing and the pinion clearance is not adjustable. If the clearance is not correct, the starter must be disassembled and checked for excessive wear of solenoid linkage, shift lever mechanism, or improper assembly of parts.

Failure of the over-running clutch drive to disengage is usually caused by binding between the armature shaft and the drive. If the drive, particularly the clutch, shows signs of overheating it indicates that it is not disengaging immediately after the engine starts. If the clutch is forced to over-run too long, it overheats and turns a bluish color. For the cause of the binding, look for rust or gum between the armature shaft and the drive, or for burred splines. Excess oil on the drive will lead to gumming, and inadequate air circulation in the flywheel housing will cause rust.

Over-running clutch drives cannot be overhauled in the field so they must be replaced. In cleaning, never soak them in a solvent because the solvent may enter the clutch and dissolve the sealed-in lubricant. Wipe them off lightly with kerosene and lubricate them sparingly with SAE 10 or 10W oil.

When Bendix Drive Fails

When a Bendix type drive doesn't engage

Fig. 95 Measuring overrunning clutch drive stop clearance. Do not compress anti-drift spring as this will give an incorrect clearance. If clearance is not present there is danger of the drive housing being broken as gear or collar slams back against it

the cause usually is one of three things: either the drive spring is broken, one of the drive spring bolts has sheared off, or the screwshaft threads won't allow the pinion to travel toward the flywheel. In the first two cases, remove the drive by unscrewing the set screw under the last soil of the drive spring and replace the broken parts. Gummed or rusty screwshaft threads are fairly common causes of Bendix drive failure and are easily cleaned with a little kerosene or steel wool, depending on the trouble. Here again, as in the case of over-running clutch drives, use light oil sparingly, and be sure the flywheel housing has adequate ventilation. There is usually a breather hole in the bottom of the flywheel housing which should be open.

The failure of a Bendix drive to disengage or to mesh properly is most often caused by gummed or rusty screwshaft threads. When this is not true, look for mechanical failure within the drive itself.

CONTENTS

INTRODUCTION

Alternators are composed of the same functional parts as the conventional D.C. generator but they operate differently: The field is called a rotor and is the turning portion of the unit. A generating part, called a stator, is the stationary member, comparable to the armature in a D.C. generator. The regulator, similar to those used in a D.C. system, regulates the output of the alternator-rectifier system.

The power source of the system is the alternator. Current is transmitted from the field terminal of the regulator through a slip ring to the field coil and back to ground through another slip ring. The strength of the field regulates the output of the alternating current. This alternating current is then transmitted from the alternator to the rectifier where it is converted to direct current.

These alternators employ a three-phase stator winding in which the phase windings are electrically 120 degrees apart. The rotor consists of a field coil encased between interleaved sections producing a magnetic field with alternate north and south poles. By rotating the rotor inside the stator the alternating current is induced in the stator windings. This alternating current is rectified (changed to D.C.) by silicon diodes and brought out to the output terminal of the alternator.

Diode Rectifiers

Six silicon diode rectifiers are used and act as electrical one-way-valves. Three of the diodes have ground polarity and are pressed or screwed into a heat sink which is grounded. The other three diodes (ungrounded) are pressed or screwed into and insulated from the end head; these diodes are connected to the alternator output terminal.

Since the diodes have a high resistance to the flow of current in one direction and a low resistance in the opposite direction, they may be connected in a manner which allows current to flow from the alternator to the battery in the low resistance direction. The high resistance in the opposite direction prevents the flow of current from the battery to the alternator. Because of this feature no circuit breaker is required between the alternator and battery.

SERVICE PRECAUTIONS

1. Be certain that battery polarity is correct when servicing units. Reversed battery polarity will damage rectifiers and regulators.

2. If booster battery is used for starting, be sure to use correct polarity in hook up.

3. When a fast charger is used to charge a vehicle battery, the vehicle battery cables should be disconnected *unless the fast charger is equipped with a special Alternator Protector,* in which case the vehicle battery cables need not be disconnected. Also the fast charger should never be used to start a vehicle as damage to rectifiers will result.

4. Lead connections to the grounded rectifiers (negative) on Chrysler units should never be soldered as the excessive heat may damage the rectifiers.

5. Unless the system includes a load relay or field relay, grounding the alternator output terminal will damage the alternator and/or circuits. This is true even when the system is not in operation since no circuit breaker is used and the battery is applied to the alternator output terminal at all times. The field or load relay acts as a circuit breaker in that it is controlled by the ignition switch.

6. When adjusting the voltage regulator, do not short the adjusting tool to the regulator base as the regulator may be damaged. The tool should be insulated by taping or by installing a plastic sleeve.

7. Before making any "on vehicle" tests of the alternator or regulator, the battery should be checked and the circuit inspected for faulty wiring or insulation, loose or corroded connections and poor ground circuits.

8. Check alternator belt tension to be sure the belt is tight enough to prevent slipping under load.

9. The ignition switch should be off and the battery ground cable disconnected before making any test connections to prevent damage to the system.

10. The vehicle battery must be fully charged or a fully charged battery may be installed for test purposes.

Bosch Type K1 Alternator

DESCRIPTION

The main components of the Bosch type K1 alternator, Figs. 1 and 2, are the front and rear housings, stator windings, rotor and rectifying diodes. Current is supplied to the rotor through slip rings and two brushes which are integral with the voltage regulator on the rear housing. The rotor is supported in the front and rear housings by ball bearings. The stator windings are assembled inside a laminated core which forms part of the alternator frame. A diode plate containing three positive and three negative diodes is soldered to the stator winding leads. Alternator field current is supplied through a diode trio which is also connected to the stator windings. A capacitor which is mounted to the rear housing, protects the diode plate assembly from high voltages

Fig. 1 Bosch Type K1 alternator

and supresses radio noises. The voltage regulator is a solid state unit which is not serviceable or adjustable. The voltage regulator can be replaced without disassembling the alternator.

IN-VEHICLE TESTING

Indicator Lamp Diagnosis

NOTE: If indicator lamp lights with engine operating, indicating a no charge condition perform the following test.

1. Check alternator belt tension and adjust as necessary.
2. Start engine and measure battery voltage

using a suitable voltmeter.
3. Raise engine speed to fast idle.
4. Ground the metal sleeve on the voltage regulator to the alternator housing and check voltage reading, Fig. 3. If voltage reading is higher than reading obtained in step 2, the regulator is defective and should be replaced. If voltage reading is lower or remains the same, the alternator must be removed and repaired.

Undercharged Battery

Refer to diagnosis charts, Figs. 4 and 5 for test procedure.

Overcharged Battery

Refer to diagnosis chart, Fig. 6 for test procedure.

ALTERNATOR DISASSEMBLY, FIG. 7

1. Scribe marks on alternator front and rear housings for use during reassembly.
2. Remove regulator and brush holder retaining screws and washers, then tilt regulator and brush holder assembly and remove from rear housing.
3. Disconnect condenser wire, then remove retaining screws, washer and condenser.
4. Remove through bolts, then separate front housing and rotor assembly from stator and rear housing assembly. Remove wave washer from rear housing.

NOTE: Place a piece of tape over rear housing bearing and slip ring end of rotor shaft to prevent entry of dirt. Do not use tape which will leave a gummy deposit on rotor shaft. If brushes are to be reused, clean with a soft dry cloth.

5. Remove battery terminal nuts and washers. Note positioning of components for reassembly.
6. Position rotor assembly in a vise, then remove shaft nut, lockwasher, pulley, key and fan from rotor shaft.

NOTE: When positioning rotor in vise, tighten vise only enough to permit loosening of shaft nut. Overtightening may cause damage to rotor.

7. Remove bearing retainer attaching screws from front housing, then remove rotor assembly.
8. Remove stator and diode assembly from rear housing.
9. Unsolder stator leads from diode plate assembly.
10. Separate drive housing from rotor shaft.
11. Press rear bearing from rotor shaft using a suitable press and support.

NOTE: The rear rotor shaft bearing must be replaced if it is found to be insufficiently lubricated. Do not attempt to lubricate or reuse a dry bearing.

12. Press front bearing from rotor shaft.

BENCH TESTS

Rotor & Slip Ring Test

To test rotor for grounds, set ohmmeter to 1000 scale, then place one ohmmeter lead on

Fig. 2 Sectional view of Bosch Type K1 alternator

rotor shaft and contact other ohmmeter lead to slip ring, Fig. 8. Repeat test with other slip ring. The ohmmeter should indicate an infinite reading. If ohmmeter indicates other than infinite reading, a short to ground exists. Inspect soldered connections at slip rings to ensure they are not grounded against the rotor coil. Inspect rotor coil and replace if damaged.

To test rotor for an open circuit, set ohmmeter to 1 scale, then contact ohmmeter leads to slip rings, Fig. 9. Ohmmeter reading should be 3.0 to 3.7 ohms. If an infinite ohmmeter reading is obtained, rotor winding has an open circuit.

To check rotor for short circuit, connect a 12 volt battery and ammeter in series with slip rings, Fig. 10. Field current at 12 volts and 80 degrees F should be between 3.5 and 5 amps. If reading is above 5 amps, shorted windings are indicated. Winding resistance and ammeter readings will vary with temperature. A reading below the specified value indicates excessive resistance. This test can also be performed by connecting an ohmmeter between the two slip rings. If resistance is below 3 ohms, at 80 degrees F, the winding is shorted. If reading is above 3.7 ohms at 80 degrees F, winding has excessive resistance.

Fig. 3 Voltage regulator grounding sleeve

Stator Winding Test

To test stator for short circuit, set ohmmeter to 1000 scale, then connect one ohmmeter to stator core and the other ohmmeter lead to one of the three stator leads, Fig. 11. The ohmmeter should indicate an infinite reading. If ohmmeter indicates other than infinite reading, the stator is grounded and should be replaced.

To test stator for continuity, set ohmmeter to 1 scale, then contact ohmmeter leads to two of the stator leads, Fig. 12. Test all three stator leads in this manner. Equal readings should be obtained for each pair. An infinite reading would indicate an open stator winding. Check junction splice for poor solder connection and resolder as necessary. Recheck stator continuity, if an open still exists replace stator. A reading of more than one ohm indicates a poor solder splice, check junction splice.

NOTE: Shorted stator windings are difficult to locate without special equipment. If other tests indicate normal, but alternator fails to supply rated output, shorted stator windings are indicated.

Diode Test

Unsolder stator winding leads at junctions. Bend lead wires as little as possible to avoid damaging wires. Set ohmmeter to 1 scale, then contact one ohmmeter lead to diode plate and the other ohmmeter lead to the individual diode junctions, Fig. 13. Each combination of terminals tested should give one high reading and one low reading. High and low readings will vary slightly with temperature. If one high and one low reading is not observed for all diodes, replace diode plate assembly.

ALTERNATOR SYSTEMS

STEP | SEQUENCE | RESULT

1 CHECK ALTERNATOR BELT

ADJUST TENSION TO 90-115 LBS. REPLACE IF NECESSARY

MAKE SURE NO ACCESSORIES ARE ON, IGNITION OFF, DOORS CLOSED, UNDER HOOD LIGHTS DISCONNECTED

DISCONNECT NEGATIVE CABLE

CONNECT TEST LIGHT BETWEEN CABLE AND BATTERY POST

TEST LIGHT ON → **2**

TEST LIGHT OFF—NO DRAIN ON BATTERY → **3**

---

2 TRACE AND CORRECT CONTINUOUS DRAIN ON BATTERY

CONNECT TEST LIGHT BETWEEN CABLE AND BATTERY POST

TEST LIGHT OFF → **STOP**

TEST LIGHT ON → **3**

---

3 RECONNECT NEGATIVE CABLE

CONNECT JUMPER (-) TERMINAL AND GROUND

CONNECT VOLTMETER (+) TERMINAL AND GROUND

CRANK ENGINE LONG ENOUGH FOR STABILIZED READING

NEEDLE ABOVE 9.0V → **6**

NEEDLE BELOW 9.0V → **4**

---

4 CHECK VOLTAGE ACROSS POST WHILE CRANKING

IF READING IS WITHIN .5 VOLT OF VOLTAGE AT ALTERNATOR

IF READING IS NOT WITHIN .5 VOLT OF READING AT ALTERNATOR, CHECK FOR BATTERY-TO-ALTERNATOR CIRCUIT RESISTANCE

TEST BATTERY USING BATTERY LOAD TEST PROCEDURE

BATTERY OK. CHARGE AS SPECIFIED BY TEST → **6**

BATTERY NOT OK → **5**

Fig. 4   Undercharged battery test chart. Part 1 of 2

Fig. 8   Rotor short to ground test

OHMMETER — SET SELECTOR AT 1000

Fig. 9   Rotor open circuit test

OHMMETER — SET SELECTOR AT 1

Fig. 10   Rotor internal short test

AMMETER — 12 VOLT BATTERY

STEP | **SEQUENCE** | **RESULT**

5 — REPLACE BATTERY → **6**

6 — DISCONNECT COIL JUMPER — CONNECT VOLTMETER ACROSS BATTERY — RECORD READING — PLACE CARBURETOR ON HIGH STEP FAST IDLE CAM — START ENGINE. DO NOT TOUCH ACCELERATOR PEDAL → **7**

7 TURN ON ACCESSORIES — HEADLIGHTS-HI / A/C – HI / RADIO / BLOWER-TYPE DEFOGGER — CHECK VOLTAGE READING
- IF VOLTAGE IS LOWER THAN PREVIOUS READING (STEP 6) → **9**
- IF VOLTAGE IS HIGHER THAN PREVIOUS READING (STEP 6) → **8**

8 TURN OFF ACCESSORIES — WAIT UNTIL UPPER RADIATOR INLET IS HOT AND VOLTMETER NEEDLE STOPS — CHECK VOLTAGE READING
- IF METER READS UNDER 12.5V → **9**
- IF METER READS OVER 15.5V → **10**
- IF METER READS 12V TO 15.5V SEE NOTE → STOP

9 GROUND ALTERNATOR. TOUCH SCREWDRIVER TO TAB AND ALTERNATOR BODY — CHECK VOLTAGE READING
- IF VOLTAGE IS HIGHER THAN PREVIOUS READING (STEP 6) → **10**
- IF VOLTAGE IS LOWER THAN PREVIOUS READING (STEP 6) → **11**

10 REPLACE VOLTAGE REGULATOR → STOP

11 OVERHAUL ALTERNATOR → STOP

Fig. 5 Undercharged battery test chart. Part 2 of 2

ALTERNATOR SYSTEMS

STEP	SEQUENCE	RESULT
1	PERFORM BATTERY HEAVY LOAD TEST PROCEDURE — BATTERY OK → **2** — BATTERY NOT OK / REPLACE BATTERY → **2**	
2	CONNECT VOLTMETER ACROSS BATTERY — PLACE CARBURETOR ON HIGH STEP FAST IDLE CAM — START ENGINE. DO NOT TOUCH ACCELERATOR PEDAL → **3**	
3	TURN OFF ALL ACCESSORIES — WAIT UNTIL UPPER RADIATOR INLET IS HOT — AND VOLTMETER NEEDLE STOPS — CHECK VOLTAGE READING: READING IS 12.5V to 15.5V → STOP; READING IS NOT 12.5V to 15.5V REPLACE VOLTAGE REGULATOR → **4**	
4	CHECK FOR SHORTED FIELD WINDINGS AS CAUSE OF VOLTAGE REGULATOR FAILURE — OHMMETER — IF SHORTED REPLACE ROTOR → STOP; IF NOT SHORTED → STOP	

Fig. 6 Overcharged battery test chart

Fig. 11 Stator short to ground test (OHMMETER — SET SELECTOR AT 1000)

Fig. 12 Stator continuity test (OHMMETER — SET SELECTOR AT 1)

Fig. 13 Diode test

Fig. 7 Exploded view of Bosch Type K1 alternator

1. PULLEY NUT	9. THROUGH-SCREW	17. REAR HOUSING
2. LOCKWASHER	10. WASHER	18. COMPRESSION SPRING
3. BEARING	11. PULLEY	19. CARBON BRUSH SET
4. COVER PLATE	12. FAN	20. REGULATOR
5. COLLAR	13. FRONT HOUSING	21. SPRING WASHER AND SCREW
6. ROTOR	14. STATOR	22. SUPPRESSION CAPACITOR
7. COLLECTOR RING	15. WASHER AND SCREW ASSEMBLY	23. SPRING WASHER AND SCREW
8. BEARING	16. RECTIFIER	24. BATTERY TERMINAL NUTS AND WASHERS

ALTERNATOR ASSEMBLY, FIG. 7

1. Fill cavity between retainer plate and bearing one quarter full with Bosch lubricant Ftv34 or equivalent. Do not overfill.
2. Install front bearing, retainer and collar into front housing. Press rear bearing onto rotor shaft. Install wave washer into rear housing.

NOTE: Use care not to misalign bearings.

3. Install rotor into front housing.
4. Solder stator leads to diode plate assembly, then install stator assembly on rear housing.
5. Remove tape from rear housing bearing and rotor shaft, then position front and rear housings together, aligning scribe marks made during disassembly.

6. Install and tighten through bolts.
7. Position key, fan, pulley and washer on rotor shaft, then install pulley nut.
8. Place rotor in a vise and tighten pulley nut. Tighten vise only enough to permit tightening of pulley nut.
9. Install nuts and washer on battery terminal.
10. Install condenser on rear housing and connect condenser lead.
11. Install voltage regulator and brush assembly on rear housing.

Chrysler Alternators

Fig. 1 Alternator assembly exc. 100 & 114 amp units. 1977—82

Fig. 3 100 & 114 amp alternator assembly. 1977—82

All Chrysler alternators except the 100 and 114 amp units are equipped with six silicon rectifiers, Figs. 1 and 2. The 100 and 114 amp alternators are equipped with twelve silicon rectifiers, Figs. 3 and 4.

TESTING SYSTEM ON VEHICLE

Charging Circuit Resistance Test

1. Disconnect battery ground cable. Disconnect "Batt" lead at the alternator.
2. Complete test connections as per Fig. 5.

NOTE: Use a 0–100 amp ammeter.

3. Connect battery ground cable, start engine and operate at idle.
4. Adjust engine speed and carbon pile to obtain 20 amps in the circuit and check voltmeter reading. Reading should not exceed .7 volts. If a voltage drop is indicated, inspect, clean and tighten all connections in the circuit. A voltage drop test at each connection can be performed to isolate the trouble.

Current Output Test

1. Disconnect battery ground cable, complete test connections as per Fig. 6 and start engine and operate at idle. *Immediately after starting, reduce engine speed to idle.*
2. Adjust the carbon pile and engine speed in increments until a speed of 1250 RPM and 15 volts are obtained on all units except 100 and 114 amp alternators. On 100 and 114 amp alternators, obtain engine speed of 900 RPM and 13 volts.

CAUTION: While increasing speed, do not allow voltage to exceed 16 volts.

3. Check ammeter reading. Output current should be within specifications.

Voltage Regulator Test

NOTE: Battery must be fully charged for test to be accurate.

1. Connect test equipment, Fig. 7.
2. Start and run engine at 1250 RPM with all lights and accessories turned "Off". Voltage should be as specified in Fig. 8.
3. It is normal for the vehicle ammeter to indicate an immediate charge, then gradually return to the normal position.
4. If voltage is below limits or is fluctuating, proceed with the following:
   a. Check voltage regulator for proper ground. The ground is obtained through the regulator case to mounting screws, then to the vehicle sheet metal.
   b. With ignition switch "Off", disconnect voltage regulator connector. Turn ig-

Fig. 2 Alternator disassembled exc. 100 & 114 amp units (typical) 1977—82

nition "On" and check for battery voltage at the wiring harness terminal. Both green and blue leads should have battery voltage.
  c. If voltage regulator was grounded properly and battery voltage was present at the green and blue leads, replace voltage regulator except on systems incorporating a field-loads relay. On systems with a field-loads relay, test the relay as outlined under "Field-Loads Relay Test". If relay tests satisfactory, replace voltage regulator. On all systems, repeat test.
5. If voltage is above limits, refer to Steps 4B and 4C.

BENCH TESTS

If the alternator performance does not meet current output specification limits, it will have to be disassembled for further tests and servicing.

To remove the alternator, disconnect the battery ground cable and the leads at the alternator. Then unfasten and remove the alternator from the vehicle.

Field Coil Draw

1. On 1979–82 units except 100 and 114 amp, place alternator on a insulated surface.
2. On all units, connect a jumper wire between one alternator field terminal and the negative terminal of a fully charged battery.
3. Connect test ammeter positive lead to the other alternator field terminal and the ammeter negative lead to the positive battery terminal.
4. On 1979–82 units except 100 and 114 amp, connect a jumper wire between alternator end shield and negative terminal of battery.
5. On all units, slowly rotate rotor by hand and note ammeter reading. On units except 100 and 114 amp, field current at 12 volts should be 4.5 to 6.5 amps. On 100 and 114 amp units, field current should be 4.75 to 6.0 amps.
6. A low rotor coil draw is an indication of high resistance in the field coil circuit, (brushes, slip rings or rotor coil). A high rotor coil draw indicates shorted rotor coil or grounded rotor. No reading indicates an open rotor or defective brushes.

ALTERNATOR REPAIRS EXCEPT 100 & 114 AMP UNITS

Disassembly

To prevent possible damage to the brush assemblies, they should be removed before disassembling the alternator. Both brushes are insulated and mounted in plastic holders.
1. Remove both brush screws, insulating nylon washers and remove brush assemblies, Fig. 2.

NOTE: The stator is laminated; do not burr it or the end shield.

2. Remove through bolts and pry between stator and drive end shield with a screwdriver. Carefully separate drive end shield, pulley and rotor from stator and diode rectifier shield, Fig. 9.
3. The pulley is an interference fit on the rotor shaft; therefore, a suitable puller must be used to remove it, Fig. 10.

Fig. 4   100 & 114 amp alternator disassembled. 1977–82

4. Pry drive end bearing spring retainer from end shield with a screwdriver, Fig. 11.
5. Support end shield and tap rotor shaft with a plastic hammer to separate rotor from end shield.
6. The drive end ball bearing is an interference fit with the rotor shaft; therefore, a suitable puller must be used to remove it, Fig. 12.
7. To remove rectifiers and heat sinks, loosen screws securing negative rectifier and heat sink assembly to end shield, remove the two outer screws and lift assembly from end shield. Remove nuts securing positive rectifier and heat sink assembly to insulated terminals in end shield. Then, remove capacitor ground screw and lift insulated washer, capacitor and positive rectifier and heat sink assembly from end shield.
8. The needle roller bearing in the rectifier end shield is a press fit. If it is necessary to remove the rectifier end frame needle bearing, protect the end shield by sup-

porting the shield when pressing out the bearing as shown in Fig. 13.

Testing Diode Rectifiers

A special Rectifier Tester Tool C-3829 provides a quick, simple and accurate method to test the rectifiers without the necessity of disconnecting the soldered rectifier leads. This instrument is commercially available and full instructions for its use are provided. Lacking this tool, the rectifiers may be tested with a 12 volt battery and a test lamp having a No. 67 bulb. The procedure is as follows:
1. Remove nuts securing stator windings, positive and negative rectifier straps to terminal block. Remove stator winding terminals and pry stator from end shield.
2. Connect one side of test lamp to positive battery post and the other side of the test lamp to a test probe. Connect another test probe to the negative battery post, Fig. 14.

Fig. 5 Charging circuit resistance test. 1977—82 alternators

does not light, the stator has an open circuit.

4. Install new stator if one tested is defective.

Testing Rotor

The rotor may be tested electrically for grounded, open or shorted field coils as follows:

Grounded Field Coil Test: Connect an ohmmeter between each slip ring and the rotor shaft. The ohmmeter should indicate infinite resistance. If reading is zero or higher, rotor is grounded.

Open or Shorted Field Coil Test: Connect an ohmmeter between slip rings and note reading. Ohmmeter reading should be between 1.5 and 2 ohms at room temperature. A reading of 2.5 to 3 ohms, would indicate that the alternator was operated at high underhood temperature, however the rotor is still satisfactory. A reading above 3.5 ohms would indicate a high resistance in rotor coils and further testing or replacement of rotor is required. If resistance is below 1.5 ohms, the field coil is shorted.

Replacing Slip Rings

NOTE: Slip rings are not serviced as a separate item. Rotor replacement is required when the slip rings are defective.

Alternator Assemble

1. Press grease retainer onto rotor shaft using tool No. C-3921, Fig. 17. The grease retainer is properly positioned when the inner bore of the installed tool bottoms on the rotor shaft.
2. Install diode end shield bearing, Fig. 18.
3. Install drive end bearing in end shield with bearing retainer plate to hold bearing in position. Place assembly on rotor shaft and press into position, Fig. 19.
4. Press pulley onto rotor shaft until it contacts inner race of bearing, Fig. 20.

NOTE: Do not exceed 6800 lbs.

5. Install output terminal stud and insulator through end shield. Then place positive heat sink assembly over studs, guiding rectifier straps over studs.
6. Place capacitor terminal over capacitor end stud and install capacitor shoulder insulator. Ground the capacitor bracket to end shield with a metal screw. Install and tighten positive heat sink lockwashers and nuts.
7. Slide negative rectifier and heat sink assembly into place, position straps on terminal block studs, then install and tighten attaching screws.
8. Position stator on diode end shield.
9. Position rotor end shield on stator and diode end shield.
10. Align through bolt holes in stator, diode end shield and drive end shield.
11. Compress stator and both end shields by hand and install through bolts, washers and nuts.
12. Install field brush into vertical and horizontal holders. Place an insulating

3. Contact heat sink with one probe and strap on top of rectifier with the other probe.
4. Reverse position of probes. If test lamp lights in one direction only, the rectifier is satisfactory. If test lamp lights in both directions, the rectifier is shorted. If test lamp lights in neither direction, the rectifier is open.

NOTE: *Possible cause of an open or a blown rectifier is a faulty capacitor or a battery that has been installed on reverse polarity. If the battery is installed properly and the rectifiers are open, test the capacitor capacity, which should be .50 microfarad plus or minus 20%.*

Testing Stator

1. Separate stator from end shields.
2. Using a 12 volt test lamp, Fig. 15, test stator for grounds. Contact one test probe to any pin on stator frame and the other to each stator lead. If lamp lights, stator is grounded.

NOTE: Remove varnish from stator frame pin to ensure proper electrical connection.

3. Use a 12-volt test lamp to test stator for continuity. Contact one stator lead with one probe and the remaining two leads with the other probe, Fig. 16. If test lamp

Fig. 6 Current output test. 1977—82 alternators

Fig. 7 Voltage regulators test. 1977-82 alternators

Ambient Temperature Near Regulator	-20°F	80°F	140°F	Above 140°F
1977-82	14.9-15.9	13.9-14.6	13.3-13.9	Less than 13.6

Fig. 8 Voltage regulator test specifications

Fig. 9 Separating drive end shield from stator

Fig. 10 Removing pulley

Fig. 11 Disengaging bearing retainer from end shield

Fig. 12 Removing bearing from rotor shaft

Fig. 13 Removing rectifier end shield bearing

washer on each field brush terminal and install lock-washers and attaching screws.

NOTE: Ensure brushes are not grounded.

13. Rotate pulley slowly by hand to be sure rotor fans do not touch diodes, capacitor lead and stator connections.
14. Install alternator and adjust drive belt.
15. Connect leads to alternator.
16. Connect battery ground cable.
17. Start and operate engine and observe alternator operation.
18. If necessary, test current output and regulator voltage setting.

100 & 114 AMP ALTERNATOR

Disassembly & Testing

Separating End Shields
1. Remove brush holder screw and insulating washer, then lift brush holder from end shield.
2. Remove the through bolts, then using a screwdriver, pry between the stator and end shield in the slot provided to separate end shields, Fig. 21.

Rectifier Testing
1. Remove stator winding leads to terminal block stud nuts, Fig. 22.
2. Lift stator winding leads and pry stator from end shield.
3. Using a 12 volt battery and a test lamp equipped with a #67 bulb, test rectifiers as follows:
   a. Connect one test probe to rectifier heat sink and the other test probe to the metal strap on top of rectifier, Fig. 23. Reverse the probes.
   b. If test lamp lights in one direction and does not light in the other, rectifier is satisfactory. If test lamp lights in both

Fig. 14   Testing diodes with a test lamp

Fig. 17   Installing bearing grease retainer

directions, rectifier is shorted. If test lamp does not light in either direction, rectifier is open.

Rectifier & Heat Sink Assembly Removal

1. Remove nut and insulator securing positive heat sink assembly to end shield stud.
2. Remove capacitor attaching screw.
3. Remove nut and insulator securing positive heat sink assembly stud to end

Fig. 21   Separating end shields. 100 & 114 amp units

Fig. 15   Testing stator for grounds

Fig. 18   Installing diode end shield bearing

Fig. 20   Installing pulley

Fig. 22   Removing stator winding leads. 100 & 114 amp units

Fig. 16   Testing stator windings for continuity (typical)

Fig. 19   Installing drive end shield and bearing

shield, then remove positive heat sink assembly, Fig. 24, noting location of the insulators.
4. Remove screws securing negative heat sink assembly to end shield, then the negative heat sink assembly, Fig. 25.
5. Remove terminal block, then the capacitor and insulator.

Stator Testing

1. Contact one test lamp probe to outer diameter of stator frame and the other probe to each of the stator lead terminals, one at a time, Fig. 26.
2. If test lamp lights, the stator lead is grounded, requiring replacement.

NOTE: The stator windings are Delta Wound, therefore the windings cannot be tested for opens or shorts using a test lamp. If the stator is not grounded, and all other electrical circuits and alternator components test satisfactory, the stator may be open or shorted.

Fig. 23   Testing rectifiers with a test lamp. 100 & 114 amp units

Fig. 24   Positive rectifier assembly.
100 & 114 amp units

Fig. 25   Negative rectifier assembly.
100 & 114 amp units

Fig. 26   Testing stator. 100 & 114 amp units

Fig. 27   Removing pulley. 100 & 114 amp
units

Fig. 28   Removing bearing from rotor shaft.
100 & 114 amp units

Fig. 29   Removing rectifier end shield
bearing. 100 & 114 amp units

Pulley & Bearing Removal

1. Remove pulley with a suitable puller, Fig. 27.
2. Remove bearing retainer to drive end shield attaching screws.
3. Support end shield and using a mallet, tap rotor from end shield.
4. Remove bearing with a suitable puller, Fig. 28.
5. If necessary to remove needle roller bearing in rectifier end shield, use tool C-4330, Fig. 29.

Rotor Testing

Grounded Field Coil Test: Connect a test lamp between each slip ring and the rotor shaft, Fig. 30. If test lamp lights, the rotor is grounded, requiring replacement.

Open Field Coil Test: Connect a test lamp between the slip rings, Fig. 31. If test lamp does not light, the rotor is open, requiring replacement.

Shorted Field Coil Test: Connect an ohmmeter between the slip rings, Fig. 31. If reading is below 1.7 ohms, the rotor is shorted.

High Resistance Test: with an ohmmeter connected across the slip rings, reading should be between 1.7 and 2.1 ohms at 80°F. If not, replace rotor.

Assembly

1. Press grease retainer onto rotor shaft, Fig. 29 (Omit tool C-4330-3).
2. Place rectifier end shield bearing on base of tool C-4330-1, Fig. 29 (Omit tool C-4330-3), then place rectifier end shield on top of bearing. Using tool C-4330-2, press end shield onto bearing until end shield contacts press base.
3. Install drive end bearing and retainer in drive end shield.
4. Position bearing and drive end shield on rotor and while supporting base of rotor shaft, press end shield onto shaft. Ensure rotor spacer is in place before pressing bearing and end shield on shaft.

Fig. 30   Testing rotor for opens or shorts
100 & 114 amp units

Fig. 31   Testing rotor for grounds
100 & 114 amp units

Fig. 32   Assembling field brushes.
100 & 114 amp units

5. Press pulley onto rotor shaft until it contacts inner race of bearing.

NOTE: Do not exceed 6800 lbs.

6. Place insulator and capacitor on positive heat sink mounting stud, then install capacitor mounting screw.
7. Place terminal block into position in rectifier end shield and install mounting screws.
8. Place negative heat sink into position, ensuring metal straps are properly located over studs on terminal block, then install negative heat sink mounting screws.

9. Place insulator over positive heat sink stud and install positive heat sink assembly into position in end shield, ensuring metal straps are properly located over terminal block studs. From inside end shield, place insulator on positive heat sink mounting stud, then install mounting nut. From outside end shield, place insulator on positive heat sink stud, then install mounting nut.
10. Place stator over rectifier end shield and install terminals on terminal block. Then, press stator pins into end shield and install terminal nuts.

NOTE: Route leads to avoid contact with

rotor or sharp edge of negative heat sink.

11. Place rotor and drive end shield assembly over stator and rectifier end shield assembly, aligning bolt holes. Compress stator and both end shields, then install and torque through bolts to 40–60 inch lbs.
12. Install field brushes into brush holder with long terminal on bottom and the short terminal on top, Fig. 32. Then, install insulators and mounting screw.
13. Place brush holder on end shield, ensure it is properly seated and tighten mounting screw.
14. Slowly rotate pulley to ensure rotor poles do not contact stator winding leads.

Delcotron Type SI Integral Charging System

DESCRIPTION

These units, Figs. 1 thru 4, feature a solid state regulator mounted inside the alternator slip ring end frame, along with the brush holder assembly. All regulator components are enclosed in a solid mold with no need or provision for adjustment of the regulator. A rectifier bridge, containing six diodes and connected to the stator windings, changes A.C. voltage to D.C. voltage which is available at the output terminal. Generator field current is supplied through a diode trio which is also connected to the stator windings. The diodes and rectifiers are protected by a capacitor which is also mounted in the end frame.

NOTE: General Motors units incorporate a resistor in the warning indicator circuit. Fig. 5.

Some alternators used on diesel engines are equipped with an R terminal for the tachometer. On these units, if the alternator pulley is to be replaced, a pulley of the same diameter as the one removed must be installed, otherwise tachometer may provide inaccurate readings.

No maintenance or adjustments of any kind are required on this unit.

TROUBLE SHOOTING

Undercharged Battery

1. Disconnect battery ground cable.
2. Disconnect wire at "BAT" terminal of alternator, connect ammeter, positive lead to "BAT" terminal and negative lead to wire.
3. Connect battery ground cable.
4. Turn on all accessories, then connect a carbon pile regulator across battery.
5. Operate engine at moderate speed, adjust carbon pile regulator to obtain maximum current output.
6. If ammeter reading is within 10 amps of rated output, alternator is not at fault.

NOTE: Alternator rated output is stamped on alternator frame.

7. If ammeter reading is not within 10 amps

of rated output, ground field winding by inserting screw driver in end frame hole, contacting tab, Fig. 6.

NOTE: Do not insert screwdriver deeper than one inch since tab is usually located within 3/4 inch of casing surface.

8. If reading is within 10 amps of rated output, regulator must be replaced. If reading is not within limits, check field winding, diode trio, rectifier bridge and stator.
9. Turn off all accessories and disconnect ammeter and carbon pile regulator.

Overcharging Battery

1. Remove alternator from vehicle and separate end frames as outlined under "Alternator Disassembly."
2. Check field winding, if shorted replace rotor and regulator.
3. Connect ohmmeter from brush clip to end

Fig. 1   Delcotron type 10 SI alternator (typical)

Fig. 1A   Cross-sectional view of 10 SI alternator

Fig. 2 Delcotron type 15 SI alternator

Fig. 3 Delcotron type 27 SI alternator

Fig. 4 Sectional view of Delcotron type SI alternator (typical)

frame, set meter on low scale and note reading. Fig. 7.

4. Reverse leads, if both readings are zero remove screw from brush clip and inspect sleeve and insulator.
5. If sleeve and insulator are in good condition, then regulator is at fault and must be replaced.

ALTERNATOR DISASSEMBLY

NOTE: When pressing bearings or seals from end frames, support frames from inside.

1. Scribe mark across end frames and stator ring so parts can be installed in same position.
2. Remove four through bolts, then using screw driver in stator slot pry end frames apart. Fig. 8.

NOTE: Brushes may fall from holders and become contaminated with bearing grease, if so they must be cleaned prior to assembly.

3. Place tape over slip ring end frame bearing and shaft at slip ring end.
4. Remove nut, washer, pulley, fan and collar from rotor shaft, then slide drive end frame from shaft.
5. Remove bearing, retainer and seal from drive and frame.
6. Remove attaching bolts, then pry stator from slip ring end frame.
7. Remove capacitor, diode trio, rectifier bridge and battery terminal stud.

NOTE: On diesel engine alternators equipped with R terminal for tachometer, the R terminal nut and jumper strap must be removed, before removing the rectifier bridge and battery terminal.

8. Remove resistor (if equipped), brush holder and regulator.
9. Remove bearing and seal from slip ring end frame.

BENCH TESTS
Rotor & Slip Ring Test

NOTE: Ohmmeter must be at low scale setting during this test.

1. Inspect rotor for wear or damage.

2. Touch ohmmeter leads to slip rings. Fig. 9.
3. If no reading is obtained an open circuit exists in windings.
4. If reading below 2.4 ohms on G.M., or 2.2 ohms on A.M.C. vehicles, is obtained, winding is shorted.
5. If a reading above 3 ohms, or 3.5 ohms on 1982 G.M. vehicles, is obtained, excessive resistance exists in windings.
6. Connect one ohmmeter lead to rotor shaft and touch slip rings with other lead, if any reading is obtained there is a ground in the circuit. Fig. 9.

NOTE: If any of the above problems are

Fig. 5 Wiring diagram of charging circuit. 1977–82 G.M. vehicles

present the rotor assembly must be replaced.

Stator Winding Test

1. Inspect stator for discolored windings, loose connections and damage.
2. Connect an ohmmeter from stator lead to frame, if any reading is obtained windings are grounded. Fig. 10.
3. On 10 SI units, connect ohmmeter between stator leads, if reading is high when connected between each pair of leads, an open circuit exists in windings. The stator windings on 15 SI and 27 SI units cannot be checked for open circuits.

NOTE: Shorted windings are difficult to locate without special equipment. If other tests indicate normal, but rated alternator output cannot be obtained the windings are probably shorted.

Diode Trio

1. With diode unit removed, connect an ohmmeter to the single connector and to one of the three connectors. Fig. 11
2. Observe the reading. Reverse ohmmeter leads.
3. Reading should be high with one connection and low with the other. If both readings are the same, unit must be replaced.
4. Repeat between the single connector and each of the three connectors.

NOTE: There are two diode units differing in appearance. These are completely interchangeable.

The diode unit can be checked for a grounded brush lead while still installed in the end frame by connecting an ohmmeter from the brush lead clip to the end frame as in Steps 1 and 2 above. If both readings are zero, check for a grounded brush or brush lead.

Rectifier Bridge Test

1. Connect ohmmeter to the grounded heat sink and one of the three terminals. Fig. 12.

Insert Screwdriver Ground Tab To End Frame

Tab

End Frame Hole

Fig. 6 Grounding field windings

OHMMETER

INSULATING WASHERS

RESISTOR (USED ON SOME MODELS)

CAPACITOR

DIODE TRIO

RECTIFIER BRIDGE

ATTACHING NUTS

Fig. 7 Testing brush clip

2. Observe the reading then reverse leads.
3. Reading should be high with one connection and low with the other. If both readings are the same, unit must be replaced.
4. Repeat test for each of the other terminals.

Voltage Regulator/Brush Lead Test

Connect an ohmmeter from the brush lead clip to the end frame, note reading, then reverse connections. If both readings are zero, either the brush lead clip is grounded or the regulator is defective.

ALTERNATOR ASSEMBLY

NOTE: When pressing bearings or seals, end frames must be supported from inside.

1. Lightly lubricate seal and position on slip ring end frame with lip facing toward rotor. Fig. 8.
2. Press seal part way into housing.
3. On 10 SI and 27 SI units, position bearing and end plug on slip ring end frame, press bearing and plug in until flush with end frame. On 15 SI units, refer to Fig. 13, when installing slip ring end frame bearing.
4. Place regulator in end frame, install

brushes and springs in brush holder, use pin to hold brushes in compressed position.

NOTE: Insulating washers are installed under two of the attaching screws, Fig. 14.

5. Install rectifier bridge and battery terminal stud.
6. On diesel engine alternators equipped with R terminal for tachometer, install plastic insulating washer on R terminal stud, then position terminal stud into end frame. Install fiber insulating washer, jumper strap and nut on R terminal stud. Position jumper strap on rectifier bridge, then tighten R terminal stud.

7. Install diode trio, ensure current only flows one way through single connector.
8. Install capacitor.

NOTE: On 15 SI units, the capacitor lead uses a push clip connector to attach to the rectifier bridge instead of a screw, Fig. 15.

9. Install stator, check the three leads for continuity, ensure stator is not grounded against case or holder.
10. On 10 SI and 27 SI units, position slinger on drive end frame, then press ball bearing

OHMMETER (CHECK FOR GROUNDS)

OHMMETER (CHECK FOR OPENS)

Fig. 9 Testing rotor & slip rings

(CHECK FOR OPENS) OHMMETER

OHMMETER (CHECK FOR OPENS)

OHMMETER (CHECK FOR GROUNDS)

Fig. 10 Testing stator winding

SINGLE CONNECTOR

OHMMETER

3 CONNECTORS

Fig. 11 Testing diode trio

Regulator

Brush unit

Terminal assembly

Spring

Insulating washer

Brush assembly

Ring end seal

Roller bearing

Through bolt

Slip ring end frame

Diode

Rotor

Stator

Capacitor bracket

Diode bridge

Capacitor

Drive end frame

Fan

Pulley

Pulley nut

Plate assembly

Bearing spacer

Washer

Roller bearing

Bearing spacer

Wave washer

Fig. 8   Alternator disassembled

ing into end frame. Fig. 16. On 15 SI units, refer to Fig. 17, when installing drive end bearing.

11. Fill seal cavity 1/4 full with special alternator lubricant, then install retainer.

12. Install rotor in drive end frame, then install collar, fan, pulley, washer and nut.

13. Align scribe marks on end frames and stator plate, install through bolts and remove brush retaining pins.

BEARING

USE THIN WALL TUBE IN SPACE BETWEEN GREASE CUP AND HOUSING TO PUSH BEARING IN FLUSH WITH HOUSING

SLIP RING END FRAME

Fig. 13   Installing slip ring end frame bearing. 15 SI units

Insulating Screws

Insulating Washers

Check For Cracked Or Worn Insulation

Fig. 14   Brush holder & regulator installation

BRUSH RETAINING PIN CAPACITOR

TEST TAB

BRUSH HOLDER ASM.

RECTIFIER BRIDGE

PUSH-IN CONNECTOR

Fig. 15   Slip ring end frame. 15 SI units

Fig. 12 Testing rectifier bridge diodes

Fig. 16 Drive end frame bearing & slinger installed

Fig. 17 Drive end frame bearing. 15 SI units

Ford Motorcraft Alternator

CONTENTS

GENERAL

A charge indicator lamp or ammeter can be used in charging system.

If a charge indicator lamp is used in the charging system, Figs. 1, 3 and 5, the system operation is as follows: when the ignition switch is turned ON, a small electrical current flows through the lamp filament (turning the lamp on) and through the alternator regulator to the alternator field. When the engine is started, the alternator field rotates and produces a voltage in the stator winding. When the voltage at the alternator stator terminal reaches about 3 volts, the regulator field relay closes. This puts the same voltage potential on both sides of the charge indicator lamp causing it to go out. When the field relay has closed, current passes through the regulator A terminal and is metered to the alternator field.

If an ammeter is used in the charging system, Figs. 2, 4 and 6, the regulator 1 terminal and the alternator stator terminal are not used. When the ignition switch is turned ON, the field relay closes and electrical current passes through the regulator A terminal and is metered to the alternator field. When the engine is started, the alternator field rotates causing the alternator to operate.

Some 1978 and all 1979–82 Ford vehicles are equipped with new electronic voltage regulators, Figs. 7 and 8. These solid state regulators are used in conjunction with other new components in the charging system such as an alternator with a higher field current requirement, a warning indicator lamp shunt resistor (500 ohms) and a new wiring harness with a new regulator connector. When replacing system components, note the following precautions:

1. Always use the proper alternator in the system. If the new 1978–82 alternator is installed on previous model systems, it will destroy the electromechanical regulator. If the older model alternator is used on the new system, it will have a reduced

Fig. 1 Indicator light rear terminal alternator charging circuit

Fig. 2 Ammeter rear terminal alternator charging circuit

output.

2. Do not use an electro-mechanical regulator in the new system since the wiring harness connector will not index properly with this type of regulator.

3. The new electronic regulators are color coded for proper installation. The black color coded unit is installed in systems equipped with a warning indicator lamp. The blue color coded regulator is installed in systems equipped with an ammeter.

4. The new systems use a 500 ohm resistor on the rear of the instrument cluster on vehicles equipped with a warning indicator lamp. Do not replace this resistor with the 15 ohm resistance wire used on previous systems.

On the new systems with an indicator lamp, closing the ignition switch energizes the warning lamp and turns on the regulator output stage. The alternator receives maximum field current and is ready to generate an output voltage. As the alternator rotor speed increases, the output and stator terminal voltages increase from zero to the system regulation level determined by the regulator setting. When the ignition switch is turned off, the solid state relay circuit turns the output stage off, interrupting current flow through the regulator so there is not a current drain on the battery.

On vehicles equipped with an ammeter, the operating principle is similar.

NOTE: The ammeter indicates current flow into (charge) or out of (discharge) the vehicle battery.

SYSTEM TESTING

NOTE: The operations and on vehicle test procedures for the side terminal alternator are same as for rear terminal alternator.

Fig. 3 Indicator light side terminal alternator charging system. 70 amp system

Fig. 4 Ammeter side terminal alternator charging system. 70 amp system

ALTERNATOR SYSTEMS

Fig. 5 Indicator light side terminal alternator charging system. 90 amp system

Fig. 6 Ammeter side terminal alternator charging system. 90 amp system

However, the internal wiring, Figs. 3 through 6, and bench test procedures differ.

In-Vehicle Voltmeter Test

NOTE: *All lights and electrical systems in the off position, parking brake applied, transmission in neutral and a charged battery (at least 1.200 specific gravity).*

1. Connect the negative lead of the voltmeter to the negative battery cable clamp (not bolt or nut).
2. Connect the positive lead of the voltmeter to the positive battery cable clamp (not bolt or nut).
3. Record the battery voltage reading shown on the voltmeter scale.
4. Connect the red lead of a tachometer to the distributor terminal of the coil and the black tachometer lead to a good ground.
5. Then, start and operate the engine at approximately 1500 rpm. With no other electrical load (foot off brake pedal and car doors closed), the voltmeter reading

should increase but not exceed (2 volts) above the first recorded battery voltage reading. The reading should be taken when the voltmeter needles stops moving.
6. With the engine running, turn on the heater and/or air conditioner blower motor to high speed and headlights to high beam.
7. Increase the engine speed to 2000 rpm. The voltmeter should indicate a minimum reading of 0.5 volts above the battery voltage, Fig. 9.

NOTE: *If the above tests indicate proper voltage*

Fig. 7 Indicator light charging system with electronic voltage regulator

Fig. 8 Ammeter charging system with electronic voltage regulator

Fig. 9 Voltmeter test scale

Fig. 10 Regulator plug voltage test

Fig. 11 Testing field circuit with ohmmeter

readings, the charging system is operating normally. Proceed to "Test Results" if a problem still exists.

TEST RESULTS

1. If voltmeter reading indicates 2 volts over battery voltage (over voltage), proceed as follows:
   a. Stop the engine and check the ground connections between the regulator and alternator and/or regulator to engine. Clean and tighten connections securely and repeat the *Voltmeter Test Procedures*.
   b. If *over voltage* condition still exists, disconnect the regulator wiring plug from the regulator and repeat the *Voltmeter Test Procedures*.
   c. If *over voltage* still exists with the regulator wiring plug disconnected, repair the short in the wiring harness between the alternator and regulator. Then, replace the regulator and connect the regulator wiring plug to the regulator and repeat the *Voltmeter Test Procedures*.
2. On 1977 units, if voltmeter does not indicate more than 1/2 volt above battery voltage, proceed as follows:
   a. Check for presence of battery voltage at alternator BAT terminal and the regulator plug A terminal, Fig. 10. Repair the wiring if no voltage is present at these terminals, and repeat the *Voltmeter Test Procedures*.

b. If voltmeter reading does not increase 1/2 volt above battery voltage, proceed to next step.
c. Before performing other tests, the field circuit (regulator plug to alternator) must be checked for a grounding condition. If the field circuit is grounded and the jumper wire is used as a check at the regulator wiring plug from the A to F terminals, Fig. 10, excessive current will cause heat damage to the regulator wiring plug terminals and may burn the jumper wire, Fig. 10. Also, if the field circuit was grounded, the connector wire inside the regulator will be burned open and an under voltage condition will result.
d. The field circuit should be checked with the regulator wiring plug disconnected and an ohmmeter connected from the *F* terminal of the regulator wiring plug to the battery ground. The ohmmeter should indicate between 4 and 250 ohms, Fig. 11.
e. A check for the regulator burned-open wire is made by connecting an ohmmeter from the *I* to *F* terminals of the regulator, Fig. 12. The reading should indicate *O* (no resistance). If the reading indicates approximately *10 ohms*, the connector wire inside the regulator is burned open. *The field circuit grounded condition must be found and repaired before installing a new regulator.*
3. On 1978–82 units, if voltmeter does not indicate more than 1/2 volt above battery voltage, proceed as follows:
   a. Disconnect voltage regulator wire connector and connect an ohmmeter between wire connector F terminal and ground. Ohmmeter reading should indicate more than 3 ohms. If reading is less than 3 ohms, repair grounded field circuit and repeat Voltmeter Test procedure.
   b. If ohmmeter reading is more than 3 ohms, connect a jumper wire between voltage regulator wire connector terminals A and F, Fig. 13, then repeat Voltmeter Test procedure. If voltmeter reading is now more than 1/2 volt above battery voltage, the voltage regulator or wiring is defective, refer Regulator Test.
   c. If voltmeter still indicates less than 1/2 volt, disconnect jumper wire from voltage regulator wire connector and leave connector disconnected from regulator. Connect a jumper wire between alternator FLD and BAT terminals, Figs. 14 and 15, then repeat Voltmeter

Test procedures.
d. If voltmeter reading now indicates 1/2 volt or more above battery voltage, repair alternator to regulator wiring harness.
e. If voltmeter still indicates less than 1/2 volt above battery voltage, stop engine and move voltmeter positive lead to alternator BAT terminal.
f. If voltmeter now indicates battery voltage, the alternator should be removed, inspected and repaired. If zero volts is indicated, repair BAT terminal wiring.

Field Circuit and Alternator Tests

1. If the field circuit is satisfactory, disconnect the regulator wiring plug at the regulator and connect the jumper wire from the A to the F terminals on the regulator wiring plug, Fig. 13.
2. Repeat the *Voltmeter Test Procedures*.
3. If the *Voltmeter Test Procedures* still indicate a problem of under voltage, remove the jumper wire at the regulator plug and leave the plug disconnected from the regulator, Figs. 14 and 15. Connect a jumper wire to the *FLD* and *BAT* terminals on the alternator, Figs. 14 and 15.
4. Repeat the *Voltmeter Test Procedures*.
5. If the *Voltmeter Test* are now satisfactory, repair the wiring harness from the alternator to the regulator. Then, remove the jumper wire at the alternator and connect the regulator wiring plug to the regulator.

Fig. 12 Testing regulator for a burned or open connector wire

Fig. 13 Regulator plug. Jumper wire connection

Fig. 14   Rear terminal alternator. Jumper wire connection

6. Repeat the *Voltmeter Test Procedures,* to be sure the charging system is operating normally.
7. If the *Voltmeter Test* results still indicate under voltage, repair or replace the alternator. With the jumper wire removed, connect the wiring to the alternator and regulator.
8. Repeat the *Voltmeter Test Procedures.*

Regulator Tests

S Circuit Test—With Ammeter

1. Connect the positive lead of the voltmeter to the *S* terminal of the regulator wiring plug Fig. 10. Turn the ignition switch to

Fig. 16   Side terminal alternator rectifier short or grounded & stator grounded test

the *ON* position. *Do not start the engine.*
2. The voltmeter reading should indicate battery voltage.
3. If there is *no* voltage reading, disconnect the positive voltmeter lead from the positive battery clamp and repair the *S* wire lead from the ignition switch to the regulator wiring plug.
4. Connect the positive voltmeter lead to the positive battery cable terminal and repeat the *Voltmeter Test Procedures.*

S and I Circuit Test—With Indicator Light

1. With the engine idling, connect the positive lead of the voltmeter to the *S* terminal and then to the *I* terminal of the regulator wiring plug. Fig. 10. The voltage of the *S* circuit should read approximately $1/2$ of the *I* circuit.
2. If no voltage is present, repair the alternator or the wiring circuit at fault. Reconnect the positive voltmeter lead to the positive battery cable terminal and repeat the *Voltmeter Test Procedures.*
3. If the above tests are satisfactory, install a new regulator.
4. Then, remove the jumper wire from the regulator wiring plug and connect the wiring plug to the regulator. Repeat the *Voltmeter Test Procedures.*

Diode Test

Test Procedure
1. Disconnect electric choke, if equipped.
2. Disconnect voltage regulator wiring connector.
3. Connect a jumper wire between the "A" and "F" terminals of the voltage regulator wiring connector, Fig. 13.
4. Connect voltmeter to battery clamps. Then, start and idle engine.
5. Observe and note voltmeter reading.
6. Move the voltmeter positive lead to the alternator "S" terminal and note voltage reading.

Test Results
1. If voltmeter reading is within $1/2$ of battery voltage, the diodes are satisfactory.
2. If voltmeter reading is approximately 1.5 volts, the alternator has a shorted negative diode or a grounded stator winding.
3. If voltmeter reading is approximately 1.5 volts less than battery voltage, the alternator has a shorted positive diode.
4. If voltage reading is approximately 1 to 1.5 volts less than $1/2$ battery voltage, the alternator has an open positive diode.
5. If voltage reading is 1 to 1.5 volts above $1/2$ battery voltage, the alternator has an open negative diode.
6. Reconnect electric choke into circuit after tests are completed, if equipped.

Bench Tests

Rectifier Short or Grounded and Stator Grounded Test

Set ohmmeter Multiply By knob at 10, and calibrate meter.
Contact one ohmmeter probe to the alternator BAT terminal, Fig. 16, the other probe to the STA terminal (rear blade terminal). Then, reverse the ohmmeter probes and repeat the test. A reading of about 60 ohms should be obtained in one direction and no needle movement with the probes reversed. A reading in both directions indicates a bad positive diode, a grounded positive diode plate or a grounded BAT terminal.

Fig. 15   Side terminal alternator. Jumper wire connector

Perform the same test using the STA and GND (ground) terminals of the alternator. A reading in both directions indicates either a bad negative diode, a grounded stator winding, a grounded stator terminal, a grounded positive diode plate, or a grounded BAT terminal.

Infinite readings (no needle movement) in all four probe positions in the preceeding tests indicates an open STA terminal lead connection inside the alternator.

Field Open or Short Circuit Test

Set the ohmmeter Multiply By knob at 1 and calibrate meter.

Contact the alternator field terminal with one probe and the ground terminal with the other probe, Fig. 17. Then, spin the alternator pulley. The ohmmeter reading should be between 3.5 and 250 ohms on 1977 units, 2.4

Fig. 17   Side terminal alternator field open or short circuit test

OHMMETER ARE 27-42

CONTACT EACH TERMINAL

CONTACT DIODE PLATE

Fig. 18   Rear terminal diode test.

stator leads and to the stator laminated core. Be sure that the probe makes a good electrical connection with the stator core. The meter should show an infinite reading (no meter movement). If the meter does not indicate an infinite reading (needle moves), the stator winding is shorted to the core and must be replaced. Repeat this test for each stator lead.

Rotor Open or Short Circuit Test

Disassemble the front housing and rotor from the rear housing and stator. Set the ohmmeter, Multiply By knob at 1 and calibrate meter.

Contact each ohmmeter probe to a rotor slip ring. The meter reading should be 3.5 to 4.5 ohms on 1977 units, 2.4 to 4.9 ohms on 1978–80 units, and 2.0 to 3.5 ohms on 1981–82 units. A higher reading indicates a damaged slip ring solder connection or a broken wire. A lower reading indicates a shorted wire or slip ring.

Contact one ohmmeter probe to a slip ring and the other probe to the rotor shaft. The meter reading should be infinite (no deflection). A reading other than infinite indicates the rotor is shorted to the shaft. Inspect the slip ring soldered terminals to be sure they are not bent and touching the rotor shaft, or that excess solder is not grounding the rotor coil connections to the shaft. Replace the rotor if it is shorted and cannot be repaired.

REGULATOR ADJUSTMENTS

1977–78 Transistorized Regulator

The only adjustment of this regulator is the voltage limiter adjustment. This adjustment is made with regulator at normal operating temperature. Remove the regulator cover and using a fiber rod, turn voltage adjusting screw clockwise to raise voltage setting or counterclockwise to lower voltage setting, Fig. 20. Refer to the "Alternator & Regulator Specifications" as listed in the individual car chapters for proper voltage setting.

OHMMETER ARE 27-42

Contact Each Terminal

Contact Diode Plate

Contact Terminal Screw

Fig. 19   Side terminal alternator diode test

1977–78 Electro-Mechanical & 1978–82 Electronic Regulators

These regulators are factory calibrated and sealed and no adjustment is possible. If regulator calibration values are not within specifications, the regulator must be replaced.

and 25 ohms on 1978–80 units 2.4 and 100 ohms on 1981–82 units, and should fluctuate while the pulley is turning. An infinite reading (no meter movement) indicates an open brush lead, worn or stuck brushes, or a bad rotor assembly. An ohmmeter reading less than 3.5 ohms on 1977 units, 2.4 ohms on 1978–81 units indicates a grounded brush assembly, a grounded field terminal or a bad rotor.

Diode Test

Remove the rectifier assembly from the alternator. Set the ohmmeter Multiply By knob at 10 and calibrate meter.

To test one set of diodes, contact one probe to the terminal bolt, Figs. 18 and 19 and contact each of the three stator lead terminals with the other probe. Reverse the probes and repeat the test. All diodes should show a low reading of about 60 ohms in one direction, and an infinite reading (no needle movement) with the probes reversed. Repeat the preceding tests for the other set of diodes except that the other terminal screw is used.

If the meter readings are not as specified, replace the rectifier assembly.

Stator Coil Open or Grounded Test

Disassemble the stator from the alternator.

Set ohmmeter Multiply By knob at 1, and calibrate meter. Connect the ohmmeter probes between each pair of stator leads (3 different ways). The ohmmeter must show equal readings for each pair or stator leads. Replace the stator if the readings are not the same.

Set ohmmeter Multiply By Knob at 1000. Connect the ohmmeter probes to one of the

Fig. 20   Transistorized regulator adjustment, 1977–78

Fig. 21 Disassembled rear terminal alternator

one of two types of rectifier assembly circuit boards, Fig. 22; one has the circuit board spaced away from the diode plates with the diodes exposed. Another type is a single circuit board with built-in diodes.

If the alternator rectifier has an exposed diode circuit board, remove the screws from the rectifier by rotating the bolt heads ¼ turn clockwise to unlock them and then remove the screws, Fig. 22. Push the stator terminal screw straight out on a rectifier with the diodes built into the circuit board, Fig. 22. Avoid turning the screw while removing to make certain that the straight knurl will engage the insulators when installing. Do not remove the grounded screw, Fig. 23.

9. Remove the drive pulley nut, Fig. 24, then, pull the lockwasher, pulley, fan, fan spacer, front housing and rotor stop from the rotor shaft.

10. Remove the three screws that hold the front end bearing retainer, and remove the retainer. If the bearing is damaged or has lost its lubricant, support the housing close to the bearing boss and press out the old bearing from the housing.

11. Perform a diode test and a field open or short circuit test.

Assembly

NOTE: Refer to "Cleaning and Inspection" procedures before reassembly.

1. The rotor, stator and bearings must not be cleaned with solvent. Wipe these parts off with a clean cloth.

2. Press the front bearing in the front housing bearing boss (put pressure on the outer race only), and install the bearing retainer, Fig. 21.

3. If the stop-ring on the rotor drive shaft was damaged, install a new stop-ring. Push the new ring on the shaft and into the groove.

NOTE: *Do not open the ring with snap ring*

Fig. 22 Rectifier assembly

ALTERNATOR REPAIRS
Rear Terminal Alternator

NOTE: Use a 100 watt soldering iron.

Disassembly

1. Mark both end housings and the stator with a scribe mark for assembly, Fig. 21.

2. Remove the three housing through bolts.

3. Separate the front housing and rotor from the stator and rear housing.

4. Remove all the nuts and insulators from the rear housing and remove the rear housing from the stator and rectifier assembly.

5. Remove the brush holder mounting screws and remove the holder, brushes, brush springs, insulator and terminal.

6. If replacement is necessary, press the bearing from the rear housing, supporting the housing on the inner boss.

7. If the rectifier assembly is being replaced, unsolder the stator leads from the printed-circuit board terminals, and separate the stator from the rectifier assembly.

8. Original production alternators will have

Fig. 23 Stator terminal installation. Integral rectifier circuit board

Fig. 24   Typical pulley removal

Fig. 25   Brush holder assembly

Fig. 26   Typical brush lead positions

pliers as permanent damage will result.

4. Position the rotor stop on the drive shaft with the recessed side against the stop-ring.
5. Position the front housing, fan spacer, fan, pulley and lock washer on the drive shaft and install the retaining nut. Torque the retaining nut, Fig. 24, to 60–100 ft lbs.
6. If the rear housing bearing was removed, support the housing on the inner boss and press in a new bearing flush with the outer end surface.
7. Place the brush springs, brushes, brush terminal and terminal insulator in the brush holder and hold the brushes in position by inserting a piece of stiff wire in the brush holder, Fig. 25.
8. Position the brush holder assembly in the rear housing and install the mounting screws. Position the brush leads in the brush holder, Fig. 26.
9. Wrap the three stator winding leads around the circuit board terminals and solder them. Position the stator neutral lead eyelet on the stator terminal screw and install the screw in the rectifier assembly, Fig. 27.
10. For a rectifier with the diodes exposed insert the special screws through the wire lug, dished washers and circuit board, Fig. 22. Turn them 1/4 turn counterclockwise to lock them. For single circuit boards with built in diodes, insert the screws straight through the wire lug, insulating washer and rectifier into the insulator, Fig. 23.

NOTE: The dished washers are to be used only on the circuit board with exposed diodes, Fig. 22. If they are used on the single circuit board, a short circuit will occur. A flat insulating washer is to be used between the stator terminal and the board when a single circuit board is used, Fig. 23.

11. Position the radio noise suppression capacitor on the rectifier terminals. On the circuit board with exposed diodes, install the STA and BAT terminal insulators, Fig. 27. On the single circuit board, position the square stator-terminal insulator in the square hole in the rectifier assembly, Fig. 23. Position the BAT terminal insulator, Fig. 28.

Position the stator and rectifier assembly in the rear housing. Make certain that all terminal insulators are seated properly in the recesses, Fig. 27. Position the STA (black), BAT (red) and FLD (orange) insulators on the terminal bolts, and install the retaining nuts, Fig. 29.

12. Wipe the rear end bearing surface of the rotor shaft with a clean lint-free rag.
13. Position the rear housing and stator assembly over the rotor and align the scribe marks made during disassembly. Seat the machined portion of the stator core into the step in both end housings. Install the housing through bolts. Remove the brush retracting wire, and put a daub of waterproof cement over the hole to seal it.

Side Terminal Alternator

Disassembly

NOTE: Use a 200 watt soldering iron.

1. Mark both end housings and the stator

Fig. 27   Stator lead connections

Fig. 28   Fiber-glass circuit board terminal insulators

Fig. 29   Alternator terminal locations

Fig. 30   Disassembled side terminal alternator

with a scribe mark for use during assembly, Fig. 30.

2. Remove the four housing through bolts, and separate the front housing and rotor from the rear housing and stator. Slots are provided in the front housing to aid in disassembly. *Do not separate the rear housing from the stator at this time.*
3. Remove the drive pulley nut, Fig. 24. Remove the lockwasher, pulley, fan and fan spacer from the rotor shaft.
4. Pull the rotor and shaft from the front housing, and remove the spacer from the rotor shaft, Fig. 30.
5. Remove three screws retaining the bearing to the front housing. If the bearing is damaged or has lost its lubricant, remove the bearing from the housing. To remove the bearing, support the housing close to the bearing boss and press the bearing from the housing.
6. Unsolder and disengage the three stator leads from the rectifier, Fig. 31.
7. Lift the stator from the rear housing.
8. Unsolder and disengage the brush holder lead from the rectifier.
9. Remove the screw attaching the capacitor lead to the rectifier.
10. Remove four screws attaching the rectifier to the rear housing, Fig. 31.
11. Remove the two terminal nuts and insulator from outside the housing, and remove the rectifier from the housing.
12. Remove two screws attaching the brush holder to the housing and remove the brushes and holder.
13. Remove sealing compound from rear housing and brush holder.
14. Remove one screw attaching the capacitor to the rear housing and remove the capacitor.
15. If bearing replacement is necessary, support the rear housing close to the bearing boss and press the bearing out of the housing from the inside.

Assembly

NOTE: Refer to "Cleaning and Inspection" procedures before reassembly.

1. If the front housing bearing is being replaced, press the new bearing in the housing.

NOTE: *Put pressure on the bearing outer race only.* Then, install the bearing retaining screws.

2. Place the inner spacer on the rotor shaft

Fig. 31   Stator lead connections

Fig. 32   Brush holder assembly

and insert the rotor shaft into the front housing and bearing.

3. Install the fan spacer, fan, pulley, lockwasher and nut on the rotor shaft, Fig. 24.
4. If the rear bearing is being replaced, press a new bearing in from inside the housing until it is flush with the boss outer surface.

Fig. 33   Brush holder and rectifier insulators installed

5. Position the brush terminal on the brush holder, Fig. 32. Install the springs and brushes in the brush holder, and insert a piece of stiff wire to hold the brushes in place, Fig. 32.
6. Position the brush holder in the rear housing and install the attaching screws. Push the brush holder toward the rotor shaft opening and tighten the brush holder attaching screws.
7. Position the capacitor to the rear housing and install the attaching screw.
8. Place the two cup shaped (rectifier) insulators on the bosses inside the housing, Fig. 33.
9. Place the insulator on the BAT (large) terminal of the rectifier, and position the rectifier in the rear housing. Place the outside insulator on the BAT terminal, and install the nuts on the BAT and GRD terminals *finger tight.*
10. Install but do not tighten the four rectifier attaching screws.
11. Tighten the BAT and GRD terminal nuts on the outside of the rear housing. Then, tighten the four rectifier attaching screws.
12. Position the capacitor lead to the rectifier and install the attaching screw.
13. Press the brush holder lead on the rectifier pin and solder securely, Fig. 31.
14. Position the stator in the rear housing and align the scribe marks. Press the three stator leads on the rectifier pins and solder securely, Fig. 31.

15. Position the rotor and front housing into the stator and rear housing. Align the scribe marks and install the four through bolts. Tighten two opposing bolts and then the two remaining bolts.
16. Spin the fan and pulley to be sure nothing is binding within the alternator.
17. Remove the wire retracting the brushes, and place a daub of waterproof cement over the hole to seal it.

Brush Replacement

Removal
1. Mark both end housings and the stator with a scribe mark for use during assembly.
2. Remove the four housing through bolts, and separate the front housing and rotor from the rear housing and stator. Slots are provided in the front housing to aid in disassembly.

NOTE: Do not separate the rear *housing and stator*.

3. Unsolder and disengage the brush holder lead from the rectifier.
4. Remove the two brush holder attaching screws and lift the brush holder from the rear housing.
5. Remove the brushes from the brush holder.

Installation
1. Insert the brushes into the brush holder and position the terminal on the brush holder.
2. Depress the brushes and insert a 1½ inch piece of stiff wire, Fig. 32, to hold the brushes in the retracted position.
3. Position the brush holder to the rear housing, inserting the wire used to retract the brushes through the hole in the rear housing.
4. Install brush holder attaching screws. Push the brush holder toward the rotor shaft opening and tighten the attaching screws.
5. Press the brush holder lead on the rectifier pin and solder securely.
6. Position the rotor and front housing into the stator and rear housing. Align the scribe marks and install the four through bolts. Tighten two opposing bolts and then the two remaining bolts.
7. Spin the fan and pulley to be sure nothing is binding within the alternator.
8. Remove the wire retracting the brushes, and place a daub of waterproof cement over the hole to seal it.

Rectifier Replacement

Removal
1. Mark both end housings and the stator with a scribe mark for use during assembly, Fig. 30.
2. Remove the four housing through bolts, and separate the front housing and rotor from the rear housing and stator. Slots are provided in the front housing to aid in disassembly.

NOTE: Do not separate the rear housing and stator at this time.

3. Unsolder and disengage the three stator leads from the rectifier, Fig. 31. Lift the stator from the rear housing.
4. Unsolder and disengage the brush holder lead from the rectifier.
5. Remove the screw attaching the capacitor lead to the rectifier.
6. Remove four screws attaching the rectifier to the rear housing, Fig. 31.
7. Remove two terminal nuts and insulator from outside the housing, and remove the rectifier from the housing.

Installation
1. Insert a piece of wire through the hole in the rear housing to hold the brushes in the retracted position.
2. Place the two cup shaped (rectifier) insulators on the bosses inside the housing, Fig. 33.
3. Place the insulator on the BAT (large) terminal of the rectifier, and position the rectifier in the rear housing. Place the outside insulator on the BAT terminal, and install the nuts on the BAT and GRD terminals finger tight.
4. Install but do not tighten the four rectifier attaching screws.
5. Tighten the BAT and GRD terminal nuts on the outside of the rear housing. Then, tighten the four rectifier attaching screws.
6. Position the capacitor lead to the rectifier and install the attaching screw.
7. Press the brush holder lead on the rectifier pin and solder securely, Fig. 31.
8. Position the stator in the rear housing and align the scribe marks. Press the three stator leads on the rectifier pins and solder securely, Fig. 31.
9. Position the rotor and front housing into the stator and rear housing. Align the scribe marks and install the four through bolts. Partially tighten all four through bolts. Then, tighten two opposing bolts and then the two remaining bolts.

10. Spin the fan and pulley to be sure nothing is binding within the alternator.
11. Remove the wire retracting the brushes in the brush holder, and place a daub of waterproof cement over the hole in the rear housing to seal it.

Cleaning and Inspection Procedures

NOTE: When rebuilding a high temperature alternator, use only high temperature rectifier assembly and bearings. If standard parts are used, alternator failure will occur.

1. The rotor, stator, and bearings must not be cleaned with solvent. Wipe these parts off with a clean cloth.
2. Rotate the front bearing on the drive end of the rotor drive shaft. Check for any scraping noise, looseness or roughness that will indicate that the bearing is excessively worn. Look for excessive lubricant leakage. If any of these conditions exist, replace the bearing.
3. Inspect the rotor shaft at the rear bearing surface for roughness or severe chatter marks. Replace the rotor assembly if the shaft is not smooth.
4. Place the rear end bearing on the slip-ring end of the shaft and rotate the bearing on the shaft. Make the same check for noise, looseness or roughness as was made for the front bearing. Inspect the rollers and cage for damage. Replace the bearing if these conditions exist, or if the lubricant is lost or contaminated.
5. Check the pulley and fan for excessive looseness on the rotor shaft. Replace any pulley or fan that is loose or bent out of shape. Check the rotor shaft for stripped or damaged threads. Inspect the hex hole in the end of the shaft for damage.
6. Check both the front and rear housing for cracks. Check the front housings for stripped threads in the mounting gear. Replace defective housings.
7. Check all wire leads on both the stator and rotor assemblies for loose soldered connections, and for burned insulation. Resolder poor connections. Replace parts that show burned insulation.
8. Check the slip rings for nicks and surface roughness. If the slip rings are badly damaged, the entire rotor will have to be replaced, as it is serviced as a complete assembly.
9. Replace any parts that are burned or cracked. Replace brushes and brush springs that are not to specification.

Mitsubishi Alternator

DESCRIPTION

On these units the regulator is incorporated into the alternator rear housing, Figs. 1 and 2. The electronic voltage regulator has the ability to vary regulated system voltage upward or downward as temperature changes. No voltage regulated adjustments are required on these units.

IN-VEHICLE TESTS

Voltage Regulator Test

1. With ignition switch in the Off position, disconnect battery positive cable and connect an ammeter between battery positive post and battery cable, Fig. 3.
2. Connect a voltmeter between alternator L terminal and ground, Fig. 3. Voltmeter should indicate zero voltage. If voltage is present, the alternator or charging system wiring is defective.
3. Place ignition switch in the On position and note voltmeter reading. Voltmeter reading should be 1 volt or less, if a higher reading is indicated, the alternator should be removed for bench tests.
4. Connect a tachometer to engine, then

NUT
LOCKWASHER
PULLEY FAN
SPACER
SCREW
DRIVE END SHIELD
BEARING RETAINER
BALL BEARING
ROTOR
BALL BEARING
CAPACITOR
DUST SHIELD
PULLEY
DUST SHIELD
BALL BEARING
VOLTAGE REGULATOR
STATOR
RECTIFIER ASSEMBLY
BOLT
INSULATOR
RECTIFIER ASSEMBLY
RECTIFIER END SHIELD
SPRING
SPRING
BRUSHES
TERMINAL SET

Fig. 1   Disassembled view of Mitsubishi alternator

start and operate engine at approximately 2000 to 3000 RPM and note ammeter reading.

NOTE: When starting engine, ensure that no starting current is applied to ammeter.

5. If ammeter reading is 5 amps or less, check voltmeter reading with engine operating at 2000 to 3000 RPM. The charging voltage should be 14.4 volts at 68 degrees F.
6. If ammeter reading is above 5 amps, continue to charge battery until reading drops to less than 5 amps and check volt-

meter reading at 2000 to 3000 RPM. If voltage is not within limits, remove alternator for bench tests.

Current Output Test

1. With ignition switch in the Off position, disconnect battery ground cable, then disconnect battery lead from alternator output terminal.
2. Connect an ohmmeter set at the 0 to 100 amp scale between alternator output terminal and the disconnected battery lead, Fig. 4.
3. Connect positive lead of voltmeter to alternator output terminal and negative lead to ground, Fig. 4.
4. Disconnect green field wire at alternator, then connect tachometer to engine and reconnect battery ground cable.
5. Connect a variable carbon pile regulator between battery terminals. When installing carbon pile regulator, ensure that regulator is in the Open or Off position.
6. Adjust carbon pile regulator and accelerate engine to the specified RPM, noting ammeter and voltmeter readings, Fig. 5.
7. If ammeter reading is less than specified, the alternator should be removed for bench tests.

ALTERNATOR, DISASSEMBLE

1. Position alternator with mounting lug in a soft jawed vise, then remove three alternator through bolts, Fig. 1.

RECTIFIERS
ARMATURE COILS
0.5 CAPACITOR
RECTIFIERS
ALTERNATOR TERMINAL
B
RECTIFIERS
TO FAN RELAY TIMER CIRCUIT
TO LOAD
L
RECTIFIERS
R
IGNITION SWITCH
ALTERNATOR TERMINAL
RECTIFIERS
FIELD COIL
RECTIFIERS
BATTERY
GROUND
GROUND
GROUND
INTEGRATED ELECTRONIC CIRCUIT REGULATOR
GROUND

Fig. 2   Wiring diagram of Mitsubishi charging system

2. Using a screwdriver, pry between stator and drive end frame, then carefully separate drive end frame and rotor from stator and rectifier end frame.

3. Remove pulley nut, pulley, fan and pulley spacer from rotor shaft, then lift drive end housing from rotor.

4. Remove front and rear dust shields from drive end housing.

5. Remove drive end housing bearing retainer, then using a suitable socket, tap bearing from drive end housing.

6. Unsolder six stator leads from rectifier terminals, then remove stator assembly from rectifier end housing.

7. Remove four screws attaching rectifiers to end housing, then remove brush holder and screw attaching regulator to end housing.

8. Remove nut from alternator B terminal and disconnect capacitor lead.

9. Remove rectifier and regulator assembly from end housing.

10. Unsolder joint attaching one of the rectifiers to the regulator, then remove the other rectifier by sliding the battery stud out of the regulator.

Fig. 3 Voltage regulator test connections

BENCH TESTS

Rotor Test

Check for continuity between field coil and slip rings. If continuity does not exist, the rotor assembly must be replaced. Check for continuity between slip rings and rotor shaft. If continuity exists, the rotor assembly should be replaced.

Stator Coil Test

Using an ohmmeter, check for continuity between stator leads. If continuity does not exist, replace stator.

Rectifier Test

Using an ohmmeter, check for continuity between stator coil lead terminal and heat sink, then reverse ohmmeter leads. Continuity should exist with only one connection. If continuity exists with both connections, the diode is short circuited and the rectifier assembly should be replaced.

Using an ohmmeter, check rectifier diodes for continuity, then reverse ohmmeter leads. If continuity or an open circuit is indicated with both connections, the diode is defective and rectifier assembly must be replaced.

Fig. 4 Current output test connections

Brush & Brush Spring Inspection

Check brush length, a brush worn to .315 inch or less should be replaced. Check brush spring tension, brush spring tension should be .7 to 1 lb.

ALTERNATOR, ASSEMBLE

Refer to Alternator, Disassemble and reverse procedure to assemble. When installing rotor, push brushes into holder and insert a suitable piece of wire, Fig. 6. After rotor has been installed, remove wire from brushes.

Engine RPM	Alternator Current Output Hot or Cold At 13.5 Volts
500	17–25 Amps
1000	63–70 Amps
2000	74 Amps

Fig. 5 Alternator output test specifications

Fig. 6 Positioning brushes for rotor installation

Hitachi LR155-12B Alternator

DESCRIPTION

This alternator is a solid state unit which incorporates an integral regulator. A vacuum pump is attached to the rear cover and is driven off the alternator shaft.

ALTERNATOR, DISASSEMBLE, FIG. 1

1. Scribe reference marks on front and rear covers for use during reassembly.
2. Remove bolts securing vacuum pump. Holding the center plate, remove pump in direction in line with rotor shaft, Fig. 1.
3. Remove brush cover, then remove the screws securing the brushes and remove.
4. Remove through bolts, and carefully separate the alternator body into front and rear sections. Ensure the stator coils remain with the rear section.

NOTE: When separating sections care must be taken not to damage the oil seal in the rear section. Taping the vacuum pump drive splines will provide some protection.

5. Clamp the rotor assembly in a suitable vise, then remove the pulley nut, pulley, front cover and rotor.
6. Remove front cover bearing retainer screws, then remove the bearing.
7. Remove nuts securing "B" terminal and diode holder, then remove the screw inside the stator.

NOTE: Use care to note the position of any insulating washers to ensure correct installation.

8. Using long-nose pliers as a heatsink, separate diodes from the stator by melting away solder on stator coils, diodes and "L" terminal leads.
9. Unsolder connections on IC regulator holder plate terminal, and remove regulator.
10. Inspect all parts for wear or abnormal damage and replace or repair as necessary.

BENCH TESTS

Rotor & Slip Ring Test

1. Visually inspect slip rings for contamination or roughness. If rings are roughened, dress with fine sandpaper. If rings are contaminated, they may be cleaned with an alcohol saturated cloth.
2. Measure outside diameter of rings. Minimum diameter is 1.181 inches.
3. Check resistance of rotor coil across slip rings, Fig. 2. Ohmmeter should read 4.2 ohms at 68 degrees F.
4. Check for continuity across slip ring and rotor core or shaft, Fig. 3. If continuity exists, replace parts as necessary.
5. Check front and rear ball bearings for binding or abnormal noise and replace as necessary.

Stator Winding Test

1. Check for continuity across stator coils, Fig. 4. If there is no continuity, replace coils.
2. Measure resistance across coil and terminal N. Ohmmeter should read .05 ohms at 68 degrees F.
3. Check for continuity across one of the stator coils and stator core, Fig. 5. If continuity exists, replace coil.

Brushes, Inspect

Measure length of brushes. Standard brush length is .787 inch and minimum length is .551 inch. Brushes are marked with a line to indicate wear limit.

Fig. 2 Testing rotor & slip rings for open circuit

Fig. 3 Testing rotor & slip rings for grounds

Disassembly order

1. Vacuum pump
2. Cover
3. Brush
4. Through bolt
5. Pulley assembly
6. Pulley nut
7. Pulley
8. Fan
9. Rotor assembly
10. Spacer
11. Ball bearing
12. Rotor
13. Front cover assembly
14. Front cover
15. Ball bearing
16. Bearing retainer
17. Screw
18. Terminal bolt and nut
19. Condenser
20. Rear cover
21. Stator
22. Diode
23. Holder plate
24. Brush holder
25. IC regulator assembly
26. Lead wire

▲ See disassembly procedures for details.

Fig. 1 Hitachi LR155-12B alternator

Fig. 4 Testing stator coils for open circuit

Fig. 5   Testing stator coils for grounds

Diode Test

1. Check for continuity across terminals, Fig. 6. If continuity exists, diode is satisfactory. If there is no continuity, replace diode.
2. Check for continuity with polarities reversed. If there is no continuity, diode is satisfactory. If there is continuity at any point, replace diode.

NOTE: Auxiliary diodes are not provided with terminal and a continuity test should be made across terminals of conventional diodes.

Regulator Test

NOTE: To perform regulator tests, the following measuring instruments will be needed: resistor (10 ohms, 3 watts).... R1, variable resistor (0–300 ohms, 3 watts).... Rv, battery (12 volts, 2 pieces).... BAT1, BAT2, DC voltmeter (0–30 volts).

1. Connect instruments as shown in Fig. 7.
2. Measure voltage at BAT1 (V1). Voltmeter reading should be 10–13 volts.
3. Measure voltage between terminals F and E (V2). Voltmeter reading should be approximately 2 volts.

Fig. 8   Testing IC regulator

U.V.W. INDICATES STATOR COIL LEAD TERMINALS

Fig. 6   Testing diodes

4. Measure voltage between BAT1 and BAT2 (V3) with terminal S disconnected. Voltmeter reading should be 20–26 volts.
5. Measure voltage between terminals E and F while varying resistance gradually with variable resistor. Voltage should increase from 2 volts to 10–13 volts without any interruption. If voltage increase is interrupted, replace regulator.
6. Measure voltage between intermediate tap on variable resistor and terminal E (V4) without actuating variable resistor. Voltmeter should read 14.0–14.6 volts, or regulator must be replaced.
7. Connect instruments as shown in Fig. 8.
8. Measure voltage between terminals B and E while gradually increasing voltage with variable resistor. Voltage should increase from approximately 2 volts to 10–13 volts. If voltage does not vary, replace regulator.
9. Check voltage between intermediate tap of variable resistor and terminal E without actuating variable resistor. Voltmeter should read 14.5–16.6 volts, or regulator must be replaced.

Vacuum Pump, Inspect

1. Measure length of vanes. Vanes should measure .511–.531 inch, or must be replaced.
2. Measure inside diameter of pump housing. Diameter should be 2.2440–2.2441 inches.
3. Apply light pressure to check valve with a screwdriver and ensure smooth operation of valve.
4. Inspect inner face of rear cover for signs of

Fig. 7   Testing IC regulator

oil leakage and inspect oil seal for excessive wear or damage.
5. If rear seal requires replacement, remove old seal from rear cover side with a screwdriver and install new seal with seal installer, Fig. 9.

ALTERNATOR, ASSEMBLE FIG. 1

1. Solder the IC regulator wires to the IC regulator, Fig. 1.
2. Using long-nose pliers as a heatsink and working as quickly as possible, solder stator coil leads and diode leads.
3. Clamp the rotor in a suitable vise, install front cover, pulley and pulley nut.
4. Install rear cover over rotor, remove tape on splines. Insert and tighten through bolts.
5. Install brushes into brush holder, and install brush cover.
6. Install vacuum pump. Torque bolts to 4–5 ft. lbs. If necessary, pour approximately 5 cc of engine oil into the vacuum pump filler port.

Fig. 9   Replacing vacuum pump oil seal

UNIVERSAL JOINTS

SERVICE NOTES

Before disassembling any universal joint, examine the assembly carefully and note the position of the grease fitting (if used). Also, be sure to mark the yokes with relation to the propeller shaft so they may be reassembled in the same relative position. Failure to observe these precautions may produce rough car operation which results in rapid wear and failure of parts, and place an unbalanced load on transmission, engine and rear axle.

When universal joints are disassembled for lubrication or inspection, and the old parts are to be reinstalled, special care must be exercised to avoid damage to universal joint spider or cross and bearing cups.

NOTE: Some late model cars use an injected nylon retainer on the universal joint bearings. When service is necessary, pressing the bearings out will sheer the nylon retainer. Replacement with the conventional steel snap ring type is then necessary.

CROSS & ROLLER TYPE

Figs. 1 and 2 illustrate typical examples of universal joints of this type. They all operate on the same principle and similar service and replacement procedures may be applied to all.

Disassembly

1. Remove snap rings (or retainer plates) that retain bearings in yoke and drive shaft.
2. Place U-joint in a vise.
3. Select a wrench socket with an outside diameter slightly smaller than the U-joint bearings. Select another wrench socket with an inside diameter slightly larger than the U-joint bearings.
4. Place the sockets at opposite bearings in

Fig. 1 Cross and roller type universal joint. Chrysler-built cars

the yoke so that the smaller socket becomes a bearing pusher and the larger socket becomes a bearing receiver when the vise jaws come together, Fig. 3. Close vise jaws until both bearings are free of yoke and remove bearings from the cross or spider.
5. If bearings will not come all the way out, close vise until bearing in receiver socket protrudes from yoke as much as possible without using excessive force. Then remove from vise and place that portion of

bearing which protrudes from yoke between vise jaws. Tighten vise to hold bearing and drive yoke off with a soft hammer.
6. To remove opposite bearing from yoke, replace in vise with pusher socket on exposed cross journal with receiver socket over bearing cup. Then tighten vise jaws to press bearing back through yoke into receiving socket.
7. Remove yoke from drive shaft and again place protruding portion of bearing be-

Fig. 2 Cross and roller universal joints & propeller shaft (Typical)

Fig. 3   Removing bearings from yoke using small and large wrench sockets as pusher and receiver tools, respectively

Fig. 4   Installing bearings into drive shaft yoke

Fig. 5   Some units have locating lugs which must face propeller shaft when installed

tween vise jaws. Then tighten vise to hold bearing while driving yoke off bearing with soft hammer.
8. Turn spider or cross 1/4 turn and use the same procedure to press bearings out of drive shaft.

Reassembly

1. If old parts are to be reassembled, pack bearing cups with universal joint grease. *Do not fill cups completely or use excessive amounts as over-lubrication may damage seals during reassembly.* Use new seals.
2. If new parts are being installed, check new bearings for adequate grease before assembling.
3. With the pusher (smaller) socket, press one bearing part way into drive shaft. Position spider into the partially installed bearing. Place second bearing into drive shaft. Fasten drive shaft in vise so that bearings are in contact with faces of vise jaws, Fig. 4. *Some spiders are provided with locating lugs which must face toward drive shaft when installed, Fig. 5.*
4. Press bearings all the way into position and install snap rings or retainer plates.
5. Install bearings in yoke in same manner. When installation is completed, check U-joint for binding or roughness. If free movement is impeded, correct the condition before installation in vehicle.

CONSTANT VELOCITY TYPE

This type of U-joint, Fig. 6, is composed of two conventional cross and roller joints connected with a special link joint. Because the two joint angles are the same, even though the usual U-joint fluctuation is present within the unit, the acceleration of the front joint (within the yoke) is always neutralized by the deceleration of the rear joint (within the yoke) and vice versa. The end result is the front and rear propeller shafts always turn at a constant velocity.

Disassemble Constant Velocity U-Joint
1. Mark yokes before disassembly to be sure reassembly is made in same relative posi-

tion of components, Fig. 7.
2. Disassemble rear section of constant velocity U-joint first as follows:
3. Remove snap rings from bearings using a punch.
4. Place rear propeller shaft yoke in a vise. Shaft must be supported horizontally and link yoke must be free to move vertically, Fig. 8.
5. Using a pipe coupling or a wrench socket with the inside diameter slightly larger than outside diameter of bearing, Fig. 8, drive link yoke downward until about 1/4" of bearing projects from yoke. *Do not attempt to drive yoke down farther than ball socket will allow easily.*
6. Rotate shaft 180 degrees and repeat Steps 3, 4 and 5.
7. Clamp 1/4" projecting portion of either bearing in vise and remove bearing by driving link yoke upward. Remove other bearing in same manner, Fig. 9.
8. Separate spider, shaft yoke and shaft from link yoke.
9. To remove bearings from shaft yoke, clamp spider in vise with its jaws bearing against ends of spider journals. Yoke must be free to move vertically between jaws of vise.
10. Using the same bearing remover tool as in Step 5, apply force on shaft yoke around bearing. Drive yoke downward until bearing is free of yoke.

Centering Ball Replacement
1. With CV joint disassembled, position inner part of tool J-23677 on centering ball, Fig. 10.
2. Install outer cylinder of tool J-23677 over inner part, thread nut onto tool and pull centering ball off stud.
3. Place replacement ball on stud and using a suitable tool, drive ball onto stud until it seats firmly against shoulder at base of stud.
4. Assemble ball seats and related parts into ball cavity as shown in Fig. 11. All parts must be adequately lubricated with lubricant provided with kit.
5. Lubricate centering ball seal with approved lubricant and install with sealing lip tipping inward. Fill ball cavity with lubricant.

Reassemble Constant Velocity U-Joint
All yokes must be carefully assembled using the marks made before disassembly for reference. Assemble front section of constant velocity joint first.

1. Position spider inside splined yoke. Install bearings by pressing between vise jaws. Make sure that spider journals enter bearings squarely to avoid damage, Fig. 12.
2. Fully install bearings and install snap rings.
3. Position splined yoke and spider inside link yoke and install bearings into link yoke in same manner as for splined yoke.
4. Position spider inside rear propeller shaft yoke and install bearings.
5. Lubricate ball and socket with a high grade of extreme pressure grease.
6. Position spider of rear propeller shaft assembly in link yoke.
7. Engage socket with ball of splined yoke assembly. *Make sure that all reference marks are properly aligned.*
8. Install bearings into link yoke in same manner as above while holding spring loaded ball and socket assembly together to make sure that spider journals enter bearing squarely.

1977 Lincoln

These vehicles incorporate a double cardan type constant velocity joint at each end of the drive shaft, Fig. 13. Each double cardan has a center yoke (cage), a centering socket yoke and a stud yoke which is welded to each end of the tube assembly. The splines on the yoke and transmission output shaft permit the drive shaft to move in and out as the axle moves up and down. All drive shaft assemblies are balanced and should be kept free of undercoating.

Disassembly
1. Mark location of spiders, center yoke and centering socket yoke as related to stud yoke.

NOTE: The spiders must be assembled with bosses in their original position to provide proper clearance.

2. Remove snap rings that secure bearings in front of center yoke, then position tool, Fig. 14, and thread clockwise until bearing protrudes about 3/8 inch out of yoke.
3. Remove drive shaft from vise and tighten bearing in vise then tap the center yoke,

Fig. 6   Cross-section of typical GM constant velocity U-joint

Fig. 8   Driving bearing from link yoke

Fig. 9   Removing bearing

Fig. 7   Marking constant velocity joint

Fig. 15, to free it from bearing.

4. Remove the two bearings from the spider, Fig. 16, then reposition the tool on the yoke and move the remaining bearing in the opposite direction so that it protrudes about ³⁄₈ inch out the yoke.
5. Grip bearing in a vise, then drive the center yoke freeing it from bearing, Fig. 15, and remove spider from center yoke.
6. Pull centering socket yoke off center stud, Fig. 17, then remove rubber seal from centering ball stud.
7. Remove the snap rings from center and drive shaft yokes, then position tool on drive shaft yoke, Fig. 18, and press bearing outward until inside of center yoke almost contacts the slinger ring at the front of the drive shaft yoke.

NOTE: Pressing beyond this point can distort the slinger ring. Fig. 19 shows the interference point.

8. Clamp exposed end of bearing in a vise and drive the center yoke with a soft face hammer freeing it from bearing, then reposition tool and press on spider to remove opposite bearing.
9. Remove center yoke from spider and remove spider from drive shaft yoke in same manner.
10. Clean all serviceable parts in cleaning solvent. If using a repair kit, use all parts supplied in kit. If driveshaft is damaged, it should be replaced to insure a balanced assembly.

Assembly

1. Position spider in shaft yoke making sure

Fig. 10   Removing centering ball with tool J-23677

that spider bosses (or lubrication plugs) will be in original position. Press in bearing cups and install snap rings.
2. Position center yoke over spider ends then press in bearing cups and install snap rings.
3. Install new seal on centering stud and position centering socket yoke on stud.
4. Place front spider in center yoke making sure that spider bosses (or lubrication plugs) are properly positioned. Press in bearing cups and install snap rings.
5. Applying pressure on centering socket, install remaining bearing cup.
6. If using a repair kit, remove plug from each spider and lubricate universal joints. Reinstall plug.

1977–80 Versailles

These models use a one-piece driveshaft with a constant velocity universal joint between the driveshaft and companion flange, Fig. 20.

Disassembly

1. Mark relative positions of the spiders, center yoke and centering socket yoke to the companion flange.
2. Install tool CJ91B, Fig. 14. Thread tool

clockwise until bearing protrudes approximately ³⁄₈ inch from yoke.
3. Remove driveshaft from vise.
4. Tighten the bearing in a vise and tap on yoke to free bearing from center yoke, Fig. 15. Do not tap on driveshaft tube.

Fig. 11   Centering ball assembly

5. Repeat steps 2 through 4 on remaining bearings.
6. Remove spider from center yoke.
7. Remove bearings from driveshaft yoke as outlined in steps 2 through 4. Remove spider from yoke.
8. Insert a screwdriver into centering ball socket, located in companion flange, and pry out rubber seal. Remove retainer, three piece ball seat, washer and spring from ball socket.

Assembly

1. Inspect centering ball socket assembly for worn or damaged components and replace the assembly if necessary.
2. Insert spring, washer, three piece ball seat and retainer into ball socket.
3. With a suitable tool, install centering ball socket seal.
4. Place spider in driveshaft yoke. Ensure that spider bosses are in the original posi-

Fig. 12   Installing bearings

Fig. 14   Partially pressing bearing from center yoke

Fig. 13   Constant velocity type universal joint 1977 Lincoln

Fig. 15   Removing bearing from center yoke

Fig. 16   Removing bearing cup from spider

UNIVERSAL JOINTS

Fig. 17   Removing center socket yoke

Fig. 18   Removing bearing from rear of center yoke

Fig. 19   Center yoke interference point

Fig. 20   Constant velocity universal joint, 1977-80 Versailles

tion. Press in bearing cups with tool CJ91B. Install snap rings.
5. Place center yoke over spider ends and press in bearing cups. Install snap rings.
6. Install spider in companion flange yoke. Ensure that spider bosses are in original positions. Press on bearing cups and install snap rings.
7. Place center yoke over spider ends and press in bearing cups. Install snap rings.

1978-79 Lincoln, Fig. 21

NOTE: Refer to the "General Motors, Centering Ball Replacement" procedure for centering ball service.

Disassembly

1. Mark position of all yokes so that original positions can be maintained during assembly.
2. Support driveshaft in a suitable vise.
3. Install tool CJ91B, Fig. 14. Tighten tool clockwise until the plastic retaining the bearing is sheared and the bearing protrudes approximately 3/8 inch from yoke.
4. Remove driveshaft from vise and tighten bearing in vise, then tap the center yoke, Fig. 15, to free yoke from bearing.
5. Repeat steps 2 through 4 on opposite bearing.
6. Remove remainder of the sheared plastic retaining rings from the grooves in the yokes. The sheared plastic may prevent the bearing cups from being properly pressed in place and seated.

Assembly

1. Ensure all alignment marks are properly positioned, then partially install one bearing cup into yoke.
2. Insert spider into yoke so the journal seats freely into bearing cup.
3. Partially install opposite bearing cup.
4. With tool CJ91B, press both bearing cups into yoke. Move the spider when pressing in the bearing cups. If any binding is felt, check the needle bearings.
5. When one of the retaining ring grooves clears the inside of the yoke, install the retaining ring.
6. Press in the remaining bearing cup until the retaining ring can be installed. If difficulty is encountered, tap the yoke with a hammer to aid in seating the retaining rings.

Fig. 21 Drive shaft and universal joints exploded view. 1978–79 Lincoln

1980–82 Cougar XR7 & Thunderbird, Fig. 22

Disassembly

1. Mark position of all yokes so that original position can be maintained during assembly.
2. Support driveshaft in suitable vise.
3. Remove two snap rings that secure rear spider bearing to center yoke.
4. Install tool T74P-4635-C, Fig. 23. Tighten tool until bearing cup extends approximately 3/8 inch from yoke.
5. Remove driveshaft from vise and grip bearing cup in vise. Tap on center yoke to free bearing from yoke.
6. Repeat steps 2 through 5 on opposite bearing.
7. Pull flanged center socket yoke off center stud.
8. Remove spider from flanged center socket yoke following steps 2 through 5.
9. Remove snap rings from center yoke and studs. Install tool T74P-4635-C on drive-shaft stud yoke and press bearing cup outward until inside of center yoke almost contacts slinger ring attached to stud yoke. Grip protruding bearing cup in vise and tap on yoke center to remove. Repeat this step on opposite bearing.

Assembly

1. Install front spider in driveshaft stud yoke. Press in bearing cups using tool T74P-4635-C and install snap rings.
2. Install center yoke over spider ends and

Fig. 22 Drive shaft and universal joint exploded view. 1980–82 Cougar & Thunderbird

UNIVERSAL JOINTS

press in bearing cup assemblies using tool T74P-4635-C. Install snap rings.

3. Install rear spider in flanged center socket yoke and press in bearing cup assemblies using tool T74P-4635-C. Install snap rings.

4. Pack inside of ball with ESW-MIC147-A and place centering spring inside ball

stud yoke.

5. Assemble flanged center socket yoke to ball stud and center yoke by guiding ball onto stud while flexing spider in flange. Press in center yoke bearing cup assemblies using tool T74P-4635-C. Install snap rings.

6. Rap center yoke to free joint.

7. Remove grease plug from each spider and lubricate all U-joints with ESW-M1C147-A. Install plugs.

NOTE: Flush type grease fittings are required to insure proper clearance during normal vehicle operation.

DISC BRAKES

CONTENTS

Fig. 1   Checking rotor for lateral runout

SERVICE PRECAUTIONS

Brake Shoes, Linings & Calipers

Remove wheels and inspect brake disc, caliper and linings. The wheel bearings should be inspected at this time and repacked if necessary. Do not get any grease on the linings.

On all models except Chevrolet Corvette, and Chrysler front wheel drive models, the brake shoe and lining assemblies should be replaced if the lining is worn to within 1/32 inch of rivet heads (riveted linings) or brake shoe (bonded linings). On Chevrolet Corvette, the brake shoe and lining assemblies should be replaced when the lining is the approximate thickness of the brake shoe. On Chrysler front wheel drive models, the brake shoe and lining assemblies should be replaced when the combined thickness of the shoe and lining is 5/16 inch or less. It is recommended that both front and/or rear wheel sets be replaced whenever a respective shoe and lining assembly is replaced.

If a visual inspection does not adequately determine the condition of the linings, the brake shoe and lining assemblies should be removed and inspected. If shoes do not require replacement, reinstall them in their original positions. Brake shoes and linings should also be replaced if cracked or damaged.

If the caliper is cracked or fluid leakage through the casting is evident, it must be replaced as a unit.

Brake Roughness

The most common cause of brake chatter on disc brakes is a variation in thickness of the disc. If roughness or vibration is encountered during highway operation or if pedal pumping

is experienced at low speeds, the disc may have excessive thickness variation. To check for this condition, measure the disc at 12 points with a micrometer at a radius approximately one inch from edge of disc. If thickness measurements vary by more than .0005″, the disc should be replaced with a new one.

Excessive lateral runout of braking disc may cause a "knocking back" of the pistons, possibly creating increased pedal travel and vibration when brakes are applied.

Before checking the runout, wheel bearings should be adjusted. The readjustment is very important and will be required at the completion of the test to prevent bearing failure. Be sure to make the adjustment according to the recommendations given under *Front Wheel Bearings, Adjust* in the car chapters.

Brake Disc Service

Servicing of disc brakes is extremely critical due to the close tolerances required in machining the brake disc to insure proper brake operation.

The maintenance of these close controls of the shape of the rubbing surfaces is necessary to prevent brake roughness. In addition, the surface finish must be non-directional and maintained at a micro inch finish. This close control of the rubbing surface finish is necessary to avoid pulls and erratic performance and promote long lining life and equal lining wear of both left and right brakes.

In light of the foregoing remarks, refinishing of the rubbing surfaces should not be attempted unless precision equipment, capable of measuring in micro inches (millionths of an inch) is available.

To check lateral runout of a disc, mount a dial indicator on a convenient part (steering knuckle, tie rod, disc brake caliper housing) so that the plunger of the dial indicator contacts the disc at a point one inch from the outer edge, Fig. 1. If the total indicated runout exceeds specifications, install a new disc.

To check parallelism (thickness variation), mount dial indicators, Fig. 2, so the plunger contacts rotor approximately 1 inch from outer edge. If parellelism exceeds specifications, replace rotor.

General Precautions

1. Grease or any other foreign material must be kept off the caliper, surfaces of the disc and external surfaces of the hub,

Fig. 2   Checking rotor parallelism (Thickness variation)

during service procedures. Handling the brake disc and caliper should be done in a way to avoid deformation of the disc and nicking or scratching brake linings.

2. If inspection reveals rubber piston seals are worn or damaged, they should be replaced immediately.
3. During removal and installation of a wheel assembly, exercise care so as not to interfere with or damage the caliper splash shield, or bleeder screw.
4. Front wheel bearings should be adjusted to specifications.
5. Be sure vehicle is centered on hoist before servicing any of the front end components to avoid bending or damaging the disc splash shield on full right or left wheel turns.
6. Before the vehicle is moved after any brake service work, be sure to obtain a firm brake pedal.
7. The assembly bolts of the two caliper housings should not be disturbed unless the caliper requires service.

Inspection of Caliper

Should it become necessary to remove the caliper for installation of new parts, clean all parts in alcohol, wipe dry using lint-free

Fig. 3   Honing caliper piston bore

Fig. 4   Gauge hook-up for testing proportioning valve (typical)

CALIPER ANCHOR PLATE

SPINDLE

CALIPER

SPRING

SCREW

CLIP

INBOARD BRAKESHOE

SUPPORT KEY

SEAL

DUST SEAL

SEAL

PISTON

OUTBOARD BRAKESHOE

NUT

NUT LOCK

WASHER

RACE

BEARING

RACE

BEARING

COTTER PIN

SEAL

GREASE CUP

HUB AND ROTOR

SPLASH SHIELD

BEARING

Fig. 5 Bendix sliding caliper disc brake (Typical)

cloths. Using an air hose, blow out drilled passages and bores. Check dust boots for punctures or tears. If punctures or tears are evident, new boots should be installed upon reassembly.

Inspect piston bores in both housings for scoring or pitting. Bores that show light scratches or corrosion can usually be cleaned with crocus cloth. However, bores that have deep scratches or scoring may be honed, provided the diameter of the bore is not increased more than .002". If the bore does not clean up within this specification, a new caliper housing should be installed (black stains on the bore walls are caused by piston seals and will do no harm).

When using a hone, Fig. 3, be sure to install the hone baffle before honing bore. The baffle is used to protect the hone stones from damage. Use extreme care in cleaning the caliper after honing. Remove all dust and grit by flushing the caliper with alcohol. Wipe dry with clean lint-less cloth and then clean a second time in the same manner.

Bleeding Disc Brakes

NOTE: Pressure bleeding is recommended for all hydraulic disc brake systems.

The disc brake hydraulic system can be bled manually or with pressure bleeding equipment. On vehicles with disc brakes the brake pedal will require more pumping and frequent checking of fluid level in master cylinder during bleeding operation.

Never use brake fluid that has been drained from hydraulic system when bleeding the brakes. Be sure the disc brake pistons are returned to their normal positions and that the shoe and lining assemblies are properly seated. Before driving the vehicle, check brake operation to be sure that a firm pedal has been obtained.

Proportioning Valve

The proportioning valve (when used), Fig. 4, provides balanced braking action between front and rear brakes under a wide range of braking conditions. The valve regulates the hydraulic pressure applied to the rear wheel cylinders, thus limiting rear braking action when high pressures are required at the front brakes. In this manner, premature rear wheel skid is prevented.

Testing Proportioning Valve

When a premature rear wheel slide is obtained on a brake application, it usually is an indication that the fluid pressure to the rear wheels is above the 50% reduction ratio for the rear line pressure and that malfunction has occured within the proportioning valve.

To test the valve, install gauge set shown in Fig. 4 in brake line between master cylinder and proportioning valve, and at output end of proportioning valve and brake line as shown. Be sure all joints are fluid tight.

Have a helper exert pressure on brake pedal (holding pressure). Obtain a reading on master cylinder output of approximately 700 psi. While pressure is being held as above, reading on valve outlet should be 550–610 psi. If the pressure readings do not meet these specifications, the valve should be removed and a new valve installed.

BENDIX SLIDING CALIPER

This sliding caliper disc brake assembly incorporates a hub and rotor assembly, caliper, brake shoes and linings, caliper anchor plate and a splash shield, Fig. 5.

Cooling fins are cast into the rotor between the two braking surfaces to ventilate and cool the rotor. The sliding caliper is positioned in, and slides on, the abutment surfaces on the leading and trailing edges of the caliper anchor plate. A caliper support key, located between the forward edge of the caliper and abutment surface, is secured with a retaining screw. A support spring is installed between the support key and caliper to maintain tension on the support key.

The caliper is a one-piece casting containing the piston, piston seal and dust seal, Fig. 6. The hydraulic seal between the caliper piston and piston bore is achieved by a square cut piston seal, located in a machined groove in the piston bore. The dust seal seats in a recess machined on the edge of the piston bore and into a groove in the caliper piston.

Caliper Removal

1. Siphon two-thirds of brake fluid from master cylinder reservoir serving front disc brakes.
2. Raise vehicle, support on jackstands and remove front wheels.
3. Bottom the caliper piston in bore. Insert a screwdriver between inboard shoe and piston, then pry piston back into bore. The piston can also be bottomed in the bore with a large "C" clamp.
4. Using a ¼ inch (1982, 7 mm) allen wrench, remove support key retaining screw, Fig. 7.
5. Drive caliper support key and spring from anchor plate with a suitable drift and hammer, Fig. 8.
6. Lift caliper from anchor plate and off rotor, Fig. 9. Hang caliper from coil spring with wire. Do not allow caliper to hang from brake hose.
7. Remove inboard brake shoe from anchor plate, then the anti-rattle spring from the brake shoe, Fig. 10. Remove teflon slipper plate from leading anchor abutment surface, if equipped.
8. Remove outboard brake shoe from caliper, Fig. 11. It may be necessary to loosen the brake shoe with a hammer to permit shoe removal.

Fig. 6 Caliper assembly

Fig. 7 Removing support key retaining screw

Caliper Disassembly

1. Drain brake fluid from caliper.
2. Position caliper with shop cloths, Fig. 12, and apply compressed air to fluid inlet port to ease piston from bore.

NOTE: Do not attempt to catch piston or to protect it when applying compressed air since personal injury is possible.

3. Remove dust seal from piston, then the piston seal from bore, Fig. 6. Use wooden or plastic tool to remove piston seal since metal tools may damage piston.
4. Remove bleeder screw.

Caliper Assembly

1. Coat square cut piston seal with clean brake fluid, then install seal into piston bore. Work seal into groove with clean fingers.
2. On 1977–81 models, install bleeder screw and plastic cap.

3. Lubricate dust seal and tool J-24387 with clean brake fluid, then place dust seal on tool, allowing 1/4 inch of tool to extend past small lip of dust seal, Fig. 13.
4. Place dust seal and tool over piston bore, then work large lip of dust seal into seal groove, Fig. 14. Ensure dust seal is fully seated.
5. Lubricate caliper piston and insert through tool. Center piston in bore and use a hammer handle to apply pressure to install piston halfway into bore, Fig. 14.

NOTE: On some models, disc brake caliper pistons may develop a light coating of rust under the dust seal and outboard of the piston seal. This rust may cause the piston to not fully retract. Before installing piston, apply a light coating of dielectric compound 8126688, or equivalent, to caliper piston bore, Fig. 14A.

6. Remove tool J-24387 and seat small lip of dust seal in caliper piston groove, then bottom piston in bore.

NOTE: On 1982 models, tool J-33028 is used to install dust seal.

Brake Shoe & Lining, Replace

The procedures to remove & install the brake shoe and lining assemblies are outlined under "caliper Removal" and "Caliper Installation". It is not necessary to disconnect the brake hose, however, use caution not to twist or kink hose.

Caliper Installation

1. Clean and lubricate abutment surfaces of caliper and the anchor plate with a suitable molydisulfide grease, Fig. 15.
2. Install inboard brake shoe anti-rattle

Fig. 8 Removing support key

Fig. 9 Removing or installing caliper

Fig. 10 Removing or installing inboard brake shoe

Fig. 11 Removing or installing outboard brake shoe

Fig. 12 Removing piston from caliper

Fig. 13. Dust seal & installer tool assembly

VIEW A

Fig. 14A Lubricating caliper piston bore

Fig. 15 Caliper & anchor plate abutment surfaces

VIEW B   A42886

Fig. 14 Installing dust seal & caliper piston

Fig. 16 Installing inboard brake shoe anti-rattle spring

Fig. 17 Single piston disc brake assembly

spring on brake shoe rear flange, ensure looped section of clip is facing away from rotor, Fig. 16. Install teflon slipper plate on leading anchor abutment surface, if equipped.

3. Install inboard brake shoe on caliper anchor plate, Fig. 10.
4. Install outboard brake shoe in caliper, Fig. 11. Ensure the shoe flange is seated fully into outboard arms or caliper. It may be necessary to use a hammer to seat the shoe.
5. Place caliper assembly over rotor and position in caliper anchor plate. Ensure dust boot is not torn or mispositioned by inboard brake shoe during caliper installation.
6. Align caliper with anchor plate abutment surfaces, then insert support key and spring between abutment surfaces, then insert support key and spring between abutment surfaces at the trailing end of caliper and anchor plate. With a hammer and brass drift, drive caliper support key and spring into position, then install and torque support key retaining screw to 15 ft. lbs.
7. Refill master cylinder to within 1/4" of rim. Press brake pedal several times to seat shoes.
8. Install front wheels and lower vehicle.

Fig. 18   Delco-Moraine single piston disc brake with single mounting bolt

Fig. 19   Removing mounting bracket from steering knuckle

DELCO-MORAINE SINGLE PISTON

w/Single Mounting Bolt

This single piston sliding caliper assembly, Figs. 17 and 18, incorporates a one piece housing with the inboard side of the housing bored for the piston. A seal within the housing bore provides a hydraulic seal between the piston and housing wall.

A spring steel scraper (wear sensor) is incorporated on each inboard shoe. When shoe lining has worn to within .030 inch of the shoe, the sensor scrapes the rotor and emits an audible high frequency sound indicating that the linings should be replaced.

The caliper assembly slides on a mounting sleeve which is secured by a mounting bolt. Upon brake application fluid pressure against the piston forces the inboard shoe against the inboard side of the rotor. This action causes the caliper to slide until the outboard shoe comes in contact with the rotor.

Caliper Removal

1. Siphon brake fluid from master cylinder to bring level to ⅓ full, discard brake fluid removed.
2. Raise vehicle and remove wheel and tire assembly.
3. Install a 7 inch C-clamp on caliper with solid end of clamp on caliper housing and screw end on metal portion of outboard brake shoe. Tighten clamp until piston bottoms in caliper bore, then remove clamp.
4. Disconnect brake hose from caliper and remove copper gaskets, cap end of brake hose.

NOTE: If only brake shoes are to be replaced do not disconnect brake hose.

---

5. Remove the two mounting brackets to steering knuckle bolts, Fig. 19.

NOTE: Do not remove socket head retaining bolt. Support caliper when removing second bolt to prevent caliper from falling.

---

6. Slide caliper from rotor.

Fig. 20   Bracket assembly installed on caliper

Fig. 21   Removing and installing cushions

Fig. 22   Removing piston boot

Fig. 23   Installing boot on caliper

DISC BRAKES

NOTE: If only brake shoes are to be replaced support caliper from suspension using wire. Do not stretch or kink brake hose.

Brake Shoe Removal

1. Remove caliper as described under "Caliper Removal".
2. Remove brake shoes, if retaining spring does not come off with inboard shoe remove it from piston.

Caliper Disassembly

1. Using clean brake fluid clean exterior of caliper.
2. Drain brake fluid from caliper.
3. Remove caliper mounting bracket bolt and slide bracket from caliper, Fig. 20, then remove sleeve and bushing from bolt and bushing from caliper mounting hole, Fig. 18.
4. Remove clips if still in place, then remove cushions, Fig. 21.
5. Pad interior of caliper with clean shop towels, then direct compressed air through caliper inlet hole to remove piston.

NOTE: Use only enough air pressure to ease piston out of bore.

CAUTION: Do not place fingers in front of piston for any reason when applying compressed air. This could result in serious personal injury.

6. Using a screwdriver carefully pry boot from caliper, Fig. 22.
7. Remove piston seal from caliper bore using a piece of wood or plastic.

NOTE: Do not use metal tool to remove piston seal as it may damage caliper bore.

8. Remove bleeder valve.

Caliper Assembly

1. Lubricate caliper bore and piston seal with clean brake fluid, then position seal in caliper bore groove.
2. Lubricate piston with clean brake fluid and install boot into piston groove with fold facing the open end of piston, Fig. 18.
3. Insert piston into caliper, then using care to avoid unseating seal, force piston into caliper.

NOTE: To force piston into caliper a force of 50–100 pounds will be required.

4. Position outside diameter of boot into caliper counterbore and seat with suitable boot installer. Fig. 23.

CAUTION: Ensure that retaining ring molded into boot is not bent and that boot is installed fully and evenly below and around the caliper, as dirt and moisture may enter caliper and cause damage and corrosion.

5. Install bleeder screw.

Fig. 24 Fitting brake pad to caliper

6. Position and stretch cushions over caliper lugs, fitting the heavy section in the lug recess and saw-tooth edges of cushions facing out, Fig. 21.
7. Using silicone lubricant, liberally lubricate sleeve and bushings and the unthreaded portion of the retainer bolt. Install the larger bushing in the caliper hole groove and install the sleeve. Install the smaller bushing in the retainer bolt groove.
8. With caliper clamped in a vise, position clips over cushions and squeeze mounting bracket over clips, aligning the bolt hole. Move bracket against retainer boss on caliper and install retainer bolt. Torque bolt to 28 ft. lbs., (38 N-m).

NOTE: Considerable force may be required to squeeze bracket over cushions and clips on caliper. Start open end of bracket over ends of clips near the boot and move the bracket toward the closed end of caliper.

Brake Shoes Installation

1. Position retaining spring on inboard shoe, place single leg in brake shoe hole, then snap two other legs over notch in shoe.

NOTE: Some inboard replacement brake pads incorporate wear sensors and have a specific left and right hand assembly. Properly installed, the wear sensor will face toward the rear of caliper.

2. Install shoe in caliper.
3. Position caliper over rotor, align mounting holes, install and torque bolts to 70 ft. lbs., (95 N-m).
4. Using suitable pliers clinch outboard shoe to caliper, place lower jaw of pliers on bottom edge of shoe, place upper jaw of pliers on shoe tab, squeeze pliers and bend tab, Fig. 24. Clinch other end of shoe in same manner. Outboard end play should be zero to .005 inch., (zero to 0.127 mm).
5. Install wheel and tire assembly and lower vehicle.
6. Add brake fluid to within ¼ inch from top of master cylinder.

NOTE: Pump brake pedal several times to ensure it is firm before moving vehicle.

Caliper Installation

1. Install caliper as described under "Brake Shoe Installation", then install brake hose with new copper gaskets, torque fitting to 21 ft. lbs., (29 N-m), if removed, bleed brake system.

NOTE: Brake hose fitting must be against machined surface on caliper to ensure proper hose positioning.

DELCO-MORAINE OPPOSED PISTONS

These brakes are used on all four wheels. The components of the disc brake system are shown in Fig. 25. The caliper assemblies replace the conventional wheel cylinder, brake shoes and linings, and the disc replaces the brake drum.

The caliper assembly contains four pistons, two acting on each shoe with one shoe on each side of the disc.

Fig. 25 Delco-Moraine opposed piston disc brake assembly

Fig. 26   Delco-Moraine parking brake components

The brake disc is riveted to the hub flange at the front wheel and to the spindle flange at the rear wheel. The disc rotates through the caliper assembly, which is bolted to a support that is attached to the steering knuckle at the front wheel and the spindle support bolts at the rear wheel. The disc has cooling fins between the two shoe reacting surfaces. When a disc must be replaced, the rivets can be drilled out and then the wheel studs will be used for disc retention purposes.

A miniature set of brake shoes, mounted on a flange plate and shield assembly attached to the rear wheel spindle support bolts, are used for vehicle parking, Fig. 26.

Removing Lining

1. To prevent overflow, remove two thirds of brake fluid from master cylinder.
2. Support vehicle on hoist and remove wheel.
3. Remove cotter pin from inboard end of retaining pin.
4. Remove inboard and outboard shoe by pulling up.

Installing Lining

1. Install inboard and outboard shoe one at a time. Use two screwdrivers to push pistons back as shoes are inserted, Fig. 27.
2. Install retaining pin through outboard caliper half, outboard shoe, inboard shoe and inboard caliper half. Insert a new $^3/_{32} \times {^5/_8}$ inch plated cotter pin through retaining pin.
3. Repeat above procedure at each wheel where shoes are to be replaced.
4. Refill master cylinder, then install wheel and lower vehicle.

CAUTION: Do not move vehicle until a firm brake pedal has been obtained.

Calipers

The caliper assembly, Fig. 28, incorporates two halves retained by bolts at the flange end. The two halves contain fluid crossover passages from one to the other, sealed with "O" rings.

The bleeder screw is threaded into a passage drilled to intersect the fluid crossover passage. The bleeder screws are located at the front of each caliper. There are two bleeder screws, one inboard, one outboard at the rear wheels, and one bleeder screw at the inboard side at the front wheel. It is necessary, therefore, to remove the rear wheel when bleeding the rear caliper.

Removing Caliper

1. Support vehicle on hoist and remove wheel.
2. On front caliper, disconnect brake hose from support bracket. On rear caliper, disconnect tubing from inboard caliper. Tape open tube or line end to prevent entry of dirt.
3. Remove caliper mounting bolts and remove caliper.

Disassembling Caliper

1. Remove brake hose from front caliper.
2. Remove cotter pin from retaining pin, then remove pin and shoe assembly from caliper.
3. Remove caliper retaining bolts and sepa-

Fig. 27   Installing Delco Moraine disc brake shoes

rate caliper halves, then remove the two O-rings from fluid transfer cavities in ends of caliper halves.

4. Push piston into caliper as far as it will move, then insert a screwdriver under inner edge of steel ring in boot and using piston as a fulcrum, pry piston boot from its seat in caliper half.

CAUTION: Use care not to puncture seal when removing pistons from caliper.

5. Remove pistons and springs from caliper half, then remove boot and seal from piston.

Cleaning & Inspection

1. Clean all metal parts using clean brake fluid, removing all traces of dirt and grease.

CAUTION: Never use mineral base cleaning solvents as they can cause deterioration of rubber parts or make them soft and swollen.

2. Using air pressure, blow out all fluid passages in caliper halves, making sure that these passages are not obstructed.
3. Discard all rubber parts and replace with new service kit parts.
4. Inspect piston bores. They must be free of scores and pits. A damaged bore will cause leaks and unsatisfactory brake operation. If either caliper half is damaged to the extent that polishing with fine crocus cloth will not restore to satisfactory condition, replace the caliper half.
5. Check fit of piston in bore using a feeler gauge. Clearance should be as follows:
   1 $^7/_8$ inch bore   .0045–.010
   1 $^3/_8$ inch bore   .0035–.009
   If bore is not damaged and clearance exceeds specifications, only a new piston will be required.

Assembling Caliper

1. Install seal in piston groove which is closest to flat end of piston. The seal lip must face toward large end of piston.

NOTE: Make certain seal lips are in

Fig. 28   Delco-Moraine disc brake caliper components

Fig. 29   Installing piston in caliper

piston groove and do not extend over step in end of groove.

2. Place spring in piston bore, then lubricate seal with brake fluid.
3. Install piston assembly in bore using tool J-22591, 22629 or 22639, Fig. 29. Use care not to damage seal lip as piston is pressed past edge of bore.
4. Install piston boot in groove closest to concave end of piston with fold in boot facing toward end of piston with seal attached.

NOTE: On 1979–82 models, apply a bead of suitable sealer (GM 1052366 or equivalent into piston boot groove, then install boot into groove.

5. Make certain that piston slides smoothly into bore until end of piston is flush with end of bore. If not, recheck piston assembly and position of piston spring and seal.
6. Using boot seal installer tool J-22592, J-22628 or J-22638, Fig. 30, over piston, seat steel boot retaining ring evenly into counterbore.

NOTE: Boot retaining ring must be flush or below machined face of caliper. Any distortion or uneven seating could allow corrosive elements to enter bore. On 1979–82 models, push pistons into bore fully and hold in place. Apply a bead of suitable sealer (GM 1052366 or equivalent) onto outer edge of boot retaining ring to form a seal between retaining ring and caliper housing.

7. Install O-rings in cavities around brake fluid transfer holes at both ends of outboard caliper halves. Lubricate caliper bolts with Delco Brake Lube #540032 (or equivalent) or clean brake fluid, then secure caliper halves together and torque front caliper housing bolts to 130 ft. lbs. and rear caliper housing bolts to 60 ft. lbs.

Installing Caliper

1. Mount caliper over disc, then using two screwdrivers, depress pistons so that caliper can be lowered into place.

NOTE: Use care not to damage boots on edge of disc as caliper is installed.

2. Install mounting bolts and torque to 70 ft. lbs.

CAUTION: If reusing old shoe assemblies, be sure to install shoes in same location

from which removed.

3. Install disc pads as outlined previously.
4. Place a new copper gasket on male end of front wheel brake hose and install brake hose in calipers. With wheels straight ahead, pass female end of hose through support bracket, then making certain that tube seat is clean, connect brake line tube nut to caliper and tighten securely.
5. Allowing hose to seek a normal position, without twist, insert hose fitting in support bracket and secure with "U" shaped retainer, then while turning steering geometry from stop to stop, check that hose does not contact other parts at anytime. If contact does occur, remove "U" shaped retainer and twist hose in a direction that will eliminate hose contact. Reinstall retainer and recheck for hose contact. If satisfactory, place steel tube connecter in hose fitting and tighten securely.
6. If rear caliper is being serviced, connect brake line to caliper.
7. Bleed brakes and install wheels.

CAUTION: Do not move vehicle until a firm pedal has been obtained.

Service Summary

1. There is no brake shoe adjustment on the disc brakes.
2. The groove in the brake shoe is an indicator of brake wear. When the groove is just about gone it is time for shoe replacement.
3. When replacing shoes it is necessary to siphon fluid from master cylinder reservoir to make room for fluid to return to the reservoir when pushing the caliper pistons back into their bores to make room for the thickness of the new shoes.
4. The shoes have a directional arrow on the back of the shoe plate. This arrow points to the forward rotation of the disc, and the purpose is for aligning the grain of the lining material in relation to the disc.
5. When bleeding the calipers, the rear wheel must be removed to reach the outboard bleeder screw.
6. A retaining clip of thin metal is used to hold the pistons into the bores while installing the new brake shoes.
7. The caliper assembly is removable, after disconnecting the brake line, by remov-

Fig. 31   Kelsey-Hayes floating caliper single piston disc brake (typical)

Fig. 30   Installing boot seal in caliper

ing the two mounting bolts and lifting the assembly off the disc.
8. The disc is riveted to the spindle flange in production. However, the rivets may be drilled out and the wheel studs and nuts are sufficient to hold the new disc in place when replacing the disc.
9. The rear wheel spindle must be removed to gain access to the parking brake shoes. It is necessary then to remove the caliper, the axle drive shaft, the spindle drive shaft yoke and remove the spindle and disc as an assembly from the wheel support. You now have access to the parking brake shoes the same as any other conventional bendix type brake shoe, Fig. 26.
10. If the car is equipped with the special optional knock-off hub assemblies, the adapters must be removed to gain access to the parking brake adjustment.

KELSEY-HAYES FLOATING CALIPER

This type brake is a floating caliper, single piston, ventilated unit, actuated by the hydraulic system, Fig. 31. The caliper assembly, Fig. 32, is made up of a floating caliper assembly and an anchor plate. The anchor plate is bolted to the wheel spindle arm by two bolts. The caliper is attached to the anchor plate through two spring steel stabilizers. The caliper slides on two guide pins which also attach to the stabilizers. A single piston is used. The cylinder bore contains a piston with a molded rubber dust boot to seal the cylinder bore from contamination and also to return the piston to the released position when hydraulic pressure is released. Also a rubber piston seal is used to provide sealing between cylinder and piston.

Service Precautions

In addition to the precautions described at the beginning of this chapter, the following must be observed:
1. If the piston is removed for any reason the piston seal must be replaced.
2. During removal and installation of a wheel assembly, use care not to interfere with and damage the caliper splash shield or the bleeder screw fitting.
3. Be sure the vehicle is centered on the

Fig. 32 Kelsey-Hayes floating caliper single piston disc brake (typical)

hoist before servicing any front end components to avoid bending or damaging the rotor splash shield on full right or left wheel turns.

4. The proportioning valve should not be disassembled or adjustments attempted on it.
5. The wheel and tire must be removed separately from the brake rotor.
6. The caliper assembly must be removed from the spindle prior to removal of shoe and lining assembly.
7. Do not attempt to clean or restore oil or grease soaked brake linings. When contaminated linings are found, linings must be replaced in complete axle sets.

Chrysler Corp.

Removing Lining & Caliper

1. Support vehicle on hoist and remove wheel assembly.
2. Remove two thirds of brake fluid from reservoir that serves disc brakes.
3. If caliper is to be removed, disconnect front brake hose from tube from mounting bracket and plug brake tube to prevent loss of fluid.

NOTE: If pistons are to be removed, leave flex brake line connected to tube at mounting bracket.

4. Remove caliper guide pins, Fig. 33. On American Motors models, remove positioners and anti-rattle clips.
5. Slide outboard and inboard shoe assembly out of caliper and adaptor.
6. Remove inner and outer bushings from caliper.

Installing Lining & Caliper

1. Install new inner and outer bushings Fig. 33, then slide shoe and lining assembly into place in caliper and adaptor making

certain that metal portion of shoe is fully in recess of caliper and adaptor.
2. Holding inboard shoe assembly in place, carefully slide caliper down into position in adaptor and over rotor. Align guide pin holes of adaptor and inboard and outboard shoes.
3. On American Motors models, install positioners over guide pins with open ends up and anti-rattle spring.
4. Press in on end of guide pin and thread pin into adaptor using extreme care not to cross threads. Torque guide pins from 33 ft. lbs. making sure that tabs of positioners are over machined surfaces of caliper.
5. If caliper was removed, connect brake hose to caliper and tighten securely, then open bleeder screw and allow caliper to fill with fluid. Make certain that all air bubbles have escaped when bleeding caliper.

CAUTION: Do not move vehicle until a firm brake pedal has been obtained.

Caliper Disassembly

1. Open bleeder screw and drain brake fluid from caliper then place caliper assembly in a soft jawed vise.

CAUTION: Do not overtighten vise as excessive pressure will cause bore distortion and binding of piston.

2. To remove piston place a cloth over piston and apply compressed air to fluid port in caliper, Fig. 34. Use extreme care to avoid damage to piston or bore. Allow dust boot to remain in caliper groove as piston is withdrawn.
3. Using a small wooden or plastic stick, work piston seal out of its groove and discard seal.

NOTE: Do not use screwdriver to remove piston seal as it could scratch bore or burr edges of seal groove.

4. Remove bleeder screw.

Cleaning & Inspection

1. Clean all parts with brake fluid and wipe

Fig. 34 Removing piston with air pressure

Fig. 33 Single piston disc brake caliper disassembled. (typical of American Motors and Chrysler Corp.)

DISC BRAKES

Fig. 35 Single piston caliper exploded view. Exc. 1980–82 Citation, Omega, Phoenix & Skylark; 1982 Cavalier, Celebrity, Century, Cimarron, Cutlass Ciera, Firenza, J2000, Skyhawk & 6000

dry, then blow out all drilled passages using compressor.

2. Inspect bore for scoring, pitting or corrosion. A deeply scored or corroded caliper should be replaced, although light scores and stains may be removed.

NOTE: If piston is pitted, scored or worn, replace piston.

3. Using crocus cloth, polish any discolored or stained area. Using finger pressure rotate crocus cloth in cylinder bore. Do not slide cloth in and out of bore under pressure or use any other form of abrasive or abrasive cloth. Black stains on bore wall are caused by piston seals and will do no harm.
4. Bores that have deep scratches or scores, should be honed providing that the diameter of the bore is not increased more than .002 inch.
5. Using a feeler gauge, check clearance of piston in bore. Clearance should be .002–.006 inch. If clearance exceeds this specification, replace caliper assembly.

Caliper Assembly

1. Dip new piston seal in clean brake fluid and install in bore groove. Seal should be positioned and gently worked around groove until properly seated.
2. Dip new dust boot in clean brake fluid and install in caliper by working into outer groove. Boot will seem larger than diameter of groove but will snap into place when properly seated in groove. Slide forefinger around inside of boot to be sure it is seated.
3. Dip piston in clean brake fluid, then with fingers spreading boot, work piston into boot and carefully down the bore until bottomed.

CAUTION: To avoid cocking, force must be uniformly applied on piston.

DELCO-MORAINE SINGLE PISTON
Dual Bolt Mounting

Exc. 1980–82 Citation, Omega, Phoenix & Skylark; 1982 Cavalier, Celebrity, Century, Cimarron, Cutlass Ciera, Firenza, J2000, Skyhawk & 6000

This single piston sliding caliper assembly, Fig. 35, incorporates a one piece housing with the inboard side of the housing bored for the piston. A seal within the housing bore provides a hydraulic seal between the piston and housing wall.

A spring steel scraper (wear sensor) is incorporated on each inboard shoe. When the shoe lining has worn to within .030 inch of the shoe, the sensor scrapes the rotor and emits an audible high frequency sound indicating that the linings should be replaced.

The caliper assembly used on all models except Astre, Monza, Skyhawk, Starfire, Sunbird and Vega, Fig. 35, slides on the mounting bolts. The caliper used on Astre, Monza, Skyhawk, Starfire, Sunbird and Vega models slide on the mounting sleeves which are secured by two mounting pins. Upon brake application, fluid pressure against the piston forces the inboard shoe and lining assembly against the inboard side of the disc. This action causes the caliper assembly to slide until the outboard lining comes into contact with the disc. As pressure builds up, the linings are pressed against the disc with increased force.

1980–82 Citation, Omega, Phoenix & Skylark; 1982 Cavalier, Celebrity, Century, Cimarron, Cutlass Ciera, Firenza, J2000, Skyhawk & 6000

The caliper has a single piston and is mounted to the support bracket by two mounting bolts, Fig. 36. The caliper assembly slides on the two mounting bolts. Upon brake application, fluid pressure against the piston forces the inboard shoe and lining assembly against the inboard side of the disc. This action causes the caliper assembly to slide until the outboard lining comes into contact with the disc. As pressure builds up the linings are pressed against the disc with increased force.

All Exc. Astre, Monza, Skyhawk, Starfire, Vega & 1980–82 Citation, Omega, Phoenix & Skylark; 1982 Cavalier, Celebrity, Century, Cimarron, Cutlass Ciera, Firenza, J2000, Skyhawk & 6000

Caliper Removal

1. Siphon enough brake fluid out of the master cylinder to bring fluid level to 1/3

Fig. 36 Single piston caliper exploded view. 1980–82 Citation, Omega, Phoenix & Skylark; 1982 Cavalier, Celebrity, Century, Cimarron, Cutlass Ciera, Firenza, J2000, Skyhawk & 6000

Fig. 37 Compressing piston and shoes with "C" clamp

Fig. 38 Caliper & mounting bolts

Brake Shoe Installation

1. Lubricate new sleeves, rubber bushings, bushing grooves and mounting bolt ends with Delco Silicone Lube or its equivalent.
2. Install new bushings and sleeves in caliper ears.

NOTE: Position the sleeve so that the end toward the shoe is flush with the machined surface of the ear.

3. Install shoe support spring by positioning single tang end of spring into notch cut at top of inboard shoe. Press remaining end of spring over bottom edge of shoe until shoe is engaged securely, Fig. 39.
4. Position inboard shoe with spring attached into caliper with ear end facing downward and bottom end facing upward with spring resting on inside diameter of piston. Press downward on both ends of shoe until shoe contacts piston and support spring contacts piston inside diameter.

NOTE: Some inboard replacement brake pads incorporate wear sensors and have a specific left and right hand assembly. Properly installed, the wear sensor will face toward the rear of caliper.

5. Position outboard shoe in caliper with shoe ears over caliper ears and tab at bottom of shoe engaged in caliper cutout.
6. With shoes installed, lift caliper and rest bottom edge of outboard lining on outer edge of brake disc to be sure there is no clearance between outboard shoe tab and caliper abutment.
7. Install caliper and torque mounting bolts to 30–40 ft. lbs. on 1977–80 models. On 1981–82 vehicles, torque to 28 ft. lbs.
8. Clinch upper ears of outboard shoe by positioning pliers with one jaw on top of upper ear and one jaw in notch on bottom shoe opposite ear, Fig. 40. Ears are to be flat against caliper housing with no radial clearance. If clearance exists, repeat clinching procedure.

full to avoid fluid overflow when the caliper piston is pushed back into its bore.
2. Raise vehicle and remove front wheels.
3. Using a "C" clamp, as illustrated in Fig. 37, push piston back into its bore.
4. Remove two mounting bolts, Fig. 38, and lift caliper away from disc.

Brake Shoe Removal

1. Remove caliper assembly as outlined above.
2. Remove inboard shoe. Dislodge outboard shoe and position caliper on the front suspension so the brake hose will not support the weight of the caliper.
3. Remove shoe support spring from piston.
4. Remove two sleeves from inboard ears of the caliper.
5. Remove four rubber bushings from the grooves in each of the caliper ears.

Disassembling Caliper

1. Remove caliper as outlined above.
2. Disconnect hose from steel line, remove U shaped retainer and withdraw hose from frame support bracket.
3. After cleaning outside of caliper, remove brake hose and discard copper gasket.
4. Drain brake fluid from caliper.
5. Pad caliper interior with clean shop towels and use compressed air to remove piston, Fig. 41.

NOTE: Use just enough air pressure to ease piston out of bore. Do not blow piston out of bore.

CAUTION: Do not place fingers in front of piston in an attempt to catch or protect it when applying compressed air. This could

Fig. 39 Installing support spring

Fig. 40 Clinching loop eared brake shoe

Fig. 41   Removing piston from caliper

result in serious injury.

6. Carefully pry dust boot out of bore.
7. Using a small piece of wood or plastic, remove piston seal from bore.

NOTE: Do not use a metal tool of any kind to remove seal as it may damage bore.

8. Remove bleeder valve.

Assembling Caliper

1. Lubricate caliper piston bore and new piston seal with clean brake fluid. Position seal in bore groove.
2. Lubricate piston with clean brake fluid and assemble a new boot into the groove in the piston so the fold faces the open end of the piston, Fig. 42.
3. Using care not to unseat the seal, insert piston into bore and force the piston to the bottom of the bore.
4. Position dust boot in caliper counterbore and install, using suitable seal installer, Fig. 43.

.012 MAX.
.005 MIN.

CALIPER

.012 MAX.
.005 MIN.

THE DIMENSION BETWEEN EACH CALIPER STOP AND THE CALIPER SHOULD BE .005"–.012"

FILE TO OBTAIN CLEARANCE

Fig. 44   Checking clearance between caliper and stops

DUST BOOT

PISTON

END OF GROOVE

Fig. 42   Installing boot to piston

NOTE: Check the boot installation to be sure the retaining ring moulded into the boot is not bent and that the boot is installed below the caliper face and evenly all around. If the boot is not fully installed, dirt and moisture may enter the bore and cause corrosion.

5. Install the brake hose in the caliper using a new copper gasket.
6. Install shoes and re-install caliper assembly.

Caliper Installation

1. Position caliper over disc, lining up holes in caliper with holes in mounting bracket. If brake hose was not disconnected during removal, be sure not to kink it during installation.
2. Start mounting bolts through sleeves in inboard caliper ears and the mounting bracket, making sure ends of bolts pass under ears on inboard shoe.

NOTE: Right and left calipers must not be interchanged.

3. Push mounting bolts through to engage holes in the outboard ears. Then thread mounting bolts into bracket.
4. Torque mounting bolts to 30–40 ft. lbs. on 1977–80 models. On 1981–82 vehicles, torque to 28 ft. lbs.
5. Check the dimensions between each caliper stop and caliper, Fig. 44.
6. If brake hose was removed, reconnect it and bleed the calipers.
7. Replace front wheels, lower vehicle and add brake fluid to master cylinder to bring level to ¼" from top.

NOTE: Before moving vehicle, pump brake pedal several times to be sure it is firm. Do not move vehicle until a firm pedal is obtained.

Astre, Monza, Starfire, Sunbird, Vega & 1977—80 Skyhawk
Lining Removal

1. Remove one half the total brake fluid capacity to front master cylinder to prevent reservoir overflow when the caliper piston is pushed back in its bore.
2. Raise and properly support vehicle.
3. Position a 7 inch C-clamp on caliper so that solid end rests against the inside of the caliper and the screw end rests on

BOOT INSTALLER

DUST BOOT

Fig. 43   Installing boot to caliper

the back side of the outer shoe. Tighten C-clamp until the caliper moves enough to push the piston to the bottom of the piston bore, then remove clamp.
4. Remove the two mounting pin snap rings or stamped nuts, Fig. 45, and slide out mounting pins, Fig. 46.
5. Lift caliper off disc and remove inner and outer by sliding out.

CAUTION: Do not permit brake hose to support weight of caliper. Support caliper by tying it to the suspension or control arm.

6. If caliper is to be removed, disconnect brake line.

Lining Installation

1. Install new sleeves with bushings on caliper grooves, Fig. 47.

NOTE: The "shouldered end" of sleeve must be installed toward outside.

2. Install inner shoe on caliper and slide shoe ears over sleeve, Fig. 47. Install the outer shoe in the same manner.

NOTE: Some inboard replacement brake pads incorporate wear sensors and have a specific left and right hand assembly. Properly installed, the wear sensor will face toward the rear of caliper.

Fig. 45   Removing stamped nuts from mounting pins

Fig. 46   Removing mounting pins

Fig. 47   Mounting sleeves and brake shoe installation

CAUTION: If pads are being re-used, they must be installed in same location as when removed.

3. Mount caliper on steering knuckle. If brake line was disconnected, reconnect and torque bolt to 22 ft. lbs.

NOTE: To avoid overflow, it may be necessary to remove half of brake fluid capacity from master cylinder.

4. Install mounting pins from outside in and install snap rings or stamped nuts, Fig. 48. Nuts should be pressed on as far as possible using a suitable size socket that just seats on outer edge of nut.
5. Install wheel assembly and lower vehicle.
6. Add brake fluid to within ¼ inch from top of master cylinder and test brake operation to insure a firm brake pedal before moving vehicle.

Caliper Disassembly

1. Remove caliper as described under "Lining Removal".
2. Drain brake fluid from caliper and clean exterior of caliper using clean brake fluid.
3. Using clean towels, pad interior of caliper and remove piston by applying just enough compressed air to fluid inlet port to ease piston out of bore.

CAUTION: Do not place fingers in front of piston in an attempt to catch or protect it when applying compressed air.

4. Carefully using a screwdriver so as not to scratch piston bore, pry dust boot out of piston bore, Fig. 49.
5. Using a piece of wood or plastic so as not to damage bore, remove piston seal from its groove in caliper bore.
6. Remove bleeder screw.

Cleaning & Inspection

1. Clean all metal parts in clean brake fluid, then using clean filtered air, dry parts and blow out all passages in caliper and bleeder valve.

NOTE: Always use clean brake fluid to clean caliper parts. Never use mineral base cleaning solvents as they can cause rubber parts to deteriorate and become soft and swollen, also the use of lubricated compressed air will leave a film of oil on metal parts that may damage rubber parts when they come in after reassembly.

2. Inspect piston surface for scoring, nicks, corrosion and worn or damaged plating. If any surface defects are detected, replace piston.

CAUTION: The piston outside surface is the primary sealing surface in the caliper. It is manufactured and plated to close tolerances, therefore refinishing by any means or the use of any abrasive is not recommended.

3. Check caliper bore for same defects as piston. The piston bore is not plated and stains or minor corrosion may be polished with crocus cloth.

CAUTION: Do not use emery cloth or any other form of abrasive and thoroughly clean caliper after use of crocus cloth. If caliper cannot be cleaned up in this manner, replace caliper.

Fig. 48   Installing stamped nuts on mounting pins

Fig. 49   Dust boot seal removal

Fig. 50 Installing piston on boot

Caliper Assembly

NOTE: The dust boot and piston seal are to be replaced each time that the caliper is disassembled.

1. Lubricate piston bore and new piston seal with clean brake fluid, then position seal in caliper bore groove.
2. Lubricate piston with clean brake fluid and assemble a new boot into groove in piston, Fig. 50.
3. Install piston into bore using care not to unseat seal, then force piston to bottom of bore.

NOTE: Approximately 50–100 pounds of force are required to push piston to bottom of bore.

4. Position dust boot in caliper counterbore and seat boot using suitable boot installer, Fig. 23.

NOTE: Check boot installation to make sure that retaining ring moulded into

boot is not bent and that boot is installed evenly all around. If boot is not fully installed, dirt and moisture may enter bore.

1980–82 Citation, Omega, Phoenix & Skylark; 1982 Cavalier, Celebrity, Century, Cimarron, Cutlass Ciera, Firenza, J2000, Skyhawk & 6000

Caliper Removal

1. Remove approximately 2/3 of brake fluid from master cylinder.
2. Raise and support front of vehicle, then remove wheel and tire assembly.
3. Position C-clamp as shown in Fig. 51, tighten C-clamp until piston bottoms in piston bore, then remove C-clamp.
4. If caliper assembly is being removed for service, remove brakeline fitting mounting bolt, Fig. 52. If only shoe and lining assemblies are to be replaced, do not disconnect brake line fitting from caliper.
5. Remove allen head caliper mounting bolts, Fig. 53. If bolts show signs of corrosion, use new bolts when installing caliper assembly.
6. Remove caliper assembly from disc. If only shoe and lining assemblies are to be replaced, using a length of wire suspend caliper from spring coil. Never allow caliper to hang from brake hose.

Shoe & Lining Removal

1. Remove caliper assembly as described under Caliper Removal.
2. Remove shoe and lining assemblies from caliper, Fig. 36.
3. Remove sleeves and bushings from grooves in caliper mounting bolt holes, Fig. 36.

Fig. 51 Compressing piston & shoes with C-clamp

Caliper Disassemble

1. Use clean shop towels to pad interior of caliper assembly, then remove piston by directing compressed air into caliper brake line inlet hole, Fig. 54.

NOTE: Use just enough air pressure to ease piston out of bore.

CAUTION: Do not place fingers in front of piston for any reason when applying compressed air. This could result in serious personal injury.

2. Remove bleeder screw from caliper body.
3. Using a suitable screwdriver, remove dust boot from caliper bore, Fig. 55.
4. Using a piece of wood or plastic, remove piston seal from groove in caliper bore.

NOTE: Do not use any type of metal tool to remove piston seal, since damage to caliper bore may result.

Fig. 52 Disconnecting brake line fitting from caliper

Fig. 53 Removing caliper mounting bolts

Fig. 54 Applying compressed air to caliper line port

Fig. 55   Removing dust boot

5. Inspect piston for corrosion, scoring, nicks, wear and damage to chrome plating. If any of the above defects are found, replace piston.
6. Inspect caliper bore for corrosion, scoring, nicks, and wear. Light corrosion can be polished out using crocus cloth. If crocus cloth fails to remove corrosion, the caliper housing must be replaced.

Caliper Assemble

1. Lubricate piston seal with clean brake fluid, then install piston seal into caliper bore groove. Check to ensure that piston seal is not twisted.
2. Lubricate caliper bore with clean brake fluid.
3. Insert piston into caliper bore of caliper, then force piston down until piston bottoms in bore.
4. Position outer diameter of dust boot in caliper housing counterbore, then seat boot as shown in Fig. 56.
5. Install bleeder screw on caliper housing.

Shoe & Lining Installation

1. Install outboard shoe and lining assembly into caliper housing.
2. Install retaining spring onto inboard shoe and lining assembly, Fig. 57, then install inboard shoe into caliper housing.
3. On 1980–81 models, using suitable pliers, clinch outboard shoe and lining assembly ears to caliper housing, Fig. 58.

Fig. 56   Seating dust boot in caliper

4. On 1982 models, to clinch caliper to brake outboard shoe proceed as follows:
   a. To seat shoe flange to caliper, tightly position a large flat blade screwdriver between outboard shoe flange and hat section of rotor, Fig. 58A.
   b. Pressurize the hydraulic system by moderately applying brake pedal, then using suitable tool, clamp the outboard shoe tightly to the caliper.
   c. Position a ball peen hammer on outboard shoe tab, Fig. 58B, then using a larger brass hammer, lightly tap the ball peen hammer to bend the outboard shoe tab. Tabs must be bent around casting to approximately 45 degrees.
   d. After both tabs have been bent pressure should be released and outboard shoe should be locked into position. If shoe is loose, repeat steps a. through d.

Fig. 57   Installing retainer spring on inboard shoe

Fig. 58   Clinching outboard shoe to caliper

NOTE: If an outboard shoe is removed from the caliper, or the tabs unclinched for any reason, then it will be necessary to replace the disc shoe and lining assemblies. Do not reclinch outboard shoe locking tabs after having removed shoe from caliper.

Caliper Installation

1. Position caliper assembly over disc and align mounting bolt holes. If brake hoses were not disconnected during removal, use care not to kink hoses during installation.

Fig. 58A   Screwdriver in position between outboard shoe flange & hat section of rotor

Fig. 58B   Ball peen hammer in position on outboard shoe tab

2. Install mounting bolts and torque to 21 to 35 ft. lbs., Fig. 53.
3. If brake line fitting was disconnected during removal, install brake line fitting and torque retaining bolt to 18 to 30 ft. lbs., Fig. 52.
4. Fill master cylinder. Bleed brake system if brake line was disconnected and recheck master cylinder fluid level.
5. Install wheel and tire assembly on vehicle, then lower vehicle and check brake system operation.

FORD SLIDING CALIPER

The caliper assembly is made up of a sliding caliper housing assembly and an anchor plate, Fig. 59.

The anchor plate is bolted to the wheel spindle arm. Two angular machined surfaces on the upper end of the caliper housing contact mating machined surfaces of the anchor plate. A steel, plated key and a caliper support spring is fitted between the angular machined surfaces of the lower end of the caliper and the machined surface of the anchor plate. The key is held in position with a retaining screw. The caliper is held in position against the mating surfaces of the anchor plate by means of the caliper support spring. A brake shoe anti-rattle spring clip is provided on the anchor plate at the lower end of the inner brake shoe and lining assembly. The inner and outer brake shoe assemblies are not interchangeable.

The sliding caliper contains a single cylinder and a piston with a molded dust boot to seal the cylinder bore from contamination. A square section rubber piston seal is positioned in a groove in cylinder bore to provide sealing between cylinder and piston.

Caliper Removal

1. Raise car and suppor with safety stands. Block both rear wheels if a jack is used.

Fig. 59 Ford sliding caliper disc brake

2. Remove wheel and tire assembly from hub.
3. Disconnect brake hose from caliper.
4. Remove retaining screw from caliper retaining key, Fig. 59.
5. Slide caliper retaining key and support spring either inward or outward from anchor plate. Use hammer and drift, if necessary, to remove the key and caliper support spring. Use care to avoid damaging the key.
6. Lift caliper assembly away from anchor plate by pushing caliper down against anchor plate and rotate upper end upward out of anchor plate, Fig. 60.
7. Remove inner shoe and lining from anchor plate. The brake shoe anti-rattle clip (inner shoe only) may become displaced at this time and if so, reposition it on anchor plate, Fig. 61. Tap lightly on outer shoe and lining to free it from caliper.

8. Clean caliper, anchor plate and rotor assemblies and inspect them for signs of fluid leakage, wear or damage. If either lining is worn to within 1/32" of any rivet head, both shoe and lining assemblies must be replaced. Also, if necessary to replace shoes and lining on one wheel, they must be replaced on both wheels to maintain equal brake action.

Caliper Disassembly

1. With caliper removed as described previously, disconnect brake hose. Cap hose and plug caliper inlet to prevent fluid loss.
2. With caliper on work bench, remove inlet plug and drain fluid from housing.
3. Place a wooden block or an old brake pad into the caliper, then place a shop cloth between wooden block and piston.
4. Apply air pressure slowly to caliper inlet port to remove piston, Fig. 62.

NOTE: If high pressure is applied quickly, piston may pop out and cause injury. A cocked or seized piston can be eased out by rapping sharply on piston end with a soft brass hammer.

5. Remove boot from piston and seal from caliper cylinder bore.

Caliper Assembly

1. Lubricate piston seal with clean brake fluid and piston seal in its cylinder bore groove.
2. Assemble dust boot on caliper housing by seating boot flange in the outer groove of cylinder bore, making sure it is fully seated.
3. Coat piston with clean brake fluid and install in cylinder bore.
4. Spread dust boot over piston as piston is installed and then bottom piston in the bore. Seat dust boot in its piston groove.

Caliper Installation

1. If new shoe and lining assemblies are to be installed, use a 4" C-clamp and a block of wood 1 3/4" × 1" and about 3/4" thick to seat the caliper piston in its bore. This must be done to provide clearance for the caliper to fit over new shoes when installed.

Fig. 60 Removing caliper assembly

Fig. 61 Caliper and outer shoe removed from anchor plate

Fig. 62   Removing piston from caliper

FIBER BLOCK   TOOL 7000-DD
CLOTH   PISTON
CALIPER

CALIPER ASSEMBLY
ANCHOR PLATE
1.

ROTATE CALIPER UNTIL PISTON DUST BOOT IS ¼" FROM EDGE OF INNER BRAKE SHOE
¼"
CALIPER ASSEMBLY
2.

ROTOR
POSITION LIGHT WEIGHT CARDBOARD OVER LOWER HALF OF PISTON & DUST BOOT
CALIPER ASSEMBLY
3.

LIGHTWEIGHT CARDBOARD
ROTATE CALIPER OVER ROTOR WHILE PULLING DOWNWARD ON CARDBOARD
CALIPER ASSEMBLY
4.

REMOVE CARDBOARD
5.

SLIDE CALIPER UP AGAINST ANCHOR PLATE ABUTMENT
ANCHOR PLATE
CALIPER ASSEMBLY
6.

Fig. 63   Installing caliper assembly

ANCHOR PLATE
CALIPER SUPPORT SPRING AND KEY

Fig. 64   Installing caliper support spring and retaining key

2. Be sure brake shoe anti-rattle clip is in place on lower inner brake shoe support on anchor plate with pigtail of clip toward inside of anchor plate. Position inner shoe and lining on anchor plate with lining toward rotor, Fig. 61.
3. Install outer shoe and lining with lower flange ends against the caliper leg abutments and the brake shoe upper flanges over the shoulders on caliper legs. The shoe upper flanges fit tightly against the shoulder machined surfaces. If the same brake shoes and linings are to be used, be sure they are installed in their original positions.
4. Remove C-clamp if used, from the caliper (the piston will remain seated in its bore).
5. Position caliper housing lower V groove on anchor plate lower abutment surface, Fig. 63. Refer to Figs. 63 and 64 to complete assembly following steps shown. Connect brake hose, bleed brakes and replace wheel.
6. Install key retaining screw and torque to 12–20 ft. lbs.

Brake Shoe & Lining, Replace

The procedure to replace the shoe and lining assemblies is the same as the caliper removal discussed previously with the exception that it is not necessary to disconnect the brake hose. Use care to avoid twisting or stretching the brake hose.

Hub & Rotor Removal

1. Remove caliper and shoes as previously described. If no repairs are necessary on the caliper it is not necessary to disconnect the brake hose. The caliper can be temporarily secured to the upper suspension arm. Do not remove the anchor plate and be careful not to stretch or twist the brake hose.
2. Remove grease cap from wheel spindle and remove cotter pin and nut lock from wheel bearing adjustment nut.
3. Remove wheel bearing adjusting nut and grasp the hub and rotor and pull it out far enough to loosen the washer and outer

wheel bearing. Then push it back in and remove the washer, outer wheel bearing and remove the hub and rotor.

KELSEY-HAYES SLIDING CALIPER

This sliding caliper single piston system uses a one piece hub and is actuated by the hydraulic system and disc assembly, Fig. 65. Alignment and positioning of the caliper is achieved by two machined guides or "ways" on the adaptor, while caliper retaining clips allow lateral movement of the caliper, Fig. 66. Outboard shoe flanges are used to position and locate the shoe on the caliper fingers, Fig. 67, while the inboard shoe is retained by the adaptor, Fig. 68. Braking force applied onto the outboard shoe is transferred to the caliper, while braking force applied onto the inboard shoe is transferred directly to the adaptor.

A square cut piston seal provides a hydraulic seal between the piston and the cylinder bore, Fig. 65. A dust boot with a wiping lip installed in a groove in the cylinder bore and

WHEEL CALIPER BOOT SEAL PISTON

SHOE AND LINING

MOUNTING BOLT

WHEEL STUD INNER BEARING SEAL

SPINDLE

ADAPTOR

MOUNTING BOLT

OUTER BEARING

STEERING KNUCKLE

BRAKING DISC AND HUB

SPLASH SHIELD

Fig. 65 Sectional view of Kelsey-Hayes sliding caliper front disc brake

STEEL BAR OR ANVIL

OUTBOARD SHOE RETAINER FLANGE

Fig. 67 Fitting outboard shoe retaining flange

piston, prevents contamination in the piston and cylinder bore area. Adjustment between the disc and the shoe is obtained automatihcally by the outward relocation of the piston as the inboard lining wears and inward movement of the caliper as the outboard lining wears.

Caliper Removal

1. Raise the vehicle and remove front wheel.
2. Remove caliper retaining clips and anti-rattle springs, Fig. 66.
3. Remove caliper from disc by slowly sliding caliper assembly out and away from disc.

NOTE: Use some means to support caliper. Do not let caliper hang from hydraulic line.

WIRE SUPPORT FOR CALIPER
INBOARD SHOE ADAPTER
"O" RINGS BRAKING DISC
CALIPER ADAPTER "WAYS"

Fig. 68 Replacing inboard shoe

Fig. 66 Caliper machined "ways" and assembly retention

Fig. 69 Removing outboard shoe

Fig. 70 Positioning outboard shoe onto caliper finger machined retainer ledge

Fig. 71 Installing outboard shoe using "C" clamp

Fig. 72 Exploded view of a Kelsey-Hayes sliding caliper disc brake

Fig. 72A Installing piston dust boot. 1981–82 models

Brake Shoe Removal

1. Remove caliper aassembly as outlined above.
2. Remove outboard shoe by prying between the shoe and the caliper fingers, Fig. 69, since flanges on outboard shoe retain caliper firmly.

NOTE: Caliper should be supported to avoid damage to the flexible brake hose.

3. Remove inboard brake shoe from the adaptor, Fig. 68.

Brake Shoe Installation

NOTE: Remove approximately ⅓ of the brake fluid out of the reservoir to prevent overflow when pistons are pushed back into the bore.

1. With care, push piston back into bore until bottomed.
2. Install new outboard shoe in recess of caliper.

NOTE: No free play should exist between brake shoe flanges and caliper fingers, Fig. 70.

If up and down movement of the shoe shows free play, shoe must be removed and flanges bent to provide a slight interference fit, Fig. 67. Reinstall shoe after modification, if shoe can not be finger snapped into place, use light "C" clamp pressure, Fig. 71.

3. Position inboard shoe with flanges inserted in adaptor "ways," Fig. 68.
4. Carefully slide caliper assembly into adaptor and over the disc while aligning caliper on machined "ways" of adaptor.

NOTE: Make sure dust boot is not pulled out from groove when piston and boot slide over the inboard shoe.

5. Install anti-rattle springs and retaining clips and torque retaining screws to 180 inch-pounds.

NOTE: The inboard shoe anti-rattle spring is to be installed on top of the retainer spring plate, Fig. 56.

Caliper Disassembly

1. With caliper and shoes removed as described previously, place caliper onto the upper control arm and slowly depress brake pedal, in turn hydraulically pushing piston out of bore.

NOTE: Pedal will fall when piston passes bore opening.

2. Support pedal below first inch of pedal travel to prevent excessive fluid loss.
3. To remove piston from the opposite caliper, disconnect flexible brake line at frame bracket, from vehicle side where piston has been removed previously and plug tube to prevent pressure loss. By depressing brake pedal this piston can also be hydraulically pushed out.
4. Mount caliper in a vise equipped with protector jaws.

NOTE: Excessive vise pressure will distort caliper bore.

5. Remove the dust boot, Fig. 72.
6. Insert a suitable tool such as a small, pointed wooden or plastic object between the cylinder bore and the seal and work seal out of the groove in the piston bore.

NOTE: A metal tool such as a screwdriver should not be used since it can cause damage to the piston bore or burr the edges of the seal groove.

Caliper Assembly

1. Dip new piston seals in clean brake fluid. Work seal gently into the groove (using clean fingers) until seal is properly seated, make sure that seal is not twisted or rolled.

NOTE: Old seals should never be reused.

2. On 1981–82 models, install piston into bore and push past seal until piston bottoms in bore.
3. Lubricate piston boot generously with clean brake fluid. On 1977–80 models, using finger pressure, install into caliper by pushing into outer groove of the caliper bore. When properly positioned in groove boot will snap into place. Double check to make sure boot is properly installed and seated by running finger around the inside of the boot. On 1981–82 models, install piston boot with tool C-4689 and handle C-4171, Fig. 72A.
4. On 1977–80 models, plug high pressure inlet to caliper and bleeder screw hole and coat piston with a generous amount of lubricant. Spread boot with finger and work piston into boot while pressing down on piston. As piston is depressed, entrapped air below piston will force boot around piston and into its groove.
5. On 1977–80 models, remove the plug and apply uniform force to the piston (avoid cocking piston) until piston bottoms in bore.
6. Install brake hose to caliper using new seal washers.
7. Install caliper and shoes as described under "Brake Shoe Installation."

DODGE ARIES, OMNI & 400; PLYMOUTH HORIZON & RELIANT & 1982 CHRYSLER LEBARON FLOATING CALIPER DISC BRAKE

Operation

The single piston floating caliper disc brake assembly consists of the hub and disc brake rotor assembly, caliper, shoes and linings, splash shield and adapter, Fig. 73.

The caliper assembly floats on two rubber bushings riding on two steel guide pins threaded into the adapter. The bushings are inserted on the inboard portion of the caliper. Two machined abutments on the adapter position and align the caliper fore and aft. Guide pins and bushings control caliper and piston seal movement to assist in maintaining proper shoe clearance.

All braking force is taken directly by the adapter. The steel piston used on Horizon and Omni models is 1.89 inches in diameter. The plastic piston used on Aries, 1982 LeBaron, Reliant and 400 models is 2.13 inches in diameter.

Fig. 73 Dodge Aries, Omni & 400; Plymouth Horizon & Reliant & 1982 Chrysler LeBaron floating caliper disc brake

Fig. 74 Removing caliper guide pins

Fig. 75 Removing caliper

Fig. 76 Removing outboard pad & lining assembly

Fig. 78 Removing inboard pad & lining assembly

Brake Shoe & Lining, Replace

Omni & Horizon

1. Raise and support front of vehicle, then remove wheel and tire assembly.
2. Remove caliper guide pins and anti-rattle spring, Fig. 74.
3. Carefully slide caliper assembly away from disc, Fig. 75. Support caliper assembly to prevent damage to brake hose.
4. Remove outboard shoe and lining assembly from adapter, Fig. 76.
5. Remove rotor from drive axle flange and studs, Fig. 77.
6. Remove inboard shoe and lining assembly from adapter, Fig. 78.
7. Carefully push piston into caliper bore.

NOTE: Remove some brake fluid from reservoir to prevent overflowing when pushing piston into caliper bore.

8. Position inboard shoe and lining on adapter. Ensure metal portion of shoe is properly positioned in recess of adapter.
9. Install rotor over studs and drive flange.
10. While holding outboard shoe in position on adapter, carefully position adapter over disc brake rotor.
11. Carefully lower caliper over disc brake rotor and adapter.
12. Install guide pins through bushings, caliper and adapter.
13. Press in on guide pins and thread pin into adapter. Torque pins to 25 to 40 ft. lbs.
14. Install wheel and tire assembly, then lower vehicle.

Aries, 1982 LeBaron, Reliant & 400

1. Raise and support vehicle, then remove wheel and tire assemblies.
2. Remove hold down spring from caliper assembly by pressing spring outward.
3. Loosen, but do not remove, caliper guide pins, then remove caliper from disc. Inboard shoe will remain inside caliper. Support caliper assembly to prevent damage to hydraulic brake hose.

NOTE: Remove caliper guide pins only if bushings or sleeves are to be replaced.

4. Remove inboard shoe from caliper and outboard shoe from adapter.
5. Push caliper piston into bore.

Fig. 77 Removing disc brake rotor from hub

NOTE: Remove some brake fluid from master cylinder reservoir to prevent overflowing when piston is pushed into bore.

6. Install new inboard shoe into caliper with retainer positioned in piston bore.
7. Install outboard shoe onto adapter.
8. Position caliper over brake disc and adapter, then torque guide pins to 18–22 ft. lbs.
9. Install hold down spring, then install tire and wheel assemblies and lower vehicle to ground.
10. Check master cylinder reservoir for proper level of brake fluid and add as necessary.

Caliper Overhaul

Disassemble, Fig. 79 & 79A

1. Remove caliper assembly as described under Brake Shoe & Lining, Replace.
2. With brake hose attached to caliper, carefully depress brake pedal to push piston out of caliper bore. Prop brake pedal to any position below first inch of brake pedal travel to prevent brake fluid loss.
3. If pistons are to be removed from both cal-

Fig. 79 Disassembled view of disc brake caliper. Omni & Horizon

Fig. 79A   Disassembled view of disc brake caliper. Aries, 1982 LeBaron, Reliant & 400

Fig. 80   Installing piston seal

Fig. 81   Installing piston dust boot

ipers, disconnect brake hose at frame bracket after removing piston, then cap brake line and repeat procedure to remove piston from other caliper.

4. Disconnect brake hose from caliper.
5. Mount caliper in a soft jawed vise.
6. Support caliper and remove dust boot and discard.
7. Using a small wooden or plastic stick, remove seal from groove in piston bore and discard.
8. Using a suitable tool, remove bushings from caliper.

Inspection

1. Clean all components using alcohol or other suitable cleaning solvent, then blow dry using compressed air. With compressed air blow out drilled passages and bores.
2. Inspect piston bore for pitting or scoring. Light scratches or corrosion can usually be cleared with crocus cloth. Bores that have deep scratches or scoring should be honed with tool No. C-4095, providing bore diameter is not increased by more than .001 in. If scratches or scoring cannot be cleared up, or if caliper bore is

Fig. 82   Installing caliper piston

Fig. 84   Installing inner brake shoe on caliper

Fig. 83   Kelsey-Hayes pin slider disc brake caliper (Typical)

Fig. 85   Installing outer brake shoe on caliper

increased by more than .001 in., replace caliper housing.

NOTE: When using hone C-4095, coat hone and caliper bore with clean brake fluid. After honing carefully clean boot and seal grooves with a stiff non-metallic brush. Flush caliper with clean brake fluid and wipe dry with a clean lintless cloth, then flush and wipe caliper dry again.

3. Replace piston if found to be scored, pitted or if plating is severely worn or if caliper bore was honed. Black stains on steel piston are caused by piston seal and are not cause for replacing piston.

Assemble, Fig. 79 & 79A

1. Mount caliper in a soft jawed vise.
2. Lubricate piston seal with clean brake fluid and install seal in caliper bore groove, Fig. 80. Ensure seal is properly seated.
3. Lubricate piston boot with clean brake fluid and install boot in caliper bore groove, Fig. 81.
4. Using a hammer and small steel plate or a suitable C-clamp, drive into caliper until seated, Fig. 82. Ensure boot is properly seated in caliper bore.
5. Plug brake hose inlet boss and bleeder screw hole, then lubricate piston with clean brake fluid.
6. Spread boot with finger and work piston into boot, then press down on piston.
7. Remove plug and carefully push piston down in bore until bottomed.
8. Compress flanges of guide pin bushings and install bushings on caliper housing. Ensure that bushing flanges extend evenly over caliper housing on both sides.

NOTE: On Aries, 1982 LeBaron, Reliant & 400 models, remove teflon sleeves from guide pin bushings prior to installing bushings into caliper. After bushings are installed into caliper, reinstall teflon sleeves into bushings.

9. Connect brake hose to brake line at frame bracket.
10. Install caliper on vehicle as described under Brake Shoe & Lining, Replace.
11. Check brake fluid level of master cylinder reservoir, then open caliper bleed screw and bleed brake system. Continue bleeding procedure until firm pedal is obtained.

KELSEY-HAYES PIN SLIDER DISC BRAKE

Operation

The caliper assembly consists of a pin slider caliper housing, inner and outer shoe and lining assemblies and a single piston, Fig. 73. The caliper slides on two pins which also act as attaching bolts between caliper and the combination anchor plate and spindle. The outer brake shoe and lining assembly is longer than the inner brake shoe and lining assembly. Inner and outer shoe and lining assemblies are attached to the caliper by spring clips riveted to the shoe surfaces. The inner shoe is attached to the caliper by installing the spring clip to the inside of the caliper piston. The outer shoe clips directly to the caliper housing. A wear indicator is incorpo-

rated which emits a noise when the lining is worn to a point when replacement is necessary. Inner and outer shoes are of left and right hand and are not interchangeable.

NOTE: The inner shoe and lining on Capri, Fairmont, Mustang, and Zephyr with V8-302 engine has a replaceable single finger anti-rattle clip and an insulator held in position by the clip. The shoe is slotted to accept the snap on clip which loads the assembly against the caliper bridge. The inner shoe on the Capri and Mustang with 2300cc and 2800cc has a single finger anti-rattle clip similar to the Fairmont and Zephyr inner shoe, holding the shoe down against the spindle ledge. The clip does not lock into the piston. The insulator is also riveted to the shoe and is not replaceable.

Brake Shoe & Lining, Replace

Removal

1. Remove brake fluid until reservoir is half full.
2. Raise and support front of vehicle, then remove wheel and tire assembly.
3. Remove caliper locating pins.
4. Lift caliper assembly from spindle and adapter plate, then remove outer shoe from caliper assembly.

NOTE: On 1982 Lincoln Continental models, slip shoe down caliper leg until clip is disengaged.

5. Remove inner shoe and lining assembly.

NOTE: On 1982 Lincoln Continental models, pull shoe straight out of piston. This could require a force as high as 20–30 lbs.

6. Suspend caliper from inner fender housing with wire to avoid damaging brake hose.
7. Remove and discard locating pin insulators and plastic sleeves.

Installation

1. Using a 4 in. C-clamp and a block of wood 2¾ × 1 in. and approximately ¾ in. thick, seat caliper piston in bore, then remove C-clamp and wooden block.

NOTE: On 1982 Lincoln Continental models, the piston is made of phenolic material. Do not seat piston in bore by applying C-clamp directly to piston.

2. Install locating pin insulators and plastic sleeves on caliper housing. Ensure insulators and sleeves are properly positioned.
3. Install inner shoe and lining assembly on caliper piston, Fig. 84.

NOTE: Inner brake shoes are marked LH (left hand) and RH (right hand) and must be installed on the proper caliper. Use care to not bend spring clips too far during installation in piston, otherwise distortion and rattles may result.

4. Install outer brake shoe and lining assembly, Fig. 85. Ensure that shoes are installed on proper caliper. Make sure that clip and buttons on shoe are properly seated.

NOTE: The outer shoe can be identified as

left hand and right hand by the wear indicator which must be installed toward front of vehicle.

5. Install locating pins and torque to 30–40 ft. lbs.

NOTE: On 1982 models except Lincoln Continental, ensure that two round torque buttons are firmly seated in the two holes of outer caliper leg and that shoe is held tightly against housing by spring clip. A temporary loss of brakes may occur if buttons are not properly seated.

6. Refill master cylinder, then install wheel and tire assembly and lower vehicle.
7. Pump brake pedal several times to position brake linings before moving vehicle.

Caliper, Replace

Removal

1. Raise and support front of vehicle, then remove wheel and tire assembly.
2. Loosen brake tube fitting which connects brake tube to fitting on frame and plug brake tube. Remove retaining clip from brake hose and bracket, then disconnect brake hose from caliper.
3. Remove caliper locating pins.
4. Lift caliper from rotor and spindle anchor plate assembly.

NOTE: Before removing calipers, mark left and right hand calipers so they can be installed in the same position.

Installation

1. Install caliper assembly over rotor with outer shoe against rotor braking surface during installation on spindle and anchor plate to prevent pinching of piston boot between inner brake shoe and piston.

NOTE: Ensure calipers are installed in the correct position.

2. Install locating pins. Torque locating pins to 30 to 40 ft. lbs.

NOTE: On 1982 Lincoln Continental and 1980–81 Ford and Mercury full size and Lincoln models, torque locating pins to 40–60 ft. lbs. On 1981–82 Escort, EXP LN7 and Lynx, torque to 18–25 ft. lbs.

3. Connect brake hose to caliper and tighten hose fitting.
4. Position upper end of brake hose in bracket and install retaining clip. Remove plug from brake line, then connect brake hose fitting to brake line. Torque fitting to 10 to 18 ft. lbs.
5. Bleed brake system and centralize pressure differential valve.
6. Install wheel and tire assembly, then lower vehicle.
7. Pump brake pedal several times to position brake shoes before moving vehicle.

Caliper Overhaul

Disassemble, Fig. 83

1. Remove caliper assembly from vehicle as described under Caliper, Replace.
2. Position fiber block and shop towels between caliper piston and caliper housing, then apply compressed air to caliper brake line fitting bore to force piston from caliper.

DISC BRAKES

SPLASH SHIELD

ANCHOR PLATE

CALIPER

ROTOR

Fig. 86   Rear disc brake

PARKING BRAKE ACTUATING LEVER
THRUST BEARING
PARKING BRAKE OPERATING SHAFT
PIN
CALIPER HOUSING
SEAL
PARKING BRAKE THRUST SCREW
PISTON
BALL
PARKING BRAKE END RETAINER

Fig. 87   Caliper housing cutaway to show parking brake mechanism

3. Remove dust boot from caliper assembly.
4. Remove pistol seal from cylinder and discard.

Inspection

Clean all metal parts with isopropyl alcohol, then clean and dry passages and grooves with compressed air. Check caliper and piston for damage and wear and replace as necessary.

Assemble, Fig. 83

1. Lubricate piston seal with clean brake fluid, then install seal in caliper bore.

NOTE: Ensure seal is firmly seated in groove.

2. Install dust boot in outer groove of caliper bore.
3. Coat piston with clean brake fluid and install piston in caliper bore. Spread dust boot over piston as it is installed. Seat dust boot in piston groove.
4. Install caliper assembly as described under "Caliper, Replace."

FORD REAR WHEEL DISC BRAKE & PARKING BRAKE

Sliding caliper rear disc brakes are used on some 1977–80 models and on the 1982 Lincoln Continental, Fig. 86. The caliper is basically the same as the larger front wheel caliper, however, a parking brake mechanism and a larger inner brake shoe anti-rattle spring have been added, Fig. 87. A hydraulically powered brake booster (Hydroboost) provides the power assist for this four wheel disc brake system.

The parking brake lever, located at the rear of the caliper, is actuated by a cable system similar to rear drum brake applications. When the parking brake is applied, the cable rotates the lever and operating shaft. Three steel balls, placed in pockets between the opposing heads of the operating shaft and

thrust screw, roll between ramps formed in the pockets and force the thrust screw away from the operating shaft, in turn, driving the caliper piston and brake shoe assembly against the rotor. An automatic adjuster in the assembly compensates for lining wear and maintains proper clearance in the parking brake mechanism.

The cast iron rotors are ventilated by curved fins located between the braking surfaces and are designed to cause the rotor to act as an air pump when the vehicle is traveling forward. The rotors are not interchangeable and are identified by a Right or Left marking cast inside the hat section of the rotor. The rotor is secured to the axle flange in the same manner as a rear brake drum. A splash shield is bolted to a forged axle adapter to protect the inboard rotor surface.

Caliper Removal

NOTE: After performing any service work, obtain a firm brake pedal before moving vehicle.

1. Raise vehicle and support on safety stands, then remove tire and wheel assemblies.
2. Disconnect fitting on rear brake tube from hose end fitting at frame mounted bracket and plug end of brake tube to prevent loss of fluid and entry of dirt. Remove horseshoe retaining clip from hose fitting and disengage hose from bracket.

NOTE: On Granada, Monarch and Versailles models, disconnect hose bracket from axle spring seat. On Lincoln Continental, Ford and Mercury models, disconnect hose end fitting from caliper. On Granada, Mark IV, Mark V, Monarch, Thunderbird and Versailles models, remove hollow retaining bolt, connecting hose fitting to caliper.

3. Disconnect parking cable from lever, Fig. 88, using care to avoid kinking or cutting

cable or return spring, then remove retaining screw from caliper retaining key, Fig. 89. On 1982 Lincoln Continental, remove caliper locating pins.
4. Slide caliper retaining key and support spring from anchor plate, Fig. 89. If necessary, use a hammer and brass drift, being careful to avoid damaging key on sliding ways or hitting parking brake lever.

NOTE: If caliper cannot be removed due to rust build-up on outer edge of rotor, scrape off loose scale, being careful not to damage braking surfaces. If rotor wear or scoring prevents removal of caliper, it will be necessary to loosen caliper end retainer 1/2 turn maximum, to allow piston to be forced back into its bore. To loosen end retainer, remove parking brake lever and mark or scribe end retainer and caliper housing to be sure that end retainer is not loosened more than 1/2 turn, then force piston back in its bore, Fig. 87, and move caliper back and forth to center rotor and remove caliper. If retainer must be loosened more than 1/2 turn, use caution, as the seal between the thrust screw and housing may be broken and brake fluid will enter parking brake mechanism chamber. In this case, the end retainer must be removed and the internal parts cleaned and lubricated.

5. On all except 1982 Lincoln Continental, remove inner shoe and lining assembly from anchor plate, then tap lightly on outer shoe and lining assembly to free it from caliper. Mark each shoe for identification if they are to be reused.
6. On 1982 Lincoln Continental, proceed as follows:
   a. Remove outer shoe and lining assembly from anchor plate, then remove rotor retainer nuts and rotor from axle shaft.
   b. Remove inner brake shoe and lining assembly from anchor plate and mark each shoe for identification if they are to be reused.
   c. Remove anti-rattle clip from anchor plate, then remove flexible hose from caliper by removing hollow retaining bolt.

Fig. 88 Parking lever & cable installation

Fig. 89 Removing rear caliper assembly

Fig. 90 Adjusting piston depth for lining installation

Cleaning & Inspection

Clean caliper, anchor plate and rotor assembly and inspect for signs of brake fluid leakage, excessive wear or damage. The caliper must be inspected for leakage both in piston boot area and operating shaft seal area. Lightly sand or wire brush any rust or corrosion from caliper and anchor plate sliding surfaces and inner brake shoe abutment surfaces in anchor plate. Inspect brake shoes for wear. If either lining is within 1/32 inch of any rivet head, replace both shoe and lining assemblies from both wheels in order to maintain equal brake action.

NOTE: On 1982 Lincoln Continental models, linings must not be worn to within less than 1/8 inch of shoe surface.

Caliper Installation

1. If end retainer has been loosened only 1/2 turn, reinstall caliper in anchor plate using key. Do not install shoe and lining assembly. Torque end retainer to 75–95 ft. lbs. and install parking brake actuating lever on its keyed spline. Lever arm must point down and rearward so that parking brake cable will pass freely under axle. Torque retainer screw to 16–22 ft. lbs.

NOTE: Parking brake lever must rotate freely after torquing retainer screw.

2. Remove caliper from anchor plate. If new shoe and lining assemblies are to be installed, the piston must be bottomed in caliper bore using tool T75P-2588-B to provide clearance. Remove rotor and install caliper without lining and shoe assemblies in anchor plate using key only. Install tool and while holding shaft, rotate tool handle counterclockwise until the tool seats firmly against piston, Fig. 90. Loosen handle about 1/4 turn, and while holding handle rotate tool shaft clockwise until piston is fully bottomed in bore (piston will continue to turn even after it is bottomed). Turn tool handle until there is no further inward movement of piston and there is a firm seating force, then remove caliper from mounting plate and reinstall rotor.

NOTE: For use on 1982 Lincoln Continental models, tool T57P-2588-B must be slightly modified, Fig. 90A.

3. Making certain that brake shoe anti-rattle clip is in place in lower inner brake shoe support on anchor plate with loop of clip toward inside of anchor plate, Fig. 89, position inner brake shoe and lining assembly on anchor plate. On 1982 Lincoln Continental models, install rotor and two retaining nuts.

4. Install outer brake shoe with lower flange ends against caliper abutments and brake shoe upper flanges over shoulders on caliper legs. The shoe upper flanges fit tightly against machined shoulder surfaces.

NOTE: If old brake shoes and lining assemblies are re-used, be certain the shoes are installed in their original positions as marked for identification during removal.

5. Lubricate caliper and anchor sliding ways with M1C-167-A (LPS-ESA-100) grease, using care to prevent lubricant from getting on braking surfaces, then position caliper housing lower V-groove on anchor plate lower abutment surfaces. On 1982 Lincoln Continental models, use D7AE-019590, or equivalent grease.

6. Rotate caliper until it is completely over rotor, being careful not to damage piston dust boot, then pull caliper outboard until inner shoe and lining is firmly seated against rotor. Measure clearance between outer lining and rotor which should be 1/16 inch or less, Fig. 91. On 1982 Lincoln

Fig. 91 Checking lining clearance

Continental models, clearance must be between 1/32 and 3/32 inch. If it is greater, remove caliper and move piston outward to narrow gap. Follow precedure in step 2 and note that 1/4 turn of the shaft counterclockwise, moves piston about 1/16 inch.

CAUTION: A clearance greater than specified limit may allow adjuster to be pulled out of piston when service brake is applied, causing parking brake to fail to adjust. It will then be necessary to replace piston/adjuster assembly.

7. While holding caliper against anchor plate upper abutment surfaces, center caliper over lower anchor plate abutment, then position caliper support spring and key in slot and slide them into opening between lower end of caliper and lower anchor plate abutment until key semicircular slot is centered over retaining screw threaded hole in anchor plate.

8. Install key retaining screw and torque to 12–16 ft. lbs., then reinstall brake hose on caliper. On Lincoln and Ford Mercury models, place a new gasket on fitting and torque to 20–30 ft. lbs. On 1982 Lincoln Continental and all Granada, Mark IV, Mark V, Monarch, Thunderbird and Versailles models, place a new gasket on each side of the fitting outlet, then install the attaching bolt through the washers and fitting and torque to 17–25 ft. lbs. (20–30 ft. lbs. on 1982 Lincoln Continental models).

NOTE: On Granada, Monarch and Versailles models, ensure the pin in the hose fitting engages the mating hole in the caliper before torquing the bolt.

9. On all except 1982 Lincoln Continental models, position upper end of flexible hose in bracket and install retaining clip, then connect brake tube to hose and torque fitting to 10–15 ft. lbs.

NOTE: Do not twist or coil brake hose, the stripe on the hose must be kept straight.

10. On 1982 Lincoln Continental models, lubricate pins and inside of insulator with D7AZ-19A331-A or equivalent silicone grease and add one drop of Loctite EOAC-19554-A, or equivalent, to locating pin threads. Install locating pins through caliper insulators and into anchor plate and torque to 29–37 ft. lbs.

11. Connect parking brake lever to lever on caliper.
12. Bleed brake system, then with engine running pump brake pedal lightly about 40 times allowing 1 second between pedal applications. An alternate with engine off is to pump brake pedal lightly about 10 times to discharge accumulator, then pump brake pedal firmly about 30 times. Check parking brake for excessive travel or very light effort, if so, repeat pumping brake pedal, and if necessary check parking brake cable tension.
13. Install wheel and torque nuts to 70–115 ft. lbs.

NOTE: Before moving vehicle, make certain that a firm brake pedal has been obtained.

Shoe & Lining Removal & Installation

To remove shoe and lining assemblies, follow "Caliper Removal" procedure and omit step 2 as it is not necessary to disconnect brake hose. After removing caliper, support it with a length of wire to avoid damaging brake hose. To install shoe and lining assemblies, follow "Caliper Installation" procedure, making certain that proper parking brake adjustment is obtained.

Caliper Overhaul

Disassemble
1. Remove caliper assembly as described previously.
2. Remove caliper end retainer, operating shaft, thrust bearing and balls, Fig. 92.
3. Remove thrust screw anti-rotation pin with a magnet or tweezers. If pin cannot be removed with a magnet or tweezers, proceed with the following procedure:
   a. With tool T75P-2588B, force piston approximately one inch from caliper bore.
   b. Push piston back into caliper housing with tool, then with tool in position, hold tool shaft in place and rotate handle counter-clockwise until thrust screw clears anti-rotation pin. Remove thrust screw and anti-rotation pin.
4. Remove thrust screw by rotating with ¼ inch allen wrench.
5. Install tool T75P-2588-A through back of caliper housing and remove piston assembly, Fig. 93.

CAUTION: Use care not to damage polished surface in thrust screw bore and do not attempt to remove or press adjuster can, as it is a press fit in piston.

6. Remove and discard piston seal, boot, thrust O-ring seal, end retainer, O-ring and end retainer lip seal.

Cleaning & Inspection
1. Clean all metal parts with alcohol, then using clean, dry compressed air, blow out and dry all grooves and passages making sure the caliper bore and component parts are free of any foreign material.
2. Inspect caliper bore for damage or excessive wear. The thrust screw must be smooth and free of pits. If piston is pitted, scored or chrome plating is worn, replace piston and adjuster assembly.
3. Adjuster can must be bottomed in piston to be properly seated and provide consis-

tent brake operation. If adjuster can is loose, appears high in piston, is damaged, or if brake adjustment is usually too tight, too loose or not functioning, replace piston/adjuster assembly. Check adjuster operation by assembling thrust screw into piston/adjuster assembly, then pull the two parts apart about ¼ inch and release them, Fig. 94. When pulling on the two parts, the brass drive ring must remain stationary causing the nut to rotate. When releasing the two parts, the nut must remain stationary and drive ring must rotate. If action does not follow this pattern, replace piston/adjuster assembly.
4. Inspect ball pockets, threads, grooves,

Fig. 92 Rear disc brake caliper assembly

bearing surfaces of thrust screw, operating shaft, balls and anti rotation pin for wear, brinnelling or pitting. Replace operating shaft, balls, thrust screw and anti rotation pin if any of these parts are worn or damaged. A polished appearance on the ball paths is acceptable if there is no sign of wear into the surface.
5. Inspect thrust bearing for corrosion, pitting or wear and replace as necessary.
6. Inspect end plug bearing surface for wear

Fig. 93 Disassembling rear disc brake caliper

Fig. 94 Checking parking brake adjuster operation

Fig. 95 Filling piston/adjuster assembly

Fig. 96 Bottoming piston in caliper

or brinnelling and replace as necessary. A polished appearance on bearing surface is acceptable if there is no sign of wear into surface.

7. Inspect operating lever for damage and replace as necessary.

Assemble

1. Coat new caliper piston seal with clean brake fluid and install it in caliper making certain that seal is not twisted and is fully seated in groove.

2. Install new dust boot by seating flange squarely in outer groove of caliper bore, then coat piston/adjuster assembly with clean brake fluid and install it in caliper bore. Spread dust boot over piston as it is installed and seat dust boot in piston groove.

3. Install caliper in vise, Fig. 95, and fill piston/adjuster assembly with clean brake fluid.

4. Coat new thrust screw O-ring with clean brake fluid and install it in thrust screw groove, then install thrust screw into piston adjuster assembly until top surface of thrust screw is flush with bottom of threaded bore, being careful to avoid cutting O-ring seal. Index notches on thrust screw and caliper housing and install anti-rotation pin.

NOTE: The thrust screw and operating shafts are not interchangeable from side to side since the ramp direction in the ball pockets are different. The pocket surfaces of the operating shaft and thrust screws are stamped "R" (Right) and "L" (Left).

5. Place a ball in each of three pockets of thrust screw and apply a liberal amount of silicone grease M1C-169-A on parking brake components, then install operating shaft on balls.

6. Coat thrust bearing with silicone grease and install it on operating shaft, then install a new lip seal and O-ring on end retainer.

7. Lightly coat O-ring seal and lip seal with silicone grease and install end retainer in caliper. Firmly hold operating shaft against internal mechanism while installing end retainer to prevent mislocation of balls. If lip seal moves out of position, reseat seal. Torque end retainer to 75–95 ft. lbs.

NOTE: Parking brake lever must rotate freely after torquing.

8. Install parking brake lever on keyed spline facing down and rearward. Torque retaining screw to 16–22 ft. lbs.

9. Bottom piston using tool T75P-2588-B, Fig. 96, and install caliper as described previously.

DELCO-MORAINE REAR DISC BRAKE

Operation, Figs. 97, 98 & 99

Upon application of brake, the cone and piston move out as one part. The nut remains stationary on the high lead screw and a gap develops between the cone and nut. When lining wear occurs, the cone and piston do not return to their original position, thereby leaving a small gap equal to the lining wear between the nut and cone. The adjusting spring causes the nut to rotate on the high lead screw to close the gap and adjust the caliper.

Upon application of parking brake, the lever rotation causes the high lead screw to turn and the nut to move down the screw, thereby loading through the cone and the cone-clutch interface of the piston, resulting in a clamp load on the linings. When the parking brake is released, the cone rotates on the clutch interface to adjust the caliper. The clutch interface prevents the cone from turning when the parking brake is applied.

Caliper Removal

CAUTION: Do not mix power steering fluid with brake fluid. If brake seals contact steering fluid or steering seals contact brake fluid, damage will result.

1. Remove two thirds of the total brake fluid capacity from the master cylinder front reservoir, to prevent overflow of brake fluid.

2. Support vehicle on a hoist and remove tire and wheel assembly.

3. Install one nut with flat side facing rotor to prevent rotor from falling out when caliper is removed.

4. Loosen parking brake cable tension at equalizer, then remove cable from parking brake lever and remove return spring, lock nut, lever, lever seal and anti-friction washer.

NOTE: Lever must be held in place while removing nut.

Fig. 97 Delco-Moraine rear disc brake

Fig. 98 Rear disc brake caliper disassembled. 1977–78 Eldorado, 1977–78 Riviera, 1977–79 Cadillac Seville & Brougham & 1978–80 Electra

5. Clean surface in area of lever seal, then using a 7 inch (or larger) C-clamp, with the solid end on lever stop and screw end on back of outboard lining, turn clamp until piston is bottomed in caliper.

NOTE: Do not position C-clamp on actuator screw.

6. Before removing clamp, lubricate housing surface under lever seal with silicone lubricant.
7. Install a new anti-friction washer, a new lever seal and lever.

NOTE: Install lever on hex with arm pointing downward.

8. Rotate lever toward front of vehicle and while holding in this position, install nut and torque to 25 ft. lbs. and rotate lever back to stop.
9. Install lever return spring and remove C-clamp.

NOTE: On Cadillac springs are color coded, red for the right hand caliper and black for the left hand caliper.

10. Disconnect brake line from caliper and plug openings to prevent loss of fluid and entry of dirt.
11. On all calipers except Eldorado and right hand Brougham remove the brass bolt from the block.

NOTE: If brake line nut is seized, brass bolt and block can be removed with brake line attached by removing bolt. Plug openings to prevent loss of fluid and entry of dirt.

12. Remove caliper mounting bolts and remove caliper.
13. Reverse procedure to install and torque caliper mounting bolts to 30 ft. lbs.

NOTE: When installing brass bolt and block, use two new copper gaskets. Torque bolt or connector to 30 foot-pounds.

Inspection

1. Clean corrosion and dirt from face of piston. Inspect piston and check valve area for fluid leakage, indicated by excessive moisture around boot area.
2. Inspect dust boot for cuts, cracks or other damage which may affect its sealing ability. If leaks are present, replace dust boot.

NOTE: Do not use compressed air to clean caliper as it may unseat the dust boot.

3. Inspect piston boot seal. Replace boot seal if leakage is indicated.
4. Inspect for leaks at threaded end of actuator screw. Replace seal if leakage is indicated. If bore is nicked or scratched, replace caliper.

Caliper Overhaul
Disassembly
1. Clamp caliper in a vise and remove the two mounting sleeves and four bushings,

Fig. 98 and 99.
2. Remove brake shoes and lever return spring.
3. Rotate parking brake lever back and forth to remove piston from housing, Fig. 100. If piston will not move from housing, remove lock nut, lever and anti-friction washer. With a 9/16 inch wrench, rotate screw clockwise on right hand caliper or counter-clockwise on left hand caliper until the piston moves from housing.

NOTE: Pad caliper with shop cloths when removing piston.

4. Remove piston assembly and balance spring.
5. Remove lock nut, lever, lever seal and anti-friction washer if not removed previously.
6. Push screw from housing, then remove piston seal and boot.

Assembly
1. Install new piston seal.
2. Install new boot onto piston assembly with lip of boot located in piston groove.
3. Install new thrust washer and seal on actuator screw.
4. Install actuator screw into piston assembly. The piston assemblies are identified by a stamped letter on the adjuster nut end. "L" denote left hand and "R" denotes right hand. The caliper housing is also marked with a letter. The parking brake will not function if the caliper and actuator screw are located on the wrong side of vehicle.
5. Coat piston seal with clean brake fluid. Install balance spring into piston and

Fig. 99 Rear disc brake caliper disassembled. 1982 Camaro, 1979–82 Eldorado, Firebird, Riviera & Toronado & 1980–82 Seville

install assembly into caliper housing, Fig. 101.

6. With tool J-23072, push piston fully into caliper housing, Fig. 102.

NOTE: The piston must be pushed straight into caliper to prevent damage to the actuator screw seal as it passes through hole in rear of piston bore.

7. Before removing tool J-23072, install lubricated anti-friction washer, new lever seal, lever and lock nut. Position lever away from stop, rotate forward and hold lever in position, then torque nut to 25 ft. lbs.

8. Remove tool J-23072, rotate lever back to stop and install return spring.

NOTE: On Cadillac the return springs are color coded red for right hand and black for left hand.

9. With tool J-26296, drive boot until seal bottoms in caliper housing, Fig. 103.

Shoe & Lining Replacement

1. Remove caliper as described previously and remove shoe and lining.

Fig. 102 Installing piston into caliper

Fig. 100 Removing piston from bore

Fig. 101 Positioning piston in caliper

Fig. 103 Driving boot into caliper

DISC BRAKES

Fig. 104 Removing piston check valve

NOTE: Sleeves are installed in inner bushings.

3. Remove and discard piston check valve and install a new one, Fig. 104.

CAUTION: Front brake shoes must not be installed on rear calipers.

4. Position new inboard shoe assembly on piston. The D-shaped tab must fit into indentation in piston. If piston requires rotation, use tool J-7642 to rotate it, Fig. 105.

NOTE: Install new spring retainers on all exc. Eldorado outboard shoe assembly.

5. Install new outboard shoe assembly onto caliper. Install caliper and torque mounting bolts to 30 ft. lbs.

Fig. 105 Rotating piston in bore

2. Remove and discard the two caliper mounting sleeves and the four bushings. Using silicone lubricant, install new bushings and seals.

Disc Brake Rotor Specifications

CAR	Year	Nominal Thickness	Minimum Refinish Thickness	Thickness Variation Parallelism	Lateral Runout (T.I.R.)	Finish (Micro-In.)
AMERICAN MOTORS						
Matador	1977–78	1.190	1.120	.0005	.003	15–80
Exc. Matador	1977–80	.880	.810	.0005	.003	15–80
Exc. Eagle	1981–82	—	.815	.0005	.003	15–80
Eagle	1981–82	—	.815	.0005	.004	15–80
BUICK (EXC. SKYHAWK, 1980–82 SKYLARK & 1982 CENTURY)						
Full Size	1977–78⑬	1.040	.980	.0005	.005	30–80
	1978–79⑭	.974	.921	.0005	.003③	—
	1979⑬	1.040	.980	.0005	.004③	30–80
	1980–82⑬	1.040	.980	.0005	.004③	⑤
	1980–82⑭	.974	.921	.0005	.004③	⑤
Intermediate	1977–78	1.040	.980	.0005	⑮	30–80
	1979–82	1.040	.980	.0005	.004	30–80
CADILLAC (EXC. CIMARRON)						
All⑬	1977	1.037	.980	.0005	.005	19.7–59
All⑭	1977	.974	.911	.0005	.003	15.7–78.7
All⑬	1978	1.038	.981	.0005	.005	19.7–59.1
All⑭	1978	.975	.911	.0005	.003	15.76–78.8
Exc. Eldorado⑬	1979	1.037	.980	.0005	.005	—
Exc. Eldorado⑭	1979	.974	.921	.0005	.003	—
Eldorado⑬	1979	1.036	—	.0005	.005	—
Eldorado⑭	1979	1.035	—	.0005	.005	—
Exc. Eldorado & Seville⑬	1980–81	1.037	—	.0005	.005	—
Eldorado & Seville⑬	1980–81	1.036	—	.0005	.005	—
Eldorado & Seville⑭	1980–81	1.036	—	.0005	.005	—
All	1982	1.000	—	.0005	.004	—
CHEVROLET (CAMARO, CHEVROLET, CORVETTE, MALIBU & MONTE CARLO)						
Corvette	1977–82	1.250	1.230	.0005	.005	20–60
All exc. Corvette	1977–82	1.030	.980	.0005	.004	20–60
1982 CHEV. CAVALIER • BUICK SKYHAWK • CAD. CIMARRON • OLDS FIRENZA • PONT. J2000						
All	1982	.885	.830	.0005	.004	—
CHEVROLET CHEVETTE & PONTIAC T1000						
All	1977	.50 (12.7 mm)	.456 (11.58 mm)	.003 (.08 mm)	.005 (.13 mm)	20–60 (.5–1.6 micro/m)
	1978–82	.4334 (11 mm)	.390 (9.9 mm)	.0005 (.013 mm)	.005 (.13 mm)	20–60 (.5–1.6 micro/m)
1980–82 CHEV. CITATION, BUICK SKYLARK, OLDS. OMEGA & PONT. PHOENIX • 1982 CHEV. CELEBRITY, BUICK CENTURY, OLDS CUTLASS CIERA & PONT. 6000						
All	1980	1.040	.980	.0005	.005	30–80
All	1981–82	.885	.830	.0005	.004	12–50
1977–80 CHEV. MONZA • BUICK SKYHAWK • OLDS. STARFIRE & PONT. SUNBIRD						
All	1977–80	.880	.830	.0005	.005	20–60
CHEVROLET VEGA & PONTIAC ASTRE						
All	1977	.500	.455	.0005	.005	20–60

Continued

DISC BRAKE ROTOR SPECIFICATIONS—Continued

CAR	Year	Nominal Thickness	Minimum Refinish Thickness	Thickness Variation Parallelism	Lateral Run-out (T.I.R.)	Finish (Micro-In.)	CAR	Year	Nominal Thickness	Minimum Refinish Thickness	Thickness Variation Parallelism	Lateral Run-out (T.I.R.)	Finish (Micro-In.)
CHRYSLER, DODGE & PLYMOUTH							Capri, Mustang, Pinto & Bobcat	1977–80	.870	.810	.0005	.003	15–80
Full Size	1977–78	1.250	1.180	.0005	.004	15–80		1981–82	.870	.810	.0005	.003	15–125
	1979–82	1.010	.940	.0005	.004	15–80	Fairmont & Zephyr	1978–80	.870	.810	.0005	.003	15–80
Imperial	1981–82	1.010	.940	.0005	.004	15–80		1981–82	.870	.810	.0005	.003	15–125
Intermediate (Exc. Below)	1977–82	1.010	.940	.0005	.004	15–80	Escort, EXP, LN7 & Lynx	1981–82	.945 (24 mm)	.882 (22.4 mm)	—	.003 (.075 mm)	16–79
Aspen, Dart, Valiant & Volare	1977–80	1.010	.940	.0005	.004	15–80							
Omni & Horizon	1978–80	.490	.431	.0005	⑪	15–80	**OLDSMOBILE (EXC. FIRENZA, STARFIRE, 1980–82 OMEGA & 1982 CUTLASS CIERA)**						
	1981–82	.498	.431	.0004	.004	15–80	88, 98 & Custom Cruiser	1977–81	1.040	.965	.0005	⑫	30–50
Aries & Reliant	1981–82	.935	.882	.0005	.005	15–80		1982	1.020	.984	.0005	.004	—
400 & LeBaron	1982	.935	.882	.0005	.005	15–80	Intermediate	1977–81	1.040	.980	.0005	.004	30–50
FORD MOTOR COMPANY								1982	1.020	.984	.0005	.004	—
Ford & Mercury Full Size	1977–78	1.180⑦	1.120⑧	.0005②	.003⑨	15–80	Toronado	1977–78	1.245	1.185	.0005	.002	30–50
	1979	1.030⑦	.972⑧	.0005	.003⑨	15–80		1979–80	1.040	1.020	.0005	.005	19–80
	1980–82	1.030	.972	.0005	.003	10–80		1981	1.020	.960	.0005	.005	19–80
Ford & Mercury Intermediate	1977–79①	1.180	1.120	.0005	.003	15–80		1982	1.020	.984	.0005	.004	19–80
	1980④	.870	.810	.0005	.003	15–80	**PONTIAC (EXC. ASTRE, SUNBIRD, T1000 & FRONT WHEEL DRIVE**						
	1981–82④	.870	.810	.0005	.003	15–125	Bonneville & Catalina	1977–80	1.040	.980	.0005	.005	20–60
Comet & Maverick	1977	.870	.810	.0005	.003	15–80		1981–82	1.030	.980	.0005	.005	30–80
Granada, Monarch & Versailles	1977–80	.870⑦	.810⑧	.0005	.003⑨	15–80	Grand Am, Grand Prix & LeMans	1977–80	1.040	.980	.0005	.005	20–60
	1981–82	.870	.810	.0005	.003	15–125		1981–82	1.030	.980	.0005	.005	30–80
Lincoln Continental, Mark V, VI & Town Car	1977–79	1.180⑦	1.120⑧	.0025⑩	.003⑨	15–80	Firebird	1977–80	1.030	.980	.0005	.004	20–60
	1980–82⑥	1.030	.972	.0005	.003	10–80		1981–82	1.030	.980	.0005	.004	30–80
	1982⑯	1.030⑦	.972⑧	.0005	.003⑨	15–125 ⑰	Phoenix & Ventura	1977–79	1.040	.980	.0005	.004	20–60

① —1977–1979 Cougar, LTD II & Thunderbird.
② —1977–78 Mercury, Front disc. .0004, 1977–78 rear disc. 0005.
③ —1979–82 Riviera, .005.
④ —Cougar, Cougar XR-7 & Thunderbird.
⑤ —Exc. Riviera, 30–80; Riviera, 19–80.
⑥ —Mark VI & Town Car.
⑦ —Rear disc. .945.
⑧ —Rear disc. .895.
⑨ —Rear disc. .004.

⑩ —Rear disc. .0004.
⑪ —1978, .003; 1979–80, .005.
⑫ —Exc. Olds 88 w/V8-403 engine, .004; Olds 88 w/V8-403 engine, .005.
⑬ —Front.
⑭ —Rear.
⑮ —1977–78 Skylark, .005; 1977–78 except Skylark, .004.
⑯ —Continental.
⑰ —Rear disc brake, 15–80.

CARBURETORS

INDEX

CARBURETION

Since carburetion is dependent in several ways on both compression and ignition, it should always be checked last when tuning an engine.

Before adjusting the carburetor, consider the factors outlined below and which definitely affect engine performance.

Performance Complaints

Flooding, flat spots or other performance complaints are often caused by dirt, or water in the carburetor. To aid in diagnosing the complaint, the carburetor should be carefully removed from the engine without draining the fuel from the bowl. The contents of the fuel bowl can then be examined for contamination as the carburetor is disassembled. A magnet moved through the fuel in the bowl will pick up any iron oxide dust that may have caused needle valve leakage.

Check float setting carefully. Too high a level will cause flooding while too low a level

will starve the engine.

Before installing carburetor, fill the bowl with clean fuel and operate the throttle by hand several times to visually check the discharge from pump jets.

Inspect gasketed surfaces between body and air horn. Small nicks or burrs should be smoothed down to eliminate air or fuel leakage. On carburetors having a vacuum piston, be especially particular when inspecting the top surface of the inner wall of the bowl around the vacuum piston passage. A poor seal at this location may contribute to a "cutting out" on turns complaint.

Dirty or Rusty Choke Housing

In cases where it is found that the interior of the choke housing is dirty, gummed or rusty while the carburetor itself is comparatively clean, look for a punctured or eroded manifold heat tube (if one is used).

Manifold Heat Control Valve

An engine equipped with a manifold heat control valve can operate with the valve stuck in either the open or closed position. Because of this, an inoperative valve is frequently overlooked at vehicle lubrication or tune-up.

A valve stuck in the "heat-off" position can result in slow warm up, deposits in combustion chamber, carburetor icing, flat spots during acceleration, low gas mileage and spark plug fouling.

A valve stuck in the "heat-on" position can result in power loss, engine knocking, sticking or burned valves and spark plug burning.

To prevent the possibility of a stuck valve, check and lubricate the valve each time the vehicle is lubricated or tuned-up. Check the operation of the valve manually. To lubricate the valve, place a few drops of penetratng oil on the valve shaft where it passes through the manifold. Then move the valve up and down a few times to work the oil in. *Do not use engine oil to lubricate the valve as it will leave a resi-*

due which hampers valve operation.

Carburetor Flange

Check the flange for looseness on the manifold. If one of the flange nuts is loose as little as one-half turn, a sufficient amount of air will enter the intake manifold below the throttle plate to destroy engine idle and all engine performance.

If a tight fit cannot be obtained by tightening the nuts, install a new gasket but be sure that all the old gasket material has been removed.

Throttle Linkage

If the throttle linkage is adjusted so that the accelerator pedal will strike the floor board before the throttle plate is wide open, it will result in low top speed.

Fuel Lines

A restriction of the fuel line will result in an apparent vapor lock action or a definite cut-off of gasoline. This can generally be corrected by

Internal idle mixture limiter

External idle mixture limiter

blowing out the line with compressed air. In some cases, it may be necessary to replace the line.

Fuel Pump

The pump should be tested to make sure that it will draw an adequate supply of fuel from the tank and deliver it to the carburetor under all conditions of operation. If the pump functions inefficiently, proper adjustment and operation of the carburetor is impossible because the fuel will not be maintained at the prescribed level in the idle passages and main discharge jet (or jets) of the carburetor under all operating conditions.

Fuel Tank

The fuel tank should not be overlooked as a possible source of trouble with carburetion. A shortage of fuel at the fuel pump or carburetor may be caused by material obstructing the mouth of the feed pipe in the tank, or by a restriction of the air vents in the filler cap and neck.

An unusual amount of dirt, water or gum in the fuel filter indicates that the tank is contaminated with these substances, which should be cleaned out to prevent future failure of the pump or carburetor.

Intake Manifold Leaks

Leakage of air into the intake manifold at any point will affect carburetion and general engine performance. Air may leak into the manifold through the joints at the carburetor or cylinder head, cracks in the manifold, cracks or poor connections in the vacuum hoses or lines, or the connections of any accessories which may be connected to the manifold. All such joints should be tested for leaks.

To test the intake manifold for leaks, apply oil from an oil can along the gasket joints with the engine idling. An air leak is indicated when oil is drawn past the gaskets by the suction of the engine. Tighten the nuts or cap screws holding the manifold to the engine and retest for leaks. If tightening fails to stop the leaks, replace the manifold gaskets. If the new gaskets fail to stop the leaks, carefully inspect the manifold for cracks and test any suspicious area with oil.

Air Cleaner

An air cleaner with a dirty element, will restrict the air flow through the carburetor and cause a rich mixture at high speeds. In such a condition the air cleaner likewise will not properly remove dirt from the air, and the dirt entering the engine will cause rapid formation of carbon, sticking valves, and wear of piston rings and cylinder bores.

Automatic Choke

The choke mechanism must be inspected and cleaned to make sure it is operating freely. Sluggish action or sticking of the choke will cause excessive fuel consumption, poor performance during warm-up, and possibly hard starting.

Choke Thermostat

If necessary to adjust the choke more than two marks from the specified setting, either rich or lean, it indicates that the thermostat spring may be bent or has lost its tension.

Carburetor Ball Checks

Whenever it becomes necessary to dismantle a carburetor be sure to account for the ball checks that may be found under pump plungers and compensating or power valves.

CARBURETOR IDLE ADJUST

The slow idle adjustment method, referred to as "Lean Roll" method, insures proper idle, ignition timing and mixture settings for greatest possible exhaust emission reduction and proper engine operation. It should be noted here that smooth idle is extremely sensitive to vacuum leaks. If rough idle is noted, check for vacuum leaks at the carburetor, manifold, etc.

Carburetor Idle Limiters

Some carburetors are equipped with idle adjustment limiters which restrict the maximum idle richness of the air/fuel mixture and prevents overly rich adjustments. There are two types of idle limiters: internal and external (see illustrations). The internal needle limiter is located in the idle channel and is not visible externally. This limiter is set and sealed at the factory and, under no circumstances, during normal service or during overhaul, should the seal be removed and adjustments made to this needle.

The other type of idle limiter is an external idle limiter cap installed on the knurled head of the idle mixture adjusting screw. Any adjustment to the idle fuel mixture on carburetors with this type of limiter must be made within the range of the limiter cap.

Under no circumstances may the limiter cap, the stop boss or the power valve cover, which the limiter caps stop against, be mutilated or deformed in any way to render the limiter inoperative. A satisfactory idle is obtainable within the range of the limiter cap.

The addition of idle limiters does not eliminate the need for adjusting idle speed and mixture. All the limiters do is prevent overly rich mixtures, which increase the amount of hydro-carbons emitted into the atmosphere.

1. With engine at operating temperature, set parking brake and block drive wheels.
2. Make sure choke valve is wide open.
3. Ensure that the air cleaner thermostatic valve is open.
4. On carburetors so equipped, hold hot idle compensator hole closed with eraser on pencil.
5. Turn air conditioner off or on according to directions given in *Tune Up Charts* in car chapters.
6. Set idle mixture screw for maximum idle rpm.
7. Adjust speed screw or solenoid to obtain the specified rpm in Drive or Neutral as specified.
8. Set ignition timing according to specifications with vacuum advance line disconnected and hole in manifold plugged.
9. Adjust mixture screw IN to obtain a 20 rpm drop (lean roll).
10. Adjust mixture screw OUT ¼ turn.
11. Repeat Steps 9 and 10 for second mixture screw (2 and 4 barrel carbs).
12. Readjust speed screw (or solenoid screw) if necessary to obtain specified rpm.
13. On model S with solenoid on carburetor, electrically disconnect solenoid and adjust carburetor idle speed screw to obtain 400 rpm in neutral, then reconnect wire to solenoid.

SERVICE BULLETINS

Carter Thermo-Quad

When installing the bowl cover on Carter TQ carburetors, it is important that the float lever pins are correctly positioned (centered in their supports). If the pins are not properly placed, they may be trapped between the gasket surfaces. When the bowl cover screws are tightened, the bowl will crack, Fig. 1.

Rochester Quadrajet

Delco/Rochester advises the possibility exists that the wrong throttle body to float bowl gaskets are being used by servicemen on Quadrajet carburetors. When this wrong substitution is made, vacuum leaks occur and cause rough idle due to air bypassing the primary throttle valves through the canister purge passage in the throttle body because the gasket will not seal this passage.

The difference between the throttle body to bowl gaskets is shown in Fig. 2.

Carter Thermo-Quad

The metering rods are preset to specifications by the manufacturer. No additional adjustment should be attempted since an accurate adjustment cannot be made in the field. An improper adjustment may result in the exhaust emissions exceeding specifications. Also, maladjustment of the metering rods may prevent the carburetor from returning to the idle position from wide open throttle (WOT) due to throttle shaft binding, resulting in poor fuel economy.

Holley 2245

Some difficulty may be encountered when adjusting curb idle speed on these carburetors. This condition may be caused by the side of the carburetor interfering with the throttle lever. To correct this condition, the throttle lever may be filed to remove excess metal causing the interference, Fig. 3.

Holley 5210-C

A possible cause of hard cold starting on vehicles equipped with this model carburetor may be binding choke linkage, preventing proper choke operation. To determine if binding choke linkage is the cause of hard starting, remove air cleaner with engine cold, then

CARBURETORS

FLOAT PIN TRAPPED BETWEEN GASKET SURFACES

Fig. 1 Carter Thermo-quad float lever pins improperly placed

UNSEALED CANISTER PURGE PASSAGE

SEALED CANISTER PURGE PASSAGE

Fig. 2 Delco/Rochester Quadrajet throttle body to float bowl gaskets

REMOVE SHADED AREA FROM THROTTLE LEVER

Fig. 3 Removing excess metal from throttle lever. Holley 2245 carburetors

fully depress and release the accelerator pedal once. If choke blade does not fully close, the linkage is binding. This binding condition may occur at the contact point between the fast idle lever and fast idle cam. To correct this condition, proceed as follows:

1. Lubricate contact surface of fast idle lever tang with Lubriplate 1050520 or equivalent.
2. Reset dechoke adjustment to .300 inch instead of the production specification of .375 inch, listed in the Holley 5210 Specification Chart.
3. Bend tang at existing bend so tang slopes toward the choke housing, Fig. 4.

NOTE: Do not bend tang at tip since this will not achieve the desired results.

Motorcraft 2150

On some applications, the clearance between the carburetor choke pulldown vacuum hose and the EGR spacer may be less than ¼ inch. If improper clearance exists, cut ½ inch off hose and recheck clearance.

1980 Rochester 2SE & E2SE

When servicing these units, care should be taken not to disturb the special friction reducing coating applied to the primary and secondary throttle shafts, the secondary actuating lever and lockout lever. On units for V6 engine, the secondary throttle bore and valve are also coated with a special graphite compound.

INCREASE THIS BEND RADIUS

ORIGINAL POSITION

ADJUSTED POSITION

Fig. 4 Revised unloader (Dechoke) adjustment. Holley 5210

Carter Carburetor Section

CARTER YF SERIES ADJUSTMENT SPECIFICATIONS

See Tune Up Chart in car chapter for curb and fast idle speeds.

Year	Carb. Model	Float Level	Float Drop	Fast Idle Cam Setting	Dechoke or Unloader Setting	Pulldown Setting	Choke Setting
AMERICAN MOTORS							
1977	7111	15/32	1 3/8	.201 ①	.275	.221	2 Rich
	7151	15/32	1 3/8	.195 ①	.275	.215	1 Rich
	7152	15/32	1 3/8	.195 ②	.275	.215	1 Rich
	7153	15/32	1 3/8	.195 ①	.275	.215	Index
	7189	15/32	1 3/8	.201 ②	.275	.215	1 Rich
	7195	15/32	1 3/8	.195 ①	.275	.221	1 Rich
	7223	15/32	1 3/8	.195 ②	.275	.215	Index
1978	7201	15/32	1 3/8	.195 ①	.275	.215	Index
	7232	15/32	1 3/8	.201 ①	.275	.221	2 Rich
	7233	15/32	1 3/8	.201 ②	.275	.221	1 Rich
	7235	15/32	1 3/8	.195 ②	.275	.215	Index
	7267	15/32	1 3/8	.195 ②	.275	.215	1 Rich
1978–79	7228	15/32	1 3/8	.195 ①	.275	.215	1 Rich
	7229	15/32	1 3/8	.195 ②	.275	.215	1 Rich

①—1600 RPM hot on 2nd step of cam with TCS solenoid & EGR disconnected.
②—1500 RPM hot on 2nd step of cam with TCS solenoid & EGR disconnected.

Year	Carb. Model	Float Level	Float Drop	Fast Idle Cam Setting	Dechoke or Unloader Setting	Pulldown Setting	Choke Setting
FORD MOTOR CO.							
1977	B7DF-ABA	25/32	1 19/32	.140	.250	.260	Index
	D7BE-BA	25/32	1 19/32	.140	.250	.260	1 Rich
	D7BE-BC	25/32	1 19/32	.140	.250	.260	1 Rich
	DDE-DA	25/32	1 19/32	.140	.250	.260	1 Rich
	D7DE-DD	25/32	1 19/32	.140	.250	.260	1 Rich
1978	D8DE-BA	25/32	1 19/32	.140	.250	.230	2 Rich
	D8DE-DA	25/32	1 19/32	.140	.250	.230	2 Rich
	D8DE-EA	25/32	1 19/32	.140	.250	.200	2 Rich
	D8KE-AA	25/32	1 19/32	.140	.250	.230	2 Rich
1979	D9BE-RA	25/32	—	.140	.250	.180	1 Rich
	D9BE-UA①	25/32	—	.140	.250	.180	1 Rich
	D9BE-UA②	25/32	—	.140	.250	.200	2 Rich
	D9DE-AA	25/32	—	.140	.250	.230	1 Rich
	D9DE-AB	25/32	—	.140	.250	.230	2 Rich
	D9DE-BA	25/32	—	.140	.250	.230	1 Rich
	D9DE-BB	25/32	—	.140	.250	.230	2 Rich
	D9DE-CA	25/32	—	.140	.250	.260	1 Rich
	D9DE-CB	25/32	—	.140	.250	.260	1 Rich
	D9DE-CC	25/32	—	.140	.250	.260	2 Rich
	D9DE-CD	25/32	—	.140	.250	.260	2 Rich
	D9DE-DA	25/32	—	.140	.250	.260	1 Rich
	D9DE-DB	25/32	—	.140	.250	.260	1 Rich
	D9DE-DC	25/32	—	.140	.250	.260	2 Rich
	D9DE-DD	25/32	—	.140	.250	.260	2 Rich
	D9DE-EA	25/32	—	.140	.250	.230	1 Rich

Continued

CARBURETORS

See Tune Up Chart in car chapter for curb and fast idle speeds.

Year	Carb. Model	Float Level	Float Drop	Fast Idle Cam Setting	Dechoke or Unloader Setting	Pulldown Setting	Choke Setting
FORD MOTOR CO.—Continued							
	D9DE-EB	25/32	—	.140	.250	.230	2 Rich
	D9DE-UA	25/32	—	.140	.250	.200	2 Rich
	D9DE-VA	25/32	—	.140	.250	.200	2 Rich
1980	DEDE-GA	25/32	—	.140	.250	.260	—
	DEDE-HA	25/32	—	.140	.250	.260	—
	EODE-GA	25/32	1½	.140	.250	.260	2 Rich
	EODE-HA	25/32	1½	.140	.250	.260	2 Rich
	EODE-JA	25/32	1½	.140	.250	.260	2 Rich
	EODE-LA	25/32	1½	.140	.250	.250	2 Rich
	EODE-MA	25/32	1½	.140	.250	.250	2 Rich
	EODE-NA	25/32	1½	.140	.250	.260	2 Rich

①—6-200 engine.   ②—6-250 engine.

MODEL YF SERIES ADJUSTMENTS

The YF Series carburetor, Figs. 1, thru 5, is a single-barrel, downdraft unit combining the fundamental features of other Carter carburetors. In addition, it features a diaphragm-type accelerating pump. It also has a diaphragm-operated metering rod, both vacuum and mechanically controlled.

Float Adjustment

Fig. 6—Invert the air horn assembly, and check the clearance from the top of the float to the bottom of the air horn with the float level gauge. Hold the air horn at eye level when gauging the float level. The float arm (lever) should be resting on the needle pin. Do not load the needle when adjusting the float. Bend the float arm as necessary to adjust the float level (clearance). Do not bend the tab at the end of the float arm. It prevents the float from striking the bottom of the fuel bowl when empty.

Float Drop Adjustment

Fig. 7—Hold air horn upright and measure maximum clearance from top of float to bottom of air horn with float drop gauge. Bend tab at end of float arm to obtain specified setting listed under YF Adjustment Specifications.

Metering Rod Adjustment

Fig. 8—Back out the idle speed adjusting screw until the throttle plate is closed tight in the throttle bore. Press down on upper end of diaphragm shaft until diaphragm bottoms in vacuum chamber. Metering rod should contact bottom of metering rod well, and metering rod should contact lifter link at the outer end nearest the springs and at supporting lug. For models not equipped with metering rod adjusting screw, adjust by bending lip of metering rod arm to which metering rod is attached, up or down as required. For models equipped with a metering rod adjusting screw, turn the adjusting screw until metering rod just bottoms in the body casting. For final adjustments turn metering rod adjusting screw in (clockwise) one additional turn.

Fast Idle Cam Linkage Adjustment

Position fast idle screw on second step of fast idle cam and against shoulder of highest step, Fig. 9. Using a drill of specified size, check clearance between lower edge of choke plate and bore, Refer to YF Specifications Chart. To adjust, bend choke connector rod as required.

Choke Plate Pulldown Adjustment

Bend a 0.026 in. diameter wire gauge at a 90 degree angle approximately 1/8-inch from one end. Insert the bent end of the gauge between the choke piston slot and the right hand slot in choke housing. Rotate the choke piston lever counterclockwise until gauge is snug in the piston slot. Exert a light pressure on choke piston lever to hold the gauge in place, then use a drill with a diameter equal to the specified pulldown clearance between the lower edge of choke plate and carburetor bore to check clearance, Fig. 10.

To adjust the choke plate pulldown clearance, bend the choke piston lever as required to obtain specified setting.

NOTE: When bending the lever, be careful not to distort the piston link. Install the choke thermostatic spring housing and gasket. Set the housing to specifications.

Dechoke Adjustment

Hold the throttle plate fully open and close the choke plate as far as possible without forcing it. Use a drill of specified diameter to check the clearance between choke plate and air horn, Fig. 11. If clearance is not within specification, adjust by bending arm on choke trip lever of the throttle lever. Bending the arm downward will decrease the clearance, bending it upward will increase the clearance.

If the choke plate clearance and fast idle cam linkage adjustment was performed with the carburetor on the engine, adjust the engine idle speed and fuel mixture. Adjust dashpot (if so equipped).

Altitude Compensator Adjustment

1977–78 American Motrs
For operation on vehicle above 4000 feet in altitude, rotate plug fully counterclockwise, Fig. 12. For operation on vehicles below 400 feet in altitude, rotate plug fully clockwise, Fig. 12.

NOTE: Whenever the position of the altitude compensator plug is changed, the ignition timing must also be corrected. Refer to the "Tune-up Specifications" in the individual car chapter.

Dashpot Adjustment

With the engine idle speed and mixture properly adjusted, and the engine at normal operating temperature, loosen the antistall dashpot lock nut, Fig. 13. Hold the throttle in the curb idle position and depress the dashpot plunger. Measure the clearance between the throttle lever and plunger tip. Turn the antistall dashpot to provide 7/64" ± 1/64" clearance between the tip of the plunger and the throttle lever. Tighten the locknut to secure the adjustment.

Automatic Choke Adjustment

Loosen choke cover retaining screws and turn choke cover so that line or index mark on cover lines up with the specified mark listed in *YF Specifications Chart* on choke housing.

AIR HORN SCREW (LONG)

AIR HORN SCREW (SHORT)

AIR HORN

AIR HORN GASKET

GASKET

NEEDLE SEAT

NEEDLE

NEEDLE SPRING

NEEDLE PIN

FLOAT PIN

LOW SPEED JET

METERING JET

MAIN BODY

BODY GASKET

PUMP CONNECTOR LINK

THROTTLE SHAFT ARM

SOLENOID & BRACKET

DASHPOT & BRACKET

UPPER PUMP SPRING RETAINER

COIL HOUSING BAFFLE PLATE

COIL HOUSING GASKET

THERMOSTATIC COIL & HOUSING

COIL HOUSING RETAINER

COIL HOUSING SCREW

UPPER PUMP SPRING

METERING ROD

METERING ROD ARM

DIAPHRAGM LIFTER LINK

WASHER

CHOKE CONNECTOR ROD RETAINER

CHOKE CONNECTOR ROD

DIAPHRAGM SPRING

DIAPHRAGM HOUSING SCREWS (4)

DIAPHRAGM HOUSING

WASHER

SPACER

FLOAT

DISCHARGE BALL WEIGHT

DISCHARGE BALL

DIAPHRAGM

BODY FLANGE SCREWS (3)

FAST IDLE CAM SCREW

FAST IDLE CAM

IDLE SCREW LIMITER CAP

IDLE MIXTURE SCREW

SPRING

THROTTLE BODY

BODY FLANGE SCREWS (3)

Fig. 1 Carter Model YF Series carburetor. 1977–78 American Motors less altitude compensation

1. AIR HORN
2. SCREW
3. CHOKE VALVE
4. SHAFT
5. PISTON
6. PIN
7. SOLENOID AND BRACKET
8. COIL HOUSING SCREW
9. COIL HOUSING RETAINER
10. CHOKE COVER
11. COIL HOUSING GASKET
12. COIL HOUSING BAFFLE PLATE
13. DIAPHRAGM LIFTER LINK
14. WASHER
15. DIAPHRAGM SPRING
16. DIAPHRAGM HOUSING SCREW (4)
17. DIAPHRAGM HOUSING
18. WASHER
19. SPACER
20. DIAPHRAGM
21. IDLE SCREW LIMITER CAP
22. IDLE MIXTURE SCREW
23. SPRING
24. THROTTLE BODY
25. BODY FLANGE SCREW (3)
26. THROTTLE SHAFT ARM
27. PUMP CONNECTOR LINK
28. BODY GASKET
29. FAST IDLE CAM
30. FAST IDLE CAM SCREW
31. MAIN BODY
32. DISCHARGE BALL
33. DISCHARGE BALL WEIGHT
34. METERING ROD JET
35. LOW SPEED JET
36. FLOAT
37. FLOAT PIN
38. NEEDLE PIN
39. NEEDLE SPRING
40. NEEDLE, NEEDLE SEAT GASKET
41. CHOKE CONNECTOR ROD
42. CHOKE CONNECTOR ROD RETAINER
43. METERING ROD
44. LEVER
45. METERING ROD ARM
46. UPPER PUMP SPRING
47. UPPER PUMP SPRING RETAINER
48. AIR HORN GASKET
49. SCREW
50. CHAMBER
51. GASKET
52. AIR HORN SCREW (SHORT)
53. AIR HORN SCREW (LONG)

Fig. 2 Carter Model YF Series carburetor. 1977-78 American Motors with altitude compensation

Fig. 8 YF metering rod adjustment

Fig. 9 YF fast idle cam linkage adjustment

Fig. 10 YF choke plate pulldown adjustment

1. AIR HORN
2. CHOKE
3. SCREW
4. SHAFT
5. PISTON
6. PIN
7. SOLENOID AND BRACKET
8. COIL HOUSING SCREW
9. COIL HOUSING RETAINER
10. CHOKE COVER
11. COIL HOUSING GASKET
12. COIL HOUSING BAFFLE PLATE
13. UPPER PUMP SPRING RETAINER
14. UPPER PUMP SPRING
15. METERING ROD ARM
16. DIAPHRAGM LIFTER LINK
17. WASHER
18. DIAPHRAGM SPRING[
19. DIAPHRAGM HOUSING SCREW (4)
20. DIAPHRAGM HOUSING
21. WASHER
22. SPACER
23. DIAPHRAGM
24. DISCHARGE BALL WEIGHT
25. DISCHARGE BALL
26. BODY FLANGE SCREW (3)
27. FAST IDLE CAM
28. FAST IDLE CAM SCREW
29. MAIN BODY
30. BODY GASKET
31. IDLE SCREW LIMITER CAP
32. IDLE MIXTURE SCREW
33. SPRING
34. THROTTLE BODY
35. WAVE WASHER
36. ARM
37. SCREW
38. PUMP CONNECTOR LINK
39. THROTTLE SHAFT ARM
40. RETAINER
41. LEVER
42. METERING ROD JET
43. LOW SPEED JET
44. FLOAT
45. FLOAT PIN
46. NEEDLE PIN
47. NEEDLE SPRING
48. NEEDLE, NEEDLE SEAT, GASKET
49. CHOKE CONNECTOR ROD
50. CHOKE CONNECTOR ROD RETAINER
51. LEVER
52. METERING ROD
53. AIR HORN GASKET
54. SPRING
55. LIFTER
56. BELLCRANK
57. RETAINER
58. SPRING
59. AIR HORN SCREW (SHORT)
60. AIR HORN SCREW (LONG)
61. STUD SUPPORT
62. SCREW

Fig. 3 Carter Model YF Series carburetor. 1979 American Motors

Fig. 6 YF float level adjustment

Fig. 7 YF float drop adjustment

AIR CLEANER BRACKET

SCREWS

SCREW

SCREW

CHOKE PLATE

AIR HORN ASSEMBLY

ANTI–STALL DASHPOT

AIR HORN ASSEMBLY

FAST IDLE CHOKE LEVER

COIL HOUSING BAFFLE PLATE

COIL HOUSING GASKET

ELECTRIC ASSIST CHOKE CAP

AIR HORN GASKET

CHOKE PISTON LEVER AND SHAFT ASSEMBLY

PISTON PIN

CHOKE PISTON

NEEDLE PIN SPRING, SEAT AND GASKET ASSEMBLY

METERING ROD ARM ASSEMBLY

METERING ROD ARM SPRING

UPPER PUMP SPRING RETAINER

COIL HOUSING RETAINER

UPPER PUMP SPRING 9D598

ATTACHING SCREW

FLOAT PIN

FLOAT AND LEVER ASSEMBLY

METERING ROD

ANTI-ROCK PLATE

PUMP LIFTER LINK

PUMP DIAPHRAGM SPRING RETAINER

PUMP DIAPHRAGM SPRING

DIAPHRAGM HOUSING ATTACHING SCREW

PUMP DIAPHRAGM HOUSING ASSEMBLY

LOW SPEED JET

METERING ROD JET

PUMP CHECK WEIGHT

PUMP CHECK BALL

MAIN BODY CASTING

SCREW

BODY FLANGE ATTACHING SCREW

BODY FLANGE GASKET

PUMP DIAPHRAGM ASSEMBLY

THROTTLE SHAFT ARM

SCREW

PUMP CONNECTOR LINK

BODY FLANGE ATTACHING SCREW

FAST IDLE CAM

BUSHING

FAST IDLE ADJUSTING SCREW

SOLENOID "OFF" OR CURB IDLE SPEED SCREW

WASHER

THROTTLE PLATE

FAST IDLE CAM LINK

LIMITER CAP

SPRING

SPRING

IDLE FUEL MIXTURE ADJUSTING SCREW AND SPRING

THROTTLE SHAFT AND LEVER ASSEMBLY

ALUMINUM THROTTLE BODY FLANGE ASSEMBLY

Fig. 4 Carter Model YF Series carburetor. 1977 Ford

Fig. 5 Carter Model YF Series carburetor. 1978-80 Ford

THROTTLE LEVER
(OPEN POSITION)

DRILL GAUGE

MAKE DECHOKE
ADJUSTMENT HERE

Fig. 11 YF dechoke adjustment

APPROX. 2½ TURNS FROM INNER SEAT
TO OUTER SEAT

HIGH ALTITUDE

LOW ALTITUDE

Fig. 12 Altitude compensator adjustment.
1977–78 American Motors

Gauge Point

Dashpot Locknut

Fig. 13 YF dashpot adjustment

CARTER BBD ADJUSTMENT SPECIFICATIONS
See Tune Up Chart in car chapter for curb and fast idle speeds.

Year	Carb. Model	Float Level	Pump Travel Inch	Bowl Vent Clearance	Choke Unloader Clearance	Initial Choke Valve Clearance	Choke Vacuum Kick Clearance	Fast Idle Cam Position Clearance	Automatic Choke Setting
AMERICAN MOTORS									
1977	8103	¼	.496	—	.280	.150	—	.120	1 Rich
	8104	¼	.520	—	.280	.128	—	.095	1 Rich
	8117	¼	.480	—	.280	.152	—	.112	1 Rich
1978	8128	¼	.496	①	.280	.150	—	.110	Index
	8129	¼	.520	①	.280	.128	—	.095	1 Rich
1979	8185	¼	.470	①	.280	.140	—	.110	1 Rich
	8186	¼	.520	①	.280	.150	—	.110	1 Rich
	8187	¼	.470	①	.280	.140	—	.110	1 Rich
	8221	¼	.530	①	.280	.150	—	.110	1 Rich
1980	8216	¼	.520	①	.280	.140	—	.090	2 Rich
	8246	¼	.520	①	.280	.140	—	.095	2 Rich
	8247	¼	.520	①	.280	.150	—	.095	1 Rich
	8248	¼	.520	①	.280	.150	—	.095	1 Rich
	8253	¼	.470	①	.280	.128	—	.095	2 Rich
	8256	¼	.470	①	.280	.128	—	.093	2 Rich
	8278	¼	.542	①	.280	.140	—	.093	Index
	8313	¼	.520	①	.280	.140	—	.095	1 Rich
1981	8302	¼	.500	①	.280	.128	—	.095	1 Rich
	8303	¼	.500	①	.280	.128	—	.090	1 Rich
	8306	¼	.500	①	.280	.128	—	.095	1 Rich
	8307	¼	.500	①	.280	.128	—	.095	1 Rich
	8308	¼	.500	①	.280	.128	—	.095	2 Rich
	8309	¼	.520	①	.280	.128	—	.093	2 Rich
	8310	¼	.525	①	.280	.140	—	.095	Index
1982	8338	¼	.520	①	.280	.140	—	.095	1 Rich
	8339	¼	.520	①	.280	.140	—	.095	1 Rich

①—Bowl vent should begin to open with fast idle cam on second step of cam.

Continued

CARTER BBD ADJUSTMENT SPECIFICATIONS—Continued

See Tune Up Chart in car chapter for curb and fast idle speeds.

Year	Carb. Model	Float Level	Pump Travel Inch	Bowl Vent Clearance	Choke Unloader Clearance	Initial Choke Valve Clearance	Choke Vacuum Kick Clearance	Fast Idle Cam Position Clearance	Automatic Choke Setting
CHRYSLER CORP.									
1977	8087S	1/4	15/32 ①	—	.280	—	.100	.070	Fixed
	8089S	1/4	15/32 ①	—	.280	—	.130	.070	Fixed
	8090S	1/4	15/32 ①	—	.280	—	.130	.070	Fixed
	8093S	1/4	15/32 ①	—	.310	—	.130	.070	Fixed
	8094S	1/4	15/32 ①	—	.310	—	.070	.070	Fixed
	8096S	1/4	15/32 ①	—	.310	—	.110	.070	Fixed
	8126S	1/4	②	—	.310	—	.110	.070	Fixed
	8127S	1/4	15/32 ①	—	.280	—	.110	.070	Fixed
	8135S	1/4	15/32 ①	—	.310	—	.070	.070	Fixed
	8145S	1/4	15/32 ①	—	.310	—	.110	.070	Fixed
	8170S	1/4	1/2 ①	.080 ①	.310	—	.110	.070	Fixed
	8171S	1/4	1/2 ①	.080 ①	.310	—	.110	.070	Fixed
	8172S	1/4	1/2 ①	.080 ①	.310	—	.110	.070	Fixed
1978	8136S	1/4	1/2 ①	.080 ①	.280	—	.110	.070	Fixed
	8137S	1/4	1/2 ①	.080 ①	.280	—	.100	.070	Fixed
	8143S	1/4	1/2 ①	.080 ①	.280	—	.150	.070	Fixed
	8175S	1/4	1/2 ①	.080 ①	.280	—	.160	.070	Fixed
	8177S	1/4	1/2 ①	.080 ①	.280	—	.100	.070	Fixed
1979	8198S	1/4	1/2 ①	.080 ①	.280	—	.100	.070	Fixed
	8199S	1/4	1/2 ①	.080 ①	.280	—	.100	.070	Fixed
1980	8233S	1/4	1/2 ①	.080 ①	.280	—	.130	.070	Fixed
	8237S	1/4	1/2 ①	.080 ①	.280	—	.110	.070	Fixed
1981	8291S	1/4	1/2 ①	—	.280	—	.130	.070	Fixed
1982	8290S	1/4	1/2	.80	.280	—	.100	.070	Fixed
	8291S	1/4	1/2	—	.280	—	.130	.070	Fixed
	8292S	1/4	1/2	.80	.280	—	.130	.070	Fixed

①—At idle.

②—Model less red tag, 15/32 inch at idle; model with red tag, 1/2 inch at idle.

MODEL BBD ADJUSTMENTS

Fig. 1 is an exploded view of a typical 1977–82 BBD two barrel carburetor. Note that American Motors units are equipped with an automatic choke coil. Fig. 2 is an external view of a typical 1977–78 unit used on Chrysler Corp. vehicles equipped with Lean Burn System. Fig. 3 is a typical view of 1977–78 units less Lean Burn and all 1979 Chrysler Corp. vehicles. Fig. 4 is an external view of units used on 1980–82 Chrysler Corp. vehicles less Electronic Feedback Carburetor System. Fig. 4A is an external view of units used on 1981–82 Chrysler Corp. vehicles equipped with Electronic Feedback Carburetor System. On some Chrysler vehicles equipped with a manual transmission, a dashpot is mounted on the carburetor. On some Chrysler vehicles equipped with an automatic transmission, an idle enrichment system is used to reduce cold engine stalling by the use of an additional metering system which enriches the mixture in the off idle position. This system is controlled by a vacuum diaphragm mounted near the top of the carburetor.

Float Level Adjustment

Fig. 5—With carburetor body inverted so that weight of floats ONLY is forcing needle against its seat, use a T-scale or the tool shown, and check the float level from surface of fuel bowl to crown of each float at center.

If an adjustment is necessary, hold floats on bottom of bowl and bend float lip as required to give the specified dimension.

CAUTION: When bending the float lip, do not allow the lip to push against the needle as the synthetic rubber tip (if used) can be compressed sufficiently to cause a false setting which will affect correct level of fuel in bowl. After being compressed, the tip is very slow to recover its original shape.

Accelerator Pump

1977–82 1¼" Bore Units, Fig. 6
1. Back off curb idle adjusting screw, completely closing throttle valve, then open choke valve, allowing throttle valves to seat in bores. Ensure accelerator pump "S" link is located in outer hole or pump arm.
2. Turn curb idle adjusting screw until screw contacts, stop, then rotate screw two additional turns.
3. Measure distance between air horn surface and top of accelerator pump shaft. Refer to BBD Specifications Chart.

4. Adjust by loosening pump arm adjusting screw and rotating sleeve until proper dimension is obtained. Tighten adjusting screw.

Bowl Vent Valve

Fig. 7

NOTE: The accelerator pump stroke and curb idle speed must be properly adjusted before making this adjustment.

1. Remove step-up piston cover plate and gasket.
2. Insert specified gauge between top of bowl vent valve and seat. Refer to the BBD Specifications Chart.
3. Adjust by bending bowl vent lever tab while supporting bowl vent lever assembly.
4. Install step-up piston cover gasket and cover.

Choke Unloader Adjustment

Fig. 8—The choke unloader is a mechanical device to partially open the choke valve at wide open throttle. It is used to eliminate

CARBURETORS

WITH AUTOMATIC TRANSMISSION

1. DIAPHRAGM CONNECTOR LINK
2. SCREW
3. CHOKE VACUUM DIAPHRAGM
4. HOSE
5. VALVE
6. METERING ROD
7. S-LINK
8. PUMP ARM
9. GASKET
10. ROLLOVER CHECK VALVE
11. SCREW
12. LOCK
13. ROD LIFTER
14. BRACKET
15. NUT
16. SOLENOID
17. SCREW
18. AIR HORN RETAINING SCREW (SHORT)
19. AIR HORN RETAINING SCREW (LONG)
20. PUMP LEVER
21. VENTURI CLUSTER SCREW

22. IDLE FUEL PICK-UP TUBE
23. GASKET
24. VENTURI CLUSTER
25. GASKET
26. CHECK BALL (SMALL)
27. FLOAT
28. FULCRUM PIN
29. BAFFLE
30. CLIP
31. CHOKE LINK
32. SCREW
33. FAST IDLE CAM
34. GASKET
35. THERMOSTATIC CHOKE SHAFT
36. SPRING
37. SCREW
38. PUMP LINK
39. CLIP
40. GASKET
41. LIMITER CAP
42. SCREW

43. THROTTLE BODY
44. CHOKE HOUSING
45. BAFFLE
46. GASKET
47. RETAINER
48. CHOKE COIL
49. LEVER
50. CHOKE ROD
51. CLIP
52. NEEDLE AND SEAT ASSEMBLY
53. MAIN BODY
54. MAIN METERING JET
55. CHECK BALL (LARGE)
56. ACCELERATOR PUMP PLUNGER
57. FULCRUM PIN RETAINER
58. GASKET
59. SPRING
60. AIR HORN
61. LEVER

Fig. 1 Exploded view of Carter model BBD 1¼" two barrel carburetor. 1977–82 (Typical)

TO EGR VACUUM AMPLIFIER

BOWL VENT

THROTTLE POSITION TRANSDUCER

CURB IDLE SCREW

FAST IDLE SPEED SCREW

I.D. TAG

IDLE STOP CARBURETOR SWITCH

TO ESA VACUUM TRANSDUCER (ON AIR CLEANER)

TO PORTED EGR SYSTEM

TO CRANKCASE PCV VALVE

TO AIR CLEANER HEATED INLET AIR SYSTEM

TO VAPOR CANISTER PURGE PORT

TO AIR PUMP DIVERTER VALVE

IDLE MIXTURE ADJ. SCREWS (2)

Fig. 2 BBD 1¼″ carburetor assembly. 1977–78 with Lean Burn (Typical)

IDLE ENRICHMENT DIAPHRAGM
TO DISTRIBUTOR OSAC VALVE

I.D. TAG

TO EGR VACUUM AMPLIFIER

TO AIR CLEANER HEATED INLET AIR SYSTEM

TO CRANKCASE PCV VALVE

TO VAPOR CANISTER PURGE PORT

IDLE MIXTURE ADJUSTING SCREWS (2)

Fig. 3 BBD 1¼″ carburetor assembly. 1977–79 less Lean Burn & 1979 All (Typical)

IDENTIFICATION TAG

BOWL VENT TO CANISTER

TO SOLENOID IDLE STOP

SOLENOID IDLE STOP

TO VAPOR CANISTER PURGE PORT

IDLE MIXTURE ADJUSTING SCREWS (2)

TO DIVERTER VALVE

TO EGR VACUUM AMPLIFIER

TO AIR CLEANER HEATED INLET AIR SYSTEM

TO CRANKCASE PCV VALVE

TO IDLE GROUND SWITCH

TO DISTRIBUTOR OSAC VALVE OR ESA VACUUM TRANSDUCER

Fig. 4   BBD 1¼" carburetor assembly. 1980—82 units less Electronic Feedback Carburetor System (Typical)

BOWL VENT TO CANISTER

TO EGR VACUUM AMPLIFIER

BOWL VENT TO CANISTER

DUTY CYCLE SOLENOID

SOLENOID IDLE STOP

TO CCEV VALVE

TO CRANKCASE PCV VALVE

TO CHOKE DIAPHRAGM

TO POWER BRAKE

TO AIR CLEANER HEATED INLET AIR CLEANER

BOWL VENT SOLENOID

Fig. 4A   BBD 1¼" carburetor assembly. 1981—82 units with Electronic Feedback Carburetor System (Typical)

Fig. 5 Checking float level. BBD carburetors

Fig. 7 Bowl vent valve adjustment. 1978–80 BBD carburetor

choke enrichment during engine cranking. Engines that have been flooded or stalled by excessive choke enrichment can be cleared by the use of the unloader. Adjust as follows:

1. Hold throttle valve in wide open position. Insert the specified drill size between upper edge of choke valve and inner wall of air horn.
2. With a finger lightly pressing against choke valve, a slight drag should be felt

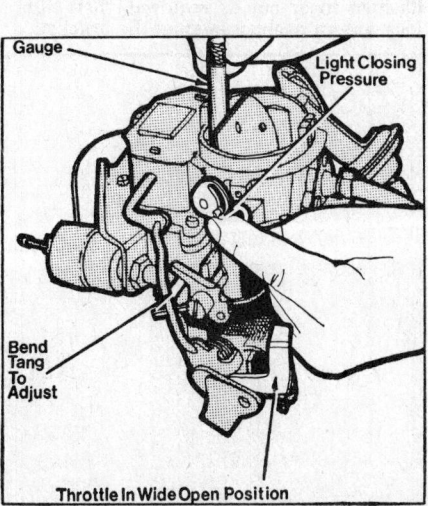

Fig. 8 Choke unloader setting. BBD carburetors

Fig. 6 Accelerator pump setting, 1977–82 BBD 1¼″

as the drill is being withdrawn.
3. If an adjustment is necessary, bend unloader tang on throttle lever until specified opening has been obtained.

Fast Idle Cam Position
Fig. 9
1. With fast idle adjusting screw contacting second highest step on fast idle cam, move choke valve toward closed position with light pressure on choke shaft lever.
2. Insert the specified size drill between top of choke valve and air horn wall. An adjustment will be necessary if a slight drag is not obtained as drill is being removed.
3. Adjust by bending fast idle connector rod at angle.

Fig. 9 Fast idle cam position adjustment. BBD 1¼″ bore carburetors

Initial Choke Valve Clearance
1977–82 American Motors
Fig. 10—Loosen choke cover and rotate ¼ turn rich, then tighten one screw. Open throttle valve slightly to place fast idle screw on high step of cam. Using, an external vacuum source, apply at least 19 inches of vacuum to pull diaphragm against stop. Measure clearance between choke plate and air horn wall. Adjust by bending diaphragm connector link.

Choke Vacuum Kick Adjustment
1978–82 Chrysler
Fig. 11—Open throttle and close choke, then close throttle to trap fast idle cam at closed choke position. Using an external vacuum source, apply 15 or more inches of vacuum to diaphragm. Apply a closing force on choke lever to completely compress spring in diaphragm stem without distorting linkage. Note that the solid rod stem of diaphragm extends to an internal stop as spring compresses. Measure clearance between top of choke valve and air horn wall at throttle lever

Fig. 10 Initial choke valve clearance adjustment. 1977–82 American Motors BBD unit

CARBURETORS

Fig. 11 Choke vacuum kick setting. BBD 1¼" bore carburetors

Fig. 12 Step-up piston adjustment

Fig. 13 Step-up piston adjustment. 1977–82 BBD 1¼" carburetors

side. Adjust clearance by bending diaphragm link at "U" bend. Remove external vacuum source and linkage for free movement.

1977 Chrysler

Fig. 11—The choke diaphragm adjustment controls the fuel delivery while the engine is running. It positions the choke valve within the air horn by action of the linkage between choke shaft and diaphragm. The diaphragm must be energized to measure the vacuum kick adjustment. Use either a distributor test machine with a vacuum source, or vacuum supplied by another vehicle.

1. If adjustment is to be made with engine running, disconnect fast idle linkage to allow choke to close to kick position with engine at curb idle. If an auxiliary vacuum source is to be used, open throttle valves (engine not running) and move choke to closed position. Release throttle first, then release choke.
2. When using an auxiliary vacuum source, disconnect vacuum hose from carburetor and connect it to hose from vacuum supply with a small length of tube to act as a fitting. Removal of hose from diaphragm may require forces which damage the system. Apply a vacuum of 15 or more inches of mercury.
3. Insert the specified drill size between choke valve and wall of air horn. Apply sufficient closing pressure on lever to which choke rod attaches to provide a minimum choke valve opening without distortion of diaphragm link. Note that the cylindrical stem of diaphragm will extend as internal spring is compressed. This spring must be fully compressed for

proper measurement of vacuum kick adjustment.

4. An adjustment will be necessary if a slight drag is not obtained as drill is being removed. Shorten or lengthen diaphragm link to obtain correct choke opening. Length changes should be made carefully by bending (opening or closing) the bend provided in the diaphragm link. *Do not apply twisting or bending force to diaphragm.*
5. Reinstall vacuum hose on correct carburetor fitting. Return fast idel linkage to its original condition if it has been disturbed as in Step 1.
6. Check as follows: With no vacuum applied to diaphragm, choke valve should move freely between open and closed positions. If movement is not free, examine linkage for misalignment or interferences caused by bending operation. Repeat adjustment if necessary.

Step-up Piston Adjustment

1977–82 1¼" BBD Units, Figs. 12 & 13

1. On 1978–82 Chrysler units and 1977 and 1979–82 American Motors units, adjust vacuum piston gap to .035 inch. On 1978 American Motors units, adjust vacuum piston gap to .040 inch. Rotate allen head screw on top of piston to adjust gap.

2. On all units, install step-up piston assembly into air horn bore, ensuring metering rods are positioned in the metering jets.
3. Back off curb idle screw until throttle valves are completely closed. Count number of turns so that screw can be returned to its original setting.
4. Fully depress piston and while applying moderate pressure on rod lifter, tighten rod lifter screw.
5. Release piston and rod lifter and reset curb idle screw.

Dashpot Adjustment

American Motors

With curb idle speed properly adjusted, hold dashpot plunger firmly against stop. Measure clearance between plunger and throttle lever with throttle in idle position. Clearance should be .104 inch. To adjust, loosen locknut and rotate dashpot.

Chrysler

To adjust the dashpot, have the curb idle speed and mixture properly adjusted, and install a tachometer. Position throttle lever so that actuating tab on lever is contacting stem of dashpot but not depressing it. Engine RPM should be 2500 RPM. If not correct, screw dashpot in or out as required, then tighten lock nut on dashpot against the bracket.

CARTER TQ ADJUSTMENT SPECIFICATIONS

See Tune Up Chart in car chapters for curb and fast idle speeds.

Year	Carb. Model	Float Setting	Secondary Throttle Linkage	Secondary Air Valve Opening	Secondary Air Valve Spring	Pump Travel	Choke Control Lever (Off Car)	Choke Vacuum Kick	Choke Unloader	Choke Setting
CHRYSLER CORP.										
1977	9076S	27/32	(1)	1/2	(4)	(5)	3 3/8	.100	.310	Fixed
	9077S	27/32	(1)	31/64	1 1/2 Turn	33/64 (2)	3 3/8	.100	.310	Fixed
	9078S	27/32	(1)	1/2	1 1/4 Turn	33/64 (2)	3 3/8	.100	.310	Fixed
	9080S	27/32	(1)	1/2	1 1/4 Turn	33/64 (3)	3 3/8	.100	.310	Fixed
	9081S	27/32	(1)	1/2	1 1/4 Turn	33/64 (2)	3 3/8	.100	.310	Fixed
	9093S	27/32	(1)	17/32	1 1/4 Turn	33/64 (3)	3 3/8	.100	.310	Fixed
	9101S	27/32	(1)	1/2	1 1/4 Turn	33/64 (2)	3 3/8	.100	.310	Fixed
	9102S	27/32	(1)	31/64	1 1/2 Turn	33/64 (2)	3 3/8	.100	.310	Fixed
	9103S	27/32	(1)	31/64	1 1/2 Turn	33/64 (2)	3 3/8	.100	.310	Fixed
	9115S	27/32	(1)	1/2	2 1/4 Turn	31/64 (2)	3 3/8	.150	.310	Fixed
	9119S	27/32	(1)	1/2	1 1/4 Turn	33/64 (2)	3 3/8	.100	.310	Fixed
1978	9104S	29/32	(1)	1/2	1 1/2 Turn	31/64 (2)	3 3/8	.150	.310	Fixed
	9109S	27/32	(1)	1/2	1 1/2 Turn	33/64 (2)	3 3/8	.100	.310	Fixed
	9110S	27/32	(1)	1/2	1 1/2 Turn	33/64 (2)	3 3/8	.100	.310	Fixed
	9112S	29/32	(1)	1/2	1 1/2 Turn	33/64 (2)	3 3/8	.100	.310	Fixed
	9134S	29/32	(1)	1/2	1 1/2 Turn	31/64 (3)	3 3/8	.100	.310	Fixed
	9140S	29/32	(1)	1/2	1 1/2 Turn	33/64 (2)	3 3/8	.150	.310	Fixed
	9147S	29/32	(1)	1/2	1 1/2 Turn	31/64 (3)	3 3/8	.100	.310	Fixed
	9148S	29/32	(1)	1/2	1 1/2 Turn	33/64 (2)	3 3/8	.100	.310	Fixed
1979	9195S	29/32	(1)	3/8	2 Turns	33/64 (2)	3 3/8	.100	.310	Fixed
	9196S	29/32	(1)	1/2	2 Turns	33/64 (2)	3 3/8	.100	.310	Fixed
	9198S	29/32	(1)	1/2	2 Turns	33/64 (2)	3 3/8	.100	.310	Fixed
	9202S	29/32	(1)	1/2	2 Turns	33/64 (2)	3 3/8	.100	.310	Fixed
	9245S	29/32	(1)	3/8	2 Turns	33/64 (2)	3 3/8	.100	.310	Fixed
	9246S	29/32	(1)	1/2	2 Turns	33/64 (2)	3 3/8	.100	.310	Fixed
1980	9244S	29/32	(1)	1/2	2 1/2 Turns	11/32 (6)	3 3/8	.100	.310	Fixed
	9234A	29/32	(1)	1/2	2 1/4 Turns	33/64 (6)(7)	3.30	.110	.310	Fixed
	9320S	29/32	(1)	3/8	2 1/4 Turns	33/64 (6)(7)	3.30	.110	.310	Fixed
1981	9372S	29/32	(1)	13/32	1 3/4 Turns	33/64 (6)(7)	3 3/8	.130	.312	Fixed
	9373S	29/32	(1)	13/32	1 3/4 Turns	33/64 (6)(7)	3 3/8	.130	.312	Fixed
	9381S	29/32	(1)	13/32	1 3/4 Turns	33/64 (6)(7)	3 3/8	.130	.312	Fixed
1982	9337S	29/32	(1)	13/32	1 3/4 Turns	33/64 (6)(7)	3 3/8	.130	.312	Fixed
	9372S	29/32	(1)	13/32	1 3/4 Turns	33/64 (6)(7)	3 3/8	.130	.312	Fixed
	9385S	29/32	(1)	13/32	1 3/4 Turns	33/64 (6)(7)	3 3/8	.130	.312	Fixed

(1)—Adjust link so primary and secondary stops both contact at same time.

(2)—Secondary stage pick/up adjustment 5/16 inch.

(3)—Secondary stage pick/up adjustment 22/64 inch.

(4)—Models less red tag. 1 1/2 turns; models with red tag, 2 1/4 turns.

(5)—Models less red tag, 33/64 inch, refer to note (2).
Models with red tag, 31/64 inch, refer to note (3).

(6)—Slot No. 2.

(7)—Secondary stage pick/up adjustment 25/64 inch.

SECONDARY AIR VALVE
CHOKE VALVE
I.D. NUMBER
IDLE ENRICHMENT VALVE ASSY.
CURB IDLE ADJUSTMENT
FAST IDLE CAM
EGR VACUUM AMP.
TO VAPOR CANISTER PURGE PORT
TO PCV VALVE
TO DISTRIBUTOR OSAC VALVE
IDLE MIXTURE SCREWS WITH LIMITER CAPS (2)
FAST IDLE ADJ.
BOWL VENT
CHOKE DIAPHRAGM
TO AIR CLEANER HEATED INLET AIR SYSTEM

Fig. 1   TQ carburetor assembly. 1977 (Typical)

CURB IDLE ADJ.
SECONDARY AIR VALVE
IDLE STOP CARBURETOR SWITCH
CURB IDLE ADJ. (ELB)
CHOKE DIAPHRAGM
IDLE MIXTURE SCREWS WITH LIMITER CAPS (2)
CHOKE VALVE
IDLE ENRICHMENT VALVE ASSEMBLY
I.D. NO.
TO ESA VACUUM TRANSDUCER
THROTTLE POSITION TRANSDUCER
ALTITUDE COMPENSATOR
FAST IDLE ADJUSTMENT
TO HEATED AIR INLET
BOWL VENT SOLENOID
TO VAPOR CANISTER
FUEL INLET HOSE
EGR VACUUM AMPLIFIER
TO AIR PUMP DIVERTER VALVE
TO PCV VALVE
TO VAPOR CANISTER PURGE PORT

Fig. 2   TQ carburetor assembly. 1978-79 (Typical)

SECONDARY AIR VALVE

CHOKE VALVE

IDLE MIXTURE SCREWS

ALITITUDE COMPENSATOR

CHOKE VALVE/AIR VALVE DIAPHRAGM

FAST IDLE SPEED SCREW

IDLE SPEED SCREW

IDLE STOP SWITCH

TO PCV VALVE

TO VAPOR CANISTER (PURGE PORT)

FUEL INLET LOCATION

IDENTIFICATION NUMBER

TO HEATED INLET AIR SYSTEM

TO VAPOR CANISTER (BOWL VENT)

AIR CONDITIONING/BACKLITE SOLENOID IDLE STOP

S/S IDLE SPEED SCREW

TO AIR PUMP DIVERTER VALVE

RY322

Fig. 3 TQ carburetor assembly. 1980–82 (Typical)

MODEL TQ ADJUSTMENTS

The TQ (Thermo-Quad) carburetor, Figs. 1 thru 4, is unique in design in that it has a black main body or fuel bowl of molded phenolic resin. This acts as an effective heat insulator. Fuel is kept cooler by about 20 degrees Fahrenheit than in carburetors of all metal design. Another reason for the lower operating temperatures is its suspended design metering system. All calibration points with the exception of the idle adjusting screws, are in the upper aluminum casting or air horn and are in effect suspended in cavities in the plastic main body.

On 1977–79 vehicles with automatic transmissions, an idle enrichment system is used to reduce cold engine stalling by the use of an additional metering system, which enriches the mixture in the off idle position. This system is controlled by a vacuum diaphragm mounted near the top of the carburetor.

Float Setting

Fig. 5—With bowl cover inverted, gasket installed and floats resting on seated needle, the dimension of each float from bowl cover gasket to bottom side of float should be as shown in *TQ Specifications Chart*. To adjust, bend float lever.

NOTE: When adjusting, do not allow lip of float lever to be pressed against needle.

Secondary Throttle Linkage

Fig. 6—Hold fast idle lever in curb idle position and invert carburetor. Open primary throttle valve until the primary and second-ary stops contact simultaneously. To adjust, bend secondary throttle operating rod at angle until correct adjustment is obtained.

Secondary Air Valve Opening

Fig. 7

1. With air valve in closed position, the opening along air valve at its long side must be at its maximum and parallel with air horn gasket surface.

2. With air valve wide open, the opening of the air valve at the short side and air horn must be as shown in *TQ Specifications Chart*. The corner of air valve is notched for adjustment. Bend the cor-

Scale

Gasket In Place

Float

Fig. 5 TQ float setting

Fig. 4 Carter TQ model exploded view (Typical)

Fig. 6   TQ secondary throttle adjustment

Fig. 7   TQ secondary air valve opening

ner with a pair of pliers to give proper opening.

Secondary Air Valve Spring Tension

Fig. 8—Loosen air valve lock plug and allow air valve to position itself wide open. With a long screwdriver that will enter center of tool C-4152 positioned on air valve adjustment plug, turn plug counter-clockwise until air valve contacts stop lightly, then turn additional turn as specified in *TQ Specifications Chart.* Hold plug with screwdriver and tighten lock plug securely with tool C-4152.

Accelerator Pump Stroke

1977–79 Units

Fig. 9—First Stage. Ensure throttle connector rod is in center hole on three hold pump arm or inner hole on two hole pump arm. With idle adjusting screw adjusted to the specified curb idle speed, measure distance from air horn surface to top of accelerator pump plunger. If equipped with an idle stop solenoid the ignition switch must be in the on position. Dimensions should be as shown in the *TQ Specifications Chart.* Bend throttle connector rod at lower angle to adjust.

Second Stage. With choke in the open position, open throttle until secondary lockout latch is just applied. Plunger downward travel stops at this point. Measure distance from air horn surface to top of accelerator pump plunger. Dimension should be shown in the *TQ Specifications Chart.* Bend tang on throttle to adjust.

1980–82 Units

Fig. 10—Ensure that throttle connector rod is in the specified hole of the pump arm. With

Fig. 8   TQ secondary air valve spring tension

Fig. 9   TQ accelerator pump stroke adjustment, with staged pump system. 1977–79 units

CARBURETORS

BEND THROTTLE CONNECTOR ROD HERE TO ADJUST

THROTTLE LEVER

TO TOP OF PUMP PLUNGER STEM

AIR HORN SURFACE

SLOT #1 SLOT #2

PUMP LEVER

LIGHT CLOSING PRESSURE

BEND HERE TO ADJUST

TOP OF HOLE

BASE OF CARBURETOR

Fig. 10 TQ accelerator pump stroke adjustment. 1980–82 units

Fig. 11 TQ choke control lever adjustment

idle adjusting screw adjusted to the specified curb idle speed, measure distance from air horn surface to top of accelerator pump plunger. Dimensions should be as shown in the TQ Specification Chart. Adjust plunger height by bending throttle connector rod in area indicated in Fig. 10.

Choke Control Lever

Fig. 11—Place carburetor on a flat surface. Close choke by pushing on choke lever with throttle partly open. Measure vertical distance between top of rod hole in control lever and base of carburetor (flat surface). Dimension should be as shown in TQ Specifications Chart. Adjust by bending link connecting the two choke shafts.

Choke Diaphragm Connector Rod

Fig. 12—Apply a vacuum of 15 inches Hg or more to fully depress diaphragm. An auxiliary source like a distributor test machine can be used for this purpose. With air valve closed, adjust connector rod to give .040" clearance between air valve and stop.

Vacuum Kick Adjustment

Fig. 13—With engine running, back off fast idle speed screw until choke can be closed to kick position at idle. Note number of screw turns so fast idle can be turned back to original adjustment. Insert a gauge or drill of specified size between long side (lower edge) of choke valve and air horn wall. Apply sufficient pressure on choke control lever to pro-

vide a minimum choke valve opening. The spring connecting the control lever to the adjustment lever must be fully extended for proper adjustment. Bend tang as shown to change contact with end of diaphragm rod. Do not adjust diaphragm rod. A slight drag should be felt as drill is being removed.

Fast Idle Cam & Linkage

Fig. 14—With fast idle adjusting screw on second step of fast idle cam, move choke valve toward closed position with light pressure on choke control lever. Clearance between choke valve lower edge and air horn wall should be .100 inch. Adjust by bending fast idle connector rod at angle.

Choke Unloader Adjustment

Fig. 15—Hold throttle valves in wide open position and insert specified drill between long side (lower edge) of choke valve and inner wall of air horn. With finger lightly

Gauge (Apply Light Down Pressure)

Stop

Air Valve

To Vacuum Source

Bend Link To Adjust

Fig. 12 TQ choke diaphragm connector rod

Gauge

Screw Driver

Bend Tang To Adjust

Light Closing Pressure

To Vacuum Source

Fig. 13 TQ vacuum kick adjustment

Fig. 14 TQ fast idle cam & linkage adjustment

Fig. 15 TQ choke unloader adjustment

pressing against choke valve control lever, a slight drag should be felt as drill is withdrawn. Refer to TQ Specification Chart for proper drill size or dimension. Adjust by bending tang on fast idle control lever.

Secondary Throttle Lockout

Fig. 16—Move choke control lever to open choke position. Measure clearance between lockout lever and stop. Clearance should be .060–.090 inch on 1977 and 1980–82 units and .075 inch on 1978–79 units. Adjust by bending tang on fast idle control lever.

Bowl Vent Valve Adjustment

1977–78 Units

Fig. 17—Remove bowl vent valve checking hole plug in bowl cover. With throttle valves at curb idle, insert a narrow ruler down through hole. Allow ruler to rest lightly on top of valve. Dimension should be .812 inch on 1977–78 units. Adjust by bending bowl vent operating lever at notch. Install a new plug.

Solenoid Bowl Vent Valve Check

Fig. 18, 1978–82

1. Remove air cleaner.

2. Disconnect vacuum hose from solenoid bowl vent diaphragm.
3. Connect an external vacuum source and apply 15 inches of vacuum to the diaphragm.
4. Observe valve movement through air horn vent tube. Valve should move when vacuum is applied.
5. Turn ignition switch "On" and disconnect external vacuum source. The valve should remain in the downward position until the ignition switch is turned "Off".
6. If the valve does not move when vacuum is applied, the diaphragm is defective and requires replacement. If the valve does not remain in the downward position when the ignition switch is turned "On" and the vacuum source removed, the solenoid or wiring is defective.
7. Install air cleaner.

Fig. 16 TQ secondary throttle lockout

Fig. 17 TQ bowl vent valve adjustment, 1977–78

Fig. 18 TQ solenoid bowl vent check.
1978–82 units

Fast Idle Speed

NOTE: On 1977 Chrysler models without Electronic Lean Burn system, remove air cleaner and plug vacuum fittings to heated air control and OSAC valves. On 1978–79 Chrysler models without Electronic Lean Burn system, remove air cleaner and eliminate vacuum ignition advance and EGR signals, then cap or plug disconnected vacuum lines. On Chrysler models with Electronic Lean Burn system, remove top of air cleaner and lift air cleaner for access to carburetor. Also, use a jumper wire to ground carburetor idle stop switch, then disconnect and plug vacuum hose to EGR valve.

Fig. 19—With engine off and transmission in Park or Neutral, open throttle slightly. Close choke valve until fast idle screw is positioned on second step of cam against shoulder of first step. Start engine and stabilize RPM, then adjust fast idle speed. Refer to Tune Up Chart located in car chapter.

Fig. 19 TQ fast idle
speed cam position

NOTE: On models with Electronic Lean Burn system, if speed continues to rise slowly, the carburetor idle stop switch has not been properly grounded.

Motorcraft Carburetor Section

MODEL 740 CARBURETOR ADJUSTMENT SPECIFICATIONS

See Tune Up Chart in car chapters for curb and fast idle speeds.

Year	Carb. Model ①	Float Level (Dry)	Float Drop	Choke Pulldown Clearance	Fast Idle Cam Clearance	Dechoke Clearance	Dashpot Clearance	Choke Setting
1981	E1EE-AAA	.250	1.693	.118	.079	.138	.138	Index
	E1EE-ACA	.250	1.693	.157	.079	.138	.157	1 Lean
	E1EE-ADA	.250	1.693	.118	.079	.138	.138	Index
	E1EE-AEA	.250	1.693	.118	.079	.138	.138	Index
	E1EE-AFA	.250	1.693	.118	.079	.138	.138	Index
	E1EE-AHA	.250	1.693	.098	.079	.138	.157	Index
	E1EE-AMA	.250	—	.157	.079	.138	.157	1 Lean
	E1EE-AVA	.250	1.693	.098	.079	.138	.157	Index
	E1EE-LA	.250	1.693	.118	.079	.138	.138	Index
	E1EE-MA	.250	1.693	.157	.079	.138	.157	1 Lean
	E1EE-PA	.250	1.693	.157	.079	.138	.157	1 Lean
	E1EE-RA	.250	1.693	.157	.079	.138	.157	1 Lean
	E1EE-SA	.250	1.693	.118	.079	.138	.138	Index
	E1EE-TA	.250	1.693	.118	.079	.138	.138	Index
1981–82	E1EE-ALA	.250	—	.157	.079	.138	.157	1 Lean
	E1EE-APA	.250	—	.157	.079	.138	.157	1 Lean
	E1EE-NA	.250	—	.157	.079	.138	.157	1 Lean
	E1EE-ZA	.250	—	.157	.079	.138	.157	1 Lean
1982	E1GE-CA	.250	—	.118	.079	.138	.138	Index
	E1GE-DA	.250	—	.118	.079	.138	.138	Index
	E1GE-EA	.250	—	.157	.079	.138	.157	1 Lean
	E1GE-GA	.250	—	.157	.079	.138	.157	1 Lean
	E2EE-AGA, AHA	.250	—	.138	.079	.138	.157	Index
	E2EE-JA	.250	—	.138	.079	.138	.059	Index
	E2EE-JC	.295	—	.256	.079	.138	.157	Index
	E2EE-GA	.250	—	.138	.079	.138	.059	Index
	E2EE-GC	.250	—	.138	.079	.138	.138	Index
	E2EE-LA	.250	—	.138	.079	.138	.157	Index
	E2EE-LC	.250	—	.177	.079	.138	.157	Index
	E2EE-MA	.250	—	.138	.079	.138	.157	Index

Continued

MODEL 740 CARBURETOR ADJUSTMENT SPECIFICATIONS—Continued

See Tune Up Chart in car chapters for curb and fast idle speeds.

Year	Carb. Model ①	Float Level (Dry)	Float Drop	Choke Pulldown Clearance	Fast Idle Cam Clearance	Dechoke Clearance	Dashpot Clearance	Choke Setting
	E2EE-MC	.250	—	.177	.079	.138	.157	Index
	E2EE-NA	.250	—	.138	.079	.138	.157	Index
	E2EE-NC	.250	—	.177	.079	.138	—	Index
	E2EE-PA	.250	—	.138	.079	.138	.157	Index
	E2EE-PC	.250	—	.177	.079	.138	—	Index
	E2EE-SA	.250	—	.138	.079	.138	.059	Index
	E2EE-VA	.250	—	.138	.079	.138	.157	1 Lean
	E2EE-YA	.250	—	.138	.079	.138	.157	1 Lean
	E2EE-ZA	.250	—	.156	.079	.138	.157	1 Lean
	E2GE-AA	.250	—	.167	.079	.138	.157	Index

①—Stamped on tag attached to bowl cover.

MODEL 740 ADJUSTMENTS

Description

The Motorcraft Model 740 carburetor, Fig. 1, consists of five basic systems: choke system, idle system, main metering system, acceleration system and power enrichment system.

The choke system is used for cold engine starting and consists of a bi-metallic spring and an electric heater. The idle system is adjustable and provides for the proper air/fuel ratio for both idle and low speed operation. The main metering system provides the correct air/fuel ratio for normal cruising speeds. A main metering system is used for primary and secondary stage operation. The acceleration system consists of a diaphragm type pump that is mechanically operated by the primary throttle linkage. This system provides fuel to the primary stage during acceleration. The power enrichment system consists of a vacuum operated power valve and a secondary stage pull over system that is regulated by airflow. This system is used together with the main metering system to provide proper vehicle operation during periods of moderate to heavy acceleration. The distributor and EGR vacuum ports are located in the primary venturi area of the carburetor.

Fuel Inlet System

The fuel inlet system maintains a specified fuel level in the fuel bowl, allowing the fuel metering system to deliver the correct air/fuel mixture to the engine. The fuel inlet needle position is controlled by a float and lever assembly hinged on the float pin. The amount of fuel entering the bowl is regulated by the distance the inlet needle is moved off its seat. When the float drops, it causes the inlet needle to drop and this allows additional fuel to enter the bowl. As the fuel level reaches a specified level, the inlet needle is raised to a position that will allow only enough fuel to enter to replace that being used by the metering systems. The float bowl uses a solenoid valve to operate the dual venting system, Fig. 2. When the ignition is On, the bowl is vented internally to the air cleaner. This balances the bowl with carburetor inlet air. When the ignition is Off, the bowl is vented externally, and fuel vapors are stored in the carbon canister to be drawn into the engine when the engine is started.

Idle System

Fuel for idle and off idle operation flows from the bowl through the primary main metering jet into the main well. Fuel then flows through an idle fuel restriction and is mixed with air entering through the primary idle air bleed. This air/fuel mixture travels past the idle transfer holes which serve as additional air bleeds during curb idle. The air/fuel mixture then moves past the idle mixture screw tip which controls the amount of mixture discharged into the engine from below the throttle plate. At speeds slightly above idle, the idle transfer holes begin discharging additional air/fuel mixture. This occurs because the increased opening of the throttle plates exposes the idle transfer holes to intake manifold vacuum. As the throttle opening and engine speed increase, airflow through the carburetor is increased. This creates a vacuum in the venturi causing the main metering system to begin operation.

Fuel Shut-Off System

When the ignition switch is in the On position, the fuel shut off system solenoid is in the operational position. This allows fuel to flow through the idle system of the carburetor. When the ignition switch is in the Off position, the solenoid releases, stopping the flow of fuel to the carburetor idle system.

Main Metering System

As engine speed increases, air velocity through the booster venturi creates a vacuum in the venturi. Fuel begins to flow through the main metering system due to high pressure in the bowl and low pressure at the main discharge nozzle. Fuel flows from the fuel bowl through the main jet and into the main well. Then the fuel travels up the main well tube where it is mixed with air. Air, supplied through the high speed air bleed, mixes with the fuel through small holes in the sides of the main well tubes. The proper air fuel ratio is maintained because the high speed air bleed meters an increased amount of air whenever venturi vacuum increases. As the air/fuel mixture moves to the discharge port, it is discharged into the booster venturi.

Secondary Progression

When the primary throttle plate is opened

approximately 45°, the secondary throttle plate begins to open, Fig. 3. The air/fuel mixture begins flowing from the secondary transfer holes as they are exposed to manifold vacuum. As the throttle plates are opened further, the secondary main metering system begins to operate. This system is similar to the primary main metering system.

Accelerator Pump System

When the throttle plates are opened quickly, air flows through the carburetor almost immediately. Because fuel is heavier than air, there is a brief time lag before fuel flow can gain enough speed to maintain proper air/fuel ratio. During this lag, the accelerator pump system supplies the necessary extra fuel to maintain correct air/fuel ratio until the other metering systems can respond. When the throttle plates are opened, the diaphragm rod is pushed upward, forcing fuel from the pump chamber into the discharge passage. Fuel under pressure moves the discharge check ball off its seat. This fuel then travels through the pump discharge valve where it enters the primary venturi through the pump discharge nozzle.

Primary Power Enrichment System

The air/fuel ratio must be increased during periods of heavy acceleration or high speed operation. The power enrichment system, controlled by intake manifold vacuum, supplies extra fuel during these operating conditions. Manifold vacuum is applied to the power valve diaphragm from an opening in the carburetor base where it is connected by passages in the main body to the diaphragm. During idle and light load conditions, high manifold vacuum overcomes the force of the power valve spring and the valve is held closed. When the throttle opening is increased and intake manifold vacuum drops, the valve opens and fuel flows from the bowl through the power valve into the primary main well. This extra fuel is then added to the main metering system fuel to provide the increased air/fuel ratio necessary for high speed or heavy load operation.

Secondary Power Enrichment System

The secondary system is provided with an

1 AIR HORN ASSEMBLY	20 CHOKE HOUSING ASSEMBLY	39 SECONDARY THROTTLE RETURN SPRING	58 POWER VALVE DIAPHRAGM WASHER
2 PRIMARY CHOKE LINK DIRT SEAL	21 CHOKE HOUSING VACUUM SEAL (O-RING)	40 PRIMARY THROTTLE RETURN SPRING "A"	59 FUEL BOWL VENT SOLENOID WASHER
3 DIRT SEAL RETAINER	22 CHOKE LEVER	41 IDLE SPEED SCREW SPRING	60 MAIN BODY ASSEMBLY
4 PRIMARY CHOKE LINK	23 CHOKE BIMETAL SHAFT LOCK WASHER	42 IDLE SPEED SCREW	61 FUEL BOWL VENT SOLENOID
5 CHOKE BIMETAL SHAFT BUSHING	24 CHOKE BIMETAL SHAFT NUT	43 IDLE FUEL SHUT OFF SOLENOID WASHER	62 BOWL VENT SPRING
6 FAST IDLE CAM SPRING	25 COVER GASKET	44 IDLE FUEL SHUT OFF SOLENOID	63 BOWL VENT ARM
7 CHOKE BIMETAL LEVER	26 FUEL BOWL FLOAT	45 IDLE MIXTURE SCREW CONCEALMENT PLUG (STEEL OUTER)	64 VITON BOWL VENT SEAL
8 CHOKE BIMETAL SHAFT	27 HIGH SPEED AIR BLEEDS	46 IDLE NEEDLE SEAL PLUG	65 "O" RING SEAL FOR PUMP NOZZLE
9 CHOKE ASSIST SPRING	28 WELL TUBES	47 IDLE MIXTURE SCREW	66 PUMP SHOOTER
10 ELECTRIC CHOKE RETAINING RIVETS (2)	29 IDLE JET HOLDER	48 IDLE MIXTURE SCREW "O" RING	67 FUEL DISCHARGE NOZZLES
11 ELECTRIC CHOKE RET. RING	30 IDLE JET	49 ACCELERATOR PUMP COVER SCREW	68 FUEL INLET SEAT AND NEEDLE
12 ELECTRIC CHOKE UNIT	31 MAIN JET	50 ACCELERATOR PUMP COVER ASSEMBLY	69 FLOAT HINGE PIN
13 CHOKE HOUSING INDEX SHIELD	32 THROTTLE LEVER	51 ACCELERATOR PUMP DIAPHRAGM	70 FUEL FILTER
14 CHOKE HOUSING SCREWS	33 FAST IDLE SPEED ADJUSTING SCREW	52 ACCELERATOR PUMP SPRING	71 FUEL RETURN LINE CHECK VALVE AND FITTING
15 CHOKE PULLDOWN SPRING	34 FAST IDLE SPEED ADJUSTING SCREW LOCK NUT	53 PRIMARY THROTTLE RETURN SPRING "B"	72 FUEL INLET SEAT GASKET
16 COVER	35 CHOKE PULL DOWN DIAPHRAGM COVER RIVET	54 ACCELERATOR PUMP CAM	73 COVER HOLD DOWN SCREWS
17 CHOKE PULLDOWN ADJUSTING SCREW	36 PRIMARY THROTTLE SHAFT NUT	55 POWER VALVE COVER SCREW	74 DASHPOT
18 CHOKE PULLDOWN ADJUSTING SCREW SEAL	37 PRIMARY THROTTLE SHAFT NUT LOCKING TAB	56 POWER VALVE COVER	75 DASHPOT MOUNTING BRACKET
18A CHOKE PULLDOWN ADJUSTING CONCEALMENT PLUG	38 SECONDARY THROTTLE OPERATING LEVER	57 POWER VALVE SPRING	76 DASHPOT ADJUSTING LOCK NUT
19 CHOKE PULLDOWN DIAPHRAGM ASSEMBLY			77 DASHPOT MOUNTING BRACKET SCREW

Fig. 1 Disassembled view of Motorcraft Model 740 carburetor

air velocity operated power system for fuel enrichment, Fig. 4. As the secondary throttle plate nears wide open position, air velocity through the secondary venturi creates a low pressure area at the discharge opening in the air horn. Fuel flows from the bowl through a vertical channel. During this time, air enters through a calibrated air bleed and mixes with the fuel, and this mixture is discharged through the opening.

Choke Plate Pulldown Adjustment

NOTE: On these units, it is necessary to remove the carburetor to remove the three

rivets retaining the choke housing cover. Using a 1/8 inch or No. 30 drill bit, remove rivet head, then drive rivet out using a 1/8 inch diameter punch.

Position fast idle adjusting screw on high step of fast idle cam. Using an external vacuum source, apply 17 inches Hg. of vacuum to vacuum channel adjacent to the primary bore on the base of the carburetor. The modulator spring should not be compressed. Using the specified drill, check clearance between choke plate and air horn wall. If clearance is not within limits as listed in the Model 740 Carburetor Adjustment Specifications, remove

choke pulldown motor adjusting screw cover and adjust as required.

Fast Idle Cam Kickdown Adjustment

Position fast idle screw on kickdown of fast idle cam against shoulder of top step. Manually close the primary choke plate and measure distance between choke plate and air horn wall. To obtain specified clearance, adjust right fork of choke bimetal shaft, which engages the fast idle cam, by bending upward or downward.

A – AIR HORN
B/C – VENTING WITH IGNITION ON
D – VENT VALVE WITH IGNITION OFF
E – VENT VALVE WITH IGNITION ON
F – FLOAT
G – VENTING WITH IGNITION OFF
H – CONNECTION FOR CANISTER
J – SOLENOID

Fig. 2   Carburetor fuel bowl vent system

A – PRIMARY AIR FLOW   B – SECONDARY AIR FLOW
C – SECONDARY POWER ENRICHMENT

Fig. 4   Carburetor secondary power enrichment system

THROTTLE PLATES AT OFF IDLE

SECONDARY PROGRESSION AS THROTTLE IS OPENED

Fig. 3   Carburetor secondary progression system

CARBURETORS

MODEL 2100, 2150-2V CARB. ADJUSTMENT SPECIFICATIONS

See Tune Up Chart in car chapters for curb and fast idle speeds.

Year	Carb. Model ①	Float Level (Dry)	Fuel Level (Wet)	Pump Setting Hole No. ②	Choke Plate Clearance (Pull down)	Fast Idle Cam Linkage Clearance	Dechoke Clearance ③	Dashpot Setting	Choke Setting
AMERICAN MOTORS									
1977	7RA2	5/16	25/32	No. 3	.136	.126	.250	—	1 Rich
	7RA2A	5/16	25/32	No. 3	.104	.089	.250	—	1 Rich
	7RA2C	5/16	25/32	No. 3	.130	.120	.250	—	1 Rich
	7RA2CP	5/16	25/32	No. 3	.136	.126	.250	—	1 Rich
	7DA2	5/16	25/32	No. 3	.136	.126	.250	—	Index
1978	8DA2	35/64	25/32	No. 3	.136	.126	.250	—	Index
	8DA2A	35/64	15/16	No. 3	.089	.078	.170	—	2 Rich
	8RA2	35/64	25/32	No. 3	.136	.126	.250	—	1 Rich
	8RA2A	35/64	25/32	No. 3	.089	.078	.170	—	2 Rich
	8RA2C	35/64	25/32	No. 3	.136	.120	.250	—	1 Rich
1979	9DA2	5/16	25/32	No. 3	.125	.113	.300	—	1 Rich
FORD MOTOR CO.									
1977	D7AE-ACA	7/16	13/16	No. 2	.156	.170	—	—	Index
	D7AE-AHA	7/16	13/16	No. 3	.179	.189	—	—	Index
	D7AE-AKA	7/16	13/16	No. 3	.179	.189	—	—	Index
	D7BE-YA	7/16	13/16	No. 2	.147	.167	—	—	1 Rich
	D7OE-LA	7/16	13/16	No. 4	.169	.189	—	—	3 Rich
	D7OE-RA	3/4	3/4	No. 3	.167	.187	—	—	2 Rich
	D7OE-TA	7/16	13/16	No. 3	.185	.205	—	—	2 Rich
	D7YE-EA	3/8	3/4	No. 3	.122	.142	—	—	2 Rich
1978	D8AE-JA	3/8	3/4	No. 3	.167	—	—	—	3 Rich
	D8BE-ACA	7/16	3/4	No. 4	.155	—	—	—	2 Rich
	D8BE-ADA	7/16	13/16	No. 2	.110	—	—	—	3 Rich
	D8BE-AEA	7/16	13/16	No. 2	.110	—	—	—	4 Rich
	D8BE-AFA	7/16	13/16	No. 2	.110	—	—	—	4 Rich
	D8BE-MB	3/8	13/16	No. 3	.122	—	—	—	Index
	D8DE-HA	7/16	13/16	No. 3	.157	—	—	—	Index
	D8KE-EA	7/16	13/16	No. 2	.135	—	—	—	3 Rich
	D8OE-BA	3/8	3/4	No. 3	.167	—	—	—	3 Rich
	D8OE-EA	7/16	13/16	No. 2	.136	—	—	—	Index
	D8OE-HA	7/16	13/16	No. 3	.180	—	—	—	2 Rich
	D8SE-CA	7/16	13/16	No. 3	.150	—	—	—	2 Rich
	D8SE-DA	7/16	13/16	No. 3	.147	—	—	—	3 Rich
	D8SE-EA	7/16	13/16	No. 3	.147	—	—	—	3 Rich
	D8SE-FA	3/8	13/16	No. 3	.147	—	—	—	3 Rich
	D8SE-GA	3/8	13/16	No. 3	.147	—	—	—	3 Rich
	D8WE-DA	7/16	13/16	No. 4	.143	—	—	—	1 Rich
	D8YE-AB	3/8	13/16	No. 3	.122	—	—	—	Index
	D8ZE-TA	3/8	3/4	No. 4	.122	—	—	—	Index
	D8ZE-UA	3/8	3/4	No. 4	.135	—	—	—	Index
	D84E-EA	7/16	13/16	No. 2	.110	—	—	—	3 Rich
1979	D9AE-AHA	7/16	13/16	No. 3	.147	—	.250	—	3 Rich
	D9AE-AJA	7/16	13/16	No. 3	.147	—	.250	—	3 Rich
	D9AE-ANB	7/16	13/16	No. 3	.129	—	—	—	1 Rich
	D9AE-APB	7/16	13/16	No. 3	.129	—	—	—	1 Rich
	D9AE-AVB	7/16	13/16	No. 3	.129	—	—	—	1 Rich
	D9AE-AYA	7/16	13/16	No. 3	.129	—	—	—	1 Rich
	D9AE-AYB	7/16	13/16	No. 3	.129	—	—	—	1 Rich
	D9AE-TB	7/16	13/16	No. 3	.129	—	—	—	2 Rich
	D9AE-UB	7/16	13/16	No. 3	.129	—	—	—	2 Rich

Continued

MODEL 2100, 2150-2V CARB. ADJUSTMENT SPECIFICATIONS—Continued

See Tune Up Chart in car chapters for curb and fast idle speeds.

Year	Carb. Model ①	Float Level (Dry)	Fuel Level (Wet)	Pump Setting Hole No.②	Choke Plate Clearance (Pull down)	Fast Idle Cam Linkage Clearance	Dechoke Clearance ③	Dashpot Setting	Choke Setting
FORD MOTOR CO.—Continued									
	D9BE-VB	7/16	13/16	No. 3	.153	—	.250	—	2 Rich
	D9BE-YB	7/16	13/16	No. 3	.153	—	—	—	2 Rich
	D9DE-NB	7/16	13/16	No. 3	.153	—	.250	—	2 Rich
	D9DE-RA	7/16	13/16	No. 2	.125	—	.115	—	3 Rich
	D9DE-RB	7/16	13/16	No. 2	.125	—	.115	—	3 Rich
	D9DE-RD	7/16	13/16	No. 2	.125	—	—	—	3 Rich
	D9DE-SA	7/16	13/16	No. 2	.125	—	.250	—	3 Rich
	D9DE-SC	7/16	13/16	No. 2	.125	—	—	—	3 Rich
	D9ME-BA	7/16	13/16	No. 2	.136	—	.115	—	Index
	D9ME-CA	7/16	13/16	No. 2	.136	—	.115	—	Index
	D9OE-CB	7/16	13/16	No. 3	.132	—	.115	—	3 Rich
	D9OE-DB	7/16	13/16	No. 3	.132	—	—	—	3 Rich
	D9OE-EA	7/16	13/16	No. 3	.132	—	.115	—	2 Rich
	D9OE-FA	7/16	13/16	No. 3	.132	—	.115	—	2 Rich
	D9SE-GA	7/16	13/16	No. 3	.150	—	.250	—	2 Rich
	D9VE-LC	3/8	3/4	No. 3	.145	—	.250	—	3 Rich
	D9VE-SA	7/16	13/16	No. 3	.147	—	—	—	3 Rich
	D9VE-UB	7/16	13/16	No. 3	.155	—	.250	—	3 Rich
	D9VE-VA	3/8	3/4	No. 3	.145	—	—	—	3 Rich
	D9VE-YB	3/8	3/4	No. 2	.145	—	.250	—	3 Rich
	D9WE-CB	7/16	13/16	No. 3	.132	—	—	—	3 Rich
	D9WE-DB	7/16	13/16	No. 3	.132	—	—	—	3 Rich
	D9WE-EB	7/16	13/16	No. 3	.132	—	—	—	2 Rich
	D9WE-FB	7/16	13/16	No. 3	.132	—	—	—	2 Rich
	D9WE-JA	7/16	13/16	No. 3	.150	—	.250	—	2 Rich
	D9WE-MB	7/16	13/16	No. 3	.132	—	—	—	1 Rich
	D9WE-NB	7/16	13/16	No. 3	.132	—	—	—	1 Rich
	D9YE-EA	7/16	13/16	No. 3	.118	—	.115	—	1 Rich
	D9YE-FA	7/16	13/16	No. 3	.118	—	.115	—	1 Rich
	D9YE-AB	7/16	13/16	No. 3	.118	—	.115	—	Index
	D9YE-BB	7/16	13/16	No. 3	.118	—	.115	—	Index
	D9YE-CA	7/16	13/16	No. 2	.118	—	.115	—	Index
	D9YE-DA	7/16	13/16	No. 2	.118	—	.115	—	Index
	D9ZE-AYA	7/16	13/16	No. 2	.138	—	.115	—	Index
	D9ZE-BFB	7/16	13/16	No. 2	.125	—	—	—	3 Rich
	D9ZE-BGB	7/16	13/16	No. 2	.125	—	—	—	3 Rich
	D9ZE-BHB	7/16	13/16	No. 2	.125	—	.250	—	3 Rich
	D9ZE-BJB	7/16	13/16	No. 2	.125	—	—	—	3 Rich
1980	D84E-TA	—	13/16	No. 2	.125	—	.250	—	3 Rich
	D84E-UA	—	13/16	No. 2	.125	—	.250	—	3 Rich
	D9AE-ANA	—	13/16	No. 3	.129	—	.250	—	1 Rich
	D9AE-APA	—	13/16	No. 3	.129	—	.250	—	1 Rich
	D9AE-AVA	—	13/16	No. 3	.129	—	.250	—	1 Rich
	D9AE-AYA	—	13/16	No. 3	.129	—	.250	—	1 Rich
	E0AE-AGA	—	13/16	No. 3	.159	—	.250	—	—
	E0BE-ASA	—	13/16	No. 2	.104	—	.250	—	3 Rich
	E0BE-ATA	—	13/16	No. 3	.116	—	.250	—	4 Rich
	E0BE-AUA	—	13/16	No. 3	.116	—	.250	—	4 Rich
	E0DE-SA	—	13/16	No. 2	.104	—	.250	—	3 Rich
	E0DE-TA	—	13/16	No. 2	.104	—	.250	—	3 Rich
	E0DE-VA	—	13/16	No. 2	.104	—	.250	—	—

CARBURETORS

See Tune Up Chart in car chapters for curb and fast idle speeds.

Year	Carb. Model ①	Float Level (Dry)	Fuel Level (Wet)	Pump Setting Hole No.②	Choke Plate Clearance (Pull down)	Fast Idle Cam Linkage Clearance	Dechoke Clearance ③	Dashpot Setting	Choke Setting
FORD MOTOR CO.—Continued									
	E0KE-CA	—	13/16	No. 3	.116	—	.250	—	3 Rich
	E0KE-DA	—	13/16	No. 3	.116	—	.250	—	3 Rich
	E0KE-GA	—	13/16	No. 3	.116	—	.250	—	4 Rich
	E0KE-HA	—	13/16	No. 3	.116	—	.250	—	4 Rich
	E0KE-JA	—	13/16	No. 3	.116	—	.250	—	4 Rich
	E0KE-KA	—	13/16	No. 3	.116	—	.250	—	4 Rich
	E0SE-GA	—	13/16	No. 2	.104	—	.250	—	3 Rich
	E0SE-HA	—	13/16	No. 2	.104	—	.250	—	3 Rich
	E0SE-LA	—	13/16	No. 2	.104	—	.250	—	3 Rich
	E0SE-MA	—	13/16	No. 2	.104	—	.250	—	3 Rich
	E0SE-NA	—	13/16	No. 2	.104	—	.250	—	3 Rich
	E0SE-PA	—	13/16	No. 2	.137	—	.250	—	3 Rich
	E0VE-FA	—	13/16	No. 2	.104	—	.250	—	—
	E0WE-BA	—	13/16	No. 2	.137	—	.250	—	3 Rich
	E0WE-CA	—	13/16	No. 2	.137	—	.250	—	3 Rich
	E04E-AAA	—	13/16	No. 2	.104	—	.250	—	4 Rich
	E04E-ABA	—	13/16	No. 2	.104	—	.250	—	4 Rich
	E04E-ACA	—	13/16	No. 2	.104	—	.250	—	4 Rich
	E04E-ADA	—	13/16	No. 2	.104	—	.250	—	4 Rich
	E04E-AEA	—	13/16	No. 2	.104	—	.250	—	4 Rich
	E04E-CA	—	13/16	No. 2	.104	—	.250	—	3 Rich
	E04E-EA	—	13/16	No. 2	.104	—	.250	—	3 Rich
	E04E-FA	—	13/16	No. 2	.104	—	.250	—	3 Rich
	E04E-KA	—	13/16	No. 2	.137	—	.250	—	3 Rich
	E04E-PA	—	13/16	No. 2	.104	—	.250	—	3 Rich
	E04E-RA	—	13/16	No. 2	.104	—	.250	—	3 Rich
	E04E-SA	—	13/16	No. 2	.104	—	.250	—	3 Rich
	E04E-VA	—	13/16	No. 2	.104	—	.250	—	3 Rich
	E04E-YA	—	13/16	No. 2	.104	—	.250	—	3 Rich
	E04E-ZA	—	13/16	No. 3	.104	—	.250	—	4 Rich
1981	E1AE-ADA	7/16	13/16	No. 3	.124	—	.250	—	V Notch
	E1AE-AEA	7/16	13/16	No. 3	.124	—	.250	—	V Notch
	E1AE-TA	—	13/16	No. 3	.104	—	.250	—	④
	E1AE-UA	—	13/16	No. 2	.104	—	.250	—	④
	E1AE-YA	Float	13/16	No. 3	.124	—	.250	—	④
	E1AE-ZA	—	13/16	No. 3	.124	—	.250	—	④
	E1KE-AA	7/16	13/16	No. 3	.120	—	.250	—	V Notch
	E1KE-BA	7/16	13/16	No. 3	.120	—	.250	—	V Notch
	E1KE-CA	7/16	13/16	No. 3	.124	—	.250	—	V Notch
	E1KE-DA	7/16	13/16	No. 3	.124	—	.250	—	V Notch
	E1KE-EA	7/16	13/16	No. 3	.124	—	.250	—	V Notch
	E1KE-FA	7/16	13/16	No. 3	.124	—	.250	—	V Notch
	E1KE-GA	7/16	13/16	No. 3	.120	—	.250	—	V Notch
	E1KE-HA	7/16	13/16	No. 3	.120	—	.250	—	V Notch
	E1KE-RA	7/16	13/16	No. 3	.124	—	.250	—	V Notch
	E1KE-SA	7/16	13/16	No. 3	.124	—	.250	—	V Notch
	E1WE-CA	7/16	13/16	No. 3	.120	—	.250	—	V Notch
	E1WE-DA	7/16	13/16	No. 3	.120	—	.250	—	V Notch
	E1WE-EA	7/16	13/16	No. 2	.120	—	.250	—	V Notch
	E1WE-FA	7/16	13/16	No. 2	.120	—	.250	—	V Notch
1982	E2AE-SA	7/16	13/16	No. 2	.172	—	.250	—	V-Notch
	E2BE-AAA, ABA	7/16	13/16	No. 2	.110	—	.250	.0045	V-Notch

Continued

MODEL 2100, 2150-2V CARB. ADJUSTMENT SPECIFICATIONS—Continued

See Tune Up Chart in car chapters for curb and fast idle speeds.

Year	Carb. Model ①	Float Level (Dry)	Fuel Level (Wet)	Pump Setting Hole No.②	Choke Plate Clearance (Pull down)	Fast Idle Cam Linkage Clearance	Dechoke Clearance ③	Dashpot Setting	Choke Setting
FORD MOTOR CO.—Continued									
	E2BE-ACA, ADA	7/16	13/16	No. 2	.113	—	.250	—	V-Notch
	E2BE-AGA, AHA	7/16	13/16	No. 2	.113	—	.250	.0041	V-Notch
	E2BE-AJA, AKA	7/16	13/16	No. 2	.110	—	.250	.0045	V-Notch
	E2BE-ALA, AMA	7/16	13/16	No. 2	.113	—	.250	—	V-Notch
	E2BE-UA	7/16	13/16	No. 2	.110	—	.250	.0045	V-Notch
	E2BE-VA	7/16	13/16	No. 2	.113	—	.250	.0045	V-Notch
	E2DE-JA	7/16	13/16	No. 2	.137	—	.250	.0045	V-Notch
	E2DE-KA	7/16	13/16	No. 2	.137	—	.250	.0045	V-Notch
	E2DE-LA	7/16	13/16	No. 2	.137	—	.250	.0045	V-Notch
	E2DE-MA	7/16	13/16	No. 2	.137	—	.250	.0045	V-Notch
	E2KE-AA, BA	7/16	13/16	No. 2	.140	—	.250	.0045	V-Notch
	E2KE-CA, DA	7/16	13/16	No. 2	.140	—	.250	.0045	V-Notch
	E2VE-CA	7/16	13/16	No. 2	.113	—	.250	.0045	V-Notch
	E2WE-EA	7/16	13/16	No. 2	.137	—	.250	.0045	V-Notch
	E2WE-FA	7/16	13/16	No. 2	.137	—	.250	.0045	V-Notch
	E2ZE-BAA, BBA	13/32	25/32	No. 2	.172	—	.250	.0045	V-Notch
	E2ZE-BCA, BDA	13/32	25/32	No. 2	.172	—	.250	.0045	V-Notch
	E2ZE-BGA, BHA	13/32	25/32	No. 2	.190	—	.250	.0045	V-Notch
	E24E-AA, BA	7/16	13/16	No. 2	.110	—	.250	.0045	V-Notch
	E24E-CA, DA	7/16	13/16	No. 2	.110	—	.250	.0045	V-Notch
	E24E-EA, FA	7/16	13/16	No. 2	.110	—	.250	.0045	V-Notch
	E24E-GA, HA	7/16	13/16	No. 2	.110	—	.250	—	V-Notch
	E24E-JA, KA	7/16	13/16	No. 2	.110	—	.250	—	V-Notch
	E25E-CA	7/16	13/16	No. 2	.137	—	.250	—	V-Notch
	E25E-DA	7/16	13/16	No. 2	.144	—	.250	.0045	V-Notch

①—Stamped on left side of fuel bowl or on tag attached to bowl cover.
②—With link in inboard hole in pump lever.
③—Minimum clearance between choke plate and air horn wall with throttle plates wide open.
④—3 Rich or V Notch.

MODEL 2100, 2150-2V ADJUSTMENTS

MECHANICAL FUEL BOWL VENT VALVE

SOLENOID OFF (TSP OFF) IDLE SPEED ADJUSTING SCREW

FAST IDLE CAM ADJUSTING SCREW

ACCELERATOR PUMP LEVER

SOLENOID THROTTLE POSITIONER

CHOKE DIAPHRAGM ASSEMBLY

FAST IDLE SPEED ADJUSTING SCREW

CHOKE THERMOSTATIC SPRING HOUSING

Fig. 1 Typical Motorcraft 2150 carburetor. 1977–82

Models 2100, 2150-2V, Figs. 1 thru 3

These carburetors have two main bodies—the air horn and throttle body. The air horn assembly, which serves as a cover for the throttle body, contains the choke plate and vents for the fuel bowl. On 1977 Ford units and 1978–79 American Motors 2100 units, an external bowl vent valve is used. On 2150 units installed on V-6 engines, the air horn assembly contains a fuel deceleration system which consists of a metered pickup orifice in the fuel bowl and air/fuel mixing orifices and bleeds.

A choke modulator assembly is incorporated in 2100 units, Fig. 4. This system, through the use of a bimetal sensor and a series of diaphragms, pulls open the choke plate within 15–60 seconds. The system operates only during times when underhood temperatures are above 60 degrees F. On Ford units, an electric choke system is incorporated which opens choke plate within 1–1½ minutes when underhood temperatures are above approximately 55° to 60°. On 1977–78 Ford units, the electric choke system is supplied current to open the choke plate when

CARBURETORS

1. MODULATOR COVER
2. MODULATOR RETAINING SCREW (3)
3. PIVOT PIN
4. MODULATOR ARM
5. CHOKE VALVE RETAINING SCREW (2)
6. CHOKE VALVE
7. CHOKE SHAFT
8. AIR HORN
9. AIR HORN RETAINING SCREW (4)
10. AIR HORN GASKET
11. FLOAT AND LEVER ASSEMBLY
12. FLOAT SHAFT RETAINER
13. FLOAT SHAFT
14. NEEDLE RETAINING CLIP
15. CURB IDLE ADJUSTING SCREW
16. CURB IDLE ADJUSTING SCREW SPRING
17. THROTTLE SHAFT AND LEVER ASSEMBLY
18. DASHPOT
19. DASHPOT LOCKNUT
20. DASHPOT BRACKET
21. DASHPOT BRACKET RETAINING SCREW
22. ADJUSTING SCREW
23. CARRIAGE
24. ELECTRIC SOLENOID
25. MOUNTING BRACKET
26. THROTTLE VALVE RETAINING SCREW (4)
27. THROTTLE VALVE (2)
28. NEEDLE AND SEAT ASSEMBLY
29. NEEDLE SEAT GASKET
30. MAIN JET (2)
31. MAIN BODY
32. ELASTOMER VALVE
33. PUMP RETURN SPRING
34. PUMP DIAPHRAGM
35. PUMP LEVER PIN
36. PUMP COVER
37. PUMP ROD
38. PUMP ROD RETAINER
39. PUMP LEVER
40. PUMP COVER RETAINING SCREW (4)
41. FUEL INLET FITTING
42. POWER VALVE GASKET
43. POWER VALVE
44. POWER VALVE COVER GASKET
45. POWER VALVE COVER
46. POWER VALVE COVER
    RETAINING SCREW (4)
47. IDLE LIMITER CAP (2)
48. IDLE MIXTURE SCREW (2)

49. IDLE MIXTURE SCREW SPRING (2)
50. RETAINER
51. RETAINER
52. FAST IDLE LEVER RETAINING NUT
53. FAST IDLE LEVER PIN
54. RETAINER
55. LEVER AND SHAFT
56. FAST IDLE CAM ROD
57. CHOKE SHIELD
58. CHOKE SHIELD RETAINING SCREW (2)
59. PISTON PASSAGE PLUG
60. HEAT PASSAGE PLUG
61. CHOKE COVER RETAINING CLAMP
62. CHOKE COVER RETAINING SCREW (3)
63. CHOKE COVER
64. CHOKE COVER GASKET
65. THERMOSTAT LEVER RETAINING SCREW
66. THERMOSTAT LEVER
67. CHOKE HOUSING RETAINING SCREW (3)
68. CHOKE HOUSING

69. CHOKE SHAFT BUSHING
70. FAST IDLE SPEED ADJUSTING SCREW
71. FAST IDLE LEVER
72. FAST IDLE CAM
73. CHOKE HOUSING GASKET
74. PUMP DISCHARGE CHECK BALL
75. PUMP DISCHARGE WEIGHT
76. BOOSTER VENTURI GASKET
77. BOOSTER VENTURI ASSEMBLY
78. AIR DISTRIBUTION PLATE
79. PUMP DISCHARGE SCREW
80. RETAINER
81. CHOKE ROD
82. CHOKE LEVER RETAINING SCREW
83. CHOKE PLATE LEVER
84. CHOKE ROD SEAL
85. STOP SCREW
86. MODULATOR RETURN SPRING
87. MODULATOR DIAPHRAGM ASSEMBLY

Fig. 2 Exploded view of Model 2100 carburetor (Typical)

UPPER BODY SCREWS (6 REQ'D)

CHOKE PLATE SCREWS (4 REQ'D)

BYPASS CHOKE PLATE

BYPASS CHOKE SHAFT AND LEVER ASSEMBLY

CHOKE PLATE

CHOKE SHAFT LINK

CHOKE PLATE LEVER

BOOSTER VENTURI SCREW

LEVER SCREW

CHOKE SHAFT AND LEVER ASSEMBLY

YOKE

CHOKE PLATE ROD

METERING RODS

RETAINER

AIR HORN

GASKET

DUST COVER

YOKE SCREW

SCREEN

GASKET

SUPPORT AND BOOSTER ASSEMBLY

SCREW (3 REQ'D)

GASKET

ADJUSTMENT SCREW

METERING VALVE ASSEMBLY

WEIGHT

ANEROID

PUMP CHECK BALL

RETAINER

FLOAT

GASKET

FLOAT SHAFT

SCREW (4 REQ'D)

GASKET

FLOAT SHAFT RETAINER

CHOKE ARM ADJUSTING SCREW

IDLE SPEED ADJUSTING SCREW (2)

FUEL INLET NEEDLE

THROTTLE SHAFT AND LEVER ASSEMBLY

SCREW (2 REQ'D)

VACUUM HOSE

SPRING

INLET NEEDLE SEAT

SHIELD

CHOKE PULLDOWN DIAPHRAGM ASSEMBLY

RESTRICTOR

MAIN BODY

FILTER SCREEN RETAINER SPRING

POSITIVE CLOSURE SPRING

RETAINER

MAIN JETS

ELASTOMER VALVE

ACCELERATOR PUMP ROD

NYLON CHOKE ARM

LOCKING CAP

RETURN SPRING

LINKAGE LEVER

PUMP DIAPHRAGM

DIAPHRAGM LINK

GASKET

ACCELERATOR PUMP COVER

FAST IDLE CAM LINK

LOCKING TAB

LOCKING PLUG

SHAFT RETAINER

FAST IDLE CAM

CHOKE HOUSING SHAFT

GASKET

SPRING

CHOKE HOUSING

FAST IDLE LEVER

ENRICHMENT VALVE

COVER SCREW (4 REQ'D)

CHOKE LEVER

SPRING

THROTTLE PLATES

GASKET

MIXTURE SCREW

PUMP OPERATING LEVER

GASKET

HIGH SPEED BLEED CAM

COVER

PIN

RETAINER

FAST IDLE ADJUSTMENT SCREW

COVER

VENT VALVE ACTUATING LEVER

SCREW (3 REQ'D)

LEVER SCREW

HOUSING SCREW (3 REQ'D)

COVER SCREW

VENT VALVE BRACKET

HOT AIR INLET

SHIELD

SHIELD SCREW (2 REQ'D)

THERMOSTATIC SPRING HOUSING

Fig. 3   Exploded view of Model 2150 carburetor (Typical)

CARBURETORS

underhood temperatures are between 80° and 110°F. On 1979–82 Ford units, the electric choke system is supplied current to open the choke when underhood temperatures are between 54 and 74°F. For service information refer to the "Emission Control System" chapter.

Some 1977–82 2150 units are equipped with an altitude compensation aneroid to improve high altitude emission control and driveability. Intake air entering the bypass valve is metered into the air flow above the throttle plates, leaning the mixture for high altitude operation. Air flow is controlled by a valve activated by an aneroid attached to the rear of the carburetor main body. Also, these units are equipped with a choke in the bypass air intake, linked to the main choke.

The throttle plate, accelerating pump, power (enrichment) valve and fuel bowl are in the throttle body. The choke housing is attached to the throttle body.

The two bodies each contain a main and booster venturi, main fuel discharge, accelerating pump discharge, idle fuel discharge, and a throttle plate. On some units, an antistall dashpot is attached to the carburetor when the vehicle is equipped with an automatic transmission.

Float Level (Dry) Adjustment

Fig. 5—This is a preliminary adjustment; the final adjustment must be made after the carburetor is mounted on the engine.

With air horn removed, float raised and fuel inlet needle seated, measure distance between top surface of throttle body and top surface of float. Take measurement near center of float at a point 1/8" from free end of float.

If a cardboard float gauge is used, place the gauge in the corner of the enlarged end section of the fuel bowl as shown. The gauge should touch the float near the end but not on the end radius.

Depress the float tab to seat the fuel inlet needle. The float height is measured from the gasket surface of the throttle body with gas-

ket removed. If the float height is not as listed in the *Ford Specifications Chart*, bend tab on float as required to achieve the desired setting.

Fuel Level (Wet) Adjustment

Fig. 6—With vehicle on a level surface, operate engine until normal temperature is reached, then stop engine and check fuel level as follows:
1. Remove carburetor air cleaner.
2. Remove air horn retaining screws and carburetor identification tag.
3. Temporarily leave air horn and gasket in position on throttle body and start engine.
4. Allow engine to idle for several minutes, then rotate air horn and remove air horn gasket to gain access to float or floats.
5. While engine is idling, use a standard depth gauge to measure vertical distance from top machined surface of throttle body to level of fuel in bowl. The measurement must be made at least 1/4" away from any vertical surface to assure an accurate reading.
6. If the fuel level is not as listed in the Specifications Chart, stop the engine to avoid any fire hazard due to fuel spray when float setting is disturbed.
7. To adjust fuel level, bend float tab (contacting fuel inlet needle) upward in relation to original position to raise the fuel level, and downward to lower it.
8. Each time an adjustment is made to the float tab to alter the fuel level, the engine must be started and permitted to idle for at least three minutes to stabilize the fuel level. Check fuel level after each adjustment until the specified level is achieved.
9. Assemble carburetor with a new air horn gasket. Then adjust idle speed and mixture, and anti-stall dashpot, if so equipped.

Accelerating Pump Adjustment

Fig. 7
The primary throttle shaft lever (Overtravel lever) has four holes on most units. However, some units have three holes. On units with three holes in the overtravel lever, the holes are numbered as shown in Fig. 7 with the No. 1 hole omitted. The accelerator pump hole has two holes, inboard and outboard.

NOTE: The stroke should not be changed from the specified setting.

1977–79 Units
1. To release rod from retainer clip, press tab end of clip toward rod. Then, at the same time, press rod away from clip until it is disengaged.
2. Position clip over specified hole in overtravel lever. Press ends of clip together and insert operating rod through clip and lever. Release clip to engage rod.

1980 Units
1. Using a suitable punch, tap retainer pin from accelerator pump cover, then rotate pump link and rod assembly until key on rod end is aligned with key hole in pump overtravel lever.
2. Position rod in specified hole in overtravel lever, then reassemble pump link and rod assembly.

1981–82 Units
1. Support accelerator pump housing at roll pin connection.
2. Using a suitable punch, tap retainer pin from accelerator pump cover and lever.
3. Rotate lever and rod assembly upward until key on rod end is aligned with key hole on pump overtravel lever.
4. Remove rod, clip and pin assembly from overtravel lever.
5. Position rod, clip and pin assembly in the specified hole, then reassemble pump link and rod assembly.

Choke Plate Clearance (Pulldown) Adjustment

2100 UNITS
1977 American Motors
1. Loosen the choke over retaining screws. Rotate the choke cover 1/4 turn counterclockwise (rich) from index and tighten the retaining screws. Disconnect the choke heat inlet tube.
2. Align the fast idle speed adjusting screw with the second step of the fast idle cam, Fig. 8.
3. Start the engine without moving the accelerator linkage. Turn the fast idle cam lever adjusting screw out counterclockwise 3 full turns.
4. Measure the clearance between the lower edge of the choke valve and the air horn wall. Refer to *2100 Specifications Chart* for the correct setting. Adjust by grasping the modulator arm securely with a pair of pliers at point "A" and twisting the arm at point "B" with a second pair of pliers. Twist toward the front of the carburetor

Fig. 4   Motorcraft 2100 choke diaphragm assembly

PIN

DIAPHRAGM LINK

COVER

DIAPHRAGM ASSEMBLY

SPRING

AIR HORN

FLOAT SHOULD JUST TOUCH AT THIS POINT

Fig. 5   Float level adjustment.

Fig. 6   Fuel level adjustment.

Fig. 7 Pump stroke adjusting points, 2100, 2150

CONVENTIONAL ONE - PIECE FAST IDLE LEVER

TWO - PIECE FAST IDLE LEVER

Fig. 8 Motorcraft fast idle adjustment 2100, 2150

Fig. 9 Choke plate pulldown clearance 2100. 1977 American Motors.

Fig. 10 Choke plate pulldown clearance adjust. 1978–79 American Motors 2100 units

to increase clearance and toward the rear to decrease clearance, Fig. 9

CAUTION: Use extreme care while twisting the modulator arm to avoid damaging the nylon piston rod of the modulator assembly.

NOTE: Connect the choke heat tube. Turn the fast idle cam lever adjusting screw in (clockwise) 3 full turns. Do not reset the choke cover until the fast idle cam linkage adjustment has been performed.

1978–79 American Motors
1. Loosen choke cover retaining screws and rotate cover 1/4 turn counterclockwise, then tighten one screw.
2. Disconnect choke heat inlet tube. Align fast idle speed adjusting screw with second step of fast idle cam.
3. Start engine without moving accelerator linkage. Turn fast idle cam lever adjusting screw counterclockwise three turns. Measure clearance between upper edge of choke valve and air horn wall, Fig. 10. Refer to 2100, 2150 Specification Chart.
4. Adjust by turning set screw on bottom of modulator.
5. Stop engine and connect choke heat tube. Adjust fast idle cam clearance.

2150 UNITS

CAUTION: Do not attempt to turn the diaphragm adjusting screw without first loosening the Loctite which has been applied to the threads of the screw. The Loctite can be softened by heating the area around the screw with an electric soldering gun or by applying Loctite to the screw. When the Loctite has softened enough, the screw can be turned without causing any damage.

1977–78 American Motors & 1977–80 Ford
1. Set throttle on fast idle cam top step, Fig. 8, then loosen choke thermostatic housing retaining screws and set housing 90° in rich direction.
2. Activate pulldown motor by manually forcing pulldown control diaphragm link in direction of applied vacuum or by applying vacuum to external vacuum tube.

3. Check clearance between lower edge of choke plate and center of carburetor air horn wall nearest fuel bowl Fig. 11. Refer to 2150 Specifications Chart. If clearance is not as specified, reset by adjusting diaphragm stop on end of choke pull-down diaphragm.

NOTE: After completing choke plate clearance adjustment, leave choke thermostatic housing in the full rich position and check fast idle cam setting as described under Fast Idle Cam Position Adjustment.

1981–82 Ford
1. Remove carburetor from engine, then using a suitable punch, center punch choke retaining cap screw heads.
2. Using a 1/4 inch drill bit, drill screw heads deep enough to remove retainer from cap, then remove choke cap by inserting a flat chisel between cap and gasket.
3. Remove remaining portion of choke cap retaining screws using pliers. Also clean epoxy sealer and gasket from choke cap and housing mating surfaces.
4. Rotate choke thermostatic housing to lightly close choke plate, then rotate housing an additional 90°.
5. Using the edge of a file, file a 1/8 inch deep groove on pulldown motor tamper resistance cover 1/4 inch from rear edge of pulldown motor.

NOTE: On 1982 models, a tamper resistance cover is not used on the pulldown motor.

6. Using a suitable awl inserted in filed groove, carefully tap plug from pulldown motor.
7. Activate pulldown motor using an external vacuum source or by manually forc-

ing the diaphragm to the retracted position.
8. Using a drill bit of the specified size, measure clearance between choke plate and carburetor air horn wall, Fig. 11.
9. Loosen pulldown motor adjusting screw as described in Caution above, then remove adjusting screw and clean remaining thread locking compound.
10. Reinstall adjusting screw and adjust. Rotate adjusting screw clockwise to decrease pulldown and counter-clockwise to increase pulldown.
11. After completing adjustment, use Loctite 240 or equivalent to lock adjusting screw in position, then tap tamper resistance cover into place on pulldown motor. Apply epoxy sealer MT13 or equivalent to edge and groove on cover.

NOTE: After completing choke plate clearance adjustment, leave choke thermostatic housing in the full rich position and check fast idle cam setting as described under Fast Idle Cam Position Adjustment.

1977–79 American Motors Units
1. Push downward on fast idle cam lever until fast idle speed adjusting screw contacts the second step of cam and is against the high step shoulder.
2. Measure clearance between lower edge of

CARBURETORS

Fig. 11 Choke plate pulldown adjustment, 2150 (Typical). 1977–82 Ford

Fig. 12 Fast idle cam clearance adjustment 2100. 1977–79 American Motors

Fig. 13 Choke unloader adjustment 1977–79 American Motors

choke valve and air horn wall. Refer to the 2100, 2150 Specifications Chart.

3. Adjust by turning fast idle cam lever screw, Fig. 12.
4. Set choke cover housing to specifications.

FAST IDLE CAM POSITION ADJUSTMENT

1977–82 Ford Units

1. With choke thermostatic housing in the rich position, cycle throttle to set fast idle cam.
2. Activate pull down by applying an external vacuum source.
3. Cycle throttle and observe fast idle cam. Fast idle cam should drop to the kickdown step and fast idle speed screw should be opposite the V notch on the cam.
4. Align screw with notch on fast idle cam by rotating screw on fast idle cam lever.
5. Reconnect vacuum hose to choke pull-down motor.
6. Reset choke thermostatic housing to specification listed in Model 2100, 2150 Car-

buretor Adjustment Specifications.

NOTE: On 1981–82 units, apply three 1/2 inch beads of MT-13 sealant to each side of choke cap gasket adjacent to choke housing screw bosses, then position gasket to housing. Position choke cap and retainer to housing, then install break-away screws finger tight. Tighten each screw until head breaks off, then reinstall carburetor.

Dechoke (Choke Unloader) Clearance

1977–79 American Motors Units

1. Hold throttle fully open and apply pressure on choke valve toward the closed position.
2. Measure clearance between lower edge of choke valve and air horn wall. Refer to

the 2100, 2150 Specifications Chart.

3. Adjust by bending the unloader tang contacting fast idle cam, Fig. 13. Bending the tang toward the cam increases the clearance and bending the tang away from the cam decreases the clearance.

NOTE: Do not bend unloader tang downward from a horizontal plane.

4. After making adjustment, open the throttle until the unloader tang is directly below the fast idle cam pivot. A clearance of .070 inch must be obtained between the unloader tang and the edge of the fast idle cam, Fig. 14.

Fig. 14 Choke unloader to fast idle cam clearance. 1977–79 American Motors

Fig. 15 Dechoke clearance adjustment. 1977–82 Ford 2150 units

Fig. 16 Automatic choke adjustment. 2100, 2150

1977–82 Ford Units

1. Hold throttle in the wide open position and measure clearance between lower edge of choke plate and air horn wall using the specified size drill. Refer to Models 2100 and 2150 Carburetor Specifications.

2. To adjust clearance, bend metal tang on fast idle speed lever attached to throttle shaft, Fig. 15.

3. Rotate throttle lever to ensure minimum throttle effort during dechoke tang engagement.

Automatic Choke Valve Tension

Turn thermostatic spring cover against spring tension until index mark on cover is aligned with mark specified in the *Ford Specifications Chart* on choke housing, Fig. 16.

MODEL 2700 & 7200 VV CARB. ADJUSTMENT SPECIFICATIONS

See Tune Up Chart for Curb and Fast idle speeds.

Year	Carb Model (Code 9510)	Float Level (Dry)	Float Drop	Internal Vent	Venturi Valve Limiter	Fast Idle Cam	Control Vacuum Regulator	Choke Setting
1977	D7Z3-AC	13/64	1 15/32	.010	61/64	①	⑲	Index
	D7Z3-BD	13/64	1 15/32	.010	13/32	②	⑲	Index
	D7ZE-GD, GE	13/64	1 15/32	.010	61/64	①	⑲	Index
	D7Z3-GE	13/64	1 15/32	.010	61/64	①	⑲	Index
	77TF-MA, NA	13/64	1 15/32	.010	61/64	①	⑲	Index
1978	D8BE-EB	13/64	1 15/32	.010	3/4	①	—	Index
	D84E-DB	13/64	1 15/32	.010	61/64	①	—	Index
1979	D84E-KA	13/64	1 15/32	.010	61/64	①	.225–.235	Index
	D84E-VA	13/64	1 15/32	.010	③	①	.225–.235	Index
	D9AE-ACA	13/64	1 15/32	.010	3/4	①	.245–.255	Index
	D9AE-CB	13/64	1 15/32	.010	③	④	.085–.095	Index
	D9AE-JB	13/64	1 15/32	.010	③	①	.085–.095	Index
	D9AE-YB	13/64	1 15/32	.010	③	①	.085–.095	Index
	D9AE-ZB	13/64	1 15/32	.010	③	④	.085–.095	Index
	D9BE-AFA	13/64	1 15/32	.010	③	④	.225–.235	Index
	D9DE-HB	13/64	1 15/32	.010	③	⑤	.225–.235	Index
	D9ME-AA	13/64	1 15/32	—	3/4	①	.245–.255	Index
	D9ME-ACA	13/64	1 15/32	.010	⑥	①	.245–.255	Index
	D9ZE-AZB	13/64	1 15/32	.010	③	④	.225–.235	Index
	D9ZE-BEA	13/64	1 15/32	.010	③	④	.225–.235	Index
	D9ZE-LB	13/64	1 15/32	.010	13/32	①	.225–.235	Index
	D9ZE-LC	13/64	1 15/32	.010	⑦	⑧	.225–.235	Index
	D94E-EB	13/64	1 15/32	.010	③	④	.225–.235	Index
	D94E-GA	13/64	1 15/32	.010	③	④	.225–.235	Index
	D94E-JA	13/64	1 15/32	.010	③	④	.225–.235	Index
	D945-FA	13/64	1 15/32	.010	③	④	.225–.235	Index
1980	E0AE-AAA	13/64	1 15/32	—	③	⑨	.070–.080	1 Rich
	E0AE-ACA	13/64	1 15/32	—	③	⑨	.070–.080	1 Rich
	E0AE-ADA	13/64	1 15/32	—	⑩	①	.270–.280	Index
	E0AE-AHA	13/64	1 15/32	—	⑩	⑪	—	—
	E0AE-APA	13/64	1 15/32	—	③	⑨	.070–.080	1 Rich
	E0AE-ATA	13/64	1 15/32	—	⑩	①	.270–.280	—
	E0AE-AVA	13/64	1 15/32	—	③	⑨	.070–.080	—
	E0AE-BA	13/64	1 15/32	—	⑩	⑫	.245–.255	Index
	E0AE-LA⑬⑭	13/64	1 15/32	—	⑩	⑫	.245–.255	Index
	E0AE-LA⑬⑮	13/64	1 15/32	—	⑩	①	.245–.255	—
	E0AE-PA	13/64	1 15/32	—	⑩	⑫	.245–.255	Index
	E0AE-ZA	13/64	1 15/32	—	③	⑨	.070–.080	1 Rich
1981	D9AE-AZA	13/64	1 15/32	—	③	①	.245–.255	Index
	E1AE-AAA	13/64	1 15/32	—	③	⑨	.070–.080	Index
	E1AE-ACA	13/64	1 15/32	—	⑯	⑰	.245–.255	Index
	E1AE-AGA	13/64	1 15/32	—	⑩	⑰	.245–.255	Index
	E1AE-KA	13/64	1 15/32	—	⑩	①	.245–.255	Index
	E1AE-LA	13/64	1 15/32	—	⑱	⑰	.245–.255	Index
	E1AE-MA	13/64	1 15/32	—	⑩	⑰	.245–.255	Index
	E1AE-SA	13/64	1 15/32	—	⑱	⑰	.245–.255	Index
	E1DE-AA	13/64	1 15/32	—	⑯	⑰	.245–.255	Index
	E1SE-EA	13/64	1 15/32	—	⑩	⑰	.245–.255	Index

Continued

CARBURETORS

Year	Carb Model (Code 9510)	Float Level (Dry)	Float Drop	Internal Vent	Venturi Valve Limiter	Fast Idle Cam	Control Vacuum Regulator	Choke Setting
	E1SE-VA	1 3/64	1 15/32	—	⑩	⑫	.245–.255	Index
	E1VE-AA	1 3/64	1 15/32	—	⑩	⑰	.245–.255	Index
1982	E1AE-ACA	1 3/64	1 15/32	—	⑩	⑰	.245–.255	Index
	E1AE-AGA	1 3/64	1 15/32	—	⑩	⑰	.245–.255	Index
	E1AE-SA	1 3/64	1 15/32	—	⑱	⑰	.245–.255	1 Rich
	E2AE-ABA, RA	1 3/64	1 15/32	—	⑩	⑰	.245–.255	Index
	E2AE-AGA, AHA	1 3/64	1 15/32	—	⑱	⑰	.245–.255	1 Rich
	E2AE-LB	1 3/64	1 15/32	—	⑩	⑰	.295–.305	Index
	E2AE-LC	1 3/64	1 15/32	—	⑩	⑰	.295–.305	Index
	E2AE-MA	1 3/64	1 15/32	—	⑱	⑰	.245–.255	1 Rich
	E2AE-MB	1 3/64	1 15/32	—	⑱	⑰	.245–.255	1 Rich
	E2AE-TA	1 3/64	1 15/32	—	⑱	⑰	.245–.255	Index
	E2AE-TB	1 3/64	1 15/32	—	⑱	⑰	.245–.255	Index
	E2DE-NA, SA, TA, UA	1 3/64	1 15/32	—	⑩	⑰	.295–.305	Index
	E2SE-DA, FA	1 3/64	1 15/32	—	⑩	⑰	.070–.080	Index
	E2SE-DB	1 3/64	1 15/32	—	⑩	⑰	.070–.080	Index
	E25E-ABA	1 3/64	1 15/32	—	⑩	⑰	.070–.080	Index
	E25E-AC, YA	1 3/64	1 15/32	—	⑩	⑰	.070–.080	Index
	E25E-FA	1 3/64	1 15/32	—	⑩	⑰	.245–.255	Index
	E25E-GA, SA, UA	1 3/64	1 15/32	—	⑩	⑰	.245–.255	Index
	E25E-GB, TA	1 3/64	1 15/32	—	⑩	⑰	.245–.255	Index

①—1 Notch rich on third step.
②—Bobcat and Pinto, 4 Notches rich on second step. Except Bobcat and Pinto, 1 notch rich on third step.
③—Limiter adjusting screw setting, .94–.98 inch; limiter stop screw setting, .99–1.01 inch.
④—5 notches rich on second highest step.
⑤—5 notches rich on highest step.
⑥—Limiter adjusting screw setting, .73–.77 inch; limiter stop screw setting, .99–1.01 inch.
⑦—Limiter adjusting screw setting, .38–.42 inch; limiter stop screw setting, .73–.77 inch.
⑧—1 notch rich on second step.
⑨—1 notch rich on forth step.
⑩—Limiter adjusting screw setting, .39–.41 inch; limiter stop screw setting, .99–1.01 inch.
⑪—.13/.14 on third highest step.
⑫—.14/.15 on third highest step.
⑬—Refer to engine calibration code on engine identification lable located at rear of left valve cover. The calibration code is located on the label after the engine code number and is preceded by the letter C and the revision code is located below the calibration code and is preceded by the letter R.
⑭—Except Calibration code 012C-R5.
⑮—Calibration code 012C-R5.
⑯—Limiter adjusting screw setting, .48–.52 inch; limiter stop screw setting .99–1.01 inch.
⑰—.355–.365 inch on second step.
⑱—Limiter adjusting screw setting, .74–.76 inch; limiter stop screw setting, .99–1.01 inch.
⑲—See text.

MODEL 2700 & 7200 VV ADJUSTMENTS

The Motorcraft model 2700 and 7200 carburetors, Figs. 1 through 4 are two bore, variable venturi units. The model 7200 carburetor is used in conjunction with EEC system. The variable venturis, located at the top of the throttle bores, are small oblong castings that slide across the throttle bores. The venturis are positioned by a spring loaded diaphragm valve regulated by a vacuum signal obtained below the venturis in the throttle bores. As the throttle is opened, the vacuum signal increases, thereby, opening the venturis and permitting more air to enter the carburetor while maintaining approximately the same venturi air velocity.

Tapered metering rods are attached to the venturi valves and fit into the metering jets. As the venturis are positioned in response to air demand, the metering rods slide in the jets to provide the proper air-fuel mixture during all modes of engine operation. By the use of the variable venturi principle, the only auxiliary fuel metering systems required are the accelerator pump, idle trim, starting enrichment and cold running enrichment.

Some 1978 2700 units are equipped with an altitude compensation feature which provides improved emission control and driveability at high altitude. This compensation is accomplished through the use of a bellows and pintle valve unit, Fig. 5. The bellows senses barometric pressure and opens the pintle valve accordingly. Opening the valve allows control vacuum to lower the pressure in the fuel bowl area, causing the fuel mixture to be leaner.

Fuel Level Adjustment

Fig. 6—Remove upper body assembly and replace the upper body gasket. With the upper body inverted, measure vertical distance from the upper body cast surface and the bottom of float. To adjust, bend float operating lever away from the fuel inlet needle to decrease the setting or toward the needle to increase the setting. After adjustment, the float pontoon must be parallel with the gasket surface. Check and adjust float drop, if necessary.

Float Drop Adjustment

Fig. 7—With upper body held in upright position, measure verticle distance between the cast surface of the upper body and the bottom of float. To adjust, bend stop tab on float lever away from hinge pin to increase setting or toward the hinge pin to decrease setting.

Cold Enrichment Metering Rod Adjustment

NOTE: On some 1979–82 vehicles, it is necessary to remove the carburetor to remove the rivets on the choke housing. Remove the top two rivets with a 1/8 inch diameter twist drill. The third bottom rivet is located in a "Blind" hole and is removed by lightly tapping the rear of the retainer ring using a punch and hammer. The rivet, retainer ring, choke housing and gasket can then be removed.

1977–79 Units
Fig. 8—Remove choke cap and install stator cap, tool T77L-9848-A as a weight to seat the cold enrichment rod. Install dial indicator with plunger contacting the top of the cold enrichment rod and zero the indicator. Remove the stator cap and reinstall at the index position. The dial indicator should read .125 inch. If rod height is not within specifications, turn adjusting nut clockwise to increase height or counterclockwise to decrease height. Reinstall choke cap and position at proper setting.

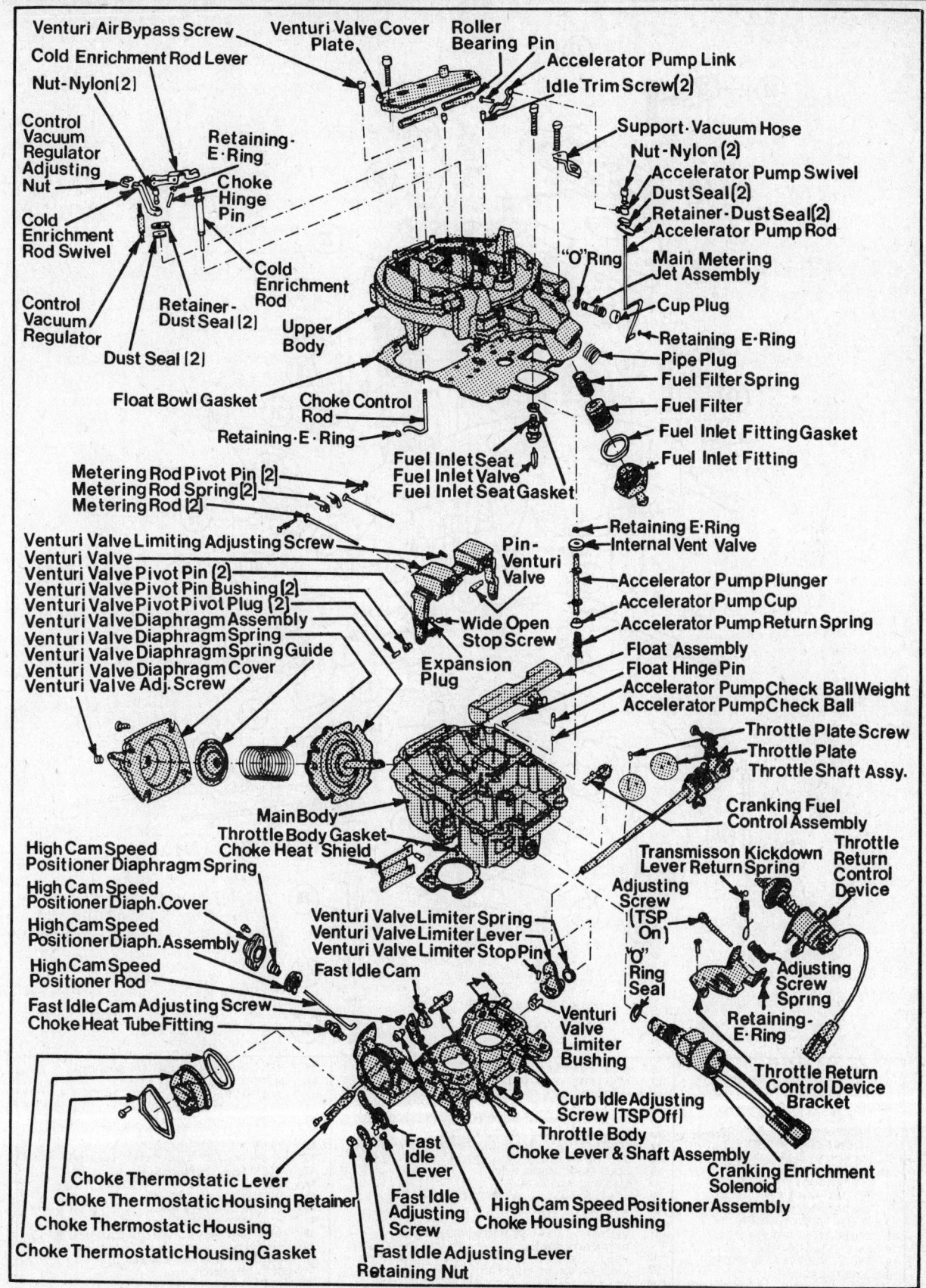

Fig. 1 Motorcraft model 2700 variable venturi carburetor, disassembled

1. FUEL INLET FITTING.	18. ACCELERATOR PUMP LINK.	35. VENTURI VALVE PIVOT PIN BUSHING.
2. FUEL INLET FITTING GASKET.	19. ACCELERATOR PUMP SWIVEL.	36. METERING ROD PIVOT PIN.
3. FUEL FILTER.	20. NUT - NYLON.	37. METERING ROD.
4. FUEL FILTER SPRING.	21. CHOKE HINGE PIN.	38. METERING ROD SPRING.
5. 1/8 RETAINING E-RING.	22. COLD ENRICHMENT ROD LEVER.	39. CUP PLUG.
6. ACCELERATOR PUMP ROD.	23. COLD ENRICHMENT ROD SWIVEL.	40. MAIN METERING JET ASSEMBLY.
7. CHOKE CONTROL ROD.	24. CONTROL VACUUM REGULATOR ADJUSTING NUT.	41. "O" RING.
8. SCREW (2). 8-32 X .88	25. CONTROL VACUUM REGULATOR.	42. ACCELERATOR PUMP RETURN SPRING.
8A. SCREW (5) 8-32 X .75	26. COLD ENRICHMENT ROD.	43. ACCELERATOR PUMP CUP.
9. UPPER BODY	27. SCREW (2) 8-32 X .75	44. ACCELERATOR PUMP PLUNGER.
10. FLOAT HINGE PIN.	28. VENTURI VALVE COVER PLATE.	45. INTERNAL VENT VALVE.
11. FLOAT ASSEMBLY.	29. GASKET	46. 3/16 RETAINING E-RING.
12. FLOAT BOWL GASKET.	30. ROLLER BEARING	47. IDLE TRIM SCREW.
13. FUEL INLET VALVE.	31. VENTURI AIR BYPASS SCREW AND TORQUE	48. VENTURI VALVE LIMITER ADJUSTING SCREW.
14. FUEL INLET SEAT.	RETENTION SPRING	49. PIPE PLUG.
15. FUEL INLET SEAT GASKET.	32. VENTURI VALVE PIVOT PLUG.	50. COLD ENRICHMENT ROD SEAL
16. DUST SEAL	33. VENTURI VALVE PIVOT PIN.	51. SEAL RETAINER
17. PIN - .12 X .69	34. VENTURI VALVE	52. HOT IDLE COMPENSATOR

Fig. 2 Upper body exploded view. Model 7200

1.	THROTTLE RETURN CONTROL DEVICE.	21.	CHOKE HEAT TUBE FITTING.
2.	THROTTLE RETURN CONTROL DEVICE BRACKET.	22.	CURB IDLE ADJUSTING SCREW (TSP OFF).
3.	MOUNTING SCREW. 10-32 X .50	23.	RETAINING NUT. 10-32
4.	ADJUSTING SCREW (TSP ON)	24.	FAST IDLE ADJUSTING LEVER.
5.	(NOT APPLICABLE 1978)	25.	FAST IDLE LEVER.
6.	SCREW (3). 8-32 X .50	26.	FAST IDLE ADJUSTING SCREW.
7.	CHOKE THERMOSTATIC HOUSING RETAINER.	27.	THROTTLE PLATE SCREWS (4).
8.	CHOKE THERMOSTATIC HOUSING.	28.	THROTTLE PLATES.
9.	CHOKE THERMOSTATIC HOUSING GASKET.	29.	VENTURI VALVE LIMITER STOP PIN.
10.	SCREW. 6-32 X .50	30.	THROTTLE SHAFT ASSEMBLY.
11.	CHOKE THERMOSTATIC LEVER.	31.	TRANSMISSION KICKDOWN ADJUSTING SCREW.
12.	CHOKE LEVER AND SHAFT ASSEMBLY.	32.	VENTURI VALVE LIMITER LEVER.
13.	FAST IDLE CAM.	33.	VENTURI VALVE LIMITER BUSHING.
14.	HIGH CAM SPEED POSITIONER ASSEMBLY.	34.	(NOT APPLICABLE 1978)
15.	SCREW (2). 8-32 X .75	35.	THROTTLE BODY.
16.	HIGH CAM SPEED POSITIONER DIAPHRAGM COVER.	36.	FAST IDLE CAM ADJUSTING SCREW.
17.	HIGH CAM SPEED POSITIONER DIAPHRAGM SPRING.	37.	TRANSMISSION KICKDOWN LEVER RETURN SPRING.
18.	HIGH CAM SPEED POSITIONER DIAPHRAGM ASSEMBLY.	38.	(NOT APPLICABLE 1978)
19.	HIGH CAM SPEED POSITIONER ROD.	39.	SCREW (5) 8-32 X .75
20.	CHOKE HOUSING BUSHING.		

Fig. 3 Lower body exploded view. Model 7200

```
                                        MAIN BODY
                              1. CRANKING ENRICHMENT        10. WIDE OPEN STOP SCREW
                                 SOLENOID                   11. PLUG EXPANSION
                              2. "O" RING SEAL              12. CRANKING FUEL CONTROL
                              3. SCREW (4) 8-32 X .56           ASSEMBLY
                              4. VENTURI VALVE DIAPHRAGM    13. ACCELERATION PUMP CHECK BALL
                                 COVER                      14. ACCELERATOR PUMP CHECK BALL
                              5. VENTURI VALVE DIAPHRAGM        WEIGHT
                                 SPRING GUIDE               15. THROTTLE BODY GASKET
                              6. VENTURI VALVE DIAPHRAGM    16. VACUUM MOTOR
                                 SPRING                     17. TORQUE RETENTION SPRING
                              7. VENTURI VALVE DIAPHRAGM
                                 ASSEMBLY
                              8. MAIN BODY
                              9. VENTURI VALVE ADJUSTING
                                 SCREW
```

Fig. 4 Main body exploded view. Model 7200

1980–82 Units

Fig. 8—Remove carburetor from vehicle, then remove choke cap. Install choke weight tool T77L-9848-A7 on choke bimetal lever, then install dial indicator with contact positioned on top of cold enrichment metering rod and zero indicator. Install stator cap and rotate to index, then note indicator reading. Reading should be between as indicated in Fig. 9, under the run position 75°F column. If reading is not within limits, adjust by turning the choke enrichment adjusting nut until reading is within limits. Do not remove or reset dial indicator to check the start position 0°F adjustment. To check this adjustment, rotate thermostat lever clockwise until cold enrichment metering rod travel stop screw is bottomed against the upper body and note indicator reading. If reading is not within limits listed in Fig. 9, under start position 0°F column, adjust by turning the travel stop screw. Without removing or resetting dial indicator, perform control vacuum regulator adjustment as described under Control Vacuum-Regulator (CVR) Adjustment, then re-check cold enrichment metering rod run position 75°F adjustment. Remove adjustment limiting diaphragm cover, then seat diaphragm using finger and note dial indicator reading, Fig. 10. If reading is not within limits listed in Fig. 9, under start position 75°F column, rotate diaphragm until dial indicator reads within specifications. Align holes on diaphragm and casting, then install diaphragm cover. Push inward on diaphragm rod until diaphragm is seated, then rotate thermostat lever clockwise until choke shaft lever pin touches fast idle intermediate lever and note indicator reading, Fig. 11. If reading is not within limits in Fig. 9, under run position 0°F column, remove lead ball from choke diaphragm cover and rotate adjusting screw clockwise to increase or counter-clockwise to decrease height, Fig. 11. After completing adjustment, install lead ball and choke cover.

Control Vacuum Adjustment

1977–79 All & 1980 2700 Units

Fig. 12—Install tachometer to engine, then start engine at set idle speed to specifications. With a 5/32 inch allen wrench, rotate venturi valve diaphram clockwise until the valve firmly closes. Connect a vacuum gauge to the vacuum tap on the venturi valve cover. With engine at curb idle, use a 1/8 inch allen wrench to rotate the venturi bypass adjusting screw to obtain the specified setting, Fig. 13. It may be necessary to readjust the idle speed at this time. Rotate the venturi valve diaphram adjusting screw until vacuum drops to the specified level, Fig. 13, however, it is necessary to open and close the throttle to obtain the vacuum drop. Check and adjust curb idle, if necessary.

Internal Vent Adjustment

1977–79 2700 Units

NOTE: This adjustment must be checked and adjusted, if necessary, whenever the curb idle is adjusted.

Fig. 5 Altitude compensator. 1978 2700 units

Fig. 6 Fuel level adjustment

Fig. 7 Float drop adjustment

Fig. 8 Cold enrichment metering rod adjustment

Year	Carb. Ident. No.	Carb. Model	Cold Enrichment Metering Rod Adjustment			
			Run Position		Start Position	
			0°F	75°F	0°F	75°F
1980	E0AE-AAA	2700	.295−.305	.115−.135	.520−.530	.460−.490
	E0AE-ACA, APA, AVA, ZA	2700	.315−.325	.115−.135	.520−.530	.460−.490
	E0AE-ADA, ATA	7200	.345−.355	.115−.135	.520−.530	.420−.450
	E0AE-BA, LA, PA, VA	7200	.345−.355	.115−.135	.520−.530	.460−.490
1981	E1AE-AAA	2700	.295−.305	.115−.135	.485−.495	.460−.490
	D9AE-AZA	7200	—	.120−.130	—	—
	E1AE-ACA, AGA, EA, LA, MA, SA	7200	.345−.355	.115−.135	.485−.495	.460−.490
	E1AE-KA, VA	7200	.345−.355	.115−.135	.520−.530	.460−.490
	E1DE-AA, E1VE-AA	7200	.345−.355	.115−.135	.485−.495	.460−.490
1982	E1AE-ACA	7200	.345−.355	.115−.135	.485−.495	.430−.460
	E1AE-AGA	7200	.345−.355	.115−.135	.485−.495	.440−.480
	E1AE-SA	7200	.345−.355	.115−.135	.485−.495	.440−.480
	E2AE-ABA, RA	7200	.345−.355	.115−.135	.485−.495	.430−.460
	E2AE-AGA, AHA	7200	.345−.355	.115−.135	.485−.495	.440−.480
	E2AE-LB	7200	.345−.355	.115−.135	.520−.530	.430−.460
	E2AE-LC	7200	.345−.355	.115−.135	.520−.530	.430−.460
	E2AE-MA	7200	.345−.355	.115−.135	.485−.495	.440−.480
	E2AE-MB	7200	.345−.355	.115−.135	.485−.495	.440−.480
	E2AE-NA, SA	7200	.345−.355	.115−.135	.520−.530	.430−.460
	E2AE-TA	7200	.345−.355	.115−.135	.485−.495	.430−.460
	E2AE-TB	7200	.345−.355	.115−.135	.485−.495	.430−.460
	E2DE-NA, SA, TA, UA	7200	.345−.355	.115−.135	.485−.495	.440−.480
	E2SE-DA, FA	7200	.345−.355	.115−.135	.520−.530	.460−.490
	E2SE-DB	7200	.345−.355	.115−.135	.520−.530	.460−.490
	E25E-ABA	7200	.345−.355	.115−.135	.485−.495	.430−.460
	E25E-AC, YA	7200	.345−.355	.115−.135	.520−.530	.460−.490
	E25E-FA	7200	.345−.355	.115−.135	.520−.530	.430−.460
	E25E-GA, SA, UA	7200	.345−.355	.115−.135	.520−.530	.430−.460
	E25E-GB, TA	7200	.345−.355	.115−.135	.520−.530	.430−.460

Fig. 9 Cold enrichment metering rod adjustment specification chart. 1980—82 Units

Fig. 14—With curb idle adjusted to specifications, place a .010 inch feeler gauge between the accelerator pump stem and the pump operating link. Rotate the nylon adjusting nut until a slight drag on the feeler gauge is obtained when removed.

Fast Idle Cam Adjustment

NOTE: On some 1979–82 California vehicles, it is necessary to remove the carburetor to remove the rivets on the choke housing. Remove the top two rivets with a ⅛ inch diameter twist drill. The third bottom rivet is located in a "Blind" hole and is removed by lightly tapping the rear of the retainer ring using a punch and hammer. The rivet, retainer ring, choke housing and gasket can then be removed.

Fig. 15—Remove choke cap and place the fast idle lever in the corner of the specified step of the fast idle cam with the high cam speed positioner retracted. If adjustment is performed on the bench, hold throttle closed with a rubber band to maintain cam position. Install stator cap, tool T77L-9848-A, and rotate clockwise until lever contacts adjusting screw. Rotate adjusting screw until index mark on stator cap aligns with the specified notch on the choke casting. Remove stator cap and reinstall choke cap.

Venturi Valve Limiter Adjustment

Fig. 16—Remove venturi valve cover and roller bearings, then the expansion plug located at rear of main body on the throttle side of carburetor. With an allen wrench, remove venturi valve wide open stop screw. Block the throttle wide open, then apply light closing pressure on the venturi valve and check gap between the valve and the air horn wall. If gap is not within specifications, adjust as follows: manually open the venturi valve to the wide open position and insert appropriate allen wrench into the hole from which the stop screw was removed. Rotate limiter adjusting screw clockwise to increase gap or counterclockwise to decrease gap. Remove allen wrench, apply light closing pressure to valve and recheck gap. If gap is within specifications, reinstall venturi valve wide open stop screw and rotate screw clockwise until screw contacts valve. Push venturi valve to wide open position and check gap between the valve and air horn wall, then rotate stop screw until gap is within specifications. Install new expansion plug in access hole. Reinstall venturi valve cover and roller bearings.

Control Vacuum Regulator (CVR) Adjustment

1977

NOTE: The cold enrichment metering rod adjustment must be performed before making this adjustment.

Fig. 10 Checking cold enrichment metering rod Start 75°F position adjustment. 1980–82 Units

Fig. 11 Adjusting cold enrichment metering rod Run 0°F position. 1980–82

Fig. 12 Control vacuum adjustment. 1977–79 All & 1980 2700 Units

Year	Carb. Ident. No.	Carb. Model	Control Vacuum Adjustment	
			Venturi Air Bypass (Inches H$_2$O)	Venturi Valve Diaphragm (Inches H$_2$O)
1977–78	All	2700	—	4.5–6.5
1979	D84E-KA	2700	—	4.5–6.5
	D84E-VA	2700	4.9–5.6	4.6–5.1
	D9AE-CB, JB, YB, ZB	2700	6.8–7.3	4.6–5.1
	D9BE-AFA	2700	4.9–5.6	4.6–5.1
	D9DE-HB	2700	4.9–5.6	4.6–5.1
	D9ZE-AZB, BEA	2700	4.9–5.6	4.6–5.1
	D9ZE-ZC	2700	6.8–7.3	4.6–5.1
	D94E-EB, GA	2700	6.8–7.3	4.6–5.1
	D94E-JA	2700	4.9–5.6	4.6–5.1
	D945-FA	2700	4.9–5.6	4.6–5.1
	D9ME-AA	7200	7.3–7.8	4.6–5.1
1980	All	2700	8	6

Fig. 13 Control vacuum adjustment specification chart. 1977–79 All & 1980 2700 Units

Fig. 14 Internal vent adjustment. 1977–79 2700 Units

Fig. 15 Fast idle cam adjustment

Fig. 16 Venturi valve limiter adjustment

Fig. 17—Rotate choke cap 180 degrees clockwise from index position and open and close the throttle to position the cam. Lightly apply pressure on the CVR rod and, if any downward travel is present, the valve is not seated and requires adjustment. If no downward travel is noted, rotate adjusting screw counter-clockwise until some downward travel is present. Rotate CVR rod clockwise until the adjusting nut starts to travel upward. Then, lightly apply pressure on the CVR rod and if any downward travel occurs, rotate adjusting screw clockwise in 1/4 turn increments until no

downward travel occurs. Reset choke cap to specified setting.

1978–82
Fig. 18—With the dial indicator installed, remove the stator cap with tool T77L-9848-A. Press downward on CVR rod until bottomed on seat. Note the dial indicator reading. If not within specifications, place a 3/8 inch box end wrench over the CVR adjusting nut and, using a

3/32 inch allen wrench, turn CVR rod to adjust the travel.

High Cam Speed Positioner Adjustment

Fig. 19—Place high cam speed positioner in the corner of the specified cam step. Then,

Fig. 17 Control vacuum regulator (CVR) adjustment. 1977 units

Fig. 18 Control vacuum regulator (CVR) adjustment. 1978—82 units

Fig. 19 High cam speed positioner adjustment

Fig. 20 Choke cap adjustment

Fig. 21 Fast idle speed adjustment

Fig. 22 Checking accelerator pump stem clearance. 1977—81 Units

Year	Carb. Model	Accelerator Pump Stem Clearance
1979	2700	.005—.015
	7200	.010—.030
1980—81	All	.010①
①—Plus one turn counter-clockwise.		

Fig. 23 Accelerator pump stem clearance specification chart. 1979—81 Units

place the fast idle lever in the corner of the high cam speed positioner and hold throttle firmly closed. Remove diaphragm cover and rotate diaphragm assembly clockwise until lightly bottomed on casting, then rotate assembly counterclockwise 1/2 to 1 1/2 turns, until the vacuum port and diaphragm hole align. Reinstall diaphragm cover.

Choke Cap Adjustment

Fig. 20—With choke cap installed, rotate choke cap clockwise until notch on cap is aligned with specified notch on housing.

Fast Idle Speed Adjustment

Fig. 21—Disconnect and plug the EGR vacuum line. With engine at curb idle and at normal operating temperature, place fast idle lever on specified step of fast idle cam. Ensure that the high cam speed positioner lever is disengaged, then rotate fast idle adjusting screw clockwise to increase speed or counterclockwise to decrease speed.

Accelerator Pump Stem Clearance

1979—81 Units
Fig. 22—After setting curb idle speed to specification, apply a slight downward pressure on

top of nylon nut located on accelerator pump stem and check clearance between pump stem and accelerator pump lever using a feeler gauge. Clearance should be as listed in Fig. 23. To adjust clearance, rotate nylon adjusting nut on top of accelerator pump stem clockwise to decrease clearance or counter-clockwise to increase clearance.

MODEL 4350-4V ADJUSTMENT SPECIFICATIONS

See Tune Up Chart in car chapters for curb and fast idle speeds.

Year	Carb. Model	Float Level (Dry)	Pump Setting (Hole No.)	Choke Plate Clearance (Pulldown)	Fast Idle Cam Linkage Setting	Auxiliary Inlet Valve Setting	Dechoke Clearance	Metering Rod Setting	Choke Setting
1977	D7VE-SA	1.00	#1	②	.140	.030	.300	—	Index
1978	D8VE-FA	1.00	#1	.160	.170	.030	.300	—	Index
	D8VE-GA	1.00	#1	.160	.170	.030	.300	—	Index

①—Initial setting; .160". Delayed setting; .210". ②—Initial setting; .140". Delayed setting; .190".

CARBURETORS

Labels on figure (left carburetor):
- DELAYED CHOKE PULLDOWN DIAPHRAGM
- "INTERNAL" FUEL BOWL VENTS
- CHOKE PLATE
- FAST IDLE SPEED ADJUSTMENT
- SOLENOID THROTTLE POSITIONER
- EGR CONNECTION
- IDLE MIXTURE ADJUSTMENT SCREWS
- SPARK PORT
- MECHANICAL FUEL BOWL VENT VALVE

Labels on figure (right carburetor):
- PCV CONNECTION
- VENTURI VACUUM (NOT USED)
- SECONDARY AIR VALVE
- CHOKE PLATE

Fig. 1   Motorcraft 4350 4V carburetor assembly

MODEL 4350-4V ADJUSTMENTS

The model 4350, Figs. 1, 2 and 2A, is a four barrel, three piece, separately cast design consisting of an upper body, main body and throttle body. The fuel bowl is vented by a mechanical fuel bowl vent valve to the carbon canister which opens when the engine is off and closes when the engine is running.

The upper main body consists of the choke plate, boost venturi assembly, secondary air valve, acceleration pump plunger, mechanical fuel vent valve and fuel inlet and float system.

The main body consists of the fuel bowl, primary fuel metering system vacuum piston and rods.

The throttle body consists of the primary and secondary throttle plates. The primary throttle is actuated by the accelerator linkage and the secondary throttle is actuated by a linkage from the primary throttle lever. A lockout tang coupled to the automatic choke linkage, prevents operation until choke is fully off. The secondary throttle shaft is split and loosely coupled in the center to permit tighter secondary plate seating.

Primary fuel metering is accomplished by tapered metering rods that are raised or lowered according to engine vacuum and are limited by a mechanical system and throttle plate opening.

Fuel inlet is controlled by twin floats on either side of the carburetor. The piston type accelerator pump is suspended into the pump well by a linkage and operating rod which are part of upper body.

The choke system consists of a bimetallic thermostatic choke system which operates when underhood temperatures are below 60°F and an electric assist choke system which operates when underhood temperatures are above 60°F. On Ford models, this carburetor is equipped with a vacuum operated delayed choke system, Fig. 6, which operates in addition to the usual pulldown system. On American Motors models, a thermostatic bypass valve, which is integral with the choke heat tube, helps prevent premature choke valve opening. For service information on the choke system, refer to the "Emission Control System" chapter.

Some carburetors are equipped with high altitude compensation to provide improved high altitude emission control and driveabil-ity. Air passing the bypass intake is metered into the air flow below the primary, thus providing the leaner air fuel mixture required at high altitudes. Air flow is controlled by a valve controlled by an aneroid attached to the rear of the carburetor. To provide improved cold engine starts at high altitudes, the bypass is equipped with a choke plate connected to the main choke system.

Accelerator Pump Adjustment

The piston-to-shaft pin position which is the only adjustment, is pre-set to deliver the cor-

Labels on Fig. 3:
- PUMP SHAFT
- PIN
- NO. 1
- NO. 2
- NO. 3
- PUMP PISTON
- ACCELERATING PUMP SPRING RETAINER
- PUMP SPRING
- PIN RETAINER

Fig. 3   Accelerator pump stroke adjustment

ADJUST

Fig. 4   Mechanical fuel vent valve adjustment

Fig. 2 Exploded view of 4350 4V carburetor without altitude compensation

Fig. 2A Exploded view of 4350 4V carburetor with high altitude compensation.

Fig. 5 Initial choke plate pulldown adjustment

Fig. 6 Choke plate delayed pulldown adjustment

rect amount of fuel for the engine on which it is installed and should not be changed from the specified setting. Do not attempt to adjust the accelerator pump stroke by turning the vacuum limiter level adjusting nut. This adjustment is pre-set and changing it could affect driveability.

1. Remove air horn assembly, then disconnect accelerator pump from operating lever by depressing spring and sliding arm out of pump shaft slot.
2. Disassemble spring and nylon keeper retaining adjustment pin. Refer to 4350 specifications chart. If pin is not in specified hole, remove it, reposition shaft in specified hole and reinstall pin, Fig. 3.
3. Slide nylon retainer over pin and position spring on shaft, then compress spring on shaft and install pump on arm.

Vent Valve Adjustment

1. With engine at curb idle speed and the solenoid throttle positioner de-energized (if used), adjust the vent valve so the adjusting screw just contacts the drive tab on the accelerator pump lever, Fig. 4. Turn adjusting screw one additional turn after screw contacts drive tab.
2. With engine off, observe that vent operating linkage pushes down on vent valve stem.

Initial Choke Pulldown

1. Remove choke housing assembly, then open throttle about half-way and position fast idle adjusting screw on high step of fast idle cam.

2. Bend a .036″ wire gauge at 90° angle, about 1/8″ from end, then insert bent end of gauge between choke piston slot and upper edge of right hand slot in choke housing, Fig. 5.
3. Rotate choke lever counterclockwise until gauge is snug in piston slot, then apply light force to lever to hold gauge and move top of choke rod away from carburetor while moving bottom of rod toward carburetor to remove end play from linkage.
4. Using a drill gauge or pin of specified size, check clearance between lower edge of choke plate and wall, Fig. 5. Refer to 4350 specifications chart.
5. Adjust clearance to specifications, by turning lock screw on choke plate shaft 3 full turns in a clockwise direction. Pry choke lever from shaft to break taper lock. Choke lever should rotate freely on choke shaft.
6. With drill gauge and .036″ wire gauge positioned as above, tighten, screw on choke shaft.
7. Install choke housing assembly.

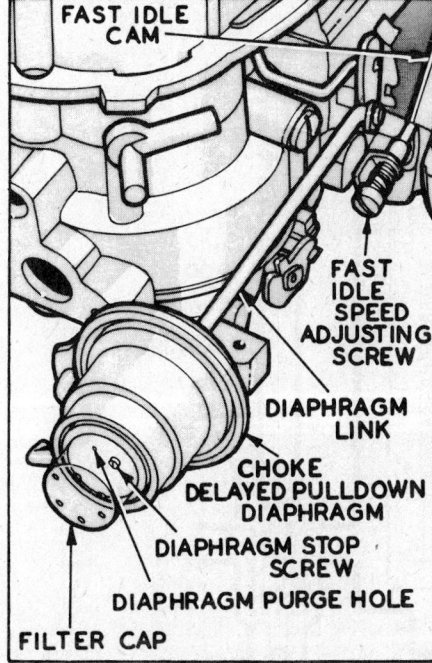

Fig. 7 Choke plate delayed pulldown stop screw adjustment

Fig. 8 Fast idle top step pulloff adjustment

Fig. 9 Dechoke clearance adjustment

Fig. 10   Float setting gauge and bending tool

Fig. 11   Float setting

Delayed Choke Pulldown

The delayed choke pulldown opens the choke to a wider setting about 6 to 18 seconds after the engine is started.

1. With throttle set on fast idle cam, note position of index marks on choke housing, loosen retaining screws and rotate cap 90° in closing (rich) direction.
2. Connect a vacuum source of 14–18 inches Hg. to vacuum supply port of delayed choke pulldown diaphragm and check clearance between lower edge of choke plate and wall, Fig. 6. Refer to 4350 specifications chart.
3. Adjust clearance to specifications by turning stop screw on delayed choke pulldown diaphragm, Fig. 7.

Fast Idle Top Step Pulloff

1. Operate delayed pulldown diaphragm manually or by applying 14 to 18 inches Hg.
2. Position fast idle speed screw on top step fast idle cam with choke plate closed. If necessary, rotate choke housing cap to close choke plate.
3. Observe that fast idle speed adjusting screw drops to second step of cam as delayed choke pulldown diaphragm is operated, Fig. 8.

Dechoke (Unloader) Clearance

1. Hold throttle plate fully open and apply pressure on choke valve toward close position.
2. Measure clearance between lower edge of choke valve and air horn wall. Fig. 9. Refer to 4350 Specifications Chart.
3. Adjust clearance to specifications by bending unloader tang which contacts fast idle cam forward to increase or rear-

ward to decrease clearance.

NOTE: Do not bend tang downward from a horizontal plane. After adjustment, make certain that there is at least .070 inch clearance between unloader tang and choke housing with throttle fully open.

Fig. 12   Auxiliary inlet valve adjustment

Fig. 13   Metering rod adjustment

Float Setting

To simplify float setting, refer to Fig. 10 for construction of an adjustable float gauge and float tab bending tool.

1. Adjust gauge to specified height and insert gauge into air horn, Fig. 11.
2. Check clearance and alignment of floats to gauge. Refer to 4350 Specifications Chart. Both floats should just touch gauge. If necessary, align floats by twisting floats slightly.
3. To raise float setting, insert open end of bending tool to right side of float lever tab between needle and float hinge. Raise float lever off needle and bend tap downward.
4. To lower float setting, insert open end of bending tool to left side of float lever tab between needle and float hinge. Support float lever and bend tap upward.
5. If above gauge is not available, invert upper body and measure distance from top of float to gasket surface of upper body. Adjust alignment and height of floats with bending tool as described previously.

Auxiliary Valve Setting

Check auxiliary valve clearance as shown in Fig. 12. If necessary to adjust clearance, use bending tool, Fig. 10.

Vacuum Piston & Metering Rods Adjustment

1. Remove air horn assembly, then depress metering rod hanger and turn vacuum piston adjusting screw and metering rod adjusting screws until metering rod hanger is fully seated against vacuum cylinder top face, Fig. 13.
2. Hold metering rod hanger in full downward position and turn each metering rod adjusting screw clockwise until the metering rod hanger starts to rise. Metering rods are now properly positioned in relation to vacuum piston.
3. Turn vacuum piston adjusting screw

GAUGE

LINK

DIAPHRAGM CANISTER

ADJUSTING SCREW

Fig. 14 Initial choke valve clearance adjustment. American Motors units with vacuum diaphragm

clockwise until specified clearance between metering rod hanger and vacuum cylinder top face is obtained.

Fast Idle Cam

1. Loosen choke cover screws and rotate cover to align index marks on cover and housing. Then, rotate cover an additional 90° counterclockwise and tighten attaching screws.
2. Place fast idle speed adjusting screw on kickdown (center) step of fast idle cam. Fully close choke plate and check clearance between air horn and lower edge of choke plate. Adjust by turning fast idle cam adjusting screw, ensuring adjusting screw remains on kickdown step during adjustment.
3. Loosen choke cove screws and rotate

cover to specified index mark and tighten cover screws.

American Motors Units With Vacuum Diaphragm

Initial Choke Valve Clearance

1. Loosen choke cover screws, open throttle and rotate choke cover until choke valve closes. Then, tighten one cover screw to hold cover in place.
2. Close throttle. The fast idle screw should be on top step of cam.
3. Bottom choke diaphragm on setscrew, however, do not press on links, Fig. 14.
4. Measure clearance between air horn and lower edge of choke valve, Fig. 14. Adjust by turning adjusting screw at rear of diaphragm housing.
5. Adjust fast idle cam linkage.
6. Loosen choke cover screw and set choke cover to specifications.

Choke Plate Indexing

1. Loosen choke lever attaching screw and pry lever from choke shaft to permit choke valve rotation.

NOTE: The choke lever attaching screw has a left hand thread.

2. Loosen choke cover screws and rotate cover 90° counterclockwise so the choke shaft lever contracts cam adjusting screw.
3. Position fast idle screw on top step of fast idle cam. Then, back off cam adjusting screw until clearance is obtained between screw and choke shaft lever.
4. Turn cam adjusting screw until it contacts choke shaft lever, then turn 6–7 additional turns.
5. Manually close choke plate and tighten choke shaft lever attaching screw.
6. Adjust initial choke valve clearance and fast idle cam linkage.
7. Set choke cover and tighten cover screws.

MODEL 5200 ADJUSTMENT SPECIFICATIONS

See Tune Up Chart in car chapters for curb and fast idle speeds.

Year	Carb. Model (9510) ①	Float Level	Pump Setting (Hole)	Choke Pulldown	Dechoke Clearance	Fast Idle Cam Clearance	Choke Setting
1977	D7EE-BGA	29/64	#2	.24	.24	.12	Index
	D7EE-BHA	29/64	#2	.24	.24	.12	Index
	D7EE-BLA	29/64	#2	.24	.24	.12	1 Rich
	D7EE-BMA	29/64	#2	.24	.24	.12	1 Rich
1978	D8BE-AKA	29/64	#2	.24	.24	.12	2 Rich
	D8EE-ANA	29/64	#2	.24	.24	.12	2 Rich
	D8BE-FA	29/64	#2	.24	.24	.12	2 Rich
	D8BE-HA	29/64	#2	.24	.24	.12	1 Rich
	D8EE-ATA	29/64	#2	.20	.24	.12	2 Rich
	D8EE-AUA	29/64	#2	.24	.24	.12	2 Rich
	D8EE-AVA	29/64	#2	.24	.24	.12	2 Rich
	D8EE-CA	29/64	#2	.24	.24	.12	1 Rich
	D8EE-DA	29/64	#2	.24	.24	.12	2 Rich
	D8EE-JA	29/64	#2	.24	.24	.12	2 Rich
	D8EE-KA	29/64	#2	.24	.24	.12	1 Rich
	D8ZE-RA	29/64	#2	.24	.24	.12	1 Rich

Continued

CARBURETORS

See Tune Up Chart in car chapters for curb and fast idle speeds.

Year	Carb. Model (9510) ①	Float Level	Pump Setting (Hole)	Choke Pulldown	Dechoke Clearance	Fast Idle Cam Clearance	Choke Setting
	D8ZE-SA	29/64	#2	.24	.24	.12	1 Rich
1979	D9BE-AAA	29/64	#2	.24	.24	.12	2 Rich
	D9BE-ABA	29/64	#2	.24	.24	.12	2 Rich
	D9BE-ACA	29/64	#2	.24	.24	.12	2 Rich
	D9BE-ADA	29/64	#2	.24	.24	.12	2 Rich
	D9BE-AGA	29/64	#2	.24	.24	.12	2 Rich
	D9EE-ALA	29/64	#2	.24	.24	.12	2 Rich
	D9EE-AMA	29/64	#2	.24	.24	.12	2 Rich
	D9EE-ANA	29/64	#2	.24	.24	.12	1 Rich
	D9EE-APA	29/64	#2	.24	.24	.12	1 Rich
	D9EE-ARA	29/64	#2	.24	.24	.12	1 Rich
	D9EE-ASA	29/64	#2	.24	.24	.12	1 Rich
	D9EE-ATA	29/64	#2	.24	.24	.12	1 Rich
	D9EE-AUA	29/64	#2	.24	.24	.12	1 Rich
	D9EE-AVA	29/64	#2	.24	.24	.12	1 Rich
	D9EE-AYA	29/64	#2	.24	.24	.12	1 Rich
	D9ZE-BCA	29/64	#2	.24	.24	.12	1 Rich
	D9ZE-BDA	29/64	#2	.24	.24	.12	1 Rich
	D9ZE-MD	29/64	#3②	.24	.24	.12	2 Rich
	D9ZE-ND	29/64	#3	.24	.24	.12	2 Rich
1980	D9EE-ANA	29/64	#2	.24	.24	.12	1 Rich
	D9EE-APA	29/64	#2	.24	.24	.12	1 Rich
	E0EE-AEA	29/64	#2	.20	.20	.08	1 Lean
	E0EE-AEB	29/64	#2	.24	.20	.06	1 Rich
	E0EE-AFA	29/64	#2	.20	.20	.08	1 Lean
	E0EE-AFB	29/64	#2	.24	.20	.06	1 Rich
	E0EE-GA	29/64	#2	.24	.20	.08	2 Rich
	E0EE-JA	29/64	#2	.20	.20	.08	1 Lean
	E0EE-JC	29/64	—	.20	.20	.08	2 Rich
	E0EE-JD	29/64	#2	.20	.20	.08	2 Rich
	E0EE-RA	29/64	#2	.24	.20	.08	2 Rich
	E0EE-TA	29/64	#2	.20	.20	.08	1 Lean
	E0EE-TC	29/64	—	.20	.20	.08	2 Rich
	E0EE-TD	29/64	#2	.20	.20	.08	2 Rich
	E0ZE-AAA	29/64	#3	.28	.24	.16	2 Rich
	E0ZE-ACA	29/64	#2	.28	.24	.16	Index
	E0ZE-ACB	29/64	—	.28	.24	.12	Index
	E0ZE-ACC	29/64	—	.28	.24	.16	Index
	E0ZE-AMA	29/64	—	.28	.24	.16	Index
	E0ZE-ATA	29/64	#2	.28	.24	.12	Index
	E0ZE-ATB	29/64	#2	.28	.24	.12	Index
	E0ZE-AZA	29/64	#3	.28	.39	.16	Index
1981	D9EE-ANA	29/64	#2	.24	.20	.12	—
	D9EE-APA	29/64	#2	.24	.20	.12	—
	E0EE-GA	29/64	#2	.20	.20	.08	—
	E0EE-RB	29/64	#2	.20	.20	.08	—
	E1ZE-VA	29/64	#2	.20	.20	.08	—
	E1ZE-YA	29/64	#2	.20	.20	.08	—
1982	E1BE-RA	15/32	#2	.197	.197	.079	—
	E1ZE-ACA	15/32	#2	.197	.197	.079	—
	E1ZE-ADB	15/32	#3	.276	.394	.236	—
	E1ZE-VA	15/32	#2	.197	.197	.079	—
	E1ZE-YA	15/32	#2	.197	.197	.079	—

Continued

MODEL 5200 ADJUSTMENT SPECIFICATIONS—Continued

See Tune Up Chart in car chapters for curb and fast idle speeds.

Year	Carb. Model (9510) ①	Float Level	Pump Setting (Hole)	Choke Pulldown	Dechoke Clearance	Fast Idle Cam Clearance	Choke Setting
	E2ZE-AAA	15/32	#2	.236	.236	.118	—
	E2ZE-ABA	15/32	#2	.236	.236	.118	—
	E2ZE-AFA	15/32	#2	.236	.236	.118	—
	E2ZE-AGA	15/32	#2	.236	.236	.118	—
	E2ZE-AHA	15/32	#2	.236	.236	.118	—

①—Tag attached to carburetor
②—Bottom.

MODEL 5200 ADJUSTMENTS

This carburetor is a two stage, two venturi carburetor, Figs. 1 and 2. The primary stage or venturi is smaller than the secondary venturi. The secondary is operated by mechanical linkage.

The primary stage includes a curb idle system, accelerator pump system, idle transfer system, main metering system and power enrichment system.

The secondary stage includes a transfer system, main metering system, and power system. Both the primary and secondary systems draw fuel from a common fuel bowl.

On 1977–80 models, the automatic choke is equipped with only the electric heater assist.

Some 1977 units are equipped with an altitude compensation feature which is controlled by the driver. This is a two piece manual system that utilizes the carburetor supplemental metering system when the dash panel control is placed in the "Sea Level" position and the normal fuel metering system when the control is in the "Altitude" position.

1978–82 units are equipped with a vacuum operated, solenoid assisted fuel bowl vent which is called a "Switching Bowl Vent". With the engine "Off", a spring holds the external vent open, closing the internal vent passage. In this position, the fuel bowl vapors pass to the evaporative emission canister. When the engine is started, manifold vacuum acting on the diaphragm overcomes the spring pressure and pulls the external vent to the seated position, uncovering the internal vent passage. A holding solenoid, connected to the ignition circuit, holding the vent closed to prevent the vent opening under low vacuum conditions. The vent will close only when the ignition is turned "Off".

Dry Float Setting

Fig. 3—With the bowl cover held in an inverted position and the float tang resting lightly on the spring loaded fuel inlet needle, measure the clearance between the edge of the float and the bowl cover. Adjust clearance by bending the float tang up or down as required, Fig. 4.

NOTE: Do not scratch or damage the tang. Adjust both floats equally.

Float Drop

1981 Units
Fig. 4A—Invert float cover and measure float drop using a suitable gauge. Float drop should be 1 inch ± 1/8 inch. If float drop is not within specifications, adjust by bending float drop tang, Fig. 4.

Fig. 1   Model 5200-2V carburetor

Fig. 2 Exploded view of model 5200 carburetor (Typical)

Fig. 3   Dry float setting

Fig. 4   Float adjusting point

Fig. 6   Choke plate pull-down

Fig. 5   De-choke adjustment

Fig. 8   Secondary throttle stop adjustment

Dechoke Clearance

Fig. 5—Hold throttle lever in wide open position and take slack out of choke linkage by applying finger pressure to top edge of choke plate. Measure clearance between lower edge of choke plate and air horn wall. Adjust by bending tab on fast idle lever where it touches the fast idle cam.

Choke Plate Vacuum Pull-Down

NOTE: On 1981–82 vehicles, it is necessary to remove the carburetor to remove rivets retaining choke cover to choke housing. Using a 1/8 inch or No. 30 drill bit, remove rivet heads, then drive rivet out using a 1/8 inch diameter punch.

Fig. 6—Remove the three screws and ring retaining choke spring cover and pull the water cover and/or choke spring cover from carburetor. On 1977 and 1981–82 units, place fast idle cam on high step. On 1978–80 units, place fast idle cam on second step. Push the diaphragm stem back against its stop. Place gauge rod or drill between the lower edge of the choke plate and the air horn wall. Remove the slack from the choke linkage by applying finger pressure to the top edge of the choke plate. Adjust the choke plate-to-air horn clearance by removing the plug from the diaphragm and turning the adjusting screw in or out as required.

Fast Idle Cam Clearance

Fig. 7—Insert specified drill or gauge between the lower edge of the choke plate and the air horn wall. With the fast idle screw held

Fig. 7   Fast idle cam clearance

CARBURETORS

on the second step of the fast idle cam, measure the clearance between the tang of the choke lever and the arm on the fast idle cam. Adjust clearance by bending choke lever tang up or down as required. Refer to *5200 Specifications Chart.*

Secondary Throttle Stop Screw Adjustment

Fig. 8—Back off the secondary throttle stop screw until the secondary throttle plate seats

in its bore. Turn the screw in until it touches the tab on the secondary throttle lever. On all units except when used on 2800 cc engines, turn the screw inward an additional 1/4 turn. On units used on 2800 cc engines, turn screw inward an additional 3/4 turn.

GM Delco/Rochester Carburetor Section

MODEL 2GC & 2GE CARBURETOR ADJUSTMENT SPECIFICATIONS

See Tune Up Chart in car chapters for curb and fast idle speeds.

Year	Carb. Production No.	Float Level	Float Drop	Pump Rod	Idle Vent	Intermediate Choke Rod	Vacuum Break Throttle Lever Side	Vacuum Break Choke Side	Choke Setting	Choke Rod	Choke Unloader
1977	17057104, 105	7/16	19/32	1 21/32	—	.120	—	②	Index	.260	.325
	17057107, 109	7/16	19/32	1 17/32	—	.120	—	②	Index	.260	.325
	17057108, 110	19/32	19/32	1 21/32	—	.120	—	②	Index	.260	.325
	17057111, 113	19/32	19/32	1 17/32	—	.120	—	②	Index	.260	.325
	17057112	19/32	19/32	1 21/32	—	.120	—	②	Index	.260	.325
	17057114	19/32	19/32	1 17/32	—	.120	—	②	Index	.260	.325
	17057121, 123	19/32	19/32	1 17/32	—	.120	—	②	Index	.260	.325
	17057140	15/32	15/32	1 9/32	—	.120	.140	.100	1 Rich	.080	.180
	17057141, 145	7/16	15/32	1 1/2	—	.120	.110	.040	1 Rich	.080	.140
	17057143, 144	7/16	15/32	1 17/32	—	.120	.130	.100	1 Rich	.080	.140
	17057146, 148	7/16	15/32	1 17/32	—	.120	.100	.040	3 Rich	.080	.140
	17057147	7/16	15/32	1 1/2	—	.120	.110	.040	1 Rich	.080	.140
	17057149	7/16	15/32	1 9/16	—	.120	.110	.040	1 Lean	.080	.140
	17057180, 182	7/16	15/32	1 17/32	—	.120	.110	.060	1 Rich	.080	.140
	17057188, 190	19/32	19/32	1 21/32	—	.120	—	②	Index	.260	.325
	17057192, 194	19/32	19/32	1 21/32	—	.120	—	②	Index	.260	.325
	17057404	1/2	19/32	1 21/32	—	.120	—	③	1/2 Lean	.260	.325
	17057405	1/2	19/32	1 5/8	—	.120	—	③	1/2 Lean	.260	.325
	17057408, 410	21/32	19/32	1 5/8	—	.120	—	③	1 Lean	.260	.325
	17057412	21/32	19/32	1 5/8	—	.120	—	③	1 Lean	.260	.325
	17057414	21/32	19/32	1 21/32	—	.120	—	③	1 Lean	.260	.325
	17057445	7/16	15/32	1 1/2	—	.120	.140	.110	1 Lean	.080	.140
	17057446, 447	7/16	15/32	1 1/2	—	.120	.130	.110	1 Rich	.080	.140
	17057448	7/16	15/32	1 1/2	—	.120	.130	.110	1 Rich	.080	.140
1978	17058102, 103	15/32	19/32	1 17/32	—	.120	—	④	Index	.260	.325
	17058104, 105	15/32	19/32	1 21/32	—	.120	—	②	Index	.260	.325
	17058107, 109	15/32	19/32	1 17/32	—	.120	—	②	Index	.260	.325
	17058108, 110	19/32	19/32	1 21/32	—	.120	—	④	Index	.260	.325
	17058111	15/32	19/32	1 17/32	—	.120	—	②	Index	.260	.325
	17058112, 114	19/32	19/32	1 21/32	—	.120	—	④	Index	.260	.325
	17058113	19/32	19/32	1 17/32	—	.120	—	②	Index	.260	.325
	17058121, 123	19/32	19/32	1 17/32	—	.120	—	②	Index	.260	.325
	17058126, 128	19/32	19/32	1 17/32	—	.120	—	.130	Index	.260	.325
	17058140	7/16	15/32	1 19/32	—	.120	.110	.070	1 Rich	.080	.140
	17058141	7/16	15/32	1 19/32	①	.120	.140	.100	1 Rich	.080	.140
	17058143	7/16	15/32	1 9/16	①	.120	.110	.080	1 Rich	.080	.140
	17058144	7/16	15/32	1 5/8	①	.120	.110	.060	1 Rich	.080	.140
	17058145	7/16	15/32	1 19/32	①	.120	.110	.060	1 Rich	.080	.140
	17058147	7/16	15/32	1 19/32	①	.120	.140	.100	1 Rich	.080	.140
	17058148, 149	7/16	15/32	1 19/32	①	.120	.110	.080	1 Rich	.080	.140
	17058182, 183	7/16	15/32	1 19/32	①	.120	.110	.080	1 Rich	.080	.140
	17058185	7/16	15/32	1 19/32	①	.120	.110	.050	1 Rich	.080	.140
	17058187, 189	7/16	15/32	1 19/32	①	.120	.110	.080	1 Rich	.080	.140

MODEL 2GC & 2GE CARBURETOR ADJUSTMENT SPECIFICATIONS—Continued

See Tune Up Chart in car chapters for curb and fast idle speeds.

Year	Carb. Production No.	Float Level	Float Drop	Pump Rod	Idle Vent	Intermediate Choke Rod	Vacuum Break		Choke Setting	Choke Rod	Choke Unloader
							Throttle Lever Side	Choke Side			
	17058188	7/16	15/32	1 19/32	①	.120	.120	.050	1 Rich	.080	.140
	17058404, 405	1/2	19/32	1 21/32	—	.120	—	③	1/2 Lean	.260	.325
	17058408, 410	21/32	19/32	1 21/32	—	.120	—	③	1/2 Lean	.260	.325
	17058412, 414	21/32	19/32	1 21/32	—	.120	—	③	1/2 Lean	.260	.325
	17058444	7/16	15/32	1 19/32	①	.120	.140	.100	1 Rich	.080	.140
	17058446	7/16	15/32	1 19/32	①	.120	.130	.110	1 Rich	.080	.140
	17058447	7/16	15/32	1 19/32	①	.120	.150	.110	1 Rich	.080	.140
	17058448	7/16	15/32	1 19/32	①	.120	.140	.110	1 Rich	.080	.140

①—With idle speed properly adjusted, the vent valve should be just closed at idle.
②—.130 inch before first scheduled tune-up;
.160 inch after first scheduled tune-up.
③—.140 inch before first scheduled tune-up;
.160 inch after first scheduled tune-up.
④—.130 inch before first scheduled tune-up;
.150 inch after first scheduled tune-up.

MODEL 2GC & 2GE ADJUSTMENTS

The Model 2GC and 2GE carburetors use a carburetor mounted choke coil, Figs. 1 and 2. The choke coil on the Model 2GE is electrically assisted.

Float Level Adjustment

Figs. 3 & 4—Adjust float level as directed for the type of float shown in the specification listed in the *Rochester Specifications Chart*.

Float Drop Adjustment

Figs. 5 & 6—Adjust float drop as directed for the type of float shown in the specification listed in the *Rochester Specifications Chart*.

Pump Rod Adjustment

Fig. 7—Back out idle stop screw and completely close throttle valves in bore. Place proper size gauge listed in the *Rochester Specifications Chart* on top of air horn ring. Bend pump rod at lower angle to obtain specified dimension to top of pump rod.

Idle Vent Adjustment

Fig. 8—Open throttle until vent valve just closes. Place proper size gauge on top of air horn ring. Dimension to top of pump rod should be as specified in the *Rochester Specifications Chart*. Adjust by bending tang on pump lever.

Bowl Vent Adjustment

Fig. 9—Set idle speed to specifications, then with the idle screw on second step of fast idle cam, vent valve should just be closed. To adjust, turn vent valve screw.

Intermediate Choke Rod Adjustment

2GC & 2GE Models, Fig. 10—Remove thermostat cover and coil assembly, then with fast idle screw on high step of cam and choke valve closed, the edge of choke lever must align with edge of .120" plug gauge as shown. To adjust, bend choke rod at point shown.

Fig. 2 Carburetor mounted automatic choke

Fig. 3 Float level adjustment (brass float)

Fig. 1 Exploded view of typical Rochester two-barrel carburetor

Fig. 4   Float level adjustment (nitrophyl float)

MEASURE FROM LIP AT TOE OF FLOAT TO AIR HORN GASKET

BEND HERE TO ADJUST

GAUGE FROM GASKET SURFACE TO BOTTOM OF FLOAT

BEND TANG TO ADJUST

Fig. 5   Float drop adjustment (brass float)

BEND FLOAT TANG TO ADJUST FOR PROPER SETTING

MEASURE SPECIFIED DISTANCE FROM GASKET SURFACE TO NOTCH AT TOE OF FLOAT

Fig. 6   Float drop adjustment (nitrophyl float)

MEASURE FROM TOP OF AIR HORN RING TO TOP OF PUMP ROD

BEND PUMP ROD TO ADJUST

THROTTLE VALVES FULLY CLOSED

Fig. 7   Pump rod adjustment

Vacuum Break Adjustment

Figs. 11 & 12—Place fast idle screw on high step of cam, then using an outside vacuum source, seat vacuum diaphragm. On purge type vacuum diaphragms, cover bleed hole so that diaphragm will not bleed down. Hold choke towards closed position, then with vacuum diaphragm seated and rod in end of slot in plunger, check clearance between upper edge of choke valve and air horn wall. Refer to *Rochester Specifications Chart*. To adjust, bend vacuum break rod at point shown.

Automatic Choke Setting

Carburetor Mounted Choke, Fig. 13—Place idle screw on high step of fast idle cam, then loosen three retaining screws and rotate choke cover against coil tension until index mark is in line with specified point on choke housing (see *Rochester Specifications Chart*).

Choke Rod Adjustment

Fig. 14—It is important to position both slow idle and fast idle screws as follows before making choke rod adjustment.

1. On models using a single idle stop screw,

turn stop screw in until it just contacts bottom step of fast idle cam. Then turn screw in one full turn farther.
2. On models using both a slow idle and a fast idle screw, turn slow idle stop screw in until it just contacts stop. Then turn this screw in one full turn from this point. Next turn the fast idle screw in until it touches bottom step of fast idle cam.
3. On all models, place idle screw on second

GAUGE ACROSS TOP OF AIR HORN RING TO TOP OF ROD

BEND TANG TO ADJUST

OPEN THROTTLE VALVES TO POINT WHERE VENT VALVE JUST CLOSES ON ITS SEAT

Fig. 8   Idle vent adjustment for 2GC carburetors

② WITH IDLE SPEED SET TO PROPER R.P.M., VENT VALVE SHOULD JUST BE CLOSED.

③ TURN VENT VALVE SCREW TO ADJUST

① WITH IDLE SPEED SET TO PROPER R.P.M., PLACE IDLE SPEED SCREW ON 2ND STEP OF FAST IDLE CAM NEXT TO HIGHEST STEP

Fig. 9   Bowl vent adjustment

Fig. 10   Intermediate choke rod adjustment

Fig. 11   Primary (throttle lever side) vacuum break adjustment

Fig. 12   Auxiliary (choke side) vacuum break adjustment

Fig. 13   Automatic choke adjustment for 2GC, 2GE carburetors

Fig. 14   Choke rod adjustment

step of fast idle cam against shoulder of high step. While holding screw in this position, check clearance between upper edge of choke valve and air horn wall as shown. Adjust to specified dimension by bending tang on choke lever and collar assembly (see *Rochester Specifications Chart*).

Choke Unloader Adjustment

Fig. 15—With throttle valves held wide open, the choke valve should be open just enough to admit the specified gauge between upper edge of choke valve and air horn wall (see *Rochester Specifications Chart*). To adjust, bend tang on throttle lever.

Fig. 15   Choke unloader adjustment for 2GC & 2GE carburetors

QUADRAJET E4M & M4M SERIES ADJUSTMENT SPECIFICATIONS

See Tune Up Chart in car chapters for curb and fast idle speeds.

Year	Carb. Production No.	Float Level	Pump Rod Hole	Pump Rod Adj.	Fast Idle (Bench) Turns	Choke Coil Lever	Choke Rod	Vacuum Break Front	Vacuum Break Rear	Air-Valve Dash-pot	Choke Setting	Choke Unleader	Air-Valve Valve Spring Wind-Up
1977	17057202, 204	15/32	Inner	9/32	3	.120	.325	②	—	.015	2 Lean	.280	7/8
	17057203	15/32	Inner	9/32	3	.120	.325	②	—	.015	3 Lean	.280	7/8
	17057210	15/32	Inner	9/32	3	.120	.325	③	—	.015	2 Lean	.280	1
	17057211	15/32	Inner	9/32	3	.120	.325	③	—	.015	3 Lean	.280	1
	17057226	15/32	Inner	9/32	3	.120	.325	.180	—	.015	2 Lean	.285	1
	17057228	13/32	Inner	9/32	3	.120	.325	③	—	.015	2 Lean	.280	1
	17057230	13/32	Inner	3/8	2	.120	.080	.140	.120	.030	2 Rich	.230	1/2
	17057231	17/32	Inner	3/8	2	.120	.080	.140	.140	.030	2 Rich	.230	3/4
	17057232	13/32	Outer	3/8	2	.120	.080	.140	.120	.030	2 Rich	.230	1/2
	17057233	13/32	Inner	3/8	2	.120	.080	.140	.140	.030	2 Rich	.230	3/4
	17057234	13/32	Inner	9/32	2	.120	.080	.140	.120	.030	2 Rich	.230	3/4
	17057235	17/32	Inner	9/32	2	.120	.080	.140	.120	.030	2 Rich	.230	3/4
	17057236	13/32	Inner	9/32	2	.120	.080	.140	.140	.030	2 Rich	.230	3/4
	17057241, 242	5/16	Outer	3/8	2	.120	.095	.120	.105	.015	1 Rich	.240	3/4
	17057248	5/16	Outer	3/8	3	.120	.095	.130	.110	.015	Index	.240	3/4
	17057250, 252	13/32	Inner	9/32	3	.120	.100	.135	.180	.030	2 Rich	.220	1/2
	17057253, 255	13/32	Inner	9/32	3	.120	.100	.135	.180	.030	2 Rich	.220	1/2
	17057256	13/32	Inner	9/32	3	.120	.100	.135	.180	.030	2 Rich	.220	1/2
	17057257, 258	15/32	Inner	9/32	3	.120	.100	.135	.225	.030	3 Rich	.220	1/2
	17057262, 266	17/32	Outer	3/8	3	.120	.130	.150	.240	.030	1 Rich	.220	1/2
	17057263	17/32	Outer	3/8	3	.120	.130	.165	.240	.030	1 Rich	.220	5/8
	17057274	17/32	Outer	3/8	3	.120	.130	.150	.240	.030	1 Rich	.220	1/2
	17057502, 504	15/32	Inner	9/32	3	.120	.325	④	—	.015	2 Lean	.280	7/8
	17057510, 528	15/32	Inner	9/32	3	.120	.325	.180	—	.015	2 Lean	.280	1
	17057530, 533	13/32	Outer	7/16	2	.120	.080	.150	.150	.030	2 Rich	.230	1/2
	17057550, 553	13/32	Inner	9/32	3	.120	.100	.135	.225	.030	2 Rich	.220	1/2
	17057552	15/32	Inner	9/32	3	.120	.100	.135	.225	.030	3 Rich	.220	1/2
	17057582, 584	15/32	Outer	3/8	3	.120	.325	③	—	.015	2 Lean	.280	7/8
1978	17058202, 204	15/32	Inner	9/32	3	.120	46°	⑤	—	.015	2 Lean	42°	7/8
	17058203	15/32	Inner	9/32	3	.120	46°	⑤	—	.015	3 Lean	42°	7/8
	17058210, 228	15/32	Inner	9/32	3	.120	46°	⑥	—	.015	2 Lean	42°	1
	17058211	15/32	Inner	9/32	3	.120	46°	⑥	—	.015	3 Lean	42°	1
	17058230	13/32	Inner	9/32	3	.120	16°	25°	39°	.030	2 Rich	35°	1/2
	17058232	13/32	Inner	9/32	2	.120	16°	26°	28°	.030	2 Rich	35°	3/4
	17058233	13/32	Inner	9/32	2	.120	16°	26°	28°	.030	2 Rich	35°	1/2
	17058240	7/32	Inner	9/32	3	.120	14 1/2°	21°	23°	.015	Index	38°	3/4
	17058241	5/16	Outer	3/8	3	.120	18°	21 1/2°	19°	.015	1 Rich	38°	3/4
	17058246	7/32	Outer	3/8	3	.120	14 1/2°	23°	23°	.015	Index	38°	3/4
	17058250, 253	13/32	Inner	9/32	3	.120	18°	23°	30 1/2°	.030	2 Rich	35°	1/2
	17058254	15/32	Inner	9/32	3	.120	19°	24°	—	.030	3 Rich	35°	1/2
	17058257, 258	13/32	Inner	9/32	3	.120	19°	24°	36 1/2°	.030	2 Rich	35°	1/2
	17058259	13/32	Inner	9/32	3	.120	19°	24°	30 1/2°	.030	2 Rich	35°	1/2
	17058263	17/32	Outer	3/8	3	.120	23°	28°	40°	.030	Index	35°	5/8
	17058264, 278	17/32	Outer	3/8	3	.120	23 1/2°	26°	40°	.030	1 Rich	35°	1/2
	17058266, 274	17/32	Outer	3/8	3	.120	23 1/2°	26°	40°	.030	Index	35°	1/2
	17058272	15/32	Outer	3/8	3	.120	14 1/2°	24°	32°	.030	2 Rich	36°	5/8
	17058276	17/32	Outer	3/8	3	.120	23 1/2°	26°	40°	.030	Index	35°	1/2
	17058282, 284	15/32	Inner	9/32	3	.120	46°	27°	—	.015	Index	42°	7/8
	17058502, 504	15/32	Inner	9/32	3	.120	46°	①	—	.015	2 Lean	42°	7/8
	17058530, 531	13/32	Inner	9/32	2	.120	16°	26°	28°	.030	2 Rich	35°	1/2
	17058532, 533	13/32	Inner	9/32	2	.120	16°	26°	28°	.030	2 Rich	35°	1/2
	17058540	7/32	Inner	9/32	3	.120	14 1/2°	21°	23°	.015	Index	38°	3/4

QUADRAJET E4M & M4M SERIES ADJUSTMENT SPECIFICATIONS—Continued

See Tune Up Chart in car chapters for curb and fast idle speeds.

Year	Carb. Production No.	Float Level	Pump Rod Hole	Pump Rod Adj.	Fast Idle (Bench) Turns	Choke Coil Lever	Choke Rod	Vacuum Break Front	Vacuum Break Rear	Air-Valve Dash-pot	Choke Setting	Choke Unleader	Air-Valve Valve Spring Wind-Up
	17058550, 553	13/32	Inner	9/32	3	.120	19°	24°	36½°	.030	2 Rich	35°	1/2
	17058555	13/32	Inner	9/32	3	.120	19°	24°	36½°	.030	2 Rich	35°	1/2
	17058559	15/32	Inner	9/32	3	.120	19°	24°	—	.030	3 Rich	36½°	1/2
	17058582, 584	15/32	Inner	9/32	3	.120	46°	⑥	—	.015	2 Lean	42°	7/8
1979	17059202, 204	15/32	Inner	1/4	2	.120	38°	28°	—	.015	1 Lean	38°	7/8
	17059203, 207	15/32	Inner	1/4	2	.120	38°	27°	—	.015	2 Lean	38°	7/8
	17059210	15/32	Inner	9/32	2	.120	38°	27°	—	.015	1 Lean	38°	1
	17059211	15/32	Inner	9/32	2	.120	38°	27°	—	.015	2 Lean	38°	1
	17059216, 217	15/32	Inner	1/4	2	.120	38°	27°	—	.015	1 Lean	38°	7/8
	17059218, 222	15/32	Inner	9/32	2	.120	38°	28°	—	.015	2 Lean	38°	7/8
	17059228	15/32	Inner	9/32	2	.120	38°	27°	—	.015	1 Lean	38°	1
	17059230	13/32	Inner	9/32	1½	.120	16°	25°	37°	.030	2 Rich	25°	1/2
	17059232	13/32	Inner	9/32	2¼	.120	16°	26°	28°	.030	2 Rich	25°	1/2
	17059240, 243	7/32	Inner	9/32	2	.120	14.5°	21°	21°	.015	1 Rich	30°	3/4
	17059241	5/16	Inner	3/8	2	.120	18°	20°	20.5°	.015	1 Rich	38°	3/4
	17059242	7/32	Inner	9/32	2	.120	14.5°	15°	13°	.015	2 Rich	30°	3/4
	17059247, 249	5/16	Outer	3/8	2	.120	18°	20°	19°	.015	1 Rich	38°	3/4
	17059250, 251	13/32	Inner	9/32	2	.120	18°	23°	30.5°	.030	2 Rich	35°	1/2
	17059253	13/32	Inner	9/32	2	.120	18°	23	30.5	.030	2 Rich	35°	1/2
	17059256, 258	13/32	Inner	9/32	2	.120	19°	24°	32°	.030	2 Rich	35°	1/2
	17059259	13/32	Inner	9/32	2	.120	18°	23°	30.5°	.030	2 Rich	35°	1/2
	17059263	17/32	Outer	3/8	2	.120	23°	28°	38°	.030	Index	35°	5/8
	17059271	7/16	Outer	3/8	2	.120	20°	25°	34°	.030	1 Rich	33°	5/8
	17059272	15/32	Outer	3/8	2	.120	14.5°	23°	29.5°	.030	2 Rich	33°	5/8
	17059282, 284	15/32	Inner	1/4	2	.120	38°	27°	—	.015	1 Lean	38°	7/8
	17059502, 504	15/32	Inner	1/4	2	.120	38°	28°	—	.015	2 Lean	38°	7/8
	17059505, 507	15/32	Inner	1/4	2	.120	38°	28°	—	.015	1 Lean	38°	7/8
	17059530, 532	13/32	Inner	9/32	2¼	.120	16°	26°	28°	.030	2 Rich	25°	1/2
	17059540, 543	7/32	Inner	9/32	2	.120	14.5°	21°	23°	.015	1 Rich	38°	3/4
	17059544	7/32	Inner	9/32	2	.120	14.5°	21°	21°	.015	1 Rich	30°	3/4
	17059546	7/32	Inner	9/32	2	.120	14.5°	21°	21°	.015	Index	30°	3/4
	17059547	7/32	Inner	9/32	2	.120	14.5°	21°	18°	.015	1 Rich	30°	3/4
	17059548	7/32	Inner	9/32	2	.120	14.5°	21°	15°	.015	1 Rich	30°	3/4
	17059553, 554	13/32	Inner	9/32	2	.120	19°	24°	36.5°	.030	2 Rich	35°	1/2
	17059555	13/32	Inner	9/32	2	.120	19°	26°	36.5°	.030	2 Rich	35°	1/2
	17059582, 584	15/32	Outer	11/32	2	.120	38°	33°	—	.015	1 Lean	46°	7/8
1980	17080202, 204	7/16	Inner	1/4	4	.120	20°	27°	—	.025	—	38°	7/8
	17080207	7/16	Inner	1/4	4	.120	20°	27°	—	.025	—	38°	7/8
	17080228	7/16	Inner	9/32	4	.120	20°	30°	—	.025	—	38°	7/8
	17080230	7/16	Inner	9/32	—	.120	16°	26°	24°	.025	—	35°	1/2
	17080240	3/16	Inner	9/32	—	.120	14.5°	16°	16°	.025	—	30°	9/16
	17080241	7/16	Inner	7/16	—	.120	18°	23°	20.5°	.025	—	38°	3/4
	17080242	13/32	Inner	9/32	—	.120	14.5°	15°	18°	.025	—	35°	9/16
	17080243	3/16	Inner	9/32	—	.120	14.5°	16°	16°	.025	—	30°	9/16
	17080244	5/16	Inner	9/32	—	.120	24.5°	18°	14°	.025	—	38°	5/8
	17080249	7/16	Inner	9/32	1½	.120	18°	23°	20.5°	.025	—	38°	3/4
	17080250, 251	13/32	Inner	9/32	3	.120	17°	26°	34°	.025	—	35°	1/2
	17080252, 253	13/32	Inner	9/32	3	.120	17°	26°	34°	.025	—	35°	1/2
	17080259, 260	13/32	Inner	9/32	3	.120	17°	26°	34°	.025	—	35°	1/2
	17080270	15/32	Outer	3/8	1½	.120	14.5°	26°	34°	.025	—	35°	5/8
	17080271	15/32	Outer	3/8	—	.120	20°	25°	34°	.025	—	33°	5/8

Continued

QUADRAJET E4M & M4M SERIES ADJUSTMENT SPECIFICATIONS—Continued

See Tune Up Chart in car chapters for curb and fast idle speeds.

Year	Carb. Production No.	Float Level	Pump Rod Hole	Pump Rod Adj.	Fast Idle (Bench) Turns	Choke Coil Lever	Choke Rod	Vacuum Break Front	Vacuum Break Rear	Air-Valve Dash-pot	Choke Setting	Choke Unleader	Air-Valve Valve Spring Wind-Up
	17080272	15/32	Outer	3/8	1½	.120	14.5°	23°	29.5°	.025	—	33°	5/8
	17080274	15/32	Outer	5/16	1½	.120	16°	20°	28°	.025	—	33°	5/8
	17080282, 284	7/16	Outer	11/32	4	.120	20°	25°	—	.025	—	38°	7/8
	17080502, 504	1/2	—	—	4	.120	20°	24°	30°	.025	—	38°	7/8
	17080530	17/32	—	9/32	—	.120	16°	25°	47°	.025	—	40°	1/2
	17080540, 543	3/8	—	—	—	.120	14.5°	19°	23°	.025	—	38°	9/16
	17080542	3/8	—	—	4	.120	14.5°	19°	13°	.025	—	38°	9/16
	17080546	—	—	—	—	—	—	—	—	—	—	—	—
	17080547	—	—	—	—	—	—	—	—	—	—	—	—
	17080548	—	—	—	—	—	—	—	—	—	—	—	—
	17080553	15/32	—	9/32	3	.120	17°	25°	35°	.025	—	35°	1/2
	17080554	15/32	—	9/32	3	.120	17°	25°	34°	.025	—	35°	1/2
1981	17081202	11/32	—	—	4½	.120	20°	26°	—	.025	—	38°	7/8
	17081203	11/32	—	—	4½	.120	20°	26°	—	.025	—	38°	7/8
	17081204	11/32	—	—	4½	.120	20°	26°	—	.025	—	38°	7/8
	17081207	11/32	—	—	4½	.120	20°	26°	—	.025	—	38°	7/8
	17081216	11/32	—	—	4½	.120	20°	26°	—	.025	—	38°	7/8
	17081217	11/32	—	—	4½	.120	20°	26°	—	.025	—	38°	7/8
	17081218	11/32	—	—	4½	.120	20°	26°	—	.025	—	38°	7/8
	17081242	5/16	—	—	4½	.120	24.5°	17°	15°	.025	—	38°	9/16
	17081243	1/4	—	—	4½	.120	24.5°	19°	17°	.025	—	38°	9/16
	17081245	3/8	—	—	3	.120	24.5°	28°	24°	.025	26°	38°	5/8
	17081247	3/8	—	—	3	.120	24.5°	28°	24°	.025	—	38°	5/8
	17081248	3/8	—	—	2	.120	24.5°	28°	24°	.025	—	38°	5/8
	17081249	3/8	—	—	3	.120	24.5°	28°	24°	.025	—	38°	5/8
	17081253	15/32	—	—	3	.120	14°	25°	36°	.025	—	35°	5/8
	17081254	15/32	—	—	3	.120	14°	25°	36°	.025	—	35°	1/2
	17081270	7/16	—	—	4½	.120	14.5°	24°	34°	.025	—	35°	5/8
	17081272	7/16	—	—	4½	.120	14.5°	24°	40°	.025	—	35°	5/8
	17081274	7/16	—	—	4½	.120	16°	24°	35°	.025	—	35°	5/8
	17081289	13/32	—	—	2	.120	24.5°	28°	24°	.025	—	38°	5/8
1982	17082202	11/32	—	—	3	.120	20°	27°	—	.025	—	38°	7/8
	17082203	11/32	—	—	3	.120	38°	27°	—	.025	—	38°	7/8
	17082204	11/32	—	—	3	.120	20°	27°	—	.025	—	38°	7/8
	17082207	11/32	—	—	3	.120	38°	27°	—	.025	—	38°	7/8
	17082244	7/16	—	—	3	.120	24.5°	21°	16°	.025	—	32°	9/16
	17082245	3/8	—	—	3	.120	24.5°	26°	26°	.025	—	32°	5/8
	17082246	3/8	—	—	3	.120	24.5°	26°	26°	.025	—	32°	5/8
	17082247	3/8	—	—	3	.120	18°	26°	26°	.025	—	32°	5/8
	17082248	13/32	—	—	3	.120	24.5°	28°	24°	.025	—	38°	5/8
	17082251	15/32	—	—	3	.120	14°	25°	45°	.025	—	35°	1/2
	17082253	15/32	—	—	3	.120	14°	25°	36°	.025	—	35°	1/2
	17082264	7/16	—	—	3	.120	24.5°	21°	16°	.025	—	32°	9/16
	17082265	3/8	—	—	3	.120	24.5°	26°	26°	.025	—	32°	5/8
	17082266	3/8	—	—	3	.120	24.5°	26°	26°	.025	—	32°	5/8
	17082267	3/8	—	—	3	.120	24.5°	28°	24°	.025	—	38°	5/8
	17082268	13/32	—	—	3	.120	24.5°	28°	24°	.025	—	38°	5/8

① —28° before first scheduled tune-up; 31° after first scheduled tune-up.

② —.160 inch before first scheduled tune-up; .245 inch after first scheduled tune-up.

③ —.180 inch before first scheduled tune-up; .275 inch after first scheduled tune-up.

④ —.165 inch before first scheduled tune-up; .260 inch after first scheduled tune-up.

⑤ —27° before first scheduled tune-up; 30° after first scheduled tune-up.

⑥ —30° before first scheduled tune-up; 33° after first scheduled tune-up.

CARBURETORS

QUADRAJET E4M & M4M SERIES CARBURETOR ADJUSTMENTS

Fig. 1 Quadrajet M4M series carburetor (Typical)

Fig. 2 Quadrajet E4M series carburetor (Typical)

The M4M Series (M4MC, M4MCA and M4MEA) Quadrajet carburetor, Fig. 1, are two stage, downdraft carburetors. These units are similar in design to the previously used Quadrajet carburetors. A triple venturi system, with $1^{7}/_{32}$ inch venturi, is used on the primary side of the carburetor with $1^{3}/_{8}$ inch primary throttle bores. The secondary side has two $2^{1}/_{4}$ inch bores.

The primary side of the carburetor has six systems of operation: float, idle, main metering, power, pump and choke. The secondary side has one metering system which supplements the primary main metering system and receives fuel from a common float chamber.

An Adjustable Part Throttle (A.P.T.) feature incorporates an adjustable metering rod assembly operating in a fixed jet. On some models, a barometric pressure-sensitive aneroid (Bellows) is an integral part of the A.P.T. metering rod assembly. This provides a close tolerance control of fuel flow to the main metering system, thereby controlling air/fuel ratios during part throttle operation.

Some units use a multiple stage power enrichment system with two power pistons. One piston is an auxiliary power piston with a single metering rod operating in a fixed jet. The primary power piston with two metering rods operates in replaceable metering jets. This system provides sensitive control of the air/fuel ratio during light engine power requirements while providing richer mixtures during moderate to heavy engine loads.

All units use a bowl mounted choke housing with a thermostatic coil assembly. Also, a dual vacuum break system is used to improve cold engine warm-up and drive-away performance. Cadillac units use a three stage electric choke with a ceramic resistor for precise timing of the choke valve opening to improve engine warm-up performance.

The E4M series (E4MC and E4ME) carburetors are used on vehicles equipped with the C4 (Computor Controlled Catalytic Converter) System or Computer Control Command System, Fig. 2. An electrically operated mixture control solenoid is mounted in the float bowl and is used to control air and fuel metered to idle and main metering systems of the carburetor. Fuel metering is controlled by two special stepped primary metering rods, operating in removable jets and positioned by a plunger in the solenoid which is controlled by an electrical signal from the Electronic Control Module. Air metering to the idle system is controlled by an idle air bleed valve located in the air horn, which follows movement of the mixture control solenoid plunger to control the amount of bleed air into the idle system. A throttle position sensor mounted in the float bowl, is used to electrically signal the Electronic Control module of various throttle position changes.

On some 1981–82 units, an idle speed control mounted on the float bowl is used to control idle speed. On these units, the curb idle speed is programmed into the Electronic Control Module and no attempt should be made to adjust idle speed. On some 1981–82 models with V8-307 engine, an idle load compensator mounted on the float bowl is used to control idle speed. The compensator uses manifold vacuum to sense changes in engine load and compensates by adjusting curb idle speed. This unit should not be adjusted, unless if during diagnosis, curb idle speed is not within specifications.

NOTE: On 1980–82 units the choke cover is retained to the choke housing by three pop rivets. With float bowl and throttle body properly supported, carefully align a No. 21 drill on pop rivet head. Drill only enough to re-

① HOLD RETAINER FIRMLY IN PLACE

③ GAUGE FROM TOP OF CASTING TO TOP OF FLOAT — GAUGING POINT 3/16" BACK) FROM END OF FLOAT AT TOE (SEE INSET)

(INSET)

— TOE

GAUGING POINT (3/16" BACK FROM TOE)

② PUSH FLOAT DOWN LIGHTLY AGAINST NEEDLE

④ REMOVE FLOAT AND BEND FLOAT ARM UP OR DOWN TO ADJUST

⑤ VISUALLY CHECK FLOAT ALIGNMENT AFTER ADJUSTING

Fig. 3 Quadrajet E4M & M4M series float level adjustment

Fig. 4 Quadrajet M4M series pump rod adjustment. 1977–80 Less C-4 System

Fig. 5 Quadrajet E4M & M4M series fast idle adjustment (Bench)

Fig. 6 Quadrajet E4M & M4M series choke coil lever adjustment

Fig. 7 Quadrajet M4M series choke rod adjustment. Plug gauge method

move the rivet heads, then using a small hammer and drift, drive remainder of rivet from choke housing. A service kit is available for choke cover installation.

Float Level Adjustment

Fig. 3—With an adjustable T-scale, measure distance from top of float bowl gasket surface, with gasket removed, to top of float at a point 3/16 inch back from toe. Dimension should be as specified in the Specification Chart. To adjust, bend float arm.

NOTE: On units equipped with Computer Controlled Catalytic Converter (C-4) System or Computer Command Control System, adjust float if level varies more than 1/16 inch from specified setting as follows:
  a. If float level is too high, hold retainer firmly in place and push downward on center of float pontoon to obtain correct setting.
  b. If float level is too low, lift out metering rods, then remove solenoid connector attaching screws. Turn lean mixture solenoid screw clockwise, noting number of turns, until screw is lightly bottomed in float bowl. Turn screw counter-clockwise and remove screw, then lift solenoid and connector from float bowl. Remove float and bend float arm to adjust. After adjusting, check float alignment. Reverse procedure to install components removed. When installing lean mix-

ture screw, ensure that screw is backed out of float bowl the exact number of turns as noted during removal.

Pump Rod Adjustment

1977–80 M4M Units
Fig. 4—With throttle valves completely closed and pump rod in specified hole, measure distance from top of choke valve wall (next to vent stack) to top of pump stem. Dimension should be as specified in the Specification Chart. To adjust, bend pump lever.

Fast Idle Adjustment

Fig. 5—With cam follower on highest step of cam, turn fast idle screw out until primary throttle valve is completely closed. Turn screw in to contact lever, then turn screw in the additional turns listed in the Specification Chart.

Choke Coil Lever Adjustment

Fig. 6—With thermostatic coil assembly removed from choke housing, push upward on coil tang to close choke valve. Insert gauge specified in the Specification Chart into hole in choke housing. The choke coil lever should contact the gauge. If not, bend choke rod to adjust.

Choke Rod Adjustment

Plug Gauge Method
Fig. 7—With the fast idle adjustment performed, and the cam follower on the second step of the fast idle cam, next to high step, close choke valve by pushing upward on choke lever. Measure dimension between the upper edge of the choke valve and air horn wall. Dimension should be as specified in the Specification Chart. To adjust, bend fast idle cam tang.

Angle Gauge Method

NOTE: On 1980–82 units, do not remove rivets and choke cover to perform this adjustment. Use a rubber band on the vacuum break lever tang to hold the choke valve in the closed position.

Fig. 8—Perform fast idle adjustment before making this adjustment. Rotate degree scale until zero is opposite pointer, then with choke valve completely closed, place magnet squarely on top of choke valve and rotate bubble until centered. Refer to Specification Chart for proper setting. Rotate scale so the specified degree for adjustment is opposite pointer. Place cam follower on second step of cam next to high step. Close choke by pushing upward on choke coil lever. To adjust, bend tang on fast idle cam until bubble is centered. Remove gauge.

Front Vacuum Adjustment

Plug Gauge Method
Fig. 9—Place cam follower on highest step of

CARBURETORS

FIGURE 1

① MAKE FAST IDLE ADJUSTMENT (BENCH OR ON-THE-CAR SETTING).

⑥ SPECIFIED ANGLE (SEE SPECS.)

⑨ TO ADJUST, BEND TANG ON FAST IDLE CAM UNTIL BUBBLE IS CENTERED.

FAST IDLE CAM

⑧ CLOSE CHOKE BY PUSHING UPWARD ON CHOKE COIL LEVER.

⑩ REMOVE GAUGE.

⑦ PLACE CAM FOLLOWER ON SECOND STEP OF CAM NEXT TO HIGH STEP.

FIGURE 2

Fig. 8   Quadrajet E4M & M4M series choke rod adjustment. Angle gauge method

NOTE: HOLD GAUGE VERTICALLY

④ PLACE GAUGE BETWEEN UPPER EDGE OF CHOKE VALVE AND INSIDE WALL OF AIR HORN

⑤ TURN SCREW TO ADJUST

② SEAT DIAPHRAGM USING OUTSIDE VACUUM SOURCE

NOTE: PLUG PURGE BLEED HOLE WITH A PIECE OF MASKING TAPE ON DELAY FEATURE MODELS

① PLACE CAM FOLLOWER ON HIGHEST STEP OF FAST IDLE CAM

③ PUSH INSIDE CHOKE COIL LEVER COUNTERCLOCKWISE UNTIL TANG ON VACUUM BREAK LEVER CONTACTS TANG ON VACUUM BREAK PLUNGER STEM

Fig. 9   Quadrajet M4M series front vacuum break adjustment. Plug gauge method

fast idle cam, then using an external vacuum source, seat diaphragm. Push choke coil lever upward until vacuum break lever tang contacts vacuum break plunger stem tang. Measure dimension between upper edge of choke valve and air horn wall. Dimension should be as specified in the M4M Series Specification Chart. To adjust, turn vacuum break plunger adjusting screw.

Angle Gauge Method

NOTE: On 1980–82 units, do not remove rivets or choke cover to place choke valve in the closed position. Use a rubber band on vacuum break lever tang to hold choke valve in the closed position. On 1981–82 units, remove vacuum break from carburetor and position bracket in a vise, then grind off weld holding adjusting screw cover. Remove adjusting screw cover, then reinstall vacuum break.

Fig. 10—Rotate degree scale until zero is opposite pointer, then with choke valve completely closed, place magnet squarely on top of choke valve and rotate bubble until centered. Refer to Specification Chart to obtain proper setting for adjustment. Rotate scale so the specified degree for adjustment is opposite pointer. Seat choke diaphragm using an external vacuum source. On some models, it will be necessary to plug air bleed with a piece of masking tape. Hold choke valve toward closed position, pushing counter-clockwise on inside coil lever. To adjust, rotate screw until bubble is centered. Remove gauge.

Rear Vacuum Break Adjustment

Plug Gauge Method
Fig. 11—Place cam follower on highest step of fast idle cam, then using an external vacuum source, seat diaphragm. Push upward on choke coil lever toward closed choke position until stem is seated. With choke rod in bottom of slot, insert gauge specified in the Specification Chart between upper edge of choke valve and air horn wall. To adjust, bend vacuum break rod.

Angle Gauge Method

NOTE: On 1981–82 units, remove vacuum

break from carburetor and position in a vise, then grind off adjusting screw cap and reinstall vacuum break. After completing adjustment, apply a suitable sealer over adjusting screw head.

Fig. 12 & 13—Rotate degree scale until zero is opposite pointer, then with choke valve completely closed, place magnet squarely on top of choke valve and rotate bubble until centered. Refer to Specification Chart for proper setting for adjustment. Rotate scale so specified degree for adjustment is opposite pointer. Seat choke diaphragm using an external vacuum source. On some models, it will be necessary to plug air bleed with a piece of masking tape. Hold choke valve toward closed position,

⑤ SPECIFIED ANGLE (SEE SPECS.)

④ LEVELING BUBBLE (CENTERED)

⑦ WITH CHOKE COIL REMOVED, ROTATE INSIDE COIL LEVER COUNTER-CLOCKWISE

① DEGREE SCALE

② POINTER

③ CHOKE VALVE CLOSED

⑧ TURN SCREW TO ADJUST UNTIL BUBBLE IS CENTERED.

MAGNET

FIGURE 1.

⑥ SEAT DIAPHRAGM USING VACUUM SOURCE.

NOTE: ON DELAY MODELS WITH AIR BLEED, PLUG END COVER WITH PIECE OF 1" SQUARE MASKING TAPE. REMOVE AFTER ADJUSTMENT

FIGURE 2

Fig. 10   Quadrajet E4M & M4M series front vacuum break adjustment. Angle gauge method

NOTE: HOLD GAUGE VERTICALLY

⑤ GAUGE BETWEEN AIR HORN WALL & UPPER EDGE OF CHOKE VALVE

④ ROD IN BOTTOM OF SLOT

CLOSING ASSIST SPRING

NOTE: PLUG PURGE BLEED HOLE WITH A PIECE OF MASKING TAPE

⑥ BEND ROD TO ADJUST

③ PUSH UP ON CHOKE COIL LEVER TOWARDS CLOSED CHOKE

② SEAT REAR VACUUM BREAK DIAPHRAGM USING OUTSIDE VACUUM SOURCE

① PLACE CAM FOLLOWER LEVER ON HIGHEST STEP OF FAST IDLE CAM

Fig. 11   Quadrajet M4M series rear vacuum break adjustment. Plug gauge method

① MAKE CHOKE COIL LEVER AND FAST IDLE ADJUSTMENT (BENCH OR ON-THE-CAR SETTING).
NOTE 1: DO NOT REMOVE RIVETS AND CHOKE COVER TO PERFORM THIS ADJUSTMENT. USE RUBBER BAND ON VACUUM BREAK LEVER TANG TO HOLD CHOKE VALVE CLOSED (STEP 8).

⑥ SPECIFIED ANGLE (SEE SPECS.)

② DEGREE SCALE
⑤ LEVELING BUBBLE (CENTERED)
③ POINTER MAGNET
④ CHOKE VALVE CLOSED
FIGURE 1

⑨ TO ADJUST, USING 1/8" HEX WRENCH TURN SCREW IN REAR COVER UNTIL BUBBLE IS CENTERED

RUBBER BAND

PLUNGER BUCKING SPRING

FIGURE 2

⑦ SEAT DIAPHRAGM USING VACUUM SOURCE

⑧ LIGHTLY CLOSE CHOKE BY PUSHING UPWARD ON CHOKE COIL LEVER OR VACUUM BREAK LEVER TANG (HOLD IN POSITION WITH RUBBER BAND). MAKE SURE PLUNGER BUCKING SPRING (IF USED) IS COMPRESSED AND SEATED (SEE NOTE 2).

NOTE 2: ON DELAY MODELS, PLUG END COVER WITH A 2GC TYPE ACCELERATOR PUMP PLUNGER CUP. REMOVE CUP AFTER ADJUSTMENT.

Fig. 12 Quadrajet E4M & M4M series rear vacuum break adjustment (units w/ adjusting screw). Angle gauge method

⑥ SEAT DIAPHRAGM USING VACUUM SOURCE.
NOTE: ON DELAY MODELS WITH AIR BLEED, PLUG END COVER WITH PIECE OF 1" SQUARE MASKING TAPE. REMOVE AFTER ADJUSTMENT

⑤ SPECIFIED ANGLE (SEE SPECS.)
④ LEVELING BUBBLE (CENTERED)
① DEGREE SCALE
② POINTER MAGNET
③ CHOKE VALVE CLOSED
FIGURE 1

PLUNGER BUCKING SPRING

FIGURE 2

⑦ WITH CHOKE COIL REMOVED, HOLD CHOKE VALVE TOWARDS CLOSED CHOKE BY PUSHING COUNTER-CLOCKWISE ON INSIDE COIL LEVER. MAKE SURE PLUNGER BUCKING SPRING (IF USED) IS COMPRESSED AND SEATED.

⑧ TO ADJUST, BEND CHOKE LINK UNTIL BUBBLE IS CENTERED.

Fig. 13 Quadrajet E4M & M4M series vacuum break adjustment (units less adjusting screw). Angle gauge method

③ PLACE GAUGE BETWEEN ROD AND END OF SLOT IN LEVER
② AIR VALVE COMPLETELY CLOSED
① SEAT CHOKE VACUUM DIAPHRAGM. USE OUTSIDE VACUUM SOURCE
④ BEND HERE FOR SPECIFIED CLEARANCE BETWEEN ROD AND END OF SLOT IN LEVER
NOTE: PLUG PURGE BLEED HOLE WITH TAPE WHERE USED. REMOVE AFTER ADJUSTMENT.

Fig. 14 Quadrajet M4M series air-valve dashpot adjustment

③ ALIGN INDEX MARKS AS SPECIFIED
② ROTATE COVER AND COIL ASSEMBLY COUNTERCLOCKWISE UNTIL CHOKE VALVE JUST CLOSES
① PLACE CAM FOLLOWER ON HIGHEST STEP OF CAM

Fig. 15 Quadrajet M4M series automatic choke coil adjustment

④ GAUGE BETWEEN UPPER EDGE OF CHOKE VALVE AND AIR HORN WALL
③ ON WARM ENGINE, CLOSE CHOKE VALVE BY PUSHING UP ON TANG ON VACUUM BREAK LEVER (HOLD IN POSITION WITH RUBBER BAND).
① INSTALL ELECTRIC CHOKE ASSEMBLY IN HOUSING. ALIGN INDEX MARK WITH SPECIFIED POINT ON HOUSING NOTE: THERE SHOULD NOT BE ANY GASKET BETWEEN CHOKE HOUSING AND CHOKE COIL ASSEMBLY
⑤ BEND TANG TO ADJUST
② HOLD PRIMARY THROTTLE VALVES WIDE OPEN

Fig. 16 Quadrajet M4M series choke unloader adjustment. Plug gauge method

⑦ HOLD PRIMARY THROTTLE VALVES WIDE OPEN.
⑤ SPECIFIED ANGLE (SEE SPECS.)
④ LEVELING BUBBLE (CENTERED)
① DEGREE SCALE
② POINTER MAGNET
③ CHOKE VALVE CLOSED
FIGURE 1
FIGURE 2

⑥ INSTALL CHOKE THERMOSTATIC COVER AND COIL ASSEMBLY IN HOUSING. ALIGN INDEX MARK WITH SPECIFIED POINT ON HOUSING.
⑨ BEND TANG TO ADJUST UNTIL BUBBLE IS CENTERED.
⑧ ON WARM ENGINE, CLOSE CHOKE VALVE BY PUSHING UP ON TANG ON VACUUM BREAK LEVER (HOLD IN POSITION WITH RUBBER BAND).

Fig. 17 Quadrajet E4M & M4M series choke unloader adjustment. Angle gauge method

Fig. 18   Quadrajet E4M & M4M series secondary throttle valve lockout adjustment

Fig. 19   Quadrajet E4M & M4M series secondary throttle valve closing adjustment

Fig. 20   Quadrajet E4M & M4M series secondary throttle valve opening adjustment

Fig. 21   Quadrajet E4M & M4M series air-valve spring wind-up adjustment

pushing counter-clockwise on inside coil lever. On units equipped with an adjusting screw, using a 1/8 in. hex wrench, turn adjusting screw in rear cover until bubble is centered, Fig. 12. On units less adjusting screw, bend choke link until bubble is centered, Fig. 13. Remove gauge.

Air Valve Dashpot Adjustment

Fig. 14—Using an external vacuum source, seat choke vacuum diaphragm. Then, with the air valve completely closed, place gauge specified in the Specification Chart between air valve rod and end of slot in air valve lever. To adjust, bend rod at air valve end.

Choke Coil Adjustment

Fig. 15—Install choke coil and cover assembly. On Cadillac units, do not install a gasket between the choke housing and electric choke assembly. Place fast idle cam follower on highest step of fast idle cam. Rotate coil and cover assembly counter-clockwise until choke just closes, then align index mark on choke

cover with the specified index mark on choke housing. Refer to the Specification Chart.

Choke Unloader Adjustment

Plug Gauge Method
Fig. 16—With the choke coil adjustment performed, close choke, valve and open throttle valve. To close choke valve on a warm engine, push upward on tang of intermediate choke lever that contacts the fast idle cam and hold in place with a rubber band. Measure dimension between upper edge of choke valve and air horn wall. To adjust, bend tang on fast idle lever.

Angle Gauge Method
Fig. 17—Rotate degree scale until zero is opposite pointer, then with choke valve completely closed, place magnet squarely on top of choke valve and rotate bubble until centered. Refer to Specification Chart for proper setting for adjustment. Rotate scale so specified degree for adjustment is opposite pointer. Install choke cover and coil assembly and align index mark with specified point on housing. Hold primary throttle valve wide open and close

choke valve by pushing upward on vacuum break lever tang. Hold in position with a rubber band. To adjust, bend tang on fast idle lever until bubble is centered. Remove gauge.

Secondary Throttle Valve Lockout Adjustment

Lockout-Pin Clearance
Fig. 18—With choke and throttle valves fully closed, measure clearance between lockout-pin and lockout lever. Maximum clearance should not exceed .015 inch. To adjust, bend lockout-pin.

Opening Clearance
Fig. 18—Push downward on fast idle cam tail to open choke valve, then push lockout lever counter-clockwise so upper end of lever contacts the round pin in fast idle cam. Measure clearance between lockout-pin and lockout lever toe. Clearance should be .015 inch. To obtain proper clearance, file metal from end of lockout-pin.

Secondary Throttle Valves Adjustment

Throttle Closing
Fig. 19—With curb idle speed set, hold choke valve open with cam follower lever off fast idle

cam steps. Measure clearance between forward edge of slot in the secondary throttle valve pick-up lever and the secondary actuating rod. On 1977 units except Pontiac and all 1978-82 units, clearance should be .020 inch. On 1977 Pontiac, clearance should be .030 in. To adjust, bend secondary closing tang on primary throttle lever.

Throttle Opening
Fig. 20—Open primary throttle lever until link lightly contacts secondary lever tang. The bottom end of the link should be in the center of the slot in secondary lever. To adjust, bend tang on secondary lever.

Air Valve Spring Wind-Up Adjustment

Fig. 21—Remove front vacuum break diaphragm unit and air valve dashpot rod. Loosen lock screw and rotate spring adjusting screw counter-clockwise until air valve is partially open. Hold air valve closed, then rotate adjusting screw clockwise specified number of turns after the spring contacts pin. Refer to the Specification Chart. Tighten lock screw and install air valve dashpot rod and the front vacuum break diaphragm unit.

Idle Load Compensator Adjustment
1981 V8-307 & 1982 Models w/E4MC Carb.

NOTE: On some 1981 models with V8-307 engine, and 1982 models with E4MC, an idle load compensator mounted on the float bowl is used to control idle speed. This unit should not be adjusted, unless if during diagnosis, curb idle speed is not within specifications. This adjustment should be performed with engine at operating temperature and choke and A/C off.

1. Remove air cleaner assembly and plug vacuum hose to thermal vacuum valve.
2. Disconnect and plug hoses to EGR valve, canister purge port and idle load compensator.
3. Apply parking brake and block wheels, then back throttle stop screw out 3 turns.
4. With engine operating, place transmission selector lever in drive position, adjust plunger to obtain 725 RPM. The jam nut on the plunger must be held in position to prevent damage to guide tabs. If a replacement idle load compensator is be-

ing installed, the plunger should be set to obtain a clearance of $^{61}/_{64}$ inch from jam nut to tip of plunger.
5. Connect vacuum hose to idle load compensator and note idle speed. If idle speed requires adjustment, stop engine and remove idle load compensator.
6. With idle load compensator removed, remove rubber and metal plug from center outlet tube.
7. Using a .090 inch allen wrench, rotate center outlet tube adjusting screw to obtain 550 RPM on 1981 models, or 500 RPM on 1982 models. Each turn of the adjusting screw will change idle speed approximately 75 to 100 RPM. Rotate adjusting screw counter-clockwise to increase engine speed and clockwise to decrease engine speed.
8. Reinstall rubber plug on center outlet tube, then install idle load compensator on carburetor. If a final adjustment is necessary it will be necessary to repeat steps 6, 7 and 8.
9. Apply a suitable vacuum source to idle load compensator to fully retract plunger.
10. Adjust throttle body idle stop screw to obtain 550 RPM on 1981 models, or 500 RPM on 1982 models, then reconnect all vacuum hoses and install air cleaner.

DUAL-JET 2MC, M2MC, M2ME 200, 210 & E2ME ADJUSTMENT SPECIFICATIONS
See Tune Up Chart in car chapters for curb and fast idle speeds.

Year	Carb. Production No.	Float Level	Pump Rod Hole	Pump Rod Adj.	Choke Coil Lever	Choke Rod	Vacuum Break Rich	Vacuum Break Lean	Vacuum Break Front	Vacuum Break Rear	Choke Un-loader	Choke Setting
1977	17057150, 151	1/8	Outer	11/32	.120	.085	.090	.160	—	—	.190	2 Rich
	17057156, 158	1/8	Outer	11/32	.120	.085	.090	.160	—	—	.190	1 Rich
	17057157	1/8	Outer	3/8	.120	.090	.100	.190	—	—	.190	1 Rich
	17057172, 176	11/32	Inner	1/4	.120	.075	—	—	①	②	.240	2 Rich
	17057173, 177	11/32	Outer	5/16	.120	.075	—	—	③	②	.240	2 Rich
1978	17058130, 131	1/4	Inner	1/4	.120	46°	—	—	24°	—	46°	Index
	17058132, 133	1/4	Inner	1/4	.120	46°	—	—	24°	—	46°	Index
	17058150, 152	3/8	Inner	1/4	.120	14°	—	—	35°	25°	35°	2 Rich
	17058151, 156	3/8	Outer	11/32	.120	14°	—	—	38°	25°	35°	2 Rich
	17058154, 155	3/8	Outer	11/32	.120	14°	—	—	27°	40°	35°	2 Rich
	17058158	3/8	Outer	11/32	.120	14°	—	—	38°	25°	35°	2 Rich
	17058160	11/32	Inner	1/4	.120	22.5°	—	—	25°	32°	33°	2 Rich
	17058192	5/16	Inner	9/32	.120	14.5°	—	—	21°	19°	50°	2 Rich
	17058450	3/8	Outer	11/32	.120	14°	—	—	27°	45°	35°	2 Rich
	17058496	1/4	Outer	3/8	.120	15°	—	—	24°	34°	38°	1 Rich
1979	17059104, 106	15/32	Inner	1/4	.120	38°	—	—	27°	—	38°	④
	17059108, 110	1/4	Inner	1/4	.120	38°	—	—	28°	—	38°	2 Lean
	17059130, 132	1/4	Inner	9/32	.120	38°	—	—	27°	—	38°	Index
	17059131	1/4	Inner	3/8	.120	38°	—	—	27°	—	38°	1 Lean
	17059133	1/4	Inner	9/32	.120	38°	—	—	27°	—	38°	1 Lean
	17059134, 135	15/32	Inner	1/4	.120	38°	—	—	27°	—	38°	1 Lean
	17059136, 137	15/32	Inner	1/4	.120	38°	—	—	27°	—	38°	1 Lean
	17059138, 139	1/4	Inner	1/4	.120	38°	—	—	28°	—	38°	1 Lean
	17059140, 141	1/4	Inner	1/4	.120	38°	—	—	28°	—	38°	1 Lean
	17059150, 152	3/8	Inner	1/4	.120	14°	—	—	32°	23°	35°	2 Rich
	17059151	3/8	Outer	11/32	.120	14°	—	—	38°	25°	35°	2 Rich
	17059154	3/8	Outer	11/32	.120	14°	—	—	27°	40°	35°	2 Rich
	17059160	11/32	Inner	1/4	.120	20°	—	—	23°	31°	32°	2 Rich
	17059170, 171	1/4	Inner	9/32	.120	38°	—	—	27°	—	38°	Index
	17059180, 190	11/32	Inner	1/4	.120	24.5°	—	—	19°	17°	38°	2 Rich
	17059184	11/32	Inner	1/4	.120	24.5°	—	—	19°	17°	35°	2 Rich
	17059191	11/32	Inner	9/32	.120	24.5°	—	—	19°	17°	38°	2 Rich

CARBURETORS

Year	Carb. Production No.	Float Level	Pump Rod Hole	Pump Rod Adj.	Choke Coil Lever	Choke Rod	Vacuum Break Rich	Vacuum Break Lean	Vacuum Break Front	Vacuum Break Rear	Choke Unloader	Choke Setting
	17059193	13/32	Inner	1/4	.120	24.5°	—	—	19°	17°	35°	2 Rich
	17059194	11/32	Inner	1/4	.120	24.5°	—	—	19°	17°	35°	2 Rich
	17059196	11/32	Inner	1/4	.120	24.5°	—	—	23°	21°	42°	1 Rich
	17059430, 432	9/32	Inner	9/32	.120	38°	—	—	27°	—	38°	1 Lean
	17059434, 436	15/32	Inner	1/4	.10	38°	—	—	29°	—	38°	1 Lean
	17059450	3/8	Outer	11/32	.120	14°	—	—	27°	45°	35°	2 Rich
	17059491, 492	11/32	Inner	9/32	.120	24.5°	—	—	23°	21°	42°	1 Rich
	17059496	5/16	Inner	3/8	.120	24.5°	—	—	21°	30°	38°	2 Rich
	17059498	11/32	Inner	9/32	.120	24.5°	—	—	23°	21°	42°	2 Rich
1980	17080108, 110	3/8	Inner	5/16	.120	20°	—	—	25°	—	38°	—
	17080130, 131	5/16	Inner	5/16	.120	20°	—	—	25°	—	38°	—
	17080132, 133	5/16	Inner	5/16	.120	20°	—	—	25°	—	38°	—
	17080138, 140	3/8	Inner	5/16	.120	20°	—	—	25°	—	38°	—
	17080146, 147	11/32	Inner	1/4	.120	20°	—	—	25°	—	38°	—
	17080148, 149	11/32	Inner	1/4	.120	20°	—	—	25°	—	38°	—
	17080150, 152	3/8	Outer	11/32	.120	14°	—	—	38°	27°	35°	—
	17080153	3/8	Outer	11/32	.120	14°	—	—	38°	27°	35°	—
	17080160	5/16	Inner	1/4	.120	14.5°	—	—	28.5°	33.5°	37.5°	—
	17080185, 187	9/32	Inner	1/4	.120	24.5°	—	—	19°	14°	38°	—
	17080190	9/32	Inner	1/4	.120	24.5°	—	—	22°	20°	38°	—
	17080191	11/32	Inner	1/4	.120	24.5°	—	—	18°	18°	38°	—
	17080192	9/32	Inner	1/4	.120	24.5°	—	—	22°	20°	38°	—
	17080195, 197	9/32	Inner	1/4	.120	24.5°	—	—	19°	14°	38°	—
	17080490, 492	5/16	—	3/8	.120	24.5°	—	—	21°	33°	38°	—
	17080491	5/16	—	3/8	.120	24.5°	—	—	21°	35°	38°	—
	17080493, 495	5/16	—	3/8	.120	24.5°	—	—	21°	30°	38°	—
	17080496, 498	5/16	—	3/8	.120	24.5°	—	—	21°	30°	38°	—
1981	17080185, 187	9/32	Inner	1/4	.120	24.5°	—	—	19°	14°	38°	—
	17080191	11/32	Inner	1/4	.120	24.5°	—	—	18°	18°	38°	—
	17080491	5/16	—	—	.120	24.5°	—	—	21°	35°	38°	—
	17080496, 498	5/16	—	—	.120	24.5°	—	—	21°	35°	38°	—
	17081130, 132	13/32	Inner	—	.120	20°	—	—	25°	—	38°	—
	17081131, 133	13/32	Inner	—	.120	20°	—	—	25°	—	38°	—
	17081138, 140	13/32	Inner	—	.120	20°	—	—	25°	—	40°	—
	17081150, 152	13/32	—	—	.120	14°	—	—	24°	36°	35°	—
	17081160	11/32	—	—	.120	14.5°	—	—	24°	37°	35°	—
	17081191, 196	5/16	—	—	.120	24.5°	—	—	28°	24°	38°	—
	17081192, 197	3/8	—	—	.120	24.5°	—	—	28°	24°	38°	—
	17081194	5/16	—	—	.120	24.5°	—	—	21°	30°	38°	—
	17081198	3/8	—	—	.120	24.5°	—	—	28°	24°	38°	—
	17081199	3/8	—	—	.120	18°	—	—	28°	24°	38°	—
1982	17082130	3/8	—	—	.120	20°	—	—	27°	—	38°	—
	17082132	3/8	—	—	.120	20°	—	—	27°	—	38°	—
	17082138	3/8	—	—	.120	20°	—	—	27°	—	38°	—
	17082140	3/8	—	—	.120	20°	—	—	27°	—	38°	—
	17082150	13/32	—	—	.120	14°	—	—	24°	38°	35°	—
	17082150⑤	13/32	—	—	.120	14°	—	—	24°	40°	35°	—
	17082182	5/16	—	—	.120	18°	—	—	28°	24°	32°	—
	17082184	5/16	—	—	.120	18°	—	—	28°	24°	32°	—
	17082186	5/16	—	—	.120	18°	—	—	21°	19°	27°	—
	17082192	5/16	—	—	.120	18°	—	—	28°	24°	32°	—
	17082194	5/16	—	—	.120	18°	—	—	28°	24°	32°	—
	17082196	5/16	—	—	.120	18°	—	—	21°	19°	27°	—
	17082497	5/16	—	—	.120	24.5°	—	—	28°	24°	32°	—
	17082916	5/16	—	—	—	25°	—	—	21°	19°	27°	—

Continued

DUAL-JET 2MC, M2MC, M2ME 200, 210 & E2ME ADJUSTMENT SPECIFICATIONS—Notes

①—With angle gauge, 24°; with plug gauge, .135 inch.
②—Before first scheduled tune up—with angle gauge, 36°; with plug gauge, .225 inch. After first scheduled tune up—with angle gauge, 38°; with plug gauge, .240 inch.
③—With angle gauge, 28°; with plug gauge, .165 inch.
④—2 notches clockwise
⑤—High Altitude

DUAL-JET 2MC, M2MC, M2ME 200, 210, E2MC & E2ME ADJUSTMENTS

The Dual Jet carburetor, Figs. 1, 2 and 3, is a two barrel, single stage unit, incorporating the design features of the primary side of the Quadrajet (four barrel) carburetor. The E2M model is used with the Computer Controlled Catalytic Converter System (C-4 System) or Computer Control Command System. The triple venturi stack up, plus the smaller 1⅜ inch bores result in good fuel metering control during all phases of operation.

The main metering system has a separate main well for each main nozzle for good fuel flow through the venturi.

On models except E2M models, an adjustable part throttle screw is used in the float bowl to aid in controlling fuel mixtures for good emission control. This screw is factory preset and should not be adjusted in service. However, if it becomes necessary to replace the float bowl, the new service float bowl will include the adjustable part throttle screw which has been preset.

On E2M models, an electrically operated mixture control solenoid, mounted in the fuel bowl, is used to control the fuel-air mixture metered to the idle and main metering systems. Fuel metering is controlled by two stepped metering rods positioned by a plunger in the mixture control solenoid. The solenoid plunger is controlled or "Pulsed" by an electrical output signal from the Electronic Control Module (ECM). The ECM, responding from a signal from the oxygen sensor, energizes the solenoid, to move the plunger and metering rods to control fuel delivery to the idle and main metering systems. At the same time, air metering to the idle system is controlled by an idle air bleed valve, located in the air horn, which follows movement of the mixture control solenoid plunger to control the amount of air bleed into the idle system to lean or richen the mixture. The movement or "Cycling" of the solenoid plunger occurs approximately 10 times per second, thereby controlling the fuel-air mixture to achieve optimum mixture ratios. The positioning of the mixture control solenoid in the float bowl, rich stop setting and idle air bleed valve in the air horn are factory adjusted and no attempt should be made to alter these settings except during major carburetor overhaul or when air horn or float bowl replacement is necessary.

Fig. 1 Rochester Dual-Jet 2MC & M2MC 200 carburetor (typical)

UPPER CHOKE LEVER
PUMP LEVER
VACUUM BREAK

REAR VACUUM BREAK
THERMOSTATIC CHOKE
FUEL FILTER
FRONT VACUUM BREAK

Fig. 2 Rochester Dual-Jet M2MC 210 carburetor

MIXTURE CONTROLS SOLENOID CONNECTOR (FROM ECM)
ELECTRIC CHOKE
VAPOR VENT TUBE (TO CANISTER)
IDLE SPEED SOLENOID
FRONT VACUUM BREAK
PLUG (IDLE MIXTURE NEEDLE)
WIDE OPEN THROTTLE SWITCH

Fig. 3 Rochester Dual-Jet model E2ME

③ GAUGE FROM TOP OF CASTING TO TOP OF FLOAT – GAUGING POINT 3/16" BACK FROM END OF FLOAT AT TOE (SEE INSET)
① HOLD RETAINER FIRMLY IN PLACE
(INSET)
TOE
② PUSH FLOAT DOWN LIGHTLY AGAINST NEEDLE
GAUGING POINT (3/16" BACK FROM TOE)
④ REMOVE FLOAT AND BEND FLOAT ARM UP OR DOWN TO ADJUST
⑤ VISUALLY CHECK FLOAT ALIGNMENT AFTER ADJUSTING

Fig. 4 Float level adjustment Exc. E2M units

CARBURETORS

① HOLD RETAINER FIRMLY IN PLACE

③ GAUGE FROM TOP OF CASTING TO TOP OF FLOAT — GAUGING POINT 3 16" BACK FROM END OF FLOAT AT TOE (SEE INSET)

② PUSH FLOAT DOWN LIGHTLY AGAINST NEEDLE

3/16

GAUGING POINT (3 16" BACK FROM TOE)

(INSET)

④ IF FLOAT LEVEL VARIES OVER ±1/16" FROM SPECIFICATIONS, ADJUST FLOAT AS FOLLOWS:
LEVEL TOO HIGH — HOLD RETAINER FIRMLY IN PLACE (① AND ②) AND PUSH DOWN ON CENTER OF FLOAT PONTOON TO OBTAIN CORRECT SETTING.
LEVEL TOO LOW — LIFT OUT METERING RODS. REMOVE SOLENOID CONNECTOR SCREWS. TURN LEAN MIXTURE SOLENOID SCREW CLOCKWISE COUNTING NUMBER OF TURNS UNTIL SCREW IS BOTTOMED LIGHTLY IN FLOAT BOWL. RECORD NUMBER OF TURNS COUNTED. TURN SCREW COUNTERCLOCKWISE AND REMOVE SCREW. LIFT SOLENOID AND CONNECTOR FROM FLOAT BOWL. REMOVE FLOAT AND BEND FLOAT ARM UP TO ADJUST. VISUALLY CHECK FLOAT ALIGNMENT AFTER ADJUSTING. REVERSE PROCEDURE TO RE-INSTALL PARTS REMOVED, MAKING SURE SOLENOID LEAN MIXTURE SCREW IS BACKED OUT OF FLOAT BOWL EXACTLY THE SAME NUMBER OF TURNS COUNTED AT DISASSEMBLY.

Fig. 5   Float level adjustment. E2M units

③ GAUGE FROM TOP OF CHOKE VALVE WALL, NEXT TO VENT STACK, TO TOP OF PUMP STEM AS SPECIFIED

④ BEND PUMP LEVER TO ADJUST

② ROD IN SPECIFIED HOLE OF PUMP LEVER

① THROTTLE VALVES COMPLETELY CLOSED

Fig. 6   Pump rod adjustment. 1977–80

On some 1981–82 E2M units, an idle speed control mounted on the float bowl is used to control idle speed. On these units, the curb idle speed is programmed into the Electronic Control Module and no attempt should be made to adjust idle speed. On some 1982 models with V8 engine, an idle load compensator mounted on the float bowl is used to control idle speed. The compensator uses manifold vacuum to sense changes in engine load and compensates by adjusting curb idle speed. This unit should not be adjusted, unless if during diagnosis, curb idle speed is not within specifications.

NOTE: On 1980-82 units, the cover is retained to the choke housing by three pop rivets. With float bowl and throttle body properly supported, carefully align a No. 21 drill on pop rivet head. Drill only deep enough to remove rivet head, then using a small hammer and drift, drive remainder of rivet from choke housing. A service kit is available for choke cover installation.

⑤ BEND CHOKE ROD AT THIS POINT TO ADJUST (SEE INSET)

CHOKE VALVE CLOSED

② PUSH UP ON THERMOSTATIC COIL TANG (COUNTERCLOCKWISE) UNTIL CHOKE VALVE IS CLOSED

④ LOWER EDGE OF LEVER SHOULD JUST CONTACT SIDE OF PLUG GAUGE

① LOOSEN THREE RETAINING SCREWS AND REMOVE THE THERMOSTATIC COVER AND COIL ASSEMBLY FROM CHOKE HOUSING

③ INSERT SPECIFIED PLUG GAUGE

Fig. 7   Choke coil lever adjustment

④ GAUGE BETWEEN UPPER EDGE OF CHOKE VALVE & INSIDE AIR HORN WALL

NOTE HOLD GAUGE VERTICALLY

⑤ BEND TANG ON FAST IDLE CAM TO ADJUST
NOTE MAKE SURE TANG LAYS AGAINST CAM AFTER BENDING

③ CLOSE CHOKE BY PUSHING UPWARD ON CHOKE COIL LEVER

② PLACE CAM FOLLOWER ON SECOND STEP OF CAM NEXT TO HIGH STEP

① MAKE FAST IDLE ADJUSTMENT

Fig. 8   Choke rod adjustment. Plug Gauge Method

Float Level Adjustment

Exc. E2M Units
Fig. 4—With adjustable T-scale, measure from top of float bowl gasket surface (gasket removed) to top of float at toe (locate gauging point 3/16" back from toe). Adjust as directed in the illustration to the dimension listed in the *Specifications Chart*. Make sure retaining pin is held firmly in place and tang of float is seated on float needle.

E2M Units
Fig. 5—With an adjustable T-scale, measure from top of float bowl gasket surface (gasket removed) to top of float at toe (locate gauging point 3/16 inch back from toe). If float level is

⑤ LEVELING BUBBLE (CENTERED)

② DEGREE SCALE

③ POINTER MAGNET

④ CHOKE VALVE CLOSED

FIGURE 1

① MAKE FAST IDLE ADJUSTMENT (BENCH OR ON-THE-CAR SETTING).

⑥ SPECIFIED ANGLE (SEE SPECS.)

⑨ TO ADJUST, BEND TANG ON FAST IDLE CAM UNTIL BUBBLE IS CENTERED.

FAST IDLE CAM

⑧ CLOSE CHOKE BY PUSHING UPWARD ON CHOKE COIL LEVER.

⑦ PLACE CAM FOLLOWER ON SECOND STEP OF CAM NEXT TO HIGH STEP.

⑩ REMOVE GAUGE.   FIGURE 2

Fig. 9   Choke rod adjustment. Angle gauge method

⑤ PLACE GAUGE BETWEEN UPPER EDGE OF CHOKE VALVE AND INSIDE WALL OF AIR HORN

NOTE HOLD GAUGE VERTICAL

③ SEAT DIAPHRAGM USING OUTSIDE VACUUM SOURCE

② PUSH BACK RUBBER CAP AND PLUG BLEED HOLE WITH TAPE. REMOVE TAPE AND REPLACE RUBBER CAP AFTER ADJUSTMENT.

⑥ BEND LOWER END OF ROD TO ADJUST

① PLACE CAM FOLLOWER ON HIGHEST STEP OF FAST IDLE CAM

④ PUSH INSIDE CHOKE COIL LEVER COUNTERCLOCKWISE UNTIL TANG ON OUTSIDE LEVER CONTACTS VACUUM BREAK ROD AND BUCKING SPRING IS COMPRESSED

Fig. 10   Vacuum break adjustment, rich setting. 2MC units

Fig. 11 Vacuum break adjustment, lean setting. 2MC units

Fig. 12 Vacuum break adjustment, rear setting (angle gauge method)

Fig. 13 Vacuum break adjustment, front setting (angle gauge method)

Fig. 14 Choke unloader adjustment. 1977 units

Fig. 15 Choke unloader adjustment. 1978–82 units

too high, hold retainer firmly in plate and lightly push down float against needle, then push downward on center of float to obtain correct setting. If float level is too low, remove metering rods and the solenoid connector screws. Turn lean mixture solenoid screw clockwise, counting the number of turns until lightly bottomed in the float bowl. Then, turn screw counterclockwise and remove screw. Remove float and bend arm upward to adjust.

Check float alignment. Install lean mixture solenoid screw until lightly bottomed, then back out screw exactly the same number of turns previously noted. Install solenoid connector screws and the metering rods.

Pump Rod Adjustment
1977–80 Units, Fig. 6
With throttle valves completely closed and pump rod in specified hole in pump lever, measure from top of choke valve wall (next to vent stack) to top of pump stem. Dimension should be as listed in the *Specifications Chart*. To adjust, bend pump lever as required.

NOTE: Support lever with a screwdriver while bending lever.

Choke Coil Lever Adjustment

Fig. 7—With thermostatic coil assembly removed, push upward on coil tang until choke valve closes. Insert gauge specified in the Specifications Chart into choke housing hole. The lower edge of choke coil lever should just contact gauge. To adjust, bend choke rod as required.

Choke Rod Adjustment

Plug Gauge Method
Fig. 8—With fast idle adjustment made, and cam follower on second step of fast idle cam and against the high step, push upward on choke coil lever until choke valve closes. Dimension between upper edge of choke valve and air horn wall should be as specified in the Specifications Chart. Adjust by bending tang on intermediate choke lever.

CARBURETORS

NOTE: On 1980–82 units, do not remove rivets or choke cover to place choke valve in the closed position. Use a rubber band on vacuum break lever tang to hold choke valve closed.

Fig. 9—Rotate degree scale until the zero is opposite pointer, then with choke valve completely closed, place magnet squarely on top of choke valve and rotate bubble until centered. Refer to the Specification Chart for proper setting for adjustment. Rotate scale so specified degree setting for adjustment is opposite pointer. Place cam follower on second step of cam, next to high step. Close choke by pushing upward on choke coil lever. To adjust, bend tang on fast idle lever until the bubble is centered.

Vacuum Break Adjustment

Rich Setting, 2MC Units
Fig. 10—With cam follower on highest step of fast idle cam, plug diaphragm bleed hole with tape, then using an external vacuum source, seat the diaphragm. Push choke coil lever counter-clockwise until outside lever tang contacts vacuum break rod and the bucking spring is compressed. Insert gauge specified in the 2MC Specification Chart between the upper edge of choke valve and air horn wall. To adjust, bend lower end of rod.

Lean Setting, 2MC Units
Fig. 11—With cam follower on highest step of fast idle cam, plug diaphragm bleed hole with tape, then using an external vacuum source, seat the diaphragm. Push choke coil lever counter-clockwise until outside lever tang lightly contacts vacuum break rod without compressing bucking spring. Insert gauge specified in the 2MC Specification Chart between upper edge of choke valve and air horn wall. To adjust, bend upper end of rod.

Rear Setting (Gauge Method), Exc. 2MC Units

NOTE: On 1980–82 units, do not remove rivets or choke cover to place choke valve in the closed position. Use a rubber band on vacuum break lever tang to hold choke valve closed. On 1981 units, remove vacuum break from carburetor and place bracket in a vise, then grind off weld holding adjusting screw cover. Remove adjusting screw cover, then reinstall vacuum break and proceed with adjustment.

Fig. 12—Rotate degree scale until zero is opposite pointer, then with choke valve completely closed, place magnet on top of choke valve and rotate bubble until it is centered. Refer to Specification Chart and rotate scale to degrees specified. Using an external vacuum source, seat choke diaphragm, then remove choke coil and rotate inside choke coil lever counterclockwise making sure bucking

Fig. 16 Choke coil adjustment

spring is compressed and seated. To make final adjustment, bend link until bubble is centered.

Front Setting (Gauge Method), Exc. 2MC Units

NOTE: On 1980–82 units, do not remove rivets or choke cover to place choke valve in the closed position. Use a rubber band on vacuum break lever tang to hold choke valve closed. On 1981–82 units, remove vacuum break and place bracket in a vise, then grind off adjusting screw cover and reinstall vacuum break. After completing adjustment apply a suitable sealer to adjusting screw head.

Fig. 13—Rotate degree scale until zero is opposite pointer, then with choke valve completely closed, place gauge on top of choke valve and rotate bubble until it is centered. Refer to Specifications Chart and rotate gauge to degrees specified. Using an external vacuum source, seat choke vacuum diaphragm, then remove choke coil and rotate inside coil lever counterclockwise. To make final adjustment, turn screw in or out until bubble is centered.

Choke Unloader Adjustment

1977 Units
Fig. 14—Install choke cover and coil assembly and align index mark with specified point on housing. Hold throttle valves wide open. On a warm engine, close choke valve by pushing upward on tang on intermediate choke lever and hold in position with a rubber band. Insert specified gauge between upper edge of choke valve and air horn wall. To adjust, bend fast idle lever tang.

1978–82 Units, Angle Gauge Method
Fig. 15—Rotate degree scale until the zero is opposite pointer, then with choke valve completely closed, place magnet squarely on top of choke valve and rotate bubble until centered. Refer to the Specification Chart for proper setting for adjustment. Rotate scale until specified degree for adjustment is opposite pointer. Install choke cover and coil assembly and align index mark with specified point on housing. Hold throttle valves wide open. On a warm engine close choke valve by pushing upward on tang on vacuum break lever and

hold in position with a rubber band. To adjust, bend fast idle lever tang until the bubble is centered.

Choke Coil Adjustment

Fig. 16—Place the fast idle cam follower on the highest step of the fast idle cam. Rotate choke cover and coil assembly counter-clockwise until the choke valve just closes and the index point on cover aligns with the specified index point on the choke housing.

Idle Load Compensator Adjustment

1981–82 E2M Units

NOTE: On some 1981–82 models with V8 engine, an idle load compensator mounted on the float bowl is used to control idle speed. This unit should not be adjusted, unless if during diagnosis, curb idle speed is not within specifications. This adjustment should be performed with engine at operating temperature and choke and A/C off.

1. Remove air cleaner assembly and plug vacuum hose to thermal vacuum valve.
2. Disconnect and plug hoses to EGR valve, canister purge port and idle load compensator.
3. Apply parking brake and block wheels, then back throttle stop screw out 3 turns.
4. With engine operating, place transmission selector lever in drive position, adjust plunger to obtain 750 RPM. The jam nut on the plunger must be held in position to prevent damage to guide tabs. If a replacement idle load compensator is being installed, the plunger should be set to obtain a clearance of 61/64 inch from jam nut to tip of plunger.
5. Connect vacuum hose to idle load compensator and note idle speed. If idle speed requires adjustment, stop engine and remove idle load compensator.
6. With idle load compensator removed, remove rubber and metal plug from center outlet tube.
7. Using a .090 inch allen wrench, rotate center outlet tube adjusting screw to obtain 550 RPM on 1981 models, or 500 RPM on 1982 models. Each turn of the adjusting screw will change idle speed approximately 75 to 100 RPM. Rotate adjusting screw counter-clockwise to increase engine speed and clockwise to decrease engine speed.
8. Reinstall rubber plug on center outlet tube, then install idle load compensator on carburetor. If a final adjustment is necessary it will be necessary to repeat steps 6, 7 and 8.
9. Apply a suitable vacuum source to idle load compensator to fully retract plunger.
10. Adjust throttle body idle stop screw to obtain 550 RPM on 1981 models, or 500 RPM on 1982 models, then reconnect all vacuum hoses and install air cleaner.

MONOJET 1ME CARBURETOR ADJUSTMENT SPECIFICATIONS

See Tune Up Chart in car chapter for curb and fast idle speeds.

Year	Carb. Part No. ①	Float Level	Metering Rod	Choke Coil Lever	Choke Rod	Vacuum Break	Unloader	Choke Setting
1977	17057013	3/8	.080	.120	.100	.125	.325	1 Rich
	17057014	3/8	.090	.120	.100	.125	.325	2 Rich
	17057015	3/8	.080	.120	.100	.125	.325	1 Rich
	17057016	3/8	.080	.120	.105	.105	.325	1 Lean
	17057018	3/8	.080	.120	.085	.120	.325	2 Rich
	17057020	3/8	.090	.120	.100	.125	.325	2 Rich
	17057030	5/32	.080	.120	.050	.080	.200	2 Rich
	17057031	5/32	.080	.120	.050	.080	.200	2 Rich
	17057032	5/32	.080	.120	.050	.080	.200	2 Rich
	17057034	5/32	.080	.120	.050	.080	.200	2 Rich
	17057035	5/32	.080	.120	.050	.080	.200	2 Rich
	17057042	5/32	.080	.120	.050	.075	.200	1 Rich
	17057044	5/32	.080	.120	.050	.075	.200	1 Rich
	17057045	5/32	.080	.120	.050	.075	.200	1 Rich
	17057310	3/8	.100	.120	—	—	—	Index
	17057312	3/8	.100	.120	—	—	—	Index
	17057314	3/8	.080	.120	.100	.110	.225	Index
	17057318	3/8	.080	.120	.100	.110	.225	Index
	17057332	5/32	.080	.120	.050	.075	.200	2 Rich
	17057334	5/32	.080	.120	.050	.075	.200	2 Rich
	17057335	5/32	.080	.120	.050	.075	.200	2 Rich
1978	17058013	3/8	.080	.120	.180	.200	.500	Index
	17058014	5/16	.100	.120	.180	.200	.500	Index
	17058020	5/16	.100	.120	.180	.200	.500	Index
	17058031	5/32	.080	.120	.105	.150	.500	2 Rich
	17058032	5/32	.080	.120	.080	.130	.500	3 Rich
	17058033	5/32	.080	.120	.080	.130	.500	2 Rich
	17058034	5/32	.080	.120	.080	.130	.500	3 Rich
	17058035	5/32	.080	.120	.080	.130	.500	3 Rich
	17058036	5/32	.080	.120	.080	.130	.500	3 Rich
	17058037	5/32	.080	.120	.080	.130	.500	2 Rich
	17058038	5/32	.080	.120	.080	.130	.500	3 Rich
	17058042	5/32	.080	.120	.080	②	.500	2 Rich
	17058044	5/32	.080	.120	.080	②	.500	2 Rich
	17058045	5/32	.080	.120	.080	②	.500	2 Rich
	17058314	3/8	.100	.120	.190	.245	.400	Index
	17058332	5/32	.080	.120	.080	②	.500	2 Rich
	17058334	5/32	.080	.120	.080	②	.500	2 Rich
	17058335	5/32	.080	.120	.080	②	.500	2 Rich
	17058339	5/32	.080	.120	.080	②	.500	2 Rich
1979	17059012	5/16	.095	.120	.180	.200	.500	Index
	17059013	3/8	.100	.120	.180	.200	.400	Index
	17059014	3/8	.100	.120	.180	.200	.400	Index
	17059020	3/8	.100	.120	.180	.200	.400	Index
	17059023	5/16	.095	.120	.180	.200	.500	Index
	17059314	3/8	.100	.120	.190	.245	.400	Index

① —On tag attached to carburetor.
② —Below 30,000 miles, .130 inch; above 30,000 miles, .160 inch.

Monojet 1ME Adjustments

This Monojet carburetor is a single bore, downdraft carburetor incorporating a triple venturi in conjunction with a plain tube nozzle. The main metering system fuel flow is controlled by a main well air bleed and a variable orifice jet. Power enrichment is provided through a mechanically operated metering rod, connected by linkage to the throttle shaft. A fuel pull-over enrichment is used to supplement main metering mixtures at higher engine RPM.

An automatic choke system using an electrically heated choke coil is incorporated into this carburetor. The vacuum diaphragm unit, mounted externally on the air horn, is connected to the thermostatic coil lever through a connecting link. The electric choke coil is contained in a housing mounted on a bracket attached to the float bowl.

Float Level Adjustment

Fig. 1
1. Hold float retaining pin firmly in place and float arm against top of float needle by pushing downward on float arm at point between needle seat and hinge pin as shown.
2. With adjustable T-scale, measure distance from top of float at toe to float bowl gasket surface (gasket removed). Measurement should be at a point 1/16" from end of flat surface at float toe (not on radius).
3. Bend float pontoon up or down at float arm junction to adjust.

Metering Rod Adjustment

Fig. 2
1. Remove metering rod by holding throttle valve wide open. Push downward on metering rod against spring tension, then slide metering rod out of slot in holder and remove from main metering jet.
2. To check adjustment, back out idle solenoid screw and rotate fast idle cam so that fast idle cam follower is not contacting steps on cam.
3. With throttle valve completely closed, apply pressure to top of power piston and hold piston down against its stop.
4. While holding downward pressure on power piston, swing metering rod holder over flat surface of bowl casting next to carburetor bore.
5. Use specified size drill and insert between bowl casting sealing bead and lower surface of metering rod holder. Drill should have a slide fit between both surfaces as shown.
6. To adjust, carefully bend metering rod holder up or down at point shown.
7. After adjustment, install metering rod.

Choke Coil Lever Adjustment

Fig. 3
1. With fast idle adjusting screw on fast idle cam high step, close choke valve.
2. Insert a .120 inch gauge pin through hole in lever and into casting. If holes do not align, bend link to adjust.

Fast Idle Adjustment

Chevette, Fig. 4
1. Adjust curb idle speed, if necessary.
2. Connect a tachometer to engine.

Fig. 1   Float level adjustment

3. Start engine, set parking brake and place transmission in Neutral.
4. With engine at normal operating temperature, turn fast idle speed screw to adjust fast idle.
5. Stop engine and remove tachometer.

Exc. Chevette, Figs. 5 & 6
1. Set normal engine idle speed.
2. Place fast idle cam follower tang on highest step of cam.
3. To adjust, insert screwdriver in slot provided in fast idle cam follower tang and bend inwards (towards cam) or outward to obtain specified dimension.

Choke Rod Adjustment

Figs. 7 & 8
1. With fast idle adjustment made, place fast idle cam follower on second step of fast idle cam and hold firmly against the rise to the high step.
2. Rotate choke towards direction of closed choke by applying force to choke coil lever.
3. Bend choke rod at point shown to obtain proper dimension between specified edge of choke valve and air horn wall.

Vacuum Break Adjustment

Figs. 9 & 10
1. With fast idle screw on fast idle cam high step, seat diaphragm using an outside vacuum source. Cover purge hole with a piece of tape.
2. Close choke valve to compress plunger bucking spring and seat plunger stem.
3. Place gauge between specified edge of choke valve and air horn wall. Bend link to adjust.

Unloader Adjustment

Figs. 11 & 12
1. With choke properly indexed and throttle valve held wide open, manually close choke valve with gauge between specified edge of choke valve and air horn wall.
2. If distance is not within specifications, bend unloader tang to adjust.

Fig. 2   Metering rod adjustment

Fig. 3   Choke coil lever adjustment

Fig. 4   Fast idle adjustment. Chevette

Fig. 5 Fast idle adjustment. 1977 exc. Chevette

Fig. 6 Fast idle adjustment. 1978–79 exc. Chevette

Fig. 7 Choke rod adjustment. 1977

Fig. 9 Vacuum break adjustment. 1977

Fig. 11 Unloader adjustment. 1977

Fig. 8 Choke rod adjustment. 1978–79

Fig. 10 Vacuum break adjustment. 1978–79

Choke Coil Adjustment

Fig. 13

1. Install electric choke assembly into housing, ensuring coil tang contacts lower side of coil lever pick-up arm.
2. Place fast cam follower on high step of cam.

3. Rotate cover and coil assembly counterclockwise until choke valve just closes, then align cover index point with the specified mark on housing.
4. Install and tighten cover retainers and screws.

NOTE: Do not install a choke cover gasket between the choke assembly and housing since the ground contact for the choke is provided by a metal plate at the rear of the choke assembly.

CARBURETORS

① INSTALL CHOKE COIL IN CHOKE HOUSING AND INDEX PROPERLY (SEE NOTE).

NOTE: IF CHOKE COIL IS WARM, COOL DOWN TO POINT WHERE CHOKE VALVE WILL CLOSE FULLY.

③ GAUGE BETWEEN LOWER EDGE OF CHOKE VALVE AND INSIDE AIR HORN WALL (SEE NOTE).

② HOLD THROTTLE VALVE WIDE OPEN.

④ BEND TANG TO ADJUST (SEE INSET).

Fig. 12 Unloader adjustment. 1978–79

① LOOSEN THREE RETAINING SCREWS

③ SET MARK ON ELECTRIC CHOKE TO SPECIFIED POINT ON CHOKE HOUSING. CHOKE VALVE TOWARDS CLOSED POSITION

② PLACE FAST IDLE CAM FOLLOWER ON HIGH STEP OF CAM

Fig. 13 Choke coil adjustment

ROCHESTER 2SE & E2SE ADJUSTMENT SPECIFICATIONS

See Tune Up Chart in car chapters for curb and fast idle speeds.

Year	Carb. Production No.	Float Level	Accel. Pump	Choke Coil Lever	Choke Rod	Vacuum Break		Air Valve Rod	Choke Setting	Unloader	Secondary Lockout
						Primary	Secondary				
AMERICAN MOTORS											
1980	17080681	3/16	17/32	.085	18°	20°	—	2°	—	32°	.065
	17080683	3/16	1/2	.085	18°	20°	—	2°	—	32°	.065
	17080686, 688	3/16	1/2	.085	18°	20°	—	2°	—	32°	.065
	17080781, 782	3/16	7/32	.085	18°	20°	—	2°	—	32°	.065
1981	17081790	.256	.128	.085	—	19°	—	2°	—	32°	.065
	17081791, 796	.208	.128	.085	—	19°	—	2°	—	32°	.065
	17081792, 793	.256	.128	.085	—	19°	—	2°	—	32°	.065
	17081794, 795	.256	.128	.085	—	19°	—	2°	—	32°	.065
	17081797	.208	.128	.065	—	19°	—	2°	—	32°	.085
	17081993	.256	.128	.085	—	19°	—	2°	—	32°	.065
1982	17082380	.125	.128	.085	—	21°	—	2°	—	34°	.050–.080
	17082383	.256	.128	.085	—	21°	—	2°	—	34°	.050–.080
	17082385	.256	.128	.085	—	21°	—	2°	—	34°	.050–.080
	17082386	.125	.128	.050–.080	—	19°	—	2°	—	34°	.050–.080
	17082387	.125	.128	.085	—	19°	—	2°	—	34°	.050–.080
	17082388	.125	.128	.085	—	19°	—	2°	—	34°	.050–.080
	17082389	.125	.128	.085	—	19°	—	2°	—	34°	.050–.080
GENERAL MOTORS											
1979	17059674	7/32	1/2	.085	18°	22°	—	.025	2 Rich	32°	.030
	17059675	7/32	17/32	.085	18°	22°	—	.025	1 Rich	32°	.030
	17059676	7/32	1/2	.085	18°	22°	—	.025	2 Rich	32°	.030
	17059677	7/32	17/32	.085	18°	22°	—	.025	1 Rich	32°	.030
	17059750	3/32	15/32	.085	21°	22°	35°	.040	Index	35°	.030
	17059751	3/16	15/32	.085	21°	22°	35°	.040	Index	35°	.030
	17059752	3/16	15/32	.085	21°	22°	35°	.040	Index	35°	.030
	17059753	3/16	15/32	.085	21°	22°	35°	.040	Index	35°	.030
1980	17059614, 616	3/16	1/2	.085	18°	17°	—	1°	—	36°	.025
	17059615, 617	3/16	17/32	.085	18°	19°	—	1°	—	36°	.025
	17059618, 620	3/16	1/2	.085	18°	17°	—	1°	—	36°	.025
	17059619, 621	3/16	17/32	.085	18°	19°	—	1°	—	36°	.025
	17059622, 624	5/32	17/32	.085	18°	17°	—	1°	—	36°	.025
	17059623, 625	5/32	17/32	.085	18°	19°	—	1°	—	36°	.025
	17059650, 652	1/4	17/32	.085	24°	30°	38°	1°	—	30°	.025

Continued

ROCHESTER 2SE & E2SE ADJUSTMENT SPECIFICATIONS—Continued

See Tune Up charts in car chapters for curb and fast idle speeds.

Year	Carb. Production No.	Float Level	Accel. Pump	Choke Coil Lever	Choke Rod	Vacuum Break		Air Valve Rod	Choke Setting	Unloader	Secondary Lockout
						Primary	Secondary				
GENERAL MOTORS—Continued											
	17059651, 653	1/4	17/32	.085	24°	30°	37°	1°	—	30°	.025
	17059660, 662	1/4	17/32	.085	24°	30°	32°	1°	—	30°	.025
	17059664, 665	1/4	17/32	.085	24°	30°	32°	1°	—	30°	.025
	17059666, 667	1/4	17/32	.085	24°	26°	32°	1°	—	30°	.025
	17059714, 716	5/32	1/2	.085	18°	19°	—	1°	—	32°	.025
	17059715, 717	5/32	1/2	.085	18°	21°	—	1°	—	32°	.120
	17059718, 720	5/32	1/2	.085	18°	19°	—	1°	—	32°	.025
	17059721, 723	5/32	17/32	.085	①	23°	—	1°	—	32°	.025
	17059722, 724	5/32	15/32	.085	①	19°	—	1°	—	32°	.025
	17059760	1/4	—	.085	16°	24°	30°	1°	—	35°	.025
	17059762, 763	1/4	—	.085	16°	24°	33°	1°	—	35°	.025
	17059768	1/4	—	.085	16°	20°	30°	1°	—	35°	.025
	17059774, 776	5/32	1/2	.085	18°	19°	—	1°	—	32°	.025
	17059775, 777	5/32	17/32	.085	18°	21°	—	1°	—	32°	.025
	17080621, 622	1/8	9/16	—	17°	22°	35°	2°	—	41°	—
	17080623, 626	1/8	9/16	—	17°	22°	35°	2°	—	41°	—
	17080674, 676	3/16	1/2	.085	18°	19°	—	2°	—	32°	.025
	17080675, 677	3/16	1/2	.085	18°	21°	—	2°	—	32°	.025
	17080720, 722	1/8	9/16	—	17°	20°	35°	2°	—	41°	—
	17080721, 723	1/8	9/16	—	17°	23.5°	35°	2°	—	41°	—
1981	17081650, 652	1/4	—	—	17°	25°	34°	1°	—	35°	.012
	17081651, 653	1/4	—	—	17°	29°	35°	1°	—	35°	.012
	17081656, 658	1/4	—	—	25°	30°	35°	1°	—	33°	.012
	17081670, 672	5/32	—	—	18°	19°	—	1°	—	32°	.012
	17081671, 673	5/32	—	—	33.5°	21°	—	1°	—	32°	.012
	17081740, 742	1/4	—	—	17°	25°	34°	1°	—	35°	.012
	17081746, 748	1/4	—	—	25°	30°	35°	1°	—	33°	.012
1982	17081600, 601	5/16	—	—	24°	20°	27°	1°	—	35°	—
	17081607	5/16	—	—	24°	20°	27°	1°	—	35°	—
	17081700, 701	5/16	—	—	24°	20°	27°	1°	—	35°	—
1982	17081600	5/16	—	—	18°	23°	27°	1°	—	35°	—
	17081601	5/16	—	—	18°	21°	27°	1°	—	35°	—
	17081606	5/16	—	—	18°	23°	27°	1°	—	35°	—
	17081607	5/16	—	—	18°	21°	27°	1°	—	35°	—
	17081609	5/16	—	—	18°	21°	27°	1°	—	35°	—
	17081700	5/16	—	—	24°	20°	27°	1°	—	35°	—
	17081701	5/16	—	—	24°	20°	27°	1°	—	35°	—
	17082300	5/16	—	—	18°	23°	27°	1°	—	35°	—
	17082301	5/16	—	—	18°	21°	27°	1°	—	35°	—
	17082303	5/16	—	—	18°	21°	27°	1°	—	35°	—
	17082304	5/16	—	—	18°	23°	27°	1°	—	35°	—
	17082305	5/16	—	—	18°	21°	27°	1°	—	35°	—
	17082316	1/4	—	—	17°	30°	34°	1°	—	45°	—
	17082317	1/4	—	—	17°	30°	35°	1°	—	45°	—
	17082320	1/4	—	—	25°	30°	35°	1°	—	45°	—
	17082321	1/4	—	—	25°	30°	35°	1°	—	45°	—

Continued

2-227

CARBURETORS

ROCHESTER 2SE & E2SE ADJUSTMENT SPECIFICATIONS—Continued

See Tune Up charts in car chapters for curb and fast idle speeds.

Year	Carb. Production No.	Float Level	Accel. Pump	Choke Coil Lever	Choke Rod	Vacuum Break Primary	Vacuum Break Secondary	Air Valve Rod	Choke Setting	Unloader	Secondary Lockout
GENERAL MOTORS—Continued											
	17082390	13/32	—	—	17°	30°	34°	1°	—	45°	—
	17082391	13/32	—	—	25°	30°	35°	1°	—	45°	—
	17082490	13/32	—	—	17°	30°	34°	1°	—	45°	—
	17082491	13/32	—	—	25°	30°	35°	1°	—	45°	—
	17082630	5/16	—	—	18°	23°	27°	1°	—	35°	—
	17082631	5/16	—	—	18°	23°	25°	1°	—	35°	—
	17082640	1/4	—	—	17°	30°	34°	1°	—	45°	—
	17082641	1/4	—	—	17°	30°	35°	1°	—	45°	—
	17082642	1/4	—	—	25°	30°	35°	1°	—	45°	—

①—Early models with three step fast idle cam,
18°; late models with two step fast idle cam,
33°.

VARAJET 2SE & E2SE ADJUSTMENTS

SECONDARY AIR VALVE LEVER
CHOKE VALVE
VACUUM BREAK
PUMP LEVER
CHOKE VALVE
SECONDARY AIR VALVE
ELECTRIC CHOKE
IDLE SPEED SOLENOID
SLOW IDLE SPEED SCREW
FAST IDLE ADJUSTING SCREW
FAST IDLE CAM
VAPOR VENT TUBE (TO CANISTER)
FUEL INLET NUT

Fig. 1 Varajet 2SE Carburetor

MIXTURE CONTROL SOLENOID
SECONDARY AIR VALVE
CHOKE VALVE
VACUUM BREAK

IDLE SPEED SOLENOID
FAST IDLE ADJUSTING SCREW
SLOW IDLE SPEED SCREW
SECONDARY AIR VALVE LEVER
VAPOR VENT TUBE (TO CANISTER)

Fig. 1A   Varajet E2SE Carburetor (Typical)

MIXTURE CONTROL SOLENOID
VENT STACK
CHOKE VALVE
AIR VALVE LEVER
PRIMARY VACUUM BREAK

CHOKE HOUSING
SECONDARY VACUUM BREAK
THROTTLE LEVER
IDLE SPEED CONTROL

Fig. 1B   E2SE carburetor equipped with idle speed control motor

The Varajet models 2SE and E2SE, Figs. 1 and 1A, are two barrel, two stage, down draft design carburetors. Aluminum die castings are used for the air horn, float bowl and throttle body. A heat insulator gasket is used between the throttle body and float bowl to reduce heat transfer to the float bowl.

The primary stage has a triple venturi, with a small 35mm bore, resulting in good fuel metering control during idle and part throttle operation. The secondary stage has a 46mm bore, providing sufficient air capacity for engine power requirements. An air valve is used in the secondary stage with a single tapered metering rod.

The float chamber is internally vented through a vertical vent cavity in the air horn. The float chamber is also externally vented through a tube in the air horn. A hose connects this tube directly to a vacuum operated vapor vent valve located in the vapor canister. When the engine is not running, the canister vapor vent valve is open, allowing fuel vapor from the float chamber to pass into the canister where the vapor is stored until normally purged.

An adjustable part throttle screw is used in the float bowl to aid emission control. This screw is factory pre-set and a plug is installed to prevent further adjustment or fuel leakage. The plug should not be removed or the screw setting disturbed. If float bowl replacement is required, the service float bowl will include a factory pre-set and plugged adjustable part throttle screw.

A hot idle compensator is used on some models and is located in the air horn. The opening and closing of the hot idle compensator valve is controlled by a bi-metal strip that

is calibrated to a specific temperature. When the valve opens, additional air is allowed to bypass the throttle valves and enter the intake manifold to prevent rough idle during periods of hot engine operation.

The idle mixture screw is recessed in the throttle body and is sealed with a hardened steel plug to prevent alteration of the factory pre-set mixture setting. The plug should not be removed and the mixture screw readjusted unless required by major carburetor overhaul or throttle body replacement.

The E2SE carburetor, includes special design features for use with the Computor Controlled Catalytic Converter (C4) System or the Computer Command System. An electrically operated mixture control solenoid mounted in the air horn, controls air and fuel metered to the idle and main metering systems of the carburetor. The plunger located at the end of the solenoid is submerged in fuel in the fuel chamber of the float bowl. This plunger is controlled by an electrical signal from the Electronic Control Module (ECM). The Electronic Control Module responding to signals from the oxygen sensor in the exhaust and other engine operating condition signals, energizes the solenoid to move the plunger down to the lean position or de-energizes the solenoid to move the plunger up to the rich position to control fuel delivery to the idle and main metering systems. When the plunger is in the lean position, fuel metering is controlled by a lean mixture screw located in the float bowl. When the plunger is in the rich position, the additional fuel is metered to the main fuel well through a rich mixture screw located at the end of the fuel supply channel in the float bowl. Air metered to the idle system is con-

trolled by the up and down movement of the mixture control solenoid plunger. The plunger increases or decreases air supplied to the idle system which is further metered by the idle air bleed screw. The plunger cycles up and down approximately 10 times per second, controlling air and fuel mixtures.

On 1981 models wth 4-151 engine and air conditioning and 1982 models with 4-112 (1.8L) engine, an idle speed control motor which is controlled by the Electronic Control Module is used to control idle speed, Fig. 1B. The curb idle speed is programmed into the Electronic Control Module and no attempt should be made to adjust idle speed using the idle speed control motor.

CAUTION: On 1980–82 units, use care not to remove the special friction reducing coating applied to the primary and secondary throttle shafts, the secondary actuating lever and lockout lever. On 1980 V6 engine units and on all 1981–82 units, a special graphite compound is also applied to the secondary throttle bore and valve.

Float Level Adjustment
Fig. 2
1. Hold float retainer firmly in place and push float lightly against needle.
2. With an adjustable T-scale, measure distance between float bowl gasket surface (gasket removed) and float toe.
3. To adjust, remove float and bend float arm.
4. Check float alignment after adjustment.

Pump Adjustment
1979–80 Units, Fig. 3

NOTE: The pump adjustment should not be altered from the specified setting.

1. Close throttle valves and ensure that fast idle screw is not contacting fast idle cam steps.
2. Measure distance between air horn cast-

CARBURETORS

① HOLD RETAINER FIRMLY IN PLACE

③ GAUGE AT TOE OF FLOAT AT POINT FURTHEST AWAY FROM FLOAT HINGE PIN (SEE INSET).

(INSET)

④ REMOVE FLOAT AND BEND FLOAT ARM UP OR DOWN TO ADJUST

② PUSH FLOAT DOWN LIGHTLY AGAINST NEEDLE

⑤ VISUALLY CHECK FLOAT ALIGNMENT AFTER ADJUSTING

Fig. 2 Float level adjustment

① THROTTLE VALVES COMPLETELY CLOSED. MAKE SURE FAST IDLE SCREW IS OFF STEPS OF FAST IDLE CAM.

③ IF NECESSARY TO ADJUST, REMOVE PUMP LEVER RETAINING SCREW AND REMOVE PUMP LEVER BY ROTATING LEVER TO REMOVE FROM PUMP ROD. PLACE LEVER IN A VISE, PROTECTING LEVER FROM DAMAGE, AND BEND END OF LEVER (NEAREST NECKED DOWN SECTION).

NOTE: DO NOT BEND LEVER IN A SIDEWAYS OR TWISTING MOTION.

② GAUGE FROM AIR HORN CASTING SURFACE TO TOP OF PUMP STEM. DIMENSION SHOULD BE AS SPECIFIED.

⑤ OPEN AND CLOSE THROTTLE VALVES CHECKING LINKAGE FOR FREEDOM OF MOVEMENT AND OBSERVING PUMP LEVER ALIGNMENT.

④ REINSTALL PUMP LEVER AND RETAINING SCREW. RECHECK PUMP ADJUSTMENT ① AND ② TIGHTEN RETAINING SCREW SECURELY AFTER THE PUMP ADJUSTMENT IS CORRECT.

Fig. 3 Pump adjustment (Typical). 1979–80 Units

① PREPARE VEHICLE FOR ADJUSTMENTS - SEE EMISSION LABEL ON VEHICLE. NOTE: IGNITION TIMING SET PER LABEL.

④ TURN FAST IDLE SCREW IN OR OUT TO OBTAIN SPECIFIED FAST IDLE R.P.M. - (SEE LABEL)

② ADJUST CURB IDLE SPEED IF REQUIRED

③ PLACE FAST IDLE SCREW ON HIGHEST STEP OF FAST IDLE CAM

Fig. 4 Fast idle adjustment

⑥ BEND INTERMEDIATE CHOKE ROD AT THIS POINT TO ADJUST

① LOOSEN THREE RETAINING SCREWS AND REMOVE THERMOSTATIC COVER AND COIL ASSEMBLY FROM CHOKE HOUSING (SEE NOTE)

NOTE: IF TAMPER-RESISTANT CHOKE (RIVETED) IS USED, REMOVE CHOKE COVER AND COIL ASSEMBLY FOLLOWING INSTRUCTIONS IN CHOKE STAT COVER RETAINER KIT.

② PLACE FAST IDLE SCREW ON HIGH STEP OF FAST IDLE CAM

③ PUSH ON INTERMEDIATE CHOKE LEVER UNTIL CHOKE VALVE IS CLOSED

④ INSERT SPECIFIED PLUG GAUGE INTO HOLE PROVIDED

⑤ EDGE OF LEVER SHOULD JUST CONTACT SIDE OF PLUG GAUGE AS SHOWN

Fig. 5 Choke coil lever adjustment (Typical)

⑤ LEVELING BUBBLE (CENTERED)

② DEGREE SCALE

③ POINTER

④ CHOKE VALVE CLOSED

MAGNET

FIGURE 1

⑥ SPECIFIED ANGLE (SEE SPECS.)

⑩ BEND ROD TO ADJUST

⑨ PUSH ON VACUUM BREAK LEVER TOWARD OPEN CHOKE UNTIL LEVER IS AGAINST REAR TANG ON CHOKE LEVER.

⑧ CLOSE CHOKE BY PUSHING ON INTERMEDIATE CHOKE LEVER

⑦ PLACE FAST IDLE SCREW ON SECOND STEP OF CAM AGAINST RISE OF HIGH STEP

FAST IDLE CAM

FIGURE 2

⑪ REMOVE GAUGE

Fig. 6 Choke rod adjustment (Typical)

② AIR VALVE COMPLETELY CLOSED

① SEAT VACUUM DIAPHRAGM USING OUTSIDE VACUUM SOURCE

③ PLACE GAUGE BETWEEN ROD AND END OF SLOT IN LEVER

④ BEND HERE FOR SPECIFIED CLEARANCE BETWEEN ROD AND END OF SLOT IN LEVER

Fig. 7 Air valve rod adjustment (Plug Gauge Method). 1979 Units

---

ing surface and top of pump stem.
3. To adjust, remove pump lever retaining screw and the pump lever. Place the lever in a vise and bend lever end. Do not bend lever in a twisting motion.
4. Install pump lever and retaining screw. Recheck pump adjustment.
5. Operate throttle valves to check for freedom of movement and pump lever alignment.

Fast Idle Adjustment

Fig. 4
1. Adjust curb idle speed, if necessary.
2. Place fast idle screw on highest step of cam.
3. Turn fast idle screw to obtain specified fast idle speed.

Choke Coil Lever Adjustment

Fig. 5
1. Loosen choke cover retaining screws, then the cover and coil assembly from choke housing. If a riveted choke cover is used, remove choke cover and coil assembly as outlined in the choke cover retainer

Fig. 7A Air valve rod adjustment (Angle Gauge Method). 1980–82 Units

Fig. 8 Primary vacuum break adjustment (Typical). 1979–80 units

Fig. 8A Primary vacuum break adjustment (Typical). 1981–82 E2SE units

Fig. 9 Secondary vacuum break adjustment. 1979–80 units

Fig. 9A Secondary vacuum break adjustment (Typical). 1981–82 units

Fig. 10 Choke setting adjustment

Choke Rod Adjustment

NOTE: The choke coil lever and fast idle adjustments must be made before performing this adjustment.

Fig. 6

1. Rotate degree scale until zero is opposite pointer, then with choke valve completely closed, place magnet on top of choke valve

kit.
2. Place fast idle screw on high step of cam.
3. Push the intermediate choke lever until the choke valve closes.
4. Insert specified gauge into hole provided in choke housing. The edge of the lever should just contact gauge.
5. To adjust, bend intermediate choke rod.

and rotate bubble until centered.
2. Rotate scale so specified degree for adjustment is opposite pointer.
3. Place fast idle screw on second step of cam against shoulder of high step.
4. Close choke by pushing intermediate choke lever.
5. Push vacuum break lever toward open choke position until lever contacts rear tang on choke lever.
6. To adjust, bend fast idle cam rod until bubble is centered.

CARBURETORS

Fig. 11 Unloader adjustment (Typical)

Fig. 12 Secondary lockout adjustment

Air Valve Rod Adjustment

1979 Units (Plug Gauge Method), Fig. 7
1. Seat vacuum diaphragm with an external vacuum source.
2. Close air valve completely.
3. Place specified gauge between rod and end of lever in slot.
4. To adjust, bend air valve rod.

1980-82 Units (Angle Gauge Method), Fig. 7A
1. Rotate gauge scale until pointer is opposite zero.
2. With air valve completely closed, place magnet on top of air valve and rotate bubble until centered.
3. Rotate scale so that specified degree for adjustment is opposite pointer.
4. Seat vacuum diaphragm using an external vacuum source.
5. Rotate air valve toward the open position by applying light pressure to the air valve shaft.
6. To adjust, bend air valve rod until bubble is centered.

Primary Vacuum Break Adjustment

1979-80 All Units & 1981 2SE Units, Fig. 8
1. Rotate degree scale until zero is opposite pointer, then with choke valve completely closed, place magnet on top of choke valve and rotate bubble until centered.
2. Rotate degree scale so specified degree for adjustment is opposite pointer.
3. Seat vacuum diaphragm with an external vacuum source.
4. Hold choke valve toward closed position by pushing on intermediate choke lever.
5. To adjust, bend vacuum break rod as shown until bubble is centered.

1981-82 E2SE Units, Fig. 8A

NOTE: Before performing adjustment procedure, remove primary vacuum break from carburetor and position bracket in vise, then grind off adjusting screw cap and reinstall vacuum break.

1. Rotate degree scale until zero is opposite

pointer, then with choke valve completely closed and fast idle screw on high step of fast idle cam, place magnet squarely on top of choke valve and rotate bubble until it is centered.
2. Rotate scale so that specified degree for adjustment is opposite pointer.
3. Seat choke vacuum diaphragm using a vacuum source with over 5 inches Hg of vacuum. Check to ensure that air valve rod is not restricting the vacuum diaphragm from being seated. It maybe necessary to bend air valve rod to obtain a slight clearance between rod and end of slot in air valve lever. If the air valve rod adjustment is disturbed, refer to the Air Valve Rod Adjustment procedure after completing the primary vacuum break adjustment.
4. Hold choke valve toward the closed position by lightly pushing on intermediate lever and note angle gauge reading.
5. If adjustment is necessary, use a 1/8 inch hex wrench to rotate adjusting screw in rear cover until bubble is centered.
6. After completing adjustment, apply a suitable sealer over adjusting screw head.

Secondary Vacuum Break Adjustment

1979-80 Units, Fig. 9
1. Rotate degree scale until zero is opposite pointer, then with choke valve completely closed, place magnet on top of choke valve and rotate bubble until centered.
2. Rotate scale so specified degree for adjustment is opposite pointer.
3. Seat vacuum diaphragm with an external vacuum source.
4. Hold choke valve toward closed position by pushing on intermediate choke lever. Ensure that bucking spring, if used, is compressed and seated.
5. To adjust, bend vacuum break rod as shown until bubble is centered.

1981-82 Units, Fig. 9A

NOTE: Before performing adjustment procedure, remove secondary vacuum break from carburetor and position bracket in a vise, then grind off adjusting screw cap and reinstall vacuum break. On 1981-82 units, plug vacuum break end cover using an accelerator

Fig. 13 Air valve spring adjustment. 1982 E2SE models

pump plunger cup or equivalent. After completing adjustment remove pump plunger cup.

1. Rotate degree scale so that zero is opposite pointer, then with choke valve completely closed and fast idle screw on high step of fast idle cam, place magnet on top of choke valve and rotate until bubble is centered.
2. Rotate scale so that specified degree for adjustment is opposite pointer.
3. Seat choke diaphragm using a vacuum source with over 5 inches Hg of vacuum.
4. Hold choke valve toward the closed position by lightly pushing on intermediate choke lever and note angle gauge reading. When noting reading check to ensure that vacuum diaphragm is seated.
5. Rotate adjusting screw in rear cover until bubble is centered. After completing adjustment, apply a suitable sealer over adjusting screw head.

NOTE: On 1981–82 units, remove pump plunger cup from end cover before applying sealer over adjusting screw head.

Choke Setting

NOTE: On 1981–82 units, the choke cover is retained to the choke housing by rivets. To remove rivets, carefully align a No. 21 drill on rivet head and drill only enough to remove rivet head. After removing rivet heads and retainers, drive remainder of rivet out using a suitable punch. A choke cover installation kit containing the proper rivets and retainers is available.

Fig. 10
1. Loosen choke cover retaining screws.
2. Place fast idle screw on high step of cam.
3. Align scribe line on choke cover with specified point on housing. Rotate cover toward closed choke position.
4. Tighten choke cover retaining screws.

Unloader Adjustment

Fig. 11
1. Rotate degree scale until zero is opposite pointer, then with choke valve completely closed, place magnet on top of choke valve and rotate bubble until centered.
2. Rotate degree scale so specified degree for adjustment is opposite pointer.
3. With choke setting properly adjusted, hold primary throttle valve wide open.
4. On warm engines, close choke valve by pushing on intermediate choke lever and hold in position with a rubber band.
5. To adjust, bend tang on throttle lever until bubble is centered.

Secondary Lockout Adjustment

Fig. 12
1. Hold choke valve wide open by pulling on intermediate choke lever.
2. Position throttle lever until end of secondary actuating lever is opposite toe of lockout lever.
3. Insert specified gauge between throttle lever and secondary lockout lever toe.
4. To adjust, bend lockout lever tang contacting fast idle cam.

Air Valve Spring Adjustment

1982 E2SE Units, Fig. 13
1. Loosen lock screw, then turn adjusting screw clockwise until air valve is partially open.
2. Turn adjusting screw counterclockwise until air valve just closes, then turn screw an additional 1/2 turn counterclockwise and tighten lock screw.
3. Lubricate air valve shaft pin and closing spring with lithium base grease.

Holley Carburetor Section

1000 & 2000 SERIES CARB. ADJUSTMENT SPECIFICATIONS

See Tune Up Chart in car chapter for curb and fast idle speeds.

Year	Carb. Part No. ①	Carb. Model	Float Level (Dry)	Fuel Level (Wet)	Pump Setting	Bowl Vent Clearance	Fast Idle Bench	Choke Unloader Clearance	Vacuum Kick Drill Size	Cam Position Drill Size	Choke Setting
CHRYSLER CORP.											
1977	R-7632A	1945	②	—	27/32 ③	1/16	.080	.250	.110	.080	Fixed
	R-7633A	1945	②	—	2²¹/₆₄ ④	1/16	.080	.250	.110	.080	Fixed
	R-7635A	1945	②	—	2²¹/₆₄ ④	—	.080	.250	.110	.080	Fixed
	R-7671A	2245	3/16	—	5/16 ⑤	.025	.110	.170	.110	.110	Fixed
	R-7744A	1945	②	—	2²¹/₆₄ ④	1/16	.080	.250	.130	.080	Fixed
	R-7745A	1945	②	—	27/32	1/16	.080	.250	.150	.080	Fixed
	R-7746A	1945	②	—	2²¹/₆₄	1/16	.080	.250	.110	.080	Fixed
	R-7764A	1945	②	—	27/32	1/16	.080	.250	.110	.080	Fixed
	R-7765A	1945	②	—	2²¹/₆₄	1/16	.080	.250	.110	.080	Fixed
1978	R-7988A	1945	②	—	27/32	1/16	.080	.250	.110	.080	Fixed
	R-7989A	1945	②	—	2²¹/₆₄	1/16	.080	.250	.110	.080	Fixed
	R-7990A	2280	9/32	—	⑥	.030	.070	.310	.150	.070	Fixed
	R-7991A	2245	3/16	—	17/64 ⑤	.025	.110	.170	.110	.110	Fixed
	R-8008A	1945	②	—	2²¹/₆₄	1/16	.080	.250	.110	.080	Fixed
	R-8010A	1945	②	—	2²¹/₆₄	1/16	.080	.250	.130	.080	Fixed
1979	R-8448A	2280	9/32	—	⑥	.030	.070	.310	.150	.070	Fixed
	R-8450A	2245	3/16	—	17/64 ⑤	.025	.110	.170	.110	.110	Fixed
	R-8452A	1945	②	—	1 5/8 ③	1/16	.080	.250	.110	.080	Fixed
	R-8523A	1945	②	—	1⁴⁵/₆₄ ⑤	1/16	.080	.250	.110	.080	Fixed
	R-8680A	1945	②	—	1 5/8 ③	1/16	.080	.250	.110	.080	Fixed
1980	R-8718A	1945	②	—	1⁴⁵/₆₄ ⑦	1/16	.090	.250	.150	.090	Fixed
	R-8831A	1945	②	—	1 5/8 ⑧	1/16	.090	.250	.140	.090	Fixed
	R-9179A	1945	②	—	1 3/4 ⑧	—	.090	—	.150	.090	Fixed
1981	R-9687A	1945	⑨	—	1³⁹/₆₄ ⑧	—	.090	.250	.150	.090	Fixed
	R-9695A	6145	⑨	—	1³⁹/₆₄ ⑧	—	.090	.250	.150	.090	Fixed

Continued

CARBURETORS

1000 & 2000 SERIES CARB. ADJUSTMENT SPECIFICATIONS—Continued

See Tune Up Chart in car chapter for curb and fast idle speeds.

Year	Carb. Part No. ①	Carb. Model	Float Level (Dry)	Fuel Level (Wet)	Pump Setting	Bowl Vent Clearance	Fast Idle Bench	Choke Unloader Clearance	Vacuum Kick Drill Size	Cam Position Drill Size	Choke Setting
CHRYSLER CORP.—Conitnued											
1982	R-9628A	1945	⑨	—	1.615⑧	—	.090	.250	.150	.090	Fixed
	R-9687A	1945	⑨	—	1.615⑧	—	.090	.250	.150	.090	Fixed
	R-9695A	6145	⑨	—	1.615⑧	—	.090	.250	.150	.090	Fixed

①—Located on tag attached to carburetor or on casting.
②—Flush with top of bowl cover gasket with bowl inverted.
③—Slot #2
④—Slot #3
⑤—Slot #1
⑥—Flush with top of bowl vent casting.
⑦—Hole position No. 1.
⑧—Hole position No. 2.
⑨—Flush with top of bowl casting to .050 inch above with bowel inverted.

Year	Carb. No.	Carb. Model	Float Level	Fuel Bowl Vent Setting	Accelerator Pump Hole No.	Pump Setting	Fast Idle Cam	Choke Pulldown	Dechoke	Choke Setting
FORD MOTOR CO.										
1978	D8BE-AAA	1946	①	½ Turn③	2	—	—	.110	.150	Index
	D8BE-AB	1946	①	½ Turn③	—	—	—	—	—	—
	D8BE-AGA	1946	①	½ Turn③	2	—	—	.110	.150	Index
	D8BE-AHA	1946	①	½ Turn③	2	—	—	.110	.150	Index
	D8BE-RA	1946	①	½ Turn③	2	—	—	.110	.150	Index
	D8BE-UC	1946	①	½ Turn③	2	—	—	.150	.150	Index
1979	D9BE-AEA	1946	①	½ Turn③	2	2.25	.055	.080	.150	Index
	D9BE-AHA	1946	②	½ Turn③	2	2.31	.130	.150	.150	Index
	D9BE-AJA	1946	②	½ Turn③	2	2.31	.130	.150	.150	Index
	D9BE-AMA	1946	①	½ Turn③	2	2.31	.070	.095	.150	Index
	D9BE-BKA	1946	①	½ Turn③	2	2.31	.055	.080	.150	Index
	D9BE-LA	1946	①	½ Turn③	2	2.21	.055	.080	.150	Index
1980	E0BE-AAA, ZA	1946-C	②	—	1	—	.090	.115	.150	2 Rich
	E0BE-ALA, AMA	1946	①	—	2	—	.070	.100	.150	Index
	E0EE-ANA, APA	1946	①	—	2	—	.070	.100	.150	—
	E0ZE-BAA, BBA	1946	①	—	2	—	.086	.120	.150	2 Rich
	E0ZE-DA, EA	1946	①	—	2	—	.070	.110	.150	2 Rich
	E0ZE-FA, GA	1946	①	—	2	—	.070	.110	.150	2 Rich
1981	E0BE-AA, CA	1946	.69	—	2	2.15	.070	.100	.150	2 Rich
	E1BE-AFA, AKA	1946	.69	—	2	2.15	.082	.113	.150	2 Rich
	E1BE-AGA	1946	.69	—	2	2.15	.086	.120	.150	2 Rich
	E1BE-ARA, ASA	1946	—	—	—	2.15	—	—	—	—
1982	E1BE-AGA	1946	.69	—	2	—	.086	.120	.150	2 Rich
	E2BE-BA	1946	.69	—	2	—	.078	.110	.150	2 Rich
	E2BE-CA	1946	.69	—	2	—	.078	.110	.150	2 Rich
	E2BE-HA	1946	.69	—	2	—	.078	.110	.150	2 Rich
	E2BE-JA	1946	.69	—	2	—	.078	.110	.150	2 Rich
	E2BE-SA	1946	.69	—	2	—	.078	.110	.150	2 Rich
	E2BE-TA	1946	.69	—	2	—	.078	.110	.150	2 Rich

①—Setting at toe. Refer to text for procedure.
②—Setting at heel. Refer to text for procedure.
③—Clockwise.

FAST IDLE CAM

TO VAPOR CANISTER PURGE PORT

TO CRANKCASE PCV VALVE

TO EGR VACUUM AMPLIFIER

BOWL VENT TUBE

TO AIR CLEANER HEATED INLET AIR SYSTEM

FAST IDLE ADJUSTMENT

CURB IDLE ADJUSTMENT

IDENTIFICATION NUMBER

IDLE MIXTURE ADJUSTMENT

TO DISTRIBUTOR OSAC VALVE

CHOKE DIAPHRAGM

ACCELERATOR PUMP OPERATING ARM

POSITIVE THROTTLE RETURN ASSEMBLY

Fig. 1 Holley model 1945 single barrel carburetor. (Typical)

DUTY CYCLE SOLENOID

BOWL VENT TUBE AND SOLENOID

CHOKE DIAPHRAGM

TO CRANKCASE PCV VALVE

FAST IDLE ADJUSTMENT

TO EGR VACUUM AMPLIFIER

TO AIR CLEANER HEATED AIR SYSTEM

SOLENOID IDLE STOP

TO VAPOR CANISTER PURGE PORT

TO CHOKE DIAPHRAGM

ACCELERATOR PUMP OPERATING ARM

Fig. 1A Holley model 6145 electronic feedback single barrel carburetor

Fig. 2 Measuring float level. 1945 & 6145 carburetor

Fig. 3 Bowl vent valve adjustment.
1977–80 1945 carburetor

MODELS 1945 & 6145

These single barrel carburetors, Figs. 1 and 1A, utilize dual nitrophyl floats to control the fuel level, thus permitting high angularity operation during the most severe operating conditions. Also, the float construction eliminates the possibility of a malfunction due to a punctured float.

On 1977–82 units, an electric choke system is incorporated to open the choke at approximately 60 degrees F.

The accelerator pump is of the piston type and is operated by a rod and a link connected to the throttle lever.

The power enrichment system on all units, consists of a power valve installed near the center of the carburetor body and a vacuum piston located in the bowl cover.

On 1977–82 units, a spring-loaded modulated power valve is used. A vacuum passage in the throttle body transmits manifold vacuum to the vacuum piston chamber in the bowl cover. Under light throttle and load conditions, vacuum acting on the vacuum piston is sufficient to overcome the spring tension. When the throttle valve is opened to 55 degrees, vacuum acting on the vacuum piston is bled to the atmosphere and manifold vacuum is closed off. The throttle shaft is provided with a small hole which aligns with a port in the base of the carburetor when the throttle valve is opened to 55 degrees. This vents the vacuum piston chamber to the atmosphere, allowing the spring tension to open the power valve.

The 6145 electronic feedback carburetor also incorporates a duty cycle solenoid which provides a limited regulation of air-fuel ratio in response to electrical signals from the spark control computer. The solenoid meters the main fuel system and operates in parallel with a conventional fixed main metering jet.

When there is no electrical signal applied to the solenoid, the valve spring pushes upward through the main system fuel valve, fully uncovering the solenoid controlled main metering orifice so that the richest condition exists within the carburetor for any given airflow. When the electrical signal is applied to the solenoid, the field windings are energized, thus causing the armature to move the push rod and main system valve downward against the valve spring. This movement will continue until the main system valve bottoms against the main system valve seat. In this position the solenoid controlled main metering orifice is fully sealed so that the leanest condition exists within the carburetor for any given airflow. This condition will remain unchanged until the signal from the spark control computer to the solenoid is switched off. The main system fuel maybe regulated between richest and leanest limits by controlling the amount of time that the solenoid is in the power on position. Under normal operating conditions, 12 volts at a frequency of 10 Hz is applied to the field windings. By controlling the duration of the voltage signal, the power on time to total time, referred to as the duty cycle, is established.

Dry Float Setting

Fig. 2—Hold float fulcrum retaining pin in position and invert carburetor bowl. Place a straight edge across surface of bowl, contracting float toes. Remove straight edge and measure distance float dropped from surface of fuel bowl. Refer to Holley Specifications Chart. Adjust by bending float tang to obtain proper dimension.

Bowl Vent Valve Adjustment

1977–80 Fig. 3—With throttle at curb idle, measure distance between the cover support surface and the flat on the plastic bowl vent lever. The distance should be 1/16 inch. If not

within specifications, turn bowl vent lever adjusting screw to obtain specified distance.

Fast Idle Cam Position Adjustment

Fig. 4—With fast idle speed adjusting screw contacting second highest step on fast idle cam, move choke valve toward closed position with light pressure on choke shaft lever. Insert specified gauge between top of choke valve and wall of air horn. Refer to *Holley Specifications Chart*. An adjustment will be necessary if a slight drag is not obtained as drill shank is being removed. Adjust by bending fast idle link at lower angle, until correct valve opening has been obtained.

Choke Vacuum Kick Adjustment

NOTE: Test can be made on or off vehicle.

Fig. 5—If adjustment is to be made with engine running, back off fast idle speed screw until choke can be closed to the kick position with engine at curb idle. (Note number of screw turns required so that fast idle can be returned to original adjustment). If an auxiliary vacuum source is to be used, open throttle valve (engine not running) and move choke to closed position. Release throttle first, then release choke.

When using an auxiliary vacuum source, disconnect vacuum hose from carburetor and connect it to hose from vacuum supply with a small length of tube to act as a fitting. Removal of hose from diaphragm may require forces which damage the system. Apply a vacuum of 15 or more inches of mercury.

Insert gauge between top of choke valve and wall of air horn. Refer to *Holley Specifications Chart*. Apply sufficient closing pressure on lever to which choke rod attaches to provide a minimum choke valve opening without distortion of diaphragm link.

GAUGE

LIGHT CLOSING PRESSURE ON CHOKE LEVER

BEND LINK HERE TO ADJUST

FAST IDLE SPEED SCREW ON 2ND HIGHEST STEP OF CAM

Fig. 4   Fast idle cam position adjustment. 1945 & 6145 carburetor

GAUGE

APPLY 15" OF VACUUM TO FULLY RETRACT DIAPHRAGM STEM

LIGHT CLOSING PRESSURE ON CHOKE LEVER

BEND LINK HERE TO ADJUST

TO VACUUM SOURCE

Fig. 5   Choke vacuum kick adjustment. 1945 & 6145 carburetor

GAUGE

LIGHT CLOSING PRESSURE ON CHOKE LEVER

BEND UNLOADER TANG HERE FOR ADJUSTMENT

THROTTLE LEVER IN WIDE OPEN POSITION

Fig. 6   Choke unloader adjustment. 1945 & 6145 carburetor

SCALE BEHIND THROTTLE LEVER

BEND LINK HERE TO ADJUST

THROTTLE LEVER IN CURB IDLE POSITION

SLOT NO. 3
SLOT NO. 2
SLOT NO. 1

Fig. 7   Accelerator pump adjustment. (1977–79) 1945 carburetor

CARBURETORS

Fig. 7A   Accelerator pump adjustment. (1980–82) 1945 & 6145 carburetor

Fig. 8   Dashpot adjustment. (1977–80) 1945 carburetor

NOTE: The cylindrical stem of diaphragm extends as the internal spring is compressed. This spring must be fully compressed for proper measurement of vacuum kick adjustment.

Adjustment is necessary if slight drag is not obtained when removing the gauge. Shorten or lengthen diaphragm link to obtain correct choke valve opening. Length changes should be made by carefully opening or closing the U-bend provided in the link. Improper bending causes contact between the U-section and the diaphragm assembly.

NOTE: Do not apply twisting or bending force to diaphragm.

After completion of adjustment, reinstall vacuum hose on correct carburetor fitting.

Return fast idle screw to its original location if disturbed. Make following check. With no vacuum applied to diaphragm, the choke valve should move freely between open and closed positions. If movement is not free, examine linkage for misalignment or interferences caused by bending operation.

NOTE: On 1982 models, adjustment is made by means of a 5/64 inch allen wrench inserted into vacuum diaphragm.

Choke Unloader (Wide Open Kick) Adjustment

Fig. 6—With throttle valves in wide open position, insert drill gauge between upper edge of choke valve and inner wall of air horn. Refer to *Holley Specifications Chart*. With a finger lightly pressing against shaft lever, a slight drag should be felt as drill is being withdrawn. Adjust by bending unloader tang on throttle lever until correct opening has been obtained.

Accelerator Pump Setting

Figs. 7 & 7A—With throttle at curb idle position, measure length of pump operating link. Refer to *Holley Specification Chart*. Adjust by bending link between throttle lever and pump operating rod.

Dashpot Setting

1977–80 Fig. 8—With curb idle speed and mixture properly set, install a tachometer on engine. Start engine and position throttle lever so actuating tab on lever contacts the dashpot stem, however, not depressing the stem. Permit the engine speed to stabilize. Engine speed should be 2300 RPM on 1979–80 models or 2500 RPM on 1977–78 models. To adjust, loosen locknut and turn the dashpot to obtain proper engine RPM.

MODEL 1946

This carburetor, Figs. 1, 2, and 2A, uses seven basic systems to provide the correct air/fuel mixture under various operating conditions. The systems are as follows: fuel inlet system, idle system, main metering system, power enrichment system, accelerator pump system, external fuel bowl vent system and automatic choke system. The carburetor is divided into three main assemblies which are the air horn assembly, the main body assembly and the throttle body assembly.

The air horn assembly contains the fuel bowl vent, enrichment valve piston and the accelerator pump piston, cup, spring and operating lever. Also contained in the air horn is the choke plate, shaft, lever, housing and choke cap. The idle air bleed and the high speed bleed restrictors are also found in the air horn assembly.

The main body assembly contains the fuel inlet system including the needle and seat assembly, the float, float hinge pin and re-tainer. The centrally located venturi contains two venturi vacuum boosters and the main discharge passage. The accelerator pump well, passages, check ball and weight, main metering jet, enrichment valve, idle tube and hot idle compensator are also located in the main body assembly. The venturi vacuum pick-up tube, manifold vacuum and EGR port vacuum pick-up tubes are incorporated in the main body assembly.

The throttle body assembly regulates air flow through the carburetor and provides the mounting flange for the carburetor. The throttle plate, shaft lever and return spring assemblies regulate air flow. Also located in the throttle body assembly are the spark vacuum port, EGR vacuum port, idle transfer slot, curb idle discharge port and the idle mixture adjusting screw.

Float Level Adjustment

Fig. 3—With air horn removed, place a finger over float hinge pin retainer and invert main body. Do not lose accelerator pump check ball and weight. Using a straight edge, check position of floats. The floats should touch the straight edge at points shown in illustration. To adjust, bend float tang.

Accelerator Pump Adjustment

Fig. 4—With the accelerator pump operating link in the specified slot, measure the length of the rod from inner side of tab to outer side of radius. To adjust, bend rod at U-joint.

Fast Idle Cam Position Adjustment

Fig. 5—With fast idle adjusting screw contacting second highest step of fast idle cam, move choke plate toward closed position. Insert specified gauge between upper edge of choke valve and air horn wall. To adjust, bend fast idle cam link.

Fig. 1   Holley model 1946 one barrel carburetor (Typical)

Choke Pulldown Adjustment

NOTE: On 1981–82 units, the carburetor must be removed from the vehicle to remove the rivets retaining the choke cap to the choke housing. Using a 1/8 inch or No. 30 drill, remove rivet heads, then drive out rivet using a 1/8 inch diameter punch.

Figs. 6 & 6A—On 1980 California 1946-C units and all 1981–82 units, remove choke thermostatic housing, retainer ring and screws, then temporarily remove choke thermostatic housing index spacer. Reinstall choke thermostatic housing, retainer and screws. On all units, loosen choke cover screw, rotate housing 90 degrees in the rich direction and tighten screws. Using an external vacuum source, apply sufficient vacuum to retract vacuum diaphragm. Push on small metal plate in the bottom of the linkage slot to ensure that the diaphragm is fully retracted. Insert specified gauge between upper edge of choke valve and air horn wall. On 1977–80 units, bend diaphragm link at U-bend to adjust. On 1981–82 units, drill a 3/32 inch hole through pull down motor adjusting screw plug, then remove plug using an easy out. Turn adjusting screw inward or outward as necessary. After completing adjustment, install a replacement plug in adjusting screw access hole.

Dechoke Adjustment

Fig. 7—With throttle held in wide open position, insert specified gauge between upper edge of choke valve and air horn wall. With light pressure against choke shaft lever, a slight drag should be felt when removing the gauge. To adjust, bend unloader tang on throttle lever.

External Fuel Bowl Vent Adjustment

1977–79 All & 1980 Units Except 1946-C
Fig. 8—Disconnect canister vent hose from

Fig. 3   Float adjustment. 1946 carburetor

Fig. 4   Accelerator pump adjustment. 1946 carburetor

Fig. 5   Fast idle cam adjustment. 1946 carburetor

1. SCREW
2. BOWL VENT COVER
3. VENT COVER GASKET
4. VENT VALVE SPRING
5. VENT VALVE HINGE PIN
6. VENT VALVE
7. VENT VALVE HINGE ATTACHING SCREW
8. AIR CLEANER BRACKET
9. VENT VALVE ARM
10. VENT VALVE ADJUSTING SCREW
11. AIR CLEANER BRACKET SCREW
12. CHOKE HEAT TUBE ADAPTER
13. AIR HORN
14. SCREW
15. CHOKE PULLDOWN LEVER
16. CHOKE SHAFT NUT
17. LOCKWASHER
18. CHOKE BIMETAL SPRING COVER
19. SCREW
20. CHOKE COVER RETAINER
21. CHOKE HOUSING GASKET
22. CHOKE SHAFT AND LEVER ASSEMBLY
23. CHOKE CONTROL LEVER
24. SCREW
25. SCREW
26. CHOKE PLATE
27. ACCELERATOR PUMP OPERATING ROD
28. ACCELERATOR PUMP ROD GROMMET
29. ROD RETAINING CLAMP
30. SCREW
31. ACCELERATOR PUMP SPRING RETAINING SPRING
32. SCREW
33. ACCELERATOR PUMP PISTON STEM
34. ACCELERATOR PUMP SPRING
35. ACCELERATOR PUMP PISTON CUP
36. FAST IDLE CAM LINK
37. ANTI-DIESEL SOLENOID
38. SCREW
39. AIR HORN GASKET
40. FLOAT HINGE RETAINER
41. ACCELERATOR PUMP OPERATING LINK
42. RETAINING CLIP
43. FAST IDLE CAM
44. FLOAT ASSEMBLY
45. POWER VALVE BODY
46. MAIN METERING JET
47. POWER VALVE PIN
48. ACCELERATOR PUMP WEIGHT
49. ACCELERATOR PUMP CHECK BALL
50. POWER VALVE SPRING
51. SPRING
52. LOW IDLE (SOLENOID OFF) ADJUSTING SCREW
53. SPEED SCREW
54. CHOKE PULLDOWN DIAPHRAGM ASSEMBLY
55. CHOKE DIAPHRAGM VACUUM HOSE
56. FUEL FILTER
57. FUEL INLET NEEDLE & SEAT ASSEMBLY
58. GASKET
59. SCREW
60. HOT IDLE COMPENSATOR COVER
61. COVER GASKET
62. HOT IDLE COMPENSATOR
63. GASKET
64. MAIN BODY ASSEMBLY
65. FLOAT HINGE PIN
66. CURB IDLE ADJUSTING SCREW
67. SPRING
68. SPRING
69. FAST IDLE ADJUSTING SCREW
70. THROTTLE SHAFT & LEVER ASSEMBLY
71. SCREW
72. THROTTLE PLATE
73. THROTTLE BODY ASSEMBLY
74. THROTTLE BODY SCREW
75. LIMITER CAP
76. IDLE FUEL MIXTURE ADJUSTING SCREW
77. SPRING
78. THROTTLE BODY GASKET
79. THROTTLE RETURN SPRING BUSHING
80. THROTTLE RETURN SPRING
81. NUT
82. LOCK WASHER
83. THROTTLE RETURN SPRING BRACKET

Fig. 2   Disassembled view of Holley Model 1946 carburetor (Typical). 1977–80 units

1. AIR CLEANER BRACKET
2. AIR CLEANER BRACKET SCREW
3. AIR HORN
4. SCREW
5. CHOKE PULLDOWN LEVER
6. CHOKE SHAFT NUT
7. LOCKWASHER
8. CHOKE BIMETAL ASSEMBLY
9. SCREW
9A. RIVET
10. CHOKE COVER RETAINER
11. CHOKE THERMOSTATIC HOUSING LOCATING DISC
12. CHOKE SHAFT AND LEVER ASSEMBLY
13. CHOKE CONTROL LEVER
14. SCREW
15. SCREW
16. CHOKE PLATE
17. ACCELERATOR PUMP OPERATING ROD
18. ACCELERATOR PUMP ROD GROMMET
19. ROD RETAINING CLAMP
20. SCREW
21. ACCELERATOR PUMP SPRING RETAINING PLATE
22. SCREW
23. ACCELERATOR PUMP PISTON STEM
24. ACCELERATOR PUMP SPRING
25. ACCELERATOR PUMP PISTON CUP
26. FAST IDLE CAM LINK
27. ANTI-DIESEL SOLENOID
28. SCREW
29. AIR HORN GASKET
30. FLOAT-HINGE RETAINER
31. ACCELERATOR PUMP OPERATING LINK
32. RETAINING CLIP
33. FAST IDLE CAM
34. FLOAT ASSEMBLY
35. POWER VALVE BODY
36. MAIN METERING JET
37. POWER VALVE PIN
38. ACCELERATOR PUMP WEIGHT
39. ACCELERATOR PUMP CHECK BALL
40. POWER VALVE SPRING
41. SPRING
42. LOW IDLE (SOLENOID OFF) ADJUSTING SCREW
43. CHOKE PULLDOWN DIAPHRAGM ASSEMBLY
44. CHOKE DIAPHRAGM VACUUM HOSE
45. FUEL FILTER
46. FUEL INLET NEEDLE & SEAT ASSEMBLY
47. GASKET
48. MAIN BODY ASSEMBLY
49. FLOAT HINGE PIN
50. CURB IDLE ADJUSTING SCREW
51. SPRING
52. SPRING
53. FAST IDLE ADJUSTING SCREW
54. THROTTLE SHAFT & LEVER ASSEMBLY
55. SCREW
56. THROTTLE PLATE
57. THROTTLE BODY ASSEMBLY
58. THROTTLE BODY SCREW
59. THROTTLE BODY GASKET
60. THROTTLE RETURN SPRING BUSHING
61. THROTTLE RETURN SPRING
62. NUT
63. LOCK WASHER
64. THROTTLE RETURN SPRING BRACKET
65. BOWL VENT SOLENOID
65A. WASHER
65B. SPRING
65C. PINTLE
65D. SEAL
66. POWER VALVE PISTON ASSEMBLY
66A. GASKET
67. SCREW
68. IDLE MIXTURE
69. CONCEALMENT PLUG
    IDLE MIXTURE NEEDLE

Fig. 2A Disassembled view of Holley Model 1946 Carburetor (Typical). 1981—82 units

CARBURETORS

Fig. 6A   Choke pulldown adjustment. 1981–82
Model 1946 carburetor

Fig. 6   Choke pulldown adjustment. 1977–80 Model 1946 carburetor

Fig. 7   Dechoke adjustment. 1946 carburetor

Fig. 8   External fuel bowl vent adjustment. 1946 carburetor

bowl vent tube. Connect an external vacuum source to bowl vent tube. Remove bowl vent cover, gasket and spring. Rotate vent adjusting screw clockwise until the adjusting screw protrudes 1/8 inch or less above vent arm. Apply vacuum to vent tube and slowly turn the adjusting screw counterclockwise in 1/8 turn increments until vacuum reading indicates that the valve is closed. Remove vacuum and rotate the adjusting screw 1/2 turn clockwise. Install bowl vent spring, gasket and cover. Connect canister vent hose.

Choke Setting Adjustment

Fig. 9—Loosen choke cover retaining screws and rotate cover to align mark on cover with specified mark on housing. Tighten choke cover retaining screws.

Fig. 9   Choke setting adjustment. 1946 carburetor

CHOKE DIAPHRAGM

BOWL VENT

IDLE STOP CARBURETOR SWITCH

CURB IDLE ADJUSTMENT SCREW

IDLE ENRICHMENT DIAPHRAGM

TO EGR VACUUM AMPLIFIER

TO ESA VACUUM TRANSDUCER

IDLE MIXTURE SCREWS (2)

TO VAPOR CANISTER

IDENTIFICATION NUMBER

THROTTLE POSITION TRANSDUCER

POSITIVE THROTTLE RETURN ASSEMBLY

FAST IDLE ADJUSTMENT SCREW

TO PCV VALVE

TO HEATED AIR INLET SYSTEM

Fig. 1 Holley model 2245 two-barrel carburetor (Typical)

MODEL 2245

This carburetor, Fig. 1, is a two-barrel unit but can be considered as two carburetors built side by side into one unit, utilizing the same fuel and air inlets. Each throat of the carburetor has its own throttle valve and main metering systems and are supplemented by the float, accelerating, idle and power systems. An electric choke system is incorporated to open choke at approximately 60° to 63°. For service information refer to the "Emission Control System" chapter. On vehicles with automatic transmissions, an idle enrichment system is used to reduce cold engine stalling by the use of an additional metering system which enrichens the mixture in the off idle position. This system is controlled by a vacuum diaphragm mounted near the top of the carburetor.

Float Adjustment

Invert air horn so that weight of float only is forcing needle against seat. Measure the clearance between top of float and float stop, Fig. 2. Be sure drill gauge is perfectly level when measuring. Refer to *Holley Specifications Chart*. Adjust by bending float lip toward or away from needle, using a narrow blade screwdriver, Fig. 3, until correct clearance of setting has been obtained.

Float Drop Adjustment

Check float drop, by holding air horn in an upright position. The bottom edge of float

should be parallel to underside surface of air horn, Fig. 4. Adjust by bending tang on float arm until parallel surfaces have been obtained.

Fast Idle Cam Position Adjustment

Fig. 5—With fast idle speed adjusting screw contacting second highest step on fast idle cam, move choke valve toward closed position with light pressure on choke shaft lever. Insert specified gauge between top of choke

valve and wall of air horn. Refer to *Holley Specifications Chart*. An adjustment will be necessary if a slight drag is not obtained as drill shank is being removed. Adjust by bending fast idle link at angle, until correct valve opening has been obtained.

Choke Vacuum Kick Adjustment

NOTE: Test can be made on or off vehicle.

FLOAT

GAUGE OR DRILL

AIR HORN INVERTED

FLOAT STOP

Fig. 2 Checking float level on 2245 carburetor

CARBURETORS

FLOAT RAISED

FLOAT ADJUSTING TANG

SMALL SCREWDRIVER

Fig. 3   Adjusting float on 2245 carburetor

UNDERSIDE SURFACE OF AIR HORN

BOTTOM EDGE OF FLOAT SHOULD BE PARALLEL

Fig. 4   Checking float drop on 2245 carburetor

LIGHT CLOSING PRESSURE

GAUGE

ADJUSTING SCREW ON 2ND HIGHEST STEP OF CAM

BEND HERE TO ADJUST

Fig. 5   Fast idle cam position adjustment on 2245 carburetor

STEM FULLY DEPRESSED

MINIMUM 15" OF VACUUM ON CHOKE DIAPHRAGM

TO VACUUM SOURCE

ADJUST HERE

LIGHT CLOSING PRESSURE

Fig. 6   Vacuum kick adjustment on 2245 carburetor

LIGHT CLOSING PRESSURE

GAUGE

THROTTLE IN WIDE OPEN POSITION

BEND TANG TO ADJUST

Fig. 7   Choke unloader adjustment on 2245 carburetor

SCALE

SLOT·1
SLOT·2

SLOT·3
SLOT·4

BEND ROD TO ADJUST

THROTTLE AT CURB IDLE

Fig. 8   Accelerator pump adjustment on 2245 carburetor

Fig. 9 Bowl vent adjustment on 2245 carburetor

Fig. 6—If adjustment is to be made with engine running, back off fast idle speed screw until choke can be closed to the kick position with engine at curb idle. (Note number of screw turns required so that fast idle can be returned to original adjustment). If an auxiliary vacuum source is to be used, open throttle valve (engine not running) and move choke to closed position. Release throttle first, then release choke.

When using an auxillary vacuum source, disconnect vacuum hose from carburetor and connect it to hose from vacuum supply with a small length of tube to act as a fitting. Removal of hose from diaphragm may require forces which damage the system. Apply 15 or more inches of vacuum to diaphragm.

Insert gauge between top of choke valve and wall of air horn. Refer to *Holley Specifications Chart*. Apply sufficient closing pressure on lever to which choke rod attaches to provide a minimum choke valve opening without distortion of diaphragm link.

NOTE: The cylindrical stem of diaphragm extends as the internal spring is compressed. This spring must be fully compressed for proper measurement of vacuum kick adjustment.

Adjustment is necessary if slight drag is not obtained when removing the gauge. Shorten or lengthen diaphragm link to obtain correct choke valve opening. Length changes should be made by carefully opening or closing the U-bend provided in the link. Improper bending causes contact between the U-section and the diaphragm assembly.

NOTE: Do not apply twisting or bending force to diaphragm.

After completion of adjustment, reinstall vacuum hose on correct carburetor fitting. Return fast idle screw to its original location if disturbed. Make following check. With no vacuum applied to diaphragm, the choke valve should move freely between open and closed positions. If movement is not free, examine linkage for misalignment or interferences caused by bending operation.

Choke Unloader (Wide Open Kick) Adjustment

Fig. 7—With throttle valves in wide open position, insert drill gauge between upper edge of choke valve and inner wall of air horn. Refer to *Holley Specifications Chart*. With a finger lightly pressing against shaft lever, a slight drag should be felt as drill is being withdrawn. Adjust by bending unloader tang on throttle lever until correct opening has been obtained.

Accelerator Pump Adjustment

Fig. 8—Back off curb idle speed adjusting screw. Open choke valve so that fast idle cam allows throttle valves to be completely seated in bores. Be sure that pump connector rod is installed in correct slot of accelerator pump rocker arm.

Using a suitable scale, measure pump travel (drop) between curb idle and wide open throttle. To adjust, bend pump operating rod until proper setting is obtained.

Bowl Vent Valve Clearance Adjustment

Fig. 9—With the throttle valves at curb idle, it should be possible to insert the specified gauge between the bowl vent valve plunger stem and operating rod. Refer to *Holley Specifications Chart*. Adjust by bending the tang on pump lever to change arc of contact with throttle lever, until correct clearance has been obtained.

MODEL 2280

This carburetor, Fig. 1, uses four basic metering systems. The basic idle system provides the proper air/fuel mixture for idle and low speed operations. The accelerator pump ystem provides additional fuel during acceleration. The main metering system provides the proper air/fuel mixture during normal cruising conditions. The power enrichment system, combining a mechanical and vacuum operated power valve, provides a richer mixture when higher engine power is required.

In addition to the four basic systems, there is a fuel inlet system which supplies fuel to the four basic systems and a choke system which temporarily enriches the mixture to aid in starting and running a cold engine.

Float Adjustment

Fig. 2—Invert main body so the weight of the floats only is forcing the needle against the seat. Hold finger against hinge pin retainer to fully seat in the float hinge cradle. Using a suitable scale, measure distance between the float bowl surface and the toe of each float. To adjust, bend the float tang. If necessary, bend either float arm to equalize individual float positions.

Accelerator Pump Adjustment

Fig. 3—Remove bowl vent cover plate and vent valve spring. Do not dislodge vent valve lever retainer. Ensure that accelerator pump rod is in the inner hole of the pump operating lever and the throttle is at curb idle. Place a straight edge on bowl vent cover surface of air horn over accelerator pump lever. Adjust until lever surface is flush with air horn surface by bending the accelerator pump connector rod. Install vent valve lever spring and bowl vent cover plate.

NOTE: If this adjustment is changed, the bowl vent and mechanical power valve adjustments must be reset.

Choke Unloader Adjustment

Fig. 4—Hold throttle valves in wide open position. Lightly press finger against control lever to move choke valve toward closed position. Insert specified gauge between top of choke valve and air horn wall. To adjust, bend tang on accelerator pump lever.

Choke Vacuum Kick Adjustment

Fig. 5—Open throttle, close choke, then close throttle to trap fast idle cam at closed choke position. Apply approximately 15 inches of vacuum to diaphragm with an external vac-

CARBURETORS

BOWL VENT

CHOKE DIAPHRAGM

FAST IDLE ADJUSTMENT

IDLE STOP CARBURETOR SWITCH

CURB IDLE ADJUSTMENT

TO PORTED EGR SYSTEM

TO VAPOR CANISTER PURGE PORT

POSITIVE THROTTLE RETURN ASSEMBLY

TO CRANKCASE PCV VALVE

TO AIR CLEANER HEATED INLET AIR SYSTEM

THROTTLE POSITION TRANSDUCER (TPT)

TO ESA VACUUM TRANSDUCER

IDLE MIXTURE ADJUSTMENT SCREWS (2)

IDENTIFICATION NUMBER

0000

Fig. 1   Holley model 2280 two barrel carburetor

uum source. Apply closing pressure on choke lever to completely compress spring in diaphragm stem without distorting linkage. The cylindrical stem of the diaphragm extends to a stop as the spring compresses. Insert specified

gauge between top of choke valve and air horn wall. Adjust by bending diaphragm link at U-bend. Check for free movement between the open and adjusted positions.

Fast Idle Cam Position Adjustment

Fig. 6—With fast idle speed adjusting screw contacting second highest step of fast idle cam, move choke valve toward closed position

FLOAT HINGE PIN RETAINER

TOE OF FLOATS

BEND TANG TO ADJUST

FLOAT

"T" SCALE

GASKET

Fig. 2   Float adjustment. 2280 carburetor

STRAIGHT EDGE

ACCELERATOR PUMP LEVER

INNER HOLE

OUTER HOLE

THROTTLE AT CURB IDLE

BEND HERE TO ADJUST

Fig. 3   Accelerator pump adjustment. 2280 carburetor

Fig. 4 Choke unloader adjustment. 2280 carburetor

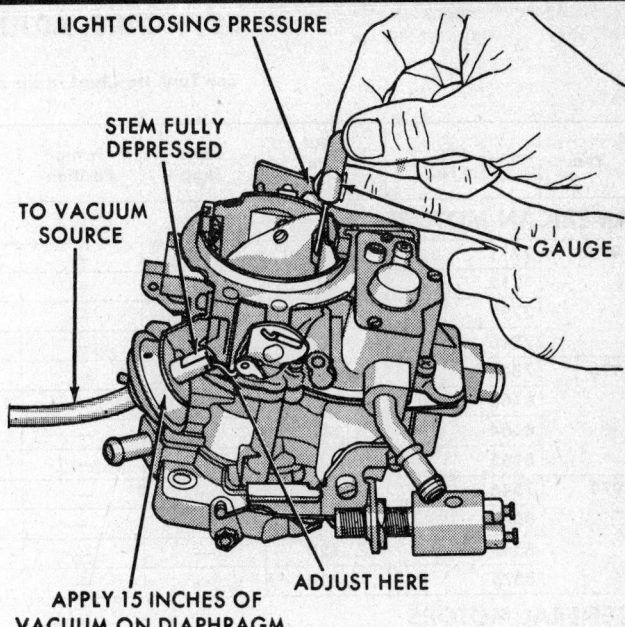

Fig. 5 Choke vacuum kick adjustment. 2280 carburetor

Fig. 6 Fast idle cam position adjustment. 2280 carburetor

Fig. 7 Bowl vent valve adjustment. 2280 carburetor

with light pressure on choke shaft lever. Insert specified gauge between top of choke valve and air horn wall. To adjust, bend the U-bend in fast idle connector link to obtain proper setting.

Bowl Vent Valve Adjustment

Fig. 7—Remove bowl vent cover plate and vent valve lever spring. Do not dislodge vent valve lever retainer. With throttle at curb idle, press downward on vent valve lever where spring seats. Measure distance between contact surfaces of vent valve tang and vent valve lever. Adjust by bending end of vent valve lever. Install vent valve lever spring and bowl vent cover plate.

Mechanical Power Valve Adjustment

Fig. 8—Remove bowl vent cover plate, vent valve lever spring and retainer, then the vent valve lever and pivot pin. Hold throttle in wide open position. Insert a 5/64 inch allen wrench in mechanical power valve adjustment screw. Push screw downward and release to determine if clearance exists. Turn screw clockwise until zero clearance is obtained. Adjust by turning screw one turn counter-clockwise. Install vent valve lever, pivot pin and retainer, then the vent valve lever spring and bowl vent cover plate.

Fig. 8 Mechanical power valve adjustment. 2280 carburetor

CARBURETORS

5210 CARB. ADJUSTMENT SPECIFICATIONS

See Tune Up Chart in car chapter for curb and fast idle speeds.

Year	Carb. Part No.	Float Level (Dry)	Float Drop	Pump Position	Fast Idle Cam Index	Vacuum Plate Pulldown	Vacuum Break Primary	Vacuum Break Secondary	Unloader Setting	Choke Setting
AMERICAN MOTORS										
1977	7711	.420	—	—	.140	.246	—	—	.300	1 Rich
	7712	.420	—	—	.140	.246	—	—	.300	1 Rich
	7799	.420	—	—	.135	.215	—	—	.300	Index
	7846	.420	—	—	.101	.204	—	—	.300	1 Rich
1978	7846	.420	—	—	.177	.180	—	—	.300	Index
	8163	.420	—	—	.193	.191	—	—	.300	1 Rich
	8164	.420	—	—	.204	.202	—	—	.300	1 Rich
	8165	.420	—	—	.101	.284	—	—	.300	1 Rich
1979	7846	.420	—	—	.193	.191	—	—	.300	1 Rich
	8548	.420	—	—	.204	.191	—	—	.300	1 Rich
	8549	.420	—	—	.191	.266	—	—	.300	1 Rich
	8675	.420	—	—	.173	.177	—	—	.300	Index
GENERAL MOTORS										
1977	458102, 04	.420	1"	①	.120	—	.250	—	.350	3 Rich
	458103, 05	.420	1"	①	.120	—	.250	—	.350	3 Rich
	458106, 08	.420	1"	#1	.120	—	.275	—	.400	3 Rich
	458107, 09	.420	1"	#2	.160	—	.275	.400	.350	3 Rich
	458110, 12	.420	1"	#1	.160	—	.325	.400	.350	3 Rich
	527200, 02	.520	1"	#2	.150	—	.300	—	.400	4 Rich
	527201, 03	.520	1"	#2	.150	—	.325	—	.400	4 Rich
	527204, 06	.520	1"	#2	.150	—	.325	—	.400	2 Rich
1978	10001047	.520	1"	—	.150	—	.325	.400	.350	1 Rich
	10001048	.520	1"	—	.150	—	.300	.400	.350	2 Rich
	10001049	.520	1"	—	.150	—	.325	.400	.350	1 Rich
	10001050	.520	1"	—	.150	—	.300	.400	.350	2 Rich
	10001052	.520	1"	—	.150	—	.325	.400	.350	2 Rich
	10001054	.520	1"	—	.150	—	.325	.400	.350	2 Rich
	10004048	.520	1"	—	.150	—	.300	—	.350	2 Rich
	10004049	.520	1"	—	.150	—	.300	—	.350	2 Rich
1979	466361	.500	—	—	.110	—	.250	—	.350	2 Rich
	466362	.500	—	—	.110	—	.250	—	.350	2 Rich
	466363	.500	—	—	.110	—	.250	—	.350	2 Rich
	466364	.500	—	—	.110	—	.250	—	.350	2 Rich
	466365	.500	—	—	.130	—	.305	—	.350	1 Rich
	466366	.500	—	—	.130	—	.305	—	.350	1 Rich
	466367	.500	—	—	.130	—	.305	—	.350	1 Rich
	466368	.500	—	—	.130	—	.305	—	.350	1 Rich
	466369	.500	—	—	.110	—	.245	—	.350	2 Rich
	466370	.500	—	—	.110	—	.250	—	.350	2 Rich
	466371	.500	—	—	.110	—	.245	—	.350	2 Rich
	466372	.500	—	—	.110	—	.250	—	.350	2 Rich
	466373	.500	—	—	.130	—	.305	—	.350	1 Rich
	466374	.500	—	—	.130	—	.305	—	.350	1 Rich
	466375	.500	—	—	.130	—	.305	—	.350	1 Rich
	466376	.500	—	—	.130	—	.305	—	.350	1 Rich
1980	14004461	.500	—	—	.110	—	.120	—	.350	—
	14004462	.500	—	—	.110	—	.120	—	.350	—
	14004463	.500	—	—	.110	—	.120	—	.350	—
	14004464	.500	—	—	.110	—	.120	—	.350	—
	14004465	.500	—	—	.110	—	.120	—	.350	—

Continued

5210 CARB. ADJUSTMENT SPECIFICATIONS—continued

See Tune Up Chart in car chapter for curb and fast idle speeds.

Year	Carb. Part No.	Float Level (Dry)	Float Drop	Pump Position	Fast Idle Cam Index	Vacuum Plate Pulldown	Vacuum Break		Unloader Setting	Choke Setting
							Primary	Secondary		
	14004466	.500	—	—	.110	—	.120	—	.350	—
	14004467	.500	—	—	.110	—	.120	—	.350	—
	14004468	.500	—	—	.110	—	.120	—	.350	—

①—Manual trans., #2; auto. trans., #1.

MODEL 5210

The Holley 5210 two-barrel carburetor, Figs. 1 and 2, has a number of unique features. An automatic choke system activated by a water heated bi-metal thermostatic coil and a primary venturi smaller in size than the secondary venturi.

An Exhaust Gas Recirculation (EGR) system is used on all applications with the EGR valve located in the intake manifold.

Carburetors used on 1977–78 vehicles use a primary and secondary vacuum break. The secondary vacuum break is used on some vehicles.

Float Adjustment

Fig. 3—With the air horn inverted and the float tang resting lightly on the spring loaded fuel inlet needle, measure the clearance between the bowl cover and the end of each float. Refer to *Holley 5210 Specifications Chart*. Adjust by bending the float tang as required.

Fig. 4   Fast idle cam index adjustment 5210 Holley carburetor

1 WITH AIR HORN INVERTED INSERT SPECIFIED PLUG GAUGE BETWEEN FLOAT AND AIR HORN

2 BEND TANG TO ADJUST

Fig. 3   Checking float level on 5210 carburetor

SOLENOID ASSISTED BOWL VENT

IDLE SOLENOID

ELECTRIC CHOKE

CHOKE VACUUM BREAK

CURB IDLE ADJUSTMENT SCREW

SOLENOID ADJUSTMENT SCREW

HOT IDLE COMPENSATOR

Fig. 1   Holley 5210 2 barrel carburetor

GAUGE

PUSH INWARD AGAINST STOP

USE ALLEN WRENCH TO ADJUST

Fig. 5   Vacuum pull down adjustment 5210 Holley carburetor

1 REMOVE THREE SCREWS AND REMOVE CHOKE COIL ASSEMBLY

4 TAKE SLACK OUT OF LINKAGE IN THE OPEN CHOKE DIRECTION

5 INSERT SPECIFIED GAUGE BETWEEN LOWER EDGE OF CHOKE VALVE & INSIDE AIR HORN WALL NOTE: HOLD GAUGE VERTICAL

3 PUSH SHAFT AGAINST STOP

6 TURN ADJUSTING SCREW TO OBTAIN CLEARANCE

7 INSTALL CHOKE COIL ASSEMBLY AND SET TO SPEC.

2 PUSH INSIDE CHOKE COIL LEVER CLOCKWISE TO CLOSE CHOKE VALVE

Fig. 5A   Primary vacuum break adjustment 5210 Holley carburetor

CARBURETORS

1. Fuel Inlet Nut
2. Gasket
3. Filter
4. Spring
5. Studs, Air Cleaner Attachment
6. Air Horn
7. Gasket
8. High Speed Bleed
9. Main Well Tube
10. Pump Discharge Nozzle
11. Gasket
12. Float Shaft
13. Discharge Check Ball
14. Float
15. Retainer
16. Secondary Idle Jet
17. Carburetor Body Assembly
18. Idle Stop Solenoid
19. Secondary Throttle Lever
20. Throttle Return Spring
21. Idle Lever
22. Secondary Operating Lever Return Spring
23. Secondary Operating Lever
24. Throttle Lever
25. Bushing
26. Fast Idle Rod
27. Fast Idle Lever
28. Bushing
29. Low Idle Screw
30. Fuel Mixture Screw
31. Retainer
32. Primary Idle Jet
33. Return Spring
34. Secondary Throttle Plate
35. Fuel Inlet Needle and Seat Assembly
36. Power Valve Economizer Assembly
37. Choke Rod Seal
38. Choke Plates
39. Choke Shaft and Lever
40. Choke Rod
41. Power Valve
42. Power Valve Assembly
43. Seat
44. Spring
45. Primary Throttle Shaft and Lever Assembly
46. Primary Throttle Plate
47. Accelerator Pump
48. Accelerator Pump Cover
49. Mixture Screw Limiter Cap
50. Choke Housing Shaft
51. Choke Lever
52. Fast Idle Cam Spring
53. Fast Idle Cam
54. Choke Housing
55. Gasket
56. Thermostatic Housing
57. Retainer
58. Gasket
59. Water Cover
60. Diaphragm and Shaft
61. Return Spring
62. Choke Diaphragm Cover
63. Hex Head Screw
64. Cover Screw

Fig. 2 Exploded view of a typical Holley 5210 carburetor

Fig. 5B   Secondary vacuum break adjustment 5210 Holley carburetor

Fig. 6   Secondary throttle plate adjustment

Fig. 7   Fast idle adjustment 5210 Holley carburetor

Fig. 8   Unloader adjustment. 1977–79 units

Fast Idle Cam Index Adjustment

Fig. 4—Place the fast idle screw on the second step of the fast idle cam and against the shoulder of the first step. Place a drill or gauge on the down stream side of the choke plate. Refer to *5210 Specifications Chart*. Adjust by bending the choke lever tang.

Vacuum Plate Pulldown Adjustment

Fig. 5—Remove the three hex headed screws and ring retaining the choke bimetal cover. Do not remove the choke water housing screw if adjusting on the car. Pull the choke water housing and bimetal cover assembly out of the way. With a screwdriver or suitable tool, push the diaphragm stem back against the stop. Place drill or gauge on the down stream side of the primary choke plate. Take all the slack out of the linkage. Refer to *5210 Specifications Chart*. Adjust by turning adjusting screw in or out with an 5/32 inch Allen wrench.

Vacuum Break

Primary, 1977–80
Fig. 5A—Remove choke coil assembly, then push inside choke coil lever clockwise to close choke valve and push shaft against stop to remove slack from linkage in open choke direction. Refer to 5210 Specifications Chart and insert specified gauge between lower edge of choke valve and inside air horn wall. Adjust by turning screw to obtain clearance.

Secondary, 1977–78
Fig. 5B—Remove choke coil assembly and place cam follower on highest step of fast idle cam. Using an outside vacuum source, seat diaphragm, then push inside choke coil lever clockwise to close choke valve. Refer to 5210 Specifications Chart and insert specified gauge between lower edge of choke valve and inside air horn wall. To adjust, bend rod.

Secondary Throttle Plate Adjustment

Fig. 6—Back out the secondary throttle stop screw, until the secondary throttle plate seats in the carburetor bore. Turn screw in until it makes contact with tab on the secondary throttle lever, then turn screw in an additional 1/4 turn.

Fast Idle Adjustment

Fig. 7—With engine at operating temperature, air cleaner off, choke off, A/C off and EGR valve free to operate, position fast idle screw on second step of fast idle cam and adjust by turning fast idle screw in or out. Refer to 5210 Specifications Chart.

Unloader (Dechoke) Adjustment

1977–80 Units
Fig. 8—Position throttle in wide open position and insert specified gauge between lower edge of choke valve and air horn wall. To adjust, bend fast idle lever tang.

CARBURETORS

MODEL 5220 ADJUSTMENT SPECIFICATIONS

See Tune Up Chart in car chapters for curb and fast idle speeds.

Year	Model No.	Float Level	Float Drop	Acc. Pump Hole No.	Choke Vacuum Kick	Choke Setting
1978	R-8376A	.480	1⅞"	2	.070	2 Rich
	R-8384A	.480	1⅞"	2	.070	2 Rich
	R-8385A	.480	1⅞"	2	.070	2 Rich
	R-8386A	.480	1⅞"	2	.070	2 Rich
	R-8387A	.480	1⅞"	2	.070	2 Rich
	R-8504A	.480	1⅞"	2	.070	2 Rich
	R-8505A	.480	1⅞"	2	.070	2 Rich
	R-8506A	.480	1⅞"	2	.070	2 Rich
	R-8507A	.480	1⅞"	2	.070	2 Rich
	R-8630A	.480	1⅞"	2	.070	2 Rich
	R-8631A	.480	1⅞"	2	.070	2 Rich
	R-8632A	.480	1⅞"	2	.070	2 Rich
1979	R-8451A	.480	1⅞"	2	.070	2 Rich
	R-8524A	.480	1⅞"	2	.040	2 Rich
	R-8525A	.480	1⅞"	2	.070	2 Rich
	R-8526A	.480	1⅞"	2	.040	2 Rich
	R-8527A	.480	1⅞"	2	.070	2 Rich
	R-8528A	.480	1⅞"	2	.040	2 Rich
	R-8529A	.480	1⅞"	2	.070	2 Rich
	R-8530A	.480	1⅞"	2	.040	2 Rich
	R-9026A	.480	1⅞"	2	.040	2 Rich
	R-9028A	.480	1⅞"	2	.040	2 Rich
1980	R-8676A	.480	1⅞"	2	.070	—
	R-8840A	.480	1⅞"	2	.070	—
	R-8841A	.480	1⅞"	2	.040	—
	R-8842A	.480	1⅞"	2	.040	—
	R-9108A	.480	1⅞"	2	.070	—
	R-9109A	.480	1⅞"	2	.100	—
	R-911A	.480	1⅞"	2	.040	—
	R-9395A	.480	1⅞"	2	.070	—
	R-9396A	.480	1⅞"	2	.070	—
	R-9397A	.480	1⅞"	2	.040	—
	R-9398A	.480	1⅞"	2	.040	—

MODEL 5220

The Holley model 5220, Figs. 1 and 2, is a staged dual venturi carburetor. The primary bore or venturi is smaller than the secondary bore. The secondary stage is mechanically operated by linkage connecting the primary and secondary throttle levers. The primary stage includes a curb idle and transfer system, diaphragm type accelerator pump system, main metering system and power enrichment system. The secondary stage includes a main metering system and power system. Both the primary and secondary venturi draw fuel from a common fuel bowl. The electric automatic choke has a bimetal two stage heating element. The carburetor also has an electronic solenoid and a vacuum operated bowl vent.

Float Level Adjustment

Figs. 3 & 4—Invert air horn and insert specified gauge between float and air horn. To adjust, use a small screwdriver to bend tang.

Float Drop Adjustment

Figs. 5 & 6—Using a suitable depth gauge, measure float drop. To adjust, use a small screwdriver to bend tang.

Choke Vacuum Kick Adjustment

Fig. 7—Open throttle, close choke, then close throttle to trap fast idle system in closed choke position. Using an external vacuum source, apply 15 inches of vacuum to choke diaphragm. Apply closing pressure to position choke at smallest opening without distorting linkage. An internal spring will compress to a stop inside choke system. Insert specified gauge between upper edge of choke valve and air horn wall at primary throttle end of carburetor. To adjust, rotate allen head screw in center of diaphragm housing.

Fast Idle Speed Adjustment

Fig. 8—Remove top of air cleaner and eliminate EGR signal. Cap or plug all disconnected vacuum fittings. Do not disconnect vacuum

HEATED AIR INLET AND VACUUM TRANSDUCER

ELECTRIC CHOKE

ELECTRIC BOWL VENT DIAPHRAGM

HARNESS CONNECTORS

CHOKE VALVES

IDLE STOP SOLENOID

TO VACUUM TRANSDUCER

CARBURETOR BOWL VENT

WIDE OPEN THROTTLE CUT-OUT SWITCH

CHOKE DIAPHRAGM

IDLE STOP SOLENOID

TO PCV VALVE

FUEL INLET

THROTTLE POSITION TRANSDUCER (MANUAL TRANSMISSION ONLY)

AIR PUMP DIVERTER VALVE

IDLE MIXTURE SCREW WITH LIMITER CAP

TO CCEGR SWITCH

TO VAPOR CANISTER

Fig. 1 Holley model 5220 carburetor. Vehicles equipped with air conditioning (Typical)

HEATED AIR INLET AND VACUUM TRANSDUCER

ELECTRIC CHOKE

ELECTRIC BOWL VENT DIAPHRAGM

HARNESS CONNECTORS

CHOKE VALVES

IDLE STOP SOLENOID

TO VACUUM TRANSDUCER

CARBURETOR BOWL VENT

CHOKE DIAPHRAGM

IDLE STOP SOLENOID

TO PCV VALVE

FUEL INLET

THROTTLE POSITION TRANSDUCER (MANUAL TRANSMISSION ONLY)

AIR PUMP DIVERTER VALVE

IDLE MIXTURE SCREW WITH LIMITER CAP

TO CCEGR SWITCH

TO VAPOR CANISTER

Fig. 2 Holley model 5220 carburetor. Vehicles less air conditioning (Typical)

CARBURETORS

Fig. 3 Measuring float level. 5220 carburetor

Fig. 4 Adjusting float level. 5220 carburetor

Fig. 5 Measuring float drop. 5220 carburetor

Fig. 6 Adjusting float drop. 5220 carburetor

Fig. 7 Choke vacuum kick adjustment. 5220 carburetor

Fig. 8 Fast idle speed adjustment. 5220 carburetor (Typical)

hose to spark control computer. Use a jumper wire to ground idle stop switch. Turn A/C "Off". Disconnect engine cooling fan at radiator and complete the circuit at plug with a jumper wire to energize fan. Apply parking brake, place transmission in Neutral with engine "Off", open throttle slightly and place lowest speed step of fast idle cam under adjusting screw. Start engine and determine stabilized speed. The choke valve must be fully open. If engine continues to rise, the idle stop switch is not grounded properly. To adjust speed, turn speed screw to obtain proper RPM. Reposition screw on cam after each adjustment to provide proper throttle closing torque and screw position.

Choke Setting Adjustment

Loosen choke coil cap retaining screws and rotate cap assembly to align mark on cap with specified mark on housing. Tighten choke coil cap retaining screws.

HOLLEY MODEL 6500 ADJUSTMENT SPECIFICATIONS

See Tune Up Chart in car chapters for curb and fast idle speeds.

Year	Carb. Model	Float Level	Pump Level Hole No.	Choke Plate Pulldown	Fast Idle Cam Clearance	Dechoke	Choke Setting
FORD MOTOR CO.							
1979	D9EE-AEC	15/32	#2	.24	.12	.24	2 Rich
	D9EE-AFC	15/32	#2	.24	.12	.24	2 Rich
	D9EE-AGC	15/32	#2	.24	.12	.24	2 Rich
	D9EE-AHC	15/32	#2	.24	.12	.24	2 Rich
	D9EE-AJC	15/32	#2	.24	.12	.24	1 Rich
	D9EE-AKC	15/32	#2	.24	.12	.24	1 Rich
	D9EE-AZA	15/32	#2	.24	.12	.24	2 Rich
	D9EE-BAA	15/32	#2	.24	.12	.24	2 Rich
	D9EE-BBA	15/32	#2	.24	.12	.24	2 Rich
	D9EE-BCA	15/32	#2	.24	.12	.24	2 Rich
	D9ZE-SB	15/32	#2	.24	.12	.24	2 Rich
	D9ZE-TB	15/32	#2	.24	.12	.24	2 Rich
	EE0E-NA	15/32	#2	.24	.12	.24	Index
	EE0E-NC	15/32	#3	.24	.12	.39	—
	EE0E-ND	15/32	#3	.24	.12	.39	—
	EE0E-VA	15/32	#2	.24	.12	.24	—

Continued

HOLLEY MODEL 6500 ADJUSTMENT SPECIFICATIONS—Continued

See Tune Up Chart in car chapters for curb and fast idle speeds.

Year	Carb. Model	Float Level	Pump Level Hole No.	Choke Plate Pulldown	Fast Idle Cam Clearance	Dechoke	Choke Setting
	EE0E-VC	15/32	#3	.24	.12	.39	Index
	EE0E-VD	15/32	#3	.24	.12	.39	—
	EEZE-AFA	15/32	#2	.24	.12	.39	Index
	EEZE-AFC	15/32	—	.24	.12	.39	—
	EEZE-SA	15/32	#2	.24	.12	.39	Index
	EEZE-SC	15/32	—	.24	.12	.39	—
1981	E1DE-DA	15/32	#3	.24	.12	.39	—
	E1DE-EA	15/32	#3	.24	.12	.39	—
	E1ZE-RA	15/32	#3	.24	.12	.39	—
	E1ZE-SA	15/32	#3	.24	.12	.39	—
1982	E2ZE-ACA	15/32	#3	.276	.118	.394	—
	E2ZE-ADA	15/32	#3	.276	.118	.394	—
	E2ZE-APA	15/32	#2	.276	.118	.394	—
	E2ZE-ARA	15/32	#2	.276	.118	.394	—
	E2ZE-UA	15/32	#3	.276	.118	.394	—
	E2ZE-VA	15/32	#3	.276	.118	.394	—

MODEL 6500

The Holley Model 6500 carburetor, Fig. 1, is used with the Ford Feedback Electronic Engine Control System. This carburetor is basically the same as the Motorcraft Model 5200 as described elsewhere in this chapter. The Model 6500 is equipped with an externally variable auxiliary fuel metering system in place of the enrichment valve used on the Motorcraft Model 5200. The auxiliary system consists of a metering valve assembly, metering valve operating piston and a diaphragm.

The feedback metering valve supplements fuel entering the main well through the conventional metering jet and channel. The amount of fuel entering the main well through the metering valve depends on the position of the tapered metering rod in the orifice. The position of the metering rod depends on the metering rod operation piston assembly.

Control vacuum from the vacuum regulator solenoid is transmitted to the cavity above the metering rod diaphragm. When no vacuum is present, the valve spring causes the valve to move to the lowest (richest) position and maximum fuel can pass through the orifice. As vacuum is applied to the diaphragm, spring pressure is overcome and the metering rod rises, reducing the orifice area and less fuel passes through the orifice. The metering valve is calibrated so the maximum vacuum signal supplied by the vacuum regulator solenoid raises the rod to the highest (leanest) position.

Adjustments

All adjustments for the Model 6500 are the same as the Motorcraft Model 5200 as described elsewhere in this chapter, however, the choke plate vacuum pulldown adjustment is different.

Choke Plate Vacuum Pulldown Adjustment

NOTE: On 1981–82 vehicles, it is necessary to remove the carburetor from the vehicle to remove rivets retaining the choke cover to choke housing. Using a 1/8 inch or No. 30 drill

Fig. 1   Model 6500 carburetor

Fig. 2   Fuel metering system

CARBURETORS

Fig. 3 Measuring choke plate vacuum pulldown

bit, remove rivet heads, then drive rivets out using a 1/8 inch diameter punch.

1. Remove choke cap, bi-metal heater assembly and plastic shield.
2. Place fast idle speed adjusting screw on top step of fast idle cam.
3. Using a suitable screwdriver, push diaphragm stem back against stop and place specified gauge between lower edge of choke valve and air horn wall, Fig. 3.
4. Remove slack from choke linkage by attaching a rubber band to choke operating lever, Fig. 3.
5. To adjust, rotate vacuum diaphragm adjusting screw as required to obtain proper setting, Fig. 4.

Fig. 4 Adjusting choke plate vacuum pulldown

MODEL 6510-C ADJUSTMENT SPECIFICATIONS

See Tune-Up chart in car chapter for curb and fast idle speeds.

Year	Carb. Model	Float level	Float Drop	Fast Idle Cam	Vacuum Break	Unloader	Choke Coil	Secondary Throttle Stop Screw
GENERAL MOTORS								
1978	10001056	.520	1	.150	.250	.350	1 Rich	①
	10001058	.520	1	.150	.250	.350	1 Rich	①
	10005603	.520	1	.150	.275	.350	2 Rich	①
	10005604	.520	1	.150	.275	.350	2 Rich	①
1979	10008489	.520	1	.150	.250	.350	2 Rich	①
	10008490	.520	1	.150	.250	.350	2 Rich	①
	10008491	.520	1	.150	.250	.350	2 Rich	①
	10008492	.520	1	.150	.250	.350	2 Rich	①
	10009973	.520	1	.150	.275	.350	2 Rich	①
	10009974	.520	1	.150	.275	.350	2 Rich	①
1980	14004469	.500	—	.130	.300	.350	—	①
	14004470	.500	—	.130	.300	.350	—	①
	14004471	.500	—	.130	.300	.350	—	①
	14004472	.500	—	.130	.300	.350	—	①
1981	14004768, 769	.500	—	.130	.300	.350	—	①
	14004770, 771	.500	—	.130	.300	.350	—	①
	14004777	.500	—	.130	.300	.350	—	①
1982	14032364	.500	—	.080	.270	.350	—	①
	14032365	.500	—	.080	.270	.350	—	①
	14032366	.500	—	.080	.270	.350	—	①
	14032367	.500	—	.080	.270	.350	—	①
	14032368	.500	—	.080	.270	.350	—	①
	14032369	.500	—	.080	.270	.350	—	①
	14032370	.500	—	.080	.270	.350	—	①
	14032371	.500	—	.080	.270	.350	—	①
	14033392	.500	—	.080	.270	.350	—	①
	14033393	.500	—	.080	.270	.350	—	①
	14047072	.500	—	.080	.270	.350	—	①

①—Refer to text for adjustment.

Fig. 1   Holley model 6510-C carburetor

Fig. 2   Holley model 6510-C carburetor

① WITH AIR HORN INVERTED INSERT SPECIFIED PLUG GAUGE BETWEEN FLOAT AND AIR HORN

② BEND TANG TO ADJUST

Fig. 3   Float level adjustment

② BEND TANG IF ADJUSTMENT REQUIRED

① WITH AIR HORN REMOVED DISTANCE FROM BOTTOM OF AIR HORN TO TOP OF FLOAT SHOULD BE 1" ±1/8"

Fig. 4   Float drop adjustment

② INSERT SPECIFIED GAUGE BETWEEN LOWER EDGE OF CHOKE VALVE & INSIDE AIR HORN WALL
   NOTE: HOLD GAUGE VERTICAL

③ BEND TANG IF ADJUSTMENT IS REQUIRED:

① SET FAST IDLE CAM SO THAT SCREW IS HELD AGAINST SECOND HIGH STEP OF CAM

Fig. 5   Fast idle cam adjustment

① REMOVE THREE SCREWS AND REMOVE CHOKE COIL ASSEMBLY

④ TAKE SLACK OUT OF LINKAGE IN THE OPEN CHOKE DIRECTION

③ PUSH SHAFT AGAINST STOP

⑤ INSERT SPECIFIED GAUGE BETWEEN LOWER EDGE OF CHOKE VALVE & INSIDE AIR HORN WALL
   NOTE: HOLD GAUGE VERTICAL

⑥ TURN ADJUSTING SCREW TO OBTAIN CLEARANCE

⑦ INSTALL CHOKE COIL ASSEMBLY AND SET TO SPEC.

② PUSH INSIDE CHOKE COIL LEVER CLOCKWISE TO CLOSE CHOKE VALVE

Fig. 6   Vacuum break adjustment. 1978–79 Units.

MODEL 6510-C

Description

The Holley Model 6510-C carburetor, Figs. 1 and 2, is a controlled air-fuel ratio carburetor of a staged two barrel design with the primary bore smaller in size than the secondary bore. The secondary throttle is mechanically operated through interconnected linkage. This carburetor is used with the Electronic Fuel Control (EFC) system described elsewhere in this manual.

This carburetor utilizes four basic fuel metering systems: idle system, feedback controlled main metering system, acceleration system and power enrichment system.

The idle system is a separate factory adjusted system which provides a proper air-fuel mixture for both idle and low speed operation. The main metering system provides the correct air-fuel mixture for all normal and cruising speeds and aids in power enrichment. Fuel for acceleration is provided by the mechanically operated acceleration system. The power enrichment system consists of the accelerator

pump discharge nozzle pullover and a secondary stage airflow regulated pullover system. These systems are used in conjunction with the main metering systems to provide adequate performance during periods of moderate to heavy acceleration.

Located in the primary bore are one or two vacuum ports for distributor vacuum spark advance, EGR vacuum and vapor canister purge depending upon emission control system usage.

A solenoid assisted vacuum operated bowl vent is used to vent the fuel vapors to the can-

Fig. 6A   Vacuum break adjustment. 1980–82 Units

Fig. 7   Unloader adjustment

Fig. 8   Choke coil adjustment

Fig. 9   Secondary throttle stop screw adjustment

ister and not into the engine when the engine is operating. The vent is used in conjunction with existing internal venting through the air horn.

A hot idle compensator is used to maintain smooth engine idle during periods of excessive high temperature operation by allowing additional air to enter the primary throttle bore.

An electrically heated automatic choke system is used to provide correct air-fuel mixtures for cold start and warm-up operation. The automatic choke system is equipped with a vacuum break controlled by an external vacuum supply and a vacuum delay valve to prevent prolonged fast idle.

Fig. 10   Fast idle speed adjustment

ADJUSTMENTS

Float Level Adjustment

Fig. 3—With air horn inverted, insert specified gauge between float and air horn. Bend tang to adjust.

Float Drop Adjustment

Fig. 4—With air horn removed, measure distance between bottom of air horn and top of float. Refer to specifications chart for correct measurement. Bend tang to adjust.

Fast Idle Cam Adjustment

Fig. 5—Set fast idle cam in position so the screw contacts second high step. Insert specified gauge between lower edge of choke valve and air horn wall. Bend tang to adjust.

Vacuum Break Adjustment

1978–79 Units
Fig. 6—Remove choke coil assembly. Push choke coil lever clockwise to close choke valve. Push vacuum break shaft against stop. Remove slack from linkage in the choke open direction. Insert specified gauge between lower edge of choke valve and air horn wall. Rotate vacuum break adjusting screw to obtain specified clearance. Install and adjust choke coil assembly.

1980–82 Units
Fig. 6A—Apply an external vacuum source to vacuum break to seat diaphragm. Rotate fast idle cam clockwise to close choke valve. Remove slack from linkage in the choke open direction. Insert the specified gauge between choke valve and air horn wall. Turn adjusting screw to obtain clearance.

Unloader Adjustment

Fig. 7—Place throttle lever in wide open position. Insert specified gauge between lower edge of choke valve and air horn wall. Bend tang at existing radius to adjust.

Choke Coil Adjustment

Fig. 8—Loosen choke coil cover retaining screws with choke coil lever located inside tang, rotate cover to align mark on cover with specified mark on choke coil housing. Tighten choke coil cover retaining screws.

Secondary Throttle Stop Screw Adjustment

Fig. 9—Back off secondary throttle stop screw until clear of throttle lever. Rotate screw inward until the screw contacts secondary throttle lever, then an additional 1/4 turn.

Fast Idle Speed Adjustment

Fig. 10—With curb idle speed adjusted, place transmission in neutral or park and place fast idle screw on high step of cam. Disconnect and plug EGR port. Rotate fast idle adjusting screw to obtain specified fast idle speed.

MODEL 6520 ADJUSTMENT SPECIFICATIONS

See Tune Up Chart in car chapter for curb and fast idle speeds.

Year	Model No.	Float Level	Float Drop	Acc. Pump Hole No.	Choke Vacuum Kick	Choke Setting
1981	R-9052A	.480	$1\frac{7}{8}$	2	.070	—
	R-9053A	.480	$1\frac{7}{8}$	2	.070	—
	R-9054A	.480	$1\frac{7}{8}$	2	.040	—
	R-9055A	.480	$1\frac{7}{8}$	2	.040	—
	R-9060A	.480	$1\frac{7}{8}$	2	.030	—
	R-9061A	.480	$1\frac{7}{8}$	2	.030	—
	R-9125A	.480	$1\frac{7}{8}$	2	.030	—
	R-9126A	.480	$1\frac{7}{8}$	2	.030	—
	R-9602A	.480	$1\frac{7}{8}$	2	.065	—
	R-9603A	.480	$1\frac{7}{8}$	2	.065	—
	R-9604A	.480	$1\frac{7}{8}$	2	.065	—
	R-9605A	.480	$1\frac{7}{8}$	2	.065	—
1982	R-9503A	.480	$1\frac{7}{8}$	3	.060	—
	R-9504A	.480	$1\frac{7}{8}$	3	.070	—
	R-9505A	.480	$1\frac{7}{8}$	3	.070	—
	R-9506A	.480	$1\frac{7}{8}$	3	.070	—
	R-9507A	.480	$1\frac{7}{8}$	3	.085	—
	R-9508A	.480	$1\frac{7}{8}$	3	.085	—
	R-9509A	.480	$1\frac{7}{8}$	3	.085	—
	R-9510A	.480	$1\frac{7}{8}$	3	.085	—
	R-9750A	.480	$1\frac{7}{8}$	3	.060	—
	R-9751A	.480	$1\frac{7}{8}$	3	.060	—
	R-9752A	.480	$1\frac{7}{8}$	3	.070	—
	R-9753A	.480	$1\frac{7}{8}$	3	.070	—
	R-9822A	.480	$1\frac{7}{8}$	2	.047	—
	R-9823A	.480	$1\frac{7}{8}$	2	.047	—
	R-9824A	.480	$1\frac{7}{8}$	2	.040	—

MODEL 6520

The Holley model 6520, Fig. 1, is a staged dual venturi electronic feedback carburetor. The primary bore is smaller than the secondary bore. The secondary stage is mechanically operated by linkage connecting the primary and secondary throttle levers. The primary stage includes a curb idle and transfer system, diaphragm type accelerator pump system, main metering system and a fuel regulator solenoid responsive to oxygen sensor. The secondary stage includes a main metering system and power system. Both the primary and secondary venturi draw fuel from a common fuel bowl. The electric automatic choke incorporates a two stage heating element. On manual transmission carburetors, only one choke valve is used, while on automatic transmission carburetors, two choke valves are used.

The 6520 electronic feedback carburetor also incorporates a duty cycle solenoid which provides a limited regulation of air-fuel ratio

Fig. 1 Holley Model 6520 Carburetor

Fig. 2   Measuring float level. 6520 carburetor

Fig. 3   Adjusting float level. 6520 carburetor

Fig. 4   Measuring float drop. 6520 carburetor

Fig. 5   Adjusting float drop. 6520 carburetor

Fig. 6   Adjusting choke vacuum kick. 6520 carburetor

in response to electrical signals from the spark control computer. The solenoid meters the main fuel system and operates in parallel with a conventional fixed main metering jet. When there is no electrical signal applied to the solenoid, the valve spring pushes upward through the main system fuel valve, fully uncovering the solenoid controlled main metering orifice so that the richest condition exists within the carburetor for any given airflow. When the electrical signal is applied to the solenoid, the field windings are energized, thus causing the armature to move the push rod and main system valve downward against the valve spring. This movement will continue until the main system valve bottoms against the main system valve seat. In this position the solenoid controlled main metering orifice is fully sealed so that the leanest condition exists within the carburetor for any given airflow. This condition will remain unchanged until the signal from the spark control computer to the solenoid is switched off. The main system fuel maybe regulated between richest and leanest limits by controlling the amount of time that the solenoid is in the power on position. Under normal operating conditions, 12 volts at a frequency of 10 Hz is applied to the field windings. By controlling the duration of the voltage signal, the power on time to total time, referred to as the duty cycle, is established.

Float Level Adjustment

Figs. 2 & 3—Invert air horn and insert specified gauge between float and air horn. To adjust, use a small screwdriver to bend tang.

Float Drop Adjustment

Figs. 4 & 5—Using a suitable depth gauge measure float drop. To adjust, use a small screwdriver to bend tang.

Choke Vacuum Kick Adjustment

Fig. 6—Open throttle and close choke valve, then close throttle to retain choke valve in the closed position. Disconnect vacuum hose from carburetor and connect an external vacuum source. Apply 15 inches Hg. of vacuum or more. Apply sufficient closing pressure to choke valve, using care not to distort linkage. Note that an internal spring will compress to a stop within the choke system. Insert the specified gauge in center area between top of choke valve and air horn wall at primary throttle end of carburetor. Adjust clearance by rotating the allen head screw in center of diaphragm housing.

MIKUNI CARBURETOR ADJUSTMENT SPECIFICATIONS

See Tune Up Chart in Car Chapter for curb and fast idle speeds.

Year	Model No.	Float Level	Fast Idle Opening At 68°F	Choke Breaker Opening At 14°F	Unloader Opening At 32°F
1981–82	MD025430	.779	14.5°	.067	.051
	MD025432	.779	14.5°	.067	.051

MIKUNI MODELS

The Mikuni carburetor, Fig. 1, is a conventional downdraft two barrel compound type carburetor. The automatic choke on these units is of the thermo-wax type which is controlled by engine coolant temperature. The main body on these units consists of a black resin compound. Other features of these units include a diaphragm type accelerator pump, bowl vent, fuel cut-off solenoid, air switching valve, sub EGR valve, coasting air valve, jet air control valve. California units also incorporate a high altitude compensation system.

Float Level Adjustment

Fig. 2—Invert air horn, with gasket removed, and measure distance from bottom of float to surface of air horn, using a suitable depth gauge. If reading is not within limits, the shim located under needle seat must be changed. Use shim kit MD606952 or equivalent, which has three shims with thicknesses of .0118 inch, .0157 inch and .0196 inch. Adding or removing a shim will change float level by three times the thickness of the shim.

Fig. 1   Mikuni carburetor assembly

Fig. 2   Float level adjustment. Mikuni carburetor

TUNE UP SERVICE

CONTENTS

Tune up service has become increasingly important to the modern automotive engine with its vastly improved power and performance. Improved fuel and electrical systems and especially the exhaust emission controls with their inherently critical settings, engines have become more sensitive to usage and operating conditions, which have a decided effect on power and performance. It is important, therefore, that this service be performed on the engine according to the recommendations of the vehicle manufacturer.

In addition to the servicing of spark plugs, ignition points and condenser, if equipped, a proper tune up includes a number of tests to check the condition of the engine and its related systems and uncover sources of future problems.

TUNE UP PROCEDURE

Since a quality tune up is dependent upon the proper operation of a number of systems, we have listed here in a logical sequence, the steps to be followed:
1. Diagnosis. This is to consist of a compression test, cylinder balance test, oscilloscope check, manifold vacuum test, charging circuit and cranking voltage test.
2. Service spark plugs.
3. Service ignition system, secondary wiring, distributor and coil.
4. Check and service battery and charging system.
5. Service manifold heat valve, if used.
6. Service carburetor, linkage, fuel and air filters and crankcase filter (if equipped).
7. Check operation of various emission control devices.

Once these mechanical checks have been performed the tune up can be finalized. The final steps are:
1. Setting the dwell on 1977–79 American Motors 4-121 engines with standard ignition distributors.
2. Setting slow idle, idle fuel mixture, choke and ignition timing if adjustments are possible and within federal and state laws.
3. Adjusting the fast idle.
4. Checking ignition output and secondary resistance.
5. Road test.

DIAGNOSIS & TESTING

Before a satisfactory tune up can be performed, the existing condition of the engine and its related systems must be determined. A tune up should not be attempted if tests indicate internal engine problems such as burnt valves, worn rings, blown head gasket, etc., until such conditions have been corrected.

Oscilloscope Test

Although oscilloscopes differ in many ways, they all display a light or "trace" on a screen which measures the voltage present at a given point and time. As the ignition system operates, its voltage creates a pattern on the screen. This pattern, when read in accordance with the manufacturer's instructions for the particular unit, indicates the condition of the entire ignition system.

Compression Test

An engine cannot be tuned to develop maximum power and smooth performance unless the proper compression is obtained in each cylinder.

CAUTION: Before cranking engine for a compression test, the ignition system should be disabled. On all ignition systems except American Motors and General Motors H.E.I. with internal ignition coil, disconnect coil wire from distributor cap and ground wire to engine block. On American Motors and General Motors H.E.I. with internal ignition coils disconnect B+ lead from distributor cap.

1. Remove any foreign matter from around spark plugs by blowing out plug area with compressed air. Then remove plugs.
2. Remove air cleaner and block throttle and choke in wide open position.
3. Insert compression gauge firmly in spark plug opening and crank engine through at least four compression strokes to obtain highest possible reading.
4. Test and record compression of each cylinder. Compression should read within the limits given in the *Tune Up Charts* in the car chapters. Refer to chart, Fig. 1, for minimum compression pressures as indicated by percentages.
5. If one or more cylinders read low, inject about a tablespoon of engine oil on top of pistons in the low reading cylinders. Crank engine several times and recheck compression.
6. If compression is higher, it indicates worn piston rings. If compression does not improve, valves are sticking or seating poorly. If two adjacent cylinders show low compression and injecting oil does not improve the condition, the cause may be a head gasket leak between cylinders.

Manifold Vacuum Test

Manifold vacuum is affected by carburetor adjustment, valve timing, ignition timing, valve condition, cylinder compression, condition of positive crankcase ventilation system

MAXIMUM PSI	MINIMUM PSI 75%	MINIMUM PSI 80%	MAXIMUM PSI	MINIMUM PSI 75%	MINIMUM PSI 80%	MAXIMUM PSI	MINIMUM PSI 75%	MINIMUM PSI 80%
134	101	107	174	131	139	214	160	171
136	102	109	176	132	141	216	162	173
138	104	110	178	133	142	218	163	174
140	105	112	180	135	144	220	165	176
142	107	114	182	136	146	222	166	178
144	108	115	184	138	147	224	168	179
146	110	117	186	140	149	226	169	181
148	111	118	188	141	150	228	171	182
150	113	120	190	142	152	230	172	184
152	114	122	192	144	154	232	174	186
154	115	123	194	145	155	234	175	187
156	117	125	196	147	157	236	177	189
158	118	126	198	148	158	238	178	190
160	120	128	200	150	160	240	180	192
162	121	130	202	151	162	242	181	194
164	123	131	204	153	163	244	183	195
166	124	133	206	154	165	246	184	197
168	126	134	208	156	166	248	186	198
170	127	136	210	157	168	250	187	200
172	129	138	212	158	170			

Fig. 1 Compression pressure limit chart

Fig. 2 Checking ignition timing with timing light

Fig. 3 Spark plug details

and leakage of manifold, carburetor, carburetor spacer or cylinder head gaskets.

Because abnormal gauge readings may indicate that more than one of the above factors is at fault, use care in analyzing an abnormal reading. For example, if the vacuum is low, the correction of one item may increase the vacuum enough to indicate that the trouble has been corrected. It is important, therefore, that each cause of an abnormal reading be investigated and further tests conducted, where necessary, to arrive at the correct diagnosis of the trouble. To check manifold vacuum, proceed as follows:

1. Bring engine to operating temperature.
2. Connect an accurate vacuum gauge to the intake manifold.
3. Operate engine at recommended idle speed.
4. Check vacuum reading on gauge.

Test Conclusions

NORMAL READING: 18 inches or more. Allowance should be made for the effect of altitude on gauge reading.
LOW & STEADY: Loss of power in all cylinders possibly caused by late ignition or valve timing, or loss of compression.
VERY LOW: Intake manifold, carburetor spacer or head gasket leak.
NEEDLE FLUCTUATES STEADILY AS SPEED INCREASES: Partial or complete loss of power in one or more cylinders caused by a leaky head or manifold gasket, burnt valve, weak valve spring or a defect in the ignition system.
GRADUAL DROP IN READING AT IDLE SPEED: Excessive back pressure in exhaust system.
INTERMITTENT FLUCTUATION: Defect in ignition system or sticking valve.
SLOW FLUCTUATION OR DRIFTING OF NEEDLE: Improper idle mixture, carburetor, carburetor spacer, intake manifold gasket leak or restricted crankcase ventilation system.

Cranking Voltage Test

The condition of the starting circuit can be checked by connecting a voltmeter across the battery posts, grounding the coil so the engine will not fire and cranking the engine. If, during cranking, the voltage reading drops below 9.6 volts, there is high resistance in the circuit.

Charging Circuit Test

The performance of the charging circuit should be checked during any tuneup. See specific unit section of this manual for test procedures.

Ignition Timing

The use of a timing light, Fig. 2, is recommended for checking and setting ignition timing.

NOTE: The use of an inductive type timing light is recommended when checking and setting ignition timing on electronic ignition systems.

Some engines have a provision for monolithic method of ignition timing utilizing a timing receptacle designed to accept an electronic probe. The receptacle is usually mounted at the front of the engine and the electronic probe is connected to electronic equipment which reads out the engine timing. These engines can also be timed using a timing light.

ROUND GAGE

RIGHT

FLAT GAGE

WRONG

Fig. 4 Correct and incorrect spark plug gauges

NOTE: The timing light should be connected to the number 1 spark plug lead by the use of an adapter. The boots around the connections should not be pierced to connect the light as this can cause spark arcing and misfiring.

Combustion Efficiency Test

This test checks the carburetor air/fuel mixture by measuring the amount of various chemicals present in the engine exhaust under different conditions. By following the manufacturer's instructions for the specific unit, the carburetor idle, intermediate, high speed and accelerator pump circuits can be checked for proper operation.

This test is especially important when working on engines equipped with exhaust emission controls because of the more critical mixture adjustments on such units.

SERVICE

Spark Plugs

1. Examine firing ends of plugs for evidence of oil fouling gas fouling, burned or overheated condition. *Oil fouling is usually identified by wet, sludgy deposits caused by excessive oil consumption. Gas fouling is identified by dry, black, fluffy deposits caused by incomplete combustion. Burned or overheated spark plugs are identified by white, burned or blistered insulator nose and badly burned electrodes. Improper fuel, insufficient cooling or improper ignition timing normally are the cause. Normal conditions are usually identified by white powdery deposits or rusty-brown to grayish-tan powdery deposits.*

2. Clean plugs with a suitable sand blast cleaner following the manufacturers instructions.
3. Remove carbon and other deposits from threads with a stiff wire brush.

NOTE: Do not use brush to clean electrodes as small pieces of wire can stick inside plug and later cause misfiring.

4. Using a small file, dress center and side electrodes to obtain flat parallel surfaces, Fig. 3.
5. If flat surfaces were obtained on used spark plugs or when installing new spark plugs, use a flat-bladed spark plug gage to check the gap. If a flat surface was not obtained due to erosion, use a wire-type spark plug gage to check the gap, Fig. 4. Refer to the Tune Up Specifications in the car chapters for spark plug gap specifications.
6. Adjust the gap to specification by bending the side electrode, never the center electrode.
7. Be sure to install gaskets, if used. Install and torque spark plugs to specifications. Refer to the Engine Tightening Torque Specifications in the car chapters for torque specifications.

NOTE: Several fuel refiners in areas of the United States have introduced a manganese compound fuel additive (MMT) for use in unleaded fuel. Fuel treated with MMT causes the entire tip of the spark plug to be coated with a rust colored deposit as a result of the combustion process. This rust colored deposit may be diagnosed incorrectly as being coolant in the combustion chamber. Spark plug performance is not affected by MMT deposits.

SERVICE NOTE

Improper installation of spark plugs is one of the greatest single causes of unsatisfactory spark plug performance. Improper installation is the result of one or more of the following practices: 1) Installation of plugs with insufficient torque to fully seat the gasket; 2) excessive torque which changes gap settings; 3) installation of plugs on dirty gasket seal; 4) installation of plugs to corroded spark plug hole threads.

Failure to install plugs properly will cause them to operate at excessively high temperatures and result in reduced operating life under mild operation or complete destruction

under severe operation where the intense heat cannot be dissipated rapidly enough.

Always remove carbon deposits in hole threads before installing plugs. When corrosion is present in threads, normal torque is not sufficent to compress the plug gasket (if used) and early failure from overheating will result.

Always use a new gasket (if required) and wipe seats in head clean. The gasket must be fully compressed on clean seats to complete heat transfer and provide a gas tight seal in the cylinder. For this reason as well as the necessity of maintaining correct plug gap, the use of correct torque is extremely important during installation.

Ignition System

1. Check to be sure all connections are clean and tight. Repair or replace any wires that are frayed, loose, or damaged. Replace brittle or damaged spark plug wires.
2. Remove distributor cap, clean and inspect for cracks, carbon tracks and burned or corroded terminals. Replace cap if necessary.
3. Clean rotor and inspect for damage or deterioration. Replace rotor if necessary.
4. Check distributor centrifugal advance mechanism (if used) by turning distributor rotor in direction of running rotation as far as possible, then release rotor to see if springs return it to its retarded position. If rotor does not return readily, the distributor must be disassembled and cause of trouble corrected.
5. Using a suitable hand operated vacuum pump, check distributor vacuum advance mechanism diaphragm for free operation.
6. On 1977–79 American Motors 4-121 engine with standard ignition distributor, examine distributor points and clean or replace if necessary. Points with an overall gray color and only slight roughness or pitting need not be replaced.
7. On 1977–79 American Motors 4-121 engine with standard ignition distributor, clean dirty points with a clean point file. Use only a few strokes of the file. The file should not be used on other metals and should not be allowed to become dirty or greasy. *Never use emery cloth or sandpaper to clean points since particles will embed and cause arcing and rapid burning of points.* Do not attempt to remove all roughness nor dress the point surfaces

down smooth. Merely remove scale or dirt.

8. On 1977–79 American Motors 4-121 engine with standard ignition distributors, replace points that are badly burned or pitted. Where burned or badly pitted points are encountered, the ignition system and engine should be checked to determine the cause of the trouble so it can be eliminated. Unless the condition causing point burning is corrected, new points will provide no better service than the old points. See "Standard Ignition Distributors" chapter for an analysis of point burning or pitting, and for proper installation of points and condensor.

Battery & Cables

Inspect for signs of corrosion on battery, cables and surrounding area, loose or broken carriers, cracked or bulged cases, dirt and acid, electrolyte leakage and low electrolyte level. Fill cells to proper level with distilled water or water passed through a "demineralizer."

The top of the battery should be clean and the battery hold-down bolts properly tightened.

For best results when cleaning batteries, wash first with a dilute ammonia or soda solution to neutralize any acid present and then flush off with clean water. Care must be taken to keep vent plugs tight so that the neutralizing solution does not enter the battery.

To insure good contact, the battery cables should be tight on the battery posts. Oil battery terminal felt washer. If the battery posts or cables terminals are corroded, the cables should be cleaned separately with a soda solution and a wire brush.

If the battery has remained undercharged, check for a loose alternator belt, defective alternator, high resistance in charging circuit, oxidized voltage regulator contact points, or a low voltage setting.

If the battery has been using too much water, the voltage regulator setting may be too high.

Fuel System

All fuel filters and the air cleaner element should be serviced during a tune up.

Since carburetion is dependent in several ways on both compression and ignition, it should always be checked last when tuning an engine. Refer to the Carburetor Chapter for pertinent data on specific units.

Service Bulletins

Chevrolet Monza 2 + 2 Spark Plug Replacement

When replacing spark plugs on V8 engines equipped with air conditioning and power steering, it is not necessary to release the engine mounts. The following procedure should be used: Have available a 1", 1½" and a 3" extension which are customarily used in spark plug servicing. Also needed are a ⅝" spark plug socket and a flex handle. Obtain a 5" to 6" length of windshield wiper hose which should be attached to a No. 3 spark plug end to facilitate installation, Fig. 5.

Insert a ¼" × 1½" stud or rod into the windshield wiper hose to achieve some rigidity in the windshield wiper hose structure as shown

in Fig. 1. Then insert a ¼" × 1" bolt into other end of hose to allow for easier rotation. Now proceed to install No. 3 spark plug. Once the spark plug is started in the threads of the cylinder head, you may then remove the hose and proceed to tighten the spark plug with the appropriate tools. All other spark plugs can be replaced in the conventional manner using an applicable extension.

1981 Cadillac 4.1L V-6 Rough Engine Operation

If conditions of rough engine operation or poor driveability are encountered at speeds of approximately 50 mph, the distributor main-

shaft washer could be faulty, Fig. 6.

To diagnose this condition, connect an ignition scope to engine, then operate engine at approximately 1900 RPM and observe scope pattern. Using a suitable timing light, check ignition timing. If the scope pattern is erratic or indicates as high as ten ignition pulses, or ignition timing is retarded −10 degrees at 1800 RPM, check distributor date code. If date code is between 1A06 and 1D29, the existing wave washer should be removed and the replacement wave washer, part # 1984360 should be installed, Fig. 6. If the distributor date code does not fall within the limits, do not replace the wave washer as the condition is probably related to the fuel or ignition system.

DO NOT ADD OR REPLACE
NEW WAVE WASHER
UNLESS DAY BUILT CODE
IS BETWEEN IA06 THRU
ID29

DO NOT REMOVE
FLAT WASHER

PART # 1984360 WAVE WASHER
MUST BE INSTALLED
BETWEEN LARGE FLAT
WASHER AND DISTRIBUTOR
GEAR

Fig. 5   Monza 2 + 2 spark plug
replacement tool

SPARK PLUG

1/4" WIPER HOSE
5-6" LONG

1/4 x 1-1/2" STUD

1/4 x 1" BOLT

Fig. 6   Correct wave washer installation

Ignition Coils & Resistors

IGNITION SWITCH

DISTRIBUTOR

IGNITION COIL

BATTERY

PENCIL   PENCIL

FLARE   FLARE

CABLE   CABLE
TERMINAL   TERMINAL

RIGHT   WRONG

Fig. 2   Checking coil polarity

Fig. 1   Wiring connections for coil with negative ground system

IGNITION COILS

1977–79 American Motors 4-121 Engine with Standard Ignition Distributor

If poor ignition performance is obtained and the coil is suspected, it may be tested on the car or it may be removed for the test.

Ignition coils are often condemned when the trouble is actually in the ignition switch. A completely defective ignition switch will produce an open primary circuit, giving the same indications as if the coil were completely dead. A partly defective ignition switch will cause a weak spark.

By cutting the ignition switch out of the circuit, it can easily be determined whether the coil is defective or the fault lies in the ignition switch.

In the absence of any testing equipment a simple check of an ignition coil can be made as follows: Turn on ignition switch with breaker points closed. Remove the high tension cable from the center socket of the distributor cap and hold it 1/4" to 1/2" away from a clean spot on the engine. If the coil and other units connected to it are in good condition a spark should jump from the wire to the engine as the points are opened. If not, use a jumper wire from the distributor terminal to the engine; if the primary is in good condition a spark will occur.

All ignition coils with metal containers can be tested for grounded windings by placing one test clip on a clean part of the metal container and touching the other clip to the primary and high tension terminals. If the lamp lights or tiny sparks appear at the points of contact, the windings are grounded and the coil should be replaced.

Coil Polarity

Most coils are marked positive and negative at the primary terminals. When installing or connecting a coil be sure to make the connections as shown in Fig. 1. A reversal of this polarity may affect the performance of the engine (or the radio).

If the coil is not marked as to its polarity, it can be checked by holding any high tension wire about 1/4" away from its spark plug terminal with the engine running. Insert the point of a wooden lead pencil between the spark plug and the wire, Fig. 2. If the spark flares and has a slight orange tinge on the spark plug side of the pencil, polarity is correct. If the spark flares on the cable side, coil connections should be reversed.

AUXILIARY BALLAST RESISTOR

NORMAL BALLAST RESISTOR

Fig. 3   Dual ballast resistor, Chrysler Corp. electronic ignition system 1977–80. All exc. 1978–79 Omni & Horizon

Fig. 4   Ballast resistor. 1978–79 Omni, Horizon & 1981–82 Chrysler Corp. exc. 1980–82 front wheel drive models

IGNITION RESISTORS

Block Type Ballast Resistors

SERVICE NOTE: If the engine fires when the ignition switch is turned on but quits when the switch is released to its running position, it indicates that the resistor is defective and must be replaced.

A dual ballast resistor is used on all 1977–80 Chrysler Corp. vehicles equipped with electronic ignition, except 1978–79 Omni and Horizon, Fig. 3. The normal side of the resistor is a compensating resistance in the primary circuit. At low engine speeds, current is maintained for a longer period of time in this side of the resistor, causing the unit to heat up, in turn increasing resistance. This increased resistance reduces the primary circuit voltage, protecting the ignition coil from high voltage at low engine speeds.

As engine speed increases, the period of time in which current is maintained in the normal side of the resistor is shorter, causing the unit to cool, in turn decreasing resistance.

This decreased resistance permits the primary circuit voltage to increase for high speed operation.

During engine start, the normal side of the ballast resistor is by-passed, allowing full battery voltage to be applied to the primary circuit.

The auxiliary side of the ballast resistor limits voltage to the control unit, thereby protecting the unit.

A single ballast resistor, Fig. 4, is used on 1978–79 Omni, Horizon and 1980–82 Chrysler Corp. except 1980–82 front wheel drive models. This resistor is bypassed during the engine starting procedure to allow full battery voltage to reach the ignition coil.

Wire Type Resistors

The special resistance wires used with 12-volt systems are five to six feet long and contained in the regular wiring harness. The wire is made of stainless steel or special alloy, plastic-coated and covered with a glass braid. There is a relatively small temperature rise and the resistance wire is switched out of the circuit for starting and back in again for running.

On Bosch and Ford systems, Fig. 5 and 6, the resistor is by-passed through a terminal on the starter relay which is connected directly to the positive terminal of the coil.

SERVICE NOTE

If the engine fires when the ignition switch is turned on but quits when the switch is released to the "run" position, it indicates that the resistance wire has lost its continuity or there is a bad connection at the resistor terminals. If the wire is defective, it must be replaced.

CAUTION: Do not attempt to operate the engine for an extended length of time with the resistor by-passed by means of a jumper wire as the breaker points will burn.

Fig. 5   Bosch ignition circuit diagram

Fig. 6   Ford ignition circuit diagram with a resistance wire connected to a three-terminal ignition switch

IGNITION COIL & RESISTOR SPECIFICATIONS

Year	Model	Coil Draw, Amps.		Coil Resistance, Ohms		Ignition Resistor Ohms @ 75°F.
		Engine Stopped	Engine Idling	Primary @ 75°F.	Secondary @ 75°F.	
AMERICAN MOTORS—All Models						
1977	4 Cyl.	4.0	2.0	1.60–1.80	9400–11700	1.8
	6 Cyl. & V8 B.I.D.①	4.0	2.0	1.25–1.40	9000–15000	—
1978–79	4 Cyl.	4.0	2.0	1.60–1.80	9400–11700	2.0
	6 Cyl. & V8 Breakerless	4.0	2.0–2.4	1.13–1.23	7700–9300	1.35
1980–82	Exc. H.E.I.	4.0	2.0–2.4	1.13–1.23	7700–9300	1.35
1981–82	H.E.I.	—	—	0	②	—

①—Breakerless Inductive Discharge.
②—Reading should be less than infinity with ohmmeter set on highest scale.

Year	Model	Engine Stopped	Engine Idling	Primary @ 75°F.	Secondary @ 75°F.	Ignition Resistor
CHRYSLER CORP.—All Models						
1977	①	—	—	1.60–1.79	9400–11700	.50–.60③
	②	—	—	1.41–1.62	8000–11200	.50–.60③
1978–79	All Models①	—	—	1.60–1.79	9400–11700	.50–.60③
	All Models Exc. Front Wheel Drive②	—	—	1.34–1.55	9000–12200	.50–.60③
	Front Wheel Drive②	—	—	1.41–1.62	8000–11200	.50–.60③
1980	All Models①	—	—	1.60–1.79	9400–11700	④
	All Models Exc. Front Wheel Drive②	—	—	1.34–1.55	9000–12200	1.12–1.38
	Front Wheel Drive②	—	—	1.41–1.62	8000–11200	—
1981–82	All Models①	—	—	1.60–1.79	9400–11700	④
	All Models Exc. Front Wheel Drive②	—	—	1.34–1.55	9000–12200	1.12–1.
	Front Wheel Drive②	—	—	1.41–1.62	9000–12200	—
	Front Wheel Drive⑤	—	—	0.7–0.85	9000–11000	—

①—Prestolite coils.
②—Essex or Echlin coils.
③—Auxiliary (control unit side) 4.75–5.75.
④—Except front wheel drive, 1.12–1.38; Front wheel drive, no resistor used.
⑤—Mitsubishi coils.

Year	Model	Engine Stopped	Engine Idling	Primary @ 75°F.	Secondary @ 75°F.	Ignition Resistor
FORD MOTOR CO.—All Models						
1977	Breakerless	—	—	1.0–2.0	7000–13000	1.30–1.40
1978–82	Dura Spark I	—	—	.71–.77	7350–8250	—
	Dura Spark II & III	—	—	1.13–1.23	7700–9300	1.05–1.15
1982	T.F.I.①	—	—	.3–1.0	8000–11500	—

①—Escort, EXP, LN7 & Lynx with auto. trans. and Thick Film Integrated Ignition.

Year	Model	Engine Stopped	Engine Idling	Primary @ 75°F.	Secondary @ 75°F.	Ignition Resistor
GENERAL MOTORS—All Models						
1977–80	H.E.I.①	—	—	0–1.0	6000–30000	—
1981–82	H.E.I.①	—	—	0	②	—

①—High Energy Ignition.
②—Reading should be less than infinity with ohmmeter set on highest scale.

STANDARD IGNITION DISTRIBUTORS

CONTENTS

BREAKER CONTACT POINTS

Contact Analysis

The normal color of points should be a light gray. If the contact surfaces are black it is usually caused by oil vapor or grease from the cam. If they are blue, the cause is usually excessive heating due to improper alignment, high resistance or open condenser circuit.

If the contacts develop a crater or depression on one point and a high spot of metal on the other, the cause is an electrolytic action transferring metal from one contact to the other, Fig. 1, due to an unbalanced ignition system, which can sometimes be improved by a slight change in condenser capacity. If the mound is on the positive point, Fig. 2, install a condenser of greater capacity; if on the negative point, Fig. 3, use a condenser of lesser capacity.

One of the most common causes of point failure is the presence of oil or grease on the contact surfaces, usually from over-lubrication of the wick at the top of the cam or too much grease on the rubbing block of the breaker arm.

Breaker Point Gap

If points are set too close, arcing and burning will occur, causing hard starting and poor low speed performance. If points are set too wide, the cam angle or dwell will be too small to allow saturation of the coil at high engine speeds, resulting in weak spark.

Contact point opening has a direct bearing on cam angle or dwell which is the number of degrees that the breaker cam rotates from the time the points close until they open again, Fig. 4. The cam angle or dwell increases as point opening is decreased and vice versa. If point gap is set with a feeler gauge, the cam angle or dwell should be checked either with a portable dwell meter or by installing the distributor in a distributor tester.

Breaker Arm Spring Tension

Breaker arm spring tension is important. If the tension is too great the arm will bounce, causing an interruption of the current in the coil and misfiring. If the spring tension is too little, the rubbing block will not follow the cam, causing a variation in cam dwell. The spring tension should always be set at the high limit as given in the *Distributor Specifications* chart in the car chapter, as it will be reduced as the rubbing block wears.

Hook a spring scale on the breaker arm and pull in a straight line as shown in Fig. 5. Take a reading as the points start to separate under the slow and steady pull of the scale. If the tension is not within specifications, loosen the screw that holds the end of the point spring and slide the end of the spring in or out as necessary. Tighten the screw and recheck the spring tension.

Breaker Point Alignment

Check alignment of points with points closed, Fig. 6. Align new points where necessary but do not attempt to align used points. Instead, replace used points where serious misalignment is observed. After aligning points, adjust point gap.

Adjusting Breaker Gap

Specifications for breaker gap, *as measured with a feeler gauge,* are listed in the *Tune Up Specifications* in the car chapters. However, if at all possible, this should be set on a distributor tester, with a dial indicator, Fig. 7, or by hooking up a portable dwell meter with the distributor cap and rotor removed and, while cranking the engine, setting the dwell.

NOTE: When setting the dwell with the engine cranking, be sure to ground the coil secondary lead and do not operate the starter for sustained periods at a time.

This eliminates the possibility of an incorrect gap because of rough points, Fig. 8.

The advantage of a distributor testing machine is that it not only measures cam angle or dwell but it also uncovers irregularities between cam lobes, point bounce, alignment of rubbing block with cam, alignment of contacts and breaker arm spring tension.

CONDENSER

A condenser should not be condemned because the points are burned or oxidized. Oil vapor, or grease from the cam, or high resistance may be the cause of such a condition.

Fig. 1 Showing how metal from one contact transfers to the other

Condensers should be tested with a good condenser tester for leakage, break-down, capacity, and resistance in series in the condenser circuit. Manufacturers of condenser testers furnish complete instructions as to their use.

CENTRIFUGAL ADVANCE

When engine speed increases, the spark must be introduced in the cylinder earlier in the cycle in order that the fuel charge can be ignited and will have time to burn and deliver its power to the piston. To provide this spark advance based on engine speed, the centrifugal advance mechanism is used.

This mechanism, Fig. 9, consists of centrifugal advance weights which throw out against spring tension as the engine speed increases. This movement imparts, through a toggle arrangement, rotational motion to the breaker cam or plate, depending on the model, causing it to rotate a number of degrees with respect to the distributor drive shaft. This

Fig. 2 Mound on positive point

Fig. 3 Mound on negative point

Fig. 4   Cam angle or dwell

Fig. 6   Breaker point alignment

Fig. 7   Dial indicator for measuring breaker gap

Fig. 5   Measuring breaker spring tension

causes the points to be opened and closed earlier in the cycle so the spark is delivered to the cylinder earlier.

In servicing the distributor, all weights should be removed from the hinge pins, cleaned and checked for excessive wear, either in the weights or pins, or the plate which is slotted for the movement of the pins on top of the governor weights. Replacement should be made if there is any appreciable wear in the slots, as any wear at this point would change the characteristic of the spark advance.

If these parts are in good condition, the hinge pins should be lubricated before being reassembled, by greasing the hinge pins and filling the pockets in the governor weights with grease. Do not use vaseline for this purpose as its melting point is comparatively low.

When installing new centrifugal advance assemblies, it is important that the spacer washers between the housing and shaft be installed correctly. If incorrectly installed, the advance assembly will be too high, causing it to rub against the bottom of the breaker plate.

On some distributors, both springs are alike, while on others there is one heavy and one light spring.

Fig. 8   Why flat feeler gauge will not provide accurate point spacing if points are rough

VACUUM ADVANCE

The vacuum advance unit consists of a spring loaded diaphragm, which is connected through linkage to the distributor breaker plate. The spring loaded side of the diaphragm is connected through a vacuum line to the carburetor or intake manifold. As vacuum increases, the diaphragm is drawn toward the source of vacuum, the diaphragm linkage is pulled with it and the breaker plate, attached to the linkage, is turned to advance the timing.

BOSCH DISTRIBUTOR SERVICE
Distributor, Replace
Removal
1. Remove air cleaner, then the distributor water shield.
2. Remove distributor cap with wires attached and position aside.
3. Disconnect vacuum hose from vacuum advance unit.
4. Disconnect distributor primary wiring connector.
5. Scribe a mark on distributor housing aligned with tip of distributor rotor.
6. Scribe a mark between distributor housing and engine block.
7. Remove distributor holddown nut and clamp.
8. Remove distributor from engine.

Installation
1. Clean distributor mounting pad on engine.
2. Install new distributor mounting gasket.
3. If engine was not cranked after distributor was removed, proceed as follows:
   a. Align rotor tip with mark scribed on housing.
   b. Slide distributor into engine, aligning the mark on distributor housing with mark on engine. It may be necessary to move distributor rotor and shaft slightly to mesh distributor gear with camshaft gear. The rotor should align with the scribe mark on housing when the distributor is fully installed into engine.
   c. Install distributor holddown clamp

Fig. 9   Exploded view of Bosch distributor. American Motors 4-121 engine

and nut.
4. If the engine was cranked after the distributor was removed, proceed as follows.
   a. Remove No. 1 spark plug.
   b. Place finger over spark plug hole and crank engine until compression pressure is felt. Then, continue to crank engine until timing mark on crankshaft pulley is aligned with "0" mark, top dead center on timing plate.
   c. Position distributor rotor tip to align with the No. 1 cylinder firing position in distributor cap. This is indicated by a manufactured mark on the edge of the distributor housing, Then, turn rotor 1/8 turn clockwise past the No. 1 firing position mark.

   d. Install distributor into engine and align scribe mark made between distributor housing and engine.
   e. Install distributor holddown clamp and nut.
5. Install distributor cap.
6. Connect vacuum hose to vacuum advance unit and the distributor primary wiring.
7. Adjust ignition timing to specifications. Refer to the individual car chapters.

Distributor Service

NOTE: Replacement parts for servicing the distributor shaft, drive gear, bushing and cam are not available. In addition, the advance weights, advance springs and breaker plate

are not serviceable since the breaker plate is permanently staked into the housing.

If distributor has been disassembled, refer to Fig. 9 at reassembly.

1. Lubricate pivot pins and install advance weights. Lubricate shaft and install cam assembly.
2. Install advance springs and advance plate, securing plate with clip and screws.
3. Insert grommet and condenser wire through hole in housing and install condenser and contact points.
4. Install vacuum advance unit. Hook vacuum advance rod over pin in advance plate and install snap ring.

ELECTRONIC IGNITION SYSTEMS

INDEX

AMERICAN MOTORS BREAKERLESS INDUCTIVE DISCHARGE (BID) IGNITION SYSTEM

Description

The BID ignition system incorporates four major units; an electronic control unit, ignition coil, distributor and high tension wires, Fig. 1. The electronic control unit is a solid-state, moisture resistant module with the components sealed in a potting compound to

Fig. 1 BID ignition system wiring

resist vibration and environmental conditions. Since the control unit has an internal current regulator, a resistance wire or ballast resistor is not necessary in the primary circuit. Battery voltage is applied to the ignition coil positive terminal when the ignition switch is in the "On" or "Start" position, therefore, an ignition system bypass is not required in this system. The primary coil circuit is electronically regulated by this unit.

The ignition coil is of standard construction and requires no special service.

The distributor is conventional except the contact points, condenser and cam are replaced by a sensor and trigger wheel, and since no wearing occurs between the trigger wheel and sensor, dwell angle remains constant. The sensor receives an alternating current signal from the electronic control unit. The sensor develops an electro-magnetic field used to detect the presence of metal which are the leading edges of the trigger wheel teeth.

Operation

When the ignition switch is placed in the "Start" or "Run" position, the control unit is activated. An oscillator within the control unit excites the sensor coil, in turn developing the electromagnetic field. When a leading edge of a trigger wheel tooth enters the electromagneticic field, the tooth reduces the sensor oscillation strength to a predetermined level, in turn activating the demodulator circuit. The demodulator circuit controls a power transistor located in series with the coil primary circuit. The power transistor switches the coil primary circuit off, thereby inducing a high voltage in the coil secondary winding. The high voltage is then delivered to the spark plugs through the distributor rotor, cap and high tension wires.

System Quick Test, Fig. 2

The BID system may be tested quickly on the vehicle using No. 57 bulb and a jumper wire. Refer to Fig. 2 for procedure.

Comprehensive testing may be performed as outlined under "Troubleshooting".

Troubleshooting, Fig. 3

1. Disconnect Electronic Control Unit (ECU) ground wire and the 4-wire connector. Using a small wire brush and solvent, clean the terminals. Leave connectors disconnected.
2. Disconnect battery cables, then momentarily move ignition switch to START and allow it to move to ON.
3. Measure resistance of entire ignition feed circuit by connecting an ohmmeter to battery positive B1 and F3 terminal in the 4-wire connector.
4. If resistance is less than 1 ohm, tighten main harness connector attaching screw to fully seat connector. If resistance is 1 ohm or more, isolate trouble area by connecting the ohmmeter and measuring the resistance of each portion of the ignition feed circuit between the following terminals: B1 and B2, B2 and A1, A1 and H1, F3 and C1, C1 and H2, H1 and H2, AV and DV. Clean, tighten or reposition connectors as needed.
5. Inspect coil primary connections for looseness and proper assembly. Wire terminals must be between channel washer and nut, channel washer tabs must be facing up. Reposition and tighten as needed.
6. Connect an ohmmeter between F3 and F4 terminals to measure coil primary circuit resistance. If resistance is 1–2 ohms, proceed to step 7. If resistance is less than 1 ohm, replace coil and proceed to step 8. If resistance is more than 2 ohms, isolate trouble and insure that the resistance between the following terminals is as follows: C1 and C2, 1–2 ohms; F3 and C1, 0 ohms; F4 and C2, 0 ohms. Replace coil or repair troubled area and proceed to step 7. If coil was replaced, proceed to step 8.
7. Measure coil secondary resistance by removing coil secondary wire from coil and connecting ohmmeter between C1 and C3.

NOTE: Set ohmmeter to the 1,000 ohm scale before testing secondary resistance.

If resistance is 9,000–15,000 ohms, reconnect coil secondary wire and proceed to step 8. If resistance is less than 9,000 ohms or more than 15,000 ohms, replace coil and reconnect coil secondary wire and proceed to Step 8.
8. Remove distributor cap, rotor and dust cover and check for 1.6–2.4 ohms resistance between F1 and F2 terminals.

NOTE: Pull and flex sensor wires, firmly squeeze molded sensor grommet at dis-

CHECK ALL CONNECTIONS BEFORE BEGINNING TEST

Fig. 2   American Motors BID system quick text

tributor, and apply firm side to side pressure on sensor post while checking resistance.

If resistance is as specified and steady, proceed to step 10. If resistance is too high or low, or if needle fluctuates or wavers, proceed to step 9.
9. Disconnect 2-wire connector and check for 1.6–2.4 ohms resistance between S1 and S2 terminals.

NOTE: Pull and flex sensor wires, firmly squeeze molded sensor wire grommet at distributor, and apply firm side to side pressure on sensor post.

If resistance is as specified and steady, proceed to step 10. If resistance is too high or too low, or if needle fluctuates or wavers, replace sensor and proceed to step 10.
10. Using a small wire brush and solvent, clean terminals S1, S2, S3 and S4.
11. Measure resistance of ECU ground circuit by connecting an ohmmeter between terminal G2 and battery negative cable G4. Resistance should be 0 ohms. Clean

and tighten connections as needed.
12. Using pliers, squeeze terminals E1, E2, E3, E4 and G1 until terminals have a distinct oval shape, thereby assuring a tight fit when terminals are connected.
13. Using petroleum jelly, coat the male terminals in the 4-wire connector and ground connectors and around the outer edge of the terminal end of the ECU 4-wire connector.
14. Connect the 4-wire and ground connectors.
15. Connect Pulse Simulator J-25331 to the S3 and S4 terminals and reconnect battery cables. Remove coil secondary wire from distributor and place end of wire ½ inch from ground, then with ignition switch ON, operate simulator and observe for spark across the ½ inch gap. If spark jumps gap, proceed to step 17. If spark does not jump gap, proceed to step 16.
16. Disconnect wire from coil negative terminal, then connect one pulse simulator clip to the coil negative terminal and connect the remaining clip to the ground. With ignition switch ON, operate pulse simulator and observe for spark across the ½

ELECTRONIC IGNITION SYSTEMS

Fig. 3 BID ignition system checkpoints

Distributor, Replace

Removal

1. Remove distributor cap with wires and position aside.
2. Disconnect vacuum advance hose and distributor primary wiring.
3. Mark position of rotor tip on distributor housing, then mark relative position of housing to engine.
4. Remove distributor holddown bolt and clamp, then remove distributor.

Installation

1. Clean distributor mounting pad on engine and install a new distributor mounting gasket.
2. Turn rotor about ⅛ of a turn counterclockwise past the mark first placed on the distributor housing.
3. Install distributor, aligning the second mark placed on the housing with the one placed on the engine. It may be necessary to move the rotor slightly or rotate the oil pump shaft with a long, flat blade screwdriver to start gear into mesh with camshaft gear, but rotor should line up with first housing mark when distributor is down in place.
4. Install distributor holddown clamp, screw and lockwasher, but do not tighten screw until ignition timing has been set. Connect vacuum line, primary wiring and install cap.

NOTE: If the engine was cranked after the distributor was removed from the engine, crank the engine to bring No. 1 piston up on its compression stroke and align the timing mark with TDC on the timing plate. Then turn rotor until it is in position to fire No. 1 cylinder. Install distributor as outlined above and adjust ignition timing to specifications. Refer to the individual car chapters.

Component Replacement

1. Place distributor in a suitable holding fixture and remove cap, rotor and dust shield, Fig. 4.
2. Using a small gear puller, remove trigger wheel. Ensure puller jaws are gripping trigger wheel inner shoulder to prevent trigger wheel damage. Also, use a thick flat washer or nut as a spacer and do not press against small center shaft.
3. Loosen sensor locking screw approximately three turns, lift sensor lead grommet from distributor bowl and pull sensor leads from slot around sensor spring pivot pin. Release sensor spring, ensure spring clears sensor leads and slide sensor from bracket.

NOTE: The sensor locking screw utilizes a tamper proof head design and requires tool J-25097 for removal. However, if special tool is not available, use a small needlenose plier to remove screw. The service (replacement) sensor has a standard slotted head screw.

4. If vacuum control unit is to be replaced, remove retaining screw and vacuum unit.
5. Install new vacuum control unit and assemble sensor, sensor guide, flat washer and retaining screw.

NOTE: Install retaining screw far enough to hold assembly together and ensure it does not protrude past bottom of sensor.

---

inch gap when button is released. If spark jumps the gap, replace ECU unit and proceed to step 17. If spark does not jump gap, replace coil before proceeding to step 17.

NOTE: If ECU unit is replaced, squeeze and lubricate the connectors as described in steps 12 and 13.

---

17. Disconnect pulse simulator. Before connecting 2-wire connector, squeeze and lubricate terminals as described in steps 12 and 13. Connect coil negative wire.
18. Inspect distributor cap for cracks and carbon tracks. Replace as necessary. Install dust cover, rotor, distributor cap and coil secondary wire.

NOTE: If the malfunction still exists after performing the above procedure, connect an engine oscilloscope and measure the ignition dwell. A scope must be used because a dwell meter will not accurately measure the dwell on this system. Start the engine and observe the dwell readings, then lower the hood being careful not to squeeze the oscilloscope leads between the fender and hood and allow the engine and wiring harness to warm up for 10 minutes. Prior to, during and after the engine warm up period, the dwell must be 23° on V8 engines and 32° for 6 cylinder engines and the dwell must not vary more than 3° at any time. If the dwell readings are as specified at all times, the malfunction may be caused by the fuel system. If the fuel system checks out OK and the malfunction still exists, replace the ECU unit and recheck the dwell. If the dwell readings are still not as specified above, replace the ignition wiring harness and recheck the dwell as above. If the dwell is below specifications, disconnect the 4-wire connector and measure the sensor circuit resistance and integrity as described in step 8. If sensor circuit resistance and integrity are within specifications, replace ECU unit. If sensor circuit resistance is too high or too low, or if needle fluctuates, replace the sensor. Be sure to squeeze and lubricate the terminals as described in steps 12 and 13.

SENSOR LOCKING SCREW

SENSOR ASSEMBLY

TO REMOVE AND REPLACE SENSOR ROUTE SENSOR LEADS AROUND PIVOT PIN

SUMMING BAR

Fig. 5 Sensor installation

POSITION GAUGE AGAINST FLAT SIDE OF YOKE

SENSOR CORE

Fig. 6 Positioning sensor

1. DISTRIBUTOR CAP
2. ROTOR
3. DUST SHIELD
4. TRIGGER WHEEL
5. FELT
6. SENSOR ASSEMBLY
7. HOUSING
8. VACUUM CONTROL SCREW
9. VACUUM CONTROL
10. SHIM
11. DRIVE GEAR
12. PIN

Fig. 4 BID distributor exploded view

ELECTRONIC IGNITION SYSTEMS

6. If vacuum control has been replaced and original sensor is being used, replace special head screw with standard slotted head screw.
7. Install sensor assembly on vacuum chamber bracket, ensuring tip of sensor is located properly in summing bar. Place sensor spring on sensor and route sensor leads around spring pivot pin, Fig. 5. Install sensor lead grommet and position leads away from trigger wheel.
8. Install sensor positioning gauge over yoke, ensure gauge is against flat of shaft, and move sensor sideways until gauge can be positioned. Snug retaining screw and check sensor position by removing and installing gauge, Fig. 6. When gauge can be removed and replaced without sensor side movement, sensor is positioned properly. Tighten retaining screw and check sensor position.
9. Place trigger wheel on yoke and check if sensor core is positioned approximately in center of trigger wheel legs. Bend a .050 inch gauge wire to dimension specified in Fig. 7, and place between trigger wheel legs and sensor base. Press trigger wheel onto yoke until legs contact gauge wire.
10. Apply 3 to 5 drops of light engine oil to felt wick in top of yoke, then install dust shield, rotor and cap.

Fig. 7 Trigger wheel installation

AMERICAN MOTORS SOLID STATE IGNITION SYSTEM

This ignition system, Figs. 8 and 8A is used on 1978–82 vehicles except those equipped with the four cylinder engine. The solid state ignition system consists of the ignition switch, electronic ignition control unit, ignition coil, primary resistance wire and bypass, distributor and spark plugs.

The electronic ignition control unit is a solid state, moisture resistant module. The component parts are sealed in a potting material to resist vibration and environmental conditions. The control unit is incorporated with reverse polarity protection and transient voltage protection.

The distributor incorporates a sensor and trigger wheel. Current flowing through the ignition coil creates a magnetic field in the primary windings. When the circuit is opened, the magnetic field collapses and induces a high voltage in the coil secondary windings. This circuit is electronically controlled by the electronic ignition control unit. The distributor sensor and trigger wheel provide the signal to operate the control unit. The trigger wheel is mounted on the distributor shaft and has one tooth for each cylinder. The sensor, a coil of fine wire mounted to a permanent magnet, develops an electromagnetic force that is sensitive to the presence of ferrous metal. The sensor detects the trigger wheel teeth as the teeth pass the sensor. When a trigger wheel tooth approaches the pole piece of the sensor, it reduces the reluctance of the magnetic field, increasing field strength. Field strength decreases as the tooth moves away from the pole piece. This increase and decrease of field strength generates an alternating current which is interpreted by the electronic ignition control unit. The control unit then opens and closes the ignition coil primary circuit.

Since there are no contacting surfaces and no wear occurs, dwell angle requires no adjustment. The dwell angle is electronically controlled by the electronic ignition control unit. When the coil circuit is switched open, an electronic timer in the control unit keeps the circuit open only long enough for the spark to discharge. Then, it automatically closes the ignition coil primary circuit.

Trouble Shooting

Secondary Circuit Test
1. Disconnect coil wire from distributor cap and, using insulated pliers, hold wire approximately 1/2 inch from a good engine ground.
2. Crank engine and observe wire for spark. If no spark occurs, proceed to Step 5. If spark occurs, proceed to Step 3.
3. Reconnect coil wire to distributor cap. Remove wire from one spark plug.

CAUTION: On 1980–82 models, do not remove ignition secondary cables from spark plugs on cylinders 1 or 5 (six cylinder engines). On 1977–79 models, do not remove ignition secondary cables on cylinders 3 or 5 on six cylinder or cylinders 3 or 4 on V8 engines while performing this test since the sensor may be damaged.

Fig. 8 1977–81 American Motors solid state ignition system schematic

Fig. 8A   1982 American Motors solid state ignition system schematic

4. Using insulated pliers, hold wire approximately 1/2 inch from a good engine ground. Crank engine and observe wire for spark. If spark occurs, check for fuel system problems or incorrect ignition timing. If no spark occurs, check for defective distributor cap, rotor or spark plug wires.

5. If no spark occurs at coil wire, measure coil wire resistance. If resistance is greater than 10,000 ohms on 1977–80 models or greater than 7700–9300 ohms at 75° F. or 12,000 ohms at 200° F. on 1981–82 models, replace wire.

6. If malfunction still exists, proceed to the following tests or diagnosis procedures.

Intermittent Failure Diagnosis

Since intermittent failure may be caused by loose or corroded terminals, defective components, poor ground connections or defective wiring, it is necessary to check all wiring connections in the ignition system. Also, refer to Fig. 9 for further diagnosis.

Ignition Coil Primary Circuit Test

1. Turn ignition switch "On" and connect a voltmeter between ignition coil positive terminal and the ground. If voltage is 5.5–6.5 volts, proceed to Step 2. If battery voltage is noted, proceed to Step 4. If voltage is below 5.5 volts, disconnect condenser lead. If voltage is now 5.5–6.5 volts, replace condenser. If voltage is still not within specifications, proceed to Step 6.

2. Turn ignition switch to "Start" and measure voltage at coil positive terminal while cranking engine. If battery voltage is present while cranking engine, the ignition coil primary circuit is satisfactory. If voltage present is less than battery voltage, proceed to Step 3.

3. Check for shorted or open circuit in wire attached to starter "I" terminal. Check for defective starter solenoid. Repair as necessary.

4. Place ignition switch in "On" position, disconnect wire from starter solenoid "I" terminal and measure voltage at ignition coil positive terminal. If voltage drops to

5.5–6.5 volts, replace starter solenoid. If voltage remains constant at battery voltage, connect a jumper wire between ignition coil negative terminal and the ground. If voltage drops to 5.5–6.5 volts, proceed to Step 5. If not, repair defective resistance wire and repeat Step 2.

5. Check continuity between ignition coil negative terminal and terminal "D4", Figs. 8 and 8A. Also, check continuity between terminal "D1" and the ground. If continuity is present, replace electronic ignition control unit. If continuity is not present, locate and repair open circuit.

6. Turn ignition switch "Off" and measure resistance between ignition coil positive terminal and the dash connector "AV" on 1977–81 models, Fig. 8, or dash connector "FW" on 1982 models, Fig. 8A. If resistance is greater than 1.40 ohms, repair or replace resistance wire. If resistance is 1.30–1.40 ohms, proceed to Step 7.

7. On 1977–81 models, with ignition "Off", measure resistance between dash connector "AV" and ignition switch terminal "I1", Fig. 8. On 1982 models, with ignition "Off", measure resistance between dash connector "FW" and ignition switch terminal "I1", Fig. 8A. If resistance is less than .1 ohm, replace ignition switch or repair switch feed wire. If resistance is greater than .1 ohm, check and repair terminal connections at dash connector or defective wiring.

Coil Test

1. Inspect ignition coil for oil leaks, exterior damage and carbon tracks. If satisfactory, proceed to Step 2. If not, replace ignition coil.

2. Disconnect ignition coil connector and connect ohmmeter between coil terminals. If resistance is 1.13–1.23 ohms at 75° F. or 1.5 ohms at 200° F., proceed to Step 3. If not, replace ignition coil.

3. Connect ohmmeter between ignition coil center tower and the plus or minus terminal. Resistance should be 7700–9300 ohms at 75° F or 12000 ohms at 200° F. If not replace ignition coil.

Sensor & Control Unit Test

1. Disconnect the four wire connector at the control unit, Figs. 8 and 8A. Disconnect coil wire from distributor and hold wire approximately 1/2 inch from a good engine ground with insulated pliers, then turn ignition "On". If spark is observed at coil wire, proceed to next step. If not, proceed to Step 5.

2. Measure resistance between terminals "D2" and "D3" of the harness connector, Figs. 8 and 8A. If resistance is 400–800 ohms, proceed to Step 6. If not, proceed to next step.

3. Disconnect and connect the three wire connector at distributor and measure resistance between terminals "D2" and "D3" of the harness connector, Figs. 8 and 8A. If resistance is now between 400–800 ohms, proceed to Step 6. If not, disconnect three wire connector at distributor and proceed to next step.

4. Measure resistance between terminals "B2" and "B3" of the distributor connector, Figs. 8 and 8A. If resistance is not 400–800 ohms, replace sensor. If resistance is 400–800 ohms, repair or replace harness between three wire and four wire connector.

5. Connect an ohmmeter between terminal "D1" of the harness connector, Figs. 8 and 8A, and the battery negative terminal. If reading is below .002 ohm, repeat Step 2. If not, check for an improper ground. Check ground cable resistance, distributor to engine block resistance and distributor ground screw to terminal "D1" resistance, Figs. 8 and 8A.

6. Using a voltmeter connected between terminals "D2" and "D3" of the harness connector, Figs. 8 and 8A, observe reading while cranking engine. If voltmeter reading fluctuates, it indicates proper sensor and trigger wheel operation. If not, the trigger wheel is defective or the distributor is not rotating.

Ignition Feed to Control Unit Test

NOTE: Perform the "Ignition Coil Primary

ELECTRONIC IGNITION SYSTEMS

Condition	Possible Cause	Correction
ENGINE FAILS TO START (No spark at plugs)	1. No voltage to ignition system.	1. Check battery, ignition switch and wiring. Repair as required.
	2. Electronic Control Unit ground lead inside distributor open, loose or corroded.	2. Clean, tighten or repair as required.
	3. Primary wiring connectors not fully engaged.	3. Clean and fully engage connectors.
	4. Coil open or shorted.	4. Test coil. Replace if faulty.
	5. Electronic Control Unit defective.	5. Replace Electronic Control Unit.
	6. Cracked distributor cap.	6. Replace cap.
	7. Defective rotor.	7. Replace rotor.
ENGINE BACKFIRES BUT FAILS TO START	1. Incorrect ignition timing.	1. Check timing. Adjust as required.
	2. Moisture in distributor.	2. Dry cap and rotor.
	3. Distributor cap faulty.	3. Check cap for loose terminals, cracks and dirt. Clean or replace as required.
	4. Ignition wires not in correct firing order.	4. Install in correct order.
ENGINE RUNS ONLY WITH KEY IN START POSITION	1. Open in resistance wire or excessive resistance.	1. Repair resistance wire.
ENGINE CONTINUES TO RUN WITH KEY OFF	1. Defective starter solenoid.	1. Replace solenoid.
	2. Shorted diode in alternator indicator lamp circuit.	2. Replace diode.
ENGINE DOES NOT OPERATE SMOOTHLY AND/OR ENGINE MISFIRES AT HIGH SPEED	1. Spark plugs fouled or faulty.	1. Clean and gap plugs. Replace as required.
	2. Ignition cables faulty.	2. Check cables. Replace as required.
	3. Spark advance system(s) faulty.	3. Check operation. Repair as required.
	4. "I" terminal shorted to starter terminal in solenoid.	4. Replace solenoid.
	5. Trigger wheel pin missing.	5. Install pin.
	6. Distributor wires installed in wrong firing order.	6. Install wires correctly.
	7. Two plug wires of consecutive firing cylinders routed next to each other.	7. Re-route plug wires away from each other.
EXCESSIVE FUEL CONSUMPTION	1. Incorrect ignition timing.	1. Check timing. Adjust as required.
	2. Spark advance system(s) faulty.	2. Check operation. Repair as required.
	3. MCU (microprocessor) faulty	3. Test system. Repair as required.
ERRATIC TIMING ADVANCE	1. Faulty vacuum advance assembly.	1. Check operation. Replace if required.
	2. Centrifugal weights sticking.	2. Remove dirt, corrosion.
TIMING NOT AFFECTED BY VACUUM	1. Defective vacuum advance unit.	1. Replace vacuum advance unit.
	2. Advance unit adjusting screw too far counterclockwise.	2. Turn screw clockwise to bring advance curve within specifications.
	3. Sensor pivot corroded.	3. Clean pivot.
INTERMITTENT OPERATION	1. Loose or corroded terminals.	1. Tighten terminals, remove corrosion, apply electrical grease.
	2. Defective pick-up coil.	2. Perform pick-up coil test.
	3. Defective control unit.	3. Perform control unit tests.
	4. Loose ground connector in distributor.	4. Clean and tighten ground connection.
	5. Wires to distributor shorted together or to ground.	5. Check for frayed, pinched, or burned wires.
	6. Trigger wheel pin missing.	6. Install new pin.

Fig. 9   American Motors solid state ignition system service diagnosis chart

Fig. 10   Distributor stator & armature segment alignment

Circuit Test" before performing this test.

1. Disconnect two wire connector from control unit and connect a voltmeter between terminal "F2" and the ground, Figs. 8 and 8A. Turn ignition "On". If voltmeter reading is within .2 volts of battery voltage, replace control unit and proceed to Step 3. If voltmeter reading is not within .2 volt of battery voltage, proceed to next step.

2. Locate and repair cause of voltage reduction as noted in Step 1. Check for a corroded dash connector or defective ignition switch. Then, check for spark at coil wire. Spark should be present at coil wire. If not, replace control unit.

3. Connect the two wire connector at control unit and disconnect the four wire connector from control unit. Connect an ammeter between terminal "C1" and the

Fig. 11   American Motors distributor used with solid state ignition system (Typical)

ground, Figs. 8 and 8A. If ammeter reading is 1 ±.1 amp., the system is satisfactory. If ammeter reading is higher or lower, replace module.

Current Flow Test
1. Remove connector from coil.
2. Depress plastic barb and remove positive wire from connector. Remove negative wire in same manner.
3. Connect an ammeter between coil positive terminal and the disconnected positive wire.
4. Connect a jumper wire between coil negative terminal and the engine ground.
5. Turn ignition "On" and note ammeter reading. Reading should be approximately 7 amps. and not exceeding 7.6 amps. If reading exceeds 7.6 amps., replace ignition coil.
6. Remove jumper wire from coil negative terminal and connect the coil green wire to negative terminal. Ammeter reading should be approximately 4 amps. If reading is less than 3.5 amps., check for poor connections at the three wire and four wire connectors or a poor ground at distributor ground screw. If reading is greater than 5 amps., the control unit is defective, requiring replacement.
7. Start and run engine. Ammeter reading should be 2–2.4 amps. If not, replace control unit.

Distributor, Replace

Removal
1. Remove No. 1 spark plug and crank

engine until compression pressure is felt. Slowly rotate engine in direction of normal rotation until timing mark on crankshaft pulley aligns with proper timing mark on timing plate. Refer to the individual car chapters for timing specifications. Remove distributor cap and ensure alignment of rotor and armature with index mark on top of magnetic pickup and mark on distributor housing, Fig. 10.
2. Disconnect vacuum advance hose and distributor primary wiring.
3. Remove distributor holddown bolt and clamp, then remove distributor.

Installation
1. Clean distributor mounting pad on engine and install a new distributor mounting gasket.
2. Ensure engine is still aligned with the proper timing marks. Align the rotor with the marks on the distributor housing and the armature with the mark on top of the magnetic pickup. It may be necessary to move the rotor slightly or rotate the oil pump shaft with a long, flat bladed screwdriver to mesh distributor gear with camshaft gear. The rotor should align with the housing mark when distributor is installed properly, Fig. 10.
3. Install distributor holddown clamp, bolt and lockwasher, but do not tighten bolt until ignition timing has been set. Connect vacuum line, primary wiring and install distributor cap. Adjust ignition

timing to specifications found in the individual car chapters.

NOTE: If the engine was cranked after the distributor was removed from the engine, refer to step 1 of removal procedure to properly position crankshaft before installing distributor.

Distributor Service

Trigger Wheel & Sensor, Replace
1. Remove distributor cap and rotor, Fig. 11.
2. Remove trigger wheel with a suitable gear puller. Use a flat washer to prevent gear puller from contacting inner shaft. The trigger wheel may also be removed by using two screwdrivers to pry trigger wheel upward. Remove pin.
3. On six cylinder distributors, remove sensor retainers and washers from pivot pin on base plate.
4. On V8 distributors, remove sensor snap ring from shaft, then the retainer from vacuum unit to sensor drive pin and position vacuum unit lever aside.
5. On all distributors, remove ground screw from harness tab.
6. Remove sensor assembly from distributor housing.
7. Reverse procedure to assemble.

Vacuum Unit, Replace
1. Disconnect vacuum hose.
2. On six cylinder distributors, remove vacuum unit attaching screws and the vac-

uum unit, Fig. 11. It is necessary to tilt the vacuum unit to disengage the link from the sensor pin and also loosen the base plate screws for clearance.
3. On V8 distributors, remove distributor cap and the retainer from the sensor pin. Remove vacuum unit attaching screws and the vacuum unit, Fig. 11.

4. Reverse procedure to install. If a new vacuum unit is installed, it must be calibrated as follows:
 a. Insert an appropriate size allen wrench into vacuum hose tube of original vacuum unit. Rotate allen wrench clockwise and note the number of turns required to bottom the adjusting

screw.
 b. Insert allen wrench into vacuum hose tube of replacement vacuum unit. Turn the allen wrench clockwise until the adjusting screw is bottomed, then rotate allen wrench counterclockwise the number of turns noted in the previous step.

Chrysler Corp. Rear Wheel Drive Models Less Electronic Spark Control (Lean Burn) System

DESCRIPTION

This system, Figs. 1 thru 2A, is composed of a magnetic distributor, an electronic control unit, a wiring harness, a production coil and a single or dual ballast resistor.

The distributor is essentially the same as the conventional type except the contacts have been replaced by a pickup coil and the cam by a reluctor. With a conventional contact type system, the voltage necessary to fire the spark plugs is developed by interrupting the current flowing through the primary of the ignition coil by opening a set of contacts. With the Electronic System, the voltage is produced the same way except that the current is interrupted by a transistor in the electronic control unit. This happens each time the control unit receives a "timing" pulse from the distributor magnetic pickup.

Since the magnetic pickup, reluctor and the control unit, which replace the contact points and cam, do not normally change or wear out with service, engine timing and dwell do not require periodic adjusting. This minimizes regular ignition maintenance of cleaning and replacing the spark plugs.

TROUBLE SHOOTING
Engine Will Not Start—Fuel System OK

1. Wiring harness electrical terminals covered with grease.
2. Faulty ballast resistor.
3. Faulty ignition coil.
4. Faulty pickup or improper pickup air gap.
5. Faulty wiring.
6. Faulty control unit.

Engine Surges Severely—Not Lean Carburetor

1. Wiring.
2. Faulty pickup leads.
3. Ignition coil.

Engine Misses—Carburetion Good

1. Spark plugs.
2. Secondary cables.
3. Ignition coil.
4. Wiring.
5. Control unit.

SYSTEM TESTING

NOTE: To completely test components and circuits of the electronic ignition system, special testers should be used. However, in event the testers are not available, the following procedures may be utilized. A voltmeter with a 20,000 volt/ohm rating and an ohmmeter using a 1.5 volt battery for power should be used for testing. Before performing any electrical tests, ensure all wiring is properly connected.

1977–80 Models
Harness Wiring Test
1. Check battery voltage and note reading.
2. Disconnect harness connector from control unit.

CAUTION: Before disconnecting or connecting harness connector, ensure ignition switch is in the "Off" position.

3. Turn ignition switch to "On" position.
4. Connect the voltmeter between harness

Fig. 1 Chrysler electronic ignition wiring. 1977–79

Fig. 2   Chrysler electronic ignition wiring. 1980

Fig. 3   Harness wiring test, No. 1 cavity. 1977—80 (Typical)

Fig. 2A   Chrysler electronic ignition wiring. 1981—82

Fig. 4   Harness wiring test, No. 2 cavity. 1977—80 (Typical)

Fig. 5   Harness wiring test, No. 3 cavity. 1977—80 (Typical)

Fig. 6   Pick-up coil test, cavity Nos. 4 & 5. 1977—80 (Typical)

ELECTRONIC IGNITION SYSTEMS

Fig. 7 Pick-up coil test, distributor lead connector. 1977–80 (Typical)

Fig. 8 Control unit ground circuit test. 1977–80 (Typical)

Fig. 8A Checking battery voltage at coil positive terminal. 1981–82

Fig. 8B Checking battery voltage at coil negative terminal. 1981–82

Fig. 8C Checking battery voltage at No. 2 cavity. 1981–82

Fig. 8D Checking continuity between coil negative terminal and No. 2 cavity. 1981–82

Fig. 8E Checking continuity between ignition switch and No. 1 cavity. 1981–82

Fig. 8F Checking resistance between cavities No. 4 & 5. 1981–82

Fig. 8G Testing pick up coil resistance. 1981–82

Fig. 8H Checking for short circuit at pick up coil terminal. 1981–82

connector cavity No. 1 and the ground. Voltage reading should be within 1 volt of battery voltage earlier noted. If not, check circuit between cavity No. 1 and the battery, Fig. 3.

5. Connect voltmeter between harness connector cavity No. 2 and ground. Voltage reading should be within 1 volt of battery voltage noted in step 1. If not, check circuit between cavity No. 2 and battery, Fig. 4.

6. On 1977–79, connect voltmeter between harness connector cavity No. 3 and ground. Voltage reading should be within 1 volt of battery voltage noted in step 1. If not, check circuit between cavity No. 3 and battery, Fig. 5

7. Turn ignition switch to off position.

Fig. 8I Dual Pick up start-run relay. 1981–82

Distributor Pick-up Coil Test

1. Connect an ohmmeter between harness connector cavities numbers 4 and 5, Fig. 6. Resistance reading should be 150 to 900 ohms.
2. If reading is not as specified in above step, disconnect distributor dual lead connector and connect ohmmeter between the two leads on distributor side of connector, Fig. 7. If resistance is not between 150 and 900 ohms, replace pick-up coil.
3. Connect one ohmmeter lead to a good ground and the other lead to either connector of the distributor. If ohmmeter shows a reading, the pickup coil must be replaced.

Control Unit Ground Circuit Test

Connect an ohmmeter between control unit connector pin No. 5 and the ground, Fig. 8. If ohmmeter indicates infinite resistance, tighten bolts securing control unit to firewall and recheck resistance. If reading is still infinite, replace control unit.

1981–82 Models

1. Visually check all spark plug cables and spark plugs for proper installation or damage.
2. Check for proper installation of primary ignition coil wire at coil terminals and at ballast resistor.
3. If above checks are satisfactory, check and record battery voltage.
4. Disconnect coil secondary lead from distributor cap. Turn ignition On, then momentarily ground negative terminal of coil using suitable jumper wire while holding coil secondary lead 1/4 inch from good ground. If no spark is observed, turn ignition Off, then disconnect four-wire electrical connector at electronic control unit. If spark is observed, proceed to step 10.

NOTE: Before connecting or disconnecting the harness connector from the control unit, check to ensure that the ignition switch is in the Off position.

5. Repeat step 4. If spark is observed, replace electronic control unit.
6. If no spark is observed, measure voltage at coil positive terminal. Reading obtained should be within one volt of previously recorded battery voltage.
7. If voltage reading is zero, replace starter relay and check wiring between battery positive terminal and coil, Fig. 8A.
8. If voltage reading obtained in step 6 is not continuous, replace ignition resistor and repeat step 6.
9. Check battery voltage at coil negative terminal, Fig. 8B. Reading obtained should be within one volt of battery voltage. If voltage reading is satisfactory, but no spark is observed when coil negative terminal is grounded, replace coil.
10. If spark was obtained in step 4 or step 9, but engine will not start, check to ensure that four-wire connector is disconnected from electronic control unit, then with ignition On check for battery voltage at cavity 2 of ECU harness connector. Reading obtained should be within one volt of battery voltage, Fig. 8C.
11. If voltage reading is not satisfactory, turn ignition Off, and check for continuity between cavity 2 and coil negative terminal using suitable ohmmeter, Fig. 8D. If

continuity is not present, check for damaged wiring or loose connections and repair as necessary.
12. If voltage reading in step 10 is satisfactory, check for battery voltage at cavity 2 of ECU connector. If battery voltage is not obtained, turn ignition Off and check for continuity between cavity 1 and ignition switch using suitable ohmmeter, Fig. 8E. If continuity is not present, check for damaged wiring or loose connections and repair as necessary.
13. If battery voltage is obtained at cavity 2 of ECU connector, turn ignition Off and check resistance between cavities 4 and 5 of ECU harness connector using suitable ohmmeter, Fig. 8F. Reading of 150–900 ohms should be obtained.
14. If reading is satisfactory, check wiring between cavities 4 and 5 for open or short circuit and repair as necessary. If wiring is satisfactory, check for proper operation of dual pick up start run relay as described under "Dual Pick Up Start-Run Relay Test".
15. If ohmmeter reading obtained in step 13 is not between 150–900 ohms, disconnect pick up leads and measure resistance at distributor side of pick up lead, Fig. 8G. If reading obtained is not between 150–900 ohms, replace pick up coils as necessary.
16. Check for short circuit at each distributor side of pick up lead by connecting ohmmeter as indicated in Fig. 8H. If ohmmeter indicates pick up is shorted, replace pick up coil and adjust air gap to .006 inch.
17. If pick up coil is satisfactory, check for proper ECU ground contact by connecting ohmmeter between pin 5 of ECU and ground. If ohmmeter indicates poor ECU ground contact, check for proper ECU installation or poor ECU electrical connections.
18. If ECU is properly grounded, reconnect all electrical connections and check again for spark. If no spark is available, replace ECU.

Dual Pick up Start-Run Relay Test, 1981–82 Models

1. Disconnect two-way connector from pins 5 and 4 of dual pick up start-run relay, Fig. 8I.
2. Connect suitable ohmmeter between pins 4 and 5 of relay.
3. If ohmmeter reading of 20–30 ohms cannot be obtained, replace relay.

Distributor Service

Distributor, Replace

Removal

1. Disconnect vacuum line at distributor.
2. Disconnect distributor pickup lead(s) at wiring harness connector, then remove distributor cap.
3. Mark position of rotor on distributor body and engine block surface so that distributor can be installed in the same position.
4. Remove holddown and/or bolt and lift distributor from engine.

Installation

1. If engine was cranked after distributor was removed from engine, rotate crankshaft to bring No. 1 piston up on its compression stroke and align timing mark on crankshaft pulley with "O" (TDC) mark on timing cover on 6 cylinder and V-8 engines. On 4 cylinder engines equipped

with manual transmission, align "O" (TDC) mark on flywheel with pointer on bell housing. On 4 cylinder engines equipped with automatic transmission, align timing mark on flywheel with "O" (TDC) mark on bell housing.
2. With distributor gasket or O-ring in place, hold distributor over mounting pad.
3. Turn rotor to a position just ahead of the No. 1 distributor cap terminal.
4. Install distributor, engaging distributor gear with camshaft drive gear on 4 and 6 cylinder engines. On V-8 engines, engage tang of distributor shaft with slot in oil pump drive gear. With distributor fully seated on engine, rotor should be under No. 1 cap terminal.
5. Install distributor holddown and/or bolt, distributor cap, pick-up lead(s) and vacuum line.
6. Adjust ignition timing to specifications found in the individual car chapters.

Distributor Shaft & Bushing Wear Test

1. Remove distributor from vehicle and clamp distributor in a vise. Use extreme caution not to damage distributor.
2. Attach a dial indicator to housing so plunger rests against reluctor sleeve.
3. Place a wire loop around reluctor sleeve and hook a spring scale on the other end of the loop. Apply a one pound pull in line with indicator plunger and read movement on indicator. Movement must not exceed .006 inch. If movement exceeds limit, replace either housing or shaft to bring movement back within tolerance.

Distributor Disassemble

1. Remove rotor and vacuum advance unit, Figs. 9 thru 10.
2. Remove reluctor by prying up from bottom of reluctor using two screwdrivers with a maximum blade width of 7/16 in. Use care not to damage or distort reluctor teeth.
3. Remove two screws and lockwashers attaching lower plate to distributor housing, then lift out lower plate, upper plate and pick-up coil as an assembly. Do not remove distributor cap clamp springs.
4. On six cylinder units, if distributor housing, or shaft and governor assembly are to be replaced, proceed as follows:
   a. If gear is worn or damaged, scribe a line on end of shaft from center to edge, so that line is centered between two gear teeth, Fig. 11. Do not scribe line completely across shaft. Remove distributor drive gear retaining pin and slide gear off end of shaft.

   NOTE: Support hub of gear so that pin can be driven out without damaging shaft.

   b. If necessary use a file to clean burrs from around pin hole area on shaft, then remove lower thrust washer.
   c. Push shaft upward and remove from distributor body.
5. On eight cylinder units, if distributor housing, shaft, reluctor sleeve or governor weights are to replace, proceed as follows:
   a. Remove distributor shaft retaining

CAP

ROTOR

RELUCTOR

SCREW

PICK-UP AND PLATE ASSEMBLY

PIN

SPACER

SNAP RING

SHAFT ASSEMBLY

VACUUM CONTROL

SEAL

HOUSING

SPRING

GASKET

WASHER

RETAINER

GEAR

PIN

PLATE

WASHER

SCREW

CAP

ROTOR

RELUCTOR

SCREW

PIN

PICK-UP AND PLATE ASSEMBLY

PIN

FELT WICK

SNAP RING

SHAFT ASSEMBLY

VACUUM CONTROL

THRUST WASHER

HOUSING AND BEARINGS

SPRING

THRUST WASHER

GEAR

PIN

SCREW

"O" RING

PLATE

WASHER

HOLD DOWN CLAMP

SCREW

Fig. 9 Disassembled view of Chrysler 6 cylinder engine electronic distributor with single pick up.

Fig. 9A Disassembled view of Chrysler 6 cylinder engine electronic distributor with dual pick up.

CAP

ROTOR

SNAP RING

RELUCTOR

SCREW

CLIP OR RETAINER

PICK UP AND PLATE ASSEMBLY

PIN

SHAFT ASSEMBLY

SPRING

SEAL

HOUSING AND BEARING

VACUUM CONTROL

COLLAR, PIN AND WASHER

Fig. 10 Disassembled view of Chrysler 8 cylinder engine electronic distributor.

CENTER LINE OF ROTOR ELECTRODE

PIN

ALIGNMENT MARK ON SHAFT

Fig. 11   Scribe line on distributor shaft. 6 cylinder units

CENTER LINE OF ROTOR ELECTRODE

GEAR ROTATED APPROX. 90°

HOLE IN SERVICE GEAR

MARK ON SHAFT

CENTER LINE OF GEAR TOOTH

Fig. 12   Aligning gear teeth with center line of rotor electrode. 6 cylinder units

pin and slide retainer off end of shaft.
b. If necessary, use a file to clean burrs from around pin hole area on shaft, then remove lower thrust washer.
c. Push shaft upward and remove from distributor housing.

Distributor Assemble

1. Lubricate and test operation of governor weights. Inspect weight springs for distortion and bearing surfaces and pins for damage.
2. Lubricate upper thrust washer and install onto shaft. Install shaft into housing, Figs. 9 thru 10.
3. On 6 cylinder units, install lower thrust washer and distributor gear and roll pin. If a replacement distributor gear is to be installed, proceed as follows:
a. Install thrust washer and replacement gear on rotor shaft. Position pin hole in replacement gear approximately 90 degrees from hole in distributor shaft, with scribed line made during disassembly between gear teeth, Fig. 11.

NOTE: On replacement distributor

Fig. 13 Air gap adjustment. Distributors equipped with dual pick up

Fig. 14 Air gap adjustment. Distributors equipped with single pick up

gears, the roll pin hole is located higher than the original gear roll pin hole, so that distributor shaft will not be weakened when the shaft is rotated 90 degrees and drilled to accommodate the replacement gear.

b. Before drilling through shaft and gear, place a .007 in. feeler gauge between gear and thrust washer and observe that centerline between two gear teeth is in line with centerline of rotor electrode, Fig. 12. Drill a .124 to .129 in. hole and install roll pin.

NOTE: Support gear hub when installing roll pin so gear teeth will not be damaged.

4. On eight cylinder units, install distributor shaft retainer and pin, Fig. 10.
5. On all units, install lower plate, upper plate and pick-up coil assembly, Figs. 9 thru 10.
6. Attach vacuum advance unit to pick-up plate, then install vacuum advance unit attaching screws and washers.
7. Position reluctor keeper pin into place on reluctor sleeve, then slide reluctor down reluctor sleeve and press firmly into position. Install keeper pin.
8. Lubricate felt pad located in top of reluctor sleeve with one drop of light engine oil, then install rotor.

Pick-up Replacement & Air Gap Adjustment

1. With distributor removed from vehicle, perform Steps 1 to 3 as outlined in Distributor Disassemble.
2. Remove pick-up coil and upper plate by depressing retainer clip and moving it away from mounting stud. Pick-up coil cannot be removed from upper plate.
3. Lightly lubricate upper plate pivot pin and lower plate support pins with distributor lubricant. Install upper plate pivot pin through smallest hole in lower plate and install retainer clip.

NOTE: The upper plate must ride on the support pins on the lower plate.

4. Install lower and upper plates and pick-up coil as an assembly and install distributor into vehicle.

NOTE: On dual pick up distributors, the start pick up may be identified by a two prong male connector and the run pick up may be identified by a male-female plug, Fig. 13.

5. To set air gap on all single pick up distributors and on start pick up of dual pick up distributors, align one reluctor tooth with pick up pole and install a .006

inch non-magnetic feeler gauge between reluctor tooth and pick up pole, Figs. 13 and 14. Rotate pick up coil until contact is made between reluctor tooth, feeler gauge and pick up pole. Tighten pick up coil hold down screw and remove feeler gauge. The feeler gauge should be removed without force. If it cannot, readjust gap.
6. To set air gap on run pick up of dual pick up distributors, first adjust start pick up as described in step 5, then adjust run pick up as described in step 5. Use a .012 inch non-magnetic feeler gauge to adjust run pick up air gap.
7. Perform a second gap check using a .008 inch feeler gauge on all single pick up distributors and on start pick up of dual pick up distributor or a .014 inch feeler gauge on run pick up of dual pick up distributors. Do not force feeler gauge between reluctor tooth and pick up pole as it is possible to do so. The feeler gauge should not be able to fit between the reluctor tooth and pick up pole if air gap is correctly set. Apply vacuum to vacuum control unit. Pick up should not contact reluctor tooth. Readjust air gap if contact occurs.

NOTE: If pick up contacts reluctor teeth on one side of shaft only, the distributor shaft is most likely bent and shaft replacement required.

Chrysler Corp. Front Wheel Drive Models Less Electronic Spark Control (Lean Burn) System, Except Horizon & Omni

DESCRIPTION

This system consists of the distributor, Fig. 1, ignition switch, ignition coil, ECU igniter and spark plugs. Primary circuit current is controlled by the ECU igniter in response to timing signals produced by the distributor pick up. The distributor consists of the power distribution section, signal generator, ECU igniter, advance mechanism and drive gear section. The signal generator is a small magneto which produces a signal that is processed by the ECU to determine the exact time to open the primary circuit and fire the spark plugs.

SYSTEM TESTING

1. Disconnect high tension lead from distributor and hold end of cable 3/16–3/8 inch from good engine ground. Crank engine and check for spark at end of high tension lead.
2. If spark is present, continue cranking engine while slowly moving coil high tension lead away from engine ground. If arcing occurs at coil tower, replace coil. If no spark is present at coil high tension lead or spark is weak, turn ignition On and check voltage at coil negative terminal using suitable voltmeter.

3. If voltage reading obtained is the same as battery voltage, system is operating satisfactorily. If reading is three volts or less, the distributor is defective and must be checked further. If zero reading is obtained, check for open circuit in ignition wiring and repair as necessary.
4. Connect one end of suitable jumper wire to coil negative terminal. Turn ignition On, position coil high tension lead as described in step 1, then momentarily touch other end of jumper wire to a good ground.
5. If no spark is observed at coil high tension lead, check for presence of voltage at coil positive terminal. If battery voltage read-

Fig. 1 Disassembled view of electronic ignition distributor. 1981–82 Aries & Reliant; 1982 400 & LeBaron

ing is obtained at coil positive terminal, replace coil. If proper voltage cannot be obtained, check for loose connections or damaged wiring and repair as necessary.

DISTRIBUTOR SERVICE

Distributor, Replace

Removal
1. Rotate engine until No. 1 cylinder is at TDC on compression stroke.
2. Disconnect battery ground cable.
3. Remove distributor cap and mark relationship of rotor to distributor housing.
4. Remove distributor wiring harness and secondary ignition cables.
5. Disconnect vacuum hose from distributor.
6. Remove distributor retaining nut, then the distributor.

Installation
1. Align mating mark on distributor housing with rotor.
2. Install distributor into engine aligning mating mark on distributor mounting flange with center of distributor retaining stud, Fig. 2.
3. Install retaining nut, vacuum hose, secondary ignition cables and distributor wiring harness.
4. Connect battery ground cable, start engine and adjust ignition timing.

Disassembly

1. Remove distributor rotor.
2. Remove governor assembly retaining screw, Fig. 1 and governor assembly.

NOTE: Governor springs are not inter-

changeable and must be installed in their original positions. Note position of each spring during disassembly for reference during assembly.

3. Remove wire retaining clamp from side of distributor.
4. Remove pick up coil and ECU igniter retaining screws, then remove pick up coil and ECU igniter as an assembly.
5. Remove vacuum chamber retaining screws, then the vacuum chamber assembly.
6. Remove breaker assembly retaining screws, then the breaker assembly.
7. Remove bearing retainer plate screws, then the bearing retainer plate.
8. Mark relationship of distributor drive gear to distributor shaft, then punch out distributor drive gear retaining pin and

Fig. 2 Aligning distributor and engine mating marks

remove gear from shaft.
9. Remove distributor shaft and bearing assembly from housing.
10. Remove distributor housing seal.

Assembly

1. Lubricate distributor housing seal with suitable grease and install into distributor housing.
2. Install distributor shaft and bearing assembly into distributor housing.
3. Install distributor drive gear onto shaft and align marks made during disassembly.
4. Install drive gear roll pin, then install bearing retainer and retaining screws.
5. Install breaker assembly and retaining screws.
6. Install vacuum chamber onto distributor housing and secure with retaining screws.
7. Install pick up coil and ECU igniter as an assembly into housing, then install retaining screws.
8. Install wire retaining clamp and governor assembly. If governor assembly was disassembled, check to ensure that governor springs are installed in original positions.
9. Install governor assembly retaining screw and rotor.

Pick Up Assembly, Replace

1. Remove distributor as described under "Distributor Service" under "Distributor, Replace".
2. Perform steps 1 thru 4 as described under "Distributor Service" under "Disassembly".
3. Reverse procedure to install.

Chrysler Corp. Horizon & Omni Less Electronic Spark Control (Lean Burn) System

This system consists primarily of the battery, ignition switch, control unit, coil, distributor and spark plugs, Fig. 1.

There are two basic circuits in this system; the primary and secondary. The primary circuit consists of the battery, ignition switch, primary windings of the ignition coil, power switching transistor of the control unit and the ground circuit. The secondary circuit consists of the coil secondary circuit, distributor rotor and cap, spark plugs, wires and ground circuit.

The compensating resistance of the circuit maintains consistant current in variation to engine speed. During starting, this resistance is by-passed and full battery voltage is supplied to the ignition coil.

In addition to the two basic circuits, there is the pick coil circuit and control unit feed circuit.

The pick up circuit senses the proper timing for the control unit switching transistor. The reluctor rotates with the distributor shaft and produces a voltage pulse in the magnetic pick up each time a spark plug is to fire. This pulse is transmitted through the pick up coil to the power switching transistor in the control unit causing the transistor to interrupt the current flow through the primary circuit. This interruption induces a high voltage in the secondary coil circuit and fires a spark plug. The length of time that the switching transistor allows the flow of current in the primary circuit is determined by the electronic circuitry in the control unit.

Fig. 1 Electronic Ignition System. 1980 Horizon & Omni

System Testing

Harness & Connections Test

1. Check battery voltage using a voltmeter. Battery voltage should be at least 12 volts.
2. Disconnect connector from control unit.

   CAUTION: The ignition switch must be in the "Off" position whenever any connector is disconnected or connected.

3. Turn ignition switch "On" and connect negative lead of voltmeter to ground.

4. Connect positive lead of voltmeter to connector cavity No. 2, Fig. 2 Voltage reading should be within 1 volt of reading taken in Step 1 with all accessories off. If there is more than 1 volt difference, check circuit shown in Fig. 2.
5. Connect positive lead of voltmeter to connector cavity No. 5, Fig. 3. Voltage reading should be within 1 volt of reading taken in Step 1 with all accessories off. If there is more than 1 volt difference, check circuit shown in Fig. 3.
6. Turn ignition switch "Off" and reconnect wiring harness to control unit.
7. Disconnect wiring harness connector from distributor and turn ignition switch to "On".
8. Connect positive lead to voltmeter to connector cavity No. 1, Fig. 4. Voltage read-

ing should be within 1 volt of reading taken in Step 1 with all accessories off. If there is more than 1 volt difference, turn ignition switch "Off" and disconnect control unit connection. Connect an ohmmeter from distributor connector cavity No. 1 to control unit connector cavity No. 1, Fig. 5. If there is no continuity, replace wiring harness.
9. Make sure that ignition switch is "Off"

Fig. 2 Cavity No. 2 and related circuitry test

Fig. 3 Cavity No. 5 and related circuitry test

Fig. 4 Cavity No. 1 and related circuitry test

Fig. 5   Cavity No. 1 continuity test

Fig. 6   Cavity No. 2 continuity test

Fig. 7   Pin No. 4 continuity test

and reconnect wiring harness to control unit.

10. Connect one ohmmeter lead to a good ground and the other lead to distributor wiring harness connector No. 2, Fig. 6. If ohmmeter does not indicate continuity, disconnect connector from control unit and connect ungrounded ohmmeter lead to control unit connector pin No. 4, Fig. 7. If ohmmeter does not indicate continuity, remove control unit mounting bolts, clean control unit surface area which comes in contact with bolts, reinstall and tighten bolts and recheck for continuity. If continuity still does not exist, replace control unit.

Ignition Secondary System Test

1. Disconnect cable from center tower of distributor and hold cable about 3/16 inch from engine.

CAUTION: Make sure that there are no fuel leaks before performing this test.

2. If arcing does not occur while cranking engine, remove wire harness connector from distributor and connect a jumper wire to wiring harness connector cavity No. 3, Fig. 8. Intermittently short the other end of jumper wire to ground. If there is a spark at cable, replace distributor pick up.

NOTE: When replacing pick up, check to make sure that rotor vanes are grounded, Fig. 9. Connect one lead of an ohmmeter to a good ground and the other lead to a shutterblade. If there is no continuity, push rotor down on shaft. If still there is no continuity, remove rotor, clean top of shaft and replace rotor. If still there is no continuity, replace rotor with one of the correct type (do not substitute rotor from previous year vehicles). Do not start engine until continuity has been obtained.

3. Crank engine again. If there is still no spark, replace control unit and recheck. If still there is no spark, replace ignition coil.

Distributor Service
Distributor, Replace

Removal
1. Disconnect distributor pickup lead wire at harness connector.
2. Remove distributor cap.
3. Rotate engine until distributor rotor faces toward cylinder block then scribe a mark

on the block to indicate rotor position.
4. Remove distributor hold down screw.
5. Remove distributor from engine.

NOTE: Do not crank engine while distributor is removed.

Installation
1. Position distributor in engine.
2. Engage distributor drive gear with camshaft drive gear so the distributor rotor will align with the scribe mark on cylinder block.
3. If the engine was cranked while the distributor was removed, proceed as follows:
   a. Rotate crankshaft until No. 1 piston is at top dead center, compression stroke. The pointer on clutch housing should align with the "0" mark on the flywheel.
   b. Rotate distributor rotor to a position ahead of the No. 1 distributor cap terminal.
   c. Install distributor into engine, engaging distributor drive gear with camshaft drive gear. The rotor should be properly positioned under the distributor cap No. 1 terminal.
4. Install distributor cap.
5. Install distributor hold down screw finger tight.
6. Connect distributor pickup lead wire.
7. Adjust ignition timing. Refer to the "Tune Up Specifications" found in the individual car chapters.

Fig. 8   Grounding cavity No. 3 to ground with jumper wire

Fig. 9   Rotor vanes

Fig. 10   Replacing vacuum chamber

Fig. 11   Replacing retaining clips

Disassembly

1. Place distributor in a short jawed vise, then remove distributor cap and rotor.
2. Remove vacuum chamber retaining screws, then lift up to disengage linking pin and remove vacuum chamber, Fig. 10.
3. Remove pick up assembly retaining clips, Fig. 11, and pick up assembly, Fig. 12.

4. Place drive gear on vise so that roll pin can be removed, then remove drive pin using a punch.
5. Remove drive gear and drive shaft from housing.
6. If necessary remove wires from distributor cap by pinching wire clips with pliers and pushing out.

Assembly

1. Clean and inspect all parts. Lubricate housing bushings with engine oil.
2. Install drive shaft into housing, then install drive gear onto shaft and retain with roll pin.
3. Install pick up assembly, Fig. 12

NOTE: Pick up assembly leads may be damaged if not properly installed. Make sure lead retainer is in locating hole properly before installing distributor cap. "T" shaped attachment on retainer must slip into locating hole. When distributor is installed, leads are behind distributor housing and cannot be easily checked for proper positioning.

4. Install pick up assembly retaining clips, Fig. 11.
5. Connect vacuum chamber linking pin and install vacuum chamber and retaining screws, Fig. 10.
6. Install rotor and distributor rotor.

HALL EFFECT PICKUP ASSEMBLY

Fig. 12   Replacing pick up assembly

Pick Up Assembly, Replace

1. Remove distributor cap and rotor.
2. Remove vacuum chamber retaining screws and vacuum chamber, Fig. 10.
3. Remove retaining clips, Fig. 11, and pick up assembly, Fig. 12.

Chrysler Corp. Rear Wheel Drive Models W/ Electronic Spark Control (Lean Burn) System

SERVICE NOTE
Ignition Timing, Adjust

1977–81
1. Connect a tachometer to engine and a suitable timing light to No. 1 cylinder.

NOTE: Do not puncture ignition cables or boots with test probes.

2. Start engine, then apply parking brake and place transmission in Neutral. Allow engine to reach operating temperature.

Fig. 1   Power & vacuum transducer tests

3. Disconnect and plug EGR vacuum hose at EGR valve and vacuum hose to Electronic Spark Control computor, then connect a jumper wire from carburetor switch to ground.
4. Disconnect PCV valve and vapor canister purge hose from carburetor. Do not plug hoses.
5. Check idle speed and adjust as necessary, then reconnect PCV valve vacuum hose and vapor canister purge hose.
6. Loosen distributor hold down bracket screw just enough so that distributor housing can be rotated.
7. Check and adjust ignition timing as necessary.
8. Tighten distributor hold down screw, then recheck idle speed and ignition timing.
9. Remove test equipment and connect vacuum hoses.

1982
1. Connect a suitable tachometer to engine and a suitable adjustable timing light to No. 1 cylinder secondary cable.

NOTE: Do not puncture ignition secondary cables or boots with test probes.

2. Set parking brake, start engine and place

gear selector in neutral. Run engine until warm.
3. On vehicles equipped with carburetor switch, connect a jumper wire between carburetor switch and a known good ground.
4. Ensure curb idle speed is set at or below specifications. Adjust as necessary.
5. Check ignition timing. If within ± 2° of specifications, shut engine "Off" and remove timing light, tachometer and carburetor ground wire. If outside of toler-

Fig. 2   Dual connector. 1977 Exc. Diplomat & LaBaron

Fig. 3 Single connector. 1977 Exc. Diplomat & LaBaron

ance, proceed to step 6.

6. Loosen distributor hold down arm screw, rotate distributor housing until correct timing marks are lined up, ensuring idle speed is still at or below specified curb idle speed.
7. Tighten distributor hold down screw, then recheck idle speed and ignition timing.
8. Turn engine "Off" and remove timing light, tachometer and carburetor ground wire.

Ignition System Starting Test

1. Remove the coil wire from distributor cap and hold end of wire about 1/4 in. from a good engine ground. Crank engine and observe spark at coil wire.
2. The spark at the coil wire must be constant and bright blue in color. If so, continue to crank engine and slowly move coil wire away from ground. If arcing occurs at the coil tower, replace coil. If spark is weak or not constant or there is no spark, proceed to the "Failure To Start Test."
3. If spark is satisfactory and no arcing occurs at coil tower, the ignition system is producing the necessary high secondary voltage. However, this voltage is transmitted to the spark plugs by checking the distributor rotor, cap, spark plug wires, and spark plugs. If satisfactory, the ignition system is not faulty. It will be necessary to check the fuel system and engine mechanical components.

Failure To Start Test

NOTE: Before proceeding with this test, perform "Ignition System Starting Test". Failure to do so may lead to unnecessary diagnostic time and incorrect test results.

1977 Exc. Diplomat & LeBaron

1. With a voltmeter, measure and note voltage at battery. Battery specific gravity must be at least 1.220, temperature corrected, to deliver the necessary voltage to operate the cranking and ignition systems properly.
2. Disconnect wiring harness connector from "Coolant Switch."
3. Place a piece of paper between curb idle adjusting screw and carburetor switch, Fig. 1, or ensure curb idle adjusting screw is not contacting switch.
4. Connect negative lead of voltmeter to an engine ground.
5. Turn ignition switch to "Run" position and measure voltage at carburetor switch terminal, Fig. 1. If voltage is greater than 5 volts but less than 10 volts, proceed to Step 7. If voltage is greater than 10 volts, check continuity between terminal 2 of

the dual connector and the ground with ignition switch in "Off" position. Continuity should be noted. If continuity does not exist, check for poor ground connection. If voltage is less than 5 volts, turn ignition switch to "OFF" and disconnect dual connector from bottom of "Spark Control Computer". Turn ignition switch to "Run" and measure voltage at terminal 4 of dual connector, Fig. 2. Voltage should be within 1 volt of battery voltage. If voltage is satisfactory, proceed to Step 6. If not, check wiring between terminal 4 of dual connector, Fig. 2, and ignition switch for opens, shorts or improper connections.

6. Turn ignition switch to "OFF" and disconnect single connector from bottom of "Spark Control Computer." Check continuity between terminal 11 of single connector, Fig. 3, and carburetor switch terminal. There should be continuity between these two points. If not, check wiring for opens, shorts or improper connections. If continuity is noted, check continuity between terminal 2 of dual connector, Fig. 2, and the ground. If continuity is noted, replace "Spark Control Computer". If not, check wiring for opens or improper connections and only proceed to Step 7 if engine still fails to start.
7. Turn ignition switch to "Run" and with positive lead of voltmeter, measure voltage at terminals 7 and 8 of disconnected leads from computer, Fig. 2. Voltage should be within 1 volt of battery voltage. If so, proceed to step 8. If not, proceed as follows:
   Terminal 7—Check wiring and connections between connector and ignition switch. Also, check 5 ohm side of ballast resistor.
   Terminal 8—Check wiring and connections between connector and ignition switch. Also, check primary windings of coil and 1/2 ohm side of ballast resistor.
8. Turn ignition switch to "OFF" position and measure resistance between terminals 5 and 6 of dual connector Fig. 2. Resistance should be between 150 and 900 ohms. If resistance is satisfactory, proceed to Step 9. If not, disconnect "Start Pick Up" coil leads from distributor and measure resistance at distributor leads, Fig. 4. If resistance is between 150 and 900 ohms, there is an open, shorted, or improper connection between distributor connector and terminals 5 and 6 of dual

Fig. 4 Distributor leads. 1977 Exc. Diplomat & LeBaron

connector, Fig. 2. If resistance is not within specifications, the "Start Pick Up" coil is faulty.

9. Connect one lead of ohmmeter to engine ground and with other lead, check for continuity at each terminal of distributor leads, Fig. 4. There should be no continuity. Reconnect distributor leads and proceed to Step 10. If there is continuity, replace "Start Pick Up" coil.
10. Remove distributor cap and check and adjust air gap of "Start Pick Up" coil outlined under "Pick-up Replacement & Air Gap Adjustment", Chrysler Corp. Rear Wheel Drive Models, Less Electronic Spark Control (Lean Burn) System. Refer to the Pick-up Air Gap Specification Chart for air gap dimensions.
11. Install distributor cap, reconnect all wiring and start engine. If engine still fails to start, replace "Spark Control Computer".
12. After installing new computer and engine still fails to start, reinstall original one and repeat test procedure, since one of the test procedures may not have been performed correctly.

1977 Diplomat & LeBaron; 1978–79 All

1. With a voltmeter, measure and note battery voltage. Battery specific gravity must be at least 1.220, temperature corrected, to deliver the necessary voltage to operate the cranking and ignition systems properly.
2. Disconnect wiring harness connector from coolant switch.
3. Place a piece of paper between curb idle adjusting screw and carburetor switch, Fig. 1, or ensure curb idle adjusting screw is not contacting carburetor switch.
4. Connect negative lead of voltmeter to an engine ground.
5. Turn ignition switch to "Run" position and measure voltage at carburetor switch, Fig. 1. If voltage is greater than 5 volts but less than 10 volts, proceed to Step 7. If voltage is greater than 10 volts, turn ignition switch to "Off" position and disconnect dual connector from bottom of "Spark Control Computer", Fig. 5, then check continuity between terminal 10 and the ground. If voltage is less than 5 volts, turn ignition switch to "Run" position and measure voltage at terminal 2 of the dual connector, Fig. 5. Voltage should be within one volt of battery voltage. If voltage is satisfactory, proceed to Step 6. If not, check wiring between terminal 2, Fig. 5, and the ignition switch for opens, shorts or improper connections.
6. With ignition switch in "Off" position, check continuity between terminal 7 of dual connector, Fig. 5, and the carburetor switch terminal. There should be continuity between these two points. If not, check wiring for opens, shorts or improper connections. If continuity is noted, check con-

Fig. 5 Dual Connector. 1977 Diplomat & LeBaron; 1978–82 All

Fig. 6 Transducer terminal resistance & idle stop solenoid checks

tinuity between terminal 10 of dual connector, Fig. 5, and the ground. If continuity is noted, replace "Spark Control Computer". If not, check wiring for opens or improper connections and only proceed to Step 7 if engine still fails to start.

7. Turn ignition switch to "Run" position and measure the voltage between terminal 1, Fig. 5, and the ground. Voltage should be within one volt of battery voltage. If so, proceed to Step 8. If not, proceed as follows:

    Terminal 1—Check wiring and connections between dual connector and ignition switch.

8. Turn ignition switch to "Off" position and measure resistance between terminals 5 and 9 of dual connector, Fig. 5. Resistance should be between 150 and 900 ohms. If so, proceed to Step 9. If not, disconnect "Pick-Up Coil" lead from distributor and measure resistance between terminals at distributor side of connector. If resistance is between 150 and 900 ohms, there is an open, shorted or improper connection between the distributor connector and terminals 5 and 9 of the dual connector. If resistance is still not within specifications, the "Pick-Up Coil" is faulty.

9. Check for continuity between each terminal on distributor side of distributor connector and the engine ground. There should be no continuity. Reconnect distributor connector and proceed to Step 10. If continuity is present, replace "Pick-Up Coil".

10. Remove distributor cap and air gap of "Pick-Up Coil". Refer to "Pick-Up Replacement & Air Gap Adjustment", Chrysler Corp. Rear Wheel Drive Models, Less Electronic Spark Control (Lean Burn) System. Adjust air gap if necessary.

11. Install distributor cap, reconnect all wiring and start engine. If engine still fails to start, replace "Spark Control Computer".

12. After installing new computer and engine still fails to start, reinstall original computer and repeat test procedure since one of the test procedures may not have been performed correctly.

1980 All Models

1. With a voltmeter, measure and note battery voltage. Battery specific gravity must be at least 1.220, temperature corrected, to deliver voltage to operate cranking and ignition system properly.

2. Place a piece of paper between curb idle adjusting screw and carb switch, Fig. 1, or ensure that carburetor idle adjusting screw is not touching carb switch.

3. Connect negative lead of voltmeter to a good engine ground.

4. Rotate ignition switch to Run position and measure voltage at carburetor switch terminal. If voltage is approximately 5 volts, proceed to step 6. If voltage is not at least 5 volts, place ignition switch in Off position and disconnect wire connector

from bottom of Spark Control Computer, Fig. 5. Rotate ignition switch back to the Run position and measure voltage at wire connector terminal 2, Fig. 5. Voltage should be within one volt of battery voltage noted previously. If voltage is correct proceed to step 5. If voltage is incorrect, check wiring between wire terminal 2 and ignition switch for open or short circuits or improper connections.

5. With ignition switch in the Off position, disconnect wire connector from Spark Control Computer. Using an ohmmeter, check for continuity between connector terminal 7, Fig. 5, and carburetor switch terminal. Continuity should exist between these two points. If not, check wiring for open or short circuit or improper connections. If continuity is noted, check for continuity between connector terminal 10 and engine ground. If continuity exist, replace Spark Control Computer. If not, check wiring for open circuit or improper connections and proceed to step 6 only if engine still fails to start.

6. Place ignition switch in the Run position and with positive lead of voltmeter, measure voltage from computer connector terminal 1 to ground Fig. 5. Voltage reading should be within one volt of battery voltage noted previously. If proper voltage reading is indicated, proceed to step 7. If improper voltage reading is indicated, check wiring and connection between connector terminal No. 1 and ignition switch.

7. Place ignition switch in the off position, then using an ohmmeter, measure resistance between terminals No. 5 and 9 for run pickup coil and terminals 3 and 9 for start pickup coil Fig. 5. Resistance should be between 150 and 900 ohms. If not, disconnect pickup coil leads from distributor and measure resistance at lead going into distributor. If resistance is now between 150 and 900 ohms, this would indicate an open or short circuit or improper connection between distributor connector and terminals 5 and 9 or terminals 3 and 9 of dual connector. If resistance is not within specifications, pickup coil is defective.

8. Connect one ohmmeter lead to engine ground and with the other lead check for continuity at each terminal going to the distributor. There should be no continuity. Reconnect distributor lead and proceed to step 9. If there is continuity, replace pickup coil.

9. Remove distributor cap and check air gap of pickup coil. Refer to Pickup Coil Replacement and Air Gap Adjustment and adjust gap as necessary.

10. Install distributor cap and reconnect all wiring, then start engine. If engine fails to start, replace spark control computer.

11. After installing new computer and engine

Fig. 8 Checking with test transducer

CORE OUT ONE INCH

1"

Fig. 7 Throttle transducer

still fails to start, reinstall original computer and repeat test procedure since one of the test procedures may have been performed incorrectly.

1981–82 All Models

1. Turn ignition "Off". Remove 10 way connector from base of Spark Control Computer. Turn ignition "On", then holding end of coil wire about 1/4" away from a ground, momentarily short coil negative wire to ground. If a spark is obtained, replace Spark Control Computer. If no spark is obtained, proceed to step 2.

2. Using a voltmeter, check for battery voltage at coil positive terminal with the ignition "On". If voltage is within 1 volt of battery voltage, proceed to step 4. If not, proceed to step 3.

3. Using an ohmmeter, check continuity of wiring between battery and coil positive, repair as necessary and repeat step 2.

4. Using a voltmeter, check for battery voltage at coil negative. If within 1 volt of battery voltage, proceed to step 5. If not, replace coil.

5. If voltage is correct, but no spark is obtained when grounding coil negative, replace coil.

6. If spark is obtained, but engine will not start, place ignition switch in "On" position. Using a suitable voltmeter, measure voltage of disconnected 10 way connector cavity 1, Fig. 5 to ground. Voltage should be within 1 volt of battery voltage. If voltage is within 1 volt of battery voltage, proceed to step 8. If not, proceed to step 7.

7. Using an ohmmeter, check continuity of wire for opens and repair as necessary (no power between coil negative and 10 way connector). Repeat step 6.

8. Place a piece of paper between curb idle adjusting screw and carburetor switch, Fig. 1, or ensure curb idle adjusting screw is not contacting carburetor switch.

9. Connect negative lead of voltmeter to a good engine ground.

10. Rotate ignition switch to "On" position and measure voltage at carburetor switch terminal. If voltage is approximately 5 volts, proceed to step 12. If voltage is not at least 5 volts, place ignition switch in "Off" position and disconnect wire connector from bottom of Spark Control Computer, Fig. 5. Rotate ignition switch back to the "On" position and measure voltage at wire connector terminal 2, Fig. 5. Voltage should be within one volt of battery voltage noted previously. If voltage is correct proceed to step 11. If voltage is incorrect check wiring between wire terminal 2 and ignition switch for open or short circuits or improper connections.

11. With ignition switch in the "Off" position, disconnect wire connector from Spark Control Computer. Using an ohmmeter, check for continuity between connector terminal 7, Fig. 5, and carburetor switch

Fig. 8A Detonation sensor location

terminal. Continuity should exist between these two points. If not, check wiring for open or short circuit or improper connections. If continuity is noted, check for continuity between connector terminal 10 and engine ground. If continuity exists, replace Spark Control Computer. If not, check wiring for open circuit or improper connections and proceed to step 12 only if engine still fails to start.

12. Place ignition switch in the "Off" position, then using an ohmmeter, measure resistance between terminals No. 5 and 9 for run pickup coil and terminals 3 and 9 for start pickup coil Fig. 5. Resistance should be between 150 and 900 ohms. If not, disconnect pickup coil leads from distributor and measure resistance at lead going into distributor. If resistance is now between 150 and 900 ohms, this would indicate an open or short circuit or improper connection between distributor connector and terminals 5 and 9 or terminals 3 and 9 of dual connector. If resistance is not within specifications, pickup coil is defective.

13. Connect one ohmmeter lead to engine ground and with the other lead check for continuity at each terminal going to the distributor. There should be no continuity. Reconnect distributor lead and proceed to step 14. If there is continuity, replace pickup coil.

14. Remove distributor cap and check air gap of pickup coil. Refer to Pickup Coil Replacement and Air Gap Adjustment and adjust gap as necessary.

15. Install distributor cap and reconnect all wiring, then start engine. If engine fails to start, replace spark control computer.

16. After installing new computer and engine still fails to start, reinstall original computer and repeat test procedure since one of the test procedures may have been performed incorrectly.

Poor Performance Tests

Run Pick-Up Function Test, 1977 Exc. Diplomat & LeBaron

1. Start and run engine for about 1½ minutes. Then, disconnect "Start Pick Up" lead from distributor. If engine continues to run, reconnect "Start Pick Up" lead and proceed to "Start Timer Advance Schedule Test." If engine stopped proceed to Step 2.

2. Reconnect "Start Pick Up" lead at distributor, turn ignition switch to "OFF" and disconnect dual connector from bottom of "Spark Control Computer." Measure resistance between terminals 3 and 5 of dual connector, Fig. 2. Resistance should be between 150 and 900 ohms. If so, proceed to Step 3. If not, disconnect "Run Pick Up" coil leads from distributor and measure resistance at distributor leads. If resistance is now between 150 and 900 ohms, check for open, shorted or improper connections of the wiring between distributor connector and terminals 3 and 5 of

dual connector, Fig. 2. If resistance is not within specifications, the "Run Pick Up" coil is faulty. Replace "Run Pick Up" coil and repeat Step 1. If engine still fails to run, proceed to Step 3.

3. Disconnect "Run Pick Up" coil from distributor. Connect one lead of ohmmeter to an engine ground and, with other lead, check for continuity at each terminal of distributor leads. There should be no continuity. If not, reconnect distributor leads and proceed to Step 4. If continuity is noted, replace "Run Pick Up" coil and repeat Step 1. If engine still fails to run, proceed to Step 4.

4. Remove distributor cap and check and adjust air gap of "Run Pick Up" coil as outlined under "Pick-up Replacement & Air Gap Adjustment", Chrysler Corp. Rear Wheel Drive Models, Less Electronic Spark Control (Lean Burn) System. Refer to the Pick-up Air Gap Specification Chart for air gap dimensions.

5. If engine still fails to run, replace "Spark Control Computer" and repeat Step 1. If engine again fails to start, reinstall original computer and repeat complete test since one of the test procedures may not have been performed correctly.

Start Timer Advance Schedule Test, 1977–79

1. Connect an adjustable timing light to engine so total timing advance at crankshaft can be checked.

2. Start engine, snap throttle open and close and immediately place gear selector in drive.

NOTE: Fully apply service brakes before placing vehicle in drive.

Observe timing mark on crankshaft damper immediately after vehicle is in drive and adjust timing light so basic timing signal is observed at timing plate. The meter on the timing light should indicate amount of advance as indicated under specifications. Continue to observe timing for 90 seconds while adjusting timing light to maintain basic timing signal. The additional advance should slowly reduce to the basic timing signal after approximately one minute. If timing did not increase and/or did not return to basic, replace "Spark Control Computer." If checked satisfactory, proceed to "Throttle Advance Schedule Test."

NOTE: Do not remove timing light since it is needed for further testing.

Speed Advance Schedule Test, 1977–80

NOTE: Before performing this test, ensure the basic timing signal and hot curb idle are within specifications. Disconnect wiring harness connector from throttle position transducer.

Start and run engine for two minutes. Increase engine speed to specified test level and adjust timing light so that basic timing is observed at timing indicator. The additional advance observed on the timing light meter should be as specified. Refer to the Chrysler Lean Burn Specification Charts. If advance is not within specifications, replace "Spark Control Computer" and repeat test.

Throttle Advance Schedule Test, 1977 Exc. Diplomat & LeBaron

NOTE: Before proceeding with test, ensure

Fig. 9 Throttle position transducer adjustment. 1978–79

"Throttle Position Transducer" is adjusted properly.

1. Place ignition switch in the "OFF" position and disconnect single connector from bottom of "Spark Control Computer."

2. Measure resistance between terminals 9 and 10 of single connector, Fig. 3. Resistance should be between 50 and 90 ohms. If so, reconnect single connector and proceed to Step 3. If not, remove connector from "Throttle Position Transducer" and measure resistance at transducer terminals, Fig. 5. If resistance is between 50 and 90 ohms, there is an open, short, or improper connection of wiring between terminals 9 and 10 of single connector, Fig. 3, and the terminals connecting to the transducer. If resistance is not within specifications, replace "Throttle Position transducer" and proceed to Step 3.

3. Reconnect all wiring and turn ignition switch to the "Run" position but do not start engine. Connect negative lead of a voltmeter to an engine ground. With positive lead of voltmeter, touch one terminal of "Throttle Position Transducer", Fig. 6, while fully opening throttle of carburetor and closing. Observe voltmeter reading. Repeat procedure with other terminal of transducer. Either of the terminals should show approximately a 2 volt change on voltmeter when throttle is opened and closed. If 2 volt change is noted, proceed to Step 4. If not, do not replace transducer since the "Spark Control Computer" can cause transducer to function improperly. It will be necessary to proceed to Step 4 to check malfunction.

4. Position throttle linkage on fast idle cam, ground carburetor switch with a jumper wire, disconnect wiring harness connector from "Throttle Position Transducer", and connect harness connector to a known good transducer of the same type suitable for testing.

5. Move core of test transducer inward to fully bottom out, start engine, wait 90 seconds, then move core outward about 1 inch, Fig. 8.

6. Adjust timing light so basic timing signal is observed at timing plate. The meter on the timing light should indicate additional amount of advance as listed under specifications. If advance is within specifications, move core back into transducer and timing should return to basic setting. If timing advanced and returned, proceed to Step 7. If timing did not advance and/or did not return, replace "Spark Control Computer." Also, after replacing computer, recheck "Throttle Position Transducer" as described in Step 3, to ensure transducer is satisfactory. If not, replace transducer.

7. Return timing light meter to zero and move core of test transducer inward and

outward about 1 inch, Fig. 8, 5 or 6 times very quickly and observe timing marks. There should be additional advance as listed under specifications for about one second and then return to basic setting. If not, replace "Spark Control Computer". Also, if "Throttle Position Transducer" failed in Step 3, replace transducer since "Spark Control Computer" is not causing it to check unsatisfactory.
8. Remove test transducer and reconnect all wiring.

Throttle Advance Schedule Test, 1977 Diplomat & LeBaron; 1978–79 All

NOTE: Before performing this test, ensure "Throttle Position Transducer" is adjusted properly.

1. With ignition switch in "Off" position, disconnect dual connector from "Spark Control Computer".
2. Measure of resistance between terminals 8 and 9 of dual connector. Resistance should be between 50 and 90 ohms. If resistance is within specifications, reconnect connector and proceed to Step 3. If not, disconnect connector from "Throttle Position Transducer" and measure resistance between transducer terminals. If resistance is between 50 and 90 ohms, there is an open, short or improper connection between terminals 8 and 9 of dual connector and the "Throttle Position Transducer". If resistance is not within specifications, replace "Throttle Position Transducer".
3. Position throttle linkage on fast idle cam, ground carburetor switch with a jumper wire, disconnect "Throttle Position Transducer" and connect connector to a known good transducer of the same type suitable for testing.
4. Move core of test transducer inward to fully bottom out, start engine, wait 90 seconds and move core outward approximately one inch.
5. Adjust timing light so basic timing signal is observed at timing plate. The timing light meter should indicate additional amount of advance as indicated in the Chrysler Lean Burn Specification Charts. If within specifications, move core back into transducer and timing should return to basic setting. If timing did not advance and/or did not return to basic setting, replace "Spark Control Computer". Retest "Throttle Position Transducer" after replacing "Spark Control Computer".

Poor Fuel Economy, Performance & Unusually High Idle Speed Tests

1. On 1977–80 models, connect suitable ohmmeter between black wire with tracer terminal of coolant switch and ground.
2. On 1981–82 models, turn ignition Off, then connect suitable ohmmeter between center terminal of temperature switch and ground for coolant temperature switch or between center terminal and ground terminal of charge temperature switch.

For Engine Cold
1. On 1977–80 models, continuity should be present at terminal. If not, replace coolant switch.

NOTE: Disregard terminal of coolant switch with orange wire connected since this wire has no function in system.

2. On 1981–82 models, continuity should be present with resistance less than 100 ohms. If not, replace switch. Charge temperature switch must be cooler than 60°F in order to perform test properly.

For Engine Hot
1. Terminal reading should show no continuity. If continuity is present, replace coolant switch.

Detonation Sensor Test, 1980–82 Models
1. Connect a suitable timing light to engine.
2. Set parking brake. Start engine and position throttle on second step of fast idle cam (at least 1200 RPM).
3. Using a suitable hand operated vacuum pump, apply 16″ of vacuum to Spark Control Computer transducer.
4. Using a small metal object, tap lightly on the intake manifold near the detonation sensor, Fig. 8A. At the same time, using the timing light, look for a decrease in spark advance at the timing marks. The decrease is proportional to the strength and frequency of the tapping. 11° is the maximum timing decrease.
5. Kick engine down to normal idle speed and turn ignition "Off". Remove timing light and vacuum pump.

Coolant Sensor Test, 1981–82 Models
1. Connect ohmmeter to terminals of coolant sensor.
2. With engine cold and ambient temperature less than 90°F., resistance should be 500–1000 ohms.
3. With engine at normal operating temperature, resistance should be greater than 1300 ohms.
4. If resistance is not as specified, replace sensor.

Vacuum Advance Schedule Test, 1977 Exc. Diplomat & LeBaron
1. Connect and adjust timing light to engine so total timing advance at crankshaft can be checked.
2. Check "Idle Stop Solenoid" by turning ignition key to "Run" position, but do not start engine. Disconnect solenoid lead wire, push plunger inward until bottomed out, and while holding throttle linkage open, reconnect solenoid lead wire, Fig. 5. The solenoid plunger should extend and remain extended. Release throttle linkage and plunger should hold throttle linkage. If not, replace "Idle Stop Solenoid". Start and run engine to reach operating temperature.
3. Ensure the transmission is in neutral and the parking brake is applied.
4. Place a piece of paper between carburetor switch and curb idle adjustment screw, Fig. 1. If curb idle adjustment screw is not contacting carburetor switch, ensure fast idle cam is not in fast idle position or is binding, linkage is not binding, or throttle stop screw is not over adjusted. Adjust timing light so basic timing signal can be observed at timing plate. The meter on the timing light should indicate additional amount of advance as listed under the specifications. If advance is not within specifications, replace "Spark Control Computer". If advance is within specifications, run engine for approximately 6 to 9 minutes and ensure a minimum of 16 inches of vacuum is available

at the transducer.
5. After 6 to 9 minutes, adjust timing light so basic timing signal can be observed at timing plate. The timing light meter should indicate additional amount of advance as listed under specifications. If advance is not within specifications, replace spark control computer. If advance is within specifications, proceed to next step.
6. Remove paper installed between carburetor switch and curb idle adjustment screw. The timing should return to the basic setting. If timing does not return to basic setting, ensure the curb idle adjustment screw is contacting carburetor switch. Then, turn engine off and check wire between Terminal 11 of single connector, Fig. 3, at bottom of computer for opens, shorts and improper connections. If wiring is satisfactory, repeat test. If timing will not return to basic setting, replace "Spark Control Computer".

Vacuum Advance Schedule Test, 1977 Diplomat & LeBaron; 1978 All
1. Connect and adjust timing light so that total timing advance at crankshaft can be checked.
2. Start engine, place transmission in neutral and apply parking brake.
3. With engine at normal operating temperature, place a piece of paper between carburetor switch and curb idle adjusting screw, Fig. 1. If curb idle adjusting screw is not contacting carburetor switch, ensure that fast idle cam is not on or is binding, linkage is not binding or throttle stop screw is not over adjusted. Adjust timing light so basic timing is observed at timing plate. Run engine for nine minutes and ensure there is a minimum of 16 inches of vacuum at the transducer. The timing light meter should indicate the additional amount of advance as listed in the Chrysler Lean Burn Specification Chart. If advance is not within specifications, replace "Spark Control Computer."
4. Remove piece of paper between carburetor switch and curb idle adjusting screw. Timing should return to basic setting. If timing does not return to basic setting, ensure that curb idle adjusting screw is not contacting carburetor switch. Then, turn engine "Off" and check wire between terminal 7 of the dual connector and carburetor switch terminal for opens, shorts or improper connections. If check is satisfactory and if timing still will not return to basic setting, replace "Spark Control Computer".

Vacuum Advance Schedule Test, 1979–80

NOTE: If computer fails to obtain specified settings, replace computer.

1. Connect timing light and tachometer to engine.
2. Start engine and allow to reach operating temperature. If engine is at operating temperature, wait at least one minute for start up advance to return to basic timing. Place transmission in Neutral and apply parking brake.
3. Check basic timing and adjust as necessary.
4. Remove vacuum line at transducer and plug line.
5. Ground carburetor switch and remove connector on throttle position transducer, if equipped.
6. Increase engine speed to 1100 rpm and

check speed advance timing. Timing should be as listed in Chrysler Lean Burn Specification Charts.

7. With engine operating at 1100 rpm, remove carburetor switch ground and connect vacuum line to vacuum transducer.
8. Check zero time offset. Timing should be as listed in Chrysler Lean Burn Specification Chart.
9. Allow accumulator to clock-up, refer to Chrysler Lean Burn Specification Chart. Operate engine at 1100 rpm and check vacuum advance. Refer to Chrysler Lean Burn Specification Chart.
10. Disconnect and plug vacuum line at vacuum transducer and operate engine at 1500 rpm.
11. Note speed advance timing.
12. Reconnect vacuum line to vacuum transducer and recheck vacuum advance.
13. Return engine to idle speed, then connect wire to carburetor switch if equipped, and install connector on throttle position transducer.

Spark Advance Of Spark Control Computer Test, 1981–82 Models

1. Ensure engine is fully warmed up and the temperature sensor is connected and operating properly.
2. Set ignition timing to specifications.
3. Place a piece of paper between curb idle adjusting screw and carburetor switch, Fig. 1, or ensure curb idle adjusting screw is not contacting carburetor switch.
4. Remove and plug vacuum transducer line.
5. Using a suitable hand operated vacuum pump, apply 16″ of vacuum to Spark Control Computer transducer.
6. Increase engine speed to 2000 RPM, wait 1 minute (or specified clock up time, see specifications). Advance specifications are in addition to basic timing advance. On systems equipped with an accumulator the specified time must be reached with the carburetor switch ungrounded before checking the specified spark advance schedule (see specifications).
7. If the computer fails to obtain specified settings, replace computer.

Carburetor Switch Test, 1981–82 Models

NOTE: On most systems, grounding the carburetor switch eliminates all spark advance.

1. Turn ignition Off, then disconnect 10-way connector from computer.
2. Check to ensure throttle is fully closed, then check continuity between pin 7 of harness connector and ground using suitable ohmmeter, Fig. 5.
3. If continuity is not present, check for open circuit in carburetor switch wiring circuit and repair as necessary.
4. Open throttle and check continuity between pin 7 of harness connector and ground. Continuity should not be present.

EGR System Test, 1981–82 Models

NOTE: The electronic EGR control is incorporated into the Spark Control Computer on 8 cylinder models and on 6 cylinder California models. On 6 cylinder models except California, the EGR control is located in a cowl mounted timer. Check to ensure that engine temperature sensors are operating properly before proceeding with test.

1. With engine cold and ignition Off, connect one lead of suitable voltmeter to gray wire terminal on EGR solenoid. Connect second voltmeter lead to ground.
2. Start engine and check voltmeter reading. Reading should be less than one volt. Reading will remain at this value until engine reaches normal operating temperature and electronic EGR schedule has timed out. EGR Solenoid will then de-energize and voltmeter will indicate charging system voltage.
3. If system does not de-energize in specified amount of time, replace solenoid.
4. If voltmeter indicates charging system voltage before EGR schedule is complete, replace Spark Control Computer or cowl mounted timer as necessary.

NOTE: V8-318 engines equipped with 2 barrel carburetors have no thermal delay at ambient temperatures below 60°F. This engine will operate according to EGR time delay schedule only. Refer to Chrysler Electronic Spark Control (Lean Burn) Specification Chart for delay schedules. Also, if vehicle is started with engine at operating temperature, EGR solenoid will be energized for length of time of time delay schedule only and will then de-energize.

Electronic Throttle Control Test, 1981–82 Models

NOTE: The electronic throttle control system is incorporated in the Spark Control Computer on 8 cylinder models and all 6 cylinder California models. On 6 cylinder models except California, the electronic throttle control is located in two cowl mounted timers. A carburetor mounted solenoid is energized whenever the air conditioner, heater, electronic heated backlite or electronic timers are activated. The timers operate with a two second delay after the throttle is closed or with an EGR time delay after an engine start condition.

1. Connect tachometer to engine, then start engine and run until operating temperature is reached.
2. Depress accelerator, then release. Curb idle speed should increase for length of time of EGR schedule.
3. Curb idle speed should increase when air conditioner, heater and/or electronic heated backlite are operated and return to normal when components are turned Off.

NOTE: Air conditioner clutch will cycle on and off as air conditioner operates and should not be mistaken as part of electronic control system operation.

4. If curb idle speed does not increase and decrease as described above, disconnect three-way electrical connector from carburetor.
5. Connect ohmmeter between carburetor solenoid black wire terminal and ground. Resistance should be 15–35 ohms. If not, replace solenoid.
6. Start engine and measure voltage between black wire of three-way connector and ground before EGR time delay has timed out. Voltmeter reading should indicate charging system voltage. If not, replace Spark Control Computer or cowl mounted gray start timer as necessary.
7. With engine operating and voltmeter connected as described in step 6, turn on air conditioner, heater and/or electronic heated backlite. Voltmeter should read

charging system voltage after time delay has timed out. If not, check wiring between three-way harness connector and instrument panel for damage and repair as necessary.

Throttle Position Transducer Adjustment

1977

This adjustment can only be performed when the "Air Temperature Sensor", located inside the computer, is below 135° F. If necessary to adjust the transducer when the engine is at operating temperature, it is necessary to cool the "Air Temperature Sensor".

NOTE: The "Air Temperature Sensor" may be cooled with a suitable cooling agent to rapidly lower the temperature of the sensor. To cool the sensor, remove the air cleaner top, insert the spray nozzle of the cooling agent into the computer and direct the spray over the sensor for approximately 15 seconds or until it is frosted.

If adjustment procedure takes longer than 3 or 4 minutes, turn engine off and re-cool "Air Temperature Sensor".

1. Start engine and wait at least 1½ minutes before proceeding with procedure.
2. Connect a jumper wire between carburetor switch terminal and the ground.
3. Disconnect electrical connector from transducer.
4. Check and adjust timing at crankshaft, if necessary.
5. Reconnect transducer electrical connector and recheck timing at crankshaft.
6. If timing is greater than specified, loosen transducer locknut and rotate transducer clockwise until timing returns to specified limits. Then, turn transducer an additional ½ turn clockwise and tighten locknut. If timing is at the specified limits, loosen transducer locknut and rotate transducer counter-clockwise until timing just starts to advance from specified limit. At that point, turn transducer an additional ½ turn and tighten locknut.

1978–79
1. Disconnect connector from transducer.
2. Loosen locknut.
3. Place special tool C-4522 between outer portion of transducer and transducer mounting bracket, Fig. 9.
4. Adjust transducer by rotating transducer until a clearance fit is obtained.
5. Tighten locknut and reconnect connector.

Distributor, Replace

Refer to "Chrysler Corp. Exc. Aries, Horizon, Omni, Reliant & 1982 400 & LeBaron & Electronic Spark Control (Lean Burn) Systems" for distributor replacement procedure.

Distributor Service

Disassembly, Figs. 10 thru 11A
1. Remove rotor. If necessary, use two screwdrivers under upper part of rotor to pry off.
2. Remove reluctor by prying up from bottom of reluctor with two screwdrivers (7/16 inch maximum width of screwdrivers). Use care not to distort or damage reluctor teeth.
3. Remove the two screws retaining plate to housing and lift out the plate and pick up coil as an assembly.

Fig. 10 Electronic spark control (Lean Burn) distributor with single pick up exploded view. 6 cylinder

Fig. 10A Electronic spark control (Lean Burn) distributor with dual pick up exploded view. 6 cylinder

NOTE: The distributor clamp springs are held in place by peened metal around the openings and should not be removed.

4. On 6 cylinder distributors, refer to "Chrysler Corp. Rear Wheel Drive Models, Less Electronic Spark Control (Lean Burn) System".
5. On V8 distributors, refer to "Chrysler Corp. Rear Wheel Drive Models, Less Electronic Spark Control (Lean Burn) System" and perform the "Distributor Shaft & Bushing Wear Test". If side play exceeds .006 inch, replace housing shaft and reluctor sleeve as follows:

a. Remove distributor shaft retaining pin and slide retainer off end of shaft.
b. Using a file, clean burrs from around pin hole in shaft and remove lower thrust washer.
c. Push shaft up and remove through top of distributor body.

Assembly, Figs. 10 thru 11A

1. Lubricate and install upper thrust washer(s) on shaft and slide shaft into distributor body.
2. Install distributor shaft retainer and pin.
3. Install plate and pick up coil assembly

and retaining screws.
4. Position reluctor keeper pin into position on reluctor sleeve.
5. Slide reluctor down reluctor sleeve and press firmly into place, then install keeper pin.

Pick Up Replacement & Air Gap Adjustment

NOTE: For pick up replacement and/or pick up air gap adjustment, refer to "Chrysler Corp. Rear Wheel Drive Models, Less Electronic Spark Control (Lean Burn) System" for procedure.

Fig. 11 Electronic spark control (Lean Burn) distributor with dual pick up exploded view. 8 cylinder

Fig. 11A Electronic spark control (Lean Burn) distributor exploded view. Electronic Fuel Injection

ELECTRONIC IGNITION SYSTEMS

1977 CHRYSLER ELECTRONIC SPARK CONTROL (LEAN BURN) SPECIFICATION CHART

Spark Control Computer	4091072①	4091073①	4091074①	4091195①
	(4094022)②	(4094008)②	(4094023)②	(4106056)②
Start Timer Advance Schedule	5°–9°	5°–9°	5°–9°	8°
Delay Time In Seconds	90	90	90	90
Throttle Advance Schedule	10°③			
a. Test Transducer Core Out 1 inch	6°–10° @ 75°F / 3°–6° @ 105°F	8°–12°	3°–5° @ 75°F / 2°–3° @ 105°F	8°–12°
b. Test transducer Core Moved Quickly In and Out	10°	10°	5°	—
Vacuum Advance Schedule				
a. Operating Vacuum Range	0 to 16 Inches Hg	0 to 16 Inches Hg	0 to 12 Inches Hg	0 to 14 Inches Hg
b. Advance Off Idle (Carb. Switch Isolated With Paper)	3°–5°	6°–8°	None	13°–15°
c. Accumulation Time in Minutes	7–9	7–9	7–9	8
d. Advance After Accumulation Time	34°	34°	28°	32°–36°
Speed Advance				
Ground Carb. Switch and Disconnect Throttle Transducer Before Checking	3°–5° @ 2000 rpm	1°–3° @ 2000 rpm	7°–9° @ 1200 rpm	1°–3° @ 2000 rpm / 3°–7° @ 4000 rpm

Spark Control Computer	4091421①	4091440①	4091468①	4091476①
	(4094021)②	(4094022)②	(4057923)②	(4094026)②
Start Timer Advance Schedule	5°–9°	5°–9°	8°	5°–9°
Delay Time In Seconds	90	90	90	90
Throttle Advance Schedule				
a. Test Transducer Core Out 1 inch	7°–9° @ 75°F / 5°–7° @ 105°F	8°–12°	8°–12°	7°–9° @ 75°F / 5°–7° @ 105°F
b. Test Transducer Core Moved Quickly In and Out	8°	10°	—	8°
Vacuum Advance Schedule				
a. Operating Vacuum Range	0 to 12 Inches Hg	0 to 16 Inches Hg	0 to 14 Inches Hg	0 to 12 Inches Hg
b. Advance Off Idle (Carb. Switch Isolated With Paper)	None	3°–5°	None	None
c. Accumulation Time in Minutes	7–9	7–9	8	7–9
d. Advance After Accumulation Time	30°	34°	32°–36°	28°
Speed Advance				
Ground Carb. Switch and Disconnect Throttle Transducer Before Checking	5°–7° @ 2000 rpm	2°–4° @ 2000 rpm	1°–3° @ 2000 rpm / 3°–7° @ 4000 rpm	0°–2° @ 2000 rpm

Spark Control Computer	4091477①	4091946①	4091447①	4091448①
	(4094023)②	(4106057)②	(4106055)②	(4106056)②
Start Timer Advance Schedule	5°–9°	8°	8°	8°
Delay Time In Seconds	90	90	90	90
Throttle Advance Schedule				
a. Test Transducer Core Out 1 inch	4°–6°	3°–5°	3°–5°	3°–5°
b. Test Transducer Core Moved Quickly In and Out	5°	—	—	—
Vacuum Advance Schedule				
a. Operating Vacuum Range	0 to 12 Inches Hg	0 to 14 Inches Hg	0 to 14 Inches Hg	0 to 14 Inches Hg
b. Advance Off Idle (Carb. Switch Isolated With Paper)	None	4°–8°	None	10°–14°
c. Accumulation Time in Minutes	7–9	8	8	8
d. Advance After Accumulation Time	28°	26°–30°	32°–36°	26°–30°
Speed Advance				
Ground Carb. Switch and Disconnect Throttle Transducer Before Checking	7°–11° @ 2000 rpm	0°–3° @ 2000 rpm / 1°–5° @ 4000 rpm	0°–3° @ 2000 rpm / 1°–5° @ 4000 rpm	0°–3° @ 2000 rpm / 1°–5° @ 4000 rpm

① —Production part number.
② —Remanufactured part number.
③ —If equipped with remanufactured spark control computer, disregard temperature specifications since there is no air temperature sensor.

1978 CHRYSLER ELECTRONIC SPARK CONTROL (LEAN BURN) SPECIFICATION CHART

Spark Control Computer	4091730①	4091731①	4091732①	4091786①
	(4106061)②	(4106067)②	(4106068)②	(4106069)②
Start Timer Advance Schedule	8°	8°	8°	8°
Delay Time In Seconds	60	60	60	60
Throttle Advance Schedule				
Test Transducer Core	7°–9° @ 100°F	4°–6° @ 100°F	5°–7° @ 100°F	5°–7° @ 100°F
Out 1 Inch	3°–6° @ 140°F	2°–4° @ 140°F	2°–5° @ 140°F	2°–4° @ 140°F
Vacuum Advance Schedule				
a. Operating Vacuum Range	0 to 12 Inches Hg	0 to 14 Inches Hg	0 to 14 Inches Hg	0 to 15.5 Inches Hg
b. Advance Off Idle (Carb. Switch Isolated With Paper)	None	7°–11°	None	5°–9°
c. Accumulation Time In Minutes	8	8	8	7
d. Advance After Accumulation Time	28°–32°	23°–27°	26°–30°	18°–22°
Speed Advance				
Ground Carb. Switch and Disconnect Throttle Transducer Before Checking	4°–8° @ 2000 rpm 8°–12° @ 4000 rpm	4°–8° @ 2000 rpm 10°–14° @ 4000 rpm	0°–3° @ 2000 rpm 2°–6° @ 4000 rpm	0°–1° @ 2000 rpm 0°–2° @ 4000 rpm

Spark Control Computer	4091787①	4091788①	4091791①	4091923①
	(4106070)②	(4106071)②	(4106073)②	
Start Timer Advance Schedule	8°	8°	8°	8°
Delay Time In Seconds	60	60	60	60
Throttle Advance Schedule				
Test Transducer Core	5°–7° @ 100°F	7°–9° @ 100°F	4°–6° @ 100°F	5°–7° @ 100°F
Out 1 Inch	2°–4° @ 140°F	4°–6° @ 140°F	1°–4° @ 140°F	2°–5° @ 140°F
Vacuum Advance Schedule				
a. Operating Vacuum Range	0 to 14 Inches Hg	0 to 14 Inches Hg	0 to 12 Inches Hg	0 to 14 Inches Hg
b. Advance Off Idle (Carb. Switch Isolated With Paper)	None	7°–11°	None	8°–12°
c. Accumulation Time In Minutes	8	8	8	8
d. Advance After Accumulation Time	23°–27°	20°–24°	20°–24°	24°–28°
Speed Advance				
Ground Carb. Switch and Disconnect Throttle Transducer Before Checking	2°–5° @ 2000 rpm 7°–11° @ 4000 rpm	1°–5° @ 2000 rpm 4°–8° @ 4000 rpm	7°–11° @ 2000 rpm 8°–12° @ 4000 rpm	1°–4° @ 2000 rpm 6°–10° @ 4000 rpm

Spark Control Computer	4091924①	4091954①	4091955①	4111012①
	(4106075)②	(4106076)②	(4106077)②	(4106079)②
Start Timer Advance Schedule	8°	8°	8°	8°
Delay Time In Seconds	60	60	60	60
Throttle Advance Schedule				
Test Transducer Core	9°–11° @ 100°F	5°–7° @ 100°F	7°–9° @ 100°F	0°
Out 1 Inch	5°–8° @ 140°F	2°–5° @ 140°F	4°–6° @ 140°F	
Vacuum Advance Schedule				
a. Operating Vacuum Range	0 to 14 Inches Hg	0 to 15.5 Inches Hg	0 to 14 Inches Hg	0 to 15.5 Inches Hg
b. Advance Off Idle (Carb. Switch Isolated With Paper)	None	None	7°–11°	None
c. Accumulation Time In Minutes	8	8	7	8
d. Advance After Accumulation Time	21°–25°	18°–22°	20°–24°	18°–22°
Speed Advance				
Ground Carb. Switch and Disconnect Throttle Transducer Before Checking	10°–15° @ 2000 rpm 16°–21° @ 4000 rpm	0°–1° @ 2000 rpm 0°–2° @ 4000 rpm	1°–5° @ 2000 rpm 4°–8° @ 4000 rpm	4°–8° @ 2000 rpm 6°–10° @ 4000 rpm

Continued

1978 CHRYSLER ELECTRONIC SPARK CONTROL (LEAN BURN) SPECIFICATION CHART—Continued

Spark Control Computer	4111013①	4111014①	4111015①	4111159①
	(4106080)②	(4106081)②	(4106082)②	(4106085)②
Start Timer Advance Schedule	8°	8°	8°	8°
Delay Time In Seconds	60	60	60	60
Throttle Advance Schedule				
Test Transducer Core Out 1 Inch	9°–11° @ 100°F 5°–8° @ 140°F	5°–7° @ 100°F 2°–5° @ 140°F	5°–7° @ 100°F 2°–5° @ 140°F	5°–7° @ 100°F 2°–5° @ 140°F
Vacuum Advance Schedule				
a. Operating Vacuum Range	0 to 14 Inches Hg	0 to 12 Inches Hg	0 to 12 Inches Hg	0 to 15.5 Inches Hg
b. Advance Off Idle (Carb. Switch Isolated With Paper)	None	2°–6°	2°–6°	None
c. Accumulation Time In Minutes	8	8	8	8
d. Advance After Accumulation Time	21°–25°	18°–22°	18°–22°	18°–22°
Speed Advance				
Ground Carb. Switch and Disconnect Throttle Transducer Before Checking	10°–14° @ 2000 rpm 16°–21° @ 4000 rpm	8°–12° @ 2000 rpm 12°–16° @ 4000 rpm	8°–12° @ 2000 rpm 12°–16° @ 4000 rpm	0–1° @ 2000 rpm 0–2° @ 4000 rpm

Spark Control Computer	4111169①	4111170①	4111172①	4111217①
	(4106086)②	(4106087)②	(4106088)②	(4106089)②
Start Timer Advance Schedule	None	None	None	8°
Delay Time In Seconds	None	None	None	60
Throttle Advance Schedule				
Test Transducer Core Out 1 Inch	5°–7° @ 100°F 2°–5° @ 140°F	5°–7° @ 100°F 2°–5° @ 140°F	5°–7° @ 100°F 2°–7° @ 140°F	0°
Vacuum Advance Schedule				
a. Operating Vacuum Range	0 to 10 Inches Hg	0 to 10 Inches Hg	0 to 10 Inches Hg	4–14 Inches Hg
b. Advance Off Idle (Carb. Switch Isolated With Paper)	5°–9°	5°–9°	5°–9°	6°–10°
c. Accumulation Time In Minutes	8	8	8	7
d. Advance After Accumulation Time	16°–20°	16°–20°	16°–20°	18°–22°
Speed Advance				
Ground Carb. Switch and Disconnect Throttle Transducer Before Checking	1°–5° @ 2000 rpm 4°–8° @ 4000 rpm	1°–5° @ 2000 rpm 4°–8° @ 4000 rpm	1°–5° @ 2000 rpm 4°–8° @ 4000 rpm	8°–12° @ 2000 rpm 12°–16° @ 4000 rpm

Spark Control Computer	4111218①	4111222①	4111253①	4111278①
Start Timer Advance Schedule	8°	8°	8°	8°
Delay Time In Seconds	60	60	60	60
Throttle Advance Scedule				
Test Transducer Core Out 1 Inch	0°	0°	5°–7° @ 100°F 2°–5° @ 140°F	7°–9° @ 100°F 4°–6° @ 140°F
Vacuum Advance Schedule				
a. Operating Vacuum Range	4–14 Inches Hg	4–14 Inches Hg	0–10 Inches Hg	0–12 Inches Hg
b. Advance Off Idle (Carb. Switch Isolated With Paper)	2°–6°	2°–6°	None	None
c. Accumulation Time In Minutes	8	8	8	8
d. Advance After Accumulation Time	18°–22°	18°–22°	23°–27°	26°–30°
Speed Advance				
Ground Carb. Switch and Disconnect Throttle Transducer Before Checking	8°–2° @ 2000 rpm 12°–16° @ 4000 rpm	8°–12° @ 2000 rpm 12°–16° @ 4000 rpm	6°–11° @ 2000 rpm 11°–16° @ 4000 rpm	0°–3° @ 2000 rpm 2°–6° @ 4000 rpm

Continued

1978 CHRYSLER ELECTRONIC SPARK CONTROL (LEAN BURN)
SPECIFICATION CHART—Continued

Spark Control Computer	4111283①	4145237①
Start Timer Advance Schedule	8°	8°
Delay Time In Seconds	60	60
Throttle Advance Schedule		
Test Transducer Core	7°–9° @ 100°F.	9°–11° @ 100°F.
Out 1 Inch	4°–6° @ 140°F.	5°–8° @ 140°F.
Vacuum Advance Schedule		
a. Operating Vacuum Range	0–12 Inches Hg	0–14 Inches Hg
b. Advance Off Idle (Carb. Switch Isolated With Paper)	None	None
c. Accumulation Time In Minutes	8	8
d. Advance After Accumulation Time	26°–30°	26°–30°
Speed Advance		
Ground Carb. Switch and Disconnect Throttle Transducer Before Checking	0°–3° @ 2000 rpm 2°–6° @ 4000 rpm	10°–14° @ 2000 rpm 16°–21° @ 4000 rpm

①—Production part number.
②—Remanufactured part number.

1979 CHRYSLER ELECTRONIC SPARK CONTROL (LEAN BURN)
SPECIFICATION CHART

Spark Control Computer	4111373① 4111697②	4111392① 4111676②	4111439① 4111677②	4111440① 4111678②	4111441① 4111679②	4111442① 4111680②
Start Up Advance (60 Seconds)	5°	5°	5°	5°	5°	5°
Crank + Electrical (Basic Timing)	10° + 5°	10° + 6°	10° + 6°	10° + 6°	12° + 0°	10° + 6°
Vacuum Advance Range (In. Hg.)	5–11	4–13	4–12	4–12	4–12	4–12
Zero Time Offset	0°–3°	8°–12°	0°–3°	8°–12°	6°–10°	6°–10°
Accumulator Time In Minutes	8	8	8	8	8	8
Vacuum Adv.—Full Accumulator						
@ 1100 rpm	11°–15°	16°–20°	8°–12°	12°–16°	11°–17°	8°–12°
@ 1500 rpm	18°–22°	23°–27°	18°–22°	18°–22°	18°–22°	18°–22°
Throttle Max. Advance (Throttle Open 20°)	6°–10°	3°–7°	6°–10°	3°–7°	0°	6°–10°
Speed Advance						
@ 1100 rpm	0°–2°	0°–1°	2°–6°	0°–1°	3°–7°	2°–6°
@ 2000 rpm	1°–4°	1°–5°	6°–10°	1°–5°	8°–12°	6°–10°
@ 4000 rpm	3°–5°	10°–14°	10°–14°	10°–14°	12°–16°	10°–14°

Spark Control Computer	4111492① 4111681②	4111540① 4111682②	4111574① 4111683②	4111575① 4111684②	4111674① 4111685②
Start Up Advance (60 Seconds)	5°	5°	5°	5°	5°
Crank + Electrical (Basic Timing)	10° + 6°	10° + 6°	10° + 6°	10° + 6°	10° + 6°
Vacuum Advance Range (In. Hg.)	4–13	4–12	4–13	4–10	4–13
Zero Time Offset	8°–12°	8°–12°	0°–3°	2°–6°	0°–3°
Accumulator Time In Minutes	8	8	8	8	8
Vacuum Adv.—Full Accumulator					
@ 1100 rpm	16°–20°	12°–16°	16°–20°	11°–15°	16°–22°
@ 1500 rpm	23°–27°	16°–22°	23°–27°	18°–22°	23°–27°
Throttle Max. Advance (Throttle Open 20°)	3°–7°	3°–7°	3°–7°	6°–10°	3°–7°
Speed Advance					
@ 1100 rpm	0°–1°	0°–1°	0°–1°	2°–6°	0°–1°
@ 2000 rpm	1°–5°	1°–5°	1°–5°	6°–10°	1°–5°
@ 4000 rpm	10°–14°	10°–14°	10°–14°	10°–14°	10°–14°

①—Production part number.
②—Remanufactured part number.

ELECTRONIC IGNITION SYSTEMS

1980 CHRYSLER ELECTRONIC SPARK CONTROL (LEAN BURN) SPECIFICATION CHART

Spark Control Computer	4105007	414500	4145003	4145004	4145087
Crank + Run (Basic Timing)	12° + 0°	8° + 8°	8° + 8°	12° + 0°	8° + 8°
Vacuum Advance (Range)	0–10	4–14	4–14	4–14	4–14
Zero Time Advance	0°–2°	23°–27°	28°–32°	23°–27°	21°–25°
Accumulator Time In Minutes	1	0	0	0	0
Vacuum Adv.—Full Accumulator					
@ 1100 rpm	0°–2°	10°–14°	14°–18°	0°–2°	0°–2°
@ 2500 rpm	20°–24°	23°–27°	28°–32°	23°–27°	21°–25°
Speed Advance					
@ 1100 rpm	0°–2°	1°–4°	0°–2°	0°–4°	0°–2°
@ 2000 rpm	1°–5°	4°–8°	1°–5°	4°–8°	4°–8°
@ 4800 rpm	1°–5°	12°–16°	12°–16°	16°–20°	12°–16°
Warm Up Schedule In Seconds	100	—	25	—	—

1981 CHRYSLER ELECTRONIC SPARK CONTROL (LEAN BURN) SPECIFICATION CHART

Spark Control Computer	4145431	4145457	4145466	4145725
Basic Timing	16°	16°	16°	12°
Vacuum Advance (Range)	3–10	4–14	1–14	2–12
Accumulator Time In Minutes	.5	0	0	0
Spark Advance Test @ 2000 RPM	20 ± 4	34 ± 4	34 ± 4	29 ± 4
Electronic EGR Time Delay	60 sec.	60 sec.	20 sec.	—
Electronic Throttle Control Time Delay	90 sec.	60 sec.	20 sec.	AIS①
Oxygen Feedback Electronic Air Switching Time	65 sec.	30 sec.	90 sec.	70 sec.

Spark Control Computer	4145726	4145788	4145817	4145850
Basic Timing	12°	16°	16°	16°
Vacuum Advance (Range)	2–12	4–14	3–10	4–14
Accumulator Time In Minutes	0	0	.5	0
Spark Advance Test @ 2000 RPM	23 ± 4	34 ± 4	20 ± 4	34 ± 4
Electronic EGR Time Delay	—	60 sec.	90 sec.	60 sec.
Electronic Throttle Control Time Delay	AIS①	60 sec.	90 sec.	60 sec.
Oxygen Feedback Electronic Air Switching Time	70 sec.	20 sec.	65 sec.	20 sec.

①—Automatic idle speed motor.

1982 CHRYSLER ELECTRONIC SPARK CONTROL (LEAN BURN) SPECIFICATION CHART

Spark Control Computer	4145452	4145701	4145726	4145907
Basic Timing	16°	12°	12°	12°
Vacuum Advance (Range)	4–14	2–12	2–12	1–14
Accumulator Time In Minutes	0	0	0	0
Spark Advance Test @ 2000 RPM	29 ± 4	23 ± 4	23 ± 4	34 ± 4
Electronic EGR Time Delay	35 sec.	—	—	20 sec.
Electronic Throttle Control Time Delay	—	AIS①	AIS①	20 sec.
Oxygen Feedback Electronic Air Switching Time	—	70 sec.	70 sec.	90 sec.

Continued

1982 CHRYSLER ELECTRONIC SPARK CONTROL (LEAN BURN)
SPECIFICATION CHART—Continued

Spark Control Computer	4145980	4145996	4145998	4289034
Basic Timing	16°	16°	16°	12°
Vacuum Advance (Range)	1–14	4–14	4–14	3–10
Accumulator Time In Minutes	0	0	0	0.5
Spark Advance Test @ 2000 RPM	34 ± 4	34 ± 4	34 ± 4	20 ± 4
Electronic EGR Time Delay	20 sec.	60 sec.	60 sec.	60 sec.
Electronic Throttle Control Time Delay	—	60 sec.	60 sec.	60 sec.
Oxygen Feedback Electronic Air Switching Time	90 sec.	20 sec.	20 sec.	65 sec.

①—Automatic idle speed motor.

Chrysler Corp. Front Wheel Drive Models W/ Electronic Spark Control (Lean Burn) System

SYSTEM TESTING

Ignition System Starting Test

1. Remove coil wire from distributor cap and hold end of wire approximately ¼ inch from a good engine ground. Crank engine and observe spark at coil wire.
2. The spark at the coil wire must be constant and bright blue in color. If so, continue to crank engine and slowly move coil wire away from the ground. If arcing occurs at the coil tower, replace coil. If spark is weak, not constant or there is no spark, proceed to the "Failure To Start Test".
3. If spark is satisfactory and no arcing occurs at the coil tower, the ignition system is producing the necessary high secondary voltage. However, this voltage is transmitted to the spark plugs by the distributor rotor, cap, spark plug wires and spark plugs and must also be checked. If satisfactory, the ignition system is not at

fault. It will be necessary to check the fuel system and engine mechanical components.

Failure To Start Test

NOTE: Before performing this test, perform the "Ignition System Starting Test". Failure to do so may lead to unnecessary diagnostic time and incorrect test results.

1978–80
1. With a voltmeter, measure and note battery voltage. Battery specific gravity must be at least 1.220, temperature corrected, to deliver the necessary voltage to operate the cranking and ignition systems properly.
2. Disconnect wire from ignition coil negative terminal.
3. Remove coil wire from distributor cap.
4. With ignition switch in "On" position and using a jumper wire, momentarily ground the ignition coil negative terminal while holding the coil wire ¼ inch from a good engine ground. A spark should be obtained.
5. If no spark was obtained in Step 4, measure voltage at ignition coil positive terminal. Voltage should be at least 9 volts. If specified voltage is noted, the ignition coil is defective, requiring replacement. If specified voltage is not noted, check ballast resistor, wiring and connections. If engine still does not start, proceed to Step 6.
6. If spark was obtained in Step 4, turn ignition switch to "Off" position, reconnect ignition coil negative terminal wire and disconnect the distributor 3-wire harness, Fig. 1.
7. Turn ignition switch to "On" position and measure voltage between pin "B" on har-

ness connector and the engine ground, Fig. 1. Voltage obtained should be battery voltage. If battery voltage is obtained, proceed to Step 11. If not, proceed to Step 8.
8. Turn ignition switch to "Off" position and disconnect the 10-wire harness connector from "Spark Control Computer", Fig. 2.

NOTE: Do not remove grease from harness connector or connector cavity since the grease is used to prevent moisture from corroding the terminals. There must be at least ¼ inch of grease on the bottom of the computer connector cavity. If not, apply a liberal amount of Mopar Multi-purpose grease, part number 2932524, or equivalent over end of connector plug before reinstallation.

9. Check continuity between pin "B" of the distributor connector, Fig. 1, and terminal 3 of the "Spark Control Computer" connector, Fig. 2. If continuity is not noted, repair wire. If continuity exists, proceed to Step 10.

COIL SECONDARY WIRE

3-WIRE HARNESS CONNECTOR GOING TO SPARK CONTROL COMPUTER

3-WIRE DISTRIBUTOR CONNECTOR

Fig. 1 Distributor 3-wire harness connector

SPARK CONTROL COMPUTER

10-WIRE HARNESS CONNECTOR

Fig. 2 Spark control computer 10-wire connector

Fig. 2A Coil negative terminal jumper wire. 1981–82 models

Fig. 2B Rotor shutter blades. 1981–82 models

10. Turn ignition switch to "On" position and measure voltage between terminals 2 and 10 of the "Spark Control Computer" connector. Battery voltage should be obtained. If not, check wiring and connections. If battery voltage is obtained, the "Spark Control Computer" is defective, requiring replacement.

11. Connect "Spark Control Computer" 10-wire harness connector, turn ignition switch to "On" position and hold coil wire ¼ inch from a good ground. Using a jumper wire, momentarily connect pins "A" and "C" of the distributor connector, Fig. 1. A spark should be obtained. If not, proceed to Step 12. If a spark is obtained, the Hall Effect Pick-up assembly is defective, requiring replacement.

12. Turn ignition to "Off" position and disconnect "Spark Control Computer" 10-wire harness connector, Fig. 2.

13. Check continuity between pin "C" of the 3-wire distributor connector, Fig. 1, and terminal 9 of the "Spark Control Computer" connector, Fig. 2. Also check continuity between pin "A" of distributor connector, Fig. 1, and terminal 5 of the "Spark Control Computer" connector, Fig. 2. If continuity exists, the "Spark Control Computer" is defective, requiring replacement. If no continuity exists, repair wiring and repeat Step 11.

1981–82

1. Perform steps 1 thru 4 as described under "Failure To Start Test" under "1978–80". Use jumper wires shown in Fig. 2A when performing tests on 1981–82 models.
2. If spark was obtained, proceed to step 5. If not, turn ignition Off, then disconnect 10-wire electrical connector at Spark Control Computer.

NOTE: Do not remove grease from harness connector or connector cavity since grease is used to prevent moisture from corroding the terminals. There must be at least ⅛ inch of grease on bottom of computer connector cavity. If not, apply a liberal amount of Mopar Multi-purpose grease, part number 2932524 or equivalent over end of connector plug before installation.

3. Turn ignition On, hold coil wire ¼ inch from ground and momentarily ground coil negative terminal using jumper wire, Fig. 2A. If spark is present, replace Spark Control Computer. If spark is not present, measure voltage at coil positive terminal using suitable voltmeter. Voltage reading should be within one volt of battery voltage.
4. If no voltage was obtained at coil positive terminal, check for open circuit between battery and coil and repair as necessary. If voltage was obtained, measure voltage

at coil negative terminal. Reading should be within one volt of battery voltage. If no voltage is present or voltage is present but spark is not, replace coil.

5. If spark was obtained in step 2, but engine will not start, hold open carburetor switch with thin piece of paper and measure voltage at carburetor switch. Reading obtained should be at least five volts. If voltage reading is satisfactory, proceed to step 9. If no voltage is present, turn ignition Off, then disconnect 10-wire connector from Spark Control Computer.

6. Turn ignition On and measure voltage between connector cavity 2 and ground, Fig. 2. Reading should be within one volt of battery voltage. If not, check for continuity between battery and cavity 2 using ohmmeter. If continuity is not present, check for open circuit between battery and cavity 2 and repair as necessary.

7. If battery voltage is present in step 6, turn ignition Off and check continuity between carburetor switch and cavity 7 on 10 way connector. If continuity is not present, check for open circuit between cavity 7 and carburetor switch and repair as necessary.

8. If continuity is present in step 7, check continuity between cavity 10 and ground. If continuity is present, replace Spark Control Computer. If continuity is not present between cavity 10 and ground, check for damaged wiring or an open circuit and repair as necessary. If wiring is satisfactory, but engine will not start, proceed to step 9.

9. Reconnect 10-wire connector into Spark Control Computer, turn ignition On and hold coil wire ¼ inch from ground. Disconnect distributor electrical connector and connect jumper wire between terminals A and C of connector, Fig. 1. Spark should be observed at coil wire.

10. If spark is present at coil wire, but engine will not start, replace pick up assembly and perform rotor test as described in step 16.

NOTE: When replacing Hall effect pick up assembly, check to ensure rotor shutter blades are grounded, Fig. 2B. Connect one lead of suitable ohmmeter to shutter blade and other lead to ground. If continuity is not present, press downward on rotor shaft and recheck continuity. If continuity is still not present, replace rotor. Check to ensure that new rotor is marked ESA on top. Do not start engine until continuity has been obtained.

---

11. If no spark is present at coil wire check voltage between cavity B of distributor connector and ground, Fig. 1. Reading obtained should be within one volt of battery voltage. If battery voltage is not present, proceed to step 13. If battery voltage is present, turn ignition off and disconnect 10-way connector from Spark Advance Computer. Check for continuity between cavity C of distributor connector, Fig. 1, and cavity 9 of 10-way connector. Repeat procedure between cavity A of distributor connector and cavity 5 of 10-way connector.

12. If continuity is not present, open circuit exists in harness wiring. Repair as necessary. If continuity is present, replace Spark Advance Computer.

13. If no battery voltage is present at cavity A of distributor connector, turn ignition Off, then disconnect 10-wire connector from Spark Control Computer.

14. Check for continuity between cavity A of distributor connector and cavity 3 of 10-wire connector. If continuity is not present, repair open circuit in wire between cavities as necessary.

15. If continuity is present, turn ignition On and check for voltage between cavity 2 and 10 of 10-wire connector. If battery voltage is present, replace Spark Control Computer. If battery voltage is not present, check for proper computer ground circuit connection and repair as necessary.

16. To perform rotor test, check to ensure that rotor is stamped ESA on top. Turn ignition Off, then using suitable ohmmeter, check for good rotor ground contact at distributor shaft. If continuity is indicated, rotor is satisfactory. If continuity is not indicated, check to ensure that rotor is properly seated on shaft.

Poor Performance Tests

Carburetor Switch Test

NOTE: On 1980–82 models, grounding the carburetor switch eliminates spark advance on most models. On models with feedback carburetor it also provides a fixed fuel/air ratio.

---

1. With ignition switch in "Off" position, disconnect 10-wire harness connector from "Spark Control Computer."
2. With throttle completely closed, check continuity between terminal 7 and the engine ground, Fig. 2. Continuity should exist. If not, check wiring and carburetor switch.
3. With throttle opened, check continuity between terminal 7 and the engine ground, Fig. 2. Continuity should not exist.

Coolant Switch Test, All Exc. 1981 2.2 L

1. With ignition switch in "Off" position, disconnect wire from coolant switch.
2. Check continuity between coolant switch terminal and the engine ground. The ohmmeter readings should be as follows: Engine cold, below 150°—Continuity should exist. If not, replace coolant switch. Engine hot, above 150°—No continuity should exist. If continuity exists, replace coolant switch.

Coolant Sensor Test, 1981 2.2 L

1. With ignition Off, disconnect coolant sensor electrical connector.
2. Connect ohmmeter leads to terminals of sensor.

Fig. 3   Throttle position transducer

3. Resistance should be 500–1000 ohms with engine cold and ambient temperature less than 90°F.
4. With engine at normal operating temperature, resistance should be 1300 ohms.
5. Replace coolant sensor if specifications cannot be obtained.

Spark Advance Test, 1981–82 Units

1. Run engine until normal operating temperature is reached, then disconnect carburetor switch electrical connector. Check to ensure that coolant sensor is operating as described under "Poor Performance Tests" under "Coolant Sensor Test".
2. Disconnect and plug vacuum transducer vacuum hose.
3. Apply 16 inches Hg. vacuum from outside vacuum source to vacuum transducer.
4. Increase engine speed to 2000 RPM, wait one minute, then check amount of advance timing. Refer to "Aries, Horizon, Omni, Reliant & 1982 400 & LeBaron Electronic Spark Control (Lean Burn) Specification Chart" for specification.

NOTE: On certain models equipped with an accumulator, the accumulator must be allowed to time out with the carburetor switch disconnected before checking spark advance.

5. If spark advance specifications cannot be obtained, replace Spark Control Computer.

Start Advance Timing Test, 1978–79 Models

1. Connect an adjustable timing light to engine so total timing advance can be checked.
2. Connect a jumper wire between carburetor switch and the engine ground.
3. Start engine and adjust timing light to align specified timing marks. The timing light meter should indicate the amount of advance listed in the Horizon & Omni Electronic Spark Control (Lean Burn) Specification Chart. Continue to observe timing for 90 seconds while adjusting timing light to maintain basic timing signal. If timing did not increase and/or did not return to basic setting, replace "Spark Control Computer".

Speed Advance Test, 1978–80 Models

1. Disconnect connector from "Throttle Position Transducer", 1978 manual transmission model. On 1980 models, remove vacuum line from vacuum transducer.
2. Start and run engine for two minutes. Increase engine speed to specified test level and adjust timing light so basic timing setting can be observed at timing indicator. The timing light meter should indicate additional advance as listed in

the Horizon and Omni Electronic Spark Control (Lean Burn) Specification Chart. If not, replace "Spark Control Computer" and repeat test.

Throttle Advance Test, 1978 Manual Trans. models

NOTE: Before performing this test, ensure the "Throttle Position Transducer" is properly adjusted.

1. With ignition switch in "Off" position, disconnect 10-wire harness connector from "Spark Control Computer", Fig. 2.
2. Measure resistance between terminals 8 and 9 of connector, Fig. 2. Resistance should be 50 to 90 ohms. If resistance is within specifications, connect connector and proceed to Step 3. If resistance is not within specifications, disconnect connector from "Throttle Position Transducer" and measure resistance between transducer terminals. If resistance is between 50 and 90 ohms, there is an open, short or improper connection between terminals 8 and 9 of "Spark Control Computer" connector and the "Throttle Position Transducer" connector. If resistance is not within specifications, replace "Throttle Position Transducer".
3. Place throttle linkage on fast idle cam, ground carburetor switch with a jumper wire, disconnect connector from "Throttle Position Transducer" and connect connector to a known good transducer of the same type suitable for testing.
4. Move core of test transducer inward until fully bottomed, Fig. 3.
5. Start engine, wait 90 seconds and move transducer core outward approximately one inch, Fig. 3.
6. Adjust timing light so timing marks are aligned. The timing light meter should indicate additional amount of advance as listed in the Horizon and Omni Electronic Spark Control (Lean Burn) Specification Chart. If within specifications, move transducer core inward and timing should return to basic setting. If timing does not advance and/or did not return to basic setting, replace Spark Control Computer. After computer replacement, repeat test.

Vacuum Advance Test, 1978 Units

1. Connect and adjust timing light to engine so total timing advance can be checked.
2. Start and run engine to obtain normal operating temperature with transmission in neutral and parking brake applied.
3. Place a piece of paper between carburetor switch and throttle lever, Fig. 4. If curb idle adjusting screw is not contacting carburetor switch, ensure fast idle cam is not on or binding, or throttle stop screw is not

Fig. 5   Throttle position transducer adjustment

Fig. 4   Carburetor switch & throttle position transducer

over adjusted. Adjust timing light so basic timing signal can be observed. Run engine for 9 minutes and ensure that a minimum of 16 inches of vacuum is present at transducer. The timing light meter should indicate additional amount of advance as listed in the Horizon and Omni Electronic Spark Control (Lean Burn) Specification Chart. If not, replace Spark Control Computer.

Vacuum Advance Test, 1979–80 Units

NOTE: If computer fails to obtain specified settings, replace computer.

1. Connect timing light and tachometer to engine.
2. Start engine and allow to reach operating temperature. If engine is at operating temperature, wait for at least one minute for start advance to return to basic timing. Place transmission Neutral and apply parking brake.
3. Check basic timing and adjust as necessary. Refer to Horizon and Omni Electronic Spark Control (Lean Burn) Specification Chart.
4. Remove and plug vacuum line at vacuum transducer.
5. Ground carburetor switch, then increase engine speed to 1100 rpm and check speed advance timing. Refer to Horizon and Omni Electronic Spark Control (Lean Burn) specifications.
6. Operate engine at 2000 rpm and remove carburetor switch ground and connect vacuum line to vacuum transducer. Check zero timing, refer to Horizon and Omni Specification Chart.
7. Allow accumulator to clock-up, refer to Horizon and Omni Electronic Spark Control (Lean Burn) Specification Chart. Operate engine at 1100 rpm, then check vacuum advance. Vacuum advance should be as listed in Horizon and Omni Electronic Spark Control (Lean Burn) Specification Chart.
8. Disconnect and plug vacuum line at transducer and increase engine speed to 3000 rpm. Note advance speed timing.
9. Reconnect vacuum line to vacuum transducer and check vacuum advance. Refer to Horizon and Omni Electronic Spark Control (Lean Burn) Specification Chart.
10. Return engine to curb idle speed. Then connect wire to carburetor switch.

Basic Advance Timing Test, 1981–82 Models

1. Connect a suitable tachometer and adjustable timing light to engine.

2. Connect a jumper wire from carburetor switch to ground.
3. Set parking brake and start vehicle, then using the timing light adjustment feature, adjust timing light so specified timing mark is lined up with pointer.
4. The adjustable timing light meter should show amount of advance as shown in "Electronic Spark Control (Lean Burn) Specifications Chart".

Throttle Position Transducer Adjustment, 1978 Units

1. Disconnect connector from transducer.
2. Loosen lock nut.
3. Place special tool C-4522 between outer portion of transducer and transducer mounting bracket, Fig. 5.
4. Adjust transducer until a clearance fit is obtained.
5. Tighten lock nut and reconnect connector.

DISTRIBUTOR SERVICE

Replacement

Refer to Aries, Horizon, Omni, Reliant & 1982 400 & LeBaron Exc. Electronic Spark Control (Lean Burn) System for distributor replacement procedure.

Disassembly

1.7 Liter Engine
1. Remove rotor from shaft, Fig. 6.
2. Remove screw holding pick-up lead.
3. Remove Hall Effect Pick-up Assembly lock springs and the pick-up assembly.
4. Remove two screws securing shield to distributor and the shield.
5. Mark position of drive gear on distributor shaft.
6. Remove roll pin with a suitable punch.
7. Remove drive gear, then the distributor shaft from housing.
8. Remove nylon spacer from shaft.

2.2 Liter Engine
1. Remove rotor from shaft and disconnect pick up electrical connector.
2. Remove Hall Effect Pick Up Assembly retaining clips.
3. Remove splash shield screws, then the splash shield.
4. Remove Hall Effect Pick Up Assembly.
5. Remove distributor drive gear roll pin using punch, then remove drive gear.
6. Remove drive gear thrust washer and distributor shaft.
7. Remove distributor to block seal.

Assembly

1.7 Liter Engine
1. Lightly lubricate housing bushings with engine oil.
2. Install shaft into housing, ensuring nylon spacer is resting on housing bushing.
3. Install drive gear onto distributor shaft in original position, aligning mating marks.
4. Drive in roll pin.
5. Install shield onto housing.
6. Place Hall Effect Pick-up Assembly into housing and secure with lock springs.
7. Secure Hall Effect Pick-up Assembly lead.
8. Install rotor onto shaft.

2.2 Liter Engine
1. Lubricate distributor housing bushings with engine oil, then install engine seal onto distributor housing.
2. Install distributor shaft thrust washer onto distributor shaft, then install shaft into distributor housing.

Fig. 6 Hall Effect electronic ignition distributor, typical

3. Install distributor drive gear thrust washer, then install distributor drive gear onto distributor shaft.
4. Install drive gear roll pin using punch.
5. Install Hall Effect Pick Up Assembly, then install splash shield.
6. Install Hall Effect Pick Up Assembly retaining clips, then install rotor.

SERVICE NOTE
Ignition Timing, Adjust

1977–81
1. Connect a tachometer to engine and a suitable timing light to No. 1 cylinder.

NOTE: Do not puncture ignition cables or boots with test probes.

---

2. Start engine, then apply parking brake and place transmission in Neutral. Allow engine to reach operating temperature.
3. Disconnect and plug EGR vacuum hose at EGR valve and vacuum hose to Electronic Spark Control computor, then connect a jumper wire from carburetor switch to

ground.

4. Disconnect PCV valve and vapor canister purge hose from carburetor. Do not plug hoses.

5. Check idle speed and adjust as necessary, then reconnect PCV valve vacuum hose and vapor canister purge hose.

6. Loosen distributor hold down bracket screw just enough so that distributor housing can be rotated.

7. Check and adjust ignition timing as necessary.

8. Tighten distributor hold down screw, then recheck idle speed and ignition timing.

9. Remove test equipment and connect vacuum hoses.

1982

1. Connect a suitable tachometer to engine and a suitable adjustable timing light to No. 1 cylinder secondary cable.

NOTE: Do not puncture ignition secondary cables or boots with test probes.

2. Set parking brake, start engine and place gear selector in neutral. Run engine until warm.

3. On vehicles equipped with carburetor switch, connect a jumper wire between carburetor switch and a known good ground. Disconnect and plug vacuum line from transducer.

4. Ensure curb idle speed is set at or below specifications. Adjust as necessary.

5. Check ignition timing. If within ±2° of specifications, shut engine "Off" and remove timing light, tachometer and carburetor ground wire. If outside of tolerance, proceed to step 6.

6. Loosen distributor hold down arm screw, rotate distributor housing until correct timing marks are lined up, ensuring idle speed is still at or below specified curb idle speed.

7. Tighten distributor hold down screw, then recheck idle speed and ignition timing.

8. Turn engine "Off" and remove timing light, tachometer and carburetor ground wire.

1978 HORIZON & OMNI ELECTRONIC SPARK CONTROL (LEAN BURN) SPECIFICATION CHART

Spark Control Computer	5206467①	5206501①	5206516①	5206525①
	(4106062)②	(4106063)②	—	(4106065)②
Start Timer Advance Schedule	8°	8°	8°	8°
Delay Time In Seconds	60	60	60	60
Throttle Advance Schedule	—	—	—	—
Test Transducer Core Out 1 Inch	0°	0°	4°–6° @ 100°F 4°–6° @ 140°F	4°–6° @ 100°F 4°–6° @ 140°F
Vacuum Advance Schedule	—	—	—	—
a. Operating Vacuum Range	0 to 14 Inches Hg	0 to 14 Inches Hg	0 to 14 Inches Hg	0 to 14 Inches Hg
b. Advance Off Idle (Carb. Switch Isolated With Paper)	None	6°–10°	2°–6°	2°–6°
c. Accumulation Time in Minutes	8	7	8	8
d. Advance After Accumulation Time	18°–22°	18°–22°	18°–22°	18°–22°
Speed Advance	—	—	—	—
Ground Carb. Switch and Disconnect Throttle Transducer Before Checking	6°–10° @ 2000 rpm 18°–22° @ 6000 rpm	6°–10° @ 2000 rpm 18°–22° @ 6000 rpm	6°–10° @ 2000 rpm 18°–22° @ 6000 rpm	5°–9° @ 2000 rpm 13°–17° @ 6000 rpm

1978 HORIZON & OMNI ELECTRONIC SPARK CONTROL (LEAN BURN) SPECIFICATION CHART—Continued

Spark Control Computer	5206526①	5206666①
	(4106066)②	(4106112)②
Start Timer Advance Schedule	8°	8°
Delay Time In Seconds	60	60
Throttle Advance Schedule	—	—
Test Transducer Core Out 1 Inch	0°	4°–6° @ 100°F 4°–6° @ 140°F
Vacuum Advance Schedule	—	—
a. Operating Vacuum Range	0 to 14 Inches Hg	0 to 14 Inches Hg
b. Advance Off Idle (Carb. Switch Isolated With Paper)	2°–6°	6°–10°
c. Accumulation Time in Minutes	8	7
d. Advance After Accumulation Time	18°–22°	18°–22°
Speed Advance	—	—
Ground Carb. Switch and Disconnect Throttle Transducer Before Checking	6°–10° @ 2000 rpm 18°–22° @ 6000 rpm	5°–9° @ 2000 rpm 13°–17° @ 6000 rpm

ELECTRONIC IGNITION SYSTEMS

1979 HORIZON & OMNI ELECTRONIC SPARK CONTROL (LEAN BURN) SPECIFICATION CHART

Spark Control Computer	5206721①	5206784①	5206785①	5206790①
	4111686②	4111687②	4111688②	4111689②
Start Up Advance (60 Seconds)	5°	5°	5°	5°
Crank + Electrical (Basic Timing)	10° + 5°	10° + 5°	10° + 5°	10° + 5°
Vacuum Advance Range (In. Hg.)	0–10	0–10	0–10	0–10
Zero Time Offset	6°–10°	2°–6°	3°–7°	0°–3°
Accumulator Time In Minutes	8	8	8	8
Vacuum Adv.—Full Accumulator				
@ 1100 rpm	18°–22°	18°–22°	18°–22°	18°–22°
@ 1500 rpm	23°–27°	23°–27°	28°–32°	28°–32°
Throttle Max. Advance (Throttle Open 20°)	0°	0°	0°	0°
Speed Advance				
@ 1100 rpm	0°–3°	0°–3°	0°–3°	0°–3°
@ 2000 rpm	8°–12°	8°–12°	8°–12°	8°–12°
@ 4000 rpm	18°–22°	18°–22°	16°–22°	18°–22°

①—Production part number.   ②—Remanufactured part number.

1980 HORIZON & OMNI ELECTRONIC SPARK CONTROL (LEAN BURN) SPECIFICATION CHART

Spark Control Computer	5213008	5213012
Crank + Run = (Basic Timing)	10° + 0°	10° + 0°
Vacuum Advance (Range)	0″ to 10″	0″ to 10″
Zero Time Advance	18° to 22°	23° to 27°
Accumulator Time (In Minutes)	0	0
Vacuum Adv.—Full Accumulator		
@ 2000 RPM	5° to 9°	5° to 9°
@ 3000 RPM	18° to 22°	23° to 27°
Speed Adv. (Ground Carb. Switch)		
@ 1100 RPM	0° to 3°	0° to 3°
@ 2000 RPM	8° to 12°	13° to 17°
@ 4800 RPM	18° to 22°	20° to 24°
Warm Up Schedule (In Seconds)	25	25
Throttle Maximum Advance (Throttle Open 20°)	0°	0°

1981 ARIES, HORIZON, OMNI & RELIANT ELECTRONIC SPARK CONTROL (LEAN BURN) SPECIFICATION CHART

Spark Control Computer	5213101	5213111	5213128	5213133
Basic Timing	12°	10°	10°	10°
Vacuum Advance (Range)	0–10	0–10	0–10	0–10
Accumulator Time (In Minutes)	0	0	0	0
Spark Advance Test @ 2000 RPM	38 ± 4	35 ± 4	28 ± 4	23 ± 4

Spark Control Computer	5213138	5213143	5213148	5213268
Basic Timing	10°	10°	10°	12°
Vacuum Advance (Range)	0–10	0–10	0–10	0–10
Accumulator Time (In Minutes)	0	0	7	0
Spark Advance Test @ 2000 RPM	23 ± 4	25 ± 4	33 ± 4	43 ± 4

Spark Control Computer	5213249	5213343	5213345	
Basic Timing	10°	10°	10°	
Vacuum Advance (Range)	0–10	0–10	0–10	
Accumulator Time (In Minutes)	0	0	0	
Spark Advance Test @ 2000 RPM	33 ± 4	25 ± 4	25 ± 4	

1982 ARIES, HORIZON, OMNI, RELIANT, 400 & LEBARON
ELECTRONIC SPARK CONTROL (LEAN BURN)
SPECIFICATION CHART

Spark Control Computer	5213437	5213438	5213480	5213481
Basic Timing	12°	20°	12°	12°
Vacuum Advance (Range)	0–10	0–12	0–12	0–12
Accumulator Time (In Minutes)	0	0	0	0
Spark Advance Test @ 2000 RPM	55 ± 4	50 ± 4	45 ± 4	47 ± 4

Spark Control Computer	5213482	5213483	5213542	5213544
Basic Timing	12°	12°	12°	12°
Vacuum Advance (Range)	0–12	0–12	0–10	0–10
Accumulator Time (In Minutes)	0	0	0	0
Spark Advance Test @ 2000 RPM	45 ± 4	.45 ± 4	55 ± 4	50 ± 4

Spark Control Computer	5213546	5213546①	5213594	
Basic Timing	12°	12°	12°	
Vacuum Advance (Range)	0–10	0–12	0–10	
Accumulator Time (In Minutes)	0	0	0	
Spark Advance Test @ 2000 RPM	43 ± 4	31 ± 4	37 ± 4	

①—High Altitude

Misar Electronic Spark Timing (E.S.T.) System

DESCRIPTION

1977 Toronado

This system uses the basic H.E.I. distributor. However, the pick-up coil, pole piece and advance mechanisms have been deleted and the rotor has been redesigned, Fig. 1. This system incorporates a crankshaft sensor, engine coolant temperature sensor and a controller unit.

The engine coolant temperature sensor resistance changes with changes in coolant temperature.

The electronic controller unit is mounted under the glove compartment and receives signals from the crankshaft sensor (crankshaft position and speed), engine coolant temperature sensor, engine vacuum and atmospheric pressure. The controller unit selects the most efficient advance as determined by the input signals and sends a signal to the distributor module to fire the spark plugs.

The electrical harness which connects these units together and to the vehicle harness, contains two vacuum hoses which are both connected to the controller unit. The white hose is connected to engine vacuum, while the black one is vented to atmospheric pressure outside of the vehicle.

The crankshaft sensor is mounted at the front of the engine with a disc located between the harmonic balancer and pulley.

A "Check Ignition" light, located in the instrument panel will go on under the following conditions:
1. Ignition switch is in start position. This mode provides a bulb check.
2. If system voltage is low and there is a heavy electrical load such as operation of power windows or other electrical accessories. Under this condition, the "check ignition" light will go off when the electrical load is removed, providing system voltage returns to normal. The alternator warning light may also go on under these conditions.
3. When checking reference timing and controller circuit is grounded.

Fig. 1   Redesigned rotor used on E.S.T. system. 1977 Tornado

NOTE EMPTY CAVITIES

4. If controller fails to advance spark timing.

1978 Toronado

This system is similar to the system used on the 1977 Toronado, except that the crankshaft sensor and pulse generator disc have been eliminated. The functions of the crankshaft sensor and pulse generator disc are performed by the pick-up coil and timer core which are located in the distributor, Fig. 2. The electronic circuitry has also been redesigned, Fig. 3. The rotor mounting plate, Fig. 2, is constructed of brass, which is a non-magnetic metal. The reason for this is so that the brass mounting plate will prevent the signal produced by the pickup coil from being affected by magnetic attraction.

With these modifications, the ignition timing can be set by turning the distributor, however the reference timing connector must be grounded with a jumper wire.

1977 TORONADO SYSTEM SERVICE & DIAGNOSIS

Adjusting Distributor Position

1. Disconnect ignition feed wire and remove distributor cap.
2. Crank engine until rotor points toward rear of engine and number one piston is almost on TDC (0 degrees on timing indicator).

Fig. 2 Electronic Spark Timing (E.S.T.) distributor. 1978 Toronado

3. Using a socket on crankshaft bolt, turn crankshaft to 0 degrees.
4. White mark on rotor should be aligned with white mark on distributor housing, Fig. 4. If not, loosen distributor clamp bolt and turn distributor to align.

NOTE: This is the final distributor position.

5. Tighten distributor clamp bolt.

Adjusting Reference Timing

NOTE: Timing should be checked with a magnetic probe timing meter.

1. With distributor postion correctly adjusted, connect the open reference timing connector (taped to harness), Fig. 5, to

ground using a jumper wire.
2. With transmission in PARK, drive wheels blocked and parking brake applied, start engine and run at low idle. Timing should be at 20 degrees.

NOTE: Engine speed will not affect timing. Also, the "check timing" light should be on.

3. If timing is incorrect, stop engine, then loosen timing adjuster clamp bolts and rotate timing adjuster bolt, Fig. 6, clockwise to retard timing. One complete turn equals about one degree.

Fig. 4 Rotor and distributor alignment mark. 1977 Toronado

Fig. 5 Reference timing connector. 1977 Toronado

HOT LIGHT

CHECK IGNITION
LIGHT

INST. CLUSTER
CONNECTORS

I. P. EXTENSION HARNESS
CONNECTOR (LEFT SIDE OF RADIO)

GAGES TRANS. FUSE
IN FUSE BLOCK

PINK

BLK. DBL. PINK STRIPE

DK. GRN.

DK. GRN.

DK. GRN.

PINK

PINK

GROUND
SCREW &
WASHER

IGNITION
SWITCH

PINK

PICK-UP COIL & MODULE

CONTROLLER

ATMOSPHERIC
PRESS.

BLK.
DBL
PINK
STR.

RED

6 WIRE
CONNECTOR

CAVITY PLUG

4 WIRE
CONNECTOR

12 VOLT
IGNITION WIRE

12V

WHITE

A B C D E F G H J K

A B C D E F G H J K

CAVITY PLUG

VOLTAGE TESTS
(Ignition Key in "RUN" Position)
■ BATTERY VOLTAGE (12 VOLTS OR MORE)
◨ .5 to 2 VOLTS (Cranking)

DK. GRN.

BROWN

HARNESS

SHIELD
DK. GRN.
WHITE
BROWN

COOLANT
TEMPERATURE
SENSOR

PICK-UP COIL

DK. GREEN

WHITE

DK. GREEN

BROWN
MODULE

PPL

SHIELD

HARNESS

BLUE

ENGINE VACUUM

REFERENCE
TIMING
CONNECTOR
(Taped to Harness)

LOCATED
AT LEFT REAR OF
ENGINE

WHITE VACUUM TUBE

Fig. 3 Electronic Spark Timing (E.S.T.) wiring circuit. 1978 Toronado

FRONT ENGINE
MOUNT

TIMING ADJUSTER BOLT

P/S PUMP
BRACKET

TURN
CW TO ADVANCE
CCW TO RETARD

DISC

.045"
.055"

CRANKSHAFT
SENSOR

.045"
.055"

TIMING ADJUSTER
CLAMP BOLTS
10 FT. LBS.

P/S PUMP
BRACKET

CLEARANCE
ADJUSTMENT
BOLTS
25 FT. LBS.

HARNESS
CONNECTOR

NOTE: TO GAUGE CLEARANCE
USE BT-5005 CARBURETOR
GAUGES.

Fig. 6 Crankshaft sensor to disc clearance. 1977 Toronado

NOTE: Do not rotate distributor in an attempt to adjust ignition timing.

4. Recheck timing. If correct, stop engine, then tighten adjuster bolt clamp bolts and disconnect jumper wire.

Crankshaft Sensor, Replace & Align

1. Turn ignition OFF and mark sensor position on mounting surfaces so that sensor can be installed in original position.
2. Disconnect sensor harness connector, then remove crankshaft sensor timing adjuster clamp bolts and sensor.
3. Install crankshaft sensor in original position and leave adjuster clamp bolts slightly loose until after checking reference timing.
4. Check clearance between disc and crankshaft sensor, Fig. 7. To adjust, loosen clearance adjustment bolts, Fig. 6.
5. Reconnect harness connector.
6. Check reference timing.

NOTE: TO GAUGE CLEARANCE USE BT-5005 CARBURETOR GAUGES.

DISC

DOWEL

4 NARROW TEETH SPACED 90° APART
76 TOTAL TEETH

.045
.055

CRANKSHAFT POSITION SENSOR

DOWEL ON FORWARD SIDE OF DISC FITS INTO HOLE IN PULLEY

DISC

.045
.055

A MINIMUM OF ½ OF EACH PIN (.059) MUST ALWAYS OVERLAP DISC IN ALL CONDITIONS

4 PINS — ENDS APPROXIMATELY FLUSH WITH THEIR RESPECTIVE SURFACES

SENSOR TO DISC RELATIONSHIP WORST CASE CONDITIONS SHOWN:

½ PIN

½ PIN

½ PIN

SENSOR OR DISC OUT OF SQUARE

SENSOR OFFSET

SENSOR NOT PARALLEL WITH DISC

Fig. 7   Crankshaft sensor alignment. 1977 Toronado

ENGINE TIMING ADVANCE IN CRANKSHAFT DEGREES

1. Engine **MUST BE** at operating temperature.

2. Connect tachometer and timing meter.

3. Disconnect controller assembly vacuum tube (white) from manifold vacuum "T". Plug "T" and connect vacuum pump and gauge to white tube. Use pump to get vacuum readings shown.

NOTE: 1400 RPM at 15" of vacuum gives maximum advance. If advance is less than specification, slowly increase vacuum to get maximum advance. If advance is now within specification, instruments/gauges used are inaccurate. If not within specification, replace controller assembly.

EXCEPT CALIFORNIA			CALIFORNIA		
ENGINE RPM	VACUUM (INCHES)	*CRANKSHAFT DEGREES	ENGINE RPM	VACUUM (INCHES)	*CRANKSHAFT DEGREES
600	16.5	29 to 34	600	13.5	17 to 20
600	15	27 to 31	600	12	17 to 20
1000	12	29 to 37	1000	12	19 to 22
1400	15	44 to 61	1400	15	44 to 61
1400	10.5	37 to 41	2000	18	31 to 49
1400	6	25 to 35	2000	0	31 to 34
2000	18	44 to 53			
2000	0	28 to 31			

*Advance specifications are approximate depending upon accuracy of tachometer, vacuum gauge and timing meter

Fig. 9   Engine timing advance specifications. 1977 Toronado

Fig. 8 Crankshaft sensor connector test connections

System Diagnosis

Engine Will Not Start (Engine Cranks Normally, Battery fully Charged)

1. Check EST fuse in fuse panel. If fuse is blown, proceed to step 2. If fuse is not blown, proceed to step 3.
2. Disconnect 3-wire connector near controller unit, then replace fuse and turn ignition ON. If fuse does not blow, locate and repair short in red wire from connector on controller unit to crankshaft sensor. If fuse blows again, locate and repair short circuit in pink wire with double-black stripes from 3-wire connector through instrument panel harness to fuse panel.
3. Check for spark at the spark plugs. If there is no spark, proceed to step 4. If there is spark, check distributor position and reference timing. If correct, trouble is not in ignition. Check fuel system and spark plugs.
4. Inspect crankshaft sensor, disc and harness for damage. Check sensor alignment and clearance at disc. Check black ground wire and screw in distributor. If connection is good, turn ignition key to RUN position and check voltage as follows:
   a. Ignition wire (black with pink stripe) at connector on distributor. If voltage is less than 12 volts, check wire from distributor to ignition switch for loose connections or open circuit. Also check ignition switch.
   b. Terminal J (pink and red) wires in connector at controller unit. If voltage is less than 12 volts, check pink wire for loose connection or open circuit from connector at controller unit to 3-wire connector near controller, then the pink wire with double-black stripes through instrument panel harness to fuse panel.
   c. Tan wire in 2-wire connector near distributor. Do not disconnect wire. Voltage should be .5–2 volts while cranking the engine. If voltage is not as specified, proceed to step 5. If voltage is as specified, check distributor, coil, and module. Replace defective parts.
5. Check voltage at terminal C (tan wire) in connector at controller unit. Voltage should be .5–2 volts. If voltage is not as specified, proceed to step 6. If voltage is as specified, check tan wire from controller to 2-wire connector near distributor for loose connection or open circuit. Replace or repair as necessary.
6. Check voltage at terminal D (light blue wire) in connector at controller unit while cranking engine. Record reading, then check voltage again with crankshaft sensor disconnected and placed aside so as not to damage it. If voltages are the same, proceed to step 7. If voltages are not the same, replace controller unit.
7. Turn ignition key to RUN position and check voltage at crankshaft sensor harness connector, Fig. 8. If voltages are as

specified, proceed to step 8. If voltages are not as specified, replace harness.
8. Turn ignition key to RUN position and check voltage at both 8–10 volt terminals. If voltage is not 8–10 volts at both terminals, proceed to step 9. If voltage is as specified, replace crankshaft sensor.
9. Turn ignition key to RUN position and check voltage at controller unit. Voltage at terminals D (light blue) and E (purple) should be 8–10 volts. If voltage is as specified, replace harness. If voltage is not as specified, replace controller unit.

Engine Detonates (Recommended Octane Rating Fuel Used)

1. Check white vacuum hose from intake manifold to controller unit for kinks, obstructions, leakage or heat damage.

NOTE: A partially obstructed hose would prevent fast drop of vacuum on acceleration.

If hose is in good condition and not leaking, disconnect coolant temperature sensor and check resistance. At engine operating temperature, the resistance should be 500 to 2,000 ohms. At 70° F., the resistance should be 25,000 to 55,000 ohms. If resistance is as specified, proceed to step 2. If resistance is not as specified or if there is an open circuit in the sensor, replace sensor.
2. With ignition off, disconnect controller unit connector and connect a jumper wire between terminals B (black wire) and F (white wire) in connector. Connect an ohmmeter to the 2 terminals in coolant temperature harness connector.
3. If ohmmeter reading is less than 1 ohm, check crankshaft sensor alignment and disc for damage, Fig. 5. Check reference timing. If no damage is found and sensor alignment and reference timing are correct, replace controller unit.
4. If ohmmeter reading is more than 1 ohm or indicates an open circuit, check for open circuit in black and white wires. Repair or replace harness as necessary.

Engine Starts Then Stops When Key Is Turned to "RUN" Position

1. Turn ignition key to RUN, then disconnect crankshaft sensor connector and check voltages as shown in Fig. 8.
2. If voltage reading at 12 volt terminal or shield terminal are not as specified, repair or replace harness.
3. If voltage reading at either 8–10 terminal are not as specified, check voltage at controller unit connector from ground to terminal D (light blue) and E (purple). Reading should be 8–10 volts at both terminals. If both readings are as specified, replace harness. If readings are not as specified, replace controller unit.
4. If all voltage readings are as specified in Fig. 8, reconnect crankshaft sensor connector and connect jumper wire to reference timing connector (purple wire) near controller and connect jumper wire to ground.
5. Start engine and run at idle. Check voltage at controller unit connector terminal E (purple). Voltage reading should be 3–5 volts. If voltage is as specified, replace controller unit. If voltage is not as specified, check disc alignment, Fig. 7. If alignment is correct, replace crankshaft sensor.

Fig. 10 Electronic Spark Timing (E.S.T.) reference timing connector. 1978 Toronado

Hard Starting, Rough Idle, Poor Performance (Battery Fully Charged)

1. Check fuel system, choke, spark plugs and cables.
2. Make sure harness connections to distributor, coolant temperature sensor and controller unit are good.
3. Inspect crankshaft sensor for alignment. Make sure clearance between sensor and disc is .045–.055 inches, Fig. 7. Also make sure harness and connector are in good condition.
4. Check all vacuum hoses for kinks, obstructions, leakage or heat damage. Repair or replace as necessary.
5. Check distributor cap and rotor for signs of arcing. Check ground wire and screw in distributor. Check module with tester J-24624.
6. Check distributor position and reference timing.
7. With engine idling, transmission in PARK and parking brakes applied, connect voltmeter to ground and touch other probe to ignition wire (black with pink stripe) in connector on distributor. If voltage is less than 12 volts, check for loose connection between distributor connector and ignition switch.
8. Connect voltmeter to ground and J terminal (pink and red wires) in controller unit. If less than 12 volts, check for loose connection through instrument panel harness connector to fuse panel.
9. If problem has not been located, proceed as follows:
10. Turn ignition key to RUN position, then disconnect crankshaft sensor connector and check voltage at 12 volt terminal and at shield terminal, Fig. 8. If voltages are as specified, proceed to step 11. If voltages are not as specified, repair or replace harness.
11. Turn ignition key to RUN position and check voltage at both 8–10 volt terminals. If voltages are as specified, proceed to step 12. If voltages are not as specified, with crankshaft sensor disconnected, check for 8–10 volts at both terminals D (light blue) and E (purple) of controller unit. If voltages are as specified, replace harness, if not, replace controller unit.
12. Reconnect crankshaft sensor connector, then with key in RUN position and engine stopped, check reference voltage at controller unit connector terminal D (light blue). Record voltage, then check voltage again with engine at idle speed. If voltage readings are different, proceed to step 13. If voltage readings are the same, replace crankshaft sensor.
13. With engine idling, check for 3–5 volts at

1. Engine **MUST BE** at operating temperature and timing set to specification.

2. Connect tachometer and timing meter. Do not ground reference timing connector.

3. Disconnect controller assembly vacuum tube (white) from manifold vacuum "T". Plug "T" and connect vacuum pump and gage to white tube. Use pump such as BT-7517 to get vacuum readings shown.

NOTE: 1400 RPM at 15" of vacuum gives maximum advance. If advance is less than specification, slowly increase vacuum to get maximum advance. If advance is now within specification, instruments/gages used are inaccurate. If not within specification, replace controller.

EXCEPT CALIFORNIA CARS			CALIFORNIA CARS		
ENGINE RPM	VACUUM (INCHES)	*CRANKSHAFT DEGREES	ENGINE RPM	VACUUM (INCHES)	*CRANKSHAFT DEGREES
600	16.5	29 to 34	600	13.5	15 to 22
600	15	27 to 31	600	12	15 to 22
1000	12	32 to 35	1000	12	17 to 25
1400	15	49 to 62	1400	15	39 to 65
1400	10.5	38 to 40	2000	18	24 to 33
1400	6	27 to 35	2000	0	23 to 32
2000	18	44 to 47			
2000	0	29 to 31			

* Advance specifications are approximate depending upon accuracy of tachometer, vacuum gage and timing meter.

Fig. 11   Electronic Spark Timing (E.S.T.) engine timing advance specifications. 1978

controller unit connector terminal E (purple). If voltage is as specified, proceed to step 14. If voltage is not as specified, replace crankshaft sensor.
14. With engine idling, check for 1-4 volts at tan wire in 2-wire connector near distributor. If voltage is as specified, proceed to step 15. If voltage is not as specified, replace controller unit assembly.
15. Check engine advance. Refer to chart in Fig. 9. If advance is not as specified, proceed to step 16. If advance is as specified, problem is not in ignition. Recheck steps 1, 3, 4, 5, and 6.
16. Disconnect coolant temperature sensor and check resistance of sensor at sensor terminals. At engine operating temperature, resistance should be 500 to 2,000 ohms. At 70° F., resistance should be 25,000 to 55,000 ohms. If resistance is as specified, proceed to step 17. If resistance is not as specified, replace coolant sensor.
17. With ignition OFF, disconnect controller unit connector and connect a jumper wire between terminals B (black wire) and F (white wire) in connector. Connect an ohmmeter to the 2 terminals in temperature sensor harness connector. If ohmmeter reads less than 1 ohm resistance, replace controller unit. If ohmmeter reads more than 1 ohm or indicates an open circuit, check for open circuit in black and white wires and repair or replace harness as necessary.

Hot Light ON (Ignition Key In "RUN" Position)
1. Check usual causes of "Hot Light On" condition. Correct as required.
2. Disconnect 2-wire connector at coolant temperature sensor and turn ignition to RUN position. If hot light remains on,

proceed to step 3. If hot light goes off, replace coolant temperature sensor.
3. Turn ignition switch OFF, then disconnect 3-wire connector near controller unit and turn ignition switch to RUN. If hot light goes off, proceed to step 4. If hot light remains on, locate and repair short in dark green wire circuit from 3-wire connector to instrument cluster and to ignition switch.
4. Disconnect controller unit connector and connect an ohmmeter to the 2 terminals in coolant temperature sensor connector. Ohmmeter should indicate an open circuit. Connect ohmmeter to ground and connector terminals. White wire terminal should indicate an open circuit. If all readings are as specified, replace controller unit. If all readings are not as specified, black and white wires are shorted together. Repair or replace harness as required.

"Check Ignition" Light "On" (Engine Running, Battery Fully Charged)
1. Check reference timing wire (purple) connector at controller unit, Fig. 3. The connector should be disconnected and not grounded.
2. With engine running, transmission in PARK and parking brakes applied, check voltage at controller unit terminal J (pink and red wires). If voltage is less than 11 volts, proceed to step 3. If voltage is above 11 volts, turn ignition key to RUN position (engine off) and disconnect 3-wire connector near controller unit. If light goes out, replace controller unit. If light remains on, circuit between H terminal and light is grounded. Repair or replace harness as required.
3. With all accessories turned off and engine running at fast idle, connect a voltmeter

to battery. If voltmeter reading is more than 12 volts, proceed to step 4. If voltmeter reading is less than 12 volts, check fan belt tension and charging system.
4. Check for loose connection from terminal J in controller unit through instrument panel harness connectors to fuse panel. Repair as required.

1978 TORONADO SYSTEM SERVICE
Adjusting Reference Timing
1. Connect reference timing connector (taped to harness), Fig. 10, to ground using a suitable jumper wire.
2. Connect timing light or magnetic probe timing meter and start engine.

NOTE: The "Check Ignition" should be on if reference timing connector is properly connected.

3. Check timing. If timing is not to specifications, loosen distributor clamp bolt and turn distributor as necessary, then tighten clamp bolt.
4. Disconnect jumper wire from reference timing connector. The "Check Ignition" light should go out.

System Diagnosis
Refer to Fig. 11 for engine timing advance specifications, and to Figs. 12 thru 15 for system diagnosis.

NOTE: Make sure controller case is grounded at all times while performing diagnosis.

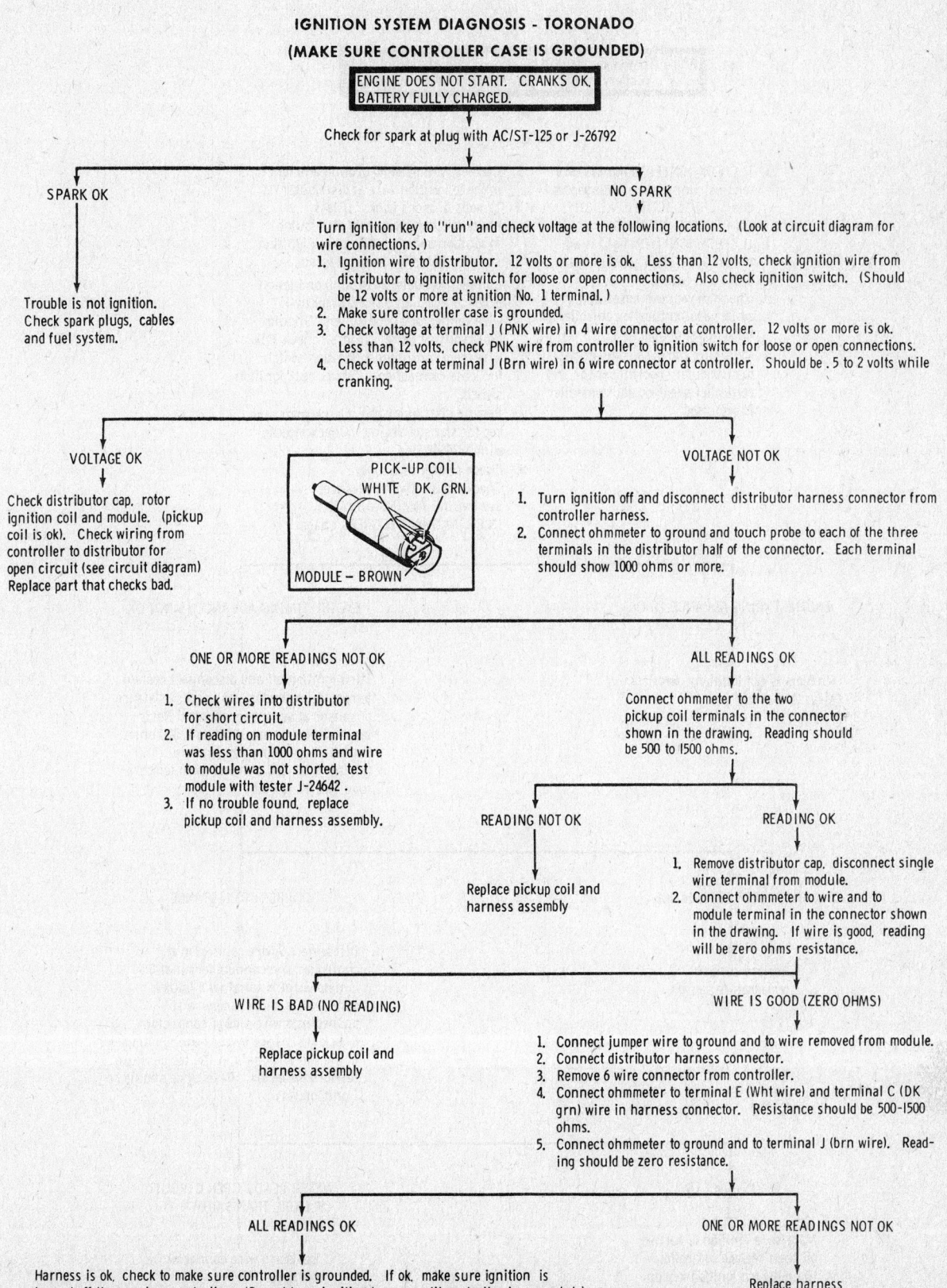

IGNITION SYSTEM DIAGNOSIS - TORONADO

(MAKE SURE CONTROLLER CASE IS GROUNDED)

ENGINE DOES NOT START.   CRANKS OK,
BATTERY FULLY CHARGED.

Check for spark at plug with AC/ST-125 or J-26792

SPARK OK

Trouble is not ignition.
Check spark plugs, cables
and fuel system.

NO SPARK

Turn ignition key to "run" and check voltage at the following locations. (Look at circuit diagram for wire connections.)
1. Ignition wire to distributor. 12 volts or more is ok. Less than 12 volts, check ignition wire from distributor to ignition switch for loose or open connections. Also check ignition switch. (Should be 12 volts or more at ignition No. 1 terminal.)
2. Make sure controller case is grounded.
3. Check voltage at terminal J (PNK wire) in 4 wire connector at controller. 12 volts or more is ok. Less than 12 volts, check PNK wire from controller to ignition switch for loose or open connections.
4. Check voltage at terminal J (Brn wire) in 6 wire connector at controller. Should be .5 to 2 volts while cranking.

VOLTAGE OK

Check distributor cap, rotor
ignition coil and module. (pickup
coil is ok). Check wiring from
controller to distributor for
open circuit (see circuit diagram)
Replace part that checks bad.

PICK-UP COIL
WHITE   DK. GRN.

MODULE – BROWN

VOLTAGE NOT OK

1. Turn ignition off and disconnect distributor harness connector from controller harness.
2. Connect ohmmeter to ground and touch probe to each of the three terminals in the distributor half of the connector. Each terminal should show 1000 ohms or more.

ONE OR MORE READINGS NOT OK

1. Check wires into distributor for short circuit.
2. If reading on module terminal was less than 1000 ohms and wire to module was not shorted, test module with tester J-24642.
3. If no trouble found, replace pickup coil and harness assembly.

ALL READINGS OK

Connect ohmmeter to the two
pickup coil terminals in the connector
shown in the drawing. Reading should
be 500 to 1500 ohms.

READING NOT OK

Replace pickup coil and
harness assembly

READING OK

1. Remove distributor cap, disconnect single wire terminal from module.
2. Connect ohmmeter to wire and to module terminal in the connector shown in the drawing. If wire is good, reading will be zero ohms resistance.

WIRE IS BAD (NO READING)

Replace pickup coil and
harness assembly

WIRE IS GOOD (ZERO OHMS)

1. Connect jumper wire to ground and to wire removed from module.
2. Connect distributor harness connector.
3. Remove 6 wire connector from controller.
4. Connect ohmmeter to terminal E (Wht wire) and terminal C (DK grn) wire in harness connector. Resistance should be 500-1500 ohms.
5. Connect ohmmeter to ground and to terminal J (brn wire). Reading should be zero resistance.

ALL READINGS OK

Harness is ok, check to make sure controller is grounded. If ok, make sure ignition is
turned off then replace controller. (Do not turn ignition key on until controller is grounded.)

ONE OR MORE READINGS NOT OK

Replace harness

Fig. 12   Electronic Spark Timing (E.S.T.) system diagnosis chart (part 1 of 4). 1978 Toronado

ELECTRONIC IGNITION SYSTEMS

IGNITION SYSTEM DIAGNOSIS - TORONADO CONTINUED
(MAKE SURE CONTROLLER CASE IS GROUNDED)

HARD STARTING, ROUGH ENGINE, POOR PERFORMANCE
(Battery fully charged – 12 Volts or more)

---

1. If CHECK IGNITION light is on (engine running), use diagnosis chart CHECK IGNITION LIGHT ON - ENGINE RUNNING.
2. If CHECK IGNITION light is off, check fuel system, choke, spark plugs and cables.
3. Check all vacuum hoses and white vacuum tube to controller for pinches or leaks.
4. Make sure harness connections to distributor, coolant sensor and controller are good and controller is grounded.

5. Connect voltmeter to ground and touch probe to ignition wire at distributor 12 volts or more is ok. If less, check ignition wire from distributor to ignition switch. Also check ignition switch. Refer to circuit diagram.
6. Connect voltmeter to ground and touch probe to terminal J (PNK wire) in 4 wire connector at controller. Should be 12 volts or more. If less, check PNK wire from controller to ignition switch for loose connections. Also check ignition switch.
7. Remove distributor cap, check rotor and cap for signs of arcing. Check module with J-24642.
8. Check reference timing.
9. Check engine timing advance. See ENGINE TIMING ADVANCE IN CRANKSHAFT DEGREES chart.

ENGINE TIMING ADVANCE IS OK

Problem is not ignition. Recheck steps 2, 3 and 5.

ENGINE TIMING ADVANCE IS NOT OK

Turn ignition off and disconnect coolant temperature sensor and check resistance of sensor at sensor terminals. Resistance should be about 500 to 2,000 ohms. Engine at operating temperature. (25,000 to 55,000 ohms at room temperature.) 70°F. (21°C).

INCORRECT RESISTANCE

Replace coolant temperature sensor.

CORRECT RESISTANCE

1. Disconnect 6 wire connector at controller and connect terminal B (shield wire) to terminal F (blue wire) with a short jumper wire pushed into wire side of connector.
2. Check resistance by connecting ohmmeter to the two terminals in the temperature sensor connector. Resistance should be 1 ohm or less.

RESISTANCE OK

Make sure ignition is turned off then replace controller. (Do not turn ignition key on until controller is grounded.)

METER READS OPEN CIRCUIT OR MORE THAN 1 OHM

Replace 6 wire connector harness.

Fig. 13 Electronic Spark Timing (E.S.T.) system diagnosis chart (part 2 of 4). 1978 Toronado

IGNITION SYSTEM DIAGNOSIS - TORONADO CONTINUED
(MAKE SURE CONTROLLER CASE IS GROUNDED)

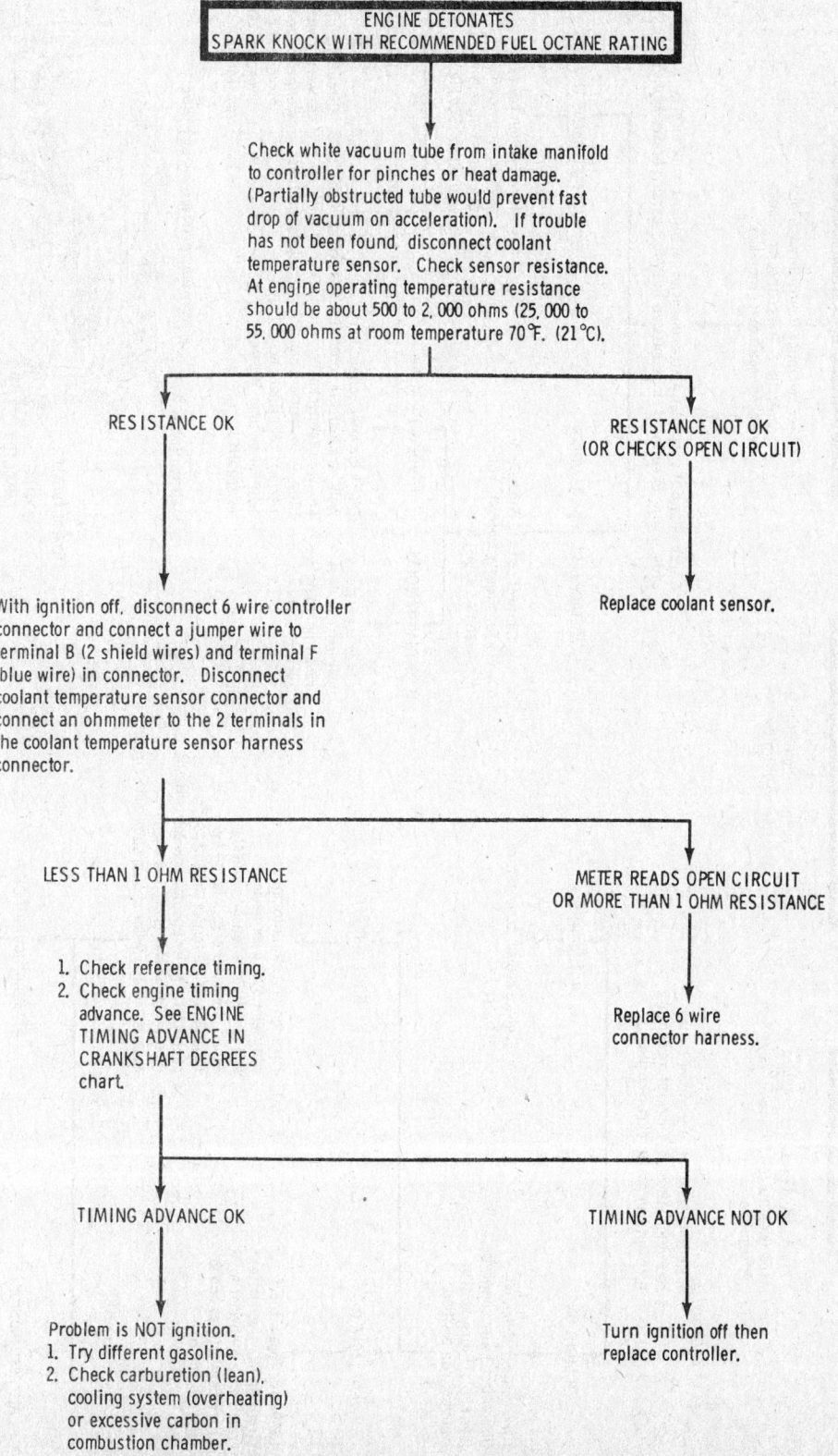

Fig. 14   Electronic Spark Timing (E.S.T.) system diagnosis chart (part 3 of 4). 1978 Toronado

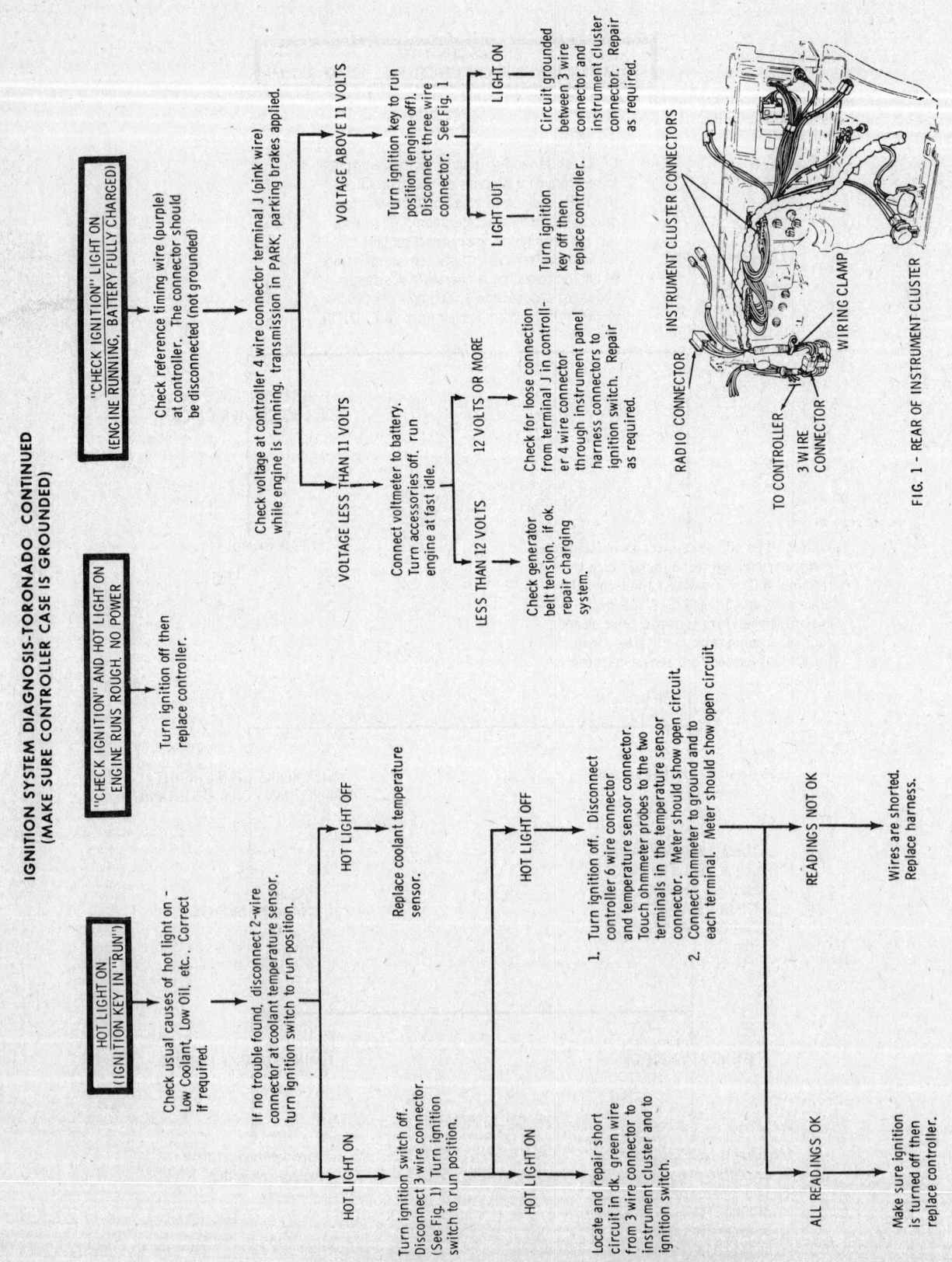

Fig. 15 Electronic Spark Timing (E.S.T.) system diagnosis chart (part 4 of 4). 1978 Toronado

Electronic Spark Selection (ESS) System

The Electronic Spark Selection (ESS) System is standard on all 1978–80 Seville, 1979–80 Eldorado, 1979 Brougham and DeVille California models less electronic fuel injection and all 1980 Brougham and DeVille. This system is able to advance or retard the entire spark curve under certain operating conditions. This improves fuel economy at cruising speeds, reduces exhaust emissions and improves hot engine restarting.

The system used on Eldorado is similar to the system used on Seville. The system used on Brougham and DeVille models less electronic fuel injection do not have EGR solenoids; a three-way coolant temperature switch is needed to signal the ESS decoder for spark retard during cold weather operation and to prevent over advance during hot engine operation.

Spark advance is retarded from normal engine timing during cranking, Fig. 1. Spark retard improved hot restarting by lessening the demand on the starting system since the spark is delivered to the cylinder when the piston is closer to top dead center. Ignition and the associated start of combustion pressure build-up in the cylinder occur closer to the point where the piston starts the downward motion at the beginning of the power stroke. This reduces demand on the starting system since the starter is not required to crank the engine a longer period of time against a high combustion pressure during engine starting.

Spark advance is also retarded from normal engine timing when coolant temperature is below approximately 130° F. (54° C.) on 1978–79 California vehicles and all 1980 vehicles. This shortens the catalytic converter warm-up time thereby reducing exhaust gas hydrocarbon emissions. The catalytic converter is brought up to operating temperature faster since higher exhaust gas temperature is obtained when the spark is retarded.

There is no modification to normal ignition timing during normal city operation when outside of the cruise mode at normal operating temperature. Cruise conditions are identified by high manifold vacuums and high engine speeds. Normal spark advance occurs any time below the cruise mode and/or manifold vacuum points. California vehicles have retarded spark when the engine is cold as described previously. All other vehicles have normal spark advance at this time.

Spark timing is advanced over normal engine timing during cruise conditions to improve fuel economy, Fig. 1. Ignition occurs earlier in the compression stroke giving the

Fig. 1   Electronic Spark Selection (ESS) system operating modes

fuel-air mixture more time to burn which increases efficiency and improves fuel economy.

This system includes an electronic decoder and a H.E.I. distributor which has been modified for the ESS system. The pick-up coil signal is sent to the electronic decoder to provide engine speed and ignition timing information. This signal is from the speed of the timer core and the relationship to the pole piece. The ESS system distributor has a five pin module in place of the 4 pin module used in conventional H.E.I. units. The electronic decoder output signal is sent to this new additional pin on the module. At this point, the decoder signal either delays or does not delay the shutting-off current in the primary winding in the ignition coil.

The spark is retarded from normal engine timing when current shut-off in the primary winding is delayed. Ignition then takes place at a later time when the piston is closer to top dead center.

Maximum delay of the primary winding current shut-off occurs when the engine is cranking and during cold engine operation on California vehicles only. This is also the point of maximum spark retard from normal ignition timing. During normal city operation, the delay is less which results in normal advance during the normal city operation mode. Spark timing advanced over normal ignition timing occurs when there is no delay in shutting-off the primary current.

Existing components are utilized to provide input to the electronic decoder to further identify engine operating conditions which influence timing for any operating mode.

Engine coolant temperature is sensed indirectly at the EGR on/off solenoid. This solenoid valve is controlled by the electronic fuel injection system electronic control unit (ECU). Engine coolant temperature is an input to the ECU on all EFI equipped vehicles. On California vehicles, the ESS circuit to the EGR solenoid activates before the solenoid. On all except California vehicles, the ESS circuit to the EGR solenoid is activated after the solenoid.

The EFI ECU sends a signal to the EGR solenoid when the engine is cold through the solenoid windings to ground and closing the valve and shutting off EGR. There are approximately 12 volts across the solenoid when the engine is cold. On California vehicles, there are approximately 12 volts at the decoder when the engine is cold. On all except California vehicles, there is a ground potential at the decoder on cold engines. The decoder recognizes the difference in voltage and processes it as an input to retard the spark from normal ignition timing on California vehicles. Spark is not retarded on cold engine on all except California vehicles.

When the engine warms up, the ECU signal to the EGR solenoid is terminated to open the EGR valve. There is now a ground potential on warm engine on all vehicles, just like there was on all vehicles except California models. Therefore, the spark is not retarded from normal spark timing.

Diagnosis of the Electronic Spark Selection (ESS) system must be accomplished through the use of a special tester, tool No. J-24642.

Electronic Spark Timing (EST) System

This system is used on 1980 Cadillac vehicles equipped with Digital Electronic Fuel Injection (DEFI) System. The H.E.I. distributor used in this system is a modified unit and does not have a vacuum advance unit or centrifugal weights. The electronic module has seven pins. A spark shield is used under the rotor to protect the electronic circuits from false impulses.

The EST system consists of a digital computer (ECM) and engine sensors. EST controls

the ignition timing in relation to crankshaft position and spark dwell. Crankshaft position is determined by distributor reference pulses received from the pick-up coil. Engine timing advance is determined by the engine speed and its load. This advance is then modified by the engine coolant temperature during starting, the actual engine coolant temperature, the barometric pressure, manifold pressure and throttle switch.

The following input signals determine the spark advance signal to the distributor:
a. System power.
b. Ignition on signal.
c. Engine crank signal.
d. Throttle switch.
e. Distributor references pulses.
f. Manifold absolute pressure (MAP).
g. Ambient pressure.
h. Engine coolant temperature.

1977–80 High Energy Ignition System (H.E.I.)

Fig. 1 H.E.I. distributor external components.
Except units with external coil

Fig. 2 H.E.I. distributor internal components.
Except units with external coil

DESCRIPTION

The H.E.I. system, Figs. 1, 2 and 3, utilizes an all-electronic module, pickup coil and timer core in place of the conventional ignition points and condenser (the condenser is used for noise suppression only). Point pitting and rubbing block wear resulting in retarded ignition timing, are eliminated.

Since the coil is part of the H.E.I. distributor there is no need for distributor-to-coil primary (breaker points to coil negative lead) or secondary lead (high voltage lead).

The magnetic pickup consists of a rotating timer core attached to the distributor shaft, a stationary pole piece, permanent magnet and pickup coil.

When the distributor shaft rotates, the teeth of the timer core line up and pass the teeth of the pole piece inducing voltage in the pickup coil which signals the all-electronic module to open the ignition coil primary circuit. Maximum inductance occurs at the moment the timer core teeth are lined up with the teeth on the pole piece. At the instant the timer core teeth start to pass the pole teeth, the primary current decreases and a high voltage is induced in the ignition coil secondary winding and is directed through the rotor and high voltage leads to fire the spark plugs.

NOTE: Since this is a full 12 volt system it does not require a resistance wire.

The vacuum diaphragm is connected by linkage to the pole piece. When the diaphragm moves against spring pressure it rotates the pole piece allowing the poles to advance relative to the timer core. The timer core is rotated about the shaft by conventional advance weights, thus providing centrifugal advance.

CAUTION: Never connect a wire directly between the "Tach" terminal, Fig. 1, of the distributor connector and the ground since this will damage the electronic circuitry of the module.

A convenient tachometer connection is incorporated in the wiring connector on the side of the distributor, Figs. 1 and 3. However due to its transistorized design, the high energy ignition system will not trigger some models of engine tachometers.

NOTE: A diagnostic connector is used on some 1977–80 vehicles. This connector is located in the engine compartment on the left front fender or skirt and can be identified by its bright orange color. On vehicles equipped with this connector, a tachometer may be connected between terminals 6 and G.

CAUTION: When using a timing light to adjust ignition timing, the connection should be made at the No. 1 spark plug. Forcing foreign objects through the boot at the No. 1 terminal of the distributor cap will damage the boot and could cause engine misfiring.

The spark plug boot has been designed to form a tight seal around the spark plug and should be twisted 1/2 turn before removal.

SYSTEM DIAGNOSIS

1980 Cadillac Electronic Spark Timing (EST)

1. With engine idling, check voltage output terminal of MAP sensor as vacuum hose is disconnected and reconnected several times.
2. If no sensor output change is indicated, inspect MAP hose for leakage or obstructions.
3. If output sensor change is indicated:

SECONDARY OUTPUT TERMINAL
TACHOMETER
BATTERY TERMINAL (CONNECTED TO IGNITION SWITCH)
TO MODULE (C−)
TO MODULE (B+)
CONNECTOR
TO SPARK PLUG
IGNITION COIL
CAP

CONNECT TACHOMETER FROM THIS TERMINAL TO GROUND. (SOME TACHOMETERS MUST CONNECT FROM THIS TERMINAL TO ENERGIZER POSITIVE (+). SOME TACHOMETERS MAY NOT WORK AT ALL. CONSULT TACHOMETER MANUFACTURER.)

LATCH (4)
VACUUM UNIT
HOUSING
GEAR

HIGH ENERGY IGNITION DISTRIBUTOR

Fig. 3   H.E.I. distributor components. 1977 Inline 4 & 6 cyl. units with external coil

a. Disconnect 4-terminal connector at distributor. Do not ground "Test" lead.
b. With engine idling, connect a jumper wire between teminals "A" and "B" in distributor side of EST connector.
c. Connect a test light from B+ supply to terminal "C" in distributor side of EST connector.
4. If engine stops running, check for an open or grounded lead to terminal "A" in distributor side of EST connector. If lead is OK, replace EST (HEI) module.
5. If engine continues running and test light is on, check for ground in lead to terminal "C" in distributor side of EST connector.
6. If engine continues running and test light is off, remove jumper wire between terminals "A" and "B" in distributor side of EST connector:
   a. If engine continues running, check for open circuit to terminal "C", or short between terminals "A" and "B" in distributor side of EST connector.
   b. If engine stops running, check for open

or short circuits or grounding on each of the leads from the ECM to the 4-terminal EST connector. Also check EST lead to ESC control, is used. If harness is OK, replace ECM.

1977–80 Units With Internal Coil Exc. 1980 Cadillac Models with EST

Refer to H.E.I. diagnosis charts, Figs. 4 and 5, for diagnosis procedures.

1977 Units with External Coil

With the wiring connector properly attached to connector at side of distributor cap and all the spark plug leads properly connected at plugs and at distributor terminals. Proceed as follows:

Engine Will Not Start
1. Connect voltmeter between "BAT" terminal lead on distributor connector and

ground and turn on ignition switch.
2. If voltage is zero, there is an open circuit between the distributor and the bulkhead connector; or between the bulkhead connector and the ignition switch; or between the ignition switch and the starter solenoid. Repair as required.
3. If reading is battery voltage, hold one spark plug lead with insulated pliers approximately 1/4 inch away from a dry area of engine block and crank engine. If a spark is visible, the distributor has been eliminated as source of trouble. Check spark plugs and fuel system.
4. If there is no visible spark, perform the "Component Checkout" and proceed as described further on.

Engine Starts But Runs Rough
1. Check for proper fuel delivery to carburetor.
2. Check all vacuum hoses for leakage.
3. Visually inspect and listen for sparks jumping to ground.
4. Check ignition timing.
5. Check centrifugal advance mechanism for proper operation.
6. Remove spark plugs and check for unusual defects, such as very wide gap, abnormal fouling, cracked insulators (inside and out), etc.
7. If no defects are found, perform the "Component Checkout" procedure as described below.

Component Checkout
1. Remove cap and coil assembly.
2. Inspect cap, coil and rotor for spark arcover.
3. On V6 and V8 engines:
   a. Connect ohmmeter, Fig. 6, step 1. If ohmmeter reading is other than zero or very near to zero, the ignition coil must be replaced.
   b. If no ohmmeter reading was observed in step 1, reconnect ohmmeter both ways, Fig. 6, step 2. If both ohmmeter readings are infinite on high scale, replace ignition coil.
4. On inline 4 and 6 cylinder engines:
   a. Connect ohmmeter, Fig. 7, step 1. If reading is not infinite, replace coil.
   b. Connect ohmmeter, Fig. 7, step 2. If reading is not zero or near zero, replace coil.
   c. Connect ohmmeter, Fig. 7, step 3. If reading is infinite, replace coil.
5. Connect an external vacuum source to the vacuum advance unit. Replace vacuum unit if inoperative.
6. If vacuum unit is operating properly, connect ohmmeter, Fig. 8, step 1. If ohmmeter reading on middle scale is not infinite at all times, pick-up coil must be replaced.
7. With ohmmeter connected, Fig. 8, step 2, reading should be within 500 to 1500 ohms.

NOTE: Tester J-24624 is required to test the module. If this tester is not available, and malfunction still exists after performing the above checks, replace module.

DISTRIBUTOR, REPLACE
Except Chevette

Removal
1. Disconnect electrical connectors from distributor cap. On Cadillac models with fuel injection, disconnect speed sensor connector at distributor trigger. Remove

ELECTRONIC IGNITION SYSTEMS

ENGINE CRANKS, BUT WILL NOT START

NOTE: IF A TACHOMETER IS CONNECTED TO THE TACHOMETER TERMINAL, DISCONNECT IT BEFORE PROCEEDING WITH THE TEST.

NOTE: VIEWS ARE IN PART 2.

Fig. 4   H.E.I. ignition system diagnosis chart (part 1 of 2). 1977–80 except units with external coil or 1980 Cadillac with EST

INTERMITTENT OPERATION OR MISS

CHECK SPARK AT TWO PLUG WIRES
WITH ST-125

SPARK ON ONE
OR BOTH

NO SPARK

CHECK FOR DWELL INCREASE
FROM LOW TO HIGH RPM

SEE NO START
PROCEDURE

CHECK PICK-UP COIL
WITH OHMMETER

BAD

REPLACE

DWELL
INCREASED

GOOD

DWELL DIDN'T
INCREASE

TROUBLE
NOT FOUND

REPLACE
MODULE

CHECK FUEL,
PLUG WIRES,
CAP AND PLUGS.

CUT A SPARK
PLUG BOOT
AS SHOWN

DISCARD

REMOVE GREEN
AND WHITE LEADS
FROM MODULE

(TO BAT +)

TEST LIGHT

CONNECT VOLTMETER,
"TACH" TERMINAL
TO GROUND

VIEW B

7/16" (11mm)
FROM TIP OF
SPARK PLUG

CONNECT TO GROUND

INSERT BOOT
OVER
PORCELAIN
END OF ST-125

LEAVE HARNESS
CONNECTED

VIEW A

Fig. 5   H.E.I. ignition system diagnosis chart (part 2 of 2). 1977-80 except units with external coil or 1980 Cadillac with EST

Fig. 6 H.E.I. distributor ignition coil ohmmeter test. Except units with external coil

Fig. 7 H.E.I. distributor ignition coil ohmmeter test. 1977 Inline 4 & 6 cyl. units with external coil

Fig. 8 Distributor pickup coil ohmmeter test

made at the No. 1 spark plug. Forcing foreign objects through the boot at the No. 1 terminal of the distributor cap will damage the boot and could cause engine misfiring.

cap and position aside.
2. Remove vacuum advance hose and mark position of distributor in engine.
3. Mark position of rotor on distributor housing, then remove distributor hold-down bolt and clamp.
4. Pull distributor up until rotor just stops turning and mark this position on housing. Remove distributor from engine.

Installation
1. If engine was not cranked after distributor was removed from engine, proceed as follows:
   a. Position rotor to align with mark made on housing in step 4 of Removal procedure.
   b. Slide distributor into engine, aligning distributor housing to engine mark made in step 2 of Removal procedure. With distributor fully seated, rotor should align with mark made on housing in step 3 of Removal procedure.

c. Install distributor cap, connect electrical connectors and attach vacuum advance hose.
   d. Adjust ignition timing to specifications found in the individual car chapters.
2. If engine was cranked after distributor was removed from engine, proceed as follows:
   a. Remove No. 1 spark plug and crank engine until compression pressure is felt in No. 1 cylinder. Slowly rotate engine until Top Dead Center (TDC) is indicated.
   b. Turn rotor to a position just ahead of the No. 1 distributor cap terminal.
   c. Slide distributor into engine. Install distributor cap, connect electrical connectors and attach vacuum advance hose.
   d. Adjust ignition timing to specifications found in the individual car chapters.

NOTE: When using a timing light to adjust ignition timing, the connection should be

Chevette
1. On models equipped with A/C, disconnect wire connector from compressor, then remove through bolt, two adjusting bolts, and upper compressor mounting bracket.
2. Raise vehicle, then remove two retaining bolts and position lower compressor bracket outward for clearance.
3. On all models, remove air cleaner and distributor cap, position distributor cap out of way.
4. Remove ignition coil cover and mounting bracket bolts.
5. Disconnect distributor primary lead from coil terminal.
6. Remove fuel pump and push rod.

NOTE: Push rod must be installed in same direction as removed.

7. Scribe a mark on engine in line with rotor, noting approximate position of distributor housing in relation to engine.
8. Remove distributor hold down bolt and clamp and remove distributor.

NOTE: Avoid rotating engine while distributor is removed.

Fig. 9 H.E.I. distributor component replacement

Fig. 10 H.E.I. wiring harness indentification

Fig. 11 Exploded view of H.E.I. distributor (Typical). All except Cadillac with fuel injecction

9. Reverse procedure to install, then adjust ignition timing.

NOTE: When using a timing light to adjust ignition timing, the connection should be made at the No. 1 spark plug. Forcing foreign objects through the boot at the No. 1 terminal of the distributor cap will damage the boot and could cause engine misfiring.

COMPONENTS, REPLACE

Ignition Coil Replacement, Fig. 2

Except Units With External Coil
1. Remove screws holding distributor cover to distributor cap and remove distributor cover.
2. Remove four screws holding coil to cap.
3. Remove harness connector and battery wire from side of distributor cap.
4. Push coil leads out of position in cap and remove coil.
5. Reverse procedure to install.

1977 Inline 4 & 6 Cyl. Unit With External Coil
1. Disconnect ignition switch to coil lead from coil.
2. Disconnect coil to distributor leads from coil.
3. Remove coil to engine retaining screws and remove coil.
4. Reverse procedure to install.

Module Replacement, Fig. 9
1. Disconnect wiring harness connector at side of distributor cap and remove distributor.
2. Remove rotor and disconnect wires from module terminals.
3. Remove two mounting screws and remove module.

NOTE: Two types of H.E.I. wiring harness are used, Fig. 10. The second type is a wiring harness, connector and capacitor which is serviced as an assembly.

4. Reverse procedure to install.

CAUTION: At installation, coat bottom of new module with dielectric lubricant (furnished with new module) to aid in heat transfer into distributor housing. Failure to apply lubricant will cause excessive heat at module and premature module failure.

Pole Piece, Magnet or Pick-Up Coil Replacement, Fig. 9

Removal
1. With distributor removed, disconnect wires at module terminals.
2. Remove roll pin from drive gear by driving out with 1/8 inch diameter drift punch.
3. Remove gear, shim and the tanged washer from distributor shaft. Remove any burrs that may be caused by removal of pin.
4. Remove distributor shaft from housing.
5. Remove washer from upper end of distributor housing.

Fig. 12 Exploded view of H.E.I. distributor. Cadillac with fuel injection

NOTE: Bushings in the housing are not serviceable.

6. Remove three screws securing pole piece to housing and remove pole piece, magnet and pick-up coil.

Installation

1. Install pick-up coil, magnet and pole piece and loosely install three screws holding pole piece.
2. With washer installed at top of housing, install distributor shaft and rotate to check for proper clearance between pole piece teeth and timer core teeth.
3. If necessary, realign pole piece to provide adequate clearance and secure properly.
4. Install tanged washer, shim and drive gear (teeth up) to bottom of shaft. Align drive gear and install new roll pin.

DISTRIBUTOR SERVICE

Disassembly, Figs. 11 & 12

NOTE: Some of the following steps do not

Fig. 13 Speed sensor location

apply to the Toronado MISAR system or Cadillac DEFI or EST systems.

1. Remove distributor.
2. Remove rotor.
3. Remove advance springs and weights.
4. Remove module retaining screws and move module to a position where connector may be removed.
5. Remove wires from module terminals. On Cadillac with DEFI, remove two connectors.
6. Support distributor gear so that distributor shaft will not be damaged, then remove roll pin by driving it out with a punch.
7. Remove gear, shim and tanged washer from shaft. Remove any burrs that may have been caused by removal of roll pin.

NOTE: Some distributors do not use a shim or tanged washer.

8. On Cadillac models with EFI:
   a. Remove the four screws retaining speed sensor, then remove speed sen-

sor and gasket.
b. Remove plug from opposite side of sensor housing on distributor.
c. Remove roll pin from magnet assembly.
9. Remove distributor shaft and magnet assembly.
10. Remove pole piece retaining screws, pole piece, magnet and pick-up coil.
11. Remove lock ring from top of housing, pick-up coil retainer and felt washer.
12. Remove vacuum advance unit.
13. Remove capacitor and wiring harness from distributor housing.

Assembly, Figs. 12 & 13
1. Install vacuum advance unit (if used) and secure with two screws.
2. Place felt washer over lubricant reservoir at top of housing.
3. Position pick up coil retainer onto housing with vacuum advance arm over actuating pin of vacuum advance mechanism and secure with lock ring.
4. Install pick up coil magnet and pole piece. Loosely install the three retaining screws.

5. Install distributor shaft and rotate to check for even clearance all around between pole piece and shaft projections.
6. Move pole piece to provide even clearance and secure with three retaining screws.
7. On Cadillac models with EFI:
a. Position distributor shaft so speed sensor rotating magnet can be installed in distributor housing, Fig. 13.
b. Engage speed sensor rotating magnet on distributor shaft and install shaft into position. Do not install roll pin.
8. Install drive with teeth up onto shaft.

NOTE: Drive gear has a dimple on one side next to drive pin hole. Align drive gear so that dimple is on same side of shaft as the rotor pointer. Temporarily install rotor to ensure correct alignment.

---

9. Install tanged washer, shim and drive gear, then retain with a new roll pin.
10. On Cadillac models with EFI:
a. Install speed sensor rotating magnet

and retain with new roll pin.
b. Using a new gasket, position speed sensor onto distributor housing with wiring harness coming out of top of sensor (directly below distributor housing) and retain with four screws.
11. Install capacitor and loosely install retaining screw.
12. Install connector on module with tab on top, then liberally apply silicone grease to bottom of module and install screws.

CAUTION: Failure to apply silicone grease to module will cause excessive heat build-up of module and premature failure.

---

13. Position wiring harness with grommet in housing notch, then connect pink wire to capacitor stud and black wire to capacitor retaining screw. Tighten screw.
14. Reconnect wires to module, then install centrifugal advance weights and springs.

1981—82 High Energy Ignition System (HEI)

DESCRIPTION

The High Energy Ignition System used on these models consists of an electronic distributor Figs. 1 and 2, with ignition coil mounted on the distributor cap on 6 and 8 cylinder models or with an externally mounted coil on 4 cylinder models. Some HEI systems use Electronic Spark Timing (EST) to change ignition timing in response to vehicle requirements. All spark timing changes in the HEI-EST system are performed electronically by the Electronic Control Module (ECM). The ECM monitors information from various engine sensors, determines the correct spark timing and signals the distributor to change timing as necessary. A secondary spark advance system is incorporated into the system to signal the ignition module in case of ECM failure. The HEI-EST system does not use vacuum or mechanical advance.

On some HEI systems equipped with EST, a Electronic Spark Control (ESC) is used to retard spark advance when detonation occurs. The spark is retarded for 20 seconds, then the spark control returns to EST.

The ESC system consists of three basic components: sensor, distributor and controller. The ESC sensor is an accelerometer or magneto-strictive device, mounted at rear of engine block. It detects presence, or absence, and intensity of detonation by vibration characteristics of the engine. The sensor's output is an electrical signal which is sent to the controller. A failure of the sensor would allow no retard.

The distributor is an HEI-EST unit with an electronic module modified so that it can respond to ESC controller signal. The command is delayed when detonation is detected, providing the level of retard required. The amount of retard is determined by the severity of detonation.

The ESC controller processes the sensor signal into a command signal to the distributor to adjust spark timing. This is a continuous process monitoring and controlling detonation. The controller is a hard-wired signal processor and amplifier which operates from 6 to 16 volts. Controller failure would be indicated by no ignition, no retard of full retard.

NOTE: Since this is a full 12 volt system, no resistance wire is used. Also, a diagnostic connector is used on some models. This connector is located in the engine compartment on the left side front fender skirt. On vehicles equipped with this connector, a tachometer may be connected between terminals 6 and G.

Fig. 1 HEI Distributor with internal coil. 1981–82 models with 6 & 8 cylinder engine

Fig. 2 HEI distributor with external coil. 1981–82 models with 4 cylinder engine

ENGINE CRANKS, BUT WILL NOT RUN

NOTE: If a tachometer is connected to the tachometer terminal, disconnect it before proceeding with the test.

1. Check spark at plug with ST-125 while cranking (if no spark on one wire, check a second wire).

Spark → Check fuel, spark plugs, etc.

No Spark → 2. Check for spark at coil wire with ST-125 while cranking. Leave ST-125 connected to coil wire for Steps 3–7.

Figure 1

Spark →
• Inspect cap for water, cracks, etc. If OK, replace rotor.

No Spark → 3. Remove dist. cap with ignition on. Check voltage at "+" term. on dist. module. See Figure 1.

10 volts or more → 4. With ign. "ON," check "C" term. voltage on HEI module. See Figure 2.

Under 10 volts → Repair wire from "+" term. on module to ign. coil "+" connection at ign. coil and primary circuit to ignition switch.

Under 1 volt → It is open or grounded lead from coil to dis. "C" term., connection or ign. coil or open primary circuit in coil.

10 volts or more →

1 to 10 volts → Replace module and check for spark from coil as in Step 6.

Spark → System OK

No Spark → Replace ign. coil, it too is faulty.

Figure 2

5. Remove pick-up coil connector from module. Check "C" term. voltage with "Ign. ON." Watch voltmeter as test light is momentarily connected from bat. + to module term. "P," not more than 5 sec. See Figure 3.

TO BAT. +
Figure 3

No Drop in Voltage → Check module ground. If OK, replace module.

Voltage Drops → 6. Check for spark from coil wire with ST-125 as test light is removed from module term.

No Spark →

Spark → It is pick-up coil or connections. Coil resistance should be 500-1500 ohms and not grounded.

If module tester is available, test mod.

OK / Bad → Replace mod.

Check coil wire from cap to coil. If OK, replace coil.

If no module tester is available:

7. Replace HEI module and repeat Step 6.

Spark → System OK

No Spark → Module removed is OK, reinstall module. Check coil wire from cap to coil. If OK, replace coil.

Fig. 3 HEI ignition system diagnostic chart (Part 1 of 5). All models with remote coil

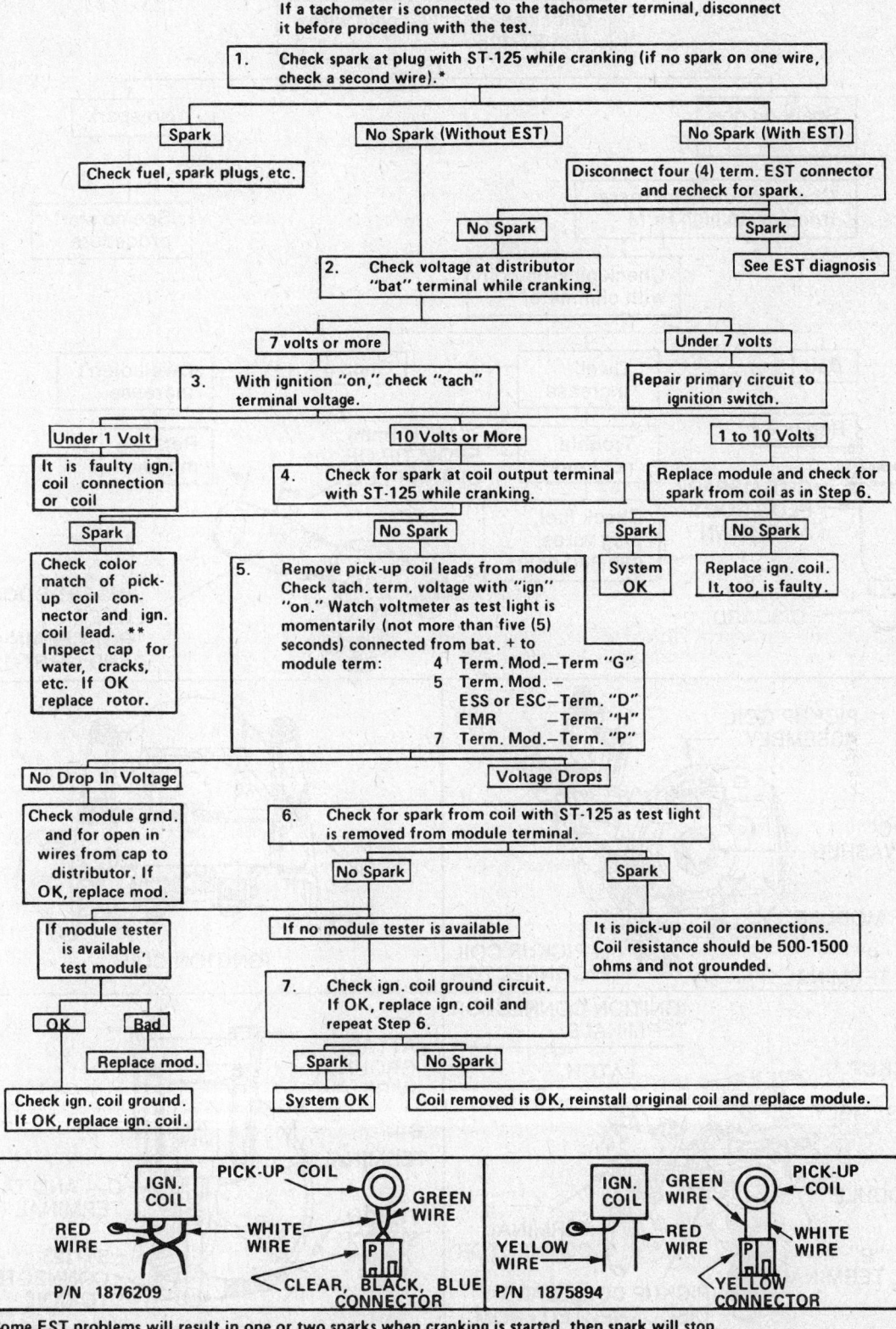

ENGINE CRANKS, BUT WILL NOT RUN

If a tachometer is connected to the tachometer terminal, disconnect it before proceeding with the test.

1. Check spark at plug with ST-125 while cranking (if no spark on one wire, check a second wire).*

Spark → Check fuel, spark plugs, etc.

No Spark (Without EST)

No Spark (With EST) → Disconnect four (4) term. EST connector and recheck for spark.
- No Spark
- Spark → See EST diagnosis

2. Check voltage at distributor "bat" terminal while cranking.

7 volts or more → 3. With ignition "on," check "tach" terminal voltage.

Under 7 volts → Repair primary circuit to ignition switch.

Under 1 Volt → It is faulty ign. coil connection or coil
- Spark → Check color match of pick-up coil connector and ign. coil lead. ** Inspect cap for water, cracks, etc. If OK replace rotor.

10 Volts or More → 4. Check for spark at coil output terminal with ST-125 while cranking.
- No Spark → 5. Remove pick-up coil leads from module Check tach. term. voltage with "ign" "on." Watch voltmeter as test light is momentarily (not more than five (5) seconds) connected from bat. + to module term:
  - 4 Term. Mod.—Term "G"
  - 5 Term. Mod. — ESS or ESC—Term. "D" / EMR —Term. "H"
  - 7 Term. Mod.—Term. "P"

1 to 10 Volts → Replace module and check for spark from coil as in Step 6.
- Spark → System OK
- No Spark → Replace ign. coil. It, too, is faulty.

No Drop In Voltage → Check module grnd. and for open in wires from cap to distributor. If OK, replace mod.

Voltage Drops → 6. Check for spark from coil with ST-125 as test light is removed from module terminal.
- No Spark
- Spark → It is pick-up coil or connections. Coil resistance should be 500-1500 ohms and not grounded.

If module tester is available, test module
- OK
- Bad → Replace mod.
- Check ign. coil ground. If OK, replace ign. coil.

If no module tester is available → 7. Check ign. coil ground circuit. If OK, replace ign. coil and repeat Step 6.
- Spark → System OK
- No Spark → Coil removed is OK, reinstall original coil and replace module.

IGN. COIL / PICK-UP COIL / GREEN WIRE / WHITE WIRE / RED WIRE / CLEAR, BLACK, BLUE CONNECTOR
P/N 1876209

IGN. COIL / GREEN WIRE / PICK-UP COIL / RED WIRE / WHITE WIRE / YELLOW WIRE / YELLOW CONNECTOR
P/N 1875894

*Some EST problems will result in one or two sparks when cranking is started, then spark will stop. This is considered a "no spark" condition.

Fig. 4   HEI ignition system diagnostic chart (Part 1 of 5). All models with integral coil

ELECTRONIC IGNITION SYSTEMS

INTERMITTENT OPERATION OR MISS

Check spark at two plug wires with ST-125

- Spark on one or both
  - Check for dwell increase from low to high RPM
    - Check pick-up coil with ohmmeter
      - Bad → Replace
      - Dwell increase → Trouble not found → Check fuel, plug wires, cap and plugs.
      - Good
      - Dwell didn't increase → Replace module
- No spark → See no start procedure

CUT A SPARK PLUG BOOT AS SHOWN

DISCARD

7/16" (11mm) FROM TIP OF SPARK PLUG

INSERT BOOT OVER PORCELAIN END OF ST-125

PICKUP COIL ASSEMBLY

"C" WASHER

MODULE

"P" TERMINAL

PICKUP COIL CONNECTOR

IGNITION COIL

IGNITION CONNECTOR TERMINALS

PICKUP COIL ASSEMBLY

LATCH

C—

B+

MODULE

"P" TERMINAL

PICKUP COIL LEADS DISCONNECTED FROM MODULE

4— TERMINAL CONNECTOR

ATTACH GROUND WIRE

B+ TERMINAL

TO IGN SWITCH

TOP VIEW

C— AND TACH TERMINAL

ST-125 CONNECTED TO COIL

Fig. 5 HEI ignition system diagnostic chart (Part 2 of 5). All models with remote coil

INTERMITTENT OPERATION OR MISS

Check spark at two plug wires with ST-125.

Spark on one or both.

No spark.

Check for dwell increase from low to high RPM.

See cranks but won't run procedure.

Check pick-up coil with ohmmeter and check for proper connection to module.

Bad

Dwell increased.

Good

Dwell didn't increase.

Replace

Trouble not found.

Replace ECM.

Check fuel, plug wires (use ST-125 on each plug wire), cap and plugs.

CUT A SPARK PLUG BOOT AS SHOWN

DISCARD

7/16" (11mm) FROM TIP OF SPARK PLUG

INSERT BOOT OVER PORCELAIN END OF ST-125

LEAVE HARNESS CONNECTED

CONNECT TO GROUND

VIEW A

REMOVE GREEN AND WHITE LEADS FROM MODULE

(TO BAT +)

TEST LIGHT

CONNECT VOLTMETER, "TACH" TERMINAL TO GROUND

VIEW B

Fig. 6   HEI ignition system diagnostic chart (Part 2 of 5). All models with integral coil

EST DIAGNOSIS

EST PERFORMANCE CHECK

Car will run with distributor connected to ECM.

- Trans. in park (A.T.) or Neutral (M.T.).
- Run engine at fast idle and note timing change as dist. EST connector is disconnected.

Changes → **No Change**

Automatic Trans.
- Engine idling in "Drive."
- Note timing change as dist. EST Connector is reconnected, then disconnected.

Changes → **No Change**

No trouble found

- With engine stopped, connect jumper from Term. "A" to "B" in dist. side of EST connector.
- Start engine, ground "test" Term. and connect test light from Bat. + to term. "C" of same connector.

Engine Stops

Check for open or grounded distributor wire to term. "A" of EST connector. If wire OK, it is faulty HEI module connection or module.

Engine Runs

Check distributor wires for:
- Open to Mod. Term. "B."
- Short between Mod. Term. "R" and "E." If wires OK, it is faulty HEI Mod. conn. or Module.

ENGINE WON'T RUN COMPLAINT

Car will not run with distributor connected to ECM.

Leave EST Connector disconnected at distributor.

Manual Trans.
With engine idling, check voltage output of map or vacuum sensor as vacuum hoses are disconnected and reconnected.

No Change-See Vacuum Sensor Chart Or Map Sensor Chart

Change

Engine Runs

Remove jumper between Term. "A" and "B."

Engine Stops

Remove test light, reconnect four (4) Term. connector and – – – –

W/O ESC | **With ESC**

No-Start complaint | **No timing change** | **See following ESC check**

Check for open from ECM Term. "U" to gn'd and open or grounded wire to ECM term. "12." If wire is OK, it is faulty ECM connection or ECM.

With P/N Sw. | **W/O P/N SW.**

Disconnect P/N switch and recheck for timing change.

Changes

- It is P/N sw. adj. or faulty P/N switch.

No Change

- Check for grounded wire from ECM Term. "H" to P/N sw.
- Check for open from ECM Term. "11" to EST Conn. Term. "C." If OK, it is faulty ECM Connector or ECM.

PICK-UP COIL

C B+

10
11
12
13
U

A
B
C
D

2.5L-L4

P N E R   + C B

A B C D

Fig. 7   EST diagnostic chart (Part 3 of 5). All 1981 models & 1982 Chevette & T1000 (if equipped)

EST PERFORMANCE CHECK

- Trans. in "Park" (A.T.) or "Neutral" (M.T.).
- Run engine at fast idle and note timing change as "test" term. is grounded.

Changes

No Change

Automatic Transmission

Manual Transmission

- Engine idling in "Drive."
- Note timing change as "test" term. is grounded.

Changes

No Change

No trouble found, clear memory.

With engine idling, check voltage at output of MAP or vacuum sensor as vacuum hose is removed and reconnected.

Voltage Changes

No Change - See Vacuum Sensor Chart or MAP Sensor Chart

Disconnect P/N switch and recheck for timing change.

Changes

No Change

It is P/N switch Adj. or faulty P/N switch.

Check for grounded wire from ECM term. 'H' to P/N switch. If not grounded, replace ECM.

ECM — H — P/N SW. — CLOSED IN PARK

Fig. 8 EST diagnostic chart (Part 3 of 5). All 1982 models (if equipped) exc. 1982 Chevette, T1000 & Corvette

ELECTRONIC IGNITION SYSTEMS

FUEL INJECTION
ELECTRONIC SPARK TIMING (EST)

- Run engine at 1800 to 2200 RPM and note timing.
- Ground diagnostic terminal and note timing; it should change.

NO CHANGE

- Disconnect HEI distributor 4-way connector.
- Using two jumpers, reconnect HEI connector term. "B" to harness connector term. "B" and HEI connector term. "D" to harness connector term. "D".
- Start and idle engine.
- Probe chassis harness connector term. "A", CKT 423, with voltmeter J-29125. Voltage should vary 2.0 to 2.8

CHANGE

No trouble found. Infrequently a rare set of circumstances during engine crank could result in a "Check Engine" light after engine starts. The light will stay on until ignition "OFF" for 10 seconds and a normal restart. EST circuits 430 and 423 should be physically checked for proper harness routing, connectors and wiring for intermittent open or short to ground. If OK, no further repairs should be made.

OK

- Ignition "OFF", engine stopped.
- Using third jumper, reconnect HEI connector term. "A" to harness connector term. "A".
- With engine idling, again probe CKT 423, with voltmeter to ground.
- Voltage should be less than 1 volt.

NOT OK

Check for open or short to ground in EST CKT 423.

CKT 423 OK.

Faulty ECM connector or ECM.

Distributor 4-Way Connector / **Black Connector**

A	423	19	EST
B	430	2	Reference
C	424	10	By Pass
D	453	3	Ground

ECM

HEI Module

NOT OK

Faulty wire or connector to HEI term. "E".

Wire and connector OK.

Replace HEI module

OK

- Engine idling.
- Again probe term. "A" with a volt meter to gnd. Note voltage while probing HEI harness conn. term. "C," CKT 424, with a test light connected to 12V. Voltage should be 1.0 to 2.8 volts.

NOT OK

Faulty HEI harness wire or connector to module term. "B". If OK, replace module.

OK

- Stop engine, ignition off for 10 seconds.
- Using fourth jumper, reconnect HEI connector term. "C" to harness connector term. "C".
- Engine idling.
- Check voltage at term. "C"; should be above 2 volts.

Clear codes and confirm "Open Loop" operation and no "Check Engine" light.

*This test requires the use of four jumpers using terminals 12014836 and 12014837.

NOT OK

Check for open or short to ground in CKT 424 to ECM.

CKT 424 OK.

Faulty ECM connector or ECM.

OK

EST OK. No trouble found.

Fig. 9 EST diagnostic chart (Part 3 of 5). All 1982 Corvette

ESC CHECK

```
NO START COMPLAINT
        |
IGN. "ON" CHECK VOLTAGE FROM ESC
CONTROLLER TERM. F TO K.
        |
   ┌────┴──────┐
UNDER 10 VOLTS   OVER 10 VOLTS
```

UNDER 10 VOLTS → CHECK FOR OPEN FROM TERM. K TO GN'D. AND TERM. F TO BAT. (INCLUDES FUSE)

OVER 10 VOLTS →
- JUMPER TERM. J AND G ON ESC CONTROLLER.
- RECONNECT EST CONNECTOR AND TRY TO START ENGINE.

```
        ┌──────┴──────┐
     STARTS         NO STARTS
```

STARTS → IT IS FAULTY ESC CONTROLLER CONNECTION OR CONTROLLER.

NO STARTS → CHECK FOR OPEN FROM ECM TERM. U TO GN'D AND OPEN OR GROUNDED WIRE TO ECM TERM. 12. IF WIRE IS OK, IT IS FAULTY ECM CONNECTION OR ECM.

```
   ┌────────┴────────┐
CHANGES           NO CHANGE
```

CHANGES → IT IS P/N SWITCH ADJUSTMENT OR FAULTY P/N SWITCH.

NO CHANGE → CHECK FOR GROUNDED WIRE FROM ECM TERM. H TO P/N SWITCH.

CHECK FOR OPEN WIRE FROM ECM TERMINAL 11 TO EST CONNECTOR TERM. C. IF OK, IT IS FAULTY ECM CONNECTION OR ECM.

```
NO TIMING CHANGE
        |
JUMPER ESC CONTROLLER TERM. C AND
D AND RECHECK FOR TIMING CHANGE.
        |
   ┌────┴─────┐
NO CHANGE    CHANGES
```

CHANGES → IT IS FAULTY ESC CONTROLLER CONNECTIONS OR CONTROLLER.

```
   ┌────────┴────────┐
WITH P/N SW.      W/O P/N SW.
```

WITH P/N SW. → DISCONNECT P/N SW. AND RECHECK FOR TIMING CHANGE.

```
ECM TERM. 12 ────── EST ──────────── EST — TERM. A ON EST CONN.
ECM TERM. 11 ────── BY-PASS ──────── BY-PASS — TERM. C ON EST CONN.
         IGN. ┤│├                    KNOCK SENSOR
                                         SHIELD

              F K D G   J C B A
              ESC CONTROLLER
```

Fig. 10 ESC diagnostic chart (Part 4 of 5). All 1981 models (if equipped)

ESC PERFORMANCE DIAGNOSTIC

This chart should only be used after other causes of knock have been
checked, i.e., timing, lack of EGR, engine temp., etc.

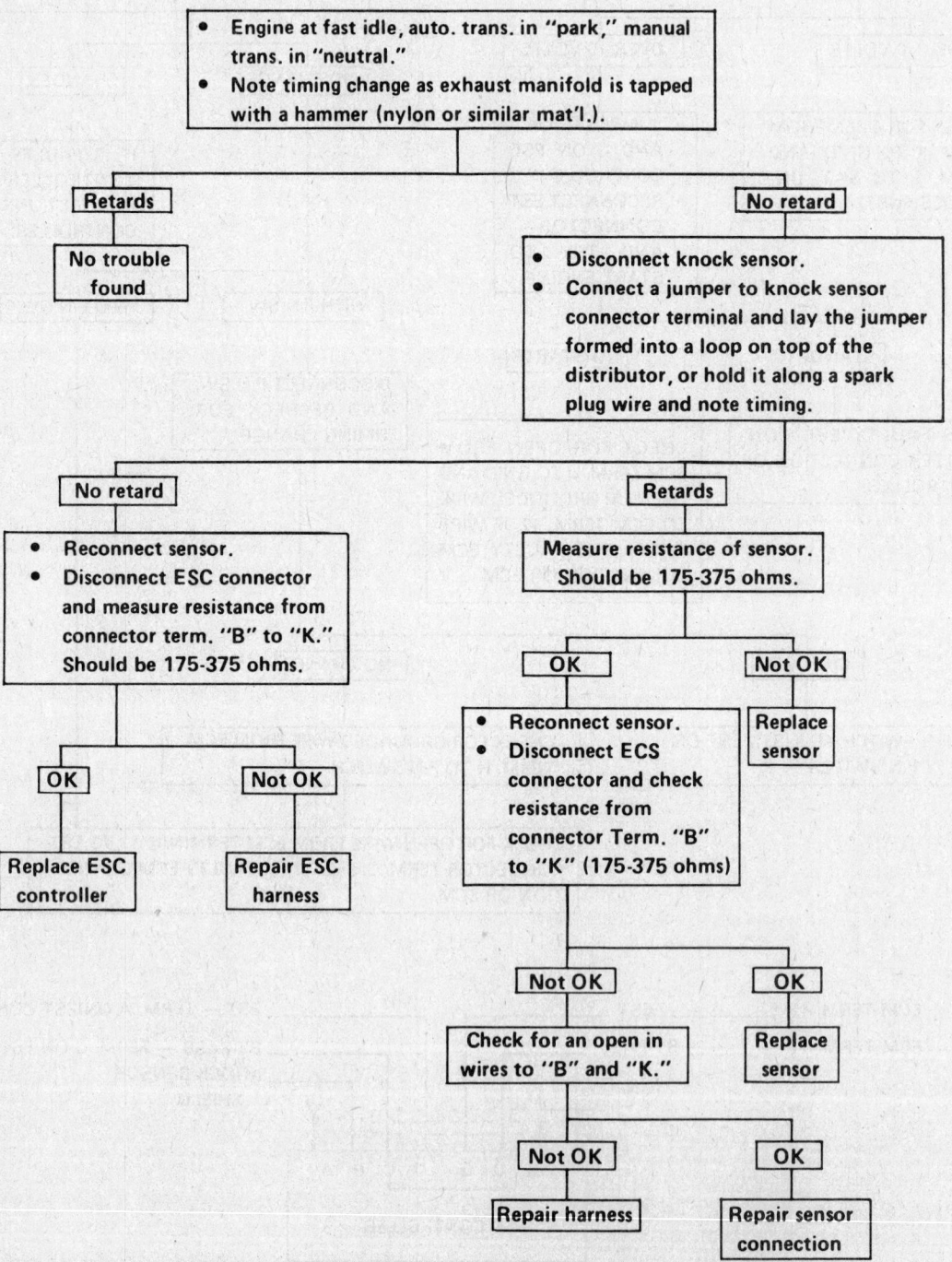

Fig. 11 ESC performance problem diagnosis (Part 4 of 5). All 1981 models (if equipped)

ENGINE CRANKS BUT DOES NOT START

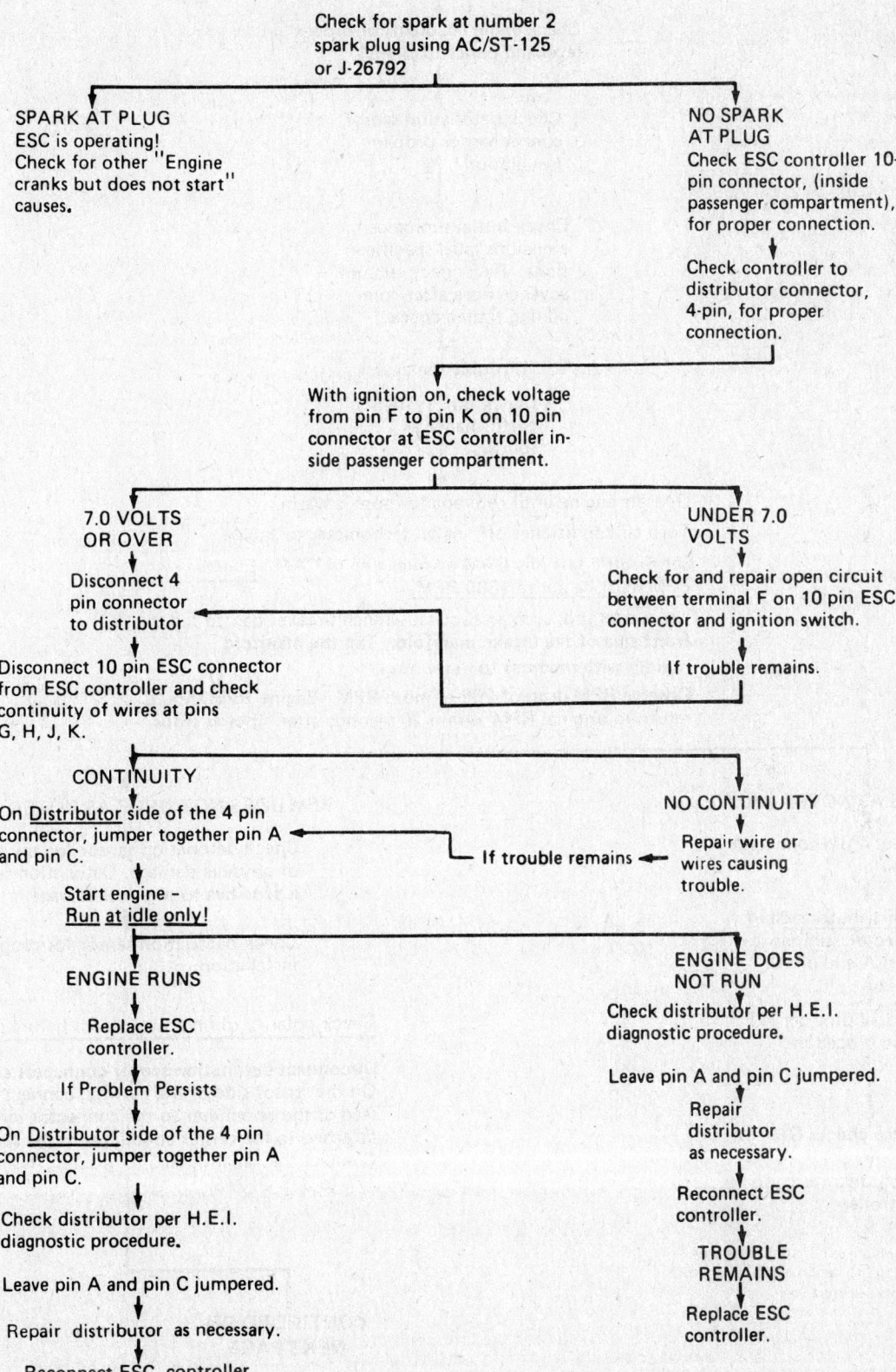

Fig. 12   ESC diagnostic chart (Part 4 of 5). 1982 Buick Electra, LeSabre, Regal & Riviera; Chevrolet Camaro; Pontiac Bonneville, Firebird & Grand Prix (if equipped)

ESC DIAGNOSTIC PROCEDURES

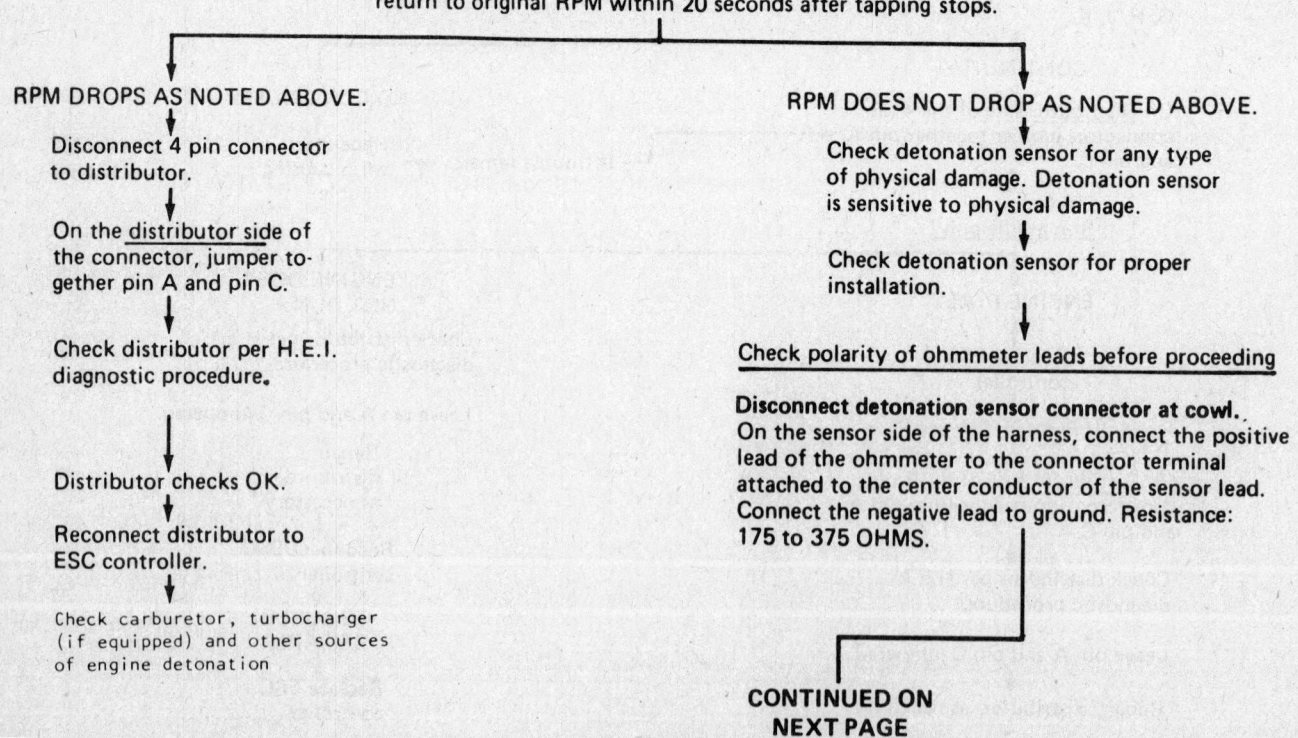

ENGINE DETONATION

Check engine coolant for proper level and concentration.

Check detonation sensor connector for proper installation.

Check initial timing per emissions label specifications. Reconnect vacuum advance hose after completing timing check.

If trouble remains

Check ESC system performance as follows:

Operate engine until top radiator hose is warm.

Turn air conditioner off, install tachometer to engine.

Set throttle fast idle CAM on high step of CAM. Engine RPM must be above 1800 RPM.

Use a steel rod, such as a socket wrench breaker bar, to tap the front area of the intake manifold. Tap the manifold rapidly with medium to heavy taps.

Observe RPM drop of 200 or more RPM. Engine RPM should return to original RPM within 20 seconds after tapping stops.

RPM DROPS AS NOTED ABOVE.

Disconnect 4 pin connector to distributor.

On the distributor side of the connector, jumper together pin A and pin C.

Check distributor per H.E.I. diagnostic procedure.

Distributor checks OK.

Reconnect distributor to ESC controller.

Check carburetor, turbocharger (if equipped) and other sources of engine detonation

RPM DOES NOT DROP AS NOTED ABOVE.

Check detonation sensor for any type of physical damage. Detonation sensor is sensitive to physical damage.

Check detonation sensor for proper installation.

Check polarity of ohmmeter leads before proceeding

Disconnect detonation sensor connector at cowl. On the sensor side of the harness, connect the positive lead of the ohmmeter to the connector terminal attached to the center conductor of the sensor lead. Connect the negative lead to ground. Resistance: 175 to 375 OHMS.

CONTINUED ON NEXT PAGE

Fig. 13 ESC diagnostic chart (Part 4 of 5). 1982 Buick Electra, LeSabre, Regal & Riviera; Chevrolet Camaro; Pontiac Bonneville, Firebird & Grand Prix (if equipped)

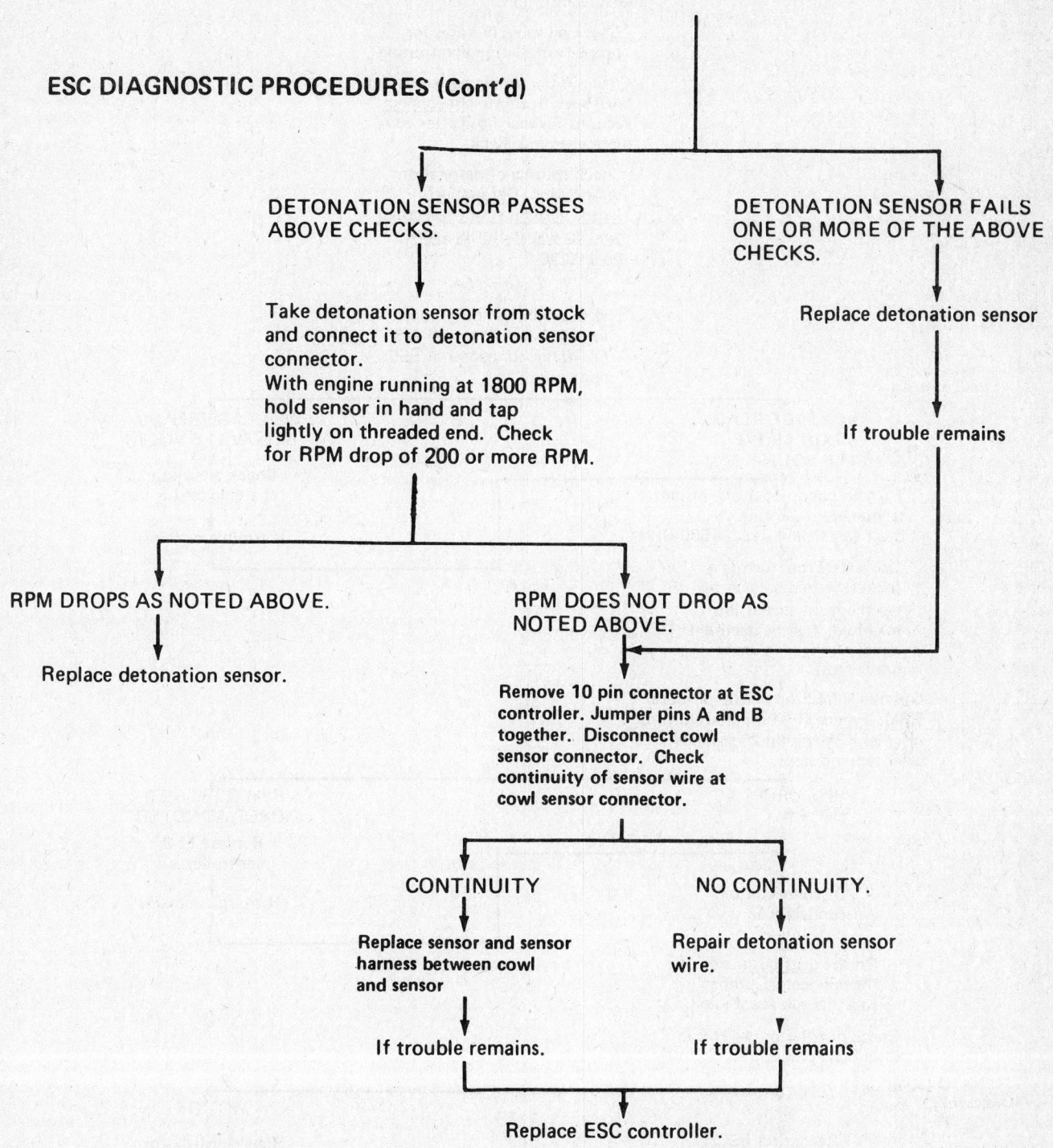

ESC DIAGNOSTIC PROCEDURES (Cont'd)

DETONATION SENSOR PASSES ABOVE CHECKS.

Take detonation sensor from stock and connect it to detonation sensor connector.
With engine running at 1800 RPM, hold sensor in hand and tap lightly on threaded end. Check for RPM drop of 200 or more RPM.

RPM DROPS AS NOTED ABOVE.

Replace detonation sensor.

RPM DOES NOT DROP AS NOTED ABOVE.

Remove 10 pin connector at ESC controller. Jumper pins A and B together. Disconnect cowl sensor connector. Check continuity of sensor wire at cowl sensor connector.

CONTINUITY

Replace sensor and sensor harness between cowl and sensor

If trouble remains.

NO CONTINUITY.

Repair detonation sensor wire.

If trouble remains

Replace ESC controller.

DETONATION SENSOR FAILS ONE OR MORE OF THE ABOVE CHECKS.

Replace detonation sensor

If trouble remains

Fig. 14   ESC diagnostic chart (Part 4 of 5). 1982 Buick Electra, LeSabre, Regal & Riviera; Chevrolet Camaro; Pontiac Bonneville, Firebird & Grand Prix (if equipped)

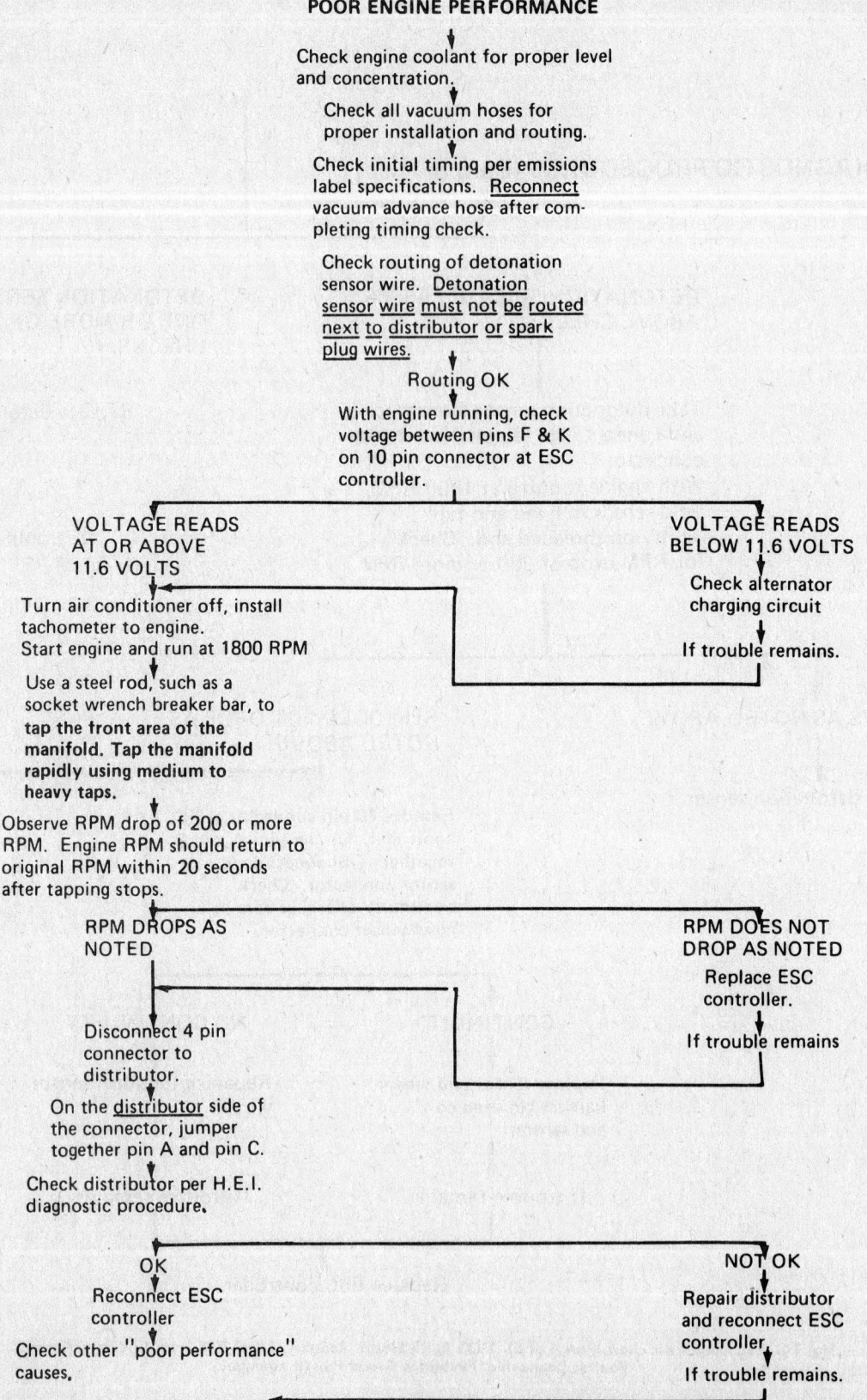

POOR ENGINE PERFORMANCE

Check engine coolant for proper level and concentration.

Check all vacuum hoses for proper installation and routing.

Check initial timing per emissions label specifications. Reconnect vacuum advance hose after completing timing check.

Check routing of detonation sensor wire. Detonation sensor wire must not be routed next to distributor or spark plug wires.

Routing OK

With engine running, check voltage between pins F & K on 10 pin connector at ESC controller.

VOLTAGE READS AT OR ABOVE 11.6 VOLTS

VOLTAGE READS BELOW 11.6 VOLTS

Check alternator charging circuit

If trouble remains.

Turn air conditioner off, install tachometer to engine. Start engine and run at 1800 RPM

Use a steel rod, such as a socket wrench breaker bar, to tap the front area of the manifold. Tap the manifold rapidly using medium to heavy taps.

Observe RPM drop of 200 or more RPM. Engine RPM should return to original RPM within 20 seconds after tapping stops.

RPM DROPS AS NOTED

RPM DOES NOT DROP AS NOTED

Replace ESC controller.

If trouble remains

Disconnect 4 pin connector to distributor.

On the distributor side of the connector, jumper together pin A and pin C.

Check distributor per H.E.I. diagnostic procedure.

OK

Reconnect ESC controller

Check other "poor performance" causes.

NOT OK

Repair distributor and reconnect ESC controller.

If trouble remains.

Fig. 15   ESC performance problem diagnosis (Part 4 of 5). 1982 Buick Electra, LeSabre, Regal & Riviera; Chevrolet Camaro; Pontiac Bonneville, Firebird & Grand Prix (if equipped)

ELECTRONIC SPARK CONTROL (ESC)
SYSTEM CHECK

This chart should only be used after all other causes of Spark Knock have been checked,
i.e., Timing, EGR, Engine Temperature or Excessive Engine Noise.

- "Test" term. ungrounded.
- Connect tachometer.
- Engine running at about 1500 RPM.
- Transmission in park or neutral and at normal operating temperature.
- Tap Engine Block in area of knock sensor and check for RPM drop.

RPM Drop

System OK

No RPM Drop

- Disconnect ESC.
- Check for RPM change.

RPM Drops

- "Ignition OFF."
- Check resistance between ESC harness connector pins 'B' and 'K.' Should be 175 – 375 ohms.

No RPM Change

Note check engine light.

OFF

"Ignition ON," engine stopped. Check voltage from ESC Term. 'J' to ground.

ON

It is most likely a faulty ESC controller, but could be the knock sensor.

Not OK

Check for open in circuit from ESC connector Pin "K" to ground.

OK

Faulty ESC connection or ESC controller.

Under 2 Volts

Replace ECM.

Over 2 Volts

Correct short to Bat. + in wire from ESC Term. 'J' to ECM term. 'L'.

Open

Repair and recheck.

Not Open

Disconnect knock sensor and check its resistance.

Not 175-375 ohms

Replace knock sensor.

175-375 ohms

Repair faulty connection, open or ground in wire from sensor to ESC term. "B."

10-PIN CONNECTOR

ECM

ESC

K J F B A

L

C

SENSOR WIRE SHIELD

IGN.

KNOCK SENSOR

Fig. 16   ESC performance problem diagnosis (Part 4 of 5). 1982 Corvette & 1982 Oldsmobile with 252 4bbl. V6

ELECTRONIC IGNITION SYSTEMS

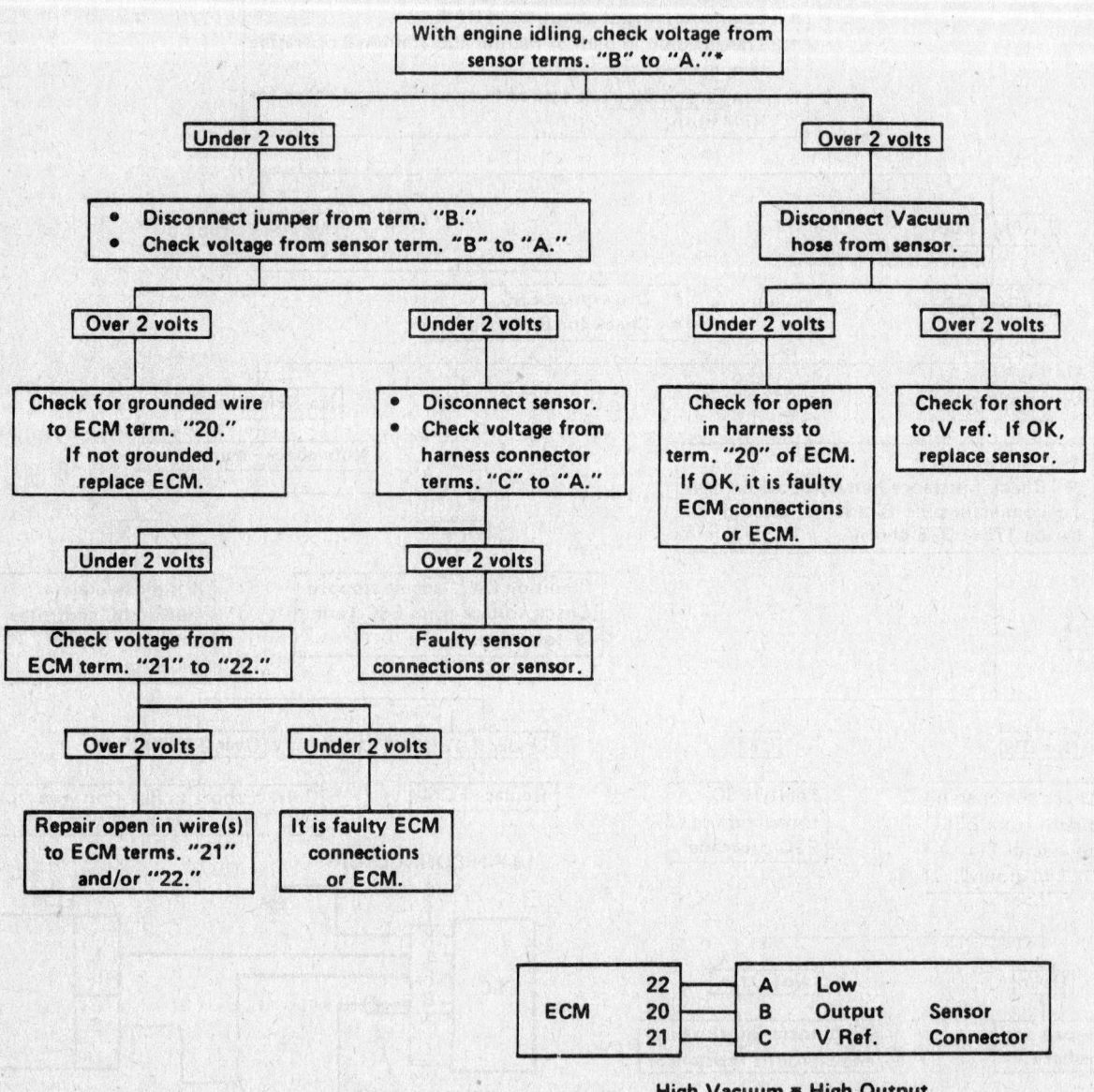

VACUUM SENSOR CIRCUIT

Check for over 34 kPa (10 inches) of vacuum at sensor with
engine idling. If not OK, repair.

With engine idling, check voltage from
sensor terms. "B" to "A."*

Under 2 volts

- Disconnect jumper from term. "B."
- Check voltage from sensor term. "B" to "A."

Over 2 volts

Check for grounded wire
to ECM term. "20."
If not grounded,
replace ECM.

Under 2 volts

- Disconnect sensor.
- Check voltage from
  harness connector
  terms. "C" to "A."

Under 2 volts

Check voltage from
ECM term. "21" to "22."

Over 2 volts

Faulty sensor
connections or sensor.

Over 2 volts

Repair open in wire(s)
to ECM terms. "21"
and/or "22."

Under 2 volts

It is faulty ECM
connections
or ECM.

Over 2 volts

Disconnect Vacuum
hose from sensor.

Under 2 volts

Check for open
in harness to
term. "20" of ECM.
If OK, it is faulty
ECM connections
or ECM.

Over 2 volts

Check for short
to V ref. If OK,
replace sensor.

	ECM		Sensor Connector
	22	A	Low
	20	B	Output
	21	C	V Ref.

High Vacuum = High Output

*This requires use of three jumpers between the sensor and the connector.
They can be made using terminals 12014836 and 12014837.

Fig. 17 Vacuum sensor diagnostic chart (Part 5 of 5). All models with ESC and vacuum sensor.

MAP SENSOR CIRCUIT

Check for over 34 kPa (10 inches) vacuum at MAP sensor with engine idling.
If not OK, repair hoses or connections.

- Ignition "on" engine stopped.
- Check voltage from sensor term. "B" to "A" *
  and refer to chart value below. **

Above table Volts

Check for short between wires to Sensor terms. "B" and "C." If not shorted, replace Sensor.

Within table Volts

Apply 34 kPa (10 inches) of vacuum sensor and note Voltage change.

Below table Volts

Disconnect jumper from term. B and check Voltage from Sensor term. "B" to "A."

More than 2.3 Volt change

Replace Sensor

Less than 1.2 Volt change

Check for short between wires to Sensor term "B" & "C." If not shorted, replace Sensor.

1.2–2.3 Volt change

Remove vacuum

Check Volts from ECM term. "20" to "22."

Under 2 Volts

Repair open in wire to ECM term. "22."

Over 2 Volts

It is faulty ECM Connection or ECM.

No change

Check Voltage from Sensor harness term. "C" to "A" with sensor disconnected.

Increases

Check for grounded wire to ECM term. "20." If not grounded, replace ECM.

Under 4.5 Volts

Check Voltage from ECM term. "21" to "22."

Over 4.5 Volts

Replace Sensor

Under 4.5 Volts

Check for grounded wire to ECM term. "21." If not grounded, it is faulty ECM Conn. or ECM.

Over 4.5 Volts

Repair open in wire to ECM terms. "21" or "22."

**Altitude	Voltage Range	
Below 1,000'	3.8 –	5.5V
1,000–2,000'	3.6 –	5.3V
2,000–3,000'	3.5 –	5.1V
3,000–4,000'	3.3 –	5.0V
4,000–5,000'	3.2 –	4.8V
5,000–6,000'	3.0 –	4.6V
6,000–7,000'	2.9 –	4.5V
7,000–8,000'	2.8 –	4.3V
8,000–9,000'	2.6 –	4.2V
9,000–10,000'	2.5 –	4.0V

sensor

	22	A	low
ECM	20	B	output
	21	C	volt. ref.

High Pressure =
High Voltage

*This requires use of three jumpers which can be made using terms. part numbers 12014836 and 12014837.

Fig. 18   MAP sensor diagnostic chart (Part 5 of 5). All models with ESC and MAP sensor

Fig. 19 Testing remote ignition coil

Fig. 20 Testing remote coil distributor pickup coil

Fig. 21 Hall Effect switch equipped distributor

A tachometer connection is incorporated in the wiring connector on the side of the distributor on 6 and 8 cylinder models, next to the coil battery terminal on Chevette and T1000 models, at the coil brown wire connector on Century, Citation, Cutlass Ciera, Omega, Phoenix, Skylark and 6000 models or at the tach connector taped to the engine wiring harness at the engine compartment side of the firewall on Cavalier, Cimarron, Firenza, J2000 and Skyhawk models. On AMC vehicles with HEI, the tach terminal is located opposite the positive terminal on the ignition coil. If vehicle is not equipped with a tachometer, there is a remote tach terminal located above the heater fan motor housing also.

CAUTION: Never connect a wire directly between the Tach terminal of the distributor connector and ground as this will damage the electronic circuitry of the module. When using a timing light to adjust ignition timing, the connection should be made at the No. 1 spark plug. Forcing foreign objects through the boot at the No. 1 spark plug terminal will damage the boot and cause engine misfire.

SYSTEM DIAGNOSIS

Refer to HEI diagnosis charts, Figs. 3 thru 18 for diagnosis procedures.

DISTRIBUTOR COMPONENT DIAGNOSIS

Units With Remote Coil

Testing Ignition Coil
1. Connect a suitable ohmmeter as shown in

Fig. 22 Testing Hall Effect switch

Fig. 19, step 1. Using the high scale, read ohmmeter. Should read very high or infinite. If not, replace coil.
2. Connect ohmmeter as shown in Fig. 19, step 2. Using the low scale, read ohmmeter. Should read very low or zero. If not, replace coil.
3. Connect ohmmeter as shown in Fig. 19, step 3. Using the high scale, read ohmmeter. Should not read infinite. If it does, replace coil.

Testing Pickup Coil
1. Remove distributor rotor, then disconnect pickup coil leads from module.
2. Connect ohmmeter as shown in Fig. 20, step 1. Connect a suitable vacuum source to vacuum advance chamber (if equipped) and note ohmmeter reading throughout entire vacuum advance range. If no vacuum advance is used, flex leads by hand to check for opens. Ohmmeter should read infinite at all times. If not, pickup coil is defective and must be replaced.
3. Connect ohmmeter as shown in Fig. 20, step 2. Repeat step 2. Ohmmeter should read one steady value between 500–1500 ohms. If not, pickup coil is defective and must be replaced.

Fig. 23 Testing integral ignition coil

NOTE: Ohmmeter may deflect if vacuum advance range causes timing core teeth to align. This is not to be considered a defect.

Testing Hall Effect Switch (If Equipped), Fig. 21
1. Carefully noting polarity, connect battery and suitable voltmeter as shown in Fig. 22.
2. Voltmeter should read less than 0.5 volts. If not, replace Hall Effect switch.
3. Insert knife blade as shown in Fig. 22. Voltmeter should read within 0.5 volts of battery voltage. If not, replace Hall Effect switch.

Units With Integral Coil

Testing Ignition Coil
1. Connect a suitable ohmmeter as shown in Fig. 23, step 1. Using the low scale, read ohmmeter. Should be near zero or zero. If not, replace coil.
2. Connect ohmmeter both ways as shown in Fig. 23, step 2. Using the high scale, read ohmmeter. If both readings are infinite, replace coil.

Testing Pickup Coil
1. Remove distributor rotor, then disconnect pickup coil leads from module.

Fig. 24 Testing integral coil distributor pickup coil

2. Connect ohmmeter as shown in Fig. 24, step 1. Connect a suitable vacuum source to vacuum advance chamber (if equipped) and note ohmmeter reading throughout entire vacuum advance range. If no vacuum advance is used, flex leads by hand to check for opens. Ohmmeter should read infinite at all times. If not, pickup coil is defective and must be replaced.

3. Connect ohmmeter as shown in Fig. 24, step 2. Repeat step 2. Ohmmeter should read one steady value between 500–1500 ohms. If not, pickup coil is defective and must be replaced.

NOTE: Ohmmeter may deflect if vacuum advance range causes timing core teeth to align. This is not to be considered a defect.

Testing Hall Effect Switch (If Equipped)
Refer to "Units With Remote Coil".

DISTRIBUTOR, REPLACE

Models Equipped With Integral Coil Distributor

1. Disconnect battery and tachometer lead from distributor cap.
2. Disconnect coil connectors from distributor cap and 4 terminal connector (if equipped).

NOTE: Do not use a tool of any kind to release coil connectors or damage to lock tabs will result.

3. Remove distributor cap with ignition high tension wires connected and position aside. Remove vacuum hose (if equipped).
4. Remove distributor clamp screw and hold down clamp.
5. Mark relationship of rotor to distributor housing, then lift distributor from engine slightly until rotor stops turning. Mark relationship of new rotor position on distributor housing, then remove distributor from engine.
6. If engine was not cranked after distributor was removed from engine, proceed as follows:
   a. Position rotor to align with second mark made on distributor housing prior to removing distributor.
   b. Install distributor into engine and align rotor with first mark made on distributor housing prior to removing distributor.
   c. Install distributor cap and connect all electrical connectors.
   d. Adjust ignition timing as specified in individual car chapters.
7. If engine was cranked after distributor was removed from engine, proceed as follows:
   a. Remove No. 1 spark plug and crank engine until compression pressure is felt in No. 1 cylinder. Slowly rotate engine until top dead center is indicated.
   b. Turn rotor to a position just ahead of No. 1 spark plug tower on distributor cap.
   c. Install distributor. Connect 4 terminal connector (if equipped).
   d. Install distributor cap, coil connectors, tachometer lead and battery feed

Fig. 25 Removing ignition coil cover. 1981–82 models with internal coil

wire.
   e. Adjust ignition timing to specifications in individual car chapters.

Models Equipped With Remote Coil Distributor

Chevette
1. Disconnect battery ground cable, then disconnect wiring harness from distributor.
2. Remove distributor cap with ignition cables connected and position aside.
3. Remove ignition coil as described under "Ignition Coil, Replace".
4. Remove air cleaner and disconnect fuel pump hoses at fuel pump.
5. Remove fuel pump and push rod.
6. Mark relationship of rotor to distributor housing and distributor housing to engine, then remove distributor hold down clamp and remove distributor from engine.
7. Install distributor checking to ensure that marks made during removal align.
8. Install hold down clamp and distributor cap.
9. Connect distributor wiring harness electrical connector.
10. Install fuel pump, air cleaner and ignition coil.
11. Adjust ignition timing as specified in individual car chapter.

1981 Citation, Omega, Phoenix & Skylark
1. Disconnect distributor harness electrical connector.
2. Loosen distributor clamp screw, then rotate distributor to gain access to distributor cap retaining latches.
3. Release latches, then remove distributor cap and position aside.
4. Remove distributor hold down clamp, then mark position of rotor in relation to distributor housing.
5. Slowly lift distributor from engine until rotor stops rotating and mark relationship of rotor to distributor housing.
6. Remove distributor from engine.
7. Reverse procedure to install. When installing distributor, align rotor with second mark made on distributor housing prior to removal. Install distributor into engine and check to ensure that rotor aligns with first mark made on distributor housing prior to removal.

1982 Celebrity, Century, Citation, Cutlass Ciera, Omega, Phoenix, Skylark & 6000
1. Raise and support vehicle.
2. Remove two bolts securing rear engine cradle.
3. Lower cradle enough to allow for access to distributor.
4. Remove five brake line support to floorpan retaining screws.
5. Remove coil wire and distributor cap and position aside.
6. Mark relationship of rotor to distributor housing and distributor housing to engine block, then remove distributor hold down clamp and remove distributor from engine.
7. Reverse procedure to install. Ensure marks made during disassembly are correctly lined up during distributor installation.
8. Adjust ignition timing as specified in individual car chapter.

Cavalier, Cimarron, Firenza, J2000 & Skyhawk Exc. 1982 Skyhawk & J2000 with 1.8L OHC Engine
1. Disconnect battery ground cable and remove air cleaner.
2. Release distributor cap latches, then remove distributor cap and position aside.
3. Disconnect AIR pipe to exhaust manifold hose at AIR Management valve.
4. Remove rear engine lift bracket bolt and nut from stud, then position assembly aside.
5. Mark relationship of rotor to distributor housing and distributor housing to block.
6. Remove distributor hold down clamp, then remove distributor from engine.
7. Reverse procedure to install. Check to ensure that marks made during removal align after distributor is installed.

1982 Skyhawk & J2000 with 1.8L OHC Engine
1. Disconnect battery ground cable.
2. Remove spark plug wires and ignition coil.
3. Disconnect distributor wiring.
4. Remove two nuts securing distributor body to cylinder head and remove distributor.
5. Reverse procedure to install. Adjust ignition timing to specifications in individual car chapters. Torque nuts 9–15 ft. lbs.

NOTE: No gear is used to drive the distributor. A lug at the distributor base engages a slot on camshaft end.

1982 AMC
1. Disconnect distributor wire connector from coil.
2. Remove distributor cap and position aside.
3. Remove vacuum advance hose.
4. Remove distributor hold down bolt and clamp.
5. Mark relationship of rotor to distributor housing and distributor housing to engine block, then pull distributor up until rotor stops turning and mark relationship of rotor to distributor housing again.
6. Remove distributor.
7. If engine was not cranked after distributor was removed from engine, proceed as follows;
   a. Position rotor to align with second mark made on distributor housing

Fig. 26 Removing distributor shield. 1981-82 models equipped with 6 & 8 cylinder engines

prior to removing distributor.

b. Install distributor into engine and align rotor with first mark made on distributor housing prior to removing distributor.

c. Install distributor cap and connect all electrical and vacuum connections.

d. Adjust ignition timing as specified in individual car chapter.

8. If engine was cranked after distributor was removed from engine, proceed as follows;

a. Remove No. 1 spark plug and crank engine until compression pressure is felt in No. 1 cylinder. Slowly rotate engine until top dead center is indicated.

b. Turn rotor to a position just ahead of No. 1 spark plug tower on distributor cap.

c. Install distributor. Connect vacuum hose.

d. Install distributor cap and connect all electrical connectors.

e. Adjust ignition timing as specified in individual car chapter.

COMPONENTS, REPLACE

Ignition Coil Replacement

Units With Internal Coil

1. Remove electrical connector from distributor cap by lifting retaining tabs.
2. Remove three coil cover attaching screws, then remove cover, Fig. 25.
3. Remove coil attaching screws, then remove ignition coil with leads from distributor cap.
4. Remove coil arc seal.
5. Reverse procedure to install.

Units With External Coil

1. On 1981-82 Citation, Omega, Phoenix & Skylark & 1982 Celebrity, Century, Cutlass Ciera & 6000, proceed as follows;
   a. Remove bolt securing radio capacitor to coil.
   b. Disconnect coil electrical connector and high tension lead.
   c. Remove three coil mounting bolts, then remove coil.
   d. Reverse procedure to install.
2. On Chevette models, proceed as follows:
   a. Remove coil cover, then disconnect ignition switch to coil lead at coil.
   b. Disconnect coil high tension lead, then remove coil retaining bolts and the coil.
   c. Reverse procedure to install.
3. On Cavalier, Cimarron, Firenza, J2000 & Skyhawk models, proceed as follows;

NOTE: On 1982 Skyhawk and J2000 with 1.8L OHC engine, the coil is located at the rear of the engine near the end of the cam cover.

   a. Disconnect battery ground cable, then raise and support vehicle.
   b. Disconnect fuel pump lines at fuel pump, then remove vacuum pipe retaining bracket nut at coil and position pipe aside.
   c. Remove fuel pump, then remove coil mounting bolts.
4. On 1982 AMC models, proceed as follows;
   a. Disconnect distributor wire connector from coil
   b. Disconnect coil high tension lead.

NOTE: When removing coil high tension lead, twist boot one half turn and pull on boot only to prevent damage to coil high tension lead.

   c. Remove coil attaching screws and coil.
   d. Reverse procedure to install.

Module Replacement

1. Remove distributor cap and rotor.
2. Remove module retaining screws, then lift module upward.
3. Disconnect module electrical connector. Note position of electrical connector prior to disconnecting. Remove module from distributor.
4. Reverse procedure to install. Check to ensure that module electrical connector is installed in proper position. If module is not being replaced, do not wipe grease from module or distributor base. If new module is to be installed, coat module and distributor base with pack of grease supplied with replacement module.

Pick Up Coil, Replace

1. Mark relationship of distributor shaft and driven gear for reference during assembly.
2. Remove roll pin and driven gear from shaft.
3. Remove distributor cap, magnetic shield (if equipped), shaft and rotor.
4. Remove C washer on top of pick up coil assembly, then disconnect pick up coil leads from module and remove pick up coil assembly.
5. Reverse procedure to install.

Fig. 27 Pick up coil disassembled. 1981-82 models equipped with 6 & 8 cylinder engines

Hall Effect Switch (If Equipped), Replace

1. Remove distributor cap and rotor.
2. Remove switch retaining screws, then while pulling switch away, remove wiring connector. Remove switch.
3. Reverse procedure to install.

NOTE: After Hall Effect switch is installed, spin distributor shaft to ensure teeth do not touch. If necessary loosen, then re-tighten pick up coil teeth and Hall Effect switch to eliminate contact.

DISTRIBUTOR SERVICE

6 & V8 Engines

1. Remove cap and coil as an assembly.
2. Remove rotor and pick up coil leads from module.
3. Mark relationship of distributor shaft and driven gear for reference during assembly.
4. Remove roll pin and driven gear.
5. Remove distributor shaft assembly.
6. Remove shield, Fig. 26.
7. Remove retaining ring, pick up coil, magnet and pole piece, Fig. 27.
8. Remove module retaining screws and capacitor screw, then remove module, capacitor and harness assembly from distributor.
9. Disconnect wiring harness from module. Reverse procedure to assemble.

4 Cylinder Engine

1. Remove rotor, then disconnect pick up coil leads from module.
2. Mark relationship of distributor shaft and driven gear for reference during assembly.
3. Remove roll pin and driven gear from distributor shaft.
4. Remove C washer retaining ring, then remove pick up coil assembly.
5. Disconnect module electrical connectors, then remove module retaining screws and the module.
6. Clean distributor base, then apply suitable silicone lubricant between module and base.
7. Reverse procedure to assemble.

Ford 1977–82 Dura Spark I & II Solid State Ignition Systems Except Escort, EXP, LN7 & Lynx

The Dura Spark ignition systems are controlled by an electronic module. The Dura Spark system uses higher spark plug voltages during the starting and running modes, permitting the use of wider spark plug gaps required to ignite the leaner air/fuel mixtures.

There are three variations of this ignition system as shown in Figs. 1 thru 3.

The distributor shaft and armature rotation, Fig. 4, causes the armature poles to pass by the core of the magnetic pick-up assembly. As an armature tooth approaches the pole piece, it reduces the reluctance of the magnetic circuit, thus increasing the field strength. The resulting alternating voltage is applied to the ignition module at a rate proportional to engine speed. The ignition module shuts off the primary circuit each time it receives a pulse from the magnetic pick-up. The timing circuitry in the module leaves the circuit "Off" just long enough for the coil to discharge into the secondary circuit then turns the primary circuit "On" again. Maximum time is allowed for the coil to discharge.

Oil filled ignition coils are used, therefore conventional ignition coils are not to be used on these systems. The ignition coil can be identified by its blue color and the terminals are marked differently, Fig. 5.

The electronic module, Fig. 6, is the brain of this system and is well protected from outside elements such as heat and shock. The heat sink containing all the electronic devices is sealed in a mixture of epoxy and sand. This module can not be disassembled and must be replaced if malfunctioning.

The ignition system is protected against electrical current produced during normal vehicle operation and against reverse polarity or high voltage accidentally applied if vehicle is jump started.

CAUTION: The ignition system will be damaged if other than volt-ohm test procedures are used to check alternator output. This alternator test procedure is outlined in the "Ford Motorcraft Alternator" section, under "Voltmeter Test."

Do not use the volt-amp test procedure or any other test that utilizes a knife switch on the battery terminal.

SYSTEM DIAGNOSIS

NOTE: When performing diagnostic or service procedures on models equipped with Dura-Spark II, the ignition switch should remain in the "Off" position unless otherwise stated in the procedure. On these units, a spark will be generated when the ignition switch is placed from the "On" position to "Off", which may inadvertently cause the engine to rotate, resulting in personal injury.

Secondary Circuit Test
Rotor Air Gap
1. Connect an oscilloscope with voltage pick-up on coil to distributor cable. Set

Fig. 1   Dura Spark Ignition system. 1977–79 California

Fig. 2   Dura Spark II ignition system. 1977–82

Fig. 3   Dura Spark II with dual mode ignition system. 1978–82

ELECTRONIC IGNITION SYSTEMS

oscilloscope to 30KV parade pattern.
2. Disconnect any spark plug wire (except no. 1) and ground it firmly to engine block.

CAUTION: While engine is running, do not disconnect spark plug wires 1 or 3 on 4 cylinder engine, 1, 3, or 5 on inline 6 cylinder engine, 1 or 4 on V6 engine or 1 or 8 on V8 engine. These contacts in the distributor cap are above the stator and arcing may result when the circuit is open.

---

3. Run engine at 1000 rpm and observe height of firing spike of disconnected cylinder. Firing spike should be 8 KV or less.
4. If firing spike is 8000 volts or less, air gap resistance is within acceptable limits. If firing spike is greater than 8000 volts, replace rotor and repeat test. If still too high, replace distributor cap.

NOTE: White deposits on rotor are normal and should not be removed. If rotor is replaced, coat new rotor with silicone grease.

Spark Plug Firing Voltage Test

1. Reconnect spark plug lead, then run engine at 2000 rpm and set oscilloscope to 30 KV parade pattern.
2. Check for firing spikes which are appreciably lower or higher (50 percent) than the other cylinders.
3. Normal firing spikes should be 6–20 KV.
4. Expand pattern to inspect individual firing spikes. If all spikes are below or above specifications, check rotor, distributor cap or coil to distributor cable.
5. To check low firing voltage, disconnect spark plug wire from spark plug and hold it so that spark cannot arc to ground:
   a. If spike does not increase to 28,000 volts or more (coil output), check for a cracked distributor cap with a grounded terminal.
   b. If spike does not rise, replace affected spark plug.
6. To check high firing voltage, disconnect spark plug wire from spark plug and ground the wire:
   a. If high spike drops, replace spark plug.
   b. If high spike remains, check spark plug wire and its connection at distributor cap.

Fig. 4 Breakerless distributor (typical)

Spark Plug Wires Continuity Test

1. Remove distributor cap and disconnect suspected wire from spark plug or coil.
2. Using an ohmmeter, check wire resistance through distributor cap. Resistance should be 100,000 ohms or less.
3. If resistance of wire is greater than 100,000 ohms, replace wire.

Spark Plug Wire Inspection

1. Clean off any deposits of road salt, dirt etc. from wires, boots, distributor cap and coil using water and a mild soap solution.
2. Inspect wires and boots for cuts, punctures, scrapes and burns. Replace as required.
3. Inspect wire terminals for corrosion. Remove corrosion with fine sandpaper.
4. Coat inside of all boots with silicone grease before reinstalling.

Primary Circuit Test

NOTE: The flow chart in Fig. 7, and test procedures provide a sequence for testing which should locate most problems in the primary ignition circuit. It is important to perform these tests in the exact order listed to check all portions of the system. A volt-ohmmeter, 15 inch jumper wire, straight pin, modified spark plug and ballast resistor, Fig. 8, are required to check the system.

Fig. 5 Ignition coil identification

The coil shows BAT and DEC labels.

Test 1, Tap Test

1. Remove distributor cap and rotor. Crank engine to align one tooth of armature with magnet in pick-up coil, Fig. 9.
2. On Dura Spark I system, install ballast resistor Motorcraft DY-36 in series with primary circuit at BAT terminal of ignition coil, Fig. 10. Using a straight pin, pierce both red and white leads of module to short these two leads together, Fig. 10.

CAUTION: Never install bypass until after the ballast resistor is in place or permanent damage to module or coil may result.

---

3. Remove coil wire from distributor cap and connect to a well grounded modified spark plug, Fig. 8, or hold wire 1/4 from engine. Turn ignition switch to Run and tap distributor body with a screwdriver handle.
4. If there are sparks, proceed to test 2. If ther are no sparks, proceed to Test 4.

Test 2, Voltage Drop On Module White Wire

1. On Dura Spark I, remove pin from red wire only, leaving pin to make contact with white wire only, Fig. 11.
2. Connect positive lead of voltmeter to positive battery terminal and negative lead of voltmeter to pin in white wire. Crank engine and observe voltmeter reading. Reading should not exceed 1 volt.
3. If reading is above 1 volt, repair circuit feeding white wire, then repeat Test 1. If reading is less than 1 volt, perform Test 3.

Test 3, Crank Test

1. Crank engine while checking for sparks.
2. If there are no sparks, perform Test 6. If there are sparks, ignition system is functioning properly. Remove pin and ballast resistor. Check fuel system and refer to "Testing for Intermittent Conditions".

Test 4, Voltage Drop On Module Red Wire

1. On Dura Spark I, remove pin from white wire only, leaving pin to make contact with red wire, Fig. 12.
2. On Dura Spark II, insert pin into red wire to make contact, Fig. 12.
3. Measure voltage drop on red wire of ignition module with key in On position. Connect positive lead of voltmeter to positive terminal and negative lead to red wire.

Fig. 6 Electronic control module (typical)

START HERE

TEST 1
TAP TEST

— Sparks →

TEST 2
VOLTAGE DROP
ON MODULE
WHITE WIRE

Voltage drop
Excessive
Repair

Voltage
drop OK

TEST 3
CRANK TEST

— Sparks →

IGNITION
PRIMARY
OK

No Sparks

No Sparks

Voltage drop
Excessive
Repair

TEST 4
VOLTAGE DROP
ON MODULE
RED WIRE

Voltage
drop OK →

TEST 5
CYCLE SWITCH

No Sparks →

TEST 6
VOLTAGE DROP
TO COIL

Voltage
Drop
OK

Sparks

PERFORM
TEST 8

Voltage drop
Excessive

REPLACE
MODULE

← Good —

TEST 11
GREEN WIRE
FROM MODULE
TO COIL

— Bad →

REPAIR
AND
REPEAT
TEST 1

REPLACE
COIL THEN
REPEAT
TEST 1

← Bad —

TEST 7
COIL
CONDITION

Good

Good

Bad

Bad

Good

TEST 10
PRIMARY GROUND
CIRCUIT TEST

REPLACE STATOR
ASSEMBLY AND
REPEAT TEST 1

← Good —

TEST 9
HARNESS TO
DISTRIBUTOR TEST

← Bad —

TEST 8
DISTRIBUTOR
AND HARNESS
TEST

Good

Fig. 7 System diagnosis flow chart

MODIFIED SPARK PLUG WITH THE SIDE
ELECTRODE REMOVED

BALLAST RESISTOR
MOTORCRAFT PART NO DY-36

Fig. 8 Test equipment

Fig. 9   Aligning armature with magnet in pick-up coil

DURASPARK I ONLY

Fig. 10   Ballast resistor installed in primary circuit. Dura Spark I system

Fig. 11   Checking voltage drop on module white wire

Fig. 12   Checking voltage drop on module red wire

Fig. 13   Checking voltage drop to coil

PRIMARY RESISTANCE	SECONDARY RESISTANCE
Dura I — 0.7-0.8 ohm Dura II — 1.15-1.25 ohm	Dura I — 7300-8200 ohms Dura II — 7700-9300 ohms

Fig. 14   Checking coil condition

4. If reading is above 1 volt, repair circuit feeding red wire, then repeat Test 1. If reading is below 1 volt, perform Test 5.

Test 5, Cycle Switch
1. On Dura Spark I, pierce both red and white wires of module to short these two leads using a straight pin, Fig. 12.

NOTE: On Dura Spark II, do not install straight pin.

2. Cycle ignition switch On and Off or turn ignition switch On and disconnect and reconnect distributor connector. A spark should be seen at the modified spark plug each time the ignition switch is cycled, or each time the connector is disconnected.
3. If there are no sparks, perform Test 6. If there are sparks, perform Test 8.

Test 6, Voltage Drop to Coil, Fig. 13.
1. Connect jumper wire from "DEC" termi-

nal to ground. Turn ignition switch to Start and then Run positions.
2. Measure voltage drop to "BAT" terminal of coil:
   a. While cranking engine, voltage drop should be no more than 1 volt.
   b. With ignition switch at Run, voltage drop should be less than 1 volt on Duraspark I, and less than 6.5 volts on Duraspark II.
3. If voltage drop is within specifications,

Fig. 15 Distributor and harness test

Fig. 16 Harness to distributor test

Fig. 17 Primary ground circuit test

Fig. 18 Checking green wire from module to coil

perform Test 7. If voltage drop is not within specifications, perform repairs as necessary and repeat test.

Test 7, Coil Condition

Refer to Fig. 14, for ohmmeter connections to check coil primary and secondary resistance. Resistance values should be as specified. If resistance values are within specifications, perform Test 8. If not, replace coil and repeat Test 1.

Test 8, Distributor & Harness Test, Fig. 15

1. Disconnect module connector with purple and orange wires. Test distributor by connecting a voltmeter to orange and purple wires at harness side of male connector.

NOTE: Do not use a voltmeter combined with a dwell-meter, as slight needle oscillations of 1/2 volt may not be detectable on this type of test equipment. Also, a digital volt-ohmmeter will not function on this test.

CAUTION: If vehicle is equipped with a catalytic converter, disconnect air supply line between by-pass valve and manifold before cranking engine with ignition off. This will prevent damage to the catalytic converter. Also, after testing, run engine for at least three minutes before reconnecting air supply line, to clear excess fuel from exhaust system.

2. Set voltmeter to its lowest scale and

crank engine. Meter needle should oscillate slightly (about 1/2 volt). Refer to "Distributor Testing" for additional information.

3. If voltmeter indications are as specified, perform Test 10. If not, perform Test 9.

Test 9, Harness To Distributor Test, Fig. 16

1. Check for open or shorted condition in orange and purple wires from module connector (harness side) to distributor connector (harness side).

2. If wires are not open or shorted, replace stator assembly and repeat test. If a shorted or open condition exists, make necessary repairs and repeat test.

Test 10, Primary Ground Circuit Test, Fig. 17

1. Connect an ohmmeter to black lead at harness side of module connector and a good ground.

2. With ohmmeter at its lowest scale, there should be no measurable resistance.

Fig. 19 Checking pick-up coil in distributor

Fig. 20 Armature roll pin

Fig. 21 Magnetic pick-up assembly and lead

Fig. 22 Module identification

3. If there is no measurable resistance, perform Test 11. If resistance can be measured, check ground in distributor and wire from module to distributor. Repair or replace as necessary and repeat test.

Test 11, Green Wire From Module To Coil, Fig. 18

1. Check green wire from module to coil for open or shorted condition.
2. If wires are open or shorted, repair or replace as necessary and repeat test. If shorted or open condition does not exist, refer to "Testing For Intermittent Conditions". If problem cannot be found, replace module.

Coil Testing

If an oscilloscope is available, connect oscilloscope and disconnect one spark plug wire not allowing it to arc to ground. Crank engine while observing coil reserve voltage. Voltage spike should be 28 KV or more.

Distributor Testing

Test 1, Fig. 19

Connect an ohmmeter to parallel blade of distributor connector. Resistance should be 400–1000 ohms. A reading of less than 400 ohms indicates a short while an infinity reading indicates an open. With ignition switch off, check resistance between orange wire and ground and purple wire and ground. Reading at each wire should be greater than 70,000 ohms.

Test 2, Fig. 20

Remove distributor cap and check that roll pin retaining armature on distributor shaft is in place. If roll pin is missing, armature can rotate in relation to distributor shaft causing timing to be out of specifications. Check for correct connection of orange and purple wires between distributor and module. If wires are reversed, distributor timing will be 22 1/2 degrees out of phase.

Test 3

If a known good distributor is available, connect it to harness, turn ignition switch "On" and spin distributor by hand while checking for sparks.

Testing For Intermittent Conditions

If the ignition system becomes operative while performing diagnosis and a repair has not been made, it indicates that a malfunctioning component has become operative. The following procedures may locate the malfunctioning components:

With engine running, try to recreate the problem by moving wires at the coil, module, distributor and other harness connectors. Start with connectors disturbed originally. Also check ground connection in distributor. Also, disconnecting and reconnecting connectors may locate an intermittent condition.

CAUTION: Do not clean compound from connectors as it is required to prevent terminal corrosion.

Pick-Up Coil

With engine off, remove distributor cap, rotor and adapter, if used. Heat stator pick-up coil using a 250 watt heat lamp placed about 1 to 2 inches from its top surface. Apply heat for 5 to 10 minutes while observing pick-up coil continuity between the parallel blades of the disconnected distributor connector. Resistance should be 400-1000 ohms. Less than 400 ohms indicates a short while infinity indicates an open. Lightly tapping distributor with a screwdriver may reveal an intermittent condition.

Ignition Module

With engine running, heat module using a 250 watt heat lamp placed about 1 to 2 inches from module. Tapping with a screwdriver may reveal an intermittent condition.

CAUTION: Do not allow module temperature to exceed 212 degrees. This can be checked after the first 10 minutes by applying drops of water to module housing. Repeat every 2 minutes thereafter until water droplets start to boil.

If the above procedure results in an ignition malfunction, substitute a known good module. If substitution corrects the malfunction, recheck old module by reconnecting it into the circuit. Refer to "Test 1" under "Primary Circuit Test" to functionally check the original and the substitute modules.

Trouble Shooting Intermittent Conditions

Engine Starts & Runs OK But Quits When Normal Operating Temperature Is Reached

1. Run engine until normal operating temperature is reached or engine quits, whichever occurs first.
2. Crank engine while checking voltage between orange and purple wires at ignition module. With voltmeter set at lowest scale, only a slight needle movement (about 1/2 volt) should be observed.
3. With ignition switch "Off", check resistance between purple and orange wires at distributor. Resistance should be 400–1000 ohms.
4. With ignition switch "Off" check resistance between purple wire at distributor and ground and between orange wire and ground. Resistance should be greater than 70,000 ohms at each wire.
5. If resistance values in step 3 and 4 are not within specifications, replace pick-up assembly.

Fig. 23 Armature tooth and stator alignment

ELECTRONIC IGNITION SYSTEMS

Engine Starts Normally At Moderate Temperature But Starts Hard Or Will Not Start In Extremely Cold Temperature

1. Check for open in feed to white lead to module.

Engine Quits Intermittently With Complete Loss Of Ignition

1. Check primary circuit ground resistance at ignition module connector black wire. Resistance should be zero ohms.
2. If resistance is not zero ohms, remove distributor cap and inspect retaining screw at rubber plug where wires enter distributor, Fig. 21. A loose or cross threaded screw or a dirty or corroded connection at this screw can cause an intermittent high resistance or a complete loss of ground.

Module Idenitification

The ignition module can be identified as to type of ignition system by the color of the sealing block, Fig. 22.

Sealing Block Color	Type Of Ignition System
Red	Dura Spark I
White	Dura Spark II (With Cranking Retard)
Blue	Dura Spark II
Yellow	Dura Spark II (Dual Mode)
Green Or Black	Early Solid State Ignition
Brown	EEC System

DISTRIBUTOR, REPLACE

Removal

NOTE: On some 4 and 6 cylinder models, it may be necessary to position thermactor air pump aside to gain access to distributor. It may also be necessary to disconnect the thermactor air filter.

1. Disconnect distributor wiring connector from the engine wiring harness.
2. Disconnect vacuum advance hose, then remove distributor cap and position aside.
3. Remove rotor and adapter, then reinstall rotor.
4. Mark position of distributor in engine and position of rotor on the distributor housing to aid installation.
5. Remove distributor hold-down and clamp, then lift distributor out of engine.

CAUTION: Do not crank engine after the distributor has been removed.

Installation

1. If engine was not cranked after distributor was removed from engine, proceed as follows:
   a. Position the distributor in the engine, aligning the housing to block marks and rotor to housing marks made before removal.
   b. Install the distributor hold-down and clamp but do not tighten bolt until timing has been adjusted.
   c. Install distributor cap and wires, then connect distributor wiring connector to engine wiring harness and attach vacuum advance hose.
   d. Adjust ignition timing to specifications found in the individual car chapters.

2. If engine was cranked after distributor was removed from engine, proceed as follows:
   a. Remove No. 1 spark plug and crank engine until compression pressure is felt in No. 1 cylinder. Slowly rotate engine until the correct initial timing mark on the crankshaft damper aligns with the timing pointer.
   b. Position the distributor in the engine with rotor at number one firing position and armature tooth aligned with stator as shown in Fig. 23.

   NOTE: Ensure oil pump intermediate shaft properly engages the distributor shaft. It may be necessary to crank the engine with the starter after the distributor drive gear is partially engaged in order to engage the oil pump intermediate shaft.

   c. Install distributor hold-down bolt and clamp but do not tighten bolt until timing has been adjusted.
   d. Install distributor cap and wires, then connect distributor wiring connector to engine wiring harness and attach vacuum advance hose.
3. Adjust ignition timing to specifications found in the individual car chapters.

CAUTION: On 1977–81 Dura Spark units, due to higher ignition system voltage, a timing light specifically designed for this system should be used when checking ignition timing. If a timing light designed for this system is not available, an inductive pickup type timing light may operate satisfactorily if a piece of split vacuum hose is first placed around the spark plug wire.

COMPONENT REPLACEMENT

Magnetic Pickup Assembly

Removal

1. Remove distributor cap and rotor, then disconnect distributor wiring harness plug, Fig. 4.
2. Using two screw drivers, pry armature from advance plate sleeve and remove roll pin.
3. Remove snap ring securing pickup assembly to base plate. On 4 and 6 cylinder models, remove washer and wave washer.
4. On all models, remove snap ring securing vacuum advance link to pickup assembly.
5. Remove pickup assembly ground screw and lift assembly from distributor.
6. Disconnect vacuum advance link from pickup assembly post.

Installation

1. Position pickup assembly over base plate and slide wiring harness into slot on side of distributor housing, Fig. 4.
2. On 4 and 6 cylinder models, install washers. On all models, install snap ring securing pickup assembly to base plate.
3. Position vacuum advance link on pickup assembly post and install snap ring.
4. Insert ground screw through wiring harness tab and install on base plate.
5. Install armature on advance plate sleeve, ensure roll pin is engaged in slot.
6. Install distributor rotor and cap, then connect distributor wiring harness plug to vehicle wiring harness.

Vacuum Advance Unit, Replace

1. Remove distributor cap and rotor.
2. Disconnect vacuum lines, then remove snap ring that secures vacuum advance link to pickup assembly.
3. Remove vacuum advance attaching screws, then tilt unit downward to disconnect link.
4. Carefully remove unit from distributor.
5. Reverse procedure to install.

Fixed Base Plate, Replace

1. Remove distributor cap and rotor.
2. Remove vacuum advance unit and magnetic pickup assembly.
3. Remove attaching screws and lift base plate from distributor.
4. Reverse procedure to install.

RESISTANCE WIRE, REPLACE

NOTE: The special resistance wire, must be of a specified length and diameter to reduce operating voltage of the ignition system. Under no circumstances should the resistance wire be replaced by any other wire but the correct service resistance wire. When a replacement resistance wire is installed, the damaged resistance wire should be isolated from the system.

1977–78 Bobcat & Pinto, Fig. 24

1. Disconnect battery ground cable.
2. From under instrument panel, detach fuse panel mounted on bracket on right hand side of steering column.
3. Pull fuse panel and wiring downward to expose damaged resistor wire.
4. From back of fuse panel, cut damaged resistor wire (single strand steel wire) close to the panel and the wiring, and insulate cut ends with D6AZ-19627-A tape, Fig. 24.
5. From same terminal (second wire), cut the circuit No. 16A red light green stripe (multiple strand copper) wire about 2 inches from fuse panel and install a C5AZ-14294-B bullet terminal on each cut end, Fig. 24.
6. Reconnect the No. 16A circuit with a B6A-14487-A double connector.
7. Connect one end of replacement D7AZ-12250-A resistor wire into the double connector and route and loop the excess length along the harness to the ignition switch. Secure resistor wire to wiring harness with tape or a strap.
8. Disconnect multiple connector from ignition switch and cut circuit no. 262 brown pink stripe wire about 2 inches from the connector.
9. Install a C5AZ-14294-B bullet terminal on each cut end, then reconnect the No. 262 circuit with a B6A-14487-A double connector.
10. Connect the remaining end of the new resistor wire into the double connector.
11. Reconnect all disassembled components and reconnect battery ground cable.
12. Turn ignition key to "Start" position and check if engine continues to run when key is released to "Run" position. If engine does not continue to run, use a voltohmmeter and check for proper voltage and or/resistance at ignition coil. With new

95874-S
ADJUSTABLE STRAP

D7AZ-12250-A RESISTOR
ASSY. IGNITION COIL (NEW)

16A

20

262

IGNITION SWITCH

16

TAPE

16A

B6A-14487-A DOUBLE
CONNECTOR (2 REQ'D.)

C5AZ-14294-B TERMINAL-
BULLET (4 REQ'D.)

CUT DAMAGED RESISTOR WIRE
FROM HARNESS - TAPE CUT ENDS

WIRE COLOR CODE

16	16A	-	RED-LT. GREEN STRIPE
262		-	BROWN-PINK STRIPE
20		-	WHITE-LT. BLUE HASH MARK

Fig. 24 Resistance wire installation. 1977–78 Bobcat & Pinto

D7AZ-12250-A resistor wire installed, the resistance should be 1.05 to 1.15 ohms at 75° F, and voltage should be 6.4 volts at the coil.

NOTE: Inspect all wiring adjacent to the resistor wire for damage, and repair as necessary.

1977–78 Mustang, Fig. 25

1. Disconnect battery ground cable.
2. From engine side of dash panel, release wiring harness connector from fuse panel.
3. From under left side of instrument panel, release connector and fuse panel from dash and pull downward to facilitate releasing multiple connector from fuse panel.
4. From multiple connector disconnected from fuse panel and dash panel, cut and remove No. 16 red-light green stripe single strand wire resistance wire close to

connector and harness.
5. Insulate cut ends of wire using tape D6AZ-19627-A or equivalent.
6. From the same terminal in connector that the resistance wire was removed, cut the No. 262 brown-pink stripe wire about 2 inches from the connector.
7. On each cut end, install bullet terminal C5AZ-14294-B or equivalent.
8. Reconnect No. 262 wire using double connector B6A-14487-A or equivalent.
9. Install one end of replacement resistance wire into the double connector, then route and loop excess length along harness to ignition switch.
10. Secure resistance wire along wiring harness using adjustable strap or suitable tape.
11. Disconnect multiple connector from ignition switch and cut red-light green stripe wire about 2 inches from ignition switch connector.
12. Install bullet terminal C5AZ-14294-B or equivalent at each cut end.
13. Reconnect cut No. 16A circuit using double connector B6A-14487-A double con-

nector or equivalent.
14. Connect remaining end of replacement resistance wire to double connector.
15. Reconnect all disassembled components and battery ground cable.
16. Rotate ignition switch to start position and check to ensure that engine will continue to operate when ignition switch is returned to the run position. If engine will not continue to operate, check for proper voltage and resistance at ignition coil. Resistance should be 1.05 to 1.15 ohms at 75° F. Voltage should be approximately 6.4 volts at the coil.

NOTE: Inspect all wiring adjacent to resistor wire for damage and repair as necessary.

1977–78 Granada, Monarch & Versailles, Fig. 26

1. Disconnect battery ground cable.
2. From inside vehicle, remove fuse panel cover, then remove two screws attaching

D7AZ-12250-A RESISTOR
ASSEMBLY IGNITION COIL
(NEW)

95874-S
ADJUSTABLE STRAP

D6AZ-19627-A TAPE

16A

262

FUSE PANEL

16C

262

262

16

TAPE

IGNITION SWITCH

CUT DAMAGED
RESISTOR WIRE
FROM HARNESS -
TAPE CUT ENDS

B6A-14487-A
DOUBLE CONNECTOR
(2 REQ'D.)

C5AZ-14294-B
TERMINAL - BULLET
(4 REQUIRED)

WIRE COLOR CODE

16   16A   16C - RED-LT. GREEN STRIPE

262 - BROWN-PINK STRIPE

Fig. 25   Resistance wire installation. 1977–78 Mustang

fuse panel to instrument panel.
3. Pull fuse panel below instrument panel, then at back of fuse panel, cut No. 16A single strand resistance wire close to panel and insulate cut ends with tap D6AZ-19627-A or equivalent.
4. From same terminal, cut No. 16 red-light green stripe multiple strand copper wire about 2 inches from fuse panel and install C5AZ-14294-B bullet terminal or equivalent on each cut end.
6. Install one end of replacement resistance wire into double connector, then route and loop excessive length of resistance wire along wiring harness to half moon shaped multiple connector that connects with harness above parking brake assembly. Secure replacement resistance wire along wiring harness using adjustable strap or suitable tape.
7. Disconnect half moon shaped connector from wiring harness above parking brake assembly, then pull wire connector downward to facilitate cutting and removal of

No. 16A red-light green stripe single strand resistance wire.
8. Insulate ends of resistance wire with tape D6AZ-19627-A or equivalent.
9. From same terminal as resistance wire was cut, cut No. 262 brown-pink strip wire about 2 inches from connector and install bullet terminal C5AZ-12294-B or equivalent on each cut end.
10. Reconnect circuit No. 262 with double connector B6A-14487-A or equivalent.
11. Install remaining end of replacement resistance wire into double connector.
12. Reconnect all disassembled components and battery ground cable.
13. Rotate ignition key to start position and check to ensure that engine will continue to operate after ignition switch is returned to run position. If engine will not continue to operate, check voltage and resistance at ignition coil. Resistance should be 1.05 to 1.15 ohms at 75° F. Voltage should be approximately 6.4 volts at coil.

NOTE: Inspect all wiring adjacent to resistor wire for damage and repairs as necessary.

1977–78 Cougar, LTD II & Thunderbird, Fig. 27

1. Disconnect battery ground cable.
2. From engine compartment, disconnect wiring connector at dash panel.
3. From inside vehicle, remove release wire connector from dash panel and disconnect from fuse panel.
4. Pull connector disconnected from fuse panel downward below instrument panel to facilitate removal of No. 16B red-light green single strand resistance wire.
5. Cut resistance wire close to fuse panel and insulate tape D6AZ-19627-A or equivalent.
6. From the same terminal as resistance wire was removed, cut No. 262 brown pink stripe multiple strand wire about 2

D7AZ-12250-A RESISTOR ASSY.
IGNITION COIL WIRE (NEW)

CUT RESISTOR
WIRE FROM HARNESS.
INSULATE CUT ENDS
WITH D6AZ-19627-A TAPE

16A

95874-S
ADJUSTABLE STRAP

16

20

262

16

16A

262

262

B6A-14487-A
DOUBLE CONNECTOR
(2 - REQ'D)

TAPE

262

IGNITION SWITCH

CONNECTS WITH
14290 HARNESS

C5AZ-14294-B
TERMINAL BULLET
(4 - REQUIRED)

WIRE COLOR CODE

16 · RED-LT. GREEN STRIPE
262 · BROWN-PINK STRIPE
20 · WHITE-LT. BLUE HASH MARK

Fig. 26 Resistance wire installation. 1977–78 Granada, Monarch & Versailles

inches from connector and install bullet terminals C5AZ-142924-B or equivalent on each cut end.

7. Reconnect circuit No. 262 using double connector B6A-14487-A or equivalent.
8. Install one end of replacement resistance wire into double connector, then route and loop excessive length along wiring harness to ignition switch. Secure resistance wire using an adjustable strap or suitable tape.
9. Remove instrument cluster as described in car chapter under Instrument Cluster, Replace.
10. Disconnect wire connector from ignition switch to facilitate removal of No. 16B red-light green single strand resistance wire. Insulate cut ends with tape D6AZ-19627-A or equivalent.
11. From the same terminal as resistance wire was removed, cut No. 16 red-light green multiple strand wire about 2 inches from connector and install bullet-connector C5AZ-14294-B or equivalent on cut ends.
12. Reconnect circuit No. 16 using double connector B6A-14487-A or equivalent.
13. Connect remaining end of replacement resistance wire into double connector.
14. Reconnect all disassembled components and battery ground cable.
15. Rotate ignition switch to start position, then check to ensure that engine will run

when ignition switch is returned to the run position. If engine fails to operate check voltage and resistance at ignition coil. Resistance should be 1.05 to 1.15 ohms at 75°F. Voltage should be approximately 6.4 volts at coil.

NOTE: Inspect all wiring adjacent to the resistor wire for damage and repair as necessary.

1977–78 Mark V, Fig. 28

1. Disconnect battery ground cable.
2. Disconnect multiple wire connector at dash panel.
3. From under left side of instrument panel, release connector and fuse panel from dash panel, then pull downward to facilitate releasing fuse panel from multiple connector.
4. After releasing fuse panel from multiple connector, cut No. 16A red-light green stripe single strand resistance wire close to fuse panel. Insulate both cut ends with tape D6AZ-19627-A or equivalent.
5. From the same terminal that the resistance wire was removed, cut No. 16 red-light green wire approximately 2 inches from fuse panel, then install bullet terminal C5AZ-14294-B or equivalent on cut ends.
6. Reconnect red-light green wire No. 16

using double connector B6A-14487-A or equivalent.
7. Install one end of replacement resistance wire into double connector and route resistance wire along wiring toward ignition switch. Loop excessive length of resistance wire and route back toward multiple connector. Secure resistance wire to wiring harness using adjustable strap or suitable tape.
8. At multiple connector, cut No. 16A red-light green stripe single strand resistance wire close to connector and insulate both cut ends with tape D6AZ-19627 B or equivalent.
9. From the same terminal that the resistance wire was removed, cut wire No. 262 brown-pink strip wire approximately 2 inches from the connector. On each cut end install bullet terminal C5AZ-14294-A or equivalent.
10. Reconnect circuit No. 262 brown-pink strip wire, using double connector B6A-14487-A or equivalent.
11. Install remaining end of resistance wire into double connector.
12. Reconnect all disassembled components and battery ground cable.
13. Rotate ignition switch to the start position, then check to ensure that engine will continue to operate when ignition switch is returned to the run position. If engine will not continue to operate, check voltage and resistance at ignition coil. Resistance should be 1.05 to 1.15 at 75° F. Voltage should be approximately 6.4 volts at coil.

NOTE: Inspect all wiring adjacent to resistor wire for damage and repair as necessary.

1977–78 Lincoln Continental, Fig. 29

1. Disconnect battery ground cable.
2. Disconnect the 14398 and 14290 wiring connector from the 14401 wiring at the dash panel, Fig. H.
3. From inside vehicle, release the 14401 wiring connector from the dash panel and fuse panel, Fig. 29.
4. Pull connector disconnected from fuse panel downward and disconnect circuit No. 16A resistor wire (red-light green stripe).
5. Release resistor wire and terminal from connector cavity, then cut resistor wire and terminal (single wire) close to harness and insulate exposed end with tape.
6. Fabricate a 4 inch long 16 GA. jumper wire, then install a D20Z-14474-C terminal wire snap-on on one end and a C5AZ-14294-B bullet terminal on the other end, Fig. 32.
7. Connect the jumper wire with the D20Z-14474-C terminal into the vacated cavity of the connector at the firewall and install a B7A-14487-A single connector on remaining bullet terminal of the jumper wire.
8. Install replacement D7AZ-12250-A resistor wire into single connector of jumper wire and route and loop the excess as shown in Fig. 29. Secure resistor wire to harness using tape or a strap.
9. Disconnect the 14401 connector from ignition switch connector and pull downward, then cut either the No. 16 or 16C red-light green stripe wire, about 2 inches from connector.
10. Install a C5AZ-14294-B bullet terminal on each cut end, then reconnect the No. 16

circuit with a B6A-14487-A double connector, and install the remaining end of the new resistor wire into the double connector.

11. Reconnect all disassembled parts and reconnect the battery ground cable.
12. Turn ignition key to "Start" position and check if engine continues to run when key is released to "Run" position. If engine does not continue to run, use a volt-ohmmeter and check for proper voltage and/or resistance at ignition coil. With new D7AZ-12250-A resistor wire installed, the resistance should be 1.05 to 1.15 ohms at 75° and voltage should be 6.4 volts at the coil.

NOTE: Inspect all wiring adjacent to the resistor wire for damage, and repair as necessary.

1979 Ford, Lincoln Continental & Mercury, Fig. 30

1. Disconnect battery ground cable.
2. From engine compartment, disconnect wire connector from fuse panel connector at left side of dash panel.
3. Remove steering column lower panel, then detach steering column from instrument panel.
4. From inside vehicle, detach wire connector that mates with connector located at rear of fuse panel.
5. Pull wire connector disconnected from fuse panel below instrument panel to facilitate removal of resistance wire.
6. Locate No. 16A red-light green stripe resistance wire in connector and retract terminal retaining tab using a small screwdriver or large paper clip, then pull terminal from connector.
7. Cut resistance wire as close to the harness as possible and insulate exposed ends with suitable electrical tape.
8. Locate ignition switch wire connector and about three inches from connector, unwrap tape to expose circuits welded to harness.
9. Cut No. 16A red-light green stripe resistance wire from wiring harness at weld. Approximately 1-1/2 inches from the wire connector, cut No. 16 red-light green stripe wire and install C5AZ-14294-B or equivalent to each cut end. Reconnect No. 16 red-light green stripe wiring circuit using double connector B6A-14487-A or equivalent.
10. Install one end of replacement resistance wire into remaining opening of double connector. Rewrap exposed welded circuits using suitable tape.
11. Route replacement resistance wire to connector behind fuse panel. Use suitable tape to support resistance wire when routing along harness.

NOTE: Do not fold, loop or overlap resistance wire onto itself under the harness covering.

12. Using a 4 inch length 16 gauge wire, strip 3/8 inch of insulation from each end, then install a D02B-14474-CB on one end and

Fig. 27 Resistance wire installation. 1977–78 Cougar, LTD II & Thunderbird

Fig. 28 Resistance wire installation. 1977–78 Mark V

Fig. 30 Resistance wire installation. 1979 Ford, Lincoln Continental & Mercury

a C5AZ-14294-B bullet connector on the other end. Install female connector into vacated cavity of fuse panel connector, where damaged resistance wire was removed. Push terminal firmly into position until lock snaps into place.
13. Connect free end of replacement wire to free end of jumper wire, using single connector B7A-14487-A.
14. Reconnect wire connector to back of fuse panel and connect with wiring harness at dash panel.
15. Reconnect battery ground cable.
16. Start vehicle and check to ensure that engine will operate when ignition switch is returned to the run position. If engine does not continue to operate, check voltage and resistance at ignition coil IGN terminal. Resistance should be 1.05 to 1.15 ohms at 75° F. Voltage should be approximately 6.4 volts.

Fig. 29 Resistance wire installation. 1977–78 Lincoln Continental

Ford 1981–82 Dura Spark II Solid State Ignition System Escort, EXP, LN7 & Lynx

DESCRIPTION

This system, Fig. 1, is described under "Ford 1977–82 Dura Spark I & II Solid State Ignition Systems Except Escort, EXP, LN7 & Lynx".

SYSTEM DIAGNOSIS

Spark Plug Firing Voltage Test

1. Connect an oscilloscope with voltage pick up on coil to distributor cable.
2. Refer to "Ford 1977–82 Dura Spark I & II Solid State Ignition System Except Escort, EXP, LN7 & Lynx" under "Spark Plug Firing Voltage Test" and perform steps 2 thru 4.

Spark Plug Wire Continuity Test

1. Remove distributor cap and disconnect suspected wire from spark plug or coil.
2. Using an ohmmeter, check wire resistance through distributor cap. Resistance should be 5000 ohms per inch. If reading is greater than as specified, replace wire.

Spark Plug Wire Inspection

1. Clean off any deposits of dirt from wires, boots, distributor cap and coil using mild soap and water solution.
2. Inspect wires and boots for cuts, punctures or other damage.
3. Inspect wire terminals for corrosion and clean with fine sandpaper.
4. Coat all boots with silicone grease before installing.

Test 1, Start Circuit

1. Connect a suitable spark tester between coil wire and a suitable ground, Fig. 2.
2. While cranking engine, check for sparks.
3. If spark is observed, start circuit is satisfactory. If spark does not occur, measure coil wire resistance. If resistance exceeds 5000 ohms per inch, replace wire.
4. If coil wire is satisfactory, inspect coil for signs of carbon tracking or external damage and inspect distributor shaft with engine cranking to ensure distributor shaft rotation. Proceed to test 5.

Test 2, Run Circuit

1. While observing spark tester, cycle ignition switch from "Off" to "Run" position several times (a spark should be generated at the spark tester each time the ignition switch is turned "Off").
2. If spark is observed;
   a. Inspect distributor cap, rotor and adapter for signs of carbon tracking and cracks, replace as necessary.
   b. Ensure armature to sleeve roll pin is correctly installed, repair as necessary.
   c. Ensure orange and purple wires are not crossed between distributor and ignition module.
   d. Check ignition timing, adjust as necessary.
3. If spark does not occur, proceed to test 3.

Test 3, Module Voltage

1. With ignition "Off", install a straight pin into module red wire, Fig. 3. Connect a suitable voltmeter positive lead to straight pin and ground negative lead. Turn ignition "On" and measure voltage.

NOTE: Do not allow straight pin to contact engine ground.

2. If reading obtained is 90% of battery voltage, module voltage is satisfactory. Proceed to test 4.
3. If reading obtained is less than 90% of battery voltage, inspect ignition switch and wiring between ignition switch and module, repair as necessary.

Test 4, Ballast Resistor

1. Disconnect module connector with red and white wires then, ignition coil connector.
2. Using a suitable ohmmeter, measure resistance between Batt. terminal of ignition coil connector and wiring harness connector wire that joins red wire in module connector.
3. If resistance is 0.8–1.6 ohms, ballast resistor is satisfactory. If resistance is less than 0.8 ohms or greater than 1.6 ohms, replace ballast resistor.

Test 5, Supply Voltage Circuit

1. Reconnect coil wire to distributor cap (if still removed).
   a. If starter relay is equipped with a I terminal, disconnect starter cable from starter relay.

Fig. 1 Dura Spark II ignition system. 1981–82

Fig. 2   Spark plug tester

b. If starter relay is equipped with a S terminal, disconnect S wire from relay.

2. With ignition "Off", install straight pins into module red and white wires.

NOTE: Do not allow straight pins to contact engine ground.

3. Using a suitable voltmeter, connect negative lead to ground.
   a. With ignition in "On" position, measure voltage at red wire pin.
   b. Place ignition in "Start" position, measure voltage at white wire pin and at coil Batt. terminal.

NOTE: When measuring voltages, wiggle wires to simulate any open circuits that might exist.

4. If readings obtained are 90% of battery voltage, supply circuits are satisfactory. Proceed to step 6.

5. If readings obtained are less than 90% of battery voltage;
   a. Defective wiring harness or connectors in supply voltage circuits.
   b. Defective ignition switch.
   c. Defective ignition coil or radio interference capacitor.

Test 6, Ignition Coil Supply Voltage
1. Connect positive lead of voltmeter to coil Batt. terminal and negative lead to ground.
2. Turn ignition switch to "On" position.
3. Observe voltmeter reading. If 6–8 volts, proceed to test 7. If less than 6 volts or more than 8 volts, proceed to test 13.

Test 7, Distributor Stator Assembly & Wiring Harness
1. Disconnect module 4 wire connector. Inspect connectors for dirt and corrosion.
2. Using a suitable ohmmeter, measure resistance of stator and wiring harness between wiring harness terminals joining orange and purple wires of module connector, Fig. 4.

NOTE: When measuring resistance, wiggle wires to simulate any open circuits that might exist.

3. If resistance is 400–1300 ohms, test results are satisfactory, proceed to test 8. If resistance is less than 400 or more than 1300 ohms, proceed to step 11.

Fig. 3   Dura Spark II ignition system module voltage test connections

Fig. 4   Dura Spark II ignition system stator assembly & wiring harness test connections

Fig. 5   Dura Spark II ignition system module to stator wiring harness test connections

Test 8, Ignition Module to Distributor Stator Assembly Wiring Harness
1. Disconnect module 4 wire connector. Inspect connectors for dirt and corrosion.
2. Using a suitable ohmmeter, connect one lead to ground. Using other lead, alternately measure resistance of harness wiring which connects to orange and purple wires of module connector to ground, Fig. 5.
3. If test results are greater than 70,000 ohms, circuits are satisfactory. If test results are less than 70,000 ohms, inspect and repair as necessary wiring harness between module connector and distribu-

tor. Also inspect distributor grommet.

Test 9, Ignition Coil Secondary Resistance
1. Disconnect and inspect ignition coil electrical connector.
2. Using a suitable ohmmeter, measure resistance between coil Batt. terminal and high tension lead terminal.
3. If resistance is between 7700–10,500 ohms, coil is satisfactory. If not between limits, replace coil.

Test 10, Coil Tach Terminal to Module Connector Circuit
1. Disconnect module 4 wire connector.

Fig. 6 Dura Spark II ignition system coil tach terminal to module connector circuit test connections

Fig. 8 Dura Spark II ignition system coil primary circuit test connections

Fig. 9 Dura Spark II ignition system ground circuit test connections

Fig. 7 Distributor electrical connector. 1981–82 Dura Spark II ignition system

tor. Inspect connectors for dirt and corrosion.
2. Using a suitable ohmmeter, measure resistance across black/orange stripe wire and black/purple stripe wire in distributor connector, Fig. 7.

NOTE: The distributor stator assembly wire connector wire colors cannot be seen without removal of connector holddown plate or distributor cap.

3. If readings obtained are within 650–1300 ohms, circuit is satisfactory. If readings are less than 650 or more than 1300 ohms, replace stator assembly.

Test 12, Ignition Coil Primary Resistance
1. Disconnect ignition coil electrical connector.
2. Using a suitable ohmmeter, measure resistance between coil Batt. terminal and Tach terminal.
3. If reading obtained is 0.8–1.6 ohms, coil is satisfactory. If not, replace coil.

Test 13, Primary Circuit
1. With ignition "Off", install a straight pin into module green wire, Fig. 8. Connect a suitable voltmeter positive lead to straight pin and ground negative lead. Turn ignition "On" and measure voltage.

NOTE: Do not allow straight pin to contact engine ground.

2. If voltage obtained is more than 1.5 volts, circuit is satisfactory. Proceed to test 14.
3. If voltage obtained is less than 1.5 volts, inspect wiring harness and connectors between ignition coil and module. Repair as necessary.

Test 14, Ground Circuit
1. With ignition "Off", install a straight pin into module black wire, Fig. 9. Connect a suitable voltmeter positive lead to straight pin and ground negative lead to distributor base. Turn ignition "On" and measure voltage.
2. If voltage obtained is more than 1.5 volts, circuit is satisfactory. Proceed to test 15.
3. If voltage obtained is less than 1.5 volts, replace ignition module.

Test 15, Distributor Ground Circuit
1. Disconnect distributor electrical connector. Inspect connections for dirt and corrosion.
2. Using a suitable ohmmeter, measure resistance between distributor base and black wire in distributor connector, Fig. 7.

Inspect connectors for dirt and corrosion.
2. Using a suitable ohmmeter, measure resistance between coil connector tach wire and the terminal in the wiring harness connector that joins the green wire of the module connector, Fig. 6.

3. If resistance is less than 1 ohm, circuit is satisfactory. If resistance is over 1 ohm, inspect and repair wiring harness as necessary.

Test 11, Distributor Stator Assembly
1. Disconnect distributor electrical connec-

NOTE: The distributor stator assembly

wire connector wire colors cannot be seen without removal of connector holddown or distributor cap.

3. If reading obtained is less than 1 ohm, circuit is satisfactory. If reading is more than 1 ohm, inspect and repair distributor ground screw.

DISTRIBUTOR, REPLACE
Removal

1. Disconnect primary circuit connector from distributor.
2. Disconnect vacuum hose from distributor vacuum advance.
3. Remove distributor cap, then mark relationship of rotor to distributor housing and relationship of distributor housing to engine for reference during installation.
4. Remove rotor, then remove distributor retaining bolts and the distributor.

Installation

1. Check to ensure that distributor base O ring is in place.
2. Install distributor into engine checking to ensure that marks made during removal align. Also check that offset tang of drive coupling seats into camshaft groove.
3. Install retaining bolts, rotor, vacuum and electrical connectors and cap.
4. Start engine and adjust ignition timing as specified in the individual car chapters.

COMPONENT REPLACEMENT
Vacuum Advance Unit, Replace

1. Remove distributor cap and position aside with ignition wires attached.
2. Disconnect vacuum advance vacuum hose.

3. Remove diaphragm retaining screws, then partially remove diaphragm assembly until it clears distributor base.
4. Tilt diaphragm assembly to disconnect rod from stator pivot pin, then remove vacuum advance assembly.
5. Check diaphragm O ring for damage, then align threaded hole in advance assembly housing with screw hole in base.
6. Rotate stator assembly clockwise to position stator pivot pin.
7. Insert vacuum advance assembly through base until rod engages stator pivot pin.
8. Continue seating advance assembly into base until threaded hole in diaphragm casting aligns with hole in base.
9. Install diaphragm retaining screw, connect vacuum hose and install distributor cap.

Stator Assembly, Replace

1. Remove distributor and vacuum advance assembly.
2. Using a small screwdriver or other suitable tool, remove drive coupling spring. Use care not to damage parts.
3. Clean distributor drive end then, using paint, make reference marks on distributor drive coupling and shaft to aid in reassembly.
4. Position distributor in a suitable holding device. Using a suitable drift and hammer, drive pin out of shaft and remove coupling.
5. Inspect end of shaft assembly and in area of drive pin hole for burrs. If necessary, use fine emery paper to polish shaft. Wipe shaft clean prior to removal to prevent damage to seal and bushing in distributor base.
6. Remove shaft assembly by gently pulling out of distributor base.
7. Inspect distributor shaft and centrifugal advance assembly. Centrifugal advance assembly should advance freely and return to original position. If binding

occurs, the entire distributor should be replaced.
8. Remove screws securing stator connector to distributor housing then screws securing the stator retainer in distributor housing.
9. Gently lift stator assembly out of distributor housing.
10. Pull stator retainer assembly from stator.
11. Inspect distributor O-rings, replace as necessary.
12. Inspect distributor base bushing for signs of wear and heat damage. if bushing is damaged, replace complete distributor.
13. Inspect distributor shaft oil seal. If oil seal is damaged, replace complete distributor.

NOTE: If seal spring retainer (inside seal) is missing or damaged, it can be replaced.

14. Inspect distributor base casting for cracks and wear. If base is cracked or worn, replace complete distributor.
15. Assemble stator retainer to stator. Position retainer so horseshoe opening of retainer is at the vacuum advance diaphragm rod pivot point.
16. Install stator assembly in distributor base with vacuum advance diaphragm pivot point positioned approximately in front of diaphragm mounting hole.
17. Install stator securing screws, ensure stator is free to rotate. If not, disassemble and check parts. Position wire connector and install securing screws.
18. Lightly lubricate distributor shaft and install.

NOTE: Do not over lubricate.

19. Reverse steps 1 through 4 to complete assembly.

Ford 1982 Thick Film Integrated (TFI) Ignition System Escort, EXP, LN7 & Lynx

DESCRIPTION

On this system the ignition module is mounted on a mounting pad located on the distributor bowl, Figs. 1 and 2. The ignition coil is potted in plastic and has external laminations similar to a transformer.

NOTE: On these units, do not reapply or remove any of the silicone coating from the distributor cap electrodes. Also when installing a replacement distributor rotor, apply a coating approximately 1/32 inch thick, of silicone dielectric compound D7AZ-19A331-A or equivalent to the brass rotor electrode.

SYSTEM DIAGNOSIS
Spark Plug Firing Voltage Test

1. Connect an oscilloscope with voltage pick up on coil to distributor cable.

2. Refer to "Ford 1977–82 Dura Spark I & II Solid State Ignition System Except Escort, EXP, LN7 & Lynx" under "Spark Plug Firing Voltage Test" and perform steps 2 thru 4.

Spark Plug Wire Continuity Test

1. Remove distributor cap and disconnect suspected wire from spark plug or coil.
2. Using an ohmmeter, check wire resistance through distributor cap. Resistance should be 5000 ohms per inch. If reading is greater than as specified, replace wire.

Spark Plug Wire Inspection

1. Clean off any deposits of dirt from wires, boots, distributor cap and coil using mild soap and water solution.
2. Inspect wires and boots for cuts, punctures or other damage.
3. Inspect wire terminals for corrosion and clean with fine sandpaper.
4. Coat all boots with silicone grease before installing.

Circuit Tests

Test 1, Start Circuit

1. Connect a suitable spark tester between coil wire and a suitable ground, Fig. 3.
2. While cranking engine, check for sparks.
3. If spark is observed, start circuit is satisfactory. If spark does not occur, measure coil wire resistance. If resistance exceeds 5000 ohms per inch, replace wire.
4. If coil wire is satisfactory, inspect coil for signs of carbon tracking or external damage and inspect distributor shaft with engine cranking to ensure distributor shaft rotation. Proceed to test 2.

Test 2, Ignition Coil Primary Circuit Switching

1. With ignition "Off", install a straight pin in ignition coil negative wire 1 inch from connector, Fig. 4.

NOTE: Do not allow straight pin to contact engine ground.

Fig. 1   Thick Film Integrated (TFI) Ignition System. 1982 Escort, EXP, LN7 & Lynx

Fig. 2   Exploded view of TFI ignition system distributor. 1982 Escort, EXP, LN7 & Lynx

2. Connect a suitable 12 volt test light between ground and straight pin. While observing test light, crank engine.

3. If test light flashes, circuit is satisfactory. Proceed to test 3. If test light glows but does not flash, proceed to test 5. If light does not glow or flash, proceed to test 7.

Test 3, Ignition Coil Primary Resistance

1. With ignition "Off", disconnect ignition coil connector. Inspect connector for dirt and corrosion.

2. Using a suitable ohmmeter, measure resistance between coil positive to negative terminals.

3. If reading is 0.3–1.0 ohm, coil is satisfactory. Proceed to test 4. If reading is less than 0.3 ohm or more than 1.0 ohm, replace coil.

Test 4, Ignition Coil Secondary Resistance

1. Disconnect and inspect ignition coil electrical connector.

2. Using a suitable ohmmeter, measure resistance between coil negative terminal and high tension lead terminal.

3. If resistance is between 8000–11,500 ohms, coil is satisfactory. If not between limits, replace coil.

Test 5, Wiring Harness

1. Disconnect wiring harness connector from distributor ignition module. Inspect connector for dirt and corrosion.

NOTE: To remove distributor connector, push connector tabs.

---

2. Connect the negative lead of a suitable voltmeter to distributor base. Connect positive lead to a straight pin to serve as a probe.

3. Turn ignition "On", probe terminals 1 and 2, Fig. 5, and record voltages.

4. Turn ignition to "Start" position and probe terminal 3, Fig. 5. Record voltage.

5. If voltages obtained are 90% of battery voltage, circuit is satisfactory. If obtained voltages are less than 90% of battery voltage, a defective wiring harness or ignition switch is indicated.

Test 6, Stator Assembly

1. Remove distributor, then remove ignition module.

2. Inspect stator wiring, wire connections and ground screw.

3. Using a suitable ohmmeter, measure stator resistance, Fig. 6

4. If resistance is 800–975 ohms, stator is satisfactory. If readings are out of specifications, replace stator.

Test 7, Primary Circuit

1. Disconnect wiring harness connector from distributor ignition module. Inspect connector for dirt and corrosion.

NOTE: To remove distributor connector, push connector tabs.

---

2. Connect the negative lead of a suitable voltmeter to distributor base. Connect positive lead to a straight pin to serve as a probe.

3. Turn ignition "On" and note voltage at terminal 1 of connector, Fig. 7.

4. If reading is within 90% of battery voltage, circuit is satisfactory. If reading is not within 90% of battery voltage, proceed to test 8.

Fig. 3   Spark plug tester

Fig. 4   TFI ignition system ignition coil primary circuit switching test connections

ELECTRONIC IGNITION SYSTEMS

Test 8, Ignition Coil Primary Voltage

1. Connect the negative lead of a suitable voltmeter to distributor base. Connect positive lead to ignition coil negative terminal.
2. Turn ignition "On" and note voltage.
3. If reading is within 90% of battery voltage, circuit is satisfactory. If reading is not within 90% of battery voltage, a defective wiring harness between ignition module and ignition coil negative terminal is indicated.

Test 9, Ignition Coil Supply Voltage

1. Connect the negative lead of a suitable voltmeter to distributor base. Connect positive lead to ignition coil positive terminal.
2. Turn ignition "On" and note voltage.
3. If reading is within 90% of battery voltage, circuit is satisfactory. If reading is not within 90% of battery voltage, a defective wiring harness or ignition switch is indicated.

DISTRIBUTOR, REPLACE

Removal

1. Disconnect primary wire connector from distributor and vacuum hose from vacuum advance unit.
2. Using a screwdriver, remove distributor cap and position aside with wires attached.

NOTE: Mark position of rotor to distributor housing and position of distributor housing to engine for reference during installation.

3. Remove rotor attaching screws, then remove rotor.
4. Remove distributor hold down bolts, then remove distributor.

NOTE: Some models use special distributor hold down bolts. To remove these bolts, tool No. T82L-12270-A or equivalent must be used.

Installation

1. Check to ensure that distributor base O-ring is in position.
2. Install distributor into engine, checking to ensure that marks made during removal are aligned. Also check to ensure that offset tang of drive coupling is seated in camshaft groove.
3. Install retaining bolts, rotor, vacuum advance hose, primary wire connector and distributor cap.
4. Start engine and adjust ignition timing.

COMPONENT REPLACEMENT, FIG. 2

Vacuum Advance Unit, Replace

1. Remove distributor cap and position aside with ignition wires attached.
2. Disconnect vacuum advance vacuum hose.
3. Remove diaphragm retaining screw, then partially remove diaphragm assembly until it clears distributor base.
4. Tilt diaphragm assembly to disconnect rod from stator pivot pin, then remove

vacuum advance assembly.
5. Check diaphragm O ring for damage, then align threaded hole in advance assembly housing with screw hole in base.
6. Rotate stator assembly clockwise to position stator pivot pin.
7. Insert vacuum advance assembly through base until rod engages stator pivot pin.
8. Continue seating advance assembly into base until threaded hole in diaphragm

casting aligns with hole in base.
9. Install diaphragm retaining screw, connect vacuum hose and install distributor cap.

TFI Ignition Module

Removal
1. Remove distributor as described under Distributor, Replace.

Fig. 5 TFI ignition system wiring harness test connections

Fig. 6 TFI ignition system stator assembly test connections

Fig. 7 TFI ignition system primary system test connections

2. Remove two screws attaching TFI module to distributor housing.
3. Pull right hand side of module downward toward distributor mounting flange, then up to disengage module terminals from connector in distributor base. Pull toward flange and away from distributor.

Installation

1. Apply a 1/32 inch thick coating of silicone grease D7A2-19A331-A or equivalent to metal base of TFI module.
2. Position TFI module on distributor mounting flange.
3. Carefully position TFI module toward distributor base to securely engage the three distributor connector pins.
4. Install two TFI module attaching screws and torque to 9 to 16 inch lbs.
5. Install distributor as described under Distributor, Replace.

Stator Assembly, Replace

1. Remove distributor and vacuum advance assembly, Fig. 2.
2. Using a small screwdriver or other suitable tool, remove drive coupling spring. Use care not to damage parts.
3. Clean distributor drive and then, using paint, make reference marks on distributor drive coupling and shaft to aid in reassembly.
4. Position distributor in a suitable holding

device. Using a suitable drift and hammer, drive pin out of shaft and remove coupling.
5. Inspect end of shaft assembly and in area of drive pin hole for burrs. If necessary use fine emery paper to polish shaft. Wipe shaft clean prior to removal to prevent damage to seal and bushing in distributor base.
6. Remove shaft assembly by gently pulling out of distributor base.
7. Inspect distributor shaft and centrifugal advance assembly. Centrifugal advance assembly should advance freely and return to original position. If binding occurs, the entire distributor should be replaced.
8. Remove screws securing stator connector to distributor housing then screws securing the stator retainer in distributor housing. Remove connector from top of module.
9. Gently lift stator assembly out of distributor housing.
10. Pull stator retainer assembly from stator.
11. Inspect distributor O-rings, replace as necessary.
12. Inspect distributor base bushing for signs of wear and heat damage. If bushing is damaged, replace complete distributor.
13. Inspect distributor shaft oil seal. If oil seal is damaged, replace complete distrib-

utor.

NOTE: If seal spring retainer (inside seal) is missing or damaged, it can be replaced.

14. Inspect distributor base casting for cracks and wear. If base is cracked or worn, replace complete distributor.
15. Assemble stator retainer to stator. Position retainer so horseshoe opening of retainer is at the vacuum advance diaphragm rod pivot point.
16. Install stator assembly in distributor base with vacuum advance diaphragm pivot point positioned approximately in front of diaphragm mounting hole.
17. Install stator securing screws, ensure stator is free to rotate. If not, disassemble and check parts. Install wire connector securing screws.
18. Position module connector on top of three pins and press down to seat the connector.
19. Lightly lubricate distributor shaft and install.

NOTE: Do not over lubricate.

20. Reverse steps 1 through 4 to complete assembly.

Ford 1981—82 Dura Spark III Solid State Ignition System

DESCRIPTION

The Dura Spark III system, Fig. 1, is used on vehicles equipped with Electronic Engine Control (EEC). The system consists of a primary side consisting of the battery, ignition switch, primary circuit, EEC system input and ignition module and a secondary side consisting of distributor cap, rotor, spark plug wires and spark plugs. When the ignition switch is in the On position, the primary circuit and the ignition coil are energized. The EEC system provides a signal which tells the ignition module to turn off the coil primary circuit. The off and on times of the primary circuit are controlled by the EEC computer. When the circuit is turned Off, the magnetic field built up in the ignition coil collapses, inducing a high voltage into the coil secondary windings. This high voltage is then delivered to the spark plugs by the secondary ignition wires.

SYSTEM DIAGNOSIS

NOTE: Before proceeding with system diagnosis, ensure battery is fully charged and all accessories are "Off". Inspect all vacuum hoses and spark plug wires for proper routing and secure connections. Inspect engine compartment ignition wiring harness and connectors for signs of insulation damage, burning, overheating and loose or broken connections.

Repair as necessary.

Secondary Circuit Tests

Spark Plug Firing Voltage Test, 1981 Models

1. Connect an oscilloscope with voltage pick up on coil to distributor cable. Set oscilloscope to 30 KV parade pattern.
2. Connect timing light to No. 1 spark plug, then start engine and operate at 2000 RPM.
3. Apply 25 inches Hg. of vacuum from outside source to BP port of MAP sensor.
4. Check oscilloscope for highest firing spikes. If highest spikes are between 6 and 20 KV, system is operating properly.
5. If reading is greater than 20 KV or highest spike is 50% greater than lowest, refer to "Primary Circuit Test" under "Test 3, Ignition Coil Primary Voltage."
6. If voltage reading is less than 6 KV, refer to "Spark Plug Wires Continuity Test."
7. Check ignition timing at 2000 RPM. If reading is not between 27 and 30° BTDC, EEC system is malfunctioning and must be repaired.

Spark Plug Firing Voltage Test, 1982 Models

1. Connect an oscilloscope with voltage pick-up on coil to distributor wire. Set oscilloscope to parade pattern.
2. Start engine, then while slowly increasing engine RPM from idle to 2000 RPM,

observe scope pattern. If the average spark plug firing voltage is 15 KV and the spark plug firing voltages do not vary more than 5 KV, the system is operating properly.
3. If the spark plug firing voltages do not vary more than 5 KV and the average spark plug firing voltage is more than 15 KV, check;
   a. Ignition coil wire for proper installation and resistance. Resistance should be less than 5000 ohms per inch. If more, replace.
   b. Spark plugs for wide gaps.
   c. Distributor cap and rotor for excessive clearance.
   d. Distributor cap and rotor for lack of silicone compound on rotor.
   e. Distributor rotor alignment. See Distributor Rotor, Replace.
4. If the spark plug firing voltages vary more than 5 KV, check;
   a. Spark plug gap(s) or worn electrodes.
   b. Correct distributor cap, adapter and rotor installation.
   c. Distributor rotor alignment. See Distributor Rotor, Replace.
5. If one or more spark plug firing voltages are unusually high, check;
   a. Disconnected spark plug wire(s).
   b. Spark plug gap(s) or open plug wire(s).
6. If one or more spark plug firing voltages are unusually low, check;
   a. Spark plug(s) for fouling or narrow gap(s).

Fig. 1 Dura Spark III ignition system, typical. 1981–82

b. Spark plug wires for grounding.
c. Distributor cap and adapter for tracking.
7. If spark plug firing voltages are inverted, check;
a. Ignition coil primary connector for improper installation. If installation is satisfactory, replace coil.

Spark Plug Wire Continuity Test, All Models
1. Remove distributor cap and disconnect suspected wire from spark plug or coil.
2. Using an ohmmeter, check wire resistance through distributor cap.
3. Resistance should be 5000 ohms per inch. If reading is greater than specified, replace wire.

Spark Plug Wire Inspection, All Models
1. Clean off any deposits of dirt from wires, boots, distributor cap and coil using mild soap and water solution.
2. Inspect wires, boots for cuts, punctures or other damage.
3. Inspect wire terminals for corrosion and clean with fine sandpaper.
4. Coat all boots with silicone grease before installing.

Secondary Circuit Voltage Drop, 1981 Models
1. Connect an oscilloscope with voltage pick up on coil to distributor cable.
2. Disconnect a spark plug wire and ground firmly to engine block.
3. Start engine and operate at idle speed.
4. If oscilloscope indicates reading of 8 KV, distributor cap voltage drop is satisfactory.
5. If reading is greater than 8 KV, check for damaged cap or rotor and replace.
6. If an abnormal scope pattern is obtained, check for worn or damaged distributor parts.

Primary Circuit Tests, 1981 Models
Test 1, Ignition Coil Output
1. Disconnect spark plug wire and ground firmly to engine block.
2. Crank engine while checking for spark.
3. If spark is observed, system is operating properly.
4. If no spark is observed, remove cap and crank engine to verify rotor movement.
5. If rotor does not move when engine is cranked, repair distributor as necessary.

Test 2, Trigger Test
1. Disconnect ignition module connector and install ignition diagnostic test adapter into wiring circuit, Fig. 2.
2. Disconnect ignition coil secondary wire at distributor and ground firmly to engine block. Turn ignition to Run position.
3. Touch diagnostic adapter lead to battery positive terminal. Spark should occur every time lead touches battery.
4. If spark occurs, system is operating properly. If not, refer to "Test 3, Ignition Coil Primary Voltage".

Test 3, Ignition Coil Primary Voltage
1. Turn ignition to Run position. Connect voltmeter between BATT terminal of ignition coil and ground.
2. If reading is between 5 and 8 volts, ignition system is satisfactory. If reading is greater than 8 volts, refer to "Test 7, Ground Circuit Check". If reading is less than 6 volts, refer to "Test 6, Wiring Harness Short Circuit" and to "Test 8, Ignition Coil Circuit".
3. In addition, check for open circuit in power supply circuit such as battery lead to ignition coil.

Test 4, Module Run Circuit
1. Turn ignition key to Run position.
2. Measure voltage between red module wire and engine ground by connecting straight pin to voltmeter positive lead and inserting into red wire.

NOTE: Do not allow straight pin to contact ground.

---

3. If reading is within 90% of battery voltage, system is operating properly.
4. If not, check for open circuit in run circuit wiring harness and repair as necessary.

Test 5, Start Circuit Voltage
1. On starter relays equipped with I terminal, disconnect cable between starter relay and starter motor.
2. On starter relays without I terminal, disconnect electrical connector at relay S terminal.
3. Hold ignition switch in Start position and measure voltage between coil BATT terminal and ground and between white module wire and ground. Connect straight pin to voltmeter lead and insert into white wire to perform test.
4. If reading is greater than 90% of battery voltage, system is satisfactory.
5. If reading is less than 90% of battery voltage, check for open circuit in ballast resistor bypass wire or module start wire and repair as necessary. Also check for defective ignition switch.

Test 6, Wiring Harness Short Circuit
1. Disconnect ignition module, ignition coil and EEC computer connectors and inspect for damage.
2. Check for damaged primary circuit wiring and repair as necessary.
3. Place transmission in Park and set parking brake. Check resistance between module connector orange wire terminal and ground, Fig. 3.
4. Measure resistance between the follow-

T79P-12127-A
OR EQUIVALENT

TD81P-6666-A
OR EQUIVALENT

Fig. 2   Installing ignition diagnostic test adapter. 1981–82 Dura Spark III ignition system

ing connector wire terminals:
a. Red to white wire terminals.
b. Red to green wire terminals.
c. Red to orange wire terminals.
d. White to green wire terminals.
e. White to orange wire terminals.
5. If any resistance reading obtained is less than 70,000 ohms, repair damaged wire in that circuit as necessary.

Test 7, Ground Circuit Check
1. Disconnect ignition module connector containing black wire and check for damage.
2. Check resistance between black wire terminal in module connector and ground.
3. If resistance is less than one ohm, system is satisfactory.
4. If resistance is greater than one ohm, check for open circuit at battery ground strap connection and repair as necessary.

Test 8, Ignition Coil Circuit
1. Disconnect ignition coil and module connectors and inspect for damage.
2. Measure resistance between green wire terminal of module connector and TACH terminal on ignition coil.
3. If resistance is greater than 2 ohms, check for open circuit in TACH wire and repair as necessary.
4. If resistance is less than 2 ohms, check resistance of ballast resistor by connecting ohmmeter between BATT terminal on coil and red wire terminal in ignition module connector.
5. If resistance is less than 2 ohms, system is operating satisfactorily. If not, check for an open circuit or replace ballast resistor as necessary.

Test 9, Module Output Check
1. Connect any connectors that were previously disconnected.
2. Connect voltmeter between coil TACH terminal and ground.
3. Set voltmeter on highest scale, then firmly ground ignition coil high tension lead to engine block.
4. Crank engine, then switch voltmeter to lowest scale.
5. If meter needle fluctuates, module is operating satisfactorily. If not, refer to "Test 10, Module Check".

NOTE: If difficulty is encountered in performing this test using a voltmeter, a test light may be substituted in its place. The light flashing would correspond to the voltmeter needle fluctuating.

Test 10, Module Check
1. Disconnect module connector containing green wire.
2. Connect voltmeter between green wire terminal of module connector and ground.
3. Turn ignition to Run position and check voltage.
4. If reading is more than 90% of battery voltage, replace ignition module.
5. If reading is less than 90% of battery voltage, refer to "Test 11, Continuity Check".

Test 11, Continuity Check
1. Check resistance between green wire terminal in harness side module connector and coil TACH terminal.

TO IGNITION COIL

SPARK TESTER

TO IGNITION COIL

ENGINE GROUND

Fig. 4   Spark tester

2. If ohmmeter indicates less than one ohm, system is operating satisfactorily.
3. If reading is greater than one ohm, check for open circuit in wire between coil TACH terminal and ignition module and repair as necessary.

Test 12, Coil Primary Circuit Check
1. Disconnect ignition coil electrical connector.
2. Measure resistance between coil BATT and TACH terminals.
3. If reading is between 1 and 2 ohms, primary circuit is satisfactory.
4. If not, replace coil.

Test 13, Coil Secondary Circuit Check
1. Check resistance between coil TACH terminal and high tension lead terminal.
2. If reading is between 7700 and 9600 ohms, secondary circuit is satisfactory.
3. If not, replace ignition coil.

Primary Circuit Tests, 1982 Models

Test 1, Run Circuit
1. Disconnect ignition module three wire-connector and install ignition diagnostic test adapter into wiring circuit, Fig. 2.
2. Connect spark tester, Fig. 4, between ignition coil and ground.
3. Turn ignition "On", then while observing spark tester, touch diagnostic test lead to battery positive terminal. Spark should occur every time lead touches battery.
4. If spark occurs, circuit is satisfactory. If not, proceed to test 2.

IGNITION SWITCH

1.1 OHMS

IGNITION COIL

BATTERY

TO EEC COMPUTER

RED
WHITE
GREEN
ORANGE
BLACK

IGNITION MODULE

NOTE:
WIRE SEQUENCE HAS BEEN ARRANGED TO SIMPLIFY SCHEMATIC.

Fig. 3   Electrical schematic. 1981–82 Dura Spark III ignition system

ELECTRONIC IGNITION SYSTEMS

Test 2, Start Circuit

1. Remove diagnostic test adapter installed in test 1 but, leave spark tester attached.
2. While cranking over engine with ignition switch, observe spark tester for sparks.
3. If sparks occur, circuit is satisfactory. If not, proceed to test 3.

Test 3, Start Voltage

1. Reconnect coil wire to distributor cap.
   a. If starter relay is equipped with a I terminal, disconnect starter cable from starter relay.
   b. If starter relay is equipped with S terminal, disconnect S wire from relay.
2. With ignition "Off", install straight pin into module white wire, Fig. 5.
3. Connect a suitable voltmeter between ground and straight pin.
4. Turn ignition switch to "Start" position and note voltage.
5. Move voltmeter positive lead to coil Batt. connector and note voltage with ignition switch in start "position".
6. If voltage obtained is 90% of battery voltage, circuit is satisfactory. If voltage obtained is less than 90% of battery voltage, a defective ignition switch or wiring harness is indicated.

Test 4, Ignition Coil Primary Circuit Switching

1. Disconnect ignition module three wire connector and install ignition diagnostic test adapter into wiring circuit, Fig. 2.
2. Connect a suitable test light between coil Tach terminal and engine ground.
3. Turn ignition "On", then while observing test light, touch diagnostic test lead to battery positive terminal. Test light should flash every time lead touches battery.
4. If test light flashes, circuit is satisfactory. If not, Proceed to test 6.

Test 5, Ignition Coil Secondary Resistance

1. Disconnect and inspect ignition coil electrical lead.
2. Using a suitable ohmmeter, measure resistance between coil Batt. terminal and high tension lead terminal.
3. If resistance is between 7700–10,500 ohms, coil is satisfactory. If not between limits, replace coil.

Test 6, Supply Voltage Circuits

1. Remove diagnostic test adapter installed in test 4 and test light, then;
   a. If starter relay is equipped with a I terminal, disconnect starter cable from starter relay.
   b. If starter relay is equipped with S terminal, disconnect S wire from relay.
2. With ignition "Off", install straight pins into module red and white wires, Fig. 6.

NOTE: Do not allow straight pins to contact engine ground.

3. Using a suitable voltmeter, connect negative lead to ground.
   a. With ignition in "On" position, measure voltage at red wire pin.
   b. Place ignition in "Start" position, measure voltage at white wire pin and at coil Batt. terminal.

NOTE: When measuring voltages, wiggle wires to simulate any open circuits that might exist.

Fig. 5   Dura Spark III ignition system start voltage test connections. 1982 models

Fig. 6   Dura Spark III ignition system supply voltage test connections. 1982 models

Fig. 7   Dura Spark III ignition system module to coil wire test connections. 1982 models

Fig. 8   Dura Spark III ignition system primary circuit continuity test connections. 1982 models

Fig. 9 Dura Spark III ignition system ballast resistor test connections. 1982 models

Fig. 10 Dura Spark III ignition system ground circuit test connections. 1982 models

4. If readings obtained are 90% of battery voltage, supply circuits are satisfactory. Proceed to test 7.
5. If readings obtained are less than 90% of battery voltage;
   a. Defective wiring harness or connectors in supply voltage circuits.
   b. Defective ignition switch.
   c. Defective ignition coil or radio interference capacitor.

Test 7, Ignition Coil Supply Voltage
1. Connect positive lead of voltmeter to coil Batt. terminal and negative lead to ground.
2. Turn ignition switch to "On" position.
3. Observe voltmeter reading. If 6–8 volts, circuit is satisfactory. If less than 6 volts or more than 8 volts, proceed to test 9.

Test 8, Testing Tach Wire
1. Disconnect and inspect module three wire connector and coil connector.
2. Using a suitable ohmmeter, connect one lead to ground and the other to the coil connector Tach. terminal. Measure resistance.
3. If readings obtained are one ohm or less, circuit is satisfactory. If readings are more than one ohm, repair short in tach wire.

Test 9, Ignition Coil Primary Resistance
1. Disconnect and inspect ignition coil connector.
2. Using a suitable tachometer, measure resistance between coil Batt. and Tach. terminals.
3. If readings are 0.8–1.6 ohms, circuit is satisfactory. If readings are out of specifications, replace coil.

Test 10, Module to Coil Wire
1. With ignition "Off", insert straight pin in module green wire, Fig. 7.

NOTE: Do not allow straight pin to contact engine ground.

2. Using a suitable voltmeter, connect negative lead to ground.
3. Turn ignition "On", then measure voltage at green wire pin and Tach. terminal of ignition coil, Fig. 7.
4. If voltmeter shows less than ½ volt difference, circuit is satisfactory. If more than ½ volt difference, inspect and repair wiring harness between coil and module.

Test 11, Primary Circuit Continuity
1. Leave straight pin in green wire as outlined in test 10.

2. Turn ignition "On", then using a suitable voltmeter connected to ground, measure voltage at green wire pin, Fig. 8.
3. If voltage exceeds 1½ volts, proceed to test 13. If voltage obtained is 1½ volts or less, proceed to test 12.

Test 12, Ballast Resistor
1. Disconnect and inspect module two wire connector and ignition coil connector, Fig. 9.
2. Using a suitable ohmmeter, measure resistance between coil connector Batt. terminal and wiring harness connector which mates with module red wire, Fig. 9.
3. If reading is 0.8–1.6 ohms, circuit is satisfactory. If reading is less than 0.8 ohms or more than 1.6 ohms, replace ballast resistor.

Test 13, Ground Circuit
1. With ignition "Off", install straight pin in module black wire, Fig. 10.

NOTE: Do not allow straight pin to touch engine ground.

2. Using a suitable ohmmeter, connect negative lead to engine ground and positive lead to black wire pin.
3. Turn ignition "On", measure voltage.
4. If voltage obtained was more than 1½ volts, proceed to test 14. If voltage obtained was less than 1½ volts, replace ignition module.

Test 14, Wiring Harness Ground Circuit
1. Disconnect module three wire connector, inspect connector for dirt and corrosion.
2. Using a suitable ohmmeter, connect one lead to engine ground. Connect other lead to wiring harness terminal which mates with black module wire terminal. Measure resistance.

NOTE: When measuring resistances, wiggle wires to simulate any open circuits that might exist.

3. If resistance is less than one ohm, inspect wiring harness connector and module black wire. If no problem is found, it is either intermittent or not in ignition system.
4. If resistance is greater than one ohm, inspect and repair wiring harness between ignition module and ground connection.

Testing For Intermittent Conditions

Refer to "Ford 1977–81 Dura Spark I & II Solid State Ignition Systems" under "Testing For Intermittent Conditions" for procedure.

Troubleshooting Intermittent Conditions

Refer to "Ford 1977–81 Dura Spark I & II Solid State Ignition Systems" under "Troubleshooting Intermittent Conditions" for procedures.

DISTRIBUTOR, REPLACE

Early Models, Fig. 11

1. Remove distributor cap. Install rotor alignment tool T78P-12200-A and remove rotor. Refer to Distributor Rotor, Replace.
2. With rotor alignment tool in position, remove distributor hold down bolt and clamp. Remove alignment tool.
3. Carefully remove distributor from engine block, noting position of rotor blades in relation to distributor housing as distributor drive gear is felt to disengage with cam gear.

NOTE: Do not rotate engine after distributor has been removed.

4. Install distributor in engine block. Ensure the distributor hold down flange slot is aligned with the clamp bolt hole and rotor upper blade slot is aligned with the slot in the distributor cap adapter.
5. Install distributor hold down bolt and clamp. Torque to 17 ft. lbs.
6. Align rotor and install distributor cap. Refer to Distributor Rotor, Replace.

Late Models, Fig. 12

1. Remove distributor cap and rotor. Position crankshaft as outlined in Distributor Rotor, Replace.

NOTE: The alignment slot in the adapter should be aligned with the alignment slot in the sleeve assembly.

2. Remove distributor hold down bolt and clamp.
3. Carefully remove distributor from engine block, noting position of the large slot in

Fig. 11 Early model Dura Spark III distributor

Fig. 12 Late model Dura Spark III distributor

the sleeve in relation to the adapter alignment slot as distributor drive gear is felt to disengage with cam gear.

NOTE: Do not rotate engine after distributor has been removed.

4. Install distributor in engine block. Ensure the distributor hold down flange slot is aligned with the clamp bolt hole and adapter alignment slot is aligned with the large sleeve alignment slot.
5. Install distributor hold down bolt and clamp. Torque to 17 ft. lbs.

DISTRIBUTOR ROTOR, REPLACE

Early Models, Fig. 11

1. Remove distributor cap.
2. Position the crankshaft to align the rotor upper blade slot with the distributor cap adapter slot to enable the rotor alignment tool T78P-12200-A to fall into place, Fig. 13.

NOTE: If alignment is not possible of rotor and adapter due to damage, position No. 1 cylinder at TDC on compression stroke with timing marks aligned at O.

3. Remove rotor alignment tool, then remove rotor retaining screws and rotor.
4. Position rotor on distributor shaft with upper rotor blade slot facing adapter slot. Install, but do not tighten rotor retaining screws.
5. Position rotor alignment tool as shown in Fig. 13, then tighten rotor retaining screws to 15–20 in. lbs.
6. Remove rotor alignment tool and install distributor cap.

Late Models, Fig. 12

1. Remove distributor cap and rotor.
2. Position No. 1 piston on compression stroke, then rotate crankshaft until rotor alignment tool, T79P-12200-A or equiva-

Fig. 13 Early model rotor alignment

Fig. 14 Late model rotor alignment

lent, can be inserted into alignment slots, Fig. 14.
3. Check vibration damper and timing pointer alignment marks. If timing pointer is within ± 4° of TDC, alignment is satisfactory. If alignment is out of specifications, position vibration damper at TDC with cylinder No. 1 at TDC. Loosen sleeve assembly adjustment screws and rotate sleeve until rotor alignment tool can be inserted into alignment slots, Fig. 14. Torque adjustment screws to 25–35 in. lbs. and remove tool.
4. Replace rotor and distributor cap.